America's History

FIFTH EDITION

America's History

James A. Henretta
University of Maryland

David Brody
University of California, Davis

Lynn Dumenil
Occidental College

Susan Ware
Radcliffe Institute for Advanced Study

Bedford / St. Martin's
Boston • New York

For Bedford / St. Martin's

Publisher for History: Patricia A. Rossi
Director of Development for History: Jane Knetzger
Executive Editor for History: Elizabeth M. Welch
Developmental Editors: Jessica N. Angell and William J. Lombardo
Production Editor: Lori Chong Roncka
Production Assistants: Tina Lai, Kristen Merrill
Senior Production Supervisor: Joe Ford
Marketing Manager: Jenna Bookin Barry
Art Director: Donna Lee Dennison
Text Design: Gretchen Tolles for Anna George Design
Cover Design: Billy Boardman and Donna Lee Dennison
Copy Editors: Barbara G. Flanagan; Susan M. Free of Reap 'n Sow
Indexer: EdIndex
Photo Research: Pembroke Herbert/Picture Research Consultants & Archives
Advisory Editor for Cartography: Gerald A. Danzer
Map Development and Coordination: Tina Samaha
Cartography: Mapping Specialists Limited
Composition: TechBooks
Printing and Binding: R.R. Donnelley & Sons Company

President: Joan E. Feinberg
Editorial Director: Denise B. Wydra
Director of Editing, Design, and Production: Marcia Cohen
Managing Editor: Elizabeth M. Schaaf

Library of Congress Control Number: 2003101705

Manufactured in the United States of America.

8   7   6   5   4   3
f   e   d   c   b   a

For information, write: Bedford / St. Martin's, 75 Arlington Street, Boston, MA 02116 (617–399–4000)

ISBN: 0–312–39879–4 (hardcover)
ISBN: 0–312–40934–6 (paperback Vol. 1)
ISBN: 0–312–40958–3 (paperback Vol. 2)

Cover and title page art: View of St. Louis, Missouri, from Lucas Place, c. 1855. Lithographer: E. Sachse & Company. Chicago Historical Society.

For Emily and Rebecca;
Siena, Cameron, Alex, Lea, and Eleanor;
Norman

In this, the fifth edition, *America's History* makes its debut as a book of the twenty-first century. When we first embarked on this edition, the country was at peace, the economy seemed invincible, and presidential candidate George W. Bush was advocating a "humble" foreign policy and no more "nation-building." The destruction of New York's World Trade Center on September 11, 2001, put an end to most Americans' hopes for a new age of normalcy; instead the nation finds itself plunged into a global war on terrorism, a war without end and without borders. As if on cue, many of our certitudes—about enduring prosperity, about the integrity of our business institutions, about an unsullied Catholic Church, about worldwide enthusiasm for America as global superpower—came crashing down. As the world becomes a threatening place, even those college students who don't think much about America's past or today's news have to wonder: How did that happen?

This question is at the heart of historical inquiry. And in asking it, the student is thinking historically. In *America's History* we aspire to satisfy that student's curiosity. We try to ask the right questions—the big ones and the not-so-big—and then write narrative history that illuminates the answers. The story, we hope, tells not only what happened, but *why*. We exclude no student from our potential audience of readers. How could we, when we hold the conviction that every student, bar none, wants to understand the world in which she lives?

From the very inception of *America's History*, we set out to write a *democratic* history, one that would convey the experiences of ordinary people even as it recorded the accomplishments of the great and powerful. We focus not only on the marvelous diversity of peoples who became American but also on the institutions—political, economic, cultural, and social—that forged a common national identity. And we present these historical trajectories in an integrated way, using each perspective to make better sense of the others. In our discussion of government and politics, diplomacy and war, we show how they affected—and were affected by—ethnic groups and economic conditions, intellectual beliefs and social changes, and the religious and moral values of the times. Just as important, we place the American experience in a global context. We trace aspects of American society to their origins in European and African cultures, consider the American Industrial Revolution within the framework of the world economy, and plot the foreign relations of the United States as part of an ever-shifting international system of impe-

rial expansion, financial exchange, and diplomatic alliances.

In emphasizing the global context, however, we had something more in mind. We wanted to remind students that America never existed alone in the world; that other nations experienced developments comparable to our own; and that, knowing this, we can better understand what was distinctive and particular to the American experience. At opportune junctures, we pause for a comparative discussion, for example about the abolition of slavery in different nineteenth-century plantation economies. This discussion enables us to explain why, in the universal struggle by emancipated slaves for economic freedom, the freedmen of the American South became sharecropping tenants in a market economy and not, as in the Caribbean, gang laborers or subsistence farmers. The operative word is *explain* and, insofar as we can make it so, explaining the past is what we intend *America's History* to do. The challenge is to write a text that has explanatory power and yet is immediately accessible to every student who enrolls in the survey course.

Organization

Accomplishing these goals means first of all grounding *America's History* in a strong conceptual framework and a clear chronology. The nation's history is divided into six **parts**, corresponding to the major phases of American development. Each part begins at a crucial turning point, such as the American Revolution or the cold war, and emphasizes the dynamic forces that unleashed it and that symbolized the era. We want to show how people of all classes and groups make their own history, but also how people's choices are influenced and constrained by circumstances: the customs and institutions inherited from the past and the distribution of power in the present. We are writing narrative history, but harnessed to historical argument, not simply a retelling of "this happened, then that happened."

To aid student comprehension, each part begins with a two-page overview. First, a **thematic timeline** highlights the key developments in politics, the economy, society, culture, and foreign affairs; then these themes are fleshed out in a corresponding **part essay**. Each part essay focuses on the crucial engines of historical change—in some eras primarily economic, in others political or diplomatic—that created new conditions of life and transformed social relations. The part organization, encapsulated in the thematic timelines and opening essays, helps students understand the major themes and periods of American history, to see how bits and pieces of historical data acquire significance as part of a larger pattern of development.

The individual chapters are similarly constructed with student comprehension in mind. A **chapter outline** gives readers an overview of the text discussion, followed by a **thematic introduction** that orients them to the central issues and ideas of the chapter. Then, at the end of the chapter, we reiterate the themes in an **analytic summary** and remind students of important events in a **chapter timeline**. A **new glossary** defines the **key concepts** boldfaced in the text where first mentioned. **Suggested references** for each chapter, now united at the back of the book and expanded to include Web sites, are annotated for students and, in another measure to facilitate research, are divided into sections corresponding to those of the chapter.

Features

The fifth edition of *America's History* contains a wealth of special features, offered not with an eye to embellishing the book but as essential components of the text's pedagogical mission. Each chapter includes two **American Voices**—excerpts from letters, diaries, autobiographies, and public testimony that convey the experience of ordinary Americans in their own words. Exciting new selections include "Red Jacket: A Seneca Chief's Understanding of Religion," "Spotswood Rice: 'Freeing My Children from Slavery,'" and "Susana Archuleta: A Chicana Youth Gets New Deal Work." In keeping with our global focus, **Voices from Abroad** similarly offers first-person testimony by foreign visitors and observers in every chapter. "Louis Antonine De Bougainville: The Defense of Canada," "The Ford Miracle: 'Slaves' to the Assembly Line," and "Fei Xiaotong: America's Crisis of Faith" are a few of the new Voices from Abroad selections in this edition. Recognizing the centrality of technology in American life, we offer in each part two **New Technology** essays in which we describe key technical innovations and their impact on American history. Examples range from the cultivation of corn and the mechanization of spinning to rural electrification and the biotech revolution. We retain our vivid **American Lives** feature—incisive biographies in every chapter of well-known, representative American figures such as founder of the African Methodist Episcopal Church Richard Allen, social reformer Dorothea Dix, newspaperman William Randolph Hearst, and Mexican American labor organizer Bert Corona.

In this fifth edition, we add a new part feature, concluding essays we entitle **Thinking about History**. In these essays we take up a major theme discussed in the preceding chapters and examine how it is currently being reconsidered by historians. The particular dynamic on which we focus is the relationship between past and present. The Thinking about History essay for Part Four, for example, deals with the Great Plains, whose settlement after the Civil War is treated in Chapter 16 as the final stage in the westward movement. This is an unexceptional perspective, with an air of the inevitable about it. But today the Great Plains are emptying out. The attempt at taming this semiarid, fragile land is increasingly seen as an ecological disaster, a terrible misstep in the nation's development. As they assimilate that knowledge, the essay asks, how are scholars rethinking the history of Great Plains settlement? And how, as a result, is that history likely to be rewritten in the future? Other Thinking about History essays deal with the tripartite colonial legacy of slavery, racism, and republicanism; the renewed scholarly debate over federalism prompted by the "Reagan Revolution" of the 1980s; the recent controversy over the words "under God" in the Pledge of Allegiance; and the role of gender in explaining the origins and character of the U.S. welfare system. We offer these new essays in hopes of alerting students to the excitement and vitality of historical inquiry and, just as important, in hopes of revealing that the past they are studying is essential to understanding the world in which they live.

Those aims similarly prompt us to offer at the close of the book an **Epilogue** subtitled "Thinking about Contemporary History." Here, however, the argument moves in a direction opposite to the earlier Thinking about History essays—not how the present influences our reading of the past, but how knowledge of the past enables us to understand the present. While we were preparing the fourth edition, the approach of the millennium suggested to us the idea of a historically reflective Epilogue on America in 2000. The Epilogue in this fifth edition, while also reflective about the uses of history, is more concerned with applying that knowledge to the fraught world that college students currently face, most particularly in the wake of September 11.

We revised with equal care the text's illustration program. *America's History* has always been noted for the rich collection of maps, figures, and pictures that help students so much to visualize the past. There is, however, always room for improvement. **One-quarter of the pictures are new** to this edition, selected to reflect changes in the text and to underscore chapter themes. Most appear in full color, with unusually **substantive captions** that actively engage students with the image and encourage them to analyze artwork as primary sources. A **new design** complements the illustrations while drawing attention to our most significant revision of the text's visual aids: a **thoroughly revised and expanded map program**. To oversee the new map program we have enlisted Professor Gerald A. Danzer of the University of Illinois at Chicago, a specialist in geographic literacy. He has worked assiduously to make our maps better teaching tools, reworking many of them, enhancing the topography, and adding map annotations that call out key points. The map program is also much expanded, with over forty new maps, covering every aspect of American life that can be captured geographically. New maps on the Ice Age, the Columbian Exchange, the National Parks and Forests, the Dust Bowl, public works projects of the New Deal, and nuclear weapons testing consider the environmental ramifications of historical events and policies. Creating new maps is an opportunity to further reinforce for students how America's history is indeed part of a broader global history, and to this end we have added maps on the settling of the Americas, fifteenth-century West Africa and the Mediterranean, European immigration to the United States at the turn of the twentieth century, and the Great Powers in East Asia in 1910. We have added new elections maps and have added map series into the narrative that show change over time, depicting, for example, Eurasian trade systems in 1500, 1650, and 1770.

This new map program is well supported by tools that teach students how to extract as much information from a map as possible and to make connections beyond the map to the narrative. The text's introduction now contains a **map primer** that walks students through a map step-by-step, offering guidance and tips on how to "read" and analyze the map. **Cross-references to online map activities**, which appear at the bottom of a key map in each chapter, encourage students to test and improve upon these skills. A **map workbook**, also written by Professor Danzer, provides skill-building exercises for a map in each chapter, effectively teaching students how to use maps to enrich their understanding of American history.

Taken together, these documents, essays, pictures, and maps offer instructors a trove of teaching materials and supply students with rich fare for experiencing the world of the American past.

Textual Changes

Of all the reasons for a new edition, of course, the most compelling is to improve the text itself—a task we have found to be never finished and yet, to our surprise, always gratifying. In this fifth edition, we are spurred on by a shift in authorial responsibility, which always brings forth much rewriting. Marilynn Johnson retires with this edition, and Lynn Dumenil of Occidental College assumes responsibility for the modern era (Chapters 22–30). Professor Dumenil is not, however, new to this project. She joined us when we undertook a concise version, assuming responsibility for the same set of chapters that are now in her charge for *America's History*. It was an opportune meeting for us because Professor Dumenil's work on the concise version makes her a seasoned practitioner of the arts of concision and clarity that, more than anything else, we hope distinguishes the writing of *America's History*.

Ask students taking the U.S. survey—or their instructors, for that matter—what's the biggest problem

with the course and they're likely to answer, "Too much to cover!" They have a point. After all, every passing year brings more American history to write about and read about. Consider the issue from a generational perspective. When the most senior of the authors of *America's History* was taking the U.S. survey in 1948–1949, most of Part Six had not yet happened! The intervening years, moreover, have seen an explosion of research into areas of our past that were invisible to earlier generations of historians—from women's history and gender roles to race and ethnicity to family life, popular culture, and work. No one, of course, would want to go back to the days when American history was essentially a chronicle of politics, diplomacy, and white men. But the inclusive, multifaceted history that we celebrate does make life harder for textbook writers. We have to resist the creep, the extra pages, that bulk up our books as we strive to incorporate what's new in the field and in contemporary America. In the fourth edition, we mounted a counteroffensive, cutting two chapters and reducing chapter length by 10 percent. In this edition, we declare victory, with even leaner chapters, 15 percent shorter than in the previous edition, so that, in effect, three words are doing the work originally of four. Our aim is to achieve a clearer, more sharply delineated narrative. Brevity, we have learned all over again, is the best antidote to imprecise language and murky argument. As textbook authors, we have always contended that if written with enough clarity and skill, the introductory survey can be made accessible to students at all levels without simplifying the story or skimping on explanation. In this fifth edition, we have enlisted the power of brevity to reach that goal.

While streamlining the narrative, we also took full advantage of the opportunity that revision affords to integrate new scholarship into our text. In the first chapter, the collision of societies now encompasses Africa as well as Europe and Native America. Our treatment of Native Americans in the colonial era incorporates recent anthropologically influenced work showing how Indian peoples maintained elements of their traditional culture in the face of European domination. We draw on new work dealing with the role of women and gender in eighteenth-century religion and antebellum politics and recent scholarship on the crisis over slavery after Independence. We offer an expanded treatment of the role of state policy during the antebellum Market Revolution, and we draw on recent Reconstruction scholarship that sees the transition from slavery to freedom as largely a battle over labor systems. We continue to incorporate more about the Far West into the nation's historical narrative, relying on the new western history for insight into the interactions among environment, peoples, and economic development. Advances in gender history enable us to offer a new discussion of bachelorhood and masculinity in the late nineteenth century and to temper our treatment of progressive welfare policy as we become aware of its patriarchal underpinnings. New scholarship on ethnic minorities similarly enables us to amplify our discussion of Native Americans during World War I and the New Deal, Asian Americans during the Great Depression, and black women during the 1920s and the later civil rights struggles. Recent scholarship based on hitherto closed Soviet and U.S. archives continues to inform our treatment of the cold war, and analysis of the turbulent 2000 presidential election and the advent of a new Republican administration bring the book to a thoughtful close. In these ways, and others, we strive to maintain the reputation of *America's History* as a fresh and timely text.

Supplements

Readers of *America's History* often cite its ancillary package as a key to the book's success in the classroom. Hence we have revised and expanded with care our array of print and electronic ancillaries for students and teachers.

For Students

Print Resources

Documents to Accompany *America's History*. Volume 1 by Melvin Yazawa (University of New Mexico), Volume 2 by Kevin Fernlund (University of Missouri, St. Louis). Revised for the fifth edition of *America's History*, this affordable documents collection offers students over 350 primary-source readings on topics covered in the main textbook, arranged to match the book's organization. One-quarter of the documents in the collection are new to this edition, giving emphasis to contested issues in American history that will spark critical thinking and class discussions. More than thirty visuals, meant to be "read" and analyzed like written sources, have been added. With many new documents emphasizing the environment, the West, and America in the context of the larger world, the collection remains a balanced assortment of political, economic, social, and cultural sources. Each document is preceded by a brief introduction and followed by questions for further thought, both of which help students analyze the documents and place them in historical context.

Maps in Context: A Workbook for American History. By Gerald A. Danzer (University of Illinois, Chicago). Published in two volumes and written by an expert in geographic literacy, these skill-building workbooks (approximately 100 pages each) correspond to the organization of *America's History* and offer instructors a powerful tool to help their students understand the essential connections between geography and history. Organized into three sections—Basic Geography, Mapping America's History, and One-Minute Quizzes—*Maps in Context* presents a wealth of in-class or take-home projects and convenient pop quizzes that give students hands-on experience working with maps from all areas of American history.

The Bedford Series in History and Culture. Natalie Zemon Davis (Princeton University); Ernest R. May (Harvard University); David W. Blight (Yale University); and Lynn Hunt (University of California at Los Angeles), advisory editors.

Over 65 American titles in this highly praised series combine first-rate scholarship, historical narrative, and important primary documents for undergraduate courses. Each book is brief, inexpensive, and focused on a specific topic or period. Package discounts are available.

Historians at Work Series. Edward Countryman (Southern Methodist University), advisory editor. Each volume in this series combines the best thinking about an important historical issue with helpful learning aids. Unabridged selections by distinguished historians, each with a differing perspective, provide a unique structure within which to examine a single question. With headnotes and questions to guide their reading and complete, original footnotes, students are able to engage in discussion that captures the intellectual excitement of historical research and interpretation. Package discounts are available.

New Media Resources

Online Study Guide at bedfordstmartins.com /henretta The *Online Study Guide* features up-to-date technology to present students with attractive and highly effective presentations and learning tools with unique self-assessment capabilities. As a student completes a practice test, the *Online Study Guide* immediately assesses his performance, targets the subject areas that need review, and refers the student back to the appropriate portions of the text. Through a series of multiple-choice, fill-in-the-blank, short-answer, and essay questions, students can gauge how well they have mastered the chapter's key events and themes. Multimedia activities on maps, visuals, and primary sources engage all types of learners and encourage critical thinking.

DocLinks at bedfordstmartins.com/doclinks DocLinks is a new, extensive database of over 750 annotated Web links to primary documents online for the study of American history. Links to speeches, legislation, U.S. Supreme Court decisions, narratives and testimony, treaties, essays, political manifestos, visual artifacts, songs, and poems provide students with a comprehensive understanding of critical events and trends in U.S. history and society. Documents are searchable by topic and date and are indexed to the chapters of *America's History*.

History Links Library at bedfordstmartins.com /historylinks Links Library is a searchable database of more than 200 carefully reviewed and annotated links to Web sites on American history. The links can be searched by topic or by specific chapters in *America's History*. Teachers can assign these links as the basis for homework assignments or research projects, or students can use them as a point of departure for their own history research.

Research and Documentation Online at bedfordstmartins.com/resdoc By Diana Hacker (Prince George's Community College). This online version of Hacker's popular booklet provides clear advice across the disciplines on how to integrate outside material into a paper, how to cite sources correctly, and how to format in MLA, APA, *Chicago*, or CBE style.

Research Assistant Hyperfolio. Delivered on CD-ROM, this intelligent tool for conducting research helps students collect, evaluate, and cite sources found both online and off.

After September 11: An Online Reader for Writers

bedfordstmartins.com/september11 This free collection of more than 100 annotated links provides social, political, economic, and cultural commentary based on the terrorist attacks of September 11, 2001, on the United States. Thoughtful discussion questions and ideas for research and writing projects are included.

For Instructors

Print Resources

Instructor's Resource Manual. By Bradley T. Gericke (U.S. Army Command and General Staff College). The *Instructor's Resource Manual,* provided free of charge with adoption of the textbook, offers an extensive collection of tools to aid both the first-time and the experienced teacher in structuring and customizing the American history course. Paralleling the textbook organization, this resource includes instructional objectives, annotated chapter outlines to guide lectures, and a chapter summary for each of the book's chapters. Lecture strategies and ideas for class discussion offer possible approaches to teaching each chapter and to presenting potentially difficult topics. A set of exercises for students includes both discussion questions and writing assignments for maps and special features. The manual also offers instructional objectives for each of the book's six parts to help instructors tie together larger sections of the book and provides critical thinking questions to pair with the part-closing Thinking about History essays. Additionally, each

chapter of the manual gives an outline of supplementary material (books from the Bedford Series in History and Culture, particular selections from *Documents to Accompany* AMERICA'S HISTORY, activities from the *Online Study Guide*) that pertains to the chapter's content.

Transparencies. A newly expanded set of over 150 full-color acetate transparencies, free to adopters, includes all the maps and many images from the text.

New Media Resources

Computerized Test Bank. A fully updated Test Bank CD-ROM offers over 80 exercises for each chapter, allowing instructors to pick and choose from a collection of multiple-choice, fill-in, map, and short and long essay questions. To aid instructors in tailoring their tests to suit their classes, every question is labeled by topic according to chapter headings and includes a textbook page number so instructors can direct students to a particular page for correct answers. Also, the software allows instructors to edit both questions and answers to further customize their tests. Correct answers are included.

Instructor's Resource CD-ROM. This easy-to-operate disc provides instructors with the resources to build engaging multimedia classroom presentations around a variety of art, photos, maps, and figures from the text. These visuals are provided in two formats: chapter-based PowerPoint files that are fully customizable and individual JPEG files.

Map Central at bedfordstmartins.com/mapcentral Map central is a searchable database of over 700 maps from Bedford/St. Martin's history survey texts that can be used to create visually striking classroom lectures.

Using the Bedford Series in the U.S. History Survey

bedfordstmartins.com/usingseries This short online guide by Scott Hovey gives practical suggestions for using the more than 65 volumes from the Bedford Series in History and Culture with *America's History* in the survey classroom. The guide not only supplies links between the text and these supplements but also provides ideas for starting discussions focused on the primary sources featured in the volumes.

Videos and multimedia. A wide assortment of videos and CD-ROMs on various topics in American history is available to qualified adopters.

Book Companion Site at bedfordstmartins.com /henretta The companion Web site for *America's History,* Fifth Edition, uses the dynamic nature of the

Web to extend the goals of the textbook and offers a convenient home base for students and instructors by gathering all the electronic resources for the text at a single Web address.

Acknowledgments

We are very grateful to the following scholars and teachers who reported on their experiences with the third edition or reviewed chapters of the fourth edition. Their comments often challenged us to rethink or justify our interpretations and always provided a check on accuracy down to the smallest detail.

Ruth M. Alexander, *Colorado State University*
Robert J. Allison, *Suffolk University*
Robin F. Bachin, *University of Miami*
Albert I. Berger, *University of North Dakota*
Neal A. Brooks, *Essex Community College (Maryland)*
Thomas Bryan, *Alvin Community College*
Montgomery Buell, *Walla Walla College*
Markus C. Cachia-Riedl, *University of California, Berkeley*
Kay J. Carr, *Southern Illinois University at Carbondale*
William Carrigan, *Rowan University*
Myles L. Clowers, *San Diego City College*
Curtis Cole, *Huron University College*
Rory T. L. Cornish, *University of Louisiana, Monroe*
John P. Daly, *Louisiana Tech University*
Thomas S. Dicke, *Southwest Missouri State University*
Jonathan Earle, *University of Kansas*
Bradley T. Gericke, *United States Military Academy*
Sally Hadden, *Florida State University*
Paul Harvey, *University of Colorado*
Lybeth Hodges, *Texas Women's University*
Nita S. Howard, *Clovis Community College*
Jen A. Huntley-Smith, *University of Nevada— Reno*
Davis D. Joyce, *East Central University (Oklahoma)*
Louisa Kilgroe, *North Carolina State University*
Keith L. King, *Houston Community College Southeast*
Norman D. Love, *El Paso Community College*
John Lyons, *Joliet Junior College*
John R. McKivigan, *West Virginia University*
Samuel T. McSeveney, *Vanderbilt University*
Rick Malmström, *The Ellis School*
M. Catherine Miller, *Texas Tech University*
Carl H. Moneyhon, *University of Arkansas— Little Rock*

Max Page, *Yale University*
Charles K. Piehl, *Mankato State University*
Edwin G. Quattlebaum III, *Phillips Academy*
Dona Reaser, *Columbus State Community College*
Steven D. Reschly, *Truman State University*
Leonard Riforgiato, *Penn State University— Shenango*
Howard B. Rock, *Florida International University*
Neil Sapper, *Amarillo College*
Timothy Shannon, *Gettysburg College*
Peter H. Shattuck, *California State University— Sacramento*
Anthony J. Springer, *Dallas Christian College*
April Summitt, *Andrews University*
Emily J. Teipe, *Fullerton College*
Suzanne R. Thurman, *Mesa State College*
Benson Tong, *Wichita State University*
Diane Tuinstra, *Kansas State University*
Ken L. Weatherbie, *Del Mar College*
Cecil E. Weller Jr., *San Jacinto College South*
Arthur J. Worrall, *Colorado State University*

As the authors of *America's History,* we know better than anyone else how much of this book is the work of other hands and other minds. We are grateful to the many scholars whose books and articles we have enjoyed and used in writing this narrative and to the editors and production staff who have provided invaluable assistance in previous editions of our text. With advice and support from Elizabeth Welch, Gretchen Boger, Louise Townsend, and Amy Langlais, Jessica Angell expertly edited our text. Charles Christensen, Joan Feinberg, Denise Wydra, Tisha Rossi, Jane Knetzger, and Marcia Cohen have been generous in providing the resources we needed to produce the fifth edition. Special thanks are due to many other individuals: Pembroke Herbert and her staff at Picture Research Associates; our project editor, Lori Chong Roncka; William Lombardo and Tina Samaha, who directed our map program, and Professor Gerald A. Danzer, a distinguished geographer and our map consultant; the fine copyeditors who worked closely with us—Barbara Flanagan and Susan M. Free; Anna George and Gretchen Tolles, who crafted our new design; our cover designers, Billy Boardman and Donna Dennison; our marketing manager, Jenna Bookin Barry; and managing editor Elizabeth Schaaf. Bradley T. Gericke diligently wrote many of the supplements for *America's History,* and Jennifer Blanksteen, Corinne McCutchen, Elizabeth Harrison, Coleen O'Hanley, and Stuart Holdsworth were of great assistance in editing and producing them. We also want to express our thanks for the valuable assistance provided by Norman S. Cohen, Michael Cohen, and Patricia Deveneau.

From the very beginning we have considered this book a joint intellectual venture, and with each edition our collaborative effort has grown. We are proud to acknowledge our collective authorship of *America's History.*

Understanding History through Maps:
An Introduction for Students

Maps and historical studies have much in common: both use art and science to create representations of things we cannot experience directly. In the case of maps, most spaces are too vast and too complex to be understood with a single look. History has an additional challenge: the past has forever slipped away and we need devices to help us recover and understand it. Both the cartographer (or mapmaker) and the historian start by gathering facts, but they are quickly overwhelmed with data, and faced with the need to select, shorten, and clarify their portrayals. The cartographer turns to symbols and visual images while the historian depends primarily on words and concepts. Working together, the historian and the cartographer combine their talents to craft a coherent narrative about the past. Their primary subjects—people, places, and times—are intimately connected. Every historical map needs a title and date, both suggested by human experience. Similarly, every historical account happened in a specific location; events, as we say, "take place."

People, places, and times are the building blocks of all history textbooks. The authors of *America's History*, Fifth Edition, selected over 150 maps designed to establish the geographic context of their story. Combined with the illustrations, figures, and narrative, the maps help readers make connections with the past and get a feel for the setting in which events happened. As in all history textbooks, the maps in *America's History* do double duty. First, they function as shorthand geography, giving readers a picture of a place. Second, maps call attention to human events that

The Common Map Projections: Orthographic, Azimuthal Equidistant, Mercator, and Gall-Peters Equal-Area

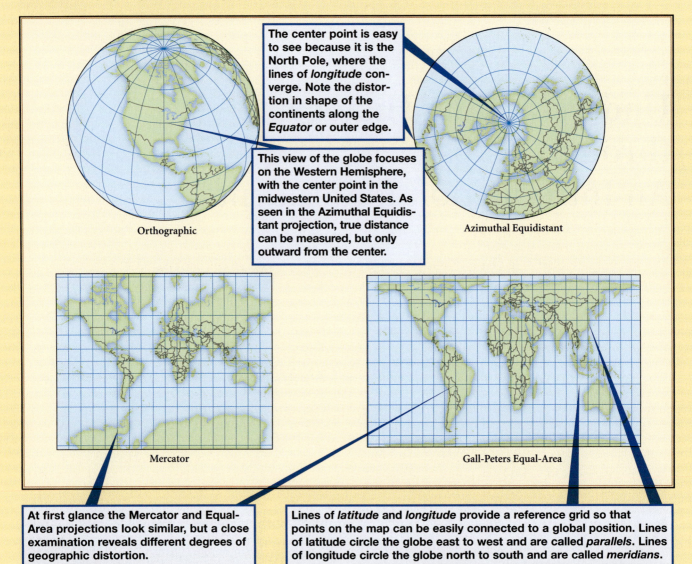

The center point is easy to see because it is the North Pole, where the lines of *longitude* converge. Note the distortion in shape of the continents along the *Equator* or outer edge.

This view of the globe focuses on the Western Hemisphere, with the center point in the midwestern United States. As seen in the Azimuthal Equidistant projection, true distance can be measured, but only outward from the center.

Orthographic

Azimuthal Equidistant

Mercator

Gall-Peters Equal-Area

At first glance the Mercator and Equal-Area projections look similar, but a close examination reveals different degrees of geographic distortion.

Lines of *latitude* and *longitude* provide a reference grid so that points on the map can be easily connected to a global position. Lines of latitude circle the globe east to west and are called *parallels*. Lines of longitude circle the globe north to south and are called *meridians*.

Figure A provides examples of several common map projections: Orthographic, Azimuthal Equidistant, Mercator, and Gall-Peters Equal-Area. All are considered world maps because they seek to depict the entire globe, or as much of it as possible. Because presenting a round image on a flat sheet of paper necessarily distorts area, shape, direction, and distance, over the years cartographers have developed numerous strategies to make their maps. Each projection is useful for a different purpose, and no single projection is the "right" one.

The Orthographic and Azimuthal Equidistant projections show the world as a globe—a three-dimensional object—but the viewer can only see two dimensions of it from any one point in space. The rounded look of the planet is retained, but only half the world can be depicted. The Orthographic projection most resembles a globe. Although it exhibits distortions in shape and area near the edges, the viewer mentally corrects these because of her familiarity with the view. Here, the shape and area of North America is relatively accurate, but to the east, across the Atlantic Ocean, western Europe is not. The Azimuthal Equidistant projection takes the skin off the globe and flattens it out to produce a two-dimensional circle. Like the Orthographic projection, it depicts half the

earth—here, the Northern Hemisphere is shown with the outer edge being the Equator. Its advantage is that it shows correct direction and distance, either of a country or continent, but only measured from the center point (in this case the North Pole). Its disadvantage is that because of the flattening and stretching, it significantly distorts (increases) the size of land forms and bodies of water near the edges.

The Mercator and Gall-Peters Equal-Area projections allow the viewer to see the entire world at a single glance. The Mercator projection accurately depicts the relative size and position of continents, countries, and bodies of water at the Equator, and fairly accurately until 45 degrees north and south latitude. Above and below these latitudes areas become distorted, as you can see from looking at Greenland, which becomes enlarged to look almost as big as North America, and Antarctica, which fills the entire bottom of the map. To correct this distortion problem, geographers developed the Gall-Peters Equal-Area projection. Its great advantage is that it depicts the areas of the continents in accurate proportion. However, its disadvantage is that it significantly distorts their shapes, as shown by the elongated views of Africa and South America.

are historically significant because they help explain change over time. To derive full benefit from the historical maps in *America's History*, readers need to view them with bifocal vision—with one eye on the physical environment and the other on the event or process depicted. A successfully read map mixes the two images, allowing for an appreciation of the human-environmental interaction that is at the root of all our experiences.

Beginning to Read Historical Maps

Readers face three challenges when looking at a map in a history textbook. First, we must discern the event being portrayed. What is the purpose of the map? Second, we must see the geography on the image, to turn the lines and symbols on the map into a picture of the physical environment in which the event took place. What area of the world are we looking at? What did it look like at the time represented? Third, maps place a major demand on our powers of understanding: How did the event and the place interact with each other? What opportunities and constraints did the environment provide? How did topography, climate, resources, or other elements of the geographic situation influence the course of events? Conversely, how did people have an impact on their environment? How did they perceive it and use it? How did a knowledge of, or attitudes toward, the physical environment differ between individuals and groups? Did these attitudes change over time? And, finally, what does it all mean? What does some insight into the experiences of people on earth tell us about who we are and where we have been?

Maps cannot tell us everything about history, and some maps are more complex than others. They have limitations as well as possibilities, and they function best when, as in *America's History*, they are accompanied by graphic aids and are integrated into the narrative flow. Maps also depend on an active reader, one who knows how to use maps and has some facility in integrating all the elements of a textbook into a meaningful educational experience. The ability to understand the strengths and limitations of maps is the core of cartographic literacy.

Developing Cartographic Literacy

The best way to start developing cartographic literacy is to review the three major shortcomings of maps. First, maps change the outer face of a globe, or a portion of it, into a flat surface. This transformation has less effect on maps that have a large scale and hence portray only a small portion of the globe. But on world maps and other small-scale portrayals the distortion created by projecting a sphere onto a plane becomes serious. The process produces exaggerations and inconsistencies of shape, direction, and/or area (Figure A).

Second, maps have a difficult time showing the irregularities on the earth's surface that are important in real life. How are mountains and valleys, plains and plateaus, hills and canyons to be indicated on a flat sheet of paper? Maps, after all, take a vantage point in the sky rather than a view toward the horizon. As Figure B illustrates, to indicate topography the cartographer must use a bag of tricks—symbols, contour lines, and suggestive shading. All of these devices rely on the reader to interpret their meaning and to translate them into landscapes.

The third limitation of maps is that they must be selective. Reducing the size of reality demands simplification, and the cartographer must focus on a few points while excluding the vast majority of details. What should be emphasized? Where should the presentation end? These choices turn any map into a very selective instrument, fashioned for a particular purpose. All maps present an argument advocating a point of view, and good maps raise more questions than they answer. Maps should not be thought of as final steps in the learning process. Instead, consider them as catalysts provided to spur active thought and raise additional issues.

These limitations of maps are directly linked to their strengths and advantages. A world map is the only way we can see all of the earth's surface at a glance. Even a round globe, a much more accurate representation of the planet, can present only a portion of its subject at one time. Paradoxically, if we want to picture the global dimension of something, only a flat world map will do. Maps help us comprehend places we cannot actually see because the distances are too vast. An ocean, a continent, a nation, a state, even a city or a town cannot be taken in by one look. Only its representation on a map enables us to see it whole.

Maps also clarify the world for us. As models of reality, they extract certain features for emphasis to make the world intelligible. Maps are instructional devices, and the cartographer always follows a lesson plan. One way to begin reading a map is to figure out the purpose of the lesson. What is the basic message the map is intended to convey? The title of the map is a good place to start, especially any dates that might be provided. Dates help readers connect the map with the narrative, placing the event described into a sequence of happenings and connecting the incident to other developments occurring at the same time. The alert reader will connect the map's title to its caption. The word *caption* is derived from the same root as the word *capture*. The sentences in every map caption in *America's History* are designed to help the reader seize the purpose of the map—and thus turn it into a valuable possession.

Working with maps also deepens our understanding of the basic themes of geography and how they relate to

FIGURE B

MAP 16.7 The Settlement of the Pacific Slope, 1860–1890

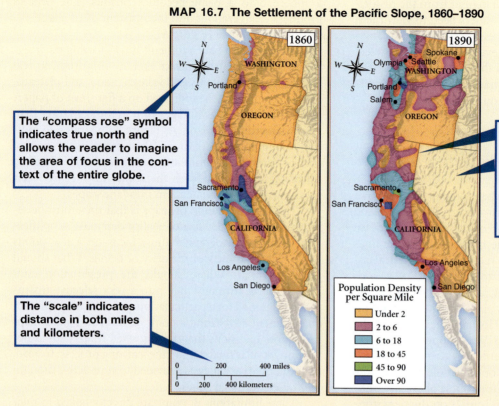

The "compass rose" symbol indicates true north and allows the reader to imagine the area of focus in the context of the entire globe.

Creative shading effectively suggests the mountainous landscape of the Pacific slope. Colored shadings are also used to indicate the change in population density per square mile from 1860 to 1890.

The "scale" indicates distance in both miles and kilometers.

Population Density per Square Mile

- Under 2
- 2 to 6
- 6 to 18
- 18 to 45
- 45 to 90
- Over 90

historical studies. Five of these themes—location, place, region, movement, and interaction—are presented as questions on the following pages, with several maps provided to illustrate how each particular theme might enrich a reader's understanding of the map and the historical situation it depicts. All of the maps reappear later in the text, and all of the questions might be called upon to enhance the value of any individual map. In the end, attention to these basic themes will fortify the reader's cartographic literacy, as well as foster her historical understanding.

Location: Where Is This Place?

"When?" and "Where?" are the first questions asked by historians and cartographers. Every event is connected to a place, and every place needs to be identified by a date. Maps are the best devices to show location, and in the final analysis any place on a map is located in reference to

the earth as a whole. Location depends, in an absolute sense, on a reference to global position, most conveniently cited in terms of latitude and longitude (see Figure A).

In a relative sense, however, location can depend on the distance, direction, or travel time from one place to another. As Figure C indicates, in 1817 Pittsburgh, Pennsylvania, was more than ten days' travel from New York City, a distance of roughly 370 miles. By 1841 improvements in travel made the trip possible in about five or six days. Relative location is also at the heart of Figure D, showing the Japanese relocation camps during World War II. Note that latitude and longitude are not used on this map because absolute location is not the point. Instead, this map is intended to show how far the Japanese Americans were forced to relocate—within the same state, several states away, or halfway across the nation. It is not necessary to show all of the states, since only those west of the Mississippi River were primarily involved. The cartographer assumes that the map reader will realize that a portion of the country is not shown and will, if needed, fill in the missing part from her mental map.

FIGURE C

MAP 10.4 The Speed of News in 1817 and 1841

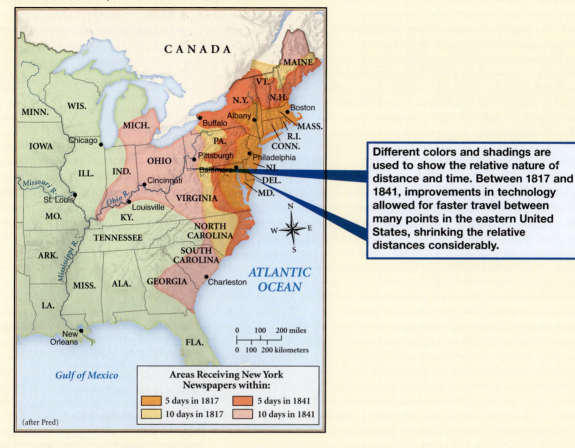

Different colors and shadings are used to show the relative nature of distance and time. Between 1817 and 1841, improvements in technology allowed for faster travel between many points in the eastern United States, shrinking the relative distances considerably.

Areas Receiving New York Newspapers within:

- 5 days in 1817
- 10 days in 1817
- 5 days in 1841
- 10 days in 1841

(after Pred)

FIGURE D

MAP 26.2 Japanese Relocation Camps

Inset maps allow the cartographer to use a large-scale map to depict the main subject area (here, the continental United States) and still show additional areas relevant to the topic. Alaska and Hawaii were territories, not states, during World War II and are included here because Japanese Americans lived in both.

This national map appears to float free of its location on the planet. Neither oceans nor continents are used to suggest a global position. The boundaries of the United States serve as the boundaries of the map, isolating the nation from its geographical position but allowing for greater focus.

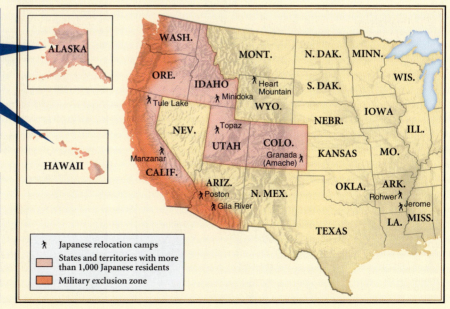

- Japanese relocation camps
- States and territories with more than 1,000 Japanese residents
- Military exclusion zone

Place: How Did This Location Become a Place?

Human activity creates places. Locations exist on their own without the presence of people, but they become places when people use them in some way. As human enterprise thickens and generation after generation use a place, it accumulates artifacts, develops layers of remains, and creates a variety of associations held in a society's history and memory.

Places have two sets of characteristics: physical and human, the products of both nature and culture. A complete physical description of a place would show the topography of the site, identify any bodies of water, and then inventory its climate, minerals, soils, plants, and animals. The human characteristics of a site would start with how people used the land, noting the settlement patterns, buildings and roads, population distribution, economic activities, social organization, language, and culture. The historian takes an additional step and considers how these have changed over time and what that change means. It would take many maps to approach a complete description of a historic place and to unravel all the characteristics and experiences that make it significant. Indeed, the very word *place* suggests a uniqueness that has emerged in large part from a particular history.

Figure E presents a pair of maps that show the settlement pattern of the Barrow plantation in Georgia in 1860 and in 1881. These illustrate how important the date is on any map. The passing of a slave society and the emergence of a sharecropping economy transformed the Barrow landscape. Only the big house remained in place between 1860 and 1881. The tight organization of a controlled society gave way to a dispersed community, but one that gained focal points on a church and a school in addition to the cotton-gin house.

FIGURE E

MAP 15.2 The Barrow Plantation, 1860 and 1881

The "key" includes symbols that make the map legible. Each item in the key is represented on the map. A pie chart that shows how ex-slave Handy Barrow made his income is also provided, allowing the map to convey additional information.

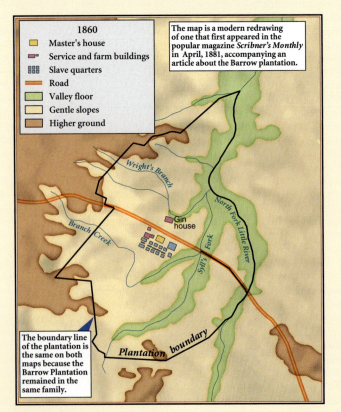

1860

- ▯ Master's house
- ▰ Service and farm buildings
- ▦ Slave quarters
- ▬ Road
- ▧ Valley floor
- ▧ Gentle slopes
- ▧ Higher ground

The map is a modern redrawing of one that first appeared in the popular magazine *Scribner's Monthly* in April, 1881, accompanying an article about the Barrow plantation.

The boundary line of the plantation is the same on both maps because the Barrow Plantation remained in the same family.

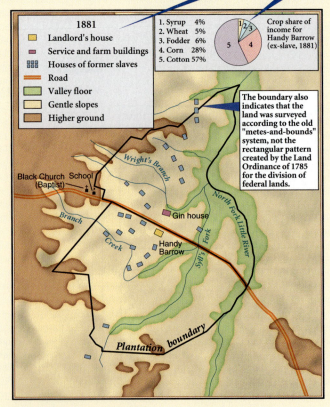

1881

- ▯ Landlord's house
- ▰ Service and farm buildings
- ▦ Houses of former slaves
- ▬ Road
- ▧ Valley floor
- ▧ Gentle slopes
- ▧ Higher ground

1. Syrup   4%
2. Wheat   5%
3. Fodder   6%
4. Corn   28%
5. Cotton   57%

Crop share of income for Handy Barrow (ex-slave, 1881)

The boundary also indicates that the land was surveyed according to the old "metes-and-bounds" system, not the rectangular pattern created by the Land Ordinance of 1785 for the division of federal lands.

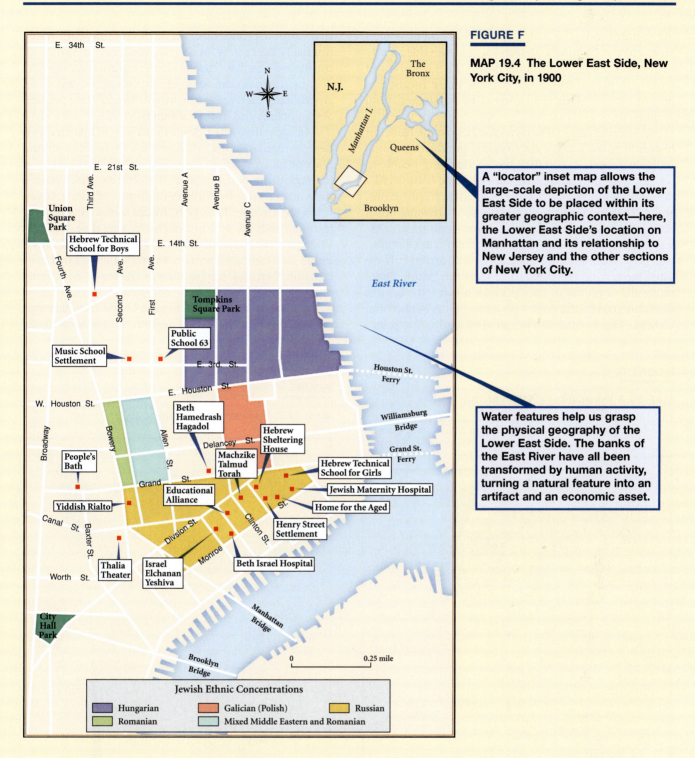

MAP 19.4 The Lower East Side, New York City, in 1900

A "locator" inset map allows the large-scale depiction of the Lower East Side to be placed within its greater geographic context—here, the Lower East Side's location on Manhattan and its relationship to New Jersey and the other sections of New York City.

Water features help us grasp the physical geography of the Lower East Side. The banks of the East River have all been transformed by human activity, turning a natural feature into an artifact and an economic asset.

Figure F maps neighborhood institutions in an urban environment. Again the date is essential to note because the Lower East Side of New York surely had a different mix of institutions in 1850 or 1950 than it did in 1900, the time of the map. In larger terms, the sense of place created here results from its waterfront location, the concentrations of ethnic groups, and the variety of neighborhood institutions.

Region: What Does a Place Have in Common with Its Surroundings?

The concept of place highlights the unique elements of every location. By contrast, the idea of a region highlights elements in common, tying certain places together as a group distinguishable from other places. New England, the cotton-producing South, the Phoenix metropolitan area, and the Columbia Plateau suggest the wide variety of groupings that help us understand the integration of particular places into larger regions. Every location is part of many regions, only a few of which share natural boundaries.

Perceiving regional ties is a great help to the reader of historical maps because they suggest the forces binding individual interests together and encouraging people to act in common. The United States could be considered a political region in which like values, shared institutions, and a common heritage create a sense of national unity. Such a region is a human construction; in contrast, physical characteristics like landforms, climate, ecosystems, and geological structures create natural regions. These often cross national boundaries. Thus the United States shares the Great Plains, the Rocky Mountains, the canyon lands, and the Pacific slope with its neighbors Mexico and Canada. Every state can be grouped with others into

larger regional entities like the Midwest or the Gulf States. Internally each state can be divided into a variety of smaller regions that represent differing interests. Upstate, downstate, urban, rural, inner city, suburban, and so on are regularly used regional concepts in analyzing political developments and historical trends.

Geographers often point to an internal pattern evident in many regions. A historical core marks a central place or point of origin for a region. Toward the edges of the region the dominance of the defining characteristic thins out, creating a periphery or frontier marking a transition zone to another region. To this useful construct the historian adds the dynamic of change over time. One way to engage the maps of the many presidential elections found in *America's History* is to apply the regional concept and then look for evidence of change by comparing maps.

Consider, for example, Figures G and H, which illuminate the importance of regions in thinking about

FIGURE G

MAP 28.3 Presidential Election of 1960

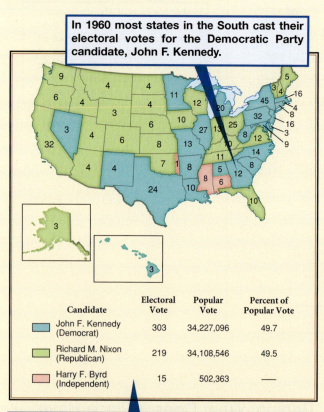

In 1960 most states in the South cast their electoral votes for the Democratic Party candidate, John F. Kennedy.

Candidate	Electoral Vote	Popular Vote	Percent of Popular Vote
John F. Kennedy (Democrat)	303	34,227,096	49.7
Richard M. Nixon (Republican)	219	34,108,546	49.5
Harry F. Byrd (Independent)	15	502,363	—

The presidential election maps in *America's History* allow the reader to quickly see the national distribution of electoral votes on a regional and state basis. Another way to depict election results graphically would be to show the winner of the popular vote per county. By shifting the focus, the results might look very different and raise further questions.

FIGURE H

MAP 31.7 Presidential Election of 2000

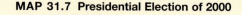
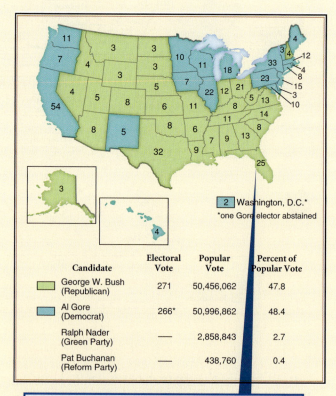

2	Washington, D.C.*

*one Gore elector abstained

Candidate	Electoral Vote	Popular Vote	Percent of Popular Vote
George W. Bush (Republican)	271	50,456,062	47.8
Al Gore (Democrat)	266*	50,996,862	48.4
Ralph Nader (Green Party)	—	2,858,843	2.7
Pat Buchanan (Reform Party)	—	438,760	0.4

Forty years later in the 2000 presidential election, the southern states cast their electoral votes for the Republican Party candidate, George W. Bush. In Alabama, Georgia, Mississippi, North and South Carolina, and Texas, Bush won easily with 55–59 percent of the popular vote; only in Florida was his victory razor-thin.

American politics. In 1960, as Figure G indicates, the South voted solidly Democratic. In 2000, the South voted just as solidly Republican, as shown by Figure H. How can such a fundamental political shift be explained? Understanding regional histories and identities explains a great deal, and presidential election maps like those placed throughout *America's History* are powerful tools that help readers focus on regional patterns and other shifts in voting behavior.

Figure I shows how a particular place—here, the Tennessee Valley—can be considered part of several overlapping regions, the significance of which changes depending on the interest of the viewer. Emerging out of the politics of the New Deal, in the 1930s the Tennessee Valley area became, for the first time, clearly defined. Figure I uses two sets of data to describe the Tennessee Valley Authority: the area served by TVA electric power (an example of a cultural region) and the actual watershed of the river (a natural region).

Movement: What Is Happening Here?

All change involves movement. People move in their daily activities, in seasonal patterns, and in migration to new places of residence. In the process they cross many boundaries. People also use products that move from one place to another through the economic system. An important type of movement is "diffusion," a concept used by geographers to describe the process by which people, animals, goods, services, ideas, and information move from a point of origin to other locations. Diffusion is sometimes a planned, purposeful activity, but it can also be accidental, like the spread of disease. To understand a map fully, the reader must always envision it as one part of a sequence, not unlike a "still" excerpted from a motion picture. To capture all of this activity on a map is a difficult undertaking. To understand the map,

FIGURE I

Map 25.4 The Tennessee Valley Authority, 1933–1952

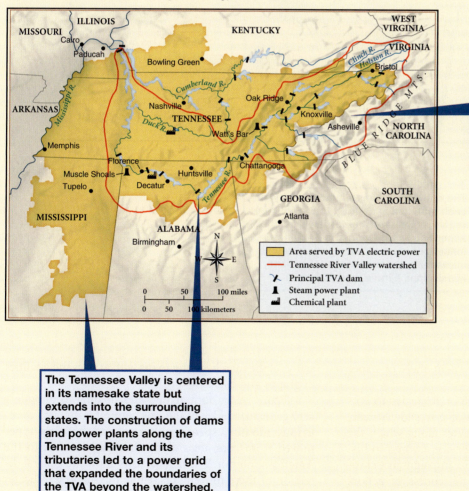

Valleys are natural regions tied together by a common drainage pattern and often sharing a variety of physical features like climate, topography, and vegetation.

The Tennessee Valley is centered in its namesake state but extends into the surrounding states. The construction of dams and power plants along the Tennessee River and its tributaries led to a power grid that expanded the boundaries of the TVA beyond the watershed.

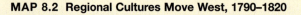

FIGURE J

MAP 8.2 Regional Cultures Move West, 1790–1820

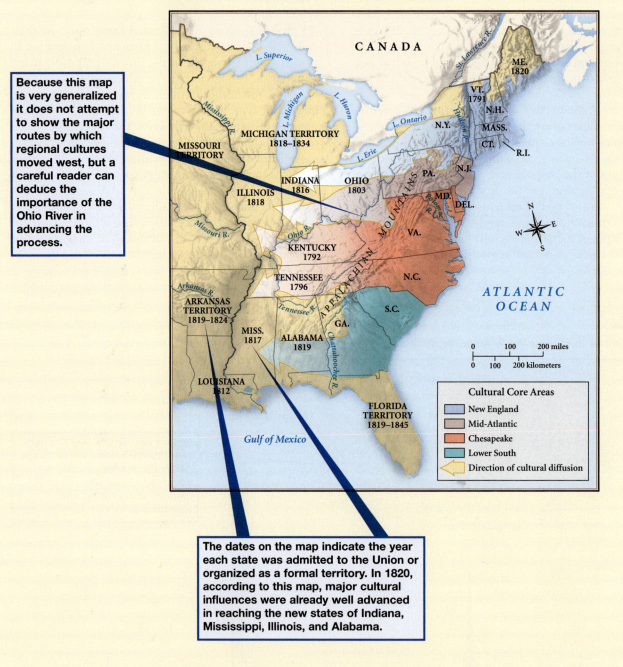

Because this map is very generalized it does not attempt to show the major routes by which regional cultures moved west, but a careful reader can deduce the importance of the Ohio River in advancing the process.

The dates on the map indicate the year each state was admitted to the Union or organized as a formal territory. In 1820, according to this map, major cultural influences were already well advanced in reaching the new states of Indiana, Mississippi, Illinois, and Alabama.

the viewer must perceive that the silent sheet of paper depicts commotion.

Cartographers employ a range of strategies to emphasize movement on maps. One way is to show, usually through color and shading, the routes along which the movement is channeled. Another device, favored in historical cartography to show military campaigns, is to provide dramatic arrows indicating the course of action. Often the width of the arrows represents the size of the army on the march, giving maps with arrows the qualities of graphs and charts.

Figure J uses both arrows and shading to provide a very generalized idea of the way cultural traits such as religious identity, speech patterns, and housing types moved from core areas along the Atlantic coast to the American interior. The large arrows show the general direction of these movements, while the shading indicates the density of the process up to 1820. The large arrows

FIGURE K

MAP 18.2 The Diffusion of the Australian Ballot

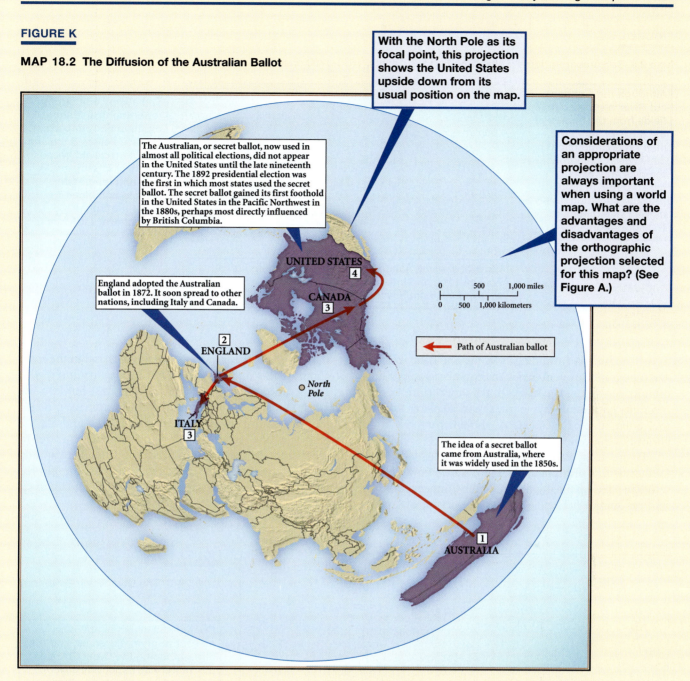

With the North Pole as its focal point, this projection shows the United States upside down from its usual position on the map.

Considerations of an appropriate projection are always important when using a world map. What are the advantages and disadvantages of the orthographic projection selected for this map? (See Figure A.)

The Australian, or secret ballot, now used in almost all political elections, did not appear in the United States until the late nineteenth century. The 1892 presidential election was the first in which most states used the secret ballot. The secret ballot gained its first foothold in the United States in the Pacific Northwest in the 1880s, perhaps most directly influenced by British Columbia.

England adopted the Australian ballot in 1872. It soon spread to other nations, including Italy and Canada.

UNITED STATES **4**

CANADA **3**

ENGLAND **2**

ITALY **3**

North Pole

The idea of a secret ballot came from Australia, where it was widely used in the 1850s.

AUSTRALIA **1**

0   500   1,000 miles
0   500   1,000 kilometers

← Path of Australian ballot

also indicate that the movement continued into the future. A creative use of cartographic symbols makes this example very dynamic.

The diffusion of a key idea in modern democratic governance—the Australian, or secret, ballot—is featured in Figure K. Note that a world map is needed for this process because the practice started in Australia in the 1850s and then spread to England. From there it was adopted in several other countries, including Italy and Canada. By the 1880s the secret ballot had gained a foothold in the United States in the Pacific Northwest. In 1892 most states used the Australian ballot for presidential elections.

Interaction: How Do People and Their Environment Influence Each Other?

The interaction between people and the environment divides into two major categories. First, people change their environment to suit their needs. The pioneer era in American history records the chopping down of great trees, followed by the clearing of land to raise crops and animals largely brought from Europe and Africa. Second, opportunities and constraints of the environment force people to change their behavior and culture as they adapt

FIGURE L

Map 2.6 Settlement Patterns within New England Towns, 1630–1700 (inset)

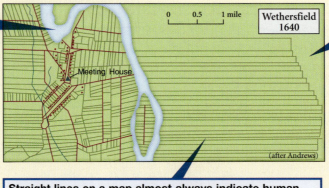

Although the Connecticut River separated many fields from the homes of the farmers along the major road, and might be considered a hindrance, the river was also an asset to the community, providing a water supply as well as a means of transportation.

The absence of strong topographical features on the map is important. Settlers selected the site for Wethersfield because the level terrain, fertile soil, and temperate climate combined to make it a fruitful agricultural settlement.

Straight lines on a map almost always indicate human activity. Here, the lots and fields are carefully arranged to take maximum advantage of the site.

to their natural surroundings. On the one hand, climate and topography present major environmental constraints on how people use the land. On the other hand, human ingenuity has found ways to put almost all places to some use, often turning elements of the environment from curiosities into valuable resources.

Figure L, a plan of the agricultural settlement of Wethersfield, Connecticut, in 1640, shows how Puritan settlers carved up the flood plain of the Connecticut River into productive fields. It seems as if every bit of land in

the settlement was put to use, even the island in the river. Contrast this image, spelling out human triumph, with the situation shown in Figure M. The dust bowl on the Great Plains in the 1930s resulted from humans pushing too hard against environmental constraints, removing the grasses of the American West and plowing the land to plant crops. In the extended period of drought beginning in 1930 crops died and winds ripped apart the plowed landscape, blowing the topsoil away in huge clouds of dust.

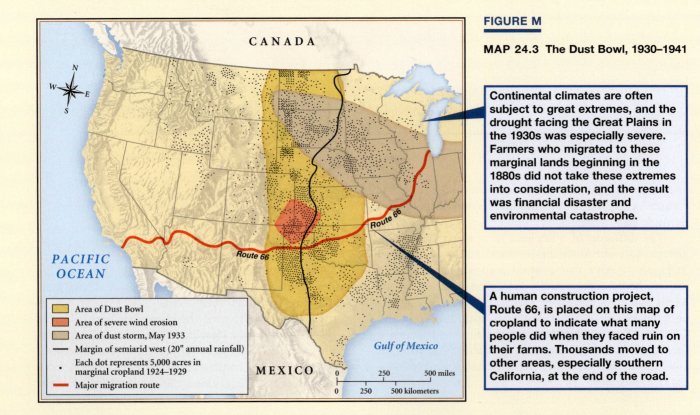

FIGURE M

MAP 24.3 The Dust Bowl, 1930–1941

Continental climates are often subject to great extremes, and the drought facing the Great Plains in the 1930s was especially severe. Farmers who migrated to these marginal lands beginning in the 1880s did not take these extremes into consideration, and the result was financial disaster and environmental catastrophe.

A human construction project, Route 66, is placed on this map of cropland to indicate what many people did when they faced ruin on their farms. Thousands moved to other areas, especially southern California, at the end of the road.

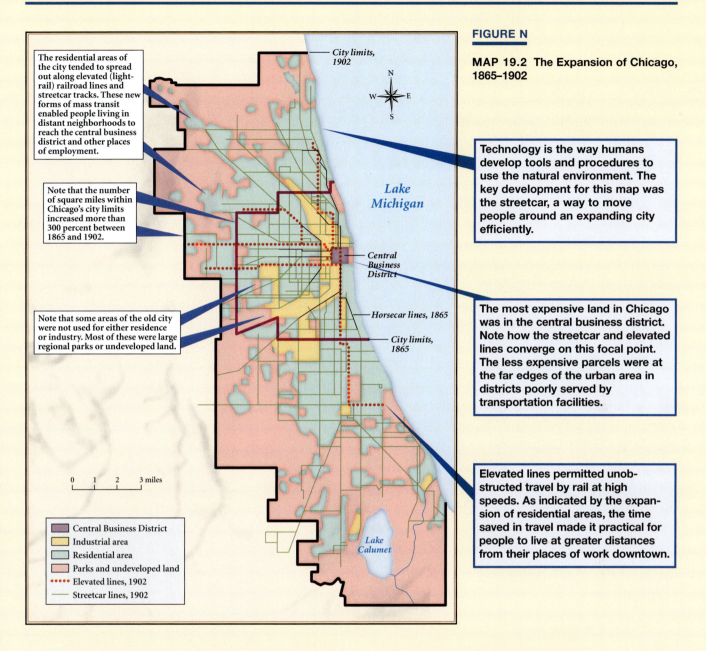

FIGURE N

MAP 19.2 The Expansion of Chicago, 1865–1902

The residential areas of the city tended to spread out along elevated (light-rail) railroad lines and streetcar tracks. These new forms of mass transit enabled people living in distant neighborhoods to reach the central business district and other places of employment.

Note that the number of square miles within Chicago's city limits increased more than 300 percent between 1865 and 1902.

Note that some areas of the old city were not used for either residence or industry. Most of these were large regional parks or undeveloped land.

Technology is the way humans develop tools and procedures to use the natural environment. The key development for this map was the streetcar, a way to move people around an expanding city efficiently.

The most expensive land in Chicago was in the central business district. Note how the streetcar and elevated lines converge on this focal point. The less expensive parcels were at the far edges of the urban area in districts poorly served by transportation facilities.

Elevated lines permitted unobstructed travel by rail at high speeds. As indicated by the expansion of residential areas, the time saved in travel made it practical for people to live at greater distances from their places of work downtown.

City limits, 1902

Lake Michigan

Central Business District

Horsecar lines, 1865

City limits, 1865

Lake Calumet

0   1   2   3 miles

Central Business District
Industrial area
Residential area
Parks and undeveloped land
Elevated lines, 1902
Streetcar lines, 1902

Figure N details the expansion of a major city, showing that human-environmental concerns operate in urban areas as well as in the countryside. In the case of Chicago, a wet, low-lying former lake bed became the site for a metropolis, which numbered about two million residents by 1900. The flat topography enabled the city to be laid out on straight lines but created sanitation and drainage problems, eventually addressed only by major human efforts, which included reversing the flow of the Chicago River.

Conclusion

Every time you encounter a map in *America's History*, ask yourself the following eight questions. With practice, you will improve your cartographic literacy, thereby deepening your historical understanding.

1. What is the purpose of the map?

2. What date is represented on the map and why is this date historically significant?

3. How does the map help explain the narrative?

4. What additional information does the caption provide?

5. What elements are emphasized on the map?

6. How does the map represent the actual landscape?

7. In what ways does the map show change over time?

8. How do the basic themes of geography—location, place, region, movement, and human-environmental interaction—help unlock the theme of the map?

—GERALD A. DANZER,
University of Illinois at Chicago

BRIEF CONTENTS

PART ONE

The Creation of American Society, 1450–1775   2

1   Worlds Collide: Europe, Africa, and America, 1450–1620   5

2   The Invasion and Settlement of North America, 1550–1700   39

3   The British Empire in America, 1660–1750   69

4   Growth and Crisis in Colonial Society, 1720–1765   101

5   Toward Independence: Years of Decision, 1763–1775   133

THINKING ABOUT HISTORY:
Slavery, Racism, and the American Republic   160

PART TWO

The New Republic, 1775–1820   162

6   War and Revolution, 1775–1783   165

7   The New Political Order, 1776–1800   193

8   Dynamic Change: Western Settlement and Eastern Capitalism, 1790–1820   221

9   The Quest for a Republican Society, 1790–1820   251

THINKING ABOUT HISTORY:
Federalism as History and Contemporary Politics   280

PART THREE

Economic Revolution and Sectional Strife, 1820–1877   282

10   The Economic Revolution, 1820–1860   285

11   A Democratic Revolution, 1820–1844   315

12   Religion and Reform, 1820–1860   341

13   The Crisis of the Union, 1844–1860   367

14   Two Societies at War, 1861–1865   397

15   Reconstruction, 1865–1877   429

THINKING ABOUT HISTORY:
Religion in American Public Life   452

PART FOUR

A Maturing Industrial Society, 1877–1914   454

16   The American West   457

17   Capital and Labor in the Age of Enterprise, 1877–1900   485

18   The Politics of Late-Nineteenth-Century America   515

19   The Rise of the City   543

20   The Progressive Era   573

21   An Emerging World Power, 1877–1914   603

THINKING ABOUT HISTORY:
The Fate of the Great Plains   632

PART FIVE
The Modern State and Society, 1914–1945   *634*

22 War and the American State, 1914–1920   *637*

23 Modern Times, The 1920s   *665*

24 The Great Depression   *695*

25 The New Deal, 1933–1939   *721*

26 The World at War, 1939–1945   *749*

┃ **THINKING ABOUT HISTORY:**
Women, Gender, and the Welfare System   *778*

PART SIX
America and the World, 1945 to the Present   *780*

27 Cold War America, 1945–1960   *783*

28 The Affluent Society and the Liberal Consensus, 1945–1965   *815*

29 War Abroad and at Home: The Vietnam Era, 1961–1975   *849*

30 The Lean Years, 1969–1980   *879*

31 A New Domestic and World Order, 1981–2001   *907*

EPILOGUE: Thinking about Contemporary History   *938*

Documents   *D–1*

Appendix   *A–1*

Glossary   *G–1*

Suggested References   *SR–1*

Credits   *C–1*

Index   *I–1*

CONTENTS

Preface for Instructors   *vii*

Understanding History through Maps:
    An Introduction for Students   *xiii*

Brief Contents   *xxvii*

Maps   *xli*

Figures and Tables   *xlvi*

Special Features   *xlviii*

About the Authors   *li*

PART ONE
The Creation of American Society, 1450–1775   *2*

Chapter 1
Worlds Collide: Europe, Africa, and America, 1450–1620   *5*

Native American Worlds   *6*
   The First Americans   6
   The Mayas and the Aztecs   9
   The Indians of the North   11

Traditional European Society in 1450   *14*
   The Peasantry   14
   Hierarchy and Authority   16
   The Power of Religion   17

Europe Encounters Africa and the Americas,
    1450–1550   *18*
   The Renaissance   19
   West African Society and Slavery   20
   Europe Reaches the Americas   22
   The Spanish Conquest   24

The Protestant Reformation and the Rise of
    England   *28*
   The Protestant Movement   29
   The Dutch and the English Challenge Spain   33
   The Social Causes of English Colonization   35

Summary   *37*

Timeline   *37*

> **AMERICAN VOICES:**
> A Navajo Emergence Story   *7*

> **VOICES FROM ABROAD:**
> Father le Petite: The Customs of the
>   Natchez   *13*
> **NEW TECHNOLOGY:**
> Indian Women and Agriculture   *14*
> **AMERICAN VOICES:**
> Friar Bernardino de Sahagún: Aztec Elders Describe
>   the Spanish Conquest   *26*
> **AMERICAN LIVES:**
> Cortés and Malinche: The Dynamics of
>   Conquest   *30*

Chapter 2
The Invasion and Settlement of North America, 1550–1700   *39*

Imperial Conflicts and Rival Colonial
    Models   *40*
   New Spain: Colonization and Conversion   40
   New France: Furs and Souls   44
   New Netherland: Commerce   46
   *The First English Model: Tobacco and
     Settlers   48*

The Chesapeake Experience   *50*
   Settling the Tobacco Colonies   50
   Masters, Servants, and Slaves   52
   The Seeds of Social Revolt   54
   Bacon's Rebellion   55

Puritan New England   *56*
   The Puritan Migration   56
   Religion and Society, 1630–1670   58
   *The Puritan Imagination and
     Witchcraft   59*
   A Yeoman Society, 1630–1700   60

The Indians' New World   *61*
   Puritans and Pequots   61
   Metacom's Rebellion   63
   The Fur Trade and the Inland Peoples   63

Summary   *67*

Timeline   *67*

> **AMERICAN LIVES:**
> Luis de Velasco/Opechancanough/Massatamohtnock:
>   A Case of Possible Multiple Identities   *42*

VOICES FROM ABROAD:
Samuel de Champlain: Going to War with
the Hurons   *45*
AMERICAN VOICES:
Richard Frethorne: Hard Times in Early Virginia   *53*
AMERICAN VOICES:
Mary Rowlandson: A Captivity Narrative   *64*

Chapter 3

The British Empire in America, 1660–1750   *69*

The Politics of Empire, 1660–1713   *70*
   The Restoration Colonies   70
   From Mercantilism to Dominion   72
   The Glorious Revolution of 1688   73
   Imperial Wars and Native Peoples   75
The Imperial Slave Economy   *76*
   The South Atlantic System   76
   Slavery in the Chesapeake and South Carolina   80
   African American Community and Resistance   85
   The Southern Gentry   89
   The Northern Maritime Economy   91
The New Politics of Empire, 1713–1750   *93*
   The Rise of Colonial Assemblies   93
   Salutary Neglect   95
   Protecting the Mercantile System of Trade   95
Summary   *99*
Timeline   *99*

VOICES FROM ABROAD:
Olaudah Equiano: The Brutal
"Middle Passage"   *81*
AMERICAN LIVES:
From a Piece of Property to a Man of Property:
The Odyssey of Robert Pearle   *82*
NEW TECHNOLOGY:
Rice: Riches, Wretchedness, and Community   *86*
AMERICAN VOICES:
Philip Fithian: Sadism under Slavery   *89*
AMERICAN VOICES:
Captain Fayrer Hall: The Impact of the
Molasses Act   *96*

Chapter 4

Growth and Crisis in Colonial Society, 1720–1765   *101*

Freehold Society in New England   *102*
   Farm Families: Women's Place   102

   Farm Property: Inheritance   103
   The Crisis of Freehold Society   104
The Middle Atlantic: Toward a New Society,
1720–1765   *105*
   Economic Growth and Social Inequality   105
   Cultural Diversity   107
   Religious Identity and Political Conflict   110
The Enlightenment and the Great Awakening,
1740–1765   *112*
   The Enlightenment in America   112
   American Pietism and the Great Awakening   114
   Religious Upheaval in the North   115
   Social and Religious Conflict in the South   119
The Midcentury Challenge: War, Trade, and Social
Conflict, 1750–1765   *121*
   The French and Indian War   121
   The Great War for Empire   124
   *British Economic Growth and the Consumer
Revolution   127*
   Land Conflicts   128
   Western Uprisings   129
Summary   *131*
Timeline   *131*

AMERICAN VOICES:
Gottlieb Mittelberger: The Perils of Migration   *109*
AMERICAN VOICES:
Jonathan Edwards: Preacher, Philosopher,
Pastor   *116*
AMERICAN VOICES:
Nathan Cole: The Power of a Preacher   *118*
VOICES FROM ABROAD:
Louis Antonine De Bougainville: The Defense of
Canada   *126*

Chapter 5

Toward Independence: Years of Decision, 1763–1775   *133*

The Imperial Reform Movement,
1763–1765   *134*
   The Legacy of War   134
   The Sugar Act and Colonial Rights   136
   An Open Challenge: The Stamp Act   138
The Dynamics of Rebellion, 1765–1766   *140*
   The Crowd Rebels   140
   Ideological Roots of Resistance   143
   Parliament Compromises, 1766   144
The Growing Confrontation, 1767–1770   *145*
   The Townshend Initiatives   145
   America Again Debates and Resists   146
   Lord North Compromises, 1770   147

The Road to War, 1771–1775   *150*
   The Compromise Ignored   150
   The Continental Congress Responds   154
   The Rising of the Countryside   154
   The Failure of Compromise   157
Summary   *159*
Timeline   *159*

| **AMERICAN VOICES:**
Samuel Adams: An American View of the
   Stamp Act   *141*
AMERICAN LIVES:
George R. T. Hewes and the Meaning
   of the Revolution   *152*
AMERICAN VOICES:
Anonymous Broadside, May 18, 1775: "To the
   Associators of the City of Philadelphia"   *156*
VOICES FROM ABROAD:
Lieutenant Colonel Francis Smith: A British View of
   Lexington and Concord   *158*

| **THINKING ABOUT HISTORY:**
Slavery, Racism, and the American
   Republic   *160*

PART TWO

The New Republic, 1775–1820   *162*

Chapter 6

War and Revolution, 1775–1783   *165*

Toward Independence, 1775–1776   *166*
   *The Second Continental Congress and
     Civil War   166*
   Common Sense   167
   Independence Declared   169
The Trials of War, 1776–1778   *170*
   War in the North   170
   Armies and Strategies   171
   Victory at Saratoga   172
   Social and Financial Perils   174
The Path to Victory, 1778–1783   *175*
   The French Alliance   175
   War in the South   177
   The Patriot Advantage   182
   Diplomatic Triumph   182
Republicanism Defined and Challenged   *184*
   *Republican Ideals under Wartime
     Pressures   185*

   The Loyalist Exodus   186
   The Problem of Slavery   187
   A Republican Religious Order   190
Summary   *191*
Timeline   *191*

| **VOICES FROM ABROAD:**
Thomas Paine: Common Sense   *168*
AMERICAN LIVES:
The Enigma of Benedict Arnold   *180*
AMERICAN VOICES:
John Adams: Making Peace with Stubborn Enemies
   and Crafty Allies   *183*
AMERICAN VOICES:
Benjamin Banneker: On Jefferson and
   Natural Rights   *188*

Chapter 7

The New Political Order, 1776–1800   *193*

Creating Republican Institutions, 1776–1787   *194*
   The State Constitutions: How Much Democracy?   194
   The Articles of Confederation   196
   Shays's Rebellion   200
The Constitution of 1787   *201*
   The Rise of a Nationalist Faction   201
   The Philadelphia Convention   202
   The People Debate Ratification   204
   The Federalists Implement the Constitution   209
The Political Crisis of the 1790s   *210*
   Hamilton's Financial Program   210
   Jefferson's Agrarian Vision   212
   The French Revolution Divides Americans   213
   The Rise of Political Parties   216
   Constitutional Crisis, 1798–1800   216
Summary   *219*
Timeline   *219*

| **AMERICAN VOICES:**
Abigail and John Adams: The Status
   of Women   *197*
AMERICAN VOICES:
Robert Yates and John Lansing: A Protest against the
   Philadelphia Convention   *203*
AMERICAN LIVES:
Gouverneur Morris: An Elitist Liberal in a
   Republican Age   *206*
NEW TECHNOLOGY:
Machine Technology and Republican Values   *214*
VOICES FROM ABROAD:
William Cobbett: Peter Porcupine Attacks
   Pro-French Americans   *217*

Chapter 8

Dynamic Change: Western Settlement and Eastern Capitalism, 1790–1820   *221*

Westward Expansion   *222*
   Native American Resistance   *222*
   Migration and the Changing Farm Economy   *225*
   The Transportation Bottleneck   *228*

The Republicans' Political Revolution   *230*
   The Jeffersonian Presidency   *230*
   Jefferson and the West   *231*
   Conflict with Britain and France   *233*
   The War of 1812   *235*

The Capitalist Commonwealth   *241*
   A Merchant-Based Economy: Banks, Manufacturing, and Markets   *241*
   Public Policy: The Commonwealth System   *244*
   Federalist Law: John Marshall and the Supreme Court   *245*

Summary   *249*
Timeline   *249*

> **AMERICAN VOICES:**
> Red Jacket: A Seneca Chief's Understanding of Religion   *224*
> **AMERICAN VOICES:**
> Noah M. Ludlow: Traveling to Kentucky, 1815   *229*
> **AMERICAN LIVES:**
> Tenskwatawa: Shawnee Prophet   *236*
> **VOICES FROM ABROAD:**
> Alexis de Tocqueville: Law and Lawyers in the United States   *248*

Chapter 9

The Quest for a Republican Society, 1790–1820   *251*

Democratic Republicanism   *252*
   Social and Political Equality for White Men   *252*
   Toward a Republican Marriage System   *253*
   Republican Motherhood   *255*
   Raising and Educating Republican Children   *257*

Aristocratic Republicanism and Slavery, 1780–1820   *261*
   The North and South Grow Apart   *261*
   Toward a New Southern Social Order   *262*
   Slave Society and Culture   *265*
   The Free Black Population   *267*
   The Missouri Crisis   *269*

Protestant Christianity as a Social Force   *272*
   The Second Great Awakening   *272*
   Women's New Religious Roles   *277*

Summary   *279*
Timeline   *279*

> **NEW TECHNOLOGY:**
> Women's Health and Fertility: From Folk Remedies to Pharmacies   *256*
> **AMERICAN VOICES:**
> Lydia Maria Child: Raising Middle-Class Children   *259*
> **AMERICAN VOICES:**
> Jacob Stroyer: A Child Learns the Meaning of Slavery   *267*
> **AMERICAN LIVES:**
> Richard Allen and African American Identity   *270*
> **VOICES FROM ABROAD:**
> Frances Trollope: A Camp Meeting in Indiana   *276*

> **THINKING ABOUT HISTORY:**
> Federalism as History and Contemporary Politics   *280*

PART THREE

Economic Revolution and Sectional Strife, 1820–1877   *282*

Chapter 10

The Economic Revolution, 1820–1860   *285*

The Coming of Industry: Northeastern Manufacturing   *286*
   Division of Labor and the Factory   *286*
   The Textile Industry and British Competition   *288*
   American Mechanics and Technological Innovation   *292*
   Wage Workers and the Labor Movement   *292*

The Expansion of Markets   *296*
   Migration to the Southwest and the Midwest   *296*
   The Transportation Revolution Forges Regional Ties   *297*
   The Growth of Cities and Towns   *302*

Changes in the Social Structure   *303*
   The Business Elite   *303*
   The Middle Class   *304*
   The New Urban Poor   *305*
   The Benevolent Empire   *306*
   Revivalism and Reform   *308*
   Immigration and Cultural Conflict   *311*

Summary   *313*

Timeline   *313*

> NEW TECHNOLOGY:
> Cotton Spinning: From Spinsters to Machines   *289*
> AMERICAN VOICES:
> Lucy Larcom: Early Days at Lowell   *291*
> AMERICAN LIVES:
> Eli Whitney: Machine Builder and Promoter   *294*
> VOICES FROM ABROAD:
> Frances Trollope: American Workers
>   and Their Wives   *307*
> AMERICAN VOICES:
> John Gough: The Vice of Intemperance   *310*

Chapter 11

A Democratic Revolution, 1820–1844   *315*

The Rise of Popular Politics, 1820–1829   *316*
*The Decline of the Notables and the
    Rise of Parties   316*
The Election of 1824   317
*The Last Notable President: John
    Quincy Adams   318*
*"The Democracy" and the
    Election of 1828   319*

The Jacksonian Presidency, 1829–1837   *321*
Jackson's Agenda: Patronage and Policy   321
The Tariff and Nullification   321
The Bank War   324
Indian Removal   326
The Jacksonian Impact   328

Class, Culture, and the Second
    Party System   *330*
The Whig Worldview   330
*Labor Politics and the
    Depression of 1837–1843   332*
"Tippecanoe and Tyler Too!"   333

Summary   *339*

Timeline   *339*

> AMERICAN VOICES:
> Margaret Bayard Smith: Republican Majesty
>   and Mobs   *322*
> VOICES FROM ABROAD:
> Alexis de Tocqueville: Parties in the
>   United States   *325*
> AMERICAN VOICES:
> Black Hawk: A Sacred Reverence
>   for Our Lands   *329*
> AMERICAN LIVES:
> Frances Wright: Radical Reformer   *336*

Chapter 12

Religion and Reform, 1820–1860   *341*

Individualism   *342*
Emerson and Transcendentalism   342
Emerson's Literary Influence   344
Brook Farm   345

Communalism   *346*
The Shakers   346
The Fourierist Phalanxes   347
*John Humphrey Noyes and the
    Oneida Community   348*
The Mormon Experience   349

Abolitionism   *352*
Slave Rebellion   352
*Garrison and Evangelical
    Abolitionism   353*
*Opposition and Internal
    Conflict   356*

The Women's Rights Movement   *358*
Origins of the Women's Movement   358
Abolitionism and Women   359
The Program of Seneca Falls   362

Summary   *365*

Timeline   *365*

> VOICES FROM ABROAD:
> Charles Dickens Assails the Shakers   *348*
> AMERICAN VOICES:
> An Illinois "Jeffersonian" Attacks
>   the Mormons   *351*
> AMERICAN LIVES:
> Dorothea Dix: Public Woman   *360*
> AMERICAN VOICES:
> Keziah Kendall: A Farm Woman Defends
>   the Grimké Sisters   *363*

Chapter 13

The Crisis of the Union, 1844–1860   *367*

Manifest Destiny   *368*
*The Mature Cotton
    Economy, 1820–1860   368*
The Independence of Texas   369
*The Push to the Pacific: Oregon and
    California   372*
The Fateful Election of 1844   375

War, Expansion, and
    Slavery, 1846–1850   376
    The War with Mexico, 1846–1848   376
    A Divisive Victory   379
    1850: Crisis and Compromise   382

The End of the Second Party
    System, 1850–1858   385
    Resistance to the Fugitive Slave Act   385
    *The Whigs' Decline and the
        Democrats' Diplomacy*   387
    *The Kansas-Nebraska Act and the
        Rise of New Parties*   387
    The Election of 1856 and Dred Scott   390

Abraham Lincoln and the Republican
    Triumph, 1858–1860   391
    Lincoln's Political Career   391
    The Party System Fragments   393

Summary   395

Timeline   395

AMERICAN VOICES:
Mary Boykin Chesnut: A Slaveholding
    Woman's Diary   370
VOICES FROM ABROAD:
Colonel José Enrique de la Peña: A Mexican View of
    the Battle of the Alamo   372
AMERICAN LIVES:
Frederick Douglass: Development of an
    Abolitionist   380
AMERICAN VOICES:
Axalla John Hoole: "Bleeding Kansas":
    A Southern View   390

Chapter 14
Two Societies at War, 1861–1865   397

Secession and Military
    Stalemate, 1861–1862   398
    Choosing Sides   398
    *Setting Objectives and Devising
        Strategies*   401

Toward Total War   407
    Mobilizing Armies and Civilians   407
    Mobilizing Resources   409

The Turning Point: 1863   413
    Emancipation   413
    Vicksburg and Gettysburg   415

The Union Victorious, 1864–1865   417
    Soldiers and Strategy   417
    *The Election of 1864 and Sherman's
        March to the Sea*   421

Summary   427

Timeline   427

VOICES FROM ABROAD:
Ernest Duveyier de Hauranne: German Immigrants and
    the Civil War within Missouri   402
NEW TECHNOLOGY:
The Rifle-Musket   410
AMERICAN VOICES:
Elizabeth Mary Meade Ingraham:
    A Vicksburg Diary   416
AMERICAN VOICES:
Spotswood Rice: Freeing My
    Children from Slavery   419
AMERICAN LIVES:
William Tecumseh Sherman:
    An Architect of Modern War   422

Chapter 15
Reconstruction, 1865–1877   429

Presidential Reconstruction   430
    Lincoln's Approach   430
    Johnson's Initiative   430
    Acting on Freedom   431
    Congress versus President   435

Radical Reconstruction   436
    Congress Takes Command   436
    Republican Rule in the South   439
    The Quest for Land   442

The Undoing of Reconstruction   444
    Counterrevolution   445
    The Acquiescent North   449
    The Political Crisis of 1877   450

Summary   451

Timeline   451

VOICES FROM ABROAD:
David Macrae: The Devastated
    South   432
AMERICAN VOICES:
Jourdon Anderson: Relishing
    Freedom   434
AMERICAN LIVES:
Nathan Bedford Forrest: Defender
    of Southern Honor   446
AMERICAN VOICES:
Harriet Hernandes: The Intimidation
    of Black Voters   448

THINKING ABOUT HISTORY:
Religion in American Public Life   452

PART FOUR

A Maturing Industrial Society, 1877–1914   *454*

Chapter 16

The American West   *457*

The Great Plains   *458*
   Indians of the Great Plains   *459*
   Wagon Trains, Railroads, and Ranchers   *460*
   Homesteaders   *464*
   The Fate of the Indians   *469*

The Far West   *474*
   The Mining Frontier   *474*
   Hispanics, Chinese, Anglos   *478*
   Golden California   *481*

Summary   *483*

Timeline   *483*

> **AMERICAN LIVES:**
> Buffalo Bill and the Mythic West   *462*
> **AMERICAN VOICES:**
> Ida Lindgren: Swedish Emigrant in
>   Frontier Kansas   *466*
> **AMERICAN VOICES:**
> Zitkala-Ša (Gertrude Simmons Bonnin): Becoming
>   White   *473*
> **VOICES FROM ABROAD:**
> Baron Joseph Alexander von Hübner:
>   A Western Boom Town   *476*

Chapter 17

Capital and Labor in the Age of Enterprise, 1877–1900   *485*

Industrial Capitalism Triumphant   *486*
   Growth of the Industrial Base   *486*
   The Railroad Boom   *488*
   Mass Markets and Large-Scale Enterprise   *491*
   The New South   *495*

The World of Work   *498*
   Labor Recruits   *498*
   Autonomous Labor   *501*
   Systems of Control   *502*

The Labor Movement   *505*
   Reformers and Unionists   *505*
   The Triumph of "Pure and Simple" Unionism   *508*

   Industrial War   *510*
   American Radicalism in the Making   *511*

Summary   *513*

Timeline   *513*

> **NEW TECHNOLOGY:**
> Iron and Steel   *488*
> **AMERICAN LIVES:**
> Jay Gould: Robber Baron?   *492*
> **VOICES FROM ABROAD:**
> Count Vay de Vaya und Luskod:
>   Pittsburgh Inferno   *503*
> **AMERICAN VOICES:**
> John Brophy: A Miner's Son   *504*
> **AMERICAN VOICES:**
> Rose Schneiderman:
>   Trade Unionist   *509*

Chapter 18

The Politics of Late-Nineteenth-Century America   *515*

The Politics of the Status Quo, 1877–1893   *516*
   The National Scene   *516*
   The Ideology of Individualism   *518*
   The Supremacy of the Courts   *519*

Politics and the People   *520*
   Cultural Politics: Party, Religion,
     and Ethnicity   *520*
   Organizational Politics   *521*
   Women's Political Culture   *523*

Race and Politics in the New South   *525*
   Biracial Politics   *526*
   One-Party Rule Triumphant   *528*
   Resisting White Supremacy   *531*

The Crisis of American Politics:
   The 1890s   *534*
   The Populist Revolt   *535*
   Money and Politics   *537*

Summary   *541*

Timeline   *541*

> **VOICES FROM ABROAD:**
> Ernst Below: Beer and German American
>   Politics   *522*
> **AMERICAN VOICES:**
> Helen Potter: The Case for Women's
>   Political Rights   *527*
> **AMERICAN VOICES:**
> Tom Watson: The Case for
>   Interracial Unity   *528*
> **AMERICAN LIVES:**
> Robert Charles: Black Militant   *532*

Chapter 19
The Rise of the City   543

Urbanization   544
   Industrial Sources of City Growth   544
   City Innovation   545
   Private City, Public City   548

Upper Class, Middle Class   550
   The Urban Elite   550
   The Suburban World   552
   Middle-Class Families   553

City Life   556
   Newcomers   557
   Ward Politics   561
   Religion in the City   562
   City Amusements   566
   The Higher Culture   569

Summary   571
Timeline   571

AMERICAN VOICES:
M. Carey Thomas: "We Did Not Know…Whether Women's Health Could Stand the Strain of College Education"   555
AMERICAN VOICES:
Anonymous: Bintel Brief   561
AMERICAN LIVES:
Big Tim Sullivan, Tammany Politician   564
VOICES FROM ABROAD:
José Martí: Coney Island, 1881   567

Chapter 20
The Progressive Era   573

The Course of Reform   574
   The Progressive Mind   574
   Women Progressives   576
   Reforming Politics   583
   Racism and Reform   587

Progressivism and National Politics   591
   The Making of a Progressive President   591
   Regulating the Marketplace   592
   The Fracturing of Republican Progressivism   595
   Woodrow Wilson and the New Freedom   597

Summary   601
Timeline   601

AMERICAN VOICES:
Charles Edward Russell: Muckraking   576
AMERICAN LIVES:
Frances Kellor: Woman Progressive   580
AMERICAN VOICES:
Dr. Alice Hamilton: Tracking Down Lead Poisoning   588
VOICES FROM ABROAD:
James Bryce: America in 1905: "Business Is King"   594

Chapter 21
An Emerging World Power, 1877–1914   603

The Roots of Expansion   604
   Diplomacy in the Gilded Age   604
   The Economy of Expansionism   606
   The Making of a "Large" Foreign Policy   608
   The Ideology of Expansionism   609

An American Empire   609
   The Cuban Crisis   612
   The Spoils of War   616
   The Imperial Experiment   618

Onto the World Stage   622
   A Power among Powers   622
   The Open Door in Asia   626
   Wilson and Mexico   628
   The Gathering Storm in Europe   629

Summary   631
Timeline   631

NEW TECHNOLOGY:
The Battleship   610
AMERICAN LIVES:
William Randolph Hearst: Jingo   614
AMERICAN VOICES:
George W. Prioleau: Black Soldiers in a White Man's War   619
AMERICAN VOICES:
Daniel J. Evans and Seiward J. Norton: Fighting the Filipinos   621
VOICES FROM ABROAD:
Jean Hess, Émile Zola, and Ruben Dario: American Goliath   624

THINKING ABOUT HISTORY:
The Fate of the Great Plains   632

PART FIVE

The Modern State and Society, 1914–1945   *634*

Chapter 22

War and the American State, 1914–1920   *637*

The Great War, 1914–1918   *638*
  War in Europe   638
  The Perils of Neutrality   640
  "Over There"   643
  The American Fighting Force   644

War on the Home Front   *647*
  Mobilizing Industry and the Economy   647
  Mobilizing American Workers   649
  *Wartime Reform: Woman Suffrage and
    Prohibition   651*
  Promoting National Unity   654

An Unsettled Peace, 1919–1920   *655*
  The Treaty of Versailles   655
  *Racial Strife, Labor Unrest, and the
    Red Scare   660*

Summary   *663*

Timeline   *663*

> **AMERICAN VOICES:**
> Harry Curtin: Trench Warfare   *641*
> **VOICES FROM ABROAD:**
> A German Propaganda Appeal to
>   Black Soldiers   *648*
> **AMERICAN VOICES:**
> Southern Migrants   *652*
> **AMERICAN LIVES:**
> George Creel: Holding Fast the
>   Inner Lines   *656*

Chapter 23

Modern Times, The 1920s   *665*

Business-Government Partnership of
  the 1920s   *666*
  Politics in the Republican "New Era"   666
  The Economy   668
  The Heyday of Big Business   669

  Economic Expansion Abroad   670
  Foreign Policy in the 1920s   672

A New National Culture   *673*
  A Consumer Culture   673
  The Automobile Culture   675
  Mass Media and New Patterns of Leisure   675

Dissenting Values and Cultural Conflict   *681*
  The Rise of Nativism   681
  *Legislating Values: The Scopes
    Trial and Prohibition   686*
  Intellectual Crosscurrents   688
  Cultural Clash in the Election of 1928   691

Summary   *693*

Timeline   *693*

> **AMERICAN VOICES:**
> Women Write the Children's Bureau   *669*
> **VOICES FROM ABROAD:**
> The Ford Miracle: "Slaves" to the
>   Assembly Line   *671*
> **AMERICAN LIVES:**
> Clara Bow: The "It" Girl   *678*
> **NEW TECHNOLOGY:**
> Aviation   *682*
> **AMERICAN VOICES:**
> Kazuo Kawai: A Foreigner in America   *686*

Chapter 24

The Great Depression   *695*

The Coming of the Great Depression   *697*
  Causes of the Depression   697
  The Deepening Economic Crisis   697
  The Worldwide Depression   698

Hard Times   *699*
  The Invisible Scar   699
  Families Face the Depression   701
  Popular Culture Views the Depression   705

Harder Times   *707*
  African Americans in the Depression   707
  Dust Bowl Migrations   709
  Mexican American Communities   711
  Asian Americans Face the Depression   714

Herbert Hoover and the Great Depression   *714*
  Hoover Responds   715
  Rising Discontent   716
  The 1932 Election: A New Order   717

Summary   *719*

Timeline   *719*

VOICES FROM ABROAD:
Mary Agnes Hamilton: Breadlines and
    Beggars   *700*
AMERICAN VOICES:
Larry Van Dusen: A Working-Class Family
    Encounters the Great Depression   *703*
AMERICAN LIVES:
Bert Corona and the Mexican American
    Generation   *712*
AMERICAN VOICES:
Public Assistance Fails a Southern Farm Family   *716*

Chapter 25
The New Deal, 1933–1939   *721*

The New Deal Takes Over, 1933–1935   *722*
    The Roosevelt Style of Leadership   *722*
    The Hundred Days   *724*
    The New Deal under Attack   *726*

The Second New Deal, 1935–1938   *728*
    Legislative Accomplishments   *728*
    The 1936 Election   *729*
    Stalemate   *730*

The New Deal's Impact on Society   *732*
    New Deal Constituencies and the Broker State   *732*
    The New Deal and the Land   *740*
    The New Deal and the Arts   *741*
    The Legacies of the New Deal   *745*

Summary   *747*
Timeline   *747*

AMERICAN VOICES:
Joe Marcus: A New Deal Activist   *723*
AMERICAN LIVES:
Mary McLeod Bethune: Black Braintruster   *736*
AMERICAN VOICES:
Susana Archuleta: A Chicana Youth Gets New Deal
    Work   *739*
VOICES FROM ABROAD:
Odette Keun: A Foreigner Looks at the
    Tennessee Valley Authority   *742*
NEW TECHNOLOGY:
Rural Electrification   *744*

Chapter 26
The World at War, 1939–1945   *749*

The Road to War   *750*
    The Rise of Facism   *750*

    Depression-Era Isolationism   *751*
    Retreat from Isolationism   *751*
    The Attack on Pearl Harbor   *753*

Organizing for Victory   *754*
    Financing the War   *755*
    *Mobilizing the American Fighting
        Force*   *758*
    Workers and the War Effort   *759*
    Civil Rights during Wartime   *760*
    Politics in Wartime   *761*

Life on the Home Front   *762*
    "For the Duration"   *762*
    Japanese Internment   *765*

Fighting and Winning the War   *767*
    Wartime Aims and Strategies   *768*
    The War in Europe   *769*
    The War in the Pacific   *771*
    Planning the Postwar World   *773*
    The Onset of the Atomic Age and the War's End   *775*

Summary   *777*
Timeline   *777*

AMERICAN LIVES:
Henry J. Kaiser: World War II's "Miracle Man"   *756*
VOICES FROM ABROAD:
German POWs: American Race Relations   *761*
AMERICAN VOICES:
Monica Sone: Japanese Relocation   *767*
AMERICAN VOICES:
Anton Bilek: The War in the Pacific   *774*

THINKING ABOUT HISTORY:
Women, Gender, and the Welfare System   *778*

PART SIX
America and the World, 1945 to the Present   *780*

Chapter 27
Cold War America, 1945–1960   *783*

The Cold War Abroad   *784*
    Descent into Cold War, 1945–1946   *784*
    The Truman Doctrine and Containment   *785*
    Containment in Asia and the Korean War   *791*
    *Eisenhower and the "New Look" of
        Foreign Policy*   *794*

The Cold War at Home   *797*
    Postwar Domestic Challenges   *797*

Fair Deal Liberalism   799
The Great Fear   799
"Modern Republicanism"   801

The Emergence of Civil Rights as a
National Issue   804
Civil Rights under Truman   804
Challenging Segregation   804
The Civil Rights Movement and the Cold War   806

The Impact of the Cold War   807
Nuclear Proliferation   807
The Military-Industrial Complex   810

Summary   813

Timeline   813

> **AMERICAN LIVES:**
> George F. Kennan: Architect of Containment   786
> **VOICES FROM ABROAD:**
> Jean Monnet: Truman's Generous Proposal   790
> **AMERICAN VOICES:**
> Mark Goodson: Red Hunting on the Quiz
> Shows; or, What's My Party Line?   802
> **AMERICAN VOICES:**
> Isaac Nelson: Atomic Witness   809
> **NEW TECHNOLOGY:**
> The Computer Revolution   810

Chapter 28

The Affluent Society and the Liberal Consensus, 1945–1965   815

The Affluent Society   816
The Economic Record   816
The Suburban Explosion   817
American Life during the Baby Boom   820

The Other America   825
Migration to Cities   825
The Urban Crisis   829

John F. Kennedy and the Politics of
Expectation   830
The New Politics   830
Activism Abroad   831
The New Frontier at Home   834
*New Tactics for the Civil Rights
Movement*   836
The Kennedy Assassination   839

Lyndon B. Johnson and the Great
Society   840
The Momentum for Civil Rights   840
Enacting the Liberal Agenda   842
War on Poverty   844

Summary   847

Timeline   847

> **VOICES FROM ABROAD:**
> Hanoch Bartov: Everyone Has a Car   821
> **AMERICAN VOICES:**
> A Woman Encounters the
> Feminine Mystique   824
> **AMERICAN LIVES:**
> Elvis Presley: Teen Idol of the 1950s   826
> **AMERICAN VOICES:**
> Anne Moody: We Would Like to Be Served   837

Chapter 29

War Abroad and at Home: The Vietnam Era, 1961–1975   849

Into the Quagmire, 1945–1968   850
*America in Vietnam: From Truman to
Kennedy*   850
Escalation: The Johnson Years   852
American Soldiers' Perspectives on the War   854

The Cold War Consensus Unravels   856
Public Opinion on Vietnam   856
Student Activism   857
The Rise of the Counterculture   859
The Widening Struggle for Civil Rights   860
The Legacy of the Civil Rights Movement   863
The Revival of Feminism   865

The Long Road Home, 1968–1975   867
1968: A Year of Shocks   867
Nixon's War   870
Withdrawal from Vietnam and Détente   871
The Legacy of Vietnam   873

Summary   877

Timeline   877

> **AMERICAN VOICES:**
> Dave Cline: A Vietnam Vet Remembers   855
> **VOICES FROM ABROAD:**
> Che Guevara: Vietnam and the World
> Freedom Struggle   859
> **AMERICAN VOICES:**
> Mary Crow Dog: The Trail of Broken Treaties   864
> **AMERICAN LIVES:**
> John Paul Vann: Dissident Patriot   874

Chapter 30

The Lean Years, 1969–1980   879

The Nixon Years   880
The Republican Domestic Agenda   880

The 1972 Election   881
Watergate   882

An Economy of Diminished Expectations   884
Energy Crisis   884
Economic Woes   884

Reform and Reaction in the 1970s   887
*The New Activism: Environmental and Consumer
    Movements*   888
*Challenges to Tradition: The Women's Movement and
    Gay Rights*   889
Racial Minorities   894
The Politics of Resentment   898

Politics in the Wake of Watergate   899
Ford's Caretaker Presidency   899
Jimmy Carter: The Outsider as President   899
The Reagan Revolution   902

Summary   905
Timeline   905

AMERICAN LIVES:
Lois Marie Gibbs: Environmental Activist   890
AMERICAN VOICES:
David Kopay: The Real Score: A Gay
    Athlete Comes Out   895
AMERICAN VOICES:
Phyllis Ellison: Busing in Boston   897
VOICES FROM ABROAD:
Fei Xiaotong: America's Crisis of Faith   900

Chapter 31

**A New Domestic
and World Order,
1981–2001**   *907*

The Reagan-Bush Years, 1981–1993   908
Reaganomics   908
Reagan's Second Term   909
The Bush Presidency   910

Foreign Relations under Reagan and Bush   912
Interventions in Developing Countries   912
The End of the Cold War   912
War in the Persian Gulf, 1990–1991   913

Uncertain Times: Economic and Social
    Trends, 1980–2000   914
The Economy   915
Popular Culture and Popular Technology   917
An Increasingly Pluralistic Society   919
Backlash against Women's and Gay Rights   925

The AIDS Epidemic   925
The Environmental Movement at Twenty-Five   927

Restructuring the Domestic Order:
    Public Life, 1992–2001   927
Clinton's First Term   928
"The Era of Big Government Is Over"   930
Second-Term Stalemates   930
An Unprecedented Election   933
George W. Bush's Early Presidency   934

Summary   937
Timeline   937

VOICES FROM ABROAD:
Saddam Hussein: Calling for a Holy War
    against the United States   915
NEW TECHNOLOGY:
The Biotech Revolution   918
AMERICAN LIVES:
Bill Gates: Microsoft's Leader in the Computer
    Revolution   922
AMERICAN VOICES:
Laurie Ouellette: A Third-Wave Feminist   926
AMERICAN VOICES:
John Lewis: We Marched to Be Counted   935

Epilogue:

**Thinking about
Contemporary
History**   *939*

Documents   *D-1*
The Declaration of Independence   *D-1*
*The Articles of Confederation and
    Perpetual Union*   *D-3*
*The Constitution of the United States
    of America*   *D-7*
*Amendments to the Constitution with Annotations
    (with Six Unratified Amendments)*   *D-12*

Appendix   *A-1*
The American Nation   *A-1*
The American People: A Demographic Survey   *A-6*
The American Government and Economy   *A-13*

Glossary   *G-1*

Suggested References   *SR-1*

Credits   *C-1*

Index   *I-1*

Chapter 1

Worlds Collide: Europe, Africa, and America, 1450–1620

∗ The Ice Age and the Settling of the Americas   8

Native American Peoples, 1492   10

West Africa and the Mediterranean in the Fifteenth Century   21

The Eurasian Trade System and European Maritime Ventures, 1500   22

The Spanish Conquest of the Great Indian Civilizations   25

The Columbian Exchange   28

Religious Diversity in Europe, 1600   32

Chapter 2

The Invasion and Settlement of North America, 1550–1700

New Spain Looks North, 1513–1610   41

The Eurasian Trade System and Overseas Spheres of Influence, 1650   46

Eastern North America in 1650   49

∗ River Plantations in Virginia, c. 1640   51

The Puritan Migration to America, 1620–1640   57

∗ Settlement Patterns within New England Towns, 1630–1700   62

Chapter 3

The British Empire in America, 1660–1750

The Dominion of New England, 1686–1689   73

∗ Britain's American Empire, 1713   77

Africa and the Atlantic Slave Trade, 1700–1810   78

∗ The Rise of the American Merchant, 1750   93

Chapter 4

Growth and Crisis in Colonial Society, 1720–1765

The Hudson River Manors   106

∗ Ethnic and Racial Diversity, 1775   110

Religious Diversity in 1750   112

European Spheres of Influence, 1754   122

The Anglo-American Conquest of New France, 1754–1760   125

Westward Expansion and Land Conflicts, 1750–1775   129

An asterisk (∗) indicates a map annotated to highlight key points and to promote map-reading skills.

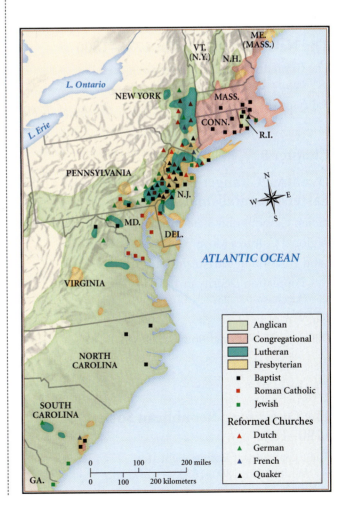

Chapter 5

Toward Independence: Years of Decision, 1763–1775

The Eurasian Trade System and European
  Colonies, c. 1770   *134*

* Britain's American Empire in 1763   *138*

British Troop Deployments, 1763–1775   *148*

British Western Policy, 1763–1774   *151*

Chapter 6

War and Revolution, 1775–1783

Patriot and Loyalist Strongholds   *170*

The War in the North, 1776–1777   *171*

Native Americans and the War in
  the West, 1778–1779   *177*

The War in the South, 1778–1781   *178*

* New Spain's Northern Empire, 1763–1800   *184*

* The Status of Slavery, 1800   *189*

Chapter 7

The New Political Order, 1776–1800

The Confederation and Western
  Land Claims   *199*

Ratifying the Constitution of 1787   *208*

Chapter 8

Dynamic Change: Western Settlement and Eastern Capitalism, 1790–1820

Indian Cessions and State Formation, to 1840   *223*

Regional Cultures Move West, 1790–1820   *226*

Land Division in the Northwest Territory   *232*

U.S. Population Density in 1803 and the Louisiana
  Purchase   *234*

* The War of 1812   *238*

Defining the National Boundaries, 1800–1820   *240*

Chapter 9

The Quest for a Republican Society, 1790–1820

The Expansion of Voting Rights for
  White Men, 1800–1830   *254*

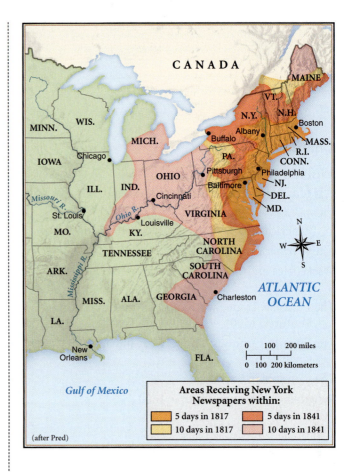

Distribution of the Slave Population
  in 1790, 1830, and 1860   *265*

The Missouri Compromise, 1820–1821   *272*

* The Second Great Awakening, 1790–1860   *275*

Chapter 10

The Economic Revolution, 1820–1860

New England's Dominance in Cotton
  Spinning, 1840   *288*

Western Land Sales, 1830–1839 and 1850–1862   *297*

The Transportation Revolution: Roads and Canals,
  1820–1850   *298*

The Speed of News in 1817 and 1841   *300*

* Railroads of the North and South, 1850–1860   *301*

The Nation's Major Cities in 1840   *302*

Chapter 11

A Democratic Revolution, 1820–1844

Presidential Election of 1824   *318*

Presidential Election of 1828   *321*

The Removal of Native Americans, 1820–1843   *327*

⋆ Anatomy of a Panic: Bank Suspensions in
    May 1837   *334*

Chapter 12

Religion and Reform, 1820–1860

Major Communal Experiments before 1860   *346*

The Mormon Trek, 1830–1848   *350*

⋆ The Underground Railroad in the 1850s   *356*

Women and Antislavery, 1837–1838   *359*

Chapter 13

The Crisis of the Union, 1844–1860

American Settlements in Texas, 1821–1836   *371*

Territorial Conflict in Oregon, 1819–1846   *373*

Routes to the West, 1835–1860   *374*

The Mexican War, 1846–1848   *378*

⋆ The Mexican Cession, 1848–1853   *382*

The California Gold Rush, 1849–1857   *385*

The Compromise of 1850 and the
    Kansas-Nebraska Act of 1854   *386*

Political Realignment, 1848–1860   *392*

Chapter 14

Two Societies at War, 1861–1865

⋆ The Process of Secession, 1860–1861   *399*

⋆ The Eastern Campaigns of 1862   *404*

The Western Campaigns, 1861–1862   *406*

Lee Invades the North, 1863   *417*

The Closing Virginia Campaign, 1864–1865   *421*

Sherman's March through the Confederacy,
    1864–1865   *425*

The Conquest of the South, 1861–1865   *426*

Chapter 15

Reconstruction, 1865–1877

Reconstruction   *437*

⋆ The Barrow Plantation, 1860 and 1881   *444*

Chapter 16

The American West

The Natural Environment of the West, 1860s   *458*

Western Trunk Lines, 1887   *461*

⋆ The Rural Ethnic Mosaic: Blue Earth County,
    Minnesota, 1880   *467*

The Indian Frontier, to 1890   *470*

The Sioux Reservations in South Dakota,
    1868–1889   *471*

The Mining Frontier, 1848–1890   *474*

The Settlement of the Pacific Slope, 1860–1890   *477*

Chapter 17

Capital and Labor in the Age of Enterprise, 1877–1900

Iron and Steel Production, 1900   *487*

The Expansion of the Railroad
    System, 1870–1890   *490*

The Dressed Meat Industry, 1900   *494*

The New South, 1900   *496*

Chapter 18

The Politics of Late-Nineteenth-Century America

Presidential Elections of 1880, 1884, and 1888   *517*

⋆ The Diffusion of the Australian Ballot   *524*

Disfranchisement in the New South   *529*

The Heyday of Western Populism, 1892   *537*

Presidential Elections of 1892 and 1896   *540*

Chapter 19

The Rise of the City

America's Cities, 1900   *545*

⋆ The Expansion of Chicago, 1865–1902   *547*

Sources of European Immigration to the
    United States, 1871–1910   *558*

The Lower East Side, New York City, 1900   *559*

Chapter 20

The Progressive Era

⋆ Woman Suffrage, 1890–1919   *582*

National Parks and Forests, 1872–1980   *592*

Presidential Election of 1912   *598*

Chapter 21

An Emerging World Power, 1877–1914

The Spanish-American War of 1898   *617*

The American Empire, 1917   *622*

The Panama Canal: The Design   *626*

Policeman of the Caribbean   *626*

The Great Powers in East Asia, 1898–1910   *627*

> **THINKING ABOUT HISTORY:**
> Population Losses: The American Plains, 1990–2000   *632*

Chapter 22

War and the American State, 1914–1920

* European Alliances in 1914   *638*

U.S. Participation on the Western Front, 1918   *644*

The Great Migration and Beyond   *650*

Prohibition on the Eve of the Eighteenth Amendment, 1919   *654*

Europe after World War I   *659*

Chapter 23

Modern Times, The 1920s

The Shift from Rural to Urban Population, 1920–1930   *681*

Ku Klux Klan Politics and Violence in the 1920s   *685*

Presidential Election of 1928   *692*

Chapter 24

The Great Depression

The Great Depression: Families on Relief, to 1933   *702*

The Spread of Radio, to 1939   *707*

The Dust Bowl, 1930–1941   *710*

Presidential Election of 1932   *718*

Chapter 25

The New Deal, 1933–1939

* Public Works in the New Deal: The PWA in Action, 1933–1939   *730*

* Popular Protest in the Great Depression, 1933–1939   *734*

* Eleanor Roosevelt's Travels, 1936–1937   *738*

The Tennessee Valley Authority, 1933–1952   *741*

Chapter 26

The World at War, 1939–1945

* World War II in the North Atlantic, 1939–1943   *752*

Japanese Relocation Camps   *766*

World War II in Europe, 1941–1943   *768*

World War II in Europe, 1944–1945   *769*

World War II in the Pacific, 1941–1942   *772*

World War II in the Pacific, 1943–1945   *773*

Chapter 27

Cold War America, 1945–1960

Cold War in Europe, 1955   *788*

* The Korean War, 1950–1953   *793*

American Global Defense Treaties in the Cold War Era   *795*

Presidential Election of 1948   *798*

Atmospheric Nuclear Weapons Testing in the Pacific and at Home, 1945–1962   *808*

The Military-Industrial Complex in Los Angeles   *812*

Chapter 28

The Affluent Society and the Liberal Consensus, 1945–1965

Metropolitan Growth, 1950–1980   *819*

Connecting the Nation: The Interstate Highway System, 1930 and 1970   *820*

Presidential Election of 1960   *831*

Decolonization and the Third World, 1943–1990   *833*

The United States and Cuba, 1961–1962   *834*

* The Civil Rights Movement, 1954–1965   *836*

Population Growth 1940–2000
- Over 200 percent
- 101–200 percent
- 51–100 percent
- 26–50 percent
- 25 percent or less

Black Voter Registration in the South, 1964 and 1975   *843*

Presidential Election of 1964   *843*

Chapter 29

War Abroad and at Home: The Vietnam Era, 1961–1975

The Vietnam War, 1954–1975   *851*

Racial Unrest in America's Cities, 1965–1968   *862*

Presidential Election of 1968   *869*

Chapter 30

The Lean Years, 1969–1980

From Rust Belt to Sun Belt, 1940–2000   *886*

States Ratifying the Equal Rights Amendment, 1972–1977   *893*

American Indian Reservations   *896*

Presidential Election of 1980   *903*

Chapter 31

A New Domestic and World Order, 1981–2001

∗ U.S. Involvement in Latin America and the Caribbean, 1954–2000   *913*

The Collapse of Communism in Eastern Europe and the Soviet Union, 1989–1991   *914*

U.S. Involvement in the Middle East, 1980–2002   *916*

Latino Population and Asian Population, 2000   *921*

Presidential Election of 1992   *928*

Ethnic Conflict in the Balkans: The Breakup of Yugoslavia, 1991–1992   *932*

Presidential Election of 2000   *934*

FIGURES AND TABLES

Figures

The Yearly Rhythm of Rural Life and Death   16

The Great Price Inflation and Living Standards in Europe   34

The Structure of English Society, 1688   35

The Growth of Slavery in South Carolina   85

Wealth Inequality in the Northern Cities   94

Family Connections and Political Power   94

Population Growth, Wheat Prices, and Imports from Britain in the Middle Colonies   105

Increasing Social Inequality in Chester County, Pennsylvania   107

Church Growth by Denomination, 1700–1780   119

Colonial Population, Imports from Britain, and the American Trade Deficit   127

The Growing Power of the British State   137

Trade as a Political Weapon, 1763–1776   149

> THINKING ABOUT HISTORY:
> Percentage of Population of African Ancestry, 1640–1790   160

Middling Men Enter the Halls of Government, 1765–1790   195

Hamilton's Fiscal Structure, 1792   211

Movement of Slaves from Upper South to Lower South, 1790–1860   263

Changes in Voting Patterns, 1824–1840   320

The Surge in Immigration, 1842–1855   338

Environment and Health: Heights of Native-born Men, by Year of Birth   343

The Surge in Cotton Production, 1835–1860   368

Economies, North and South, 1860   409

Freight Rates for Transporting Nebraska Crops   469

Business Activity and Wholesale Prices, 1869–1913   486

Changes in the Labor Force, 1870–1910   498

American Immigration, 1870–1914   499

Ethnocultural Voting Patterns in the Midwest, 1870–1892   521

Distributions of Weekly Wages for Black and White Workers in Virginia, 1907   535

Floor Plan of a Dumbbell Tenement   549

The Federal Bureaucracy, 1890–1917   600

Balance of U.S. Imports, 1870–1914   607

American Immigration after World War I   684

Statistics of the Depression   698

Unemployment, 1915–1945   699

Government Spending as a Percentage of GDP   755

National Defense Spending, 1940–1965   807

Labor Union Strength, 1900–1997   817

Gross Domestic Product, 1930–1972   817

The Declining American Birthrate, 1860–1980   823

Legal Immigration to the United States by Region, 1931–1984   828

Americans in Poverty, 1959–2000   845

U.S. Troops in Vietnam, 1960–1973   854

U.S. Energy Consumption, 1900–2000   885

The Inflation Rate, 1960–2000   885

The Escalating Federal Debt, 1939–2000   910

Productivity and Wages, 1982–1995   917

Tables

Important Native American Cultures   6

Spanish Monarchs, 1474–1598   29

European Colonies in North America before 1660   40

Environment, Disease, and Death in Virginia, 1618–1624   51

Indentured Servants in the Chesapeake Labor Force   54

English Colonies Created in North America, 1660–1750   70

Navigation Acts, 1651–1751   72

English Wars, 1650–1750   75

Slave Imports in the Americas, 1520–1810   77

African Slaves Imported into North America, by Ethnicity, 1700–1775   85

Estimated European Migration to the British Mainland
Colonies, 1700–1780   *107*

Colonial Colleges   *119*

Ministerial Instability in Britain   *144*

Patriot Resistance, 1762–1775   *155*

Major Acts Involving Land Sales of National Domain,
1785–1862   *231*

Major Decisions of the Marshall Court   *246*

Number of Lawyers in Three Selected States,
to 1820   *253*

African Slaves Imported into North America by
Ethnicity, 1776–1809   *265*

Number of Church Congregations by Denomination,
1780 and 1860   *273*

Leading Branches of Manufacture, 1860   *287*

Government Investment in Canals in Three
States   *299*

Slavery and Secession   *401*

The Cost of the War: Union Finances, 1860 and
1864   *412*

Primary Reconstruction Laws and Constitutional
Amendments   *438*

Ten Largest Cities by Population, 1870 and
1900   *544*

High School Graduates, 1870–1910   *557*

Newspaper Circulation   *569*

Progressive Legislation and Supreme Court
Decisions   *578*

Exports to Canada and Europe Compared with
Exports to Asia and Latin America,
1875–1900   *607*

American Banks and Bank Failures, 1920–1940   *724*

Major New Deal Legislation   *731*

Major Great Society Legislation   *841*

SPECIAL FEATURES

American Lives

Cortés and Malinche: The Dynamics of
   Conquest   *30*

Luis de Velasco/Opechancanough/Massatamohtnock:
   A Case of Possible Multiple Identities   *42*

From a Piece of Property to a Man of Property: The
   Odyssey of Robert Pearle   *82*

Jonathan Edwards: Preacher, Philosopher,
   Pastor   *116*

George R. T. Hewes and the Meaning of the
   Revolution   *152*

The Enigma of Benedict Arnold   *180*

Gouverneur Morris: An Elitist Liberal in a
   Republican Age   *206*

Tenskwatawa: Shawnee Prophet   *236*

Richard Allen and African American Identity   *270*

Eli Whitney: Machine Builder and Promoter   *294*

Frances Wright: Radical Reformer   *336*

Dorothea Dix: Public Woman   *360*

Frederick Douglass: Development of an
   Abolitionist   *380*

William Tecumseh Sherman: An Architect of Modern
   War   *422*

Nathan Bedford Forrest: Defender of Southern
   Honor   *446*

Buffalo Bill and the Mythic West   *462*

Jay Gould: Robber Baron?   *492*

Robert Charles: Black Militant   *532*

Big Tim Sullivan: Tammany Politician   *564*

Frances Kellor: Woman Progressive   *580*

William Randolph Hearst: Jingo   *614*

George Creel: Holding Fast the Inner Lines   *656*

Clara Bow: The "It" Girl   *678*

Bert Corona and the Mexican American
   Generation   *712*

Mary McLeod Bethune: Black Braintruster   *736*

Henry J. Kaiser: World War II's "Miracle Man"   *756*

George F. Kennan: Architect of Containment   *786*

Elvis Presley: Teen Idol of the 1950s   *826*

John Paul Vann: Dissident Patriot   *874*

Lois Marie Gibbs: Environmental Activist   *890*

Bill Gates: Microsoft's Leader in the Computer
   Revolution   *922*

American Voices

A Navajo Emergence Story   *7*

Friar Bernardino de Sahagún: Aztec Elders Describe
   the Spanish Conquest   *26*

Richard Frethorne: Hard Times in Early
   Virginia   *53*

Mary Rowlandson: A Captivity Narrative   *64*

Philip Fithian: Sadism under Slavery   *89*

Captain Fayrer Hall: The Impact of the Molasses
   Act   *96*

Gottlieb Mittelberger: The Perils of Migration   *109*

Nathan Cole: The Power of a Preacher   *118*

Samuel Adams: An American View of the Stamp
   Act   *141*

Anonymous Broadside, May 18, 1775: "To the
   Associators of the City of Philadelphia"   *156*

John Adams: Making Peace with Stubborn Enemies
   and Crafty Allies   *183*

Benjamin Banneker: On Jefferson and Natural
   Rights   *188*

Abigail and John Adams: The Status of Women   *197*

Robert Yates and John Lansing: A Protest against the
   Philadelphia Convention   *203*

Red Jacket: A Seneca Chief's Understanding of
   Religion   *224*

Noah M. Ludlow: Traveling to Kentucky, 1815   *229*

Lydia Maria Child: Raising Middle-Class
   Children   *259*

Jacob Stroyer: A Child Learns the Meaning of
   Slavery   *267*

Lucy Larcom: Early Days at Lowell   *291*

John Gough: The Vice of Intemperance   *310*

Margaret Bayard Smith: Republican Majesty and
   Mobs   *322*

Black Hawk: A Sacred Reverence for Our Lands   *329*

An Illinois "Jeffersonian" Attacks the Mormons   *351*

Keziah Kendall: A Farm Woman Defends the Grimké Sisters   *363*

Mary Boykin Chesnut: A Slaveholding Woman's Diary   *370*

Axalla John Hoole: "Bleeding Kansas": A Southern View   *390*

Elizabeth Mary Meade Ingraham: A Vicksburg Diary   *416*

Spotswood Rice: Freeing My Children from Slavery   *419*

Jourdon Anderson: Relishing Freedom   *434*

Harriet Hernandes: The Intimidation of Black Voters   *448*

Ida Lindgren: Swedish Emigrant in Frontier Kansas   *466*

Zitkala-Ša (Gertrude Simmons Bonnin): Becoming White   *473*

John Brophy: A Miner's Son   *504*

Rose Schneiderman: Trade Unionist   *509*

Helen Potter: The Case for Women's Political Rights   *527*

Tom Watson: The Case for Interracial Unity   *528*

M. Carey Thomas: "We Did Not Know . . . Whether Women's Health Could Stand the Strain of College Education"   *555*

Anonymous: Bintel Brief   *561*

Charles Edward Russell: Muckraking   *576*

Dr. Alice Hamilton: Tracking Down Lead Poisoning   *588*

George W. Prioleau: Black Soldiers in a White Man's War   *619*

Daniel J. Evans and Seiward J. Norton: Fighting the Filipinos   *621*

Harry Curtin: Trench Warfare   *641*

Southern Migrants   *652*

Women Write the Children's Bureau   *669*

Kazuo Kawai: A Foreigner in America   *686*

Larry Van Dusen: A Working-Class Family Encounters the Great Depression   *703*

Public Assistance Fails a Southern Farm Family   *716*

Joe Marcus: A New Deal Activist   *723*

Susana Archuleta: A Chicana Youth Gets New Deal Work   *739*

Monica Sone: Japanese Relocation   *767*

Anton Bilek: The War in the Pacific   *774*

Mark Goodson: Red Hunting on the Quiz Shows; or, What's My Party Line?   *802*

Isaac Nelson: Atomic Witness   *809*

A Woman Encounters the Feminine Mystique   *824*

Anne Moody: We Would Like to Be Served   *837*

Dave Cline: A Vietnam Vet Remembers   *855*

Mary Crow Dog: The Trail of Broken Treaties   *864*

David Kopay: The Real Score: A Gay Athlete Comes Out   *895*

Phyllis Ellison: Busing in Boston   *897*

Laurie Ouellette: A Third-Wave Feminist   *926*

John Lewis: We Marched to Be Counted   *935*

Voices from Abroad

Father le Petite: The Customs of the Natchez   *13*

Samuel de Champlain: Going to War with the Hurons   *45*

Olaudah Equiano: The Brutal "Middle Passage"   *81*

Louis Antonine De Bougainville: The Defense of Canada   *126*

Lieutenant Colonel Francis Smith: A British View of Lexington and Concord   *158*

Thomas Paine: Common Sense   *168*

William Cobbett: Peter Porcupine Attacks Pro-French Americans   *217*

Alexis de Tocqueville: Law and Lawyers in the United States   *248*

Frances Trollope: A Camp Meeting in Indiana   *276*

Frances Trollope: American Workers and Their Wives   *307*

Alexis de Tocqueville: Parties in the United States   *325*

Charles Dickens Assails the Shakers   *348*

Colonel José Enrique de la Peña: A Mexican View of the Battle of the Alamo   *372*

Ernest Duveyier de Hauranne: German Immigrants and the Civil War within Missouri   *402*

David Macrae: The Devastated South   *432*

Baron Joseph Alexander von Hübner: A Western Boom Town   *476*

Count Vay de Vaya und Luskod: Pittsburgh Inferno   *503*

Ernst Below: Beer and German American Politics   *522*

José Martí: Coney Island, 1881   *567*

James Bryce: America in 1905: "Business Is King"   594

Jean Hess, Émile Zola, and Ruben Dario: American Goliath   624

A German Propaganda Appeal to Black Soldiers   648

The Ford Miracle: "Slaves" to the Assembly Line   671

Mary Agnes Hamilton: Breadlines and Beggars   700

Odette Keun: A Foreigner Looks at the Tennessee Valley Authority   742

German POWs: American Race Relations   761

Jean Monnet: Truman's Generous Proposal   790

Hanoch Bartov: Everyone Has a Car   821

Che Guevara: Vietnam and the World Freedom Struggle   859

Fei Xiaotong: America's Crisis of Faith   900

Saddam Hussein: Calling for a Holy War against the United States   915

New Technology

Indian Women and Agriculture   14

Rice: Riches, Wretchedness, and Community   86

Machine Technology and Republican Values   214

Women's Health and Fertility: From Folk Remedies to Pharmacies   256

Cotton Spinning: From Spinsters to Machines   289

The Rifle-Musket   410

Iron and Steel   488

The Battleship   610

Aviation   682

Rural Electrification   744

The Computer Revolution   810

The Biotech Revolution   918

JAMES A. HENRETTA is Priscilla Alden Burke Professor of American History at the University of Maryland, College Park. He received his undergraduate education at Swarthmore College and his Ph.D. from Harvard University. He has taught at the University of Sussex, England; Princeton University; UCLA; Boston University; as a Fulbright lecturer in Australia at the University of New England; and at Oxford University as the Harmsworth Professor of American History. His publications include *The Evolution of American Society, 1700–1815: An Interdisciplinary Analysis; "Salutary Neglect": Colonial Administration under the Duke of Newcastle; Evolution and Revolution: American Society, 1600–1820;* and *The Origins of American Capitalism.* Recently he coedited and contributed to a collection of original essays, *Republicanism and Liberalism in America and the German States, 1750–1850,* as part of his larger research project on "The Liberal State in America: New York, 1820–1975." In 2002–2003, he held the John Hope Franklin Fellowship at the National Humanities Center in North Carolina.

DAVID BRODY is Professor Emeritus of History at the University of California, Davis. He received his B.A., M.A., and Ph.D. from Harvard University. He has taught at the University of Warwick in England, at Moscow State University in the former Soviet Union, and at Sydney University in Australia. He is the author of *Steelworkers in America; Workers in Industrial America: Essays on the 20th Century Struggle;* and *In Labor's Cause: Main Themes on the History of the American Worker.* He has been awarded fellowships from the Social Science Research Council, the Guggenheim Foundation, and the National Endowment for the Humanities. He is past president (1991–1992) of the Pacific Coast branch of the American Historical Association. His current research is on labor law and workplace regimes during the Great Depression.

LYNN DUMENIL is Robert Glass Cleland Professor of American History at Occidental College in Los Angeles. She is a graduate of the University of Southern California and received her Ph.D. from the University of California, Berkeley. She has written *The Modern Temper: American Culture and Society in the 1920s* and *Freemasonry and American Culture: 1880–1930.* Her articles and reviews have appeared in the *Journal of American History;* the *Journal of American Ethnic History: Reviews in American History;* and the *American Historical Review.* She has been a historical consultant to several documentary film projects and is on the Pelzer Prize Committee of the Organization of American Historians. Her current work, for which she received a National Endowment for the Humanities Fellowship, is on World War I, citizenship, and the state. In 2001–2002 she was the Bicentennial Fulbright Chair in American Studies at the University of Helsinki.

SUSAN WARE specializes in twentieth-century U.S. history and the history of American women. She is affiliated with the Radcliffe Institute for Advanced Study, Harvard University, where she is editing the next volume of the noted biographical dictionary *Notable American Women.* Ware received her undergraduate degree from Wellesley College and her Ph.D. from Harvard University and from 1986 to 1995 taught in the history department at New York University. Her publications include *Beyond Suffrage: Women in the New Deal; Holding Their Own: American Women in the 1930s; Partner and I: Molly Dewson, Feminism, and New Deal Politics; Modern American Women: A Documentary History; Still Missing: Amelia Earhart and the Search for Modern Feminism;* and *Letter to the World: Seven Women Who Shaped the American Century.* She has served on the national advisory boards of the Franklin and Eleanor Roosevelt Institute and the Schlesinger Library at Radcliffe and has been a historical consultant to numerous documentary film projects. Her most recent project is a biography of radio talk show pioneer Mary Margaret McBride.

America's History

The Creation of American Society

1450–1775

ECONOMY	SOCIETY	GOVERNMENT	RELIGION	CULTURE
From Staple Crops to Internal Growth	Ethnic, Racial, and Class Divisions	From Monarchy to Republic	From Hierarchy to Pluralism	The Creation of American Identity
1450 ▶ Native American subsistence economy Europeans fish off North American coast	▶ Sporadic warfare among Indian peoples Spanish conquest of Mexico (1519–1521)	▶ Rise of monarchical nation-states in Europe	▶ Protestant Reformation begins (1517)	▶ Diverse Native American cultures in eastern woodlands
1600 ▶ First staple export crops: furs and tobacco	▶ English-Indian warfare African servitude begins in Virginia (1619)	▶ James I claims divine right to rule England Virginia House of Burgesses (1619)	▶ Persecuted English Puritans and Catholics migrate to America	▶ Puritans implant Calvinism, education, and freehold ideal
1640 ▶ New England trade with sugar islands Mercantilist regulations: first Navigation Act (1651)	▶ White indentured servitude in Chesapeake Indians retreat inland	▶ Puritan Revolution Stuart restoration (1660) Bacon's Rebellion in Virginia (1675)	▶ Religious liberty in Rhode Island	▶ Aristocratic aspirations in the Chesapeake
1680 ▶ Tobacco trade stagnates Rice cultivation expands	▶ Indian slavery in the Carolinas Ethnic rebellion in New York (1689)	▶ Dominion of New England (1686–1689) Glorious Revolution ousts James II (1688–1689)	▶ Rise of toleration	▶ Emergence of African American language and culture
1720 ▶ Mature yeoman farm economy in North Imports from Britain increase	▶ Scots-Irish and German migration Growing rural inequality	▶ Rise of the colonial representative assemblies Challenge to "deferential" politics	▶ German and Scots-Irish Pietists in Middle Atlantic region Great Awakening	▶ Expansion of colleges, newspapers, and magazines Franklin and the American Enlightenment
1760 ▶ Trade boycotts encourage domestic manufacturing	▶ Uprisings by tenants and backcountry farmers Artisan protests	▶ Ideas of popular sovereignty Battles of Lexington and Concord (1775)	▶ Evangelical Baptists in Virginia Quebec Act allows Catholicism (1774)	▶ First signs of an American identity Republican innovations in political theory

Societies are made, not born. They are the creation of decades, even centuries, of human endeavor and experience. The first American societies were formed by hunting and gathering peoples who migrated to the Western Hemisphere from Asia many centuries ago. Over many generations these migrants—the Native Americans—came to live in a wide variety of environments and cultures. In much of North America they developed kinship-based societies that relied on farming and hunting. But in the lower Mississippi Valley, Native Americans developed a hierarchical social order similar to that of the great civilizations of the Aztecs, Mayas, and Incas of Mesoamerica. The coming of Europeans and their diseases tore the fabric of most Native American cultures into shreds. Native Americans increasingly confronted a new American society, one dominated by men and women of European origins.

The Europeans who settled America sought to transplant their traditional societies to the New World—their farming practices, their social hierarchies, their culture and heritage, and their religious ideas. But in learning to live in the new land, the Europeans who came to England's North American colonies eventually created societies that were distinctly different from those of their homelands in their economies, social character, political systems, religion, and culture.

ECONOMY Many European settlements were very successful in economic terms. Traditional Europe was made up of poor, overcrowded, and unequal societies that periodically suffered devastating famines. But with few people and a bountiful natural environment, the settlers in North America replaced poverty with plenty, creating a bustling economy and, in the northern mainland colonies, prosperous communities of independent farm families. Indeed, this region became know as "the best poor man's country" for migrants from the British Isles and Germany.

SOCIETY However, some of the European settlements became places of oppressive captivity for Africans. Aided by African slave traders, Europeans transported hundreds of thousands of workers, from many African regions, to the West Indies and the southern mainland colonies and forced them to labor as slaves on sugar, tobacco, and rice plantations. Slowly and with great effort, they and their descendants created an African American culture within a social order dominated by Europeans.

GOVERNMENT In the meantime, whites in the emerging American societies created an increasingly free and competitive political system. The first English settlers transplanted authoritarian institutions to America, and the English government continued to manage their lives. But after 1689 traditional controls gradually gave way to governments based in part on representative assemblies. Eventually, the growth of self-rule would lead to demands for political independence from England.

RELIGION The American experience profoundly changed religious institutions and values. Many migrants left Europe because of the conflicts of the Protestant Reformation and came to America seeking to practice their religion without interference. The societies they created became increasingly religious, especially after the evangelical revivals of the 1740s. By this time many Americans had rejected the harshest tenets of Calvinism (a strict Protestant faith), and others had embraced the rationalist view of the European Enlightenment. As a result, American Protestant Christianity became increasingly tolerant, democratic, and optimistic.

CULTURE The new American society witnessed the appearance of new forms of family and community life. The first English settlers lived in patriarchal families ruled by dominant fathers and in communities controlled by men of high status. By 1750, however, many American fathers no longer strictly managed their children's lives. As these communities became more diverse and open, many men and some women began to enjoy greater personal independence. This new American society was increasingly pluralistic, composed of migrants from many European ethnic groups—English, Scots, Scots-Irish, Dutch, and Germans—as well as enslaved West Africans and many different Native American peoples. Distinct regional cultures developed in New England, the Middle Atlantic colonies, and the Chesapeake and Carolina areas. Consequently, an overarching American identity based on the English language, British legal and political institutions, and shared experiences emerged very slowly.

The story of the colonial experience is thus both tragic and exciting. The settlers created a new American world but one that warred with Native Americans and condemned most African Americans to bondage even as it offered Europeans rich opportunities for economic security, political freedom, and spiritual fulfillment.

CHAPTER 1

Worlds Collide: Europe, Africa, and America

1450–1620

Native American Worlds
The First Americans
The Mayas and the Aztecs
The Indians of the North

Traditional European Society in 1450
The Peasantry
Hierarchy and Authority
The Power of Religion

Europe Encounters Africa and the Americas, 1450–1550
The Renaissance
West African Society and Slavery
Europe Reaches the Americas
The Spanish Conquest

The Protestant Reformation and the Rise of England
The Protestant Movement
The Dutch and the English Challenge Spain
The Social Causes of English Colonization

"**B**EFORE THE FRENCH CAME AMONG US**,**" an elder of the Natchez people of Mississippi exclaimed, "we were men . . . and we walked with boldness every road, but now we walk like slaves, which we shall soon be, since the French already treat us . . . as they do their black slaves." Before the 1490s the Indian peoples of the Western Hemisphere knew absolutely nothing about the light-skinned inhabitants of Europe and the dark-complexioned peoples of Africa. However, Europeans hungry for the trade and riches of Asia had already sailed along the west coast of Africa and were deeply involved in the long-established trade in African slaves. When Christopher Columbus, another European searching for a sea route to Asia, encountered the lands and peoples of the Americas, the destinies of four continents quickly became intertwined. On his second voyage to the Western Hemisphere, Columbus carried a cargo of enslaved Africans, beginning the centuries-long process that created a multitude of triracial societies in the Americas.

◀ **Orbis Typus Universalis**

This map of 1507, drawn by the German cartographer Martin Waldseemüller, is one of the first to use "America" as the name of the western continents. Only the northwestern area of present-day Brazil and a few (mislocated) Caribbean islands appear on Waldseemüller's map. Europeans had not yet comprehended the size and shape of the New World.
John Carter Brown Library, Brown University.

As the Natchez elder knew well, the resulting mixture of peoples from the far-flung continents was based not on equality but on exploitation. By the time he urged his people to resist the invaders, the Europeans were too numerous and too well positioned to be dislodged. The French and their Indian allies killed hundreds of those who joined the Natchez uprising and sold many of the survivors into slavery on the sugar plantations of the West Indies.

The fate of the Natchez was hardly unique. Over the course of the three centuries following Columbus's voyage, many Native American peoples came under the domination of the various Europeans—Spanish, Portuguese, French, English, Dutch—who colonized the Western Hemisphere and imported enslaved Africans to work on agricultural plantations. In the new societies—new to all their inhabitants—race became a prime determinant of people's status and lives. How did this happen? How did Europeans become leaders in world trade and extend their influence across the Atlantic? What was the character of the Native Americans' life and culture, and what made their societies vulnerable to conquest by European adventurers? And what led to the transatlantic trade in African slaves? In the answers to these questions lie the origins of the United States and, beyond that, the dominant position of people of European descent in the modern world.

Native American Worlds

When the Europeans arrived, the great majority of Native Americans—about 40 million—lived in Mesoamerica (present-day Mexico and Guatemala), and another 15 million resided in lands to the north (present-day United States and Canada). Some lived in simple hunter-gatherer or agricultural communities governed by kin ties, but the majority resided in societies ruled by warrior-kings and priests. In Mesoamerica and Peru, Indian peoples created

civilizations whose art, religion, society, and economy were as complex as those of Europe and the Mediterranean (Table 1.1).

The First Americans

According to the elders of the Navajo people, history began when their ancestors emerged from under the earth (see American Voices, "A Navajo Emergence Story," p. 7); for the Iroquois, the story of their Five Nations began when people fell from the sky. However, most twenty-first-century anthropologists and historians believe that the first people to live in the Western Hemisphere were migrants from Asia. Some migrants came by water, but most probably came by land. Strong archaeological and genetic evidence suggests that late in the last Ice Age, which lasted from 25,000 B.C. until 11,000 B.C., small bands of hunters—residents of Siberia—followed herds of game across a hundred-mile-wide land bridge between Siberia and Alaska. An oral history of the Tuscarora Indians, who lived in present-day North Carolina, tells of a famine in the old world and a journey over ice toward where "the sun rises," a trek that brought their ancestors to a lush forest with abundant food and game.

Most anthropologists believe that the main migratory stream from Asia lasted from about 13,000 B.C. to 11,000 B.C., until the glaciers melted and the rising ocean waters submerged the land bridge and created the

TABLE 1.1 Important Native American Cultures						
	Mesoamerica		Andes		North America	
Time Period	Coastal Lowlands	Highlands	Coastal Lowlands	Highlands	Southwest	Mississippi & Ohio Valleys
Pre–Classic Era 900 B.C.–A.D. 300	Olmec			Chavin		Hopewell
Classic Era A.D. 300–900	Mayan (Tikal)	Teotihuacán	Mochica	Tiwanaku	Mogollon Hohokam Anasazi	
Post–Classic Era A.D. 900–1500	Mayan (Chichén Itzá)	Toltec Aztec	Nazca	Inca (Cuzco)		Mississippian (Cahokia)

The Olmec were the "mother culture" to the Mayans and the Teotihuacáns, and the Chavin to the Mochica and Tiwanaku, influencing subsequent cultures in both the coastal lowlands and the highlands of the Classic and post–Classic Eras. These subsequent cultures drew additional influences from the surrounding Native American groups.

A Navajo Emergence Story

Every culture has a story—part factual, part mythical—that expresses the meaning of its past. This story was told to Sandoval, whose Navajo name was Hastin Tlo'tsi hee, by his grandmother, herself the descendant of a long line of medicine women. It locates the homeland of the Navajo people in the Plateau country of northwestern Arizona near Abalone Shell Mountain (San Francisco Peak), where the tribe apparently settled sometime between A.D. 1200 and 1500.

Here are the stories of the Four Worlds that had no sun, and of the Fifth, the world we live in. . . . The First World, Ni'hodilquil, was black as black wool. It had four corners and over these appeared four clouds. These four clouds contained within themselves the elements of the First World. They were in color, black, white, blue, and yellow.

The Black Cloud represented the Female Being or Substance. For as a child sleeps when being nursed, so life slept in the darkness of the Female Being. The white Cloud represented the Male Being or Substance. He was the Dawn, the Light-Which-Awakens, of the First World.

In the East, at the place where the Black Cloud and the White Cloud met, First Man, Atse'hastqin, was formed; and with him was formed the white corn, perfect in shape, with kernels covering the whole ear. . . . The First World was small in size, a floating island in mist or water. On it there grew one tree, a pine tree, which was later brought to the present world for firewood. . . . The creatures of the First World are thought of as the Mist People; they had no definite form, but were to change to men, beasts, birds, and reptiles of this world.

Now on the western side of the First World, in a place that later was to become the Land of Sunset, there appeared the Blue Cloud, and opposite it there appeared the Yellow Cloud. Where they came together, First Woman was formed, and with her the yellow corn. This ear of corn was also perfect. With First Woman there came the white shell and the turquoise and the yucca. . . .

Because of the strife in the First World, First Man, First Woman . . . climbed up from the world of Darkness and Dampness to the Second or Blue World. They found a number of people already living there: blue birds, blue hawks, blue jays, blue herons, and all the blue-feathered beings. The powerful swallow people lived there also, and these people made the Second World unpleasant. . . . There was fighting and killing. . . .

The bluebird was the first to reach the Third or Yellow World. After him came . . . all the others. There were six mountains in the Third World. . . . In the West . . . Dichi'li dzil, the Abalone Shell Mountain. . . .

[After climbing to the Fourth World, which was filled with other animals] First Man and his people saw four dark clouds and four white clouds pass, and then they sent the badger up the reed. This time when the badger returned he said he had come out on solid earth. So First Man and First Woman led the people to the Fifth World, which some call the Many Colored Earth and some the Changeable Earth. They emerged through a lake [said to be near Pagosa Springs, Colorado] surrounded by four mountains. The water bubbles in this lake when anyone goes near. . . .

Some medicine men tell us that there are two worlds above us, the first is the World of the Spirits of Living Things, the second is the Place of Melting into One.

Source: Aileen O'Bryan, "The Diné: Origin Myths of the Navaho Indians," *Bureau of American Ethnology*, Bulletin 163 (Washington, D.C.: U.S. Government Printing Office, 1956), 1–13.

Bering Strait. A second movement of peoples around 6000 B.C., now traveling by water across the narrow strait, brought the ancestors of the Navajo and the Apaches to North America, while a third migration around 3000 B.C. introduced the forebears of the Aleut and Inuit peoples—the "Eskimos." Subsequently, the people of the Western Hemisphere, who by that time had moved as far south as the tip of South America and as far east as the Atlantic coast of North America, were largely cut off from the rest of the world for three hundred generations (Map 1.1).

For many centuries the first Americans lived as hunter-gatherers, subsisting on the abundant vegetation and wildlife. Over time, many of the larger species of animals—mammoths, giant beaver, and horses—died out, victims of overhunting and climatic change; their demise forced hunters to become adept at killing more elusive and faster rabbits, deer, and elk. About

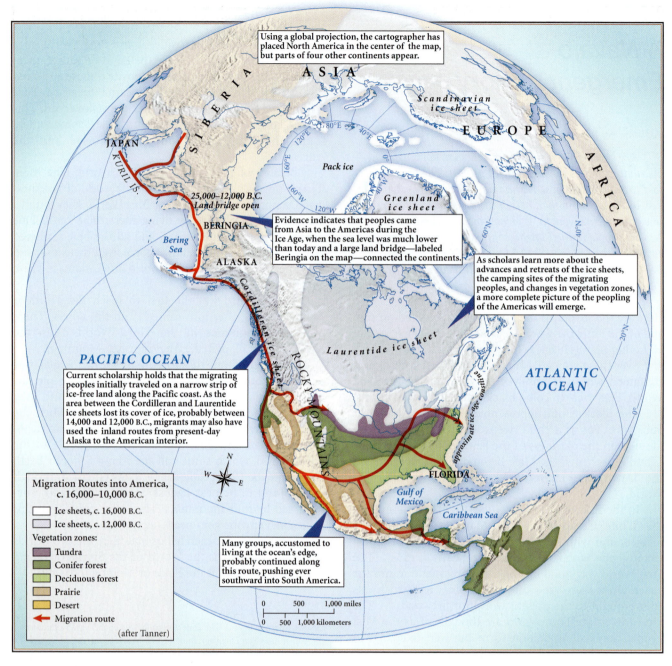

Using a global projection, the cartographer has placed North America in the center of the map, but parts of four other continents appear.

Scandinavian ice sheet

EUROPE

AFRICA

Pack ice

Greenland ice sheet

25,000–12,000 B.C. Land bridge open

BERINGIA

Bering Sea

ALASKA

Evidence indicates that peoples came from Asia to the Americas during the Ice Age, when the sea level was much lower than today and a large land bridge—labeled Beringia on the map—connected the continents.

As scholars learn more about the advances and retreats of the ice sheets, the camping sites of the migrating peoples, and changes in vegetation zones, a more complete picture of the peopling of the Americas will emerge.

JAPAN

KURIL IS.

SIBERIA

ASIA

Cordilleran ice sheet

Laurentide ice sheet

ROCKY MOUNTAINS

approximate ice-age coastline

PACIFIC OCEAN

ATLANTIC OCEAN

Current scholarship holds that the migrating peoples initially traveled on a narrow strip of ice-free land along the Pacific coast. As the area between the Cordilleran and Laurentide ice sheets lost its cover of ice, probably between 14,000 and 12,000 B.C., migrants may also have used the inland routes from present-day Alaska to the American interior.

FLORIDA

Gulf of Mexico

Caribbean Sea

N
W E
S

Migration Routes into America, c. 16,000–10,000 B.C.

- ☐ Ice sheets, c. 16,000 B.C.
- ☐ Ice sheets, c. 12,000 B.C.

Vegetation zones:
- ■ Tundra
- ■ Conifer forest
- ■ Deciduous forest
- ■ Prairie
- ■ Desert
- → Migration route

(after Tanner)

Many groups, accustomed to living at the ocean's edge, probably continued along this route, pushing ever southward into South America.

0   500   1,000 miles
0   500   1,000 kilometers

MAP 1.1 The Ice Age and the Settling of the Americas

Some sixteen thousand years ago, a sheet of ice covered much of Europe and North America. Taking advantage of a broad bridge of land connecting Siberia and Alaska, hunting peoples from Asia migrated into North America, searching for large game animals, such as woolly mammoths, and ice-free habitats. By 10,000 B.C. the descendants of the migrant peoples had moved as far south as present-day Florida and central Mexico.

3000 B.C. some Native American peoples began to develop horticulture, most notably in the region near present-day Mexico. These inventive farmers planted beans, squashes, and cotton and learned how to breed maize, or Indian corn, as well as tomatoes, potatoes, and manioc—crops that would eventually enrich the food supply of the entire world. Over the centuries the Indian peoples bred maize into a much larger, extremely nutritious plant that was hardier and had more varieties and a higher yield per acre than wheat, barley, and rye, the staple cereals of Europe. They also learned to cultivate beans and squash and plant them together with corn, creating a mix of crops that provided a nutritious diet, preserved soil fertility, and produced intensive farming and high yields. The resulting agricultural surplus laid the economic foundation for populous and wealthy societies in Mexico, Peru, and the Mississippi River Valley.

The Mayas and the Aztecs

The flowering of civilization in Mesoamerica began among the Mayan peoples of the Yucatán Peninsula of Mexico and the neighboring rain forests of Guatemala during the long Olmec era (900 B.C.–A.D. 300). The Mayas built large religious centers, urban communities with elaborate systems of water storage and irrigation. By A.D. 300 the Mayan city of Tikal had at least 20,000 inhabitants, mostly farmers who worked the nearby fields and whose labor was used to build huge stone temples. An elite class claiming descent from the gods ruled Mayan society, living in splendor on goods and taxes extracted from peasant families. Drawing on religious and artistic traditions that stretched back to the Olmec people, who had lived along the Gulf of Mexico around 700 B.C., skilled Mayan artisans decorated temples and palaces with art depicting warrior-gods and complex religious rituals. Mayan astronomers created a calendar that recorded historical events and predicted eclipses of the sun and the moon with remarkable accuracy. The Mayas also developed hieroglyphic writing to record royal lineages and noteworthy events, including wars. These skills in calculation and writing facilitated the movement of goods and ideas, allowing the creation of complex society.

Beginning around A.D. 800, Mayan civilization went into decline. Some evidence suggests that a two-century-long dry period caused a loss in population and an economic crisis that prompted overtaxed peasants to desert the temple cities and retreat into the countryside. By A.D. 900 many religious centers had been abandoned, but some Mayan city-states lasted until the Spanish invasion in the 1520s.

As the Mayan peoples flourished in the Yucatán region, a second major Mesoamerican civilization

Gold Piece from Peru
Skilled Inca artisans created gold jewelry and artifacts of striking beauty. Found in a tomb, this figurine may be a stylized image of the dead man, who was undoubtedly a noble of considerable status. Note the intricate detail on the man's headdress and garment.
Dumbarton Oaks Research Library and Collections, Washington, DC.

developed in the central highlands of Mexico around the city of Teotihuacán, with its magnificent Pyramid of the Sun. At its zenith about A.D. 500, Teotihuacán had more than one hundred temples, about four thousand apartment buildings, and a population of at least 100,000. By A.D. 800 Teotihuacán had also declined, probably because of a long-term drop in rainfall and recurrent invasions by seminomadic warrior peoples. Eventually one of these peoples, the Aztecs, established an even more extensive empire.

The Aztecs entered the highlands of Mexico from the north and settled on an island in Lake Texcoco. There, in A.D. 1325, they began to build a new city, Tenochtitlán (present-day Mexico City). They learned the settled ways of the resident peoples, mastered their complex irrigation systems and written language, and established an elaborate culture with a hierarchical social order. Priests and warrior-nobles ruled over twenty clans of free Aztec commoners who farmed communally owned land, and the nobles used huge numbers of non-Aztec slaves and serfs to labor on their private estates. Artisans worked in stone, pottery, cloth, leather, and

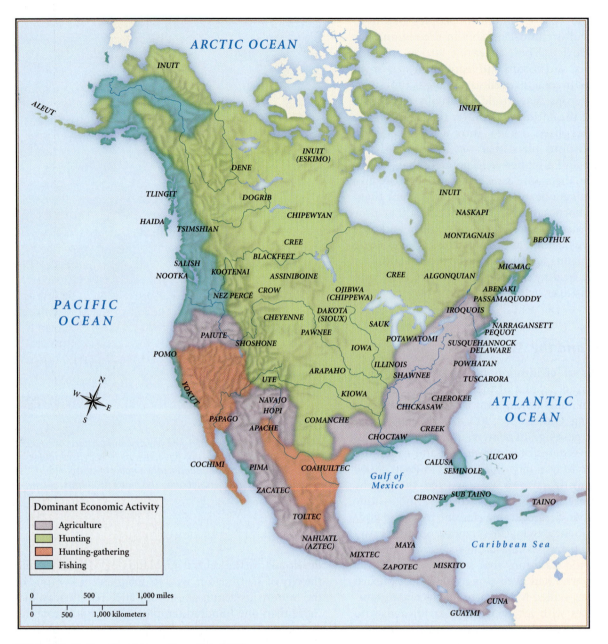

MAP 1.2 Native American Peoples, 1492

Native Americans populated the entire Western Hemisphere at the time of Columbus's arrival, having learned how to live in many environments. They created diverse cultures that ranged from the centralized agriculture-based empires of the Mayas and the Aztecs to seminomadic tribes of hunter-gatherers. The sheer diversity among Indians—of culture, language, tribal identity—usually prevented united resistance to the European invaders.

especially obsidian (hard volcanic glass used to make sharp-edged weapons and tools).

The Aztecs remained an aggressive tribe and soon subjugated most of central Mexico. Their rulers demanded both economic and human tribute from scores of subject tribes, gruesomely sacrificing untold thousands of men and women to ensure agricultural fertility and the daily return of the sun. Aztec merchants created far-flung trading routes and imported

furs, gold, textiles, food, and obsidian. By A.D. 1500, Tenochtitlán had grown into a great metropolis with splendid palaces and temples and over 200,000 inhabitants, dazzling the first Spanish soldiers who saw it: "These great towns and pyramids and buildings arising from the water, all made of stone, seemed like an enchanted vision." The Aztecs' wealth, strong institutions, and military power posed a formidable challenge to any adversary, at home or from afar.

The Indians of the North

The Indians who resided north of the Rio Grande were fewer in number and lived in less coercive societies than those to the south. In A.D. 1500 these Indians lived in dispersed communities of a few thousand people and spoke many different languages—no fewer than sixty-eight east of the Mississippi River (Map 1.2). Most were organized in self-governing tribes composed of **clans**—groups of related families that had a common identity and a real or legendary common ancestor. Tribal members lived in scattered settlements composed of various clans and led by a local chief, who, aided by the clan elders, conducted ceremonies and regulated personal life. For example, elders encouraged individuals to share food and other scarce goods, promoting an ethic of reciprocity rather than one of accumulation. "You are covetous, and neither generous nor kind," the Micmac Indians of Nova Scotia told acquisitive-minded French fur traders around 1600. "As for us, if we have a morsel of bread, we share it with our neighbor." The individual ownership of land was virtually unknown in Indian culture; as a French missionary among the Iroquois noted, they "possess hardly anything except in common." However, Indian elders granted families exclusive use-rights over certain planting grounds and hunting areas. Clan leaders also resolved personal feuds, disciplined individuals who violated customs, decided whether to go to war, and banned marriage between members of the same clan, a rule that helped prevent inbreeding. Nonetheless, the elders' and chiefs' power was far less than that of the Mayan and Aztec nobles because their kinship system of government was locally based and worked by consensus, not by coercion.

The Hopewell Culture. Over the centuries some Indian peoples exerted influence over their immediate neighbors through trade or conquest. The earliest expansive Indian cultures appeared in the eastern woodlands of North America as the inhabitants increased the food supply by domesticating plants and were thus able to settle in large villages. By A.D. 100 the vigorous Hopewell people in the area of present-day Ohio had spread their influence through trade from Wisconsin to Louisiana, importing obsidian from the Yellowstone region of the Rocky Mountains, copper from the Great Lakes, and pottery and marine shells from the Gulf of Mexico. They built large burial mounds and surrounded them with extensive circular, rectangular, or octagonal earthworks that in some cases still survive. The Hopewell people buried their dead with striking ornaments fashioned by their craftsmen: copper beaten into intricate artistic designs, crystals of quartz, mica cut into the shapes of serpents and human hands, and stone pipes carved to represent frogs, hawks, bears, and other animals—figurines evidently representing spiritually

powerful beings. For unknown reasons, the elaborate trading network of the Hopewell gradually collapsed around A.D. 400.

The Peoples of the Southwest.   A second complex culture developed among the Pueblo peoples of the Southwest—the Hohokams, Mogollons, and Anasazis. By A.D. 600 Hohokam peoples in the highland region along the border of present-day Arizona and New Mexico were using irrigation to grow two crops a year, fashioning fine pottery with red-on-buff designs, and, under Mesoamerican influence, worshiping their gods on platform mounds; by A.D. 1000, they were living in elaborate multiroom stone structures (or pueblos). To the east, in the Mimbres Valley of New Mexico, the Mogollon peoples developed a distinctive black-on-white pottery. In the north of present-day New Mexico, the Anasazi culture developed around A.D. 900. The Anasazis were master architects, building residential-ceremonial villages in steep cliffs and a pueblo in Chaco Canyon that housed 1,000 people. Over four hundred miles of straight roads radiated out of Chaco Canyon, making it

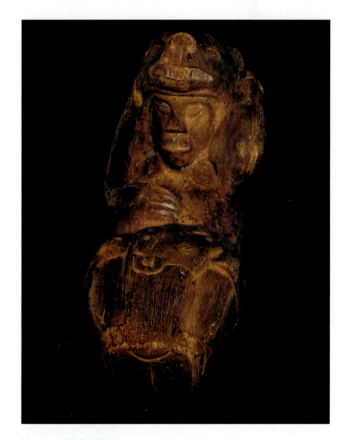

Hopewell Artifact

The Wray figurine is one of the rare representations of a person from the Hopewell mound-building culture. It may depict a noble or a priest or, if the two circles below the chin are stylized breasts, may be a female fertility icon. Note the wolf mask atop the human head and the clawlike fingers of the right hand.
Ohio Historical Society.

a center for trade. However, the culture of the Anasazis, Mogollons, and Hohokams gradually collapsed after A.D. 1150 as long periods of drought and soil exhaustion disrupted maize production and prompted the abandonment of Chaco Canyon and other long-established communities. The descendants of these Pueblo peoples—including the Zunis and the Hopis—later built strong but smaller and more dispersed village societies.

Mississippian Civilization. The last large-scale culture to emerge north of the Rio Grande was the Mississippian civilization. Beginning about A.D. 800, the advanced farming technology of Mesoamerica spread into the Mississippi River Valley, perhaps carried by emigrants fleeing across the Gulf of Mexico from warfare among the Mayas in the Yucatán Peninsula. The Mississippian peoples planted new strains of maize and beans on fertile river bottomland, providing a protein-rich diet and creating an agricultural surplus. A robust culture based on small, fortified temple cities quickly emerged. By A.D. 1150 the largest city, Cahokia (near present-day St. Louis), had a population of 15,000 to 20,000 and more than one hundred temple mounds, one of them as large as the great Egyptian pyramids. As in Mesoamerica, the tribute paid by peasant cultivators supported a privileged class of nobles and priests who waged war against neighboring chiefdoms, patronized skilled artisans, and may have been worshiped as quasi-sacred beings related to the sun god.

However, by A.D. 1350 this six-hundred-year-old Mississippian civilization was in rapid decline, undermined by overpopulation, warfare over fertile bottomlands, and urban diseases such as tuberculosis. Nonetheless, the values and institutions of this culture endured for centuries east of the Mississippi River. When the Spanish adventurer Hernán de Soto invaded the region in the 1540s, he found the Apalachee and Timucua Indians living in permanent settlements, harvesting their fields twice a year, and fiercely resistant to his commands. "If you desire to see me, come where I am," a paramount chief told de Soto, "neither for you, nor for any man, will I set back one foot." A century and a half later French traders and priests who encountered the Natchez people in the area of present-day Mississippi found a society rigidly divided among hereditary chiefs, two groups of nobles and honored people, and a bottom class of peasants. Undoubtedly influenced by Mayan or Aztec rituals, the Natchez practiced human sacrifice; the death of a chief called for the sacrifice of his wives and the enlargement of a ceremonial mound to bury their remains (see Voices from Abroad, "Father le Petite: The Customs of the Natchez," p. 13).

Other peoples in the region retained some Mesoamerican practices and also exhibited traces of the earlier mound-building Hopewell culture. Thus, the

Casa Grande Pot
The artistically and architecturally talented Mogollon and Anasazi peoples of Arizona and New Mexico took utilitarian objects—such as this ordinary pot—and decorated them with black-on-white designs. Their cultures flourished from 1000 to 1250, after which they slowly declined, probably because the climate became increasingly arid.
Courtesy, The Amerind Foundation, Inc., Dragoon, AZ / Photo by Robin Stancliff.

Choctaws regarded a mound in present-day Winston County, Mississippi, as *ishki chito*, the "great mother." There, according to a Choctaw legend, "the Great Spirit created the first Choctaws, and through a hole or cave, they crawled forth into the light of day." However, the Choctaws and others peoples of this region (such as the Creeks, Chickasaws, Cherokees, and Seminoles) lived in small and dispersed agricultural communities and thus escaped the devastating environmental damage and disease that destroyed the impressive city-states of the Mississippian peoples.

The Eastern Woodland Peoples. Although farming in Mesoamerica was the province of both sexes, among eastern Woodland Indians it was the work of women. Over the centuries North American Indian women became adept horticulturists, using flint hoes and more productive strains of corn, squash, and beans to reduce the dependence of their peoples on gathering and hunting (see New Technology, "Indian Women and Agriculture," p. 14). Because of the importance of farming, a matrilineal inheritance system developed among many eastern Indian peoples, including the Five Nations of the Iroquois. Women cultivated the fields around semipermanent settlements, passing the right to use them to their daughters. In these matrilineal societies, fathers stood outside the main lines of kinship, and the main responsibility for childraising fell upon the mother and her brothers, who lived with her. The ritual lives of these

Father le Petite

The Customs of the Natchez

B*eliefs and institutions from the earlier Mississippian culture (*A.D. *1000–1450) lasted for centuries among the Natchez, who lived in present-day Mississippi. This letter was written around 1730 by Father le Petite, one of the hundreds of Jesuits who lived among the Indians in the French colonies of Louisiana and Canada and wrote detailed accounts of what they saw. Father le Petite accurately describes many Indian customs but misinterprets the rules governing the succession of the chief, which simply followed the normal practice of descent and inheritance in a matrilineal society.*

My Reverend Father, The peace of Our Lord.

This Nation of Savages inhabits one of the most beautiful and fertile countries in the World, and is the only one on this continent which appears to have any regular worship. Their Religion in certain points is very similar to that of the ancient Romans. They have a Temple filled with Idols, which are different figures of men and of animals, and for which they have the most profound veneration. Their Temple in shape resembles an earthen oven, a hundred feet in circumference. They enter it by a little door about four feet high, and not more than three in breadth. Above on the outside are three figures of eagles made of wood, and painted red, yellow, and white. Before the door is a kind of shed with folding-doors, where the Guardian of the Temple is lodged; all around it runs a circle of palisades, on which are seen exposed the skulls of all the heads which their Warriors had brought back from the battles in which they had been engaged with the enemies of their Nation. . . .

The Sun is the principal object of veneration to these people; as they cannot conceive of anything which can be above this heavenly body, nothing else appears to them more worthy of their homage. It is for the same reason that the great Chief of this Nation, who knows nothing on the earth more dignified than himself, takes the title of brother of the Sun, and the credulity of the people maintains him in the despotic authority which he claims. To enable them better to converse together, they raise a mound of artificial soil, on which they build his cabin, which is of the same construction as the Temple.

The old men prescribe the Laws for the rest of the people, and one of their principles is . . . the immortality of the soul, and when they leave this world they go, they say, to live in another, there to be recompensed or punished.

In former times the Nation of the *Natchez* was very large. It counted sixty Villages and eight hundred Suns or Princes; now it is reduced to six little Villages and eleven Suns. [Its] Government is hereditary; it is not, however, the son of the reigning Chief who succeeds his father, but the son of his sister, or the first Princess of the blood. This policy is founded on the knowledge they have of the licentiousness of their women. They are not sure, they say, that the children of the chief's wife may be of the blood Royal, whereas the son of the sister of the great Chief must be, at least on the side of the mother.

Source: The Jesuit Relations and Allied Documents, ed. Reuben Gold Thwaites (Cleveland: Murrow Brothers, 1900), 68:121–35.

---

farming peoples focused on religious ceremonies related to the agricultural cycle, such as the Iroquois green corn and strawberry festivals. Indian peoples ate better because of women's labor and long-term advances in their farming practices, but they enjoyed few material comforts, and their populations grew slowly.

In A.D. 1500 most Indians north of the Rio Grande had resided on the same lands for generations, but the elaborate civilizations and strong city-states that had once flourished in the Southwest and in the great river valleys in the heart of the continent had vanished.

Consequently, when the European adventurers, traders, and settlers came ashore from the Atlantic, there were no great Indian empires or religious centers that could lead a campaign of military and spiritual resistance. "When you command, all the French obey and go to war," the Chippewa chief Chigabe told a European general, but "I shall not be heeded and obeyed by my nation." Because household and lineage were the basis of his society, Chigabe explained, "I cannot answer except for myself and for those immediately allied to me."

Indian Women and Agriculture

Corn was the dietary staple of most Native Americans, and its cultivation shaped their vision of the natural world. The Agawam Indians of Massachusetts began their year with the month of Squannikesas, a word that meant "when they set Indian corn," and subsequent months had names that referred to the weeding, hilling, and ripening of corn. To appease the spirit forces in nature and ensure a bountiful harvest, the Seneca Indians of New York held a corn-planting ceremony. They asked the Thunderers, "our grandfathers," to water their crops and beseeched the sun, "our older brother," not to burn them.

Among the eastern Woodland tribes, growing corn was women's work. The French priest Gabriel Sagard spoke of Huron women doing "more work than the men. . . . They have the care of the household, of sowing and gathering corn, grinding flour, . . . and providing the necessary wood." Indian women prepared the ground for planting with wooden hoes tipped with bone, flint, or clamshells. According to a Dutch traveler, they made "heaps like molehills, each about two and a half feet from the others" and planted "in each heap five

or six grains." As the tall slender plants appeared, the women piled on more dirt to support the roots. They also "put in each hill three or four Brazilian [kidney] beans. When they grow up, they interlace with the corn, which reaches to a height of from five to six feet; and they keep the ground free of weeds."

The planting of corn and beans together represented a major technological advance, dramatically increasing total yields and human nutrition. The beans fixed nitrogen in the soil, preserving fertility, and conserved moisture, preventing erosion. Beans and corn provided a diet rich in vegetable proteins. By intensively cultivating two acres, an Indian woman typically harvested sixty bushels of shelled corn—half the calories required by five persons for a year.

This economic contribution enhanced the political influence of women in some tribes, especially those in which names and inheritance rights passed through women (matrilinealism). Thus, among the matrilineal Iroquois, women chose the clan leaders. To preserve their status, women jealously guarded their productive role. A Quaker missionary reported as late as 1809 that "if a man took hold of a hoe to use it, the Women would get down his gun by way of derision & laugh and say such a Warrior is a timid woman."

In seventeenth-century America, English farmers appropriated Indian corn technology and made it part of their own culture. Now Protestant ministers (as well as Indian shamans) prayed for a bountiful harvest of corn. After clearing their fields of tree stumps, English farmers

Traditional European Society in 1450

In A.D. 1450 few observers would have predicted that the European peoples would become the overlords of the Western Hemisphere. A thousand years after the fall of the magnificent Roman empire, Europe had become a backward society, devastated around 1350 by a vicious epidemic from the subcontinent of India—the Black Death—that killed one-third of its peoples. Other areas of the world were much more economically advanced and were expanding their seaborne trade. Indeed, the ruling dynasty in China had recently dispatched a major commercial fleet to the eastern coast of Africa.

The Peasantry

There were only a few large cities in Western Europe before A.D. 1450—only Paris, London, and Naples had

100,000 residents and thus equaled the size of Teotihuacán at its zenith. More than 90 percent of the European population consisted of **peasants** living in small rural communities. Peasant families usually owned or leased a small dwelling in the village center and had the right to farm strips of land in the surrounding fields. The fields were "open"—not divided by fences or hedges—making cooperative farming a necessity. The village community decided which crops would be grown, and every family followed its dictates. Because there were few merchants or good roads to carry goods to distant markets, most families exchanged surplus grain and meat with their neighbors or bartered their farm products for the services of local millers, weavers, and blacksmiths. Most peasants yearned to live in a **yeoman** family—a household that was under no obligation to a landlord and owned enough land to support its members in comfort—but relatively few achieved that goal.

plowed furrows at three-foot intervals from north to south. Then they cut east-west furrows, heaping up the soil into Indian-style cornhills at the intersecting points. English planting methods were less labor-intensive than Indian techniques and far less productive, averaging from ten to fifteen bushels per acre, not thirty.

Equally significant, among European settlers men—not women—planted, tended, and harvested the crop. In combination with patrilineal naming and inheritance practices, the dominance of men in agriculture confined colonial women to a subordinate role in economic and political life.

Among Europeans as well as Indians, corn soon became the premier crop, and with good reason. As a Welsh migrant to Pennsylvania noted, corn "produced more increase than any other Graine whatsoever." Pigs and chickens ate its kernels, and cows munched its stalks and leaves. Ground into flour and made into bread, cakes, or porridge, corn became the dietary staple of poor people in the northern English colonies and of white tenant farmers and enslaved blacks in the South and the West Indies.

Iroquois Women at Work, 1724

As this European engraving suggests, Iroquois women took the major responsibility for growing food crops. The women in the background are hoeing the soil into small hillocks, in which they are planting corn and beans. Most of the other workers are tapping sugar maples and boiling the sweet sap to create maple syrup. However, the woman at the left is probably grinding corn into flour and, by adding water, making flat patties for baking.
Newberry Library.

The Seasonal Cycle. As among the Native Americans, many aspects of European peasant life followed a seasonal pattern (Figure 1.1). The agricultural year began in March or April, when the ground thawed and dried and the villagers began the exhausting work of spring plowing and the planting of wheat, rye, and oats. During these busy months men sheared the thick winter wool of their sheep, which the women washed and spun into yarn. Peasants cut the first crop of hay in June and stored it as winter fodder for their livestock. In the summer, life became more relaxed, and families mended their fences or repaired their barns. August and September often were marked by grief as infants and old people succumbed to epidemics of fly-borne dysentery. Fall brought the strenuous harvest time, followed by solemn feasts of thanksgiving and riotous bouts of merrymaking. As winter approached, peasants slaughtered excess livestock and salted or smoked the meat. During the cold months peasants completed the tasks of threshing grain and weaving textiles and had time to visit friends and relatives in nearby villages. Just before the farming cycle began again in the spring, rural residents held carnivals to celebrate with drink and dance the end of the long winter night.

Many rural people died in January and February, victims of viral diseases and the cold. More mysteriously, in European villages (and later in rural British America), the greatest numbers of babies were born in February and March, with a smaller peak in September and October. The precise causes of this pattern are unknown. Religious practices, such as the abstention from sexual intercourse by devout Christians during Lent, might have increased the number of conceptions in the months following the Easter holy day. Even more likely, seasonal fluctuations in female work patterns or the food supply might have altered a woman's ability to carry a child to full term. One thing is certain. This

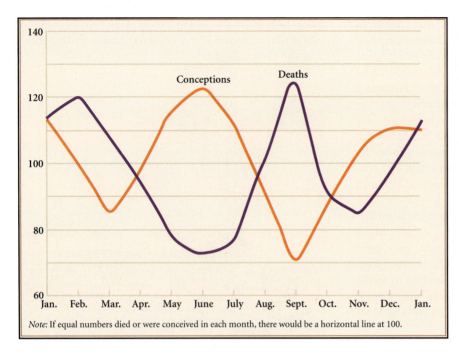

FIGURE 1.1 The Yearly Rhythm of Rural Life and Death
The annual cycle of nature profoundly affected life in the traditional agricultural world. The death rate soared by 20 percent in February and September. Summer was the healthiest season, with the fewest deaths and the greatest number of successful conceptions (as measured by births nine months later).

pattern of births does not exist in modern urban societies, so it must have been a reflection of the rigors of the traditional agriculture cycle.

The Peasant's Lot. For most peasants survival required unremitting labor. Horses and oxen strained to break the soil with primitive wooden plows, while workers harvested hay, wheat, rye, and barley with hand sickles. Because of the lack of high-quality seeds, chemical fertilizers, and pesticides, output was pitifully small—less than one-tenth of present-day yields. The margin of existence was thin, corroding family relations. Malnourished mothers fed their babies sparingly, calling them "greedy and gluttonous," and many newborn girls were "helped to die" so that their older brothers would have enough to eat. About half of all peasant children died before the age of twenty-one. Violence—assault, murder, rape—was much more prevalent than in most modern industrialized societies, and hunger and disease were constant companions. "I have seen the latest epoch of misery," a French doctor reported as famine and plague struck. "The inhabitants . . . lie down in a meadow to eat grass, and share the food of wild beasts."

Often destitute, usually exploited and dominated by landlords and aristocrats, many peasants simply accepted their condition, but others did not. It would be the deprived rural classes of Britain, Spain, and Germany, hoping for a better life for themselves and their children, who would supply the majority of white migrants to the Western Hemisphere.

Hierarchy and Authority

In the traditional European social order, as among the Aztec and Mayan peoples, authority came from above. Kings and princes owned vast tracts of land, conscripted men for military service, and lived in splendor off the labor of the peasantry. Yet rulers were far from supreme, given the power of the nobles, each of whom also owned large estates and controlled hundreds of peasant families. Collectively, these noblemen had the power to challenge royal authority. They had their own legislative institutions, such as the French *parlements* and the English House of Lords, and enjoyed special privileges, such as the right to a trial before a jury of other noblemen. However, after 1450 kings began to undermine the power of the nobility and to create more centralized states, laying the administrative basis for overseas expansion.

Just as kings and nobles ruled the state, so the men in peasant families ruled their women and children. The man was the head of the house, his power justified by the teachings of the Christian Church. As one English clergyman put it, "The woman is a weak creature not embued with like strength and constancy of mind"; law and custom consequently "subjected her to the power of man." On marriage, an English woman assumed her husband's surname and was required (under the threat of legally sanctioned physical "correction") to submit to his orders. Moreover, she surrendered to her husband the legal right to all her property; on his death she received a **dower**, usually the use during her lifetime of one-third of the family's land and goods.

A father controlled the lives of his children with equal authority, demanding that they work for him until their middle or late twenties. Then a landowning peasant would try to provide land to sons and dowries to daughters and choose marriage partners of appropriate wealth and status for them. In many regions fathers bestowed most of the land on the eldest son, an inheritance practice known as "primogeniture," which forced many younger children to join the ranks of the roaming poor. In such a society few men—and even fewer women—had much personal freedom or individual identity.

Hierarchy and authority prevailed in traditional European society both because of the power of established institutions and because, in a violent and unpredictable world, they offered ordinary people a measure of security. These values of order and security, which migrants carried with them to America, would shape the character of family life and the social order there well into the eighteenth century.

The Power of Religion

The Roman Catholic Church served as one of the great unifying forces in Western European society. By A.D. 1000 Christian priests had converted most of pagan Europe. The pope, as head of the Catholic Church, directed a vast hierarchy of cardinals, bishops, and priests. Latin, the great language of classical scholarship, was preserved by Catholic institutions, and Christian dogma provided a common understanding of God, the world, and human history. Equally important, the Church provided another bulwark of authority and discipline in society. Every village had a church, and holy shrines dotted the byways of Europe.

Christian doctrine penetrated deeply into the everyday lives of peasants. Over the centuries the Church had devised a religious calendar that followed the agricultural cycle and transformed pagan festivals into Christian holy days. The pagans of Europe, like many of the Indians of North America, were animists who believed that the entire natural world contained unpredictable spiritual forces that had to be paid ritual honor. Conversely, Christian priests taught that spiritual power came from outside nature, from a great God located above the earth who had sent his divine son, Jesus Christ, into the world to save humanity from its sins. They turned the winter solstice, which for pagans marked the return of the sun, into the feast of Christmas, to mark the coming of the Savior. Likewise the feast of Easter, celebrating Christ's resurrection from the dead, imparted a new meaning to the pagans' spring fertility festivals. To avert famine and plague, Christian peasants did not make ritual offerings to nature but

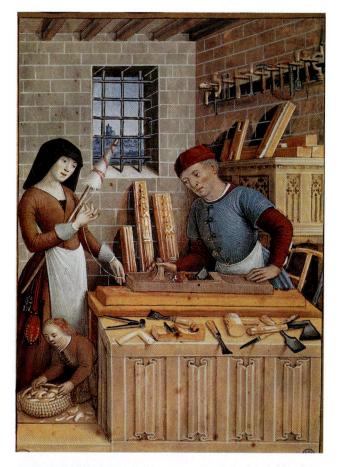

Artisan Family

Work was slow and output was limited in the preindustrial world, and survival required the efforts of all family members. Here a fifteenth-century French woodworker planes a panel of wood while his wife twists flax fibers into linen yarn for the family's clothes and their son fashions a basket out of reeds.
Giraudon / Art Resource, NY.

turned to priests for spiritual guidance and offered prayers to Christ and the saints.

The Church also taught that Satan, a lesser and evil supernatural being, constantly challenged God by tempting people into sin and wrongdoing. If prophets spread unusual doctrines, or **heresies**, they were surely the tools of Satan. If a devout Christian fell mysteriously ill, the sickness might be the result of an evil spell cast by a witch in league with Satan. Combating other religions and suppressing false doctrines among Christians became an obligation of rulers and a principal task of the new orders of Christian knights. In the centuries after the death in A.D. 632 of the prophet Muhammad, the founder of Islam, the newly converted peoples of the Mediterranean used force and persuasion to spread the Islamic faith and Arab civilization into sub-Saharan Africa, India, and Indonesia and deep into Spain and the Balkan region of eastern Europe. Between 1096 and 1291 successive armies of Christians, led by European kings and nobles, embarked on a series of Crusades to halt the advance of Islam and expel Arab Muslims from the Holy Land in the eastern Mediterranean, where Jesus had lived. Within Europe, Crusader armies crushed heretical Christian sects, such as the Albigensians of southern France.

The crusaders temporarily gained control of much of Palestine, but the impact of the Crusades on Europe was more profound. Religious warfare reinforced and intensified its Christian identity, resulting in renewed persecution of Jews and their expulsion from many European countries. The Crusades also broadened the intellectual and economic horizons of the privileged classes of Western Europe, bringing them into contact with the Mediterranean region of North Africa and its Arabic-speaking peoples. Arab Muslims led the world in scholarship, and their language and merchants dominated the trade routes that stretched from Mongolia to Constantinople and from the East Indies to the Mediterranean.

Europe Encounters Africa and the Americas, 1450–1550

Around A.D. 1400 Europeans shook off the lethargy of their traditional agricultural society with a major revival of learning—the Renaissance (from the French word for "rebirth"). Drawing inspiration from classical Greek and Roman (rather than Christian) sources, Renaissance intellectuals were optimistic in their view of human

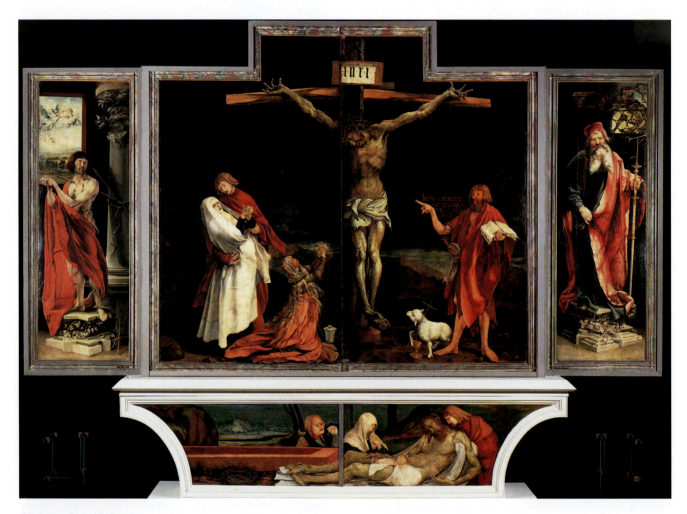

Christ's Crucifixion

This graphic portrayal by the German painter Grünewald of Christ's death on the cross and subsequent burial reminded believers not only of Christ's sacrifice but also of the ever-present prospect of their own death. The panel to the left depicts the martyr St. Sebastian, killed by dozens of arrows, while that to the right probably portrays the abbot of the monastery in Isenheim, Germany, that commissioned the altarpiece.
Colmar, Musée Unterlinden, Colmar-Giraudon/Art Resource.

nature and celebrated individual potential. They saw themselves not as prisoners of blind fate or victims of the forces of nature but as many-sided individuals with the capacity to change the world. Inspired by new knowledge and a new optimism, the rulers of Portugal and Spain commissioned Italian navigators to find new trade routes to India and China. These maritime adventurers soon brought Europeans into direct contact with the peoples of Africa, Asia, and the Americas, beginning a new era in world history.

The Renaissance

Stimulated by the wealth and learning of the Arab world, first Italy and then the countries of northern Europe experienced the rebirth of learning and cultural life now known as the Renaissance. Arab traders had access to the fabulous treasures of the East, such as silks and spices, and Arab societies had acquired magnetic compasses, water-powered mills, and mechanical clocks. In great cultural centers such as Alexandria and Cairo in Egypt, Arab scholars carried on the legacy of Christian Byzantine civilization, which had preserved the great achievements of the Greeks and Romans in religion, medicine, philosophy, mathematics, astronomy, and geography. Through Arab learning, the peoples of Europe reacquainted themselves with their own classical heritage.

Innovations in Economics, Art, and Politics. The Renaissance had the most profound impact on the upper classes. Merchants from the Italian city-states of Venice, Genoa, and Pisa dispatched ships to Alexandria, Beirut, and other eastern Mediterranean ports, where they purchased goods from China, India, Persia, and Arabia and sold them throughout Europe. The enormous profits from this commerce created a new class of merchants, bankers, and textile manufacturers who conducted trade, lent vast sums of money, and spurred technological innovation in silk and wool production. This moneyed elite ruled the republican city-states of Italy and created the concept of **civic humanism**, an ideology that celebrated public virtue and service to the state and would profoundly influence European and American conceptions of government.

In addition to new civic ideals, perhaps no other age in European history has produced such a flowering of artistic genius. Michelangelo, Andrea Palladio, and Filippo Brunelleschi designed and built great architectural masterpieces, while Leonardo da Vinci and Raphael produced magnificent religious paintings, creating styles and setting standards that have endured into the modern era.

This creative energy inspired Renaissance rulers. In *The Prince* (1513), Niccolò Machiavelli provided unsentimental advice on how monarchs could increase their political power. The kings of Western Europe followed his advice, creating royal law courts and bureaucracies to reduce the power of the landed classes and seeking alliances with merchants and urban artisans. Monarchs allowed merchants to trade throughout their realms and granted privileges to artisan guilds, encouraging both domestic manufacturing and foreign trade. In return, these rulers extracted taxes from towns and loans from merchants to support their armies and officials. This alliance of monarchs, merchants, and royal bureaucrats (which eventually became known as **mercantilism**) challenged the power of the agrarian nobility, while the increasing wealth of monarchical nation-states such as Spain and Portugal propelled Europe into its first age of overseas expansion.

Maritime Expansion. Under the direction of Prince Henry (1394–1460), Portugal led the great surge of

Astronomers at Istanbul, 1581
Arab and Turkish scholars transmitted ancient texts and learning to Europeans during the Middle Ages and provided much of the geographical and astronomical knowledge used by European explorers during the sixteenth century, the great Age of Discovery. Ergun Cagutay, Istanbul.

Renaissance Architecture

In the painting The Ideal City, *the Renaissance artist Piero della Francesca uses columned buildings to recall the classical world of Greece and Rome and emphasizes symmetrical forms to create a world of ordered beauty.* Scala/Art Resource.

maritime commercial expansion. Henry was at once a Christian warrior and a Renaissance humanist. As a general of the Crusading Order of Christ, he had fought the Muslims in North Africa, an experience that reinforced his desire to extend the bounds of Christendom—and Portuguese power. As a humanist, Henry patronized Renaissance thinkers; as an explorer, he relied on Arab and Italian geographers for the latest knowledge about the shape and size of the continents. Imbued with the spirit of the Renaissance, he tried to fulfill the mission assigned to him by an astrologer: "to engage in great and noble conquests and to attempt the discovery of things hidden from other men."

Because Arab and Italian merchants dominated trade in the Mediterranean, Henry sought an alternative oceanic route to the wealth of Asia. In the 1420s he established a center for exploration and ocean mapping near Lisbon and sent newly developed, strongly constructed three-masted ships (caravels) to sail the African coast. His seamen soon discovered and settled three sets of islands—the Madeiras, Canaries, and the Azores. By 1435 Portuguese sea captains were roaming the coast of West Africa, seeking ivory and gold in exchange for salt, wine, and fish. By the 1440s they were trading in humans as well, the first Europeans to engage in the long-established African slave trade.

West African Society and Slavery

Vast and diverse, West Africa stretches along the coast from present-day Senegal to Angola. In the 1400s tropical rain forest covered much of the coast, but a series of great rivers—the Senegal, Gambia, Volta, Niger, and Congo—provided relatively easy access to the woodlands, plains, and savanna of the interior (Map 1.3).

West African Life.   Most of the people of West Africa farmed modest plots and lived in extended families in small villages. Normally, men cleared the land and women planted and harvested the crops. On the plains of the savanna, millet, cotton, and livestock were the primary products, while the forest peoples grew yams and harvested oil-rich palm nuts. Forest dwellers exchanged palm oil and kola nuts, a mild stimulant, for the textiles and leather goods produced by savanna dwellers. Similarly, salt produced along the seacoast was traded for iron or gold mined in the hills of the interior.

West Africans spoke many different languages and lived in hundreds of distinct cultural and political groups. A majority of the people resided in hierarchical, socially stratified societies ruled by princes. Other West Africans dwelled in stateless societies organized by household and lineage (much like those of the Woodland Indians of eastern North America). Most peoples had secret societies, such as the Poro for men and the Sande for women, that united people from different lineages and clans and exercised political influence by checking the powers of rulers in princely states. These societies provided sexual education for the young, conducted adult initiation ceremonies, and, by shaming individuals and officials, enforced codes of public conduct and private morality.

Spiritual beliefs varied greatly. Although some West Africans had been converted by Arab missionaries from the north to the Muslim faith and believed in a single god, most recognized a variety of deities—ranging from a remote creator-god who seldom interfered in human affairs to numerous animistic spirits that lived in the earth, animals, and plants. Africans viewed their ancestors with great respect, believing that they inhabited a spiritual world from which they could intercede on behalf of their descendants. Royal families in particular paid elaborate homage to their ancestors, hoping to give themselves an aura of divinity.

At first European traders had a positive impact on life in West Africa by introducing new plants and animals. Portuguese merchants carried coconuts from East Africa, oranges and lemons from the Mediterranean, pigs from Western Europe, and (after 1500) maize, manioc, and tomatoes from the Americas. Portuguese merchants also expanded existing African trade networks, stimulating the economy. From small, fortified trading posts on the coast, iron bars and metal products joined kola nuts and salt moving inland; in return, grain, gold, ivory, pepper, cotton textiles, and, eventually, slaves flowed down the rivers to oceangoing ships. Because of disease, the inland trade remained in the hands of Africans; Europeans who lived in the interior of West Africa were quickly

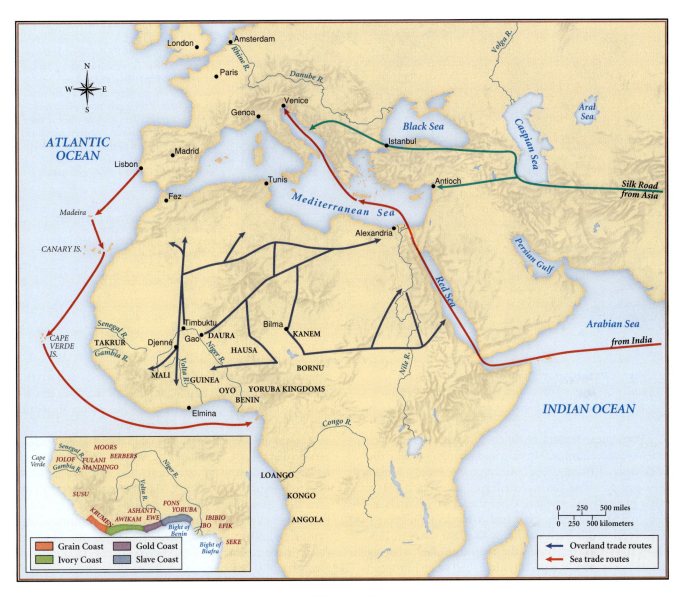

MAP 1.3 West Africa and the Mediterranean in the Fifteenth Century
*Trade routes across the Sahara Desert had long connected West Africa with the
Mediterranean region. Gold, ivory, and slaves moved northward; fine textiles, spices, and
the Muslim faith traveled to the south. Beginning in the 1430s, the Portuguese opened up
a maritime trade with the coastal regions of West Africa, which were home to many
peoples and dozens of large and small states.*

stricken by yellow fever, malaria, and dysentery, and their
death rate often reached 50 percent a year.

The Slave Trade. Europeans soon joined in the trade
in humans. Unfree status had existed for many centuries
in West Africa. Some people were held in bondage as
security for debts; others had been sold into servitude by
their kin, often in exchange for food in times of famine;
still others were war captives. Although treated as
property and exploited as agricultural laborers, slaves
usually were considered members of the society that had
enslaved them and sometimes were treated as kin. Most
retained the right to marry, and their children were

often free. A small proportion of unfree West Africans
were **trade slaves**, mostly war captives and criminals
sold from one kingdom to another or carried overland
in caravans by Arab traders to the Mediterranean
region. Thus, the first Portuguese in Senegambia found
that the Wolof king there had created a slave-trading
society:

> *[The king] supports himself by raids which re-*
> *sult in many slaves from his own as well as*
> *neighboring countries. He employs these slaves*
> *in cultivating the land allotted to him; but*
> *he also sells many to the Azanaghi [Arab]*

Fulani Village in West Africa

Around 1550 the Fulani people conquered the lands to the south of the Senegal River. To protect themselves from subject peoples and neighboring tribes, the Fulani constructed fortified villages, such as the one depicted here. Previously the Fulani had been nomadic herders and, as the enclosed pasture shows, continued to keep livestock. Note the cylindrical houses of mud brick, surmounted by thatched roofs.

Frederic Shoberl, ed., *The World in Miniature,* 1821.

For more help analyzing this image, see the ONLINE STUDY GUIDE at bedfordstmartins.com/henretta.

merchants in return for horses and other goods, and also to the Christians, since they have begun to trade with these blacks.

Portuguese traders established "forts" at small port cities—Gorée, Elmina, Mpinda, and Loango—where they bought slaves from African princes and warlords. Initially they carried a few thousand African slaves each year to sugar plantations in Madeira and the Canary Islands and also to Lisbon, which soon had a black population of 9,000, and Seville in Spain, home to 6,000 slaves in 1550. From this small beginning the maritime slave trade expanded enormously, especially after 1550 when Europeans set up sugar plantations in Brazil and the West Indies. By 1700 slave traders were carrying hundreds of thousands of slaves to toil and die on American plantations.

Europe Reaches the Americas

As they traded with Africans, Portuguese adventurers continued to look for a direct ocean route to Asia. In 1488 Bartholomeu Dias rounded the Cape of Good Hope, the southern tip of Africa, and ten years later Vasco da Gama reached India. Although the Arab, Indian, and Jewish merchants who controlled the trade along India's Malabar Coast tried to exclude him, da Gama acquired a highly profitable cargo of cinnamon and pepper—spices that were especially valuable because they could be used to flavor and preserve meat. To capture the trade in spices and Indian textiles for Portugal, da Gama returned to India in 1502 with twenty-one fighting vessels, which outmaneuvered and outgunned the Arab fleets. Soon the Portuguese government set up fortified trading posts for its merchants at key points around the Indian Ocean and

opened trade routes from Africa to Indonesia and up the coast of Asia to China and Japan. In a momentous transition, Portuguese replaced Arabs as the leaders in world commerce and the trade in African slaves.

Spain quickly followed Portugal's example. As Renaissance rulers, King Ferdinand of Aragon and Queen Isabella of Castile saw national unity and commerce as the keys to power and prosperity. Married in their teens in an arranged match, the young rulers (r. 1474–1516) combined their kingdoms and completed the centuries-long campaign known as the **reconquista** to oust the Muslims from their realm. In 1492 their armies reconquered Granada, the last outpost of Islam in Western Europe. Continuing their effort to use the Catholic religion to build a sense of "Spanishness," Ferdinand and Isabella launched a brutal Inquisition against suspected Christian heretics and expelled or forcibly converted thousands of Jews. Simultaneously they sought new opportunities for trade and empire (Map 1.4).

Because Portugal controlled the southern, or African, approach to Asia, Isabella and Ferdinand listened with interest to proposals for an alternative, western route to

▶ **MAP 1.4 The Eurasian Trade System and European Maritime Ventures, 1500**

For centuries the Mediterranean port cities of Antioch and Alexandria served as the western termini of the great Eurasian trading routes—the silk route from China and the spice trade from India and Indonesia. Between 1480 and 1550, European explorers subsidized by the monarchs and merchants of Portugal, Spain, and Holland opened new maritime connections to Africa, India, and the Americas, challenging the primacy of the Arab-dominated routes through the lands and waterways of the eastern Mediterranean. (To trace changes in trade and empires over time, see also Map 2.2 on p. 46 and Map 5.1 on p. 134.)

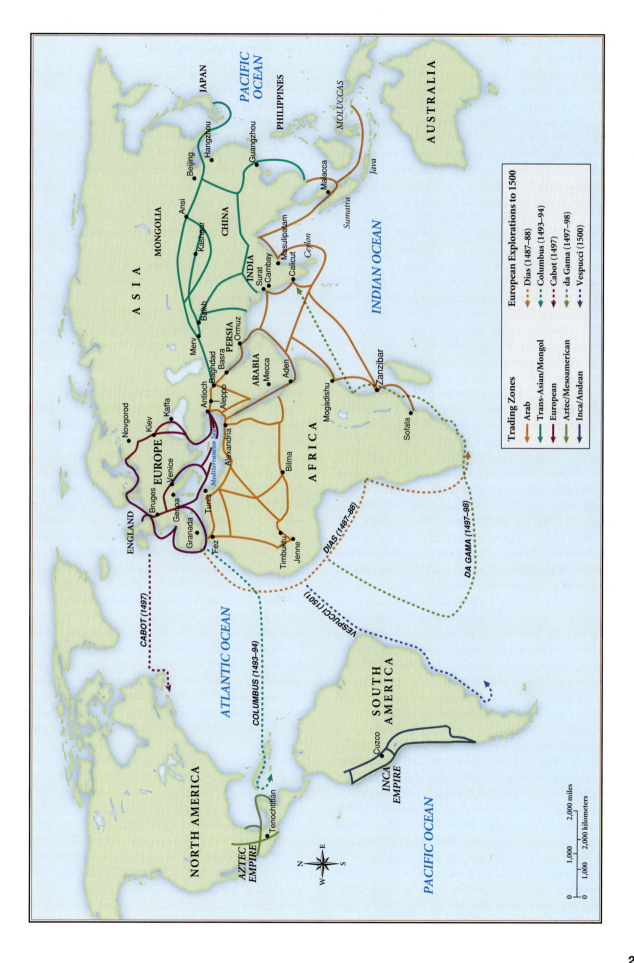

PACIFIC OCEAN

JAPAN
Hangzhou
Beijing
Ansi
Kashgar
MONGOLIA
CHINA
Guangzhou
PHILIPPINES
MOLUCCAS
Java
Malacca
Sumatra
AUSTRALIA

A S I A

Merv
Balkh
INDIA
Surat
Cambay
Calicut
Masulipatam
Ceylon

INDIAN OCEAN

PERSIA
Ormuz
Baghdad
Basra
Antioch
Aleppo
ARABIA
Mecca
Aden
Zanzibar

Novgorod
Kiev
Kaffa
EUROPE
Bruges
Venice
Genoa
Granada
ENGLAND
Fez
Tunis
Mediterranean Sea
Alexandria
Bilma
Timbuktu
Jenne
AFRICA
Mogadishu
Sofala

DIAS (1487–88)
DA GAMA (1497–98)

CABOT (1497)

ATLANTIC OCEAN

COLUMBUS (1493–94)

VESPUCCI (1501)

NORTH AMERICA

Tenochtitlán
AZTEC EMPIRE

SOUTH AMERICA
Cuzco
INCA EMPIRE

PACIFIC OCEAN

N
W E
S

0   1,000   2,000 miles
0   1,000   2,000 kilometers

European Explorations to 1500
- Dias (1487–88)
- Columbus (1493–94)
- Cabot (1497)
- da Gama (1497–98)
- Vespucci (1500)

Trading Zones
- Arab
- Trans-Asian/Mongol
- European
- Aztec/Mesoamerican
- Inca/Andean

the riches of the East. The main advocate for such a route was Christopher Columbus, a devout Catholic and a struggling Genoese sea captain who was determined to become rich and to convert the peoples of Asia to Christianity. Misinterpreting the findings of Italian geographers, Columbus believed that the Atlantic Ocean, long feared by Arab sailors as a ten-thousand-mile-wide "green sea of darkness," was little more than a narrow channel of water separating Europe from Asia. Dubious at first about Columbus's theory, Ferdinand and Isabella finally agreed to arrange financial backing from Spanish merchants. They charged Columbus with the task of discovering a new trade route to China and, in an expression of the crusading mentality of the *reconquista*, of carrying Christianity to the peoples of Asia.

Columbus set sail with three small ships in August 1492. Six weeks later, after a perilous voyage of three thousand miles, he finally found land, disembarking on October 12, 1492, on one of the islands of the present-day Bahamas. Although surprised by the rude living conditions of the natives, Columbus expected them to "easily be made Christians, for it appeared to me that they had no religion." With ceremony and solemnity, he bestowed the names of the Spanish royal family and Catholic holy days on the islands, intending thereby to claim them for Spain and for Christendom.

Believing he had reached Asia—"the Indies," in fifteenth-century parlance—Columbus called the native inhabitants Indians and the islands the West Indies. He then explored the neighboring Caribbean islands, demanding gold from the local Taino, Arawak, and Carib peoples. Buoyed by the natives' stories of rivers of gold lying "to the west," Columbus left forty men on the island of Hispaniola (present-day Haiti and the Dominican Republic) and returned triumphantly to Spain, taking several Tainos to display to Isabella and Ferdinand.

Although Columbus brought back no gold, the Spanish monarchs were sufficiently impressed by his discovery to support three more voyages over the next twelve years. During those expeditions Columbus began the colonization of the West Indies, transporting more than a thousand Spanish settlers—all men—and hundreds of domestic animals. He also began the transatlantic trade in slaves, carrying hundreds of Indians to bondage in Europe and importing black slaves from Africa to work as artisans and farmers in the new Spanish settlements. However, Columbus failed to find either golden treasures or great kingdoms, so that his death in 1506 went virtually unrecognized. Other explorers soon followed Columbus, and a German geographer named the continents not after their European discoverer but after a Genoese mariner, Amerigo Vespucci, who had traveled to South America around 1500 and called it a *nuevo mundo*, a new world: America. For its part, the Spanish crown continued to call the new lands Las Indias (the Indies) and determined to make them a Spanish world.

The Spanish Conquest

Columbus and other Spanish adventurers ruled the peoples of the Caribbean islands with an iron hand, seizing their goods and exploiting their labor to grow sugarcane. After subduing the Arawaks and Tainos on Hispaniola, the Spanish probed coastal settlements on the mainland in search of booty. In 1513 Juan Ponce de León searched for gold and slaves along the coast of Florida and gave the peninsula its name. That same year Vasco Núñez de Balboa crossed the Isthmus of Darien (Panama), becoming the first European to see the Pacific Ocean. Although these greedy adventurers found no gold, rumors of riches to the west encouraged others to launch an invasion of the interior. These men were not explorers or merchants but hardened veterans of the wars against the Muslims who were eager to do battle and get rich. To encourage these adventurers to expand its American empire, the Spanish crown offered them plunder, landed estates and Indian laborers in the conquered territory, and titles of nobility.

The Fall of the Aztecs and the Incas. The first great success of the Spanish **conquistadors** (conquerors) occurred in present-day Mexico (Map 1.5). In 1519 the ambitious and charismatic adventurer Hernán Cortés landed on the Mexican coast with 600 men and marched toward the Aztec capital of Tenochtitlán. Fortuitously for the Spaniards, Cortés arrived in the very year in which Aztec mythology had predicted the return of the god Quetzalcoatl to his earthly kingdom. Believing that Cortés might be the returning god, Moctezuma, the Aztec ruler, acted indecisively. After an Aztec ambush against the conquistadors failed, Moctezuma allowed Cortés to proceed without challenge to Tenochtitlán and received him with great ceremony, only to become Cortés's captive. When Moctezuma's forces finally attempted to expel the invaders, they were confronted by superior European military technology. The sight of the Spaniards in full armor, with guns that shook the heavens and inflicted devastating wounds, made a deep impression on the Aztecs, who had learned how to purify gold and fashion it into ornate religious objects but did not produce iron tools or weapons. Moreover, the Aztecs had no wheeled carts or cavalry, and their warriors, fighting on foot with flint- or obsidian-tipped spears and arrows, were no match for mounted Spanish conquistadors wielding steel swords and aided by vicious attack dogs. Although heavily outnumbered and suffering great losses, Cortés and his men were able to fight their way out of the Aztec capital.

At this point, the vast population of the Aztec empire could easily have crushed the European invaders if the Indian peoples had remained united. But Cortés exploited the widespread resentment against the Aztecs, forming military alliances and raising thousands of

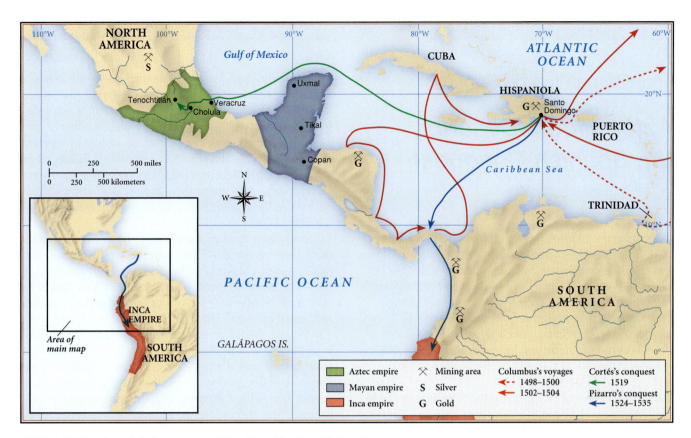

MAP 1.5 The Spanish Conquest of the Great Indian Civilizations

The Spanish first invaded the islands of the Caribbean. Rumors of a magnificent golden civilization led to Cortés's invasion of the Aztec empire in 1519. By 1535 other Spanish conquistadors had conquered the Mayan temple cities and the Inca empire in Peru, completing one of the great conquests in world history.

troops from subject peoples who had seen their wealth expropriated by Aztec nobles and their people sacrificed to the Aztec sun god. The Aztec empire collapsed, the victim not of superior Spanish military technology but of a vast internal rebellion of Indian peoples (see American Voices, "Aztec Elders Describe the Spanish Conquest," p. 26).

As the Spanish sought to impose their dominion over the peoples of the Aztec empire, they had a silent ally— disease. Separated from Eurasia for thousands of years, the inhabitants of the Western Hemisphere had no immunities to common European diseases. A massive smallpox epidemic lasting seventy days ravaged Tenochtitlán following the Spanish exodus, "striking everywhere in the city," according to an Aztec source, killing Moctezuma's brother and many others. "They could not move, they could not stir. . . . Covered, mantled with pustules, very many people died of them." Subsequent outbreaks of smallpox, influenza, and measles killed hundreds of thousands of Aztecs and their subject peoples and sapped the morale of the survivors. Exploiting this demographic weakness, Cortés quickly extended Spanish rule over the entire Aztec

empire, and his lieutenants then moved against the Mayan city-states in the Yucatán Peninsula, eventually conquering them as well (see American Lives, "Cortés and Malinche: The Dynamics of Conquest," p. 30).

In 1524 the Spanish conquest entered a new phase, when Francisco Pizarro led a military expedition to the mountains of Peru, home of the rich and powerful Inca empire that stretched 2,000 miles along the Pacific coast of South America. To govern this far-flung empire, the Inca rulers built 24,000 miles of roads and dozens of carefully placed administrative centers, which were constructed of finely crafted stone. A semidivine Inca king ruled the empire, assisted by a hierarchical bureaucracy staffed by noblemen, many of whom were his relatives. By the time Pizarro and his small force of 168 men and 67 horses reached Peru, half of the Inca population had died from European diseases, which had been spread by Indian traders. Weakened militarily and fighting over succession to the throne, the Inca nobility was easy prey for Pizarro's army. In little more than a decade Spain had become the master of the wealthiest and most populous regions of the Western Hemisphere.

Friar Bernardino de Sahagún

Aztec Elders Describe the Spanish Conquest

During the 1550s Friar Bernardino de Sahagún published the Florentine Codex: General History of New Spain. *According to Sahagún, the authors of the Codex were Aztec elders who lived through the conquest. Here the elders describe their reaction to the invading Europeans and the devastating impact of smallpox. They told their stories to Sahagún in a repetitive style, using the conventions of Aztec oral histories, and he translated them into Spanish.*

Moctezuma enjoyed no sleep, no food, no one spoke to him. Whatsoever he did, it was as if he were in torment. Ofttimes it was as if he sighed, became weak, felt weak. . . . Wherefore he said, "What will now befall us? Who indeed stands [in charge]? Alas, until now, I. In great torment is my heart; as if it were washed in chili water it indeed burns." . . .

And when he had so heard what the messengers reported, he was terrified, he was astounded. . . . Especially did it cause him to faint away when he heard how the gun, at [the Spaniards'] command, discharged: how it resounded as if it thundered when it went off. It indeed bereft one of strength; it shut off one's ears. And when it discharged, something like a round pebble came forth from within. Fire went showering forth; sparks went blazing forth. And its smoke smelled very foul; it had a fetid odor which verily wounded the head. And when [the shot] struck a mountain, it was as if it were destroyed, dissolved . . . as if someone blew it away.

All iron was their war array. In iron they clothed themselves. With iron they covered their heads. Iron were their swords. Iron were their crossbows. Iron were their shields. Iron were their lances. And those which bore them upon their backs, their deer [horses], were as tall as roof terraces.

And their bodies were everywhere covered; only their faces appeared. They were very white; they had chalky faces; they had yellow hair, though the hair of some was black. . . . And when Moctezuma so heard, he was much terrified. It was as if he fainted away. His heart saddened; his heart failed him. . . .

[Soon] there came to be prevalent a great sickness, a plague. It was in Tepeilhuitl that it originated, that there spread over the people a great destruction of men. Some it indeed covered [with pustules]; they were spread everywhere, on one's face, on one's head, on one's breast. There was indeed perishing; many indeed died of it. No longer could they walk; they only lay in their abodes, in their beds. No longer could they move. . . . And when they bestirred themselves, much did they cry out. There was much perishing. Like a covering, covering-like, were the pustules. Indeed, many people died of them, and many just died of hunger. There was death from hunger; there was no one to take care of another; there was no one to attend to another.

Source: Friar Bernardino de Sahagún, *Florentine Codex: General History of New Spain*, trans. Arthur J. O. Anderson and Charles E. Dibble (Santa Fe and Salt Lake City: School of American Research and University of Utah Press, 1975), 12:17–20, 26, 83.

The Legacy of the Conquest.   The Spanish invasion and European diseases changed life forever throughout the Americas. Virtually all the Indians of Hispaniola—at least 300,000 people—were wiped out by disease and warfare. In Peru the population plummeted from 9 million in 1530 to fewer than half a million a century later. Likewise, diseases unintentionally introduced by early Spanish expeditions in the present-day United States inflicted equally catastrophic losses on the Pueblo peoples of the Southwest and the Mississippian chiefdoms of the Southeast. In 1500 Mesoamerica as a whole had probably 40 million Indians; by 1650 its Native American population had fallen to a mere 3 million people—one of the greatest demographic disasters in world history.

Once the conquistadors had triumphed, the Spanish government quickly created an elaborate bureaucratic empire, headed in Madrid by the Council of the Indies, which issued laws and decrees to viceroys and other Spanish-born officials in America. However, the conquistadors remained powerful because they held grants (**encomiendas**) from the crown giving them legal

Premonition of Disaster

In 1570 Fray Diego Durán, a Spanish Dominican monk, recorded the history of Aztec people. This leaf from his manuscript captures the moment when Moctezuma first hears of the arrival of white-skinned strangers on the coast of the empire that he ruled. The watercolor shows the comet that Moctezuma reportedly saw plunging to the earth, an event that according to Aztec belief was a harbinger of disaster. Library of Congress.

control of the native population. They ruthlessly exploited the surviving Native Americans, forcing them to work on vast plantations to raise crops and cattle for local consumption and export to Europe. The Spaniards also altered the natural environment by introducing grains and grasses that supplanted the native flora. Horses, first brought to the mainland by Cortés, gradually spread throughout the Western Hemisphere and in the following centuries dramatically changed the way of life of many Indian peoples, especially on the Great Plains of the United States.

The Spanish invasion of the Americas had a significant impact on life in Europe and Africa as well. In a process of transfer known as the **Columbian Exchange**, the food products of the Western Hemisphere—especially maize, potatoes, and cassava (manioc)—became available to the peoples of other continents, significantly increasing agricultural yields and stimulating the growth of population (Map 1.6). Similarly, the livestock and crops—and weeds and human diseases—of African and Eurasian lands became part of the lives of residents

of the Americas. Nor was that all. In addition to this ecological revolution, the gold and silver that had honored Aztec gods flowed into the countinghouses of Spain and into the treasury of its monarchs, making that nation the most powerful in Europe.

By 1550 the once magnificent civilizations of Mexico and Peru lay in ruins. "Of all these wonders"—the great city of Tenochtitlán, rich orchards, overflowing markets—"all is overthrown and lost, nothing left standing," recalled the Spanish chronicler Bernal Díaz, who had been a young soldier in Cortés's army. Moreover, those Native Americans who survived had lost vital parts of their cultural identity. Spanish priests suppressed their worship of traditional gods and converted them to Catholicism. As early as 1531 an Indian convert reported a vision of a dark-skinned Virgin Mary, later known as the Virgin of Guadalupe, a Christian version of the "corn mother" who traditionally protected the maize crop.

Soon Spanish bureaucrats imposed taxes and supervised the lives of the Indians, as no fewer than 350,000

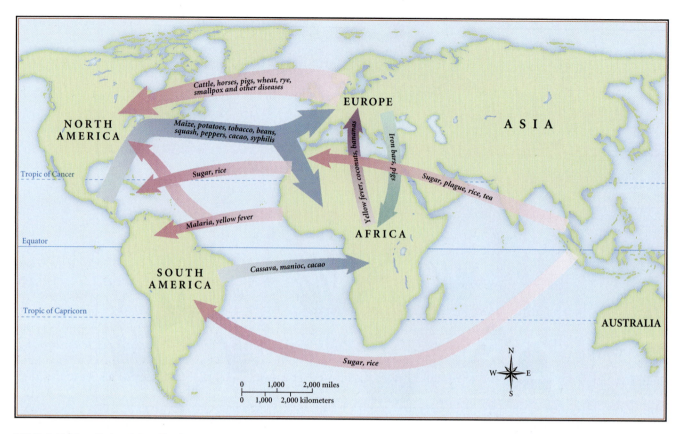

MAP 1.6 The Columbian Exchange

As European traders and adventurers traveled to Africa, the Americas, and Asia between 1430 and 1600, they began what historians call the "Columbian Exchange," a vast intercontinental movement of the plants, animals, and diseases that changed the course of historical development. As the nutritious, high-yielding American crops of corn and potatoes enriched the diets of Europeans and Africans, the Eurasian and African diseases of smallpox, diphtheria, malaria, and yellow fever nearly wiped out the native inhabitants of the Western Hemisphere and virtually ensured that they would lose control of their lands.

For more help analyzing this map, see the ONLINE STUDY GUIDE at bedfordstmartins.com/henretta.

Spanish migrants settled between 1500 and 1650 on lands previously occupied by the native peoples of Mesoamerica and South America. Because nearly 90 percent of the Spanish settlers were men who took Indian women as wives or mistresses, the result was a substantial **mestizo** (mixed-race) population and an elaborate system of race-based caste distinctions. Around 1800, at the end of the colonial era, Spanish America had about 17 million people: 7.5 million Indians, 3.2 million Europeans, 1 million enslaved Africans, and 5.5 million people of mixed race and cultural heritage.

Some Indians resisted assimilation by retreating into the mountains, but they lacked the numbers or the power to oust the Spanish invaders or their descendants. Today only a single Indian tongue, Guarani in Paraguay, is a recognized national language, and no Native American state has representation in the United Nations. For

the original Americans the consequences of the European intrusion in 1492 were tragic and irreversible.

The Protestant Reformation and the Rise of England

Religion was a central aspect of European life and, because of a major crisis in Western Christendom, played a crucial role in the settlement of America. Even as Christian fervor drove Portugal and Spain to expel Muslims and Jews from their nations and to convert the peoples of Mesoamerica to Catholicism, Christianity ceased to be a unifying force in European society. New religious doctrines preached by Martin Luther and other reformers divided Christians into armed ideological camps of

TABLE 1.2 Spanish Monarchs, 1474–1598		
Monarch	Dates of Reign	Achievements
Ferdinand and Isabella	1474–1516	Expelled Muslims from Spain; dispatched Columbus
Charles I	1516–1556	Holy Roman Emperor, 1519–1556
Philip II	1556–1598	Attacked Protestantism; mounted Spanish Armada

Catholics and Protestants and plunged the continent into religious wars that lasted for decades.

These struggles set the stage for Protestant dominance of North America. In the 1560s a Protestant rebellion in the Spanish Netherlands led to Holland's emergence as a separate nation and a major commercial power in both Asia and the Americas. England likewise experienced a religious revolution and a major economic transformation that gave it the physical resources and spiritual energy to establish Protestant settlements in North America.

The Protestant Movement

Over the centuries the Catholic Church had become a large and wealthy institution, controlling vast resources throughout Europe. Renaissance popes and cardinals were among the leading patrons of the arts, but some also misused the Church's wealth. Pope Leo X (r. 1513–1521) was the most notorious, receiving half a million ducats a year from the sale of religious offices. Ordinary priests and monks regularly used their authority to obtain economic or sexual favors. One English reformer denounced the clergy as a "gang of scoundrels" who should be "rid of their vices or stripped of their authority," but he was ignored. Other reformers, such as Jan Hus of Bohemia, were tried and executed as heretics.

Martin Luther's Attack on Church Doctrine. In 1517 Martin Luther, a German monk and professor at the university in Wittenberg, nailed his famous Ninety-five Theses to the door of the castle church. That widely reprinted document condemned the sale of **indulgences**—church certificates that purportedly pardoned a sinner from punishments in the afterlife. Luther argued that heavenly salvation could come only from God through grace, not from the Church for a fee. He was excommunicated by the pope and threatened with punishment by King Charles I of Spain (r. 1516–1556), the head of the Holy Roman Empire, which included most of Germany (Table 1.2). Northern German princes, who were resisting the emperor's authority for political reasons, embraced Luther's teachings and protected him from arrest, thus allowing the Protestant movement to flourish.

Luther broadened his attack, articulating positions that differed from Roman Catholic doctrine in three major respects. First, Luther rejected the doctrine that Christians could win salvation through good deeds, arguing that people could be saved only by grace, which came as a free gift from God. Second, he downplayed the role of clergy and the pope as mediators between God and the people, proclaiming, "Our baptism consecrates us all without exception and makes us all priests." Third, Luther said that believers must look to the Bible (not Church doctrine) as the ultimate authority in matters of faith. So that every German-speaking believer could read the Bible, he translated it from Latin into German.

Peasants as well as princes heeded Luther's attack on authority and, to his dismay, mounted social protests of their own. In 1524 some German peasants rebelled against their manorial lords and were ruthlessly suppressed. Fearing social revolution, Luther urged obedience to established political institutions and condemned the teachings of new groups of religious dissidents, such as the Anabaptists (so called because they rejected infant baptism).

Embracing Luther's views, most princes in northern Germany broke from Rome, in part because they wanted the power to appoint bishops and control the Church's property within their own domains. In response, Emperor Charles dispatched armies to Germany to restore Catholic doctrine and his political authority, unleashing a generation of warfare. Eventually the Peace of Augsburg (1555) restored order by allowing princes to decide the religion of their subjects. Most southern German rulers installed Catholicism as the official religion, while those in the north made Lutheranism the state creed (Map 1.7).

The Teachings of John Calvin. The most rigorous Protestant doctrine was established in Geneva, Switzerland, under the leadership of the French theologian John Calvin. Even more than Luther, Calvin stressed the omnipotence of God and the corruption of human nature. His *Institutes of the Christian Religion* (1536) depicted God as an awesome and absolute sovereign who

Cortés and Malinche: The Dynamics of Conquest

Hernán Cortés conquered an empire and destroyed a civilization, an achievement that was both magnificent and tragic. The immensity of Cortés's dual triumph was partly accidental, owing to the rebellion of the non-Aztec peoples and the extraordinarily devastating impact of European diseases, but it also reflected his burning ambition and political vision. Unlike most other gold-hungry Spanish adventurers, Cortés had a sense of politics and of history. Once he learned from the Maya, in whose territory he first landed, of the existence of Moctezuma and his kingdom, Cortés's priority became the pursuit of power rather than of plunder. As Bernal Díaz del Castillo, one of his soldiers, reported in the *History of the Conquest of New Spain*, Cortés immediately declared his intention "to serve God and the king" by subjugating the Aztec king and his great empire.

Could this be done? Six hundred Spanish troops might plunder the lands at the far reaches of an empire of millions, but what chance did they stand against an Aztec army of tens of thousands? The odds of conquering the Aztec empire were so low that a less audacious man would not even have tried. But Cortés was no ordinary man. A person of great presence—intelligent and ruthless, courageous yet prudent, decisive yet flexible—the Spanish chieftain inspired fear and respect among his enemies and unthinking loyalty among his followers, who time and again risked their lives at his command. No one was more loyal to Cortés—and, at crucial points in the conquest of Mexico, more important—than the native woman known as La Malinche, who became his interpreter and mistress. Had he not conquered her affections, he might have failed to conquer the empire.

As a child, the girl who became Malinche was called Malinali, the name of the twelfth month in the Nahuatl language spoken by the Aztec and other Mexican peoples. Her father was the local lord of Painala, a village near the Gulf of Mexico in the far southern reaches of the Aztec empire, and her mother was the ruler of Xatipan, a small nearby settlement. As the daughter of minor nobles, Malinali lived in comfort and no doubt developed the sense of confidence that would serve her so well in the future. But she lived her adolescent years as a mere slave. Following the death of her father and the remarriage of her mother, Malinali was sold into bondage by her mother and stepfather, who wanted to enhance the succession rights of their newborn son. Owned first by merchants, she ended up as an enslaved worker in the Mayan settlement of Potonchan on the Gulf of Mexico. There, in March 1519 when she was about seventeen years old, Malinali had her rendezvous with destiny.

Initially the confrontation between Spaniards and Native Americans took place with gestures and misunderstandings, for the two peoples could not comprehend each other's language, intentions, and values. But Cortés was lucky, for his expedition had chanced upon Father Gerónimo de Aguilar, a shipwrecked Spanish priest who had lived for a decade as a slave among the Mayas and knew their language. And he was doubly lucky when the Mayas of Potonchan, whom he had defeated in battle, presented him with twenty slave women, one of whom was Malinali. Cortés treated these women as servants and concubines, assigning them to his commanders; and because Malinali was "of pleasing appearance and sharpwitted and outward-going" (according to Díaz del Castillo), she was given to his chief lieutenant, Alonso Puertocarrero. Learning that the young woman could speak Nahuatl, Cortés soon took her as his own servant and mistress. At his command she conversed with Nahuatl-speaking peoples and then used Mayan to convey what she had learned to Aguilar, who translated it into Spanish. The process was cumbersome, but it worked. Now Cortés could negotiate directly with both Moctezuma's officials and the leaders of the non-Aztec peoples whose help he needed to conquer the empire.

Of Malinali's motives in providing aid to the Spanish invaders there is no record. Like other Mexican peoples, including Moctezuma, at first she may have viewed Cortés as a returning god. Or, like his Spanish followers, she may have been dazzled by his powerful presence and personality. Or, quite likely, Malinali may have calculated that Cortés was her best hope of escaping slavery and reclaiming a noble status. Whatever the reasons, Malinali's loyalty to her new master was complete and unbending. Rejecting an opportunity to betray the Spanish on their march to the Aztec capital of Tenochtitlán in 1519, she risked her life by warning Cortés of a surprise attack by the Cholulans. In 1520 she stood by him when the Spanish cause seemed lost following the disastrous retreat from Tenochtitlán. And in 1524 and 1525 she helped him survive a catastrophic military campaign in the jungles of present-day Honduras.

There is no question about Malinali's importance to the Spanish cause. As Bernal Díaz del Castillo concluded, "without her we never should have understood the Mexican language and, upon the whole, [would] have been unable to surmount many difficulties." The Aztecs likewise acknowledged her eminence. They called her Malinche, addressing her with respect by adding the suffix *-che* to her original name, and they often referred to Cortés as "the captain of Malinche," defining the Spaniard in terms of the interpreter through whom he spoke.

Yet there is no evidence that Cortés felt indebted to Malinche or developed a deep emotional bond with the young woman. In 1522 or 1523 she bore him a son (whom he named Martin after his father), but by then he had taken many other mistresses, including the daughters of Moctezuma, and in succeeding years sired numerous illegitimate children by other Mexican women. Moreover, in 1525 Cortés again gave the services of Malinali, now known by the respectful Spanish name of Doña Marina, to one of his commanders, Juan Jaramillo, with whom she lived in marriage until her death in 1551. A mere native woman was not what the great conqueror had in mind as a wife. To solidify his achievement and lay the foundation for a great family dynasty, in 1528 Cortés won entry into the ranks of the Spanish nobility, taking as his wife Juana, daughter of the count of Aguilar and a niece of the duke of Béjar, one of the richest and most politically powerful men in Spain. After living with Juana in Mexico for a decade Cortés returned to his native land, where he died in 1647 at the age of sixty-two, a respected and colossally wealthy man.

Malinche fared less well than her former master did, in death as well as in life. Because she was among the first native women to bear mixed-race (mestizo) children, Malinche has sometimes been celebrated as the symbolic mother of the post-conquest Mexican people. More often, she has seemed to subsequent generations of Mexicans as a traitor to her people, a mere instrument in the hands of greedy invaders who subjugated a society and destroyed a civilization. Within the dynamics of sexual and military conquest, both views are correct.

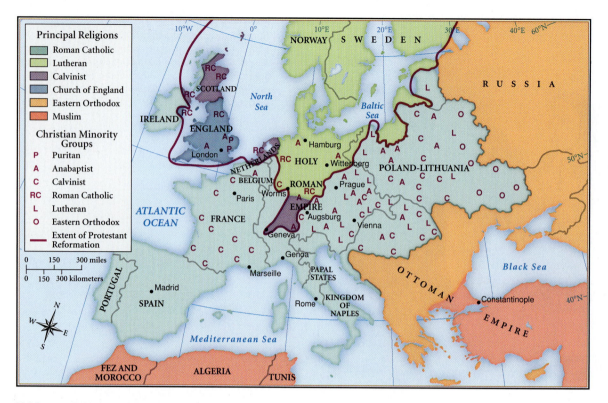

MAP 1.7 Religious Diversity in Europe, 1600

By 1600 Europe was permanently divided. Catholicism remained dominant in the south, but Lutheran princes and monarchs ruled northern Europe, and Calvinism had strongholds in Switzerland, Holland, and Scotland. Radical sects were persecuted by legally established Protestant churches as well as by Catholic clergy and monarchs. These religious conflicts encouraged the migration of minority sects to America.

governed the "wills of men so as to move precisely to that end directed by him." Calvin preached the doctrine of **predestination**—the idea that God had chosen certain people for salvation even before they were born, condemning the rest to eternal damnation. In Geneva he set up a model Christian community, eliminating bishops and placing spiritual power in the hands of ministers chosen by the members of each congregation. These ministers and pious laymen ruled the city, prohibiting frivolity and luxury and imposing religious discipline on the entire society. "We know," wrote Calvin, "that man is of so perverse and crooked a nature, that everyone would scratch out his neighbor's eyes if there were no bridle to hold them in." Despite widespread persecution, Calvinists won converts all over Europe. Calvinism was adopted by the Huguenots in France, by the Protestant (or Reformed) churches in Belgium and Holland, and by Presbyterians and Puritans in Scotland and England.

Protestantism in England. In England, King Henry VIII (r. 1509–1547) initially opposed the spread of Protestantism in his kingdom. But when the pope denied his request for an annulment of his marriage to Catherine of Aragon, Henry broke with Rome in 1534 and made

himself the head of a national Church of England (which promptly granted the annulment). Although Henry made few changes in Church doctrine, organization, and ritual, his daughter Queen Elizabeth I (r. 1558–1603) approved a Protestant confession of faith that incorporated both the Lutheran doctrine of salvation by grace and the Calvinist belief in predes-tination. To mollify traditionalists Elizabeth retained the Catholic ritual of Holy Communion—now conducted in English rather than in Latin—as well as the hierarchy of bishops and archbishops.

Elizabeth's compromises angered radical Protestants, who condemned the power of bishops as "anti-Christian and devilish and contrary to the Scriptures" and demanded major changes in Church organization. Many of these reformers took inspiration from the Presbyterian system pioneered in Calvin's Geneva and developed fully by John Knox for the Church of Scotland; in Scotland local congregations elected lay elders (presbyters), who assisted ministers in running the Church, and sent delegates to synods (councils) that decided Church doctrine. By 1600, at least five hundred ministers in the Church of England wanted to eliminate bishops and install a Presbyterian form of church government.

Other radical English Protestants were calling themselves "unspotted lambs of the Lord" or "Puritans." More intensely than most Protestants they wanted to "purify" the Church of "false" Catholic teachings and practices. Following radical Calvinist principles, Puritans condemned many traditional religious rites as magical or idolatrous. Puritan services avoided appeals to dead saints or the burning of incense and instead focused on a carefully argued sermon on ethics or dogma. Puritans also placed special emphasis on the idea of a "calling," the duty to serve God in one's work. To ensure that all men and women had access to God's commands, they encouraged everyone to read the Bible, thus promoting widespread literacy. Finally, most Puritans wanted authority over spiritual and financial matters to rest primarily with the local congregation, not with bishops or even Presbyterian synods (church councils). Eventually thousands of Puritan migrants would establish churches in North America based on these radical Protestant doctrines.

The Dutch and the English Challenge Spain

Luther's challenge to Catholicism in 1517 came just two years before Cortés conquered the Aztec empire, and the two events remained linked. Gold and silver from Mexico and Peru made Spain the wealthiest nation in Europe and King Philip II (r. 1556–1598), the successor to Charles I, its most powerful ruler. In addition to Spain, Philip presided over wealthy city-states in Italy, the commercial

and manufacturing provinces of the Spanish Netherlands (present-day Holland and Belgium), and, after 1580, Portugal and all its possessions in America, Africa, and the East Indies. "If the Romans were able to rule the world simply by ruling the Mediterranean," a Spanish priest boasted, "what of the man who rules the Atlantic and Pacific oceans, since they surround the world?"

Philip, an ardent Catholic, tried to root out Protestantism in the Netherlands, which had become wealthy from trade with the vast Portuguese empire and from the weaving of wool and linen. To protect their Calvinist faith and political liberties, the Dutch and Flemish provinces revolted in 1566, and in 1581 the seven northern provinces declared their independence, becoming the Dutch Republic (or Holland). When Elizabeth I of England dispatched 6,000 troops to assist the Dutch cause, Philip found a new enemy. In 1588 he sent the Spanish Armada—130 ships and 30,000 men—against England. Philip planned to reimpose Catholicism in England and then wipe out Calvinism in Holland. However, the Armada failed utterly, as English ships and a fierce storm destroyed the Spanish fleet. Philip continued to spend his American gold on foreign wars, undermining the Spanish economy and prompting the migration of hundreds of thousands of Spaniards to America. By the time of his death in 1598, Spain was in serious decline.

As Spain faltered, Holland prospered, the economic miracle of the seventeenth century. Amsterdam emerged as the financial capital of northern Europe, and the Dutch Republic became the leading commercial power of Europe, replacing Portugal as the dominant trader in

Dutch Merchant Family
This painting of Pierre de Moucheron and his family by the Dutch artist Cornelius de Zeeuw captures the prosperity and the severe Calvinist ethos of Holland in the sixteenth century. It also suggests the character of the traditional patriarchal family, in which status reflected a rigid hierarchy of gender and age. Rijksmuseum, Amsterdam.

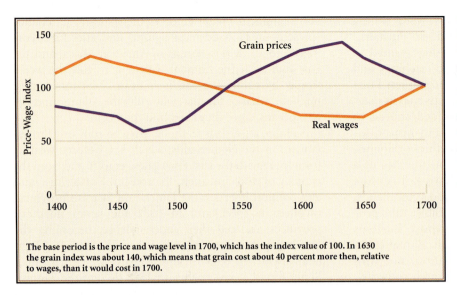

FIGURE 1.2 The Great Price Inflation and Living Standards in Europe

As American gold and silver poured into Europe after 1520, there was more money in circulation and people used it to bid up the price of grain. Grain prices also rose because of increasing demand; the result of growth in Europe's population. Because prices rose faster than wages living standards fell from a high point about 1430 to a low point about 1630. As "real wages" rose after 1630, people lived better.

The base period is the price and wage level in 1700, which has the index value of 100. In 1630 the grain index was about 140, which means that grain cost about 40 percent more then, relative to wages, than it would cost in 1700.

Asia and coastal Africa. The Dutch also looked across the Atlantic, creating the West India Company, which invested in sugar plantations in Brazil and the Caribbean and established the fur-trading colony of New Netherland in North America.

England also emerged as an important European state, its economy stimulated by a rise in population from 3 million in 1500 to 5 million in 1630. An equally important factor was the state-supported expansion of the merchant community. English merchants had long supplied high-quality wool to European weavers, and around 1500 they created their own system of textile production. In this **outwork** (or putting-out) system merchants bought wool from the owners of great estates and provided it to landless peasants, who spun and wove the wool into cloth. The merchants then sold the finished product in English and foreign markets. The government helped manufacturers to expand production by setting low rates for wages and assisted merchants to increase exports by granting special monopoly privileges to the Levant Company (Turkey) in

Elizabeth I (r. 1558–1603)

Attired in richly decorated clothes that symbolize her power, Queen Elizabeth I relishes the destruction of the Spanish Armada (pictured in background) and proclaims her nation's imperial ambitions. The queen's hand rests on a globe, asserting England's claims in the Western Hemisphere.

Woburn Abbey Collection, by permission of the Marquess of Tavistock and the Trustees of the Bedford Estates.

1581, the Guinea Company (Africa) in 1588, and the East India Company in 1600.

This system of state-assisted manufacturing and trade became known as mercantilism. Mercantilist-minded monarchs like Elizabeth I encouraged merchants to invest in domestic manufacturing, thereby increasing exports and reducing imports, in order to give England a favorable balance of trade. The queen and her advisors wanted gold and silver to flow into the country in payment for English manufactures, stimulating further economic expansion and enriching the merchant community. Increased trade also meant higher revenues from import duties, which swelled the royal treasury and enhanced the power of the national government. By 1600 the success of these merchant-oriented policies had laid the foundations for overseas colonization. The English (as well as the Dutch) now had the merchant fleets and economic wealth needed to challenge Spain's monopoly in the Western Hemisphere.

The Social Causes of English Colonization

England's monarchs and ministers of state had long been interested in America. Now economic changes in England (as well as continuing religious conflict) provided a large body of settlers willing to go to America. The massive expenditure of American gold and silver by Philip II and the Spanish conquistadors had doubled the money supply of Europe and sparked a major inflation between 1530 and 1600—known today as the Price Revolution—that brought about profound social changes in the English countryside (Figure 1.2).

The Decline of the Nobility.   In England the nobility was the first casualty of the **Price Revolution**. Aristocrats had customarily rented out their estates on long leases for fixed rents, gaining a secure income and plenty of leisure. As one English nobleman put it, "We eat and drink and rise up to play and this is to live like a gentleman." Then inflation struck. In less than two generations the price of goods more than tripled while the nobility's income from the rents on its farmlands barely increased. As the wealth and status of the aristocracy declined in relative terms, that of the **gentry** and the yeomen rose. The gentry (nonnoble landholders with substantial estates) kept pace with inflation by renting land on short leases at higher rates. Yeomen, described by a European traveler as "middle people of a condition between gentlemen and peasants," owned small farms that they worked with family help. As wheat prices tripled, yeomen used the profits to build larger houses and provide their children with land.

Economics influenced politics. As aristocrats lost wealth, their branch of Parliament, the House of Lords, declined in influence. At the same time, members of the rising gentry entered the House of Commons, the political voice of the propertied classes. Supported by the yeomen, the gentry demanded new rights and powers for the Commons, such as control of taxation. Thus the Price Revolution encouraged the rise of governing institutions in which rich commoners and small property owners had a voice, a development with profound consequences for English—and American—political history.

The Dispossession of the Peasantry.   Peasants and landless farm laborers made up three-fourths of the population of England (Figure 1.3), and their lives also were transformed by the Price Revolution. Many of these rural folk lived in open-field settlements, but the rise of domestic manufacturing increased the demand for wool, prompting profit-minded landlords and wool merchants to persuade Parliament to pass **enclosure acts**. These acts allowed owners to fence in open fields and put sheep to graze on them. Thus dispossessed of their land, peasant families lived on the brink of poverty, spinning and weaving wool or working as wage laborers on large estates. Wealthy men had "taken farms into their hands," an observer noted in 1600, "and rent them to those that will give most, whereby the

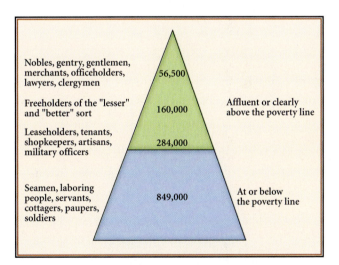

FIGURE 1.3 The Structure of English Society, 1688
This famous table, the work of Gregory King, an early statistician, shows the result of centuries of aristocratic rule. It depicts a social structure shaped like a thin pyramid, with a small privileged elite at the top and a mass of poor working people at the bottom. The majority of English families (some 849,000, according to King) lived at or below the poverty line and, he thought, were "Decreasing the Wealth of the Kingdom." In fact, the labor of the poor produced much of the wealth owned by the 500,500 families at the middle and the top of the social scale.

peasantry of England is decayed and become servants to gentlemen."

These changes, and a series of crop failures caused by cold weather between 1590 and 1640, set the stage for a substantial migration to America. As the danger of starvation increased and land prices continued to rise, thousands of yeomen families looked across the Atlantic for land for their children. Dispossessed peasants and weavers, their livelihoods threatened by a decline in the cloth trade, were likewise on the move. "Thieves and rogues do swarm the highways," warned Justice of the Peace William Lamparde, "and bastards be multiplied in parishes." Seeking food and security, tens of thousands of young propertyless laborers contracted to go to America in the lowly condition of indentured servants. This massive migration of English yeomen families and impoverished laborers would bring about

a new collision between the European and Native American worlds.

FOR FURTHER EXPLORATION

▶ For definitions of key terms boldfaced in this chapter, see the glossary at the end of the book.

▶ To assess your mastery of the material covered in this chapter, see the Online Study Guide at **bedfordstmartins.com/henretta**.

▶ For suggested references, including Web sites, see page SR-1 at the end of the book.

▶ For map resources and primary documents, see **bedfordstmartins.com/henretta**.

SUMMARY

The first inhabitants of the Western Hemisphere were hunter-gatherers who migrated from Asia some thirty thousand years ago. Their descendants settled throughout the Americas, establishing a great variety of cultures. In Mesoamerica, the Mayan and Aztec peoples created populous agricultural societies with sophisticated systems of art, religion, and politics, while the Incas set up an empire along the western coast of South America. In North America, the Hopewell and Mississippian peoples created elaborate ceremonial and urban sites, as did the Pueblo peoples of the Southwest. However, in 1500 most Indians north of the Rio Grande lived in small-scale communities of hunters and farmers.

The Europeans who invaded America came from a traditional agricultural society ruled by a privileged elite. Christianity provided unity and spiritual meaning to European civilization. Both church and state endorsed hierarchy and authority, demanding that peasants submit to strict discipline. Carried by settlers to America, these values of order and security strongly influenced colonial life.

The Crusades exposed Europeans to the learning of the Arab Muslim world, while the Italian Renaissance and the rise of monarchical nation-states imparted dynamism to European society. Portugal sent explorers and merchants to Africa and Asia and sold enslaved West Africans to sugar planters in the Mediterranean and later in Brazil. Spain conquered Mexico and Peru, the wealthiest areas of the "new world" found by Christopher Columbus. The coming of Europeans—and their diseases, crops, horses, government, and religion—brought death to millions of Native Americans and altered the ecology of Western Hemisphere. Likewise, the Columbian exchange and mass emigration of Europeans and enslaved Africans to the Americas changed the character of the "old world."

Thus, gold and silver from America disrupted Europe's economy and society, which was already reeling from the Protestant Reformation. Religious warfare and the Price Revolution undermined Catholic Spain while assisting the rise of Holland, France, and England. In England, monarchs used mercantilist policies to promote domestic manufacturing and foreign trade, while the enclosure acts and religious conflicts prompted a mass migration to America.

English migrants carried both traditional and modern ideas and institutions across the Atlantic—a contrast between old and new that was sharpened in America: in England's Chesapeake colonies a new form of aristocratic rule would emerge, based first on white indentured servitude and then on African slavery, while in New England the settlers would establish a yeoman society that had few European antecedents.

TIMELINE

13,000– 3000 B.C.	Main settlement of North America
3000– 2000 B.C.	Cultivation of crops begins in Mesoamerica
100–400	Flourishing of Hopewell culture
300	Rise of Mayan civilization
500	Zenith of Teotihuacán civilization
600	Emergence of Pueblo cultures
700–1100	Spread of Arab Muslim civilization
800–1350	Development of Mississippian culture
1096–1291	Crusades link Europe with Arab learning
1300–1450	Italian Renaissance
1325	Aztecs establish capital at Tenochtitlán
1440s	Portugal enters trade in African slaves
1492	Christopher Columbus's first voyage to America
1513	Juan Ponce de León explores Florida
1517	Martin Luther begins Protestant Reformation
1519–1521	Hernán Cortés conquers Aztec empire
1531–1538	Francisco Pizarro vanquishes Incas in Peru
1534	Henry VIII establishes Church of England
1536	John Calvin, *Institutes of Christian Religion*
1550–1630	Price Revolution English mercantilism Enclosure acts
1556–1598	Philip I, king of Spain
1558–1603	Elizabeth I, queen of England
1560s	English Puritan movement begins

The manner of their fishing.

CHAPTER 2

The Invasion and Settlement of North America

1550–1700

Imperial Conflicts and Rival Colonial Models
New Spain: Colonization and Conversion
New France: Furs and Souls
New Netherland: Commerce
The First English Model: Tobacco and Settlers

The Chesapeake Experience
Settling the Tobacco Colonies
Masters, Servants, and Slaves
The Seeds of Social Revolt
Bacon's Rebellion

Puritan New England
The Puritan Migration
Religion and Society, 1630–1670
The Puritan Imagination and Witchcraft
A Yeoman Society, 1630–1700

The Indians' New World
Puritans and Pequots
Metacom's Rebellion
The Fur Trade and the Inland Peoples

ESTABLISHING COLONIES IN THE DISTANT LAND OF NORTH AMERICA was not for the faint of heart. First came a long voyage in small ships over stormy, dangerous waters. Then the migrants, weakened by weeks of travel, spoiled food, and shipboard diseases, faced the challenges of life in an alien land inhabited by potentially hostile Indian peoples. "We neither fear them or trust them," declared Puritan settler Francis Higginson, but rely for protection on "our musketeers." Although the risks were great and the rewards uncertain, tens of thousands of Europeans crossed the Atlantic during the seventeenth century, driven by poverty and persecution at home or drawn by the lures of the New World: land, gold, and—as another Puritan migrant put it—the hope of "propagating the Gospel to these poor barbarous people."

◀ **Carolina Indians Fishing, 1585**
The artist John White was one of the English settlers in Sir Walter Raleigh's ill-fated colony on Roanoke Island, and his watercolors provide a rich visual record of Native American life. Here the Indians who resided near present-day Albemarle Sound in North Carolina are harvesting a protein-rich diet of fish from its shallow waters.
Trustees of the British Museum.

For Native Americans, the European invasion was nothing short of catastrophic. "Our fathers had plenty of deer and skins, . . . and our coves were full of fish and fowl," the Narragansett chief Miantonomi warned the neighboring Montauk people in 1642, "but these English having gotten our land . . . their cows and horses eat the grass, and their hogs spoil our clam banks, and we shall all be starved." Whether they came as settlers or missionaries or fur traders, the white-skinned people spread havoc, bringing new diseases and religions and threatening Indian peoples with the loss of their cultures, lands, and lives. The stakes of the contest were enormous and demanded united resistance. "We [are] all Indians," Miantonomi continued, and must "say brother to one another, . . . otherwise we shall all be gone shortly." The first century of cultural contact foretold the course of North American history: the advance of the European invaders and the dispossession of the Indian peoples.

Imperial Conflicts and Rival Colonial Models

In Mesoamerica the Spanish colonial regime forced the Indians to convert to Catholicism and to work digging gold and farming large estates. But in the sparsely populated Indian lands north of the Rio Grande, other Europeans founded different types of colonies (Table 2.1). In the fur-trading empires created by the French and the Dutch, the native peoples retained their lands and political autonomy, while in the English colonies the rapidly multiplying settlers expelled the resident Indians, who were pushed ever farther to the west. Despite the differing goals of these colonial regimes—the exploitation of native labor by the Spanish, the trading of furs by the French and the Dutch, the creation of farming communities by the English—nearly everywhere the Indian peoples eventually rose in revolt.

New Spain: Colonization and Conversion

In their ceaseless quest for gold, Spanish adventurers became the first Europeans to explore the southern and western United States. In the 1540s Francisco Vásquez de Coronado searched in vain for Cíbola, the fabled seven golden cities said to lie north of present-day Albuquerque. Continuing his search, Coronado dispatched expeditions that discovered the Grand Canyon in Arizona, the Pueblo peoples of New Mexico, and the grasslands of central Kansas. Simultaneously, Hernán de Soto and a force of 600 adventurers cut a bloody swath across the densely populated Southeast, doing battle with the Apalachees of northern Florida and the Coosas of northern Alabama but finding no gold and few other riches (Map 2.1).

By the 1560s few Spanish officials still dreamed of finding rich Indian empires north of Mexico. Now their main goal was to prevent other European nations from establishing settlements. Roving English "sea dogs" were already plundering Spanish possessions in the Caribbean, and French corsairs were attacking Spanish treasure ships, halving the Spanish crown's revenue. Equally ominously, French Protestants began to settle in Florida, long claimed by Spain. In response King Philip II ordered that the Frenchmen in Florida be "cast . . . out by the best

TABLE 2.1 European Colonies in North America before 1660

	Date	First Settlement	Type	Religion	Chief Export or Economic Activity
New France	1608	Quebec	Royal	Catholic	Furs
New Netherland	1613	New Amsterdam	Corporate	Dutch Reformed	Furs
New Sweden	1628	Fort Christina	Corporate	Lutheran	Furs; farming
English Colonies					
Virginia	1607	Jamestown	Corporate (Merchant)	Anglican	Tobacco
Plymouth	1620	Plymouth	Corporate (Religious)	Separatist-Puritan	Mixed farming; livestock
Massachusetts Bay	1630	Boston	Corporate (Religious)	Puritan	Mixed farming
Maryland	1634	St. Mary's	Proprietary	Catholic	Tobacco; grain
Connecticut	1635	Hartford	Corporate (Religious)	Puritan	Mixed farming; livestock
Rhode Island	1636	Providence	Corporate (Religious)	Separatist-Puritan	Mixed farming; livestock

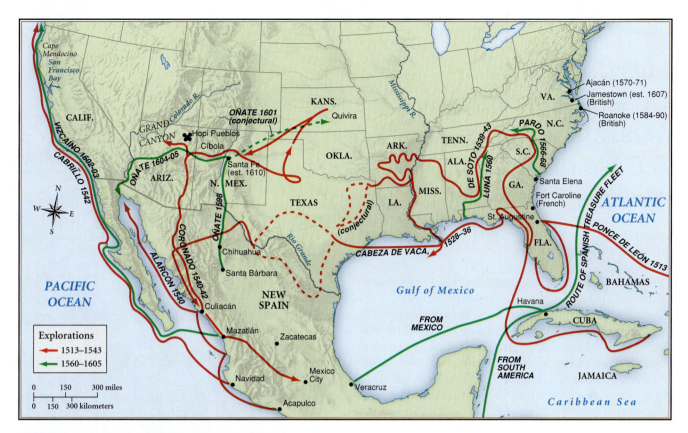

MAP 2.1 New Spain Looks North, 1513–1610

The quest for gold drew Spanish adventurers first to Florida and then deep into the present-day United States. When the wide-ranging expeditions of Hernán de Soto and Francisco Vásquez de Coronado failed to find gold or flourishing Indian civilizations, authorities in New Spain confined northern settlements to St. Augustine in Florida (to protect the treasure fleet) and Santa Fe in the upper Rio Grande Valley.

For more help analyzing this map, see the ONLINE STUDY GUIDE at
bedfordstmartins.com/henretta.

means," and Spanish troops massacred 300 members of the "evil Lutheran sect."

To safeguard Florida, in 1565 Spain established a fort at St. Augustine, the first permanent European settlement in the future United States (see American Lives, "Luis de Velasco/Opechancanough/Massatamohtnock: A Case of Possible Multiple Identities," p. 42). It also founded a dozen other military outposts and religious missions, one as far north as Chesapeake Bay, but these were soon destroyed by Indian attacks. Spain also confronted a new threat from the Atlantic. In 1586 the English sea captain Sir Francis Drake sacked the important port city of Cartagena (in present-day Colombia) and nearly wiped out St. Augustine.

Franciscan Missions. Military setbacks at the hands of Native Americans prompted the Spanish crown to adopt a new policy toward the Indian peoples. The Comprehensive Orders for New Discoveries, issued in 1573, placed the "pacification" of new lands primarily in

the hands of missionaries, not conquistadors. Franciscan friars promptly established missions in the Pueblo world visited by Coronado two generations before, naming the area Nuevo México (Map 2.1). The friars built their missions and churches near existing Indian pueblos and farming villages and often learned Indian languages. Protected by Spanish soldiers, the robed and sandaled Franciscans smashed the religious idols of the Native Americans and, to win their allegiance to the Christian God, dazzled them with rich vestments, gold crosses, and silver chalices.

For the Franciscans, religious conversion and cultural assimilation went hand in hand. They introduced the European practice of having men instead of women grow most of the crops and encouraged the Indians to talk, cook, dress, and walk like Spaniards. The friars' rule was hardly benevolent. Sexual sinners and spirit worshipers were whipped, and monks generally ignored Spanish laws intended to protect the native peoples from coerced labor. This neglect allowed privileged Spanish landowners

Luis de Velasco/ Opechancanough/ Massatamohtnock: A Case of Possible Multiple Identities

Long before the Chesapeake Bay took its present name, it was known as the Bahía de Santa María (the Bay of Saint Mary), claimed by Spain and part of the giant colony of Florida that stretched from present-day Texas to Newfoundland. And long before the first English adventurers set foot in the colony they called Virginia, Spanish Jesuits established a mission there (in 1571) at Ajacán; they came to convert the local Algonquian inhabitants—the Powhatan people—to the Catholic faith.

For eighty years, from the 1560s to the 1640s, this land would be contested ground, as Spanish conquistadors, English adventurers, and native chiefs vied with one another for control of the land and its people. Strong but not conclusive evidence suggests that the life of one man spanned this eighty-year struggle and shaped its course. The Spanish knew him as Don Luis de Velasco, a young Indian cacique (chief) who had lived in Spain for a time and had apparently become a pious convert to the Catholic faith. A generation later the English probably encountered the same man as Opechancanough, a local chief, "the King of the Pamaunches" (Pamunkeys), and an astute negotiator who seemed to favor interracial peace. Finally, when Opechancanough succeeded his elder brother as the Powhatan, or main chief, in 1621, he assumed a new name, Massatamohtnock, and a new role: a diplomat-warrior who led two Indian uprisings.

Spanish Catholic convert, pacific leader and diplomat, zealous Native American patriot: Was this a case of several individuals or was there only one man? If so, what accounts for his multiple identities? A confused response to contradictory cultural pressures? Simple deception?

C.Smith taketh the King of Pamaunkee prisoner 1608

John Smith and Chief Opechancanough
The powerful Indian chief Opechancanough towers over the English adventurer John Smith in this engraving of their confrontation in 1609 over English access to Indian supplies of food. Library of Congress.

This puzzle has its origins in 1561, when two vessels commanded by the Spanish mariner and adventurer Pedro Menéndez de Avilés sailed into the Bahía de Santa María. Like other conquistadors Menéndez came looking for gold and plunder, but he also sought good harbors for naval garrisons to protect Spanish treasure ships from pirates. Menéndez went away without riches but bearing the youthful son of a local chief, an Indian "of fine presence and bearing," whom he promised to take to Europe "that the King of Spain, his lord, might see him." King Philip II was equally impressed by the imposing young cacique, who stood more than six feet tall. He granted the young Indian an allowance and had

Dominican friars teach him the Spanish language and the principles of the Catholic faith.

Three years later the young man was in Mexico, where he acquired a new patron, Don Luis de Velasco, the viceroy of New Spain, who became his godfather and gave the Indian his own name. Eager to return to his people, in 1566 the Indian Don Luis accompanied an expedition to the Bahía de Santa María that was blown off course, and he found himself once again in Spain. Under Jesuit instruction, a contemporary chronicler noted, "he was made ready and they gave him the holy sacraments of the altar and Confirmation." For his part, the Indian Don Luis convinced the Jesuit father Juan Baptista de Segura of his "plan and determination . . . of converting his parents, relatives, and countrymen to the faith of Jesus Christ, and baptizing them and making them Christians as he was."

Thus it was that the young Christianized Indian and eight Jesuit missionaries landed in 1571 in Ajacán, five miles from the later site of Jamestown. Once restored to the land of his childhood, Don Luis readopted its customs, taking a number of wives. Publicly chastised for adultery by Father Segura, he took refuge in his native village. When three missionaries came to fetch him, Don Luis had them killed with a "shower of arrows"; then, according to one account, he murdered Father Segura and the rest of the Jesuits by his own hand. The massacre brought quick retribution. In 1572 Menéndez personally led a punitive expedition that killed dozens of Indians, but his former protégé escaped his wrath.

At this point the historical record becomes cloudy, but there is strong circumstantial evidence that the young cacique, Don Luis, now took the name Opechancanough and became chief of the Pamunkeys. Both chiefs are described in the records as imposing in size, much taller than most Indians and most Europeans. And there is a chronological fit between their lives. When Don Luis returned to America in 1571, he was about twenty-five years old; in 1621, when Opechancanough succeeded Powhatan as chief, he was an elderly man. Finally, there is the translation of Opechancanough's name: "He whose soul is white"— perhaps a reference to his life as a Christian Indian or his remorse about Father Segura's fate.

As Spanish dreams of an eastern North American empire faded in the face of fierce Native American resistance, England dispatched its own adventurers to search for gold and promote "the Christian religion to such People as yet live in Darkness." Opechancanough first confronted the new invaders in December 1607, when he captured Captain John Smith but spared his life. Two years later, after Smith grabbed Opechancanough "by the long lock of his head; and with my pistol at his breast . . . made him fill our bark with twenty tuns of corn," the chief did not seek revenge. Instead, for the next decade, the Pamunkeys' leader pursued a complicated diplomatic strategy: he "stood aloof" from the English and "would not be drawn to any Treaty." In particular, he strongly resisted proposals to take Indian children from their parents so that they might be "brought upp in Christianytie." At the same time, Opechancanough promoted interracial peace by accepting the marriage of his niece Pocahontas to John Rolfe and by arranging a treaty between the English and a Chesapeake tribe. The chief's allegiance may have been divided between two worlds: Algonquian and European. An Indian in culture and outlook, he was also a person whose soul was "white."

Then, in 1621, this man assumed a new identity, taking the name Massatamohtnock. And he took up a new cause. The number of English migrants had greatly increased, leading many Algonquians to believe that the English would soon take up "all their lands and would drive them out the country." To prevent this, the aging Massatamohtnock played a double game. While assuring Governor Wyatt of Virginia that "the Skye should sooner falle than Peace be broken, on his parte," he secretly mobilized the Pamunkeys and more than two dozen other Indian peoples. In 1622 these tribes launched a surprise attack that took the lives of 347 English men, women, and children. Urging the chief of the Potomacks to continue the onslaught, Massatamohtnock declared his goal: "before the end of two Moons there should not be an Englishman in all their Countries."

Finally defeated in the late 1620s when the English systematically burned Indian cornfields, the old chief reappeared in 1644, orchestrating another surprise assault that took the lives of "near five hundred Christians." Now a hundred years old, "so decrepit that he was not able to walk alone but was carried about by his men," Massatamohtnock was captured by the English and taken to Jamestown. There, an English official reported, an angry soldier "basely shot him through the back . . . of which wound he died."

The absence of Algonquian sources makes it unlikely that we will ever know the complete history or the real motives of this remarkable man. But the violent treatment Don Luis meted out to Father Segura and the uprisings Massatamohtnock instigated in 1622 and 1644 suggest that ultimately he defined himself as an Indian patriot, a resolute enemy of the European invaders and their Christian religion.

Conversion in New Mexico

Franciscan friars introduced Catholicism to the Indian peoples north of the Rio Grande, assisted by nuns of various religious orders. This 1631 engraving shows one of those nuns, María de Jesús de Agreda, preaching to a nomadic people (los chichimecos) *in New Mexico.*

Nettie Lee Benson Latin American Collection, University of Texas at Austin.

(**encomenderos**) who lived near the missions to collect tribute from the native population, both in goods and in forced labor. The Franciscan missions also depended on Indian workers, who grew the crops and carried them to market, often on their backs. Most Native Americans tolerated the Franciscans out of fear of military reprisals or in hopes of learning their spiritual secrets. But when Christian prayers failed to prevent European diseases, extended droughts, and Apache raids from devastating their communities, many Indians returned to their ancestral religions and began to blame Spanish rule for their ills. Thus, the chief and people of Hawikuh refused to become "wetheads" (as Indians called baptized Christians) "because with the water of baptism they would have to die."

Indian Revolts. In 1598 the already tense relations between Indians and Spaniards deteriorated when Juan de Oñate led an expedition of 500 Spanish soldiers and settlers into New Mexico to establish a fort and a trading villa. Oñate's men seized corn and clothing from the Pueblo peoples and murdered or raped those who resisted. When Indians of the Acoma pueblo killed 11 soldiers, the remaining troops destroyed the pueblo, killing 500 men and 300 women and children. Faced by now-hostile Indian peoples, most of the settlers withdrew. In 1610 the Spanish returned, founding the town of Santa Fe and reestablishing the system of missions and forced labor.

By 1680 nearly a hundred years of European diseases, forced tribute, and raids by Navajos and Apaches threatened many pueblos in New Mexico with extinction. Their population, which had once numbered 60,000, had declined to a mere 17,000. In desperation the Indian shaman (priest) Popé led the peoples of two dozen pueblos in a carefully coordinated rebellion, killing over 400 Spaniards and forcing the remaining 2,000 colonists to flee three hundred miles down the Rio Grande to El Paso. Repudiating Christianity, the Pueblo peoples desecrated churches and tortured and killed twenty-one missionaries. Reconquered a decade later, the Indians rebelled again in 1696, only to be subdued. Exhausted by war but having won the right to practice their own religion and avoid forced labor, the Pueblo peoples accepted their dependent position, joining with the Spanish to defend their lands against attacks by nomadic Indians.

Spain had managed to maintain its northern empire but had largely failed to achieve its goals of religious conversion and cultural assimilation. Taken aback by the military costs of expansion, Spanish officials decided not to undertake the settlement of the distant region of California, delaying until 1769 the permanent European occupation of that area. For the time being, Florida and New Mexico stood as the defensive outposts of Spain's American empire.

New France: Furs and Souls

Far to the northeast the French likewise tried to convert the native peoples to Catholicism. In the 1530s Jacques Cartier had claimed the lands bordered by the Gulf of St. Lawrence for France, but the first permanent French settlement came only in 1608, when Samuel de Champlain founded Quebec. Despite a series of brutal famines in northwestern France and the availability of attractive leaseholds in the fertile St. Lawrence Valley, few peasants migrated to America. Government policy was partly to blame. France's Catholic monarchs wanted an ample supply of military recruits at home. They also barred Huguenots (French Protestants) from settling in Quebec, fearing they would not be loyal to the crown. Moreover, the French peasantry held strong legal rights to their village lands and feared the short growing seasons and long bitter winters in Quebec. As one official remarked in 1684, Canada was "regarded as a country at the end of the world," a virtual sentence of "civil death." Of the 27,000 French men and women who migrated to Quebec, nearly

Samuel de Champlain

Going to War with the Hurons

Best known as the founder of Quebec, Samuel de Champlain was primarily a soldier and an adventurer. After fighting in the French religious wars, Champlain joined the Company of New France, determined to create a French empire in North America. In 1603 he traveled down the St. Lawrence River as far as Quebec, lived for three years in the company's failed settlement in Maine, and in 1608 returned to Quebec. To ensure French access to western fur trade, the following year Champlain joined the Hurons in a raid against the Iroquois, which he later described in a book of his American adventures.

Pursuing our route, I met some two or three hundred savages, who were encamped in huts near a little island called St. Eloi. . . . We made a reconnaissance, and found that they were tribes of savages called Ochasteguins [Hurons] and Algonquins, on their way to Quebec to assist us in exploring the territory of the Iroquois, with whom they are in deadly hostility. . . . [We joined with them and] went to the mouth of the River of the Iroquois [the Richelieu River, where it joins the St. Lawrence], where we stayed two days, refreshing ourselves with good venison, birds, and fish, which the savages gave us.

In all their encampments, they have their Pilotois, or Ostemoy, a class of persons who play the part of soothsayers, in whom these people have faith. One of these builds a cabin, surrounds it with small pieces of wood and covers it with his robe: after it is built, he places himself inside, so as not to be seen at all, when he seizes and shakes one of the posts of his cabin, muttering some words between his teeth, by which he says he invokes the devil, who appears to him in the form of a stone, and tells them whether they will meet their enemies and kill many of them. . . . They frequently told me that the shaking of the cabin, which I saw, proceeded from the devil, who made it move, and not the man inside, although I could see the contrary. . . . They told me also that I should see fire come out from the top, which I did not see at all.

Now, as we began to approach within two or three days' journey of the abode of our enemies, we advanced only at night. . . . By day, they withdraw into the interior of the woods, where they rest, without straying off, neither making any noise, even for the sake of cooking, so as not to be noticed in case their enemies should by accident pass by. They make no fire, except in smoking, which amounts to almost nothing. They eat baked Indian meal, which they soak in water, when it becomes a kind of porridge. . . .

In order to ascertain what was to be the result of their undertaking, they often asked me if I had had a dream, and seen their enemies, to which I replied in the negative. . . . [Then one night] while sleeping, I dreamed that I saw our enemies, the Iroquois, drowning near a mountain, within sight. When I expressed a wish to help them, our allies, the savages, told me we must let them all die. . . . This, upon being related [to our allies], gave them so much confidence that they did not doubt any longer that good was to happen to them. . . .

[After our victory over the Iroquois] they took one of the prisoners, to whom they made a harangue, enumerating the cruelties which he and his men had already practiced toward them without any mercy, and that, in like manner, he ought to make up his mind to receive as much. They commanded him to sing, if he had courage, which he did; but it was a very sad song.

Meanwhile, our men kindled a fire; and, when it was well burning, they brand, and burned this poor creature gradually, so as to make him suffer greater torment. Sometimes they stopped, and threw water on his back. Then they tore out his nails, and applied fire to the extremities of his fingers and private member. Afterwards, they flayed the top of his head, and had a kind of gum poured all hot upon it. . . .

Source: Samuel de Champlain, *Voyages of Samuel de Champlain, 1604–1618*, ed. W. L. Grant (New York: Charles Scribner's Sons, 1907), 79–86.

two-thirds eventually returned to their homeland. In 1698 the European population of New France was only 15,200, compared with 100,000 settlers in the English colonies.

Rather than developing as a settler colony, New France instead became a vast fur-trading enterprise, and French explorers traveled deep into the continent to seek new suppliers. In return for French support against the Five Nations of the Iroquois, the Huron Indians (who lived just to the north of the Great Lakes) allowed Champlain and his fur traders into their territory (see Voices from Abroad, "Samuel de Champlain: Going to War with the Hurons," above). By 1673 another French explorer,

Jacques Marquette, reached the Mississippi River in present-day Wisconsin and traveled as far south as Arkansas. Seeking fortune as well as fame, in 1681 Robert de La Salle traveled down the Mississippi to the Gulf of Mexico, completing exploration of the majestic river. As a French priest noted with disgust, La Salle's expedition hoped "to buy all the Furs and Skins of the remotest Savages, who, as they thought, did not know their Value; and so enrich themselves in one single voyage." To honor Louis XIV, the Sun King, La Salle named the region he explored Louisiana; soon it included the small but thriving port of New Orleans on the Gulf of Mexico.

Despite their small numbers, French traders had a disastrous impact on Native Americans living near the Great Lakes. By introducing European diseases, they unwittingly triggered epidemics that killed 25 to 90 percent of the residents of many Indian villages, including those of their Huron allies. Moreover, by providing a market for deerskins and beaver pelts, the French set in motion a devastating series of Indian wars. Beginning in the 1640s, the New York Iroquois seized control of the fur trade by launching aggressive expeditions against the Hurons, forcing them to migrate to the north and west.

While French traders amassed furs, French priests sought converts among both the defeated Hurons and the belligerent Iroquois. Between 1625 and 1763 hundreds of Jesuit priests lived among the Indians and, to a greater extent than the Spanish Franciscans, came to understand their values. One Jesuit reported a Huron belief that "our souls have desires which are inborn and concealed, yet are made known by means of dreams"; he then used this belief to explain the Christian doctrines of immortality and salvation to the native peoples. At first many Indians welcomed the French "Black Robes" as powerful spiritual beings with magical secrets, such as the ability to forge iron, but, as in New Mexico, skepticism grew when prayers to the Christian God did not protect them from disease and enemy attack. A Peoria chief charged that the priest's "fables are good only in his own country; we have our own [religious beliefs], which do not make us die as his do."

Unlike the Spanish Franciscans, the French Jesuits did not use Indians for forced labor and tried to keep alcoholic beverages, which wreaked havoc among Indian peoples, from becoming a bargaining item in the French fur trade. Moreover, the French Jesuits won converts by addressing Indian needs. In the 1690s young women of the Illinois people in the Mississippi River Valley embraced the cult of the Virgin Mary, using its emphasis on chastity to assert the Algonquian belief that unmarried women were "masters of their own body."

Still, the French fur-trading system brought war and cultural devastation to the Indian peoples of eastern North America. According to an oral history of the Iroquois, "Everywhere there was peril and everywhere mourning. Feuds with outer nations, feuds with brother nations, feuds of . . . sister towns and feuds of families and of clans made every warrior a stealthy man who liked to kill."

New Netherland: Commerce

Unlike the French and Spanish, the Dutch in North America had little interest in religious conversion. Their eyes were fastened on commerce, for the Dutch Republic was the trading hub of Europe. In 1609 Henry Hudson, an Englishman employed by the Dutch East India Company, found and named the Hudson River in the area of present-day New York, and a few years later the Dutch established fur-trading posts on Manhattan Island and at Fort Orange (present-day Albany). In 1621 the Dutch government chartered the West India Company, giving it a trade monopoly in West Africa and exclusive authority to establish outposts in America. Three years later the company founded the town of New Amsterdam on Manhattan Island, the capital of New Netherland (Map 2.2).

The wilderness fur-trading posts attracted few Dutch settlers, and their small size made them vulnerable to invasion by rival European nations. To encourage migration of permanent settlers, the West India Company granted huge estates along the Hudson River to wealthy Dutchmen, stipulating that each proprietor settle fifty tenants on his land within four years or lose it; by 1646 only one proprietor, Kiliaen Van Rensselaer, had succeeded. The population in Dutch North America remained small, reaching only 1,500 in 1664.

Although New Netherland failed as a settler colony, it flourished briefly as a fur-trading enterprise. In 1633 Dutch traders at Fort Orange exported thirty thousand beaver and otter pelts. Subsequently, the Dutch seized prime farming land from the Algonquian-speaking peoples and took over their trading network, in which corn and wampum from Long Island were exchanged for furs from Maine. The Algonquians responded with force. By the end of a bloody two-year war more than 200 Dutch residents and 1,000 Indians had been killed, many in brutal massacres of women, children, and elderly men. After the war the Dutch traders expanded their profitable links with the Mohawks, one of the Iroquois Nations of New York and a long-time foe of the Algonquians, exchanging guns and other manufactures

▶ **MAP 2.2 The Eurasian Trade System and Overseas Spheres of Influence, 1650**

Between 1550 and 1650 Spanish, Portuguese, and Dutch merchants took control of the maritime trade of the Southern Hemisphere, carrying goods to Europe from China, the Philippines, Indonesia, and India. They also created the South Atlantic system (see Chapter 3), transporting African slaves to European-run plantations in Brazil and the Caribbean and returning to Europe with valuable cargoes of sugar. After 1600 the Spanish and the Dutch began to settle and trade in North America as well. (To trace changes in trade and empires over time, see also Map 1.4 on p. 22 and Map 5.1 on p. 134.)

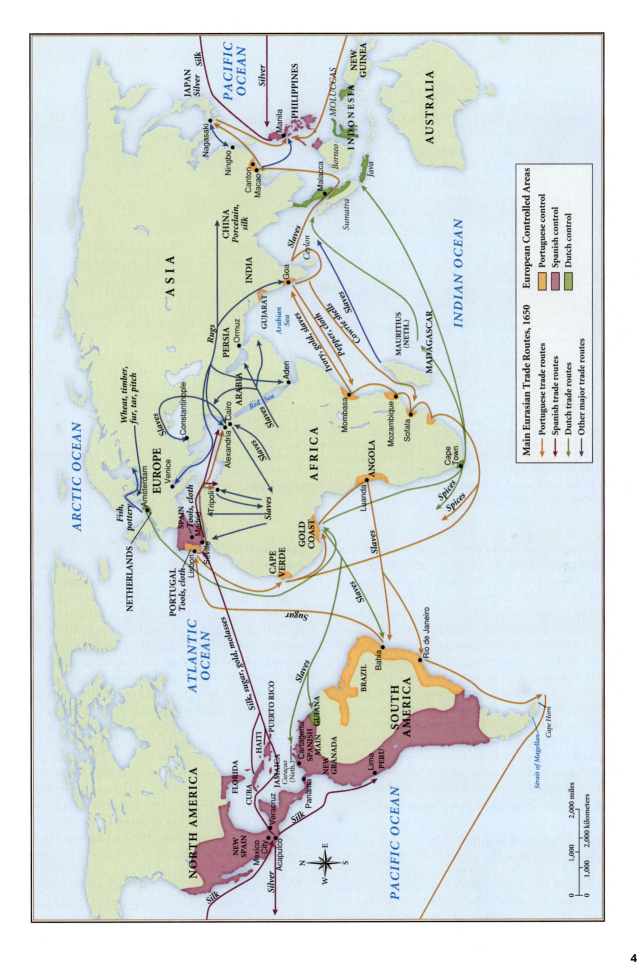

Main Eurasian Trade Routes, 1650

European Controlled Areas
- Portuguese trade routes
- Spanish trade routes
- Dutch trade routes
- Other major trade routes

European Controlled Areas
- Portuguese control
- Spanish control
- Dutch control

PACIFIC OCEAN

JAPAN *Silver Silk*

Silver

PHILIPPINES

Nagasaki

Ningbo

Canton
Macao

NEW GUINEA

MOLUCCAS

INDONESIA

Borneo

AUSTRALIA

Java

Sumatra

Malacca

CHINA
Porcelain, silk

INDIA

GUJARAT

Rugs

PERSIA

Ormuz

Arabian Sea

Goa

Slaves

Ceylon

ASIA

Slaves

Cowrie shells

Pepper, cloth

Ivory, gold, slaves

MAURITIUS
(NETH.)

MADAGASCAR

INDIAN OCEAN

Aden

ARABIA

Red Sea

Cairo

Alexandria

Slaves

Constantinople

Venice

Slaves

EUROPE

Slaves

Wheat, timber, fur, tar, pitch

ARCTIC OCEAN

NETHERLANDS
Amsterdam

Fish, pottery

Tripoli

Slaves

Slaves

SPAIN
Madrid
Tools, cloth

Lisbon
PORTUGAL
Tools, cloth

Seville

CAPE VERDE

AFRICA

GOLD COAST

Mombasa

Mozambique

Sofala

Cape Town

Spices

Spices

Luanda
ANGOLA

Slaves

Slaves

ATLANTIC OCEAN

Silk, sugar, gold, molasses

Sugar

Slaves

BRAZIL

Bahia

Rio de Janeiro

SOUTH AMERICA

PERU
Lima

NEW GRANADA

SPANISH MAIN

Cartagena

GUIANA

PUERTO RICO

HAITI

JAMAICA

Curaçao (Neth.)

Panama

CUBA

FLORIDA

Silk

Veracruz

Mexico City

Acapulco

NEW SPAIN

NORTH AMERICA

Silver

Silk

PACIFIC OCEAN

Strait of Magellan

Cape Horn

N E S W

0 1,000 2,000 miles
0 1,000 2,000 kilometers

47

New Amsterdam, c. 1640

As the wooden palisade surrounding the town indicates, New Amsterdam was a frontier settlement, a fortlike trading post at the edge of vast lands populated by alien Indian peoples. The first settlers, remembering the architecture and waterways of Amsterdam and other Dutch cities, built houses in the Dutch style, with their gable ends facing the street (note the middle two houses), and excavated a canal across lower Manhattan Island, connecting the Hudson and East Rivers. Library of Congress.

for furs. However, the West India Company now largely ignored its crippled North American settlement, concentrating instead on the profitable importation of African slaves to its sugar plantations in Brazil.

Moreover, Dutch officials in New Amsterdam ruled shortsightedly. Governor Peter Stuyvesant rejected the demands of English Puritan settlers on Long Island for a representative system of government and alienated the colony's increasingly diverse population of Dutch, English, and Swedish migrants. Consequently, in 1664, during an Anglo-Dutch war, the population of New Amsterdam offered little resistance to an English invasion and subsequently accepted English rule. For the rest of the century the renamed towns of New York and Albany remained small fur-trading centers, Dutch-English outposts in a region still dominated by Native Americans. In Albany, Mohawk remained the language of business until the 1720s.

The First English Model: Tobacco and Settlers

The first English ventures in North America, undertaken by minor nobility in the 1580s, were abject failures. Sir Humphrey Gilbert's settlement in Newfoundland collapsed for lack of financing, and Sir Ferdinando Gorges's colony along the coast of Maine foundered because of inadequate supplies and the harsh climate. Sir Walter Raleigh's three expeditions to North Carolina likewise ended in disaster when the colony he financed at Roanoke vanished without a trace (today it is known as the "lost" colony). After these failures, merchants replaced landed gentry as the leaders of English expansion; initially, their main goal was trade rather than settlement. To provide adequate funding, the merchants formed **joint-stock companies** that sold shares to many investors and sought royal support. In 1606 the new monarch, King James I (r. 1603–1625), granted a group of ambitious London merchants the right to exploit North America from present-day North Carolina to southern New York. To honor the memory of Elizabeth I, the "Virgin Queen," the company's directors named the region Virginia. They promised to settle the land and "propagate the *Christian* religion" among the "infidels and Savages" (Map 2.3).

The Jamestown Settlement.   However, trade for gold and other valuable goods remained the main goal of the Virginia Company, and the first expedition in 1607

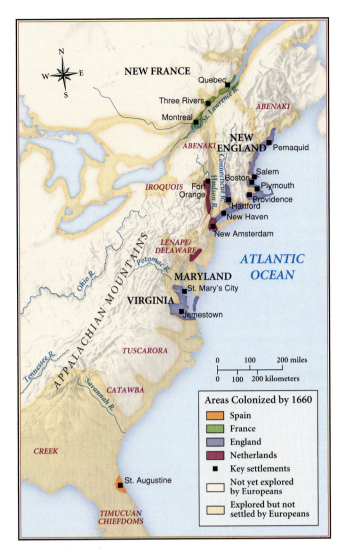

MAP 2.3 Eastern North America in 1650

Four European nations had permanent settlements in eastern North America by 1650, but only England had substantial numbers of settlers, some 25,000 in New England and another 15,000 in the Chesapeake region. However, the European presence extended into the interior, as colonial authorities established diplomatic and commercial relations with neighboring Indian peoples and as French and Dutch fur traders carried European goods and diseases to distant tribes.

included only traders and adventurers—no settlers, ministers, or women. The company retained ownership of all the land and appointed a governor and a small council to direct the adventurers, who were its employees or "servants." They were expected to procure their own food and ship anything of value to England—gold, exotic crops, and Indian merchandise. Some of the employees were young gentlemen with personal ties to the shareholders of the company but no experience in living off the land: a bunch of "unruly Sparks, packed off by their Friends to escape worse Destinies at home." The rest were cynical adventurers bent on seizing gold from the Indians or turning a quick profit from trade in

English cloth and metalware. All they wanted, as one of them said, was to "dig gold, refine gold, load gold."

Unfortunately, such traders were unprepared for the challenges of the new environment. Arriving in Virginia after a hazardous four-month voyage, the newcomers settled on a swampy peninsula on a river. They named both their new home (Jamestown) and the waterway (James River) after the king. Because the adventurers had chosen an unhealthful location with little fresh water and refused to plant crops, their fate was sealed. Of the 120 Englishmen who embarked on the expedition, only 38 were alive nine months later, and death continued to take a high toll. By 1611 the Virginia Company had sent 1,200 settlers to Jamestown, but fewer than half had survived. "Our men were destroyed with cruell diseases, as Swellings, Fluxes, Burning Fevers, and by warres," reported one of the leaders, "but for the most part they died of meere famine."

Native American hostility was a major threat to the survival of the settlement. Upon their arrival, the traders had been immediately confronted by the Pamunkey chief Powhatan, the leader of the Algonquian-speaking tribes of the region, some 14,000 people in all. Powhatan, whom the adventurer John Smith described as a "grave majestical man," allowed his followers to exchange their corn for English cloth and iron hatchets but treated the English as one of the dependent peoples of his chiefdom.

As conflicts over food and land increased, Powhatan threatened war, accusing the English of coming "not to trade but to invade my people and possess my country." In 1614 the Indian leader tried another strategy to integrate the newcomers into his chiefdom, allowing the marriage of his daughter Pocahontas to the adventurer John Rolfe. This tactic also failed, in part because Rolfe imported tobacco seeds from the West Indies and began to cultivate the crop, which was already popular in England. Tobacco quickly became the basis of economic life in Virginia, setting in motion the creation of a settler society.

New Political Institutions. To attract migrants to its increasingly valuable colony, the Virginia Company instituted a new and far-reaching set of policies. In 1617 it allowed individual settlers to own land, granting one hundred acres to every freeman in Virginia, and established a **headright** system giving every incoming head of a household a right to fifty acres of land and fifty additional acres for every servant. The following year the company issued a "great Charter" that swept away the military-style regime of Governor Sir Thomas Dale, laying the basis for a system of representative government. The House of Burgesses, which first convened in Jamestown in 1619, had the authority to make laws and levy taxes, although the governor or the company council in England could veto its legislative acts. By 1622 these incentives of land ownership for ordinary settlers, self-government by local leaders, and a court system based on "the lawes of the realme of England" had attracted about 4,500 new recruits. Virginia was on the verge of becoming an established colony.

However, the influx of settlers sparked all-out war with the Indians. Land-hungry farmers demanded access to land that the Native Americans had cleared and were using, alarming Opechancanough, Powhatan's brother and successor. Mobilizing the peoples of many Chesapeake tribes, in 1622 Opechancanough launched a surprise attack, killing nearly a third of the white population and vowing to drive the rest into the ocean. The English retaliated by harvesting the Indians' cornfields, providing food for themselves while depriving their enemies of sustenance, a strategy that gradually secured the safety of the colony.

The cost of the war was high for both sides. The Indians killed many settlers and destroyed much property, but Opechancanough's strategy had failed; rather than ending the English invasion, the uprising accelerated it. As one English militiaman put it, "[We now felt we could] by right of Warre, and law of Nations, invade the Country, and destroy them who sought to destroy us; whereby wee shall enjoy their cultivated places . . . possessing the fruits of others' labour." The invaders sold captured warriors into slavery and took control of huge areas of land. By 1630 the colonists in Virginia had created a flourishing tobacco economy and a stable English-style local polity, controlled by landed gentlemen sitting as justices of the peace.

The Chesapeake Experience

The English colonies in the Chesapeake brought wealth to some people but poverty and moral degradation to many more. Settlers forcefully dispossessed Indians of their lands, and prominent families ruthlessly pursued their dreams of wealth by exploiting the labor of English indentured servants and enslaved African laborers.

Settling the Tobacco Colonies

Distressed by the Indian uprising of 1622, James I dissolved the Virginia Company, accusing its directors of mismanagement, and created a royal colony in 1624. Under the terms of the charter, the king and his ministers appointed the governor and a small advisory council. The king allowed the House of Burgesses to remain, but any legislation it enacted required ratification by his Privy Council. James also legally established the Church of England in Virginia, so that all property owners had to pay taxes to support the clergy. These institutions—a royal governor, an elected assembly, and an established

Anglican church—became the model for royal colonies throughout English America.

Catholics in Maryland. However, a second tobacco-growing settler colony, which developed in neighboring Maryland, had a different set of institutions. In 1632 King Charles I (r. 1625–1649), the successor to James I, conveyed most of the territory bordering the vast Chesapeake Bay to Cecilius Calvert, an aristocrat who carried the title Lord Baltimore. As the proprietor of Maryland (named in honor of Queen Henrietta Maria, Charles's wife), Baltimore could sell, lease, or give this land away as he wished. He also had the authority to appoint public officials and to found churches and appoint ministers.

Baltimore wanted Maryland to become a refuge from persecution for his fellow English Catholics. He therefore devised a policy of religious toleration intended to minimize confrontations between Catholics and Protestants, instructing the governor (his brother, Leonard Calvert) to allow "no scandall nor offence to be given to any of the Protestants" and to "cause All Acts of Romane Catholicque Religion to be done as privately as may be." In 1634, twenty gentlemen (mostly Catholics) and two hundred artisans and laborers (mostly Protestants) established St. Mary's City, which overlooked the mouth of the Potomac River. The population grew quickly, for the Calverts carefully planned and supervised the colony's development, hiring skilled artisans and offering ample grants of land to wealthy migrants. However, political and religious conflict constantly threatened Maryland's stability. When Governor Leonard Calvert tried to govern without the "Advice, Assent, and Approbation" of the freemen of the colony, as the charter specified, a representative assembly elected by the freemen insisted on the right to initiate legislation, which Lord Baltimore grudgingly granted. Uprisings by Protestant settlers also endangered Maryland's religious mission. To protect his Catholic coreligionists, who remained a minority, Lord Baltimore persuaded the assembly to enact a Toleration Act (1649) granting religious freedom to all Christians.

Tobacco and Disease. In Maryland, as in Virginia, tobacco was the basis of the economy. Indians had long used tobacco, a substance unknown in Europe before the Columbian Exchange, as a medicine and a stimulant. By the 1620s English men and women were craving tobacco and the nicotine it contained, smoking, chewing, and snorting it with abandon. Initially James I condemned the use of this "vile Weed" and warned that its "black stinking fumes" were "baleful to the nose, harmful to the brain, and dangerous to the lungs." But the king's attitude changed as revenues from an import tax on tobacco filled the royal treasury.

European demand for tobacco set off a forty-year economic boom in the Chesapeake, attracting thousands

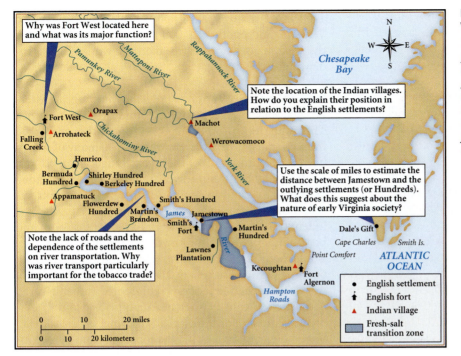

MAP 2.4 River Plantations in Virginia, c. 1640

The first migrants settled in widely dispersed plantations—and different disease environments—along the James River. The growth of the tobacco economy continued this pattern as wealthy planter-merchants traded with English ship captains from their riverfront plantations. Consequently, few substantial towns or trading centers developed in the Chesapeake region.

of profit-hungry migrants. "All our riches for the present do consist in tobacco," a planter remarked in 1630. Exports rose from about 3 million pounds in 1640 to 10 million pounds in 1660. Planters moved up the river valleys, establishing large farms (plantations) that were distant from one another but easily reached by water (Map 2.4). The scarcity of towns meant a much weaker sense of community than existed in the open-field villages of rural England.

For most of the seventeenth century life in the Chesapeake colonies remained harsh, brutish, and short. Most men never married because there were few women settlers, and families were often disrupted by early death. Mosquitoes as well as tobacco flourished in the mild Chesapeake climate, spreading malaria and weakening people's resistance to other diseases (Table 2.2). Pregnant women were especially hard hit. Many died after bearing a first or second child. In Middlesex County, Virginia, more than 60 percent of children lost one or both of their parents by the time they were thirteen. Orphaned children and unmarried young men constituted a large fraction of the society,

TABLE 2.2 Environment, Disease, and Death in Virginia, 1618–1624

Zone of James River Estuary	Percentage of Colony Population in Zone	Annual Mortality in Zone	Percentage of All Deaths in Colony
Freshwater	28.5%	16.7%	16.9%
Freshwater/Saltwater Mix	49.3%	37.1%	64.6%
Saltwater	22.2%	23.3%	18.4%
Estimated Annual Mortality Rate for Virginia: 28.3%			

Early Virginia was a deadly place, with no less than 28 percent of the population dying *each and every* year, mostly from typhoid fever and dysentery (the "bloody flux"). Only a constant stream of migrants allowed slow population growth. Most settlers lived along the James River estuary, and their place of residence determined their chances of survival. The most dangerous environment was the zone of water that was fresh in the spring, when the river ran fast, and mixed fresh and salt in the summer—when the inflow of saltwater from the Atlantic Ocean trapped human and animal waste from upriver and contaminated the water and its fish, oysters, and crabs. The year-round saltwater zone was the next most deadly, because of both fecal contamination and salt poisoning from drinking "brackish" well water.

Source: Adapted from Carville V. Earle, "Environment, Disease, and Mortality in Early Virginia," in *The Chesapeake in the Seventeenth Century*, ed. Thad W. Tate and David L. Ammerman (New York: W. W. Norton, 1979), Table 3.

The Tobacco Economy

Most poor farmers raised tobacco, for it grew just as well in small fields as on vast plantations. Large-scale operations, such as the one pictured here, used indentured servants and slaves to grow and process the crop. The workers cured the tobacco stalks by hanging them for several months in a well-ventilated shed; then they stripped the leaves and packed them tightly into large plantation-made barrels, or "hogsheads," for shipment to Europe. Library of Congress.

For more help analyzing this image, see the ONLINE STUDY GUIDE at **bedfordstmartins.com/henretta.**

inhibiting population growth. Although 15,000 settlers arrived in Virginia between 1622 and 1640, the number of English settlers rose only from 2,000 to 8,000.

Masters, Servants, and Slaves

Despite the dangers, the prospect of owning land continued to lure migrants to the Chesapeake region. By

1700 more than 80,000 English settlers had moved to Virginia, and another 20,000 had arrived in Maryland, the great majority not as free men and women but as indentured servants.

Indentured Servants. English shipping registers provide insight into the background of these servants. Three-quarters of the 5,000 servants who embarked from the port of Bristol were young men, many of whom had traveled hundreds of miles searching for work. Once in Bristol, these penniless wanderers were persuaded by merchants and sea captains to sign labor contracts called **indentures** and embark for the Chesapeake. The indentures bound them to work in return for room and board for a period of four or five years, after which they would be free, able to marry and work for themselves, planting corn for sustenance and tobacco for sale.

For merchants, servants represented valuable cargo because their contracts fetched high prices from Chesapeake planters. For the plantation owners, they were an incredible bargain. During the tobacco boom a male indentured servant could produce five times his purchase price in a year. Furthermore, imported servants were counted as household members, and so planters in Virginia received fifty acres of land for each one.

Most masters ruled their servants with an iron hand, beating them for bad behavior and withholding permission to marry. If a servant ran away or became pregnant, a master went to court to increase the term of service. Female servants were especially vulnerable to abuse, from both male servants and their owners. As a Virginia law of 1692 stated, "dissolute masters have gotten their maids with child; and yet claim the benefit of their service." Planters got rid of uncooperative servants by selling their contracts to new masters. As an Englishman remarked in disgust, in Virginia "servants were sold up and down like horses."

For most indentured servants this ordeal did not provide the escape from poverty they had sought (see American Voices, "Richard Frethorne: Hard Times in Early Virginia," p. 53). Half the men died before receiving their freedom, and another quarter remained poor. The remaining quarter benefited from their ordeal, acquiring property and respectability (Table 2.3). If they survived, female servants generally fared better because men in the Chesapeake had grown "very sensible of the Misfortune of Wanting Wives." Many such servants married their masters or other well-established men. By migrating to the Chesapeake, these few—and very fortunate—men and women escaped a life of landless poverty in England.

African Laborers. The first African workers fared worse. In 1619 John Rolfe noted that "a Dutch man of warre . . . sold us twenty Negars," but for a generation the numbers of Africans remained small. About 400 Africans lived in the Chesapeake colonies in 1649,

Richard Frethorne

Hard Times in Early Virginia

The lot of an indentured servant in Virginia was always hard, especially before 1630, when food was scarce and Indians were a constant danger. In 1623 Richard Frethorne wrote a letter to his parents begging them to buy out the remaining years of his labor contract so that he could return to England. Richard Frethorne's fate is unknown, but documentary evidence indicates that more than half of the English men and women who went to Virginia as indentured servants died during their four years of service.

Loving and kind father and mother . . . this is to let you understand that I your child am in a most heavy case by reason of the nature of the country . . . it causes much sickness, as the scurvy and the bloody flux [severe dysentery], and diverse other diseases, which make the body very poor and weak, and when we are sick there is nothing to comfort us. For since I came out of the ship, I never ate anything but peas and loblollie [gruel]. As for deer or venison I never saw any since I came into this land. There is indeed some fowl, but we are not allowed to go and get it, but must work hard both early and late for a mess of water gruel and a mouthful of bread and beef.

People cry out day and night, Oh that they were in England without their limbs and would not care to lose any limb to be in England again . . . we live in fear of the enemy every hour. . . . We are in great danger, for our plantation is very weak, by reason of the dearth, and sickness of our company. . . .

I have nothing to comfort me, nor there is nothing to be gotten here but sickness and death, except that one had money to lay out in some things for profit; but I have nothing at all, no not a shirt to my back, but two rags nor no clothes, but one poor suit, nor but one pair of shoes . . . my cloak is stolen by one of my own fellows, and to his dying hours would not tell me what he did with it, but some of my fellows saw him have butter and beef out of a ship, which my cloak [no] doubt paid for. . . .

I am not half, a quarter, so strong as I was in England, and all is for want of victuals, for I do protest unto you, that I have eaten more in a day at home than [is] allowed me here for a week. . . . Good father, do not forget me, but have mercy and pity my miserable case. I know if you did but see me you would weep. . . . The answer of this letter will be life or death to me; therefore, good father, send as soon as you can. . . .

Source: Susan M. Kingsbury, ed., *The Records of the Virginia Company of London* (Washington, D.C.: Library of Congress, 1935), 4:58–60.

making up 2 percent of the population, and by 1670 the proportion of blacks had reached only 5 percent. Although many Africans served their masters for life, they were not legally enslaved. English common law acknowledged indentured servitude but not chattel slavery—the ownership as property of one human being by another. Moreover, many of these early workers had labored as slaves in African seaports and had some knowledge of European traders and Atlantic commerce. By cunning calculation, hard work, or conversion to Christianity many of them escaped bondage. Some ambitious African Christian freemen even purchased slaves, bought the labor contracts of white servants, or married English women, suggesting that at this time religion and personal initiative were as important as race in determining social status. By becoming a Christian and a planter, an enterprising African could aspire to near equality with the English settlers.

This mobility came to end in the 1660s because legislatures in the Chesapeake colonies enacted laws that lowered the status of Africans. The motives for these laws are not clear. Perhaps the English-born elite grew more conscious of race as the number of Africans increased or, with the end of the tobacco boom, used race to divide workers. By 1671 the Virginia House of Burgesses had forbidden Africans to own guns or join the militia. It had also barred them—"tho baptized and enjoying their own Freedom"—from buying the labor contracts of white servants and specified that conversion to Christianity did not qualify Africans for eventual freedom. Being black was becoming a mark of inferior legal status, and slavery was becoming a permanent and hereditary condition. As an English clergyman observed around 1680, "These two words, Negro and Slave had by custom grown Homogeneous and convertible."

The Seeds of Social Revolt

By the 1660s the growing size of the Chesapeake tobacco crop triggered a collapse of the market. During the boom years of the 1620s tobacco sold for 24 pence a pound; forty years later it was fetching barely one-tenth as much. As the economic boom turned into a "bust," long-standing social conflicts flared up in political turmoil.

Political decisions in England had a lot to do with the decline of tobacco prices. In 1651, in an effort to exclude Dutch ships and merchants from England's overseas possessions, Parliament passed an Act of Trade and Navigation. Revised and extended in 1660 and 1663, the Navigation Acts permitted only English or colonial-owned ships to enter American ports. They also required the colonists to ship certain "enumerated articles," including tobacco, only to England. Chesapeake planters could no longer legally trade with Dutch merchants, who paid the highest prices. Moreover, to increase royal revenues the English monarchs continually raised the import duty on tobacco, thereby increasing the price to consumers and stifling growth of the market. By the 1670s planters were getting only one penny a pound for their crop.

Nonetheless, the number of planters in Virginia and Maryland grew, and tobacco exports doubled from 20 million pounds annually in the 1670s to 41 million pounds between 1690 and 1720. Profit margins were now thin, and the Chesapeake ceased to offer upward social mobility to whites as well as to blacks. Yeomen families painstakingly raised about 10,000 tobacco plants each year but earned just enough to scrape by, and many fell into debt. Even worse off were newly freed indentured servants. Low tobacco prices made it nearly impossible for them to pay the necessary fees to claim the 50 acres of land to which they were entitled and buy the tools and seed needed to plant it. Many former servants had to sell their labor again, signing new indentures or becoming wageworkers or tenant farmers.

Gradually the Chesapeake colonies came to be dominated by an elite of planter-landlords and merchants. Landowners prospered by dividing their ample estates and leasing small plots to the growing army of former servants. They also lent money at high interest rates to hard-pressed yeomen families. Some well-to-do planters became commercial middlemen, setting up small retail stores or charging a commission for storing the tobacco of their poorer neighbors and selling it to English merchants. In Virginia this elite accumulated nearly half the land by soliciting favors from royal governors; on average, the 215 justices of the peace in four counties owned more than 1,000 acres apiece. In Maryland well-connected Catholic planters were equally dominant; by 1720 Charles Carroll owned 47,000 acres of land, farmed by scores of tenants, indentured servants, and slaves.

As these aggressive planter-entrepreneurs confronted a growing number of young, landless laborers, social divisions intensified, reaching a breaking point in Virginia during the corrupt regime of Governor William Berkeley. Berkeley first served as governor between 1642 and 1652, winning fame in 1644 by putting down the second major Indian revolt led by Opechancanough. Serving as governor again beginning in 1660, he made large land grants to himself and to members of his council, who promptly exempted their own lands from taxation and appointed friends as local justices of the peace and county judges. Berkeley suppressed dissent in the House of Burgesses by assigning land grants to friendly legislators and appointing their relatives to lucrative positions that charged fees for services, such as sheriffs, tax collectors, constables, and estate appraisers. Social and political unrest increased

Decade Ending	White Population	Percent of Population in Labor Force	White Labor Force	White Servant Population	Servants as Percent of Labor Force
TABLE 2.3 Indentured Servants in the Chesapeake Labor Force					
1640	8,000	75	6,000	1,790	29.6
1660	24,000	66	15,800	4,300	27.2
1680	55,600	58	32,300	5,500	17.0
1700	85,200	46	38,900	3,800	9.7

The population of the Chesapeake increased tenfold between 1640 and 1700, and its character changed significantly. As more women migrated to Virginia and bore children, the percentage of the population in the labor force declined dramatically. The importance of indentured servants also declined; before 1660 white servants formed about 30 percent of the labor force but by 1700 accounted for only 10 percent of the workers.

Source: Adapted from Christopher Tomlins, "Reconsidered Indentured Servitude" (unpublished paper, 2001), Table 3.

when the corrupt Burgesses changed the voting system to exclude landless freemen, who constituted half of all adult white men. Property-holding yeomen retained the vote but—distressed by tobacco prices, rising taxes, and political corruption—were no longer willing to support the rule of increasingly corrupt and power-hungry landed gentry.

Bacon's Rebellion

An Indian conflict suddenly sparked the flame of social rebellion. By 1675 the native inhabitants of Virginia were few and weak, their numbers having dwindled from 30,000 in 1607 to a mere 3,500, as compared to 38,000 Europeans and about 2,500 Africans. Although most Indians now lived along the frontier, their presence remained controversial among English settlers. Hundreds of impoverished English freeholders and aspiring tenants wanted cheap land and insisted that the natives be expelled from their treaty-guaranteed lands or simply exterminated. Wealthy planters on the seacoast, who wanted a ready supply of white labor, opposed expansion into Indian territory, as did the planter-merchants who traded with the Native Americans for furs.

Fighting broke out when a band of Virginia militiamen murdered 30 Indians. Defying orders from Governor Berkeley, a larger force of 1,000 militiamen then surrounded a fortified Susquehannock village and killed five chiefs who had come out to negotiate. The militarily strong Susquehannocks, who had recently migrated from present-day northern Pennsylvania, retaliated by raiding outlying plantations and killing 300 whites. Berkeley did not want war, which would disrupt the fur trade, and proposed a defensive military policy, asking the House of Burgesses in March 1676 to raise taxes for a series of frontier forts. Western settlers dismissed this strategy as useless, a plot by planters and merchants to impose high taxes and, in the words of one yeoman, to take "all our tobacco into their own hands."

Nathaniel Bacon emerged as the leader of the protesters. A bold and wealthy man, he had recently arrived from England and settled on a frontier estate. Although he was only twenty-eight, Bacon commanded the respect of his neighbors because of his vigor and his English connections, which had made him a member of the governor's council. When Berkeley refused to grant Bacon a military commission, the headstrong planter marched his frontiersmen against the Indians anyway, slaughtering some of the peaceful Doeg people and triggering a political upheaval. Condemning the frontiersmen as "rebels and mutineers," Berkeley expelled Bacon from the council and placed him under arrest. When Bacon's followers threatened to free their leader by force, the governor quickly changed course, agreeing to legislative elections that brought many new men into

Nathaniel Bacon

Reviled as a rebel and a traitor in his own time, Nathaniel Bacon emerged in the late nineteenth century as an American hero, a harbinger of the Patriots of 1776. This stained-glass window, possibly the creation of the famed jeweler and glassmaker Tiffany & Co. of New York, was installed in a church, endowing Bacon with a semisacred status.
The Association for the Preservation of Virginia Antiquities.

government. The new House of Burgesses promptly enacted far-reaching political reforms that curbed the powers of the governor and the council and restored voting rights to landless freemen.

These much-needed reforms failed to end the rebellion. Bacon was bitter about Berkeley's arbitrary actions, and the poor farmers and indentured servants in his army resented years of exploitation by arrogant justices of the peace and politically well-connected families. As one yeoman rebel put it, "A poor man who has only his labour to maintain himself and his family pays as much [in taxes] as a man who has 20,000 acres." Backed by 400 armed men, Bacon seized control of the colony and issued a "Manifesto and Declaration of the People," demanding the death or removal of all Indians and an end to the rule of wealthy "parasites." "All the power and sway is got into the hands of the rich," Bacon proclaimed, as his army burned Jamestown to the ground and plundered the plantations of Berkeley's allies. When Bacon died suddenly from dysentery in October 1676, the governor took his revenge, dispersing the rebel army, seizing the estates of well-to-do rebels, and hanging 23 men.

Bacon's Rebellion was a pivotal event in the history of Virginia. Although landed planters continued to dominate the economy and polity, they curbed corruption and found public positions for politically ambitious yeomen. The planter-merchant elite appeased the lower social orders by cutting their taxes and supporting the expansion of settlement onto Indian lands. The uprising also contributed to the expansion of African slavery. To forestall another rebellion by poor whites, planters in Virginia and Maryland turned away from indentured servitude. To provide labor for their expanding plantations, they explicitly legalized slavery and imported thousands of Africans, committing their descendants to a social system based on racial exploitation.

Puritan New England

The Puritan exodus from England from 1620 to 1640 was both a worldly quest for land and a spiritual effort to preserve the "pure" Christian faith. By creating a "holy commonwealth" in America, these pious migrants hoped to promote reform within the established Church of England. By distributing land broadly, they tried to build a society of independent property-owning farm families. And by defining their mission in spiritual terms, the Puritans gave a moral dimension to American history.

The Puritan Migration

From the beginning New England differed from other European settlements. New Spain and Jamestown were populated initially by unruly male adventurers, New France and New Netherland by commercial-minded fur traders. By contrast, women and children as well as men settled Plymouth, the first permanent community in New England, and its leaders were pious Protestants—the Pilgrims.

The Pilgrims. The Pilgrims were Puritans who had left the Church of England, thus earning the name "Separatists." When King James I embraced hierarchical religious policies in the 1610s and threatened to harry Puritans "out of the land, or else do worse," the Pilgrims left England and settled among like-minded Dutch Calvinists in Holland. Subsequently, 35 of these exiles

resolved to migrate to America to maintain their English identity. Led by William Bradford and joined by 67 other migrants from England, they sailed to America aboard the *Mayflower* in 1620 (Map 2.5).

Before departing, the Pilgrims organized themselves into a joint-stock corporation with backing from sympathetic Puritan merchants. Arriving in America without a royal charter, they created their own covenant of government, the Mayflower Compact, to "combine ourselves together into a civill body politick." This document was the first "constitution" adopted in North America and used the Puritan model of a self-governing religious congregation as the blueprint for political society.

The first winter in America tested the Pilgrims. As in Virginia, hunger and disease took a heavy toll; of the 102 migrants who arrived in November, only half survived until the spring. Thereafter the Plymouth colony—unlike Virginia—became a healthy and thriving community. The cold climate inhibited the spread of mosquito-borne diseases, and the Pilgrims' religious discipline established a strong work ethic. Moreover, because a severe smallpox epidemic in 1618 had killed 90 percent of the local Wampanoag people, the migrants faced few external threats. The Pilgrims quickly built solid houses, planted ample crops, and entered the fur trade. Their numbers grew rapidly to 3,000 by 1640, prompting the creation of ten new self-governing towns. A legal code embodied their social ethics, providing for a colonywide system of representative self-government, broad political rights, and a prohibition of government interference in spiritual matters.

Meanwhile, England was plunging deeper into religious turmoil. King Charles I supported the Church of England but personally repudiated some Protestant doctrines, such as the role of grace in salvation. English Puritans, who had gained many seats in Parliament, accused the king of "popery"—holding Catholic beliefs. Charles's response was to dissolve Parliament in 1629, claiming that he ruled by "divine right." He began to raise money through royal edicts, customs duties, and the sale of monopolies. The king's arbitrary rule struck at the power of the landed gentry, who expected to exercise authority through the House of Commons, and cut away at the profits of the merchant community, a stronghold of Puritanism. Then in 1633 the king chose William Laud, who loathed Puritans, to head the Church of England. Laud removed hundreds of Puritan ministers and forced Anglican rituals on their congregations, prompting thousands to seek refuge in America.

The Massachusetts Bay Colony. The exodus began in 1630, when 900 Puritans boarded eleven ships and sailed across the Atlantic under the leadership of John Winthrop, a well-educated country squire. Calling England morally corrupt and "overburdened with people," Winthrop sought land and opportunity for his

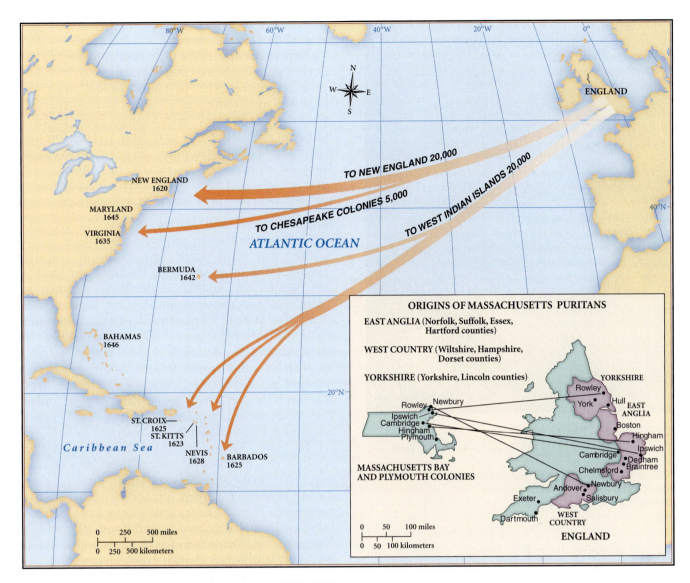

MAP 2.5 The Puritan Migration to America, 1620–1640

Nearly fifty thousand Puritans left England between 1620 and 1640, but they managed to create Puritan-dominated societies only in the New England colonies of Plymouth, Massachusetts Bay, and Connecticut. Within New England, migrants from the three major areas of English Puritanism—Yorkshire, East Anglia, and the West Country—commonly settled among those from their own region. They named American communities after their English towns of origin and transplanted regional customs to New England, such as the open-field agriculture practiced in Rowley in Yorkshire and Rowley in Massachusetts Bay.

children and a place in Christian history for his people. "We must consider that we shall be as a City upon a Hill," Winthrop told his fellow passengers aboard the ship *Arbella* in 1630. "The eyes of all people are upon us." Like the Pilgrims, this larger wave of Puritans envisioned a reformed Christian society, a genuinely "New" England. They saw themselves as a "saving remnant" chosen by God to preserve the true faith in America and inspire religious change in England.

Winthrop and his associates established the Massachusetts Bay colony in the area around Boston and transformed their joint-stock business corporation, the

General Court of shareholders, into a colonial legislature. Over the next decade about 10,000 Puritans migrated to the Massachusetts Bay colony, along with 10,000 others fleeing hard times in England. The Puritans created representative political institutions that were locally based, with the governor as well as the assembly and council elected by the colony's freemen. However, to ensure rule by the godly, the Puritans limited the right to vote and hold office to men who were church members. Eschewing the religious toleration of the Pilgrims, they established Puritanism as the state-supported religion and barred members of other faiths from conducting services.

Governor John Winthrop
This portrait, painted in the style of the Flemish artist Anthony Van Dyke, captures the gravity and intensity of Winthrop, whose policies of religious orthodoxy and elite rule shaped the early history of the Massachusetts Bay colony.
Courtesy, American Antiquarian Society.

Massachusetts Bay became a religious commonwealth with the Bible as its legal as well as spiritual guide. Following a biblical rule, Massachusetts Bay Puritans divided inheritances among all children in a given family, with a double portion going to the oldest son. "Where there is no Law," the colony's government advised local magistrates, they should rule "as near the law of God as they can."

Religion and Society, 1630–1670

In establishing their churches, the Puritans in New England tried to re-create the simplicity of the first Christians. They eliminated bishops and devised a democratic church structure controlled by the laity, or the ordinary members of the congregation—hence their name, Congregationalists. Influenced by John Calvin, Puritans embraced **predestination**, the doctrine that God had decided, or "predestined," the fates of all people before they were born and chosen a few "elect" men and women (the Saints) for salvation and condemned the rest to damnation. Most congregations set extraordinarily high standards for church membership, rigorously examining those who applied. Even so, many Saints lived in great anxiety, for they could never be sure that God had predestined them for salvation.

Puritans dealt with the uncertainties of divine election in three ways. Some congregations stressed the conversion experience: when God infused a soul with grace, the person was "born again" and knew that salvation was at hand. Other Puritans stressed "preparation," the confidence in redemption that came from years of spiritual guidance and church discipline. Still others believed that God had entered into a covenant, or contract, with them, promising to treat them as a divinely "chosen people" as long as they lived according to his laws.

Roger Williams and Rhode Island. To maintain God's favor, the Puritan magistrates of Massachusetts Bay felt they must purge their society of religious dissidents. One target was Roger Williams, who in 1634 had become the minister of the Puritan church in Salem. Williams preferred the Pilgrims' separation of church and state in Plymouth colony and condemned the legal establishment of Congregationalism in Massachusetts Bay. He taught that political magistrates should have authority over only the "bodies, goods, and outward estates of men," not their spiritual lives. Moreover, he questioned the Puritans' seizure (rather than purchase) of Indian lands. In response, the Puritan magistrates banished him from Massachusetts Bay.

In 1636 Williams and his followers resettled in Rhode Island, founding the town of Providence on land acquired from the Narragansett Indians. Other religious dissidents founded Portsmouth and Newport. In 1644 these towns obtained a corporate charter from the English Parliament that granted them full authority "to rule themselves." In Rhode Island as in Plymouth there was no legally established church; every congregation was autonomous, and individual men and women could worship God as they pleased.

Anne Hutchinson. Puritan magistrates in Massachusetts Bay also felt threatened by Anne Hutchinson, the wife of a merchant and a mother of seven who worked as a midwife. Hutchinson held weekly prayer meetings in her house—attended by as many as sixty women—in which she accused certain Boston clergymen of placing undue emphasis on church laws and good behavior. In words that recalled Martin Luther's rejection of indulgences, Hutchinson argued that salvation could not be earned through good deeds; there was no "covenant of works." Rather, God bestowed salvation through the "covenant of grace." Hutchinson stressed the importance of revelation: God directly revealing truth to the individual believer. Since the doctrine of revelation diminished the role of ministers and, indeed, of all established authority, Puritan magistrates found it heretical.

The magistrates also resented Hutchinson because of her sex. Like other Christians, Puritans believed in the

Changing Images of Death

Death—sudden and arbitrary—was a constant presence in the preindustrial world, but it was given various cultural meanings. In the Calvinistic world of pre-1700 New England, gravestones often depicted death as a frightening skull, warning sinners to repent of their sins. After 1700, a smiling cherub adorned many gravestones, suggesting that later generations of Puritans held a more optimistic view of the afterlife. Peabody & Essex Museum.

equality of souls: both men and women could be saved. When it came to the governance of church and state, however, women were seen as being clearly inferior to men. As the Pilgrim minister John Robinson put it, women "are debarred by their sex from ordinary prophesying, and from any other dealing in the church wherein they take authority over the man." Puritan women could never be ministers, lay preachers, or even voting members of the congregation.

In 1637 the Massachusetts Bay magistrates put Hutchinson on trial for heresy, accusing her of believing that inward grace freed an individual from the rules of the church. Hutchinson defended her views with great skill and tenacity, and even Winthrop admitted that she was "a woman of fierce and haughty courage." But the judges found her guilty and berated her for not attend-

ing to "her household affairs, and such things as belong to women." Banished, she followed Roger Williams into exile in Rhode Island.

The coercive policies of the magistrates, along with the desire for better land, prompted some Puritans to leave Massachusetts Bay. In 1636 Thomas Hooker led a hundred settlers to the Connecticut River Valley, where they established the town of Hartford. Others followed, settling along the river at Wethersfield and Windsor. In 1639 the Connecticut Puritans adopted the Fundamental Orders, a plan of government that included a representative assembly and a popularly elected governor. Connecticut was patterned after Massachusetts Bay, with a firm union of church and state and a congregational system of church government, but voting rights were extended to most property-owning men—not just church members.

The English Puritan Revolution. As Puritans established themselves in America, England fell into a religious war. When Archbishop Laud imposed a Church of England prayer book on Presbyterian Scotland in 1642, a Scottish army invaded England. Thousands of English Puritans joined the revolt, demanding greater authority for Parliament and reform of the established church, and hundreds more Puritans returned from America to join the conflict. After four years of civil war the Parliamentary forces led by Oliver Cromwell were victorious. In 1649 Parliament executed Charles I, proclaimed a republican commonwealth, and banished bishops and elaborate rituals from the Church of England.

The Puritan triumph was short-lived. Popular support for the Commonwealth ebbed, especially after 1653 when Cromwell took dictatorial control of the government. Following Cromwell's death, moderate Protestants and a resurgent aristocracy summoned the son of Charles I from Europe, restoring the monarchy and the power of bishops in the Church of England. For many Puritans, Charles II's accession in 1660 represented the victory of the Antichrist—the false prophet described in the last book of the New Testament.

For the Puritans in Massachusetts Bay, the restoration of the monarchy began a new phase of their "errand into the wilderness." They had come to New England to preserve the "pure" Christian church, expecting to return to Europe in triumph. When that sacred mission was dashed by the failure of the English Revolution, Puritan ministers articulated a new vision: they exhorted their congregations to create a permanent new society in America based on their faith and ideals.

The Puritan Imagination and Witchcraft

Like the Native Americans they encountered in New England, the Puritans thought that the physical world was full of supernatural forces. This belief in "spirits" stemmed in part from Christian teachings, such as the Catholic belief in miracles and the Protestant faith in the powers of "grace." Devout Christians saw signs of God's (or Satan's) power in blazing stars, birth defects, and other unusual events. Noting that "more Ministers' Houses than others proportionally had been smitten with Lightning," Cotton Mather, a prominent Massachusetts minister, wondered "what the meaning of God should be in it."

The Puritans' respect for spiritual forces also reflected certain pagan assumptions shared by nearly everyone. When Samuel Sewall, a well-educated Puritan merchant and judge, moved into a new house, he tried to fend off evil spirits by driving a metal pin into the floor. Thousands of ordinary Puritan farmers followed the pagan astrological charts printed in almanacs to determine the best times to plant crops, marry, and make other important decisions.

Zealous ministers attacked many of these beliefs and practices as "superstition" and condemned "cunning" individuals who claimed to have special powers as healers or prophets. Indeed, many Christians looked on folk doctors or conjurers as "wizards" or "witches" who acted at the command of Satan. The people of Andover, Massachusetts, "were much addicted to sorcery," claimed one observer, and "there were forty men in it that could raise the Devil as well as any astrologer." Between 1647 and 1662 civil authorities in Massachusetts and Connecticut hanged 14 people for witchcraft, mostly older women who, their accusers claimed, were "double-tongued" or "had an unruly spirit."

The most dramatic episode of witch-hunting took place in Salem, Massachusetts, in 1692. Initially, a few young girls experienced strange seizures and accused various neighbors of bewitching them. When judges allowed the introduction of "spectral" evidence—visions seen only by the young accusers—the number of accusations spun out of control. Eventually, Massachusetts authorities arrested 175 people and executed 20 of them. The causes of this mass hysteria were complex and are still hard to fathom. Some historians stress group rivalries, pointing out that many of the accusers were the daughters and young female servants of poor farmers in a rural area of Salem, whereas many of the accused witches were wealthier church members or their friends. Because 19 of those executed were women, other historians view the witchcraft trials as part of a broader attempt to keep women, especially those who had inherited property, as subordinate "helpmates" to their husbands. Still other scholars focus on the fears raised by recent Indian attacks in nearby Maine, raids that killed the parents of the young girls whose accusations sparked the Salem prosecutions.

Whatever the cause, the Salem episode marked a turning point for New England. Popular revulsion against the executions weakened the ties between state and church; there would be no more legal prosecutions for

An Affluent Puritan Woman
This well-known painting (c. 1671) of Elizabeth Freake and her daughter Mary is perhaps the finest portrait of a seventeenth-century American. The skill of the artist, probably a visiting English portraitist, and the finery of Mrs. Freake's dress and bonnet suggest the growing cosmopolitanism and prosperity of Boston's merchant community. Worcester Art Museum.

witchcraft or heresy. The European Enlightenment, a major intellectual movement that began around 1675, also helped to limit the number of witchcraft accusations by promoting a more rational view of the world. Increasingly, educated people explained accidents and sudden deaths through theories that drew upon the "laws of nature," not through religion, astrology, or witchcraft. In contrast to Cotton Mather (d. 1728), who believed that lightning might be a supernatural sign, well-read men of the next generation—such as Benjamin Franklin—would conceive of lightning as a natural phenomenon.

A Yeoman Society, 1630–1700

In creating their communities in New England, Puritans consciously shunned the worst features of traditional Europe. They had no wish to live in towns dominated by a few wealthy landowners or controlled by a distant government that levied oppressive taxes. Consequently, they devised land-distribution policies that created self-governing towns and encouraged broad property ownership. Instead of granting thousands of acres to wealthy planters (as occurred in the Chesapeake colonies), the

General Courts of Massachusetts Bay and Connecticut bestowed the title to a township on a group of settlers, or **proprietors**, who distributed the land among themselves. Legal title passed in **fee simple**, which meant that the proprietors' families held the land outright, free from manorial obligations or feudal dues; they could sell, lease, or rent it as they pleased.

Widespread ownership of land did not mean equality of wealth or status. Like most seventeenth-century Europeans, Puritans believed in a social and economic hierarchy. "God had Ordained different degrees and orders of men," proclaimed the wealthy Boston merchant John Saffin, "some to be Masters and Commanders, others to be Subjects, and to be commanded." Town proprietors normally bestowed the largest plots of land on men of high social status, who often became selectmen and justices of the peace. However, all male heads of families received some land, laying the basis for a society of independent yeomen, and landowners had a voice in the town meeting, the main institution of local government (Map 2.6).

Consequently, ordinary farmers in New England communities had much more political power than did most peasants in European villages and most yeomen in the planter-dominated local governments of the Chesapeake colonies. Each year the town meeting chose selectmen to manage its affairs. The meeting also levied taxes; enacted ordinances regarding fencing, lot sizes, and road building; and regulated the use of common fields for grazing livestock and cutting firewood. Beginning in 1634 each town in Massachusetts Bay elected its own representatives to the General Court, a political innovation that gradually shifted authority away from the governor and into the hands of the towns' representatives in the General Court.

As one generation gave way to the next, the farming communities of New England became more socially divided. The larger proprietors owned enough land to divide among all their sons, who usually numbered three or four. Smallholding farmers could provide land for only some of their sons, forcing the rest to begin adult life as propertyless laborers. Newcomers who lacked the rights of proprietors were the least well off, for they had to buy land or work as tenants or laborers. By 1702 in Windsor, Connecticut, landless sons and newcomers accounted for 30 percent of the male taxpayers. It would take years of saving or migration to a new town for these men and their families to become freeholders.

Despite these inequalities, nearly all New Englanders had an opportunity to acquire property, and even those at the bottom of the social scale enjoyed some economic security. When he died in the 1690s, Nathaniel Fish was one of the poorest men in Barnstable, Massachusetts, yet he owned a two-room cottage, eight acres of land, an ox, and a cow. For him and thousands of other settlers, New England had proved to be the promised land, a new world of opportunity.

The Indians' New World

Native Americans along the Atlantic coast were also living in a new world, but for them it was a bleak, dangerous, and conflict-ridden place. Some Indian peoples, like the Pequots, resisted the invaders by force. Others retreated into the Appalachian Mountains to preserve their traditional culture or to band together in new tribes.

Puritans and Pequots

Seeing themselves as God's chosen people, the Puritans justified their intrusions on Native American lands on moral grounds. "By what right or warrant can we enter into the land of the Savages," they asked themselves while still in England, "and take away their rightfull inheritance from them?" John Winthrop provided a clear answer by seeing God's hand in a disastrous smallpox epidemic that reduced the Indian population from 13,000 to 3,000. "If God were not pleased with our inheriting these parts," he asked, "why doth he still make roome for us by diminishing them as we increase?" Citing the Book of Genesis, the magistrates of Massachusetts Bay declared that the Indians had not "subdued" their land and therefore had no "just right" to it.

Imbued with moral righteousness, the Puritans often treated Native Americans with a brutality equal to that of the Spanish conquistadors and Nathaniel Bacon's frontiersmen. When Pequot warriors attacked English farmers who had intruded onto their lands in 1636, Puritan militiamen and their Indian allies led a surprise attack on a Pequot village and massacred about 500 men, women, and children. "God laughed at the Enemies of his People," one soldier boasted, "filling the Place with Dead Bodies." Many of the survivors were ruthlessly tracked down and sold into slavery in the Caribbean.

Like most Europeans, English Puritans viewed the Indians as "savages," culturally inferior people who did not deserve civilized treatment. But the Puritans were not racist as the term is understood today. To them, Native Americans were not genetically inferior—they were white people with sun-darkened skins—and "sin" or Satan, rather than race, accounted for their degenerate condition. "Probably the devil" delivered these "miserable savages" to America, wrote the Puritan minister Cotton Mather, "in hopes that the gospel of the Lord Jesus Christ would never come here to destroy or disturb his absolute empire over them."

This interpretation of the Indians' history inspired the Puritan minister John Eliot to convert them to Christianity. Eliot translated the Bible into Algonquian and undertook numerous missions to Indian villages in eastern Massachusetts. Because Puritans demanded that Indians understand the complexities of Protestant

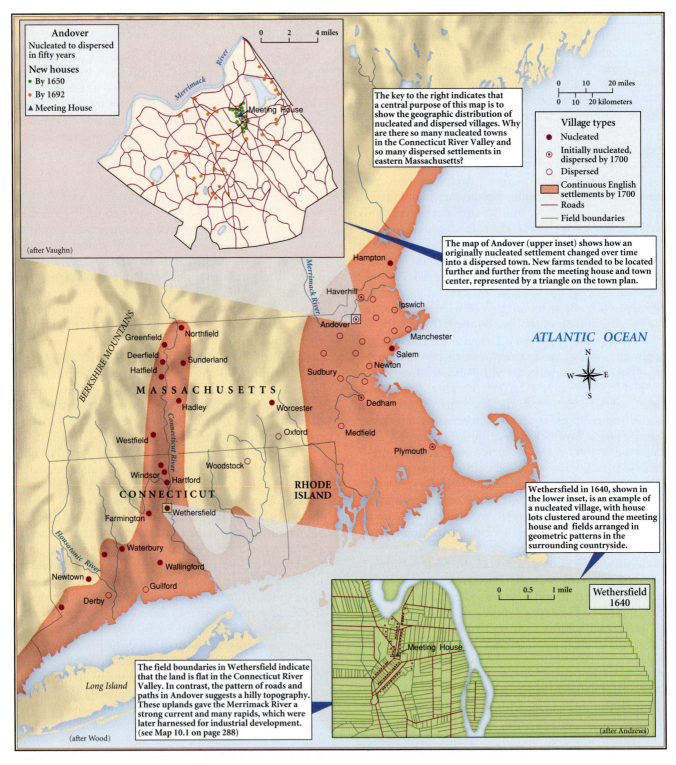

Andover
Nucleated to dispersed in fifty years
New houses
● By 1650
● By 1692
▲ Meeting House

(after Vaughn)

The key to the right indicates that a central purpose of this map is to show the geographic distribution of nucleated and dispersed villages. Why are there so many nucleated towns in the Connecticut River Valley and so many dispersed settlements in eastern Massachusetts?

The map of Andover (upper inset) shows how an originally nucleated settlement changed over time into a dispersed town. New farms tended to be located further and further from the meeting house and town center, represented by a triangle on the town plan.

Village types
● Nucleated
◉ Initially nucleated, dispersed by 1700
○ Dispersed
Continuous English settlements by 1700
Roads
Field boundaries

ATLANTIC OCEAN

Wethersfield in 1640, shown in the lower inset, is an example of a nucleated village, with house lots clustered around the meeting house and fields arranged in geometric patterns in the surrounding countryside.

The field boundaries in Wethersfield indicate that the land is flat in the Connecticut River Valley. In contrast, the pattern of roads and paths in Andover suggests a hilly topography. These uplands gave the Merrimack River a strong current and many rapids, which were later harnessed for industrial development. (see Map 10.1 on page 288)

(after Wood)

Wethersfield 1640

(after Andrews)

MAP 2.6 Settlement Patterns within New England Towns, 1630–1700

Initially, most Puritan towns were compact; regardless of the local topography (hills or plains), families lived close to one another in the nucleated village center and traveled daily to work in the surrounding fields. This pattern is clearly apparent in the 1640 map of Wethersfield, Connecticut, which is situated on the broad plains of the Connecticut River Valley. The first settlers of Andover, Massachusetts, also chose to live in the village center. However, the rugged topography of eastern Massachusetts encouraged a dispersed form of settlement, and by 1692 many residents of Andover lived on their own farms.

theology to become full members of Puritan congregations, only a few Native Americans did so. However, the Puritans created "**praying towns**" that, like the Spanish Franciscans' missions in New Mexico, supervised the Indian population; more than 1,000 Indians lived in fourteen special mission towns. By 1670 the combination of European diseases, military force, and Christianization had pacified most of the Algonquian-speaking peoples who lived along the seacoast of New England, guaranteeing, at least temporarily, the safety of the white settlers.

Metacom's Rebellion

By the 1670s there were three times as many whites as Indians in New England. As the English population grew from 20,000 in 1640 to 55,000, the number of Indians plummeted: from an estimated 120,000 in 1570, to 70,000 in 1620, to barely 16,000. To Metacom, leader of the Wampanoags, the future looked grim. When his people copied English ways, raising hogs and selling pork in Boston, Puritan officials accused them of selling at "an under rate" and placed restrictions on their trade. When they killed wandering livestock that damaged their cornfields, authorities denounced them for violating English property rights. Like Opechancanough in Virginia and Popé in New Mexico, Metacom finally concluded that only military resistance could save Indian lands and culture. So in 1675 Metacom (whom the English called King Philip) forged a military alliance with the Narragansetts and Nipmucks and attacked white settlements throughout New England. Bitter fighting continued into 1676, ending only when Indian warriors ran short of guns and powder, and Mohegans and Mohawks allied with the Massachusetts Bay government ambushed and killed Metacom.

The rebellion was a deadly affair. The Indians burned 20 percent of the English towns in Massachusetts and Rhode Island and killed 1,000 whites, about 5 percent of the adult population. Almost every day, recalled settler William Harris, he had heard new reports of the Indians' "burneing houses, takeing cattell, killing men & women & Children: & carrying others captive." But the Indians' own losses—from famine and disease as well as battle—were much larger: as many as 4,500, or 25 percent of an already diminished population. Many survivors were sold into slavery in the Caribbean, including Metacom's wife and nine-year-old son.

Other members of the defeated Algonquian peoples migrated farther into the New England backcountry, where they intermarried with tribes tied to the French. They had suffered a double tragedy, losing both their land and the integrity of their traditional cultures. Over the next century, these displaced peoples would take their revenge, allying with the French to attack their Puritan enemies (see American Voices, "Mary Rowlandson: A Captivity Narrative," p. 64).

Metacom (King Philip), Chief of the Wampanoag
The Indian uprising of 1675 left an indelible mark on the historical memory of New England. This painting from the 1850s, done on semitransparent cloth and lit from behind for dramatic effect, was used by traveling performers during the 1850s to tell the story of King Philip's War. Note that Metacom is not depicted as a savage but as a dignified man; freed from fear of Indian attack, nineteenth-century New England whites could adopt a romanticized version of their region's often brutal history. Shelburne Museum.

The Fur Trade and the Inland Peoples

As English settlers slowly advanced up the river valleys from the Atlantic coast, the Indians who lived near the Appalachian Mountains and in the great forested areas beyond remained independent. Yet even these distant Indian peoples felt the European presence, as they entered the fur trade to obtain guns and manufactures. Partly because of their location in present-day central New York, the militarily aggressive and diplomatically astute Iroquois peoples were the most successful. Iroquois warriors moved quickly to the east and south along the Mohawk, Hudson, Delaware, and Susquehanna Rivers to exchange goods with (or threaten) the English and Dutch colonies. They traveled north via Lake Champlain and the Richelieu River to French traders in Quebec and west by means

Mary Rowlandson

A Captivity Narrative

Mary Rowlandson, a minister's wife in Lancaster, Massachusetts, was one of many settlers taken captive by the Indians during Metacom's war. Mrs. Rowlandson spent twelve weeks in captivity, traveling constantly, until her family ransomed her for the considerable sum of £20. Her account of this ordeal, The Sovereignty and Goodness of God, *published in 1682, became one of the most popular prose works of its time.*

On the tenth of February 1675, came the Indians with great numbers upon Lancaster: their first coming was about sunrising; hearing the noise of some guns, we looked out; several houses were burning, and the smoke ascending to heaven. . . . [T]he Indians laid hold of us, pulling me one way, and the children another, and said, "Come go along with us"; I told them they would kill me: they answered, if I were willing to go along with them, they would not hurt me. . . .

The first week of my being among them I hardly ate any thing; the second week I found my stomach grow very faint for want of something; and yet it was very hard to get down their filthy trash; but the third week . . . they were sweet and savory to my taste. I was at this time knitting a pair of white cotton stockings for my [Indian] mistress; and had not yet wrought upon a sabbath day. When the sabbath came they bade me go to work. I told them it was the sabbath-day, and desired them to let me rest, and told them I would do as much more tomorrow; to which they answered me they would break my face. . . .

During my abode in this place, Philip [Metacom] spake to me to make a shirt for his boy, which I did, for which he gave me a shilling. I offered the money to my master, but he bade me keep it; and with it I bought a piece of horse flesh. Afterwards he asked me to make a cap for his boy, for which he invited me to dinner. I went, and he gave me a pancake, about as big as two fingers. It was made of parched wheat, beaten, and fried in bear's grease, but I thought I never tasted pleasanter meat in my life. . . .

Hearing that my son was come to this place, I went to see him. . . . He told me also, that awhile before, his master (together with other Indians) were going to the French for powder; but by the way the Mohawks met with them, and killed four of their company, which made the rest turn back again, for which I desire that myself and he may bless the Lord; for it might have been worse with him, had he been sold to the French, than it proved to be in his remaining with the Indians. . . .

My master had three squaws, living sometimes with one, and sometimes with another one. . . . [It] was Weetamoo with whom I had lived and served all this while. A severe and proud dame she was, bestowing every day in dressing herself near as much time as any of the gentry of the land: powdering her hair, and painting her face, going with necklaces, with jewels in her ears, and bracelets upon her hands. When she had dressed herself, her work was to make girdles of wampom and beads. . . .

On Tuesday morning they called their general court (as they call it) to consult and determine, whether I should go home or no. And they all as one man did seemingly consent to it, that I should go home. . . .

Source: C. H. Lincoln, ed., *Original Narratives of Early American History: Narratives of Indian Wars, 1675–1699* (New York: Barnes and Noble, 1952), 14: 139–41.

of the Great Lakes and the Allegheny-Ohio river system to the rich fur-bearing lands of the Mississippi Valley.

The rise of the Iroquois was breathtakingly rapid, just as their subsequent decline was tragically sobering. In 1600 the Iroquois in New York numbered about 30,000 and lived in large towns of 500 to 2,000 inhabitants. Two decades later they had organized themselves in a great "longhouse" confederation of the Five Nations: the Senecas, Cayugas, Onondagas, Oneidas, and Mohawks.

Although a virulent smallpox epidemic in 1633 cut their numbers by a third, the Iroquois waged a successful series of wars against the Iroquoian-speaking Hurons (1649), Neutrals (1651), Eries (1657), and Susquehannocks. The victorious Iroquois warriors carried hundreds of captives to New York, where villagers tortured them with firebrands to atone for those lost in battle.

These triumphs gave the Iroquois control of the fur trade with the French in Quebec and the Dutch in New

York. Equally important, it replenished the populations of villages hard hit by epidemics and wartime losses. Taking control of those war captives that were not tortured and killed, Iroquois families conducted "requickening" ceremonies that transferred to them their dead relatives' names, along with social roles and duties. By 1667 half of the population of many Mohawk towns consisted of adopted prisoners. The cultural diversity within Iroquoia further increased as the Five Nations made peace with their traditional French foes and allowed Jesuit missionaries to live among them. Soon about 20 percent of the Iroquois were Catholics, some living under French protection in separate mission-towns.

In 1680 the Iroquois repudiated the treaty with the French. To obtain furs to trade for guns and goods with the English and Dutch merchants in New York, they embarked on a new series of western wars. Warriors of the Five Nations pushed a dozen Algonquian-speaking peoples allied with the French—the Ottawas, Foxes, Sauks, Kickapoos, Miamis, and Illinois—out of their traditional lands north of the Ohio River and into a newly formed multitribal region (present-day Wisconsin) west of Lake Michigan. The cost of these victories was high;

Algonquian Beaver Bowl

In part because of the importance to the fur trade, the beaver played a significant role in Native American cultural life. This beaver-shaped bowl, carved from the root of an ash tree, was the work of an eighteenth-century Algonquian artisan in present-day Ohio or Illinois.

Peabody Museum, Harvard University. Photo by Hillel Burger.

after losing about 2,200 warriors, in 1701 the Iroquois again made peace with the French, bringing peace to the inland region for two generations.

However, the character of Indian society in the eastern woodlands had been permanently altered. Most tribes had become smaller as the fighting and European diseases devastated their peoples and as the rum and corn liquor sold by fur traders took their toll. "Strong spirits . . . Causes our men to get very sick," a Catawba leader protested, "and many of our people has Lately Died by the Effects of that Strong Drink." Many Indian peoples also lost their economic and cultural independence. As they exchanged furs for European-made iron utensils and cloth blankets, they neglected traditional artisan skills—each year making fewer flint hoes, clay pots, and skin garments. As a Cherokee chief complained in the 1750s, "Every necessity of life we must have from the white people." Moreover, as French missionaries won converts among the Hurons, Iroquois, and inland peoples, they divided communities into hostile religious factions.

The commitment to constant warfare altered tribal politics. Most strikingly, it increased the influence of those who made war, shifting political power from cautious elders, the sachems, to headstrong young warriors. The sachems, one group of Seneca warriors said with scorn, "were a parcell of Old People who say much but who Mean or Act very little." Equally important, the position and status of women changed in complex and contradictory ways. Traditionally, eastern Woodland women had asserted authority as the chief providers of food and

An English View of Pocahontas

By depicting the Indian princess Pocahontas as a well-dressed European woman, the artist casts her as a symbol of peaceful assimilation to English culture. In actuality, marriages between white men (often fur traders) and Indian women usually created bilingual families that absorbed elements from both cultures.

National Portrait Gallery, Smithsonian Institution / Art Resource, NY.

handcrafted goods. As a French Jesuit noted of the Iroquois, "The women are always the first to deliberate . . . on private or community matters. They hold their councils apart and . . . advise the chiefs . . . , so that the latter may deliberate on them in their turn." The influx of European goods and the disruptive impact of warfare on agricultural production threatened the economic basis of women's power. At the same time, the influence of women in victorious tribes increased as they assumed responsibility for assimilating hundreds of captive peoples into the culture.

Finally, the sheer extent of the fur industry—the trapping and killing of hundreds of thousands of beaver, deer, otter, and other animals—profoundly altered the environment. Streams ran faster because there were fewer beaver dams, and the winter hunt for food became more arduous and less fruitful. Death from trapping and hunting severely depleted the animal population of North America, just as death from disease and warfare cut down its Indian inhabitants. The native animals as well as the native peoples now lived in a new American world.

FOR FURTHER EXPLORATION

▶ For definitions of key terms boldfaced in this chapter, see the glossary at the end of the book.

▶ To assess your mastery of the material covered in this chapter, see the Online Study Guide at **bedfordstmartins.com/henretta**.

▶ For suggested references, including Web sites, see page SR-2 at the end of the book.

▶ For map resources and primary documents, see **bedfordstmartins.com/henretta**.

SUMMARY

Beginning in 1565, first Spain and then England, France, and Holland established permanent settlements in North America. Spain claimed most of the continent, but settled military garrisons and Franciscan missions only in present-day Florida and New Mexico. Both soldiers and friars exploited native laborers, prompting Indian revolts that by 1700 had temporarily expelled most Spaniards from New Mexico. The fur trade became the lifeblood of the Dutch colony of New Netherland and the far-flung French settlements in Canada and Louisiana, where Jesuit priests extended France's influence among the native peoples. The English came primarily as settlers, and their relentless quest for land led to frequent conflict with the Indian peoples.

The English created two types of colonies in North America. Settlers in the Chesapeake region created plantation societies that raised tobacco for export to Europe and were controlled by wealthy planters who exploited the labor of thousands of white indentured servants. In Virginia, economic hardship and political corruption by Governor Berkeley prompted Nathaniel Bacon's unsuccessful rebellion of 1675–1676. Subsequently, Chesapeake planters turned increasingly to slave labor from Africa, creating full-scale slave societies.

The Puritan migrants to New England created a society of freehold farmers who raised crops mostly for their own consumption. Reacting against hierarchical institutions in England, the Puritans set up self-governing churches and towns. At first Puritan magistrates in Boston enforced religious orthodoxy, banishing Roger Williams, Anne Hutchinson, and other religious dissidents, but they gradually relinquished power to a town-based representative assembly.

Wherever Europeans intruded, native peoples died from epidemic diseases, fur-trade-related wars, and political revolts. The Pueblo peoples rose against the Spanish in 1598 and 1680, the Chesapeake Indians nearly wiped out the Virginia colony in 1622, and Metacom's forces dealt New England a devastating blow in 1675–1676. However, by 1700 many Indian communities in New Mexico and along the Atlantic seaboard had been nearly annihilated by disease and warfare, and native peoples in the Ohio and Mississippi Valleys had experienced grave cultural damage.

TIMELINE

1539–1543	Coronado and de Soto explore northern lands
1565	Spain establishes St. Augustine, Florida
1598	Acoma rebellion in New Mexico
1603–1625	James I, king of England
1607	English adventurers settle Jamestown, Virginia
1608	Samuel de Champlain founds Quebec
1613	Dutch set up fur-trading post on Manhattan Island
1619	First Africans arrive in the Chesapeake region Virginia House of Burgesses convened
1620	Pilgrims found Plymouth colony
1620–1660	Tobacco boom in Chesapeake colonies
1621	Dutch West India Company chartered
1622	Opechancanough's uprising
1624	Virginia becomes a royal colony
1625–1649	Charles I, king of England
1630	Puritans found Massachusetts Bay colony
1634	Maryland settled
1636–1637	Pequot war Roger Williams and Anne Hutchinson banished
1640s	Puritan revolution in England Iroquois go to war over fur trade
1651	First Navigation Act
1660	Restoration of English monarchy Poor tobacco market begins
1664	English conquer New Netherland
1675–1676	Bacon's Rebellion Metacom's uprising Expansion of African slavery in the Chesapeake region
1680	Popé's rebellion in New Mexico
1692	Salem witchcraft trials

CHAPTER 3

The British Empire in America

1660–1750

The Politics of Empire, 1660–1713
The Restoration Colonies
From Mercantilism to Dominion
The Glorious Revolution of 1688
Imperial Wars and Native Peoples

The Imperial Slave Economy
The South Atlantic System
*Slavery in the Chesapeake and
    South Carolina*
*African American Community and
    Resistance*
The Southern Gentry
The Northern Maritime Economy

The New Politics of Empire,
1713–1750
The Rise of Colonial Assemblies
Salutary Neglect
*Protecting the Mercantile System of
    Trade*

BETWEEN 1660 AND 1750 BRITAIN CREATED A DYNAMIC COMMERCIAL EMPIRE IN AMERICA. When Charles II came to the throne in 1660 England was a second-class trading country, picking up the crumbs left by Dutch merchants who dominated the Atlantic. "What we want is more of the trade the Dutch now have," declared the duke of Albemarle. To win commercial power the English government passed the Acts of Trade and Navigation, which excluded Dutch merchants from its growing American colonies, and then went to war first against the Dutch and then against the French to enforce the new legislation. By the 1720s the newly unified kingdom of Great Britain (comprising England and Scotland) controlled the North Atlantic trade. "We have within ourselves and in our colonies in America," a British pamphleteer boasted, "an inexhaustible fund to supply ourselves, and perhaps Europe." A generation later British officials celebrated the American trade as a leading source of the nation's prosperity. As the ardent imperialist Malachy Postlethwayt proclaimed in 1745, the British empire "was a magnificent superstructure of American commerce and naval power on an African foundation."

As Postlethwayt observed, the wealth of the empire stemmed primarily from the predatory trade in African slaves and the profits generated by slave labor, mainly on the sugar plantations of the West Indies. To protect Britain's increasingly valuable sugar colonies from European rivals— the Dutch in New Netherland, the French in Quebec and the

◄ **Power and Race in the Chesapeake**
Lord Baltimore holds a map of his proprietary colony, Maryland, in this 1670 painting by Gerard Soest. The colony will soon belong to his grandson Cecil Calvert, who points to his magnificent inheritance. The presence of an African servant foreshadows the importance of slave labor in the post-1700 Chesapeake economy.
Enoch Pratt Free Library of Baltimore.

West Indies, and the Spanish in Florida—British officials expanded the navy and repeatedly went to war. Increasingly, economic power came from the barrels of its naval guns and calculated diplomatic policies. Boasted one English pamphleteer, "We are, of any nation, the best situated for trade, . . . capable of giving maritime laws to the world."

To solidify these commercial gains, the British government extended financial and political control over its American settlements. Beginning in the 1660s it successfully controlled the course of colonial commerce through the Navigation Acts and, with less success, tried to subordinate colonial political institutions to imperial direction. These initiatives made Britain a dominant power in Europe and the Western Hemisphere, bringing modest prosperity to most of the white colonists on the North American mainland while condemning thousands of enslaved Africans to brutal work and early death.

The Politics of Empire, 1660–1713

In the first decades of settlement England governed its Chesapeake and New England colonies in a haphazard fashion. Taking advantage of this laxity and the upheaval produced by religious conflict and civil war in England, local oligarchies of Puritan magistrates and

tobacco-growing planters ran their societies as they wished. However, with the restoration of the monarchy in 1660 royal bureaucrats imposed order on the unruly settlements and, with the aid of Indian allies, went to war against rival European powers.

The Restoration Colonies

In 1660 Charles II ascended the English throne and promptly gave away millions of acres of American land. A generous but extravagant man who was always in debt, Charles rewarded eight aristocrats who had supported his return to power with a gift of the Carolinas, an area long claimed by Spain and populated by thousands of Indians. Then in 1664 he granted all the territory between the Delaware and Connecticut Rivers to his brother James, the duke of York. That same year James took possession of the conquered Dutch province of New Netherland, renaming it New York, and conveyed the ownership of the adjacent province of New Jersey to two of the Carolina proprietors (Table 3.1).

In one of the great land grabs in history, a few English aristocrats had taken title to vast provinces. Like Lord Baltimore's Maryland, their new colonies were proprietorships; the aristocrats owned all the land and could rule as they wished as long as the laws conformed broadly to those of England. Most proprietors envisioned a traditional social order presided over by a

TABLE 3.1 English Colonies Created in North America, 1660–1750					
	Date	Type	Religion	Status in 1775	Chief Export or Economic Activity
Carolinas	1663	Proprietary	Church of England	Royal	
North	1691				Mixed farming; naval stores
South	1691				Rice; indigo
New Jersey	1664	Proprietary	Church of England	Royal	Wheat
New York	1664	Proprietary	Church of England	Royal	Wheat
Pennsylvania	1681	Proprietary	No established church	Proprietary	Wheat
Georgia	1732	Trustees	Church of England	Royal	Rice
New Hampshire (separated from Massachusetts)	1739	Royal	Congregationalist	Royal	Mixed farming; lumber; naval stores
Nova Scotia	1749	Royal	Church of England	Royal	Fishing; mixed farming; naval stores

William Penn, Quaker Proprietor

As a member of the Society of Friends, Penn dressed in a plain and simple style, as this portrait shows. However, because of his proprietorship, the young Quaker was a wealthy man, the sole owner of millions of acres of land. This 1685 indenture, or contract, authorized the sale of five hundred acres of land along the Delaware River to John Dwight, a "Gentleman" of Fulham in England. Historical Society of Pennsylvania / Jonathan Horne.

gentry class and a legally established Church of England. Thus, the Fundamental Constitutions of Carolina (1669) prescribed a manorial system with a powerful nobility and a mass of serfs.

The Carolinas. This aristocratic scheme proved to be a pure fantasy. The first settlers in North Carolina, poor families from Virginia, refused to work on large manors and chose to live on modest family farms, raising grain and tobacco. Indeed, farmers in Albemarle County, inspired by Bacon's Rebellion in Virginia and angered by taxes on tobacco exports, rebelled in 1677. They deposed the governor and forced the proprietors to abandon most of their financial claims.

The colonists of South Carolina refused to accept the Fundamental Constitutions and created their own version of the hierarchical social order of Europe. White settlers, many of them migrants from the overcrowded sugar-producing island of Barbados, imported enslaved African workers and used them to raise cattle and food crops for export to the West Indies. They also opened a lucrative trade with Native Americans, exchanging English manufactured goods for furs and Indian slaves. Because of the Carolinians' growing reliance on Indian slaves, they encouraged their native allies to take captives from Indian settlements in Florida, raising the threat of war with Spain. In 1715 these slave raids prompted a brutal war with the Yamasee people, which took the lives

of four hundred settlers. Until the 1720s South Carolina remained an ill-governed, violence-ridden frontier settlement.

William Penn and Pennsylvania. In dramatic contrast to the Carolinas, the new proprietary colony of Pennsylvania (which included present-day Delaware) pursued a pacifistic policy toward Native Americans and quickly became prosperous. In 1681 Charles II bestowed the colony on William Penn in payment of a large debt owed to Penn's father. Born to wealth and seemingly destined for courtly pursuits, the younger Penn had converted to the Society of Friends (Quakers), a radical Protestant sect, and used his wealth and prestige to spread its influence. He designed Pennsylvania as a refuge for Quakers, who were persecuted in England because they refused to serve in the army and would not pay taxes to support the Church of England.

Like the Puritans, the Quakers wanted to restore the simplicity and spirituality of early Christianity. However, the Quakers rejected the pessimistic religious doctrines of Puritans or other Calvinists, who restricted salvation to a small elect. Rather, Quakers followed the teachings of the English visionaries George Fox and Margaret Fell, who argued that all men and women had been imbued by God with an inner "light" of grace or understanding that opened salvation to everyone. Quakers did not have ministers, and when they met for worship there were no sermons; members sat in silence until moved to speak by the inner light.

Penn's Frame of Government (1681) extended Quaker radicalism into politics. In a world dominated by established churches, Penn's constitution guaranteed religious freedom to Christians of all denominations and allowed all property-owning men to vote and hold office. Thousands of Quakers, primarily from the ranks of middling farmers in northwestern England, flocked to Pennsylvania, settling along the Delaware River in or near the city of Philadelphia, which Penn himself laid out in a rational grid pattern of main streets and back alleys. The proprietor sold land at low prices and, to attract Protestant settlers from Europe, published pamphlets in Dutch and German advertising the advantages of his colony. In 1683 migrants from the German province of Saxony founded Germantown (just outside Philadelphia) and thousands of other Germans soon joined them, attracted by cheap, fertile land and the prospect of freedom from religious warfare and persecution. Ethnic diversity, pacifism, and freedom of conscience made Pennsylvania the most open and democratic of the Restoration colonies.

From Mercantilism to Dominion

Since the 1560s, Elizabeth I and her successors had used government subsidies and charters to stimulate English manufacturing and foreign trade. Beginning in the 1650s, the English government extended these policies—known as **mercantilism**—to its American colonies, where they created a generation of political controversy.

The Navigation Acts. The new mercantilist policies regulated colonial commerce and manufacturing. According to mercantilist theory, the American colonies were to produce agricultural goods and raw materials, which English merchants would carry to the home country, where they would be reexported or manufactured into finished products. Consequently, the Navigation Act of 1651 prohibited Dutch merchants from the colonial trade and gave English traders a monopoly by requiring that goods imported into England or its American settlements be carried on English-owned ships. New parliamentary acts in 1660 and 1663 strengthened the ban on foreign merchants and stipulated that colonial sugar, tobacco, and indigo could be shipped only to England. To provide even more business for English merchants, the acts also required that European exports to America pass through England. To enforce these mercantilist laws and raise money, the Revenue Act of 1673 imposed a "plantation duty" on sugar and tobacco exports and created a staff of customs officials to collect the duty (Table 3.2).

The English government backed its mercantilist policy with the force of arms. In three commercial wars between 1652 and 1674 the English navy drove the Dutch from New Netherland and ended Dutch supremacy in the West African slave trade. Meanwhile, English merchants expanded their fleets and dominated Atlantic commerce.

Many Americans resisted these mercantilist laws as burdensome and intrusive. Edward Randolph, an English customs official in Massachusetts, reported that the colony's Puritan-dominated government took

TABLE 3.2 Navigation Acts, 1651–1751			
	Date	Purpose	Result
Act of 1651	1651	Cut Dutch trade	Mostly ignored
Act of 1660	1660	Ban foreign shipping; enumerated goods only to England	Partially obeyed
Act of 1663	1663	Require European imports to pass only through England	Partially obeyed
Staple Act	1663	Require enumerated goods to pass through England	Mostly obeyed
Revenue Act	1673	Impose "plantation duty"; create customs system	Mostly obeyed
Act of 1696	1696	Prevent frauds; create Vice-Admiralty Courts	Mostly obeyed
Woolen Act	1699	Prevent export or intercolonial sale of textiles	Partially obeyed
Hat Act	1732	Prevent export or intercolonial sale of hats	Partially obeyed
Molasses Act	1733	Cut American imports of molasses from French West Indies	Extensively violated
Iron Act	1750	Prevent manufacture of finished iron products	Extensively violated
Currency Act	1751	End use of paper currency as legal tender in New England	Mostly obeyed

"no notice of the laws of trade," welcoming Dutch merchants, importing goods from the French sugar islands, and claiming that its royal charter exempted it from most of the new regulations. Outraged, Randolph called for English troops to "reduce Massachusetts to obedience." Instead of using force, the Lords of Trade—the administrative body charged with colonial affairs—pursued a punitive legal strategy. In 1679 they denied the claim of Massachusetts Bay to the adjoining province of New Hampshire and created a separate colony there with a royal governor. To bring the Puritans in Massachusetts Bay directly under their control, in 1684 English officials persuaded the English Court of Chancery to annul the colony's charter on the grounds that the Puritan government had violated the Navigation Acts and virtually outlawed the Church of England.

The Dominion of New England.

The accession to the throne of James II (r. 1685–1688), who had grown up in France during the reign of Oliver Cromwell, brought new demands for imperial reform. An admirer of France's authoritarian Louis XIV and of "divine-right" monarchy, James instructed the Lords of Trade to create a centralized imperial system in America. Backed by the king, in 1686 they revoked the corporate charters of Connecticut and Rhode Island and merged them with the Massachusetts Bay and Plymouth colonies to form a new royal province, the Dominion of New England. Two years later the home government added New York and New Jersey to the Dominion, creating a single colony that stretched from the Delaware River to Maine (Map 3.1).

This administrative innovation went far beyond mercantilism, which had respected the political autonomy of the various colonies while regulating their trade, and extended to America the authoritarian model of colonial rule imposed on Catholic Ireland. When James II had taken control of New York in 1674, he had refused to allow an elective assembly and ruled by decree. Now he extended absolutist rule to the entire Dominion, appointing Sir Edmund Andros, a former military officer, as governor and empowering him to abolish the existing colonial legislative assemblies. In Massachusetts, Andros immediately banned town meetings, angering villagers who prized local self-rule, and advocated public worship in the Church of England, offending Puritan Congregationalists. Even worse from the colonists' perspective, the governor imposed new taxes and challenged all land titles granted under the original Massachusetts charter. Andros offered to provide new deeds but only if the colonists would agree to pay an annual fee (or quitrent). The Puritans protested to the king, but James was determined to impose absolutist rule and refused to restore the old charter.

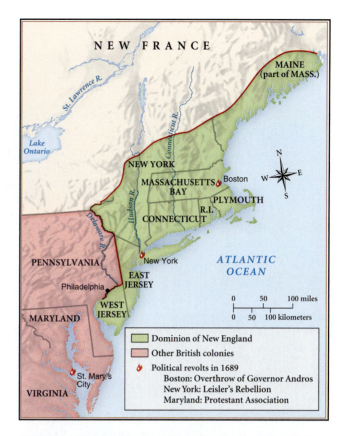

MAP 3.1 The Dominion of New England, 1686–1689

The Dominion created a vast new royal colony stretching nearly five hundred miles along the Atlantic coast. After the Glorious Revolution in England, revolts led or instigated by local politicians and ministers in Boston and New York City ousted royal officials, effectively ending the Dominion. In Maryland, a Protestant association mounted a third revolt, deposing the Catholic proprietary governor. The new governments instituted by King William III balanced the power held by imperial authorities and local political institutions.

The Glorious Revolution of 1688

Fortunately for the colonists, James II angered English political leaders as much as Andros alienated the Americans. The king revoked the charters of many English towns, rejected the advice of Parliament, and aroused popular opposition by openly practicing Roman Catholicism. Then in 1688 James's foreign-born Catholic wife gave birth to a son, raising the prospect of a Catholic heir to the throne. Fearing political persecution similar to that inflicted by King Louis XIV on French Protestants (the Huguenots) in France in 1685, English parliamentary leaders supported the quick and bloodless coup known as the Glorious Revolution. Backed by popular protests and the army, they forced James into exile and enthroned Mary, his Protestant daughter by his first wife, and her Protestant Dutch husband, William of Orange. Queen Mary II and King William III agreed to rule as constitutional monarchs, accepting a bill of rights that limited

A Prosperous Dutch Farmstead

Many Dutch farmers in the Hudson River Valley prospered because of easy access to market and their exploitation of black slaves, which they owned in much greater numbers than their neighbors of English ancestry did. To record his good fortune, Martin Van Bergen of Leeds, New York, had this mural painted over his mantelpiece.
New York State Historical Association, Cooperstown, NY.

royal prerogatives and increased personal liberties and parliamentary powers.

To justify their coup, parliamentary leaders relied on the political philosopher John Locke. In his *Two Treatises on Government* (1690) Locke rejected divine-right theories of monarchical rule; he argued that the legitimacy of government rests on the consent of the governed and that individuals have inalienable natural rights to life, liberty, and property. Locke's celebration of individual rights and representative government had a lasting influence in America, where many political leaders wanted to expand the powers of the colonial assemblies.

More immediately, the Glorious Revolution sparked rebellions by colonists in Massachusetts, Maryland, and New York in 1689. When the news of the coup reached Boston in April 1689, Puritan leaders seized Governor Andros and shipped him back to England. Responding to American protests, the new monarchs broke up the

Dominion of New England. However, they refused to restore the old Puritan-dominated government, creating instead a new royal colony of Massachusetts (which included Plymouth and Maine). According to the new charter of 1692, the king would appoint the governor (as well as naval officers who were charged with enforcing customs regulations), and members of the Church of England would enjoy religious freedom. The charter restored the Massachusetts assembly but stipulated that it be elected by all male property owners (not just Puritan church members).

The uprising in Maryland had both economic and religious causes. Since 1660 tobacco prices had been falling, threatening the livelihoods of small holders, tenant farmers, and former indentured servants, most of whom were Protestants. They resented the rising taxes and the high fees imposed by wealthy proprietary officials, who were primarily Catholics. When Parliament ousted James II, a Protestant association in Maryland quickly removed the Catholic officials appointed by Lord Baltimore. The Lords of Trade suspended Baltimore's proprietorship, imposed royal government, and established the Church of England as the colony's official church. This arrangement lasted until 1715, when Benedict Calvert, the fourth Lord Baltimore, renounced Catholicism and converted to the Anglican faith, prompting the crown to restore the proprietorship to the Calvert family.

In New York the rebellion against the Dominion of New England began a decade of violence and political conflict. New England settlers on Long Island, angered by James's prohibition of representative institutions, began the uprising, and they quickly won the support of Dutch Protestant artisans in New York City, who welcomed the succession of Queen Mary and her Dutch husband. The Dutch militia ousted Lieutenant Governor Nicholson, an Andros appointee and an alleged Catholic sympathizer, and rallied behind a new government led by Jacob Leisler, a militant Protestant merchant and former army officer who had married into a prominent New York Dutch family. Leisler hoped to win the support of all classes and ethnic groups, but his outbursts of religious rage, as he denounced his political rivals as "popish dogs" and "Roages, Rascalls, and Devills," alienated many New Yorkers. When Leisler imprisoned his opponents, imposed new taxes, and championed the interests of Dutch artisans, the wealthy merchants who had traditionally controlled the city government condemned his rule. In 1691 the merchants won the support of a newly appointed royal governor, who instituted a representative assembly and supported a merchant-dominated Board of Aldermen that lowered artisans' wages. The governor had Leisler indicted for treason. He was convicted by a jury, hanged, and then decapitated, an act of political violence that corrupted New York politics for a generation.

In both America and England the Glorious Revolution of 1688 and 1689 began a new phase in imperial history. The uprisings in Boston and New York toppled the authoritarian Dominion of New England and, because William I wanted colonial support for a war against France, won the restoration of internal self-government. In England, the new constitutional monarchs promoted an empire based on commerce, launching a period of "salutary neglect" that gave free rein to enterprising merchants and financiers who developed the American colonies as a source of trade. Although Parliament created a new Board of Trade (1696) to supervise the American settlements, it had little success. Settlers and proprietors resisted the board's attempt to install royal governments in every colony, as did many English political leaders, who feared an increase in monarchical power. Consequently, the empire remained diverse. Colonies that were of minor economic and political importance retained their corporate governments (Connecticut and Rhode Island) or proprietary institutions (Pennsylvania, Maryland, and the Carolinas) while royal governors ruled the lucrative staple-producing settlements in the West Indies and Virginia.

Imperial Wars and Native Peoples

Between 1689 and 1815 Britain vied with France for dominance in western Europe. Prompted by this series of wars, British political leaders created a powerful state that devoted three-quarters of its revenue to military expenses. As these wars spread to the Western Hemisphere, they involved increasing numbers of Native American warriors, who were now armed with European guns and steel knives and hatchets (Table 3.3). By this time many Indian peoples were familiar enough with European goals and diplomacy to turn the fighting to their own advantage.

TABLE 3.3 English Wars, 1650–1750

	Date	Purpose	Result
Anglo-Dutch	1652–1654	Develop commercial markets	Stalemate
Anglo-Dutch	1664	Acquire markets—conquest	England conquers New Netherland
Anglo-Dutch	1673	Develop commercial markets	England makes maritime gains
King William's (War of the League of Augsburg)	1689–1697	Maintain European balance of power	Stalemate in North America
Queen Anne's (War of the Spanish Succession)	1702–1713	Maintain European balance of power	British acquire Hudson Bay, Nova Scotia, and strategic sites in Europe
Jenkins' Ear	1739	Expand markets in Spanish America	Stalemate
King George's (War of Austrian Succession)	1740–1748	Maintain European balance of power	British capture and return Louisbourg (on Cape Breton Island)

The first significant fighting in North America occurred during the War of the Spanish Succession (1702–1713), which pitted Britain against France and Spain. Taking advantage of this European conflict, English settlers in the Carolinas tried to protect their growing settlements by launching an attack against Spanish Florida. Seeking military allies, the Carolinians armed the Creeks, a 15,000-member agrarian people who lived in matrilineal clans on the fertile lands along the present-day Georgia-Alabama border. A joint English-Creek expedition burned the Spanish town of St. Augustine but failed to capture the nearby fort. Fearing that future Carolinian-backed Indian raids would endanger its colony of Florida and pose a threat to Havana in nearby Cuba, the Spanish reinforced St. Augustine and launched unsuccessful attacks against Charleston, South Carolina.

The Creeks had their own quarrels to settle with the pro-French Choctaws to the west and the Spanish-allied Apalachees to the south, and they took this opportunity to become the dominant tribe in the region. Beginning in 1704 a force of Creek and Yamasee warriors destroyed the remaining Franciscan missions in northern Florida, attacked the Spanish settlement at Pensacola, and massacred the Apalachees, selling 1,000 Apalachee prisoners to South Carolinian traders, who carried most of them to slavery in the West Indies. "In all these extensive dominions and provinces," a Spanish official lamented, "the law of God and the preaching of the Holy Gospel have now ceased." Simultaneously, a Carolina-supplied and Creek-led army attacked the Iroquois-speaking Tuscarora people of North Carolina, killing hundreds, executing 160 male captives, and sending 400 women and children into slavery. The Tuscaroras who survived migrated to the north and joined the New York Iroquois, who now became the Six Nations. Having ruled by the guns and hatchets of their Indian allies, the Carolinians now died by them. In 1715, when traders demanded the payment of debts, the Yamasee and Creek revolted, killing 400 colonists before being overwhelmed by the Carolinians and their new Cherokee allies.

Native Americans also played a central role in the fighting in the Northeast, where French Catholics from Canada confronted English Puritans from New England. Aided by the French, Abenaki and Mohawk warriors took revenge on their Puritan enemies. They destroyed English settlements along the coast of Maine and in 1704 attacked the western Massachusetts town of Deerfield, where they killed 48 residents and carried 112 into captivity. New England responded to these raids by launching attacks against French settlements, joining with British naval forces and troops in 1710 to seize Port Royal in French Acadia (Nova Scotia). However, in the following year a major British-American expedition against the French stronghold at Quebec failed miserably.

The New York frontier remained quiet because France and England did not want to disrupt the lucrative fur trade and because most of the Iroquois Nations had adopted a new policy of "aggressive neutrality." In 1701, after a decade of heavy losses, the Iroquois concluded a peace with France and its Indian allies. Simultaneously, they reinterpreted their "covenant chain" of military alliances with the English governors of New York and the Algonquian tribes of New England. For the next half-century the Iroquois exploited their central geographic location by trading with the English and the French but refusing to fight for either side. The Delaware leader Teedyuscung explained this strategy by showing his people a pictorial message from the Iroquois: "You see a Square in the Middle, meaning the Lands of the Indians; and at one End, the Figure of a Man, indicating the English; and at the other End, another, meaning the French. Let us join together to defend our land against both."

Despite the military stalemate in the colonies, Britain used victories in Europe to win major territorial and commercial concessions in the Americas in the Treaty of Utrecht (1713). From France, Britain obtained Newfoundland, Acadia, the Hudson Bay region of northern Canada, and access to the western Indian trade. From Spain, Britain acquired the strategic fortress of Gibraltar at the entrance to the Mediterranean and a thirty-year contract to supply slaves to Spanish America. These gains solidified Britain's commercial supremacy and brought peace to eastern North America for a generation (Map 3.2).

The Imperial Slave Economy

Britain's increasing administrative and military interest in American affairs reflected the growing importance of its Atlantic trade in slaves and staple crops. European merchants had created a new agricultural and commercial order—the South Atlantic system, as historians call it—that produced sugar, tobacco, rice, and other subtropical products. At the core of the new productive regime stood plantations staffed by enslaved labor from Africa (Table 3.4).

The South Atlantic System

The South Atlantic system had three major components: fertile lands seized from Indians, enslaved laborers purchased from Africans, and capital and ships provided by Europeans. In Brazil and the West Indies—the core of the South Atlantic system—European adventurers and settlers used Indian lands to produce sugar. Before 1500 Europeans had few sweeteners—mostly honey and apple juice—and quickly developed a craving for the

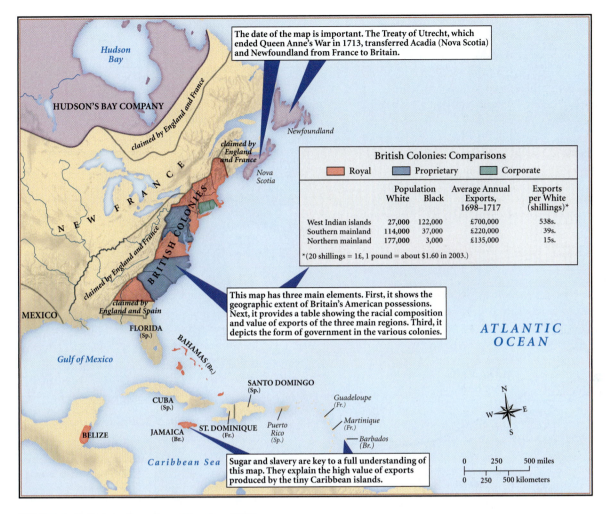

The date of the map is important. The Treaty of Utrecht, which ended Queen Anne's War in 1713, transferred Acadia (Nova Scotia) and Newfoundland from France to Britain.

British Colonies: Comparisons

	Royal	Proprietary	Corporate

	Population		Average Annual Exports, 1698–1717	Exports per White (shillings)*
	White	Black		
West Indian islands	27,000	122,000	£700,000	538s.
Southern mainland	114,000	37,000	£220,000	39s.
Northern mainland	177,000	3,000	£135,000	15s.

*(20 shillings = 1£, 1 pound = about $1.60 in 2003.)

This map has three main elements. First, it shows the geographic extent of Britain's American possessions. Next, it provides a table showing the racial composition and value of exports of the three main regions. Third, it depicts the form of government in the various colonies.

Sugar and slavery are key to a full understanding of this map. They explain the high value of exports produced by the tiny Caribbean islands.

MAP 3.2 Britain's American Empire, 1713

Britain's West Indian possessions were small—mere dots on the Caribbean Sea. However, in 1713 they were by far the most valuable parts of the empire. Their sugar crops brought wealth to English merchants, trade to the northern colonies, and a brutal life (and early death) to African workers.

TABLE 3.4 Slave Imports in the Americas, 1520–1810

Destination	Number of Africans Arriving
South America	
Brazil	3,650,000
Dutch America	500,000
West Indies	
British	1,660,000
French	1,660,000
Central America	
Spanish	1,500,000
North America	
British colonies	500,000
Europe	175,000
TOTAL	**9,645,000**

potent new sweetener. Demand for sugar soared, outrunning supply for decades and guaranteeing high profits to producers.

A new agricultural economy quickly sprang into existence in the semitropical lands of the Western Hemisphere. European merchants and investors provided the organizational skill, ships, and money needed to grow and process sugarcane, carry the refined sugar to market, and supply the plantations with European tools and equipment. To provide labor for the sugar plantations, the merchants relied primarily on slaves from Africa. Between 1550 and 1700 Portuguese and Dutch traders annually transported about 10,000 Africans across the Atlantic. Subsequently, British and French merchants took over this commerce, developing African-run slave-catching systems that extended far into the interior of Africa and funneled captives to the slave ports of Elmina, Whydah, Loango, and Cabinda. Between 1700 and 1810 they

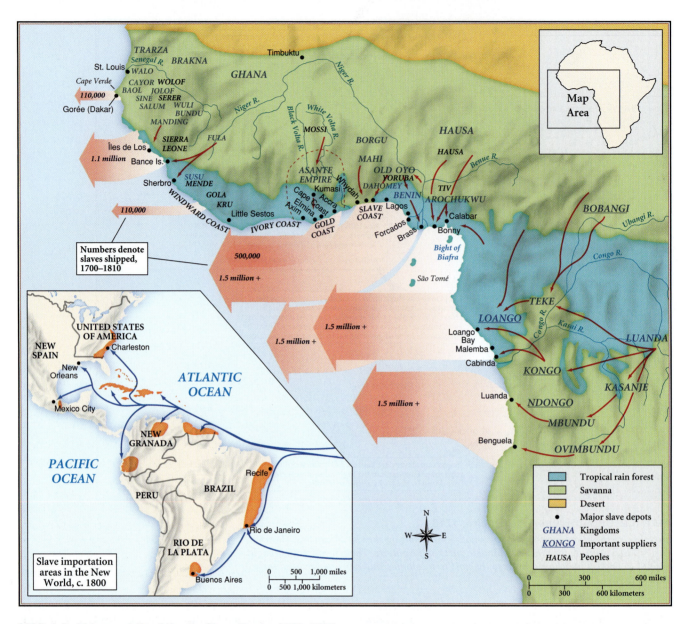

MAP 3.3 Africa and the Atlantic Slave Trade, 1700–1810

The tropical rainforest region of West Africa was home to scores of peoples and dozens of kingdoms. Some kingdoms, such as Dahomey, became aggressive slavers, taking tens of thousands of war captives and funneling them to the seacoast, where they were sold to European traders. About 15 percent of the Africans died on the transatlantic voyage, the grueling Middle Passage, between enslavement in Africa and slavery in the Americas. Most of the survivors labored on sugar plantations in Brazil and the British and French West Indies (see Table 3.4).

For more help analyzing this map, see the ONLINE STUDY GUIDE at bedfordstmartins.com/henretta.

carried about 7 million Africans—800,000 in the 1780s alone—to toil in the Americas (Map 3.3).

Portuguese and Dutch planters developed sugar plantations in Brazil and, beginning in the 1620s, English and French merchants carried the new industry to the subtropical islands of the West Indies. In the 1650s

the island of Barbados had a white population of 30,000, consisting of planters and their indentured servants, who exported tobacco and livestock hides to England. Then came the "sugar revolution," financed initially by Dutch merchants, which quickly converted Barbados into an island of slaves. By 1660 Africans formed a

Shipping Sugar from Antigua
Sugar was a valuable commodity but also a heavy one that was shipped to European markets in giant barrels. Because it was difficult and expensive to build wharves that could accommodate large transports, the barrels were conveyed in small boats to the oceangoing ships, which used winches and pulleys to lift them on board.
National Maritime Museum, London.

majority of the population, and English settlers were departing for the Carolinas. By 1700 English sugar planters were investing heavily in the Leeward Islands and Jamaica, which soon had populations that were 85 to 90 percent African. In 1750, Jamaica—the largest island in the British West Indies—had seven hundred large sugar plantations worked by more than 105,000 slaves, who labored for ten hours a day, slept in flimsy huts, lived on a starchy diet of corn, yams, and dried fish, and were subject to brutal discipline.

Sugar production required fertile land, many laborers to plant and cut the cane, and heavy equipment to process cane into raw sugar and molasses. Because only wealthy merchants or landowners had the capital to outfit a plantation, a planter-merchant elite financed the sugar industry and drew annual profits of more than 10 percent on investments. As the Scottish economist Adam Smith declared in his famous treatise *The Wealth of Nations* (1776), sugar was the most profitable crop in Europe and America.

The South Atlantic system brought wealth to the entire European economy. To take England as an example, the owners of most of the plantations in the British West Indies lived as absentees in England, spending their profits there. Moreover, the British Navigation Acts required that American sugar be sold to English consumers or sent through England to continental markets, thus raising the level of trade. By 1750 reexports of sugar and tobacco from America accounted for half of all British exports. Substantial profits also came from the slave trade, for the Royal African Company and other English traders sold male slaves in the West Indies for three to five times what they paid for them in Africa. Finally, the trade in American sugar and tobacco stimulated manufacturing. To transport slaves (and machinery and settlers) to America, English shipyards built hundreds of vessels. Thousands of English and Scottish men and women worked in related industries: building port facilities and warehouses, refining sugar and tobacco, distilling rum from molasses (a by-product of sugar), and manufacturing textiles and iron products for the growing markets in Africa and America. Commercial expansion also provided a supply of experienced sailors, helping to make the Royal Navy the most powerful fleet in Europe.

As the South Atlantic system enhanced prosperity in Europe, it brought economic decline, political change, and human tragedy to West Africa and the parts of East Africa, such as Madagascar, where slavers were also active. Between 1550 and 1870 the Atlantic slave trade uprooted about 15 million Africans, diminishing the population and wealth of the continent. Overall, the guns, iron, tinware, rum, cloth, and other European products that entered the African economy in exchange for slaves were worth from one-tenth (in the 1680s) to one-third (by the 1780s) as much as the goods those slaves subsequently produced in America.

Equally important, the slave trade changed the nature of West African society by promoting centralized states and military conquest. In 1739 an observer noted that "whenever the King of Barsally wants Goods or Brandy . . . the King goes and ransacks some of his enemies' towns, seizing the people and selling them." War and slaving became a way of life in Dahomey, where the royal house made the sale of slaves a state monopoly and used the resulting access to European guns to create a regime of military despotism. Dahomey's army, which included a contingent of 5,000 women, systematically raided the interior for captives, and exported thousands of slaves each year (Map 3.3). The Asante kings also used the firearms and wealth acquired through the Atlantic trade to create a bureaucratic empire of 3 million

Olaudah Equiano

This 1780 portrait by an unknown artist in England shows the freed slave and journal writer Olaudah Equiano. Equiano was among the first Africans to develop a consciousness of an African identity that transcended traditional ethnic and national boundaries. Royal Albert Memorial Museum, Exeter, England.

to 5 million people. Yet slaving remained a choice for Africans, not a necessity. The old and still powerful kingdom of Benin, famous for its cast bronzes and carved ivory, resolutely opposed the slave trade, prohibiting the export of male slaves for over a century.

The trade in humans produced untold misery—taking tens of thousands of lives and subjecting millions to slavery. In many African societies class divisions hardened as people of noble birth enslaved and sold those of lesser status. Gender relations shifted as well. Men constituted two-thirds of the slaves sent across the Atlantic both because European planters paid more for "men and stout men boys," "none to exceed the years of 25 or under 10," and because African traders directed women captives into local slave markets for sale as agricultural workers and house servants. The resulting imbalance between the sexes in Africa allowed some men to take several wives, changing the nature of marriage. Moreover, the Atlantic trade prompted harsher forms of slavery in Africa, eroding the dignity of human life there as well as in the Western Hemisphere.

But those Africans sold into the heart of the South Atlantic system had the bleakest fate. Torn from their village

homes, captives were marched in chains to coastal ports such as Elmina on the Gold Coast. From there they made the perilous **Middle Passage** to the New World in hideously overcrowded ships. There was little to eat and drink, and the stench of excrement was nearly unbearable. Some captives jumped overboard, choosing to drown rather than endure more suffering (see Voices from Abroad, "Olaudah Equiano: The Brutal 'Middle Passage,'" p. 81). Nearly a million (15 percent of the 8 million who crossed the Atlantic between 1700 and 1810) died on the journey, mostly from dysentery, smallpox, or scurvy.

For the survivors of the Middle Passage, life only got worse on arrival in northwest Brazil or the West Indies because sugar plantations were based on relentless exploitation and systematic violence. Planting and harvesting sugarcane required intense labor under a tropical sun, with a pace set by the overseer's whip. With sugar prices high and the cost of slaves low, many planters worked slaves to death and then imported more. For example, between 1708 and 1735 about 85,000 Africans were brought into Barbados, but the island's black population increased only from 42,000 to 46,000 during these decades.

Slavery in the Chesapeake and South Carolina

As the British slave trade increased after 1700, planters in Virginia and Maryland imported thousands of Africans into the Chesapeake. In what historian Ira Berlin has termed a "tobacco revolution," leading planters created a slave-based economy and a new plantation regime, buying as many black workers as they could afford and sending them to toil under the direction of overseers on far-flung "quarters." By 1720 Africans numbered 20 percent of the Chesapeake population, and slavery had become a defining principle of the social order, not just one of several forms of labor. Equally important, slavery was increasingly defined in racial terms. A Virginia law of 1692 prohibited sexual intercourse between English and Africans, and in 1705 another statute explicitly defined virtually all resident Africans as slaves: "All servants imported or brought into this country by sea or land who were not Christians in their native country shall be accounted and be slaves" (see American Lives, "From a Piece of Property to a Man of Property: The Odyssey of Robert Pearle," p. 82).

Nonetheless, living conditions for Africans in Maryland and Virginia were much less severe than in the West Indies, and slaves lived relatively long lives. In terms of labor to produce a harvest, tobacco was not as physically demanding a crop as sugar. Slaves planted the young tobacco seedlings in the spring, hoed and weeded the crop throughout the summer, and in the fall picked and hung up the leaves to cure over the winter. Epidemic diseases did not spread easily in the Chesapeake because the plantation quarters were small and dispersed. Also,

Olaudah Equiano

The Brutal "Middle Passage"

Olaudah Equiano, known during his life in London as Gustavus Vassa, claimed to have been born in the ancient kingdom of Benin (in present-day southern Nigeria). However, in separate scholarly articles, two researchers have recently suggested that Equiano was actually born into slavery in America and used information from conversations with African-born slaves to create a fictitious history of an idyllic childhood, kidnapping and enslavement at the age of eleven, and a traumatic Middle Passage across the Atlantic. Whatever the truth of this controversial interpretation, Equiano apparently endured plantation slavery in Barbados and Virginia, where he was purchased by an English sea captain. Buying his freedom in 1766, Equiano lived in London and became an antislavery activist; twenty years later he published the memoir from which this selection has been taken.

My father, besides many slaves, had a numerous family of which seven lived to grow up, including myself and a sister who was the only daughter. . . . I was trained up from my earliest years in the art of war, my daily exercise was shooting and throwing javelins, and my mother adorned me with emblems after the manner of our greatest warriors. One day, when all our people were gone out to their works as usual and only I and my dear sister were left to mind the house, two men and a woman got over our walls, and in a moment seized us both, and without giving us time to cry out or make resistance they stopped our mouths and ran off with us into the nearest wood. . . .

At length, after many days' travelling, during which I had often changed masters, I got into the hands of a chieftain in a very pleasant country. This man had two wives and some children, and they all used me extremely well and did all they could to comfort me, particularly the first wife, who was something like my mother.

Although I was a great many days' journey from my father's house, yet these people spoke exactly the same language with us. This first master of mine, as I may call him, was a smith, and my principal employment was working his bellows.

I was again sold and carried through a number of places till . . . at the end of six or seven months after I had been kidnapped I arrived at the sea coast.

The first object which saluted my eyes when I arrived on the coast was the sea, and a slave ship which was then riding at anchor and waiting for its cargo. I now saw myself deprived of all chance of returning to my native country . . . ; and I even wished for my former slavery in preference to my present situation, which was filled with horrors of every kind. . . . I was soon put down under the decks, and there I received such a salutation in my nostrils as I had never experienced in my life; so that with the loathsomeness of the stench and crying together, I became so sick and low that I was not able to eat, nor had I the least desire to taste any thing. I now wished for the last friend, death, to relieve me; but soon, to my grief, two of the white men offered me eatables, and on my refusing to eat, one of them held me fast by the hands and laid me across I think the windlass, and tied my feet while the other flogged me severely. I had never experienced anything of this kind before, and although, not being used to the water, I naturally feared that element the first time I saw it, yet nevertheless could I have got over the nettings, I would have jumped over the side, but I could not. . . . One day, when we had a smooth sea and moderate wind, two of my wearied countrymen who were chained together (I was near them at the time), preferring death to such a life of misery, somehow made it through the nettings and jumped into the sea.

At last we came in sight of the island of Barbados; the white people got some old slaves from the land to pacify us. They told us we were not to be eaten but to work, and were soon to go on land where we should see many of our country people. This report eased us much; and sure enough soon after we were landed there came to us Africans of all languages.

Source: The Interesting Narrative of the Life of Olaudah Equiano, or Gustavus Vassa, the African, Written by Himself (London, 1789), 15, 22–23, 28–29.

From a Piece of Property to a Man of Property: The Odyssey of Robert Pearle

When Robert Pearle died in 1765 at the age of seventy-five, he owned an extensive estate that included fourteen slaves, whom he divided among his three sons. The father's financial skills apparently rubbed off on his son James. When James Pearle died in 1774, he owned nine slaves, nine thousand pounds of tobacco, and personal goods worth £782, an estate that placed him among the top tenth of all Maryland property owners. Unlike these other wealthy men, the Pearles were not solely European by ancestry. Robert Pearle was a mulatto, "born of a negroe slave" (as a court report put it) and a slave himself until the age of thirty-five. His son James was born free, the son of Nanny Pearle, who was also a mulatto and a former slave.

According to law, Robert Pearle was the product of an illegal union. By 1700 Maryland law strictly prohibited miscegenation, sexual relations between those of European and African descent, labeling such unions "Unnatural and Inordinate Copulations." However, planters handled their human property pretty much as they pleased. For decades planters had flogged the young English indentured servants who worked their lands and had forced themselves on servant women—callously adding a year to the woman's time of service if she became pregnant. The coming of racial slavery only increased this physical and sexual exploitation, as scores of English planters fathered children by enslaved African women. A Maryland census of 1755 listed 42,000 enslaved blacks (28 percent of the total population) and 3,592 mulattos (2 percent), a majority of whom were slaves.

Whatever the brutality of forced interracial sex, it opened the door to freedom. Robert Pearle was undoubtedly the son of his owner, Richard Marsham, a wealthy Catholic planter in Prince George's County who, at his death in 1713, owned thirty-six slaves. Pearle's mother was probably the "Negro woman Sarah" who received special treatment in Marsham's will. Sarah obtained her freedom and the right to receive "good sufficient Dyet and apparill . . . and every year

Robert Pearle's Will, 1765

"In the Name of God Amen." Apart from this ritualistic phrase, Robert Pearle's last Testament—unlike other colonial wills—is completely devoid of religious sentiments, suggesting that he may not have imbibed the Catholic faith of his father and his patrons. In businesslike fashion, the will divides his most valuable property—fourteen slaves—among his sons Daniel, James, and Basill, and provides a token sum of money, a mere five shillings, to each of Pearle's other children—two sons and two daughters.
Maryland Historical Society.

during her natural Life the Sum of two Pounds Sterling." Marsham's will also granted the prospect of freedom to Sarah's mulatto offspring. Robert and his mulatto wife Nanny—perhaps another of Marsham's children—along with their two-year-old son Daniel—were "to be fully discharged and set free" in 1720, provided they remained "vigilent and faithful" to his executors, members of the influential Waring family. In the sins of the white father lay the salvation of the mulatto son and daughter.

Robert Pearle used his freedom wisely. Initially propertyless, he employed his skills as a carpenter to make his way in the world. In 1726 he won a legal suit for a debt against innkeeper Edward Bradshaw, receiving a judgment of 3,200 pounds of tobacco, and collected similar debts from many others: despite Pearle's background, the justices of the Prince George's County court enforced his contractual agreements. On the one occasion when they denied his right to sue, "Considering the Circumstances of the Plaintiff who is a Molatto (born of a Negro slave)," Pearle successfully petitioned the Maryland Assembly for the right "to Recover his Just Debts," eventually winning a substantial judgment of £45.

Something—his carpentry skills, solid character and ambition, or ties to the Marshams and Warings—smoothed Pearle's way through the white world. By 1724 he had acquired 100 acres of land; three years later he owned a white servant; and two years after that he held title to African slaves, mortgaging "negro man Harry" and "negro woman Lucy" to sheriff Richard Lee for 8,400 pounds of tobacco. For the next decade Pearle lived quietly, enjoying his property and raising his children.

Then interracial sex, the source of Robert Pearle's freedom, threatened his family with legal disaster. In 1742 a grand jury indicted William Marshall, a white planter, for marrying a mulatto: Ann Pearle, Robert's daughter. Just as this case was coming to trial, the county court charged Elizabeth Graves, a white woman, with the crime of marrying Daniel Pearle, Robert's mulatto son. For some reason—perhaps a personal vendetta, perhaps increasing racial tension—the Pearles and their spouses found themselves facing severe legal penalties. The justices tried William Marshall, found him guilty of miscegenation, and sentenced him to "Become a Servant for Seven Years"—the fate that awaited Elizabeth Graves as well. If convicted of interracial marriage, the two Pearle children faced a much harsher prospect: to "become a Slave during Life."

Mysteriously, none of these sentences was ever imposed. Marshall successfully appealed his conviction to the Provincial Court, while "by order of [the] Attorney General," the case against Elizabeth Graves was never prosecuted. The young Pearles—Ann and Daniel—were never even indicted. Apparently Robert Pearle's influential white friends had intervened to protect his family. As Pearle's biographer, Mary Jeske, has suggested, their success demonstrated that race relations in the small and intimate world of plantation society were much more fluid and complex than the statutes dictated.

However, the lines of racial caste were steadily hardening. When Robert Pearle won his freedom in 1720, slaves constituted about 20 percent of the population of Prince George's County; by 1740, the proportion was twice as great, and blacks formed the majority in many Tidewater districts. Fearing slave revolts, whites were no longer willing to tolerate free blacks and mulattos, especially those who threatened white supremacy by marrying across racial lines. Aware of this ominous change, in 1744 Robert Pearle, his son Daniel, and his son-in-law William Marshall moved their families west to the Monocacy Valley, a sparsely settled region in what would soon become Frederick County. There, each man took a seventeen-year lease on 100-acre farmsteads on the Carrollton Manor, a vast estate owned by Charles Carroll and populated primarily by German and English tenants. At one stroke the Pearles had escaped the racially charged atmosphere of the Tidewater region and secured a new powerful white Catholic ally. Following in the religious footsteps of his owner-father, Robert Pearle was a Catholic—as were the Warings and the Carrolls. The ties of religion, like those of kinship, counterbalanced the antagonisms of race.

Migration to Carrollton Manor offered the prospect of family cohesion and economic mobility. Land was plentiful, and eventually all of Robert Pearle's sons secured manorial leases. Taking advantage of low rents, high prices for tobacco and wheat, and slave labor, the Pearles attained substantial prosperity.

We can only wonder if the Pearles had any qualms about owning enslaved Africans. Having been raised in a "society with slaves" in which racial boundaries were blurred, the family may have identified with successful planters and regretted only that it did not own more slaves. As biographer Mary Jeske notes: "Had he been the legitimate son of his white father rather than a mulatto bastard, Pearle might well have joined the ranks of the Chesapeake elite." As it was, Robert Pearle had to scrape and struggle for decades, first for freedom, then for economic prosperity, and finally for family security. Racial slavery and the caste system exacted a high price even from those who attained their freedom.

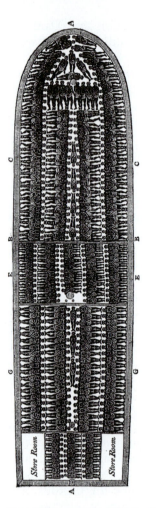

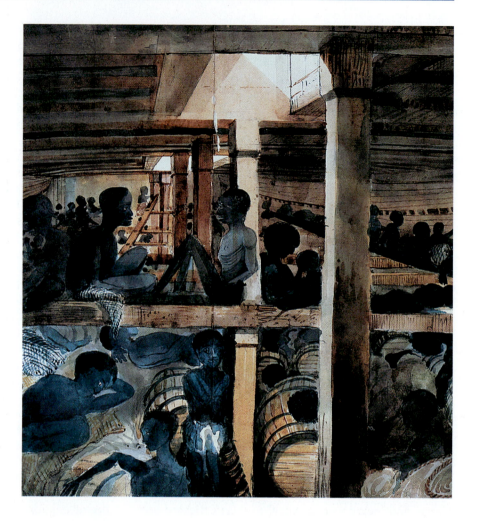

Two Views of the Middle Passage
As the slave trade boomed during the eighteenth century, ship designers packed in more and more human cargo, treating enslaved Africans with no more respect than hogsheads of sugar or tobacco. By contrast, a watercolor of 1846, painted by a ship's officer on a voyage to Brazil, captures the humanity and dignity of the enslaved Africans.
Peabody & Essex Museum / Royal Albert Memorial Museum, Exeter, England / Bridgeman Art Library.

because tobacco profits were low, planters could not afford to buy new slaves and therefore treated those they had less harshly than West Indian planters did. Some tobacco planters attempted to increase their workforce through reproduction, purchasing a high proportion of female slaves and encouraging large families. In 1720 women made up about a third of the African population of Maryland, and the black population had begun to increase naturally. One absentee owner instructed his plantation agent "to be kind and indulgent to the breeding wenches, and not to force them when with child upon any service or hardship that will be injurious to them." And, he added, "the children are to be well looked after." By midcentury slaves made up 40 percent of some parts of the Chesapeake, and over three-quarters of them were American born.

Slaves in South Carolina labored under conditions that were much more oppressive. The colony had grown slowly until 1700, when Africans from rice-growing societies, who knew how to plant, harvest, and process that nutritious grain, turned it into a profitable export crop (see New Technology, "Rice: Riches, Wretchedness, and Community," p. 86). To expand production, white planters imported tens of thousands of slaves—and a "rice revolution" quickly brought an extraordinary change to the colony (Figure 3.1). By 1720 Africans made up a majority of the population of South Carolina as a whole and constituted 80 percent of the residents of the rice-growing areas, where they lived on plantations of fifty or more slaves. However, many workers met an early death. Growing rice in inland swamp areas required months of work in ankle-deep mud, weeding the crop amidst pools of putrid water. Mosquito-borne epidemic diseases swept through these lowlands, taking thousands of African lives. Overwork killed many more slaves because moving tons of dirt to build irrigation works was brutally hard labor. As a Scottish traveler noted, "the labour required for it is only fit for slaves, and I think the hardest work I have seen them

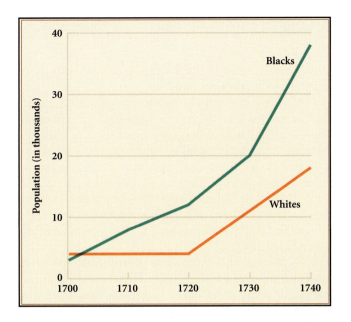

FIGURE 3.1 The Growth of Slavery in South Carolina
To grow more rice, white planters imported thousands of African slaves, giving South Carolina a black majority and prompting the development of an African-influenced language and culture.

Coast and Gambia, who had a reputation as hard workers with farming experience (Map 3.3). However, as African sources of slaves shifted southward after 1730, more than 30 percent of the colony's workforce came from the Congo and Angola. Because of such changes in the trade, no African people or language group formed a majority of the slaves in any American colony (Table 3.5). Moreover, many white planters consciously enhanced this cultural diversity to prevent slave revolts. "The safety of the Plantations," declared a widely read English pamphlet, "depends upon having Negroes from all parts of Guiny, who do not understand each other's languages and Customs and cannot agree to Rebel."

The Emergence of an African American Culture. In fact, slaves initially did not regard each other as "Africans" or "blacks" but as members of a specific family, clan, or people—Mende, Hausa, Ibo, Yoruba—and they associated mostly with those who shared their language or culture. Gradually, however, enslaved peoples found it in their interest to transcend these cultural barriers. Especially in the West Indies and in the lowlands of South Carolina, the largely African-born population created new languages, such as the Gullah dialect in South Carolina, that combined English and African words in an African grammatical structure. "They have a language peculiar to themselves," a missionary reported, "a wild confused medley of Negro and corrupt English, which makes them very unintelligible except to those who have conversed with them for many years." In South Carolina, another missionary complained as late as 1754 that "our negros are so Ignorant of the English Language . . . it is a great while before you can get them to understand . . . the Meaning of

engaged in." As in the West Indies, there were many deaths and few births, and the importation of new slaves constantly "re-Africanized" the black population.

African American Community and Resistance

Slaves came from many regions of West Africa. South Carolina slave owners preferred laborers from the Gold

TABLE 3.5 African Slaves Imported into North America, by Ethnicity, 1700–1775			
African Region of Departure	Ethnicity	Number	Percent
Senegambia	Mandinka, Fulbe, Serer, Jola, Wolof, and Bambara	47,300	17
Sierra Leone	Vai, Mende, Kpelle, and Kru	33,400	12
Gold Coast	Ashanti and Fanit	19,500	7
Bight of Benin, Bight of Biafra	Ibo and Ibibio	47,300	17
West-Central	Kongo, Tio, and Matamba	44,600	16
Southeast Africa	Unknown	2,800	1
Other or Unknown		83,500	30
TOTAL		**278,400**	**100**

The numbers are estimated from known voyages involving 195,000 Africans. Ethnic origins should be considered as very tentative because slaves from many regions left from the same port and because the ethnic and regional origins of 83,500 slaves (30 percent) are not known.

Source: Aaron S. Fogleman, "From Slaves, Convicts, and Servants to Free Passengers: The Transformation of Immigration in the Era of the American Revolution," *Journal of American History* 85 (June 1998), Table A4.

Rice: Riches, Wretchedness, and Community

Two technological innovations—one African, one European—shaped the evolution of the South Carolina rice industry and black life during the eighteenth century. Because rice was an exotic crop to them, the first English settlers in the Carolinas failed in their attempts to grow the nutritious grain. As one planter recalled, "The people being unacquainted with the manner of cultivating rice, many difficulties attended to the first planting and preparing it, as a vendable commodity."

West Africans soon provided the requisite knowledge. Along the semitropical western coast of Africa, a traveler noted, rice "forms the chief part of the African's sustenance." Eager to have ready access to a familiar food, enslaved blacks in South Carolina took up rice cultivation during the 1690s, teaching their English owners not only how to plant and tend the crop but how to process it. To separate the tough husk of the rice seed from the nutritious grain inside, English settlers had experimented with a "rice mill," a "Pendulum Engine, which doeth much better, and in lesser time and labour, huske rice." When these machines did not prove equal to the task, English planters turned to African women and their traditional husking technology. The women placed the grain in large wooden mortars hollowed from the trunks of pine or cypress trees and then pounded it with long wooden pestles, removing the husks and whitening the grains. Their labor was prodigious. By the 1770s slaves were annually processing 75 million tons of rice for export and millions more for their own consumption.

African labor and technology brought both wealth and wretchedness to South Carolina. The planter-merchant aristocracy that controlled the rice industry became immensely wealthy, while the tens of thousands of enslaved Africans who grew the rice in putrid inland swamps lived hard and brutal lives that ended in early death. There were few marriages among blacks, few children, and a weak sense of community life as the surviving slaves clung to their diverse African ethnic identities.

Following the American Revolution, planters transformed rice production by introducing tidal irrigation. Moving their operations to coastal areas, the planters had their slave laborers build high dikes to keep salt water out of the rice fields and elaborate floodgates and irrigation ditches to admit fresh river water. As the well-irrigated rice grew taller, workers raised the level of the water until the crop had shoots with three leaves (about three weeks after planting). Then they drained the field, hoed away the weeds, and reflooded the fields until harvest time.

The new system was more expensive in terms of initial capital but much more productive. The average yield per acre on a prewar inland swamp plantation was about 800 pounds, while on a postwar tidal plantation it was around 1,300 pounds. Equally important, a worker could now cultivate five times as much rice, dramatically reducing day-to-day labor costs. Finally, planters devised mills that used the tidal flow to power the pestle-and-mortar machines, removing the heavy burden of hulling the rice from slave women.

The new tidal technology permitted the flowering of the task system of labor that was unique to the South Carolina slave economy. Exploiting the weight of their overwhelming numbers, enslaved laborers had gradually won control over their work lives and staged minor rebellions when it was challenged. "All my

Words." In the Chesapeake, where there were more American-born blacks (and in the northern colonies, which had small numbers of slaves), many Africans gradually gave up their native tongues for English. A European visitor to mid-eighteenth-century Virginia reported with surprise that "all the blacks spoke very good English."

The acquisition of a common language, whether Gullah or English, was a prerequisite for the creation of an African American community. A more equal sex ratio, which would encourage stable families, was another. In South Carolina a high death rate undermined ties of family and kinship, but after 1725 blacks in the Chesapeake colonies created strong nuclear families and extended kin relationships. For example, all but 30 of the 128 slaves on the home quarter of Charles Carroll's estate in Maryland were members of two extended families. These "African Americans" had gradually developed a culture of their own, passing on family names, traditions, and knowledge to the next generation. As one observer noted, blacks had

working Negroes left me last Night," one planter complained in 1786. However, as the carefully laid-out irrigation system on tidal plantations gradually imposed an orderly grid on the landscape, slaves and masters found it easier to negotiate the tasks a worker would perform each day: hoeing a square of 105 feet, digging 75 trenches, harvesting a half-acre. As slaves settled in to a regular work routine, they also lived longer and bore more children, primarily because tidal plantations were less disease-ridden than inland swamps. Even before the end of the Atlantic slave trade in 1808, they had begun to create a cohesive African American community. Technological change had affected the course of cultural life.

Rice Hulling in West Africa and Georgia
The eighteenth-century engraving shows West African women hulling rice using huge wooden mortars and pestles, the same technology employed in the photograph of early-twentieth-century African American women in Georgia.
Library of Congress / Georgia Department of Archives and History, Atlanta.

For more help analyzing these images, see the ONLINE STUDY GUIDE at bedfordstmartins.com/henretta.

created a cultural world of their own, "a Nation within a Nation."

As enslaved blacks forged an identity in an alien land, their lives became a mixture of old African forms and new American experiences. Many Africans arrived in the colonies with filed teeth and ritual scars that white planters called "country markings" or "negro markings." Because slaves could not re-create traditional ethnic-based communities, these marks of tribal or group identity fell into disuse. However, the African heritage took tangible form in wood carvings inspired by traditional motifs, the large wooden mortars and pestles that slaves used to hull rice, and the design of shacks, which often had rooms arranged from front to back in a distinctive "I" pattern (not side by side, as was common in English houses). African values also persisted, as some slaves retained Muslim religious beliefs and many more relied on the spiritual powers of conjurers, who knew the ways of African gods. As an English missionary reported from Georgia in the 1750s, many slaves clung to "the old

African Culture in South Carolina
The dance and the musical instruments are of Yoruba origin, the contribution of Africans from the Niger River–Gold Coast region. This Yoruba-dominated area accounted for one-sixth of the slaves imported into South Carolina. Colonial Williamsburg Foundation.

Superstition of a false Religion." Other slaves adopted Protestant Christianity but reshaped its doctrines, ethics, and rituals to fit their needs and create a spiritually rich and long-lasting religious culture of their own.

Yet there were drastic limits on African American creativity because slaves were denied education and accumulated few material goods. A well-traveled European who visited a slave hut in Virginia in the late eighteenth century found it to be

more miserable than the most miserable of the cottages of our peasants. The husband and wife sleep on a mean pallet, the children on the ground; a very bad fireplace, some utensils for cooking. . . . They work all week, not having a single day for themselves except for holidays.

Oppression and Resistance. Slaves resisted the rigorous work routine at their peril. To punish slaves who disobeyed, refused to work, or ran away, planters resorted to the lash and the amputation of fingers, toes, and ears (see American Voices, "Philip Fithian: Sadism under Slavery," p. 89). Declaring the chronic runaway Ballazore an "incorrigeble rogue," a Virginia planter ordered all his toes cut off: "nothing less than dismembering will reclaim him." Thomas Jefferson, who witnessed such cruelty on his father's plantation in mid-eighteenth-century

Virginia, noted that each generation of whites was "nursed, educated, and daily exercised in tyranny," for the relationship "between master and slave is a perpetual exercise of the most unremitting despotism on the one part, and degrading submission on the other."

The extent of violence by whites depended on the size and density of the slave population. Because their numbers were so small, blacks in rural areas of New York, Pennsylvania, and other northern colonies endured low status but little violence. Conversely, assertive slaves in the predominantly African-populated West Indian islands routinely suffered branding with hot irons. In the lowlands of South Carolina, where Africans outnumbered Europeans eight to one, planters prohibited their black workers from leaving the plantation without special passes and organized their poor white neighbors into armed patrols to police the countryside. Slaves dealt with their plight in a variety of ways. Some newly arrived Africans fled to the frontier, where they tried to establish African villages or, more often, married into Indian tribes. Blacks familiar with white ways, especially those fluent in English, fled to towns, where they tried to pass as free blacks. But the great majority of African Americans worked out their destinies as enslaved laborers on rural plantations, continually bargaining over the terms of their bondage. Some blacks agreed to do extra work in return for better food and clothes; at other times they seized a small privilege

Philip Fithian

Sadism under Slavery

Planters relied on various incentives to get work from their African slaves. A few used rewards, providing cooperative laborers with food, leisure, and relatively good treatment. Many more planters wanted to maximize their profits and relied on force, extracting work by whipping recalcitrant laborers. Some brutal owners and overseers were so determined to demonstrate their power that they went much further, as described by Philip Fithian, a young Princeton College graduate who was employed as a tutor by Robert Carter III, one of the wealthiest Virginia planters.

[1773] This Evening, after I had dismissed the Children, & was sitting in the School-Room cracking Nuts, [I asked] . . . Mr. Carters Clerk, a civil, inoffensive agreeable young Man . . . what their [the slaves' food] allowance is? He told me that, excepting some favourites around the table their weekly allowance is a peck of Corn, & a pound of Meat a Head!—And Mr. Carter is allowed by all . . . [to be] by far the most humane to his Slaves of any in these parts! Good God! are these Christians?

While I am on the Subject, I will relate further, what I heard George Lee's Overseer, one Morgan, say the other day that he himself had often done to Negroes, and found it useful. He said that whipping of any kind does them no good, for they will laugh at your greatest Severity; But he told us he had invented two things, and by several experiments had proved their success.

For Sullenness, Obstinacy, or Idleness, says he, Take a Negro, strip him, tie him fast to a post; take then a sharp Curry-Comb, and curry him severely till he is well scrap'd; and call a Boy with some dry Hay, and make the Boy rub him down for several Minutes, then salt him, & unlose him. He will attend to his Business (said the inhuman Infidel) afterwards!

But savage Cruelty does not exceed His next diabolical Invention—To get a Secret from a Negro, says he, take the following Method—Lay upon your Floor a large thick plank, having a peg about eighteen inches long, of hard wood, & very Sharp, on the upper end, fixed fast in the plank—then strip the Negro, tie the Cord to a staple in the Ceiling, [and suspend the Negro from that cord] so that his foot may just rest on the sharpened Peg then turn him briskly around, and you would laugh (said our informer) at the Dexterity of the Negro, while he was relieving his Feet on the sharpen'd Peg!

I need say nothing of these seeing there is a righteous God, who will take vengeance on such Inventions.

Source: Philip Vickers Fithian, *Journals and Letters, 1773–1774,* ed. Hunter Dulsingon Farish (Williamsburg, VA: Colonial Williamsburg Press, 1943), 50–51.

and dared the master to revoke it. By such means Sundays became a day free of labor—a right rather than a privilege. When bargaining failed to yield results, slaves protested silently by working slowly or stealing. Other blacks, provoked beyond endurance, attacked their owners or overseers, although such assaults were punishable by mutilation or death. And despite the fact that whites were armed and, outside of coastal South Carolina, more numerous than Africans, some blacks plotted rebellion.

Predictably, South Carolina became the setting for the largest slave uprising of the eighteenth century—the Stono Rebellion of 1739. The governor of the Spanish (and Catholic) colony of Florida helped to instigate the revolt by promising freedom and land to slaves who ran away from their English owners. By February 1739 at least sixty-nine slaves had escaped to St. Augustine, and rumors circulated "that a Conspiracy was formed by Negroes in Carolina to rise and make their way out of the province."

When war between England and Spain broke out later in September, seventy-five Africans—some of them Portuguese-speaking Catholics from the African kingdom of Kongo—rose in revolt and killed a number of whites near the Stono River. Displaying their skills as former soldiers in the war-torn Kongo, the rebels took up arms and marched south toward Florida "with Colours displayed and two Drums beating." Unrest swept the countryside, but the white militia killed many of the Stono rebels and dispersed the rest, preventing a general uprising. Frightened whites imported fewer new slaves and tightened plantation discipline. For Africans the price of active resistance was high.

The Southern Gentry

As the southern colonies became full-fledged slave societies, the character of life changed for whites as well as

"Virginia Luxuries"

This painting by an unknown artist (c. 1810) depicts the exploitation inherent in a slave society. On the right, an owner chastises a male slave by beating him with a cane; on the left, ignoring the cultural and legal rules prohibiting such affairs, a white master prepares to engage in sex with his black mistress.

Abby Aldrich Rockefeller Folk Art Collection, Colonial Williamsburg Foundation.

blacks. After 1675 settlement in the Chesapeake region moved inland, away from the disease-ridden swampy lowlands, allowing English migrants to live much longer lives and form stable families and communities. Similarly, many white planters in South Carolina improved their health by transferring their residence to Charleston during the hot, mosquito-ridden summer months. As their longevity increased, men reassumed their customary control of family property. When death rates had been high, many husbands had named their wives as executors of their estates and legal guardians of their children and had given their widows large inheritances. After 1700 most wealthy planters named male kin as executors and guardians and again gave priority of inheritance to male children, limiting a widow's portion to the traditional one-third share during her lifetime.

The reappearance of strict patriarchy within the family mirrored broader social developments. The planter and merchant elite now stood at the top of a social hierarchy somewhat like that of Europe, exercising authority over a yeoman class, a larger group of white tenant farmers, and a growing host of enslaved black laborers—the American equivalent of oppressed peasants and serfs. Wealthy planters used Africans to plant orchards and grow food as well as tobacco; build houses, wagons, and tobacco casks; and make shoes and clothes. By increasing the self-sufficiency of their plantations, the planter elite survived the depressed tobacco market between 1660 and 1720. Small-scale planters who used family labor to grow tobacco fared less well, falling deeper into debt to their creditors among the elite.

To prevent another rebellion like Bacon's uprising, which had brought a short military occupation by English troops, the Chesapeake gentry paid attention to the concerns of middling and poor whites. They urged smallholders to invest in land and slaves. By 1770 no fewer than 60 percent of the English families in the Chesapeake owned at least one slave and therefore had a personal stake in this exploitative labor system. In addition, the gentry gradually reduced the taxes paid by poorer whites; in Virginia the annual poll tax paid by every free man fell from 45 pounds of tobacco in 1675 to 5 pounds in 1750. The political elite also allowed poor yeomen and some tenants to vote. The strategy of the leading families—the Carters, Lees, Randolphs, Robinsons—was to curry favor with these voters at election time, bribing them with rum, money, and the promise of favorable legislation and minor offices in county governments. In return, they expected yeomen and tenants to elect them to political office and defer to their authority. This "horse trading" solidified the social position of the planter elite, which used its control of the Virginia House of Burgesses to cut the political power of the royal governor—bargaining with him over patronage and land grants. Hundreds of yeoman farmers benefited as well, tasting political power and garnering substantial fees and salaries as deputy sheriffs, road surveyors, estate appraisers, and grand jurymen.

Even as the expansion of officeholding and slave ownership created new ties between rich planters and yeoman farmers, wealthy Chesapeake gentlemen consciously set themselves apart from their less affluent neighbors. Until the 1720s the ranks of the gentry were filled with boisterous, aggressive men who enjoyed many of the amusements of common folk—from hunting, hard drinking, and gambling on horse races to sharing tales of their manly prowess in seducing female servants and slaves. As time passed, however, affluent

Chesapeake landholders took on the trappings of wealth, modeling themselves after the English aristocracy. Beginning in the 1720s they replaced their modest wooden houses with mansions of brick and mortar. The plantation dwelling of Robert "King" Carter was over seventy-five feet long, forty-four feet wide, and forty feet high. Genteel planters entertained their neighbors in lavish style and sent their sons to London to be educated as lawyers and gentlemen. Most of the southern men who were educated in England returned to America, married well-to-do heiresses, and followed in their fathers' footsteps, managing plantations, socializing with other members of the gentry class, and participating in politics.

Wealthy Chesapeake and South Carolina women also emulated the elegant and refined ways of the English gentry. They read English newspapers and fashionable magazines, wore English clothes, and dined in the English fashion, with an elaborate afternoon tea. To improve their daughters' chances of finding a desirable marriage partner, they hired English tutors to teach them etiquette. Once married, affluent gentry women deferred to their husbands' authority, reared pious children, and maintained elaborate social networks—gradually creating the new ideal of the southern genteel woman. Using the profits of the South Atlantic system, the planter elite formed an increasingly well-educated, refined, and stable ruling class.

The Northern Maritime Economy

The South Atlantic system had a broad geographic reach. As early as the 1640s, New England farmers provided bread, lumber, fish, and meat to the sugar islands. As a West Indian explained in 1647, planters in the islands "had rather buy food at very dear rates than produce it by labour, so infinite is the profit of sugar works." By 1700 the economies of the West Indies and New England were tightly interwoven. After 1720 farmers and merchants in New York, New Jersey, and Pennsylvania entered the West Indian trade, shipping wheat, corn, and bread to the sugar islands.

The South Atlantic system tied the whole British empire together economically. In return for the sugar they exported to England, West Indian planters received bills of exchange (credit slips) from London merchant houses. The planters used those bills to buy slaves from transatlantic slavers and to reimburse North American farmers and merchants for their provisions and shipping services. Farmers and merchants then exchanged the bills for British manufactures, primarily textiles and iron goods, thus completing the cycle.

Urban Development. The West Indian trade created the first American merchant fortunes and the first urban industries (Map 3.4). Merchants in Boston, Newport, Providence, Philadelphia, and New York invested their profits from the West Indian trade in new ships and in factories that refined raw sugar into finished loaves (which previously had been imported from England) and distilled West Indian molasses into rum. By the 1740s Boston distillers were exporting more than half a million gallons of rum annually. In addition, merchants in smaller ports, such as Salem and Marblehead, built a major fishing industry, providing salted mackerel and cod to feed the slaves of the sugar islands and to export to southern Europe. Southern merchants transformed Baltimore into a major port by developing a bustling trade in wheat, while Charleston traders exported deerskins, indigo, and rice to European markets.

The expansion of Atlantic commerce in the eighteenth century fueled rapid growth in American port cities and coastal towns. By 1750 Newport, Rhode Island, and Charleston, South Carolina, had nearly 10,000 residents apiece, Boston had 15,000, and New York had almost 18,000. The largest port was Philadelphia, whose population by 1776 reached 30,000, the size of a large European provincial city. Smaller coastal towns emerged as centers of the shipbuilding and lumber industries. By the 1740s seventy sawmills dotted the Piscataqua River in New Hampshire, providing low-cost wood for homes, warehouses, and especially shipbuilding. Taking advantage of the Navigation Acts, which allowed colonists to build and own trading vessels, scores of shipwrights turned out oceangoing vessels, while hundreds of other artisans made ropes, sails, and metal fittings for the new fleet. Shipyards in Boston and Philadelphia launched about 15,000 tons of oceangoing vessels annually; eventually colonial-built ships made up about one-third of the British merchant fleet.

The impact of the South Atlantic system extended into the interior of North America. A small fleet of trading vessels sailed back and forth between Philadelphia and the villages along the Delaware Bay, exchanging cargoes of European goods for barrels of flour and wheat for sale in both the West Indies and Europe. By the 1750s hundreds of professional teamsters in Maryland moved 370,000 bushels of wheat and corn and 16,000 barrels of flour to market each year—over 10,000 wagon trips. To service this traffic, entrepreneurs and artisans set up taverns, horse stables, and barrel-making shops in small towns along the wagon roads, providing additional jobs. The prosperous interior town of Lancaster, Pennsylvania, boasted more than 200 artisans, both German and English. The South Atlantic system thus provided not only markets for farmers (by far the largest group of northern residents) but also opportunities for merchants, artisans, and workers in country towns and seaport cities.

Seaport Society. At the top of seaport society stood a small group of wealthy landowners and prosperous merchants. By 1750 about forty merchants controlled over

A View of Boston in 1738

In this painting of Boston by John Smibert (1738), church spires dominate the skyline and long wharves extend far into the harbor, offering anchorage for oceangoing vessels. This mixture of religious piety and maritime prosperity gave Boston—and, to a lesser extent, Philadelphia—a distinctive tone, with greater moral discipline than the other large seaport cities of New York, Baltimore, and Charleston. Courtesy, Childs Gallery, Boston.

50 percent of Philadelphia's trade and had taxable assets averaging £10,000, a huge sum at the time (Figure 3.2). Like the Chesapeake gentry, these urban merchants imitated the British upper classes, importing design books from England and building Georgian-style mansions to showcase their wealth. Their wives created a genteel culture, decorating their houses with fine furniture and entertaining guests at elegant dinners.

Artisan and shopkeeper families formed the middle ranks of seaport society and numbered nearly half the population. Innkeepers, butchers, seamstresses, shoemakers, weavers, bakers, carpenters, masons, and dozens of other specialists socialized among themselves, formed mutual self-help societies, and worked to gain a competency—an income sufficient to maintain their families in modest comfort and dignity. Wives and husbands often worked as a team, teaching the "mysteries of the craft" to their children. Some artisans aspired to wealth and status, an entrepreneurial ethic that prompted them to hire apprentices and expand production, and the most prosperous owned their own houses and shops (sometimes run by widows continuing a family business). However, most

craft workers were not well-to-do, and many of them were quite poor. In his entire lifetime a tailor was lucky to accumulate £30 worth of property—far less than the £2,000 owned at death by an ordinary merchant or the £300 listed in the probate inventory of a successful blacksmith.

Laboring men and women formed the lowest ranks of urban society. Merchants needed hundreds of dockworkers to unload manufactured goods and molasses from inbound ships and reload the ships with barrels of wheat, fish, and rice for export. They often filled these demanding jobs with black slaves—who numbered 10 percent of the workforce in Philadelphia and New York City—or they hired unskilled men who worked for wages. Poor women—whether single, married, or widowed—could eke out a living by washing clothes, spinning wool, or working as servants or prostitutes. To make ends meet, most laboring families sent their children out to work at an early age. Indispensable to the economy yet without homes of their own, these urban laborers lived in crowded tenements in back alleys. In good times hard work brought family security or enough money to drink cheap New England rum in waterfront taverns.

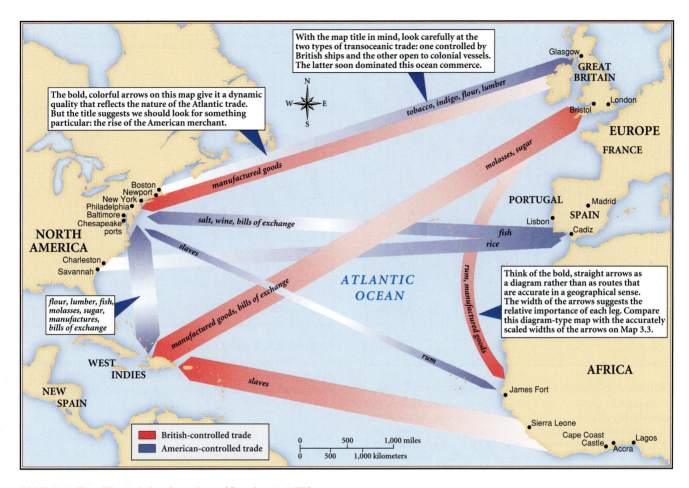

With the map title in mind, look carefully at the two types of transoceanic trade: one controlled by British ships and the other open to colonial vessels. The latter soon dominated this ocean commerce.

The bold, colorful arrows on this map give it a dynamic quality that reflects the nature of the Atlantic trade. But the title suggests we should look for something particular: the rise of the American merchant.

Think of the bold, straight arrows as a diagram rather than as routes that are accurate in a geographical sense. The width of the arrows suggests the relative importance of each leg. Compare this diagram-type map with the accurately scaled widths of the arrows on Map 3.3.

flour, lumber, fish, molasses, sugar, manufactures, bills of exchange

tobacco, indigo, flour, lumber

molasses, sugar

manufactured goods

salt, wine, bills of exchange

slaves

fish rice

manufactured goods, bills of exchange

rum, manufactured goods

rum

slaves

British-controlled trade
American-controlled trade

0   500   1,000 miles
0   500   1,000 kilometers

MAP 3.4 The Rise of the American Merchant, 1750

In accordance with mercantilist doctrine, British merchants controlled most of the transatlantic trade in manufactures, sugar, tobacco, and slaves. However, merchants in Boston, New York, and Philadelphia seized control of the West Indian trade, while Newport traders imported some slaves from Africa, and Boston and Charleston merchants carried fish and rice to southern Europe.

Periods of stagnant commerce affected everyone, threatening merchants with bankruptcy and artisans with irregular work. For laborers and seamen, whose household budgets left no margin for sickness or unemployment, depressed trade meant hunger, dependence on charity handed out by town-appointed overseers of the poor, and—for the most desperate—a life of petty thievery. Involvement in the South Atlantic system between 1660 and 1750 brought economic uncertainty as well as jobs and opportunities to northern workers and farmers.

The New Politics of Empire, 1713–1750

The triumph of the South Atlantic system of production and trade changed the politics of empire. British ministers, pleased with the prosperous commerce in staple crops, were content to rule the colonies with a gentle hand. The colonists enjoyed a significant degree of self-government

and economic autonomy, which put them in a position to challenge the rules of the mercantilist system.

The Rise of Colonial Assemblies

Before 1689 the authority of the representative assemblies in most colonies was weak. Political power rested in the hands of proprietors, royal governors, and authoritarian elites, reflecting the traditional view that "Authority should Descend from Kings and Fathers to Sons and Servants," as a royal-minded political philosopher put it. In the Glorious Revolution of 1688 the political faction known as the Whigs challenged that hierarchical outlook in England, winning the fight for a constitutional monarchy that limited the authority of the crown. English Whigs did not advocate democracy but did believe that the substantial property owners represented by the House of Commons should have some political power, especially over the levying of taxes. When Whig politicians forced William and Mary to accept a Declaration of Rights in

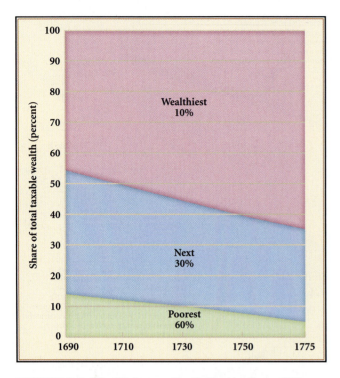

FIGURE 3.2 Wealth Inequality in the Northern Cities

As commerce expanded, the wealth of merchants grew much more rapidly than did that of artisans and laborers. By the 1770s the poorest 60 percent of the taxable inhabitants of Boston, New York, and Philadelphia owned less than 5 percent of the taxable wealth, whereas the top 10 percent—the merchant elite and its allies—controlled 65 percent.

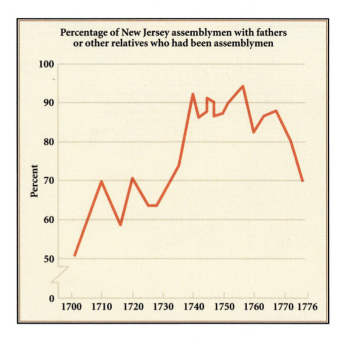

FIGURE 3.3 Family Connections and Political Power

By the 1750s nearly every member of the New Jersey assembly came from a family with a history of political leadership. This is clear testimony to the emergence of an experienced governing elite in the colonies.

1689, they strengthened the powers of the Commons at the expense of the crown.

American representative assemblies also wished to limit the powers of the crown and insisted on maintaining their authority over taxes, refusing to fund military projects and other programs advocated by royal governors. Gradually the colonial legislatures won partial control of the budget and the appointment of local officials, angering imperial bureaucrats and absentee proprietors. "The people in power in America," complained the proprietor William Penn during a struggle with the Pennsylvania Assembly, "think nothing taller than themselves but the Trees." In Massachusetts during the 1720s the assembly refused repeatedly to obey the king's instructions to provide a permanent salary for the royal governor; subsequently legislatures in North Carolina, New Jersey, and Pennsylvania declined to pay their governors any salary for several years.

The rising power of the colonial assemblies created an elitist rather than a democratic political system. Although most property-owning white men had the right to vote after 1700, only men of considerable wealth and status stood for election (Figure 3.3). In Virginia in the 1750s seven members of the influential slave-owning Lee family sat in the House of Burgesses and, along with other powerful families, dominated its major commit-

tees. In New England descendants of the original Puritans had intermarried and formed a core of political leaders. "Go into every village in New England," John Adams said in 1765, "and you will find that the office of justice of the peace, and even the place of representative, have generally descended from generation to generation, in three or four families at most."

However, neither elitist assemblies nor wealthy property owners could impose unpopular edicts on the people. The crowd actions that had overthrown the Dominion of New England in 1689 were a regular part of political life in America and were used to enforce community values. In New York mobs closed houses of prostitution, while in Salem, Massachusetts, they ran people with infectious diseases out of town. In Boston in 1710 crowds prevented merchants from exporting grain during a wartime shortage, and in New Jersey in the 1730s and 1740s angry mobs obstructed proprietors who were forcing tenants from disputed lands. When officials in Boston attempted to restrict the sale of farm produce to a designated public marketplace, a crowd destroyed the building and defied the authorities to arrest them. "If you touch One you shall touch All," an anonymous letter warned the sheriff, "and we will show you a Hundred Men where you can show one." Such expressions of popular power, combined with the growing power of the assemblies, undermined the old authoritarian system. By the 1750s most colonies had representative political institutions that were broadly responsive to popular pressure and increasingly immune to British control.

Salutary Neglect

British colonial policy during the reigns of George I (r. 1714–1727) and George II (r. 1727–1760) contributed significantly to the rise of American self-government. Royal bureaucrats relaxed their supervision of internal colonial affairs, focusing instead on defense and trade. Two generations later the British political philosopher Edmund Burke would praise this strategy as "**salutary** [healthy] **neglect**."

Salutary neglect was a by-product of the political system developed by Sir Robert Walpole, the leader of the British Whigs in the House of Commons and the king's chief minister between 1720 and 1742. By strategically dispensing appointments and pensions in the name of the king, Walpole won parliamentary support for his policies. However, Walpole's politically driven use of patronage weakened the imperial system by filling the Board of Trade and the royal governorships with men of little talent. When Governor Gabriel Johnson went to North Carolina in the 1730s, he vowed to curb the powers of the assembly and "make a mighty change in the face of affairs." However, Johnson was soon discouraged by the lack of support from the Board of Trade. Forsaking reform, Johnson decided "to do nothing which can be reasonably blamed, and leave the rest to time, and a new set of inhabitants."

Walpole's tactics also weakened the empire by undermining faith in the integrity of the political system. Radical-minded English Whigs were the first to raise the alarm. They argued that Walpole had betrayed the constitutional monarchy established by the Glorious Revolution by using patronage and bribery to create a strong **Court (or Crown) Party**. A Country Party of landed gentlemen likewise warned that Walpole's policies of high taxes and a bloated royal bureaucracy threatened the liberties of the British people. Politically minded colonists adopted these arguments as their own, maintaining that royal governors likewise abused their patronage powers. To preserve American liberty, they tried to enhance the powers of the provincial representative assemblies, thus preparing the way for later demands for political equality within the British empire.

Protecting the Mercantile System of Trade

During the years of salutary neglect Walpole's main preoccupation was to protect British commercial interests in America from the military threats posed by the Spanish and French colonies and from the economic dangers posed by the unwillingness of the American colonists to abide by the acts of Trade and Navigation.

Georgia and War with Spain. Initially, Walpole pursued a cautious foreign policy to allow Britain to

Sir Robert Walpole, the King's Minister
All eyes are on Walpole (left) as he offers advice to the Speaker of the House of Commons. A brilliant politician, Walpole used patronage to command a majority in the Commons and to win the support of George I and George II—the German-speaking monarchs from the duchy of Hanover. Walpole's personal motto, "Let sleeping dogs lie," helps to explain his colonial policy of salutary neglect. © National Trust Photographic Library / John Hammond.

recover from the huge expense of the long wars against Louis XIV of France that finally ended in 1713. However, in 1732 he agreed to provide a subsidy for the new colony of Georgia, a settlement designed by social reformers as a refuge for Britain's poor. Envisioning a society of small farms worked by independent landowners and white indentured servants, the trustees of Georgia limited most land grants to 500 acres and initially outlawed slavery.

Walpole arranged for Parliament to subsidize Georgia because he wanted to protect the valuable rice colony of South Carolina. Spain had long resented the British presence in Carolina and was outraged by the expansion into Georgia, where Spanish Franciscans had Indian missions. In addition, English merchants had steadily increased their trade in slaves and manufactured goods to Spain's colonies in Mesoamerica, eventually controlling two-thirds of that trade. To resist Britain's commercial and geographic expansion, in 1739 Spanish naval forces sparked the so-called War of Jenkins' Ear by mutilating Robert Jenkins, an English

Captain Fayrer Hall

The Impact of the Molasses Act

Before Parliament enacted the Molasses Act of 1733, it conducted a long investigation about its possible effects. One of those testifying was Captain Fayrer Hall, who for many years carried grain, lumber, and horses from the mainland colonies to the West Indies and returned with cargoes of sugar and molasses. Despite considerable evidence that the act would harm the mainland economy and the British export trade, Parliament bowed to the demands of the West Indian Interest—the politically powerful sugar planters and merchants—and passed the legislation.

Capt. Fayrer Hall, you will acquaint the Committee whether you know the Trade between the West-Indies and Northern Colonies?

I have lived in and traded for twenty Years past to the West-Indies, and the Northern Colonies. . . .

What Quantities of Lumber do the French take off from the northern colonies?

Martineco, Gardaloupa, Grand-terre, Marigalant & Granada, these Islands all together, I believe, may take off as much, or more than the British-owned islands do. . . .

Is there a sufficient Quantity of Molasses made at our [British] Sugar Islands to supply the Northern Colonies?

No, they have a Demand for a much greater Quantity than they can make, for they take all that is made at our own [British] islands, and, if I am rightly informed, as much or more from the foreign Settlements; . . . and the Demand is so much increased, that the Northern People could use and vend more, if they knew where to get more, even notwithstanding what they have from the French. . . .

Have our [British] Sugar Islands a demand for all their northern colonial Lumber & Horses?

It is impossible; I have known many losing Voyages from the northern colonies by sending of Lumber and Horses, and they the [British] Islanders have [sent the unsold portions of the goods] to other Islands. The Northern Colonies are capable of selling and sending a thousand Times as much [as the British islands can buy]; the District of Land is Larger than all Europe.

Supposing they were confined only to sell their Lumber and Horses to our [British] Islands?

It would destroy the Employment of three hundred sail of Ships and Vessels; we have three sail to one of any other Nation's. It is not long ago that the Dutch . . . had ten to our one, but the Act of Navigation put an end to that; we are now what the Dutch were at that Time, we have three sail to one, we are the Carriers as they used to be; but if this [Molasses] Act passes, the French will have the far greater Number of Ships, as we have now.

How is the Balance [of payments] in regard to the Northern Colonies? Do they take more Goods [from English merchants] than they send us [from the colonies]?

Yes, they have no other way of paying [English merchants] but by the Remittance of Money which they have from the Dutch & French [trade in the West Indies].

Supposing the Northern Colonies are not suffered to take their Molasses, will not that put a Stop to the Trade of their Lumber and Horses?

Yes. . . . We receive Money from [the French] now, and we never got so much from any of our own [British] Islands; besides, they produce more Sugar, Rum, and Molasses lately, then they used to do. . . .

Source: New York Gazette, 17–31 July 1732.

sea captain who was trading illegally with the Spanish West Indies.

Yielding to Parliamentary pressure Walpole used this provocation to launch a predatory war against Spain's increasingly vulnerable American empire. In 1740 British regulars commanded by Governor Oglethorpe of Georgia attacked St. Augustine without success, in part because South Carolina whites—still shaken by the Stono revolt—refused to commit militia units to the expedition. In 1741 the governors of the other mainland colonies raised 2,500 volunteers, who joined a British naval force in an assault on the prosperous Spanish seaport of Cartagena (in present-day Colombia). The attack failed and, instead of enriching themselves with Spanish

Bristol Docks and Quay

The triangular trade with Africa, the West Indies, and the mainland colonies made Bristol, in southwest England, into a bustling and prosperous seaport. In this detail from an eighteenth-century painting, horses draw large hogsheads of West Indian sugar to local factories and workers prepare smaller barrels of rum and other goods for export to Africa. City of Bristol Museum and Art Gallery.

booty, hundreds of colonial troops died of tropical diseases.

The War of Jenkins' Ear quickly became part of a general European conflict, the War of the Austrian Succession (1740–1749), bringing a new threat from France. Massive French armies battled German forces subsidized by Britain in Europe, and French naval forces roamed the West Indies, seeking without success to conquer a British sugar island. However, there were only minor Indian raids along the long frontier between the Anglo-American colonies and French Canada until 1745, when 3,000 New England militiamen, supported by a British naval squadron, captured the powerful French naval fortress of Louisbourg at the entrance to the St. Lawrence River. To the dismay of New England

Puritans, the Treaty of Aix-la-Chapelle (1748) returned Louisbourg to France, but it also secured the territorial integrity of Georgia by reaffirming British military superiority over Spain.

The Politics of Mercantilism.   At the same time, Walpole and other British officials confronted an unexpected American threat to British economic ascendancy. According to the mercantilist Navigation Acts, the colonies were expected to produce agricultural goods and other raw materials that British merchants would carry to England and Scotland, where they would be consumed, exported to Europe, or turned into manufactured goods. To enforce the monopoly enjoyed by British manufacturers, Parliament passed a series of acts that prohibited Americans from selling colonial-made textiles (1699), hats (1732), and iron products such as plows, axes, and skillets (1750).

However, the Navigation Acts had a major loophole because they allowed Americans to own ships and transport goods. Colonial merchants exploited those provisions, securing 95 percent of the commerce between the mainland and the West Indies and 75 percent of the trade in manufactures shipped from London and Bristol. Quite unintentionally, the Atlantic trade had created a dynamic community of colonial merchants (see Map 3.4).

Moreover, by the 1720s the British sugar islands could not use all of the flour, fish, and meat produced by the rapidly growing mainland colonies, and so colonial merchants sold them in the French West Indies. These supplies helped French planters produce low-cost sugar, enabling them to capture control of the European sugar market. When American rum distillers began to buy cheap French molasses rather than molasses from the British sugar islands, planters petitioned Parliament for help. The resulting Molasses Act of 1733 permitted the mainland colonies to export fish and farm products to the French islands but—to enhance the competitiveness of British molasses—placed a high tariff on imports of French molasses (see American Voices, "Captain Fayrer Hall: The Impact of the Molasses Act," p. 96).

American merchants and public officials protested that the act would cut farm exports and cripple their distilling industry, making it more difficult for colonists to purchase British goods. When Parliament ignored their petitions, American merchants turned to smuggling, importing French molasses and bribing customs officials to ignore the new tax. Luckily for the Americans, sugar prices rose sharply in the late 1730s, enriching planters in the British West Indies, so the act was not enforced.

The lack of adequate currency in the colonies led to another confrontation. American merchants sent most of the gold and silver coins and **bills of exchange** they earned in the West Indian trade to Britain to pay for manufactured goods, draining the domestic money supply. To remedy this problem, the assemblies of ten colonies established land banks that lent paper money to farmers, taking their land as collateral. Farmers used the paper money to buy tools or livestock or to pay their creditors, thereby stimulating trade. However, some assemblies, such as that of Rhode Island, issued large amounts of currency, causing it to fall in value, and required merchants to accept it as legal tender. Creditors, especially English merchants, rightly complained that they were being forced to accept worthless currency. In 1751 Parliament passed the Currency Act, which prevented all the New England colonies from establishing new land banks and prohibited the use of public currency to pay private debts.

These economic conflicts and the growing assertiveness of the colonial assemblies angered a new generation of British political leaders, who believed that the colonies already had too much autonomy. In 1749 Charles Townshend of the Board of Trade charged that American assemblies had assumed many of the "ancient and established prerogatives wisely preserved in the Crown." Townshend and other officials were determined to replace salutary neglect with a more rigorous system of imperial control.

The wheel of empire had come full circle. In the 1650s England set out to build a centralized colonial empire and, over the course of a century, achieved the economic part of that goal through the use of sweeping mercantilist legislation, warfare against the Dutch, French, and Spanish, and the forced labor of more than a million African slaves. However, as a result of the Glorious Revolution and the era of salutary neglect that followed, the empire unexpectedly devolved into a group of politically self-governing colonies linked together primarily by trade. And so in the 1740s British officials vowed once again to create a politically centralized colonial system.

FOR FURTHER EXPLORATION

▶ For definitions of key terms boldfaced in this chapter, see the glossary at the end of the book.

▶ To assess your mastery of the material covered in this chapter, see the Online Study Guide at **bedfordstmartins.com/henretta.**

▶ For suggested references, including Web sites, see page SR-3 at the end of the book.

▶ For map resources and primary documents, see **bedfordstmartins.com/henretta.**

S U M M A R Y

Upon becoming king of England in 1660, Charles II pursued contradictory colonial policies. On the one hand, he diminished imperial authority by relinquishing control of Carolina to eight aristocrats, New York to his brother James, and Pennsylvania to William Penn. On the other hand, Charles pursued mercantilist policies, securing the enactment of Navigation Acts that regulated colonial exports and imports. In 1685 his absolutist-minded successor, James II, imposed tighter political controls, abolishing the existing charters of the northern mainland colonies and creating the absolutist Dominion of New England. The Glorious Revolution of 1688 cost James his throne, and revolts in Maryland, Massachusetts, and New York secured the restoration of colonial self-government.

The Navigation Acts ensured that Britain would secure its share of the profits of the South Atlantic system and its valuable commerce in sugar, rice, indigo, and tobacco. To work the sugar plantations of the British West Indies and rice and indigo plantations of South Carolina, planters imported 1.5 million African slaves and brutally exploited their labor. In the Chesapeake colonies, where Africans raised tobacco and grains, the black population grew dramatically through natural increase, resulting in the creation of an African American community. By providing markets for farm products, the South Atlantic system also brought prosperity to farmers and merchants in the northern mainland colonies.

Beginning in the 1690s, the unofficial British policy of salutary neglect allowed American political leaders to strengthen the power of the provincial assemblies. These institutions were dominated by wealthy men but were responsive to the views of ordinary people, who wanted paper money and increased trade with the West Indies. These goals conflicted with British interests and policies and prompted greater imperial scrutiny of American affairs. In 1733, alarmed by the decline of the British sugar industry because of colonial trade with the French West Indies, the British Parliament passed the Molasses Act, which tightened mercantilist controls. By 1750, Parliament had also restricted American manufacturing and regulated the colonists' issue of paper currency. This legislation signaled that the era of salutary neglect was rapidly ending.

T I M E L I N E

1651	First Navigation Act
1660s	Virginia moves toward slave system
1663	Charles II grants Carolina proprietorship
1664	English capture New Netherland, rename it New York
1681	William Penn founds Pennsylvania
1686–1689	Dominion of New England
1688–1689	Glorious Revolution in England; William and Mary ascend throne
	Revolts in Massachusetts, Maryland, and New York
1689–1713	England, France, and Spain at war
1696	Parliament creates Board of Trade
1705	Virginia enacts slavery legislation
1714–1750	British follow policy of "salutary neglect"
	American assemblies gain power
1720–1742	Sir Robert Walpole serves as chief minister
1720–1750	African American community forms
	Rice exports from Carolina soar
	Planter aristocracy emerges
	Seaport cities expand
1732	Parliament charters Georgia, challenging Spain
	Hat Act
1733	Molasses Act
1739	Stono Rebellion in South Carolina
	War with Spain in the Caribbean
1740	Veto of Massachusetts land bank
1750	Iron Act
1751	Currency Act

Susanna Truax
Geboorenden 8 9b. 1726,
Geschildert Maart 1730

CHAPTER 4

Growth and Crisis in Colonial Society

1720–1765

Freehold Society in New England
Farm Families: Women's Place
Farm Property: Inheritance
The Crisis of Freehold Society

The Middle Atlantic: Toward a New Society, 1720–1765
Economic Growth and Social Inequality
Cultural Diversity
Religious Identity and Political Conflict

The Enlightenment and the Great Awakening, 1740–1765
The Enlightenment in America
American Pietism and the Great Awakening
Religious Upheaval in the North
Social and Religious Conflict in the South

The Midcentury Challenge: War, Trade, and Social Conflict, 1750–1765
The French and Indian War
The Great War for Empire
British Economic Growth and the Consumer Revolution
Land Conflicts
Western Uprisings

◄ **Young Dutch American Girl, 1730**
This painting of four-year-old Susanna Truax of Albany, New York, was the work of the "Gansevoort Limner," an unknown Dutch portrait painter. Following the artistic conventions of the time, the limner rendered Susanna as a mature young woman adding a lump of sugar to her tea. Born in 1726 (as noted in the upper left corner), Susanna never married; by the time she died in 1805, at age seventy-nine, Albany had lost much of its character as a "Dutch" city.
National Gallery of Art, Washington, DC; gift of Edgar William and Bernice Chrysler Garbisch.

I N 1736 ALEXANDER MACALLISTER LEFT THE HIGHLANDS OF SCOTLAND to settle in the backcountry of North Carolina, where he was soon joined by his wife and three sisters. Over the years MacAllister prospered as a landowner and mill proprietor and had only praise for his new home. Carolina was "the best poor man's country I have heard in this age," he wrote to his brother Hector, urging him to "advise all poor people . . . to take courage and come." In North Carolina there were no landlords to keep "the face of the poor . . . to the grinding stone," and so many Highlanders were arriving that "it will soon be a new Scotland." Here, on the margin of the British empire, people could "breathe the air of liberty, and not want the necessarys of life." Tens of thousands of European migrants—Highland Scots, English, Scots-Irish, Germans—heeded such advice, helping to swell the size of Britain's North American settlements from 400,000 people in 1720 to almost 2 million by 1765.

The rapid and continuous increase in the number of settlers—and slaves—transformed the character of life in every region of British America. Long-settled towns in New England became densely settled and then overcrowded.

Antagonistic ethnic and religious communities jostled uneasily with one another in the Middle Atlantic region, and the influx of the MacAllisters and thousands of other settlers into the southern backcountry altered the traditional dynamics of politics and social conflict in that region as well. Moreover, in every colony the growing influence of a European spiritual movement called Pietism changed the tone of religious life. Finally, and perhaps most important, as the new immigrants and the landless children of long-settled families moved inland, they sparked warfare with the native peoples and with the other European powers contesting for dominance of North America—France and Spain. A generation of growth produced a decade of crisis.

Freehold Society in New England

In the 1630s the Puritans had migrated from a country where a handful of nobles and gentry owned 75 percent of the arable land and farmed it by using servants, leaseholding tenants, and wage laborers. In their new home the Puritans consciously created a yeoman society composed primarily of independent farm families who owned their lands as **freeholders**—without feudal dues or leases. By 1750, however, the rapidly growing population outstripped the supply of easily farmed land, posing a severe challenge to the freehold ideal.

Farm Families: Women's Place

The Puritans' commitment to individual autonomy did not extend to gender relations, and by law and custom men dominated their families. As the Reverend Benjamin Wadsworth of Boston advised women in *The Well-Ordered Family* (1712), being richer, more intelligent, or of higher social status than their husbands mattered little: "Since he is thy Husband, God has made him the head and set him above thee." Therefore, Wadsworth concluded, it was a woman's duty "to love and reverence him." Puritan ideology celebrated the husband as head of the household, according him nearly complete control over his dependents.

Throughout their lives women saw firsthand that their role was a subordinate one. Small girls watched their mothers defer to their fathers. As young women they saw the courts prosecute few men and many women for the crime of fornication, especially those who bore an illegitimate child. And they learned that their marriage portions would be inferior in kind and size to those of their brothers; usually daughters received not highly prized land but rather livestock or household goods. Thus, Ebenezer Chittendon of Guilford, Connecticut, left all his land to his sons, decreeing that "Each Daughter have half so much as Each Son, one half in money and the other half in Cattle." Thanks to

the English Statute of Wills of 1540, which eliminated many customary restrictions over the disposition of wealth, fathers had nearly complete freedom to devise their property as they pleased.

In rural New England—indeed, throughout the colonies—women were raised to be dutiful helpmeets (helpmates) to their husbands. Farmwives spun thread and yarn from flax or wool and wove it into shirts and gowns. They knitted sweaters and stockings, made candles and soap, churned milk into butter and pressed curds into cheese, fermented malt for beer, preserved meats, and mastered dozens of other household tasks. The most exemplary or "notable" practitioners of these domestic arts won praise from the community, for their physical labor was crucial to the rural household economy.

Bearing and rearing children were equally central tasks. Most women married in their early twenties; by their early forties many had given birth to six or seven children, usually delivered with the assistance of midwives. A large family sapped the physical and emotional strength of even the most energetic wife, focusing her attention on domestic activities for about twenty of her most active years. A Massachusetts mother explained that she had less time than she would have liked for religious activities because "the care of my Babes takes up so large a portion of my time and attention." Yet more women than men became full members of the Puritan congregations of New England. As the revivalist Jonathan Edwards explained, they joined so "that their children may be baptized" in the church and because they feared the dangers of childbirth.

As the size of farms shrank in long-settled communities, many couples chose to have fewer children. After 1750 women in the typical farm village of Andover, Massachusetts, bore an average of only four children and thus gained the time and energy to pursue other tasks. Farm women made extra yarn, cloth, or cheese to exchange with neighbors or sell to shopkeepers, enhancing their families' standard of living. Or like Susan Huntington of Boston (the wife of a prosperous merchant), they spent more time in "the care & culture of children, and the perusal of necessary books, including the scriptures."

Yet women's lives remained tightly bound by a web of legal and cultural restrictions. While ministers often praised the piety of women, they excluded them from an equal role in the life of the church. When Hannah Heaton grew dissatisfied with her Congregationalist minister, thinking him unconverted and a "blind guide," she sought out Quaker and Baptist churches that welcomed questioning women and allowed them to become spiritual leaders. But by the 1760s even evangelical Baptist congregations were emphasizing traditional male prerogatives. "The government of Church and State must be . . . family government" controlled by its "king,"

The Character of Family Life: The Cheneys

Life in a large colonial-era family was very different from that in a small modern one. Mrs. Cheney's face shows the rigors of having borne many children, a task that has occupied her entire adult life (and may continue still, if the child she holds is her own). Her eldest daughter has married the man standing at the rear and holds two of her own children, who are not much younger than the last of her mother's brood. In such families, the lines between the generations were blurred.

National Gallery of Art, Washington, DC; gift of Edgar William and Bernice Chrysler Garbisch.

declared the Danbury (Connecticut) Baptist Association. Willingly or not, most New England women lived according to the conventional view that, as the essayist Timothy Dwight put it, they should be "employed only in and about the house and in the proper business of the sex."

Farm Property: Inheritance

By contrast, men who migrated to the colonies escaped many traditional constraints of European society, including the curse of landlessness. "The hope of having land of their own & becoming independent of Landlords is what chiefly induces people into America," an official noted in the 1730s. For men who had been peasants in Europe, owning property was a key element of their social identity, justifying their position as heads of the community's households.

Indeed, property ownership and family authority were closely related, because most migrating Europeans wanted farms that were large enough to provide sustenance for the present generation and land for the next one.

Parents with small farms could not provide their children with a start in life and had to adopt a different strategy. Many indentured their sons and daughters as servants and laborers in more prosperous households, where they would have enough to eat. When the indentures ended at age eighteen or twenty-one, their propertyless sons faced the daunting challenge of a ten-to-twenty-year climb up the agricultural ladder, from laborer to tenant and finally to freeholder.

Luckier sons and daughters in successful farm families received a **marriage portion** when they reached the age of twenty-three to twenty-five. The marriage portion—land, livestock, or farm equipment—repaid children for their past labor and allowed parents to choose their children's partners, which they did not hesitate to do. The family's prosperity and the parents' security during old age depended on a wise choice of a wife or husband. Normally, children had the right to refuse an unacceptable match, but they did not have the luxury of "falling in love" with whomever they pleased.

Marriage under English common law was hardly a contract between equals. A bride relinquished to her

Tavern Culture
By the eighteenth century, many taverns were run by women, such as this "Charming Patroness," who needed all her charm to deal with her raucous clientele. It was in taverns, declared puritanical John Adams, that "diseases, vicious habits, bastards, and legislators are frequently begotten."
Connecticut Historical Society.

husband the legal ownership of her land and personal property. After his death, she received her dower right—the right to use (but not to sell) a third of the family's estate. The widow's death or remarriage canceled this use-right, and her portion was divided among the children. In this way the widow's property rights were subordinated to those of the family "line," which stretched, through the children, across the generations.

It was the cultural duty of the father to provide inheritances for his children, and men who failed to do so lost status in the community. Some fathers willed the family farm to a single son, providing their other children with money, apprenticeship contracts, or uncleared land along the frontier or requiring the inheriting son to do so. Alternatively, yeomen moved their families to the New England frontier or to other unsettled regions, where life was hard but land for the children was cheap and abundant. "The Squire's House stands on the Bank

of the Susquehannah," the traveler Philip Fithian reported from the Pennsylvania backcountry in the early 1760s. "He tells me that he will be able to settle all his sons and his fair Daughter Betsy on the Fat of the Earth."

The historic accomplishment of these farmers was the creation of whole communities composed of independent property owners. A French visitor remarked on the sense of personal worth and dignity in this rural world, which contrasted sharply with European peasant life. Throughout the northern colonies, he wrote, he had found "men and women whose features are not marked by poverty, by lifelong deprivation of the necessities of life, or by a feeling that they are insignificant subjects and subservient members of society."

The Crisis of Freehold Society

How long would this happy circumstance last? Because of high rates of natural increase, the population of New England doubled with each generation, a rate of growth that raised the specter of landlessness and poverty. The Puritan colonies had about 100,000 people in 1700, nearly 200,000 in 1725, and almost 400,000 in 1750. In long-settled areas farms had been divided and subdivided and now often consisted of fifty acres or less. Many parents found themselves in a quandary because they could not provide an adequate inheritance. In the 1740s the Reverend Samuel Chandler of Andover, Massachusetts, was "much distressed for land for his children," seven of whom were male. A decade later in the neighboring town of Concord, about 60 percent of farmers owned less land than their fathers had.

Because parents had less to give their sons and daughters, they had less control over their children's lives. The system of arranged marriages broke down as young people engaged in premarital sex and used the urgency of pregnancy to win their fathers' permission to marry. Throughout New England the number of first-born children conceived before marriage rose spectacularly, from about 10 percent in the 1710s to 30 percent or more in the 1740s. Given another chance, young people "would do the same again," an Anglican minister observed, "because otherwise they could not obtain their parents' consent to marry."

New England families met the threat to the freeholder ideal through a variety of strategies. Many parents chose to have smaller families by using primitive methods of birth control. Others joined with neighbors to petition the provincial government for land grants, moving inland and hacking new farms out of the forests of central Massachusetts and western Connecticut—and eventually New Hampshire and the future Vermont. Still other farmers learned to use their small plots more productively, replacing the traditional English crops of wheat and barley with high-yielding potatoes and Indian corn. Corn offered a hearty food for humans, and its leaves furnished feed for cattle and pigs, which in turn provided milk and meat. New England developed a livestock economy, becoming the major supplier of salted and pickled meat to the slave plantations of the West Indies.

Finally, New England farmers made do on their smaller farms by exchanging goods and labor, developing the full potential of what historian Michael Merrill has called the "**household mode of production.**" Men lent each other tools, draft animals, and grazing land. Women and children joined other families in spinning yarn, sewing quilts, and shucking corn. Farmers plowed fields owned by artisans and shopkeepers, who repaid them with shoes, furniture, or store credit. Typically, no money changed hands; instead farmers, artisans, and shopkeepers recorded their debts and credits in personal account books and every few years "balanced" the books by transferring small amounts of cash to one another. The system of community exchange allowed households—and the entire economy—to achieve maximum output, thereby preserving the freehold ideal.

The Middle Atlantic: Toward a New Society, 1720–1765

Unlike New England, which was settled mostly by English Puritans, the Middle Atlantic colonies of New York, New Jersey, and Pennsylvania became home to peoples of differing origins, languages, and religions. These settlers—Scots-Irish Presbyterians, English and Welsh Quakers, German Lutherans, Dutch Reformed Protestants, and others—created ethnic and religious communities that coexisted uneasily with one another. New York was particularly unsettled as a result of a fairly sizable African populace—in 1756 slaves constituted more than 15 percent of its population.

Economic Growth and Social Inequality

Ample fertile land and a long growing season attracted migrants to the Middle Atlantic colonies of New York, New Jersey, and Pennsylvania, and profits from wheat financed their rapid settlement. Between 1720 and 1770 a population explosion in Western Europe doubled the price of wheat; American farmers profited from the growing demand by increasing their exports of wheat, corn, flour, and bread. This boom in exports helped the population of the Middle Atlantic region to surge from 50,000 in 1700 to 120,000 in 1720 and 450,000 in 1765 (Figure 4.1).

Tenancy in New York. As the population rose, so did the demand for land. Nonetheless, many migrants

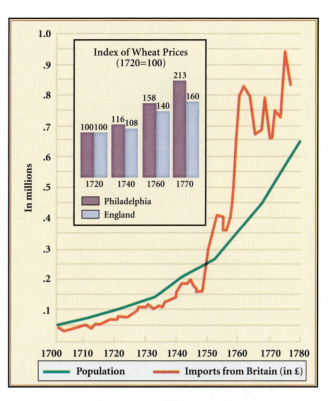

FIGURE 4.1 Population Growth, Wheat Prices, and Imports from Britain in the Middle Colonies
Wheat prices soared in Philadelphia because of demand in the West Indies and Europe. Exports of grain and flour paid for British manufactures, which were imported in large quantities after 1750.

refused to settle in New York's fertile Hudson River Valley. There, Dutch families presided over long-established manors created by the Dutch West India Company and wealthy British families, such as the Clarke and Livingston clans, dominated vast tracts granted by English governors between 1700 and 1714 (Map 4.1). Like the slave-owning planters in the Chesapeake, these landlords tried to live like European gentry, but few migrants wanted to labor as poor and dependent peasants. However, as freehold land became scarce in eastern New York, manorial lords were able to attract tenants, but only by granting them long leases and the right to sell their improvements—their houses and barns—to the next tenant. The number of tenants on the vast Rensselaer estate, for example, rose from 82 in 1714 to 345 in 1752 to nearly 700 by 1765.

Most tenant families hoped that with hard work and luck they could sell enough wheat to buy freehold farmsteads. However, preindustrial technology limited their output, especially during the crucial harvest season. As the wheat ripened, it had to be harvested quickly; any ripe uncut grain promptly sprouted and became useless. Yet a worker with a hand sickle could reap only half an acre a day, limiting the number of acres a family could

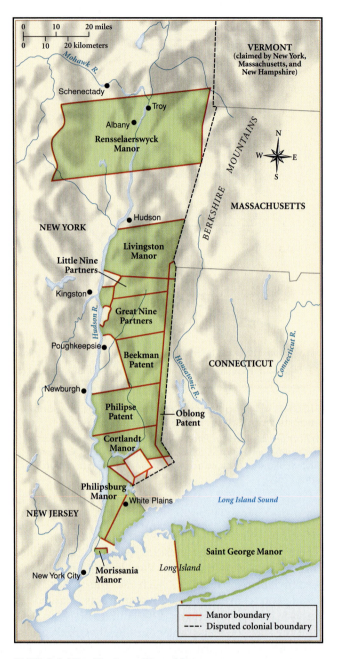

MAP 4.1 The Hudson River Manors

Dutch and English manorial lords dominated the fertile eastern shores of the Hudson River Valley, leasing small farms to German tenant families and refusing to sell land to freehold-seeking migrants from overcrowded New England. This powerful elite produced Patriot leaders, such as Gouverneur Morris (see American Lives, p. 206), and leading American families, such as the Roosevelts.

plant. The **cradle scythe**, an agricultural tool introduced during the 1750s, doubled or tripled the amount of grain a worker could cut. Even so, a family with two adult workers could not reap more than about twelve acres of grain each harvest season, a yield of perhaps 150 to 180 bushels of wheat and rye. After family needs were met, the remaining grain might be worth £15—enough to buy salt and sugar, tools, and cloth but little else. The road to land ownership was not an easy one.

Quaker Pennsylvania. Unlike New York, rural Pennsylvania and New Jersey were initially marked by relative economic equality because the original Quaker migrants arrived with approximately equal resources (Figure 4.2). The first settlers lived simply in small houses with one or two rooms, a sleeping loft, a few benches or stools, some wooden trenchers (platters), and a few wooden noggins (cups). Only the wealthiest families ate off pewter or ceramic plates imported from England or Holland. However, the rise of the wheat trade and an influx of poor settlers introduced marked social divisions. By the 1760s some farmers in eastern Pennsylvania had grown wealthy by buying slaves and hiring propertyless laborers to raise large quantities of wheat for market sale. Others had bought up land and subdivided it into small farms, which they let out on lease. Still others had become successful commercial entrepreneurs, providing newly arrived settlers with farming equipment, sugar and rum from the West Indies, and financial services. Gradually a new class of wealthy agricultural capitalists—large-scale farmers, rural landlords, speculators, storekeepers, and gristmill operators—accumulated substantial estates that included mahogany tables, four-poster beds, couches, table linen, and imported Dutch dinnerware.

By 1760 there were also many people at the bottom of the Middle Atlantic social order, for half of all white men were propertyless. Some landless men were the sons of property owners and would eventually inherit at least part of the family estate, but just as many were Scots-Irish **inmates**—single men or families "such as live in small cottages and have no taxable property, except a cow." In the predominantly German settlement of Lancaster, Pennsylvania, a merchant noted an "abundance of Poor people" who "maintain their Families with great difficulty by day Labour." Although Scots-Irish and German migrants hoped to become tenants and eventually landowners, sharply rising land prices prevented many from realizing their dreams.

Merchants and artisans took advantage of the ample supply of labor by organizing an outwork system. They bought wool or flax from farmers and paid propertyless workers and land-poor farm families to spin it into yarn or weave it into cloth. In the 1760s an English traveler reported that hundreds of Pennsylvanians had turned "to manufacture, and live upon a small farm, as in many parts of England." Indeed, eastern areas of the Middle Atlantic colonies had become as crowded and socially divided as rural England, and many farm families feared a return to the lowly status of the European peasant. Although some wealthy men heaped abuse on "shitten farmers," a letter to the *Pennsylvania Gazette* celebrated the old Quaker ideal of social equality: it was simply

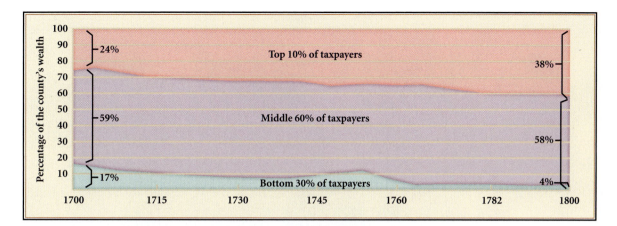

FIGURE 4.2 Increasing Social Inequality in Chester County, Pennsylvania
By renting land and selling goods to a growing population, the county's landed and commercial elite grew rich. Eventually the top 10 percent of taxpayers commanded nearly 40 percent of the wealth, far above the paltry 4 percent owned by the poorest 30 percent.

"impudence to tell another animal like myself that I came into the world his superior; none is born with the right to control another."

Cultural Diversity

The middle colonies were not a melting pot in which European cultures blended into a homogeneous "American" society; rather, they were a patchwork of ethnically and religiously diverse communities (Table 4.1). A traveler in Philadelphia in 1748 found no fewer than twelve religious denominations, including Anglicans, Quakers, Swedish and German Lutherans, Scots-Irish Presbyterians, and even Roman Catholics.

Migrants usually tried to preserve their cultural identities, marrying within their own ethnic groups or maintaining the customs of their native lands. The major exception was the Huguenots—Protestant Calvinists who were expelled from Catholic France. They settled in New York and various seacoast cities and gradually lost their French ethnic identity by intermarrying with other Protestants. More typical were the Welsh Quakers. Seventy percent of the children of the original Welsh migrants to Chester County, Pennsylvania, married other Welsh Quakers, as did 60 percent of the third generation.

Members of the Society of Friends (Quakers) became the dominant social group in Pennsylvania, at first because of their numbers and later because of their wealth and influence. Quakers controlled Pennsylvania's representative assembly until the 1750s and exercised considerable power in New Jersey as well. Because

TABLE 4.1 Estimated European Migration to the British Mainland Colonies, 1700–1780

Period	Germany	Northern Ireland	Southern Ireland	Scotland	England	Wales	Other	Total
1700–1719	4,000	2,000	2,500	700	1,700	1,200	300	12,400
1720–1739	17,900	6,900	10,400	2,800	7,100	4,700	1,000	50,800
1740–1759	52,700	25,400	18,200	6,800	16,300	10,700	2,300	132,400
1760–1779	23,700	36,200	13,400	25,000	19,000	12,400	2,300	132,000
TOTAL	**98,300**	**70,500**	**44,500**	**35,300**	**44,100**	**29,000**	**5,900**	**327,600**

After 1720, European migration to British America increased dramatically, reaching its climax between 1740 and 1780, when over 264,000 settlers arrived in the mainland colonies. Immigration from Germany peaked in the mid-1750s, while that from Ireland, Scotland, England, and Wales continued to increase during the 1760s and early 1770s. Most migrants were Protestants, including those from southern Ireland.

Source: Adapted from Aaron S. Fogleman, "Migrations to the Thirteen British North American Colonies, 1700–1775: New Estimates," *Journal of Interdisciplinary History* 22 (1992).

Quaker Meeting for Worship

Quakers dressed plainly and met in unadorned buildings, sitting in silence until inspired to speak by the "inner light." Women spoke with near-equality to men, a tradition that prepared Quaker women to take a leading part in the nineteenth-century women's rights movement. In this English work, entitled Quaker Meeting, *an elder (his hat on a peg above his head) conveys his thoughts to the congregation.* Museum of Fine Arts, Boston.

Quakers were pacifists, they dealt peaceably with Native Americans, negotiating treaties and buying land rather than seizing it by force. These conciliatory policies enabled Pennsylvania to avoid a major war with the Indian peoples until the 1750s. Some Quakers extended the egalitarian values emphasized by their faith to their relations with blacks. After 1750 many Quaker meetings condemned the institution of slavery, and some expelled members who continued to keep slaves.

The Quaker vision of a "peaceable kingdom" attracted many German settlers who were fleeing their homelands because of war, religious persecution, and poverty. First to arrive, in 1683, was a group of religious dissenters—the Mennonites—attracted by a pamphlet promising religious freedom. In the 1720s religious upheaval and population growth in southwestern Germany and Switzerland stimulated another wave of migrants. "Wages were far better" in Pennsylvania, Heinrich Schneebeli reported to his friends in Zurich after an exploratory trip, and "one also enjoyed there a free unhindered exercise of religion." Beginning in 1749 thousands of Germans and Swiss fled their overcrowded societies; by 1756, nearly 37,000 of these migrants had landed in Philadelphia. Some of these newcomers were redemptioners—a type of indentured servant—but many more were propertied farmers and artisans who

Gottlieb Mittelberger

The Perils of Migration

Gottlieb Mittelberger was a Lutheran minister who migrated to Pennsylvania with thousands of other Germans in the 1740s. Dismayed by the lax religious behavior of the colonial population and the lack of state support for religious authority, he returned to his homeland after a few years. In a book published in Germany in 1750, Mittelberger viewed America with a critical eye, warning his readers of the difficulties of migration and of life in a harsh, competitive society.

[The journey from Germany to Pennsylvania via Holland and England] lasts from the beginning of May to the end of October, fully half a year, amid such hardships as no one is able to describe adequately with their misery. Both in Rotterdam and in Amsterdam the people are packed densely, like herrings so to say, in the large sea-vessels. One person receives a place of scarcely 2 feet width and 6 feet length in the bedstead, while many a ship carries four to six hundred souls. . . .

During the journey the ship is full of pitiful signs of distress—smells, fumes, horrors, vomiting, various kinds of sea sickness, fever, dysentery, headaches, heat, constipation, boils, scurvy, cancer, mouth-rot, and similar afflictions, all of them caused by the age and the highly-salted state of the food, especially of the meat, as well as by the very bad and filthy water, which brings about the miserable destruction and death of many. . . .

Children between the ages of one and seven seldom survive the sea voyage; and parents must often watch their offspring suffer miserably, die, and be thrown into the ocean, from want, hunger, thirst, and the like. I myself, alas, saw such a pitiful fate overtake thirty-two children on board our vessel, all of whom were finally thrown into the sea. Their parents grieve all the more, since their children do not find repose in the earth, but are devoured by the predatory fish of the ocean. . . .

When the ships finally arrive in Philadelphia after the long voyage only those are let off who can pay their sea freight or can give good security. The others, who lack the money to pay, have to remain on board until they are purchased and until their purchasers can thus pry them loose from the ship. In this whole process the sick are the worst off, for the healthy are preferred and are more readily paid for. . . . Every day Englishmen, Dutchmen and High-German people select among the healthy persons; . . . adult persons bind themselves in writing to serve 3, 4, 5, or six years for the amount due to them. . . . Many parents must sell and trade away their children like so many head of cattle; for if their children take the debt upon themselves, the parents can leave the ship free and unrestrained. It often happens that whole families, husband, wife, and children, are separated by being sold to different purchasers, especially when they have not paid any part of their passage money. . . .

Thus let him who wants to earn his piece of bread honestly and in a Christian manner and who can only do this by manual labor in his native country stay there rather than come to America.

Source: Gottlieb Mittelberger, *Journey to Pennsylvania* (1756), ed. and trans. Oscar Handlin and John Clive (Cambridge: Harvard University Press, 1960), 11–21.

---

migrated to secure ample land for their children (American Voices, "Gottlieb Mittelberger: The Perils of Migration," above).

German settlements soon dominated certain districts of eastern Pennsylvania, and thousands of Germans moved down the Shenandoah Valley into the western parts of Maryland, Virginia, and the Carolinas (Map 4.2). The migrants carefully guarded their language and cultural heritage, encouraging their American-born children to marry within the community. A minister in North Carolina admonished his

congregation "not to contract any marriages with the English or Irish," explaining that "we owe it to our native country to do our part that German blood and the German language be preserved in America." Well beyond 1800 these settlers spoke German, read German-language newspapers, conducted church services in German, and preserved German agricultural practices, which included women taking an active part in plowing and harvesting. English travelers remarked that German women were "always in the fields, meadows, stables, etc. and do not dislike any work whatsoever." Most German

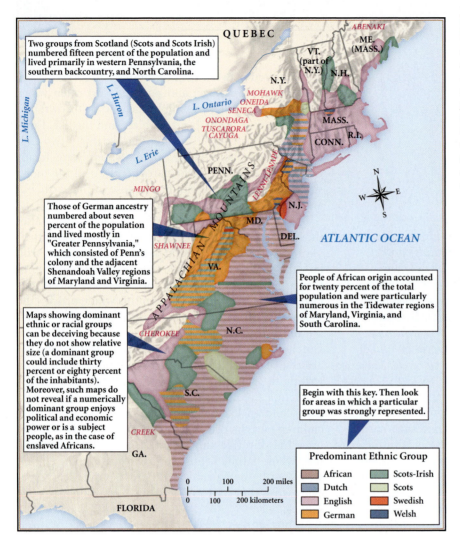

Two groups from Scotland (Scots and Scots Irish) numbered fifteen percent of the population and lived primarily in western Pennsylvania, the southern backcountry, and North Carolina.

Those of German ancestry numbered about seven percent of the population and lived mostly in "Greater Pennsylvania," which consisted of Penn's colony and the adjacent Shenandoah Valley regions of Maryland and Virginia.

Maps showing dominant ethnic or racial groups can be deceiving because they do not show relative size (a dominant group could include thirty percent or eighty percent of the inhabitants). Moreover, such maps do not reveal if a numerically dominant group enjoys political and economic power or is a subject people, as in the case of enslaved Africans.

People of African origin accounted for twenty percent of the total population and were particularly numerous in the Tidewater regions of Maryland, Virginia, and South Carolina.

Begin with this key. Then look for areas in which a particular group was strongly represented.

Predominant Ethnic Group

African	Scots-Irish
Dutch	Scots
English	Swedish
German	Welsh

0   100   200 miles
0   100   200 kilometers

MAP 4.2 Ethnic and Racial Diversity, 1775

In 1700 most colonists in British North America were of English origin, but by 1775 settlers of English descent constituted a minority of the total nonaboriginal population. African Americans now accounted for one-third of the residents of the South, while thousands of Germans and Scots-Irish migrants created ethnic and religious diversity in the Middle Atlantic colonies and southern backcountry (see Table 4.1).

migrants felt at ease living in a British-controlled colony, for few of them came from the politically active classes and many rejected political involvement on religious grounds. They engaged in politics only to protect their churches and cultural practices—insisting, for example, that as in Germany, married women should have the right to hold property and write wills.

Migrants from Ireland formed the largest group of incoming Europeans, about 150,000 in number. Some were Catholic but most were the descendants of the Presbyterian Scots who had been sent to Ireland between 1608 and 1650 to bolster English control of its Catholic population. In Ireland the Scots faced discrimination and economic regulation from the dominant English. The Irish Test Act of 1704 excluded Scottish Presbyterians as well as Irish Catholics from holding public office; English mercantilist regulations placed heavy import duties on the woolens made by Scots-Irish weavers; and Scots-Irish farmers faced heavy taxes. "Read this letter, Rev. Baptist Boyd," a migrant to New York wrote back to his minister, "and tell all the

poor folk of ye place that God has opened a door for their deliverance . . . all that a man works for is his own; there are no revenue hounds [tax collectors] to take it from us here." Lured by such reports, thousands of Scots-Irish sailed for Philadelphia beginning in the 1720s and then moved to central Pennsylvania and southward down the Shenandoah Valley into the backcountry of Maryland and Virginia. Like the Germans, the Scots-Irish vowed to keep their culture, holding firm to their Presbyterian faith and promoting marriage within the church.

Religious Identity and Political Conflict

In Western Europe the leaders of church and state condemned religious diversity, and some German ministers in Pennsylvania carried these sentiments to America, criticizing the separation of church and state in the colony. "The preachers do not have the power to punish anyone, or to force anyone to go to church," complained

German Farm in Western Maryland

Beginning in the 1730s, wheat became a major export crop in Maryland and Virginia. This engraving probably depicts a German farm, because the harvesters are using oxen, not horses, and women are working in the field alongside men. Using "a new method of reaping" that is possibly of German origin, the harvester cuts only the grain-bearing tip and leaves the wheat stalks in the fields, to be eaten by livestock. Library of Congress.

For more help analyzing this image, see the ONLINE STUDY GUIDE at bedfordstmartins.com/henretta.

the minister Gottlieb Mittelberger. As a result, "Sunday is very badly kept. Many people plough, reap, thresh, hew or split wood and the like." Thus, Mittelberger concluded, "Liberty in Pennsylvania does more harm than good to many people, both in soul and body."

Mittelberger ignored the fact that religious sects in Pennsylvania enforced moral behavior among their members through communal self-discipline. For example, each Quaker family attended a weekly worship meeting and a monthly discipline meeting. Four times a year a committee met with each family to make certain the children were receiving proper religious instruction, a reminder that fathers heeded. "If thou refuse to be obedient to God's teachings," Walter Faucit of Chester admonished his son, "thou will be a fool and a vagabond." The committee also supervised the moral behavior of adults; a Chester County meeting disciplined one of its members "to reclaim him from drinking to excess and keeping vain company." More important, Quaker meetings regulated marriages, granting permission only to couples with land and livestock sufficient to support a family. As a result, the children of well-to-do friends usually married within the sect, while poor Quakers remained unmarried, wed at later ages, or married without permission—in which case they were usually barred

from Quaker meetings. These communal sanctions effectively sustained a self-contained and prosperous Quaker community.

However, in the 1750s Quaker dominance in Pennsylvania came under attack. Scots-Irish Presbyterians living in frontier settlements west of the Susquehanna River challenged the pacifism of the Quaker-dominated assembly by urging a more aggressive Indian policy. Many of the newer German migrants also opposed the Quakers, demanding laws that respected their inheritance customs and fair representation in the provincial assembly. As a European visitor noted, Scots-Irish Presbyterians, German Baptists, and German Lutherans had begun to form "a general confederacy" against the Quakers, but they found it difficult to unite because of "a mutual jealousy, for religious zeal is secretly burning" (Map 4.3).

These ethnic passions embittered the politics of the Middle Atlantic region. In Pennsylvania Benjamin Franklin disparaged the "boorish" character and "swarthy complexion" of German migrants, while in New York a Dutchman declared that he "Valued no English Law no more than a Turd." The Quaker-inspired experiment in cultural and religious diversity prefigured the passionate ethnic and social conflicts that would characterize much of American society in the centuries to come.

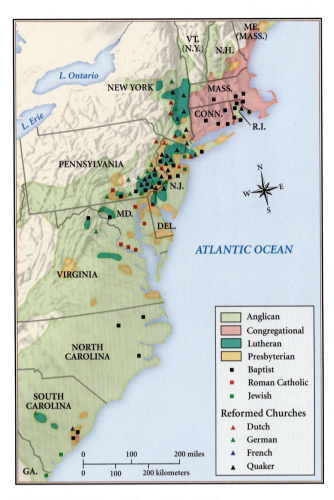

MAP 4.3 Religious Diversity in 1750

By 1750 religious diversity among European Colonists was on the rise and not only in the ethnically disparate Middle Atlantic colonies. Baptists had increased their numbers in New England, long the stronghold of Congregationalism, and would soon be important in Virginia. Already there were good-sized pockets of Presbyterians, Lutherans, and German Reformed in the South, where the Church of England (Anglicanism) was the established religion.

For more help analyzing this map, see the ONLINE STUDY GUIDE at bedfordstmartins.com/henretta.

The Enlightenment and the Great Awakening, 1740–1765

Two great European cultural movements reached America between the 1720s and the 1760s: the Enlightenment and Pietism. The Enlightenment, which emphasized the power of human reason to understand and shape the world, appealed especially to well-educated men and women from merchant or planter families and to urban artisans. **Pietism**, an emotional, evangelical religious movement that stressed a Christian's personal relation to God, attracted many adherents, especially among farmers and urban laborers. The two move-

ments promoted independent thinking in different ways; together they transformed American intellectual and cultural life.

The Enlightenment in America

Most early Americans relied on religious teachings or folk wisdom to explain the workings of the natural world. Thus, Swedish settlers in Pennsylvania attributed medicinal powers to the great white mullein, a common wildflower, tying the leaves around their feet and arms when they had a fever. Even highly educated people believed that events occurred for reasons that today would be considered magical. When a measles epidemic struck Boston in the 1710s, the Puritan minister Cotton Mather thought that only God could end it. Like most Christians of his time, Mather believed that the earth stood at the center of the universe and that God intervened directly in human affairs.

The European Enlightenment.   Early Americans held to these beliefs despite the scientific revolution of the sixteenth and seventeenth centuries, which had challenged both traditional Christian and folk worldviews. As early as the 1530s the astronomer Copernicus had observed that the earth traveled around the sun rather than vice versa, implying a more modest place for humans in the universe than had previously been assumed. Other scholars had conducted experiments using empirical methods—actual observed experience— to learn about the natural world. Eventually the English scientist Isaac Newton, in his *Principia Mathematica* (1687), used mathematics to explain the movement of the planets around the sun. Newton's laws of motion and concept of gravity described how the universe could operate without the constant intervention of a supernatural being, undermining traditional Christian explanations of the cosmos.

In the century between the publication of Newton's book and the outbreak of the French Revolution in 1789, the philosophers of the European Enlightenment applied scientific reasoning to all aspects of life, including social institutions and human behavior. Enlightenment thinkers believed that men and women could observe, analyze, and improve their world. They advanced four fundamental principles: the lawlike order of the natural world, the power of human reason, the natural rights of individuals (including the right to self-government), and the progressive improvement of society.

In his *Essay Concerning Human Understanding* (1690), the English philosopher John Locke emphasized the impact of environment, experience, and reason on human behavior, proposing that the character of individuals and societies was not fixed by God's will but could be changed through education and purposeful

Franklin's Influence
Benjamin Franklin's work as a scientist and inventor captivated subsequent generations of Americans. This painted panel (c. 1830) from a fire engine of the Franklin Volunteer Fire Company of Philadelphia depicts Franklin's experiment in 1752 that demonstrated the presence of electricity in lightning. Cigna Museum and Art Collection / Photo by Joseph Painter.

action. Locke's *Two Treatises on Government* (1690) advanced the revolutionary theory that political authority was not given by God to monarchs (as kings such as James II had insisted) but was derived from social compacts that people made to preserve their "natural rights" to life, liberty, and property. In Locke's view, the people should have the right to change government policies—or even their form of government—through the decision of a majority.

The ideas of Locke and other Enlightenment thinkers came to America through books, travelers, and educated migrants and quickly affected the beliefs of influential colonists about religion, science, and politics. As early as the 1710s the Reverend John Wise of Ipswich, Massachusetts, used Locke's political principles to defend the Puritans' decision to vest power in the ordinary members of their churches. Wise argued that just as the social compact formed the basis of political society, the religious covenant made the congregation—not the bishops of the Church of England or even the ministers—the proper interpreter of religious truth. And when a smallpox epidemic threatened Boston in the 1720s, the Puritan minister Cotton Mather sought a scientific rather than a religious remedy, joining with a prominent Boston physician to support the new technique of inoculation.

Franklin in Philadelphia.   Benjamin Franklin was the epitome of the American Enlightenment. Born in Boston in 1706 to a devout Calvinist family and apprenticed to a printer as a youth, Franklin was a self-taught, self-made man. While working as a tradesman, printer, and journalist in Philadelphia he formed "a club of mutual improvement" that met weekly to discuss "Morals, Politics, or Natural Philosophy." These dis-cussions and Enlightenment literature, rather than the Bible, shaped Franklin's imagination. As Franklin explained in his *Autobiography*, written in 1771, "from the different books I read, I began to doubt of Revelation [God-revealed truth] itself." Like many urban artisans, wealthy Virginia planters, and affluent seaport merchants, Franklin became a **deist**. Influenced by Enlightenment science, deists believed that God had created the world but allowed it to operate in accordance with the laws of nature. The deists' God was a rational being, a divine "watchmaker" who did not intervene directly in history or in people's lives. Rejecting the authority of the Bible, deists relied on people's "natural reason" to define a moral code. Adherence to the code, they believed, would be rewarded in life and after death. A sometime slave owner himself, Franklin used natural ethics to question the moral legitimacy of racial bondage, eventually repudiating the institution as he became a defender of

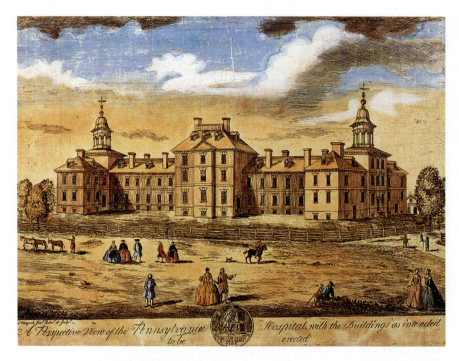

Enlightenment Philanthropy: The Philadelphia Hospital

This imposing structure, built in 1753 with public funds and private donations, embodied two Enlightenment principles— that purposeful action could improve society and that the world should express reason and order (exhibited here in the symmetrical facade). Etchings such as this one, drawn about 1761, circulated widely, bolstering Philadelphia's reputation as the center of the American Enlightenment. Historical Society of Pennsylvania.

American freedom from the threat of British political "slavery."

Franklin popularized this practical-minded outlook of the Enlightenment in *Poor Richard's Almanack* (1732–1757), an annual publication read by thousands. In 1743 he helped found the American Philosophical Society, an institution devoted to "the promotion of useful knowledge," and proceeded to invent bifocal lenses for eyeglasses, the Franklin stove, and the lightning rod. Franklin's book on electricity, first published in England in 1751, won praise from the English scientist Joseph Priestley as the greatest contribution to science since Newton. Following in Franklin's footsteps, other ambitious printers in Philadelphia and other American cities published newspapers and gentleman's magazines, the first significant nonreligious publications to appear in the colonies. Thus, the European Enlightenment added a secular dimension to colonial intellectual life, preparing the way for the great American contributions to republican political theory by John Adams, James Madison, and other Patriots during the Revolutionary era.

American Pietism and the Great Awakening

As some influential Americans—merchants and wealthy Virginia planters—and various urban artisans turned to deism, many other colonists embraced the European devotional movement known as Pietism. Pietists emphasized devout, or "pious," behavior, emotional church services, and a striving for a mystical union with God— appealing to the hearts, rather than the minds, of their congregations. Their teachings came to America with German migrants in the 1720s and sparked a religious revival among many farmers, artisans, and laborers. In Pennsylvania and New Jersey the Dutch minister Theodore Jacob Frelinghuysen moved from church to church, preaching rousing, emotional sermons to German settlers. In private prayer meetings he encouraged lay members to carry a message of spiritual urgency to growing congregations. A decade later William Tennent and his son Gilbert, Presbyterian clergymen who copied Frelinghuysen's approach, led revivals among Scots-Irish migrants throughout the Middle Atlantic region.

Simultaneously, a native-born Pietistic movement appeared in Puritan New England. Puritanism had taken root in England as part of a Pietistic upsurge, and the first migrants to America had sustained that intensity. However, over the decades many New England congregations had lost their religious zeal. In the 1730s the minister Jonathan Edwards restored spiritual enthusiasm to the Congregational churches in the Connecticut River Valley. An accomplished philosopher as well as an effective preacher, Edwards urged his hearers—especially young men and women—to commit themselves to a life of piety and prayer (see American Lives, "Jonathan Edwards: Preacher, Philosopher, Pastor," p. 116).

George Whitefield, a young English revivalist with what one historian has called a "flamboyant, highly sexualized style," transformed the local revivals into a "Great Awakening" that spanned the mainland settlements. Whitefield had experienced conversion after reading German Pietistic tracts and became a follower of John Wesley, the founder of English Methodism, who

George Whitefield, c. 1742
No painting captured Whitefield's magical appeal, although this image conveys his open demeanor and religious intensity. When Whitefield spoke to a crowd near Philadelphia, an observer noted, his words were "sharper than a two-edged sword. . . . Some of the people were pale as death; others were wringing their hands . . . and most lifting their eyes to heaven and crying to God for mercy." Courtesy, Trustees of the Boston Public Library.

making striking use of biblical metaphors, and even at times assuming a female persona—as a woman in labor struggling to deliver the word of God. The young preacher evoked a deep emotional response, telling his listeners they had all sinned and must seek salvation. Hundreds of men and women suddenly felt the "new light" of God's grace within them. As "the power of god come down," Hannah Heaton recalled, "my knees smote together . . . it seemed to me I was a sinking down into hell . . . but then I resigned my distress and was perfectly easy quiet and calm . . . it seemed as if I had a new soul & body both." Strengthened and self-confident, these "New Lights" were prepared to follow in Whitefield's footsteps.

Religious Upheaval in the North

Like all cultural explosions, the Great Awakening was controversial. Conservative (or "Old Light") ministers such as Charles Chauncy of Boston condemned the "cryings out, faintings and convulsions" produced by emotional preachers. Chauncy denounced the willingness of the New Lights to allow women to speak in public as "a plain breach of that *commandment of the LORD*, where it is said, *Let your WOMEN keep silence in the churches.*" In Connecticut the Old Lights persuaded the legislative assembly to prohibit evangelists from speaking to established congregations without the ministers' permission. When Whitefield returned to Connecticut in 1744, he found many pulpits closed to him. But the New Lights resisted attempts by civil officials to silence them. Dozens of farmers, women, and artisans roamed the countryside, condemning the Old Lights as "unconverted" sinners and willingly accepting imprisonment: "I shall bring glory to God in my bonds," a dissident preacher wrote from jail.

As the Awakening proceeded, it undermined support for traditional churches and challenged the authority of governments to impose taxes that supported them. In New England many New Lights left the established Congregational Church. By 1754 they had founded 125 "separatist" churches, supporting their ministers through voluntary contributions. Other religious dissidents joined Baptist congregations, which favored a greater separation of church and state (see Figure 4.3). According to the Baptist preacher Isaac Backus, "God never allowed any civil state upon earth to impose religious taxes." In New York and New Jersey the Dutch Reformed Church split in two, as New Lights resisted conservative church authorities in the Netherlands.

The Awakening also challenged the authority of ministers, whose education and biblical knowledge had traditionally commanded respect. In an influential pamphlet, *The Dangers of an Unconverted Ministry* (1740), Gilbert Tennent maintained that the minister's authority came not from theological training but through the conversion experience. Reasserting Martin

combined enthusiastic sermons with disciplined "methods" of worship. In 1739 Whitefield carried Wesley's preaching style to America and over the next two years attracted huge crowds of "enthusiasts" from Georgia to Massachusetts. "Religion is become the Subject of most Conversations," the *Pennsylvania Gazette* reported. "No books are in Request but those of Piety and Devotion." The usually skeptical and restrained Benjamin Franklin was so impressed by Whitefield's oratory that when the preacher asked for contributions, Franklin emptied the coins in his pockets "wholly into the collector's dish, gold and all." By the time the evangelist reached Boston, the Reverend Benjamin Colman reported, the people were "ready to receive him as an angel of God."

Whitefield owed his appeal partly to his compelling personal presence. "He looked almost angelical; a young, slim, slender youth . . . cloathed with authority from the Great God," wrote a Connecticut farmer (see American Voices, "Nathan Cole: The Power of a Preacher," p. 118). Like most evangelical preachers, Whitefield did not read his sermons but spoke from memory as if inspired, raising his voice for dramatic effect, gesturing eloquently,

Jonathan Edwards: Preacher, Philosopher, Pastor

Jonathan Edwards did not mince words. Echoing the harsh theology of John Calvin, Edwards preached that men and women were helpless creatures completely dependent on God: "There is Hell's wide gaping mouth open; and you have nothing to stand upon, nor any thing to take hold of: there is nothing between you and Hell but the air; 'tis only the power and mere pleasure of God that holds you up."

Edwards spoke "without much noise of external emotion" and without a single gesture, a listener noted, but his intense "inner fervor" underlined the torments that awaited those who fell into the eternal flames:

> *How dismal will it be . . . to know assuredly that you never, never shall be delivered from them; . . . after you shall have endured these torments millions of ages . . . your bodies, which shall have been burning and roasting all this while in these glowing flames, yet shall not have been consumed, but will remain to roast through an eternity yet.*

Such was the terrible—and inevitable—fate that Edwards the preacher promised to complacent Christians in his most famous sermon, *Sinners in the Hands of an Angry God* (1742). But Edwards the pastor preached a more hopeful message of personal repentance and spiritual rebirth, telling congregations that this fate awaited only those who "never passed under a great change of heart, by the mighty power of the spirit of God upon your souls; all that were never born again, and made new creatures."

Blending passionate warnings with compassionate forgiveness, Edwards inspired a religious revival in the Connecticut River Valley in the mid-1730s and helped George Whitefield stir up an even greater one in the 1740s. This Connecticut minister, one of the leading revivalists of his age, was also a profound and original philosopher, perhaps the most intellectually brilliant colonial American.

Jonathan Edwards, 1720
This portrait, painted by Joseph Badger when Edwards was seventeen, shows that even as a young man the great preacher and philosopher was grave and dignified.
Yale University Art Gallery, Bequest of Eugene Philips Edwards.

Jonathan Edwards was born in 1703 in East Windsor, Connecticut, the fifth child and only son among the eleven children of Timothy and Esther Stoddard Edwards. His father came from a wealthy family but ended up a poorly paid rural minister who fought constantly with his congregation over his salary and authority, battles that Jonathan would later fight with his own church. His mother was the daughter of Solomon Stoddard, a famous Connecticut preacher and revivalist—a family legacy that would both help and haunt Jonathan Edwards throughout his life.

As a youth Jonathan embraced his grandfather Stoddard's theology, rejecting the Calvinist belief in God's omnipotence over people's lives and labeling it "a horrible doctrine." But at the age of seventeen Edwards became a committed Calvinist, explaining in his *Personal Narrative*, written later in life, that he had then experienced "a delightful conviction" of the Almighty's absolute sovereignty, of "sweetly conversing with Christ, and wrapt and swallowed up in God." In fact, Edwards's autobiography distorted the truth, for he found his Calvinist God only after many years of personal torment and a series of physical and emotional collapses.

The Enlightenment came more easily to the intellectually minded Edwards. While studying for the ministry at Yale College, he read the works of Isaac Newton, John Locke, and other Enlightenment thinkers, beginning a lifetime of philosophical inquiry into the meaning of words and things. He accepted Locke's argument in *An Essay Concerning Human Understanding* (1690) that ideas are not innate at birth but are the product of experience as conveyed through the senses—our ability to see, hear, feel, and taste the world around us. A person who has never tasted a pineapple, said Locke, will never have "the true idea of the relish of that celebrated and delicious fruit."

However, Locke's theory of knowledge was less successful in explaining abstract ideas—such as God, love, salvation—and here Edwards made an original contribution. Locke had suggested that abstract ideas resulted when the mind rationally analyzed various sense experiences. Edwards knew better. He had worked out his theological doctrines through intense personal torment and he knew they had an emotional component. "Love" (whether of God or a fellow human being) was "felt" and not merely understood. It followed that abstract ideas were emotional as well as rational, the product of the passions as well as the senses.

Edwards used his theory of knowledge to justify his style of preaching, arguing that vivid words promoted conversions. As he put it in *A Treatise Concerning Religious Affections* (1746), "true religion, in great part, consists in holy affection." He would save his congregation through powerful sermons: "to fright persons away from Hell." In the end, the philosopher was at one with the preacher.

In 1729 Edwards put these ideas into practice as pastor of the Congregational church in Northampton, Massachusetts, taking over that ministry from his grandfather Solomon Stoddard and matching Stoddard's success as a revivalist. Beginning in 1734, Edwards reported, "the number of true saints multiplied . . . the town seemed to be full of the presence of God," especially among young people. News of the Northampton revival stimulated religious fervor up and down the Connecticut River Valley "till there was a general awakening."

Edwards interpreted his success as "a remarkable Testimony of God's Approbation of the Doctrine . . . that we are justified only by faith in Christ, and not by any manner of virtue or goodness of our own." He maintained that uncompromising Calvinist position during the widespread revivals of the 1740s. Also seeking to restore an older communal order, he took issue with those New Lights who asserted "the absolute Necessity for every Person to act singly . . . as if there was not another human Creature upon earth." Repudiating that spirit of individualism, Edwards insisted that aspiring Saints should heed their pastors, who were "skilful guides," and then make a "credible Relation of their inward Experience" to the congregation, thereby strengthening the covenant bonds that knit members together in a visible church. Edwards extended his critique of individualism to economic affairs, speaking out against "a narrow, private spirit" of greedy merchants and landlords, men who "are not ashamed to hit and bite others [and] grind the faces of the poor."

Edwards's rigorous standards and assault on individualism deeply offended the wealthiest and most influential members of his congregation. In 1750 struggles over his salary and disciplinary authority culminated in a final battle, when Edwards repudiated Stoddard's practice of admitting almost all churchgoers to the sacrament of Communion; he would offer full church membership only to those whom God had chosen as Saints. By a vote of 200 to 20, the Northampton congregation dismissed the great preacher and philosopher from his pastorate. Impoverished and with a family of ten children to support, Edwards moved to Stockbridge, Massachusetts, a small frontier outpost. There he ministered, without great success, to the Housatonic Indians and wrote an impressive philosophical work, *Freedom of the Will* (1752).

In 1757, as Edwards was about to take up the presidency of the College of New Jersey (Princeton), he was inoculated against smallpox, had a severe reaction, and died. He left a pair of spectacles, two wigs, three black coats, and some three hundred books, including twenty-two written by himself—but not much else in the way of earthly goods.

As he lay dying, this turn of fate puzzled America's first great philosopher. Why had God called him to Princeton only to give him no time to undertake his duties? As a preacher and pastor Edwards had always responded to such questions by stressing God's arbitrary power and the "insufficiency of reason" to understand God's purpose. Now he himself had to accept that grim and unsatisfying answer, showing through his personal experience why Calvinism was such a hard faith by which to live . . . and die.

Nathan Cole

The Power of a Preacher

The evangelist George Whitefield transformed the lives of thousands of Americans, such as the Connecticut farmer Nathan Cole, by convincing them of their sinfulness. In his reflections on his life (a short unpublished manuscript now in the archives of the Connecticut Historical Society), Cole described the impact that Whitefield's preaching made on his life in 1741 and his months of agony as he prayed for a sign that he was worthy enough to merit God's grace.

Now it please God to Send Mr. Whitefield into this land; and my hearing of his preaching at Philadelphia, like one of the old apostles, . . . I felt the Spirit of God drawing me by conviction; I longed to see and hear him and wished he would come this way. . . . Then of a sudden, in the morning about 8 or 9 of the clock there came a messenger and said Mr. Whitefield . . . is to preach at Middletown this morning at ten of the clock. I was in my field at work. I dropped my tool that I had in my hand and ran home to my wife, telling her to make ready quickly. . . .

When I saw Mr. Whitefield come upon the scaffold, he looked almost angelical; a young, slim, slender youth before some thousands of people with a bold undaunted countenance. And my hearing how God was with him everywhere as he came, it solemnized my mind and put me into a trembling fear before he began to preach; for he looked as if he was clothed with authority from the Great God, and a sweet solemnity sat upon his brow, and my hearing him preach gave me a heart wound. By God's blessing my old foundation was broken up, and I saw that my righteousness would not save me.

Then I was convinced of the doctrine of Election: and went right to quarrelling with God about it; because that all I could do would not save me, and he had decreed from Eternity who should be saved and who not: I began to think I was not Elected, and that God had made some for heaven and me for hell. And I thought God was not Just in so doing. . . . Now this distress lasted Almost two years—Poor—Me—Miserable me. . . .

Hell fire was most always in my mind; and I have hundreds of times put my fingers into my pipe when I have been smoking to feel how fire felt: And to see how my Body could bear to lye in Hell fire for ever and ever. . . .

And while these thoughts were in my mind God appeared unto me and made me Skringe [cringe]. . . . I seemed to hang in open Air before God, and he seemed to Speak to me in an angry and Sovereign way: What won't you trust your Soul with God? My heart answered Oh yes, yes, yes. I was set free, my distress was gone. . . . Then I began to pray and praise God.

Source: Richard Bushman, *The Great Awakening: Documents on the Revival of Religion, 1740–1745* (Chapel Hill: University of North Carolina Press, 1989), 67–71.

Luther's commitment to the priesthood of all believers, Tennent suggested that anyone who had experienced the saving grace of God could speak with ministerial authority. Not long afterward, Isaac Backus celebrated this spiritual democracy, noting that "the common people now claim as good a right to judge and act in matters of religion as civil rulers or the learned clergy."

Religious revivalism carried a social message, reaffirming the communal ethic of many farm families and questioning the growing competition and pursuit of wealth that accompanied the expansion of the American economy. "In any truly Christian society," Tennent explained, "mutual Love is the Band and Cement"—not the mercenary values of the marketplace. Suspicious of merchants and land speculators and dismayed by the erosion of traditional morality, Jonathan Edwards spoke for many rural Americans when he charged that a "private niggardly [miserly] spirit" was more suitable "for wolves and other beasts of prey, than for human beings."

As religious enthusiasm spread, churches founded new colleges to educate their youth and train ministers. New Light Presbyterians established the College of New Jersey (Princeton) in 1746, and New York Anglicans founded King's College (Columbia) in 1754. Baptists set up the College of Rhode Island (Brown) and the Dutch Reformed Church subsidized Queen's College (Rutgers) in New Jersey (Table 4.2). The true intellectual legacy of the Awakening, however, was not education for the few but a new sense of religious—and ultimately political—authority among the many. As a European visitor to Philadelphia remarked in surprise, "the poorest day-laborer on the bank of the Delaware hold it his right

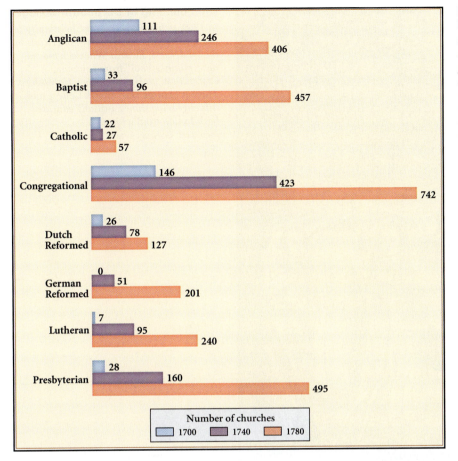

FIGURE 4.3 Church Growth by Denomination, 1700–1780

Some churches, such as the Anglican and Dutch Reformed, grew slowly as parents passed their faith down to their children. After 1740, the fastest-growing denominations were the immigrant churches—German Lutheran, German Reformed, and Scots-Irish Presbyterian—and those with an evangelical message, such as the Baptists.

to advance his opinion, in religious as well as political matters, with as much freedom as the gentleman."

Social and Religious Conflict in the South

In the southern colonies religious enthusiasm also sparked social conflict. In Virginia the Church of England was the legally established religion, supported by public taxes. However, Anglican ministers generally ignored the spiritual needs of African Americans (about 40 percent of the population), and landless whites (another 20 percent) attended irregularly. Middling white freeholders, who accounted for about 35 percent of the population, formed the core of most Anglican congregations. Prominent planters and their families (a mere 5 percent of the

TABLE 4.2 Colonial Colleges

	Date of Founding	Colony	Religious Affiliation
Harvard	1636	Massachusetts	Puritan
William and Mary	1693	Virginia	Church of England
Yale	1701	Connecticut	Puritan
College of New Jersey (Princeton)	1746	New Jersey	Presbyterian
King's (Columbia)	1754	New York	Church of England
College of Philadelphia (University of Pennsylvania)	1755	Pennsylvania	None
College of Rhode Island (Brown)	1764	Rhode Island	Baptist
Queen's (Rutgers)	1766	New Jersey	Dutch Reformed
Dartmouth	1769	New Hampshire	Congregationalist

The Founding of Dartmouth College

In 1769, to bring Protestant Christianity to European settlers and Native Americans in the wilderness, Eleazar Wheelock moved his "Indian School" from Lebanon, Connecticut, to Hanover, New Hampshire. There it became Dartmouth College and, as this engraving shows, initially educated both Indians and whites.
Dartmouth College Library.

population) held real power in the church and used their control of parish finances to discipline Anglican ministers. One clergyman complained that dismissal awaited any minister who "had the courage to preach against any Vices taken into favor by the leading Men of his Parish."

The Presbyterian Revival.

The Great Awakening challenged both the Church of England and the power of the southern planter elite. In 1743 the bricklayer Samuel Morris, inspired by his reading of George Whitefield's sermons, led a group of Virginia Anglicans out of the established Church. Seeking a more vital religious experience, Morris and his followers invited New Light Presbyterian ministers from Scots-Irish settlements along the Virginia frontier to lead their prayer meetings. Soon these Presbyterian revivals spread across the backcountry and into the Tidewater region along the Atlantic coast, threatening the social authority of the Virginia gentry. Planters and their well-dressed families were accustomed to arriving at Anglican services in elaborate carriages drawn by well-bred horses, and they often flaunted their power by marching in a body to their

seats in the front pews. These potent reminders of the gentry's social superiority would vanish if freeholders attended New Light Presbyterian rather than Church of England services. Moreover, religious pluralism would threaten the government's ability to tax the population to support the established church.

To prevent the spread of New Light doctrines, Virginia's governor denounced them as "false teachings," and Anglican justices of the peace closed down Presbyterian meetinghouses. This harassment kept most white yeomen families and poor tenants within the Church of England, as did the fact that most Presbyterian ministers were highly educated and sought converts mainly among skilled workers and propertied farmers.

The Baptist Insurgency.

Baptists succeeded where Presbyterians failed. The evangelical Baptist preachers who came to Virginia in the 1760s drew their congregations primarily from poor farmers by offering them solace and hope in a troubled world. The Baptists' central ritual was adult baptism, often involving complete immersion in water. Once men and women had experienced the infusion of grace—had been "born again"—they were baptized in an emotional public ceremony that celebrated the Baptists' shared fellowship. During the 1760s thousands of yeomen and tenant farm families in Virginia were drawn to revivalist meetings by the enthusiasm and democratic ways of Baptist preachers.

Even slaves were welcome at Baptist revivals. As early as 1740 George Whitefield had openly condemned the brutality of slaveholders and urged that blacks be brought into the Christian fold. In South Carolina and Georgia a handful of New Light planters took up Whitefield's challenge, but the hostility of the white population and the commitment of many Africans to their ancestral religions kept the number of converts low. Virginia in the 1760s witnessed the first significant conversion of slaves to Christianity, as second- and third-generation African Americans who knew the English language and English ways responded positively to the Baptist message that all people were equal in God's eyes.

The ruling planters reacted violently to the Baptists, viewing them as a threat to social authority and the gentry's way of life. The Baptists emphasized spiritual equality by calling one another "brother" and "sister," and their preachers condemned the customary pleasures of Chesapeake planters—gambling, drinking, whoring, and cockfighting. Hearing Baptist Dutton Lane condemn "the vileness and danger" of drunkenness, planter John Giles took the charge personally: "I know who you mean! and by God I'll demolish you." To maintain traditional practices and Anglican power, sheriffs and justices of the peace broke up Baptist services by force. In Caroline County, Virginia, an Anglican posse attacked a prayer meeting led by Brother John Waller, who, a fellow Baptist reported, "was violently jerked off the stage; they caught him by the back part of his neck, beat his head against the ground, and a gentleman gave him twenty lashes with his horsewhip."

Despite such attacks, Baptist congregations continued to multiply. By 1775 about 20 percent of Virginia's whites and hundreds of enslaved blacks had joined Baptist churches, bringing cultural as well as religious change. To signify their state of grace, some Baptist men "cut off their hair, like Cromwell's round-headed chaplains." Many others refused to attend "a horse race or other unnecessary, unprofitable, sinful assemblies." Still others forged a new ethic of evangelical masculinity, "crying, weeping, lifting up the eyes, groaning" when touched by the Holy Spirit but defending themselves with vigor. "Not able to bear the insults" of heckler Robert Ashby, a group of Baptists "took Ashby by the neck and heels and threw him out of doors," sparking a bloody fray. In the South as in the North, Protestant revivalism was on the way to becoming a powerful American religious movement.

However, the revival in the Chesapeake did not bring radical changes to the social order. Rejecting the requests of evangelical women, Baptist men kept authority within the church in the hands of "free born male members." Anglican slaveholders likewise retained power within the polity. Nonetheless, the Baptist insurgency gave spiritual meaning to the lives of the poor and powerless and influenced some yeomen and tenants to defend their economic interests. Moreover, as Baptist ministers spread Christianity among slaves, the cultural gulf between blacks and whites shrank, undermining one justification for slavery and giving blacks a new sense of religious identity. Within a generation African Americans would develop their own versions of Protestant Christianity.

The Midcentury Challenge: War, Trade, and Social Conflict, 1750–1765

Between 1750 and 1765 colonial life was transformed not only by Pietism and the Enlightenment but also by a major war, a boom-and-bust economy, and brutal frontier violence. First, Britain embarked on a war in America, the French and Indian War, which became a worldwide conflict—the Great War for Empire. Second, a rapid surge in trade boosted colonial prosperity but put Americans deeply in debt to British creditors. Third, a great westward migration sparked new battles with Indian peoples, armed conflicts between settlers and landowners, and frontier rebellions against eastern governments.

The French and Indian War

In 1750 Indian peoples remained dominant throughout the interior regions of eastern North America—the great valleys of the Ohio and Mississippi Rivers. Most Spanish colonists lived far to the west, along the Rio Grande in present-day New Mexico. French settlers lived along the St. Lawrence River, near the fur-trading centers of Montreal and Quebec (see Map 4.4). The more numerous residents of the British colonies inhabited the Atlantic coastal plain. Only a few pioneers had ventured across the Appalachian Mountains, both because there were few natural transportation routes and because of Indian resistance. For more than a generation the Iroquois and other Native Americans had firmly opposed the intrusion of white settlers, using their control of the fur trade to bargain for guns and subsidies from British and French officials.

The Failure of Diplomacy. However, the Iroquois strategy of playing off the French against the British was gradually breaking down as the European governments resisted the rising cost of "gifts" of arms and money.

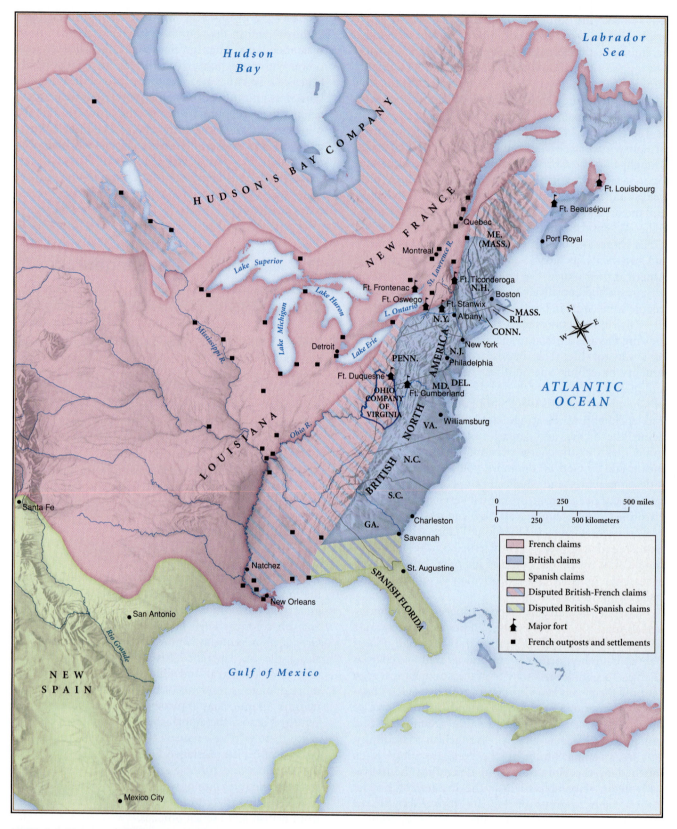

MAP 4.4 European Spheres of Influence, 1754

France and Spain laid claim to vast areas of North America and used their Indian allies to combat the numerical superiority of British settlers. For their part, Native Americans played off one European power against another. As a British official observed: "To preserve the Ballance between us and the French is the great ruling Principle of Modern Indian Politics." By expelling the French from North America, the Great War for Empire disrupted this balance, leaving Indian peoples on their own to resist encroaching Anglo-American settlers.

Equally important, crucial Indian alliances began to crumble. Along the upper Ohio River the Delawares and Shawnees declared that they would no longer abide by Iroquois policies. In part, this Indian discontent stemmed from escalating Anglo-American demand for Indian lands from colonial speculators and recent European migrants. In the late 1740s the Mohawks rebuffed attempts by Sir William Johnson, a British Indian agent and land speculator, to settle Scottish migrants west of Albany. To the south, the Iroquois were infuriated when Governor Dinwiddie of Virginia and a group of prominent planters laid plans for "the Extension of His Majesties Dominions" into the upper Ohio River Valley, an area that they had traditionally controlled. Supported by influential London merchants, the Virginia speculators formed the Ohio Company in 1749 and obtained a royal grant of 200,000 acres along the upper Ohio River. "We don't know what you Christians, English and French intend," the outraged Iroquois complained, "we are so hemmed in by both, that we have hardly a hunting place left."

To shore up the alliance with the Iroquois Nations, the British Board of Trade, the body charged with supervising American affairs, called for a great inter-colonial meeting with the Indians at Albany, New York, in June 1754. At the meeting the American delegates assured the Iroquois that they had no designs on their lands and asked for their assistance against the French. To bolster colonial defenses, Benjamin Franklin proposed a Plan of Union among the colonies with a continental assembly that would manage all western affairs: trade, Indian policy, and defense. But neither the Albany Plan nor a similar proposal by the Board of Trade for a political "union between ye Royal, Proprietary, & Charter Governments" ever materialized because both the provincial assemblies and the imperial government feared that a consolidated colonial government would undermine their authority.

Britain's movement into the Ohio River Valley alarmed the French. They countered by constructing a series of forts, including Fort Duquesne at the point where the Monongahela and Allegheny Rivers join to

The Siege of Louisbourg, 1745

Assisted by British redcoats, blue-coated New England militiamen swarmed ashore on Cape Breton Island in May 1745 and laid siege to the formidable French citadel at Louisbourg. By late June the colonists' artillery had silenced a strategic French battery, allowing British warships to enter the harbor. Faced with a combined assault from land and sea, the French surrendered. Yale University Art Gallery, Mabel Brady Garvan Collection.

Pipe of Peace

In 1760 the Ottawa chief Pontiac welcomed British troops to his territory, offering a pipe of peace to their commander, Major Robert Rogers. Three years later, Pontiac led a coordinated uprising against British troops, traders, and settlers, accusing them of cheating Native American peoples of their furs and lands. Library of Congress.

form the Ohio (present-day Pittsburgh). The confrontation escalated when Governor Dinwiddie dispatched an expedition led by Colonel George Washington, a young planter and Ohio Company stockholder, to support the company's claims. In July 1754 French troops seized Washington and his men and expelled them from the region, prompting expansionists in Virginia and Britain to demand war. The British prime minister, Henry Pelham, urged calm: "There is such a load of debt, and such heavy taxes already laid upon the people, that nothing but an absolute necessity can justifie our engaging in a new War."

Expansionism Triumphant. Pelham could not control the march of events. In Parliament William Pitt, a rising British statesman, and Lord Halifax, the new head of the Board of Trade, strongly advocated a policy of expansionism in the colonies. They persuaded Pelham to dispatch naval and military forces to America, where they joined with colonial militia in attacking French forts. In June 1755 British and New England troops captured Fort Beauséjour in Nova Scotia (Acadia). Equally significant, in a carefully planned military operation of dubious morality, troops from Puritan Massachusetts seized nearly 10,000 French Catholic Acadians, permanently deported them to various destinations—France, Louisiana, the West Indies, South Carolina—and settled English and Scottish Protestants on their farms.

This Anglo-American triumph was quickly offset by a stunning defeat. As 1,400 British regulars and Virginia militiamen advanced on Fort Duquesne in July 1755, they came under attack by a small force of French and a larger group of Delawares and Shawnees, who had decided to side with the French. In the ensuing battle the British commander, General Edward Braddock, lost his life and nearly two-thirds of his troops. "We have been beaten, most shamefully beaten, by a handfull of Men," Washington complained bitterly as he led the militiamen back to Virginia.

The Great War for Empire

By 1756 the fighting in America had spread to Europe, where the conflict aligned Britain and Prussia against France and Austria and was known as the Seven Years' War. When Britain decided to mount major offensives in India and West Africa as well as in North America and the West Indies, the conflict became a "great war for empire." Since 1700 Britain had reaped unprecedented profits from its overseas trading empire and was determined to crush France, the main obstacle to further expansion.

William Pitt, who was appointed secretary of state in 1757, was the grandson of the East Indies merchant "Diamond" Pitt and a committed expansionist. A haughty man, Pitt was constantly at odds with his colleagues. "I know that I can save this country and that I alone can," he declared. Indeed, Pitt was a master of strategy, both commercial and military, and planned to cripple France by attacking its colonies. In designing the critical campaign against New France, Pitt exploited a demographic advantage: on the North American mainland, King George II's 2 million subjects outnumbered the French by 14 to 1. To mobilize the colonists, Pitt agreed to pay half the cost of their troops and supply them with arms and equipment, an expenditure in America of nearly £1 million a year. He then committed

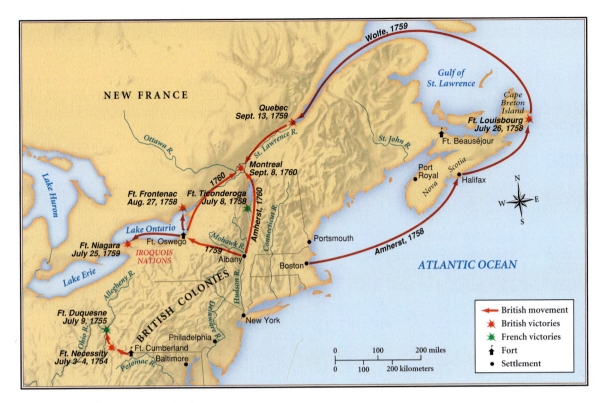

MAP 4.5 The Anglo-American Conquest of New France, 1754–1760

After full-scale war broke out in 1756, it took three years for the British ministry to equip colonial forces and dispatch a British army to America. Then British and colonial troops attacked the heartland of New France, capturing Quebec in 1759 and Montreal in 1760. The conquest both united and divided the allies. Colonists celebrated the great victory— "The Illuminations and Fireworks exceeded any that had been exhibited before," reported the South Carolina Gazette*—but British officers viewed provincial soldiers with disdain: "the dirtiest, most contemptible, cowardly dogs you can conceive."*

a major British fleet and 30,000 British regulars to the American conflict, appointing three young officers— James Wolfe, Jeffrey Amherst, and William Howe—as the top commanders (Map 4.5).

Beginning in 1758 the British moved from one triumph to the next. They forced the French to abandon Fort Duquesne (which they renamed Fort Pitt) and then captured the major fortress of Louisbourg at the mouth of the St. Lawrence (see Voices from Abroad, "Louis Antoinne De Bougainville: The Defense of Canada," p. 126). The following year Wolfe sailed down the St. Lawrence to attack Quebec, the heart of France's American empire. After several failed attacks, 4,000 British troops scaled the high cliffs protecting the city and defeated the French. Quebec's fall was the turning point of the war. The Royal Navy prevented French reinforcements from crossing the Atlantic, and when British forces captured Montreal in 1760, the conquest of Canada was complete.

Elsewhere the British also went from success to success. Fulfilling Pitt's dream, the East India Company captured French commercial outposts and took control of trade in large sections of India. British forces seized French

Senegal in West Africa, the French sugar islands of Martinique and Guadeloupe, and the Spanish colonies of Cuba and the Philippine Islands. The Treaty of Paris of 1763 confirmed this triumph, granting Britain sovereignty over half the continent of North America, including French Canada, all French territory east of the Mississippi River, and Spanish Florida. Spain received Louisiana west of the Mississippi, along with the restoration of Cuba and the Philippines. The French empire in North America was reduced to a handful of sugar islands in the West Indies and two rocky islands off the coast of Newfoundland.

As British armies and traders occupied French forts, Indian peoples from New York to Michigan grew increasingly concerned. Fearing an influx of Anglo-American settlers, the Ottawa chief Pontiac hoped for a return of the French, declaring, "I am French, and I want to die French." Neolin, a Delaware prophet, went further, teaching that the suffering of the Indian peoples stemmed from their dependence on the Europeans and their goods, guns, and rum. He called for the expulsion of all Europeans. Inspired by Neolin's vision and his own anti-British sentiments, in 1763 Pontiac led a group of loosely confederated tribes in a major uprising,

Louis Antonine De Bougainville

The Defense of Canada

Following the outbreak of the Seven Years' War in Europe in 1756, the resident French governor in New France mobilized local troops to defend the colony. As Britain poured 11,000 regular troops into the conflict in America, the French government dispatched the marquis de Montcalm and a few thousand soldiers to Quebec. In July 1758 they met an invading British army at Fort Carrillon on Lake Champlain. In his journal Louis Antonine De Bougainville, Montcalm's chief of staff, recorded the following account of the battle. Like most European officers, British as well as French, Bougainville had nothing but contempt for the colonists and their leaders.

July 1, 1758. The Marquis de Montcalm went this morning . . . to reconnoiter the surroundings of Fort Carrillon in order to select a battlefield and the place for an entrenched camp. We lack manpower, and perhaps time is also lacking. Our situation is critical. Action and audacity are our sole resources. . . .

July 2. It has been decided to occupy the heights which dominate Carillon with an entrenched camp, with redoubts and abatis [a defensive line of felled trees and sharpened posts]. . . . But to carry out these works strong arms are needed, as well as the arrival of the colony troops, and time granted us by the enemy. . . .

July 8. Half an hour after noon the English army advanced on us. . . . The left was first attacked by two columns, one of which tried to outflank the defenses and found itself under fire of La Sarre, the other directed its efforts on a salient between [the battalions from] Languedoc and Berry. The center, where Royal Roussillon was, was attacked at almost the same time by a third column, and a fourth carried its attack toward the right between Bearn and La Reine. These different columns were intermingled with their light troops and better marksmen who, protected by trees, delivered a most murderous fire on us. . . . The different attacks, almost all afternoon and almost everywhere, were made with the greatest of vigor. . . .

July 9. The day was devoted to . . . burying our dead and those the enemy had left on the field of battle. Our companies of volunteers went out, advanced up to the falls, and reported that the enemy had abandoned the posts at the falls and even at the portage.

This victory which, for the moment, has saved Canada, is due to the sagacity of the dispositions, to the good maneuvers of our generals before and during the action, and to the unbelievable valor of our troops. . . .

July 29: Certain people [French colonists] are talking a lot of going home. They never made war [European-style] in Canada before 1755. They never had gone into camp. To leave Montreal with a party, to go through the woods, to take a few scalps, to return at full speed once the blow was struck, that is what they called war, a campaign, a success, victory. . . .

Now war is established here on the European basis. Projects for the campaign, for armies, for artillery, for sieges, for battles. It no longer is a matter of making a raid, but of conquering or being conquered. What a revolution! What a change! One would believe that the people of this country, at the novelty of these objects, would ask some time to accustom themselves to it, some more time to reflect on what they have seen. . . . On the contrary, townsmen, bankers, merchants, officers, bishops, parish priests, Jesuits, all plan this [war against English troops], speak of it, discuss it, pronounce on it.

Great misfortune for this country: it will perish, victim of its prejudices, the stupidity or of the roguery of its chiefs.

Source: *Adventure in the Wilderness: The American Journals of Louis Antonine De Bougainville*, trans. and ed. Edward P. Hamilton (Norman: University of Oklahoma Press, 1964).

capturing nearly every British garrison west of Fort Niagara, besieging the fort at Detroit, and killing or capturing over 2,000 frontier settlers. But the Indian alliance gradually weakened, and British military expeditions defeated the Delawares near Fort Pitt and broke the siege of Detroit. In the peace settlement that followed, Pontiac and his allies accepted the British as their new political "fathers." In return, the British addressed some of the Indians' concerns, temporarily barring Anglo-Americans from settling west of the Appalachians by establishing the Proclamation Line of 1763. Thus, in the aftermath of the Great War for Empire, the British crown took control of Canada and decided not to provide land for the expansion-minded American colonists.

British Economic Growth and the Consumer Revolution

Britain owed its military and diplomatic success in large part to its unprecedented economic resources. Since 1700, when it had wrested control of many oceanic trade routes from the Dutch, Britain had been the dominant commercial power in the Atlantic and Indian Oceans. By 1750 it was becoming the first country to undergo industrialization. Its new technology and work discipline made Britain the first—and for over a century the most powerful—industrial nation in the world.

The new machines and new business practices of the Industrial Revolution allowed Britain to produce more wool and linens, more iron tools, paper, chinaware, and glass than ever before—and to sell those goods at lower prices. British artisans had designed and built water- and steam-driven machines that powered lathes for shaping wood, jennies and looms for spinning and weaving textiles, and hammers for forging iron. The new machines produced goods far more rapidly than human hands could. Furthermore, the entrepreneurs who ran the new factories drove their employees hard, forcing them to keep pace with the machines and work long hours. To market the resulting products, English and Scottish merchants launched aggressive campaigns in the rapidly growing mainland colonies, extending a full year's credit to American traders instead of the traditional six months.

This first "consumer revolution" raised the living standard of many Americans, who soon were purchasing 20 percent of all British exports and paying for them by increasing their exports of wheat, rice, and tobacco (Figure 4.4). For example, Scottish merchants

financed the settlement of the Virginia Piedmont, a region of plains and rolling hills just inland from the Tidewater counties. They granted planters and Scots-Irish migrants ample credit to purchase land, slaves, and equipment and took their tobacco crop in payment, exporting it to expanding markets in France and central Europe. In South Carolina planters supported their luxurious lifestyle by using British government subsidies to develop indigo plantations. By the 1760s they were exporting large quantities of the deep blue dye to English textile factories as well as exporting about 65 million pounds of rice a year to Holland and southern Europe. Simultaneously, New York, Pennsylvania, Maryland, and Virginia became the breadbasket of the Atlantic world, supplying Europe's exploding population with wheat at ever-increasing profits. In Philadelphia wheat prices jumped almost 50 percent between 1740 and 1765.

This first American spending binge, like most subsequent splurges, landed many consumers in debt. Even during the boom times of the 1750s and early 1760s exports paid for only 80 percent of imported British goods. The remaining 20 percent—millions of pounds—was financed by Britain, both by the extension of mercantile credit and by Pitt's military expenditures in the colonies. As the war wound down, the loss of military supply contracts and cash subsidies made it more difficult for Americans to purchase British goods. Colonial merchants looked anxiously at their overstocked warehouses and feared bankruptcy. "I think we have a gloomy prospect before us," a Philadelphia trader noted in 1765, "as there are of late some Persons failed, who were in no way suspected." The increase in transatlantic trade had

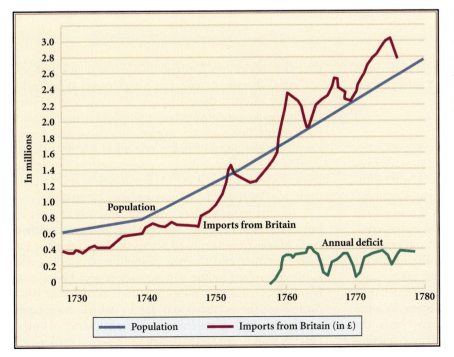

FIGURE 4.4 Colonial Population, Imports from Britain, and the American Trade Deficit

Around 1750 the rate of growth of imports from Britain into the American colonies outpaced the settlers' rate of population growth, indicating that consumption per capita was increasing. The colonists then went into debt to pay for these goods, running an annual deficit with their British suppliers.

New York Manor

The Philipse Manor stretched over ninety thousand acres and included mills and warehouses as well as a grand manor house. In this unattributed painting, the artist garbs the women in the foreground in classical costumes, thereby linking the Philipses to the noble families of the Roman republic. To preserve their aristocratic lifestyle and the quasi-feudal leasehold system of agriculture, the Philipses joined other Hudson River manorial lords in suppressing the tenant uprisings of the 1760s.
Historic Hudson Valley, Tarrytown, New York.

raised living standards but also had made Americans more dependent on overseas creditors and international economic conditions.

Land Conflicts

In good times and bad the colonial population continued to grow, causing increased conflicts over land rights. The families who founded the town of Kent, Connecticut, in 1738 had lived in the colony for a century. Each generation sons and daughters had moved westward to establish new farms, but now they lived at the generally accepted western boundary of the colony. To provide for the next generation, Kent families joined other Connecticut farmers in 1749 to form the Susquehanna Company, a land-speculating venture. Hoping to settle the Wyoming Valley in northeastern Pennsylvania, the company petitioned the legislature to assert jurisdiction

over that region on the basis of Connecticut's "sea-to-sea" royal charter of 1662. But King Charles II had subsequently granted these lands to William Penn, whose family invoked its proprietary rights and issued its own land grants. Soon settlers from Connecticut and Pennsylvania were burning down one another's houses. To avert further violence the two governments referred the dispute to the authorities in London, where it remained undecided at the time of independence (Map 4.6).

Simultaneously, three different land disputes broke out in the Hudson River Valley. First, groups of settlers from Massachusetts moved across the imprecise border with New York and claimed freehold estates on manor lands controlled by the Van Rensselaer and Livingston families. Second, the Wappinger Indians asserted legal claims to their traditional lands, which had been granted by English governors to various manorial lords. Finally, Dutch and German tenants asserted ownership

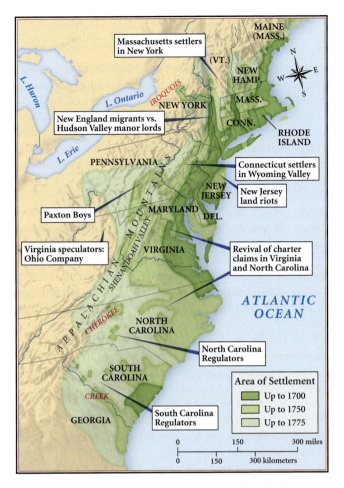

MAP 4.6 Westward Expansion and Land Conflicts, 1750–1775

Between 1750 and 1775 the mainland population doubled— from 1.2 million to 2.5 million—sparking westward migration and legal battles over land, which had become increasingly valuable. Violence broke out in many areas, as tenant farmers and smallholders contested landlord titles in eastern areas and backcountry settlers fought with Indians, rival claimants, and eastern-dominated governments.

proprietors of 1660, to collect an annual tax on land in North Carolina; another decision awarded ownership of the entire northern neck of Virginia (along the Potomac River) to Lord Fairfax.

This revival of proprietary power underscored the growing strength of the landed gentry and the increasing resemblance between rural societies in Europe and America. High-quality land on the Atlantic coastal plain was getting more expensive, and English aristocrats, manorial landlords, and wealthy speculators had control of much of it. Tenants and even yeomen farmers feared they soon might be reduced to the status of European peasants and searched for cheap freehold land in western regions near the Appalachian Mountains.

Western Uprisings

Movement to the western frontier created new disputes over Indian policy, political representation, and debts. During the war with France, Delaware and Shawnee warriors had attacked farms throughout central and western Pennsylvania, destroying property and killing and capturing hundreds of residents. Subsequently, the Scots-Irish who lived along the frontier wanted to push the Indians out of the colony, but pacifistic Quakers prevented such military action. In 1763 a band of Scots-Irish farmers known as the Paxton Boys took matters into their own hands and massacred twenty members of the peaceful Conestoga tribe. When Governor John Penn tried to bring the murderers to justice, about 250 armed Scots-Irish advanced on Philadelphia, prompting mobilization of the militia. Benjamin Franklin intercepted the angry mob at Lancaster and arranged a truce, narrowly averting a pitched battle. Prosecution of the accused men failed for lack of witnesses. Although the Scots-Irish dropped their demand for the expulsion of the Indians, the episode left a legacy of racial hatred and political resentment.

The South Carolina Regulators. Violence also broke out in the backcountry of South Carolina, where land-hungry Scottish and Anglo-American settlers had clashed repeatedly with Cherokees during the war with France. After the war ended in 1763, a group of landowning vigilantes, the Regulators, tried to suppress outlaw bands of whites that were roaming the countryside and stealing cattle and other property. The Regulators also wanted greater political rights for their region and demanded that the eastern-controlled government provide them with more local courts, fairer taxes, and greater local representation in the provincial assembly. The South Carolina government, which was dominated by lowland rice planters, decided to compromise with the Regulators because it feared slave revolts if the militia was away in the backcountry. In 1767 the assembly agreed to create locally controlled courts in the western counties of the colony

rights to farms they had long held by lease and, when the landlords ignored their claims, refused to pay rent. By 1766 the tenants in Westchester, Dutchess, and Albany Counties were in open rebellion against their landlords and used mob violence to close the courts. At the behest of the royal governor, General Thomas Gage and two British regiments joined local sheriffs and manorial bailiffs to suppress the tenant uprising, intimidate the Wappinger Indians, and evict the Massachusetts squatters.

Other land disputes erupted in New Jersey and the southern colonies, where resident landowners and English aristocrats successfully asserted legal claims based on long-dormant seventeenth-century charters. For example, one court decision upheld the right of Lord Granville, an heir of one of the original Carolina

and reduce the fees for legal documents. However, it refused to reapportion the assembly or lower western taxes. Eventually a rival backcountry group, the Moderators, raised an armed force of its own and forced the Regulators to accept the authority of the colonial government. Like the Paxton Boys in Pennsylvania, the South Carolina Regulators attracted attention to western needs but ultimately failed to wrest power from the eastern elite.

Civil Strife in North Carolina. In 1766 another Regulator movement arose in the newly settled backcountry of North Carolina. After the Great War for Empire tobacco prices plummeted, and many debt-ridden farmers were forced into court. Eastern judges directed sheriffs to seize the property of bankrupt farmers and auction it off to pay creditors and court costs. Backcountry farmers—many of them migrants from Germany—resented merchants' lawsuits, not just because they generated high fees for lawyers and court officials but also because they violated rural custom. In both the Old

and New Worlds, smallholding farmers made loans among neighbors on trust and often allowed the loans to remain unpaid for years.

To save their farms from grasping creditors and tax-hungry local officials, North Carolina debtors joined together in a Regulator movement. Disciplined mobs of farmers intimidated judges, closed down courts, and broke into jails to free their comrades. Their leader, Herman Husband, focused his attention on misbehavior of local officials, urging his followers not to vote for "any Clerk, Lawyer, or Scotch merchant. We must make these men subject to the laws or they will enslave the whole community." But the North Carolina Regulators also proposed a coherent program of reforms, demanding passage of a law allowing them to pay their taxes in the "produce of the country" rather than in cash. They insisted on lower legal fees, greater legislative representation, and fairer taxes, proposing that each person be taxed "in proportion to the profits arising from his estate." In May 1771 Royal Governor William Tryon mobilized British troops and the eastern militia and defeated a large Regulator force at the Alamance River; at the end of the fighting thirty men lay dead and seven insurgent leaders were summarily executed. Not since Leisler's revolt in New York in 1689 (see Chapter 3) had a domestic political conflict caused so much bloodshed in America.

In 1770 as in 1689, colonial conflicts became intertwined with imperial politics. In Connecticut the Reverend Ezra Stiles defended the North Carolina Regulators. "What shall an injured & oppressed people do," he asked, when faced with "Oppression and tyranny (under the name of Government)?" Stiles's remarks reflected growing resistance to British imperial control, a result of the profound changes that had occurred in the mainland colonies between 1720 and 1765. America was still a dependent society closely tied to Britain by trade, culture, and politics, but it was also an increasingly complex society with the potential for an independent existence. British policies would determine the direction the maturing colonies would take.

History and Memory
This visually striking highway marker, erected by a government agency in North Carolina, offers an official—and only partially correct—view of the past. Rather than assail the Regulators as extralegal vigilantes or outright lawbreakers (as many observers did at the time), the marker shrouds them in patriotism, as innocent victims of a vengeful British governor.
Alamance Battle Field, photo by Mike Mayse.

FOR FURTHER EXPLORATION

▶ For definitions of key terms boldfaced in this chapter, see the glossary at the end of the book.

▶ To assess your mastery of the material covered in this chapter, see the Online Study Guide at **bedfordstmartins.com/henretta**.

▶ For suggested references, including Web sites, see page SR-4 at the end of the book.

▶ For map resources and primary documents, see **bedfordstmartins.com/henretta**.

Between 1700 and 1760 Britain's mainland colonies grew dramatically in numbers and wealth. A freeholding yeoman society flourished in New England. Men exercised firm authority within families, controlling their wives' property and providing inheritances for their children. As population growth threatened the freehold ideal, New England farmers averted a crisis by planting higher-yielding crops, sharing their labor and goods with one another, or moving to new frontier settlements.

In the Middle Atlantic colonies, farmers prospered because of the rising European demand for wheat. A great influx of Germans and Scots-Irish created an ethnically and religiously diverse society and led to sharp conflicts with the Quakers over Indian policy and access to political power. Economic inequality increased as gentlemen farmers and entrepreneurs grew wealthy and a substantial group of landless workers appeared at the bottom of the social order.

As the American colonies developed closer ties with Europe, they partook of its intellectual life. The rationalism of the European Enlightenment prompted educated Americans such as Benjamin Franklin to become deists and social reformers, while pietistic religion from Germany and England reinvigorated colonial churches. In the 1740s, the preaching of George Whitefield prompted a Great Awakening that brought spiritual renewal and cultural conflict. In the northern colonies enthusiastic New Lights condemned traditional Old Lights, while in Virginia evangelical Baptists converted white tenant farmers and enslaved blacks, challenging the dominance of the Anglican elite.

At midcentury a variety of conflicts disrupted American life. Rival claims to the trans-Appalachian west sparked a major war between Britain and France that ended with the British conquest of Canada. The peace treaty excluded the French from North America, destroying the "playoff system" of the Iroquois and other native American peoples. Within the British colonies, landed proprietors battled with dissident tenants in New York and used the courts to uphold their land claims in Pennsylvania, Virginia, and the Carolinas. In the backcountry of Pennsylvania and the Carolinas yeomen farmers fought with Indians and formed Regulator movements to challenge eastern-controlled governments. Britain's North American settlements had become mature, conflict-ridden provinces.

1700– 1714	New Hudson River manors created
1710s– 1730s	Enlightenment ideas spread from Europe to America
	Deists rely on "natural reason" to define a moral code
1720s	Germans and Scots-Irish settle in the Middle Atlantic colonies
	Theodore Jacob Frelinghuysen preaches Pietism to German migrants
1730s	William and Gilbert Tennent lead Presbyterian revivals among Scots-Irish
	Jonathan Edwards preaches in New England
1739	George Whitefield sparks the Great Awakening
1740s– 1760s	Growing shortage of farmland in New England
	Religious and ethnic pluralism in the Middle Atlantic colonies
	Rising grain and tobacco prices
	Increasing rural inequality
1740s	Great Awakening sparks conflict between Old Lights and New Lights
	Colleges established by religious denominations
1743	Benjamin Franklin founds the American Philosophical Society
1749	Virginia speculators create the Ohio Company
	Connecticut farmers form the Susquehanna Company
1750s	Industrial Revolution begins in England
	Consumer revolution increases American imports and debt to Britain
1754	French and Indian War begins
	Meeting of Iroquois and Americans at Albany; Plan of Union
1756	Britain begins the Great War for Empire
1759	Britain captures Quebec
1760s	Land conflict along the border between New York and New England
	Regulator movements in the Carolinas suppress outlaw bands and seek power
	Baptist revivals in Virginia
1763	Pontiac's uprising leads to the Proclamation of 1763
	Treaty of Paris ends the Great War for Empire
	Scots-Irish Paxton Boys massacre Indians in Pennsylvania

CHAPTER 5

Toward Independence: Years of Decision

1763–1775

The Imperial Reform Movement, 1763–1765
The Legacy of War
The Sugar Act and Colonial Rights
An Open Challenge: The Stamp Act

The Dynamics of Rebellion, 1765–1766
The Crowd Rebels
Ideological Roots of Resistance
Parliament Compromises, 1766

The Growing Confrontation, 1767–1770
The Townshend Initiatives
America Again Debates and Resists
Lord North Compromises, 1770

The Road to War, 1771–1775
The Compromise Ignored
The Continental Congress Responds
The Rising of the Countryside
The Failure of Compromise

As THE GREAT WAR FOR EMPIRE ENDED IN 1763, Seth Metcalf and many other American colonists rejoiced over the triumph of British arms. A Massachusetts veteran just returned from the war, Metcalf thanked "the Great Goodness of God" for the "General Peace" that was so "percularly Advantageous to the English Nation." Two years later, Metcalf saw God's dialogue with his chosen Puritan people in very different terms. "God is angry with us of this land," the pious Puritan wrote in his journal, "and is now Smiting [us] with his Rod Especially by the hands of our [British] Rulers."

The rapid disintegration of the bonds uniting Britain and America—events that Metcalf explained in terms of Divine Providence—mystified many Americans. How had it happened, asked the president of King's College in New York in 1775, that such a "happily situated" people had armed themselves and were ready to "hazard their Fortunes, their Lives, and their Souls, in a Rebellion"? Unlike other colonial peoples of the time, the majority of white Americans had enjoyed life in a prosperous and relatively free society with a strong tradition of self-government. They had little to gain and much to lose by rebelling.

◀ **British Troops Occupy Concord**
In April 1775, hundreds of British troops stationed in Boston marched to Lexington and Concord, Massachusetts, searching houses for arms and munitions. The raid prompted a violent and deadly confrontation with the Patriot militia, an outcome prefigured by the unknown artist's depiction of a graveyard in the foreground.
Courtesy, Concord Museum.

Britain Triumphant

Celebrating the Great War for Empire, this painting honors George III, "The Best of Kings," and praises two wartime heroes, Prime Minister William Pitt and General James Wolfe, who was killed in the battle of Quebec. The artist also offers a political message with real Whig overtones, warning the king against "Evil and Corrupt Ministers."
Courtesy, American Antiquarian Society.

Or so it seemed in 1765, before the British government attempted to reform the imperial system. The long overdue but disastrous administrative reforms prompted a violent response, beginning a downward spiral of ideological debate and political conflict that ended in civil war. "This year Came an act from England Called the Stamp Act . . . ," Metcalf reflected, "which is thought will be very oppressive to the Inhabitants of North America . . . But Mobbs keep it back." This course of events was far from inevitable. Careful British statecraft and political compromise could have saved the empire. Instead, inflexible negative responses to passionate Patriot agitation brought about its demise.

The Imperial Reform Movement, 1763–1765

The Great War for Empire left a mixed legacy. By driving the French out of Canada, Britain had achieved dominance over eastern North America (Map 5.1). But the cost of the triumph was high: a mountain of debt that prompted the British ministry to impose new taxes on its American possessions. More fundamentally, the war spurred Parliament to redefine the character of the empire, moving from an administrative system based on self-government and trade to one centered on rule by imperial officials.

The Legacy of War

The war fundamentally changed the relationship between Britain and its American colonies. During the fighting, there were major conflicts between colonial leaders and British generals over funding, military appointments, and policy objectives. Moreover, the massive presence of British troops revealed sharp cultural differences between colonies and the home country. In particular, the arrogance of British officers and their demands for social deference shocked many Americans. A Massachusetts militiaman wrote in his diary that British soldiers "are but little better than slaves to their officers." The disdain was mutual. General James Wolfe complained that colonial troops were drawn from the dregs of society and that "there was no depending on them in action."

Disputes over Trade and Troops.   The war also exposed the weak political position of British royal governors and other officials. In theory governors had extensive political powers, including command of the provincial militia; in reality they had to share power with the colonial assemblies, outraging British officials. The Board of Trade complained that in Massachusetts "almost every act of executive and legislative power is ordered and directed by votes and resolves of the General Court." To enhance the authority of the crown in America, British officials began a strict enforcement of

▶ **MAP 5.1 The Eurasian Trade System and European Colonies, c. 1770**

Western European dominance of maritime trade after 1650 spurred the creation of overseas colonies. By 1770 Spain controlled the western halves of North and South America, Portugal dominated Brazil, and Holland ruled Indonesia. Britain, a newcomer on the imperial scene, boasted a far-flung empire, with settler societies in eastern North America, rich Caribbean sugar islands, slave ports in West Africa, and a growing presence on the Indian subcontinent. Only France had failed to sustain a significant colonial empire. (To trace changes in trade and empires over time, see also Map 1.4 on p. 22 and Map 2.2 on p. 46.)

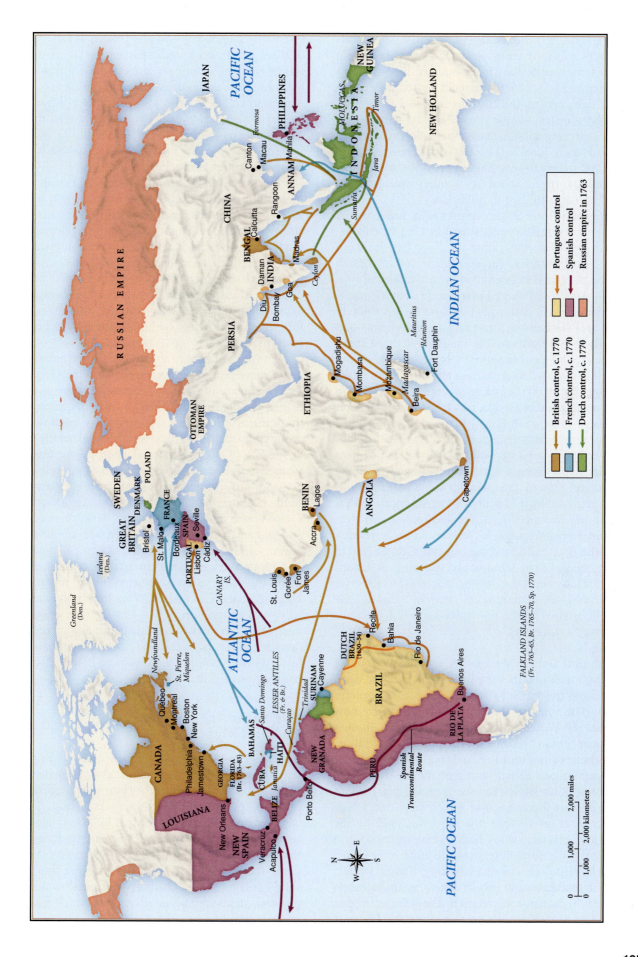

PACIFIC OCEAN

JAPAN

RUSSIAN EMPIRE

CHINA

Canton
Macau

PHILIPPINES

Manila

ANNAM

Rangoon

INDONESIA

MOLUCCAS

NEW GUINEA

NEW HOLLAND

Calcutta

BENGAL

Daman
Diu
INDIA

Bombay
Goa

Madras

Ceylon

Sumatra

Java

Timor

Formosa

PERSIA

OTTOMAN EMPIRE

ETHIOPIA

Mogadishu

Mombasa

Mozambique
Madagascar

Beira

Fort Dauphin

Mauritius

Réunion

INDIAN OCEAN

BENIN
Lagos

Accra

ANGOLA

Capetown

SWEDEN
DENMARK
POLAND

GREAT BRITAIN

Bristol

St. Malo
Bordeaux
FRANCE
SPAIN
Seville
Lisbon
PORTUGAL
Cádiz

CANARY IS.

St. Louis
Gorée
Fort James

ATLANTIC OCEAN

Iceland (Den.)

Greenland (Den.)

Newfoundland

St. Pierre,
Miquelon

Québec
Montreal
Boston
New York
CANADA

Philadelphia
Jamestown
GEORGIA
FLORIDA
(Br. 1763–83)

CUBA
BAHAMAS
Santo Domingo
Jamaica
HAITI
LESSER ANTILLES
(Fr. & Br.)
Curaçao

BELIZE

NEW SPAIN
Veracruz
Acapulco
New Orleans
LOUISIANA

Porto Bello

NEW GRANADA

PERU

Trinidad
SURINAM
Cayenne

Recife
Bahia
DUTCH BRAZIL
(1630–54)
Rio de Janeiro

BRAZIL

Buenos Aires
RIO DE LA PLATA

Spanish Transcontinental Route

FALKLAND ISLANDS
(Fr. 1763–65, Br. 1765–70, Sp. 1770)

PACIFIC OCEAN

N
E
W
S

0   1,000   2,000 miles
0   1,000   2,000 kilometers

Portuguese control
Spanish control
Russian empire in 1763

British control, c. 1770
French control, c. 1770
Dutch control, c. 1770

135

the Navigation Acts. Before the war colonial merchants had routinely bribed customs officials to avoid paying the duties imposed by the Molasses Act of 1733. To curb such corruption, in 1762 Parliament passed a Revenue Act that tightened up the customs service. In addition, the ministry instructed the Royal Navy to seize vessels that were carrying goods between the mainland colonies and the French islands. The fact that French armies attempting "to Destroy one English province, are actually supported by Bread raised in another" was absurd, declared an outraged British politician.

The victory over France provoked a fundamental shift in imperial military policy, and in 1763 Britain deployed a large peacetime army of about ten thousand men in North America. The decision to station British troops on the mainland stemmed from a variety of motives. King George III wanted to maintain a large army so that he would have patronage positions for his military friends, and he needed someplace to put them—and somebody to pay for them. His ministers worried about the defense of the newly acquired colonies of Quebec and Florida. They wanted to discourage any thought of rebellion among the 60,000 French residents of Canada and to prevent an invasion of Florida, which Spain wanted back. Moreover, Pontiac's rebellion had nearly overwhelmed Britain's frontier forts. It underscored the need for substantial military garrisons both to restrain the Indians and to deter land-hungry whites from settling west of the Proclamation Line of 1763. Finally, some British politicians worried about the loyalty of the American settlers now that they no longer needed protection from an invasion from French Canada. As William Knox, a treasury official who once had served the crown in Georgia, put it: "The main purpose of Stationing a large Body of Troops in America is to secure the Dependence of the Colonys on Great Britain." By stationing an army in America, the British ministry was indicating its willingness to use force to preserve its authority.

The National Debt.   Yet another significant result of the war was the rapid increase in Britain's national debt, which soared from £75 million in 1754 to £133 million in 1763. The interest charges on the war debt now consumed 60 percent of the annual budget, forcing cutbacks in other government expenditures. Lord Bute, who became prime minister in 1760, needed to raise taxes—certainly in Britain and perhaps in America as well. However, his advisors in the Treasury Department advised against increasing the British land tax, which was already at an all-time high and was paid by the propertied classes, who had great influence in Parliament. Therefore, Bute taxed the underrepresented poor and middling classes, imposing higher import duties on tobacco and sugar, which manufacturers passed on to British consumers in the form of higher prices. The ministry also increased **excise levies**—

essentially sales taxes—on goods such as salt, beer, and distilled spirits, once again passing on the costs of the war to the king's ordinary subjects. Left unresolved for the moment was the question of imposing taxes on the American colonists, who also had little political power in Parliament. However, ministers knew that free Americans paid only about five shillings a year in imperial taxes, while British taxpayers were liable for nearly five times as much.

To collect these taxes and duties, the British government doubled the size of its bureaucracy and increased its powers. Customs agents and informers patrolled the coasts of southern Britain, arresting smugglers and seizing tons of goods, such as French wines and Flemish textiles, on which import duties had not been paid. Convicted smugglers faced heavy penalties, including death or "transportation" to America as indentured servants. Despite protests by colonial assemblies, nearly fifty thousand English criminals had already been banished to America.

The price of empire abroad had turned out to be debt and a more powerful government at home (Figure 5.1). The emergence of a big and expensive government confirmed the predictions of the British opposition parties, the **Radical Whigs** and Country Party landlords. Both groups argued that the huge war debt had left the treasury at the mercy of the "monied interest," the banks and financiers who were reaping millions of pounds in interest from government bonds. Moreover, the expansion of the tax bureaucracy had created thousands of patronage positions that were filled with "worthless pensioners and placemen." To reverse the growth of government power—and the consequent threats to personal liberty and property rights—reformers demanded that Parliament be made more representative of the property-owning classes. The Radical Whig John Wilkes called for an end to **rotten boroughs**—tiny districts whose voters were controlled by wealthy aristocrats and merchants. In domestic affairs as in colonial policy, the war had transformed British political life, creating a more active and intrusive government.

The Sugar Act and Colonial Rights

The active exercise of government power was particularly apparent in American affairs as a new generation of British officials undertook a systematic reform of the imperial system. The first to act was George Grenville, who became prime minister in 1763. Grenville quickly won Parliamentary approval of a Currency Act (1764) that protected British merchants by banning the use of paper money (which was often worth less than its face value) as legal tender. Ordinary colonists would have to pay their debts in gold or silver coin, which was always in short supply.

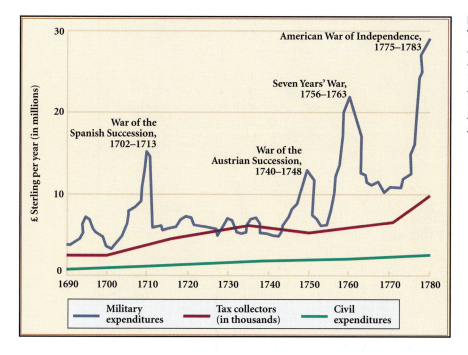

FIGURE 5.1 The Growing Power of the British State

As Britain built a great navy and subsidized the armies of its European allies, the government's military expenditures soared, as did the number of tax collectors. The tax bureaucracy more than doubled in size between 1700 and 1735 and increased sharply again between 1750 and 1780.

The Sugar Act. Then Grenville proposed a new Navigation Act, the Sugar Act of 1764, to replace the widely evaded Molasses Act of 1733. The new legislation was well thought-out. Treasury officials who understood the pattern of colonial trade convinced Grenville that the mainland settlers had to sell some of their wheat, fish, and lumber in the French islands. Without the molasses, sugar, and bills of exchange those sales brought, the officials pointed out, the colonists would lack the funds to buy British manufactured goods. Armed with this knowledge, Grenville resisted demands from British sugar planters for a duty of 6 pence per gallon that would completely cut off colonial imports of French molasses. Instead, he settled on a smaller duty of 3 pence per gallon, arguing that it would allow molasses from the British islands to compete with the cheaper French product without destroying the trade of the North American mainland colonies or their distilling industry (Map 5.2).

This carefully crafted policy garnered little support in America. Many New England merchants, such as John Hancock of Boston, had made their fortunes by smuggling French molasses and thus had never paid the duty. Their profits would be cut severely if the new regulations were enforced. These merchants and New England distillers, who feared a rise in the price of molasses, campaigned publicly against the Sugar Act, claiming that the new tax would wipe out trade with the French islands. Privately, they vowed to evade the duty by smuggling or by bribing officials.

Constitutional Issues. More important, the merchants and their allies raised constitutional objections to the new legislation. The speaker of the Massachusetts House of Representatives argued that the duties constituted a tax, making the Sugar Act "contrary to a fundamental Principall of our Constitution: That all Taxes ought to originate with the people." The Sugar Act raised other constitutional issues as well. Merchants accused of violating the act would be tried by **vice-admiralty courts**—maritime tribunals composed only of a judge—and not by a local common-law jury. For half a century American legislatures had vigorously opposed vice-admiralty courts, expanding the jurisdiction of colonial courts to cover customs offenses occurring in the seaports. As a result, most merchants charged with violating the Navigation Acts were tried in common-law courts and were often acquitted by friendly local juries. By extending the jurisdiction of vice-admiralty courts to all customs offenses, the Sugar Act closed this loophole.

The new powers given to the vice-admiralty courts revived old American fears and complaints. The influential Virginia planter Richard Bland reminded his fellow settlers that for many decades the colonies had been subject to the Navigation Acts, which restricted their manufactures and commerce. But, he protested, the colonists "were not sent out to be the Slaves but to be the Equals of those that remained behind." John Adams, a young Massachusetts lawyer who was defending merchant John Hancock on a charge of smuggling, similarly condemned the new vice-admiralty courts, saying that they "degrade every American . . . below the rank of an Englishman."

While the logic of these arguments was compelling, some of the facts were wrong. The Navigation Acts certainly discriminated against the colonists; indeed, they were expressly intended to assist British-based merchants

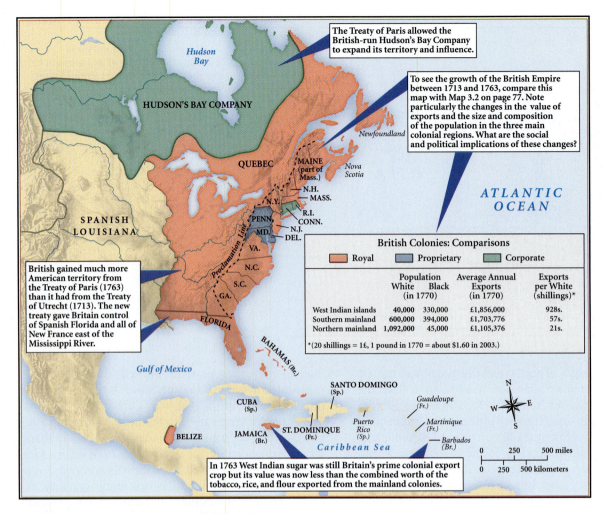

The Treaty of Paris allowed the British-run Hudson's Bay Company to expand its territory and influence.

To see the growth of the British Empire between 1713 and 1763, compare this map with Map 3.2 on page 77. Note particularly the changes in the value of exports and the size and composition of the population in the three main colonial regions. What are the social and political implications of these changes?

British gained much more American territory from the Treaty of Paris (1763) than it had from the Treaty of Utrecht (1713). The new treaty gave Britain control of Spanish Florida and all of New France east of the Mississippi River.

British Colonies: Comparisons

Royal   Proprietary   Corporate

	Population White Black (in 1770)		Average Annual Exports (in 1770)	Exports per White (shillings)*
West Indian islands	40,000	330,000	£1,856,000	928s.
Southern mainland	600,000	394,000	£1,703,776	57s.
Northern mainland	1,092,000	45,000	£1,105,376	21s.

*(20 shillings = 1£, 1 pound in 1770 = about $1.60 in 2003.)

In 1763 West Indian sugar was still Britain's prime colonial export crop but its value was now less than the combined worth of the tobacco, rice, and flour exported from the mainland colonies.

MAP 5.2 Britain's American Empire in 1763

Following the Great War for Empire and the Treaty of Paris of 1763, Britain held a dominant position in the West Indies and controlled all of eastern North America. British ministers dispatched troops to the conquered colonies of Florida and Quebec and, with the Proclamation Line of 1763, tried to prevent Anglo-American settlement west of the Appalachian Mountains.

and manufacturers. However, the new vice-admiralty legislation did not penalize Americans; those in Britain had long been subject to the same rules. The real issue was the new spirit of imperial reform and the growing administrative power of the British state. Having lived for decades under a policy of "salutary neglect," Americans were quick to charge that the new British policies challenged the existing constitutional structure of the empire. As a committee of the Massachusetts House of Representatives put it, the Sugar Act and other British edicts "have a tendency to deprive the colonies of some of their most essential Rights as British subjects."

For their part, British officials insisted on the supremacy of Parliamentary laws and denied that the colonists were entitled to special privileges or even the traditional legal rights of Englishmen. When Royal Governor Francis Bernard of Massachusetts heard that the Massachusetts House had objected to the Sugar Act,

claiming no taxation without representation, he asserted that Americans did not have that constitutional right. "The rule that a British subject shall not be bound by laws or liable to taxes, but what he has consented to by his representatives," Bernard argued, "must be confined to the inhabitants of Great Britain only." In the eyes of most officials and politicians who now held power in Britain, the Americans were second-class subjects of the king, their rights limited by the Navigation Acts and the interests of the British state, as determined by Parliament.

An Open Challenge: The Stamp Act

The issue of taxation sparked the first great imperial crisis. When Grenville introduced the Sugar Act in 1764, he planned to seek a stamp tax the following

George Grenville, Architect of the Stamp Act
As prime minister from 1764 to 1766, Grenville assumed leadership of the movement for imperial reform and taxation. This portrait of 1763 suggests Grenville's energy and ambition. As events were to show, the new minister was determined to reform the imperial system and ensure that the colonists shared the cost of the empire. The Earl of Halifax, Garrowby, Yorkshire.

The Stamp Act
The official document that would fan the flames of resistance in America begins in Latin, the ancient language of law and authority: "In the fifth year of the reign of George III. . . ." By imposing a direct tax on the colonists, the new legislation ignited a storm of opposition, much of it violent, and began a decade-long political confrontation between British ministers and American Patriots. Library of Congress.

year. This new levy would cover part of the cost of keeping ten thousand British troops in America—some £200,000 per year (about $20 million today). The tax would raise revenue by requiring small embossed markings (somewhat like today's postage stamps) on all court documents, land titles, contracts, playing cards, newspapers, and other printed items. A similar tax in England was yielding an annual revenue of £290,000; Grenville hoped the American levy would raise at least £60,000 a year. The prime minister knew that some Americans would object to the tax on constitutional grounds, and so he asked explicitly whether any member of the House of Commons doubted "the power and sovereignty of Parliament over every part of the British dominions, for the purpose of raising or collecting any tax." No one rose to object.

Confident of Parliament's support, Grenville vowed to impose a stamp tax in 1765 unless the colonists would tax themselves. This challenge threw the London representatives of the colonial legislatures into confusion because they did not see how the American assemblies could collectively raise and apportion their defense budget. Representatives from the various colonies had met together officially only once, at the Albany Congress of 1754, and not a single assembly had accepted that body's proposals. Benjamin Franklin, who was in Britain as the representative of the Pennsylvania assembly, proposed another solution to Grenville's challenge: American representation in Parliament. "If you chuse to tax us," he suggested to an influential British friend, "give us Members in your Legislature, and let us be one People."

With the exception of William Pitt, British politicians rejected Franklin's radical idea. They argued that the colonists were already **"virtually" represented** in the home legislature by the merchants who sat in Parliament and by other members with interests in America. Colonial leaders were equally skeptical. Americans were "situate at a great Distance from their Mother Country," the Connecticut assembly declared, and therefore "cannot participate in the general Legislature of the Nation." Influential merchants in Philadelphia, worried that a handful of colonial delegates would be powerless in Parliament, warned Franklin "to beware of any measure that might extend to us seats in the Commons."

The way was now clear for Grenville to introduce the Stamp Act. His goal was not only to raise revenue but also to assert a constitutional principle: "the Right of Parliament to lay an internal Tax upon the Colonies," as his chief assistant declared. The ministry's plan worked smoothly. The House of Commons refused to accept American petitions opposing the act and passed the new legislation by an overwhelming vote of 205 to 49. At the request of General Thomas Gage, commander of the British military forces in America, Parliament also passed a Quartering Act directing colonial governments to provide barracks and food for the British troops stationed in the colonies. Finally, Parliament approved Grenville's proposal that violations of the Stamp Act be tried in vice-admiralty courts.

The design was complete. Using the doctrine of Parliamentary supremacy, Grenville had begun to fashion a genuinely imperial administrative system run by British officials without regard for the American assemblies. He thus provoked a constitutional confrontation not only on the specific issues of taxation, jury trials, and quartering of the military but also on the fundamental question of representative self-government.

The Dynamics of Rebellion, 1765–1766

Grenville had thrown down the gauntlet to the Americans. Although the colonists had often opposed unpopular laws and arbitrary governors, they had faced an all-out attack on their institutions only once—in 1686 when James II had arbitrarily imposed the Dominion of New England. Now the danger was even greater, because the new reforms were backed not only by the king and his ministers but also by the Parliament. However, the Patriots—as the defenders of American rights came to be called—took up Grenville's challenge, organizing protest meetings, rioting in the streets, and articulating an ideology of resistance.

The Crowd Rebels

In May 1765 the eloquent young Patrick Henry addressed the Virginia House of Burgesses and blamed the new king, George III (r. 1760–1820) for naming—and supporting—the ministers who designed the new legislation. Comparing George to the tyrannical Charles I who had sparked the Puritan Revolution of the 1640s, Henry seemed to call for a new republican revolution.

The Intensity of Patrick Henry

This portrait, painted in 1795 when Henry was in his sixties, captures his lifelong seriousness and intensity. As an orator, Henry drew on evangelical Protestantism to create a new mode of political oratory. "His figures of speech . . . were often borrowed from the Scriptures," a contemporary noted, and the content of his speeches mirrored "the earnestness depicted in his own features." Mead Art Museum, Amherst College.

Although Henry's remarks against the king (which bordered on treason) dismayed most of the Burgesses, they endorsed his attack on the Stamp Act, declaring that any attempt to tax the colonists without their consent "has a manifest Tendency to Destroy American freedom." In Massachusetts, James Otis, another republican-minded firebrand, persuaded the House of Representatives to call for a general meeting of all the colonies "to implore Relief" from the act.

The Stamp Act Congress. Nine colonial assemblies sent delegates to the Stamp Act Congress, which met in New York City in October 1765. The Congress issued a set of Resolves protesting against the loss of American "rights and liberties," especially trial by jury. The Resolves also challenged the constitutionality of the Stamp and Sugar Acts, declaring that only the colonists' elected representatives could impose taxes on them (see American Voices, "Samuel Adams: An American View of the Stamp Act," p. 141). However, most of the delegates were moderate men who sought compromise, not confrontation. They concluded by assuring Parliament

Samuel Adams

An American View of the Stamp Act

Thanks to his education at Harvard College, distiller Samuel Adams had impressive intellectual and literary skills. In this private letter to an English friend, Adams presents the various arguments used by British ministers to defend the new measures of imperial taxation and control. Then, in dispassionate, reasoned prose, Adams undertakes to refute them.

To John Smith
December 19, 1765

Your acquaintance with this country . . . makes you an able advocate on her behalf, at a time when her friends have everything to fear for her. . . . The [British] nation, it seems, groaning under the pressure of a very heavy debt, has thought it reasonable & just that the colonies should bear a part; and over & above the tribute which they have been continually pouring into her lap, in the course of their trade, she now demands an internal tax. The colonists complain that this is both burdensome & unconstitutional. They allege, that while the nation has been contracting this debt solely for her own interest, detached from theirs, they have [been] subduing & settling an uncultivated wilderness, & thereby increasing her power & wealth at their own expense. . . .

But it is said that this tax is to discharge the colonies' proportion of expense in carrying on the [recent] war in America, which was for their defense. To this it is said, that it does by no means appear that the war in America was carried on solely for the defense of the colonies. Had the [British] nation been only on the defensive here, a much less expense would have been sufficient; there was evidently a view of making conquests, [thereby] . . . advancing her dominion & glory. . . .

There are other things which perhaps were not considered when the nation determined this to be a proportionate tax upon the colonies. . . . The [British] nation constantly regulates their trade, & lays it under what restrictions she pleases. The duties upon the goods imported from her & consumed here . . . amount to a very great sum. . . .

There is another consideration which makes the Stamp Act obnoxious to the people here, & that is, that it totally annihilates, as they apprehend, their essential rights as Englishmen. The first settlers . . . immediately after their arrival here . . . solemnly recognized their allegiance to their sovereign in England, & the Crown graciously acknowledged them, granted them charter privileges, & declared them & their heirs forever entitled to all the liberties & immunities of free & natural born subjects of the realm. . . .

The question then is, what the rights of free subjects of Britain are? . . . It is sufficient for the present purpose to say, that the main pillars of the British Constitution are the right of representation & trial by juries, both of which the Colonists lose by this act. Their property may be tried . . . in a court of Admiralty, where there is no jury. [As for representation], no man of common sense can easily be made to believe that the colonies all together have one representative in the House of Commons, *upon their own free election.* If the colonists are free subjects of Britain, which no one denies, it should seem that the Parliament cannot tax them consistent with the Constitution, because they are not represented. . . .

Source: Harry Alonzo Cushing, ed., *The Writings of Samuel Adams* (New York: G. P. Putnam, 1904).

that Americans "glory in being subjects of the best of Kings" and humbly petitioning for repeal of the Stamp Act. Other influential Americans advocated nonviolent resistance through a boycott of British goods.

Popular resentment was not so easily contained. When the act went into effect on November 1, disciplined mobs immediately took action. Led by men who called themselves the **Sons of Liberty**, the mobs demanded the resignation of newly appointed stamp tax collectors, most of whom were native-born colonists. In Boston the Sons of Liberty made an effigy of the collector Andrew Oliver, which they beheaded and burned, and then they destroyed a new brick building he owned. Two weeks later Bostonians attacked the house of Lieutenant Governor Thomas Hutchinson, a defender of social privilege and imperial authority, breaking the furniture, looting the wine cellar, and burning the library.

A British View of American Mobs

This satiric view of the Sons of Liberty attacks their brutal treatment of John Malcolm, the commissioner of the customs in Boston, who was threatened with death (note the noose hanging from the tree) and then tarred and feathered and forced to drink huge quantities of tea. See the men in the background, disregarding property rights by pouring tea into Boston Harbor. The presence of a "Liberty Tree" implicitly poses the question Does Liberty mean Anarchy? Courtesy, John Carter Brown Library at Brown University.

The leaders of the mobs were usually middling artisans. "Spent the evening with the Sons of Liberty," John Adams wrote in his diary, "John Smith, the brazier [metalworker], Thomas Crafts, the painter, Edes, the printer, Stephen Cleverly, the brazier; Chase, the distiller; [and] Joseph Field, Master of a vessel." Some of these men had met through their work; more often they were drinking buddies, meeting nightly in the many taverns that dotted the streets and byways of the major port cities and soon became centers of political debate and Patriot agitation.

However, resistance to the Stamp Act spread far beyond the port cities. In nearly every colony crowds of angry people—the "rabble," as their detractors called them—intimidated royal officials. Near Wethersfield, Connecticut, five hundred farmers and artisans held tax collector Jared Ingersoll captive until he resigned his

office. This was "the Cause of the People," shouted one rioter, and he would not "take Directions about it from any Body." In New York nearly three thousand shopkeepers, artisans, laborers, and seamen marched through the streets, breaking street lamps and windows and crying "Liberty!"

The Motives of the Crowd.   Although the strength of the Liberty mobs was surprising, such plebeian crowd actions were a fact of life in both Britain and America. Every November 5, Protestant mobs on both sides of the Atlantic marched through the streets celebrating Guy Fawkes Day. They burned effigies of the pope to commemorate the failure in 1605 of a plot by Fawkes and other English Catholics to blow up the Houses of Parliament. Likewise, colonial mobs regularly destroyed houses used as brothels and rioted to protest the impressment of merchant seamen by the Royal Navy.

If rioting was traditional, its political goals were new. The leaders of the Sons of Liberty in New York City were Radical Whigs who feared that reform of the imperial system would undermine political liberty. These men, minor merchants such as Isaac Sears and Alexander McDougall, tried to direct the raw energy of the crowd against the new tax measures. However, the mobs drew support from established artisans, struggling journeymen, and poor laborers and seamen who had different agendas and goals. Some artisans joined the crowds because imports of low-priced British shoes and other manufactured goods threatened their livelihood, and they feared the additional burden of a stamp tax. Unlike "the Common people of England," a well-traveled colonist observed, "the people of America . . . never would submitt to be taxed that a few may be loaded with palaces and Pensions and riot in Luxury and Excess, while they themselves cannot support themselves and their needy offspring with Bread."

Other members of the crowd were stirred by the religious passions of the Great Awakening. As evangelical Protestants who led disciplined, hardworking lives, they resented the arrogance of British military officers and the corruption of royal bureaucrats. In New England, some protesters looked back to the English Puritan Revolution, reviving antimonarchical and prorepublican sentiments of their great-grandparents. A letter sent to a Boston newspaper promising to save "all the Freeborn Sons of America" from "tyrannical ministers" was signed "Oliver Cromwell," the English republican revolutionary of the 1640s. And a masked and costumed figure known as "Joyce, Jr."—named after Cornet George Joyce, who had captured King Charles I—led crowds through the Boston streets. Finally, the mobs in all areas included apprentices, journeymen, day laborers, and unemployed sailors—young men seeking adventure and excitement who, when fortified by drink, were ready to resort to violence.

Throughout the colonies popular resistance nullified the Stamp Act. Fearing a massive assault on Fort George on Guy Fawkes Day (November 5, 1765), New York lieutenant governor Cadwallader Colden called on General Gage to use his small military force to protect the stamps stored in the fort. Gage refused. "Fire from the Fort might disperse the Mob, but it would not quell them," he told Colden, and the result would be "an Insurrection, the Commencement of Civil War." Frightened collectors gave up their stamps, and angry Americans coerced officials into accepting legal documents without them. This popular insurrection gave a democratic cast to the emerging American Patriot movement, extending it far beyond the ranks of merchants, lawyers, and elected officials. "Nothing is wanting but your own Resolution," a New York Son of Liberty declared during the upheaval, "for great is the Authority and Power of the People."

Slow communication across the Atlantic meant that the ministry's response to the Stamp Act Congress and the Liberty mobs would not be known until the spring of 1766. But it was already clear that royal officials could no longer count on the deferential political behavior that had ensured the empire's stability for three generations. As the collector of the customs in Philadelphia lamented, "What can a Governor do without the assistance of the Governed?"

Ideological Roots of Resistance

Initially the American resistance movement had no acknowledged leaders and no central organization. It had arisen spontaneously in the seaport cities because urban residents were directly affected by British policies. The Stamp Act taxed the newspapers sold by printers and the contracts and court documents used by merchants and lawyers, the Sugar Act raised the cost of molasses to distillers, and the flood of British manufactures threatened the livelihood of urban artisans. All in all, an official in Rhode Island reported, the interests of Britain and the colonies were increasingly "deemed by the People almost altogether incompatible in a Commercial View." As urban merchants and crowds protested against the new measures, they found some allies in the colonial assemblies—the traditional defenders of local interests against royal governors—but the movement was slow to develop a coherent outlook and organization.

Consequently, the first protests focused narrowly on particular economic and political matters. One pamphleteer complained that colonists were being compelled to give the British "our money, as oft and in what quantity they please to demand it." Other writers alleged that the British had violated specific "liberties and privileges" embodied in colonial charters. But American Patriot publicists gradually focused the debate by defining "liberty" as an abstract ideal—a natural right of all people—rather than a set of historical privileges. Men trained as lawyers took the lead, in part because

merchants hired them to contest the seizure of their goods by customs officials. The lawyers' own professional values and training provided another motive; as practitioners of the common law they opposed extension of vice-admiralty courts and favored trial by juries. Composing pamphlets of remarkable political sophistication, Patriot publicists provided the resistance movement with an intellectual rationale, a political agenda, and a visible cadre of leaders.

Patriot publicists drew on three intellectual traditions. The first was English **common law**—the centuries-old body of legal rules and procedures that protected the king's subjects against arbitrary acts by the government. In 1761 the Boston lawyer James Otis had cited English legal precedent in the famous *Writs of Assistance* case. In that instance Otis disputed the legitimacy of a general search warrant permitting customs officials to inspect the property and possessions of any and all persons. Similarly, in demanding a jury trial for John Hancock, John Adams invoked common-law tradition. "This 29th Chap. of Magna Charta," Adams argued, referring to an ancient English document that had established the right to trial by jury, "has for many Centuries been esteemed by Englishmen, as one of the . . . firmest Bulwarks of their Liberties." Other lawyers protested when the terms of appointment for colonial judges were altered from "during good behavior" to "at the pleasure" of the royal governor, arguing that the change in wording compromised the independence of the judiciary.

A second major intellectual resource for educated Americans was the rationalist thought of the Enlightenment. Unlike American common-law attorneys, who used legal precedents to criticize British measures, the Virginia planter Thomas Jefferson invoked Enlightenment philosophers, such as David Hume and Francis Hutcheson, who questioned the past and relied on reason to discover and correct social ills. Jefferson and other Patriot authors also drew on the political philosopher John Locke, who argued that all individuals possessed certain "natural rights," such as life, liberty, and property, which government was responsible for protecting. And they celebrated the French theorist Montesquieu, who praised institutional curbs, such as the separation of powers among government departments, to prevent the arbitrary exercise of political power.

The republican and Whig strands of the English political tradition provided the third ideological basis for the American Patriot movement. In some places, particularly Puritan New England, Americans had long venerated the Commonwealth era—the brief period between 1649 and 1660 when England was a republic. After the Glorious Revolution of 1688, many colonists had welcomed the constitutional restrictions placed on the monarchy by English Whigs, such as the ban on royally imposed taxes. Later, educated Americans such as Samuel Adams of Boston absorbed the arguments of

Sam Adams, Boston Agitator

This painting by John Singleton Copley (c. 1772) shows the radical Patriot pointing to the Massachusetts Charter of 1692, suggesting that "charter rights" accounted for Samuel Adams's opposition to British policies. But Adams also was influenced by the natural rights tradition.

Deposited by the City of Boston. Courtesy, Museum of Fine Arts, Boston.

Radical Whig spokesmen who denounced political corruption. "Bribery is so common," John Dickinson of Pennsylvania had complained during a visit to London in the 1750s, "that there is not a borough in England where it is not practiced." These republican and Radical Whig sentiments made many Americans suspicious of royal officials. Joseph Warren, a physician and Patriot, reported that many Bostonians believed the Stamp Act

was part of a well-planned political conspiracy. They alleged that the new tax was intended "to force the colonies into rebellion," after which the ministry would use "military power to reduce them to servitude." As historian Alan Taylor has noted, the colonists "were quick to speak of 'slavery' because they knew from their own practice on Africans where unchecked dominion ultimately led."

These writings—swiftly disseminated thanks to the presence of a well-developed colonial printing industry and regularly published newspapers—provided the developing Patriot movement with a sense of identity and an ideological agenda, turning a series of impromptu riots and tax protests into a coherent political coalition.

Parliament Compromises, 1766

In Britain, Parliament was in turmoil, with different political factions advocating radically different responses to the American challenge. George III had replaced Grenville with a new prime minister, Lord Rockingham, who was allied with the Old Whigs and opposed Grenville's tough policies toward the colonies (Table 5.1). But hard-liners in Parliament, outraged by the popular rebellion in America, demanded that imperial reform continue. After listening to Benjamin Franklin tell Parliament that Americans would "never" pay a stamp tax "unless compelled by force of arms," they wanted to dispatch British soldiers to suppress the riots and compel the colonists to submit to the constitutional supremacy of Parliament. "The British legislature," declared Chief Justice Sir James Mansfield, "has authority to bind every part and every subject, whether such subjects have a right to vote or not."

Three factions were willing to repeal the Stamp Act, but for different reasons. The Old Whigs advocated repeal for reasons of policy: they believed that America was more important for its "flourishing and increasing trade" than for its tax revenues. Some Old Whigs even agreed with the colonists that the new tax was unconstitutional. British merchants favored repeal out of self-interest because the American boycott of British goods had caused a

TABLE 5.1 Ministerial Instability in Britain		
Leading Minister	Dates of Ministry	American Policy
Lord Bute	1760–1763	Mildly reformist
George Grenville	1763–1765	Ardently reformist
Lord Rockingham	1765–1766	Accommodationist
William Pitt/Charles Townshend	1766–1770	Ardently reformist
Lord North	1770–1782	Coercive

drastic fall in their sales. A committee of "London Merchants trading to America" mobilized support for repeal in the capital, and in January 1766 the leading commercial centers of Liverpool, Bristol, and Glasgow deluged Parliament with petitions, pointing out the threat to their prosperity. "The Avenues of Trade are all shut up," a Bristol merchant with large inventories on hand complained. "We have no Remittances and are at our Witts End for want of Money to fulfill our Engagements with our Tradesmen." Finally, former prime minister William Pitt demanded that "the Stamp Act be repealed absolutely, totally, and immediately" as a failed policy. Pitt's view of the constitutional issues was confusing. On the one hand, he argued that Parliament could not tax the colonies; on the other hand, he maintained that British authority over America was "sovereign and supreme, in every circumstance of government and legislation whatsoever." The Americans' challenge had raised new and difficult constitutional questions, to which there were few clear answers.

Rockingham gave each group just enough to feel satisfied. To assist British merchants and mollify colonial opinion, he repealed the Stamp Act and ruled out the use of troops against colonial crowds. He also modified the Sugar Act, reducing the duty on French molasses from 3 pence to 1 penny a gallon but extending it to British molasses as well. Thus, the revised Sugar Act regulated foreign trade, which most American officials accepted, but it also taxed a British product, which some colonists saw as unconstitutional. Finally, Rockingham pacified imperial reformers and hard-liners with the Declaratory Act of 1766, which explicitly reaffirmed the British Parliament's "full power and authority to make laws and statutes . . . to bind the colonies and people of America . . . in all cases whatsoever."

Because the Stamp Act crisis ended quickly, it might have been forgotten just as quickly. As of 1766 political positions had not yet hardened. Leaders of goodwill could still hope to work out an imperial relationship that was acceptable to British officials and American colonists.

The Growing Confrontation, 1767–1770

The compromise of 1766 was short lived. Within a year political rivalries in Britain sparked a new and more prolonged struggle with the American provinces, reviving the passions of 1765. The newfound ideological rigidity of key British ministers and American officials aggravated the conflict and dashed prospects for a quick resolution.

The Townshend Initiatives

Often the course of history is changed by a small event—a leader's illness, a personal grudge, a chance remark. So it was in 1767, when Rockingham's Old Whig ministry collapsed and George III named William Pitt to head the new ministry. Pitt, the master strategist of the Great War for Empire, was chronically ill with gout and frequently missed Parliamentary debates, leaving Chancellor of the Exchequer Charles Townshend in command. Pitt was sympathetic toward America; Townshend was not. Indeed, as a member of the Board of Trade in the 1750s, he had backed measures restricting the power of the colonial assemblies. So when Grenville attacked Townshend's military budget in 1767, demanding that the colonists pay for the British troops in America, Townshend made an unplanned, fateful policy decision. Long convinced of the necessity of imperial reform and eager to reduce the English land tax, he promised that he would find a new source of revenue in America.

The Townshend Act. The new tax legislation, known as the Townshend Act of 1767, had a political as well as a financial goal. The legislation imposed duties on paper, paint, glass, and tea imported into the colonies and was expected to raise about £40,000 a year. To pacify Grenville, part of this revenue would defray military expenses in America. However, the act reserved the major part of the new tax revenue to create a colonial civil list—a fund to pay the salaries of royal governors, judges, and other imperial officials. Once freed from financial dependence on the American legislatures, royal officials would be able to enforce Parliamentary laws and the king's instructions.

To increase royal power still further, Townshend also devised the Revenue Act of 1767. This act created a Board of American Customs Commissioners in Boston and vice-admiralty courts in Halifax, Boston, Philadelphia, and Charleston. These administrative innovations posed a greater threat to the autonomy of American political institutions than did the small sums raised by the import duties.

The Restraining Act. The full implications of Townshend's policies became clear in New York, where the assembly refused to comply with the Quartering Act of 1765, which required Americans to house and feed British troops. Fearing an unlimited drain on its treasury, the New York legislature first denied General Gage's requests for barracks and supplies and then limited its assistance. Pointing out that most British troops were in New York to protect against raids by hostile Indians, the ministry instructed the colony to comply fully with the Quartering Act. If the assembly refused, some members of Parliament threatened to impose a special duty on New York's imports and exports. The earl of Shelburne, the new secretary of state, was prepared to go even further. He proposed the appointment of a military governor with authority to seize funds from New York's treasury to pay for

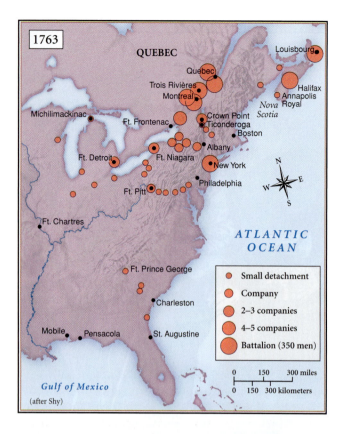

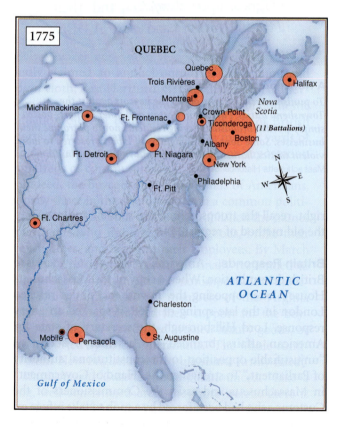

MAP 5.3 British Troop Deployments, 1763–1775

As the imperial crisis deepened, British military priorities changed. In 1763 most British battalions were stationed in Canada to deter Indian uprisings and French-Canadian revolts. After the Stamp Act riots of 1765, the British established larger garrisons in New York and Philadelphia. By 1775 eleven battalions of British regulars occupied Boston, the center of the American Patriot movement.

tenants deserted their farms and sought landed independence in America, aggravating a series of natural disasters that cut grain production. As food shortages mounted, riots spread across the English countryside. In

the highly publicized Massacre of Saint George Fields, troops killed seven demonstrators. The Radical Whig John Wilkes, supported by associations of merchants, tradesmen, and artisans, stepped up his attacks on

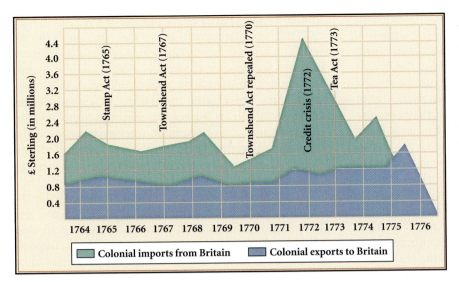

FIGURE 5.2 Trade as a Political Weapon, 1763–1776

Political upheaval did not affect the mainland colonies' exports to Britain, which remained steady (and rose slightly) over the period, but imports fluctuated greatly. The American boycott of 1768–1769 brought a sharp decline in the importation of British manufactures, which then soared after the repeal of the Townshend duties.

government corruption and won election to Parliament. Overjoyed, American Patriots drank toasts in Wilkes's honor and purchased thousands of teapots and drinking mugs emblazoned with his picture. Riots in Ireland over the growing military budget there added to the ministry's difficulties.

Nonimportation Succeeds. The American trade boycott also began to hurt the British economy. Normally the colonies had an annual trade deficit with the home country of £500,000, but in 1768 they imported less from Great Britain, cutting the deficit to £230,000. In 1769 the boycott had a major economic impact. By continuing to export tobacco, rice, fish, and other goods to Britain while refusing to buy its manufactured goods, Americans accumulated a trade surplus of £816,000 (Figure 5.2). To revive their flagging fortunes, British merchants and manufacturers petitioned Parliament for repeal of the Townshend duties. British government revenues, which were heavily dependent on excise taxes and duties on imported goods, had also suffered. By late 1769 merchants' petitions had persuaded some ministers that the Townshend duties were a mistake, and the king had withdrawn his support for Hillsborough's plan to coerce the colonies with military force.

Early in 1770 Lord North became prime minister and arranged a new compromise. Arguing that it was foolish to tax British exports to America, raising their price and decreasing consumption, North persuaded Parliament to repeal the duties on glass, paper, paint, and other manufactured items. However, he retained the tax on tea as a symbol of Parliament's supremacy. Gratified by North's initiative, merchants in New York and Philadelphia rejected pleas from Patriots in Boston to continue the boycott. Rather than contesting the symbolic levy on tea, most Americans simply avoided the tax by drinking smuggled tea provided by Dutch merchants.

Even the outbreak of violence in New York City and Boston did not rupture the compromise. During the boycott New York artisans and workers had taunted British troops, mostly with words but occasionally with stones and fists. In retaliation the soldiers tore down a Liberty Pole (a Patriot flagpole), setting off a week of street fighting. In Boston friction between the residents and British soldiers over constitutional principles and everyday issues, such as competition for part-time jobs, sparked the Boston Massacre. In March 1770, a group of soldiers fired into a rowdy crowd, killing five men, including one of the leaders, Crispus Attucks, an escaped slave who was working as a seaman. Reviving fears of a ministerial conspiracy against liberty, a Radical Whig pamphlet accused the British of deliberately planning the massacre.

Sovereignty Debated. Although most Americans ignored such charges and remained loyal to the empire, five years of conflict over taxes and constitutional principles had taken its toll. In 1765 American leaders had accepted Parliament's authority; the Stamp Act Resolves had opposed only certain "unconstitutional" legislation. By 1770 the most outspoken Patriots—Benjamin Franklin in Pennsylvania, Patrick Henry in Virginia, and Samuel Adams in Massachusetts—had repudiated Parliamentary supremacy, claiming equality for the American assemblies. Beginning from this premise, Franklin looked for a way to redefine the imperial relationship so that the colonies would have political equality within the empire. Perhaps thinking of various European "composite monarchies" (in which kings ruled far-distant and semiautonomous provinces acquired by inheritance or conquest), Franklin suggested that the colonies were now "distinct and separate states" but ones that had "the same Head, or Sovereign, the King."

Franklin's proposal horrified Thomas Hutchinson, the American-born royal governor of Massachusetts, who rejected the idea of "two independent legislatures in one and the same state." For Hutchinson, the British empire was a single whole, its sovereignty indivisible. "I know of no line," he told the Massachusetts House of Representatives, "that can be drawn between the supreme authority of Parliament and the total independence of the colonies."

There the matter rested. The British had twice tried to impose taxes on the colonies, and American Patriots had twice forced them to retreat. If Parliament or the king insisted on exercising Britain's claim to sovereign power, at least some Americans were prepared to resist by force. Nor did they flinch when reminded that George III condemned their agitation. As the Massachusetts House told Hutchinson, "There is more reason to dread the consequences of absolute uncontrolled supreme power, whether of a nation or a monarch, than those of total independence." Fearful of civil war, the ministry hesitated to take the final fateful step.

The Road to War, 1771–1775

The repeal of the Townshend duties in 1770 restored harmony to the British empire. For the next three years most disputes were resolved peacefully. Yet below the surface lay strong fears and passions and mutual distrust. Suddenly, in 1773 those undercurrents erupted, overwhelming any hope for compromise. In less than two years the Americans and the British stood on the brink of war.

The Compromise Ignored

Once roused, political passions were not easily quelled. Radical Boston Patriots who wanted greater rights for the colonies continued to warn Americans of the dangers of imperial domination. In November 1772 Samuel Adams persuaded the Boston town meeting to establish a Committee of Correspondence to urge Patriots in other towns "to state the Rights of the Colonists of this Province." Within a few months eighty Massachusetts towns had similar committees, all in communication with one another. Other colonies organized similar networks when the British government set up a royal commission to investigate the burning of the *Gaspée*, a British customs vessel, in Rhode Island. The commission's broad powers, particularly its authority to send Americans to Britain for trial, aroused the Virginia House of Burgesses to set up a Committee of Correspondence "to communicate with the other colonies" about the situation in Rhode Island. By July 1773 committees had sprung up in Connecticut, New Hampshire, and South Carolina.

The Tea Act.   Parliament's passage of a Tea Act in May 1773 initiated the chain of events that led directly to civil war. The act had little to do with America. Its primary purpose was to provide financial relief for the British East India Company, which was deeply in debt because of military expeditions undertaken to extend British trade in India. The Tea Act provided the company with a government loan and, more important, relieved the company of paying tariffs on the tea it imported into Britain or exported to the colonies. Only the American consumers would pay the duty.

Lord North failed to understand how unpopular the Tea Act would be in America. Since 1768, when the Townshend Act had placed a duty of 3 pence a pound on tea, the colonies had evaded the tax by illegally importing tea from Dutch sources. By relieving the East India Company of English tariffs, the Tea Act gave its tea a competitive price advantage over that sold by Dutch merchants. In this way the act encouraged Americans to drink East India tea—and in the process pay the Townshend duty. Radical Patriots smelled a plot and accused the ministry of bribing Americans to give up their principled opposition to British taxation. As an anonymous woman wrote in the *Massachusetts Spy*, "the use of [British] tea is considered not as a private but as a public evil . . . a handle to introduce a variety of . . . oppressions amongst us." American merchants also voiced their opposition because the East India Company planned to distribute its tea directly to shopkeepers, excluding most colonial merchants from the profits of the trade. "The fear of an Introduction of a Monopoly in this Country," General Haldimand reported from New York, "has induced the mercantile part of the Inhabitants to be very industrious in opposing this Step and added Strength to a Spirit of Independence already too prevalent."

The newly formed Committees of Correspondence took the lead in organizing resistance to the Tea Act. They held public bonfires at which they persuaded their fellow citizens (sometimes gently, sometimes not) to consign British tea to the flames. The Sons of Liberty patrolled the harbors, preventing East India Company ships from landing new supplies. By forcing the company's captains to return the tea to Britain or store it in public warehouses, the Patriots effectively nullified the legislation.

The Tea Party and the Coercive Act.   Governor Thomas Hutchinson of Massachusetts was determined to uphold the Tea Act and hatched a scheme to land the tea and collect the tax. When a shipment of tea arrived on the *Dartmouth*, Hutchinson had the ship passed through customs immediately so that the Sons of Liberty could not prevent its landing. If necessary, he was prepared to use the British army to unload the tea and supervise its sale by auction. But Patriots foiled the governor's plan by raiding the *Dartmouth*: a group of artisans and laborers disguised as Indians boarded the ship, broke open the 342 chests of tea (valued at about £10,000, or roughly $800,000 today), and threw them into the harbor (see American Lives, "George R. T. Hewes and the Meaning of the Revolution," p. 152). "This destruction of the Tea is so bold and it must have so important Consequences," John Adams wrote in his diary, "that I cannot but consider it as an Epoch in History."

The British Privy Council was outraged, as was the king. "Concessions have made matters worse," George III declared. "The time has come for compulsion." Early in 1774 Parliament decisively rejected a proposal to repeal the duty on American tea; instead, it enacted four Coercive Acts to force Massachusetts into submission. A Port Bill closed Boston Harbor until the East India Company received payment for the destroyed tea. A Government Act annulled the Massachusetts charter and prohibited most local town meetings. A new Quartering Act required the colony to build barracks or accommodate soldiers in private houses. Finally, to protect royal officials from Patriot-dominated juries in Massachusetts, a Justice Act allowed the transfer of trials for capital crimes to other colonies or to Britain.

Patriot leaders throughout the mainland colonies condemned these measures, branding them as the "Intolerable Acts" and rallying support for Massachusetts. In far-off Georgia, a Patriot warned the "Freemen of the Province" that "every privilege you at present claim as a birthright, may be wrested from you by the same authority that blockades the town of Boston." "The cause of Boston," George Washington declared from Virginia, "now is and ever will be considered as the cause of America." The activities of the Committees of Correspondence had created a firm sense of unity among those with Patriot sympathies.

In 1774 Parliament passed the Quebec Act, which heightened the sense of common danger among Americans of European Protestant descent who lived in the seaboard colonies. The law extended the boundaries of Quebec into the Ohio River Valley, thus restricting the western boundaries of Virginia and other coastal colonies and angering influential land speculators and politicians with western land claims (Map 5.4). The act also gave legal recognition in Quebec to Roman Catholicism. This humane concession to the predominantly Catholic population aroused latent religious hatreds, especially in New England, where Puritans associated Catholicism with arbitrary royal government and popish superstition. Although the ministry had not intended the Quebec Act as

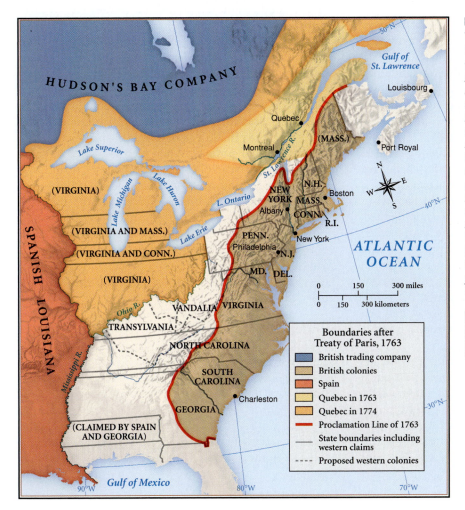

MAP 5.4 British Western Policy, 1763–1774

The Proclamation Line of 1763 restricted white settlement west of the Appalachian Mountains, but colonial land speculators and resident settlers proposed the new colonies of Vandalia and Transylvania. However, the Quebec Act of 1774 designated most western lands as Indian reserves and, by vastly enlarging the boundaries of Quebec, eliminated the sea-to-sea land claims of many seaboard colonies. The act, which also allowed French residents to practice Catholicism, angered many Americans: settlers and land speculators who wanted easy access to the West, New England Protestants who had long feared Catholicism, and colonial political leaders who condemned its failure to provide a representative assembly in Quebec.

For more help analyzing this map, see the ONLINE STUDY GUIDE at **bedfordstmartins.com/henretta.**

George R. T. Hewes and the Meaning of the Revolution

George Hewes

In this portrait (c. 1835) Joseph Cole presents the elderly Hewes as a dignified gentleman, not the impoverished shoemaker and farmer that he actually was. Bostonian Society / Old State House.

George Robert Twelves Hewes was born in Boston in 1742. He was named George for his father, Robert for a paternal uncle, and Twelves for his maternal grandmother, whose family name was Twelves. Apart from his long name, Hewes received little from his parents—not size, for he was unusually short, at five feet, one inch; not wealth, for his father, a failed leather tanner, died a poor soap boiler when Hewes was seven years old; not even love, for Hewes spoke of his mother only as someone who whipped him for disobedience. When he was fourteen she apprenticed him to a shoemaker, one of the lower trades.

This harsh upbringing shaped Hewes's outlook on life. As an adult he spoke out against all brutality, even the tarring and feathering of a Loyalist who had almost killed him. And throughout his life he was extremely sensitive about his class status. He was "neither a rascal nor a vagabond," Hewes retorted to a Boston gentleman who pulled rank on him, "and though a poor man was in as good credit in town as he [the gentleman] was."

In 1768 the occupation of Boston by four thousand British soldiers drew the twenty-six-year-old Hewes into the resistance movement. At first his concerns were personal: he took offense when British sentries challenged him and when a soldier refused to pay for a pair of shoes. Then they became political: Hewes grew angry when some of the poorly paid British soldiers moonlighted, taking jobs away from Bostonians, and even angrier when a Loyalist merchant fired into a crowd of apprentices who were picketing his shop, killing one of them. So on March 5, 1770, when British soldiers came out in force to clear the streets of rowdy civilians, Hewes joined his fellow townspeople: "They were in the king's highway, and had as good a right to be there" as the British troops, he said.

Fate—and his growing political consciousness—placed Hewes in the middle of the Boston Massacre. He claimed to know four of the five workingmen shot down that night by British troops, and one of them, James Caldwell, was standing by his side. Hewes caught him as he fell. Outraged, Hewes armed himself with a cane, only to be confronted by Sergeant Chambers of the 29th British Regiment and eight or nine soldiers, "all with very large clubs or cutlasses." Chambers seized his cane, but as Hewes stated in a legal deposition, "I told him I had as good a right to carry a cane as they had to carry clubs." This deposition, which told of the soldiers' threats to kill more civilians, was included in *A Short Narrative of the Horrid Massacre in Boston* (1770), published by a group of Boston Patriots.

Hewes had chosen sides, and his political radicalism did not go unpunished. His deposition roused the ire of one of his creditors, a Loyalist merchant tailor. Hewes had never really made a go of it as a shoemaker and lived on the brink of poverty. When he was unable to make good on a two-year-old debt of 6 pounds, 8 shillings, 3 pence in Massachusetts currency, about $300 today, for "a sappled coat & breeches of fine cloth," the merchant sent him to debtors' prison for over a month. Hewes's extravagance was not in character; his purchase of the suit had been the desperate ploy of a propertyless artisan to win the hand of Sally Summer, the daughter of the sexton of the First Baptist Church, whom Hewes married in 1768.

Prison did not blunt Hewes's enthusiasm for the Patriot cause. On the night of December 16, 1773, he volunteered for the raid on the British tea ship being organized by the radical Patriots of Boston. He "daubed his face and hands with coal dust in the shop of a blacksmith" and then found, to his surprise, that "the commander of the division to which I belonged, as soon as we were on board the ship, appointed me boatswain, and ordered me to go to the captain and demand of him the keys to the hatches."

Hewes had been singled out and made a minor leader, and he must have played the part well. Thompson Maxwell, a volunteer sent to the raid by John Hancock, recalled that "I went accordingly, joined the band under one Captain Hewes; we mounted the ships and made tea in a trice." In the heat of conflict the small man with the large name had been elevated from a poor shoemaker to "Captain Hewes."

A man of greater ability or ambition might have seized the moment, using his reputation as a Patriot to win fame or fortune, but that was not Hewes's destiny. During the War of Independence he fought as an ordinary sailor and soldier, shipping out twice on privateering voyages and enlisting at least four times in the militia, about twenty months of military service in all. He did not win riches as a privateer (although, with four children to support, that was his hope). Nor did he find glory in battle or even adequate pay: "we received nothing of the government but paper money, of very little value, and continually depreciating." Indeed, the war cost Hewes his small stake in society: "The shop which I had built in Boston, I lost"; it was pulled down and burned by British troops.

In material terms, the American Revolution did about as much for Hewes as his parents had. When a journalist found the shoemaker in New York State in the 1830s, he was still "pressed down by the iron hand of poverty." The spiritual reward was greater. As his biographer, Alfred Young, aptly put it: "He was a nobody who briefly became a somebody in the Revolution and, for a moment near the end of his life, a hero." Because Americans had begun to celebrate the memory of the Revolution, in 1835 Hewes was brought back to Boston in triumph as one of the last surviving participants in the Tea Party—the guest of honor on Independence Day.

But an even more fundamental spiritual reward had come to Hewes when he became a revolutionary, casting off the deferential status of a "subject" in a monarchy and becoming a proud and equal "citizen" in a republic. What this meant to Hewes, and to thousands of other poor and obscure Patriots, appeared in his relationship—both real and fictitious—with John Hancock. As a young man Hewes had sat rapt and tongue-tied in the rich merchant's presence. But when he related his story of the Tea Party, Hewes elevated himself to the same level as Hancock, placing the merchant at the scene (which was almost certainly not the case) and claiming that he "was himself at one time engaged with him [Hancock] in the demolition of the same chest of tea." In this lessening of social distance—this declaration of equality—lay one of the profound meanings of the American Revolution.

The Boston "Tea Party"

Led by radical Patriots disguised as Mohawk Indians, Bostonians dump taxed British tea into the harbor. The rioters underlined their "pure" political motives by punishing those who sought personal gain; a Son of Liberty who stole some of the tea was "stripped of his booty and his clothes together, and sent home naked." Library of Congress.

PART ONE

Slavery, Racism, and the American Republic

The creation in British North America of racially based slave-labor societies was one of the most significant—and lasting—legacies of the colonial era. In 1775, what historian Ira Berlin has called "societies with slaves" existed throughout the northern colonies, from the Puritan settlements of New England to the Quaker colonies of Pennsylvania and Delaware. Farther south, in the Chesapeake and the Carolinas, were "slave societies," colonies whose character was shaped by slavery and the sheer number of Africans. The "best poor man's country" for many whites, British North America—like the rest of the Western Hemisphere—was a land of oppression for most blacks.

Patriot demands for freedom from British rule exposed the moral flaw in the colonial social order. "How is it that we hear the loudest yelps for liberty among the drivers of Negroes?" asked British author Samuel Johnson. Many Americans, especially in the North but also in the South, recognized the contradiction between their pursuit of republican freedom and the institution of slavery. Consequently, one northern state after another abolished slavery or provided for gradual emancipation. This outcome was also a legacy of the North's colonial heritage, which had produced a relatively egalitarian society. Most whites enjoyed extensive liberties. They worshiped in the Christian church of their choice. They owned their own farms, paid low taxes, and resided in self-governing communities. Because there was no powerful landowning gentry demanding deference, no impoverished peasantry or sizable slave population threatening chaos, the dominant yeoman and artisan classes could confidently legislate an end to slave labor (see figure).

Drawing inspiration from the North's relatively egalitarian rural world of independent farm families, Thomas Jefferson declared that "the small land holders are the most precious part of a state." But in 1775, Jefferson's own colony of Virginia—and every colony from Maryland to Georgia—was a "slave society," one based on inequality and racial bondage. Throughout the South, Anglican ministers and gentry demanded allegiance to the established Church of England, suppressing the more egalitarian Presbyterian and Baptist churches. Politically influential landlords monopolized thousands of acres of land, grew rich by leasing farms to poor tenant families, and worked vast plantations with slave labor. Some 500,000 Africans and African Americans—over one-third of the region's

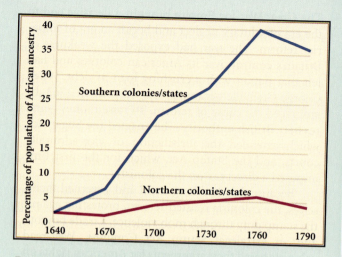

Percentage of Population of African Ancestry, 1640–1790

As enslaved Africans replaced English indentured servants in the tobacco and rice fields after 1680, the Chesapeake and Carolina colonies became "slave societies." The northern colonies remained "societies with slaves," facilitating emancipation there after 1776. Source: U.S. Bureau of the Census, *Historical Statistics of the United States: Colonial Times to 1970* (Washington, DC, 1975), A:195–209, Z:1–19.

population—labored on tobacco, corn, and rice plantations, receiving only their subsistence in return. In this slave-based society, powerful plantation-owning families—roughly 5 to 10 percent of the population—dominated the new republican institutions of government and refused to end the slave system that made them rich.

These divergent social and political orders shaped the character of American history. Between 1800 and 1860 the North and the South engaged in increasingly bitter battles over economic policy, westward expansion, and the extension of slavery to new territories, culminating in a devastating Civil War that took the lives of over 600,000 soldiers.

The Union victory in 1865 preserved the nation and ended slavery for four million African Americans, but it did not end racial discrimination—either in the North or in the South—until another century had passed. Only in the aftermath of World War II, a struggle waged by the United States and its allies against Nazi Germany and its ideology of racial superiority, would most white Americans begin to reconsider their nation's history of racism. Only then—and only grudgingly—were they prepared to make good on what historian C. Vann Woodward in 1960 called "The Deferred Commitment" of the Civil War: the promise of full equality for black citizens. "Equality was a far more revolutionary aim than freedom," Woodward explained, because it required fundamental alterations in racial attitudes that had deep colonial roots. As the civil rights movement gathered force, scholars probed the early history of American racism in such works as Winthrop Jordan's *White over Black: American Attitudes toward the Negro,*

1550–1812 (1968). Indeed, in 1975 the distinguished historian Edmund Morgan argued in *American Slavery, American Freedom: The Ordeal of Colonial Virginia* that the gentlemen planters who led that colony into the American Revolution were ardent republicans in part *because* they were ardent racists and slave owners.

To understand this paradox—how slavery for blacks enhanced freedom for whites—Morgan turned to the history of republican ideology. Beginning around 1600, Morgan pointed out, radical thinkers and members of the English middling classes began to embrace republicanism and its promise of a popularly elected representative government. However, because a majority of the people were either propertyless or poor, republicanism based on popular sovereignty had a fatal weakness. To grant suffrage to the poor would threaten the entire social order—not only the inherited wealth and privileges of the gentry and aristocracy but also the modest possessions and social status enjoyed by hardworking yeomen farmers and shopkeepers. Events during the English Puritan Revolution of the 1640s confirmed the danger. During that social upheaval, radical Christian Levelers demanded not only equal political rights for all men but also an end to private property. In Virginia itself, during Bacon's Rebellion of 1676, discontented white freemen and rebellious indentured servants spoke from the barrels of their guns, demanding an end to rule by wealthy "parasites." Only bloody repression quelled that uprising. For the Virginia planter-gentry to give votes to this "rabble" would be social suicide.

And, yet exactly a century later, the great leaders of the Virginia gentry—George Mason, Thomas Jefferson, Landon Carter, George Washington—became firm Patriots and ardent republicans, committed to the doctrine of popular sovereignty. What had changed? According to Morgan, the answer lay in the rise of a slave-based society. In 1676, men and women of African origin or descent had numbered about 5 percent of Virginia's population, and most poor people were English indentured servants and free laborers. A century later enslaved blacks formed nearly 40 percent of the population, changing the color of Virginia's poor. More important, racial slavery effectively excluded a majority of the propertyless from the political system and made republicanism a possibility. As antiblack prejudice united rich and poor whites, it laid the social foundation for what historian George Frederickson has called a *herrenvolk* (or master-race) republic.

Was Morgan right? Did slavery for blacks bring freedom for whites? Does the nation owe its heritage of republican liberty to its history of racial oppression?

The answers to these questions, like those to most historical puzzles, are complex. It is certainly true that slavery shaped the contours of southern politics, making the region "safe" for gentry-republicanism before 1775 and for white men's democracy thereafter. However, the social landscape of the northern colonies was far different. There, the number of slaves—and of poor whites—was too small to determine the course of eighteenth-century politics, and the broad ownership of property formed the foundations for a democratic republican society. Morgan had it half-right. Whatever the role of slavery in the South, it was freehold farming that enabled northern whites to embrace a regime of republican liberty—for blacks as well as whites.

But not republican equality. For the colonial era imbued most white northerners with a racial ideology that repudiated political equality for African Americans. As Stephen Douglas, a leading northern politician and future presidential candidate, put it in 1858, "this government was made by our fathers, by white men for the benefit of white men and their posterity forever." That colonial legacy of racial superiority would remain strong—in the North as well as the South—until the mid-twentieth century, and is not yet extinguished.

Plantation Overseer, Mississippi, 1936

This well-known photograph by Dorothea Lange captures the persistence of racial inequality long after the end of slavery. Standing with one foot on his car, the white overseer dominates the visual image, just as he dominates the working lives of the blacks whose jobs depend on his whim.
Courtesy, Hallmark Photographic Collection, Hallmark Cards, Inc., Kansas City, MO.

The New Republic

1775–1820

GOVERNMENT	DIPLOMACY	ECONOMY	SOCIETY	CULTURE
Creating Republican Institutions	**European Entanglements**	**Expanding Commerce and Manufacturing**	**Defining Liberty and Equality**	**Pluralism and National Identity**
1775 ▸ States constitutions devised and implemented	▸ Independence declared (1776) French alliance (1778)	▸ Wartime expansion of manufacturing	▸ Emancipation of slaves in the North Judith Sargent Murray, *On the Equality of the Sexes* (1779)	▸ Thomas Paine's *Common Sense* calls for a republic
1780 ▸ Articles of Confederation ratified (1781) Legislative supremacy in states Philadelphia convention drafts U.S. Constitution (1787)	▸ Treaty of Paris (1783) British trade restrictions in West Indies U.S. government signs treaties with Indian peoples	▸ Bank of North America (1781) Commercial recession (1783–1789) Western land speculation	▸ Virginia Statute of Religious Freedom (1786) Idea of republican motherhood French Revolution sparks ideological debate	▸ Land ordinances create a national domain in the West German settlers preserve own language Noah Webster defines American English
1790 ▸ Bill of Rights ratified (1791) First national parties: Federalists and Republicans	▸ Wars of the French Revolution Jay's and Pinckney's Treaties (1795) Undeclared war with France (1798)	▸ First Bank of the United States (1792–1812) States charter business corporations Outwork system grows	▸ Sedition Act limits freedom of the press (1798)	▸ Indians form Western Confederacy Sectional divisions emerge between South and North
1800 ▸ Revolution of 1800 Activist state legislatures Chief Justice Marshall asserts judicial power	▸ Napoleonic wars (1802–1815) Louisiana Purchase (1803) Embargo of 1807	▸ Cotton expands into Old Southwest Farm productivity improves Embargo encourages U.S. manufacturing	▸ Youth choose own marriage partners New Jersey decrees male-only suffrage (1807) Atlantic slave trade legally ended (1808)	▸ African Americans absorb Protestant Christianity Tenskwatawa and Tecumseh revive Indian identity
1810 ▸ Triumph of Republican Party State constitutions democratized	▸ War of 1812 Treaty of Ghent (1816) ends war Monroe Doctrine (1823)	▸ Second Bank of the United States (1816–1836) Supreme Court protects business Emergence of a national economy	▸ Expansion of suffrage for white men New England abolishes established churches (1820s)	▸ War of 1812 tests national unity Second Great Awakening shapes American culture

"The American war is over," the Philadelphia Patriot Benjamin Rush declared in 1787, "but this is far from being the case with the American Revolution. On the contrary, nothing but the first act of the great drama is closed. It remains yet to establish and perfect our new forms of government." The job was even greater than Rush imagined, for the republican revolution of 1776 challenged nearly all the values and institutions of the colonial social order, forcing changes not only in politics but also in economic, religious, and cultural life.

GOVERNMENT The first and most fundamental task was to devise a republican system of government. In 1775, no one in America knew how the governments in the new republican states should be organized and if there should be a permanent central authority along the lines of the Continental Congress. It would take time and experience to find out. It would take even longer to assimilate a new institution—the political party—into the workings of government. By 1820 these years of constitutional experiment and party strife had produced a successful republican system on both the state and national levels. This system of political authority had three striking characteristics: popular sovereignty: government of the people; activist legislatures that pursued the public good: government for the people; and democratic decision making by most white adult men: government by the people.

DIPLOMACY To create and preserve their new republic, Americans of European descent had to fight two wars against Great Britain, an undeclared war against France, and many battles with Indian peoples and confederations. The wars against Britain divided the country into bitter factions—Patriots against Loyalists in 1776, and prowar Republicans against antiwar Federalists in 1812—and expended much blood and treasure. Tragically, the extension of American sovereignty and settlement into the trans-Appalachian West brought cultural disaster to many Indian peoples, as their lives were cut short by European diseases and alcohol and their lands were seized by white settlers. Despite the costs, by 1820 the United States had emerged as a strong independent state, free from a half century of entanglement in the wars and diplomacy of Europe and prepared to exploit the riches of the continent.

ECONOMY By this time the expansion of commerce and the market system had established the foundations for a strong national economy. Beginning in the 1780s northern merchants financed a banking system and organized a rural-based system of manufacturing, while state governments used charters and legal incentives to assist business entrepreneurs and provide improved transportation. Simultaneously, southern planters carried slavery westward to Alabama and Mississippi and grew rich by exporting a new staple crop—cotton—to markets in Europe and the North. Some yeoman farm families migrated to the West while others diversified, producing raw materials such as leather and wool for the burgeoning manufacturing enterprises and working part-time as handicraft workers. As a result of these efforts, by 1820 the young American republic had begun to achieve economic as well as political independence.

SOCIETY As Americans defined the character of their new republican society, they divided along lines of gender, race, religion, and class, disagreeing on fundamental issues: legal equality for women, the status of slavery, the meaning of free speech and religious liberty, and the extent of public responsibility for social inequality. They resolved some of these disputes, extinguishing slavery in the North and broadening religious liberty by allowing freedom of conscience and (except in New England) ending the system of established churches. However, they continued to argue over social equality, in part because their republican creed placed authority in the family and society in the hands of men of property and thus denied power not only to slaves but also to free blacks, women, and poor white men.

CULTURE The efforts of political and intellectual leaders to define a distinct American culture and identity was complicated by the diversity of peoples and regions. Native Americans still lived in their own clans and nations, while black Americans, one-fifth of the enumerated population, were developing a new, African American culture. The white inhabitants created vigorous regional cultures and preserved parts of their ancestral heritage—English, Scottish, Scots-Irish, German, and Dutch. Nevertheless, political institutions began to unite Americans, as did their increasing participation in the market economy and in evangelical Protestant churches. By 1820 to be an American meant, for many members of the dominant white population, being a republican, a Protestant, and an enterprising individual in a capitalist-run market system.

CHAPTER 6

War and Revolution
1775–1783

Toward Independence, 1775–1776
*The Second Continental Congress
    and Civil War*
Common Sense
Independence Declared

The Trials of War, 1776–1778
War in the North
Armies and Strategies
Victory at Saratoga
Social and Financial Perils

The Path to Victory, 1778–1783
The French Alliance
War in the South
The Patriot Advantage
Diplomatic Triumph

**Republicanism Defined and
Challenged**
*Republican Ideals under Wartime
    Pressures*
The Loyalist Exodus
The Problem of Slavery
A Republican Religious Order

WHEN THE PATRIOTS OF FREDERICK COUNTY, MARYLAND, demanded allegiance to the American cause in 1776, Robert Gassaway would have none of it. "It was better for the poor people to lay down their arms and pay the duties and taxes laid upon them by King and Parliament," he told the local Council of Safety, "than to be brought into slavery and commanded and ordered about as they were." The story was much the same in Farmington, Connecticut, where the Patriot officials imprisoned Nathaniel Jones and seventeen other men for a month for "remaining neutral" and failing to join their militia unit in opposing a British raid. Everywhere, the logic of events was forcing families to choose sides between the Loyalists and the Patriots.

In this battle for the hearts and minds of ordinary men and women, the Patriots' control of local governments gave them an edge. Combining physical threats with monetary incentives, they organized some of their neighbors into Patriot militia units and recruited others for service in the Continental army. Gradually the Patriots forged an army that, despite its ragged appearance and diverse origins, held its own on the field of battle. "I admire the American troops tremendously!" exclaimed a French officer toward the end of the war.

◀ **Washington at Verplank's Point**
Arrayed in the ceremonial uniform of the Continental army (in the traditional Whig colors of buff and blue), General Washington watches the reunion of the American and French armies in New York in 1782, following their victory the previous September over Cornwallis at Yorktown, Virginia. The artist, John Trumbull (1756–1843), served as an aide-de-camp to Washington during the war, then studied painting in London with the American-born artist Benjamin West, and executed this picture in 1790.
Courtesy, Winterthur Museum.

"It is incredible that soldiers composed of every age, even children of fifteen, of whites and blacks, almost naked, unpaid, and rather poorly fed, can march so well and withstand fire so steadfastly."

Military mobilization created political commitment. To encourage ordinary Americans to support the war—as soldiers, taxpayers, and hardworking citizens—the Patriot leadership prompted them to participate actively in forming and maintaining the new republican governments. The locus of power shifted, as common men became the rulers rather than the ruled. "From subjects to citizens the difference is immense," remarked the South Carolina physician and Patriot David Ramsay. "Each citizen of a free state contains . . . as much of the common sovereignty as another." By repudiating aristocratic and monarchical rule and raising a democratic army, the Patriots placed sovereignty in the people, launching the age of democratic revolutions.

Toward Independence, 1775–1776

The Battle of Concord took place on April 19, 1775, but fourteen months would elapse before the rebels formally broke with Britain. In the meantime Patriot legislators in most of the thirteen colonies stretching from New Hampshire to Georgia threw out their royal governors and created the two essentials for independence: a government and an army.

The Second Continental Congress and Civil War

Armed struggle in Massachusetts lent urgency to the deliberations of the Second Continental Congress, which met in Philadelphia in May 1775. Soon after the Congress opened, more than 3,000 British troops attacked new American fortifications on Breed's Hill and Bunker Hill overlooking Boston. After three assaults and 1,000 casualties they finally dislodged the Patriot militia. Inspired by his countrymen's valor, John Adams exhorted the Congress to rise to the "defense of American liberty" by creating a Continental army and nominated George Washington of Virginia to lead it. More cautious delegates and those with Loyalist sympathies warned that these measures would commit the colonists irretrievably to rebellion. After bitter debate Congress approved the proposals—but as Adams lamented, only "by bare majorities."

Congress versus the King.   Despite the blood that had been shed, a majority in Congress still hoped for reconciliation with Britain. Led by John Dickinson of Pennsylvania, these moderates passed a proposal known as the Olive Branch petition, expressing loyalty to

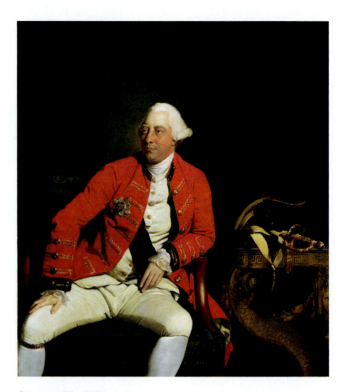

George III, 1771

This portrait of George III was painted by Johann Zoffany in 1771. Like George Washington (b. 1732), King George III (b. 1738) was a young man when the American troubles began in 1765. A headstrong monarch, he tried to impose his will on Parliament, sparking political confusion and contributing to the inept policymaking that led to war. But George III strongly supported Parliament's attempts to tax the colonies and continued the war long after most of his ministers agreed that it had been lost. The Royal Collection. © Her Majesty Queen Elizabeth II.

George III and requesting the repeal of oppressive Parliamentary legislation. But zealous Patriots such as Samuel Adams of Massachusetts and Patrick Henry of Virginia mobilized anti-imperial sentiment and won passage of the Declaration of the Causes and Necessities of Taking Up Arms. Americans dreaded the "calamities of civil war," the declaration asserted, but were "resolved to die Freemen rather than to live [as] slaves." George III chose not to exploit these divisions among the Patriots, refusing even to receive the moderates' petition. Instead, in August 1775 he issued the Proclamation for Suppressing Rebellion and Sedition.

Even before the king's proclamation reached America, the radicals in Congress had won support for an invasion of Canada that they hoped would unleash a popular uprising and add a fourteenth colony to the rebellion. Patriot forces easily took Montreal, but in December 1775 they failed to capture Quebec City. To aid the Patriot cause American merchants waged financial warfare, implementing the resolution of the First Continental Congress to cut off all exports to Britain and its West Indian sugar islands. By ending the tobacco trade and disrupting sugar production, they hoped to undermine the British economy. Parliament retaliated at the end of 1775 with the Prohibitory Act, which outlawed all trade with the rebellious colonies.

Rebellion in the South. Meanwhile, skirmishes between Patriots and Loyalists broke out in many colonies. Acting with great purpose, Patriot militia forcibly disarmed hundreds of Loyalist sympathizers in Delaware, southern New Jersey, and Queens County, New York. In June 1775 the Patriot-dominated House of Burgesses in Virginia forced the royal governor, Lord Dunmore, to take refuge on a British warship in Chesapeake Bay. Branding the Patriots "traitors," the governor organized two military forces—one white, the Queen's Own Loyal Virginians, and one black, the **Ethiopian Regiment**, which enlisted about 1,000 slaves who had fled from their Patriot owners and were eager to fight for their freedom. In November 1775 Dunmore issued a controversial proclamation, offering to emancipate all slaves and indentured servants who joined the Loyalist cause. White planters denounced Dunmore's "Diabolical scheme" as "pointing a dagger to their Throats, thru the hands of their slaves." Faced with black unrest and pressed by yeoman and tenant farmers demanding independence, Patriot planters called for a final break with Britain.

In North Carolina, military conflict likewise prompted demands for independence. Early in 1776 North Carolina's royal governor, Josiah Martin, raised a force of 1,500 Scottish Highlanders from the Carolina backcountry. In response, low-country Patriots mobilized the militia and in February defeated Martin's army at the Battle of Moore's Creek Bridge, capturing more than 800 Highlanders. By April radical Patriots had transformed the North Carolina assembly into an independent Provincial Congress, which instructed its representatives in Philadelphia "to concur with the Delegates of other Colonies in declaring Independency, and forming foreign alliances." Virginia followed suit. In May, led by James Madison, Edmund Pendleton, and Patrick Henry, Virginia Patriots met in convention and resolved unanimously to support independence.

Common Sense

Americans moved slowly toward independence because many colonists retained a deep loyalty to the crown. Joyous crowds had toasted the health of George III when he ascended the throne in 1760 and when he appointed a new ministry that repealed the Stamp Act. Even as the imperial crisis worsened, Benjamin Franklin had proposed that the king rule over autonomous American assemblies. The very structure of society supported this loyalty to the crown, because Americans used the same metaphors of age and family to describe both social authority and imperial rule. According to the Stoning-

ton (Connecticut) Baptist Association, a father should act "as a king, and governor in his family." Just as the settlers followed the lead of respected male elders in town meetings, churches, and families, so they should obey the king as the father of his people. Denial of the king's legitimacy might threaten all paternal authority and disrupt the hierarchical social order.

Nonetheless, by 1775 many Americans had turned against the monarch. Responding to the escalating military conflict, they accused George III of supporting oppressive legislation and ordering armed retaliation against them. Surprisingly, agitation against the king became especially intense in Philadelphia, the largest but hardly the most tumultuous and Patriot-minded seaport city. Because many Philadelphia merchants harbored Loyalist sympathies, the city had been slow to join the boycott against the Townshend duties. But artisans, who accounted for about half the city's population, had become a powerful force in the Patriot movement. Worried that British imports threatened their small-scale manufacturing enterprises, they organized a Mechanics Association to protect America's "just Rights and Privileges." By February 1776 forty artisans sat with forty-seven merchants on the Philadelphia Committee of Resistance, the extralegal body that enforced the latest trade boycott.

Many Scots-Irish artisans and laborers in Philadelphia became Patriots for cultural and religious reasons. They came from Presbyterian families who had fled British-controlled northern Ireland to escape economic and religious discrimination. Moreover, many of them had embraced the egalitarian message preached by Gilbert Tennent and other New Light ministers. As pastor of Philadelphia's Second Presbyterian Church, Tennent had told his congregation that all men and women were equal before God. Applying that idea to politics, New Light Presbyterians shouted in street demonstrations that they had "no king but King Jesus." Republican ideas derived from the European Enlightenment also circulated freely in Pennsylvania. Well-educated scientists and political leaders such as Benjamin Franklin and Benjamin Rush questioned not only the wisdom of George III but also the idea of monarchy itself.

With popular sentiment in flux, a single pamphlet tipped the balance toward the Patriot side. In January 1776 Thomas Paine published *Common Sense*, a call for independence and republicanism phrased in language that aroused the public. Paine had been a minor bureaucrat in the Customs Service in England when he was fired for protesting low wages. He found his way to London, where he wangled a meeting with Benjamin Franklin. In 1774, armed with a letter of introduction from Franklin, Paine migrated to Philadelphia, where he met Benjamin Rush and other Patriots who shared his republican sentiments. In *Common Sense* Paine launched a direct assault on the traditional political order in language that the public could understand and respond to.

Thomas Paine

Common Sense

Thomas Paine was a sharp critic and an acute observer. Before arriving in Philadelphia from his native England in mid-1774, Paine had already rejected the legitimacy of monarchical rule. And he quickly came to understand that the existing system of American politics was republican in spirit and localist in character. In the widely read political pamphlet Common Sense *(1776), he showed the colonists that their customary practices of self-rule had intellectual validity and could easily be adapted to create independent republican governments.*

I draw my idea of the form of government from a principle in nature, which no art can overturn, viz. [that is] that the more simple any thing is, the less liable it is to be disordered, and the easier repaired when disordered; and with this maxim in view, I offer a few remarks on the much boasted constitution of England....

If we will suffer ourselves to examine the component parts of the English constitution, we shall find them to be the base remains of two ancient tyrannies, compounded with some new republican materials.

First.—The remains of monarchical tyranny in the person of the king.

Secondly.—The remains of aristocratical tyranny in the person of the peers.

Thirdly.—The new republican materials in the persons of the commons, on whose virtue depends the freedom of England....

The plain truth is, that it is wholly owing to the constitution of the people, and not to the constitution of the government, that the crown is not as oppressive in England as in Turkey.... For it is the republican and not the monarchical part of the constitution of England which Englishmen glory in, viz. the liberty of choosing a house of commons from out of their own body—and it is easy to see that when republican virtue fails, slavery ensues....

If there is any true cause of fear respecting independence, it is because no plan is yet laid down. Men do not see their way out—Wherefore, ... I offer the following hints....

Let the assemblies [in all of the former colonies] be annual, with a President only ... their business wholly domestic, and subject to the authority of a Continental Congress.

Let each colony be divided into six, eight, or ten convenient districts, each district to send a proper number of delegates to Congress, so that each colony send at least thirty. The whole number in Congress will be at least 390....

But where, say some, is the King of America? I'll tell you. Friend, he reigns above, and doth not make havoc of mankind like the Royal Brute of Britain. Yet that we may not appear to be defective even in earthly honors, let a day be solemnly set apart for proclaiming the charter [of the new Continental republic]; let it be brought forth placed on the divine law, the word of God; let a crown be placed thereon, by which the world may know ... that in America THE LAW IS KING. For as in absolute governments the King is law, so in free countries the law ought to be King; and there ought to be no other.... Let the crown at the conclusion of the ceremony, be demolished, and scattered among the people whose right it is.

Source: Thomas Paine, *Common Sense* (Philadelphia: W. & T. Bradford, 1776), n.p.

"Monarchy and hereditary succession have laid the world in blood and ashes," Paine proclaimed, leveling a personal attack against George III, "the hard hearted sullen Pharaoh of England." Mixing insults with biblical quotations, Paine blasted the British system of "mixed government" among the three estates of king, lords, and commoners. "That it was noble for the dark and slavish times in which it was created," Paine granted, but now this system of governance yielded only "monarchical tyranny in the person of the king" and "aristocratical tyranny in the persons of the peers" (see Voices from Abroad, "Thomas Paine: *Common Sense*," above).

Paine also made a compelling case for American independence. Suggesting that it was absurd for the small island of England to rule a great continent, he turned the traditional metaphor of patriarchal authority on its head: "Is it the interest of a man to be a boy all his life?" Within six months *Common Sense* went through twenty-five editions and reached hundreds of thousands of people throughout the colonies. "There is great talk of independence," a worried New York Loyalist wrote in March 1776, "and the unthinking multitude are mad for it.... A pamphlet called Common Sense has carried off ... thousands." Paine's message was not only popular but also clear: reject the arbitrary powers of king and Parliament and create independent republican states. "A government of our own is our natural right, 'TIS TIME TO PART."

Independence Declared

Throughout the colonies Patriot conventions, inspired by Paine's arguments and beset by armed Loyalists, called urgently for a break from Britain. In June 1776 Richard Henry Lee presented the Virginia Convention's resolution to the Continental Congress: "That these United Colonies are, and of right ought to be, free and independent states . . . absolved from all allegiance to the British Crown." Faced with certain defeat, staunch Loyalists and anti-independence moderates withdrew from the Congress, leaving committed Patriots to take the fateful step. On July 4, 1776, the Congress approved a Declaration of Independence (see Documents, p. D-1).

The main author of the Declaration was Thomas Jefferson, a young Virginia planter and legislative leader who had mobilized resistance to the Coercive Acts with the pamphlet *A Summary View of the Rights of British America.* To persuade Americans and foreign observers of the need to create an independent republic, Jefferson justified the revolt by blaming the rupture on George III rather than on Parliament: "He has plundered our seas, ravaged our coasts, burned our towns, and destroyed the lives of our people. . . . A prince, whose character is thus marked by every act which may define a tyrant," Jefferson concluded, conveniently ignoring his own actions as a slave owner, "is unfit to be the ruler of a free people."

Jefferson, who was steeped in the ideas and rhetoric of the European Enlightenment, preceded these accusations with a proclamation of "self-evident" truths: "that all men are created equal"; that they possess the "unalienable rights" of "Life, Liberty, and the pursuit of Happiness";

Independence Declared

In this painting by John Trumbull, Thomas Jefferson and the other drafters (John Adams of Massachusetts, Roger Sherman of Connecticut, Robert Livingston of New York, and Benjamin Franklin of Pennsylvania) present the Declaration of Independence to John Hancock, the president of the Continental Congress. When the Declaration was read at a public meeting in New York City on July 10, Patriot Lieutenant Isaac Bangs reported, a massive statue of George III was "pulled down by the Populace" and its four thousand pounds of lead melted down to make "Musquet balls" for use against the British troops massed on Staten Island. Yale University Art Gallery, Mabel Brady Garven Collection.

that government derives its "just powers from the consent of the governed" and can rightly be overthrown if it "becomes destructive of these ends." By linking these doctrines of individual liberty and popular sovereignty with independence, Jefferson established revolutionary republicanism as a defining value of the new nation.

For Jefferson as for Paine the pen proved mightier than the sword. In rural hamlets and seaport cities crowds celebrated the Declaration by burning George III in effigy and toppling statues of the king. These acts of destruction broke the Patriots' psychological ties to the father monarch and established the legitimacy of republican state governments that derived their authority from the people. On July 8, 1776, a "great number of spectators" heard a reading of the Declaration at Easton, Pennsylvania, and "gave their hearty assent with three loud huzzahs, and cried out, 'May God long preserve and unite the Free and Independent States of America.'"

The Trials of War, 1776–1778

The Declaration of Independence coincided with Britain's decision to launch a full-scale military assault against the Patriots. For the next two years British forces outfought the Continental army commanded by George Washington, winning nearly every battle. A few inspiring American victories kept the rebellion alive, but in late 1776 and during the winter of 1777 at Valley Forge the Patriot cause hung in the balance.

War in the North

When the British resorted to military force to crush the American revolt, few European observers gave the rebels a chance. Great Britain had 11 million people, compared with the colonies' 2.5 million, nearly 20 percent of whom were enslaved Africans. The British also had a profound economic advantage in the immense profits created by the South Atlantic system and the emerging Industrial Revolution. These financial resources paid for the most powerful navy in the world, a standing army of 48,000 men, and thousands of German mercenaries, soldiers hired to fight for the British cause. British military officers had been tested in combat during the Seven Years' War, and their soldiers were well armed. Finally, the imperial government had the support of tens of thousands of American Loyalists as well as many Indian tribes. The Cherokees in the Carolinas had long opposed the expansion of white settlement and were firmly committed to the British side. So also were four of the six Iroquois Nations of New York—the Mohawks, Senecas, Cayugas and Onondagas—who were led by the pro-British Mohawk chief Joseph Brant; only the Oneida and Tuscarora peoples supported the rebel side (Map 6.1).

By contrast, the rebellious Americans were militarily weak. They had no navy, and General Washington's poorly trained army consisted of about 18,000 troops, mostly short-term recruits hastily assembled by state governments in Virginia and New England. The Patriots could field thousands more militiamen but only for short periods and only near their own farms and towns. Although many American officers had fought during the French and Indian War, even the most experienced had never commanded a large force or faced a disciplined army skilled in the intricate maneuvers of European warfare.

To exploit this military advantage Britain's prime minister, Lord North, responded quickly to the unexpected American invasion of Canada in 1775. Assembling a large invasion force, he selected General William Howe, who had served in the colonies during the French and Indian War, to lead it. North ordered Howe to capture New York City and seize control of the Hudson River, thereby isolating the radical Patriots in New England

MAP 6.1 Patriot and Loyalist Strongholds

Patriot supporters formed the dominant faction throughout most of the thirteen colonies and used their control of local governments to funnel men, money, and supplies to the rebel cause. Loyalists were powerful only in Nova Scotia, eastern New York, and New Jersey and in certain areas in the South. However, most Native Americans favored the British cause and joined with Loyalist militia to fight Patriot forces in the backcountry of the Carolinas and in central New York (see Map 6.3).

For more help analyzing this map, see the ONLINE STUDY GUIDE at bedfordstmartins.com/henretta.

from the other colonies. In July 1776, as the Continental Congress was declaring independence in Philadelphia, Howe was beginning to land 32,000 troops—British regulars and German **mercenaries**—outside New York City.

British superiority was immediately apparent. In August 1776 Howe attacked the Americans in the Battle of Long Island and forced their retreat to Manhattan Island. There Howe outflanked Washington's troops, nearly trapping them on several occasions. Outgunned and outmaneuvered, the Continental army again retreated, first to Harlem Heights, then to White Plains, and finally across the Hudson River to New Jersey. By December the British army had pushed the rebels out of New Jersey and across the Delaware River into Pennsylvania, forcing Congress to flee from Philadelphia to Baltimore (Map 6.2).

From the Patriots' perspective winter came just in time, for the British halted their campaign for the cold months, according to eighteenth-century military custom. The respite allowed the Americans to catch them off guard and score a few triumphs. On Christmas night in 1776 Washington crossed the Delaware River and staged a surprise attack on Trenton, New Jersey, forcing the surrender of 1,000 German mercenaries. In early January 1777 the Continental army won another victory in a small engagement at nearby Princeton, raising Patriot morale and allowing the Continental Congress to return to Philadelphia. Bright stars in a dark night, these minor triumphs could not mask British military superiority. These are the times, wrote Tom Paine, that "try men's souls."

Armies and Strategies

British superiority did not break the will of the Continental army and, partly because of Howe's tactical decisions

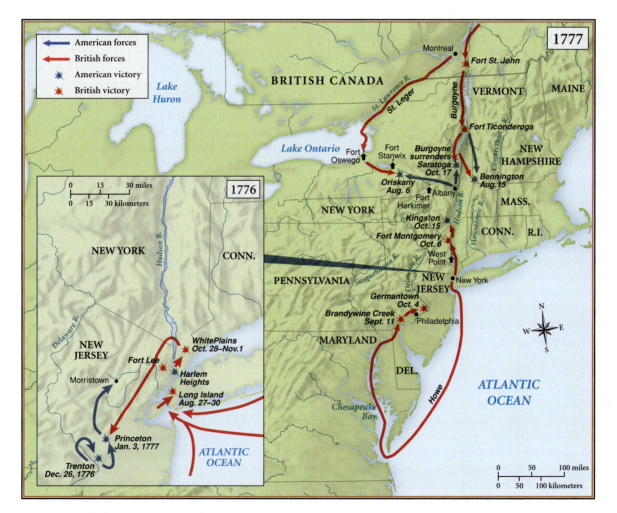

MAP 6.2 The War in the North, 1776–1777

In 1776 the British army drove Washington's forces across New Jersey into Pennsylvania. The Americans counterattacked successfully at Trenton and Princeton and then set up winter headquarters at Morristown. In 1777 British forces stayed on the offensive. General Howe attacked the Patriot capital of Philadelphia from the south, capturing it in early October. Meanwhile, General Burgoyne and Colonel St. Leger launched simultaneous invasions from Canada. Aided by thousands of New England militia, American troops commanded by General Horatio Gates defeated Burgoyne at Bennington, Vermont, and then in October at Saratoga, New York, the military turning point of the war.

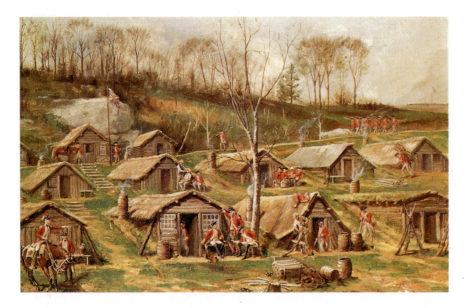

A British Camp, c. 1778

While American troops at Valley Forge huddled from the cold in thin tents, British troops stationed just outside New York City (on upper Manhattan Island) lived in simple but well-constructed and warm log cabins. Each hut housed either a few officers or as many as ten soldiers of the 17th Regiment of Foot. This painting, based on careful archaeological fieldwork, was executed in 1915 by John Ward Dunsmore. New-York Historical Society.

and mistakes, the rebellion continued. Howe had opposed the Coercive Acts of 1774, and as the British military commander he still hoped for a political compromise—indeed, he had authority from Lord North to negotiate with the rebels and allow them to surrender on honorable terms. Consequently, instead of following up his early victories with a ruthless pursuit of the retreating American army, Howe was content to show his superior power and tactics, hoping to convince the Continental Congress that resistance was futile. Howe's caution also reflected the conventions of eighteenth-century warfare, which prescribed outmaneuvering the opposing forces and winning their surrender rather than destroying them. Moreover, the British general knew that his troops were 3,000 miles from supplies and reinforcements. In case of a major defeat, replenishing his force would take six months. Although Howe's prudent tactics were understandable, they cost the British the opportunity to nip the rebellion in the bud.

Howe's failure to win a decisive victory was paralleled by Washington's success in avoiding a major defeat. He too was cautious, challenging Howe on occasion but retreating in the face of superior strength. As Washington advised Congress, "On our Side the War should be defensive." His strategy was to draw the British away from the seacoast, extend their lines of supply, and sap their morale while keeping the Continental army intact as a symbol and instrument of American resistance.

Congress had promised Washington a regular force of 75,000 men, but the Continental army never reached a third of that number. Yeomen preferred to serve in the local militia, and so the regular army drew most of its recruits from the lower ranks of society. General William Smallwood of Maryland commanded soldiers who were either poor American-born youths or older foreign-born men—often British ex-convicts and former indentured servants. Such men enlisted not out of patriotism but for a bonus of $20 in cash (about $2,000 today) and

the promise of 100 acres of land. Molding such recruits into a fighting force took time. In the face of a British artillery bombardment or flank attack many men panicked; hundreds of others deserted, unwilling to submit to the discipline and danger of military life. The soldiers who stayed resented the contemptuous way Washington and other American officers treated the "camp followers," the women who fed and cared for the troops.

Such personal support was crucial, for the Continental army was poorly supplied and faintly praised. Radical Whig Patriots had long viewed a peacetime standing army as a threat to liberty, and even in wartime they preferred the militia to a professional force. General Philip Schuyler of New York complained that his troops were "weak in numbers, dispirited, naked, destitute of provisions, without camp equipage, with little ammunition, and not a single piece of cannon." Given these handicaps, Washington was fortunate to have escaped an overwhelming defeat in the first year of the war.

Victory at Saratoga

Howe's failure to achieve a quick victory dismayed Lord North and his colonial secretary, Lord George Germain. Accepting the challenge of a long-term military commitment, the British leaders increased the land tax to finance the war and prepared to mount a major campaign in 1777.

The isolation of New England remained the primary British goal and was to be achieved by a three-pronged attack converging on Albany, New York. General John Burgoyne was to lead a large contingent of British regulars from Quebec to Albany. A second, smaller force of Iroquois warriors, who had allied themselves with the British to protect their land from American settlers, would attack from the west under Colonel Barry St. Leger. To assist Burgoyne from the south, Germain ordered Howe to dispatch a force northward from New York City (see Map 6.2).

American Militiamen
Because of the shortage of cloth, the Patriot army dressed in a variety of fashions that used many different kinds of fabrics. This German engraving, based on a drawing by a German officer, shows two barefoot American militiamen arrayed in hunting shirts and trousers made of ticking, a strong woven linen fabric that was often used as the coverings for mattresses and pillows.
Anne S. K. Brown Military Collection, Brown University.

Joseph Brant
The Mohawk chief Thayendanegea, known to the whites as Joseph Brant, was a devout member of the Church of England who had helped to translate the Bible into the Iroquois language. An influential leader, Brant secured the support of four of the six Iroquois Nations for the British. In 1778 and 1779, he led Iroquois warriors and Tory Rangers in devastating attacks on American settlements in the Wyoming Valley of Pennsylvania and Cherry Valley in New York. This portrait by Charles Willson Peale was painted in 1797. Independence National Historic Park.

For more help analyzing this image, see the ONLINE STUDY GUIDE at bedfordstmartins.com/henretta.

Howe had a different scheme and it led to a disastrous result. Howe wanted to attack Philadelphia, the home of the Continental Congress, and end the rebellion with a single victory over Washington's army. With Germain's apparent approval, the British commander set his plan in motion—but only very slowly. Rather than march quickly through New Jersey, British troops sailed south from New York, then up the Chesapeake Bay. Approaching Philadelphia from the south, Howe's troops easily outflanked the American positions along Brandywine Creek in Delaware and forced Washington to withdraw. On September 26 the British marched triumphantly into Philadelphia, hoping that the capture of the rebels' capital would end the uprising. But the Continental Congress fled into the interior, determined to continue the struggle.

The British paid a high price for Howe's victory in Philadelphia, for it contributed directly to the defeat of Burgoyne's army from Canada. Initially Burgoyne's troops had sped across Lake Champlain, overwhelming the American defenses at Fort Ticonderoga and driving

toward the upper reaches of the Hudson River. Then they stalled, for Burgoyne—"Gentleman Johnny," as he was called—fought with style, not speed, weighed down by comfortable tents and ample stocks of food and wine. The American troops led by General Horatio Gates further impeded Burgoyne's progress by felling huge trees across the crude wagon trail used by Burgoyne and by raiding his long supply lines to Canada.

By the end of the summer Burgoyne's army—6,000 regulars (half of them German mercenaries) and 600 Loyalists and Indians—was in trouble, bogged down in the wilderness near Saratoga, New York. In August 2,000 American militiamen left their farms to fight a bitter battle at nearby Bennington, Vermont, that cost Burgoyne 900 casualties and deprived him of much-needed supplies of food and horses. Meanwhile, Patriot forces in the Mohawk Valley forced St. Leger and the Iroquois to retreat. To make matters worse, the British commander in New York City recalled the 4,000 troops he had sent toward Albany and dispatched them instead to bolster Howe's force in Philadelphia. While Burgoyne waited in vain for help, thousands of Patriot militiamen from Massachusetts, New Hampshire, and New York joined Gates's forces. They "swarmed around the army like birds of prey," an alarmed English sergeant wrote in his journal, and in October 1777 forced Burgoyne to surrender.

The battle at Saratoga proved to be the turning point of the war. The Americans captured more than 5,000 British troops and their equipment. Their victory virtually ensured the success of American diplomats in Paris, who were seeking a military alliance with France. Patriots on the home front were delighted, though their joy was muted by wartime difficulties.

Social and Financial Perils

The war exposed tens of thousands of civilians to deprivation, displacement, and death. "An army, even a friendly one, are a dreadful scourge to any people," a Connecticut soldier wrote from Pennsylvania. "You cannot imagine what devastation and distress mark their steps." New Jersey was particularly hard hit by the fighting, as British and American armies marched back and forth across the state. Families with reputations as Patriots or Loyalists fled their homes to escape arrest—or worse. Soldiers and partisans looted farms, seeking food or political revenge. Wherever the armies went, drunk and disorderly troops harassed and raped women and girls. Families lived in fear of their approach. When British warships sailed up the Potomac River, women and children fled from Alexandria, Virginia, and "stowed themselves into every Hut they can get, out of the reach of the Enemys canon."

In some areas, the War of Independence became a bloody partisan conflict. In New England mobs of Patriot farmers beat suspected Tories or destroyed their property. "Every Body submitted to our Sovereign Lord the Mob," a Loyalist preacher lamented. Patriots organized local Committees of Safety to collect taxes, send food and clothing to the Continental army, and impose fines or jail sentences on those who failed to support the cause. But in some areas of Maryland, the number of "non-associators"—those who refused to join either side—was so large that they successfully defied Patriot organizers. "Stand off you dammed rebel sons of bitches," Robert Davis of Anne Arundel County shouted, "I will shoot you if you come any nearer."

Financial Crisis.   Such defiance reflected the weakness of the new state governments, which teetered on the brink of bankruptcy. To feed, clothe, and pay their troops, state officials borrowed gold, silver, or British currency from wealthy individuals. When those funds ran out, Patriot officials were afraid to raise taxes, knowing how unpopular that would be. Instead, individual states printed paper money, issuing $260 million in currency and transferable bonds. Theoretically, the new notes could be redeemed in gold or silver, but since they were printed in huge quantities and were not backed by tax revenues or mortgages on land, many Americans refused to accept them at face value. North Carolina's paper money came to be worth so little that even the state government's tax collectors refused it.

The finances of the Continental Congress collapsed too, despite the efforts of the Philadelphia merchant Robert Morris, the government's chief treasury official.

Paper Currency

To symbolize their independent status, the new state governments printed their own currency. Initially Pennsylvania retained the British system of pounds and shillings; Virginia chose the Spanish gold dollar as the basic unit of currency but included the equivalent in pounds ($1,200 was £360, a ratio of 3.3 to 1). By 1781, Virginia had printed so much paper money to pay its soldiers and wartime expenses that the value of the currency had depreciated. It now took 40 Virginia paper dollars to buy the same amount of goods as one Spanish gold dollar (a 40 to 1 ratio).
American Numismatic Society.

The Congress lacked the authority to impose taxes and so depended on funds requisitioned from the states, which frequently paid late or not at all. The Congress therefore borrowed $6 million in specie from France, using it as security to encourage wealthy Americans to purchase Continental loan certificates. When those funds and other French and Dutch loans were exhausted, the Congress followed the lead of the states and printed currency and bills of credit. Between 1775 and 1779 it issued notes with a face value of $191 million, but when funds received from the states retired only $3 million, the actual value of the bills fell dramatically.

Indeed, the excess of currency helped to spark the worst inflation in American history. The amount of goods available for purchase—both domestic foodstuffs and foreign manufactures—had shrunk significantly because of the fighting and the British naval blockade, while the money in circulation had multiplied. Because more currency was chasing fewer goods, prices rose rapidly. In Maryland a bag of salt that had cost $1 in 1776 sold for $3,900 in currency a few years later. Unwilling to accept nearly worthless currency, farmers refused to sell their crops, even to the Continental army. Instead, merchants and farmers turned to barter—trading wheat for tools or clothes—or sold goods only to those who could pay in gold or silver. The result was social upheaval. In Boston a mob of women accused merchant Thomas Boyleston of hoarding goods, "seazd him by his Neck," and forced him to sell—at the traditional prices. In rural Ulster County, New York, women surrounded the Patriot Committee of Safety, demanding steps to end the food shortages; otherwise, they said, "their husbands and sons shall fight no more." Civilian morale and social cohesion crumbled, causing some Patriot leaders to doubt that the rebellion could succeed.

Valley Forge. Fears reached their peak during the winter of 1777–78. Howe camped in Philadelphia and with his officers partook of the finest wines, foods, and entertainment the city could offer. Washington's army retreated to Valley Forge, some twenty miles to the west, where about 12,000 soldiers and hundreds of camp followers suffered horribly. "The army . . . now begins to grow sickly," a surgeon confided to his diary. "Poor food—hard lodging—cold weather—fatigue—nasty clothes—nasty cookery. . . . Why are we sent here to starve and freeze?" Nearby farmers refused to help. Some were pacifists—Quakers and German sectarians—unwilling to support either side. Others pursued the self-interest of their families, hoarding their grain in hopes of higher prices in the spring or willing to accept only the gold and silver offered by British quartermasters. "Such a dearth of public spirit, and want of public virtue," Washington complained—but to no effect. By spring 1,000 of his hungry soldiers had vanished into the countryside and another 3,000 had died from malnutrition and disease.

One winter at Valley Forge took as many American lives as had two years of fighting against General Howe.

In this dark hour Baron von Steuben raised the self-respect and readiness of the American army at Valley Forge. A former Prussian military officer, von Steuben was one of a handful of foreigners who had volunteered their services to the American cause. To counter falling morale, he instituted a standardized system of drill and maneuver and encouraged officers to become more professional in their demeanor and behavior. Thanks to von Steuben, the smaller Continental army that emerged from Valley Forge in the spring was a much tougher and better-disciplined force with a renewed sense of purpose.

The Path to Victory, 1778–1783

Wars are often won as much by astute diplomacy as by sheer firepower, and the War of Independence was no exception. The Patriots' prospects for victory improved dramatically in 1778, when the United States formed a military alliance with France, the most powerful European nation. The alliance brought the Americans money, troops, and supplies and changed the conflict from a colonial rebellion to an international war.

The French Alliance

France and America were unlikely partners. France was Catholic and a monarchy; the United States, largely Protestant and a federation of republics. Moreover, the two peoples had been on opposite sides in wars from 1689 to 1763, and New Englanders had just inflicted enormous suffering on the French population of Acadia (Nova Scotia). But France was intent on avenging its loss of Canada to Britain in the French and Indian War. In 1776 the Comte de Vergennes, the French foreign minister, persuaded King Louis XVI to extend a secret loan to the rebellious colonies and, equally important, to supply them with much-needed gunpowder. Early in 1777 Vergennes opened official commercial and military negotiations with Benjamin Franklin and two other American diplomats, Arthur Lee and Silas Deane. When news of the American victory at Saratoga reached Paris in December 1777, Vergennes sought a formal alliance with the Continental Congress.

Negotiating the Treaty. Franklin and his associates craftily exploited the rivalry between France and Britain, using the threat of a negotiated settlement with Britain to win an explicit French commitment to American independence. The Treaty of Alliance of February 1778 specified that once France had entered the war against Great Britain, neither partner would sign a separate peace before the "liberty, sovereignty, and independence" of the United States were ensured. In return, the American

***Marion Crossing the Pedee*, William T. Ranney, 1851**
In 1780 the war in the South went badly for the Patriots. General Lincoln surrendered one American army at Charleston, South Carolina, in May and General Gates lost another at Camden, South Carolina, in August. Then the tide turned, thanks in part to Patriot guerrilla forces led by Francis Marion, known as the "Swamp Fox," whose raids on enemy forts and supply lines forced the British to withdraw from the interior of South Carolina. Here Marion (on the chestnut horse) and his men cross the Pee Dee River on their way to a raid. Amos Carter Museum of Western Art.

diplomats pledged that their government would recognize any French conquests in the West Indies.

The alliance with France gave new life to the Patriots' cause. With access to military supplies and European loans, the American army soon strengthened and hopes soared. "There has been a great change in this state since the news from France," a Patriot soldier reported from Pennsylvania. Farmers—"mercenary wretches," he called them—"were as eager for Continental Money now as they were a few weeks ago for British gold."

The alliance also bolstered the resources and confidence of the Continental Congress. Acting with energy and purpose the Congress addressed the continuing demands of the officer corps for military pensions. Most officers came from the upper ranks of society and had used their own funds to equip themselves and sometimes their men as well. In return they demanded lifetime military pensions at half pay. John Adams condemned the petitioners for "scrambling for rank and pay like apes for nuts," but General Washington urged Congress to grant the pensions, warning the lawmakers that "the salvation of the cause depends upon it." Congress reluctantly agreed to grant the officers half pay after the war, but only for seven years.

The British Response.   Meanwhile, the war was becoming increasingly unpopular in Britain. Radical agitators and republican-minded artisans supported American demands for greater rights and campaigned for political reform at home, including broadened voting rights and more equitable representation for cities in Parliament. The landed gentry and urban merchants protested increases in the land tax and new levies on carriages, wine, and imported goods. "It seemed we were to be taxed and stamped ourselves instead of inflicting taxes and stamps on others," a British politician complained.

But George III remained determined to crush the rebellion, afraid it would lead to the collapse of the empire. If America won independence, he warned Lord North, "the West Indies must follow them. Ireland would soon follow the same plan and be a separate state, then this island would be reduced to itself, and soon would be a poor island indeed." Following the British defeat at Saratoga the king assumed a more pragmatic attitude. To head off an American alliance with France, the king authorized North to seek a negotiated settlement. In February 1778 North persuaded Parliament to repeal the Tea and Prohibitory Acts and, in an amazing concession, to renounce its power to tax the colonies. The prime minister then opened discussions with the Continental Congress, offering a return to the constitutional "condition of 1763," before the Sugar and Stamp Acts. But the Patriots, now allied with France, rejected the overture.

War in the South

The French alliance expanded the war but did not rapidly conclude it. When France entered the conflict in June 1778, it hoped to capture a rich sugar island and therefore concentrated its naval forces in the West Indies. Spain, which joined the war in 1779, also had its own agenda: in return for naval assistance to France, it wanted to regain Florida and Gibraltar. The Patriot cause had become enmeshed in a web of European territorial quarrels and complex diplomatic intrigue.

Britain's Southern Strategy. The British ministry, by 1778 beset by many enemies on many fronts, settled on a modest strategy in North America. It decided to use its army to recapture the rich tobacco- and rice-growing colonies of Virginia, the Carolinas, and Georgia and rely on local Loyalists to hold and administer them. The British knew that Scottish Highlanders in North Carolina retained a strong allegiance to the crown and hoped to recruit other Loyalists from the ranks of the Regulators, the enemies of the low-country Patriot planters. The ministry also hoped to take advantage of racial divisions in the plantation regions of the South and potential Indian allies in the backcountry (Map 6.3). In 1776 over 1,000 slaves had fought for Lord Dunmore under the banner "Liberty to Slaves!"; a British military offensive might prompt thousands more to flee from their Patriot owners.

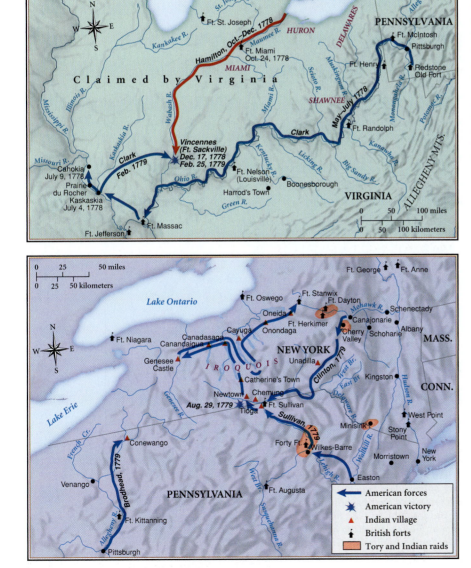

MAP 6.3 Native Americans and the War in the West, 1778–1779

Most Indian peoples remained neutral or, fearing land-hungry Patriot farmers, used British guns to raid American settlements. To thwart attacks on the southern backcountry by militant groups of Shawnees, Cherokees, and Delawares, George Rogers Clark and Patriot militia captured the British fort and supply depot at Vincennes in the Illinois country in late 1778 and again in early 1779. To the north, Patriot Generals John Sullivan and James Clinton defeated pro-British Indian forces near Tioga in August 1779 and then systematically destroyed villages throughout Iroquoia.

In fact, because African Americans formed 30 to 50 percent of the population, Patriot planters refused to allow their sons or white overseers to leave the plantations and join the Patriot forces. South Carolina could not defend itself, its representative told the Continental Congress, "by reason of the great proportion of citizens necessary to remain at home to prevent insurrection among the Negroes." The policy was a wise one. Whenever British warships appeared along the coast, blacks would row out to sell provisions and many stayed as volunteers.

Implementing Britain's southern military strategy became the responsibility of Sir Henry Clinton. In June 1778 Clinton moved the main British army from Philadelphia to more secure quarters in New York. In December he launched his southern campaign, capturing Savannah, Georgia, and mobilizing hundreds of blacks to build

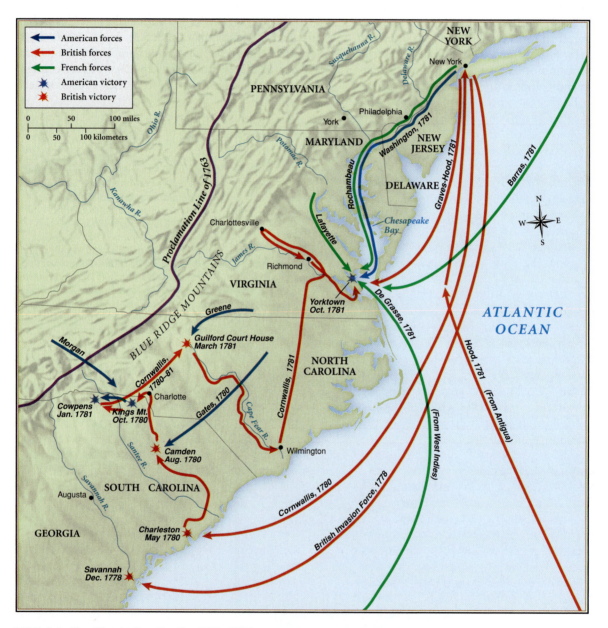

MAP 6.4 The War in the South, 1778–1781

The British ministry's southern strategy started well. British forces captured Savannah in December 1778 and Charleston in May 1780. Brutal warfare raged in the interior over the next eighteen months, fought more by small bands of irregulars than by disciplined armies, and ended in a stalemate between British forces and their Loyalist supporters and the American army and militia. Hoping to break the deadlock, in 1781 British General Charles Cornwallis carried the battle into Virginia. A Franco-American army led by Washington and Lafayette, aided by the French fleet under Admiral de Grasse, surrounded Cornwallis's forces on the Yorktown peninsula and forced their surrender.

barricades and unload supplies. Then Clinton moved inland, capturing Augusta early in 1779. By the end of the year, with the help of local Loyalists, Clinton's forces had taken control of Georgia, and 10,000 troops were poised for an assault on South Carolina. To counter this threat the Continental Congress suggested that South Carolina raise 3,000 black troops, but the state assembly overwhelmingly rejected the proposal.

During most of 1780 British forces marched from victory to victory (Map 6.4). In May Clinton surrounded the city of Charleston, South Carolina, forcing the surrender of General Benjamin Lincoln and his garrison of 5,000 troops. Then Lord Cornwallis assumed control of the British forces and sent out expeditions to secure the countryside. In August Cornwallis defeated an American force at Camden, South Carolina, commanded by General Horatio Gates, the hero of Saratoga. Only about 1,200 Patriot militiamen joined Gates at the battle in Camden—a fifth of the number at Saratoga—and many of them panicked, handing the British control of South Carolina. Hundreds of African Americans fled to freedom in British-controlled Florida, while hundreds more found refuge with the British army, providing labor in return for their liberty.

Then the tide of battle turned. The Dutch declared war against Britain, and France finally dispatched troops to America. The French decision was partly the work of the Marquis de Lafayette, a republican-minded aristocrat who had long supported the American cause. In 1780 Lafayette persuaded Louis XVI to send General Comte de Rochambeau and 5,500 men to Newport, Rhode Island, where they posed a threat to the British forces in New York City.

Partisan Warfare in the Carolinas. Meanwhile, Washington dispatched General Nathanael Greene to recapture the Carolinas. There the fighting had led to social anarchy, making it difficult to distinguish military units from criminal gangs. The words of a Patriot soldier captured the confusion: "Heard of a party of tories on the Sandy River, we killed three and wounded three most notorious villains." Given this social disarray, Greene faced a difficult task. His troops, he reported, "are almost naked and we subsist by daily collections and in a country that has been ravaged and plundered by both friends and enemies." To make use of local militiamen, who were "without discipline and addicted to plundering," Greene devised a new military strategy. He divided the militia into small groups with strong leaders and directed them to harass less-mobile British forces. In October 1780 a militia force of Patriot farmers defeated a regiment of Loyalists at King's Mountain, South Carolina, taking about 1,000 prisoners. Led by the "Swamp Fox," General Francis Marion, American guerrillas won a series of small but fierce battles in South Carolina, while General Daniel Morgan led another band to a bloody victory at Cowpens, South Carolina, in January 1781. But Loyalist garrisons and militia units remained powerful, assisted by the well-organized Cherokees, who protected their lands by attacking American settlers and troops. "We fight, get beaten, and fight again," General Greene declared doggedly. In March 1781 Greene's soldiers fought Cornwallis's seasoned army to a draw at North Carolina's Guilford Court House.

Weakened by this war of attrition and Patriot successes in restoring authority, Cornwallis decided to concede the southernmost states to Greene and seek a decisive victory in Virginia. Aided by reinforcements from New York, the British general invaded Virginia's Tidewater region. There Benedict Arnold, the infamous traitor to the Patriot cause (see American Lives, "The Enigma of Benedict Arnold, p. 180), led British troops in raids up and down the James River, where they met only slight resistance from an American force commanded by Lafayette. Then in May 1781, as the two armies sparred near the York Peninsula, France ordered its large fleet from the West Indies to North America.

Emboldened by the naval forces at his disposal, Washington launched a well-coordinated attack. Feinting

Lafayette at Yorktown

This painting, executed by the French artist J. B. Le Paon in 1780, shows Lafayette and James Armistead, an enslaved African American who served as a spy for the Patriot army commanded by the French general. Receiving his freedom as a reward for his exploits, James took Lafayette's surname, becoming James Lafayette. The two Lafayettes met again in 1824, when the Frenchman visited the United States.

Lafayette College Art Collection, Easton, PA. Gift of Mrs. John Hubbard.

The Enigma of Benedict Arnold

Benedict Arnold was an exceptional man, and so too was his military career. During the American War of Independence, Arnold became a hero for both the Patriot and the Loyalist sides.

Arnold began his military exploits as an American Patriot. In May 1775 he devised a plan to capture Fort Ticonderoga on Lake Champlain and then joined with Ethan Allen and the Green Mountain Boys of Vermont to do it. Arnold's heroics continued in September when he led an expedition of 1,150 riflemen against Quebec City, the capital of British Canada. He drove his men hard through the Maine wilderness, overcoming leaky boats, spoiled provisions, treacherous rivers, and near starvation to arrive at Quebec in November, his force reduced to 650 men. These losses did not deter Arnold. Joined by General Richard Montgomery, who had arrived with 300 troops after capturing Montreal, Arnold's forces attacked the strongly fortified city, only to have the assault end in disaster. The British defenders killed 100 Americans, including Montgomery; captured 400 more; and wounded many others—among them Arnold, who fell as he stormed over a barricade, a musket ball through his leg.

Ticonderoga and Quebec were only the beginning. For the next five years Arnold served the Patriot side with distinction, including a dangerous assault against the center of the British line at Saratoga, where he was again wounded in the leg. No general was more imaginative than Arnold, no field officer more daring, no soldier more courageous.

Yet Arnold has become immortalized not as a Patriot hero but as a villain, a military traitor who, as commander of the American fort at West Point, New York, in 1780, schemed to hand it over to the British. Of his role in this conspiracy there is no doubt. His British contact, Major John André, was caught with incriminating documents in Arnold's handwriting, including routes of access to the fort. Fleeing down the Hudson River on a British ship, Arnold defended his conduct in a letter to George Washington, declaring that "love to my country actuates my present conduct, however it may appear inconsistent to the world, who very seldom judge right of any man's actions."

Benedict Arnold, 1776
This engraving depicts Arnold prior to the American assault on Quebec City (pictured in the background). Arnold's portrait is an imaginary representation, issued by a London bookseller to capitalize on British interest in the American revolt.
Anne S. K. Brown Military Collection, Brown University.

But judge we must. Why did Arnold desert the cause for which he had fought so gallantly and twice been wounded? Was there any justification for his conduct?

Arnold grew up in modest circumstances, a member of a respectable Puritan family, and served in a Connecticut regiment during the French and Indian War. When the fighting began at Lexington and Concord in April 1775, he was thirty-four years old, a minor merchant in New Haven, Connecticut, and a militia captain. Eager to support the Patriot rebellion, Arnold marched off with his militiamen to besiege the British forces in Boston. Along the way he remembered seeing the cannon at Fort Ticonderoga during the French war and realized the Patriots could seize these weapons in order to bombard General Thomas Gage's army. Once his ingenious plan forced the British out of Boston, Arnold submitted an inflated claim for expenses (£1,060 in Massachusetts currency, or about $60,000 today), then protested vehemently when suspicious legislators closely examined each item.

This adventure revealed Arnold's great strengths and equally great flaws. Bold and creative, he thought quickly and acted decisively. Ambitious and thin-skinned, he craved power and money but reacted badly to criticism. Intrepid and ruthless, he risked his life—and the lives of others—to get what he wanted.

Such larger-than-life figures are often resented as much as they are admired, and so it was with Benedict Arnold. At Quebec some New England officers accused him of arrogance, but Congress rewarded the colonel's bravery by making him a brigadier general. When Arnold again distinguished himself in battle in early 1777—having his horse shot out from under him—Congress promoted him to major general "as a token of their admiration of his gallant conduct." Then, in the middle of the struggle at Saratoga, General Horatio Gates relieved Arnold of his command, partly for insubordination and partly because the American commander considered him a "pompous little fellow." Nonetheless, George Washington rewarded Arnold, appointing him commandant at Philadelphia following the British evacuation of the city in July 1778.

By then Arnold was an embittered man, disdainful of his fellow officers and resentful toward Congress for not promoting him more quickly and to even higher rank. A widower, he threw himself into the social life of Philadelphia, courting and marrying Margaret Shippen—a much younger woman from a wealthy merchant family—and falling deeply into debt. Arnold's financial extravagance drew him into shady schemes and into disrepute with Congress, which investigated his accounts and recommended a court-martial—which Arnold managed to dodge. "Having . . . become a cripple in the service of my country, I little expected to meet [such] ungrateful returns," he complained to Washington.

Faced with financial ruin, uncertain of future promotion, and disgusted with congressional politics, Arnold made a fateful decision: he would seek fortune and fame in the service of Great Britain. With cool calculation Arnold initiated correspondence with Sir Henry Clinton, the British commander, promising to deliver West Point and its 3,000 defenders for £20,000 sterling (about $1 million today), a momentous act that he hoped would spark the collapse of the American cause. Persuading Washington to place the fort under his command, in September 1780 Arnold began to execute his audacious plan, only to see it fail when André was captured and executed as a spy. The British ministry nonetheless rewarded Arnold, giving him £6,000 and appointment as a brigadier general.

Arnold served George III with the same skill and daring he had shown in the Patriot cause. In 1781 in Virginia he led an army that looted Richmond and destroyed munitions and grain intended for the American army opposing Lord Cornwallis. Then he fell upon Connecticut, the colony of his birth, burning ships, warehouses, and much of the town of New London, a major port for Patriot privateers.

In the end, Benedict Arnold's moral failure lay not in his disenchantment with the Patriot cause—for many other American officers left the army in disgust. Nor did his infamy result from his decision to join the British side—for other Patriots chose to become Loyalists, sometimes out of principle but just as often for personal gain. Arnold's treason lay in the abuse of his position of authority: he would betray West Point and its garrison to secure his own success. His treachery was not that of a principled man but of a selfish one, and he never lived that down. Hated in America as a consort of "Beelzebub . . . the Devil," after the war Arnold was treated with coldness and even contempt in Britain. He died as he lived—a man without a country.

Major John André Executed as a British Spy
Unable to catch the traitor Benedict Arnold, the American army executed his British accomplice, whose elegance, intelligence, and dignity won the hearts of his captors. "He died universally esteemed and universally regretted," noted Alexander Hamilton.
Library of Congress.

an assault on New York City, he secretly marched General Rochambeau's army from Rhode Island to Virginia, where it joined his Continental army. Simultaneously, the French fleet massed off the coast, establishing control of Chesapeake Bay. By the time the British discovered Washington's audacious plan, Cornwallis was surrounded, his 9,500-man army outnumbered two to one on land and cut off from reinforcement or retreat by sea. Abandoned by the British navy, Cornwallis surrendered at Yorktown in October 1781.

The Franco-American victory at Yorktown broke the resolve of the British government. "Oh God! It is all over!" Lord North exclaimed when he heard the news. The combined French and Spanish fleet was menacing the British sugar islands, Dutch merchants were capturing European markets from British traders, and a group of European states—the League of Armed Neutrality—was demanding an end to Britain's commercial blockade of France. Isolated diplomatically in Europe, stymied militarily in America, and lacking public support at home, the British ministry gave up active prosecution of the war.

The Patriot Advantage

Angry members of Parliament demanded an explanation. How could mighty Britain, victorious in the Great War for Empire, be defeated by a motley group of colonists? The ministry blamed the military leadership, pointing with some justification to a series of blunders. Why had Howe not been more ruthless in pursuing Washington's army in 1776? How could Howe and Burgoyne have failed to coordinate the movement of their armies in 1777? Why had Cornwallis marched deep into the Patriot-dominated state of Virginia in 1781?

Historians have also criticized these blunders while emphasizing the high odds against British success, given broad-based American support for the rebel cause. Although only a third of the white colonists were zealous Patriots, another third were supportive enough to pay the taxes imposed by state governments. Unlike most revolutionaries the Patriots were led by experienced politicians who commanded public support. The more than 55,000 Tories and thousands of Native Americans who joined the British side could not offset these advantages. Once the rebels had the financial and military support of France, they could reasonably hope for victory. While Britain suffered mediocre generals, Americans had the inspired leadership of George Washington as commander of the Continental army. An astute politician, Washington deferred to the civil authorities, winning respect and support from the Congress and the state governments alike. Confident of his own abilities, he recruited outstanding military officers to instill discipline in the ranks of the fledgling Continental army. Thanks to their efforts, the Continental army emerged as a respectable fighting force that was crucial to the American success. Alone, the Patriot militia lacked the organization necessary to defeat the British army. However, in combination with the Continental forces, it proved potent, providing the margin of victory at Saratoga and other important battles. Militarily flexible, Washington came to understand that warfare in a lightly governed agricultural society required the deft use of rural militia units.

But Washington also had a greater margin for error than the British generals did because Patriots controlled local governments and at crucial moments could mobilize the militia to assist his Continental army. Thousands of militiamen had besieged General Gage in Boston in 1775, surrounded Burgoyne at Saratoga in 1777, and forced Cornwallis from the Carolinas in 1781. In the end the American people decided the outcome of the conflict. Preferring Patriot rule, they refused to support Loyalist forces or accept imperial control in British-occupied areas. Consequently, while the British won many military victories, they achieved little, and their defeats at Saratoga and Yorktown proved catastrophic.

Diplomatic Triumph

After Yorktown diplomats took two years to conclude the war. Peace talks began in Paris in April 1782, but the French and Spanish stalled for time, hoping for a major naval victory or territorial conquest. Their delaying tactics infuriated the American diplomats—Benjamin Franklin, John Adams, and John Jay—who feared that France might sacrifice American interests (see American Voices, "John Adams: Making Peace with Stubborn Enemies and Crafty Allies," p. 183). For this reason the Americans negotiated secretly with the British, prepared if necessary to cut their ties to France and sign a separate peace. The British ministry was also eager to obtain a quick settlement, for the war had little support in Parliament and officials feared the loss to France of a rich West Indian sugar island.

Exploiting the rivalry between Britain and France, the American diplomats finally secured peace on very favorable terms. In the Treaty of Paris, signed in September 1783, Great Britain formally recognized the independence of its seaboard colonies and, while retaining Canada, also relinquished its claims to all the lands south of the Great Lakes between the Appalachian Mountains and the Mississippi River—the domain of undefeated, pro-British Indian peoples. Leaving the Native Americans to their fate, the British negotiators did not insist on a separate Indian territory and promised to withdraw their garrisons "with all convenient speed." "In endeavouring to assist you," a Wea Indian complained to a British general, "it seems we have wrought our own ruin."

Other treaty provisions were equally favorable to the American side. They granted Americans fishing rights off Newfoundland and Nova Scotia, forbade the British from "carrying away any negroes or other property," and guaranteed freedom of navigation on the Mississippi to

John Adams

Making Peace with Stubborn Enemies and Crafty Allies

*M*aking peace proved to be as difficult as winning the war. Negotiations commenced following the Franco-American victory at Yorktown in October 1781, but a year later American diplomats Benjamin Franklin, John Jay, and John Adams were still haggling with their British counterparts (Richard Oswald and Richard Strachey) over control of the fisheries off Nova Scotia, navigation of the Mississippi, reparations for confiscated Loyalist property, and prewar American debts owed to British merchants. As the following entries from John Adams's diary show, the Americans could not rely on their Spanish and French allies, who were pursuing their own diplomatic agendas.

September 14, 1782. The Hague [The Netherlands]. Fell into conversation naturally with Don Joas Theolomico de Almeida, Envoy extraordinary of Portugal. He said to me, "The peace is yet a good way off; there will be no peace this winter. . . . Spain will be the most difficult to satisfy of all the powers. Her pretensions will be the hardest for England to agree to. As to the independence of America, that is decided."

November 2. [Paris]. Almost every moment of this week has been employed in negotiation with the English gentlemen concerning peace. . . .

November 3. I proposed to them [Jay and Franklin] that we should agree, that Congress should recommend to the States to open their courts of justice for the recovery of all just debts. They gradually fell into this opinion, and we all expressed these sentiments to the English gentlemen, who were much pleased with it; and with reason, because it silences the clamors of all the British [merchant] creditors against the peace, and prevents them from making common cause with the [Tory] refugees. . . .

November 4. Mr. Strachey is as artful and insinuating a man as they could send; he pushes and presses every point as far as it can possibly go. . . .

November 5. Mr. Jay likes Frenchmen as little as Mr. Lee and Mr. Izard did. He says they are not a moral people; they know not what it is. . . . Our allies don't play fair, he told me; they were endeavoring to deprive us of the fishery, the western lands, and the navigation of the Mississippi; they would even bargain with the English to deprive us of them; they want to play the western lands, Mississippi, and the whole Gulf of Mexico into the hands of Spain.

November 18. I returned Mr. Oswald's visit. We went over the old ground concerning the Tories. . . . I told him he . . . must bend all his thoughts to convince and persuade his Court to give it up; that if the terms now before his Court were not accepted, the whole negotiation would be broken up. "You are afraid," says Mr. Oswald today, "of being made the tools of the powers of Europe." "Indeed I am," says I.

November 20. Dr. Franklin came in [and said] that the fisheries and Mississippi could not be given up; that nothing was clearer to him than that the fisheries were essential to the Northern States, and the Mississippi to the Southern. . . .

November 25. Strachey told us he had been to London, and waited personally on every one of the King's Cabinet Council, and . . . every one of them, unanimously condemned [our proposal] respecting the Tories. . . .

November 26. The rest of the day was spent in endless discussions about the Tories. Dr. Franklin is very staunch against them. . . .

November 29. Strachey [said that] he had determined to advise Mr. Oswald to strike with us, according to the terms we had proposed as our ultimatum respecting the fisheries and the loyalists. Accordingly, we . . . read over the whole treaty, and corrected it, and agreed to meet tomorrow, at Mr. Oswald's house, to sign and seal the treaties.

November 30. The unravelling of the plot has been to me the most affecting and astonishing part of the whole piece. As soon as I arrived in Paris I waited on Mr. Jay, and learned from him the rise and progress of negotiations. Nothing that has happened since the beginning of the controversy [with Britain] in 1761, has ever struck me more forcibly, or affected me more intimately, than that entire coincidence of principles and opinions between him and me.

Source: Charles Francis Adams, ed., *The Works of John Adams, Second President of the United States* (Boston: Little, Brown, 1850), 2: 227–35.

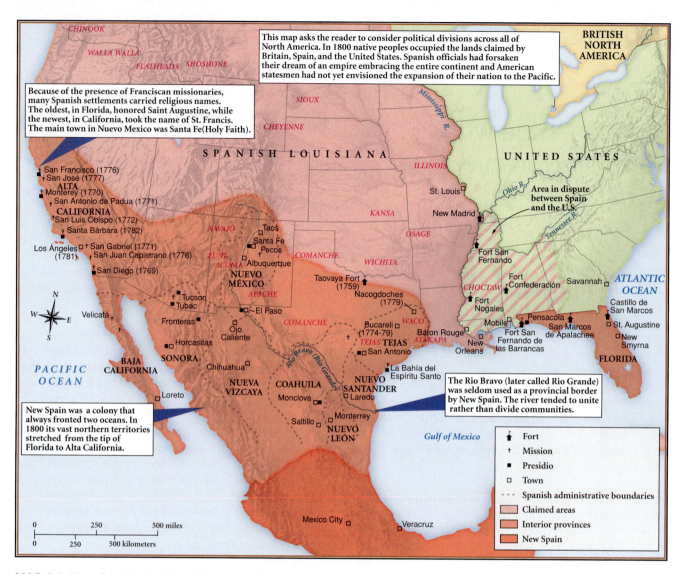

This map asks the reader to consider political divisions across all of North America. In 1800 native peoples occupied the lands claimed by Britain, Spain, and the United States. Spanish officials had forsaken their dream of an empire embracing the entire continent and American statesmen had not yet envisioned the expansion of their nation to the Pacific.

Because of the presence of Franciscan missionaries, many Spanish settlements carried religious names. The oldest, in Florida, honored Saint Augustine, while the newest, in California, took the name of St. Francis. The main town in Nuevo Mexico was Santa Fe (Holy Faith).

New Spain was a colony that always fronted two oceans. In 1800 its vast northern territories stretched from the tip of Florida to Alta California.

The Rio Bravo (later called Rio Grande) was seldom used as a provincial border by New Spain. The river tended to unite rather than divide communities.

MAP 6.5 New Spain's Northern Empire, 1763–1800

Following its acquisition of Louisiana from France in 1763, Spain tried to create a great northern empire. It established missions and forts in California (such as that at Monterey), expanded its settlements in New Mexico, and, by joining in the American War of Independence, won the return of Florida from Britain. By the early nineteenth century, this dream had been shattered by Indian uprisings in California and Texas, Napoleon's seizure of Louisiana, and an imminent American takeover of Florida.

both British subjects and American citizens "forever." In its only concessions the American government promised to allow British merchants to recover prewar debts and to encourage the state legislatures to return confiscated property to Loyalists and grant them citizenship.

In the Treaty of Versailles, signed at the same time as the Treaty of Paris, Britain made peace with France and Spain. Neither American ally gained very much. Spain reclaimed Florida from Britain but failed in its main objective of regaining the fortress of Gibraltar (Map 6.5). France had the pleasure of reducing British power, but its only territorial gain was the Caribbean island of Tobago. Moreover, the war had quadrupled France's national debt; only six years later cries for tax relief and political liberty would spark the French Revolution. Only Americans profited handsomely from the treaties, which gave them independence from Britain and opened up the interior of the North American continent for settlement.

Republicanism Defined and Challenged

From the moment they became revolutionary republicans, Americans began to define the character of their new social order. In the Declaration of Independence Thomas Jefferson had turned to John Locke, the philosopher of private liberty, when he declared a universal human right to "Life, Liberty, and the pursuit of Happiness." But Jefferson and many other Americans also lauded "republican virtue," an enlightened quest for the public good. As the New Hampshire constitution phrased it, "Government [was] instituted for the common benefits, protection, and security of the whole community." The tension between individual self-interest and the public interest would shape the future of the new nation.

Republican Ideals under Wartime Pressures

Simply put, a **republic** is a state without a monarch and with a representative system of government. For many Americans republicanism was also a social philosophy. "The word republic" in Latin, wrote Thomas Paine, "means the public good," which citizens have a duty to secure. "Every man in a republic is public property," asserted the Philadelphia Patriot Benjamin Rush, who eventually extended the notion to include women as well. "His time and talents—his youth—his manhood—his old age—nay more, life, all belong to his country." Reflecting this sense of community, members of the Continental Congress praised the militiamen who fought and fell at Lexington and Concord, Saratoga and Camden. And they applauded Henry Laurens of South Carolina, who condemned as a "total loss of virtue" the wartime demand by Continental officers for lifetime pensions. Raised as gentlemen, officers were supposed to be exemplars of virtue who gave freely to the republic.

Republican Ideals Tested. However, the hardships of war undermined selfless idealism, and during the war Patriot military forces became increasingly restive and unruly. Continental troops stationed at Morristown, New Jersey, in the winters of 1779 and 1780 mutinied, unwilling any longer to endure low pay and sparse rations. To restore military authority Washington ordered the execution of several leaders of the revolt but urged Congress to pacify the soldiers with back pay and new clothing. Later in the war unrest among officers erupted at Newburgh, New York, and Washington had to use his personal authority to thwart a dangerous challenge to the Congress's policies.

Economic distress tested the republican virtue of ordinary citizens. The British naval blockade disrupted the New England fishing industry and cut the supply of European manufactures. British occupation of Boston, New York, and Philadelphia also trimmed domestic trade and manufacturing. As unemployed shipwrights, dock laborers, masons, coopers, and bakers deserted the cities and drifted into the countryside, New York City's population declined from 21,000 residents in 1774 to less than half that number by the war's end. In the Chesapeake the British blockade deprived tobacco planters of European markets, forcing them to cultivate grain, which could be sold to the contending armies. All across the land the character of commercial activity changed as farmers and artisans adapted to a war economy.

Mobilizing for War

This 1779 woodcut illustrated a poem by Molly Guttridge, a Daughter of Liberty in Marblehead, Massachusetts, and symbolized the many different wartime contributions of American women. A few Patriot women disguised themselves as men and fought in the war, and thousands more traveled with the Continental army, providing the troops with food and support. Many others took over the farm chores of their soldier-husbands. New-York Historical Society.

Women and Household Production. Faced with a shortage of goods and constantly rising prices, government officials found it necessary to requisition goods directly from the people. In 1776 Connecticut officials called on the citizens of Hartford to provide 1,000 coats and 1,600 shirts and assessed smaller towns on a proportionate basis. In 1777 Connecticut officials again pressed the citizenry to provide shirts, stockings, and shoes for their men serving in the Continental army. Soldiers added personal pleas. During the Battle of Long Island in 1776, Captain Edward Rogers lost "all the shirts except the one on my back." "The making of cloath," he wrote to his wife, " . . . must go on. . . . I must have shirts and stockings & a jacket sent me as soon as possible & a blankit."

In those difficult times Patriot women contributed to the war effort by increasing production of homespun cloth. One Massachusetts town produced 30,000 yards of homespun, while women in Elizabeth, New Jersey, promised "upwards of 100,000 yards of linnen and woolen cloth." Other women assumed the burdens of farm production while their men were away at war.

Some went into the fields, plowing, harvesting, and loading grain, while others supervised hired laborers or slaves, in the process acquiring a taste for decision making. "We have sow'd our oats as you desired," Sarah Cobb Paine wrote to her absent husband. "Had I been master I should have planted it to Corn." Taught from childhood to value the welfare of their fathers, brothers, and husbands above their own, women were expected to act "virtuously" and often did so. Their wartime efforts not only increased farm household productivity but also boosted self-esteem, prompting some women to claim greater rights in the new republican society.

Inflation and Regulation. Despite the women's efforts, goods remained in short supply, bringing a sharp rise in prices and widespread appeals for government regulation. Hard-pressed consumers decried merchants and traders as "enemies, extortioners, and monopolizers." But in 1777, when a convention of New England states limited price increases to 75 percent, many farmers and artisans refused to sell their goods at the set prices. In the end, a government official admitted, consumers had to pay the much higher market price "or submit to starving."

The struggle over regulation came to a head in Philadelphia. Following the British withdrawal in 1778, food shortages led to soaring prices and demands by the city's artisans and laborers to establish a Committee on Prices. In May 1779 the committee set prices for thirty-two commodities, invoking the traditional concept of the "just price" and urging citizens to act with "republican virtue." Patriot financier Robert Morris and the merchant community condemned the price controls and espoused "classical liberal" ideas of free trade. They argued that regulation would encourage farmers to hoard their crops, whereas allowing prices to rise would bring more goods to market. Most farmers agreed with Morris, as did Benjamin Franklin, who condemned price controls as "contrary to the nature of commerce."

Nonetheless, most Philadelphians favored "fair" trade rather than "free" trade—at least in principle. At a town meeting in August 1779, over 2,000 Philadelphians voted for regulation, and fewer than 300 opposed it. In practice, however, many artisan-republicans—shoemakers, tanners, and bakers—found that they could not support their families on fixed prices and so refused to abide by them. In civilian life as in the military, self-interest tended to triumph over republican virtue.

Spiraling inflation posed a severe challenge to American families. By 1778 so much currency had been printed that a family needed $7 in Continental bills to buy goods worth $1 in gold or silver. The ratio steadily escalated—to 42 to 1 in 1779, 100 to 1 in 1780, and 146 to 1 in 1781, when not even the most dedicated Patriots would accept paper money. To restore the value of Continental currency, the Congress asked the states to accept tax payments in depreciated Continental bills (with $40 in paper money counting as $1 in specie). This plan redeemed $120 million in Continental bills, but at the end of the war speculators still held $71 million in currency, hoping they could eventually redeem it at face value. "Private Interest seemed to predominate over the public weal," a leading Patriot complained.

Ultimately, this currency inflation transferred most of the costs of the war to ordinary Americans. The tens of thousands of farmers and artisans who received Continental bills as payment for supplies and the soldiers who took them as pay found that the currency literally depreciated in their pockets. Every time they received a paper dollar and kept it for a week, the money lost value and could buy less, thus imposing a hidden currency tax on them. Each individual "tax" was small—a few pennies on each dollar they handled. But taken together—as millions of dollars changed hands multiple times—these currency taxes paid the huge cost of the war.

The Loyalist Exodus

As the war turned in favor of the Patriots, more than 100,000 Loyalists, fearing for their lives, emigrated to the West Indies, Canada, and Britain. Among the more prominent refugees only a few found happiness in exile in England; the majority felt out of place and complained of "their uneasy abode in this country of aliens." Many suffered severe financial losses. John Tabor Kempe, the last royal attorney general of New York,

A Black Loyalist Pass, 1783
White Patriots claimed their freedom by fighting against the British, while thousands of black slaves won liberty by fighting for them. This pass certifies that Cato Rammsay, "a Negro," supported the Loyalist cause in New York and is now a free man, able to migrate to British Nova Scotia "or wherever else He may think proper." Nova Scotia Archives and Record Management.

sought £65,000 sterling (about $5 million today) in compensation from the British government but received only £5,000. The great mass of Loyalist refugees received nothing and tried desperately to create new lives. Watching "sails disappear in the distance," an exiled Loyalist woman in Nova Scotia had "such a feeling of loneliness come over me that . . . I sat down on the damp moss with my baby on my lap and cried bitterly."

The Loyalist exodus disrupted the social hierarchy in many communities because, like Kempe, a significant minority of Loyalists came from the ranks of wealthy officials, merchants, and landowners. Although some angry Patriots demanded that the state governments seize the property of these "traitors," most public officials argued that confiscation would be contrary to Patriot principles. In Massachusetts officials cited the state's constitution of 1780, which declared that every citizen should be protected "in the enjoyment of his life, liberty, and property, according to the standing laws."

Consequently, the new republican governments did not seek to change the existing social order. Most states seized only a limited amount of Loyalist property and usually sold it to the highest bidder, who was often a wealthy Patriot rather than a yeoman or a propertyless foot soldier. But in a few cases confiscations did produce a democratic result. In North Carolina about half the new owners of Loyalist lands were small-scale farmers. And on the former Philipse manor in New York many Patriot tenants used their hard-earned savings to buy the seized land and become fee-simple owners. When Philipse tried to reclaim his land, former tenants told him they had "purchased it with the price of their best blood" and "will never become your vassals again." But in general the revolutionary upheaval did not drastically alter the structure of rural society.

Social turmoil was greater in the cities, as Patriot merchants replaced Tories at the top of the economic ladder. In Massachusetts the Lowell, Higginson, Jackson, and Cabot families moved their trading enterprises to Boston to fill the vacuum created by the departure of the Loyalist Hutchinson and Apthorp clans. In Philadelphia, small-scale traders stepped into the vacancies created by the collapse of Anglican and Quaker mercantile firms. In the countinghouses as on the battlefield, Patriots emerged triumphant. The War of Independence replaced a tradition-oriented economic elite—one that invested its profits from trade in real estate, becoming landlords—with a group of entrepreneurial-minded republican merchants who promoted new trading ventures and domestic manufacturing.

The Problem of Slavery

Slavery revealed a contradiction in the Patriots' republican ideology. "How is it that we hear the loudest yelps for liberty among the drivers of Negroes?" the British

Symbols of Slavery—and Freedom

The scar on the forehead of this black woman, who was widely known as "Mumbet," underlined the cruelty of slavery. Winning emancipation through a legal suit in Massachusetts, she chose a name befitting her new status: Elizabeth Freeman. This watercolor, by Susan Sedgwick, was painted in 1811.
Massachusetts Historical Society.

author Samuel Johnson chided the rebellious white Americans, a point some Patriots took to heart. "I wish most sincerely there was not a Slave in the province," Abigail Adams confessed to her husband, John, as Massachusetts went to war. "It always appeared a most iniquitous Scheme to me—to fight ourselves for what we are daily robbing and plundering from those who have as good a right to freedom as we have."

In fact, the struggle of white Patriots for independence raised the prospect of freedom for enslaved Africans. Many slaves hoped for a British invasion that would free them. As the war began, a black preacher in Georgia told his fellow slaves that King George III "came up with the Book [the Bible], and was about to alter the World, and set the Negroes free." Similar rumors circulated among slaves in Virginia and the Carolinas, prompting thousands of African Americans to seek freedom by fleeing behind British lines. Two neighbors of Richard Henry Lee, the Virginia Patriot, lost "every slave they had in the world," as did many other planters. When the British army evacuated Charleston, more than 6,000 former slaves went with them; another 4,000 left from Savannah. All told, some 30,000 blacks may have fled their owners. Hundreds of black Loyalists settled permanently in Canada. Over 1,000 others, poorly treated by British officials and settled on inferior land in Nova Scotia, sought a better life in the abolitionist settlement in Sierra Leone, West Africa (see Chapter 9, American Lives, "Richard Allen and the African American Identity," p. 270).

Benjamin Banneker

On Jefferson and Natural Rights

In his Notes on Virginia *(1785), Thomas Jefferson suggested the inherent inferiority of the black race. In 1791 Benjamin Banneker, a free African American farmer and mathematician who helped to survey the District of Columbia, sent Jefferson a manuscript copy of his forthcoming* Almanac, *an annotated and illustrated guide to the coming agricultural year. In the accompanying letter Banneker asks Jefferson, now the secretary of state in the new federal government, to reconsider his view of Africans, pointing out the contradiction between Jefferson's racial beliefs and the doctrine of natural rights that he had articulated in the* Declaration of Independence.

I suppose it is a truth too well attested to you, to need a proof here, that we are a race of Beings who have long laboured under the abuse and censure of the world . . . considered rather as brutish than human, and Scarcely capable of mental endowments. . . .

Sir, I hope . . . that you are a man far less inflexible in Sentiments of this nature, than many others. . . . Now, Sir, if this is founded in truth, I apprehend you will readily embrace every opportunity to eradicate that train of absurd and false ideas and opinions which so prevail with respect to us, and that your Sentiments are concurrent with mine, which are that the one universal Father has given to us all, and that he hath not only made us all of one flesh, but that he hath also without partiality afforded us all the Same Sensations, and imbued us all with the same faculties, and that however diversified in Situation or colour, we are all of the Same Family, and Stand in the Same relation to him. . . .

Sir, Suffer me to recall to your mind that time in which the Arms and tyranny of the British Crown were exerted with very powerful effort in order to reduce you to a State of Servitude. . . . This, Sir, was a time in which you clearly saw into the injustice of a State of Slavery [and] . . . that you publickly held forth this true and invaluable doctrine . . . : "We hold these truths to be Self evident, that all men are created equal . . ."; but Sir, how pitiable it is to reflect, that . . . in detaining by fraud and violence so numerous a part of my brethren under groaning captivity and cruel oppression that you should at the Same time be found guilty of that most criminal act, which you professedly detested in others, with respect to yourselves.

Source: John J. Patrick, ed., *Founding the Republic: A Documentary History* (Westport, CT: Greenwood Press, 1995), 102–5.

Gradual Emancipation in the North.   For a variety of reasons thousands of African Americans decided to serve the Patriot cause. Knowing firsthand the meaning of slavery and eager to raise their status in society, free blacks in New England volunteered for military service in the First Rhode Island Company and the Massachusetts "Bucks." In Maryland a large number of slaves also took up arms for the Patriot cause in return for a promise of freedom. Elsewhere in the South slaves struck informal bargains with their Patriot masters, trading loyalty in wartime for a promise of eventual liberty. In 1782 the Virginia assembly passed an act allowing **manumission** (liberation); within a decade planters had freed 10,000 slaves.

The Quakers, whose belief in religious and social equality had made them sharp critics of many inequities, took the lead in condemning slavery. Beginning in the 1750s the Quaker evangelist John Woolman had urged Friends to free their slaves, and during the war many did so. Other rapidly growing pietistic groups, notably the Methodists and the Baptists, also advocated emancipation and admitted both enslaved and free blacks to their congregations. In 1784 a conference of Virginia Methodists declared that slavery was "contrary to the Golden Law of God on which hang all the Law and Prophets."

Enlightenment philosophy also worked to undermine slavery and racism. John Locke had argued that ideas were not innate but stemmed from a person's experiences in the world. Accordingly, Enlightenment thinkers suggested that the oppressive conditions of slavery, not inherent inferiority, accounted for the debased situation of Africans in the Western Hemisphere. As one American put it, "A state of slavery has a mighty tendency to shrink and contract the minds of men." Anthony Benezet, a Quaker philanthropist who funded a school for blacks in Philadelphia, defied popular opinion in declaring that African Americans were "as capable of improvement as White People" (see American Voices, "Benjamin Banneker: On Jefferson and Natural Rights," above).

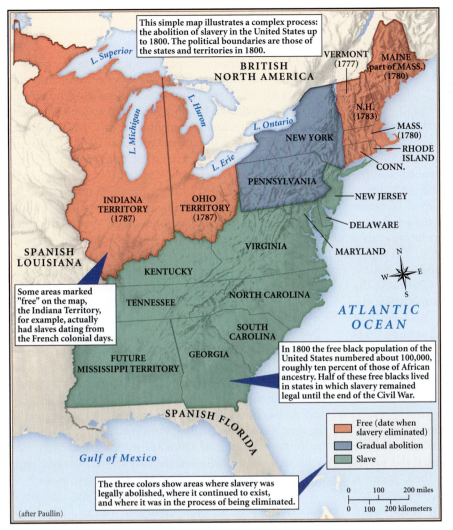

This simple map illustrates a complex process: the abolition of slavery in the United States up to 1800. The political boundaries are those of the states and territories in 1800.

Some areas marked "free" on the map, the Indiana Territory, for example, actually had slaves dating from the French colonial days.

In 1800 the free black population of the United States numbered about 100,000, roughly ten percent of those of African ancestry. Half of these free blacks lived in states in which slavery remained legal until the end of the Civil War.

The three colors show areas where slavery was legally abolished, where it continued to exist, and where it was in the process of being eliminated.

Free (date when slavery eliminated)
Gradual abolition
Slave

0   100   200 miles
0   100   200 kilometers

(after Paullin)

MAP 6.6 The Status of Slavery, 1800

In 1775 racial slavery was legal in every British American colony. By the time the American states achieved their independence in 1783, most African Americans in New England had also become free. By 1800 nearly all of the states north of Maryland had provided for the gradual abolition of slavery, a slow process that was not completed until the 1830s. After the Revolution, some slave owners in the Chesapeake region had also manumitted their slaves, leaving only the whites of the Lower South firmly committed to racial bondage.

By 1784 Massachusetts abolished slavery outright, and three other states—Pennsylvania, Connecticut, and Rhode Island—provided for its gradual termination. Within another twenty years every state north of Delaware had enacted similar laws (Map 6.6). Gradual emancipation laws compensated white owners by requiring more years—even decades—of servitude; the New York Emancipation Act of 1799 granted freedom to slave children only when they reached the age of twenty-five. As late as 1810, almost 30,000 blacks in the northern states—nearly a fourth of their African American residents—were still enslaved. Emancipation came slowly because whites feared competition for jobs and housing and the prospect of race melding. To keep the races separate, in 1786 Massachusetts reenacted an old law prohibiting whites from marrying blacks, Indians, or mulattos.

The White South Grapples with Slavery. The tension between the republican values of liberty and property was greatest in the South, where slaves made up 30 to 60 percent of the population and represented a huge financial investment. Some planters, moved by religious principles or oversupplied with workers on declining tobacco plantations, allowed blacks to buy their freedom through paid work as artisans or laborers. In Maryland, manumission and self-purchase gradually brought freedom to a third of its African American residents, but in 1792 in Virginia the legislature made manumission more difficult. Following the lead of Thomas Jefferson, who owned more than 100 slaves, the Chesapeake gentry argued that slavery was a "necessary evil" required to maintain white supremacy and the luxurious planter lifestyle. Resistance to freedom for blacks was even greater in North Carolina, where the legislature condemned Quaker manumissions as "highly criminal and reprehensible." The rice-growing states of South Carolina and Georgia rejected emancipation out of hand.

The debate over emancipation among southern whites ended in 1800, when Virginia authorities thwarted an uprising planned by the enslaved artisan Gabriel Prosser and hanged him and thirty of his followers. "Liberty and equality have brought the evil upon us," a letter to the *Virginia Herald* proclaimed, for such doctrines are "dangerous and extremely wicked in this country, where every white man is a master, and every black man is a slave." To preserve their privileged social position, whites redefined republicanism so that it applied only to the "master race."

A Republican Religious Order

Political revolution broadened the appeal of religious liberty, forcing Patriot lawmakers to devise a new relationship between church and state. During the colonial era only the Quaker- and Baptist-controlled governments of Pennsylvania and Rhode Island had repudiated the idea of an established church. Then in 1776 James Madison and George Mason used Enlightenment principles to undermine the traditional commitment to a single state-supported church in Virginia. They persuaded the state's constitutional convention to issue a Declaration of Rights guaranteeing all Christians the "free exercise of religion." To win broad support for the war, the Virginia Anglican elite put this doctrine into practice, accepting the legitimacy of the dissenting Presbyterian and Baptist churches that they had previously persecuted. In 1778 Virginia Anglicans launched their own religious revolution by severing ties with the hierarchy of the Church of England in London and creating the Protestant Episcopal Church of America.

After the Revolution an established church and compulsory religious taxes were no longer the norm in the United States. Baptists in particular opposed the use of taxes to support religion. In Virginia their political influence prompted lawmakers to reject a bill supported by George Washington and Patrick Henry, which would have imposed a general tax to fund all Christian churches. Instead, in 1786 the Virginia legislature enacted Thomas Jefferson's Bill for Establishing Religious Freedom, which made all churches equal before the law and granted direct financial support to none. In New York and New Jersey the sheer number of churches—Episcopalian, Presbyterian, Dutch Reformed, Lutheran, and Quaker, among others—prevented legislative agreement on an established church or compulsory religious taxes. In New England Congregationalism remained the official state church until the 1830s, but state law allowed Baptists and Methodists to pay religious taxes to their own churches.

However, even in Virginia, the separation of church and state was never complete. Many Americans still believed that firm connections between church and state were necessary to promote morality and respect for authority. "Pure religion and civil liberty are inseparable companions," a group of North Carolinians advised their minister. "It is your particular duty to enlighten mankind with the unerring principles of truth and justice, the main props of all civil government." Accepting this premise, most state governments provided churches with indirect aid by exempting their property and ministers from taxation.

Freedom of conscience proved equally difficult to achieve. In Virginia Jefferson's Bill for Establishing Religious Freedom instituted the principle of liberty of conscience by outlawing religious requirements for political and civil officeholding. But many states enforced religious criteria for voting and officeholding, penalizing individuals who dissented from the doctrines of Protestant Christianity. The North Carolina constitution of 1776 disqualified from public office any citizen "who shall deny the being of God, or the Truth of the Protestant Religion, or the Divine Authority of the Old or New Testament." New Hampshire's constitution contained a similar provision until 1868.

Americans influenced by the Enlightenment and by evangelical Protestantism condemned such restrictions on freedom of conscience, but for different reasons. Leading American intellectuals, including Thomas Jefferson and Benjamin Franklin, argued that God had given humans the power of reason so that they could determine moral truths for themselves. To protect society from "ecclesiastical tyranny," they demanded complete freedom of expression. Many evangelical Protestants also wanted religious liberty, but their goal was to protect their churches from the government. The New England minister Isaac Backus warned Baptists not to incorporate their churches under the law or accept public funds because that might lead to state control. In Connecticut a devout Congregationalist welcomed voluntarism (the voluntary funding of churches by their members) for another reason: it allowed the laity to control the clergy, thereby furthering "the principles of republicanism."

In religion as in politics, independence provided Americans with the opportunity to fashion a new institutional order. In each case they repudiated the hierarchical ways of the past—monarchy and establishment—in favor of a republican alternative. These choices reflected the outlook and increased influence of ordinary citizens, who had fought and financed the long, difficult military struggle. True to the prediction of a wealthy Virginia planter in April 1776, independence and revolution had allowed yeomen to promote "their darling Democracy."

FOR FURTHER EXPLORATION

▶ For definitions of key terms boldfaced in this chapter, see the glossary at the end of the book.

▶ To assess your mastery of the material covered in this chapter, see the Online Study Guide at **bedfordstmartins.com/henretta**.

▶ For suggested references, including Web sites, see page SR-6 at the end of the book.

▶ For map resources and primary documents, see **bedfordstmartins.com/henretta**.

S U M M A R Y

The War of Independence changed the course of American history by creating the United States as a separate nation with a republican system of government. This dramatic change gathered momentum in April 1775, when the American colonists challenged British authority with military force. Thomas Paine's *Common Sense* attacked the monarchical system and persuaded many Americans to support republicanism and independence, which was formally declared by the Continental Congress on July 4, 1776.

The British ministry dispatched a large British army under General Howe to put down the rebellion. Howe's force defeated Washington's Continental army in a series of battles during 1776, but Patriot triumphs at Trenton and Princeton revived American morale. Howe captured Philadelphia, the Patriots' capital, in the summer of 1777, but the rebels won a major victory at Saratoga, New York, in October. The Patriots nearly lost their main army to cold and hunger at Valley Forge, Pennsylvania, during the winter of 1777–78. Simultaneously, a severe inflation caused by an excess of paper money undermined public support for the new republican governments.

The tide turned in February 1778, when an alliance with France aided the Patriot cause. Congress rejected British overtures for a negotiated settlement, and Lord North embarked on a southern military strategy. British troops won important victories in Georgia and the Carolinas during 1779 and 1780, but Patriot troops finally forced General Cornwallis and his army into Virginia, where they suffered a stinging defeat at Yorktown in October 1781. The Treaty of Paris in 1783 acknowledged the independence of the United States and defined its western boundary at the Mississippi River. Thousands of Loyalists fled to various parts of the British empire, and thousands of slaves won their freedom by assisting the British or escaping to Spanish Florida.

Some Patriots defined republicanism as pursuit of the common good, while others embraced the liberal outlook inspired by John Locke and celebrated the pursuit of individual self-interest. Wartime hardships—such as currency inflation, the hidden tax that paid for the Patriots' military effort—increased the tension between these republican and liberal ideals.

Long after the war ended, Americans continued to debate the social and cultural implications of republicanism. State governments in the North began the gradual abolition of slavery, but those in the South refused to extend freedom to most African Americans. However, throughout the new nation there was growing commitment to freedom of religious worship and the separation of church and state.

T I M E L I N E

1775   Second Continental Congress meets in Philadelphia (May)

Battle of Bunker Hill

Congressional moderates submit Olive Branch petition; King rejects it

Lord Dunmore's proclamation offers freedom to slaves and servants (November)

American invasion of Canada

1776   Patriots and Loyalists skirmish in the South

Thomas Paine publishes *Common Sense* (January)

Declaration of Independence (July 4)

Howe forces Washington to retreat from New York and New Jersey

Virginia Declaration of Rights

1777   Patriot women become important in war economy

Howe occupies Philadelphia (September)

Gates defeats Burgoyne at Saratoga (October)

Continental army suffers at Valley Forge during winter

Severe inflation of paper currency begins

1778   Franco-American alliance (February)

Lord North seeks political settlement; Congress rejects negotiations

British begin southern strategy; capture Savannah (December)

1780   Sir Henry Clinton seizes Charleston (May)

French army lands in Rhode Island

1781   Lord Cornwallis invades Virginia (April); surrenders at Yorktown (October)

Large-scale Loyalist emigration

Partial redemption of Continental currency at 40 to 1

1782   Virginia passes law allowing slave manumission (reversed in 1792)

1783   Treaty of Paris (September 3) officially ends war

1786   Virginia enacts Bill for Establishing Religious Freedom

1800   Gabriel Prosser organizes slave rebellion in Virginia

CHAPTER 7

The New Political Order

1776–1800

Creating Republican Institutions,
1776–1787
*The State Constitutions: How
    Much Democracy?*
The Articles of Confederation
Shays's Rebellion

The Constitution of 1787
The Rise of a Nationalistic Faction
The Philadelphia Convention
The People Debate Ratification
*The Federalists Implement the
    Constitution*

The Political Crisis of the 1790s
Hamilton's Financial Program
Jefferson's Agrarian Vision
*The French Revolution Divides
    Americans*
The Rise of Political Parties
Constitutional Crisis, 1798–1800

LIKE AN EARTHQUAKE THE AMERICAN REVOLUTION SHOOK the foundations of the traditional European political order, and its aftershocks were felt far into the nineteenth century. By "creating a new republic based on the rights of [the] individual, the North Americans introduced a new force into the world," the eminent German historian Leopold von Ranke explained to the king of Bavaria in a private lecture in 1854, warning that the ideology of republicanism might cost the monarch his throne:

This was a revolution of principle. Up to this point, a king who ruled by the grace of God had been the center around which everything turned. Now the idea emerged that power should come from below [from the people]. . . . These two principles are like opposite poles, and it is the conflict between them that determines the course of the modern world.

◀ **Congress Hall, Philadelphia**
As the elegant Georgian edifice depicted (left foreground) in William Birch's 1800 painting suggests, Philadelphia boasted the most distinguished architecture of all the American port cities. Between 1790 and 1800, the Quaker city served as the home of the national government. Huntington Library.

Previous republican revolutions—such as that of the Puritan Commonwealth in England in the 1650s—had ended in political chaos and military rule, and many Europeans expected the new American states to experience the same fate. But General George Washington stunned the world in 1783 when he voluntarily left public life to return to his plantation.

193

"Tis a Conduct so novel," the American painter John Trumbull reported from London, "so inconceivable to People [here], who, far from giving up powers they possess, are willing to convulse the empire to acquire more." Washington's retirement bolstered the authority of elected Patriot leaders, who were firmly committed to representative government.

Fashioning republican institutions absorbed the energy and intellect of an entire generation. Between 1776 and 1800 Americans wrote new state and federal constitutions and devised a system of politics that was responsive to the popular will. Controversies arose at every step in the process. When a bill was introduced into a state legislature, conservative Ezra Stiles grumbled that every elected official "instantly thinks how it will affect his constituents" rather than what its impact would be on the welfare of the public as a whole. What Stiles criticized as an excess of democracy, most ordinary Americans welcomed. For the first time the interests of middling citizens were represented in the halls of government, and the monarchs of Europe trembled.

Creating Republican Institutions, 1776–1787

Once independence had been won, Patriots had to allocate political power among themselves. "Which of us shall be the rulers?" asked a Philadelphia newspaper. The question was complex: Where would power reside, in the national government or the states? Who would control the new republican institutions, traditional elites or average citizens?

The State Constitutions: How Much Democracy?

In May 1776 the Continental Congress had urged Americans to suppress royal authority and establish new governing institutions. Most states quickly complied. Within six months Virginia, Maryland, North Carolina, New Jersey, Delaware, and Pennsylvania had written new constitutions, and Connecticut and Rhode Island had transformed their colonial charters into republican documents by deleting references to the king. "Constitutions employ every pen," an observer noted.

The Meaning of Popular Sovereignty. However, republicanism meant more than ousting the king. The Declaration of Independence had stated the principle of popular sovereignty: that governments derive "their just powers from the consent of the governed." In the heat of revolution many Patriots gave this clause a democratic twist. In North Carolina the backcountry farmers of Mecklenburg County instructed their delegates to the state's constitutional convention to "oppose everything that leans to aristocracy or power in the hands of the rich and chief men exercised to the oppression of the poor." In Virginia voters elected a new assembly that, an observer remarked, "was composed of men not quite so well dressed, nor so politely educated, nor so highly born," while Delaware's constitution declared that "the Right of the People to participate in the Legislature, is the Foundation of Liberty and of all free government."

This democratic outlook received its fullest expression in Pennsylvania, thanks to a coalition of Scots-Irish farmers, Philadelphia artisans, and Enlightenment-influenced intellectuals. Pennsylvania's constitution abolished property owning as a test of citizenship and granted all men who paid taxes the right to vote and hold office. It also created a **unicameral** (one-house) legislature with complete power. No council or upper house was reserved for the wealthy, and no governor exercised veto power. Other constitutional provisions mandated an extensive system of elementary education, protected citizens from imprisonment for debt, and called for a society of economically independent freemen. Pennsylvania's democratic constitution alarmed many leading Patriots, who believed that voting and especially office-holding should be restricted to "men of learning, leisure and easy circumstances." From Boston John Adams denounced Pennsylvania's unicameral legislature as "so democratical that it must produce confusion and every evil work." "Remember," Adams continued, "democracy never lasts long. It soon wastes, exhausts, and murders itself." He and other conservative Patriots feared that popular rule would lead to ordinary citizens using their numerical advantage to tax the rich: "If you give [democrats] the command or preponderance in the . . . legislature, they will vote all property out of the hands of you aristocrats. . . ."

To counter the appeal of the Pennsylvania constitution, Adams published his *Thoughts on Government* (1776) and sent the treatise to friends at constitutional conventions in other states. In his treatise Adams adapted the British Whig theory of **mixed government** (in which power was shared by the king, lords, and commons) to a republican society. To preserve liberty his system dispersed authority by assigning the different functions of government—lawmaking, administering, and judging—to separate branches. Thus, legislatures would make the laws and the executive and the judiciary would enforce them. Adams also called for a **bicameral** (two-house) legislature in which the upper house would be restricted to men who owned substantial property; its role would be to check the power of popular majorities in the lower house. As a further curb on democracy, he proposed an elected governor with the power to veto laws and an appointed—not elected—judiciary to review them. Adams argued that his plan was republican because the people would elect both the chief executive and the legislature.

Leading Patriots endorsed Adams's scheme because it preserved representative government while restricting popular power. Consequently, they wrote state constitutions providing for bicameral legislatures in which membership in both houses was elective. However, only three constitutions gave the veto power to governors; many Patriots recalled the arbitrary conduct of royal governors and had no wish to enhance the power of the executive. In line with Adams's suggestions, many states also retained traditional property qualifications for voting. In New York 90 percent of white men could vote in elections for the assembly, but only 40 percent could vote for the governor and the upper house. The most flagrant use of property to maintain the power of the elite occurred in South Carolina, where the 1778 constitution required candidates for governor to have a debt-free estate of £10,000 (about $600,000 today), senators to be worth £2,000, and assemblymen to own property valued at £1,000. These provisions ruled out officeholding for about 90 percent of white men.

Nonetheless, post-Revolutionary politics had a distinctly democratic tinge (Figure 7.1). The legislature emerged as the dominant branch of government, and state constitutions apportioned seats on the basis of population, giving farmers in rapidly growing western areas the fair representation they had long demanded. Indeed, because of backcountry pressure some legislatures moved the state capital from merchant-dominated seaports such as New York City and Philadelphia to inland cities such as Albany and Harrisburg. Even conservative South Carolina moved its seat of government inland, from Charleston to Columbia.

Moreover, most of the state legislatures were filled by new sorts of political leaders. Rather than electing their social "betters" to office, ordinary citizens increasingly chose men of "middling circumstances" who knew "the wants of the poor." By the mid-1780s middling farmers and urban artisans controlled the lower houses in most northern states and formed a sizable minority in southern assemblies. These middling men took the lead in opposing the collection of back taxes and other measures that tended "toward the oppression of the people."

The political legacy of the Revolution was complex. Only in Pennsylvania and Vermont were radical Patriots able to take power and create democratic institutions. Yet everywhere representative legislatures had more power, and the day-to-day politics of electioneering and interest-group bargaining became much more responsive to the demands of average citizens.

The Political Status of Women.   The extraordinary excitement of the Revolutionary era also tested the dictum that only men could engage in politics. While men continued to control all public institutions—legislatures, juries, government offices—upper-class women entered into political debate, filling their letters and diaries (and undoubtedly their conversations) with opinions on public issues. "The men say we have no business [with politics]," Eliza Wilkinson of South Carolina complained in 1783. "They won't even allow us liberty of thought, and that is all I want" (see American Voices, "Abigail and John Adams: The Status of Women," p. 197).

These American women did not insist on complete civic equality with men, but they wanted to eliminate certain restrictive customs and laws. Abigail Adams demanded equal legal rights for married women, pointing out that under existing common law wives could not own most forms of property and could not enter into a contract or initiate a lawsuit without their husbands' action. "Men would be tyrants" if they continued to hold such power over women, Adams declared to her husband, criticizing him and other Patriots for "emancipating all nations" from monarchical despotism while "retaining absolute power over Wives."

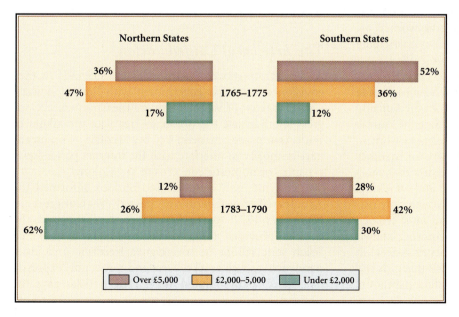

Northern States / Southern States

	Over £5,000	£2,000–5,000	Under £2,000
Northern 1765–1775	36%	47%	17%
Southern 1765–1775	52%	36%	12%
Northern 1783–1790	12%	26%	62%
Southern 1783–1790	28%	42%	30%

FIGURE 7.1 Middling Men Enter the Halls of Government, 1765–1790

Before the Revolution, wealthy men dominated the colonial assemblies. In the new republic, the proportion of men of middling property (as measured by tax lists and probate records) increased dramatically, especially in the northern states.
Source: Adapted from Jackson T. Main, "Government by the People: The American Revolution and the Democratization of the Legislatures," *William and Mary Quarterly,* 3rd ser., vol. 23 (1966).

John and Abigail Adams

Both Adamses had strong personalities and often disagreed in private about political and social issues. In 1794 John playfully accused his wife of being a "Disciple of Wollstonecraft," but (as the American Voices selection on p. 197 shows) Abigail's commitment to legal equality for women long predated Wollstonecraft's A Vindication of the Rights of Woman *(1792).*

Boston Athenaeum / New York State Historical Association, Cooperstown, NY.

Most men paid little attention to women's requests, and most husbands remained patriarchs, dominating their households. Even young men who embraced the republican ideal of "companionate" marriage did not support reform of the common law or a public role for their wives and daughters. With the partial exception of New Jersey, which until 1807 granted the vote to unmarried and widowed women of property, women remained second-class citizens, unable to participate directly in American political and economic life.

The republican quest for an educated citizenry provided the avenue for the most important advances made by American women. In her 1779 essay "On the Equality of the Sexes" (published in 1790), Judith Sargent Murray compared the intellectual faculties of men and women, arguing that women had an equal capacity for memory and superior imagination. Murray conceded that most women were inferior to men in judgment and reasoning, but only because of a lack of training: "We can only reason from what we know," she argued, and most women had been denied "the opportunity of acquiring knowledge." To remedy this situation, the attorney general in Massachusetts persuaded a jury in the 1790s that girls had an equal right to schooling under the state constitution.

With greater access to public elementary schools and the rapid creation of girls' academies (private high schools), many young women became literate and knowledgeable. By 1850 as many women as men in the northeastern states would be able to read and write, and literate women would again challenge their subordinate legal and political status.

The Articles of Confederation

As the Patriots moved toward independence in 1776, they envisioned a central government with limited powers. Carter Braxton of Virginia thought the Continental Congress should have the power to "regulate the affairs of trade, war, peace, alliances, &c." but "should by no means have authority to interfere with the internal police [governance] or domestic concerns of any Colony."

This intensely state-focused outlook informed the Articles of Confederation, passed by Congress in November 1777. As the first national constitution, the Articles provided for a loose confederation in which "each state retains its sovereignty, freedom, and independence" as well as all powers and rights not "expressly delegated" to the United States. The Articles gave the

Abigail and John Adams

The Status of Women

Most American women of European descent accepted the subordinate status of their sex; it was the way life had always been and, many believed, the way God intended it to be. Yet the rhetoric of liberty and equality prompted a few women, including Abigail Adams, the wife of the prominent Massachusetts Patriot John Adams, to challenge men's dominant position. However, as this exchange between the Adamses suggests, most of these challenges were very tentative and very brief.

March 31, 1776 Abigail Adams to John Adams
I long to hear that you have declared an independancy—and by the way in the new Code of Law . . . be more generous and favorable to [the Ladies] than your ancestors. Do not put such unlimited power into the hands of Husbands. Remember all Men would be tyrants if they could. If perticuliar care and attention is not paid to the Ladies we are determined to foment a Rebellion, and will not hold ourselves bound by any Laws in which we have no voice, or Representation. . . . Men of Sense in all Ages abhor those customs which treat us only as the vassals of your Sex. Regard us then as Beings placed by providence under your protection. . . .

April 14, 1776 John Adams to Abigail Adams
As to your extraordinary Code of Laws, I cannot but laugh. We have been told that our Struggle [for independence] has loosened the bonds of Government every where. That Children and Apprentices were disobedient—that schools and Colledges were grown turbulent—that Indians slighted their Guardians and Negroes grew insolent to their Masters. But your letter was the first Intimation that another Tribe more numerous and powerful than all the rest were grown discontented. . . .

Depend on it, We know better than to repeal our Masculine System. Altho they are in full Force, you know they are little more than Theory. We dare not exert our Power in its full Latitude. We are obliged to go fair, and softly, and in Practice you know We are the subjects. We have only the Name of Masters, and rather than give up this, which would compleatly subject Us to the Despotism of the Peticoat, I hope General Washington, and all our brave Heroes would fight. . . .

May 7 and August 14, 1776 Abigail Adams to John Adams
Notwithstanding all your wise Laws and Maxims we have it in our power not only to free ourselves but to subdue our Masters, and without violence to throw both your natural and legal authority at our feet—

> "Charm by accepting, by submitting sway
> Ye have our Humour most when we obey."

I most sincerely wish that some more liberal plan might be laid or executed for the Benefit of the rising Generation, and that our new constitution may be distinguished for Learning and Virtue. If we mean to have Heroes, Statesmen and Philosophers, we should have learned women. The world would laugh at me, and accuse me of vanity, But you I know have a mind too enlarged and liberal. . . . If much depends as is allowed upon the early Education of youth and the first principles which are instilld take the deepest root, great benifit must arise from litirary accomplishments in women.

Source: Lyman H. Butterfield, ed., *Adams Family Correspondence*, 4 vols. (Cambridge: Harvard University Press, 1963), 1: 370, 382–83, 402–3; 2: 94.

confederation government considerable authority; it could declare war and peace, make treaties with foreign nations, adjudicate disputes between the states, borrow and print money, and requisition funds from the states "for the common defense or general welfare." These powers were to be exercised by a central legislature, Congress, in which each state had one vote regardless of its wealth or population. Important laws needed approval by at least nine of the thirteen states, and changes in the Articles required unanimous consent. In the new national government there was no separate executive branch or judiciary.

Because of disputes over western lands, some states did not ratify the Articles until 1781. Some states, such as Virginia, Massachusetts, and Connecticut, invoked their royal charters to claim boundaries that stretched to the Pacific Ocean. States with no claims to land in the West, such as Maryland and Pennsylvania, refused to accept the

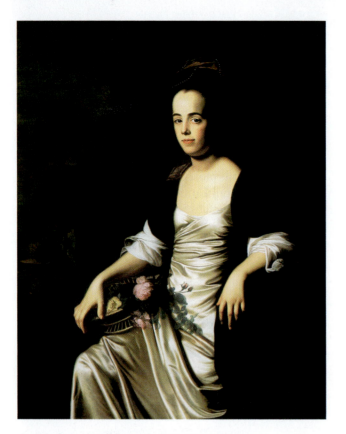

Judith Sargent (Murray), Age Nineteen
The well-educated daughter of a wealthy Massachusetts merchant, Judith Sargent enjoyed a privileged childhood. She endured a difficult seventeen-year marriage to John Stevens, who ultimately went bankrupt, fled from his creditors, and died in the West Indies. In 1788 she wed the Reverend John Murray, who became a leading American Universalist. Her portrait, painted around 1771 by the renowned artist John Singleton Copley, captures Sargent's skeptical view of the world, an outlook that enabled her to question customary gender roles.
Terra Museum of American Art, Chicago, Illinois. Daniel J. Terra Collection.

Articles until the land-rich states relinquished their claims and allowed Congress to create a common national domain. Threatened by Cornwallis's army in 1781, Virginia finally agreed to give up its land claims, and Maryland, the last holdout, then ratified the Articles (Map 7.1).

Ongoing Fiscal Crisis. Formal approval of the Articles was anticlimactic. Congress had been exercising de facto constitutional authority for four years, raising the Continental army and negotiating with foreign nations. Despite its successes, the Confederation government had a major weakness. Congress lacked the authority to impose taxes and therefore had to requisition funds from the state legislatures and hope they would pay, which they usually failed to do. Indeed, by 1780 the Confederation was nearly bankrupt. Facing imminent disaster, General Washington called urgently for a national system of taxation, warning Patriot leaders that otherwise "our cause is lost."

In response, nationalist-minded members of Congress tried to expand the Confederation's authority. Robert Morris, who became superintendent of finance in 1781, persuaded Congress to charter the Bank of North America, a private institution in Philadelphia, hoping to use its notes to stabilize the inflated Continental currency. Morris also developed a comprehensive financial plan that apportioned some war expenses among the states while centralizing control of army expenditures and foreign debt. He hoped that the existence of a national debt would underline the Confederation's need for an import duty. But some state legislatures refused to support an increase in the Confederation's powers, which required the unanimous consent of the states. In 1781 Rhode Island rejected Morris's proposal for an import duty of 5 percent, and two years later New York refused to accept a similar plan, pointing out that it had opposed British-imposed import duties and would not accept them from Congress.

The Northwest Ordinance. Despite its limited powers, Congress successfully planned the settlement of the trans-Appalachian West. In fact, Congress strongly asserted the Confederation's title to the lands in the West in part because it wanted to sell them to farmers and speculators and thereby raise revenue for the government. In 1783 Congress began to negotiate with Indian tribes, hoping to persuade them that the Treaty of Paris had extinguished their land rights. Congress also bargained with white squatters—"white savages," John Jay called them—who had illegally settled on unoccupied land, allowing them to stay only if they paid for the property. Given the natural barrier of the Appalachian Mountains, many members of Congress also feared that an uncontrolled surge of settlers into the West might result in the creation of separate republics. Such governments might then ally themselves with Spain in order to export their crops via the Mississippi River and Spanish-controlled Louisiana. The danger was real: in 1784 settlers in what is now eastern Tennessee organized the new state of Franklin and the worry about Spanish influence increased. To preserve its authority over the West, Congress refused to recognize Franklin or consider its application to join the Confederation. Instead, the delegates directed the states of Virginia, North Carolina, and Georgia to administer the process of creating new states south of the Ohio River, a decision that indirectly encouraged the expansion of slavery into that vast region.

To the north of the Ohio River, Congress established the Northwest Territory and issued three ordinances affecting the settlement and administration of western lands. The Ordinance of 1784, written by Thomas Jefferson, called for the admission of states as soon as the population of a territory equaled that of the smallest existing state. To deter squatters the Land Ordinance of 1785

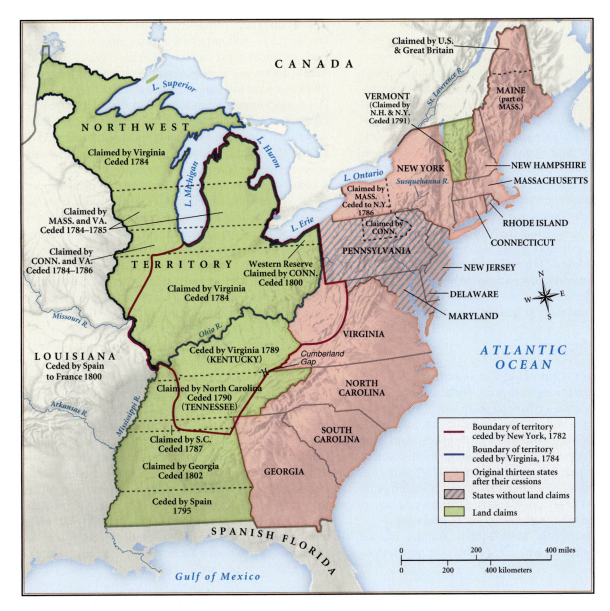

MAP 7.1 The Confederation and Western Land Claims

The Confederation Congress resolved the conflicting land claims of the states by creating a "national domain" west of the Appalachian Mountains. Between 1781 and 1802 all of the seaboard states with western land claims ceded them to the national government. In the Northwest Ordinances, the Confederation Congress laid out rules for establishing territories with democratic political institutions in this domain and declared that all territories were open to settlement by citizens from all the states.

For more help analyzing this map, see the ONLINE STUDY GUIDE at bedfordstmartins.com/henretta.

required that the lands be surveyed before settlement and mandated a grid surveying system that would allow the work to be done quickly (although without attention to the contours and characteristics of the environment). The ordinance also specified a minimum price of $1 per acre and required that 50 percent of the townships be sold in single blocks of 23,040 acres each, which only

large-scale investors and speculators could afford, and the rest in parcels of 640 acres each, which only well-to-do farmers could manage to buy (see Map 8.3).

Finally, the Northwest Ordinance of 1787 provided for the creation of three to five territories that would eventually become the states of Ohio, Indiana, Illinois, Michigan, and Wisconsin. Reflecting the Enlightenment social philosophy of Jefferson and other Patriots, the ordinance prohibited slavery in those territories and earmarked funds from the sale of some land for the support of schools. It also specified that initially Congress should appoint a governor and judges to administer a new territory. Once the number of free adult men reached 5,000 settlers could elect their own legislature. When the population grew to 60,000 residents could write a republican constitution and apply to join the Confederation. On admission a new state would enjoy all the rights and privileges of the existing states.

The ordinances of the 1780s were a great and enduring achievement. They provided for the orderly settlement of the West while reducing the prospect of secessionist movements and preventing the emergence of dependent "colonies." The ordinances also added a new "western" dimension to the national identity. The United States was no longer confined to thirteen governments on the eastern seaboard. It had space to expand.

Shays's Rebellion

However bright the futures of the western states, in the East postwar conditions were grim. Peace had brought a recession rather than a return to prosperity. The war had destroyed many American merchant ships and disrupted the export of tobacco and other farm goods. And now the British Navigation Acts, which had nurtured colonial commerce, barred Americans from trading with the British West Indies. Moreover, low-priced British manufactures flooded American markets, driving many urban artisans and wartime textile firms out of business.

State governments were equally fragile, having emerged from the war with large debts that now had to be paid off. Speculators—mostly wealthy merchants and landowners—had purchased huge quantities of state debt certificates for far less than face value. They demanded that the state governments redeem the bonds quickly, and at full value, despite the fact that such policies would require high taxes. Simultaneously, yeomen farmers and artisans, hard hit by the postwar recession, demanded tax relief. Most state legislatures followed the sentiments of the farmer-majority. To assist indebted yeomen, they enacted laws allowing debtors to pay their creditors in installments. Other states printed more paper currency in an effort to extend credit. Although wealthy men deplored these actions as destructive of "the just rights of creditors," these stopgap measures probably prevented a major social upheaval.

In Massachusetts the lack of debtor-relief legislation provoked the first armed uprising in the new nation. Merchants and creditors had persuaded the Massachusetts legislature to impose taxes to repay the state's war debt and not to issue more paper currency. When cash-strapped farmers could not pay their private debts, creditors threatened them with court suits and high legal fees. Debtor Ephraim Wetmore heard that merchant Stephan Salisbury threatened that he "would have my Body Dead or Alive in case I did not pay." In 1786 residents of central and western counties called extralegal meetings not only to protest the taxes and property seizures but also to demand abolition of imprisonment for debt, property qualifications for officeholding, and the upper house of the state legislature. To back up these radical political demands, bands of angry farmers—including men of status and substance—closed the courts by force. "[I] had no Intensions to Destroy the Publick Government," declared Captain Adam Wheeler, a former town selectman; rather,

History and Memory: Shays's Rebellion

Unlike the North Carolina Regulators (see the illustration on p. 130), the debt-ridden farmers who joined Daniel Shays have not won a place in the pantheon of American heroes. Only a worn, tilting stone hidden away at the side of a field marks the final battle of their struggle against creditor lawsuits, high taxes, and an unresponsive state government. While some Americans have viewed the Shaysites as fighters for freedom, many more have seen them as dangerous political radicals. As Sam Adams, a onetime Patriot radical put it, "The man who dares to rebel against the laws of a republic ought to suffer death." To escape the gallows, Shays fled to New York State, where he died in 1821, still a poor farmer.

Jim Abell, National Geographic Image Collection.

he had rioted to prevent "Valuable and Industrious members of Society [being] dragged from their families to prison [because of their debts], to the great damage . . . [of] the Community at large." The resistance gradually grew into a full-scale revolt led by Captain Daniel Shays, a former Continental army officer who had received a sword for gallant service during the war.

As a struggle against taxes imposed by the distant state government in Boston, Shays's Rebellion resembled colonial resistance to the British Stamp Act. To drive home that point, members of Shays's army placed twigs from pine trees in their hats, just as the Continental army had done. "The people have turned against their teachers the doctrines which were inculcated to effect the late revolution," complained the conservative Massachusetts political leader Fisher Ames. But even the Radical Patriots of 1776 condemned the Shaysites as antirepublican. "Those Men, who . . . would lessen the Weight of Government lawfully exercised must be Enemies to our happy Revolution and Common Liberty," charged onetime revolutionary Samuel Adams. To preserve its authority the Massachusetts legislature passed a Riot Act outlawing illegal assemblies. Governor James Bowdoin, supported by eastern merchants, equipped a formidable fighting force to put down the rebellion and called for additional troops from the Continental Congress. But Shays's army dwindled during the winter of 1786–87, falling victim to freezing weather and inadequate supplies, and Bowdoin's military force easily dispersed the rebels.

The collapsed rebellion provided graphic proof that the costs of war and the fruits of independence were not being shared evenly. Many middling families who had suffered while supporting the struggle for independence felt they had exchanged one tyranny for another. Angry Massachusetts voters turned Governor Bowdoin out of office, and debt-ridden farmers in New York, northern Pennsylvania, Connecticut, and New Hampshire closed courthouses, demanding economic relief. As British officials in Canada predicted the imminent demise of the United States, many Americans feared for the fate of their republican experiment. At this dire moment nationalists redoubled their efforts to create a central government equal to the challenges facing the new republic. Events in Massachusetts, declared Henry Knox, formed "the strongest arguments possible" for the creation of "a strong general government."

The Constitution of 1787

From the moment of its creation, the Constitution was a controversial document, praised by advocates as a solution to the nation's economic woes and condemned by critics as a perversion of republicanism. Simply put, the issue was whether the institutions of self-government were suited only to relatively small states or could be extended across a vast nation. This debate, begun in 1787, would not be finally resolved until the Civil War.

The Rise of a Nationalist Faction

Money questions—debts, taxes, and tariffs—dominated the postwar political agenda, and men who had served the Confederation government during the war as military officers, diplomats, and officials looked at them from a "national" rather than a "state" perspective. National leaders such as General Washington, financier Robert Morris, and diplomats Benjamin Franklin, John Jay, and John Adams became advocates of a stronger central government with the power to control foreign commerce and impose tariffs. They knew that without tariff revenue Congress would be unable to pay the interest on the foreign debt and the nation's credit would collapse. However, key commercial states in the North—New York, Massachusetts, Pennsylvania—resisted national tariffs because they already had trade policies that subsidized local merchants and imposed state taxes on imported goods. Most southern planters also opposed tariffs because they were eager to import British textiles and ironware at the lowest possible prices.

However, some southern planters took a strong nationalist stance because they were deeply worried about the financial policies of the state governments. Legislatures in Virginia and other southern states had responded to the economic hard times of the 1780s by lowering taxes and granting tax relief to various groups of citizens. Such measures troubled wealthy creditors because they diminished public revenue and delayed the redemption of state debts. Taxpayers were being led to believe they would "never be compelled to pay" the public debt, lamented Charles Lee of Virginia, a wealthy bondholder. Private creditors had similar complaints against debtors who persuaded state governments to enact laws that stayed (delayed) the payment of debts. "While men are madly accumulating enormous debts, their legislators are making provisions for their non-payment," a South Carolina creditor complained. To these nationalists, the democratic majorities in the state legislatures constituted a grave threat to republican government.

In 1786 nationalists took an important initiative when James Madison persuaded the Virginia legislature to ask states to attend a special commercial convention to discuss tariff and taxation policies. Only five state governments responded, sending twelve delegates to a meeting in Annapolis, Maryland; undeterred by their small numbers, the delegates called for another meeting in Philadelphia to undertake an even broader review of the Confederation government. Spurred on by Shays's

Rebellion, nationalists in Congress secured a resolution supporting the Philadelphia convention and calling for a revision of the Articles of Confederation "adequate to the exigencies of government and the preservation of the Union." "Nothing but the adoption of some efficient plan from the Convention," a fellow nationalist wrote to James Madison, "can prevent anarchy first & civil convulsions afterwards."

The Philadelphia Convention

In May 1787 fifty-five delegates arrived in Philadelphia, representing every state except Rhode Island, whose legislature opposed any increase in central authority. Some delegates, such as Benjamin Franklin of Pennsylvania, had been early leaders of the independence movement. Others, including George Washington and Robert Morris, had become prominent during the war. Several famous Patriots missed the convention. John Adams and Thomas Jefferson were in Europe, serving as the American ministers to Britain and France, respectively. The radical Samuel Adams had not been chosen as a delegate by the Massachusetts legislature, while the firebrand Patrick Henry refused to attend because he favored a strictly limited national government and "smelt a rat." Their places were taken by capable young nationalists such as James Madison and Alexander Hamilton; both believed that the decisions of the convention would "decide for ever the fate of Republican Government."

Most delegates to the Philadelphia convention were men of property: merchants, slaveholding planters, or "monied men." There were no artisans, backcountry settlers, or tenants and only a single yeoman farmer. Consequently, most delegates supported the property rights of creditors. The majority also favored a stronger central government that would protect the republic from "the imprudence of democracy," as Hamilton put it.

The Virginia and New Jersey Plans. The delegates elected Washington as the presiding officer and, to forestall popular opposition, decided to deliberate behind closed doors (in fact, Americans learned of the proceedings only in the 1840s, when Madison's notebooks were published). They agreed that each state would have one vote, as in the Confederation, and that a majority of states would decide an issue. Then the delegates exceeded their mandate to revise the Articles of Confederation and considered the Virginia Plan, a scheme for a truly national government devised by James Madison. Madison had arrived in Philadelphia determined to fashion a new political order run by men of high character. A graduate of Princeton, he had read classical and modern political theory and served in both the Confederation Congress and the Virginia assembly. Once an optimistic Patriot and republican, Madison had grown increasingly pessimistic. His experience in the

Virginia legislature had convinced him of the "narrow ambition" and lack of public virtue of many state political leaders. He wanted to design a national government that would inhibit petty factional disputes, what he called the "Vices of the Political System."

Madison's Virginia Plan differed from the Articles of Confederation in three crucial respects. First, it rejected state sovereignty in favor of the "supremacy of national authority." The central government would have the power not only to "legislate in all cases to which the separate States are incompetent" but also to overturn state laws. Second, the plan called for a national republic that drew its authority directly from all the people and had direct power over them. As Madison explained, the new central government would bypass the states, operating directly "on the individuals composing them." Third, the plan created a three-tier national government with a lower house elected by voters, an upper house elected by the lower house, and an executive and judiciary chosen by the entire legislature.

From a political perspective Madison's plan had two fatal flaws. First, state politicians and many ordinary citizens would strongly oppose the provision allowing the national government to veto laws enacted by state legislatures. Second, by assigning great power to the lower house, whose composition was based on population, Madison's plan would increase the influence of voters who lived in the large states. Consequently, delegates from the less populous states rejected the plan out of hand, fearing, as a Delaware delegate put it, that the states with many inhabitants would "crush the small ones whenever they stand in the way of their ambitious or interested views."

Delegates from the smaller states rallied behind a plan devised by William Paterson, a delegate from New Jersey. The New Jersey Plan, as it came to be called, strengthened the Confederation by giving the central government the power to raise revenue, control commerce, and make binding requisitions on the states. But it preserved the states' control over their own laws and guaranteed their equality: each state would have one vote in a unicameral legislature, as in the Confederation. Delegates from the populous states rejected this provision of Paterson's plan and, after a month of debate, mustered a bare majority in favor of the principles of the Virginia Plan.

This decision raised the prospect of a dramatically new constitutional system and prompted two New York representatives—Robert Yates and John Lansing—to accuse the delegates of exceeding their mandate and to leave the convention (see American Voices, "Robert Yates and John Lansing: A Protest against the Philadelphia Convention," p. 203). During the hot, humid summer of 1787 the remaining delegates met six days a week, debating high principles and discussing a multitude of technical details. Experienced and realistic

Robert Yates and John Lansing

A Protest against the Philadelphia Convention

Robert Yates and John Lansing attended the Philadelphia convention as delegates from New York but left in protest when the Virginia Plan became the basis for a new constitutional order. In a letter to the governor of New York, Yates and Lansing explained their reasons: the convention lacked the authority to create the "consolidated" government implicit in the Virginia Plan, and a centralized system of rule would undermine civil liberties and republican principles of representative government. These Antifederalist arguments failed to prevent ratification of the Constitution, but they remained powerful and were restated by hundreds of American politicians—from the North as well as the South—for the next seventy years and beyond.

We beg leave, briefly, to state some cogent reasons, which, among others, influenced us to decide against a consolidation of the states. . . .

Our powers were explicit, and confined to the sole and express purpose of revising the Articles of Confederation. . . . [We believed] that a system of consolidated government could not, in the remotest degree, have been in contemplation of the legislature of this state; for that so important a trust, as adopting measures which tended to deprive the state government of its most essential rights of sovereignty, could not have been confided by implication. . . .

Reasoning in this manner, we were of opinion that the leading feature of every amendment ought to be the preservation of the individual states in their uncontrolled constitutional rights, and that, in reserving these, a mode might have been devised of granting to the Confederacy, the moneys arising from a general system of revenue, the power of regulating commerce and enforcing the observance of foreign treaties, and other necessary matters of less moment.

[We also] entertained an opinion that a general government, however guarded by declarations of rights, or cautionary provisions, must unavoidably, in a short time, be productive of the destruction of the civil liberty of such citizens who could be coerced by it, by reason of the extensive territory of the United States, the dispersed situation of its inhabitants, and the insuperable difficulty of controlling or counteracting the views of a set of men (however unconstitutional and oppressive their acts might be) possessed of all the power of government, and who [were remote] . . . from their constituents. . . . [Moreover, we believed] that however wise and energetic the principles of the general government might be, the extremities of the United States could not be kept in due submission and obedience to its laws, at the distance of so many hundred miles from the seat of government;

[And finally] that, if the general legislature was composed of so numerous a body of men as to represent the interests of all the inhabitants of the United States, in the usual and true ideas of representation, the expense of supporting it would become intolerably burdensome; and that, if a few only were vested with a power of legislation, the interests of a great majority of the inhabitants of the United States must necessarily be unknown. . . . These reasons were, in our opinion, conclusive against any system of consolidated government.

Source: J. Elliot, ed., Debates in the Several State Conventions on the Adoption of the Constitution (New York, 1861), 1: 480–83.

---

politicians, they knew that their final plan had to be acceptable to existing political interests and powerful social groups. Pierce Butler of South Carolina invoked a classical Greek precedent: "We must follow the example of Solon, who gave the Athenians not the best government he could devise but the best they would receive."

The Great Compromise. Representation remained the central problem. To satisfy both large and small states the Connecticut delegates suggested amending the Virginia Plan so that the upper house, the Senate, would always have two members from each state, while seats in the lower chamber, the House of Representatives, would be apportioned on the basis of population. In addition, the size of the states' delegations would be altered every ten years on the basis of a national census. After bitter debate, this "Great Compromise" was accepted, but only reluctantly; to some delegates from populous states it seemed less a compromise than a victory for the smaller states.

Other issues that would directly affect the interests of the existing states were quickly settled by restricting (or leaving ambiguous) the extent of central authority. Some delegates opposed establishing national courts within the states, warning that "the states will revolt at such encroachments." The convention therefore defined the judicial power of the United States in broad terms, vesting it "in one supreme Court" and leaving the new national legislature to decide whether to establish lower courts within the states. The convention also decided against requiring voters in national elections to own a certain amount of land. "Eight or nine states have extended the right of **suffrage** beyond the freeholders [landowners]," George Mason of Virginia pointed out. "What will people there say if they should be disfranchised?" The convention also curried favor with the existing state governments by placing the selection of the president in an **electoral college** chosen on a state-by-state basis and specifying that state legislatures, not the voters at large, would elect members of the U.S. Senate. By giving states an important role in the new constitutional system, the delegates encouraged their citizens to accept a reduction in state sovereignty.

Slavery hovered in the background of the delegates' debates, rarely discussed but always a factor. When the issue came to the fore, speakers divided along regional lines. Speaking for many northerners Gouverneur Morris of New York condemned slavery as "a nefarious institution" and hoped for its eventual demise (see American Lives, "Gouverneur Morris: An Elitist Liberal in a Republican Age," p. 206). Reflecting the outlook of many Chesapeake planters, who wanted to retain the institution but already owned ample numbers of slaves, George Mason of Virginia advocated an end to the Atlantic slave trade. However, delegates from the rice-growing states of South Carolina and Georgia insisted that slave imports must continue, warning that otherwise their states "shall not be parties to the Union." At their insistence the delegates denied Congress the power to regulate slave imports for twenty years; thereafter the slave trade could be abolished by legislative action (which Congress proceeded to do in 1808).

For the sake of national unity, the delegates likewise treated other slavery-related issues as political rather than moral questions. To protect the property of southern slave owners, they agreed to a "fugitive" clause that allowed masters to reclaim enslaved blacks (or white indentured servants) who took refuge in other states. To mollify the northern states the delegates did not mention slavery explicitly in the Constitution (referring instead to citizens and "all other Persons"), thus denying the institution national legal status. They also refused southern demands to count slaves and citizens equally in determining states' representation in Congress, accepting a compromise proposal in which a slave would be counted as three-fifths of a free person for purposes of representation and taxation.

National Power.   Having allayed the concerns of small states and slave states, the delegates proceeded to create a powerful national government that favored the interests of creditors over those of debtors. The finished document declared that the Constitution and all national legislation and treaties made under its authority would be the "supreme" law of the land. It gave the national government broad powers over taxation, military defense, and external commerce as well as the authority to make all laws "necessary and proper" to implement those and other provisions. To protect creditors and establish the fiscal integrity of the new government, the Constitution mandated that the United States honor the existing national debt. Finally, it restricted the ability of state governments to assist debtors by forbidding the states to issue money or enact "any Law impairing the Obligation of Contracts."

The proposed Constitution was not a "perfect production," Benjamin Franklin admitted on September 17, 1787, as he urged the forty-one delegates still present to sign it. Yet the great diplomat confessed his astonishment at finding "this system approaching so near to perfection as it does." His colleagues apparently agreed; all but three signed the document.

The People Debate Ratification

The procedures for ratifying the new Constitution were as controversial as its political proposals. The delegates hesitated to submit the Constitution to the state legislatures for their unanimous consent, as required by the Articles of Confederation, because they knew that Rhode Island (and perhaps a few other states) would reject it. So they specified that the Constitution would go into effect on ratification by special conventions in at least nine of the thirteen states. Because of its nationalist sympathies the Confederation Congress winked at this extralegal procedure; surprisingly, so too did most state legislatures, which promptly called the ratification conventions.

As a great national debate began, the nationalists seized the initiative with two bold moves. First, they called themselves Federalists, a term that suggested a loose, decentralized system of government and partially obscured their quest for a strong central authority. Second, they launched a coordinated political campaign, publishing dozens of pamphlets and newspaper articles supporting the proposed Constitution.

The Antifederalists.   The opponents of the Constitution, who became known as Antifederalists, had diverse backgrounds and motives. Some, like

Governor George Clinton of New York, feared losing their power at the state level. Others were rural democrats who predicted that a powerful central government controlled by merchants and creditors would produce a new aristocracy. "These lawyers and men of learning and monied men expect to be managers of this Constitution," worried a Massachusetts farmer, "and get all the power and all the money into their own hands and then they will swallow up all of us little folks . . . just as the whale swallowed up Jonah." Melancton Smith of New York warned that the large electoral districts prescribed by the Constitution would encourage the election of a few wealthy upper-class men, whereas the smaller state districts produced "a representative body, composed principally of respectable yeomanry." Smith and other Antifederalists pointed out that the Constitution, unlike most state constitutions, lacked a declaration of individual rights.

Well-educated Americans with a traditional republican outlook also opposed the new system. To keep government "close to the people," they wanted the nation to remain a collection of small sovereign republics tied together only for trade and defense—not the "United States" but the "States United." Citing the French political philosopher Montesquieu, Antifederalists argued that republican institutions were best suited to cities or small states—a localist outlook that shaped American political thinking well into the twentieth century. "No extensive empire can be governed on republican principles," James Winthrop of Massachusetts declared. Patrick Henry predicted the Constitution would re-create the worst features of British rule: high taxes, an oppressive bureaucracy, a standing army, and a "great and mighty President . . . supported in extravagant munificence."

In New York, where ratification was hotly contested, James Madison, John Jay, and Alexander Hamilton countered these arguments in a series of eighty-five essays collectively called *The Federalist*. Although not widely read at the time outside of New York City (as only a few of the essays were reprinted in newspapers elsewhere), *The Federalist* was subsequently recognized as a classic work of republican political theory. Its authors stressed the need for a strong government to conduct foreign affairs and denied that it would foster domestic tyranny. Citing Montesquieu's praise for mixed government (and drawing on John Adams's *Thoughts on Government*), Madison, Jay, and Hamilton pointed out that national authority would be divided among a president, a bicameral legislature, and a judiciary. Each branch of government would check and balance the others, thus preserving liberty.

Indeed, in *The Federalist*, No. 10, Madison made a significant contribution to the theory of republicanism by denying it was suited only to small states. It was "sown in the nature of man," Madison wrote, that individuals would seek power and form factions to advance

their interests. Indeed, "a landed interest, a manufacturing interest, a mercantile interest, a moneyed interest, with many lesser interests, grow up of necessity in civilized nations." He argued that a free society should not suppress those groups but simply prevent any one of them from becoming dominant—an end best achieved in a large republic. "Extend the sphere," Madison concluded, "and you take in a greater variety of parties and interests; you make it less probable that a majority of the whole will have a common motive to invade the rights of other citizens."

The Ratification Conventions. The delegates who met at the state ratifying conventions between December 1787 and June 1788 represented a wide spectrum of Americans, from untutored farmers and middling artisans to well-educated gentlemen. Generally, delegates from the backcountry were Antifederalists, whereas those from the seacoast were Federalists. Thus, a coalition of merchants, artisans, and commercial farmers from Philadelphia and its vicinity spearheaded an easy Federalist victory in Pennsylvania. Other early Federalist successes came in the less populous states of Delaware, New Jersey, Georgia, and Connecticut, where delegates counted on a strong national government to offset the power of their larger neighbors.

The Constitution's first real test came in January 1788 in Massachusetts, one of the most populous states and a hotbed of Antifederalist sentiment (Map 7.2). Influential Patriots, including Samuel Adams and Governor John Hancock, opposed the new constitution, as did Shaysite sympathizers in the western part of the state. But Boston artisans, who wanted tariff protection from British imports, supported ratification. Astute Federalist politicians finally persuaded wavering delegates by promising that the new government would consider a national guarantee of individual rights. By a close vote of 187 to 168, the Federalists carried the day.

Spring brought new Federalist victories in Maryland and South Carolina. When New Hampshire ratified by the narrow margin of 57 to 47 in June, the required nine states had approved the Constitution. Still, the essential states of Virginia and New York had not yet acted. Writing in *The Federalist*, Madison, Jay, and Hamilton used their superb rhetorical skills to win support in those states. Addressing a powerful Antifederalist argument, leading Federalists reiterated their promise to amend the Constitution with a bill of rights. In the end the Federalists won narrowly in Virginia, 89 to 79, and that success carried them to victory in New York by the even smaller margin of 30 to 27. Suspicious of centralized power, the yeomen of North Carolina and Rhode Island ratified only in 1789 and 1790, respectively.

Ratification of the Constitution brought an end to the Antifederalist agitation and marked a temporary

Gouverneur Morris: An Elitist Liberal in a Republican Age

The life of Gouverneur Morris (1752–1814) reveals the personal and ideological complexity of the American Revolution. Morris was born into the comfortable world of the New York aristocracy and quickly imbibed its values. Even as a young man he understood the dangers to his class posed by a "democratic" revolution supported by social nobodies such as George Robert Twelves Hewes (see Chapter 5, American Lives, p. 154). Responding to agitation for independence in 1774, Morris advised New York's political elite "to seek for reunion with the parent state." Otherwise, "I see, and I see it with fear and trembling, that . . . we shall be under the worst of all possible dominions . . . the domination of a riotous mob." "The mob begin to think and reason," he warned again in 1775, and soon "they will bite, depend on it."

His family situation had a lot to do with Morris's fear and disdain of ordinary men and women. His grandfather Lewis Morris was the first lord of Morrisania, a large estate in Westchester County, New York, and the king's governor of New Jersey. His father, Lewis Jr., was also a royal official, a judge of the vice-admiralty court, who vowed on his deathbed that Gouverneur should have "the best Education that is to be had in Europe or America." In fact, education was a consolation prize, provided to younger sons who had no prospects of a valuable landed inheritance. So Gouverneur studied at King's College in New York and then took up an apprenticeship with William Smith Jr., an eminent New York lawyer. Socially privileged yet economically deprived, Morris feared downward mobility and hurled abuse on his social inferiors.

The sharpening struggle with Britain forced Gouverneur Morris to make a fateful decision. Breaking with his mother, many relatives, and his legal mentor, all of whom remained loyal to the crown, Morris became a Patriot—of the most conservative stripe. At the Provincial Convention that drafted the New York State constitution of 1777, Morris argued strenuously for maintaining the old aristocratic method of voting by public declaration, but more republican-minded members mandated voting by ballot. Still, the convention heeded Morris's call to impose high property qualifications for voting: a freehold worth £20 to vote for the assembly and one valued at £100 to vote for the senate or governor.

Morris was equally conservative—but much more innovative—in Patriot politics at the national level. As one of New York's delegates to the Continental Congress, Morris worked hard to remedy the financial weaknesses of the Confederation. As early as 1778 Morris proposed the elimination of state currencies, the creation of a national domain in the West, and national tariffs to pay off the growing war debt. Three years later he happily enlisted as the assistant to the new superintendent of finance, the merchant Robert Morris. Together the Morrises (who were not related) devised measures to restore the government's credit. In 1781 they won approval for the Bank of North America and then issued a "Report on Public Credit" that called for the Confederation government to assume the entire national debt, issue new interest-bearing debt certificates, and impose tariffs and internal taxes to pay the interest costs. Here in outline was the fiscal program implemented a decade later by Alexander Hamilton.

Like Hamilton, Gouverneur Morris was a man of "spirit and nerve" who never doubted his own judgment and rarely respected that of others. George Washington chastised Morris for displaying his "brilliant imagination" too quickly and recklessly. Never humbled, not even by an accident in 1780 that left him with a wooden leg, Morris used his personal charm and intellectual brilliance to compensate for these flaws in his character. He played a prominent role at the Philadelphia convention in 1787, insisting that "property was the sole or primary object of Government & Society." To protect property rights, Morris demanded an elitist Senate whose members would serve for life, a national freehold property qualification for voting, and a strong president with the power of the veto.

Nevertheless, Morris rejected the legitimacy of two traditional types of property rights—the feudal dues paid by tenants to landowners and the ownership of slaves. In debates over the New York constitution Morris called for the end of "domestic slavery . . . so that in future ages, every human being who breathes the air of the State, shall enjoy the privileges of a freeman," a proposition he reiterated with great force at the Philadelphia convention.

Morris's defense of freedom for individuals—in their personal lives, their property rights, and their ability to form legal contracts—aligned him with those Patriots who gave a "classical liberal" definition to the American Revolution (rather than the Patriots who gave greater weight to "classical republican" values of public virtue and the public good). Valuing individual liberty more highly than majority rule, liberal Patriots such as Morris hoped the new Constitution would protect property rights from popularly elected state legislatures and encourage economic growth.

Indeed, Morris's outlook—and increasingly his life—reflected the emergent principles of a free-market capitalism. After serving as Robert Morris's assistant, Gouverneur became his business partner. The two men invested jointly in land in New York and Pennsylvania, a maritime venture in Massachusetts, and the sale of tobacco to the French tobacco monopoly. Such speculations landed Robert Morris in debtors' prison but made Gouverneur Morris a rich man, able at last to live in the elegant style to which he had been bred.

Beginning in 1788, Morris resided in Europe for ten years, first as a speculating merchant, then as the American minister to France (1792–1794), and finally as a cultured man of independent wealth. Fluent in French, polished in manners, confident of his talents, Morris fit easily into Parisian high society. He took as his mistress the young wife of an aging aristocrat, formed a lifelong friendship with the formidable Madame de Staël (a leading figure in Paris society), and came to share the hopes and fears of the endangered French monarch and his aristocratic supporters. While disparaging the French nobility for "Hugging the Privileges of Centuries long elapsed," Morris refused to support the constitutional monarchy proposed by the Marquis de Lafayette and other republican-minded French reformers. Indeed, as republicans seized control of France in 1792, Morris joined an unsuccessful aristocratic plot to smuggle King Louis XVI out of Paris.

In the end Gouverneur Morris stands forth as an elitist classical liberal, an American precursor of Alexis de Tocqueville (see Chapter 8, Voices from Abroad, p. 247). Patrician in manners and fearful of mob rule, Morris was a political conservative, "opposed to the Democracy from Regard to Liberty." More egalitarian in his economic views, he celebrated the classical liberal principles of personal freedom, entrepreneurial enterprise, and equal opportunity.

Gouverneur Morris, Federalist Statesman
Morris almost became a Loyalist because he was a snob who liked privilege and feared the people. ("The mob begins to think and reason," he once noted with disdain.) He became a Federalist for similar reasons, helping to write the Philadelphia Constitution and, after 1793, strongly supporting the Federalist Party.
National Portrait Gallery, Smithsonian Institution / Art Resource, NY.

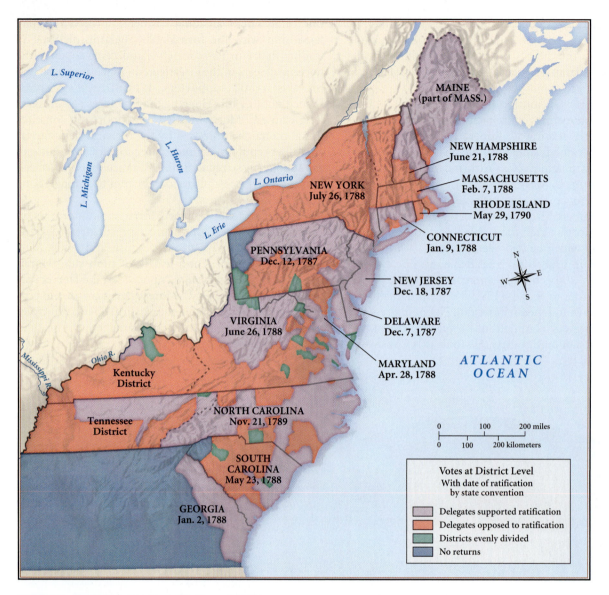

MAP 7.2 Ratifying the Constitution of 1787

In 1907 the geographer Owen Libby mapped the votes of members of the state ratification conventions. His map shows that most delegates from seaboard or commercial farming districts favored the Constitution, while those from backcountry areas opposed it. Subsequent research has confirmed Libby's socioeconomic interpretation in North and South Carolina and Massachusetts; however, other factors influenced delegates in some states with frontier districts, such as Georgia, where the Constitution was ratified unanimously.

decline in ascendancy of the democratically inclined state legislatures. "A decided majority" of the New Hampshire General Assembly had long opposed the "new system" of centralized authority, reported Joshua Atherton, but had now bowed to the inevitable, saying, "It is adopted, let us try it." In Virginia, Antifederalist firebrand Patrick Henry likewise vowed to "submit as a quiet citizen" and fight for amendments "in a constitutional way."

Working against great odds the Federalists had created a national republic that restored the political authority of established leaders. To celebrate their victory Federalists organized great processions in the seaport cities. By marching in an orderly fashion—in a conscious effort to contrast themselves to the riotous Revolutionary mobs—Federalist-minded citizens affirmed their commitment to a self-governing republican community based on law. Floats carried a copy of the Constitution on an "altar of liberty," using sacred symbols to endow the new national regime with moral legitimacy and lay the foundations for a secular "civil religion."

The Federalists Implement the Constitution

The Constitution expanded the dimensions of American political life, allowing voters to fill national as well as local and state offices. The Federalists swept the election of 1788, placing forty-four supporters in the first Congress; only eight Antifederalists won election. As expected, members of the electoral college chose George Washington as president. John Adams received the second highest number of electoral votes and became vice president. The two men took up their posts in New York City, the temporary home of the national government.

Devising the New Government. Washington, the military savior of his country, became its political father as well. At fifty-seven he was a man of great personal dignity and influence. Instinctively cautious, he generally followed the administrative practices of the Confederation, asking Congress to reestablish the existing executive departments: Foreign Affairs (State), Finance (Treasury), and War. However, he made one important innovation. The Constitution gave the president the power to appoint major officials with the consent of the Senate, but Washington insisted that only he—and not the Senate—could remove them, thus ensuring the chief executive's control over the bureaucracy. To head the

Department of State Washington chose Thomas Jefferson, a fellow Virginian and an experienced diplomat. For secretary of the treasury he turned to Alexander Hamilton, a lawyer and wartime military aide. The new president designated Jefferson, Hamilton, and Secretary of War Henry Knox as his **cabinet**, or advisory body.

The Constitution had created a Supreme Court but left the establishment of the court system to Congress. Because the Federalists wanted national institutions to act directly on individual citizens within the various states, they enacted a far-reaching Judiciary Act in 1789. The act created a hierarchical federal court system with thirteen district courts, one for each state, and three circuit courts to hear appeals from the districts, with the Supreme Court having the final say. Moreover, the Judiciary Act permitted appeals to the Supreme Court of federal legal issues that arose in state-run courts, ensuring that national (and not state) judges would decide the meaning of the Constitution.

The Bill of Rights. The Federalists kept their promise to add a declaration of rights to the Constitution. Drawing on proposed lists of rights submitted by the states' ratifying conventions, James Madison, who had been elected to the House of Representatives, submitted nineteen amendments to the first Congress, and ten of them were approved by that Congress and ratified by the

The First "White House"

In 1790 New York City became the home of the new national government. To keep the capital at New York, the city began to build an imposing mansion for the president. To symbolize the nation's commitment to republicanism, the architects gave the residence a classical columned facade like those of the Roman Republic, creating a sharp contrast with nearby Dutch-influenced buildings. Shortly before the completion of the mansion, the national government moved to the District of Columbia, a federal territory created by cessions from Maryland and Virginia. New-York Historical Society.

states in 1791. These ten amendments, which became known as the Bill of Rights, safeguarded certain fundamental personal rights, such as freedom of speech and religion, and mandated certain legal procedures that protected the individual, such as trial by jury. The Second Amendment gave the people the right to bear arms so that they might serve in the militia and defend their liberties, while the Tenth Amendment limited the authority of the national government by reserving powers not otherwise addressed to the states or the people.

As a safeguard against improper governmental authority, the amendments have had a complex history. Like all constitutional clauses and ordinary laws, they are subject to judicial interpretation, which has changed with time and circumstance. For example, the Second Amendment, which gives the people the right "to keep and bear Arms," has been interpreted by most twentieth-century courts to allow the states and Congress to forbid citizens from owning certain types of guns (such as automatic weapons) and to require the registration of others (such as handguns in cities). Moreover, in 1833 the Supreme Court (in the important case of *Barron v. Baltimore*) declared that the amendments safeguarded rights only from infringement by the national government; for protection from state authorities, citizens would have to rely on the state constitutions. But nearly a century later, in the 1920s, federal courts began to enforce the Fourteenth Amendment (1868), which prohibited the states from depriving "any person of life, liberty, or property, without due process of law," against state and local governments.

Whatever their ultimate fate, the amendments addressed Antifederalists' concerns, securing the legitimacy of the new government and ensuring broad political support for the Constitution.

The Political Crisis of the 1790s

The final decade of the century brought fresh political challenges. The Federalists divided into two irreconcilable factions over financial policy, and the ideological impact of the French Revolution widened this split. In the course of these struggles Alexander Hamilton and Thomas Jefferson offered contrasting ideological visions of the American future.

Hamilton's Financial Program

One of George Washington's most important decisions was his choice of Alexander Hamilton as secretary of the treasury. An ambitious self-made man of great charm and intelligence, Hamilton had served as Washington's personal aide during the war. He married into the rich and influential Schuyler family of Hudson River landowners and during the 1780s became a leading lawyer in New York

City. At the Philadelphia convention Hamilton condemned the "amazing violence and turbulence of the democratic spirit," calling for an authoritarian government headed by a president with nearly monarchical powers.

As treasury secretary Hamilton devised bold policies to enhance the authority of the national government and favor wealthy financiers and seaport merchants (Figure 7.2). He outlined his plans in three path-breaking and interrelated reports to Congress: on public credit (January 1790), a national bank (December 1790), and manufactures (December 1791).

Public Credit.   The financial and social implications of Hamilton's "Report on the Public Credit" made it instantly controversial. The report called for Congress to buy ("redeem") at face value the millions of dollars in securities issued by the Confederation, a plan that would bolster the government's credit but also provide windfall profits to speculators. For example, the Massachusetts merchant firm of Burrell & Burrell had paid about $600 for Confederation notes with a face value of $2,500; their redemption at full value would bring the firm an enormous profit of $1,900. Equally controversial, Hamilton proposed to create a permanent **national debt** to pay the Burrells and other note holders. Their Confederation notes would not be paid off in gold or silver coins but with new government-issued securities bearing the relatively high annual interest rate of 6 percent.

Hamilton's plan for a permanent national debt owned by wealthy families reawakened Radical Whig and republican fears of scheming British financiers. Speaking for the Virginia House of Burgesses Patrick Henry condemned the plan, arguing that "in an agricultural country like this, to erect, and concentrate, and perpetuate a large monied interest [must prove] . . . fatal to the existence of American liberty." Challenging the morality of Hamilton's proposal, James Madison asked Congress to assist the thousands of shopkeepers, farmers, and soldiers who had accepted Confederation securities during the dark days of the war and then been forced by hard times to sell them to speculators. Madison proposed giving the present bondholders only "the highest price which has prevailed in the market" and distributing the remaining funds to the original owners. But finding the original owners would have been difficult; moreover, nearly half the members of the House of Representatives owned Confederation securities and would personally profit from Hamilton's plan. Melding practicality with self-interest the House rejected Madison's innovative proposal. By way of protest, an angry citizen composed an ode, "On the Rejection of Mr. Madison's Motion":

A soldier's pay are rags and fame,
A wooden leg—a deathless name.
To specs, both in and out of Cong.
The four and six per cents belong.

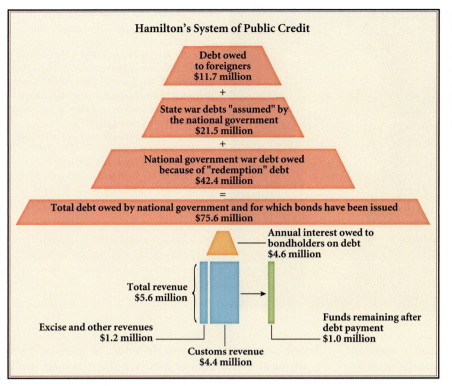

Hamilton's System of Public Credit

Debt owed
to foreigners
$11.7 million

+

State war debts "assumed" by
the national government
$21.5 million

+

National government war debt owed
because of "redemption" debt
$42.4 million

=

Total debt owed by national government and for which bonds have been issued
$75.6 million

Annual interest owed to
bondholders on debt
$4.6 million

Total revenue
$5.6 million

Excise and other revenues
$1.2 million

Funds remaining after
debt payment
$1.0 million

Customs revenue
$4.4 million

FIGURE 7.2 Hamilton's Fiscal Structure, 1792

Alexander Hamilton used the revenue from excise taxes and customs duties to defray the annual interest on the national debt. He did not pay off the debt because he wanted to tie wealthy American bondholders to the new national government.

Hamilton then advanced a second proposal that favored wealthy creditors, a plan by which the national government would take over ("assume") the war debts of the states. Rumors of this plan unleashed a flurry of speculation and some governmental corruption. Before Hamilton's announcement, Assistant Secretary of the Treasury William Duer used insider knowledge to buy up the depreciated war bonds of southern states; if Congress approved the assumption plan, Duer and his speculator associates would reap an enormous profit. Concerned members of Congress condemned such speculation and pointed out that some state legislatures had already levied high taxes to pay off their states' war debts. Responding to that argument, Hamilton modified his plan to reimburse those states. Other representatives, particularly those from Virginia and Maryland, argued that assumption would further enhance the already excessive powers of the national government. To quiet their fears about a runaway central government, the treasury chief backed their bid to locate the national capital (which the Constitution specified would consist of a special "district") along the banks of the Potomac—where they could easily watch its operations. Such astute political bargaining gave Hamilton the votes he needed in the House of Representatives to enact his assumption plan.

A National Bank. In December 1790 Hamilton issued a second report, asking Congress to charter a national financial institution, the Bank of the United States. The bank would be jointly owned by private stockholders and the national government. Hamilton argued that the bank, by making loans to merchants, handling government funds, and issuing financial notes, would provide a respected currency for the specie-starved American economy and make the new national debt easier to fund. These benefits persuaded Congress to enact Hamilton's bill and send it to the president for approval.

At this critical juncture Secretary of State Thomas Jefferson joined ranks with Madison against Hamilton. Jefferson had condemned the shady dealings in southern war bonds and the "corrupt squadron of paper dealers" who had arranged them. Now he charged that Hamilton's scheme for a national bank was unconstitutional. "The incorporation of a Bank," Jefferson told President Washington, was not a power "delegated to the United States by the Constitution." Giving a *strict* interpretation to the national charter, Jefferson maintained that the central government had only the limited powers explicitly assigned to it. In response, Hamilton articulated a *loose* interpretation, noting that Article 1, Section 8, empowered Congress to make "all Laws which shall be necessary and proper" to carry out the Constitution's provisions. Washington agreed with his treasury secretary and signed the legislation creating the bank.

Revenue and Tariffs. Hamilton turned now to the final element of his financial system: a national revenue that would be used to pay the annual interest on the permanent debt. In 1792, at Hamilton's insistence, Congress imposed a variety of domestic excise taxes, including a duty on whiskey distilled in the United States.

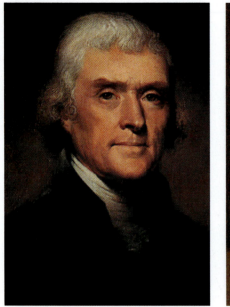

Two Visions of America

Thomas Jefferson and Alexander Hamilton confront each other in these portraits, as they did during the political battles of the 1790s. Jefferson was pro-French, Hamilton pro-British. Jefferson favored farmers and artisans; Hamilton supported merchants and financiers. Jefferson believed in democracy and rule by legislative majorities; Hamilton argued for a strong executive and for judicial review. But in 1800 Hamilton's timely support for Jefferson in his postelection struggle with Aaron Burr, whom Hamilton detested, secured the presidency for his longtime political foe.

Jefferson, by Rembrandt Peale, © White House Historical Association / Photo by National Geographic Society; Yale University Art Gallery, Mabel Brady Garven Collection.

But the revenue from those taxes was small, a mere $1 million a year. To raise another $4–5 million the treasury secretary proposed to raise tariffs on foreign imports. Although his "Report on Manufactures" (1791) called for a nation that was self-sufficient in manufactured goods, he did not ask Congress to impose high protective tariffs that would exclude foreign products. Such **tariffs** would inhibit foreign commerce, and so Hamilton settled for a modest increase in customs duties, a tariff that would allow trade and provide revenue for the national government.

Hamilton's carefully designed plan worked brilliantly. As American trade increased, customs revenue rose steadily (providing about 90 percent of the U.S. government's income from 1790 to 1820), allowing the treasury to pay for the redemption and **assumption** programs. In less than two years Hamilton had devised a strikingly modern fiscal system that provided the new national government with financial stability.

Jefferson's Agrarian Vision

Hamilton paid a high price for this success. By the time Washington began his second four-year term in 1793, Hamilton's financial measures had split the Federalists who wrote and ratified the Constitution into two irreconcilable factions. Most northern Federalists adhered to the political alliance led by Hamilton, and most southerners to a rival group headed by Madison and Jefferson. By the elections of 1794 the two **factions** had acquired names. Hamilton's supporters retained their original name: Federalists; Madison and Jefferson's supporters called themselves Democratic-Republicans or simply Republicans.

The southern planters and western farmers who became Republicans rejected Hamilton's economic and social philosophy. Thomas Jefferson, a man of great learning as well as an able politician and diplomat, spoke for them. Well read in architecture, natural history, scientific farming, and political theory, Jefferson embraced the optimistic spirit of the Enlightenment, declaring his belief in the "improvability of the human race." But he knew that progress was not inevitable and deplored both the long-standing speculative practices of merchants and financiers and the emerging social divisions of an urban industrial economy. Having seen the masses of property-less laborers in the manufacturing regions in Britain, Jefferson had concluded that workers who depended on wages lacked the economic independence required to sustain a republic (see New Technology, "Machine Technology and Republican Values," p. 214).

Jefferson's vision of the American future was agrarian and democratic. Although he had grown up (and remained) a privileged slave owner, he understood the needs of yeomen farmers and other ordinary white Americans. When Jefferson drafted the Ordinance of 1784, he pictured a West settled by productive yeomen farm families. His vision took form in his *Notes on the State of Virginia* (1785): "Those who labor in the earth are the chosen people of God," he wrote. Their grain and meat would feed European nations, which "would manufacture and send us in exchange our clothes and other comforts" in an international division of labor similar to that proposed by the Scottish economist Adam Smith in *The Wealth of Nations* (1776).

Turmoil in Europe created new opportunities for American farmers, bringing Jefferson's vision closer to reality. The French Revolution began in 1789, and four years later France's new republican government went to war against a British-led coalition of monarchical states. As warfare disrupted European farming, wheat prices

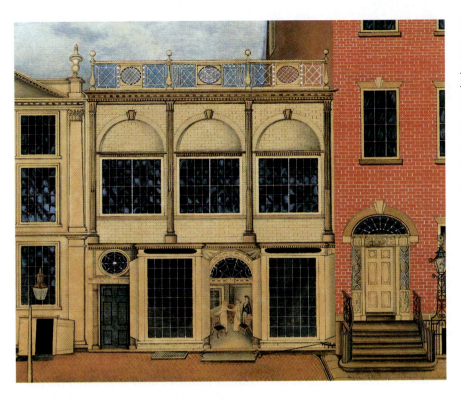

Urban Affluence

Beginning in the 1790s, New York merchants built large town houses and furnished them with fine pieces of furniture. This detail of John Rubens Smith's watercolor The Shop and Warehouse of Duncan Phyfe *(c. 1816) illustrates the success of America's most skillful furniture designer and manufacturer. Phyfe employed more than a hundred skilled joiners and carvers in his New York factory.*
Metropolitan Museum of Art, Rogers Fund, 1922.

leaped from 5 to 8 shillings a bushel and remained high for twenty years, bringing substantial profits to export-minded Chesapeake and Middle Atlantic farmers. Simultaneously, a boom in the export of raw cotton, fueled by the invention of the cotton gin and mechanization of cloth production in Britain, boosted the economy of Georgia and South Carolina. As Jefferson had hoped, European markets brought prosperity to American farmers and planters.

The French Revolution Divides Americans

American merchants profited even more handsomely from the European war. President Washington issued a Proclamation of Neutrality, which allowed U.S. citizens to trade with both sides. As neutral carriers, American ships claimed the right to pass through the British naval blockade along the French coastline and soon took over the lucrative sugar trade between France and its West Indian islands. The American merchant fleet became one of the largest in the world, increasing from 355,000 tons in 1790 to more than 1.1 million tons in 1808. Commercial earnings rose spectacularly, averaging $20 million annually in the 1790s—twice the value of cotton and tobacco exports. To keep up with demand, northern shipowners invested in new vessels, providing work for thousands of shipwrights, sail makers, laborers, and seamen. Hundreds of carpenters, masons, and cabinetmakers in Boston, New York, and Philadelphia found work building warehouses and fashionable town houses,

in what became known as the Federal style, for newly affluent merchants. In Philadelphia, a European visitor reported, "a great number of private houses have marble steps to the street door, and in other respects are finished in a style of elegance."

Ideological Conflict and Rebellion. Even as they prospered from the European struggle, Americans argued passionately over its ideologies. Most Americans had welcomed the French Revolution of 1789 because it abolished feudalism and established a constitutional monarchy. But the creation of the democratic French republic in 1792 and the execution of King Louis XVI the following year divided public opinion. Many American artisans praised the egalitarianism of the radical French Jacobins and followed their example, addressing each other as "citizen" and founding political clubs modeled on the radical democratic societies in Paris—the controversial Jacobin clubs. But Americans with strong religious beliefs condemned the new French regime for abandoning Christianity in favor of atheism. Wealthy Americans likewise denounced Robespierre and his radical republican followers for executing King Louis XVI, 3,000 of his aristocratic supporters, and 14,000 other citizens (see Voices from Abroad, "William Cobbett: Peter Porcupine Attacks Pro-French Americans," p. 217).

These ideological conflicts sharpened the debate over Hamilton's economic policies and even helped foment a domestic insurrection. In 1794 farmers in western Pennsylvania mounted the Whiskey Rebellion

Federalist Gentry

A prominent New England Federalist, Oliver Ellsworth served as chief justice of the United States (1796–1800). His wife, Abigail Wolcott Ellsworth, was the daughter of a Connecticut governor. In 1792 the portraitist Ralph Earl captured the aspirations of the Ellsworths by giving them an aristocratic demeanor and prominently displaying their mansion (in the window). Like other Federalists who tried to reconcile their wealth and social authority with republican values, Ellsworth dressed with restraint, and his manners, remarked Timothy Dwight, were "wholly destitute of haughtiness and arrogance."
Wadsworth Atheneum, Hartford.

The Rise of Political Parties

The appearance of Federalists and Republicans marked a new stage in American politics. Although colonial legislatures had often divided into temporary factions based on family alliances, ethnicity, or region, they lacked well-organized parties. The new state and national constitutions made no provision for organized political bodies; indeed, most politically minded Americans considered parties unnecessary and dangerous. Following classical republican principles, they wanted voters and legislators to act independently and in the interest of the public—not a party. Thus, Senator Pierce Butler of South Carolina criticized his colleagues in Congress as "men scrambling for partial advantage, State interests, and in short, a train of narrow, impolitic measures."

However, the revolutionary ideology of popular sovereignty drew average citizens into politics and created a contest for their votes. Simultaneously, the financial and ideological conflicts of the 1790s divided the political elite. The result was a competitive—and potentially destructive—**party system**. Merchants, creditors, and urban artisans favored Federalist policies, as did wheat-exporting slaveholders in the Tidewater districts of the Chesapeake. The emerging Republican coalition was more diverse and drew supporters from across the social spectrum. It included not only southern tobacco and rice planters and debt-conscious western farmers but also German and Scots-Irish in the southern backcountry, and subsistence-oriented eastern farmers.

Party identity crystallized during the election of 1796. To prepare for the election Federalist and Republican leaders called legislative caucuses in Congress and conventions in the states to discuss policies and nominate candidates. To mobilize the citizenry the parties organized public festivals and processions, with the Federalists celebrating Washington's achievements and the Republicans invoking the egalitarian principles of the Declaration of Independence.

Federalist candidates triumphed in the 1796 election, winning a majority in Congress and electing John Adams as the new president. Adams continued Hamilton's pro-British foreign policy and reacted sharply when the French navy seized American merchant ships. When the French foreign minister Talleyrand solicited a loan and a bribe from American diplomats to stop the seizures, Adams urged Congress to prepare for war. He charged that Talleyrand's agents, whom he dubbed X, Y, and Z, had insulted the honor of the United States. Responding to the "XYZ Affair," the Federalist-controlled Congress cut off trade with France in 1798 and authorized American privateers to seize French ships. Party conflict, which had begun over Hamilton's financial policies, now extended to foreign affairs.

Constitutional Crisis, 1798–1800

For the first time in American history (but not the last) a controversial foreign policy prompted domestic protest and governmental repression. As the United States

William Cobbett

Peter Porcupine Attacks Pro-French Americans

T*he Democratic-Republican followers of Thomas Jefferson declared that "he who is an enemy to the French Revolution, cannot be a firm republican." William Cobbett, a British journalist who settled in Philadelphia and wrote under the pen name "Peter Porcupine," contested this definition of republicanism. A strong supporter of the Federalist Party, Cobbett was eager to attack its opponents and did so frequently in caustic and widely read pamphlets and newspaper articles. Here he evokes the horrors of the Terror in France, during which thousands of aristocrats and ordinary citizens were executed, and warns that the triumph of Radical Republicanism would bring the same fate to the United States.*

France is a republic, and the decrees of the Legislators were necessary to maintain it a republic. This word outweighs, in the estimation of some persons (I wish I could say they were few in number), all the horrors that have been and that can be committed in that country. One of these modern republicans will tell you that he does not deny that hundreds of thousands of innocent persons have been murdered in France; that the people have neither religion nor morals; that all the ties of nature are rent asunder; . . . that its riches, along with millions of the best of the people, are gone to enrich and aggrandize its enemies; that its commerce, its manufactures, its sciences, its arts, and its honour, are no more; but at the end of all this, he will tell you that it must be happy, because it is a republic. I have heard more than

one of these republican zealots declare, that he would sooner see the last of the French exterminated, than see them adopt any other form of government. Such a sentiment is characteristic of a mind locked up in a savage ignorance.

Shall we say that these things never can take place among us? . . . We are not what we were before the French revolution. Political projectors from every corner of Europe, troublers of society of every description, from the whining philosophical hypocrite to the daring rebel, and more daring blasphemer, have taken shelter in these States.

We have seen the guillotine toasted to three times three cheers. . . . And what would the reader say, were I to tell him of a Member of Congress, who wished to see one of these murderous machines employed for lopping off the heads of the French, permanent in the State-house yard of the city of Philadelphia?

If these men of blood had succeeded in plunging us into a war; if they had once got the sword into their hands, they would have mowed us down like stubble. The word Aristocrat would have been employed to as good account here, as ever it had been in France. We might, ere this, have seen our places of worship turned into stables; we might have seen the banks of the Delaware, like those of the Loire, covered with human carcasses, and its waters tinged with blood: ere this we might have seen our parents butchered, and even the head of our admired and beloved President rolling on a scaffold.

I know the reader will start back with horror. His heart will tell him that it is impossible. But, once more, let him look at the example before us. The attacks on the character and conduct of the aged Washington, have been as bold, if not bolder, than those which led to the downfall of the unfortunate French Monarch [Louis XVI, executed in 1793]. Can it then be imagined, that, had they possessed the power, they wanted the will to dip their hands in his blood?

Source: William Cobbett, *Peter Porcupine in America,* ed. David A. Wilson (Ithaca: Cornell University Press, 1994), 150–54.

fought an undeclared maritime war against France, pro-Republican and anti-British immigrants from Ireland vehemently attacked Adams's foreign policy. Some Federalists responded in kind: "Were I president, I would hang them for otherwise they would murder me," declared a Philadelphia Federalist pamphleteer. To silence its critics, in 1798 the administration enacted coercive measures. The Naturalization Act increased the residency requirement for American citizenship from five to fourteen years; the Alien Act authorized the deportation of foreigners; and the Sedition Act prohibited the publication of ungrounded or malicious attacks on the president or Congress. "He that is not for us is against us," thundered the Federalist *Gazette of the United States.* Prosecutors arrested more than twenty Republican newspaper editors and politicians, accused them of sedition, and won convictions and jail sentences against some of them.

The Federalists' repressive actions created a constitutional crisis. Republicans charged that the Sedition Act violated the First Amendment's prohibition against "abridging the freedom of speech, or of the press." However, they did not appeal to the Supreme Court, both because the Court's power to review congressional legislation had not been established and because the Court was packed with Federalists. Instead Madison and Jefferson looked to the federal system—and the state legislatures—to remedy unconstitutional laws. "The powers of the federal government" resulted "from the compact to which the states are parties," Madison declared. At Jefferson's urging, in 1798 the Kentucky legislature declared the Alien and Sedition Acts to be "unauthoritative, void, and of no force," arguing that the states had a "right to judge" the constitutionality of national laws. The Virginia legislature passed a similar resolution that also followed Madison's **states' rights** interpretation of the Constitution.

The debate over the Sedition Act set the stage for the election of 1800. Jefferson, once opposed in principle to political parties, now saw them as a valuable way "to watch and relate to the people" the activities of an oppressive government. Republicans strongly supported Jefferson's bid for the presidency, pointing to the wrongful imprisonment of newspaper editors and championing states' rights. President Adams responded to these attacks by reevaluating his foreign policy. Adams was a complicated man who was dogmatic and easily offended, but he also possessed great personal strength and determination. Rejecting the advice of Hamilton and other belligerent-minded Federalists to declare war against France (and benefit from an upsurge in patriotism), Adams put country ahead of party and entered into diplomatic negotiations that brought an end to the fighting.

Nonetheless, the election of 1800 was the first "dirty" political campaign. The Federalists attacked Jefferson's character, branding him as an irresponsible pro-French radical, "the arch-apostle of irreligion and free thought," and both parties forced changes in state election laws to favor their candidates. A low Federalist turnout in Virginia and Pennsylvania and the three-fifths rule for slave representation (which boosted the number of electoral votes in the southern states) gave Jefferson a narrow 73 to 65 victory in the electoral college. But the Republican electors unexpectedly also gave seventy-three votes to Aaron Burr of New York (Jefferson's choice for vice president), throwing the presidential election into the House of Representatives. (The Twelfth Amendment, ratified in 1804, would remedy this constitutional defect by requiring electors to vote separately for president and vice president.)

Ironically, as the era of Federalism and its aristocratic outlook came to an end, Alexander Hamilton ushered in a more democratic era. For thirty-five ballots, Federalists in the House of Representatives blocked Jefferson's election. Then Hamilton intervened. Calling Burr an "embryo Caesar" and the "most unfit man in the United States for the office of president," he persuaded key Federalists to permit Jefferson's selection. The Federalists' concern for political stability also played a role. As Senator James Bayard of Delaware explained, "It was admitted on all hands that we must risk the Constitution and a Civil War or take Mr. Jefferson."

Jefferson called the election the "Revolution of 1800," and so it was. The bloodless transfer of power demonstrated that governments elected by the people could be changed in an orderly way, even in times of bitter partisan conflict and foreign crisis. In his inaugural address in 1801 Jefferson praised this achievement, declaring: "We are all Republicans, we are all Federalists." Despite the predictions of European conservatives, the new republican constitutional order of 1776 had survived a quarter century of economic and political turmoil.

FOR FURTHER EXPLORATION

▶ For definitions of key terms boldfaced in this chapter, see the glossary at the end of the book.

▶ To assess your mastery of the material covered in this chapter, see the Online Study Guide at **bedfordstmartins.com/henretta**.

▶ For suggested references, including Web sites, see page SR-8 at the end of the book.

▶ For map resources and primary documents, see **bedfordstmartins.com/henretta**.

The republican revolution began in the states, which between 1776 and 1780 wrote new constitutions. Most states established property qualifications for voting and a separation of powers that inhibited popular rule. The Pennsylvania and Vermont constitutions were more democratic, with a powerful one-house legislature and voting rights for most free men. The New Jersey constitution allowed property-owning women to vote, but most American women were excluded from the political sphere. A few women asserted claims of intellectual and social equality and sought greater legal rights, mostly without success. On the national level the government created by the Articles of Confederation began the orderly settlement of the trans-Appalachian West, but it lacked the authority to regulate foreign trade or raise enough revenue to pay off wartime debts. Clashes over debts and taxes also disrupted the state governments and culminated in 1786 in Shays's Rebellion, an uprising of indebted farmers in Massachusetts.

The perceived weaknesses of the Confederation led nationalists and creditors to convene a constitutional convention in Philadelphia in 1787. The delegates devised a new constitution that derived its authority not from the states but from the people, who were directly represented in the lower house of the legislature. The delegates created a strong national government with the power to levy taxes, issue money, and control trade. Its legislation was to be the supreme law of the land. In several important states the Constitution was ratified by narrow margins because it diminished the sovereignty of the states and seemed to create a potentially oppressive central government immune from popular control.

In 1789 George Washington became the first president under the new government and, working with the first Congress, established the executive and judicial departments. The economic policies of Washington's secretary of the treasury, Alexander Hamilton, favored northern merchants and financiers and led to the creation of the Federalist Party. Thomas Jefferson and James Madison organized farmers, planters, and artisans into a rival Republican Party. The French Revolution prompted bitter ideological struggles in the United States and, during an undeclared war with France, political repression in the form of the Alien and Sedition Acts of 1798. The peaceful transfer of power to Jefferson and the Republicans in 1800 ended a decade of political strife.

1776	Pennsylvania approves a democratic constitution
	John Adams, *Thoughts on Government*
	Propertied women allowed to vote in New Jersey (retracted in 1807)
1777	Articles of Confederation (ratified 1781)
1779	Judith Sargent Murray, "On the Equality of the Sexes" (published in 1790)
1780s	Postwar commercial recession increases creditor-debtor conflicts in the states
1781	Confederation Congress charters Bank of North America
1784–1785	Political and Land Ordinances outline settlement policy for new states
1785	Thomas Jefferson, *Notes on the State of Virginia*
1786	Commercial convention in Annapolis, Maryland
	Shays's Rebellion roils Massachusetts
1787	Northwest Ordinance
	Constitutional convention in Philadelphia
1787–1788	States hold ratification conventions
	John Jay, James Madison, and Alexander Hamilton write the *Federalist* essays
1789	George Washington inaugurated as first president
	Judiciary Act establishes federal court system
	Outbreak of French Revolution
1790	Hamilton wins Congress's approval of redemption and assumption
1791	Bill of Rights ratified
1792	Mary Wollstonecraft, *A Vindication of the Rights of Woman*
1793	French create Republic and execute King Louis XVI
	Madison and Jefferson found Republican Party
	War between Britain and France; Washington's Proclamation of Neutrality
1794	Whiskey Rebellion in western Pennsylvania
1795	Jay's Treaty with Great Britain
1798	XYZ Affair (1797) prompts war with France
	Alien, Sedition, and Naturalization Acts
	Kentucky and Virginia Resolutions contest federal authority
1800	Jefferson elected president in "Revolution of 1800"

CHAPTER 8

Dynamic Change: Western Settlement and Eastern Capitalism

1790–1820

Westward Expansion
Native American Resistance
Migration and the Changing Farm
   Economy
The Transportation Bottleneck

The Republicans' Political Revolution
The Jeffersonian Presidency
Jefferson and the West
Conflict with Britain and France
The War of 1812

The Capitalist Commonwealth
A Merchant-Based Economy:
   Banks, Manufacturing, and
   Markets
Public Policy: The Commonwealth
   System
Federalist Law: John Marshall and
   the Supreme Court

◄ **The Fairview Inn, by Thomas Cole Ruckle (detail)**
Scores of inns dotted the roads of the new republic, providing food, accommodations, and livery services for settlers moving west and for cattle drovers and teamsters carrying western produce to eastern markets. Although executed in 1889, this painting accurately depicts the architecture of an early-nineteenth-century Maryland inn and captures the character of its workforce—with free and enslaved African Americans driving cattle and tending to horses. Maryland Historical Society.

"IT IS A COUNTRY IN FLUX," a French aristocrat observed of the United States in 1799, "that which is true today as regards its population, its establishments, its prices, its commerce will not be true six months from now." Indeed, the coming of the nineteenth century would produce a dramatic change in American society and politics. In 1800, the American republic stood on the edge of a period of dynamic westward expansion and eastern economic development that would soon change its very character. "If movement and the quick succession of sensations and ideas constitute life," another French observer wrote a few decades later, "here one lives a hundred fold more than elsewhere; here, all is circulation, motion, and boiling agitation."

Circulation and motion were especially evident along the western frontier. Standing on the eastern edge of the continent in 1766, a white observer noted that "the thirst after Indian lands, is become almost universal." When the Treaty of Paris in 1783 gave the United States access to the trans-Appalachian West, hundreds of thousands of extraordinarily self-confident Americans trekked into the interior to farm its rich soils with a nearly complete disregard for Indian property rights. As George Washington put it, members of the Sons of Liberty in the East became "the lords and proprietors of a vast tract of continent" in the West.

Unfortunately for Washington's Federalist Party, the votes of these western farmers helped to ensure the political ascendancy of Republican president Thomas Jefferson and his western-oriented policies. To provide even more land for American farmers, Jefferson doubled the country's size through the Louisiana Purchase in 1803. "[No] territory can be too large," declared Dr. David Ramsay of South Carolina, "for a people, who multiply with such unequalled rapidity."

While Republican policy encouraged homesteading in the West, state legislatures in the East promoted banking, manufacturing, and commercial growth. This governmental stimulus unleashed a cumulative process of capitalist-financed economic growth. "Experiment follows experiment; enterprise follows enterprise," a European traveler noted, and "riches and poverty follow." Of the two, riches were the more apparent. Beginning around 1800 per capita income in the United States increased by more than 1 percent per year—over 30 percent in a single generation. By the 1820s the nation was well on its way to becoming a republic that was continental in scope and capitalist in character.

Westward Expansion

In 1803 Shawnee diplomats told American officials that long ago their ancestors had stood on the shores of the Atlantic Ocean and seen a strange object. "At first they took it for a great bird, but they soon found it to be a monstrous canoe filled with . . . white people." Soon thereafter, the Indian emissaries continued, the white people robbed the Shawnees of their wisdom and then "usurped their land," purchasing it with goods that "were more the property of the Indians than the white people because the knowledge which enabled them to manufacture these goods actually belonged to the Shawnees."

Whatever the truth of this legend, by 1803 the expansionist-minded American republic clearly threatened the Shawnees and other native peoples. The first national census in 1790 counted 3.9 million people, both white and black, with 200,000 of them living west of the Appalachian Mountains. By 1820 there were 9.6 million white and black Americans, and no fewer than 2 million inhabited nine new states and three new territories west of the Appalachians. The country was moving west at an astonishing pace.

Native American Resistance

In the Treaty of Paris of 1783 Great Britain relinquished its claims to the trans-Appalachian region and, as one British statesman put it, left the Indian nations "to the care of their [American] neighbours." "Care" was hardly the right term, for some influential Americans wanted to exterminate the native peoples. "Cut up every Indian Cornfield and burn every Indian town," proclaimed William Henry Drayton of South Carolina, so that their "nation be extirpated and the lands become the property of the public." Many others, including Henry Knox, President Washington's first secretary of war, favored assimilating the Indians into American society. Knox wanted commonly held tribal lands to become the private property of individual Indian families, who would become citizens of the various states. Most Indians rejected these policies out of hand and continued to view themselves as members of a particular clan or tribe. Without much success, a few Native American leaders raised the notion of a broader, pan-Indian identity.

Conflict over Land Rights. Not surprisingly, the major struggle between Indians and whites concerned

Red Jacket or Sagoyewatha, c. 1758–1830
Like most Senecas, Sagoyewatha fought for the British during the American War for Independence, acquiring his English name from the coat given him by a British officer. In 1792 Red Jacket journeyed to Philadelphia as a member of a delegation that ceded Iroquois lands to the United States. There he met with President Washington, who presented him with the silver peace medal depicted in this painting by an unknown artist (based on a portrait by Robert W. Weir, c. 1828). Subsequently, Red Jacket became the leader of the Seneca faction that opposed Christian missionary efforts and called for a return to the traditional Indian way of life.

Fenimore Art Museum / © New York State Historical Association, Cooperstown, NY.

land rights. Invoking the Paris treaty and claiming that pro-British Indians were conquered peoples, the United States government asserted ownership over all Indian lands in the West. Native Americans rejected this claim, pointing out that they had not signed the treaty and had never been conquered. The Confederation Congress and the state governments brushed aside those arguments. In 1784 U.S. commissioners used military threats to force pro-British Iroquois peoples— the Mohawks, Onondagas, Cayugas, and Senecas—to sign the Treaty of Fort Stanwix and relinquish much of their land in New York and Pennsylvania. New York officials and land speculators used liquor and bribes to take title to additional millions of acres. By 1800 the once powerful Iroquois were confined to relatively small reservations.

American negotiators employed similar tactics farther to the west. In 1785 they induced the Chipewyans, Delawares, Ottawas, and Wyandots to sign away most of the future state of Ohio. The tribes quickly repudiated the agreements, claiming—justifiably—that they were made under duress. Those peoples, along with the Shawnees, Miamis, and Potawatomis, formed a Western Confederacy to defend themselves against aggressive

settlers. Led by Little Turtle, a Miami chief, they defeated American armies in 1790 and again in 1791.

Fearing an alliance between the Western Confederacy and the British in Canada, President Washington doubled the size of the U.S. Army and ordered General "Mad Anthony" Wayne to lead a new expedition. In August 1794 Wayne defeated the Indians in the Battle of Fallen Timbers (near present-day Toledo, Ohio). Nevertheless, the Western Confederacy remained strong, forcing a compromise peace in the Treaty of Greenville (Ohio) in 1795. American negotiators acknowledged Indian ownership of the lands of the trans-Appalachian West, while the members of the confederacy accepted American political sovereignty and agreed to place themselves "under the protection of the United States, and no other Power whatever." In practice this agreement encouraged American officials and settlers to pressure Native Americans to give up their lands but allowed Indian peoples to demand money or goods in return. Indeed, during the Greenville negotiations the Indians ceded ownership of most of Ohio and certain strategic areas along the Great Lakes, including Detroit and the future site of Chicago (Map 8.1). Recognizing the gains made by the United States, Britain cut some of

MAP 8.1 Indian Cessions and State Formation, to 1840

By virtue of the Treaty of 1783 with Britain, the United States claimed sovereignty over the entire trans-Appalachian West. The Western Indian Confederacy contested this claim, which the U.S. government upheld by military force. As Native American peoples were coerced by armed diplomacy to cede most of their domain, white settlers occupied the land, formed territorial governments, and eventually entered the Union as members of separate—and equal—states. Gradually, the new western region emerged as an important economic and political force.

Red Jacket

A Seneca Chief's Understanding of Religion

The Seneca chief Red Jacket (c. 1758–1830) acquired his name during the Revolutionary War, when he fought for the British "redcoats" to protect his people from the threat posed by American settlers. Although reconciled to American rule, Red Jacket strongly adhered to Indian values and rejected Christianity. In 1805 he explained why to a group of missionaries, whom he addressed as "Brother."

Brother: Continue to listen. You say that you are sent to instruct us how to worship the Great Spirit agreeably to his mind; and, if we do not take hold of the religion which you white people teach, we shall be unhappy hereafter. You say that you are right, and we are lost. How do we know this to be true? We understand that your religion is written in a book. If it was intended for us as well as you, why has not the Great Spirit given to us, and not only to us, but why did He not give to our forefathers, the knowledge of the book, with the means of understanding it rightly?

Brother: The Great Spirit has made us all, but he has made a great difference between his white and red children. He has given us different complexions and different customs. To you He has given the arts [i.e., manufacturing]. To these He has not opened our eyes. We know these things to be true. Since He has made a great difference between us in other things, why may we not conclude that He has given us different religion according to our understanding? The Great Spirit does right. He knows what is best for his children; we are satisfied.

Source: David J. Rothman and Sheila Rothman, eds., *Sources of the American Social Tradition* (New York: Basic Books, 1975), 182.

---

its trading ties with the Indians and, in Jay's Treaty of 1795, reaffirmed its (still unfulfilled) obligation under the Treaty of Paris to remove its military garrisons from the region.

American westward migration increased as soon as the fighting ended. In 1805 the two-year-old state of Ohio had more than 100,000 residents. Thousands more farm families moved into the future states of Indiana and Illinois, sparking new conflicts with native peoples over land and hunting rights. As a Delaware Indian declared, "The Elks are our horses, the buffaloes are our cows, the deer are our sheep, & the whites shan't have them."

Attempts at Assimilation. To alleviate these tensions the U.S. government encouraged Native Americans to become farmers and assimilate into white society. The goal, as one Kentucky Protestant minister put it, was to make the Indian "a farmer, a citizen of the United States, and a Christian." Most Native Americans resisted these efforts. As a Munsee prophet put it, "There are two ways to God, one for the whites and one for the Indians." To preserve their traditional cultures, many Indian peoples drove out white missionaries and forced Christianized Indians to participate in tribal rites. A few Indian leaders tried to find a middle path between ancestral ways and European practices. Among the Senecas of New York the prophet Handsome Lake promoted traditional Iroquois ceremonies that gave thanks to the earth, plants, animals, water, and sun. But he also incorporated some Christian beliefs, such as heaven and hell, into his teachings and used them to deter his followers from drinking alcohol, gambling, and practicing witchcraft. Handsome Lake's rejection of some Indian beliefs and his support of Quaker missionaries divided the tribe into hostile religious factions. More conservative Senecas, led by Chief Red Jacket, condemned Indians who accepted white ways and beliefs and demanded a return to ancestral customs (see American Voices, "Red Jacket: A Seneca Chief's Understanding of Religion," above).

Most Indian women also rejected European farming practices. Among the Iroquois and many other Eastern Woodland peoples, women had long been responsible for growing staple foods; partly as a result, they controlled the inheritance of cultivation rights and exercised considerable political power. Shawnee women had even more authority, because women "war" chiefs decided whether to dispatch a war party or to torture captives. Even those Indians who embraced Christian teachings retained many traditional values. To view themselves as individuals, as the Europeans demanded, meant repudiating the clan, the essence of Indian life.

Migration and the Changing Farm Economy

Native American resistance did not deter the advance of white farmers and planters, who poured across the Appalachians and moved along the Atlantic coastal plain in search of fertile lands. This migratory upsurge brought financial rewards to many settlers and an increasing diversity of crops to the American farm economy.

Movement Out of the South. Between 1790 and 1820 two great streams of migrants moved out of the southern states. One stream of migrants, composed primarily of white tenant farmers and struggling yeomen families, flocked through the Cumberland Gap into Kentucky and Tennessee. They were fleeing the depleted soils and planter elite of the Chesapeake region, confident that they would prosper by growing cotton and hemp, which were in great demand. The second stream, dominated by slave-owning planters and their enslaved workers, moved along the coastal plain of the Gulf of Mexico into the future states of Alabama and

Mississippi. A worried eastern landlord lamented the massive loss of farm labor, writing to the *Maryland Gazette* that "boundless settlements open a door for our citizens to run off and leave us, depreciating all our landed property and disabling us from paying taxes."

Many migrants to Kentucky and Tennessee were poor, without ready cash to buy land. To gain title to farmland, they relied upon "the ancient cultivation law" governing frontier tracts. Invoking the argument of the North Carolina Regulators (see Chapter 4), they argued that poor settlers had a customary right "from time out of Mind" to occupy "back waste vacant Lands" sufficient "to provide a subsistence for themselves and their posterity." The Virginia government, which administered the Kentucky Territory, had a more elitist vision. While it allowed poorer settlers to purchase up to 1,400 acres of land at reduced prices, it also sold or granted estates of 20,000 to 200,000 acres to scores of wealthy individuals and partnerships. Consequently, when Kentucky became a state in 1792, a handful of **speculators** owned one-fourth of the state, while half the adult white men owned no land and lived as **squatters** or tenant farmers.

Slave Auction in Charleston, South Carolina, 1833
As one slave departs with his new master (far right), the auctioneer tries to interest the assembled planters in his next sale item, a black family. The artist, a British Canadian named Henry Byam Martin, showed his disdain for these proceedings in the sketch itself (compare the family's dignified bearing with the planters' slouching postures) and in its sarcastic title: The Land of the Free and the Home of the Brave.
National Archives of Canada.

to replenish eastern soils, farm families increased their productivity. Westward migration had boosted the entire American economy.

The Transportation Bottleneck

American geography threatened to cut short this economic advance: water transport was the quickest and cheapest way to get goods to market, but no rivers cut through the Appalachian Mountains. It cost Pennsylvania farmers as much to send crops fifty miles by road to Philadelphia as to ship them from Philadelphia to London. Without access to waterways or other cheap means of transportation, settlers west of the Appalachian Mountains would be unable to send goods to markets in the East, Europe, and the West Indies (see American Voices, "Noah M. Ludlow: Traveling to Kentucky, 1815," p. 229).

Improved inland trade therefore became a high priority for the new state governments, which actively encouraged transportation ventures. Between 1793 and 1812 the Pennsylvania legislature granted fifty-five corporate charters to private turnpike companies, and Massachusetts chartered over a hundred. Turnpike companies built level gravel roads that significantly reduced travel time and transport costs and charged tolls for their use. State governments and private entrepreneurs constructed even more cost-efficient inland waterways, dredging rivers to make them navigable and constructing short canals to bypass waterfalls or rapids. By 1816 the United States had about 100 miles of canals, but only three of these artificial waterways were more than 2 miles long and none breached the great Appalachian barrier. Only after 1819, when the Erie Canal began to connect the central and western counties of New York to the Hudson River, could inland farmers sell their produce in eastern markets (see Chapter 10).

For farmers farther west the great streams that connected to the Mississippi River represented the great hope. Western settlers paid premium prices for land along navigable rivers, while speculators bought up property in growing towns—such as Cincinnati, Louisville, Chattanooga, and St. Louis—along the Ohio, Tennessee, and Mississippi Rivers. Western farmers and merchants built barges to float cotton, surplus grain, and meat down this great interconnected river system to the port of New Orleans, which by 1815 was processing about $5 million in agricultural products yearly.

But many western settlers in the trans-Appalachian West lacked access to these waterways and had no choice but to be self-sufficient. "A noble field of Indian corn

View of Cincinnati, by John Casper Wild, c. 1835
Thanks to its location on the Ohio River, Cincinnati quickly became one of the major commercial cities of the trans-Appalachian West. By the 1820s passenger steamboats as well as freight barges connected the city with Pittsburgh to the north and the ocean port of New Orleans to the far south. Museum of Fine Arts, Boston.

Noah M. Ludlow

Traveling to Kentucky, 1815

In 1815, Noah Ludlow (1795–1886) was an actor in a traveling theatrical troupe headed by Samuel Drake, one of the first cultural entrepreneurs to bring entertainment to the trans-Appalachian West. As Ludlow ventured from Albany, New York, to Frankfort, Kentucky, he encountered firsthand the hazards of water transportation and the slow and difficult course of travel by land—adventures he recounted in a memoir published in 1880.

With the commencement of the year 1815, Mr. Drake was looking around for some actors and actresses bold and adventurous enough to risk their lives and fortunes in a Western wilderness. . . . His course was to travel northwest in the State of New York, until he should reach Canandaigua; then to deflect to the south-west, strike the head waters of the Allegheny river, descend by boat to Pittsburgh, and perform there until the assembling of the State Legislature of Kentucky, early in December. . . .

Sometime about the latter part of July, 1815, our party started from Canandaigua for the head waters of the Allegheny River. Our means of transportation were a road wagon, drawn by two horses, owned by Mr. Drake, and a light spring-wagon . . . [for the] comfort of his wife. . . . The other portions of the company . . . were expected to walk the greater part of the way . . . [to] Olean, a settlement on the Allegheny . . . about one hundred and fifty miles south-west.

Olean . . . was a wild-looking place. . . . Mr. Drake immediately made a trade, disposing of his wagons and horses, and purchasing a flat-bottomed boat, known in those days as an "Ark," or "broad-horn." It was about twenty-five feet long by fifteen wide, boarded up at the sides, and covered with an elliptical roof about high enough to allow a man . . . to stand erect. . . . In one end of this boat were two rooms, partitioned off as bedrooms, one for Mr. Lewis and wife; the other for the three single young ladies. . . . The men . . . were expected to "rough it." . . .

The good "broadhorn" wended her slow but steady way wherever it pleased the current of old Allegheny to carry her . . . [until] an alarming cry that the boat was going over a waterfall. Five [men] . . . plunged into the river . . . and . . . succeeded in getting the boat safely to shore. After resting a little, we set to work to retrace the course we had come, until we should reach that point at which . . . the boat had taken the wrong "chute," or fork of the river. This we effected with much labor by passing a rope to the shore . . . [and] those on shore pulled it along. . . .

At Pittsburgh another "broad-horn" boat had been purchased, larger and more conveniently arranged [and] . . . we commenced our voyage down the Ohio. . . . There was a great sameness in this water journey of about four hundred miles. . . . [We reached] Maysville, on the Kentucky side of the river . . . about a week from the time we left Pittsburgh. . . .

I do not recollect how many days we were journeying to Frankfort, but it was . . . a very slow method of travelling. We did not make more than from twenty to twenty-five miles each day.

Source: Noah M. Ludlow, *Dramatic Life as I Found It* (St. Louis: G. I. Jones and Company, 1880), 5–14, 17–21, 76–78.

---

stretched away into the forest on one side," an English visitor to an isolated Ohio farm in the 1820s noted,

and immediately before the house was a small potato garden, with a few peach and apple trees. The woman told me that they spun and wove all the cotton and woollen garments of the family, and knit all the stockings; her husband, though not a shoemaker by trade, made all the shoes. She manufactured all the soap and candles they use.

Self-sufficiency meant a low standard of living. As late as 1840 per capita income in states formed out of the Northwest Territory was only 70 percent of the national average.

Despite these financial hardships and transportation bottlenecks white Americans continued to migrate westward. They knew it would take a generation to clear land, build houses, barns, and roads and plant orchards, and yet they were confident that their sacrifices and the expansion of the canal and road system would yield future security for themselves and their children. The

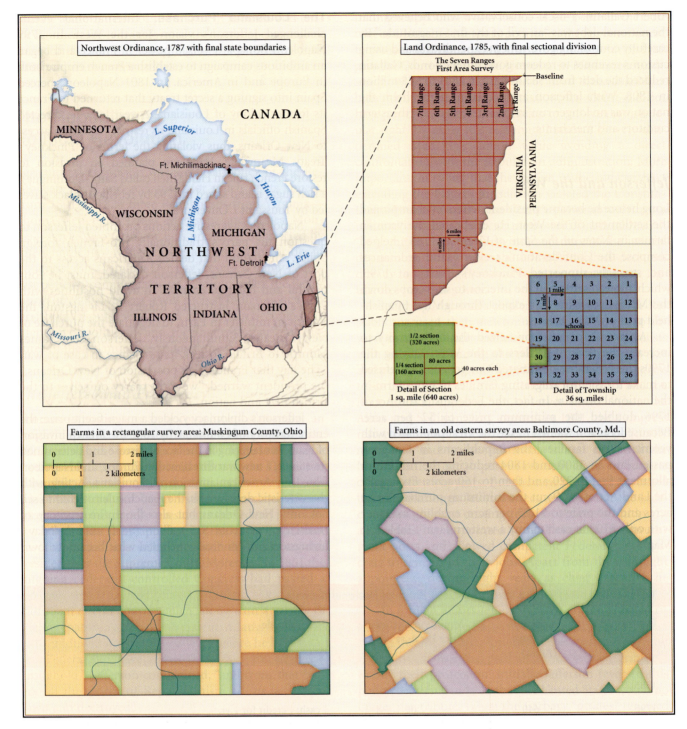

Northwest Ordinance, 1787 with final state boundaries

CANADA

MINNESOTA

L. Superior

Ft. Michilimackinac

L. Huron

WISCONSIN

L. Michigan

MICHIGAN

N O R T H W E S T

Ft. Detroit

L. Erie

Mississippi R.

T E R R I T O R Y

OHIO

ILLINOIS   INDIANA

Missouri R.

Ohio R.

Land Ordinance, 1785, with final sectional division

The Seven Ranges
First Area Survey

Baseline

7th Range · 6th Range · 5th Range · 4th Range · 3rd Range · 2nd Range · 1st Range

VIRGINIA

PENNSYLVANIA

6 miles

6 miles

Detail of Section
1 sq. mile (640 acres)

1/2 section
(320 acres)

1/4 section
(160 acres)

80 acres

40 acres each

Detail of Township
36 sq. miles

6	5	4	3	2	1
7	8	9	10	11	12
18	17	16 schools	15	14	13
19	20	21	22	23	24
30	29	28	27	26	25
31	32	33	34	35	36

1 mile

1 mile

Farms in a rectangular survey area: Muskingum County, Ohio

0   1   2 miles

0   1   2 kilometers

Farms in an old eastern survey area: Baltimore County, Md.

0   1   2 miles

0   1   2 kilometers

MAP 8.3 Land Division in the Northwest Territory

Throughout the Northwest Territory, government surveyors imposed a rectangular grid on the landscape, regardless of the local topography, so that farmers bought neatly defined properties. The right-angled property lines in Muskingum County, Ohio (lower left), contrasted sharply with those in Baltimore County, Maryland (lower right), where—as in most of the eastern and southern states—boundaries followed the contours of the land.

The Continent Described

Meriwether Lewis and William Clark fulfilled Jefferson's injunction to explore the trans-Mississippi West by filling their journals with drawings and descriptions of its topography, plants, and animals. Clark drew this picture of the white salmon trout along the Columbia River (in present-day Washington State) in his diary in March 1806.

Missouri Historical Society, Voorhis Number 2, William Clark Papers.

as the Louisiana Purchase. "We have lived long," Livingston remarked to Monroe, "but this is the noblest work of our lives."

The Louisiana Purchase forced the president to reconsider his interpretation of the Constitution. Jefferson had always been a strict constructionist, maintaining that the national government possessed only the powers "expressly" delegated to it in the Constitution. There was no provision in the Constitution for adding new territory, however, so to fulfill his dreams for the West Jefferson pragmatically accepted a loose interpretation of the treaty-making powers granted by the Constitution to complete the deal with France.

A scientist as well as a statesman, Jefferson wanted detailed information about the physical features of the new territory and its plant and animal life. In 1804 he sent his personal secretary, Meriwether Lewis, to explore the region with William Clark, an army officer. Aided by Indian guides Lewis and Clark and their group of American soldiers and frontiersmen traveled up the Missouri River, across the Rocky Mountains, and (venturing beyond the bounds of the Louisiana Purchase) down the Columbia River to the Pacific Ocean. After two years they returned with the first maps of the immense wilderness and vivid accounts of its natural resources and inhabitants (Map 8.4).

Threats to the Union. The Louisiana Purchase was a stunning accomplishment, doubling the size of the nation at a single stroke, but it brought a new threat. New England Federalists, fearing that western expansion would diminish the power of their states and their party, talked openly of leaving the Union. When Alexander Hamilton refused to support their plan for a separate Northern Confederacy, the secessionists turned to Aaron Burr, the ambitious vice president, who was seeking election as governor of New York. In July 1804 Hamilton accused Burr of participating in a conspiracy to destroy the Union, and Burr challenged him to a pistol duel. Hamilton died by gunshot in the illegal confrontation, and state courts in New York and New Jersey indicted Burr for murder.

This tragic event propelled Burr into yet another secessionist scheme. After his vice presidential term ended early in 1805, Burr moved west to avoid prosecution. There he conspired with General James Wilkinson, the military governor of the Louisiana Territory. Their plan remains a mystery, but it probably involved either the capture of territory in New Spain or a rebellion to establish Louisiana as a separate nation headed by Burr. Wilkinson betrayed Burr, however, and arrested him for treason as the former vice president led an armed force down the Ohio River. In a highly politicized trial presided over by Chief Justice John Marshall, the jury acquitted Burr of treason. The verdict was less important than the dangers to national unity that it revealed. The Republicans' policy of western expansion had increased sectional tension and party conflict, generating states' rights sentiment in New England and secessionist schemes in the West.

Conflict with Britain and France

As the Napoleonic Wars ravaged Europe between 1802 and 1815, they threatened the commercial interests of the American republic. Great Britain and France, the major belligerents, refused to respect the neutrality of American merchant vessels. Napoleon imposed the "Continental System" on European ports under French

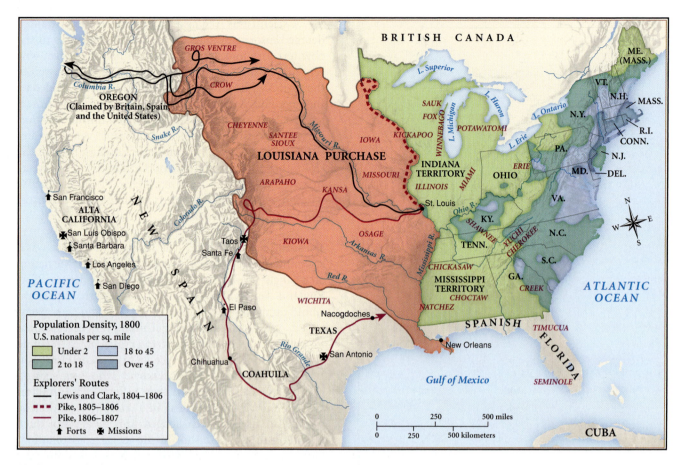

MAP 8.4 U.S. Population Density in 1803 and the Louisiana Purchase

When the United States purchased Louisiana from France in 1803, much of the land between the Appalachian Mountains and the Mississippi River remained in Indian hands, with only a few residents of European or African descent. The vast lands beyond the Mississippi were virtually unknown, even after the epic explorations of Zebulon Pike and Meriwether Lewis and William Clark. Nonetheless, President Jefferson predicted (quite accurately, as it turned out) that the vast Mississippi Valley "from its fertility . . . will ere long yield half of our whole produce, and contain half of our whole population."

control, requiring customs officials to seize neutral ships that had stopped in Britain. For its part, the British ministry set up a naval blockade, seizing ships carrying goods to Europe, including American vessels filled with sugar and molasses from the French West Indies. The British navy also searched American ships for British deserters and **impressed** (forced) them back into service. Between 1802 and 1811 British officers seized nearly eight thousand sailors, many of whom were American citizens. American resentment turned to outrage in 1807, when a British warship attacked the U.S. Navy vessel *Chesapeake*, killing or wounding twenty-one men and seizing four alleged deserters. "Never since the battle of Lexington have I seen this country in such a state of exasperation as at present," Jefferson declared.

The Embargo. To protect American interests while avoiding war Jefferson pursued a policy of **peaceful coercion**. Working closely with Secretary of State James

Madison, the president devised the Embargo Act of 1807, which prohibited American ships from leaving their home ports until Britain and France repealed their restrictions on U.S. trade. Though the embargo was a creative diplomatic measure—an economic weapon similar to the nonimportation movements between 1765 and 1775—it overestimated the dependence of France and Britain on American shipping and underestimated resistance from New England merchants, who feared it would ruin them.

The embargo was a disaster for the American economy. Exports plunged from $108 million in 1806 to $22 million in 1808, hurting farmers as well as merchants and prompting Federalists to demand its repeal. When the Republican Congress passed a Force Act giving customs officials extraordinary powers to prevent smuggling into Canada, Federalists railed against government tyranny. "Would to God," exclaimed one Federalist, "that the Embargo had done as little evil to ourselves as it has done to foreign nations."

Despite discontent over the embargo voters elected James Madison, one of its authors, to the presidency in 1808. As the main architect of the Constitution, an advocate of the Bill of Rights, and a prominent congressman and party leader, Madison had served the nation well. But as John Beckley, a loyal Republican, complained in 1806, he had performed poorly as secretary of state: "Madison is deemed by many too timid and indecisive as a statesman." Thus, at a crucial juncture in foreign affairs, a man with little understanding of the devious, cutthroat world of international politics became president. Madison quickly acknowledged the embargo's failure and replaced it with a series of new economic restrictions, none of which succeeded in persuading France and Britain to respect America's neutral rights. "The Devil himself could not tell which government, England or France, is the most wicked," an exasperated congressman declared.

Republican War Hawks. Republican congressmen from the West—the future "war hawks" of 1812—thought Britain was the major offender, pointing in particular to its assistance to the Indians in the Ohio River Valley. Bolstered by British guns and supplies, in 1809 the Shawnee chief Tecumseh, assisted by his brother, the prophet Tenskwatawa, had revived the Western Confederacy of the 1790s (see American Lives, "Tenskwatawa: Shawnee Prophet," p. 236). Their goal was to exclude whites from all lands west of the Appalachian Mountains. Responding to this threat, expansionists in Congress condemned British support of Tecumseh and threatened to invade Canada. In 1811, following a series of clashes between settlers and the Confederacy, William Henry Harrison, the governor of the Indiana Territory, led an army against Tenskwatawa's village of Prophetstown (on the Wabash River in present-day Indiana). After fending off the confederacy's warriors at the Battle of Tippecanoe, Harrison burned the village to the ground.

Henry Clay of Kentucky, the new Speaker of the House of Representatives, and John C. Calhoun, a rising young congressman from South Carolina, pushed Madison toward war with Great Britain. Southern and western Republican congressmen eyed new territory in British Canada and Spanish Florida, part of which had already been seized by American militia. They also hoped that war would discredit the Federalists, who had long pursued a pro-British foreign policy. With national elections approaching, Madison demanded British respect for American sovereignty in the West and neutral rights on the Atlantic. When the British did not respond quickly, Madison asked Congress for a declaration of war. In June 1812 a sharply divided Senate voted 19 to 13 for war, and the House of Representatives concurred, 79 to 49. To mobilize support for the war, Republicans emphasized Britain's disregard for American rights. As President Madison put it, "National honor is national property of the highest value."

The underlying causes of the War of 1812 have been much debated. Officially, the United States went to war because of violations of its neutral rights: the seizure of merchant ships and the impressment of their sailors. But the Federalists who represented merchants' and seamen's interests in Congress voted against the war declaration, and in the subsequent election voters in New England and the Middle Atlantic states cast their ballots (and 89 electoral votes) for the Federalist candidate for president, De Witt Clinton of New York. Madison amassed most of his 128 electoral votes in the South and West, where Republican congressmen and their constituents supported the war. Because of this regional split, more than one historian has argued that the conflict was "a western war with eastern labels."

The War of 1812

The War of 1812 was a near disaster for the United States, both militarily and politically. Predictions of an easy victory over British forces in Canada ended when a first invasion resulted in a hasty American retreat back to Detroit. But Americans stayed on the offensive in the West, as Commodore Oliver Hazard Perry defeated a small British flotilla on Lake Erie. Then in October 1813 General William Henry Harrison triumphed over a combined British and Indian force at the Battle of the Thames, killing Tecumseh, who had become a general in the British army. Another American expedition burned York (present-day Toronto) but lacking sufficient men and supplies quickly withdrew.

Political divisions in the United States prevented a major invasion of Canada in the East. New Englanders opposed the war and prohibited their militias from fighting outside their states. Boston merchants and banks declined to lend money to the federal government, making the war difficult to finance. In Congress Daniel Webster, a dynamic young representative from New Hampshire, led Federalist opposition to higher taxes and tariffs and to the national conscription of state militiamen.

Partly because of these domestic conflicts, the tide of battle gradually began to turn in Britain's favor. Initially the British had lost scores of merchant vessels to American privateers, but the Royal Navy redeployed its forces and British commerce moved in relative safety. By 1813 a flotilla of British warships moved up and down the American coastline, harassing American shipping and threatening seaport cities. In 1814 a British fleet sailed up Chesapeake Bay and British troops stormed ashore to attack the District of Columbia, burning government buildings. Then the troops advanced on Baltimore, where they were finally repulsed at Fort McHenry. After two years of sporadic warfare the United States had made little military progress along the Canadian frontier and was on the defensive along the Atlantic,

Tenskwatawa: Shawnee Prophet

By 1800 Indian peoples in the interior of North America were in a state of crisis—their warriors dying at the hands of aggressive frontiersmen, their communities disintegrating from the violence and sexual promiscuity that flowed from the white man's whiskey, their very existence threatened by the European diseases of influenza, measles, and smallpox. War, alcoholism, disease—the trilogy of social disasters that had virtually wiped out the eastern Indian peoples—now ravaged the tribes of the American heartland.

Everywhere along the frontier new Indian leaders arose to explain these disastrous happenings and to prescribe solutions. The religious prophet Handsome Lake urged the Senecas of New York to abstain from alcohol and revive traditional Indian spiritual beliefs. Eight hundred miles to the west, the eloquent shaman Main Poc denounced whites for disrupting Indian life and spread his message of Indian renewal not only among his fellow Potawatomis in Illinois and Wisconsin but also among the neighboring Sac, Winnebago, and Chippewa peoples.

The most important Indian prophet was Tenskwatawa (pronounced *Tens-qua-ta-wa*). He was born in 1775 at Old Piqua, a Shawnee village on the Mad River in western Ohio. His father, a prominent Shawnee warrior, had died four months before his birth, killed in battle against the Virginia militia; four years later his Creek mother abandoned the village, leaving her young children to be raised by kinfolk. As a young man the future prophet was known as Lalawethika ("Rattle" or "Noisemaker") because of his boastful ways, blatant alcoholism, and flagrant disrespect for sacred Shawnee laws. Then in 1805, at age thirty, he had a profound emotional experience, lapsing for hours into an unconscious state resembling death.

Upon awakening Lalawethika claimed to have died and to have visited the Master of Life, the Good Spirit and main Shawnee god, who allowed him a glimpse of heaven: "a rich fertile country, abounding in game, fish, pleasant hunting grounds and fine corn fields," where virtuous Shawnee would go after death. He also observed the spirits of sinful Indians suffering fiery tortures (similar to those described by the Puritan preacher Jonathan Edwards). Transformed by this experience, Lalawethika renounced his wicked ways and old

identity, taking the name Tenskwatawa ("The One That Opens the Door"). He settled at Greenville in western Ohio, where he lived as a holy man, vowing to deliver the Shawnees from their present woes.

Like other Indian prophets, Tenskwatawa preached a nativist message, urging his followers to shun Americans, "the children of the Evil Spirit . . . who have taken away your lands." He denounced the consumption of alcohol, a "poison and accursed" drink, and called for a return to traditional food and clothes: "You must not dress like the White Man . . . you must go naked Excepting the Breach cloth, and when you are clothed, it must be in skins or leather." To spread these teachings, Tenskwatawa founded a new religion, deriving some of its rituals from Catholicism, which French Jesuits had spread among the Indian peoples of the region. Converts were to confess their sins and then to worship an effigy of Tenskwatawa, fingering a string of beads (similar to a rosary) and thereby "shaking hands with the Prophet."

The new religion spread like wildfire among the Delawares of Indiana, who in 1806 showed their zeal by burning alive six suspected Indian witches. Shocked by these deaths, William Henry Harrison, the American governor of the Indiana Territory, denounced Tenskwatawa as a "pretended prophet" who was leading the Shawnees down "a dark, crooked, and thorny road." "If he is really a prophet," Harrison told the Indians, "ask of him to cause the sun to stand still . . . or the dead to rise from their graves." Harrison soon regretted these words. Learning from visiting American astronomers of an imminent eclipse of the sun in Indiana and Illinois, Tenskwatawa announced that on June 16 he would darken the sun at midday. "Did I not speak the truth?" he asked those— Delawares and Wyandots as well as Shawnees—who gathered at Greenville at the appointed time. "See, the sun is dark." As reports of this "miracle" circulated, warriors and wise men from many western tribes—Kickapoo, Potawatomi, Winnebago, Ottawa, Chippewa—journeyed to Greenville to learn the Prophet's teachings.

In 1808 the new religion took on a political cast. Fearing attacks by Americans and seeking closer proximity to his western followers, Tenskwatawa founded a new holy village, Prophetstown, near the juncture of the Tippecanoe and Wabash Rivers. There, he said, "they would be able to watch the Boundary Line between the Indians and white people—and if a white man put his foot over it [the Wabash River] then the warriors could easily put him back." To defend this newly defined boundary, the Prophet dispatched his older brother Tecumseh to Canada, where he secured food, manufactures, and guns from British officials. The determination of the Shawnee brothers stiffened in September 1809 when "government

Tenskwatawa, "The Prophet," 1836

Tenskwatawa added a spiritual dimension to Native American resistance, urging a holy war against the invading whites. His religious message transcended differences among Indian peoples, helping to create a formidable political and military alliance.

Smithsonian American Art Musuem, Washington, D.C. / Art Resource, NY.

chiefs" (Miami, Delaware, and Potawatomi leaders who received annuities from U.S. officials) ceded more than 3 million acres of land in Indiana and Illinois to the United States. Arguing that the land belonged to all Indians, Tenskwatawa declared that "no sale was good unless made by all the Tribes." Tecumseh demanded that the governor "restore the land"; otherwise he would "kill all the chiefs that sold you this land" and form a great confederation that would unite with the British to expel American invaders. What had begun as a movement of religious revitalization had become a crusade for Indian political unity and land rights.

As the movement changed its focus, Tecumseh seized the reins of leadership. After meeting Tecumseh in August 1811, Harrison reported to the secretary of war that he was "really the efficient man—the Moses of the family . . . a bold, active, sensible man, daring in the extreme and capable of any undertaking." When Tecumseh left for the South (to persuade the Chickasaws, Choctaws, and Creeks to join the Indian Confederation), Harrison took advantage of his absence, quickly mobilizing an army of 1,000 men and marching on Prophetstown. Ignoring his

brother's instructions to avoid conflict, Tenskwatawa assured his force of 600 warriors that the Master of Life would make them invulnerable and attacked Harrison's camp near the Tippecanoe River. In a bitter but inconclusive battle, the Americans suffered 62 dead and 124 wounded while the Indians lost 50 dead and 80 wounded. But the victory went to Harrison. Shocked by their losses, Tenskwatawa's followers now scoffed at his claims of religious power, threatened him with death, and melted away, allowing the American troops to burn Prophetstown.

The Prophet's religion suffered a severe wound on the battlefield at Tippecanoe, and it died during the War of 1812, as American bullets took the lives of Tecumseh and many of Tenskwatawa's remaining followers. After a decade of exile in British Canada, Tenskwatawa returned to the United States in 1824 as one of the "government chiefs" he had long despised, working for U.S. officials and persuading hundreds of Shawnees to leave Indiana and move with him to a reservation on the plains of eastern Kansas. He died there in 1836, without power, influence, or followers.

MAP 8.5 The War of 1812

Unlike the War for Independence, the War of 1812 had few large-scale military campaigns. The most extensive fighting took place along the Canadian border. In 1812 and 1813, American armies led by Generals Hull, Harrison, and Dearborn and a naval force commanded by Commodore Perry attacked British targets with mixed success. The British took the offensive in 1814, launching a successful raid on Washington and Baltimore but suffering heavy losses when they invaded the United States along Lake Champlain. Near the Gulf of Mexico, American forces moved from one success to another, as General Andrew Jackson defeated the pro-British Creek Indians at the Battle of Horseshoe Bend and, in the major battle of the war, an invading British army at New Orleans.

Map labels:

CANADA

Quebec

MAINE (part of Mass.)

Montreal

Chrysler's Farm Nov. 11, 1813

2. Americans burn York (Toronto), April 27, 1813

Lake Ontario

Dearborn

6. British invasion stopped at Plattsburgh on Lake Champlain, Sept. 11, 1814

VT. N.H.

Boston

MASS.

CONN. R.I.

Ft. Mackinac

Lake Superior

Lake Huron

Lake Michigan

4. Harrison defeats British, Battle of the Thames, Oct. 5, 1813

Lundy's Lane July 25, 1814

NEW YORK

MICHIGAN TERRITORY

1. Hull's invasion of Canada fails, then he loses Detroit, Aug. 16, 1812

Ft. Detroit

Hull

Lake Erie

Erie

Perry

N.J.

New York

PENNSYLVANIA

7. British seige of Baltimore, Sept. 13–14, 1814

Fort Dearborn

Harrison

3. Perry defeats British, Put-In-Bay, Sept. 10, 1813

OHIO

Philadelphia

Godly Wood Sept. 12, 1814

Baltimore

DEL.

Ft. McHenry

1814

Tippecanoe Nov. 7, 1811

ILLINOIS TERRITORY

INDIANA TERRITORY

Washington, D.C.

MD.

St. Louis

Ohio R.

5. British burn Washington, D.C., Aug. 24–28, 1814

VIRGINIA

Chesapeake Bay

KENTUCKY

UNORGANIZED TERRITORY

Mississippi R.

NORTH CAROLINA

ATLANTIC OCEAN

TENNESSEE

SOUTH CAROLINA

8. Jackson defeats Creek Indians, Horseshoe Bend, March 27, 1814

Jackson

MISSISSIPPI TERRITORY

GEORGIA

Charleston

Savannah

Jackson

9. Jackson invades Spanish Florida to attack the British at Pensacola, Nov. 7, 1814

Jackson

LOUISIANA

Pensacola

SPANISH FLORIDA

New Orleans

10. Jackson defeats British at New Orleans, Jan. 8, 1815

1814

Gulf of Mexico

Scale:
0 — 150 — 300 miles
0 — 150 — 300 kilometers

Legend:
- U.S. states in 1812
- U.S. territories in 1812
- American movements
- British movements
- British blockade
- American victories
- British victories
- Forts

with its new capital city in ruins. The only positive news came from the Southwest. There a rugged slave-owning planter named Andrew Jackson led an army of militiamen from Tennessee to victory over the British-supported Creek Indians in the Battle of Horseshoe Bend (1814), forcing the Indians to cede 23 million acres of land (Map 8.5).

American military setbacks strengthened opposition to the war, especially in New England. In 1814 Federalists in the Massachusetts legislature called for a convention "to lay the foundation for a radical reform in the National Compact," and New England Federalists met in Hartford, Connecticut, to discuss strategy. Some delegates to the Hartford convention proposed secession by their states, but the majority favored revising the Constitution. To end domination of the presidency by Virginians the delegates proposed a constitutional amendment that would limit the office to a single four-year term and require it to rotate among citizens from different states. Other delegates suggested amendments restricting commercial embargoes to sixty days and requiring a two-thirds majority in Congress to declare war, prohibit trade, or admit a new state to the Union.

As a minority party in Congress and the nation, the Federalists could prevail only if the war continued to go badly—a very real prospect. In late summer of 1814 a planned British invasion of the Hudson River Valley was narrowly averted by an American naval victory at the Battle of Lake Champlain. Then while the Federalists were meeting in Hartford in December, thousands of seasoned British troops landed at New Orleans, threatening to cut off the access of western settlers to the sea. The United States was under military pressure from both north and south.

Fortunately for the young American republic, Britain wanted peace. The twenty-year struggle against France had sapped its wealth and energy, and so it entered into negotiations with the United States in Ghent, Belgium. At

Battle of New Orleans, by Jean Hyacinthe de Laclotte (detail)
As their artillery (right center) bombarded the American lines, British troops attacked the center of General Andrew Jackson's troops while a column of redcoats (foreground) tried to turn the right flank of the American fortifications. Secure behind their battlements, Jackson's forces repelled the assaults, leaving the ground littered with British casualties and taking thousands of prisoners.
New Orleans Museum of Art, gift of Edgar William and Bernice Chrysler Garbisch.

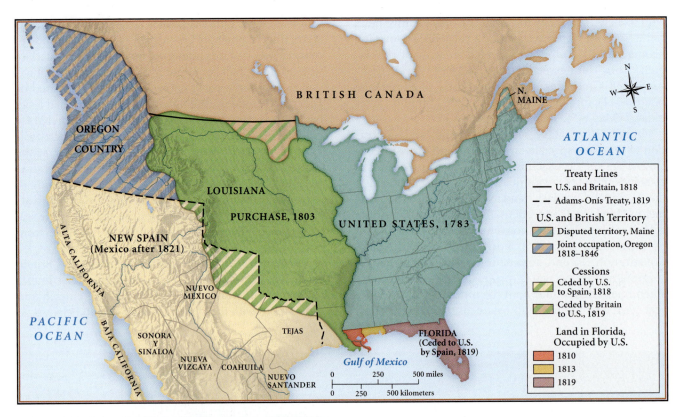

MAP 8.6 Defining the National Boundaries, 1800–1820

After the War of 1812 American diplomats negotiated treaties with Great Britain and Spain that defined the boundaries of the Louisiana Purchase with British Canada to the north and New Spain (which in 1821 became the independent nation of Mexico) to the south and west. These treaties eliminated the threat of border wars with neighboring states for a generation, providing the United States with a much-needed period of peace and security.

For more help analyzing this map, see the ONLINE STUDY GUIDE at bedfordstmartins.com/henretta.

first the American commissioners—John Quincy Adams, Albert Gallatin, and Henry Clay—demanded territory in Canada and Florida, and British diplomats insisted on an Indian buffer state between the United States and Canada. Ultimately, both sides realized that small concessions won at the bargaining table were not worth the costs of prolonged warfare. The Treaty of Ghent, signed on Christmas Eve 1814, restored the prewar borders of the United States.

This result hardly justified three years of fighting, but a final victory in combat lifted Americans' morale. Before news of the Treaty of Ghent reached the United States, newspaper headlines proclaimed an "ALMOST INCREDIBLE VICTORY!! GLORIOUS NEWS": on January 8, 1815, General Andrew Jackson's troops (including a contingent of French-speaking black Americans, the Corps d'Afrique) crushed the British forces attacking New Orleans. The Americans fought from carefully constructed breastworks and were amply supplied with cannon, which rained "grapeshot and cannister bombs" on the massed British formations. The British lost some of

their finest troops, with seven hundred dead and two thousand wounded or taken prisoner. By contrast the Americans sustained only thirteen dead and fifty-eight wounded. The victory made Jackson a national hero and a symbol of the emerging West. It also redeemed the nation's battered pride and, together with the coming of peace, undercut the Hartford convention's demands for a significant revision of the Constitution.

Just as Jackson emerged as a war hero, John Quincy Adams rose to national prominence for his diplomatic efforts at Ghent and his subsequent success in resolving boundary disputes. The son of Federalist president John Adams, John Quincy had joined the Republican Party before the war and in 1817 became secretary of state under President James Monroe (1817–1825). In 1817 Adams negotiated the Rush-Bagot Treaty with Great Britain, which limited both nations' naval forces on the Great Lakes; the following year he concluded another agreement that set the border between the Louisiana Purchase and British Canada at the forty-ninth parallel. Then in 1819

Adams persuaded Spain to cede Florida to the United States in the Adams-Onís Treaty. In return the American government took responsibility for its citizens' financial claims against Spain, renounced Jefferson's earlier claim that Spanish Texas was part of the Louisiana Purchase, and agreed on a compromise boundary between New Spain and the state of Louisiana, which had entered the Union in 1812 (Map 8.6). As a result of Adams's efforts the United States gained undisputed possession of nearly all the land south of the forty-ninth parallel and between the Mississippi River and the Rocky Mountains.

The Capitalist Commonwealth

The increasing size of the American republic was paralleled by the growth of its economic institutions and wealth. Before 1790 the United States was an agricultural society, dependent on Great Britain for markets, credit, and manufactured goods. Over the next generation the nation gradually developed a more diverse economy as some rural Americans became manufacturers, bankers supplied credit to expand trade, merchants developed regional markets, and state governments actively encouraged economic development.

The emerging American economic order was capitalist in character because it was based on private property and market exchanges and because capitalists—investors, bankers, and wealthy entrepreneurs—shaped many of its political and financial policies. But this capitalist political economy was still influenced by the political ideology of the republican commonwealth, which elevated the public good over private gain.

A Merchant-Based Economy: Banks, Manufacturing, and Markets

America was "a Nation of Merchants," a British visitor reported from Philadelphia in 1798, "always alive to their interests; and keen in the pursuit of wealth in all the various modes of acquiring it." And acquire it they did, especially during the European wars that lasted from 1792 to 1815 and provided opportunities for spectacular profits. Entrepreneurs such as the fur trader John Jacob Astor and the merchant Robert Oliver became the nation's first millionaires. Migrating from Germany to New York in 1784, Astor became wealthy by carrying furs from the Pacific Northwest to markets in China. He soon became the largest landowner in New York City. Oliver started in Baltimore as an agent for Irish linen merchants and then opened his own mercantile firm. Exploiting the wartime shipping boom, he reaped enormous profits in the West Indian coffee and sugar trade.

Banking and Credit. To finance such enterprises Americans needed a banking system. Before 1776

Cloth Merchant

Elijah Boardman (1760–1832) was a prosperous storekeeper in New Milford, Connecticut, who eventually became a United States senator. Along with other American traders, he imported huge quantities of cloth from Britain. When war cut off trade, some merchants financed the domestic production of textiles. Others, including Boardman, turned to speculation in western lands; in 1795 he joined the Connecticut Land Company and bought huge tracts in Connecticut's "Western Reserve," including the present towns of Medina, Palmyra, and Boardman, Ohio. Ralph Earl painted this portrait of Boardman in 1789. Metropolitan Museum of Art, bequest of Susan W. Tyler, 1979.

ambitious colonists found it difficult to secure loans. Farmers relied on government-sponsored land banks, while merchants arranged partnerships, borrowed funds from other merchants, or obtained credit from British suppliers. Then in 1781 Philadelphia merchants persuaded the Confederation Congress to charter the Bank of North America to provide short-term commercial loans; traders in Boston and New York founded similar banks in 1784. Those institutions provided merchants with the credit they needed to finance their transactions. "Our monied capital has so much increased from the Introduction of Banks, & the

Circulation of the Funds," the Philadelphia merchant William Bingham boasted as early as 1791, "that the Necessity of Soliciting Credits from England will no longer exist, & the Means will be provided for putting in Motion every Specie of Industry."

In 1791, on Alexander Hamilton's initiative, Congress chartered the First Bank of the United States. The bank had the power to issue notes and make commercial loans, and although the bank's managers used their lending powers cautiously, profits still averaged a handsome 8 percent annually. By 1805, in response to the continuing demand for commercial credit, the bank had branches in eight major cities. Despite this success the First Bank of the United States did not survive. Jeffersonians, who were suspicious of corruption by monied men, accused the bank of encouraging "a consolidated, energetic government supported by public creditors, speculators, and other insidious men lacking in public spirit of any kind." When the bank's charter expired in 1811, President Madison did not seek renewal, forcing merchants, artisans, and farmers to ask their state legislatures to charter new banks. By 1816, when Madison adopted a more "national" stance with respect to economic policy and signed the congressional legislation creating the Second Bank of the United States, there were 246 state-chartered banks with $68 million in banknotes in circulation.

Many state banks were shady operations, issuing notes without adequate specie reserves and making ill-advised loans to insiders. Such poorly managed state banks were one cause of the Panic of 1819, a credit crisis sparked by a sharp drop in world agricultural prices. As farm income plummeted by one-third, many farmers could not pay their bills, causing bankruptcies among local storekeepers, wholesale merchants, and overextended state banks. By 1821, those state banks that were still solvent had only $45 million in circulation and court dockets were crowded with thousands of cases, as creditors tried to save their own businesses by taking possession of the devalued property of their debtors. The panic gave Americans their first taste of the business cycle—the periodic expansion and contraction of profits and employment that is an inherent part of a market economy.

Rural Manufacturing. The panic also revealed that artisans and yeomen as well as merchants now depended on regional or national markets. Before 1790 most artisans in New England and the Middle Atlantic region sold their handicrafts locally or bartered them with neighbors. For example, John Hoff of Lancaster, Pennsylvania, sold his fine wooden-cased clocks locally and bartered them with his neighbors for such things as a dining table, a bedstead, and labor on his small farm. But others—shipbuilders in seacoast towns, iron smelters in Pennsylvania and Maryland, and shoemakers in Lynn, Massachusetts—already sold their products in far-flung markets. Indeed, merchant-entrepreneurs were

hard at work developing a rural-based manufacturing system similar to the European outwork, or putting-out, system (see Chapter 1) and selling its products in all parts of the nation. Merchants stood at the center of this system, buying raw materials, organizing workers to make goods, and selling finished products. At the periphery were hundreds of thousands of farm families that supplied the labor. When a French traveler visited central Massachusetts in 1795, he found "almost all these houses . . . inhabited by men who are both cultivators and artisans; one is a tanner, another a shoemaker, another sells goods, but all are farmers."

By the 1820s thousands of New England farm families produced shoes, brooms, palm-leaf hats, and tinware—baking pans, cups, utensils, lanterns. Merchants shipped these products to cities and slave plantations, while New England peddlers, equipped "with a horse and a cart covered with a box or with a wagon," blanketed the South and acquired a reputation as crafty, hard-bargaining "Yankees." The success of these peddlers and merchants expanded the commercial sector of the American domestic economy.

This economic advance stemmed initially from innovations in organization and marketing rather than in technology. Water-powered machines—the product of the Industrial Revolution in Britain—were adopted slowly in America, beginning in the textile industry. In the 1780s merchants built small mills along the waterways of New England and the Middle Atlantic states. They installed water-powered machines and hired workers to card and comb wool—and later cotton—into long strands. For several decades the next steps in the manufacturing process were accomplished under the outwork system rather than in water-powered factories. Wage-earning farm women and children spun the strands into yarn by hand, and men in other households used foot-powered looms to weave the yarn into cloth. In his *Letter on Manufactures* (1810) Secretary of the Treasury Albert Gallatin estimated that there were 2,500 outwork weavers in New England. A decade later more than 12,000 household workers in that region wove woolen cloth, which then went to water-powered fulling mills to be pounded flat and finished smooth. Thus, even before textile production was centralized in factories, the nation had a profitable and expanding preindustrial outwork system of manufacturing.

Toward a Market Economy. The penetration of the market economy into rural areas motivated farmers to produce more goods. Ambitious farm families switched from mixed-crop agriculture to raising cattle, in order to sell their hides to the booming shoe industry, and to keeping dairy cows to provide milk for cheese making. As a Polish traveler in central Massachusetts reported in 1798, "Along the whole road from Boston, we saw women engaged in making cheese" for sale in cities. Hatmaking emerged as another new industry. "Straw hats and

The Yankee Peddler, c. 1830

Even in 1830 most Americans lived too far from market towns to go there regularly to buy needed goods. Instead, farm families, such as this relatively prosperous one depicted by an unknown artist, purchased most of their tinware, clocks, textiles, and other manufactures from peddlers, often from New England, who traveled far and wide in small horse-drawn vans such as that pictured in the doorway. Collection IBM Corporation, Armonk, NY.

For more help analyzing this image, see the ONLINE STUDY GUIDE at bedfordstmartins.com/henretta.

Bonnets are manufactured by many families," a Maine official commented, while another observer noted that "probably 8,000 females" in the vicinity of Foxborough, Massachusetts, braided rye straw into hats for market sale. Other farm families began to raise sheep and sold raw wool to textile manufacturers. Processing these raw materials brought new businesses to many farming towns. In 1792 Concord, Massachusetts, had one slaughterhouse and five small tanneries; a decade later the town had eleven slaughterhouses and six large tanneries.

As the rural economy produced more goods, it also produced significant changes in the environment. For example, foul odors from stockyards and tanning pits now wafted over Concord and many other leather-producing towns. Moreover, the multiplication of livestock—dairy cows, cattle, and especially sheep—created a new landscape as farmers cut down hundreds of thousands of acres of trees to provide pasturage. By the mid-nineteenth century, most of the forests in southern New England were

gone, leaving a barren visual landscape. Likewise, New England's rivers were now dotted with scores of textile milldams that altered the flow of rivers, and made it difficult if not impossible for fish to reach their upriver spawning grounds. Even as the income of many farmers rose, the quality of their natural environment deteriorated.

At first, barter transactions were a central feature of the emergent market system. When Ebenezer and Daniel Merriam of Brookfield, Massachusetts, began publishing books in the 1810s and distributing them to booksellers and publishers in New York City, Philadelphia, and Boston, they received neither cash nor credit in return. Rather, they received other books, which they had to exchange with local storekeepers to get supplies for their business. The Merriams also paid their employees on a barter basis; a journeyman printer received a third of his "wages" in books, which he had to peddle himself. Gradually a cash economy replaced this complex barter system. As farm families sold more and more goods in the market,

Voting Box

Elections in Pennsylvania were often contentious affairs, marred by riots and fistfights as rival political groups tried to keep their opponents from the polls. Once safely inside the voting place, citizens deposited their ballots in containers such as this nicely crafted late-eighteenth-century walnut box from the Delaware Valley. Independence National Historic Park.

they stopped making their own textiles and shoes and bought them instead, using the cash or store credit they had earned.

The new capitalist-run market economy had some drawbacks. Rural parents and their children now worked longer and harder, making specialized products during the winter in addition to their regular farming chores during the warmer seasons. Perhaps more important, they lost some of their economic independence. Instead of working solely for themselves as yeomen farm families, they toiled as part-time wage earners for merchants and manufacturers. The new market system decreased the self-sufficiency of families and communities even as it made them more productive. But the tide of change was unstoppable.

Public Policy: The Commonwealth System

Throughout the nineteenth century state governments were the most important political institutions in the United States and were the leading lawmaking bodies. They enacted legislation governing criminal and civil affairs, established taxation systems, and oversaw county, city, and town officials. Consequently, state governments had a much greater impact on the day-to-day lives of Americans than did the national government.

As early as the 1790s many state legislatures devised an American plan of mercantilism, known to historians as the commonwealth system (because its goal was to increase the common wealth, or common good, of the society). Just as the British Parliament had promoted the imperial economy through the Navigation Acts

(1651–1696), state legislatures enacted measures to stimulate commerce and economic development. In particular, they granted hundreds of corporate charters to private businesses to build roads, bridges, and canals, enterprises that were intended to be "of great public utility," as the act establishing the Massachusetts Bank put it. For example, in 1794 the Pennsylvania assembly chartered the Lancaster Turnpike Company to lay a graded gravel road between Lancaster and Philadelphia, a distance of sixty-five miles. The venture was expensive—nearly $500,000 (about $8 million today)—but the road made a modest profit for the investors and greatly enhanced the regional economy by allowing a rapid movement of goods and people. "The turnpike is finished," noted a farm woman, "and we can now go to town at all times and in all weather." A boom in turnpike construction soon connected dozens of inland market centers to seaport cities.

By 1800 state governments had granted more than three hundred corporate charters. Incorporation often included a grant of **limited liability** that made it easier to attract investors; in the event the business failed, the personal assets of the shareholders could not be seized to pay the corporation's debts. Most transportation charters also included the power of **eminent domain**, giving turnpike, bridge, and canal corporations the use of the judicial system to force the sale of privately owned land along proposed routes. State legislatures also came to the aid of capitalist flour millers or textile manufacturers whose dams flooded adjacent land, thereby infringing on the property rights of farmers or constituting a public "nuisance" under **common law**. In Massachusetts, the

Mill Dam Act of 1795 overrode common law and required farmers to accept "fair compensation" for their lost acreage.

To some critics such uses of state power by private companies ran contrary to republicanism, "which does not admit of granting peculiar privileges to any body of men." Charters not only violated the "equal rights" of all citizens, opponents argued, but also restricted the sovereignty of the people. As a Pennsylvanian put it, "Whatever power is given to a corporation, is just so much power taken from the State" and therefore the citizenry. Nonetheless, state courts consistently upheld corporate charters and routinely approved grants of eminent domain to private corporations. "The opening of good and easy internal communications is one of the highest duties of government," a New Jersey court declared.

State mercantilism soon encompassed much more than transportation. Following the embargo of 1807, which cut off goods and credit from Europe, New England states awarded charters to two hundred iron-mining, textile-manufacturing, and banking firms, and the Pennsylvania legislature granted more than eleven hundred. Thus by 1820 innovative state governments had created a new political economy: the commonwealth system. The use of state incentives to encourage business and improve the general welfare would continue for another generation.

Federalist Law: John Marshall and the Supreme Court

Both Federalists and Republicans endorsed the commonwealth idea but in different ways. Federalists looked

***John Marshall,* by Chester Harding, c. 1830**
Even at age seventy-five, John Marshall (1755–1835) had a commanding personal presence. Upon becoming chief justice of the U.S. Supreme Court in 1801, Marshall elevated the Court from a minor department of the national government to a major institution in American legal and political life. His constitutional decisions dealing with judicial review, contract rights, the regulation of commerce, and national banking permanently shaped the character of American law. Boston Athenaeum.

to the national government for economic leadership and supported Alexander Hamilton's program of national mercantilism: a funded debt, tariffs, and a central bank. Jeffersonian Republicans generally opposed such policies, preferring state-based initiatives, but following the War of 1812 some Republicans began to support national economic policies. As Speaker of the House of Representatives, Republican Henry Clay of Kentucky supported the creation of the Second Bank of the United States in 1816. In the following year Clay won passage of the Bonus Bill, sponsored by Representative John C. Calhoun of South Carolina, to establish a national fund for roads and other internal improvements. But most Republicans still believed that such policies exceeded the powers delegated to the national government by the Constitution. They welcomed President Madison's veto of the Bonus Bill and urged state legislatures to take the lead in promoting economic development. This fundamental disagreement over the role of the national government remained a key issue of political debate for the next thirty years (see Chapter 11).

The difference between Federalist and Jeffersonian Republican conceptions of public policy emerged during John Marshall's tenure on the Supreme Court. Appointed chief justice by President John Adams in January 1801, Marshall was a committed Federalist from Virginia who dominated the Court until 1822 and upheld nationalist principles on the Court until his death in 1835. His success stemmed not from a mastery of legal principles and doctrines but from the power of his logic and the force of his personality. By winning the support of Joseph Story and other nationalist-minded Republican judges on the Court, Marshall shaped the evolution of the Constitution. Three principles formed the basis of his jurisprudence: a commitment to judicial authority, the supremacy of national over state legislation, and a traditional, static view of property rights (Table 8.2).

After Marshall proclaimed the power of judicial review in *Marbury v. Madison* (see Chapter 7), the doctrine evolved slowly. During the first half of the nineteenth century the Supreme Court and the state courts used it sparingly and then only to overturn state laws that clearly conflicted with constitutional principles. Not until the *Dred Scott* decision of 1857 would the Supreme Court void another law passed by Congress (see Chapter 13).

Federal-State Relations. The position of the Marshall Court on federal-state relations was most eloquently expressed in *McCulloch v. Maryland* (1819). In 1816 Congress created the Second Bank of the United States, giving it authority to handle the notes of state-chartered banks and thus to monitor their financial reserves. To preserve the competitive position of its state-chartered banks, the Maryland legislature imposed an annual tax of $15,000 on notes issued by the Baltimore branch office of the Second Bank. In response, the Second Bank contested the constitutionality of the Maryland law, claiming that it infringed on the powers of the national government. To make their case, lawyers for the state of Maryland adopted Jefferson's argument against the First Bank of the United States, maintaining that Congress lacked the constitutional authority to charter a national bank. Even if such a bank could be created, the lawyers argued, Maryland had a right to tax its activities within the state.

Marshall and the nationalist-minded Republicans on the Court firmly rejected both arguments. The Second Bank was constitutional, said the chief justice, because it was "necessary and proper," given the national government's responsibility to control currency and credit. Like Alexander Hamilton and other Federalists, Marshall preferred a loose construction of the Constitution. If the goal of a law is "legitimate [and] . . . within the scope of the Constitution," he wrote, then "all means which are appropriate" to secure that goal are also constitutional, even if they are not explicitly mentioned. As for Maryland's right to tax the national bank, the chief justice stated that "the power to tax involves the power to destroy," suggesting that Maryland's bank tax would render the national government "dependent on the states"—an outcome that "was not intended by the American people" who ratified the Constitution.

TABLE 8.2 Major Decisions of the Marshall Court		
Date	Case	Significance of Decision
1803	*Marbury v. Madison*	Asserts principle of judicial review
1810	*Fletcher v. Peck*	Protects property rights by a broad reading of "contract" clause
1819	*Dartmouth College v. Woodward*	Safeguards property rights of chartered corporations
1819	*McCulloch v. Maryland*	Interprets Constitution to give broad powers to national government
1824	*Gibbons v. Ogden*	Gives national government jurisdiction over interstate commerce

The Marshall Court asserted the dominance of national statutes over state legislation again in *Gibbons v. Ogden* (1824), which struck down a monopoly that the New York legislature had granted to Aaron Ogden for steamboat passenger service across the Hudson River to New Jersey. Asserting that the Constitution gave the federal government the authority to regulate interstate commerce, the chief justice sided with Thomas Gibbons, who held a federal license to transport people and goods between the two states.

Property Rights. Marshall also turned to the Constitution to uphold his view of property rights. During the 1790s Thomas Jefferson and other Republicans had celebrated the primacy of statute (or "positive") law enacted by representatives of the people. As a Republican jurist put it, a magistrate "should be governed himself by positive law" while executing and enforcing "the will of the supreme power, which is the will of THE PEOPLE." In response, Federalist judges and politicians warned that popular sovereignty had to be curbed to prevent the "tyranny of the majority"—the passage of statutes that would infringe on the property rights of individual citizens. To prevent state legislatures from overriding property rights, Federalist lawyers asserted that judges had the power to void laws that violated traditional common-law principles or were contrary to "natural law" or "natural rights" (see Chapter 4).

Marshall shared the goal of protecting individuals' property from government interference but used another legal strategy. He seized on the contract clause of the Constitution (Article 1, Section 10; see Documents, p. D-9), which prohibits the states from passing any law "impairing the obligation of contracts." Delegates at the 1787 Philadelphia convention had included this clause primarily to allow creditors to overturn state laws that prevented them from seizing the lands and goods of debtors, but Marshall expanded it to defend other property rights.

To extend the reach of this constitutional provision, Marshall gave an exceedingly broad definition to the term *contract*, enlarging it to embrace grants and charters made by the state governments. The case of *Fletcher v. Peck* (1810) involved a large grant of land made by the Georgia legislature to the Yazoo Land Company. A newly elected state legislature canceled the grant, alleging it had been obtained through fraud and bribery; in response, speculators who had already purchased Yazoo lands appealed to the Supreme Court to uphold their titles. Marshall ruled that the legislative grant to Yazoo Land Company was a contract that could not subsequently be abridged by the state. The property rights of the company and the purchasers had become "vested" in the new owners. This far-reaching decision not only gave constitutional protection to those who purchased state-owned lands but also promoted the development of a national capitalist economy by protecting out-of-state investors.

The court extended its defense of vested property rights even further in *Dartmouth College v. Woodward* (1819). Dartmouth College was a private institution established by a charter granted by King George III. In 1816 the Republican-dominated legislature of New Hampshire tried to convert the college into a public university that would educate more of the state's citizens, thereby enhancing the commonwealth. The Dartmouth trustees resisted the legislature and engaged Daniel Webster, a renowned constitutional lawyer as well as a leading Federalist politician, to plead their case. Citing the Court's decision in *Fletcher v. Peck*, Webster argued that the royal charter constituted a contract and therefore could not be tampered with by the New Hampshire legislature. Marshall and Story agreed, upholding the rights of the college. Marshall's triumph seemed complete. Many Federalist principles, such as judicial review and corporate property rights, had been permanently incorporated into the American legal system (see Voices from Abroad, "Alexis de Tocqueville: Law and Lawyers in the United States," p. 248).

The "Era of Good Feeling." Yet even as Marshall announced the *Dartmouth* and *McCulloch* decisions in 1819, the political fortunes of his Federalist Party were in severe decline. Nationalist-minded Republicans had won the allegiance of many Federalist voters in the East, while the pro-agrarian policies of Jeffersonian Republicans commanded the support of most western farmers and southern planters. "No Federal character can run with success," Gouverneur Morris of New York lamented, and the election results of 1818 bore out his pessimism. Following the election Republicans outnumbered Federalists 37 to 7 in the Senate and 156 to 27 in the House of Representatives. Westward expansion and the transformation in American government begun by Jefferson's Revolution of 1800 had brought the tumultuous era of Federalist-Republican conflict to an end.

The decline of political controversy prompted contemporary observers to dub James Monroe's two terms as president (1817–1825) the "Era of Good Feeling." Actually, national political harmony was more apparent than real, for the Republican Party was now divided into a National faction and a Jeffersonian (or "state"-oriented) faction. The two groups fought bitterly over patronage and policy, especially the issue of federal support for internal improvement projects such as roads and canals. As the aging Jefferson himself complained about the National Republicans, "You see so many of these new republicans maintaining in Congress the rankest doctrines of the old federalists." This division in the ranks of the Republican Party would soon produce a second party system—in which Whigs faced off against Democrats. One cycle of American politics and economic debate had ended and another was about to begin.

Alexis de Tocqueville

Law and Lawyers in the United States

A French aristocrat and lawyer, Alexis de Tocqueville came to the United States to study its innovative prison system but ended up writing Democracy in America (1835), a comprehensive and astute analysis of its dynamic society. Here argues that the raw vigor of American democracy was restrained by the ingrained conservatism of men of the law, who dominated the political system.

The political activity that pervades the United States must be seen in order to be understood. No sooner do you set foot upon American ground than you are stunned by a kind of tumult . . . everything is in motion around you; here the people of one quarter of a town are met to decide upon the building of a church; there the election of a representative is going on; . . . in another place, the laborers of a village quit their plows to deliberate upon the project of a road or a public school. . . .

The political agitation of American legislative bodies, which is the only one that attracts the attention of foreigners, is a mere episode, or a sort of continuation, of that universal movement which originates in the lowest classes of the people and extends successively to all the ranks of society. . . .

In visiting the Americans and studying their laws, we perceive that the authority they have entrusted to the members of the legal profession, and the influence that these individuals exercise in the government, are the most powerful existing security against the excesses of democracy. This effect seems to me to result from a general cause, which it is useful to investigate. . . . Men who have made a special study of the laws derive from [that] occupation certain habits of order, a taste for formalities, and a kind of instinctive regard for the regular connection of ideas, which naturally render them very hostile to the revolutionary spirit and the unreflecting passions of the multitude. . . .

[Moreover,] the government of democracy is favorable to the political power of lawyers; for when the wealthy, the noble, and the prince are excluded from the government, the lawyers take possession of it, in their own right, as it were, since they are the only men of information and sagacity, beyond the sphere of the people, who can be the object of popular choice. . . .

The people in democratic states do not mistrust the members of the legal profession, because it is known that they are interested to serve the popular cause. . . . Lawyers belong to the people by birth and interest, and to the aristocracy by habit and taste; they may be looked upon as the connecting link between the two great classes of society. . . . When the American people are intoxicated by passion or carried away by the impetuosity of their ideas, they are checked and stopped by the almost invisible influence of their legal counselors.

As most public men are legal practitioners, they introduce the customs and technicalities of their profession into the management of public affairs. The jury extends this habit to all classes. The language of the law thus becomes, in some measure, a vulgar tongue . . . so that at last the whole people contract the habits and the tastes of the judicial magistrate.

Source: Alexis de Tocqueville, Democracy in America, ed. Philip Bradley (New York: Vintage, 1945), 1: 283–90.

FOR FURTHER EXPLORATION

▶ For definitions of key terms boldfaced in this chapter, see the glossary at the end of the book.

▶ To assess your mastery of the material covered in this chapter, see the Online Study Guide at **bedfordstmartins.com/henretta**.

▶ For suggested references, including Web sites, see page SR-9 at the end of the book.

▶ For map resources and primary documents, see **bedfordstmartins.com/henretta**.

Between 1790 and 1820 the United States acquired immense new lands in the West and developed a capitalist economy in the East. The pace of westward expansion was rapid despite determined resistance by Indian peoples, the difficulties of transport and trade across the Appalachian Mountains, and the high price of land sold by both the U.S. government and speculators. Nonetheless, by 1820, fully 2 million Americans, white and black, were living west of the Appalachians.

Led by Thomas Jefferson, who strongly favored westward expansion, the Republicans wrested political power from the Federalists. While retaining the Bank of the United States and many Federalist officeholders, Jefferson eliminated excise taxes, reduced the national debt, cut the size of the army, and lowered the price of national lands in the West. Faced with British and French seizures of American ships and sailors, he devised the embargo of 1807, but it failed to change the policies of the warring nations. Eventually, Indian uprisings and expansionist demands by western Republicans led President James Madison into the War of 1812 against Britain. The war split the nation, prompting a secessionist movement in New England, but a negotiated peace ended the military conflict and Andrew Jackson's victory at New Orleans preserved American honor. The diplomacy of John Quincy Adams won the annexation of Florida to the United States in 1819 and the settlement of boundaries with British Canada and Spanish Texas. Western expansion helped to seal the fate of the Federalist Party, which faded from the scene, leaving a divided Republican Party in charge of the affairs of the nation.

As white Americans imposed European agricultural practices and private property rights on the lands of the West, they developed a capitalist economy in the East. Beginning in the 1790s merchant capitalists created a flourishing outwork system of rural manufacturing, and state governments devised the commonwealth system—awarding corporate charters and subsidies to assist transportation companies, manufacturers, and banks. Republican-minded state legislatures enacted statutes that promoted economic development by redefining common-law property rights. Led by the Federalist John Marshall, the Supreme Court protected the vested rights of property owners and the charter privileges of business corporations. Entrepreneurs took advantage of state legislation and judicial protection to create new business enterprises, strong regional economies, and the beginnings of a national market system.

1783	Treaty of Paris gives Americans access to the trans-Appalachian West
1787	Northwest Ordinance
1790s	State mercantilism: states grant corporation charters
	Entrepreneurs build turnpikes and short canals
	Merchants create a rural outwork system
1790–1791	Little Turtle defeats American armies in Northwest Terrritory
1791	First Bank of the United States founded; charter expires in 1811
1792	Kentucky joins Union; Tennessee follows (1796)
1794	Battle of Fallen Timbers
1795	Treaty of Greenville recognizes Indian land rights
	Massachusetts Mill Dam Act promotes textile industry
	Pinckney's Treaty with Spain allows U.S. use of Mississippi River
1801	Spain restores Louisiana to France
	John Marshall becomes chief justice of the Supreme Court
1801–1807	Treasury Secretary Albert Gallatin reduces national debt
	Seizures of American ships by France and Britain
1803	Louisiana Purchase; Lewis and Clark expedition
	Marshall asserts judicial review in *Marbury v. Madison*
1807	Embargo Act cripples American shipping
	Congress bans importation of slaves
1809	Tecumseh and Tenskwatawa mobilize Indians
1810	*Fletcher v. Peck* extends contract clause
1810s	Expansion of slavery into Old Southwest
1811	Battle of Tippecanoe
1812–1815	War of 1812
1817–1825	Era of Good Feeling during Monroe's presidency
1819	Adams-Onís Treaty annexes Florida and defines Texas boundary
	McCulloch v. Maryland enhances power of national government
	Dartmouth College v. Woodward protects property rights

CHAPTER 9

The Quest for a Republican Society

1790–1820

Democratic Republicanism
Social and Political Equality for White Men
Toward a Republican Marriage System
Republican Motherhood
Raising and Educating Republican Children

Aristocratic Republicanism and Slavery, 1780–1820
The North and South Grow Apart
Toward a New Southern Social Order
Slave Society and Culture
The Free Black Population
The Missouri Crisis

Protestant Christianity as a Social Force
The Second Great Awakening
Women's New Religious Roles

B Y THE 1820s A SENSE OF OPTIMISM pervaded white American society. "The temperate zone of North America already exhibits many signs that it is the promised land of civil liberty, and of institutions designed to liberate and exalt the human race," a Kentucky judge declared in a Fourth of July speech. Not even the deaths on July 4, 1826, of both John Adams and Thomas Jefferson shook people's optimism. Rather, most took it as a divine sign. Two great founding fathers had died, but the republic lived on.

There were good reasons for this enthusiasm. A half century after independence, white Americans lived in a self-governing society that was free from both arbitrary taxes and a dogmatic, established church. Moreover, many citizens had come to consider themselves "republicans" not simply in their legal order and their constitutional system of representative government but also in their political behavior, social outlook, and cultural habits.

However, Americans defined republicanism in different ways. Many white Americans in the North subscribed to "democratic republicanism," an ideology that encouraged individuals to aspire to greater equality in politics and within the family. However, they often failed to achieve this goal because of the strength of entrenched cultural values and economic interests.

◀ **The Fourth of July in Philadelphia, c. 1811**

By the early nineteenth century July Fourth had become a popular holiday, a time for political speeches, leisurely conversations, and youthful revelry. This detail from a painting by J. Krimmel shows a crowd celebrating the holiday. The young man buying an alcoholic drink from a street vendor (left side) may well engage in some rowdy behavior before Independence Day is over.

Pennsylvania Academy of the Fine Arts, Philadelphia. Pennsylvania Academy Purchase (from the estate of Paul Beck Jr.).

In the South many whites shared these democratic aspirations, but their society was so sharply divided along the lines of class and race that such ideals were impossible to sustain. Consequently, southern leaders gradually devised an aristocratic-republican ideology that better represented the hierarchical character and deferential values of their society. Yet a third vision of American republican society took shape in the wake of the massive religious revival that swept through the nation during the first half of the nineteenth century. For the many Americans—white and black, southern and northern—who embraced this vision, the United States was both a great experiment in republican government and the seedbed of a new Christian civilization that would redeem the world.

Democratic Republicanism

After independence, leading Americans developed a political system based on the principle of "ordered liberty," which in practice meant rule by the traditional elite. Gradually, white men of modest means deserted these patrician political leaders and embraced the republican doctrines of political equality and social mobility. Many citizens also reorganized traditional institutions such as families and schools, pursuing more egalitarian marriages and more affectionate ways of rearing and educating their children.

Social and Political Equality for White Men

Between 1780 and 1820 hundreds of well-educated Europeans visited the United States. Coming from countries with monarchical governments, established churches, patriarchal families, and profound divisions between social classes, they thought that the American republic represented a genuinely different and more just social order. In his famous *Letters from an American Farmer* (1782) the French-born essayist St. Jean de Crèvecoeur wrote that European society was composed "of great lords who possess everything, and of a herd of people who have nothing." America, by contrast, had "no aristocratical families, no courts, no kings, no bishops."

Social Mobility. This absence of a hereditary aristocracy encouraged Americans to condemn inherited social privilege, and republican ideology proclaimed legal equality for all free men. "The law is the same for everyone both as it protects and as it punishes," noted one European traveler. Yet Americans willingly accepted social divisions if they were based on personal achievement. As one letter to a newspaper put it, people should be valued not for their "wealth, titles, or connections" but for their "talents, integrity, and virtue."

As individuals amassed wealth, they gained a higher social standing, a result that astounded some Europeans. "In Europe to say of someone that he rose from nothing is a disgrace and a reproach," remarked an aristocratic Polish visitor. "It is the opposite here. To be the architect of your own fortune is honorable. It is the highest recommendation."

Changes in the legal profession exemplify the popular belief in the superiority of a competitive, achievement-oriented society. During the Revolutionary era American attorneys had won legislation that prevented untrained lawyers from practicing law. By 1800 most states required at least three years of formal schooling or a long apprenticeship in a law firm, training available only to young men from well-established families. As legal rules and the legal profession became more central to American life, republican-minded critics attacked what they called the "professional aristocracy" of lawyers. They demanded that legislatures regulate attorneys' fees, create small-claims courts in which ordinary citizens could represent themselves, and lower educational requirements for admission to the bar. Legislatures met many of these demands; by the 1820s only eleven of the twenty-six states required lawyers to complete a fixed period of legal education. These changes lowered the intellectual quality of the legal profession even as they made it more democratic in composition and spirit (Table 9.1).

Some Americans from long-distinguished families questioned the morality of a social order based on mobility and financial success. "The aristocracy of Kingston [New York] is more one of money than any village I have ever seen," complained Nathaniel Booth, whose family had once ruled Kingston but had lost its prominence. "Man is estimated by dollars," he lamented; "what he is worth determines his character and his position at once." For most white men such a system meant the opportunity to better themselves.

A Wider Franchise for Men. By the 1810s republicanism also meant voting rights for all free white men. As early as 1776 the state constitutions of Pennsylvania and Vermont allowed all taxpayers to vote, which opened up political participation to propertyless young men who paid a "poll" (or head) tax and artisans who did not own land but paid an occupational tax. By 1810 Maryland and South Carolina had extended the vote to all adult white men, and the new states of Indiana (1816), Illinois (1818), and Alabama (1819) provided for a broad male franchise in their constitutions. Within another decade fifteen states allowed all white male taxpayers to vote, and another seven instituted universal white manhood suffrage, leaving only three states with property qualifications (Map 9.1).

This expansion of suffrage changed the tone of politics. Most conservative politicians accepted popular

TABLE 9.1 Number of Lawyers in Three Selected States, to 1820		
	Number of Lawyers	Lawyers per 10,000 Population
Massachusetts (including Maine)		
1740	15	10
1775	71	24
1780	34	11
1785	92	24
1790	112	24
1800	200	35
1810	492	70
1820	710	87
Connecticut		
1790	129	54
1800	169	67
1820	248	90
South Carolina		
1771	24	19
1820	200	40

Source: George Dargo, *Law in the New Republic: Private Law and the Public Estate* (New York: Knopf, 1983), 49. Reprinted by permission of McGraw-Hill, Inc.

suffrage but insisted upon an elite-dominated political system. As Samuel Stone put it, the Federalist ideal was "a speaking aristocracy in the face of a silent democracy." However, Americans increasingly rejected this hierarchical system. They refused to vote for politicians who flaunted their high social status by wearing "top boots, breeches, and shoe buckles," their hair in "powder and queues." Instead, voters elected politicians who dressed simply and endorsed democracy, even if those leaders still favored policies that benefited those with substantial wealth.

As the political power of middling and poor white men grew, the rights and status of white women and free blacks declined. In 1802 Ohio disfranchised African Americans, and in 1821 New York kept property-holding requirements for black voters while eliminating them for whites. The most striking case of racial and sexual discrimination occurred in New Jersey, where the state constitution of 1776 had granted suffrage to all property holders. As Federalists and Republicans competed for votes after 1800, they challenged political custom by encouraging property-owning blacks and unmarried women and widows to vote. Sensing a threat to the polit-

ical dominance of white men, in 1807 the New Jersey legislature enacted legislation that defined full citizenship (and therefore voting rights) as an attribute of white men only. To justify the exclusion of women, legislators invoked both biology and custom. As one letter to a newspaper put it, "Women, generally, are neither by nature, nor habit, nor education, nor by their necessary condition in society fitted to perform this duty with credit to themselves or advantage to the public."

Toward a Republican Marriage System

European and American husbands had long dominated their wives and controlled the family's property. However, as John Adams had lamented on behalf of husbands in 1776, the revolutionary doctrine of political equality had "spread where it was not intended," encouraging some white women to demand the right to control their inheritances or speak out on public matters. These women maintained that the subordination of women was at odds with a belief in equal natural rights. Patriarchy was not "natural," the Patriot author and historian Mercy Otis

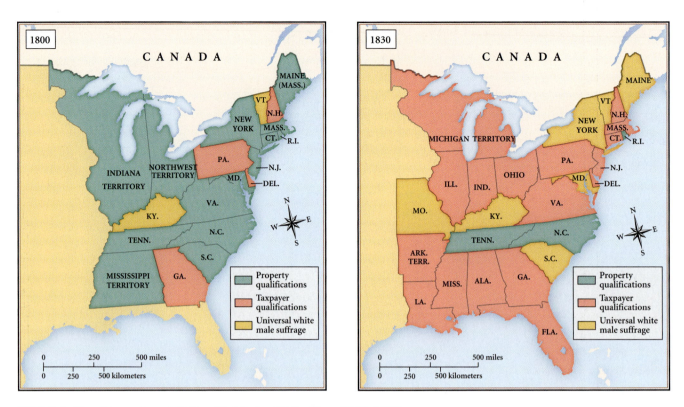

MAP 9.1 The Expansion of Voting Rights for White Men, 1800–1830

Between 1800 and 1830 the United States moved steadily toward political democracy for white men. Many existing states revised their constitutions, replacing property ownership with taxpaying or militia service as a qualification for voting. Some new states in the West extended the suffrage to all adult white men. As parties sought votes from a broader electorate, the tone of politics became more open and competitive—swayed by the interests and values of ordinary people.

Warren argued; making men the heads of households could be justified only "for the sake of order in families."

Economic and cultural changes also eroded customary paternal authority. Traditionally, landowning fathers had arranged their children's marriages to ensure the economic well-being of themselves and their wives during old age. As land holdings shrank in long-settled rural communities, yeomen fathers could no longer bequeath substantial farms—the economic incentives they had used to influence their children's selection of a spouse. Young men and women began to choose their own partners, influenced by the new cultural attitude of **sentimentalism**.

The Effects of Sentimentalism. Sentimentalism was an outlook that originated in Europe during the Romantic movement of the late eighteenth century and spread quickly among all classes of American society. Sentimentalism celebrated the importance of "feeling"— that is, a physical, sensuous appreciation of God, nature, and other human beings. This new sensibility found many forms of expression. It dripped from the pages of German and English literary works, fell from the lips of

actors in popular tear-jerking melodramas, and infused the emotional rhetoric of revivalist preachers.

As the passions of the heart overwhelmed the cool logic of the mind, a new marriage system appeared. Parents had always considered physical attraction and emotional compatibility as they arranged marriages for their children, but they were primarily concerned with the personal character and financial resources of a prospective son- or daughter-in-law. Now magazines encouraged marriages "contracted from motives of affection, rather than of interest." Many young people began to seek a spouse who was, as Eliza Southgate of Maine put it, "calculated to promote my happiness."

As young people arranged their own marriages, fathers gave up the goal of complete patriarchal control and instead became paternalists, protecting the interests of their children. To guard against free-spending sons-in-law, wealthy fathers placed their daughters' inheritances in legal trust—out of their husbands' control. As a Virginia planter wrote to his lawyer, "I rely on you to see the property settlement properly drawn before the marriage, for I by no means consent that Polly shall be left to the Vicissitudes of Life."

The Wedding, 1805
The unknown artist who painted this watercolor depicts the bride and groom staring intently into each other's eyes as they exchange marriage vows, suggesting that their union stems more from love than from economic calculation. Given the plain costumes of the assembled guests and the sparse furnishing of the room, this may be a rural Quaker wedding. Philadelphia Museum of Art.

Companionate Marriages. Theoretically the new republican ideal of **"companionate" marriage** gave wives "true equality, both of rank and fortune," with their husbands, as one Boston man suggested. However, husbands continued to occupy a privileged position because of deeply ingrained habits and laws that gave them control of the family's property. The new marriage system also discouraged parents from becoming too involved in their children's married lives, making young wives more dependent on their husbands than their mothers had been. In addition, governments accepted no obligation to prevent domestic abuse; as a lawyer noted, women who would rather "starve than submit" to the orders of their husbands were left to their fate. The marriage contract "is so much more important in its consequences to females than to males," a young man at the Litchfield Law School in Connecticut concluded in 1820, "for besides leaving everything else to unite themselves to one man, they subject themselves to his authority. He is their all—their only relative—their only hope."

Young adults who chose partners unwisely were severely disappointed when their spouses failed as providers or faithful companions, and a few sought divorces. Before 1800 most petitioners for divorce had charged their spouses with neglect, abandonment, or adultery—serious offenses against the moral order of society. After 1800 emotional grounds dominated divorce petitions. One woman complained that her husband had "ceased to cherish her," while a man grieved that his wife had "almost broke his heart." Reflecting these changed cultural values, some states expanded the legal grounds for divorce to include personal cruelty and drunkenness.

Republican Motherhood

In all societies, marriage has many purposes: it channels sexuality, facilitates the inheritance of property, and, by creating strong family and kinship ties, eases the rearing of children. Traditionally, most American women had focused their lives on family duties: work in the home or farm and the bearing and nurture of children. However, by the 1790s the birthrate in the northern seaboard states was dropping dramatically. In the farm village of Sturbridge, Massachusetts, women who had married around 1750 gave birth on average to eight or nine children, whereas women who married around 1810 had only about six. An even greater decline occurred in urban areas, where native-born white women bore an average of only four children.

Women's Health and Fertility: From Folk Remedies to Pharmacies

"I once was verry Bad with a violent pain in my Back and Bowells and three months Gone with Child," Philadelphia shopkeeper Elizabeth Coates Pascall noted in her Receipt Book around 1760. As her condition steadily worsened from this "violent Chollick Pain," Pascall consulted medical professionals, who advised an abortion. "It was Judged Both By the Doctor and midwife that if I was not Speedily Delivered I should Dye." The midwife "tryed to Deliver me butt found it impossible," so Pascall turned to a folk healer, "an Elderly woman [who] proposed Giving me a Glister [an herbal potion]. . . . I took it and Lay Still Near an hour after it: Being presently Eased and the Child came from me [and] the after Birth all together and with very Little pain."

Like most American women in the eighteenth century, Elizabeth Pascall was not trying to control her fertility or restrict the number of her offspring. She would bear and rear the number of children that her husband and her God gave her. However, to do so she needed to protect her health, and like countless other Americans of her time she turned to folk medicine.

The general state of medical knowledge was low. Most women understood that the lack of menstruation might be a sign of conception. As Dr. Samuel Jennings's *The Married Lady's Companion* (1808) put it, "An entire suppression of the menses attends almost every case of pregnancy." But they also believed that the absence of menstruation might simply be a sign of illness, either "mental despondency" that took the form of "Grief and Distress," or "hysteria," characterized by "lowness of spirits, oppression and anxiety" as well as by stomach pains that caused "inflation, sickness and sometimes vomiting." In 1805 Lydia Tallender "had not had the female customs for 2 mos [months], and had been unwell," so she took medicines to cure her "illness."

In popular discourse, Lydia Tallender had "taken a cold"—the absence of "hot" menstrual blood indicated that a cold "humor" had taken control of her body. To restore her flow, an afflicted woman normally drank a medicine made of water suffused with herbs and minerals such as savin (a variety of juniper), red cedar, rue, aloes, or seneca snakeroot. When Elizabeth Drinker found her daughter Molly Rhoads "disorder'd and in pain . . . oweing to takeing colds," she administered "mint water," probably peppermint and magnesia.

Health manuals and diaries written in English did not mention the abortive qualities of such potions, but German publications were more forthright. *The Small*

The United States was one of the first countries in the world to experience this sharp decline in the birthrate—what historians have termed "demographic transition." There were several causes. Beginning in the 1790s thousands of young men migrated to the trans-Appalachian West, leaving some women without partners and delaying the marriage of many more. Women who married later in life had fewer children. Also, thousands of white American couples in the emerging middle class deliberately limited the size of their families. After having four or five children, they used birth control or abstained from sexual intercourse. Fathers wanted to provide each of their children with an adequate inheritance and so favored smaller families; mothers, affected by new ideas of individualism and self-achievement, were no longer willing to spend all of their active years bearing and rearing children (see New Technology, "Women's Health and Fertility: From Folk Remedies to Pharmacies," above).

As women looked for new opportunities, they found support from changes in Christian thought. Traditionally, most religious writers had viewed women as morally inferior to men—as sexual temptresses or witches—but by 1800 Protestant ministers, probably influenced by the numerical dominance of women in their congregations, had begun to place responsibility for sexual misconduct primarily on men. In fact, Christian moralists now claimed that modesty and purity were inherent in women's nature, making women uniquely qualified to educate the spirit.

Reflecting this sentiment, political leaders called on women to become "republican wives" and "republican mothers" who would correctly shape the characters of American men. In his *Thoughts on Female Education* (1787) the Philadelphia physician Benjamin Rush argued that a young woman should receive intellectual training so that she would be "an agreeable companion for a sensible man" and ensure "his perseverance in the

Herbal of Little Cost, printed in Germantown, Pennsylvania, between 1762 and 1778 by Christopher Sauer, provided women with recipes "to expel the dead fruit," and German midwifery manuals explained that such tonics would expel the fetus, "be it dead or alive." However, English women clearly understood the potions' effect. Nursing mothers commonly drank savin tea to delay a new pregnancy—both to preserve their own health and to ensure a supply of milk for their nursing babies. However, the cost of taking such tonics was high, for they caused physical pain and might identify a woman as weak, dependent, and "hysterical."

By the late eighteenth century, American women no longer had to turn to folk healers for such medicines. Pharmacists in England and America had learned how to make pills and tonics to promote menstruation (or induce abortions), and energetic entrepreneurs quickly marketed them. One of the most popular was Hooper's Female Pills, which were composed of Barbados aloes, iron sulfate, hellebore, and myrrh. Such patent medicines— including rosemary-laced Hungary Water, Dr. Ryans's Sugar Plums, and Fraunce's Female Elixir—were advertised in newspapers as "highly serviceable to the Female Sex" and, by the beginning of the nineteenth century, were widely available in rural shops as well as urban pharmacies.

This advance in technology, along with the importation in the 1790s of French syringes (a douche used to clean the vagina that could be used to prevent conception), assisted some American women in limiting their fertility. Previously, women had used folk remedies to preserve their health or lengthen the interval between births. Now some upper-class women and Quaker women in Pennsylvania used patent medicines and other means in a conscious program of family planning. "It gives me great pleasure to hear of your prudent resolution of not increasing your family," Margaret Shippen Arnold of Philadelphia wrote to her sister around 1790. "I have determined upon the same plan; and when our Sisters have had five or six [children], we will likewise recommend it to them."

Dr. Hooper's Female Pills
As early as the 1740s English women had access to patent medicines that, the makers alleged, would address their special needs. Within a few decades, these medicines (and competing American brands) were widely available in the United States.
Science, Medicine, and Society Division, National Museum of American History, Smithsonian.

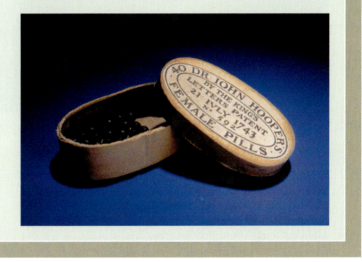

paths of rectitude." Rush also called for loyal "republican mothers" who would instruct "their sons in the principles of liberty and government." As the author of a list of "Maxims for Republics" commented, "Some of the first patriots of ancient times were formed by their mothers."

Christian ministers readily embraced the idea of **republican motherhood**. "Preserving virtue and instructing the young are not the fancied, but the real 'Rights of Women,'" the Reverend Thomas Bernard told the Female Charitable Society of Salem, Massachusetts. He urged his audience to dismiss the public roles for women advocated by English activist Mary Wollstonecraft and others. Instead, women should be content to care for their children, a responsibility that gave them "an extensive power over the fortunes of man in every generation." Although Bernard wanted women to remain in their traditional domestic sphere, he campaigned to enhance its value. A few ministers went further and envisioned a public role for women based on their domestic virtues. As South Carolina minister Thomas Grimké asserted, "Give me a host of educated pious mothers and sisters and I will revolutionize a country, in moral and religious taste."

Raising and Educating Republican Children

Republican social thought also altered assumptions about inheritance and childrearing. Under English common law, property owned by a father who died without a will passed to his eldest son, a practice known as **primogeniture**. However, legislators in most American states enacted statutes that required such estates to be divided equally among all the offspring. Most American parents supported these statutes because they had already begun to treat all of their children as equals and to

teach all of them—including the eldest son—how to make their own way in the world.

Encouraging Independence. Foreign visitors believed that republican ideology encouraged American parents to relax parental discipline and give their children greater freedom. Because of the "general ideas of Liberty and Equality engraved on their hearts," suggested a Polish aristocrat who traveled through the United States around 1800, American children had "scant respect" for their parents. Several decades later a British traveler was dumbfounded when an American father excused his son's "resolute disobedience" with a smile and the remark, "a sturdy republican, sir." The traveler guessed that American parents encouraged such independence to assist young people to "go their own way" in the world.

However, these relatively permissive childrearing habits were not universal. Foreign visitors interacted primarily with well-to-do Americans, who were often members of Episcopal or Presbyterian churches. These parents often followed the teachings of rationalist-minded religious writers influenced by John Locke and the Enlightenment. In their minds children were "rational creatures" who should be encouraged to act correctly by means of praise, advice, and reasoned restraint. Training should develop the children's consciences and stress self-discipline so that young people would learn to control their own behavior and to think and act responsibly

(see American Voices, "Lydia Maria Child: Raising Middle-Class Children," p. 259).

By contrast, many yeomen and tenant farmers influenced by the Second Great Awakening followed the precepts of authoritarian-minded writers. These parents, especially those in Calvinist-oriented churches, raised their children using strict rules and harsh discipline. Evangelical Baptists and Methodists believed that infants were "full of the stains and pollution of sin" and needed strict discipline. Fear was a "useful and necessary principle in family government," the minister John Abbott advised parents; a child "should submit to your authority, not to your arguments or persuasions." Abbott told parents to instill humility in children and to teach them to subordinate their personal desires to God's will. Both of these modes of childrearing—the authoritarian and the rationalist—persisted, with the rationalists' emphasis on self-discipline becoming the preference among families in the rapidly expanding middle class.

Expanding Education. The values transmitted within families were crucial because until the 1820s most education still took place within the household. In New England locally funded public schools provided most boys and some girls with basic instruction in reading and writing. In other regions fewer white children and virtually no African American children received schooling; about a quarter of the boys and perhaps 10 percent of the

Lydia Maria Child

Raising Middle-Class Children

Violence was pervasive in traditional Europe and colonial America. Masters whipped servants and slaves and challenged one another to duels; husbands beat wives and cowed children into submission; fistfights and brawls spilled out of taverns and into the streets. Gentry and plebeians alike paid homage to the codes of physical strength and personal honor.

In the late eighteenth century evangelical ministers and middle-class moralists challenged the dominant ethos of violence. Ministers urged believers to "turn the other cheek" if assaulted and respect the bodies of others as temples of God. Mothers taught their children to control their passions and to fight with words rather than fists.

Lydia Maria Child (1802–1880) was a social reformer who combined middle-class values and religious principles. In the following selection from The Mother's Book *(1831), Child accepts John Locke's theory of knowledge that the mind at birth is a "blank slate" ("a vessel empty and pure") and is shaped by its environment. Melding Lockean psychology with religious sentimentalism (the child as "the beautiful little image of God"), she sets forth an affectionate-rationalist approach to childrearing for the emerging middle class.*

I once saw a mother laugh very heartily at the distressed face of a kitten, which a child of two years old was pulling backward by the tail. At last, the kitten, in self-defense, turned and scratched the boy. He screamed, and his mother ran to him, kissed the wound, and beat the poor kitten, saying all the time, "Naughty kitten, to scratch John." . . .

This little incident, trifling as it seems, no doubt had important effects on the character of the child. . . .

In the first place, the child was encouraged in cruelty, by seeing that it gave his mother amusement. . . .

In the next place, the kitten was struck for defending herself; this was injustice to the injured animal, and a lesson of tyranny to the boy. In the third place, striking the kitten because she had scratched him, was teaching him retaliation. . . . The influence upon him is, that it is right to injure when we are injured. . . .

The mind of a child is not like that of a grown person . . . it is a vessel empty and pure—always ready to receive, and always receiving. Every look, every movement, every expression, does something toward forming the character of the little heir to immortal life. . . .

The rule, then, for developing good affections in a child is, that he never be allowed to see or feel the influence of bad passions, even in the most trifling things; and in order to effect this, you must drive evil passions from your own heart. Nothing can be real that has not its home within us. The only sure way, as well as the easiest, to appear good, is to be good.

It is not possible to indulge anger, or any other wrong feeling, and conceal it entirely. If not expressed in words, a child feels the baneful influence. Evil enters into his soul, as the imperceptible atmosphere he breathes enters into his lungs: and the beautiful little image of God is removed farther and farther from his home in heaven.

Source: Lydia Maria Child, *The Mother's Book* (Boston: Carter and Hendee, 1831), 45–46.

---

girls attended privately funded schools or had personal tutors. Even in New England only a small fraction of the men and almost no women went on to grammar (high) school. Only 1 percent of men graduated from college.

In the 1790s Bostonian Caleb Bingham, an influential textbook author, called for "an equal distribution of knowledge to make us emphatically a 'republic of letters.'" Thomas Jefferson and Benjamin Rush separately proposed ambitious schemes for a comprehensive system of primary and secondary schooling, followed by college attendance for young men. They also advocated the establishment of a university in which distinguished scholars would lecture on law, medicine, theology, and political economy.

To ordinary citizens such educational proposals smacked of elitism. Farmers, artisans, and laborers looked to schools for basic instruction in the "three Rs": reading, 'riting, and 'rithmetic. They supported public funding for primary schools but not for secondary schools or colleges, because their own teenage children had already joined the workforce. "Let anybody show what advantage the poor man receives from colleges," an anonymous "Old Soldier" wrote to the Maryland *Gazette*. "Why should they support them, unless it is to serve those who are in affluent circumstances, whose children can be spared from labor, and receive the benefits?"

The Battle over Education

The artist pokes fun at a tyrannical schoolmaster and, indirectly, at the evangelicals' strict approach to childrearing. The students' faces reflect the rationalist outlook of the artist. As one Enlightenment-influenced minister put it, we see in their eyes "the first dawn of reason, beaming forth its immortal rays." Copyright, The Frick Collection.

Although many state constitutions encouraged the use of public resources to fund primary schools, there was not much progress until the 1820s. Then a new generation of reformers, led primarily by merchants and manufacturers, successfully campaigned to raise standards by certifying qualified teachers and appointing state superintendents of education. To encourage self-discipline and individual enterprise in the students, the reformers chose textbooks, such as *The Life of George Washington* by "Parson" Mason Weems, that praised honesty and hard work while condemning gambling, drinking, and laziness. They also required the study of American history, believing that patriotic instruction would foster shared cultural ideals. As Thomas Low, a New Hampshire schoolboy, recalled, "We were taught every day and in every way that ours was the freest, the happiest, and soon to be the greatest and most powerful country of the world."

Promoting Cultural Independence. The author Noah Webster had long championed the goal of American intellectual greatness. Asserting that "America must be as independent in *literature* as she is in politics," he called on his fellow citizens to detach themselves "from the dependence on foreign opinions and manners, which is fatal to the efforts of genius in this country."

Webster's *Dissertation on the English Language* (1789) introduced American spelling (such as *labor* for the British *labour*) and defined words according to American usage. His "blue-backed speller," first published in 1783, sold 60 million copies over the next half century and helped give Americans of all backgrounds a common vocabulary and grammar. "None of us was 'lowed to see a book," an enslaved African American recalled, "but we gits hold of that Webster's old blue-back speller and we . . . studies [it]."

Though Webster and others promoted an independent, republican literary culture, it was slow to develop. Ironically, the most accomplished and successful writer in the new republic was Washington Irving, an elitist-minded Federalist in politics and an expatriate. His essays and histories, including *Salmagundi* (1807) and *Diedrich Knickerbocker's History of New York* (1809), had substantial American sales and won fame abroad. Impatient with the slow pace of American literary development, Irving lived in Europe for seventeen years, drawn to its aristocratic manners and intense intellectual life.

Apart from Irving no American author was well known in Europe, partly because most American writers followed primary careers as planters, merchants, or lawyers. "Literature is not yet a distinct profession with

Women's Education

Even in education-conscious New England, few girls attended the free public primary school for more than a few years. After 1800, as this scene from A Seminary for Young Ladies *(c. 1810–1820) indicates, some girls stayed in school into their teenage years and were exposed to a wide variety of subjects, such as geography. Many of the graduates of these female academies became teachers, entering a new field of employment for women.*
St. Louis Art Museum.

us," Thomas Jefferson told an English friend. "Now and then a strong mind arises, and at its intervals from business emits a flash of light. But the first object of young societies is bread and covering." Not until the 1830s and 1840s, in the works of Ralph Waldo Emerson and novelists of the American Renaissance, would American-born authors make a significant contribution to the great literature of the Western world (see Chapter 12).

Aristocratic Republicanism and Slavery, 1780–1820

Both in theory and in practice, republicanism in the South differed significantly from that in the North. Republican theorists had traditionally defined governmental tyranny as the greatest political evil and slave-owning planters, fearing political attacks on their landed wealth or slave property, were in full agreement. To prevent despotic rule by tyrants or demagogues, they wanted to place authority in the hands of independent and incorruptible men of "virtue." Indeed, planters came to see themselves as the practical embodiment of this ideal, men whose private wealth from slave owning freed them from dependence on government favors and whose education and training equipped them to discern and protect the welfare of the entire white community. Some consciously cast themselves as republican aristocrats. "The planters here are essentially what the nobility are in other countries," declared John Henry Hammond of South Carolina. "They stand at the head of society & politics . . . [and form] an aristocracy of talents, of virtue, of generosity and courage."

The North and South Grow Apart

European visitors to the new American republic commonly noted profound social differences among the regions. New England was home to religious "fanaticism," according to a British observer, but "the lower orders of citizens" there had "a better education, are more intelligent, and better informed" than those he met in the South. "The state of poverty in which a great number of white people live in Virginia" surprised the Marquis de Chastellux, and other visitors to the South commented on the rude manners, heavy drinking, and lack of a strong work ethic they found there. White tenant farmers and small freeholders seemed only to have a "passion for gaming at the billiard table, a cock-fight or cards."

Some southerners felt that slavery was a major cause of the ignorance and poverty of their region. The wealthy planters who controlled southern society wanted a compliant labor force, content with the drudgery of agricultural work. Consequently, they trained most of their slaves as field hands (allowing only a few to learn the arts of the blacksmith, carpenter, or bricklayer), and they made little or no effort to provide ordinary whites with elementary instruction in reading or arithmetic. In 1800 the leadership of Essex County, Virginia, spent about twenty-five cents per person for local government, including schooling, while their counterparts in Acton, Massachusetts, expended about one dollar per person. As a result, over one-third of white southerners could not read or write, compared with less than 1 percent of New Englanders. A South Carolina merchant likewise linked slavery to a weak work ethic: "Where there are Negroes a White Man despises to work, saying what, will you have me a Slave and work like a Negroe?"

Slavery and National Politics.   Slavery quickly found its way into national politics. At the Philadelphia Convention in 1787 most delegates accepted slavery as a fact of American life that, like the state governments, would have to be accommodated to secure approval of the new national constitution. To assure the accession of

Georgia and South Carolina to the Union, they inserted a clause that prevented Congress from restricting the importation of people (including enslaved workers) for twenty years. The delegates also included a fugitive clause that prevented state governments from offering a safe haven to runaway slaves and indentured servants. Southerners sought additional protection for slavery in the second session of the new national legislature, winning approval of James Madison's resolution that "Congress have no authority to interfere in the emancipation of slaves, or in the treatment of them within any of the States."

Slavery remained a contested issue nationally. The slave revolts in Haiti and other French sugar islands during the 1790s brought a flood of white refugees to the United States and prompted congressional debates about diplomatic relations with the new black-run government of Haiti. Simultaneously, northern political leaders attacked the British impressment of American sailors as "to all intents and purposes a practice as unjust, as immoral, as base, as oppressive and tyrannical as the slave trade," and called for the end of both. When Congress ended legal American participation in the Atlantic slave trade in 1807, northern representatives tried to regulate the coastal trade in slaves and provide for the emancipation of illegally imported slaves. In response, the southern congressmen asserted a strong defense of their labor system. "A large majority of people in the Southern states do not consider slavery as even an evil," declared one congressman, and the South's political clout—its domination of the presidency and the Senate—ensured that the national government would protect its central institution. American diplomats vigorously—and successfully—demanded compensation for slaves freed by the British during the War of 1812, and Congress secured the existence of slavery in the District of Columbia by enforcing the property rights of slave owners who lived there.

Political conflict over slavery increased as the northern states emancipated more and more of their African American laborers and the South expanded its slave-based agricultural economy into new territories and states in the lower Mississippi Valley. Antislavery advocates grew increasingly concerned as Louisiana (1812), Mississippi (1816), and Alabama (1818) joined the Union with state constitutions permitting slavery. They had hoped that African bondage would "die a natural death" following the demise of the Atlantic slave trade and the decline of the tobacco economy.

Colonization. In 1817 the founders of the American Colonization Society, who included President James Monroe and Speaker of the House Henry Clay, proposed another means of ending slavery. The society would encourage southern planters to emancipate their slaves—who now numbered nearly 1.5 million people—and the society would arrange for their resettlement in Africa. The society's leaders believed, as Clay put it, that racial bondage had placed his state of Kentucky and the other slaveholding states "in the rear of our neighbors . . . in the state of agriculture, the progress of manufactures, the advance of improvement, and the general prosperity of society." Slavery had to go, as did the freed slaves. Emancipation without colonization, the Kentucky congressman predicted, "would be followed by instantaneous collisions between the two races, which would break out into a civil war that would end in the extermination or subjugation of the one race or the other." Northerners who joined the Colonization Society had much the same outlook. They regarded the 250,000 free blacks in the northern states as "notoriously ignorant, degraded and miserable, mentally diseased, brokenspirited," as one society report put it. Hoping to create a "white man's country," what they wanted was "African removal."

The American Colonization Society was a dismal failure. Despite appeals to wealthy individuals, churches, and state governments, the society raised enough money to purchase freedom for only a few hundred slaves. Moreover, most free blacks rejected colonization, agreeing with Bishop Richard Allen of the African Methodist Episcopal Church that "this land which we have watered with our tears and our blood is now our mother country." Three thousand African Americans met in Philadelphia's Bethel Church to condemn colonization, declaring that their goal was to advance in American society using "those opportunities . . . which the Constitution and the laws allow to all." Lacking significant support from either blacks or whites, the society transported only 6,000 African Americans to Liberia, a colony it established on the west coast of Africa.

Toward a New Southern Social Order

Colonization failed in part because the South was changing in a dramatic fashion—and in ways that encouraged the expansion of slavery. In 1780 the western boundary of the plantation system ran through the middle of Georgia; by 1820 the plantation frontier stretched through the middle of Louisiana. That jump of six hundred miles had doubled the geographic area cultivated by slave labor. Moreover, many of the workers on those plantations were African-born slaves who had been imported into the United States between 1780 and 1808, when the Atlantic slave trade legally ended. During those three decades nearly 250,000 Africans had been added to the workforce—a total that equaled the number of slaves imported into Britain's mainland settlements during the entire colonial period. Most of these Africans labored on cotton and sugar plantations in the newly settled southwestern states and territories.

Despite this influx of new slaves, the demand for labor in the Southwest far exceeded the supply. "The Negro business is a great object with us," one merchant declared, because "the Planter will as far in his power sacrifice every thing to attain Negroes." To acquire workers for their plantations, white owners purchased or moved

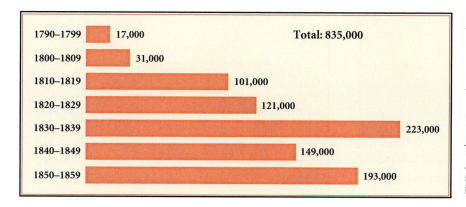

1790–1799	17,000
1800–1809	31,000
1810–1819	101,000
1820–1829	121,000
1830–1839	223,000
1840–1849	149,000
1850–1859	193,000

Total: 835,000

FIGURE 9.1 Movement of Slaves from Upper South to Lower South, 1790–1860

The cotton boom that began in the 1810s set in motion a great redistribution of the African American population. Between 1810 and 1860 white planters moved or sold nearly 800,000 slaves from the Upper to the Lower South, a process that broke up families and long-established black communities.

Source: Adapted from Robert William Fogel and Stanley Engerman, *Time on the Cross* (Boston: Little, Brown, 1974), figure 12.

African American workers from long-settled regions that had a surplus of labor. Between 1790 and 1820 whites relocated more than 150,000 African Americans from Maryland, Virginia, and parts of North and South Carolina (Figure 9.1). Some of these forced migrants—perhaps as many as one-half—moved with relatives and friends when their owners sold their old plantations and began anew on the fertile plains of Alabama, Mississippi, and Louisiana (Map 9.2). Thousands of others were sold, and separation became a common experience for black families. "I am Sold to a man by the name of Peterson a trader," lamented a Georgia slave. "My Dear wife for you and my Children my pen cannot Express the griffe I feel to be parted from you all." Some of these slaves forever lost touch with their families. "Dey sole [sold] my sister Kate," Anna Harris remembered decades later, ". . . and I ain't seed or heard of her since." Planters who remained on their estates in Maryland, Virginia, the Carolinas, and Georgia reaped impressive profits by selling their "surplus" blacks to slave traders. The profits to be gained by planting cotton in the Southwest and selling enslaved laborers from the Southeast doomed both the colonization movement and many well-established African American communities.

Westward movement also changed the character of white society. Following the tobacco and rice revolutions of the early eighteenth century (see Chapter 3), a wealthy planter elite exercised considerable political power in much of the South. However, particularly in tobacco-growing areas, slave owning remained broadly diffused. During the 1770s about 60 percent of the white families in the Chesapeake region owned at least one African American worker and benefited directly from slavery. By 1820 a much smaller proportion of white families in all regions of the South owned slaves, and the percentage continued to fall. For example, in Alabama in 1830 only 30 percent of the voters owned slaves. Among those 30 percent were the owners of the new cotton plantations that, like the rice-growing plantations in South Carolina and Georgia, were large-scale operations using dozens of enslaved black workers. Their wealthy and influential owners dominated society and gave an aristocratic republican definition to politics. In Alabama a majority of the legislators owned more than 20 African Americans, and one-quarter held more than 50. "Inequality is the fundamental law of the universe," proclaimed one southern politician. "Slavery does indeed create an aristocracy."

The Internal Slave Trade

Mounted whites escort a convoy of slaves from Virginia to Tennessee in Lewis Miller's Slave Trader, Sold to Tennessee *(1853). For white planters, the trade was a lucrative one, pumping money into the declining Chesapeake economy and providing workers for the expanding plantations of the cotton belt. For blacks it was a traumatic journey, a new Middle Passage that broke up families and long-settled slave communities.*

Abby Aldrich Rockefeller Folk Art Center.

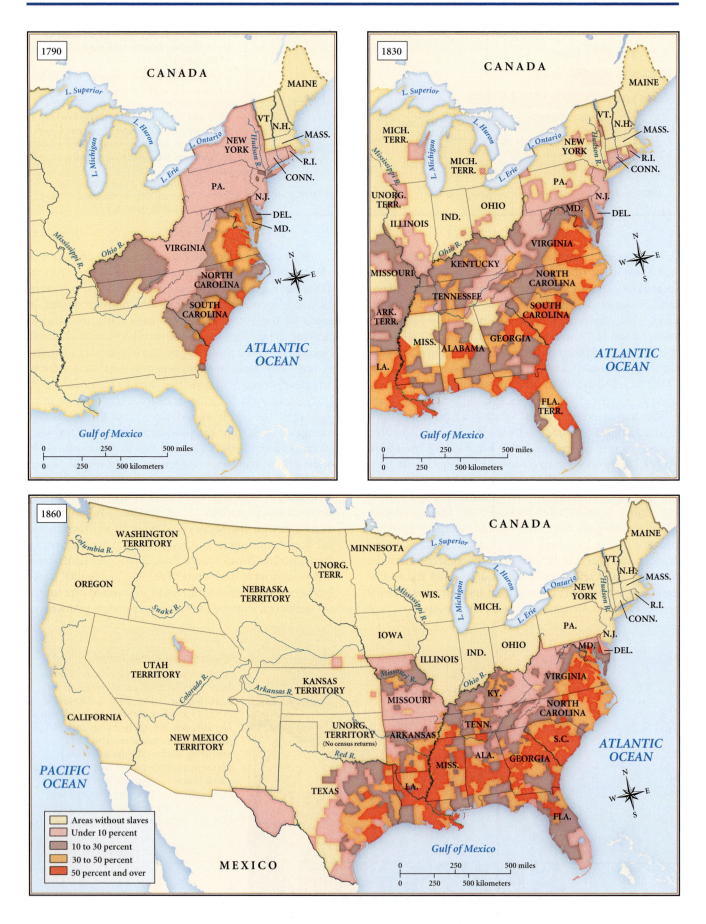

◀ **MAP 9.2 Distribution of the Slave Population in 1790, 1830, and 1860**

The cotton boom shifted enslaved African Americans to the Old Southwest. In 1790 most slaves lived and worked on the tobacco plantations of the Chesapeake and in the rice and indigo areas of South Carolina. By 1830, tens of thousands were laboring on the cotton and sugar lands of the lower Mississippi Valley and on cotton plantations in Georgia and Florida. Three decades later, the centers of slavery lay along the Mississippi River and in an arc of fertile cotton land—the "black belt"—sweeping from Mississippi through Georgia.

For more help analyzing this map, see the ONLINE STUDY GUIDE at bedfordstmartins.com/henretta.

As cotton production consolidated in fewer and fewer hands, some white yeomen in plantation regions became the tenants of wealthy landlords. Other white families scraped by on small farms, growing foodstuffs for sustenance and a few bales of cotton for cash. Influenced by the patriarchal ideology of the planter class, the husbands in these households asserted traditional male authority over their wives and children, ruling their small worlds with a firm hand. Other yeomen families retreated into the backcountry near the Appalachian Mountains, hoping to maintain their economic independence and to control local county governments. Owning hilly farms of fifty to one hundred acres, these families grew some cotton but primarily raised corn and livestock, especially hogs. Their goal was modest: to preserve their holdings and secure enough new land or goods to set up all of their children as small-scale farmers.

In the new southwestern economy, prosperity was limited primarily to the shrinking minority of the white population that owned plantations and slaves. The prospect of a more equal political and social order raised by the democratic impulses of the Revolutionary era had been counterbalanced by an expanding aristocratic republican plantation society based on cotton and sugar.

Slave Society and Culture

As planters ruled over a class-divided white social order, African Americans created a distinct and relatively unified rural culture. A major cause was the end of the transatlantic slave trade in 1808, which gradually created an entirely American-born black population. Even in South Carolina—the point of entry of most of the slaves imported since independence—in 1820 only about 20 percent of the black inhabitants had been born in Africa. Second, the rapid movement of slavery into the Mississippi Valley reduced cultural differences among slaves. For example, the Gullah dialect spoken by slaves from the Carolina low country gradually died out on the cotton plantations of Alabama and Mississippi, replaced by the black English spoken by slaves from the Chesapeake.

African Influences. Even as the black population became more homogeneous, African cultural elements remained important. At least one-third of the slaves who entered the United States between 1776 and 1809 were from the Congo region of west-central Africa, and they brought their culture with them (Table 9.2). As the traveler Isaac Holmes reported in 1821, "In Louisiana,

TABLE 9.2 African Slaves Imported into North America by Ethnicity, 1776–1809

African Region of Departure	Ethnicity	Number	Percentage of Imported Slaves
Senegambia	Mandinka, Fulbe, Serer, Jola, Wolof, and Bambara	8,000	7
Sierra Leone	Via, Mende, Kpelle, and Kru	18,300	16
Gold Coast	Ashanti and Fanit	15,000	13
Bight of Benin; Bight of Biafra	Ibo and Ibibio	5,700	5
West Central Africa	Kongo, Tio, and Matamba	37,800	33
Southeast Africa	Unknown	1,100	1
Other or Unknown		28,700	25
TOTAL		**114,600**	**100**

Note: The numbers are estimated from known voyages involving 65,000 Africans. Ethnic origins should be considered as very tentative because slaves from many regions left from the same port and because the ethnic and regional origins of 28,700 slaves (25 percent) are not known.

Source: Aaron S. Fogleman, "From Slaves, Convicts, and Servants to Free Passengers: The Transformation of Immigration in the Era of the American Revolution," *Journal of American History* (June 1998): table A.6.

Sugar Harvest in Louisiana

In Louisiana, as in the West Indies, cultivating and harvesting sugarcane was backbreaking work that took the lives of many workers. Throughout the nineteenth century, death rates in sugar-growing areas of Louisiana rivaled those in the crowded, disease-ridden immigrant districts in northern cities. This watercolor, by an unknown artist, shows that enslaved women joined men in the fields during harvest time.
Glenbow Museum, Calgary, Alberta, Canada.

and the state of Mississippi, the slaves . . . dance for several hours during Sunday afternoon. The general movement is in what they call the Congo dance." Similar descriptions of blacks who "danced the Congo and sang a purely African song to the accompaniment of . . . a drum" appeared as late as 1890.

Enslaved blacks in South Carolina and elsewhere continued to respect African incest taboos, shunning marriage between cousins. On the Good Hope plantation in South Carolina nearly half of the slave children born between 1800 and 1857 were related by blood to one another, yet only one marriage had taken place between cousins. By contrast, many wealthy planter families in South Carolina and Georgia encouraged marriage between cousins to keep inherited property in the family.

However, southern state legislatures and law courts prohibited legal marriages between slaves, so that they could be sold without breaking a legal bond. African Americans therefore devised their own marriage rituals, first asking their parents' consent to marry and then seeking their owner's permission to live together. Following African custom, many couples symbolized their married state by jumping over a broomstick together in a public ceremony. Christian slaves often had a religious service performed by a white or black preacher, but these rites never ended with the customary phrase "until death do you part." Everyone knew that black marriages could end with the sale of one or both of the spouses. To maintain their cultural identity, recently imported slaves often gave their children African names. Males born on Friday were often called Cuffee—the name of that day in several West African languages. Most Chesapeake slaves chose names of British origin and named sons after fathers, uncles, or grandfathers and daughters after grandmothers. Like incest rules and marriage rituals, these

naming patterns solidified kinship ties, creating order in a harsh and arbitrary world.

A World of Limited Choices. By forming stable families and strong communities, African Americans were better able to control their own lives. In the rice-growing lowlands of South Carolina blacks won the right to labor by the **task** rather than work under constant supervision. Each day a worker had to complete a precisely defined task—for example, turn over a quarter acre of land, hoe half an acre, or pound seven mortars of rice. By working hard, many finished their tasks "by one or two o'clock in the afternoon," a Methodist preacher reported, and had "the rest of the day for themselves, which they spend in working their own private fields . . . planting rice, corn, potatoes, tobacco &c. for their own use and profit." These private efforts provided slaves with better clothes and food, and on some large plantations planters gave decent health care to children, the sick, and the elderly. But few enslaved African Americans enjoyed a comfortable standard of living, and slaves clearly understood that planters gave them material favors not out of benevolence but to protect their investment (see American Voices, "Jacob Stroyer: A Child Learns the Meaning of Slavery," p. 267).

A few blacks, such as Gabriel and Martin Prosser in Virginia (1800), definitely plotted mass uprisings and murders, and others, such as Denmark Vesey in South Carolina (1822), may have done so. But in most areas blacks accounted for less than half the population, and everywhere they lacked the strong institutions—such as the communes of free peasants or serfs in Europe—needed to organize a successful rebellion. Moreover, whites were well armed, unified, and militant. Escape was equally problematic. Blacks in the Lower South

Jacob Stroyer

A Child Learns the Meaning of Slavery

Jacob Stroyer, born into slavery in South Carolina, was emancipated and became a minister in Salem, Massachusetts, and an abolitionist. In My Life in the South *(1885), he relates a dramatic incident that revealed his family's subordinate and powerless status as slaves.*

Father had a surname, Stroyer, which he could not use in public, as the surname Stroyer would be against the law; he was known only by the name of William Singleton, because that was his master's name. . . . Mother's name was Chloe. She belonged to Colonel M. R. Singleton too; she was a field hand, and was never sold, but her parents once were. . . .

Father . . . used to take care of horses and mules. I was around with him in the barnyard when but a small boy; of course that gave me an early relish for the occupation of hostler, and soon I made known my preference to Colonel Singleton, who was a sportsman and had fine horses. . . . Hence I was allowed to be numbered among those who took care of the fine horses, and learned to ride. . . .

It was not long after I had entered my new work before they put me upon the back of a horse which threw me to the ground almost as soon as I reached his back. . . .

When I got up there was a man standing near with a switch in hand, and he immediately began to beat me. . . . This was the first time I had been whipped by anyone except Mother and Father, so I cried out in a tone of voice as if I would say, this is the first and last whipping you will give me when Father gets hold of you.

When I got away from him I ran to Father with all my might, but soon my expectation was blasted, as Father very coolly said to me, "Go back to your work and be a good boy, for I cannot do anything for you." But that did not satisfy me, so I went on to Mother with my complaint and she came out to the man who whipped me. He was a groom, a white man whom master hired to train his horses . . . [and] he took a whip and started for her, and she ran from him, talking all the time. . . .

Then the idea first came to me that I, with my dear father and mother and the rest of my fellow Negroes, was doomed to cruel treatment through life and was defenseless. . . .

One day, about two weeks after Boney Young and Mother had the conflict, he . . . gave me a first-class flogging. That evening when I went home to Father and Mother, I said to them, "Mr. Young is whipping me too much now; I shall not stand it. I shall fight him." Father said to me, "You must not do that, because if you do he will say that your mother and I advised you to do it, and it will make it hard for your mother and me, as well as yourself. You must do as I told you my son. . . . I can do nothing more than pray to the Lord to hasten the time when these things shall be done away."

Source: Linda R. Monk, ed., *Ordinary Americans: U.S. History through the Eyes of Everyday People* (Alexandria, VA: Close Up Publications, 1994), 71–72.

could seek freedom in Spanish Florida until 1819, when the United States annexed the territory.

Even then, hundreds of blacks continued to flee to Florida, where they intermarried with the Seminole Indians. Elsewhere in the South small groups of escaped slaves eked out a living in deserted marshy areas or in mountain valleys, hoping that they would not be killed, enslaved, or returned by Indian warriors. Given these limited options most slaves had no choice but to build the best possible lives for themselves on the plantations where they lived.

The Free Black Population

Between 1790 and 1820 the number of free blacks rose steadily from 8 percent of the total African American population to about 13 percent, but few of them were truly free. One-third of all free blacks—some 50,000 in 1810—lived in the North, where they performed the most menial and low-paying work and were treated as second-class citizens. In rural areas of the North free blacks worked as farm laborers or tenant farmers; in towns and cities, as domestic servants, laundresses, or day laborers. Only a small minority of free African Americans owned land. "You do not see one out of a hundred . . . that can make a comfortable living, own a cow, or a horse," a traveler in New Jersey noted. In addition, blacks were usually forbidden to vote, attend public schools, or sit next to whites in churches. Of the states admitted to the Union between 1790 and 1821 only Vermont and Maine extended the vote to free blacks,

CLASS No. 1.

Comprises those prisoners who were found guilty and executed.

Prisoners Names.	Owners' Names.	Time of Commit.	How Disposed of.
Peter	James Poyas	June 18	
Ned	Gov. T. Bennett,	do.	Hanged on Tuesday
Rolla	do.	do	the 2d July, 1822,
Batteau	do.	do.	on Blake's lands,
Denmark Vesey	A free black man	22	near Charleston.
Jessy	Thos. Blackwood	23	
John	Elias Horry	July 5	Do. on the Lines near
Gullah Jack	Paul Pritchard	do.	Ch.; Friday July 12.
Mingo	Wm. Harth	June 21	
Lot	Forrester	27	
Joe	P. L. Jore	July 6	
Julius	Thos. Forrest	8	
Tom	Mrs. Russell	10	
Smart	Robt. Anderson	do.	
John	John Robertson	11	
Robert	do.	do.	
Adam	do.	do.	
Polydore	Mrs. Faber	do.	Hanged on the Lines
Bacchus	Benj. Hammet	do.	near Charleston,
Dick	Wm. Sims	13	on Friday, 26th
Pharaoh	— Thompson	do.	July.
Jemmy	Mrs. Clement	18	
Mauidore	Mordecai Cohen	19	
Dean	— Mitchell	do.	
Jack	Mrs. Purcell	12	
Bellisle	Est. of Jos. Yates	18	
Naphur	do.	do.	
Adam	do.	do.	
Jacob	John S. Glen	16	
Charles	John Billings	18	
Jack	N. McNeill	22	
Cæsar	Miss Smith	do.	
Jacob Stagg	Jacob Lankester	23	Do. Tues. July 30.
Tom	Wm. M. Scott	24	
William	Mrs. Garner	Aug. 2	Do. Friday, Aug. 9.

"An Account of the Late Intended Insurrection, Charleston, South Carolina"

In 1822 Charleston had a free black population of 1,500, which boasted an array of its own institutions, including a Brown Fellowship Society (for those of mixed racial ancestry) and an African Methodist Episcopal (AME) church. Historians have long thought that one of these free African Americans, Denmark Vesey, organized a conspiracy to free the city's slaves. However, recent studies have suggested that the prospect of slave rebellion reflected white fears rather than historical fact. In any event, South Carolina authorities hanged Vesey and thirty-four co-conspirators and tore down the AME church where they had allegedly plotted the insurrection.
Rare Book, Manuscript & Special Collections, Duke University Library.

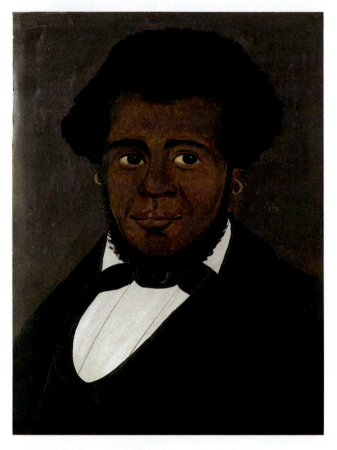

Captain Absalom Boston

Absalom Boston was born in 1785 on the island of Nantucket, the heart of the American whaling industry. A member of a community of free black whalers manumitted from slavery by their Quaker owners, Boston went to sea at age fifteen. By the age of thirty he had used his earnings to become the proprietor of a public inn. In 1822 Boston became the first black master with an all-black crew to undertake a whaling voyage from Nantucket. In later years he became an important leader of the island's black community, serving as a trustee of the African School.
Nantucket Historical Association.

and they could testify against whites in court only in Massachusetts. The federal government did not allow free African Americans to work for the postal service, claim public lands, or hold a U.S. passport.

Nonetheless, a few free blacks in the North were able to make full use of their talents, and some achieved great distinction. The mathematician and surveyor Benjamin Banneker published an almanac and helped lay out the new national capital in the District of Columbia. Joshua Johnston, a skilled painter, won praise for his portraiture, and merchant Robert Sheridan acquired a small fortune from his business enterprises. More impressive and enduring were the community institutions created by

this first generation of free African Americans. In many northern communities they founded schools, mutual-benefit organizations, and fellowship groups, often with the title Free African Society. Discriminated against in white Protestant churches, they also formed their own congregations and an independent religious denomination—the African Methodist Episcopal (AME) Church. These institutions gave free African Americans a sense of cultural, if not political, autonomy (see American Lives, "Richard Allen and African American Identity," p. 270).

Most free blacks who lived in slave states resided in the Upper South—some 110,000 in 1810. In Maryland a quarter of the black population was free; in Delaware free blacks outnumbered slaves by three to one. Free blacks accused of crimes were often denied a jury trial, and many others had to contend with vagrancy and apprenticeship laws intended to force them back into slavery. To prove their free status blacks had to carry manumission documents and in some states needed official permission to travel across county lines. Even with valid papers free African Americans in the South had to be careful; kidnapping and sale were constant threats. Yet the shortage of skilled workers in southern cities created opportunities for many blacks, who became the backbone of the region's urban workforce. Trained African American carpenters, blacksmiths, barbers, butchers, and shopkeepers in Baltimore, Richmond, Charleston, and New Orleans formed benevolent societies and churches, providing education, recreation, and social welfare programs for their communities.

As a privileged group among African Americans, free blacks felt both loyalty to the welfare of their families, which often meant assimilating white culture, and loyalty to their race, which meant identifying with the great mass of enslaved African Americans. Some wealthier free blacks, particularly the mulatto children of white masters and black women, drew apart from common laborers and field hands and adopted the outlook of the planter class. In Charleston and New Orleans a few free African Americans even owned slaves.

Generally, however, both free and enslaved African Americans saw themselves as one people. "We's different [from whites] in color, in talk and in 'ligion and beliefs," as one put it. Knowing their own freedom was not secure as long as slavery existed, free blacks sought to win freedom for all those of African ancestry. Free blacks in the South aided fugitive slaves, while free black northerners supported the antislavery movement. In the rigid caste system of American race relations, free blacks stood as symbols of hope to enslaved African Americans and as omens of danger to the majority of whites.

The Missouri Crisis

White society was increasingly divided over the question of the wisdom and morality of a republican society based on slave labor. The rapid advance of plantation society into the Southwest heightened the tension and added a new dimension to the debate. In a speech opposing nationally financed internal improvements in 1818, Congressman Nathaniel Macon of North Carolina warned that radical-minded members of the "colonizing bible and peace societies" wanted to increase the federal power in order "to try the question of emancipation." Indeed, a major conflict over emancipation came even more quickly than Macon had anticipated. When Missouri applied for admission to the Union as a slave state in 1819, Congressman James Tallmadge of New York proposed a ban on the importation of slaves into Missouri and the gradual emancipation of its black inhabitants. When Missouri whites rejected those conditions, the northern majority in the House of Representatives blocked the territory's admission to the Union.

Southerners were horrified. "It is believed by some, & feared by others," Alabama Senator John Walker reported from Washington, that Tallmadge's amendment was "merely the entering wedge and that it points already to a total emancipation of the blacks." The outlook was grim. "You conduct us to an awful precipice, and hold us over it," Mississippi Congressman Christopher Rankin warned his northern colleagues. To underline their determination to protect slavery, southerners used their power in the Senate (where they held half the seats) to withhold statehood from Maine, which was seeking to separate itself from Massachusetts.

In the ensuing debate, southerners advanced three constitutional arguments. First, they raised the principle of "equal rights," arguing that Congress could not impose conditions for statehood on the citizens of Missouri that it had not imposed on other new states. Second, they argued that slavery was purely an internal affair, a matter that fell under the sovereignty of the state government. Finally, they maintained that Congress had no authority to infringe on the property rights of slaveholders. Going beyond these constitutional issues, southern leaders abandoned the traditional argument that slavery was a "necessary evil" and now championed the institution as a "positive good." "Christ himself gave a sanction to slavery," declared Senator William Smith of South Carolina, and many southern religious leaders agreed. "If it be offensive and sinful to own slaves," a prominent Mississippi Methodist remarked, "I wish someone would just put his finger on the place in Holy Writ."

Controversy raged for two years before Henry Clay of Kentucky put together a series of political agreements known collectively as the Missouri Compromise. A series of legislative measures allowed Maine to enter the Union as a free state in 1820 and Missouri to be admitted as a slave state in 1821. By admitting both states, the compromise preserved the existing balance between North and South in the Senate and set a precedent for the future admission of states in pairs—one free and one slave. To mollify northern antislavery activists in the House of Representatives, southern congressmen accepted legislation that prohibited slavery in the rest of the Louisiana Purchase north of latitude 36°30′, the southern boundary of Missouri (Map 9.3).

Just as in the Constitutional Convention of 1787, white leaders in both the North and the South had given first priority to the Union, finding complex but workable ways to reconcile regional interests. But the task had become more difficult. The Philadelphia delegates had resolved sectional and other differences in two months. Congress took two years to work out the Missouri Compromise, with no guarantee that it would work. The fate of the western lands, the Union, and the black race had become inextricably intertwined and the specter of civil war lurked in the background. As the aging Thomas Jefferson exclaimed in the midst of the Missouri crisis,

Richard Allen and African American Identity

Richard Allen lived a full life. Born into slavery in Philadelphia in 1760 and sold with his family as a child to a farmer in Delaware, he died in 1831 not only free but influential, a founder of the African Methodist Episcopal Church and its first bishop. Allen's rise to fame is a classic American success story, but it bears a larger significance: As one of the first African Americans to be emancipated during the Revolutionary era, Allen worked to forge an identity for his people as well as for himself.

Allen began his ascent in 1777, when Freeborn Garretson, an itinerant preacher, converted him to Methodism. A powerful foe of slavery, Garretson also converted Allen's master and convinced him that on Judgment Day slaveholders would be "weighted in the balance, and . . . found wanting." Allowed by his repentant owner to buy his freedom, Allen earned a living sawing cordwood and driving a wagon during the Revolutionary War. After the war he enlisted in the Methodist cause, becoming a "licensed exhorter" and preaching to blacks and whites from New York to South Carolina.

Allen's success as a preacher attracted the attention of white Methodist leaders, including Francis Asbury, the first American bishop of the Methodist Church. In 1786 Allen won appointment as an assistant minister in Philadelphia, serving the racially mixed congregation of St. George's Methodist Church. The following year he and Absalom Jones, another black preacher, joined other former slaves and Quaker philanthropists to establish the Free African Society, a benevolent organization that offered fellowship and mutual aid to "free Africans and their descendants."

Allen remained a staunch Methodist throughout his life. In 1789, when the Free African Society adopted the Quaker custom of having fifteen minutes of silence at its meetings, Allen led a withdrawal of those who preferred more enthusiastic Methodist practices. Five years later he rejected an offer to become the pastor of St. Thomas's African Church, the Episcopal-affiliated church that the Free African Society had built and that a majority of its members had joined. "I informed them that I could not be anything else but a Methodist, as I was born and awakened under them," Allen recalled.

Now Allen confronted a more difficult challenge: reconciling his Methodist faith with the fact that many white Methodists were prejudiced against African Americans. Allen's solution was to form a separate congregation. Gathering a group of ten black Methodists, Allen formed the Bethel African Methodist Episcopal Church in the increasingly black southern section of Philadelphia. There its tiny congregation worshiped "separate from our white brethren." A few years later Allen helped to found another all-black institution, the Society of Free People of Colour for Promoting the Instruction and School Education of Children of African Descent. By 1811 there were no fewer than eleven black schools in the city.

Allen's decision to found separate black institutions was partly a response to white racism. Although most white Methodists in the 1790s favored emancipation, they did not treat free blacks as social equals. They refused to allow African Americans to be buried in the regular Methodist cemetery and, in a famous incident in 1792, segregated black worshipers in a newly built gallery of St. George's Methodist Church. Allen's initiative also reflected a desire among African Americans to control their religious lives, "to call any brother that appears to us adequate to the task to preach or exhort as a local preacher." By 1795 the congregation of Allen's Bethel Church numbered 121; a decade later it had grown to 457, and by 1813 it had reached 1,272.

Bethel's rapid expansion reflected that of Philadelphia's free black population, which numbered nearly 10,000 by 1810, as well as the appeal of Methodist practices. Blacks welcomed Methodist "love feasts," which allowed the full expression of emotions repressed under slavery, and the church's strict system of discipline—its communal sanctions against drinking, gambling, and marital infidelity—which helped them bring order to their lives.

Nonetheless, Allen and his congregation grew dissatisfied with Methodism, as white ministers retreated from their antislavery principles and the Church hierarchy curbed the autonomy of African American congregations. In 1807 the Bethel Church added an "African Supplement" to its articles of incorporation, and in 1816 it won legal recognition as an independent church. In the same year Allen and representatives from four other black Methodist congregations (in Baltimore, Maryland; Wilmington, Delaware; Salem, New Jersey; and Attleboro, Pennsylvania) organized a new denomination—the African Methodist Episcopal Church. The delegates chose Allen as the first bishop of the church, the first fully independent black denomination in America.

But where did Allen think "free people of colour" should look for their future? This question had arisen in Philadelphia as early as 1787, in a debate over a plan to settle free American and West Indian blacks in Sierra Leone, a settlement on the west coast of Africa founded

**The Mount Bethel African Methodist Episcopal Church and
Its First Minister, the Reverend Richard Allen**

*During the 1790s Allen founded a separate congregation for Philadelphia's African
American Methodists, who eventually established the Mount Bethel Church. In 1816 Allen
invited ministers from other black Methodist congregations to Mount Bethel where they
founded the first independent black denomination in the United States: the African
Methodist Episcopal Church.* Library of Congress; Mount Bethel A.M.E. Church, Philadelphia.

For more help analyzing these images, see the ONLINE STUDY GUIDE at
bedfordstmartins.com/henretta.

by British abolitionists. Many blacks in Boston and
Newport had endorsed this scheme, but the members of
Philadelphia's Free African Society had rejected it. While
acknowledging the racism that kept blacks in a subordinate position, they declared their intention to seek
advancement in America.

To pursue their goal, Philadelphia's blacks adopted a
dual strategy. As a social group, they embraced their
ancestry by forming "African" churches and benevolent
societies. However, as individuals they asserted their
American identity by taking English names (although
virtually never those of their former owners). Although
these efforts yielded few significant gains in wealth or status, Philadelphia's African Americans again rejected colonization when the issue was revived around 1800. Only
four people signed up for immigration to Sierra Leone.

Instead, the city's black community turned to political action to improve the social and legal condition of
the race. Hundreds of African Americans signed petitions asking Congress to end the Atlantic slave trade and
to repeal the Fugitive Slave Act of 1793, which allowed
slave owners to seize blacks without a warrant.
Underlining the importance of the latter issue, in 1806
Allen himself was held temporarily as a fugitive slave,
showing that even the most prominent northern blacks
could not be sure of their freedom.

Allen's brush with slavery may account for his initial
support for the American Colonization Society. But a
mass meeting of nearly 3,000 Philadelphia blacks condemned the society's plan to settle free blacks in Africa.
Instead, it set forth a different vision of the African
American future: "Whereas our ancestors (not of
choice) were the first successful cultivators of the wilds
of America, we their descendants feel ourselves entitled
to participate in the blessings of her luxuriant soil."

Philadelphia's black community, including Allen, was
more favorably inclined toward the Haitian Emigration
Society, founded in 1824 to help African Americans settle
in the black-run republic of Haiti. When this venture
failed in 1827, Allen forcefully urged blacks to remain in
the United States, writing in *Freedom's Journal,* the nation's
first black newspaper: "This land which we have watered
with our tears and our blood is now our mother country."

Born a slave of African ancestry, Allen had won freedom for himself and had helped to fashion an African
American religious identity for his people. Tempted by
emigration but ultimately rejecting that option, Allen
cast his lot and that of his descendants with a society
pervaded by racism. It was a brave decision, characteristic of the man who made it, but indicative of the very
limited choices available to men and women freed from
the bonds of slavery.

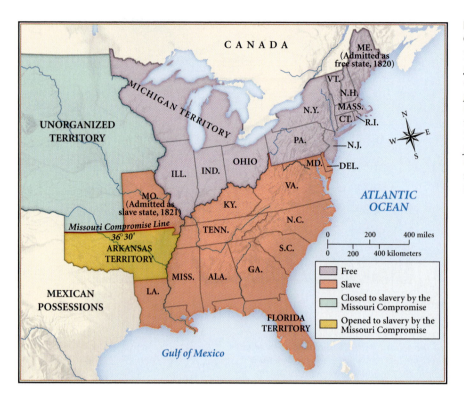

MAP 9.3 The Missouri Compromise, 1820–1821

The Missouri Compromise resolved for a generation the issue of slavery in the lands of the Louisiana Purchase. The agreement prohibited slavery north of the Missouri Compromise line (36°30′ north latitude), with the exception of the state of Missouri. To maintain an equal number of senators from free and slave states in the U.S. Congress, the compromise provided for the nearly simultaneous admission to the Union of Maine and Missouri.

"This momentous question, like a fire-bell in the night, awakened and filled me with terror."

Protestant Christianity as a Social Force

Religion had always been a significant part of American life. However, beginning in 1790 a series of religious revivals planted the values of Protestant Christianity deep in the national character and gave a spiritual definition to American republicanism. The revivals also changed African American life. Free and enslaved blacks became Christians, absorbing the faith of white Baptists and Methodists and creating a distinctive and powerful institution—the black church. Evangelical Christianity also created new public roles for women, especially in the North, and set in motion a long-lasting movement for social reform.

The Second Great Awakening

The revivals that began around 1790 were much more complex than those of the First Great Awakening. In the 1740s most revivals had occurred in existing congregations; fifty years later they took place in frontier camp meetings as well and often involved the creation of new churches and denominations. More striking, the Second Great Awakening spawned new organizations dedicated to social and political reform.

Republican Churches and Revivalism. Churches that prospered in the new nation were those that adopted a republican outlook, proclaiming the spiritual equality of all believers and creating relatively democratic church organizations (Table 9.3). Because the Roman Catholic Church was dominated by bishops and priests, it attracted few converts among Protestants, who adhered to Luther's doctrine of the priesthood of all believers, or among the unchurched—the great number of Americans who had never belonged to churches and who feared clerical power. The number of Catholic congregations grew primarily through immigration. Likewise, few ordinary native-born Americans joined the Episcopal Church (created by former members of the Church of England), which had a hierarchical structure similar to that of Catholicism and was dominated by its wealthiest members. The Presbyterian Church was more popular, in part because the membership elected laymen to the synods (congresses) where doctrine and practice were formulated. The Methodist and Baptist Churches attracted even more Americans because most of their preachers were fervent evangelists and promoted an egalitarian religious culture, encouraging lay preaching and communal singing.

A continuous wave of revivalism fueled the expansion of Protestant Christianity. Beginning in the 1790s Baptists and Methodists evangelized the cities and the backcountry of New England. A new sect of Universalists, who repudiated the Calvinist doctrine of predestination and preached universal salvation, attracted thousands of converts, especially in Massachusetts and

TABLE 9.3 Number of Church Congregations by Denomination, 1780 and 1860

	1780	1860	Increase
Anglican / Episcopalian	406	2,100	5-fold
Baptist	457	12,150	26-fold
Catholic	50	2,500	50-fold
Congregational	742	2,200	3-fold
Lutheran	240	2,100	8-fold
Methodist	50	20,000	400-fold
Presbyterian	495	6,400	13-fold

northern New England. After 1800 enthusiastic camp meeting revivals swept the frontier regions of South Carolina, Kentucky, Tennessee, and Ohio (Map 9.4).

When frontier preachers got together at a revival meeting, they were electrifying. James McGready, a Scots-Irish Presbyterian preacher, "could so array hell before the wicked," an eyewitness reported, "that they would tremble and Quake, imagining a lake of fire and brimstone yawning to overwhelm them." James Finley described the Cane Ridge, Kentucky, revival of 1802:

The noise was like the roar of Niagara. The vast sea of human beings seemed to be agitated as if by a storm. I counted seven ministers, all preaching at one time, some on stumps, others on wagons. . . . Some of the people were singing, others praying, some crying for mercy.

Through such revivals, Baptist and Methodist preachers reshaped the spiritual landscape of the South and the Old Southwest. Because of their emotional message, revivalists were particularly successful in attracting the unchurched. The evangelicals' promise of religious fellowship also appealed to young men and women and geographically mobile families who had few social ties in their new communities. With the assistance of black ministers, they began to implant evangelical Protestant Christianity among African Americans as well (see Voices from Abroad, "Frances Trollope: A Camp Meeting in Indiana," p. 276).

The Second Great Awakening changed the denominational base of American religion. The leading churches of the colonial period—the Congregationalists, Episcopalians, and Quakers—declined in relative membership because they were content to maintain existing congregations or to grow slowly through natural increase. Because of their evangelical activities and democratic outlook, Methodist and Baptist churches grew

spectacularly. By the early nineteenth century they had become the largest religious denominations in the United States. In New England and the Middle Atlantic states, pious women supplemented the work of preachers and lay elders by holding prayer meetings and providing material aid and spiritual comfort to poorer members of the congregation, doubling the amount of organized spiritual energy. In the South and West, Baptist and Methodist preachers traveled constantly. A Methodist minister followed a circuit, "riding a hardy pony or horse . . . with his Bible, hymn-book, and Discipline." These "circuit riders" established new churches by searching out devout families, bringing them together for worship, and then appointing lay elders to lead the congregation and enforce moral discipline until the circuit rider returned.

Evangelical ministers copied the techniques of George Whitefield and other eighteenth-century revivalists, codifying their methods in manuals on "practical preaching." To attract converts, preachers were advised to adopt theatrical gestures and a flamboyant style, to throw away their precise but stodgy written sermons and to speak extemporaneously. "Preach without papers" and emphasize piety rather than theology, advised one minister, "seem earnest & serious; & you will be listened to with Patience, & Wonder; both of your hands will be seized, & almost shook off as soon as you are out of the Church."

In the South evangelical religion became increasingly important. Initially revivalism was a disruptive force; by proclaiming the spiritual equality of all people—women and blacks as well as white men—it threatened the traditional authority wielded by husbands and planters and incurred their wrath. In response Methodist and Baptist preachers adapted the social content of their religious message so that it supported the rule of yeomen patriarchs and slave-owning planters. "We hold that a Christian slave must be submissive,

A Baptist Ceremony

Unlike many other Christian churches, which practiced infant baptism, Baptists reserved this sacred ceremony for adults who had been born again by the infusion of God's grace. Some Baptist congregations, such as the one depicted in this 1819 painting, required complete immersion in water, symbolizing the cleansing of all sins. Such communal practices, along with an egalitarian atmosphere and an intense religiosity, attracted tens of thousands of converts and quickly made the Baptists one of the largest American denominations. Chicago Historical Society.

faithful, and obedient," a Methodist conference proclaimed, while a Baptist minister declared that a man was naturally at "the head of the woman." Ultimately Christian republicanism in the South added a sacred dimension to the ideology of aristocratic republicanism, while in the North it pushed forward the movement toward a democratic republican society.

Black Protestantism. After the family, the religious community played the most important role in the lives of enslaved African Americans. Initially most blacks maintained the practices of their African homeland. "At the time I first went to Carolina," remembered Charles Ball, an escaped slave, "there were a great many African slaves in the country. . . . Many of them believed there were several gods [and] I knew several . . . Mohamedans [Muslims]."

When the First Great Awakening swept through the Upper South in the 1750s and 1760s, some blacks joined

Christian churches, but the first major wave of conversions began along the James River in Virginia in the mid-1780s. Evangelical white Baptists and Methodists won the conversion of hundreds of slaves and free blacks, who absorbed the white churches' teachings and adapted them to their needs. Black Christians generally preferred to envision God as a warrior who had liberated the Jews, his chosen people. Their cause was similar to the Israelites', Martin Prosser told his fellow slave conspirators as they plotted rebellion in Virginia in 1800. "I have read in my Bible where God says, if we worship him, we should have peace in all our land and five of you shall conquer a hundred and a hundred of you a hundred thousand of our enemies." Confident of their special relationship with God, the slaves prepared themselves spiritually for emancipation, which they saw as deliverance to the Promised Land.

Blacks generally ignored the doctrines of original sin and predestination as well as biblical passages that encouraged unthinking obedience to authority or

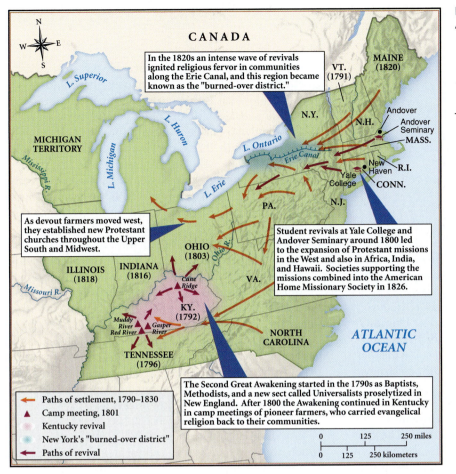

MAP 9.4 The Second Great Awakening, 1790–1860

The awakening lasted for decades and invigorated churches in every part of the nation. However, the revivals in Kentucky and in New York State were particularly intense and influential. As thousands of farm families migrated to the South and West (see Map 8.2), they carried with them the fervor generated by the Cane Ridge revival in Kentucky in 1802 and the religious wildfires that swept through the "burned-over district" along the Erie Canal in New York between 1825 and 1835.

CANADA

In the 1820s an intense wave of revivals ignited religious fervor in communities along the Erie Canal, and this region became known as the "burned-over district."

As devout farmers moved west, they established new Protestant churches throughout the Upper South and Midwest.

Student revivals at Yale College and Andover Seminary around 1800 led to the expansion of Protestant missions in the West and also in Africa, India, and Hawaii. Societies supporting the missions combined into the American Home Missionary Society in 1826.

The Second Great Awakening started in the 1790s as Baptists, Methodists, and a new sect called Universalists proselytized in New England. After 1800 the Awakening continued in Kentucky in camp meetings of pioneer farmers, who carried evangelical religion back to their communities.

Paths of settlement, 1790–1830
Camp meeting, 1801
Kentucky revival
New York's "burned-over district"
Paths of revival

portrayed the church as a lawgiver. When a white minister urged slaves in Liberty County, Georgia, to obey their masters, he noted that "one half of my audience deliberately rose up and walked off." Slaves identified not only with the powerful Father-God but also with his persecuted Savior-Son, who had suffered and died so that his followers might gain salvation. By offering eventual liberation from life's sorrows, the Christian message helped many slaves endure their bondage. Amid the manifest injustice of their own lives African Americans used Christian principles to affirm their spiritual equality with whites and to hope for ultimate justice in the afterlife. Black Christianity thus developed as a religion of emotional fervor and stoical endurance.

New Religious Thought and Institutions. Like African Americans, whites responded more positively to certain Christian doctrines than to others. The Calvinist preoccupation with human depravity and weakness had shaped the thinking of many colonial-era writers, teachers, and statesmen. By the early nineteenth century, ministers (whether or not they were revivalists) placed greater stress on human ability and individual free will, making the religious culture of the United States more optimistic and more compatible with republican doctrines of liberty and equality.

In New England many educated, well-off Congregationalists reacted against the emotionalism of Methodist and Baptist services by stressing the power of human reason. Rejecting the concept of the Trinity—God the Father, Son, and Holy Spirit—they worshiped an indivisible and "united" God; hence their name: Unitarians. "The ultimate reliance of a human being is, and must be, on his own mind," argued the famous Unitarian minister William Ellery Channing, "for the idea of God is the idea of our own spiritual nature, purified and enlarged to infinity." This emphasis on a believer's reason, a legacy of the Enlightenment, gave Unitarianism a humanistic and individualistic aspect.

Lyman Beecher, the preeminent New England Congregationalist clergyman, accepted the doctrine of universal salvation. Although Beecher continued to believe that humans had a natural tendency to sin, he retreated from the Calvinist doctrine of predestination still held by many ministers, declaring that men and women had the capacity to choose God. In emphasizing choice—the free will of the believer—Beecher testified to the growing confidence in the power of human action.

Frances Trollope

A Camp Meeting in Indiana

Frances Trollope, a successful English author and the mother of novelist Anthony Trollope, resided in the United States during the late 1820s. She lived for a time in Cincinnati, where she owned a bazaar that sold imported goods from Europe. Unsuccessful as a storekeeper, she won great acclaim as a social commentator. Her critical and at times acerbic Domestic Manners of the Americans *(1832) was a best-seller in both Europe and the United States. Here she provides her readers with a vivid description of a revivalist meeting in Indiana around 1830.*

We reached the ground about an hour before midnight, and the approach to it was highly picturesque. The spot chosen was the verge of an unbroken forest, where a space of about twenty acres appeared to have been partially cleared for the purpose. Tents of different sizes were pitched very near together in a circle round the cleared space. . . .

Four high frames, constructed in the form of altars, were placed at the four corners of the inclosure; on these were supported layers of earth and sod, on which burned immense fires of blazing pine-wood. On one side a rude platform was erected to accommodate the preachers, fifteen of whom attended this meeting, and with very short intervals for necessary refreshment and private devotion, preached in rotation, day and night, from Tuesday to Saturday.

When we arrived, the preachers were silent; but we heard issuing from nearly every tent mingled sounds of praying, preaching, singing, and lamentation. . . . The floor [of one of the tents] was covered with straw, which round the sides was heaped in masses, that might serve as seats, but which at that moment were used to support the heads and arms of the close-packed circle of men and women who kneeled on the floor.

Out of about thirty persons thus placed, perhaps half a dozen were men. One of these [was] a handsome-looking youth of eighteen or twenty. . . . His arm was encircling the neck of a young girl who knelt beside him, with her hair hanging dishevelled upon her shoulders, and her features working with the most violent agitation; soon after they both fell forward on the straw, as if unable to endure in any other attitude the burning eloquence of a tall grim figure in black, who, standing erect in the center, was uttering with incredible vehemence an oration that seemed to hover between praying and preaching. . . .

One tent was occupied exclusively by Negroes. They were all full-dressed, and looked exactly as if they were performing a scene on a stage. . . . The men were in snow white pantaloons, with gay colored linen jackets. One of these, a youth of coal-black comeliness, was preaching with the most violent gesticulations. . . .

At midnight, a horn sounded through the camp, which, we were told, was to call the people from private to public worship; and we presently saw them flocking from all sides to the front of the preacher's stand. . . . There were about two thousand persons assembled.

One of the preachers began in a low nasal tone, and, like all other Methodist preachers, assured us of the enormous depravity of man. . . . Above a hundred persons, nearly all females, came forward, uttering howlings and groans so terrible that I shall never cease to shudder when I recall them. They appeared to drag each other forward, and on the word being given, "let us pray," they fell on their knees . . . and they were soon all lying on the ground in an indescribable confusion of heads and legs.

Source: Frances Trollope, *Domestic Manners of the Americans* (London: Whittaker, Treacher and Co., 1832), 139–42.

Reflecting this optimistic outlook, the minister Samuel Hopkins linked individual salvation with social reform through the concept of religious benevolence. Benevolence was the practice of disinterested virtue, to be undertaken by those who had received God's sanctifying grace. According to the New York Presbyterian minister John Rodgers, fortunate individuals who had received God's grace had a duty "to dole out charity to their poorer brothers and sisters." Heeding this message pious merchants founded the New York Humane Society and other charitable organizations. By the 1820s some conservative church leaders were complaining that lay men and women were devoting themselves to secular reforms, such as the prevention of pauperism, to the neglect of spiritual goals. Their criticism underlined a key element of the new religious outlook: its emphasis on improving society. It was her belief, the social reformer Lydia Maria Child later recalled, that "the only true church organization [is] when heads and hearts unite in working for the welfare of the human-race."

Unlike the First Great Awakening of the 1740s, which split churches into factions, the Second Great Awakening fostered cooperation among the denominations. Five interdenominational societies were founded between 1815 and 1826: the American Education Society (1815), the American Bible Society (1816), the American Sunday School Union (1824), the American Tract Society (1824), and the American Home Missionary Society (1826). The new organizations were based in New York, Boston, and Philadelphia, but they ministered to a national congregation. Each year these societies dispatched hundreds of missionaries to small towns and rural villages and distributed tens of thousands of religious pamphlets, organizing thousands of church members in a great collective undertaking and diminishing the importance of differences over religious doctrine. Many congregations abandoned books and pamphlets that took controversial stances on old theological debates over predestination and replaced them, a layman explained, with publications that would not give "offense to the serious Christians of any denomination."

This unity among Protestants had a galvanizing effect, as men and women scattered across the expanding nation saw themselves as part of a single religious movement that could change the course of history. "I want to see our state evangelized," declared one pious New York layman: "Suppose the great State of New York in all its physical, political, moral, commercial, and pecuniary resources should come over to the Lord's side. Why it would turn the scale and could convert the world. I shall have no rest until it is done."

As a result of the Second Awakening, religion became a central force in American political life. On July 4, 1827, the Reverend Ezra Stiles Ely called on the members of the Seventh Presbyterian Church in Philadelphia to begin a "Christian party in politics." In his sermon, entitled "The Duty of Christian Freemen to Elect Christian Rulers," Ely set out for the American republic a new religious goal—one that the recently deceased Thomas Jefferson and John Adams would have found strange if not troubling. The two founders had believed that America's mission was to spread political republicanism. In contrast Ely urged the United States to become an evangelical Christian nation, dedicated to religious conversion at home and abroad. As Ely put it, "All our rulers ought in their official capacity to serve the Lord Jesus Christ."

Women's New Religious Roles

Pious women assumed a new leading role in many Protestant churches in the North and even founded new sects. Mother Ann Lee organized the Shaker sect in Britain and migrated in 1774 to America, where she and a handful of followers attracted numerous recruits; by the 1820s Shaker communities dotted the American countryside from New Hampshire to Kentucky and Indiana (see Chapter 12). In 1776 in Rhode Island, Jemima Wilkinson, a young Quaker woman stirred by reading the sermons of George Whitefield, had a vision that she had died and been reincarnated as the second coming of Christ:

> The heavens were open'd and she saw [two] Archangels descending from the east . . . and the Angels said, the Spirit of Life from God had descended to earth. . . . And according to the declaration of the Angels, the Spirit took full possession of the Body it now Animates.

Repudiating her birth name, Wilkinson declared herself to be the Publick Universal Friend and won scores of converts to her new religion, which blended the Calvinist warning of "a lost and guilty, gossiping, dying World" with Quaker-inspired plain dress, pacifism, and abolitionism.

Increasing Public Activities. Far more important were the activities undertaken by women in mainstream churches. To give but a few examples, in New Hampshire women managed more than fifty local "cent" societies to raise funds for the Society for Promoting Christian Knowledge. Evangelical women in New York City founded the Society for the Relief of Poor Widows. And young Quaker women in Philadelphia ran the Society for the Free Instruction of African Females.

Women became active in religion and charitable work partly because they were excluded from other spheres of public life and partly because ministers were forced to rely on female members, who formed a substantial majority in some denominations, to do the work of the church. After 1800 over 70 percent of the members of New England Congregational churches were female. Ministers acknowledged their presence by changing long-standing practices such as gender-segregated seating at services and separate prayer meetings for each sex, while evangelical Methodist and Baptist preachers actively encouraged mixed seating and praying. "Our prayer meetings have been one of the greatest means of the conversion of souls," a minister in central New York reported in the 1820s, "especially those in which brothers and sisters have prayed together."

Far from promoting promiscuity, as critics feared, these new practices were accompanied by greater moral self-discipline. Absorbing the principle of female virtue, many young women and the men who courted them postponed sexual intercourse until after marriage—a form of self-restraint uncommon in the eighteenth century. In Hingham, Massachusetts, and many other New England towns, about 30 percent of the women who married between 1750 and 1800 had borne a child within eight months of their wedding day. By the 1820s the proportion had dropped to 15 percent.

Nevertheless, as women exercised their new spiritual authority, men scrutinized their behavior and tried to curb their power. Evangelical Baptist churches that had once stressed spiritual equality now denied women the right to vote on church affairs or to offer testimonies of faith before the congregation. Such activities, declared one layman, were "directly opposite to the apostolic command in Cor[inthians] xiv, 34, 35, 'Let your women learn to keep silence in the churches.'" "Women have a different *calling*," claimed another, "That they *be chaste, keepers at home* is the Apostle's direction." Seizing on that role, by the 1820s mothers throughout the United States had founded local maternal associations to encourage Christian childrearing. Newsletters such as *Mother's Magazine* were widely read in hundreds of small towns and villages, giving women a sense of shared purpose and identity as women.

Women's Education. Religious activism also advanced female education. Churches established scores of seminaries and academies where girls from the middling classes received sound intellectual training and moral instruction. Emma Willard, the first American to advocate higher education for women, opened the Middlebury Female Seminary in Vermont in 1814 and later founded girls' schools in Waterford and Troy, New York. Women educated in these seminaries and academies gradually displaced men as public-school teachers. By the 1820s women taught the summer session in many schools; in the following decade they took on the more demanding winter term as well. Women were able to usurp these formerly male roles because women had few other opportunities and would therefore accept lower pay than men. Female schoolteachers earned from $12 to $14 per month with room and board—less than a farm laborer. However, as schoolteachers women had an acknowledged place in public life, one that had been beyond their reach in colonial and Revolutionary times. Here too, the Second Great Awakening had transformed the scope of women's lives. Just as the ideology of democratic republicanism had expanded voting rights and the political influence of ordinary men in the North, so the values of Christian republicanism had encouraged women to take a more active role in the affairs of their communities.

FOR FURTHER EXPLORATION

▶ For definitions of key terms boldfaced in this chapter, see the glossary at the end of the book.

▶ To assess your mastery of the material covered in this chapter, see the Online Study Guide at **bedfordstmartins.com/henretta**.

▶ For suggested references, including Web sites, see page SR-10 at the end of the book.

▶ For map resources and primary documents, see **bedfordstmartins.com/henretta**.

SUMMARY

Three variants of republican society developed in the United States in the early nineteenth century: democratic republicanism in the North, aristocratic republicanism in the South, and an evangelical Protestant vision of republicanism that was embraced by many people in both regions. In the North the ideals of liberty and equality encouraged the emergence of a white male citizenry that demanded voting rights, pursued social mobility, and looked with suspicion on those with aristocratic pretensions. Political and religious leaders promoted a different path for women, developing the notion of a separate sphere consisting primarily of domestic responsibilities. Republicanism and sentimentalism encouraged young people to marry for love as well as for economic security and prompted parents to rear their children using reason as well as authority.

White society in the South changed as southern planters extended the slave regime into the Old Southwest in response to the demand for cotton. Ownership of slaves became concentrated in fewer hands, and smallholding white farmers moved into the hilly backcountry. Southern society developed an aristocratic republican system of politics dominated by slaveholders. Distressed by the rapid geographic growth of plantation society, northern representatives in Congress delayed for two years the entry of Missouri into the Union. Finally, the Missouri Compromise temporarily resolved the crisis, by dividing the lands of the Louisiana Purchase into free and slave territory.

Enslaved blacks gradually forged a distinct African American culture, melding together various African traditions with the English language and Christian religious practices. Slaves developed increasingly strong family, community, and religious values, which helped them survive the forced migration to the cotton South and the relentless work of carving new plantations out of the wilderness. In the northern cities, free blacks founded independent churches and benevolent institutions.

The Second Great Awakening made Americans a fervently Protestant people and dramatically increased the influence of the evangelical Baptist and Methodist Churches. Religious revivalism also enhanced the status of women, whose moral activism broadened their sphere to encompass teaching in public schools and managing charitable groups and religious societies. The shared religious experience of hundreds of thousands of Americans between the 1770s and the 1820s formed the core of an emerging national identity, even as the citizens of the North and the South defined republicanism in distinctly different ways.

TIMELINE

1782   St. Jean de Crèvecoeur publishes *Letters from an American Farmer*

1787   Benjamin Rush, *Thoughts on Female Education*

1790s   Parents limit family size as farms shrink

Second Great Awakening expands church membership

Ministers encourage "Republican motherhood"

1800   Gabriel Prosser plots a slave rebellion in Virginia

1800s   Rise of sentimentalism and republican marriage system

Women's religious activism; founding of female academies

Spread of evangelical Baptists and Methodists

Religious benevolence sparks social reform

Chesapeake blacks adopt Protestant beliefs

1807   New Jersey excludes propertied women from suffrage

1810s   Expansion of suffrage for men

Slavery defended as a "necessary evil"

Expansion of cotton South and domestic slave trade

1819–1821   Conflict over admission of Missouri as a slave state ends with Missouri Compromise

1820s   Reform of public education

Women become schoolteachers

PART TWO

Federalism as History and Contemporary Politics

People sometimes wonder why they need to know about what seems like ancient history—events that took place, as in Part Two, hundreds of years ago or more. Not politicians. They root around avidly in the nation's past to find traditions and precedents to justify their policies. No era is more heavily exploited than the nation-building decades recounted in the chapters you have just read. Take, for example, the "Reagan Revolution" of the 1980s. President Ronald Reagan (1981–1989) was bent on diminishing the power of the national government by cutting its tax revenue and transferring policymaking and spending authority to the state and local levels. In 1987 he issued Executive Order 12612 instructing all executive departments and agencies to "refrain, to the maximum extent possible, from establishing uniform, national standards for programs and . . . defer to the States to establish standards." Entitled "Federalism," Order 12612 laid down some of the general principles underlying the Reagan Revolution, including its basic premise that "our political liberties are best assured by limiting the size and scope of the national government." As the historical grounding for this argument, the order quoted the words of none other than the author of the Declaration of Independence, Thomas Jefferson, that the states are "the most competent administrations for our domestic concerns and the surest bulwarks against antirepublican tendencies."

In appealing to Jefferson, Reagan was setting himself against the reigning scholarly consensus. Historians had long debated the merits of the Antifederalists—those who had opposed the U.S. Constitution of 1789 and defended states' rights—as against those of the Federalists—supporters of the Constitution and activist national policies. By Reagan's time, most historians thought that the Federalists had the stronger case. In a famous article of 1955, the highly respected constitutional historian Cecilia Kenyon had denigrated the Antifederalists as "men of little faith" who had misread the course of history and the meaning of the American experiment by refusing to support a strong national government. Influenced by the New Deal, a wide-ranging set of federal programs that had rescued the nation from the Great Depression of the 1930s, many other historians—and especially those with a "liberal" outlook—likewise praised activist governments. During the 1940s historians Oscar Handlin, Louis Hartz, and Carter Goodrich celebrated those state governments that had actively subsidized economic development between 1790 and 1840; subsequently, scholars of the Progressive Era (1890–1914) praised reformers who strengthened regulatory powers on the state and national levels. In their eyes, stronger government was the wave of the future.

The actual results of the Reagan Revolution would seem to have sustained the interpretation of these liberal historians. For all his rhetoric of states' rights and personal liberty, Reagan failed to reverse the centralizing tendencies of American government. The anti-Communist crusade of his administration was too vigorous, the entitlements of federal programs were too valued, even by his own conservative constituents, to allow Reagan to dismantle the powerful national regulatory, Social Security, and military bureaucracies created during the New Deal and the cold war.

If the Reagan Revolution fell short of its political objectives, it succeeded remarkably as an intellectual movement. The Antifederalists have again become respectable in scholarly circles. In part this result has been the fruit of a sustained effort by Reagan's followers to breathe new life into conservative American thought by means of think tanks like the Heritage Foundation and the Cato Institute. Conservative and libertarian scholars such as Gary L. McDowell (*Reason and Republicanism: Thomas Jefferson's Legacy of Liberty*, 1997) and David A. J. Richards (*Foundations of American Constitutionalism*, 1989) reinvigorated the study of the Antifederalists and the doctrines of state-based federalism, individualism, and limited government. They have been joined by such mainstream scholars as Saul Cornell, who explains in *The Other Founders: Anti-Federalism and the Dissenting Tradition in America, 1788–1828* (1999) how Jeffersonian Republicans embraced the strong localist impulses represented by the Antifederalists and devised a new constitutional doctrine, the "compact" or "states' rights" theory of federalism. Even on the left the values of the Antifederalists have drawn sympathy. In *The Transformation of American Law, 1780–1860* (1976), legal scholar Morton Horwitz shows how activist state government systematically favored entrepreneurs and capitalists in the nineteenth century, throwing the costs of economic development on workers and taxpayers.

Once they began to explore, moreover, historians had no difficulty identifying the long-standing strength—and political integrity—of the traditions of limited government and local self-rule. Consider the following examples from the period covered in Part Two, The New Republic, 1775–1820:

▶ In theory and law, the British Constitution declared the supremacy of central authority: the king-in-

Implementing Reagan's Federalist Agenda

Upon becoming president in 1989, George H. Bush continued President Ronald Reagan's efforts to cut the size of the national government. Unable to reduce taxes because of spiraling budget deficits, Bush used the television commercial shown here to promise Americans there would be "NO New Taxes." Bush's inability to keep that pledge helped to prevent his reelection in 1992. Ken Hawking / Sygma.

Parliament. However, many American political leaders rejected the primacy of imperial law, for they had long governed according to what John Phillip Reid (*In a Defiant Stance,* 1977) has called "Whig Law," rules enacted by local institutions and enforced by local officials. Why should we be governed by "strangers *ignorant* of the interests and laws of the Colonies?" asked William Henry Drayton of South Carolina, a future leader of the Patriot localist revolt against British centralized authority.

▶ Having vanquished a distant, powerful government in London, the Antifederalists were determined not to allow a new one in America. Their leaders subjected the centralizing Constitution of 1787 to thorough, coherent criticism. Massachusetts Antifederalist James Winthrop spoke for them when supporting the existing system of "Whig Law": "It is necessary that there should be local laws and institutions," he argued, "for a people inhabiting various climates will unavoidably have local habits and different modes of life."

▶ When the Antifederalists failed to block ratification of the Constitution of 1787, they limited its authority by insisting on a Bill of Rights to protect individual liberty. Subsequently, when Alexander Hamilton as secretary of the treasury expanded the powers of the new national government, former Antifederalists joined James Madison and Thomas Jefferson in the Democratic Republican Party, which in turn adopted their localist outlook (see Chapter 7) and articulated a new interpretation of the Constitution, a compact theory of federalism. In the Kentucky Resolution of 1798, Jefferson suggested that each state had "an equal right to judge for itself" whether an act of the national government was unconstitutional. In addition to this ideological contribution to the theory of federalism, Jefferson laid the institutional foundations for a limited central government. As president from 1801 to 1809, he systematically dismantled the energetic national government created by Hamilton.

As in the contest between Jefferson and Hamilton, President Reagan's ideologically charged statement of administrative policy inevitably evoked a political counterresponse. Speaking for those who favored an activist central government, in 1998 President William Jefferson Clinton (1993–2001) issued Executive Order 13083, also entitled "Federalism," which offered a nationalist reading of American constitutional history. "Preserving the supremacy of Federal law," it asserted, "provides an essential balance to the power of the States. "Clinton's executive order justified national action in many circumstances, including those in which "there is a need for uniform national standards" and in which "States have not adequately protected individual rights and liberties."

What are we to make of these political and historical controversies? In the first place they remind us that the established facts of "history" were once the contested terrain of "politics." In seeking to reverse Hamilton's policies, Jefferson was just as much a politician as Clinton. Second, these episodes warn us about the frequent abuse of the historical record by self-interested politicians. In celebrating Jefferson's ideology and achievements, Reagan consciously ignored Hamilton's great contributions to the American political tradition. Finally, the struggle over federalism shows us the intimate connection between contemporary politics and historians' views of the past. If history is always more complex than political rhetoric suggests, historians' interpretations often reflect the political wisdom of the moment.

Economic Revolution and Sectional Strife

1820–1877

ECONOMY	SOCIETY	GOVERNMENT	CULTURE	SECTIONALISM
The Economic Revolution Begins	A New Class Structure Emerges	Creating a Democratic Polity	Reforming People and Institutions	From Compromise to Civil War and Reconstruction
1820 ▸ Waltham textile factory (1814) Erie Canal completed (1825); market economy expands	▸ Business class emerges Rural women and girls recruited as factory workers	▸ Spread of universal white male suffrage Rise of Jackson and Democratic Party	▸ American Colonization Society (1817) Benevolent Reform Movements Revivalist Charles Finney	▸ Missouri Compromise (1820) David Walker's *Appeal to the Colored Race* (1829)
1830 ▸ Protective tariffs aid owners and workers Panic of 1837 U.S. textile makers outcompete British	▸ Mechanics form craft unions Depression shatters labor movement	▸ Anti-Masonic movement Whig Party formed (1834); Second Party System emerges	▸ Joseph Smith founds Mormonism Female Moral Reform Society (1834) Temperance Crusade expands	▸ Nullification crisis (1832) W. L. Garrison forms American Anti-Slavery Society (1833)
1840 ▸ Irish join labor force *Commonwealth v. Hunt* (1842) legalizes unions Manufacturing grows	▸ Working-class districts emerge in cities Irish immigration accelerates	▸ Log Cabin campaign mobilizes voters Antislavery parties: Liberty and Free Soil	▸ Fourierist and other communal settlements founded Seneca Falls convention (1848)	▸ Texas annexation, Mexican War, and Wilmot Proviso (1846) increase sectional conflict
1850 ▸ Growth of cotton output in South and railroads in the North and Midwest Panic of 1857	▸ Expansion of farm society into Midwest and Far West Free labor ideology justifies inequality	▸ Whig Party disintegrates; Republican Party founded (1854): Third Party System begins	▸ Harriet Beecher Stowe's *Uncle Tom's Cabin* (1852) Anti-immigrant nativist movement	▸ Compromise of 1850 Kansas-Nebraska Act (1854) and Bleeding Kansas *Dred Scott* decision (1857)
1860 ▸ Republicans enact agenda: Homestead Act, railroad aid, high tariffs, national banking	▸ Emancipation Proclamation (1863) Free blacks struggle for control of land	▸ Thirteenth Amendment (1865) ends slavery; Fourteenth Amendment (1868) extends legal and political rights	▸ U.S. Sanitary Commission and American Red Cross founded	▸ South Carolina leads secession movement (1860) Confederate States of America (1861–1865)
1870 ▸ Panic of 1873	▸ Rise of sharecropping in the South	▸ Fifteenth Amendment extends vote to black men (1870)	▸ Freed African Americans create schools and churches	▸ Compromise of 1877 ends Reconstruction

Between 1820 and 1877 the United States changed from a predominantly agricultural society into one of the world's most powerful manufacturing economies. This profound transformation began slowly in the Northeast and then accelerated after 1830, affecting every aspect of life in the northern and midwestern states and bringing important changes to the South as well.

ECONOMY Two revolutions in industrial production and the market system transformed the nation's economy. Factory owners used high-speed machines and a new system of labor discipline to boost production, and enterprising merchants employed a newly built network of canals and railroads to create a vast national market. The manufacturing sector produced an ever-increasing share of the country's wealth: from less than 5 percent in 1820 to more than 30 percent in 1877.

SOCIETY The new economic system spurred the creation of a class-based society. A wealthy elite of merchants, manufacturers, bankers, and other entrepreneurs emerged at the top of the social order and tried to maintain social stability through a paternalistic program of religious reform. However, an urban middle class with a distinct material and religious culture grew in size and political importance. Equally striking was the increasing number of propertyless workers, many of them immigrants from Germany and Ireland, who labored for wages in the new factories and built the new canals and railroads. By 1860 half the nation's free workers labored for wages, and wealth had become concentrated in the hands of relatively few families.

GOVERNMENT Economic growth and social diversity facilitated the development of political parties and a more open, democratic polity. To enhance their economic prospects, farmers, workers, and entrepreneurs turned to politics, seeking improved transportation, shorter work days, and special corporate charters. Catholic immigrants from Ireland and Germany also entered the political arena in order to protect their religion and culture from attacks by nativists and reformers. Led by Andrew Jackson, the Democratic party took the lead in advancing the interests of southern planters, farmers, and urban workers. It did so primarily by carrying through a democratic political and constitutional revolution that cut governmental aid to financiers, merchants, and business corporations. To compete with the Democrats, the Whig party (and, beginning in the 1850s, the Republican party) promoted reform and a vision of a society with few class barriers and a high rate of individual social mobility. The result was a two-party system that engaged the energies of the vast majority of the electorate and unified the fragmented social order.

CULTURE During these decades, a series of reform movements, many with religious roots and goals, swept across America. Dedicated men and women preached the gospel of temperance, observance of Sunday, prison reform, and dozens of other causes. Some Americans pursued their social dreams in utopian communities in the Midwestern states, but most reformers worked within society. Two interrelated groups—abolitionists and women's rights activists—called for radical changes in the social order, the immediate end of slavery and reform of the patriarchal legal and cultural order. Abolitionist attacks prompted southern leaders to defend slavery as beneficial to slaves as well as planters. During the 1840s and 1850s, antislavery advocates turned to political action, campaigning for free soil in the western territories and alleging that the southern slave power threatened free labor and republican values.

SECTIONALISM These economic, political, and cultural changes combined to sharpen sectional divisions: the North developed into an urbanizing and industrializing society based on free labor, whereas the South remained a rural, slaveholding society dependent on the production and export of cotton. Following the conquest of vast areas of the West during the Mexican War (1846–1848), northern and southern politicians argued vigorously over the issue of permitting slavery in these newly acquired territories. These conflicts could not be resolved by political compromise, leading in 1861 to the secession of the South from the Union and, thereafter, civil war. The conflict became a total war, a struggle between two societies as well as two armies. Because of new technology and the mass mobilization of armies, the two sides endured unprecedented casualties and costs before the North emerged victorious.

The fruits of victory were substantial. During Reconstruction, the Republican Party ended slavery, imposed its economic policies and constitutional doctrines on the nation, and began to extend full democratic rights to the former slaves. Faced by massive resistance from white southerners, northern leaders lacked the will to undertake the fundamental transformation of the economic and political order of the South that was required to provide African Americans with the full benefits of freedom.

ART IS THE HANDMAID OF HUMAN GOOD. · LOWELL ·

CHAPTER 10

The Economic Revolution
1820–1860

The Coming of Industry: Northeastern Manufacturing
Division of Labor and the Factory
The Textile Industry and British Competition
American Mechanics and Technological Innovation
Wage Workers and the Labor Movement

The Expansion of Markets
Migration to the Southwest and the Midwest
The Transportation Revolution Forges Regional Ties
The Growth of Cities and Towns

Changes in the Social Structure
The Business Elite
The Middle Class
The New Urban Poor
The Benevolent Empire
Revivalism and Reform
Immigration and Cultural Conflict

◄ **Technology Celebrated**
Artists joined with manufacturers in praising the new industrial age. In this 1836 emblem, a proposed seal for the city of Lowell, Massachusetts, a cornucopia (horn of plenty) spreads its bounty over the community, as bales of raw cotton (in the foreground) await their transformation in the city's textile factories into smooth cloth for shipment to far-flung markets via the new railroad system. The image of prosperity was deceptive; two years earlier, 2,000 women textile workers had gone on strike in Lowell, claiming that their wages were too low to provide a decent standard of living. Private collection.

For more help analyzing this image, see the ONLINE STUDY GUIDE at bedfordstmartins.com/henretta.

IN 1804 LIFE SUDDENLY TURNED GRIM for eleven-year-old Chauncey Jerome. Following the death of his farmer-blacksmith father, Jerome was hired out as an indentured servant to a farmer. Aware that few farmers "would treat a poor boy like a human being," Jerome bought out his indenture by finding a job making dials for clocks and eventually ended up working as a journeyman for clockmaker Eli Terry. A manufacturing wizard, Terry had turned Litchfield, Connecticut, into the clock-making center of the United States by designing an enormously popular desk-model clock with brass parts. Jerome followed in Terry's footsteps, setting up his own clock business in 1816. By organizing work more efficiently and using new machines to make interchangeable metal parts, Jerome drove down the price of a simple clock from $20 to $5 and then to less than $2. By the 1840s he was selling his clocks in England, the center of the Industrial Revolution; two decades later his workers were turning out 200,000 clocks a year, testimony to American industrial enterprise. By 1860 the United States was not only the world's leading exporter of cotton and wheat but also the third-ranking manufacturing nation, behind only Great Britain and France.

The French aristocrat Alexis de Tocqueville captured a key feature of Chauncey Jerome's experience and the American economic revolution in his treatise *Democracy in America* (1835). "What most astonishes me," Tocqueville remarked after a two-year stay in the United States, "is not so much the marvelous grandeur of some undertakings, as the innumerable magnitude of small ones." The individual efforts of tens of thousands of artisan-inventors like Eli Terry and Chauncey Jerome had propelled the country into a new economic era. As the editor of *Niles' Weekly Register* in Baltimore put it, there was an "almost universal ambition to get forward."

Not all Americans embraced the new ethic of enterprise, and many who did failed to share in the new prosperity. The Industrial Revolution and the Market Revolution created a class-divided society that challenged the founders' vision of an agricultural republic with few distinctions of wealth or power. As the philosopher Ralph Waldo Emerson warned in 1839, "The invasion of Nature by Trade with its Money, its Credit, its Steam, [and] its Railroad threatens to . . . establish a new, universal Monarchy."

The Coming of Industry: Northeastern Manufacturing

Together the Industrial Revolution and the Market Revolution created a new economy. Industrialization came to the United States after 1790 as American merchants and manufacturers increased the output of goods by reorganizing work and building factories. The rapid construction of turnpikes, canals, and railroads by state governments and private entrepreneurs allowed manufactured goods and farm products from many regions to be sold throughout the land. Thanks to these innovations in production and transportation, the average per capita wealth of Americans increased by nearly 1 percent per year—30 percent over the course of a generation. Goods that once had been luxury items became part of everyday life (Table 10.1).

Division of Labor and the Factory

This impressive gain in living standards stemmed initially from changes in the organization of production. Consider the shoe industry. Traditionally New England shoemakers worked in small wooden shacks called "ten-footers," where they turned leather hides into finished shoes and boots. During the 1820s and 1830s merchants and manufacturers centered in Lynn, Massachusetts, took over the shoe industry and increased output through a **division of labor**. The employers hired semiskilled journeymen and set them to work in large central shops cutting the leather into soles and uppers. They then sent out the upper sections to shoe binders, women in dozens of Massachusetts towns who worked at home sewing in fabric linings. Finally, the manufacturers had other journeymen assemble the shoes and return them to the central shop for inspection and packing. The new system made the manufacturer into a powerful "shoe boss" and eroded the workers' control over the pace and conditions of labor. "I guess you won't catch me to do that little thing again," vowed one Massachusetts binder. Whatever the cost to workers, the division of labor dramatically increased the output of shoes while cutting their price.

For tasks that were not suited to the outwork system, entrepreneurs created an even more important new organization, the modern **factory**, which concentrated production under one roof and divided the work into

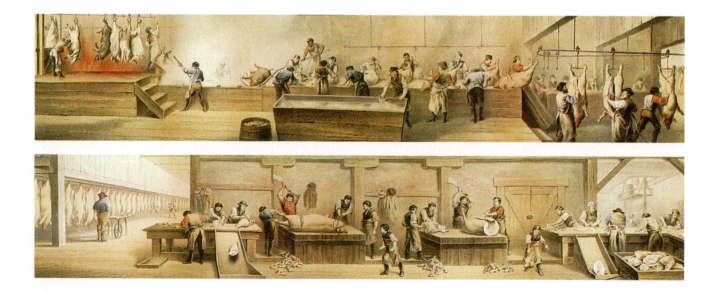

TABLE 10.1 Leading Branches of Manufacture, 1860

Item	Number of Workers	Value of Product	Value Added by Manufacture	Rank by Value Added
Cotton Textiles	115,000	$107.3 million	$54.7 million	1
Lumber	75,600	104.9 million	53.8 million	2
Boots and Shoes	123,000	91.9 million	49.2 million	3
Flour and Meal	27,700	248.6 million	40.1 million	4
Men's Clothing	114,800	80.8 million	36.7 million	5
Iron (cast, forged, etc.)	49,000	73.1 million	35.7 million	6
Machinery	41,200	52.0 million	32.5 million	7
Woolen Goods	40,600	60.7 million	25.0 million	8
Leather	22,700	67.3 million	22.8 million	9
Liquors	12,700	56.6 million	32.5 million	10

Source: Adapted from Douglass C. North, *Growth and Welfare in the American Past,* 2nd ed. (Paramus, NJ: Prentice-Hall, 1974), table 6.1.

specialized tasks performed under supervision by different individuals. For example, in the 1830s Cincinnati merchants built slaughterhouses that rationalized the process of butchering hogs—that is, subdivided the process into a series of specific tasks. A simple system of overhead rails moved the hog carcasses past workers who split the animals, removed various organs, and trimmed the carcasses into pieces. Then packers stuffed the cuts of pork into barrels and pickled them to prevent spoilage. The system was efficient and quick—sixty hogs per hour—and by the 1840s Cincinnati was butchering so many hogs that the city became known as "Porkopolis."

Some factories boasted impressive new technology. The prolific Delaware inventor Oliver Evans built a highly automated flour mill driven by waterpower. His machinery lifted the grain to the top of the mill, cleaned the grain as it fell into hoppers, ground it into flour, conveyed the flour back to the top of the mill, and then cooled the flour during its descent into barrels. Evans's factory, remarked one observer, "was as full of machinery as the case of a watch." It needed only six men to mill 100,000 bushels of grain a year.

Subsequently, factory owners used newly improved stationary steam engines to power their mills and began to

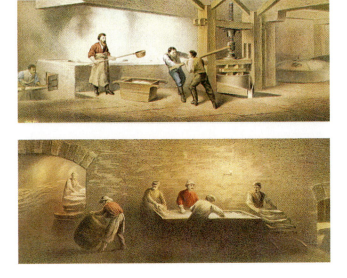

Pork Packing in Cincinnati
The only form of modern technology in this Cincinnati pork-packing plant was the overhead pulley system that carried hog carcasses past the workers. The plant's efficiency came from organization, a division of labor in which each worker performed a specific task. Such plants pioneered the design of the moving assembly lines that reached a high level of sophistication in the early-twentieth-century automobile factories of Henry Ford.
Cincinnati Historical Society.

manufacture new types of products. Before 1830 power-driven machines and assembly lines mainly processed agricultural goods—pork, leather, wool, and cotton; subsequently they were used to fabricate goods and machines made of metal. Cyrus McCormick of Chicago developed power-driven conveyor belts to assemble reaping machines, and Samuel Colt built an assembly-line factory in Hartford, Connecticut, to produce his invention—the "six-shooter" revolver, as it became known. As a team of British observers noted apprehensively, "The contriving and making of machinery has become so common in this country, and so many heads and hands are at work with extraordinary energy, that . . . it is to be feared that American manufacturers will become exporters not only to foreign countries, but even to England."

The Textile Industry and British Competition

British textile manufacturers were particularly worried about American competition. To protect its industrial leadership, the British government prohibited the export of textile machinery and the emigration of mechanics who knew how to build it. However, lured by high wages or offers of partnerships, thousands of British mechanics disguised themselves as ordinary laborers and set sail for the United States. By 1812 there were more than 300 British mechanics at work in the Philadelphia area alone.

Samuel Slater was the most important of the immigrants. Slater came to America in 1789 after working for Richard Arkwright, the inventor and operator of the most advanced British machinery for spinning cotton. Having memorized the design of Arkwright's machinery, the young Slater introduced his innovations in merchant Moses Brown's cotton mill in Providence, Rhode Island. The opening of Slater's factory in 1790 marks the advent of the American Industrial Revolution (see New Technology, "Cotton Spinning: From Spinsters to Machines," p. 289).

American and British Advantages.   In competing with British mills, American manufacturers had one major advantage: an abundance of natural resources. America's rich agriculture produced a wealth of cotton and wool, and from Maine to Delaware its rivers provided a cheap source of energy. As rivers cascaded downhill from the Appalachian foothills to the Atlantic coastal plain, they were easily harnessed to run power machinery. Industrial villages and towns sprang up along these waterways, dominated by massive textile mills—150 feet long, 40 feet wide, and four stories high (Map 10.1).

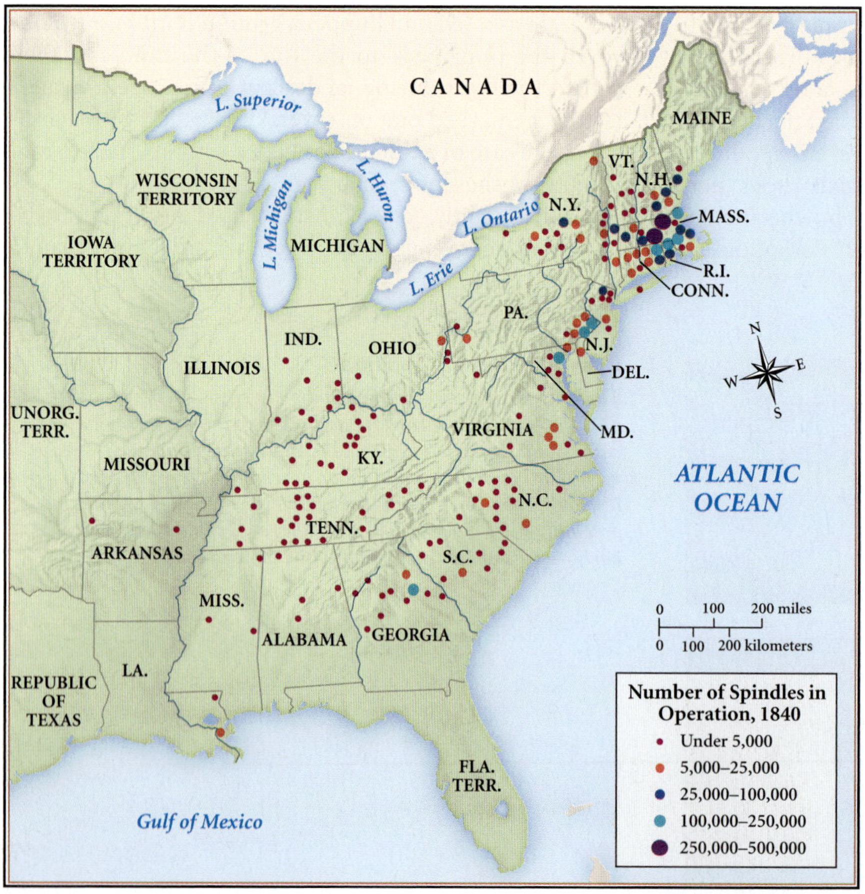

MAP 10.1 New England's Dominance in Cotton Spinning, 1840

Although the South grew the nation's cotton, Boston and Rhode Island entrepreneurs built most of the factories for spinning and weaving the cotton into cloth in New England, using the abundant waterpower of the region. The new factories relied on the labor of young farm women and, later, of immigrants from Ireland and French-speaking regions of Canada.

Cotton Spinning: From Spinsters to Machines

For centuries the making of cloth had been slow and laborious work, mostly done by women. Taking raw wool or cotton, women pulled out burrs and seeds and separated the fibers into strands by running over them with a comb or "card," a flat paddle studded with twigs or nails. Next they began the even more time-consuming task of spinning the fibers into cotton or woolen thread (or more bulky woolen yarn) by using hand- or foot-powered spinning machines. Finally, the women fitted hundreds of these threads into hand-powered looms so that they could be woven into cloth, sometimes by women but more often by men.

Despite its importance in cloth making, spinning had a low social value, in part because it was drudge work—slow, repetitive, and uninteresting. It became the work of women without power: young girls, grandmothers, and especially unmarried women. Living in the households of their fathers or brothers, unmarried women sat at the bottom of the family hierarchy, condemned to the menial tasks of cleaning, mending, and especially spinning. Indeed, the connection between spinning and never-married older women was so close that such women became (and remain) known as "spinsters."

The name should not have survived the Industrial Revolution, which transformed the processing of cotton and wool and made spinsters obsolete. By 1800 carding was no longer handwork, as water- or hand-powered carding machines turned raw cotton into clean fibers. Consisting of two or more cylinders covered with wire pins, the machines combed the fibers into parallel strands and fed them into other machines that wound the carded cotton into a long, loose rope called "roving."

Mechanization also revolutionized the technology of spinning. The key tool in spinning had always been the spindle, which first elongated the strands of fiber and then twisted them together to make strong threads or yarn. In 1765 the British inventor James Hargreaves devised a "spinning jenny" that imitated the function of spinning wheels. The jenny's operator manually turned a wheel that spun a series of spindles—from twenty-four to one hundred—each of which simultaneously drew out the roving and twisted it into thread. Using a jenny, one person could now do the work of dozens of spinsters, and in less time.

However, American textile manufacturers preferred another British invention—the spinning frame, patented by Richard Arkwright in 1769 and pirated to the United States by Samuel Slater. The spinning frame separated the functions of drawing and twisting. After two pairs of rollers had elongated the roving, it was passed down the arm of a flier, a device attached to a spindle. The flier twisted the roving into thread and wound it onto a bobbin attached to the spindle.

The spinning frame lowered production costs dramatically. The machine ran hundreds of spindles continuously on inexpensive waterpower and produced threads and yarn that were strong enough to be woven on the fast-moving, waterpowered looms that came into use during the 1820s. Most important from the manufacturers' perspective, the spinning frame required only low-skilled and low-priced labor. The operative had only to affix the roving to the frame and tie any threads that broke. In many American factories, tending spinning frames became the ill-paid work of young women and girls—such as the two hundred girls between the ages of six and thirteen employed at the Union Manufactory and McKim's Cotton Factory in Baltimore in 1820.

By a cruel twist of fate, spinning had once again become drudge work—repetitive, uninteresting, and low-paid. But now it was the work not of family-dependent "spinsters" but of wage-dependent juvenile "proletarians" (workers who had nothing to sell but their labor). In myriad such small transformations, the Industrial Revolution changed the character of American economic—and social—life.

Samuel Slater's Spinning Frame

Samuel Slater's frame for spinning wool was powered by water and could spin thread simultaneously onto ninety-six bobbins (forty-eight on each side of the lower part of the machine). The introduction of the spinning frame revolutionized textile manufacturing by dramatically increasing the output of a single worker.
Museum of History and Technology, Smithsonian Institution, Washington, DC.

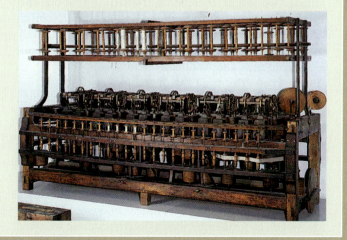

Nevertheless, the British producers easily undersold their American competitors. Thanks to cheap shipping and lower interest rates in Britain, they could import raw cotton from the United States, manufacture it into cloth, and sell it in America at a low price. Moreover, because British companies were better established, they could engage in cutthroat competition, cutting prices briefly but sharply to drive the newer American firms out of business. The most important British advantage was cheap labor. Britain had a larger population—about 12.6 million in 1810 compared with 7.3 million Americans—and thousands of landless laborers who were willing to take low-paying factory jobs. Since unskilled American workers could obtain good pay for farm or construction work, American manufacturers had to pay them higher wages.

To offset these British advantages American entrepreneurs sought assistance from the federal government. In 1816 Congress passed a tariff that gave manufacturers protection from low-cost imports of cotton cloth. New protective legislation in 1824 levied a tax of 35 percent on imported iron products, higher-grade woolen and cotton textiles, and various agricultural products, and the rate rose to 50 percent in 1828. But in 1833, under pressure from southern planters, western farmers, and urban consumers—who wanted to buy inexpensive imported manufactures—Congress began to reduce tariffs (see Chapter 11), causing some American textile firms to go out of business.

Improved Technology and Women Workers.
American producers adopted two other strategies to compete with their British rivals. First, they improved on British technology. In 1811 Francis Cabot Lowell, a wealthy Boston merchant, spent a holiday touring British textile mills. A well-educated and charming young man, he flattered his hosts by asking many questions, but his easy manner hid a serious purpose. Lowell secretly made detailed drawings of power machinery, and Paul Moody, an experienced American mechanic, then copied the machines and made improvements. In 1814 Lowell joined two other merchants, Nathan Appleton and Patrick Tracy Jackson, to form the Boston Manufacturing Company. Raising the staggering sum of $400,000, they built a textile plant on the Charles River in Waltham, Massachusetts. The Waltham factory was the first in America to perform all the operations of cloth making under one roof. Thanks to Moody's improvements, Waltham's power looms operated at higher speeds than British looms and needed fewer workers.

The second American strategy was to find less expensive workers. In the 1820s the Boston Manufacturing Company pioneered a labor system that became known as the "Waltham plan." The company recruited thousands of farm girls and women, who would work at low wages, as textile operatives. To attract these workers, the company provided boardinghouses and cultural activities such as evening lectures. The mill owners reassured anxious parents by enforcing strict curfews, prohibiting alcoholic beverages, and requiring regular church attendance. At Lowell (1822), Chicopee (1823), and other sites in Massachusetts and New Hampshire, the company built new cotton factories on the Waltham plan; other Boston-owned firms quickly followed suit.

By the early 1830s more than 40,000 New England women were working in textile mills. Lucy Larcom became an operative when she was eleven so that she would not be "a trouble or burden or expense" to her widowed mother. Other women sent their savings home to help their fathers pay off farm mortgages, defray the cost of schooling for their brothers, or accumulate a dowry for themselves. A few just had a good time. Susan Brown, who worked as a Lowell weaver, spent half of her earnings on food and lodging and much of the rest for entertainment—attending fifteen plays, concerts, and

Mill Girl, c. 1850
This fine daguerreotype (an early form of photography) shows a neatly dressed textile worker about twelve years old. The harsh working conditions in the mill have taken a toll on her spirit and body: the young girl's eyes and mouth show little joy or life and her hands are rough and swollen. She probably worked either as a knotter, tying broken threads on spinning jennies, or a warper, straightening out the strands of cotton or wool as they entered the loom. Jack Naylor Collection.

Lucy Larcom

Early Days at Lowell

Lucy Larcom (1824–1893) went to work in a textile mill in Lowell, Massachusetts, when she was eleven years old and remained there for a decade. She then migrated to Illinois with her sisters and a great tide of other New Englanders. In later life Larcom became a teacher and a writer; in her autobiography she decribed the impact of industrial labor on the lives and outlook of women from farms and rural villages.

I never cared much for machinery. The buzzing and hissing and whizzing of pulleys and rollers and spindles and flyers around me often grew tiresome. I could not see into their complications, or feel interested in them. But in a room below us we were sometimes allowed to peer in through a sort of blind door at the great water-wheel that carried the works of the whole mill. It was so huge we could only watch a few of its spokes at a time, and part of its dripping rim, moving with a slow, measured strength through the darkness that shut it in. It impressed me with something of the awe which comes to us in thinking of the great Power which keeps the mechanism of the universe in motion. . . .

We did not call ourselves ladies. We did not forget that we were working girls, wearing coarse aprons suitable to our work, and that there was some danger of our becoming drudges. I know that sometimes the confinement of the mill became very wearisome to me. In the sweet June weather I would lean far out of the window, and try not to hear the unceasing clash of sound inside.

Looking away to the hills, my whole stifled being would cry out

Oh, that I had wings!

Still I was there from choice, and

The prison unto which we doom ourselves,
No prison is.

I regard it as one of the privileges of my youth that I was permitted to grow up among these active, interesting girls, whose lives were not mere echoes of other lives, but had principle and purpose distinctly their own. Their vigor of character was a natural development. The New Hampshire girls who came to Lowell were descendants of the sturdy backwoodsmen who settled that State scarcely a hundred years before. Their grandmothers had suffered the hardships of frontier life. . . . Those young women did justice to their inheritance. They were earnest and capable; ready to undertake anything that was worth doing. My dreamy, indolent nature was shamed into activity among them. They gave me a larger, firmer ideal of womanhood. . . .

Country girls were naturally independent, and the feeling that at this new work the few hours they had of every-day leisure were entirely their own was a satisfaction to them. They preferred it to going out as "hired help." It was like a young man's pleasure in entering upon business for himself. Girls had never tried that experiment before, and they liked it. It brought out in them a dormant strength of character which the world did not previously see.

Source: Lucy Larcom, *A New England Girlhood* (Boston: Houghton Mifflin, 1889), 153–55, 181–83, 196–200.

lectures and taking a two-day excursion to Boston. Like many other textile operatives, Brown's spirits were gradually ground down by the monotony and never-ending rigor of factory labor—twelve hours a day, six days a week. After eight months she quit, probably to take a break at home and then to move to another mill. Whatever the hardships, waged work gave many young women a new sense of freedom and autonomy. "Don't I feel independent!" a mill worker wrote to her sister in the 1840s. "The thought that I am living on no one is a happy one indeed to me" (see American Voices, "Lucy Larcom: Early Days at Lowell," above).

The owners of the Boston Manufacturing Company were even happier. By combining improved technology, female labor, and **tariff** protection, they could sell cheap textiles for a lower price than their British rivals could. They also had an advantage over textile manufacturers in New York and Pennsylvania, where farmworkers were better paid than in New England and textile wages consequently were higher. Manufacturers in those states pursued a different strategy, modifying traditional technology to produce higher-quality cloth, also with good results. In 1825 Thomas Jefferson, once a critic of industrialization, expressed his pride in the American achievement: "Our manufacturers are now very nearly on a footing with those of England."

American Mechanics and Technological Innovation

By the 1820s American-born craftsmen had replaced British immigrants at the cutting edge of technological innovation. Although few of these mechanics had a formal education and once had been viewed as "mean" or even "servile" workers, they now claimed respect as "men professing an ingenious art." In 1837 one such inventor, Richard Garsed, experimented with improvements on power looms in his father's factory and in three years nearly doubled their speed. By 1846 Garsed had patented a cam and harness device that allowed fabrics such as damask (which contains elaborate designs) to be woven by machine.

In the Philadelphia region the most important inventors came from the remarkable Sellars family. Samuel Sellars Jr. invented a machine for twisting worsted woolen yarn. His son John devised more efficient ways of using waterpower to run the family's sawmills and built a machine to weave wire sieves. John's sons and grandsons built machine shops that turned out a variety of new products: riveted leather fire hoses, papermaking equipment, and eventually locomotives. In 1824 the Sellars family and other mechanics founded the Franklin Institute in Philadelphia. Named after Benjamin Franklin, whom the mechanics admired for his scientific accomplishments and idealization of hard work, the institute fostered a sense of professional identity. The Franklin Institute published a journal; provided high-school-level instruction in mechanics, chemistry, mathematics, and mechanical drawing; and organized annual fairs to exhibit new products. Craftsmen in Ohio and other states soon established their own mechanics institutes, which played a crucial role in disseminating technical knowledge and encouraging innovation. Around 1820 the United States Patent Office had issued about two hundred patents on new inventions each year, mostly to gentlemen and merchants. By 1850 it was awarding a thousand patents annually, mostly to mechanics from modest backgrounds, and by 1860 more than four thousand.

During these years American craftsmen pioneered the development of **machine tools**—machines for making other machines—thus facilitating the rapid spread of the Industrial Revolution. **Mechanics** in the textile industry invented lathes, planers, and boring machines that turned out standardized parts, making it possible to manufacture new spinning jennies and weaving looms at a low cost and to repair broken machines. Moreover, this machinery was precise enough in design and construction to operate at higher speeds than British equipment.

Technological innovation swept through the rest of American manufacturing. For example, in 1832 the mechanics employed by Samuel W. Collins in his Connecticut ax-making company built a vastly improved die-forging machine—a device that pressed and hammered hot metal into dies, or cutting forms. Using the improved machine, a skilled worker could increase the production of ax heads from twelve to three hundred a day. In the South, Welsh- and American-born mechanics at the Tredegar Iron Works helped to make Richmond, Virginia, a regional manufacturing center. Especially important technical advances came in the firearms industry. To fill large-scale contracts for guns from the federal government, Eli Whitney and his coworkers in Connecticut developed machine tools that produced interchangeable, precision-crafted parts (see American Lives, "Eli Whitney: Machine Builder and Promoter," p. 294). After Whitney's death his partner, John H. Hall, an engineer at the federal armory at Harpers Ferry, Virginia, built a series of sixteen special-purpose lathes to make a gun stock out of sawn lumber and an array of machine tools to work metal: turret lathes, milling machines, and precision grinders. Thereafter, manufacturers could use those machine tools to produce complicated machinery with great speed, at low cost, and in large quantities.

With this expansion in the availability of machines, the American Industrial Revolution came of age. The sheer volume of output caused some products—Remington rifles, Singer sewing machines, and Yale locks—to become household names in the United States and abroad. After showing their machine-tooled goods at the Crystal Palace Exhibition in London in 1851 (the first major international display of industrial goods), Remington, Singer, and other American businesses built factories in Great Britain and soon dominated many European markets.

Wage Workers and the Labor Movement

As the Industrial Revolution gathered momentum, it changed the nature of work and of workers' lives. Each decade, more and more white Americans ceased to be self-employed and took jobs as wage-earning workers. They had little security of employment or control over their working conditions.

The Emergence of Unions.   Some wageworkers labored as journeymen, having acquired some of the skills of a traditional artisan craft. These carpenters,

Woodworker, c. 1850
Skilled cabinetmakers took great pride in their work, which was often intricately designed and beautifully executed. To underline the dignity of his occupation, this woodworker poses in formal dress and proudly displays the tools of his craft. A belief in the value of labor was an important ingredient of the artisan-republican ideology held by many workers. Library of Congress.

house painters, stonecutters, masons, nailers, and cabinetmakers had both valuable skills and a strong sense of craft identity. Consequently, they were able to form unions and bargain with the master artisans who employed them. The journeymen's main concern was the increasing length of the workday, which deprived them of time to spend with their families or improve their education. During the eighteenth century the workday for apprentices and journeymen workers in the building trades had averaged about twelve hours, including breaks for meals. By the 1820s masters were demanding a longer day during the summer, when it stayed light longer, while paying journeymen the old daily rate. In response, 600 carpenters in Boston went on strike in 1825, demanding a ten-hour workday, 6 A.M. to 6 P.M., with an hour each for breakfast and a noontime meal. Although the Boston protest failed, two years later journeymen carpenters in Philadelphia won a similar strike and then helped found the Mechanics' Union of Trade Associations. This citywide organization of fifty unions and 10,000 Philadelphia wage earners set forth a broad program of reform, demanding "a just balance of power . . . between all the various classes." To secure this

goal, in 1828 the Philadelphia artisans founded the Working Men's Party, which campaigned for the abolition of banks, equal taxation, and a universal system of public education. By the mid-1830s skilled building-trades workers had forced many urban employers to accept a ten-hour workday and persuaded President Andrew Jackson to set a similar standard at the Philadelphia navy yard.

Artisans whose occupations were threatened by industrialization were less successful in controlling their work lives. As aggressive entrepreneurs and machine technology changed the nature of work, shoemakers, hatters, printers, furniture makers, and weavers faced declining incomes, unemployment, and loss of status. To avoid the regimentation of factory work some artisans in these trades moved to small towns or set up specialized shops. In New York City, 800 highly skilled cabinetmakers worked in artisan-like shops that made fashionable or custom-made furniture. In status and income they outranked a much larger group of 3,200 semitrained workers—derogatively called "botches"—who labored in factories and turned out cheap, mass-produced tables and chairs. The coming of the new industrial system had divided the traditional artisan class into two groups: self-employed craftsmen and wage-earning workers.

In many industries these wage-earning workers banded together to form unions and bargain for higher wages. However, under English and American common law, workers' organizations for raising wages were illegal—"a government unto themselves," in the words of a Philadelphia judge—because they prevented other workers from hiring out for whatever wages they wished. Despite such legal obstacles, unions sprang up whenever wages fell and working conditions became intolerable. In 1830 in Lynn, Massachusetts, journeymen shoemakers founded a Mutual Benefit Society, which quickly spread to other shoemaking centers. "The division of society into the producing and nonproducing classes," the journeymen explained, had made workers like themselves into a mere "commodity" whose labor could be bought and sold without regard for their welfare. As another group of workers put it, "The capitalist has no other interest in us, than to get as much labor out of us as possible. We are hired men, and hired men, like hired horses, have no souls." In 1834 local unions from Boston to Philadelphia combined their resources in the National Trades' Union, the first regional union of different trades.

Labor Ideology and Strikes. Union leaders mounted a critique of the new industrial order, devising an artisan-republican ideology that celebrated the labor and autonomy of working people. Worried that waged workers were becoming "slaves to a monied aristocracy," they condemned the new outwork and factory systems in

Eli Whitney: Machine Builder and Promoter

Eli Whitney

Eli Whitney posed for this portrait in the 1820s, when he had achieved both prosperity and social standing. Whitney's success as an inventor prompted the artist, his young New Haven neighbor Samuel F. B. Morse, to turn his creative energies from painting to industrial technology. By the 1840s Morse had devised the first successful commercial telegraph.
Yale University Art Gallery, gift of George Hoadley, B.A. 1801.

Eli Whitney (1765–1825) thought life was "a Lottery in which many draw blanks," but thanks to the opportunities offered by the Industrial Revolution, that was not to be his fate. Whitney's luck, combined with intense social ambition and exceptional talents for self-advertisement and mechanical innovation, allowed him to rise in the world and to exert a significant influence on the development of industry in America.

Born into a middling farm family in Massachusetts, Eli Whitney found routine farming chores boring and even depressing. As often as he could, the young lad fled to the farm's workshop to repair household furniture and farm tools. As his sister recalled, Eli "possessed a great measure of affability" and enjoyed talking with his family's neighbors. Those conversations sharpened Whitney's awareness of the limits of New England's mature farm economy—how its poor soil and overcrowded towns condemned most young people to lives of unrelenting labor and meager economic rewards.

The outbreak of the American Revolution opened new doors for the restless youth. In 1779, when he was fourteen, Eli went into business for himself. Persuading his father to install a forge in the workshop, he manufactured nails and knife blades. This enterprise flourished during the war, but peace brought an avalanche of cheap nails from Britain, ruining Eli's market. So the young entrepreneur began producing women's hatpins and men's walking sticks.

Despite his success, Whitney realized that his workshop and his father's small farm would not provide a living for himself, two younger brothers, and four sisters. Moreover, the young man aspired to wealth and high social status, ambitious goals that would be facilitated by a college education—then the privileged preserve of a mere 1 percent of American men. To acquire the necessary training in English grammar, classics, and mathematics, Eli enrolled at Leicester Academy, financing his studies by teaching primary school. By 1789, at age twenty-four, Whitney finally had the skills and the social connections necessary to win admission to Yale College.

At Yale, Whitney pursued a traditional curriculum, with a heavy emphasis on ancient languages, history, rhetoric, and religion. The absence of courses in science or engineering was of little concern because Eli wanted to exploit the social advantages of his college education. Upon Whitney's graduation in 1792, the president of Yale found him a position as a tutor on a Georgia plantation. In traveling south Whitney met Catherine Greene, the young widow of the Revolutionary War general Nathanael Greene, who was charmed by Whitney's "affability" and Yale-bred manners. When Whitney's tutoring position fell through, she invited him for an extended visit to her Georgia plantation, Mulberry Grove.

The exclusive social world of the southern planters fascinated the young New Englander and he paid close attention to their efforts to expand cotton production. Encouraged by Catherine Greene, he set up a workshop and built a simple machine to separate cottonseeds from the delicate fibers that surrounded them. Applying techniques learned in producing women's hatpins, Whitney fashioned thin tines of metal and arrayed them in ranks to

An Early Cotton Gin

As the worker turned the crank of the gin, brushes at the back of the machine pushed the bolls of cotton through an array of wire teeth, which separated the seeds in the bolls from the cotton fiber. The gin processed cotton rapidly and cheaply, and its efficiency facilitated the dramatic expansion of the cotton textile industry. Smithsonian Institution.

create a rudimentary cotton gin, the machine that would revolutionize the processing of cotton. In 1793 Whitney returned to New Haven and began manufacturing gins in quantity. "One of the most Respectable Gentlemen in N. Haven," the young manufacturer proudly reported to his father, said "he would rather be the author of the [my] Invention than the prime minister of England."

If the cotton gin brought prestige, it did not yield wealth. Although Whitney had patented his invention in 1794, he was unable to control the market. Exploiting Whitney's ideas, numerous planters built their own gins, while other manufacturers made slight improvements on his design and competed with him for sales. In a futile bid to assert his patent rights and collect royalties, Whitney filed scores of lawsuits, using up the profits from the sales of his own gins and falling into debt.

To restore his finances, Whitney decided to manufacture military weapons—a product with a guaranteed government market. His Yale connections again served him well. While patenting his cotton gin, he had formed a friendship with a Yale alumnus, Oliver Wolcott, who had become secretary of the treasury. In 1798 Whitney convinced Wolcott that he could mechanize the production of firearms and turn out guns at an unprecedented

scale and pace. Whitney's timing was superb. The new national government had established two armories— in Springfield, Massachusetts, and Harpers Ferry, Virginia—but their production was dismal. To prepare for a possible war with France, Congress had just authorized the Treasury Department to contract for arms with private parties. Almost immediately Wolcott engaged Whitney to manufacture ten thousand muskets within twenty-eight months.

Whitney knew little about muskets, but he had a clear understanding of machine tools and was confident that his tools could produce interchangeable musket parts. As he wrote to Wolcott, "[I will] form the tools so that the tools themselves shall fashion the work and give to every part its just proportion." The young inventor quickly devised improved forms and jigs to guide the hands of mechanics; crafted the first milling machine, which used sharp teeth on a gearlike wheel to cut metal; and achieved a greater interchangeability of parts than previous manufacturers.

Despite these technical advances, Whitney was unable to fulfill his original contract on time. It took ten years—not twenty-eight months—to produce the ten thousand muskets, and even then some components had to be made by hand. But Wolcott continued to support the young inventor, as did the government inspector in New Haven, yet another Yale alumnus, and a group of ten prominent citizens of New Haven, including Pierpont Edwards, the wealthy son of the preacher and philosopher Jonathan Edwards (see Chapter 4).

Whitney also won the backing of Thomas Jefferson, who had been interested in interchangeable parts since the 1780s. Because of his curiosity about science, Jefferson knew of Whitney's cotton gin and in 1800 had witnessed his dramatic public demonstration of interchangeability. Understanding that these techniques would vastly increase the productivity of American manufacturers, Jefferson helped Whitney to win new contracts for military weapons during the War of 1812. These contracts, along with shrewd investment advice from Oliver Wolcott, gave Eli the wealth and social position that he had long craved. Yale awarded him an honorary master's degree and in 1817 he joined one of New England's most respected families, marrying Henrietta Edwards, the daughter of Pierpont Edwards.

When Whitney died in 1825, he had still not achieved his goal of mass production. But his revolutionary technical advances in the design of machine tools had provided a great stimulus to industrial production in the United States. By midcentury American manufacturers led the world in the output of goods that used standardized, interchangeable parts. As a team of British observers noted with admiration, many American products were made "with machinery applied to almost every process . . . all reduced to an almost perfect system of manufacture."

which "capital and labor stand opposed." To restore a just society, they devised a **labor theory of value**, arguing that the price of a product should reflect the labor required to make it. Moreover, they wanted artisans and farmers (and not merchants and factory owners) to reap most of the profit from the sales of products, to enable them "to live as comfortably as others." Appealing to the spirit of the American Revolution, which had destroyed the aristocracy of birth, they called for a new revolution to destroy the aristocracy of capital. Armed with this artisan-republican ideology, in 1836 union men organized nearly fifty strikes for higher wages.

Women textile operatives were equally active. Competition in the cotton textile industry was fierce as output grew (at 5 percent per year) and prices fell (about 1 percent per year). As prices and profits declined, employers reduced workers' wages and imposed more stringent work rules. In 1828 women mill workers in Dover, New Hampshire, struck against new rules, winning some relief; six years later more than 800 Dover women walked out to protest wage cuts. In Lowell, Massachusetts, 2,000 women operatives backed a strike by withdrawing their savings from an employer-owned bank. The Boston *Transcript* reported that "one of the leaders mounted a pump, and made a flaming . . . speech on the rights of women and the iniquities of the 'monied aristocracy.'" When conditions did not improve, young New England women refused to enter the mills, and impoverished Irish (and later French Canadian) immigrants took their places. Many of the new textile workers were men, foreshadowing the emergence of a predominantly male system of factory labor (see Chapter 17).

By the 1850s workers faced yet another threat to their jobs. As machines produced more goods, the supply of manufactures exceeded the demand for them, prompting employers to lay off or dismiss workers. One episode of overproduction preceded the Panic of 1857—a financial crisis sparked by excess railroad investments—and resulted in a major recession. Unemployment rose to 10 percent, reminding Americans of the social costs of the new—and otherwise very successful—system of industrial production.

The Expansion of Markets

As American factories and farms turned out more goods, merchants and legislators created faster and cheaper ways to get those products to consumers—setting in motion a **Market Revolution**. Beginning in the 1820s they promoted the construction of a massive system of canals and roads to link the Atlantic coast states with one another and with the new states in the trans-Appalachian West. By 1860 nearly one-third of the nation's people lived in the Midwest (the five states carved out of the Northwest Territory—Ohio, Indiana,

Illinois, Michigan, and Wisconsin—along with Missouri, Iowa, and Minnesota), where they created a complex society and economy that increasingly resembled that of the Northeast.

Migration to the Southwest and the Midwest

After 1820 vast numbers of men and women migrated to the West, following in the footsteps of the thousands who had already left the seaboard states (Map 10.2). Abandoned farms and homes dotted the countryside of the Carolinas, Vermont, and New Hampshire. "It is useless to seek to excite patriotic emotions" for one's state of birth, complained an easterner, "when self-interest speaks so loudly." Some migrant families wanted to acquire enough land to settle their children on nearby farms, recreating traditional rural communities. Others were more entrepreneurial and hoped for greater profits from the fertile soil of the western territories. By 1840 about 5 million people lived west of the Appalachians.

As in the past the new pioneers migrated in three great streams. In the South plantation owners encouraged by the voracious demand for raw cotton moved more slaves into the Old Southwest (see Chapter 9), expanding the cotton kingdom in Louisiana, Mississippi, and Alabama and pushing on to Missouri (1821) and Arkansas (1836). "The Alabama Feaver rages here with great violence," a North Carolina planter remarked, "and has carried off vast numbers of our Citizens."

Small-scale farmers from the Upper South, especially Virginia and Kentucky, created a second stream as they crossed the Ohio River into the Northwest Territory. Some of these migrants were fleeing planter-dominated slave states. In a free community, thought Peter Cartwright, a Methodist lay preacher from southwestern Kentucky, "I would be entirely clear of the evil of slavery . . . [and] could raise my children to work where work was not thought a degradation." These southerners introduced corn and hog farming to the southern regions of Ohio, Indiana, and Illinois.

A third stream of migrants continued to pour out of the overcrowded farming communities of New England. Thousands of settlers flowed first into upstate New York and then into the fertile farmlands of the Old Northwest, establishing wheat farms throughout the Great Lakes Basin: northern Ohio, northern Illinois, Michigan (admitted in 1837), Iowa (1846), and Wisconsin (1848).

To meet the demand for cheap farmsteads, in 1820 Congress reduced the price of federal land from $2.00 an acre to $1.25—just enough to cover the cost of the survey and sale. For $100 a farmer could buy eighty acres, the minimum required under federal law. Many American families saved enough in a few years to make the minimum purchase and used money from the sale of an old farm to finance the move. By 1860 the

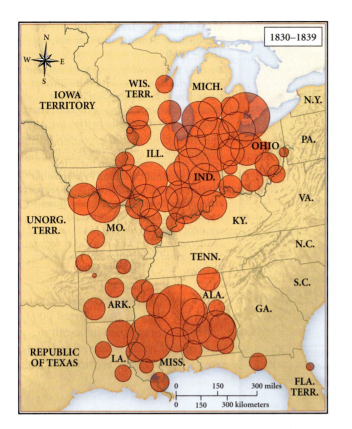

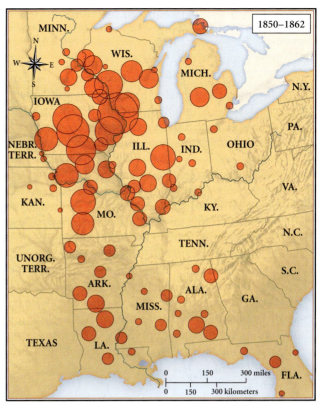

MAP 10.2 Western Land Sales, 1830–1839 and 1850–1862

The federal government set up land offices to sell farmland to western settlers. During the 1830s the offices sold huge amounts of land in the corn and wheat belt of the Old Northwest (Ohio, Indiana, Illinois, and Michigan) and the cotton belt of the Old Southwest (especially Alabama and Mississippi). By the 1850s most government land sales were in the upper Mississippi River Valley (particularly Iowa and Wisconsin). Each circle centers on a government land office and depicts the relative amount of land sold at that office.

population center of American society had shifted significantly to the west.

The Transportation Revolution Forges Regional Ties

To enhance the "common wealth" of their citizens, the federal and state governments took measures to create a larger market. Beginning in the 1790s they chartered private companies to build toll-charging turnpikes in well-populated areas and subsidized road construction in the West. The most significant feat was the National Road, which started in Cumberland, Maryland, passed Wheeling (then in Virginia) in 1818, crossed the Ohio River in 1833, and reached Vandalia, Illinois, in 1839 (Map 10.3). The National Road and other interregional highways carried migrants and their heavily loaded wagons to the West, where they passed herds of livestock being driven to eastern markets. However, such long-distance road travel was too slow and expensive to transport manufactured goods and heavy farm crops.

Canals and Steamboats. To carry wheat, corn, and manufactured goods to far-flung markets, Americans developed a water-borne transportation system of unprecedented size, complexity, and cost, beginning with the Erie Canal. When the New York legislature approved the building of the canal in 1817, no artificial waterway in the United States was longer than 28 miles—a reflection of their huge capital cost and the lack of American engineering expertise. The New York project had three things in its favor: the vigorous support of New York City merchants, who wanted access to western markets; the backing of New York's governor, DeWitt Clinton, who persuaded the legislature to finance the waterway from tax revenues, tolls, and bond sales to foreign investors; and the relative gentleness of the terrain west of Albany. Even so, the task was enormous. Workers—many of them Irish immigrants—had to dig out millions of cubic yards of soil, quarry thousands of tons of rock to build huge locks to raise and lower boats, and construct vast reservoirs to ensure a steady supply of water.

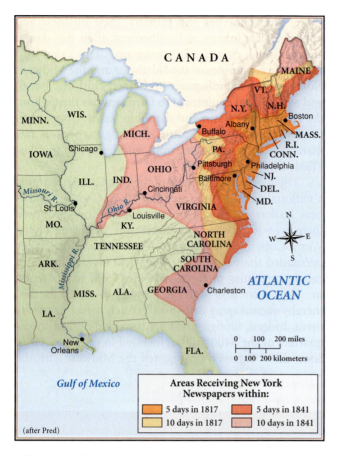

MAP 10.4 The Speed of News in 1817 and 1841

The transportation revolution increased the speed of trade and communication between the Atlantic seaports and the towns of the interior. Aggressive entrepreneurs provided for the national circulation of daily New York City newspapers, and by 1841 many parts of the country received economic and other news from New York in less than ten days. By 1860 telegraph lines ran between major cities in the Northeast, allowing for instantaneous communication.

For more help analyzing this map, see the ONLINE STUDY GUIDE at bedfordstmartins.com/henretta.

interior. In 1830 a traveler or a letter from New York could go by water to Buffalo or Pittsburgh in less than a week and to Detroit or St. Louis in two weeks. Thirty years earlier the same journeys, by road or sail, had taken twice as long (Map 10.4).

Various agencies of the national government played key roles in the creation of this interregional system of transportation. Following the passage of the Post Office Act of 1792, the mail network grew rapidly—to eight hundred post offices by 1800 and more than eight thousand by 1830—and safely carried thousands of letters and millions of dollars of banknotes from one end of the country to the other. The Supreme Court, headed by John Marshall, likewise encouraged interstate communication and trade by striking down state restrictions on commerce. In the crucial case of *Gibbons v. Ogden* (1824) the Court voided a New York law that created a monopoly on steamboat travel into New York City, ruling that the federal government had paramount authority over interstate commerce (see Chapter 8). This decision meant that no local or state monopolies—or tariffs—would impede the flow of goods and services across the nation.

Railroads and Regional Ties. Another product of industrial technology—the railroad—created close ties between the Northeast and the Midwest (Map 10.5). As late as 1852 canals were carrying twice the tonnage of railroads, but over the next six years track mileage increased dramatically and railroads became the nation's main carriers of freight. Serviced by a vast network of locomotive and freight-car repair shops, the Erie Railroad, the Pennsylvania Railroad, and other major long-distance railroad lines connected the Atlantic ports—New York, Philadelphia, and Boston—with the Great Lakes cities of Cleveland and Chicago. Each year more and more midwestern grain moved east by rail rather than south by barge down the Ohio and Mississippi Rivers.

Tied together by the steel rails that ran along the route of New England migration, the Midwest and the Northeast increasingly resembled each other in ethnic composition, cultural values, and technical skills. The first migrants to the Midwest had relied on manufactured goods made in Britain or in the Northeast. They bought high-quality shovels and spades fabricated at the Delaware Iron Works, axes forged in Connecticut factories, and steel horseshoes manufactured in Troy, New York. By the 1830s midwestern entrepreneurs were producing many of these goods. As a blacksmith in Grand Detour, Illinois, John Deere made his first steel plow out of old saws in 1837; ten years later he opened a factory in Moline, Illinois, that used mass-production techniques. His steel plows, superior in strength to the cast-iron model developed earlier in New York by Jethro Wood, soon dominated the midwestern market. Other midwestern companies—McCormick and Hussey—mass-produced self-raking reapers that allowed a farmer

great port cities of New York and Philadelphia (via the Erie and Pennsylvania Canals) and New Orleans (via the Ohio and Mississippi Rivers).

The steamboat, another product of the industrial age, ensured the success of this vast transportation system. The engineer-inventor Robert Fulton had built the first American steamboat, the *Clermont*, which he navigated up the Hudson River in 1807. However, the first steamboats consumed huge amounts of wood or coal and could not navigate shallow western rivers. During the 1820s engineers broadened the hulls of these boats, thereby enlarging their cargo capacity and giving them a shallower draft. The improved design cut the cost of upstream river transport in half and dramatically increased the flow of goods, people, and news into the

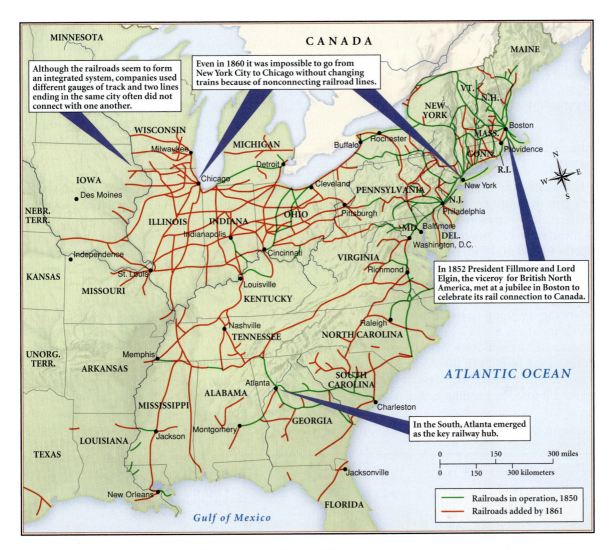

MINNESOTA

CANADA

MAINE

Although the railroads seem to form an integrated system, companies used different gauges of track and two lines ending in the same city often did not connect with one another.

Even in 1860 it was impossible to go from New York City to Chicago without changing trains because of nonconnecting railroad lines.

WISCONSIN

MICHIGAN

Milwaukee

Detroit

Chicago

Buffalo

Rochester

NEW YORK

VT.

N.H.

MASS.

Boston

Providence

CONN.

R.I.

Cleveland

PENNSYLVANIA

New York

N.J.

IOWA

Des Moines

ILLINOIS

INDIANA

OHIO

Pittsburgh

Philadelphia

NEBR. TERR.

Indianapolis

Cincinnati

MD.

Baltimore

DEL.

Washington, D.C.

In 1852 President Fillmore and Lord Elgin, the viceroy for British North America, met at a jubilee in Boston to celebrate its rail connection to Canada.

Independence

St. Louis

KANSAS

MISSOURI

Louisville

KENTUCKY

VIRGINIA

Richmond

UNORG. TERR.

Nashville

TENNESSEE

Raleigh

NORTH CAROLINA

ATLANTIC OCEAN

Memphis

ARKANSAS

Atlanta

SOUTH CAROLINA

ALABAMA

MISSISSIPPI

Montgomery

Jackson

GEORGIA

Charleston

In the South, Atlanta emerged as the key railway hub.

TEXAS

LOUISIANA

0   150   300 miles

0   150   300 kilometers

New Orleans

Jacksonville

FLORIDA

Gulf of Mexico

—— Railroads in operation, 1850
—— Railroads added by 1861

MAP 10.5 Railroads of the North and South, 1850–1860

In the decade before the Civil War, entrepreneurs in the Northeast and the Midwest laid thousands of miles of new railroad lines, providing those regions with extensive and dense transportation systems that stimulated economic development. The South built a much simpler system. In all regions, railroad companies used different track gauges, which hindered the efficient flow of traffic.

to harvest twelve acres of grain a day (rather than the two or three acres he could cut by hand).

The maritime trade that linked northeastern cotton brokers and textile plants with southern planters increased the wealth of these two regions as well but did not produce a similar social and economic order. Southern investors continued to concentrate their capital in the plantation economy, investing in land and slaves, with impressive economic results. By the 1840s the South was producing more than two-thirds of the world's cotton and accounted for almost two-thirds of the total value of American exports. Except in Richmond, Virginia, planters did not invest the profits from the cotton trade in local industries but continued to buy manufactures from the Northeast and Britain. Moreover, the

South did not develop a well-educated workforce. Planters wanted compliant workers who would be content with the drudgery of agricultural work, so they trained most of their slaves as field hands (allowing only a few to learn the arts of the blacksmith, carpenter, or bricklayer). Likewise, they made few efforts to provide blacks or ordinary whites with elementary instruction in reading or arithmetic. At the height of the prosperity of the slave regime, most African Americans and about 20 percent of white southerners could not read or write (as compared with less than 1 percent in New England). Lacking cities, factories, and highly trained workers, the South remained an agricultural economy that brought higher living standards only to the 25 percent of the white population who owned plantations and slaves. By

1860 the southern economy generated an average annual per capita income of $103, while the more productive economic system of the North created an average income of $141. The national system of commerce had accentuated the agricultural character of the South even as it helped to create a diversified economy in the Midwest.

The Growth of Cities and Towns

The expansion of industry and trade led to a dramatic increase in the urban population. In 1820 there were only 58 towns in the nation with more than 2,500 inhabitants; by 1840 there were 126 urban centers, located mostly in the Northeast and Midwest. During those two decades the total number of city dwellers grew fourfold, from 443,000 to 1,844,000.

The most rapid growth occurred in the new industrial towns that sprang up along rivers at the fall line (the point at which the rivers began a rapid descent to the coastal plain). In 1822 the Boston Manufacturing Company built a complex of mills in the sleepy Merrimack River village of East Chelmsford, Massachusetts, quickly transforming it into the bustling textile factory town of Lowell. Hartford, Connecticut; Trenton, New Jersey; and Wilmington, Delaware, also became urban centers as mill owners exploited the waterpower of the nearby rivers and recruited workers from the surrounding countryside.

Western commercial cities such as New Orleans, Pittsburgh, Cincinnati, and Louisville grew almost as rapidly. The initial expansion of these cities resulted from their location at points where goods were transferred from one mode of transport, such as canal boats or farmers' wagons, to another, such as steamboats or sailing vessels. As the midwestern population grew during the 1830s and 1840s, St. Louis, Rochester, Buffalo, and Detroit emerged as dynamic centers of commerce. Merchants and bankers settled in those cities, developing the marketing, provisioning, and financial services that were essential to farmers and small-town merchants in the hinterland (Map 10.6).

Within a few decades these midwestern commercial hubs—joined by Cleveland and Chicago—became manufacturing centers as well. Exploiting these cities' locations as key junctions for railroad lines and steamboats, entrepreneurs established flour mills, packing plants, and docks and provided work for hundreds of

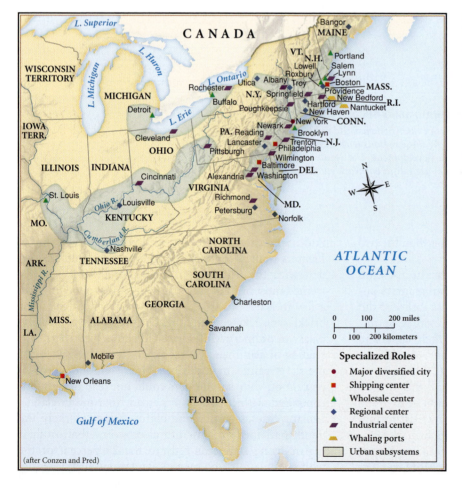

MAP 10.6 The Nation's Major Cities in 1840

By 1840 the United States boasted three major networks of cities. The string of port cities on the Atlantic—from Boston to Baltimore—served as centers for import merchants, banks, insurance companies, ready-made clothing manufacturers, and many other businesses, and their reach extended far into the interior—nationwide in the case of New York City. A second group of cities stretched along Lake Erie and included the wholesale distribution hubs of Buffalo and Detroit and the manufacturing center of Cleveland. A third urban system extended along the Ohio River, comprising the industrial cities of Cincinnati and Pittsburgh and the wholesale hubs of Louisville and St. Louis.

artisans and laborers. In 1846 Cyrus McCormick moved his reaper factory from western Virginia to Chicago to be closer to his midwestern customers. St. Louis and Chicago were the fastest-growing boom towns and by 1860 had become the nation's third and fourth largest cities, respectively, after New York and Philadelphia.

Yet the old Atlantic seaports—Boston, Philadelphia, Baltimore, Charleston, and especially New York—remained important for their foreign commerce and increasingly as centers of finance and manufacturing. In 1817 New York merchants founded the New York Stock Exchange, which soon became the nation's chief market for securities. The New York metropolis grew at a phenomenal rate; between 1820 and 1860 the population quadrupled to more than 800,000 as tens of thousands of German and Irish immigrants poured into the city. Drawing on the abundant supply of labor, New York became a center of small-scale manufacturing. Entrepreneurs also developed the ready-made clothing industry, which relied on the labor of thousands of low-paid seamstresses, both native- and foreign-born. "The wholesale clothing establishments are . . . absorbing the business of the country," a "Country Tailor" complained to the New York *Tribune*, "casting many an honest and hardworking man out of employment [and allowing] . . . the large cities to swallow up the small towns."

New York's growth stemmed primarily from its dominant position in foreign trade. It had the best harbor in the United States, and oceangoing vessels could sail or steam up the Hudson River to Albany and the Erie Canal. The city's merchants exploited these natural advantages. In 1818 four Quaker merchants founded the Black Ball Line, a service that operated on a regular schedule and carried cargo, people, and mail between New York and the European ports of Liverpool, London, and Le Havre. New York merchants likewise gained an unassailable lead in commerce with the newly independent Latin American nations of Brazil, Peru, and Venezuela. New York–based traders also took over the cotton trade by offering finance, insurance, and shipping to cotton exporters in southern ports. And by persuading the state government to build the Erie Canal, the city's merchants acquired a dominant position in the export of western grain to European markets. By 1840 the port of New York handled almost two-thirds of foreign imports into the United States, almost half of all foreign trade, and much of the immigrant traffic.

Changes in the Social Structure

The Industrial and Market Revolutions transformed the material lives of many Americans, allowing them to live in larger houses, cook on iron stoves, and wear better-made clothes. But the new economic order created distinct social classes: a wealthy industrial and commercial elite, a substantial urban middle class, and a mass of propertyless wage earners. By creating a class-divided society, industrialization posed a momentous challenge to American republican ideals.

The Business Elite

Before industrialization white American society had been divided into various ranks, with "notables" ruling over the "lower orders." But in rural society the different ranks shared a common culture: gentlemen farmers talked easily with yeomen about crop yields, while their wives conversed about the art of quilting. In the South humble tenants and aristocratic slave owners shared the same amusements: gambling, cockfighting, and horse racing. Rich and poor attended the same Quaker meetinghouse or Presbyterian church. "Almost everyone eats, drinks, and dresses in the same way," a European visitor to Hartford, Connecticut, reported in 1798, "and one can see the most obvious inequality only in the dwellings."

The Industrial Revolution shattered this traditional order and created a society of classes, each with its own culture. The new economic system pulled many Americans into cities and made a few of them—the business elite of merchants, manufacturers, bankers, and landlords—very rich. In 1800 the top 10 percent of the nation's families owned about 40 percent of the wealth; by 1860 the wealthiest 10 percent owned nearly 70 percent. In large cities—New York, Chicago, Baltimore, New Orleans—the richest 1 percent of the population held more than 40 percent of all tangible property—such as land and buildings—and an even higher share of intangible property—such as stocks and bonds.

Government tax policies allowed this accumulation of wealth. The U.S. Treasury raised most of its revenue from tariffs—taxes on imported goods such as textiles that were purchased mostly by ordinary citizens. State and local governments also favored the wealthier classes. They usually taxed real estate (farms, city lots, and buildings) and tangible personal property (such as furniture, tools, and machinery) but almost never taxed the stocks and bonds owned by the rich or the inheritances they passed on to their children.

Over time the wealthiest families consciously set themselves apart from the rest of the population. They dressed in well-tailored clothes, rode around town in fancy carriages pulled by fine horses, and lived in expensively furnished houses tended by butlers, cooks, coachmen, and other servants. The women of the family no longer socialized with those of lesser wealth, and the men no longer labored side by side with their journeymen. Instead, they became managers and directors, issuing orders through trusted subordinates to hundreds of factory operatives. Increasingly merchants, manufacturers, and bankers chose to live in separate residential areas, turning away from traditional practices such as boarding unmarried workers in their own homes. By the 1830s most employers had moved their families to distinct upper-class enclaves, often at the edge of the city. The desire for greater privacy by privileged families and the massive flow of immigrants into many cities created fragmented communities, divided geographically along the lines of class, race, and ethnicity.

The Middle Class

Standing between wealthy owners and entrepreneurs at one end of the social spectrum and nonpropertied wage earners at the other was a growing middle class—the product of the Market Revolution. As a Boston printer and publisher explained, the "middling class" was made up of "the farmers, the mechanics, the manufacturers, the traders, who carry on professionally the ordinary operations of buying, selling, and exchanging merchandize." The growth of cities likewise fostered the rise of various professional groups—building contractors, lawyers, and surveyors—who suddenly found their services in great demand and financially profitable. Middle-class business owners, employees, and professionals were most numerous in the Northeast, where they numbered about 30 percent of the population in 1840, but they could be found in every American town and village, even in the agrarian South. In the boom town of Oglethorpe, Georgia (population 2,500), in 1854, there were no fewer than eighty "business houses" and eight hotels.

The size, wealth, and cultural influence of the middle class continued to grow, fueled by a dramatic rise in prosperity. Between 1830 and the Panic of 1857, the per capita income of Americans increased by about 2.5 percent a year, a remarkable rate that the United States has never since matched. This surge in income, along with the availability of inexpensive mass-produced goods, facilitated the creation of a distinct middle-class culture, especially in urban areas of the Northeast. Middle-class husbands had sufficient earnings so that their wives did not have to seek paid work. Typically these men saved about 15 percent of their income, depositing it in banks and then using it to buy a well-built house in a "respectable part of town." They purchased handsome clothes for themselves and their families and drove about town in smart carriages. Their wives and daughters were literate and accomplished, buying books and pianos as well as commodious furniture for their front parlors. Rather than hiring servants to perform menial tasks, they turned to the new industrial technology, outfitting their residences with furnaces that heated water for bathing and radiators that warmed entire rooms; stoves with ovens, including broilers and movable grates; treadle-operated sewing machines; and iceboxes, which ice company wagons filled periodically, to preserve perishable food. They also bought packaged goods: as early as 1825 the Underwood Company of Boston was marketing well-preserved Atlantic salmon in jars. Following the introduction of the airtight Mason jar in 1858, housewives bought perishable farm produce when it was cheap and preserved it, thereby providing their families with a varied diet even in winter.

If material comfort was one distinguishing mark of the middle class, moral and mental discipline was another. Seeking to pass on their status to their children, successful parents usually provided them with a high school education (in an era when most white children

Middle-Class Family Life, 1836

The family of Azariah Caverly boasted many of the amenities of middle-class life—handsome clothes, finely decorated furniture, and a striking floor covering. Underlining the social conventions of the time, the husband and his son hold a newspaper and a square, symbolizing the worlds of commerce and industry, while the wife and her daughter are pictured next to a Bible, indicating their domestic and moral vocations.

New York State Historical Association, Cooperstown, NY.

received only five years of schooling). Ambitious parents were equally concerned with their children's character and stressed discipline, morality, and hard work. Puritans and other American Protestants had long believed that work in an earthly "calling" was a duty people owed to God. Now the business elite and the middle class gave this idea a secular twist: they celebrated work as socially beneficial, the key to a higher standard of living for the nation and social mobility for the individual.

Benjamin Franklin gave classical expression to the secular work ethic in his *Autobiography*, which was published in full in 1818 and immediately found a huge audience. Heeding Franklin's suggestion that an industrious man would become a rich one, tens of thousands of young American men worked hard, saved their money, adopted temperate habits, and practiced honesty in their business dealings. Countless magazines, children's books, self-help manuals, and novels taught the same lessons. The ideal of the "**self-made man**" became a central theme of American popular culture. Just as a rural-producer ethic had united the social ranks in pre-1800 America, this new goal of personal achievement and social mobility tied together the upper and middle classes of the new industrializing society. Knowing that many affluent families had risen from modest beginnings, middle-class men and women took them as models and shunned the rapidly increasing numbers of working families who owned nothing and had to struggle just to survive.

The New Urban Poor

As thoughtful business leaders surveyed the emerging social landscape, they concluded that the old yeoman society of independent families no longer seemed possible or even advisable. "Entire independence ought not to be wished for," Ithamar A. Beard, the paymaster of the Hamilton Manufacturing Company, told a mechanics' association in 1827. "In large manufacturing towns, many more must fill subordinate stations and must be under the immediate direction and control of a master or superintendent, than in the farming towns."

Beard had a point. In 1840 all of the nation's slaves and about half of its native-born free workers were laboring for others rather than for themselves. The bottom 10 percent of this wage-earning labor force consisted of casual workers—those hired on a short-term basis for the most arduous jobs. Poor women washed clothes, while their husbands and sons carried lumber and bricks for construction projects, loaded ships and wagons, and dug out dirt and stones to build canals. When they could find work, these men earned "their dollar *per diem*," an "Old Inhabitant" wrote to the *Baltimore American,* but he reminded readers that most workers could never save enough "to pay rent, buy fire wood and eatables" for their families when the harbor froze up. During business depressions they bore the brunt of unemployment, and even in the best of times their jobs were unpredictable, seasonal, and dangerous.

Other laborers had greater security of employment, but few were prospering. In Massachusetts in 1825 the daily wage of an unskilled worker was about two-thirds that of a mechanic; two decades later it was less than half as much. The 18,000 native-born and immigrant women who made men's clothing in New York City in the 1850s were even worse off, averaging less than $80 a year. These meager wages paid for food and rent and not much more, so many wage earners were unable to take advantage of the rapidly falling prices of manufactured goods. Only the most fortunate working families could afford to educate their children, pay the fees required for an apprenticeship, or accumulate small dowries so that their daughters could marry men with better prospects. Most families sent their children out to work, and the death of one of the parents often threw the survivors into dire poverty. As a charity worker noted, "What can a bereaved widow do, with 5 or 6 little children, destitute of every means of support but what her own hands can furnish (which in a general way does not amount to more than 25 cents a day)."

By the 1830s most urban factory workers and unskilled laborers resided in well-defined neighborhoods. Single men and women lived in large, crowded boardinghouses, while families inhabited tiny apartments carved out of the living quarters, basements, and attics of small houses. As immigrants poured into the nation after 1840, urban populations soared and developers squeezed more and more buildings onto a single lot, interspersed with outhouses and connected by foul-smelling courtyards. Venturing into the slums of New York City in the 1850s, state legislators were shocked to find gaunt, shivering people with "wild ghastly faces" living amid "hideous squalour and deadly effluvia, the dim, undrained courts oozing with pollution, the dark, narrow stairways, decayed with age, reeking with filth, overrun with vermin."

Living in such distressing conditions, many wage earners turned to the dubious solace of alcohol. Alcohol had long been an integral part of American life; beer and rum had lubricated ceremonies, work breaks, barn raisings, and games. But during the 1820s native-born urban wage earners led Americans to new heights of alcohol consumption. Aiding them were western farmers, who distilled corn and rye into gin and whiskey as a low-cost way to get their grain to market. By 1830 drinkers consumed enormous amounts of liquor every year—enough to provide every man, woman, and child in the United States with five gallons, more than three times present-day levels (see Voices from Abroad, "Frances Trollope: American Workers and Their Wives," p. 307).

Drinking patterns changed as well. Workers in many craft unions "swore off" liquor, convinced that it would undermine their skilled work as well as their health and finances. But other workers began to drink on the job—

The Eastern State Penitentiary, Philadelphia, 1836
Today it is unusual to see prisons celebrated on postcards or, as here, in a color lithograph meant to be hung on a living room wall. However, in the 1820s and 1830s, American penitentiaries were world famous, their physical layout and methods of discipline studied by Alexis de Tocqueville and hundreds of other foreign observers and penal experts. Benevolent reformers pledged that the new institutions would turn criminals into model citizens by using methods of mental conditioning rather than physical punishment. In fact, most prisons quickly became places of incarceration rather than reform.
Paul Eisenhauer.

and not just during the traditional 11 A.M. and 4 P.M. "refreshers." Journeymen used apprentices to smuggle whiskey into shops, and then, as one baker recalled, "One man was stationed at the window to watch, while the rest drank." Even before the appearance of spirit-drinking Irish and beer-drinking German immigrants, grogshops and tippling houses had appeared on almost every block in working-class districts. The saloons became focal points for crimes and urban disorder. Fueled by unrestrained drinking, a fistfight among young men one night could turn into a brawl the second night and a full-scale riot the third. The urban police forces, consisting of low-paid watchmen and untrained constables, were unable to contain the lawlessness.

The Benevolent Empire

The disorder among native-born urban wage earners sparked concern among well-to-do Americans. Inspired by the religious ideal of benevolence—doing good for

the less fortunate—they created a number of organizations that historians refer to collectively as the "**Benevolent Empire.**" During the 1820s Congregational and Presbyterian ministers united with like-minded merchants and their wives to launch a program of social reform and regulation. Their purpose, announced leading Presbyterian minister Lyman Beecher, was to restore "the moral government of God." The reformers introduced new forms of moral discipline into their own lives and tried to infuse them into the lives of working people as well. They would regulate popular behavior—by persuasion if possible, by law if necessary.

Although the Benevolent Empire targeted age-old evils such as drunkenness, prostitution, and crime, its methods were new. Instead of relying on church sermons and moral suasion by community leaders, the reformers set out in a systematic fashion to institutionalize charity and combat evil. They established large-scale organizations, such as the Prison Discipline Society and the American Society for the Promotion of Temperance, among

Frances Trollope

American Workers and Their Wives

During her four-year stay in the United States, British businesswoman Frances Trollope traveled widely and proved to be an acute social commentator. Her book Domestic Manners of the Americans *(1832) was a best-seller on both sides of the Atlantic. She frequently compared life in America with that in Britain, as in this discussion of the living conditions and habits of working people.*

Mohawk [in southern Ohio], as our little village was called, gave us an excellent opportunity of comparing the peasants of the United States with those of England, and of judging the average degree of comfort enjoyed by each. . . .

Mechanics, if good workmen, are certain of employment, and good wages, rather higher than with us; the average wages of a labourer throughout the Union is ten dollars a month, with lodging, boarding, washing, and mending; if he lives at his own expense he has a dollar a day. It appears to me that the necessaries of life, that is to say, meat, bread, butter, tea, and coffee (not to mention whiskey), are within the reach of every sober, industrious, and healthy man who chooses to have them; and yet I think that an English peasant, with the same qualifications, would, in coming to the United States, change for the worse [because American men indulge in various vices that consume their money and their health]. . . .

Tobacco grows at their doors, and is not taxed: yet this too costs something, and the air of heaven is not in more general use among the men of America than chewing tobacco. . . . Ardent spirits, though lamentably cheap, still cost something, and the use of them among the men . . . is universal. . . . I am not now pointing out the evils of dram-drinking, but it is evident, that where this practice prevails universally, and often to the most frightful excess, the consequence must be, that the money spent to obtain the dram [a small glass of whiskey] is less than the money lost by the time consumed in drinking it.

Long, disabling, and expensive fits of sickness are incontestably more frequent in every part of America than in England, and the sufferers have no aid to look to, but what they have saved, or what they may be enabled to sell. I have never seen misery exceeded what I have witnessed in an American cottage where disease has entered.

But if the condition of the labourer be not superior to that of the English peasant, that of his wife and daughters is incomparably worse. It is they who are indeed the slaves of the soil. One has but to look at the wife of an American cottager, and ask her age, to be convinced that the life she leads is one of hardship, privation, and labour. It is rare to see a woman in this station who has reached the age of thirty, without losing every trace of youth and beauty.

Even the young girls, though often with lovely features, look pale, thin, and haggard. . . . The horror of domestic service, which the reality of slavery, and the fable of equality, have generated, excludes the young women from that sure and most comfortable resource of decent English girls; and the consequence is . . . the daughters are, to the full extent of the word, domestic slaves.

Source: Frances Trollope, *Domestic Manners of the Americans* (New York: Whittaker, Treacher & Co., 1832), n.p.

many others. Each organization had a managing staff, a network of volunteers and chapters, and a newspaper.

Often working in concert, these benevolent groups set out to improve society. First they encouraged people to lead well-disciplined lives, campaigning for temperance in drinking habits and an end to prostitution. To encourage orderly behavior, they persuaded local governments to ban carnivals of drink and dancing, such as Negro Election Day (mock festivities in which African Americans symbolically took over the government), which had been enjoyed by whites as well as blacks. Second, they devised new institutions to control people who were threats to society and to assist those who were unable to handle their own affairs. Reformers provided homes of refuge for the abandoned children of the poor and removed the insane from isolation in attics and cellars and placed them in newly built asylums. They also campaigned to end corporal punishment for criminals, advocating instead their confinement and moral rehabilitation in penitentiaries—a largely unsuccessful experiment in social engineering.

Women played an increasingly active role in the Benevolent Empire. Since the 1790s upper-class women had sponsored a number of charitable organizations, such as the Society for the Relief of Poor Widows with Small Children, founded in New York by Isabella Graham, a devout Presbyterian widow. By the 1820s Graham's society was assisting hundreds of widows and their children in New York City. Her daughter Joanna Bethune set up other charitable institutions, including the Orphan Asylum Society and the Society for the Promotion of Industry, which found hundreds of poor women jobs as spinners and seamstresses.

Some reformers came to believe that one of the greatest threats to the "moral government of God" was the decline of the traditional Sabbath. As the pace of commercial activity accelerated, merchants and shippers began to conduct business on Sunday, since they did not want their goods and equipment to lie idle one day in every seven. To restore traditional values, in 1828 Lyman Beecher and other ministers formed the General Union for Promoting the Observance of the Christian Sabbath. General Union chapters—usually with women's auxiliaries—sprang up from Maine to the Ohio Valley. Seeking a symbolic issue to rally Christians to their cause, the General Union focused on a law Congress had enacted in 1810 allowing mail to be transported—though not delivered—on Sunday. To secure its repeal the Union adopted the tactics of a political party, organizing rallies and circulating petitions. Its members also boycotted shipping companies that did business on the Sabbath and campaigned for municipal laws forbidding games and festivals on the Lord's day.

Not everyone agreed with the program of the Benevolent Empire. Men who labored twelve or fourteen hours a day for six days a week refused to spend their one day of leisure in meditation and prayer. Shipping company managers demanded that the Erie Canal provide lockkeepers on Sundays and joined those Americans who argued that using boycotts and laws to enforce morality was "contrary to the free spirit of our institutions." And when the evangelical reformers proposed to teach Christianity to slaves, many white southerners were outraged. Such popular resistance or indifference limited the success of the Benevolent Empire. A different kind of message was required if religious reformers were to do more than preach to the already converted and discipline the already disciplined.

Revivalism and Reform

The Presbyterian minister Charles Grandison Finney brought just such a message to Americans. Finney was not part of the traditional religious elite. Born into a poor farming family in Connecticut, he hoped to join the new middle class as a lawyer. But in 1823 Finney underwent an intense conversion experience and decided

Charles Finney, Evangelist (1792–1875)
When this portrait was painted in 1834, Finney was forty-two years old and at the height of his career as an evangelist. Handsome and charismatic, Finney had just led a series of enormously successful revivals in Rochester, New York, and other cities along the Erie Canal. In 1835 he established a theology department at the newly founded Oberlin College in Ohio, where he helped train a generation of ministers and served as its president from 1851 to 1866. Oberlin College Archives.

to become a minister. Beginning in towns along the Erie Canal, the young minister conducted emotional revival meetings that stressed conversion rather than instruction; what counted for Finney was the will to be saved. Repudiating traditional Calvinist beliefs, he maintained that God would welcome any sinner who submitted to the Holy Spirit. Finney's ministry drew on—and greatly accelerated—the Second Great Awakening, the wave of Protestant revivalism that had begun after the Revolution (see Chapter 9).

Evangelical Ideology.   Finney's message that "God has made man a moral free agent" who could choose salvation was particularly attractive to members of the new middle class, who had already chosen to improve their material lives. But he became famous for converting those at the ends of the social spectrum: the haughty rich, who had placed themselves above God, and the abject poor, who seemed lost to drink, sloth, and misbehavior. To humble the pride of the rich and relieve the shame of the poor, Finney celebrated their common fellowship in Christ and identified them spiritually with earnest, pious middle-class respectability.

Finney's most spectacular triumph came in 1830, when he moved his revivals from small towns to Rochester, New York, now a major milling and commercial city on the Erie Canal. Preaching every day for six months he won over the influential merchants and manufacturers of Rochester, who pledged to reform their lives and those of their workers. They promised to attend church, join the Cold Water movement by giving up intoxicating beverages, and work steady hours. To encourage their employees to follow suit, wealthy businessmen founded a new Free Presbyterian Church—"free" because members did not have to pay for pew space. Other evangelical Protestants founded two similar churches to serve canal laborers, transients, and the settled poor. To reinforce the work of the churches, Rochester's business elite established a savings bank to encourage thrift, Sunday schools to instruct poor children, and the Female Charitable Society to provide relief for the families of the unemployed.

However, these initiatives to create a harmonious community of morally disciplined Christians were not altogether effective. To reach as many nonbelievers as possible, Finney added a new tactic—group prayer meetings in family homes—in which women played an active role. Finney's wife, Lydia, and other pious middle-class women carried the Christian message to the wives of the unconverted, often while their husbands were at work. But skilled workers who belonged to strong crafts organizations—bootmakers, carpenters, stonemasons, and boat builders—resisted the message, arguing that workers needed higher wages and schools more urgently than sermons and prayers. And Finney's revival seldom moved poor people, especially the Irish Catholic immigrants who had recently begun arriving in American cities, including Rochester, and who thought of Protestants as religious heretics and as their political oppressors in Ireland.

Ignoring these setbacks, revivalists in cities and towns from New England to the Midwest duplicated Finney's evangelical message and techniques. In New York City, the wealthy silk merchants Arthur and Lewis Tappan founded a magazine, *The Christian Evangelist*,

"The Drunkard's Progress: From the First Glass to the Grave"
This lithograph of 1846, published by the firm of N. Currier, depicts the inevitable fate of those who partake of alcoholic beverages. The drunkard's descent into "Poverty and Disease" ends with "Death by Suicide," leaving a grieving and destitute wife and child. Temperance reformers urged Americans to take the "Cold Water Cure," drinking water instead of liquor. To promote abstinence among the young, the Reverend Thomas Hunt founded the Cold Water Army, an organization that grew to embrace several hundred thousand children, all of whom pledged "perpetual hate to all that can Intoxicate."
Library of Congress.

John Gough

The Vice of Intemperance

*J*ohn Gough (1817–1886) was twelve years old when his impoverished English parents shipped him to New York City, where he found work as a bookbinder—and eventually turned to drink. In 1842, at age twenty-five, Gough converted to temperance. For the next four decades he used his eloquence as a lecturer—and his considerable talents as an actor—to command high fees and persuade thousands to join the temperance movement. The following selection is taken from his Autobiography (1869).

Will it be believed that I again sought refuge in rum? Yet so it was. Scarcely had I recovered from the fright, than I sent out, procured a pint of rum, and drank it all in less than an hour. And now came upon me many terrible sensations. Cramps attacked me in my limbs, which racked me with agony; and my temples throbbed as if they would burst. . . . Then came on the drunkard's remorseless torturer—delirium tremens, in all its terrors, attacked me. For three days I endured more agony than pen could describe, even were it guided by the mind of Dante. . . . I was at one time surrounded by millions of monstrous spiders, that crawled slowly over every limb, whilst the beaded drops of perspiration would start to my brow, and my limbs would shiver until the bed rattled. . . . All at once, whilst gazing at a frightful creation of my distempered mind, I seemed struck with sudden blindness. I knew a candle was burning in the room, but I could not see it—all was so pitchy dark. . . . And then the scene would change: I was falling—falling swiftly as an arrow—far down into some terrible abyss. . . .

By the mercy of God, I survived this awful seizure; and when I rose, a weak, broken-down man, and surveyed my ghastly features in the glass, I thought of my mother, and asked myself how I had obeyed the instructions received from her lips, and to what advantage I had turned the lessons she taught me. I remembered her countless prayers and tears. . . . Oh! how keen were my rebukes; and, in the excitement of the moment, I resolved to lead a better life, and abstain from the accursed cup.

For about a month, terrified by what I had suffered, I adhered to my resolution; then my wife came home, and, in my joy at her return, I flung my good resolutions to the wind, and, foolishly fancying that I could now restrain my appetite, which had a whole month remained in subjugation, I took a glass of brandy. That glass aroused the slumbering demon, who would not be satisfied by so tiny a libation. Another and another succeeded, until I was again far advanced in the career of intemperance. The night of my wife's return, I went to bed intoxicated.

Source: David Brion Davis, ed., *Antebellum American Culture: An Interpretive Anthology* (Lexington, MA: Heath, 1979), 402–3.

which promoted Finney's ideas across the country. Soon converts in towns in many states—North Carolina, Tennessee, Indiana, Pennsylvania—reported that "You could not go upon the street and hear any conversation, except upon religion." The success of the revival "has been so general and thorough," concluded a General Assembly of Presbyterians, "that the whole customs of society have changed."

Temperance. The temperance movement proved to be the most effective arena for national evangelical reform. In 1832 evangelicals gained control of the American Temperance Society; within a few years it had grown to two thousand chapters with more than 200,000 members. The society adapted the methods that had worked so well in the revivals—group confession and prayer, a focus on the family and the spiritual role of women, and sudden, emotional conversion—and took them into virtually every town in the North and rural hamlet in the South. On one day in New York City in 1841, more than 4,000 people took the temperance "pledge." The average annual consumption of spirits fell from about five gallons per person in 1830 to about two gallons in 1845 (see American Voices, "John Gough: The Vice of Intemperance," above).

Evangelical reformers used religion to reinforce the traditional moral foundations of the American work ethic. Laziness and drinking could not be cured by following Benjamin Franklin's method of self-discipline, they argued; rather, people had to experience the profound change of heart achieved through religious conversion. As this evangelical message spread, it fostered a commitment to individual enterprise and moral discipline not only among middle-class Americans but also among many wage earners. Religion and the ideology of social mobility served as powerful cement, holding society together in the face of the massive changes brought by the spread of industrial enterprise and the market economy.

Immigration and Cultural Conflict

Between 1840 and 1860 about 2 million Irish immigrants, 1.5 million Germans, and 750,000 Britons poured into the United States, placing new strains on the American social order. Most immigrants avoided the South because they opposed slavery, shunned blacks, or feared competition from enslaved workers. Many German migrants settled on farms or in the growing cities of the midwestern states of Wisconsin, Iowa, and Missouri, often comprising a majority of the local residents. Other Germans and most of the Irish settled in the Northeast, where by 1860 they accounted for nearly one-third of white adults.

Irish Poverty.   The most prosperous immigrants were the British, many of whom were professionals, propertied farmers, and skilled workers. The majority of German immigrants also came from farming and artisan families and could afford to buy land in America. The poorest migrants were Irish peasants and laborers, fleeing a widespread famine caused by severe overpopulation and a devastating blight on the potato crop. Arriving in dire poverty the Irish found new homes in the cities of New England and New York and took low-skilled, low-paying jobs as laborers in factories and on construction projects and as servants in private residences. Many Irish immigrants lived in crowded tenements with primitive sanitation systems and were the first to die when epidemics swept through American cities. In the summer of 1849 a cholera epidemic took the lives of thousands of poor immigrants in St. Louis and New York.

In times of hardship and sorrow immigrants turned to their churches. Many Germans and virtually all the Irish were Catholics, and they fueled the growth of the Catholic Church. In the 1840s there were sixteen Catholic dioceses and seven hundred churches in the United States; by 1860 the number had increased to forty-five dioceses and twenty-five hundred churches. Under the guidance of their priests and bishops the Irish built an impressive network of institutions—charitable societies, orphanages, militia companies, parochial schools, and political organizations—that helped them maintain their cultural identity.

Nativism.   Owing in part to the religious fervor raised by the Second Great Awakening, the immigrants' Catholic beliefs and institutions stirred up fear and distaste among native-born citizens. A rash of anti-Catholic publications greeted the first Irish immigrants in the 1830s. One of the most militant critics of Catholicism was Samuel F. B. Morse (who would later make the first commercial adaptation of the telegraph). In 1834 Morse published *Foreign Conspiracy against the Liberties of the United States*, which warned of a Catholic threat to American republican institutions. Morse believed that Catholic immigrants would obey the dictates of Pope Pius IX, who had condemned republicanism as a false political ideology based on the sovereignty of the people rather than on the sovereignty of God. Republican-minded Protestants of

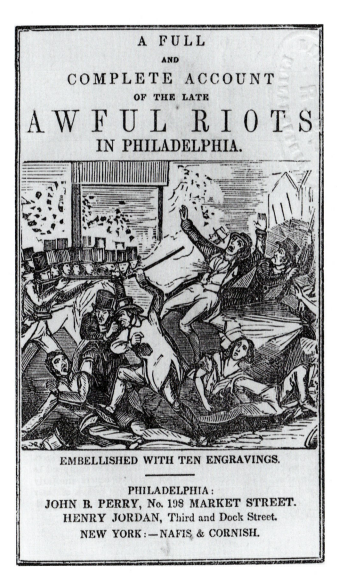

An Anti-Catholic Riot
When riots against Irish Catholics broke out in Philadelphia in 1844, the governor of Pennsylvania called out the militia to protect Catholic churches and residential neighborhoods. In the foreground, two Protestant rioters, depicted by the artist as well-dressed gentlemen, attack an Irish family with sticks, while in the background the militia exchanges musket fire with other members of the mob. Library Company of Philadelphia.

many denominations shared Morse's fears, and *Foreign Conspiracy* became their textbook.

The social tensions stemming from industrialization intensified anti-Catholic sentiment. Unemployed Protestant mechanics and factory workers joined mobs that attacked Catholics, accusing them of taking jobs and driving down wages; other Protestants organized Native American Clubs, which called for limits on immigration, the restriction of public office to native-born citizens, and the exclusive use of the Protestant version of the Bible in public schools. Many reformers supported the anti-Catholic movement for reasons of public policy—to prevent the diversion of tax resources to Catholic schools and to oppose alcohol abuse by many Irish men. These cultural conflicts also inhibited the growth of a strong labor movement because Protestant wage earners felt they had more in common with their Protestant employers than with their Catholic co-workers.

In almost every large northeastern city religious and cultural conflicts led to violence. In 1834 in Charlestown, Massachusetts, a quarrel between Catholic laborers repairing a convent owned by the Ursuline order of nuns and Protestant workers in a neighboring brickyard turned into a full-scale riot and the burning of the convent. In Philadelphia the violence peaked in 1844 when the Catholic bishop persuaded public school officials to use the Catholic as well as the Protestant version of the Bible. Anti-Irish rioting incited by the city's Native American Clubs lasted for two months and escalated into open warfare between Protestants and the Pennsylvania militia.

Thus, even as economic revolution brought prosperity to many Americans, it divided the society along the lines of class and, by encouraging the influx of immigrants, created new ethnic and religious tensions. Differences of class and culture now split the North in much the same way that race and class had long divided the South. Yet overall the majority of white Americans shared a common commitment to a dynamic economic system based on private property and a vibrant political culture of democratic republicanism.

FOR FURTHER EXPLORATION

▶ For definitions of key terms boldfaced in this chapter, see the glossary at the end of the book.

▶ To assess your mastery of the material covered in this chapter, see the Online Study Guide at **bedfordstmartins.com/henretta**.

▶ For suggested references, including Web sites, see page SR–11 at the end of the book.

▶ For map resources and primary documents, see **bedfordstmartins.com/henretta**.

S U M M A R Y

Between 1820 and 1860 the United States experienced an "industrial" and a "market" revolution that created a new economic structure. Merchants and manufacturers organized increasingly efficient systems of production and, aided by skilled mechanics, introduced water- and steam-powered machines to turn out huge quantities of goods. Simultaneously merchants, traders, and shopkeepers created a vast market system in which they exchanged these manufactures for grain, meat, cotton, leather, and wool produced by a rapidly growing—and westward-moving—farm population.

Three streams of migrants transplanted the cultures of the plantation South, the Middle Atlantic, and yeoman New England into the Old Southwest, the Ohio River Valley, and the Old Northwest. State governments promoted this westward movement—and the creation of regional and national markets—by subsidizing the building of roads, canals, and railroads and creating a transportation system that was unprecedented in size and complexity. As domestic markets and production grew, urbanization accelerated in the Northeast, where industrial towns dotted the landscape, and New York City became the nation's largest city and leading trading center.

Economic growth fostered the creation of new social classes: a wealthy urban business elite of merchants and manufacturers; a prosperous, educated, and well-housed middle class; and a mass of wage-earning laborers with little or no property. Some artisans and workers formed trade unions in generally unsuccessful efforts to improve their economic welfare; other working people lived in poverty and sought solace in drink.

To improve the living conditions and the morals of the poor, upper-class Americans formed benevolent reform societies that promoted temperance, dispensed charity, and encouraged respect for the Christian Sabbath. Simultaneously, Charles Grandison Finney and other evangelical clergymen gave new life to the Second Great Awakening, enlisting millions of propertied farmers and middle-class Americans in a massive religious revival. Preaching the doctrine of "free moral agency," Finney urged Americans both to assist in their own salvation and to reform the world in which they lived.

Protestant evangelicalism heightened the cultural conflict between native-born Americans and millions of Catholic immigrants from Ireland and Germany. Nativist writers attacked Irish Catholics as antirepublican, and American workers blamed immigrant labor for their economic woes—attitudes that led to ethnic riots in many northern cities. By 1860 the United States was a more prosperous society than ever before, and a more socially divided one.

T I M E L I N E

1782 Oliver Evans develops automated flour mill

1790 Samuel Slater opens spinning mill in Providence, Rhode Island

1793 Eli Whitney manufactures cotton gins

1807 Robert Fulton launches the *Clermont,* the first American steamboat

1810s Cotton kingdom begins in Old Southwest

1814 Boston Manufacturing Company opens cotton mill in Waltham, Massachusetts

1817 Erie Canal begun; completed in 1825

1820 Minimum federal land price reduced to $1.25 per acre

1820s New England women become textile operatives

Building-trade workers seek ten-hour workday

Rise of Benevolent Empire

1821 End of Panic of 1819; fifteen-year boom begins

1824 Congress raises tariffs; increased again in 1828

Gibbons v. Ogden promotes interstate trade

1830s Expansion of western commercial cities

Labor movement gains strength

Class-segregated cities

Growth of temperance movement

Creation of middle-class culture

1830 Charles Grandison Finney begins Rochester revival

1837 Panic of 1837

John Deere invents steel plow

1839 European financial crisis begins four-year depression in United States

1840s Irish and German immigration; ethnic riots

1850s Expansion of railroads

Rise of machine-tool industry

1857 Financial panic after fourteen-year boom

CHAPTER 11

A Democratic Revolution
1820–1844

**The Rise of Popular Politics,
1820–1829**
*The Decline of the Notables and
    the Rise of Parties*
The Election of 1824
*The Last Notable President: John
    Quincy Adams*
*"The Democracy" and the Election
    of 1828*

**The Jacksonian Presidency,
1829–1837**
*Jackson's Agenda: Patronage and
    Policy*
The Tariff and Nullification
The Bank War
Indian Removal
The Jacksonian Impact

**Class, Culture, and the Second
Party System**
The Whig Worldview
*Labor Politics and the Depression
    of 1837–1843*
"Tippecanoe and Tyler Too!"

I F AMERICANS BELIEVED their political institutions were ordained by God, visiting Europeans thought them the work of the Devil. "The gentlemen spit, talk of elections and the price of produce, and spit again," Mrs. Frances Trollope reported in *Domestic Manners of the Americans* (1832). In her view American politics was the sport of party hacks who reeked of "whiskey and onions." Other European visitors used more refined language but likewise found little to celebrate. Harriet Martineau was "deeply disgusted" by the "clap-trap of praise and pathos" uttered by a leading Massachusetts politician, while Basil Hall could only shake his head in astonishment at the shallow arguments, the "conclusions in which nothing was concluded," that were advanced by the inept "farmers, shopkeepers, and country lawyers" who sat in the New York assembly.

◄ **The Inauguration of President
William Henry Harrison, March 4,
1841 (detail)**

*After being sworn into office, President
Harrison stands on the steps of the U.S.
Capitol reviewing a parade of military
units. Despite the fact that they could not
vote, many women attended the ceremony
not only to enjoy the festivities but also
because the Whig Party actively solicited
their support for its policies of moral
reform.*
Anne S. K. Brown Military Collection, Brown
University.

The verdict was unanimous and negative. As the French aristocrat Alexis de Tocqueville put it in *Democracy in America* (1835): "The most able men in the United States are very rarely placed at the head of affairs," a result he ascribed to the character of democracy itself. Ordinary citizens were jealous of their intellectual superiors and so refused to elect them to office; moreover, because most voters had little time to consider important policy issues, they assented to "the clamor of a mountebank [charlatan] who knows the secret of stimulating [their] tastes."

The European visitors were witnesses to the unfolding of the American democratic revolution. In the early years of the nation the ruling ideology had been *republicanism*, rule by property-owning "men of TALENTS and VIRTUE." By the 1820s and 1830s the watchword was becoming *democracy*, which in the nineteenth-century United States meant power exercised by party politicians elected by the people as a whole. "That the majority should govern was a fundamental maxim in all free governments," declared Martin Van Buren, the most talented of the new breed of middle-class professional politicians who had taken over the halls of government. The new party politicians were often crude and usually self-interested, but by uniting ordinary Americans in "election fever," they held together an increasingly fragmented social order.

The Rise of Popular Politics, 1820–1829

Expansion of the **franchise** was the most dramatic expression of the democratic revolution. Beginning in the late 1810s many states revised their constitutions to eliminate property qualifications, giving the franchise to nearly every farmer and wage earner. Nowhere else in the world did ordinary men have so much political power; in England, even after passage of the Reform Bill of 1832, only 600,000 out of 6 million men—a mere 10 percent—had the right to vote.

The Decline of the Notables and the Rise of Parties

In America's traditional agricultural society, people from the low and middle ranks of society deferred to their "betters," and wealthy notable men—northern landlords, slave-owning planters, and seaport merchants—dominated the political system. As former Supreme Court justice John Jay—himself a notable—put it in 1810, "Those who own the country are the most fit persons to participate in the government of it." The notables managed local elections by building up an "interest": lending money to small farmers, giving business to storekeepers and artisans, and treating their workers and tenants to rum at election time. An outlay of $20 for refreshments, according to an experienced poll watcher, "may produce about 100 votes." Martin Van Buren, whose father was a tavern keeper, knew from personal experience that this gentry-dominated system excluded men of modest means who lacked wealth and "the aid of powerful family connections" from running for office.

The Rise of Democracy.   The first assaults on the traditional political order came in the Midwest and Southwest. As smallholding farmers and ambitious laborers settled the trans-Appalachian region, they broke free of control by the notables. In Ohio, a traveler

reported, "no white man or woman will bear being called a servant." Influenced by this social egalitarianism, the constitutions of the new states of Indiana (1816), Illinois (1818), and Alabama (1819) prescribed a broad male franchise. Once armed with the vote, ordinary citizens in the western states usually elected middling men to local and state offices. A well-to-do migrant in Illinois noted with surprise that the man who plowed his fields "was a colonel of militia, and a member of the legislature." Once in public office, men from modest backgrounds listened to the demands of their ordinary constituents, enacting laws that restricted imprisonment for debt, kept taxes low, and allowed farmers to claim "squatters' rights" to unoccupied land.

To deter migration to the western states and unrest at home, the notables who ran most eastern legislatures grudgingly accepted a broader franchise. Responding to reformers who condemned property qualifications as a "tyranny" that endowed "one class of men with privileges which are denied to another," in 1810 the Maryland legislature extended the vote to all adult white men. By the mid-1820s only a few states—North Carolina, Virginia, Rhode Island—required the ownership of freehold property for voting. A solid majority of the states had instituted universal white manhood suffrage, and most of the others, such as Ohio and Louisiana, excluded only the relatively few men who did not pay taxes (on their property, persons, or occupations) or serve in the militia. Moreover, between 1818 and 1821 the eastern states of Connecticut, Massachusetts, and New York revised their entire constitutions, reapportioning the representation of legislative districts on the basis of population and instituting more democratic forms of local government, such as the election (rather than the appointment) of judges and justices of the peace.

The politics of the new democracy was more complex and contentious than the traditional politics of deference. Powerful entrepreneurs and speculators—whether they were notables or self-made men—demanded government assistance for their business enterprises and paid bribes to legislators to get it. Bankers sought charters from the state and opposed laws that placed limits on interest rates, while land speculators demanded the eviction of squatters and the building of roads and canals to enhance the value of their holdings. Other Americans turned to politics to advance religious and cultural causes. In 1828 evangelical Presbyterians in Utica, New York, campaigned for a town ordinance to restrict secular activities on Sunday. In response a member of the local Universalist Church (a freethinking Protestant denomination) attacked this effort at coercive reform and called for "Religious Liberty."

Parties Take Command.   Political parties allowed the voices of diverse interest groups—and even individual voters—to be heard. The founders of the American republic had condemned political "factions" and "parties" as antirepublican and therefore refused to give parties a role in the new constitutional system. But as the power of notables declined, the political party emerged as the central organizing force in the American system of government. The new parties were disciplined groups run by professional politicians from middle-class back-grounds, especially lawyers and journalists. To some observers the parties resembled the mechanical inno-vations of the Industrial Revolution, **political "machines"** that, like a well-designed textile loom, wove the diverse threads of social groups and economic interests into an elaborate tapestry—a coherent legislative program.

Martin Van Buren of New York was the chief architect—and advocate—of the emerging system of party government. Between 1817 and 1821 the "Little Magician" created the first statewide political machine, the Albany Regency; a few years later he organized the first nationwide political party, the Jacksonian Democrats. Van Buren repudiated the republican principle that political parties were dangerous to the commonwealth. Indeed, he argued, the opposite was true: "All men of sense know that political parties are inseparable from free government" because they checked the government's "disposition to abuse power . . . [and curbed] the passions, the ambition, and the usurpations" of potential tyrants.

One key to Van Buren's success as a politician in New York was his systematic use of the *Albany Argus* and other party newspapers to promote a platform and drum up the vote. **Patronage** was even more important to the success of Van Buren's party because the Albany Regency's control of the legislature gave Van Buren and his followers a greater "interest" than any landed no-table—some six thousand appointments to the legal bu-reaucracy of New York (judges, justices of the peace, sheriffs, deed commissioners, and coroners) carrying salaries and fees worth $1 million. Finally, Van Buren in-sisted on party discipline, requiring state legislators to follow the majority decisions of a party meeting, or **cau-cus.** On one crucial occasion, Van Buren pleaded with seventeen legislators to "magnanimously sacrifice indi-vidual preferences for the general good" and rewarded their party loyalty with patronage and a formal banquet where, an observer wrote, they were treated with "some-thing approaching divine honors."

The Election of 1824

The advance of political democracy disrupted the old system of national politics and undermined the power of the leading notables who ran it. The aristocratic Federalist Party virtually disappeared, and the Republi-can Party broke up into competing factions. As the election of 1824 approached, no fewer than five candi-dates, all calling themselves Republicans, campaigned for the presidency. Three were veterans of President James Monroe's cabinet: Secretary of State John Quincy Adams, the son of former president John Adams; Secretary of War John C. Calhoun; and Secretary of the

John Quincy Adams (1767–1848)
This famous daguerreotype of the former president, taken about 1843 by Philip Haas, conveys his rigid personality and high moral standards. These personal attributes hindered Adams's effectiveness as the nation's chief executive but contributed to his success as an antislavery congressman from Massachusetts in the 1830s and 1840s.
Metropolitan Museum of Art. Gift of I. N. Phelps Stokes, Edward S. Hawes, Alice Mary Hawes, Marion Augusta Hawes.

Treasury William H. Crawford. The fourth candidate was Henry Clay of Kentucky, the dynamic Speaker of the House of Representatives, and the fifth was General An-drew Jackson, now a senator from Tennessee. Although a caucus of the Republicans in Congress had selected Crawford as the "official" nominee, the other candidates refused to accept that result.

Instead they introduced democracy to national poli-tics by seeking support among ordinary voters. As a result of democratic reforms, eighteen of the twenty-four states used popular elections (rather than a vote of the state leg-islature) to choose members of the electoral college. Thus in three-quarters of the states the contest for the presi-dency depended directly on the votes of ordinary men.

The battle was closely fought. Thanks to his diplo-matic successes as secretary of state (see Chapter 10), John Quincy Adams enjoyed national recognition and, because of his Massachusetts origins, commanded most of the electoral votes of the New England states. Henry Clay framed his candidacy around domestic issues.

During his many years in Congress, Clay had gradually articulated a program known as the **American System**, a plan for economic development in which the national government would use the Second Bank of the United States to regulate state banks and would spend tariff revenues to subsidize internal improvements such as roads and canals. Clay's nationalistic program won him great popularity in the West, where such transportation improvements would have a strong impact, and equally great criticism in the South, which could rely on rivers to carry its cotton to market and did not have manufacturing industries to protect. William Crawford of Georgia led a strong southern contingent of "Old Republicans," heirs of the political principles of Thomas Jefferson. Fearing the "consolidation" of all political power in Washington, the Old Republicans attacked the American System as a danger to the authority and powers of the state governments. Recognizing Crawford's strength in his home region, John C. Calhoun of South Carolina withdrew his candidacy, endorsing Andrew Jackson for the presidency and seeking the vice presidency for himself.

As the hero of the Battle of New Orleans, Jackson surged to prominence on the wave of nationalistic pride that flowed from the War of 1812. Born in the Carolina backcountry, Jackson had settled in Nashville, Tennessee, where he formed ties to influential families through marriage and his career as an attorney and slave-owning cotton planter. His reputation as a man of civic virtue and "plain solid republican utility" attracted many voters, and his rise from common origins fit the tenor of the new democratic age. Nominated for the presidency by the Tennessee legislature, Jackson soon commanded nationwide support.

Still, Jackson's strong showing in the election surprised most political leaders, who had predicted a dead heat among Adams, Jackson, and Crawford. The Tennessee senator received 99 votes in the electoral college; Adams garnered 84 votes; Crawford, who suffered a stroke during the campaign, won 41; and Clay finished with 37 (Map 11.1). Since no candidate had received an absolute majority, the Constitution specified that the House of Representatives would choose the president from among the three leading contenders. Throwing the election into the House hurt Jackson, because many congressmen rebelled at the thought of a rough-hewn westerner in the White House and feared that this "military chieftain" might become a political tyrant. Personally out of the race, Henry Clay used his powers as Speaker to thwart Jackson's election. By the time the House met in February 1825, Clay had assembled a coalition of congressmen from New England and the Ohio Valley that voted Adams into the presidency. Adams showed his gratitude by appointing Clay as secretary of state, the traditional steppingstone to the presidency.

Clay's appointment was a fatal mistake for both men. Convinced Adams and Clay had made a deal before the election was decided, John C. Calhoun

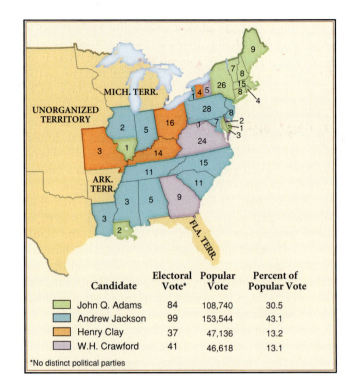

MAP 11.1   Presidential Election of 1824

Regional ties decided the presidential election of 1824. John Quincy Adams captured every electoral vote in New England and most of those in New York. Henry Clay carried Ohio and Kentucky, the most populous trans-Appalachian states, and William Crawford took the southern states of Virginia and Georgia. Only Andrew Jackson claimed a national constituency, winning Pennsylvania and New Jersey in the East, Indiana and Illinois in the Midwest, and most of the South. Only about 356,000 Americans voted, about 27 percent of the eligible electorate.

Candidate	Electoral Vote*	Popular Vote	Percent of Popular Vote
John Q. Adams	84	108,740	30.5
Andrew Jackson	99	153,544	43.1
Henry Clay	37	47,136	13.2
W.H. Crawford	41	46,618	13.1

*No distinct political parties

accused Adams of subverting the popular will by using "the power and patronage of the Executive" to select his successor. It was, he wrote, "the most dangerous stab, which the liberty of this country has yet received." Jackson's many supporters in Congress likewise suspected that Clay had made a preelection deal to become secretary of state. Condemning this "corrupt bargain," they vowed that Clay would never become president.

The Last Notable President: John Quincy Adams

As president, Adams called for a government based on "talent and virtue alone" and bold national leadership. "The moral purpose of the Creator," he told Congress, was to use the president and every other public official to "improve the conditions of himself and his fellow men." Adams called for the establishment of a national university in Washington, extensive scientific explorations in the Far West, and the adoption of a uniform standard of weights and measures. Most important of all, he embraced the American System of national economic development proposed by Henry Clay: (1) a protective tariff to stimulate manufacturing, (2) federally subsidized internal improvements (roads and canals) to aid commerce, and (3) a national bank to provide a uniform currency and control credit.

Internal Improvements Rejected.   Adams's policies favored the business elite of the Northeast and also assisted entrepreneurs and commercial farmers in the Midwest. They won little support among southern planters, who opposed protective tariffs, and among smallholding farmers, who feared powerful banks. From his deathbed Thomas Jefferson condemned Adams for promoting "a single and splendid government of [a monied] aristocracy . . . riding and ruling over the plundered ploughman and beggared yeomanry." Other politicians objected to the American System on constitutional grounds. In 1817 President Madison had vetoed a Bonus Bill, proposed by Henry Clay and John C. Calhoun, that would have used the federal government's income from the Second Bank of the United States to fund internal improvement projects in the various states. In his veto message Madison had argued that such projects fell into the province of the states and exceeded the national government's constitutional powers, a sentiment that was widely shared. Declaring his allegiance on "Constitutional questions . . . with the doctrines of the Jefferson School," Martin Van Buren joined with the Old Republicans in voting against federal subsidies for roads and canals and proposed constitutional amendments to limit them. A hostile Congress defeated most of Adams's ambitious proposals for a nationally financed system of economic development, approving only a few navigation improvements and a short extension of the National Road from Wheeling, Virginia, into Ohio.

The Tariff Battle.   The most far-reaching battle of the Adams administration came over tariffs. The Tariff of 1816 effectively excluded imports of cheap English cotton cloth, giving control of that market to New England textile producers. In 1824 a new tariff had imposed a protective tax of 35 percent on more expensive types of woolen and cotton cloth as well as iron goods. Adams and Clay now demanded even higher duties to protect the iron and textile industries in Pennsylvania and New England. When Van Buren and his Jacksonian allies took control of Congress in 1826, they also supported higher tariffs but for different reasons. By imposing tariffs on imported raw materials, such as wool and hemp, Van Buren hoped to win the support of farmers in New York, Ohio, and Kentucky for Jackson's presidential candidacy in 1828. The tariff had become a prisoner of politics. "I fear this tariff thing," remarked Thomas Cooper of South Carolina, "by some strange mechanical contrivance . . . it will be changed into a machine for manufacturing Presidents, instead of broadcloths, and bed blankets." Disregarding southern opposition, northern Jacksonians joined with the supporters of Adams and Clay to enact the Tariff of 1828, which raised duties on both raw materials and manufactures.

A CARTOON COMPARING CONDITIONS UNDER FREE TRADE AND PROTECTIVE TARIFF

From "The United States Weekly Telegram," November 5, 1832.

The Tariff of Abominations

Political cartoons were widely used in eighteenth-century England and became popular in the United States during the political battles of the First Party System (1794–1815). By the 1820s newspapers, most of which were subsidized by political parties, published daily cartoons. This political cartoon of 1828 attacks the new tariff as hostile to the interests and prosperity of the South. The gaunt figure on the left represents a southern planter, starved by exactions of the tariff, while the northern textile manufacturer on the right has grown stout by feasting on the bounty of protection. Corbis-Bettmann.

The new tariff enraged the South, which gained nothing from the legislation. As the world's cheapest producer of raw cotton, the South did not need a protective tariff, and by raising the price of British manufactures, the tariff cost southern planters about $100 million a year. Now they had to buy either higher-cost American textiles and iron goods, thus enriching northeastern businesses and workers, or highly taxed British goods, thus paying the cost of the national government. The new tariff was "little less than legalized pillage" declared an Alabama legislator, a "Tariff of Abominations."

"The Democracy" and the Election of 1828

Despite the Jacksonians' support for the tariff, most southerners blamed President Adams for the new act and, also offended by his Indian policy, refused to support Adams's bid for a second term. A deeply moralistic man, Adams had supported the land rights of Native Americans against expansionist-minded southern whites. In 1825 U.S. commissioners had secured a treaty from one faction of Creeks that ceded the remaining Creek lands in Georgia to the United States. When the Creek National Council repudiated the treaty as fraudulent, Adams called for new negotiations. In response Governor George M. Troup vowed to take the lands by force. Troup attacked the president as a "public enemy . . . the unblushing ally of the savages" and persuaded Congress to pass legislation that extinguished the Creeks' land titles, forcing most Creeks to leave the state.

Elsewhere in the nation Adams's primary weakness was political. He was the last notable to serve in the White House, and he acted the part: aloof, moralistic, paternalistic. When Congress rejected his activist economic policies, Adams questioned the wisdom of the people and advised elected officials not to be "palsied by the will of our constituents." Ignoring his waning popularity, the president failed to use patronage to reward his supporters; indeed, he allowed hostile federal officeholders to keep their appointed positions as long as they were competent. As the election of 1828 approached, Adams did not mount a full-scale campaign. Rather than "run" for reelection, he "stood" for it, telling supporters, "If my country wants my services, she must ask for them."

Martin Van Buren and the professional politicians handling Andrew Jackson's campaign for the presidency had no reservations about "running" for office. Now a U.S. senator from New York, Van Buren began to fashion the first national campaign organization. His goal was to re-create the old Jeffersonian coalition, uniting northern farmers and artisans (the "plain Republicans of the North") with the southern slave owners and smallholding farmers who had voted Jefferson, Madison, and Monroe into the presidency. John C. Calhoun, Jackson's semiofficial running mate, brought his South Carolina allies into Van Buren's party, and Jackson's close friends in Tennessee rallied voters in the Old Southwest to the cause. Directed by Van Buren, state politicians orchestrated a massive newspaper campaign; in New York fifty newspapers declared their support for Jackson on the same day. Local Jacksonians organized mass meetings, torchlight parades, and barbecues to excite public interest. They celebrated Jackson's frontier origins and his rise to fame without the advantages of birth, education, or political intrigue. Old Hickory—the nickname came from the toughest American hardwood tree—was a "natural" aristocrat, a self-made man. "Jackson for ever!" was their cry.

Initially the Jacksonians called themselves Democratic Republicans, but as the campaign wore on, they became Democrats or "the Democracy." The name conveyed their message. The American republic had been corrupted by "special privilege" and corporate interests that, as Jacksonian Thomas Morris told the Ohio legislature, gave "a few individuals rights and privileges not enjoyed by the citizens at large." Morris promised that his party would destroy "artificial distinction in society" and ensure rule by the majority—the Democracy. As Jackson himself declared, "Equality among the people in the rights conferred by government" was the "great radical principle of freedom."

Jackson's message of equal rights and popular rule appealed to a variety of social groups. His hostility to special privileges for business corporations and to Clay's American System won support among urban workers and artisans in the Northeast who felt threatened by industrialization. In the Southeast and the Midwest Old Hickory's well-known animus toward Native Americans reassured white farmers who favored Indian removal. On the controversial Tariff of Abominations, Jackson benefited from the financial boost it gave to Pennsylvania ironworkers and New York farmers, but he declared his personal preference for a "judicious" tariff, thus appealing for southern votes by suggesting that the existing rates were too high.

The Democrats' strategy of seeking votes from a variety of social and economic groups worked like a charm. In 1824 only about a fourth of the eligible electorate had voted; in 1828 more than half went to the polls, and they voted overwhelmingly for Jackson (Figure 11.1). The senator from Tennessee received 178 of 261 electoral votes and became the first president from a western state, indeed from any state other than Virginia and Massachusetts (Map 11.2). As Jackson traveled to Washington to take up the reins of government, an English visitor noted, he "wore his hair carelessly but not ungracefully arranged, and in spite of his harsh, gaunt features looked like a gentleman and a soldier." However, the massive outpouring of popular support for Jackson had frightened men of wealth and influence. As the ex-Federalist and corporate lawyer Daniel Webster warned his clients, the new president would "bring a breeze with him. Which way it will blow, I cannot tell [but] . . . my fear is stronger than my hope." Watching an unruly crowd clamber over the elegant furniture in the White House to shake the hand of the newly inaugurated president, Supreme Court

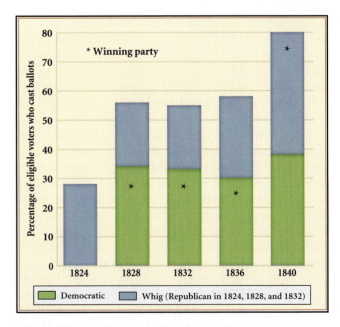

FIGURE 11.1 Changes in Voting Patterns, 1824–1840

Because of the return of two-party competition, voter participation soared in the critical presidential elections of 1828 and 1840.

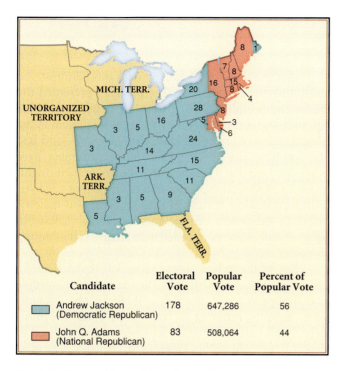

Candidate	Electoral Vote	Popular Vote	Percent of Popular Vote
Andrew Jackson (Democratic Republican)	178	647,286	56
John Q. Adams (National Republican)	83	508,064	44

MAP 11.2 Presidential Election of 1828

As in 1824, John Quincy Adams carried all of New England and some of the Middle Atlantic states. However, Andrew Jackson swept the rest of the nation and won a resounding victory in the electoral college. Nearly 1.2 million American men cast ballots in 1828, three times the number who voted in 1824.

Justice Joseph Story thought he knew the answer, lamenting that "the reign of King 'Mob' seemed triumphant" (see American Voices, "Margaret Bayard Smith: Republican Majesty and Mobs," p. 322).

The Jacksonian Presidency, 1829–1837

Political democracy—a broad franchise, a disciplined political party, and policies tailored to specific social groups—had carried Andrew Jackson to the presidency. Jackson used his popular mandate to enhance the authority of the president over that of Congress, destroy the nationalistic American System of Adams and Clay, and ordain a new ideology for the Democracy. An Ohio supporter outlined Jackson's vision: "the Sovereignty of the People, the Rights of the States, and a Light and Simple Government."

Jackson's Agenda: Patronage and Policy

To decide policy, Jackson relied primarily on an informal group of advisors, his so-called Kitchen Cabinet. Its most influential members were Francis Preston Blair of Kentucky, who edited the *Washington Globe*; Amos Kendall, also from Kentucky, who helped Jackson write

his public addresses; Roger B. Taney of Maryland, who became attorney general and then chief justice of the United States; and, the most influential, Secretary of State Martin Van Buren.

Following Van Buren's example in New York, Jackson used patronage to create a loyal and disciplined national party. He insisted on rotation in office: when a new administration came to power, bureaucrats would have to leave government service and return "to making a living as other people do." Dismissing the argument that forced rotation would eliminate expertise, Jackson suggested that most public duties were "so plain and simple that men of intelligence may readily qualify themselves for their performance." William L. Marcy, a New York Jacksonian, put it more bluntly: government jobs were like the spoils of war, and there was "nothing wrong in the rule that to the victor belong the spoils of the enemy." Using the **spoils system**, Jackson dispensed government jobs to aid his friends and win support for his legislative program.

Jackson's main priority was to destroy the American System. As Henry Clay noted apprehensively, the new president wanted "to cry down old constructions of the Constitution . . . to make all Jefferson's opinions the articles of faith of the new Church." Declaring that the "voice of the people" called for "economy in the expenditures of the Government," Jackson rejected federal support for transportation projects, which he also opposed on constitutional grounds. In 1830 he vetoed four internal improvement bills, including an extension of the National Road, arguing in part that the proposed extension would lie entirely within Kentucky and therefore amounted to "an infringement of the reserved powers of states." Then Jackson turned his attention to two complex and equally politically-charged parts of the American System: protective tariffs and the national bank.

The Tariff and Nullification

The Tariff of 1828 had helped Jackson win the presidency, but it saddled him with a major political crisis. Fierce opposition to the tariff arose in South Carolina, where slave owners faced the prospect of slave rebellion and suffered from chronic insecurity. South Carolina was the only state with an African American majority—56 percent of the population in 1830—and, like the white planters in the predominantly black sugar islands of the West Indies, its slave owners lived in fear of a black rebellion. They also worried about the legal abolition of slavery. The British Parliament had promised to end slavery in the West Indies (and did so in August 1833), and South Carolina planters worried that the U.S. government might do the same. "If the general government shall continue to stretch their powers," a southern congressman had warned as early as 1818, antislavery societies "will undoubtedly put them to try the question of emancipation." To rule out this

Margaret Bayard Smith

Republican Majesty and Mobs

As Andrew Jackson ascended to the presidency in 1829, he threatened the established political and social system by questioning the legitimacy of a powerful central government and calling for democracy and "equal rights." Writing to her son, the Washington socialite Margaret Bayard Smith revealed a mixture of pride and anxiety about the new president and the coming of popular democracy.

The inauguration . . . was one grand whole—an imposing and majestic spectacle. . . . Thousands and thousands of people, without distinction of rank, collected in an immense mass around the Capitol, silent, orderly, and tranquil, with their eyes fixed on the front of the Capitol, waiting the appearance of the president. . . . The door from the Rotunda opens, preceded by the marshall surrounded by the judges of the Supreme Court, the old man [President Jackson] with his grey hair, that crown of glory, advances, bows to the people, who greet him with a shout that rends the air. The cannon, from the heights around from Alexandria and Fort Washington, proclaim the [oath of office] he has taken and all the hills around reverberate the sound. It was grand; it was sublime! An almost breathless silence succeeded and the multitude was still—listening to catch the sound of his voice, though it was so low as to be heard only by those nearest to him.

After reading his speech, the oath was administered to him by the chief justice. The marshall presented the Bible. The president took it from his hand, pressed his lips to it, laid it reverently down, then bowed again to the people. Yes, to the people in all their majesty—and had the spectacle closed here, even Europeans must have acknowledged that a free people, collected in their might, silent and tranquil, restrained solely by a moral power, without a shadow around of military force, was majesty, rising to sublimity, and far surpassing the majesty of kings and princes, surrounded with armies and glittering in gold. . . .

[But at the White House reception that followed,] what a scene did we witness!! The majesty of the people had disappeared, and [instead] a rabble, a mob . . . scrambling, fighting, romping . . . [crowded around] the president, [who,] after having literally been nearly pressed to death . . . escaped to his lodgings at Gadsby's. Cut glass and bone china to the amount of several thousand dollars had been broken in the struggle to get refreshments. . . . Ladies fainted, men were seen with bloody noses. . . . Ladies and gentlemen only had been expected at this [reception], not the people en masse. . . . But it was the people's day, and the people's president. . . .

God grant the people do not put down all rule and rulers. I fear . . . as they have been found in all ages and countries where they get power in their hands, that of all tyrants, they are the most ferocious, cruel, and despotic. The . . . rabble in the president's house brought to my mind descriptions I had read of the mobs in the Tuileries and at Versailles [during the French Revolution].

Source: M. B. Smith to J. B. H. Smith, March 1829, Smith Family Correspondence, Library of Congress, in Linda R. Monk, ed., *Ordinary Americans: U.S. History through the Eyes of Ordinary People* (Alexandria, VA: Close Up Foundation, 1993), 49–50.

possibility, South Carolina politicians tried to limit the power of the central government and chose the tariff as their target.

The crisis began in 1832, when high-tariff congressmen ignored southern warnings that they were "endangering the Union" and passed legislation retaining the duties imposed by the Tariff of Abominations. In November leading South Carolinians called a state convention, which boldly adopted an Ordinance of Nullification. The ordinance declared the tariffs of 1828 and 1832 null and void, forbade the collection of those

duties in the state after February 1, 1833, and threatened secession if federal bureaucrats tried to collect them.

South Carolina's act of **nullification** rested on the constitutional arguments developed in a tract published in 1828, *The South Carolina Exposition and Protest*. Written anonymously by Vice President John C. Calhoun, the *Exposition* denied that majority rule lay at the heart of republican government. "Constitutional government and the government of a majority are utterly incompatible," Calhoun wrote. "An unchecked majority is a despotism." To devise a mechanism to check congressional

Fashion and Fear in South Carolina, c. 1831

This painting, executed by South Carolina artist S. Bernard around the time of the nullification crisis, shows fashionably dressed whites strolling along the East Battery of Charleston. To the left, two African Americans resort to fisticuffs, while other blacks sit and watch. Although the scene is tranquil, many whites feared an uprising by enslaved blacks, who formed a majority of the state's population. Yale University Art Gallery.

majorities, Calhoun turned to the arguments advanced by Jefferson and Madison in the Kentucky and Virginia Resolutions of 1798. Developing a constitutional theory that states' rights advocates would use well into the twentieth century, Calhoun maintained that the U.S. Constitution had been ratified by the people in state conventions. Consequently, he argued, a state convention could determine whether a congressional law was unconstitutional and declare it null and void within the state's borders.

Although Jackson wanted to limit the powers of the national government, he believed it should be done through the existing constitutional system. Confronting Calhoun at a banquet in 1830, Jackson publicly repudiated his vice president's ideas by proposing a formal toast: "Our Federal Union—it must be preserved." Two years later the president's response to South Carolina's Nullification Ordinance was equally forthright. "Disunion by armed force is treason," he declared in December 1832. Appealing to patriotism, Jackson asserted that

nullification violated the Constitution and was "unauthorized by its spirit, inconsistent with every principle on which it is founded, and destructive of the great object for which it was formed." At Jackson's request, Congress passed a Force Bill early in 1833 authorizing him to use the army and navy to compel South Carolina to obey national laws. Simultaneously, Jackson met the South's objections to high import duties by winning passage of a compromise Tariff Act that provided for a gradual reduction in rates. By 1842 import taxes would revert to the modest levels set in 1816, eliminating another part of Clay's American System.

The compromise worked. Having won a gradual reduction in duties, the South Carolina convention rescinded its nullification of the tariff (while defiantly nullifying the now meaningless Force Act). Jackson was satisfied. He had upheld the principle that no state could nullify a law of the United States, a position that Abraham Lincoln would embrace in defense of the Union during the secession crisis of 1861.

The Bank War

In the middle of the tariff crisis Jackson faced another major challenge, this one from the supporters of the Second Bank of the United States. The Second Bank stood at the center of the American financial system. A privately managed entity, it had operated since 1816 under a twenty-year charter from the federal government, which owned 20 percent of its stock. The bank's most important role was to stabilize the nation's money supply. Most American money consisted of notes and bills of credit—in effect, paper money—issued by state-chartered banks. The banks promised to redeem the notes on demand with "hard" money—that is, gold or silver coins (also known as **specie**). By collecting those notes and regularly demanding specie, the Second Bank kept the state banks from issuing too much paper money and thereby prevented monetary inflation and higher prices.

During the prosperous 1820s the Second Bank had maintained monetary stability by restraining some expansion-minded banks in the western states and forcing others to close. This tight-money policy pleased bankers and entrepreneurs in Boston, New York, and Philadelphia, whose capital investments were underwriting economic development, but aroused considerable popular hostility. Most Americans did not understand the regulatory role of the Second Bank and feared its ability to force bank closures, which left ordinary citizens holding worthless paper notes. Some wealthy Americans also opposed the Second Bank because they resented the financial clout wielded by its arrogant president, Nicholas Biddle. "As to mere power," Biddle wrote to a friend, "I have been for years in the daily exercise of more personal authority than any President habitually enjoys." Fearing Biddle's power, New York bankers wanted the specie owned by the federal government to be deposited in their institutions rather than in the Second Bank. Likewise, expansion-minded bankers in western cities, including friends of Jackson in Nashville, wanted to escape supervision by a central bank.

Jackson Vetoes the Rechartering Bill.

However, it was a political miscalculation by the supporters of the Second Bank that brought about its downfall. In 1832 Jackson's opponents in Congress, led by Henry Clay and Daniel Webster, persuaded Biddle to request an early recharter of the bank. They had the votes to get a rechartering bill through Congress and hoped to lure Jackson into a veto that would split the Democrats just before the 1832 elections.

Jackson turned the tables on Clay and Webster. He vetoed the bill that rechartered the bank and became a public hero by justifying his action in a masterful public statement. His veto message blended constitutional arguments with class rhetoric and patriotic fervor. Adopting the position that Jefferson had taken in 1792, Jackson declared that Congress had no constitutional authority to charter a national bank, which was "subversive of the rights of the States." Then, using the populist republican rhetoric of the American Revolution, he attacked the Second Bank as "dangerous to the liberties of the people," a nest of special privilege and monopoly power that promoted "the advancement of the few at the expense of the many . . . the farmers, mechanics, and laborers." Finally, the president evoked national patriotism by pointing out that British aristocrats owned much of the bank's stock; any such powerful institution should be "purely American," he declared.

Jackson's attack on the bank carried him to victory in the presidential election of 1832. He jettisoned Calhoun as a running mate because of the South Carolinian's support for nullification and Calhoun's refusal to welcome Peggy Eaton, a cabinet wife accused of sexual improprieties, into Washington society. As his new vice president, Jackson chose his longtime political ally and advisor Martin Van Buren. Together Old Hickory and Little Van overwhelmed Henry Clay, who headed the National Republican ticket, by 219 to 49 electoral votes. Jackson's most fervent supporters were eastern workers and western farmers, whose lives had been disrupted by falling wages or price fluctuations and who blamed their fate on the Second Bank. "All the flourishing cities of the West are mortgaged to this money power," charged Senator Thomas Hart Benton of Missouri. "They may be devoured by it at any moment. They are in the jaws of the monster." But just as many Jacksonians were the beneficiaries of a decade of strong economic growth and rising living standards and wanted more of the same. Expansion-minded state bankers hoped to benefit from the demise of the Second Bank, and thousands of middle-class Americans—lawyers, clerks, shopkeepers, artisans—cheered Jackson's attacks on privileged corporations. They wanted equal opportunity to rise in the world (see Voices from Abroad, "Alexis de Tocqueville: Parties in the United States," p. 325).

The Bank Destroyed.

Shortly after his reelection and in the midst of the tariff struggle with South Carolina, Jackson launched a new assault on the Second Bank, which still had four years left on its charter. He appointed Roger B. Taney, a strong opponent of corporate privilege, as secretary of the treasury and directed Taney to withdraw the government's gold and silver from the bank and deposit it in state institutions, which critics called his "pet banks." To justify this abrupt (and probably illegal) act Jackson claimed that his own reelection represented "the decision of the people against the bank," giving him a mandate to destroy it. This was the first time a president had claimed that victory at the polls allowed him to act independently of Congress.

The "bank war" escalated. In March 1834 Jackson's opponents in the Senate passed a resolution written by

Alexis de Tocqueville

Parties in the United States

*I*n the late 1820s Alexis de Tocqueville visited the United States to inspect its innovative system of prisons and ended up writing a brilliant memoir. In Democracy in America (1835) Tocqueville presented both a philosophical analysis of the society of the United States and an astute description of its political institutions. Here the republican-minded French aristocrat explains why "great political parties" are not to be found in the United States and how regional interests and individual ambitions threaten the stability of the political system.

The political parties that I style great are those which cling to principles rather than to their consequences; to general and not to special cases; to ideas and not to men.... In them private interest, which always plays the chief part in political passions, is more studiously veiled under the pretext of the public good....

Great political parties ... are not to be met with in the United States at the present time. Parties, indeed, may be found which threaten the future of the Union; but there is none which seems to contest the present form of government or the present course of society. The parties by which the Union is menaced do not rest upon principles, but upon material interests. These interests constitute, in the different provinces of so vast an empire, rival nations rather than parties. Thus, upon a recent occasion [the Tariff of 1832 and the nullification crisis] the North contended for the system of commercial prohibition, and the South took up arms in favor of free trade, simply because the North is a manufacturing and the South an agricultural community; and the restrictive system that was profitable to the one was prejudicial to the other.

In the absence of great parties the United States swarms with lesser controversies.... The pains that are taken to create parties are inconceivable, and at the present day it is no easy task. In the United States there is no religious animosity, ... no jealousy of rank, ... no public misery.... Nevertheless, ambitious men will succeed in creating parties.... A political aspirant in the United States begins by discerning his own interest ... [and] then contrives to find out some doctrine or principle that may suit the purposes of this new organization, which he adopts in order to bring forward his party and secure its popularity....

The deeper we penetrate into the inmost thought of these parties, the more we perceive that the object of the one is to limit and that of the other to extend the authority of the people. I do not assert that the ostensible purpose or even that the secret aim of American parties is to promote the rule of aristocracy or democracy in the country; but I affirm that aristocratic or democratic passions may easily be detected at the bottom of all parties....

To quote a recent example, when President Jackson attacked the Bank of the United States, the country was excited, and parties were formed; the well-informed classes rallied round the bank, the common people round the President. But it must not be imagined that the people had formed a rational opinion upon a question which offers so many difficulties to the most experienced statesmen. By no means. The bank is a great establishment, which has an independent existence; and the people ... are startled to meet with this obstacle to their authority [and are] led to attack it, in order to see whether it can be shaken, like everything else.

Source: Alexis de Tocqueville, *Democracy in America* (1835; New York: Random House, 1981), 1:94–99.

Henry Clay censuring the president and warning of executive tyranny: "We are in the midst of a revolution, hitherto bloodless, but rapidly descending towards a total change of the pure republican character of the Government, and the concentration of all power in the hands of one man." Jackson was not deterred by widespread congressional opposition and was determined to succeed, "regardless of who goes with me." As he vowed to Van Buren, "The Bank is trying to kill me but I will kill it!" And so he did. In 1836 the Second Bank lost its national charter and became a state bank in Pennsylvania, still a wealthy institution but one without public responsibilities.

Jackson had destroyed both national banking—the creation of Alexander Hamilton—and the American System of protective tariffs and internal improvements favored by John Quincy Adams and Henry Clay. The result was a profound change in the policies and powers of the national government. "All is gone," observed a Washington newspaper correspondent. "All is gone,

Jackson Destroys the Bank

In this political cartoon Jackson proudly orders the withdrawal of "Public Money" from the privately run Second Bank of the United States. Crushed by the subsequent collapse of the bank are its director Nicholas Biddle, depicted as the Devil, wealthy British and American investors, and the newspapers that supported Biddle during the bank war. Standing behind the president is "Major Jack Downing," the pseudonym for Seba Smith, a pro-Jackson humorist. Library of Congress.

For more help analyzing this image, see the ONLINE STUDY GUIDE at bedfordstmartins.com/henretta.

which the General Government was instituted to create and preserve."

Indian Removal

The status of the Native American peoples was as difficult a political issue as the tariff and the bank, and it also raised issues of national versus state power. In the late 1820s white voices throughout the western states and territories called for the resettlement of Indians to the west of the Mississippi River (Map 11.3). Many easterners also favored removal. Even to those whites who were sympathetic to the Native American peoples, resettlement seemed the only way to protect Indians from alcoholic degradation and economic sharp dealing and to preserve their traditional cultures.

Most Indians had no wish to leave their ancestral lands. The Old Southwest was the home of the so-called Five Civilized Tribes: the Cherokees and Creeks in Georgia, Tennessee, and Alabama; the Chickasaws and Choctaws in Mississippi and Alabama; and the Seminoles in Florida. During the War of 1812 Jackson's military expeditions had forced the Creeks to relinquish millions of acres. But Indian peoples still controlled vast tracts of land and, led by the mixed-blood descendants of white traders and Indian women, strongly resisted removal. Growing up in a bicultural world, mixed-blood Indians had learned the political ways of whites and some of them emulated the lifestyle of southern planters. James Vann, a Georgia Cherokee, owned more than twenty black slaves, two trading posts, and a gristmill. Forty other Cherokee mixed-blood families owned a total of more than a thousand slaves. To protect their property and the lands of their people, the mixed-bloods attempted to forge a strong national identity. Sequoyah, a mixed-blood, developed a system of writing for the Cherokee language, and the tribe published a newspaper. In 1827 the Cherokees introduced a new

charter of government modeled directly on the U.S. Constitution. Full-blooded Cherokees, who made up 90 percent of the population, resisted many of the mixed-bloods' cultural and political innovations but were equally determined to retain their ancestral lands. "We would not receive money for land in which our fathers and friends are buried," one chief declared. "We love our land; it is our mother."

The Cherokees' preferences carried no weight with the Georgia legislature. In 1802 Georgia had given up its land claims in the West in return for a federal promise to extinguish Indian landholdings in the state. Now it demanded the fulfillment of that promise, declaring that the Cherokees were merely tenants on state-owned land. Having spent most of his military life fighting Indians and seizing their lands, Jackson gave full support to Georgia. On assuming the presidency, he withdrew the federal troops that had protected Indian enclaves there and in Alabama and Mississippi. The states, he argued, were sovereign within their borders.

Jackson then pushed through Congress the Indian Removal Act of 1830, which provided territory in present-day Oklahoma and Kansas to Native Americans who would give up their ancestral holdings. To persuade Indians to move, government officials promised that they could live on the new lands, "they and all their children, as long as grass grows and water runs." When Chief Black Hawk and his Sauk and Fox followers refused to move from rich farmland along the Mississippi River in western Illinois in 1832, Jackson sent troops to expel them (see American Voices, "Black Hawk: A Sacred Reverence for Our Lands," p. 329). Rejecting Black Hawk's offer to surrender, the American army pursued him into the Wisconsin Territory and, in the brutal eight-hour Bad Axe Massacre, killed 850 of Black Hawk's 1,000 warriors. Over the next five years diplomatic pressure and military power forced seventy Indian peoples to sign treaties and move west of the Mississippi. Those

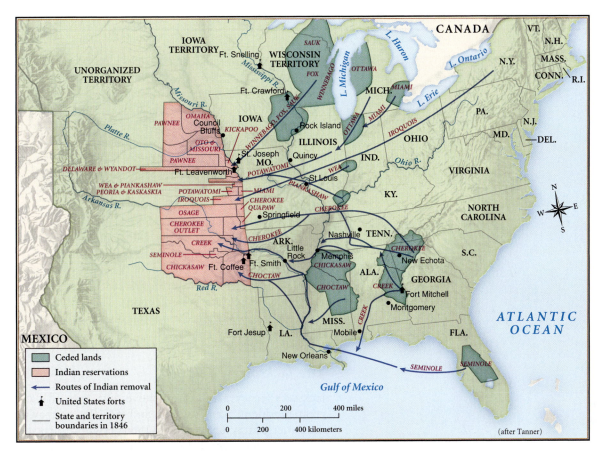

MAP 11.3 The Removal of Native Americans, 1820–1843

Beginning in the 1820s the U.S. government coerced scores of Native American peoples to sign treaties that exchanged Indian lands in the East for money and designated tracts west of the Mississippi River. During the 1830s the government used military force to expel the Cherokees, Chickasaws, Choctaws, Creeks, and many Seminoles from their ancestral homes in the Old Southeast and resettle them on reservations in the Indian Territory in the present-day states of Oklahoma and Kansas.

Raising Public Opinion against the Seminoles

During the eighteenth century hundreds of enslaved Africans from South Carolina and Georgia sought refuge in Spanish Florida, where they lived among and intermarried with the Seminole people. This graphic color engraving of the 1830s, intended to bolster political support for the forced removal of the Seminoles to the Indian Territory, shows red and black Seminoles butchering respectable white families. By the mid-1840s, after a decade of warfare, the U.S. Army had forced 2,500 Seminoles—about half the total number—to migrate to Oklahoma; the remainder continued to live in Florida, protected by a new treaty. Granger Collection.

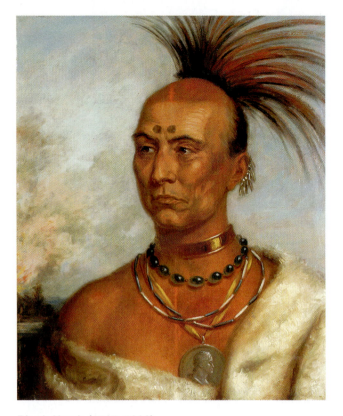

Black Hawk (1767–1838)

This portrait of Black Hawk, by Charles Bird King, shows the Indian leader as a young warrior, wearing a medal commemorating an early-nineteenth-century agreement with the U.S. government. Later, in 1830, when Congress approved Andrew Jackson's Indian Removal Act, Black Hawk mobilized Sauk and Fox warriors to protect ancestral lands in Illinois. "It was here, that I was born—and here lie the bones of many friends and relatives," the aging chief declared, "I . . . never could consent to leave it." Newberry Library.

agreements exchanged 100 million acres of land in the East for $68 million and 32 million acres in the West.

In the meantime the Cherokees had carried their case to the Supreme Court, claiming the status of a "foreign nation" under the U.S. Constitution. In *Cherokee Nation v. Georgia* (1831) Chief Justice John Marshall denied their claim to national independence. Speaking for a majority of the justices Marshall declared that Indian peoples enjoyed only partial autonomy and were "domestic dependent nations." However, in *Worcester v. Georgia* (1832) Marshall sided with the Cherokees, voiding Georgia's extension of state law over them and holding that Indian nations were "distinct political communities, having territorial boundaries, within which their authority is exclusive . . . [and this is] guaranteed by the United States." When Jackson heard the outcome, he reputedly responded, "John Marshall has made his decision; now let him enforce it."

Rather than guaranteeing the Cherokees' territory, Jackson moved purposefully to take it from them. U.S. commissioners signed a removal treaty with a minority

faction and insisted that all Cherokees abide by it. By the deadline in May 1838 only 2,000 of the 17,000 Cherokees had departed. During the summer, Martin Van Buren, who had succeeded Jackson as president, ordered General Winfield Scott to enforce the treaty. Scott's army rounded up about 14,000 Cherokees and forcibly marched them 1,200 miles to the new Indian Territory, an arduous journey they remembered as the Trail of Tears (see Map 11.3). Along the way 3,000 Indians died of starvation and exposure. After the Creeks, Chickasaws, and Choctaws moved west of the Mississippi, the only remaining Indian people in the Old Southwest were the Seminoles in Florida. Aided by runaway slaves who had married into the tribe, a portion of the Seminoles fought a successful guerrilla war during the 1840s and remained in Florida. They were the exceptions. The national government had asserted its control over most eastern Indian peoples and forced their removal.

The Jacksonian Impact

Jackson's legacy as chief executive, like that of every great president, was complex and rich. By destroying the American System, he disrupted the movement toward stronger central direction of American life and reinvigorated the Jeffersonian tradition of a limited, frugal national government. Having restrained the reach of the Union government, the president firmly defended it during the nullification crisis, threatening the use of military force to uphold laws enacted by the national legislature. Finally, Jackson permanently expanded the authority of the nation's chief executive, using the rhetoric of popular sovereignty to declare that "the President is the direct representative of the American people."

The Taney Court. Jackson and his Democratic Party used their political predominance to infuse American institutions with their principles. Following the death in 1835 of John Marshall, Jackson appointed Roger B. Taney as chief justice of the Supreme Court. During his long tenure (1835–1864), Taney persuaded the Court to give constitutional legitimacy to Jackson's policies of antimonopoly and states' rights. Writing for a majority of the Court in the landmark case *Charles River Bridge Co. v. Warren Bridge Co.* (1837) Taney declared that the legislative charter held by the Charles River Bridge Company in Massachusetts did not convey a monopoly because an exclusive right was not explicitly stated in the charter. Consequently, the legislature retained the power to charter a competing bridge company. As Taney put it: "While the rights of private property are sacredly guarded, we must not forget that the community also has rights." This decision qualified John Marshall's interpretation of the contract clause of the Constitution in *Dartmouth College v. Woodward* (1819), which had emphasized the binding nature of public charters and

Black Hawk

A Sacred Reverence for Our Lands

*B*lack Hawk (1767–1838), or Makataimeshekiakiak in the language of his people, was a chief of the Sauk and Fox. In 1833 he dictated his life story to a government interpreter, and a young newspaper editor published it. Here Black Hawk describes the coming of white settlers to his village, near present-day Rock Island, Illinois, and his decision to resist removal to lands west of the Mississippi River.

We had about eight hundred acres in cultivation. The land around our village . . . was covered with bluegrass, which made excellent pasture for our horses. . . . The rapids of Rock river furnished us with an abundance of excellent fish, and the land, being good, never failed to produce good crops of corn, beans, pumpkins, and squashes. We always had plenty—our children never cried with hunger, nor our people were never in want. Here our village had stood for more than a hundred years.

[In 1828] Nothing was now talked of but leaving our village. Ke-o-kuck [the principal chief] had been persuaded to consent to . . . remove to the west side of the Mississippi. . . . [I] raised the standard of opposition to Ke-o-kuck, with full determination not to leave my village. . . . I was of the opinion that the white people had plenty of land and would never take our village from us. . . .

During the [following] winter, I received information that three families of whites had arrived at our village and destroyed some of our lodges, and were making fences and dividing our corn-fields for their own use. . . . I requested them [to remove, but some weeks later] we came up to our village, and found that the whites had not left it—but that others had come, and that the greater part of our corn-fields had been enclosed. . . . Some of the whites permitted us to plant small patches in the fields they had fenced, keeping all the best ground for themselves. . . . The white people brought whiskey into our village, made people drunk, and cheated them out of their homes, guns, and [beaver] traps!

That fall [1829] I paid a visit to the agent, before we started to our hunting grounds. . . . He said that the land on which our village stood was now ordered to be sold to individuals; and that, when sold, our right to remain, by treaty, would be at an end, and that if we returned next spring, we would be forced to remove! I refused . . . to quit my village. It was here, that I was born—and here lie the bones of many friends and relatives. For this spot I felt a sacred reverence, and never could consent to leave it, without being forced therefrom.

[In the spring of 1831] I directed my village crier to proclaim, that my orders were, in the event of the [Indian] war chief coming to our village to remove us [to honor the treaty], that not a gun should be fired, nor any resistance offered. That if he determined to fight, for them to remain quietly in their lodges, and let them kill them if he chose.

Source: David Jackson, ed., *Black Hawk: An Autobiography* (Urbana: University of Illinois Press, 1964), 88–90, 95–97, 111–13.

had limited the power of states to alter or repeal them (see Chapter 8). Taney's decision encouraged competitive enterprise, opening the way for legislatures to charter railroads that would vie for business with existing canal and turnpike companies.

Other decisions by the Taney Court refused to broaden Marshall's nationalistic interpretation of the commerce clause. Instead, it enhanced the regulatory role of state governments. For example, in *Mayor of New York v. Miln* (1837) the Taney Court ruled that New York State could use its "police power" to inspect the health of arriving immigrants. The new Jacksonian Court also restored to the states some of the economic powers they had exercised before 1787. In *Briscoe v. Bank of Kentucky* (1837) the Court approved the issuance of currency by a bank owned and controlled by the state of Kentucky, ruling that it did not violate the provision (in Article 1, Section 10, of the U.S. Constitution; see p. D-9) that forbade states from issuing "bills of credit."

State Government Reform. Jacksonian Democrats in the various states mounted their own constitutional revolution. Between 1830 and 1860 twenty states called conventions to revise their basic charters. Most states extended the vote to all white men and reapportioned their legislatures on the basis of population. The revised constitutions also brought government "near to the people" by mandating the election, rather than the appointment, of most public officials—including sheriffs, justices of the peace, and judges.

By inserting Jacksonian ideals into the new constitutions, the delegates changed their character from "republican" governments that undertook public projects to "liberal" regimes that limited the power of the state. Thus most Jacksonian-era constitutions prohibited states from granting exclusive charters to corporations or extending loans or credit guarantees to private businesses. "If there is any danger to be feared in . . . government," declared a New Jersey Democrat, "it is the danger of associated wealth, with special privileges." The revised state constitutions also protected taxpayers by setting strict limits on state debts and encouraging judges to enforce them. As a New York reformer put it, "We will not trust the legislature with the power of creating indefinite mortgages on the people's property." Just as Jackson had destroyed the American System's program of government subsidies on the national level, so his disciples in the states undermined the "commonwealth" philosophy of using chartered corporations and state funds to promote economic development. Declaring that "the world is governed too much," Jacksonians attacked government-granted special privileges and embraced a small-government, laissez-faire outlook. The first American "populists," they celebrated the power of ordinary people to make decisions in the marketplace and the voting booth.

Class, Culture, and the Second Party System

The rise of the Democracy and Jackson's tumultuous presidency sparked the creation in the mid-1830s of a second national party—the Whigs. For the next two decades Whigs and Democrats dominated American politics, forming what historians call the Second Party System. Many evangelical Protestants became Whigs, while most Catholics and nonevangelical Protestants joined the Democrats. The two parties competed fiercely for votes, debating issues of economic policy, class power, and moral reform and offering Americans a clear choice between political programs.

The Whig Worldview

The Whig Party began in Congress in 1834, when opponents of Andrew Jackson banded together to protest his policies and high-handed "kinglike" actions. They took the name **Whigs** to identify themselves with the pre-Revolutionary American and British parties—also called Whigs—that had opposed the arbitrary actions of British monarchs. The congressional Whigs charged that "King Andrew I" had violated the Constitution by creating a "spoils system" and increasing presidential authority, an "executive usurpation" that had undermined

government by elected legislators, the true representatives of the sovereign people.

Whig Ideology. The Whigs were a diverse group, a "heterogeneous mass of old National Republicans and former Jackson men; Masons and Antimasons; abolitionists and proslavery men; bank men and antibank men," according to Whig congressman Millard Fillmore. However, led by Senators Webster of Massachusetts, Clay of Kentucky, and Calhoun of South Carolina, the Whigs gradually elaborated a distinct political vision. Beginning in the congressional elections of 1834 they sought votes especially among evangelical Protestants and upwardly mobile middle- and working-class citizens in the North. Their goal, like that of the Federalists of the 1790s, was a political world dominated by men of ability and wealth;

BORN TO COMMAND.

OF VETO MEMORY.

HAD I BEEN CONSULTED.

KING ANDREW THE FIRST.

A Whig Cartoon

Attacking the president as "KING ANDREW THE FIRST," this political cartoon accuses Andrew Jackson of acting arbitrarily, like a monarch, and trampling on the principles of the Constitution. It emphasizes Jackson's contempt for Congress, expressed in his vetoes of legislation on banking and internal improvements. Seeking to turn democratic fervor to the advantage of the Whig Party, the caption asked: "Shall he reign over us, or shall the PEOPLE RULE?" New-York Historical Society.

unlike the Federalists, the Whig elite would be chosen by talent, not birth.

The Whigs celebrated the role played by enterprising entrepreneurs. "This is a country of self-made men," they boasted, pointing to the relative absence of permanent distinctions of class and status among white citizens of the United States. Arguing that the Industrial Revolution had increased social harmony, they welcomed the investments of "moneyed capitalists" as providing the poor with jobs, "bread, clothing and homes" and stressed the role of activist governments in increasing the nation's wealth. Whig congressman Edward Everett told a Fourth of July crowd in Lowell, Massachusetts, that there was a "holy alliance" among laborers, owners, and governments. Many workers agreed, especially those holding jobs in the New England textile factories and Pennsylvania iron mills that benefited from state subsidies and protective tariffs. To ensure continued economic progress, Everett and northern Whigs called for a return to the American System of Henry Clay and John Quincy Adams.

Support for the Whigs in the South was fragmentary and rested on the appeal of specific policies rather than agreement with the Whigs' social vision. Some southern Whigs were wealthy planters who invested in railroads and banks or sold their cotton to New York merchants. The majority were yeomen whites in the backcountry who wanted to break the grip over state politics held by low-country planters, most of whom were Democrats. In addition, some states' rights Democrats in Virginia and South Carolina became Whigs because, like John C. Calhoun, they condemned Andrew Jackson's crusade against nullification. Like Calhoun, most southern Whigs did not share their party's enthusiasm for high tariffs and social mobility. Indeed, Calhoun argued that the northern Whig ideal of equal opportunity was contradicted not only by slavery, which he considered a fundamental American institution, but also by the wage-labor system of industrial capitalism. "There is and always has been in an advanced state of wealth and civilization a conflict between labor and capital," he argued in 1837, urging southern slave owners and northern factory owners to unite in a defensive alliance against their common foe: the working class composed of enslaved blacks and propertyless whites.

Most Whig leaders rejected Calhoun's class-conscious vision. "A clear and well-defined line between capital and labor" might fit the slave South or class-ridden Europe, Daniel Webster conceded, but in the North "this distinction grows less and less definite as commerce advances." Webster focused on the growing size and affluence of the northern middle class. Indeed, in the election of 1834 the Whigs won a majority in the House of Representatives by appealing to middling groups—the prosperous farmers, small-town merchants, and skilled industrial workers in New England, New York, and the new communities along the Great Lakes.

Anti-Masonry Influence. Many Whig voters had previously been Anti-Masons, members of a powerful but short-lived political movement of the late 1820s. As their name implies, Anti-Masons opposed the Order of Freemasonry, a secret deistic and republican organization that began in eighteenth-century Europe. Spreading rapidly to America it attracted leading political leaders—including George Washington, Henry Clay, and Andrew Jackson—and ambitious businessmen. By the mid-1820s there were 20,000 Masons in New York State alone, organized into 450 local lodges. Following the kidnapping and murder of William Morgan, a New York Mason who had threatened to reveal the order's secrets, Thurlow Weed, a Rochester newspaper editor, spearheaded an Anti-Masonic political party. Attacking Masonry as a secret aristocratic fraternity, the Anti-Masons drove its members from local and state offices. Having achieved its goals, the movement collapsed.

Picking up on Anti-Masonic themes—temperance, equality of opportunity, evangelical religious values— the Whigs recruited Anti-Masons by advocating legal curbs on the sale of alcohol and local bylaws that preserved Sunday as a day of worship. The Whigs also won congressional seats in the Ohio and Mississippi Valleys, where farmers, bankers, and shopkeepers favored Henry Clay's policies for governmental subsidies for roads, canals, and bridges.

The Election of 1836. In the election of 1836 the Whig Party faced Martin Van Buren, the architect of the Democratic Party and Jackson's handpicked successor. Van Buren emphasized his opposition to the American System, declaring its revival would undermine the rights of the states and create an oppressive system of "consolidated government." Positioning himself as a defender of individual rights, Van Buren likewise opposed the plans of Whigs and moral reformers to use governmental power to impose temperance, evangelical religious values, and the abolition of slavery. "The government is best which governs least" became his motto.

To oppose Van Buren the Whigs ran four regional candidates, hoping to garner enough electoral votes to throw the contest into the House of Representatives, which they controlled. The plan failed. The Whig tally— 73 electoral votes collected by William Henry Harrison of Ohio, 26 by Hugh L. White of Tennessee, 14 by Daniel Webster of New Hampshire, and 11 by W. P. Magnum of Georgia—fell far short of Van Buren's 170 votes. Still, the size of the popular vote for the four Whig candidates—49 percent of the total—showed that the party's message of economic improvement and moral uplift appealed not only to middle-class Americans but

Celebrating a Political Triumph, 1836

To commemorate Martin Van Buren's election to the presidency and to reward friends for their support, the Democratic Party distributed thousands of snuffboxes inscribed with his portrait. By using such innovative measures to enlist the loyalty of voters, Van Buren and his allies transformed American politics from an upper-class avocation to a democratic contest for votes and ***power.*** Collection of Janice L. and David J. Frent.

also to farmers and workers with little or no property. Most important, the election of 1836 witnessed the creation of the Second Party System, a closely fought struggle between Whigs and Democrats that would define American political life for the next two decades.

Labor Politics and the Depression of 1837–1843

As the Democratic and Whig Parties battled for power, they faced challenges from new worker-based political parties. Moreover, a set of sudden catastrophic financial upheavals threw the American economy into a sustained depression, which further increased class tensions and political conflicts.

Working Men's Parties and the Rise of Unions. In seeking the votes of workers, the established parties had to compete with radical reformers, such as Frances Wright (see American Lives, "Frances Wright: Radical Reformer," p. 336) and the Working Men's Parties that had sprung up in fifteen states between 1827 and 1833. Rising prices and stagnant wages had lowered the standard of living of many urban artisans and wage earners, who feared what they called "the glaring inequality of society" and began to organize politically.

"Past experience teaches us that we have nothing to hope from the aristocratic orders of society," declared the New York Working Men's Party, which vowed "to send men of our own description, if we can, to the Legislature at Albany." It called for the end to private banks, chartered monopolies, and imprisonment for debt. The Philadelphia Working Men's Party demanded higher taxes on the wealthy and in 1834 persuaded the Pennsylvania legislature to authorize free, tax-supported schools so that workers' children could advance into the ranks of the propertied classes.

The Working Men's Parties embraced the ideology of artisan republicanism. Their goal was a society in which (as the radical thinker Orestes Brownson put it) there would be no dependent wage earners and "all men will be independent proprietors, working on their own capitals, on their own farms, or in their own shops." This vision led the Working Men's Parties to join the Jacksonians in demanding equal rights and attacking chartered corporations and monopolistic banks. "The only safeguard against oppression," argued William Leggett, a leading member of the New York Loco-Foco (Equal Rights) Party, "is a system of legislation which leaves to all the free exercise of their talents and industry." At first the Working Men's Parties prospered at the polls, but divisions over policy and voter apathy soon took a toll. By the mid-1830s most politically active workers had joined the Democratic Party, urging it to oppose protective tariffs and to tax the stocks and bonds owned by wealthy capitalists.

Taking advantage of the economic boom of the early 1830s, which increased the demand for skilled labor, workers formed unions to bargain for higher wages. Employers responded by attacking the union movement. In 1836 clothing manufacturers in New York City agreed not to hire workers belonging to the Union Trade Society of Journeymen Tailors and circulated a list—a so-called **blacklist**—of its members. The employers also brought lawsuits to overturn **closed-shop agreements** that required them to hire only union members. They argued that such contracts violated both the common law and legislative statutes that prohibited "conspiracies" in restraint of trade.

Judges usually agreed. In 1835 the New York Supreme Court found that a shoemakers' union in Geneva had illegally caused "an industrious man" to be "driven out of employment." "It is important to the best interests of society that the price of labor be left to regulate itself," the Court declared. When a court in New York City upheld a conspiracy verdict against a tailors' union, a crowd of 27,000 people demonstrated outside city hall, and tailors circulated handbills proclaiming that the "Freemen of the North are now on a level with the slaves of the South." In 1836 popular demonstrations prompted local juries to acquit shoemakers in Hudson, New York, carpet makers in Thompsonville, Connecticut, and plasterers in Philadelphia of similar conspiracy charges.

The Panic and the Depression. At this juncture the Panic of 1837 threw the American economy into disarray. The panic began early in the year, when the Bank of England, hoping to boost the faltering British economy, sharply curtailed the flow of money and credit to the United States. For the previous decade and a half British manufacturers and investors had stimulated the American economy, providing southern planters with credit to expand cotton production and purchasing millions of dollars of the canal bonds issued by northern states. Suddenly deprived of British funds, American planters, merchants, and canal corporations had to withdraw specie from domestic banks to pay their foreign loans and commercial debts. Moreover, because the Bank of England refused to advance credit to American cotton brokers, the price of raw cotton in the South collapsed from 20 cents a pound to 10 cents or less.

Falling cotton prices and the drain of gold and silver set off a general financial crisis. On May 8 the Dry Dock Bank of New York City closed its doors, and panicked depositors withdrew more than $2 million in gold and silver coins from other city banks, forcing them to suspend all payments in specie. Within two weeks every bank in the United States had followed suit, shocking high-flying entrepreneurs and ordinary citizens and sending the economy into a steep decline (Map 11.4). "This sudden overthrow of the commercial credit and honor of the nation" had a "stunning effect," observed Henry Fox, the British minister in Washington. "The conquest of the land by a foreign power could hardly have produced a more general sense of humiliation and grief."

A second, longer-lasting economic downturn began in 1839. Following the Panic of 1837, state governments had increased their investments in canals and other transportation ventures. As more and more bonds to finance these ventures were sold in Europe, their prices fell sharply, sparking an international financial crisis in 1839 that lasted for four years. The crisis soon engulfed state governments, which were unable to meet the substantial interest payments on their bonds. Nine states defaulted on their obligations to foreign creditors; other states declared a moratorium on debt payments, undermining the confidence of British investors and cutting the flow of capital. Bumper crops drove down cotton prices even further, bringing more bankruptcies.

The American economy fell into a deep depression. By 1843 canal construction had dropped 90 percent and prices nearly 50 percent. Unemployment reached almost 20 percent of the workforce in seaports and industrial centers. From his pulpit, minister Henry Ward Beecher described a land "filled with lamentation . . . its inhabitants wandering like bereaved citizens among the ruins of an earthquake, mourning for children, for houses crushed, and property buried forever."

By creating a surplus of unemployed workers the depression devastated the labor movement. In 1837, six thousand masons, carpenters, and other building-trades workers lost their jobs in New York City, depleting union membership and destroying unions' bargaining power. By 1843 most local unions and all the national labor organizations had disappeared, along with their newspapers.

However, two events during the depression years improved the long-term prospects of the labor movement. One was a major legal victory. In *Commonwealth v. Hunt* (1842), a case decided by the Massachusetts Supreme Judicial Court, Chief Justice Lemuel Shaw upheld the rights of workers to form unions and enforce a closed shop. Shaw, one of the great jurists of the nineteenth century, overturned common-law precedents by making two critical rulings: (1) a union was not an inherently illegal organization, and (2) union members could legally attempt to enforce a closed shop, even by striking. Courts in other states generally accepted Shaw's opinion, but judges (who were mostly Whigs) found other methods, such as court injunctions, to restrict strikes and boycotts. Labor's second success was political. Continuing Jackson's effort to attract workers to the Democratic Party, in 1840 President Van Buren signed an executive order establishing a ten-hour day for all federal employees. Significantly, this achievement came after the unions had been defeated in the marketplace, underlining the fact that the outcome of workers' struggles—like conflicts over tariffs, banks, and internal improvements—would depend not only on economic factors but also on political decisions.

"Tippecanoe and Tyler Too!"

The depression had a major impact on American politics. Few people understood the complex workings of the international economy, and thus many Americans blamed the Democrats for their economic woes. In particular, they derided Jackson for destroying the Second Bank and for issuing the Specie Circular of 1836, which required western settlers to use gold and silver coins to pay for land purchases. Not realizing that shipment of specie to Britain (to pay off past debts) was the main cause of the financial panic, the Whigs blamed Jackson's policies.

The public turned its anger on Van Buren, who entered office just as the panic began. Ignoring the pleas of influential bankers, the new president refused to revoke the Specie Circular or take other actions that might reverse the downturn. Holding to his philosophy of limited government, Van Buren advised Congress that "the less government interferes with private pursuits the better for the general prosperity." As a major depression settled upon the nation in 1839, this laissez-faire outlook commanded less and less political support. Worse, Van Buren's major piece of economic legislation, the Independent Treasury Act of 1840, actually delayed recovery. The act pulled federal specie out of Jackson's "pet banks" (which had used it to back loans) and placed it in government vaults (where it did no economic good at

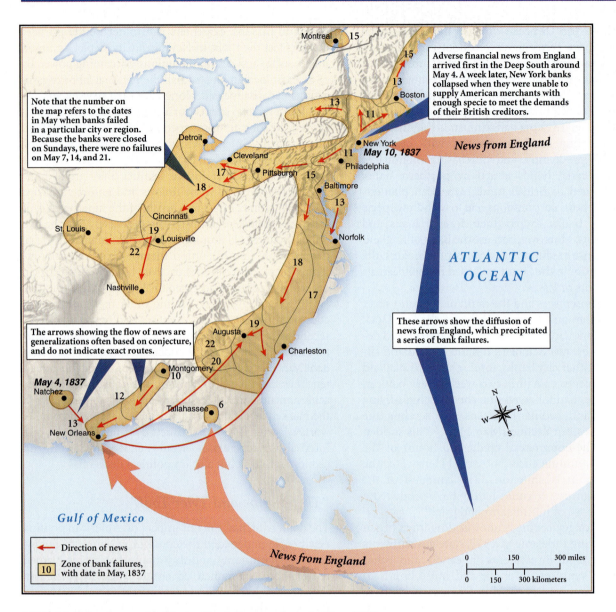

Note that the number on the map refers to the dates in May when banks failed in a particular city or region. Because the banks were closed on Sundays, there were no failures on May 7, 14, and 21.

Adverse financial news from England arrived first in the Deep South around May 4. A week later, New York banks collapsed when they were unable to supply American merchants with enough specie to meet the demands of their British creditors.

The arrows showing the flow of news are generalizations often based on conjecture, and do not indicate exact routes.

These arrows show the diffusion of news from England, which precipitated a series of bank failures.

News from England

News from England

ATLANTIC OCEAN

Gulf of Mexico

May 10, 1837

May 4, 1837

← Direction of news

10 Zone of bank failures, with date in May, 1837

0   150   300 miles
0   150   300 kilometers

MAP 11.4 Anatomy of a Panic: Bank Suspensions in May 1837

The first failures occurred in cotton belt banks (Natchez, Tallahassee, Montgomery), prompted by news that the Bank of England would no longer advance credit to American cotton brokers. A few days later, when British bankers and creditors demanded repayment of loans in specie, New York City merchants withdrew millions of dollars in gold from the city's banks, forcing them to close. This collapse precipitated a chain reaction; within twelve days most banks along the Atlantic coast, the Erie Canal, and the Ohio River had shut their doors. This pattern of bank failures clearly reveals the central importance of New York in the economic nerve system of the nation. (See Map 10.4, on p. 300, for an additional illustration of New York's growing importance.)

For more help analyzing this map, see the ONLINE STUDY GUIDE at bedfordstmartins.com/henretta.

all). Whatever its value in placing the nation's financial reserves above politics, the Independent Treasury Act did little to enhance Van Buren's popularity.

The Election of 1840.   Determined to exploit Van Buren's weakness, in 1840 the Whigs organized their first national convention and nominated William Henry

Harrison of Ohio for president and John Tyler of Virginia for vice president. A military hero of the Battle of Tippecanoe and the War of 1812, Harrison was well advanced in age (sixty-eight) and had little political experience. But the Whig leaders in Congress, Clay and Webster, did not want a strong president; they planned to have Harrison rubber-stamp their program for protective tariffs and a national bank. Party strategists such as Thurlow Weed of New York had chosen Harrison primarily because of his military record and western background, promoting him as the Whig version of Andrew Jackson. An unpretentious, amiable man, Harrison warmed to that task, telling voters that Whig policies were "the only means, under Heaven, by which a poor industrious man may become a rich man without bowing to colossal wealth."

Panic and depression stacked the political cards against Van Buren, but the contest itself turned as much on style as on substance. It became the great "log cabin" campaign—the first occasion on which two well-organized parties competed for the loyalties of a mass electorate by projecting vivid images of their candidates and creating a new style of festive political celebrations. Whig pamphleteering, songfests, parades, and well-orchestrated mass meetings dominated the contest, drawing new voters and new social groups into the political arena. Whig speakers assailed "Martin Van Ruin" as a manipulative politician with aristocratic tastes—a devotee of fancy wines and elegant clothes, as indeed he was. With less candor they praised Harrison, actually the son of a wealthy planter who had signed the Declaration of Independence, as a self-made soldier and statesman who lived in a simple log cabin and enjoyed hard cider, a drink of the common man.

The Whigs boosted their electoral hopes by welcoming women to their festivities. Previously women had been systematically excluded not only from voting and jury duty but also from nearly every other aspect of political life, even marching in July 4 and Washington's Birthday parades. Jacksonian Democrats celebrated politics as a "manly" affair, likening the women who ventured into the political arena to the ordinary run of "public" women—the prostitutes who plied their trade in theaters and other public places. However, the Whigs recognized that women from Yankee families, a core Whig constituency, were deeply involved in American public life through religious revivalism, the temperance movement, and other benevolent activities. So in October 1840 Daniel Webster addressed a special meeting of 1,200 Whig women, perhaps the first mass meeting of women in American politics. Noting women's benevolent efforts, Webster praised their moral perceptions as "both quicker and juster" than those of men and identified their concerns with the Whig programs for moral reform. "This way of making politicians of their women is something new under the sun," noted one Democrat, worried that it would bring more Whig men to the polls. Whatever the cause, more than 80 percent of the eligible male voters cast ballots in 1840 (up from less than 60 percent in 1832 and 1836). Heeding the Whig slogan "Tippecanoe and Tyler Too," they voted Harrison into the White House as

The Log Cabin Campaign, 1840

During the Second Party System, politics became more responsive to the popular will as ordinary people voted for candidates who shared their values and lifestyles. The barrels of hard cider surrounding this homemade campaign banner evoke the drink of the common man, while the central image falsely portrays William Henry Harrison as a poor and simple frontier farmer—a man of the people.
New-York Historical Society.

Frances Wright: Radical Reformer

Frances Wright (1795–1852) arrived in New York City on January 1, 1829, intending to begin the New Year with a new life and a new message. Born into a wealthy, republican-minded merchant family in Glasgow, Scotland, Wright had first learned about America at age sixteen. "From that moment on," she recalled, "my attention became rivetted on this country as upon the theatre where man might first awake to the full knowledge and exercise of his powers." Of the many Europeans drawn to the United States by the egalitarian doctrines of the Declaration of Independence, Wright was among the most radical and controversial. She was an advocate of deism, black emancipation, the abolition of private property, and women's rights.

In 1818 Wright first crossed the Atlantic to her promised land. Returning to Britain three years later, she published an enthusiastic account of republican society, *Views of Society and Manners in America* (1821), which was translated into three languages. Among her readers was the Marquis de Lafayette, the French hero of the American Revolution, who became Wright's friend and patron. She and her sister moved to France, residing at the country estate of the sixty-four-year-old widower. Ignoring the objections of Lafayette's family, Wright stayed with the aging aristocrat for almost two years, at one point begging him either to marry her or adopt her as a daughter.

Wright's tie to Lafayette provided a new link to the United States. In 1824 she accompanied the French general on his triumphal tour of the United States and exploited his social contacts. During a six-week stay with Thomas Jefferson at Monticello, the young Scotswoman outlined a bold plan to set up a community of whites and freed slaves who would live together in full equality. Like other visionaries who believed in human perfectibility, Wright had great ambitions.

Encouraged by Jefferson, in 1825 Wright founded her utopian community, called Nashoba, in the wilderness of western Tennessee. Joined by young white idealists, Wright purchased about thirty enslaved African Americans. Believing in the dignity of labor and self-reliance, she required the slaves to earn their freedom by working the land. While the slaves labored in the fields, the Nashoba community educated their children. A genuine egalitarian, Wright joined in the arduous task of clearing and ditching the marshy land. But she soon lost the willing support of the black workers, who saw little improvement in their lives.

Wright remained undaunted. She embraced the ideals of Robert Owen, a Scottish manufacturer and philanthropist who in 1824 had founded his own utopian community in New Harmony, Indiana. Endorsing Owen's criticism of marriage, organized religion, and private property, Wright called on those at Nashoba to form a society "where affection shall form the only marriage, kind feelings and kind action the only religion, . . . and reunion of interest the bond of peace and security." However, the rude conditions at Nashoba repelled potential recruits, and its numbers dwindled.

By 1828 Wright had concluded that the solution to society's ills required a general campaign to reform the "collective body politic." Forsaking Nashoba, Wright joined forces with Owen's son Robert Dale Owen who had become infatuated with her. Together they launched a lecture campaign that brought her to New York, the high temple of the emerging American capitalist system and a center of trade unionism.

Wright took New York by storm. Preceded by rumors of free love and racial mixing at Nashoba, she attracted large audiences and lived up to her advance billing. Sweeping onto the stage with a group of women apostles, Wright would throw off her cloak to reveal her unorthodox attire—a tunic of white muslin. Then she would wave a copy of the Declaration of Independence and elaborate on its ideals in a resonant, musical voice. The poet Walt Whitman, who heard Wright lecture when he was a young lad, remembered that "we all loved her; fell down before her: her very appearance seemed to enthrall us." Echoing Robert Dale Owen's socialist ideas, Wright told her listeners that a "monied aristocracy" of bankers and a "professional aristocracy" of ministers, lawyers, and politicians was oppressing the "laboring class." She lashed out at evangelical ministers, describing the Benevolent Empire of religious-minded social reformers as the "would-be Christian Party in politics."

Wright preached peaceful reform, not violent revolution. To promote the gradual transition to a better society, she called for the compulsory training in boarding schools of all children between the ages of two and sixteen. Such an educational system would encourage social equality, insulate children from organized religion, and benefit young women, who would learn to break their "mental chains" and seek equality under the law. To nurture a radical culture, Wright and Owen took over an abandoned church in a working-class neighborhood and

Frances Wright

Wright not only preached radical doctrine but also lived by its precepts. This portrait, painted in 1826 at the Nashoba community in Tennessee, broadcasts a culturally subversive message. Wright dresses in masculine attire, wearing the simple and practical costume for women adopted by Robert Owen's socialist community at New Harmony, Indiana—pantaloons covered by a tunic. She also poses next to a horse, a traditional symbol of masculine virility; note the similarity between Wright's pose and that of General George Washington on page 164.

Miriam and Ira D. Wallach Division of Art, Prints and Photographs. The New York Public Library. Astor, Lenox and Tilden Foundations.

transformed it into a "Hall of Science." They established a newspaper, *The Free Enquirer*, a reading room and lecture auditorium, a free medical dispensary, and a deist Sunday school. The two reformers hoped that rationalist science—the religion of the Enlightenment—would displace Protestant dogma as the guiding principle of workers' lives. Wright won a significant following among artisans and journeymen, some of whom turned to politics and energized the Working Men's Party. In 1829 twenty devotees wrote her name on their ballots for the New York assembly.

But most New York workers rejected Wright's message. They believed that a skewed distribution of wealth and opportunity—not traditional religion—was the primary cause of their poverty and powerlessness. Disheartened, in 1831 Wright and Owen sold the Hall of Science to a Methodist congregation and went their separate ways. Owen returned to New Harmony and became a Jacksonian politician. Wright transported the African Americans at Nashoba to the black-run nation of Haiti and then sailed for Paris, where she married a French reformer.

Wright never abandoned her dreams. Inspired by Andrew Jackson's war against the Second Bank, she returned to America in 1835. But her time had passed. Audiences greeted her lectures and her speeches for presidential candidate Martin Van Buren with indifference or hostility. Newspaper editors labeled her the "Red Harlot of Infidelity" (a phrase that simultaneously condemned her socialism, feminism, and deism), and Christian parents compared her to Satan, invoking her name to frighten their children.

Wright settled in Cincinnati, where she lived out her life in obscurity. She became increasingly pessimistic about the American republic, which appeared to have squandered its republican ideals in a mad quest for wealth. Wright no longer felt at home in her chosen land. It seemed, she mused, as if she had "fallen from a strange planet among a race whose sense and perceptions are all different from my own."

the nation's first Whig president and gave the Whigs a majority in Congress.

The Tyler Administration. The Whig triumph was short-lived. One month after his inauguration Harrison died of pneumonia, and the nation got "Tyler Too." Vice President John Tyler of Virginia, who became president, had joined the Whig Party primarily because he opposed Jackson's stance against nullification. On economic issues Tyler was really a Democrat, sharing Jackson's hostility to the Second Bank and the American System. Consequently, he vetoed bills that would have raised tariffs and created a new national bank. Also like Jackson, Tyler favored the common man and the rapid settlement of the West. He approved the Preemption Act of 1841, which allowed cash-poor settlers to stake a free claim to 160 acres of federal land. By building a house and farming the land, they could buy the property later at a set price of $1.25 an acre.

The split between Tyler and the Whigs allowed the Democrats to regroup. The party vigorously recruited supporters among subsistence farmers in the North and smallholding planters in the South. It cultivated the votes of the urban working class and was particularly successful among Irish and German Catholic immigrants—whose numbers had increased rapidly during the 1830s—supporting their demands for religious and cultural freedom (Figure 11.2). Thanks to these recruits, the Democrats remained the majority party in most parts of the nation. Their program of equal rights, states' rights, and cultural liberty was more attractive than the Whig platform of economic nationalism, moral reform, and individual mobility.

The continuing struggle between Whigs and Democrats, each claiming to speak for "the people," completed the democratic revolution that European visitors found so troubling. The new system perpetuated many problematic political customs—denying women, Indians, and most African Americans an effective voice in public life—and introduced a few more dubious practices, such as the spoils system and a coarser standard of public debate. Yet the United States now boasted universal suffrage for white men as well as a highly organized system of representative government that was responsive to ordinary citizens. In their scope and significance these political initiatives matched the economic advances of the Industrial and Market Revolutions.

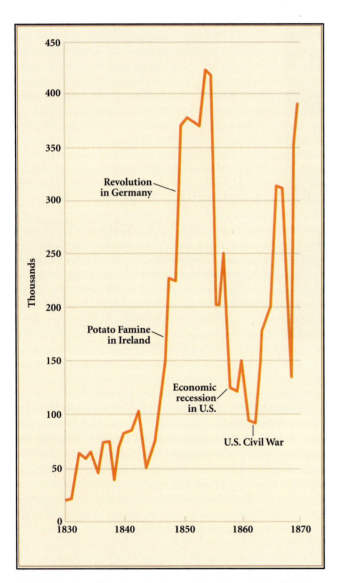

FIGURE 11.2 The Surge in Immigration, 1842–1855

The failure of the potato crop prompted a wholesale migration of peasants from the overcrowded farms of western Ireland. Population pressure likewise spurred the migration of tens of thousands of German peasants, while the failure of the liberal political revolution of 1848 prompted hundreds of prominent German politicians and intellectuals to settle in the United States.

Source: David M. Potter, *Division and the Stresses of Reunion, 1845–1876.* Copyright © 1973 Scott, Foresman and Company. Reprinted by permission.

FOR FURTHER EXPLORATION

▶ For definitions of key terms boldfaced in this chapter, see the glossary at the end of the book.

▶ To assess your mastery of the material covered in this chapter, see the Online Study Guide at **bedfordstmartins.com/henretta.**

▶ For suggested references, including Web sites, see page SR-12 at the end of the book.

▶ For map resources and primary documents, see **bedfordstmartins.com/henretta.**

With the rise of popular politics in the states, the power of notable men declined, and political parties and professional politicians assumed control of American public life. Martin Van Buren and other party leaders used patronage to enact legislation favorable to powerful social groups.

Political democracy came to national politics in 1824, as John Quincy Adams, Henry Clay, William Crawford, and Andrew Jackson competed for the presidency. Jackson received the most electoral votes but, because he lacked a majority, the House of Representatives decided the contest. A "corrupt bargain" between Adams and Clay elevated Adams to the presidency and made Clay his secretary of state. As president, Adams failed to win congressional approval for the American System because many citizens opposed the expansion of federal power. The high rates imposed by the Tariff of 1828 caused many southerners to oppose Adams's reelection, and Andrew Jackson won an overwhelming victory in 1828.

During his eight years as president, Jackson carried through a political revolution, dramatically reducing the economic agenda of the national government. He ended federal subsidies for internal improvements and won a gradual reduction in tariff rates. Jackson likewise eliminated national banking by refusing to recharter the Second Bank of the United States. However, Jackson used the military power of the national government to carry through his policy of Indian removal and to coerce South Carolina to renounce nullification. He was the first "modern" president, in claiming that his victory at the polls gave him a political mandate.

Charging that "King Andrew I" had abused his powers, Henry Clay, Daniel Webster, and John C. Calhoun formed the Whig Party. It drew support from the growing middle class and from former Anti-Masons, who were attracted by the Whigs' ideology of social mobility, and moral reform. For the next two decades Whigs and Democrats struggled for dominance in the Second Party System.

The Panic of 1837 and the depression of 1839 destroyed the workingmen's parties and most labor unions. The depression helped the Whigs to victory in the log cabin campaign of 1840, but when the new president, William Henry Harrison, suddenly died, President John Tyler pursued Democrat-like policies that prevented the Whigs from instituting Clay's American System. By the early 1840s the American democratic revolution was complete, and the new political system was about to be tested by the growing conflict over slavery.

1810s Revision of state constitutions and expansion of voting rights for men

Martin Van Buren creates a disciplined party in New York

1825 John Quincy Adams elected president by House; advocates Henry Clay's American System

1827 Philadelphia Working Men's Party organized

1828 "Tariff of Abominations" raises duties on imported materials and manufactures

The South Carolina Exposition and Protest challenges idea of majority rule

1830 Andrew Jackson vetoes extension of National Road

Congress enacts Jackson's Indian Removal Act

1831 *Cherokee Nation v. Georgia* denies Indians' claim of national independence

1832 Expulsion of Sauk and Fox peoples; Bad Axe Massacre by American troops

Jackson vetoes the rechartering of the Second Bank

South Carolina nullifies Tariff of 1832

Worcester v. Georgia upholds political autonomy of Indian peoples

1833 Force Bill and compromise Tariff Act

1834 Whig Party formed by Henry Clay, John C. Calhoun, and Daniel Webster

1835 Roger Taney named Supreme Court chief justice

1837 *Charles River Bridge Co. v. Warren Bridge Co.* weakens legal position of chartered monopolies

Panic of 1837 ends long period of economic expansion.

1838 Trail of Tears: thousands of Cherokees die on forced march to new Indian Territory

1839 American borrowings spark international financial crisis and four-year economic depression

1840 Van Buren finally wins Independent Treasury Act

Whig victory in "log cabin" campaign

1841 John Tyler succeeds William Henry Harrison as president

Preemption Act promotes purchase of federal land

1842 *Commonwealth v. Hunt* legitimates trade unions

CHAPTER 12

Religion and Reform

1820–1860

Individualism
Emerson and Transcendentalism
Emerson's Literary Influence
Brook Farm

Communalism
The Shakers
The Fourierist Phalanxes
*John Humphrey Noyes and the
    Oneida Community*
The Mormon Experience

Abolitionism
Slave Rebellion
*Garrison and Evangelical
    Abolitionism*
Opposition and Internal Conflict

The Women's Rights Movement
Origins of the Women's Movement
Abolitionism and Women
The Program of Seneca Falls

"THE SPIRIT OF REFORM IS IN EVERY PLACE," the children of legal reformer David Dudley Field wrote in their handwritten monthly *Gazette* in 1842:

the labourer with a family says "reform the common schools"; the merchant and the planter say, "reform the tariff"; the lawyer "reform the laws," the politician "reform the govern-ment," the abolitionist "reform the slave laws," the moralist "reform intemperance," . . . the ladies wish their legal privileges extended, and in short, the whole country is wanting reform.

◀ **"Pieties Quilt," by Maria Cadman Hubbard, 1848**

Maria Hubbard may have been a Quaker because "No Cross, No Crown" (an inscription on the far right) was the title of William Penn's pamphlet of the 1670s attacking the Church of England. Whatever Hubbard's affiliation, she used her skills as a quilt maker to express deeply held religious beliefs. By inscribing her name and age on the quilt, Maria Cadman Hubbard also created an artifact of material culture that would perpetuate her memory among descendants and provide a historical document for future generations. Unlike most women of her time, she would not vanish from the record of the past.

Collection of the American Folk Art Museum, New York. Gift of Cyril Irwin Nelson in loving memory of his parents, Cyril Arthur and Elise Macy Nelson.

Like many Americans, the young Field children sensed that a whirlwind of political change in the 1830s had transformed the way people thought about themselves as individuals and as a society. It encouraged men and women to believe that they could improve not just their personal lives but society as a whole. Some people dedicated themselves to societal reform. Beginning as an antislavery advocate, William Lloyd Garrison went on to embrace women's rights, pacifism, and the abolition of prisons. Such individuals, the Unitarian minister Henry W. Bellows warned, were obsessed, pursuing "an object, which in its very nature is unattainable—the perpetual improvement of the outward condition."

Many obstacles stood in the way of the reformers' quest for a better society. The American social order was still rigidly divided by race and gender as well as by wealth and religious belief. Moreover, recent social changes brought hardships to some individuals even as they enhanced the standard of living for many others. Most strikingly, the emergent economic system imposed greater discipline on many workers, as slave owners compelled enslaved African Americans to work in labor gangs and factory managers prescribed strict routines for factory operatives. In fact, the first wave of American "improvers," the benevolent reformers of the 1820s, seized on social discipline as the answer to the nation's ills, championing regular church attendance, temperance, and the strict moral codes of the evangelical churches.

Then in the 1830s and 1840s a more powerful wave of reform spilled out of these conservative religious channels and washed over American society, threatening to submerge traditional values and institutions. Mostly middle-class northerners and midwesterners in origin, the new reformers propounded a bewildering assortment of radical ideals—extreme individualism, common ownership of property, the immediate emancipation of slaves, and sexual equality—and demanded immediate action to satisfy their visions. Although they formed a small minority of the American population, the reformers launched a far-reaching intellectual and cultural debate that challenged the premises of the social order and won the attention, but not the respect, of the majority. As a fearful southerner saw it, the goal of the reformers was a world in which there would be "No-Marriage, No-Religion, No-Private Property, No-Law and No Government."

The Founder of Transcendentalism

As this painting of Ralph Waldo Emerson by an unknown artist indicates, the young New England philosopher was an attractive man, his face brimming with confidence and optimism. Because of his radiant personality and incisive intellect, Emerson deeply influenced dozens of influential writers, artists, and scholars and enjoyed great success as a lecturer among the emerging middle class.
The Metropolitan Museum of Art, bequest of Chester Dale, 1962 [64.97.4].

Individualism

The reform movement reflected the social conditions and intellectual currents of American life. In 1835 Alexis de Tocqueville coined a new word, **individualism**, to describe the condition and values of native-born white Americans. He argued that Americans lived a more solitary existence than their European ancestors, "no longer attached to each other by any tie of caste, class, association, or family." Unlike Tocqueville, an aristocrat who feared the disintegration of society, the New England transcendentalist Ralph Waldo Emerson (1803–1882) celebrated this liberation of the individual from traditional social and institutional constraints. Emerson's vision of individual freedom—balanced by a strong sense of personal responsibility—influenced thousands of ordinary Americans and a generation of important artists and writers.

Emerson and Transcendentalism

Emerson was the leading spokesman for **transcendentalism**, an intellectual movement rooted in the religious soil of New England. Its first advocates were spiritually inclined young men, often Unitarian ministers from well-to-do New England families, who questioned the constraints imposed by their Puritan heritage. For inspiration they turned to Europe, drawing on a new conception of self and society known as *Romanticism*. Romantic thinkers, such as the English poet Samuel Taylor Coleridge, rejected the ordered, rational world of the eighteenth-century Enlightenment. Instead they tried to capture the passionate character of the human spirit and sought deeper insights into the mysteries of existence. Drawing on ideas borrowed from the German philosopher Immanuel Kant, English Romantics and Unitarian radicals believed that behind the concrete world of the senses was an ideal world. To reach this deeper reality people had to "transcend," or go beyond, the rational ways in which they normally comprehended the world. By tapping mysterious intuitive powers people could soar beyond the limits of ordinary experience and gain mystical knowledge of ultimate and eternal things.

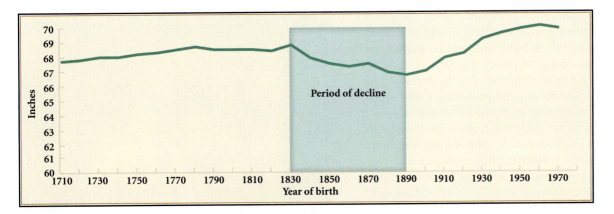

FIGURE 12.1 Environment and Health: Heights of Native-born Men, by Year of Birth

The Transcendentalists sensed that the new commercial and industrial economy would bring a decline in living standards, and modern research suggests they were right. Military records and other sources show that men born in America from the 1830s to the 1890s had average heights as adults that were significantly lower than those of men born between 1710 and 1830. Important causes seem to be a decline in the quality of childhood nutrition and an increase in diseases, especially in urban areas. Better nutrition, public health regulations, and higher living standards in the twentieth century ushered in a rise in the average height of men.
Source: Richard Steckel, "Health and Nutrition in the Preindustrial Era," National Bureau of Economic Research, Working Paper 8452 (2001), figure 3.

Emerson had followed in the footsteps of his father and had become a Unitarian minister, thus placing himself outside the religious mainstream. Unlike most Christians, Unitarians held that God was a single being and not a trinity of Father, Son, and Holy Spirit. In 1832 Emerson moved still further from orthodox Christianity, resigning his Boston pulpit and rejecting organized religion. Moving to Concord, Massachusetts, he gradually articulated the philosophy of transcendentalism in a series of influential essays. His focus was what he called "the infinitude of the private man," the idea of the radically free individual.

The young philosopher saw people as being trapped in inherited customs and institutions. They wore the ideas of people from earlier times—the tenets of New England Calvinism, for example—as a kind of "faded masquerade" and needed to shed those values and practices. "What is a man born for but to be a Reformer, a Remaker of what man has made?" he asked. For Emerson an individual's remaking depended on the discovery of his or her own "original relation with Nature," an insight that would lead to a mystical private union with the "currents of Universal Being." The ideal setting for such a discovery was solitude under an open sky, among nature's rocks and trees.

Emerson's genius lay in his capacity to translate such abstract ideas into examples that made sense to ordinary middle-class Americans. His essays and lectures conveyed the message that all nature was saturated with the presence of God—a pantheistic spiritual outlook that departed from traditional Christian doctrine and underlay his attack on organized religion. Emerson also criticized the new industrial society, predicting that a preoccupation with work, profits, and the consumption of factory-made goods would drain the nation's spiritual energy (Figure 12.1). "Things are in the saddle," Emerson wrote, "and ride mankind."

The transcendentalist message of inner change and self-realization reached hundreds of thousands of people, primarily through Emerson's writings and lectures. Public lectures had become a spectacularly successful way of spreading information and fostering discussion among the middle classes. Beginning in 1826 the **American Lyceum** undertook to "promote the general diffusion of knowledge." Named in honor of the place where the ancient Greek philosopher Aristotle taught, the Lyceum organized lecture tours by all sorts of speakers—poets, preachers, scientists, reformers—and soon achieved great popularity, especially in the North and Midwest. In 1839, nearly 150 local Lyceums in Massachusetts invited lecturers to their towns to speak to more than 33,000 subscribers. Among the hundreds of lecturers on the Lyceum circuit, Emerson was the most popular. Between 1833 and 1860 he gave 1,500 lectures in more than 300 towns in twenty states.

Emerson celebrated individuals who rejected traditional social restraints but were self-disciplined and responsible members of society. His outlook tapped currents that already ran deep in the predominantly middle-class members of his audience, because many of them had made their own way in the world. The publication of Benjamin Franklin's *Autobiography* in 1818 had given many of them a down-to-earth model of an individual seeking social mobility and "moral perfection" through self-discipline. Charles Grandison Finney's widely known account of his religious conversion also pointed in Emersonian directions. Finney, the foremost business-class evangelist, pictured his conversion as a mystical union of an individual, alone in the woods, with God. The great revivalist's philosophical outlook, like that of Emerson, affirmed the importance of individual action. As Finney put it, "God has made man a moral free agent," thereby endowing individuals with the ability—and the responsibility—to determine their spiritual fate.

Emerson's Literary Influence

Emerson took as one of his tasks the remaking of American literature. In an address entitled "The American Scholar" (1837) the philosopher issued a literary declaration of independence from the "courtly muse" of Old Europe. He urged American writers to celebrate democracy and individual freedom and find inspiration not in the doings and sayings of aristocratic courts but in the "familiar, the low . . . the milk in the pan; the ballad in the street; the news of the boat; the glance of the eye; the form and gait of the body."

Henry David Thoreau and Margaret Fuller. A young New England intellectual, Henry David Thoreau (1817–1862), heeded Emerson's call by turning to the American environment for inspiration. In 1845, depressed by his beloved brother's death, Thoreau turned away from society and embraced self-reliance and the natural world, building a cabin at the edge of Walden Pond near Concord, Massachusetts, and living alone there for two years. In 1854 he published *Walden, or Life in the Woods*, an account of his spiritual search for meaning beyond the artificiality of "civilized" life:

> I went to the woods because I wished to live deliberately, to front only the essential facts of life, and see if I could not learn what it had to teach, and not, when I came to die, discover that I had not lived.

Although Thoreau's book had little impact outside transcendentalist circles during his lifetime, *Walden* has become an essential text of American literature and an inspiration to those who reject the dictates of society. Its most famous metaphor provides an enduring justification for independent thinking: "If a man does not keep pace with his companions, perhaps it is because he hears a different drummer." Beginning from this premise, Thoreau became an advocate of social nonconformity and civil disobedience against unjust laws.

Margaret Fuller, by Thomas Hicks, 1848
At the age of thirty-eight, Fuller moved to Italy, where she worked as a correspondent for a New York newspaper reporting on the Italian Revolution of 1848. There Fuller became enamored of Thomas Hicks (1823–1890), a much younger American artist. Hicks rebuffed Fuller's advances but painted this rather flattering portrait, softening her features and giving her a pensive look. Fuller married a Roman nobleman, Giovanni Angelo, Marchese d'Ossoli, and gave birth to a son in September 1848. Constance Fuller Threinen.

As Thoreau sought independence and self-realization for men, Margaret Fuller (1810–1850) explored the possibilities of freedom for women. Born into a wealthy Boston family, Fuller mastered six languages, read broadly in the classic works of literature, and educated her four siblings. While teaching in a school for girls, she became interested in Emerson's ideas and in 1839 began a transcendental "conversation," or discussion group, for educated Boston women. Soon Fuller was editing the leading transcendentalist journal, the *Dial*, and in 1844 she published *Woman in the Nineteenth Century*, which proclaimed that a "new era" was coming in the relations between men and women.

Fuller's philosophy began with the transcendental belief that women, like men, had a mystical relationship with God that gave them identity and dignity. It followed that every woman deserved psychological and social independence—the ability "to grow, as an intellect to discern, as a soul to live freely and unimpeded." Thus, she declared, "We would have every arbitrary barrier thrown down" and "every path laid open to Woman as freely as to Man." Embracing that vision, Fuller became the literary critic of the *New York Tribune* and went to Italy to report on the Revolution of 1848. Her adventurous life led to an early death; returning to the United States at the age of forty, she drowned in a shipwreck. Nonetheless, Fuller's example and writings inspired a rising generation of women writers and reformers.

Walt Whitman. Another writer who responded to Emerson's call was the poet Walt Whitman (1819–1892). When Whitman first encountered Emerson, he later recalled, he had been "simmering, simmering." Then Emerson "brought me to a boil." Whitman had been a teacher, a journalist, an editor of the *Brooklyn Eagle* and other newspapers, and an active publicist for the Democratic Party. But poetry was the "direction of his dreams." In *Leaves of Grass*, first published in 1855 and constantly revised and expanded for almost four decades afterward, he recorded in verse his attempt to pass a number of "invisible boundaries": between solitude and community, between prose and poetry, and even between the living and the dead. It was a wild, exuberant poem in both form and content, self-consciously violating every poetic rule and every canon of respectable taste. Unlike the cautious Emerson, Whitman dared readers to shut the book in revulsion or accept his idiosyncratic vision.

At the center of *Leaves of Grass* is the individual—the figure of the poet, "I, Walt." He begins alone: "I celebrate myself, and sing myself." But because he has what Emerson called an "original relation" with nature, Whitman claims not solitude but perfect communion with others: "For every atom belonging to me as good belongs to you." Whitman celebrates democracy as well as himself, arguing that a poet can claim a profoundly intimate, mystical relationship with a mass audience. For Emerson, Thoreau, and Fuller the individual had a divine spark. For Whitman the individual had expanded to become divine, and democracy assumed a sacred character.

The transcendentalists were not naive optimists. Whitman wrote about human suffering with passion, and Emerson's accounts of the exhilaration that could come in natural settings were tinged with anxiety. "I am glad," he once said, "to the brink of fear." Thoreau's gloomy judgment of everyday life is well known: "The mass of men lead lives of quiet desperation." Still, such dark murmurings were muted in their work, woven into triumphant and expansive assertions that nothing was impossible for an individual who could break free from tradition, law, and other social restraints and discover an "original relation with Nature."

Darker Visions. Emerson's writings also influenced two great novelists, Nathaniel Hawthorne and Herman Melville, who had more pessimistic outlooks. They addressed the opposition between individual transcendence and the legitimate requirements of social order, discipline, and responsibility. Both sounded powerful warnings that unfettered egoism could destroy individuals and those around them. Hawthorne's most brilliant exploration of the theme of excessive individualism appeared in his novel *The Scarlet Letter* (1850). The two main characters, Hester Prynne and Arthur Dimmesdale, challenge their seventeenth-century New England community in the most blatant way—by committing adultery and producing a child. The result of their assertion of individual freedom from social discipline is not liberation but degradation—a profound sense of personal guilt and condemnation by the community.

Herman Melville explored the limits of individualism in even more extreme and tragic terms and emerged as a scathing critic of transcendentalism. He made his most powerful statement in *Moby Dick* (1851), the story of Captain Ahab's obsessive hunt for a mysterious white whale that ends in death not only for Ahab but for all but one member of his crew. Here the quest for spiritual meaning in nature brings death, not transcendence, because Ahab, the liberated individual, lacks inner discipline and self-restraint.

Moby Dick was a commercial failure. The middle-class audience that was the primary target of American publishers refused to follow Melville into the dark, dangerous realms of individualism gone mad. Readers also were unenthusiastic about Thoreau's advocacy of civil disobedience and Whitman's boundless claims for a mystical union between the man of genius and the democratic masses. What American readers emphatically preferred were the more modest examples of individualism offered by Emerson—personal improvement through spiritual awareness and self-discipline.

Brook Farm

To escape the constraints of life in America's emerging market society, transcendentalists and other radical reformers created ideal communities, or **utopias**. They hoped that these planned societies, which organized life in new ways, would allow members to realize their spiritual and moral potential. The most important communal experiment of the transcendentalists was Brook Farm, founded in 1841. Once freed from the tension and demands of an urban, competitive society, its members hoped to develop their minds and souls and uplift society through inspiration. The Brook Farmers supported themselves by selling milk, vegetables, and hay for cash but organized their farming so that they could remain relatively independent of the market, with its unpredictable cycles of boom and bust. Residents who did not work on the farm made cash payments—in effect, tuition for what was virtually a transcendentalist boarding school.

The intellectual life at Brook Farm was electric. Hawthorne lived there for a time and later used the setting for his novel *The Blithedale Romance* (1852). All the major transcendentalists, including Emerson, Thoreau, and Fuller, were residents or frequent visitors. A former member recalled that they "inspired the young with a passion for study, and the middle-aged with deference and admiration, while we all breathed the intellectual grace that pervaded the atmosphere." Music, dancing, games, plays, parties, picnics, and dramatic readings filled the leisure hours.

If Brook Farm offered intellectual bliss, it failed to prosper economically. At first most of its members were ministers, teachers, writers, and students who had few productive skills; to succeed as a farming enterprise it needed practical men and women. A reorganization in 1844 attracted more farmers and artisans but yielded only marginal economic gains. And these changes resulted in a more disciplined routine that, as one resident put it, suppressed "the joyous spirit of youth." After a devastating fire in 1846 the organizers disbanded and sold the farm.

After the failure of Brook Farm the transcendentalists abandoned their attempts to fashion a new system of social organization. Most accepted the brute reality of the coming industrial order and tried to reform it, especially through the education of workers. However, the passion of the transcendentalists for individual freedom and social progress lived on in the movement to abolish slavery, which many of them actively supported.

Communalism

Even as Brook Farm faded, thousands of Americans joined other communal settlements during the 1840s, primarily in the rural areas of the Northeast and Midwest (Map 12.1). Most communalists were ordinary farmers and artisans seeking refuge and security from the seven-year economic depression that had begun with the Panic of 1837. These rural utopias were also symbols of social protest. By organizing themselves along socialist lines with common ownership of property or by experimenting with unconventional forms of marriage and family life, the members questioned acquisitive capitalist values and traditional gender roles.

The Shakers

The Shakers, whose origins dated back to the Revolutionary era, were the first successful American communal movement. In 1770 Ann Lee Stanley (Mother Ann), a young cook in Manchester, England, had a vision that she was an incarnation of Christ and that Adam and Eve had been banished from the Garden of Eden because of their sexual lust. Four years later she led a band of eight followers to America, where they established a church near Albany, New York. Because of the ecstatic dances that became part of their worship, the sect became known as "Shaking Quakers" or, more simply, "Shakers." After Mother Ann's death in 1784, the Shakers venerated her as the Second Coming of Christ and decided to withdraw

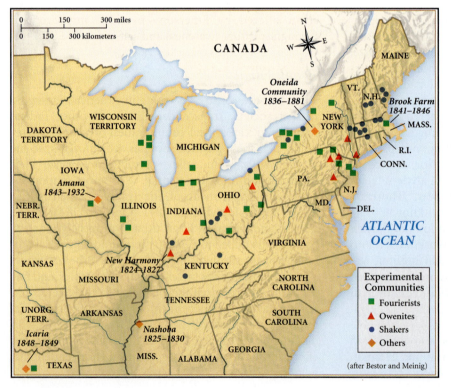

MAP 12.1 Major Communal Experiments before 1860

Some experimental communities settled along the frontier, but the vast majority chose relatively secluded areas in well-settled regions of the North and West. Because of their opposition to slavery, communalists avoided the South. Most secular experiments failed within a few decades, as the founders lost their reformist enthusiasm or died off; religious communities—such as the Shakers and the Mormons—were longer-lived.

The Shaker Community at Poland Hill, Maine (detail)

Like all Shaker communities, the settlement at Poland Hill, Maine, painted by Joshua H. Bussell around 1850, was built on a regular gridlike plan. There was a large dwelling for communal living, surrounded by various workshops and farm buildings. The design of the architecture, like that of Shaker furniture, was plain and sparse.

Collection of the United States of Shakers, Sabbathday Lake, ME.

For more help analyzing this image, see the ONLINE STUDY GUIDE at bedfordstmartins.com/henretta.

from the evils of the world into strictly run communities of believers. They embraced the common ownership of property, accepted strict government by the church, and pledged to abstain from alcohol, tobacco, politics, and war. Shakers also eliminated marriage and made a commitment to celibacy, in accordance with Mother Ann's testimony against "the lustful gratifications of the flesh as the source and foundation of human corruption."

The Shakers believed that God was "a dual person, male and female," and that Mother Ann represented God's female element. These doctrines provided the underpinning for their attempt to eliminate distinctions between the sexes. Community governance was the dual responsibility of women and men, the Eldresses and Elders, but in other respects Shakers maintained a traditional division of labor between men and women.

Beginning in 1787 Shakers founded twenty communities, mostly in New England, New York, and Ohio. Their agriculture and crafts, especially furniture making, acquired a reputation for quality that enabled most of these communities to become self-sustaining and even comfortable. Thanks to this economic success and their ideology of sexual equality, Shaker communities attracted more than three thousand converts during the 1830s, with women outnumbering men more than two to one. They welcomed blacks as well as whites; to Rebecca Cox Jackson, an African American seamstress from Philadelphia who joined their community, the Shakers seemed to be "loving to live forever." Because the Shakers had no children of their own, they had to rely on converts and the adoption of young orphans to replenish their numbers. As these sources dried up in the 1840s and 1850s, the communities stopped growing and eventually began to decline (see Voices from Abroad, "Charles Dickens Assails the Shakers," p. 348). By the end of the nineteenth century most Shaker communities had virtually disappeared, leaving as their material legacy a distinctive and much-imitated furniture style.

The Fourierist Phalanxes

The rise of the American Fourierist movement in the 1840s was one cause of the Shakers' decline. Charles Fourier (1777–1837) was a French utopian reformer who devised an eight-stage theory of social evolution, predicting the imminent decline of individualism and capitalism. As interpreted by his idealistic American disciple Arthur Brisbane, Fourierism would complete "our great political movement of 1776" through new social institutions that would end the "menial and slavish system of Hired Labor or Labor for Wages." In the place of capitalist waged labor there would be cooperative work in communities called **phalanxes**. The members of a phalanx would be its shareholders; they would own all its property in common, including stores and a bank as well as a school and a library.

Fourier and Brisbane saw the phalanx as a practical, more humane alternative to a society based on private property and capitalist values, and one that would liberate women as well as men. "In society as it is now constituted," Brisbane wrote, "Woman is subjected to unremitting and slavish domestic duties"; in the "new Social Order . . . based upon Associated households" women's domestic labor would be shared with men.

Brisbane skillfully promoted Fourier's ideas in his influential book *The Social Destiny of Man* (1840), a regular column in Horace Greeley's *New York Tribune*, and hundreds of lectures, many of them in towns along the Erie Canal. These ideas found a receptive audience among educated farmers and craftsmen, who yearned for economic stability and communal solidarity in the wake of the Panic of 1837. In the 1840s Brisbane and his followers started nearly one hundred cooperative communities, mostly in western New York and the midwestern states of Ohio, Michigan, and Wisconsin, but almost all were unable to

Charles Dickens Assails the Shakers

The English novelist Charles Dickens enjoyed a meteoric rise to fame and by 1837, at the age of twenty-five, was a major literary figure in his home country. Five years later he ventured to the United States intending, like Alexis de Tocqueville, to investigate the prison system. Unlike his French predecessor, Dickens showed little sympathy for Americans and their institutions. In this excerpt from his American Notes, the English novelist recounts his visit to the Shaker community in New Lebanon, New York, and assails the sect's way of life, which he views as grim and repressive.

As we rode along, we passed a party of Shakers, who were at work upon the road; who wore the broadest of all broad brimmed hats; and were in all visible respects such very wooden men, that I felt about as much sympathy for them, and as much interest in them, as if they had been so many figure-heads of ships. Presently we came to the beginning of the village, and . . . requested permission to see the Shaker worship.

Pending the conveyance of this request to some person in authority, we walked into a grim room, where several grim hats were hanging on grim pegs, and the time was grimly told by a grim clock which uttered every tick with a kind of struggle, as if it broke the grim silence reluctantly, and under protest. Ranged against the wall were six or eight stiff high-backed chairs. . . .

Presently, there stalked into this apartment, a grim old Shaker, with eyes as hard, and dull, and cold, as the great round metal buttons on his coat and waistcoat; a sort of calm goblin. Being informed of our desire, he [informed us] . . . that in consequence of certain unseemly interruptions which their worship had received from strangers, their chapel was closed to the public for the space of one year. . . .

All the possessions and revenues of the [Shaker] settlement are thrown into a common stock, which is managed by the elders. As they have made converts among people who were well to do in the world, and are frugal and thrifty, it is understood that this fund prospers. . . .

They eat and drink together, after the Spartan model, at a great public table. There is no union of the sexes, and every Shaker, male and female, is devoted to a life of celibacy. . . .

This is well enough, but nevertheless I cannot, I confess, incline towards the Shakers; view them with much favour, or extend towards them any very lenient construction. I so abhor, and from my soul detest that bad spirit, no matter by what class or sect it may be entertained, which would strip life of its healthful graces, rob youth of its innocent pleasures, pluck from maturity and age their pleasant ornaments, and make existence but a narrow path towards the grave: that odious spirit which, if it could have had full scope and sway upon the earth, must have blasted and made barren the imaginations of the greatest men, and left them . . . no better than the beasts: that, in these very broad brimmed hats and very sombre coats, in [their] stiff-necked solemn visaged piety . . . I recognise the worst among the enemies of Heaven and Earth, who turn the water at the marriage-feasts of this poor world, not into wine, but gall. . . .

Source: Charles Dickens, American Notes (New York: Harper & Brothers, 1842), 71–72.

support themselves and quickly collapsed. Despite its failure to establish viable communities, the Fourierist movement underscored both the extent of the social dislocation caused by the economic depression and the difficulty of establishing a utopian community in the absence of charismatic leaders or a compelling religious vision.

John Humphrey Noyes and the Oneida Community

The radical minister John Humphrey Noyes (1811–1886) was both charismatic and deeply religious. He believed that the Fourierists had failed because their communities lacked the strong religious ethic required for sustained altruism and cooperation and pointed to the success of the Shakers, praising them as the true "pioneers of modern Socialism." Noyes was also attracted by the Shakers' marriageless society and set about creating a community that defined sexuality and gender roles in radically new ways.

Noyes was a well-to-do graduate of Dartmouth College in New Hampshire who was inspired to join the ministry by the preaching of Charles Finney. When Noyes was expelled from his Congregational church for holding unorthodox beliefs, he became a leader of **perfectionism**. Perfectionism was an evangelical movement that attracted thousands of followers during the 1830s, primarily among religiously minded New Englanders who had settled in New York. Perfectionists believed that the Second Coming of Christ had already occurred and that people could therefore aspire to perfection in their earthly lives, attaining complete freedom from sin. Unlike most perfectionists (who lived conventional personal lives), Noyes believed that the major barrier to achieving this ideal state was marriage, which did not exist in heaven and should not exist on earth. "Exclusiveness, jealousy, quarreling have no place at the marriage supper of the Lamb," Noyes wrote. Like the Shakers, Noyes wanted to liberate individuals from sin by reforming relations between men and women. However, his solution was dramatically different: instead of Shaker celibacy, Noyes and his followers embraced **complex marriage**—all the members of his community were married to one another.

Complex marriage was a complex doctrine designed to attain various social goals. Noyes rejected monogamy partly because he wished to free women from being regarded as the property of their husbands, as they were by custom and by common law. To give women even more freedom, he sought to limit childbirth by urging men to have intercourse without orgasm. For those children they did have, Noyes set up communal nurseries. By freeing women from endless childbearing and childraising, Noyes gave them the time and energy to become full and equal members of the community. To symbolize their equality with men the women cut their hair short and wore pantaloons under their calf-length skirts.

In the 1830s Noyes established a community in his hometown of Putney, Vermont. In 1848, as local opposition to the practice of complex marriage grew increasingly intense, Noyes moved his followers to an isolated settlement in Oneida, New York. By the mid-1850s more than two hundred people were living at Oneida, and it became financially self-sufficient when the inventor of a highly successful steel animal trap joined the community. With the profits from the production of traps Oneida diversified into making silverware. After Noyes fled to Canada in 1879 to avoid prosecution for adultery, the community abandoned complex marriage and founded a joint-stock silver manufacturing company, the Oneida Community, Ltd., which survived as an independent business well into the twentieth century.

As with the Shakers and Fourierists, the historical significance of Noyes and his followers does not lie in their numbers, which were small, or in their fine crafts. Rather, these alternative communities were important because, in an even more radical way than Emerson, they questioned traditional customs and repudiated the class divisions and sexual norms of the emergent capitalist society. They stood as countercultural blueprints for a more egalitarian social order.

The Mormon Experience

The Shakers and the Oneidians challenged marriage and family life—two of the most deeply rooted institutions in American society—but their small communities aroused little hostility. The Mormons, or the Church of Jesus Christ of Latter-day Saints, provoked much more animosity because of their equally controversial doctrines and their success in attracting thousands of members.

Joseph Smith. Like many social movements of the era, Mormonism emerged from the religious ferment

Mob Violence against Mormons
In this lithograph, Martyrdom of Joseph and Hiram Smith in Carthage Jail, June 27, 1844, *the artist G. N. Fasel after C. G. Crehen evokes sympathy for the fallen Mormon leader by depicting an assailant as a masked ruffian, prevented from mutilating the corpse only by the intervention of a gentleman. In fact, many leading Illinois politicians and businessmen feared Smith and welcomed the mob's action. The murders prompted Brigham Young, the leader of a large group of Mormons, to move his followers into territory claimed by Mexico, where they hoped to escape religious persecution.*
Library of Congress.

among families of Puritan descent who lived along the Erie Canal. The founder of the Mormon Church was Joseph Smith (1805–1844), a vigorous, powerful individual. Born in Vermont, he moved at the age of ten with his very religious but rather poor farming and shopkeeping family to Palmyra in central New York. In a series of religious experiences that began in 1820, Smith came to believe that God had singled him out to receive a special revelation of divine truth. In 1830 he published *The Book of Mormon*, claiming he had translated it from ancient hieroglyphics on gold plates shown to him by an angel named Moroni. *The Book of Mormon* told the story of ancient civilizations from the Middle East that had migrated to the Western Hemisphere and of the visit of Jesus Christ, soon after the Resurrection, to one of them.

Smith proceeded to organize the Church of Jesus Christ of Latter-day Saints. Seeing himself as a prophet to a sinful, excessively individualistic society, Smith affirmed traditional patriarchal authority within the family and Church control over many aspects of life. Like many Protestant ministers, he encouraged his followers to work hard, save their earnings, and become entrepreneurs—practices central to success in the age of capitalist markets and factories. Unlike other ministers, Smith placed equal emphasis on a communal framework that would protect the Mormon "New Jerusalem" from individualism and outside threats. His goal was a Church-directed society that would inspire moral perfection.

Smith struggled for years to establish a secure home for his new religion. Facing persecution from anti-Mormons, Smith and his growing congregation trekked west, eventually settling in Nauvoo, Illinois, a town they founded on the Mississippi River (Map 12.2). By the early 1840s Nauvoo had become the largest utopian community in the United States, with 30,000 inhabitants. The rigid discipline and secret rituals of the Mormons, along with their prosperity, hostility to other

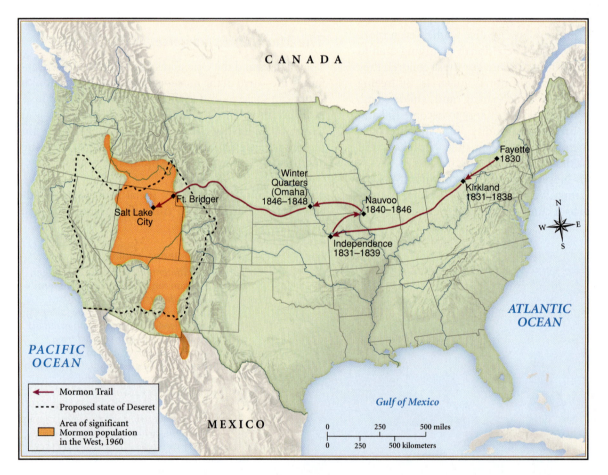

MAP 12.2 The Mormon Trek, 1830–1848

Because of their unorthodox religious views and communal solidarity, Mormons faced hostility first in New York and then in Missouri and Illinois. Following the murder of Joseph Smith, Brigham Young led the polygamist faction of Mormons into lands thinly populated by Native American peoples. From Omaha, the migrants followed the path of the Oregon Trail to Fort Bridger and then struck off to the Southwest, settling in Mexican territory along the Wasatch Mountains in the basin of the Great Salt Lake in present-day Utah.

An Illinois "Jeffersonian" Attacks the Mormons

The corporate solidarity of the Mormon community enraged many Illinois residents, who feared both the political power wielded by the Mormons' large and nearly independent city-state at Nauvoo and the military might of the two-thousand-strong "Legion" commanded by Joseph Smith. In 1844 a mob led by "respectable citizens" assassinated Smith and his brother, and some Illinois residents—such as the author of this letter to the Warsaw Signal, *a newspaper in a town near Nauvoo—called for the forcible expulsion of the Mormons from the state.*

Mr. Editor,

. . . It is a low pitiable contemptable kind of electioneering, that old Tom Jefferson would have been ashamed of—when a body of men acting under the garb of religion (as the Mormons themselves say they are) shall decide our elections and act together as a body politically, we might as well bid a final farewell to our liberties and the common rights of man.

Now Sir, under all these circumstances, it is high time that every individual should come out and clearly define the position that he occupies. I too am an Anti-Mormon both in principle and in practice. . . . Mr. Editor when I speak harshly of the Mormons, I wish it to be perfectly understood I do not mean every individual that advocates the Mormon cause. By no means; that

there are some good, law-abiding peaceable citizens belonging to the Mormon profession I verily believe . . . but I am opposed to them because of the unprincipled manner in which the leaders of that fanatical sect, set at defiance the laws of the land . . . (as was the case in Missouri) claiming to be the chosen people of God; not subject to the laws of the state in any respect whatever, and receiving revelations direct from Heaven almost daily commanding them to take the property of the older citizens of the county and confiscate it to the use of the Mormon church. . . .

It was for the commission of such deeds together with deeds ten fold more dark and damning in their nature that finally led to their expulsion from that state, and one of the brightest pages in the history of Missouri is that, on which is written "Governor Boggs's exterminating order" directing that the lawless rabble should be driven beyond the limits of the state, or exterminated at their own option. They chose the former, [which was] a most unfortunate thing for the state of Illinois.

Strange to tell, yet such is the fact, they have commenced nearly the same operation here that they did in Missouri . . . they have attempted to subsidize the press, thereby attempting to corrupt the very fountains of public virtue,—they have went [*sic*] into the legislative halls and attempted to bribe the representatives of the people in their seats and made them their tools.

They have in short, by a long series of high handed outrages . . . forfeited all claims (if any they ever had) to confidence and respect, and ought justly to receive the condemnation of every individual, not only in this community, but in this nation.

Source: David Brion Davis, *Antebellum America: An Interpretive Anthology* (University Park: Pennsylvania State University Press, 1997), 226–27.

sects, and bloc voting in Illinois elections, fueled resentment among their neighbors. This resentment turned to overt hostility when Smith refused to abide by any Illinois law that he did not approve of, asked Congress to turn Nauvoo into a separate federal territory, and in 1844 declared himself a candidate for president of the United States (see American Voices, "An Illinois 'Jeffersonian' Attacks the Mormons," above).

Moreover, Smith had received a new revelation that justified **polygamy**—the practice of a man having more than one wife at one time. A few leading Mormon men began to practice polygamy, dividing the community,

while Christian outrage encouraged assaults from outside the Mormon Church. In 1844 Illinois officials arrested Smith and charged him with treason for allegedly conspiring with foreign powers to create a Mormon colony in Mexican territory. An anti-Mormon mob stormed the jail in Carthage, Illinois, where Smith and his brother were being held and murdered them.

Brigham Young and Utah. Now led by Brigham Young, a large contingent of Mormons sought religious freedom by leaving the United States. In 1846 Young led a phased migration of more than 10,000 people across the Great Plains into Mexican territory. Eventually the settlers reached their destination, the Great Salt Lake Valley in present-day Utah. Using communal labor and an elaborate irrigation system based on communal water rights, the Mormon pioneers transformed the region. They quickly spread planned agricultural communities along the base of the Wasatch Range.

Most Mormons who did not support polygamy remained in the United States rather than travel to Utah. Led by Smith's son Joseph Smith III, they formed the Reorganized Church of Jesus Christ of Latter-day Saints and settled throughout the Midwest.

When the United States acquired Mexico's northern territories in 1848 (see Chapter 13), the Mormons petitioned Congress to create a vast new state, Deseret, stretching from present-day Utah to the Pacific coast. Instead, Congress tried to confine Mormon influence, setting up the much smaller Utah Territory in 1850 and naming Brigham Young as territorial governor. In 1858 President James Buchanan removed Young from the governorship and, responding to pressure from Protestant Christian churches to eliminate polygamy, sent a small army to Salt Lake City. However, the "Mormon War" proved bloodless. Fearing that the forced abolition of the "domestic institution" of polygamy would serve as a precedent for the ending of slavery, Buchanan pursued a pro-southern policy and withdrew the troops. The national government did not succeed in pressuring the Utah Mormons to make polygamy illegal until 1890, six years before Utah became a state.

Mormons had succeeded where other social experiments and utopian communities had failed. By endorsing the private ownership of property and encouraging individualistic economic enterprise, they became prosperous contributors to the new market society. However, Mormon leaders resolutely used strict religious controls to create disciplined communities and patriarchal families, reaffirming traditional values inherited from the eighteenth century. This blend of economic innovation, social conservatism, and hierarchical leadership created a wealthy church with a strong missionary impulse.

Abolitionism

In most cities and farm villages, the communalists attracted far less attention than the abolitionists, whose demand for the immediate end to racial slavery led to fierce political debates, riots, and sectional conflict. Like other reform movements, abolitionism drew on the religious energy and ideas generated by the Second Great Awakening, which altered the attitude of many northern and midwestern whites toward the South's "peculiar institution." Early-nineteenth-century reformers had criticized human bondage as contrary to the tenets of republicanism and liberty. Now abolitionists condemned slavery as a sin and saw it as their moral duty to end this violation of God's law.

Slave Rebellion

During the first decades of the nineteenth century, African American leaders in the North had encouraged free blacks to "elevate" themselves. They hoped that a majority of free blacks, by securing "respectability"—through education, temperance, moral discipline, and hard work—could rise to a position of equality with the white citizenry. To promote that goal, black leaders such as James Forten, a Philadelphia sail maker; Prince Hall, a Boston barber; and ministers Hosea Easton and James Allen founded an array of churches, schools, and self-help associations. Testifying to the success of these efforts, in 1827 John Russwurm and Samuel D. Cornish published the first African American newspaper, *Freedom's Journal*, in New York.

However, the black quest for respectability threatened many whites, who organized antiblack mobs in Boston, Pittsburgh, and other northern cities during the 1820s. White mobs in Cincinnati were so violent and destructive that they prompted several hundred African Americans to flee to Canada.

Partly in response to these attacks, in 1829 David Walker published a stirring pamphlet entitled *An Appeal . . . to the Colored Citizens of the World*. Walker was a free black from North Carolina who had moved to Boston, where he sold secondhand clothes and served as the agent for *Freedom's Journal*. A self-educated man, Walker studied the speeches of Thomas Jefferson and other slave owners and devoured volumes of history, seeking to place racial slavery within a coherent historical context. His pamphlet ridiculed the religious pretensions of slaveholders, justified slave rebellion, and in biblical language warned white Americans that the slaves would revolt if justice was delayed. "We must and shall be free," he told white Americans. "And woe, woe, will be it to you if we have to obtain our freedom by fighting. . . . Your DESTRUCTION is at hand, and will be speedily consummated unless you REPENT." Within a year Walker's *Appeal* had gone through three printings and, carried by black merchant seamen, had begun to reach free African Americans in the South.

In 1830 Walker and other African American activists called a national convention in Philadelphia. The delegates did not adopt Walker's radical call for revolt but made collective equality for all blacks—enslaved as well as free—their fundamental demand. Stressing "race-equality" rather than individual uplift and respectability, a new generation of African American leaders such as Martin Delaney urged free blacks to use every legal means to improve the condition of their race and asked for divine assistance in breaking "the shackles of slavery."

As Walker was predicting violent black rebellion from Boston, Nat Turner, a slave in Southampton County, Virginia, staged a bloody revolt—a coincidence

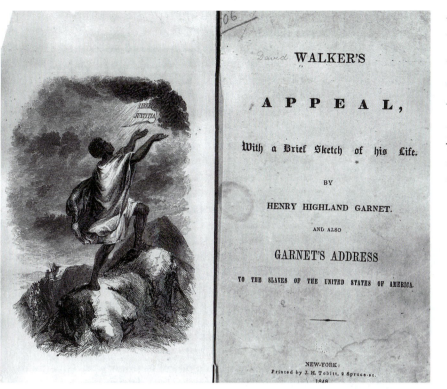

A Call for Revolution
David Walker (1785–1830), who ran a used-clothing shop in Boston, Massachusetts, spent his own savings to issue An Appeal . . . to the Colored Citizens of the World, *a learned and passionate attack against racial slavery. In the* Appeal, *published in 1829, Walker depicts Christ as an avenging "God of justice and of armies" and raises the banner of slave rebellion. A year later he was found in his shop, dead from unknown causes.* Library of Congress.

that had far-reaching consequences. As a child Turner had taught himself to read and had hoped to be emancipated, but a new master forced him into field work and another master separated him from his wife. Turner became deeply spiritual and had considerable success as a preacher. Then, in a religious vision, "the Spirit" told him that "Christ had laid down the yoke he had borne for the sins of men, and that I should take it on and fight against the Serpent, for the time was fast approaching when the first should be last and the last should be first." Taking an eclipse of the sun as an omen, Turner and a handful of relatives and close friends plotted to meet the masters' terror with a terror of their own. In August 1831 Turner and his followers rose in rebellion and killed almost sixty whites, in many cases dismembering and decapitating them. Turner hoped that a vast army of slaves would rally to his cause, but he had mustered only sixty men by the time a white militia dispersed his poorly armed and exhausted force. Vengeful whites now took slaves' lives at random. One company of cavalry killed forty blacks in two days, putting the heads of fifteen on poles to warn "all those who should undertake a similar plot." Fifty slaves were prosecuted, and twenty were hanged. After hiding for nearly two months Turner was captured and hanged, still identifying his mission with that of the Savior. "Was not Christ crucified?" he asked.

Deeply shaken by Turner's Rebellion, the Virginia legislature debated a bill providing for gradual emancipation and colonization. When the bill was rejected in 1832 by a vote of 73 to 58, the possibility that southern planters would legislate an end to slavery faded forever. Instead, the southern states marched down another path, toughening their slave codes, limiting the movement of slaves, and prohibiting anyone from teaching them to read. They would meet Walker's radical *Appeal* with radical measures of their own.

Garrison and Evangelical Abolitionism

The prospect of a bloody racial revolution mobilized a dedicated cadre of northern and midwestern whites who belonged to evangelical churches. Inspired by the antislavery efforts of free blacks, they launched a moral crusade to abolish slavery. Previously many Quakers—and some pious Methodists and Baptists—had freed their own slaves and campaigned for the gradual emancipation of all blacks. Now radical Christian abolitionists demanded that southerners free their slaves immediately. The evangelical abolitionists believed the issue was absolute: if the slave owners did not repent and allow slaves their God-given status as free moral agents, they faced the prospect of revolution in this world and damnation in the next. "The conviction that SLAVERY IS A SIN is the Gibraltar of our cause," declared abolitionist Wendell Phillips.

William Lloyd Garrison, Theodore Weld, and Angelina and Sarah Grimké.   The most uncompromising leader of the abolitionist movement was William Lloyd Garrison (1805–1879). A Massachusetts-born printer, Garrison had

William Lloyd Garrison, c. 1835

As this portrait suggests, William Lloyd Garrison was an intense and righteous man. In 1831, his hatred of slavery prompted Garrison to demand its immediate end, thereby beginning the abolitionist movement. His attack on slavery led him eventually on a passionate quest to destroy all institutions and cultural practices that prevented individuals—whites as well as blacks, women as well as men—from discovering their full potential. Garrison demanded civic equality for women and, believing it upheld slavery, publicly burned the U.S. Constitution, declaring: "So perish all compromises with tyranny."
Trustees of the Boston Public Library.

worked in Baltimore during the 1820s with a Quaker, Benjamin Lundy, the publisher of the *Genius of Universal Emancipation,* the leading antislavery newspaper of the decade. In 1830 Garrison went to jail, convicted of writing and publishing an article that libeled a New England merchant engaged in the domestic slave trade; after seven weeks he was released when a wealthy moral reformer paid his fine. In 1831 Garrison moved to Boston and founded his own antislavery weekly, *The Liberator,* which attracted many free-black subscribers. The next year he spearheaded the formation of the New England Anti-Slavery Society.

From the outset *The Liberator* took a radical stance, demanding the immediate abolition of slavery without reimbursement to slaveholders. In pursuing this goal, Garrison declared, "I *will be* as harsh as truth, and as uncompromising as justice . . . I will not retreat a single

inch—AND I WILL BE HEARD." He lived up to his word, condemning the American Colonization Society and charging that its real aim was to strengthen slavery by removing troublesome African Americans who were already free. He assailed the U.S. Constitution for its implicit acceptance of racial bondage, labeling it "a covenant with death, an agreement with Hell." As time went on, Garrison concluded that slavery was a sign of deep corruption infesting all American institutions and called for comprehensive reform of society. He demanded not only the equality of women but also the repudiation of all governments because their rule, like that of slave owners, rested ultimately on force.

Theodore Dwight Weld, who joined Garrison as a leading abolitionist, came to the movement from the religious revivals of the 1830s. The son of a Congregationalist minister and inspired by Charles Finney, Weld became an advocate of temperance and educational reform. Turning to abolitionism, he worked in northern Presbyterian and Congregational churches, preaching the moral responsibility of all Americans for the denial of liberty to slaves. In 1834 Weld inspired a group of students at Lane Theological Seminary in Cincinnati to form an antislavery society. Weld's crusade gathered force, buttressed by the theological arguments he advanced in *The Bible against Slavery* (1837). Collaborating closely with Weld were Angelina Grimké, whom he married in 1838, and her sister, Sarah. The Grimkés had left their father's South Carolina slave plantation and converted to Quakerism and taken up the cause of abolitionism in Philadelphia.

Weld and the Grimkés provided the abolitionist movement with a mass of evidence in *American Slavery as It Is: Testimony of a Thousand Witnesses* (1839). The book set out to answer a simple question—"What is the actual condition of the slaves in the United States?"—with evidence from southern newspapers and firsthand testimonies. In one account Angelina Grimké told of a treadmill that slave owners used for punishment: "One poor girl, [who was] sent there to be flogged, and who was accordingly stripped naked and whipped, showed me the deep gashes on her back—I might have laid my whole finger in them—large pieces of flesh had actually been cut out by the torturing lash." The book sold over 100,000 copies in its first year alone.

The American Anti-Slavery Society.   In 1833 Weld and Garrison met in Philadelphia with sixty delegates, black and white, from local abolitionist groups and established the American Anti-Slavery Society. The society received financial support from Arthur and Lewis Tappan, wealthy silk merchants in New York City. Women abolitionists quickly established separate organizations, such as the Philadelphia Female Anti-Slavery Society, founded by Lucretia Mott in 1833, and the Anti-Slavery Conventions of American Women,

Antislavery Card

"Buy us too," cries the enslaved mother with her child, as a trader leads her husband away in chains. This card was one of a series of twelve issued in 1863 by H. T. Helmbold, a drug and chemical company, to promote its products (such as "Helmbold's Rose Wash") while also mobilizing support among its customers for abolition. Scenes showing the breakup of African American families were among the most effective antislavery images, because the spread of sentimentalism had enhanced the importance of family ties for many middle-class northerners.
Library of Congress.

formed by a network of local societies in the late 1830s. The women's societies raised money for *The Liberator* and were a major force in the movement, especially in the farm villages and rural areas of the Midwest, distributing abolitionist literature and collecting tens of thousands of signatures on antislavery petitions.

Abolitionist leaders developed a three-pronged plan of attack, beginning with an appeal to public opinion. To foster intense public condemnation of slavery they adopted the tactics of the religious revivalists: large rallies led by stirring speakers, constant agitation by local anti-slavery chapters, and home visits by agents of the movement. The abolitionists also used the latest techniques of mass communication. Assisted by new steam-powered printing presses, the American Anti-Slavery Society distributed more than 100,000 pieces of literature in 1834. In 1835 the society launched its "great postal campaign," which flooded the nation, including the South, with a million abolitionist pamphlets. In July 1835 alone abolitionists mailed more than 175,000 items at the New York City post office.

The abolitionists' second strategy was to assist the African Americans who fled from slavery. Those blacks who lived near a free state had the greatest chance of success, but fugitives from plantations deeper in the South received aid from the "underground railroad," an informal network of whites and free blacks in Richmond, Charleston, and other southern cities (Map 12.3). In Baltimore a free African American sailor lent his identification papers to the future abolitionist Frederick Douglass, who used them to escape to New York. Many escaped slaves, such as Harriet Tubman, returned repeatedly to the South, risking reenslavement or death to help others escape. As Tubman wrote, "I should fight for . . . liberty as long as my strength lasted, and when the time came for me to go, the Lord would let them take me." Thanks to the "railroad," by the 1840s about a thousand African Americans reached freedom in the North each year.

There they faced an uncertain future. Whites in the northern and midwestern states did not support civic equality for free blacks. Five New England states extended suffrage to African American men, but six northern and midwestern states changed their constitutions to deny the franchise to free blacks. Moreover, the Fugitive Slave Law (1793) allowed masters and hired slave catchers to capture suspected fugitives and carry them back to bondage. To thwart these efforts, white abolitionists in northern cities joined with crowds of free blacks to seize recaptured slaves and drive slave catchers out of town.

The third element of the abolitionists' program was to seek support among state and national legislators. In 1835 the American Anti-Slavery Society encouraged local chapters and members to bombard Congress with petitions demanding the abolition of slavery in the District of Columbia, an end to the domestic slave trade, and a ban on the admission of new slave states. By 1838 petitions with nearly 500,000 signatures had arrived in Washington.

This agitation drew thousands of deeply religious people to abolitionism—farmers, wage earners, and small proprietors, many of whom lived in rural villages and small towns. During the 1830s the number of local abolitionist societies grew swiftly, from about two hundred in 1835 to more than five hundred in 1836 and nearly two thousand by 1840—when they had nearly 200,000 members, including many leading transcendentalists. Emerson condemned American society for tolerating slavery;

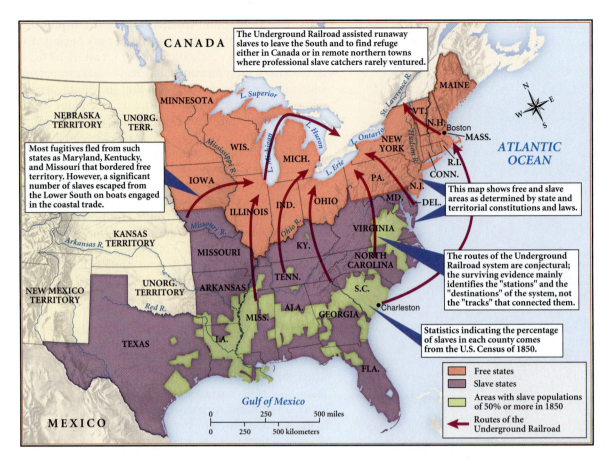

The Underground Railroad assisted runaway slaves to leave the South and to find refuge either in Canada or in remote northern towns where professional slave catchers rarely ventured.

Most fugitives fled from such states as Maryland, Kentucky, and Missouri that bordered free territory. However, a significant number of slaves escaped from the Lower South on boats engaged in the coastal trade.

This map shows free and slave areas as determined by state and territorial constitutions and laws.

The routes of the Underground Railroad system are conjectural; the surviving evidence mainly identifies the "stations" and the "destinations" of the system, not the "tracks" that connected them.

Statistics indicating the percentage of slaves in each county comes from the U.S. Census of 1850.

Free states
Slave states
Areas with slave populations of 50% or more in 1850
Routes of the Underground Railroad

MAP 12.3 The Underground Railroad in the 1850s

Before 1840, most blacks who fled slavery did so on their own or with the aid of their family and friends. Thereafter, they could count on support from members of the underground railroad, a loose network of black and white antislavery activists. Provided with food, directions, and guides by free blacks in the South, fugitive slaves crossed into free states, where they received protection and shelter from sympathetic whites and blacks, who arranged for their transportation to Canada or to "safe" American cities and towns.

Thoreau was even more assertive. Seeing the Mexican War (see Chapter 13) as an attempt to extend slavery, in 1846 he refused to pay his taxes and submitted to arrest. Two years later he published an anonymous essay entitled "Civil Disobedience," which outlined how individuals, by resisting governments because of loyalty to a higher moral law, could redeem themselves and the state. "A minority is powerless while it conforms to the majority," Thoreau declared, but it becomes "irresistible when it clogs by its whole weight."

Opposition and Internal Conflict

As Thoreau recognized, despite the thousands drawn to its cause, the abolitionist crusade had won the whole-hearted allegiance of only a small minority of white Americans. Perhaps 10 percent of northerners and mid-westerners strongly supported the movement; another 20 percent were sympathetic to its goals. Its opponents were much more numerous and no less aggressive. Men of wealth feared that the abolitionist attack on slave property might become a general assault on all property rights; tradition-minded clergymen condemned the public roles assumed by abolitionist women; and northern merchants and textile manufacturers rallied to the support of the southern planters who supplied them with cotton. Northern wage earners feared that freed slaves would work for subsistence wages and take their jobs. Finally, whites almost universally opposed the prospect of "amalgamation"—racial mixing and intermarriage—that Garrison seemed to support by encouraging joint meetings of black and white abolitionists of both sexes.

Attacks on Abolitionism.   Moved by such sentiments, northern opponents of abolitionism turned to violence, often led or instigated by "gentlemen of property and standing." In 1833 an antiabolitionist mob of fifteen hundred New Yorkers stormed a church in search of

Retribution, Southern Style

Jonathan Walker, a Massachusetts shipwright, paid a high price for his abolitionist activities by being branded, as this daguerreotype shows. Captured off the coast of Florida in 1844 while trying to smuggle seven slaves to freedom in the Bahama islands, Walker had the initials "SS" (for "slave stealer") burned into his hand. Massachusetts Historical Society.

Garrison and Arthur Tappan, and in 1834 a group of laborers vandalized and set fire to Lewis Tappan's house. Another white mob swept through Philadelphia's African American neighborhoods, clubbing and stoning residents, destroying homes and churches, and forcing crowds of black women and children to flee the city. In 1835 in Utica, New York, a group of lawyers, local politicians, merchants, and bankers broke up an abolitionist convention and beat several delegates. Two years later in Alton, Illinois, a mob shot and killed an abolitionist editor, Elijah P. Lovejoy. By pressing the issues of emancipation and equality, the abolitionists had exposed the extent of racial prejudice and the near-impossibility of creating in the North a biracial middle class of "respectable" whites and blacks. Indeed, their initiative had heightened race consciousness, encouraging whites—and blacks—to identify across class lines with those of their own race.

Racial solidarity was particularly strong in the South, where whites reacted to abolitionism with fury. Southern legislatures banned the movement and passed resolutions demanding that northern states follow suit. The Georgia legislature offered a $5,000 reward to anyone who would kidnap Garrison and bring him south to be tried for inciting rebellion. In Nashville vigilantes whipped a northern college student for distributing abolitionist pamphlets, and a mob in Charleston attacked the post office and destroyed sacks of abolitionist mail. After 1835 southern postmasters simply refused to deliver mail suspected to be of abolitionist origin.

Politicians joined the fray. President Andrew Jackson, though a radical on many issues, was a longtime slave owner and a firm supporter of the southern social order. Jackson privately approved of South Carolina's removal of abolitionist pamphlets from the U.S. mail, and in 1835 he asked Congress to restrict the use of the mails by abolitionist groups. Congress did not comply, but in 1836 the House of Representatives adopted the so-called **gag rule**. Under this informal rule, which remained in force until 1844, antislavery petitions were automatically tabled when they were received so that they could not become the subjects of debate in the House.

Internal Divisions.   Assailed by racists from the outside, abolitionists were also divided among themselves. Many antislavery clergymen denounced the public lecturing to mixed audiences by the Grimké sisters and other abolitionist women as "promiscuous" and immoral. Other supporters abandoned the Anti-Slavery Society because of Garrison's advocacy of further social reforms.

Indeed, Garrison had broadened his agenda and now supported pacifism and the abolition of prisons and asylums. Arguing that "our object is universal emancipation, to redeem women as well as men from a servile to an equal condition," he demanded that the American Anti-Slavery Society adopt a broad statement of policy that included support for women's rights. At the convention of the American Anti-Slavery Society in 1840 Garrison precipitated a split with more conservative abolitionists by insisting on equal participation by women and helping to elect Abby Kelley to the organization's business committee. When the movement split, Kelley and fellow women's rights activists Lucretia Mott and Elizabeth Cady Stanton remained with Garrison in the American Anti-Slavery Society. They recruited new women agents, including Lucy Stone, to proclaim the common interests of enslaved blacks and free women.

Garrison's opponents founded a new organization, the American and Foreign Anti-Slavery Society, which received financial backing from Lewis Tappan and focused its energies on ending slavery. Some of its members worked through their churches to win public support while others turned to electoral politics, establishing the Liberty Party and nominating James G. Birney for president in 1840. Birney was a former Alabama slave owner who had been converted to abolitionism by Theodore Weld and had founded an antislavery newspaper in Cincinnati. Birney and the Liberty Party argued that the Constitution did not recognize slavery; that the Fifth Amendment, by barring any congressional deprivation of "life, liberty, or property," prevented the federal government from supporting slavery; and that slaves became automatically free when they entered areas of federal authority, such as the District of Columbia and national territories. However, Birney won few votes in the election of 1840, and the future of the Liberty Party and political abolitionism appeared dim.

Coming hard on the heels of popular violence in the North and governmental suppression in the South, these schisms and electoral failures stunned the abolitionist movement. By melding the energies and ideas of thousands of evangelical Protestants, moral reformers, and transcendentalists, it had raised the banner of antislavery to new heights. Indeed, the very strength of abolitionism had proved its undoing because its radical program had aroused the hostility of a substantial majority of the white population. "When we first unfurled the banner of *The Liberator*," Garrison admitted in 1837, ". . . it did not occur to us that nearly every religious sect, and every political party would side with the oppressor."

The Women's Rights Movement

The prominence of women among the abolitionists was the product of a broad shift in American culture. After the American Revolution women began to play a significant role in public life, joining religious revivals and reform movements such as the temperance crusade. Suddenly issues involving gender—sexual behavior, marriage, family authority—rose to the surface not only among communal groups such as Mormons and Shakers but also among the white citizenry. However, it was the public activities of abolitionist women that created the greatest controversy over gender issues and made some reformers into women's rights activists. They argued that women had rights as individuals and within marriage that were equal to those of men.

Origins of the Women's Movement

"Don't be afraid, not afraid, fight Satan; stand up for Christ; don't be afraid." So spoke Mary Walker Ostram on her deathbed in 1859. Her religious convictions were as firm at the age of fifty-eight as they had been in 1816, when she helped found the first Sabbath School in Utica, New York. Married to a lawyer-politician but childless, Ostram had devoted her life to evangelical Presbyterian religion and the benevolent social reform that it helped spawn. Her minister, the Reverend Philemon Fowler, celebrated her as a "living fountain" of faith, an exemplar of "Women's Sphere of Influence" in the world.

Such a public presence had been won only grudgingly. Even as Reverend Fowler heaped praise on Ostram, he reiterated the precepts of Revolutionary era Patriot leaders that women should limit their political role to that of "republican mothers" who would instruct "their sons in the principles of liberty and government." As Fowler put it, women inhabited a "separate sphere" and had no place in "the markets of trade, the scenes of politics and popular agitation, the courts of justice and the halls of legislation. Home is her peculiar sphere and members of her family her peculiar care."

As Ostram's life suggested, many middle-class women transcended these rigid boundaries, by joining in the Second Great Awakening and becoming guardians of morality. Such spiritual activities bolstered their authority within the household, enabling many wives to enlarge their influence over all areas of family life, including the timing of pregnancies. Publications such as *Godey's Lady's Book* and Catharine Beecher's *Treatise on Domestic Economy* (1841) taught women how to make their homes more efficient and justified a life of middle-class domesticity. To protect their homes and husbands from the evils of alcoholic excess, farm women joined the Independent Order of Good Templars, a temperance organization that granted them full membership and sought to safeguard family life.

For most middle-class women a greater influence within the household was enough, but some women used their newfound religious authority to increase their public activities. Moral reform was among the first of their efforts. In 1834 a group of middle-class women founded the New York Female Moral Reform Society and elected Lydia Finney, the wife of the evangelical minister Charles Finney, as its president. Its goals were to end prostitution, redeem "fallen" women, and protect single women from moral corruption. Eschewing the culturally embedded male double standard, the society advocated a single moral code, demanding chastity for men as well as for women. By 1840 it had grown into a national association, the American Female Moral Reform Society, with 555 chapters and 40,000 members throughout the North and Midwest. Employing only women as its agents, bookkeepers, and staff, the society attempted to provide moral "government" for factory girls, seamstresses, clerks, and servants who lived away from their families. Women reformers even visited brothels, where they sang hymns, offered prayers, searched for runaway girls, and noted the names of clients. They also founded homes of refuge for prostitutes and homeless women and won the passage of laws regulating men's sexual behavior—including making seduction a crime—in Massachusetts in 1846 and New York in 1848.

Women also turned their energies to the reform of social institutions, working to improve conditions in almshouses, asylums, hospitals, and jails, all of which grew in number in the 1830s and 1840s. The Massachusetts reformer Dorothea Dix was a leader in these efforts, persuading legislatures in many states to expand state hospitals to accommodate poor people and mentally ill women rather than jail them with criminals (see American Lives, "Dorothea Dix: Public Woman," p. 360). Other female reformers also enlisted the aid of the government in their projects. In New York in 1849 the Female Guardian Society secured the authority to take charge of the children of "dissipated and vicious parents" and to supervise their upbringing and education.

Both as reformers and as teachers, northern women played a major role in education. From Maine to Wisconsin women vigorously supported the movement led by Horace Mann to increase the number of public elementary schools and improve their quality. As secretary of the newly created Massachusetts Board of Education from 1837 to 1848, Mann lengthened the school year; established teaching standards in reading, writing, and arithmetic; and improved instruction by recruiting well-educated women as teachers. The intellectual leader of the new corps of women educators was Catharine Beecher, who founded academies for young women in Hartford and Cincinnati. In a series of publications Beecher argued that "energetic and benevolent women" were the best qualified to impart moral and intellectual instruction to the young. By the 1850s most teachers were women both because school boards heeded Beecher's arguments and because women could be paid less than men.

Abolitionism and Women

The public accomplishments of moral reformers such as Dix and Beecher inspired other women to assume an active role in the movement to end slavery (Map 12.4). During the Revolutionary era, Quaker women in Philadelphia had established schools for freed slaves, and subsequently many Baptist and Methodist women in the Upper South endorsed religious arguments against slavery. When William Lloyd Garrison began his radical campaign for abolition, a number of women rallied to his cause. One of the first Garrisonian abolitionists was Maria W. Stewart, an African American who spoke to mixed audiences of men and women in Boston in the early 1830s. As the abolitionist movement mushroomed, scores of white women delivered lectures condemning slavery and thousands more conducted home "visitations" to win converts.

Influenced by abolitionist ideas and their own experience of discrimination, a few women challenged the subordinate status of their sex. The most famous were Angelina and Sarah Grimké, who had become antislavery lecturers. When some Congregationalist clergymen demanded in 1836 that they cease lecturing on slavery to mixed male and female audiences, Sarah Grimké turned to the Christian Bible for justification: "The Lord Jesus defines the duties of his followers in his Sermon on the Mount . . . without any reference to sex or condition," she wrote. "Men and women are CREATED EQUAL! They

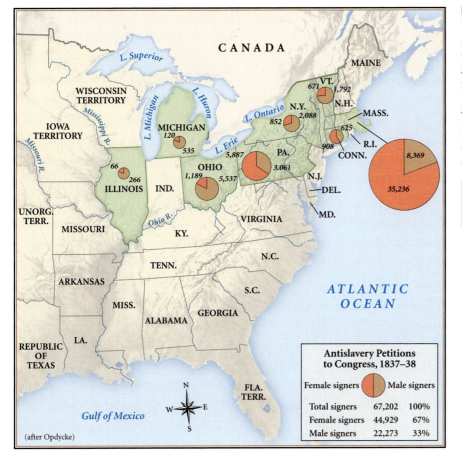

MAP 12.4 Women and Antislavery, 1837–1838

Beginning in the 1830s, abolitionists and antislavery advocates dispatched dozens of petitions to Congress, which, to avoid sectional conflict, refused to discuss them. Women made up two-thirds of the 67,000 people signing the petitions submitted in 1837–1838, suggesting not only their influence in the antislavery movement but also the extent of female organizations and social networks.

For more help analyzing this map, see the ONLINE STUDY GUIDE at bedfordstmartins.com/henretta.

Dorothea Dix: Public Woman

At the time of Dorothea Dix's birth in 1802 women were second-class citizens, excluded by law and custom from voting and from most civic activities. They could not sit on juries, attend secondary school or college, or speak in public about the issues of the day. At her death in 1887 the world had changed significantly. Some women were demanding complete civic equality with men, and many more were already playing active roles in society. Although she never fully endorsed the goals of this social revolution, Dorothea Dix had a lot to do with it—as a teacher, author, moral reformer, and political activist.

"I never knew childhood," Dix once remarked, because she had always been forced to fend for herself. Her paternal grandparents, Elijah and Dorothy Dix, were prominent Bostonians, but her father, Joseph Dix, had dropped out of Harvard and never made much of his life. After marrying an older woman, he moved to Maine to manage his father's land developments. There he suffered one business failure after another, ending up an itinerant (and alcoholic) Methodist minister. For Dorothea and her two brothers, family life meant poverty, frequent moves, and emotional abuse. Dorothea's grandmother came to the rescue, bringing the twelve-year-old girl to Boston. But Grandmother Dix was a rigid and remote person and a poor mentor for a precocious and willful child.

These emotionally scarring early experiences made Dix into a compassionate young woman with a strong sense of moral purpose. At the age of nineteen she set up a school for young children at her grandmother's Boston mansion. Like other "dame" or "marm" schools, it prepared young boys for further education in secondary schools and provided young girls with the only intellectual training most of them would ever get. Drawing again on her grandparents' financial resources, Dorothea opened a "charity school" to "rescue some of America's miserable children from vice," urging them to become responsible adults through individual moral uplift. For the next seventeen years she ran such schools, taking time off only to recover from bouts of physical illness and mental stress.

When she was too weak to teach, Dix would write. In 1824 she published *Conversations on Common Things*, an enormously successful book on natural science and moral improvement that went through sixty editions over the next four decades. By 1832 Dix had published six more books, establishing herself as a public personality. Substantial royalties, along with an inheritance from her grandmother, gave her financial independence.

Dix's literary achievements—and her family background—gave her access to the highest reaches of Boston society. William Ellery Channing, the most prominent Unitarian minister in the nation, invited Dix to teach his children and soon became a close friend. When Dorothea's health and spirits broke again in 1836, she spent eighteen months on the English estate of William Rathbone, a wealthy Unitarian merchant and philanthropist. There she met British reformers who were addressing the maladies of industrial society, and they inspired her to look for similar possibilities in America.

In March 1841 Dix found her cause. Outraged by her discovery that insane women were jailed alongside male criminals, she petitioned the Massachusetts courts for separate facilities for the women. Expanding her goals, Dix spent two years studying the institutions that treated the insane and mentally retarded. She praised reformers for founding new asylums that cared compassionately for mentally ill patients but worried that those institutions served only the families of New England's elite and that poorer patients continued to endure neglect and punishment. In a petition to the Massachusetts legislature in 1843, she presented "the condition of the miserable, the desolate, the outcast" in detail and persuaded the lawmakers to enlarge the state hospital in Worcester to accommodate indigent mental patients.

Exhilarated by this success, Dix began a national movement to establish separate, well-funded state hospitals for the mentally ill. Between 1843 and 1854 she traveled more than thirty thousand miles and visited eighteen state penitentiaries, three hundred county jails and houses of correction, and more than five hundred almshouses in addition to innumerable hospitals. Issuing dozens of reports and memorials, she aroused public support and prompted many states to expand their state hospitals. To secure additional funding, Dix turned to the national legislature, declaring that "the insane poor, through the Providence of God, are wards of the nation." In 1848 she asked Congress to place five million acres of land into a national trust to fund asylums for the mentally ill. If canal and railroad developers could lobby for public lands to subsidize their ventures, "why can I not too, go in with this selfish, struggling throng, and plead for God's poor . . . that they shall not be forgotten?"

Dorothea Dix (1802–1887)
This daguerreotype captures Dix's firm character, which helped her endure emotional abuse as a child and accounted for her great success as a social reformer. Her call for government action to address social problems anticipated twentieth-century reform and social welfare measures. Boston Athenaeum.

At first, Dix's relentless lobbying seemed to work. In 1850 the House of Representatives passed her funding proposal, but the Senate failed to act; the next year her legislation got through the Senate but not the House. On both occasions President Millard Fillmore, a Whig sympathetic to moral reform and Dix's friend, was ready to sign her bill. But when Dix finally persuaded both houses of Congress to pass the measure in 1854, President Franklin Pierce vetoed the bill. A small-government Democrat, Pierce argued that the legislation was unconstitutional because it exceeded the prescribed powers of the national government and encroached on the responsibilities of the states. Amidst the crisis over slavery, Pierce and other pro-southern Democrats feared any measure that might enhance national authority. Although temporarily depressed by this defeat, Dix continued her reform work at the state level and founded an international movement to improve the treatment of the mentally ill.

During the Civil War, Dix accepted a presidential appointment as superintendent of hospital nurses for the entire Union army, making her the highest-ranking woman in the federal government. These responsibilities revealed the limits of Dix's talents and outlook. She was a mediocre administrator, and her old-fashioned expec-

tations about the role and character of "proper" nurses hampered the recruitment of an adequate medical staff. Moreover, Dix quarreled with younger women activists who wanted to press for significant advances in women's rights. Her energy drained and her reputation shattered, Dix returned to private life in 1866. She remained active in reform for another fifteen years and then, as her health deteriorated, retired to the New Jersey state hospital in Trenton, an institution she had helped establish.

Dix's career embodied the temper of her age. During her lifetime, thousands of women became active participants in moral and social reform, and she was in the forefront of that movement, one of the first "public women." If her "proper" views of women's place stamped her as a lady of the early nineteenth century, Dix's political activism placed her far in advance of her time. More politically aware than most women reformers, Dix became a successful legislative lobbyist. Her systematic investigations of social problems were also pathbreaking, making Dix a precursor of the scientific-minded social reformers of the late nineteenth century. Finally, in her campaign for a nationally funded social welfare program, Dorothea Dix was genuinely innovative, anticipating the reform movements of the twentieth century.

are both moral and accountable beings and whatever is right for man to do is right for woman." In a debate with Catharine Beecher (who wanted women to exercise power primarily as wives, mothers, and schoolteachers) Angelina Grimké pushed the argument beyond religion, using Enlightenment principles to claim equal civic rights for women:

> It is a woman's right to have a voice in all the laws and regulations by which she is governed, whether in Church or State. . . . The present arrangements of society, on these points are a violation of human rights, a rank usurpation of power, *a violent seizure and confiscation of what is sacredly and inalienably hers.*

By 1840 the Grimkés and other female abolitionists were asserting that traditional gender roles amounted to the "domestic slavery" of women. "How can we endure our present marriage relations," asked Elizabeth Cady Stanton, since they give woman "no charter of rights, no individuality of her own?" As another female reformer put it, "the radical difficulty . . . is that women are considered as *belonging* to men" (see American Voices, "Keziah Kendall: A Farm Woman Defends the Grimké Sisters," p. 363).

As abolitionists paid increasing attention to issues of gender during the 1840s and 1850s, they emphasized the special horrors of slavery for women. Apologists for slavery had exalted the sexual purity of white plantation women, contrasting them with stereotypical descriptions of passionately sexual black men and women. Critics pointed out that the reality of plantation life was much more complex and contradictory. Speaking of forced sexual relations with her white owner, the black abolitionist Harriet Jacobs confessed in anguish in her autobiography, *Incidents in the Life of a Slave Girl* (1861), "I cannot tell how much I suffered in the presence of these wrongs." As Jacobs and other former slaves testified, sexual assault by their masters was compounded by cruel treatment at the hands of mistresses enraged by their husbands' promiscuity. In *Uncle Tom's Cabin* (1852), Harriet Beecher Stowe charged that among the greatest moral failings of slavery was its destruction of the slave family and the degradation of slave women. Sojourner Truth, a former slave who lectured to both antislavery and women's rights conventions, hammered home the point that women slaves were denied both basic human rights and the protected separate sphere enjoyed by free women. "I have ploughed and planted and gathered into barns, and no man could head me—and ain't I a woman?" she asked. Drawn into public life by abolitionism, thousands of northern women had become firm advocates of greater rights not only for enslaved African American women but also for themselves.

Sojourner Truth

Few women had as interesting a life as Sojourner Truth. Born as "Isabella" in Dutch-speaking rural New York about 1797, she labored as a slave until 1827. Following a religious vision, Isabella moved to New York City, learned English, and worked for deeply religious—and ultimately fanatical—Christian merchants. In 1843, seeking further spiritual enlightenment, she took the name "Sojourner Truth" and left New York. After briefly joining the Millerites (who believed the world would end in 1844), Truth became famous as a forceful speaker on behalf of abolitionism and women's rights. This illustration, showing Truth addressing an antislavery meeting, suggests her powerful personal presence.

Miriam and Ira D. Wallach Division of Art, Prints and Photographs, the New York Public Library.

The Program of Seneca Falls

The commitment to full civil equality for women emerged during the 1840s as activists devised a pragmatic program of reform. While championing the rights of women, they did not challenge the institution of marriage or even the conventional division of labor within the family. Instead, harking back to the efforts of Abigail Adams and other Revolutionary era women, they tried to strengthen the legal rights of married women, especially with respect to property. This initiative won crucial support from affluent men, who wanted to protect their wives' assets in case their own businesses went into bankruptcy, a constant threat in the volatile economy of mid-nineteenth-century America. By giving property rights to married women, they

Keziah Kendall

A Farm Woman Defends the Grimké Sisters

The Grimké sisters' lecture tour of New England on behalf of abolitionism sparked a huge outcry from orthodox ministers and social conservatives, who questioned the propriety of women taking public roles and speaking to "mixed" audiences of men and women. In a lecture titled "The Legal Rights of Women," Simon Greenleaf, Royall Professor of Law at Harvard College, added his voice to those advocating a restricted role for women. Replying to Greenleaf, Keziah Kendall—possibly the fictional creation of a contemporary women's rights advocate—sent the following letter to her local newspaper.

My name is Keziah Kendall. I live not many miles from Cambridge, on a farm with two sisters, one older, one younger than myself. I am thirty two. Our parents and only brother are dead—we have a good estate—comfortable house—nice barn, garden, orchard &c and money in the bank besides. . . . Under these circumstances the whole responsibility of our property, not less than twenty five thousand dollars rest upon me.

Well—our milkman brought word when he came from market that you were a going to lecture on the legal rights of women, and so I thought I would go and learn. Now I hope you wont think me bold when I say, I did not like that lecture much . . . [because] there was nothing in it but what every body knows. . . .

What I wanted to know, was good reasons for some of those laws that I cant account for. . . . One Lyceum lecture that I heard in C[ambridge] stated that the Americans went to war with the British, because they were taxed without being represented in Parliament. Now we [women] are taxed every year to the full amount of every dollar we possess—town, county, state taxes—taxes for land, for movable [property], for money and all. Now I don't want to [become a legislative] representative . . . any more than I do to be a "constable or a sheriff," but I have no voice about public improvements, and I don't see the justice of being taxed any more than the "revolutionary heroes" did.

Nor do I think we are treated as Christian women ought to be, according to the Bible rule of doing to others as you would others should do unto you. . . . Another thing . . . women have joined the Antislavery societies, and why? Women are kept for slaves as well as men—it is a common cause, deny the justice of it, who can! To be sure I do not wish to go about lecturing like the Misses Grimkie, but I have not the knowledge they have, and I verily believe that if I had been brought up among slaves as they were . . . I should run the venture of your displeasure, and that of a good many others like you.

Source: Dianne Avery and Alfred S. Konefsky, "The Daughters of Job: Property Rights and Women's Lives in Mid-Nineteenth-Century Massachusetts," *Law and History Review* 10 (Fall 1992): 323–56.

also hoped to guard against irresponsible sons-in-law who might waste their daughters' inheritances. Such considerations influenced legislatures in three states—Mississippi, Maine, and Massachusetts—which enacted Married Women's Property Acts between 1839 and 1845. In New York, women activists entered the campaign and won a more comprehensive statute (1848), which gave a woman full legal control over the property she brought to a marriage and became the model for similar laws in fourteen other states.

To advance the nascent women's movement, Elizabeth Cady Stanton and Lucretia Mott, who had become friends at the World Anti-Slavery Convention in London in 1840, organized a gathering in Seneca Falls in central New York in 1848. Seventy women activists and thirty men, mostly from the local area, attended the meeting, which devised a coherent statement of women's equality. Taking the republican ideology of the Declaration of Independence as a starting point, the attendees declared that "all men and women are created equal." "The history of mankind is a history of repeated injuries and usurpations on the part of man toward woman," their Declaration of Sentiments continued, "having in direct object the establishment of an absolute tyranny over her." To persuade Americans to right this long-standing wrong, the activists resolved to "use every instrumentality within our power . . . [to] employ agents, circulate tracts, petition the State and National legislatures, and endeavor to enlist the pulpit and the press on our behalf." By staking out claims for equality for women in public life, the Seneca Falls reformers repudiated the idea that the assignment of separate spheres for men and women was the natural order of society.

Most men dismissed the Seneca Falls Declaration as nonsense, and many women repudiated the activists and their message. Writing in her diary, one small-town mother and housewife lashed out at the female reformer who "aping mannish manners . . . wears absurd and barbarous attire, who talks of her wrongs in harsh tone, who struts and strides, and thinks that she proves herself superior to the rest of her sex."

Nonetheless, the women's rights movement attracted a committed group of female reformers and a few radical men to its ranks. In 1850 the activists convened the first national women's rights convention in Worcester, Massachusetts, and began to hammer out a program. Local and state conventions of women called on churches to revise concepts of female inferiority in their theology. They also proposed legal changes to allow married women to control their property and earnings, guarantee the custody rights of mothers in the event of divorce or the husband's death, and ensure women's rights to sue and testify in court. Finally, and above all else, they began a concerted campaign to win the vote for women. In 1851 the national convention declared that suffrage was "the corner-stone of this enterprise, since we do not seek to protect woman, but rather to place her in a position to protect herself."

The struggle for legislation required leaders who had talents as organizers and lobbyists. The most prominent political operative was Susan B. Anthony (1820–1906). Anthony came from a Quaker family and as a young woman had been active in temperance and antislavery efforts. Her experience in the temperance movement, Anthony explained, had taught her "the great evil of woman's utter dependence on man." In 1851 she joined the movement for women's rights and forged an enduring friendship with Elizabeth Cady Stanton. Anthony created a network of political "captains," all women, who relentlessly lobbied the legislature in New York and other states. In 1860 her efforts culminated in a New York law granting women the right to collect and spend their own wages (which fathers or husbands previously could insist on controlling), bring suit in court, and, if widowed, acquire full control of the property they had brought to the marriage. Such successes would provide the basis for more aggressive reform attempts after the Civil War.

The attack by women's rights activists against the traditional legal and social prerogatives of husbands, like the abolitionists' assault on the power and property of southern slaveholders, prompted many Americans to fear that social reform might not perfect their society but destroy it. The various movements for reform, begun with such confidence and religious zeal, had raised legal and political issues that threatened the fabric of society and the unity of the nation.

FOR FURTHER EXPLORATION

▶ For definitions of key terms boldfaced in this chapter, see the glossary at the end of the book.

▶ To assess your mastery of the material covered in this chapter, see the Online Study Guide at **bedfordstmartins.com/henretta**.

▶ For suggested references, including Web sites, see page SR-13 at the end of the book.

▶ For map resources and primary documents, see **bedfordstmartins.com/henretta**.

After 1820 rapid economic and political change prompted many Americans to question traditional values and to support social reform movements. Ralph Waldo Emerson and other transcendentalists urged men—and women—to reject the outworn ideas of the past and realize their complete potential as individuals. To promote full spiritual growth, transcendentalists founded utopian communities such as Brook Farm. Transcendental thought influenced a generation of American writers, many of whom probed the tensions between individual freedom and social responsibility.

Thousands of other Americans joined utopian communities that questioned traditional gender roles and the acquisitive capitalist values of the market-oriented, industrializing society. Shakers, Fourierists, and members of the Oneida Community endorsed the communal ownership of property and devised various schemes—celibacy, phalanxes, complex marriage—to promote greater equality between men and women.

Joseph Smith and his Mormon followers created the most successful communal enterprise. They encouraged their members to pursue capitalist enterprise but subjected them to strict religious controls. Mormons celebrated the traditional patriarchal family, and some practiced polygamy. The Mormons' unorthodox marriage practices, along with their bloc voting, resulted in mob attacks on their communities and the migration of many Mormons to Utah.

During the 1830s thousands of middle-class white women also questioned traditional social practices. Many women became active in moral reform, attacking the sexual double standard and trying to eliminate prostitution. Other women enlisted in the abolitionist movement and, when denied an equal role, demanded complete political and civil equality for women. In 1848 they issued a "Declaration of Sentiments," beginning the modern women's rights movement.

The most dramatic expression of reform was a new attack on slavery by William Lloyd Garrison, who demanded the immediate, uncompensated emancipation of slaves. His crusade soon attracted the support of thousands of reformers. In 1835 the nationwide postal campaign of the American Anti-Slavery Society prompted widespread mob violence against abolitionists. In 1840 some abolitionists turned to politics, forming the Liberty Party. Over the next two decades, political struggles over slavery would gradually come to dominate the nation's history.

1817	American Colonization Society founded
1829	David Walker's *Appeal . . . to the Colored Citizens* encourages slave rebellion
1830	Joseph Smith publishes *The Book of Mormon*
1831	William Lloyd Garrison founds *The Liberator*
	Nat Turner's uprising in Virginia
1832	Ralph Waldo Emerson rejects organized religion and embraces transcendentalism
1833	American Anti-Slavery Society founded
1834	New York Female Moral Reform Society established
1835	Abolitionists launch mail campaign; antiabolitionists riot against them
1836	House of Representatives adopts gag rule on antislavery petitions
	Grimké sisters defend public roles for women
1840	Liberty Party runs James G. Birney for president
1840s	Fourierist communities founded in Midwest
1841	Transcendentalists found Brook Farm, a utopian community
	Dorothea Dix promotes hospitals for the insane
1844	Margaret Fuller publishes *Woman in the Nineteenth Century*
1845	Henry David Thoreau withdraws to Walden Pond
1846	Mormon followers of Brigham Young trek to Salt Lake
1848	John Humphrey Noyes founds Oneida Community
	Seneca Falls convention proposes women's equality
1850	Nathaniel Hawthorne publishes *The Scarlet Letter*
1851	Herman Melville's *Moby-Dick*
1852	Harriet Beecher Stowe writes *Uncle Tom's Cabin*
	Walt Whitman issues *Leaves of Grass*
1858	The "Mormon War" over polygamy

CHAPTER 13

The Crisis of the Union

1844–1860

Manifest Destiny
*The Mature Cotton Economy,
    1820–1860*
The Independence of Texas
*The Push to the Pacific: Oregon
    and California*
The Fateful Election of 1844

**War, Expansion, and Slavery,
1846–1850**
The War with Mexico, 1846–1848
A Divisive Victory
1850: Crisis and Compromise

**The End of the Second Party
System, 1850–1858**
Resistance to the Fugitive Slave Act
*The Whigs' Decline and the
    Democrats' Diplomacy*
*The Kansas-Nebraska Act and the
    Rise of New Parties*
*The Election of 1856 and
    Dred Scott*

**Abraham Lincoln and the
Republican Triumph, 1858–1860**
Lincoln's Political Career
The Party System Fragments

DURING THE 1850S THE CRUSADERS in the temperance and antislavery movements faced off against the defenders of traditional rights. The resulting struggle was nowhere more intense than in South Carolina. When local temperance activists demanded a law like that in Maine to prohibit the sale of intoxicants, Randolph Turner was outraged: any such "legislation upon Liquor would cast a shade on my character which as a Caucassian [*sic*] and a white man, I am not willing to bear." A candidate for the South Carolina assembly, Turner vowed to shoulder his musket and, along with "hundreds of men in this district, . . . fight for individual rights, as well as State Rights."

In Washington, Congressman Preston Brooks and other South Carolinians likewise battled against abolitionists to defend "Southern Rights." In an inflammatory speech in 1856, Senator Charles Sumner of Massachusetts denounced the South and accused Senator Andrew P. Butler of South Carolina of having taken "the harlot slavery" as his mistress. Outraged by Sumner's verbal attack on his uncle, Brooks accosted the Massachusetts senator at his desk and beat him unconscious with a walking cane. As Brooks struck down Sumner in Washington in 1856, Axalla Hoole of South Carolina and

◄ **War News from Mexico, by Richard Caton Woodville, 1848**
In this painting of a crowd gathered on the porch of the "American Hotel" in an unknown town, artist Richard Caton Woodville (1825–1855) captures the public's hunger for news of the Mexican War, the first military conflict with a foreign nation since the War of 1812. As a journalist in Woodville's hometown of Baltimore noted, "People begin to collect every evening, about 5 o'clock at the telegraph and newspaper offices, waiting for extras and despatches, where they continue even to 12 or 1 o'clock at night, discussing the news that may be received."
National Gallery of Art, Washington, DC.

other proslavery migrants in the Kansas Territory leveled their guns at an armed force of abolitionist settlers. Passion and violence had replaced political compromise as the hallmark of American public life.

The immediate events that sparked the political violence of the 1850s were the admission of Texas to the Union in 1845 and the war with Mexico that followed. The ultimate causes lay much deeper in the process of economic and cultural change that had widened the long-standing differences between North and South. By midcentury these sectional differences were keenly felt, especially in the South. As John C. Calhoun declared explicitly in 1850, white southerners feared the North's wealth, political power, and moral righteousness, especially its "long-continued agitation of the slavery question."

Now a massive surge of westward migration accentuated the importance of those divisions. To many Americans it was the nation's "manifest destiny" to extend republican institutions to the Pacific Ocean. But whose republican institutions: the aristocratic traditions and practices of the slaveholding South or the more democratic customs and culture of the reform-minded North and Midwest? The answer to this question would determine the future of the nation.

Manifest Destiny

Between 1820 and 1860 the white planters in the South grew rich and powerful as they developed a cotton economy. Shaken by the crisis over Missouri (see Chapter 9), the two major political parties prevented another confrontation over slavery by devising programs that were national in appeal. The compromise worked as long as the geographic boundaries of the United States remained unchanged, but by the 1840s the people of the nation were again on the move.

The Mature Cotton Economy, 1820–1860

By 1820 the American South produced more raw cotton than any other country in the world—160 million pounds a year—and by the 1840s grew over two-thirds of the world's supply (Figure 13.1). Family labor by thousands of white families accounted for hundreds of thousands of bales of the prized fiber, but most cotton came from large plantations employing slave labor. To increase output, profit-conscious slave owners in the upland regions of South Carolina and Georgia and in Alabama and Mississippi devised a new gang-labor system. Previously planters had either supervised their workers sporadically while attending to other tasks or assigned them a daily quota and let them work at their own pace. Now masters with twenty or more slaves organized the hands into disciplined teams, or "gangs,"

supervised by black "drivers" or white overseers, and assigned them specific tasks. They instructed drivers and overseers to use the lash to work the gangs at a steady pace, clearing and plowing the land or hoeing and picking cotton. A traveler glimpsed two gangs returning from work in Mississippi:

> First came, led by an old driver carrying a whip, forty of the largest and strongest women I ever saw together; they were all in a simple uniform dress of a bluish check stuff, the skirts reaching little below the knee; their legs and feet were bare; they carried themselves loftily, each having a hoe over the shoulder, and walking with a free, powerful swing.

Next marched the plow hands with their mules, "the cavalry, thirty strong, mostly men, but a few of them women." Finally, "a lean and vigilant white overseer, on a brisk pony, brought up the rear." By 1860 nearly two million enslaved African Americans were laboring on the cotton and sugar lands of the lower Mississippi Valley and along an arc of fertile cotton land—the "black belt"—sweeping from Mississippi through Georgia.

The slaveholding elite who owned great plantations and scores of slaves described themselves as natural aristocrats and indulged in displays of conspicuous consumption. They married their children to one another,

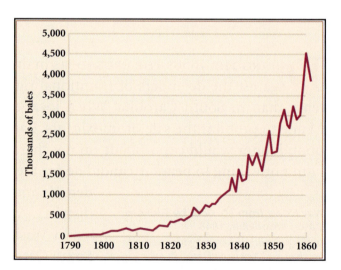

FIGURE 13.1 The Surge in Cotton Production, 1835–1860

Between 1835 and the mid-1840s, southern cotton planters doubled their output from one to two million 500-pound bales per year. Another dramatic rise came in the 1850s, as production doubled again—reaching four million bales per year by the end of the decade. Because the price of raw cotton rose slightly (from about 11 cents a pound in the 1830s to 13 cents in the 1850s), planters reaped substantial profits—reinforcing their commitment to the slave system.

Source: Robert William Fogel and Stanley L. Engerman, *Time on the Cross* (Boston: Little, Brown, 1974), figure 25.

and their sons and daughters became commercial and cultural leaders—the men working as planters, merchants, lawyers, newspaper editors, and ministers and the women hosting plantation balls and church bazaars. John Henry Hammond, a leading South Carolina planter and politician, inhabited a Greek Revival mansion with a center hall fifty-three feet by twenty feet, its floor embellished with stylish Belgian tiles and expensive Brussels carpets. "Once a year, like a great feudal landlord," a guest recounted, Hammond "gave a fete or grand dinner to all the country people."

The planters justified their power by endowing it with moral purpose. Before the Missouri crisis, southern apologists defended slavery as a "necessary evil" to maintain white living standards and prevent racial warfare; subsequently they argued that slavery was a "positive good" that allowed a civilized lifestyle for leading whites and provided tutelage for genetically inferior Africans. Seeking a religious justification, southern ministers pointed out that the Hebrews, God's chosen people, had owned slaves and that Jesus Christ had never condemned slavery. As Hammond told a British abolitionist in 1845: "What God ordains and Christ sanctifies should surely command the respect and toleration of man." Some defenders of slavery also depicted planters and their wives as aristocratic models of "disinterested benevolence" whose workers were adequately fed, housed, and cared for in old age (see American Voices, "Mary Boykin Chesnut: A Slaveholding Woman's Diary," p. 370).

Seeing themselves as a republican aristocracy, the elite planters encouraged ambitious men from modest backgrounds to buy slaves and grow rich as they had. In fact, white politics and society in the South remained deeply divided along the lines of class and region. Slave owners used their political power to exempt their slave property from taxation and to impose land taxes by acreage rather than by value, shifting the tax burden to yeoman farmers in the backcountry. Planters also enacted laws that forced yeomen to "fence in" their livestock, sparing themselves the cost of building fences around their large properties. Finally, legislatures forced all white men—whether they owned slaves or not—to serve in patrols and militias that deterred slaves from running away or rising in rebellion. Warning of race warfare, John Henry Hammond told his poor white neighbors that "in a slave country every freeman is an aristocrat."

Control of enslaved African Americans—a majority of the population throughout the "black belt"—was a matter of overriding concern for planters. In theory masters had virtually unlimited power over their slaves. By law enslaved individuals were personal property, subject to discipline at the will of their owners and bought and sold as if they were horses. As Thomas Ruffin, a justice of the North Carolina Supreme Court, declared in a court decision in 1829, "The power of the master must be absolute to render the submission of the slave perfect." In practice, both social conventions and black resistance limited the power of masters. Especially after 1830, when abolitionists subjected slavery to critical scrutiny, masters resorted less frequently to the lash and searched for positive incentives—food, visiting privileges, specified workloads—to manage their American-born laborers.

To resist the demands of their white masters, slaves used various strategies. They slowed the pace of work by feigning illness and were deliberately careless with the master's property, losing or breaking tools and setting fire to houses and barns. They also challenged the arbitrary breakup of communities, insisting that people be sold "in families" and defying their masters when they were not (see Figure 9.1, p. 263). One Maryland slave, faced with transport to Mississippi and separation from his wife, "neither yields consent to accompany my people, or to be exchanged or sold," his owner reported. Masters ignored such resistance at their peril because a slave's relatives might retaliate with arson, poison, or destruction of crops or equipment. Slavery was never a regime of equality but over the decades many masters and slaves had come to be tied to one another by complex personal—and often biological—bonds that reduced the extent of day-to-day violence. The institution of slavery had become part of the fiber of American life, and white southerners wanted to extend its sway across the entire continent.

The Independence of Texas

Beginning in the 1820s northeastern farmers and European migrants moved by the tens of thousands into the Midwest. Simultaneously thousands of farmers from the Ohio Valley and the South carried both yeoman farming and plantation slavery into Arkansas and Missouri, pushing just beyond their western boundaries to the ninety-fifth meridian. Beyond this north–south line stretched the semiarid Great Plains. An army explorer, Major Stephen H. Long, described the area between the Missouri River and the Rocky Mountains as a Great American Desert, "almost wholly unfit for cultivation." Sharing this assumption, land-hungry southern planters looked toward the west and the Mexican province of Texas (see Map 13.3, p. 374).

American Settlements.   Texas had long been a zone of conflict between European nations. During the eighteenth century the Spanish had used Texas as a buffer against the French. After the Louisiana Purchase in 1803, Texas became Spain's buffer against Americans. Although adventurers from the United States did settle in Texas, the Adams-Onís Treaty of 1819 guaranteed Spanish sovereignty over the region.

Mary Boykin Chesnut

A Slaveholding Woman's Diary

During the 1850s, in response to Harriet Beecher Stowe's Uncle Tom's Cabin and Republican celebrations of free labor, proslavery advocate George Fitzhugh wrote Sociology for the South; or, the Failure of Free Society. In this influential book and in his other writings, Fitzhugh contrasted the slave owners' benevolent concern for their enslaved workers with the factory owners' indifference toward the welfare of their wage laborers. Mary Boykin Chesnut (1823–1886), wife of South Carolina senator James Chesnut, held a more complex view. Although believing that blacks were innately inferior and celebrating the benevolence of white women, she hated slavery, in part because she thought that it oppressed the women of both races. Chesnut recorded her views in notes made during the Civil War, later revised into a beautifully written diary.

March 18, 1861 . . . I wonder if it be a sin to think slavery a curse to any land. [Massachusetts senator Charles] Sumner said not one word of this hated institution which is not true. Men and women are punished when their masters and mistresses are brutes and not when they do wrong—and then we live surrounded by prostitutes. An abandoned woman is sent out of any decent house elsewhere. Who thinks any worse of a negro or mulatto woman for being a thing we can't name? God forgive us, but ours is a monstrous system and wrong. . . . Like the patriarchs of old our men live all in one house with their wives and their concubines, and the mulattoes one sees in every family exactly resemble the white children—and every lady tells you who is the father of all the mulatto children in everybody's household, but those in her own she seems to think drop from the clouds, or pretends so to think. Good women we have . . . the purest women God ever made. Thank God for my countrywomen—alas for the men! No worse than men everywhere, but the lower their mistresses, the more degraded they must be.

November 27, 1861 . . . Now what I have seen of my mother's life, my grandmother's, my mother-in-law's: These people were educated at Northern schools mostly—read the same books as their Northern condemners, the same daily newspapers, the same Bible—have the same ideas of right and wrong—are highbred, lovely, good, pious—doing their duty as they conceive it. They live in negro villages. They do not preach and teach hate as a gospel and the sacred duty of murder and insurrection, but they strive to ameliorate the condition of these Africans in every particular. . . . These women are more troubled by their duty to negroes, have less chance to live their own lives in peace than if they were African missionaries. They have a swarm of blacks about them as children under their care—not as Mrs. Stowe's fancy paints them, but the hard, unpleasant, unromantic, undeveloped savage Africans. And they hate slavery worse than Mrs. Stowe. . . .

We are human beings of the nineteenth century—and slavery has to go, of course. All that has been gained by it goes to the North and to negroes. The slave-owners, when they are good men and women, are the martyrs. And as far as I have seen, the people here are quite as good as anywhere else. I hate slavery.

Source: C. Vann Woodward, Mary Chesnut's Civil War (New Haven: Yale University Press, 1981), 29–30, 245–46.

After winning independence from Spain in 1821, the Mexican government encouraged the settlement of Texas by both its citizens and migrants from the United States. To win the allegiance of the American settlers, officials granted them some of the best land (Map 13.1). One early grantee was Moses Austin, who moved to Texas to create an aristocratic-like landed estate, occupied by tenants or smallholders: "one great family who are under my care." His son, Stephen F. Austin, later acquired about 180,000 acres, which he sold to new migrants. Most American settlers did not assimilate Mexican culture and in 1829 won special exemption from a law ending slavery in Mexico. By 1835, about 27,000 white Americans and their 3,000 African American slaves were raising cotton and cattle in eastern and central Texas; they far outnumbered the 3,000 Mexican residents, most of whom lived, along with a few Americans, in the southwestern towns of Goliad and San Antonio.

When the Mexican government asserted greater control over Texas in the mid-1830s, the Americans split into two groups. The "peace party," led by Stephen

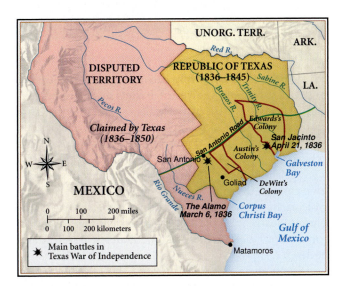

MAP 13.1 American Settlements in Texas, 1821–1836

During the 1820s Mexican authorities granted huge tracts of land in the province of Texas to American empresarios (essentially land entrepreneurs), who were expected to encourage immigration. Stephen F. Austin managed the largest "colony"; by 1835 he had issued land titles to more than 1,000 families, who grew cotton and exported it from Galveston and other Gulf ports. By the mid-1830s, there were nearly 30,000 Americans in Texas, far outnumbering the Mexican settlers, who lived primarily in the town of Goliad and areas south.

Austin and other longtime settlers with substantial interests to protect, worked to win more self-government for the province, while the "war party," led by recent migrants from Georgia, demanded independence. Austin won significant concessions from Mexican authorities, but the new president, General Antonio López de Santa Anna, nullified these measures. A strong nationalist, Santa Anna appointed a military commandant for Texas, prompting the American war party to provoke a rebellion that most of the American settlers ultimately supported. On March 2, 1836, the rebels proclaimed the independence of Texas and adopted a constitution legalizing slavery.

Rebellion and War. Santa Anna vowed to put down the rebellion. On March 6 his army wiped out the rebel garrison defending the Alamo in San Antonio and soon thereafter captured the settlement of Goliad (see Voices from Abroad, "Colonel José Enrique de la Peña: A Mexican View of the Battle of the Alamo," p. 372). With these victories Santa Anna thought he had crushed the rebellion, but the battle of the Alamo had captured the attention of New Orleans and New York newspapers. Their correspondents romanticized the heroism of the Texans and the deaths at the Alamo of folk heroes Davy Crockett and Jim Bowie. Using strong anti-Catholic rhetoric, the newspapers described the Mexicans as tyrannical butchers in the service of the pope. Hundreds of American adventurers, lured by Texan offers of land bounties, flocked in from neighboring states. Reinforced by the new arrivals and led by General Sam Houston, in April 1836 the rebels routed the Mexicans in the Battle of San Jacinto, establishing de facto independence. The

SIEGE OF THE ALAMO.

Assault on the Alamo

After a thirteen-day siege, on March 6, 1836, a Mexican army of 4,000 stormed the small mission in San Antonio, Texas. "The first to climb were thrown down by bayonets . . . or by pistol fire," reported a Mexican officer. Only a half hour of continuous assaults gave the attackers control of the wall. This contemporary woodcut shows the fierceness of the battle, which took the lives of all 250 American defenders; the Mexicans suffered 1,500 dead or wounded.

Archives Division, Texas State Library.

For more help analyzing this image, see the ONLINE STUDY GUIDE at **bedfordstmartins.com/henretta**

Colonel José Enrique de la Peña

A Mexican View of the Battle of the Alamo

In February 1836 a Mexican army led by General Antonio López de Santa Anna laid siege to the Alamo, an old San Antonio mission building held by about 250 Texas rebels and some American supporters, all of whom were commanded by William B. Travis. In his personal narrative of the war in Texas, Colonel José Enrique de la Peña offers a dramatic and critical account of the ensuing events, in which he played a prominent role.

Our commander [Santa Anna] became more furious when he saw that the enemy resisted the idea of surrender. He believed as others did that the fame and honor of the army were compromised the longer the enemy lived.... But prudent men ... were of the opinion that victory over a handful of men concentrated in the Alamo did not call for a great sacrifice. In fact, it was necessary only to await the artillery's arrival at Béjar for these to surrender....

Travis's resistance was on the verge of being overcome, for several days his followers had been urging him to surrender, giving the lack of food and the scarcity of munitions as reasons.... [O]n the 5th he promised them if no help arrived on that day they would surrender the next day or would try to escape under the cover of darkness.... [I]t was said as a fact ... that the president-general [Santa Anna] knew of Travis's decision, and it was for this reason that he precipitated the assault, because he wanted to create a sensation and would have regretted taking the Alamo without clamor and without bloodshed, for some believed that without these there is no glory....

The columns, bravely storming the fort in the midst of a terrible shower of bullets and cannon-fire, had reached the base of the walls.... A lively rifle fire coming from the roof ... caused painful havoc.... [Finally] our soldiers, some stimulated by courage and others by fury, burst into the quarters ... our losses were grievous.... [But our men] turned the enemy's own cannon to bring down the [inner] doors ... a horrible carnage took place, and some [rebels] were trampled to death.... This scene of extermination went on for an hour before the curtain of death covered and ended it....

Some seven men had survived the general carnage and, under the protection of General Castrillon, they were brought before Santa Anna. Among them was one of great stature, well proportioned, with regular features, in whose face there was the imprint of adversity, but in whom one noticed a degree of resignation and nobility that did him honor. He was the naturalist David Crockett, well known in North America for his unusual adventures, who had undertaken to explore the country and who, finding himself at Béjar at the very moment of surprise, had taken refuge in the Alamo, fearing his status as a foreigner might not be respected. Santa Anna answered Castrillon's intervention in Crockett's behalf with a gesture of indignation and ... ordered his execution. The commanders and officers were outraged at this action and did not support the order.... [But several officers] thrust themselves forward, in order to flatter their commander, and with swords in hand, fell upon these unfortunate, defenseless men just as a tiger leaps upon his prey....

To whom was this sacrifice useful and what advantage was derived by increasing the number of victims? ... [T]he taking of the Alamo was not considered a happy event, but rather a defeat that saddened us all.

Source: José Enrique de la Peña, *With Santa Anna in Texas: A Personal Narrative of the Revolution,* trans. Carmen Perry (College Station: Texas A&M University Press, 1975), 40–57.

Mexican government refused to recognize the new republic but abandoned efforts to reconquer it.

The Texans quickly voted by plebiscite for annexation by the United States, but Presidents Andrew Jackson and Martin Van Buren refused to act. They knew that adding Texas as a slave state would divide the Democratic Party and the nation and almost certainly lead to war with Mexico.

The Push to the Pacific: Oregon and California

The annexation of Texas became a more pressing issue in the 1840s, as American expansionists developed continental ambitions. Those dreams were captured by the term **Manifest Destiny**, coined in 1845 by John L. O'Sullivan, the editor of the *Democratic Review.* As O'Sullivan

Sam Houston, by Martin Johnson Heade, 1846
Military hero, president of the Lone Star Republic of Texas, and senator from the state of Texas: Sam Houston cut an impressive figure and had many admirers both inside and outside politics. According to a Nashville belle who knew the Texan as a young man, "two classes of people pursued Sam Houston all his life— artists and women." Heade's portrait, painted when Houston was a senator, conveys the Texan's flamboyant character and personal charm. Texas State Library and Archives Collection.

MAP 13.2 Territorial Conflict in Oregon, 1819–1846
As thousands of American settlers poured into the "Oregon Country" in the early 1840s, British authorities tried to confine them south of the Columbia River. But the migrants—and fervent midwestern expansionists—asserted that Americans could settle anywhere in the territory. In 1846 British and American diplomats resolved the dispute by dividing the region at the forty-ninth parallel.

put it, "Our manifest destiny is to overspread the continent allotted by Providence for the free development of our yearly multiplying millions." Behind the rhetoric of Manifest Destiny was a sense of cultural and even racial superiority; "inferior" peoples—Native Americans and Mexicans—were to be brought under American dominion, taught about republican forms of government, and converted to Protestantism.

Oregon.   Already many residents of the Ohio River Valley were casting their eyes westward to the fertile valleys of the Oregon Country. This region stretched along the Pacific Coast from the forty-second parallel in the south (the border with Mexican California) to the fifty-fourth parallel in the north (54°40′, the border with Russian Alaska) and was claimed by both Great Britain and the United States. Since 1818 a British-American convention had allowed both the British and Americans to settle anywhere in the disputed region. The British-run Hudson's Bay Company developed a

lucrative fur trade north of the Columbia River, while several hundred Americans settled to the south, mostly in the Willamette Valley. On the basis of this settlement, the United States established a claim to the zone between the forty-second parallel and the Columbia River (Map 13.2).

In 1842 American interest in Oregon increased dramatically. Navy Lieutenant Charles Wilkes published glowing reports of the potential harbors he had found in the area of Puget Sound, news of great interest to New England merchants plying the China trade. In the same year a party of a hundred settlers journeyed along the Oregon Trail that fur traders and explorers had blazed through the Great Plains and the Rocky Mountains (Map 13.3). Their reports from Oregon told of a mild climate and fertile soil.

"Oregon fever" suddenly raged. In May 1843 over a thousand men, women, and children—with more than a hundred wagons and five thousand oxen and cattle— gathered in Independence, Missouri, for the trek to Oregon. The migrants were mostly farming and trading families from Missouri, Kentucky, and Tennessee. With military-style organization, the pioneers overcame flooding streams, dust storms, dying livestock, and encounters with Indians. After a journey of six months they reached the Willamette Valley, more than two

MAP 13.3 Routes to the West, 1835–1860

By the mid- to late 1840s a variety of trails spanned the arid zone west of the ninety-fifth meridian and the Pacific Coast. From the south, El Camino Real linked Mexico City to the California coast, Santa Fe, and the breakaway province of Texas. From the east, the Santa Fe, Oregon, California, and Mormon Trails carried tens of thousands of Americans from departure points on the Mississippi and Missouri Rivers to new communities in Utah and along the Pacific Coast. By the 1860s both the Pony Express and the Butterfield Overland Mail provided reliable communication between the eastern United States and California.

thousand miles across the continent. During the next two seasons another 5,000 people reached Oregon, and numbers continued to grow.

By 1860 about 350,000 Americans had braved the Oregon Trail. More than 34,000 of them died in the effort, mostly from disease and exposure; only 400 deaths came from Indian attacks. The walking migrants wore three-foot-deep paths and their wagons carved five-foot-deep ruts across sandstone formations in southern Wyoming—tracks that are visible today. Women found the trail especially difficult, for it exaggerated the authority of their husbands and added to their traditional chores the labor of driving wagons and animals.

California.   Some pioneers ended up in the Mexican province of California. They left the Oregon Trail at the Snake River and struggled southward down the California Trail, settling in the interior valley along the Sacramento River. California had been the remotest corner of Spain's American empire, and Spain had established a significant foothold there only in the 1770s, when it built a chain of religious missions and forts (presidios) along the coast (see Chapter 8). New England merchants soon struck up trade with the settlers in California, buying sea otter pelts that they carried to China. Commerce increased after

Mexico won independence. To promote California's development the new Mexican government took over the Franciscan-run missions, liberating more than 20,000 Indians who worked on them, and promoted large-scale cattle ranching.

The rise of cattle ranching in California created a new society and economy. While some mission Indians joined Native American peoples in the interior, many remained in the coastal region. They intermarried with the local mestizos (Mexicans of mixed Spanish and Indian ancestry) and worked as laborers and cowboys. New England merchants carried the leather and tallow produced on the large California ranches to the booming Massachusetts boot and shoe industry. To handle the increased business, New England firms dispatched dozens of resident agents to California. Unlike the American settlers in Texas, many of those New Englanders assimilated Mexican culture. They married into the families of the elite Mexicans—the Californios—and adopted their dress, manners, outlook, and Catholic religion. A crucial exception was Thomas Oliver Larkin, the most successful merchant in the coastal town of Monterey. Larkin established a close working relationship with Mexican authorities, but he remained an American citizen and plotted for the peaceful annexation of California to the United States.

The Promised Land—The Grayson Family, **by William S. Jewett, 1850**

For adventurous nineteenth-century Americans, the West symbolized a brighter future. Here Andrew Jackson Grayson (1819–1869) and his family catch their first glimpse of the fertile lands of California's Sacramento Valley. The Graysons had traveled west with the ill-fated migrants who perished in a blizzard at the Donner Pass; fortunately, they had left the main group and made their own way over the Sierra Nevada. To celebrate his family's safe arrival, Andrew Grayson commissioned this painting by William S. Jewett, who executed it at the very spot the Graysons first saw their new home.
Terra Museum of American Art, Chicago, Illinois. Daniel J. Terra Collection.

Like Larkin, American migrants in the Sacramento Valley had no desire to assimilate into Mexican society. Moreover, their legal standing was uncertain; many were squatters and others held land grants of dubious validity. Some of them hoped to emulate the Americans in Texas by colonizing the country, overwhelming what they regarded as an inferior culture and then seeking annexation to the United States. However, these settlers numbered only about 700 in the early 1840s, compared with the coastal population of 7,000 Mexicans and 300 American traders.

The Fateful Election of 1844

The election of 1844 determined the course of the American government's policy toward California, Oregon, and Texas. Since 1836, when Texas requested annexation, some southern leaders had favored territorial expansion to extend the slave system. They had been opposed not only by cautious party politicians and northern abolitionists but also, southerners came to think, by British antislavery advocates. In 1839 Britain and France had intervened in Mexico to force payment of foreign debts, and there were rumors that Britain wanted California as payment. Southern leaders also believed that Britain was encouraging Texas to remain independent and had designs on Spanish Cuba, which some southerners wanted to annex. To thwart any such British schemes southern expansionists demanded the immediate annexation of Texas.

At this crucial moment "Oregon fever" and Manifest Destiny altered the political and diplomatic landscape in the North. In 1843 Americans throughout the Ohio Valley and the Great Lakes states called on the federal government to renounce the joint occupation of Oregon. Democrats and Whigs jointly organized "Oregon conventions," and in July a bipartisan national convention demanded that the United States seize Oregon all the way to 54°40′ north latitude, the southern limit of Russian Alaska.

Now that northern Democrats were demanding expansion, southern Democrats could champion the annexation of Texas without threatening party unity. Moreover, they had the support of President John Tyler. Disowned by the Whigs because of his opposition to Henry Clay's nationalist economic program, Tyler hoped to win reelection in 1844 as a Democrat. To curry favor among expansionists Tyler proposed to annex Texas and seize Oregon to the 54°40′ line. In April 1844 Tyler and John C. Calhoun, his new secretary of state, submitted to the Senate a treaty to annex Texas. Two political leaders with presidential ambitions, Democrat Martin Van Buren and Whig Henry Clay, quickly declared their opposition. They knew that annexation would alienate many northern voters and persuaded Whig and northern Democratic senators to defeat the treaty.

Texas became the central issue in the election of 1844. The Democrats passed over Tyler, whom they did not trust, and Van Buren, whom southern Democrats despised for his opposition to annexation. They selected former Governor James K. Polk of Tennessee, a slave owner who favored annexation and who, as Andrew Jackson's personal favorite, was nicknamed "Young

A Californio Patriarch

The descendant of a Spanish family that had lived—and prospered—in Mexico since the Spanish conquest, Mariano Guadalupe Vallejo served in Mexican California as a military officer. In the 1820s he acquired 270,000 acres of land in the Sonoma Valley north of San Francisco. Vallejo, the father of nine children, presents himself in this photograph as a proud patriarch, surrounded by two daughters and three granddaughters. During the American takeover in 1846, he was imprisoned for a short period and subsequently suffered severe financial setbacks, losing most of his vast landholdings to squatters and rival claimants.
Bancroft Library, University of California, Berkeley.

Hickory." Unimpressive in appearance, Polk was a man of iron will and boundless ambition for the nation. "Fifty-four forty or fight!" became the patriotic cry of his expansionist campaign.

The Whigs nominated Henry Clay, who again championed his American System of internal improvements, high tariffs, and national banking. Initially Clay dodged the issue of Texas, finally suggesting that he might support annexation. His evasive position disappointed thousands of northern Whigs and Democrats who strongly opposed any expansion of slavery. Rather than vote for Clay, some antislavery advocates supported the Liberty Party's candidate, James G. Birney of Kentucky. Birney garnered less than 3 percent of the total vote but probably claimed enough Whig votes in New York to cause Clay to lose that state. By taking New York's 36 electoral votes, Polk won the presidency by a

margin of 170 to 105 in the electoral college (otherwise Clay would have won, by a margin of 141 to 134).

Following Polk's victory, congressional Democrats closed ranks and moved immediately to bring Texas into the Union. Unable to secure a two-thirds majority in the Senate for a treaty with the Republic of Texas, they approved annexation by a joint resolution of Congress, which required only a majority vote in each house. Polk's strategy of linking Texas and Oregon had put him in the White House and Texas in the Union.

War, Expansion, and Slavery, 1846–1850

Polk had even greater territorial ambitions than Texas and Oregon: he wanted all of Mexico between Texas and the Pacific Ocean and was prepared to go to war to get it. What he was not prepared for, though he should have been, was the major crisis over slavery unleashed by the success of his expansionist dreams.

The War with Mexico, 1846–1848

Mexico had not prospered in the twenty-five years since it won independence from Spain in 1821. Its population remained small at 7 million people, and its stagnant economy yielded only modest tax revenue, which was eaten up by interest payments on foreign debts and a bloated government bureaucracy. Consequently, the Mexican government lacked the people and the money to settle its distant northern provinces. The Spanish-speaking population of California and New Mexico remained small—about 75,000 in 1840—and contributed little to the national economy. Still, Mexican officials were determined to retain all their nation's historical territories, and when the breakaway Texas Republic accepted American statehood on July 4, 1845, Mexico broke off diplomatic relations with the United States.

Polk's Expansionist Program.   Taking advantage of the rupture, President James Polk put into action a secret plan he had devised to acquire Mexico's far northern provinces. To intimidate the Mexican government he ordered General Zachary Taylor and an American army of 2,000 soldiers to occupy the disputed lands between the Nueces River (the historical boundary of the Mexican province of Texas) and the Rio Grande, which the expansionist-minded Texas Republic had claimed as its southern and western border (see Map 13.1). Then Polk launched a diplomatic initiative, dispatching John Slidell on a secret mission to Mexico City. Slidell was instructed to secure Mexico's acceptance of the Rio Grande boundary and buy the Mexican provinces of New Mexico and California, paying as much as $30 million. When Slidell arrived in December 1845, Mexican officials refused to see him, declaring that the American annexation of Texas was illegal.

Anticipating the failure of Slidell's mission, Polk had already embarked on an alternative plan to take California. The president's strategy was to foment a revolution that, as in Texas, would lead to the creation of an independent republic and a request for annexation. In October 1845 Secretary of State James Buchanan told merchant Thomas O. Larkin, now the U.S. consul in the port of Monterey, to encourage leading Mexican residents to declare independence and support peaceful annexation. To add military muscle to his plan, Polk sent orders to American naval commanders in the Pacific to seize San Francisco Bay and California's coastal towns in

case of war. The president also had the War Department dispatch Captain John C. Frémont and an "exploring" party of heavily armed soldiers deep into Mexican territory. By December 1845 Frémont had reached California's Sacramento Valley.

Events now moved quickly toward war. When Polk learned of the failure of Slidell's mission, he ordered General Taylor to build a fort near the Rio Grande, hoping to incite an armed response by Mexico. As Ulysses S. Grant, a young officer serving with Taylor, said much later, "We were sent to provoke a fight, but it was essential that Mexico should commence it." When Mexican and American forces clashed near the Rio Grande in May 1846, Polk delivered the war message he had drafted long before. Taking liberties with the truth, the president declared that

Street Fighting in the Calle de Iturbide, 1846
The American conquest of Monterrey, which Spain's troops had been unable to capture during Mexico's war for independence in 1820–1821, came after bloody house-to-house fighting. Protected by thick walls and shuttered windows, Mexican defenders pour a withering fire on dark-uniformed American troops and buckskin-clad frontier fighters. A spacious Catholic cathedral looms in the background, its foundations obscured by the smoke from Mexican cannon. West Point Museum, United States Military Academy, West Point, NY.

Frederick Douglass: Development of an Abolitionist

Frederick Douglass was born a slave in 1818. Thirty years later he was a famous man, author of the acclaimed *Narrative of the Life of Frederick Douglass* (1845) and a leading moral abolitionist. Within another five years Douglass had become a political activist, convinced that only the power of the government would end slavery.

His white father's sense of paternity—or guilt—played a crucial role in Frederick Douglass's life, but his own abilities and determination accounted for his rapid ascent to fame: he was a man of remarkable talents. Born on a Maryland plantation, Douglass grew up as Frederick Bailey, having been given his enslaved mother's family name. He never knew the identity of his father, though talk in the slave quarters pointed toward a man Douglass later described as "his master." This rumor was probably true, given the course of Frederick Bailey's early life. In 1827 his owner, Thomas Auld, sent nine-year-old Frederick to Baltimore to live with his brother Hugh Auld.

There were no other slaves in Hugh Auld's household and, quite remarkably, for the next five years Frederick was treated much like the Auld children. He listened to Sophia Auld read the Bible, learned to read from a spelling book, figured out the meaning of abolition from newspapers, and heard about slaves running away to the North. At age twelve he purchased a copy of *The Columbian Orator,* a collection of speeches expounding the virtues of the American republic—including its devotion to "the rights of man." Enthralled, Frederick memorized and recited the speeches to his friends, including the free blacks he sought out at Methodist and Baptist churches. Despite his legal status, the young Frederick Bailey had begun to think and act like a free man.

In 1833 Thomas Auld returned Frederick to the sleepy rural town of St. Michaels, perhaps to keep him

Frederick Douglass, c. 1848

The daguerreotype of Douglass was taken when he was about thirty years old. Describing Douglass, an admirer wrote: "He was more than six feet in height, and his majestic form . . . straight as an arrow, muscular, yet lithe and graceful, his flashing eye, and more than all, his voice, that rivaled Webster's in its richness and in the depth . . . of its cadences, made up such an ideal of an orator as the listeners never forgot."
Chester County Historical Society.

from running away or becoming mixed up in antislavery agitation. Frederick became rebellious, organizing a Sabbath school and refusing to work. So in 1834 Auld hired him out to Edward Covey, a farmer with a reputation for "breaking" unruly slaves. After enduring six months of heavy labor and regular beatings, Frederick reached his own breaking point and had it out with Covey. Their brutal fight "was the turning point in my 'life as a slave,'" Douglass recalled. "I was nothing before; I WAS A MAN NOW." Determined "to be a FREEMAN" as well, Frederick hatched an escape plan. Betrayed by a fellow conspirator, he found himself in jail, faced with being sold into the harsh slavery of the Deep South. Once again Thomas Auld intervened, returning Frederick to his brother's charge in Baltimore and promising him freedom in eight years, at the age of twenty-five. Becoming a journeyman caulker in the shipyards, the young slave soon worked independently, giving Hugh Auld a weekly payment.

Frederick plunged enthusiastically into the life of Baltimore's free African American community, which numbered almost 30,000. He courted a free black woman, Anna Murray, and joined the East Baltimore Mental Improvement Society, a self-help organization set up by free black caulkers. This stimulating life came to an abrupt end when Frederick fell behind in his payments to Hugh Auld. Rather than face the loss of his independence, Frederick decided to run away. In the fall of 1838 he borrowed the identification papers of a free African American sailor and sailed to New York City.

Frederick Bailey began his life of freedom by taking the new name Douglass, marrying Anna Murray, and settling in the seaport town of New Bedford, Massachusetts. Inspired by the lectures of William Lloyd Garrison, he became a public antislavery speaker. Hearing Douglass deliver a powerful address in 1841, Garrison hired him as a lecturer for the American Anti-Slavery Society. Soon Douglass became a celebrity. His partly African origins drew crowds to his lectures, as did his commanding personal presence, dramatic rhetoric, and forceful intellect. He lectured in hundreds of communities in the Northeast, holding audiences spellbound. Hearing Douglass speak in Boston, the future women's rights activist Elizabeth Cady Stanton was deeply impressed:

> *Around him sat the great antislavery orators of the day watching the effect of his eloquence on that immense audience, that laughed and wept by turns, completely carried away by the wondrous gifts of his pathos and humor. On this occasion, all the other speakers seemed tame after Frederick Douglass.*

In his speeches Douglass denounced slavery in the South and racial discrimination in the North. Gradually his views diverged from those of Garrison. To rid America of the sin of slavery, Garrison was prepared to expel the southern states from the Union. To Douglass this policy was madness because it would perpetuate slavery. Following a triumphal British lecturing tour from 1845 and 1847, Douglass founded an antislavery newspaper, the *North Star*. Departing from Garrison's moral radicalism, the *North Star* gravitated toward political abolitionism. In 1848 Douglass attended the Buffalo convention that established the Free-Soil Party and ignored Garrison's condemnation of the party as a species of "whitemanism," a racist effort to keep the territories white. Douglass also attended the women's rights convention at Seneca Falls, and subsequently he endorsed a wider public role for women. "In respect to political rights," he declared in the *North Star*, "we hold woman to be justly entitled to all we claim for men."

In 1851 Douglass publicly separated himself from Garrison and the American Anti-Slavery Society by defending the Constitution, which Garrison had previously condemned as "a covenant with death." A year later in his influential "Fifth of July" speech, Douglass celebrated the Constitution as a vehicle for black liberation. "In that instrument, I hold there is no warrant, license, nor sanction of the hateful thing [of slavery]; but, interpreted as it ought to be interpreted, the Constitution is a GLORIOUS LIBERTY DOCUMENT."

Douglass's involvement in practical politics deepened during the 1850s. Although he believed that violence would be necessary to abolish slavery, he was cautious in encouraging slave insurrections, declining to join John Brown's raid on Harpers Ferry. Nonetheless, popular suspicion that he was a key conspirator led Douglass to flee to Canada and then to Britain. When he resumed speech making in America in 1860, the victory of the Republican Party and its program of free soil seemed imminent.

During and after the Civil War Douglass remained a respected African American leader. He pressed the Republicans to embrace the abolition of slavery as a war aim, celebrated Lincoln's Emancipation Proclamation, and assisted the War Department in recruiting black soldiers. Throughout Reconstruction he spoke and lobbied effectively for equal treatment for African Americans, especially for the right to vote. Finally rewarding Douglass's service to its cause, the Republican Party secured his appointment in 1888 as the American minister to the black nation of Haiti.

By the time of his death in 1895 Douglass's optimism about race relations had waned, as Jim Crow laws in the southern states fastened new bonds of discrimination on African Americans. In his last major speech he warned that the "presence of eight millions of people . . . constituting an aggrieved class, smarting under terrible wrongs, denied the exercise of the commonest rights of humanity . . . [is] a disgrace and scandal to . . . the whole country."

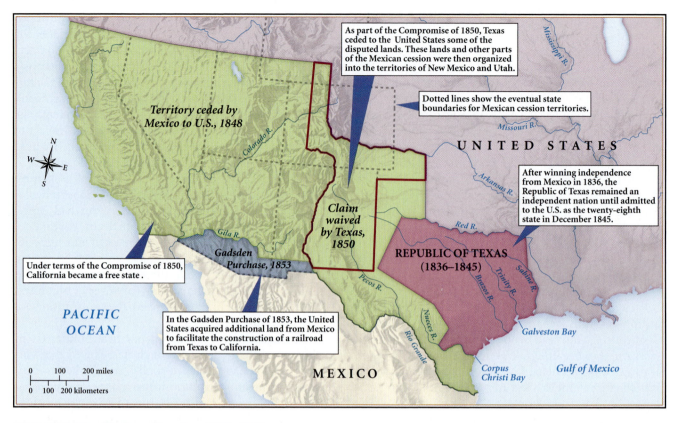

MAP 13.5 The Mexican Cession, 1848–1853

In the Treaty of Guadalupe Hidalgo (1848), Mexico ceded to the United States its vast northern territories—the present-day states of California, Nevada, Utah, Arizona, New Mexico, and half of Colorado and Texas. These new territories, President Polk boasted to Congress, "constitute of themselves a country large enough for a great empire, and the acquisition is second in importance only to that of Louisiana in 1803."

Yucatán Peninsula, and taking all of Oregon. To maintain party unity Cass was deliberately vague on the question of slavery in the West. He promoted a new idea—squatter sovereignty—that would give settlers in each territory the power to determine its status as free or slave.

The Election of 1848.   Cass's political ingenuity failed to hold the party together. Demanding unambiguous opposition to the expansion of slavery, some northern Democrats joined the newly formed Free-Soil Party, which nominated Martin Van Buren for president. Van Buren's conversion to free soil was genuine, but he also wanted to punish southern Democrats for having denied him the presidential nomination in 1844. To attract Whig votes, the Free-Soil Party chose conscience Whig Charles Francis Adams as its candidate for vice president.

To avoid divisions in their ranks, the Whigs nominated General Zachary Taylor. Taylor was a southerner and a Louisiana slave owner, but he had not taken a position on the politically charged issue of slavery in the territories. Equally important, the general's exploits during the war with Mexico had made him a popular hero.

Known as "Old Rough and Ready," Taylor possessed a common touch that had won him the affection of his troops. "Our Commander on the Rio Grande," wrote Walt Whitman, "emulates the Great Commander of our revolution"—George Washington.

In 1848, as in 1840, running a military hero worked for the Whigs. Taylor and his vice presidential running mate, Millard Fillmore, took 47 percent of the popular vote against 42 percent for Cass, but the margin in the electoral college was thin: 163 to 127. The Free-Soil ticket of Van Buren and Adams made the difference in the election. They won 10 percent of the popular vote and, crucially, deprived the Democrats of enough votes in New York to cost Cass that state and the presidency. The bitter debate over the Wilmot Proviso had fractured the Democratic Party in the North and changed the dynamics of American politics.

1850: Crisis and Compromise

Even before President Zachary Taylor took office, events in California sparked a major political crisis that threatened the Union. In January 1848 workmen building a

A General Runs for President

Of the first nine presidents, three—Washington, Jackson, and Harrison—owed their political success to their exploits as military commanders. Fresh from the battlefields of the Mexican War, General Zachary Taylor followed in their footsteps, posing for this daguerreotype campaign portrait in his uniform. In part because of his popular appeal as a military hero, Taylor— running on the Whig ticket—won a narrow victory over Democrat Lewis Cass. Collection of Janice L. and David J. Frent.

mill for John A. Sutter in the Sierra Nevada foothills in northern California discovered flakes of gold. Sutter was a Swiss immigrant who arrived in California in 1839, became a Mexican citizen, and established an estate in the Sacramento Valley. He tried to keep the discovery a secret, but by May Americans from San Francisco were pouring into the foothills. When President Polk confirmed the discovery in December, the gold rush was on. By January 1849 sixty-one crowded ships had departed from northeastern ports to sail around Cape Horn for San Francisco, and by May, nearly twelve thousand wagons had crossed the Missouri River, also bound for the gold fields. In 1849 alone more than 80,000 migrants—the "forty-niners"—arrived in California (Map 13.6).

Statehood for California. The rapid influx of settlers revived the national debate over free soil. The forty-niners, who lived in crowded, chaotic towns and mining camps, demanded the formation of a territorial government to protect their lives and property. To avoid an

extended debate over slavery, President Taylor advised the Californians to apply for statehood immediately, and in November 1849 they ratified a state constitution that prohibited slavery. Few of the many southerners who flocked to the gold fields or to San Francisco owned slaves or wanted to. For his part Taylor wanted to attract Free-Soilers and northern Democrats into the Whig Party and urged Congress to admit California as a free state.

The swift victory of the antislavery forces in California alarmed southern politicians. The admission of California as a free state would not only cut off the expansion of slavery to the Pacific but also threaten the carefully maintained balance in the Senate. In 1845 the entry of Texas and Florida had raised the total of slave states to fifteen, against thirteen free states. However, the entry of Iowa in 1846 and Wisconsin in 1848 had reestablished the balance. Fearing that the South would be placed at a political disadvantage from which it would never recover, southern politicians decided to block California's admission unless the federal government guaranteed the future of slavery.

Constitutional Conflict. The resulting political impasse produced long and passionate debates in Congress and four different positions with respect to the status of slavery in the territories. As usual John C. Calhoun took an extreme stance. He began by asserting the right of states to secede from the Union and warning that, to protect their slave property, the southern states might exercise that right. To avoid that outcome he proposed a constitutional amendment that would permanently balance power between the sections. Calhoun also advanced the radically new doctrine that Congress had no constitutional authority to regulate slavery in the territories. This argument ran counter to a half century of practice. In 1787 Congress had prohibited slavery in the Northwest Territory, and in the Missouri Compromise of 1821 it had extended this ban to most of the Louisiana Purchase.

Although Calhoun's controversial constitutional doctrine that all the territories were open to slavery won support in the Deep South, many southerners were prepared to accept a second—more moderate—position: an extension of the Missouri Compromise line to the Pacific Ocean. This extension would guarantee slave owners access to some western territory, including a separate state in southern California. Some northern Democrats, including former secretary of state James Buchanan, also favored this plan as a way to resolve the crisis.

A third alternative for resolving the status of slavery in the territories was squatter sovereignty, the plan advanced by Lewis Cass in 1848 and now championed by Democratic senator Stephen Douglas of Illinois. Douglas called his plan "**popular sovereignty**" to emphasize

California Gold Prospectors

Beginning in 1849, thousands of fortune seekers from all parts of the world converged on the California gold fields. By 1852 the state had 200,000 residents, including 25,000 Chinese, many of whom toiled in the gold fields as wage laborers. Working at the head of the Auburn Ravine in 1852, these prospectors are using a primitive technique—panning— to separate gold from sand and gravel. California State Library.

its roots in republican ideology, and it had considerable appeal. Popular sovereignty would place decisions about slavery in the hands of local settlers and their territorial governments, removing the explosive issue from national politics. However, popular sovereignty was a vague and slippery concept. For example, did popular sovereignty mean that residents could accept or ban slavery when a territory was first organized or only when a territory had enough people to frame a constitution and apply for statehood?

For their part, antislavery advocates were unwilling to accept any plan that might involve the expansion of slavery and stood firm for complete exclusion. In 1850 Senator Salmon P. Chase of Ohio, elected by a Democratic–Free-Soil coalition, and Senator William H. Seward, a New York Whig, urged federal authorities to restrict slavery within its existing boundaries and then extinguish it completely. Condemning slavery as "morally unjust, politically unwise, and socially pernicious" and invoking "a higher law than the Constitu-

tion," Seward demanded bold action to protect freedom, "the common heritage of mankind."

A Complex Compromise. Standing on the brink of disaster, senior Whigs and Democrats desperately sought a compromise to preserve the Union. Through a long and complex legislative process, Whig leaders Henry Clay and Daniel Webster and Democrat Stephen A. Douglas organized an interrelated package of six laws known collectively as the Compromise of 1850. To mollify the South, the Compromise included a new Fugitive Slave Act allowing slave owners to demand that federal magistrates in the free states help return runaway slaves. To satisfy the North, the legislation admitted California as a free state, resolved a boundary dispute between New Mexico and Texas in favor of New Mexico, and abolished the slave trade (but not slavery) in the District of Columbia. Finally, the Compromise organized the rest of the lands acquired from Mexico into the territories of New Mexico and Utah on the basis of popular sovereignty (Map 13.7).

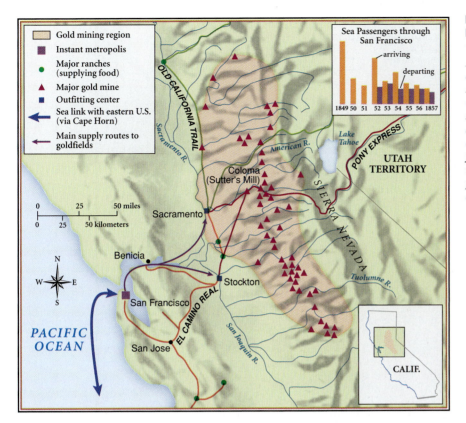

MAP 13.6 The California Gold Rush, 1849–1857

Traveling from all parts of the world—Europe, China, and Australia as well as the eastern United States—hundreds of thousands of bonanza seekers converged on the California gold fields. Miners traveling by sea landed at San Francisco, which became an instant metropolis; many others trekked overland to the gold fields on the Old California Trail. By the mid-1850s the gold rush was over; almost as many people departed by sea from San Francisco each year as arrived to seek their fortune.

The Compromise averted a secession crisis in 1850—but only barely. In the midst of the struggle the governor of South Carolina declared that there was not "the slightest doubt" that his state would secede from the Union. He and other "**fire-eaters**" in Georgia, Mississippi, and Alabama organized special conventions to protect "Southern Rights" and demand secession. To persuade these conventions to support the Compromise, moderate southern politicians agreed to support secession in the future if Congress abolished slavery anywhere or refused to grant statehood to a territory with a proslavery constitution. Lacking sufficient popular support, the "fire-eaters" drew back from secession, averting a constitutional crisis.

The End of the Second Party System, 1850–1858

The architects of the Compromise of 1850 hoped that their agreement would resolve the issue of slavery for a generation. Their hopes were quickly dashed. Demanding freedom for fugitive slaves and free soil in the West, some northerners refused to accept the letter or the spirit of the Compromise. Some southerners were equally hostile to the agreement and plotted to expand slavery in the West and the Caribbean. These resulting disputes destroyed the Second Party System, deepening the crisis of the Union.

Resistance to the Fugitive Slave Act

The most controversial element of the Compromise proved to be the Fugitive Slave Act, which ensured federal protection for slavery and made no concessions to the humanity of African Americans. Under its terms federal judges or special commissioners in the northern states determined the status of blacks who were accused of being runaway slaves. The accused blacks were denied jury trials and even the right to testify. Because federal marshals were legally required to support slave catchers, the new legislation was effective, and about two hundred fugitives (as well as some free northern blacks) were sent to the South and enslaved.

The plight of runaways and the appearance of slave catchers aroused popular hostility in the North and Midwest, and free blacks and abolitionists defied the new law. In October 1850 Boston abolitionists helped two slaves escape to freedom and drove a Georgia slave catcher out of town. The following year rioters in Syracuse, New York, broke into a courthouse to free a fugitive slave. Abandoning his commitment to nonviolence, Frederick Douglass declared that "the only way to make a Fugitive Slave Law a dead letter is to make half a dozen or more dead kidnappers." As if in response, in September 1851 a deadly confrontation took place in the Quaker village of Christiana, Pennsylvania. About twenty African Americans exchanged gunfire with a group of slave catchers from Maryland, killing two of them. Federal

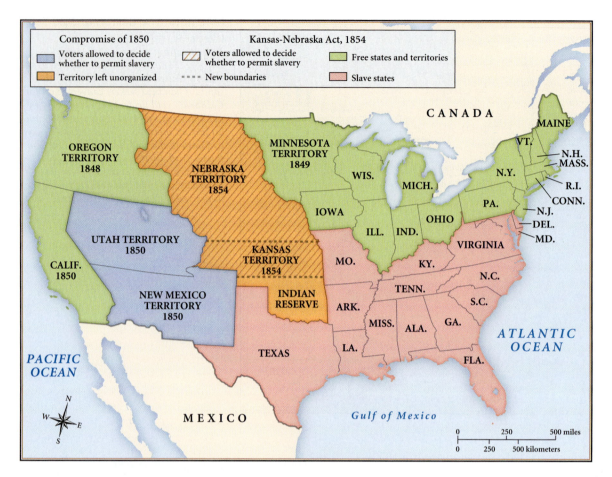

MAP 13.7 The Compromise of 1850 and the Kansas-Nebraska Act of 1854

Vast territories were at stake in the contest over the extension of slavery. The Compromise of 1850 resolved the status of lands in the Far West: California would be a free state, and the settlers of the Utah and New Mexico Territories would decide their own fate by voting for or against slavery. But the implementation of popular sovereignty in Kansas and Nebraska in 1854 sparked a bitter local war between the advocates of free soil and slavery, revealing a fatal flaw in the concept.

For more help analyzing this map, see the ONLINE STUDY GUIDE at bedfordstmartins.com/henretta.

marshals arrested thirty-six blacks and four whites and had them indicted for treason for defying the law. But a Pennsylvania jury acquitted one defendant, and northern public opinion forced the government to drop its charges against the rest.

Harriet Beecher Stowe's abolitionist novel *Uncle Tom's Cabin* (1852) increased northern opposition to the Fugitive Slave Act. By translating the moral principles of abolitionism into heartrending personal situations, Beecher's novel evoked empathy and outrage throughout the North. Members of northern state legislatures were equally outraged that the South was using the federal government as an agent of the slaveholding interest within their states. In response, they enacted **personal-liberty laws** that extended legal rights in their states to accused fugitives. In 1857 the

Wisconsin Supreme Court went even further, ruling in *Ableman v. Booth* that the Fugitive Slave Act was void in Wisconsin because it was contrary to state law and resulted in the illegal federal confinement of a Wisconsin citizen accused of violating it. Continuing to assert a state's rights position, the Wisconsin court rejected the authority of federal courts to review its decision. When the case reached the U.S. Supreme Court in 1859, Chief Justice Roger B. Taney led a unanimous court in affirming the supremacy of federal over state courts—a position that has stood the test of time—and upheld the constitutionality of the Fugitive Slave Act. By that time popular opposition in the North had made it nearly impossible to catch fugitive blacks. As Frederick Douglass had hoped, the act had become a "dead letter."

Uncle Tom's Cabin, 1852

The cover of this "Young Folks Edition" of Uncle Tom's Cabin *shows Tom as an old man, worn down by his life as a slave and the brutal punishments of overseer Simon Legree. Little Eva, whom Tom had saved from drowning, rests her hand compassionately on his knee. Like the book's text, this image offered whites a sympathetic view of African Americans, challenging generations of negative stereotypes.* Picture Research Consultants & Archives.

The Whigs' Decline and the Democrats' Diplomacy

The conflict over fugitive slaves split the Whig Party, which went into the election of 1852 weakened by the death of Henry Clay, one of its greatest leaders. Rejecting Millard Fillmore, who had become president on the death of Zachary Taylor, the Whigs nominated General Winfield Scott, another hero of the war with Mexico. However, about a third of southern Whigs threw their support to the Democrats, refusing to support Scott because northern members of the Whig Party refused to support slavery.

The Democrats too were divided. Southerners wanted a candidate who would support Calhoun's position that all territories should be open to slavery. But northern and midwestern Democrats advocated the principle of popular sovereignty, as did the three leading candidates—Lewis Cass of Michigan, Stephen Douglas of Illinois, and James Buchanan of Pennsylvania. At the national convention no candidate could secure the necessary two-thirds majority. Exhausted after forty-eight ballots, the convention settled on a compromise nominee, Franklin Pierce of New Hampshire, a congenial man reputed to be sympathetic to the South.

The Democrats' cautious strategy paid off, and they swept the election. Pleased by the admission of California

as a free state, Martin Van Buren and many other Free-Soilers voted for Pierce, reuniting the Democratic Party. Conversely, the election fragmented the Whig Party into sectional wings; it would never again wage a national campaign.

As president, Pierce pursued an expansionist foreign policy. To assist northern merchants he sent a mission to Japan to negotiate a commercial treaty. Pierce was even more solicitous of southern interests. To resolve a dispute over the southern boundary of New Mexico, the president revived Polk's plan to annex a large amount of territory south of the Rio Grande and named James Gadsden as his negotiator. Mexican officials rejected Pierce's annexation bid but agreed to sell a small amount of land that Gadsden, a railroad promoter, wanted to construct a southern-based transcontinental railroad to the Pacific (see Map 13.5).

Pierce's most dramatic foreign policy initiative came in the Caribbean. Southern expansionists had previously funded three clandestine military expeditions to Spanish Cuba, where they hoped to prod the slave-owning elite into declaring independence and then joining the United States. In 1853 Pierce covertly supported a new Cuban expedition led by John A. Quitman, a former governor of Mississippi. While Quitman was building up his forces, the Pierce administration threatened war with Spain over the seizure of an American ship, demanding an apology and a large indemnity. When northern Democrats in Congress refused to support this aggressive diplomacy, Pierce and Secretary of State William L. Marcy had to back down. Still determined to seize Cuba, Marcy tried to buy the island from Spain and then prompted American diplomats in Europe to pressure Pierce to seize it. In the Ostend Manifesto (1854), the diplomats sent a message to Pierce declaring that the United States would be justified in seizing Cuba "by every law, human and Divine." Quickly leaked to the press by antiexpansionists, the Ostend Manifesto triggered a new wave of northern resentment against the South and forced Pierce to halt his efforts. But his expansionist policy had already revived northern fears of a "**Slave Power**" conspiracy.

The Kansas-Nebraska Act and the Rise of New Parties

In the wake of the Ostend Manifesto a new struggle over westward expansion inflamed sectional divisions. Because the Missouri Compromise prohibited slavery in the Louisiana Purchase north of 36°30′, southern senators had delayed the political organization of that area. However, westward-looking residents of the Ohio River Valley and the Upper South demanded its settlement. Senator Stephen A. Douglas of Illinois became their spokesman, in part because he supported a northern transcontinental railroad from Chicago to California. In

Presidential Election of 1852

In this cartoon, Franklin Pierce races toward the White House on a fleet Democratic horse while General Winfield Scott futilely beats his stubborn Whig mule, which is pulled by members of the Know-Nothing Party ("Native Americans") and prodded by a group of African Americans. By identifying Scott and the Whigs as anti-foreigner and pro-black (because many Whigs opposed the Fugitive Slave Act of 1850), the cartoonist seeks to garner votes for Pierce and the Democrats from New York's large population of Irish and German immigrants. Collection of Janice L. and David J. Frent.

1854 Douglas introduced a bill to extinguish Native American rights on the central Great Plains and organize a large territory to be called Nebraska. Because Nebraska was north of 36°30′, it would be a free territory.

Douglas's bill conflicted with the plans of southern senators and representatives, who wanted to extend slavery throughout the Louisiana Purchase. Moreover, like James Gadsden, southern leaders hoped that one of their cities—New Orleans, Memphis, or St. Louis—would become the eastern terminus of a transcontinental railroad. To win southern support for the organization of Nebraska, Douglas made two major concessions. First, he amended his bill so that it explicitly repealed the Missouri Compromise and organized the region on the basis of popular sovereignty. Second, Douglas agreed to the formation of two new territories, Nebraska and Kansas, giving slaveholders a chance to dominate the settlement of Kansas, the more southern territory (see Map 13.7). To persuade northerners and midwesterners, Douglas argued that Kansas would be settled primarily by nonslaveholders because its climate and terrain were not suited to plantation agriculture.

After weeks of bitter debate, the Senate enacted the Kansas-Nebraska Act, which was strongly supported by President Pierce. However, the House of Representatives initially voted to kill the measure, as sixty-six northern Democrats defied party policy. Using all the powers at his disposal—patronage pressure, newspaper propaganda, floor management—Pierce persuaded twenty-two members to change their votes, and the measure squeaked through.

Republicans and Know-Nothings. The price of this victory was enormous because passage of the Kansas-Nebraska Act completed the destruction of the Whig Party and nearly wrecked the Democratic Party. Abolitionists and Free-Soilers denounced the act, calling it "part of a great scheme for extending and perpetuating supremacy of the slave power," and their message now fell on receptive ears. Antislavery northern Whigs and "anti-Nebraska" Democrats abandoned their respective parties to create a new Republican Party, named after the party headed by Thomas Jefferson. Emphasizing uncompromising opposition to the

"Bleeding Kansas"

The confrontation between North and South in Kansas took many forms. In the spring of 1859 Dr. John Doy (seated) slipped across the border into Missouri and tried to lead thirteen escaped slaves to freedom in Kansas, only to be captured and jailed in St. Joseph, Missouri. This serious-minded band of antislavery men, well armed with guns and Bowie knives, attacked the jail and carried Doy back to Kansas. Kansas State Historical Society.

expansion of slavery, the Republicans ran a slate of candidates in the congressional election of 1854.

Like most American parties, the Republican Party was a coalition of diverse groups—Free-Soilers, antislavery Democrats, conscience Whigs—but most of its founders shared a common philosophy. They opposed slavery because it degraded manual labor, enslaving blacks and thereby driving down the wages and working conditions of free white workers. In contrast, Republicans as diverse as farmer Abijah Beckwith of Herkimer, New York, and Senator Thaddeus Stevens of Pennsylvania celebrated the moral virtues of a society based on "the middling classes who own the soil and work it with their own hands." Abraham Lincoln, an Illinois Whig who became a Republican, articulated the party's vision of social mobility. "There is no permanent class of hired laborers among us," he argued, and every man had a chance to become a property owner. In the face of increasing class divisions in the industrializing North and Midwest, Lincoln and his fellow Republicans asserted the values of republican freedom and individual enterprise.

Competing for Whig and Democratic votes was another new party, the American, or "Know-Nothing," Party. The American Party had its origins in the anti-immigrant and anti-Catholic organizations of the 1840s (see Chapter 10). In 1850 these secret societies banded together as the Order of the Star-Spangled Banner and the following year they formed the American Party. The secrecy-conscious members sometimes answered outsiders' questions by saying, "I know nothing," giving the party its nickname, but its program was far from secret. Know-Nothings hoped to unite native-born Protestants against the "alien menace" of Irish and German Catholics, banning further immigration and instituting literacy tests for voting. In 1854 the Know-Nothings gained control of the state governments of Massachusetts and Pennsylvania and, allied with the Whigs, commanded a majority in the U.S. House of Representatives. The emergence of a

new major party led by nativists suddenly became a real possibility.

"Bleeding Kansas."   At the same time, the Kansas-Nebraska Act had created yet another political crisis. In 1854 thousands of settlers rushed into the Kansas Territory, putting Douglas's theory of popular sovereignty to the test. On the side of slavery Senator David R. Atchison of Missouri organized residents of his state to cross into Kansas and vote in crucial elections there. Opposing him were agents of the abolitionist New England Emigrant Aid Society, which dispatched hundreds of Free-Soilers to Kansas. In March 1855 the Pierce administration stepped into the fray by accepting the legitimacy of the territorial legislature sitting in Lecompton, Kansas, which had been elected primarily by border-crossing Missourians and had adopted proslavery legislation. However, the majority of Kansas residents were Free-Soilers and refused allegiance to the Lecompton government.

In May 1856 both sides turned to violence. A proslavery gang, seven hundred strong, sacked the free-soil town of Lawrence, destroying two newspaper offices, looting stores, and burning down buildings (see American Voices, "Axalla John Hoole: 'Bleeding Kansas': A Southern View," p. 390). The attack enraged John Brown, an abolitionist from New York and Ohio, whose free-state militia force arrived too late to save the town. Brown was a complex man with a checkered past. Born in 1800, he had started more than twenty businesses in six states and had often been sued by his creditors. Despite his record of business failures, Brown had an intelligence and a moral intensity that won the trust of influential people, including leading abolitionists. Taking vengeance for the sack of Lawrence, he and a few followers murdered and mutilated five proslavery settlers. We must "fight fire with fire" and "strike terror in the hearts of the proslavery people," Brown declared. The sack of Lawrence and the "Pottawatomie massacre," as

Axalla John Hoole

"Bleeding Kansas": A Southern View

Early in 1856 Axalla John Hoole and his bride left South Carolina to build a new life in the Kansas Territory (K.T.). These letters from Hoole to his family show that things did not go well from the start and gradually got worse; after eighteen months the Hooles returned to South Carolina. A Confederate militia captain during the Civil War, Axalla Hoole died in the Battle of Chickamauga in September 1863.

Kansas City, Missouri, Apl. 3d., 1856. The Missourians . . . are very sanguine about Kansas being a slave state & I have heard some of them say it shall be . . . but generally speaking, I have not met with the reception which I expected. Everyone seems bent on the Almighty Dollar, and as a general thing that seems to be their only thought. . . . [T]he supper bell has rung and I must close. Give my love to [the family] and all the Negroes. . . .

Lecompton, K.T., Sept. 12, 1856. I have been unwell ever since the 9th of July. . . . I thought of going to work in a few days, when the Abolitionists broke out and I have had to stand guard of nights when I ought to have been in bed, took cold which . . . caused diarrhea. . . . Betsie is well—

You perceive from the heading of this that I am now in Lecompton, almost all of the Proslavery party between this place and Lawrence are here. We brought our families here, as we thought that we would be better able to defend ourselves. . . .

Lane [and a force of abolitionists] came against us last Friday (a week ago to-day). As it happened we had about 400 men with two cannon—we marched out to meet him, though we were under the impression at the time that we had 1,000 men. We came in gunshot of each other, but the regular [U.S. Army] soldiers came and interfered, but not before our party had shot some dozen guns, by which it is reported that five of the Abolitionists had been killed or wounded. We had strict orders . . . not to fire until they made the attack, but some of our boys would not be restrained. I was a rifleman and one of the skirmishers, but did all that I could to restrain our men though I itched all over to shoot myself. . . . [B]ut we were acting on the defensive, and did not think it prudent to commence the engagement. I firmly believe we would have whipped them, though we would have lost a good many men. . . .

July the 5th., 1857. I fear, Sister, that [our] coming here will do no good at last, as I begin to think that this will be made a Free State at last. 'Tis true we have elected Proslavery men to draft a state constitution, but I feel pretty certain, if it is put to a vote of the people, it will be rejected, as I feel pretty confident that they have a majority here at this time. The South has ceased all efforts, while the North is redoubling her exertions. We nominated a candidate for Congress last Friday—Ex-Gov. Ransom of Michigan. I must confess I have not much faith in him, tho he professes to hate the abolitionists bitterly. . . . If we had nominated a Southern man, he would have been sure to have been beaten. . . .

Source: William Stanley Hoole, ed., "A Southerner's Viewpoint of the Kansas Situation, 1856–1857," *Kansas Historical Quarterly* 3 (1934): 43–65, 149–71, passim.

the killings became known, initiated a guerrilla war in Kansas that cost about two hundred lives.

The Election of 1856 and Dred Scott

The violence in Kansas dominated the presidential election of 1856. The two-year-old Republican Party counted on anger over "Bleeding Kansas" to boost its fortunes. The party's platform denounced the Kansas-Nebraska Act and, alleging a "Slave Power" conspiracy, insisted that the federal government prohibit slavery in all the territories. Its platform also called for federal subsidies to transcontinental railroads, reviving the element of the Whig economic program that was most popular among midwestern Democrats. For president the Republicans nominated Colonel John C. Frémont, a Free-Soiler famous for his role in the conquest of California. The American Party entered the election with high hopes, but it quickly split into sectional factions over Kansas. The southern faction of the American Party nominated former Whig President Millard Fillmore. The Republicans cleverly maneuvered the northern faction of the American Party into endorsing Frémont, and they won the support of many Know-Nothing workingmen by adding anti-Catholic nativism to the Republican Party's program of high tariffs on foreign manufactures. As a Pennsylvania Republican declared, "Let our motto be, protection to everything American, against everything foreign." In

New York Republicans likewise shaped their policies "to cement into a harmonious mass . . . all of the Anti-Slavery, Anti-Popery and Anti-Whiskey" voters.

The Democrats reaffirmed their support for popular sovereignty and the Kansas-Nebraska Act and nominated James Buchanan of Pennsylvania. A tall, dignified figure of sixty-four, Buchanan was an experienced but unimaginative and timid politician. Drawing upon his party's organizational strength and the loyalty of Democratic voters, Buchanan won the three-way race, amassing 174 votes in the electoral college and winning the popular vote—1.8 million votes (45 percent) to 1.3 million (33 percent) for Frémont. Nonetheless, Frémont demonstrated the appeal of the new Republican Party in the North by carrying eleven free states with 114 electoral votes. Buchanan took only five free states, and a small shift of the popular vote to Frémont in Illinois and Pennsylvania would have given him the presidency. Fillmore, the candidate of the southern members of the American Party, won 21 percent of the national vote but only 8 electoral votes.

The dramatic restructuring of parties was now apparent (Map 13.8). With the splintering of the Know-Nothings, the Republicans had replaced the Whigs as the second major party. Moreover, because they had no support in the South, a Republican victory in the next presidential election might mean the end of the Union. The fate of the republic hinged on the ability of President Buchanan to defuse the passions of the past decade and achieve a new compromise that would protect free soil in the West and slavery in the South.

Events—and his own values and weaknesses—conspired against Buchanan. Shortly after the election the Supreme Court prepared to render a decision on the case of Dred Scott, which involved the bitterly controversial issue of Congress's constitutional authority to regulate slavery in the territories. Scott was an enslaved African American who had lived for a time with his owner, an army surgeon, in the free state of Illinois and at Fort Snelling, then in the Wisconsin Territory, where the Northwest Ordinance (1787) prohibited slavery. In his suit Scott claimed that his residence in a free state and a free territory had made him free. In March 1857, after Buchanan had pressured several northern justices to vote in tandem with their southern colleagues, the Court announced its decision in *Dred Scott v. Sandford*.

Seven of the nine members of the Court concurred on one critical point: Scott remained a slave. Because they could not agree on the legal issues, each justice wrote a separate opinion. In the most influential opinion, Chief Justice Roger B. Taney of Maryland declared that Negroes, whether enslaved or free, could not be citizens of the United States and that Scott therefore had no right to sue in federal court. That argument was controversial enough, since free blacks could be citizens of a state and therefore presumably had access to the federal courts. But Taney went on to make two even more controversial points. First, he endorsed John C. Calhoun's argument that because the Fifth Amendment prohibited the taking of property without due process of law, Congress could not prevent southern citizens from taking their slave "property" into the territories or owning it there. Consequently, the chief justice concluded, the Northwest Ordinance and the Missouri Compromise—which prohibited slavery in the territories—had never been constitutional. Second, Taney declared that Congress could not give to territorial governments any powers that Congress itself did not possess. Since Congress had no authority to prohibit slavery in a territory, neither did a territorial government. Taney thereby endorsed Calhoun's interpretation of popular sovereignty: only when settlers wrote a constitution and requested statehood could they prohibit slavery. In a single stroke a Democrat-dominated Supreme Court had declared the Republicans' antislavery platform to be unconstitutional, a decision the Republicans could never accept. Led by Senator William H. Seward of New York, they accused the Supreme Court and President Buchanan of participating in the "Slave Power" conspiracy.

Buchanan then added new fuel to the raging constitutional fire. In early 1858 he recommended the admission of Kansas as a slave state under the Lecompton constitution. Many observers—including the influential Democratic senator Stephen Douglas—believed that the constitution had been enacted by fraudulent means. Angered that Buchanan would not permit a referendum in Kansas on the Lecompton constitution, Douglas broke with the president and his southern allies and persuaded Congress to deny statehood to Kansas. (Kansas would enter the Union as a free state in 1861.) By pursuing a proslavery agenda—first in the *Dred Scott* decision and then in Kansas—Buchanan had helped to split his party and the nation.

Abraham Lincoln and the Republican Triumph, 1858–1860

The crisis of the Union intensified as the national Democratic Party fragmented into sectional factions and the Republicans gained the support of a majority of northern voters. During this transition Abraham Lincoln emerged as the pivotal figure in American politics, the only Republican leader whose policies and temperament might have saved the Union. But few southerners trusted Lincoln, and his election threatened to unleash the secessionist movement that had menaced the nation since 1850.

Lincoln's Political Career

The flourishing of the middle class of storekeepers, lawyers, and entrepreneurs in the small towns of the Ohio River Valley shaped Lincoln's early career. He came from an illiterate yeoman farming family that had moved from

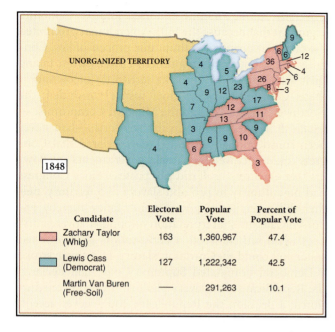

Candidate	Electoral Vote	Popular Vote	Percent of Popular Vote
Zachary Taylor (Whig)	163	1,360,967	47.4
Lewis Cass (Democrat)	127	1,222,342	42.5
Martin Van Buren (Free-Soil)	—	291,263	10.1

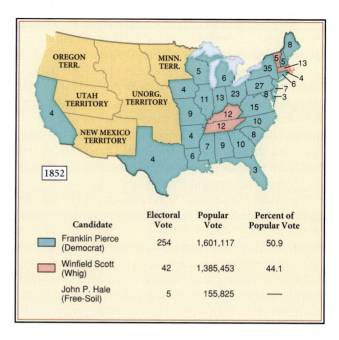

Candidate	Electoral Vote	Popular Vote	Percent of Popular Vote
Franklin Pierce (Democrat)	254	1,601,117	50.9
Winfield Scott (Whig)	42	1,385,453	44.1
John P. Hale (Free-Soil)	5	155,825	—

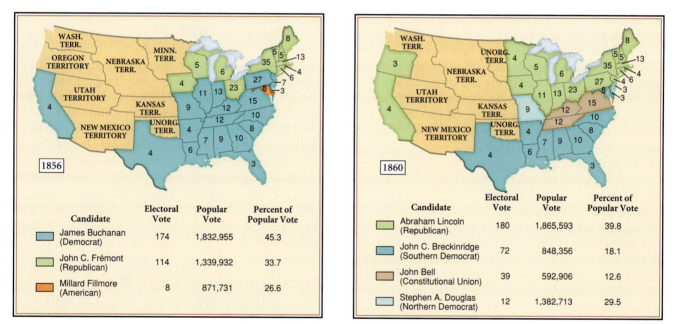

Candidate	Electoral Vote	Popular Vote	Percent of Popular Vote
James Buchanan (Democrat)	174	1,832,955	45.3
John C. Frémont (Republican)	114	1,339,932	33.7
Millard Fillmore (American)	8	871,731	26.6

Candidate	Electoral Vote	Popular Vote	Percent of Popular Vote
Abraham Lincoln (Republican)	180	1,865,593	39.8
John C. Breckinridge (Southern Democrat)	72	848,356	18.1
John Bell (Constitutional Union)	39	592,906	12.6
Stephen A. Douglas (Northern Democrat)	12	1,382,713	29.5

MAP 13.8 Political Realignment, 1848–1860

In 1848 both the Whigs and the Democrats boasted national *parties, with strong support in most parts of the nation. Then political conflict over slavery and the Compromise of 1850 destroyed the Whig Party in the South, making the Democrats the only nationwide party and giving them an easy victory in 1852. The Democratic supremacy was short-lived: by 1856 the passions aroused by "Bloody Kansas" resulted in the creation of the Republican Party, which carried most of the states of the Northeast and Midwest. By 1860 a new* regionally based *party system had taken shape and would persist for the next seventy years, with Democrats dominant in the South and Republicans in the Northeast and Midwest.*

Kentucky, where Lincoln was born in 1809, to Indiana and then to Illinois. In 1831 Lincoln rejected the farmer's life of his father and became a store clerk in New Salem, Illinois. Socially ambitious, Lincoln sought entry into the middle class, joining the New Salem Debating Society and reading Shakespeare and other literary works.

Lincoln's ambition was "a little engine that knew no rest," his closest associate later remarked. Admitted to the bar in 1837, Lincoln moved to Springfield, the small country town that had become the new state capital. There he met Mary Todd, the cultured daughter of a Kentucky banker; they married in 1842. The couple were a picture in contrasts. Her tastes were aristocratic; his were humble. She was volatile in temperament; he had an easygoing manner but suffered bouts of depression that tried her patience and tested his character. Entering political life, Lincoln served four terms as a Whig in the Illinois assembly, where he promoted education, state banking, and internal improvements such as canals and railroads. In 1846 the rising lawyer-politician won election to Congress.

As a congressman during the war with Mexico, Lincoln had to take a stand on the contentious issue of slavery. He had long felt that slavery was unjust but did not believe that the federal government had the constitutional authority to tamper with slavery in the South. With respect to the war with Mexico, Lincoln took the middle ground. He endorsed military appropriation bills but voted to restrict slavery, throwing his support behind the Wilmot Proviso. He also proposed that Congress follow the lead of the northern states and enact legislation for the gradual (and therefore compensated) emancipation of slaves in the District of Columbia. Lincoln argued that such measures—firm opposition to the expansion of slavery, gradual emancipation, and the colonization of freed slaves in Africa and elsewhere—represented the only practical way to address the issue. In the highly emotional political atmosphere of the time, both abolitionists and proslavery activists derided these pragmatic policies. Dismayed, Lincoln withdrew from politics and devoted his energies to a lucrative legal practice representing railroads and manufacturers.

Lincoln returned to the political fray after the passage of Stephen Douglas's Kansas-Nebraska Act. Attacking Douglas's doctrine of popular sovereignty, Lincoln reaffirmed his position on slavery. He would not threaten the institution in the states where it existed but would use national authority to exclude it from the territories. Confronting the moral issue, Lincoln declared that if the nation was to uphold its republican ideals, then it must eventually cut out slavery like a "cancer."

Abandoning the Whig Party in favor of the Republicans, Lincoln quickly emerged as their leader in Illinois. Campaigning for the U.S. Senate against Stephen Douglas in 1858, Lincoln alerted his audiences to the dangers of the "Slave Power" conspiracy. He warned that the proslavery Supreme Court might soon declare that the Constitution "does not permit a state to exclude slavery from its limits," just as it had decided (in *Dred Scott*) that "neither Congress nor the territorial legislature can do it." In that event, he continued, "we shall awake to the reality . . . that the Supreme Court has made Illinois a slave state." This fear of the spread of slavery into the North informed Lincoln's famous "House Divided" speech. Quoting from the Bible, "A house divided against itself cannot stand," he predicted a constitutional crisis: "I believe this government cannot endure permanently half slave and half free. . . . It will become all one thing, or all the other." The contest in Illinois between Lincoln and Douglas in 1858 attracted

Abraham Lincoln and Stephen Douglas, 1860
When Douglas and Lincoln squared off in the presidential election of 1860, they distributed thousands of silk campaign ribbons bearing their portraits and signatures. The well-known photographer Matthew Brady took their pictures and retouched the images to make them more flattering—smoothing out Lincoln's gaunt and well-lined face and slimming down Douglas's ample cheeks. Collection of Janice L. and David J. Frent.

national interest because of Douglas's prominence and Lincoln's reputation as a formidable speaker. During a series of seven debates Douglas declared his support for white supremacy and attacked Lincoln for his alleged belief in "negro equality." Put on the defensive by Douglas's racist tactics, Lincoln advocated economic opportunity for blacks (but not equal political rights) and asked Douglas how he could accept the *Dred Scott* decision (which protected slave owners' property in the territories) and at the same time advocate popular sovereignty (which asserted settlers' power to exclude slavery). Douglas responded with the so-called Freeport Doctrine, asserting that the residents of a territory could exclude slavery simply by not adopting local legislation to protect it. Douglas's statement upset both proslavery advocates, who feared they would be denied the victory won in the *Dred Scott* decision, and abolitionists, who were not convinced that local regulations would halt the expansion of slavery. Nonetheless, the Democrats won a narrow victory in Illinois, and the state legislature re-elected Douglas to the U.S. Senate.

The Party System Fragments

The election of 1858 established the Republican Party as a formidable political force, as it won control of the House of Representatives and gave Lincoln a national reputation, making him a potential presidential candidate.

The Rise of Radicalism. In the wake of these Republican gains, southern Democrats divided into two groups. Moderates such as Senator Jefferson Davis of Mississippi, who were known as Southern Rights Democrats, pursued the traditional policy of seeking ironclad commitments to protect slavery in the states and territories. Radical southern leaders, such as Robert Barnwell Rhett of South Carolina and William Lowndes Yancey of Alabama, repudiated the Union and actively promoted secession. Radical antislavery northerners played into their hands. Senator William Seward of New York declared that freedom and slavery were locked in "an irrepressible conflict." That battle, whether inevitable or not, seemed to have begun in October 1859 when the militant abolitionist John Brown led eighteen heavily armed black and white men in an unsuccessful raid on the federal arsenal at Harpers Ferry, Virginia. Brown's announced purpose was to provide arms for a slave rebellion that would establish an African American state in the South.

Republican leaders disavowed Brown's raid, but Democrats called his plot "a natural, logical, inevitable result of the doctrines and teachings of the Republican party." Fueling the Democratic charges were letters that linked six leading abolitionists to the financing of Brown's raid. Brown was charged with treason, sentenced to death, and hanged—only to be praised by reformer Henry David Thoreau as "an angel of light." Slaveholders were horrified by northern admiration of Brown and looked toward the future with fear. "The aim of the present black republican organization is the destruction of the social system of the Southern States, without regard to consequences," warned one newspaper.

Nor could the South count on the Democratic Party to protect its interests. At its April 1860 convention, northern Democrats rejected Jefferson Davis's program to protect slavery in the territories, prompting the delegates from eight southern states to leave the hall. At a second Democratic convention in Baltimore, northern and western delegates nominated Stephen Douglas; southern Democrats met separately and nominated Buchanan's vice president, John C. Breckinridge of Kentucky. At odds with each other since the *Dred Scott* decision, the sectional factions of the Democratic Party now separated into two distinct organizations.

The Election of 1860. The Republicans sensed victory. They courted white voters by opposing both slavery and racial equality: "Missouri for white men and white men for Missouri," declared that state's Republican platform. On the national level the Republican convention chose Lincoln as its presidential candidate. Lincoln's position on

slavery was more moderate than that of the best-known Republicans, Senator William H. Seward of New York and Salmon P. Chase of Ohio, who demanded its abolition. Lincoln also conveyed a compelling egalitarian image that appealed to smallholding farmers and wage earners. And Lincoln's home territory—the rapidly growing Midwest—was crucial in the competition between Democrats and Republicans. The Republican Party's campaign slogan of "free soil, free speech, free labor, and free men" focused on liberty and had radical overtones. However, the party's platform endorsed Lincoln's moderate views, upholding free soil in the West and denying the right of states to secede but ruling out direct interference with slavery in the South. In addition, the platform endorsed the old Whig program of economic development, which had gained increasing support in the Midwest, especially after the economic Panic of 1857.

The Republican strategy was successful. Lincoln received only 40 percent of the popular vote but won every northern and western state except New Jersey, giving him a majority in the electoral college. Douglas took 30 percent of the total vote, drawing support from all regions except the South, but won electoral votes only in Missouri and New Jersey. Breckinridge captured every state in the Deep South as well as Delaware, Maryland, and North Carolina, while John Bell, a former Tennessee Whig who became the nominee of the compromise-seeking Constitutional Union Party, carried the Upper South states where the Whigs had been strongest: Kentucky, Tennessee, and Virginia.

The Republicans had united the Northeast, the Midwest, and the Far West behind free soil and had seized national power. A revolution was in the making. Slavery had permeated the American federal republic for so long and so thoroughly that southerners had come to see it as part of the constitutional order—an order now under siege. To many southerners it seemed time to think carefully about the meaning of Lincoln's words of 1858 that the Union must "become all one thing, or all the other."

FOR FURTHER EXPLORATION

▶ For definitions of key terms boldfaced in this chapter, see the glossary at the end of the book.

▶ To assess your mastery of the material covered in this chapter, see the Online Study Guide at **bedfordstmartins.com/henretta**.

▶ For suggested references, including Web sites, see page SR-14 at the end of the book.

▶ For map resources and primary documents, see **bedfordstmartins.com/henretta**.

SUMMARY

Westward expansion carried American settlers into the disputed Oregon Country, parts of California, and the Mexican province of Texas, where they mounted a successful rebellion and petitioned for annexation to the United States. The popular appeal of Manifest Destiny prompted southern leaders such as John Tyler and John C. Calhoun to advocate the immediate annexation of Texas and to support northern politicians who laid claim to all of Oregon. This expansionist program carried Democrat James K. Polk to the presidency in the election of 1844.

Polk's expansionist schemes led the United States into a successful war of conquest against Mexico, but the acquisition of new territory in the West undermined the long-standing political compromise over the spread of slavery and threatened to split the Union. Democratic and Whig leaders joined in framing a political settlement known as the Compromise of 1850; its most important aspects were laws admitting California as a free state and providing federal assistance to planters seeking the return of fugitive slaves.

The Compromise and the Second Party System died in the political conflicts and armed violence of the 1850s. Antislavery northerners defied the Fugitive Slave Act by battling southern slave catchers in the courts and on the streets. When northern Whigs refused to support the act and the westward expansion of slavery, southerners deserted the Whig Party, killing it as a national organization. The Democratic Party also lost support as its leaders conspired to add slave states in northern Mexico and the Caribbean and as Stephen Douglas's doctrine of popular sovereignty failed to allow for the peaceful settlement of Kansas and Nebraska. As a guerrilla war festered in "Bleeding Kansas," northern Whigs and Free-Soilers established the Republican Party, which also attracted anti-Nebraska Democrats and former Know-Nothings. By 1856 the Second Party System of Democrats and Whigs had given way to a new alignment in which proslavery Democrats confronted antislavery Republicans.

The national Democratic Party disintegrated following the Supreme Court's decision in the *Dred Scott* case and President James Buchanan's support for a proslavery constitution in Kansas. Following John Brown's attempt to raise a major black rebellion, southern Democrats unsuccessfully demanded ironclad protection for the institution of slavery. In the 1860 election the Democrats divided along sectional lines, facilitating the election of Abraham Lincoln and the Republican Party. The nation stood poised on the brink of secession and civil war.

TIMELINE

1820s	Expansion of cattle raising in Mexican California
1821	Mexico wins independence from Spain
1836	Texas proclaims independence from Mexico
1842	Overland migration to Oregon begins
1844	Fate of Texas and Oregon dominate presidential election
1845	John O'Sullivan coins term *Manifest Destiny*
	Texas admitted to Union as a slave state
	John Slidell's diplomatic mission to Mexico fails
1846	United States declares war on Mexico
	Treaty with Britain divides Oregon Country at forty-ninth parallel
	Wilmot Proviso to prohibit slavery in any territories acquired from Mexico dies in the Senate
1847	General Winfield Scott captures Mexico City
1848	Gold discovered in California
	In Treaty of Guadalupe Hidalgo Mexico cedes its provinces of California, New Mexico, and Texas to the United States
	Free-Soil Party organized
1850	Compromise of 1850 seeks to preserve the Union
	Fugitive Slave Act rejected by northern abolitionists
1851	American (Know-Nothing) Party formed
1852	Harriet Beecher Stowe publishes *Uncle Tom's Cabin*
1854	Ostend Manifesto seeks expansion of slavery in Caribbean
	Kansas-Nebraska Act implements popular sovereignty
	Republican Party formed
1856	"Bleeding Kansas" undermines popular sovereignty
1857	*Dred Scott v. Sandford* allows slavery in the territories
1858	James Buchanan backs Lecompton constitution
	Lincoln-Douglas debates
1860	Abraham Lincoln elected president in four-way contest

CHAPTER 14

Two Societies at War

1861–1865

Secession and Military Stalemate, 1861–1862
Choosing Sides
Setting Objectives and Devising Strategies

Toward Total War
Mobilizing Armies and Civilians
Mobilizing Resources

The Turning Point: 1863
Emancipation
Vicksburg and Gettysburg

The Union Victorious, 1864–1865
Soldiers and Strategy
The Election of 1864 and Sherman's March to the Sea

"**W**HAT A SCENE IT WAS," the Union soldier Elisha Hunt Rhodes wrote in his diary in July 1863 as the battle of Gettysburg ended. "Oh the dead and the dying on this bloody field." The passions kindled by southern rights and the northern nationalism had inspired thousands of men to die in battle, and the slaughter would continue for two more years. "What is this all about?" asked Confederate lieutenant R. M. Collins at the end of another gruesome battle. "Why is it that 200,000 men of one blood and tongue . . . [should be] seeking one another's lives? We could settle our differences by compromising and all be at home in ten days." But there was no compromise—not in 1861 nor even in 1865.

To explain why Southerners seceded and then fought the war to the bitter end is not simple, but racial slavery is an important part of the answer. For political leaders in the South, the Republican victory in 1860 presented a clear and immediate danger to the slave-owning republic that had existed since 1776. Lincoln was the only president elected without a single electoral vote from the South, and Southerners knew that his Republican Party would prevent the extension of slavery into the territories.

◀ **Fields of Death**

Fought with mass armies and new weapons, the Civil War took a huge toll in human lives, as evidenced by grisly photographs like this one of a battlefield at Antietam, Maryland. At Shiloh, Tennessee, General Ulysses Grant surveyed a field "so covered with dead that it would have been possible to walk . . . in any direction, stepping on dead bodies, without a foot touching the ground." Library of Congress.

The Bombardment of Fort Sumter, 1861
Currier and Ives, a New York publishing house, brought colorful art into thousands of middle-class homes by printing inexpensive lithographs of pastoral scenes and dramatic historical events. This fairly realistic depiction of the Confederate bombardment of Fort Sumter in Charleston harbor in April 1861 was especially popular in the South.
Library of Congress.

during the nullification crisis—promised to use it. The choice was the South's: return to the Union or face war.

The Seizure of Fort Sumter. The decision came quickly. Within a month of Lincoln's inauguration the garrison at Fort Sumter urgently needed supplies. To maintain his credibility, the new president dispatched a relief expedition, promising that it would not land troops or arms unless the rebels disrupted the delivery of food and medicine. Jefferson Davis and his government welcomed Lincoln's decision, believing that a confrontation would turn the wavering Upper South against the North and win foreign support for the Confederate cause. Resolving to take the fort immediately, Davis demanded its surrender. When Major Robert Anderson refused to comply, the Confederate forces opened fire on April 12, forcing the surrender of the fort two days later. The next day Lincoln called 75,000 state militiamen into federal service for ninety days to put down an insurrection "too powerful to be suppressed by the

ordinary course of judicial proceedings." All talk of compromise was past.

Northerners responded to Lincoln's call to arms with enthusiasm. Asked to provide thirteen regiments of volunteers, Republican Governor William Dennison of Ohio sent twenty. "Our fathers made this country," declared an enlisted man in the 12th Ohio Regiment, "we their children are to save it." Many northern Democrats were equally committed to the Union cause. As Stephen Douglas declared six weeks before his death: "Every man must be for the United States or against it. There can be no neutrals in this war, only patriots—or traitors."

The Contest for the Upper South. The white residents of the Upper South now had to choose between the Union and the Confederacy, and their decision was crucial. Those eight states accounted for two-thirds of the South's white population, more than three-fourths of its industrial production, and well over half of its food and fuel. They were home to many of the nation's best military leaders, including Colonel Robert E. Lee of Virginia, a career officer whom General in Chief Winfield Scott recommended to Lincoln as field commander of the new Union army. And they were geographically strategic. Kentucky, with its 500-mile border on the Ohio River, was essential to the movement of troops and supplies. Maryland was vital to the Union's security because it surrounded the nation's capital on the north.

The weight of history decided the outcome in Virginia, the original home of American slavery. Three days after the fall of Fort Sumter, a Virginia convention passed an ordinance of secession by a vote of 88 to 55. The dissenting votes came mainly from the yeoman-dominated northwestern counties (see Map 14.1); elsewhere in Virginia whites rallied to the Confederate cause. As William Poague, a former Unionist lawyer, explained his decision to enlist in a Virginia artillery unit: "The North was the aggressor. The South resisted her invaders." Refusing Scott's offer to command the Union troops, Robert E. Lee resigned from the army. "Save in defense of my native state," Lee told Scott, "I never desire again to draw my sword." Arkansas, Tennessee, and North Carolina quickly joined Virginia in the Confederacy.

Lincoln moved aggressively to hold the rest of the Upper South. In May he ordered General George B. McClellan to take control of northwestern Virginia, thus securing the railway line between Washington and the Ohio Valley. In October voters in that predominantly yeoman region overwhelmingly approved the creation of a breakaway state, West Virginia, which was admitted to the Union in 1863. The Union cause also triumphed in Delaware but received much less support in Maryland, where slavery was well entrenched. A pro-Confederate mob attacked Massachusetts troops marching between railroad stations in Baltimore, causing the war's first combat deaths: four soldiers and twelve civilians. When other Maryland secessionists destroyed railroad bridges and telegraph lines, Lincoln ordered military occupation of the state and imprisoned suspected secessionists, including members of the state legislature. He released them only in November 1861, after Unionists had gained control of the Maryland legislature.

In Missouri, the key to communications and trade on the Missouri and upper Mississippi Rivers, Lincoln mobilized support among the large German American community. In July a force of German American militia defeated Confederate sympathizers commanded by the governor. Despite continuing raids by Confederate guerrilla bands led by William Quantrill and Jesse and Frank James, the Union retained control of Missouri (see Voices from Abroad, "Ernest Duveyier de Hauranne, German Immigrants and the Civil War within Missouri," p. 402).

In Kentucky secessionist and Unionist sentiment was evenly balanced, so Lincoln moved cautiously. He waited until August, when Unionists took control of the state government, before ordering federal troops to halt Kentucky's thriving trade with the Confederacy in horses, mules, whiskey, and foodstuffs. When the Confederates responded to this cutoff by moving troops into Kentucky, the Unionist legislature asked for federal protection. In September Illinois volunteers under the command of the relatively unknown Brigadier General Ulysses S. Grant crossed the Ohio River and drove out the Confederates. Of the eight states of the Upper South, Lincoln had kept four (Delaware, Maryland, Kentucky, and Missouri) and a portion of a fifth (western Virginia) in the Union (Table 14.1).

Setting Objectives and Devising Strategies

Following the creation of the Confederacy, its leaders called on their people to defend its independence. At his inauguration in February 1861 Jefferson Davis identified the Confederate cause with that of the American Revolution: like their grandfathers, white Southerners were fighting against tyranny and for the "sacred right of

TABLE 14.1 Slavery and Secession		
Group	Percentage of Whites in Slave-owning Families	Percentage of Slaves in Population
Original Confederate States	38%	47%
Border States that Later Joined the Confederacy	24%	32%
Border States that Remained in Union	14%	15%

Ernest Duveyier de Hauranne

German Immigrants and the Civil War within Missouri

Tens of thousands of German immigrants settled in Missouri and other midwestern states in the two decades before the Civil War and, as the following letter by the Frenchman Ernest Duveyier de Hauranne indicates, most of them supported the Union cause. De Hauranne traveled widely, and his letters home offer an intelligent commentary on American politics and society during the Civil War.

St. Louis, September 12, 1864

Missouri is to all intents and purposes a rebel state, an occupied territory where the Federal forces are really nothing but a garrison under siege; even today it is not certain what would happen if the troops were withdrawn. Party quarrels here are poisoned by class hatreds. . . . The old Anglo-French families, attached to Southern institutions, harbor a primitive, superstitious prejudice in favor of slavery. Conquered now, but full of repressed rage, they exhibit the implacable anger peculiar to the defenders of lost causes. . . .

The more recent German population is strongly abolitionist. They have brought to the New World the instincts of European democracy, together with its radical attitudes and all-or-nothing doctrines. Ancient precedents and worn-out laws matter little to them. They have not studied history and have no respect for hallowed injustices; but they do have, to the highest degree, that sense of moral principle which is more or less lacking in American democracy. They aren't afraid of revolution: to destroy a barbarous institution they would, if necessary, take an axe to the foundations of society. Furthermore, their interests coincide with their principles. . . .

The immigrant arrives poor and lives by his work. A newcomer, having nothing to lose and caring little for the interests of established property owners, sees that the subjection of free labor to the ruinous competition of slave labor must be ended. At the same time, his pride rebels against the prejudice attached to work in a land of slavery; he wants to reestablish its value. . . .

There is no mistaking the hatred the two parties, not to say the two peoples, have for each other. . . . As passions were coming to a boil, the Federal government sent General [John C.] Frémont here as army commander and dictator. . . . An abolitionist and a self-made man, he put himself firmly at the head of the German party, determined to crush the friends of slavery. He formed an army of Germans who are completely devoted to their chief. . . .

[However,] bands of guerrillas hold the countryside, where they raid as much as they please; politics serves as a fine pretext for looting. Their leaders are officers from the army of the South who receive their orders from the Confederate government. . . . These "bushwackers," who ordinarily rob indiscriminately, maintain their standing as political raiders by occasionally killing some poor, inoffensive person. Finally, people bent on personal vengeance take advantage of the state of civil war: sometimes one hears of villages divided against themselves so bitterly that massacres are carried on from door to door with incredible ferocity. . . . You can see what emotions are still boiling in this region that is supposed to be pacified.

Source: Ernest Duveyier de Hauranne, *A Frenchman in Lincoln's America* (Chicago: Lakende Press, 1974), 305–9.

---

self-government." As Davis put it, the Confederacy sought "no conquest, no aggrandizement, no concession of any kind from the states with which we were lately confederated; all we ask is to be let alone." The decision to focus on the defense of the Confederacy and not to conquer western territories gave southern leaders a strong advantage: they needed only a military stalemate to guarantee independence. However, the Confederacy's firm commitment to slavery undermined its support in Europe, where opposition to forced labor was strong. Alexander Stephens of Georgia, the vice president of the Confederacy, ruled out any plan for gradual emancipation, declaring that his nation's "cornerstone rests upon the great truth that the Negro is not equal to the white man, that slavery—subordination to the superior race—is his natural or normal condition."

Lincoln made his first major statement on Union goals and strategy in a speech to Congress on July 4,

1861. He portrayed secession as an attack on popular government, America's great contribution to world history, telling his audience that the issue at stake was "whether a constitutional republic, or a democracy—a government of the people, by the same people—can or cannot maintain its territorial integrity against its domestic foe." Convinced that the nation could preserve its republican principles only by crushing the rebellion, Lincoln rejected General Winfield Scott's plan to use economic sanctions and a naval blockade to persuade the Confederates to return to the Union. Instead, the president insisted on an aggressive military strategy and a policy of unconditional surrender.

The Union Thrust toward Richmond.   The president hoped that a successful strike against the Confederate capital of Richmond, Virginia, would end the rebellion. He therefore dispatched General Irwin McDowell and an army of 30,000 men to attack P. G. T. Beauregard's force of 20,000 troops at Manassas, a major rail junction thirty miles southwest of Washington. In July McDowell launched a strong attack near Manassas Creek (also called Bull Run), but panic swept through his troops during a Confederate counterattack. For the first time Union soldiers heard the hair-raising rebel yell. "The peculiar corkscrew sensation that it sends down your backbone under these circumstances can never be told,"

one Union veteran wrote. "You have to feel it." McDowell's troops retreated in disarray to Washington, along with the many civilians who had come to observe the battle. The victorious Confederate troops also dispersed, confused and without the wagons and supplies they needed to pursue McDowell's army.

The rout of the Union army at Bull Run made it clear that the rebellion would not be easily crushed. To bolster northern morale, Lincoln replaced McDowell with General George B. McClellan and signed bills for the enlistment of an additional million men, who would serve for three years in the newly created Army of the Potomac. A cautious military engineer, McClellan spent the winter of 1861 training raw recruits, and early in 1862 he launched the first major offensive of the war, a thrust toward Richmond. In a maneuver that required skillful logistics, the Union general transported about 100,000 troops by boat down the Potomac River and Chesapeake Bay, putting them ashore on the peninsula between the York and James Rivers (Map 14.2). Ignoring Lincoln's advice to "strike a blow" quickly, McClellan advanced slowly up the peninsula toward the South's capital, tactics that allowed the Confederates to mount a counterstroke. To relieve the pressure on Richmond, a Confederate army under Thomas J. ("Stonewall") Jackson marched rapidly north up the Shenandoah Valley in western Virginia, threatening Washington. Lincoln recalled 30,000 troops from

The Battle of Antietam: The Fight for Burnside's Bridge

Nearly 8,000 soldiers lost their lives at Antietam on September 17, 1862, many of them in the struggle for the Rohrback Bridge, which crossed Antietam Creek. One of those who survived the battle, Captain James Hope of the Second Vermont Volunteers, recorded the event in this painting, giving the bridge the name of the Union general who sacrificed many of his troops trying to capture it.

Antietam National Battlefield, National Park Service, Sharpsburg, Maryland.

McClellan's army to protect the Union's capital, but Jackson, a brilliant general, won a series of small engagements, tying down the larger Union forces. Then Jackson quickly joined the Confederates' formidable commanding general, Robert E. Lee, who had confronted McClellan outside Richmond. Lee launched a ferocious attack that lasted for seven days (June 25–July 1), suffering 20,000 casualties (to the Union's 10,000). McClellan failed to exploit the Confederates' weakness, refusing to renew the offensive unless he received fresh troops. Lincoln ordered the withdrawal of the Army of the Potomac, and Richmond remained secure.

Lee Moves North.   Lee promptly went on the offensive, hoping for victories that would humiliate Lincoln's government. Joining with Jackson in northern Virginia, Lee routed Union troops in the Second Battle of Bull Run (August 1862) and then struck north

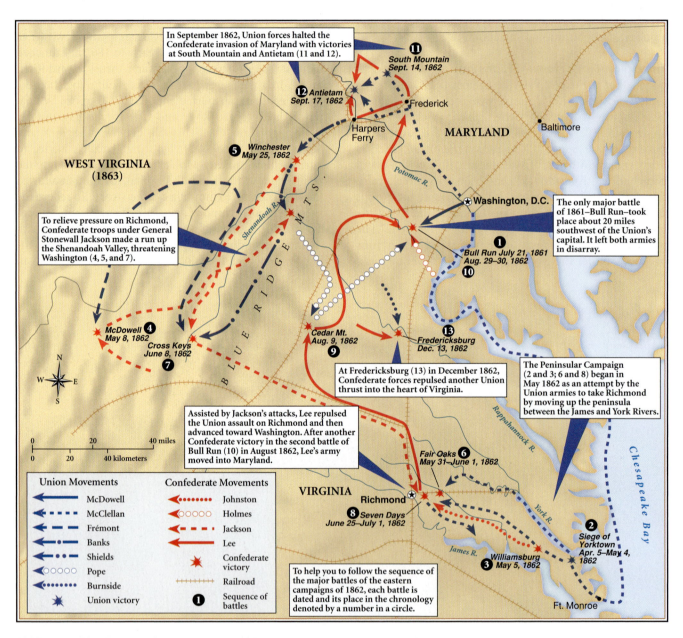

MAP 14.2   The Eastern Campaigns of 1862

Many of the great battles of the Civil War took place in the 125 miles between the Union capital of Washington and the Confederate capital of Richmond. During the eastern campaigns of 1862, Confederate Generals Robert J. "Stonewall" Jackson and Robert E. Lee secured victories that were almost decisive; they also suffered a defeat—at Antietam, in Maryland—that was almost fatal. As was often the case in the Civil War, the victors in these battles were either too bloodied or too timid to exploit their advantage.

through western Maryland, where he met with near disaster. When Lee divided his force—sending Jackson to capture Harpers Ferry in West Virginia—a copy of his orders fell into McClellan's hands. But the Union general again failed to pursue his numerical advantage, delaying his attack against Lee's depleted army and thereby allowing it to occupy a strong defensive position behind Antietam Creek, near Sharpsburg, Maryland. Outnumbered 87,000 to 50,000, Lee desperately fought off McClellan's attacks. Just as Union regiments were about to overwhelm his right flank, Jackson's troops arrived, saving the Confederates from a major defeat. Appalled by the number of Union casualties, McClellan let Lee retreat to Virginia.

The fighting at Antietam was savage. A Wisconsin officer described his men as "loading and firing with demoniacal fury and shouting and laughing hysterically." At a critical point in the battle a sunken road, nicknamed Bloody Lane, was filled with Confederate bodies two and three deep, and the attacking Union troops knelt on "this ghastly flooring" to shoot at the retreating Confederates. The battle at Antietam on September 17, 1862, remains the bloodiest single day in U.S. military history. Together the Confederate and Union dead numbered 4,800 and the wounded 18,500, of whom 3,000 soon died. (In comparison, 6,000 Americans were wounded or killed on D-Day, which began the invasion of Nazi-occupied France in World War II.)

In public Lincoln declared Antietam a victory, but privately he declared that McClellan should have fought Lee to the finish. A masterful organizer of men and supplies, McClellan lacked the stomach for an all-out attack. Dismissing McClellan as commander of the Army of the Potomac, Lincoln began a long search for an effective replacement. His first choice was Ambrose E. Burnside, who proved to be more daring but less competent than his predecessor. In December, after heavy losses in futile attacks against well-entrenched Confederate forces at Fredericksburg, Virginia, Burnside resigned his command and Lincoln replaced him with Joseph ("Fighting Joe") Hooker. As 1862 ended, the Confederates had some reason to be content: the war in the East was a stalemate.

The War in the West. In the West, Union forces had been more successful. The goal of the Union commanders was to control the Ohio, Mississippi, and Missouri Rivers, dividing the Confederacy and reducing the mobility of its armies (Map 14.3). The decision of Kentucky not to join the rebellion had already given the Union dominance in the Ohio River Valley. In 1862 the Union army launched a series of highly innovative land

Lincoln Visits the Army of the Potomac, 1862
Following the battle of Antietam, President Lincoln journeyed to the headquarters of General McClellan. Supported by his military advisors (standing to his rear), the towering commander in chief vigorously urged his principal general to exploit the opportunity offered by Lee's heavy casualties and launch an all-out attack against Richmond. When McClellan did not undertake this offensive, Lincoln removed him as commander of the Army of the Potomac. Library of Congress.

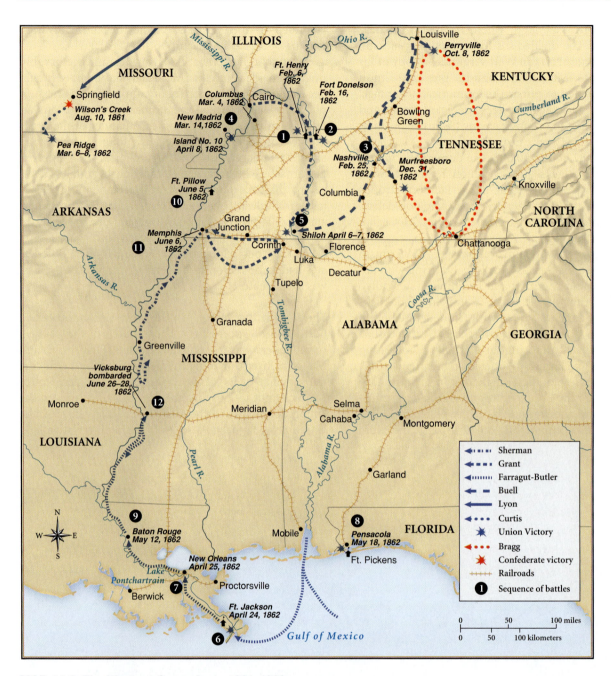

MAP 14.3 The Western Campaigns, 1861–1862

As the Civil War intensified in 1862, Union and Confederate military and naval forces fought to control the great valleys of the Ohio, Tennessee, and Mississippi Rivers. Between February and April, Union armies moved south through western Tennessee (#1, 2, 3, and 5). By the end of June, Union naval forces controlled the Mississippi River north of Memphis (#4, 10, and 11) and from the Gulf of Mexico to Vicksburg (#6, 7, 9, and 12). These victories gave the Union control of crucial transportation routes, kept Missouri in the Union, and carried the war to the borders of the states of the Deep South.

and water operations to gain control of the Tennessee and Mississippi Rivers as well. In the north, General Ulysses S. Grant used riverboats clad with iron plates to take Fort Henry on the Tennessee River and Fort Donelson on the Cumberland. Grant then moved south along the Tennessee to seize critical railroad lines. A

Confederate army under Albert Sidney Johnston and P. G. T. Beauregard caught Grant by surprise on April 6 near a small log church named Shiloh. Grant relentlessly threw troops into the battle, forcing a Confederate withdrawal but taking huge casualties. When the fighting ended, Grant looked out over a large field "so covered with dead that it would have been possible to walk over the clearing in any direction, stepping on dead bodies, without a foot touching the ground." The cost in lives was high, but Lincoln was pleased. "What I want . . . is generals who will fight battles and win victories." Grant had done that, creating military momentum for the Union in the West.

Three weeks later Union naval forces commanded by David G. Farragut struck from the south, moving through the Mississippi Delta from the Gulf of Mexico to capture New Orleans. The Union now held the South's financial center and largest city as well as a major base for future naval operations. Union victories in the West had significantly undermined Confederate strength in the Mississippi Valley.

Toward Total War

The carnage at Antietam and Shiloh had made it clear that the war would be long, costly, and fought to the finish. After Shiloh, Grant later noted, he "gave up all idea of saving the Union except by complete conquest." The conflict became a **total war**—arraying the entire resources of the two societies against each other and eventually resulting in warfare against enemy civilians. Aided by a strong party and a talented cabinet, Lincoln skillfully mobilized the North for all-out war, organizing an effective central government. Jefferson Davis was less successful in harnessing the resources of the South because the eleven states of the Confederacy remained deeply suspicious of centralized rule.

Mobilizing Armies and Civilians

Initially, patriotic fervor filled both armies with eager volunteers. The widowed mother of nineteen-year-old Elisha Hunt Rhodes of Pawtuxet, Rhode Island, sent her son to war, saying, "My son, other mothers must make sacrifices and why should not I?" The call for soldiers was especially successful in the South, which had a strong military tradition, an ample supply of trained officers, and a culture that stressed duty and honor. "Would you, My Darling, . . . be willing to leave your Children under such a [despotic Union] government?" James B. Griffin of Edgefield, South Carolina, asked his wife, "No—I know you would sacrifice every comfort on earth, rather than submit to it." However, the initial surge of enlistments fell off as potential recruits learned of the realities of mass warfare: heavy losses to epidemic diseases in the camps and dreadful carnage on the battlefields. Soon both governments faced the necessity of forced enlistment.

The Military Draft.   The Confederacy was the first to act. In April 1862, after the bloody defeat at Shiloh, the Confederate Congress imposed the first legally binding draft in American history. One law extended all existing enlistments for the duration of the war; another required three years of military service from all able-bodied men between the ages of eighteen and thirty-five. In September, after the heavy casualties at Antietam, the age limit was raised to forty-five. The Confederate draft had two loopholes, both controversial. First, it exempted one white man—the planter, a son, or an overseer—for each twenty slaves, allowing men on large plantations to avoid military service. Second, drafted men could hire substitutes. Before this provision was repealed in 1864, the price for a substitute had risen to $300 in gold, about three times the annual wages of a skilled worker. Laborers and yeomen farmers angrily complained that it was "a rich man's war and a poor man's fight."

Consequently, some Southerners refused to serve, and the Confederate government lacked the power to compel them. Because the Confederate constitution vested sovereignty in the individual states, strong governors such as Joseph Brown of Georgia and Zebulon Vance of North Carolina simply ignored Davis's first draft call in early 1862. Elsewhere state judges issued writs of **habeas corpus** (a legal process designed to protect people from arbitrary arrest) and ordered the Confederate army to release protesting draftees. Reluctantly the Confederate Congress overrode the judges' authority to free conscripted men, enabling the Confederacy to keep substantial armies in the field well into 1864.

The Union government took a more authoritarian stance toward potential foes and ordinary citizens. To prevent sabotage and concerted resistance to the war effort, Lincoln suspended habeas corpus and over the course of the war imprisoned about 15,000 Confederate sympathizers without trial. The president also extended martial law to civilians who discouraged enlistment or resisted the draft, making them subject to military courts rather than local juries. This firm policy had the desired effect. The Militia Act of 1862 set a quota of volunteers for each state, which was increased by the Enrollment Act of 1863. States and towns enticed volunteers with cash bounties, prompting the enlistment or reenlistment of almost a million men. As in the South, wealthy men could avoid military service by providing a substitute or paying a $300 **commutation**, or exemption, fee.

The Enrollment Act sparked significant opposition, as thousands of recent immigrants from Germany and Ireland refused to serve in the Union army, saying it was not their fight. Northern Democrats exploited this resentment by charging that Lincoln was drafting poor whites to free the slaves and flood the cities with black laborers who would take their jobs. Some northern Democrats opposed the war, believing that the South should be allowed to secede, while others simply wanted to protect the interests of immigrants, most of whom

Draft Riots and Antiblack Violence in New York City

The Enrollment Act of 1863 enraged many workers and recent Irish and German immigrants who did not want to go to war. In July in New York City they took out their anger on free blacks in a week-long series of riots. This engraving depicts the burning by a mob of the Colored Orphan Asylum on Fifth Avenue, home to two hundred African American children. All of the children escaped before the mob set fire to the building; the fire spread to adjoining structures, forcing residents to flee with whatever possessions they could carry. Library of Congress.

were Democratic voters. In July 1863 hostility to the draft and to African Americans turned to violence on the streets of New York City. For five days immigrant Irish and German workers ran rampant, burning draft offices, sacking the homes of important Republicans, and attacking the police. The rioters lynched and mutilated a dozen African Americans, drove hundreds of black families from their homes, and burned down the Colored Orphan Asylum. Lincoln rushed in Union troops, fresh from the battle of Gettysburg, who killed more than a hundred rioters and suppressed the insurrection.

The Civilian War Effort. The Union government's determination to wage total war won greater support among native-born middle-class citizens. In 1861 prominent New Yorkers established the United States Sanitary Commission. Its task was to provide medical services and prevent the spread of epidemic diseases,

which had accounted for three-fourths of the deaths in the recently concluded Crimean War between Britain and Russia. Through its network of 7,000 local auxiliaries, the Sanitary Commission gathered supplies; distributed clothing, food, and medicine to the army; improved the sanitary standards of camp life; and recruited battlefield nurses and doctors for the Union Army Medical Bureau. Despite these measures, epidemic diseases took a fearful toll. Dysentery, typhoid, and malaria spread through the camps, as did childhood viruses such as mumps and measles, to which many rural men had not developed an immunity. Diseases and infections killed about 250,000 Union soldiers, about twice the number who died in combat. Still, better sanitation and high-quality food substantially lowered the mortality rate among Union troops compared with the rate in major nineteenth-century wars in Europe. Confederate soldiers were less fortunate. Although thousands of women volunteered as nurses, the Confederate health system was poorly organized. Thousands of southern soldiers contracted scurvy because of the lack of vitamin C in their diets, and they died from camp diseases at higher rates than did Union soldiers.

Women took a leading role in the Sanitary Commission and other wartime agencies. As superintendent

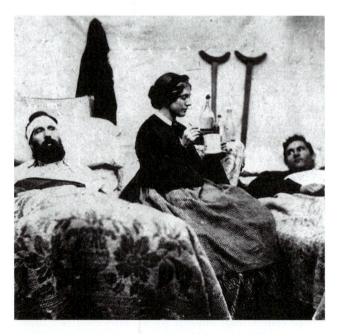

Hospital Nursing

Working as nurses in battlefront hospitals, thousands of Union and Confederate women gained firsthand experience of the horrors of war. A sense of calm prevails in this behind-the-lines Union hospital in Nashville, Tennessee, as nurse Anne Belle tends to the needs of soldiers recovering from their wounds. Most Civil War nurses served as unpaid volunteers and spent time cooking and cleaning for their patients as well as tending their injuries. U.S. Army Military History Institute.

of female nurses, Dorothea Dix became the first woman to receive a major federal appointment (see Chapter 12, American Lives, "Dorothea Dix: Public Woman," p. 360). Dix used her influence to combat the prejudice against women treating men, opening a new occupation to women. Thousands of educated Union women also joined the war effort as clerks in the expanding government bureaucracy, while in the South women staffed the efficient Confederate postal service. Indeed, in both sections millions of women assumed new economic responsibilities and worked with far greater intensity. They took over many farm tasks previously done by men and filled jobs not only in schools and offices but also in textile, clothing, and shoe factories. A number of women even took on military duties as spies, scouts, and (disguising themselves as men) soldiers. As the nurse Clara Barton, who later founded the American Red Cross, recalled, "At the war's end, woman was at least fifty years in advance of the normal position which continued peace would have assigned her."

Mobilizing Resources

Wars are usually won by the side with superior resources and economic organization, and in this regard the Union entered the war with a distinct advantage. With nearly two-thirds of the American people, about two-thirds of the nation's railroad mileage, and nearly 90 percent of American industrial output, the North's economy was far superior to the South's (Figure 14.1). The North had an especially great advantage in the manufacture of cannon and rifles because many of its arms factories were equipped for mass production.

However, the Confederate position was far from weak. Virginia, North Carolina, and Tennessee had substantial industrial capacity. Richmond, with its Tredegar Iron Works, was an important industrial center, and in 1861 the Confederacy transported to Richmond the gun-making machinery from the U.S. armory at Harpers Ferry. The production of the Richmond armory, the purchase of Enfield rifles from Britain, and the capture of 100,000 Union guns enabled the Confederacy to provide every infantryman with a modern rifle-musket by 1863 (see New Technology, "The Rifle-Musket," p. 410).

Moreover, with 9 million people, the Confederacy could mobilize enormous armies. Although one-third of that number were slaves, their masters kept them in the fields, producing food for the army and cotton for export. In fact, Confederate leaders counted on "**King Cotton**" to provide the revenue to purchase clothes, boots, blankets, and weapons from abroad. They also counted on cotton as a diplomatic weapon, hoping that Britain, which depended on the South to supply its textile factories, would grant diplomatic recognition and provide military aid. Although the British government never

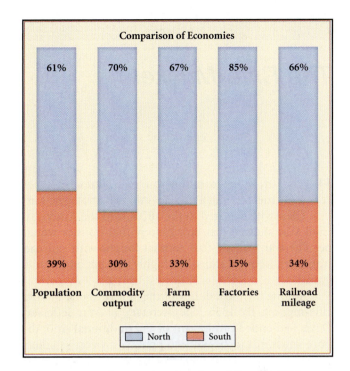

FIGURE 14.1 Economies, North and South, 1860
The military advantages of the North were even greater than this chart suggests because the population figures included slaves whom the South feared to arm and because its commodity output was dominated by farm goods rather than manufactures. Moreover, southern factories were, on average, much smaller than those in the North.
Source: Stanley Engerman, "The Economic Impact of the Civil War," in Robert W. Fogel and Stanley L. Engerman, *The Reinterpretation of American Economic History* (New York: Harper & Row, 1971), U.S. Census data.

recognized the Confederacy as an independent nation, it regarded the conflict as a war (rather than a domestic insurrection), thereby giving the rebels the status of a belligerent power with the right under international law to borrow money and purchase weapons. Thus the odds did not necessarily favor the Union, despite its superior resources.

Forging New Economic Policies. The outcome ultimately depended on the success of the rival governments in mobilizing their societies. To build political support for their fledgling party and boost industrial output, Lincoln and the Republicans enacted the program of national mercantilism previously advocated by Henry Clay and the Whig Party. First the Republicans raised tariffs, winning praise from northeastern manufacturers and laborers who feared competition from cheap foreign goods. Then Secretary of the Treasury Salmon P. Chase created a national banking system—an important element of every modern centralized government—by linking thousands of local banks. This integrated banking system was far more

The Rifle-Musket

"War is the continuation of politics by other means," the Prussian military strategist Karl Von Clauswitz declared in the 1820s, and the American Civil War showed just how bloody that politics would be. The war was the first conflict fought with railroad transport, ironclad ships, and highly efficient and deadly guns.

Among the most deadly of the new weapons was the rifle-musket. By 1855 U.S. Secretary of War Jefferson Davis had ended production of the traditional smoothbore musket and begun equipping American soldiers with the new type of gun. During the Civil War most Union infantrymen used Springfields, rifle-muskets manufactured by the U.S. armory at Springfield, Massachusetts. Many Confederate soldiers carried Enfields, a similar weapon made in Britain. In many

1861 Springfield Rifle-Musket
Private Collection.

respects, the rifle-musket was a traditional weapon. Like a musket, it had a long barrel (usually forty inches), fired a single shot, and was loaded through the muzzle, a cumbersome process. Before aiming and firing, a soldier had to rip open a paper-wrapped cartridge of gunpowder with his teeth, pour the powder and a bullet down the barrel, jam them tight with a ramrod, half-cock the hammer to insert a percussion cap, and then—finally—cock the hammer. Some soldiers could do all this lying on their backs, but to fire two or three times a minute, most men had to load from a kneeling or standing position, exposing themselves to enemy fire.

That fire was now much more accurate because the rifle-muskets used the advanced technology of eighteenth-century hunting weapons: tapered barrels that were rifled—lined with spiral grooves—to give the bullet greater speed and accuracy. These hunting rifles had given Daniel Boone his reputation as a "Kentucky sharpshooter" but they had not previously been issued to combat soldiers because the grooved barrel quickly accumulated gunpowder and required frequent cleaning.

A technological innovation solved that problem. In the early 1850s James S. Burton, an American mechanic working at the Harpers Ferry armory in Virginia, developed a new bullet based on an earlier French model. Burton's cylindro-conoidal bullet had a radically different shape from the round bullets of the day and was cast with a cavity at its base. When the gunpowder in the barrel exploded, hot gas expanded the soft-metal cavity and forced the bullet to engage the grooves of the rifling, cleaning them as it sped through the barrel.

The rifle-musket revolutionized warfare and military strategy by enormously strengthening defensive forces. Infantrymen could now kill reliably at three hundred yards—triple the previous range—and thus keep attackers from getting close enough for hand-to-hand combat. As a result, bayonets accounted for less than 1 percent of all wounds in the Civil War.

Elaborate entrenchments strengthened defensive positions even more. Firing from deep trenches, infantrymen with rifle-muskets could easily turn back assaults by forces three to four times their size, as the great success of the depleted Confederate forces defending Atlanta and Richmond in 1864 and 1865 clearly showed. Indeed, the grinding trench warfare around Petersburg, Virginia, provided a chilling preview of World War I, when quick-firing breech-loaded rifles and machine guns strengthened defensive positions even more.

The new rifle technology baffled most Civil War commanders, who continued to use the tactics perfected during the heyday of the musket and bayonet. They ordered thousands of infantrymen into dense close-order formations and sent them against enemy positions in successive waves. The result was brutally tragic. In battle after battle charging infantrymen went down like harvested wheat. Finally, the terrible losses at Gettysburg forced officers to search for ways to cope with the rifle-musket—the new and deadly weapon of war.

Industrial Richmond
Exploiting their city's location at the falls of the James River, Richmond entrepreneurs developed a wide range of industries: flour mills, tobacco factories, railroad and port facilities, and, most important, a profitable and substantial iron industry. In 1861 the Tredegar Iron Works employed nearly a thousand workers and, as the only facility in the South that could manufacture large machinery and heavy weapons, made a major contribution to the Confederate war effort. Virginia State Library.

effective in raising capital and controlling inflation than earlier efforts by the First and Second Banks of the United States had been. Finally, the Lincoln administration implemented Clay's program for a nationally financed system of internal improvements. In 1862 the Republican Congress began to build transcontinental railroads, chartering the Union Pacific and Central Pacific Railroads and subsidizing them lavishly. In addition, the Republicans moved aggressively to provide northern farmers with "free land" in the West. The Homestead Act of 1862 gave heads of families or individuals age twenty-one or older the title to 160 acres of public land after five years of residence and improvement. This economic program sustained the allegiance of many Northerners to the Republican Party while bolstering the Union's ability to fight the war.

In contrast, the Confederate government had a much less coherent economic policy. True to its states' rights philosophy, the Confederacy initially left most economic matters in the hands of the state governments. As the realities of total war became clear, the Davis administration took some extraordinary measures: it built and operated shipyards, armories, foundries, and textile mills; commandeered food and scarce raw materials such as coal, iron, copper, and lead; requisitioned slaves to work on fortifications; and exercised direct control over foreign trade. As the war wore on, ordinary southern citizens resented these measures, especially in areas where Confederate leaders failed to manage wartime shortages. To sustain the war effort, the Confederacy increasingly counted on white solidarity: Jefferson Davis warned whites that a Union victory would destroy slavery "and reduce the whites to the degraded position of the African race."

Raising Money in the North.   For both the North and the South the cost of fighting a total war was enormous. In the Union, government spending shot up from less than 2 percent of gross national product to about 15 percent (Table 14.2). To meet those expenses the Republicans established a powerful modern state that raised money in three ways. First, the government increased tariffs on consumer goods and imposed direct taxes on business corporations, large inheritances, and incomes. These levies paid for about 20 percent of the cost of the war. The sale of treasury bonds financed

TABLE 14.2 **The Cost of the War: Union Finances, 1860 and 1864**

	1860	1864
Income	$56.1 million	$264.6 million
Expenditures	$63.1 million	$865.3 million
General	32.0 million	35.1 million
Army and Navy	27.9 million	776.5 million
Interest on Debt	3.2 million	53.7 million
Total Public Debt	$64.8 million	$1,815.8 million

In 1864, the Union government received five times as much revenue as it had in 1860, but it spent nearly fourteen times as much, mostly to pay soldiers and buy military supplies. In four years the public debt had risen twenty-eight-fold, so that interest payments in 1865 nearly equaled the level of all federal government expenditures in 1860.

another 65 percent of the northern war effort. Led by Jay Cooke, a Philadelphia banker, the treasury used newspaper advertisements and 2,500 subagents to persuade nearly a million northern families to buy war bonds. In addition, the National Banking Acts of 1863 and 1864 forced state banks to accept national charters, which, in turn, required them to purchase treasury bonds and thereby finance the war.

The Union paid the remaining cost of the war by printing paper money. The Legal Tender Act of 1862 authorized the issue of $150 million in treasury notes—which soon became known as **greenbacks**—and required the public to accept them as legal tender. As with the "Continentals" issued during the War of Independence, these treasury notes were backed by faith in the government rather than by specie. Unlike the Continentals, this paper money did not depreciate disastrously in value. Although $450 million in greenbacks had been issued by the end of the war, this paper money funded only 15 percent of wartime expenses (as opposed to 80 percent during the Revolutionary War) and consequently did not spark an inflationary rise in prices. By imposing broad-based taxes, borrowing from the middle classes, and creating a national monetary system, the Union government had created the financial foundations of a modern nation-state.

The South Resorts to Inflation. The financial demands on the South were just as great, but it lacked a powerful central government that could tax and borrow.

The War's Toll on Civilians
Fighting along the Mississippi River in the spring of 1862 and the Union blockade along the Gulf of Mexico disrupted the supply of foodstuffs to New Orleans. By the time Union troops captured the city in May, foodstocks were severely depleted. In June, hungry citizens—men in top hats and fashionably dressed women as well as barefoot children and white and black working people—stormed the stores and emptied them of their last supplies of food. This engraving, titled Starving People of New Orleans, *appeared in* Harper's Weekly, *a prominent New York journal.*
Library of Congress.

The Confederate Congress fiercely opposed taxes on cotton exports and slaves, the most valuable property of wealthy planters. Taxes fell primarily on urban middle-class and nonslaveholding yeomen farm families, who often refused to pay. Consequently, the Confederacy covered less than 5 percent of its expenditures through taxation. The government paid for another 35 percent by borrowing, although many wealthy planters refused to buy large quantities of Confederate bonds, and foreign bankers were equally wary.

Thus the Confederacy was forced to finance about 60 percent of its expenses with unbacked paper money. The flood of currency created a spectacular inflation, which was compounded by the widespread circulation of counterfeit Confederate notes. As the huge supply of money (and shortages of goods) caused food prices to soar, riots broke out in more than a dozen southern cities and towns. In Richmond several hundred women broke into bakeries, crying, "Our children are starving while the rich roll in wealth." By the spring of 1865 prices had risen to ninety-two times their 1861 levels. Inflation not only undermined civilians' morale but also prompted them to refuse Confederate money, sometimes with serious consequences. When South Carolina store clerk Jim Harris refused to accept Confederate notes from a group of soldiers, they raided his storehouse and "robbed it of about five thousand dollars worth of goods." Army supply officers did the same, offering payment in worthless IOUs. Fearful of a strong government and taxation, the Confederacy was forced to violate the property rights of its citizens to sustain the war.

The Turning Point: 1863

By 1863 the Lincoln administration had mobilized northern society, creating a complex war machine and a coherent financial system. "Little by little," the young diplomat Henry Adams noted at his post in London, "one began to feel that, behind the chaos in Washington power was taking shape; that it was massed and guided as it had not been before." Slowly but surely the tide of the struggle shifted toward the Union.

Emancipation

From the beginning of the conflict antislavery Republicans had tried to persuade their party to make abolition—as well as restoration of the Union—a central war aim. They based their argument not just on morality but also on "military necessity," pointing out that slave-grown crops sustained the Confederate war effort. As Frederick Douglass put it, "the very stomach of this rebellion is the Negro in the form of a slave. Arrest that hoe in the hands of the Negro, and you smite the rebellion in the very seat of its life." Lincoln initially refused to consider the war as a struggle for black freedom, telling Horace Greeley of the *New York Tribune* that "if I could save the Union without freeing any slave, I would do it." As war casualties mounted in 1862, Lincoln and some Republican leaders moved closer to Douglass's position and began to redefine the war as a struggle against slavery—the cornerstone of southern society.

"Contrabands." However, it was enslaved African Americans who forced the issue by seizing freedom for themselves. Exploiting the disorder of wartime, tens of thousands of slaves escaped and sought refuge behind Union lines. The first Union official to confront this issue was General Benjamin Butler. When three slaves reached his army camp on the Virginia coast in May 1861, he labeled them "contraband of war" and refused to return them to their owner. His term stuck, and for the rest of the war slaves behind Union lines were known as **contrabands**. Within a few months a thousand contrabands were camping with Butler's army. To define their status and undermine the Confederate war effort, in August 1861 Congress passed the First Confiscation Act, which authorized the seizure of all property—including slaves—used to support the rebellion.

Radical Republicans, who had long condemned slavery, now saw a way to use the war to end it. By the spring of 1862 leading Radicals—Treasury Secretary Chase; Charles Sumner, chair of the Senate Committee on Foreign Relations; and Thaddeus Stevens, chair of the House Ways and Means Committee—had pushed moderate Republicans toward abolition. A longtime Pennsylvania congressman and an uncompromising foe of slavery, Stevens was a masterful politician, adept at fashioning legislation that commanded majority support. In April 1862 Stevens and his Radical allies persuaded Congress to end slavery in the District of Columbia, with compensation for owners. In June it outlawed slavery in the federal territories, finally enacting into law the Wilmot Proviso and the Republicans' free-soil policy. And in July Congress passed the Second Confiscation Act. This far-reaching legislation overrode the property rights of Confederate slave owners, declaring "forever free" all fugitive slaves and all slaves captured by the Union army. Emancipation had become an instrument of war.

The Emancipation Proclamation. Lincoln now seized the initiative from the Radicals. In July 1862 he prepared a general proclamation of emancipation and, viewing the battle of Antietam as "an indication of the Divine Will," issued it on September 22, 1862. Based on the president's powers as commander in chief, the proclamation declared Lincoln's intention to fight the rebellion by ending slavery in all states that remained out of the Union on January 1, 1863. The rebel states

***First Reading of the Emancipation Proclamation,* by Francis Bicknell Carpenter**

Treasury Secretary Salmon P. Chase (far left) and Secretary of State William H. Seward (center foreground) were longtime foes of slavery. As thousands of black contrabands sought freedom behind Union lines, Chase and Seward pressed Lincoln to make abolition one of his war aims. In July 1862 the president drew up a draft proclamation but Seward, himself a successful politician who knew the importance of timing, persuaded Lincoln to "postpone its issue until you can give it to the country supported by military success." On September 21, four days after the battle of Antietam, Lincoln read the Emancipation Proclamation to his cabinet and the next day issued it to the public.
U.S. Capitol Historical Society.

had a hundred days in which to preserve slavery by renouncing secession. None chose to do so.

The proclamation was politically astute. Because Lincoln needed to keep the loyalty of the border states still in the Union, the proclamation left slavery intact there. He also wanted to secure the allegiance of the areas occupied by Union armies—western and central Tennessee, western Virginia, and southern Louisiana, including New Orleans—so he left slavery untouched there. Consequently, the Emancipation Proclamation did not actually free a single slave. Yet, as the abolitionist Wendell Phillips perceived, Lincoln's proclamation had moved the institution of slavery to "the edge of Niagara," where it would soon be swept over the brink, bringing freedom to all enslaved African Americans. Indeed, Union troops soon became agents of liberation, freeing slaves as they advanced into the South. "I became free in 1863, in the summer, when the yankees come by and said I could go work for myself," Jackson Daniel of Maysville, Alabama, recalled. "I was farming after that

[and also] . . . making shoes." The conflict was no longer simply a struggle to preserve the Union but, as Lincoln put it, a war of "subjugation" in which "the old South is to be destroyed and replaced by new propositions and ideas."

As a war aim, emancipation was controversial. In the Confederacy, Jefferson Davis labeled it the "most execrable measure recorded in the history of guilty man," while in the North it produced the backlash among whites that the moderate Republicans had feared. During the congressional election of 1862 the Democrats denounced emancipation as unconstitutional, warned of slave uprisings and massive bloodshed in the South, and claimed that a "black flood" would wash away the jobs of northern workers. Democrat Horatio Seymour won the governorship of New York by declaring that if abolition was the purpose of the war, the South should not be conquered. Other Democrats swept to victory in Pennsylvania, Ohio, and Illinois, and the party gained thirty-four seats in Congress. However, the Republicans still held a twenty-five-seat majority in the House and had gained five seats in the Senate. Lincoln refused to retreat. On New Year's Day 1863 he signed the Emancipation Proclamation. To reassure Northerners who sympathized with the South or feared race warfare, Lincoln urged slaves to "abstain from all violence." He now justified emancipation as an "act of justice." "If my name ever goes into history," he said, "it was for this act."

Vicksburg and Gettysburg

The fate of the proclamation would depend on the success of Union armies and the Republicans' ability to win political support for their war policies. The outlook was not encouraging. Not only had Democrats registered gains in the election of 1862 but there was also increased popular support for Democrats who favored a negotiated peace. Two brilliant victories by Lee, whose army defeated Hooker's forces at Fredericksburg (December 1862) and Chancellorsville, Virginia (May 1863), caused further erosion of northern support for the war, as did rumors of a new draft.

The Crucial July Battles.   At this critical juncture General Grant mounted a major offensive in the West designed to split the Confederacy in two. Grant drove south along the west bank of the Mississippi and then moved his troops across the river near Vicksburg, Mississippi, where he defeated two Confederate armies and laid siege to the city. After repelling Union assaults for six weeks, the exhausted and starving Vicksburg garrison surrendered on July 4, 1863. Five days later Union forces took Port Hudson, Louisiana, establishing Union control of the Mississippi River. Grant had taken 31,000 prisoners, cut off Louisiana, Arkansas, and Texas from the rest of the Confederacy, and prompted hundreds of slaves to desert their plantations (see American Voices, "Elizabeth Mary Meade Ingraham: A Vicksburg Diary," p. 416).

Grant's initial advance down the Mississippi had created an argument over strategy within the Confederate leadership. Jefferson Davis and other civilian leaders wanted to throw in reinforcements to defend Vicksburg and send troops to Tennessee to draw Grant out of Mississippi. But Robert E. Lee, buoyed by his recent victories over Hooker, favored a new invasion of the North. He argued that a military thrust into the free states would relieve the pressure on Vicksburg by drawing the Union armies east. Beyond that Lee hoped for a major victory that would undermine northern support for the war.

Lee won out. In June 1863 he maneuvered his army north through Maryland into Pennsylvania. The Union's Army of the Potomac moved along with him, positioning itself between Lee and the federal capital of Washington. Early in July the two great armies met in an accidental but decisive confrontation at Gettysburg, Pennsylvania (Map 14.4). On the first day of battle, July 1, Lee drove the Union's advance guard to the south of town. There General George G. Meade, who had just taken over command of the Union forces from Hooker, placed his troops in well-defended hilltop positions and called up reinforcements. By the morning of the second day Meade had 90,000 troops to Lee's 75,000. Aware that he was outnumbered but bent on victory, Lee attacked both of Meade's flanks but failed to turn them. General Richard B. Ewell, assigned to attack the Union right, was unwilling to risk his men in an all-out assault, and General Longstreet, on the Union left, was unable to dislodge Meade's forces from a hill known as Little Round Top.

On July 3 Lee decided to attempt a frontal assault on the center of the Union lines. He recognized the danger of this tactic but felt this might be his last chance to inflict a crushing defeat on the North. Moreover, he had enormous confidence in his troops. After the heaviest artillery barrage of the war, Lee ordered 14,000 men under General George E. Pickett to take Cemetery Ridge. Anticipating this attack, Meade had reinforced the center of his line with artillery and his best troops. When Pickett's men charged across a mile of open terrain, they were met by massive fire from artillery and rifle-muskets; thousands were killed, wounded, or captured. By the end of the battle Lee had suffered 28,000 casualties, one-third of the Army of Northern Virginia, while 23,000 of Meade's soldiers lay killed or wounded, making Gettysburg the most lethal battle of the Civil War. Shocked by the bloodletting, Meade allowed the remaining Confederate soldiers to escape, thus losing an opportunity to end the war. "As it is," Lincoln brooded, "the war will be prolonged indefinitely."

Political and Diplomatic Effects.   Nonetheless, Gettysburg was a great Union victory and, in combination with the triumph at Vicksburg, represented a major turning point in the conflict. Never again would a southern army invade the North. In the fall of 1863 Republicans reaped the political gains from those victories by sweeping state and local elections in Pennsylvania, Ohio, and New York. In the South the military setbacks accentuated war weariness. The Confederate elections of 1863 went sharply against the politicians who supported Jefferson Davis, and a large minority in the new Confederate Congress were outspokenly hostile to his policies. A few advocated peace negotiations, and many more criticized the ineffectiveness of the war effort, with the Confederate vice president, Alexander Stephens, comparing Davis to "my poor old blind and deaf dog."

Vicksburg and Gettysburg also represented a great diplomatic triumph for the North, ending the Confederacy's prospect of winning foreign recognition and acquiring advanced weapons. In 1862 British shipbuilders

Elizabeth Mary Meade Ingraham

A Vicksburg Diary

Elizabeth Mary Meade Ingraham (1806–?) was the sister of Union General George Meade but, having become a plantation mistress, she sided with the Confederacy. In 1831 Ingraham and her husband, who had been an agent of the Second Bank of the United States, moved from Philadelphia to Mississippi and purchased Ashwood Plantation, thirty miles from Vicksburg. Her diary, which covers the six weeks between May 2 and June 13, 1863, describes how Ulysses S. Grant's Vicksburg campaign dramatically changed the relationship between masters and slaves.

May 4. [Union General] Osterhaus' Division, scum of St. Louis, camped in the big field. All the corn ruined in the field, and nearly all consumed in the granaries. . . . Nancy [a slave] sent me a little. Elsy, faithful and true, and Jack and Emma [all slaves] very attentive.

May 8. The last thing Eddens [a slave] did was to save some meat for me. He slept in the spare room Sunday night, and Monday at noon he had quit our service. . . . Parker, Sol, Mordt, Jim Crow, Isaiah, and Wadloo, have quit us, but the rest are here, and very attentive and willing. . . .

May 13. Elsy still faithful, feeds us, and does what she can; Rita Jane too; Bowlegs very attentive. Emma beginning to tire of waiting on me, did not come up at noon; Nancy not true.

May 15. Edward's [Ingraham's son] sash and six pairs of gloves taken out of my wardrobe. I am afraid Emma has done this; don't feel as if I could trust any one but Elsy; she feeds and takes care of me.

May 18. [We] have reason to think the hands will all leave; only a question of time, they are not quite ready; Elsy still true; but Jack doubtful. . . .

May 27. Negro meetings are being held, and the few whites left begin to be very anxious. . . . Powers was burnt out by his own negroes. I fear the blacks more than I do the Yankees. Jack trying to persuade Elsy to leave. . . . She tells him to get her a home and a way of earning a living, and she is ready to go, but [I] told her, if he left here, to move up into the wash-house with her children. I would give her $12 a month and free her four children.

June 3. Our darkeys in great commotion, yesterday, on account of Secesh [secessionists], who, about twenty-five in number, have been going the rounds, and setting the negroes to work; they whipped one fellow . . . and hung another; and we thought last evening all ours but a few meant to go. . . . I wish the Secesh would come [here]. . . .

June 6. Martha with her three children and Emma, left at midnight Friday . . . and the rest are packing today. Hays resolved to go, and I dread lest he take his wife with him, for I can hardly get along as it is, and shall die if I have the cooking to do.

June 10. Fanny, John Smith, and the children, Buck and his family, Dave and his, Kate and hers, making in all thirteen who have gone—Dave intending to come back, but the Yankees would not let him. . . . [T]hose who have stayed are utterly demoralized; if they work for you, the job is only half done.

Source: W. Maury Darst, "The Vicksburg Diary of Mrs. Alfred Ingraham," *Journal of Mississippi History* 44 (May 1982): 148–79.

---

had begun to supply armed cruisers to the Confederacy, and one of them, the *Alabama*, had sunk or captured more than a hundred Union merchant ships. Charles Francis Adams, the son of John Quincy Adams and the American minister in London, despaired of preventing the scheduled delivery of two more ironclad cruisers in mid-1863. News of the Union victories changed everything, and Adams persuaded the British government to impound the ships.

Moreover, cotton had not become an effective diplomatic weapon, as the South had hoped. British manufacturers had stockpiled raw cotton before the war, and when those stocks were depleted, they found new sources in Egypt and India. Equally important, the dependence of British consumers on cheap wheat from the North deterred the government from supporting the Confederacy. Finally, British workers and reformers were enthusiastic champions of abolition, which the Emancipation Proclamation had established as a Union war aim. The results at Vicksburg and Gettysburg confirmed British neutrality by demonstrating the military might of the Union. The British did not want to risk Canada or their merchant marine by provoking a strong, well-armed United States.

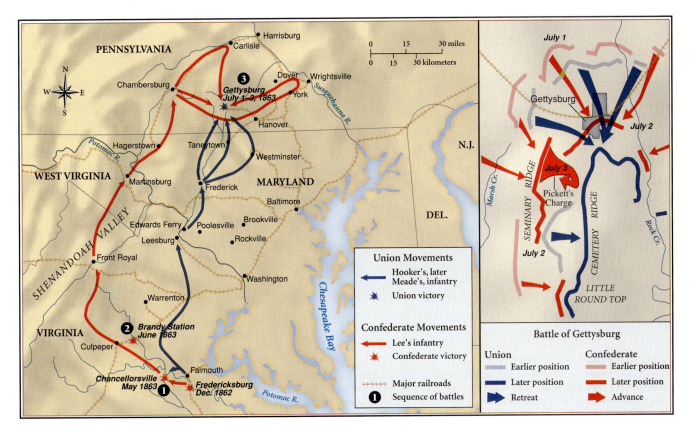

MAP 14.4 Lee Invades the North, 1863

After Lee's victory at Chancellorsville and Brandy Station (#1 and 2), the Confederate forces moved northward, constantly shadowed by the Union army, until the two armies met accidentally near Gettysburg, Pennsylvania, in early July. In the ensuing battle (#3), the Union army, commanded by General George Meade, emerged victorious, primarily because it was much larger than the Confederate force and held well-fortified positions along Cemetery Ridge, which gave its units a major tactical advantage.

The Union Victorious, 1864–1865

The Union victories of 1863 made it clear that the South could not win the war on the battlefield, but the Confederacy still hoped for a military stalemate and a negotiated peace. Lincoln and his generals faced the daunting task of winning a quick and decisive victory; otherwise a majority of northern voters might well desert the Republican Party and its policies.

Soldiers and Strategy

Two developments allowed the Union to prosecute the war with continued vigor and eventually to prevail: the enlistment of African American soldiers and the emergence of generals capable of fighting a modern war.

The Impact of Black Troops. Free African Americans and fugitive slaves had tried to enlist in the Union army as early as 1861, and the black abolitionist Frederick Douglass had embraced their cause: "Once

let the black man get upon his person the brass letters, 'U.S.' . . . a musket on his shoulder and bullets in his pockets, and there is no power on earth which can deny that he has earned the right to citizenship in the United States." The possibility of such an outcome frightened many northern whites, who were determined to keep blacks in a position of political inferiority. Moreover, most Union generals doubted that former slaves would make good soldiers, and so the Lincoln administration initially refused to consider blacks for military service. Nonetheless, by 1862 free and contraband blacks had formed regiments in South Carolina, Louisiana, and Kansas and waited for orders to join the fighting.

The Emancipation Proclamation changed popular thinking and military policy. If blacks were to benefit from a Union victory, some northern whites argued, they should share in the fighting and dying. The valor exhibited by the first African American regiments also influenced northern opinion. In January 1863 Thomas Wentworth Higginson, the white abolitionist commander of the black First South Carolina Volunteers,

Black Soldiers in the Union Army
Determined to end racial slavery, tens of thousands of African Americans volunteered for service in the Union army in 1864 and 1865, boosting the northern war effort at a critical time. These proud soldiers were members of the 107th Colored Infantry, stationed at Fort Corcoran near Washington, D.C. In January 1865 their regiment participated in the daring capture of Fort Fisher, which protected Wilmington, North Carolina, the last Confederate port open to blockade runners. Library of Congress.

wrote a glowing newspaper account of their military prowess: "No officer in this regiment now doubts that the key to the successful prosecution of the war lies in the unlimited employment of black troops." In July the heroic but costly attack on Fort Wagner, South Carolina, by another black regiment, the Fifty-fourth Massachusetts Infantry, convinced many white Northerners, including Union officers, of the value of black soldiers. The War Department authorized the enlistment of free blacks and contraband slaves, and as white resistance to conscription increased, the Lincoln administration recruited as many African Americans as it could. Without black soldiers, the president suggested in the autumn of 1864, "we would be compelled to abandon the war in three weeks." By the spring of 1865 there were nearly 200,000 African American soldiers and sailors.

Military service did not end racial discrimination. Black soldiers served under white officers in segregated regiments and were used primarily to build fortifications, garrison forts, and guard supply lines. At first they were paid less than white soldiers ($7 versus $13 per month) and won equal pay only by threatening to lay down their arms. Despite such treatment African Americans volunteered for military service in disproportionate numbers and diligently served the Union cause. They knew they were fighting for freedom and the possibility of a new social order. "Hello, Massa," said one black

soldier to his former master, who had been taken prisoner. "Bottom rail on top dis time." The worst fears of the secessionists had come true: through the agency of the Union army, blacks had enlisted in a great rebellion against slavery (see American Voices, "Spotswood Rice: Freeing My Children from Slavery," p. 419).

New Generals Take Command. As African Americans joined the ranks, Lincoln finally found a commanding general in whom he had confidence. Impressed with General Ulysses S. Grant's victories in the West, in March 1864 Lincoln placed Grant in charge of all the Union armies and created a command structure appropriate to the large, complex organization that the Union army had become. From then on, the president would determine general strategy and Grant would decide how best to implement it. Lincoln directed Grant to advance simultaneously against all the major Confederate forces, a strategy Grant had long favored. Both the general and the president wanted a decisive victory before the election of 1864.

As the successful western campaigns of mid-1863 showed, Grant understood how to fight a modern war—a war relying on industrial technology and directed at an entire society. At Vicksburg he had besieged an entire city and forced its surrender. Then, in November 1863, he had used the North's superior technology, utilizing railroad

Spotswood Rice

Freeing My Children from Slavery

The face of the war changed in 1864 as tens of thousands of blacks—many of them ex-slaves—joined the Union army, which now began to occupy significant parts of the Confederacy. In February, Spotswood Rice, a tobacco roller and the slave of Benjamin Lewis, fled from his owner near Glasgow, Missouri, and became a Union soldier. In September, although hospitalized with rheumatism, Rice wrote the following letters to his still enslaved children and to Kittey Diggs, who owned one of them.

[Benton Barracks Hospital, St. Louis, Mo., September 3, 1864]

My Children I take my pen in hand to rite you a few lines to let you know that I have not forgot you and that I want to see you as bad as ever. Now my Dear Children . . . be assured that I will have you if it cost me my life.

on the 28th of the mounth, 8 hundred White and 8 hundred blacke solders expects to start up the rivore to Glasgow and [will] . . . be jeneraled by a jeneral that will give me both of you. When they Come I expect to be with them and expect to get you both in return. Dont be uneasy my children I expect to have you.

If Diggs dont give you up this Government will [take you from Diggs] and I feel confident that I will get you Your Miss Kaitty said that I tried to steal you But I'll let her know that god never intended for man to steal his own flesh and blood. . . . If I ever had any Confidence in her I have none now and never expect to have And I want her to remember if she meets me with ten thousand soldiers she [will] meet her enemy I once [thought] that I had some respect for them but now my respects is worn out and have no sympathy for Slaveholders. And as for her cristianantty I expect the Devil has Such in hell. You tell her from me that She is the frist Christian that I ever hard say that a man could Steal his own child especially out of human bondage. . . .

now my Dear children I am a going to close my letter to you. . . . Oh! My Dear children how I do want to see you

[To Kittey Diggs]

I received a leteter from Cariline telling me that you say I tried to steal, to plunder my child away from you now I want you to understand that mary is my Child and she is a God given rite of my own . . . the longor you keep my Child from me the longor you will have to burn in hell and the qwicer [quicker] youll get their

for we are now making up a bout one thoughsand blacke troops to . . . come through Glasgow and when we come wo [woe] be to Copperhood rabbels and to the Slaveholding rebbels for we dont expect to leave them there. . . .

I want you to understand kittey diggs that where ever you and I meets we are enmays to each orthere I offered once to pay you forty dollers for my own Child but I am glad now that you did not accept it. . . . my Children is my own and I expect to get them and . . . to exacute vengencens on them that holds my Child

I have no fears about geting mary out of your hands this whole Government gives chear to me and you cannot help your self

Spotswood Rice

Source: Ira Berlin, Joseph P. Reidy, and Leslie S. Rowland, eds., *Freedom's Soldiers: The Black Military Experience in the Civil War* (New York: Cambridge University Press, 1998), 131–33.

transport to charge to the rescue of a Union army near Chattanooga, Tennessee, and drive an invading Confederate army back into Georgia. Moreover, Grant was willing to accept heavy casualties in assaults on strongly defended positions, abandoning the caution of earlier Union commanders. Their attempts "to conserve life" had in fact prolonged the war, Grant argued. These aggressive tactics earned Grant a reputation as a butcher both of his own men and of enemy armies, which he pursued relentlessly.

To crush the South's will to resist, the new Union commander was willing to terrorize the civilian population.

In May 1864 Grant ordered major new offensives on two fronts. Personally taking charge of the 115,000-strong Army of the Potomac, he set out to destroy Lee's force of 75,000 troops in Virginia. Simultaneously he instructed General William Tecumseh Sherman, who shared his views on warfare, to invade Georgia and take Atlanta. As Sherman prepared for battle, he wrote that

William Tecumseh Sherman: An Architect of Modern War

The Civil War rescued William Tecumseh Sherman (1820–1891) from a life of disappointment and failure, giving him the opportunity to use his talents as a ruthless soldier and military strategist. By the end of the war Sherman had emerged not only as a major force in the Union victory but also as an important architect of modern warfare.

Disappointment had come early in Sherman's life. He was born into a socially prominent clan in Connecticut, but his immediate family fell on hard times when his parents moved west to Lancaster, Ohio. His father's law practice did not prosper, and his early death in 1829 shattered the family. Able to support only two of her eleven children, Sherman's mother sent the rest to be raised by friends and relatives. The sixth child, Tecumseh (named after the great Indian chief), went to live with Thomas Ewing, a close family friend and a wealthy Lancaster lawyer.

Life with the Ewings brought many privileges but not much pleasure. His foster mother insisted that Tecumseh be baptized into her Catholic faith and take the Christian name William. Embarrassed by his father's financial failure, Sherman never adjusted to his new life. In 1836 he gladly left Ohio to enter the United States Military Academy at West Point, an appointment arranged by Thomas Ewing, who was now a U.S. senator.

Sherman flourished at West Point and adopted the army as his real family, finding in the corps of professional officers the sense of identity, order, and belonging that he had missed as a child. After his graduation in 1840, the young officer used assignments in Florida, Alabama, South Carolina, and Georgia to travel widely. However, the Ewings had grandiose plans for their foster son, approving his marriage to their daughter Ellen and encouraging him to enter the world of business. Sherman refused to leave the army, hoping he would rise in the ranks during the Mexican War. But by the time he reached California in 1847 there was little to do except paperwork. Six years later, he resigned his commission.

Sherman had no more success as a businessman than he had as a soldier. Unstable financial times ruined

William Tecumseh Sherman

Sherman was a nervous man who smoked cigars and talked continuously. When he was seated, he crossed and uncrossed his legs incessantly, and a journalist described his fingers as constantly "twitching his red whiskers—his coat buttons— playing a tattoo on the table—or running through his hair." But Sherman was a decisive general who commanded the loyalty of his troops. This photograph was taken in 1865, after Sherman's devastating march through Georgia and the Carolinas.
Library of Congress.

his budding career as a banker, and he was forced to accept a junior partnership in a business run by two of his foster brothers. Unwilling to remain a dependent of the Ewings, in 1860 Sherman rejoined the army as superintendent of the brand-new Louisiana Military Seminary.

The new superintendent's earlier assignments in the South had made him sympathetic to the planter class and its institutions. In particular, he believed that slavery was necessary to maintain the stability of southern social order. However, Sherman remained a staunch Unionist. A Whig in politics and a soldier by profession, he was convinced that a strong national government was the key to American greatness. In 1861 there was no question on which side William Tecumseh Sherman would stand. When Louisiana troops seized the U.S. arsenal at Baton Rouge in January 1861, Sherman resigned his position.

Secession meant "anarchy," he told his southern friends, and had to be crushed. "There can be no peaceable secession," he continued. "If war comes, as I fear it surely will, I must fight your people whom I best love."

Sherman understood how costly and bloody the war would be, and he doubted that Abraham Lincoln and his administration would pay the price. But his family was firmly committed to the war effort and, urged on by Senator Ewing and his younger brother John Sherman, who had just been elected as a Republican senator from Ohio, William Tecumseh became a colonel in a newly formed Union brigade.

Bull Run was Sherman's first taste of combat, and the rout of the Union army confirmed his long-standing doubts about democratic individualism. "The want of organization and subordination of our people is a more dangerous enemy than the armies of the South," he wrote. By October 1861 Sherman had risen to the rank of brigadier general and had command of the Union forces in Kentucky, but he remained so darkly pessimistic about Union prospects that Lincoln relieved him of his command. Thanks to his military friends and his powerful family, by February 1862 Sherman was back in Kentucky, serving under Ulysses S. Grant. A quiet, confident general, Grant provided the sense of determination that Sherman needed. Moreover, Grant agreed with Sherman's emphasis on strict military discipline and on the swift and decisive deployment of forces. Under Grant's guidance, Sherman enjoyed a string of successes. He distinguished himself at Shiloh, winning a promotion to major general. As military governor of Memphis he pacified a strategic sector along the Mississippi River and then in 1863 joined Grant in the successful campaign against the Confederate stronghold at Vicksburg.

Now experienced and increasingly self-confident, Sherman developed his innovative military ideas. Assuming command of a Union army in Tennessee, he turned his troops loose against prosouthern civilians suspected of assisting anti-Union guerrillas. "When one nation is at war with another, all the people of one are enemies of the other," he declared. After guerrillas fired on a boat with Unionist passengers near Randolph, Tennessee, Sherman sent a regiment to level the town, asserting, "We are justified in treating all inhabitants as combatants."

In March 1864 Sherman assumed command of all military operations in the West and worked closely with Grant on a coordinated plan to destroy the Confederacy. Over the next year, Sherman's army dealt the secessionist cause a series of major blows, taking and burning the strategic railway hub of Atlanta, devastating the countryside as he marched through Georgia to the sea, and then sweeping quickly across the Carolinas. These campaigns demonstrated both his tactical military genius and his understanding of psychological warfare: he would destroy the rebels' army and morale by laying waste to southern society.

Following the Union victory Sherman received international acclaim. His former troops revered him, grateful American businessmen made him wealthy, and world leaders honored him. Unlike Grant and other Union generals who pursued political careers, Sherman remained a military man, leading a war against the Great Plains Indians and serving as commanding general of the army from 1869 to 1883. Contemptuous of democratic politics, Sherman rebuffed all overtures from Democratic and Republican leaders. Asked to run for the presidency in 1883, Sherman replied with the oft-quoted words "If nominated, I will not accept; if elected, I will not serve." A stickler for order and discipline, Sherman had no stomach for the anarchic and increasingly corrupt world of American politics.

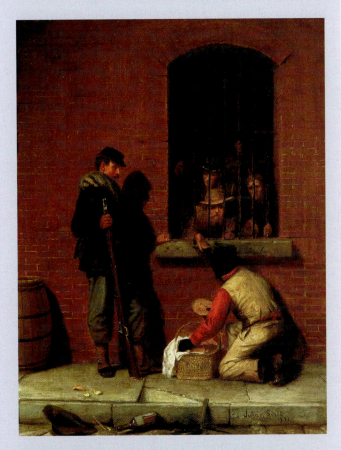

Imprisoned Confederate Troops, by Julian Scott
As the Union armies advanced, they captured tens of thousands of Confederate soldiers. This 1873 painting depicts an African American orderly distributing meager rations to Confederate soldiers, who are crowded into a small cell.
West Point Museum, U.S. Military Academy / Photo by Ted Speigel.

For more help analyzing this image, see the ONLINE STUDY GUIDE at bedfordstmartins.com/henretta.

by both Republicans and Unionist Democrats endorsed Lincoln's war measures, demanded the unconditional surrender of the Confederacy, and called for a constitutional amendment to abolish slavery. Attempting to attract border-state voters to their northern- and midwestern-based party and create a genuinely national organization, Lincoln and the Republican leadership took a new name, the National Union Party, and chose as Lincoln's vice presidential running mate Andrew Johnson, a slave owner and a Unionist Democrat from Tennessee.

The Democratic convention met in late August and nominated General George B. McClellan, whom Lincoln had removed from a military command because of his opposition to emancipation. Like McClellan, the Democratic delegates rejected freedom for blacks and condemned Lincoln's uncompromising repression of domestic dissent. Then they split into two camps over the issue of continuing the war. By threatening to bolt the convention, the "Peace Democrats" forced through a platform calling for "a cessation of hostilities" and for a constitutional convention to restore peace "on the basis of the Federal Union." Although personally a **War Democrat**," McClellan promised if elected to recommend an immediate armistice and a peace convention. Rejoicing in "the first ray of real light I have seen since the war began," Confederate vice president Alexander Stephens declared that if Atlanta and Richmond held out, then Lincoln could be defeated and northern Democrats persuaded to accept an independent Confederacy.

The Fall of Atlanta and Lincoln's Victory. However, on September 2, 1864, Atlanta fell to Sherman's army. In a stunning move the Union general pulled his troops from the trenches and swept around the city to destroy its roads and rail links to the rest of the Confederacy. Fearing that Sherman would be able to trap and destroy his army, Hood abandoned the city. "Atlanta is ours, and fairly won," Sherman telegraphed Lincoln, sparking 100-gun salutes and wild Republican celebrations in northern cities. A deep pessimism settled over the Confederacy. In her diary Mary Chesnut, a slave-owning plantation mistress, confessed that she "felt as if all were dead within me, forever," and foresaw the end of the Confederacy: "We are going to be wiped off the earth." Acknowledging the dramatic change in the military situation, McClellan repudiated the Democratic peace platform, and dissident Republicans abandoned all efforts to dump Lincoln. Instead, the Republican Party went on the offensive, charging that McClellan was still a peace candidate and attacking Peace Democrats as "copperheads" (poisonous snakes) who were hatching treasonous plots.

Sherman's success in Georgia gave Lincoln a clear-cut victory in November. The president took 212 of 233 electoral votes, winning 55 percent of the popular vote and carrying all of the free states as well as the border states of Maryland, Tennessee, and Missouri. Republicans won 145 of the 185 seats in the House of Representatives and increased their Senate majority to 42 of 52 seats. Many of those victories came from the votes of Union troops, most of whom wanted the war to continue until the Confederacy met every Union demand, including emancipation.

Already legal emancipation was under way at the edges of the Confederacy. In 1864 Maryland and Missouri amended their constitutions to free their slaves, and the three occupied states of Tennessee, Arkansas, and Louisiana followed suit. Abolitionists still worried that the Emancipation Proclamation, based on the president's wartime powers, would lose its force at the end of the war and that southern states would reestablish slavery. Urged on by Lincoln, the Republican-dominated Congress took a major step to guarantee black freedom. On January 31, 1865, it approved the Thirteenth Amendment, which prohibited slavery throughout the United States, and sent it to the states for ratification. Slavery was nearly dead.

Sherman's Total War. Thanks to William Tecumseh Sherman, the Confederacy was nearly dead as well. After the capture of Atlanta Sherman declined to follow the retreating Confederate army into Tennessee and decided on a bold strategy. Rather than spread his troops dangerously thin by protecting supply lines to the rear, he would "cut a swath through to the sea," living off the land. To persuade Lincoln and Grant to approve this unconventional plan, Sherman pointed out that such a march would devastate Georgia and score a major psychological victory. It would be "a demonstration to the world, foreign and domestic, that we have a power [Jefferson] Davis cannot resist."

Sherman carried out the concept of total war he and Sheridan had pioneered: destruction of the enemy's economic resources and will to resist. "We are not only fighting hostile armies," Sherman wrote, "but a hostile people, and must make old and young, rich and poor, feel the hard hand of war." He left Atlanta in flames and during his three-hundred-mile march to the sea destroyed railroads, property, and supplies (Map 14.6). A Union veteran wrote that "[we] destroyed all we could not eat, stole their niggers, burned their cotton & gins, spilled their sorghum, burned & twisted their R.Roads and raised Hell generally." The havoc so demoralized Confederate soldiers that many deserted their units and fled home to protect their farms and families. When Sherman reached Savannah, Georgia, in mid-December, the 10,000 Confederate defenders left without a fight.

In February 1865 Sherman invaded South Carolina. He planned to link up with Grant at Petersburg and along the way punish the state where secession had begun. "The truth is," Sherman wrote, "the whole army

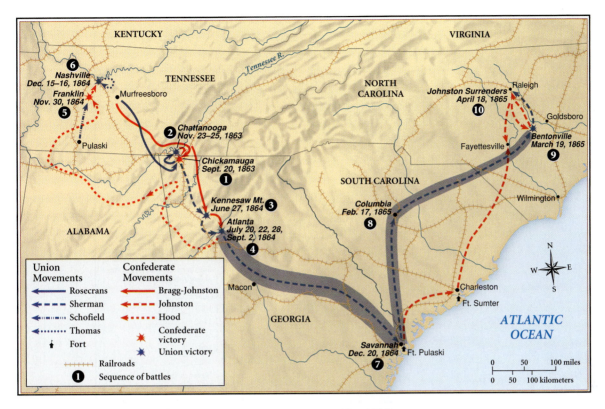

MAP 14.6 Sherman's March through the Confederacy, 1864–1865

The Union victory (#2) in November 1863 at Chattanooga, Tennessee, was almost as critical as the victories in July at Gettysburg and Vicksburg. The Union was now in position to invade the heart of the Confederacy by advancing on the railway hub of Atlanta (#3 and 4). After finally taking the city in September 1864, General William Tecumseh Sherman relied on other Union armies to repulse General John B. Hood's invasion of Tennessee (#5 and 6). Sherman swept on to Savannah in a devastating "March to the Sea" (#7) and then in 1865 cut a swath through the Carolinas (#8, 9, and 10).

For more help analyzing this map, see the ONLINE STUDY GUIDE at bedfordstmartins.com/henretta.

is burning with an insatiable desire to wreak vengeance upon South Carolina." His troops cut a comparatively narrow swath across the state but ravaged the countryside even more thoroughly than they had in Georgia. After capturing South Carolina's capital, Columbia, they burned the business district, most churches, and the wealthiest residential neighborhoods. "This disappointment to me is extremely bitter," lamented Jefferson Davis. By March Sherman had reached North Carolina and was on the verge of linking up with Grant and crushing Lee's army.

The Confederate Collapse. Sherman's march exposed an internal Confederate weakness: rising class resentment on the part of poor whites. Long angered by the "twenty-negro" exemption from military service given to slave owners and fearing that the Confederacy was doomed, ordinary southern farmers resisted

military service. "It is no longer a reproach to be known as a deserter," a Confederate officer in South Carolina complained in late 1863. "I am now going to work instead of to the war," declared David Harris, a backcountry farmer. "I think I will like it the best." By early 1865 the Confederacy was experiencing such a severe manpower crisis that its leaders decided to take an extreme measure: arming the slaves. Urged on by Lee, the Confederate Congress voted to enlist black soldiers; Davis issued an executive order granting freedom to all blacks who served in the Confederate army. But the war ended too soon to reveal whether any slaves would have fought for the Confederacy.

The symbolic end of the war took place in Virginia. In April 1865 Grant finally forced Lee into a showdown by gaining control of the crucial railroad junction at Petersburg and cutting off his supplies. Lee abandoned the defense of Richmond and turned west, hoping to join

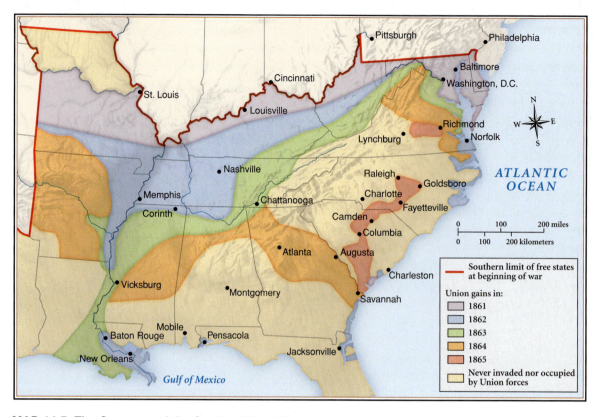

MAP 14.7 The Conquest of the South, 1861–1865

It took four years for the Union armies to defeat those of the Confederacy. Until the last year of the long conflict, most of the South remained in Confederate hands, and even at the end of the war Union armies had never entered many parts of the rebellious states. Most of the Union's territorial gains came on the vast western front, where its control of strategic lines of communication—rivers and railways—gave its forces a decisive advantage.

Confederate forces in North Carolina. While Lincoln visited the ruins of the Confederate capital, mobbed by joyful former slaves, Grant cut off Lee's escape route. On April 9, almost precisely four years after the attack on Fort Sumter, Lee surrendered to Grant at Appomattox Court House, Virginia. In accepting the surrender of the Confederate general, Grant set a tone of generosity, allowing Lee's men to take their horses home for spring planting. By late May all the Confederate generals had ceased to fight, and the Confederate army and government simply dissolved (Map 14.7; see also Map 14.5).

The armies of the Union had destroyed the Confederacy and much of the South's economy. Its factories, warehouses, and railroads were in ruins, as were many of its farms and some of its most important cities. Almost 260,000 Confederate soldiers had paid for secession with their lives. Most significant, the Union had been preserved and slavery destroyed. But the cost of victory was enormous in money, resources, and lives. More than

360,000 Union soldiers were dead, and hundreds of thousands were maimed and crippled. The hard and bitter war was over, and a reunited nation turned to the tasks of peace. These were to be equally hard and bitter.

FOR FURTHER EXPLORATION

▶ For definitions of key terms boldfaced in this chapter, see the glossary at the end of the book.

▶ To assess your mastery of the material covered in this chapter, see the Online Study Guide at **bedfordstmartins.com/henretta**.

▶ For suggested references, including Web sites, see page SR-15 at the end of the book.

▶ For map resources and primary documents, see **bedfordstmartins.com/henretta**.

Following the victory of Abraham Lincoln and the antislavery Republican Party in the election of 1860, secessionists led the cotton-producing states of the Deep South out of the Union. After fighting began at Fort Sumter, South Carolina, in April 1861, other southern and border states joined the rebellious Confederate states, but owing mainly to Lincoln's efforts, four border states and a portion of a fifth (western Virginia) remained loyal to the United States.

In the East, the first major military battles were inconclusive. In the spring of 1862 Confederate forces commanded by Robert E. Lee repulsed a Union advance on Richmond, and in September northern forces halted Lee's first invasion of the North at Antietam in Maryland. In the West, Union forces under Ulysses S. Grant scored significant victories.

The conflict became a total war, one of unsurpassed cost in lives and resources. To staff their armies, the Union and Confederate governments resorted to a draft, which sparked resistance and riots. The Lincoln administration pursued a coherent economic policy, instituting Henry Clay's American System. It also created an efficient system of taxation and borrowing to finance most of its war effort, whereas Jefferson Davis's Confederate government had to pay its troops and suppliers primarily by printing paper money, which produced a runaway inflation.

The turning point of the war came in 1863, which began with Lincoln's Emancipation Proclamation, establishing abolition as a Union policy. Tens of thousands of African American slaves fled behind Union lines, and many of those eventually enlisted in the northern army. In July 1863 Grant's capture of Vicksburg gave the Union control of the Mississippi and split the Confederacy. Simultaneously, George Meade's victory over Lee at Gettysburg ended the Confederate hope for a military victory.

The war turned into a stalemate, threatening Lincoln's bid for reelection and raising the prospect of a negotiated peace that would give independence to the Confederacy. Then in September 1864 Union forces under William Tecumseh Sherman captured the key city of Atlanta, Georgia, giving military momentum to the North and ensuring Lincoln's reelection. Sherman's devastating "march to the sea" undermined Confederate morale, and Grant's capture of Petersburg in early 1865 led to the surrender of Lee's army.

The Union victory ended the secessionist rebellion and ensured the triumph of nationalist constitutional principles. The Republicans enacted and ratified the Thirteenth Amendment, which ended slavery.

1861 Confederate States of America formed (February 4)

Abraham Lincoln inaugurated (March 4)

Confederates fire on Fort Sumter (April 12)

Virginia leads Upper South out of Union (April 17)

General Benjamin Butler declares runaway slaves "contraband of war" (May)

Confederates rout Union forces at first Battle of Bull Run (July 21)

1862 Congress passes Legal Tender Act, begins to print greenbacks

Homestead Act provides free land to settlers

Congress extends federal subsidies to transcontinental railroads

Battle of Shiloh advances Union cause in West (April 6–7)

Confederacy introduces first draft

Union halts Confederate offensive at Antietam, Maryland (September 17)

Lincoln issues preliminary Emancipation Proclamation (September 22)

1863 Lincoln signs Emancipation Proclamation (January 1)

Enrollment Act begins draft in North; riots in New York City (July)

Union victories at battles of Gettysburg (July 1–3) and Vicksburg (July 4)

1864 Ulysses S. Grant given command of all Union armies (March)

Grant advances on Richmond and lays seige to Petersburg (May)

William T. Sherman takes Atlanta (September 2)

Lincoln reelected (November)

Sherman marches through Georgia (November and December)

1865 Congress approves Thirteenth Amendment, which outlaws slavery (January)

Robert E. Lee surrenders at Appomattox Court House, Virginia (April 9)

Ratification of Thirteenth Amendment

CHAPTER 15

Presidential Reconstruction
Lincoln's Approach
Johnson's Initiative
Acting on Freedom
Congress versus President

Radical Reconstruction
Congress Takes Command
Republican Rule in the South
The Quest for Land

The Undoing of Reconstruction
Counterrevolution
The Acquiescent North
The Political Crisis of 1877

Reconstruction

1865–1877

I N HIS SECOND INAUGURAL ADDRESS, President Lincoln spoke of the need to "bind up the nation's wounds." No one knew better than Lincoln how daunting a task that would be. Foremost, of course, were the terms on which the rebellious states would be restored to the Union. But America's Civil War had opened more fundamental questions. Slavery was finished. That much was certain. But what system of labor should replace plantation slavery? What rights should the freedmen be accorded beyond emancipation? How far should the federal government go to settle these questions? And who should decide—the president or Congress?

◀ **Chloe and Sam** (1882)

After the Civil War the country went through the wrenching peacemaking process known as Reconstruction. The struggle between the victorious North and the vanquished South was fought out on a political landscape, but Thomas Hovenden's heartwarming painting reminds us of the deeper meaning of Reconstruction: that Chloe and Sam, after lives spent in slavery, might end their days in the dignity of freedom.

Thomas Colville Fine Art.

The last speech Lincoln delivered, on April 11, 1865, demonstrated his grasp of these issues. Reconstruction, he said, had to be regarded as a practical, not a theoretical, problem. It could be solved only if Republicans remained united, even if that meant compromising on principled differences dividing them, and only if the defeated South gave its consent, even if that meant forgiveness of the South's transgressions. The speech showed, above all, Lincoln's sense of the fluidity of events, of policy toward the South as an evolving, not a fixed, position.

429

What course Reconstruction might have taken had Lincoln lived is one of the unanswerable questions of American history. On April 14, 1865—five days after Lee's surrender at Appomattox—Lincoln was shot in the head at Ford's Theatre in Washington by a fanatic actor named John Wilkes Booth. Ironically, Lincoln might have been spared if the war had dragged on longer, for Booth and his Confederate associates had originally plotted to kidnap the president to force a negotiated settlement. After Lee's surrender, Booth became bent on revenge. Without regaining consciousness, Lincoln died on April 15.

With one stroke John Wilkes Booth had sent Lincoln to martyrdom, hardened many Northerners against the South, and handed the presidency to a man utterly lacking in Lincoln's moral sense and political judgment, Vice President Andrew Johnson.

Presidential Reconstruction

The procedure for Reconstruction—how to restore rebellious states to the Union—was not addressed by the Founding Fathers. The Constitution does not say which branch of government handles the readmission of rebellious states or, for that matter, even contemplates the possibility of secession. It was an open question whether, on seceding, the Confederate states had legally left the Union. If so, their reentry surely required legislative action by Congress. If not, if even in defeat they retained their constitutional status, then the terms for restoring them to the Union might be defined as an administrative matter best left to the president. The ensuing battle between the White House and Capitol Hill was one of the fault lines in Reconstruction's stormy history.

Lincoln's Approach

Lincoln, as wartime president, had the elbow room to take the initiative, offering in December 1863 a general amnesty to all but high-ranking Confederates willing to pledge loyalty to the Union. When 10 percent of a state's 1860 voters had taken this oath, the state would be restored to the Union, provided that it abolished slavery. The Confederate states (save those like Louisiana and Tennessee that were under Union control) rebuffed Lincoln's generous offer, ensuring that the war would have to be fought to the bitter end.

What the Ten Percent Plan also revealed was the rocky road that lay ahead for Reconstruction. In Louisiana, for example, the Unionist government restored under Lincoln's offer employed curfew laws to restrict the movements of the freed slaves and vagrancy regulations to force them back to work. But the Louisiana freedmen fought back. Led by the free black community of New Orleans, they began to agitate for political rights. No less than their former masters, ex-slaves intended to be actors in the savage drama of Reconstruction.

With the struggle in Louisiana in mind, congressional Republicans proposed a stricter substitute for Lincoln's Ten Percent Plan. The initiative came from the Radical wing of the party—those bent on a stern peace and full rights for the freedmen—but with broad support among more moderate Republicans. The Wade-Davis Bill, passed on July 2, 1864, laid down, as conditions for the restoration of the rebellious states to the Union, an oath of allegiance by a majority of each state's adult white men, new state governments formed only by those who had never carried arms against the Union, and permanent disfranchisement of Confederate leaders. The Wade-Davis bill served notice that the congressional Republicans were not about to hand over Reconstruction policy to the president.

Rather than openly challenging Congress, Lincoln executed a **pocket veto** of the Wade-Davis bill by not signing it before Congress adjourned. At the same time he initiated informal talks with congressional leaders aimed at finding common ground. Lincoln's successor, however, had no such inclinations. Andrew Johnson held the view that Reconstruction was the president's prerogative, and by an accident of timing he was free to act on his convictions: under leisurely rules that went back to the early republic, the 39th Congress elected back in November 1864 was not scheduled to convene until December 1865.

Johnson's Initiative

Andrew Johnson was a self-made man from the hills of eastern Tennessee. A Jacksonian Democrat, he saw himself as the champion of the common man. He hated what he called the "bloated, corrupt aristocracy" of the Northeast, and he was equally disdainful of the southern planters, whom he blamed for the poverty of the South's small farmers. It was the poor whites that he championed; Johnson, a slave owner himself, had little sympathy for the enslaved blacks. Johnson's political career had taken him to the U.S. Senate, where he remained when the war broke out, loyal to the Union. After federal forces captured Nashville, Johnson became Tennessee's military governor. The Republicans nominated him for vice president in 1864 in an effort to promote wartime unity and to court the support of southern Unionists.

In May 1865, just a month after Lincoln's death, Johnson launched his own Reconstruction plan. He offered amnesty to all Southerners who took an oath of allegiance to the Constitution, except for high-ranking Confederate officials and wealthy planters, whom he held responsible for secession. Such persons could be pardoned only by the president. Johnson appointed provisional governors for the southern states and, as conditions for their restoration, required only that they revoke their ordinances of secession, repudiate their Confederate debts, and ratify the Thirteenth Amendment, which abolished slavery. Within months all the former Confederate

Andrew Johnson

The president was not an easy man. This photograph of Andrew Johnson (1808–1875) conveys some of the prickly qualities that contributed so centrally to his failure to reach an agreement with Republicans on a moderate Reconstruction program.
Library of Congress.

states had met Johnson's requirements and had functioning, elected governments.

At first Republicans responded favorably. The moderates among them were sympathetic to Johnson's argument that it was up to the states, not the federal government, to settle what civil and political rights the freedmen should have. Even the Radicals held their fire. They liked the stern treatment of Confederate leaders, and they hoped that the new southern governments would show good faith by generous treatment of the freed slaves.

Nothing of the sort happened. The South lay in ruins (see Voices from Abroad, "David Macrae: The Devastated South," p. 432). But Southerners held fast to the old order. The newly seated legislatures moved to restore slavery in all but name. They enacted laws—known as **Black Codes**—designed to drive the former slaves back to the plantations and deny them elementary civil rights. The new governments had mostly been formed by southern Unionists, but when it came to racial attitudes, little distinguished these loyalists from the Confederates. The latter, moreover, soon filtered back into the corridors of power. Despite his hard words against them, Johnson forgave ex-Confederate leaders easily, so long as he got the satisfaction of humbling them in their appeals to him for pardons.

His perceived indulgence of their efforts to restore white supremacy emboldened the ex-Confederates. They packed the delegations to the new Congress with

old comrades—nine members of the Confederate Congress, seven former officials of Confederate state governments, four generals and four colonels, and even the vice president of the Confederacy, Alexander Stephens. This was the last straw for the Republicans.

Under the Constitution Congress is "the judge of the Elections, Returns and Qualifications of its own Members" (Article 1, Section 5; see Documents, p. D-8). With this power the Republican majorities in both houses refused to admit the southern delegations when Congress convened in early December 1865, effectively blocking Johnson's Reconstruction program. Seeking to formulate the terms on which the South would be readmitted to Congress, the Republicans established a House-Senate committee—the Joint Committee on Reconstruction—and began public hearings on conditions in the South.

In response the southern states backed away from the most flagrant of the Black Codes, replacing them with regulatory ordinances silent on race yet not different in effect; in practice they applied to blacks, not to whites. On top of that a wave of violence erupted across the South against the freedmen. In Tennessee a Nashville paper reported that white gangs "are riding about whipping, maiming and killing all negroes who do not obey the orders of their former masters, just as if slavery existed." Listening to the testimony of officials, observers, and victims, Republicans concluded that the South had embarked on a concerted effort to circumvent the Thirteenth Amendment. The only possible response was for the federal government to intervene.

Back in March 1865, before adjourning, the 38th Congress had established the Freedmen's Bureau to provide emergency aid to ex-slaves during the transition from war to peace. Now in early 1866, under the leadership of the moderate Republican Senator Lyman Trumbull, Congress voted to extend the Freedmen's Bureau's life, gave it direct funding for the first time, and authorized its agents to investigate mistreatment of blacks.

More extraordinary was Trumbull's proposal for a Civil Rights Act declaring all persons born in the United States to be citizens and granting them—without regard to race—equal rights of contract, access to the courts, and protection of person and property. Trumbull's bill nullified all state laws depriving citizens of these rights, authorized U.S. attorneys to bring enforcement suits in the federal courts, and provided for fines and imprisonment for violators, including public officials. Provoked by an unrepentant South, Republicans of the most moderate persuasion demanded that the federal government assume responsibility for securing the basic civil rights of the freedmen.

Acting on Freedom

While Congress debated, emancipated slaves acted on their own idea of freedom. News that their bondage was

David Macrae

The Devastated South

In this excerpt from The Americans at Home *(1870), an account of his tour of the United States, the Scottish clergyman David Macrae describes the war-stricken South as he found it in 1867–1868.*

I was struck with a remark made by a Southern gentleman in answer to the assertion that Jefferson Davis [the president of the Confederacy] had culpably continued the war for six months after all hope had been abandoned.

"Sir," he said, "Mr. Davis knew the temper of the South as well as any man in it. He knew if there was to be anything worth calling peace, the South must win; or, if she couldn't win, she wanted to be whipped—well whipped—thoroughly whipped."

The further south I went, the oftener these remarks came back upon me. Evidence was everywhere that the South had maintained the desperate conflict until she was utterly exhausted.... Almost every man I met at the South, especially in North Carolina, Georgia, and Virginia, seemed to have been in the army; and it was painful to find many who had returned were mutilated, maimed, or broken in health by exposure. When I remarked this to a young Confederate officer in North Carolina, and said I was glad to see that he had escaped unhurt, he said, "Wait till we get to the office, sir, and I will tell you more about that." When we got there, he pulled up one leg of his trousers, and showed me that he had an iron rod there to strengthen his limb, and enable him to walk without limping, half of his foot being off. He showed me on the other leg a deep scar made by a fragment of a shell; and these were two of but seven wounds which had left their marks upon his body. When he heard me speak of relics, he said, "Try to find a North Carolina gentleman without a Yankee mark on him."

Nearly three years had passed when I travelled through the country, and yet we have seen what traces the war had left in such cities as Richmond, Petersburg, and Columbia. The same spectacle met me at Charleston. Churches and houses had been battered down by heavy shot and shell hurled into the city from Federal batteries at a distance of five miles. Even the valley of desolation made by a great fire in 1861, through the very heart of the city, remained unbuilt. There, after the lapse of seven years, stood the blackened ruins of streets and houses waiting for the coming of a better day.... Over the country districts the prostration was equally marked. Along the track of Sherman's army especially, the devastation was fearful—farms laid waste, fences burned, bridges destroyed, houses left in ruins, plantations in many cases turned into wilderness again.

The people had shared in the general wreck, and looked poverty-stricken, careworn, and dejected. Ladies who before the war had lived in affluence, with black servants round them to attend to their every wish, were boarding together in half-furnished houses, cooking their own food and washing their own linen, some of them, I was told, so utterly destitute that they did not know when they finished one meal where they were to find the next.... Men who had held commanding positions during the war had fallen out of sight and were filling humble situations—struggling, many of them, to earn a bare subsistence.... I remember dining with three cultured Southern gentlemen, one a general, the other, I think, a captain, and the third a lieutenant. They were all living together in a plain little wooden house, such as they would formerly have provided for their servants. Two of them were engaged in a railway office, the third was seeking a situation, frequently, in his vain search, passing the large blinded house where he had lived in luxurious ease before the war.

Source: Allan Nevins, ed., *America through British Eyes* (Gloucester, MA: Peter Smith, 1968), 345–47.

over left them exultant and hopeful (see American Voices, "Jourdon Anderson: Relishing Freedom," p. 434). Freedom meant many things—the end of punishment by the lash, the ability to move around, the reuniting of families, the opportunity to begin schools, to form churches and social clubs, and, not least, to engage in politics. Across the South blacks held mass meetings, paraded, and formed organizations. Topmost among

their demands were equality before the law and the right to vote—"an essential and inseparable element of self-government."

Struggling for Economic Independence. First of all, however, came ownership of land, which emancipated blacks believed was the basis for true freedom. During the Civil War they had acted on this assumption whenever

Union armies drew near. In the chaotic final months of the war, as plantation owners fled Union forces, freedmen seized control of land where they could. Most famously, General William T. Sherman reserved large coastal tracts in Georgia and South Carolina—the Sea Islands and abandoned plantations within thirty miles of the coast—for liberated slaves and settled them on forty-acre plots. Sherman only wanted to be rid of the responsibility for the refugees as his army drove across the lower South. But the freedmen assumed that Sherman's order meant that the land would be theirs. When the war ended, resettlement became the responsibility of the Freedmen's Bureau, which was charged with feeding and clothing war refugees, distributing confiscated land to "loyal refugees and freedmen," and regulating labor contracts between freedmen and planters.

Encouraged by the Freedmen's Bureau, blacks across the South occupied confiscated or abandoned land. Many families stayed on their old plantations, awaiting redistribution of the land to them after the war. When the South Carolina planter Thomas Pinckney returned home, his freed slaves told him: "We ain't going nowhere. We are going to work right here on the land where we were born and what belongs to us."

Johnson's amnesty plan, entitling pardoned Confederates to recover property seized during the war, shattered these hopes. In October 1865 Johnson ordered General Oliver O. Howard, head of the Freedmen's Bureau, to tell Sea Islands' blacks that the land they occupied would have to be restored to the white owners. When Howard reluctantly obeyed, the dispossessed farmers protested: "Why do you take away our lands? You take them from us who have always been true, always true to the Government! You give them to our all-time enemies! That is not right!"

In the Sea Islands and elsewhere, former slaves resisted efforts to remove them. Led by black veterans of the Union army, they fought pitched battles with plantation owners and bands of ex-Confederate soldiers. Landowners struck back hard. One black veteran wrote from Maryland: "The returned colard Solgers are in Many cases beten, and their guns taken from them, we darcent walk out of an evening. . . . They beat us badly and Sumtime Shoot us." Often aided by federal troops, the local whites generally prevailed in this land war.

Resisting Wage Labor. As planters prepared for a new growing season, a great battle took shape over the labor system that would replace slavery. Convinced that blacks needed supervision, planters wanted to retain the gang labor of the past, only now with wages replacing the food, clothing, and shelter their slaves had once received. The Freedmen's Bureau, although watchful against exploitative labor contracts, sided with the planters. The main thing, its designers had always felt, was that the bureau not encourage dependency "in the guise of guardianship." Rely upon your "own efforts and

exertions," an agent told a large crowd of freedmen in North Carolina, "make contracts with the planters" and "respect the rights of property."

This was advice given with little regard for the world in which those North Carolina freedmen lived. It was not only their unequal bargaining power they worried about, or even that their ex-masters' real desire was to re-enslave them under the guise of "free" contracts. In their eyes the condition of wage labor was itself, by definition, debasing. The rural South was not like the North, where working for wages was the norm and qualified a man as independent. In the South, selling one's labor to another—and in particular, selling one's labor to work another's land—implied not freedom, but dependency. To be a "freeman"—a fully empowered citizen—meant heading a household, owning some property, conducting one's own affairs.

So the issue of wage labor cut to the very core of the former slaves' struggle for freedom. Nothing had been more horrifying than that as slaves their persons had been the property of others. When a master cast his eye on a slave woman, her husband had no recourse, nor, for that matter, was rape of a slave a crime. In a famous oration celebrating the anniversary of emancipation, the Reverend Henry M. Turner spoke bitterly of the time when his people had "no security for domestic happiness," when "our wives were sold and husbands bought, children were begotten and enslaved by their fathers," and "we therefore were polygamists by virtue of our condition." That was why formalizing marriage was so urgent a matter after emancipation and why, when hard-pressed planters demanded that freedwomen go back into the fields, they resisted so resolutely. If the ex-slaves were to be free as white folk, then their wives could not, any more than white wives, labor for others. "I seen on some plantations," one freedman recounted, "where the white men would . . . tell colored men that their wives and children could not live on their places unless they work in the fields. The colored men [answered that] whenever they wanted their wives to work they would tell them themselves; and if he could not rule his own domestic affairs on that place he would leave it and go someplace else."

The reader will see the irony in this definition of freedom: it assumed the wife's subordinate role and designated her labor the husband's property. But if that was the price of freedom, freedwomen were prepared to pay it. Far better to take a chance with their own men than with their ex-masters.

Many freedpeople voted with their feet, abandoning their old plantations and seeking better lives and more freedom in the towns and cities of the South. Those who remained in the countryside refused to work the cotton fields under the hated gang-labor system or negotiated tenaciously over the terms of their labor contracts. Whatever system of labor finally might emerge, it was clear that the freedpeople would never settle for anything resembling the old plantation system.

Jourdon Anderson

Relishing Freedom

Folklorists have recorded the sly ways that slaves found, even in bondage, for "puttin' down" their masters. But only in freedom—and beyond reach in a northern state at that—could Anderson's sarcasm be expressed so openly, with the jest that his family might consider returning if they first received the wages due them, calculated to the dollar, for all those years in slavery. Yet intermixed with the bitterness, and the pride in personal dignity, is an admission of affection for "the dear old home" that helps explain why, even after the horror of bondage, ex-slaves often chose to remain in familiar surroundings and even work for their former masters. Anderson's letter, although probably written or edited by a white friend in Dayton, surely is faithful to what the ex-slave wanted to say.

Dayton, Ohio. August 7, 1865.
To My Old Master, Colonel P. H. Anderson, Big Spring, Tennessee.
Sir:

I got your letter, and was glad to find that you had not forgotten Jourdon, and that you wanted me to come back and live with you again, promising to do better for me than anybody else can. I have often felt uneasy about you. I thought the Yankees would have hung you long before this, for harboring Rebs they found at your house. I suppose they never heard about your going to Colonel Martin's to kill the Union soldier that was left by his company in their stable. Although you shot at me twice before I left you, I did not want to hear of your being hurt, and am glad you are still living. It would do me good to go back to the dear old home again, and see Miss Mary and Miss Martha and Allen, Esther, Green, and Lee. Give my love to them all, and tell them I hope we will meet in the better world, if not in this. I would have gone back to see you all when I was working in the Nashville Hospital, but one of the neighbors told me that Henry intended to shoot me if he ever got a chance.

I want to know particularly what the good chance is you propose to give me. I am doing tolerably well here.

I get twenty-five dollars a month, with victuals and clothing; have a comfortable home for Mandy,—the folks call her Mrs. Anderson,—and the children—Milly, Jane, and Grundy—go to school and are learning well. The teacher says Grundy has a head for a preacher. They go to Sunday school, and Mandy and me attend church regularly. We are kindly treated. Sometimes we overhear others saying, "Them colored people were slaves" down in Tennessee. The children feel hurt when they hear such remarks; but I tell them it was no disgrace in Tennessee to belong to Colonel Anderson. Many darkeys would have been proud, as I used to be, to call you master. Now if you will write and say what wages you will give me, I will be better able to decide whether it would be to my advantage to move back again. . . .

Mandy says she would be afraid to go back without some proof that you were disposed to treat us justly and kindly; and we have concluded to test your sincerity by asking you to send us our wages for the time we served you. This will make us forget and forgive old scores, and rely on your justice and friendship in the future. I served you faithfully for thirty-two years, and Mandy twenty years. At twenty-five dollars a month for me and two dollars a week for Mandy, our earnings would amount to eleven thousand six hundred and eighty dollars. Add to this the interest for the time our wages have been kept back, and deduct what you paid for our clothing, and three doctor's visits to me, and pulling a tooth for Mandy, and the balance will show what we are in justice entitled to. . . .

In answering this letter, please state if there would be any safety for my Milly and Jane, who are now grown up, and both good-looking girls. You know how it was with poor Matilda and Catherine. I would rather stay here and starve—and die, if it come to that—than have my girls brought to shame by the violence and wickedness of their young masters. You will also please state if there has been any schools opened for the colored children in your neighborhood. The great desire of my life now is to give my children an education, and have them form virtuous habits.

Say howdy to George Carter, and thank him for taking the pistol from you when you were shooting at me.

From your old servant,
Jourdon Anderson

Source: Stanley I. Kutler, ed., *Looking for America*, 2nd ed. (New York: W. W. Norton, 1979), 2: 4–6.

Wage Labor of Former Slaves
This photograph, taken in South Carolina shortly after the Civil War, shows former slaves leaving the cotton fields. Ex-slaves were organized into work crews probably not that different from earlier slave gangs, although they now worked for wages and their plug-hatted boss bore little resemblance to the slave drivers of the past.
New-York Historical Society.

The efforts of former slaves to control their own lives challenged deeply entrenched white attitudes. "The destiny of the black race," asserted one Texan, could be summarized "in one sentence—subordination to the white race." Southern whites, a Freedmen's Bureau official observed, could not "conceive of the negro having any rights at all." And when freedmen resisted, white retribution was swift and often terrible. In Pine Bluff, Arkansas, "after some kind of dispute with some freedmen," whites set fire to their cabins and hanged twenty-four of the inhabitants—men, women, and children. The toll of murdered and beaten blacks mounted into untold thousands. The governments established under Johnson's plan only put the stamp of legality on the pervasive efforts to enforce white supremacy. Blacks "would be *just as well* off with no law at all or no Government," concluded a Freedmen's Bureau agent, as with the justice they got under the restored white rule.

In this unequal struggle, blacks turned to Washington. "We stood by the government when it wanted help," a black Mississippian wrote President Johnson. "Now . . . will it stand by us?"

Congress versus President

Andrew Johnson was, alas, not the man to ask. In February 1866 he vetoed the Freedmen's Bureau bill. The bureau, Johnson charged, was an "immense patronage," showering benefits on blacks never granted to "our own people." Republicans could not muster enough votes to override his veto. A month later, further rebuffing his critics, Johnson vetoed Trumbull's civil rights bill, arguing that federal protection of black civil rights constituted "a stride toward centralization." His racism, hitherto muted, now blazed forth. In his view granting blacks the privileges of citizenship was discriminatory, operating "in favor of the colored and against the white race," and threatening all manner of evil consequences, including racial mixing.

Galvanized by Johnson's attack on the civil rights bill, the Republicans went into action. In early April they got the necessary two-thirds majorities in both houses to override a presidential veto. The enactment of the civil rights bill into law was a truly historic event, the first time Congress had prevailed over a presidential veto on a major piece of legislation. Republican resolve was reinforced by news of mounting violence in the South, culminating in three days of rioting in Memphis. Forty-six blacks and two whites were left dead, and hundreds of black homes, churches, and schools were looted and burned. In July an angry Congress renewed the Freedmen's Bureau over a second Johnson veto.

The Fourteenth Amendment. Eager to consolidate their gains, Republicans moved to enshrine black civil rights in an amendment to the Constitution. The heart of the Fourteenth Amendment was Section 1, which declared that "all persons born or naturalized in the United States" were citizens. No state could abridge "the privileges or immunities of citizens of the United States," deprive "any person of life, liberty, or property, without due process of law," or deny anyone "the equal protection of the laws." These phrases were vague, intentionally so, but they established the constitutionality of the Civil Rights Act and, more important, the basis on which the courts and Congress could establish an enforceable standard of equality before the law in the states.

For the moment, however, the Fourteenth Amendment was most important for its impact on national politics. With the 1866 Congressional elections approaching, Johnson somehow figured he had a winning issue in the Fourteenth Amendment. He urged the states not to ratify it. Months earlier, Johnson had begun to maneuver politically against the Republicans, aiming to build a coalition of white Southerners, northern Democrats, and conservative Republicans under the banner of National Union. Any hope of creating a new party, however, was shattered by Johnson's intemperate behavior and by escalating violence in the South. A dissension-ridden National Union convention in July ended inconclusively, and Johnson's campaign against the Fourteenth Amendment became, effectively, a campaign for the Democratic Party.

Republicans responded furiously, unveiling a practice that would become known as "waving the bloody shirt." The Democrats were traitors, charged Indiana governor Oliver Morton, and their party was "a common sewer and loathesome recepticle, into which is emptied every element of treason North and South, every element of inhumanity and barbarism which has dishonored this age." In late August Johnson embarked on a disastrous "swing around the circle"—a railroad tour from Washington to Chicago and St. Louis and back. It was unprecedented for a president to campaign personally, and Johnson made matters worse by engaging in shouting matches with hecklers and insulting the hostile crowds.

The 1866 Congressional elections inflicted a humiliating defeat on Johnson. The Republicans won a three-to-one majority in Congress, so that, to begin with, the Republicans considered themselves "masters of the situation," free to proceed "entirely regardless of [Johnson's] opinions or wishes." As a referendum on the Fourteenth Amendment, moreover, the election registered overwhelming popular support for the civil rights of the former slaves. The Republican Party emerged with a new sense of unity—a unity coalescing not at the center, but on the left, around the unbending program of the Radical minority.

Radical Republicans. The Radicals represented the abolitionist strain within the Republican Party. Most of them hailed from New England or from the area of the upper Midwest settled by New Englanders. In the Senate they were led by Charles Sumner of Massachusetts; in the House, by Thaddeus Stevens from Pennsylvania. For them Reconstruction was never primarily about restoring the Union but about remaking southern society. "The foundations of their institutions . . . must be broken up and relaid," declared Stevens, "or all our blood and treasure will have been spent in vain."

Only a handful went as far as Stevens in demanding that the plantations be treated as "forfeited estates of the enemy" and broken up into small farms for the former slaves. About the need to guarantee the freedmen's civil and political rights, however, there was agreement. In this endeavor Radicals had no qualms about expanding the powers of the national government. "The power of the great landed aristocracy in those regions, if unrestrained by power from without, would inevitably reassert itself," warned Congressman George Julian. Radicals were aggressively partisan. They regarded the Republican Party as the instrument of the Lord and black votes as the means by which the party would bring regeneration of the South.

At first, in the months after Appomattox, few but the Radicals themselves imagined that so extreme a program had any chance of enactment. Black suffrage especially seemed beyond reach, since the northern states (excepting in New England) denied blacks the vote at this time. And yet as fury mounted against the intransigent South, Republicans became ever more radicalized until, in the wake of the smashing victory of 1866, they embraced the Radicals' vision of a reconstructed South.

Radical Reconstruction

Afterward, thoughtful Southerners admitted that the South had brought radical Reconstruction on itself. "We had, in 1865, a white man's government in Alabama," remarked the man who had been Johnson's provisional governor, "but we lost it." The state's "great blunder" was not to "have at once taken the negro right under the protection of the laws." Remarkably, the South remained defiant even after the 1866 elections. Every state legislature but Tennessee's rejected the Fourteenth Amendment, mostly by virtual acclamation. It was as if they could not imagine that governments installed under the presidential imprimatur and fully functioning might be swept away. But that, in fact, is just what the Republicans intended to do.

Congress Takes Command

The Reconstruction Act of 1867, enacted in March by the Republican Congress, organized the South as a conquered land, dividing it into five military districts, each under the command of a Union general (Map 15.1). The price for reentering the Union was granting the vote to the freedmen and disfranchising those of the South's prewar leadership class who had participated in the rebellion. Each military commander was ordered to register

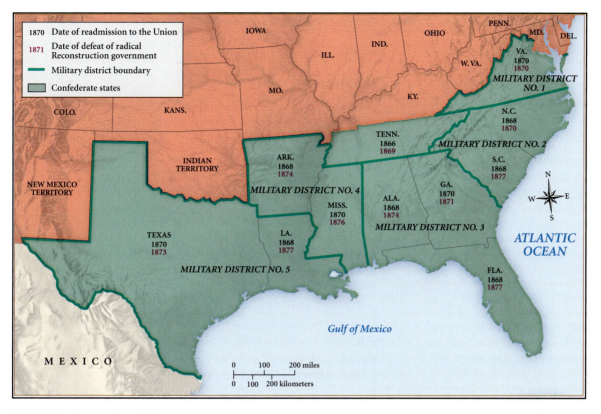

MAP 15.1 Reconstruction

The federal government organized the Confederate states into five military districts during radical Reconstruction. For each state the first date indicates when that state was readmitted to the Union; the second date shows when Radical Republicans lost control of the state government. All the ex-Confederate states rejoined the Union from 1868 to 1870, but the periods of radical rule varied widely. Republicans lasted only a few months in Virginia; they held on until the end of Reconstruction in Louisiana, Florida, and South Carolina.

all eligible adult males (black as well as white), supervise the election of state conventions, and make certain that the new constitutions contained guarantees of black suffrage. Congress would readmit a state to the Union if its voters ratified the constitution, if that document proved acceptable to Congress, and if the new state legislature approved the Fourteenth Amendment (thus insuring the needed ratification by three-fourths of the states). Johnson vetoed the Reconstruction Act, but Congress overrode the veto (Table 15.1).

Impeachment. Republicans also restricted President Johnson's room for maneuver. The Tenure of Office Act, a companion to the Reconstruction Act, required Senate consent for the removal of any official whose appointment had required Senate confirmation. Congress chiefly wanted to protect Secretary of War Edwin M. Stanton, a Lincoln holdover and the only member of Johnson's cabinet who favored radical Reconstruction. In his position Stanton could do much to frustrate Johnson's anticipated efforts to undermine Reconstruction. The law also required the president to issue all orders to the army through its commanding general, Ulysses S. Grant. In effect

Congress was attempting to reconstruct the presidency as well as the South.

Seemingly defeated, Johnson appointed generals recommended by Stanton and Grant to command the five military districts in the South. But he was just biding his time. In August 1867, after Congress had adjourned, he "suspended" Stanton and replaced him with Grant, believing that the general would act like a good soldier and follow orders. Next Johnson replaced four of the commanding generals. Johnson, however, had misjudged Grant, who publicly objected to the president's machinations. When the Senate reconvened in the fall, it overruled Stanton's suspension. Grant, now an open enemy of Johnson's, resigned so that Stanton could resume his office.

On February 21, 1868, Johnson formally dismissed Stanton. The feisty secretary of war, however, barricaded the door of his office and refused to admit the replacement Johnson had appointed. Three days later, House Republicans introduced articles of **impeachment** against the president, employing the power granted the House of Representatives by the Constitution to charge high federal officials with "Treason, Bribery, or other high Crimes and Misdemeanors." The House overwhelmingly approved

TABLE 15.1 Primary Reconstruction Laws and Constitutional Amendments	
Law (Date of Congressional Passage)	Key Provisions
Thirteenth Amendment (January 1865*)	Prohibited slavery
Civil Rights Act of 1866 (April 1866)	Defined citizenship rights of freedmen Authorized federal authorities to bring suit against those who violated those rights
Fourteenth Amendment (June 1866†)	Established national citizenship for persons born or naturalized in the United States Prohibited the states from depriving citizens of their civil rights or equal protection under the law Reduced state representation in House of Representatives by the percentage of adult male citizens denied the vote
Reconstruction Act of 1867 (March 1867‡)	Divided the South into five military districts, each under the command of a Union general Established requirements for readmission of ex-Confederate states to the Union
Tenure of Office Act (March 1867)	Required Senate consent for removal of any federal official whose appointment had required Senate confirmation
Fifteenth Amendment (February 1869)	Forbade states to deny citizens the right to vote on the grounds of race, color, or "previous condition of servitude"
Ku Klux Klan Act (April 1871)	Authorized the president to use federal prosecutions and military force to suppress conspiracies to deprive citizens of the right to vote and enjoy the equal protection of the law

*Ratified by three-fourths of all states in December 1868.
†Ratified by three-fourths of all states in July 1868.
‡Ratified by three-fourths of all states in March 1870.

eleven counts of presidential misconduct, nine of which dealt with violations of the Tenure of Office Act.

The case went to the Senate, which acts as the court in impeachment cases, with Chief Justice Salmon P. Chase presiding. After an eleven-week trial, thirty-five senators on May 15 voted for conviction, one vote short of the two-thirds majority required. Seven moderate Republicans broke ranks, voting for acquittal along with twelve Democrats. The dissenting Republicans felt that the Tenure of Office Act was of dubious validity (in fact, the Supreme Court subsequently declared it unconstitutional), that the motives of the impeachers were really political, and that removing a president for defying Congress was too extreme and too threatening to constitutional checks and balances, even for the sake of punishing Johnson.

Despite his acquittal, however, Johnson had been defanged. For the remainder of his term he was powerless to alter the course of Reconstruction.

The Election of 1868. The impeachment controversy made Grant, already the North's war hero, a Republican hero as well, and he easily won the party's presidential nomination in 1868. In the fall campaign he supported radical Reconstruction, but he also urged reconciliation between the sections. His Democratic opponent Horatio Seymour, a former governor of New York, almost declined the nomination because he doubted that the Democrats could overcome the stigma of their ties with the disloyal South.

As Seymour feared, the Republicans "waved the bloody shirt," stirring up old wartime emotions against the Democrats to great effect. Grant won about the same share of the northern vote (55 percent) that Lincoln had won in 1864 and received 214 of 294 electoral votes. The Republicans also retained two-thirds majorities in both houses of Congress.

The Fifteenth Amendment. In the wake of their smashing victory, the Republicans quickly produced the last major piece of Reconstruction legislation—the Fifteenth Amendment, which forbade either the federal government or the states from denying citizens the right to vote on the basis of race, color, or "previous condition of servitude" (see Documents, p. D-17). The amendment left room for **poll taxes** and property or literacy tests that might be used to discourage blacks from voting, which

Resistance in the South

This engraving, entitled "If He Is a Union Man or Freedman: Verdict, Hang the D———— Yankee and Nigger," appeared in Harper's Weekly *on March 23, 1867, just as the Reconstruction Act was being adopted. Thomas Nast's cartoon encapsulated the outrage at the South's murderous intransigence that led even moderate Republicans to support radical Reconstruction.* Library of Congress.

> For more help analyzing this image, see the ONLINE STUDY GUIDE at bedfordstmartins.com/henretta.

was necessary because its authors did not want to alienate northern states that already relied on such qualifications to keep immigrants and the "unworthy" poor from the polls. A California senator warned that in his state, with its rabidly anti-Chinese sentiment (see Chapter 16), any restriction on that power would "kill our party as dead as a stone."

Despite grumbling by Radical Republicans, the amendment passed without modification in February 1869. Congress required the states still under federal control—Virginia, Mississippi, Texas, and Georgia—to ratify it as a condition for being readmitted to the Union. A year later the Fifteenth Amendment became part of the Constitution.

Woman Suffrage Denied. If the Fifteenth Amendment troubled some proponents of black suffrage, this was nothing compared to the outrage felt by women's rights advocates. They had fought the good fight for the abolition

of slavery for so many years, only to be abandoned when the chance finally came to get the vote for women. All it would have taken was one more word in the Fifteenth Amendment so that the protected categories for voting would have read "race, color, *sex*, or previous condition." Leading suffragists such as Susan B. Anthony and Elizabeth Cady Stanton did not want to hear from Radical Republicans that this was "the Negro's hour" and that women would have to wait for another day. How could suffrage be granted to ex-slaves, Stanton demanded to know, but not to them?

In her despair Stanton lashed out in ugly racist terms against "Patrick and Sambo and Hans and Ung Tung," ignorant as they were about the Declaration of Independence, yet entitled to vote, while the best and most accomplished of American women remained voteless. In 1869 the annual meeting of the Equal Rights Association, the champion of both black and woman suffrage, broke up in acrimony, and Stanton and Anthony came out against the Fifteenth Amendment.

At this searing moment a schism opened in the ranks of the women's movement. The majority, led by Lucy Stone and Julia Ward Howe, reconciled themselves to disappointment and accepted the priority of black suffrage. Organized into the American Woman Suffrage Association, these moderates remained allied to the Republican Party, in hopes that once Reconstruction had been settled it would be time for the woman's vote. The Stanton-Anthony group, however, struck out in a new direction. The embittered Stanton declared that woman "must not put her trust in man" in fighting for her rights. The new organization she headed, the New York–based National Woman Suffrage Association, accepted only women, focused exclusively on women's rights, and resolutely took up the battle for a federal woman suffrage amendment.

The fracturing of the women's movement obscured the common ground the two sides shared. Both now realized that a constituency had to be built beyond the narrow confines of abolitionism and evangelical reform. Both elevated suffrage into the preeminent women's issue. And both were energized by a shared anger not evident in earlier times. "If I were to give vent to all my pent-up wrath concerning the subordination of woman," Lydia Maria Child wrote the Republican warhorse Charles Sumner in 1872, "I might frighten *you*. . . . Suffice it, therefore, to say, either the theory of our government is *false*, or women have a right to vote." If radical Reconstruction seemed a barren time for women's rights, in fact it had planted the seeds of the modern feminist movement.

Republican Rule in the South

Between 1868 and 1871 all the southern states met the congressional stipulations and rejoined the Union. Protected by federal troops and encouraged by northern party leaders, state Republican organizations took hold

A Woman Suffrage Quilt

Homemade quilts provided funds and a means of persuasion for the temperance and antislavery movements. Suffragists, however, regarded quilts and needlework as symbols of the domestic subjugation of women, so woman suffrage quilts, such as this one (c. 1860–1880) depicting a women's rights lecture, were rare.

Collections of Mrs. Nancy W. Livingston and Mrs. Elizabeth Livingston Jaeger / Photo courtesy, Los Angeles County Museum of Art.

across the South and won control of the newly established Reconstruction governments. These Republican administrations remained in power for periods ranging from a few months in Virginia to nine years in South Carolina, Louisiana, and Florida (see Map 15.1). Their core support came from African Americans, who constituted a majority of registered voters in Alabama, Florida, South Carolina, and Mississippi.

Carpetbaggers and Scalawags. Southern white Republicans faced the scorn of Democratic ex-Confederates, who mocked them as **scalawags**—an ancient Scots-Irish term for runty, worthless animals. Whites who had come from the North they denounced as **carpetbaggers**—self-seeking interlopers who carried all their property in cheap suitcases called carpetbags. Such labels glossed over the actual diversity of these white Republicans.

Some carpetbaggers, while motivated by personal profit, also brought capital and skills. Others were Union army veterans taken with the South—its climate, people, and economic opportunities. And interspersed with the self-seekers were many idealists anxious to advance the cause of emancipation.

The scalawags were even more diverse. Some were former slave owners, ex-Whigs and even ex-Democrats, drawn to Republicanism as the best way to attract northern capital to southern railroads, mines, and factories. In southwest Texas the large population of Germans was strongly Republican. They sent to Congress Edward Degener, an immigrant San Antonio grocer whom Confederate authorities had imprisoned and whose sons had been executed for treason. But most numerous among the scalawags were yeomen farmers from the backcountry districts who wanted to rid the South of its slaveholding aristocracy. Scalawags had generally fought against, or at least refused to support, the Confederacy; they believed that slavery had victimized whites as well as blacks. "Now is the time," a Georgia scalawag wrote, "for every man to come out and speak his principles publickly [*sic*] and vote for liberty as we have been in bondage long enough."

African American Leadership. The Democrats' scorn for black political leaders as ignorant field hands was just as false as stereotypes about white Republicans. The first African American leaders in the South came from an elite of blacks freed before the Civil War. They were joined by northern blacks who moved south when radical Reconstruction offered the prospect of meaningful freedom. Like their white allies, many were Union army veterans. Some had participated in the antislavery crusade; a number were employed by the Freedmen's Bureau or northern missionary societies. Others had escaped from slavery and were returning home. One of these was Blanche K. Bruce, who had been tutored on the Virginia plantation of his white father. During the war Bruce escaped and established a school for ex-slaves in Missouri. In 1869 he moved to Mississippi, became active in politics, and in 1874 became Mississippi's second black U.S. senator.

As the reconstructed Republican governments of 1867 began to function, this diverse group of ministers, artisans, shopkeepers, and former soldiers reached out to the freedmen. African American speakers, some financed by the Republican Party, fanned out into the old plantation districts and recruited ex-slaves for political roles. Still, few of the new leaders were field hands; most had been preachers or artisans. The literacy of one ex-slave, Thomas Allen, who was a Baptist minister and shoemaker, helped him win election to the Georgia legislature. "In my county," he recalled, "the colored people came to me for instructions, and I gave them the best instructions I could. I took the *New York Tribune* and other papers, and in that way I found out a great deal, and I told them whatever I thought was right."

Although never proportionate to their numbers in the population, black officeholders were prominent across the South. In South Carolina African Americans constituted a majority in the lower house of the legislature in 1868. Three were elected to Congress, another joined the state supreme court. Over the entire course of Reconstruction, twenty African Americans served in

THE FIRST COLORED SENATOR AND REPRESENTATIVES.
In the 41st and 42nd Congress of the United States.

African American Congressional Delegation, 1872

This Currier and Ives lithograph celebrates one of the notable achievements of radical Reconstruction—the representation that ex-slaves won, however briefly, in the U.S. Congress. Hiram Revels of Mississippi, the Senate's first African American member, is seated at the extreme left.
Granger Collection.

state administrations as governor, lieutenant governor, secretary of state, treasurer, or superintendent of education, more than six hundred served as state legislators, and sixteen as congressmen.

The Radical Program. The Republicans who took office had ambitious plans for a reconstructed South. They wanted to end its dependence on cotton agriculture and build an entrepreneurial economy like the North's. They fell far short of achieving this vision but accomplished more than their critics gave them credit for.

The Republicans modernized state constitutions, eliminated property qualification for the vote, and made more offices elective. They attended especially to the personal freedom of the ex-slaves, sweeping out the shadow Black Codes that coerced the freedmen and limited their mobility. Women also benefited from the Republican defense of personal liberty. Nearly all the new constitutions expanded the rights of married women, enabling them to hold property and earnings independent of their husbands—"a wonderful reform," a Georgia woman wrote, for "the cause of Women's Rights." Republican social programs called for hospitals, more humane penitentiaries, and asylums for orphans and the insane. Republican governments built roads in areas where roads had never existed. They poured money into rebuilding the region's railroad network. And they did all this without federal financing.

To pay for their ambitious programs the Republican governments copied taxes that Jacksonian reformers had earlier introduced in the North—in particular, gen-

eral property taxes on both real estate and personal wealth. The goal was to make planters pay their fair share and to broaden the tax base. In many plantation counties, former slaves served as tax assessors and collectors, administering the taxation of their one-time owners.

Higher tax revenues never managed to overtake the burgeoning obligations assumed by the Reconstruction governments. State debts mounted rapidly and, as interest payments on bonds fell into arrears, public credit collapsed. On top of that, much of the spending was wasted or ended in the pockets of state officials. Corruption was endemic to American politics, present in the southern states before the Republicans came on the scene, and rampant everywhere in this era, not least in the Grant administration itself. Still, in the free-spending atmosphere of the southern Republican regimes, corruption was especially luxuriant and damaging to the cause of radical Reconstruction.

Nothing, however, could dim the achievement in public education. Here the South had lagged woefully; only Tennessee had a system of public schooling before the Civil War. Republican state governments vowed to make up for lost time, viewing education as the foundation for a democratic order. African Americans of all ages rushed to attend the newly established schools, even when they had to pay tuition. An elderly man in Mississippi explained his hunger for education: "Ole missus used to read the good book [the Bible] to us . . . on Sunday evenin's, but she mostly read dem places where it says, 'Servants obey your masters.' . . . Now we is free, there's heaps of tings in that old book we is just suffering to learn." By 1875 about half of all the children in Florida, Mississippi, and South Carolina were in school.

The Role of Black Churches. The building of schools was part of a larger effort by African Americans to fortify the institutions that had sustained their spirit during the days before emancipation. Religious belief had struck deep roots in nineteenth-century slave society. Now, in freedom, the African Americans left their old white-dominated congregations, where they had been relegated to segregated balconies and denied any voice in church governance, and built churches of their own. These churches joined together to form African American versions of the Southern Methodist and Southern Baptist denominations, including, most prominently, the National Baptist Convention and the African Methodist Episcopal Church. Everywhere the robust black churches served not only as places of worship but as schools, social centers, and political meeting halls.

Black clerics were community leaders and often, political leaders as well. As Charles H. Pearce, a Methodist minister in Florida, declared, "A man in this State cannot do his whole duty as a minister except he looks out for the political interests of his people." Calling forth the special destiny of the ex-slaves as the new "Children of Israel," black ministers provided a powerful religious underpinning for the Republican politics of their congregations.

The Quest for Land

In the meantime the freedmen were locked in a great economic struggle with their former owners. In 1869 the Republican government of South Carolina had established a land commission empowered to buy property and resell it on easy terms to the landless. In this way about 14,000 black families acquired farms. South Carolina's land distribution plan showed what was possible, but it was the exception and not the rule. Despite a lot of rhetoric, Republican regimes elsewhere did little to help the freedmen fulfill their dreams of becoming independent farmers. Federal efforts proved equally feeble. The Southern Homestead Act of 1866 offered eighty-acre grants to settlers, limited for the first year to freedmen and southern Unionists. The advantage was strictly symbolic, however, since the public land made available to homesteaders was off the beaten track in swampy, infertile parts of the Lower South. Only about a thousand families succeeded.

Sharecropping. There was no reversing President Johnson's order restoring confiscated lands to ex-Confederates. Property rights, it seemed, trumped everything else, even for most Radical Republicans. The Freedman's Bureau, which had earlier championed the land claims of the ex-slaves, now devoted itself to teaching them how to be good agricultural laborers.

While they yearned for farms of their own, most freedmen started out landless and with no option but to work for their former owners. But not, they vowed, under the conditions of slavery—no gang work, no overseers, no fines or punishments, no regulation of their private lives. In certain parts of the agricultural South wage work became the norm—for example, on the great sugar plantations of Louisiana taken over after the war by northern investors. The problem was that cotton planters lacked the money to pay wages, at least not until the crop came in, and sometimes, in lieu of a straight wage, they offered a share of the crop. As a wage,

Freedmen's School, c. 1870

This rare photograph shows the interior of one of the 3,000 freedmen's schools established across the South after the Civil War. Although many of these schools were staffed by white missionaries, a main objective of northern educators was to prepare black women to take over the classrooms. The black teacher shown here is surely one of the first. Library of Congress.

this was a bad deal for the freedmen, but if they could be paid in shares for their work, why could they not pay in shares to rent the land they worked?

This form of land tenantry was already familiar in parts of the white South, and the freedmen now seized on it for the independence it offered them. Planters resisted, believing, as one wrote, that "wages are the only successful system of controlling hands." But, in a battle of wills that broke out all across the cotton South, the planters yielded to "the inveterate prejudices of the freedmen, who desire to be masters of their own time."

Thus there sprang up the distinctive laboring system of cotton agriculture—**sharecropping**, in which the freedmen worked as renters, exchanging their labor for the use of land, house, implements, sometimes seed and fertilizer, typically turning over half to two-thirds of their crops to the landlord (Map 15.2). The sharecropping system joined laborers and the owners of land and capital in a common sharing of risks and returns. But it was a very unequal relationship, given the force of southern law and custom on the white landowner's side, and given the sharecroppers' dire economic circumstances. Starting out penniless, they had no way of making it through the first growing season without borrowing for food and supplies.

Country storekeepers stepped in. Bankrolled by their northern suppliers, they "furnished" the sharecropper and took as collateral a **lien** on the crop, effectively assuming ownership of the cropper's share and leaving him only the proceeds that remained after his debts had been paid. Once indebted at one store, the sharecropper was no longer free to shop around and became an easy target for exorbitant prices, unfair interest rates, and crooked bookkeeping. As cotton prices declined during the 1870s, more and more sharecroppers failed to settle accounts and fell into permanent debt.

And if the merchant was also the landowner, or conspired with the landowner, the debt became a pretext for forced labor, or **peonage**, although evidence now suggests that sharecroppers generally managed to pull up stakes and move on once things became hopeless. Sharecroppers always thought twice about moving, however, because part of their "capital" was being known and well reputed in their home communities. Freedmen who lacked that local standing generally found sharecropping hard going and ended up in the ranks of agricultural laborers.

In the face of so much adversity, black families struggled to better themselves. Being that it enabled *family*, struggle was, in truth, the saving advantage of sharecropping because it mobilized husbands and wives in common enterprise while shielding both from personal subordination to whites. Freedwomen were doubly blessed, neither field hands for their ex-masters, nor dependent housewives, but partners laboring side by side with their husbands. The trouble with sharecropping, one planter grumbled, was that "it makes the laborer too independent; he becomes a partner, and has to be consulted." By the end of Reconstruction, about one-quarter of sharecropping families had managed to save enough to rent with cash payments, and eventually black farmers owned about a third of the land they cultivated.

A Comparative Perspective. The battle between planters and freedmen over the land was by no means unique to the American South. Whenever slavery ended—in Haiti after the slave revolt of 1791, in the British Caribbean by abolition in 1833, in Cuba and Brazil by gradual emancipation during the 1880s—a fierce struggle ensued between planters bent on restoring a gang-labor system and ex-slaves bent on gaining economic autonomy. The outcome of this universal

Sharecroppers

This sharecropping family stands proudly in front of their new cabin and young cotton crop, which is planted nearly up to the cabin door. But the presence of the white landlord in the background casts a shadow on them, suggesting their hard struggle for economic freedom. Brown Brothers.

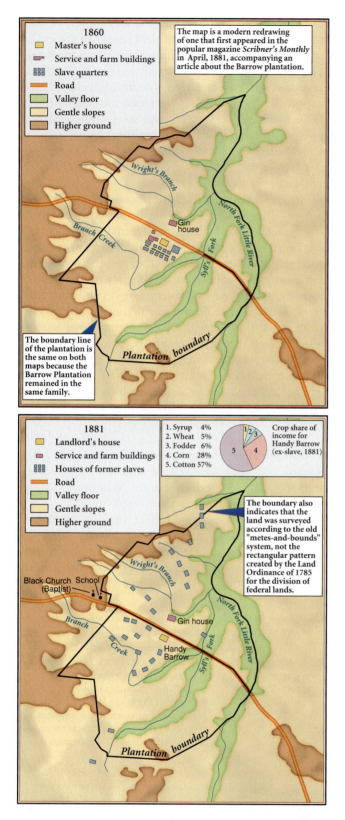

1860
- ☐ Master's house
- ▭ Service and farm buildings
- ▦ Slave quarters
- ━ Road
- ▥ Valley floor
- ▢ Gentle slopes
- ▨ Higher ground

The map is a modern redrawing of one that first appeared in the popular magazine *Scribner's Monthly* in April, 1881, accompanying an article about the Barrow plantation.

Wright's Branch

Branch Creek

Syll's Fork

North Fork Little River

Gin house

The boundary line of the plantation is the same on both maps because the Barrow Plantation remained in the same family.

Plantation boundary

1881
- ☐ Landlord's house
- ▭ Service and farm buildings
- ▦ Houses of former slaves
- ━ Road
- ▥ Valley floor
- ▢ Gentle slopes
- ▨ Higher ground

1. Syrup 4%
2. Wheat 5%
3. Fodder 6%
4. Corn 28%
5. Cotton 57%

Crop share of income for Handy Barrow (ex-slave, 1881)

The boundary also indicates that the land was surveyed according to the old "metes-and-bounds" system, not the rectangular pattern created by the Land Ordinance of 1785 for the division of federal lands.

Wright's Branch

Black Church School (Baptist)

Branch Creek

Syll's Fork

North Fork Little River

Gin house

Handy Barrow

Plantation boundary

◄ **MAP 15.2 The Barrow Plantation, 1860 and 1881**

Comparing the 1860 map of this central Georgia plantation with the 1881 map reveals the impact of sharecropping on patterns of black residence. In 1860 the slave quarters were clustered near the planter's house. The sharecroppers scattered across the plantation's 2,000 acres, building cabins on the ridges of land between the low-lying streams. The name Barrow was common among the sharecropping families, which means almost certainly that they had been slaves on the Barrow plantation who, years after emancipation, still had not moved on. For all the croppers freedom surely meant not only their individual lots and cabins, but the school and church shown on the map.

so by the importation of indentured servants from India and China. Where land could not be had, as in British Barbados or Antigua, the ex-slaves returned to plantation labor as wage workers, although often in some combination with customary rights to housing and garden plots. The cotton South fit neither of these broad patterns. The freedmen did not get the land, but neither did the planters get field hands. What both got was sharecropping.

The reason for this exceptional outcome was ultimately political. Elsewhere, emancipation almost never meant civil or political equality for the freed slaves. Even in the British islands, where substantial self-government existed, high property qualifications effectively disfranchised the ex-slaves. In the United States, however, hard on the heels of emancipation came civil rights, manhood suffrage and, for a brief era, a real measure of political power for the freedmen. Sharecropping took shape during Reconstruction, and there was no going back afterward.

For the freedmen sharecropping was not the worst choice; it certainly beat laboring for their former owners. But for southern agriculture the costs were devastating. Sharecropping committed the South inflexibly to cotton, despite soil depletion and low prices. Crop diversification declined, costing the South its self-sufficiency in grains and livestock. And with farms leased year-to-year, neither tenant nor owner had much incentive to improve the property. The crop-lien system lined merchants' pockets with unearned profits that might otherwise have gone into agricultural improvement. The result was a stagnant farm economy, blighting the South's future and condemning it to economic backwardness—a kind of retribution, in fact, for the fresh injustices visited on the people it had once enslaved.

The Undoing of Reconstruction

Ex-Confederates were blind to the benefits of radical Reconstruction. Indeed, no amount of achievement could have persuaded them that it was anything but an abomination, undertaken without their consent and intended

conflict depended on the ex-slaves' access to land. Where vacant land existed, as in British Guiana, or where plantations could be seized, as in Haiti, the ex-slaves became subsistence farmers, and insofar as the Caribbean plantation economy survived without the ex-slaves, it did

to deny them their rightful place in southern society. Led by the planters, ex-Confederates staged a massive counterrevolution—one designed to "redeem" the South and restore them to political power under the banner of the Democratic Party. But the **Redeemers** could not have succeeded on their own. They needed the complicity of the North. The undoing of Reconstruction is as much about northern acquiescence as it is about southern resistance.

Counterrevolution

Insofar as they could win at the ballot box, southern Democrats took that route. They worked hard to get ex-Confederates restored to the rolls of registered voters, they appealed to racial solidarity and southern patriotism, and they campaigned against black rule as a threat to white supremacy. But force was equally acceptable. Throughout the Deep South, especially where black voters were heavily concentrated, ex-Confederate planters and their supporters organized secret societies and waged campaigns of terrorism against blacks and their white allies.

The Ku Klux Klan. The most widespread of these groups, the Ku Klux Klan, first appeared in 1866 as a Tennessee social club but quickly became a paramilitary force under the aegis of Nathan Bedford Forrest, the Confederacy's most decorated cavalry general (see *American Lives,* "Nathan Bedford Forrest: Defender of Southern Honor," p. 446). By 1870 the Klan was operating almost everywhere in the South as a terrorist organization serving the Democratic Party. The Klan murdered and whipped Republican politicians, burned black schools and churches, and attacked party gatherings (see *American Voices,* "Harriet Hernandes: The Intimidation of Black Voters," p. 448). Such terrorist tactics enabled the Democrats to seize power in Georgia and North Carolina in 1870 and make substantial gains elsewhere. An African American politician in North Carolina wrote, "Our former masters are fast taking the reins of government."

Congress responded by passing enforcement legislation, including the Ku Klux Klan Act of 1871, authorizing President Grant to use federal prosecutions, military force, and martial law to suppress conspiracies to deprive citizens of the right to vote, hold office, serve on juries, and enjoy equal protection of the law. In South Carolina, where the Klan was most deeply entrenched, federal troops occupied nine counties, made hundreds of arrests, and drove as many as 2,000 Klansmen from the state.

The Grant administration's assault on the Klan raised the spirits of southern Republicans, but it also emphasized how dependent they were on the federal government. The potency of the Ku Klux Klan Act, a Mississippi Republican wrote, "derived alone from its

Klan Portrait

Two armed Klansmen pose in their disguises, which they donned not only to hide their identity but also to intimidate their black neighbors. Northern audiences saw a lithograph based on this photograph in Harper's Weekly *on December 28, 1868.*
Rutherford B. Hayes Presidential Center.

source" in the federal government. "No such law could be enforced by state authority, the local power being too weak." If they were to prevail over antiblack terrorism, Republicans needed what one carpetbagger described as "steady, unswerving power from without."

The Failure of Federal Enforcement. But northern Republicans were growing weary of Reconstruction and the endless bloodshed it seemed to produce. Prosecuting Klansmen was an uphill battle. U.S. attorneys usually faced all-white juries, and the Justice Department lacked the resources to handle the cases. After 1872 prosecutions began to drop off, and many Klansmen received hasty pardons; few served significant prison terms.

In a kind of self-fulfilling prophecy, the unwillingness of the Grant administration to shore up Reconstruction guaranteed that it would fail. Republican governments that were denied federal help found themselves overwhelmed by the massive resistance of

Nathan Bedford Forrest: Defender of Southern Honor

Nathan Bedford Forrest in Uniform, c. 1865
Library of Congress.

As a boy Nathan Bedford Forrest had little stake in the old plantation order of the South. His father was a blacksmith who followed the frontier to Tennessee, where Nathan, the oldest of eleven children, was born on July 13, 1821. When he was only sixteen, his father died, leaving Forrest the primary breadwinner. With hardly any schooling, the boy took charge of the family's rented Mississippi farm; he also became an adept horse-trader. At age twenty-one, when his mother remarried, Forrest left for Hernando, Mississippi, where his uncle ran a livery business.

Tall and physically imposing, Forrest was normally soft-spoken, the soul of courtesy, but he had a violent temper. When four men attacked his uncle, Forrest leapt to his defense. The uncle died from a bullet meant for his nephew, but the young Forrest had shown his mettle. Admiring his raw courage, Hernando citizens rewarded Forrest by electing him town constable. Equally implacable in love, Forrest so insistently wooed a young lady from a well-connected local family that at their third meeting she agreed to marry him.

For a hard-driving young man like Forrest, the booming cotton economy offered much opportunity. He took over his uncle's business, ran a stagecoach service, traded livestock and—in due course—slaves. In 1851 ambition took him and his family to Memphis, Tennessee, where he became a well-known slave trader. With his profits he purchased a large plantation in Mississippi. By now he had become a man of substance, a leading Memphis citizen. In the sectional crisis brewing in the late 1850s, Forrest fiercely championed southern rights and, of course, slavery.

When war came in 1861, Forrest immediately organized a Tennessee cavalry regiment. In April 1862 he distinguished himself at the bloody battle of Shiloh, where he was badly wounded. Promoted to brigadier general, he began a brilliant career as a cavalry raider, fighting mostly behind Union lines. His warrior spirit often led him into the thick of battle, oblivious to the fact that he was a general and not a trooper. That same explosiveness ignited one of the war's worst atrocities, the slaughter by his men of black troops at Fort Pillow, Tennessee, on April 12, 1864, evidently because of rumors that the Fort Pillow garrison had been harassing local whites loyal to the Confederacy.

The Fort Pillow massacre anticipated the civil strife that would consume Tennessee over the next half-decade. The Republican governor William G. Brownlow, a former Confederate prisoner, was not shy about calling his enemies to account. Elected in March 1865, he disfranchised ex-Confederates, leaving political power in the hands of a minority of Unionist whites and freed slaves. Foreshadowing the reaction to radical Reconstruction a few years later, ex-Confederates around the state concluded that they could regain power only by waging a secret campaign of terror against Brownlow's black supporters. This was the genesis, among other things, of the first den of the Ku Klux Klan in Pulaski, Tennessee, sometime in late 1865 or early 1866.

Home safe from the war, Forrest was absorbed by his own damaged fortunes. The wealth represented by his slaves had been wiped out by emancipation, and he was heavily in debt. With the aid of the Freedmen's Bureau, Forrest managed to put his former slaves back to work on his plantation. But flooding over war-damaged levies wiped out his cotton crop. In August 1866 he gave up, surrendering his plantation to his creditors, swept down, like so many others, by the war-devastated economy. In desperation, he considered leading an expedition of former Confederate comrades to seize the riches of Mexico.

A more promising avenue for Forrest's energies, however, had by now opened up. From its obscure beginnings after the war, the Ku Klux Klan proliferated wildly across Tennessee and into neighboring states. What the Klan needed was a tough, respected figure able to impose order on the Invisible Empire and prevent it from spinning out of control—none other than Nathan Bedford Forrest. At a clandestine meeting in Nashville sometime in late 1866, he accepted the job and donned the robes of Grand Wizard, the Klan's highest office. Forrest's activities are mostly unknown because he worked in secrecy, but there is no mystery about why he gravitated to the Klan. For him, the Klan was politics by other means, the vehicle by which disfranchised former Confederates like himself might strike a blow against the despised Republicans who ran Tennessee.

In many towns, including Memphis, the Klan became virtually identical to the Democratic clubs; in fact, Klan members—including Forrest—dominated the state's delegation to the Democratic national convention of 1868. On the ground the Klan unleashed a murderous campaign of terror against Republican sympathizers. Governor Brownlow responded resolutely, threatening to mobilize the state militia and root out the Klan. If Brownlow tried, answered Forrest, "there will be war, and a bloodier one than we have ever witnessed. . . . If the militia attack us, we will resist to the last; and, if necessary, I think I could raise 40,000 men in five days, ready for the field."

For many months, Tennessee endured a high state of tension. In September 1868 a new law identified membership in the Klan as a felony, and the following February martial law was declared in nine Klan-ridden counties. But it was the Republicans, not the Klan, who cracked. In March 1869 Brownlow retreated to the U.S. Senate. The Democrats were on their way back to power, and the Klan, having served its purpose, was officially disbanded in Tennessee.

Like many other Confederate heroes, Forrest might now have anticipated a comfortable life in politics. But he had too much blood on his hands. He was among the very last to be pardoned by President Johnson. His appearance at the Democratic convention in 1868 brought forth bitter Republican denunciations against "the Fort Pillow Butcher." Physical violence, moreover, still dogged his life, including the killing (he claimed self-defense) of a sharecropper on his plantation. What sealed Forrest's political fate, however, was the Ku Klux Klan. Forrest had regarded the Klan's mission in strictly political terms, its violence calibrated to the task of driving the Republicans from power. In this Forrest only reflected what conservative Southerners generally favored.

KKK Flag

Striking fear in the hearts of its enemies was a favorite tactic of Forrest's Ku Klux Klan—hence this menacing ceremonial flag from Tennessee, with its fierce dragon and mysterious Latin motto, "Because it always is, because it is everywhere, because it is abominable." Chicago Historical Society.

But he could not curb the senseless brutality against blacks done in the Klan's name. Any ruffian, he complained, could put on a white sheet and go after his neighbors. But Forrest was the Grand Wizard, and even after he resigned, his name could not be dissociated from Klan savagery. Celebrated though he might have been, when it came to supporting him for political office, Democratic leaders kept their distance.

So Forrest had to cash in his chips elsewhere, which he did as president and chief promoter of the Memphis & Selma Railroad. Beginning in 1869 he hawked bonds to communities along the proposed right of way and lobbied for state and county subsidies, expending his considerable reputation on an ambitious project linking Memphis by rail to northern Alabama and eastern Mississippi: all in vain. The unfinished Memphis & Selma collapsed after the Panic of 1873, and Forrest was left with nothing. Resilient to the end, he contracted with Selby County for convicts to work 1,700 acres of land he had rented on President's Island, four miles from Memphis. Leasing convicts was a practice notorious for horrendous abuses, but none were reported on President's Island. The swamp-ridden island, however, proved hard on him; he contracted a debilitating intestinal illness that ultimately proved fatal. After so many setbacks, his luck turned at least in this regard: against all odds, Nathan Bedford Forrest died peacefully in his bed on October 29,1877. The legacy he left, however, gave the South no peace. Racial violence plagued the land, and in 1915 the Ku Klux Klan revived, its victims extending beyond the black community to include Jews, Catholics, and immigrants.

Harriet Hernandes

The Intimidation of Black Voters

The following testimony was given in 1871 by Harriet Hernandes, a black resident of Spartanburg, South Carolina, to the Joint Congressional Select Committee investigating conditions in the South. The terrorizing of black women through rape and other forms of physical violence was among the means of oppression used by the Ku Klux Klan.

Question: How old are you?
Answer: Going on thirty-four years. . . .
Q: Are you married or single?
A: Married.
Q: Did the Ku-Klux come to your house at any time?
A: Yes, sir; twice. . . .
Q: Go on to the second time. . . .
A: They came in; I was lying in bed. Says he, "Come out here, sir; come out here, sir!" They took me out of bed; they would not let me get out, but they took me up in their arms and toted me out—me and my daughter Lucy. He struck me on the forehead with a pistol, and here is the scar above my eye now. Says he, "Damn you, fall." I fell. Says he, "Damn you, get up." I got up. Says he, "Damn you, get over this fence!" and he kicked me over when I went to get over; and then he went on to a brush pile, and they laid us right down there, both together. They laid us down twenty yards apart, I reckon. They had dragged and beat us along. They struck me right on top of my head, and I thought they had killed me; and I said, "Lord o'mercy, don't, don't kill my child!" He gave me a lick on the head, and it liked to have killed me; I saw stars. He threw my arm over my head so I could not do anything with it for three weeks, and there are great knots on my wrist now.

Q: What did they say this was for?
A: They said, "You can tell your husband that when we see him we are going to kill him. . . . "
Q: Did they say why they wanted to kill him?
A: They said, "He voted the radical ticket [slate of candidates], didn't he?" I said, "Yes," that very way. . . .
Q: When did [your husband] get back home after this whipping? He was not at home, was he?
A: He was lying out; he couldn't stay at home, bless your soul! . . .
Q: Has he been afraid for any length of time?
A: He has been afraid ever since last October. He has been lying out. He has not laid in the house ten nights since October.
Q: Is that the situation of the colored people down there to any extent?
A: That is the way they all have to do—men and women both.
Q: What are they afraid of?
A: Of being killed or whipped to death.
Q: What has made them afraid?
A: Because men that voted radical tickets they took the spite out on the women when they could get at them.
Q: How many colored people have been whipped in that neighborhood?
A: It is all of them, mighty near.

Source: Report of the Joint Congressional Select Committee to Inquire into the Condition of Affairs in the Late Insurrectionary States, House Report, 42nd Cong., 2nd sess. (Washington, DC: U.S. Government Printing Office, 1872), vol. 5, South Carolina, December 19, 1871.

their ex-Confederate enemies. Democrats overthrew Republican governments in Texas in 1873, in Alabama and Arkansas in 1874, and in Mississippi in 1875.

The Mississippi campaign showed all too clearly what the Republicans were up against. As elections neared in 1875, paramilitary groups such as the Rifle Clubs and Red Shirts operated openly. Often local Democrats paraded armed, as if they were militia companies. They identified black leaders in assassination lists called "dead books," broke up Republican meetings, provoked rioting that left hundreds of African Americans dead, and threatened voters. Mississippi's Republican governor, Adelbert Ames, a Congressional Medal of Honor winner from Maine, appealed to President Grant for federal troops, but Grant refused. Ames then contemplated organizing a state militia but ultimately decided against it, believing that only blacks would join and that the state would be plunged into racial war. Brandishing their guns and stuffing the ballot boxes, the Redeemers swept the 1875 elections and took control of Mississippi. Facing impeachment by the new Democratic legislature, Governor Ames resigned his office and returned to the North.

By 1876 Republican governments, backed by token U.S. military units, remained in only three states—Louisiana, South Carolina, and Florida. Elsewhere, the former Confederates were back in the saddle.

The Acquiescent North

The faltering of Reconstruction stemmed from more than discouragement about prosecuting the Klan, however. Sympathy for the freedman began to wane. The North was flooded with one-sided, often racist reports, such as James M. Pike's *The Prostrate State* (1873), describing extravagant, corrupt Republican rule and a South in the grip of "a mass of black barbarism." The impact of this propaganda could be seen in the fate of the civil rights bill, which Charles Sumner introduced in 1870 at the height of radical Reconstruction. Sumner's bill was a remarkable application of federal power against discrimination in the country, guaranteeing citizens equal access to public accommodation, schools, and jury service. By the time the bill passed in 1875, it had been stripped of its key provisions and was of little account as a weapon against discriminatory treatment of African Americans. The Supreme Court finished the demolition job when it declared the remnant Civil Rights Act unconstitutional in 1883.

The political cynicism that overtook the Civil Rights Act signaled the Republican Party's reversion to the practical politics of earlier days. In many states a second generation took over the party—men like Roscoe Conkling of New York, who treated the Manhattan Customs House, with its regiment of political appointees, as an auxiliary of his machine. Conkling and similarly minded politicos had little enthusiasm for Reconstruction, except as it benefited the Republican Party. As the party lost headway in the South, they abandoned any interest in the battle for black rights. In Washington President Grant presided benignly over this transformation of his party, turning a blind eye on corruption even as it began to lap against the White House.

The Liberal Republicans and Election of 1872. As Grant's administration lapsed into cronyism, a revolt took shape inside the Republican Party, led by an influential collection of intellectuals, journalists, and reform-minded businessmen. The first order of business for them was civil service reform that would replace corrupt patronage with a merit-based system of appointments. The reformers also, however, disliked the government activism spawned by the Civil War crisis. They regarded themselves as liberals—believers in free trade, market competition, and limited government. And, with unabashed elitism, they spoke out against universal suffrage, which "can only mean in plain English the government of ignorance and vice." So it followed that liberal reformers would have little patience with the former slaves. Although mostly veterans of the antislavery movement, they now became strident critics of radical Reconstruction.

Unable to deny Grant renomination for a second term, the dissidents broke away and formed a new party under the name Liberal Republican. Their candidate was Horace Greeley, longtime editor and publisher of the *New York Tribune* and a warhorse of American reform in all its variety, including antislavery. The Democratic Party, still in disarray, also nominated Greeley, notwithstanding his editorial diatribes against Democrats as "murderers, adulterers, drunkards, liars, thieves." A poor campaigner, Greeley was assailed so bitterly during the campaign that, as he said, "I hardly knew whether I was running for the Presidency or the penitentiary."

Grant won overwhelmingly, capturing 56 percent of the popular vote and every electoral vote. Yet the Liberal Republicans had managed to shift the terms of political debate in the country. The new agenda they had established—civil service reform, limited government, reconciliation with the South—was adopted by the Democrats as they shed their disloyal reputation and reclaimed their place as a legitimate national party. In the 1874 elections the Democrats dealt the Republicans a heavy blow, gaining control of the House of Representatives for the first time since secession and capturing seven normally Republican states.

Scandal and Depression. Charges of Republican corruption, mounting ever since Grant's reelection, came to a head in 1875. The scandal involved the Whiskey Ring, a network of liquor distillers and treasury agents who defrauded the government of millions of dollars of excise taxes on whiskey. The ringleader was a Grant appointee, and Grant's own private secretary, Orville Babcock, had a hand in the thievery. The others went to prison, but Grant stood by Babcock, possibly perjuring himself to save his secretary from jail. The stench of scandal, however, had engulfed the White House.

On top of this the economy had fallen into a severe depression after 1873. The precipitating event was the bankruptcy of the Northern Pacific Railroad and its main investor, Jay Cooke. Both Cooke's privileged role as financier of the Civil War and the generous federal subsidies to the Northern Pacific suggested to many economically pressed Americans that Republican financial manipulations had caused the depression. Grant's administration responded ineffectually, rebuffing the pleas of debtors for relief by increasing the money supply (see Chapter 18). In 1874 Democrats gained enough Republican support to push through Congress a bill that would have increased the volume of currency in circulation and eased the money pinch. But President Grant vetoed it, fueling Democratic charges that the Republicans served only the business interests.

Among the casualties of the bad economy was the Freedman's Savings and Trust Company, which held the small deposits of thousands of ex-slaves. When the bank failed in 1874, Congress refused to compensate the depositors, and many lost their life savings. In denying their pathetic pleas, Congress was signaling also that Reconstruction had lost its moral claim on the country. National politics had moved on; other concerns absorbed the voter as another presidential election approached in 1876.

The Political Crisis of 1877

Abandoning Grant, the Republicans nominated Rutherford B. Hayes, governor of Ohio, a colorless figure, but untainted by corruption or by strong convictions—in a word, a safe man. His Democratic opponent was Samuel J. Tilden, governor of New York, a wealthy lawyer with ties to Wall Street and a reform reputation for helping to break the grip of the thieving Tweed Ring on New York City politics. The Democrat Tilden, of course, favored "**home rule**" for the South but so, more discreetly, did the Republican Hayes. Reconstruction actually did not figure prominently in the campaign and was mostly subsumed under broader Democratic charges of "corrupt centralism" and "incapacity, waste, and fraud." By now Republicans had essentially written off the South and scarcely campaigned there. Not a lot was said about the states still ruled by Reconstruction governments—Florida, South Carolina, and Louisiana.

Once the returns started coming in on election night, however, those three states began to loom very large indeed. Tilden led in the popular vote and, victorious in key northern states, he seemed headed for the White House. But sleepless politicians at Republican headquarters realized that if they kept Florida, South Carolina, and Louisiana, Hayes would win by a single electoral vote. The campaigns in those states had been bitterly fought, replicating the Democratic assaults on blacks that had overturned Republican regimes everywhere else in the South. But Republicans still controlled the election machinery in those states, and, citing Democratic fraud and intimidation, they certified Republican victories. The audacious announcement came forth from Republican headquarters: Hayes had carried the three southern states and won the election. But, of course, newly elected Democratic officials in the three states also sent in electoral votes for Tilden, and, when Congress met in early 1877, it faced two sets of electoral votes from those states.

The Constitution does not provide for this contingency. All it says is that the President of the Senate (in 1877, a Republican) opens the electoral certificates before the House (Democratic) and the Senate (Republican) and that "the Votes shall then be counted" (Article 2, Section 1; see Documents, p. D-9). An air of crisis gripped the country. There was talk of inside deals, of a new election, even of a violent coup and civil war. Just in case, the commander of the army, General William T. Sherman, deployed four artillery companies in Washington. Finally, Congress decided to appoint an electoral commission to settle the question. The commission included seven Republicans, seven Democrats, and, as the deciding member, David Davis, a Supreme Court justice not known to have fixed party loyalties. But Davis disqualified himself by accepting an Illinois seat in the Senate. He was replaced by Republican justice Joseph P. Bradley, and by 8 to 7 the commission awarded the disputed votes to Hayes.

Outraged Democrats had one more trick up their sleeves. They controlled the House, and they set about stalling a final count of the electoral votes so as to prevent Hayes's inauguration on March 4. But a week before, secret Washington talks had begun between southern Democrats and Ohio Republicans representing Hayes. Other issues may have been on the table, but the main thing was the situation in South Carolina and Louisiana, where rival governments were encamped at the state capitols, with federal soldiers holding the Democrats at bay. Exactly what deal was struck or how involved Hayes himself was will probably never be known, but on March 1 the House Democrats suddenly ended their filibuster, the ceremonial counting of votes went forward, and Hayes was inaugurated on schedule. He soon ordered the Union troops back to their barracks and the Republican regimes in South Carolina and Louisiana fell. Reconstruction had ended.

In 1877 political leaders on all sides seemed ready to say that what Lincoln had called "the work" was complete. But for the freedpeople, the work had only begun. Reconstruction turned out to have been a magnificent aberration, a leap beyond what most white Americans actually felt was due their black fellow citizens. Redemption represented a sad falling back to the norm. Still, something real had been achieved—three rights-defining amendments to the Constitution, some elbow room to advance economically, and, not least, a stubborn confidence among blacks that, by their own efforts, they could lift themselves up. Things would, in fact, get worse before they got better, but the work of Reconstruction was imperishable and could never be erased.

FOR FURTHER EXPLORATION

► For definitions of key terms boldface in this chapter, see the glossary at the end of the book.

► To assess your mastery of the material covered in this chapter, see the Online Study Guide at **bedfordstmartins.com/henretta**.

► For suggested references, including Web sites, see page SR-17 at the end of the book.

► For map resources and primary documents, see **bedfordstmartins.com/henretta**.

When the Civil War ended in 1865, no one could have foreseen the future course of Reconstruction. The slaves had been emancipated, but there was no consensus about their future status as citizens. The South had been defeated, but there was no consensus about its restoration to the Union. Had Abraham Lincoln lived, these great questions might have been settled peaceably, but with his assassination they were left to the mercy of unfolding events.

Without consulting Congress, Lincoln's successor, Andrew Johnson, offered the South easy terms for reentering the Union. This might have succeeded had the South responded with restraint, but instead a concerted effort was made to reenslave the freedmen through the Black Codes. In this opening round of freedom's struggle, the ex-slaves showed their determination to be agents of their own fate, resisting the Black Codes and demanding equal civil and political rights. Infuriated by southern intransigence, congressional Republicans closed ranks behind the Radicals, embraced the freedmen's demand for full equality, placed the South under military rule in 1867, and inaugurated radical Reconstruction.

The new Republican state governments that undertook to reconstruct the South through ambitious programs of economic and educational improvement. No amount of accomplishment, however, could have reconciled the ex-Confederates to Republican rule, and they staged a violent counterrevolution in the name of white supremacy and "redemption."

Despite an initially stern response, the Grant administration had no stomach for a protracted guerrilla war in the South. Northern politics moved on, increasingly absorbed by Republican scandals and, after depression hit in 1873, by the nation's economic problems. By allying with the Liberal Republicans in 1872, the discredited Democrats scrambled back into the political mainstream and began to compete on even terms with the Republicans. So close was the presidential election of 1876 that both parties claimed victory. The constitutional crisis was resolved only by Democratic agreement to accept the Republican Hayes as president in exchange for an end to Republican rule in South Carolina and Louisiana, signaling the conclusion of Reconstruction.

1863   Lincoln announces his Ten Percent Plan

1864   Wade-Davis Bill passed by Congress

Lincoln gives Wade-Davis Bill a "pocket" veto

1865   Freedmen's Bureau established

Lincoln assassinated; Andrew Johnson succeeds as president

Johnson implements his restoration plan

Joint Committee on Reconstruction formed

1866   Civil Rights Act passes over Johnson's veto

Memphis riots

Johnson makes disastrous "swing around the circle"; defeated in congressional elections

1867   Reconstruction Act

Tenure of Office Act

1868   Impeachment crisis

Fourteenth Amendment ratified

Ulysses S. Grant elected president

1870   Ku Klux Klan at peak of power

Fifteenth Amendment ratified

1872   Grant's reelection as president

1873   Panic of 1873 ushers in depression of 1873–1877

1874   Democrats win majority in House of Representatives

1875   Whiskey Ring scandal undermines Grant administration

1877   Compromise of 1877; Rutherford B. Hayes becomes president

Reconstruction ends

PART THREE

Religion in American Public Life

For Americans, reciting the Pledge of Allegiance is the most personal way they have for affirming their national identity. So students must think the words are in the same league with the Declaration of Independence and the Constitution. In fact, the pledge is of much later origin, composed in 1892 by Francis Bellamy, a Boston cleric-turned-social critic, who used its final words to promote his personal philosophy of "liberty and justice for all." Originally, it was an entirely secular document. Only in 1954 did "under God" become part of the pledge, inserted by Congress to further the cold war crusade against "godless Communism." Once in, however, that phrase, like the pledge itself, came to seem timeless and beyond questioning.

It therefore came as a shock in 2002 when a three-judge panel of the 9th U.S. Circuit Court of Appeals declared that a California law requiring students to recite the pledge was unconstitutional because of the words "under God." The political reaction to *Newdow v. U.S. Congress et al.* was quick and harsh. The Republican president George W. Bush denounced the decision, asserting, "America is a nation that values our relationship with an Almighty." Senator Joseph Lieberman, the Democratic vice presidential candidate in 2000 and an orthdox Jew, called for a constitutional amendment to make clear that "we are one nation because of our faith in God."

We have been down this road before. In 1863 the House of Representatives considered amending the Preamble of the Constitution to read: "Acknowledging the Lord Jesus Christ as the Governor among nations, His revealed will as the supreme law of the land, in order to constitute a Christian government, we the people of the United States. . . ." Like Senator Lieberman, living in the shadow of the terrorist attacks on America of September 11, 2001, the U.S. congressmen of 1863 were acting at a time of great national crisis, when Americans were pitted against their fellow citizens in a bloody civil war.

These professions of faith occupy one side of a great fault line in American public life. On the other side stands a secular constitutional tradition that goes back to the Revolutionary era and to the document that founded the national republic, the U.S. Constitution. The Constitution is a thoroughly secular document, containing no reference to God and mentioning religion in Article VI only to prohibit religious tests for federal office. Then came the Bill of Rights, the original ten amendments ratified in 1793. The First Amendment begins: "Congress shall make no law respecting an establishment of religion, or prohibiting the free exercise thereof. . . ." The first of these prohibitions, known as the Establishment Clause, mandates the separation of church and state and is the basis for the decision by the 9th Circuit Court in the *Newdow* case. The second, the "free exercise clause," also is germane, because freedom of conscience seems incompatible with state-mandated expressions of faith—like the phrase "under God" in the Pledge of Allegiance—that touch every citizen. These two provisions are, like freedom of speech and assembly, at the core of American civil liberties protected by the Bill of Rights.

This constitutional triumph was, however, by no means unqualified. The state constitutions of the 1770s and 1780s already in place were far from secular. Most New England states imposed taxes for the support of religion, and various states required elected officials to profess belief in "the Christian religion." Moreover, even at the federal level the secularist triumph was not quite what it seemed. As Akhil Reed Amar argues in *The Bill of Rights* (1998), many churchgoing Americans actually favored the Establishment Clause in hopes that it would shield state support of religion from federal interference. Separation of church and state, if a remarkable achievement, was tempered from the start by an abiding sense that the cohesion of the nation rested on Christian faith.

Ever since those nation-building years, religious belief and constitutional secularism have coexisted in this state of tension. And what determines which has the relative advantage? Primarily, scholars suggest, the varying intensity of religious belief. The Revolutionary era had been an age of rationalism. Thereafter, as the Second Great Awakening took hold, religious enthusiasm again swept the country. In *Southern Cross: The Beginnings of the Bible Belt* (1997), Christine Heyrman estimates that the number of white Southerners who attended evangelical churches jumped from 25 percent in 1776 to 65 percent in 1835. Alexis de Tocqueville remarked in

Democracy in America (1835) that the Great Awakening gave "the Christian religion . . . a greater influence over the souls of men" in the United States than in any other society. Modern scholars concur with Tocqueville. As we have shown in the preceding chapters, religious fervor prompted political activism on many fronts in the antebellum years—from abolitionism to temperance to the condemnation by 8,000 federal postmasters of mail delivery on Sunday, the Christian Sabbath, as "a disgrace to the nation, and an insult to the Supreme Lawgiver."

What this age of faith also revealed, however, was the staying power of constitutional secularism. Americans were coming to regard the Constitution itself as an inviolable document and a model for the states. Even in these fervent years, the bastions of public religion began to fall as churches were disestablished in the New England states and religious tests for officeholders were abandoned. New political realities set in. Irish Catholics arrived in great numbers and, ironically, the Second Great Awakening itself stimulated denominational diversity. Politicians took heed of President Andrew Jackson's warning that religiously inspired public policies would disturb "the security which religion now enjoys in this country in its complete separation from the political concerns of the General Government." Similar concerns sealed the fate of the Civil War amendment seeking to make Christianity the official federal creed.

As religious fervor waned after the Civil War, so did efforts to breach the wall of church/state separation. It is telling that the man who wrote the Pledge of Allegiance without invoking the Almighty was a Baptist minister. Moreover, the Establishment Clause proved not to be the shield for state support for religion that some of its original supporters had hoped for. In the twentieth century the courts began to move aggressively on this front. In *Everson v. Board of Education* (1947), a New Jersey case involving the use of public funds to transport students to Catholic schools, Justice Hugo Black declared that the Constitution erected "a wall of separation between church and state" that the courts would enforce. Then, in the landmark New York case of *Engel v. Vitale* (1962), the Court held that prayer in the public schools was "wholly inconsistent with the Establishment Clause," a decision that was a precedent for the *Newdow* decision and aroused even more controversy.

In each age, as the pendulum swings, a new balance has to be struck between the contradictory traditions of constitutional secularism and religious belief. That, at any rate, is what the history of church/state relations in America suggests. In our own time, a new age of faith, the courts have looked for legal accommodation. Thus laws limiting Sunday activities have been allowed on the secular grounds that they "provide a uniform day of rest for all citizens"; similarly, using a legal theory of "child benefit," judges have approved the use of public taxes to buy textbooks or defray tuition at religious schools. Such a strategy may be in the offing with respect to the pledge. Unlike President Bush and those who proclaim the centrality of faith in American public life, the Department of Justice has sought reconsideration of the *Newdow* case on the grounds that the words "under God" are essentially ritualistic, one of "many ceremonial references to our religious heritage and do not establish a religious faith." Such a legal tactic could well resolve the pledge controversy and satisfy the country. What do *you* think the outcome will be? And if, by the time you read this essay, the Supreme Court has decided this case, what did the judges actually do—and why?

Inculcating . . . What???

Three young children stare reverently at the American flag as they say (or listen to) the Pledge of Allegiance. Intended originally to promote national identity and social justice, during the twentieth century the pledge became a vehicle for inculcating patriotism and religious belief. Should children be required to recite the pledge? If so, what beliefs should it promote? Newsweek.

A Maturing Industrial Society

1877–1914

ECONOMY	SOCIETY	CULTURE	GOVERNMENT	DIPLOMACY
The Triumph of Industrialization	**Racial, Ethnic, and Gender Divisions**	**The Rise of the City**	**From Inaction to Progressive Reform**	**An Emerging World Power**
1877 ▸ Andrew Carnegie launches modern steel industry Knights of Labor becomes national movement (1878)	▸ Struggle for black equality defeated Nomadic Indian life ends	▸ National League founded (1876) Dwight L. Moody pioneers urban revivalism	▸ Election of Rutherford B. Hayes ends Reconstruction	▸ United States becomes net exporter
1880 ▸ Gustavus Swift pioneers vertically integrated firm American Federation of Labor (1886)	▸ Chinese Exclusion Act (1882) Dawes Act divides tribal lands (1887)	▸ Electrification transforms city life First Social Register defines high society (1888)	▸ Ethnocultural issues dominate state and local politics Civil service reform (1883)	▸ Diplomacy of inaction Naval buildup begins
1890 ▸ United States surpasses Britain in iron and steel output Economic depression (1893–1897) Era of farm prosperity begins	▸ Black disfranchisement and segregation in the South Immigration from southeastern Europe rises sharply	▸ Settlement houses spread progressive ideas to cities William Randolph Hearst's *New York Journal* pioneers yellow journalism	▸ Populist Party founded (1892) William McKinley wins presidency; defeats Bryan's free-silver crusade (1896)	▸ Social Darwinism and Anglo-Saxonism promote expansion Spanish-American War (1898–1899); conquest of the Philippines
1900 ▸ Great industrial merger movement Immigrants dominate factory work Industrial Workers of the World (1905)	▸ Women lead social reform Struggle for civil rights revived	▸ Muckraking journalism Movies begin to overtake vaudeville	▸ Progressivism in national politics Theodore Roosevelt attacks the trusts Hepburn Act regulates railroads (1906)	▸ Panama cedes Canal Zone to United States (1903) Roosevelt Corollary to Monroe Doctrine (1904)
1910 ▸ Henry Ford builds first automobile assembly line	▸ NAACP (1910) Women vote in western states World War I ends European migration	▸ Urban liberalism	▸ Woodrow Wilson elected (1912) New Freedom legislation creates Federal Reserve, FTC	▸ Taft's diplomacy promotes U.S. business Wilson proclaims U.S. neutrality in World War I

While the nation was absorbed by the political drama of Reconstruction, few people noticed an equally momentous watershed in American economic life. For the first time, as the decade of the 1870s passed, farmers no longer constituted a majority of working Americans. Henceforth America's future would be linked to its development as an industrial society.

ECONOMY The effects of accelerating industrialization were felt, first of all, in the manufacturing sector. Production became increasingly mechanized and increasingly directed at making the capital goods that undergirded economic growth. As the railroad system was completed, the vertically integrated model began to dominate American enterprise. The labor movement became firmly established, and as immigration surged the foreign-born and their children became America's workers. What had been partial and limited now became general and widespread; America turned into a land of factories, corporate enterprise, and industrial workers.

THE WEST The final surge of western settlement across the Great Plains was largely driven by the pressures of this industrializing economy. Cities demanded new sources of food; factories needed the Far West's mineral resources. Defending their way of life, western Indians were ultimately defeated not so much by army rifles as by the unceasing encroachment of railroads, mines, ranches, and proliferating farms. These same forces disrupted the old established Hispanic communities of the Southwest but spurred Asian, Mexican, and European migrations that made for a multiethnic western society.

THE CITY Industrialization also transformed the nation's urban life. By 1900 one in five Americans lived in cities. That was where the jobs were—as workers in the factories; as clerks and salespeople; as members of a new, salaried middle class of managers, engineers, and professionals; and at the apex as a wealthy elite of investors and entrepreneurs. The city was more than just a place to make a living, however. It provided a setting for an urban lifestyle unlike anything seen before in America.

GOVERNMENT The unfettered, booming economy of the Gilded Age tended at first to marginalize political life. The major parties remained robust not because they stood for much programmatically but because they exploited a culture of popular participation and embraced the ethnocultural interests of their constituencies. The depression of the 1890s triggered a major challenge to the political status quo by the agrarian Populist Party, with its demand for free silver. The election of 1896 turned back that challenge and established the Republicans as the dominant national party.

Still unresolved was the threat that corporate power posed to the marketplace and democratic politics. How to curb the trusts dominated national debate during the Progressive Era. In those years as well, the country took a critical look at its institutions and began to address its social ills. From different angles political reformers, women progressives, and urban liberals went about the business of cleaning up machine politics and making life better for America's urban masses. African Americans, victimized by disfranchisement and segregation, found allies among white Progressives and launched a new drive for racial equality.

DIPLOMACY Finally, the dynamism of America's economic development decisively altered the country's foreign relations. In the decades after the Civil War, America had been inward-looking, neglectful of its navy and inactive diplomatically. The business crisis of the 1890s, however, brought home the need for a more aggressive foreign policy that would advance the nation's overseas economic interests. In short order the United States went to war with Spain, acquired an overseas empire, and became actively engaged in Latin America and Asia. There was no mistaking America's standing as a Great Power and, as World War I approached, no evading the responsibilities and entanglements that came with that status.

CHAPTER 16

The American West

The Great Plains
Indians of the Great Plains
Wagon Trains, Railroads, and
  Ranchers
Homesteaders
The Fate of the Indians

The Far West
The Mining Frontier
Hispanics, Chinese, Anglos
Golden California

DURING THE LAST DECADES of the nineteenth century, America seemed like two nations. One was an advanced industrial society—the America of great factories and sprawling cities. But another America still remained frontier country, with pioneers streaming onto the Great Plains, repeating the old dramas of "settlement" they had been performing ever since Europeans had first set foot on the continent. Not until 1890 did the U.S. Census declare that a "frontier of settlement" no longer existed: the country's "unsettled area has been so broken into . . . that there can hardly be said to be a frontier line."

Eighteen-ninety also marked the year the country surpassed Great Britain in the production of iron and steel. Newspapers carried reports of Indian wars and industrial strikes in the same edition. The last tragic episode in the suppression of the Plains Indians, the massacre at Wounded Knee, South Dakota, occurred only eighteen months before the great Homestead steel strike of 1892. This alignment of events from the distant worlds of factory and frontier was not accidental. The final surge of settlement across the Great Plains and the Far West was powered primarily by the dynamism of American industrialism.

◀ **The Yo-Hamite Falls, 1855**
This is one of the earliest artistic renderings of Yosemite Valley, drawn, in fact, before the place came to be called Yosemite. The scale of the waterfall, which drops 2,300 feet to the valley below, is dramatized by artist Thomas A. Ayres's companions in the foreground. In this romantic lithograph one can already see the grandeur of the West that Yosemite came to represent for Americans.
University of California at Berkeley, Bancroft Library, Honeyman Collection.

457

The Great Plains

During the 1860s agricultural settlement reached the western margins of the tall-grass prairie. Beyond, roughly at the ninety-eighth meridian (Map 16.1), stretched vast, dry country, uninviting to farmers accustomed to woodlands and ample rainfall. They saw it much as did the New York publisher Horace Greeley on his way to California in 1859: "a land of starvation," "a treeless desert," baking in heat in the daytime and "chill and piercing" cold at night.

Greeley was describing the Great Plains. The geologic event creating the Great Plains occurred sixty million years ago when the Rocky Mountains arose out of the ocean covering western North America. With no outlet, the shallow inland sea to the east dried up, forming a hard pan on which sediment washing down from the mountains built up a loose, featureless surface layer. The mountain barrier also made for a dry climate because the moisture-laden winds from the Pacific spent themselves on the western slopes. Only vegetation capable of withstanding the bitter winters and periodic cycles of severe drought could take hold on the plains. The short grama grass, the linchpin of this fragile ecosystem, matted the easily blown soil into place and sustained a rich wildlife dominated by grazing antelope and buffalo. What the dry short-grass country had not sustained, until the past few centuries, was human settlement.

MAP 16.1 The Natural Environment of the West, 1860s

As settlers pushed into the Great Plains and beyond the line of semiaridity, they sensed the overwhelming power of the natural environment. In a landscape without trees for fences and barns, and without adequate rainfall, ranchers and farmers had to relearn their business. The Native Americans peopling the plains and mountains had in time learned to live in this environment, but this knowledge counted for little against the ruthless pressure of the settlers to domesticate the West.

Indians of the Great Plains

Probably 100,000 Native Americans lived on the Great Plains at mid-nineteenth century. They were a diverse people, divided into six linguistic families and at least thirty tribal groupings. On the eastern margins and along the Missouri River, the Mandans, Arikaras, and Pawnees planted corn and beans and lived in permanent villages. Smallpox and measles introduced by Europeans ravaged these settled tribes. Less vulnerable to epidemics because they were dispersed were the hunting tribes that had first arrived on the Great Plains in the seventeenth century: Kiowas and Comanches in the southwest; Arapahos and Cheyennes on the central plains; and, to the north, Blackfeet, Crows, Cheyennes, and the great Sioux nation.

The Teton Sioux.   Originally the Sioux had been eastern prairie people, occupying settlements in the lake country of northern Minnesota. With fish and game dwindling, some Sioux tribes drifted westward and around 1760 began to cross the Missouri River. These Sioux became nomadic, living in portable skin tepees and hunting the buffalo. From tribes to the southwest, they acquired horses. Once mounted, the Sioux became splendid hunters and formidable fighters, claiming the entire Great Plains north of the Arkansas River as their hunting grounds and driving out or subjugating longer-settled tribes.

A society that celebrates the heroic virtues of hunting and war is likely to define gender roles sharply. But before the Sioux had horses, chasing down the buffalo demanded the cooperation of the entire community, so that hunting could not be an exclusively male enterprise. It took the efforts of both men and women to construct the "pounds," into which, beating the brush side by side, they endeavored to stampede the herds. Once they had horses, however, the men rode off to the hunt while the women stayed behind to prepare the mounting piles of buffalo skins. This was laborious, painstaking work. Fanny Kelly, who had been a Sioux captive, considered the women's lives "a servitude"; but she noticed also that they were "very rebellious, often displaying ungovernable and violent temper." Subordination to the men was not how Sioux women understood their unrelenting labor; this was their allotted share in a partnership on which the proud, nomadic life of the Teton depended.

Teton Religion.   Living so close to wild nature, depending on its bounty for survival, the Sioux saw sacred meaning in every manifestation of the natural world. Unlike Europeans, they conceived of God not as a supreme being but, in the words of the pioneering ethnologist Clark Wissler, as a "series of powers pervading the universe"—Wi, the sun; Skan, the sky; Maka, the earth; Inyan, the rock. Below these came the moon, wind, and buffalo down through a hierarchy embodying the entire natural order.

By prayer and fasting Sioux prepared themselves to commune with these mysterious powers. Medicine men provided instruction, but the religious experience was personal and open to both sexes. The vision, when a supplicant achieved it, attached itself to some object—a feather, an animal skin, or a shell—that was tied into a sacred bundle and became the person's lifelong talisman. In the **Sun Dance** the entire tribe celebrated the rites of coming of

Tepee Liner
For the Plains Indians, tribal life revolved around the buffalo hunt and the battleground. These were the themes with which an unknown Indian artist decorated this dewcloth, which was hung inside a tepee to shield the occupants and provide some insulation from the cold. American Hurrah, New York City.

age, fertility, the hunt and combat, followed by four days of fasting and dancing in supplication to Wi, the sun.

The world of the Teton Sioux was not self-contained. All along they had exchanged pelts and buffalo robes for the produce of agriculturalist Pawnees and Mandans. When white traders appeared on the upper Missouri River during the eighteenth century, the Sioux began to trade with them. Although the buffalo remained their staff of life, the Sioux came to rely as well on the traders' pots, kettles, blankets, knives, and guns. The trade system they entered was linked to the Euro-American market economy, yet it was also integrated into the Sioux way of life. Everything depended on the survival of the Great Plains as the Sioux had found it—wild grassland on which the antelope and buffalo ranged free.

Wagon Trains, Railroads, and Ranchers

On first encountering the Great Plains, Euro-Americans thought these unforested lands best left to the Indians. After exploring a drought-stricken stretch in 1820, Major Stephen H. Long declared it "almost wholly unfit for cultivation, and of course uninhabitable by a people depending upon agriculture for their subsistence."

For years thereafter maps marked the plains as the **Great American Desert**. With that notion in mind Congress formally designated the Great Plains in 1834 as permanent Indian country. The army general in charge, Edmund Gaines, wanted the border forts, stretching from Lake Superior to Fort Worth, Texas, to be constructed of stone because they would be there forever. Trade with the Indians would continue, but now closely supervised and licensed by the federal government, with the Indian country otherwise off limits to whites.

Events swiftly overtook the nation's solemn commitment to the Native Americans. During the 1840s

Killing the Buffalo
This woodcut shows passengers shooting buffalo from a Kansas Pacific Railroad train—a small thrill added to the modern convenience of traveling west by rail. North Wind Picture Archives.

settlers began moving westward to Oregon and California. Instead of serving as a buffer against the Mexicans and British, Indian country became a bridge to the Pacific. The first wagon train headed west for Oregon from Missouri in 1842. Soon thousands of emigrants traveled the Oregon Trail to the Willamette Valley or cut south beyond Fort Hall down into California. Approaching Fort Hall in 1859, it seemed to Horace Greeley as if "the white coverings of the many emigrant and transport wagons dott[ing] the landscape" gave "the trail the appearance of a river running through great meadows, with many ships sailing on its bosom." Only these "ships" left behind, not a trailing wake of foam, but a rutted landscape devoid of grass and game and littered with abandoned wagons and rotting garbage.

The Railroads.   Talk about the need for a railroad to the Pacific soon began to be heard in Washington. How else could the distant territories formally acquired from Mexico and Britain in 1848 (see Chapter 13) be firmly linked to the Union or the ordeal of the overland journey by wagon train be alleviated? The project languished while North and South argued over the terminus for the route. Meanwhile, the Indian country was criss-crossed by overland freight lines and Pony Express riders delivered mail between Missouri and California. In 1861 telegraph lines brought San Francisco into instant communication with the East. The next year, with the South in rebellion, the federal government finally moved forward with the transcontinental rail project (Map 16.2).

No private company could be expected to foot the bill by itself. The construction costs were staggering, and in the short run not much traffic could be expected along the thinly populated route. So the federal government awarded generous land grants plus millions of dollars in loans to the two companies that undertook the transcontinental project.

The Union Pacific, building westward from Omaha, made little headway until the Civil War ended but then advanced rapidly across Indian country, reaching Cheyenne, Wyoming, in November 1867. It took the Central Pacific nearly that long moving eastward from Sacramento, California, to cross the crest of the Sierra Nevada. Both then worked furiously—since the government subsidy was based on miles of track laid—until, to great fanfare, the tracks met at **Promontory Point**, Utah, in 1869. None of the other railroads following other westward routes made it as far as the Rockies before the Panic of 1873 hit, throwing them into bankruptcy and bringing work to an abrupt halt.

By then, however, railroad tycoons had changed their minds about the Great Plains. No longer did they see it through the eyes of the Oregon-bound settlers— as a place to be gotten through en route to the Pacific. They realized rail transportation was laying the basis for the economic exploitation of the Great Plains. This

MAP 16.2 Western Trunk Lines, 1887

In the 1850s the talk in Washington had been about the need for a transcontinental rail-road to bind the West to the Union. This map shows vividly how fully that talk had turned into reality in a matter of three decades. By 1887 no portion of the Pacific Coast lacked a rail connection to the East.

calculation spurred the railroad boom that followed economic recovery in 1878. Construction soared. During the 1880s, 40,000 miles of track were laid west of the Mississippi, including links from southern California via the Southern Pacific to New Orleans and via the Santa Fe to Kansas City, and from the Northwest via the Northern Pacific to St. Paul, Minnesota.

The Cattle Kingdom. Of all the opportunities beckoning, the most obvious was cattle raising. Grazing buffalo made it easy to imagine the plains as cow country. But first the buffalo had to go. A small market for buffalo robes had existed for years. And buffalo hunters like William F. Cody (see American Lives, "Buffalo Bill and the Mythic West," p. 462) made a good living provisioning army posts and leading hunting parties. Then in the early 1870s eastern tanneries discovered how to cure the hides, sparking a huge demand by shoe and harness manufacturers. Parties of professional hunters with high-powered

rifles swept across the plains and began a systematic slaughter of the buffalo. Already diminished by disease and shrinking pasturage, the great herds almost vanished within ten years. Many people spoke out against this mass killing, but no way existed to stop people bent on making a quick dollar. Besides, as General Philip H. Sheridan pointed out, exterminating the buffalo would starve the Indians into submission.

In south Texas about five million head of longhorn cattle grazed on Anglo ranches, hardly worth bothering about because they could not be profitably marketed. In 1865, however, the Missouri Pacific Railroad reached Sedalia, Missouri, far enough west to be accessible to Texas ranchers and their herds. At the Sedalia terminus, which connected to eastern markets, a longhorn worth $3 in Texas might command $40. With this incentive Texas ranchers inaugurated the famous **Long Drive**, hiring cowboys to herd the longhorn cattle hundreds of miles north to the railroads that were pushing west across Kansas.

Buffalo Bill and the Mythic West

Scott County, Iowa, was still frontier country when William F. Cody was born there on February 26, 1846. His family moved to Kansas in 1854, where it was even wilder, for it was not only frontier country but racked by bloody conflict between proslavery and free-soil settlers. Bill's father, Isaac Cody, was active on the free-soil side, serving in the Topeka legislature and frequently in harm's way from neighboring southern sympathizers and marauding Border Ruffians. One of Bill's first exploits was a wild gallop, with proslavery men in hot pursuit, to warn his father of a trap set for him near the family farm. Isaac Cody was less an idealist, however, than a typical enterprising westerner on the lookout for the main chance. He had been an Indian trader, a farm manager, a stagecoach operator, and, in Kansas, a land speculator around Grasshopper Falls. When he died suddenly in 1857, Cody left the family with a pile of land titles but little money.

Bill, never much for schooling anyway, had to find work. At age eleven he was taken on by Majors and Waddell, the firm that transported goods from Fort Leavenworth to army posts west of the Missouri River. Bill worked as a messenger boy, livestock herder, and teamster helper on the freight wagons. When his employers organized the short-lived Pony Express in 1860, Cody became a stock tender and an occasional rider in the Colorado–Nebraska division. Most of this was hard and tedious labor, but there were flashes of excitement—scrapes with Indians and with bandits (at fifteen, Bill killed one), buffalo stampedes, and brief encounters with Wild Bill Hickok and other tough western characters on whom Bill modeled himself. In the early part of the Civil War, Cody was at loose ends. Among other things, he engaged in horse thieving disguised as guerrilla activity in Missouri, and he became a heavy drinker. After a stint in the Seventh Kansas Cavalry and a halfhearted effort to settle down after the war (in what turned out to be an unhappy marriage), Cody got his lucky break in 1867.

The Kansas Pacific Railroad was building a line through Indian country to Sheridan, Kansas. To provision the work crews, the contractors hired Cody at $500 a month—excellent pay—to supply the cooks with buffalo meat. Cody was a crack shot and an excellent horseman, and he knew buffalo hunting. This assignment was duck soup for him, and the aplomb with which he carried it off soon gave him the name "Buffalo Bill."

Indian war broke out in Kansas in the summer of 1868, and Cody got his second claim to fame. He was hired as chief scout for the U.S. Fifth Cavalry. Cody knew the Kansas landscape intimately, he seemed to have a remarkable instinct for following a trail, and he was intrepid in the face of danger. At the height of the fighting in 1868 and 1869, Cody saw repeated action. In the climactic Battle of Summit Springs, his scouting played a decisive role, and he himself shot the Cheyenne chief Tall Bull. Although the legends later built up around Buffalo Bill have inclined scholars to be skeptical, he was in fact an authentic hero. Perhaps the best testimony was the extra $100 awarded him by the normally tight-fisted army "for extraordinarily good services as a trailer and fighter in the pursuit of hostile Indians."

Out of these promising materials there began to emerge a mythic figure. In July 1869 the dime novelist Ned Buntline (Edward Zane Carroll Judson) came through Kansas, met Cody, and, after returning to New York, wrote Buffalo Bill, the King of the Border Men—the first of some 1,700 potboilers to feature Cody's name and exploits. Then there were the buffalo-hunting parties of the rich and famous that Cody periodically led, including a royal hunt in 1872 with Grand Duke Alexis of Russia that had the entire country agog. With his white horse, buckskin suit, crimson shirt, and broad sombrero, Buffalo Bill began to play his part to the hilt. "He realized to perfection the bold hunter and gallant sportsman of the plains," wrote one appreciative participant. In 1872 Cody was persuaded to appear as himself in a play Ned Buntline proposed to put on in New York. Buntline was said to have dashed off The Scouts of the Prairie in four hours. Critics pronounced it "execrable." But Buffalo Bill, who mostly ad-libbed, was a great hit, and so was the production. Cody was launched on his career as a showman.

From then on the lines between reality and make-believe began to blur. Not only did Buffalo Bill draw on his past exploits when he went on stage, but he had the stage in mind when he returned to the real world. During the Sioux wars of 1875 and 1876 Cody was again out in the field as an army scout. (Fortunately, the fighting took place during the theatrical off-seasons in the East.) Shortly after

I AM COMING

COL. W. F. CODY

Buffalo Bill's Wild West Show

Advertising the arrival of his troupe was a key function of Buffalo Bill's business enterprise. This brilliantly executed poster must have done duty all across the country, supplemented by flyers and newspaper ads announcing the date and place of the performance. The buffalo stampeding in the background were of course long gone by the time this poster appeared in the early twentieth century (judging by Buffalo Bill's gray beard). Library of Congress.

For more help analyzing this image, see the ONLINE STUDY GUIDE at bedfordstmartins.com/henretta.

the annihilation of Custer's troops at Little Big Horn, Cody gained a measure of vengeance in a famous skirmish in which he killed and scalped a Sioux chief named Yellow Hand. Cody rode into that engagement wearing his stage vaquero outfit—black velvet and scarlet with lace—so that when he reenacted the mayhem on stage, he could say he was wearing the very clothes in which he had seen action. Over time and with some help from Cody, the fight with Yellow Hand assumed legendary proportions, becoming a formal duel, with a challenge laid down by the Indian chief and troopers and Indian warriors lined up on opposing sides watching Buffalo Bill and Yellow Hand fight it out.

The mythic West that Cody was creating became full blown in his Wild West Show, first staged in 1883. Taking the circus and rodeo as his model, Cody put on an open-air extravaganza with displays of horsemanship, sharpshooting by Little Annie Oakley, real Indians (in one season Chief Sitting Bull toured with the company), and reenactments of stagecoach robberies and great events such as Custer's Last Stand. The Wild West Show toured the country every year and was a smashing success in Europe as well.

Buffalo Bill had been keen enough to see the hunger of city people for a legendary West. He traded on his talents as a showman, but he relied as well on his grasp of the authentic world behind the make-believe. When Cody died in 1917 that world was long gone, but his Wild West Show kept it alive in legend, where it still remains in the mythic figures of cowboys and Indians that populate our movies and television screens.

Cowboys on the Open Range

In open-range ranching, cattle from different ranches grazed together. At the roundup, cowboys separated the cattle by owner and branded the calves. Cowboys, celebrated in dime novels, were really farmhands on horseback, with the skills to work on the range. An ethnically diverse group, including blacks and Hispanics, they earned twenty-five dollars a month, plus meals and a bed in the bunkhouse, in return for long hours of grueling, lonesome work. Library of Congress.

At Abilene, Ellsworth, and Dodge City, ranchers sold their cattle, and trail-weary cowboys went on a binge. These cattle towns captured the nation's imagination as symbols of the Wild West. The reality was much more ordinary. The cowboys, many of them African Americans and Hispanics, were in fact farmhands on horseback who worked long hours under harsh conditions for small pay. Colorful though it seemed, the Long Drive was actually a makeshift method of bridging a gap in the developing transportation system. As soon as railroads reached the Texas range country during the 1870s, ranchers abandoned the Long Drive.

The Texas ranchers owned or leased the land they used, sometimes in huge tracts. North of Texas, where the land was in the public domain, cattlemen simply helped themselves. Hopeful ranchers would spot a likely area along a creek and claim as much land as they could qualify for as settlers under federal homesteading laws, plus what might be added by the fraudulent claims taken out by one or two ranch hands. By a common usage that quickly became established, ranchers had a "range right" to all the adjacent land rising up to the divide—the point where the land sloped down to the next creek.

News of easy money traveled fast. Calves cost $5; steers sold for maybe $60 on the Chicago market. Rail connections were in place or coming in. The grass was free. Profits of 40 percent per year seemed sure. The rush was on, drawing from as far away as Europe both hard-headed investors and romantics (like the recent Harvard graduate Teddy Roosevelt) eager for a taste of the Wild West. By the early 1880s the plains overflowed with cattle—as many as 7.5 million head decimating the grass and trampling the water holes.

A cycle of good weather only postponed the inevitable disaster. When it came—a hard winter in 1885, a severe drought the following summer, then record blizzards and bitter cold—cattle died by the hundreds of thousands. An awful scene of rotting carcasses greeted the cowhands riding out onto the range the following spring. Beef prices plunged when hard-pressed ranchers dumped the surviving cattle on the market. The boom collapsed and investors fled, leaving behind a more enduring ecological catastrophe: the destruction of native grasses from the relentless overgrazing in the drought cycle.

Open-range ranching came to an end. Ranchers fenced their land and planted hay. No longer would cattle be left to fend for themselves over the winters. Hispanic shepherds from New Mexico brought sheep in to feed on the mesquite and prickly pear that supplanted the native grasses. Sheep raising, previously scorned by ranchers as unmanly and resisted as a threat to cattle, became a major enterprise in the sparser high country. Some ranchers even sold out to the despised "nesters"—those who wanted to try farming the Great Plains.

Homesteaders

Potential settlers, of course, needed first to be persuaded that crops would grow in that dry country. Powerful interests worked hard to overcome the popular notion that the plains was a Great American Desert. Foremost were the railroads, eager to sell off the public land they had been granted—180 million acres of it—and develop traffic for their routes. They aggressively advertised, offered cut-rate tickets, and sold off their land holdings at bargain prices. Land speculators, transatlantic steamship lines, and the western states and territories did all they could to encourage settlers. And so did the federal government, which offered 160 acres of public land to all comers under the Homestead Act (1862).

"Why emigrate to Kansas?" asked a testimonial in *Western Trail*, the Rock Island Railroad's gazette. "Because it is the garden spot of the world. Because it will grow anything that any other country will grow, and with less work. Because it rains here more than any other place, and at just the right time."

As if to confirm the optimists, an exceptionally wet cycle occurred between 1878 and 1886. "As the plains are settled up we hear less and less of drouth, hot winds, alkali and other bugbears that used to hold back the adventurous," remarked one Nebraska man. Some settlers attributed the increased rainfall to soil cultivation and tree planting. Others credited God. As a settler on the southern plains remarked, "The Lord just knowed we needed more land an' He's gone and changed the climate."

No amount of optimism, however, could dispel the pain of migration. "That last separating word of *Farewell!* sinks deeply into the heart," one pioneer woman recorded in her diary, thinking of family and friends left behind. But then came the treeless plains. "Such an air of desolation," wrote a Nebraska-bound woman; from another woman in Texas, "such a lonely country." One old hand likened these despairing feelings to an illness. "A stranger travelling on the prairie would get his hopes up, expecting to see something different on making the next rise." But all he found was "grass and then more grass—the monotonous, endless prairie! . . . To him the disappointment and monotony were terrible. 'He's got loneliness,' we would say of such a man." For a Swedish emigrant like Ida Lindgren (see American Voices, "Ida Lindgren: Swedish Emigrant in Frontier Kansas," p. 466) no place could have seemed so far from home and loved ones, and with so little hope of ever seeing family again.

Some women were liberated by this hard experience. Prescribed gender roles broke down as women shouldered men's work on new farms and became self-reliant in the face of danger and hardship. When husbands died or gave up, wives operated farms on their own. Under the Homestead Act, which accorded widows and single women the same rights as men, women filed 10 percent of the claims. "People afraid of coyotes and work and loneliness had better leave ranching alone," advised one woman homesteader. "At the same time, any woman who can stand her own company . . . and is willing to put in as much time at careful labor as she does at the washtub, will certainly succeed; will have independence, plenty to eat all the time, and a home of her own in the end."

Even with a man around, women contributed crucially to the farm enterprise. Farming might be thought of as a dual economy in which men's labor brought in the big wage at harvest time, while women provisioned the family day by day and produced a steady bit of money for groceries by selling eggs or butter. If the crop failed, it was women's labor that carried the family through. No wonder farming placed a high premium on marriage: a mere 2.4 percent of Nebraska women in 1900 had never married.

Male or female, the vision of new land beckoned people onto the plains. By the 1870s the older agricultural states had filled up, and farmers looked hungrily westward. "Hardly anything else was talked about," recalled the short-story writer Hamlin Garland about his Iowa neighbors. "Every man who could sell out had gone west or was going. . . . Farmer after farmer joined the march to Kansas, Nebraska, and Dakota. . . . The movement . . . had . . . become an exodus, a stampede."

The same excitement took hold in northern Europe, as Norwegians and Swedes for the first time joined the older German migration. At the peak of the "American fever" in 1882, over 105,000 Scandinavians emigrated to the United States. Swedish and Norwegian became the primary languages in parts of Minnesota and the Dakotas. Roughly a third of the farmers on the northern plains were foreign-born (Map 16.3).

The motivation for most settlers, American or European, was to better themselves economically. But for some southern blacks, Kansas briefly represented something more precious—the Promised Land of racial freedom. In the spring of 1879, with Reconstruction over and federal protection withdrawn, black communities fearful of white vengeance were swept by enthusiasm for Kansas. Within a month or so, some 6,000 blacks left Mississippi and Louisiana, most of them with nothing more than the clothes on their backs and faith in the Lord. They called themselves **Exodusters**, participants in the exodus to the dry prairie. How many of them remained is hard to say, but the 1880 census reported 40,000 blacks in Kansas—by far the largest African American concentration in the West aside from Texas—whose expanding cotton frontier attracted hundreds of thousands of black migrants during the 1870s and 1880s.

Farming the Plains. No matter where they came from, homesteaders found the plains an alien place. A cloud of grasshoppers might descend and destroy a crop in a day; a brushfire or hailstorm could do the job in an hour. What forested land had always provided—ample water, lumber for cabins and fencing, firewood—was absent. For shelter settlers often cut dugouts into hillsides and after a season or two erected houses made of turf cut from the ground.

The absence of trees, on the other hand, meant an easier time clearing the land. New technology overcame obstacles once thought insurmountable: steel plows enabled homesteaders to break the tightly matted ground, and barbed wire provided cheap, effective fencing against roaming cattle. Strains of hard-kernel wheat tolerant of the extreme temperatures of the plains came in from Europe. Homesteaders had good crops while the wet cycle held and began to anticipate the wood-frame house, deep well, and full coal bin that might make life tolerable on the plains.

In the later 1880s the dry years came and wrecked those hopeful calculations. "From day to day," reported the budding novelist Stephen Crane from Nebraska, "a wind hot as an oven's fury . . . raged like a pestilence,"

Ida Lindgren

Swedish Emigrant in Frontier Kansas

Like many emigrants, Ida Lindgren did not find it easy to adjust to the harsh new life on the frontier. Her diary entries and letters home show that the adjustment for the first generation was never complete.

May 15, 1870 [Lake Sibley, Nebraska]
What shall I say? Why has the lord brought us here? Oh, I feel so oppressed, so unhappy! Two whole days it took us to get here and they were not the least trying part of our travels. We sat on boards in the work-wagon packed in so tightly that we could not move a foot, and we drove across endless, endless prairies, on narrow roads; no, no, not roads, tracks like those in the fields at home when they harvested grain. No forest but only a few trees which grow along the rivers and creeks. And then here and there you see a homestead and pass a little settlement. The Indians are not so far away from here, I can understand, and all the men you see coming by, riding or driving wagons, are armed with revolvers and long carbines, and look like highway robbers.

No date [probably written July 1870]
Claus and his wife lost their youngest child at Lake Sibley and it was very sad in many ways. There was no real cemetery but out on the prairie stood a large, solitary tree, and around it they bury their dead, without tolling of bells, without a pastor, and sometimes without any coffin. A coffin was made here for their child, it was not painted black, but we lined it with flowers and one of the men read the funeral service, and then there was a hymn, and that was all.

August 25, 1874 [Manhattan, Kansas]
It has been a long time since I have written, hasn't it? . . . When one never has anything fun to write about, it is no fun to write. . . . We have not had rain since the beginning of June, and then with this heat and often strong winds as well, you can imagine how everything has dried out. There has also been a general lamentation and fear for the coming year. We are glad we have the oats (for many don't have any and must feed wheat to the stock) and had hoped to have the corn leaves to add to the fodder. But then one fine day there came millions, trillions of grasshoppers in great clouds, hiding the sun, and coming down into the fields, eating up everything that was still there, the leaves on the trees, peaches, grapes, cucumbers, onions, cabbage, everything, everything. Only the peach stones still hung on the trees, showing what had once been there.

July 1, 1877 [Manhattan, Kansas]
. . . It seems so strange to me when I think that more than seven years have passed since I have seen you all. . . . I can see so clearly that last glimpse I had of Mamma, standing alone amid all the tracks of Eslov station. Oliva I last saw sitting on her sofa in her red and black dress, holding little Brita, one month old, on her lap. And Wilhelm I last saw in Lund at the station, as he rolled away with the train, waving his last farewell to me. . . .

Source: H. Arnold Barton, ed., *Letters from the Promised Land* (Minneapolis: University of Minnesota Press, 1975), 143–45, 150–56.

destroying the crops and leaving farmers "helpless, with no weapon against this terrible and inscrutable wrath of nature." Land only recently settled emptied out as homesteaders fled in defeat. The Dakotas lost 50,000 settlers between 1885 and 1890, and comparable departures occurred up and down the drought-stricken plains.

Other settlers held on grimly. Stripped of the illusion that rain followed the plow, the survivors came to terms with the semiarid climate prevailing west of the ninety-eighth meridian. Mormons around the Great Salt Lake (see Chapter 12) had demonstrated how irrigation could turn a wasteland into a garden. But the Great Plains generally lacked the water reserves needed for irrigation. The answer lay in dry-farming methods, which involved deep planting to bring subsoil moisture to the roots and quick harrowing after rainfalls to turn over a dry mulch that slowed evaporation. Dry farming developed most fully on the corporate farms that covered up to 100,000 acres in the Red River Valley of North Dakota. But even family farms, which remained the norm elsewhere, could not survive with less than 300

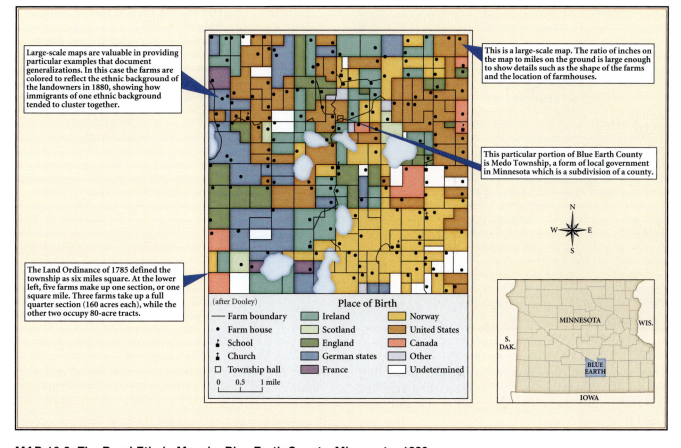

Large-scale maps are valuable in providing particular examples that document generalizations. In this case the farms are colored to reflect the ethnic background of the landowners in 1880, showing how immigrants of one ethnic background tended to cluster together.

This is a large-scale map. The ratio of inches on the map to miles on the ground is large enough to show details such as the shape of the farms and the location of farmhouses.

This particular portion of Blue Earth County is Medo Township, a form of local government in Minnesota which is a subdivision of a county.

The Land Ordinance of 1785 defined the township as six miles square. At the lower left, five farms make up one section, or one square mile. Three farms take up a full quarter section (160 acres each), while the other two occupy 80-acre tracts.

(after Dooley)

Place of Birth

— Farm boundary
• Farm house
School
Church
☐ Township hall

0   0.5   1 mile

Ireland
Scotland
England
German states
France

Norway
United States
Canada
Other
Undetermined

MINNESOTA   WIS.
S. DAK.
BLUE EARTH
IOWA

MAP 16.3 The Rural Ethnic Mosaic: Blue Earth County, Minnesota, 1880

What could have been more natural for emigrants such as Ida Lindgren (see American Voices, p. 466) than to settle next to others sharing common ties to a homeland? This map of Medo township reveals that in rural America, no less than in the cities, ethnicity strongly influenced where people lived.

acres of grain crops and machinery for plowing, planting, and harvesting. Dry farming was not for the unequipped homesteader.

By the turn of the century, the Great Plains had fully submitted to agricultural development. About half the nation's cattle and sheep, a third of its cereal crops, and nearly three-fifths of its wheat came from the newly settled lands. In this process there was little of the "pioneering" that Americans associated with the westward movement. The railroads came before the settlers, eastern capital financed the ranching bonanza, and agriculture depended on sophisticated dry-farming techniques and modern machinery.

Where was the economic capital of the Great Plains? Far off in Chicago. There, at the hub of the nation's rail system, the wheat pit traded western grain and consigned it to world markets; the great packing houses slaughtered western livestock and supplied the nation with sausage, bacon, and sides of beef. In return western ranchers and farmers received lumber, barbed wire, McCormick reapers, and Sears, Roebuck catalogues. Chicago was truly "nature's metropolis."

Farmers' Woes. American farmers embraced this commercial world. They relished the innovations of the industrial age, and supported whatever incentives it took, even public purchase of railway bonds, to attract rail lines to their towns. They had little of the passionate identification with the soil that tied European peasants to their inherited plots, regarding their acreage instead as a commodity. In frontier areas, where newly developed land appreciated rapidly, they anticipated as much profit, if not more, from the rising value of the land as from the crops it produced. American farmers were not averse to borrowing money. In boom times they rushed into debt to acquire more land and better farm equipment. All these enthusiasms—for cash crops, for land speculation, for borrowed money, for new technology—bore witness to the conviction that farming was, as one agricultural journal remarked, a business "like all other business."

Somehow, however, farmers went unrewarded for their faith in free enterprise. The basic problem was that they remained individual operators in an ever more complex and far-flung economic order. And they were, in certain ways, acutely aware of their predicament.

The Shores Family, Custer County, Nebraska, 1887

Whether the Shores family came west as Exodusters, we do not know. But in 1887, when this photograph was taken, they were well settled on their Nebraska farm, although still living in sod houses. The patriarch of the family, Jerry Shores, an ex-slave, is second from the right.
Nebraska State Historical Society.

They understood, for example, the disadvantages they faced in dealing with the big businesses that supplied them with machinery, arranged their credit, and marketed their products.

One answer was cooperation. In 1867 Oliver H. Kelley, a government clerk, founded the National Grange of the Patrons of Husbandry mainly in hopes of improving the social life of farm families. Local granges spread by the thousands across rural America, providing meeting places and a rich array of dances, picnics, and lectures. The Grange soon added cooperative programs, purchasing in bulk from suppliers and setting up its own

banks, insurance companies, grain elevators, and processing plants. The Iowa Grange even attempted to manufacture farm implements. But private businesses fought back hard and generally got the better of the poorly managed and underfinanced Grange cooperatives. The cooperative idea was highly resilient, however, and would be embraced by every successive farmers' movement. Rural hostility to middlemen also left as a legacy the great mail-order house of Montgomery Ward, which had been founded in 1872 to serve Grange members.

The power of government might also be enlisted to counterbalance the organizational weakness of the

Buffalo Chips

With no trees around for firewood, settlers on the plains had to make do with dried cow and buffalo droppings. Gathering the "buffalo chips" must have been a regular chore for Ada McColl and her daughter on her homestead near Lakin, Kansas, in 1893. Kansas State Historical Society.

farmer in the marketplace. In the early 1870s the Grange encouraged independent political parties that ran on antimonopoly platforms. In a number of prairie states these agrarian parties enacted so-called Granger laws regulating grain elevators, fixing maximum railroad rates, and prohibiting discriminatory treatment of small and short-haul shippers.

Farmers turned to cooperatives and state regulation out of a deep sense of organizational disadvantage. But that disadvantage, tangible though it was, did not really account for the unprofitability of farming in this period. Manufacturers and banks lacked the degree of market control ascribed to them by angry farmers. The much-maligned mortgage companies actually could not rig credit markets in the western states; interest rates here matched those in the rest of the country. Nor for the period 1865 to 1890 could manufacturers establish a relative price advantage over agriculture. In fact, the wholesale prices of all commodities fell at a slightly faster pace than did farm prices during those years. As for the railroads, freight rates fell steadily as improved technology reduced operating costs and the volume of western traffic increased (Figure 16.1).

The general fall in prices, or deflation (see Chapter 17), did have dire consequences, however, for wheat farmers, who were subject to the wider, more unpredictable price swings of the international commodity markets. Also at risk in deflationary periods were farmers in debt, since falling prices forced them to pay back in real terms

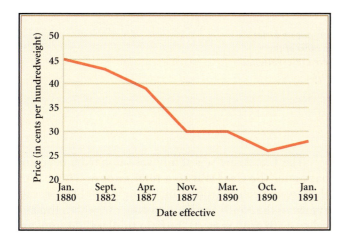

FIGURE 16.1 Freight Rates for Transporting Nebraska Crops

In railroading, a standard measure of operating efficiency is what it costs to move a given volume of goods a given distance. Thanks to improved technology and increasing traffic, costs so measured fell by 50 percent from 1870 to 1890 (see Chapter 17). Freight charges for shipping wheat from Grand Island, Nebraska, to Chicago fell at roughly the same rate (calculated for the years 1880 to 1891), an indication that savings from improved operations were being passed on to customers and that, at least in this respect, western farmers were benefiting from advances in the industrial economy.

more than they had borrowed. And who was most deeply in debt? The same group: wheat farmers.

In the 1870s the major wheat-growing states had been Illinois, Wisconsin, and Minnesota. These states had been at the center of the Granger agitation of that decade. By the 1880s wheat had moved onto the Great Plains. Among the indebted farmers of Kansas, Nebraska, and the Dakotas, the deflationary economy of the 1880s made for stubbornly hard times. All that was needed to bring on a real crisis was a sharp drop in world prices for wheat.

The Fate of the Indians

What of the Native Americans who had inhabited the Great Plains? Basically, their history has been told in the foregoing account of western settlement. "The white children have surrounded me and have left me nothing but an island," lamented the great Sioux chief Red Cloud in 1870, the year after the completion of the transcontinental railroad. "When we first had all this land we were strong; now we are all melting like snow on a hillside, while you are grown like spring grass."

Settlement occurred despite the provisions for a permanent Indian country that had been written into federal law and ratified by treaties with various tribes. As incursions into their lands increased from the late 1850s onward, the Indians resisted as best they could, striking back all along the frontier: the Apache in the Southwest, the Cheyenne and Arapaho in Colorado, and the Sioux in the Wyoming and Dakota territories. The Indians hoped that, if they resisted stubbornly enough, the whites would tire of the struggle and leave them in peace. This reasoning seemed not altogether fanciful given the country's exhaustion after the Civil War. But the federal government did not give up; instead it formulated a new policy for dealing with the western Indians.

The Reservation Solution. Few whites questioned the necessity of moving the Native Americans out of the path of settlement and into reservations. That, indeed, had been the fate of the eastern and southern tribes. Now, however, Indian removal included something new: a planned approach for weaning the Indians from their tribal way of life. The first step was a peace commission appointed in 1867 to negotiate an end to the fighting and sign treaties by which the western Indians would cede their lands and move to reservations. There, under the guidance of the Office of Indian Affairs, they would be wards of the government until they learned "to walk on the white man's road."

The government set aside two extensive areas. It allocated the southwestern quarter of the Dakota Territory—present-day South Dakota west of the Missouri River—to the Teton Sioux tribes. And it assigned what is now Oklahoma to the southern plains Indians, along with the major southern tribes—the Choctaw, Cherokee,

MAP 16.4 The Indian Frontier, to 1890

As settlement pushed onto the Great Plains after the Civil War, the Indians put up bitter resistance but ultimately to no avail. Over a period of decades, they ceded most of their lands to the federal government, and by 1890 they were confined to scattered reservations where the most they could expect was an impoverished and alien way of life.

For more help analyzing this map, see the ONLINE STUDY GUIDE at bedfordstmartins.com/henretta.

Chickasaw, Creek, and Seminole—and eastern Indians who had been removed there thirty years before. Scattered reservations went to the Apache, Navaho, and Ute in the Southwest and to the mountain Indians in the Rockies and beyond (Map 16.4).

That the Plains Indians would resist was inevitable. "You might as well expect the rivers to run backward as that any man who was born a free man should be contented when penned up and denied liberty to go where he pleases," said Chief Joseph of the Nez Percé, who led his people in 1877, including women and children, on an epic 1,500-mile march from eastern Oregon to escape confinement in a small reservation. In a series of heroic engagements, the Nez Percé fought off the pursuing U.S. Army until, after four months of extraordinary hardship, the remnants of the tribe were finally cornered and forced to surrender in Montana near the Canadian border.

The U.S. Army was thinly spread, having been cut back after the Civil War to a total force of 27,000. But these were veteran troops, including 2,000 black cavalrymen of the Ninth and Tenth regiments, whom Indians called, with grim respect, "**buffalo soldiers.**" Technology also favored the army. Telegraph communications and railroads enabled the troops to be quickly concentrated; repeating rifles and Gatling machine guns increased their firepower. As fighting intensified in the mid-1870s, a reluctant Congress appropriated funds for more western troops. Because of tribal rivalries, the army could always find Indian allies. Worst of all, however, beyond the formidable U.S. Army or the Indians' disunity, was the overwhelming impact of white settlement.

Resisting the reservation solution, the Indians fought on for years—in Kansas in 1868 and 1869, in the Red River Valley of Texas in 1874, and sporadically among the fierce Apache, who made life miserable for white settlers in the Southwest until their wily chief Geronimo was finally captured in 1886. On the northern plains the crisis came in 1875, when the Indian Office—despite an 1868 treaty guaranteeing their Powder River rights—ordered the Sioux to vacate their Powder River hunting grounds and withdraw to the reservation.

Led by Sitting Bull, Sioux and Cheyenne warriors gathered on the Little Big Horn River to the west of the Powder River country. In a typical concentrating maneuver, army columns from widely separated forts converged on the Little Big Horn. The Seventh Cavalry, commanded by famous Civil War hero George A. Custer, came upon the Sioux encampment on June 25, 1876. Disregarding orders, the reckless Custer sought out battle on his own. He attacked from three sides, hoping to capitalize on the element of surprise. But his forces were spread too thin. The other two contingents fell back with heavy losses to defensive positions, but Custer's own force of 256 men was surrounded and annihilated by Crazy Horse's Sioux warriors. It was a great victory but not a decisive one. The day of reckoning was merely postponed.

Pursued by the military and physically exhausted, the Sioux bands one by one gave up and moved onto the reservation. Last to come in were Sitting Bull's followers. They had retreated to Canada, but in 1881 after five hard years they recrossed the border and surrendered at Fort Buford, Montana.

Not Indian resistance but white land hunger wrecked the reservation solution. In the mid-1870s prospectors began to dig for gold in the Black Hills, sacred land to the Sioux and entirely inside their Dakota reservation. Unable to hold back the prospectors or to buy out the Sioux, the government opened up the Black Hills to gold seekers at their own risk. In 1877, after Sioux resistance had crumbled, federal agents forced the tribes to cede the western third of their Dakota reservation (Map 16.5).

The Indian Territory of Oklahoma met the same fate. Two million acres in the heart of the territory had not been assigned to any tribe, and white homesteaders coveted that fertile land. The "Boomer" movement, stirred up initially by railroads operating in the Indian Territory, agitated tirelessly to open this so-called Oklahoma District to settlers. In 1889 the government gave in and placed the Oklahoma District under the Homestead Act. On April 22, 1889, a horde of claimants rushed in and staked out the entire district within a few hours. Two tent cities—Guthrie with 15,000 people and Oklahoma City with 10,000—were in full swing by nightfall.

Undermining Tribal Culture. In the meantime the campaign to move the Indians on to "the white man's road" relentlessly went forward. During the 1870s the Office of Indian Affairs developed a program to train Indian children for farm work and prepare them for citizenship. Some

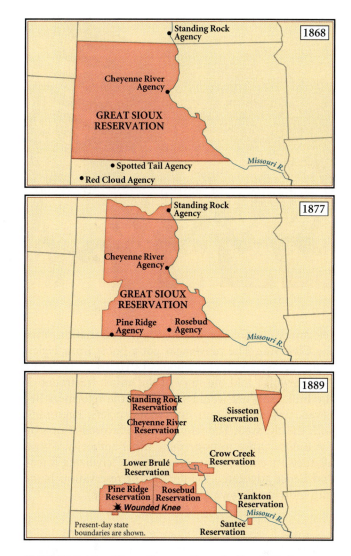

MAP 16.5 The Sioux Reservations in South Dakota, 1868–1889

In 1868, when they bent to the demand that they move onto the reservation, the Sioux thought they had gained secure rights to a substantial part of their ancestral hunting grounds. But as they learned to their sorrow, fixed boundary lines only increased their vulnerability to the land hunger of the whites and sped up the process of expropriation.

attended reservation schools, while the less lucky were sent to boarding schools far from home. Children as young as five were taken from their families and sent to Indian schools that taught them the rudiments of English while discouraging traditional tribal ways. The pupils were shorn of their braids and deprived of their moccasins and blankets. Mother Hubbard dresses and shirts and trousers visibly demonstrated that these bewildered children were being inducted into white society (see American Voices, "Zitkala-Ša [Gertrude Simmons Bonnin]: Becoming White," p. 473).

And not a moment too soon, believed many avowed friends of the Native Americans. The Indians had never lacked sympathizers—especially in the East, where

Indian School

In this photograph taken at the Riverside Indian School in Anadarko, Oklahoma Territory, the pupils have been shorn of their braids and dressed in laced shoes, Mother Hubbard dresses, and shirts and trousers—one step on the journey into the mainstream of white American society. Children as young as five were separated from their families and sent to Indian schools like this one that taught them new skills while encouraging them to abandon traditional Indian ways.
University of Oklahoma, Western History Collections.

reformers created the Indian Rights Association after the Civil War. The movement got a boost from Helen Hunt Jackson's influential book *A Century of Dishonor* (1881), which told the story of the unjust treatment of the Indians. What would save them, the reformers believed, was assimilation into white society, beginning with the children. The reformers also favored efforts by the Indian Office to undermine tribal authority. Above all, they esteemed private property as a "civilizing force" and hence advocated the division of reservation lands into individually owned parcels.

The result was the Dawes Act of 1887, authorizing the president to carve up tribal lands, with each family head receiving an allotment of 160 acres and individuals receiving smaller parcels. The land would be held in trust by the government for twenty-five years, and the Indians would become U.S. citizens. Remaining reservation lands would be sold off, with the proceeds placed in an Indian education fund.

The Last Battle: Wounded Knee. The Sioux were among the first to bear the brunt of the Dawes Act. The

The Dead at Wounded Knee

In December 1890 U.S. soldiers massacred 146 Sioux men, women, and children in the Battle of Wounded Knee in South Dakota. It was the last big fight on the northern plains between the Indians and the whites. Black Elk, a Sioux holy man, related that "after the soldiers marched away from their dirty work, a heavy snow began to fall . . . and it grew very cold." The body of Yellow Bird lay frozen where it had fallen.
National Anthropological Archives, Smithsonian Institution, Washington, DC.

Zitkala-Ša (Gertrude Simmons Bonnin)

Becoming White

Zitkala-Ša, known later as the author Gertrude Simmons Bonnin, recalled in 1900 her painful transformation from Sioux child to pupil at a mission school.

The first day . . . a paleface woman, with white hair, came up after us. We were placed in a line of girls who were marching into the dining room. These were Indian girls, in stiff shoes and closely clinging dresses. The small girls wore sleeved aprons and shingled hair. As I walked noiselessly in my soft mocassins, I felt like sinking into the floor, for my blanket had been stripped from my shoulders. . . . Late in the morning, my friend Judewin gave me a terrible warning. Judewin knew a few words of English; and she had overheard the paleface woman talk about cutting our long, heavy hair. Our mothers had taught us that only unskilled warriors who were captured had their hair shingled by the enemy. Among our people, short hair was worn by mourners, and shingled hair by cowards! . . . In spite of myself, I was carried downstairs and tied fast in a chair. I cried aloud, shaking my head all the while until I felt the cold blades of the scissors against my neck, and heard them gnaw off one of my thick black braids. Then I lost my spirit. . . .

Now, as I look back upon the recent past, I see it from a distance, as a whole. I remember how, from morning till evening, many specimens of civilized peoples visited the Indian school. The city folks with canes and eyeglass, the countrymen with sunburned cheeks and clumsy feet . . . alike astounded at seeing the children of savage warriors so docile and industrious. . . .

In this fashion many have passed through the Indian schools during the last decade, afterward to boast of their charity to the North American Indian. But few there are who have paused to question whether real life or long lasting death lies beneath this semblance of civilization.

Source: Linda K. Kerber and Jane De-Hart Mathews, eds., *Women's America: Refocusing the Past,* 2nd ed. (New York: Oxford University Press, 1987), 254–57.

---

federal government, announcing it had gained tribal approval, opened their "surplus" land to white settlement on February 10, 1890. But no surveys had been made nor any provision for land allotments for the Indians living in the ceded areas. On top of these signs of bad faith by the whites, drought wiped out the Indians' crops that summer. It seemed beyond endurance. They had lost their ancestral lands. They faced a future as farmers, which was alien to their traditions. And immediately confronting them was a winter of starvation.

But news of salvation had also come. An Indian messiah, a holy man who called himself Wovoka, was preaching a new religion on a Paiute reservation in Nevada. In a vision Wovoka had gone to heaven and received God's word that the world would be regenerated. The whites would disappear, all the Indians of past generations would return to earth, and life on the Great Plains would be as it was before the white man appeared. All this would come to pass in the spring of 1891. Awaiting that great day the Indians should follow Wovoka's commandments and practice the **Ghost Dance**, a day-long ritual that sent the spirits of the dancers rising to heaven. As the frenzy of the Ghost Dance swept through some Sioux encampments in the fall of 1890, resident whites became alarmed and called for army intervention.

Wovoka had an especially fervent following among the Minneconjou, where the medicine man Yellow Bird held sway. But their chief, Big Foot, had fallen desperately ill with pneumonia, and the Minneconjou agreed to come in under military escort to an encampment at Wounded Knee Creek on December 28. The next morning, when the soldiers attempted to disarm the Indians, a battle exploded in the encampment. Among the U.S. troopers 25 died; among the Indians 146 men, women, and children perished, many of them shot down as they fled.

Wounded Knee was the final episode in the war against the Plains Indians but not the end of their story. The division of tribal lands now proceeded without hindrance. In the Dakota Territory the Teton Sioux fared relatively well, and many of the younger generation settled down as small farmers and stock grazers. Ironically, the more fortunate tribes were probably those occupying infertile land that did not attract white settlement and thus were spared the allotment process. The flood of whites into South Dakota and Oklahoma, on the other hand, left the Indians as small minorities in lands once wholly theirs—20,000 Sioux in a South Dakotan population of 400,000 in 1900; 70,000 of various tribes in a population of a million when Oklahoma became a state in 1907.

Even so, tribal life survived until, with the restoration of the reservation policy in 1934, it once again rested on a communal territorial basis. All along, Native American cultures had been adaptive, changing in the face of adversity and even absorbing features of white society including, in some cases, developing written languages. This cultural resilience persisted—in religion, in tribal structure, in crafts—but the fostering Native American world was gone, swept away, as an Oklahoma editor put it in the year of statehood, by "the onward march of empire."

The Far West

On the western edge of the Great Plains, the Rocky Mountains rise up to form a great barrier between the mostly flat eastern two-thirds of the country and the rugged Far West (see Map 16.1). Beyond the Rockies lie two vast plateaus: in the north the Columbia plateau, extending into eastern Oregon and Washington, and, flanking the southern Rockies, the Colorado plateau. Where they break off, the plateaus carve out the desert-like Great Basin that covers western Utah and all of Nevada. Separating this arid interior from the Pacific Ocean are two great mountain ranges—the Sierra Nevada and, to the north, the Cascades—beyond which lies a coastal region that is cool and rainy in the north but increasingly dry southward, until in southern California rainfall becomes almost as sparse as in the interior.

What most impressed white Americans about this far western country was its sheer inhospitability. The transmountain West could not be occupied in the standard American fashion—that is, by a multitude of settlers moving westward along a broad front, blanketing the land and, homestead by homestead, bringing it under cultivation. The wagon trains moving to Oregon's Willamette Valley adopted an entirely different strategy of occupation—the planting of scattered settlements in a vast, mostly barren landscape.

New Spain had pioneered this strategy when in 1598 it had sent the first wagon trains 700 miles northward from Mexico into the upper Rio Grande Valley. When the United States seized the Southwest 250 years later major Hispanic settlements existed in New Mexico and California, with lesser settlements scattered along the borderlands into south Texas. At that time, aside from Oregon, the only significant Anglo settlement was around the Great Salt Lake in Utah, where Mormons had moved to escape persecution and plant a New Zion. Fewer than 100,000 Euro-Americans—roughly 25,000 of them Anglo, the rest Hispanic—lived in the entire Far West when it became U.S. territory in 1848.

The Mining Frontier

More emigrants would be coming, certainly, but the Far West seemed unlikely to be much of a magnet. California was "hilly and mountainous," noted a U.S. naval officer in 1849, too dry for farming and surely not "susceptible of supporting a very large population." He had not taken account of the recent discovery of gold in the Sierra foothills, however. California would indeed support a very large population, drawn not by arable land but by dreams of gold.

Extraction of mineral wealth became the basis for the Far West's development (Map 16.6). First of all, this meant explosive growth. By 1860, when the Great Plains was still Indian country, California was a booming state with 300,000 residents. There was also a burst of city building. Overnight San Francisco became a bustling metropolis—it had 57,000 residents by 1860—and was

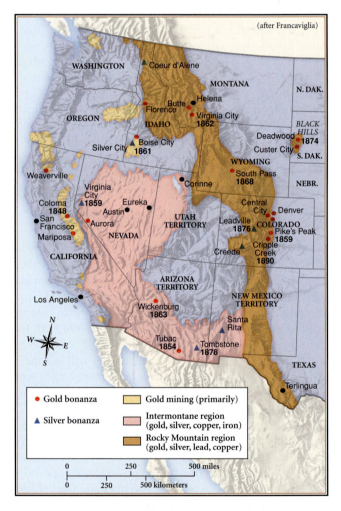

MAP 16.6 The Mining Frontier, 1848–1890

The Far West was America's gold country because of its geological history. Veins of gold and silver form when molten material from the earth's core is forced up into fissures caused by the tectonic movements that create mountain ranges, such as the ones that dominate the far western landscape. It was these veins, the product of mountain-forming activity many thousands of years earlier, that prospectors began to discover after 1848 and furiously exploit. Although widely dispersed across the Far West, the lodes that they found followed the mountain ranges bisecting the region and bypassing the great plateaus not shaped by the ancient tectonic activity.

the hub of a mining empire that stretched to the Rockies. Similarly, Denver mushroomed into the metropolis for the mining camps on the eastern slope.

In its swift urbanization the Far West resembled Australia, whose gold rush began in 1851, much more than it resembled the American Midwest. Like San Francisco, Melbourne was a city incongruously grand amid the empty spaces and rough mining camps of the Australian "outback." The distinctive pattern of isolated settlement persisted in the Far West, driven now, however, by a proliferation of mining sites and by people moving not east to west but west to east, coming mainly from California.

By the mid-1850s, as easy pickings in the California gold country diminished, prospectors began to pull out and spread across the West in hopes of striking it rich

elsewhere. Gold was discovered on the Nevada side of the Sierra Nevada, in the Colorado Rockies, and along the Fraser River in British Columbia. New strikes occurred in Montana and Wyoming during the 1860s, a decade later in the Black Hills of South Dakota, and in the Coeur d'Alene region of Idaho during the 1880s.

As the news of each gold strike spread, a wild, remote area turned almost overnight into a mob scene of prospectors, traders, gamblers, prostitutes, and saloonkeepers. At least 100,000 fortune seekers flocked to the Pike's Peak area of Colorado in the spring of 1859. Trespassers on government or Indian land, the prospectors made their own law. The mining codes devised at community meetings limited the size of a mining claim to what a person could reasonably work. This kind of informal lawmaking also

Hydraulic Mining

When surface veins of gold were played out, miners turned to hydraulic mining, which was invented in California in 1853. The technology was simple, using high-pressure streams of water to wash away hillsides of gold-bearing soil. Although building the reservoirs, piping systems, and sluices cost money, the profits from hydraulic mining helped transform western mining into big business. But, as this daguerreotype suggests, hydraulic mining wreaked havoc on the environment. Collection of Matthew Isenburg.

Baron Joseph Alexander von Hübner

A Western Boom Town

During a leisurely trip around the world in 1871 Baron von Hübner, a distinguished Austrian diplomat, traveled across the United States, taking advantage of the newly completed transcontinental railroad to see the Wild West. After observing Mormon life in Salt Lake City, he went northward to Corinne, Utah, near the juncture where the Central and Union Pacific railroads met. He was struck not only by the crudeness of Corinne (see Map 16.6) but also by the tough "rowdies" inhabiting the place.

Corinne has only existed for four years. Sprung out of the earth as if by enchantment, this town now contains upwards of 2,000 inhabitants, and every day increases in importance. It is a victualing center for the advanced posts of the [miners] in Idaho and Montana. A coach runs twice a week to Virginia City and to Helena, 350 and 500 miles to the north. Despite the serious dangers and the terrible fatigue of the journeys, these diligences are always full of passengers. Various articles of consumption and dry goods of all sorts are sent in wagons. The "high road" is but a rough track in the soil left by the wheels of the previous vehicles.

The streets of Corinne are full of white men armed to the teeth, miserable looking Indians dressed in the ragged shirts and trousers furnished by the federal government, and yellow Chinese with a business-like air and hard, intelligent faces. No town in the Far West gave me so good an idea as this little place of what is meant by "border life," the struggle between civilization and savage men and things. . . .

All commercial business centers in Main Street. The houses on both sides are nothing but boarded huts. I have seen some with only canvas partitions. . . . The lanes alongside of the huts, which are generally the resort of Chinese women of bad character, lead into the desert, which begins at the doors of the last houses. . . .

To have on your conscience a number of man-slaughters committed in full day, under the eyes of your fellow citizens; to have escaped the reach of justice by craft, audacity, or bribery; to have earned a reputation for being "sharp," that is, for knowing how to cheat all the world without being caught—those are the attributes of the true rowdy in the Far West. . . . Endowed as they often are with really fine qualities—courage, energy, and intellectual and physical strength—they might in another sphere and with the moral sense which they now lack, have become valuable members of society. But such as they are, these adventurers have a reason for being, a providential mission to fulfill. The qualities needed to struggle with and conquer savage nature have naturally their corresponding defects. Look back, and you will see the cradles of all civilization surrounded with giants of Herculean strength ready to run every risk and to shrink from neither danger nor crime to attain their ends. It is only by the peculiar temper of the time and place that we can distinguish them from the backwoodsman and rowdy of the United States.

Source: Oscar Handlin, ed., *This Was America* (Cambridge, MA: Harvard University Press, 1949), 313–15.

became an instrument for excluding or discriminating against Mexicans, Chinese, and African Americans in the gold fields. It turned into hangman's justice for the many outlaws who infested the mining camps. Supplying these camps were rough depots like Corinne, Utah (see Voices from Abroad, "Baron Joseph Alexander von Hübner: A Western Boom Town," above).

The heyday of the prospectors was always brief. They were equipped only to skim gold from the surface outcroppings and stream beds. Extracting the metal locked in underground lodes required mine shafts and crushing mills—hence capital, technology, and business organization. The original claim holders quickly sold out when a generous bidder came along. At every gold-rush site the prospector soon gave way to entrepreneurial development and large-scale mining. Rough mining camps turned into big towns.

Virginia City. Nevada's Virginia City started out as a bawdy, ramshackle mining camp, but with the opening of the Comstock silver lode in 1859 it soon boasted a stock exchange, mansions for the mining kings, fancy hotels, and even Shakespearean theater. Virginia City remained a rough **boomtown** nonetheless. It was a magnet for job seekers of both sexes: the men laboring as miners below ground for $4 a day, many of the wage-earning women becoming dance-hall entertainers and prostitutes because that was the best they could do in Virginia City. In 1870 a hundred saloons operated day and night, brothels lined D Street, and men outnumbered women two to one.

When James Galloway arrived looking for work on February 4, 1875, however, he brought his family with him, as did many other miners. Galloway's diary describes a family life that was entirely ordinary—church-going, picnics, the purchase of a lot for a small house. But Galloway was infected by Virginia City's pervasive gambling fever: he speculated regularly in mining stock and always lost money. In the end, he fell victim to the extraordinary hazards of hard-rock mining. He was killed when his sleeve got caught in the gears of a mine machine. He might have survived had he permitted rescuers to hack off his arm, but he took a long chance on being cut loose and coming out whole, and lost.

In Galloway's time Virginia City became respectable and gave the appearance, with its churches and fine public buildings, of a place that would last forever. But in fact when the Comstock lode played out in the early 1880s, Virginia City declined and, in a fate all too familiar in bonanza mining, became a ghost town.

Industrialization of Western Mining. In its final stage the mining frontier passed into the industrial world. At some sites gold and silver proved less important than the commoner metals—copper, lead, and zinc—for which there was a huge demand in eastern manufacturing. Copper mining thrived in the Butte district of Montana. In the 1890s Idaho's Coeur d'Alene silver district became the nation's main source of lead and zinc.

Entrepreneurs raised capital, built rail connections, financed the technology for treating the lower-grade copper deposits, constructed smelting facilities, and recruited a labor force. As with other workers, western miners organized trade unions (see Chapter 17). As elsewhere in corporate America, the western mining industries went through a process of consolidation. The Anaconda Copper Mining Company and other Montana mining firms came under the control of the Amalgamated Copper Company in 1899. Also in that year the American Smelting and Refining Company brought together the bulk of the nation's lead-mining and copper-refining properties. Blackfeet and Crow country in the 1860s, the Butte copper district was a center of industrial capitalism thirty years later.

The Pacific Slope. But for its mineral wealth the Far West's history would certainly have been very different. Before the discovery of gold at Sutter's Mill in 1848, Oregon's Willamette Valley, not dry California, mostly attracted westward-bound settlers. And, but for the gold rush, California would likely have remained like the Willamette Valley—an agricultural backwater with no markets for its products and a slow-growing population. In 1860, although already a state, Oregon had scarcely 25,000 inhabitants, and its principal city, Portland, was little more than a village. Booming California and its tributary mining country pulled Oregon from the doldrums by creating a market for the state's produce and timber. During the 1880s Oregon and Washington (which became a state in 1899) grew prodigiously. Where scarcely 100,000 settlers had lived twenty years earlier, there were nearly 750,000 by 1890 (Map 16.7). Portland and, even more dramatically, Seattle blossomed into important commercial centers, both prospering from a mixed economy of farming, ranching, logging, and fishing.

At a certain point, especially as railroads opened up eastern markets, this diversified growth became self-sustaining. But what had triggered it—what had provided the first markets and underwritten the economic infrastructure—was the bonanza mining economy, at the hub of which stood San Francisco, the metropolis for the entire Far West.

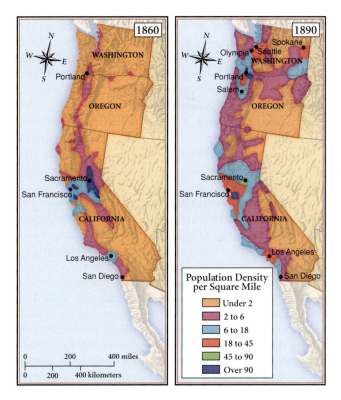

MAP 16.7 The Settlement of the Pacific Slope, 1860–1890

In 1860 the settlement of the Pacific slope was remarkably uneven—fully underway in northern California and scarcely begun anywhere else. By 1890 a new pattern had begun to emerge, with the swift growth of southern California foreshadowed and the settlement of the Pacific Northwest well launched.

Hispanics, Chinese, Anglos

California was the anchor of two distinct far western regions. First, it joined with Oregon and Washington to form the Pacific slope. Second, by climate and Hispanic heritage, California was linked to the Southwest, which today includes Arizona, New Mexico, and Texas.

The Hispanic Southwest. The first Europeans to enter the Far West—two centuries before the earliest Anglos—were Hispanics moving northward out of Mexico. There, along a 1,500-mile borderland, outposts had been planted over many years by the viceroys of New Spain. Most populous and best established were the settlements along New Mexico's upper Rio Grande Valley; the main town, Santa Fe, was over 200 years old and contained 4,635 residents in 1860. Farther down the Rio Grande was El Paso, nearly as old but much smaller, and, to the west in present-day Arizona, Tucson, an old presidio, or garrison, town. At the western end of this Hispanic crescent, in California, a Spanish-speaking population was spread thinly in the old presidio towns along the coast and on a patchwork of great ranches.

The economy of this Hispanic crescent was pastoral, consisting primarily of cattle and sheep ranching. In south Texas there were family-run ranches. Everywhere else the social order was highly stratified. At the top stood an elite—the beneficiaries of royal land grants, who were proudly Spanish and devoted to the traditional life of a landed aristocracy. Below them, with little in between, was a laboring class of servants, artisans, vaqueros (cowboys), and farmworkers. New Mexico also contained a large mestizo population—people of mixed Hispanic and Indian blood. They were a Spanish-speaking and Catholic peasantry but still faithful in their village life and farming methods to their Pueblo heritage.

Pueblo Indians, although their dominance over the Rio Grande Valley had long passed, still occupied much of the region, living in the old ways in adobe villages and making the New Mexico countryside a patchwork of Hispanic and Pueblo settlements. To the north a vibrant new people, the Navajo, had appeared, warriors like the Apache from which they descended but also skilled at crafts and sheep raising.

New Mexico was one place where European and Native American cultures managed a successful, if uneasy, coexistence and where the Indian inhabitants were equipped to hold their own against the Anglo challenge. In California, by contrast, the Hispanic occupation had been harder on the indigenous hunter-gatherer peoples, undermining their tribal structure, reducing them to forced labor, and making them easy prey for the aggressive Anglo miners and settlers, who, in short order, nearly wiped out California's once numerous Indian population.

Anglo-Hispanic Conflict. The fate of the Hispanic Southwest after its incorporation into the United States in 1848 depended on the rate of Anglo immigration. In New Mexico, which remained off the beaten track even after the arrival of railroads in the 1880s, the Santa Fe elite more than held its own, incorporating the Anglo newcomers into Hispanic society through intermarriage and business partnerships. In California, however, expropriation of the great ranches was relentless, even though the 1848 treaty with Mexico had recognized the property rights of the Californios and had made them U.S. citizens. Around San Francisco the great ranches disappeared almost in a puff of smoke. Farther south, where Anglos were slow to arrive, the dons held on longer, but by the 1880s just a handful of the original families still retained their Mexican land grants.

The New Mexico peasants found themselves equally embattled. Crucial to their livelihood were grazing rights on communal lands. But these were customary rights that could not withstand legal challenge when Anglo ranchers established title and began putting up fences. The peasants responded as best they could. Their subsistence economy relied on a division of labor that gave women a productive role in the village economy. Women tended the small gardens, engaged in village bartering, and maintained the households. With the loss of the communal lands, the men began migrating seasonally to railway work or the Colorado mines and sugar-beet fields, earning dollars while leaving the village economy in their wives' hands.

Elsewhere, hard-pressed Hispanics struck back for what they considered rightfully theirs. When Anglo ranchers began to fence in communal lands in San Miguel County, the New Mexicans long settled there, *los pobres* (the poor ones) organized themselves into masked night-riding raiders and in 1889 and 1890 mounted an effective campaign of harassment against the interlopers. After 1900, when Anglo farmers swarmed into south Texas bent on exploiting new irrigation methods, the displaced Tejanos responded with sporadic but persistent night-riding attacks. Much of the raiding by Mexican "bandits" from across the border in the years before World War I was really more in the nature of a civil war by embittered Tejanos who had lived north of the Rio Grande for generations.

But they, like the New Mexico villagers who became seasonal wage laborers, could not avoid being driven into the ranks of a Mexican American working class as the Anglo economy developed. This same development also began to attract increasing numbers of immigrants from Old Mexico.

Mexican Migrants. All along the Southwest borderlands, economic activity was picking up in the late nineteenth century. Railroads were being built, copper mines were opening in Arizona, cotton and

Mexican Miners

When large-scale mining began to develop in Arizona and New Mexico in the late nineteenth century, Mexicans crossed the border to earn Yankee dollars. In this unidentified photograph from the 1890s, the men are wearing traditional clothing, indicating perhaps that they are recent arrivals at the mine.

Division of Cultural Resource, Wyoming Department of Commerce.

vegetable agriculture was developing in south Texas, and orchards were planted in southern California. In Texas the Hispanic population increased from about 20,000 in 1850 to 165,000 in 1900. Some came as contract workers for railway gangs and harvest crews; virtually all were relegated to the lowest-paying and most back-breaking work; and everywhere they were discriminated against and reviled by Anglo workers.

What stimulated the Mexican migration was the enormous demand for workers by a region undergoing explosive development, which also accounted for the exceptionally high number of European immigrants in the West. In California, where they were most heavily concentrated, roughly one-third of the population was foreign-born, more than twice the level for the country as a whole. Most numerous were the Irish, followed by the Germans and British. But there was another group unique to the West—the Chinese.

The Chinese Migration. Attracted first by the California gold rush, 200,000 Chinese came to the United States between 1850 and 1880. In those years they constituted a considerable minority of California's population—around 9 percent—and because virtually all were actively employed, they represented a much larger proportion of the state's labor force—probably a quarter. Elsewhere in the West, at the crest of mining activity, their presence could surge remarkably, to over 25 percent of Idaho's population in 1870, for example.

The arrival of the Chinese in North America was part of a worldwide Asian migration that had begun in the mid-nineteenth century. Driven by poverty, the Chinese went to Australia, Hawaii, and Latin America; Indians to Fiji and South Africa; and Javanese to Dutch colonies in the Caribbean. Most of these Asians migrated as indentured servants, which in effect made them the property of others. In America, however, indentured servitude was no longer lawful—by the 1820s state courts were banning it as involuntary servitude—so the Chinese came as free workers, going into debt for their passage money but not surrendering their personal freedom or right to choose their employers.

Once in America, Chinese immigrants normally entered the orbit of the Six Companies, a powerful confederation of Chinese merchants in San Francisco's Chinatown. Most of the arrivals were young unmarried men eager to earn a stake and return to their native Cantonese villages. The Six Companies acted not only as an employment agency but provided new arrivals with the social and commercial services they needed to survive in an alien world. The few Chinese women—the male/female ratio was thirteen to one—worked mostly as servants and prostitutes, sad victims of the desperate poverty that drove the Chinese to America. Some were sold by impoverished parents; others were enticed or kidnapped by procurers and transported to America.

Until the early 1860s, when surface mining played out, Chinese men labored mainly in the California gold fields—as prospectors where white miners permitted it and as laborers and cooks where they did not. Then, when construction began on the transcontinental railroad, the Central Pacific hired Chinese workers. Eventually they constituted four-fifths of the railroad's labor force, doing most of the pick-and-shovel work laying the track across the Sierra Nevada. Many were recruited by labor agents and worked in labor gangs run

Kitty Tatch and Friend on Glacier Point, Yosemite
From the time the Yosemite Valley was set aside in 1864 as a place "for public pleasuring, resort, and recreation," it attracted a stream of tourists eager to experience the grandeur of the American West. As is suggested by this photograph taken sometime in the 1890s, the magic of Yosemite was enough to set even staid young ladies dancing. The Yosemite Museum.

devoted to studying the High Sierras and protecting them from "despoiling gain-seekers . . . eagerly trying to make everything immediately and selfishly commercial." One result was the creation of California's national parks

in 1890—Yosemite, Sequoia, and General Grant (later part of King's Canyon). Another was the formation in 1892 of the Sierra Club, which became a powerful voice for the defenders of California's wilderness.

They won some and lost some. Advocates of water-resource development insisted that California's irrigated agriculture and thirsty cities could not grow without tapping the abundant snowpack of the Sierra Nevada. By the turn of the century, Los Angeles faced a water crisis that threatened its growth. The answer was a 238-mile aqueduct to the Owens River in the southern Sierra. A bitter controversy blew up over this immense project, driven by the resistance of local residents to the flooding of the beautiful Owens Valley. More painful for John Muir and his **preservationist** allies was their failure to save the Hetch Hetchy gorge north of Yosemite National Park. After years of controversy the federal government in 1913 approved the damming of Hetch Hetchy to serve the water needs of San Francisco.

When the stakes became high enough, nature lovers like John Muir generally came out on the short end. Even so, something original and distinctive had been added to California's heritage—the linking of a society's well-being with the preservation of its natural environment. This realization, in turn, said something important about the nation's relationship to the West. If the urge to conquer and exploit persisted, at least it was now tempered by a sense that nature's bounty was not limitless. And this, more than any announcement by the U.S. Census that a "frontier line" no longer existed, registered the country's acceptance that the age of heedless westward expansion had ended.

FOR FURTHER EXPLORATION

▶ For definitions of key terms boldfaced in this chapter, see the glossary at the end of the book.

▶ To assess your mastery of the material covered in this chapter, see the Online Study Guide at **bedfordstmartins.com/henretta**.

▶ For suggested references, including Web sites, see page SR-18 at the end of the book.

▶ For map resources and primary documents, see **bedfordstmartins.com/henretta**.

SUMMARY

In 1860 the Great Plains was still ancestral home to nomadic Indian tribes that had built a vibrant society based on the horse and the buffalo. By 1890 the Indians had been crowded onto reservations and forced to abandon their tribal way of life. With railroads leading the way, cattle ranchers and homesteaders in short order displaced the Indians and domesticated the Great Plains. Beyond the Rockies a different pattern of settlement occurred. Because so much of this region was arid and uninhabitable, occupation took the form of oases of settlement rather than progressive occupation along a broad frontier that had prevailed east of the Rockies. And while arable land had been the lure for settlers up to that point, what drove settlement beyond the Rockies was the discovery of mineral wealth. For the entire trans-Mississippi West, the pace of occupation was accelerated by the nation's economic development. Industry needed the West's mineral resources; the cities demanded agricultural products; and from railroads to barbed wire, the industrial economy provided the means for a swift and decisive conquest of the West. For Great Plains farmers suffering from weak markets, however, integration into this modern economy was no guarantee of prosperity.

By population, economy, and strategic position, California was the regional power dominating the Far West in the late nineteenth century. It was the anchor both of a crescent of Hispanic settlement to the Southwest and of the Pacific slope region stretching up to the Canadian border. The discovery of gold had set off a huge migration that overwhelmed the thinly spread Hispanic inhabitants and swiftly transformed California into a populous state with a large urban sector. California developed a distinctive culture that capitalized on its rediscovered Hispanic heritage and its climate and natural environment. The treatment of the Chinese, Japanese, and Mexicans who provided the state's cheap labor, however, infused a dark streak of racism into its society.

TIMELINE

1849	California gold rush
	Chinese migration begins
1862	Homestead Act
1864	Yosemite Valley reserved as public park
1865	Long Drive of Texas longhorns begins
1867	Patrons of Husbandry (the Grange) founded
	U.S. government adopts reservation policy for Plains Indians
1868	Indian treaty confirms Sioux rights to Powder River hunting grounds
1869	Union Pacific–Central Pacific transcontinental railroad completed
1875	Sioux ordered to vacate Powder River hunting grounds; war breaks out
1876	Battle of Little Big Horn
1877	San Francisco anti-Chinese riots
1879	Exoduster migration to Kansas
1882	Chinese Exclusion Act
1884	Helen Hunt Jackson's novel *Ramona*
1886	Dry cycle begins on the Great Plains
1887	Dawes Act
1889	Oklahoma opened to white settlement
1890	Indian massacre at Wounded Knee, South Dakota
	U.S. Census declares end of the frontier

CHAPTER 17

Industrial Capitalism Triumphant
Growth of the Industrial Base
The Railroad Boom
Mass Markets and Large-Scale
   Enterprise
The New South

The World of Work
Labor Recruits
Autonomous Labor
Systems of Control

The Labor Movement
Reformers and Unionists
The Triumph of "Pure and Simple"
   Unionism
Industrial War
American Radicalism in the
   Making

Capital and Labor in the Age of Enterprise

1877–1900

THE YEAR THAT RECONSTRUCTION ENDED, 1877, also marked the end of the first great crisis of American industrial capitalism. In 1873, four years earlier, a severe depression had set in, bankrupting 47,000 firms and driving wholesale prices down by 30 percent. Railroad building ground to a halt. Orders for industrial goods disappeared. Hundreds of thousands of workers lost their jobs, and suffering was widespread. Across the country workers demanded "bread for the needy, clothing for the naked, and houses for the homeless." Before long the foundations of the social order began to shake.

On July 16, 1877, railroad workers went on strike to protest a wage cut at the Baltimore and Ohio Railroad. In towns along the B&O tracks, crowds cheered as the strikers attacked company property and prevented trains from running. The strike rippled across the country. In Pittsburgh the Pennsylvania Railroad's roundhouse went up in flames on July 21, and at many rail centers rioters and looters roamed freely. Only the arrival of federal troops restored order. On August 15 President Rutherford B. Hayes wrote in his diary: "The strikers have been put down *by force*." The Great Strike of 1877 had been crushed but only after raising the specter of social revolution.

And then recovery came. Within months the economy was booming again. In the next fifteen years, the output of manufactured goods increased by over 150 percent. Confidence in the nation's industrial future rebounded. "Upon [material progress] is founded all other progress," asserted a railroad president in 1888. "Can there be any doubt that cheapening the cost of necessaries and conveniences of life is the most powerful agent of civilization and progress?"

◀ **Homestead at Twilight**
In this evocative painting Aaron Henry Gorson (1872–1933) looks across the Monongahela River at Andrew Carnegie's great steel mill, a symbol of America's industrial prowess but also, as the clouds of smoke lighting the sky suggest, a major source of the Pittsburgh district's polluted air. Westmorland Museum of Art.

The rail magnate's boast represents the confident face of America's industrial revolution. President Hayes's anxious diary entries suggest a grimmer face, manifest for example in the armories built in cities across the country after 1877. They were fortresses designed to withstand assault by future strikers and rioters. It was a paradox of the nation's industrial history that an economy celebrated for its dynamism and inventiveness—a wealth-creating machine beyond anything the world had ever seen—was also brutally indifferent to the many who fell by the wayside, hence never secure and never free of social conflict.

Industrial Capitalism Triumphant

Economic historians speak of the late nineteenth century as the age of the Great Deflation. Prices fell steadily not only in the United States but worldwide (Figure 17.1). Falling prices normally signal economic stagnation: there is not enough demand for the available goods and services. For England, a mature industrial power, the Great Deflation did indeed signal economic decline. But not for the United States. Industrial expansion went into high gear during the Great Deflation. Because of increasing manufacturing efficiencies, American firms could cut prices and yet earn profits for financing still better equipment. This achievement meant higher real income for Americans, which increased by nearly 50 percent (from $388 in 1877 to $573 in 1900) in scarcely a quarter of a century.

Growth of the Industrial Base

By the 1870s factories were a familiar sight in America. But early manufacturing had really been an extension of the agricultural economy, producing consumer goods—textiles, shoes, paper, and furniture—that replaced articles made at home or by individual artisans. Gradually, however, a different kind of demand developed as the country's economy surged. Railroads needed locomotives; new factories needed machinery; cities needed trolley lines, sanitation systems, and commercial buildings. Railroad equipment, machinery, and construction materials were **capital goods**, that is, goods themselves adding to the nation's productive capacity. Although consumer goods remained very important, it was the manufacture of capital goods that now drove America's industrial economy.

Central to the capital-goods sector was technological revolution in steel making. The country already produced large quantities of wrought iron, a malleable metal easily worked by rural blacksmiths and farmers. But wrought iron was expensive—it was produced in small batches by skilled puddlers—and did not stand up under heavy use as railway track. In 1856 the British inventor Henry Bessemer designed a furnace—the Bessemer converter—that refined raw pig iron into an essentially new product, steel, a metal harder and more durable than wrought iron (see New Technology, "Iron and Steel," p. 488). Others adopted Bessemer's invention, but it was Andrew Carnegie who fully exploited its revolutionary potential.

Carnegie arrived from Scotland in 1848 at the age of twelve with his poverty-stricken family. He became a telegraph operator, then went to work for the Pennsylvania Railroad and rapidly climbed the managerial ladder. In 1865, having amassed a fortune in wartime speculation, Carnegie struck out on his own as an iron manufacturer. His main customers were his former associates in the railroad business.

In 1872 Carnegie erected a massive steel mill outside Pittsburgh, with the Bessemer converter as its centerpiece. The converter broke a bottleneck at the refining stage and enabled Carnegie's engineers to design a mill that functioned on the basis of integrated operation. Iron ore entered the blast furnaces at one end and emerged without interruption at the other end as finished steel rails.

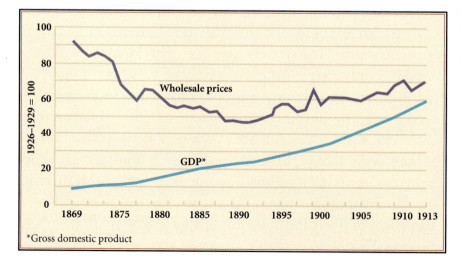

*Gross domestic product

FIGURE 17.1 Business Activity and Wholesale Prices, 1869–1913

This graph shows the key feature of the performance of the late-nineteenth-century economy: while output was booming, the price of goods was falling.

Named after Carnegie's admired boss at the Pennsylvania Railroad, the Edgar Thompson Works became a model for the modern steel industry. Giant integrated steel plants swiftly replaced the puddling mills that had once dotted western Pennsylvania.

The technological breakthrough in steel spurred the intensive exploitation of the country's rich mineral resources. Once iron ore began to be shipped down the Great Lakes from the rich Mesabi Range in northern Minnesota, the industry was assured of an ample supply of its primary raw material. The other key ingredient, coal, came from the great Appalachian field that stretched from Pennsylvania to Alabama (Map 17.1). A minor enterprise before the Civil War, coal production doubled every decade after 1870, exceeding 400 million tons a year by 1910.

As steam engines became the nation's energy workhorse, prodigious amounts of coal began to be consumed by railroads and factories. Industries previously dependent on waterpower rapidly converted to steam. The turbine, utilizing continuous rotation rather than the steam engine's back-and-forth motion, marked another major advance during the 1880s. With the coupling of the steam turbine to the electric generator, the nation's energy revolution was completed, and after 1900 America's factories began a massive conversion to electric power.

▲ **The Corliss Engine**

The symbol of the Philadelphia Centennial in 1876 was the great Corliss engine, which towered over Machinery Hall and powered all the equipment on exhibit there. Yet the Corliss engine also signified the incomplete nature of American industrialism at that time; it soon became obsolete. Westinghouse turbines generating electricity would be the power source for the nation's next World's Fair in Chicago in 1893. Culver Pictures.

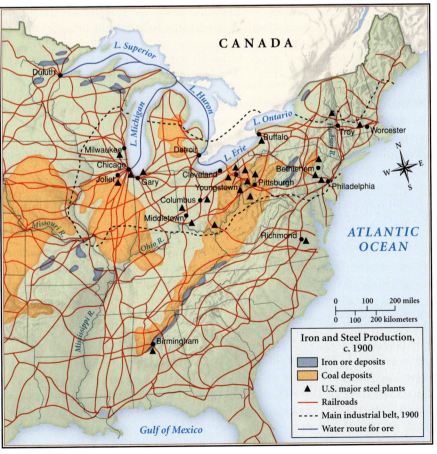

◄ **MAP 17.1 Iron and Steel Production, 1900**

Before the Civil War, the iron industry was concentrated in eastern Pennsylvania and northern New Jersey. With the shift to steel and the westward movement of population and industry, production moved first to western Pennsylvania and then to Ohio, Indiana, Illinois, and southward into Alabama. The specific locations—Pittsburgh, Youngstown, Chicago, and Birmingham—were dictated by the rail network, new sources of coal and iron ore, and markets for steel.

Iron and Steel Production, c. 1900

- Iron ore deposits
- Coal deposits
- ▲ U.S. major steel plants
- Railroads
- Main industrial belt, 1900
- Water route for ore

Iron and Steel

Iron was not a product new to the nineteenth century in the way that plastic was new to the twentieth century. Early Europeans had made iron tools and weapons at least a thousand years before Christ, and in the years since those remote times, the underlying processes did not change, for they are dictated by the nature of iron metallurgy. What did change were the techniques for carrying out those processes.

The first break from ancient methods came when blast furnaces appeared in Belgium around 1340. Ore was melted in a charcoal-burning furnace to which limestone had been added. A blast of air then set off a combustion process that combined carbon from the charcoal with the molten iron while the impurities combined with the limestone to form a slag. The slag was drawn off from the top while the molten iron was tapped from the bottom into sand forms resembling piglets feeding from a sow—hence the term *pig iron*.

By the late eighteenth century, Great Britain was running out of wood for charcoal. The substitution of coke, made by superheating coal, saved the industry and gave Britain the competitive edge it needed to launch the Industrial Revolution. Endowed with ample forests, the United States was slow to adopt coke-using furnaces, but by 1860 it had caught up with Britain technologically.

The search for a metal harder and more durable than wrought iron resulted in the invention in 1856 of an entirely different refining process by the Englishman Henry Bessemer. The Bessemer converter was a pear-shaped vessel that was open at the top and had a bottom perforated with many holes. Molten pig iron flowed into the top while the converter was tilted on its side. Air was blasted through the perforated bottom with great force, and the converter then swung back to its upright position. The resulting combustion set off a spectacular display of flame and smoke. Within fifteen minutes the impurities in the molten iron burned off, and the flames died down. The converter was again tilted on its side, and after manganese and other chemicals had been added, the purified iron was emptied into ingot molds. The refined metal, called *steel*, was ideally suited for use as railroad track.

Bessemer's device, though invented primarily with the aim of gaining a more durable metal, also proved vastly more efficient than the hand-operated puddling furnaces that produced wrought iron. The Bessemer converter turned out great quantities of steel with virtually no labor, and this forced changes up and down the line. To feed the converters' appetite for pig iron, blast furnaces were built larger and, with the introduction of the hot blast, became much faster. To handle the flow of steel from the converters, rolling mills became increasingly mechanized and automatic. Finally, blast furnaces, converters, and rolling mills were brought together and linked into a single processing operation. The integrated

---

Thus in the decades after the Civil War, the steel industry was established, the nation's mineral resources came under intensive development, and energy was harnessed to the manufacturing system. All these basic elements of modern industrialism—steel, coal, and energy—grew after 1870 at rates far exceeding manufacturing.

The Railroad Boom

Before the Civil War moving goods by water satisfied the country's transportation needs. But it was love at first sight when locomotives arrived from Britain in the early 1830s. Americans were impatient for the year-round, on-time service that canal barges and riverboats could not provide. By 1860, with a network of tracks already criss-crossing the country east of the Mississippi, the railroad clearly was on the way to being industrial America's mode of transportation (Map 17.2).

Constructing the Railroads. The question was, who would pay for it? Railroads could be state enterprises like the canals. Alternatively they could be financed by private investors. Unlike most European countries the United States chose free enterprise. Even so, government played a big role. Eager for the economic benefits, many states and localities lured railroads with offers of financial aid, mostly by buying railroad bonds. Land grants were the principle means by which the federal government encouraged interregional railroads; huge tracts went to the transcontinental railroads tying the Far West to the rest of the country.

The most important boost that government gave the railroads, however, was not money or land but a legal form of organization—the **corporation**—that enabled private capital to be raised in prodigious amounts. Investors who bought stock in the railroads enjoyed limited liability: they risked only the money they had invested and were not personally liable for the railroad's

steel plant of 1900—capable of producing 2,500 tons or more a day—became a voracious consumer of ore and coal.

The commanding lead the United States had built up by 1900 rested on the world's best reserves of coking coal in western Pennsylvania and the vast ore deposits in Minnesota's Mesabi Range, northern Michigan's older fields, and Alabama. The geographical face of American industrialism changed as the places best located in relation to raw materials, transportation, and markets—Pittsburgh, the steel towns along the Great Lakes, and Birmingham, Alabama—became the great centers of steel production. American cities relied on steel for the construction of skyscrapers, trolley lines, subways, and the vast underground complexes of pipe that supplied the urban millions with water and gas and carried away their sewage. Without steel the emerging automobile industry would not have grown, nor would a host of other industries.

It is no wonder that historians have called the last decades of the nineteenth century America's Age of Steel. What was overlooked at the time and for long afterward was the fact that the nation's natural resources were not inexhaustible. It is the exhaustion of the great Mesabi Range that has leveled the playing field among global competitors and helps explain the recent decline of the American steel industry.

Bessemer Converter, Bethlehem Works, Steelton, Pennsylvania, 1885

Workers for Bethlehem Steel in Steelton, Pennsylvania, pose for this 1885 photograph with a Bessemer converter. The late nineteenth century in America came to be known as "America's Age of Steel," thanks to the increased steel production that the Bessemer converter helped generate. Hagley Museum and Library.

debts. A corporation could also borrow money by issuing interest-bearing bonds, which was how the railroads actually raised most of the money they needed.

Railroad building generally was handed over to construction companies, which, despite the name, were primarily another arm of the complex financing system. Hiring contractors and suppliers often involved persuading them to accept the railroad's bonds as payment and, when that failed, wheeling and dealing to raise cash by selling or borrowing on the bonds. Since the railroad promoters actually ran the construction companies, the opportunities for plunder were enormous. The most notorious, the Union Pacific's Credit Mobilier, siphoned probably half the money it paid out into the pockets of the promoters.

The railroad business was not for the faint of heart. Most successful were promoters with the best access to capital, such as John Murray Forbes, a great Boston merchant in the China trade who developed the

Chicago, Burlington, and Quincy Railroad in the Midwest; or Cornelius Vanderbilt, who started with the fortune he had made in the steamboat business. Vanderbilt was primarily a consolidator, linking previously independent lines crossing New York State and ultimately developing the New York Central into a trunk line to Chicago. James J. Hill, who without federal subsidy made the Great Northern into the best of the transcontinental railroads, was certainly the nation's champion railroad builder. In contrast Jay Gould, at various times owner of the Erie, Wabash, Union Pacific, and Missouri Pacific systems, always remained a stock-market speculator at heart (see American Lives, "Jay Gould: Robber Baron?" p. 492).

Railroad development in the United States was often sordid, fiercely competitive, and subject to boom and bust. Yet vast sums of capital were raised and a network built exceeding that of the rest of the world combined. By 1900 virtually no corner of the country lacked rail service.

Jay Gould: Robber Baron?

Jay Gould was an operator pure and simple. . . . It would be at least very difficult to show that the Nation as a whole is a dollar richer by the existence of JAY GOULD, while he himself has become the richer . . . from the expansion of the city and the Nation. He has simply absorbed what would have been made in spite of him.

Thus did the *New York Times* bid farewell to Jay Gould at his death on December 3, 1892. There was a name for the kind of businessman the *Times* thought Gould was: robber baron. In the Middle Ages the term described renegade knights who exacted tribute from all who passed by; by extension to Gould's time, robber baron referred to capitalists who extracted riches from the economic system while contributing nothing in return. By that definition was Gould a robber baron? Yes, said historians for many years, following the thesis first advanced by Matthew Josephson in his book *The Robber Barons* (1934). Today historians are no longer so sure.

Jay Gould was born on May 27, 1836, in Roxbury, New York, in the mountainous Catskill region. John Gould wanted Jay, his only son, to take over the family farm, but the boy was small and sickly, and he detested farmwork. By sheer tenacity Jay got more education than most farm boys, but even tenacity could not get him to Yale, which had been his dream. At sixteen he became a surveyor, at nineteen he wrote a flowery history of Delaware County for the money, and then at twenty he got a big break. An eccentric but wealthy tanner, Zadock Pratt, befriended Gould, taking him as a partner to set up a tannery in Pennsylvania, where Gould had located a rich new source of tanning bark. The venture succeeded thanks to Pratt's money and Gould's hard work, but after two years there was a falling-out and Pratt proposed terminating the partnership. He would buy Gould's share for $10,000 or sell out to the young man for $60,000. Gould found backers among the leather merchants who marketed the tannery's output and bought out the surprised Pratt. This was a typical Gould maneuver—bold, unexpected, and decisive. The new partnership quickly turned sour, primarily because of the collapse of the leather market. The damage to

Jay Gould, c. 1882
Culver Pictures.

well-reputed merchants left Gould discredited in the leather trade. He had made money amid the wreckage of other people's fortunes, another Gould trademark. In 1860 he settled in New York, bent on satisfying what had become his obsession: he wanted to be rich.

Enlisting in the Union army probably never occurred to him. The Civil War was too good a chance for turning quick profits; and besides, Gould had no taste for fighting. In 1863 he married the daughter of a wealthy New York merchant, sired six children in rapid succession, and became a devoted family man. These were, above all, schooling years for Gould. He learned about the railroads from a controlling interest he gained in a small Vermont railroad. And—no one knows exactly how—he developed a consummate mastery of Wall Street finance. Few could have been aware of this when Gould was elected in 1867 to the board of the Erie Railroad just as a titanic battle was taking shape for control of the Erie.

The aggressor was Cornelius Vanderbilt, who wanted to ally the Erie with his emerging New York

Central system. Vanderbilt began secretly buying up Erie stock, a maneuver by which he had captured other key railroad properties. This time, however, Erie stock mysteriously kept entering the market even though no more could legally be issued by the Erie. Gould was exploiting a dubious loophole: freshly minted convertible bonds that could immediately be converted to stock. Vanderbilt countered with court injunctions, forcing Gould and his confederates to decamp to New Jersey, while in Albany Vanderbilt lobbied to prevent legalization of the convertible-bond gambit. A bidding war began for legislators' votes, which, with the Erie dollars overflowing his satchel, Gould finally won. To settle things, Vanderbilt and his allies had to be compensated for their losses, which Gould ingeniously arranged by spending $9 million from the Erie treasury to buy back their stock at inflated prices. The Erie was effectively bankrupted, but it was now firmly in Gould's hands.

Gould was never able to shed the unsavory reputation he acquired during the Erie years. But even in that buccaneering period, there was another side to him as a railroad man. Indifferent to day-to-day operations, Gould had a brilliant strategic sense for how railroads should grow. The key, he knew, was integrated development, with trunk-line service between major centers. Right off Gould moved to take over the local western roads and make the Erie the dominant system linking the Atlantic seaboard and the Midwest. But he lacked the resources, and the Pennsylvania and the New York Central, spurred by his challenge, beat him out, capturing the key western lines and leaving the Erie a weak secondary system.

Yet the vision had been Gould's, and in 1879 he found greener fields for his strategic talents west of St. Louis and southward into Texas. The railroads in this region were a jumble of incomplete and disconnected lines. Gould began buying control, finishing the lines, and linking them into a regional system under his parent company, the Missouri Pacific. He also moved aggressively in other parts of the country, challenging established railroads and cutting rates ruthlessly to take traffic from them. By 1882 he controlled 15 percent of the nation's entire trackage, and Western Union and the New York Elevated besides.

The economic boom that fostered this empire building did not last, however, and after 1881 Gould found himself on the wrong side of the stock market, overextended in holdings that were falling in value. On the verge of ruin in early 1884, he managed to get a "corner" on the stock of the Missouri Pacific, forcing up its price and thus saving himself. But Gould was not the same man after that. He lost his iron nerve, and his health began to fail. He swore off speculation. His business dealings, while still far-flung, became more cautious and defensive. But to the end he remained a tough

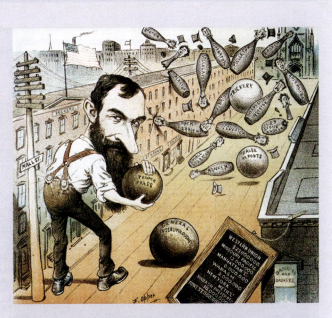

Wall Street: Gould's Private Bowling Alley
This 1882 cartoon testifies vividly to Gould's unsavory reputation as a financial manipulator, bowling over his adversaries with Trickery and False Reports and keeping score of his ill-gotten gains on the slate at lower right. Granger Collection.

customer, never justifying himself, never cloaking himself in religious piety, not even seeking to make amends by a show of philanthropy. In death he thumbed his nose at the world: his entire fortune—$75 million—went in trust to his family.

A century later historians can perhaps appreciate better than Gould's obituarists the positive side of Gould's amazing business career. The nation's railroad network bore in some considerable degree Gould's mark by virtue of his own system building and by virtue of the spur he gave to others. Moreover, his forays broke open monopoly markets and drove shipping prices down. Even Gould's purely speculative ventures may have contributed to the nation's economic growth. Economists say that money made in speculation is an especially efficient source of fresh capital, which is what Gould's winnings were to America's capital-hungry railroads.

Let us suppose that Gould never understood this. Let us grant further that he was motivated by greed, that his methods were unscrupulous, and that, had he lived at a later time, he probably would have ended up in prison. Are we justified in calling him a robber baron?

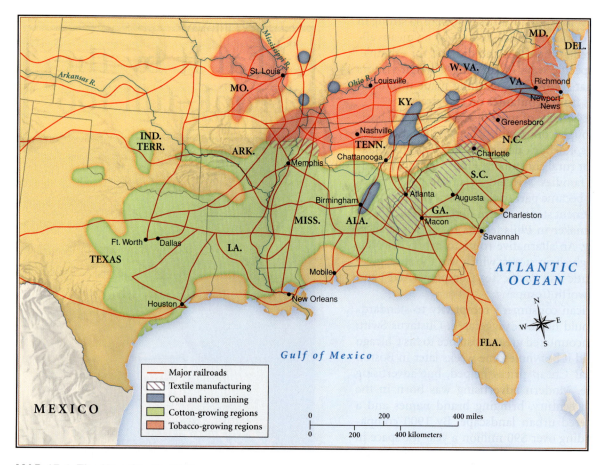

MAP 17.4 The New South, 1900

The economy of the Old South focused on raising staple crops, especially cotton and to-bacco. In the New South staple agriculture continued to dominate, but there was marked industrial development as well. Industrial regions developed, producing textiles, coal and iron, and wood products. By 1900 the South's industrial pattern was well defined.

South Carolina and Georgia in the mid-1870s. The mills recruited workers from the surrounding hill farms, where people struggled to make ends meet. To attract them mill wages had to exceed farm earnings but not by much. Paying rock-bottom wages the new mills had a competitive advantage over the long-established New England industry—as much as 40 percent in labor costs in 1897.

The labor system that evolved was based on hiring whole families. "Papa decided he would come because he didn't have nothing much but girls and they had to get out and work like men," recalled one woman. It was not Papa, in fact, but his girls whom the mills wanted, to work as spinners and loom tenders. Only they could not be recruited individually: no right-thinking parent would have permitted that. Hiring by families, on the other hand, was already familiar; after all everyone had been expected to work on the farm. So the family system of mill labor developed, with a labor force that was half female and very young. In the 1880s a quarter of all southern textile workers were under fifteen years of age.

The hours were long—twelve hours a day—but life in the mill villages was, in the words of one historian, "like a family." Employers tended to be paternalistic, providing company housing and a variety of services. The mill workers built close-knit, supportive communities, but for whites only. Although blacks sometimes worked as day laborers and janitors, they hardly ever got jobs as operatives in the cotton mills.

Cheap, abundant labor might have been termed the South's most valuable natural resource. But the region was blessed with other resources as well. From its rich soil came tobacco, the South's second cash crop. When cigarettes became fashionable in the 1880s, the young North Carolina entrepreneur James B. Duke seized the new market by taking advantage of a southern invention—James A. Bonsack's machine for producing cigarettes automatically. Blacks stemmed and stripped the leaf as they always had, but Duke followed the textile example and restricted machine tending to white women.

Lumbering, by contrast, was racially integrated, with a labor force evenly divided between black and

Houston's Cotton Depot

After the Civil War cotton-raising blossomed on the virgin lands of east Texas, and Houston simultaneously blossomed as the region's commercial center. This photograph from the 1890s reveals the tremendous volume of traffic that came through Houston as Texas cotton was unloaded and transshipped to be made into cloth in the mills of the Southeast and across the ocean in Britain.

Houston Public Library, Houston Metropolitan Research Center.

white men. Cutting down the South's pine forests was a growth business in these years. Alabama's coal and iron ore deposits also attracted investors; by 1890 the Birmingham district was producing nearly a million tons of iron and steel annually.

Economic Retardation. Despite the South's high hopes, this burst of industrial development did not lift the region out of poverty. In 1900 two-thirds of all southerners made their living from the soil, just as they had in 1870. Moreover the industries that did develop produced raw materials (forestry and mining) or engaged in the low-tech processing of coarse products. Industry by industry, the key statistic—the value added by manufacturing—showed the South lagging behind the North.

Southerners tended to blame the North: the South was a "colonial" economy controlled by New York and Chicago. There was some truth to this charge. Much of the capital—by no means all—did come from the North. And the integrating processes of the economy did subordinate regional to national interests. When the railway network moved to a uniform gauge in 1886, the southern railroads converted to the northern standard.

Northern firms did not hesitate to use their muscle to maintain the interregional status quo. Railroads, for example, manipulated freight rates so that it was cheap for southern cotton and timber to flow out and for northern manufactured goods to flow in.

Yet in the end the South's economic backwardness was mostly of its own making. The crowning irony was that the great advantage of the South—its cheap labor— also kept it from becoming a more technologically advanced economy. First, low wages discouraged employers from replacing workers with machinery. Second, low wages attracted labor-intensive industry, such as textiles. Third, a cheap labor market inhibited investment in education because of the likelihood that better-educated workers would flee to higher-wage markets.

What distinguished the southern labor market was that it was insulated from the rest of the country. Northern workers and European immigrants steered clear of the South because wages were too low and attractive jobs too scarce. Harder to explain is why so few southerners, black or white, left for the higher-wage North prior to World War I. At its core the explanation is that the South was a place apart, with social and racial mores that discouraged all but the most resourceful

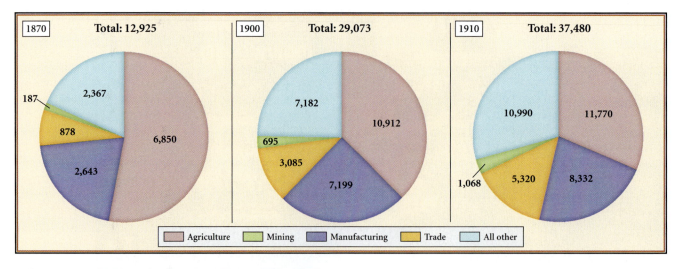

FIGURE 17.2 Changes in the Labor Force, 1870–1910

The numbers represent thousands of people (for example, 12,925 = 12,925,000 workers).
They reveal both the enormous increase in the labor force between 1870 and 1910 and the
dramatic shift from agriculture to industry and other nonagricultural jobs.

from seeking opportunity elsewhere. The result was that a normal flow of workers back and forth did not occur, and wage differentials did not narrow. So long as this isolation persisted, the South would remain a tributary economy, a supplier on unequal terms to the advanced industrial heartland of the North.

The World of Work

In a free-enterprise system, profit drives the entrepreneur. But the industrial order is not populated only by profit makers. It includes—in vastly larger numbers—wage earners. Economic change always affects working people but never so drastically as it did in the late nineteenth century.

Labor Recruits

Industrialism invariably set people in motion. Farm folk migrated to cities. Artisans entered factories. An industrial labor force emerged. This happened in the United States just as it did in Europe but with a difference: the United States did not rely primarily on its own population for a supply of workers.

The demand for labor was ravenous, tripling between 1870 and 1900 (Figure 17.2). Rural Americans were highly mobile in the late nineteenth century, and of those who moved, half ended up in cities. But the higher-paid jobs—puddlers, rollers, molders, machinists—required industrial skills not held by rural Americans. Except in the South, moreover, native-born whites

mostly rejected factory work. They had a basic education, they could read and calculate, and they understood American ways of doing things. City-bound white Americans found their opportunities in the multiplying white-collar jobs in offices and retail stores.

Modest numbers of blacks began to migrate out of the South—roughly 80,000 between 1870 and 1890 and another 200,000 between 1890 and 1910. Most of them settled in cities, but men were restricted to casual labor and janitorial work, while women were restricted to domestic service. Employers turned black applicants away from the factory gates—and away from their one best chance for a fair shake at American opportunity—because immigrant workers already supplied companies with as much cheap labor as they needed.

Immigrant Workers. The great migration from the Old World started in the 1840s, when over a million Irish fled the potato famine. In the following years, as European agriculture became increasingly commercialized, the peasant economies began to fail, first in Germany and Scandinavia and then, later in the nineteenth century, across Austria-Hungary, Russia, Italy, and the Balkans. This upheaval set off a great migration of Europeans, some of them going to Europe's own industrial centers, others heading for South America and Australia, but most coming to the United States.

Ethnic origin largely determined the work the immigrants took in America. Seeking the jobs in which they were already experienced, the Welsh labored as tinplate workers, the English as miners, the Germans as machinists and traditional artisans (for example, bakers and carpenters), the Belgians as glass workers, and

Scandinavians as seamen on Great Lakes boats. For common labor employers had long counted on the brawn of Irish rural immigrants, although all emigrating groups contributed to the pool of unskilled workers.

As technology advanced American employers needed fewer European craftsmen, while the demand for ordinary labor skyrocketed. The sources of immigration began to shift, and by the early twentieth century arrivals from southern and eastern Europe far outstripped immigration from western Europe (Figure 17.3). Italian and Slavic immigrants without industrial skills flooded into American factories. Heavy, low-paid labor became the domain of the recent immigrants (see Voices from Abroad, "Count Vay de Vaya und Luskod: Pittsburgh Inferno," p. 503). Blast-furnace jobs, a job-seeking investigator heard, were "Hunky work," not suitable for him or any other American. The derogatory term *Hunky* refers to Hungarian workers, but it was applied indiscriminately to Poles, Slovaks, and all other Slavic groups arriving in America's industrial districts.

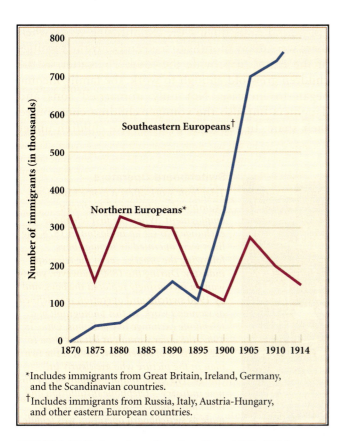

FIGURE 17.3 American Immigration, 1870–1914

This graph shows the surge of European immigration in the late nineteenth century. While northern Europe continued to send substantial numbers, it was overshadowed after 1895 by southern Europeans pouring into America to work in mines and factories. (See Map 19.3, Sources of European Immigration to the United States, 1871–1910, on p. 558.)

Not only skill determined where immigrants ended up in American industry. The newcomers, although generally not traveling in groups, moved within well-defined networks, following relatives or fellow villagers already in America and relying on them to land a job. A high degree of ethnic clustering resulted, even within a single factory. At the Jones and Laughlin steel works in Pittsburgh, for example, the carpentry shop was German, the hammer shop Polish, and the blooming mill Serbian. Immigrants also had different job preferences. Men from Italy, for instance, liked outdoor work, often laboring in gangs under a *padrone* (boss), much as they had in Italy.

Immigrants entered a modern industrial order, but it was not a world they wanted. They were peasants, displaced by the breakdown of traditional rural economies. Many had lost their land and fallen into the class of dependent, propertyless servants. They could escape that bitter fate only if they had money to buy property. In Europe job-seeking peasants commonly tried seasonal agricultural labor or temporary work in nearby cities. America represented merely a larger leap, made possible by cheap and speedy steamships across the Atlantic. The peasant immigrants, most of them young and male, never intended to stay permanently. About half did return, departing in great numbers during depression years. No one knows how many left because they had saved enough and how many left for lack of work. For their American employers it scarcely mattered. What did matter was that the immigrants took the worst jobs and were always available when they were wanted. For the new industrial order, they made an ideal labor supply.

Working Women and the Family Economy. Over four million women worked for wages in 1900. Representing a quarter of the nonfarm labor force, they played a vital part in the industrial economy. The opportunities they found were shaped by gender—by the fact that they were women. Contemporary beliefs about womanhood largely determined which women took jobs and how they were treated once they became wage earners.

Wives were not supposed to work outside the home, and in fact fewer than 5 percent did so in 1890. Only among African Americans did many married women—above 30 percent—work for wages. Among whites the typical working woman at that time was under twenty-four and unmarried. When older women worked, remarked one observer, it "was usually a sign that something had gone wrong"—their husbands had died, deserted them, or lost their jobs.

Since women were held to be inherently different from men, it followed that they not be permitted to do "men's work." Nor, regardless of their skills, could they be paid a man's wage. The dominant view was that a woman did not require a "living wage" because, as one investigator

Ironworkers—Noontime

The qualities of the nineteenth-century craft worker—dignity, "unselfish brotherhood," a "manly" bearing—shine through in this painting by Thomas P. Anschutz. Ironworkers—Noontime *became a popular painting when it was reproduced as an engraving in* Harper's Weekly *in 1884.* Fine Arts Museum of San Francisco.

To some degree their youthful preoccupations made it easier for working women to accept the miserable terms under which they labored. But this did not mean that they lacked a sense of solidarity or self-respect. A pretty dress might appear frivolous to the casual observer, but also conveyed the message that the working girl considered herself as good as anyone. Rebellious youth culture sometimes united with job grievances to produce astonishing strike movements, as demonstrated, for example, by the Jewish garment workers of New York and the Irish-American telephone operators of Boston.

Rarely, however, did women workers wield the kind of craft power that the skilled male worker commonly enjoyed. He hired his own helpers, supervised their work, and paid them from his earnings. In the late nineteenth century, when increasingly sophisticated production called for closer shop-floor supervision, many factory managers deliberately shifted this responsibility to craft workers. In metal-fabricating firms that did precise machining and complex assembling, a system of inside contracting developed in which skilled employees bid for a production run, taking full responsibility for the operation, paying their crew and pocketing the profits.

Dispersal of authority was characteristic of nineteenth-century industry. The aristocracy of the workers—the craftsmen, inside contractors, and foremen—enjoyed a high degree of autonomy. However, their subordinates often paid dearly for that independence. Any worker who paid his helpers from his own pocket might be tempted to exploit them. In the Pittsburgh area foremen were known as "pushers," notorious for driving their gangs mercilessly. On the other hand industrial labor in the nineteenth century remained on a human scale. People dealt with each other face to face, often developing cohesive ties within the shop. Striking craft workers commonly received the support of helpers and laborers, and labor gangs sometimes walked out on behalf of a popular foreman.

Systems of Control

As technology advanced, workers increasingly lost the proud independence characteristic of nineteenth-century craft work. One cause of this deskilling process was a new system of production—Henry Ford called it "**mass production**"—that lent itself to mechanization. Agricultural implements, typewriters, bicycles, and,

Count Vay de Vaya und Luskod

Pittsburgh Inferno

Count Vay de Vaya und Luskod, a Hungarian nobleman and high functionary in the Catholic Church, crossed the United States several times between 1903 and 1906 en route to his post as the Vatican's representative to Asia. In a book about his travels, he expresses his distress at the plight of his countrymen laboring in the mills of the Pittsburgh steel district.

The bells are tolling for a funeral. The modest train of mourners is just setting out for the little churchyard on the hill. Everything is shrouded in gloom, even the coffin lying upon the bier and the people who stand on each side in threadbare clothes and with heads bent. Such is my sad reception at the Hungarian workingmen's colony at McKeesport. Everyone who has been in the United States has heard of this famous town, and of Pittsburgh, its close neighbor. . . .

Fourteen-thousand tall chimneys are silhouetted against the sky . . . discharg[ing] their burning sparks and smok[ing] incessantly. The realms of Vulcan could not be more somber or filthy than this valley of the Monongahela. On every hand are burning fires and spurting flames. Nothing is visible save the forging of iron and the smelting of metal. . . .

And this fearful place affects us very closely, for thousands of immigrants wander here from year to year. Here they fondly seek the realization of their cherished hopes, and here they suffer till they are swallowed up by the inferno. He whom we are now burying is the latest victim. Yesterday he was in full vigor and at work at the foundry, toiling, struggling, hoping—a chain broke, and he was killed. . . .

This is scarcely work for mankind. Americans will hardly take anything of the sort; only [the immigrant] rendered desperate by circumstances . . . and thus he is at the mercy of the tyrannous Trust, which gathers him into its clutches and transforms him into a regular slave.

This is one of the saddest features of the Hungarian emigration. In making a tour of these prisons, wherever the heat is most insupportable, the flames most scorching, the smoke and soot most choking, there we are certain to find compatriots bent and wasted with toil. Their thin, wrinkled, wan faces seem to show that in America the newcomers are of no use except to help fill the moneybags of the insatiable millionaires. . . . In this realm of Mammon and Moloch everything has a value—except human life. . . . Why? Because human life is a commodity the supply of which exceeds the demand. There are always fresh recruits to supply the place of those who have fallen in battle; and the steamships are constantly arriving at the neighboring ports, discharging their living human cargo still further to swell the phalanx of the instruments of cupidity.

Source: Oscar Handlin, ed., *This Was America* (Cambridge, MA: Harvard University Press, 1949), 407–10.

---

after 1900, automobiles were assembled from standardized parts. The machine tools that cut, drilled, and ground these metal parts were originally operated by skilled machinists. But because they produced long runs of a single item, these machine tools became more specialized; they became *dedicated* machines—machines set up to do the same job over and over—and the need for skilled operatives disappeared. In the manufacture of sewing machines, one machinist complained in 1883, "the trade is so subdivided that a man is not considered a machinist at all. One man may make just a particular part of a machine and may not know anything whatever about another part of the same machine." Such a worker, noted an observer, "cannot be master of a craft, but only master of a fragment."

Employers were attracted to automatic machinery because it increased output; the impact on workers was not uppermost in their minds. Employers recognized that mechanization made it easier to control workers, but that was only an incidental benefit. Gradually, however, the idea took hold that managing workers might itself be a way to reduce the cost of production.

The pioneer in this field was Frederick W. Taylor. An expert on metal-cutting methods, Taylor believed that the engineer's approach might be applied to managing workers, hence the name for his method: **scientific management**. To get the maximum work from the individual worker, Taylor suggested two basic reforms. The first would eliminate the brain work from manual labor. Managers would assume "the burden of

John Brophy

A Miner's Son

*J*ohn Brophy (1883–1963), an important mine union official, recalls in an oral history what mining was like in his boyhood, a time when mining was strictly pick-and-shovel work and machinery had not yet eroded the prized skills of the miner.

I got a thrill at the thought of having an opportunity to go and work in the mine, to go and work along side my father. After . . . I got experience and some strength, and the ability to work with a little skill, I was conscious of the fact that my father was a good workman; that he had pride in his calling. . . . It was a great satisfaction to me that my father was a skilled, clean workman with everything kept in shape, and the timbering done well—all of these things: the rib side, the roadway, the timbering, the fact that you kept the loose coal clean rather than cluttered all over the workplace, the skill with which you undercut the vein, the judgment in drilling the coal after it had been undercut and placing the exact amount of explosive so that it would do an effective job of breaking the coal from the solid—indicated the quality of his work. . . .

It was skill in handling the pick and the shovel, the placing of timbers, and understanding the vagaries of the workplace—which is subject to certain pressures from the overhanging strata as you advance into the seam. It's an awareness of roof conditions. And it's something else too. Under the older conditions of mining under which I went to work with my father, the miner exercised considerable freedom in his working place in determining his pace of work and the selection of the order of time in the different work operations. Judgment was everywhere along the line, and there was also necessary skill. It was the feel of all this. You know that another workman in another place was a good miner, a passable miner, or an indifferent one. . . . I think that was one of the great satisfactions that a miner had—that he was his own boss within his workplace. . . .

The miner is always aware of danger, that he lives under dangerous conditions in the workplace, because he's constantly uncovering new conditions as he advances in the workingplace, exposing new areas of roof, discovering some weakened condition or break which may bring some special danger. There is also the danger that comes from a piece of coal slipping off the fast and falling on the worker as he lays prone on the bottom doing his cutting. The worker has got to be aware of all these conditions that may be in the coal, that may be in the roof. . . .

Then there is the further fact that the miners by and large lived in purely mining communities which were often isolated. They developed a group loyalty under all these circumstances. They were both individualists and they were group conscious. . . . It made them an extraordinary body of workers, these miners, because of these very special conditions, because involved in it was not only earning a living, but a matter of health and safety, life and death were involved in every way. You find time and again miners, in an effort to rescue their fellow workers, taking chances which quite often meant death for themselves. . . .

Along with that is a sense of justice. There was the very fact the miner was a tonnage worker and that he could be short weighed and cheated in various ways, and that the only safeguard against it was [union] organization. In that case it was important to have a representative of the miners to see that the weight was properly done and properly credited to the individual miner. There was the whole complex of circumstances that had been in the mining industry for generations which had been their experience. The miner in my day in the United States was aware that all knowledge didn't start with his generation. . . . At least on one side of my family there are at least four generations of [British] miners, and I say this with a sense of pride; very much so. I'm very proud of the fact that there is this long tradition of miners who have struggled with the elements.

Source: Jerold S. Auerbach, ed., *American Labor: The Twentieth Century* (Indianapolis: Bobbs-Merrill, 1969), 44–48.

gathering together all of the traditional knowledge which in the past has been possessed by the workmen and then of classifying, tabulating, and reducing this knowledge to rules, laws, and formulae." The second reform, a logical consequence of the first, would deprive workers of the authority they had exercised on the shop floor. Workers would "do what they are told promptly and without asking questions or making suggestions. . . . The duty of enforcing . . . rests with the management alone."

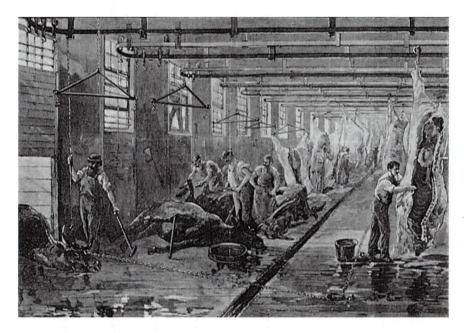

The Killing Floor
To the modern eye the labor process depicted in this 1882 engraving of a Chicago meatpacking plant seems primitive and inefficient, but it contains the seeds of America's mass-production revolution. At the far left the steer has already been stunned by one specialist, killed by a second, and attached to a chain that will lift it onto the overhead conveyor. The division of labor is already in place (each of the workers on the line does a single repetitive task), and the process is continuous. It would be only a small step from the killing floors of the Chicago packing plants to Henry Ford's assembly line. Library of Congress.

Once managers had the knowledge and the power, they would put labor on a "scientific" basis. This meant subjecting each task to **time-and-motion study** by an engineer who would analyze and time each job with a stopwatch. Workers would be paid at a differential rate—that is, a certain amount if they met the stopwatch standard and a higher rate for additional output. Taylor claimed that his techniques would guarantee optimum worker efficiency. His assumption was that only money mattered to workers and that they would automatically respond to the lure of higher earnings.

Scientific management was not, in practice, a roaring success. Implementing it proved to be very expensive, and workers stubbornly resisted the job-analysis method. "It looks to me like slavery to have a man stand over you with a stopwatch," complained one iron molder. A union leader insisted that "this system is wrong, because we want our heads left on us." Far from solving the labor problem, as Taylor claimed it would, scientific management embittered relations on the shop floor.

Yet Taylor achieved something of fundamental importance. He was a brilliant publicist, and his teachings spread throughout American industry. Taylor's disciples moved beyond his simplistic economic psychology, creating the new fields of personnel work and industrial psychology, whose practitioners purported to know how to extract more and better labor from workers. A threshold had been crossed into the modern era of labor management.

So the circle closed on American workers. With each advance the quest for efficiency eroded their cherished autonomy, diminishing them and cutting them down to fit the industrial system. The process occurred unevenly. For textile workers the loss had come early. Miners and ironworkers felt it much more slowly. Others, such as construction workers, escaped almost entirely. But increasing numbers of workers found themselves in an environment that crushed any sense of mastery or even understanding.

The Labor Movement

Wherever industrialization took hold, workers organized and formed labor unions. However, the movements they built varied from one industrial society to another. In the United States workers were especially uncertain about the path they wanted to take. Only in the 1880s did the American labor movement settle into a steady course.

Reformers and Unionists

Thomas B. McGuire, a New York wagon driver, was ambitious. He had saved $300 from his wages "so that I might become something of a capitalist eventually." But his venture as a cab driver in the early 1880s soon failed:

> *Corporations usually take that business themselves. They can manage to get men, at starvation wages, and put them on a hack, and put a livery on them with a gold band and brass buttons, to show that they are slaves—I beg pardon; I did not intend to use the word slaves; there are no slaves in this country now—to show that they are merely servants.*

Slave or liveried servant, the symbolic meaning was the same to McGuire. He was speaking of the crushed aspirations of the independent American worker.

Terence V. Powderly, Labor Peacemaker

The Knights of Labor, unlike their trade union rivals, in principle opposed strikes. In this cartoon from Puck, *dated April 7, 1886, the little man depicted in the middle is Master Workman Powderly, leader of the Knights of Labor. The cartoon shows Powderly offering Capital and Labor the Knights' proposal for the peaceful settlement of labor disputes by means of "arbitration," which in those days meant mediation and negotiation rather than resolution by a third party. Powderly's judicious stance, however, could not keep the two sides from each other's throats, and in the national strikes soon to break out, Powderly's own members joined the picket lines.* Puck, April 17, 1886.

Labor Reform and the Knights of Labor. What would satisfy the Thomas McGuires of the nineteenth century? Only the establishment of an egalitarian society, one in which every citizen might hope to become economically independent. This republican goal did not mean returning to the agrarian past, but rather replacing the existing wage system with a more just order that did not distinguish between capitalists and workers. All would be "producers" laboring together in what was commonly called the "cooperative commonwealth." This was the ideal that inspired the Noble and Holy Order of the Knights of Labor.

Founded in 1869 as a secret society of garment workers in Philadelphia, the Knights of Labor spread to other cities and by 1878 emerged as a national movement. The Knights boasted an elaborate ritual calculated to appeal to the fraternal spirit of nineteenth-century workers. The local assemblies of the Knights engendered a spirit of comradeship very much like that offered by the Masons or Odd Fellows. For the Knights, however, fraternalism was harnessed to labor reform. The goal was to "give voice to that grand undercurrent of mighty thought, which is today [1880] crystallizing in the hearts of men, and urging them on to perfect organization through which to gain the power to make labor emancipation possible."

But how was "emancipation" to be achieved? Through cooperation, the Knights argued. They intended to set up factories and shops that would be owned and run by the employees. As these cooperatives flourished, American society would be transformed into a cooperative commonwealth. But little was actually done. Instead the Knights devoted themselves to "education." Their leader, Grand Master Workman Terence V. Powderly, regarded the organization as a vast labor

college open to all but lawyers and saloonkeepers. The cooperative commonwealth would arrive in some mysterious way as more and more "producers" became members and learned the group's message from lectures, discussions, and publications. Social evil would not end in a day but "must await the gradual development of educational enlightenment."

Trade Unionism. The labor reformers expressed the higher aspirations of American workers. Another kind of organization—the trade union—tended to their everyday needs. Unions had long been at the center of the lives of craft workers. Apprenticeship rules regulated entry into a trade, and the **closed shop**—by reserving all jobs for union members—kept out lower-wage and incompetent workers. Union rules specified the terms of work, sometimes in minute detail. Above all, trade unionism defended the craft worker's traditional skills and rights.

The trade union also expressed the social identity of the craft. Hatters took pride in their alcoholic consumption, an on-the-job privilege that was jealously guarded. More often craft unions had an uplifting character. A Birmingham iron puddler claimed that his union's "main object was to educate mechanics up to a standard of morality and temperance, and good workmanship." Some unions emphasized mutual aid. Because operating trains was a high-risk occupation, the railroad brotherhoods provided accident and death benefits and encouraged members to assist one another. On and off the job, the unions played a big part in the lives of craft workers.

The earliest unions were local organizations of workers in the same craft, that, especially among German workers, were sometimes limited to a single ethnic group. As expanding markets intruded, breaking down

A Railroad Brotherhood

Locomotive firemen, who fed the boilers on nineteenth-century steam engines, ranked below locomotive engineers but still considered theirs a privileged occupation. This union certificate conveys the respectable values to which locomotive firemen adhered and, as depicted in the scenes on the right-hand side, the need they felt to protect their families (through the affordable insurance provided by their union) in the event of accidents that were so much a part of the dangerous trade they followed.
Library of Congress.

their ability to control local conditions, unions began to form national organizations. The first was the International Typographical Union in 1852. By the 1870s molders, ironworkers, bricklayers, and about thirty other trades had done likewise. The national union, uniting local unions of the same trade, was becoming the dominant organizational form for American trade unionism.

The practical job interests that trade unions espoused might have seemed a far cry from the idealism of the Knights of Labor. But both kinds of motives arose from a single workers' culture. Seeing no conflict many workers carried membership cards in both the Knights of Labor and a trade union. For many years little separated a trade assembly of the Knights from a local trade union; both engaged in fraternal and job-oriented activities. And because the Knights, once established in a town or city, tended to become politically active and

field independent slates of candidates, that too became a magnet attracting trade unionists.

Trade unions generally barred women, and so did the Knights until 1881, when women shoe workers in Philadelphia struck in support of their male coworkers and won the right to form their own local assembly. By 1886 probably 50,000 women belonged to the Knights of Labor. Their courage on the picket line prompted Powderly's rueful remark that women "are the best men in the Order." For a handful of women, such as the hosiery worker Leonora M. Barry, the Knights provided a rare chance to take up leadership roles as organizers and officials.

Similarly, the Knights of Labor grudgingly opened the door for black workers, out of the need for solidarity and, just as important, in deference to the Order's egalitarian principles. The Knights could rightly boast that

Samuel Gompers
This is a photograph of the labor leader in his forties taken when he was visiting striking miners in West Virginia, an area where mine operators resisted unions with special fierceness. The photograph was taken by a company detective.
George Meany Memorial Archives.

their "great work has been to organize labor which was previously unorganized."

The Triumph of "Pure and Simple" Unionism

In the early 1880s the Knights began to act more and more like trade unions. Boycott campaigns against the products of "unfair" employers achieved impressive results. With the economy booming and workers in short supply, the Knights began to win strikes, including a major victory against Jay Gould's Southwestern railway system in 1885. Workers flocked to the organization, and its membership jumped from 100,000 to perhaps 700,000. For a brief time the Knights stood poised as a potential industrial-union movement capable of bringing all workers into its fold.

The rapid growth of the Knights frightened the national trade unions. They began to insist on a clear

separation of roles, with the Knights confined to labor reform. This was partly a battle over turf, but it reflected also a deepening divergence of labor philosophies.

Samuel Gompers, a cigar maker from New York City, led the ideological assault on the Knights. Gompers hammered out the philosophical position that would become known as "pure and simple" unionism. His starting point was that grand theories and schemes like those that excited the labor reformers should be strictly avoided. Unions, Gompers thought, should focus on concrete, achievable gains, and they should organize workers not as an undifferentiated mass of "producers" but by craft and occupation. The battleground should be at the workplace, where workers could best mobilize their power, not in the quicksands of politics.

Gompers developed these views as general propositions, but they were grounded in the hard experience of ordinary workers like Rose Schneiderman, striving to organize fellow workers and bring employers to the bargaining table (see American Voices, "Rose Schneiderman: Trade Unionist," p. 509). Schneiderman would have nodded in agreement with Gompers's assertion that "no matter how just . . . unless the cause is backed up with power to enforce it, it is going to be crushed and annihilated."

The struggle for the eight-hour day crystallized the conflict between the rival movements. Both, of course, favored a shorter workday but for different reasons. For the Knights more leisure was desirable because workers had duties "to perform as American citizens and members of society." Trade unionists took a more hard-boiled view: the eight-hour day would spread the available jobs among more workers, protect them against overwork, and give them an easier life. When the trade unions set May 1, 1886, as the deadline for achieving the eight-hour day, the leadership of Knights objected. But workers everywhere responded enthusiastically, and as the deadline approached, a wave of strikes and demonstrations broke out across the country.

At one such eight-hour strike, at the McCormick reaper works in Chicago, a battle erupted on May 3, leaving four strikers dead. Chicago was a hotbed of **anarchism**—the revolutionary advocacy of a stateless society—and local anarchists, most of them German immigrants, called a protest meeting the next evening at Haymarket Square. When police moved in to break it up, someone threw a bomb that killed and wounded several of the police, who responded with wild gunfire. Most of the casualties, including some police, came from police bullets. Despite no evidence of their involvement, the anarchists were tried and found guilty of murder and criminal conspiracy. Four were executed, one committed suicide, and the others received long prison sentences. They were victims of one of the great miscarriages of American justice.

Seizing on the antiunion hysteria set off by the Haymarket affair, employers took the offensive. They

Rose Schneiderman

Trade Unionist

Rose Schneiderman (1882–1972) typified the young Jewish garment workers who became the firebrands of their Manhattan industry. Schneiderman went on to an illustrious career as a labor organizer and social reformer (see photo on p. 579). At the time of her initiation, recorded below, she was twenty-one years old.

We had no idea that there was a union in our industry and that women could join it. Nor did we have a full realization of the hardships we were needlessly undergoing. There was the necessity of owning a sewing machine before you could work. Then you had to buy your own thread. But the worst of it was the incredibly inefficient way in which work was distributed. Because we were all pieceworkers, any time lost during the season was a real hardship. But because of poor management there never seemed to be any synchronizing between our available time and the supplying of materials we needed. . . .

[My friend] Bessie Braut pointed out all these things and more, insisting that it was possible to have all these hardships corrected if we complained as a group. An employer would think twice before telling a group what he would not hesitate to tell an individual employee: that if she didn't like it, she was free to take herself and her machine and go somewhere else where things would most likely be just as bad or perhaps worse. . . .

As her word began to sink in, we formed a committee composed of my friend Bessie Mannis, who worked with me, myself, and a third girl. Bravely we ventured into the office of the United Cloth Hat and Cap Makers Union and told the man in charge that we would like to be organized. . . .

We were told we would have to have least twenty-five women from a number of factories before we could acquire a charter. Novices that we were, we used the simplest methods. We waited at the doors of factories and, as the girls were leaving for the day, we would approach them and speak our piece. We had blank pledges of membership ready in case some could be persuaded to join us. Within days we had the necessary number. . . .

The only cloud in the picture was mother's attitude toward my being a trade unionist. She kept saying I'd never get married because I was so busy—a prophecy which came true. Of course, what she resented most of all was my being out of the house almost every evening. But for me it was the beginning of a period that molded all my subsequent life and opened wide many doors that might otherwise have remained closed to me. . . .

That June we decided to put our strength to the test. In the summer the men usually worked only a half-day on Saturdays, which was pay day. But even when there was no work we women had to hang around until three or four o'clock before getting our pay. I headed a committee which informed Mr. Fox that we wanted to be paid at the same time as the men. . . . He didn't say outright that he agreed, he wouldn't give us that much satisfaction. But on the first Sunday in July, when we went for our pay at twelve noon, there it was for us. . . .

Source: Rose Schneiderman, *All for One* (1967), reprinted in Irving Howe and Kenneth Lebo, eds., *How We Lived* (New York: New American Library, 1979), 139–41.

---

broke strikes violently, compiled blacklists of strikers, and forced workers to sign **yellow-dog contracts** guaranteeing that, as a condition of employment, they would not join a labor organization. If trade unionists needed any confirmation of the tough world in which they lived, they found it in Haymarket and its aftermath.

In December 1886, having failed to persuade the Knights of Labor to desist from union activity, the national trade unions formed the American Federation of Labor (AFL), with Samuel Gompers as president. The AFL in effect locked into place the trade union structure as it had evolved by the 1880s. Underlying this structure was the conviction that workers had to take the world as it was, not as they dreamed it might be. At this point the American movement definitely diverged from the European model, for fundamental to Gompers's AFL was opposition to a political party for workers.

The Knights of Labor never recovered from the Haymarket affair. Powderly retreated to the rhetoric of labor reform, but wage earners had lost interest, and he was unable to formulate a viable new strategy. By the mid-1890s the Knights of Labor had faded away. In the meantime the AFL took firm root, justifying Gompers's

In 1897 WFM president Ed Boyce called on all union members to arm themselves with rifles, and his rhetoric—he called the wage system "slavery in its worst form"—had a hard edge. Any lingering faith in the political process died in the Colorado state elections of 1905, which the miners thought they had won, only to have the state supreme court overturn the results and reinstall their archenemy, Republican governor George H. Peabody.

In 1905 the Western Federation of Miners joined with left-wing socialists to create a new movement, the Industrial Workers of the World (IWW). The Wobblies, as IWW members were called, fervently supported the Marxist class struggle—but at the workplace rather than in politics. By resistance at the point of production and ultimately by means of a general strike, they believed that the workers would bring about a revolution. A new society would emerge, run directly by the workers through their industrial unions. The term **syndicalism** describes this brand of workers' radicalism.

In both its major forms—politically oriented Socialism and the syndicalist IWW—American radicalism flourished after the crisis of the 1890s but only on a limited basis and never with the possibility of seizing power. Nevertheless, Socialists and Wobblies served a larger purpose. American radicalism, by its sheer vitality, bore witness to what was exploitative and unjust in the new industrial order.

FOR FURTHER EXPLORATION

▶ For definitions of key terms boldfaced in this chapter, see the glossary at the end of the book.

▶ To assess your mastery of the material covered in this chapter, see the Online Study Guide at **bedfordstmartins.com/henretta**.

▶ For suggested references, including Web sites, see page SR-19 at the end of the book.

▶ For map resources and primary documents, see **bedfordstmartins.com/henretta**.

SUMMARY

American industrialism took modern shape during the last decades of the nineteenth century. Central to this development were the shift from iron making to the manufacture of steel, the great expansion of coal mining, and the technology for generating steam and electrical power. These advances made possible the production of capital goods and energy required by an expanding manufacturing economy. An efficient railway system provided access to national markets. The scale of enterprise grew very large, and the vertically integrated firm became the predominant form of business organization. Only in the South did prevailing conditions—in particular the insulated low-wage labor market—retard the growth of an advanced industrial economy.

In the North the enormous demand for labor led to a great influx of immigrants, making ethnic diversity a distinctive feature of the American working class. Gender likewise defined occupational opportunity. Women joined the labor force in growing numbers but were almost universally subjected to a sex-typing process that relegated them to "women's work," always at the wage rates below those of men. Mass production—the volume output of standardized products—vastly improved the productivity of American manufacturing but also deskilled workers and mechanized their jobs. Scientific management, the brainchild of Frederick W. Taylor, cut further into the traditional autonomy of American workers by systematizing the labor process and shifting control into the hands of supervisors.

The late nineteenth century gave rise to the American labor movement in its modern form. In the Knights of Labor, labor reform enjoyed one final surge during the mid-1880s and then succumbed to the "pure and simple" unionism of the American Federation of Labor. The AFL was conservative in that it accepted the economic order, but its insistence on a larger share for workers guaranteed that employers would fiercely resist collective bargaining. The resulting industrial warfare of the 1890s stirred new radical impulses, leading both to the political socialism of Eugene Debs and to the industrial radicalism of the IWW.

TIMELINE

1869 Knights of Labor founded in Philadelphia

1872 Andrew Carnegie starts construction of Edgar Thomson steelworks near Pittsburgh

1873 Panic of 1873 ushers in economic depression

1875 John Wanamaker establishes first department store in Philadelphia

1877 Baltimore and Ohio workers initiate nationwide railroad strike

1878 Gustavus Swift introduces refrigerator car

1879 Jay Gould begins to build Missouri Pacific railway system

1883 Railroads establish national time zones

1886 Haymarket Square bombing in Chicago

American Federation of Labor (AFL) founded

1892 Homestead steel strike crushed

Wave of western miners' strikes begins

1893 Panic of 1893 leads to national depression

Surge of railroad bankruptcies; reorganization by investment bankers begins

1894 President Cleveland sends troops to break Pullman boycott

1895 Southeastern European immigration exceeds northern European immigration for first time

F. W. Taylor formulates scientific management

1901 Eugene V. Debs helps found Socialist Party of America

1905 Industrial Workers of the World (IWW) launched

CHAPTER 18

The Politics of Late-Nineteenth-Century America

The Politics of the Status Quo, 1877–1893
The National Scene
The Ideology of Individualism
The Supremacy of the Courts

Politics and the People
Cultural Politics: Party, Religion, and Ethnicity
Organizational Politics
Women's Political Culture

Race and Politics in the New South
Biracial Politics
One-Party Rule Triumphant
Resisting White Supremacy

The Crisis of American Politics: The 1890s
The Populist Revolt
Money and Politics

EVER SINCE THE FOUNDING OF THE REPUBLIC, foreign visitors had been coming to America to study its political system. Most famous of the early observers was the French aristocrat Alexis de Tocqueville, the author of *Democracy in America* (1832). When an equally brilliant visitor, the Englishman James Bryce, sat down to write his own account fifty years later, he decided that Tocqueville's great book could not serve as his model. For Tocqueville, Bryce noted, "America was primarily a democracy, the ideal democracy, fraught with lessons for Europe." In his own book, *The American Commonwealth* (1888), Bryce was much less rhapsodic. Tocqueville's robust democracy had devolved into the dreary machine politics of post–Civil War America.

Bryce was anxious, however, that his readers not misunderstand him. Europeans would find in his book "much that is sordid, much that will provoke unfavourable comment." But they needed to be aware of "a reserve of force and patriotism more than sufficient to sweep away all the evils now tolerated, and to make a politics of the country worthy of its material grandeur and of the private virtues of its inhabitants." Bryce was ultimately an optimist: "A hundred times in writing this book have I been disheartened by the facts I was stating; a hundred times has the recollection of the abounding strength and vitality of the nation chased away these tremours."

◀ **Bandanna, 1888 Election**
During the late nineteenth century, politics was a vibrant part of America's culture. Party paraphernalia, such as this colorful bandanna depicting the Democratic presidential nominee Grover Cleveland and his running mate, A. G. Thurman, flooded the country.
Collection of Janice L. and David J. Frent.

515

Politics and the People

The country may have felt, as Kansas editor William Allen White wrote, "sick with politics" and "nauseated at all politicians," but somehow this did not reduce the people's appetite for politics. Proportionately more voters turned out in presidential elections from 1876 to 1892 than at any other time in American history. People voted Democratic or Republican loyally for a lifetime. National conventions attracted huge crowds. "The excitement, the mental and physical strains," remarked an Indiana Republican after the 1888 convention, "are surpassed only by prolonged battle in actual warfare, as I have been told by officers of the Civil War who latter engaged in convention struggles." The convention he described had nominated the colorless Benjamin Harrison on a routine platform. What was all the excitement about?

Cultural Politics: Party, Religion, and Ethnicity

In the late nineteenth century, politics was a vibrant part of the nation's culture. America "is a land of conventions and assemblies," a journalist noted, "where it is the most natural thing in the world for people to get together in meetings, where almost every event is the occasion for speechmaking." During the election season the party faithful marched in torchlight parades. Party paraphernalia flooded the country—handkerchiefs, mugs, posters, and buttons emblazoned with the Democratic donkey or the Republican elephant, symbols that had been adopted in the 1870s. In the 1888 campaign the candidates were featured on cards, like baseball players, packed into Honest Long Cut tobacco. In an age before movies and radio, politics ranked as one of the great American forms of entertainment.

Party loyalty was a deadly serious matter, however. Long after the killing ended, Civil War emotions ran high. Among family friends in Cleveland, recalled the urban reformer Brand Whitlock, the Republican Party was "a synonym for patriotism, another name for the nation. It was inconceivable that any self-respecting person should be a Democrat"—or, among ex-Confederates in the South, that any self-respecting person could be a Republican.

Beyond these sectional differences the most important determinants of party loyalty were religion and ethnicity (Figure 18.1). Statistically northern Democrats tended to be foreign-born and Catholic, while Republicans tended to be native-born and Protestant. Among Protestants, the more *pietistic* a person's faith—that is the more personal and direct the believer's relationship to God—the more likely he or she was to be a Republican and to favor using the powers of the state to uphold social values and regulate personal behavior.

During the 1880s, as ethnic tensions built up in many cities, education became an arena of bitter conflict. One issue was whether instruction would be in

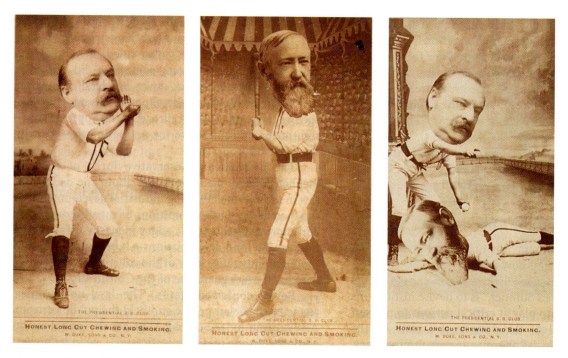

The Presidential B.B. Club (1888)
On the left Grover Cleveland is the baseman; at center Benjamin Harrison is at bat; and on the right Cleveland tags Harrison out—not, alas, the right prediction, since Harrison won the 1888 election. Collection of Janice L. and David J. Frent.

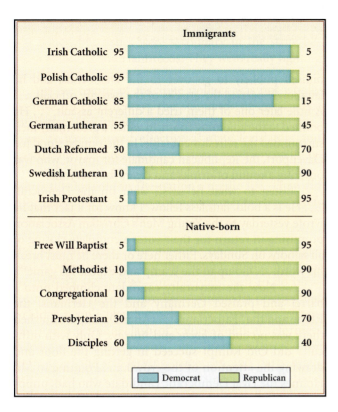

FIGURE 18.1 Ethnocultural Voting Patterns in the Midwest, 1870–1892

These figures demonstrate how voting patterns among Midwesterners reflected ethnicity and religion in the late nineteenth century. Especially striking is the overwhelming preference by immigrant Catholics for the Democratic Party. Among Protestants there was an equally strong preference for the Republican Party by certain groups of immigrants (Swedish Lutherans and Irish Protestants) and native born (Free Will Baptists, Methodists, and Congregationalists), but other Protestant groups were more evenly divided in their party preferences.

English. Immigrant groups often wanted their children taught in their own languages. In St. Louis, a heavily German city, the long-standing policy of teaching German to all students was overturned after a heated campaign. Religion was an even more explosive educational issue. Catholics fought a losing battle over public aid for parochial schools, which by 1900 was prohibited by twenty-three states. In Boston a furious controversy broke out in 1888 over the use of an anti-Catholic history textbook. When the school board withdrew the offending book, angry Protestants elected a new board and returned the text to the curriculum.

Then there was the regulation of public morals. In many states so-called **blue laws** restricted activity on Sundays. When Nebraska banned Sunday baseball, the state supreme court approved the law as a blow struck in "the contest between Christianity and wrong." But German and Irish Catholics, who saw nothing evil in a bit of fun on Sunday, considered blue laws a violation of their personal freedom. Ethnocultural conflict also flared

over the liquor question (see Voices from Abroad, "Ernst Below: Beer and German American Politics," p. 522). Many states adopted strict licensing and local-option laws governing the sale of alcoholic beverages. Indiana permitted drinking but only joylessly in rooms containing "no devices for amusement or music . . . of any kind."

Because the hottest social issues of the day—education, the liquor question, and observance of the Sabbath—were also party issues, they lent deep significance to party affiliation. And because these issues were fought out mostly at the state and local levels, they hit very close to home. Crusading Methodists thought of Republicans as the party of morality. For embattled Irish and German Catholics, who favored "the largest individual liberty consistent with public order," the Democratic Party was the defender of their freedoms.

Organizational Politics

Politics was also important because of the organizational activity it generated. By the 1870s both major parties had evolved formal, well-organized structures. At the base lay the precinct or ward, where party meetings were open to all members. County, state, and national committees ran the ongoing business of the parties. Conventions determined party rules, adopted platforms, and selected the party's candidates.

At election time the party's main job was to get out the vote. Wherever elections were close and hard fought, the parties mounted intensive efforts organized down to the individual voter. In Indiana, for example, the Republicans appointed ten thousand "district men," each responsible for turning out a designated group of voters.

Machine Politics. Party governance seemed, on its face, highly democratic, since in theory all power derived from the party members in the precincts and wards. In practice, however, the parties were run by unofficial internal organizations—**political machines**—which consisted of insiders willing to do party work in exchange for public jobs or the sundry advantages of being connected. The machines tended toward one-man rule, although the "boss" ruled more by the consent of the secondary leaders than by his own absolute power.

Absorbed in the tasks of power brokerage, party bosses treated public issues as somewhat irrelevant. The high stakes of money, jobs, and influence made for intense factionalism. After Ulysses S. Grant left the White House in 1877, the Republican Party divided into two warring factions—the Stalwarts, led by Senator Roscoe Conkling of New York, and the Halfbreeds, led by James G. Blaine of Maine. The split was sparked by a personal feud between Conkling and Blaine, but it persisted because of a furious struggle over patronage. The Halfbreeds represented a newer Republican generation that was more favorably disposed than the Stalwarts to

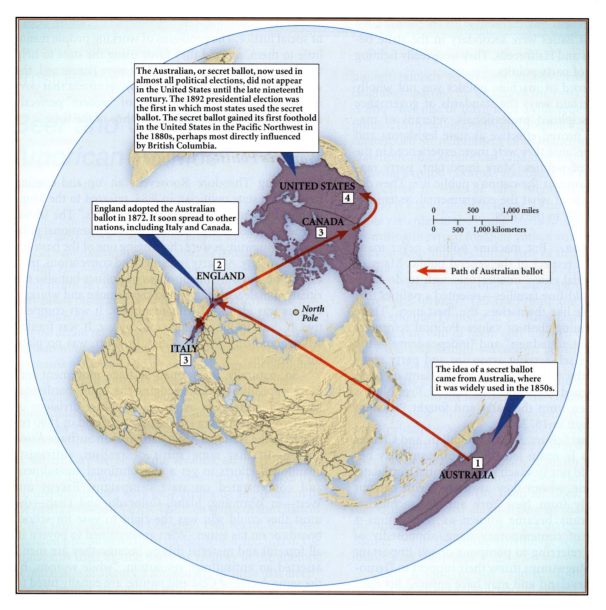

The Australian, or secret ballot, now used in almost all political elections, did not appear in the United States until the late nineteenth century. The 1892 presidential election was the first in which most states used the secret ballot. The secret ballot gained its first foothold in the United States in the Pacific Northwest in the 1880s, perhaps most directly influenced by British Columbia.

England adopted the Australian ballot in 1872. It soon spread to other nations, including Italy and Canada.

UNITED STATES **4**

CANADA **3**

ENGLAND **2**

ITALY **3**

AUSTRALIA **1**

North Pole

| 0 | 500 | 1,000 miles |
| 0 | 500 | 1,000 kilometers |

⟵ Path of Australian ballot

The idea of a secret ballot came from Australia, where it was widely used in the 1850s.

MAP 18.2 The Diffusion of the Australian Ballot
Although the foreign influences have not generally been acknowledged, many reforms that we think of as American are actually transnational phenomena, more often than not with the United States the beneficiary of advances elsewhere in the world. This was the case with the secret ballot, which originated in Australia in the 1850s and took four decades to reach the United States.

the contrary: women were bent on creating their own political sphere.

No issue joined home and politics more poignantly than did the liquor question. Just before Christmas in 1873 the women of Hillsboro, Ohio, began to hold vigils in front of the town's saloons, pleading with the owners to close and end the suffering of families of hard-drinking fathers. Thus began a spontaneous uprising of women that spread across the country. From this agitation came the Women's Christian Temperance Union (WCTU), which after its formation in 1874 rapidly blossomed into the largest women's organization in the country.

Because it excluded men, the WCTU was the spawning ground for a new generation of women leaders. Under the guidance of Frances Willard, who became president in 1879, the WCTU moved beyond temperance and adopted a "Do-Everything" policy. Women recognized that alcoholism was not simply a personal failing; it stemmed from larger social problems in American society. Willard also wanted to attract women who had no particular interest in the liquor question. Local affiliates were encouraged to undertake causes that were important in their own communities. By 1889 the WCTU had thirty-nine departments concerned with

The Levi P. Morton Association

The top-hatted gentlemen in this photograph constituted the local Republican Party organization of Newport, Rhode Island, named in honor of Levi P. Morton, Republican leader and vice president during the Benjamin Harrison administration (1889–1893). The maleness of party politics leaps from the photograph and asserts more clearly than a thousand words why the suffragist demand for the right to vote was met with ridicule and disbelief. Newport Historical Society.

labor, prostitution, health, international peace, and other issues.

Most important, the WCTU was drawn to woman suffrage. This was necessary, Willard argued, "because the liquor traffic is entrenched in law, and law grows out of the will of majorities, and majorities of women are against the liquor traffic." The WCTU began by stressing moral suasion and personal discipline—hence the word "temperance" in its name—but expanded its attack on liquor to include prohibition by law. Women needed the vote, said Willard, to fulfill their social responsibilities *as women* (see American Voices, "Helen Potter: The Case for Women's Political Rights," p. 527). This was very different from the claim made by the suffragists—that the ballot was an inherent right of all citizens *as individuals*—and was less threatening to masculine pride.

Not much changed in the short run. The WCTU was divided on the suffrage issue and did not become a major participant in later struggles for women's right to vote. But by linking women's social concerns to women's political participation, the WCTU helped lay the groundwork for a fresh attack on male electoral politics in the early twentieth century. And in the meantime, even without the vote, the WCTU demonstrated how potent a voice women could find in the public arena and how vibrant a political culture they could build.

Race and Politics in the New South

When Reconstruction ended in 1877, so did the hopes of African Americans that they would enjoy the equal rights of citizenship promised them by the Fourteenth and Fifteenth Amendments. Southern schools were strictly segregated. Access to jobs, the courts, and social services was racially determined and unequal. However, public accommodations were not yet legally segregated, and practices varied a good deal across the South. Only on the railroads, as rail travel became more common, did whites demand that blacks be excluded from first-class cars, with the result that southern railroads became after 1887 the first public accommodation subject to segregation laws.

In politics the situation was still more fluid. Blacks had not been driven from politics. On the contrary their turnout at elections was not far behind the turnout by whites. But blacks did not participate on equal terms with whites. In the Black Belt areas, where African Americans sometimes outnumbered whites, voting districts

political clubs were for men only. Populism, on the other hand, arose from a network of local alliances that had formed for largely social purposes and that welcomed women. Although they participated actively and served prominently as speakers and lecturers, few women became leaders of the alliance movement, and their role diminished with the shift into politics. In deference to the southern wing, the Populist platform was silent on woman suffrage. Still, neither Democrats nor Republicans would have countenanced a spokeswoman such as the fiery Mary Elizabeth Lease, who became famous for calling on farmers "to raise less corn and more hell." Mrs. Lease insisted just as strenuously on Populism's "grand and holy mission . . . to place the mothers of this nation on an equality with the fathers."

Populist Ideology.   Populism was driven as much by ideology as by the quest for political power. Populists felt that the problems afflicting farmers could stem only from some basic evil. They identified this evil with the business interests controlling the levers of the economic system. "There are but two sides," proclaimed a Populist manifesto. "On the one side are the allied hosts of monopolies, the money power, great trusts and railroad corporations. . . . On the other are the farmers, laborers, merchants and all the people who produce wealth. . . . Between these two there is no middle ground."

By this reasoning farmers and workers formed a single producer class. The claim was not merely rhetorical. Texas railroad workers and Colorado miners cooperated with the farmers' alliances, got their support in strikes, and actively participated in forming state Populist parties. The national platform contained strong labor planks, and party leaders earnestly sought the support of the labor movement. In its explicit class appeal—in recognizing that "the irrepressible conflict between capital and labor is upon us"—Populism parted company from the two mainstream parties.

In an age dominated by laissez-faire doctrine, what most distinguished Populism from the major parties was its positive attitude toward the state. In the words of the Populist platform: "We believe that the power of government—in other words, of the people—should be expanded as rapidly and as far as the good sense of an intelligent people and the teachings of experience shall justify, to the end that oppression, injustice and poverty should eventually cease in the land." Spokesmen such as Lorenzo Dow Lewelling, Populist governor of Kansas, considered it to be "the business of the government to make it possible to live and sustain the life of my family."

At the founding Omaha convention in 1892 Populists called for nationalization of the railroads and communications; protection of the land, including natural resources, from monopoly and foreign ownership; a graduated income tax; the Texas Alliance's subtreasury plan; and the free and unlimited coinage of silver. From this array of issues, the last—free silver—emerged as the overriding demand of the Populist Party.

Free Silver.   In the early 1890s, reeling from rock-bottom prices, embattled farmers gravitated to free silver because they hoped that an increase in the money supply would raise farm prices and give them some relief. In addition the party's slim resources would be fattened by hefty contributions from silver-mining interests who, scornful though they might be of Populist radicalism, yearned for the day when the government would buy at a premium all the silver they could produce.

Free silver triggered a debate for the soul of the Populist Party. Social democrats such as Henry Demarest Lloyd of Chicago and agrarian radicals such as Georgia's Tom Watson argued that free silver, if it became the

En Route to a Populist Rally, Dickinson County, Kansas

Farm people traveled miles to rallies and meetings for the chance to voice their grievances and socialize with like-minded folks. This tradition infused Populism with a special fervor. Gatherings such as the one these Kansans were heading to were a visible sign of what Populism meant—a movement of the "people."
Kansas State Historical Society.

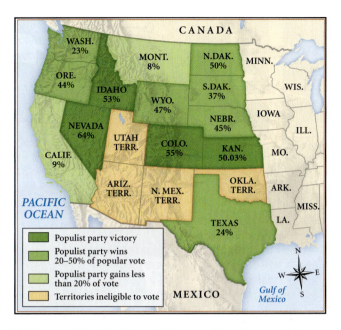

MAP 18.4 The Heyday of Western Populism, 1892

This map shows the percentage of the popular vote won by James B. Weaver, the People's Party candidate, in the presidential election of 1892. Except in California and Montana, the Populists won broad support across the West and genuinely threatened the established parties in that region.

Mary Elizabeth Lease

As a political movement the Populists were short on cash and organization but long on rank-and-file zeal and tub-thumping oratory. No one was more rousing on the stump than Mary Elizabeth Lease, who came from a Kansas homestead and pulled no punches. "What you farmers need to do," she proclaimed in her speeches, "is to raise less corn and more Hell!" Kansas State Historical Society.

defining party issue, would undercut the broader Populist program and alienate wage earners, who had no enthusiasm for inflationary measures. Any chance of a farmer-labor alliance that might transform Populism into an American version of the social-democratic parties of Europe would be doomed. The practical appeal of free silver, however, was simply too great.

But once Populists made that choice, they had fatally compromised their party's capacity to maintain an independent existence. Free silver was not an issue over which the Populists held a monopoly, but, on the contrary, a question at the very center of mainstream politics in the 1890s.

Money and Politics

In a rapidly developing economy, the money supply is bound to be a big political issue. Money has to increase rapidly enough to meet the economy's needs or growth will be stifled. How fast the money supply should grow, however, is a divisive question. Debtors and commodity producers want a larger money supply: more money in circulation inflates prices and reduces the real cost of borrowing. The "sound-money" people—creditors, individuals on fixed incomes, those in the slower-growing sectors of the economy—have an opposite interest.

Before the Civil War the main source of the nation's money supply had been state-chartered banks, several thousand of them, all issuing banknotes to borrowers that then circulated as money. The economy's need for money was amply met by the state banks, although the

soundness of the banknotes—the ability of the issuing banks to stand behind their notes and redeem them at face value—was always uncertain. This freewheeling activity was sharply curtailed by the U.S. Banking Act of 1863. However, because the Lincoln administration itself was printing paper money—**greenbacks**, so-called—to finance the Civil War, the economic impact of the Banking Act was not immediately felt.

After the war the sound money interests lobbied for a return to the traditional national policy, which was to base the federal currency on the amount of **specie**—gold and silver—held by the U.S. Treasury. The issue was hotly contested for a decade, but in 1875 the inflationists were defeated, and the circulation of greenbacks as legal tender—that is, backed by nothing more than the good faith of the federal government—came to an end. With state banknotes also in short supply, the country entered an era of chronic deflation and tight credit.

This was the context out of which the silver question emerged. The country had always operated on a bimetallic standard, but the supply of silver had gradually

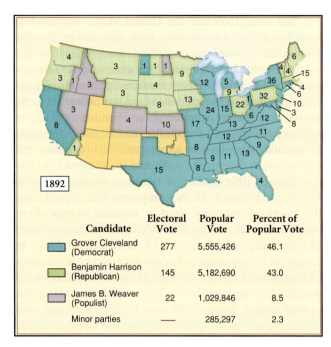

Candidate	Electoral Vote	Popular Vote	Percent of Popular Vote
Grover Cleveland (Democrat)	277	5,555,426	46.1
Benjamin Harrison (Republican)	145	5,182,690	43.0
James B. Weaver (Populist)	22	1,029,846	8.5
Minor parties	—	285,297	2.3

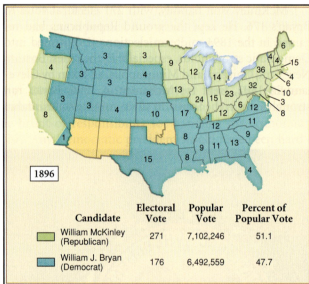

Candidate	Electoral Vote	Popular Vote	Percent of Popular Vote
William McKinley (Republican)	271	7,102,246	51.1
William J. Bryan (Democrat)	176	6,492,559	47.7

MAP 18.5 Presidential Elections of 1892 and 1896

In the 1890s the age of political stalemate came to an end. Students should compare the 1892 map with Map 18.1 on page 517 and note especially Cleveland's breakthrough in the normally Republican states of the upper Midwest. In 1896 the pendulum swung in the opposite direction, with McKinley's consolidation of Republican control over the Northeast and Midwest far overbalancing the Democratic advances in the thinly populated western states. The 1896 election marked the beginning of forty years of Republican dominance in national politics.

the Populist West (Map 18.5). But the gains his evangelical style brought him in some Republican rural areas did not compensate for his losses in traditionally Democratic urban districts.

The paralyzing equilibrium in American politics ended in 1896. The Republicans skillfully turned both economic and cultural challenges to their advantage. They persuaded the nation that they were the party of prosperity, and they persuaded many traditionally Democratic urban voters that they were sympathetic to ethnic diversity. In so doing the Republicans became the nation's majority party. In 1896, too, electoral politics regained its place as an arena for national debate.

The Decline of Agrarian Radicalism. As for Populism, it simply faded away. Fusion with the Democrats in 1896 deprived the People's Party of its identity and undermined its organizational structure. After the election the issue on which Populism had staked its fate—free silver—vanished. During the 1890s gold was discovered in South Africa, Colorado, and the Yukon, and the new cyanide refining process greatly increased ore yields. The newly abundant gold supply took the sting out of the lost battle for free silver. In 1897, moreover, the world market for agricultural commodities turned favorable. Wheat went from 72 cents a bushel in 1896 to 98 cents in 1909, corn from 27 cents a bushel to 57 cents, and cotton from 6 cents a pound to 14 cents. Farm prices rose faster than the prices of other products, and, as a result, so did the real income of farmers. A new spirit of optimism took hold in the "golden age" of American agriculture before World War I.

There would be times when distressed farmers would turn again to insurgent politics but never with the potency of the Populist Party. By 1900 scarcely a third of the labor force earned a living from the soil; the proportion would shrink in each succeeding census until, in our own time, less than 3 percent of the labor force is engaged in agriculture (see Appendix, p. A-14). It would be as an organized interest group, not as a protest movement, that farmers would ultimately find a way of advancing their interests in politics.

Agriculture had long been at the heart of American life. In the twentieth century agriculture became just one more economic interest—important but subordinate in the modern industrial order.

FOR FURTHER EXPLORATION

▶ For definitions of key terms boldfaced in this chapter, see the glossary at the end of the book.

▶ To assess your mastery of the material covered in this chapter, see the Online Study Guide at **bedfordstmartins.com/henretta**.

▶ For suggested references, including Web sites, see page SR-20 at the end of the book.

▶ For map resources and primary documents, see **bedfordstmartins.com/henretta**.

When Reconstruction ended in 1877, national politics became less issue oriented and, as a formal process, less important in American life. This situation resulted from weaknesses in governmental institutions, from the prevailing philosophy of laissez faire, and from the paralysis of evenly matched political parties. Yet post-Reconstruction politics displayed great vigor, as can be seen in the high levels of popular participation. For one thing, politics was the arena in which the nation's ethnic and religious conflicts were largely fought out. Equally important, the party machines were robust, engaging the energies of political activists and performing crucial functions that properly belonged to, but were still beyond the capacity of, governmental institutions. Finally, despite the slow headway made toward woman suffrage, women's organizations carved out for themselves a broader sphere of social reform activity.

In the South the political aftermath of Reconstruction was one-party rule by the "Redeemer" Democrats. Their appeal to sectional pride and white supremacy, potent though it was, could not quite contain the South's class tensions, which with the rise of Populism burst out in a full-fledged, biracial challenge to conservative Democratic rule. The defeat of southern Populism turned into a grim reaction that disfranchised African Americans, completed a rigid segregation system, and let loose a terrible cycle of racial violence. Blacks resisted but had to bend to overwhelming white power. The accommodationist strategy of Booker T. Washington seemed to offer the best hope for black survival in an age of extreme racism.

Elsewhere in the country the Populist challenge stirred new life into the two-party system. Seizing free silver from the Populists, the Democratic Party made the election of 1896 a contest of real programmatic significance. The Republicans won decisively, ending the paralyzing party stalemate of the previous twenty years. With electoral politics once more an arena of national debate, the stage was set for the reform politics of the Progressive Era.

1874 Woman's Christian Temperance Union founded

1877 Rutherford B. Hayes inaugurated as president, marking end of Reconstruction

1881 President James A. Garfield assassinated

1883 Pendleton Civil Service Act

Supreme Court strikes down Civil Rights Act of 1875

1884 Mugwump reformers leave Republican Party to support Grover Cleveland, first Democrat elected president since 1856

1887 Florida adopts first law segregating railroad travel

1888 James Bryce's *The American Commonwealth*

1890 McKinley Tariff

Democrats sweep congressional elections, inaugurating brief era of Democratic Party dominance

Mississippi becomes first state to adopt literacy test to disfranchise blacks

1892 People's (Populist) Party founded

1893 Panic of 1893 leads to national depression

Repeal of Sherman Silver Purchase Act (1890)

1894 "Coxey's army" of unemployed fails to win federal relief

1895 Booker T. Washington sets out Atlanta Compromise

1896 Election of Republican president William McKinley; free-silver campaign crushed

Plessy v. Ferguson upholds constitutionality of "separate but equal" facilities

Economic depression ends; era of agricultural prosperity begins

CHAPTER 19

The Rise of the City

Urbanization
Industrial Sources of City Growth
City Innovation
Private City, Public City

Upper Class, Middle Class
The Urban Elite
The Suburban World
Middle-Class Families

City Life
Newcomers
Ward Politics
Religion in the City
City Amusements
The Higher Culture

◄ **Mulberry Street, New York City, c. 1900**

The influx of southern and Eastern Europeans created teeming ghettos in the heart of New York City and other major American cities. The view is of Mulberry Street, with its pushcarts, street peddlers, and bustling traffic. The inhabitants are mostly Italians, and some of them, noticing the photographer preparing his camera, have gathered to be in the picture.
Library of Congress.

For more help analyzing this image, see the ONLINE STUDY GUIDE at bedfordstmartins.com/henretta.

VISITING HIS FIANCÉE'S MISSOURI HOMESTEAD IN 1894, Theodore Dreiser was struck by "the spirit of rural America, its idealism, its dreams." But this was an "American tradition in which I, alas!, could not share." Said Dreiser, "I had seen Pittsburgh. I had seen Lithuanians and Hungarians in their [alleys] and hovels. I had seen the girls of the city—walking the streets at night." Only twenty-three at the time, Dreiser would go on to write one of the great American urban novels, *Sister Carrie* (1900), about one young woman in the army of small-town Americans flocking to the Big City. But Dreiser, part of that army, already knew that between rural America and Pittsburgh an unbridgeable chasm had opened up.

In 1820, after two hundred years of settlement, fewer than one in twenty Americans lived in a city of 10,000 people or more. After that, decade by decade, the urban population swelled until, by 1900, one of every five Americans was a city dweller. Nearly 6.5 million inhabited just three great cities: New York, Chicago, and Philadelphia (Table 19.1).

The city was the arena of the nation's vibrant economic life. Here the factories went up, and here the new immigrants settled, constituting in 1900 a third of the residents of the

543

TABLE 19.1 Ten Largest Cities by Population, 1870 and 1900

1870		1900	
City	Population	City	Population
1. New York	942,292	New York	3,437,202
2. Philadelphia	674,022	Chicago	1,698,575
3. Brooklyn*	419,921	Philadelphia	1,293,697
4. St. Louis	310,864	St. Louis	575,238
5. Chicago	298,977	Boston	560,892
6. Baltimore	267,354	Baltimore	508,957
7. Boston	250,526	Cleveland	381,768
8. Cincinnati	216,239	Buffalo, N.Y.	352,387
9. New Orleans	191,418	San Francisco	342,782
10. San Francisco	149,473	Cincinnati	325,902

*Brooklyn was consolidated with New York in 1898.
Source: U.S. Census data.

major American cities. Here, too, lived the millionaires and a growing white-collar middle class. For all these people the city was more than a place to make a living. It provided the setting for an urban culture unlike anything seen before in the United States. City people, although differing vastly among themselves, became distinctively and recognizably urban.

Urbanization

The march to the cities seemed irresistible to nine-teenth-century Americans (Map 19.1). "The greater part of our population must live in cities—cities much greater than the world has yet known," declared the Congregational minister Josiah Strong. "There was no resisting the trend," said another writer. Urbanization became inevitable because of another inevitability of American life—industrialism.

Industrial Sources of City Growth

Until the Civil War cities were centers of commerce, not industry. They were the places where goods were bought and sold for distribution into the interior or shipment out to world markets. Early industry sprang up in the countryside because factories needed water power from

streams, access to fuel and raw materials, and workers recruited from the countryside.

But once steam engines came along, mill operators no longer depended on water-driven power. In the iron industry coal replaced charcoal as the primary fuel, so it was not necessary to be near forests. Improved trans-portation, especially railroads, enabled entrepreneurs to locate in places most convenient to suppliers and mar-kets. The result was a geographic concentration of indus-try. Iron makers gravitated to Pittsburgh because of its superior access to coal and ore fields and also to markets for iron products. Chicago, midway between western livestock suppliers and eastern markets, became a great meatpacking center (see Map 17.3 on p. 494).

The increasing size of factories contributed to urban growth. A plant that employed thousands of workers instantly created a small city in its vicinity, sometimes in the form of a company town like Aliquippa, Pennsylvania, which became body and soul the property of the Jones and Laughlin Steel Company. Many firms built plants near a large city so they could draw on its labor supply and transportation facilities, as George Pullman did in 1880 when he located his sleeping-car works and model town southwest of Chicago.

Sometimes the metropolis spread and absorbed nearby factory towns, which was the fate of Pullman. Elsewhere, as in northern New Jersey or along Lake

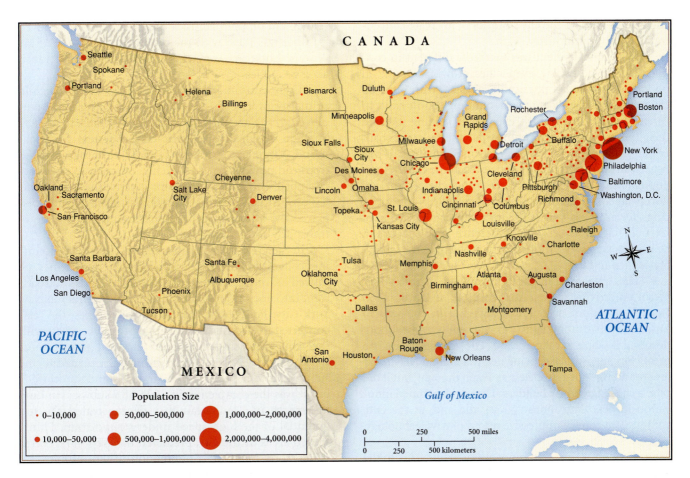

MAP 19.1 America's Cities, 1900

The number of Americans living in urban places more than doubled between 1880 and 1900, with the most dramatic increases in the largest metropolitan centers. New York grew from 1.2 million to 3.4 million, Chicago from 500,000 to 1.7 million.

For more help analyzing this map, see the ONLINE STUDY GUIDE at bedfordstmartins.com/henretta.

Michigan south of Chicago, the lines between industrial towns blurred and an extended urban-industrial area emerged. The same process occurred in Europe, where industrial regions were emerging in northeastern France around Lille and in Germany's Ruhr Valley.

Older commercial cities also became more industrial. Warehouse districts could readily be converted to small-scale manufacturing; a distribution network was right at hand. In addition, as gateways for immigrants, port cities offered abundant cheap labor. Boston, Philadelphia, Baltimore, and San Francisco became hives of small-scale, labor-intensive industrial activity. New York's enormous pool of immigrant workers made that city a magnet for the garment trades, cigarmaking, and diversified light industry. Preeminent as a city of trade and finance, New York also ranked as the nation's largest manufacturing center.

City Innovation

The commercial cities of the early nineteenth century had been compact places, densely settled around harbors or riverfronts. As late as 1850, when it had 565,000 people, Philadelphia covered only ten square miles. From the foot of Chestnut Street on the Delaware River, a person could walk almost anywhere in the city within forty-five minutes. Thereafter, as it developed, Philadelphia spilled out and, like American cities everywhere, engulfed the surrounding countryside.

A downtown area emerged, usually on the site of the original commercial city. Downtown in turn broke up into shopping, financial, warehousing, manufacturing, hotel and entertainment, and red-light districts. Moving out from the center, industrial development tended to follow the arteries of transportation—railroads, canals, and rivers—and, at the city's outskirts, to create concentrations of heavy industry.

Urban development was markedly different in continental Europe, where even cities growing rapidly in population remained physically compact, with built-up areas ending abruptly at the surrounding countryside. In America cities constantly expanded, spilling beyond their boundaries and forming what the federal census began to designate in 1910 as metropolitan areas. While American cities were highly congested at the center, their population density was actually much below that of European cities: 22 persons per acre for fifteen American cities, for example, versus 158 for a comparable group of German cities. Given this difference efficient urban transportation was a more urgent problem in the United States than in Europe.

"The only trouble about this town," wrote Mark Twain on arriving in New York in 1867, "is that it is too large. You cannot accomplish anything in the way of business, you cannot even pay a friendly call without devoting a whole day to it. . . . [The] distances are too great." Finding ways of moving nearly a million New Yorkers around was not as hopeless as Twain thought, but it did pose a challenge to city builders. The city demanded innovation no less than industry itself did and, in the end, compiled an equally impressive record of new technology.

Mass Transit. The first innovation, dating back to the 1820s, was the omnibus, an elongated version of the horse-drawn carriage. Much better was the horsecar, whose key advantage was that it ran on iron tracks so that the horses could pull more passengers and move them at a faster clip through congested city streets. All this happened because of a modest but crucial refinement on railroad track design in 1852—a grooved rail that was flush with the pavement. From the 1840s onward horsecars were the mainstay of urban transit across America.

Then came the electric trolley car, the brainchild primarily of Frank J. Sprague, an engineer once employed by the great inventor Thomas A. Edison. In 1887 Sprague designed an electric-driven system for Richmond, Virginia: a "trolley" carriage running along an overhead power line was attached by cable to streetcars equipped with an electric motor—hence the name "trolley car." After Sprague's success, the trolley swiftly displaced the horsecar and became the primary mode of transportation in most American cities.

In the great metropolitan centers, however, mounting congestion led to demands that transit lines be moved off the streets. In 1879 the first elevated railroads went into operation on Sixth and Ninth Avenues in New York City. Powered at first by steam engines, the "els" converted to electricity following Sprague's success with the trolley. Chicago developed elevated transit most fully (Map 19.2). New York, meanwhile, turned to the subway. Boston opened a short underground line in 1897, but it was the completion in 1904 of a subway running the length of Manhattan that demonstrated the full potential of the high-speed underground train. Thinly settled areas of the city, predicted the *New York Times*, would soon boast of "a population of ten millions . . . housed comfortably, healthfully and relatively cheaply." The subway would especially delight "all who travel with the sole purpose of 'getting there' in the least possible time." Mass transit had become *rapid* transit.

By 1890 the number of passengers carried on American street railways was more than 2 billion per

The Chicago Elevated, 1900
This is Wabash Avenue, looking north from Adams Street. For Americans from farms and small towns, this photograph by William Henry Jackson captured something of the peculiarity of the urban scene. What could be stranger than a railroad suspended above the streets in the midst of people's lives?
KEA Publishing Services Ltd.

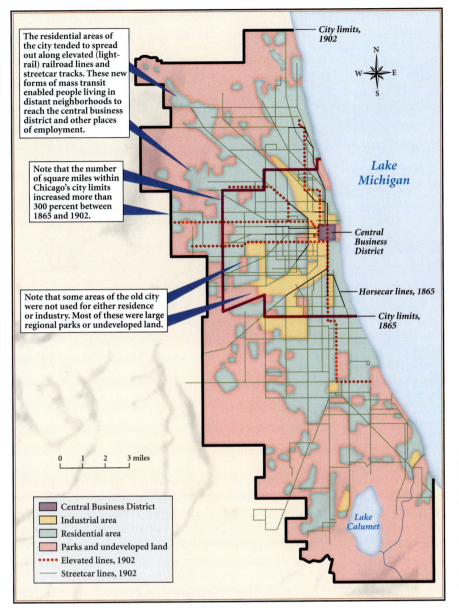

The residential areas of the city tended to spread out along elevated (light-rail) railroad lines and streetcar tracks. These new forms of mass transit enabled people living in distant neighborhoods to reach the central business district and other places of employment.

Note that the number of square miles within Chicago's city limits increased more than 300 percent between 1865 and 1902.

Note that some areas of the old city were not used for either residence or industry. Most of these were large regional parks or undeveloped land.

City limits, 1902

N
W E
S

Lake Michigan

Central Business District

Horsecar lines, 1865

City limits, 1865

Lake Calumet

0   1   2   3 miles

Central Business District
Industrial area
Residential area
Parks and undeveloped land
Elevated lines, 1902
Streetcar lines, 1902

MAP 19.2 The Expansion of Chicago, 1865–1902

In 1865 Chicagoans depended on horsecar lines to get around town. By 1900 the city limits had expanded enormously, accompanied by an equally dramatic expansion of streetcar service, which was by then electrified. Elevated trains also helped to ease congestion in the urban core. New streetcar lines, some extending beyond the city limits, were important to suburban development in the coming years.

year, over twice that of the rest of the world combined. In Great Britain the horsecar remained dominant long after it had disappeared from American streets. In Tokyo, the largest Asian city, the horsecar was not even introduced until 1882, and electric streetcars first appeared there in 1903.

Skyscrapers. Equally remarkable was the architectural revolution sweeping metropolitan business districts. With steel girders, durable plate glass, and the passenger elevator available by the 1880s, a wholly new way of construction opened up. A steel skeleton supported the building, while the walls, previously weight bearing, served as curtains enclosing the structure. The sky, so to speak, became the limit.

The first "skyscraper" to be built on this principle was William Jenney's ten-story Home Insurance Building

(1885) in Chicago. Although this pioneering effort appeared unremarkable—it looked just like the other downtown buildings—the steel-girdered technology it contained liberated the aesthetic perceptions of American architects. A Chicago school sprang up, dedicated to the design of buildings whose form expressed, rather than masked, their structure and function. Chicago pioneered skyscraper construction, but New York, with its unrelenting need for prime downtown space, took the lead after the mid-1890s. The fifty-five story Woolworth Building, completed in 1913, marked the beginning of the modern Manhattan skyline.

The Electric City. For ordinary citizens the electric lights that dispelled the gloom of the city at night offered the most dramatic evidence that times had changed. Gaslight—illuminating gas produced from

Thomas Edison's Laboratories in Menlo Park, New Jersey, c. 1880
Thomas Edison's dream of illuminating the world is illustrated by this fanciful drawing of his laboratories in Menlo Park, New Jersey. For the time being, however, it was the American home that was the primary beneficiary of Edison's wonderful light bulb, since electricity was slow to arrive in many parts of the world.
U.S. Department of the Interior, National Park Service, Edison National Historic Site.

coal—had been in use since the early nineteenth century but, at 12 candlepower, the lamps were too dim to brighten the downtown streets and public spaces of the city. The first use of electricity, once generating technology made it commercially feasible in the 1870s, was for better city lighting. Charles F. Brush's electric arc lamps, installed in Wanamaker's department store in Philadelphia in 1878, threw a brilliant light and soon replaced gaslight on city streets and public buildings across the country. Electric lighting then entered the American home, thanks to Thomas Edison's invention of a serviceable incandescent bulb in 1879. Edison's motto—"Let there be light!"—truly described the experience of the modern city.

Before it had any significant effect on industry, electricity gave the city its modern tempo, lifting elevators, powering streetcars and subway trains, turning night into day. Meanwhile, Alexander Graham Bell's telephone (1876) sped communication beyond anything imagined previously. Twain's complaint of 1867 that it was impossible to carry on business in New York had been answered: all he needed to do was pick up the phone.

Private City, Public City

City building was very much an exercise in private enterprise. The lure of profit spurred the great innovations—the trolley car, electric lighting, the skyscraper, the

elevator, the telephone—and drove urban real estate development. The investment opportunities looked so tempting that new cities sprang up almost overnight from the ruins of the Chicago fire of 1871 and the San Francisco earthquake of 1906. Real estate interests, eager to develop subdivisions, often were instrumental in pushing streetcar lines outward from the central districts of cities.

Urban transit became big business. In the early 1880s the streetcar lines of Philadelphia were merged into the Philadelphia Traction Company. The promoters, Peter A. B. Widener and William L. Elkins, then joined with financiers in Chicago and New York and built an immense syndicate that by 1900 controlled streetcar systems in over a hundred cities as well as utilities supplying gas and electricity to urban residents. The city, like industry, became an arena for enterprise and profit.

America gave birth to what one urban historian has called the "private city"—whose growth was shaped primarily by the actions of many individuals, all pursuing their own goals and bent on making money. The prevailing belief was that the sum of such private activity would far exceed what the community could accomplish through public effort.

Yet constitutionally it was up to the cities to draw the line between public and private. New York City was entirely within its rights to operate a municipally owned subway, the State Supreme Court ruled in 1897. Even the use of private land was subject to whatever regulations the city might impose. Thus the skylines of Chicago and Boston did not resemble Manhattan's because of the limits those cities imposed on the heights of buildings. Moreover, city governance improved impressively in the late nineteenth century. Though by no means free of the corruption of earlier days, municipal agencies became far better organized and staffed and, above all, more expansive in the functions they undertook. Nowhere in the world, indeed, were there more massive public projects—aqueducts, sewage systems, bridges, and spacious parks.

The Urban Environment. In the space between public and private, however, was an environmental no-man's land. City streets were often filthy and poorly maintained. "Three or four days of warm spring weather," remarked a New York journalist, would turn Manhattan's garbage-strewn, snow-clogged streets into "veritable mud rivers." Air quality likewise suffered. A visitor to Pittsburgh noted "the heavy pall of smoke which constantly overhangs her . . . until the very sun looks coppery through the sooty haze." As for the lovely hills rising from the rivers, "they have been leveled down, cut into, sliced off, and ruthlessly marred and mutilated." Pittsburgh presented "all that is unsightly and forbidding in appearance, the original beauties of nature having been ruthlessly sacrificed to utility."

Hardest hit by urban growth were the poor. In earlier times they had mainly lived in makeshift wooden structures in alleys and back streets and then, as more prosperous families moved away, in the subdivided homes left behind. As land values climbed after the Civil War, speculators tore down these houses and began to erect buildings specifically designed for the urban masses. In New York City the dreadful result was five- or six-story **tenements** housing twenty or more families in cramped, airless apartments (Figure 19.1). In New York's Eleventh Ward, an average of 986 persons occupied each acre, a density matched only in Bombay, India.

Reformers recognized the problem but seemed unable to solve it. Some favored model tenements financed by public-spirited citizens willing to accept a limited return on their investment. When private philanthropy failed to make much of a dent, cities turned to housing codes. The most advanced of these was New York's Tenement House Law of 1901, which required interior courts, indoor toilets, and fire safeguards for new structures but did little for existing housing stock. Commercial development had pushed up land values in downtown areas. Only high-density, cheaply built housing could earn a sufficient profit for the landlords of the poor. This economic fact defied nineteenth-century solutions.

It was not that America lacked an urban vision. On the contrary an abiding rural ideal had influenced American cities for many years. Frederick Law Olmsted, who designed New York's Central Park, wanted cities that exposed people to the beauties of nature. One of Olmsted's projects, the Chicago Columbian Exposition of 1893, gave rise to the influential "City Beautiful" movement. The results included larger park systems, broad boulevards and parkways, and after the turn of the century, zoning laws and planned suburbs.

But cities usually heeded urban planners too little and too late. "Fifteen or twenty years ago a plan might have been adopted that would have made this one of the most beautiful cities in the world," Kansas City's park commissioners reported in 1893. At that time "such a policy could not be fully appreciated." Nor, even if Kansas City had foreseen its future, would it have shouldered the "heavy burden" of trying to shape its development. The American city had placed its faith in the

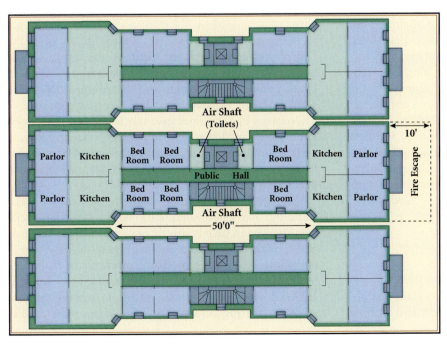

FIGURE 19.1 Floor Plan of a Dumbbell Tenement

In a contest for a design that met an 1879 requirement that every room have a window, the dumbbell tenement won. The interior indentation, which created an airshaft between adjoining buildings, gave the tenement its "dumbbell" shape. What was touted as a "model" tenement demonstrated instead the futility of trying to reconcile maximum land usage with decent housing. Each floor contained four apartments of three or four rooms, the largest only 10 by 11 feet. The two toilets in the hall became filthy or broke down under daily use by forty or more people. The narrow airshaft provided almost no light for the interior rooms and served mainly as a dumping ground for garbage. So deplorable were these tenements that they became the stimulus for the next wave of New York housing reform.

dynamics of the marketplace, not the restraints of a planned future. The pluses and minuses are perhaps best revealed by the following comparison.

A Balance Sheet: Chicago and Berlin. Chicago and Berlin had virtually equal populations in 1900. But they had very different histories. Seventy years earlier, when Chicago had been a muddy frontier outpost, Berlin was already a city of 250,000 and the royal seat of the Hohenzollerns of Prussia.

With German unification in 1871, the imperial authorities rebuilt Berlin on a grander scale. "A capital city is essential for the state, to act as a pivot for its culture," proclaimed the Prussian historian Heinrich von Treitschke. Berlin served that national purpose—"a center where Germany's political, intellectual, and material life is concentrated, and its people can feel united." Chicago had no such pretensions. It was strictly a place of business, made great by virtue of its strategic grip on the commerce of America's industrial heartland. Nothing in Chicago evoked the grandeur of Berlin's boulevards or its monumental palaces and public buildings, nor were Chicagoans witness to the pomp and ceremony of the imperial parades up broad, tree-lined Unter den Linden to the national cathedral.

Yet as a functioning city Chicago was in many ways superior to Berlin. Chicago's waterworks pumped 500 million gallons of water a day, or 139 gallons of water per person, while Berliners had to make do with 18 gallons. Flush toilets, a rarity in Berlin in 1900, could be found in 60 percent of Chicago's homes. Chicago's streets were lit by electricity, while Berlin still relied mostly on gaslight. Chicago had a much bigger streetcar system, twice as much acreage devoted to parks, and a public library containing many more volumes. And Chicago had just completed an amazing sanitation project, reversing the course of the Chicago River so that its waters—and the city's sewage—would flow away from Lake Michigan and southward down into the Illinois and Mississippi Rivers.

Giant sanitation projects were one thing; an inspiring urban environment was something else. For well-traveled Americans admiring of things European, the sense of inferiority was palpable. "We are enormously rich," admitted the journalist Edwin L. Godkin, "but . . . what have we got to show? Almost nothing. Ugliness from an artistic point of view is the mark of all our cities." Thus the urban balance sheet: a utilitarian infrastructure that was superb by nineteenth-century standards, but "no municipal splendors of any description, nothing but population and hotels."

Upper Class, Middle Class

In the compact city of the early republic, class distinctions had been expressed by the way men and women dressed and by the deference they demanded from or granted to others. As the industrial city grew, these interpersonal marks of class began to lose their force. In the anonymity of a large city, recognition and deference no longer served as mechanisms for conferring status. Instead, people began to rely on external signs: conspicuous display of wealth, membership in exclusive clubs, and above all, choice of neighborhood.

For the poor, place of residence depended, as always, on being close to their jobs. But for higher-income urbanites, where to live became a matter of personal means and social preference.

The Urban Elite

As early as the 1840s, Boston merchants had taken advantage of the new railway service to escape the congested city. Fine rural estates appeared in Milton, Newton, and other outlying towns. By 1848 roughly 20 percent of Boston's businessmen were making the trip by train to their downtown offices. Ferries that plied the harbor between Manhattan and Brooklyn or New Jersey served the same purpose for New Yorkers.

Lifestyles of the Rich. As commercial development engulfed downtown residential areas, the exodus by the well-to-do spread across America. In Cincinnati wealthy families settled on the scenic hills rimming the crowded, humid tableland that ran down to the Ohio River. On those hillsides, a traveler noted in 1883, "the homes of Cincinnati's merchant princes and millionaires are found . . . elegant cottages, tasteful villas, and substantial mansions, surrounded by a paradise of grass, gardens, lawns, and tree-shaded roads." Residents of the area, called Hilltop, founded country clubs, five downtown gentlemen's clubs, and a host of other institutions that sustained an exclusive social life for Cincinnati's elite.

Despite the attractions of country life, many of the very richest preferred the heart of the city. Chicago boasted its Gold Coast; San Francisco, Nob Hill; Denver, Quality Hill; and Manhattan, Fifth Avenue. New York novelist Edith Wharton recalled how the comfortable midcentury brownstones gave way to the "'new' millionaire houses," which spread northward on Fifth Avenue along Central Park. Great mansions, emulating the aristocratic houses of Europe, lined Fifth Avenue at the turn of the century.

But great wealth did not automatically confer social standing. An established elite dominated the social heights, even in such relatively raw cities as San Francisco and Denver. It had taken only a generation—and sometimes less—for money made in commerce or real estate to shed its tarnish and become "old" and genteel. In long-settled Boston, wealth passed intact through several generations, creating a closely knit tribe of Brahmin families that kept moneyed newcomers at bay. Elsewhere urban elites tended to be more open, but only to the socially ambitious who were prepared to make visible and energetic use of their money.

New York's Metropolitan Opera was one product of this ongoing struggle among the wealthy. The Academy of Music, home to the city's opera since 1854, was controlled by the Livingstons, the Bayards, the Beekmans, and other old New York families. Denied boxes at the Academy, the Vanderbilts and their allies sponsored a rival opera house. In 1883, with its glittering opening to the strains of Gounod's *Faust,* the Metropolitan Opera proclaimed its ascendancy in the music world and in due course won the patronage even of the Beekmans and Bayards. During this war of the opera houses the Vanderbilt circle achieved social recognition.

"High Society."   New York City became the home of a national elite as the most ambitious gravitated to this preeminent capital of American finance and culture. Manhattan's extraordinary vitality in turn kept the city's high society fluid and relatively open. In Theodore Dreiser's novel *The Titan* (1914), the tycoon Frank Cowperwood reassures his unhappy wife that if Chicago society will not accept them, "there are other cities. Money will arrange matters in New York—that I know. We can build a real place there, and go in on equal terms, if we have money enough." New York thus came to be a magnet for millionaires. The city attracted them not only because of its importance as a business center but for the opportunities it offered for display and social recognition.

This infusion of wealth shattered the older elite society of New York. Seeking to be assimilated into the upper class, the flood of moneyed newcomers simply overwhelmed it. There followed a curious process of reconstruction, a deliberate effort to define the rules of conduct and identify those who properly "belonged" in New York society.

The key figure was Ward McAllister, a southern-born lawyer who had made a quick fortune in gold-rush San Francisco and then devoted himself to a second career as the arbiter of New York society. In 1888 McAllister compiled the first *Social Register,* which announced that it would serve as a "record of society, comprising an accurate

Going to the Opera, 1873

In this painting by Seymour J. Guy, William H. Vanderbilt, eldest son and successor of the railroad tycoon Cornelius Vanderbilt, has gathered with his family and friends preparatory to attending the opera. It was the sponsorship of New York's Metropolitan Opera that helped the Vanderbilts achieve social recognition among the older, more established moneyed families of New York City. Courtesy, Biltmore Estate, Asheville, NC.

and careful list" of all those deemed eligible for New York society. McAllister instructed the socially ambitious on how to select guests, set a proper table, arrange a party, and launch a young lady into society. He presided over a round of assemblies, balls, and dinners that defined the boundaries of an elite society. At the apex stood "The Four Hundred"—the true cream of New York society. McAllister's list corresponded to those invited to Mrs. William Astor's gala ball of February 1, 1892.

Americans were adept at making money, remarked the journalist Edwin L. Godkin in 1896, but they lacked the aristocratic traditions of Europe for spending it. "Great wealth has not yet entered our manners," Godkin remarked. In their struggle to find the rules and establish the manners, the moneyed elite made an indelible mark on urban life. If there was magnificence in the American city, that was mainly their handiwork. And if there was conspicuous waste and display, that too was their doing.

The Suburban World

The middle class left a smaller imprint on the public face of urban society. Its members, unlike the rich, preferred privacy and retreated into the domesticity of suburban comfort and family life.

Since colonial times the American economy had spawned a robust middle class of mostly self-employed lawyers, doctors, merchants, and proprietors. This older middle class remained important, but it was joined by a new salaried middle class brought forth by industrialism. Corporate organizations required managers, accountants, and clerks. Technology advances called for engineers, chemists, and designers, while the distribution system needed salesmen, advertising executives, and accountants. These salaried ranks increased sevenfold between 1870 and 1910—much faster than any other occupational group. Nearly 9 million people held **white-collar** jobs in 1910, more than a fourth of all employed Americans.

Some members of this salaried class lived in the row houses of Baltimore and Boston or the comfortable apartment buildings of New York City. But more preferred to escape the clamor and congestion of the city. They were attracted by a persisting "rural ideal," agreeing with the landscape architect Andrew Jackson Downing that "nature and domestic life are better than the society and manners of town." As trolley service expanded out from the central city, middle-class Americans followed the wealthy into the countryside. All sought what one Chicago developer promised for his North Shore subdivision in 1875—"qualities of which the city is in a large degree bereft, namely, its pure air, peacefulness, quietude, and natural scenery."

No major American city escaped **suburbanization** during the late nineteenth century. City limits everywhere expanded rapidly, but even so, much of the suburban growth took place beyond city limits. By 1900 more than half of Boston's people lived in "streetcar suburbs" outside Boston proper; nationwide, according to the 1910 census, about 25 percent of the urban population lived in such autonomous suburbs.

On the European continent, by contrast, cities remained highly concentrated. When expansion did occur, it was the poor and not the well-to-do who inhabited the margins. Unlike its American counterpart, the European middle class was not attracted to the rural ideal and valued urban life for its own sake. The preconditions for suburbanization were likewise weaker in Europe: mass transit developed more slowly; traditional beam-and-post construction did not give way to the cheaper balloon frame techniques; and there was less of the freewheeling real estate development that spurred American suburbanization.

The geography of the suburbs was truly a map of class structure because where a family lived told where it ranked. The farther out from the city center, the finer the houses and the larger the lots. Affluent businessmen and professionals had the time and flexibility to travel a long distance into town. People closer in wanted transit lines that went straight into the city center and carried them quickly between home and office. Lower-income commuters were more likely to have more than one wage earner in the family, less secure employment, and jobs requiring movement around the city. It was better for them to be closer to the city center because they then had access to crosstown lines that afforded the mobility they needed for their work.

Suburban boundaries were ever shifting, as working-class city residents who wanted to better their lives moved to the cheapest suburbs, prompting an exodus of older residents who in turn pushed the next higher group farther out in search of space and greenery. Suburbanization was the sum of countless individual decisions. Each family's move represented an advance in living standards—not only more light, air, and quiet but better accommodation than the city afforded. Suburban houses were typically larger for the same money and came equipped with flush toilets, hot water, central heating, and, by the turn of the century, electricity.

The suburbs also restored an opportunity that rural Americans thought they had lost when they moved to the city. In the suburbs home ownership again became the norm. "A man is not really a true man until he owns his home," propounded the Reverend Russell H. Conwell in his famous sermon on the virtues of making money, "Acres of Diamonds."

The small towns of rural America had fostered community life. Not so the suburbs. The grid street pattern, while efficient for laying out lots, offered no natural focus for group life. Nor did the stores and services that lay scattered along the trolley-car streets. Suburban development conformed to the economics of real estate and transportation, and so did the thinking of middle-class home seekers entering the suburbs. They wanted a house that gave them good value and convenience to the trolley line.

The need for community had lost some of its force for middle-class Americans. Two other attachments assumed greater importance: one was work; the other, family.

Middle-Class Families

In the preindustrial economy there was little separation between work and family life. Farmers, merchants, and artisans generally worked at home, and everyone employed there, not only blood relatives, was considered part of the household. As industrialism progressed economic activity left the home. For the middle class in particular, the family became dissociated from employment. The father departed every morning for the office, and children spent more years in school. Clothing was bought ready made, and food came increasingly in cans and packages. Middle-class families became smaller, excluding all but nuclear members and consisting typically by 1900 of husband, wife, and three children.

Within this family circle relationships became intense and affectionate. "Home was the most expressive experience in life," recalled the literary critic Henry Seidel Canby of his growing up in the 1890s. "Though the family might quarrel and nag, the home held them all, protecting them against the outside world." The suburb provided a fit setting for such middle-class families. The quiet, tree-lined streets created a domestic space insulated from the hurly-burly of commerce and enterprise.

The Wife's Role. The burdens of this domesticity fell heavily on the wife. It was nearly unheard of for her to seek an outside career—that was her husband's role. Her job was to manage the household. "The woman who could not make a home, like the man who could not support one, was condemned," Canby remembered. But with fewer children, the wife's workload declined. Moreover servants still played an important part in middle-class households. In 1910 there were about 2 million domestic servants, the largest job category for women.

As the physical burdens of household work eased, higher-quality homemaking became the new ideal. This was the message of Catharine Beecher's best-selling book *The American Woman's Home* (1869) and of such magazines as the *Ladies' Home Journal* and *Good Housekeeping*,

Middle-Class Domesticity

For middle-class Americans the home was a place of nurture, a refuge from the world of competitive commerce. Perhaps that explains why their residences were so heavily draped and cluttered with bric-a-brac. All of it emphasized privacy and pride of possession.

Culver Pictures.

which first appeared during the 1880s. This advice literature told wives that, in addition to their domestic duties, they were responsible for bringing sensibility, beauty, and love to the household. "We owe to women the charm and beauty of life," wrote one educator. "For the love that rests, strengthens and inspires, we look to women." In this idealized view the wife made the home a refuge for her husband and a place of nurture for their children.

Womanly virtue, even if much glorified, by no means put wives on equal terms with their husbands. Although the legal status of married women—their right to own property, control separate earnings, make contracts, and get a divorce—improved markedly during the nineteenth century, law and custom still dictated a wife's submission to her husband. She relied on his ability as the family breadwinner, and despite her superior virtues and graces she was thought below him in vigor and intellect. Her mind could be employed "but little and in trivial matters," wrote one prominent physician, and her proper place was as "the companion or ornamental appendage to man" (see American Voices, "M. Carey Thomas: 'We Did Not Know . . . Whether Women's Health Could Stand the Strain of College Education,'" p. 555).

Not surprisingly, many bright, independent-minded women rebelled against marriage. The marriage rate fell to its lowest point during the last forty years of the nineteenth century. More than 10 percent of women of marriageable age remained single, and the rate was much higher among college graduates and professionals. "I know that something perhaps, humanly speaking, supremely precious has passed me by," remarked the writer Vida Scudder. "But how much it would have excluded!" Married life "looks to me often as I watch it terribly impoverished, for women."

The Cult of Masculinity. If fewer women were marrying, of course, so were fewer men. We can, thanks to the census, trace the tardy progression into marriage of the male cohort born just after the Civil War: in 1890, when they were in their early thirties, two-fifths of this group remained unmarried; a decade later, in their early forties, a quarter still had not married; and ultimately, a hard-core, over 10 percent, never did. One historian has labeled the late nineteenth century the Age of the Bachelor, a time when being an unattached male lost its social stigma and, especially in large cities, became a happy alternative for many men of marriageable age.

A bachelor's counterpart to Vida Scudder's dim view of marriage was this ditty making the rounds in the early 1880s:

> *No wife to scold me*
> *No children to squall*
> *God bless the happy man*
> *Who keeps bachelor's hall.*

With its residential hotels, restaurants, and multifarious personal services, the urban scene afforded bachelors all the comforts of home and, doubtless more important, an ample array of men's clubs, saloons, and sporting events on which to erect a robust male subculture.

The appeal of the manly life was not, however, confined to confirmed bachelors. A larger crisis was overtaking American males, especially middle-class males. They inherited a pride in independence and autonomy, achieved above all by being one's own boss, but in the salaried jobs they increasingly held middle-class men were distinctly not their own bosses. Nor were they capable, once work and household had been severed, of exerting the patriarchal hold over family life that had empowered their fathers and grandfathers. A palpable anxiety arose that the American male was becoming, as one magazine editor warned, "weak, effeminate, decaying." There was a telling shift in language. While people had once spoken of *manhood*, which meant leaving *childhood* behind, they now spoke of *masculinity*, the opposite of *femininity*: being a man meant surmounting the feminizing influences of modern life.

And how was this to be accomplished? By engaging in competitive sports like football and boxing, which became hugely popular in this era. By working out and becoming fit because, as the psychologist G. Stanley Hall put it, "you can't have a firm will without firm muscles." By resorting to the great outdoors—preferably out West—and engaging in Theodore Roosevelt's "strenuous life." Or, vicariously, by reading Roosevelt's books or Owen Wister's best-selling cowboy novel, *The Virginian* (1902), or that paean to primitive man, Edgar Rice Burroughs's *Tarzan of the Apes* (1912). The surging popularity of westerns and adventure novels was surely a marker of the fears by urban dwellers that theirs was not a life for real men.

Changing Views of Sexuality. In earlier times sexuality and reproduction had been more or less in harmony. A large family was considered a good thing, and the heavy toll of repeated pregnancies on the wife was accepted as God's will. In middle-class families especially, this fatalism began to wane. Birth control, however, was not an easy matter. Beginning in the 1830s information about contraception became widely available, as did an array of commercial products. But the knowledge purveyed was imperfect or, like advice about the rhythm method, absolutely wrong (doctors thought women were fertile around the menstrual period). And contraceptive products were for the most part not very effective or, as in the case of the condom, stigmatized by association with the brothel.

Before these barriers could be surmounted, birth control was swept up by the social-purity campaign championed by Anthony Comstock. From the 1870s onward contraceptive devices and birth control information

M. Carey Thomas

"We Did Not Know . . . Whether Women's Health Could Stand the Strain of College Education"

President of Bryn Mawr College for many years, M. Carey Thomas (1857–1935) recalls in a retrospective essay her dreams of college as a girl growing up in Baltimore in the 1870s.

The passionate desire of women of my generation for higher education was accompanied thruout its course by the awful doubt, felt by women themselves as well as by men, as to whether women as a sex were physically and mentally fit for it. . . . I was always wondering whether it could be really true, as everyone always said, that boys were cleverer than girls. . . . I often remember praying about it, and begging God that if it were true that because I was a girl I could not successfully master Greek and go to college and understand things to kill me at once, as I could not bear to live in such an unjust world. When I was a little older I read the Bible entirely thru with passionate eagerness because I had heard it said that it proved that women were inferior to men. . . . To this day I can never read many parts of the Pauline epistles without feeling again the sinking of the heart with which I used to hurry over the verses referring to women's keeping silence in the churches and asking their husbands at home. . . .

It was not to be wondered at that we were uncertain in those old days as to the ultimate result of women's education. We did not know when we began whether women's health could stand the strain of college education. We were haunted in those early days by the clanging chains of that gloomy little specter, Dr. Edward H. Clarke's *Sex in Education*. With trepidation of spirit I made my mother read it, and was much cheered by her remark that, as neither she, nor any of the women she knew, had ever seen girls or women of the kind described in Dr. Clarke's book, we might as well act as if they did not exist. Still, we did not know whether college might not produce a crop of just such invalids. . . .

Before I myself went to college I had never seen but one college woman. I had heard that such a woman was staying at the house of an acquaintance. I went to see her with fear. Even if she had appeared in hoofs and horns I was determined to go to college all the same. But it was a relief to find this Vassar graduate tall and handsome and dressed like other women. When, five years later, I went to Leipzig to study after graduating from Cornell, my mother used to write me that my name was never mentioned to her by the women of her acquaintance. I was thought by them to be as much a disgrace to my family as if I had eloped with the coachman. . . .

We are now [1908] living in the midst of great and, I believe on the whole beneficent, social changes which are preparing the way for the coming economic independence of women. . . . The passionate desire of the women of my generation for a college education seems, as we study it now in the light of coming events, to have been part of this greater movement.

Source: Linda K. Kerber and Jane De Hart-Mathews, eds., *Women's America: Refocusing the Past*, 2nd ed. (New York: Oxford University Press, 1987), 263–65.

were legally classified as obscene, barred from the mails, and criminalized by many states. Abortion, long accepted by common law, became illegal except to save the mother's life. Although the practice of abortion remained widespread, it was expensive and dangerous—and considered shameful besides.

Around 1890 a change set in. Although the birthrate continued to decline, more young people married, and at an earlier age. These developments reflected the beginnings of a sexual revolution in the American middle-class family. Experts began to abandon the notion, put forth by one popular medical text, that "the majority of women (happily for society) are not very much troubled by sexual feeling of any kind." In succeeding editions of his book *Plain Home Talk on Love, Marriage, and Parentage*, physician Edward Bliss Foote began to favor a healthy sexuality that gave pleasure to women as well as men.

During the 1890s the artist Charles Dana Gibson created the image of the "new woman." In his drawings

The New Woman

John Singer Sargent's painting Mr. and Mrs. Isaac Newton Phelps Stokes *(1897) captures on canvas the essence of the "new woman" of the 1890s. Nothing about Mrs. Phelps Stokes, neither how she is dressed nor how she presents herself, suggests physical weakness or demure passivity. She confidently occupies center stage, a fit partner for her husband, who is relegated to the shadows of the picture.*

The Metropolitan Museum of Art. Bequest of Edith Minturn Phelps Stokes (Mrs. I. N.), 1938 (38.104). Photo © 1992 The Metropolitan Museum of Art.

the **Gibson girl** was tall, spirited, athletic, and chastely sexual. She rejected bustles, hoop skirts, and tightly laced corsets, preferring shirtwaists and other natural styles that did not disguise her female form. In the city women's sphere began to take on a more public character. Among the new urban institutions catering to women, the most important was the department store, which became a temple for their emerging role as consumers.

Attitudes toward Children. The offspring of the middle class experienced their own revolution. In the past children had been regarded as an economic asset—added hands for the family farm, shop, or countinghouse. Especially for the urban middle class, that no longer held true. Parents stopped expecting their children to be working members of the family. In the old days Ralph Waldo Emerson remarked in 1880, "children had been repressed and kept in the background; now they are considered, cosseted, and pampered." There was such a thing as "the juvenile mind," lectured Jacob Abbott in his book *Gentle Measures in the Management and Training of the Young* (1871). The family was responsible for providing a nurturing environment in which the young personality could grow and mature.

Preparation for adulthood became increasingly linked to formal education. School enrollment went up 150 percent between 1870 and 1900. High school attendance, while still encompassing only a small percentage of teenagers, increased at the fastest rate (Table 19.2). As the years between childhood and adulthood began to stretch out, a new stage of life—adolescence—emerged. While rooted in longer years of family dependency, adolescence shifted much of the socializing role from parents to peer group. A youth culture—one of the hallmarks of American life in the twentieth century—was starting to take shape.

City Life

With its soaring skyscrapers, jostling traffic, and hum of business, the city symbolized energy and enterprise. When the budding writer Hamlin Garland and his brother arrived in Chicago from Iowa in 1881, they knew immediately that they had entered a new world: "Everything interested us. . . . Nothing was commonplace, nothing was ugly to us." In one way or another every city-bound migrant, whether from the American countryside or from a foreign land, experienced something of this sense of wonder.

But with the boundless variety came disorder and uncertainty. The city was utterly unlike the rural world the newcomers had left. In the countryside every person had been known to his or her neighbors. Mark Twain found New York "a splendid desert, where a stranger is lonely in

TABLE 19.2 High School Graduates, 1870–1910

Year	Numbers	Percent 17-Year-Olds	Male	Female
1870	16,000	2.0	7,000	9,000
1890	44,000	3.0	19,000	25,000
1910	156,000	8.6	64,000	93,000

Source: Historical Statistics of the United States (1975), 1: 386.

the midst of a million of his race. . . . Every man rushes, rushes, rushes, and never has time to be companionable [or] to fool away on matters which do not involve dollars and duty and business." If rural roles and obligations had been well understood, in the city the only predictable relationships were those dictated by the marketplace.

Rural people could never re-create in the city the communities they had left behind. But they found ways to gain a sense of belonging, they built a multitude of new institutions, and they learned how to function in an impersonal, heterogeneous environment. An urban culture emerged, and through it there developed a new breed of American who was entirely at home in the modern city.

Newcomers

At the turn of the century, upwards of 30 percent of the residents of New York, Chicago, Boston, Cleveland, Minneapolis, and San Francisco were foreign-born. The biggest ethnic group in Boston was Irish; in Minneapolis, Swedish; in most other northern cities, German. But by 1910 the influx from southern and eastern Europe had changed the ethnic complexion of many of these cities (Map 19.3). In Chicago, Poles took the lead; in New York, eastern European Jews; in San Francisco, Italians.

For these later arrivals there was less intermingling with the resident populations than in the earlier "walking cities." By the 1880s observers were noticing that only immigrants lived in the dingier downtown areas. "One may find for the asking" ghettos of every kind, remarked Jacob Riis in his book about New York's poor, *How the Other Half Lives* (1890). "The one thing you shall vainly ask for in the chief city of America is a distinctly American community."

The arrivals from southern and eastern Europe had little choice about where they lived; they needed to find cheap housing near their jobs. Some gravitated to the outlying factory districts; others settled in the congested downtown **ghettos**. The immigrants tended to settle by ethnic group. In New York Italians crowded into the Irish neighborhoods west of Broadway, and Russian and Polish Jews pushed the Germans out of the Lower East Side (Map 19.4). A colony of Hungarians lived around Houston Street, and Bohemians occupied the poorer stretches of the Upper East Side between Fiftieth and Seventy-sixth Streets.

Within ethnic groups one could spot clusters from the same province or town. Among New York Italians, for example, Neapolitans and Calabrians populated the Mulberry Bend district, while Genoese lived on Baxter

Italian Bread Peddlers, New York City

Because of crowded conditions in East Side tenements, immigrant life spilled out onto the streets, which offered a bit of fresh air, a chance to socialize with neighbors, and a place to shop for food, including bread.
KEA Publishing Services Ltd.

Big Tim Sullivan: Tammany Politician

Big Tim Sullivan Culver Pictures.

Timothy D. Sullivan was born on July 23, 1863, near the Hudson River docks in lower Manhattan. His parents were Irish immigrants, part of the mass migration of potato famine victims who flooded into New York in the 1840s. Four years later Tim's father died, leaving his young widow, Catherine Connelly Sullivan, with four small children. Soon after, Catherine married Lawrence Mulligan, an Irish laborer, and the family moved to the notorious Five Points district on the Lower East Side. There the 1870 census found them, a household of ten (including three boarders) living in an overcrowded tenement at 25 Baxter Street.

Tim had a harsh childhood. His stepfather drank heavily and beat his wife and children regularly. To make ends meet Catherine took in washing, and Tim went to work at age seven bundling papers for $1.50 a week on Newspaper Row across from City Hall. Tim got through grammar school, but his family needed his earnings too much for him to go on to high school. "Free as it was, he later remarked, "it was not free enough for me to go there." Instead—Horatio Alger style—he made his way up in the newspaper business and by age eighteen was well established as a wholesale newspaper dealer. He soon became the proprietor of two saloons and in his early twenties was ready for politics. A handsome fellow, over six feet tall, Sullivan was quick with his fists. He gained a local reputation by thrashing a tough he had encountered on the street beating up a woman. True or not, the story helped him win the Democratic nomination at age twenty-three for the New York State assembly from the Second District.

In 1889 Sullivan opposed a bill granting Manhattan's police virtually unlimited powers to detain people with jail records. The champion of the bill was Thomas F. Byrnes, chief inspector of the New York Police Department and the most celebrated detective in the country. Byrnes did not take kindly to opposition from small-time politicians. He raided Sullivan's saloons, arrested two barkeepers for excise tax violations, and denounced Sullivan as someone who consorted with criminals. Against the advice of friends, Sullivan took the assembly floor to answer the charge.

In tearful tones Sullivan cast himself as an "honest Bowery boy," describing his impoverished childhood, his saintly mother, and his struggle to rise in the world. "When, at the conclusion [so a reporter recorded], he asked if he had any time or money to spend with thieves, there was a 'No' on nearly every member's lips." The performance was the making of the obscure assemblyman. Although he gained notoriety with uptown New Yorkers that would dog him throughout his career, he won the hearts of his own constituents, who reveled in the success story of one of their own. They thought "Big Tim" a fine fellow, and so did the Tammany leaders.

When the Tammany machine swept into power in the 1892 elections, Boss Richard Croker tapped Sullivan to run the new Third Assembly District centering on the Bowery. Sullivan swiftly consolidated his power. His inner circle was all Irish, but for election district captains he appointed Jews, Italians, and Germans who were well connected in the immigrant communities that populated his fiefdom. Sullivan became famous for his summer "chowders," when he transported his constituents by riverboat to the country for a rowdy day of picnicking. At Christmas there was a fine dinner for all who were in

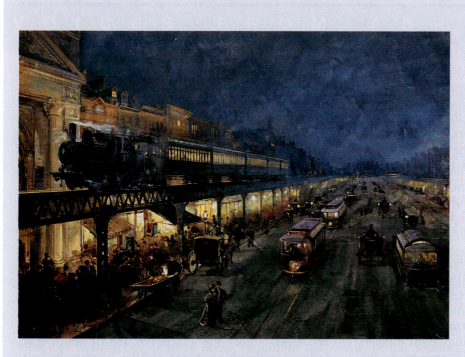

The Bowery at Night, 1895

This painting by W. Louis Sonntag Jr. shows Big Tim's stomping ground—the Bowery—crowded with shoppers and pleasure seekers. It was during this time that the Bowery gained its raffish reputation. Museum of the City of New York.

need. And in February Sullivan handed out wool socks and shoes—always with the sentimental tale of how a teacher had given him free shoes one cold winter.

Big Tim also attended assiduously to the nitty-gritty business of running a political machine. He got jobs for his supporters, visited the jails regularly to offer bail and other aid to the inmates, and on election day made sure his strong-arm crews patrolled the polling places. Sullivan's district became the best organized in the city, and Tammany hailed him as "the most popular man on the East Side."

In the meantime Sullivan was making his fortune. His particular form of "honest graft" was commercial entertainment. Big Tim knew instinctively how important a good time was to city people. Besides, the main street of his district, the Bowery, was the gaudy center of low-life entertainment for the entire city, lined with burlesque houses, concert saloons, restaurants, and cheap hotels. In the mid-1890s Sullivan formed a partnership with two theatrical producers and began to invest in vaudeville houses. He contributed not only money and a shrewd head but the political contacts that ensured lax enforcement of building codes and easy access to liquor licenses. Sullivan also became involved in professional boxing, horse racing, and, more illicitly, the gambling dens that dotted his district.

Sullivan was accused of trafficking in East Side prostitution, but this he indignantly denied: "Nobody who knows me well will believe I would take a penny from any woman, much less from the poor creatures who are more to be pitied than any other human beings

on earth. I'd be afraid to take a cent from a poor woman of the streets for fear my old mother would see me. I'd a good deal rather break into a bank and rob the safe. That would be a more manly and decent way of getting money."

When Boss Croker resigned in 1902, Sullivan might have succeeded him, but Big Tim preferred his own district and threw his support to Charles F. Murphy, who ruled Tammany for the next twenty-two years. Sullivan served briefly in Congress, made a lot more money investing in the early movie industry and in vaudeville syndicates across the country, and in the final phase of his career became a champion of progressive social legislation in the New York Senate. In 1912 Sullivan suffered a severe mental breakdown, possibly caused by tertiary syphilis. A year later he died under the wheels of a freight train after running off from his brother's house outside New York. His funeral procession down the Bowery was one of the largest in memory and brought out an immense crowd from every stratum of New York society, from statesmen to prizefighters to scrubwomen.

The National Pastime

In 1897, as today, the end-of-season games filled the bleachers. Here the Boston Beaneaters are playing the Baltimore Orioles. Boston won. The Baltimore stadium would soon be replaced by a bigger concrete and steel structure, but what is happening on the field needs no updating. The scene is virtually identical to today's game. Library of Congress.

over courtship broke down, and amid the bright lights and lively music of the dance hall and amusement park working-class youth forged a more easygoing culture of sexual interaction and pleasure seeking.

The geography of the big city carved out ample space for commercialized sex. Prostitution was not new to urban life, but in the late nineteenth century it became more open and more intermingled with other forms of public entertainment. In New York the red-light district was the Tenderloin, running northward from Twenty-third Street between Fifth and Eighth Avenues.

The Tenderloin and the Bowery farther downtown were also the sites of a robust gay subculture. The long-held notion that homosexual life was covert, in the closet, in Victorian America appears not to be true, at least not in the country's premier city. In certain corners of the city, a gay world flourished, with a full array of saloons, meeting places, and drag balls, which were widely known and patronized by uptown "slummers."

Baseball. Of all forms of (mostly) male diversion, none was more specific to the city, or so spectacularly successful, as professional baseball. The game's promoters decreed that baseball had been created in 1839 by Abner Doubleday in the village of Cooperstown, New York. Actually, baseball was neither of American origin—it developed from the British game of rounders—nor a product of rural life. The game apparently first appeared in the early 1840s in New York City, where a group of

gentlemen enthusiasts competed on an empty lot. Over the next twenty years, the aristocratic tone of baseball disappeared. Clubs sprang up across the country and intercity competition developed on a scheduled basis. In 1868 baseball became openly professional, following the lead of the Cincinnati Red Stockings in signing players to contracts for the season.

Big-time commercial baseball came into its own with the launching of the National League in 1876. The team owners were profit-minded businessmen who shaped the sport to please the fans. Wooden grandstands gave way to the concrete and steel stadiums of the early twentieth century, such as Fenway Park in Boston, Forbes Field in Pittsburgh, and Shibe Park in Philadelphia.

For the urban multitudes baseball grew into something more than an afternoon at the ballpark. By rooting for the home team, fans found a way of identifying with the city in which they lived. Amid the diversity and anonymity of urban life, the common experience and language of baseball acted as a bridge among strangers.

Newspapers. Most efficient at this task, however, was the newspaper. James Gordon Bennett, founder of the *New York Herald* in 1835, wanted "to record the facts . . . for the great masses of the community." The news was whatever interested city readers, starting with crime, scandal, and sensational events. After the Civil War the *New York Sun* added the human-interest story, which made news of ordinary happenings. Newspapers also

TABLE 19.3 Newspaper Circulation	
Year	Total Circulation
1870	2,602,000
1880	3,566,000
1890	8,387,000
1900	15,102,000
1909	24,212,000

Source: Historical Statistics of the United States (1975), 2: 810.

targeted specific audiences. A women's page offered recipes and fashion news, separate sections covered sports and high society, and the Sunday supplement helped fill the weekend hours.

The competition for readers became fierce when Joseph Pulitzer, the owner of the *St. Louis Post-Dispatch*, invaded New York in 1883 by buying the *New York World*. Pulitzer was in turn challenged by William Randolph Hearst, who arrived from San Francisco in 1895 prepared to beat the *New York World* at its own game (see Chapter 21, American Lives, "William Randolph Hearst: Jingo," p. 614). Hearst's sensationalist style of newspaper reporting became known as **yellow journalism**. The term, linked to the first comic strip to appear in color, *The Yellow Kid* (1895), meant a type of reporting in which accuracy came second to eliciting a "Gee Whiz!" feeling in the reader.

"He who is without a newspaper," said the great showman P. T. Barnum, "is cut off from his species." Barnum was speaking of city people and their hunger for information. By meeting this need, newspapers revealed their sensitivity to the public they served (Table 19.3).

The Higher Culture

In the midst of this popular ferment, new institutions of higher culture were taking shape in America's cities. A desire for the cultivated life was not, of course, specifically urban. Before the Civil War the lyceum movement had sent lecturers to the remotest towns, bearing messages of culture and learning. Chautauqua, founded in upstate New York in 1874, carried on this work of cultural dissemination. However, great institutions such as museums, public libraries, opera companies, and symphonic orchestras could flourish only in metropolitan centers.

Cultural Institutions. The nation's first major art museum, the Corcoran Gallery of Art, opened in Washington, D.C., in 1869. New York's Metropolitan Museum of Art started in rented quarters two years later, then moved in 1880 to its permanent site in Central Park and launched an ambitious program of art acquisition. When J. P. Morgan became chairman of the board in 1905, the Metropolitan's preeminence was assured. The Boston Museum of Fine Arts was founded in 1876 and Chicago's Art Institute in 1879.

Symphony orchestras also appeared, first in New York under the conductors Theodore Thomas and Leopold Damrosch in the 1870s and then in Boston and Chicago during the next decade. National tours by these leading orchestras planted the seeds for orchestral societies in many other cities. Public libraries grew from modest collections (in 1870 only seven had as many as fifty thousand books) into major urban institutions. The greatest library benefactor was Andrew Carnegie, who announced in 1881 that he would build a library in any town or city that was prepared to maintain it. By 1907 Carnegie had spent more than $32.7 million to establish about a thousand libraries throughout the country.

The late nineteenth century was the great age not only of moneymaking but of money *giving*. Generous with their surplus wealth, new millionaires patronized the arts partly as a civic duty and partly, as in the founding of the Metropolitan Opera, as a vehicle for establishing themselves in society. But museums and symphony orchestras also received support as an expression of national aspirations.

"In America there is no culture," pronounced the English critic G. Lowes Dickinson in 1909. Science and the practical arts, yes, "every possible application of life to purposes and ends," but "no life for life's sake." Such condescending remarks received a respectful American hearing out of a sense of cultural inferiority to the Old World. In 1873 Mark Twain and Charles Dudley Warner published a novel, *The Gilded Age*, satirizing America as a land of money grubbers and speculators. This enormously popular book touched a nerve in the American psyche. Its title has in fact been appropriated by historians to characterize the late nineteenth century—America's "Gilded Age"—as an era of materialism and cultural shallowness.

Some members of the upper class, like the novelist Henry James, despaired of the country and moved to Europe. But the more common response was to try to raise the nation's cultural level. The newly rich had a hard time of it. They did not have much opportunity to cultivate a taste for art, and a great deal of what they collected was mediocre and garish. On the other hand George W. Vanderbilt, grandson of the rough-hewn Cornelius Vanderbilt, was an early champion of French Impressionism, and the coal and steel baron Henry Clay Frick built a brilliant art collection that is still housed, as a public museum, in his mansion in New York City. The enthusiasm of moneyed Americans largely fueled the great cultural institutions that sprang up during the Gilded Age.

CHAPTER 20

The Progressive Era

The Course of Reform
The Progressive Mind
Women Progressives
Reforming Politics
Racism and Reform

Progressivism and National Politics
The Making of a Progressive President
Regulating the Marketplace
The Fracturing of Republican Progressivism
Woodrow Wilson and the New Freedom

◀ **Reba Owen, Settlement-House Worker**

The settlement house was a hallmark of progressive America. Columbus, Ohio, had five, including Godman Guild House, where Reba Owen served as a visiting nurse, tending the pregnant mothers and children of the neighborhood.

LifeCare Alliance / Courtesy, Ohio Historical Society.

O N THE FACE OF IT, the political ferment of the 1890s ended with the election of 1896. After the bitter struggle over free silver, the victorious Republicans had no stomach for political crusades. The McKinley administration devoted itself to maintaining business confidence: sound money and high tariffs were the order of the day. The main thing, as party chief Mark Hanna said, was to "stand pat and continue Republican prosperity."

Yet beneath the surface a deep unease had set in. The depression of the 1890s had unveiled truths not acknowledged in better days. The fury of the decade's industrial disputes, for example, revealed a frightening chasm between America's social classes. In Richard Olney's view, the great Pullman strike of 1894 had brought the country "to the ragged edge of anarchy." As Cleveland's attorney general, it had been Olney's job to crush the strike, which he had done with ruthless efficiency (see Chapter 17). But Olney took little joy in his success. He asked himself what might be done to avoid such repressive government actions in the future. His answer: by federal regulation of labor relations on the railroads so that crippling rail strikes would not happen. As a first step toward Olney's goal, Congress adopted the Erdman Mediation Act in 1898. In such ways did the crisis of the 1890s turn the nation's thinking to reform.

573

Frances Kellor: Woman Progressive

From the day its doors opened in 1892, the University of Chicago was a major center of American learning. Financed by John D. Rockefeller, the university modeled itself on the great German research universities and, unlike Yale and Harvard, concentrated on graduate education. At Chicago and other American universities, modern social science was taking shape, breaking from its nineteenth-century moral foundations and seeking a scientific basis for the study of society. Economics, political science, and sociology demanded a rigorous course of study certified by the granting of the Ph.D. But if the social sciences were becoming professional, their guiding purpose was not yet disinterested research but the improvement of society. The University of Chicago saw the city surrounding it as a great laboratory for social betterment. Its students were being prepared, whether they knew it or not, to be in service to the American progressivism of the next decade. The University of Chicago, moreover, was receptive to the admission of women, and for them in particular, graduate education was a breeding ground for careers as social reformers.

Among the women entering in 1898 was Frances Alice Kellor, a recent graduate of Cornell University. Kellor was born in Columbus, Ohio, in 1873. Her father abandoned the family before she was two, and her mother made a hard living as a domestic and laundress. In 1875 her family moved to Coldwater, Michigan, a former abolitionist center (and station on the underground railroad) and a stronghold of Yankee culture. From the Coldwater community, with its high moral standards and strong educational institutions, Kellor received the reformist values that other budding progressives learned from their families. Her first patrons were the well-to-do librarians of Coldwater, Mary and Frances Eddy, who befriended her and took her into their home. Born Alice, Kellor began to call herself "Frances" as a sign that she considered herself adopted by the Eddy sisters. She graduated from high school, became a reporter for the *Coldwater Republican*, and then, with the backing of the Eddys, enrolled at Cornell in 1895. A natural athlete, Kellor made her first mark as a fighter for equal rights on a sports issue: she led the campaign for a women's crew. She got a

solid education in the social sciences at Cornell and decided to become a criminologist.

When Frances Kellor arrived in Chicago in 1898, sociology was an infant discipline, with an emphasis on high-minded investigations of social problems. Kellor's interest in crime was encouraged by the Chicago faculty. The prevailing theory of the time, advanced by the Italian Cesare Lombroso, was that criminality was an inherited trait—that criminals were born criminal and that this tendency was manifest in their physical features. Skeptical, Kellor conducted a study of the female inmates of five midwestern prisons. Comparing them with a control group of college women, she could find no physical differences. Kellor concluded that not heredity but social environment, economic disadvantage, and poverty produced criminality. Kellor also rejected "the prevailing opinion that when women are criminal they are more degraded and more abandoned than men." People thought so, she asserted, only because of "the difference in the standards which we set for the two sexes."

A project on criminality among southern blacks likewise rejected heredity and stressed environmental factors, but Kellor's conclusions were pessimistic and racially conservative: centuries of slavery and indolent southern life had left blacks so morally weakened that "the Negro at present has neither the perceptions nor the solidity of character that would enable him to lead his race." She considered the southern restrictions on blacks' legal and political rights unfortunate but necessary, and she believed that "the free intermingling of the two races is impossible, at least for many generations." In drawing these illiberal conclusions, Kellor was echoing the views of her teachers and indeed of most white progressives of her generation.

Despite her precocious record, Kellor left the university in 1902 without a degree. The reasons are not altogether clear but doubtless had something to do with the fact that the University of Chicago almost never placed its female graduate students in university teaching jobs. To be a professor, it seemed, was still a male prerogative. There was, however, a positive side to Kellor's decision. Like many of her fellow students, she had fallen under the spell of Jane Addams. Kellor lived periodically at Hull House and joined the circle of social reformers that congregated there. When she left Chicago, it was to do social research for New York's College Settlement Association.

Her first project was a study of unemployment. Kellor was among the first investigators to see that unemployment was an economic problem, not, as was generally believed, the result of individual shiftlessness or

Frances Kellor

This photograph of Kellor was taken in her early twenties when she was a student at Cornell University.

incompetence, but of the impersonal operations of the labor market. Her book *Out of Work* (1904) was a pioneering investigation, paving the way for the modern study of unemployment. Kellor was especially concerned with the plight of jobless women and their exploitation by commercial employment agencies. Representing the Women's Municipal League of New York, Kellor lobbied successfully for state regulation of these agencies. Kellor thus employed her research to bring about social change. The combination of professional investigation and robust political advocacy became the hallmark of Kellor's progressivism. Her next study, on the problems of immigrants in New York, led to the establishment of the New York State Bureau of Industries and Immigration in 1910. Kellor was chosen to be its head, the first woman to hold so high a post in New York State government.

The high point of Kellor's career came two years later, when Theodore Roosevelt launched the Progressive Party. Convinced that social reform required strong government, Kellor was drawn to the New Nationalism. She linked it with her own fervent advocacy of women's political rights. Always a fighter, she was entirely at ease in the rough-and-tumble of partisan politics. After Roosevelt's defeat in 1912, the Progressive Party set up the National Progressive Service, a kind of think tank for studying social problems and formulating legislative proposals. The idea was mainly Kellor's, and she was tapped to chair the service. This was truly a pinnacle for a woman in American politics at a time when women in most states could not vote in national elections. Unfortunately, Kellor's emphasis on scientific investigation put her at odds with the practical politicians, and she was forced out in early 1914. Hers was a brief run in national politics, exhilarating while it lasted and unique for a woman of her generation.

Kellor never married. Like many other woman progressives, she found personal fulfillment in an enduring relationship with another woman. This was Mary Dreier, one of two wealthy sisters who played leading roles in New York progressivism. From the time Kellor moved into the Dreier home in Brooklyn Heights in 1904 until her death almost fifty years later, she and Mary were constant companions. Kellor's later professional life was devoted to a distinguished career with the American Arbitration Association.

in honorable company until, by his own account, a Republican boss offered him a bribe to fix a judge in a railroad case. Awakened by this "awful ordeal," La Follette broke with the Wisconsin machine in 1891 and became a tireless advocate of political reform, which for him meant restoring America's democratic ideals. "Go back to the first principles of democracy; go back to the people," he told his audience when he launched his campaign against the state Republican machine. In 1900, after battling for a decade, La Follette won the Wisconsin governorship on a platform of higher taxes for corporations, stricter utility and railroad regulation, and political reform.

The key to party reform, La Follette felt, was to deny bosses the power to choose the party's candidates. This could be achieved by requiring that nominations be decided not in party conventions but by popular vote. Enacted in 1903, the direct primary expressed La Follette's democratic idealism, but it also suited his particular political talents. The party regulars opposing him were insiders, more comfortable in the caucus room than out on the stump. But that was where La Follette, a superb campaigner, excelled. The direct primary gave La Follette an iron grip on Republican politics in Wisconsin that lasted until his death twenty-five years later.

What was true of La Follette was more or less true of all successful progressive politicians. They typically described their work as political restoration, frequently confessing that they had converted to reform after discovering how far party politics had drifted from the ideals of representative government. Like La Follette, Albert B. Cummins of Iowa, Harold U'Ren of Oregon, and Hiram Johnson of California all espoused democratic ideals, and all skillfully used the direct primary as the stepping stone to political power. They practiced a new kind of popular politics, which in a reform age could be a more effective way to power than the backroom techniques of the old-fashioned machine politicians.

Even the most democratizing of reforms espoused by the progressives—the initiative and recall—were really exercises in power politics. The initiative enabled citizens to have issues placed on the ballot; recall empowered them to remove officeholders who had lost the public's confidence. It soon became clear, however, that direct democracy did not supplant organized politics. Initiative and recall campaigns required organization, money, and expertise, and these were attributes not of the people at large but of well-financed interests. Like the direct primary, the initiative and recall had as much to do with power relations as with political reform.

Municipal Reform. And so, in many cities, did the demand for more efficient government. Taxes went up, local businessmen complained, but services always lagged. There had to be an end, as one manufacturer said, to "the inefficiency, the sloth, the carelessness, the

injustice and the graft of city administrations." By making aldermanic elections citywide, municipal reformers attacked the ward politics that underlay the corrupting patronage system. A more radical strategy focused on the very structure of city governance that gave the masses a voice.

After a hurricane devastated Galveston, Texas, in 1901, business leaders impatient to rebuild the city persuaded voters to replace the mayor and board of aldermen with a nonpartisan five-member commission. This was the opening wedge in a nationwide drive to put municipal affairs, as John Patterson of the National Cash Register Company said, "on a strict business basis." In Dayton, Ohio, where Patterson was a leading citizen, the elected commission was combined with an appointed city manager, and this became the model for municipal reformers in medium-sized cities across the country. The commission-manager system aimed at running the city "in exactly the same way as a private business corporation." But of course there was nothing democratic about how private corporations operated. Some municipal reformers thought that was just as well. "Ignorance should be excluded from control," said former mayor Abram Hewitt of New York in 1901. "City business should be carried on by trained experts selected on some other principle than popular suffrage."

Urban Liberalism. The antidemocratic strain in municipal reform was powerfully counterbalanced by the activation of the urban masses in progressive politics. When the Republican Hiram Johnson ran for California governor in 1910, he was the reform candidate of the state's middle class. Famous as prosecutor of the corrupt San Francisco boss Abe Ruef, Johnson pledged to purify California politics and curb the Southern Pacific Railroad—the dominating economic power in the state. By his second term, Johnson was championing social and labor legislation. His original base in the middle class had eroded, and he had become the champion of California's working class.

Johnson's career reflected a shift in the center of gravity of progressivism, which had begun as a movement of the middle class but then took on board America's working people. A new strain of progressive reform emerged that historians have labeled **urban liberalism**. To understand this phenomenon, we have to begin with city machine politics.

Thirty minutes before quitting time on Saturday afternoon, March 25, 1911, fire broke out at the Triangle Shirtwaist Company in downtown New York. The flames trapped the workers, who were mostly young immigrant women. Forty-seven leapt to their deaths; another ninety-nine never reached the windows.

In the wake of the tragedy, the New York State Factory Commission developed a remarkable program of labor reform over a four-year period: fifty-six laws dealing with

Triangle Shirtwaist Factory Fire

The doors were the problem. Most were locked (to keep the working girls from leaving early); the few that were open became jammed by bodies as the flames spread. When the fire trucks finally came, the ladders were too short. Compared with those caught inside, the girls who leapt to their deaths were the lucky ones. "As I looked up I saw a love affair in the midst of all the horror," a reporter wrote. A young man was helping girls leap from a window. The fourth "put her arms about him and kiss[ed] him. Then he held her out into space and dropped her." He immediately followed. "Thud—dead, Thud—dead . . . I saw his face before they covered it. . . . He was a real man. He had done his best."

New York Tribune, March 26, 1911.

fire hazards, unsafe machines, industrial homework, and wages and hours for women and children. The chairman of the commission was Robert F. Wagner; the vice chairman, Alfred E. Smith. Both were Tammany Hall politicians, serving at the time as leaders in the state legislature. They established the commission, participated fully in its work, and marshaled the party regulars to pass the proposals into law—all with the approval of the Tammany machine.

In thus responding to the Triangle fire, Tammany was conceding that social problems had grown too big to be handled informally by party machines. Only the

Dr. Alice Hamilton

Tracking Down Lead Poisoning

Alice Hamilton (1869–1970) studied medicine over the objections of her socially prominent family in Fort Wayne, Indiana. When she finally landed a job teaching pathology in Chicago in 1897, Dr. Hamilton at last had her chance to fulfill a girlhood dream of living at Jane Addams's Hull House. That experience launched her on an illustrious career as a pioneer in industrial medicine—one of the many paths to social reform opened up by settlement-house work.

When I look back on the Chicago of 1897 I can see why life in a settlement seemed so great an adventure. It was all so new, this exploring of the poor quarters of a big city. The thirst to know how the other half lives had just begun to send people pioneering in the unknown parts of American life. . . . To settle down to live in the slums of a great city was a piece of daring as great as trekking across the prairie in a covered wagon. . . .

It was also my experience at Hull House that aroused my interest in industrial diseases. Living in a working-class quarter, coming in contact with laborers and their wives, I could not fail to hear tales of the dangers that working men faced, of cases of carbon-monoxide poisoning in the great steel mills, of painters disabled by lead palsy, of pneumonia and rheumatism among the men in the stockyards. Illinois then had no legislation providing compensation for accident or disease caused by occupation. (There is something strange in speaking of "accident and sickness compensation." What could "compensate" anyone for an amputated leg or paralyzed arm, or even an attack of lead colic, to say nothing of the loss of a husband or son?)

At the time I am speaking of [1910] Professor Charles Henderson . . . persuaded [the governor] to appoint an Occupational Disease Commission, the first time a state had ever undertaken such a survey. . . . We were staggered by the complexity of the problem we faced and we soon decided to limit our field almost entirely to the occupational poisons, for at least we knew what their action was, while the action of various kinds of dust, and of temperature extremes and heavy exertion, was only vaguely understood at the time. The only poisons we had to cover were lead, arsenic, brass, carbon monoxide, the cyanides, and turpentine. Nowadays [1943], the list involved in a survey of the painters' trade alone is many times as long as that.

But to us it seemed far from a simple task. We could not even discover what were the poisonous occupations in Illinois. The Factory Inspector's Office was blissfully ignorant, yet that was the only governmental body concerned with working conditions. There was nothing to do but begin with trades we knew were dangerous and hoped that as we studied them, we would discover others less well known. My field was to be lead. . . .

One case, of colic and double wristdrop,* which was discovered in the Alexian Brothers' Hospital, took me on a pretty chase. The man, a Pole, said he had worked in a sanitary-ware factory, putting enamel on bathtubs. I had not come across this work in the English or German authorities on lead poisoning, and had no idea it was a lead trade. . . . The management assured me that no lead was used in the coatings and invited me to inspect the workrooms. . . . Completely puzzled, I made a journey to the Polish quarter to see the palsied man and heard from him I had not even been in the enameling works, only the one for final touching up. The real one was far out on the Northwest Side. I found it and discovered that enameling means sprinkling a finely ground enamel over a red hot tub where it melts and flows over the surface. I learned that the air is thick with enamel dust . . . rich in red oxide of lead. A specimen . . . proved to contain as much as 20 per cent soluble lead—that is, lead that dissolves into solution in the stomach. Thus I nailed down the fact that sanitary-ware enameling is a dangerous lead trade in the United States, whatever was true of England or Germany.

---

*Paralysis of the wrist muscles, causing the hand to droop.

Source: Exploring the Dangerous Trades: The Autobiography of Alice Hamilton (Boston: Little, Brown and Co., 1943).

as an attack on back-room party rule, but it also served to deprive blacks of their political rights.

White Supremacy in the Progressive Vein.

How could democratic reform and white supremacy be thus wedded together? By the racism of the age. In a 1902 book on Reconstruction, Professor John W. Burgess of Columbia University denounced the Fifteenth Amendment: granting blacks the vote after the Civil War had been a "monstrous thing." Burgess was southern born, but he was confident that his northern audience saw the "vast differences in political capacity" between blacks and whites and approved of black disfranchisement. Even the Republican Party offered no rebuttal. Indeed, as president-elect in 1908, William Howard Taft applauded the southern laws as necessary to "prevent entirely the possibility of domination by . . . an ignorant electorate." Taft assured southerners that "the federal government has nothing to do with social equality."

Racial tensions were on the rise in the North. Over 200,000 blacks migrated from the South between 1900 and 1910. Their arrival in northern cities invariably sparked white resentment. Attacks on blacks became widespread, capped by a bloody race riot in Springfield, Illinois, in 1908. Equally reflective of racist sentiment was the huge success of D. W. Griffith's epic film *Birth of a Nation* (1915), which depicted Reconstruction as a moral struggle between rampaging blacks and a chivalrous Ku Klux Klan. Woodrow Wilson found the film's history "all so terribly true." His Democratic administration marked a low point for the federal government as the ultimate guarantor of equal rights: during Wilson's tenure, segregation of the U.S. civil service would have gone into effect but for an outcry among black leaders and influential white allies.

The Civil Rights Struggle Revived.

In these bleak years a core of young black professionals, mostly northern born, began to fight back. The key figure was William Monroe Trotter, the pugnacious editor of the *Boston Guardian* and an outspoken critic of Booker T. Washington. "The policy of compromise has failed," Trotter argued. "The policy of resistance and aggression deserves a trial." In this endeavor Trotter was joined by W. E. B. Du Bois, a Harvard-trained sociologist and author of *The Souls of Black Folk*. In 1906, after breaking with Washington, they called a meeting of twenty-nine supporters at Niagara Falls—but on the Canadian side because no hotel on the U.S. side would admit blacks.

The **Niagara Movement** resulting from that meeting had an impact far beyond the scattering of members and local bodies it organized. The principles it affirmed would define the struggle for the rights of African Americans: first, encouragement of black pride by all possible means; second, an uncompromising demand for full political and civil equality; and above all, the resolute denial "that the Negro-American assents to inferiority, is submissive under oppression and apologetic before insults."

W. E. B. Du Bois

No activity undertaken by the NAACP in the early years was more important than the publication of its journal, The Crisis, *which under the brilliant editorship of W. E. B. Du Bois became the strongest voice for equal rights and black pride in the country. In this photograph Du Bois is pictured at his desk at the magazine's editorial office.*

Schomburg Center for Research in Black Culture, New York Public Library.

MAP 20.2 National Parks and Forests, 1872–1980

Close inspection of the above map illustrates that the national park system did not begin with the Progressive Era. Indeed, Yellowstone, the first park, dates from 1872. In 1893, the federal government began the protection of national forests. Without Roosevelt, however, the national forest program might have languished, and during his presidency he added 125 million acres to the forest system plus six national parks. More importantly, Roosevelt endowed these systems with a progressive, public-spirited stamp that has remained a principle resource of environmentalists striving to preserve the nation's natural heritage from over-development and destructive exploitation. In the list of progressive triumphs, a robust national park and forest system is one of the most enduring.

considerable influence. At that point the coal operators caved in. The strike ended with the appointment by Roosevelt of an arbitration commission—another unprecedented step. While not especially sympathetic to organized labor, Roosevelt blamed the crisis on the "arrogant stupidity" of the mine owners.

"Of all the forms of tyranny the least attractive and the most vulgar is the tyranny of mere wealth," Roosevelt wrote in his autobiography. He was prepared to deploy all his presidential authority against the "tyranny" of irresponsible business.

Regulating the Marketplace

The economic issue that most troubled Roosevelt was the threat posed by big business to competitive markets. The drift toward large-scale enterprise was itself not new; for many years efficiency-minded entrepreneurs had been building vertically integrated national firms (see Chapter 17). But bigger business, they knew, also meant power to control markets. And when, in the aftermath of the depression of the 1890s, promoters scrambled to merge

rival firms, the primary motive was not efficiency but the elimination of competition. These mergers—**trusts**, as they were called—greatly increased business concentration in the economy. By 1910, 1 percent of the nation's manufacturers accounted for 44 percent of the nation's industrial output (see Voices from Abroad, "James Bryce: America in 1905: 'Business Is King,'" p. 594).

As early as his first annual message, Roosevelt acknowledged the nation's uneasiness with the "real and grave evils" of economic concentration. But what weapons could the president use in response?

The legal principles upholding free competition were already firmly established under common law: anyone injured by monopoly or illegal restraint of trade could sue for damages. With the passage of the Sherman Antitrust Act of 1890, these common-law rights entered the U.S. statute books and could be enforced by the federal government where offenses involved interstate commerce. Neither Cleveland nor McKinley showed much interest, but the Sherman Act was there waiting to be used. Its potential consisted above all in the fact that it incorporated common-law principles of unimpeachable validity. In the

J. Pierpont Morgan

J. P. Morgan was a giant among American financiers. He had served an apprenticeship in investment banking under his father, a leading Anglo-American banker in London. A gruff man of few words, Morgan had a genius for instilling trust and the strength of will to persuade others to follow his lead and do his bidding—qualities the great photographer Edward Steichen captured in this portrait. Courtesy, George Eastman House, reprinted with permission of Joanna T. Steichen.

Jack and the Wall Street Giants

In this vivid cartoon from the humor magazine Puck, *Jack (Theodore Roosevelt) has come to slay the giants of Wall Street. To the country, trust-busting took on the mythic qualities of the fairy tale—with about the same amount of awe for the fearsome Wall Street giants and hope in the prowess of the intrepid Roosevelt. J. P. Morgan is the giant leering at front right.* Library of Congress.

For more help analyzing this image, see the ONLINE STUDY GUIDE at bedfordstmartins.com/henretta.

right hands the Sherman Act could be a mighty weapon against the abuse of economic power.

Trust-Busting. Roosevelt made his opening move in 1903 by establishing a Bureau of Corporations empowered to investigate business practices and bolster the Justice Department's capacity to mount antitrust suits. The department had already filed such a suit in 1902 against the Northern Securities Company, a combination of the railroad systems of the Northwest. In a landmark decision the Supreme Court ordered Northern Securities dissolved in 1904.

In the presidential election that year, Roosevelt handily defeated a weak conservative Democratic candidate, Judge Alton B. Parker. Now president in his own right, Roosevelt stepped up the attack on the trusts. He took on forty-five of the nation's giant firms, including Standard Oil, American Tobacco, and DuPont. His rhetoric rising, Roosevelt became the nation's trust-buster, a crusader against "predatory wealth."

But Roosevelt was not antibusiness. He regarded large-scale enterprise as a natural tendency of modern industrialism. Only firms that abused their power deserved punishment. But how would those companies be identified? Under the Sherman Act, following common-law

practice, the courts decided whether an act in restraint of trade was "unreasonable"—that is, excessive and harmful of the public interest—on a case-by-case basis. In the *Trans-Missouri* decision of 1897, however, the Supreme Court abandoned this discretionary "rule of reason," holding now that actions that restrained or monopolized trade, regardless of the public impact, automatically violated the Sherman Act.

Little noticed at first, *Trans-Missouri* placed Roosevelt in a quandary. He had no desire to hamstring legitimate business activity, but he could not rely on the courts to distinguish between "good" and "bad" trusts. The only solution was for Roosevelt to do so himself, a power he had because as president it was up to him to

James Bryce

America in 1905: "Business Is King"

James Bryce, British author of The American Commonwealth *(1888), a great treatise on American politics, visited the United States regularly over many years. In an essay published in 1905, Lord Bryce took stock of the changes he had seen during the previous quarter century. What most impressed him, beyond the sheer growth of material wealth, was the loss of individualism and the intensifying concentration of corporate power. In this he was at one with his old friend Theodore Roosevelt, who at that very time was gearing up to do battle with the trusts.*

That which most strikes the visitor to America today is its prodigious material development. Industrial growth, swift thirty or forty years ago, advances more swiftly now. The rural districts are being studded with villages, the villages are growing into cities, the cities are stretching out long arms of suburbs, which follow the lines of road and railway in every direction. The increase of wealth, even more remarkable than the increase of population, impresses the European more than ever before because the contrast with Europe is greater. The huge fortunes, the fortunes of those whose income reaches or exceeds a million dollars a year, are of course far more numerous than in any other country. . . . With this extraordinary material development it is natural that in the United States, business, that is to say, industry, commerce, and finance, should have more and more come to overshadow and dwarf all other interests, all other occupations. . . . Business is king.

Commerce and industry themselves have developed new features. Twenty-two years ago there were no trusts. . . . Even then, however, corporations had covered a larger proportion of the whole field of industry and commerce in America than in Europe, and their structure was more flexible and efficient. Today this is still more the case; while as for trusts, they have become one of the most salient phenomena of the country. They fix the attention, they excite the alarm of economists and politicians as well as of traders in the Old World, while they exercise and baffle the ingenuity of American legislators. Workingmen follow, though hitherto with unequal steps, the efforts at combination which the lords of production and distribution have been making. The consumer stands, if not with folded hands, yet so far with no clear view of the steps he may make for his own protection. Perhaps his prosperity— for he is prosperous— helps him to be quiescent.

The example of the United States, the land in which individualism has been most conspicuously vigorous, may seem to suggest that the world is passing out of the stage of individualism and returning to that earlier stage in which groups of men formed the units of society. The bond of association was, in those early days, kinship, real or supposed, and a servile or quasi-servile dependence of the weak upon the strong. Now it is the power of wealth which enables the few to combine so as to gain command of the sources of wealth. . . . Is it a paradox to observe that it is because the Americans have been the most individualistic of peoples that they are now the people among whom the art of combination has reached its maximum? The amazing keenness and energy, which were stimulated by the commercial conditions of the country, have evoked and ripened a brilliant talent for organization. This talent has applied new methods to production and distribution and has enabled wealth, gathered into a small number of hands, to dominate even the enormous market of America.

Source: Allan Nevins, ed., *America through British Eyes* (Gloucester, MA: Peter Smith, 1968), 384–87.

decide whether to initiate antitrust prosecutions in the first place. It was his negative power that counted here: he could choose not to prosecute a trust.

In November 1904, with an antitrust suit looming, the United States Steel Corporation's chairman Elbert H. Gary approached Roosevelt with a deal: cooperation in exchange for preferential treatment. The company would open its books to the Bureau of Corporations; if it found evidence of wrongdoing, the company would be warned privately and given a chance to set matters right. Roosevelt accepted this "gentlemen's agreement" because it met his interest in accommodating the realities of the modern industrial order while maintaining his public image as slayer of the trusts.

Railroad Regulation.   The railroads posed a different kind of problem. As quasi-public enterprises, they had always been subject to state regulation; in 1887 they came under federal regulation by the Interstate Commerce Commission (ICC). As with the Sherman Act, this assertion of federal authority was mostly symbolic at first. Convinced that the railroads needed firmer oversight, Roosevelt pushed through the Elkins Act of 1903, which prohibited discriminatory rates that gave an unfair advantage to preferred or powerful customers; and then, with the 1904 election behind him, he launched a drive for real railroad regulation.

In 1906, after nearly two years of wrangling, Congress passed the Hepburn Railway Act, which empowered the ICC to set maximum shipping rates and prescribe uniform methods of bookkeeping. As a concession to the conservative Republican bloc, however, the courts retained broad powers to review the ICC's rate decisions.

The Hepburn Act was a triumph of Roosevelt's skills as a political operator. He had maneuvered brilliantly against determined opposition and come away with the essentials of what he wanted. Despite grumbling by Senate progressives, Roosevelt was satisfied. He had achieved a landmark expansion of the government's regulatory powers over business.

Consumer Protection.   The protection of consumers, another signature issue for progressives, was very much the handiwork of muckraking journalism. What sparked the issue was a riveting series of articles in *Collier's*. Samuel Hopkins Adams exposed the patent-medicine business as "undiluted fraud" dangerous to the nation's health and "exploited by the skillfullest of advertising bunco men." For a time industry lobbyists stymied legislative action.

Then, in 1906, Upton Sinclair's novel *The Jungle* appeared. Sinclair thought he was writing about the exploitation of workers in Chicago meatpacking plants, but what caught the nation's attention was his descriptions of rotten meat and filthy conditions. President Roosevelt, weighing into the legislative battle, authorized a federal investigation of the stockyards. Within months the Pure Food and Drug and the Meat Inspection Acts passed, and another administrative agency joined the expanding federal bureaucracy: the Food and Drug Administration.

The Square Deal.   During the 1904 presidential campaign, Roosevelt had taken to calling his program the **Square Deal**. This kind of labeling was new to American politics, emblematic of a political style that dramatized issues, mobilized public opinion, and asserted leadership. But the label identified something of substance as well. After many years of passivity and weakness, the federal government was reclaiming the role it had abandoned after the Civil War. Now, however,

Campaigning for the Square Deal
When William McKinley ran for president in 1896, he sat on his front porch in Canton, Ohio, and received delegations of voters. That was not Theodore Roosevelt's way. He considered the presidency a "bully pulpit," and he used the office brilliantly to mobilize public opinion and to assert his leadership. The preeminence of the presidency in American public life begins with Roosevelt's administration. Here, at the height of his crusading power, Roosevelt stumps for the Square Deal in the 1904 election. Library of Congress.

the target was the new economic order. When companies abused their corporate power, the government would intercede to assure ordinary Americans a "square deal."

During his two terms as president, Roosevelt had struggled to bring a modern corporate economy under public control. He was well aware, however, that his Square Deal was built on nineteenth-century foundations. In particular, antitrust doctrine, which aimed at enforcing competition, seemed inadequate when the economy's tendency was toward industrial concentration. Better, Roosevelt felt, for the federal government to regulate big business than try to break it up. In his final presidential speeches, Roosevelt dwelled on the need for a reform agenda for the twentieth century. This was the task he bequeathed to his chosen successor, William Howard Taft.

The Fracturing of Republican Progressivism

William Howard Taft was an estimable man in many ways. An able jurist and superb administrator, he had served Roosevelt loyally as governor-general of the Philippines and as secretary of war. He was an avowed Square Dealer. But he was not by nature a progressive politician. He disliked the give-and-take of politics, he distrusted power, and he revered the processes of law. He could not, for example, have imagined intruding into the 1902 anthracite strike, as Roosevelt had done, or taken so flexible a view of the Sherman Act. He was, in fundamental ways, a conservative.

Taft's Democratic opponent in the 1908 campaign was William Jennings Bryan. This was Bryan's last hurrah, his third attempt at the presidency, and he made the most of it. Eloquent as ever, Bryan attacked the Republicans as the party of the "plutocrats" and outdid them in urging tougher antitrust legislation, lower tariffs, stricter railway regulation, and advanced labor legislation. Bryan's campaign moved the Democratic Party into the mainstream of national progressive politics, but it was not enough to offset Taft's advantages as Roosevelt's candidate.

Taft won comfortably, and he entered the White House with a mandate to pick up where Roosevelt left off. That, alas, was not to be.

Taft's Troubles.   By 1909 the ferment of reform had unsettled the Republican Party. On the right the conservatives were girding themselves against further losses. Led by the formidable Senator Nelson W. Aldrich of Rhode Island, they were still a force to be reckoned with. On the left progressive Republicans were rebellious. They had broad popular support—especially in the Midwest—and in Robert La Follette, a fiery leader. The progressives felt that Roosevelt had been too easy on business, and with him gone from the White House, they intended to make up for lost time. Reconciling these conflicting forces within the Republican Party would have been a daunting task for the most accomplished politician. For Taft it spelled disaster.

First there was the tariff. Progressives considered protective tariffs a major reason why competition had declined and the trusts had taken hold. Although Taft had campaigned for tariff reform, he was won over by the conservative Republican bloc and ended up approving the protectionist Payne-Aldrich Tariff Act of 1909, which critics charged sheltered eastern industry from foreign competition.

Next came the Pinchot-Ballinger affair. U.S. Chief Forester Gifford Pinchot, an ardent conservationist and a chum of Roosevelt's, accused Secretary of the Interior Richard A. Ballinger of conspiring to transfer Alaskan public land—rich in natural resources—to a private syndicate. When Pinchot aired these charges in January 1910, Taft fired him for insubordination. Despite Taft's strong conservationist credentials, in the eyes of the progressives the Pinchot-Ballinger affair marked him as a friend of the "interests" bent on plundering the nation's resources.

Taft found himself propelled into the conservative Republican camp, an ally of "Uncle Joe" Cannon, the dictatorial Speaker of the House of Representatives. When a House revolt finally broke Cannon's power in 1910, it was regarded as a defeat for the president as well. Galvanized by Taft's defection, the reformers in the Republican Party became a dissident faction, calling themselves "Progressives," or in more belligerent moments, "Insurgents." Taft answered by backing their conservative foes in the Republican primaries that year.

The Taft-Roosevelt Split.   The Progressives emerged from the 1910 elections stronger and angrier. In January 1911 they formed the National Progressive Republican League and began a drive to take over the Republican Party. Though La Follette was their leader, the Progressives knew that their best chance to topple Taft lay with Theodore Roosevelt.

Home from a year-long safari in Africa, Roosevelt yearned to reenter the political fray. Taft's dispute with the Progressives gave Roosevelt the cause he needed. But Roosevelt was a loyal party man and too astute a politician not to recognize that a party split would benefit the Democrats. He could be spurred into rebellion only by a true clash of principles. On the question of the trusts, just such a clash materialized.

By distinguishing between good and bad trusts, Roosevelt had managed to reconcile public policy (the Sherman Act) and economic reality (the tendency toward corporate concentration). But this was a makeshift solution that depended on a president who was willing to stretch his powers to the limit. Taft had no such inclination. His legalistic mind rebelled at the notion that as president he should decide which trusts should be prosecuted. The Sherman Act was on the books. "We are going to enforce that law or die in the attempt," Taft promised grimly.

In the *Standard Oil* decision (1911), the Supreme Court eased Taft's problem by reasserting the rule of reason, which meant that, once again, the courts themselves would distinguish between good and bad trusts. With that burden lifted from the executive branch, Attorney General George W. Wickersham stepped up the pace of antitrust actions.

The United States Steel Corporation became an immediate target. Among the charges against the steel trust was that it had violated the antimonopoly provision of the Sherman Act by acquiring the Tennessee Coal and Iron Company in 1907. Roosevelt had personally approved the acquisition, believing this was necessary—so U.S. Steel representatives had told him—to prevent a financial collapse on Wall Street. Taft's suit against U.S. Steel thus amounted to an attack on Roosevelt that he could not, without dishonor, ignore.

The New Nationalism.   Ever since leaving the White House, Roosevelt had been pondering the trust problem. There was, he concluded, a third way between breaking up big business and submitting to corporate rule. The federal government could be empowered to oversee the nation's industrial corporations to make sure they acted in the public interest. They would be regulated by a federal trade commission as if they were natural monopolies or public utilities.

In a speech in Osawatomie, Kansas, in August 1910, Roosevelt made the case for what he called the **New Nationalism**. The central issue, he argued, was human welfare versus property rights. In modern society, property had to be controlled "to whatever degree the public welfare may require it." The government would become "the steward of the public welfare."

This formulation unleashed Roosevelt's reformist bent. He took up the cause of social justice, adding to his program a federal child labor law, regulation of labor relations, and a national minimum wage for women. Most radical, perhaps, was Roosevelt's attack on the legal system. Insisting that the courts stood in the way of reform, Roosevelt proposed sharp curbs on their powers, even raising the possibility of popular recall of court decisions.

Early in 1912 Roosevelt announced his candidacy for the presidency and immediately swept the Progressive Republicans into his camp. A bitter party battle ensued. Roosevelt won the states that held primary elections, but Taft controlled the party machinery elsewhere. Dominated by the party regulars, the Republican convention chose Taft. Considering himself cheated out of the nomination, Roosevelt led his followers into a new Progressive Party, soon nicknamed the "Bull Moose" party. In a crusading campaign Roosevelt offered the New Nationalism to the people.

Woodrow Wilson and the New Freedom

While the Republicans battled among themselves, the Democrats were on the move. The scars caused by the free-silver campaign of 1896 had faded, and in the 1908 campaign William Jennings Bryan established the party's progressive credentials. The Democrats made

On to the White House

At the Democratic convention of 1912, Woodrow Wilson only narrowly defeated the front-runner, Champ Clark of Missouri. Harper's Weekly *triumphantly depicted Wilson immediately after his nomination—the scholar turned politician riding off on the Democratic donkey, with his running mate, Thomas R. Marshall, hanging on behind. The magazine's editor, George Harvey, had identified Wilson as presidential timber back in 1906, long before the Princeton president had thought of politics, and had worked on his behalf from then on.* Newberry Library.

dramatic gains in 1910, taking over the House of Representatives for the first time since 1892 and capturing a number of traditionally Republican governorships. After fourteen years as the party's standard-bearer, Bryan made way for a new generation of leaders.

The ablest was Woodrow Wilson of New Jersey, a noted political scientist who, as university president, had brought Princeton into the front rank of American universities. In 1910, with no political experience, he accepted the Democratic nomination for governor of New Jersey and won. Wilson compiled a sterling reform record, including the direct primary, workers' compensation, and stringent utility regulation. Wilson went on to win the Democratic presidential nomination in 1912 in a bruising battle.

Forging the New Freedom. Wilson possessed, to a fault, the moral certainty that characterized the progressive politician. A brilliant speaker, he instinctively assumed the mantle of righteousness. Only gradually, however, did Wilson hammer out, in reaction to Roosevelt's New Nationalism, a coherent reform program, which he called the **New Freedom**.

As he warmed to the debate, Wilson cast his differences with Roosevelt in fundamental terms of slavery and freedom. "This is a struggle for emancipation," he proclaimed in October 1912. "If America is not to have free enterprise, then she can have freedom of no sort whatever." Wilson also scorned Roosevelt's social program. Welfare might be benevolent, he declared, but it also would be paternalistic and contrary to the traditions of a free people. The New Nationalism represented a future of collectivism, Wilson warned, whereas the New Freedom would preserve political and economic liberty.

Wilson actually had much in common with Roosevelt. "The old time of individual competition is probably gone by," Wilson admitted. Like Roosevelt, he opposed not bigness but the abuse of economic power. Wilson agreed that the abuse of power could not be prevented without a strong federal government. He parted company from Roosevelt over *how* government should restrain private power.

Despite all the rhetoric, the 1912 election fell short of being a referendum on the New Nationalism versus the New Freedom. The outcome turned on a more humdrum reality: Wilson was elected because he kept the traditional Democratic vote, while the Republicans split between Roosevelt and Taft (Map 20.3). Despite a landslide in the electoral college, Wilson received only 42 percent of the popular vote. At best the 1912 election signified that the American public was in the mood for reform. Only 23 percent, after all, had voted for the one candidate who stood for the status quo, President Taft. Wilson's own program, however, had received no clear mandate from the people.

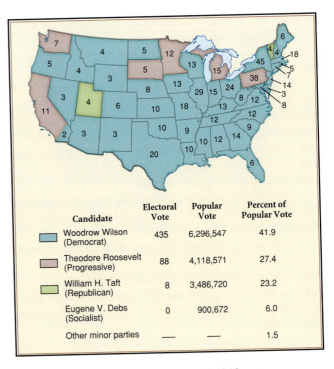

Candidate	Electoral Vote	Popular Vote	Percent of Popular Vote
Woodrow Wilson (Democrat)	435	6,296,547	41.9
Theodore Roosevelt (Progressive)	88	4,118,571	27.4
William H. Taft (Republican)	8	3,486,720	23.2
Eugene V. Debs (Socialist)	0	900,672	6.0
Other minor parties	—	—	1.5

MAP 20.3 Presidential Election of 1912

The 1912 election reveals why the two-party system is so strongly rooted in American politics. The Democrats, though a minority party, won an electoral landslide because the Republicans divided their vote between Roosevelt and Taft. This result indicates what is at stake when major parties splinter. The Socialists, despite a record vote of 900,000, received no electoral votes. To vote Socialist in 1912 meant in effect to throw away one's vote.

Yet the 1912 election proved decisive in the history of economic reform. The debate between Roosevelt and Wilson had brought forth, in the New Freedom, a program capable of finally resolving the crisis over corporate power that had gripped the nation for a decade. Just as important, the election created a rare legislative opportunity in Washington. With Congress in Democratic hands, the time was ripe to act on the New Freedom.

The First Phase: Tariff Reform and the Federal Reserve. Long out of power, the Democrats were hungry for tariff reform. From the prevailing average of 40 percent, the Underwood Tariff Act of 1913 pared rates down to 25 percent. Targeting especially the trust-dominated industries, Democrats confidently expected the Underwood Tariff to spur competition and reduce prices for consumers.

Wilson's administration then turned to the nation's banking system, whose key weakness was the absence of a central bank, or federal reserve. The main function of central banks at that time was to regulate commercial banks and back them up in case they could not meet their obligations to depositors. In the past this backup role had been assumed by the great New York banks that handled the accounts of outlying banks. If the New York banks weakened, the entire system could collapse. This nearly happened in 1907, when the Knickerbocker Trust Company failed and panic swept the nation's financial markets.

While the need for a central bank was clear, the form it should take was hotly disputed. Wall Street wanted a unified system run by the bankers. Rural Democrats and their spokesman, Senator Carter Glass of Virginia, preferred a decentralized network of reserve banks. Progressives in both parties agreed that the essential feature should be strong public control. The bankers, whose practices were already under scrutiny by Congress, were on the defensive.

President Wilson, initially no expert, learned quickly and reconciled the reformers and bankers. The monumental Federal Reserve Act of 1913 gave the nation a banking system that was resistant to financial panic. The act delegated financial functions to twelve district reserve banks that would be controlled by their member banks. The Federal Reserve Board imposed public regulation on this regional structure. In one stroke the act strengthened the banking system and placed a measure of restraint on Wall Street.

Settling the Trust Question.   Having dealt with tariff and banking reform, Wilson turned to the big question of how to curb the trusts. In this effort Wilson relied heavily on a new advisor, Louis D. Brandeis, famous as the "people's lawyer" for his public service in many progressive causes (including the landmark *Muller* case). Brandeis denied that bigness meant efficiency. On the contrary, he argued, trusts were wasteful compared with firms that vigorously competed in a free market. The main thing was to prevent the trusts from unfairly using their power to curb free competition.

This could be done by strengthening the Sherman Act, but the obvious course—defining with precision what constituted anticompetitive practices—proved hard to implement. Was it feasible to say exactly when interlocking directorates, discriminatory pricing, or exclusive contracts became illegal? Brandeis decided that it was not, and Wilson assented. In the Clayton Antitrust Act of 1914, amending the Sherman Act, the definition of illegal practices was left flexible, subject to the test of whether an action "substantially lessen[ed] competition or tend[ed] to create a monopoly."

This retreat from a definitive antitrust prescription meant that a federal trade commission would be needed to back up the Sherman and Clayton Acts. Wilson was understandably hesitant, given his principled opposition to Roosevelt's powerful trade commission in the campaign. At first Wilson favored an advisory, information-gathering agency. But ultimately, under the 1914 law establishing it, the Federal Trade Commission (FTC) received broad powers to investigate companies and issue "cease and desist" orders against unfair trade practices that violated antitrust law.

Despite a good deal of commotion, this arduous legislative process was actually an exercise in consensus building. Wilson opened the debate in a conciliatory way. "The antagonism between business and government is over," he said, and the time ripe for a program representing the "best business judgment in America." Afterward, Wilson felt he had brought the long controversy over corporate power to a successful conclusion, and in fact he had. Steering a course between Taft's conservatism and Roosevelt's radicalism, Wilson had carved out a middle way that brought to bear the powers of government without threatening the constitutional order and curbed abuse of corporate power without threatening the capitalist system.

What few Americans recognized, in the midst of this protracted struggle, was how very odd it seemed from a European standpoint. Neither Britain nor Germany, America's industrial rivals, made such a fuss over competitive markets. It was true that the fundamental concept—restraint of trade—originated in English common law, but the British, free traders and export-oriented, lacked the opportunity to engage in market-controlling behavior and hence had no need for antitrust legislation. Germany, by contrast, was a veritable hotbed of conspiracies in restraint of trade, only they were called "cartels"—business groups that divided the market and set prices, operating with the approval of the imperial government.

Wilson's Social Program.   On social policy, as with antitrust policy, Wilson charted a middle way. Having denounced Roosevelt's paternalism, he was at first unreceptive to what he saw as special-interest demands by labor and farm organizations. On the leading issue—that they be exempt from antitrust prosecution—the most Wilson was willing to accept was cosmetic language in the Clayton Act that did not grant them the immunity they sought.

The labor vote had grown increasingly important to the Democratic Party, however. Wilson's tenure in the White House, moreover, coincided with a burst of industrial conflict, including dramatic strikes by textile workers, mostly immigrant women, at Lawrence, Massachusetts, in 1912, and Paterson, New Jersey, in 1913, and a violent coal miners' strike in 1914 in Colorado, which climaxed with the torching of a tent city at Ludlow by state militia. The resulting asphyxiation of strikers' wives and children hiding in the tents horrified the nation and made Ludlow the focus of a wide-ranging investigation into the troubled industrial relations of the country. The "labor question" was suddenly prominent on the progressive agenda.

As his second presidential campaign drew near, Wilson lost some of his scruples about prolabor legislation.

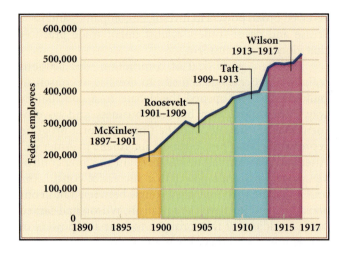

FIGURE 20.1 The Federal Bureaucracy, 1890–1917

The surge in federal employment after 1900 mirrored the surge in government authority under Theodore Roosevelt's progressive leadership. Not even Wilson, although he ran on a platform of limited government, could stem the tide. Numerically, in fact, the federal bureaucracy grew most rapidly during Wilson's first term.

In 1915 and 1916 he championed a host of bills beneficial to American workers: a federal child labor law, the Adamson eight-hour law for railroad workers, and the landmark Seamen's Act, which eliminated age-old abuses of sailors aboard ship. Likewise, after earlier resistance, Wilson approved in 1916 the Federal Farm Loan Act, which provided the low-interest rural credit system long demanded by farmers. Nor was it lost on observers that, his New Freedom rhetoric notwithstanding, Wilson presided over an ever more active federal government, and an ever-expanding federal bureaucracy (Figure 20.1).

Wilson encountered the same dilemma that confronted all successful progressives: the claims of moral principle versus the unyielding realities of political life. Progressives were high-minded but not radical. They saw evils in the system, but they did not consider the system itself to be evil. They also prided themselves on being realists as well as moralists. So it stood to reason that Wilson, like other progressives who achieved power, would find his place at the center.

But it would be wrong to underestimate their achievement. Progressives made presidential leadership important again, they brought government back into the nation's life, and they laid the foundation for twentieth-century social and economic policy.

FOR FURTHER EXPLORATION

► For definitions of key terms boldfaced in this chapter, see the glossary at the end·of the book.

► To assess your mastery of the material covered in this chapter, see the Online Study Guide at **bedfordstmartins.com/henretta**.

► For suggested references, including Web sites, see page SR-22 at the end of the book.

► For map resources and primary documents, see **bedfordstmartins.com/henretta**.

SUMMARY

A new chapter in American reform began at the start of the twentieth century. For decades the problems resulting from industrialization and urban growth had been mounting. Now, after 1900, reform began to dominate the nation's public life. The unifying element in progressivism was a common intellectual outlook, highly principled and idealistic as to goals and confident of the human capacity to find the means to achieve those goals.

Beyond this shared belief, progressives broke up into diverse and sometimes conflicting groups. Social welfare became the province of American women and that effort reinvigorated the struggle for women's voting rights. Suffragists divided over tactics, however, and the rise of feminism generated further strains in the women's movement. Political reformers included business groups concerned chiefly with improving the efficiency of city government. Other progressives, such as Robert La Follette, opposed privilege and wanted to democratize the political process. Both groups worked to enhance their power at the expense of entrenched party machines. In the cities working people and immigrants also became reform minded and set in motion a new political force—urban liberalism. While progressivism was infected by the endemic racism of American life, there was a reform wing that joined with black activists to forge the major institutions of black protest and uplift of the twentieth century: the NAACP and the Urban League.

At the national level, progressives focused primarily on controlling the economic power of corporate business. This overriding problem led to Theodore Roosevelt's Square Deal, then to his New Nationalism, and finally to Woodrow Wilson's New Freedom. The role of the federal government expanded dramatically but in service to a cautious and pragmatic approach to the country's problems.

TIMELINE

1889 Jane Addams and Ellen Gates Starr found Hull House

1893 Panic of 1893 starts depression of the 1890s

1899 National Consumers' League founded

1900 Robert M. La Follette elected Wisconsin governor

Commission form of city government first appears, in Galveston, Texas

1901 President McKinley assassinated; Theodore Roosevelt succeeds him

1902 President Roosevelt settles national anthracite strike

1903 National Women's Trade Union League founded

1904 Supreme Court dissolves the Northern Securities Company

1905 *Lochner v. New York* overturns law restricting length of bakers' workday

1906 Upton Sinclair's *The Jungle*

Hepburn Railway Act

AFL adopts "Bill of Grievances"

1908 *Muller v. Oregon* upholds regulation of working hours for women

William Howard Taft elected president

1909 NAACP formed

1910 Roosevelt announces the New Nationalism

Woman suffrage movement revives

1911 *Standard Oil* decision restores "rule of reason"

Triangle Shirtwaist fire

1912 Progressive Party formed

Woodrow Wilson elected president

1913 Federal Reserve Act

Underwood Tariff Act

1914 Clayton Antitrust Act

CHAPTER 21

An Emerging World Power

1877–1914

The Roots of Expansion
Diplomacy in the Gilded Age
The Economy of Expansionism
The Making of a "Large" Foreign Policy
The Ideology of Expansionism

An American Empire
The Cuban Crisis
The Spoils of War
The Imperial Experiment

Onto the World Stage
A Power among Powers
The Open Door in Asia
Wilson and Mexico
The Gathering Storm in Europe

IN 1881 Great Britain sent a new envoy to Washington. He was Sir Lionel Sackville-West, son of an earl and brother-in-law of the Tory leader Lord Denby, but otherwise distinguished only as the lover of a celebrated Spanish dancer. His well-connected friends wanted to park Sir Lionel somewhere comfortable, but out of harm's way. So they made him minister to the United States.

Twenty years later such an appointment would have been unthinkable. All the European powers had by then elevated their missions in Washington to embassies and staffed them with top-of-the-line ambassadors. And they treated the United States, without question, as a fellow Great Power.

In Sir Lionel's day the United States scarcely cast a shadow on world affairs. America's army was smaller than Bulgaria's; its navy ranked thirteenth in the world and was a threat mainly to the crews manning its unseaworthy ships. By 1900, however, the United States was flexing its muscles. It had just made short work of Spain in a brief but decisive war and acquired for itself an empire stretching from Puerto Rico to the Philippines. America's standing as a rising naval power was manifest, and so was its muscular assertion of national interest in the Caribbean and the Pacific.

◄ **Battle of Santiago de Cuba, 1898**
James G. Tyler's dramatic painting of the final sea battle of the Spanish-American War showcased America's newest weapon of war, the battleship.
Franklin D. Roosevelt Library.

In practice the United States still acted as a regional power, but Europeans were keenly aware of its capacity to cut a wider swath whenever it chose to do so. The notion of an "American peril" became a lively topic after 1900 among Europeans surveying America's industrial and military potential. No one could be sure what America's role would be, since the United States retained its traditional policy of nonalignment in European affairs. But by 1914, when a great war engulfed Europe, there was no question but that the United States would have a big role to play. How the United States emerged onto the world stage in the decades before World War I is the subject of this chapter.

The Roots of Expansion

In 1880 the United States had a population of 50 million, and by that measure ranked with the great European powers. In industrial production the nation stood second only to Britain and was rapidly closing the gap. Anyone who doubted the military prowess of Americans needed only to recall the ferocity with which they had fought one another in the Civil War. The great campaigns of Lee, Sherman, and Grant had entered the military textbooks and were closely studied by army strategists everywhere.

And when vital interests were at stake, the United States had not shown itself lacking in diplomatic vigor. The Civil War had put the United States at odds with both France and Britain. The dispute with France involved the establishment in Mexico of a French-sponsored regime under Archduke Maximilian, a move regarded by the United States as a threat to its security in the Southwest. When American troops under General Philip Sheridan began to mass on the Mexican border in 1867, the French military withdrew, abandoning Maximilian to a Mexican firing squad.

With Britain, the thorny issue involved damages to Union shipping by the *Alabama* and other Confederate sea raiders operating from English ports. American hopes of taking Canada as compensation were dashed by Britain's grant of dominion status to Canada in 1867. But four years later, after lengthy negotiations, Britain expressed regret for its unneutral acts and agreed to the arbitration of the *Alabama* claims, settling to America's satisfaction the last outstanding diplomatic issue of the Civil War.

Diplomacy in the Gilded Age

In the years that followed, the United States lapsed into diplomatic inactivity, not out of weakness but for lack of any clear national purpose in world affairs. The business of building the nation's industrial economy absorbed Americans and turned their attention inward. And while the new international telegraphic cables provided the country with swift overseas communication after the 1860s, wide oceans still kept the world at a distance and gave Americans a sense of isolation and security.

European power politics, which centered on Franco-German rivalry and on ethnic conflict in the Balkans, did not seem to matter very much. As far as President Cleveland's secretary of state, Thomas F. Bayard, was concerned, "we have not the slightest share or interest [in] the small politics and backstage intrigues of Europe."

As for the empires that the European powers were avidly building in Africa and Asia, this expression of national prowess did not tempt the United States. Even so ardent an American nationalist as the young Theodore Roosevelt saw the folly of overseas expansion. "We want no unwilling citizens to enter our Union," he wrote in 1886. "European nations war for possession of thickly settled districts. . . . We, wiser in our generation, have seized the waste solitudes that lay near us."

In these circumstances, with no external threat to be seen, why maintain a big navy? After the Civil War, the fleet gradually deteriorated. Of the 125 ships on the navy's active list, only about 25 were seaworthy at any one time. No effort was made to keep up with European advances in weaponry or battleship design; the American fleet consisted mainly of sailing ships and obsolete ironclads modeled on the *Monitor* of Civil War fame.

During the administration of Chester A. Arthur (1881–1885), the navy began a modest upgrading program, commissioning new ships, raising the standards for the officer corps, and founding the Naval War College. But the fleet remained small, without a unified naval command, and with little more to do than maintain coastal defenses.

The conduct of diplomacy was likewise of little account. Appointment to the foreign service was mostly through the spoils system. American envoys and consular officers were a mixed lot, with many idlers and drunkards among the hard working and competent. Domestic politics, moreover, made it difficult to develop a coherent foreign policy. Although diplomacy was a presidential responsibility, the U.S. Senate jealously guarded its constitutional right to give "advice and consent" on treaties and diplomatic appointments. For its part the State Department tended to be inactive, exerting little control over either policy or its missions abroad. In distant places the American presence was likely to be Christian missionaries proselytizing among the native populations of Asia, Africa, and the Pacific islands.

Latin American Diplomacy.   In the Caribbean, the expansionist enthusiasms of the Civil War era subsided. William H. Seward, Lincoln and Andrew Johnson's secretary of state, had dreamed of an American empire extending from the Caribbean across Mexico to Hawaii.

Sugarcane Plantation, Hawaii

Over 300,000 Asians from China, Japan, Korea, and the Philippines came to work in the Hawaiian cane fields between 1850 and 1920. The hardships they endured are reflected in plantation work songs, such as this one by Japanese laborers:

> *Hawaii, Hawaii*
> *But when I came what I saw was Hell*
> *The boss was Satan*
> *The lunas [overseers] his helpers.*

George Bacon Collection, Hawaii State Archives.

Nothing came of his grandiose plans, nor of President Grant's efforts to purchase Santo Domingo (the future Dominican Republic) in 1870, and the Senate regularly blocked later moves to acquire bases in Haiti, Cuba, and Venezuela. The long-cherished interest in a canal across Central America also faded. Despite its claims of exclusive rights, the United States stood by when a French company headed by the builder of the Suez Canal, Ferdinand de Lesseps, started to dig across the Panama isthmus in 1880. That project failed after a decade, but the reason was bankruptcy and not American opposition.

Diplomatic activity quickened when the energetic James G. Blaine became secretary of state in 1881. He got involved in a border dispute between Mexico and Guatemala, tried to settle a war Chile was waging against Peru and Bolivia, and called the first Pan-American conference. Blaine's interventions in Latin American disputes went badly, however, and his successor canceled the Pan-American conference after Blaine left office in late 1881. This was a characteristic example of Gilded Age diplomacy, driven largely by partisan politics and carried out without any clear sense of national purpose.

Pan-Americanism—the notion of a community of western-hemispheric states—took root, however, and Blaine, returning in 1889 for a second stint at the State Department, took up the plans of the outgoing Cleveland administration for a new Pan-American conference. But little came of it, except for provisions for an agency in Washington that became the Pan-American

Union. Any South American goodwill won by Blaine's efforts was soon blasted by the humiliation the United States visited upon Chile because of a riot against American sailors in the port of Valparaiso in 1891. Threatened with war, Chile was forced to apologize to the United States and pay an indemnity of $75,000.

Pacific Episodes. In the Pacific, American interest centered on Hawaii, where prospects for raising sugarcane had attracted a horde of American planters and investors. Nominally an independent nation, Hawaii fell increasingly under American dominance. Under an 1875 treaty Hawaiian sugar gained duty-free entry in to the American market and the islands were declared off limits to other powers. A second treaty in 1887 granted the United States naval rights at Pearl Harbor.

When Hawaii's favored access to the American market was abruptly canceled by the McKinley Tariff of 1890, sugar planters began to plot an American takeover of Hawaii. They organized a revolt in January 1893 against Queen Liliuokalani and quickly negotiated a treaty of annexation with the Harrison administration. Before the Senate could approve, however, Grover Cleveland returned to the presidency and withdrew the treaty. To annex Hawaii, he declared, would violate America's "honor and morality" and an "unbroken tradition" against acquiring territory far from the nation's shores.

Meanwhile, the American presence elsewhere in the Pacific was growing. The purchase of Alaska from imperial

Russia in 1867 gave the United States not only a huge territory with vast natural resources but an unlooked-for presence stretching across the northern Pacific. And far to the south, in the Samoan islands, the United States secured rights in 1878 to a coaling station at Pago Pago harbor—a key link on the route to Australia—and established an informal protectorate there. In 1889, after some jostling with Germany and Britain, the rivalry over Samoa ended in a tripartite protectorate, with America retaining its rights in Pago Pago.

American diplomacy in these years has been characterized as a series of incidents, not the pursuit of a foreign policy. Many things happened, but intermittently and without any well-founded conception of national objectives. This was possible because, as the Englishman James Bryce remarked in 1888, America still sailed "upon a summer sea." In the stormier waters that lay ahead, a different kind of diplomacy would be required.

The Economy of Expansionism

"A policy of isolation did well enough when we were an embryo nation," remarked Senator Orville Platt of Connecticut in 1893. "But today things are different. . . . We are 65 million people, the most advanced and powerful on earth, and regard to our future welfare demands an abandonment of the doctrines of isolation." What especially demanded that Americans look outward was their enormously productive economy.

The Search for Foreign Markets. America's gross domestic product—the total value of goods and services—quadrupled between 1870 and 1900. But were there markets big enough to absorb the output of America's farms and factories? Over 90 percent of American goods in the late nineteenth century were consumed at home. Even so, foreign markets mattered. Roughly a fifth of the nation's agricultural output was exported, and as the industrial economy expanded, so did manufactured goods. Between 1880 and 1900, the industrial share of total exports jumped from 15 percent to over 30 percent.

American firms began to plant themselves overseas. As early as 1868 the Singer Sewing Machine Company established its first foreign factory in Glasgow, Scotland. The giant among American firms doing business abroad was Rockefeller's Standard Oil, with European branches operating tankers and marketing kerosene across the continent. In Asia Standard Oil cans, converted into utensils and roofing tin, became a visible sign of American market penetration. Brand names like Kodak (cameras), McCormick (agricultural equipment), and Ford (the Model T) became household words around the world.

Foreign trade was important partly for reasons of international finance. As a developing economy the United States attracted a lot of foreign capital. The result was a heavy outflow of dollars to pay interest and dividends to foreign investors. To balance this account, the United States needed to export more goods than it imported. In fact, a favorable import-export balance was achieved in 1876 (Figure 21.1). But because of its dependence on foreign capital, America had to be constantly vigilant about its export trade.

Even more important, however, was the relationship that many Americans perceived between foreign markets and the nation's social stability. Hard times always sparked agrarian unrest and labor strife. The problem, many thought, was that the nation's capacity to produce was outrunning its capacity to consume. When the economy

The Singer Sewing Machine

The sewing machine was an American invention that swiftly found markets abroad. The Singer Company, the dominant firm, not only exported large quantities but produced 200,000 machines annually at a Scottish plant that employed 6,000 workers. Singer's advertising rightly boasted of its prowess as an international company and of a product that was "The Universal Machine." New-York Historical Society.

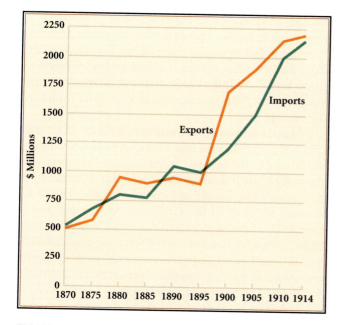

FIGURE 21.1 Balance of U.S. Imports, 1870–1914

By 1876 the United States had become a net exporting nation. The brief reversal after 1888 aroused fears that the United States was losing its foreign markets and helped fuel the expansionist drive of the 1890s.

slowed, cutbacks in domestic demand drove down farm prices and caused layoffs across the country. The answer was to make sure there would always be enough buyers for America's surplus products, and this meant, more than anything else, buyers in foreign markets.

Overseas Trade and Foreign Policy.   How did these concerns about overseas trade relate to America's foreign policy? The bulk of American exports in the late nineteenth century—over 80 percent—went to Europe and Canada (Table 21.1). In these countries the normal instruments of diplomacy sufficed to protect the nation's economic interests. But in Asia, Latin America, and other regions that Americans considered "backward," a tougher brand of intervention seemed necessary because there the United States was competing with other industrial powers.

Asia and Latin America represented only a modest part of America's export trade—roughly an eighth of the total in the late nineteenth century. Still, this trade was growing—it was worth $200 million in 1900—and parts of it mattered a great deal to specific industries—for example, the Chinese market for American textiles. The real importance of these non-Western markets, however, was not so much their current value as their future promise. China especially exerted a powerful hold on the American mercantile imagination. Many felt that the China trade, although quite small at the time, would one day be the key to American prosperity. Therefore, China and other beckoning markets must not be closed to the United States.

In the mid-1880s the pace of European imperialism picked up. After the Berlin Conference of 1884, Africa was rapidly carved up by the European powers. In a burst of modernizing energy, Japan transformed itself into a major power and began to challenge China's claims to Korea. In the Sino-Japanese War of 1894–1895, Japan won an easy victory and started a scramble among the great powers, including Russia, to divide China up into spheres of influence. In Latin America, U.S. interests began to be challenged more aggressively by Britain, France, and Germany.

On top of all this came the Panic of 1893, setting in motion industrial strikes and agrarian protests that Cleveland's secretary of state, Walter Q. Gresham, like many other Americans, took to be "symptoms of revolution." With the nation's stability seemingly at risk, securing the markets of Latin America and Asia became an urgent necessity, inspiring the expansionist diplomacy of the 1890s.

TABLE 21.1 Exports to Canada and Europe Compared with Exports to Asia and Latin America, 1875–1900

Year	Exports to Canada and Europe ($)	Percentage of Total	Exports to Asia and Latin America ($)	Percentage of Total
1875	494,000,000	86.1	72,000,000	12.5
1885	637,000,000	85.8	87,000,000	11.7
1895	681,000,000	84.3	108,000,000	13.4
1900	1,135,000,000	81.4	200,000,000	14.3

Source: Compiled from information in *Historical Statistics of the United States* (1960); U.S. Department of Commerce, *Long Term Growth, 1860–1965* (1966); National Bureau of Economic Research, *Trends in the American Economy in the Nineteenth Century* (1960).

The Making of a "Large" Foreign Policy

"Whether they will or no, Americans must now begin to look outward. The growing production of the country requires it." So wrote Captain Alfred T. Mahan, America's leading naval strategist, in his book *The Influence of Seapower upon History* (1890). The key to imperial power was control of the seas, Mahan perceived, and from this insight he developed a naval analysis that became the cornerstone of American strategic thinking.

A Global Strategy. "When a question arises of control over distant regions . . . it must ultimately be decided by naval power," Mahan advised. The United States should regard the oceans not as barriers, but as "a great highway . . . over which men pass in all directions." Traversing that highway required a robust merchant marine (America's had fallen on hard times since its heyday in the 1850s), a powerful navy to protect American commerce, and strategic overseas bases. Having converted from sail to steam, navies required coaling stations far from home. Without such stations, Mahan warned, warships were "like land birds, unable to fly far from their own shores."

Mahan advocated a canal across Central America connecting the Atlantic and Pacific Oceans. Such a canal would enable the eastern United States to "compete with Europe, on equal terms as to distance, for the markets of East Asia." The canal's approaches would need to be guarded by bases in the Caribbean Sea. Hawaii would have to be annexed to extend American power into the Pacific. What Mahan envisioned was a form of colonialism different from Europe's—not rule over territories and populations but control over strategic points in defense of America's trading interests.

Other enthusiasts of a powerful America flocked to Mahan, including such up-and-coming politicians as Theodore Roosevelt and Henry Cabot Lodge. The influence of these men, few in number but well connected, increased during the 1890s. They pushed steadily for what Lodge called a "large policy." But mainstream politicians also accepted Mahan's arguments, and from the inauguration of Benjamin Harrison in 1889 onward, a surprising consistency emerged in the conduct of American foreign policy.

Alfred T. Mahan

Mahan's theory about the influence of sea power on history came to him while he was killing time on a tour of naval duty, reading Roman history in a library in Lima, Peru, in 1885. His insight was personal as well as intellectual: embarrassed by the decrepit ships on which he served, Mahan thought the United States should have a modern fleet in which officers like himself could serve with pride (and with some hope of professional advancement). U.S. Naval Historical Foundation.

Rebuilding the Navy. Mahan wanted a battleship fleet capable of roaming the high seas and striking a decisive blow against an enemy. In 1890 Congress appropriated funds for three battleships as the first installment on a two-ocean navy. Battleships might be expensive, said Benjamin F. Tracy, Harrison's ambitious secretary of the navy, but they were "the premium paid by the United States for the insurance of its acquired wealth and its growing industries." The battleship took on a special aura for those—like the young Roosevelt—who had grand dreams for the United States. "Oh, Lord! if only the people who are ignorant about our Navy could see those great warships in all their majesty and beauty, and could realize how [well fitted they are] to uphold the honor of America!" (see New Technology, "The Battleship," p. 610).

The incoming Cleveland administration was less spread-eagled, and by canceling Harrison's scheme for annexing Hawaii, established its antiexpansionist credentials. But after hesitating briefly Cleveland picked up the naval program of his Republican predecessor, pressing Congress just as forcefully for more battleships (five were authorized) and making the same basic argument. The nation's commercial vitality—"free access to all markets," in the words of Cleveland's second secretary of state, Richard Olney—depended on its naval power.

While rejecting the territorial aspects of Mahan's thinking, Cleveland absorbed the underlying strategic arguments about where America's vital interests lay. This explains the remarkable crisis that suddenly blew up in 1895 over Venezuela.

The Venezuela Crisis. For years a border dispute had simmered between Venezuela and British Guiana. Now the United States demanded that it be resolved. The European powers were carving up Africa and Asia. How could the United States be sure that Europe did not have similar designs on Latin America? Secretary of State Olney made that point in a bristling note to London on July 25, 1895, insisting that Britain accept arbitration or face the consequences. Invoking the Monroe Doctrine, Olney warned that the United States would brook no challenge to its vital interests in the Caribbean. These vital interests were America's, not Venezuela's; Venezuela was not consulted during the entire dispute.

Despite its suddenness the pugnacious stand of the Cleveland administration was no aberration but a logical step in the new American foreign policy. Once the British realized that Cleveland meant business, they backed off and agreed to arbitration of the boundary dispute. Afterward, Olney remarked with satisfaction that, as a great industrial nation, the United States needed "to accept [a] commanding position" and take its place "among the Powers of the earth." Other countries would have to accommodate America's need for access to "more markets and larger markets for the consumption and products of the industry and inventive genius of the American people."

The Ideology of Expansionism

As policymakers hammered out a new foreign policy, a sustaining ideology took shape. One source of expansionist dogma was the Social Darwinist theory that dominated the political thought of this era (see Chapter 18). If, as Charles Darwin had shown, animals and plants evolved through the survival of the fittest, so did nations. "Nothing under the sun is stationary," warned the American social theorist Brooks Adams in *The Law of Civilization and Decay* (1895). "Not to advance is to recede." By this criterion the United States had no choice; if it wanted to survive, it had to expand.

Linked to Social Darwinism was a spreading belief in the inherent superiority of the Anglo-Saxon "race." In the late nineteenth century, Great Britain basked in the glory of its representative institutions, industrial prosperity, and far-flung empire—all ascribed to the supposed racial superiority of its people and, by extension, of their American cousins as well. On both sides of the Atlantic, **Anglo-Saxonism** was in vogue. Thus did John Fiske, an American philosopher and historian, lecture the nation on its future responsibilities: "The work

which the English race began when it colonized North America is destined to go on until every land on the earth's surface that is not already the seat of an old civilization shall become English in its language, in its religion, in its political habits, and to a predominant extent in the blood of its people."

Fiske titled his lecture "Manifest Destiny." A half century earlier this term had expressed the sense of national mission—America's "manifest destiny"—to sweep aside the Native American peoples and occupy the continent. In his widely read book *The Winning of the West* (1896), Theodore Roosevelt drew a parallel between the expansionism of his own time and the suppression of the Indians. To Roosevelt, what happened to "backward peoples" mattered little because their conquest was "for the benefit of civilization and in the interests of mankind." More than historical parallels, however, linked the Manifest Destiny of past and present.

In 1890 the U.S. Census reported the end of the westward movement on the North American continent: there was no longer a frontier beyond which land remained to be conquered. The psychological impact of that news on Americans was profound, spawning among other things a new historical interpretation that stressed the importance of the frontier in shaping the nation's character. In a landmark essay setting out this thesis— "The Significance of the Frontier in American History" (1893)—the young historian Frederick Jackson Turner suggested a link between the closing of the frontier and overseas expansion. "He would be a rash prophet who should assert that the expansive character of American life has now entirely ceased," Turner wrote. "Movement has been its dominant fact, and, unless this training has no effect upon a people, the American energy will continually demand a wider field for its exercise." As Turner predicted, Manifest Destiny did turn outward.

Thus a strong current of ideas, deeply rooted in American experience and traditions, justified the new diplomacy of expansionism. The United States was eager to step onto the world stage. All it needed was the right occasion.

An American Empire

Ever since Spain had lost its South American empire in the early nineteenth century, still-subjugated Cubans yearned to join their mainland brothers and sisters in freedom. In February 1895, inspired by the poet José Martí, Cuban patriots rebelled against Spain. Although Martí died in an early skirmish and no mass uprising occurred, the rebels built up substantial fighting forces and launched a guerrilla war. A standoff developed; the Spaniards controlled the towns, the insurgents much of the countryside. In early 1896 the newly appointed Spanish commander, Valeriano Weyler, adopted a harsh

The Battle of San Juan Hill
On July 1, 1898, the key battle for Cuba took place on heights overlooking Santiago. African American troops bore the brunt of the fighting. Although generally overlooked, the black role in the San Juan battle is done justice in this contemporary lithograph, without the demeaning stereotypes by which blacks were normally depicted in an age of intensifying racism. Even so, the racial hierarchy is maintained. The blacks are the foot soldiers; their officers are white. Library of Congress.

to the United States. American forces occupied Manila pending a peace treaty.

The Imperial Experiment

The big question was the Philippines, an archipelago of over 7,000 islands populated—as William R. Day, McKinley's secretary of state, put it in the racist language of that era—by "eight or nine millions of absolutely ignorant and many degraded people." Not even avid American expansionists had advocated colonial rule over subject peoples—that was European-style imperialism, not the strategic bases that Mahan and his followers had in mind. Mahan and Lodge initially advocated keeping only Manila. It gradually became clear, however, that Manila was not defensible without the whole of Luzon, the large island on which the city was located.

Taking the Philippines. McKinley and his advisors surveyed the options. One possibility was to return most

of the islands to Spain, but the reputed evils of Spanish rule made that a "cowardly and dishonorable" solution. Another possibility was to partition the Philippines with one or more of the Great Powers. But as McKinley observed, to turn over valuable territory to "our commercial rivals in the Orient—that would have been bad business and discreditable."

Most plausible was the option of Philippine independence. As in Cuba, Spanish rule had already stirred up a rebellion, led by the fiery patriot Emilio Aguinaldo. An arrangement might have been possible like the one being negotiated with the Cubans over Guantanamo Bay: the lease of a naval base to the Americans as the price of freedom. But after some hesitation McKinley was persuaded that "we could not leave [the Filipinos] to themselves—they were unfit for self-rule—and they would soon have anarchy and misrule over there worse than Spain's was."

As for the Spaniards, they had little choice against what they considered "the immoderate demands of a

George W. Prioleau

Black Soldiers in a White Man's War

The chaplain of the Ninth Cavalry regiment expresses his bitterness toward the racism experienced by black troopers in the South on their way to battle in Cuba.

Hon. H. C. Smith
Editor, *Gazette*

Dear Sir:

The Ninth Cavalry left Chickamauga on the 30th of April for Tampa, Fla. We arrived here (nine miles from Tampa) on May 3. From this port the army will sail for Cuba. We have in this camp here and at Tampa between 7,000 and 8,000 soldiers, artillery, one regiment of cavalry (the famous fighting Ninth) and the Twenty-fourth and Twenty-fifth infantries. The Ninth Cavalry's bravery and their skillfulness with weapons of war . . . is well known by all who have read the history of the last Indian war. . . .

Yesterday, May 12, the Ninth was ordered to be ready to embark at a moment's notice for Cuba. . . .These men are anxious to go. The country will then hear and know of the bravery of these sable sons of Ham.

The American Negro is always ready and willing to take up arms, to fight and to lay down his life in defense of his country's flag and honor. All the way from northwest Nebraska this regiment was greeted with cheers and hurrahs. At places where we stopped the people assembled by the thousands. While the Ninth Cavalry band would play some national air the people would raise their hats, men, women and children would wave their handkerchiefs, and the heavens would resound with their hearty cheers. The white hand shaking the black hand. The hearty "goodbyes," "God bless you," and other expressions aroused the patriotism of our boys. . . . These

demonstrations, so enthusiastically given, greeted us all the way until we reached Nashville. At this point we arrived about 12:30 A.M. There were about 6,000 colored people there to greet us (very few white people) but not a man was allowed by the railroad officials to approach the cars. From there until we reached Chattanooga there was not a cheer given us, the people living in gross ignorance, rags and dirt. Both white and colored seemed amazed; they looked at us in wonder. Don't think they have intelligence enough to know that Andrew Jackson is dead. . . .

The prejudice against the Negro soldier and the Negro was great, but it was of heavenly origin to what it is in this part of Florida, and I suppose that what is true here is true in other parts of the state. Here, the Negro is not allowed to purchase over the same counter in some stores that the white man purchases over. The southerners have made their laws and the Negroes know and obey them. They never stop to ask a white man a question. He (Negro) never thinks of disobeying. You talk about freedom, liberty, etc. Why sir, the Negro of this country is a freeman and yet a slave. Talk about fighting and freeing poor Cuba and of Spain's brutality; of Cuba's murdered thousands, and starving reconcentradoes. Is America any better than Spain? Has she not subjects in her very midst who are murdered daily without a trial of judge or jury? Has she not subjects in her own borders whose children are half-fed and half-clothed, because their father's skin is black. . . . Yet the Negro is loyal to his country's flag. . . .

The four Negro regiments are going to help free Cuba, and they will return to their homes, some then mustered out and begin again to fight the battle of American prejudice. . . .

Yours truly,
Geo. W. Prioleau
Chaplain, Ninth Cavalry

Source: Cleveland Gazette (May 13, 1898), reprinted in Willard B. Gatewood, *"Smoked Yankees" and the Struggle for Empire, 1898–1902* (Urbana: University of Illinois Press, 1971), 27–29.

conquerer." In the Treaty of Paris they ceded the Philippines to the United States for a payment of $20 million. The treaty encountered harder going at home and was ratified by the Senate (requiring a two-thirds majority) on February 6, 1899, with only a single vote to spare.

The Anti-Imperialists. The administration's narrow margin signaled the revival of an antiexpansionist tradition that had been briefly silenced by the passions of a nation at war. In the Senate opponents of the treaty invoked the country's republican principles. Under the

Emilio Aguinaldo

At the start of the war with Spain, U.S. military leaders brought the Filipino patriot Emilio Aguinaldo back from Singapore because they thought he would stir up a popular uprising that would help defeat the Spaniards. Aguinaldo came because he thought the Americans favored an independent Philippines. These differing intentions—it has remained a matter of dispute what assurances Aguinaldo received—were the root cause of the Filipino insurrection that proved far costlier in American and Filipino lives than the war with Spain that preceded it.
Corbis-Bettmann.

Constitution, argued the conservative Republican George F. Hoar, "no power is given to the Federal Government to acquire territory to be held and governed permanently as colonies" or "to conquer alien people and hold them in subjugation." The alternative—making 8 million Filipinos American citizens—was equally unpalatable to the anti-imperialists, who were no more champions of "these savage people" than were the expansionists who denigrated the self-governing capacity of the Filipinos.

Leading citizens enlisted in the anti-imperialist cause, including the steel king Andrew Carnegie, who offered a check for $20 million to purchase the independence of the Philippines; the labor leader Samuel Gompers, who feared the competition of cheap Filipino labor; and Jane Addams, who believed that women

should stand for peace. The key group, however, was a social elite of old-line Mugwump reformers such as Carl Schurz, Charles Eliot Norton, and Charles Francis Adams. In November 1898 a Boston group formed the first of the Anti-Imperialist Leagues that began to spring up around the country.

Although skillful at publicizing their cause, the anti-imperialists never became a popular movement. They shared little but their anti-imperialism and, within the Mugwump core, lacked the common touch. Nor was anti-imperialism easily translated into a viable political cause because the Democrats, once the treaty had been adopted, waffled on the issue. Although an outspoken anti-imperialist, William Jennings Bryan, the Democratic standard-bearer, confounded his friends by favoring ratification of the treaty and afterward hesitated to stake his party's future on a crusade against a national policy he privately believed to be irreversible. Still, if it was an accomplished fact, Philippine annexation lost the moral high ground because of the grim events that began to unfold in the Philippines.

War in the Philippines. On February 4, 1899, two days before the Senate ratified the treaty, fighting broke out between American and Filipino patrols on the edge of Manila. Confronted by American annexation, Aguinaldo asserted his nation's independence and turned his guns on the occupying American forces.

The ensuing conflict far exceeded in ferocity the war just concluded with Spain. Fighting tenacious guerrillas, the U.S. Army resorted to the reconcentration tactic the Spaniards had employed in Cuba, moving people into towns, carrying out indiscriminate attacks beyond the perimeters, and burning crops and villages (see American Voices, "Daniel J. Evans and Seiward J. Norton: Fighting the Filipinos," p. 621). Atrocities became commonplace on both sides. In three years of warfare, 4,200 Americans and many thousands of Filipinos died. The fighting ended in 1902, and William Howard Taft, who had been appointed governor-general, set up a civilian administration. He intended to make the Philippines a model of American road-building and sanitary engineering.

Uneasy Aftermath. McKinley's convincing victory over William Jennings Bryan in the 1900 election, though by no means a referendum on American expansionism, suggested popular satisfaction with America's overseas adventure. Yet a strong undercurrent of misgivings was evident. Americans had not anticipated the brutal methods needed to subdue the Filipino guerrillas. "We are destroying these islanders by the thousands, their villages and cities," protested the philosopher William James. "No life shall you have, we say, except as a gift from our philanthropy after your unconditional surrender to our will. . . . Could there be any more damning

Daniel J. Evans and Seiward J. Norton

Fighting the Filipinos

When Arthur MacArthur, the commanding general of U.S. forces in the Philippines, appeared in 1902 before a Senate committee investigating the conduct of the war, he boasted of "planting the best traditions, the best characteristics of Americanism . . . deep down in that fertile soil." Two enlisted men offered the Senate committee a different picture of the implanting of American ideals in Filipino soil.

Daniel J. Evans, Twelfth Infantry

Q: The committee would like to hear . . . whether you were the witness to any cruelties inflicted upon the natives of the Philippine Islands; and if so, under what circumstances.—A. The case I had reference to was where they gave the water cure to a native in the Ilicano Province at Ilocos Norte . . . about the month of August 1900. There were two native scouts with the American forces. They went out and brought in a couple of insurgents. . . . They tried to get from this insurgent . . . where the rest of the insurgents were at that time. . . . The first thing one of the Americans—I mean one of the scouts for the Americans—grabbed one of the men by the head and jerked his head back, and then they took a tomato can and poured water down his throat until he could hold no more. . . . Then they forced a gag into his mouth; they stood him up . . . against a post and fastened him so that he could not move. Then one man, an American soldier, who was over six feet tall, and who was very strong, too, struck this native in the pit of the stomach as hard as he could. . . . They kept that operation up for quite a time, and finally I thought the fellow was about to die, but I don't believe he was as bad as that, because finally he told them he would tell, and from that on he was taken away, and I saw no more of him.

Seiward J. Norton, Eighteenth Infantry

Q: Did you witness the burning of any towns by the United States soldiers over there?—A. Oh, yes.

Q: Just state what towns you saw burned.—A. Well, we were out on an expedition this time; we started one morning at three o'clock and rode around the country to the north of Jaro to San Miguel, and came back down this road. It was not the town of San Miguel, but the houses built along the road side by side—barrios—and we burned that old string of houses there, it is my impression, to San Miguel. . . . Brown was acting corporal in the scouts and was ordered to go out with his squad and burn houses there, and he obeyed the order. . . .

Q: What other barrios and towns were burned besides those you mentioned, within your knowledge?—A. We burned a great many barrios which I did not know the names of. We burned a good deal of the country as were fired upon. It was the practice, in fact, if a column was marching along and was fired upon to burn the buildings in that neighborhood. That impressed the natives with the fact that they could not fire upon us with impunity, although they did not often do great damage. . . .

Q: Were the people in the houses warned to get out and then their houses were burned?—A. Oh, yes.

Q: You allowed the inmates to get out and then their houses were burned?—A. Yes, sir.

Q: You have stated that with the exception of isolated cases the treatment of Filipinos by the American soldiers was humane?—A. Yes, sir; very much so.

Q: And considerate?—A. So humane and considerate it was deemed a weakness on the part of the natives.

Source: Henry F. Graff, ed., *American Imperialism and the Philippine Insurrection* (Boston: Little, Brown, 1969), 80–81, 132–34.

indictment of that whole bloated ideal termed 'modern civilization'?"

There were, moreover, disturbing constitutional issues to be resolved. Did the Constitution extend to the acquired territories? Did their inhabitants automatically become U.S. citizens? In 1901 the Supreme Court ruled negatively on both questions; these were matters for Congress to decide. A special commission appointed by McKinley recommended independence for the islands after an indefinite period of U.S. rule, during which the Filipinos would be prepared for self-government. In 1916 the Jones Act formally committed the United States to granting Philippine independence but set no date.

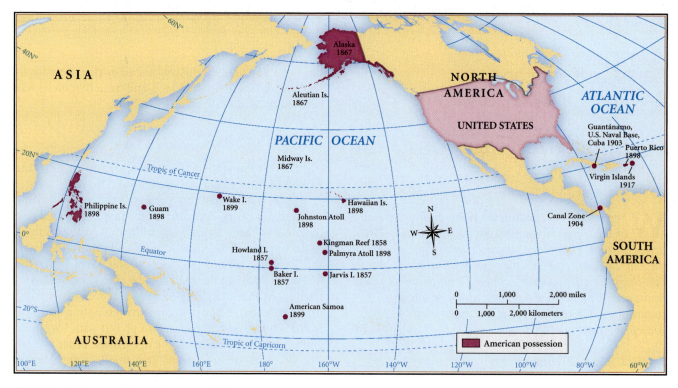

MAP 21.2 The American Empire, 1917

In 1890 Alfred T. Mahan wrote that the United States should regard the oceans as "a great highway" across which America would carry on world trade. That was precisely what resulted from the empire the United States acquired after the Spanish-American War. The Caribbean possessions, the strategically located Pacific islands, and, in 1903, the Panama Canal Zone gave the United States commercial and naval access to a wider world.

The brutal war in the Philippines rubbed off some of the moralizing gloss but left undeflected America's global aspirations. In a few years the United States had acquired the makings of an overseas empire: Hawaii, Puerto Rico, Guam, the Philippines, and finally, in 1900, several of the Samoan islands that had been jointly administered with Germany and Britain (Map 21.2). The United States, remarked the legal scholar John Bassett Moore in 1899, had moved "from a position of comparative freedom from entanglements into a position of what is commonly called a world power."

Onto the World Stage

In Europe the flexing of America's muscles against Spain caused a certain amount of consternation. At the instigation of Kaiser Wilhelm II of Germany, the major powers had tried before war broke out to intercede on Spain's behalf—but tentatively, because no one was looking for trouble with the Americans. President McKinley had listened politely to their envoys and had then proceeded with his war.

The decisive outcome confirmed what the Europeans already suspected. After Dewey's naval victory, the semiofficial French paper *Le Temps* observed that "what passes before our eyes is the appearance of a new power of the first order." And the *London Times* concluded: "This war must . . . effect a profound change in the whole attitude and policy of the United States. In the future America will play a part in the general affairs of the world such as she has never played before" (see Voices from Abroad, "Jean Hess, Émile Zola, and Ruben Dario: American Goliath," p. 624).

A Power among Powers

The politician most ardently agreeing with the *London Times*'s vision of America's future was the man who, with the assassination of William McKinley, became president on September 14, 1901. Unlike his predecessors in the White House, Theodore Roosevelt was an avid student of world affairs, widely traveled and acquainted with many European leaders. He had no doubt about America's role in the world.

It was important, first of all, to uphold the country's honor in the community of nations. "I am not

VOLUME XXXI.   NEW YORK, JUNE 16, 1898.   NUMBER 810.

Entered at the New York Post Office as Second-Class Mail Matter.
Copyright, 1898, by Life Publishing Company.

HURRAH FOR IMPERIALISM!

Hurrah for Imperialism!

Amid the patriotic frenzy over Dewey's naval victory, cooler heads wondered whether the United States knew what it was getting into with all the talk about creating an American empire. Here, Life *magazine, often a skeptical commentator on American public life, pictures a blindfolded Uncle Sam stepping off a cliff.*
Life, *1898, Newbury Library.*

For more help analyzing this image, see the ONLINE STUDY GUIDE at bedfordstmartins.com/henretta.

farsighted about the likelihood—in this he was truly exceptional among Americans—of a catastrophic world war. He believed in American responsibility for helping to maintain the balance of power.

Anglo-American Friendship. After the Spanish-American War, the European powers had been uncertain about how to deal with the victor. Germany toyed briefly with the notion of an American alliance, but only Great Britain had a clear view of what it wanted from the United States. In the late nineteenth century, Britain's position in Europe was steadily worsening in the face of a rising challenge from Germany and soured relations with France and Russia over clashing imperial ambitions in North Africa and across Asia.

In its growing isolation Britain turned to the United States. This explains why Britain bowed to American demands in the Venezuela dispute of 1895. From that time onward, after a century of cool relations (or worse) with its former colonies in North America, Britain strove for *rapprochement* (literally, a "coming together") with the United States. In the Hay-Pauncefote Agreement (1901), Britain gave up its treaty rights to participate in any Central American canal project, clearing the way for a canal under exclusive U.S. control. And two years later the last of the vexing U.S.–Canadian border disputes—this one involving British Columbia and Alaska—was settled, again to American satisfaction.

No formal alliance was forthcoming, but Anglo-American friendship had been placed on such a firm basis that after 1901 the British admiralty designed its war plans on the assumption that America was "a kindred state with whom we shall never have a parricidal war." Roosevelt heartily agreed: "England and the United States, beyond any other two powers, should be friendly." In his unflagging efforts to maintain a global balance of power, the cornerstone of Roosevelt's policy was the British relationship.

The Big Stick. Among nations, however, what counted was strength, not merely goodwill. Roosevelt wanted "to make all foreign powers understand that when we have adopted a line of policy we have adopted it definitely, and with the intention of backing it up with deeds as well as words." As Roosevelt famously said: "Speak softly and carry a big stick." By a "big stick" he meant above all naval power.

The battleship program went on apace under Roosevelt. By 1904 the U.S. Navy stood fifth in the world; by 1907 it was third. At the top of Roosevelt's agenda, however, was a canal across Central America. The Spanish-American War had graphically demonstrated the strategic need: the entire country had waited anxiously while the battleship *Oregon* steamed at full speed from the Pacific around the tip of South America to join the final action against the Spanish fleet in Cuba.

hostile to any European power in the abstract," Roosevelt once wrote. "I am simply American first and last, and therefore hostile to any power which wrongs us." Nor should the country shrink from righteous battle. "All the great masterful races have been fighting races," Roosevelt declared. But when he spoke of war, Roosevelt had in mind actions by the "civilized" nations against "backward peoples." Roosevelt felt "it incumbent on all the civilized and orderly powers to insist on the proper policing of the world." That was why Roosevelt sympathized with European imperialism and how he justified American dominance in the Caribbean.

As for the "civilized and orderly" policemen of the world, the worst thing that could happen was for them to fall to fighting among themselves. Roosevelt had an acute sense of the fragility of world peace, and he was

Jean Hess, Émile Zola, and Ruben Dario

American Goliath

America's emergence as an imperial power provoked much anxious comment abroad. Not surprisingly, this commentary tended to mirror the concerns of the commentators. What was unexpected, as the following excerpts suggest, was that they took seriously America's high estimate of itself. If its actions violated professed ideals, foreign critics were not averse to calling the United States to account.

Jean Hess, a Frenchman well traveled in East Asia, questioned American motives for intervening in the Philippines (1899).

Nowhere, in my opinion, better than in the Philippines, has it been shown that modern wars are simply "deals." The American intervention in the struggle engaged in by the revolutionary Tagals against the Spanish government has turned out to be nothing but a speculation of "business men," and not the generous effort of a people paying a debt in procuring for others the liberty that it concedes belongs to all. . . . Back of all these battles, this devastation and mourning, in spite of the newly-born Yankee imperialism, there was only, there is only, what the people of the Bourse [stock market] call a deal.

Émile Zola, the great French novelist, feared that America's military adventurism was dealing a blow to the cause of world peace (1900).

I know that, for belief in peace and future disarmament, the time is scarcely auspicious, as we are now beholding an alarming recrudescence of militarism. Nations which till now seem to have held aloof from the contagion, to have escaped this madness so prevalent in Europe, now appear to be attacked. Thus, since the Spanish war, the United States seems to have become a victim of the war fever. . . . I can see in that great nation a dangerous inclination toward war. I can detect the generation of vague ideas of future conquest. Until the present time that country wisely occupied itself with its domestic affairs and let Europe severely alone, but now it is donning plumes and epaulets, and will be dreaming of possible campaigns and be carried away with the idea of military glory—notions so perilous as to have been responsible for the downfall of nations.

In 1905, a year after the promulgation of the Roosevelt Corollary, the acclaimed Nicaraguan poet Ruben Dario issued an impassioned challenge from a small Central American country under the shadow of the Goliath. (Nicaragua was in fact occupied by U.S. Marines four years later.) Dario addressed his poem "To Roosevelt."

You are primitive and modern, simple and
        complex;
you are one part George Washington and one
        part Nimrod.
You are the United States,
future invader of our naive America
with its Indian blood, an America
that still prays to Christ and still speaks
        Spanish.
. . . .
The United States is grand and powerful.
. . . A wealthy country,
joining the cult of Mammon to the cult of
        Hercules;
while Liberty, lighting the path
to easy conflict, raises her torch in New York.

But our own America . . .
has lived, since the earliest moments of its life,
in light, in fire, in fragrance, and in love—
the America of Moctezuma and Atahuelpa. . . .
O men with Saxon eyes and barbarous souls,
our America lives. And dreams. And loves.
And it is the daughter of the Sun. Be Careful.
Long live Spanish America!

Sources: Philip S. Foner and Robert C. Winchester, eds., *The Anti-Imperialist Reader: A Documentary History of Anti-Imperialism in the United States,* 2 vols. (New York: Holmes and Meier Publishers, 1984), 1: 98–99, 417–18; Thomas G. Paterson and Dennis Merrill, eds., *Major Problems in American Foreign Relations,* 2 vols. (Lexington, MA: D. C. Heath Co., 1995), 1: 508–9; *Selected Poems of Ruben Dario,* tr. Lysander Kemp (Austin: University of Texas Press, 1965).

The Panama Canal. Having secured Britain's surrender of its joint canal rights in 1901, Roosevelt proceeded to the more troublesome task of leasing from Colombia the needed strip of land across Panama, a Colombian province. Furious when the Colombian legislature voted down the proposed treaty, Roosevelt contemplated outright seizure of Panama but settled on a more devious solution. With an independence movement brewing in Panama, the United States lent covert assistance that ensured the success of a bloodless revolution against Colombia. On November 7, 1901, the United States recognized Panama and received two weeks later a perpetually renewable lease on a canal zone. Roosevelt never regretted the victimization of Colombia, although the United States, as a kind of conscience money, paid Colombia $25 million in 1922.

Building the canal, one of the heroic engineering feats of the century, involved a swamp-clearing project to rid the area of malaria and yellow fever, the construction of a series of great locks, and the excavation of 240 million cubic yards of earth. It took the U.S. Army Corps of Engineers and the digging by thousands of hired laborers eight years to finish the huge project. When the Panama Canal opened in 1914, it gave the United States a commanding commercial and strategic position in the Western Hemisphere (Map 21.3).

Policeman of the Caribbean. Next came the task of making the Caribbean basin secure. The countries there, said Secretary of State Elihu Root, had been placed "in the front yard of the United States" by the Panama Canal. Therefore, as Roosevelt put it, they had to "behave themselves."

In the case of Cuba, good behavior was readily managed by the settlement following the Spanish-American War. Before withdrawing in 1902 the United States reorganized Cuban public finances and concluded a swamp-clearing program that eliminated yellow fever, a disease that had ravaged Cuba for many years. As a condition for gaining independence, Cuba

The Panama Canal: Excavating the Culebra Cut
The Canal Zone was acquired through devious means from which Americans could take little pride (and which led in 1978 to the Senate's decision to restore the property to Panama). But the building of the Panama Canal itself was a triumph of American ingenuity and drive. Dr. William C. Gorgas cleaned out the malarial mosquitoes that had earlier stymied the French. Under Colonel George W. Goethals, the U.S. Army overcame formidable obstacles in a mighty feat of engineering. This photograph shows the massive effort under way in December 1904 to excavate the Culebra Cut so that oceangoing ships would be able to pass through. Corbis-Bettmann.

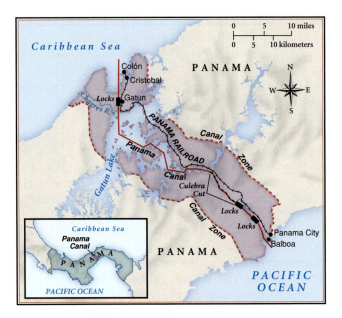

MAP 21.3 The Panama Canal: The Design

The forty-mile-long canal route zigzags to take maximum advantage of the regional topography, including an existing internal waterway via Gatun Lake. The lake is situated 85 feet above sea level, necessitating the use of locks to raise and lower ships as they approach the lake and the section known as the Culebra Cut, pictured on the previous page.

accepted a proviso in its constitution called the Platt Amendment, which gave the United States the right to intervene if Cuban independence was threatened or if internal order broke down. Cuba also granted the

United States a lease on Guantanamo Bay (which is still in effect), where the U.S. Navy built a large base.

Claiming that instability in the Caribbean invited the intervention of European powers, Roosevelt announced in 1904 that the United States would act as "policeman" of the region, stepping in, "however reluctantly, in flagrant cases . . . of wrong-doing or impotence" (Map 21.4). This policy, which became known as the Roosevelt Corollary to the Monroe Doctrine, transformed that doctrine's broad principle against European interference in Latin America into an unrestricted American right to regulate Caribbean affairs. The **Roosevelt Corollary** was not a treaty with other states; it was a unilateral declaration sanctioned only by American power and national interest.

Citing the Roosevelt Corollary, the United States intervened regularly in the internal affairs of Caribbean states. In 1905 American personnel took over the customs and debt management of the Dominican Republic, and, similarly, Nicaragua in 1911 and Haiti in 1916. When domestic order broke down, the U.S. Marines occupied Cuba in 1906, Nicaragua in 1909, and Haiti and the Dominican Republic in later years.

The Open Door in Asia

Commercial interest dominated American policy in East Asia, especially the prospect of the huge China market. By the late 1890s Japan, Russia, Germany, France, and Britain had all carved out spheres of influence in China (Map 21.5). Fearful of being frozen out, U.S. Secretary of

MAP 21.4 Policeman of the Caribbean

After the Spanish-American War, the United States vigorously asserted its interest in the affairs of its neighbors to the south. As the record of interventions shows, the United States truly became the "policeman" of the Caribbean.

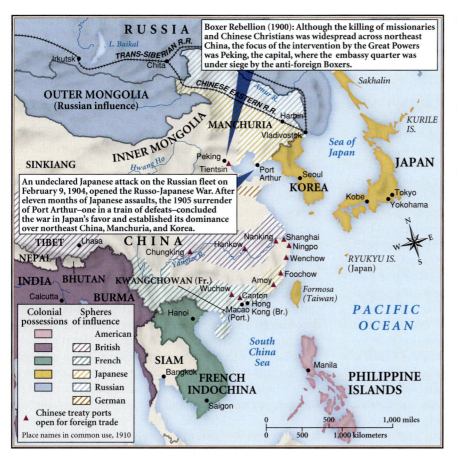

Boxer Rebellion (1900): Although the killing of missionaries and Chinese Christians was widespread across northeast China, the focus of the intervention by the Great Powers was Peking, the capital, where the embassy quarter was under siege by the anti-foreign Boxers.

An undeclared Japanese attack on the Russian fleet on February 9, 1904, opened the Russo-Japanese War. After eleven months of Japanese assaults, the 1905 surrender of Port Arthur—one in a train of defeats—concluded the war in Japan's favor and established its dominance over northeast China, Manchuria, and Korea.

Colonial possessions / Spheres of influence

American
British
French
Japanese
Russian
German
▲ Chinese treaty ports open for foreign trade

Place names in common use, 1910

MAP 21.5 The Great Powers in East Asia, 1898–1910

The pattern of foreign dominance over China was via "treaty ports," where the powers based their naval forces, and "spheres of influence" extending from the ports into the hinterland. This map reveals why the United States had a weak hand; it lacked a presence on this colonized terrain. The Boxer Rebellion, by bringing an American expeditionary force to Peking, gave the United States a chance to insert itself onto the Chinese mainland, and American diplomats made the most of the opportunity to defend its commercial interest in China.

State John Hay in 1899 sent them an **Open Door note** claiming the right of equal trade access—an open door—for all nations that wanted to do business in China. Despite its Philippine bases, the United States lacked real leverage in East Asia and elicited only noncommittal responses from the occupying powers. But Hay chose to interpret them as accepting the American open-door position.

When a secret society of Chinese nationalists, the Boxers, rebelled against the foreigners in 1900, the United States sent 5,000 troops from the Philippines and joined the multinational campaign to break the Boxers' siege of the diplomatic missions in Peking (Beijing). America took this opportunity to assert a second principle of the Open Door: that China would be preserved as a "territorial and administrative entity." As long as the legal fiction of an independent China survived, so would American claims to equal access to the China market.

The European powers had acceded to American dominance in the Caribbean. But Britain, Germany, France, and Russia were strongly entrenched in East Asia and not inclined to defer to American interests. The United States also confronted a powerful Asian nation—Japan—that had its own vital interests. Although the open-door policy was important to him, Roosevelt sensed that there were higher stakes at risk in the Pacific.

Japan had unveiled its military strength in the Sino-Japanese War of 1894–1895, which began the dismemberment of China. A decade later, provoked by Russian rivalry in Manchuria and Korea, Japan suddenly attacked the tsar's fleet at Port Arthur, Russia's leased port in China. In a series of brilliant victories, the Japanese smashed the Russian forces in Asia. Anxious to restore a balance of power, Roosevelt mediated a settlement of the Russo-Japanese War at Portsmouth, New Hampshire, in 1905. Japan emerged as the dominant power in East Asia.

Contemptuous of other Asian nations, Roosevelt admired the Japanese—"a wonderful and civilized people . . . entitled to stand in absolute equality with all the other peoples of the civilized world." He conceded that Japan had "a paramount interest in what surrounds the Yellow Sea, just as the United States has a paramount interest in what surrounds the Caribbean." But American strategic and commercial interests in the Pacific had to be accommodated. The United States approved of Japan's protectorate over Korea in 1905, and then of its declaration of full sovereignty six years later. However, a surge of anti-Asian feeling in California complicated Roosevelt's efforts. In 1906 San Francisco's school board placed all Asian students in a segregated school, infuriating Japan. The "Gentlemen's Agreement" of 1907, in which Japan agreed to restrict immigration to the United States, smoothed matters over, but periodic racist slights by Americans made for continuing tensions with the Japanese.

Roosevelt meanwhile moved to balance Japan's military power by increasing American naval strength in the Pacific. American battleships visited Japan in 1908 on a global tour that impressively displayed U.S. sea power. Late that year, near the end of his administration, Roosevelt achieved a formal accommodation with Japan. The Root-Takahira Agreement confirmed the status quo in the Pacific, as well as the principles of free oceanic commerce and equal trade opportunity in China.

William Howard Taft, however, entered the White House in 1909 convinced that the United States had been short-changed. He pressed for a larger role for American investors, especially in the railroad construction going on in China. An exponent of **dollar diplomacy**—the aggressive coupling of American political and economic interests abroad—Taft hoped that American capital would counterbalance Japanese power and pave the way for increased commercial opportunities. When the Chinese Revolution of 1911 toppled the ruling Manchu dynasty, Taft supported the victorious Chinese Nationalists, who wanted to modernize their country and liberate it from Japanese domination. The United States thus entered a long-term rivalry with Japan that would end in war thirty years later.

The United States had become embroiled in a distant struggle heavy with future liabilities but little by way of the fabulous profits that had lured Americans to Asia.

Wilson and Mexico

When Woodrow Wilson became president in 1913, he was bent on reform in American foreign policy no less than in domestic politics. Wilson did not really differ with his predecessors on the importance of America's economic interests overseas. He applauded the "tides of commerce" that would arise from the Panama Canal. But he opposed dollar diplomacy, which he believed bullied weaker countries financially and gave undue advantage to American business. It seemed to Wilson "a very perilous thing to determine the foreign policy of a nation in terms of material interest."

The United States, Wilson insisted, should conduct its foreign policy in conformity with its democratic principles. He intended to foster the "development of constitutional liberty in the world," and above all in the nation's neighbors in Latin America. In a major foreign-policy speech in 1913, Wilson promised those nations that the United States would "never again seek one additional foot of territory by conquest." He was committed to advancing "human rights, national integrity, and opportunity" in

Latin America. To do otherwise would make "ourselves untrue to our own traditions."

Mexico became the primary object of Wilson's ministrations. A cycle of revolution had begun there in 1911. The dictator Porfirio Díaz was overthrown by Francisco Madero, who spoke much as Wilson did about liberty and constitutionalism. But before Madero got very far with his reforms, he was deposed and murdered in February 1913 by one of his generals, Victoriano Huerta. Other powers recognized Huerta's provisional government but not the United States, despite a long-standing tradition of granting quick recognition to new governments. Wilson abhorred Huerta, called him a murderer, and pledged "to force him out."

By intervening in this way, Wilson insisted, "we act in the interest of Mexico alone. . . . We are seeking to counsel Mexico for its own good." Wilson meant that he intended to put the Mexican Revolution back on the constitutional path started by Madero. Wilson was not deterred by the fact that American business interests, with big investments in Mexico, favored Huerta.

The emergence of armed opposition in northern Mexico under Venustiano Carranza strengthened Wilson's hand. But Carranza's Constitutionalist movement was ardently nationalist and had no desire for American intervention in Mexican affairs. Carranza angrily rebuffed Wilson's efforts to bring about elections by means of a compromise with the Huerta regime. He also vowed to fight any intrusion of U.S. troops in his country. All he wanted from Wilson, Carranza asserted, was recognition of the Constitutionalists' belligerent status, so that they could purchase arms in the United States. In exchange for vague promises to respect property rights and "fair" foreign concessions, Carranza finally got his way in 1914. American weapons began to flow to his troops.

When it became clear that Huerta was not about to fall, the United States threw its own forces into the conflict. On the pretext of a minor insult to the U.S. Navy at Tampico, Wilson ordered the occupation of the port of Veracruz on April 21, 1914, at the cost of 19 American and 126 Mexican lives. At that point the Huerta regime began to crumble. Carranza nevertheless condemned the United States, and his forces came close to engaging the Americans. When he entered Mexico City in triumph in August 1914, Carranza had some cause to thank the Yankees. But if any sense of gratitude existed, it was overshadowed by the anti-Americanism inspired by Wilson's insensitivity to Mexican pride and revolutionary zeal.

No sooner had the Constitutionalists triumphed than Carranza was challenged by his northern general, Pancho Villa, with some encouragement by American interests in Mexico. Defeated and driven northward, Villa began to stir up trouble along the border, killing sixteen American civilians taken from a train in January 1916 and two months later raiding the town of Columbus,

In Pursuit of Pancho Villa

Pancho Villa's attack on American citizens prompted General Pershing's punitive expedition into Mexico in 1916. U.S. troops captured some of Villa's followers, but he and his main force escaped. It was an early lesson about the difficulties Great Powers have against a guerrilla foe able to melt away into a larger civilian society.
Corbis-Bettmann.

New Mexico. Wilson sent troops led by General John J. Pershing across the border after the elusive Villa. Soon Pershing's force resembled an army of occupation more than a punitive expedition. Mexican public opinion demanded that Pershing withdraw, and armed clashes with Mexican troops began. At the brink of war, the two governments backed off, and U.S. forces began to withdraw in early 1917. Soon after, with a new constitution ratified and elections completed, the Carranza government finally received official recognition from Washington.

The Gathering Storm in Europe

In the meantime Europe had begun to drift toward war. There were two main sources of tension. One was the rivalry between Germany, the new superpower of Europe, and the European states threatened by its might—above all France, which had been humiliated in the Franco-Prussian War of 1870. The second danger zone was the Balkans, where the Ottoman Empire was disintegrating and where, in the midst of explosive ethnic rivalries, Austria-Hungary and Russia were maneuvering for dominance. Out of these conflicts an alliance system had emerged, with Germany, Austria-Hungary, and Italy (the Triple Alliance) on one side and France and Russia (the Dual Alliance) on the other.

The tensions in Europe were partially released by European imperial adventures, especially by France in Africa and by Russia in Asia. These activities made France and Russia rivals of imperial Britain, effectively excluding Britain from the European alliance system. Fearful of Germany, however, Britain in 1904 resolved her differences with France, and the two countries reached a friendly understanding, or *entente*. When Britain came to a similar understanding with Russia in 1907, the basis was laid for the Triple Entente. A deadly confrontation between two great European power blocs became possible.

In these European quarrels Americans had no obvious stake nor any inclination, in the words of a cautionary Senate resolution, "to depart from the traditional American foreign policy which forbids participation . . . [in] political questions which are entirely European in scope." But on becoming president, Theodore Roosevelt took a lively interest in European affairs and was eager, as the head of a Great Power, to make a contribution to the cause of peace there. In 1905 he got his chance.

The Moroccan Crisis.   The Anglo-French entente of the previous year was based partly on an agreement over spheres of influence in North Africa: the Sudan went to Britain, Morocco to France. Then Germany suddenly challenged France over Morocco—a disastrous move, conflicting with Germany's self-interest in keeping France's attention diverted from Europe. The German ruler, Kaiser Wilhelm, turned to Roosevelt for help. Roosevelt arranged an international conference, which was held in January 1906 at Algeciras, Spain. With U.S. diplomats playing a key role, the crisis was defused. Germany got a few token concessions, but France's dominance over Morocco was sustained.

Algeciras marked an ominous turning point—the first time the power blocs that would become locked in battle in 1914 squared off against one another. But in 1906 the outcome of the conference seemed a diplomatic triumph. Roosevelt's secretary of state, Elihu Root, boasted of America's success in "preserv[ing] world peace because of the power of our detachment."

Root's words prefigured how the United States would define its role among the Great Powers: it would be the apostle of peace, distinguished by its "detachment," by its lack of selfish interest in European affairs. Opposing this internationalist impulse, however, was America's traditional isolationism.

The Peace Movement.   Americans had applauded the international peace movement launched by the Hague Peace Conference of 1899. The Permanent Court of Arbitration that resulted offered new hope for the peaceful settlement of international disputes. Both the Roosevelt and the Taft administrations negotiated arbitration treaties with other countries, pledging to submit their disputes to the Hague Court, only to have the treaties emasculated by a Senate unwilling to permit any erosion of the nation's sovereignty. Nor was there any sequel to Roosevelt's initiative at Algeciras. It was coolly received in the Senate and by the nation's press.

When Wilson became president, he chose William Jennings Bryan to be secretary of state. An apostle of world peace, Bryan devoted himself to negotiating a series of "cooling off" treaties with other countries—so called because the parties agreed to wait for one year while disputed issues were submitted to a conciliation process. Although admirable, these bilateral agreements had no bearing on the explosive power politics of Europe. As tensions there reached the breaking point in 1914, the United States remained effectively on the sidelines.

Yet at Algeciras Roosevelt had correctly anticipated what the future would demand of America. So did the French journalist Andre Tardieu, who remarked in 1908:

> *The United States is . . . a world power. . . . Its power creates for it . . . a duty—to pronounce upon all those questions that hitherto have been arranged by agreement only among European powers. . . . The United States intervenes thus in the affairs of the universe. . . . It is seated at the table where the great game is played, and it cannot leave it.*

FOR FURTHER EXPLORATION

▶ For definitions of key terms boldfaced in this chapter, see the glossary at the end of the book.

▶ To assess your mastery of the material covered in this chapter, see the Online Study Guide at **bedfordstmartins.com/henretta**.

▶ For suggested references, including Web sites, see page SR-23 at the end of the book.

▶ For map resources and primary documents, see **bedfordstmartins.com/henretta**.

S U M M A R Y

In 1877 the United States was, by any economic or demographic measure, already a great power. But America was inward looking. The lax conduct of its foreign policy and neglect of its naval power reflected the absence of significant overseas concerns. America's rapid economic development, however, began to force the country to look outward, in particular because of the felt need for outlets for its surplus products. By the early 1890s a new strategic outlook had taken hold, shaped mainly by the writings of Alfred T. Mahan. Mahan called for a battleship navy, an interoceanic canal, and overseas bases. Supporting this new expansionism were arguments drawn from Social Darwinism, Anglo-Saxon racism, and America's earlier tradition of Manifest Destiny.

The Spanish-American War created an opportunity for acting on these imperialist impulses. Swift victory enabled the United States to seize from Spain the key possessions it wanted, while wartime patriotism briefly silenced America's traditional anti-imperialism. In taking the Philippines, however, the United States overstepped the bounds of the colonialism palatable to the country. The result was a resurgence of anti-imperialist sentiment that was intensified by the sight of native patriots fighting Americans in the Philippines. Even so, the McKinley administration achieved the strategic goals it had set, and the United States entered the twentieth century poised to fulfill its destiny as a Great Power.

In Europe the immediate consequences were few. Only in its budding alliance with Britain and Roosevelt's involvement in the Moroccan crisis did the United States depart from its traditional policy of avoiding European entanglements. But in the Caribbean and Asia, where it had strong interests, the United States moved more decisively, building the Panama Canal, asserting its dominance over the nearby states, and pressing for an open door in China. In Japan the United States encountered a formidable opponent with interests not easily reconciled with America's. When Woodrow Wilson became president, he tried to conduct America's foreign policy more in conformity with the nation's political ideals, only to discover the limits of that approach when he intervened in the Mexican Revolution. As world war engulfed Europe in 1914, Wilson's idealism was about to receive a much harder test.

T I M E L I N E

1875 Treaty brings Hawaii within U.S. orbit

1876 United States achieves favorable balance of trade

1881 Secretary of State James G. Blaine inaugurates Pan-Americanism

1889 Conflict with Germany in Samoa

1890 Alfred Thayer Mahan's *The Influence of Seapower upon History*

1893 Annexation of Hawaii fails

Frederick Jackson Turner's "The Significance of the Frontier in American History"

1894 Sino-Japanese War begins breakup of China into spheres of influence

1895 Venezuela crisis

Cuban civil war

1898 Spanish-American War

Hawaii annexed

Anti-imperialist movement launched

1899 Treaty of Paris

Guerrilla war in the Philippines

Open-door policy in China

1901 Theodore Roosevelt becomes president; diplomacy of the "big stick"

Hay-Pauncefote Agreement

1902 United States withdraws from Cuba; Platt Amendment gives United States right of intervention

1903 United States recognizes Panama and receives grant of Canal Zone

1904 Roosevelt Corollary

1906 United States mediates Franco-German crisis over Morocco at Algeciras

1907 Gentlemen's Agreement with Japan

1908 Root-Takahira Agreement

1913 Wilson asserts new principles for American diplomacy

Intervention in the Mexican Revolution

1914 Panama Canal opens

World War I begins

PART FOUR

The Fate of the Great Plains

The founder of scientific management, Frederick W. Taylor, used to talk about "the one best way." There were many ways to organize work, said Taylor, but only one best, most efficient way (which of course only industrial engineers trained in his methods were capable of finding). More than one might think the writing of American history is infused with this kind of confident assumption: that there was "one best way" for history to unfold and that the historian's task is to explain why that way, and no other, was the one the nation had to take.

For in no period is this sense of inevitability more engrained than in the Age of Industrialism that you have just read about. Not in all its aspects, to be sure. On overseas expansion, which in some ways went contrary to the nation's self-conception, one can readily imagine paths other than to American empire. And, broadly speaking, this is true for politics generally. The abandonment of the southern blacks by the Republicans was not inevitable; nor was the failure of Populism; nor the progressive presidency of Theodore Roosevelt, who might have ended up just another obscure vice president but for McKinley's untimely death. But on the great social and economic developments—the onset of modern industrialism, the nation's urbanization, the settlement of the Great Plains—historians do indeed write as if it could not have been otherwise.

What might shake this sense of inevitability? Consider the settlement of the Great Plains. Every ten years the U.S. Census generates a new statistical portrait of American society. Always there are surprises, but none ever exceeded the discovery by the 2000 census that the Great Plains are emptying out. Sixty percent of the counties there lost population during the 1990s and huge stretches, equal in size to the original Louisiana Purchase, nearly 900,000 square miles, now count so few inhabitants as to meet the nineteenth-century census definition of frontier, with fewer than six people per square mile. There are, indeed, substantial areas even less populated than in the pre-settlement era, qualifying under the census definition as vacant, with fewer than two persons per square mile.

As the native grasses and wildlife return, the plains increasingly resemble the land it was before the settlers arrived, although their marks are still evident in abandoned farmhouses and ghost towns. The Native American popu-

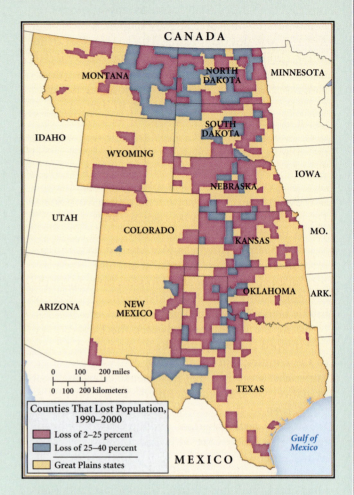

Population Losses: The American Plains, 1990–2000

The population losses shown on this map represent only the later stage in a long-term decline, especially among farmers, whose numbers in the northern plains states peaked in 1920. By mid-century, the farming population had already shrunk by a third.

Counties That Lost Population, 1990–2000

- Loss of 2–25 percent
- Loss of 25–40 percent
- Great Plains states

lation meanwhile is returning—there are as many Indians on the Great Plains today as in the 1870s—although not of course as portrayed in the nomadic life they once led. Their ties to the buffalo, however, have revived. Roughly 300,000 head now graze on the northern plains, tended by more than 30 tribes, and buffalo management is being taught at many Indian colleges. We are realizing, as the Rutgers social scientists Frank and Deborah Popper who first identified this grand reversal in 1987 have said, that settlement of the Great Plains was "the largest, longest-run agricultural and environmental miscalculation in American history."

That conclusion, insofar as it is accepted, will surely prompt a rethinking of western history. For many years the dominant interpretation was Frederick Jackson Turner's frontier thesis, which celebrated the westward movement as an ever-renewable source of American democracy and individualism. Readers of Chapter 16's bibliographical essay will know that the Turnerian interpretation has come

Abandoned Farmhouse, North Dakota, 1996

Judging by the house depicted above, this had once been a large and prosperous farm. Now the cultivated acres have gone back to wild grass, and so, eventually, will the spacious house. For the long-departed family, the glorious sunsets will only be a memory. Annie Griffiths Belt / Corbis.

under fire in recent years from "new" western historians such as Patricia Nelson Limerick and Richard White, who have emphasized the rapacious and environmentally destructive underside of the westward movement. News that the Great Plains is emptying out will surely strengthen this critical assessment, but it will also expand what needs to be explained: not only why white settlement has not lasted but why it happened on the Great Plains in the first place.

Maps once called the Great Plains the "Great American Desert." This label has long been a source of mild amusement among historians, who regarded it as the error of easterners unaccustomed to the flat, unforested vistas of the Great Plains. Climatologists now tell us that there was something to the notion of a Great American Desert. A long-term drought cycle gripped the Great Plains in the early nineteenth century that in fact reduced much of it to shifting sands; eastern visitors did indeed see desert. Although that cycle ended before white settlement began, dry spells since then have produced incipient desert conditions, and another long-term drought cycle is only a matter of time, if indeed, under current conditions, it has not already arrived. So the question of a Great American Desert takes on new significance—why the truth it told was overridden and lands unsuitable for cultivation were put to the plow.

Or consider the question of why settlers undertook that ruinous task. The Turnerian view is that they acted as individuals, driven by pluck and courage to remake their lives on the frontier. To this day it remains an article of faith among westerners that they are the exemplars of American individualism and self-reliance. Nothing could be further from the truth, argue the new western historians. "More than any other region," says Richard White flatly, "the West has been historically a dependency of the federal government" (*It's Your Misfortune and None of My Own*, 1991), and this, indeed, in a nineteenth-century society otherwise remarkably free of any state presence.

Now that we know the Great Plains are emptying out—and that the ranching and farming remaining survive mostly on federal subsidies—the debunking argument opened by the new western historians is surely going to be pressed harder. The peopling of the Great Plains is increasingly going to be a history of how public subsidy, army protection, and federal land policy fostered a movement onto semiarid plains unlikely to have succeeded, or perhaps even attempted, by its individual members acting on their own.

In this textbook the westward movement, in its final phases, is linked to the industrial revolution and is likely to remain so linked in future editions. The industrial economy needed the mineral resources of the Far West, and once that region became economically important, railroads were certainly going to be built tying the Far West into the country. It does not follow, however, that railroads meant agricultural settlement of the Great Plains.

In the twenty-first century superhighways are still going to be crossing the Great Plains, but out the car windows travelers more and more will be seeing grasslands and buffalo. Some will be stopping on vacation to enjoy the sights as well as the casinos now undergirding many tribal economies. So it does not strain the mind to imagine a nineteenth-century counterpart—the Indian Country that was once American policy surviving in some fashion side by side with the railroads. And once we can imagine alternatives, we can no longer think of what actually happened as inevitable.

Historians know that the history they write is shaped by the times in which they live. That—as much as the uncovering of new facts—explains why history is constantly being revised. The question of inevitability we have been discussing is a central strand in this ongoing process of historical revision. Historians often speak of *contingency*. We call an event contingent if we find that prior events admit of more than one outcome. We can be sure that a sense of contingency will figure more strongly in future histories of the Age of Industrialism, including the treatment of that age in *America's History*.

SEPT 29th 1917

Leslie's
Illustrated Weekly Newspaper

Price 10 Cents
In Canada, 15 Cents

Paul Stahr

Be Patriotic
sign your country's pledge to save the food

★

CHAPTER 22

War and the American State

1914–1920

The Great War, 1914–1918
War in Europe
The Perils of Neutrality
"Over There"
The American Fighting Force

War on the Home Front
Mobilizing Industry and the
*   Economy*
Mobilizing American Workers
Wartime Reform: Woman Suffrage
*   and Prohibition*
Promoting National Unity

An Unsettled Peace, 1919–1920
The Treaty of Versailles
Racial Strife, Labor Unrest, and
*   the Red Scare*

"IT'S UP TO YOU—Protect the Nation's Honor—Enlist Now." "Turn Your Silver into Bullets at the Post Office." "Rivets Are Bayonets—Drive Them Home!" "Women! Help America's Sons Win the War: Buy U.S. Government Bonds." "Food Is Ammunition—Don't Waste It." At every turn during the eighteen months of U.S. participation in the Great War—at the movies, in schools and libraries, in shop windows and post offices, at train stations and factories—Americans encountered dramatic posters urging them to do their share. More than the colorful reminders of a bygone era they seem today, these propaganda tools were meant to unify the American people in voluntary, self-sacrificing service to the nation. They suggest not only that the federal government had increased its presence in the lives of Americans but also that in modern war victory demanded more than armies. On the home front, businessmen, workers, farmers, housewives, and even children had important roles to play.

Although the United States' participation in the conflict was of short duration, the war would have a lasting impact on the nation's domestic life as well as on its international position. The American decision to enter the conflict in 1917 confirmed one of the most important shifts of power in the twentieth century.

◀ **America and the War Effort**
Popular magazines like Leslie's Illustrated Weekly Newspaper *teamed up with the federal government to promote food conservation. This image features an idealized woman representing America and is directed at women. Eager to avoid food rationing and instead encourage voluntary sacrifice, the government mobilized 500,000 volunteers to go door to door to secure housewives' signatures on cards that pledged them to follow food conservation guidelines.*
Leslie's, *September 29, 1917 / Picture Research Consultants & Archives.*

Before the outbreak of the Great War in 1914, the world had been dominated by Europe; the postwar world was increasingly dominated by the United States as it spread its political, economic, and cultural influence across the globe. Related changes that shaped the country for the rest of the twentieth century also emerged at home. New federal bureaucracies had to be created to coordinate the efforts of business, labor, and agriculture—a process that hastened the emergence of a national administrative state. War meant new opportunities, albeit temporary, for white women and for members of ethnic minorities. It also meant new divisions among Americans and new hatreds, first of Germans and Austrians and then of "Bolshevik" Reds. When the war ended, the United States was forced to confront the deep class, racial, and ethnic divisions that had surfaced during wartime mobilization.

The Great War, 1914–1918

When war erupted in August 1914, most Americans saw no reason to involve themselves in the struggle among Europe's imperialistic powers. No vital U.S. interests were at stake. Indeed the United States had a good relationship with both sides, and its industries benefited from providing war material for the combatants. Many Americans placed their faith in what historians call *U.S. exceptionalism*—the belief that their superior democratic values and institutions made their country immune from the corruption and chaos of other nations. Horrified by the carnage and sympathetic to the suffering, Americans nevertheless expected that they would be able to follow their president's dictum "to be neutral in fact as well as in name."

War in Europe

Almost from the moment France, Russia, and Britain formed the Triple Entente in 1907 to counter the Triple Alliance of Germany, Austria-Hungary, and Italy (see Chapter 21), European leaders began to prepare for what they saw as an inevitable conflict. The spark that ignited the war came in Europe's perennial tinderbox, the Balkans, where Austria-Hungary and Russia competed for power and influence. Austria's seizure of the

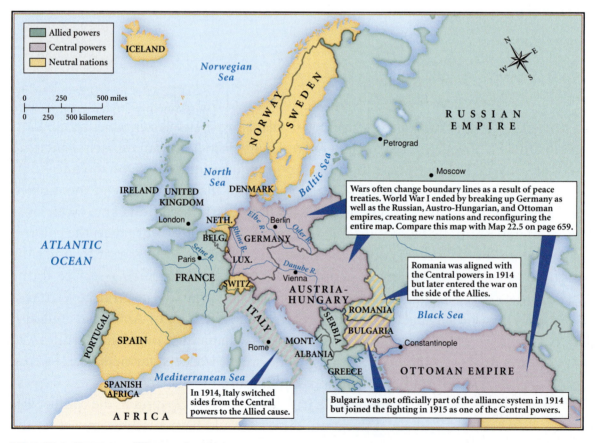

MAP 22.1 European Alliances in 1914

In early August 1914 a complex set of interlocking alliances drew the major European powers into war. At first the United States avoided the conflict. Not until April 1917 did America enter the war on the Allied side.

provinces of Bosnia and Herzegovina in 1908 had enraged Russia and its client, the independent state of Serbia. Serbian terrorists responded by recruiting Bosnians to agitate against Austrian rule. On June 28, 1914, a nineteen-year-old Bosnian student, Gavrilo Princip, assassinated Franz Ferdinand, the heir to the Austro-Hungarian throne, and his wife, the Duchess of Hohenberg, in the town of Sarajevo.

After the assassination the complex European alliance system, which had for years maintained a fragile peace, drew all the major powers into war. Austria-Hungary, blaming Serbia for the assassination, declared war on Serbia on July 28. Russia, which had a secret treaty with Serbia, mobilized its armies; Germany responded by declaring war on Russia and its ally, France, and by invading neutral Belgium. The brutality of the invasion, and Britain's commitment to Belgian neutrality, prompted Great Britain to declare war on Germany on August 4. Within a few days all the major European powers had formally entered the conflict.

The combatants were divided into two rival blocs. The Allied Powers—Great Britain, France, Japan, Russia, and, in 1915, Italy—were pitted against the Central Powers—Germany, Austria-Hungary, Turkey, and, in 1915, Bulgaria (Map 22.1). Because the alliance system encompassed competing imperial powers, the conflict spread to parts of the world far beyond Europe, including the Middle East, Africa, and China. Its worldwide scope gave it the name the Great War, or later, World War I.

The term *Great War* also suggested the terrible devastation the conflict produced. It was the first modern war in which extensive harm was done to civilian populations. New military technology, much of it from the United States, made armies more deadly than ever before. Soldiers carried long-range, high-velocity rifles that could hit a target at 1,000 yards—a vast technical improvement over the 300-yard range of the rifle-musket used in the American Civil War. Another innovation was the machine gun, whose American-born inventor, Hiram Maxim, moved to Great Britain in the

The Landscape of War
World War I devastated the countryside: this was the battleground at Ypres in western Belgium in 1915. The carnage of trench warfare also scarred the soldiers who served in these surreal settings, causing "gas neurosis," "burial-alive neurosis," and "soldiers' heart"—all symptoms of shell shock. Imperial War Museum, London.

The 1916 Campaign
This campaign van sponsored by the Women's Bureau of the Democratic National Committee linked Woodrow Wilson to the themes of progressivism, prosperity, and preparedness. Note the variation on the popular slogan, "He kept us out of war."
Corbis-Bettmann.

the election of 1916. The Republican Party passed over the belligerently prowar Theodore Roosevelt in favor of Supreme Court Justice Charles Evans Hughes, a former governor of New York. The Democrats renominated Wilson, whose campaign emphasized his progressive reform record (see Chapter 20) but whose telling campaign slogan was "He kept us out of war." Wilson won reelection by only 600,000 popular votes and by 23 votes in the electoral college, a slim margin that limited his options in mobilizing the nation for war.

The events of early 1917 diminished Wilson's lingering hopes of staying out of the conflict. On January 31 Germany announced the resumption of unrestricted submarine warfare, a decision dictated by the impasse in the land war. In response Wilson broke off diplomatic relations with Germany on February 3. A few weeks later, newspapers published an intercepted communication from Germany's foreign secretary, Arthur Zimmermann, to the German minister in Mexico City, in which Zimmermann urged Mexico to join the Central Powers

in the war. In return Germany promised to help Mexico recover "the lost territory of Texas, New Mexico, and Arizona." This threat to the territorial integrity of the United States jolted both congressional and public opinion, especially in the West, where opposition to entering the war was strong. Combined with the resumption of unrestricted submarine warfare, the Zimmermann telegram inflamed anti-German sentiment. Although the likelihood of Mexico's reconquering the border states was small, the continued instability there in the final phases of the Mexican Revolution (see Chapter 21) had led to border raids that killed sixteen U.S. citizens in January 1916 and made American policymakers take the German threat seriously.

Throughout March, U-boats attacked American ships without warning, sinking three on March 18 alone. On April 2, 1917, after consulting his cabinet, Wilson appeared before a special session of Congress to ask for a declaration of war. The rights of the nation had been trampled, and its trade and citizens' lives imperiled, he charged. But while U.S. self-interest shaped the decision to go to war, Americans' long-standing sense of their exceptionalism, coupled with Progressive Era zeal to right social injustices, also played a part. Believing that the United States, in sharp contrast to other nations, was uniquely high minded in the conduct of its international affairs, many Americans accepted Wilson's claim that America had no selfish aims: "We desire no conquest, no dominion. We seek no indemnities for ourselves, no material compensation for the sacrifices we shall freely make. We are but one of the champions of the rights of mankind." In a memorable phrase intended to ennoble the nation's role, Wilson proposed that U.S. participation in the war would make the world "safe for democracy."

Four days after Wilson's speech, on April 6, 1917, the United States declared war on Germany. Reflecting the divided feelings of the country as a whole, the vote was far from unanimous. Six senators and fifty members of the House voted against the action, including Representative Jeannette Rankin of Montana, the first woman elected to Congress. "I want to stand by my country," she declared, "but I cannot vote for war."

First Woman in Congress

In 1916 Jeannette Rankin, a former suffrage organizer, became the first woman elected to Congress. Her vote against U.S. entry into World War I cost her a chance for election to the Senate in 1918. In 1940 Rankin again won election to Congress from Montana. True to her lifelong pacifism, she cast the only vote against American entry into World War II. Corbis-Bettmann.

"Over There"

To native-born Americans, Europe seemed a great distance away—literally "over there," as the lyrics of George M. Cohan's popular song described it. After the declaration of war, many citizens were surprised to learn that the United States planned to send troops to Europe, optimistically having assumed that the nation's participation could be limited to military and economic aid. In May 1917 General John J. Pershing traveled to London and Paris to determine how the United States could best support the war effort. The answer, as Marshal Joseph Joffre of France put it, was clear: "Men, men, and more men."

Conscription. The problem was that the United States had never maintained a large standing army in peacetime. To field a fighting force strong enough to enter a global war, the government turned to conscription. The passage of the Selective Service Act in May 1917 demonstrated the increasing impact of the state on ordinary citizens. Though draft resistance had been common during the Civil War, no major riots occurred in 1917. The Selective Service system worked in part because it combined central direction from Washington with local administration and civilian control and thus did not tread on the nation's tradition of individual freedom and local autonomy. Draft registration also demonstrated the potential bureaucratic capacity of the American state. On a single day, June 5, 1917, more than 9.5 million men between the ages of twenty-one and thirty were processed for military service in their local voting precincts. By the end of the war almost 4 million men, popularly known as doughboys, plus a few thousand female navy clerks and army nurses, were in uniform. Another 300,000 men, called slackers, evaded the draft, and 4,000 were classified as conscientious objectors.

Wilson chose Pershing to head the American Expeditionary Force (AEF). But the newly raised army did not have an immediate impact on the fighting. The fresh recruits had to be trained and outfitted and then wait for transport across the submarine-infested Atlantic. The nation's first significant contribution was to secure the safety of the seas. Aiming for safety in numbers in the face of mounting German submarine activity, the government began sending armed **convoys** across the Atlantic. The plan worked: no American soldiers were killed on the way to Europe, and Allied shipping losses were cut dramatically.

The Western Front. Meanwhile, trench warfare on the Western Front continued its deadly grind. Allied commanders pleaded for American reinforcements, but Pershing was reluctant to put his soldiers under foreign commanders, preferring to delay introducing American troops until the AEF could be brought up to full strength and combat readiness. Thus, until May 1918, the brunt of the fighting continued to fall on the French and British.

Flying Aces

One of America's best-known aces was former professional race-car driver Eddie Ricken-backer (middle) of the Ninety-fourth Aero Pursuit Squadron. Note the insignia on the plane. The Ninety-fourth was known as the hat-in-the-ring squadron for the American custom of throwing a hat into the ring as an invitation to fight. Corbis-Bettmann.

army dropped the test in 1919, but revised versions of intelligence tests soon became a standard part of assessment measures in the American educational system.

The "Americanization" of the army remained imperfect at best, with African American soldiers receiving the worst treatment. Blacks were organized into rigidly segregated units, almost always under the control of white officers. In addition blacks were assigned to the most menial tasks, working as stevedores (workers who loaded and unloaded the ships) and messboys (workers who cleaned up kitchen and dining facilities). Although the policy of segregation minimized contact between black and white recruits, racial violence erupted at several camps. The worst incident occurred in Houston in August 1917, when black members of the Twenty-fourth Infantry's Third Battalion killed fifteen white soldiers and police officers in retaliation for a string of racial incidents, including the beating of a black woman by a white police officer. Sixty-four soldiers were tried in military courts, and nineteen were hanged. The army quickly disbanded the battalion, but the legacy of racial mistrust lingered throughout the rest of the war.

Racial equality had never been a central concern on the progressive agenda, and the black experience in World War I reflected the persistent gap between democratic rhetoric and reality. Over 400,000 black men served in the military, accounting for 13 percent of the armed forces; 92 percent were draftees, a far higher rate than that of whites. Black soldiers often found the French more willing to socialize with them on an equal basis than white American soldiers. Despite documented cases of extreme heroism, no blacks received the Congressional Medal of Honor, the nation's highest military award, even though they had been so honored in the Civil War and the Spanish-American War. The French, however, had no qualms about awarding the Croix de Guerre (Legion of Honor) to several hundred African American soldiers (see Voices from Abroad, "A German Propaganda Appeal to Black Soldiers," p. 648).

Demobilization. Just as it had taken months to get American troops to Europe to join the fighting, similar delays slowed demobilization at the war's end. June 1919 was the peak month for returns, with 368,000 men—plus the women who had served in France as telephone operators, canteen workers, and nurses—coming home to begin the process of readjusting to civilian life.

After the armistice the war lived on, however, in the minds of the men and women who had gone "over

World War I Veteran Fred Fast Horse

In contrast to the segregation African Americans experienced, Native Americans served in integrated combat units in the military. Ironically, racial stereotypes about their natural abilities as warriors, their adroit tactics, sense of strategy, and feats of camouflage both enhanced the reputation of Native Americans' military ability and meant that officers gave them hazardous duties as advance scouts, messengers, and snipers. Casualties were high. Roughly 5 percent died, compared to 1 percent for the military as a whole. Fred Fast Horse, a Rosebud Sioux, pictured here, was partially paralyzed in the Meuse-Argonne campaign. William Hammond Mathers Museum, Indiana University.

there." Spared the trauma of sustained battle, many members of the AEF had experienced the war more as tourists than as soldiers. Before joining the army most recruits had barely traveled beyond their hometowns, and for them the journey across the ocean to Europe was a monumental, once-in-a-lifetime event. In 1919 a group of former AEF officers formed the American Legion "to preserve the memories and incidents of our association in the great war." The word *legion* perfectly captured the romantic, almost chivalric memories that many veterans held of their wartime service. Only later did disillusionment set in over the contested legacy of World War I.

War on the Home Front

Fighting World War I required extraordinary economic mobilization on the home front in which corporations, workers, and the general public cooperated. Although the federal government did expand its power and presence during the emergency, the watchword was voluntarism. The government avoided compulsion as much as possible. Ambivalence about expanding state power, coupled with the pressures of wartime mobilization, severely damaged the impetus for progressive reforms that had characterized the prewar era. Yet even in the context of international crisis, some reformers expected that the war could serve the cause of improving American society.

Mobilizing Industry and the Economy

Even before the formal declaration of war, the United States had geared up as the arsenal for the Allied Powers. As hundreds of tons of American grain and military supplies crossed the Atlantic and the Allies paid for their purchases in gold, the United States reversed its historical position as a debtor and became a leading creditor. In addition, U.S. financial institutions increasingly provided capital for investment in the world market when British financial reserves started to be diverted to the war effort. This shift from debtor to creditor status, which would last until the 1980s, guaranteed the nation a major role in international financial affairs after the war and confirmed the new role of the United States as a world power.

Paying for the War.   The continuing impact of the prewar progressive reform movement was evident in the financing of the war, the cost of which would eventually mount to $33 billion. The government paid for the war in part by using the Federal Reserve System established in 1913 (see Chapter 20) to expand the money supply, making it easier to borrow money. Two-thirds of the funds came from loans, especially the popular liberty bonds. Treasury Secretary William McAdoo encouraged the small, heavily advertised bond sales as a way of widening support for the war and demonstrating the voluntary self-sacrifice of the nation's citizenry. To augment the funds raised by bonds, McAdoo increased the federal income tax. Income taxes had been instituted by Congress after the passage of the Sixteenth Amendment to the Constitution in 1913. Now the War Revenue Bills of 1917 and 1918 transformed the tax into the foremost method of federal fund-raising. The Wilson administration took a progressive approach, rejecting a tax on all wages and salaries in favor of a tax on corporations and wealthy individuals. The **excess-profits tax** signaled a direct and unprecedented intrusion of the state into the workings of corporate capitalism. By 1918 U.S. corporations were paying over $2.5 billion in excess-profits taxes per year—more than half of all federal taxes.

Wartime Economic Regulation.   The revenue bills should not mask the fact that the federal government for the most part took a collaborative rather than a coercive

Organized Labor. Besides mobilizing armies and businesses to wage war, the federal government also needed to ensure a reliable workforce, especially in war industries. Acute labor shortages, caused by the demands of the draft, the abrupt decline in European immigration, and the urgency of war production, had enhanced workers' bargaining power. The National War Labor Board (NWLB), formed in April 1918, also helped to improve labor's position. Composed of representatives of labor, management, and the public, the NWLB established an eight-hour day for war workers, with time and a half for overtime, and endorsed equal pay for women workers. Workers were not allowed to disrupt war production through strikes or other disturbances. In return the NWLB supported the workers' right to organize unions, required employers to deal with shop committees, and arbitrated labor disputes.

After years of federal hostility toward labor, the NWLB's actions brought a welcome change in labor's status and power. From 1916 to 1919 AFL membership grew by almost 1 million workers, reaching over 3 million at the end of the war. Few of the wartime gains lasted, however. Like other agencies, the NWLB was quickly disbanded. Wartime inflation ate up most of the wage hikes, and a virulent postwar antiunion movement caused a rapid decline in union membership that lasted into the 1930s.

Black and Mexican American Workers. While the war emergency benefited labor in general, it had a special effect on workers who were traditionally excluded from many industrial jobs. For the first time northern factories actively recruited African Americans, spawning the "Great Migration" (Map 22.3). Over 400,000 African Americans from the South moved northward to cities such as St. Louis, Chicago, New York, and Detroit during the war. The lure of decent jobs was potent. As one Mississippi man said in anticipation of working in northern meatpacking

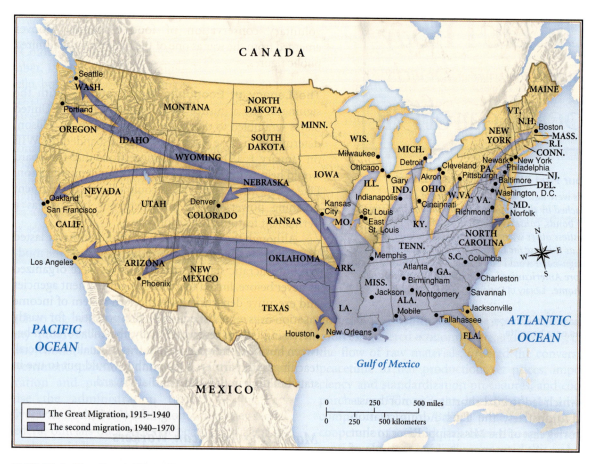

MAP 22.3 The Great Migration and Beyond

Employment opportunities that opened up during World War I and World War II served as catalysts for "great migrations" out of the rural South. In the first migration that began in 1915, African Americans headed primarily to industrial cities of the North and Midwest, such as Chicago, New York, and Pittsburgh. With the Second World War, their destinations expanded to include the West, especially Los Angeles, the San Francisco Bay area, and Seattle.

For more help analyzing this map, see the ONLINE STUDY GUIDE at bedfordstmartins.com/henretta.

houses: "You could not rest in your bed at night for thoughts of Chicago." African Americans encountered discrimination in the North—in jobs, housing, and education—but most were able to better their circumstances as they found new opportunities and an escape from the repressive southern agricultural system (see American Voices, "Southern Migrants," p. 652).

Mexican Americans in California, Texas, New Mexico, and Arizona also found new opportunities. Wartime labor shortages prompted many Mexican Americans to leave farm labor for industrial jobs in rapidly growing southwestern cities. Continuing political instability in Mexico following the revolution encouraged many Mexicans to relocate, temporarily or permanently, across the border, a process facilitated by newly opened railroad lines. At least 100,000 Mexicans entered the United States between 1917 and 1920, often settling in segregated neighborhoods (barrios) in urban areas, meeting discrimination similar to that faced by African Americans.

Women and the War Effort.   Women were the largest group to take advantage of new wartime opportunities. White women and, to a lesser degree, black and Mexican American women found that factory jobs usually reserved for men had been opened to them. About 1 million women joined the labor force for the first time, while many of the 8 million women who already held jobs switched from low-paying fields like domestic service to higher-paying industrial work. Americans soon got used to the sight of female streetcar conductors, train engineers, and defense workers. But everyone—including most working women—believed that those jobs would return to men after the war.

Wartime Reform: Woman Suffrage and Prohibition

Many progressive reformers had been active in the mobilization for war, hoping to keep alive the progressive spirit by pushing for a wide range of social reforms. They

Wartime Opportunities

Women took on new jobs during the war, working as mail carriers, police officers, drill-press operators, and farm laborers attached to the Women's Land Army. These women are riveters at the Puget Sound Navy Yard in Washington. Black women in particular, who customarily were limited to employment as domestic servants or agricultural laborers, found that the war opened up new opportunities and better wages in industry. When the war ended, black and white women alike usually lost jobs deemed to be men's work.

National Archives.

Southern Migrants

The Great Migration of southern African Americans to the cities of the North disrupted communities and families, but the migrants kept in touch with friends and kin through letters and visits. Cities like Chicago offered new opportunities and experiences, as these letters suggest, and migrants eagerly promoted their promise to the folks back home.

CHICAGO, ILLINOIS.

My dear Sister: I was agreeably surprised to hear from you and to hear from home. I am well and thankful to say I am doing well. The weather and everything else was a surprise to me when I came. I got here in time to attend one of the greatest revivals in the history of my life—over 500 people joined the church. We had a Holy Ghost shower. You know I like to have run wild. It was snowing some nights and if you didnt hurry you could not get standing room. Please remember me kindly to any who ask of me. The people are rushing here by the thousands and I know if you come and rent a big house you can get all the roomers you want. You write me exactly when you are coming. I am not keeping house yet I am living with my brother and his wife. My son is in California but will be home soon. He spends his winter in California. I can get a nice place for you to stop until you can look around and see what you want. I am quite busy. I work in Swifts packing Co. in the sausage department. My daughter and I work for the same company— We get $1.50 a day and we pack so many sausages we dont have much time to play but it is a matter of a dollar with me and I feel that God made the path and I am walking therein.

Tell your husband work is plentiful here and he wont have to loaf if he want to work. . . . Well goodbye from your sister in Christ.

CHICAGO, ILLINOIS, 11/13/17.

Mr. H————
Hattiesburg, Miss.
Dear M————: Yours received sometime ago and found all well and doing well. hope you and family are well.

I got my things alright the other day and they were in good condition. I am all fixed now and living well. I certainly appreciate what you done for us and I will remember you in the near future.

M, old boy, I was promoted on the first of the month I was made first assistant to the head carpenter when he is out of the place I take everything in charge and was raised to $95. a month. You know I know my stuff.

Whats the news generally around H'burg? I should have been here 20 years ago. I just begin to feel like a man. It's a great deal of pleasure in knowing that you have got some privilege My children are going to the same school with the whites and I dont have to umble to no one. I have registered—Will vote the next election and there isnt any "yes sir" and "no sir"—its all yes and no and Sam and Bill.

Florine says hello and would like very much to see you.

All joins me in sending love to you and family. How is times there now? Answer soon, from your friend and bro.

Source: Journal of Negro History 4, no. 4 (1919): 457, 458–59.

anticipated that the wartime expansion of federal power would lead to a more dramatic governmental activism in the postwar era. Their efforts met with limited success, but the war did help to get two amendments to the Constitution adopted that many reformers had long supported: woman suffrage and prohibition.

Suffrage Victory. Supporters of woman suffrage hoped that the war would reinvigorate their cause. The National American Woman Suffrage Association (NAWSA) continued to lobby for the proposed woman suffrage amendment to the Constitution. It also threw the support of its 2 million members behind the Wilson administration, encouraging women to do their part to win the war. Women in communities all over the country labored exhaustively to promote food conservation, to protect children and women workers, and to distribute emergency relief through organizations like the Red Cross. Many agreed with Carrie Chapman Catt, president of NAWSA, that women's patriotic service could advance the cause of woman's suffrage.

Alice Paul and the National Woman's Party (NWP) took a more militant tack. To the dismay of NAWSA leaders, NWP militants began picketing the White House in July 1917 to protest their lack of the vote. Arrested and sentenced to seven months in jail, Paul and other women prisoners went on a hunger strike, which prison authorities met with forced feeding. Public shock

Woman Suffrage Triumphant

This 1919 poster celebrating the passage of the Nineteenth Amendment by Congress promised that woman suffrage was coming, but it took still another year of intense lobbying to win the necessary ratification by the states. Then, finally, the woman's hour struck.

Poster Collection, US5084, Hoover Institution Archives, Stanford University, CA.

at the women's treatment made them martyrs, drawing attention to the issue of woman's suffrage.

The combination of the NWP's and NAWSA's policy of patient persuasion finally brought results. In January 1918 Woodrow Wilson withdrew his opposition to a federal woman suffrage amendment. The constitutional amendment quickly passed the House but took eighteen months to get through the Senate. Then came another year of hard work for ratification by the states. Finally, on August 26, 1920, Tennessee gave the Nineteenth Amendment the last vote it needed. The goal that had first been declared publicly at the Seneca Falls convention in 1848 was finally achieved seventy-two years later, in large part because of women's contributions to the war effort.

Moral Reform, Family Welfare, and Prohibition.
Other activists also saw the war as an opportunity to further their long-standing goals. Moral reformers, concerned with vice and prostitution found that their

agenda meshed with the military's interest in army efficiency. With the slogan "Keeping fit to fight," the federal government launched an ambitious campaign against sexually transmitted diseases, forcing the shutdown of "red-light" districts in cities with military training camps. With the cooperation of the YMCA and the YWCA, the government undertook a far-reaching sex education program, designed to enlighten both men and women about the dangers of sexual activity and the value of "social purity."

While some reformers worried about soldiers' physical and moral welfare, others acted to protect the families they left behind. Responding to concerns about familial disruption and deprivation among working-class families, Congress enacted the War Risk Insurance Act in 1917, which required that enlisted men and noncommissioned officers allot $15 monthly from their military pay to their dependents, who also received allowances from the federal government, which disbursed almost $570 million for the program between 1917 and its end in 1921. The funds gave women some degree of financial security and even independence, but the program also reinforced expectations that women's proper role was in the home and men's was as the family breadwinner. This unprecedented expansion of the federal government into the private lives of families, although short lived, would shape the assumptions of the welfare programs established in the New Deal era (see Chapter 25).

A more dramatic enlargement of federal power resulted from the efforts of Prohibitionists who viewed alcoholic beverages as the nation's key social evil. In the early twentieth century, many Americans viewed the legal prohibition of alcohol as a progressive reform and not a denial of individual freedom. Urban reformers, concerned about good government, poverty, and public morality, supported a nationwide ban on drinking. The drive for Prohibition also had substantial backing in rural communities. Many people equated liquor with all the sins of the city: prostitution, crime, immigration, machine politics, and public disorder. The churches with the greatest strength in rural areas, including the Methodists, the Baptists, and the Mormons, also strongly condemned drinking. Protestants from rural areas dominated the membership of the Anti-Saloon League, which supplanted the Women's Christian Temperance Union as the leading proponent of Prohibition early in the century.

Temperance advocates were right in identifying cities as the sites of resistance to Prohibition. Alcoholic beverages, especially beer and whiskey, played an important role in the social life of certain ethnic cultures in the nation's heavily urbanized areas, especially those of German Americans and Irish Americans. Most saloons were in working-class neighborhoods and served as gathering places for workers. Machine politicians indeed conducted much of their business in bars. Thus many immigrants and working-class people opposed Prohibition, not only

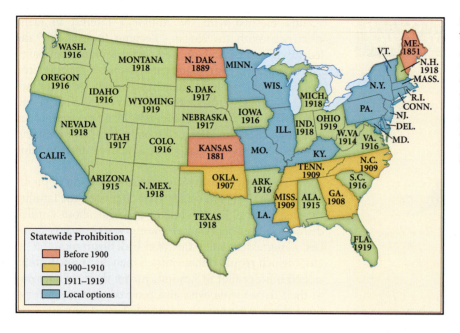

MAP 22.4 Prohibition on the Eve of the Eighteenth Amendment, 1919
Prohibition had already made headway in the states before the adoption of the Eighteenth Amendment in 1919. States such as Maine, North Dakota, and Kansas had been dry since the nineteenth century; by 1919 two-thirds of the states had passed laws banning liquor. Most states that resisted the trend were industrial centers or had large immigrant populations.

as an attack on drinking but as an attempt to impose middle-class cultural values on them.

Numerous states—mostly southern and midwestern states without a significant immigrant presence—already had Prohibition laws (Map 22.4), but World War I offered the impetus for national action. Because several major breweries had German names (Pabst and Busch, for example), beer drinking became unpatriotic in many people's minds. To conserve food Congress prohibited the use of foodstuffs such as hops and barley in breweries and distilleries. Finally, in December 1917, Congress passed the Eighteenth Amendment, which prohibited the "manufacture, sale, or transportation of intoxicating liquors." Ratified in 1919 and effective on January 16, 1920, the Eighteenth Amendment demonstrated the widening influence of the state in matters of personal behavior.

The Eighteenth Amendment was an example of how progressive reform efforts could benefit from the climate of war. But despite the stimulus the Great War gave to some types of reform, for the most part it blocked rather than furthered reforms. Though many Progressives had anticipated that the stronger federal presence in wartime would lead to stronger economic controls and corporate regulation, federal agencies were quickly disbanded once the war was over, reflecting the unease most Americans felt about a strong bureaucratic state. The wartime collaboration between government and business gave corporate leaders more influence in shaping the economy and government policy, not less.

Promoting National Unity

For the liberal reformers convinced that the war for democracy could promote a more just society at home, perhaps the most discouraging development was the campaign to promote "One Hundred Percent Americanism," which meant an insistence on conformity and an intolerance of dissent. It was Woodrow Wilson who had predicted what came to pass: "Once lead this people into war, and they'll forget there ever was such a thing as tolerance." The president recognized the need to manufacture support for the war, but ironically his efforts encouraged a repressive spirit hostile to reform.

Wartime Propaganda.   In April 1917 Wilson formed the Committee on Public Information (CPI) to promote public support for the war. This government **propaganda** agency, headed by the journalist George Creel, quickly attracted progressive reformers and muckraking journalists (see American Lives, "George Creel: Holding Fast the Inner Lines," p. 656). Professing lofty-sounding goals such as educating citizens about democracy, promoting national unity, assimilating immigrants, and breaking down the isolation of rural life, the committee also acted as a nationalizing force by promoting the development of a common ideology.

During the war the CPI touched the lives of practically every American. It distributed 75 million pieces of patriotic literature and sponsored speeches at local movie theaters, reaching cumulative audiences estimated at more than 300 million—three times the population of the United States at the time. In its zeal the committee often ventured into hatemongering. In early 1918, for example, it encouraged speakers to use inflammatory stories of alleged German atrocities to build support for the war effort.

A Climate of Suspicion.   As a spirit of conformity pervaded the home front, many Americans found themselves targets of suspicion. Local businesses paid for newspaper and magazine ads that asked citizens to report to the Justice Department "the man who spreads pessimistic stories, cries for peace, or belittles our efforts to win the war." Posters encouraged Americans to be on the lookout for German spies. And quasi-vigilante groups such as the American Protective League mobilized about 250,000 self-appointed agents, furnished with badges issued by the Justice Department, to spy on neighbors and coworkers.

The CPI also urged ethnic groups to give up their Old World customs in the spirit of One Hundred Percent Americanism. German Americans bore the brunt of this campaign. In an orgy of hostility generated by propaganda about German militarism and outrages, everything associated with Germany became suspect. German music, especially opera, was banished from the concert halls. Publishers removed pro-German references from textbooks, and many communities banned the teaching of the German language. Sauerkraut was renamed "liberty cabbage," and hamburgers were transformed into "liberty sandwiches." Though anti-German hysteria dissipated when the war ended, hostility toward the "hyphenated" American survived into the 1920s.

Curbing Dissent. In law enforcement officials tolerated little criticism of established values and institutions. The main legal tools for curbing dissent were the Espionage Act of 1917 and the Sedition Act of 1918. The Espionage Act imposed stiff penalties for antiwar activities and allowed the federal government to ban treasonous materials from the mails. The postmaster general revoked the mailing privileges of groups considered to be radical, virtually shutting down their publications.

Individuals suffered as well. Because these acts defined treason and sedition loosely, they led to the conviction of more than a thousand people. The Justice Department focused particularly on socialists, who criticized the war and the draft, and on radicals like the Industrial Workers of the World (see Chapter 17), whose attacks on militarism threatened to disrupt war production in the western lumber and copper industries. Socialist party leader Eugene Debs was sentenced to ten years in jail for stating that the master classes declared war while the subject classes fought the battles. (Debs was pardoned by President Warren G. Harding in 1921.) Victor Berger, a Milwaukee socialist who had been jailed under the Espionage Act, was twice prevented from taking the seat to which he had been elected in the U.S. House of Representatives.

The courts rarely resisted these wartime excesses. In *Schenck v. United States* (1919), the Supreme Court upheld the conviction of the general secretary of the Socialist Party, Charles T. Schenck, who had been convicted of mailing pamphlets urging draftees to resist induction. In a unanimous decision Justice Oliver Wendell Holmes ruled that an act of speech uttered under circumstances that would "create a clear and present danger to the safety of the country" could be constitutionally restricted. Because of the national war emergency, then, the Court upheld limits on freedom of speech that would not have been acceptable in peacetime. In wartime, the drive for conformity reigned, dashing reformers' optimistic hopes that war could be what philosopher John Dewey had called a "plastic juncture," in which the country would be more open to progressive ideas.

An Unsettled Peace, 1919–1920

The war's end did not bring the tranquility Americans had hoped for. Demobilization proceeded with little planning, in part because Wilson was so preoccupied with the peacemaking process and his efforts to promote a league of nations. Spending only ten days in the United States between December 1918 and June 1919, for more than six months he was virtually an absentee president. Unfortunately, many urgent domestic issues demanded strong leadership that never emerged. In particular, racial, ethnic, and class tensions racked the nation as it attempted to adjust to a postwar order.

The Treaty of Versailles

In January 1917 Woodrow Wilson had proposed a "peace without victory," since only a "peace among equals" could last. His goal was "not a balance of power, but a community of power; not organized rivalries, but an organized common peace." The keystone of Wilson's postwar plans was a permanent league of nations. But he would first have to win over a Senate that was Republican controlled and openly hostile to the treaty he had brought home.

Negotiating the Treaty. President Wilson brought to the 1919 peace negotiations in France an almost missionary zeal. Confident in his own vision for a new world order, he believed that if necessary, "I can reach the peoples of Europe over the heads of their rulers." He scored an early victory when the Allies accepted his Fourteen Points as the basis for the peace negotiations that began in January 1919. In this blueprint for the postwar world, the president called for open diplomacy, "absolute freedom of navigation upon the seas," arms reduction, the removal of trade barriers, and an international commitment to national self-determination. Essential to Wilson's vision was the creation of a multinational organization "for the purpose of affording mutual guarantees of political independence and territorial integrity to great and small States alike." The League of Nations became Wilson's obsession.

The **Fourteen Points** were imbued with the spirit of progressivism. Widely distributed as propaganda during

George Creel:
Holding Fast the
Inner Lines

Woodrow Wilson called George Creel, his choice to lead the Committee on Public Information (CPI), a man with a "passion for adjectives." The forty-one-year-old Creel had already made a name for himself as a muckraking journalist and unabashed progressive, picking up a number of detractors along the way for his impetuous and flamboyant style. "A little shrimp of a man with burning dark eyes set in an ugly face under a shock of curly black hair" was how one critic described him; another called him "a fascinating talker who looked like a gargoyle." Whether it concerned his appearance or his politics, no one was neutral about George Creel.

George Creel was born on December 1, 1876, in Lafayette County, Missouri, the son of a Confederate officer who had moved west from Virginia after the Civil War. His mother, who ran a boardinghouse while his father brooded and drank, made sure that her son heard the Southern version of the War Between the States. "The battle of Antietam, indeed!" she exclaimed after he recounted one history lesson from school. "Why, honey, it was the battle of Sharpsburg, and we whipped them." The young boy concluded about his upbringing, "The open mind was no part of my inheritance. I took in prejudice with mother's milk, and was weaned on partisanship."

Quitting high school after one year, Creel worked briefly on a Kansas City newspaper before hopping on a cattle train to New York City to try his luck as a writer and freelance journalist. By 1900 he was back in the Midwest to found the *Kansas City Independent*, a weekly paper whose slogan was "A Clean, Clever Paper for Intelligent People." With zeal shared by early-twentieth-century urban progressives all around the country, he lead battles to clean up municipal government, pass laws to protect workers, and stop prostitution.

In 1909 Creel moved to Denver, which was a hotbed of progressive activity. When reformers won a majority in the 1912 city elections, he became police commissioner but was fired from the job a year later when his

George Creel
George Creel in 1917, at the time of his appointment as head of the Committee on Public Information. Corbis-Bettmann.

campaigns to dismiss political holdovers and rehabilitate criminals went too far even for his fellow progressives. Freed from the straitjacket of public office, he intensified his muckraking activities, exposing, for example, the glowing personal endorsements that often accompanied advertisements for quack medical remedies by printing the death dates of these supposedly cured patients. He was an ardent woman suffragist, and he coauthored a book on child labor with Edwin Markham and Denver's crusading judge, Ben Lindsey. Along the way he married Hollywood actress Blanche

Bates, star of *The Darling of the Gods* and other films, and starred in a cowboy movie himself. He also boxed professionally. Who says progressive reformers have to be dull?

Creel had been impressed by Woodrow Wilson's idealism as far back as 1905, and he became an enthusiastic backer of Wilson's presidential ambitions in 1912. In the 1916 campaign Creel wrote an influential pamphlet called *Wilson and the Issues*, which stressed Wilson's reform record and endorsed his stand of neutrality toward the European war. In return the reelected president offered him a position in Washington, but Creel declined. When America was on the verge of entering the war in the spring of 1917, Creel had a change of heart. If there was going to be someone in charge of public opinion, he told a Wilson aide, he wanted "to be it."

Reaction to Creel's appointment was decidedly mixed. Many newspapers, including the *New York Times*, saw him as "a radical writer" and questioned whether such an outspoken and thin-skinned figure would be able to work effectively with the press. Creel brushed these criticisms aside and promptly got down to work.

The jurisdiction of the Committee on Public Information was "everything related to public opinion, both at home and abroad," and Creel enlisted the cooperation of journalists, moviemakers, advertising executives, and others in the common battle of "holding fast the inner lines" of American public opinion during wartime. His goal was affirmative propaganda, not rank appeals to emotion—to "inspire, not inflame." So confident was he of "the absolute justice of America's cause, the absolute selflessness of America's aims," that he believed "no other argument was needed than the simple, straightforward presentation of the facts." "Words evaporate," he said repeatedly, but "facts remain."

Creel later called the CPI "the world's greatest adventure in advertising." In the days before radio, printed publicity played a crucial role in reaching, and then binding together, a diverse nation. By the end of 1917, the CPI was sending each newspaper in California an average of six pounds of publicity copy a day. One unintended by-product of this government-sponsored media campaign was the stimulation of the advertising industry, which became a major force in shaping patterns of consumption in the 1920s. The war also stimulated the nascent film industry, which cooperated wholeheartedly with CPI efforts.

George Creel quickly demonstrated that he aimed not just to shape the minds of American citizens but to "fight for the mind of mankind" worldwide. The foreign section of the CPI exported ideas about American life and values to three target audiences: neutral nations, America's allies, and the civilian populations of the Central Powers. German and Austrian citizens were bombarded with propaganda leaflets dropped from balloons and airplanes or smuggled behind enemy lines. And in the newly formed Soviet Union, the CPI distributed a million pamphlets, "sounding alarms against typhus as well as against Lenin and Trotsky." Propaganda became part of a global network.

At war's end the CPI was quickly dismantled and Creel returned to journalism. Always the publicist, he wrote a book about his CPI experiences entitled *How We Advertised America* (1920) in which he took great delight in settling old scores with his opponents, especially Republican members of Congress. He also ardently defended, to no avail, the Treaty of Versailles out of loyalty to his friend Woodrow Wilson. In 1926 he and his family moved to San Francisco, where he continued to write for national publications such as *Collier's* magazine, as well as publish books of popular history and biography.

The upheavals of the 1930s and 1940s drew Creel back into public life. He warmly supported Franklin Roosevelt's efforts to end the Great Depression and served on a variety of New Deal advisory boards. He was far more critical, however, of the administration's conduct of World War II, especially the "blundering" (in his words) propaganda efforts undertaken by the Office of War Information. With his usual inflated pride and self-justification, he commented, "A full twenty organizations now spend more than $130,000,000 a year to do the work that I did with $2,500,000 a year." By the 1940s he was moving away from his former progressive belief in reform, fearing that the federal government had gotten so big that it was stifling individual initiative. Creel died in 1951, having spent the last years of his life battling what he saw as a huge international conspiracy of Communists and their sympathizers.

George Creel always thought of himself as a "rebel at large," the title he chose for his 1947 autobiography. Reflecting on the changes that had occurred in America during his lifetime, he concluded, "At twenty, when I enlisted in the progressive movement, I was appalled at the magnitude of the task of reform. Today, at seventy, I am amazed at the swiftness of our approach to equal justice." Despite his ideological journey away from progressivism toward the end of his life, Creel never deviated from his wartime creed: "Democracy is a religion with me, and throughout my adult life I have preached America as the hope of the world."

The Peace at Versailles
This painting by Sir William Orpen of the signing of the peace treaty in the Hall of Mirrors at Versailles in June 1919 captures the solemnity of the occasion and the grandeur of the surroundings. Wilson was justifiably proud of his role in the peace negotiations, but he faced strong opposition in the Senate. Imperial War Museum, London.

the final months of the war, Wilson's plan proposed to extend the ideals of America—democracy, freedom, and peaceful economic expansion—to the rest of the world. The League of Nations, acting as a kind of international Federal Trade Commission, would supervise disarmament and—according to the crucial Article X of its covenant—curb aggressor nations through collective military action. More grandiosely, Wilson anticipated that the league would mediate disputes between nations, preventing future wars, and thus ensuring that the Great War would be "the war to end all wars." By emphasizing these lofty goals, Wilson set the stage for disappointment: his ideals for world reformation proved too far-reaching to be practical or attainable.

Twenty-seven countries sent representatives to the peace conference in Versailles, near Paris. Distrustful of the new Bolshevik regime in Russia and its call for proletarian revolution against capitalism and imperialism, the Allies deliberately excluded its representatives. Nor was Germany invited. The Big Four—Wilson, Prime Minister David Lloyd George of Great Britain, Premier Georges Clemenceau of France, and Prime Minister Vittorio Orlando of Italy—did most of the negotiating. The three European leaders sought a peace that differed radically from Wilson's plan. They wanted to punish Ger-

many and treat themselves to the spoils of war by demanding heavy **reparations**. In fact, before the war ended, Britain, France, and Italy had already made secret agreements to divide up the German colonies.

It is a tribute to Wilson that he managed to influence the peace settlement as much as he did. He was able to soften some of the harshest demands for reprisal against Germany. National self-determination, a fundamental principle of Wilson's Fourteen Points, bore fruit in the creation of the independent states of Austria, Hungary, Poland, Yugoslavia, and Czechoslovakia from the defeated empires of the Central Powers (Map 22.5). The establishment of the new nations of Finland, Estonia, Lithuania, and Latvia not only upheld the principle of self-determination but also served Wilson's (and the Allies') desire to isolate Soviet Russia from the rest of Europe.

The Battle for Ratification and the League. Wilson had less success in achieving other goals. He won only limited concessions regarding the colonial empires of the defeated powers. The old central and eastern European colonial empires in Africa, Asia, and the Middle East were dismantled, but instead of becoming independent countries the colonies were assigned to victorious Allied

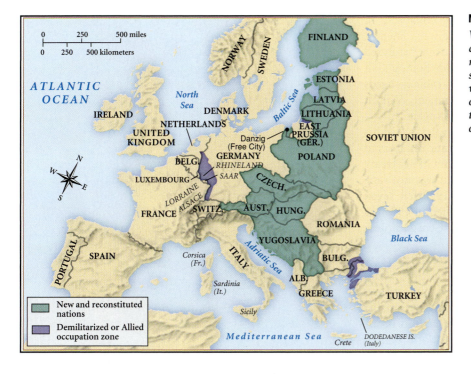

MAP 22.5 Europe after World War I

World War I and its aftermath dramatically altered the landscape of Europe, most notably with the reunification of countries such as Poland, Yugoslavia, and Czechoslovakia from territory of the defeated powers of Germany and Russia. Twenty years later, these new countries were the battlegrounds of the next world war.

nations to administer as trustees, a far cry from Wilson's ideal of national self-determination. Certain topics, such as freedom of the seas and free trade, never even appeared on the agenda because of Allied resistance. Finally Wilson had only partial success in scaling back French and British demands for reparations from Germany, which eventually were set at $33 billion.

In the face of these disappointments, Wilson consoled himself with the negotiators' commitment to his proposed League of Nations. He acknowledged that the peace treaty had defects but expressed confidence that they could be resolved by a permanent international organization dedicated to the peaceful resolution of disputes.

On June 28, 1919, representatives gathered in the Hall of Mirrors at the Palace of Versailles to sign the peace treaty. Wilson sailed home to a public enthusiastic about a league of nations in principle. Major newspapers and the Federal Council of Churches of Christ of America supported the treaty, and even an enemy of the proposed league, Senator Henry Cabot Lodge of Massachusetts, acknowledged that "[T]he people of the country are very naturally fascinated by the idea of eternal preservation of the world's peace."

But by the time Wilson presented the treaty to the Senate on July 10, it was clear that the treaty was in trouble, with support in the Senate being far short of the two-thirds vote necessary for ratification. Wilson had not paid much attention to the political realities of building support for the League of Nations and the treaty in the Senate. He had failed to include a prominent Republican in the American commission that represented the United States at Versailles. Stubbornly convinced of his own rectitude and ability, he had kept

the negotiations firmly in his own hands. When the Senate balked at the treaty, Wilson adamantly refused to compromise. "I shall consent to nothing," he told the French ambassador. "The Senate must take its medicine."

The Senate, however, did not oblige. And despite the president's attempt to make the 1918 congressional elections a referendum for his peace plans, Americans returned a Republican majority to Congress. Wilson and the league faced stiff opposition in the Senate. Some progressive senators, who endorsed the idea of American internationalism, felt that the peace agreement was too conservative, that it served to "validate existing empires" of the victorious Allies. The "irreconcilables," including progressive senators William E. Borah of Idaho, Hiram W. Johnson of California, and Robert M. La Follette of Wisconsin, disagreed fundamentally with the premise of permanent U.S. participation in European affairs. More influential was a group of Republicans led by Lodge. They proposed a list of amendments that focused on Article X, the section of the league covenant that called for collective security measures when a member nation was attacked. This provision, they argued, would restrict Congress's constitutional authority to declare war and would limit the freedom of the United States to pursue a unilateral foreign policy.

Defeat. Wilson refused to budge, especially not to placate Lodge, his hated political rival. Hoping to mobilize support for the treaty, in September 1919 the president launched an extensive speaking tour during which he brought large audiences to tears with his impassioned defense of the treaty. But the strain proved too much, and the ailing sixty-two-year-old president collapsed in Pueblo, Colorado, late in September. One week later, in Washington, Wilson suffered a severe stroke that paralyzed one side of his body. While his wife, Edith Bolling Galt Wilson, his physician, and the various cabinet heads oversaw the routine business of government, Wilson slowly recovered, but he was never the same again.

From his sickbed Wilson remained inflexible in his refusal to compromise, ordering Democratic senators to vote against all Republican amendments. The treaty came up for a vote in November 1919 but was not ratified. When another attempt in March 1920 fell seven votes short, the issue was dead. Wilson died in 1924 "as much a victim of the war," David Lloyd George noted, "as any soldier who died in the trenches."

The United States never ratified the Versailles treaty or joined the League of Nations. Many wartime issues were only partially resolved, notably Germany's future, the fate of the colonial empires, and rising nationalist demands for self-determination. These unsolved problems played a major role in the coming of World War II; some, like the competing ethnic nationalisms in the Balkans, remain unresolved today.

Racial Strife, Labor Unrest, and the Red Scare

Shortly after the end of the war, an author in the popular periodical *World's Work* observed that "the World War has accentuated all our differences. It has not created those differences, but it has revealed and emphasized them." These differences virtually exploded in the aftermath of war. Race riots exposed white resistance to the rising expectations of African Americans. Thousands of strikes signified class tensions, and a witch hunt for foreign radicals reflected anxieties about social order and the nation's ethnic pluralism.

Riots in Chicago. Many African Americans emerged from the war determined to stand up for their rights, and they contributed to a spirit of black militancy that characterized the early 1920s. The volatile mix of black migration and raised expectations of blacks as a result of service in World War I combined to exacerbate white racism. In the South the number of lynchings rose from forty-eight in 1917 to seventy-eight in 1919. Several African American men were lynched while wearing military uniforms. In the North race riots broke out in more than twenty-five cities, with one of the first and most deadly occurring in 1917 in East St. Louis, Illinois, where nine whites and more than forty blacks died in a conflict sparked by competition over jobs at a defense plant.

By the summer of 1919, the death toll from racial violence had reached 120. One of the worst race riots in American history took place in Chicago in July, where five days of rioting left twenty-three blacks and fifteen whites

Chicago Race Riot
Racial violence exploded in Chicago during the summer of 1919, and photographer Jun Fujita was on the scene to capture it. As one of the few Japanese immigrants in Chicago at the time, Fujita was probably no stranger to racism, but it took personal courage to put himself in the midst of the escalating violence. When the riot finally ended, thirty-eight people were dead and more than five hundred were injured.
Chicago Historical Society / Photo by Jun Fujita.

dead. A variety of tensions were at work in cities where violence erupted. Black voters often determined the winners of close elections, thereby enraging white racists who resented black political influence. Blacks also competed with whites for jobs and scarce housing. Even before the July riot, blacks in Chicago had suffered the bombing of their homes and other forms of harassment. They did not sit meekly by as whites destroyed their neighborhoods: they fought back in self-defense and for their rights as citizens. Wilson's rhetoric about democracy and self-determination had raised their expectations, too.

1919—A Year of Strikes. Workers of all races harbored similar hopes for a better life after the war. The war years had brought them higher pay, shorter hours, and better working conditions. Yet many native-born Americans continued to identify unions with radicalism and foreigners, and soon after the armistice many employers resumed their attacks on union activity. In addition rapidly rising inflation—in 1919 the cost of living was 77 percent higher than its prewar level—threatened to wipe out workers' wage increases. Nevertheless, workers hoped to hold onto and perhaps even expand their wartime gains.

General Strike in Seattle

Seattle was a strong union town, and 110 local unions took part in the 1919 general strike that paralyzed the city. Although the strike was peaceful, city officials deputized local citizens for police duty, such as this ragtag group of volunteers being issued guns.
Museum of History and Industry, Seattle, WA.

The result of workers' determination—and employers' resistance—was a dramatic wave of strikes. More than four million workers—one in every five—went on strike in 1919, a proportion never since equaled. The year began with a walkout by shipyard workers in Seattle, a strong union town. Their action spread into a general strike that crippled the city. Another hard-fought strike disrupted the steel industry when 350,000 steel workers demanded union recognition and an end to twelve-hour shifts and the seven-day workweek. And in the fall the Boston police force shocked many Americans by going on strike. Governor Calvin Coolidge of Massachusetts propelled himself into the political spotlight by declaring, "There is no right to strike against the public safety by anybody, anywhere, any time." Coolidge fired the entire police force, and the strike failed. The public supported this harsh reprisal, and Coolidge was rewarded with the Republican vice presidential nomination in 1920.

The Red Scare and the Palmer Raids.   A crucial factor in organized labor's failure to win many of its strikes in the postwar period was the pervasive fear of radicalism. This concern coincided with mainstream Americans' long-standing anxiety about unassimilated immigrants—an anxiety the war had made worse. The Russian Revolution of 1917 so alarmed the Allies that Wilson sent several thousand troops to Russia in the summer of 1918 in hopes of weakening the Bolshevik regime. When the Bolsheviks founded the Third International (or Comintern) in 1919 to export Communist doctrine throughout the world, American fears deepened. As domestic labor unrest increased, Americans began to see

radicals everywhere. Hatred of the German Hun was quickly replaced by hostility toward the Bolshevik Reds.

Ironically, as public concern about domestic Bolshevism increased, radicals were rapidly losing members and political power. No more than 70,000 Americans belonged to either the fledgling U.S. Communist Party or the Communist Labor Party in 1919. Both the IWW and the Socialist Party had been weakened by wartime repression and internal dissent. Yet the public and the press continued to blame almost every disturbance, especially labor conflicts, on alien radicals. "REDS DIRECTING SEATTLE STRIKE—TO TEST CHANCE FOR REVOLUTION," warned a typical newspaper headline.

Tensions mounted with a series of bombings in the early spring. "The word 'radical' in 1919," as one historian observed, "automatically carried with it the implication of dynamite." In June a bomb detonated outside the Washington townhouse of the recently appointed attorney general, A. Mitchell Palmer. His family escaped unharmed, but the bomber was blown to bits. Angling for the presidential nomination, Palmer capitalized on the event, fanning fears of domestic radicalism.

In November 1919, on the second anniversary of the Russian Revolution, the attorney general staged the first of what became known as "Palmer raids." Federal agents stormed the headquarters of radical organizations, capturing supposedly revolutionary booty such as a set of blueprints for a phonograph (at first thought to be sketches for a bomb). The dragnet pulled in thousands of aliens who had committed no crime but were suspect because of their anarchist or revolutionary beliefs or their immigrant backgrounds. Lacking the protection of U.S.

Through her dealings as business manager of the home, the modern woman brings sound commercial sense to bear on her judgment of a Ford closed car.

She knows that its low first cost, its small upkeep and operation costs, and its long-sustained usefulness make it a genuine economy. She is aware that the ease with which she can get expert attention for it anywhere and at any time is an asset of great dollar-and-cents value to her.

And she is delighted to find this value in a car that she drives so easily, and whose outward style and inward comfort she so whole-heartedly approves.

TUDOR SEDAN, $590   FORDOR SEDAN, $685   COUPE, $525   (All prices f. o. b. Detroit)

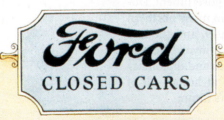

Ford
CLOSED CARS

CHAPTER 23

Modern Times

The 1920s

Business-Government Partnership
of the 1920s
*Politics in the Republican
"New Era"*
The Economy
The Heyday of Big Business
Economic Expansion Abroad
Foreign Policy in the 1920s

A New National Culture
A Consumer Culture
The Automobile Culture
*Mass Media and New Patterns of
Leisure*

Dissenting Values and Cultural
Conflict
The Rise of Nativism
*Legislating Values: The Scopes
Trial and Prohibition*
Intellectual Crosscurrents
*Cultural Clash in the
Election of 1928*

I N 1924 SOCIOLOGISTS ROBERT LYND AND HELEN MERRELL LYND arrived in Muncie, Indiana, to study the life of a small American city. They observed how the citizens of Middletown (the fictional name they gave the city) made a living, maintained a home, educated their young, practiced their religion, organized community activities, and spent their leisure time. As the Lynds' fieldwork proceeded, they were struck by how much had changed over the past thirty-five years—the lifetime of a middle-aged Middletown resident—and decided to contrast the Muncie of the 1890s with the Muncie of the 1920s. When *Middletown* was published in 1929, this "study in modern American culture" became an unexpected best-seller. Its success spoke to

Americans' desire to understand the forces that were transforming their society.

This transformation began with World War I. The United States emerged from the war as a powerful modern state and a major player in the world economy. The 1920s, however, rather than World War I were the watershed in the development of a mass national culture. Only then did the Protestant work ethic and the old values of self-denial and frugality begin to give way to the fascination with consumption, leisure, and self-realization that is the essence of modern American culture.

◄ **Selling Mrs. Consumer**

No other image captures the spirit of the consumer culture of the 1920s more emphatically than the Ford Model T. With the Ford Company in the lead, automobiles revolutionized Americans' patterns of spending money and spending leisure—with the help of the rapidly expanding advertising industry. This 1924 ad in the Ladies' Home Journal, *reflects advertisers' sense of the growing importance of the role of the "modern" housewife as the family's purchasing agent.*
Ladies' Home Journal, August 1924.

In economic organization, political outlook, and cultural values, the 1920s had more in common with the United States today than with the industrializing America of the late nineteenth century.

Business-Government Partnership of the 1920s

The business-government partnership fostered by World War I continued on an informal basis throughout the 1920s. As the *Wall Street Journal* enthusiastically proclaimed, "Never before, here or anywhere else, has a government been so completely fused with business." While the *Journal* exaggerated the fusion, it did convey the way in which business interests exerted powerful influence on public policy. From 1922 to 1929 the nation's prosperity seemed to confirm the economy's ability to regulate itself with minimal government regulation. Gone or at least submerged was the reform impulse of the Progressive Era. Business leaders were no longer villains but respected public figures. President Warren G. Harding captured the prevailing political mood when he offered the American public "not heroics but healing, not nostrums but normalcy."

Politics in the Republican "New Era"

Except for Woodrow Wilson's two terms, the Republican Party had controlled the presidency since 1896. When Wilson's progressive coalition floundered in 1918, the Republicans had a chance to regain the White House. With the ailing Wilson out of the picture, in the 1920 election the Democrats nominated Governor James M. Cox of Ohio for president and Assistant Secretary of the Navy Franklin D. Roosevelt as vice president. The Democratic platform called for U.S. participation in the League of Nations and a continuation of Wilson's progressivism. The Republicans, led by Warren G. Harding and Calvin Coolidge, promised a return to "normalcy," which meant a strong probusiness stance and conservative cultural values. Reflecting many Americans' desire to put the war and the stresses of 1919 behind them, voters rejected the party in power. Harding and Coolidge won in a landslide, marking the beginning of a Republican dominance that would last until 1932.

Government-Business Cooperation. Central to what Republicans termed the "New Era" was business-government cooperation. Although Republican administrations generally opposed expanding state power to promote progressive reforms, they had no qualms about using federal policy and power to assist corporations. In other words, some extensions of government activity seemed acceptable, while others did not. Thus Harding's

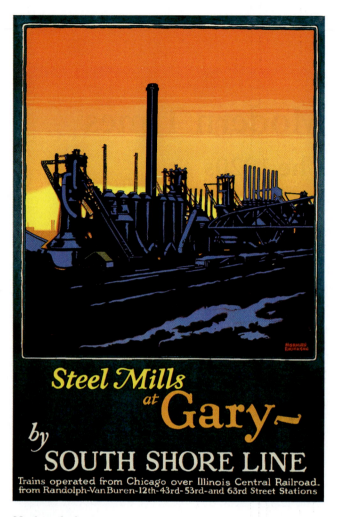

Modern Industry
This highly stylized 1928 poster promotes the steel mills of Gary, Indiana, as a tourist attraction on par with Yellowstone or Yosemite. The Gary that steelworkers experienced was more likely to be full of soot, grime, and hard work than recreation or beauty. The sky in Gary was often similar in color to that eerie shade of orange shown in the poster due to the high levels of pollution generated by the steel mills. Chicago Historical Society.

secretary of the treasury, financier Andrew W. Mellon, engineered a tax cut that undercut the wartime Revenue Acts, benefiting wealthy individuals and corporations. The Republican-dominated Federal Trade Commission (FTC) for the most part ignored the antitrust laws rather than using federal power to police industry. In this the commission followed the lead of the Supreme Court, which in 1920 had dismissed the long-pending antitrust case against U.S. Steel, ruling that largeness in business was not against the law as long as some competition remained.

Perhaps the best example of government-business cooperation emerged in the Department of Commerce, headed by Herbert Hoover. Hoover thought that with the offer of government assistance, businessmen would voluntarily run their enterprises in ways that would benefit the public interest, thereby benefiting the entire country. Under Hoover the Commerce Department expanded dramatically, offering new services like the compilation and distribution of trade and production statistics to American business. It also assisted private trade associations in their efforts to rationalize and make more efficient major sectors of industry and commerce by using such tools as product standardization and wage and price controls.

Unfortunately, not all government-business cooperation was as high minded as Hoover had anticipated. President Harding was basically an honest man, but some of his political associates were not. When Harding died suddenly of a heart attack in San Francisco in August 1923, evidence of widespread fraud and corruption in his administration had just come to light. In 1924 a particularly damaging scandal concerned the secret leasing of government oil reserves in Teapot Dome, Wyoming, and in Elk Hills, California, without competitive bidding. Secretary of the Interior Albert Fall was eventually convicted of taking $300,000 in bribes; he became the first cabinet officer in American history to serve a prison sentence.

After Harding's death, the taciturn vice president, Calvin Coolidge, moved into the White House. In contrast to his predecessor's political cronyism and outgoing style, Coolidge personified an austere rectitude. As vice president "Silent Cal" often sat through official functions without uttering a word. A dinner partner once challenged him by saying, "Mr. Coolidge, I've made a rather sizable bet with my friends that I can get you to speak three words this evening." Responded Coolidge icily, "You lose." Although Coolidge was quiet and unimaginative, his image of unimpeachable integrity reassured voters, and he soon announced his candidacy for the presidency in 1924.

The 1924 Election. When the Democrats gathered that July in the sweltering heat of New York City, they faced a divided party that drew its support mainly from the South and from northern urban political machines like Tammany Hall in New York. These two constituencies often collided. They disagreed mightily over Prohibition, immigration restriction, and most seriously, the mounting power of the racist and anti-immigrant Ku Klux Klan. The resolutions committee remained deadlocked for days over whether the party should condemn the Klan, eventually reaching a weak compromise that affirmed its general opposition to "any effort to arouse religious or racial dissension."

With this contentious background, the convention took 103 ballots to nominate John W. Davis, a Wall Street lawyer, for the presidency. To attract rural voters the Democrats chose as their vice presidential candidate Governor Charles W. Bryan of Nebraska, William Jennings Bryan's brother. But the Democrats could not mount an effective challenge to their more popular and

On the Campaign Trail

Although Calvin Coolidge was a man of few words, with little charisma, he recognized the importance of modern campaigning. In 1924 he hired advertising man Bruce Barton as a consultant to his presidential campaign. Here, Coolidge is pictured with an automobile decked out with radio equipment for broadcasting to potential voters in the streets. Library of Congress.

better-financed Republican rivals, whose strength came chiefly from the native-born Protestant middle class, augmented by small-business people, skilled workers, farmers, northern blacks, and wealthy industrialists. Until the Democrats could overcome their sectional and cultural divisions and build an effective national organization to rival that of the Republicans, they would remain a minority party.

The 1924 campaign also featured a third-party challenge by Senator Robert M. La Follette of Wisconsin, who ran on the Progressive Party ticket. La Follette's candidacy mobilized reformers and labor leaders as well as disgruntled farmers in an effort to reinvigorate the reform movement both major parties had abandoned. Their platform called for nationalization of railroads, public ownership of utilities, and the right of Congress to overrule Supreme Court decisions. It also favored the direct election of the president by the voters rather than by indirect election through the electoral college.

In an impressive Republican victory, Coolidge received 15.7 million popular votes to Davis's 8.4 million and won a decisive margin in the electoral college. La Follette chalked up almost 5 million popular votes, but he carried only Wisconsin in the electoral college.

Perhaps the most significant aspect of the election was the low voter turnout. Only 52 percent of the electorate cast their ballots in 1924, compared to more than 70 percent in presidential elections of the late nineteenth century. Newly enfranchised women voters were not to blame, however; a long-term drop in voting by men, rather than apathy among women, caused the decline.

Women in Politics. Instead of resting after their suffrage victory, women increased their political activism in the 1920s. African American women struggled for voting rights in the Jim Crow South and pushed unsuccessfully for a federal antilynching law. Many women tried to break into party politics, but Democrats and Republicans granted them only token positions on party committees. Women were more influential as lobbyists. The Women's Joint Congressional Committee, a Washington-based coalition of ten major white women's organizations, including the newly formed League of Women Voters, lobbied actively for reform legislation (see American Voices, "Women Write the Children's Bureau," p. 669). Its major accomplishment was the passage in 1921 of the Sheppard-Towner Federal Maternity and Infancy Act, which appropriated $1.25 million for well-baby clinics, educational programs, and visiting nurse projects. Such major reform legislation was rare in the 1920s, however, and its success was short lived. The Sheppard-Towner Act had passed in part because politicians feared that if it did not pass, women would vote them out of office. Once politicians realized that women did not vote as a bloc, they stopped listening to the women's lobby, and in 1929 Congress cut off the act's funding.

The roadblocks women activists faced were part of a broader public antipathy to ambitious reforms. Although some states—such as New York, where an urban liberalism was coalescing under leaders like Al Smith—did enact a flurry of legislation that promoted workmen's compensation, public health programs, and conservation measures, on the national level reforms that would strengthen federal power made little headway. After years of progressive reforms and an expanded federal presence in World War I, Americans were unenthusiastic about increased taxation or more governmental bureaucracy. The Red Scare had given ammunition to opponents of reform by making it easy to claim that legislation calling for governmental activism was the first step toward Bolshevism. The general prosperity of the 1920s further hampered the reform spirit. With a strong economy, the Republican policy of an informal partnership between business and government seemed to work and made reforms regulating corporations and the economy seem unnecessary and even harmful.

The Economy

Although prosperity and the 1920s seem almost synonymous, the decade got off to a bumpy start in the transition from a wartime to a peacetime economy. In the immediate postwar years, the nation suffered rampant inflation: prices jumped by a third in 1919, accompanied by feverish business activity. Federal efforts to halt inflation—through spending cuts and a contraction of the supply of credit—produced the recession of 1920 and 1921, the sharpest short-term downturn the United States had ever faced. Unemployment reached 10 percent. Foreign trade dropped by almost half as European nations resumed production after the disruptions of war. Prices fell dramatically—more than 20 percent—and reversed much of the wartime inflation.

The recession was short. In 1922, stimulated by an abundance of consumer products, particularly automobiles, the economy began a recovery that continued with only brief interruptions through 1929. Between 1922 and 1929 the gross domestic product (GDP) grew from $74.1 billion to $103.1 billion, approximately 40 percent. Per capita income rose from $641 in 1921 to $847 in 1929. Soon the federal government was recording a budget surplus. This economic expansion provided the backdrop for the partnership between business and government.

As industries churned out an abundance of new consumer products—cars, appliances, chemicals, electricity, radios, aircraft, and movies—manufacturing output expanded 64 percent. Behind the growth lay new techniques of management and mass production, which brought a 40 percent increase in workers' productivity. The demand for goods and services kept unemployment low in most industries throughout the decade. High employment rates combined with low inflation enhanced the spending power of many Americans, especially skilled workers and the middle class.

The economy had some weaknesses, however. Income distribution reflected significant disparity: 5 percent of the nation's families received one-third of all income. In addition a number of industries were unhealthy. Agriculture never fully recovered from the 1920 and 1921 recession. During the inflationary period of 1914 to 1920, farmers had borrowed heavily to finance mortgages and equipment in response to government incentives, increased demand, and rising prices. When the war ended, European countries resumed agricultural production, glutting the world market. The price of wheat dropped 40 percent as the government withdrew wartime price supports. Corn prices fell 32 percent, and hog prices declined 50 percent. Farmers were not the only ones whose incomes plunged. Certain "sick industries," such as coal and textiles, had also expanded in response to wartime demand, which dropped sharply at war's end. Their troubles foreshadowed the Great Depression of the 1930s.

Women Write the Children's Bureau

The Children's Bureau in the Department of Labor was in charge of administering the Sheppard-Towner Act from 1921 to 1929. In addition to setting up clinics and offering correspondence courses, the staff answered letters from anxious mothers, such as the two excerpted here—yet another example of how the state was becoming part of everyday life.

Dear Doctor Sherbon:

You can not imagine how much I have enjoyed the Course. As soon as I received it I lay down and never stopped until I read it through. It is splendid, and if every woman could follow each lesson to the letter there would be less suffering. But how are we going to convince our families that such care is necessary? Of course the children can be taught these things, but the husbands and our mothers think it is foolishness to take such care of ourselves.

Do you think it proper to explain to children where they come from and the science of life? I have told my stepson, age 18, all of these things and how he should take care of himself, and also how he should treat girls and how much suffering there was to childbirth, and I was very much criticized by some of the family.

I must close. I am taking up your valuable time and am losing much time of my own. Thank you for all the help and the good you are doing, not only for myself but others.

Dear Madam:

I took your correspondence course last winter and enjoyed it very much although I have been a mother three times and expect to be again as [I] am pregnant three months now. Maybe you have something for me or that might help me in some way, so [I] thot that I would drop you a line.

We are a poor family and live in western Kansas and [are] heavily in debt, so this ordeal is hard for me at present. But what I would like to ask you is if a poor mother can get any county or state aid. My teeth are badly in need of dental work, and [I have] no money to pay the bill and the doctor bill worries me too. The doctor we have gone to is so high I don't see how we can afford it. We owe $125 in doctor bills in another county . . . and I dread any more until back ones are paid.

Isn't there a law in Kansas that unless a confinement case is obstetrical the limit charge is $15 and if obstetrical the limit is $25? He says he charges $25 for a confinement case and $1.00 mileage which would make a total of $37 for us for doctor bill, besides a nurse or lady to nurse and do the work too. But if you know anything about such things you know that mother and babe are sadly neglected if the nurse has all the house work to do too. . . .

Does the county doctor tend to such cases and look to the community for his money? It looks like we ought to be able to do and care for such things without asking for help, but you know there are just lots and lots of mothers in my fix that just drag along and worry because they have no way of buying the most needy things at such a time and are too proud to find out if there is any way to get help. My husband thinks it's awful to get help in any way besides paying for it, but when I know he is not financially able to help, I don't see why I should suffer if there is any way to help me, as any mother or doctor knows at that time a mother needs the best of care in every way. And it's because I have always had to work too soon after childbirth that I am broken down now.

I will see what I hear from you before going into details any more. Hoping you will not think it too trifling a matter to interest you and will answer me as soon as possible. Yours truly.

Source: Molly Ladd-Taylor, Raising a Baby the Government Way: Mothers' Letters to the Children's Bureau, 1915–1932 (New Brunswick, NJ: Rutgers University Press, 1986), 131–32, 136–38.

The Heyday of Big Business

But for the most part, despite these ominous signs, the nation was in a confident mood about the economy and the corporations that shaped it. Throughout the decade business leaders enjoyed enormous popularity and respect; their reputations often surpassed those of the era's lackluster politicians. The most revered businessman of the decade was Henry Ford, whose rise from poor farm boy to corporate giant embodied both the traditional value of individualism and the triumph of mass production. Success stories like Ford's prompted

were being paid for on the installment plan. Once people saw how easy it was to finance a car, they bought radios, refrigerators, and sewing machines on credit. "A dollar down and a dollar forever," a cynic remarked. By 1929 banks, finance companies, credit unions, and other institutions were lending consumers over $7 billion a year, and consumer lending had become the tenth largest business in the United States.

Many of the new products were household appliances, made feasible by the rapid electrification that had reached 85 percent of American nonfarm households by 1930. Irons and vacuum cleaners were the most popular appliances, followed by phonographs, sewing machines, and washing machines. Radios, whose production increased twenty-five-fold in the 1920s, sold for around $75. One of the most expensive items was a refrigerator, which cost $900 at the beginning of the decade. Technological improvements soon brought the price down to

$180, but many families still had to make do with an old-fashioned icebox, which supplied cooling through blocks of ice delivered to the house.

Because much of the new technology was concentrated in the home, it had a dramatic impact on women's lives, especially prosperous white women. Despite enfranchisement and participation in the work force, the primary role for most women remained that of housewife. Electric appliances made housewives' chores less arduous: plugging in an electric iron was far easier than heating an iron on the stove; using a vacuum cleaner was quicker and easier than wielding a broom and a rug beater. Paradoxically, however, the time women spent on housework did not decline. More middle-class women began to do their own housework and laundry as electric servants replaced human ones. Technology also raised standards of cleanliness so that a man could wear a clean shirt every day instead of just on

Sunday, and a house could be vacuumed daily rather than swept weekly.

Few of the new consumer products could be considered necessities, so the advertising industry spent billions of dollars (in 1929 an average of $15 annually on every man, woman, and child in the United States) to entice consumers to buy their products. Advertisements appealed to people's social aspirations by projecting images of successful and elegant sophisticates who smoked a certain brand of cigarettes or drove a recognizable make of car. Ad writers also sold products by preying on people's insecurities, coming up with a variety of socially unacceptable "diseases," including "office hips," "ashtray breath," and the dreaded "BO" (body odor). After the term *halitosis* was discovered in a British medical journal, many consumers rushed out to buy Listerine mouthwash. Advertising became a big business in the 1920s, accounting for 3 percent of the gross national product, comparable to its share after World War II.

Yet consumers were not merely passive victims. Advertisers recognized that the buying public made choices and struggled to offer messages that appealed to their targeted audiences. In the process they made consumption a cultural ideal for most of the middle class. Character, religion, and social standing, once the main criteria for judging self-worth, became less important than the gratification of personal desires through the acquisition of more and better possessions.

The Automobile Culture

No possession typified the new consumer culture better than the automobile. "Why on earth do you need to study what's changing this country?" a Muncie, Indiana, resident asked sociologists Robert and Helen Lynd. "I can tell you what's happening in just four letters: A-U-T-O!" The showpiece of modern capitalism, the automobile revolutionized the way Americans spent their money and leisure time. In the wake of the automobile, the isolation of rural life broke down. Cars touched so many aspects of American life that the word *automobility* was coined to describe their impact on production methods, the landscape, and American values.

Mass production of cars stimulated the prosperity of the 1920s. Before the introduction of the moving assembly line in 1913, Ford workers took twelve and a half hours to put together an auto; on an assembly line they took only ninety-three minutes. By 1927 Ford was producing a car every twenty-four seconds. Auto sales climbed from 1.5 million in 1921 to 5 million in 1929, a year in which Americans spent $2.58 billion on cars. By the end of the decade, Americans owned about 80 percent of the world's automobiles—an average of one car for every five people.

The success of the auto industry had a ripple effect on the American economy. In 1929, 3.7 million workers owed their jobs to the automobile, either directly or indirectly. Auto production stimulated the steel, petroleum, chemical, rubber, and glass industries. Highway construction became a billion-dollar-a-year enterprise, financed by federal subsidies and state gasoline taxes. Car ownership also spurred the growth of suburbs, contributed to real-estate speculation, and in 1924 spawned the first shopping center, Country Club Plaza in Kansas City. Not even the death of 25,000 people a year in traffic accidents—70 percent of them pedestrians—could dampen America's passion for the automobile.

The auto also changed the way Americans spent their leisure time. They took to the roads, becoming a nation of tourists. The American Automobile Association, founded in 1902, reported that in 1929 about 45 million people—almost a third of the population—took vacations by automobile, patronizing the "autocamps" and tourist cabins that were the forerunners of motels. And like movies and other products of the new mass culture, cars changed the dating patterns of young Americans. Contrary to many parents' views, premarital sex was not invented in the backseat of a Ford, but a Model T offered more privacy and comfort than did the family living room or the front porch and contributed to increased sexual experimentation among the young.

Mass Media and New Patterns of Leisure

Equal in importance to the automobile in transforming American culture were the increasingly significant mass media. Innovations in the movies, radio, and the print media helped to spread common values and attitudes throughout the United States and offered Americans new ways to "spend" their leisure time.

Moving Pictures. The movie industry probably did more than anything else to disseminate common values and attitudes. In contrast to Europe where cinema developed as an avant-garde, highbrow art form, in America movies were part of popular culture almost from the start. They began around the turn of the century in nickelodeons, where for a nickel the mostly working-class audience could see a one-reel silent film like the spectacularly successful *The Great Train Robbery* (1903). Because the films, mostly comedies and melodramas, were silent, they could be understood by immigrants who did not speak English. Both democratic and highly lucrative, the new medium quickly became popular.

By 1910 the moviemaking industry had concentrated in southern California, which had cheap land, plenty of sunshine, and varied scenery—mountains, deserts, cities, and the Pacific Ocean—within easy reach. Another attraction was Los Angeles's reputation as an antiunion town. By war's end the United States was producing 90 percent of the world's films. Foreign distribution of

makeshift rural honky-tonks, showing off elaborate gowns as well as their musical talent, blues women offered a glamorous image of successful black womanhood that belied the difficult lives that many of them experienced. Novelist Ralph Ellison expressed their importance to the black community in his description of Bessie Smith, noting that she "might have been a 'blues Queen' to the society at large, but within the tighter Negro community where the blues were a total way of life, and major expression of an attitude toward life, she was a priestess, a celebrant who affirmed the values of the group and man's ability to deal with chaos."

Phonograph records increased the appeal of jazz and the blues by capturing its spontaneity and distributing it to a wide audience; jazz, in turn, boosted the infant recording industry. Soon this uniquely American art form had caught on in Europe, especially in France. That jazz, which often expressed black dissent in the face of mainstream white values, also appealed to white audiences signifies the role that African Americans played in shaping the contours of American popular culture.

Journalism and the Radio. Other forms of mass media also helped to establish national standards of taste and behavior. In 1922 ten magazines claimed a circulation of at least 2.5 million, including the *Saturday Evening Post*, the *Ladies' Home Journal, Collier's Weekly*, and *Good Housekeeping. Reader's Digest, Time*, and the *New Yorker*, still found today in homes throughout the country, all started publication in the 1920s. Tabloid newspapers, which were half the size of standard papers and highlighted crime, sports, comics, and scandals, also became part of the national scene. Thanks to syndicated newspaper columns and features, people across the United States could read the same articles. They could also read the same books, preselected by a board of expert judges for the Book-of-the-Month Club, founded in 1926.

The newest instrument of mass culture, professional radio broadcasting, took off on November 2, 1920, when station KDKA in Pittsburgh carried the presidential election returns. By 1929 about 40 percent of the nation's households owned a radio. More than 800 stations, most affiliated with the Columbia Broadcasting Service (CBS) or the National Broadcasting Company (NBC), were on the air. Unlike European networks, which were government monopolies, American radio stations operated for profit. Though the federal government licensed the stations, their revenue came primarily from advertisers and corporate sponsors.

Americans loved radio. They listened avidly to the World Series and other sports events and to variety shows sponsored by advertisers. One of the most popular radio shows of all time, *Amos 'n' Andy* premiered on NBC in 1928, featuring two white actors playing stereotypical black characters. Soon fractured phrases from *Amos 'n' Andy*, such as "check and double check," became part of everyday speech. So many people "tuned in" (another new phrase of the 1920s) that the country seemed to come to a halt during popular programs—a striking example of the pervasiveness of mass media.

Leisure and Sports. The automobile and new forms of entertainment like movies and radio pointed to a new emphasis on leisure. As the workweek shrank and some workers won the right to paid vacations, Americans had more time and energy to spend on recreation. Like so much else in the 1920s, leisure became increasingly tied to consumption and mass culture. Public recreation flourished as cities and suburbs built baseball diamonds, tennis courts, swimming pools, and golf courses. Americans not only played sports but had the time and money to watch professional athletes perform in increasingly commercialized enterprises. They could see a game in a comfortable stadium, listen to it on the radio, or catch highlights in the newsreel at the local movie theater.

Americans reveled vicariously in the accomplishments of the superb athletes of the 1920s. Baseball continued to be the national pastime, drawing as many as 10 million fans a year. Tarnished in 1919 by the "Black Sox" scandal, in which some Chicago White Sox players took bribes to throw the World Series, baseball bounced back with the rise of stars like Babe Ruth of the New York Yankees. African Americans, however, had different heroes from whites. Excluded from the white teams, black athletes like Satchel Paige played in Negro leagues formed in the 1920s.

Thanks to the media's attention, the popularity of sports figures rivaled that of movie stars. In football Red Grange of the University of Illinois was a major star, while Jack Dempsey and Gene Tunney attracted a loyal following in boxing and Bobby Jones helped to popularize golf. Bill Tilden dominated men's tennis, while Helen Wills and Suzanne Lenglen reigned in the women's game. The decade's best-known swimmer was Gertrude Ederle, who crossed the English Channel in 1926 in just over fourteen hours.

The decade's most popular hero, however, was neither an athlete nor a movie star. On May 20, 1927, aviator Charles Lindbergh, flying the small plane *The Spirit of St. Louis*, made the first successful nonstop solo flight between New York and Paris, a distance of 3,610 miles, in $33\frac{1}{2}$ hours (see New Technology, "Aviation," p. 682). Returning home to tickertape parades and effusive celebrations, he became *Time* magazine's first Man of the Year in 1928. Lindbergh captivated the nation by combining his mastery of the new technology (the airplane) with the pioneer virtues of individualism, self-reliance, and hard work. He symbolized Americans' desire to

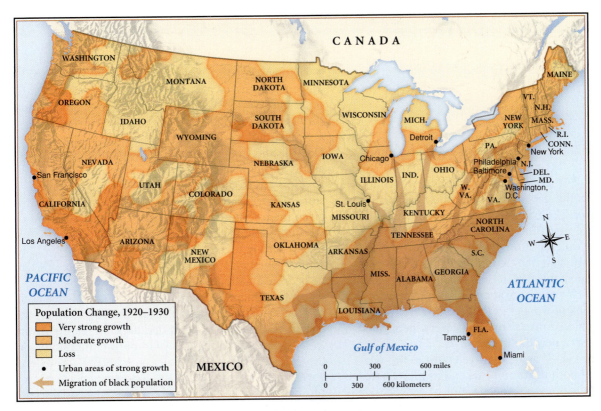

MAP 23.1 The Shift from Rural to Urban Population, 1920–1930

Despite the increasingly urban tone of modern America after 1920, regional patterns of population growth and decline were far from uniform. Cities in the South and West grew most dramatically as southern farmers moved to more promising areas with familiar climates. An important factor in the growth of northern cities, such as New York and Chicago, was the migration of southern blacks set in motion by World War I (see Map 22.3).

For more help analyzing this map, see the ONLINE STUDY GUIDE at bedfordstmartins.com/henretta.

enjoy the benefits of modern industrialism without renouncing their traditional values.

Dissenting Values and Cultural Conflict

As movies, radio, advertising, and mass-production industries helped to transform the country into a modern, cosmopolitan nation, many Americans welcomed them as exciting evidence of progress. But others were uneasy. Flappers dancing to jazz, youthful sexual experimentation in the back of Ford Model Ts, hints of a decline in religious values: these harbingers of a new era worried more tradition-minded folk. In the nation's cities the powerful presence of immigrants and African Americans suggested the waning of white Protestant cultural dominance. Beneath the clichés of the Roaring Twenties were deeply felt tensions that surfaced in conflicts over immigration, religion, Prohibition, and race relations.

The Rise of Nativism

Tensions between the fast-paced city and the traditional, small-town values of the country partially explain the decade's conflicts. As farmers struggled with severe economic problems, rural communities lost residents to the cities at an alarming rate. The 1920 census revealed that for the first time in the nation's history city people outnumbered rural people: 52 percent of the population lived in urban areas, compared with just 28 percent in 1870. Though the census exaggerated the extent of urbanization—its guidelines classified towns with only 2,500 people as cities—there was no mistaking the trend (Map 23.1). By 1929 ninety-three cities had populations over 100,000. The mass media generally reflected the cosmopolitan values of these urban centers, and many old-stock Americans worried that the cities and the immigrants who clustered there would soon dominate the culture.

Yet the polarities between city and country should not be overstated. Rural and small-town people were affected

Aviation

Charles Lindbergh captivated an American public that was already captivated by aviation. In the 1910s and 1920s, many Americans embraced this new technology, investing in the airplane almost utopian hopes for a new world order. There was something about seeing an airplane for the first time that called forth these feelings—it was so different from anything that anyone had ever seen before that they could only describe it in miraculous, almost mystical, terms. As a Chicago minister said of his first experience at an airshow, "Never have I seen such a look of wonder in the faces of a multitude. From the gray-haired man to the child, everyone seemed to feel that it was a new day in their lives."

World War I acted as a great accelerator to the aviation industry in both its commercial and its military applications. When the war ended, a glut of inexpensive training planes became available, and these craft became the vehicles of choice for the barnstorming pilots of the 1920s. With their open cockpits, canvas wings, and rudimentary controls, these planes were tricky and often dangerous to fly, but that did not stop the pilots from spreading the "winged gospel" through stunts, shows, and air races. These "birdmen"—and a fair number of "birdwomen"—brought aviation to towns and hamlets all across America. Said Amelia Earhart, who learned to fly in 1921, "Not to have had a ride in an airplane today is like not having heard the radio."

Hollywood discovered aviation in the 1920s, cranking out dozens of aviation-related films whose plots, often on World War I themes, featured production thrillers like dogfights and fiery crashes. Flying became a popular hobby for Hollywood celebrities like Cecil B. DeMille and Colleen Moore, which further added to its allure. In newspapers and tabloids across the country, aviation was front-page news precisely because aviation stories, especially crashes (of which there were many, given the technologically unsophisticated equipment of the time), sold papers. So did coverage of long-distance record-setting flights. When Admiral Richard Byrd became the first person to fly over the North Pole in 1926, he became a national hero.

It took railroads half a century to complete a cycle of pioneering, merger, regulation, and stabilization; the airlines did it in just over a decade, culminating in the 1938 Civil Aeronautics Act. An important milestone was the 1925 Contract Air Mail Act, whereby the federal government awarded contracts for airmail delivery on a competitive basis. These contracts were essential to the emergence of modern airlines because they offered a guaranteed profit at a time when neither the technology nor the demand existed for commercial transport of passengers. Charles Lindbergh had been both a stunt pilot and an airmail pilot in Minnesota before his record-breaking flight.

Lindbergh's transatlantic solo set off a boom—often called the Lindbergh boom—that saw the number of airlines expand from sixteen in 1927 to forty-seven in 1930. But commercial air travel was still very much in its infancy. In 1929 Lindbergh joined other investors to

by the same forces that influenced urban residents. Much of the new technology—especially automobiles—enhanced rural life. Country people, like their urban counterparts, were tempted by the materialistic new values proclaimed on the radio, in magazines, and in movies. Moreover, many urban residents—immigrant Catholics, for example—were just as alarmed about declining moral standards as rural Protestants were. A simplified urban-rural dichotomy misrepresents the complexity of the decade's cultural and ethnic conflicts.

Immigration Restriction. These conflicts often centered on the question of growing racial and ethnic pluralism. When native-born white Protestants—both rural and city dwellers—looked at their communities in

1920, they saw a nation that had changed dramatically in only forty years. During that time more than 23 million immigrants had come to America, many of them Jews or Catholics, most of peasant stock. Senator William Bruce of Maryland branded them "indigestible lumps" in the "national stomach," implying that mainstream society could not absorb their large numbers and foreign customs. This sentiment, termed **nativism**, was widely shared.

Nativist animosity fueled a new drive against immigration. The Chinese had been excluded in 1882, and Theodore Roosevelt had negotiated a "gentleman's agreement" to limit Japanese immigration in 1908. Yet efforts to restrict European immigration did not meet with much success until after World War I, which had heightened

customers.) TAT was not that much more efficient than the fastest train, however, and was much more expensive, so it never turned much of a profit despite its nickname of "the Lindbergh line." The airline was soon absorbed into Trans World Airlines (TWA). In fact by the early 1930s, the outlines of the other major airline dynasties, including United, Eastern, and Northwest, were firmly in place. These companies would dominate the domestic and, in the case of Pan American, the international markets until airline deregulation in the 1970s.

Aviation technology took a quantum leap forward with the introduction in 1936 of the DC-3. With its seating capacity of twenty-one passengers, the DC-3 offered airlines the possibility of generating profits through passenger travel rather than being dependent on airmail contracts. The DC-3, manufactured by the Douglas Aircraft Company, proved to be the most influential piece of aircraft in history as well as one of the most dependable. Hundreds of its models are still flying today.

found Transcontinental Air Transport (TAT), which promised passengers coast-to-coast passage in forty-eight hours by flying during the day and taking the train at night. (Night flying, especially over mountainous regions, was considered too dangerous a risk to paying

suspicion of "hyphenated" Americans. During the Red Scare, nativists had played up the supposed association of the immigrants with radicalism and labor unrest, charging that southern and eastern European Catholics and Jews were incapable of becoming true Americans.

In response Congress passed an emergency bill in 1921, limiting the number of immigrants to 3 percent of the foreign born from each national group as represented in the 1910 census. President Woodrow Wilson refused to sign it, but the bill was reintroduced and passed under Warren Harding. In 1924 a more restrictive measure, the National Origins Act, reduced immigration until 1927 to 2 percent of each nationality's representation in the 1890 census—which had included relatively small numbers of people from southeastern Europe and Russia. After 1927

(later postponed to 1929) the law set a cap of 150,000 immigrants per year and continued to tie admission into the United States to the quota system. Japanese immigrants were excluded entirely. While limiting all immigration, the act clearly privileged older immigrant groups whose "national origins" were northern and western European at the expense of more recent southern and eastern Europeans. By placing Japanese immigrants outside the quota system, the act also drew sharp racial lines as to who was welcome to American shores (see American Voices, "Kazuo Kawai: A Foreigner in America," p. 686).

Puerto Rico provided a different source of immigration. After the Jones Act of 1917 conferred U.S. citizenship on Puerto Ricans, they could go to and from the mainland without restriction. Most of the movement

Kazuo Kawai

A Foreigner in America

Before the 1920s the laws regulating immigration from Asia contained more loopholes for the Japanese than the Chinese. As a result there were approximately 110,000 Japanese living in the United States in 1920. Asian immigrants' experience of prejudice was much sharper than that of Europeans; in California, for example, the Alien Land Law of 1913 barred foreign-born Japanese from purchasing land or leasing it for more than three years. At the same time the experiences of Japanese immigrants such as Kazuo Kawai echoed the problems that many young ethnic Americans faced in the 1920s as they recognized that they did not belong in the old country but were not accepted as "One Hundred Percent Americans."

Then, for the first time, I began to think about my trip to Japan. I found myself wondering if I could prepare myself for some work there. . . . I began to feel that no matter for what position I prepared myself for in America, I would be unrecognized and handicapped. I would be able to go just so high and no higher. But thinking of my trip to Japan, I realized that there was a nation, complete in itself, great, wonderful, with a glorious future, where every position from the bottom to the top was filled by Japanese. There, I would meet no cool unrecognition. If I had the ability, I could go to the top,

and set the limit myself. . . . For the first time, I felt myself becoming identified with Japan, and began to realize that I was a Japanese. But there was another side. Was I a Japanese? What could I be able to do in Japan? I couldn't read or write Japanese. I didn't know any of the customs or traditions of Japan. How could I do anything there? I realized with a shock that I was not a Japanese. Thus, at the same time that I came to realize that I was a Japanese, I came to realize also that I was not a Japanese. Where did I belong? I realized with a pang that I was a "man without a country." . . . [I]t hurt because I couldn't say: "This is my own, my native land." What was my native land? Japan? True, I was born there. But it had seemed a queer, foreign land to me when I visited it. America? I had, until now, thought so. I had even told my father once that even in case of war between Japan and America, I would consider America as my country. In language, in thought, in ideals, in custom, in everything, I was American. But America wouldn't have me. She wouldn't recognize me in high school. She put the pictures of those of my race at the tail end of the year book. (I was a commencement speaker, so they had to put my picture near the front.) She won't let me play tennis on the courts in the city parks of Los Angeles, by city ordinance. She won't give me service when I go to a barber's shop. She won't let me own a house to live in. She won't give me a job, unless it is a menial one that no American wants. I thought I was American, but America wouldn't have me. Once I was American, but America made a foreigner out of me—not a Japanese, but a foreigner—a foreigner to any country, for I am just as much a foreigner to Japan as to America.

Source: Stanford Survey of Race Relations (Stanford, CA: Stanford University, 1924), Hoover Institute Archives.

---

of the National Origins Act in 1924 reduced the nativist fervor, robbing the Klan of its most potent issue.

Legislating Values: The Scopes Trial and Prohibition

Other cultural tensions erupted over religion. The debate between modernist and fundamentalist Protestants, which had been simmering since the 1890s (see Chapter 19), came to a boil in the 1920s. Modernists, or liberal Protestants, tried to reconcile religion with Charles Dar-

win's theory of evolution and recent technological and scientific discoveries. **Fundamentalists** clung to a literal interpretation of the Bible. Most major Protestant denominations, especially the Baptists and the Presbyterians, experienced heated internal conflicts over these issues. However, the most conspicuous evangelical figures came from outside mainstream denominations. Popular preachers like Billy Sunday and Aimee Semple McPherson used revivals, storefront churches, and open-air preaching to popularize their own blends of charismatic fundamentalism and traditional values.

Ku Klux Klan Women Parade in Washington, D.C.

The Ku Klux Klan was so well integrated into the daily life of some white Protestants that one woman from rural Indiana remembered her time in the KKK in the 1920s as "just a celebration . . . a way of growing up." Perhaps as many as 500,000 women joined the Women of the Ku Klux Klan (WKKK) in the 1920s, including these women who paraded down Pennsylvania Avenue in Washington, D.C., in 1928. National Archives at College Park, MD.

For more help analyzing this image, see the ONLINE STUDY GUIDE at **bedfordstmartins.com/henretta.**

The Scopes Trial. Religious controversy soon entered the political arena when fundamentalists, worried about increasing secularism and declining morality, turned to the law to shore up their vision of a righteous Protestant nation. Some states enacted legislation to block the teaching of evolution in the schools. In 1925, for instance, Tennessee passed a law declaring that "it shall be unlawful . . . to teach any theory that denies the story of the Divine creation of man as taught in the Bible, and to teach instead that man has descended from a lower order of animals." In a test case involving John T. Scopes, a high school biology teacher in Dayton, Tennessee, the fledgling American Civil Liberties Union (ACLU) challenged the constitutionality of that law. Clarence

Darrow, the famous criminal lawyer, defended Scopes; the spellbinding orator William Jennings Bryan, three-time presidential candidate and ardent fundamentalist, was the most prominent member of the prosecution's team.

The Scopes trial was quickly dubbed the "monkey trial," referring both to Darwin's theory that human beings and primates share a common ancestor and to the circus atmosphere in the courtroom. In July 1925 more than 100 journalists crowded the sweltering courthouse in Dayton, Tennessee, giving massive publicity to the knotty questions of faith and scientific theory that the trial addressed. The jury took only eight minutes to deliver its verdict: guilty. Though the Tennessee Supreme Court later overturned the conviction on a technicality,

the reversal prevented further appeals of the case, and the controversial law remained on the books for more than thirty years. Historically, the trial symbolizes the conflict between the two competing value systems, cosmopolitan and traditional, that clashed in the 1920s. It suggests that despite the period's image as a frivolous and decadent time, traditional religious values of spirituality and morality continued to matter deeply to many Americans.

Prohibition. Like the dispute over evolution, Prohibition involved the power of the state to enforce social values. Americans did drink less overall after passage of the Eighteenth Amendment, which took effect in January of 1920 (see Chapter 22). Yet more than any other issue, Prohibition gave the decade its reputation as the Roaring Twenties. In major cities, whose ethnic populations had always opposed Prohibition, noncompliance was widespread. People imitated rural moonshiners by distilling "bathtub gin." Illegal saloons called **speakeasies** sprang up everywhere—more than 30,000 of them in New York City alone. Liquor smugglers operated with ease along borders and coastlines. Organized crime, already a presence in major cities, supplied a ready-made distribution network for the bootleg liquor, using the "noble experiment," as Prohibition was called, to entrench itself more deeply in city politics. Said the decade's most notorious gangster, Al Capone, "Everybody calls me a racketeer. I call myself a businessman. When I sell liquor, it's bootlegging. When my patrons serve it on a silver tray on Lake Shore Drive, it's hospitality."

By the middle of the decade, Prohibition was clearly failing. Government appropriations for its enforcement were woefully inadequate; the few highly publicized raids hardly made a dent in the liquor trade. Forces for repeal—the "wets," as opposed to the "drys," who continued to support the Eighteenth Amendment—began the long process to obtain the necessary votes in Congress and state legislatures to amend the Constitution once more. The wets argued that Prohibition had undermined respect for the law and had seriously impinged on individuals' liberty. The onset of the Great Depression hastened the repeal process, as politicians began to see alcohol production as a way to create jobs and prop up the faltering economy. On December 5, 1933, the Eighteenth Amendment was repealed. Ironically, drinking became more socially acceptable, though not necessarily more widespread, than it had been before the experiment began.

Intellectual Crosscurrents

The most articulate and embittered dissenters of the 1920s were writers and intellectuals disillusioned by the horrors of World War I and the crass materialism of the new consumer culture. Some artists were so repelled by what they saw as the complacent, moralistic, and anti-intellectual tone of American life that they settled in Europe—some temporarily, like the novelists Ernest Hemingway and F. Scott Fitzgerald, others permanently, like writer Gertrude Stein. Prominent African American artists, such as dancer Josephine Baker and writer

Ignoring Prohibition

Despite their popularity, speakeasies were rarely drawn or photographed; after all, they were supposed to be private clubs tucked away beyond the reach of the law. Fancy hotels were unable to compete with speakeasies once their bars were shut down, and many went out of business in the 1920s. But John Sloan's 1928 painting shows the rich enjoying themselves at New York's posh Lafayette Hotel. It is likely that these gentlemen and ladies had flasks concealed somewhere in their evening finery.

John Sloan, *The Lafayette*, 1928, Metropolitan Museum of Art, New York. Gift of Friends of John Sloan, 1929 (28.18).

Langston Hughes, sought temporary escape from racism in France. The poet T. S. Eliot, who left the United States before the war, ultimately became a British citizen. His despairing poem *The Waste Land* (1922), with its images of a fragmented civilization in ruins after the war, influenced a generation of writers.

Other writers also made powerful statements against war and contemporary culture, including John Dos Passos, whose first novel, *The Three Soldiers* (1921), was inspired by the war, and whose *1919* (1932), the second volume in his *USA* trilogy, railed against the obscenity of "Mr. Wilson's war." Ernest Hemingway's novels *In Our Time* (1924), *The Sun Also Rises* (1926), and *A Farewell to Arms* (1929) also powerfully described the dehumanizing consequences and the futility of war. In 1925 F. Scott Fitzgerald published *The Great Gatsby*, which showed the corrosive consequences of the mindless pursuit of wealth.

But the artists and writers who migrated to Europe, particularly Paris, were not simply a "lost generation" fleeing America. They were also drawn to Paris as the cultural and artistic capital of the world and a beacon of modernism. Paris, as Gertrude Stein put it, was "where the twentieth century was happening." Indeed, the **modernist movement**, which was marked by skepticism and technical experimentation in literature, art, and music, invigorated American writing both abroad and at home. Many American writers, whether they settled in Paris or remained in their home country, joined the movement, which had begun before the war as intellectuals reacted with excitement to the cultural and social changes that science, industrialization, and urbanization had brought.

In the 1920s the business culture and political corruption of the Harding years caused intellectuals to cast a more critical eye on American society. One of the sharpest critics, the Baltimore journalist H. L. Mencken, directed his mordant wit against mass culture, small-town America with its guardians of public morals, and the *booboisie*, his contemptuous term for the middle class. In the *American Mercury*, the journal he founded in 1922, Mencken championed writers like Sherwood Anderson, Sinclair Lewis, and Theodore Dreiser, who satirized the provincialism of American society.

The literature of the 1920s was rich and varied. Poetry enjoyed a renaissance in the works of Robert Frost, Wallace Stevens, Marianne Moore, and William Carlos Williams. Edith Wharton won a Pulitzer Prize—the first woman so honored—for *The Age of Innocence* (1920). Influenced by Freudian psychology, William Faulkner achieved his first critical success with *The Sound and the Fury* (1929), set in the fictional Mississippi county of Yoknapatawpha, where inhabitants clung to the values of the old agrarian South as they struggled to adjust to modern industrial capitalism. Playwright Eugene O'Neill showed the influence of Freudian psychology in his experimental plays, including *The Hairy Ape* (1922) and *Desire Under the Elms* (1924). Although both Faulkner and O'Neill went on to produce additional major works in the 1930s, on the whole the creative energy of the literary renaissance of the 1920s did not survive into the 1930s. The Great Depression, social and ideological unrest, and the rise of totalitarianism would reshape the intellectual landscape.

Harlem Renaissance. A different kind of cultural affirmation took place in the African American community of Harlem in the 1920s. In the words of the Reverend Adam Clayton Powell Sr., pastor of the influential Abyssinian Baptist Church, Harlem loomed as "the symbol of liberty and the Promised Land to Negroes everywhere." The migration of African Americans out of the South and into the cities during the war years had continued into the 1920s, helping to make Harlem in particular a vital place that attracted talented artists and writers. Here they created the Harlem Renaissance, which broke with older genteel traditions of black literature to reclaim a cultural identity with African roots. Alain Locke, editor of the anthology *The New Negro* (1926), summed up the movement when he stated that, through art, "Negro life is seizing its first chances for group expression and self-determination."

The Harlem Renaissance championed racial pride and cultural identity in the midst of white society. The poet Langston Hughes, who became a leading exponent of the Harlem Renaissance, captured its affirmative spirit when he asserted, "I am a Negro—and beautiful." Authors such as Claude McKay, Jean Toomer, Jessie

The Harlem Renaissance

The Crisis, edited by W. E. B. Du Bois, was the magazine of the National Association for the Advancement of Colored People (NAACP). This 1929 cover suggests the cultural and political awakenings associated with the Harlem Renaissance.
Henry Lee Moon Library and Civil Rights Archive, NAACP, Washington, DC.

Fauset, and Zora Neale Hurston explored the black experience and represented the "**New Negro**" in fiction. Countee Cullen and Langston Hughes turned to poetry, and Augusta Savage used sculpture to draw attention to black accomplishments. Their production of creative work showed the ongoing African American struggle to find a way, as W. E. B. Du Bois put it, "to be both a Negro and an American."

The artistic outpouring encouraged a wide range of creative expression. Jean Toomer, a writer passionately committed to black self-expression, wrote the influential novel *Cane* in 1923. With its poems, sketches, and stories about a northern black's discovery of the rural black South, it inspired other African American artists and writers. Langston Hughes drew on the black artistic forms of blues and jazz in *The Weary Blues* (1926), a groundbreaking collection of poems. Considered the most original black poet and the most representative African American writer of the time, Hughes also wrote novels, plays, and essays. Zora Neale Hurston, born in

Florida to a family of poor tenant farmers, attended Howard University in Washington, D.C., and won a scholarship to study anthropology at Barnard College in New York City. She spent a decade collecting folklore in the South and the Caribbean and incorporated that material into her short stories and novels. Her genius for storytelling won her acclaim.

The vitality of the Harlem Renaissance was short-lived. Although the NAACP's magazine *The Crisis* was a forum for the Harlem writers, the black middle class and the intellectual elite in Harlem were relatively small and could not support the group's efforts. Its main audience consisted of white intellectuals and philanthropists, and many writers were ambivalent about depending on white patronage as they struggled to attain an authentic voice in their fiction. Langston Hughes became disillusioned with his white patron when she withdrew support as he began to write about common black people in Kansas and New York rather than keeping with African themes.

During the Jazz Age, when Harlem was in vogue, the publishing industry courted its writers, but the stock market crash of 1929 brought that interest to a sudden end. The movement waned in the 1930s as the depression deepened. Nonetheless, the writers of the Harlem Renaissance would influence a future generation of black writers when their works were rediscovered by black intellectuals during the civil rights movement of the 1960s.

Marcus Garvey and the UNIA. Although the Harlem Renaissance had little impact on the masses of African Americans, other movements built racial pride and challenged white political and cultural hegemony. The most successful was the Universal Negro Improvement Association (UNIA), which championed black separatism under the leadership of the Jamaican-born Marcus Garvey. Based in Harlem, the UNIA was the black working class's first mass movement. At its height it claimed 4 million followers, many of whom were recent migrants to northern cities. Like several nineteenth-century reformers, Marcus Garvey urged blacks to return to Africa because, he reasoned, blacks would never be treated justly in countries ruled by whites. Although he did not anticipate a massive migration, he did envision a strong black Africa that could use its power to protect blacks everywhere. Garvey's wife, Amy Jacques Garvey, appealed to black women by combining black nationalism with an emphasis on women's contributions to culture and politics.

The UNIA grew rapidly in the early 1920s. It published a newspaper called *Negro World* and undertook extensive business ventures to support black enterprise. The most ambitious project, the Black Star Line steamship company, was supposed to ferry cargo between the West Indies and the United States and take African Americans back to Africa. Irregularities in fund-raising for the project, however, led to Garvey's conviction for mail fraud in

1925, and he was sentenced to five years in prison. President Coolidge commuted his sentence in 1927, but Garvey was deported to Jamaica. Without his charismatic leadership, the movement collapsed.

Cultural Clash in the Election of 1928

The works of the lost generation and the Harlem Renaissance touched only a small minority of Americans in the 1920s, but emotionally charged issues like Prohibition, fundamentalism, and nativism eventually spilled over into national politics. The Democratic Party, which attracted both rural Protestants in the South and the West and ethnic minorities in northern cities, was especially vulnerable to the cultural conflicts of the time. The 1924 Democratic National Convention had revealed an intensely polarized party, split between the urban machines and the rural wing.

In 1928 the urban wing held sway and succeeded in nominating New York's Governor Alfred E. Smith, a descendant of Irish immigrants and a product of Tammany Hall. Proud of his background, Smith adopted "The Sidewalks of New York" as his campaign song. His candidacy troubled many voters, however. His heavy New York accent, his brown derby, and his colorful style highlighted his urban, ethnic, working-class origins, and his early career in Tammany Hall suggested incorrectly that he was little more than a cog in the machine. Smith's stand on Prohibition—although he promised to enforce it, he wanted it repealed—alienated even more voters.

An equally serious handicap, however, was his religion. In 1928 most Protestants were not ready for a Catholic president. Although Smith insisted that his religion would not interfere with his duties as president, his perceived allegiance to Rome cost him the support of Democrats and Republicans alike. Protestant clergymen, who already opposed Smith because he supported the repeal of Prohibition, led the drive against him. "No Governor can kiss the papal ring and get within gunshot of the White House," declared one Methodist bishop.

Smith's candidacy met with much opposition, but for his supporters he embodied a new America. Throughout the decade, attacks on immigrants, Catholics, and Jews had repeatedly labeled them as unwelcome outsiders. Ethnic and religious leaders and communities had vehemently countered these criticisms by offering a more inclusive vision of citizenship. One Catholic bishop summed it up neatly in 1921, stating that "National aspirations constitute Americanism. We are the blend of all the peoples of the world, and I think we are much the better for that. Americanism is not a matter of birth, Americanism is a matter of faith, of consecration to the ideals of America." That Al Smith, a man of Catholic immigrant stock, could be the Democratic Party's nominee for president suggested to many in 1928 that the country might yet embrace a more pluralistic conception of American identity.

Just as Smith was a new kind of presidential candidate for the Democrats, so was Herbert Hoover for the Republicans. As a professional administrator and engineer who had never before been elected to political office, Hoover embodied the new managerial and technological elite that was restructuring the nation's economic order. During his campaign, in which he gave only seven speeches, Hoover asserted that his vision of individualism and cooperative endeavor would banish poverty from the United States. That rhetoric, as well as his reputation for organizing a drive for humanitarian relief during the war, caused many voters to see him as more progressive than Smith. Hoover won a stunning victory, receiving 58 percent of the popular vote to Smith's 41 percent and 444 electoral votes to Smith's 87 (Map 23.3). The election suggested important underlying political changes. Despite the

overwhelming loss, the Democrats' turnout increased substantially in urban areas with significant concentrations of ethnic voters. Smith also won the industrialized states of Massachusetts and Rhode Island. The Democrats were on their way to fashioning a new identity as the party of the urban masses, a reorientation the New Deal would complete in the 1930s.

It is unlikely that any Democratic candidate, let alone a Catholic, could have won the presidency in 1928. With a seemingly prosperous economy, national consensus on foreign policy, and strong support from the business community, the Republicans were unbeatable. Ironically, Herbert Hoover's victory would put him in the unenviable position of leading the United States when the Great Depression struck in 1929. Having claimed credit for the prosperity of the 1920s, the Republicans could not escape blame for the depression; twenty-four years would pass before a Republican won the presidency again.

But as Hoover began his presidency in early 1929, most Americans expected progress and prosperity to continue. The New Era the Republicans had touted meant more than Republican ascendancy in politics, more than business-government cooperation, and more than a decline in the progressive reform movement. To most Americans the New Era embodied the industrial productivity and technological advances that made consumer goods widely available and the movies and the radio an exciting part of American life. At home and abroad the nation seemed unprecedentedly vigorous and powerful. Despite disruptive cultural conflicts and a changing workplace that undermined workers' power, despite inequities in the racial order and in the distribution of income, the general tone was one of optimism, of faith in the modern society the country had become.

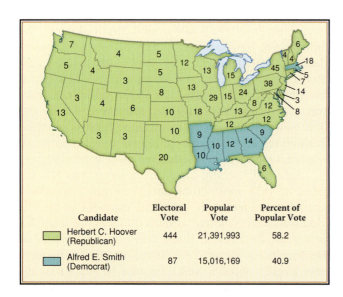

Candidate	Electoral Vote	Popular Vote	Percent of Popular Vote
Herbert C. Hoover (Republican)	444	21,391,993	58.2
Alfred E. Smith (Democrat)	87	15,016,169	40.9

MAP 23.3 Presidential Election of 1928

Historians still debate the extent to which 1928 was a critical election—an election that produced a significant realignment in voting behavior. Although the Republican Herbert Hoover swept the electoral college, Democrats were heartened by the fact that Alfred E. Smith won the heavily industrialized states of Rhode Island and Massachusetts. Not evident in this map is that Democratic turnout increased substantially in urban areas with a significant concentration of ethnic voters, a trend that would eventually lead to a new identity for the Democrats as the party of the urban masses.

FOR FURTHER EXPLORATION

► For definitions of key terms boldfaced in this chapter, see the glossary at the end of the book.

► To assess your mastery of the material covered in this chapter, see the Online Study Guide at **bedfordstmartins.com/henretta**.

► For suggested references, including Web sites, see page SR-25 at the end of the book.

► For map resources and primary documents, see **bedfordstmartins.com/henretta**.

By the 1920s modern America had arrived, a transformation that had begun with World War I. The Republican Party controlled the national government and cemented the partnership between business and government that had been accelerated by the war and that characterized the pattern of state building during the era. In foreign policy the United States promoted disarmament and the reduction of German war reparations but otherwise generally steered clear of European political affairs. The chief U.S. interest was to ensure a stable environment for economic expansion abroad, especially in the Western Hemisphere. With the exception of the 1920–1921 recession, the economy performed well, although agriculture never recovered from the postwar slump, and some industries remained overextended after their wartime expansion. The automobile industry typified the new mass-production techniques that dominated economic life in the United States and revolutionized American society.

During the 1920s a national culture began to develop. It was characterized by new ways of spending leisure time, a heightened emphasis on consumption and advertising, and the wide diffusion of new, more secular ideas and values through movies, radio, and other mass media. The new lifestyles of the decade, often called the Roaring Twenties or the Jazz Age, captured the popular imagination but were limited to a minority of the population. Families needed a middle-class income to buy cars, radios, vacuum cleaners, and toasters. Those left outside the circle of prosperity included farmers, blacks, and Mexican Americans.

Not everyone welcomed the new secular values of the 1920s. Conflicts arose over Prohibition, religion, race, and immigration. Those cultural disputes spilled over into politics, disrupting the already fractured Democratic Party. The 1928 election showed that the nation could not yet accept a Catholic as president. The Republican ascendancy continued under Herbert Hoover, who looked forward to a term filled with even greater prosperity and progress. The advances of the New Era, and the expectation that the nation would continue to be vigorous and powerful at home and abroad, made the harsh realities of the Great Depression that would follow all the more shocking.

1920	Eighteenth Amendment outlawing alcohol takes effect
	First commercial radio broadcast
	Warren G. Harding elected president
	Census reveals shift in population from farms to cities
	Edith Wharton, *The Age of Innocence*
1920–1921	National economic recession
1921	Sheppard-Towner Act
	Immigration Act limits immigration
	Washington Conference supports naval disarmament
1922	T. S. Eliot, *The Waste Land*
1922–1929	Record economic expansion
1923	Harding dies in office: succeeded by Calvin Coolidge as president
	Time magazine founded
	Jean Toomer, *Cane*
1924	Dawes Plan reduces German reparation payments
	Teapot Dome scandal
	U.S. troops withdraw from Dominican Republic
	National Origins Act further limits immigration
1925	F. Scott Fitzgerald, *The Great Gatsby*
	Height of Ku Klux Klan's power
	Scopes ("monkey") trial
1926	Alain Locke, *The New Negro*
	The Book-of-the-Month Club is founded
1927	First "talkies"
	Charles Lindbergh's solo flight
	Ford's Model A car
1928	Herbert Hoover elected president
	Kellogg-Briand Pact condemning militarism signed
1929	*Middletown* published
	Ernest Hemingway, *A Farewell to Arms*
	William Faulkner, *The Sound and the Fury*

CHAPTER 24

The Great Depression

The Coming of the Great Depression
Causes of the Depression
The Deepening Economic Crisis
The Worldwide Depression

Hard Times
The Invisible Scar
Families Face the Depression
*Popular Culture Views the
    Depression*

Harder Times
*African Americans in the
    Depression*
Dust Bowl Migrations
Mexican American Communities
*Asian Americans Face the
    Depression*

**Herbert Hoover and the Great
Depression**
Hoover Responds
Rising Discontent
The 1932 Election: A New Order

OUR IMAGES OF THE 1920s and the decade that followed are polar opposites. Flappers and movie stars, admen and stockbrokers, caught up in what F. Scott Fitzgerald called the "world's most expensive orgy"—these are our conceptions of the Jazz Age. The 1930s we remember in terms of breadlines and hobos, dust bowl devastation and hapless migrants piled into dilapidated jalopies. Almost all our impressions of that decade are black and white, in part because widely distributed photographs taken by Farm Security Administration photographers etched this dark visual image of depression America on the popular consciousness.

But this contrast between the flush times of the 1920s and the hard times of the 1930s is too stark. The vaunted prosperity of the 1920s was never as widespread or as deeply rooted as many believed. Though America's mass-consumption economy was the envy of the world, many people lived on its margins. However, not all Americans were devastated by the depression. Those with secure jobs or fixed incomes survived the economic downturn in relatively good shape. Yet few could escape the depression's wide-ranging social, political, and cultural effects. Whatever their personal situation was, Americans understood that the nation was deeply scarred by the pervasive struggle to survive and overcome "hard times."

◄ **Looking for Work**
This detail of Moses Soyer's painting Employment Agency *(1940) captures the despair and bleak resignation of a victim of the Great Depression—a white male, down on his luck but still trying to keep up appearances and hope.*
Collection of Philip J. and Suzanne Schiller.

Wall Street, October 1929
Crowds gather in front of the New York Stock Exchange on October 25, 1929, the day after "Black Thursday." The mood would be even darker after "Black Tuesday," October 29, the day the bubble burst. Corbis-Bettmann.

The Coming of the Great Depression

Booms and busts are a permanent feature of the business cycle in capitalist economies. Since the beginning of the Industrial Revolution early in the nineteenth century, the United States had experienced recessions or panics at least once every twenty years. But none was as severe as the Great Depression of the 1930s. The country would not recover from the depression until World War II put American factories and people back to work.

Causes of the Depression

The downturn began slowly and almost imperceptibly. After 1927 consumer spending declined, and housing construction slowed. Soon inventories piled up; in 1928 manufacturers began to cut back production and lay off workers, reducing incomes and buying power and reinforcing the slowdown. By the summer of 1929, the economy was clearly in recession.

Stock Market Speculation and the Great Crash. Yet stock market activity continued unabated. By 1929 the stock market had become the symbol of the nation's prosperity, an icon of American business culture. In a *Ladies' Home Journal* article titled "Everyone Ought to Be Rich," financier John J. Raskob advised that $15 a month invested in sound common stocks would grow to $80,000 in twenty years. Not everyone was playing the market, however. Only about 4 million Americans, or roughly 10 percent of the nation's households, owned stock in 1929.

Stock prices had been rising steadily since 1921, but in 1928 and 1929 they surged forward, rising on average over 40 percent. At the time market activity was essentially unregulated. **Margin buying** in particular proceeded at a feverish pace, as customers were encouraged to buy stocks with a small down payment and finance the rest with a broker loan. But then on "Black Thursday," October 24, 1929, and again on "Black Tuesday," October 29, the bubble burst. On those two bleak days, more than 28 million shares changed hands in frantic trading. Overextended investors, suddenly finding themselves heavily in debt, began to sell their portfolios. Waves of panic selling ensued. Practically overnight stock values fell from a peak of $87 billion (at least on paper) to $55 billion.

The impact of what became known as the Great Crash was felt far beyond the trading floors of Wall Street. Commercial banks had invested heavily in corporate stock. Speculators who had borrowed from banks to buy their stocks could not repay their loans because they could not sell their shares. Throughout the nation bank failures multiplied. Since bank deposits were uninsured, a bank collapse meant that depositors lost all their money. The sudden loss of their life savings was a tremendous shock to members of the middle class,

many of whom had no other resources to cope with the crisis. More symbolically, the crash destroyed the faith of those who viewed the stock market as the crowning symbol of American prosperity, precipitating a crisis of confidence that prolonged the depression.

Structural Weaknesses. Although the stock market crash triggered the Great Depression, long-standing weaknesses in the economy accounted for its length and severity. Agriculture, in particular, had never recovered from the recession of 1920 and 1921. Farmers faced high fixed costs for equipment and mortgages, which they had incurred during the inflationary war years. When prices fell because of overproduction, many farmers defaulted on their mortgage payments, risking foreclosure. Because farmers accounted for about a fourth of the nation's gainfully employed workers in 1929, their difficulties weakened the general economic structure.

Certain basic industries also had economic setbacks during the prosperous 1920s. Textiles, facing a steady decline after the war, abandoned New England for cheaper labor in the South but suffered still from decreased demand and overproduction. Mining and lumbering, which had expanded in response to wartime demand, confronted the same problems. The railroad industry, damaged by stiff competition from trucks, faced shrinking passenger revenues and stagnant freight levels, worsened by inefficient management. While these older sectors of the economy faltered, newer and more successful consumer-based industries, such as chemicals, appliances and food processing, proved not yet strong enough to lead the way to recovery.

Unequal Distribution of Wealth. The unequal distribution of the nation's wealth was another underlying weakness of the economy. During the 1920s the share of national income going to families in the upper- and middle-income brackets increased. The tax policies of Secretary of the Treasury Andrew Mellon contributed to a concentration of wealth by lowering personal income tax rates, eliminating the wartime excess-profits tax, and increasing deductions that favored corporations and the affluent. In 1929 the lowest 40 percent of the population received only 12.5 percent of aggregate family income, while the top 5 percent of the population received 30 percent. Once the depression began, this skewed income distribution left the majority of people unable to spend the amount of money that was needed to revive the economy.

The Deepening Economic Crisis

The Great Depression became self-perpetuating. The more the economy contracted, the longer people expected the depression to last. The longer they expected it to last, the more afraid they became to spend or invest their money, if they had any—and spending and investment was exactly what was needed to stimulate economic recovery. The economy showed some improvement in the summer of 1931, when low prices encouraged consumption but plunged again late that fall.

The nation's banks, already weakened by the stock market crash, continued to collapse. When agricultural prices and income fell more steeply than usual in 1930, many farmers went bankrupt, causing rural banks to fail. By December 1930 so many rural banks had defaulted on their obligations that urban banks too began to collapse. The wave of bank failures frightened depositors, who withdrew their savings, deepening the crisis.

In 1931 a change in the nation's monetary policy compounded the banks' problems. In the first phase of the depression, the Federal Reserve System had reacted cautiously. But in October 1931 the Federal Reserve Bank of New York significantly increased the **discount rate**— the interest rate charged on loans to member banks—and reduced the amount of money placed in circulation through the purchase of government securities. This miscalculation squeezed the money supply, forcing prices down and depriving businesses of funds for investment. In the face of the money shortage, the American people could have pulled the country out of the depression only by spending faster. But because of falling prices, rising unemployment, and a troubled banking system, Americans preferred to keep their dollars, stashing them under the mattress rather than depositing them in the bank, further limiting the amount of money in circulation. Economic stagnation solidified.

The Worldwide Depression

President Hoover later blamed the severity of the depression on the international economic situation. Although domestic factors far outweighed international causes of America's protracted decline, Hoover was correct in surmising that economic problems in the rest of the world affected the United States and vice versa. Indeed, the international economic system had been out of kilter since World War I. It functioned only as long as American banks exported enough capital to allow European countries to repay their debts and to buy U.S. manufactured goods and foodstuffs. By the late 1920s European economies were staggering under the weight of huge debts and trade imbalances with the United States, which effectively undercut their recovery from the war. By 1931 most European economies had collapsed.

In an interdependent world the economic downturn in America had enormous repercussions. When U.S. companies cut back production, they also cut their purchases of raw materials and supplies abroad, devastating many foreign economies. When American financiers sharply reduced their foreign investment and consumers bought fewer European goods, debt repayment became even more difficult, straining the gold standard, the foun-

dation of international commerce in the interwar period. As European economic conditions worsened, demand for American exports fell drastically. Finally, when the Hawley-Smoot Tariff of 1930 went into effect, raising rates to all-time highs, foreign governments retaliated by imposing their own trade restrictions, further limiting the market for American goods and intensifying the worldwide depression.

No other nation was as hard hit as the United States (Figure 24.1). From the height of its prosperity before the stock market crash in 1929 to the depths of the

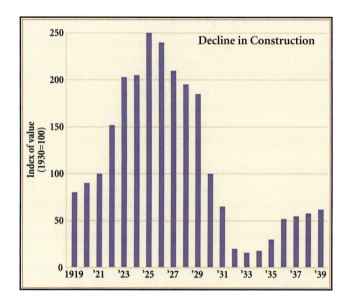

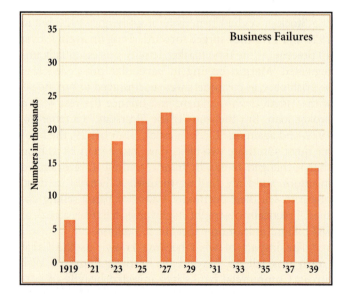

FIGURE 24.1 Statistics of the Depression

The top graph shows the decline in construction, as reflected in the value of new building permits; the bottom graph shows the number of business failures.

Source: Historical Statistics of the United States, Colonial Times to 1970 (Washington, DC: U.S. Government Printing Office, 1975), 626, 912.

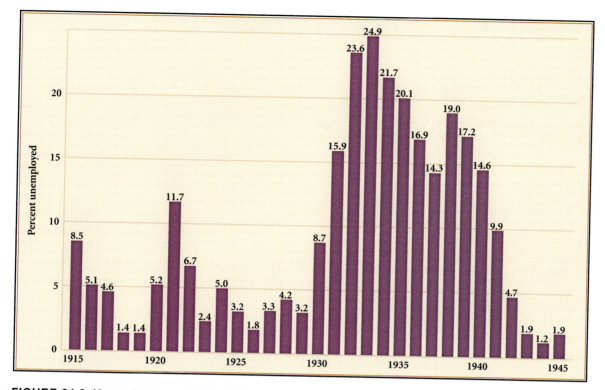

FIGURE 24.2 Unemployment, 1915–1945

This graph shows how the historically low unemployment levels of the 1920s began to rise in 1930. By 1933 one in four American workers was out of a job.

depression in 1932 and 1933, the U.S. gross domestic product (GDP) was cut almost in half, declining from $103.1 billion to $58 billion in 1932. Consumption expenditures dropped by 18 percent, construction by 78 percent; private investment plummeted 88 percent, and farm income, already low, was more than halved. In this period 9,000 banks went bankrupt or closed their doors and 100,000 businesses failed. The consumer price index (CPI) declined by 25 percent, and corporate profits fell from $10 billion to $1 billion.

Most tellingly, unemployment rose from 3.2 percent to 24.9 percent, affecting approximately 12 million workers (Figure 24.2). Statistical measures at the time were fairly crude, so the figures were probably understated. At least one in four workers was out of a job, and even those who had jobs faced wage cuts, work for which they were overqualified, or layoffs. Their stories put a human face on the almost incomprehensible dimensions of the economic downturn.

Hard Times

"We didn't go hungry, but we lived lean." That statement sums up the experiences of many families during the Great Depression. The majority of Americans were neither very rich nor very poor. For most the depression did not mean losing thousands of dollars in the stock market or pulling children out of boarding school; nor did it mean going on relief or living in a shantytown. In a typical family in the 1930s, the husband still had a job, and the wife was still a homemaker. Families usually managed to "make do." But life was far from easy, and most Americans worried about an uncertain future that might bring even harder times into their lives.

The Invisible Scar

"You could feel the depression deepen," recalled the writer Caroline Bird, "but you could not look out the window and see it." Many people never saw a breadline or a man selling apples on the corner. The depression caused a private kind of despair that often simmered behind closed doors. "I've lived in cities for many months broke, without help, too timid to get in breadlines," the writer Meridel LeSueur remembered. "A woman will shut herself up in a room until it is taken away from her, and eat a cracker a day and be as quiet as a mouse" (see Voices from Abroad, "Mary Agnes Hamilton: Breadlines and Beggars," p. 700).

Many variables—race, ethnicity, age, class, and gender—influenced how Americans experienced the depression. Blacks, Mexican Americans, and others already on the economic margins saw their opportunities shrink

Mary Agnes Hamilton

Breadlines and Beggars

British writer and Labor Party activist Mary Agnes Hamilton arrived in the United States on a gloomy morning in December 1931 for a lecture tour that eventually took her as far west as Nebraska and as far south as Virginia. Her observations of conditions in New York during that grim winter confirm the devastation and despair gripping urban America.

One does not need to be long in New York (or for that matter in Chicago, in Cleveland, in Detroit, in Kansas, or in Buffalo) to see that there are plenty of real tragedies, as well as plenty of not-so-real ones. If those who have turned in the second or third car talk the most, the others talk—when they get the chance. In New York, one has only to pass outside the central island bounded by Lexington and Sixth Avenues to see hardship, misery, and degradation, accentuated by the shoddy grimness of the shabby houses and broken pavements. Look down from the Elevated, and there are long queues of dreary-looking men and women standing in "breadlines" outside the relief offices and the various church and other charitable institutions. Times Square, at any hour of the day and late into the evening, offers an exhibit for the edification of the theater-goer, for it is packed with shabby, utterly dumb and apathetic-looking men, who stand there, waiting for the advent of the coffee wagon run by Mr. W. R. Hearst of the New York American. Nowhere, in New York or any other city, can one escape from the visible presence of those who with perhaps unconscious cruelty are called "the idle." At every street corner, and wherever taxi or car has to pause, men try to sell one apples, oranges, or picture papers. Not matches—matches, in book form, are given away with every fifteen-cent package of cigarettes, lie on every restaurant table, litter the street, half used, and exemplify how little, as yet, the depression has done to overcome the national habit of easy-going wastefulness. On a fine day, men will press on one gardenias at fifteen cents apiece; on any day, rows of them line every relatively open space, eager to shine one's shoes. It is perhaps because so many people are doing without this "shine," or attempting with unfamiliar hands and a sense of deep indignity to shine their own, that the streets look shabby and the persons on them so much less well-groomed than of yore. The well-shod feet of the States struck me forcibly on my first visit; the ill-cleaned feet of New York struck me as forcibly in January and April 1932. In 1930 an English friend, long domesticated in New England, told me that she hesitated to bring her children to London, since the sight of beggars would make so painful an impression on them; in 1932 there are more beggars to be met with in New York than in London. Yes, distress is there; the idle are there. How many, no one really knows. Ten million or more in the country; a million and a half in New York are reported. They are there; as is, admittedly a dark undergrowth of horrid suffering that is certainly more degraded and degrading than anything Britain or Germany knows. Their immense presence makes a grim background to the talk of depression: there is an obscure alarm as to what they may do "if this goes on," and the charitable relief funds (about which more later) dry up, as they are in many centers already doing; their existence, in numbers that grow instead of diminishing, constitutes the fact that largely justifies the feeling of gloom. . . .

The American people, unfamiliar with suffering, with none of that long history of catastrophe and calamity behind it which makes the experience of European nations, is outraged and baffled by misfortune. Depression blocks its view: it cannot see round it. Misled in the onset by leaders who assured it, in every soothing term and tone, that reverse was to last but for a little while; that it was the preliminary to recovery; that American institutions were immune to the ills that had laid the countries of the rest of the world upon their backs; that prosperity was native to the soil of the Union, and all that was needed was to wait till the clouds, blown up by the wickedness of other lands, rolled by, as they were bound to do, and that speedily; the nation now suffers from a despair of any and every kind of leadership. Every institution is assailed; even the sacred foundations of democracy are being undermined. The defeatism that has been so lamentably evidenced in Congress is not peculiar to Congressmen, any more than is the crude individualism of their reactions. It lies like a pall over the spirit of the nation. It is felt by most people to be, in fact, the greatest obstacle to recovery, to that restoration of confidence for which everybody pleads, which everybody sees as necessary. But how to break it nobody knows.

Source: Mary Agnes Hamilton, *In America Today* (1932), in Allan Nevins, ed., *America through British Eyes* (Gloucester, MA: Peter Smith, 1968), 443–44.

further. Often the last hired they were the first fired. Hard times weighed heavily on the nation's senior citizens of all races, many of whom faced destitution. Many white middle-class Americans experienced downward mobility for the first time. An unemployed man in Pittsburgh told the journalist Lorena Hickok, "Lady, you just can't know what it's like to have to move your family out of the nice house you had in the suburbs, part paid for, down into an apartment, down into another apartment, smaller and in a worse neighborhood, down, down, down, until finally you end up in the slums." People like this, who strongly believed in the Horatio Alger ethic of upward mobility through hard work, suddenly found themselves floundering in a society that did not reward them for that work as they had expected. Thus the depression challenged basic American tenets of individualism and success. Yet even in the midst of pervasive unemployment, many people blamed themselves for their misfortune. This sense of damaged pride pervaded letters written to President Franklin D. Roosevelt and his wife Eleanor, summed up succinctly in one woman's plea for assistance: "Please don't think me unworthy."

After exhausting their savings and credit, many families found the traditional path of turning to relatives, neighbors, church, and mutual-aid societies in time of need blocked. Private charities and benefit societies were overwhelmed by the needy, and individuals often had too few resources to share. For many the only alternative was the humiliation of going on relief—seeking aid from state or local governments (Map 24.1). Even if families endured the demeaning process of certification for state or local relief, the amount they received was a pittance. In New York State, where benefits were among the highest in the nation, a family on relief received only $2.39 a week. Such hardships left a deep wound: one historian described it as the "invisible scar." And the scar branded more than those who were forced onto the relief rolls. For the majority of Americans, the fear of losing control over their lives was the crux of the Great Depression.

Families Face the Depression

Sociologists who studied family life during the 1930s found that the depression usually intensified existing behavior. If a family had been stable and cohesive before the depression, then members pulled together to overcome the new obstacles. But if a family had shown signs of disintegration, the depression made the situation worse. On the whole far more families hung together than broke apart.

Gender Roles. Men and women experienced the Great Depression differently, partly because of the gender roles that governed male and female behavior in the 1930s. From childhood men had been trained to be

The Breadline

Some of the most vivid images from the depression were breadlines and men selling apples on street corners. Note that all the people in this breadline are men. Women rarely appeared in breadlines, often preferring to endure private deprivation rather than violate standards of respectable behavior by appearing in public to ask for help.

Franklin D. Roosevelt Library, Hyde Park, NY.

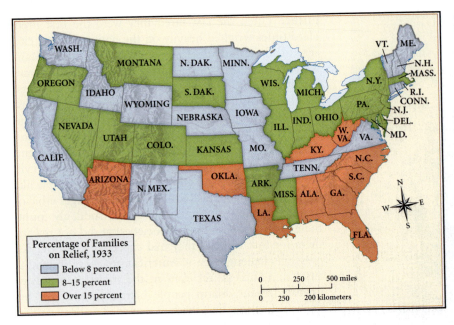

breadwinners; they considered themselves failures if they could no longer support their families (see American Voices, "A Working-Class Family Encounters the Great Depression," p. 703). But while millions of men lost their jobs, few of the nation's 28 million homemakers lost their positions in the home. In contrast to men, women's sense of self-importance increased as they struggled to keep their families afloat. Sociologists Robert and Helen Lynd noticed this phenomenon in their follow-up study of *Middletown* (Muncie, Indiana), published in 1937: "The men, cut adrift from their usual routine, lost much of their sense of time and dawdled helplessly and dully about the streets; while in the homes the women's world remained largely intact and the round of cooking, housecleaning, and mending became if anything more absorbing."

Even if a wife took a job when her husband lost his, she retained almost total responsibility for housework and child care. To economize women sewed their own clothes and canned fruits and vegetables. They bought day-old bread and heated several dishes in the oven at once to save fuel. Women who had once employed servants did their own housework. Eleanor Roosevelt described the stressful effects of the depression on these women's lives: "It means endless little economies and constant anxiety for fear of some catastrophe such as accident or illness which may completely swamp the family budget." Housewives' ability to watch every penny often made the difference in a family's survival.

Consumption Trends. Despite hard times Americans as a whole maintained a fairly high level of consumption. As in the 1920s households in the middle-income range—in 1935 the 50.2 percent of American families

with an annual income of $500 to $1,500—did much of the buying. Several trends allowed those families to maintain their former standard of living despite pay cuts and unemployment. Between 1929 and 1935 deflation lowered the cost of living almost 20 percent. And buying on the installment plan increased in the 1930s, permitting many families to stretch their reduced incomes.

Americans spent their money differently in the depression, though. Telephone use and clothing sales dropped sharply, but cigarettes, movies, radios, and newspapers, once considered luxuries, became necessities. The automobile proved one of the most depression-proof items in the family budget. Though sales of new cars dropped, gasoline sales held stable, suggesting that families bought used cars or kept their old models running longer.

Demographics of the Great Depression. Another measure of the impact of the depression on family life was the change in demographic trends. The marriage rate fell from 10.14 per thousand persons in 1929 to 7.87 per thousand in 1932. The divorce rate decreased as well because couples could not afford the legal expense of dissolving failed unions. And between 1930 and 1933, the birthrate, which had fallen steadily since 1800, dropped from 21.3 live births per thousand to 18.4, a dramatic 14 percent decrease. The new level would have produced a decline in population if maintained. Though it rose slightly after 1934, by the end of the decade it was still only 18.8. (In contrast, at the height of the baby boom following World War II, the birthrate was 25 per thousand.)

The drop in the birthrate during the Great Depression could not have happened without increased access to effective contraception. In 1936, in *United States v.*

Larry Van Dusen

A Working-Class Family Encounters the Great Depression

Although many families endured the privations of the Great Depression with equanimity, others, like Larry Van Dusen's family, experienced tremendous strains. In this passage from his oral history account to journalist Studs Terkel, he describes the pressures on male wage earners and their children.

One of the most common things—and it certainly happened to me—was this feeling of your father's failure. That somehow he hadn't beaten the rap. Sure things were tough, but why should I be the kid who had to put a piece of cardboard into the sole of my shoe to go to school? It was not a thing coupled with resentment against my father. It was simply this feeling of regret, that somehow he hadn't done better, that he hadn't gotten the breaks. Also a feeling of uneasiness about my father's rage against the way things are.

My father was very much of an individualist, as craftsmen usually are. He would get jobs he considered beneath his status during this period. Something would happen: he'd quarrel with the foreman, he'd have a fight with the boss. He was a carpenter. He couldn't be happy fixing a roadbed or driving a cab or something like that. He was a skilled tradesman and this whole thing had him beat. I think it bugged the family a lot.

Remember, too, the shock, the confusion, the hurt that many kids felt about their fathers not being able to provide for them. This reflected itself very often in bitter quarrels between father and son. I recall I had one. I was the oldest of six children. I think there was a special feeling between the father and the oldest son. . . .

My father led a rough life: he drank. During the Depression, he drank more. There was more conflict in the home. A lot of fathers—mine, among them—had a habit of taking off. They'd go to Chicago to look for work. To Topeka. This left the family at home, waiting and hoping that the old man would find something. And there was always the Saturday night ordeal as to whether or not the old man would get home with his paycheck. Everything was sharpened and hurt more by the Depression.

Heaven would break out once in a while, and the old man would get a week's work. I remember he'd come home at night, and he'd come down the path through the trees. He always rode a bicycle. He'd stop and sometimes say hello, or give me a hug. And that smell of fresh sawdust on those carpenter overalls, and the fact that Dad was home, and there was a week's wages—well, this is something you remember, too. That's the good you remember.

And then there was always the bad part. That's when you'd see your father coming home with the toolbox on his shoulder. Or carrying it. That meant the job was over. The tools were home now, and we were back on the treadmill again.

I remember coming back home, many years afterwards. Things were better. It was after the Depression, after the war. To me, it was hardly the same house. My father turned into an angel. They weren't wealthy, but they were making it. They didn't have the acid and the recriminations and the bitterness that I had felt as a child.

Source: Studs Terkel, *Hard Times* (New York: Pantheon Books, 1986), 107–18.

One Package of Japanese Pessaries, a federal court struck down all federal restrictions on the dissemination of contraceptive information. The decision gave doctors wide discretion in prescribing birth control for married couples, making it legal everywhere except the heavily Catholic states of Massachusetts and Connecticut. While abortion remained illegal the number of women who underwent the procedure increased. Because many abortionists operated under unsafe or unsanitary condi-tions, between 8,000 and 10,000 women died each year from the illegal operations.

Margaret Sanger played a major role in encouraging the availability and popular acceptance of birth control (see Chapter 20). Sanger began her career as a public-health nurse in the 1910s in the slums of New York City. At first she joined forces with socialists trying to help working-class families to control their fertility. In the 1920s and 1930s, however, she appealed to the middle

It's Up to the Women

Ironically, as women struggled to cope with their own unemployment or to help their families weather the hard times, advertisers relentlessly urged middle-class women to maintain their consumption patterns as a means of stimulating the economy and bringing about recovery. This 1932 cover for Ladies' Home Journal *not only emphasizes the perception of women's pivotal role as consumers but also evokes the patriotism of World War I through use of the icon of Uncle Sam, so familiar in World War I posters. The analogy between fighting a war and fighting the depression was a common theme throughout the decade.* Ladies' Home Journal, *February 1932.*

class for support, identifying those families as the key to the movement's success. Sanger also courted the medical profession, pioneering the establishment of professionally staffed birth control clinics and winning the American Medical Association's endorsement of contraception in 1937. As a result of Sanger's efforts, birth control became less a feminist issue and more a medical question. And in the context of the depression it became an economic issue as well, as financially pressed couples sought to delay or limit their childbearing while they weathered hard times.

Women and Work.   One way for families to make ends meet was to send an additional member of the household to work. Whereas in African American families that role already often fell to a married woman by the turn of the century, it was not until the 1930s that married white women expanded their presence in the labor market, too, and the total number of married women employed outside the home rose 50 percent. Working women, especially white married women, encountered sharp resentment and outright discrimination in the workplace. When asked in a 1936 Gallup poll whether wives should work when their husbands had jobs, 82 percent of those interviewed said no. Such public disapproval encouraged restrictions on women's right to work. From 1932 to 1937 the federal government would not allow a husband and a wife to hold government jobs at the same time. Many states adopted laws that prohibited married women from working.

Married or not, most women worked because they had to. A sizable minority were the sole support of their families because their husbands had left home or lost their jobs. Single, divorced, deserted, or widowed women had no husbands to support them. This was especially true of poor black women. A survey of Chicago revealed that two-fifths of adult black women in the city were single. These working women rarely took jobs away from men. "Few of the people who oppose married women's employment," observed one feminist in 1940, "seem to realize that a coal miner or steel worker cannot very well fill the jobs of nursemaids, cleaning women, or the factory and clerical jobs now filled by women." Custom made gender crossovers from one field to another rare.

The division of the workforce by gender gave white women a small edge during the depression. Many fields where they had concentrated—including clerical, sales, and service and trade occupations—reinforced the traditional stereotypes of female work but suffered less from economic contraction than heavy industry, which employed men almost exclusively. As a result unemployment rates for white women, although extremely high, were somewhat lower than those for their male counterparts. This small bonus came at a high price, however. When the depression ended, women were even more concentrated in low-paying, dead-end jobs than when it began. White women also benefited at the expense of minority women. To make ends meet white women willingly sought jobs usually held by blacks or other minority workers—domestic service jobs, for example—and employers were quick to act on their preference for white workers.

White men also took jobs once held by minority males. Contemporary observers' concerns about the crisis of the male breadwinner or married women in the workforce rarely extended to blacks. Most commentators paid scant attention to the impact of the depression on the black family, focusing instead on the perceived threats to the stability of white households. As historian Jacqueline Jones explains it, few leaders worried "over the baneful effects of economic independence on the male ego when the ego in question was that of a black husband."

During the Great Depression there were few feminist demands for equal rights, at home or on the job. On an individual basis, women's self-esteem probably rose because of the importance of their work to family survival. Most men and women, however, continued to believe that the two sexes should have fundamentally different roles and responsibilities and that a woman's life cycle should be shaped by marriage and her husband's career.

Hard Times for Youth.   The depression hit another segment of the family—the nation's 21 million young people—especially hard. Though small children often escaped the sense of bitterness and failure that gripped their elders, hard times made children grow up fast. About 250,000 young people became so demoralized that they took to the road as hobos and "sisters of the road," as female tramps were called. Others chose to stay in school longer: public schools were free, and they were warm in the winter. In 1930 less than half the nation's youth attended high school, compared with three-fourths in 1940, at the end of the depression. College, however, remained the privilege of a distinct minority. About 1.2 million young people, or 7.5 percent of the population between eighteen and twenty-four, attended college in the 1930s. Forty percent of them were women. After 1935 college became slightly more affordable when the National Youth Administration (NYA) gave part-time employment to more than 2 million college and high school students. The government agency also provided work for 2.6 million out-of-school youths.

College students worked hard in the 1930s; financial sacrifice encouraged seriousness of purpose. Interest in fraternities and sororities declined as many students became involved in political movements. Fueled by disillusionment with World War I, thousands of youth took the "Oxford Pledge" never to support United States involvement in a war. In 1936 the Student Strike against War drew support from several hundred thousand students across the country.

Although many youths enjoyed more education in the 1930s, the depression damaged their future prospects. Studies of social mobility confirm that young men who entered their twenties during the depression era had less successful careers than those who came before or after. After extensive interviews with these youths all over the nation, the writer Maxine Davis described them as "runners, delayed at the gun," adding, "The depression years have left us with a generation robbed of time and opportunity just as the Great War left the world its heritage of a lost generation."

Popular Culture Views the Depression

Americans turned to popular culture to alleviate some of the trauma of the Great Depression. In June 1935 a Chicago radio listener wrote station WLS, "I feel your music and songs are what pulled me through this

winter." She explained that "Half the time we were blue and broke. One year during the depression and no work. Kept from going on relief but lost everything we possessed doing so. So thanks for the songs, for they make life seem more like living." Mass culture flourished in the 1930s, offering not just entertainment but commentary on the problems that beset the nation. Movies and radio served as a forum for criticizing the system—especially politicians and bankers—as well as vehicles for reaffirming traditional ideals.

Movies.   Despite the closing of one-third of the country's theaters by 1933, the movie industry and its studio system flourished. Sixty percent of Americans—some 60 to 75 million people—flocked to the cinema each week, seeking solace from the pain of the depression. In the early thirties moviegoers might be

Dancing Cheek to Cheek
During the Great Depression Americans turned to inexpensive recreational activities such as listening to the radio and going to the movies. One of the most popular attractions in Hollywood movies was the dance team of Fred Astaire and Ginger Rogers, who starred together in ten movies. Steve Schapiro.

titillated or scandalized by Mae West, who was noted for her sexual innuendoes: "I used to be Snow White, but I drifted." But in response to public outcry against immorality in the movies, especially from the Protestant and Catholic churches, the industry established a means of self-censorship, the Production Code Administration. After 1934 somewhat racy films were supplanted by sophisticated, fast-paced, screwball comedies like *It Happened One Night*, which swept the Oscars in 1934. The musical comedies of Fred Astaire and Ginger Rogers, including *Top Hat* (1935) and *The Gay Divorcee* (1934), in which the two dancers seemed to glide effortlessly through opulent sets, provided a stark contrast with most moviegoers' own lives.

But Hollywood, which produced 5,000 films during the decade, offered much more than what on the surface might seem to be escapist entertainment. Many of its movies contained complex messages that reflected a real sense of the societal crisis that engulfed the nation. Depression-era films repeatedly portrayed politicians as cynical and corrupt. In *Washington Merry-Go-Round* (1932), lobbyists manipulated weak congressmen to undermine democratic rule. The Marx Brothers' irreverent comedies more humorously criticized authority—and most everything else. In *Duck Soup* (1933) Groucho Marx played Rufus T. Firefly, president of the mythical Freedonia, who sings gleefully:

The last man nearly ruined this place,
He didn't know what to do with it.
If you think this country's bad off now,
Just wait till I get through with it.

Even if they did not deal specifically with the economic or political crisis, many films reaffirmed traditional values like democracy, individualism, and egalitarianism. They also contained criticisms—suggestions that the system was not working or that law and order had broken down. Thus popular gangster movies, such as *Public Enemy* (1931), with James Cagney, or *Little Caesar* (1930), starring Edward G. Robinson, could be seen as perverse Horatio Alger tales, in which the main character struggled to succeed in a harsh environment. Often these movies suggested that incompetent or corrupt politicians, police, and businessmen were as much to blame for organized crime as the gangsters themselves.

Few filmmakers left more of a mark on the decade than Frank Capra. An Italian immigrant who personified the possibilities for success that the United States offered, Capra made films that spoke to Americans' idealism. In movies like *Mr. Deeds Goes to Town* (1936) and *Mr. Smith Goes to Washington* (1939), he pitted the virtuous small-town hero against corrupt urban shysters—businessmen, politicians, lobbyists, and newspaper publishers—whose machinations subverted the nation's ideals. Though the hero usually prevailed, Capra was realistic enough to suggest that the victory

Mr. Smith Goes to Washington

In this classic 1939 film, directed by Frank Capra, actor Jimmy Stewart plays an idealistic young senator who exposes the unscrupulous political machine that dominates his home state. In response, the machine frames Senator Smith for corruption, and he must struggle to vindicate himself. Although the movie has a romantic subplot as Stewart's character wins over the cynical woman played by costar Jean Arthur, this light-hearted advertising poster belies the more serious tone of the movie. Collection of Hershenson-Allen Archives.

was not necessarily permanent and that the problems the nation faced were serious.

Radio.   Radio occupied an increasingly important place in popular culture during the 1930s (Map 24.2). At the beginning of the decade, about 13 million households had radios; by the end 27.5 million owned them. Listeners tuned in to daytime serials like *Ma Perkins*, picked up useful household hints on *The Betty Crocker Hour*, or enjoyed the Big Band "swing" of Benny Goodman, Duke Ellington, and Tommy Dorsey. Weekly variety shows featured Jack Benny; George Burns and Gracie Allen; and the ventriloquist Edgar Bergen and his impudent dummy, Charlie McCarthy. And millions of listeners followed the adventures of the Lone Ranger, Superman, and Dick Tracy.

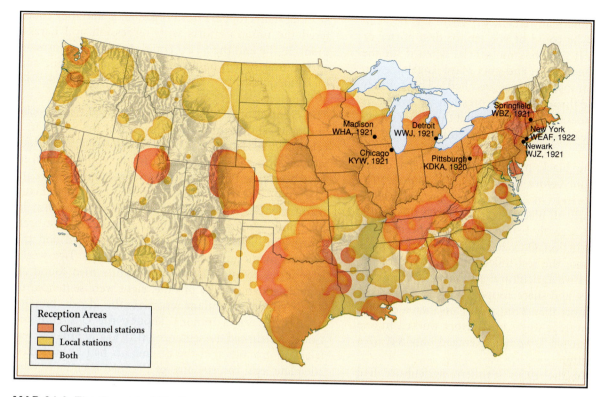

MAP 24.2 The Spread of Radio, to 1939

In 1938 more than 26 million American households, or about three-quarters of the population, had a radio. Four national networks dominated the field, broadcasting news and entertainment across the country. Powerful clear-channel stations reached listeners hundreds of miles away. By 1939, only sparsely populated areas were beyond radio's reach.

Like movies, radio offered Americans more than escape. A running gag in comedian Jack Benny's show was his stinginess; audiences could identify with an unwillingness—or inability—to spend money. Even more relevant was Benny's distrust of banks. He kept his money in an underground vault guarded by a pet polar bear named Carmichael—presumably a more reliable place than the nation's financial institutions. *Amos 'n' Andy* (see Chapter 23) is remembered primarily for its racial stereotyping. But the exceptionally popular show also dealt with hard times, often referring explicitly to the depression. A central theme was the contrast between Amos's hard work and Andy's more carefree approach to life. Amos, tending to believe that the nation's economic crisis had been brought about by the extravagant spending of the 1920s, criticized his friend's fiscal irresponsibility. Though *Amos 'n' Andy* reinforced racial stereotypes, it also reaffirmed the traditional values of "diligence, saving, and generosity."

Americans did not spend all their leisure time in commercial entertainment. In a resurgence of traditionalism, attendance at religious services rose, and the home again became a center for pleasurable pastimes. Amateur photography and stamp collecting enjoyed tremendous vogues, as did the new board game Monopoly, invented in 1934 by an unemployed Germantown, Pennsylvania,

man. Reading aloud from books borrowed from the public library was another affordable diversion. But Americans bought books, too. Taking advantage of new manufacturing processes that made books cheaper, they made best-sellers of Margaret Mitchell's *Gone with the Wind* (1936), James Hilton's *Lost Horizon* (1933), and Pearl Buck's *The Good Earth* (1932).

Harder Times

Much writing about the 1930s has focused on white working-class or middle-class families caught suddenly in a downward spiral. For African Americans, farmers, Mexican Americans, and Asian Americans, times had always been hard; during the 1930s they got much harder. As the poet Langston Hughes noted, "The depression brought everybody down a peg or two. And the Negroes had but few pegs to fall."

African Americans in the Depression

The African American worker had always known discrimination and limited opportunities and thus viewed the depression differently from most whites. "It didn't mean too much to him, the Great American Depression, as you call it," one man remarked. "There was no such thing. The best he could be is a janitor or a porter or shoeshine boy. It only became official when it hit the white man." The novelist and poet Maya Angelou, who grew up in Stamps, Arkansas, recalled, "The country had been in the throes of the Depression for two years before the Negroes in Stamps knew it. I think that everyone thought the Depression, like everything else, was for the white folks."

Despite the black migration to northern cities, which had begun before World War I, as late as 1940 more than 75 percent of African Americans still lived in the South. Nearly all black farmers lived in the South, their condition scarcely better than it had been at the end of Reconstruction. Only 20 percent of black farmers owned their land; the rest toiled at the bottom of the South's exploitative agricultural system as tenant farmers, farm hands, and sharecroppers. African Americans rarely earned more than $200 a year, less than a quarter of the annual average wages of a factory worker. In one Louisiana parish black women averaged only $41.67 a year picking cotton.

Throughout the 1920s southern agriculture had suffered from falling prices and overproduction. The depression made an already desperate situation worse. Some black farmers tried to protect themselves by joining the Southern Tenant Farmers Union (STFU), which was founded in 1934. The STFU was one of the few southern groups that welcomed both blacks and whites. "The same chain that holds you hold my people, too," an elderly black farmer reminded whites on the organizing committee. Landowners, however, had a stake in keeping sharecroppers from organizing, and they countered the union's efforts with repression and harassment. In the end the STFU could do little to reform an agricultural system based on such deep economic and racial inequities.

The Scottsboro Case.   All blacks faced harsh social and political discrimination throughout the South. In a celebrated 1931 case in Scottsboro, Alabama, two white women who had been riding a freight train claimed to have been raped by nine black youths, all under twenty years old. The two women's stories contained many inconsistencies, and one woman later recanted. But in the South when a white woman claimed to have been raped by a black, she was taken at her word and the accused man's guilt was taken for granted. Two weeks later juries composed entirely of white men found all nine defendants guilty of rape; eight were sentenced to death. (One defendant escaped the death penalty because he was a minor.) Though the U.S. Supreme Court overturned the sentences in 1932 and ordered new trials on grounds that the defendants had been denied adequate legal counsel, five of the men eventually were again convicted and sentenced to long prison terms.

The hasty trials and the harsh sentences, especially given the defendants' young age, stirred public protest, prompting the International Labor Defense (ILD), a labor organization tied closely to the Communist Party, to take over the defense. Though the Communist Party had targeted the struggle against racism as a priority in the early 1930s, it was making little headway recruiting African Americans. "It's bad enough being black, why be red?" was

Lynching

The threat of lynching remained a terrifying part of life for African Americans in the 1930s and not just in the South. Artist Joe Jones set this canvas in 1933, perhaps influenced by the fact that twenty-four blacks were lynched that year. He gave it the ironic title of American Justice, 1933 *(White Justice).*

Collection of Philip J. and Suzanne Schiller.

Drought Refugees

Like the Joad family in John Steinbeck's powerful novel The Grapes of Wrath *(1939), many thousands of poor people hit hard by the drought, dust, and debt of farm life in the Great Plains loaded all their possessions in a pick-up truck and set out for a new start in the West. In this 1937 photograph of Missouri drought refugees on Highway 99 near Tracy, California, photographer Dorothea Lange vividly captured the migrants' bleak circumstances.* Library of Congress.

For more help analyzing this image, see the ONLINE STUDY GUIDE at bedfordstmartins.com/henretta.

a common reaction. White southerners resented radical groups' interference, noting that almost all those involved in the Scottsboro defense were northerners and Jews. Declared a local solicitor, "Alabama justice cannot be bought and sold with Jew money from New York." The Scottsboro case received wide coverage in black communities across the country. Along with an increase in lynching in the early 1930s (twenty blacks were lynched in 1930, twenty-four in 1933), it gave black Americans a strong incentive to head for the North and the Midwest.

Harlem in the 1930s. Harlem, one of their main destinations, was already strained by the enormous influx of African Americans in the 1920s. The depression only aggravated the housing shortage. Residential segregation kept blacks from moving elsewhere, so they paid excessive rents to live in deteriorating buildings where crowded living conditions fostered disease and premature death. As whites clamored for jobs traditionally held by blacks—as waiters, domestic servants, elevator operators, and garbage collectors—unemployment in Harlem rose to 50 percent, twice the national rate. At the height of the depression, shelters and soup kitchens staffed by the Divine Peace Mission, under the leadership of the charismatic black religious leader Father Divine, provided 3,000 meals a day for Harlem's destitute.

In March 1935 Harlem exploded in the only major race riot of the decade. Anger about the lack of jobs, a slowdown in relief services, and economic exploitation of the black community had been building for years. Although white-owned stores were entirely dependent on black trade, store owners would not employ blacks. The arrest of a black shoplifter, followed by rumors that he had been severely beaten by white police, triggered the riot. Four blacks were killed, and $2 million worth of property was damaged.

There were some signs of hope for African Americans in the 1930s. Partly in response to the 1935 riot but mainly in return for growing black allegiance to the Democratic Party (see Chapter 25), the New Deal would channel significant amounts of relief money toward blacks outside the South. And the National Association for the Advancement of Colored People (NAACP) continued to challenge the status quo of race relations. Though calls for racial justice went largely unheeded during the depression, World War II and its aftermath would further the struggle for black equality.

Dust Bowl Migrations

A distressed agricultural sector had been one of the causes of the Great Depression. In the 1930s conditions

Bert Corona and the Mexican American Generation

Bert Corona always considered himself a child of the revolution—the Mexican Revolution. His father, Noe Corona, had crossed the border from Mexico to the United States around 1915 or 1916, seeking safety after being wounded while fighting in Pancho Villa's army. Settling temporarily in El Paso, he married Margarita Escápite Salayandia, and they had four children, including Humberto (his Anglo teachers later Americanized his name to Bert), who was born in 1918.

The border is an apt metaphor for Mexican American life, capturing the fluidity of crossing back and forth between two countries and two cultures. Bert's family returned to Mexico in 1922, where two years later Noe Corona was assassinated by unknown assailants, presumably political enemies. This loss had a profound effect on Noe's six-year-old son: "The Revolution, my father's role in it, and his martyrdom symbolized the struggle for social justice. This would be the same struggle I would later pursue."

Strong female role models influenced Bert as well. The Corona family resettled in El Paso, where Bert's mother secured a job at the Mexican customs house on the El Paso–Ciudad Juarez border, and his grandmother, a doctor, pursued her practice of medicine and midwifery. The El Paso school system provided a searing introduction to the discrimination and unequal treatment that Mexican immigrants in the Southwest faced. Corona's segregated "Mexican" school in the barrio, geared primarily toward vocational education, was far inferior to white schools. Although he attended an integrated high school with a good academic reputation, racism and discrimination remained very much a part of his education, both in daily encounters with his Anglo teachers and classmates and in the general lack of respect for Mexican history and culture in the curriculum. His grandmother said tartly, "Well, you have to understand that the United States writes its history to its own convenience. It always has, and these people always will."

Bert Corona
Bert Corona addresses a press conference at the National Chicano Political Caucus in 1972. Bert Corona.

When Bert graduated from high school in 1934 at age sixteen, it was the height of the Great Depression, and El Paso was hard hit. Fortunately, his mother kept her job at the Juarez customs house, but hard times forced many Mexicans to leave. El Paso was a major border crossing for *los repatriados* (those returning to their old country), as they fled the depression and the threat of deportation, but Mexicans were not the only group on the move. The Corona backyard faced the train tracks, and Bert vividly remembered the thousands of Dust Bowl migrants traveling through El Paso on their way west. A hundred-car freight train could carry a thousand Dust Bowlers, and there were three trains in the morning and three in the evening. "It was like the population of a small town coming in every day," he later recalled.

After working for two years in El Paso, Bert headed to the University of Southern California, where he hoped to play basketball and continue his education on an athletic scholarship. But an injury cut short his sports career, and he soon found new interests that took him away from his studies, although he later regretted not getting a college degree. What took precedence over his family's strong belief in education? Participating in the revitalized labor movement and fostering Mexican American political consciousness—the two causes that shaped the rest of Corona's life.

The Congress of Industrial Organizations, or CIO (see Chapter 25), became his vehicle for labor activism: "I had a sense of the historical importance of the CIO, and I viewed the CIO as a movement whose time had come. Nothing could stop it, and—for a time—nothing did." In the 1930s many labor activists focused on organizing Mexican American migrant workers in the fields, but Corona concentrated on recruiting Los Angeles industrial workers into the newly constituted International Longshoremen's and Warehousemen's Union (ILWU). His organizing was not restricted to Mexican workers, however. Like the CIO, he wanted the entire working class to join unions to work for social change in the workplace and in society as a whole. While organizing at an aviation plant in 1941, he met his future wife, Blanche Taff. The daughter of Polish Jewish immigrants, she shared his commitment to progressive social change. Their marriage fit right in with the interracial and interethnic culture of the CIO. So great was their commitment to organized labor that they gave up their honeymoon to participate in a major CIO organizing drive.

In addition to labor organizing, Bert Corona felt a deep commitment to the political mobilization of Spanish-speaking peoples throughout the United States. In 1939 he joined El Congreso Nacional del Pueblo de Habla Español (the National Congress of Spanish-Speaking Peoples), a militant organization founded to fight for the rights of Mexican Americans and other Latinos as part of the larger struggle against racial and class oppression. There he worked with noted activists such as Luisa Moreno, a Guatemalan-born CIO organizer who had been active in the cannery industry, and Josefina Fierro, a radical young Mexican American married to the screenwriter John Bright, who was part of Hollywood's leftist community. Their activist agenda was far to the left of that of organizations such as the League of United Latin American Citizens (LULAC), founded in 1929, which focused on assimilation and citizenship from a distinctly middle-class perspective.

After serving in the armed forces during World War II, Corona continued to be a labor and community activist. In the 1960s he became involved in the Mexican American Political Association, or MAPA, which mobilized Latino political power to force the Kennedy and Johnson administrations to do more for those constituencies. Since then he has been involved in community organizing, especially of undocumented Mexican workers, arguing that they have just as legitimate claims to live, work, and be protected by the basic guarantees of American law as any other workers.

Bert Corona exemplifies what the historian Mario Garcia has called the "Mexican-American Generation." These men and women, who were born and raised in the United States, came of political age between the 1930s and the 1950s. They filled the leadership vacuum created when *los repatriados*, mainly older and Mexican-born, returned permanently to that country in the 1930s. Even before terms such as *Mexican American, Hispanic,* and *Latino* were widely used, this generation had the "double consciousness" that W. E. B. Du Bois described in African Americans: a sense of being both *Mexicanos* and American citizens. Many members of the Mexican American Generation shared Corona's commitment to organizing for social change—in their communities, on the job, and in the wider political arena. Tracing their political activism over the years provides a window on the changing character of Mexican American communities in the United States.

Since the 1930s Bert Corona has seen a dramatic expansion of Latino empowerment, but he remains modest about his role in this story. "It's hard for me to think how I would like to be remembered by history," he told Mario Garcia as they collaborated on a book about his life. "I never planned my life. It just happened the way it did. . . . If my life has meant anything, I would say that it shows that you can organize workers and poor people if you work hard, are persistent, remain optimistic, and reach out to involve as many people as possible. . . . But my life is not over yet, and I continue *la lucha*, the struggle." For Bert Corona, that commitment to *la lucha* had its roots in his Mexican heritage, but it first began to flower during the turbulent 1930s.

unusually democratic union in which women, the majority of the rank-and-file workers, played a leading role.

Activism in the fields and factories demonstrated how a second generation of Mexican Americans, born in the United States, had turned increasingly to the struggle for political and economic justice in the United States rather than retaining primary allegiance to Mexico. Joining American labor unions and becoming more involved in American politics (see Chapter 25) were important steps in the creation of a distinct Mexican American ethnic identity.

Asian Americans Face the Depression

Men and women of Asian descent—mostly from China, Japan, and the Philippines—constituted a tiny minority that concentrated primarily in the western states. Their experiences during the depression were as diverse as the people themselves, although all were subject to a pervasive anti-Asian racism. Second-generation Japanese Americans, for example, had eagerly pursued higher education, finishing an average of two years of college during the period of 1925 to 1935, but relatively few professional jobs were open to them as white firms refused to hire them. They and their families concentrated in farming and small ethnic enterprises, often linked to agriculture, such as fruit and vegetable vendors. They had carved out a modest success by the time of the depression, despite a 1913 California law, strengthened in 1920, that prohibited Japanese immigrants from owning land. Having circumvented the laws by various devices—including putting land titles in the names of their citizen children—during the depression, most Japanese farmers managed to hold on to their land, and the amount of acreage owned actually increased. But times were hard, and many farm families barely eked out a decent subsistence. Twenty-two percent of the immigrant population—presumably the poorest—returned to Japan during the depression. And toward the end of the decade, economic anxieties were compounded by renewed anti-Japanese sentiment, stemming from mounting tensions between the United States and Japan over the latter's aggression in Asia (see Chapter 26).

Chinese Americans as a rule had not prospered as much as the Japanese. For example statistics show that as late as 1940, only around 3 percent of Chinese Americans were engaged in professional and technical occupations. But ironically the discrimination that had kept them isolated from the mainstream economy may have proved somewhat beneficial as they weathered the 1930s. In San Francisco, where Chinese were excluded from most industrial jobs, they clustered in ethnic enterprises in the city's Chinatown. Like the rest of the nation's small enterprises, Chinatown's businesses and their employees suffered during the depression, but they bounced back much more quickly. And similar to the experience of white working women, Chinese women found that the labor market that had limited them to a handful of low-paid job categories in light industry and service work in good times worked to their advantage in hard times. They were far less likely to be unemployed than Chinese men. Despite these factors that may have meliorated the hardships of the depression, most Chinese immigrants and their families were on the margins economically. In hard times they turned inward to the community, getting assistance from traditional Chinese social organizations such as *huiguan* (district associations) and kin networks until San Francisco finally extended relief assistance to them—approximately one-sixth of the city's Chinese population was on public assistance in 1931. The New Deal aided them as well, although many programs were limited to citizens and thus barred Chinese immigrants who were "aliens ineligible for citizenship" until the repeal of the Chinese Exclusion Act in 1943.

Filipinos differed from the Japanese and Chinese in that they alone were not affected by the ban on Asian immigration passed in 1924 (see Chapter 23) because the Philippines were a U.S. territory. Consequently their numbers swelled during the 1920s, and by 1930 over 45,000 had emigrated, concentrating mostly along the Pacific Coast. Relegated primarily to menial labor, 60 percent found jobs in agriculture, where they were preferred for the arduous stoop labor for which growers believed they were exceptionally well suited. When the depression struck, Filipinos were among the most militant of the agricultural workers who organized to try to extract decent pay from their employers. Although their first major strike in 1933 was broken, in part by the use of Mexican, Japanese, and Asian Indian strikebreakers, they later enjoyed some success in extracting wage concessions. In 1936 Filipinos and Mexican workers came together in a Field Workers Union chartered by the American Federation of Labor.

Just as the depression focused attention on Mexican immigration, hard times also led to demands that Filipino immigration be restricted. Racial hostility, as well as a concern about Filipinos as competitors for jobs and public relief, fueled the drive to bring about immigration exclusion by making the Philippines an independent nation. In 1934 Congress passed the Tydings-McDuffie Act, which granted independence, classified all Filipinos in the United States as aliens, and restricted immigration to fifty persons per year. By the time the act passed, immigration had slowed to a trickle, but their new status as aliens ineligible for citizenship—or most New Deal assistance programs—had a powerful impact on the Filipinos who remained as unwelcome interlopers.

Herbert Hoover and the Great Depression

Had Herbert Hoover been elected in 1920 instead of 1928, he probably would have been a popular president. As the director of successful food conservation programs at home and charitable food relief abroad during World War I, he was respected as an intelligent and able administrator. Although Hoover's name frequently emerged as a possible candidate in 1920, he did not run for president until the end of the decade. Timing was against him. Although his optimistic predictions in the 1928 campaign—that "the poorhouse is vanishing from among us" and that America was "nearer to the final triumph over poverty than ever before in the history of any land"—reflected beliefs that many Americans shared, that prosperity and Hoover's reputation were soon to be dramatically undermined. When the stock market crashed in 1929, Hoover stubbornly insisted that the downturn was only temporary. In June 1930 he greeted a business delegation with the words "Gentlemen, you have come sixty days too late. The Depression is over." As the country hit rock bottom in 1931 and 1932, the president finally acted, but by then it was too little, too late.

Hoover Responds

Hoover's approach to the Great Depression was shaped by his priorities as secretary of commerce. Hoping to avoid coercive measures on the part of the federal government, he turned to the business community for leadership in overcoming the economic downturn. Hoover asked business executives to maintain wages and production levels voluntarily and to work with the government to build people's confidence in the economic system.

Fiscal Policy. Hoover did not rely solely on public pronouncements, however; he also used public funds and federal action to encourage recovery. Soon after the stock market crash, he cut federal taxes and called on state and local governments to increase their expenditures on public construction projects. He signed the 1929 Agricultural Marketing Act, which gave the federal government an unprecedented role in stabilizing agriculture. In 1930 and the first half of 1931, Hoover raised the federal budget for public works to $423 million, a dramatic increase in expenditures not traditionally considered to be the federal government's responsibility. Hoover also eased the international crisis by declaring a moratorium on the payment of Allied debts and reparations early in the summer of 1931. The depression continued, however. When the president, alarmed about the federal deficit, asked Congress for a 33-percent tax increase to balance the budget, the ill-advised move choked investment and, to a lesser extent, consumption, contributing significantly to the continuation of the depression.

Not all the steps taken by the Hoover administration were so ill conceived. The president pushed Congress to create a system of government home-loan banks in 1932 and supported the Glass-Steagall Banking Act of 1932, which made government securities available to guarantee Federal Reserve notes and thus temporarily propped up the ailing banking system. The federal government under Hoover also spent $700 million—an unprecedented sum for the time—on public works.

The Reconstruction Finance Corporation. Hoover's most innovative program to aid the economy—one the New Deal would later draw on—was the Reconstruction Finance Corporation (RFC), approved by Congress in January 1932. Modeled on the War Finance Corporation of World War I and developed in collaboration with the business and banking communities, the RFC was the first federal institution created to intervene directly in the economy during peacetime. To alleviate the credit crunch for business, the RFC would provide federal loans to railroads, financial institutions, banks, and insurance companies in a strategy that has been called **pump priming**. In theory, money lent at the top of the economic structure would stimulate production, creating new jobs and increasing consumer spending. These benefits would eventually "trickle down" to the rest of the economy.

Unfortunately, the RFC lent its funds too cautiously to make a significant difference. Nonetheless, it represents a watershed in American political history and the growth of the federal government: when voluntary cooperation failed, the president turned to federal action to stimulate the economy. Yet Hoover's break with the past had clear limits. In many ways his support of the RFC was just another attempt to encourage business confidence. Compared with previous chief executives—and in contrast to his popular image as a "do-nothing" president—Hoover responded to the national emergency on an unprecedented scale. But the nation's needs were also unprecedented, and Hoover's programs failed to meet them (see American Voices, "Public Assistance Fails a Southern Farm Family," p. 716).

In particular, federal programs fell short of helping the growing ranks of the unemployed. Hoover remained adamant in his refusal to consider any plan for direct federal relief to those out of work. Throughout his career he had believed that privately organized charities were sufficient to meet the nation's social welfare needs. During World War I he had headed the Commission for Relief of Belgium, a private group that distributed 5 million tons of food to Europe's suffering civilian population. And in 1927 he had coordinated a rescue and cleanup operation after a devastating flood of the Mississippi River left 16.5 million acres of land under water in seven states. The success of these and other predominantly voluntary responses to public emergencies had confirmed Hoover's belief that private charity, not federal aid, was the "American way" of solving social problems. He would not undermine the country's hallowed faith in individualism, even in the face of evidence that charities and state and local relief agencies could not meet the needs of a growing unemployed population.

Public Assistance Fails a Southern Farm Family

When times were bad, even public assistance could be bad for a family in dire straits. Here a young mother living in the farming community of Commerce, Georgia, relates how relief efforts ironically proved to be a burden to her family of eight. She also indicates the strains that "making do" put on poor women.

I've just met with a problem I cannot solve alone. I am a Mother of six children the oldest is only 11 years old the youngest 18 months and I'm expecting another in March. We couldn't get any crop for 1936 because we could neither furnish ourselves or had any stock. So here we are having made out on a little work once in a while all summer. And then in Aug I had to have a serious operation and now I'm not able to feed & clothe our six children as my husband couldnt find anything at all to do was compelled to get on relief job at $1.28 a day 16 days a month. Well you take 8 meals 3 times a day out of $1.28 and what will you have left is 24 meals and what kind of meals do you have? We have to buy everything we eat. We have nothing except what we buy. Our bedclothes are threadbare our clothes the same. No shoes and no money to buy yet the relief say that cant help us as he is working. Can he work naked. Can he sleep cold. I don't know of any one at all that can help me and I know we cant go on like this.

We have four children in school and they cant go on unless thay [sic] have some warm clothes when cold weather sets in.... Do you know of any people in Atlanta that have any used clothes they would give in exchange for piecing quilts or quilting. Id be glad to do anything I can in exchange for clothes to keep our children in school.

I hate to be like this but can a person that is willing to work for a living and that honest and disable to help themselves sit idle and see their small children suffer day after day without enough food or clothes to keep their bodies warm when there are thousands of people with plenty to give if they knew your need.

How it hurts to know that you are almost starving in the land of plenty.

Source: Julia Kirk Blackwelder, "Letters from the Great Depression," in *Southern Exposure* 6, no. 3 (Fall 1978): 77.

Rising Discontent

As the depression deepened many citizens came to hate Herbert Hoover. Once the symbol of business prosperity, he became the scapegoat for the depression. "In Hoover we trusted, now we are busted," declared the hand-lettered signs carried by the down and out. New terms entered the vocabulary: *Hoovervilles* (shantytowns where people lived in packing crates and other makeshift shelters), *Hoover flags* (empty pockets turned inside out), and *Hoover blankets* (newspapers). Hoover's declarations that nobody was starving, that hobos were better fed than ever before, seemed cruel and insensitive. His apparent willingness to bail out businesses and banks while leaving individuals to fend for themselves added to his reputation for coldheartedness.

As the country entered the fourth year of depression, signs of rising discontent and rebellion emerged. Farmers were among the most vocal protestors, banding together to harass the bank agents and government officers who enforced evictions and foreclosures and to protest the low prices they received for their crops. Midwestern farmers had watched the price of wheat fall from $3 a bushel in 1920 to barely 30 cents in 1932. Now they formed the Farm Holiday Association, barricaded local roads, and dumped milk, vegetables, and other farm produce in the dirt rather than accept prices that would not cover their costs. Nothing better captured the cruel irony of maldistribution than farmers destroying food at a time when thousands were going hungry.

Protest was not confined to rural America, however. Bitter labor strikes occurred in the depths of the depression, despite the threat that strikers would lose their jobs. In Harlan County, Kentucky, in 1931 miners struck over a 10 percent wage cut. Their union was crushed by mine owners and the National Guard. In 1932 at Ford's River Rouge factory outside Detroit, a demonstration provoked violence from police and Ford security forces; three demonstrators were killed, and fifty more were seriously injured. Later some 40,000 people viewed the coffins under a banner charging that "Ford Gave Bullets for Bread."

Hoovervilles
By 1930 shantytowns had sprung up in most of the nation's cities. In New York City squatters camped out along the Hudson River railroad tracks, built makeshift homes in Central Park, or lived in the city dump. This scene from the old reservoir in Central Park looks east toward the fancy apartment buildings of Fifth Avenue and the Metropolitan Museum of Art, at left. Grant Smith / Corbis.

In 1931 and 1932 violence broke out in the nation's cities. Groups of the unemployed battled local authorities over inadequate relief, staging rent riots and hunger marches. Some of these actions were organized by the Communist Party—still a tiny organization with only 12,000 members—as a challenge to the capitalist system, such as "unemployment councils" that agitated for jobs and food and a hunger march on Washington, D.C., in 1931. Though the marches were well attended and often got results from local and federal authorities, they did not necessarily win converts to communism.

Not radicals but veterans staged the most publicized—and most tragic—protest. In the summer of 1932, the "Bonus Army," a ragtag group of about 15,000 unemployed World War I veterans, hitchhiked to Washington to demand immediate payment of their bonuses, originally scheduled for distribution in 1945. While their leaders lobbied Congress, the Bonus Army camped out in the capital. "We were heroes in 1917, but we're bums now," one veteran complained bitterly. When the marchers refused to leave their Anacostia Flats camp, Hoover called out riot troops to clear the area. Led by General Douglas MacArthur, and assisted by Major Dwight D. Eisenhower and Major George S. Patton, the troops burned the encampment to the ground. In the fight that followed, more than a hundred marchers were injured. Newsreel footage captured the deeply disturbing spectacle of the U.S. Army moving against its own veterans, and Hoover's popularity plunged even lower.

The 1932 Election: A New Order

Despite the evidence of discontent, the nation overall was not in a revolutionary mood as it approached the 1932 election. Having internalized Horatio Alger's ideal of the self-made man, many Americans initially blamed themselves rather than the system for their hardship. Despair and apathy, not anger, was their mood. The Republicans, who could find no credible way to dump an incumbent president, unenthusiastically again nominated Hoover. The Democrats turned to Governor Franklin Delano Roosevelt of New York, who won the nomination by capitalizing on that state's reputation for innovative relief and unemployment programs.

Roosevelt, born into a wealthy New York family in 1882, had attended Harvard College and Columbia Law School. He had served in the New York State legislature and as assistant secretary of the navy in the Wilson administration, a post that had earned him the vice presidential nomination on the Democratic ticket in 1920. Roosevelt's rise to the presidency was interrupted in 1921 by an attack of polio that left both his legs paralyzed for life. But he fought back from illness, emerging from the ordeal a stronger, more resilient man. "If you had spent two years in bed trying to wiggle your toe, after that anything would seem easy," he explained. His wife, Eleanor, strongly supported his return to public life and helped to mastermind his successful campaign for the governorship of New York in 1928.

The 1932 campaign for the presidency foreshadowed little of the New Deal. Roosevelt hinted only vaguely at new approaches to alleviating the depression: "The country needs and, unless I mistake its temper, the country demands bold, persistent experimentation." He won easily, receiving 22.8 million votes to Hoover's 15.7 million. Despite the nation's economic collapse, Americans remained firmly committed to the two-party system. The Socialist Party candidate, Norman Thomas, got fewer than a million votes, and the Communist Party candidate, party leader William Z. Foster, drew only 100,000 votes (Map 24.4).

The 1932 election marked a turning point in American politics—the emergence of a Democratic coalition that would help to shape national politics for the next four decades. Roosevelt won the support of the Solid South, which returned to the Democratic fold after defecting in 1928 because of Al Smith's Catholicism and his views on Prohibition. Roosevelt drew substantial support in the West and in the cities, continuing a trend first noticed in 1928, when the Democrats appealed successfully to recent immigrants and urban ethnic groups. However, Roosevelt's election was hardly a mandate to reshape American political and economic institutions. Many people voted as much against Hoover as for Roosevelt.

Having spoken, the voters had to wait until Roosevelt's inauguration in March 1933 to see him put his ideas into action. (The four-month interval between the election and the inauguration was shortened by the Twentieth Amendment in 1933.) In the worst winter of the depression, Americans could do little but hope that things would get better. According to the most conservative estimates, unemployment stood at 20 to 25 percent nationwide. The rate was 50 percent in Cleveland, 60 percent in Akron, and 80 percent in Toledo—cities dependent on manufacturing jobs in industries that had essentially shut down. The nation's banking system was so close to collapse that many state governors closed banks temporarily to avoid further panic.

By the winter of 1932–33, the depression had totally overwhelmed public welfare institutions. Private charity and public relief, both of whose expenditures had risen dramatically, still reached only a fraction of the needy. Hunger haunted cities and rural areas alike. When a teacher tried to send a coal miner's daughter home from school because she was weak from hunger, the girl replied, "It won't do any good . . . because this is sister's day to eat." In New York City hospitals reported ninety-five deaths from starvation. This was the America that Roosevelt inherited when he took the oath of office on March 4, 1933.

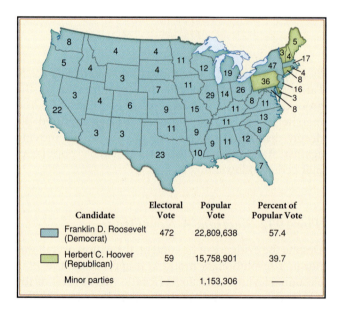

Candidate	Electoral Vote	Popular Vote	Percent of Popular Vote
Franklin D. Roosevelt (Democrat)	472	22,809,638	57.4
Herbert C. Hoover (Republican)	59	15,758,901	39.7
Minor parties	—	1,153,306	—

MAP 24.4 Presidential Election of 1932

Franklin Roosevelt's convincing electoral victory over Herbert Hoover in 1932 resulted from a political realignment and dissatisfaction with the incumbent president. Even in the midst of the gravest crisis capitalism ever faced, candidates of the Communist and Socialist Parties received fewer than 1 million votes out of almost 40 million cast.

FOR FURTHER EXPLORATION

▶ For definitions of key terms boldfaced in this chapter, see the glossary at the end of the book.

▶ To assess your mastery of the material covered in this chapter, see the Online Study Guide at **bedfordstmartins.com/henretta**.

▶ For suggested references, including Web sites, see page SR-26 at the end of the book.

▶ For map resources and primary documents, see **bedfordstmartins.com/henretta**.

The Great Depression of the 1930s was the longest and most severe economic downturn the United States had ever faced, and it had wide-ranging social, political, and cultural effects. The economic prosperity of the 1920s had rested on shaky ground. After the stock market crash of 1929, the economy entered a downward spiral that did not bottom out until 1932 to 1933. In addition to the collapse of the stock market, the main causes of the depression were underconsumption, an unequal distribution of wealth, an unstable international financial situation, a legacy of "sick industries" and agricultural distress from the 1920s, and the flawed monetary policies of the Federal Reserve System. At first President Hoover did not want to intervene in the economy because of his reliance on private charities and his adamant stance on maintaining a balanced budget. Then in 1932 the Hoover administration authorized the first direct federal intervention in the economy during peacetime, the Reconstruction Finance Corporation, to win business and public confidence. Though unprecedented, such measures did not end the Great Depression. In 1932 the nation turned to Franklin D. Roosevelt and the Democrats.

The Great Depression left an invisible scar on many people who lived through the 1930s, especially white middle-class Americans. Those who wanted to work blamed themselves if they could not find a job. The impact of the depression was especially catastrophic for African Americans and Mexican Americans, for whom times had always been hard, and left a scar with many Asian Americans as well. And for farmers in the Midwest, things got even worse than they had been in the 1920s. Misguided agricultural practices and drought created the Dust Bowl, forcing many farmers off their land.

Despite the devastating impact of the depression, many aspects of American life and culture continued to conform to traditional patterns. Families pulled together, with women taking on expanded roles—and often new jobs—to help support their households. Young people stayed in school longer. Families sought relief in popular culture, especially movies and radio programs, which played an especially important role in reaffirming—and obliquely criticizing—traditional American ideals and institutions.

1929   Stock market crash

Agricultural Marketing Act to stabilize agriculture

1930   Midwestern drought begins

Hawley-Smoot Tariff

1931   *Scottsboro* case

Hoover declares moratorium on Allied war sdebts

Miners strike in Harlan County, Kentucky

1932   Reconstruction Finance Corporation created

Bonus Army rebuffed in Washington

Height of deportation of Mexican migrant workers

Farm Holiday Association dumps produce

Strike at Ford's River Rouge plant in Michigan

Communist-led hunger marches

1933   Unemployment rises to highest level

Franklin Delano Roosevelt becomes president

Birthrate drops to lowest level due to depression

The Marx Brothers in *Duck Soup*

1934   Southern Tenant Farmers Union founded

It Happened One Night sweeps Oscars

Tydings-McDuffie Act grants Philippine independence and curtails immigration

1935   National Youth Administration created

Harlem race riot

1936   Student Strike against War

Margaret Mitchell, *Gone with the Wind*

Birth control legalized

1939   John Steinbeck, *The Grapes of Wrath*

Frank Capra, *Mr. Smith Goes to Washington*

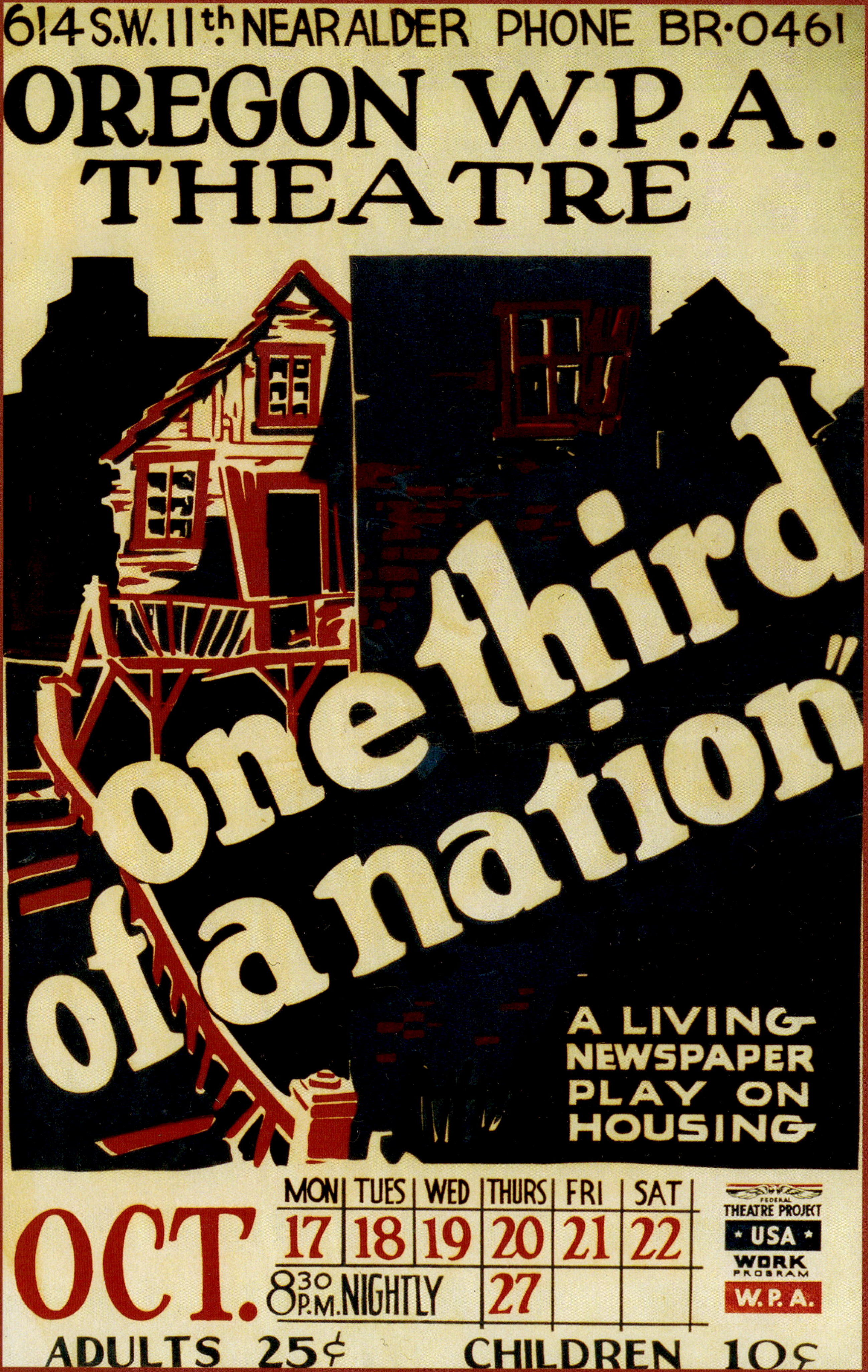

614 S.W. 11th NEAR ALDER PHONE BR·0461
OREGON W.P.A. THEATRE
"one third of a nation"
A LIVING NEWSPAPER PLAY ON HOUSING
MON TUES WED THURS FRI SAT
OCT. 17 18 19 20 21 22
8:30 P.M. NIGHTLY 27
FEDERAL THEATRE PROJECT
USA
WORK PROGRAM
W.P.A.
ADULTS 25¢ CHILDREN 10¢

CHAPTER 25

The New Deal

1933–1939

The New Deal Takes Over,
1933–1935
The Roosevelt Style of Leadership
The Hundred Days
The New Deal under Attack

The Second New Deal, 1935–1938
Legislative Accomplishments
The 1936 Election
Stalemate

The New Deal's Impact on Society
*New Deal Constituencies and the
    Broker State*
The New Deal and the Land
The New Deal and the Arts
The Legacies of the New Deal

IN HIS BOLD INAUGURAL ADDRESS on March 4, 1933, President Franklin Delano Roosevelt told a despondent, impoverished nation, "The only thing we have to fear is fear itself." That memorable phrase rallied a nation that had already endured almost four years of the worst economic contraction in its history, with no end in sight. His demeanor grim and purposeful, Roosevelt preached his first inaugural address like a sermon. Issuing ringing declarations of his vision of governmental activism—"This Nation asks for action, and action now"—he repeatedly compared combating the Great Depression to fighting a war. The new president was willing to ask Congress for "broad Executive power to wage a war against the emergency, as great as the power that would be given to me if we were in fact invaded by a foreign foe." He promised to "assume unhesitatingly the leadership of this great army of our people dedicated to a disciplined attack upon our common problems."

To wage this war Roosevelt proposed the *New Deal*, a term that he first used in his acceptance speech at the Democratic National Convention in 1932 and that eventually came to stand for his administration's complex set of responses to the nation's economic collapse. The New Deal was never a definitive plan of action but rather evolved and expanded over the course of Roosevelt's presidency.

◀ **"One Third of a Nation"**
One of the more innovative New Deal programs was the Federal Theatre Project. Its director, Hallie Flanagan, envisioned a nationwide network of community theaters that would produce plays of social relevance. "Living Newspaper" productions, such as the one advertised in this 1938 poster for a performance in Oregon, were documentary plays designed to expose Americans to contemporary social problems. One Third of a Nation by Arthur Arent tackled the history of New York City's housing problems, while at the same time it promoted New Deal housing legislation. National Archives.

In a time of major crisis, it was meant to relieve suffering yet conserve the nation's political and economic institutions through unprecedented activity on the part of the national government. Its legacy would be an expanded federal presence in the economy and in the lives of ordinary citizens.

The New Deal Takes Over, 1933–1935

The Great Depression destroyed Herbert Hoover's political reputation and helped to make Roosevelt's. Although some Americans—especially wealthy conservatives—hated Roosevelt, he was immensely popular and beloved by many. Ironically, the ideological differences between Hoover and Roosevelt were not that vast. Both were committed to maintaining the nation's basic institutional structure. Both believed in the basic morality of a balanced budget and extolled the values of hard work, cooperation, and sacrifice. But Roosevelt's personal charisma, his political savvy, and his willingness to experiment made all the difference. Above all, his New Deal programs put people to work, instilling hope and restoring the nation's confidence.

The Roosevelt Style of Leadership

While the New Deal involved hundreds of programs and thousands of people, the leadership of Franklin Roosevelt tied it all together. A superb and pragmatic politician, Roosevelt crafted his administration's program in response to shifting political and economic conditions rather than according to a set ideology or plan. He experimented with an idea; if it did not work, he tried another. "I have no expectation of making a hit every time I come to bat," Roosevelt told his critics. "What I seek is the highest possible batting average."

Roosevelt established an unusually close rapport with the American people. "Mr. Roosevelt is the only man we ever had in the White House who would understand that my boss is a son of a bitch," remarked one worker. Many ordinary citizens credited Roosevelt with the positive changes in their lives, saying "He gave me a job" or "He saved my home." Roosevelt's masterful use of the new medium of radio, typified by the "**fireside chats**" he broadcast during his first two terms, fostered this personal identification. In the week after the inauguration, more than 450,000 letters, many of which addressed Roosevelt as a friend or a member of the family, poured into the White House. An average of 5,000 to 8,000 arrived weekly for the rest of the decade. Whereas one person had handled public correspondence during the Hoover administration, a staff of fifty was required under Roosevelt.

Roosevelt's charisma allowed him to continue the expansion of presidential power begun in the administrations of Theodore Roosevelt and Woodrow Wilson. From the beginning he dramatically enlarged the role of the executive branch in initiating policy, thereby helping to create the modern presidency. For policy formulation he turned to his talented cabinet, which included Secretary of the Interior Harold Ickes, Frances Perkins at Labor, Henry A. Wallace at Agriculture, and an old friend, Henry Morgenthau Jr. at Treasury. During the interregnum (the period between election and inauguration), Roosevelt relied so heavily on the advice of the Columbia University

FDR

President Franklin Delano Roosevelt was a consummate politician who loved the adulation of a crowd, such as this one greeting him in Warm Springs, Georgia, in 1933. He consciously adopted a cheerful mien to keep people from feeling sorry for him because of his infirmity, knowing that he could not be a successful politician if the public pitied him. He so zealously avoided having photographs taken that might show his leg braces or limited mobility that many Americans thought FDR had recovered from the polio that had stricken him in 1921. Corbis-Bettmann.

Joe Marcus

A New Deal Activist

As an economist working for Harry Hopkins, Joe Marcus was one of thousands who formed the growing New Deal bureaucracy. Marcus's account, as told to Studs Terkel, captures some of the excitement that the New Deal generated. Marcus also suggests the way in which Roosevelt's administration expanded opportunities for Jews and other "outsiders."

I graduated college in '35. I went down to Washington and started to work in the spring of '36. The New Deal was a young man's world. Young people, if they showed any ability, got an opportunity. I was a kid, twenty-two or twenty-three. In a few months I was made head of the department. We had a meeting with hot shots: What's to be done? I pointed out some problems: let's define what we're looking for. They immediately had me take over. I had to set up the organization and hire seventy-five people. Given a chance as a youngster to try out ideas, I learned a fantastic amount. The challenge itself was great.

It was the idea of being asked big questions. The technical problems were small. These you had to solve by yourself. But the context was broad: Where was society going? Your statistical questions became questions of full employment. You were not prepared for it in school. If you wanted new answers, you needed a new kind of people. This is what was exciting.

Ordinarily, I might have had a job at the university, marking papers or helping a professor. All of a sudden, I'm doing original research and asking basic questions about how our society works. What makes a Depression?

What makes for pulling out of it? Once you start thinking in these terms, you're in a different ball game.

The climate was exciting. You were part of a society that was on the move. You were involved in something that could make a difference. Laws could be changed. So could the conditions of people.

The idea of being involved close to the center of political life was unthinkable, just two or three years before all this happened. Unthinkable for someone like me, of lower middle-class, close to ghetto, Jewish life. Suddenly you were a significant member of society. It was not the kind of closed society you had lived in before.

. . . You were really part of something, changes could be made. Bringing immediate results to people who were starving. You could do something about it: that was the most important thing. This you felt.

A feeling that if you had something to say, it would get to the top. As I look back now, memoranda I had written reached the White House, one way or another. The biggest thrill of my life was hearing a speech of Roosevelt's, using a selection from a memorandum I had written.

Everybody was searching for ideas. A lot of guys were opportunists, some were crackpots. But there was a search, a sense of values . . . that would make a difference in the lives of people.

We weren't thinking of remaking society. That wasn't it. I didn't buy this dream stuff. What was happening was a complete change in social attitudes at the central government level. The question was: How can you do it within this system? People working in all the New Deal agencies were dominated by this spirit. . . .

It was an exciting community, where we lived in Washington. The basic feeling—and I don't think this is just nostalgia—was one of excitement, of achievement, of happiness. Life was important, life was significant.

Source: Studs Terkel, *Hard Times* (New York: Pantheon Books, 1986), 265–66.

professors Raymond Moley, Rexford Tugwell, and Adolph A. Berle Jr. that the press dubbed them the "Brain Trust."

When searching for new ideas and fresh faces, Roosevelt was just as likely to turn to advisors and administrators scattered throughout the New Deal bureaucracy. Eager young people flocked to Washington to join the New Deal—"men with long hair and women with short hair," wags quipped (see American Voices, "Joe Marcus: A New Deal Activist," above). Lawyers in their mid-

twenties and fresh out of Harvard found themselves drafting legislation or being called to the White House for strategy sessions with the president. Paul Freund, a Harvard Law School professor who worked in the Department of Justice, remembered, "It was a glorious time for obscure people." Many young New Dealers who went on to distinguished careers in government or public service later recalled that nothing could match the excitement of the early New Deal.

The Hundred Days

The first problem the new president confronted was the banking crisis, which, far more than the stock market crash, had brought the depression home to the middle class. Since the onset of the depression, about 9 million people had lost their savings. On the eve of the inauguration, thirty-eight states had closed their banks, and the remaining ten had restricted their hours of operation. On March 5, the day after the inauguration, the president declared a national "**bank holiday**"—a euphemism for closing all the banks—and called Congress into special session. Four days later Congress, which responded enthusiastically to most early New Deal legislative proposals, passed Roosevelt's proposed emergency banking bill, which permitted banks to reopen beginning on March 13 but only if a Treasury Department inspection showed they had sufficient cash reserves. The House approved the plan after only thirty-eight minutes of debate.

The Emergency Banking Act. The Emergency Banking Act, which Roosevelt developed in consultation with banking leaders, was a conservative document that mirrored Herbert Hoover's proposals. The difference was the public's reaction. On the Sunday evening before the banks reopened, Roosevelt broadcast his first fireside chat to a radio audience estimated at 60 million. In simple terms he reassured citizens that the banks were safe, and Americans believed him. When the banks reopened on Monday morning, deposits exceeded withdrawals. "Capitalism was saved in eight days," observed Raymond Moley, who had served as Roosevelt's speech writer in the 1932 campaign. By using the federal government to investigate the nation's banks and restore confidence in the system, the banking act did its job. Though more than 4,000 banks failed in 1933—the majority in the months before the law was passed—only 61 closed their doors in 1934 (Table 25.1).

The banking act was the first of fifteen pieces of major legislation enacted by Congress in the opening months of the Roosevelt administration. This legislative session, known as the "Hundred Days," remains one of the most productive ever. Congress created the Home Owners Loan Corporation to refinance home mortgages threatened by foreclosure. A second banking law, the Glass-Steagall Act, curbed speculation by separating investment banking from commercial banking and created the Federal Deposit Insurance Corporation (FDIC), which insured deposits up to $2,500. Another act established the Civilian Conservation Corps (CCC), which sent 250,000 young men to do reforestation and conservation work. The Tennessee Valley Authority (TVA) received legislative approval for its innovative plan of government-sponsored regional development and public energy. And in a move that lifted public spirits immeasurably, Roosevelt legalized beer in April. Full repeal of Prohibition came eight months later in December 1933.

TABLE 25.1 American Banks and Bank Failures, 1920–1940

Year	Total Number of Banks	Total Assets ($ billion)	Bank Failures
1920	30,909	53.1	168
1929	25,568	72.3	659
1931	22,242	70.1	2,294
1933	14,771	51.4	4,004
1934	15,913	55.9	61
1940	15,076	79.7	48

Source: Historical Statistics of the United States: Colonial Times to 1970 (Washington, DC: U.S. Government Printing Office, 1975), 1019, 1038–39.

The Agricultural Adjustment Act. To speed economic recovery the Roosevelt administration targeted three pressing problems: agricultural overproduction, business failures, and unemployment relief. Roosevelt considered a healthy farming sector crucial to the nation's economic well-being. As he put it in 1929, "If farmers starve today, we will all starve tomorrow." Thus he viewed the Agricultural Adjustment Act (AAA) as a key step toward the nation's recovery. The AAA established a system for seven major commodities (wheat, cotton, corn, hogs, rice, tobacco, and dairy products) that provided cash subsidies to farmers who cut production—a policy that continues to the present day. These benefits were financed by a tax on processing (such as the milling of wheat), which was passed on to consumers. New Deal planners hoped prices would rise in response to the federally subsidized scarcity, spurring a general recovery.

Though the AAA stabilized the agricultural sector, its benefits were distributed unevenly. Subsidies for reducing production went primarily to the owners of large and medium-size farms, who often cut production by reducing their renters' and sharecroppers' acreage rather than their own. In the South, where many sharecroppers were black and the landowners and government administrators were white, that strategy had racial overtones. As many as 200,000 black tenant farmers were displaced from their land by the AAA. Thus New Deal agricultural policies fostered the migration of marginal farmers in the South and Midwest to northern cities and California, while they consolidated the economic and political clout of larger landholders.

The National Recovery Administration. The New Deal's major response to the problem of economic recovery, the National Industrial Recovery Act, launched the National Recovery Administration (NRA). The NRA, which drew on the World War I experience of Bernard Baruch's War Industries Board, established a system of industrial self-government to handle the problems of overproduction, cutthroat competition, and price instability that had caused business failures. Each industry—ranging from large industries such as coal, cotton, and steel to small ones such as dog food, costume jewelry, and even burlesque theaters—hammered out a code of prices and production quotas, similar to those for farm products. In effect, these legally enforceable agreements suspended the antitrust laws. The codes also established minimum wages and maximum hours and outlawed child labor. One of the most far-reaching provisions, Section 7(a), guaranteed workers the right to organize and bargain collectively, "through representatives of their own choosing." These union rights dramatically spurred the growth of the labor movement in the 1930s.

Yet trade associations, controlled by large companies, tended to dominate the code-drafting process, thus solidifying the power of large businesses at the expense of smaller enterprises. Labor had little input, and consumer interests almost none. To sell the program to skeptical consumers and businesspeople, the NRA launched an extensive public relations campaign, complete with plugs in Hollywood films and stickers with the NRA slogan, "We Do Our Part."

Unemployment Legislation. The early New Deal also addressed the critical problem of unemployment. In the fourth year of the depression, the total exhaustion of private and local sources of charity made some form of federal relief essential. Reluctantly, Roosevelt moved toward federal assumption of responsibility for the unemployed. The Federal Emergency Relief Administration (FERA), set up in May 1933 under the direction of Harry Hopkins, a social worker from New York, offered federal money to the states for relief programs. FERA was designed to keep people from starving until other recovery measures took hold. In his first two hours in office, Hopkins distributed $5 million. When told that some of the projects he had authorized might not be sound in the long run, Hopkins replied, "People don't eat in the long run—they eat every day." Over the program's two-year existence, FERA spent $1 billion.

Roosevelt and his advisors maintained a strong distaste for the **dole**. As Hopkins worried, "I don't think anybody can go year after year, month after month, accepting relief without affecting his character in some ways unfavorably. It is probably going to undermine the independence of hundreds of thousands of families." Whenever possible New Deal administrators promoted work relief over cash subsidies, and they consistently favored jobs that would not compete directly with the private sector. When the Public Works Administration (PWA), under Secretary of the Interior Harold L. Ickes, received a $3.3 billion appropriation in 1933, Ickes's cautiousness in initiating public works projects limited the agency's effectiveness. But in November 1933 Roosevelt established the Civil Works Administration (CWA) and named Harry Hopkins its head. Within thirty days the CWA had put 2.6 million men and women to work; at its peak in January 1934, it employed 4 million in jobs such as repairing bridges, building highways, constructing public buildings, and setting up community projects. The CWA, regarded as a stopgap measure

"Gulliver's Travels"

So many new agencies flooded out of Washington in the 1930s that one almost needed a scorecard to keep them straight. Here a July 1935 Vanity Fair *cartoon by William Gropper substitutes Uncle Sam for Captain Lemuel Gulliver, tied to the ground by Lilliputians, in a parody of Jonathan Swift's* Gulliver's Travels.
Courtesy, *Vanity Fair.* © 1935 (renewed 1963) by The Conde Nast Publications, Inc.

The Second New Deal, 1935–1938

As the depression continued and attacks on the New Deal mounted, Roosevelt and his advisors embarked on a new course, which historians have labeled the Second New Deal. By 1935, frustrated by his inability to win the support of big business, Roosevelt began to openly criticize the "money classes," proudly stating of his administration that "We have earned the hatred of entrenched greed." Pushed to the left by the popularity of movements like Long's as well as by signs of militancy among workers, Roosevelt, his eye fixed firmly on the 1936 election, began to construct a new coalition and broaden the scope of his response to the depression.

Legislative Accomplishments

Unlike the First New Deal, which focused on recovery, the Second New Deal emphasized reform and promoted legislation to increase the role of the federal government in providing for the welfare of citizens. While one of the most dramatic programs, the Works Progress Administration, did not last beyond the crisis of the depression, the Wagner Act and the Social Security Act would become permanent features of American life.

The Wagner Act and Social Security. The first beneficiary of Roosevelt's change in direction was the labor movement. The rising number of strikes in 1934— about 1,800 involving a total of 1.5 million workers— reflected the dramatic growth of rank-and-file militancy. After the Supreme Court declared the NRA unconstitutional in 1935, invalidating Section 7(a), labor representatives demanded effective legislation that would protect the right to organize and bargain collectively. Named for its sponsor, Senator Robert F. Wagner of New York, the Wagner Act (1935) offered a degree of protection to labor. It upheld the right of industrial workers to join a union (farm workers were not covered) and outlawed many unfair labor practices used to squelch unions, such as firing workers for union activities. The act also established the nonpartisan National Labor Relations Board (NLRB) to protect workers from employer coercion, supervise elections for union representation, and guarantee the process of collective bargaining.

The Social Security Act signed by Roosevelt on August 14, 1935, was partly a response to the political mobilization of the nation's elderly through the Townsend and Long movements. But it also reflected prodding from social reformers like Grace Abbott, head of the Children's Bureau, and Secretary of Labor Frances Perkins. The Social Security Act provided pensions for most workers in the private sector, although originally agricultural workers and domestics were not covered, a limitation that disproportionately disadvantaged poor blacks, especially women. Pensions were to be financed

General Strike, San Francisco, 1934
A general strike in San Francisco began with the longshoremen and soon spread to almost every union member (and some middle-class supporters as well) in the city. This striker has been shot in the head during an altercation with police. On July 19, union leaders voted to accept government arbitration, and the strike ended. Corbis-Bettmann.

by a federal tax that both employers and employees would pay. The act also established a joint federal-state system of unemployment compensation, funded by an unemployment tax on employers.

The Social Security Act was a milestone in the creation of the modern **welfare state**. Now the United States joined industrialized countries like Great Britain and Germany in providing old-age pensions and unemployment compensation to citizens. (The Roosevelt administration chose not to push for national health insurance, even though most other industrialized nations offered such protection.) The act also mandated categorical assistance to the blind, deaf, and disabled and to dependent children—the so-called deserving poor, who clearly could not support themselves. Categorical assistance programs, only a small part of the New Deal, gradually expanded over the years until they became an integral part of the American welfare system.

The Works Progress Administration.   Roosevelt was never enthusiastic about large expenditures for social welfare programs. But in the sixth year of the depression, 10 million Americans were still out of work, creating a pressing moral and political issue for FDR and the Democrats. Under Harry Hopkins the Works Progress Administration (WPA) became the main federal relief agency for the rest of the depression. While FERA had supplied grants to state relief programs, the WPA put relief workers directly onto the federal payroll. Between 1935 and 1943 the WPA employed 8.5 million Americans, spending $10.5 billion. The agency's employees constructed 651,087 miles of roads, 125,110 public buildings, 8,192 parks, and 853 airports and built or repaired 124,087 bridges (Map 25.1).

Though the WPA was an extravagant operation by the standards of the 1930s (it inspired nicknames such as "We Putter Around" and "We Poke Along"), it never reached more than a third of the nation's unemployed. The average wage of $55 a month—well below the government-defined subsistence level of $100 a month—barely enabled workers to eke out a living. In 1941 the government cut the program severely. It ended in 1943 when the economy returned to full employment during World War II.

The Revenue Act of 1935.   The Revenue Act of 1935, a tax reform bill that increased estate and corporate taxes and instituted higher personal income tax rates in the top brackets, showed Roosevelt's willingness to push for reforms that were considered too controversial earlier in his presidency. Much of the business community had already turned violently against Roosevelt in reaction to the NRA, the Social Security Act, and the Wagner Act. Now wealthy conservatives quickly labeled the Revenue Act an attempt to "soak the rich." Roosevelt, seeking to defuse the popularity of Huey Long's Share Our Wealth plan, was just as interested in the political mileage of the tax bill as in its actual results, which increased federal revenue by only $250 million a year.

The 1936 Election

As the 1936 election approached, the broad range of New Deal programs (Table 25.2) brought new voters into the Democratic coalition. Many had been personally helped by federal programs. Others benefited because their interests had found new support in the federal expansion: Roosevelt could count on a potent coalition of urban-based workers, organized labor, northern blacks, farmers, white ethnic groups, Catholics, Jews, liberals, intellectuals, progressive Republicans, and middle-class families concerned about unemployment and old-age dependence. The Democrats also held on, though with some difficulty, to their traditional constituency of white southerners.

The Republicans realized that they could not directly oppose Roosevelt and the New Deal. To run against the president, they chose the progressive governor of Kansas, Alfred M. Landon, who accepted the general precepts of the New Deal. Landon and the Republicans concentrated on criticizing the inefficiency and expense of many New Deal programs, stridently accusing FDR of harboring dictatorial ambitions.

Roosevelt's victory in 1936 was one of the biggest landslides in American history. The assassination of Huey Long in September 1935 had deflated the threat of a serious third-party challenge; the candidate of the combined Long-Townsend-Coughlin camp, Congressman William Lemke of North Dakota, garnered fewer than 900,000 votes (1.9 percent) for the Union Party ticket. Roosevelt received 60.8 percent of the popular vote and carried every state except Maine and Vermont. Landon fought such an uphill battle that the columnist Dorothy Thompson quipped, "If Landon had given one more speech, Roosevelt would have carried Canada." The New Deal was at high tide.

See America

During the New Deal, the United States Travel Bureau encouraged Americans to explore the nation's wide variety of vacation destinations and commissioned travel posters from the WPA's Federal Art Project. This example highlighting Montana was typical of the emphasis on regional distinctiveness as well as natural beauty. The imagery also often invoked a sense of power and encouraged Americans not just to "see America" but to see its strength and potential, a message designed to offset the pessimism created by the economic crisis. Library of Congress.

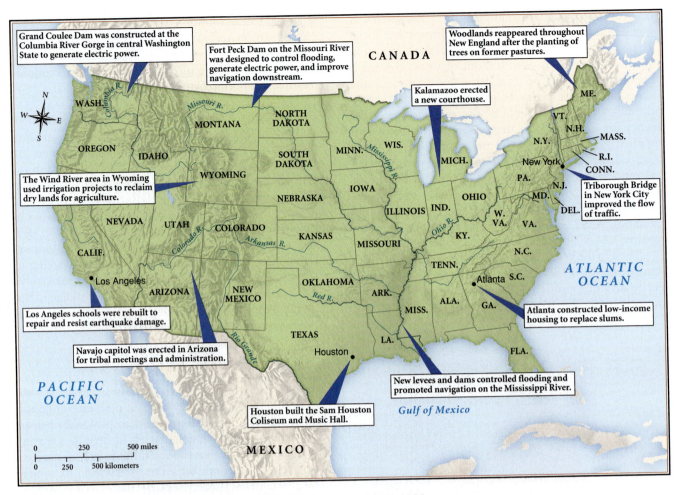

MAP 25.1 Public Works in the New Deal: The PWA in Action, 1933–1939

Between 1933 and 1939, the New Deal agencies of the Civilian Conservation Corps (CCC), the Works Progress Administration (WPA), and the Public Works Administration (PWA) created public works projects designed to put unemployed Americans to work and prime the economy with federal dollars, while simultaneously making lasting contributions to the nation's communities. The PWA, established in 1933 and directed by Harold Ickes, was the first federal agency to undertake extensive public projects that ranged from courthouses to swimming pools, airports to aircraft carriers, the Triborough Bridge to the Grand Coulee Dam.

Stalemate

"I see one-third of a nation ill-housed, ill-clad, ill-nourished," the president declared in his second inaugural address in January 1937. Roosevelt's appraisal suggested that he was considering further expansion of the welfare state that had begun to form late in this first term. However, retrenchment, controversy, and stalemate—not further reform—marked the second term.

The Supreme Court Fight. Only two weeks after his inauguration, Roosevelt stunned Congress and the nation by asking for fundamental changes in the structure of the Supreme Court. Shortly after finding the NRA unconstitutional in *Schechter v. United States*, the Court had struck down the Agricultural Adjustment

Act, a coal conservation act, and New York State's minimum wage law. With the Wagner Act, the TVA, and Social Security coming up on appeal, the future of New Deal reform measures seemed in doubt.

Roosevelt responded by proposing the addition of one new justice for each sitting justice over the age of seventy—a scheme that would have increased the number of justices from nine to fifteen. Roosevelt's opponents quickly protested that he was trying to "pack" the Court with justices who favored the New Deal. The president's proposal was also regarded as an assault on the principle of the separation of powers. Congress blocked the proposal, but Roosevelt ultimately achieved some part of what he wanted, as the Supreme Court upheld several key pieces of New Deal legislation, and a series of resignations created vacancies on the Court. Within four

TABLE 25.2 Major New Deal Legislation

Agriculture

1933	Agricultural Adjustment Act (AAA)
1935	Resettlement Administration (RA) Rural Electrification Administration
1937	Farm Security Administration (FSA)
1938	Agricultural Adjustment Act of 1938

Business and Industry

1933	Emergency Banking Act Glass-Steagall Act (FDIC) National Industrial Recovery Act (NIRA)
1934	Securities and Exchange Commission (SEC)
1935	Banking Act of 1935 Revenue Act (wealth tax)

Conservation and the Environment

| 1933 | Tennessee Valley Authority (TVA) Civilian Conservation Corps (CCC) |
| 1936 | Soil Conservation and Domestic Allotment Act |

Labor and Social Welfare

1933	Section 7(a) of NIRA
1935	National Labor Relations Act (Wagner Act) National Labor Relations Board (NLRB) Social Security Act
1937	National Housing Act
1938	Fair Labor Standards Act (FLSA)

Relief

| 1933 | Federal Emergency Relief Administration (FERA) Civil Works Administration (CWA) Public Works Administration (PWA) |
| 1935 | Works Progress Administration (WPA) National Youth Administration (NYA) |

he will soon be out of office. No one yet suspected that FDR would break with tradition by seeking a third term.

Congressional Opposition. Congressional conservatives had long opposed the direction of the New Deal, but the court-packing episode galvanized them by demonstrating that Roosevelt was no longer politically invincible. Throughout Roosevelt's second term a conservative coalition composed mainly of southern Democrats and Republicans from rural areas blocked or impeded social legislation. Two pieces of reform legislation that did win passage were the National Housing Act of 1937, which mandated the construction of low-cost public housing, and the Fair Labor Standards Act of 1938, which made permanent the minimum wage, maximum hours, and anti–child labor provisions in the NRA codes.

Roosevelt's attempts to reorganize the executive branch met a different fate. When Roosevelt inherited the presidency, the executive branch was still relatively weak. The enormity of the economic crisis gave the president far more influence in proposing and passing legislation, and the administration of New Deal programs significantly expanded the executive's influence. Congress resisted this accrual of power, however. In both 1937 and 1938, it refused to consider a plan to consolidate all independent agencies into cabinet-rank departments, extend the civil service system, and create the new position of auditor general. Conservatives effectively played on lawmakers' fears that centralized executive management would dramatically reduce congressional power and linked the plan to popular fears of fascism and dictatorship abroad, fears fanned by Hitler's rise to power in Germany. Roosevelt settled for a less ambitious bill in 1939 that allowed him to create the Executive Office of the President and name six administrative assistants to the White House staff. The White House also took control of the all-important budget process by moving the Bureau of the Budget to the Executive Office from its old home in the Treasury department.

The Roosevelt Recession. The "Roosevelt recession" of 1937 to 1938 dealt the most devastating blow to the president's political standing in the second term. Until that point the economy had made steady progress. From 1933 to 1937 the gross domestic product had grown at a yearly rate of about 10 percent, and by 1937 industrial output and real income had finally returned to 1929 levels. Unemployment had declined from 25 percent to 14 percent. Many Americans agreed with Senator James F. Byrnes of South Carolina that "the emergency has passed."

The steady improvement of the economy cheered Roosevelt, who had never been comfortable with large federal expenditures. Accordingly, Roosevelt slashed the federal budget in 1937. Between January and August Congress cut the WPA's funding in half, causing layoffs

years, retirements allowed Roosevelt to reshape the Supreme Court to suit his liberal philosophy through seven new appointments, including Hugo Black, Felix Frankfurter, and William O. Douglas. Yet his court scheme was a costly blunder at a time when his second-term administration was vulnerable to the lame-duck syndrome, in which Congress traditionally is less responsive to the proposals of a second-term president, knowing

of about 1.5 million workers. Fearing inflation, the Federal Reserve tightened credit, creating a sharp drop in the stock market. Unemployment soared to 19 percent, which translated into more than 10 million workers without jobs. Roosevelt soon found himself in the same situation that had confounded Hoover. Having taken credit for the recovery between 1933 and 1937, he had to take the blame for the recession.

Shifting gears, Roosevelt spent his way out of the downturn. Large WPA appropriations and a resumption of public works projects poured enough money into the economy to lift it out of the recession by early 1938. Roosevelt and his economic advisors were groping their way toward the general theory advanced by John Maynard Keynes, a British economist who proposed that governments use **deficit spending** (the spending of public funds obtained by borrowing rather than through taxation) to stimulate the economy when private spending proves insufficient. But Keynes's theory would not be widely accepted until a dramatic increase in defense spending for World War II finally ended the Great Depression.

Still struggling with attacks on the New Deal, Roosevelt decided to "purge" the Democratic Party of some of his most conservative opponents as the 1938 election approached. In the spring primaries he campaigned against members of his own party who had been hostile or unsympathetic to New Deal initiatives. The purge failed abysmally and widened the liberal-conservative rift in the party. In the general election of 1938, Republicans capitalized on the "Roosevelt recession" and the backlash against the court-packing attempt: they picked up eight seats in the Senate and eighty-one in the House. The Republicans also gained thirteen governorships.

Even without these political reversals, the reform impetus of the New Deal probably would not have continued. Roosevelt had always set clear limits on how far he was willing to go. His instincts were basically conservative, not revolutionary; he had wanted only to save the capitalist economic system by reforming it. The new activism of the Second New Deal was a major step beyond the informal, one-sided business-government partnership of the preceding decade, but it was a step Roosevelt took only because the emergency of the depression had pushed him in that direction.

The New Deal's Impact on Society

Despite the limits of the New Deal, it had a tremendous impact on the nation and fundamentally altered Americans' relationship to their government. With an optimistic faith in using government for social purposes, New Dealers sponsored programs in the arts. They created vast projects to conserve the country's natural beauty and resources and to make them more accessible to its citizens. The broker state that emerged in the New Deal also brought the voices of more citizens—women, blacks, labor, Mexican Americans—into the public arena, helping to promote the view that Roosevelt and his party represented and mediated for the common people.

New Deal Constituencies and the Broker State

The New Deal accelerated the expansion of the federal bureaucracy that had been under way since the turn of the century. In a decade the number of civilian government employees increased 80 percent, exceeding a million by 1940. The number of federal employees who worked in Washington grew at an even faster rate, doubling between 1929 and 1940. Power was increasingly centered in the nation's capital and not in the states. In 1939 a British observer summed up the new orientation: "Just as in 1929 the whole country was 'Wall Street conscious', now it is 'Washington conscious'."

The growth of the federal government increased the potential impact of its decisions (and spending) on various constituencies. During the 1930s the federal government operated as a broker state, mediating between contending pressure groups seeking power and benefits. Democrats recognized the importance of satisfying certain blocs of voters to cement their allegiance to the party. Even before the depression they had begun to build a coalition based on urban political machines and white ethnic voters. In the 1930s organized labor, women, African Americans, and other groups joined that coalition, receiving increased attention from the Democrats and the federal government they controlled.

Organized Labor. During the 1930s, after decades of federal hostility or inattention to the rights of workers, labor relations became a legitimate arena for federal action and intervention, and organized labor claimed a place in national political life. Labor's dramatic growth in the 1930s represented one of the most important social and economic changes of the decade, an enormous contrast to its demoralized state at the end of the 1920s. Several factors encouraged the growth of the labor movement: the inadequacy of welfare capitalism in the face of the depression, New Deal legislation like the Wagner Act, the rise of the Congress of Industrial Organizations (CIO), and the growing militancy of rank-and-file workers. By the end of the decade, the number of unionized workers had tripled to almost 9 million, or 23 percent of the nonfarm workforce. Organized labor won the battle not only for union recognition but for higher wages, seniority systems, and grievance procedures.

The CIO served as the cutting edge of the union movement by promoting "industrial unionism"—that is, organizing all the workers in an industry, both skilled and unskilled, into one union. John L. Lewis, leader of the United Mine Workers (UMW) and the foremost exponent of industrial unionism, broke with the American Federation of Labor, which favored organizing workers on a craft-by-craft basis, and in 1935 helped to found the CIO. The CIO achieved some of its momentum through the presence in its ranks of members of the Communist Party. The rise of fascism in Europe had prompted the Soviet Union to mobilize support in democratic countries. In Europe and the United States, Communist parties called for a "popular front," welcoming the cooperation of any group concerned about the threat of fascism to civil rights, organized labor, and world peace. Under the popular front Communists softened their revolutionary rhetoric and concentrated on becoming active leaders in many CIO unions. While few workers actually joined the Communist Party, its influence in labor organizing in the

Organize

The Steel Workers Organizing Committee was one of the most vital labor organizations contributing to the rise of the CIO. Note that artist Ben Shahn chose a male figure to represent the American labor movement in this poster from the late 1930s. Such iconography reinforced the notion that the typical worker was male, despite the large number of women who joined the CIO. Library of Congress.

For more help analyzing this image, see the ONLINE STUDY GUIDE at bedfordstmartins.com/henretta.

thirties was far greater than its numbers, which in 1936 reached 40,000.

The CIO's success also stemmed from the recognition that unions must be more inclusive in order to succeed. The CIO worked deliberately to attract new groups to the labor movement. Mexican Americans and African Americans found the CIO's commitment to racial justice a strong contrast to the AFL's long-established patterns of exclusion and segregation. And about 800,000 women workers also found a limited welcome in the CIO. Few blacks, Mexican Americans, or women held leadership positions, however.

The CIO scored its first major victory in the automobile industry. On December 31, 1936, General Motors workers in Flint, Michigan, staged a sit-down strike, vowing to stay at their machines until management agreed to collective bargaining. The workers lived in the factories and machine shops for forty-four days before General Motors recognized their union, the United Automobile Workers (UAW). Shortly thereafter the CIO won another major victory, at the U.S. Steel Corporation. Despite a long history of bitter opposition to unionization, as demonstrated in the 1919 steel strike (see Chapter 22), Big Steel executives capitulated without a fight and recognized the Steel Workers Organizing Committee (SWOC) on March 2, 1937.

The victory in the steel industry was not complete, however. A group of companies known as "Little Steel" chose not to follow the lead of U.S. Steel in making peace with the CIO, causing steelworkers to strike the Republic Steel Corporation plant in South Chicago. On Memorial Day, May 31, 1937, strikers and their families gathered for a holiday picnic and rallied outside the plant's gates. Tension mounted, rocks were thrown, and the police fired on the crowd, killing ten protesters. All were shot in the back. A newsreel photographer recorded the scene, but Paramount Pictures considered the film of the "Memorial Day Massacre" too inflammatory for distribution. Workers in Little Steel did not win union recognition until 1941. The road to recognition for labor, even with New Deal protections, was still long and violent.

The 1930s constituted one of the most active periods of labor solidarity in American history (Map 25.2). The sit-down tactic spread rapidly. In March 1937 a total of 167,210 workers staged 170 sit-down strikes. Labor unions called for nearly 5,000 strikes that year and won favorable terms in 80 percent of them. Yet large numbers of middle-class Americans felt alienated by sit-down strikes, which they considered attacks on private property. The Supreme Court agreed and in 1939 upheld a law that banned the practice.

Labor's new vitality spilled over into political action. The AFL generally had stood aloof from partisan politics, but the CIO quickly allied itself with the Democratic Party, hoping to use its influence to elect candidates sympathetic to labor and social justice. Establishing a

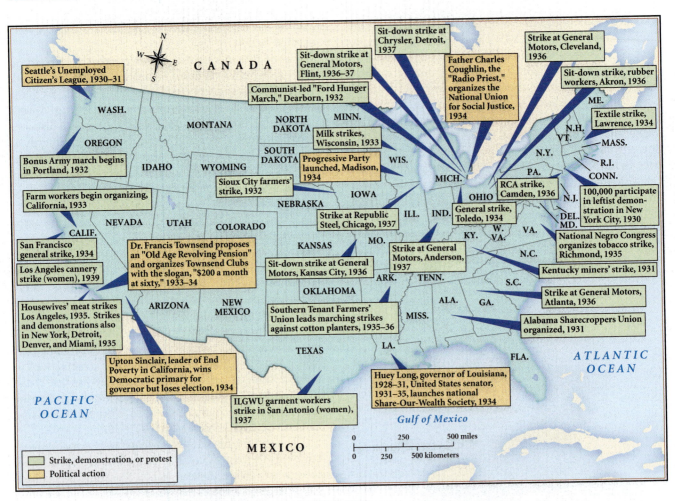

MAP 25.2 Popular Protest in the Great Depression, 1933–1939

Throughout the Depression, Americans protested the harsh conditions brought about by economic collapse. Some expressed their discontent through large social movements like Upton Sinclair's EPIC (End Poverty in California) or Huey Long's Share Our Wealth movement. Others turned to Communist-led demonstrations such as the 1932 "Ford Hunger March" in Dearborn, Michigan. Independent farmers in Iowa's Farm Holiday Association organized to bring about higher prices in 1932, while in 1935, the socialist-led Southern Tenant Farmers' Union challenged cotton planters over their restriction of tenants' rights. Also in 1935, militant housewives staged meat strikes in cities countrywide to protest high meat prices. Everywhere, it seemed, American workers were striking against their employers. Despite this wellspring of popular protest, discontent in the 1930s did not lead to a radical restructuring of politics or the economy, in large measure because Franklin Roosevelt's New Deal shored up confidence and deflected dissent.

group it rather misleadingly called Labor's Nonpartisan League, the CIO gave $770,000 to Democratic campaigns in 1936. Labor also provided solid support for Roosevelt's plan to reorganize the Supreme Court.

Despite the breakthroughs of the New Deal, the labor movement never developed into a dominant force in American life. Roosevelt never made the growth of the labor movement a high priority, and many workers remained indifferent or even hostile to unionization. And although the Wagner Act guaranteed unions a permanent place in American industrial relations, it did not revolutionize working conditions. The right to collective bargaining, rather than redistributing power in Ameri-

can industry, merely granted labor a measure of legitimacy. Management even found that unions could be used as a buffer against rank-and-file militancy. New Deal social welfare programs also tended to diffuse some of the pre-1937 radical spirit by channeling economic benefits to workers whether or not they belonged to unions. The road to union power, even with New Deal protection, continued to be a rocky and uncertain one.

Women and the New Deal. Like organized workers white women achieved new influence in the experimental climate of the New Deal, as unprecedented numbers of them were offered positions in the Roosevelt

A First Lady without Precedent

Reflecting Eleanor Roosevelt's tendency to turn up in odd places, a famous 1933 New Yorker *cartoon has one coal miner saying to another, "For gosh sakes, here comes Mrs. Roosevelt." Life soon imitated art. Here, the first lady emerges from a coal mine in Dellaire, Ohio, still carrying her miner's cap in her left hand, while speaking with Joseph Bainbridge on May 22, 1935.*
Wide World Photos, Inc.

administration. Frances Perkins, the first woman named to a cabinet post, served as secretary of labor throughout Roosevelt's presidency. Molly Dewson, a social reformer turned politician, headed the Women's Division of the Democratic National Committee, where she pushed an issue-oriented program that supported New Deal reforms. Roosevelt's woman appointees also included the first female director of the mint, the head of a major WPA division, and a judge on a circuit court of appeals. Many of those women were close friends as well as professional colleagues and cooperated in an informal network to advance feminist and reform causes.

Eleanor Roosevelt exemplified the growing prominence of women in public life. In the 1920s she had worked closely with other reformers to increase women's power in political parties, labor unions, and education. The experience proved an invaluable apprenticeship for her White House years, when her marriage to FDR developed into one of the most successful political partnerships of all time. He was the pragmatic politician, always aware of what could be done; she was the idealist, the gadfly, always pushing him—and the New Deal—to

do more. Eleanor Roosevelt served as the conscience of the New Deal.

Despite the advocacy by a female political network for equal opportunity for women, grave flaws still marred New Deal programs. A fourth of the NRA codes set a lower minimum wage for women than for men performing the same jobs. New Deal agencies like the Civil Works Administration and the Public Works Administration gave jobs almost exclusively to men: only 7 percent of CWA workers were female. And the CCC excluded women entirely, prompting critics to ask, "Where is the 'she-she-she'?"

When they did hire women, New Deal programs tended to reinforce the broader society's gender and racial attitudes. Thus program administrators resisted placing women in nontraditional jobs. Under the WPA, sewing rooms became a sort of dumping ground for unemployed women. African American and Mexican American women, if they had access to work relief at all, often found themselves shunted into training as domestics, whose work was not covered by the Social Security and Fair Labor Standards Acts. For the most part, progress for women did not come from specific attempts to recognize them as a group but occurred as part of a broader effort to improve the economic security of all Americans.

Blacks and the New Deal. Just as the New Deal did not seriously challenge gender inequities, it did little to battle racial discrimination. In the 1930s the majority of the American people did not regard civil rights as a legitimate area for federal intervention. Indeed many New Deal programs reflected prevailing racist attitudes. CCC camps segregated blacks and whites, and many NRA codes did not protect black workers. Most tellingly, Franklin Roosevelt repeatedly refused to support legislation to make lynching a federal crime, claiming it would antagonize southern members of Congress whose support he needed to pass New Deal measures.

Nevertheless, blacks did receive significant benefits from those New Deal relief programs that were directed toward the poor regardless of their race or ethnic background. Blacks made up about 18 percent of the WPA's recipients, although they constituted only 10 percent of the population. The Resettlement Administration, established in 1935 to help small farmers buy land and to resettle sharecroppers and tenant farmers on more productive land, fought for the rights of black tenant farmers in the South, until angry southerners in Congress drastically cut its appropriations. Still, many blacks reasoned that the tangible aid from Washington outweighed the discrimination that marred many federal programs.

African Americans were also pleased to see blacks appointed to federal office. Mary McLeod Bethune, an educator who ran the Office of Minority Affairs of the National Youth Administration, headed the "black cabinet" (see American Lives, "Mary McLeod Bethune: Black Braintruster," p. 736). This informal network worked for

Mary McLeod Bethune: Black Braintruster

The New Deal brought many remarkable people to Washington, but few had traveled as far as Mary McLeod Bethune. As the Reverend Adam Clayton Powell Sr. wrote to her in 1935 when she received the prestigious Spingarn Medal from the National Association for the Advancement of Colored People, "It is a long way from the rice and cotton fields of South Carolina to this distinguished recognition, but you have made it in such a short span of years that I am afraid you are going to be arrested for breaking the speed limit." In terms of her contributions to black history, Mary McLeod Bethune deserves to be remembered alongside such luminaries as Frederick Douglass, W. E. B. Du Bois, and Martin Luther King Jr.

Born on July 10, 1875, near Mayesville, South Carolina, Mary was the fifteenth of seventeen children born to Sam and Patsy McLeod, former slaves liberated after the Civil War. She was educated at the Scotia Seminary in Concord, North Carolina, and the Bible Institute for Home and Foreign Missions in Chicago (later the Moody Bible Institute) in preparation for her chosen career as a missionary. Turning from her original plan to go to Africa, she redirected her missionary zeal to the United States and the field of education and racial uplift. In 1898 she married Albertus Bethune, and their only child, Albert McLeod Bethune, was born in 1899. The family moved to Florida, but the marriage foundered and the couple separated in 1907. She never remarried, and Albertus Bethune died in 1918.

In 1904, "with $1.50 and a prayer," Mary McLeod Bethune opened the school in Daytona Beach, Florida, that eventually became the prestigious Bethune-Cookman College, the only historically black college founded by a black woman that continues to thrive today. The initial student body consisted of five girls and her son; by 1923 the school had more than 300 students and a faculty and staff of twenty-five. Bethune was intimately involved with this institution—and by extension with the issue of providing expanded educational opportunities for African Americans—for the rest of her life. Through her extensive civic involvement in Daytona

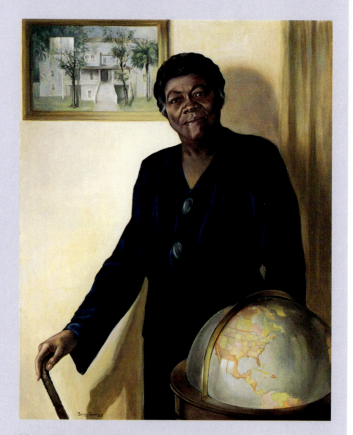

Mary McLeod Bethune

This 1943 painting by Betsy Graves Reyneau captures the strength and dignity of one of the twentieth century's most important African Americans. Behind Bethune is a picture of the first building at the Daytona Literary and Industrial School for Training of Negro Girls, which later became Bethune-Cookman College.

National Portrait Gallery, Smithsonian Institution / Art Resource, NY.

Beach and the constant fundraising needed to keep her school afloat, she was quickly drawn into wider national networks, especially through the National Association of Colored Women (NACW)—the leading black women's organization in the first quarter of the twentieth century. Bethune served as president of that organization from 1924 to 1928. In 1935 she organized the National Council of Negro Women (NCNW), a coalition of the major national black women's associations, serving as its president until 1949.

Mary McLeod Bethune was a forceful personality and a born leader. The New Deal offered her a national platform through which to promote her agendas on race, education, women, and youth when she was named—at Eleanor Roosevelt's suggestion—to the advisory committee of the National Youth Administration in 1935. In the next year she was named director of the division of Negro Affairs in the NYA, where she served until 1944. One of her greatest contributions was the leadership she provided to the other black administrators who found opportunities in the New Deal. The Federal Council of Negro Affairs, known informally as the Black Cabinet, met on Sunday nights at her home in Washington. As the Washington correspondent for the Associated Negro Press noted, "Mrs. Bethune has gathered everything and everybody under her very ample wing since her arrival last June." Along with NAACP general secretary Walter White, she was the only ranking black administrator who had access to the White House.

Bethune recognized the limits of the New Deal's commitment to civil rights, but she remained a loyal supporter of Franklin Roosevelt, with whom she enjoyed an easy friendship. But it was Eleanor Roosevelt who became her staunchest political ally. When funding for a black housing project in Daytona Beach was stalled by bureaucratic red tape, local activists contacted Bethune, who in turn reached Eleanor Roosevelt, who with one call to the head of the Federal Housing Authority had the project back on track. On several occasions the first lady opened the White House to Bethune for conferences, thereby ensuring that they would receive national attention. Along the way the two women became personal friends as well as allies, although Roosevelt admitted that it took her a while to feel comfortable giving Bethune the customary peck on the cheek she bestowed when greeting white friends. Not until she kissed Mrs. Bethune without thinking about it, she told her daughter, did she feel that she had overcome the racial prejudice that was so much a part of Roosevelt's—and many white Americans'—background.

Bethune's basic strategy was to win policymaking positions for African Americans and then use those bases to work for more equitable treatment for blacks throughout the New Deal. Sometimes her small gestures were just as telling as her larger public stances. She always insisted on being called "Mrs. Bethune" as a term of respect, refusing to go down in history as "Mary from Florida." When a White House guard addressed her as "Auntie," a name whites often used indiscriminately for older black women, she looked at him sweetly and asked, "Which one of my brother's children are you?" Her entire adult life was devoted to improving conditions and access for her race. "The drums of Africa beat in my heart," she often said. "I cannot rest while there is a single Negro boy or girl lacking a chance to prove his worth."

There must have been many times when Bethune, a deeply religious woman, had to suppress personal feelings of disappointment or outright anger at the pace of change, but she always favored conciliation and compromise over confrontation. "I am diplomatic about certain things. I let people infer a great many things, but I am careful about what I say because I want to do certain things." But she also knew when to apply pressure, twist arms, appeal to publicity, and move a group toward concensus. As she once said forthrightly, "The White man has been thinking for us too long. We want him to think with us instead of for us."

When the National Youth Administration ceased operation in 1944, Bethune left government service but continued to be active in educational and charitable work. In 1952 she fulfilled a lifelong dream when she visited Liberia as an official U.S. representative at the inauguration of William Tubman as that country's president. She died of a heart attack in 1955 and was buried on the Bethune-Cookman campus. In 1974, on the ninety-ninth anniversary of her birth, the National Council of Negro Women dedicated the Mary McLeod Bethune Memorial Statue at Lincoln Park in Washington, D.C., just a short distance from the Capitol.

"Most people think I am a dreamer," Mary McLeod Bethune once said. "Through dreams many things come true." A dream come true was the 1938 gathering organized in conjunction with the National Council of Negro Women that brought sixty-seven black women leaders to the White House. Bethune recalled its significance soon thereafter:

> It certainly was history-making. . . . The pressure we have been making, the intercessions . . . they are finding their way. . . . The position I hold now—I give you that as an example. The first time in history that a Negro woman filled a national, federal position with the leeway, the opportunity . . . the contacts. Because one got in there, sixty-seven got in one day and many others are getting in here and there and there and there.

"A door has been sealed up for two hundred years," she concluded. "You can't open it overnight but little crevices are coming." Mary McLeod Bethune cracked open that door, and generations of African American activists, male and female, have been opening it wider and wider ever since.

In 1936–1937, Eleanor visited 33 of the 48 states. Most of her visits were on her own initiative, rather than accompanying FDR. She used these visits to schools, factories, and town meetings to bring back to the White House first-hand accounts of how the Depression affected peoples' lives.

California and the Southwest as well as Florida and the Southeast did not appear on the itinerary in 1936–1937, but Eleanor did visit those areas later in her tenure as First Lady.

Eleanor Roosevelt traveled mostly by train, and one can almost fill in train tracks to connect the dots on this map.

(after Opdycke)

MAP 25.3 Eleanor Roosevelt's Travels, 1936–1937

First Lady Eleanor Roosevelt quickly achieved a reputation as a seemingly inexhaustible traveler, who often served as "the eyes and ears of the New Deal." The high public profile produced by her heavily publicized appearances throughout the nation helped to create an image of both Eleanor and Franklin as caring, humane people. Throughout FDR's twelve years as president, it is not surprising that many of the millions of letters that poured into the White House addressed Eleanor as though she was a friend or family member.

fairer treatment of blacks by New Deal agencies in the same way the white women's network advocated feminist causes. Both groups benefited greatly from the support of Eleanor Roosevelt. The first lady's promotion of equal treatment for blacks ranks as one of her greatest legacies.

Help from the WPA and other New Deal programs and a belief that the White House—or at least Eleanor Roosevelt—cared about their plight, caused a dramatic change in African Americans' voting behavior (Map 25.3). Since the Civil War, blacks had voted Republican, a loyalty based on Abraham Lincoln's freeing of the slaves. As late as 1932 black voters in northern cities overwhelmingly supported Republican candidates. But in 1936 black Americans outside the South (where blacks were still

largely prevented from voting) gave Roosevelt 71 percent of their votes. In Harlem, where relief dollars increased dramatically in the wake of the 1935 riot (see Chapter 24), their support for Roosevelt was an extraordinary 81.3 percent. Black voters have remained overwhelmingly Democratic ever since.

The Politicization of Mexican Americans. The election of Franklin Roosevelt also had an immediate effect on Mexican American communities, demoralized by the depression and the deportations of the Hoover years. In cities like Los Angeles and El Paso, Mexican Americans qualified for relief more easily under New Deal guidelines, and there was more relief to go around (see American Voices, "Susana Archuleta: A Chicana

Susana Archuleta

A Chicana Youth Gets New Deal Work

Although African Americans and Chicanos often experienced discrimination in New Deal programs, many did find opportunities in agencies like the Civilian Conservation Corps, the National Youth Administration, or the Works Progress Administration. They attributed the help they received directly to Franklin Delano Roosevelt's election, as Susana Archuleta's reminiscence of life in Wyoming suggests.

I was born in New Mexico, on a farm up North in Mora County. I was the fifth of eight children. When I was very little, my dad moved us all to Wyoming. You see, he heard that they had free textbooks in Wyoming, while here in New Mexico the parents had to pay for the books. Daddy didn't have much money, and he felt that we all needed an opportunity for education. We left the farm—the animals, the machinery, everything—and he went to work in the mines up in Rock Springs, Wyoming. . . .

During the Depression, things got bad. My dad passed away when I was about twelve, leaving my mother with eight children and no means of support. There wasn't any welfare. My mother took in washings to make a living, and our job was to pick up the washings on the way home from school. We'd pick up clothes from the school-teachers, the attorney, and what-have-you. Then, at night, we'd help iron them and fold them. On Saturdays we'd help with the wash, too. We'd put a big old fire out in the patio and a big old tub of water on top of it. Then we'd bring the tub in and wash the clothes.

Summer months would come along and everybody had their chores. My oldest brother always went out and worked, delivering papers, things like that. Two of my sisters did the housework. My next oldest brother and I used to fill up the coal bin for the winter months. We'd go down to the pits where the coal cars would come out. They'd come out loaded full, and some of the coals would fall off. So during the hours when the cars weren't working, we'd go with the other kids from town and fill up our sacks with the coal from the tracks. It took a long time, because that coal bin would hold about three tons of coal. I used to carry a good fifty-pound sack on my back.

When I was a teenager, the Depression began to take a turn. Franklin Roosevelt was elected, and the works projects started. The boys and young men who'd been laid off at the mines went to the CCC camps, and the girls joined the NYA. When school was over, we'd go and work right there in the school building. We'd help out in the office, do filing and other things. Actually, we didn't do much work—it was our first job. But we learned a lot. It was good experience.

They paid us about twenty-one dollars a month. Out of that we got five and the other sixteen was directly issued to our parents. The same was true of the boys working in the camps. They got about thirty dollars a month. They were allowed to keep five of it. The rest was sent to their families. All of us were hired according to our family income. If a man with a lot of children was unemployed, he was given preference over someone who had less children. They also had projects for women who were widows. They made quilts and mattresses. Those programs were great. Everybody got a chance to work. I think there should be more training programs like that, instead of giveaway programs like welfare. . . .

Source: Nan Elsasser, "Susana Archuleta," in Nan Elsasser et al., *Las Mujeres: Conversations from a Hispanic Community* (New York: Feminist Press, 1980), 36–37.

Youth Gets New Deal Work," above). Even though New Deal regulations prohibited discrimination based on an immigrant's legal status, the new climate encouraged a marked rise in requests for naturalization papers. Mexican Americans also benefited from New Deal labor policies; joining the CIO was an important stage for many in becoming Americans. Inspired by New Deal rhetoric about economic recovery and social progress through cooperation, Mexican Americans increasingly identified with the United States rather than with Mexico. This shift was especially evident among American-born children of Mexican immigrants.

Participating in the political system increasingly became part of Mexican American life. Los Angeles activist Beatrice Griffith noted, "Franklin D. Roosevelt's name was the spark that started thousands of Spanish-speaking

Odette Keun

A Foreigner Looks at the Tennessee Valley Authority

French writer Odette Keun visited the United States in 1936 and was so impressed by the Tennessee Valley Authority (TVA) that she wrote a book about it. Among other observations, Keun felt that experiments like the TVA might help inhibit the development of an American variety of fascism.

The vital question before democracy is, therefore, not how to bring back an economic freedom which is irretrievably lost, but how to prevent the intellectual freedom, which is still our heritage, from being submerged. It is already threatened. It will be threatened more and more strongly in the years ahead—and the menace, of course, is dictatorship. But to fight dictatorship it is necessary first to understand in what circumstances it arises, and then to think out the counterattack which democracy can launch against its approaching force.

Dictatorship springs from two very clear causes. One is the total incapacity of parliamentary government: total, as in Germany in 1933 and in Spain in 1935. To such a breakdown neither the democratic nations of Europe nor America have yet been reduced, although everywhere there are very ominous creaks and cracks, and the authority and prestige of parliamentary institutions have greatly and perilously diminished. The other cause, infinitely closer to us and more dynamic, is the failure of the economic machine to function properly, and by functioning properly I mean ensuring a livelihood for the entire population. No system can survive if it cannot procure food and wages for the people who live under it. Man has to get subsistence from his rulers, for the most immediate and the most imperious law of our nature is that the belly must be filled. It is perfectly futile to orate on fine, high, and abstract principles to human beings who are permanently hungry, permanently harassed, permanently uncertain, who hear their wives begging for the rent and their children crying out for nourishment. . . .

One of the main tenets of liberalism—I reiterate this like a gramophone, but I must get it to sink in—is that all necessary overhauling and adjustment ought to be done in a manner which will minimize the shock to the greatest number, and soften as much as possible the unavoidable human suffering which these changes entail. This opposition to extremes, this practice of a graduated change, we can call "the middle of the road in time and space." But it is not nearly enough to conceive it and to bestow upon it a name. We must reach it. It is unutterably foolish to look at the middle of the road, to talk of the middle of the road, to hope for the middle of the road—and never get there.

Now I have tried to show that the middle of the road is already being laid down in America. The Tennessee Valley Authority is laying it down. Handicapped and restricted though it is in all sorts of ways, it is the noblest, the most intelligent, and the best attempt made in this country or in any other democratic country to economize, marshal, and integrate the actual assets of a region, plan its development and future, ameliorate its standards of living, establish it in a more enduring security, and render available to the people the benefits of the wealth of their district, and the results of science, discovery, invention, and disinterested forethought. In its inspiration and its goal there is goodness, for goodness is that which makes for unity of purpose with love, compassion, and respect for every life and every pattern of living. The economic machine, bad though it is, has not been smashed in the Tennessee Watershed; it is being very gradually, very carefully, very equitably reviewed and amended, and the citizens are being taught and directed, but not bullied, not coerced, not regimented, not frightened, within the constitutional frame the nation itself elected to build. It is not while the Tennessee Valley Authority has the valley in its keeping that despair or disintegration can prepare the ground for a dictatorship and the loss of freedom. The immortal contribution of the TVA to liberalism, not only in America but all over the world, is the blueprint it has drawn, and that it is now transforming into a living reality, of the road which liberals believe is the only road mankind should travel.

Source: Odette Keun, *A Foreigner Looks at the TVA* (1937), in Oscar Handlin, ed., *This Was America* (Cambridge, MA: Harvard University Press, 1949), 547–49.

"The Promise of the New Deal"

This 1936 mural by noted artist Ben Shahn depicts the beginnings of Roosevelt, New Jersey, originally called "Jersey Homesteads." The product of a New Deal planning initiative, the town included a cooperative consisting of retail stores, a factory, and a farm, and was designed for poor immigrants from New York City. While the mural includes the intended beneficiaries of the new community in the background and acknowledges the powerful presence of Franklin D. Roosevelt with the image on the wall, it focuses on the New Deal planners themselves, capturing some of the faith in experts and social planning of the New Deal era. Roosevelt Arts Project.

sculptors at a point in their careers when the lack of private patronage might have prevented them from continuing their artistic production. Under the direction of Holger Cahill, an expert on American folk art, the FAP commissioned murals for public buildings and post offices across the country. Jackson Pollock, Alice Neel, Willem de Kooning, and Louise Nevelson all received support from the FAP.

The Federal Music Project employed 15,000 musicians under the direction of Nicholas Sokoloff, the conductor of the Cleveland Symphony Orchestra. Government-sponsored orchestras toured the country, presenting free concerts of both classical and popular music. Like many New Deal programs, the Music Project emphasized American themes. The composer Aaron Copland wrote his ballets *Billy the Kid* (1938) and *Rodeo* (1942) for the WPA, basing the compositions on western folk motifs. The distinctive "American" sound and athletic dance style of these works made them immensely appealing to audiences. The federal government also employed the musicologist Charles Seeger and his wife, the composer Ruth Crawford Seeger, to catalog hundreds of American folk songs.

The former journalist Henry Alsberg headed the Federal Writers' Project (FWP), which at its height employed about 5,000 writers. Young FWP employees who later achieved fame included Saul Bellow, Ralph Ellison, Tillie Olsen, and John Cheever. The black folklorist and novelist Zora Neale Hurston finished three novels while on the Florida FWP, among them *Their Eyes Were Watching God* (1937). And Richard Wright won the 1938 *Story* magazine prize for the best tale by a WPA writer. Wright used his spare time to complete his novel *Native Son* (1940).

Of all the New Deal arts programs, the Federal Theatre Project (FTP) was the most ambitious. American drama thrived in the 1930s, the only time at which the United States had a federally supported national theater. Under the gifted direction of Hallie Flanagan, former head of Vassar College's Experimental Theater, the FTP reached an audience of 25 to 30 million people in the four years of its existence. Talented directors, actors, and playwrights, including Orson Welles, John Houseman, and Arthur Miller, offered their services. The tendency to take a hard and critical look at social problems, however, made the program vulnerable to **red-baiting**. After a series of

Rural Electrification

In 1935 fewer than one-tenth of the nation's 6.8 million farms had electricity. For millions of farm families, that stark fact meant a life of unremitting toil made even harsher by the lack of simple conveniences. Farm families used an average of 200 gallons of water a day. Any chore requiring water—and most did—meant pumping the water from a distant well and carrying it to the house or barn in a pair of buckets that weighed as much as 30 pounds each. Water had to be heated on a woodstove that required constant tending. Meeting a family's yearly water needs took 63 eight-hour days and involved carrying water a distance of 1,750 miles.

Rural women suffered especially from the lack of electricity. Canning, a necessity before refrigeration, kept women standing over steaming vats of fruit or vegetables, often in the worst summer heat, before the freshly harvested produce spoiled. Wash day, traditionally Monday, called for three large zinc washtubs for washing, rinsing, and bleaching. A week's wash consisted of four to eight loads, each requiring three washtubs of clean water hauled from the well. Few rural households could afford commercial soap, so women used lye, which barely removed ground-in dirt from soiled clothes and was very harsh on hands. But if farm women dreaded Monday, they hated Tuesday even more. Tuesday meant ironing, another all-day job. The iron, a 6- or 7-pound wedge of metal, had to be heated on the stove, and, because it did not retain heat for more than a few minutes, it took several irons to do a shirt. The women in Texas's hill country called them "sad irons."

A day that began in darkness and was given over to twelve hours of backbreaking toil brought few comforts in the evening. Reading by kerosene lamps strained the eyes. Children's eyes might be strong enough to read in the semidarkness, but few older people could read without squinting. The absence of electricity also meant no radios, which meant no contact with the outside world.

Studies showed that farmers would find many uses for electricity and would make good customers, but power companies balked at the prospect of bringing electricity to the countryside, claiming that it was not economically feasible to run lines to individual farms. In 1935 the federal government made a commitment to bring power to rural America. The Rural Electrification Administration, an independent agency, promoted the formation of nonprofit farm cooperatives to bring electricity to their regions. For a $5 down payment, local farmers could join an association and become eligible for low-interest federal loans covering the cost of installing power lines. Each household was committed to a monthly minimum usage, usually about $3, but as usage increased, the rates came down. By 1940, 40 percent of the nation's farms had electricity; in 1950 the rate reached 90 percent.

Electricity brought relief from the drudgery and isolation of farm life. An electric milking machine saved hours of manual labor, most of it previously done before dawn by the faint glow of a kerosene lamp so farmers could devote the daylight hours to outdoor chores. An electric water pump lightened many chores, especially the hauling of water. Electric irons, vacuum cleaners, and washing machines eased women's burdens.

People's responses to rural electrification were poignant. A small child told his mother, "I didn't realize how dark our house was until we got electric lights." One farm woman remembered, "I just turned on the light and kept looking at Paw. It was the first time I'd ever really seen him after dark." Another family, caught unaware by the timing of the hookup, saw their house from a distance and thought it was on fire. Schoolteachers noticed that children did better at school when they had light to do homework by at night. Along with the automobile, electricity probably did more than any other technological innovation to break down the barriers between urban and rural life in twentieth-century America.

"Blue Monday"

Laundry was one of women's hardest household chores. Although this woman did not have to haul water from an outdoor well, she still had to pump it by hand in order to do the wash because her home lacked electricity. She also had to wring out the wet clothes manually—another arduous task. Corbis-Bettmann.

investigations as to alleged Communist influence, Congress terminated the FTP in 1939. Director Flanagan wryly remarked, "I could see why certain powers would not want even 10% of the Federal Theatre plays to be the sort to make people in our democracy think. Such forces might well be afraid of thinking people."

The WPA arts projects were influenced by a broad artistic trend called the "**documentary impulse**." Combining social relevance with distinctively American themes, this approach, which presented actual facts and events in a way that aroused the interest and emotions of the audience, characterized the artistic expression of the 1930s. The documentary, probably the decade's most distinctive genre, influenced practically every aspect of American culture—literature, photography, art, music, film, dance, theater, and radio. It is evident in John Steinbeck's fiction (see Chapter 24) and in John Dos Passos's *USA* trilogy, which used actual newspaper clippings, dispatches, and headlines in its fictional story. *The March of Time* newsreels, which movie audiences saw before feature films, presented the news of the world for the pretelevision age. The filmmaker Pare Lorentz commissioned the composer Virgil Thompson to create music that set the mood for documentary movies such as *The Plow That Broke the Plains* (1936) and *The River* (1936). The new photojournalism magazines, including *Life* and *Look*, also reflected this documentary approach. And the New Deal institutionalized the trend by sending investigators like the journalist Lorena Hickok and the writer Martha Gellhorn into the field to report on the conditions of people on relief.

Finally, the federal government played a leading role in compiling the photographic record of the 1930s. The Historical Section of the Resettlement Administration had a mandate to document and photograph the American scene for the government. Through their haunting images of sharecroppers, Dust Bowl migrants, and the urban homeless, photographers Dorothea Lange, Walker Evans, Ben Shahn, and Margaret Bourke-White permanently shaped the image of the Great Depression. The government hired photographers solely for their professional skills, not to provide them relief, as in Federal One projects. Their photographs, collected by the Historical Section, which in 1937 became part of the newly created Farm Security Administration (FSA), rank as the best visual representation of life in the United States during the depression years.

The Legacies of the New Deal

The New Deal set in motion far-reaching changes, notably the growth of a modern state of significant size. For the first time people experienced the federal government as a concrete part of everyday life. During the 1930s more than a third of the population received direct government assistance from new federal programs, including Social Security payments, farm loans, relief work, and mortgage guarantees. Furthermore, the government had made a commitment to intervene in the economy when the private sector could not guarantee economic stability. New legislation regulated the stock market, reformed the Federal Reserve System by placing more power in the hands of Washington policymakers, and brought many practices of modern corporate life under federal regulation. Thus the New Deal accelerated the pattern begun during the Progressive Era of using federal regulation to bring order and regularity to economic life, a pattern that would persist for the rest of the twentieth century, despite recurring criticism about the increased presence of the state in American life.

One particularly important arena of expansion was the development of America's welfare state—that is, the federal government's acceptance of primary responsibility for the individual and collective welfare of the people. Although the New Deal offered more benefits to American citizens than they had ever received before, its safety net had many holes, especially in comparison with the far more extensive welfare systems of Western Europe.

The Human Face of the Great Depression
Migrant Mother by Dorothea Lange is perhaps the most famous documentary photograph of the 1930s. Lange spent only ten minutes in the pea-picker's camp in California where she captured this image and did not even get the name of the woman whose despair and resignation she so powerfully recorded. She was later identified as Florence Thompson, a full-blooded Cherokee from Oklahoma. Library of Congress.

The Social Security Act did not include national health care. Another serious defect of the emerging welfare system was its failure to reach a significant minority of American workers, including domestics and farm workers, for many years. Since state governments administered the programs, benefits varied widely, with southern states consistently providing the lowest amounts.

Another shortcoming of the welfare system stemmed from male and female New Dealers' gendered conceptions of the "family wage," an ideal that assumed men were workers and women were homemakers. The old-age pensions and unemployment compensation provisions in the Social Security Act, which were designed primarily with men in mind and with the hope of maintaining the dignity of the male breadwinner, tended to be more generous and applied universally, regardless of need. Moreover, Social Security policies discriminated against married women until the 1970s. The programs for dependent children of poor women, usually referred to as simply "welfare," by contrast, applied means and morals tests and provided funds to keep women out of the workforce and in their proper place in the home. Denying the growing presence of women in the workforce, welfare made no provisions for helping poor working women sustain their families. A highly stigmatized program, welfare rarely offered enough for a decent standard of living or a means for poor women to get out of poverty (see Thinking about History, "Women, Gender, and the Welfare System," p. 778).

To its credit the New Deal recognized that poverty was an economic problem and not a matter of personal failure. However, it did not come up with the perfect economic solution. Reformers assumed that once the depression was over, full employment and an active economy would take care of the nation's welfare needs, and poverty would wither away. It did not. When later administrations confronted the persistence of inequality and unemployment, they grafted welfare programs onto the jerry-built system left over from the New Deal. Thus the American welfare system would always be marked by its birth during the crisis atmosphere of the Great Depression.

Even if the depression-era welfare system had some serious flaws, it was brilliant politics. The Democratic Party courted the allegiance of citizens who benefited from New Deal programs. Organized labor aligned itself with the administration that had made it a legitimate force in modern industrial life. Blacks voted Democratic in direct relation to the economic benefits that poured into their communities. At the grassroots level the Women's Division of the Democratic National Committee mobilized 80,000 women who recognized what the New Deal had done for their communities. The unemployed also looked kindly on the Roosevelt administration. According to one of the earliest Gallup polls, 84 percent of those on relief voted the Democratic ticket in 1936.

But the Democratic Party did not attract only the down-and-out. Roosevelt's magnetic personality and the dispersal of New Deal benefits to families throughout the social structure brought middle-class voters, many of them first- or second-generation immigrants, into the Democratic fold. Thus the New Deal completed the transformation of the Democratic Party that had begun in the 1920s toward a coalition of ethnic groups, city dwellers, organized labor, blacks, and a broad cross section of the middle class. Those voters would form the backbone of the Democratic coalition for decades to come and would provide support for liberal reforms that extended the promise of the New Deal.

The New Deal coalition contained potentially fatal contradictions involving mainly the issue of race. Because Roosevelt depended on the support of southern white Democrats to pass New Deal legislation, he was unwilling to challenge the economic and political marginalization of blacks in the South. At the same time New Deal programs were changing the face of southern agriculture by undermining the sharecropping system and encouraging the migration of southern blacks to northern and western cities. Outside the South blacks were not prevented from voting, guaranteeing that civil rights would enter the national agenda. The resulting fissures would eventually weaken the coalition that seemed so invincible at the height of Roosevelt's power.

With all its shortcomings the New Deal nonetheless had a profound impact on the nation, all the more remarkable in light of its short duration—most of its legislation passed between 1933 and 1936. While the Supreme Court–packing scheme, the "Roosevelt recession," and the political successes of Republicans in 1938 helped to bring an end to the New Deal, the darkening international scene also played a part. As Europe moved toward war, and Japan flexed its muscles in the Far East, Roosevelt became increasingly preoccupied with international relations and pushed domestic reform further and further into the background.

FOR FURTHER EXPLORATION

▶ For definitions of key terms boldfaced in this chapter, see the glossary at the end of the book.

▶ To assess your mastery of the material covered in this chapter, see the Online Study Guide at **bedfordstmartins.com/henretta**.

▶ For suggested references, including Web sites, see page SR-27 at the end of the book.

▶ For map resources and primary documents, see **bedfordstmartins.com/henretta**.

The New Deal was the response of Franklin Roosevelt and the Democratic Party to the crisis of the Great Depression. It offered a broad-based program of political and economic reform, but its programs were hardly revolutionary. President Hoover had taken the first steps toward involving the federal government more actively in economic life, a trend that Roosevelt continued and expanded, pushed in part by growing protest on the part of the workers, the elderly, and supporters of programs like Huey Long's Share Our Wealth movement. The New Deal never cured the depression, but it restored confidence that Americans could overcome hard times. It provided a measure of economic security against the worst depression in American history by relieving many of its tragic effects. Legislation such as the Social Security Act of 1935 laid the foundation of the modern welfare state, bringing the United States more in line with other industrialized countries in its acceptance of responsibility for the collective welfare of its citizens.

The New Deal dramatically expanded the size and power of the federal government, continuing a trend that had begun in the late nineteenth and early twentieth centuries. Decisions made in Washington touched millions of individual lives. The New Deal provided new opportunities and a larger role in public life for blacks, women, Mexican Americans, and the labor movement. The collapse of the economy encouraged a reassertion of American values in literature and the arts. This artistic flowering was partly supported by a unique experiment in government patronage of the arts through the WPA. In politics the Democratic coalition of white southerners and the urban working class that had begun to emerge in the 1920s reached a climax in the landslide presidential victory of 1936. The coalition provided the Democrats with electoral success but also contained the seeds of future conflict, especially over the issue of race.

Although the hard times were far from over, by 1938 the New Deal had run out of steam. It was not until the United States entered the war in 1941 that Roosevelt made the end of his depression program official when he announced in 1943 that it was time for "Dr. Win the War" to take the place of "Dr. New Deal." But in reality the New Deal had long ceased to propel the nation toward social reform.

1933 FDR's inaugural address and first fireside chat

Emergency Banking Act begins the Hundred Days

Glass-Steagall Act establishes Federal Deposit Insurance Corporation (FDIC)

Civilian Conservation Corps (CCC)

Agricultural Adjustment Act (AAA)

National Industrial Recovery Act (NIRA)

Tennessee Valley Authority (TVA)

United States abandons gold standard

Townsend Clubs promote Old Age Revolving Pension Plan

Twenty-First Amendment repeals Prohibition

1934 Securities and Exchange Commission (SEC)

Indian Reorganization Act

Share Our Wealth Society established by Senator Huey Long

1935 Supreme Court finds the NRA unconstitutional in *Schechter v. United States*

National Union for Social Justice (Father Charles Coughlin)

National Labor Relations (Wagner) Act

Social Security Act

Works Progress Administration (WPA)

Huey Long assassinated

Rural Electrification Administration (REA)

Supreme Court finds Agricultural Adjustment Act unconstitutional

Congress of Industrial Organizations (CIO) formed

1935–1939 Communist Party at height of influence

1936 General Motors sit-down strike

Landslide reelection of FDR marks peak of New Deal power

The Plow That Broke the Plains and *The River*, documentary movies by Pare Lorentz

1937 FDR's attempted Supreme Court reorganization fails

1937–1938 "Roosevelt recession"

1938 Aaron Copland's *Billy the Kid*

Fair Labor Standards Act (FLSA)

1939 Federal Theatre Project terminated

CHAPTER 26

The World at War
1939–1945

The Road to War
The Rise of Fascism
Depression-Era Isolationism
Retreat from Isolationism
The Attack on Pearl Harbor

Organizing for Victory
Financing the War
Mobilizing the American Fighting Force
Workers and the War Effort
Civil Rights during Wartime
Politics in Wartime

Life on the Home Front
"For the Duration"
Japanese Internment

Fighting and Winning the War
Wartime Aims and Strategies
The War in Europe
The War in the Pacific
Planning the Postwar World
The Onset of the Atomic Age and the War's End

◄ **A B-17 Crew "Somewhere in England"**

The cheerful camaraderie evident in this photograph of crew members as they rode to their B-17G "Flying Fortress" bomber on an airfield in England is the type of image that fuels Americans' memories of World War II as "The Good War." With over 100 bombing missions over Germany, their plane, named I'll Get By, chalked up one of the highest records of the war. Boeing manufactured 12,713 B-17s during World War II, of which 4,753 were lost in combat.
National Archives.

TIMES SQUARE IN NEW YORK CITY on August 15, 1945, was awash with people celebrating V-J (Victory over Japan) Day. World War II was over. Civilians and soldiers "jived in the streets and the crowd was so large that traffic was halted and sprinkler trucks were used to disperse pedestrians." The spontaneous street party seemed a fitting end to what had been the country's most popular war. For many Americans World War II had been what one man described to journalist Studs Terkel as "an unreal period for us here at home. Those who lost nobody at the front had a pretty good time."

Americans had many reasons to view World War II as the "good war." Shocked by the Japanese attack on Pearl Harbor on December 7, 1941, they united in their determination to fight German and Japanese totalitarianism in defense of their way of life. When evidence of the grim reality of the Jewish Holocaust came to light, U.S. participation in the war seemed even more just. And despite their sacrifices, many people found the war a positive experience because it ended the devastating Great Depression, bringing full employment and prosperity. The unambiguous nature of the victory and the subsequent emergence of the United States as an unprecedentedly powerful nation further contributed to the sense of the war as one worth fighting.

Pearl Harbor
The U.S. destroyer West Virginia *exploded into flames after receiving a direct hit during the surprise Japanese attack on Pearl Harbor on December 7, 1941. It was early Sunday morning, and many of the servicemen were still asleep. More than 2,400 Americans were killed; the Japanese suffered only light losses.* U.S. Navy.

intelligence knew that Japan was planning an attack but did not know where it would come. Early on Sunday morning, December 7, 1941, Japanese bombers attacked Pearl Harbor in Hawaii, killing more than 2,400 Americans. Eight battleships, three cruisers, three destroyers, and almost two hundred airplanes were destroyed or heavily damaged.

Although the attack was devastating, it infused the American people with a determination to fight. Pearl Harbor Day is still etched in the memories of millions of Americans who remember precisely what they were doing when they heard about the attack. The next day Roosevelt went before Congress. Calling December 7 "a date which will live in infamy," he asked for a declaration of war against Japan. The Senate voted unanimously for war, and the House concurred by a vote of 388 to 1. The lone dissenter was Jeannette Rankin of Montana, who had also opposed American entry into World War I.

Three days later Germany and Italy declared war on the United States, and the United States in turn declared war on those nations.

Organizing for Victory

The task of fighting a global war accelerated the growing influence of the state on all aspects of American life. A dramatic expansion of power occurred at the presidential level when Congress passed the War Powers Act of December 18, 1941, giving Roosevelt unprecedented authority over all aspects of the conduct of the war. Coordinating the changeover from civilian to war production, raising an army, and assembling the necessary workforce taxed government agencies to the limit. Mobilization on such a scale demanded cooperation between business executives and political leaders in

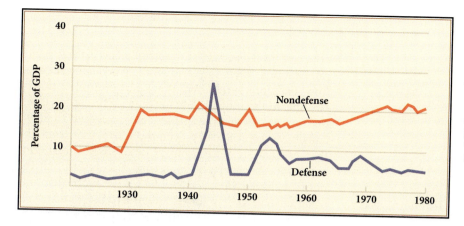

FIGURE 26.1 Government Spending as a Percentage of GDP

Government defense spending was a minuscule percentage of the gross domestic product in the 1930s, but it ballooned during World War II and rose again during the Korean War and, to a lesser degree, during the Vietnam War. Nondefense government spending did not display such wild fluctuations—just a steady, upward trend.

Washington, solidifying a partnership that had been growing since World War I.

Financing the War

Defense mobilization had a powerful impact on the federal government's role in the economy (Figure 26.1). The federal budget of $95.2 billion in 1945 was ten times that of 1939, and the national debt grew sixfold, topping out at $258.6 billion in 1945. Along with huge federal budgets came greater acceptance of Keynesian economics, that is, the use of government fiscal policy to stimulate economic growth. At the same time, the national government became more closely tied to its citizens' pocketbooks. The Revenue Act of 1942 continued the income tax reform that had begun during World War I by taxing not just wealthy individuals and corporations but average citizens as well. Tax collections rose from $2.2 billion to $35.1 billion, facilitated by payroll deductions and tax withholding instituted in 1943. This system of mass taxation, a revolutionary change in the financing of the modern state, was sold to the taxpayers as a way to express their patriotism.

The war also brought significant changes in the federal bureaucracy. The number of civilians employed by the government increased almost fourfold, to 3.8 million—a far more dramatic growth than the New Deal period had witnessed. Leadership of federal agencies also changed as the Roosevelt administration turned to business executives to replace the reformers who had staffed New Deal relief agencies in the 1930s. The executives became known as "**dollar-a-year men**" because they volunteered for government service while remaining on the corporate payroll. Many wartime agencies extended the power of the federal government. The Office of Price Administration (OPA) supervised the domestic economy, allocating resources and trying to keep inflation down. By February 1942 retail prices were rising by 2 percent a month, as consumers had more income to spend than there were available goods and services. In April the OPA froze most prices and rents at their March 1942 levels. When loopholes, especially regarding food prices, undermined that effort, Congress passed the Anti-Inflation Act, which stabilized prices, wages, and salaries. The consumer price index rose by 28.3 percent between 1940 and 1945, but most of the inflation occurred before 1943.

One of the most important wartime agencies was the War Production Board (WPB), which awarded defense contracts, evaluated military and civilian requests for scarce resources, and oversaw the conversion of industry to military production. The WPB used the carrot more often than the stick. To encourage businesses to convert to war production, the board granted generous tax write-offs for plant construction and approved contracts with **cost-plus provisions** that guaranteed a profit and promised that businesses could keep the new factories after the war. As Secretary of War Henry Stimson put it, in capitalist countries at war "you had better let business make money out of the process or business won't work."

In the interest of efficiency and maximum production, the WPB preferred to deal with major corporations rather than with small businesses. The fifty-six largest corporations received three-fourths of the war contracts; the top ten received a third. This system of allocating contracts, along with the suspension of antitrust prosecution during the war, hastened the trend toward large corporate structures. In 1940 the hundred largest companies manufactured 30 percent of the nation's industrial output; by 1945 their share was 70 percent. These very large businesses would form the core of the military-industrial complex of the postwar years, which linked the federal government, corporations, and the military in an interdependent partnership (see Chapter 27).

Together business and government produced an astonishing number of military goods. By 1945 the United States had turned out 86,000 tanks, 296,000 airplanes, 15 million rifles and machine guns, 64,000 landing craft, and 6,500 ships. Henry J. Kaiser, a West coast shipbuilder, performed shipyard production miracles. Using the mass-production techniques of the automobile industry, Kaiser cut the time needed to build a transport ship from 300 days to 17 (see American Lives, "Henry J. Kaiser: World War II's 'Miracle Man,'" p. 756). Mobilization on this gigantic scale gave a tremendous boost to the economy, causing it to more than double, rising from a gross

Henry J. Kaiser: World War II's "Miracle Man"

Henry Kaiser was a workaholic. His motto was "Find a Need and Fill It." He hated being alone and hated taking vacations. He worked twenty-hour days and expected his top managers to do the same. If ordinary mortals were trying to sleep in California, he made long-distance calls to associates in other time zones. "Whenever he had a new idea—and he commonly had a score or so daily—he reached for the telephone," noted his biographer, Mark Foster. As early as 1942 his company was running up then-extravagant phone bills of $250,000 a year.

Kaiser was one of the most widely known figures of the 1940s, a genuine folk hero to many for his ability to get things done. After shipyard triumphs such as the construction of an entire Liberty ship in four days, fifteen hours, and twenty-six minutes in November 1942, the press dubbed him the "Miracle Man." He was a special darling of media mogul Henry Luce: 40 percent of the popular articles on Kaiser between 1941 and 1943 appeared in *Time*, *Life*, and *Fortune*, Luce's three major publications. Even the staid *Wall Street Journal* called him "Fabulous Mr. Kaiser." Franklin Roosevelt seriously considered the industrialist for the vice presidential slot on the 1944 Democratic ticket and, according to FDR's cousin Margaret Suckley, even thought Kaiser would be the best man to succeed him if he chose not to run for reelection. A Roper poll in spring 1945 found that the public believed Henry Kaiser had done more than any other civilian to help the president win the war.

Kaiser's career and the rise of the modern American West went hand in hand. Born in upstate New York in 1882 to German immigrant parents, he left school at age thirteen to make his way in the world. In 1906 he headed west to Spokane, Washington, to establish himself in business so that he could marry his fiancée; in 1921 he and his family settled permanently in Oakland, California. From 1914 to 1931 Kaiser's contracting business built roads, trying to keep up with the West's insatiable demand for highways for the new cars rolling off the assembly lines in Detroit. In the 1930s Kaiser was part of a six-company partnership that successfully bid for massive engineering projects such as building the Hoover and Grand Coulee Dams, federally funded public works projects that permanently changed the western landscape. In the 1930s he also lobbied extensively in Washington, developing contacts with New Deal bureaucrats that would prove invaluable during the war years.

The Miracle Man

In November 1942 Henry Kaiser used an 81-piece, 14-foot-long model of the 10,400-ton Liberty freighter to show shipowners and navy representatives how it was built in the amazing time of 4 days, 15 hours, and 26 minutes. Corbis-Bettmann.

Moved largely by wartime opportunities, Kaiser left construction to launch a career as an industrialist. He made his first big splash—literally—building Liberty ships faster and better than anyone else. Shipbuilding was an ideal choice for an inveterate self-promoter like Henry Kaiser. The World War II era boasted few photo opportunities better than a ship launching, and Kaiser invited Hollywood stars, members of the president's family, and a host of other celebrities to christen the ships, always with the newsreel cameras rolling and the photographers' flash bulbs popping. Thanks to his public relations machine, Kaiser's name was all over the news.

But before Kaiser could build ships, he had to build shipyards. Drawing on the availability of vacant tracts of West Coast waterfront (something the older shipyards in the East did not have), he constructed work spaces large enough to accommodate the assembly of prefabricated ship components. Kaiser's shipyards in Richmond, California, were designed like a city grid, complete with numbered and lettered streets. "It was a city without houses," remembered one worker, "but the traffic was heavy. Cranes, trucks, trains noised by." Recalled a recent migrant from a small Iowa town, "It was such a huge place, something I had never been in. People from all walks of life, all coming and going and working, and the noise. The whole atmosphere was overwhelming to me."

Although Kaiser did not invent the subassembly technique, he was the most successful at applying mass production to shipbuilding. Previously, most jobs in shipbuilding had been skilled or semiskilled, requiring apprenticeship and training far too lengthy for the wartime emergency. To train new workers more quickly, the work process was broken down into small, specialized tasks, in effect removing the skill from what had previously been a craft. As Kaiser put it, "production is not labor anymore, but a process."

The Kaiser shipyards were known as much for their corporate welfare programs as for their bureaucratized work climate. Kaiser offered his workers day care, financial and job counseling, subsidized housing, and especially health care, his most significant long-term contribution. The Kaiser Permanente Medical Care Program was founded in 1942, an outgrowth of prepaid health-care plans first tried on remote federal construction projects in the 1930s. This health-care system, the forerunner of today's health maintenance organizations (HMOs), was available to Kaiser workers for a nominal paycheck deduction of 50 cents a week. Almost 90 percent of his workers chose that option. Kaiser provided health care for both philanthropic and business reasons. The initial investment was quickly repaid in the form of healthier workers, lower absenteeism, and greater productivity. As a Permanente executive explained, "To the private physician, a sick person is an asset. To Permanente, a sick person is a liability. We'd go bankrupt if we didn't keep most of our members and their families well most of the time."

At the core of Kaiser's popularity was a dichotomy. The public saw him as a man who broke the rules for them, a self-made outsider who made things happen in wartime Washington despite the bureaucrats. Yet Kaiser could never have achieved his business miracles without a close working relationship with the federal government, which, for example, allowed him to borrow $300 million from the Reconstruction Finance Corporation during World War II to construct new plants. Noting the symbiotic relationship between business and government that increasingly characterized the twentieth century, historian Stephen B. Adams called Henry Kaiser a government entrepreneur. But the public persisted in seeing him as an individualist, a symbol of a "can-do" age.

While many business executives faced the postwar period with caution, Kaiser looked forward to peacetime reconversion with the boundless optimism of a far-sighted entrepreneur. He was especially excited about opportunities for industrial expansion in the West. Between 1944 and 1946 he identified opportunities in areas such as steel, magnesium, and aluminum as well as foresaw a demand for mass-produced suburban tract housing. In the 1950s he headed a multinational corporate empire that included many companies with assets close to $1 billion. In 1965 he became the first industrialist to win the AFL-CIO's highest honor, the Philip Murray–William Green Award.

To many Americans Henry Kaiser was a twentieth-century incarnation of Horatio Alger, even though he was a portly sixty years old in 1942 when he launched the Richmond shipyards. In terms of managerial style, he was more an old-style "seat-of-the-pants" entrepreneur than a modern corporate bureaucrat. He was a maverick, challenging traditional ways of doing business at every stage of his career at the same time that he seized the opportunities presented by the growth of the administrative state. He was a visionary in the role that he saw for an industrial West, a dream that was amply fulfilled during the postwar era. But he was also lucky, his success being the product of a highly favorable set of economic conditions both regionally in the West and globally during World War II and its aftermath. After his death in 1967, his industrial empire largely disappeared, but Kaiser Permanente lives on, one of the country's largest and most successful health maintenance organizations.

domestic product in 1940 of $99.7 billion to $211 billion by the end of the war. After years of depression, Americans' faith in the capitalist system was restored. But it was a transformed system that relied heavily on the federal government's participation in the economy.

Mobilizing the American Fighting Force

An expanded state presence was also evident in the government's mobilization of a fighting force. By the end of World War II, the armed forces of the United States numbered more than 15 million men and women. Draft boards had registered about 31 million men between the ages of eighteen and forty-four. More than half the men failed to meet the physical standards: many were rejected because of defective teeth or poor vision. The military

This is the Enemy

WINNER R. HOE & CO., INC. AWARD – NATIONAL WAR POSTER COMPETITION
HELD UNDER AUSPICES OF ARTISTS FOR VICTORY, INC.—COUNCIL FOR DEMOCRACY–MUSEUM OF MODERN ART

Why We Fight
This 1942 award-winning lithograph by Karl Koehler and Victor Ancona painted a sinister, menacing portrait of a Nazi officer, leaving little room for doubt as to why it was necessary to end Nazism.
National Museum of American Art, Smithsonian Institution, Washington, DC.

also tried to screen out homosexuals, but its attempts were ineffectual. Once in service homosexuals found opportunities to participate in a gay subculture more extensive than that in civilian life, where they were often channeled into marriage and heterosexual societal roles.

Racial discrimination prevailed in the armed forces, directed mainly against the approximately 700,000 blacks who fought in all branches of the armed forces in segregated units. Though the National Association for the Advancement of Colored People (NAACP) and other civil rights groups chided the government with reminders such as "A Jim Crow army cannot fight for a free world," the military continued to segregate African Americans and to assign them the most menial duties. In contrast Mexican Americans were never officially segregated. Unlike blacks they were welcomed into combat units, and seventeen Mexican Americans won the Congressional Medal of Honor. Native Americans also served in nonsegregated combat, and some, like the Navajo Code Talkers, played a unique role in circumventing Japanese code-breaking efforts by using their native language to send military messages.

Women found both opportunities and discrimination in the armed services. Approximately 350,000 American women enlisted in the armed services and achieved a permanent status in the military. There were about 140,000 WAC (Women's Army Corps) members; 100,000 naval WAVES (Women Accepted for Volunteer Emergency Service); 23,000 members of the Marine Corps Women's Reserve; and 13,000 SPARs (for *Semper Paratus*, or Always Ready, the coast guard's motto) in the coast guard. One-third of the nation's registered nurses, almost 75,000 overall, volunteered for military duty. In addition about 1,000 WASPs (Women's Airforce Service Pilots) ferried planes and supplies in noncombat areas. The government refused to incorporate the WASPs as part of the military, primarily because male pilots resented women's encroachment on their high-status preserve. Not until 1977 did a congressional act accord them veterans' benefits, a belated recognition of their wartime service.

The armed forces limited the types of duty assigned to women, as it did with blacks. Women were barred from combat, although nurses and medical personnel sometimes served close to the front lines, risking capture or death. The social lives of women soldiers, most of whom were single, were more strictly regulated than those of their male counterparts, mainly to prevent sexual impropriety. Most military jobs reflected stereotypes of women's roles in civilian life—clerical work, communications, and health care. The widely distributed pin-ups of Betty Grable in a bathing suit, Rita Hayworth in a flimsy nightgown, and, for the black soldiers, the singer Lena Horne were probably closer to the average GI's view of women than was a WAC or a WAVE.

The WACs Overseas
Not all military women were relegated to stateside duty. These eager WACs, members of the first Women's Army Corps unit to go overseas, have just arrived in North Africa in 1943 to begin their assignments, most likely as nurses, clerks, drivers, or telephone operators. Archive Photos.

Workers and the War Effort

When millions of citizens entered military service, a huge hole opened in the American workforce. The backlog of depression-era unemployment quickly disappeared, and the United States faced a critical labor shortage. The nation's defense industries provided jobs for about 7 million new workers, including great numbers of women, who were given employment opportunities for the first time.

Rosie the Riveter. Government planners "discovered" women while looking for workers to fill the jobs vacated by departing servicemen. Well-organized government propaganda stressed patriotism as it urged women into the workforce. "Longing won't bring him back sooner . . . GET A WAR JOB!" one poster beckoned, while the artist Norman Rockwell's famous "Rosie the Riveter" appealed to women from the cover of the *Saturday Evening Post.*

Although the government directed its propaganda at housewives, women who were already employed gladly abandoned low-paying "women's" jobs as domestic servants or file clerks for higher-paying jobs in the defense industry. Suddenly the nation's factories were full of women working as riveters, welders, and drill-press operators. Women made up 36 percent of the labor force in 1945, compared with 24 percent at the beginning of the war.

Government planners and employers regarded women as just "filling in" while the men were away. Employers rarely offered day care or flexible hours, and government child-care programs established by the 1940 Lanham Act reached only 10 percent of those who needed them. Because women were responsible for home care as well as their jobs, they had a higher absentee rate than did men. Often, the only way to get shopping done or take a child to the doctor was to skip work. Women war workers also faced discrimination on the job. In shipyards women with the most seniority and responsibility earned $6.95 a day, whereas the top men made as much as $22.

When the men came home from war, and the nation's plants returned to peacetime operations, Rosie the Riveter was out of a job. But many women refused to put on aprons and stay home. Though women's participation in the labor force dropped temporarily when the war ended, it rebounded steadily for the rest of the 1940s, especially among married women (see Chapter 27).

Organized Labor. Wartime mobilization also opened up opportunities to advance the labor movement. Organized labor responded to the war with an initial burst of patriotic unity. On December 23, 1941, representatives of the major unions made a "no-strike" pledge—though it was nonbinding—for the duration of the war. In January 1942 Roosevelt set up the National War Labor Board (NWLB), composed of representatives of labor, management, and the public. The NWLB established wages, hours, and working conditions and had the authority to order government seizure of plants that did not comply. Forty plants were seized during the war.

During its tenure the NWLB handled 17,650 disputes affecting 12 million workers. It resolved the controversial issue of union membership through a compromise. New hires did not have to join a union, but those who already belonged had to maintain their membership over the life of a contract. Agitation for wage increases caused a more serious disagreement. Because managers wanted to keep production running smoothly and profitably, they were willing to pay higher wages. However, pay raises would conflict with the government's efforts to combat inflation, which drove up prices dramatically in the early war years. Incomes rose as much as 70 percent during the war because workers earned overtime pay, which was not covered by wage ceilings.

Although incomes were higher than anyone could have dreamed during the depression, many union members felt cheated as they watched corporate profits soar in relation to wages. Dissatisfaction peaked in 1943. That year a nationwide railroad strike was narrowly averted. Then John L. Lewis led more than half a million United Mine Workers out on strike, demanding an increase in wages over that recommended by the NWLB.

Though Lewis won concessions, he alienated Congress, and because he had defied the government, he became one of the most disliked public figures of the 1940s.

Congress countered Lewis's action by overriding Roosevelt's veto of the Smith-Connally Labor Act of 1943, which required a thirty-day cooling-off period before a strike and prohibited entirely strikes in defense industries. Nevertheless, about 15,000 walkouts occurred during the war. Though less than one-tenth of 1 percent of working hours were lost to labor disputes, the public perceived the disruptions to be far more extensive. Thus although union membership increased dramatically during the war, from 9 million to almost 15 million workers—a third of the nonagricultural workforce—the labor movement also evoked significant public and congressional hostility that would hamper it in the postwar years.

Civil Rights during Wartime

Just as labor sought to benefit from the war, African Americans manifested a new mood of militancy. "A wind is rising throughout the world of free men everywhere," Eleanor Roosevelt wrote during the war, "and they will not be kept in bondage." Black leaders pointed out parallels between anti-Semitism in Germany and racial discrimination in America and pledged themselves to a "Double V" campaign: victory over Nazism abroad and victory over racism and inequality at home.

Even before Pearl Harbor, black activism was on the rise. In 1940 only 240 of the nation's 100,000 aircraft workers were black, and most of them were janitors. Black leaders demanded that the government require defense contractors to integrate their workforces. When the government took no action, A. Philip Randolph, head of the Brotherhood of Sleeping Car Porters, a black union, announced plans for a "March on Washington" in the summer of 1941. Though Roosevelt was not a strong supporter of civil rights, he feared the embarrassment of a massive public protest. Even more, he worried about a disruption of the nation's war preparations.

In June 1941, in exchange for Randolph's cancellation of the march, Roosevelt issued Executive Order 8802, declaring "that there shall be no discrimination in the employment of workers in defense industries or government because of race, creed, color, or national origin," and established the Fair Employment Practices Commission (FEPC). Though this federal commitment to minority employment rights was unprecedented, it was limited in scope; for instance, it did not affect segregation in the armed forces. Moreover, the FEPC could not require compliance with its orders and often found that the needs of defense production took precedence over fair employment practices. The committee resolved only about a third of the more than 8,000 complaints it received.

Fighting for Freedom at Home and Abroad
This protester from the Negro Labor Relations League pointedly drew the parallel between blacks serving in the armed forces and a 1941 labor discrimination dispute at a Chicago dairy.
Library of Congress.

Encouraged by the ideological climate of the war years, civil rights organizations increased their pressure for reform. The League of United Latin American Citizens (LULAC) built on their community's patriotic contributions to national defense and the armed services to challenge long-standing patterns of discrimination and exclusion. In Texas, where it was still common to see signs reading, "No Dogs or Mexicans Allowed," the organization protested segregation in schools and public facilities. African American groups also flourished. The NAACP grew ninefold to 450,000 by 1945. Although the NAACP generally favored lobbying and legal strategies, a student chapter of the NAACP at Howard University

German POWs

American Race Relations

During World War II Nazi prisoners of war were assigned to various army camps throughout the United States, where their labor was often contracted out to help with the acute shortage of workers caused by war mobilization. German prisoners thus had a unique opportunity to observe American life. Here are some of their observations, mainly centered on the issue of race.

We picked cotton the length of the Mississippi. I'm an agriculturalist, and I know how to handle hard work, but there it was truly very, very hard. It was terribly hot, and we had to bend over all day. We had nothing to drink. . . . There were a great number of Blacks on the plantation. They required us to gather 100 lbs. of cotton a day; but of the Blacks, they demanded two or three times more. . . . For them it was worse than for us. And you have to see how they lived. Their farms: very ugly, very primitive. These people were so exploited. . . .

Me, I was in peas; picking and the canning factory. The farmers liked me, and wanted me to stay after the war, but I wasn't sure. . . . I met some old people of German origin one day, and these poor old people told me: "We feel alone here. It's sad. It's too big. If we could, we would walk back to Germany on foot. . . ." And the Blacks! They were always saying: "We are just like you: Prisoners; Oppressed; Second-class men. . . ."

There was a plumber who came to work in the camp. His name was Gutierrez, and he was Mexican. . . . He was a very nice guy. When he went to the barbershop, he stood in the corner, he did not move, and, as he was "colored," he had to wait until all the Whites were done. You know, things like that upset us very much. . . .

I was in a camp near Miami in Florida. I was one of the scavenger commandos; every morning we went to gather the garbage in the city. . . . People of German origin were the least nice to us. . . . Those who helped us the most, on the contrary, were the Jews. . . . Ah, the Jews and the Blacks.

Source: Arnold Krammer, *Nazi Prisoners of War in America* (New York: Stein and Day, 1979), 92–93.

---

used direct tactics. In 1944 it forced several restaurants in Washington, D.C., to serve blacks after picketing them with signs that read "Are You for Hitler's Way or the American Way? Make Up Your Mind." In Chicago James Farmer helped to found the Congress of Racial Equality (CORE), a group that became known nationwide for its use of direct action like demonstrations and sit-ins. These wartime developments—both federal intervention and resurgent African American militancy—laid the groundwork for the civil rights revolution of the 1950s and 1960s (see Voices from Abroad, "German POWs: American Race Relations," above).

Politics in Wartime

Although the federal government expanded dramatically during the war years, there was little attempt to use the state to promote social reform on the home front, as in World War I. An enlarged federal presence was justified only insofar as it assisted war aims. During the early years of the war, Roosevelt rarely pressed for social and economic change, in part because he was preoccupied with the war but also because he wanted to counteract Republican political gains. Republicans had picked up ten seats in the Senate and forty-seven seats in the House in the 1942 elections, thus bolstering conservatives in Congress who sought to roll back New Deal measures. With little protest Roosevelt agreed to drop several popular New Deal programs, including the Civilian Conservation Corps and the National Youth Administration, which were less necessary once war mobilization brought full employment.

Later in the war Roosevelt began to promise new social welfare measures. In his State of the Union address in 1944, he called for a second bill of rights, which would serve as "a new basis of security and prosperity." This extension of the New Deal identified jobs, adequate food and clothing, decent homes, medical care, and education as basic rights. But the president's commitment to them remained largely rhetorical; congressional support for this vast extension of the welfare state did not exist in 1944. Some of those rights did become realities for veterans, however. The Servicemen's Readjustment Act (1944), known as the GI Bill of Rights, provided education, job training, medical care, pensions, and mortgage loans for men and women who had served in the armed forces during the war. An extraordinarily influential program, particularly in making higher education more widely available, it distributed almost four billion dollars worth of benefits to 9 million veterans between 1944 and 1949 and in the 1950s would be extended to veterans of the Korean War era.

Roosevelt's renewed call for social legislation was part of a plan to woo Democratic voters after the congressional setbacks of the 1942 elections. The Democrats realized they would have to work hard to maintain their strong coalition in 1944. Once again Roosevelt headed the ticket, reasoning that the continuation of the war made a fourth term necessary. Democrats, concerned about Roosevelt's health and the need for a successor, dropped Vice President Henry Wallace, whose outspoken support for labor, civil rights, and domestic reform was too extreme for many party leaders. In his place they chose Senator Harry S Truman of Missouri, known for heading a Senate investigation of government efficiency in awarding wartime defense contracts.

The Republicans nominated Governor Thomas E. Dewey of New York. Only forty-two years old, Dewey had won fame fighting organized crime as a U.S. attorney. He accepted the broad outlines of the welfare state and was among those Republicans who rejected isolationism in favor of an internationalist stance. The 1944 election was the closest since 1916: Roosevelt received only 53.5 percent of the popular vote. The party's margin of victory came from the cities: in urban areas of more than 100,000 people the president drew 60 percent of the vote, reflecting in part ethnic minorities' loyalty to the Democratic Party. A significant segment of this urban support came from organized labor. The CIO's Political Action Committee made substantial contributions to the party, canvassed door to door, and conducted voter registration campaigns—a role organized labor would continue to play after the war.

Life on the Home Front

Although the United States did not suffer the physical devastation that ravaged much of Europe and the Pacific, the war affected the lives of those who stayed behind. Every time relatives of a loved one overseas saw the Western Union boy on his bicycle, they feared a telegram from the War Department saying that their son, husband, or father would not be coming home. All Americans tolerated small deprivations daily. "Don't you know there's a war on?" became the standard reply to any request that could not be fulfilled. People accepted the fact that their lives would be different "for the duration." They also accepted, however grudgingly, the increased role of the federal government in shaping their daily lives.

"For the Duration"

Just like the soldiers in uniform, people on the home front had a job to do. They worked on civilian defense committees, collected old newspapers and scrap material, and served on local rationing and draft boards. About 20 million home "Victory gardens" produced 40 percent of the nation's vegetables. All these endeavors were encouraged by various federal agencies, especially the Office of War Information (OWI), which strove to disseminate information and promote patriotism. Working closely with advertising agencies, the OWI urged them to link their clients' products to the "four freedoms," explaining that patriotic ads would not only sell goods but would "invigorate, instruct and inspire [the citizen] as a functioning unit in his country's greatest effort."

Popular Culture. Popular culture, especially the movies, reinforced the connections between the home front and troops serving overseas. Average weekly movie attendance soared to over 100 million during the war. Demand was so high that many theaters operated around the clock to accommodate defense workers on the swing and night shifts. Many movies, encouraged in part by the OWI, had patriotic themes; stars such as John Wayne, Anthony Quinn, and Spencer Tracy portrayed the heroism of American fighting men in films like *Back to Bataan* (1945), *Guadalcanal Diary* (1943), and *Thirty Seconds over Tokyo* (1945). Other movies, such as *Watch on the Rhine* (1943), warned of the danger of fascism at home and abroad, while the Academy Award–winning *Casablanca* (1943) demonstrated the heroism and patriotism of ordinary citizens. *Since You Went Away* (1943), starring Claudette Colbert as a wife who took a war job after her husband left for war, was one of many films that portrayed struggles on the home front. Newsreels accompanying the feature films kept the public up-to-date on the war, as did on-the-spot radio broadcasts by commentators such as Edward R. Murrow. Thus popular culture reflected America's new international involvement at the same time that it built morale on the home front.

Consumption Patterns and Rationing. Perhaps the major source of Americans' high morale was wartime prosperity. Federal defense spending had solved the depression; unemployment had disappeared, and per capita income had risen from $691 in 1939 to $1,515 in 1945. Despite geographical dislocations and shortages of many items, about 70 percent of Americans admitted midway through the war that they had personally experienced "no real sacrifices." A Red Cross worker put it bluntly: "The war was fun for America. I'm not talking

Entertaining the Troops

The original Stage Door Canteen opened in the basement of a Broadway theater in 1942. It provided servicemen with coffee, doughnuts, and big-time entertainment volunteered by Broadway and Hollywood stars. The canteen's popular weekly radio show was the inspiration for the 1943 movie Stage Door Canteen. Lee Boltin Picture Library.

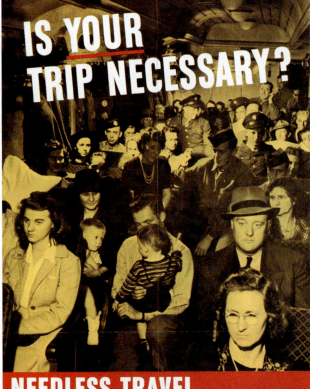

Please Stay Home

With the economy booming and most citizens reporting no great hardships or dislocations, Americans sometimes had to be reminded that there was a war on. A poster from the Office of Defense Transportation pointing out that needless travel interfered with the war effort jogged their memory. Picture Research Consultants & Archives.

about the poor souls who lost sons and daughters. But for the rest of us, the war was a hell of a good time."

For many Americans the major inconveniences of the war were the limitations placed on their consumption. In contrast to the largely voluntaristic approach used during World War I, federal agencies such as the Office of Price Administration subjected almost everything Americans ate, wore, or used during World War II to rationing or regulation. In response to depleted domestic gasoline supplies and a shortage of rubber—the Japanese had conquered Malaysia and Netherlands' East Indies, the source of 97 percent of American rubber—the government restricted the sale of tires, rationed gas, and imposed a nationwide speed limit of 35 miles per hour, which cut highway deaths dramatically. By 1943 the amount of meat, butter, sugar, and other foods Americans could buy was also regulated. Most people cooperated with the complicated system of restrictions, but almost a fourth occasionally bought items on the black market, especially meat, gasoline, and cigarettes. People found it especially hard to

cut back on sugar. When sugar disappeared from grocery shelves, the government rationed it at a rate of 1 to 1½ cups per person a week. However, the manufacturers of products such as Coca-Cola and Wrigley's chewing gum received unlimited quantities of sugar by convincing the government that the products helped the morale of the men and women in the armed forces.

Migration and Family Life. The war and the government affected not only what people ate, drank, and wore, but also where they lived. When men entered the armed services, their families often followed them to training bases or points of debarkation. The lure of high-paying defense jobs encouraged others—Native Americans on reservations, white southerners in the hills of Appalachia, African Americans in the rural South—to move. About 15 million Americans changed residence during the war years, half of them moving to another state.

A Family Effort

After migrating from the Midwest to Portland, Oregon, fifteen members of the family of John R. Brauckmiller (sixth from left) found jobs at Portland's Swan Island shipyard. A local newspaper pronounced them "the shipbuildingest family in America."
Ralph Vincent, *The Journal*, Portland, OR.

As a center of defense production, California was affected by wartime migration more than any other state. The western mecca welcomed nearly 3 million new residents during the war, a 53 percent growth in population. "The Second Gold Rush Hits the West," headlined the *San Francisco Chronicle* in 1943. During the war one-tenth of all federal dollars went to California, and the state turned out one-sixth of the total war production. People went where the defense jobs were—to Los Angeles, San Diego, and the San Francisco Bay area. Some towns grew practically overnight: just two years after the Kaiser Corporation opened a shipyard in Richmond, California, the population quadrupled.

Migration and relocation often caused strains. In many towns with defense industries, housing was scarce and public transportation inadequate. Conflicts over public space and recreation erupted between old-timers and newcomers. Of special concern were the young people the war had set adrift from traditional commu-

nity safeguards. Newspapers were filled with stories of "latchkey" children who stayed home alone while their mothers worked in defense plants. Adolescents were even more of a problem. Teenage girls who hung around army bases looking for a good time became known as "victory girls." In 1942 and 1943 juvenile delinquency seemed to be reaching epidemic proportions.

Another significant result of the growth of war industries was the migration of more than a million African Americans to defense centers in California, Illinois, Michigan, Ohio, and Pennsylvania. The migrants' need for jobs and housing led to racial conflict in several cities. Early in 1942 black families encountered resistance and intimidation when they tried to move into the Sojourner Truth housing project in the Polish community of Hamtramck near Detroit, the new home of a large number of southern migrants, both black and white. In June 1943 similar tensions erupted in Detroit, where a major race riot left thirty-four people dead.

Zoot Suits
Zoot suits gained wide popularity among American youth during the war. In 1943 this well-dressed teenager greased his hair in a ducktail and wore a loosely cut, midthingh-length coat with padded shoulders ("fingertips"), baggy pleated pants cut tight ("pegged") around the ankles, and a long gold watch chain. Corbis-Bettmann.

Racial conflicts broke out in forty-seven cities across the country during 1943.

Other Americans also experienced racial violence. In Los Angeles male Latinos who belonged to *pachuco* (youth) gangs dressed in "zoot suits"—broad-brimmed felt hats, pegged trousers, and clunky shoes—wore their long hair slicked down and carried pocket knives on gold chains. The young women they hung out with favored long coats, huarache sandals, and pompadour hairdos. Blacks and some working-class white teenagers in Los Angeles, Detroit, New York, and Philadelphia also wore zoot suits as a symbol of alienation and self-assertion. To adults and to many Anglos, however, the zoot suit symbolized wartime juvenile delinquency.

In Los Angeles white hostility toward Mexican Americans had been smoldering for some time, and zoot-suiters soon became the targets. In July 1943 rumors that a *pachuco* gang had beaten a white sailor set off a four-day riot, during which white servicemen entered Mexican American neighborhoods and attacked zoot-suiters, taking special pleasure in slashing their pegged pants. The attacks occurred in full view of white police officers, who did nothing to stop the violence.

Although racial confrontations and zoot-suit riots recalled the widespread racial tensions of World War I, the mood on the home front was generally calm in the 1940s. German Americans generally did not experience the intense prejudice of World War I nor did Italian Americans, though some aliens in both groups were interned. Leftists and Communists faced little repression, mainly because after Pearl Harbor the Soviet Union became an ally of the United States.

Japanese Internment

The internment of Japanese Americans on the West Coast was a glaring exception to this record of tolerance, a reminder of the fragility of civil liberties in wartime. California had a long history of antagonism toward both Japanese and Chinese immigrants (see Chapters 16, 21, and 24). The Japanese Americans, who clustered together in highly visible communities, were a small, politically impotent minority, numbering only about 112,000 in the three coastal states. But unlike German and Italian Americans, the Japanese stood out. "A Jap's a Jap," snapped General John DeWitt. "It makes no difference whether he is an American citizen or not." This sort of sentiment, coupled with fears of the West Coast's vulnerability to attack and the inflammatory rhetoric of newspapers and local politicians, fueled mounting demands that the region be rid of supposed Japanese spies.

In early 1942 Roosevelt issued Executive Order 9066, which gave the War Department the authority it needed for its plan to evacuate Japanese Americans from the West Coast and intern them in relocation camps for the rest of the war. Despite the lack of any evidence of their disloyalty or sedition—no Japanese American was ever charged with espionage—few public leaders opposed the plan. The announcement shocked Japanese Americans, more than two-thirds of whom were native-born American citizens. (They were *Nisei*, children of the foreign-born *Issei*.) Most had to sell their property and possessions at cut-rate prices and were then rounded up in temporary assembly centers and sent by the War Relocation Authority to internment camps in California, Arizona, Utah, Colorado, Wyoming, Idaho, and Arkansas (Map 26.2)—places "where nobody had lived before and no one has lived since," a historian commented (see American Voices, "Monica Sone: Japanese Relocation," p. 767).

Almost every Japanese American in California, Oregon, and Washington was involuntarily detained for some period during World War II. Ironically, the Japanese

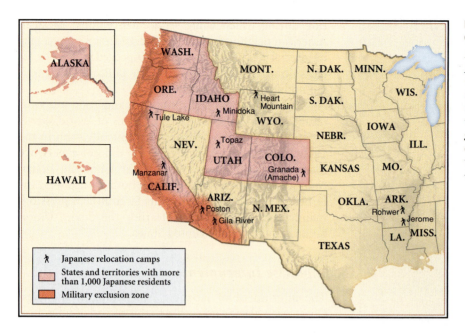

MAP 26.2 Japanese Relocation Camps

In 1942 the government ordered 112,000 Japanese Americans living on the West Coast into internment camps in the nation's interior because of their supposed threat to public safety. Some of the camps were as far away as Arkansas. The federal government had rescinded the mass evacuation order in December 1944, but when the war ended in August 1945, 44,000 people still remained in the camps.

Americans who made up one-third of the population of Hawaii, and presumably posed a greater threat because of their numbers and proximity to Japan, were not interned. Less vulnerable to suspicion because of the islands' multiracial heritage, the Japanese also provided much of the unskilled labor in the island territory. The Hawaiian economy simply could not function without them.

Cracks soon appeared in the relocation policy. A labor shortage in farming led the government to furlough seasonal agricultural workers from the camps as early as 1942. About 4,300 young people who had been in college when they were interned were allowed to return to school if they would transfer out of the West Coast military zone. Another route out of the camps was enlistment in the armed services. The 442nd Regimental Combat Team, a segregated unit composed almost entirely of Nisei volunteers, served in Europe and became one of the most decorated units in the armed forces.

Behind Barbed Wire

As part of the forced relocation of 112,000 Japanese Americans, Los Angeles photographer Toyo Miyatake and his family were sent to Manzanar, a camp in the California desert east of the Sierra Nevada. Miyatake secretly began shooting photographs of the camp, although he eventually received permission from the authorities to document life in the camp. This photograph of three young boys behind barbed wire with a watchtower in the distance must have been shot with official sanction because the photographer is on the other side of the barbed wire. It gives new meaning to the phrase "prisoners of war." Toyo Miyatake.

For more help analyzing this image, see the ONLINE STUDY GUIDE at **bedfordstmartins.com/henretta.**

Monica Sone

Japanese Relocation

Monica (Itoi) Sone's autobiography, Nisei Daughter *(1953), tells the story of Japanese relocation from the perspective of a young woman in Seattle, Washington. Here, she describes the Itoi family's forced evacuation to a temporary encampment called Camp Harmony; later they were moved to a settlement in Idaho. Although her parents spent the entire war in the camp, Monica Sone was allowed to leave in 1943 to attend college in Indiana.*

We felt fortunate to be assigned to a room at the end of the barracks because we had just one neighbor to worry about. The partition wall separating the rooms was only seven feet high with an opening of four feet at the top, so at night, Mrs. Funai next door could tell when Sumi was still sitting up in bed in the dark, putting her hair up. "Mah, Sumi-chan," Mrs. Funai would say through the plank wall, "are you curling your hair tonight again? Do you put it up every night?" Sumi would put her hands on her hips and glare defiantly at the wall.

The block monitor, an impressive Nisei who looked like a star tackle with his crouching walk, came around the first night to tell us that we must all be inside our room by nine o'clock every night. At ten o'clock, he rapped at the door again, yelling, "Lights out!" and Mother rushed to turn the light off not a second later.

Throughout the barracks, there were a medley of creaking cots, whimpering infants and explosive night coughs. Our attention was riveted on the intense little wood stove which glowed so violently I feared it would melt right down to the floor. We soon learned that this condition lasted for only a short time, after which it suddenly turned into a deep freeze. Henry and Father took turns at the stove to produce the harrowing blast which all but singed our army blankets, but did not penetrate through them. As it grew quieter in the barracks, I could hear the light patter of rain. Soon I felt the "splat! splat!" of raindrops digging holes into my face. The dampness on my pillow spread like a mortal bleeding, and I finally had to get out and haul my cot toward the center of the room. In a short while Henry was up. "I've got multiple leaks, too. Have to complain to the landlord first thing in the morning."

All through the night I heard people getting up, dragging cots around. I stared at our little window, unable to sleep. I was glad Mother had put up a makeshift curtain on the window for I noticed a powerful beam of light sweeping across it every few seconds. The lights came from high towers placed around the camp where guards with Tommy guns kept a twenty-four hour vigil. I remembered the wire fence encircling us, and a knot of anger tightened in my breast. What was I doing behind a fence like a criminal? If there were accusations to be made, why hadn't I been given a fair trial? Maybe I wasn't considered an American anymore. My citizenship wasn't real, after all. Then what was I? I was certainly not a citizen of Japan as my parents were. On second thought, even Father and Mother were more alien residents of the United States than Japanese nationals for they had little tie with their mother country. In their twenty-five years in America, they had worked and paid their taxes to their adopted government as any other citizen.

Of one thing I was sure. The wire fence was real. I no longer had the right to walk out of it. It was because I had Japanese ancestors. It was also because some people had little faith in the ideas and ideals of democracy. They said that after all these were but words and could not possibly insure loyalty. New laws and camps were surer devices. I finally buried my face in my pillow to wipe out burning thoughts and snatch what sleep I could.

Source: Monica Sone, *Nisei Daughter* (Boston: Little, Brown and Co., 1953), 176–78.

In a series of three cases dealing with curfews and other discriminatory treatment of the Japanese related to the relocation process, *United States v. Minoru Yasui* (1943), *Hirabayashi v. United States* (1943), and *Korematsu v. United States* (1944), the Supreme Court legitimated internment, while not expressly ruling on its constitutionality. In 1944 it held in *Ex Parte Endo* that U.S. citizens who could be proved to be loyal could not be detained, but it was not until 1988 that Congress decided to issue a public apology and to give $20,000 in cash to each of the 80,000 surviving internees.

Fighting and Winning the War

World War II, noted military historian John Keegan, was "the largest single event in human history." Fought on six continents at a cost of 50 million lives, it was far more

MAP 26.3 World War II in Europe, 1941–1943

Hitler's Germany reached its greatest extent in 1942, when Nazi forces stalled at Leningrad and Stalingrad. The tide of battle turned in the fall, when the Soviet army launched a massive counterattack at Stalingrad and Allied forces began to drive the Germans from North Africa. In 1943 the Allies invaded Sicily and the Italian mainland.

For more help analyzing this map, see the ONLINE STUDY GUIDE at **bedfordstmartins.com/henretta.**

global than World War I. At least 405,000 Americans were killed and 671,000 wounded in the global fighting—less than half of 1 percent of the U.S. population. In contrast the Soviets lost as many as 21 million soldiers and civilians during the war, or about 8 percent of their population.

Wartime Aims and Strategies

The Allied coalition was composed mainly of Great Britain, the United States, and the Soviet Union; other nations, notably China and France, played lesser roles. President Franklin Roosevelt, Prime Minister Winston Churchill of Britain, and Premier Joseph Stalin of the Soviet Union took the lead in setting overall strategy. The Atlantic Charter, which Churchill and Roosevelt had drafted in August 1941, formed the basis of the

Allies' vision of the postwar international order. But Stalin had not been part of that agreement, a fact that would later cause disagreements over its goals.

One way to wear down the Germans would have been to open a second front on the European continent, preferably in France. The Russians argued strongly for this strategy because it would draw German troops away from Russian soil. In 1941 the German army had reached the outskirts of Leningrad and Moscow, but the Russians had pushed them back from Moscow in the winter of 1941–42. The issue came up so many times that the Soviet foreign minister, Vyacheslav Molotov, was said to know only four English words: *yes, no,* and *second front.* Though Roosevelt assured Stalin informally that the Allies would open a second front in 1942, British opposition and the need first to raise American war production to full capacity

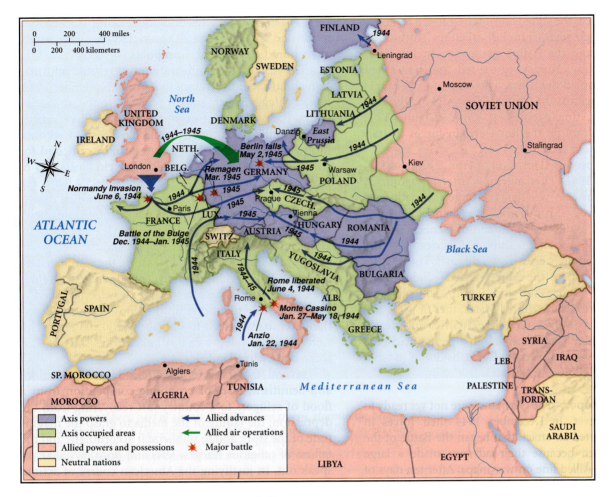

MAP 26.4 World War II in Europe, 1944–1945

On June 6, 1944 (D-Day), the Allies finally invaded France. It took almost a year for the Allied forces to close in on Berlin—the Soviets from the east and the Americans, British, and French from the west. Germany surrendered on May 8, 1945.

For more help analyzing this map, see the ONLINE STUDY GUIDE at bedfordstmartins.com/henretta.

stalled the effort. At a conference in Tehran, Iran, in late November 1943, Churchill and Roosevelt agreed to open a second front within six months in return for Stalin's promise to join the fight against Japan after the war in Europe ended. Both sides kept their promises. However, the long delay in creating a second front meant that for most of the war the Soviet Union bore the brunt of the land battle against Germany. Roosevelt and Churchill's foot-dragging angered Stalin, who was suspicious about American and British intentions. His mistrust and bitterness carried over into the cold war that followed the Allied victory.

The War in Europe

During the first seven months of 1942, the military news was so bad that it threatened to swamp the Grand Alliance. The Allies suffered severe defeats on land and sea in both Europe and Asia. German armies pushed deeper into Soviet territory, into the Ukraine and the oil-rich Caucasus, moving toward Stalingrad. Simultaneously they began an offensive in North Africa aimed at seizing the Suez Canal. At sea German submarines were crippling Allied convoys carrying vital supplies to Britain and the Soviet Union.

The major turning point of the war in Europe occurred in the winter of 1942 to 1943, when the Soviets halted the German advance in the Battle of Stalingrad (Map 26.3). By 1944 Stalin's forces had driven the German army out of the Soviet Union. Meanwhile, the Allies launched a major offensive in North Africa, Churchill's substitute for a second front in France. Between November 1942 and May 1943, Allied troops under the leadership of General Dwight D. Eisenhower and General George S. Patton defeated Germany's crack *Afrika Korps*, led by General Erwin Rommel.

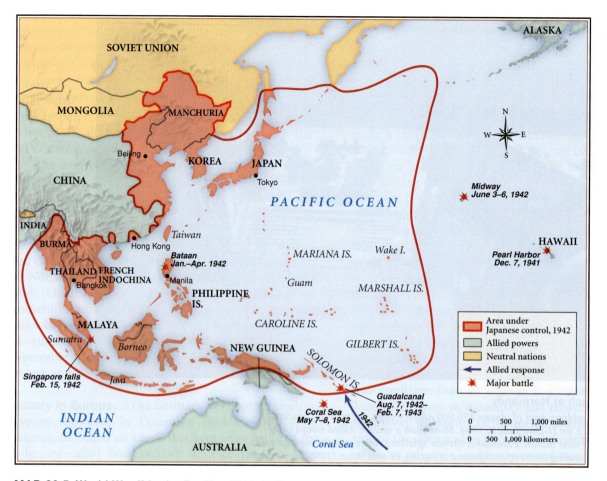

MAP 26.5 World War II in the Pacific, 1941–1942
*After the attacks on Pearl Harbor in December 1941, the Japanese rapidly extended their
domination in the Pacific. The Japanese flag soon flew as far east as the Marshall and
Gilbert Islands and as far south as the Solomon Islands and parts of New Guinea. Japan
also controlled the Philippines, much of Southeast Asia, and parts of China, including
Hong Kong. American naval victories at the Coral Sea and Midway stopped further
Japanese expansion.*

the next eighteen months, American forces advanced ar-
duously from one island to the next, winning major victories at Tulagi and Guadalcanal in the Solomon Islands
and at Tarawa and Makin in the Gilberts. They reached
the Marshall Islands in early 1944. In October 1944 the
reconquest of the Philippines began with a victory in the
Battle of Leyte Gulf, a massive naval encounter in which
the Japanese lost practically their entire fleet whereas the
Americans suffered only minimal losses (Map 26.6).

By early 1945 victory over Japan was in sight. The
campaign in the Pacific moved slowly toward what military leaders anticipated would be a massive and costly invasion of Japan. A stunning victory in the Mariana Islands
in July 1944 had given them a strategic location for constructing airfields to serve as a base for the "flying super-
fortress" B-29s that would bomb Japan. But bases closer to
Japan were essential. In the spring of 1945, the focus was

on two islands, Iwo Jima and Okinawa, that could provide
some protection for the B-29s' bombing raids launched
from the Marianas and could serve as the base for American fighter planes. In some of the fiercest fighting of the
war, the marines sustained more than 20,000 casualties at
Iwo Jima, including 6,000 dead; at Okinawa the toll
reached 7,600 dead and 32,000 wounded. The closer U.S.
forces got to the Japanese home islands, the more fiercely
the Japanese fought. On Iwo Jima almost all of the 21,000
Japanese died.

By mid-1945 Japan's army, navy, and air force had
suffered devastating losses. American bombing of the
mainland had killed about 330,000 civilians and crippled
the Japanese economy. In a last-ditch effort to stem the
tide, Japanese pilots began suicidal **kamikaze** missions,
crashing their planes and boats into American ships. This
desperate action, combined with the Japanese military

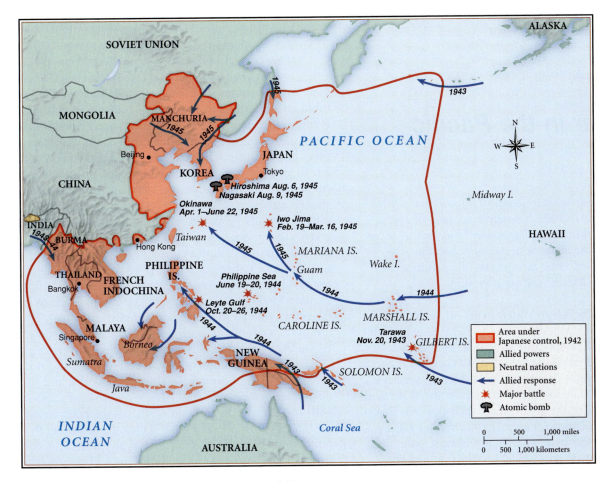

MAP 26.6 World War II in the Pacific, 1943–1945

Allied forces retook the islands in the central Pacific in 1943 and 1944 and the Philippines early in 1945. The capture of Iwo Jima and Okinawa put bombers in position to attack Japan itself. At Yalta, Stalin pledged that following Germany's defeat, the Soviet Union would join the Allies fighting in the Pacific. Before the Soviets could act, the Japanese offered to surrender on August 10, after the United States dropped atomic bombs on Hiroshima and Nagasaki.

leadership's refusal to surrender, suggested that Japan would keep up the fight despite overwhelming losses. Based on the fighting at Okinawa and Iwo Jima, American military commanders grimly predicted millions of casualties in the upcoming invasion.

Planning the Postwar World

When Roosevelt, Churchill, and Stalin met in February 1945 at Yalta, a resort on the Black Sea, victory in Europe and the Pacific was in sight, but no agreement had been reached on the peace to come. Roosevelt focused on maintaining Allied unity, the key to postwar peace and stability. The fate of British colonies such as India, where an independence movement had already begun, caused friction between Roosevelt and Churchill. Some of the tensions with the Russians were resolved when, in return for additional possessions in the Pacific, Stalin agreed to

enter the war against Japan within three months of the German surrender.

A more serious source of conflict was Stalin's desire for a band of Soviet-controlled satellite states to protect the Soviet Union's western border. With Soviet armies in control of much of Eastern Europe, Stalin had become increasingly inflexible about that region, insisting that he needed friendly (that is, Soviet-dominated) governments there to provide a buffer zone that would guarantee the Soviet Union's national security. Roosevelt acknowledged the legitimacy of that demand but, with the Atlantic Charter's principle of self-determination in mind, hoped for democratically elected governments in Poland and the neighboring countries. Unfortunately, the two goals proved mutually exclusive.

At Yalta Roosevelt and Churchill agreed in principle on the idea of a Soviet sphere of influence in Eastern Europe but deliberately left its dimensions vague. Stalin in

Anton Bilek

The War in the Pacific

Anton Bilek grew up in southern Illinois and enlisted in the army in 1939 at nineteen because jobs were hard to get. Sent to the Philippines in 1940, he was taken prisoner when the Japanese overran the Bataan peninsula in April 1942. He describes the infamous "Bataan Death March" and its aftermath.

The next morning, we got orders to get rid of all our arms and wait for the Japanese to come. General King had surrendered Bataan. They came in. First thing they did, they lined us up and started searchin' us. Anybody that had a ring or a wristwatch or a pair of gold-rimmed spectacles, they took 'em. Glasses they'd throw on the floor and break 'em and put the gold rims in their pockets. If you had a ring, you handed it over. If you couldn't get it off, the guy'd put the bayonet right up against your neck. Fortunately I never wore a ring. I couldn't afford one.

They moved us about on the road. Here was a big stream of Americans and Filipinos marchin' by. They told us to get in the back of this column. This was the start of the Death March. (A long, deep sigh.) That was a sixty-mile walk. Here we were, three, four months on half-rations, less. The men were already thin, in shock. Undernourished, full of malaria. Dysentery is beginning to spread. This is even before the surrender. We had two hospitals chuck-full of men. Bataan peninsula was the worst malaria-infected province of the Philippines.

The Japanese emptied out the hospitals. Anybody that could walk, they forced 'em into line. You found all kinda bodies along the road. Some of 'em bloated, some had just been killed. If you fell out to the side, you were either shot by the guards or you were bayoneted and left there. We lost somewhere between six hundred and seven hundred Americans in the four days of the march. The Filipinos lost close to ten thousand. At San Fernando, we were stuffed into boxcars and taken about thirty-five miles further north. The cars were closed, you couldn't get air. In the hot sun, the temperature got up there. You couldn't fall down because you were held up by the guys stacked around you. You had a lot of guys blow their top, start screamin'. From there, they marched us another seven, eight miles to Camp O'Donnell, which was built hurriedly for the Philippine army. It was built like the huts were built, of native bamboo and nipa and grass. There must've been about nine thousand of us and about fifty thousand Filipinos. Americans in one camp, Filipinos in the other. We had to leave after a month and a half. The monsoon season was starting. A hurricane blew down two of the barracks. Eighty men were killed. Just crushed.

I went blind, momentarily. It scared the hell out of me. I was at the hospital for about two weeks, and the doctor, an American, said, "There's nothing I can do with you. Rest is the only thing. Eat all the rice you can get. That's your only medicine." That's the one thing that pulled me through. He said, "You won't have to go on details." The Japanese were comin' in and they'd take two, three hundred and start 'em repairing a bridge that was blown up. We were losin' a lot of men there. They couldn't work any more. They were dyin'. . . .

I'm back home. It's all over with. I'd like to forget it. I had nothin' against the Japanese. But I don't drive a Toyota or own a Sony. . . . A lotta friends I lost. We had 185 men in our squadron when the war started. Three and a half years later, when we were liberated from a prison camp in Japan, we were 39 left. It's them I think about. Men I played ball with, men I worked with, men I associated with. I miss 'em.

Source: Studs Terkel, "The Good War": An Oral History of World War Two (New York: Pantheon Books, 1984), 85, 90–91, 95–96.

return pledged to hold "free and unfettered elections" at an unspecified time. (Those elections never took place.) The compromise reached by the three leaders at Yalta was open to multiple interpretations. Admiral William D. Leahy, Roosevelt's chief military aide, described the agreement as "so elastic that the Russians can stretch it all the way from Yalta to Washington without ever technically breaking it."

The three leaders proceeded with plans to divide Germany into four zones to be controlled by the United States, Great Britain, France, and the Soviet Union. The capital city, Berlin, which lay in the middle of the Soviet zone, would also be partitioned among the four powers. The issue of German reparations remained unsettled.

The Big Three made further progress toward the establishment of an international organization in the form of the United Nations. They agreed that the Security Council of the United Nations would include the five

The Big Three at Yalta

With victory in Europe at hand, Roosevelt journeyed in 1945 to Yalta, on the Black Sea, to meet one last time with Churchill and Stalin. It was here that they discussed the problems of peace settlements. The Yalta agreement mirrored a new balance of power and set the stage for the cold war. Franklin D. Roosevelt Library.

major Allied powers—the United States, Britain, France, China, and the Soviet Union—plus six other nations elected on a rotating basis. They also decided that the permanent members of the Security Council should have veto power over decisions of the General Assembly, in which all nations would be represented. Roosevelt, Churchill, and Stalin announced that the United Nations would convene in San Francisco on April 25, 1945.

Roosevelt returned to the United States in February, visibly exhausted by his 14,000-mile trip. He neglected to inform the American public of the concessions he had made to maintain the increasingly fragile wartime alliance. When he reported to Congress on the Yalta agreements, he made an unusual acknowledgment of his physical infirmity. Referring to the heavy steel braces he wore on his legs, he asked Congress to excuse him for giving his speech while sitting down. The sixty-three-year-old president was a sick man, suffering from heart failure and high blood pressure. On April 12, 1945, during a short visit to his vacation home in Warm Springs, Georgia, Roosevelt suffered a cerebral hemorrhage and died.

The Onset of the Atomic Age and the War's End

When Harry S Truman assumed the presidency, he learned about the top-secret Manhattan Project, charged with developing an atomic bomb. The project, which cost $2 billion and employed 120,000 people, culminated in Los Alamos, New Mexico, where the country's top physicists assembled the first bomb. Not until the first test—at Alamogordo, New Mexico, on July 16, 1945—did scientists know that the bomb would work. A month later Truman ordered the dropping of atomic bombs on two Japanese cities, Hiroshima on August 6 and Nagasaki on August 9.

Many later questioned why the United States did not warn Japan about the attack or choose a noncivilian target; the rationale for dropping the second bomb was even less clear. Some historians have argued that American

Hiroshima

This aerial view of Hiroshima after the dropping of an atomic bomb on August 6, 1945, shows the terrible devastation of the city. A U.S. Army report prepared in 1946 describes the bomb exploding "with a blinding flash in the sky, and a great rush of air and a loud rumble of noise extended for many miles around the city; the first blast was soon followed by the sounds of falling buildings and of growing fires, and a great cloud of dust and smoke began to cast a pall of darkness over the city." With the exception of around 50 concrete-reinforced buildings designed to withstand earthquakes, every structure within one mile of the center of the bomb blast was reduced to rubble. The physical destruction was second to the human cost: with a population estimated at between 300,000 and 400,000 people, Hiroshima lost 100,000 in the initial explosion and many thousands more died slowly of radiation poisoning. U.S. Air Force.

policymakers, already worried about potential conflicts with the Soviets over the postwar order, used the bomb to intimidate the Soviets. Others have suggested the fact that the Japanese were a nonwhite race facilitated the momentous decision to use the new, alarming weapon. At the time, however, the belief that Japan's military leaders would never surrender unless their country was utterly devastated convinced policymakers that they had to deploy the atom bomb. One hundred thousand people died at Hiroshima and sixty thousand at Nagasaki; tens of thousands more died slowly of radiation poisoning. Japan offered to surrender on August 10 and signed a formal treaty of surrender on September 2, 1945.

FOR FURTHER EXPLORATION

▶ For definitions of the key terms boldfaced in this chapter, see the glossary at the end of the book.

▶ To assess your mastery of the material covered in this chapter, see the Online Study Guide at **bedfordstmartins.com/henretta**.

▶ For suggested references, including Web sites, see page SR-28 at the end of the book.

▶ For map resources and primary documents, see **bedfordstmartins.com/henretta**.

SUMMARY

World War II was a global war, consisting of massive military campaigns in both Europe and the Pacific. With the rise of fascism and imperialism in Germany, Italy, and Japan, the world was at war by 1939. Although most Americans clung to strong isolationist sentiment, as evidenced by the series of Neutrality Acts during the 1930s, by the end of the decade President Roosevelt had begun mobilizing public opinion for intervention and converting the economy to war production. The Japanese attack on Pearl Harbor on December 7, 1941, brought the nation into World War II.

Defense mobilization ended the Great Depression and caused the economy to rebound. As with World War I, mobilization led to a dramatic expansion of the state. On the home front the war resulted in rationing and shortages of many items but no serious hardships. Geographical mobility increased as labor shortages opened job opportunities for women, blacks, and Mexican Americans. The labor movement surged, and the ideological climate of fighting Nazism aided the cause of civil rights. However, Japanese Americans on the West Coast suffered a devastating denial of civil liberties when the government moved them into internment camps.

The war news was bleak at first, but by 1943 the Allies had started to move toward victory, first in Europe and then in the Pacific. Soviet forces bore the brunt of the fighting in the European theater, while American forces primarily orchestrated the war effort in the Pacific. More than 15 million American men and women served in the armed forces, and at least 405,000 lost their lives.

While the Allied forces mobilized to defeat Germany and Japan, Roosevelt attempted to maintain harmony among the United States, Great Britain, and the Soviet Union. Many of the disagreements over wartime diplomacy would become serious problems in the postwar world, especially the fate of Eastern Europe and the intentions of the Soviet Union. Of all the major powers that fought in World War II, only the United States emerged physically unharmed. And at the end of the war, only the United States had a powerful new weapon—the atomic bomb. But the most enduring legacy of World War II was the onset of the cold war, which would dominate American foreign policy for the next four decades.

TIMELINE

1933 Adolf Hitler becomes chancellor of Germany

1935 Italy invades Ethiopia

1935–1937 U.S. Neutrality Acts

1936 Germany reoccupies Rhineland demilitarized zone

Rome-Berlin Axis established

Japan and Germany sign Anti-Comintern Pact

1937 Japan invades China

1938 Munich agreement between Germany, Britain, and France

1939 Nazi-Soviet Nonaggression Pact

Germany invades Poland

Britain and France declare war on Germany

1940 American conscription reinstated

Germany, Italy, and Japan sign Tri-Partite Pact

1941 Roosevelt promulgates Four Freedoms

Germany invades Soviet Union

Lend-Lease Act passed

Fair Employment Practices Commission

Atlantic Charter

Japanese attack Pearl Harbor

1942 Allies suffer severe defeats in Europe and Asia

Executive Order 9066 leads to Japanese internment camps

Battles of Coral Sea and Midway halt Japanese advance

Women recruited for war industries

1942–1945 Rationing

1943 Race riots in Detroit and Los Angeles

Fascism falls in Italy

1944 D-Day

GI Bill of Rights

1945 Yalta Conference

Battles of Iwo Jima and Okinawa

Germany surrenders

Harry S Truman becomes president after Roosevelt's death

United Nations convenes

Atomic bombs dropped on Hiroshima and Nagasaki

Japan surrenders

PART FIVE

Women, Gender, and the Welfare System

Would it surprise you to learn that as recently as twenty-five years ago the experiences of women were virtually absent from U.S. history books? Now, thanks in large part to the feminist movement that began in the 1960s, women's history is flourishing. Initially, the aim was simply to include women in the central narrative of the nation's history—to make them visible. This effort continues, but as scholars have discovered that women's experience often cannot be extricated from men's experience, they have increasingly made *gender*, encompassing both women's and men's roles, a preferred strategy of analysis. Gendered analysis has, in turn, proved to have life of its own, spilling from its original confines in women's history and illuminating subjects seemingly far removed from the intimate realm of sexual identity. The welfare system that originated in the New Deal era is a key case in point.

The cornerstone for welfare was the Social Security Act of 1935, which provided old-age pensions for most workers, a joint federal-state system of unemployment compensation, and direct federal assistance for the blind, deaf, and disabled and for single mothers with dependent children. The first generation of scholars after the New Deal, such as the eminent historian Arthur Schlesinger Jr., not surprisingly identified the Social Security Act with the progressive thrust of the federal government under Franklin D. Roosevelt. As witnesses to the Great Depression, these historians celebrated the Social Security Act for providing Americans with a much needed safety net.

Subsequent interpretation has been more critical, however. Some scholars have stressed how business interests managed to reshape the proposed legislation so that its pension and unemployment provisions were much more limited than Social Security advocates had intended. Other scholars noted the denial of coverage to farm workers because of the power of the farm lobby, dominated by agribusiness leaders who wanted no federal interference with their control over the farm labor force. That decision, along with the exclusion of domestic household workers from coverage, meant that two-thirds of African American workers were left out of the Social Security system in 1935. A rich body of literature has emerged, contrasting the conservative tone of the Roosevelt administration's approach with the more generous and comprehensive systems of Western European nations and stressing the powerful impact of American racial inequality in shaping social welfare legislation.

Now gendered analysis has come into play, focusing through works of such feminist scholars as Alice Kessler-Harris (*In Pursuit of Equity: Women, Men, and the Quest for Economic Citizenship in Twentieth-Century America,* 2001), Gwendolyn Mink (*The Wages of Motherhood: Inequality in the Welfare State, 1917–1942,* 1995), and Linda Gordon (*Pitied But Not Entitled: Single Mothers and the History of Welfare,* 1994) on the way policymakers' assumptions about men's and women's proper roles framed the initial Social Security legislation and its implementation. The starting point for this critique is the distinction embedded in the Social Security Act of 1935 between *social security*, which applies to old-age pensions, and *welfare*, which usually describes aid to families with dependent children. In *Pitied But Not Entitled,* Gordon traces welfare's beginnings to the white women's social reform network established in the late nineteenth and early twentieth centuries, which supported a wide range of government programs to assist the urban poor (see Chapter 20). Between 1910 and 1920, pressure from these reformers led most states to enact mothers' pension programs that provided cash subsidies to poor women and their children in the absence of a male breadwinner.

With the coming of the Great Depression, welfare issues, traditionally the sphere of women, moved to the center of public policy. Men dominated the planning of Social Security and relegated the women within the

Creating the Welfare System
When FDR signed the Social Security bill on August 14, 1935, he set in motion a system that shaped social benefits, including social security and welfare, for decades. Behind him is Frances Perkins, the first woman to hold a cabinet position. The Children's Bureau, so crucial to the framing of the provisions for Aid to Dependent Children, was housed in Perkins's Department of Labor. Associated Press.

Job Training for Welfare Recipients

One of the most widely touted aspects of President Clinton's 1996 Personal Responsibility and Work Opportunity Act was the requirement that welfare recipients find work within two years. This act gave states more discretion in running welfare programs, and many implemented job-training programs, such as this one in California. It is still too soon to evaluate the long-term impact of the welfare reforms put in place in the 1990s. Lava Jo Regan / Saba.

Children's Bureau—Grace Abbott, Katherine Lenroot, Martha Eliot, and others—to planning one small piece of the omnibus legislation, a federal program for dependent mothers and children.

Although the planning process suggests marginalization of the women's network and the poor mothers who were the objects of their concern, both male and female New Dealers believed in the concept of the "family wage"—in which the husband earned enough money to support his family, preventing the need for the wife to enter the work force. Concerned about the crippling impact of joblessness and aging on the masculine role of breadwinner, New Dealers hoped to ensure that men—and, through them, their families—could weather unemployment and have a cushion for old age. They created social insurance programs tied to a payroll tax system, still in use today, that enabled supporters to describe old-age pensions and unemployment compensation as "rights" based on payroll taxation and therefore "earned."

In contrast to these programs designed primarily for male breadwinners, Gordon argues that the system established for poor women and children was not portrayed as a "right" linked to participation in the workforce but rather as aid founded on "need." Drawing upon the family wage concept, which had also shaped the mothers' pension programs enacted earlier by states, women New Dealers designed the policy of Aid to Dependent Children (ADC, later called AFDC) to keep poor women out of the workforce and in the home with their children—a policy that ignored the growing numbers of working mothers and reinforced notions of women's dependence. Rather than develop a program that would make it feasible for single mothers to work to support their families (for example, through subsidies to supplement their low wages or child

care), New Dealers opted for one that would keep women in the home at a bare subsistence. It stigmatized these mothers as "needy" and failed to protect poor children.

Other factors contributed to the stigma attached to AFDC, Gordon points out. Initially, relatively few black women received welfare benefits, primarily because southern congressmen had balked at national welfare standards, insisting instead on local control of welfare payments. This demand led to a shared federal-state program that in the short term gave localities the power to refuse aid to poor black women, making them more easily exploitable as farm labor. By the 1960s, however, in part because of black migration to the cities of the north, African American women began to swell the ranks of welfare mothers. Never a majority, their numbers were nonetheless proportionately higher than other groups, and racist attitudes, intersecting with the association of black women with welfare, led to further stigmatization of AFDC.

By the 1980s welfare was widely condemned, both by feminist and welfare-rights activists for its failure to provide for the needs of the poor and by conservatives who criticized it for supporting "irresponsible" mothers at taxpayers' expense and undermining the work ethic. Bowing to demands for reform, in 1996 President Bill Clinton signed the Personal Responsibility and Work Opportunity Act, which he promised "would end welfare as we know it." The new program eliminated the federal guarantee of cash assistance to poor children by abolishing AFDC, required most adult recipients to find work within two years, set a five-year limit on payments to any one family, and gave states wide discretion in running their welfare programs.

Gordon wrote her book in 1994, when the older order was still in effect. What might she say today about gender and the reform of welfare? To some extent, the 1996 act continued to rely on traditional gender assumptions, especially in urging states to "encourage the formation and maintenance of two-parent families." However, in their emphasis on putting welfare mothers to work, contemporary policymakers have clearly broken with early reformers who idealized women in the home, supported by a family wage. Gordon would likely argue that the long-term success of welfare reform, measured not just in reducing the welfare rolls but in reducing poverty itself, will rest on its ability to address what the original Social Security Act of 1935, with its assumptions about men's and women's proper roles, neglected: the problem of providing poor working mothers access to jobs that offer adequate wages and benefits as well as to affordable child and medical care, a proposal that for many Americans would seem almost as contentious as welfare itself. Feminist scholars like Gordon may have limited success in influencing contemporary public policy, but they have made important contributions to the history of the American welfare state. Introducing gender into our analysis of Social Security legislation is, moreover, just one example of how women's history has broadened our understanding of the factors shaping politics and policy.

PART SIX

America and the World

1945 to the Present

DIPLOMACY	GOVERNMENT	ECONOMY	SOCIETY	CULTURE
The Cold War— and After	Redefining the Role of the State	Ups and Downs of U.S. Economic Dominance	Social Movements and Demographic Diversity	Consumer Culture and the Information Revolution
1945 ▶ Truman Doctrine (1947) Marshall Plan (1948) NATO founded (1949)	▶ Truman's Fair Deal liberalism Taft-Hartley Act (1947)	▶ Bretton Woods system established: World Bank, IMF, GATT	▶ Migration to cities accelerates Armed forces desegregated (1948)	▶ End of wartime rationing Rise of television
1950 ▶ Permanent mobilization: NSC-68 (1950) Korean War (1950–1953)	▶ Eisenhower's modern Republicanism Warren Court activism	▶ Rise of military-industrial complex Service sector expands	▶ *Brown v. Board of Education* (1954) Montgomery bus boycott (1955)	▶ Growth of suburbia Baby boom
1960 ▶ Cuban missile crisis (1962) Nuclear test ban treaty (1963) Vietnam War escalates (1965)	▶ High tide of liberalism: Great Society, War on Poverty Nixon ushers in conservative era	▶ Kennedy-Johnson tax cut, military expenditures fuel economic growth	▶ Student activism Civil Rights Act (1964); Voting Rights Act (1965) Revival of feminism	▶ Shopping malls spread Baby boomers swell college enrollment Youth counterculture
1970 ▶ Nixon visits China (1972) SALT initiates détente (1972) Paris Peace Accords (1973)	▶ Watergate scandal; Nixon resigns (1974) Deregulation begins under Ford and Carter	▶ Arab oil embargo (1973–1974); inflation surges Deindustrialization brings unemployment to "Rust Belt" Income stagnation	▶ *Roe v. Wade* (1973) Televangelists mobilize evangelical Protestants New Right urges conservative agenda	▶ Rise of consumer and environmental protection movements Gasoline shortages Apple introduces first personal computer (1977)
1980 ▶ Reagan begins arms buildup INF treaty (1988) Berlin Wall falls (1989)	▶ Reagan Revolution Supreme Court conservatism	▶ Reaganomics Budget and trade deficits soar Savings and loan bailout	▶ New Latino and Asian immigration AIDS epidemic	▶ MTV debuts Compact discs and cell phones invented
1990– 2002 ▶ War in the Persian Gulf (1990) USSR disintegrates; end of the cold war U.S. peacekeeping forces in Bosnia Radical Muslim terrorists destroy New York's World Trade Center and attack the Pentagon	▶ Democratic party adopts "moderate" policies Republican Congress shifts federal government tasks to states George W. Bush narrowly elected President	▶ Corporate downsizing Boom of the mid-1990s gives way to weakening economy	▶ "Culture Wars" over affirmative action, feminism, and gay rights Affirmative action challenged Welfare reform	▶ Health care crisis Information superhighway Biotech revolution

In 1945 the United States entered an era of unprecedented international power. Unlike the period after World War I, American leaders did not avoid international commitments; instead they aggressively pursued U.S. interests abroad, vowing to contain communism around the globe. The consequences of that struggle profoundly influenced the nation's domestic economy, political affairs, and social and cultural trends for the next half century.

DIPLOMACY First, the United States took a leading role in global diplomatic and military affairs. When the Soviet Union challenged America's vision of postwar Europe, the Truman administration responded by crafting the policies and alliances that came to define the cold war. That struggle lasted for more than forty years, spawned two "hot" wars in Korea and Vietnam, and fueled a terrifying nuclear arms race. The cold war mentality prevailed until the collapse of the Soviet Union in 1991. In the absence of bipolar superpower confrontations, international conflicts persisted, arising from regional, religious, and ethnic differences, and brought new challenges to the nation. In 1990 it fought the Gulf War against Iraq and ten years later sent peacekeeping troops to war-torn Bosnia. And, as a devastating attack on New York's World Trade Center in September 2001 so powerfully indicated, the problem of international terrorism looms menacingly.

GOVERNMENT Second, America's global commitments had dramatic consequences for American government, as liberals and conservatives generally agreed on keeping the country in a state of permanent mobilization and maintaining a large military establishment.

The end of the cold war brought modest cutbacks but with new diplomatic challenges, military expenditures remained a high priority and competed with spending for domestic needs. In the area of economic policy, both Republicans and Democrats were willing to intervene in the economy when private initiatives could not maintain steady growth, but liberals also pushed for a larger role for the federal government in the areas of social welfare and environmental protection. In the 1960s Lyndon B. Johnson's "Great Society" erected an extensive federal and state apparatus to provide for social welfare. In subsequent years, particularly under the presidency of Ronald Reagan in the 1980s and the Republican control of Congress in the mid-1990s, conservatives cut back on many of the major programs and tried to delegate federal powers to the states.

ECONOMY Third, thanks to the growth of a military-industrial complex and the expansion of consumer culture, the quarter century after 1945 represented the heyday of American capitalism. Economic dominance abroad translated into unparalleled affluence at home. In the early 1970s, however, competition from other countries began to challenge America's economic supremacy, and for the next two decades, many American workers experienced high unemployment, declining real wages, stagnant incomes, and a standard of living that could not match that of their parents. Following this period of global economic restructuring, the U.S. economy rebounded in the mid-1990s, reclaiming a position of undisputed dominance. By 2002, however, this sense of extraordinary American prosperity was undercut by a weakening economy and a volatile stock market as well as concerns that

disparities in wealth and opportunity were growing.

SOCIETY Fourth, the victory over fascism in World War II led to renewed calls for America to make good on its promise of liberty and equality for all. In great waves of protests in the 1950s and 1960s, African Americans—and then women, Latinos, and other groups—challenged the political status quo. The resulting hard-won reforms brought concrete gains for many Americans, but since the late 1970s, conservatives have challenged many of these initiatives. As the century drew to a close, the promise of true equality remained unfulfilled.

CULTURE Fifth, American economic power in the postwar era accelerated the development of a consumer society based on suburbanization and technology. As millions of Americans migrated to new suburban developments after World War II, growing baby boom families provided an expanded market for household products of all types. Among the most significant were new technological devices—television, video recorders, and personal computers—that helped break down the isolation of suburban and rural living. In the 1990s the popularization of the Internet initiated an "information revolution" that expanded and challenged the power of corporate-sponsored consumer culture.

Today, more than a half century after the end of World War II, Americans are living in an increasingly interwoven network of national and international forces. Outside events shape ordinary lives in ways that were inconceivable a century ago. As the cold war era fades into history, the United States remains the sole military superpower, but it shares economic leadership in the new interdependent global system.

CHAPTER 27

Cold War America

1945–1960

The Cold War Abroad
Descent into Cold War, 1945–1946
The Truman Doctrine and
Containment
Containment in Asia and the
Korean War
Eisenhower and the "New Look" of
Foreign Policy

The Cold War at Home
Postwar Domestic Challenges
Fair Deal Liberalism
The Great Fear
"Modern Republicanism"

The Emergence of Civil Rights as a National Issue
Civil Rights under Truman
Challenging Segregation
The Civil Rights Movement and
the Cold War

The Impact of the Cold War
Nuclear Proliferation
The Military-Industrial Complex

WHEN HARRY TRUMAN ARRIVED at the White House on April 12, 1945, after Franklin Roosevelt died, he asked the president's widow, "Is there anything I can do for you?" Eleanor Roosevelt responded, "Is there anything we can do for you? For you are the one in trouble now." Truman inherited the presidency at one of the most perilous times in modern history. Unscathed by bombs and battles on the home front, U.S. industry and agriculture had grown rapidly during World War II. The nation wielded enormous military power as the sole possessor of the atomic bomb. The most powerful country in the world, the United States had become a preeminent force in the international arena. Only the Soviet Union represented an obstacle to American **hegemony**, or dominance, in global affairs. Soon the two superpowers were locked in a cold war of economic, political, and military rivalry but no direct engagement on the battlefield.

Soviet-American confrontations during the postwar years had important domestic repercussions. The cold war boosted military expenditures, fueling a growing arms race. It fostered a climate of fear and suspicion of "subversives" in government, education, and the media who might undermine American

◀ **Protect Them**

The cold war and nuclear arms race pervaded American culture in the post–World War II years. The government's Civil Defense Agency, founded in 1950, mounted an extensive campaign to alert the nation to the need for civil defense plans, including the construction of public shelters and the development of emergency evacuation strategies. This Teaneck, New Jersey, poster not only reminded Americans of the potential for attack, but also, by picturing a mother and child in need of protection, reinforced the era's emphasis on family and traditional gender roles.
Collection of Janice L. and David J. Frent.

democratic institutions. It both constrained and assisted the emerging civil rights movement. The economic benefits of internationalism also gave rise to a period of unprecedented affluence and prosperity during which the United States enjoyed the highest standard of living in the world (see Chapter 28). That prosperity helped to continue and in some cases to expand federal power, perpetuating the New Deal state in the postwar era.

The Cold War Abroad

The defeat of Germany and Japan did not bring stability to the world. Six years of devastating warfare had destroyed prewar governments and geographical boundaries, creating new power relationships that helped to dissolve colonial empires. Even before the war ended, the United States and the Soviet Union were struggling for advantage in those unstable areas; after the war they engaged in a protracted global conflict. Hailed as a battle between communism and capitalism, the cold war was in reality a more complex power struggle covering a range of economic, strategic, and ideological issues. As each side tried to protect its own national security and way of life, its actions aroused fear in the other, contributing to a cycle of distrust and animosity that would shape U.S.-Soviet relations for decades to come.

Descent into Cold War, 1945–1946

During the war Franklin Roosevelt worked effectively with Soviet leader Joseph Stalin and determined to continue

Postwar Devastation

Berlin, Germany, was one of many European cities reduced to rubble during World War II. Both Allied bombing and brutal fighting in April 1945, when Soviet troops entered Berlin, devastated the once impressive capital city. Here, in a telling statement about the collapse of Hitler's Third Reich, German refugees walk in front of what was once Goebbels's Propaganda Ministry. U.S. policymakers feared that this type of destruction and the economic disorder that accompanied it would make many areas of postwar Europe vulnerable to Communist influence. National Archives.

For more help analyzing this image, see the ONLINE STUDY GUIDE at bedfordstmartins.com/henretta.

good relations with the Soviet Union in peacetime. In particular he hoped that the United Nations would provide a forum for resolving postwar conflicts. Avoiding the disagreements that had doomed American membership in the League of Nations after World War I, the Senate approved America's participation in the United Nations in December 1945. Coming eight months after Roosevelt's death, the vote was in part a memorial to the late president's hopes for peace.

Shortly before his death, however, Roosevelt had been disturbed by Soviet actions in Eastern Europe. As the Soviet army drove the Germans out of Russia and back through Eastern Europe, the Soviet Union sponsored provisional governments in the occupied countries. Since the Soviet Union had been a victim of German aggression in both world wars, Stalin was determined to prevent the rebuilding and rearming of its traditional foe, and he insisted on a security zone of friendly governments in Eastern Europe for further protection. At the Yalta Conference in February, both America and Britain had agreed to recognize this Soviet "**sphere of influence**," with the proviso that "free and unfettered elections" would be held as soon as possible. But in succeeding months the Soviets made no move to hold elections and rebuffed Western attempts to reorganize the Soviet-installed governments.

When Truman assumed the presidency after Roosevelt's death, he took a belligerent stance toward the Soviet Union. Recalling Britain's disastrous appeasement of Hitler in 1938, he had decided that the United States had to take a hard line against Soviet expansion. "There isn't any difference in totalitarian states," he said, "Nazi, Communist, or Fascist." At a meeting held shortly after he took office, the new president berated the Soviet foreign minister, V. M. Molotov, over the Soviets' failure to honor their Yalta agreement to support free elections in Poland. Truman used what he called "tough methods" that July at the Potsdam Conference, which brought together the United States, Britain, and the Soviet Union. After learning of the successful test of America's atomic bomb, Truman "told the Russians just where they got off and generally bossed the whole meeting," recalled British prime minister Winston Churchill. Negotiations on critical postwar issues deadlocked, revealing serious cracks in the Grand Alliance.

One issue tentatively resolved at Potsdam was the fate of occupied Germany. At Yalta the defeated German state had been divided into four zones of occupation, controlled by the United States, France, Britain, and the Soviet Union. At Potsdam the Allies agreed to disarm the country, dismantle its military production facilities, and permit the occupying powers to extract reparations from the zones they controlled. Plans for future reunification stalled, however, as the United States and the Soviet Union each worried that a united Germany would fall into the other's sphere. The foundation was

thus laid for what would become the political division into East and West Germany four years later (Map 27.1).

As tensions over Europe divided the former Allies, hopes of international cooperation in the control of atomic weapons faded as well. In the Baruch Plan, submitted to the United Nations in 1946, the United States proposed a system of international control that relied on mandatory inspection and supervision but preserved American nuclear monopoly. The Soviets, profoundly uneasy about this monopoly, rejected the plan and worked assiduously to complete their own bomb. Meanwhile, the Truman administration pursued plans to develop nuclear energy and weapons further. Thus the failure of the Baruch Plan signaled the hardening of tensions and the beginning of a frenzied nuclear arms race between the two superpowers.

The Truman Doctrine and Containment

As tensions mounted between the superpowers, the United States increasingly perceived Soviet expansionism as a threat to its own interests, and a new American policy, **containment**, began to take shape. The most influential expression of the policy came in February 1946 from George F. Kennan in an 8,000-word cable, dubbed the "Long Telegram," from his post at the U.S. embassy in Moscow to his superiors in Washington. Kennan, who was identified only as "X," warned that the Soviet Union was moving "inexorably along the prescribed path, like a persistent toy automobile wound up and headed in a given direction, stopping only when it meets unanswerable force" (see American Lives, "George F. Kennan: Architect of Containment," p. 786). To stop Soviet expansionism, Kennan argued, the United States should pursue a policy of "firm containment . . . at every point where [the Russians] show signs of encroaching upon the interests of a peaceful and stable world."

The Truman Doctrine and the National Security Act. The emerging policy of containment crystallized in 1947 over a crisis in Greece. In the spring of 1946, several thousand local Communist guerrillas, whom American advisors mistakenly believed were taking orders from Moscow, launched a full-scale civil war against the government and the British occupation authorities. In February 1947 the British informed Truman that they could no longer afford to assist anti-Communists in Greece. American policymakers worried that Soviet influence in Greece threatened American and European interests in the eastern Mediterranean and the Middle East, especially in strategically located Turkey and the oil-rich state of Iran.

In response the president announced what would be known as the Truman Doctrine. In a speech to the Republican-controlled Congress on March 12, he

George F. Kennan: Architect of Containment

On February 22, 1946, a diplomatic advisor named George Kennan dictated an 8,000-word telegram from the U.S. embassy in Moscow. Responding to a Department of State request for an assessment of Soviet foreign policy, Kennan described the Soviet Union as an insecure state intent on expansion, subversion, and the export of Communist revolution. It was, he argued, "a political force committed fanatically to the belief that with the U.S. there can be no permanent modus vivendi." A preliminary blueprint of the containment theory, this "Long Telegram" was a confidential communiqué to President Harry Truman and Secretary of State James Byrnes. Within weeks, however, it became required reading for hundreds of U.S. military and diplomatic personnel around the world.

Kennan's Long Telegram found an enthusiastic audience among Washington policymakers who were eager to redefine U.S.-Soviet relations in the early postwar period. Its alarmist language helped convince the Truman administration to take a harder line against the Soviet Union and provided the ideological foundations for the emerging cold war. Summoned back to Washington a few months later, Kennan became one of the most influential advisors in the Truman administration. Writing and lecturing continuously for the next forty years, he would also become one of the foremost foreign policy theorists of the twentieth century.

Kennan's containment theory was shaped by his many years of experience in the diplomatic corps. Born in Milwaukee in 1904, Kennan graduated from Princeton University in 1925 and entered the foreign service the following year. After holding minor positions in Switzerland and Germany, he was offered training as a Soviet specialist in 1929. Under the tutelage of anti-Communist Russian émigrés in Berlin, Kennan studied Russian history, language, and literature and later served as a Soviet expert at the U.S. embassy in Latvia. In 1933, when Franklin Roosevelt initiated diplomatic relations with the Soviet Union, Kennan helped open the new U.S. embassy in Moscow and joined the embassy staff. During his four years in the Soviet Union, he witnessed the horrors of the Stalinist purges, an experience that fueled his animosity toward the Russian leader Joseph Stalin and the Soviet Communist regime. Between 1937 and 1944 Kennan occupied a variety of diplomatic posts in the United States and Europe, none of which truly satisfied him. When the new ambassador to the Soviet Union, Averell Harriman, requested him as an advisor in 1944, he jumped at the opportunity to return to Moscow.

Still deeply antagonistic toward the Soviet Union, Kennan disagreed with Roosevelt's wartime alliance with Stalin and issued a steady stream of anti-Soviet memoranda. During the war most of these pronouncements fell on deaf ears. With the end of the war and the rise of Soviet-American conflict over Poland, however, Harriman and other members of the Truman administration became more receptive to Kennan's views. Widespread praise for his Long Telegram won Kennan an offer to lecture at the National War College in Washington in April 1946. A year later, Secretary of State George Marshall appointed him director of the department's new Policy Planning Staff (PPS), which helped devise the Marshall Plan and other long-range foreign-policy initiatives.

While serving as PPS director from 1947 to 1950, Kennan refined his ideas about containment. His best-known articulation of the theory appeared in a July 1947 article in *Foreign Affairs*, which he wrote anonymously as "Mr. X." Kennan's identity, however, was soon revealed, and his views of an antagonistic and deceitful Soviet state won wide currency. Conceding Soviet influence in Eastern Europe, he urged the United States and its Allies to contain the Soviet threat through "the adroit and vigilant application of counter-force at a series of constantly shifting geographical and political points." By pursuing such a policy, Kennan speculated, Soviet power could be diminished since it "bears within it the seeds of its own decay."

As Kennan himself would later admit, his formulation of containment was ambiguous and imprecise. His use of the term *force* was vague; he failed to specify whether the United States should use political, economic, or military force to contain the Soviets. And he placed no geographical limits on American intervention. Although Kennan later claimed that containment was primarily a political/economic strategy intended to protect the world's key industrial areas, the ambiguity of the 1947 article invited American policymakers to interpret containment in the broadest possible fashion.

By 1950 Truman's increasingly hard-line approach toward the Soviet Union had alienated Kennan. He criticized the open-ended commitment of the Truman Doctrine, the militarization of containment under NSC-68, and the division of Europe under the NATO treaty. Increasingly marginalized by the new secretary of state, Dean Acheson, Kennan took a leave of absence to attend the Institute for Advanced Study at Princeton University.

George F. Kennan

As a diplomat, foreign policy theorist, and historian, George F. Kennan has enjoyed a long and distinguished career spanning more than seventy years. This portrait by Guy Rowe dates from 1955.

National Portrait Gallery, Smithsonian Institution / Art Resource, NY.

In 1952 he returned to the administration to serve as ambassador to the Soviet Union; within months, however, he was forced to resign after making disparaging remarks comparing Stalin's regime to Nazism.

With the election of Republican Dwight D. Eisenhower in 1952, Kennan's influence in Washington was further diminished. Eisenhower's secretary of state, the staunchly conservative John Foster Dulles, condemned containment as immoral and denounced Kennan for his "appeasement" of the Soviets in Eastern Europe. Kennan briefly returned to the diplomatic corps in 1961 as ambassador to Yugoslavia under President John F. Kennedy. Two years later, however, Congress revoked that country's most-favored-nation trading status, undermining Kennan's work and prompting his permanent retirement from government service.

As Kennan's diplomatic career waned, he became a renowned historian and theorist of American foreign relations. Working from his office at the Institute for Advanced Studies, he produced dozens of books and articles, including two Pulitzer Prize–winning works, *Russia Leaves the War* (1950) and his often-quoted *Memoirs* (1967). His popular historical text *American Diplomacy, 1900–1950* (1951) introduced millions of Americans to the "realist" critique of foreign policy—an approach that stresses national interests and power politics over the idealistic motives of both conservatives and liberals.

On numerous occasions Kennan aired his realist views of controversial cold war developments. During the 1950s he condemned McCarthyism and advocated Soviet and U.S. disengagement from Europe. Later he became an outspoken opponent of the Vietnam War, testifying before the Senate Foreign Relations Committee in 1966 that the containment doctrine was poorly suited to Indochina. Opposing moralistic foreign policy, he criticized Jimmy Carter's preoccupation with human rights in the 1970s and Ronald Reagan's dramatic arms buildup and anti-Soviet pronouncements in the 1980s. As an outspoken critic of the nuclear arms race, he called for "no first use" of nuclear weapons in 1984 and pressed for comprehensive arms control agreements.

The demise of the Soviet Union in 1991 seemed to fulfill Kennan's prophecy in the 1947 article and brought him renewed public attention. But historians continue to debate the usefulness of containment in ending the cold war. During his long career, Kennan served as both chief architect and key critic of containment. His evolving views highlight the complexities and perils of cold war policymaking in the late twentieth century.

Jean Monnet

Truman's Generous Proposal

*J*ean Monnet was an eminent French statesman and a tireless promoter of postwar European union. As head of a French postwar planning commission, he helped oversee the dispersal of Marshall Plan funds, the importance of which he described in his memoirs.

So we had at last concerted our efforts to halt France's economic decline; but now, once more, everything seemed to be at risk. Two years earlier [1947], we thought that we had plumbed the depths of material poverty. Now we were threatened with the loss of even basic essentials. . . . Our dollar resources were melting away at an alarming rate, because we were having to buy American wheat to replace the crops we had lost during the winter. This alone cost us $200m. instead of the $30m. we had expected to pay. In addition, we had to increase our coal imports at a time when prices had risen in the United States. In June, we met the cost with gold bullion from the Bank of France; in August, we cut off inessential imports. A further American loan was soon exhausted.

Nor was this grim situation confined to France. Britain too had come to the end of her resources. In February 1947 she had abruptly cancelled her aid to Greece and Turkey, whose burdens she had seemed able to assume in 1945. Overnight, this abrupt abdication gave the United States direct responsibility for part of Europe. Truman did not hesitate for a moment: with the decisiveness that was to mark his actions as President, he at once asked for credits and arms for both Turkey and Greece. . . . [Soon after], he announced the Truman Doctrine of March 12, 1947. Its significance was general: it meant that the United States would prevent Europe from becoming a depressed area at the mercy of Communist advance. On the very same day, the Four-Power Conference began in Moscow. There, for a whole month, George Marshall, Ernest Bevin, and Georges Bidault argued with Vyacheslav Molotov about all the problems of the peace, and above all about Germany.

When Marshall returned to Washington, he knew that for a long time there would be no further genuine dialogue with Stalin's Russia. The "cold war," as it was soon to be known, had begun. . . . Information from a number of sources convinced Marshall and his Under-Secretary Dean Acheson that once again, as in 1941, the United States had a great historic duty. And once again there took place what I had witnessed in Washington a few years earlier: a small group of men brought to rapid maturity an idea which, when the Executive gave the word, turned into vigorous action. This time, it was done by five or six people, in total secrecy and at lightning speed. Marshall, Acheson, Clayton, Averell Harriman, and George Kennan worked out a proposal of unprecedented scope and generosity. It took us all by surprise when we read the speech that George Marshall made at Harvard on June 5, 1947. Chance had led him to choose the University's Commencement Day to launch something new in international relations: helping others to help themselves.

Source: Jean Monnet, *Memoirs*, trans. Richard Mayne (New York: Doubleday, 1978), 264–66.

for each resident. On May 12, 1949, Stalin lifted the blockade, which had made West Berlin a symbol of resistance to communism.

The coup in Czechoslovakia and the crisis in Berlin convinced U.S. policymakers of the need for a collective security pact. In April 1949, for the first time since the end of the American Revolution, the United States entered into a peacetime military alliance, the North Atlantic Treaty Organization (NATO). Truman asked Congress for $1.3 billion in military assistance to NATO and authorized the basing of four U.S. Army divisions in Western Europe. Under the NATO pact, twelve nations—the United States, Canada, Britain, France, Italy, Belgium, the Netherlands, Luxembourg, Denmark, Norway, Portugal, and Iceland—agreed that "an armed attack against one or more of them in Europe or North America shall be considered an attack against them all." In May 1949 those nations also agreed to the creation of the Federal Republic of Germany (West Germany), which joined NATO in 1955.

In October 1949, in response to the creation of NATO, the Soviet Union tightened its grip on Eastern Europe by creating a separate government for East Germany, which became the German Democratic

Republic. The Soviets also organized an economic association, the Council for Mutual Economic Assistance (COMECON) in 1949, and a military alliance for Eastern Europe, the Warsaw Pact, in 1955. The postwar division of Europe was nearly complete.

Containment Militarized: NSC-68.   New impetus for the policy of containment came in September 1949, when American military intelligence detected a rise in radioactivity in the atmosphere—proof that the Soviet Union had detonated an atomic bomb. The American atomic monopoly, which some military and political advisors had argued would last for decades, had ended in just four years, forcing a major reassessment of the nation's foreign policy.

To devise a new diplomatic and military blueprint, Truman turned to the National Security Council (NSC), an advisory body established in 1947 to set defense and military priorities. In April 1950 the NSC delivered its report, known as "NSC-68," to the president. Filled with alarmist rhetoric and exaggerated assessments of Soviet capabilities, the document made several specific recommendations, including the development of a hydrogen bomb, an advanced weapon a thousand times more destructive than the atomic bombs that had destroyed Hiroshima and Nagasaki. (The United States would explode its first hydrogen bomb in November 1952 and the Soviet Union its first in 1953.) NSC-68 also supported increases in U.S. conventional forces and the establishment of a strong system of alliances. Most important, it called for increased taxes to finance "a bold and massive program of rebuilding the West's defensive potential to surpass that of the Soviet world."

Though Truman was an aggressive anti-Communist, he was reluctant to commit to a major defense buildup, fearing that it would overburden the budget. But the Korean War, which began just two months after NSC-68 was completed, helped to transform the report's recommendations into reality, as the cold war spawned a hot war.

Containment in Asia and the Korean War

As mutual suspicion deepened between the United States and the Soviet Union, cold war doctrines began to influence the American position in Asia as well. American policy there was based on Asia's importance to the world economy as much as on the desire to contain communism. At first American plans for the region centered on a revitalized China, but political instability there prompted the Truman administration to focus on developing the Japanese economy instead. After dismantling Japan's military forces and weaponry, American occupation forces under General Douglas MacArthur began the job of transforming the country into a bulwark of Asian

capitalism. MacArthur drafted a democratic constitution and oversaw the rebuilding of the economy, paving the way for the restoration of Japanese sovereignty in 1951.

The "Fall" of China.   In China the situation was more precarious. Since the 1930s a civil war had been raging, as Communist forces led by Mao Zedong (Mao Tse-tung) and Zhou Enlai (Chou En-lai) contended for power with conservative Nationalist forces under Jiang Jieshi (Chiang Kai-shek). Although dissatisfied with the corrupt and inefficient Jiang regime, officials for the Truman administration did not see Mao as a good alternative, and they resigned themselves to working with the Nationalists. Between 1945 and 1949 the United States provided more than $2 billion to Jiang's forces but to no avail. In 1947 General Albert Wedemeyer, who had tried to work with Jiang, reported to President Truman that, until the "corrupt, reactionary, and inefficient Chinese National government" undertook "drastic political and economic reforms," the United States could not accomplish its purpose. In August 1949, when those reforms did not occur, the Truman administration cut off aid to the Nationalists, sealing their fate. The People's Republic of China was formally established under Mao on October 1, 1949, and what was left of Jiang's government fled to Taiwan.

Although nothing less than a massive U.S. military commitment could have stopped the Chinese Communists, many Americans viewed Mao's success as a defeat for the United States. A pro-Nationalist "China lobby," supported by the powerful publisher Henry R. Luce and by Republican senators Karl Mundt of South Dakota and William S. Knowland of California, protested that under Truman's newly appointed secretary of state, Dean Acheson, the State Department was responsible for the "loss of China." The China lobby's influence led to the United States' refusal to recognize what it called "Red China"; instead, the nation recognized the exiled Nationalist government in Taiwan. The United States also used its influence to block China's admission to the United Nations. For almost twenty years U.S. administrations treated mainland China, the world's most populous country, as a diplomatic nonentity.

The Korean War Begins.   In Korea as in China, cold-war confrontation grew out of World War II roots. Both the United States and the Soviet Union had troops in Korea at the end of the war and had agreed to occupy the nation jointly. They divided Korea into competing spheres of influence at the thirty-eighth parallel. The Soviets supported a Communist government, led by Kim Il Sung, in North Korea; the United States backed a long-time Korean nationalist, Syngman Rhee, in South Korea. Soon sporadic fighting broke out along the thirty-eighth parallel, and a civil war began.

The Korean War

These men of the Second Infantry Battalion, shown here in Korea in 1950, helped pave the way for the formal integration of all U.S. Army units by 1954. The Korean War marked the first time in the nation's history that all troops served in racially integrated combat units.
National Archives.

On June 25, 1950, the North Koreans launched a surprise attack across the thirty-eighth parallel (Map 27.2). The attack was part of an initiative for Korean reunification that came from Kim Il Sung, with Stalin's support (although the extent of Soviet involvement was unknown at the time). Soviet and North Korean leaders may have expected Truman to ignore this armed challenge, but the president felt that the United States must take a firm stance against the spread of communism. "There's no telling what they'll do if we don't put up a fight now," he said. Truman immediately asked the U.N. Security Council to authorize a "**police action**" against the invaders. Because the Soviet Union was temporarily boycotting the Security Council to protest the exclusion of the People's Republic of China from the United Nations, it could not veto Truman's request. Three days after the Security Council voted to send what was called a "peacekeeping force," Truman ordered U.S. troops to Korea.

Fighting the War. Though fourteen other non-Communist nations sent troops, the rapidly assembled United Nations army in Korea was overwhelmingly American. At the request of the Security Council, President Truman named General Douglas MacArthur

to head the U.N. forces. At first the North Koreans held an overwhelming advantage, controlling practically the entire peninsula except for the area around Pusan. But on September 15, 1950, MacArthur launched a surprise amphibious attack at Inchon, far behind the North Korean front line, while U.N. forces staged a breakout from Pusan. Within two weeks the U.N. forces controlled Seoul, the South Korean capital, and almost all the territory up to the thirty-eighth parallel.

Encouraged by this success MacArthur sought the authority to lead his forces across the thirty-eighth parallel and into North Korea. Truman's initial plan had been to restore the 1945 border, but he managed to win U.N. support for the broader goal of creating "a unified, independent and democratic Korea." Though the Chinese government in Beijing warned repeatedly that such a move would provoke retaliation, American officials ignored the warnings. MacArthur's troops crossed the thirty-eighth parallel on October 9, reaching the Chinese border at the Yalu River by the end of the month. Just after Thanksgiving a massive Chinese counterattack of almost 300,000 troops forced MacArthur to retreat south of the thirty-eighth parallel. Then on January 4, 1951, Communist troops reoccupied Seoul.

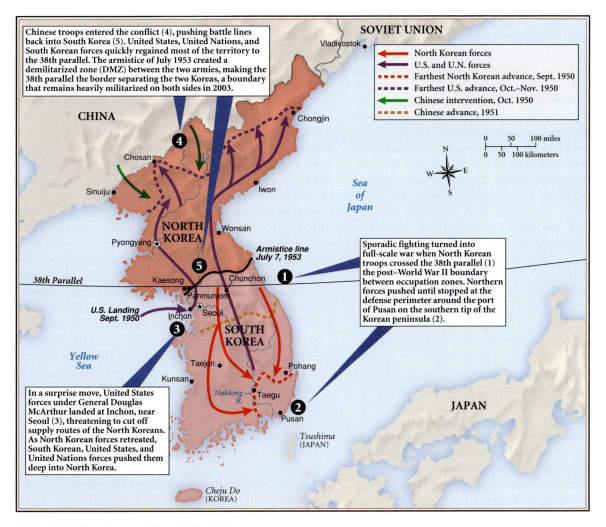

Chinese troops entered the conflict (4), pushing battle lines back into South Korea (5). United States, United Nations, and South Korean forces quickly regained most of the territory to the 38th parallel. The armistice of July 1953 created a demilitarized zone (DMZ) between the two armies, making the 38th parallel the border separating the two Koreas, a boundary that remains heavily militarized on both sides in 2003.

Legend:
North Korean forces
U.S. and U.N. forces
Farthest North Korean advance, Sept. 1950
Farthest U.S. advance, Oct.–Nov. 1950
Chinese intervention, Oct. 1950
Chinese advance, 1951

Sporadic fighting turned into full-scale war when North Korean troops crossed the 38th parallel (1) the post–World War II boundary between occupation zones. Northern forces pushed until stopped at the defense perimeter around the port of Pusan on the southern tip of the Korean peninsula (2).

In a surprise move, United States forces under General Douglas MacArthur landed at Inchon, near Seoul (3), threatening to cut off supply routes of the North Koreans. As North Korean forces retreated, South Korean, United States, and United Nations forces pushed them deep into North Korea.

MAP 27.2 The Korean War, 1950–1953

The Korean War, which the United Nations officially deemed a "police action," lasted three years and cost the lives of over 36,000 U.S. troops. South and North Korean deaths were estimated at over 900,000. Although hostilities ceased in 1953, the U.S. military and the North Korean army faced each other across the Demilitarized Zone for the next fifty years.

Two months later American forces and their Allies counterattacked, regained Seoul, and pushed back to the thirty-eighth parallel. Then stalemate set in. Public support in the United States had dropped after Chinese intervention increased the likelihood of a long war. A poll revealed in early January 1951 that 66 percent of Americans thought the United States should withdraw; 49 percent felt intervening in the war had been a mistake. Given domestic opinions and the stalemate in Korea, Truman and his advisors decided to work for a negotiated peace. They did not want to tie down large numbers of U.S. troops in Asia, far from what were considered more strategically important trouble spots in Europe and the Middle East.

The Fate of Douglas MacArthur. MacArthur disagreed. Headstrong, arrogant, and brilliant, the general

fervently believed that the nation's future lay in Asia, not Europe. Disregarding Truman's instructions MacArthur traveled to Taiwan and urged the Nationalists to join in an attack on mainland China. He pleaded for permission to use the atomic bomb against China. In an inflammatory letter to the House minority leader, Republican Joseph J. Martin of Massachusetts, he denounced the Korean stalemate. "We must win," MacArthur declared. "There is no substitute for victory."

Martin released MacArthur's letter on April 6, 1951, as part of a concerted Republican campaign to challenge Truman's conduct of the war. The strategy backfired. On April 11 Truman relieved MacArthur of his command in Korea and Japan, accusing him of insubordination—a decision the Joint Chiefs of Staff supported. Truman's decision was nonetheless highly unpopular. But when the shouting subsided, Truman had the last word. After failing to win the Republican presidential nomination in 1952, MacArthur faded from public view.

The war dragged on for more than two years after MacArthur's dismissal. Truce talks began in Korea in July 1951, but a final armistice was not signed until July 1953. Approximately 45 percent of American casualties were sustained during this period. The final settlement left Korea divided very near the original border at the thirty-eighth parallel, with a demilitarized zone between the two countries. North Korea remained firmly allied with the Soviet Union; South Korea signed a mutual defense treaty with the United States in 1954.

The Impact of the Korean War. The three-year conflict was costly for the United States: 36,516 American soldiers died, 103,000 were wounded, and military expenditures totaled $54 billion. Defense mobilization helped stimulate the American economy but did not foster the patriotic fervor that had characterized World War II. Struggling against heavy snow and subzero cold, American troops in Korea grew to hate the endless fighting that characterized the stalemate. "I'll fight for my country," a corporal from Chicago complained, "but I'm damned if I see why I'm fighting for this hell-hole." When the armistice was signed, there were few public celebrations.

The Korean War had a lasting impact on the conduct of American foreign policy. Truman's decision to commit troops to Korea without congressional approval set a precedent for future undeclared wars. The war also expanded American involvement in Asia, transforming containment into a truly global policy. During and after the war, the United States stationed large numbers of troops in South Korea and increased military aid to French forces fighting Communist insurgents in Indochina (see Chapter 29). Such commitments were costly. Overall defense expenditures grew from $13 billion in 1950, roughly one-third of the federal budget, to $50 billion in 1953, nearly two-thirds of the budget. Although military expenditures dropped briefly after the Korean War, defense spending remained at over $35 billion annually throughout the 1950s. American foreign policy had become more global, more militarized, and more expensive. Even in times of peace, the United States now functioned in a state of permanent mobilization.

Eisenhower and the "New Look" of Foreign Policy

The election of 1952 brought Republican Dwight D. Eisenhower to the White House. Despite his lack of political experience, Eisenhower's military reputation—he had been Supreme Commander of Allied forces in Europe—engendered confidence in his leadership. Although Eisenhower shared many of Truman's and the Democrats' assumptions about the cold war, his administration's policies were distinctive. Eisenhower's "New Look" in foreign policy continued the nation's commitment to containment but sought less expensive ways of implementing the nation's predominance in the cold war struggle against international communism.

One of Eisenhower's first acts as president was to use his negotiating skills to bring an end to the Korean War. As he had pledged in the campaign, Eisenhower visited Korea in December 1952. The final settlement was signed in July 1953, after the parties reached a compromise on the tricky issue of prisoner exchange. With the Korean War concluded, Eisenhower turned his attention to Europe and the Soviet Union. Stalin's death in March 1953 precipitated an intraparty struggle in the Soviet Union, which lasted until 1956, when Nikita S. Khrushchev emerged as Stalin's successor. Although Khrushchev surprised westerners by calling for "**peaceful coexistence**" between Communist and capitalist societies, he made certain that the Soviet Union's Eastern European satellites did not deviate too far from the Soviet path. When nationalists revolted in Hungary in 1956 and moved to take the country out of the Warsaw Pact, Soviet tanks moved rapidly into Budapest—an action the United States could condemn but could not realistically resist. Soviet repression of the Hungarian revolt showed that American policymakers had few, if any, options for rolling back Soviet power in Eastern Europe, short of going to war with the Soviet Union.

Massive Retaliation. Although Eisenhower strongly opposed communism, he hoped to keep the cost of containment at a manageable level. Under his "New Look" defense policy, Eisenhower and Secretary of State John Foster Dulles decided to economize by developing a massive nuclear arsenal as an alternative to more expensive conventional forces. Nuclear weapons delivered "more bang for the buck," explained Defense Secretary Charles E. Wilson. To that end the Eisenhower administration expanded its commitment to the hydrogen bomb, approving extensive atmospheric testing in the South Pacific and in western states such as Nevada, Colorado, and Utah. To improve the nation's defenses against an air attack from the Soviet Union, the administration made a commitment to develop the long-range bombing capabilities of the Strategic Air Command and installed the Distant Early Warning line of radar stations in Alaska and Canada in 1958.

Those measures did little to improve the nation's security, however, as the Soviets matched the United States weapon for weapon in an escalating arms race. The Soviet Union carried out its own atmospheric tests of hydrogen bombs between 1953 and 1958 and developed a fleet of long-range bombers. By 1958 both nations had intercontinental ballistic missiles (ICBMs). When an American nuclear submarine launched an atomic-tipped Polaris missile in 1960, Soviet engineers raced to produce

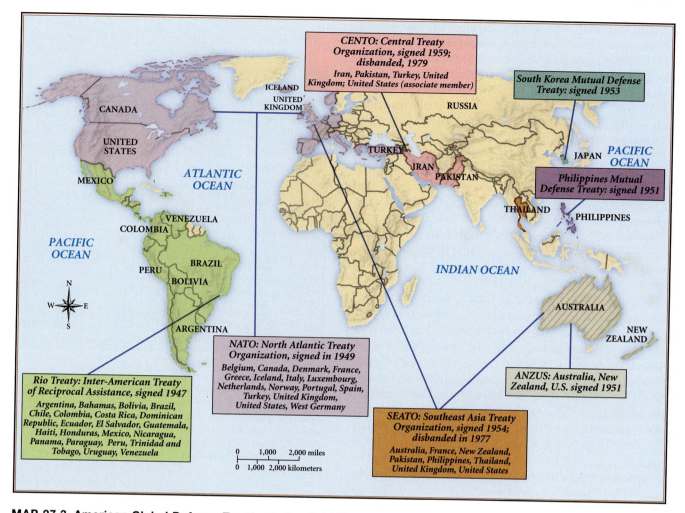

MAP 27.3 American Global Defense Treaties in the Cold War Era

The experience of World War II and the advent of the cold war led to a major shift in American foreign policy—the signing of mutual defense treaties. Dating back to George Washington's call "to steer clear of permanent alliances with any portion of the foreign world," the United States had remained officially neutral in conflicts between other nations. As late as 1919, the U.S. Senate had rejected the principle of "collective security," the centerpiece of the League of Nations established by the Treaty of Versailles that ended World War I. In response to fears of Soviet expansion globally, in the late 1940s and 1950s, the United States pledged to defend much of the non-Communist world. As illustrated by the map, major treaty organizations to which the United States belonged included NATO, SEATO, CENTO, ANZUS, and the Rio Treaty.

an equivalent weapon. While the arms race boosted the military-industrial sectors of both nations, it debilitated their social welfare programs by funneling immense resources into soon-to-be-obsolete weapons systems.

Collective Security. The New Look policy also extended collective security agreements between the United States and its Allies. To complement the NATO alliance in Europe, for example, Secretary of State Dulles orchestrated the creation of the Southeast Asia Treaty Organization (SEATO), which in 1954 linked America and its major European allies with Australia, Pakistan, Thailand, New Zealand, and the Philippines. This extensive system of defense tied the United States to more than forty other countries (Map 27.3).

U.S. policymakers tended to support stable governments, no matter how repressive, as long as they were overtly anti-Communist. Some of America's staunchest Allies—the Philippines, Iran, Cuba, South Vietnam, and Nicaragua—were governed by dictatorships or repressive right-wing regimes that lacked broad-based popular support. In fact, Dulles often resorted to **covert interventions** against governments that were, in his opinion, too closely aligned with communism.

For such tasks he used the newly formed Central Intelligence Agency (CIA), which had moved beyond its original mandate of intelligence gathering into active, albeit covert, involvement in the internal affairs of foreign countries, even to the extent of overthrowing several governments. When Iran's nationalist premier, Muhammad Mossadegh, seized British oil properties in 1953, CIA agents helped the young shah of Iran, Muhammad Reza Pahlavi, depose him. In 1954 the CIA supported a coup in Guatemala against the popularly elected Jacobo Arbenz Guzman, who had expropriated 250,000 uncultivated acres held by the American-owned United Fruit Company and accepted arms from the Communist government of Czechoslovakia. Eisenhower specifically approved those efforts. "Our traditional ideas of international sportsmanship," he wrote privately in 1955, "are scarcely applicable in the morass in which the world now flounders."

The Cold War in the Middle East. American leaders had devised the containment policy in response to Soviet expansion in Eastern Europe, but they soon extended it to the new nations that were emerging in the Third World. Before World War II, nationalism, socialism, and religion had inspired powerful anticolonial movements; in the 1940s and 1950s those forces intensified and spread, especially in the Middle East, Africa, and Asia. Between 1947 and 1962 the British, French, Dutch, and Belgian empires all but disintegrated. Seeking to draw the newly created countries into an American-led world system, U.S. policymakers encouraged the development of stable market economies in those areas. They also sought to further the ideal of national self-determination. But under the growing East-West tensions of the cold war, both the Truman and the Eisenhower administrations often failed to recognize that indigenous nationalist or socialist movements in emerging nations had their own goals and were not necessarily under the control of either local Communists or the Soviet Union.

The Middle East, an oil-rich area that was playing an increasingly central role in the strategic planning of the United States and the Soviet Union, presented one of the most complicated challenges. Zionism, the Jewish nationalist movement, had long encouraged Jews to return to their ancient homeland of Israel (Palestine). After World War II, many Jewish survivors of the Nazi extermination camps had resettled in Palestine, which was still controlled by Britain under a World War I mandate. On November 29, 1947, the U.N. General Assembly voted to partition Palestine into two states, Jewish and Arab—a decision that Egypt, Jordan, and other Arab League states resisted. On May 14, 1948, the British mandate ended, and Zionist leaders proclaimed the state of Israel. President Truman quickly recognized the new state, alienating the Arabs but winning crucial support from Jewish voters in the 1948 election.

Egypt was another site of conflict with the Arab nations, one that reflected the way in which Third World

Future Israelis

In 1945 these survivors of the Buchenwald concentration camp, like many other Jewish survivors of the Holocaust, resettled in Palestine. International outrage over Hitler's effort to exterminate the Jewish people was one of the factors that led the United Nations in 1947 to partition Palestine into two states, Jewish and Arab. The state of Israel was established in 1948.
National Archives.

countries became embroiled in the cold war. When Gamal Abdel Nasser came to power in Egypt in 1954, two years after independence from Britain, he pledged to lead not just his country but the entire Middle East out of its dependent, colonial relationship through a form of pan-Arab socialism. Nasser obtained arms and promises of economic assistance from the Soviet Union, including help in building the Aswan Dam on the Nile, a major water and energy development project. Secretary of State Dulles countered with an offer of American assistance, but Nasser refused to distance himself from the Soviets, declaring Egypt's neutrality in the cold war. Unwilling to accept this stance of nonalignment, Dulles abruptly withdrew his offer in July 1956.

A week later Nasser retaliated against the withdrawal of Western financial aid by seizing and nationalizing the Suez Canal, over which Britain had retained administrative authority and through which three-quarters of Western Europe's oil was transported. Nasser said he would use the tolls from the canal to build the dam himself. After several months of fruitless negotiation, Britain and France, in alliance with Israel, attacked Egypt and retook the canal. Their attack occurred at the same time as the Soviet repression of the Hungarian revolt, placing the United States in the potentially awkward position of denouncing Soviet aggression while tolerating a similar action by its own Allies. Eisenhower and the United Nations forced France and Britain to pull back. Egypt retook the Suez Canal and built the Aswan Dam with Soviet support. In the end the Suez crisis increased Soviet influence in the Third World, intensified anti-Western sentiment in Arab countries, and produced dissension among leading members of the NATO alliance.

The Eisenhower Doctrine. In early 1957, in the aftermath of the Suez crisis, the president persuaded Congress to approve the Eisenhower Doctrine. Addressing concerns over declining British influence in the Middle East, the policy stated that American forces would assist any nation in the region "requiring such aid, against overt armed aggression from any nation controlled by International Communism." Later that year Eisenhower invoked the doctrine when he sent the U.S. Sixth Fleet to the Mediterranean Sea to aid King Hussein of Jordan against a Nasser-backed revolt. A year later he landed 14,000 troops to back up a pro-U.S. government in Lebanon.

The attention that the Eisenhower administration paid to developments in the Middle East in the 1950s demonstrated how the desire for access to steady supplies of oil increasingly affected foreign policy. More broadly, attention to the Middle East confirmed the global scope of American interests. Just as the Korean War had stretched the application of containment from Europe to Asia, the Eisenhower Doctrine revealed U.S. intentions to influence events in the Middle East as well.

The Cold War at Home

As the cold war took shape, Americans had to grapple with a new and often alarming world order. Fears about the menace of Soviet communism pervaded the culture, as did anxieties about the destructive capabilities of nuclear weaponry. These factors would have a powerful impact on domestic politics, especially in the hunt for internal Communist subversives, but other issues, including the conversion to a peacetime economy, the call for black civil rights, and the legacy of the New Deal, also influenced politics on the "home front" of the cold war.

Postwar Domestic Challenges

The public's main fear in 1945—that the depression would return once war production had ended—proved unfounded. Despite a drop in government spending after the war, consumer spending increased; workers had amassed substantial wartime savings and were eager to spend them. The Servicemen's Readjustment Act of 1944, popularly known as the GI Bill, also put money into the economy by providing educational and economic assistance to returning veterans. Despite some temporary dislocations as war production shifted back to civilian production and veterans entered the workforce, unemployment did not soar.

Economic Policy. But the transition was hardly trouble free. The main domestic problem was inflation. Consumers wanted to end wartime restrictions and price rationing, but Truman feared economic chaos if he lifted all controls immediately. In the summer of 1945, he eased industrial controls but retained the wartime Office of Price Administration (OPA). When he disbanded the OPA and lifted almost all the remaining controls in the following year, prices soared, producing an annual inflation rate of 18.2 percent. Rising prices and persistent shortages of food and household goods irritated consumers.

With the Employment Act of 1946, the federal government began developing mechanisms to pursue a more coherent economic policy. The legislation introduced federal fiscal planning on a permanent basis—not just in times of economic crisis—to achieve full employment. Besides supporting the Keynesian notion of government spending to spur economic growth, the act promoted the use of tax policy as a tool for managing the economy, using tax cuts to spur economic growth and tax increases to slow inflation. Yet the legislation was weak. It merely advocated rather than mandated such planning measures and gave the new three-member Council of Economic Advisors only an advisory role. It also failed to establish clear economic priorities, such as the proper relationship between the commitment to full employment and the need for a balanced budget. Nevertheless, the Employment Act of 1946 was an important milestone in establishing federal responsibility for the performance of the economy.

Postwar Strikes. The rapidly rising cost of living prompted workers' demands for higher wages. Under government-sanctioned agreements the labor movement held the line on salary increases during the war. But after the war ended, union leaders expressed frustration. Corporate profits had doubled while real wages had declined as a result of inflation and the loss of overtime pay. Determined to make up for their war-induced sacrifices, workers mounted crippling strikes in the automobile, steel, and coal industries. General strikes effectively closed down business in more than a half dozen cities in 1946. By the end of that year, 5 million workers had idled factories and mines for a total of 107,476,000 workdays.

Truman responded dramatically. In the face of a devastating railway strike, he used his executive authority to place the nation's railroad system under federal control and asked Congress for the power to draft striking workers into the army—a move that infuriated labor leaders but pressured strikers to go back to work. Three days later he seized control of the nation's coal mines to end a strike by the United Mine Workers. Such actions won Truman support from many Americans but outraged organized labor, an important partner in the Democratic coalition.

The Taft-Hartley Act. These domestic upheavals did not bode well for the Democrats at the polls. In 1946 the Republicans gained control of both houses of Congress and set about undoing New Deal social welfare measures, especially targeting labor legislation. In 1947 Congress passed the Taft-Hartley Act, a rollback of several provisions of the 1935 National Labor Relations Act. Unions especially disliked Section 14b of Taft-Hartley, which outlawed the closed shop and allowed states to pass "right-to-work" laws that further limited unions' operations. The act also restricted unions' political power by prohibiting use of their dues for political activity and allowed the president to declare an eighty-day cooling-off period in strikes that had a national impact. Truman issued a ringing veto of the Taft-Hartley bill in June 1947, calling it "bad for labor, bad for management, and bad for the country." Congress easily overrode the veto, but Truman's actions countered some of workers' hostility to his earlier antistrike activity and kept labor in the Democratic fold.

The 1948 Election. Most observers believed that Truman faced an impossible task in the presidential campaign of 1948. The Republicans were united, and with Thomas E. Dewey, the politically moderate governor of New York, as their candidate once again, they had a good chance of attracting traditional Democratic voters. To increase their appeal in the West, the Republicans nominated Earl Warren, governor of California, for vice president. In their platform they promised to continue most New Deal reforms and to support a bipartisan foreign policy.

Truman, in contrast, led a party in disarray. Both the left and the right wings of the Democratic Party split off and nominated their own candidates. Henry A. Wallace, a former New Deal liberal whom Truman had fired as secretary of commerce in 1946 because he was perceived as too "soft" on communism, ran as the candidate of the new Progressive Party. Wallace advocated increased government intervention in the economy, more power for labor unions, and cooperation with the Soviet Union. The right-wing challenge came from the South. At the Democratic national convention, northern liberals such as Mayor Hubert H. Humphrey of Minneapolis had pushed through a platform calling for the repeal of the Taft-Hartley Act and increased federal commitment to civil rights. Southern Democrats, unwilling to tolerate federal interference in race

relations, bolted the convention and created the States' Rights Party, popularly known as the "Dixiecrats." They nominated Governor J. Strom Thurmond of South Carolina for president.

Truman responded to these challenges with one of the most effective presidential campaigns ever waged. He launched a strenuous cross-country speaking tour in which he hammered away at the Republicans' support for the antilabor Taft-Hartley Act. He also criticized Republicans for opposing legislation for housing, medical insurance, and civil rights. By combining these issues with attacks on the Soviet menace abroad, Truman began to salvage his troubled campaign. At his rallies enthusiastic listeners shouted, "Give 'em hell, Harry!"

Truman won a remarkable victory, receiving 49.6 percent of the vote to Dewey's 45.1 percent (Map 27.4). The Democrats also regained control of both houses of Congress. Strom Thurmond carried only four southern states, and Henry Wallace failed to win any electoral votes. Truman retained the support of organized labor. Jewish and Catholic voters in the big cities and black voters in the North offset his losses to the Dixiecrats. Most importantly, Truman appealed effectively to people like himself from the farms, towns, and small cities in the nation's heartland.

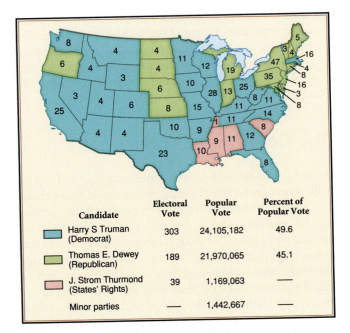

Candidate	Electoral Vote	Popular Vote	Percent of Popular Vote
Harry S Truman (Democrat)	303	24,105,182	49.6
Thomas E. Dewey (Republican)	189	21,970,065	45.1
J. Strom Thurmond (States' Rights)	39	1,169,063	—
Minor parties	—	1,442,667	—

MAP 27.4 Presidential Election of 1948
Political advisor Clark Clifford planned Truman's electoral strategy in 1948, arguing that the president should concentrate his campaign in urban areas where the Democrats had their greatest strength. In an election with a low turnout, Truman held onto enough support from the Roosevelt coalition of blacks, union members, and farmers to defeat Dewey by more than 2 million votes. In December 2002, Mississippi senator Trent Lott's comments suggesting approval of Strom Thurmond's support for segregation sparked a political uproar and cost Lott the position of majority leader in the 108th Congress.

Fair Deal Liberalism

Shortly after becoming president Truman proposed to Congress a twenty-one-point plan for expanded federal programs based on individual "rights," including the right to a "useful and remunerative" job, controls over monopolies, good housing, "adequate medical care," "protection from the economic fears of old age," and a "good education." Later Truman added support for civil rights and in his 1949 State of the Union address christened his program the Fair Deal. Although to some extent the Fair Deal represented an extension of the New Deal's liberalism—with faith in the positive influence of government and the use of federal power to ensure public welfare—it also took some new directions. Its attention to civil rights reflected the growing importance of African Americans to the Democratic Party's coalition of urban voters. And the desire to extend a high standard of living and other benefits of capitalism to an ever-greater number of citizens reflected a new liberal vision of the role of the state. Economically, the liberals of Truman's era were more moderate than the Progressive Era and New Deal reformers who had proposed extensive federal regulation of corporations and intrusive planning of the economy. They believed that the essential role of the federal government was to manage the economy indirectly through fiscal policy. Drawing on the Keynesian notion of using government spending to spur economic growth, they expected that welfare

Truman Triumphant

In one of the most famous photographs in American political history, Harry S Truman gloats over an inaccurate headline in the Chicago Daily Tribune. *Pollsters had predicted an overwhelming victory for Thomas E. Dewey. Their primitive techniques, however, did not reflect the dramatic surge in support for Truman during the last days of the campaign.*
Corbis-Bettmann.

programs not only would provide a safety net for disadvantaged citizens but also would maintain consumer purchasing power, keeping the economy healthy.

Truman's agenda met with a generally hostile Congress, despite the Democratic majority. The same conservative coalition that had blocked Roosevelt's initiatives in his second term and dismantled or cut popular New Deal programs during wartime continued to fight against Truman's proposals. Only parts of the Fair Deal won adoption: the minimum wage was raised; the Social Security program was extended to cover 10 million new workers; and Social Security benefits were increased by 75 percent. The National Housing Act of 1949 called for the construction of 810,000 units of low-income housing, but only half that number were actually built.

Interest groups successfully opposed other key items in the Fair Deal. The American Medical Association (AMA) quashed a labor-backed movement for national health insurance by denouncing it as the first step toward "**socialized medicine**." Catholics successfully opposed aid to education because it did not include subsidies for parochial schools. Trade associations, the National Association of Manufacturers, and other business groups also actively opposed what they called "creeping socialism." Though most corporate leaders recognized that some state involvement in the economy was necessary and even beneficial to business interests, they felt the Fair Deal went too far. As a lobbyist for the National Association of Real Estate Boards explained, "In our country we prefer that government activity shall take the form of assisting and aiding private business rather than undertake great public projects of a governmental character." Through extensive lobbying and public relations campaigns, business groups agitated not only to defeat specific pieces of Fair Deal legislation but also to forestall increased taxes, antitrust activity, and other unwanted federal interference in corporate affairs. Their activities helped to block support for enlarged federal responsibilities for economic and social welfare. The outbreak of the Korean War in 1950 also limited the chances of the Fair Deal being passed by diverting national attention and federal funds from domestic affairs. So did the nation's growing paranoia concerning internal subversion, the most dramatic manifestation of the cold war's effect on American life.

The Great Fear

As American relations with the Soviet Union deteriorated, fear of communism at home fueled a widespread campaign of domestic repression. Americans often call this phenomenon "McCarthyism," after Senator Joseph R. McCarthy of Wisconsin, the decade's most vocal anti-Communist, but more was involved than the work of just one man. The Great Fear built on the long-standing distrust of radicals and foreigners that had exploded in the Red Scare after World War I. Worsening cold war tensions intersected with both those deep-seated anxieties and partisan politics to spawn an obsessive concern with internal subversion. Ultimately, few Communists were found in positions of power; far more Americans became innocent victims of false accusations and innuendos.

HUAC. The roots of postwar anticommunism dated back to 1938, when Congressman Martin Dies of Texas and other conservatives launched the House Committee on Un-American Activities (HUAC) to investigate alleged fascist and Communist influence in labor unions and New Deal agencies. HUAC gained heightened visibility after the war, especially after revelations in 1946 of a Soviet spy ring operating in Canada and the United States' accentuated fears of Soviet subversion.

In 1947 HUAC helped spark the "Great Fear" by holding widely publicized hearings on alleged Communist infiltration in the film industry. A group of writers and directors, soon dubbed the Hollywood Ten, went to jail for contempt of Congress when they cited the First Amendment while refusing to testify about their past associations. Hundreds of other actors, directors, and writers whose names had been mentioned in the HUAC investigation or whose associates and friends the committee had labeled as "reds" were unable to get work, victims of an unacknowledged but very real **blacklist** honored by industry executives. HUAC also investigated playwrights, authors, university professors, labor activists, organizations, and government officials thought to be "left wing."

Truman's Loyalty Program. Although HUAC bore much of the responsibility for spawning the witch hunt, its effects spread far beyond the congressional committee. In March 1947 President Truman issued an executive order initiating a comprehensive investigation into the loyalty of federal employees. Following Washington's lead many state and local governments, universities, political organizations, churches, and businesses undertook their own antisubversion campaigns, including the requirement that employees take loyalty oaths. In the labor movement, which Communists had been active in organizing in the 1930s, charges that Soviet-led Communists were taking over American unions led to a purge of Communist members. Civil rights organizations such as the NAACP and the National Urban League also expelled Communists or "fellow travelers"—words used to describe people viewed as left-wing—or as Communist sympathizers who were not members of the Communist Party. Thus the Great Fear was particularly devastating to the political left; accusations of guilt by association affected progressives of all stripes.

The anti-Communist crusade intensified in 1948 when HUAC began an investigation of Alger Hiss, a former New Dealer and a State Department official who had accompanied Franklin Roosevelt to Yalta. A former Communist, Whittaker Chambers, claimed that Hiss was a member of a secret Communist cell operating within the government and had passed him classified documents in the 1930s. Hiss categorically denied the allegations and denied even knowing Chambers. HUAC's investigation was orchestrated by Republican congressman Richard M. Nixon of California. Because the statute of limitations on the crime of which Hiss was accused had expired, he was charged instead with perjury for lying about his Communist affiliations and acquaintance with Chambers. In early 1950 Hiss was found guilty and sentenced to five years in federal prison. Although recently released evidence from Soviet archives has helped to harden the case against Hiss, the question of his guilt continues to be a contentious one among historians and journalists.

The Rise and Fall of McCarthy. Hiss's conviction fueled the paranoia about a Communist conspiracy in the federal government, contributing to the meteoric rise of Senator Joseph McCarthy of Wisconsin. In February 1950 McCarthy delivered a bombshell during a speech in Wheeling, West Virginia: "I have here in my hand a list of the names of 205 men that were known to the Secretary of State as being members of the Communist Party and who nevertheless are still working and shaping the policy of the State Department." McCarthy later reduced his numbers, first to fifty-seven, then to one "policy risk," and he never released any names or proof, but he had gained the attention he sought. For the next four years, he was the central figure in a virulent campaign of anticommunism. Like other Republicans in the late 1940s, McCarthy leveled accusations of Communist subversion in the government to embarrass President Truman and the Democratic Party. Critics who disagreed with him exposed themselves to charges of being "soft" on communism. Because McCarthy charged that his critics were themselves part of "this conspiracy so immense," few political leaders challenged him. Truman called McCarthy's charges "slander, lies, character assassination" but could do nothing to curb them. When Republican Dwight D. Eisenhower was elected president in 1952, he refrained from publicly challenging his party's most outspoken senator.

Despite McCarthy's failure to identify a single Communist in government, a series of national and international events allowed him to retain credibility. Besides the Hiss case, the sensational 1951 espionage trial of Julius and Ethel Rosenberg fueled McCarthy's allegations. Convicted of passing atomic secrets to the Soviet Union in a highly controversial trial, the Rosenbergs were executed in 1953. (As in the case of Hiss, their convictions continue to be debated; the recent release of declassified documents from a top-secret intelligence

McCarthy's Assault on Civil Liberties

Senator Joseph McCarthy's reckless attacks on alleged Communists in the U.S. government stirred widespread public fears of Soviet subversion in the 1950s. His critics, such as cartoonist Al Hirschfeld, expressed alarm at what they saw as McCarthy's assault on American liberty.

© Al Hirschfeld. Drawing reproduced by special arrangement with The Margo Feiden Galleries, NY.

mission has provided some new evidence of Julius Rosenberg's guilt.) The Korean War, which embroiled the United States in a frustrating fight against communism in a faraway land, also made Americans susceptible to McCarthy's claims. Blaming disloyal individuals rather than complex international factors for the problems of the cold war undoubtedly helped many Americans make sense of a disordered world of nuclear bombs, "police actions," and other world crises that seemed to come with alarming regularity.

In early 1954 McCarthy overreached himself by launching an investigation into possible subversion in the U.S. Army. When the lengthy televised hearings brought McCarthy's smear tactics and leering innuendoes into the nation's living rooms, support for him declined. The end of the Korean War and the death of Stalin in 1953 also undercut public interest in McCarthy's red-baiting campaign. In December 1954 the Senate voted sixty-seven to twenty-two to censure McCarthy for unbecoming conduct. He died from an alcohol-related illness three years later at the age of forty-eight, his name forever attached to a period of political repression of which he was only the most flagrant manifestation (see American Voices, "Mark

Goodson: Red Hunting on the Quiz Shows; or, What's My Party Line?," p. 802).

"Modern Republicanism"

At the height of the Great Fear, Dwight D. Eisenhower became president. Having secured the 1952 Republican nomination, he asked Senator Richard M. Nixon of California to be his running mate. Nixon, young, tirelessly partisan, and with a strong anti-Communist record from his crusade against Alger Hiss, brought an aggressive campaign style as well as regional balance to the Republican ticket. The new administration set the tone for what historians have called "modern Republicanism," an updated party philosophy that emphasized a slowdown, rather than a dismantling, of federal responsibilities. Compared with their predecessors in the 1920s and their successors in the 1980s and 1990s, modern Republicans were more tolerant of government intervention in social and economic affairs, though they did seek to limit the scope of federal action.

The 1952 Election. The Democrats never seriously considered renominating Harry Truman, who by 1952

Mark Goodson

Red Hunting on the Quiz Shows; or, What's My Party Line?

Active in the television industry from its earliest days, Mark Goodson was a highly successful producer whose game shows included What's My Line?, To Tell the Truth, Password, *and* Family Feud. *In this interview Goodson recalls his experience in the industry in the early 1950s when rampant anticommunism plagued the entertainment business.*

I'm not sure when it began, but I believe it was early 1950. At that point I had no connection with the blacklisting that was going on, although I heard about it in the motion picture business and heard rumors about things that had happened on other shows, like *The Aldrich Family.* . . .

Soon afterwards, CBS installed a clearance division. There wasn't any discussion. We would just get the word—"drop that person"—and that was supposed to be it. Whenever I booked a guest or a panelist on *What's My Line?* or *I've Got a Secret*, one of our assistants would phone up and say, "We're going to use so-and-so." We'd either get the okay, or they'd call back and say, "Not clear," or "Sorry, we can't use them." Even advertising agencies—big ones, like Young & Rubicam and BBD&O—had their own clearance departments. They would never come out and say it. They would just write off somebody by saying, "He's a bad actor." You were never supposed to tell the person what it was about;

you'd just unbook them. They never admitted there was a blacklist. It just wasn't done. . . .

Anna Lee was an English actress on a later show of ours called *It's News to Me*. The sponsor was Sanka Coffee, a product of General Foods. The advertising agency was Young & Rubicam. One day, I received a call telling me we had to drop one of our panelists, Anna Lee, immediately. They said she was a radical, that she wrote a column for the *Daily Worker*. They couldn't allow that kind of stuff on the air. They claimed they were getting all kinds of mail. It seemed incongruous to me that this little English girl, someone who seemed very conservative, would be writing for a Communist newspaper. It just didn't sound right.

I took her out to lunch. After a little social conversation, I asked her about her politics. She told me that she wasn't political, except she voted Conservative in England. Her husband was a Republican from Texas.

I went to the agency and said, "You guys are really off your rocker. Anna Lee is nothing close to a liberal." They told me, "Oh, you're right. We checked on that. It's a different Anna Lee who writes for the *Daily Worker*." I remember being relieved and saying, "Well, that's good. You just made a mistake. Now we can forget this." But that wasn't the case. They told me, "We've still got to get rid of her, because the illusion is just as good as the reality. If our client continues to get the mail, no one is going to believe him when he says there's a second Anna Lee." At that point I lost it. I told them their demand was outrageous. They could cancel the show if they wanted to, but I would not drop somebody whose only crime was sharing a name. When I got back to my office, there was a phone call waiting for me. It was from a friend of mine at the agency. He said, "If I were you, I would not lose my temper like that. If you want to argue, do it quietly. After you left, somebody said, 'Is Goodson a pinko?'"

Source: Griffin Fariello, *Red Scare* (New York: Norton, 1995), 320–24.

---

was a thoroughly discredited leader. Lack of popular enthusiasm for the Korean War had dealt the most severe blow to Truman's support, but a series of scandals involving federal officials in bribery, kickback, and influence-peddling schemes also had caused a public outcry about the "mess in Washington." With a certain relief the Democrats turned to Governor Adlai E. Stevenson of Illinois, who enjoyed the support of respected liberals such as Eleanor Roosevelt and of organized labor. To appease southern voters who feared Stevenson's liberal agenda, the Democrats nominated Senator John A. Sparkman of Alabama for vice president.

Throughout the 1952 campaign Stevenson advocated New Deal and Fair Deal policies with an almost literary eloquence. But Eisenhower's artfully unpretentious speeches and "I Like Ike" slogan were more

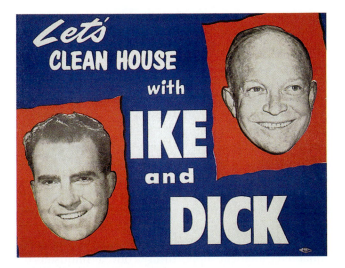

The 1952 Presidential Campaign

The 1952 Republican ticket of Dwight D. Eisenhower and Richard M. Nixon launched an effective attack on the Democratic leadership by stressing the Truman administration's involvement in bribery and influence-peddling scandals and by capitalizing on Truman's failure to end the war in Korea.
Collection of Janice L. and David J. Frent.

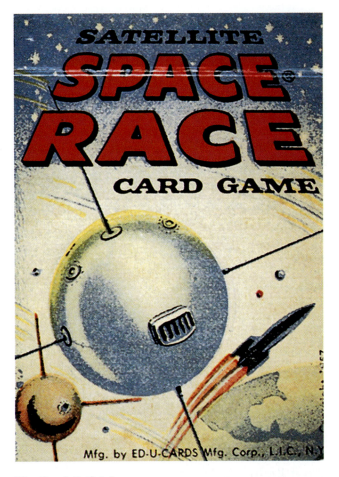

The *Sputnik* Crisis

The Soviet launching of the Sputnik *space satellite in 1957 precipitated a crisis of confidence in American science and education. That sense of crisis was reflected in a 1950s "Space Race" card game, in which those dealt the* Sputnik *card would lose two turns.* The Michael Barson Collection / Past Perfect.

effective with voters. Eager to win the support of the broadest electorate possible, Eisenhower played down specific questions of policy. Instead, he attacked the Democrats with the "K_1C_2" formula—"Korea, Communism, and Corruption."

That November Eisenhower won 55 percent of the popular vote, carrying all the northern and western states and four southern states. Republican candidates for Congress did not fare quite as well. They regained the Senate from the Democrats but took the House of Representatives by a slender margin of only four seats. In 1954 they would lose control of both houses to the Democrats. Even though the enormously popular Eisenhower would easily win reelection over Adlai Stevenson in 1956, the Republicans would remain in the minority in Congress.

The Hidden-Hand Presidency.   The political scientist Fred Greenstein has characterized Eisenhower's style of leadership as the "hidden-hand presidency," pointing out that the president maneuvered deftly behind the scenes while seeming not to concern himself in public with partisan questions. Seeking a middle ground between liberalism and conservatism, Eisenhower did his best to set a quieter national mood, hoping to decrease the need for federal intervention in social and economic issues, while avoiding conservative demands for a complete rollback of the New Deal.

Eisenhower nonetheless presided over new increases in federal activity. When the Soviet Union launched the first satellite, *Sputnik,* in 1957, Eisenhower

supported a U.S. space program to catch up in this new cold war competition. The National Aeronautics and Space Administration (NASA) was founded the following year. Alarmed that the United States was falling behind the Soviets in technological expertise, the president also persuaded Congress to appropriate additional money for college scholarships and for research and development at universities and in industry. After 1954, when the Democrats took over control over Congress, the Eisenhower administration also acceded to legislation promoting social welfare. Federal outlays for veterans' benefits, unemployment compensation, housing, and Social Security were increased, and the minimum wage was raised from 75 cents an hour to $1. The creation of the new Department of Health, Education, and Welfare (HEW) in 1953 consolidated government control of social welfare programs, confirming federal commitments in that area. Congress also passed the Interstate Highway Act of 1956, which authorized $26 billion over a ten-year period for the construction of a nationally integrated highway system. This enormous public works program surpassed anything undertaken during the New Deal.

Thus Republicans, though they resisted the unchecked expansion of the state, did not generally cut back federal power. In social welfare programs and defense expenditures, modern Republicanism signaled an abandonment of the traditional Republican commitment to limited government. When Eisenhower retired from public life in 1961, the federal government had become an even greater presence in everyday life than it had been when he took office. Some of the most controversial federal initiatives occurred in the area of civil rights.

The Emergence of Civil Rights as a National Issue

The civil rights movement was arguably the most important force for change in postwar America, and its accelerating momentum had profound implications for the federal government. The movement built upon a long tradition of African American protest but was also shaped by the climate of the cold war that so pervaded American politics and society.

Civil Rights under Truman

Beginning with World War II, the National Association for the Advancement of Colored People (NAACP) had redoubled its efforts to combat segregation in housing, transportation, and other areas. Black demands for justice continued into the postwar years, spurred by symbolic victories such as Jackie Robinson's breaking through the color line in major league baseball by joining the Brooklyn Dodgers in 1947. African American leaders were cautiously optimistic about extracting support from President Truman. Although capable of using racist language in private, Truman was moderately sympathetic to civil rights on moral grounds, a sympathy that was reinforced not just by cold war considerations but also by the realization that black voters were playing an increasingly large role in the Democratic Party as they migrated from the South, where they were effectively disenfranchised, to northern and western cities.

Lacking a popular mandate on civil rights, Truman turned to executive action. In 1946 he appointed a National Civil Rights Commission. Basing its arguments on moral, economic, and international grounds, its 1947 report called for an expanded federal role in civil rights that foreshadowed much of the civil rights legislation of the 1960s. Truman also ordered the Justice Department to prepare an amicus curiae ("friend of the court") brief in the Supreme Court case of *Shelley v. Kraemer* (1948),

which ruled that states that enforced restrictive covenants maintaining residential segregation by barring home buyers of a certain race or religion violated the Fourteenth Amendment. In this and other briefs, the Justice Department explicitly referred to the way in which "the United States has been embarrassed in the conduct of foreign relations by acts of discrimination taking place in this country." Also in 1948, under pressure from the Committee Against Jim Crow in Military Service organized by World War II's March on Washington's founder, A. Philip Randolph, Truman signed an executive order desegregating the armed forces. His administration also proposed a federal antilynching law, federal protection of voting rights (such as an end to poll taxes), and a permanent federal agency to guarantee equal employment opportunity, but a filibuster by southern conservatives blocked the legislation.

Challenging Segregation

In addition to exerting pressure on white politicians like Truman, civil rights leaders in the early 1950s continued their long-standing battle to challenge segregation in the courts and adopted a new strategy of nonviolent protest. They were determined to overturn the legal segregation of the races that still governed southern society in the early 1950s. In most southern states whites and blacks could not eat in the same rooms at restaurants and luncheonettes or use the same waiting rooms and toilets at bus and train stations. All forms of public transportation were rigidly segregated by custom or by law. Even drinking fountains were labeled "White" and "Colored."

Brown v. Board of Education of Topeka. The first significant victory came in 1954, when the Supreme Court handed down its most far-reaching decision in *Brown v. Board of Education of Topeka*. The NAACP's chief legal counsel, Thurgood Marshall, had argued that the segregated schools mandated by the Board of Education in Topeka, Kansas, were inherently unconstitutional because they stigmatized an entire race, denying black children the "equal protection of the laws" guaranteed by the Fourteenth Amendment. In a unanimous decision announced on May 17, 1954, the Supreme Court, following the lead of Chief Justice Earl Warren (see Chapter 30), agreed with Marshall and overturned the long-standing "separate but equal" doctrine of *Plessy v. Ferguson* (see Chapter 19).

Over the next several years, in response to NAACP suits, the Supreme Court used the *Brown* precedent to overturn segregation at city parks, public beaches, and golf courses; in interstate and intrastate transportation; and in public housing. In the face of these Court decisions, white resistance to integration solidified. In 1956,

Integration at Little Rock, Arkansas

With chants such as "Two-four-six-eight, we ain't gonna integrate," angry crowds taunted Elizabeth Eckford (shown here walking past white students and National Guardsmen) and eight other black students who tried to register at the previously all-white Central High School in Little Rock, Arkansas, on September 4, 1957. The court-ordered integration proceeded only after President Eisenhower reluctantly nationalized the Arkansas National Guard to protect the students. Francis Miller, LIFE Magazine, © Time, Inc.

101 members of Congress signed the Southern Manifesto, denouncing the *Brown* decision as "a clear abuse of judicial power" and encouraging their constituents to defy it. That same year, 500,000 southerners joined White Citizens' Councils dedicated to blocking school integration and other civil rights measures. Some whites revived old tactics of violence and intimidation, swelling the ranks of the Ku Klux Klan to levels not seen since the 1920s.

Eisenhower and Civil Rights. Unlike Harry Truman, Eisenhower showed little interest in civil rights. Though he proved extremely reluctant to intervene in what was widely seen as a state issue, entrenched southern resistance to federal authority eventually forced his hand. In 1957 in response to the *Brown* decision, racial moderates on the Little Rock, Arkansas, school board had designed a desegregation plan. But pressure from Citizens' Councils and others groups led the governor of Arkansas, Orval Faubus, to defy a federal court order to desegregate Little Rock's Central High School. Faubus called out the National Guard to bar nine black students who were attempting to enroll in the all-white school. When scenes of vicious mobs harassing the determined students aired on television,

the crisis rocked the nation and provoked a storm of criticism abroad. President Eisenhower—concerned about the nation's international image and Faubus's defiance of federal authority—reluctantly intervened, sending 1,000 federal troops and 10,000 nationalized members of the Arkansas National Guard to protect the students. Eisenhower thus became the first president since Reconstruction to use federal troops to enforce the rights of blacks.

The Montgomery Bus Boycott. White resistance to the *Brown* decision, as well as Eisenhower's hesitancy to act in Little Rock, showed that court victories were not enough to overturn segregation. In 1955 a single act of defiance gave black leaders an opportunity to implement a new strategy—nonviolent protest. On December 1 Rosa Parks, a seamstress and a member of the NAACP in Montgomery, Alabama, refused to give up her seat on a city bus to a white man. "I felt it was just something I had to do," Parks stated. She was promptly arrested and charged with violating a local segregation ordinance. When the black community in Montgomery met to discuss the proper response, they turned to the Reverend Martin Luther King Jr., who had become the

Martin Luther King in Montgomery

After the arrest of Rosa Parks in December 1955, the black community of Montgomery, Alabama, organized a citywide bus boycott with the help of Dr. Martin Luther King Jr., a local Baptist pastor. Many black women served as grassroots organizers of the boycott, but it was King who rose to prominence as an eloquent and highly respected spokesperson for the emerging civil rights movement in the region.

Dan Weiner / Courtesy, Sandra Weiner.

(SCLC), based in Atlanta. The black church had long been the center of African American social and cultural life. Through the SCLC the church lent its moral and organizational strength, as well as the voices of its most inspirational preachers, to the civil rights movement. Black churchwomen flocked to the movement, transferring the skills they had honed through years of church work to the fight for racial change. Soon the SCLC joined the NAACP as one of the major advocates for racial justice. While the two groups achieved only limited victories in the 1950s, they laid the organizational groundwork for the dynamic civil rights movement that would become one of the defining issues of the 1960s and would open the door to wide-ranging dissent from America's cold war culture of consensus and conformity.

The Civil Rights Movement and the Cold War

One effect of the cold war on civil rights was the way in which the hunt for internal subversives stifled dissent in American culture in the late 1940s and 1950s. Black activists were often "red-baited," branded as "Communist agitators," and harassed in a variety of ways. Paul Robeson, a charismatic actor and singer who had long sympathized with the political left and had made positive statements about the Soviet Union, had his passport revoked in 1950. State Department officials explained that allowing him to "travel abroad . . . would be contrary to the best interests of the United States," because of "his frequent criticism of the treatment of blacks in the United States." When Communists and fellow travelers were ousted from the NAACP and labor unions, other militant voices were silenced. This suppression helped to shape the direction of the civil rights movement in the postwar era, minimizing the attention given to class and economic issues and focusing attention on the legal discrimination and violence African Americans faced in the South.

But if the cold war constrained the postwar civil rights movement, it also engendered support for reforms. The fight against the spread of international communism was in many ways a war of words, and American leaders were well aware that the world press reported on incidents of lynching and other violence as well as on the disenfranchisement and segregation of blacks in the South. Chester Bowles, U.S. ambassador to India, noted in 1952 that "the colored peoples of Asia and Africa, who total two-thirds of the world's population, seldom think about the United States without considering the limitations under which our 13 million Negroes are living." The Soviets capitalized on the issue, repeatedly hammering on the fact that the United States fell far short of realizing its ideals of democracy and equality. Black activists invoked the cold war as a justification for pursuing racial reform, increasingly forcing U.S. presidents and

pastor at a local church the year before. King endorsed a plan by a Montgomery black women's organization to boycott the city's bus system until it was integrated. For the next 381 days, members of a united black community formed carpools or walked to work. The bus company neared bankruptcy, and downtown stores saw their business decline. But not until the Supreme Court ruled in November 1956 that bus segregation was unconstitutional did the city of Montgomery finally relent, prompting one woman boycotter to proclaim, "My feets is tired, but my soul is rested."

The Montgomery bus boycott catapulted King to national prominence. In 1957, with the Reverend Ralph Abernathy and other southern black clergy, King founded the Southern Christian Leadership Conference

their administrations to view black civil rights at home in the context of international politics.

The Impact of the Cold War

The cold war extended to the most distant areas of the globe, but it also had powerful effects on the domestic economy, politics, and cultural values of the United States. It permeated domestic politics, helped to shape the response to the civil rights movement, and created an atmosphere that stifled dissent. Moreover, the implications of the nation's extensive military mobilization, even in times of peace, were far ranging. For the first time in the nation's history, there was a peacetime draft. In the past the armed forces had shrunk to a skeleton volunteer force at the end of each war or foreign engagement. But when World War II ended, the draft was kept in place to meet the military commitments associated with the cold war: occupation forces in defeated Axis countries, missile deployment operations in Europe, and counterinsurgency forces in the Third World.

The postwar expansion of the military produced a dramatic shift in the country's economic priorities, as military spending took up a greater percentage of national income. Between 1900 and 1930, except for the two years that the United States fought in World War I, the country spent less than 1 percent of its GDP for military purposes. When Eisenhower left office in January 1961, the figure was closer to 10 percent, fully half of the federal budget (Figure 27.1). Even though the country was at peace during most of his administration, the

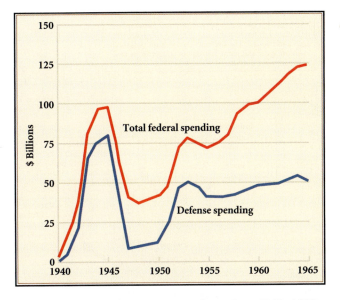

FIGURE 27.1 National Defense Spending, 1940–1965
In 1950 the defense budget was $13 billion, less than a third of total federal outlays. In 1961 defense spending reached $47 billion, fully half of the federal budget and almost 10 percent of the gross domestic product.

economy and the government operated practically on a war footing.

Nuclear Proliferation

One of the most alarming aspects of the nation's militarization was the dangerous cycle of nuclear proliferation

Duck and Cover
The nation's Civil Defense Agency's efforts to alert Americans to the threat of a nuclear attack extended to children in schools, where repeated drills taught them to "duck and cover" as protection against the impact of an atomic blast. Variations of this 1954 scene at Franklin Township School in Quakertown, New Jersey, were repeated all over the nation.
Paul F. Kutta / Courtesy, *Reminiscences* Magazine.

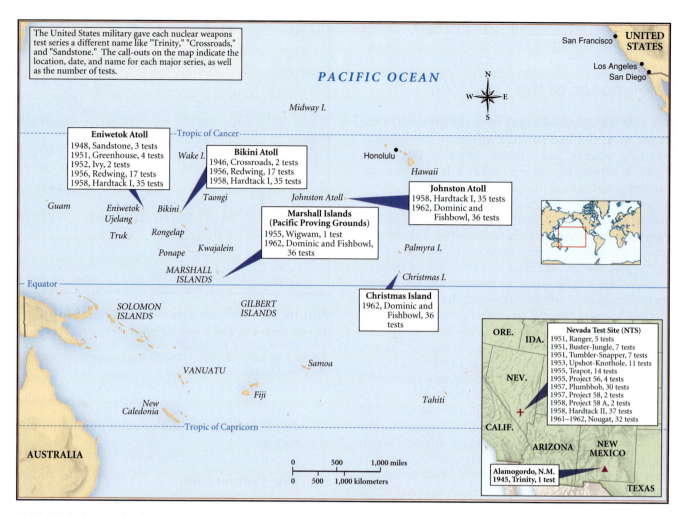

The United States military gave each nuclear weapons test series a different name like "Trinity," "Crossroads," and "Sandstone." The call-outs on the map indicate the location, date, and name for each major series, as well as the number of tests.

PACIFIC OCEAN

San Francisco • **UNITED STATES**

Los Angeles •
San Diego •

Midway I.

Eniwetok Atoll
1948, Sandstone, 3 tests
1951, Greenhouse, 4 tests
1952, Ivy, 2 tests
1956, Redwing, 17 tests
1958, Hardtack I, 35 tests

Tropic of Cancer

Wake I.

Bikini Atoll
1946, Crossroads, 2 tests
1956, Redwing, 17 tests
1958, Hardtack I, 35 tests

Honolulu •

Hawaii

Guam

Taongi

Johnston Atoll

Johnston Atoll
1958, Hardtack I, 35 tests
1962, Dominic and Fishbowl, 36 tests

Eniwetok   Bikini
Ujelang

**Marshall Islands
(Pacific Proving Grounds)**
1955, Wigwam, 1 test
1962, Dominic and Fishbowl, 36 tests

Truk   Rongelap

Palmyra I.

Ponape   Kwajalein

MARSHALL ISLANDS

Christmas I.

Equator

Christmas Island
1962, Dominic and Fishbowl, 36 tests

SOLOMON ISLANDS

GILBERT ISLANDS

ORE.   IDA.

Nevada Test Site (NTS)
1951, Ranger, 5 tests
1951, Buster-Jungle, 7 tests
1951, Tumbler-Snapper, 7 tests
1953, Upshot-Knothole, 11 tests
1955, Teapot, 14 tests
1955, Project 56, 4 tests
1957, Plumbbob, 30 tests
1957, Project 58, 2 tests
1958, Project 58 A, 2 tests
1958, Hardtack II, 37 tests
1961–1962, Nougat, 32 tests

VANUATU   Samoa

NEV.

New Caledonia   Fiji

Tahiti

CALIF.

Tropic of Capricorn

ARIZONA   **NEW MEXICO**

AUSTRALIA

0   500   1,000 miles
0   500   1,000 kilometers

Alamogordo, N.M.
1945, Trinity, 1 test

TEXAS

MAP 27.5 Atmospheric Nuclear Weapons Testing in the Pacific and at Home, 1945–1962

On July 16, 1945, with the detonation of the world's first atomic bomb at the Trinity test site in Alamogordo, New Mexico, the United States began, as a critical part of its growing cold war conflict with the Soviet Union, what would become nearly two decades of nuclear weapons testing in the atmosphere (as opposed to underground explosions). While the U.S. military conducted numerous aboveground tests at the Nevada Test Site, the majority of atmospheric tests were conducted in the Pacific in the area of Bikini, Eniwetok, and Christmas Islands. In response to mounting scientific evidence and a growing worldwide fear of radioactive nuclear "fallout," the United States and the Soviet Union signed a test-ban treaty in 1963 pledging a halt to atmospheric weapons testing, although nations like France and China continued to test above ground. Underground testing by all nations possessing nuclear weapons continued into the 1990s.

For more help analyzing this map, see the ONLINE STUDY GUIDE at bedfordstmartins.com/henretta.

that would outlive the Soviet-American conflict that spawned it. The nuclear arms race affected all Americans by fostering a climate of fear and uncertainty. Bomb shelters and civil defense drills provided a daily reminder of the threat of nuclear war, and atomic research and testing had a devastating impact on human health. In the late 1950s a small but growing number of citizens

became concerned about the effects of radioactive fallout from above-ground bomb tests (Map 27.5). In later years federal investigators documented a host of illnesses, deaths, and birth defects among families of veterans who had worked on weapons tests and among "down-winders"—people who lived near nuclear test sites and weapons facilities (see American Voices, "Isaac Nelson:

Isaac Nelson

Atomic Witness

Isaac Nelson, a naval veteran of World War II, returned to his hometown of Cedar City, Utah, in 1945 and went to work for a nearby hardware company. Like many other residents of southern Utah, he and his wife Oleta lived downwind from the Nevada Test Site, where the U.S. government detonated 126 atomic bombs into the atmosphere between 1951 and 1963.

After 1951 they were going to start the testing in Nevada, and everybody was really excited, and thought maybe we'd get a part to play in it and show our patriotism. We wanted to help out what little we could. My wife and I and a hundred or so residents of Cedar drove out to see the first one. We huddled up, our blankets around us because it was cold, so early in the morning before daylight, and we were chattering like chipmunks, so excited! Pretty soon, why, the whole sky just flared up in an orange-red flash, and it was so brilliant that you could easily see the trees ten miles across the valley, and if you had a newspaper you could have easily read it, it was so bright. . . .

Later on in the day, you'd see these fallout clouds drifting down in Kanarraville, and up through Cedar, and if you'd ever seen one you'd never mistake it because it was definitely different from any rain cloud, kind of a pinkish-tan color strung out all down through the valley there for several miles. They'd float over the city and everyone would go out and ooh and aah just like a bunch of hicks. We was never warned that there was any danger involved in going out and being under these fall-out clouds all the time I lived here. . . .

Along about 1955 a cloud came over Cedar, and my wife and I, the kids and the neighbors stood outside looking at it and talking about it. Later on towards evening, my wife, her skin, her hands, arms, neck, face, legs, anything that was exposed just turned a beet red. . . . She got a severe headache, and nausea, diarrhea, really miserable. We drove out to the hospital, and the doctor said, "Well it looks like sunburn, but then it doesn't." Her headache persisted for several months, and the diarrhea and nausea for a few weeks.

Four weeks after that I was sittin' in the front room reading the paper and she'd gone into the bathroom to wash her hair. All at once she let out the most ungodly scream, and I run in there and there's about half her hair layin' in the washbasin! You can imagine a woman with beautiful, raven-black hair, so black it would glint green in the sunlight just like a raven's wing. . . . She was in a state of panic. . . . After that she kept getting weaker, and listless, and she didn't even have any desire to go out in the garden to work with her flowers. . . . Finally [the doctors] said it looked like a large tumor in her brain, and they operated and removed a tumor about the size of a large orange or softball, but they couldn't get it all out, it was too embedded in the brain tissue. Oleta lived two years or so after that operation. She started going downhill from 1955 and died in 1965 at 41.

Source: Carole Gallagher, *American Ground Zero* (Cambridge, MA: MIT Press, 1993), 133–35.

Atomic Witness," above). The most shocking revelations, however, came to light in 1993, when the Department of Energy released millions of previously classified documents on human radiation experiments conducted in the late 1940s and 1950s under the auspices of the Atomic Energy Commission (AEC) and other federal agencies. Many of the subjects were irradiated without their consent or understanding.

By the late 1950s, public concern over nuclear testing and fallout had become a high-profile issue, and new antinuclear groups such as SANE (the National Committee for a Sane Nuclear Policy) and Physicians for Social Responsibility called for an international test ban.

Eisenhower himself had second thoughts about a nuclear policy based on the premise of annihilating the enemy even if one's own country was destroyed—the aptly named **MAD** (**Mutually Assured Destruction**) policy. He also found spiraling arms expenditures a serious hindrance to balancing the federal budget, one of his chief fiscal goals. Consequently, Eisenhower tried to negotiate an arms-limitation agreement with the Soviet Union. Progress along those lines was cut short, however, when on May 5, 1960, the Soviets shot down an American U-2 spy plane over their territory and captured and imprisoned its pilot, Francis Gary Powers. Eisenhower at first denied that the plane was engaged in

The Computer Revolution

The first modern computers—information-processing machines capable of storing and manipulating data according to specified programs—appeared in the 1940s. During World War II engineers and mathematicians at the University of Pennsylvania developed a general-purpose, programmable electronic calculator called ENIAC (Electronic Numerical Integrator and Computer), which could add 5,000 ten-digit decimal numbers in one second. It stood 8 feet tall, measured 80 feet long, and weighed 30 tons; it used 18,000 vacuum tubes for computations. When it performed complex mathematical computations, one scientist noted, ENIAC sounded "like a roomful of ladies knitting." Although ENIAC lacked a central memory and could not store a program, it was the bridge to the modern computer revolution.

Six computers were under construction by 1947, including UNIVAC (Universal Automatic Computer), the first commercial computer system. To the general public in the 1950s, the word UNIVAC was synonymous with computer. UNIVAC was basically a data-processing system that could be tailored to a customer's needs. In 1951 the U.S. Census Bureau bought the first UNIVAC. Soon CBS-TV signed on, using a UNIVAC to predict the outcome of the 1952 presidential election. At 9 P.M., after only the East Coast polls had closed and with only 7 percent of the votes counted, UNIVAC predicted that Dwight D. Eisenhower would sweep the election with 438 electoral votes. CBS programmers and network executives, who had expected a closer election, got jittery

and altered the program to give Eisenhower a far narrower margin. When the final tally gave him 442 electoral votes, only 4 votes off the original projection, commentator Edward R. Murrow observed, "The trouble with machines is people."

Computers are essentially collections of switches; the programs tell the machine which switches to turn on and off. The puzzle early computer scientists had to solve was how to increase the speed of this basic operation while lowering the cost. The first generation of computers needed vacuum tubes for computation power and used punched cards for writing programs and analyzing data. Computers such as ENIAC were room-size machines, and programming them could take several days because the programmers had to manually set thousands of switches in the on or off position. The vacuum tubes were the weakest part of early computers; the burnout of just a few of them could shut down the entire system. Furthermore, the tubes gave off enormous amounts of heat, necessitating noisy and cumbersome air-conditioning units wherever computers operated. After a critical signal relay stopped one early program, scientists finally located the problem—a dead moth trapped in the apparatus, the origin of the term *debugging*.

The 1948 invention of the transistor revolutionized computers and the whole field of electronics, making the second generation of computers possible. Like vacuum tubes, transistors served as on-off switches, but they did not generate heat, burn out, or consume a lot of energy. They also were inexpensive to manufacture. The invention of integrated circuits in 1959 ushered in the third computer generation, characterized by greater sophistication in miniaturization: the number of transistors that could be installed on a silicon chip increased dramatically, with a corresponding increase in computational power. The fourth computer generation arrived

espionage but later admitted that he had authorized the mission and other secret flights over the Soviet Union. In the midst of the dispute, a proposed summit meeting was canceled, and Eisenhower's last chance to negotiate an arms agreement evaporated.

The Military-Industrial Complex

With its headquarters at the sprawling Pentagon in Arlington, Virginia, the Department of Defense

evolved into a massive bureaucracy that profoundly influenced the postwar economy. Federal money underwrote 90 percent of the cost of research on aviation and space and also subsidized the scientific instruments, automobile, and electronics industries. With the government paying part of the bill, corporations developed products with unprecedented speed. After the Pentagon backed IBM's investment in integrated circuits in the 1960s, these new devices—crucial to the computer revolution (see New Technology, "The

in 1971 with the development of the microprocessor, which placed the entire central processing unit (CPU) of a computer on a single silicon chip (about the size of the letter "O" on this page).

Miniaturization progressed so rapidly that by the mid-1970s a $1 chip provided as much processing power as had the ENIAC of thirty years earlier. Since then, transistor size has continued to shrink, resulting in chips with twice as many transistors roughly every eighteen months. The increased speed and memory of these chips, together with the immense data storage capabili-

ties of the Internet (an online network first established by the Department of Defense in 1969), have made today's compact personal computers incredibly powerful tools. At the same time, scientists have been developing large-scale "supercomputers"—an integrated series of smaller computers that can be used to simulate complex natural and human phenomena such as weather, transportation systems, and genetics. Computers and computer technology have become so much a part of modern life that it is hard to remember how recent are the origins of this technological revolution.

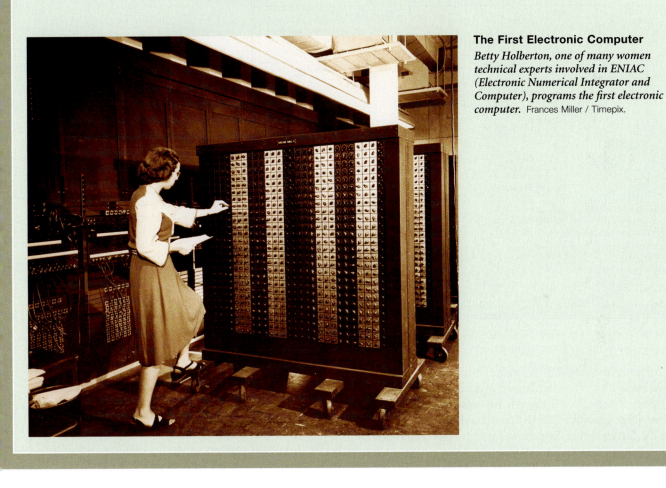

The First Electronic Computer
Betty Holberton, one of many women technical experts involved in ENIAC (Electronic Numerical Integrator and Computer), programs the first electronic computer. Frances Miller / Timepix.

Computer Revolution," above)—were in commercial production within three years. More directly, Pentagon spending created a powerful defense industry. Aircraft companies such as Boeing and Lockheed did so much of their business with the government that they became dependent on Defense Department orders. By the 1960s perhaps as many as one American in seven owed his or her job to the military-industrial complex. In the South and West, where much of the new military

activity was concentrated, dependence on federal defense spending was even greater (Map 27.6). That increased spending put money in the pockets of the millions of people working in defense-related industries, but it also limited the resources available for domestic needs.

In his final address to the nation, Eisenhower warned against the power of what he called the "military-industrial complex," which by then was employing

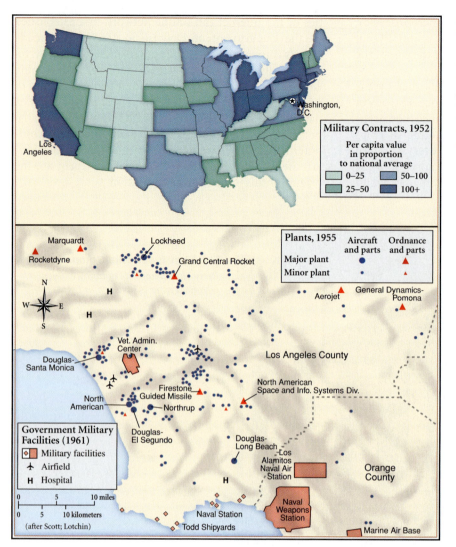

MAP 27.6 The Military-Industrial Complex in Los Angeles

The development and expansion of military facilities and defense contracting during the cold war helped boost the populations and economies of Los Angeles and other Sun Belt cities. Large defense contracts made the economies of California and other states highly dependent on defense expenditures.

3.5 million Americans. Its pervasive influence, he said, "is felt in every city, every statehouse, every office of the federal government." Even though his administration had fostered this growth in the defense establishment to contain the Soviet threat, Eisenhower was gravely concerned about its implications for a democratic people: "We must guard against the acquisition of unwarranted influence, whether sought or unsought, by the military-industrial complex," he warned. "We must never let the weight of this combination endanger our liberties or democratic processes." With those words Dwight Eisenhower showed how well he understood the major transformations that the cold war had brought to American life.

FOR FURTHER EXPLORATION

▶ For definitions of key terms boldfaced in this chapter, see the glossary at the end of the book.

▶ To assess your mastery of the material covered in this chapter, see the Online Study Guide at **bedfordstmartins.com/henretta**.

▶ For suggested references, including Web sites, see page SR-29 at the end of the book.

▶ For map resources and primary documents, see **bedfordstmartins.com/henretta**.

S U M M A R Y

Emerging from World War II as the world's most powerful nation, the United States soon became embroiled in a conflict with the Soviet Union over Eastern Europe. Twice a victim of German aggression, the Soviet Union used its occupation forces to establish a buffer zone of friendly governments in the region. The Truman administration set out to contain Communist influence and to support non-Communist governments that shared America's commitment to a free-market system. Originally intended to curb the Communist threat in Europe through economic and political aid, containment soon became a policy of military aid against Communist and left-wing movements around the world.

Tension over communism abroad fostered a period of domestic repression and fear at home. The government, unions, schools, and other organizations instituted loyalty oaths as a requirement for employment; media organizations blacklisted suspected Communists; and congressional committees conducted sensationalized public investigations of alleged Communist subversion. Red-hunting activities peaked during the anti-Communist crusade of Senator Joseph McCarthy in the early 1950s, shattering the lives and careers of many innocent victims.

The cold war also enhanced the power of the presidency and the national security state. The president gained greater latitude in foreign policymaking and increasingly relied on covert operations of the Central Intelligence Agency to maintain friendly governments in the Third World. The national security state required increased defense expenditures, which consumed an ever larger part of the gross national product. Americans now lived in a world where small foreign wars were a constant possibility and fear of a nuclear attack and radioactive fallout was part of daily life.

Under both Democratic and Republican presidents, New Deal reforms were modestly expanded during the postwar era. Harry Truman's Fair Deal proposed a sweeping program of social and economic reform but won only limited legislative victories. The Republican administration of Dwight Eisenhower did not roll back the New Deal and in fact presided over cautious increases in federal power through new initiatives in aerospace, education, and transportation. A growing civil rights movement in the South spurred federal activism on behalf of racial equality and put civil rights back on the national political agenda. Ultimately the civil rights movement would usher in a broader wave of social activism in the 1960s, a development that was rooted in the anxieties as well as the affluence of the cold war era.

T I M E L I N E

1945   Yalta and Potsdam conferences

Harry S Truman succeeds Roosevelt as president

End of World War II

Senate approves U.S. participation in United Nations

1946   George Kennan sends "Long Telegram" outlining containment policy

Baruch Plan for international control of atomic weapons fails

1947   Taft-Hartley Act limits union power

Jackie Robinson becomes first black player in Major League Baseball

House Un-American Activities Committee (HUAC) investigates film industry

Truman Doctrine promises aid to governments resisting communism

Marshall Plan aids economic recovery in Europe

1948   Communist coup in Czechoslovakia

Truman signs executive order desegregating armed forces

State of Israel created

Stalin blockades West Berlin; Berlin airlift begins

1949   North Atlantic Treaty Organization (NATO) founded

Soviet Union detonates atomic bomb

Mao Zedong establishes People's Republic of China

1950– 1953   Korean War

1950   Joseph McCarthy's "list" of Communists in government

NSC-68 calls for permanent mobilization

1952   Dwight D. Eisenhower elected president

1954   Army-McCarthy hearings on army subversion

Brown v. Board of Education of Topeka

1955   Montgomery bus boycott begins

1956   Crises in Hungary and at Suez Canal

Southern Manifesto defies *Brown* decision

Interstate Highway Act

1957   Eisenhower Doctrine commits aid to Middle East

Eisenhower sends U.S. troops to enforce integration of Little Rock Central High School

Southern Christian Leadership Conference founded

Soviet Union launches *Sputnik*

1958   National Aeronautics and Space Administration (NASA) established

CHAPTER 28

The Affluent Society and the Liberal Consensus

1945–1965

The Affluent Society
The Economic Record
The Suburban Explosion
American Life during the Baby Boom

The Other America
Migration to Cities
The Urban Crisis

John F. Kennedy and the Politics of Expectation
The New Politics
Activism Abroad
The New Frontier at Home
New Tactics for the Civil Rights Movement
The Kennedy Assassination

Lyndon B. Johnson and the Great Society
The Momentum for Civil Rights
Enacting the Liberal Agenda
War on Poverty

IN 1959 VICE PRESIDENT RICHARD NIXON TRAVELED to Moscow to open the American National Exhibit, one of several efforts to reduce cold war tensions in the period. While touring the kitchen of a model American home, Nixon and Soviet Premier Nikita Khrushchev got into a heated debate about the relative merits of Soviet and American societies. Instead of discussing rockets, submarines, and missiles, however, they talked dishwashers, toasters, and televisions. In what was quickly dubbed the "kitchen debate," Nixon used the exhibit and its representation of American affluence and mass consumption to assert the superiority of capitalism over communism and inevitable American victory in the cold war.

◀ **The Growing Middle Class**

Postwar affluence resulted in an unprecedented standard of living for the rapidly expanding middle class of the 1950s and 1960s. This 1951 photograph shows DuPont worker Steve Czekalinski and his family amid a year's supply of food. Prior to the 1950s, most families relied on a diet of starches and smoked meats. The newfound prosperity of the growing middle class enabled families like the Czekalinskis to enrich their diets with fresh meats and vegetables and frozen food. The cost to the Czekalinskis in 1951 for a year's supply of food: $1,300.
Alexander Henderson / Hagley Museum and Library.

During the postwar era millions of Americans, enjoying the highest standard of living in the nation's history, pursued the promise of consumer society in the burgeoning suburbs. But affluence was never as widespread as the Moscow exhibit implied. The middle-class suburban lifestyle was beyond the reach of many poor and nonwhite Americans, particularly those in the decaying central cities. Hoping to spread the abundance of a flourishing economy to greater numbers of Americans, the Democratic administrations of the early 1960s pressed for the expansion of New Deal social welfare programs.

815

The administrations of John F. Kennedy and—to a much greater extent—Lyndon B. Johnson tried to use federal power to ensure the public welfare in areas such as health care, education, and civil rights. In the Great Society program—a burst of social legislation in 1964 and 1965 that marked the high tide of postwar liberalism—the Johnson administration attempted to use the fiscal powers of the state to redress the imbalances of the economy without directly challenging capitalism.

Liberal politicians also pursued an activist stance abroad. Continuing and in some cases expanding the cold war policies of Truman and Eisenhower, the Kennedy and Johnson administrations took aggressive action against Communist influence in Europe, the Caribbean, Vietnam (see Chapter 29), and other areas. The growing financial and political costs of that ambitious agenda, however, hampered further progress on the domestic front and revealed ominous cracks in the postwar liberal coalition.

The Affluent Society

By the end of 1945, war-induced prosperity had made the United States the richest country in the world, a pre-eminence that would continue unchallenged for twenty years. U.S. corporations and banking institutions so dominated the world economy that the period has been called the *Pax Americana* (American peace). U.S. military policy and foreign aid, as well as the absence of major economic competitors, were vital factors in extending the global reach of American corporate capitalism, which enjoyed remarkable growth in productivity and profits. American economic leadership abroad translated into affluence at home. As many Americans, especially whites, moved to home ownership in new suburban communities, it was clear that domestic prosperity was benefiting a wider segment of society than anyone would have dreamed possible in the dark days of the Great Depression.

The Economic Record

The predominant thrust of modern corporate life in this period was the consolidation of economic and financial resources by **oligopolies**—a few large producers that controlled the national and, increasingly, the world market. In 1970, for example, the top four American firms produced 91 percent of the motor vehicles sold in the domestic market. Large firms maintained their dominance by diversifying. Combining companies in unrelated industries, these **conglomerates** ensured for themselves protection from instability in any single market, making them more effective international competitors. International Telephone and Telegraph became a diversified conglomerate by acquiring companies in unrelated industries, including Continental Baking, Sheraton Hotels, Avis Rent-a-Car, Levitt and Sons home builders, and Hartford Fire Insurance. This pattern of corporate acquisition developed into a great wave of mergers that peaked in the 1960s.

The development of giant corporations also depended on the penetration of foreign markets. Unlike the Soviet Union, Western Europe, and Japan, America emerged physically unscathed from the war, with its defense industries eager to convert to consumer production. The weakness of the competition enabled American business to enter foreign regions when domestic markets became saturated or when American recessions cut into sales. Soon American companies provided products and services for war-torn European and Asian markets, giving the nation a trade surplus close to $5 billion in 1960.

The Bretton Woods System. American global supremacy rested in part on decisions made at a United Nations economic conference held in Bretton Woods, New Hampshire, in July 1944, which established the U.S. dollar as the capitalist world's principal reserve currency. Two global institutions—the International Bank for Reconstruction and Development (commonly known as the World Bank) and the International Monetary Fund (IMF)—resulted from this meeting. The World Bank provided private loans for the reconstruction of war-torn Europe as well as for the development of Third World countries. The IMF was set up to stabilize the value of currencies, providing a secure and predictable monetary environment for trade. It did this by encouraging fixed exchange rates, which facilitated the free convertibility of currencies to gold or to the currencies of other trading nations; the strong U.S. dollar served as the benchmark. In 1947 multinational trade negotiations resulted in the first General Agreement on Tariffs and Trade (GATT), which led to the establishment of an international body to oversee trade rules and practices.

The World Bank, the IMF, and GATT were the cornerstones of the so-called Bretton Woods system, which guided the world economy after the war. The United States dominated the World Bank and the IMF because it contributed the most capital to them and because the U.S. dollar had a pivotal role in international currency exchange. Thus these independent international organizations worked along lines that favored American-style internationalism over the economic nationalism that was traditional in most other countries. The World Bank, the IMF, and GATT encouraged stable prices, the liberalization of trade barriers and the reduction of tariffs, flexible domestic markets, and free trade based on fixed exchange rates. As long as the U.S. dollar remained the strongest currency, the Bretton Woods system would effectively serve America's global economic interests.

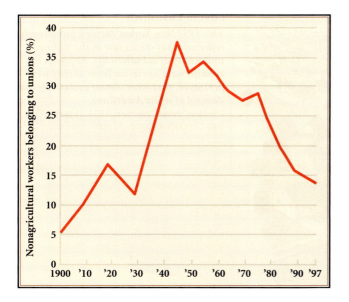

FIGURE 28.1 Labor Union Strength, 1900–1997
Labor unions reached their peak strength immediately after World War II. For the next thirty years, they consistently represented more than a quarter of the nonfarm workforce. After 1975 the influence of labor unions declined dramatically.
Source: AFL-CIO Information Bureau, Washington, DC.

Postwar Prosperity. U.S. economic supremacy abroad helped boost the domestic economy, creating millions of new jobs. One of the fastest-growing groups was salaried office workers, whose numbers increased by 61 percent between 1947 and 1957. Growing corporate bureaucracies and increased access to a college education through the GI Bill helped expand the male white-collar ranks. These "organization men," as sociologist William Whyte called them, were joined by millions of women who moved into clerical work and other lower-paying service-sector occupations. Although the percentage of blue-collar manufacturing jobs declined slightly during this period, the power of organized labor reached an all-time high (Figure 28.1). In 1955 the Congress of Industrial Organizations made a formal alliance with its old adversary, the American Federation of Labor. That merger created a single organization—the AFL-CIO—which represented more than 90 percent of the nation's 17.5 million union members. In exchange for labor peace and stability—that is, fewer strikes—corporate managers often cooperated with unions, agreeing to contracts that gave many workers secure, predictable, and steadily rising incomes, guaranteeing them a share in the new prosperity.

As the income of many American workers grew, consumer spending soared. That spending, combined with federal outlays for defense and domestic programs, seemed to promise a continuously rising standard of living. The gross domestic product (GDP) grew from $213 billion in 1945 to more than $500 billion in 1960 (Figure 28.2). With the inflation rate under 3 percent in

the 1950s, this steady economic growth meant a 25 percent rise in real income between 1946 and 1959. American homeownership rates reflected the rising standard of living: in 1940, 43 percent of American families owned their homes; by 1960, 62 percent owned them. The postwar boom was marred, however, by periodic bouts of recession and unemployment that particularly hurt low-income and nonwhite workers. Moreover, the rising standard of living was not accompanied by a redistribution of income: the top 10 percent of Americans still earned more than the bottom 50 percent. Nevertheless, most Americans had more money to spend than ever before.

The Suburban Explosion

Although Americans had been gravitating toward urban areas throughout the twentieth century, the postwar period was characterized by two new patterns: one was a shift away from older cities in the Northeast and Midwest and toward newer urban centers in the South and West; the other, a mass defection from the cities to the suburbs. Both processes were stimulated by the dramatic growth of a car culture and the federal government's support of housing and highway initiatives.

The Housing Boom. At the end of World War II, many cities were surrounded by pastures and working farms, but just five to ten years later those cities were surrounded by tract housing, factories, and shopping centers. By 1960 more Americans—particularly whites—lived in suburbs than in cities. People flocked to the suburbs in part because they followed the available housing. Few new dwellings had been built during the depression or war years, and the returning veterans and their families faced a critical housing shortage. The difficulty was partly resolved by an innovative Long Island building contractor. Arthur Levitt revolutionized the suburban housing market by applying mass-production techniques to home construction. Levitt's company could build 150 homes per week. In Levittown a basic four-room house, complete with kitchen appliances and an attic that

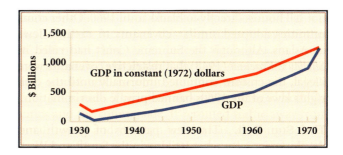

FIGURE 28.2 Gross Domestic Product, 1930–1972
After a sharp dip during the Great Depression, the gross domestic product (GDP) rose steadily in both real and constant dollars in the postwar period.

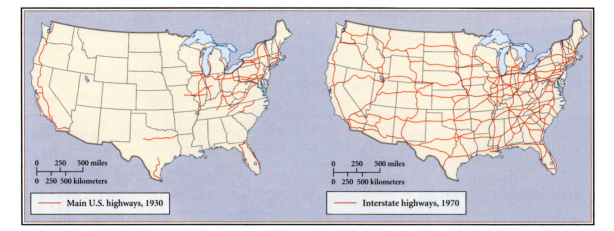

MAP 28.2 Connecting the Nation: The Interstate Highway System, 1930 and 1970

The 1956 Interstate Highway Act paved the way for an extensive network of federal highways throughout the nation. The act pleased American drivers and enhanced their love affair with the automobile, and also benefited the petroleum, construction, trucking, real estate, and tourist industries. The new highway system promoted the nation's economic integration and contributed to the erosion of distinct regional identities within the United States.

Highway construction had far-reaching effects on patterns of consumption and shopping. Instead of taking a train into the city or walking to a corner grocery store, people drove to suburban shopping malls and supermarkets. The first mall appeared in Kansas City in the 1920s, and there were still only eight in 1945; by 1960 the number mushroomed to almost 4,000. When a 110-store complex at Roosevelt Field on suburban Long Island opened in 1956, it was conveniently situated at an expressway exit and had parking for 11,000 cars. Downtown department stores and other retail outlets soon declined, helping to precipitate the decay of American central cities.

At the time few Americans understood that trade-offs were involved in the postwar economic boom. With a strong economic position internationally and government spending to help fuel expansion at home, Americans expected an unending trajectory of progress. Their faith led to complacency—an unwillingness to look beneath the surface for the hidden implications of the forces that were transforming America.

American Life during the Baby Boom

Hula Hoops and poodle skirts, sock hops and rock 'n' roll, and shiny cars and gleaming appliances—all signify the "fifties," a period that really stretched from 1945 through the early 1960s. The postwar years are remembered as a time of affluence and stability, a time when Americans enjoyed an optimistic faith in progress and technology and a serene family-centered culture, reflected in a booming birthrate known as the baby

boom and enshrined in television sitcoms such as *Father Knows Best.* This powerful myth, like many myths, has some truth to it, but there were other sides to the story. Focusing solely on affluence, popular culture, and consumption does not do justice to this complex period of economic and social transformation, which included challenges to the status quo as well as conformity.

Consumer Culture.   The new prosperity of the 1950s was aided by a dramatic increase in consumer credit, which enabled families to stretch their incomes. Between 1946 and 1958 short-term consumer credit rose from $8.4 billion to almost $45 billion. The Diners Club introduced the first credit card in 1950, followed by the American Express card and Bank Americard in 1959. By the 1970s the omnipresent plastic credit card had revolutionized personal and family finances.

Aggressive advertising contributed to the massive increase in consumer spending. In 1951 businesses spent more on advertising ($6.5 billion) than taxpayers did on primary and secondary education ($5 billion). The 1950s gave Americans the Marlboro man; M&Ms that "melt in your mouth, not in your hand"; Wonder Bread to "build strong bodies in twelve ways"; and the "Does she or doesn't she?" Clairol woman.

Consumers had more free time in which to spend their money than ever before. In 1960 the average worker put in a five-day week, with eight paid holidays a year (double the 1946 standard) plus a two-week paid vacation. Americans took to the interstate highway system by the millions, encouraging dramatic growth in motel chains, roadside restaurants, and fast-food eateries.

Hanoch Bartov

Everyone Has a Car

O*ne of Israel's foremost writers and journalists, Hanoch Bartov spent two years in the United States working as a correspondent for the newspaper* Lamerchav. *As a newcomer to Los Angeles in the early 1960s, he was both fascinated and appalled by Americans' love affair with the automobile.*

Our immediate decision to buy a car sprang from healthy instincts. Only later did I learn from bitter experience that in California, death was preferable to living without one. Neither the views from the plane nor the weird excursion that first evening hinted at what I would go through that first week.

Very simple—the nearest supermarket was about half a kilometer south of our apartment, the regional primary school two kilometers east, and my son's kindergarten even farther away. A trip to the post office—an undertaking, to the bank—an ordeal, to work—an impossibility.

Truth be told: the Los Angeles municipality . . . does have public transportation.

Buses go once an hour along the city's boulevards and avenues, gathering all the wretched of the earth, the poor and the needy, the old ladies forbidden by their grandchildren to drive, and other eccentric types. But few people can depend on buses, even should they swear never to deviate from the fixed routes. . . . There are no tramways. No one thought of a subway. Railroads—not now and not in the future.

Why? Because everyone has a car. A man invited me to his house, saying, "We are neighbors, within ten minutes of each other." After walking for an hour and a half

I realized what he meant—"ten minute drive within the speed limit." Simply put, he never thought I might interpret his remark to refer to the walking distance. The moment a baby sees the light of day in Los Angeles, a car is registered in his name in Detroit. . . .

At first perhaps people relished the freedom and independence a car provided. You get in, sit down, and grab the steering wheel, your mobility exceeding that of any other generation. No wonder people refuse to live downtown, where they can hear their neighbors, smell their cooking, and suffer frayed nerves as trains pass by bedroom windows. Instead, they get a piece of the desert, far from town, at half price, drag a water hose, grow grass, flowers, and trees, and build their dream house. . . .

The result? A widely scattered city, its houses far apart, its streets stretched in all directions. Olympic Boulevard from west to east, forty kilometers. Sepulveda Boulevard, from Long Beach in the south to the edge of the desert, forty kilometers. Altogether covering 1,200 square kilometers. As of now.

Why "as of now"? Because greater distances mean more commuting, and more commuting leads to more cars. More cars means problems that push people even farther away from the city, which chases after them.

The urban sprawl is only one side effect. Two, some say three, million cars require an array of services. . . .

. . . Why bother parking, getting out, getting in, getting up and sitting down, when you can simply "drive in"? Mailboxes have their slots facing the road, at the level of the driver's hand. That is how dirty laundry is deposited, electricity and water bills paid. That is how love is made, how children are taken to school. That is how the anniversary wreath is laid on the graves of loved ones. There are drive-in movies. And, yes, we saw it with our own eyes: drive-in churches. Only in death is a man separated from his car and buried alone. . . .

Source: Oscar and Lilian Handlin, eds., *From the Outer World* (Cambridge, MA: Harvard University Press, 1997), 293–96.

(The first McDonald's restaurant opened in 1954 in San Bernardino, California; the Holiday Inn motel chain started in Memphis in 1952.) Among the most popular destinations were state and national parks and Disneyland, which opened in Anaheim, California, in 1955.

Television. Perhaps the most significant hallmark of postwar consumer culture was television. Television's leap

to cultural prominence was swift and overpowering. There were only ten broadcasting stations in the country and a meager 7,000 sets in American homes in 1947. By 1960, 87 percent of American families had at least one television set. Soon television supplanted radio as the chief diffuser of popular culture, its national programming promoting shared interests and tastes and reducing regional and ethnic differences.

A Woman Encounters the Feminine Mystique

The power of the feminine mystique in the 1950s made it difficult for middle-class women who challenged the view that women's proper place was in the home. In this oral history account, "Sylvia" describes her struggle to pursue a career as an ophthalmologist. She began her medical training in nursing, even though she knew when she entered college at Adelphi University that she wanted to become a doctor.

My mother's notion was, "You don't know anything about being a doctor. Become a nurse first and then if you like it, become a doctor." This dean [at Adelphi] said to me, "Well, what do you want to be, a doctor or a nurse?" What came out of my mouth was, "I want to be a nurse." To this day I'm not sure why. In a way I was trying to be practical. We didn't have that much money and I thought I could pay for medical school with a profession. You know, what women earned in those days was pathetic. One of my classmates worked in a bank and made two hundred to three hundred dollars a month. I had no artistic talent and I didn't like teaching, that was the other women's profession. What else was there? And then, I thought, what if I didn't get accepted into medical school?

[She worked for four years as a nurse. Here she describes her first, unsuccessful interview for medical school.] I'd traveled all day to get there, and I was anxious and it was a rigorous interview. At the end of the interview, that man said to me, "You know, I don't know if I could ever recommend accepting a woman here. She'd have to be better than the best man . . . and even then, I'm not sure." This was in 1957. You don't forget things like that.

. . . Of course, all this time my mother was hocking [nagging] me to get married. She told me that the more education I got the harder it would be for me to get married. I did date a little, but since I was always either in school or working, I didn't have much time. One fellow I was dating in medical school, he was a veterinarian and he wanted to get married. I said, but you're going to be moving to Minneapolis, and he said, oh, you can quit and I'll take care of you. I said, "Go."

[After medical school, she interviewed for a residency in ophthalmology.]

We sat on a bench in the middle of the lobby there—I remember it looked like a train station—and he [her professor] said, "Do you plan to get pregnant or married?" I promised him I wouldn't do either. I felt like I was about ten years old. They gave me a year's trial in the research department and after that I could get a residency. Most people there, the men, had a three-year residency. I was only the second woman they'd ever accepted, and I was the only woman out of twenty men.

I had a fellowship, so when I finished with my work I'd have to go over to see how my research projects were coming along. I never, never, goofed off. These guys were watching me all the time and complaining that I wasn't doing my work. It was hard enough to be a first-year resident, where you're the bottom person who gets kicked by everybody. I had no friends. My fellow physicians were constantly telling me I should switch to obstetrics or pediatrics, I should be home having babies, that a man could earn a wonderful living for his family in my place. Finally I was at my wits' end and I called my old ophthalmology professor and told him I didn't know if I could psychologically take this for another two and a half years. He said, "You know, if you give up now I'll never be able to get another woman in there." So I went on.

Source: Brett Harvey, *The Fifties: A Women's Oral History* (New York: Harper, 1993), 154–55.

norms of suburban domesticity, ideals that were out of reach of or irrelevant to many racial minorities, inner-city residents, recent immigrants, rural Americans, and homosexuals. At the height of the postwar period, more than one-third of American women held jobs outside the home (see American Voices, "A Woman Encounters the Feminine Mystique," above). The increase in the number of working women coincided with another change of equal significance—a dramatic rise in the number of older, married middle-class women who took jobs.

How could the society of the 1950s cling so steadfastly to the domestic ideal while an increasing number of wives and mothers worked? Often women justified their jobs as an extension of their family responsibilities, enabling their families to enjoy more of the fruits of the consumer culture. Working women also still bore full responsibility for child care and household management, allowing families and society to avoid facing the implications of their new roles. Thus the reality of women's lives departed significantly from the cultural stereotypes glorified in advertising, sitcoms, and women's magazines.

Youth Culture. Beneath the surface of family togetherness lay other tensions—those between parents and children. Dating back to the 1920s, the emergence of a mass youth culture had its roots in the democratization of education and the increasing purchasing power of teenagers in an age of affluence. Youth, eager to escape the climate of suburban conformity of their parents, had become a distinct new market that advertisers eagerly exploited. In 1956 advertisers projected an adolescent market of $9 billion for items such as transistor radios (introduced in 1952), clothing, and fads such as Hula Hoops (1958).

What really defined this generation's youth culture, however, was its music. Rejecting the rigid boundaries of traditional popular music, teenagers in the 1950s discovered **rock 'n' roll**, an amalgam of white country and western music and the black urban music known as rhythm and blues. The Cleveland disc jockey Alan Freed played a major role in introducing white America to the new African American sound by playing rhythm and blues records on white radio stations beginning in 1954. Young white performers such as Bill Haley, Buddy Holly, and especially Elvis Presley incorporated the new mixture into their own music and capitalized on the new youth market. Between 1953 and 1959 record sales increased from $213 million to $603 million, with 45-rpm rock 'n' roll records as the driving force (see American Lives, "Elvis Presley: Teen Idol of the 1950s," p. 826). The new teen music shocked many white adults, who saw rock 'n' roll as an invitation to race-mixing, sexual promiscuity, and juvenile delinquency.

Cultural Dissenters. The youth rebellion was only one aspect of a broader undercurrent of discontent with the conformist culture of the 1950s. In major cities across the nation, gay men and women, many of whom had served in the military during World War II, fought back against homophobic laws and personal attacks. In Los Angeles homosexual men founded the Mattachine Society, a gay rights organization, in 1951, and in 1954 lesbians established the Daughters of Bilitis. While for the most part the gay subculture remained closeted, this did not stop gay baiting or local police raids on gay bars. And because homosexuals were viewed as emotionally unstable or vulnerable to blackmail, they were assumed to be security risks. As a result of publicity attached to raids, as well as government investigations, many gays lost their jobs, a testament to the perceived threat they represented to mainstream sexual and cultural norms.

Postwar artists, musicians, and writers expressed their alienation from mainstream society through intensely personal, introspective art forms. In New York Jackson Pollock and other painters rejected the social realism of the 1930s for an unconventional style that became known as abstract expressionism. Swirling and splattering paint onto giant canvases, Pollock emphasized self-expression in the act of painting, capturing the chaotic atmosphere of the nuclear age.

A similar trend developed in jazz, as black musicians originated a hard-driving improvisational style known as "bebop." Black jazz musicians found eager fans not only in the African American community but among young white Beats in New York and San Francisco. Disdaining middle-class conformity, corporate capitalism, and suburban materialism, the Beats were a group of writers and poets who were both literary innovators and outspoken social critics. In his poem "Howl" (1956), which became a manifesto of the Beat generation, Allen Ginsberg lamented: "I saw the best minds of my generation destroyed by madness, starving hysterical naked, dragging themselves through the angry negro streets at dawn looking for an angry fix." In works such as Jack Kerouac's novel *On the Road* (1957) the Beats glorified spontaneity, sexual adventurism, drug use, and spirituality. Although they were most often apolitical—their rebellion was strictly cultural—in the 1960s they inspired a new generation of rebels who would champion both political and cultural change.

The Other America

As middle-class whites flocked to the suburbs, a diverse group of poor and working-class migrants, many of them nonwhite, moved into the central cities. With jobs and financial resources flowing to the suburbs, urban newcomers inherited a declining economy and a decaying environment. To those enjoying new prosperity, "the Other America"—as the social critic Michael Harrington called it in 1962—remained largely invisible.

Migration to Cities

Newly arrived immigrants were one of several groups moving into the nation's cities in the postwar era. Although until 1965 U.S. immigration policy followed the restrictive national origins quota system set up in 1924 (see Chapter 23), Congress modified the law during and after World War II. The War Brides Act of 1945, permitting the entry and naturalization of the wives and children of Americans living abroad (mainly servicemen), brought thousands of new immigrants between 1950 and 1965, including some 17,000 Koreans. Three years later the Displaced Persons Act admitted approximately 415,000 European refugees. The repeal of the Chinese Exclusion Act in 1943, in deference to America's wartime alliance with China, and the passage of the

Elvis Presley: Teen Idol of the 1950s

When Elvis Presley performed on *The Ed Sullivan Show* in 1956, the television cameras zoomed in on his head and shoulders. The closeups were inspired not by the young singer's good looks but by a desire to conceal his lower body. After several scandalous TV appearances earlier that season, CBS decided that Presley's sexually suggestive bumping and grinding were unsuitable for family viewing. Despite the censorship, Presley's performance was an unprecedented success, claiming over 80 percent of the television audience. His records sold 10 million copies that year alone and would account for a quarter of RCA's record sales over the next decade. More than any other recording artist of the 1950s, Presley popularized the new hybrid music known as "rock 'n' roll."

Born in East Tupelo, Mississippi, in 1935, Elvis Aron Presley grew up in a white working-class family that keenly felt the hardships of the Great Depression. Like many poor southerners, the Presleys moved frequently in search of work as laborers and mill hands. When Elvis was thirteen, his father found a job at a paint factory in Memphis, and the Presleys settled in one of that city's new public-housing projects.

Elvis's earliest exposure to music came through gospel singing at the Pentecostal First Assembly of God Church, where his uncle was pastor. Later, when his family lived in or adjacent to the black districts of Tupelo and Memphis (as the South's poorest whites often did), Elvis gravitated toward local churches, bars, and clubs, where he gained a lifelong love of blues, gospel, and other black music.

Local radio was an equally powerful force in his musical education. In the late 1940s commercial radio offered a diverse selection of musical programming, catering to the growing audience of rural migrants who had been moving to southern cities since World War II. Although there had always been significant cross-fertilization between white and black musical styles, industry promoters maintained an artificial distinction between "hillbilly" and "race" music. After World War II, those derogatory labels gave way to the more respectable labels "country and western" and "rhythm and blues," but the programming remained rigidly segregated.

Young white southerners like Presley listened to both types of programs. They admired the traditional vocal styles and guitar picking they heard on *The Grand Ole Opry* and other country shows, and they developed a keen appreciation for the blues progressions and driving rhythms of black music. White youngsters' growing fascination with rhythm and blues was not generally acknowledged and was considered somewhat scandalous. But a small group of disc jockeys and record promoters spotted the potential of the new market. As Memphis record producer Sam Phillips once said, "If I could find a white man who had the Negro sound and the Negro feel, I could make a billion dollars."

Phillips found that man in Elvis Presley. In 1953 nineteen-year-old Presley was working as a truck driver and occasionally stopped by Phillips's Sun Studios to make sample recordings for his friends and family. Phillips remembered his unusual vocal style and later asked him to cut a record with a local band. The result was an eclectic mix of musical styles: on one side a white version of a black blues song, "That's All Right," on the other side a black-influenced interpretation of a bluegrass number, "Blue Moon of Kentucky." The record was an overnight local sensation and launched Presley into a national recording career the following year. Over the next decade he produced dozens of hits for RCA, including "Hound Dog," "Heartbreak Hotel," "Jailhouse Rock," and "Blue Suede Shoes."

Presley's success was based not only on his music but also on his stage presence and his relationship with the audience. With his slicked-back hair, long sideburns, and tight pants, Presley cultivated a lower-class "greaser" look that proved immensely popular with teenage fans. His quivering legs, gyrating pelvis, and playful sneer drove young female fans wild; they frequently mobbed the stage, grabbing at his clothes for souvenirs. Many adults, however, condemned such antics, associating them with juvenile delinquency, sexual immorality, and race-mixing. After his first television appearance, one critic described Presley's performance as "suggestive and vulgar, tinged with the kind of animalism that should be

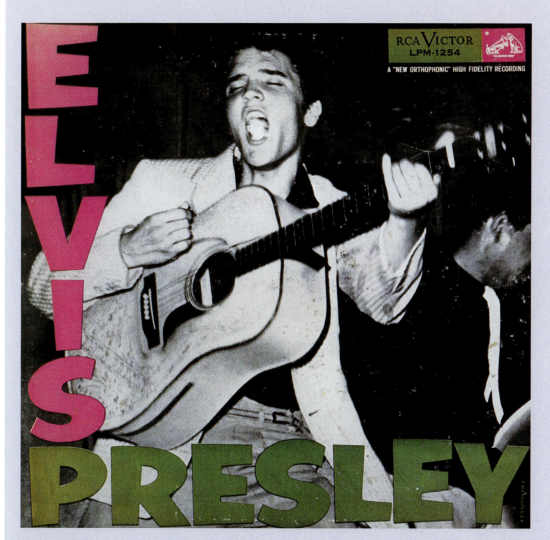

Elvis Presley
The young Elvis Presley, shown here on the cover of his first album in 1956, embodied cultural rebellion against the conservatism and triviality of adult life in the 1950s.
© 1956 BGM Music.

confined to dives and bordellos," and another critic called it "a strip-tease with clothes on." To many adults rock 'n' roll seemed an invitation to rebellion by the younger generation.

African Americans found Presley's success and notoriety somewhat ironic. Chuck Berry and other black musicians had been performing such music for years—but with little commercial success among white audiences. Many of them viewed the appropriation of black rhythm and blues by white artists as out-and-out theft. In the long run, however, the popularity of rock 'n' roll introduced black performers such as Little Richard, Fats Domino, and James Brown to white as well as black audiences.

Presley's musical popularity declined with his induction into the army in 1958 (the long arm of the state reached even the most popular stars). Afterward he headed for Hollywood, acting and singing in dozens of mostly mediocre teen-oriented movies. He enjoyed a comeback starting in 1968, but his career was hampered by personal problems. In 1977 he died of an accidental drug overdose. Since then he has become a cult figure, spawning hundreds of books and articles and a spate of Elvis impersonators. Graceland, his ornate home in Memphis, attracts more visitors per year than does George Washington's estate at Mount Vernon.

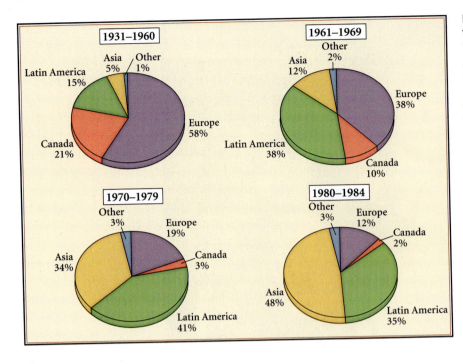

FIGURE 28.4 Legal Immigration to the United States by Region, 1931–1984

As immigration law shifted in the postwar era, the sources of immigration to the United States shifted from Europe to Latin America and Asia.

Source: Robert W. Gardner, Bryant Robie, and Peter C. Smith, "Asian Americans: Growth, Change, and Diversity," *Population Bulletin*, vol. 40, no. 4 (Washington, DC: Population Reference Bureau, 1985), 2.

McCarran-Walter Act in 1952 ended the exclusion of Chinese, Japanese, Korean, and Southeast Asian immigrants. Finally, in recognition of the freeing of the Philippines from American control in 1946, Filipinos received their own quota (Figure 28.4).

Latino Immigration. One of the largest groups of postwar migrants came from Mexico. Nearly 275,000 Mexicans came in the 1950s and almost 444,000 in the 1960s. They moved primarily to western and southwestern cities such as Los Angeles, El Paso, and Phoenix, where they found jobs as migrant workers or in the expanding service sector. Before World War II most Mexican Americans had lived in rural areas and engaged in agricultural work; by 1960 a majority were living in urban areas where they joined more settled communities of service and manufacturing workers.

Part of the stimulus for Mexican immigration was the reinstitution of the bracero program from 1951 to 1964. Originally devised as a means of importing temporary labor during World War II, the program brought 450,000 Mexican workers to the United States at its peak in 1959. But even as the federal government welcomed braceros, it deported those who stayed on illegally. In response to the recession of 1953 to 1954 and the resulting high rate of unemployment throughout the nation, federal authorities deported nearly 4 million Mexicans in a program called "Operation Wetback." The deportations discouraged illegal immigration for a few years, but the level increased again after the bracero program ended.

Another group of Spanish-speaking migrants came from the American-controlled territory of Puerto Rico. Residents of that island had been American citizens since 1917, so their migration was not subject to immigration laws. The inflow from the territory increased dramatically after World War II, when mechanization of the island's sugarcane industry pushed many rural Puerto Ricans off the land. When airlines began to offer cheap direct flights between San Juan and New York City (in the 1940s the fare was about $50, or two weeks' wages), Puerto Ricans—most of whom settled in New York—became this country's first group to immigrate by air.

Cuban refugees constituted the third large group of Spanish-speaking immigrants. In the six years after Communist Fidel Castro's overthrow of the Batista dictatorship in 1959, an estimated 180,000 people fled Cuba for the United States. The Cuban refugee community grew so quickly that it turned Miami into a cosmopolitan, bilingual city almost overnight. Unlike most new immigrants, Miami's Cubans prospered, in large part because they had arrived with more resources.

Internal Migration. Internal migration from rural areas also brought large numbers of people to the cities, especially African Americans, continuing a trend that had begun during World War I (see Chapter 22). Although both whites and blacks left the land, the starkest decline was among black farmers. Their migration was hastened by the transformation of southern agriculture, especially by the introduction of innovations like the mechanical cotton picker, which significantly reduced the demand for farm labor.

Some of the migrants settled in southern cities, where they found industrial jobs. White southerners from Appalachia moved north to "hillbilly" ghettos such as Cincinnati's Over the Rhine neighborhood and Chicago's

Uptown. As many as 3 million blacks headed to Chicago, New York, Washington, Detroit, Los Angeles, and other cities between 1940 and 1960. So pervasive were the migrants that certain sections of Chicago seemed like the Mississippi Delta transplanted. By 1960 about half of the nation's black population was living outside the South, compared with only 23 percent before World War II.

In western cities an influx of Native Americans also contributed to the rise in the nonwhite urban population. Seeking to end federal responsibility for Indian affairs, Congress in 1953 authorized a "termination" program aimed at liquidating the reservation system and integrating Native Americans into mainstream society. The program, which reflected a cold war preoccupation with conformity and assimilation, enjoyed strong support from mining, timber, and agricultural interests that wanted to open reservation lands for private development. The Bureau of Indian Affairs encouraged voluntary relocation to urban areas with a program subsidizing moving costs and establishing relocation centers in San Francisco, Denver, Chicago, and other cities. The relocation program proved problematic, however, as many Native Americans found it difficult to adjust to an urban environment and culture. Although forced termination was halted in 1958, by 1960 some 60,000 Native Americans had moved to the cities. Despite the program's stated goal of assimilation, most Native American migrants settled together in poor urban neighborhoods alongside other nonwhite groups.

The Urban Crisis

American cities thus saw their nonwhite populations swell at the same time that whites were flocking to the suburbs. From 1950 to 1960 the nation's twelve largest cities lost 3.6 million whites and gained 4.5 million nonwhites. As affluent whites left the cities, urban tax revenues shrank, leading to the decay of services and infrastructure, which, coupled with growing racial fears, accelerated white suburban flight in the 1960s.

By the time that blacks, Latinos, and Native Americans moved into the inner cities, urban America was in poor shape. Housing continued to be a crucial problem. City planners, politicians, and real estate developers responded with urban renewal programs, razing blighted city neighborhoods to make way for modern construction projects. Local residents were rarely consulted about whether they wanted their neighborhoods "renewed," and redevelopment programs often produced grim high-rise housing projects that destroyed community bonds and created anonymous open areas that were vulnerable to crime. Between 1949 and 1967 **urban renewal** demolished almost 400,000 buildings and displaced 1.4 million people.

Postwar urban areas were increasingly becoming places of last resort for the nation's poor. Lured to the

Harlem in the Fifties

During and after World War II, thousands of African Americans left the rural South for northern and western cities, expanding the population of Harlem and other black neighborhoods. Ironically, the migrants arrived just as declining employment, deteriorating housing, and shrinking tax revenues were making life more difficult for inner-city residents. Henry Hammond.

cities by the promise of plentiful jobs, migrants found that many of those opportunities had relocated to the suburban fringe, putting steady employment out of reach for those who needed it most. Migrants to the city, especially blacks, also faced racial hostility and institutional barriers to mobility—biased school funding, hiring and promotion decisions, and credit practices. Two separate Americas were emerging: a largely white society in suburbs and peripheral areas and an inner city populated by blacks, Latinos, and other disadvantaged groups.

The stereotypes of boundless affluence and contentment in the 1950s—of "Happy Days"—are thus misleading, for they hide those persons who did not share equally in the American dream—displaced factory workers, destitute old people, female heads of households, blacks and other racial minority groups. In the turbulent decade to come, the contrast between suburban affluence and the "other America," between the lure of the city for the poor and minorities and its grim, segregated reality, and between a heightened emphasis on domesticity and the widening opportunities for women

The Other America
While many celebrated the "affluent society" of the postwar era, critics like Michael Harrington noted that thousands of Americans remained in poverty. Among them were many elderly people who struggled to survive on fixed incomes and without medical insurance. Cincinnati Historical Society.

second Amendment prevented them from doing so. Passed in 1951 by a Republican-controlled Congress to prevent a repetition of Franklin Roosevelt's four-term presidency, the amendment limited future presidents to two full terms. So in 1960 the Republicans turned to Vice President Richard M. Nixon, who campaigned for an updated version of Eisenhower's policies but was hampered by lukewarm support from the popular president.

The Democrats chose Senator John F. Kennedy of Massachusetts, with the Senate majority leader, Lyndon B. Johnson of Texas, as the vice presidential nominee. First elected to Congress in 1946, John Kennedy moved to the Senate in 1952. Ambitious and hard driven, Kennedy launched his campaign in 1960 with a platform calling for civil rights legislation, health care for the elderly, aid to education, urban renewal, expanded military and space programs, and containment of communism abroad.

At forty-three Kennedy was poised to become the youngest man ever elected to the presidency and the nation's first Catholic chief executive. Turning his age into a powerful campaign asset, Kennedy practiced what came to be called the "**new politics**," an approach that emphasized youthful charisma, style, and personality more than issues and platforms. Using the power of the media—particularly television—to reach voters directly, practitioners of the new politics relied on professional media consultants, political pollsters, and mass fund-raising.

A series of four televised debates between the two principal candidates, a major innovation of the 1960 campaign, showed how important television was becoming to political life. Nixon, far less photogenic than

would spawn growing demands for social change that the nation's leaders in the 1960s could not ignore.

John F. Kennedy and the Politics of Expectation

In his 1961 inaugural address President John Fitzgerald Kennedy challenged a "new generation of Americans" to take responsibility for the future: "Ask not what your country can do for you, ask what you can do for your country." Few presidents came to Washington more primed for action than John F. Kennedy. His **New Frontier** program promised to "get America moving again" through vigorous governmental activism at home and abroad. But the legislative achievements of Kennedy's New Frontier, particularly in domestic affairs, were modest.

The New Politics

The Republicans would have been happy to renominate Dwight D. Eisenhower for president, but the Twenty-

The Kennedy Magnetism
John Kennedy, the Democratic candidate for president in 1960, used his youth and personality to attract voters. Here, the Massachusetts senator draws an enthusiastic crowd on a campaign stop in Elgin, Illinois. Wide World Photos, Inc.

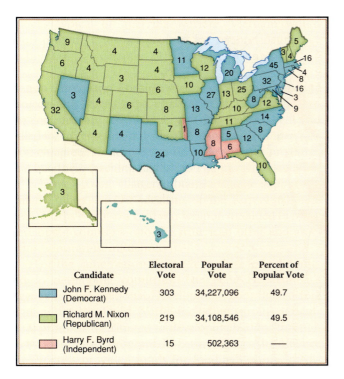

Candidate	Electoral Vote	Popular Vote	Percent of Popular Vote
John F. Kennedy (Democrat)	303	34,227,096	49.7
Richard M. Nixon (Republican)	219	34,108,546	49.5
Harry F. Byrd (Independent)	15	502,363	—

MAP 28.3 Presidential Election of 1960

The Kennedy-Nixon contest was the closest since 1884. Kennedy won twelve states, including Illinois, by less than 2 percent of the two-party vote tally; he lost six others, including California, by a similarly small margin. Fifteen electors cast their votes for the Independent Democrat, Harry F. Byrd. Despite his razor-thin margin of victory, Kennedy won 303 electoral votes, the same number Truman had won in 1948, showing that the electoral college vote can be a misleading indicator of popular support.

Kennedy, looked sallow and unshaven under the intense studio lights. Kennedy, in contrast, looked vigorous, cool, and self-confident on screen. Polls showed that television did sway political perceptions: voters who listened to the first debate on the radio concluded that Nixon had won, but those who viewed it on television judged in Kennedy's favor.

Despite the edge Kennedy enjoyed in the debates, he won only the narrowest of electoral victories, receiving 49.7 percent of the popular vote to Nixon's 49.5 percent (Map 28.3). Kennedy successfully appealed to the diverse elements of the Democratic coalition, attracting large numbers of Catholic and black voters and a significant sector of the middle class; the vice presidential nominee, Lyndon Johnson, brought in southern white Democrats. Yet only 120,000 votes separated the two candidates, and the shift of a few thousand votes in key states such as Illinois (where there were confirmed cases of voting fraud) would have reversed the outcome.

Activism Abroad

Kennedy's greatest priority as president was foreign affairs. A resolute cold warrior, Kennedy took a hard line against Communist expansionism. In contrast to Eisenhower, whose cost-saving New Look program had built up the American nuclear arsenal at the expense of conventional weapons, Kennedy proposed a new policy of "**flexible response**," stating that the nation must be prepared "to deter all wars, general or limited, nuclear or conventional, large or small." Congress quickly granted Kennedy's military requests, and by 1963 the defense budget reached its highest level as a percentage of total federal expenditures in the cold war era, greatly expanding the military-industrial complex.

Flexible response measures were designed to deter direct attacks by the Soviet Union. To prepare for a new kind of warfare, evident in the **wars of national liberation** that had broken out in many developing countries, Kennedy adopted a new military doctrine of **counterinsurgency**. Soon U.S. Army Special Forces, called "Green Berets" for their distinctive headgear, were receiving intensive training in repelling the random, small-scale

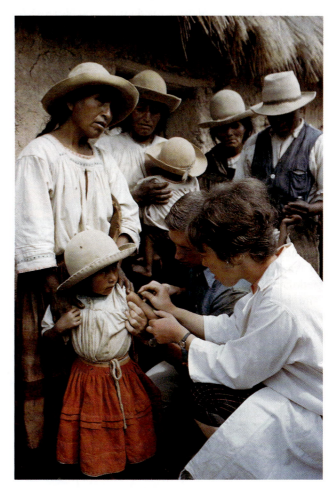

The Peace Corps

The Peace Corps, a New Frontier program initiated in 1961, attracted thousands of idealistic young Americans, including these volunteers who worked in a vaccination program in Bolivia. David S. Boyer / National Geographic Society Image Collection.

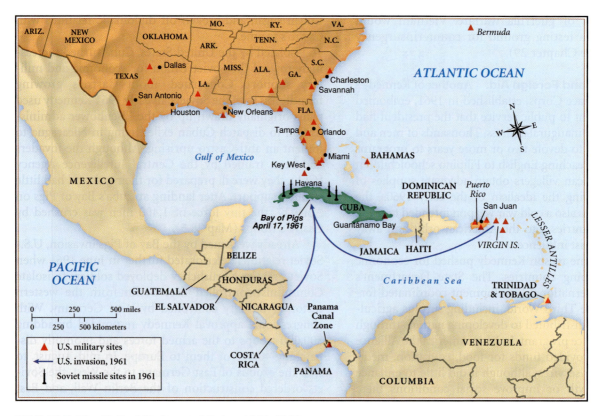

MAP 28.5 The United States and Cuba, 1961–1962
Fidel Castro's takeover in Cuba in 1959 brought cold war tensions to the Caribbean. In 1961 the United States tried unsuccessfully to overthrow Castro's regime by supporting the Bay of Pigs invasion of Cuban exiles launched from Nicaragua and other points in the Caribbean. In 1962 a major confrontation with the Soviet Union occurred over Soviet construction of nuclear missile sites in Cuba. The Soviets removed the missiles after President Kennedy ordered a naval blockade of the island, which lies just 90 miles south of Florida. Despite the fall of the Soviet Union in 1991 and the official end of the cold war, the United States continues to view Cuba, still governed in 2003 by Fidel Castro, as an enemy nation.

relations. In the words of national security advisor Mc-George Bundy, "having come so close to the edge, the leaders of the two governments have since taken care to keep away from the cliff." Kennedy softened his cold war rhetoric and began to strive for peaceful coexistence. Soviet leaders, similarly chastened, were willing to talk. In August 1963 the three nuclear powers—the United States, the Soviet Union, and Great Britain—agreed to ban the testing of nuclear weapons in the atmosphere, in space, and under water. Underground testing, however, was allowed to continue. The new emphasis on peaceful coexistence also led to the establishment of a Washington-Moscow telecommunications "hot line" in 1963 so that leaders could contact each other quickly during potential crises.

But no matter how often American leaders talked about opening channels of communication with the Soviets, the preoccupation with the Soviet military threat to American security remained a cornerstone of U.S. policy. And Soviet leaders did not moderate their concern over the threat that they believed the United States posed to the survival of the Soviet Union. The cold war, and the escalating arms race that accompanied it, would continue for another twenty-five years.

The New Frontier at Home

The expansive vision of presidential leadership that Kennedy and his advisors brought to the White House worked less well at home than it did abroad. Hampered by the lack of a popular mandate in the 1960 election, Kennedy could not mobilize public support for the domestic agenda of the New Frontier. A conservative coalition of southern Democrats and western and midwestern Republicans effectively stalled most liberal initiatives. More important, Kennedy was not nearly as impassioned about domestic reform as he was about foreign policy.

One program that did win both popular and congressional support was increased funding for the National Aeronautics and Space Administration (NASA),

Following the Cuban Missile Crisis

In the tense days of the Cuban missile crisis in October 1962, Americans, fearful that the Soviet Union and the United States were on the verge of war, followed the news intently. In this photograph Cuban refugees in a New York hotel room watched as President Kennedy outlined his plans to impose a quarantine of Cuba and warned of U.S. instant retaliation if the Soviet Union launched an attack from Cuba on any Western Hemisphere nation. Corbis-Bettmann.

whose Mercury space program had begun in 1958. On May 5, 1961, just three months after Kennedy took office, Alan Shepard became the first American in space. (The Soviet cosmonaut Yuri Gagarin became the first person in space when he made a 108-hour flight in April 1961.) The following year, American astronaut John Glenn manned the first space mission to orbit the earth. At the height of American fascination with space flight, Kennedy proposed that the nation commit itself to landing a man on the moon within the decade. To support this mission (accomplished in 1969), Kennedy persuaded Congress to greatly increase NASA's budget.

Kennedy's most striking domestic achievement was his use of modern economic theory to shape government fiscal policy. New Dealers had gradually moved away from the ideal of a balanced budget, turning instead to deliberate deficit spending to stimulate economic growth. In addition to relying on federal spending to create the desired deficit, Kennedy and his advisors proposed a reduction in income taxes. A tax cut, they argued, would put more money in the hands of taxpayers, who would

spend it, thereby creating more jobs. For a time federal expenditures would exceed federal income, but after a year or two the expanding economy would raise American incomes and generate higher tax revenues.

Congress balked at this unorthodox proposal, and the measure failed to pass. But Lyndon Johnson pressed for it after Kennedy's assassination, signing it into law in February 1964. The Kennedy-Johnson tax cut—the Tax Reduction Act (1964)—marked a milestone in the use of fiscal policy to encourage economic growth, an approach that Republicans and other fiscal conservatives would later embrace.

Kennedy's interest in stimulating economic growth did not include a commitment to spending for domestic social needs, although he did not entirely ignore the liberal legislative agenda of Franklin Roosevelt and Harry Truman. Kennedy managed to push through legislation raising the minimum wage and expanding Social Security benefits. But on other issues—federal aid to education, wilderness preservation, federal investment in mass transportation, and medical insurance for the elderly—he ran into determined congressional

The success of SNCC's unorthodox tactics encouraged the Congress of Racial Equality (CORE), an interracial group founded in 1942, to organize a series of **freedom rides** in 1961 on interstate bus lines throughout the South, riding in integrated groups to call attention to the continuing segregation of public transportation. The activists who rode the buses, mostly young and both black and white, were brutally attacked by white mobs in Anniston, Montgomery, and Birmingham, Alabama. Governor John Patterson refused to intervene, claiming, "I cannot guarantee protection for this bunch of rabble rousers."

Although the Kennedy administration generally opposed the freedom riders' activities, films of their beatings and the bus burning shown on the nightly news prompted Attorney General Robert Kennedy to send federal marshals to Alabama to restore order. Faced with Department of Justice intervention against those who defied the Interstate Commerce Commission's prohibition of segregation in interstate vehicles and facilities, most southern communities quietly acceded to the changes. And civil rights activists learned that nonviolent protest could succeed if it provoked vicious white resistance and generated publicity. Only when forced to, it appeared, would the federal authorities act.

Birmingham. This lesson was confirmed in Birmingham, Alabama, when Martin Luther King Jr. and the Reverend Fred Shuttlesworth called for a protest against conditions in what King called "the most segregated city in the United States." In April 1963 thousands of black demonstrators marched downtown to picket Birmingham's department stores. They were met by Eugene ("Bull") Connor, the city's commissioner of public safety, who used snarling dogs, electric cattle prods, and high-pressure fire hoses to break up the crowd. Television cameras captured the scene for the evening news.

President Kennedy, realizing that he could no longer postpone decisive action, decided to step up the federal government's role in civil rights. On June 11, 1963, Kennedy went on television to promise major legislation banning discrimination in public accommodations and empowering the Justice Department to enforce

Racial Violence in Birmingham

When thousands of blacks marched through downtown Birmingham, Alabama, to protest racial segregation in April 1963, they were met with fire hoses and attack dogs unleashed by Police Chief "Bull" Connor. The violence, which was televised on the national evening news, shocked many Americans and helped build sympathy for the civil rights movement among northern whites. Bill Hudson / Wide World Photos, Inc.

The March on Washington

The Reverend Martin Luther King Jr. (1929–1968) was one of the most eloquent advocates of the civil rights movement. For many, his "I have a dream" speech of the 1963 March on Washington was the high point of the event, but the focus on the charismatic King has meant that the importance of other civil rights leaders is frequently overlooked.

Bob Adelman / Magnum Photos, Inc.

desegregation. Black leaders hailed the speech as the "Second Emancipation Proclamation," but for one person Kennedy's speech came too late. That night, Medgar Evers, president of the Mississippi chapter of the NAACP, was shot in the back and killed in his driveway in Jackson. The martyrdom of Evers became a spur to further action.

The March on Washington. To rouse the conscience of the nation and to marshal support for Kennedy's bill, civil rights leaders adopted a tactic that A. Philip Randolph had first suggested in 1941 (see Chapter 26): a massive march on Washington. Martin Luther King Jr. of the SCLC, Roy Wilkins of the NAACP, Whitney Young of the National Urban League, and the black socialist Bayard Rustin were the principal organizers. On August 28, 1963, about 250,000 black and white demonstrators—the largest crowd at any demonstration up to that time—gathered at the Lincoln Memorial. The march culminated in a memorable speech delivered, indeed preached, by King, in the evangelical style of the black church. He ended with an exclamation from an old Negro spiritual: "Free at last! Free at last! Thank God almighty, we are free at last!"

King's eloquence and the sight of blacks and whites marching solemnly together did more than any other event to make the civil rights movement acceptable to white Americans. The March on Washington marked the highpoint of the nonviolent phase of the civil rights movement and confirmed King's position, especially among white liberals, as the leading speaker for the black cause. In 1964 King won the Nobel Peace Prize for his leadership.

The attention focused on King, however, has often obscured the dynamics of the civil rights movement, especially the importance of thousands of activists working within their communities, particularly women in church groups and organizations like SNCC. It also has minimized the role of other leaders, including Bayard Rustin, Roy Wilkins, and Ella Baker, as well as the young activists in SNCC, and those such as John Lewis, who were more radical than King and becoming impatient with the federal government's failure to act decisively to protect black lives and rights. At the march Lewis was pressured to modify the militant tone of the speech he was to give, and the episode foreshadowed the conflicts among black activists over tactics and goals that were to transform the civil rights movement in the next few years (see Chapter 30).

Although the March on Washington had a positive impact on public opinion about King and the civil rights movement, it changed few congressional votes. Southern senators continued to block Kennedy's legislation by threatening a filibuster. Even more troubling was a new outbreak of violence by white extremists who were determined to oppose equality for blacks at all costs. In September a Baptist church in Birmingham was bombed, and four black Sunday school students were killed. The violence shocked the nation and stiffened the resolve of civil rights activists to escalate their demands for change. Two months later President Kennedy was assassinated.

The Kennedy Assassination

Although the first two years of Kennedy's presidency had been plagued by foreign-policy crises and domestic inaction, many political observers believed that by 1963 Kennedy was maturing as a national leader. On November

22, 1963, Kennedy went to Texas. As he and his wife, Jacqueline, rode in an open car past the Texas School Book Depository in Dallas, he was shot through the head and neck by a sniper. Kennedy died a half-hour later. (Whether accused killer Lee Harvey Oswald, a twenty-four-year-old loner who had spent three years in the Soviet Union, was the sole gunman is still a matter of controversy.) Before Air Force One left Dallas to take the president's body back to Washington, a grim-faced Lyndon Johnson was sworn in as president. Kennedy's stunned widow, still wearing her bloodstained pink suit, looked on.

Kennedy's youthful image, the trauma of his assassination, and the collective sense that Americans had been robbed of a promising leader contributed to a powerful mystique. This romantic aura has overshadowed what most historians agree was at best a mixed record. Kennedy exercised bold presidential leadership in foreign affairs, but his initiatives in Cuba and Berlin marked the height of superpower confrontation during the cold war. Moreover, his enthusiasm for fighting communism abroad had no domestic equivalent. Kennedy's proposals for educational aid, medical insurance, and other liberal reforms stalled, and his tax-cut bill languished in Congress until after his death. Perhaps his greatest domestic failure was his reluctance to act boldly on civil rights.

Lyndon B. Johnson and the Great Society

Lyndon Baines Johnson, a seasoned politician who was best at negotiating in the back rooms of power, was no match for the Kennedy style, but less than a year after assuming office, Johnson won the 1964 presidential election in a landslide that far surpassed Kennedy's meager mandate in 1960. Johnson then used his astonishing energy and genius for compromise to bring to fruition many of Kennedy's stalled programs and more than a few of his own. Those legislative accomplishments—Johnson's "Great Society"—fulfilled and in many cases surpassed the New Deal liberal agenda of the 1930s (Table 28.1).

The Momentum for Civil Rights

On assuming the presidency, Lyndon Johnson promptly pushed the passage of civil rights legislation as a memorial to his slain predecessor—an ironic twist in light of Kennedy's lukewarm support for the cause. Johnson's motives were a combination of the political and the personal. As a politician he hoped to maintain the loyalty of African Americans and northern white liberals to the Democratic Party. As an unelected president from the South, he sought to appeal to a broad national audience,

especially on the issue of race. Achieving historic civil rights legislation would not only be an impressive legislative accomplishment, but would, he hoped, place his mark on the presidency.

The Civil Rights Act of 1964. The Civil Rights Act, passed finally in June 1964, was a landmark in the history of American race relations. Its keystone, Title VII, outlawed discrimination in employment on the basis of race, religion, national origin, or sex. Another section barred discrimination in public accommodations. But while the act forced the desegregation of public facilities throughout the South, including many public schools, obstacles to black voting rights remained.

Freedom Summer. Although Johnson's political acumen in pushing the legislation through Congress was crucial, his role should not obscure the importance of the relentless efforts of the civil rights activists themselves. In 1964, with the Civil Rights Act on the brink of passage, black organizations and churches mounted a major civil rights campaign in Mississippi. Known as "Freedom Summer," the effort drew several thousand volunteers from across the country, including many idealistic white college students. Freedom Summer workers established freedom schools, which taught black children traditional subjects as well as their own history; conducted a major voter registration drive; and organized the Mississippi Freedom Democratic Party, a political alternative to the all-white Democratic organization in Mississippi.

Some white southerners reacted swiftly and violently to those efforts. In June James Chaney, a CORE volunteer from Mississippi; Andrew Goodman, a student from New York; and Michael Schwerner, a New York social worker, disappeared from Philadelphia, Mississippi, and were presumed murdered. As public demand for an investigation grew, Rita Schwerner, Michael's wife, noted, "We all know that this search . . . is because Andrew Goodman and my husband are white. If only Chaney was involved, nothing would have been done." Six weeks later the FBI discovered the three bodies inside a newly constructed dam five miles away. Goodman and Schwerner had been killed by a single bullet each; Chaney had been brutally beaten with a chain and shot several times. An investigation later determined that members of the Ku Klux Klan had committed the crime. During Freedom Summer fifteen civil rights workers were murdered and only about twelve hundred black voters were registered.

The Voting Rights Act of 1965. The need for federal action to support voting rights became even clearer in March 1965, when Martin Luther King Jr. and other black leaders called for a massive march from Selma,

TABLE 28.1	Major Great Society Legislation	
Civil Rights		
1964	Twenty-fourth Amendment	Outlawed poll tax in federal elections
	Civil Rights Act	Banned discrimination in employment and public accommodations on the basis of race, religion, sex, or national origin
1965	Voting Rights Act	Outlawed literacy tests for voting; provided federal supervision of registration in historically low-registration areas
Social Welfare		
1964	Economic Opportunity Act	Created Office of Economic Opportunity (OEO) to administer War on Poverty programs such as Head Start, Job Corps, and Volunteers in Service to America (VISTA)
1965	Medical Care Act	Provided medical care for the poor (Medicaid) and the elderly (Medicare)
1966	Minimum Wage Act	Raised hourly minimum wage from $1.25 to $1.40 and expanded coverage to new groups
Education		
1965	Elementary and Secondary Education Act	Granted federal aid for education of poor children
	National Endowment for the Arts and Humanities	Provided federal funding and support for artists and scholars
	Higher Education Act	Provided federal scholarships for postsecondary education
Housing and Urban Development		
1964	Urban Mass Transportation Act	Provided federal aid to urban mass transit
	Omnibus Housing Act	Provided federal funds for public housing and rent subsidies for low-income families
1965	Housing and Urban Development Act	Created Department of Housing and Urban Development (HUD)
1966	Metropolitan Area Redevelopment and Demonstration Cities Acts	Designated 150 "model cities" for combined programs of public housing, social services, and job training
Environment		
1964	Wilderness Preservation Act	Designated 9.1 million acres of federal lands as "wilderness areas," barring future roads, buildings, or commercial use
1965	Air and Water Quality Acts	Set tougher air quality standards; required states to enforce water quality standards for interstate waters
Miscellaneous		
1964	Tax Reduction Act	Reduced personal and corporate income tax rates
1965	Immigration Act	Abandoned national quotas of 1924 law, allowing more non-European immigration
	Appalachian Regional Development Act	Provided federal funding for roads, health clinics, and other public works projects in economically depressed regions

Civil Rights Protesters in Selma

Protesting the killing of a black voting-rights advocate, thousands of civil rights activists staged a 54-mile march from Selma to Montgomery, Alabama, on March 7, 1965. The men and women in this photograph, shown here singing songs of freedom, were part of the historic march. The peaceful protest turned violent when state troopers clubbed and tear-gassed demonstrators on the Pettus Bridge outside Selma. Public outrage over the violence on "Bloody Sunday," as the incident became known, helped Johnson push the Voting Rights Act through Congress that summer. Bob Adelman / Magnum Photos, Inc.

Alabama, to the state capital in Montgomery to protest the murder of a voting-rights activist. As soon as the marchers left Selma, mounted state troopers attacked them with tear gas and clubs. The scene was shown on national television that night.

Calling the episode "an American tragedy," President Johnson redoubled his efforts to persuade Congress to pass the pending voting-rights legislation. In a televised speech to a joint session of Congress on March 15, quoting the best-known slogan of the civil rights movement, "We shall overcome," he proclaimed voting rights a moral imperative.

On August 6 Congress passed the Voting Rights Act of 1965, which suspended the literacy tests and other measures most southern states used to prevent blacks from registering to vote. The act authorized the attorney general to send federal examiners to register voters in any county where less than 50 percent of the voting-age population was registered. Together with the adoption in 1964 of the Twenty-fourth Amendment to the Constitution, which outlawed the poll tax in federal elections, and successful legal challenges to state and local poll taxes, the Voting Rights Act allowed millions of blacks to register and vote for the first time. Congress reauthorized the Voting Rights Act in 1970, 1975, and 1982.

In the South the results were stunning. In 1960 only 20 percent of blacks of voting age had been registered to vote; by 1964 the figure had risen to 39 percent, and by 1971 it was 62 percent (Map 28.7). As Hartman Turnbow, a Mississippi farmer who risked his life to register in 1964, later declared, "It won't never go back where it was."

Enacting the Liberal Agenda

Johnson's success in pushing through the 1965 Voting Rights Act stemmed in part from the 1964 election, in which he won the presidency in his own right by defeating the conservative Republican senator Barry Goldwater of Arizona. With his running mate, Senator Hubert H. Humphrey of Minnesota, Johnson achieved one of the largest margins in history, 61.1 percent of the popular vote (Map 28.8). And Johnson's coattails were long—his sweeping victory brought democratic gains in both Congress and the state legislatures. Thus strengthened politically, he used this mandate not only to promote a civil rights agenda but also to bring to fruition what he called the "Great Society."

Like most New Deal liberals, Johnson took an expansive view of presidential leadership and the role of the federal government. Johnson's first major success came in education. The Elementary and Secondary Education Act, passed in 1965, authorized $1 billion in federal funds to benefit impoverished children. The same year the Higher Education Act provided the first federal scholarships for college students. The Eighty-ninth Congress also gave Johnson enough votes to enact the federal health insurance legislation first proposed by Truman. The result was two new programs: Medicare, a health plan for the elderly funded by a surcharge on Social Security payroll taxes, and Medicaid, a health plan for the poor paid for by general tax revenues.

Although the Great Society is usually associated with programs for the disadvantaged, many Johnson administration initiatives actually benefited a wide spectrum of Americans. Federal urban renewal and home mortgage assistance helped those who could afford to live in single-family homes or modern apartments. Medicare covered every elderly person eligible for Social Security, regardless of need. Much of the federal aid to

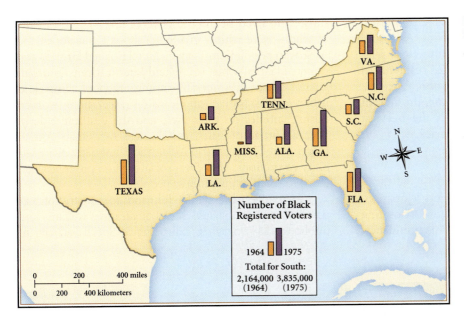

MAP 28.7 Black Voter Registration in the South, 1964 and 1975

After passage of the Voting Rights Act of 1965, black registration in the South increased dramatically. The bars on the map show the number of blacks registered in 1964, before the act was passed, and in 1975, after it had been in effect for ten years. States in the Deep South, such as Mississippi, Alabama, and Georgia, had the biggest rises.

education benefited the children of the middle class. Finally, the creation of the National Endowment for the Arts and the National Endowment for the Humanities in 1965 supported artists and historians in their efforts to understand and interpret the nation's cultural and historical heritage.

Another aspect of public welfare addressed by the Great Society was the environment. President Johnson pressed for expansion of the national park system, improvement of the nation's air and water, and increased land-use planning. At the insistence of his wife, Lady Bird Johnson, he promoted the Highway Beautification Act of 1965. His approach marked a significant break

with past conservation efforts, that had tended to concentrate on maintaining natural resources and national wealth. Under Secretary of the Interior Stewart Udall, Great Society programs emphasized quality of life, battling the problem "of vanishing beauty, of increasing ugliness, of shrinking open space, and of an overall environment that is diminished daily by pollution and noise and blight."

Taking advantage of the Great Society's reform climate, liberal Democrats also brought about significant changes in immigration policy. The Immigration Act of 1965 abandoned the quota system of the 1920s that had discriminated against Asians and southern and Eastern

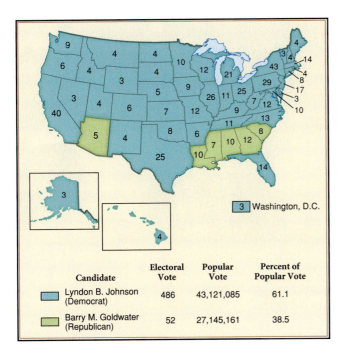

Candidate	Electoral Vote	Popular Vote	Percent of Popular Vote
Lyndon B. Johnson (Democrat)	486	43,121,085	61.1
Barry M. Goldwater (Republican)	52	27,145,161	38.5

◄ **MAP 28.8 Presidential Election of 1964**

A landslide victory in 1964, along with significant Democratic gains in Congress and the states, helped President Lyndon B. Johnson to claim that he had a mandate for social reform. Johnson's ambitious "Great Society" led to extensive federal programs in the areas of education, housing, health, transportation, welfare, civil rights, and the environment. Although the conservative Republican senator Barry Goldwater of Arizona was soundly defeated in 1964, a Republican resurgence in the 1980s would be based on Goldwater's critique of the "big government" unleashed by the Great Society.

Europeans, replacing it with more equitable numerical limits on immigration from Europe, Africa, Asia, and countries in the Western Hemisphere. Since close relatives of individuals who were already legal residents of the United States could be admitted over and above the numerical limits, the legislation led to an immigrant influx far greater than anticipated, with the heaviest volume coming from Asia and Latin America.

War on Poverty

In the midst of his campaign for civil rights legislation, Johnson was also pursuing his ambitious goal of putting "an end to poverty in our time." During his presidency, those who lived below the poverty line—three-fourths of whom were white—made up about a quarter of the American population. They included isolated farmers and miners in Appalachia, blacks and Puerto Ricans in urban ghettos, Mexican Americans in migrant labor camps and urban *barrios*, Native Americans on reservations, women raising families on their own, and the destitute elderly. Because programs such as Old Age Assistance, Aid to Dependent Children, and Aid to the Blind had strict eligibility restrictions, New Deal social welfare programs had failed to reach many of these people.

To reduce poverty, the Johnson administration expanded long-established social insurance, welfare, and public works programs. It broadened Social Security to

Project Head Start

Project Head Start, which offered free early education programs for poor children, was one of the most acclaimed programs of Lyndon Johnson's War on Poverty. In 1965 folk singer Tom Glazer staged a series of concerts for the more than 25,000 children enrolled in Head Start throughout New York City. Wide World Photos, Inc.

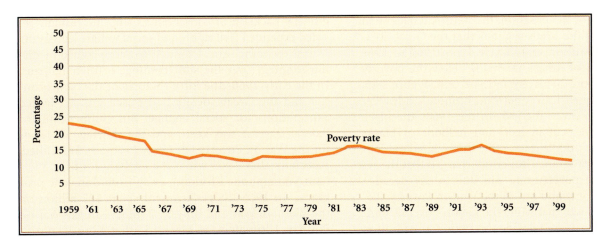

FIGURE 28.5 Americans in Poverty, 1959–2000
During the 1960s the poverty rate among American families dropped from 20 percent to 11 percent, suggesting that the War on Poverty was bringing more Americans into the economic mainstream. Critics charged, however, that economic growth spurred by the Vietnam War accounted for the decrease.

include waiters and waitresses, domestic servants, farmworkers, and hospital employees. Social welfare expenditures increased rapidly, especially for Aid to Families with Dependent Children (AFDC), as did public housing and rent subsidy programs. Food Stamps, begun in 1964 largely to stabilize farm prices, grew into a major program of assistance to low-income families. The Appalachian Regional Development Act of 1965 provided federal funding for local roads, health clinics, and other public works projects in that poverty-stricken region. As during the New Deal, these social welfare programs developed in piecemeal fashion, without overall coordination.

The Office of Economic Opportunity (OEO), established by the Economic Opportunity Act of 1964, was the Great Society's showcase in the War on Poverty. Built around the twin strategies of equal opportunity and community action, OEO programs were so numerous and diverse that they recalled the alphabet agencies of the New Deal. Sargent Shriver, who moved from the Peace Corps to head the new agency, admitted, "It's like we went down to Cape Kennedy [the NASA space center in Florida] and launched a half dozen rockets at once."

OEO programs produced some of the most innovative measures of the Johnson administration. Head Start provided free nursery schools to prepare disadvantaged preschoolers for kindergarten. The Job Corps and the Neighborhood Youth Corps provided jobs and vocational training for young people. Upward Bound gave low-income teenagers the skills and motivation to go to college. Volunteers in Service to America (VISTA), modeled on the Peace Corps, promoted community service among youths in impoverished rural and urban areas. The Community Action Program encouraged the poor

to demand "maximum feasible participation" in decisions that affected them. Community Action organizers worked closely with 2,000 lawyers employed by the Legal Services Program to provide the poor with free legal aid.

By the end of 1965, the Johnson administration had compiled the most impressive legislative record of liberal reforms since the New Deal. It had put issues of poverty, justice, and access at the center of national political life, and it had expanded the federal government's role in protecting citizens' welfare. Yet the Great Society never quite measured up to the extravagant promises made for it, and by the end of the decade, many of its programs were under attack.

In part the political necessity of bowing to pressure from various interest groups hampered Great Society programs. For example, the American Medical Association (AMA) used its influence to shape the Medicare and Medicaid programs to ensure that Congress did not impose a cap on medical expenses. Its intervention produced escalating federal expenditures and contributed to skyrocketing medical costs. And Democratic-controlled urban political machines criticized VISTA and Community Action Program agents who encouraged poor people to demand the public services long withheld by unresponsive local governments. In response to such political pressure, the Johnson administration gradually phased out the Community Action Program and instead channeled spending for housing, social services, and other urban poverty programs through local municipal governments.

Another inherent problem was the limited funding of Great Society programs. The annual budget for the War on Poverty was less than $2 billion. Despite the limited nature of the program, the statistical decline in poverty during the 1960s suggests that the Great Society was successful on some levels. From 1963 to 1968 the proportion of Americans living below the poverty line dropped from 20 percent to 13 percent (Figure 28.5, p. 845). Among African Americans economic advancement was even more marked. In the 1960s the black poverty rate was cut in half, and millions of blacks moved into the middle class, some through federal jobs in antipoverty programs. But critics charged that the reduction in the poverty rate was due to the decade's booming economy and not to the War on Poverty. Another criticism was that while the nation's overall standard of living increased during this period, distribution of wealth was still uneven. The poor were better off in an absolute sense, but they remained far behind the middle class in a relative sense.

Other factors also hampered the success of the Great Society. Following in the steps of Roosevelt's New Deal coalition, Kennedy and Johnson had gathered an extraordinarily diverse set of groups—middle-class and poor; white and nonwhite; Protestant, Jewish, and Catholic; urban and rural—in support of an unprecedented level of federal activism. For a brief period between 1964 and 1966, the coalition held together. But inevitably the demands of certain groups—such as blacks' demands for civil rights and the urban poor's demands for increased political power—conflicted with the interests of other Democrats, such as white southerners and northern political bosses. In the end the Democratic coalition could not sustain a consensus on the purposes of governmental activism powerful enough to resist a growing backlash of conservatives who increasingly resisted expanded civil rights and social welfare legislation.

At the same time, Democrats were plagued by disillusionment over the shortcomings of their reforms. In the early 1960s the lofty rhetoric of the New Frontier and the Great Society had raised unprecedented expectations for social change. But competition for federal largesse was keen, and the shortage of funds for the War on Poverty left many promises unfulfilled, especially after 1965 when the escalation of the Vietnam War siphoned funding away from domestic programs. In 1966 the government spent $22 billion on the Vietnam War and only $1.2 billion on the War on Poverty. Ultimately, as Martin Luther King Jr. put it, the Great Society was "shot down on the battlefields of Vietnam."

FOR FURTHER EXPLORATION

▶ For definitions of key terms boldfaced in this chapter, see the glossary at the end of the book.

▶ To assess your mastery of the material covered in this chapter, see the Online Study Guide at **bedfordstmartins.com/henretta**.

▶ For suggested references, including Web sites, see page SR-30 at the end of the book.

▶ For map resources and primary documents, see **bedfordstmartins.com/henretta**.

In the postwar era, American dominance of the global economy ensured an unprecedented level of domestic prosperity. Increased levels of spending on defense and consumer goods led to new economic development concentrated in the southern and western states and in the suburbs. Federal intervention in the economy, especially cold war defense spending, boosted the economies and populations of California, Texas, Florida, and other emerging Sun Belt states. Federal home loan programs and highway construction spurred rapid suburban development, siphoning jobs and middle-class residents out of the central cities. At the same time, many blacks, Latinos, Native Americans, and other low-income groups were migrating into these declining urban areas, where they encountered growing unemployment, rising crime, and deteriorating housing and education.

After years of depression and war-induced insecurity, Americans turned inward toward religion, home, and family. Postwar couples married young, had several children, and—if they were white and middle class—raised their children in a climate of suburban affluence and consumerism. The profamily orientation of the 1950s celebrated social conformity and traditional gender roles, even though millions of women entered the workforce in those years. Many of the smoldering contradictions of the postwar period—unequally shared affluence, institutionalized racism, tensions in women's lives—helped spur the civil rights movement and other social reform efforts of the 1960s.

As Americans looked to Washington for solutions to the nation's social and economic ills, the Democrats offered a diverse array of federal programs designed to appeal to a broad range of constituencies. John F. Kennedy first set the agenda for this politics of expectation in his 1960 presidential bid, but the domestic accomplishments of his New Frontier were limited. Kennedy's activism was more evident in foreign policy, where he proved a resolute Cold Warrior. Following Kennedy's assassination in 1963, Lyndon Johnson played a critical role in pushing civil rights legislation through Congress. Moreover, Johnson used his formidable political skills to usher in the most ambitious legislative reform program since the New Deal. Congress funded an array of Great Society programs in education, medical care, social welfare, housing, transportation, and environmental protection. But although the Great Society raised hopes, it could not always deliver on its promises. Increasing military expenditures for the Vietnam conflict limited federal funds for domestic programs. And as federal functions and responsibilities grew, accommodating the diverse and often competing constituencies in the Democratic coalition became increasingly difficult. By the mid-1960s the liberal consensus was breaking apart.

1944	Bretton Woods economic conference
	World Bank and International Monetary Fund (IMF) founded
1947	Levittown, New York, built
1953–1958	Operation Wetback and Indian termination programs
1954	*Brown v. Board of Education of Topeka*
1955	AFL and CIO merge
	Montgomery bus boycott
1956	National Interstate and Defense Highway Act
1957	Peak of postwar baby boom
	School desegregation battle in Little Rock, Arkansas
	Southern Christian Leadership Conference (SCLC) founded
1960	Sit-ins in Greensboro, North Carolina
	John F. Kennedy elected president
1961	Peace Corps established
	Freedom rides
	Bay of Pigs invasion
	Berlin Wall erected
1962	Michael Harrington's *The Other America*
	Cuban missile crisis
1963	Betty Friedan's *The Feminine Mystique*
	Civil rights protest in Birmingham, Alabama
	March on Washington
	Nuclear test-ban treaty
	John F. Kennedy assassinated; Lyndon B. Johnson assumes presidency
1964	Freedom Summer
	Civil Rights Act
	Economic Opportunity Act inaugurates War on Poverty
	Johnson elected president
1965	Immigration Act abolishes national quota system
	Civil rights march from Selma to Montgomery
	Voting Rights Act
	Medicare and Medicaid programs established
	Elementary and Secondary Education Act

CHAPTER 29

War Abroad and at Home: The Vietnam Era

1961–1975

Into the Quagmire, 1945–1968
America in Vietnam: From Truman to Kennedy
Escalation: The Johnson Years
American Soldiers' Perspectives on the War

The Cold War Consensus Unravels
Public Opinion on Vietnam
Student Activism
The Rise of the Counterculture
The Widening Struggle for Civil Rights
The Legacy of the Civil Rights Movement
The Revival of Feminism

The Long Road Home, 1968–1975
1968: A Year of Shocks
Nixon's War
Withdrawal from Vietnam and Détente
The Legacy of Vietnam

IN FEBRUARY 1969, while conducting his first mass as a Catholic priest, James Carroll seized the opportunity to criticize the U.S. war in Vietnam. Carroll's public pronouncement against the war, delivered in a U.S. Air Force base chapel before an audience of high-ranking officers, among them his father, opened a rift in his family that never healed. Carroll's stand was not unique; he joined countless other ministers and priests who used their pulpits to condemn the war. His experience provides a dramatic example of the ruptures the Vietnam War brought to families, institutions, and the American social fabric.

Vietnam spawned a vibrant antiwar protest movement, which intersected with a broader youth movement that questioned traditional American political and cultural values. The challenges posed by youth, together with the revival of feminism, the rise of the black and Chicano power movements, and explosive riots in the cities, produced a profound sense of social disorder at home. Vietnam split the Democratic Party and shattered the liberal consensus. The high monetary cost of the war diverted resources from domestic uses, spelling an end to the Great Society. Beyond its domestic impact the war wreaked extraordinary damage on the country of Vietnam and undermined U.S. credibility abroad. For the first time average Americans began to question their assumptions about the nation's cold war objectives and the beneficence of American foreign policy.

◀ **The Longest War**
American combat troops fought in Vietnam from 1965 to 1973, making it the longest war in the nation's history. Ambushed during a search-and-destroy mission, these soldiers await the arrival of a medical evacuation helicopter. The red smoke, produced by a grenade, designated the clearing in the jungle where the helicopter could land. More than 58,000 Americans lost their lives in the conflict, while another 300,000 were injured.
© Tim Page.

849

Into the Quagmire, 1945–1968

Like many new nations that emerged from the dissolution of European empires after World War II, Vietnam was characterized by a volatile mix of nationalist sentiment, religious and cultural conflict, economic need, and political turmoil. The rise of communism there was just one phase of the nation's larger struggle, which would eventually climax in a bloody civil war. But American policymakers viewed these events through the lens of the cold war, interpreting them as part of an international Communist movement toward global domination. Their failure to understand the complexity of Vietnam's internal conflicts led to a long and ultimately disastrous attempt to influence the course of the war.

America in Vietnam: From Truman to Kennedy

Vietnam had been part of the French colony of Indochina since the late nineteenth century but had been occupied by Japan during World War II. When the Japanese surrendered in 1945, Ho Chi Minh and the Vietminh, the Communist nationalist group that had led Vietnamese resistance to the Japanese, took advantage of the resulting power vacuum. With words drawn from the American Declaration of Independence, Ho proclaimed the establishment of the independent republic of Vietnam that September. The next year, when France rejected his claim and reasserted control over the country, an eight-year struggle ensued that the Vietminh called the Anti-French War of Resistance. Appealing to American anticolonial sentiment Ho called on President Truman to support the struggle for Vietnamese independence. But Truman ignored his pleas and instead offered covert financial support to the French, in hopes of stabilizing the politically chaotic region and rebuilding the French economy.

By the end of the decade cold war developments had prompted the United States to step up its assistance to the French. After the Chinese Revolution of 1949, the United States became concerned that China—along with the Soviet Union—might actively support anticolonial struggles in Asia and that newly independent countries might align themselves with the Communists. At the same time Republican charges that the Democrats had "lost" China influenced Truman to take a firmer stand against perceived Communist aggression in Korea and Vietnam. Truman also wanted to maintain good relations with France, whose support was crucial to the success of the new NATO alliance. Finally, Indochina played a strategic role in Secretary of State Dean Acheson's plans for an integrated Pacific Rim economy centered on a reindustrialized Japan.

For all these reasons, when the Soviet Union and the new Chinese leaders recognized Ho's republic early in 1950, the United States—along with Great Britain—recognized the French-installed puppet government of Bao Dai. Subsequently, both the Truman and the Eisenhower administrations provided substantial military support to the French in Vietnam. President Eisenhower argued that such aid was essential to prevent the collapse of all non-Communist governments in the area, in a chain reaction he called the **domino effect**: "You have a row of dominoes set up, you knock over the first one, and what will happen to the last one is the certainty that it will go over very quickly."

Despite joint French-American efforts, the Vietminh forces gained strength in northern Vietnam. In the spring of 1954, they seized the isolated administrative fortress of Dienbienphu after a fifty-six-day siege. The spectacular victory gave the Vietminh negotiating leverage in the 1954 Geneva accords, which partitioned Vietnam temporarily at the seventeenth parallel (Map 29.1) and committed France to withdraw its forces from the area north of that line. The accords also provided that within two years, in free elections, the voters in the two sectors would choose a unified government for the entire nation. The United States considered the agreements a "disaster," especially provisions for elections that it feared would be won by the Communists. It refused to sign the accords and instead issued a separate protocol acknowledging them and promising to "refrain from the threat or use of force to disturb them."

Eisenhower had no intention of allowing a Communist victory in Vietnam's upcoming election. With the help of the CIA, he made sure that a pro-American government took power in South Vietnam in June 1954, just before the accords were signed. Ngo Dinh Diem, an anti-Communist Catholic who had spent eight years in the United States, returned to Vietnam as the premier of the French-backed South Vietnamese government. The next year, in a rigged election, Diem became president of an independent South Vietnam. Realizing that the popular Ho Chi Minh would easily win in both the north and south, Diem called off the reunification elections that were scheduled for 1956—a move the United States supported.

In March 1956 the last French soldiers left Saigon, the capital of South Vietnam, and the United States replaced France as the dominant foreign power in the region. American policymakers quickly asserted that a non-Communist South Vietnam was vital to U.S. security interests. In reality, Vietnam was too small a country to upset the international balance of power, and its Communist movement was regional and intensely nationalistic rather than expansionist. Nevertheless, Eisenhower and subsequent U.S. presidents persisted in viewing Vietnam as part of the cold war struggle to contain the Communist threat to the free world. Between 1955 and 1961 the Eisenhower administration sent

MAP 29.1 The Vietnam War, 1954–1975

The Vietnam War was a guerrilla war, fought in skirmishes and inconclusive encounters rather than decisive battles. Supporters of the National Liberation Front filtered into South Vietnam along the Ho Chi Minh Trail, which wound through Laos and Cambodia. In January 1968 Vietcong forces launched the Tet offensive, a surprise attack on several South Vietnamese cities and provincial centers. American vulnerability to these attacks served to undermine U.S. credibility and fueled opposition to the war. After a 1973 cease-fire was signed, the United States withdrew its troops, and in 1975 South Vietnam fell to the northern forces. The country was reunited under Communist rule in April of that year.

Diem an average of $200 million a year in aid and stationed approximately 675 American military advisors in Saigon. Having stepped up U.S. involvement there considerably, Eisenhower left office, passing the Vietnam situation to his successor, John F. Kennedy.

President Kennedy saw Vietnam as an ideal testing ground for the counterinsurgency techniques that formed the centerpiece of his military policy (see Chapter 28). But he first had to prop up Diem's unpopular regime, which faced a growing military threat. In December 1960 the Communist Party in North Vietnam organized most of Diem's opponents in South Vietnam into a revolutionary movement known as the National Liberation Front (NLF). In response, Kennedy increased the number of American military "advisors" (an elastic term that included helicopter units and special forces), raising it to more than 16,000 by November 1963. To win the "hearts and minds" of Vietnamese peasants away from the insurgents and to increase agricultural production, he also sent economic development specialists. But Kennedy refused to send combat troops to assist the South Vietnamese in what had become a guerrilla-style civil war with the north.

American aid did little good in South Vietnam. Diem's political inexperience and corruption, combined with his Catholicism in a predominantly Buddhist country, prevented him from creating a stable popular government. The NLF's guerrilla forces—called the Vietcong by their opponents—made considerable headway against Diem's regime, using the revolutionary tactics of the Chinese leader Mao Zedong to blend into South Vietnam's civilian population "like fish in the water." They found a receptive audience among peasants who had been alienated by Diem's "strategic hamlet" program, which uprooted families and whole villages and moved them into barbed-wire compounds in a vain attempt to separate them from Ho Chi Minh's sympathizers.

Anti-Diem sentiment also flourished among Buddhists, who charged the government with religious persecution. Starting in May 1963 militant Buddhists staged a dramatic series of demonstrations against Diem, including several self-immolations that were recorded by American television crews. Diem's regime retaliated with raids on temples and mass arrests of Buddhist priests in August, prompting more antigovernment demonstrations.

Buddhist Protesters, 1966

Beginning in 1963, militant Buddhist monks staged a series of protests against the war that helped bring down the American-backed regime of Ngo Dinh Diem. Here, robed monks, part of a group of 250 Buddhist protesters, stage an antigovernment demonstration in Saigon. They are surrounded by barbed wire put there by government troops. Strongly nationalistic, the monks appealed for peace talks with the Vietcong and for free elections that would allow the Vietnamese to decide their fate. The South Vietnamese military government arrested Buddhist leaders in 1966 and effectively crushed their movement. Wide World Photos, Inc.

As opposition to Diem deepened, Kennedy decided that he would have to be removed. Ambassador Henry Cabot Lodge Jr. let it be known in Saigon that the United States would support a military coup that had "a good chance of succeeding." On November 1, 1963, Diem was driven from office and assassinated by officers in the South Vietnamese army. America's role in the coup reinforced the links between the United States and the new regime in South Vietnam, making the prospect of withdrawal from the region less acceptable to U.S. policymakers.

Less than a month later, Kennedy was assassinated. Although historians continue to debate whether Kennedy would have withdrawn American forces from Vietnam had he lived, his administration's actions clearly accelerated U.S. involvement. When Lyndon Johnson became president, he retained many of Kennedy's foreign-policy advisors. Asserting that "I am not going to be the President who saw Southeast Asia go the way China went," he quickly declared he would maintain U.S. support for South Vietnam.

Escalation: The Johnson Years

The removal of Diem did not improve the efficiency or popularity of the Saigon government. Secretary of Defense Robert McNamara and other top advisors argued that only a rapid, full-scale deployment of U.S. forces could prevent the imminent defeat of the South Vietnamese. But Johnson would need at least tacit congressional support, perhaps even a declaration of war, to commit U.S. forces to an offensive strategy. Originally, Johnson wanted to wait until after the 1964 election to place this controversial request before Congress, but events gave him an opportunity to win authorization sooner.

The Gulf of Tonkin Resolution.   During the summer of 1964, American naval forces conducted surveillance missions off the North Vietnamese coast to aid amphibious attacks by the South Vietnamese. When the North Vietnamese resisted the attacks, President Johnson told the nation that on two separate occasions North Vietnamese torpedo boats had fired on American destroyers in international waters in the Gulf of Tonkin. At Johnson's request, Congress authorized him to "take all necessary measures to repel any armed attack against the forces of the United States and to prevent further aggression." On August 7 the Gulf of Tonkin Resolution passed by 88 to 2 votes in the Senate and 416 to 0 in the House. Only Senators Wayne Morse of Oregon and Ernest Gruening of Alaska opposed it as a "predated declaration of war" that further increased the president's ability to carry out foreign policy without consulting Congress.

Many questions were later raised about the resolution. A draft version had been ready for several months, awaiting just such an incident. The evidence of a North Vietnamese attack was sketchy at best. As the president admitted to his advisors soon afterward, "For all I know, our navy was shooting at whales out there." But this unverified attack got Johnson what he wanted—a sweeping mandate to conduct Vietnam operations as he saw fit. It was the only formal approval of American intervention in Vietnam that Congress ever granted.

During the 1964 presidential campaign, Johnson declared, "We are not going to send American boys nine or ten thousand miles away from home to do what Asian boys ought to be doing for themselves." Yet plans were already being drawn up for a possible escalation of American efforts. With congressional support assured and the 1964 election safely over, the Johnson administration began the fateful move toward the total Americanization of the war. The escalation, which was accomplished during the first several months of 1965, took two forms: the initiation of direct bombing campaigns against North Vietnam and the deployment of ground troops.

Operation Rolling Thunder. The first phase of escalation began on March 2, 1965, with Operation Rolling Thunder, a protracted campaign of bombing attacks against North Vietnam designed to cripple the economy and force the Communists to the bargaining table. A special target was the Ho Chi Minh Trail, an elaborate network of paths, bridges, and shelters that stretched from North Vietnam through Cambodia and Laos into South Vietnam (see Map 29.1). By 1967 some 20,000 Vietnamese soldiers were moving southward along that route each month, along with the military equipment and other resources necessary to supply them.

Between 1965 and 1968 Operation Rolling Thunder (named for a Protestant hymn) dropped a million tons of bombs on North Vietnam, 800 tons a day for three and a half years. Each B-52 bombing sortie cost $30,000, and by early 1966 the direct costs of the air war had exceeded $1.7 billion. From 1965 to 1973 the United States dropped three times as many bombs on North Vietnam, a country roughly the size of Texas, as had fallen on Europe, Asia, and Africa during World War II. The several hundred captured American pilots downed in the raids then became pawns in negotiations with the North Vietnamese over the fate of prisoners of war.

To the amazement of American advisors, the bombing had little effect on the ability of the Vietnamese to wage war. Despite continuous sorties and the use of chemical defoliants to deny the Vietcong cover, the flow of troops and supplies to the south continued. The North Vietnamese quickly rebuilt roads and bridges, moved munitions plants underground, and constructed a network of tunnels and shelters. Instead of destroying enemy morale and bringing the North Vietnamese to the bargaining table, Operation Rolling Thunder intensified their will to fight. The bombing continued nevertheless.

The Arrival of U.S. Ground Troops. A week after the launch of Operation Rolling Thunder, the United States sent its first official ground troops into combat duty. Soon U.S. Marines were skirmishing with the enemy. Over the next three years, the number of American troops in Vietnam grew dramatically. Although U.S. troops were accompanied by military forces from Australia, New Zealand, and South Korea, the war increasingly became an American war, fought for American aims. By 1966 more than 380,000 American soldiers were stationed in Vietnam; by 1967, 485,000; by 1968, 536,000 (Figure 29.1).

The massive commitment of troops and air power threatened to destroy Vietnam's countryside. The defoliation campaign had seriously damaged agricultural production, undercutting the economic and cultural base of Vietnamese society. After one devastating but not unusual engagement, a commanding officer reported, using the logic of the time, "It became necessary to destroy the town in order to save it." Graffiti on a plane that dropped defoliants read "Only you can prevent forests." (In later years defoliants such as Agent Orange were found to have highly toxic effects on both humans and the environment.) The destruction was not limited to North Vietnam; South Vietnam, America's ally, absorbed more than twice the bomb tonnage dropped on the North, as U.S. forces tried to flush out

Aerial Bombing in Vietnam
The bombs dropped by U.S. forces in an attempt to root out Vietcong sympathizers inflicted heavy damage on the countryside and caused many civilian deaths. B-52 jets dropped most of the bombs.
Larry Burrows / LIFE Magazine © Time, Inc.

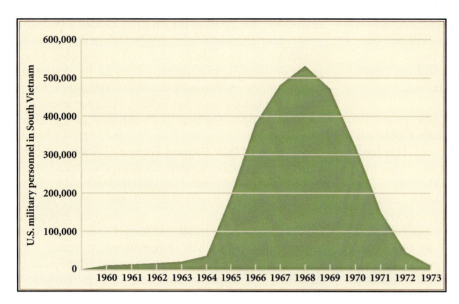

FIGURE 29.1 U.S. Troops in Vietnam, 1960–1973

When Lyndon Johnson escalated the Vietnam War, troop levels rose from 23,300 in December 1964 to 184,300 a year later. Troop levels eventually peaked at more than 543,000 personnel. Under Richard Nixon's Vietnamization program, beginning in the summer of 1969, levels drastically declined; the last U.S. military forces left South Vietnam on March 29, 1973.

Vietcong sympathizers. In Saigon and other South Vietnamese cities, the influx of American soldiers and dollars distorted local economies, spread corruption and prostitution, and triggered uncontrollable inflation and black-market activity.

Why did the dramatically increased American presence in Vietnam fail to turn the tide of the war? Some advisors argued that military intervention could accomplish little without simultaneous reform in Saigon and increased popular support in the countryside. Other critics claimed that the United States never fully committed itself to a "total victory"—although what that term meant was never settled. Military strategy was inextricably tied to political considerations. For domestic reasons policymakers often searched for an elusive "middle ground" between all-out invasion of North Vietnam (and the possibility of sparking a nuclear exchange between the two superpowers) and the politically unacceptable alternative of disengagement. Hoping to win a war of attrition, the Johnson administration assumed that American superiority in personnel and weaponry would ultimately triumph. But that limited commitment was never enough to ensure victory—however it was defined.

American Soldiers' Perspectives on the War

Approximately 2.8 million Americans served in Vietnam. At an average age of only nineteen, most of those servicemen and women were too young to vote or drink (the voting age was twenty-one until passage of the Twenty-sixth Amendment in 1971), but they were old enough to fight and die. Some were volunteers, including 7,000 women enlistees. Many others served because they were drafted. Until the nation shifted to an all-volunteer force in 1973, the draft stood as a concrete

reminder of the government's impact on the lives of ordinary Americans. Even more than in other recent wars, sons of the poor and the working class shouldered a disproportionate amount of the fighting, forming an estimated 80 percent of the enlisted ranks. Young men from more affluent backgrounds were more likely to avoid combat through student deferments, medical exemptions, and appointments to National Guard and reserve units—alternatives that made Johnson's Vietnam policy more acceptable to the middle class. Although over the course of the war blacks were drafted and died roughly in the same proportion as their share of the draft-age population (about 12 to 13 percent), black casualty rates were significantly higher than average in the early 1960s.

At first many draftees and enlistees shared common cold war assumptions about the need to fight communism and the superiority of the American military. However, their experience in Vietnam quickly challenged simple notions of patriotism and the inevitability of victory (see American Voices, "Dave Cline: A Vietnam Vet Remembers," p. 855). In "Nam" long days of boring menial work were punctuated by brief flashes of intense fighting. "Most of the time, nothing happened," a soldier recalled, "but when something did, it happened instantaneously and without warning." Rarely were there large-scale battles, only skirmishes; rather than front lines and conquered territory, there were only daytime operations in areas the Vietcong controlled at night.

Racism was a fact of everyday life. Because differentiating between friendly South Vietnamese and Vietcong sympathizers was difficult, many soldiers lumped them together as "gooks." As a draftee noted of his indoctrination, "The only thing they told us about the Vietcong was they were gooks. They were to be killed.

Dave Cline

A Vietnam Vet Remembers

Born in 1947, Dave Cline grew up in a working-class family outside Buffalo, New York. Drafted by the army in 1967, the twenty-year-old Cline was eager to help fight Communist aggression in Vietnam. But after his arrival in Danang seven months later, his attitude toward the war quickly changed. Cline described this transformation in an interview conducted in 1992.

I went to basic training at Fort Dix. . . .

Down there, they used to give you basically two raps on why you were going to Vietnam. One was that rap about we're going to help the heroic South Vietnamese people. We're going to go fight for freedom [and repel] communist aggression. They'd show you the maps and stuff, the domino theory, the Red Chinese are trying to engulf all of southeast Asia. The other rap was: killing communists was your duty. . . .

The boat came into Danang, and then they flew us from Danang to Cu Chi. I remember it was humid and hot and smelled. First thing you do when you get in-country is, they give you these indoctrination classes and they say, "Forget all that shit they told; you can't trust any of these people. They're not really people anyway; they're gooks." . . . In other words: You see anyone with slant eyes, that's your potential enemy—don't trust them. That sort of blows away any "help the people" thing. . . .

I got wounded the last time out near the Cambodian border. This happened on December 20, 1967. Again, we were doing these sweeps and we were overrun about two in the morning. The North Vietnamese launched a massive human wave attack. We could hear them yelling orders maybe 25, 30 feet away, and these guys were charging. . . .

A guy came running up to my foxhole. We saw him coming from the next hole over and we didn't know if it was an American retreating over to us or a Vietnamese, because it was two in the morning. So we didn't shoot him.

I was sitting there with my rifle waiting to see, and all of a sudden he stuck his rifle in. I saw the front side of an AK-47 and a muzzle flash, and then I pulled my trigger. I shot him through his chest. I blacked out initially, but then I came to and found a round went right through my knee. They threw me in a foxhole and gave me a bottle of Darvons. I lay there until the battle ended. In the morning they medivaced me out.

They carried me over to this guy I had shot. He was sitting up against this tree stump. He was just sitting there with his rifle across his lap. He was dead. The sergeant started giving me this pep talk, "Here's the gook you killed!" In my unit they had a big thing about confirmed kills. If you had a confirmed kill and the person had an automatic weapon, then you were supposed to get a three-day in-country pass. . . .

This kid looked about the same age as me. The first thing I started thinking was, Why is he dead and I'm alive? . . .

Then after going into the hospital, I started thinking about that guy. I wonder if his mother knows he's dead? I wonder if he had a girlfriend? Looking back, I think I was retaining the sense that he was a human being.

Source: Richard Stacewicz, *Winter Soldiers: An Oral History of the Vietnam Veterans against the War* (New York: Twayne Publishers, 1997), 135–36, 140–41.

Nobody sits around and gives you their historical and cultural background. They're the enemy. Kill, kill, kill."

Fighting and surviving under such conditions took its toll. One veteran explained that "the hardest thing to come to grips with was the fact that making it through Vietnam—surviving—is probably the only worthwhile part of the experience. It wasn't going over there and saving the world from communism or defending the country." Cynicism and bitterness were common. The pressure of waging war under such conditions drove many soldiers to seek escape in alcohol or drugs, which were cheap and readily available.

The women who served in Vietnam shared many of these experiences. As WACs, nurses, and civilians serving with organizations such as the USO, women volunteers witnessed death and mutilation on a massive scale. Though they tried to maintain a professional distance, as a navy nurse recalled, "It's pretty damn hard not getting involved when you see a nineteen- or twenty-year-old blond kid from the Midwest or California or the East Coast screaming and dying. A piece of my heart would go with each."

The Cold War Consensus Unravels

In the twenty years following World War II, despite widespread affluence and confidence in the nation's cold war leadership, there had emerged a variety of challenges to the status quo. From the nonconforming Beats came a critical assault on corporate capitalism. Teenagers' embrace of rock 'n' roll defied the cultural norms of their elders. African Americans' boycotts, sit-ins, and freedom rides signaled a rising wind of protest against racial injustice. By 1965 such angry expressions of disaffection from mainstream America had multiplied dramatically. Criticism of the war in Vietnam mounted, as youthful protesters rebelled against traditional respect for the "system." The civil rights movement took on a more militant thrust and expanded beyond African Americans to other minority groups, while the feminist movement revived to challenge social values and the family structure itself. Together the various movements forced Americans to reassess basic assumptions about the nature of their society.

A Televised War

This harrowing scene from Saigon during the Tet offensive in 1968 was broadcast on U.S. network news. The NBC bureau chief described the film in a terse telex message: "A VC officer was captured. The troops beat him. They bring him to [Brigadier General Nguyen Ngoc] Loan who is head of South Vietnamese national police. Loan pulls out his pistol, fires at the head of the VC, the VC falls, zoom on his head, blood spraying out. If he has it all it's startling stuff." Wide World Photos, Inc.

Public Opinion on Vietnam

President Kennedy and at first President Johnson enjoyed broad support for their conduct of foreign affairs. Both Democrats and Republicans approved Johnson's escalation of the war, and public opinion polls in 1965 and 1966 showed strong popular support for his policies. But in the late 1960s, public opinion began to turn against the war. In July 1967 a Gallup poll revealed that for the first time a majority of Americans disapproved of Johnson's Vietnam policy and believed the war had reached a stalemate. Television had much to do with these attitudes. Vietnam was the first war in which television brought film of the fighting directly into the nation's living rooms.

The Credibility Gap. Despite the glowing reports filed by the media and the administration on the progress of the war, by 1967 many administration officials had privately reached a more pessimistic conclusion. In November Secretary of Defense Robert McNamara sent a memo to the president arguing that continued escalation "would be dangerous, costly in lives, and unsatisfactory to the American people," but President Johnson continued to insist that victory in Vietnam was vital to U.S. national security and prestige. Journalists, especially those who had spent time in Vietnam, soon began to warn that the Johnson administration suffered from a "**credibility gap.**" The administration, they charged, was concealing important and discouraging information about the war's progress. In February 1966 television coverage of hearings by the Senate Foreign Relations Committee (chaired by J. William Fulbright, an outspoken critic of the war) raised further questions about the administration's policy.

Economic developments put Johnson and his advisors even more on the defensive. In 1966 the federal deficit was $9.8 billion; in 1967 the Vietnam War cost the taxpayers $27 billion, and the deficit jumped to $23 billion. Although the war consumed just 3 percent of the gross national product, its costs became more evident as the growing federal deficit nudged the inflation rate upward. Only in the summer of 1967 did Johnson ask for a 10 percent surcharge on individual and corporate income taxes, an increase that Congress did not approve until 1968. By then the inflationary spiral that would plague the U.S. economy throughout the 1970s was well under way.

The Rise of the Antiwar Movement. As a result of these troubling political and economic developments, more Americans than during previous American wars began to question the war effort in Vietnam. As in every American military conflict, a small group of dissenters opposed the war from the beginning, including pacifist organizations such as the War Resisters League and the

Women's International League for Peace and Freedom and religious groups such as the Quakers and the Fellowship for Reconciliation. Those groups were joined by a new generation of activists who had emerged in the 1950s in groups such as SANE (the National Committee for a Sane Nuclear Policy), Physicians for Social Responsibility, and Women Strike for Peace. These activists opposed the accelerating arms race in general and atmospheric testing in particular and lobbied successfully for the 1963 nuclear test-ban treaty between the United States and the Soviet Union (see Chapter 28).

Between 1963 and 1965, peace activists in both older and newer organizations staged protests, vigils, and letter-writing campaigns against U.S. involvement in the war. After the escalation in the spring of 1965, various antiwar coalitions, swelled by growing numbers of students, clergy, housewives, politicians, artists, and others opposed to the war, organized several mass demonstrations in Washington, bringing out 20,000 to 30,000 people at a time. A diverse lot, participants in these rallies shared a common skepticism about the means and aims of U.S. policy. The war was morally wrong, they argued, and antithetical to American ideals; the goal of an independent, anti-Communist South Vietnam was unattainable; and American military involvement would not help the Vietnamese people.

Student Activism

Youth were among the key protestors of the era. Not all youth challenged authority in the 1960s, but those who did had a powerful impact. It was primarily college students—many of whom had been raised in a privileged environment, showered with consumer goods, and inculcated with faith in American institutions and leaders—who began to question U.S. foreign policy, racial injustice, and middle-class morals and conformity.

In June 1962 forty students from Big Ten and Ivy League universities, disturbed by the gap they perceived between the ideals they had been taught to revere and the realities in American life, met in Port Huron, Michigan, to found Students for a Democratic Society (SDS). Tom Hayden wrote their manifesto, the Port Huron Statement, which expressed their disillusionment with the consumer culture and the gulf between the prosperous and the poor. These students rejected cold war ideology and foreign policy, including but not limited to the Vietnam conflict. The founders of SDS referred to their movement as the "**New Left**" to distinguish themselves from the "Old Left"—Communists and socialists of the 1930s and 1940s. Consciously adopting the activist tactics pioneered by members of the civil rights movement, they turned to grassroots organizing in cities and on college campuses.

The Free Speech Movement. The first major student protests erupted in the fall of 1964 at the University of California at Berkeley, after administrators banned political activity near the Telegraph Avenue entrance, where student groups had traditionally distributed leaflets and recruited volunteers. In protest the major student organizations formed a coalition called the Free Speech Movement (FSM) and organized a sit-in at the administration building. The FSM owed a strong debt to the civil rights movement. Some students had just returned from Freedom Summer in Mississippi, radicalized by their experience. Mario Savio spoke for many of them:

> Last summer I went to Mississippi to join the struggle there for civil rights. This fall I am engaged in another phase of the same struggle, this time in Berkeley. The two battlefields may seem quite different to some observers, but this is not the case. The same rights are at stake in both places—the right to participate as citizens in a democratic society and to struggle against the same enemy. In Mississippi an autocratic and powerful minority rules, through organized violence, to suppress the vast, virtually powerless majority. In California, the privileged minority manipulates the university bureaucracy to suppress the students' political expression.

Free Speech at Berkeley, 1964
Students at the University of California's Berkeley campus protested the administration's decision to ban political activity in the school plaza. Free speech demonstrators, many of them active in the civil rights movement, relied on tactics and arguments that they learned during that struggle.
University of California at Berkeley, Bancroft Library.

Columbia University Protests, 1968
At the height of the Vietnam War in 1968, Columbia University students launched a series of protests against military research contracts, university governance, and the construction of a gymnasium in a nearby Harlem neighborhood. Steve Schapiro / Black Star.

On a deeper level Berkeley students were challenging a university that in their view had grown too big and was too far removed from the major social issues of the day. Emboldened by the Berkeley movement, students across the nation were soon protesting their universities' academic policies and then, more passionately, the Vietnam War.

The Antiwar Movement. The highly politicized activists of the New Left, who had developed a wide-ranging critique of American society, increasingly focused on the war, and they were joined by thousands of other students in protesting American participation in the Vietnam conflict. When President Johnson escalated the war in March 1965, faculty and students at the University of Michigan organized a **teach-in** against the war. Abandoning their classes, they debated the political, diplomatic, and moral aspects of the nation's involvement in Vietnam. Teach-ins quickly spread to other universities as students turned from their studies to protest the war.

Many protests centered on the draft, especially after the Selective Service system abolished automatic student deferments in January 1966. To avoid the draft some young men enlisted in the National Guard or the reserves; others declared themselves conscientious objectors. Several thousand young men ignored their induction notices, risking prosecution for draft evasion.

Others left the country, most often for Canada or Sweden. In public demonstrations of civil disobedience, opponents of the war burned their draft cards, closed down induction centers, and on a few occasions broke into Selective Service offices.

As antiwar and draft protests multiplied, students realized that their universities were deeply implicated in the war effort. In some cases as much as 60 percent of a university's research budget came from government contracts, especially those of the Defense Department. Protesters blocked recruiters from the Dow Chemical Company, the producer of napalm and Agent Orange. Arguing that universities should not train students for war, they demanded that the Reserve Officer Training Corps (ROTC) be removed from college campuses.

After 1967 nationwide student strikes, mass demonstrations, and other organized protests became commonplace. In October 1967 more than 100,000 antiwar demonstrators marched on Washington, D.C., as part of "Stop the Draft Week." The event culminated in a "siege of the Pentagon," in which protesters clashed with police and federal marshals. Hundreds of people were arrested and several demonstrators beaten. Lyndon Johnson, who had once dismissed antiwar protesters as "nervous Nellies," rebellious children, or Communist dupes, now had to face the reality of large-scale public opposition to his policies. Criticism of American policy also came

Che Guevara

Vietnam and the World Freedom Struggle

Che Guevara, a leader of the Cuban Revolution, later worked with revolutionary nationalist movements in Africa and Latin America. Between his departure from Cuba in 1965 and his death in Bolivia in 1967, he made only one public statement. His message, "Vietnam and the World Freedom Struggle," helped convince some young American radicals of the necessity of armed struggle at home and abroad.

This is the painful reality: Vietnam, a nation representing the aspirations and the hopes for victory of the entire world of the disinherited, is tragically alone. . . .

And—what grandeur has been shown by this people! What stoicism and valor in this people! And what a lesson for the world their struggle holds!

It will be a long time before we know if President Johnson ever seriously thought of initiating some of the popular reforms necessary to soften the sharpness of the class contradictions that are appearing with explosive force and more and more frequently.

What is certain is that the improvements announced under the pompous label of the Great Society have gone down the drain in Vietnam.

The greatest of the imperialist powers feels in its own heart the drain caused by a poor, backward country; and its fabulous economy feels the effect of the war. . . .

And for us, the exploited of the world, what should our role be in this? . . .

Our part, the responsibility of the exploited and backward areas of the world, is to eliminate the bases sustaining imperialism—our oppressed peoples, from whom capital, raw materials, technicians and cheap labor are extracted, and to whom new capital, means of domination, arms and all kinds of goods are exported, submerging us in absolute dependence.

The fundamental element of this strategic goal will be, then, the real liberation of the peoples, a liberation that will be obtained through armed struggle in the majority of cases, and which, in the Americas, will have almost unfailingly the property of becoming converted into a socialist revolution.

In focusing on the destruction of imperialism, it is necessary to identify its head, which is none other than the United States of North America. . . .

The adversary must not be underestimated; the North American soldier has technical ability and is backed by means of such magnitude as to make him formidable. He lacks the essential ideological motivation which his most hated rivals of today have to the highest degree—the Vietnamese soldiers. . . .

Over there, the imperialist troops encounter the discomforts of those accustomed to the standard of living which the North American nation boasts. They have to confront a hostile land, the insecurity of those who cannot move without feeling that they are walking on enemy territory; death for those who go outside of fortified redoubts; the permanent hostility of the entire population.

All this continues to provoke repercussions inside the United States; it is going to arouse a factor that was attenuated in the days of the full vigor of imperialism—the class struggle inside its own territory.

Source: Ernesto C. Guevara, *Che Guevara Speaks* (New York: Pathfinder Press, 1967), 144–59.

---

from abroad. Cuban revolutionary leader Che Guevara denounced the war as an imperialist struggle, a view embraced by a growing number of young American radicals (see Voices from Abroad, "Che Guevara: Vietnam and the World Freedom Struggle," above).

The Rise of the Counterculture

While the New Left took to the streets in protest, a growing number of young Americans embarked on a general revolution against authority and middle-class respectability. The "**hippie**"—attired in ragged blue jeans, tie-dyed T-shirt, beads, and army fatigues, with long, unkempt hair—symbolized the new counterculture, a youthful movement that glorified liberation from traditional social strictures.

Not surprisingly, given the importance of rock 'n' roll to 1950s youth culture, popular music formed an important part of the counterculture. The folk singer Pete Seeger set the tone for the era's political idealism with songs such as the antiwar ballad "Where Have All the Flowers Gone?" Another folk singer, Joan Baez, gained national prominence for her rendition of the African American protest song "We Shall Overcome" and other folk and political anthems she performed at protest rallies in the mid-1960s. In 1963, the year of the Birmingham demonstrations and President Kennedy's assassination, Bob Dylan's "Blowin' in the Wind" reflected the impatience of people whose faith in "the system" was wearing thin.

Other winds of change in popular music came from the Beatles, four English working-class youths who burst onto the American scene early in 1964. The Beatles' music, by turns lyrical and driving, was phenomenally successful, spawning a commercial and cultural phenomenon called "Beatlemania." American youth's eager embrace of the Beatles deepened the generational divide between teenagers and their elders already set in motion by the popularity of rock 'n' roll in the 1950s. The Beatles also helped to pave the way for the more rebellious, angrier music of other British groups, notably the Rolling Stones, whose raunchy 1965 "(I Can't Get No) Satisfaction" not only signaled a new openness about sexuality but also made fun of the consumer culture ("He can't be a man 'cause he doesn't smoke the same cigarettes as me").

Drugs intertwined with music as a crucial element of the youth culture. The recreational use of drugs—especially marijuana and lysergic acid diethylamide, the hallucinogen popularly known as LSD, or "acid"—was celebrated in popular music. San Francisco bands such as the Grateful Dead and Jefferson Airplane and musicians like the Seattle-born guitarist Jimi Hendrix developed a musical style known as "acid rock," which was characterized by long, heavily amplified guitar solos accompanied by psychedelic lighting effects. In August 1969, 400,000 young people journeyed to Bethel, New York, to "get high" on music, drugs, and sex at the three-day Woodstock Music and Art Fair. Despite torrential rain and numerous drug overdoses, most enjoyed the festival, which was heralded as the birth of the "Woodstock nation."

For a brief time adherents of the counterculture believed a new age was dawning. They experimented in communal living and glorified uninhibited sexuality. In 1967 the "world's first Human Be-In" drew 20,000 people to Golden Gate Park in San Francisco. The Beat poet Allen Ginsberg "purified" the site with a Buddhist ritual, and the LSD advocate Timothy Leary, a former Harvard psychology instructor, urged the gathering to "turn on to the scene, tune in to what is happening, and drop out." That summer—dubbed the "Summer of Love"—San Francisco's Haight-Ashbury, New York's East Village, and Chicago's Uptown neighborhoods swelled with young dropouts, drifters, and teenage runaways dubbed "flower children" by observers. Their faith in instant love and peace quickly turned sour, however, as they suffered bad drug trips, sexually transmitted diseases, loneliness, and violence. Although many young people kept their distance from both the counterculture and the antiwar movement, to many adult observers it seemed that all of American youth were rejecting political, social, and cultural norms.

The Widening Struggle for Civil Rights

The counterculture and the antiwar movement were not the only social movements to challenge the status quo in the 1960s. The frustration and anger of blacks boiled

Jimi Hendrix at Woodstock
The three-day outdoor "Woodstock" concert in August 1969 was a defining moment in the counterculture as 400,000 young people journeyed to Bethel, New York, for music, drugs, and sex. Jimi Hendrix closed the show with an electrifying version of "The Star Spangled Banner." More overtly political than most counterculture music, Hendrix's rendition featured sound effects that seemed to evoke the violence of the Vietnam War. Michael Wadleigh, who directed the documentary Woodstock, *called Hendrix's performance "his challenge to American foreign policy."*
Allan Koss / Image Bank.

over in a new racial militance as the civil rights struggle moved outside the South and took on the more stubborn problems of entrenched poverty and racism. The rhetoric and tactics of the emerging black-power movement shattered the existing civil rights coalition and galvanized white opposition.

Rising Militance.   Once the system of legal, or de jure, segregation had fallen, the civil rights movement turned to the more difficult task of eliminating the de facto segregation, enforced by custom, that made blacks second-class citizens throughout the nation. Outside the South racial discrimination was less flagrant, but it was pervasive, especially in education, housing, and employment. Although the *Brown* decision outlawed separate schools, it did nothing to change the educational system in areas where schools were all-black or all-white because of residential segregation. Not until 1973 did federal judges begin to extend the desegregation of schools, which had begun in the South two decades earlier, to the rest of the country.

As civil rights leaders took on northern racism, the movement fractured along generational lines. Some younger activists, eager for confrontation and rapid social change, questioned the very goal of integration into white society. Black separatism, espoused by earlier black leaders such as Marcus Garvey in the 1920s (see Chapter 23), was revived in the 1960s by the Nation of Islam, a religious group with more than 10,000 members and many more sympathizers. Popularly known as the Black Muslims, the organization was hostile to whites and stressed black pride, unity, and self-help.

The Black Muslims' most charismatic figure was Malcolm X. A brilliant debater and spellbinding speaker, Malcolm X preached a philosophy quite different from Martin Luther King's. He advocated militant protest and separatism, though he condoned the use of violence only for self-defense. Hostile to the traditional civil rights organizations, he caustically referred to the 1963 March on Washington as the "Farce on Washington." In 1964, after a power struggle with the founder of the Black Muslims, Elijah Muhammad, Malcolm X broke with the Nation of Islam. Following a pilgrimage to Mecca and a tour of Africa, he embraced the liberation struggles of all colonized peoples. But before he could fully pursue his new agenda, he was assassinated while delivering a speech at the Audubon Ballroom in Harlem on February 21, 1965. Three Black Muslims were later convicted of his murder.

Black Power.   A more secular black nationalist movement emerged in 1966 when young black SNCC and CORE activists, following the lead of Stokely Carmichael, began to call for black self-reliance and racial pride under the banner of "Black Power." Amid growing distrust of

white domination, SNCC effectively ejected its white members. In the same year Huey Newton and Bobby Seale, two college students in Oakland, California, founded the Black Panthers, a militant self-defense organization dedicated to protecting local blacks from police violence. The Panthers' organization quickly spread to other cities, where members undertook a wide range of community organizing projects, including interracial efforts, but their affinity for Third World revolutionary movements and armed struggle became their most publicized attribute.

Among the most significant legacies of black power was the assertion of racial pride. Many young blacks insisted on using the term *Afro-American* rather than *Negro*, a term they found demeaning because of its historical association with slavery and racism. Rejecting white tastes and standards, blacks wore African clothing and hairstyles and helped to awaken interest in black history, art, and literature. By the 1970s many colleges and universities were offering programs in black studies.

The new black assertiveness alarmed many white Americans. They had been willing to go along with the moderate reforms of the 1950s and early 1960s but became wary when blacks began demanding immediate access to higher-paying jobs, housing in white neighborhoods, proactive integration of public schools, and increased political power. Another major reason for the erosion of white support was a wave of riots that struck the nation's cities. Lacking education and skills, successive generations of blacks had moved out of the rural South in search of work that paid an adequate wage. In the North many remained unemployed. Resentful of white landlords, who owned the substandard housing they were forced to live in, and white shopkeepers, who denied them jobs in their neighborhoods, many blacks also hated police, whose violent presence in black neighborhoods seemed that of "an occupying army." Stimulated by the successes of southern blacks who had challenged whites and gotten results, young urban blacks expressed their grievances through their own brand of direct action.

Summer in the City.   The first "long hot summer" began in July 1964 in New York City, when police shot a young black criminal suspect in Harlem. Angry youths looted and rioted there for a week. Over the next four years, the volatile issue of police brutality set off riots in dozens of cities. In August 1965 the arrest of a young black motorist in the Watts section of Los Angeles sparked six days of rioting that left thirty-four blacks dead. The riots of 1967 were the most serious, engulfing twenty-two cities in July and August (Map 29.2). The most devastating outbreaks occurred in Newark and Detroit. Forty-three people were killed in Detroit alone, nearly all of them

MAP 29.2 Racial Unrest in America's Cities, 1965–1968

American cities suffered through four "long hot summers" of rioting in the mid-1960s. In 1967, the worst year, riots broke out across the United States, including numerous locations in the South and West. The 1968 report of the National Advisory Commission on Civil Disorders targeted racism as the source of black rage: "What white Americans have never fully understood—but what the Negro can never forget—is that white society is deeply implicated in the ghetto. . . . White institutions created it, white institutions maintain it, and white society condones it." The riots' major impact on white America was to create a climate of fear that helped drain support from the larger civil rights movement.

For more help analyzing this map, see the ONLINE STUDY GUIDE at bedfordstmartins.com/henretta.

black, and $50 million worth of property was destroyed. As in most of the riots, the arson and looting in Detroit targeted white-owned stores and property, but there was little physical violence against white people.

On July 29, 1967, President Johnson appointed a special commission to investigate the riots. The final report of the National Advisory Commission on Civil Disorders (also known as the Kerner Commission), released in March 1968, detailed the continuing inequality and racism of urban life. It also issued a warning: "Our nation is moving toward two societies, one black, one white—separate and unequal. . . . What white Americans have never fully understood—but what the Negro can never forget—is that white society is deeply implicated in the ghetto. White institutions created it, white institutions maintain it, and white society condones it."

The Assassination of Martin Luther King Jr.   On April 4, 1968, barely a month after the Kerner

Commission released its report, Martin Luther King Jr. was assassinated in Memphis, Tennessee, where he had gone to support a strike by predominantly black sanitation workers. King's death set off an explosion of urban rioting, with major violence breaking out in more than a hundred cities.

With King's assassination, the civil rights movement lost the black leader best able to stir the conscience of white America. At the time of his death, King was only thirty-nine years old. During the last years of his life, he had moved toward a broader view of the structural problems of poverty and racism faced by blacks in contemporary America. He spoke out eloquently against the Vietnam War, and in 1968 he was planning a poor people's campaign to raise issues of economic injustice and inequality. How successful King would have been in those endeavors will never be known, but his death marked the passing of an important national leader and symbolized the troubled course of the civil rights movement.

The Legacy of the Civil Rights Movement

The 1960s brought permanent, indeed revolutionary, changes in American race relations. Jim Crow segregation was overturned and federal legislation passed to ensure protection of black Americans' most basic civil rights. The enfranchisement of blacks in the southern states ended political control by all-white state Democratic parties and allowed black candidates to enter the political arena. White candidates who had once been ardent segregationists began to court the black vote. In time Martin Luther King Jr.'s greatness was recognized even among whites in the South; in 1986 his birthday became a national holiday.

Yet much remained undone. The more entrenched forms of segregation and discrimination persisted. African Americans, particularly those in the central cities, continued to make up a disproportionate number of the poor, the unemployed, and the undereducated. As the civil rights movement gradually splintered, its agenda remained unfinished. Yet, even as African Americans experienced frustration with the slow rate of change, their movement provided a fresh and innovative model for other groups seeking to expand their rights.

The Chicano Movement. Although Mexican Americans had been working actively for civil rights since the 1930s (see Chapter 24), poverty, an uncertain legal status, and language barriers made their political mobilization difficult. That situation began to change when the Mexican American Political Association (MAPA) mobilized support for John F. Kennedy; in return Kennedy appointed several Mexican American leaders to posts in Washington. Over the next four years, MAPA and other political organizations worked successfully to elect Mexican American candidates to Congress: Edward Roybal of California and Henry González and Elizo de la Garza of Texas in the House, and Joseph Montoya of New Mexico in the Senate.

Younger Mexican Americans quickly grew impatient with MAPA, however. The barrios of Los Angeles and other western cities produced the militant Brown Berets, modeled on the Black Panthers (who wore black berets). Rejecting the assimilationist approach of their elders, 1,500 Mexican American students met in Denver in 1969 to hammer out a new nationalist political and cultural agenda. They proclaimed a new term, *Chicano*, to replace *Mexican American*, and later organized a new political party, La Raza Unida (The United Race), to promote Chicano interests and candidates. In California and other southwestern states, students staged demonstrations and boycotts to press for bilingual education, the hiring of more Chicano teachers, and the creation of Chicano studies programs. By the 1970s dozens of such programs were offered at universities throughout the region.

Chicano strategists also pursued economic objectives. Working in the fields around Delano, California, labor leader César Chávez organized the United Farm Workers (UFW), the first union to represent migrant workers successfully. A 1965 grape pickers' strike and a nationwide boycott of table grapes brought Chávez and his union national publicity and won support from the AFL-CIO and from Senator Robert F. Kennedy of New York. Victory came in 1970 when California grape growers signed contracts recognizing the UFW.

The Native American Movement. North American Indians also found a model in the civil rights movement. Numbering nearly 800,000 in the 1960s, Native Americans were an exceedingly diverse group, divided by language, tribal history, region, and degree of integration into the mainstream of American life. The termination policy that had begun in the 1950s had accelerated the breakdown of tribal life and the dispersal of Native American populations—although it could also be said to have fostered a sense of "American Indian" identity by bringing diverse Native Americans together. As a group, they shared an unemployment rate ten times the national average as well as the worst poverty, the most inadequate housing, the highest disease rates, and the least access to education of any group in the United States.

As early as World War II, the National Council of American Indians had lobbied for improvement of those conditions. In the 1960s some Indian groups became more assertive. Like the young militants in the black civil rights movement, they challenged the accommodationist approach of their elders. Proposing a new name for themselves—*Native Americans*—they organized protests and demonstrations to build support for their cause. In 1968 several Chippewas from Minnesota organized the militant American Indian Movement (AIM), which drew its strength from the third of the Native American population who lived in "red ghettos" in cities throughout the West.

In November 1969 a group calling themselves "Indians of All Tribes" seized the deserted federal penitentiary on Alcatraz Island in San Francisco Bay, offering the government $24 worth of trinkets to pay for it, supposedly the sum the Dutch had paid the native inhabitants for Manhattan Island in 1626. The occupation of Alcatraz lasted until the summer of 1971. A year later a thousand protesters occupied the headquarters of the Federal Bureau of Indian Affairs in Washington, D.C., which was to many Native Americans a hated symbol of the inconsistent federal policy on tribal welfare (see American Voices, "Mary Crow Dog: The Trail of Broken Treaties," p. 864).

In February 1973, 200 Sioux organized by AIM leaders began an occupation of the tiny village of Wounded Knee, South Dakota, the site of an army massacre of the Sioux in 1890 (see Chapter 16). They were protesting the light sentences given to a group of white men convicted

Mary Crow Dog

The Trail of Broken Treaties

*I*n November 1972, nineteen-year-old Mary Crow Dog *traveled to Washington, D.C., with several hundred other Sioux from the Rosebud and Pine Ridge reservations in South Dakota. As she explains in her autobiography, their group was one of several caravans participating in a protest known as the "Trail of Broken Treaties," which ended in a six-day occupation of the Bureau of Indian Affairs headquarters.*

When we arrived in Washington we got lost. We had been promised food and accommodation, but due to government pressure many church groups which had offered to put us up and feed us got scared and backed off. . . .

Somebody suggested, "Let's all go to the BIA." It seemed the natural thing to do, to go to the Bureau of Indian Affairs building on Constitution Avenue. They would have to put us up. It was "our" building after all. Besides, that was what we had come for, to complain about the treatment the bureau was dishing out to us. . . . Next thing I knew we were in it. We spilled into the building like a great avalanche. Some people put up a tipi on the front lawn. . . . The building finally belonged to us and we lost no time turning it into a tribal village. . . .

We pushed the police and guards out of the building. Some did not wait to be pushed but jumped out of the ground-floor windows like so many frogs. We had formulated twenty Indian demands. These were all rejected by the few bureaucrats sent to negotiate with us. . . . Soon we listened to other voices as the occupation turned into a siege. I heard somebody yelling, "The pigs are here." I could see from the window that it was true. The whole building was surrounded by helmeted police armed with all kinds of guns. A fight broke out between the police and our security. Some of our young men got hit over the head with police clubs and we saw the blood streaming down their faces. . . .

We barricaded all doors and the lowest windows with document boxes, Xerox machines, tables, file cabinets, anything we could lay our hands on. . . .

From then on, every morning we were given a court order to get out by six P.M. Come six o'clock and we would be standing there ready to join battle. I think many brothers and sisters were prepared to die right on the steps of the BIA building. . . .

In the end a compromise was reached. The government said . . . they would appoint two high administration officials to seriously consider our twenty demands. Our expenses to get home would be paid. Nobody would be prosecuted. Of course, our twenty points were never gone into afterward. From the practical point of view, nothing had been achieved. . . . But morally it had been a great victory. We had faced White America collectively, not as individual tribes. We had stood up to the government and gone through our baptism of fire. We had not run.

Source: Mary Crow Dog, *Lakota Woman* (New York: Grove Weidenfeld, 1990), 84–85, 88–91.

of killing a Sioux in 1972. To dramatize their cause the protesters took eleven hostages and occupied several buildings. But when a gun battle with the FBI left one protester dead and another wounded, the seventy-one-day siege collapsed. Although the new Native American activism helped to alienate many white onlookers, it did spur government action on tribal issues (see Chapter 31).

Identity Politics.   Civil rights, once seen as a movement exclusively for the rights of black people, also sparked a new awareness among some predominantly white groups. Americans of Polish, Italian, Greek, and Slavic descent, most of them working class and Catholic, proudly embraced their ethnic identities. Through groups like the Grey Panthers, elderly Americans organized to demand better health, Social Security, and other benefits.

Homosexual men and women also banded together to protest legal and social oppression based on their sexual orientation. In 1969 the gay liberation movement gained momentum in the "Stonewall riot" in New York City, when patrons of a gay bar fought back against police harassment. The assertion of gay pride that followed the incident drew heavily on the language and tactics of the civil rights movement. Activists took the new name of *gay* rather than *homosexual*; founded advocacy groups, newspapers, and political organizations to challenge

Wounded Knee Revisited

In 1973 members of the American Indian Movement staged a seventy-one-day protest at Wounded Knee, South Dakota, the site of the 1890 massacre of 200 Sioux by U.S. soldiers. (See Map 16.4, The Indian Frontier, to 1890, p. 470.) The takeover was sparked by the murder of a local Sioux by a group of whites but quickly expanded to include demands for basic reforms in federal Indian policy and tribal governance.
Corbis-Bettmann.

discrimination and prejudice; and offered emotional support to those who "came out" and publicly affirmed their homosexuality. For gays as well as members of various ethnic and cultural groups, political activism based on heightened group identity represented one of the most significant legacies of the African American struggle.

The Revival of Feminism

The black civil rights movement also helped to reactivate **feminism**, a movement that had been languishing since the 1920s. Just as the abolition movement had been the training ground for women's rights advocates in the nineteenth century, the black struggle became an inspiration for young feminists in the 1960s. But the revival of feminism also sprang from social and demographic changes that affected women young and old.

Changing Social Conditions.   By 1970, 42.6 percent of women were working, and four out of ten working women were married. Especially significant was the growth in the number of working women with preschool children—up from 12 percent in 1950 to 30 percent in 1970.

Another significant change was increased access to education for women. Immediately after World War II, the percentage of college students who were women declined, as the GI Bill gave men a temporary advantage in access to higher education. At the height of the baby boom, many college women dropped out of school to marry and raise families. By 1960, however, the percentage of college students who were women had risen to 35 percent; in 1970 it reached 41 percent.

The meaning of marriage was changing, too. The baby boom turned out to be only a temporary interruption of a century-long decline in the birthrate. The introduction of the birth control pill, first marketed in 1960, and the intrauterine device (IUD) helped women control their fertility. Women had fewer children, and because of an increased life expectancy (seventy-five years in 1970, up from fifty-four years in 1920), they devoted proportionally fewer years to raising children. At the same time the divorce rate, which had risen slowly throughout the twentieth century, rose markedly as the states liberalized divorce laws. As a result of these changes, traditional gender expectations were dramatically undermined. American women's lives now usually included work and marriage, often childrearing and a career, and possibly bringing up children alone after a divorce. Those changing social realities created a major constituency for the emerging women's movement of the 1960s.

Older, politically active professional women sought change by working through the political system. This group was galvanized in part by a report by the Presidential Commission on the Status of Women (1963), which documented the employment and educational discrimination women faced. More important than the report's rather conservative recommendations was the rudimentary nationwide network of women in public life that formed in the course of the commission's work.

Another spark that ignited the revival of feminism was Betty Friedan's pointed indictment of suburban domesticity, *The Feminine Mystique*, published in 1963 (see Chapter 28). Women responded enthusiastically to Friedan's book—especially white, college-educated, middle-class women. The book sold 3 million copies and was excerpted in many women's magazines. *The Feminine Mystique* gave women a vocabulary with which to express their dissatisfaction and promoted women's self-realization through employment, continuing education, and other activities outside the home.

Like so many other constituencies in postwar America, women's rights activists looked to the federal government for help. Especially important was the Civil Rights Act of 1964, which had as great an impact on women as it did on blacks and other minorities. Title VII, which barred discrimination in employment on the basis of race, religion, national origin, or sex, eventually became a powerful tool in the fight against sex discrimination. At first, however, the Equal Employment Opportunity Commission (EEOC) avoided implementing it.

The National Organization for Women.

Dissatisfied with the Commission's reluctance to defend women's rights, Friedan and others founded the National Organization for Women (NOW) in 1966. Modeling itself on groups such as the NAACP, NOW aimed to be a civil rights organization for women. "The purpose of NOW," an early statement declared, "is to take action to bring women into full participation in the mainstream of American society now, exercising all the privileges and responsibilities thereof in truly equal partnership with men." Under Friedan, who served as NOW's first president, membership grew from 1,000 in 1967 to 15,000 in 1971. Men made up a fourth of NOW's early membership. The group is still the largest feminist organization in the United States.

Women's Liberation.

Another group of new feminists, the women's liberationists, came to the women's movement through their civil rights work. White college women had made up about half the students who went south with SNCC in the Freedom Summer project of 1964. Young women like Casey Hayden and Mary King found role models in older southern women like Ella Baker, Anne Braden, and Virginia Foster Durr, who were prominent in the civil rights movement. They also appreciated the work of local black women who were in the forefront of community organizing and who put their lives on the line by housing SNCC workers. As Dorothy Burlage noted, these women "inspired me to think that women could do anything." As the white college women developed self-confidence and organizational skills working in the South, some of them began to question what would later be called the sexism of the male-dominated leadership.

After 1965 black militants made whites unwelcome in the civil rights movement. But when white women transferred their energies to the antiwar groups that were emerging in that period, they found the New Left even more male dominated. When the antiwar movement adopted draft resistance as a central strategy, women found themselves marginalized. Those women who tried to raise feminist issues at conventions were shouted off the platform with jeers such as "Move on, little girl, we have more important issues to talk about here than women's liberation."

Around 1967 the contradiction between the New Left's lip service to egalitarianism and women's treatment by male leaders caused women radicals to realize

Women's Liberation

Arguing that beauty contests were degrading to women, members of the National Women's Liberation Party staged a protest against the Miss America pageant held in Atlantic City, New Jersey, in September 1968. Wide World Photos, Inc.

that they needed their own movement. In contrast to groups such as NOW, which had traditional organizational structures and dues-paying members, these women formed loose collectives whose shifting membership often lacked any formal structure. They organized independently in five or six different cities, including Chicago, San Francisco, and New York.

Members of the women's liberation movement (or "women's lib," as it was dubbed by the somewhat hostile media) went public in 1968 in a protest at the Miss America pageant. Their demonstration featured a "freedom trash can" into which they encouraged women to throw false eyelashes, hair curlers, brassieres, and girdles—all of which they branded as symbols of female oppression. An activity with a more lasting impact was "consciousness raising"—group sessions in which women shared their experiences of being female. Swapping stories about being passed over for a promotion, needing a husband's signature on a credit card application, or enduring the whistles and leers of men while walking down the street helped participants to realize that their individual problems were part of a wider pattern of oppression. The slogan "The personal is political" became a rallying cry of the movement.

By 1970 a growing convergence of interests began to blur the distinction between women's rights and women's liberation. Radical women realized that key feminist goals—child care, equal pay, and abortion rights—could best be achieved in the political arena. At the same time more traditional activists developed a broader view of the women's movement, tentatively including divisive issues such as abortion and lesbian rights. Although the movement remained largely white and middle class, feminists were beginning to think of themselves as part of a broad, growing, and increasingly influential social crusade that would continue to grow.

The Long Road Home, 1968–1975

The United States in 1968 was deeply polarized. Riots in the cities, black and Chicano power, campus unrest, and a host of protests and challenges were, in the eyes of many citizens, tearing the country in two. But Vietnam remained the central domestic and foreign-policy issue. Although the Johnson administration insisted that there was "light at the end of the tunnel," the reality was otherwise. The war would continue, at home and in Vietnam, for another five years.

1968: A Year of Shocks

In 1968, as Lyndon Johnson planned his reelection campaign, antiwar protests and rising battlefield casualties had begun to erode public support for a war that seemed to have no end. Since Diem's assassination in 1963, South Vietnam had undergone a confusing series of military coups and countercoups. In the spring of 1966, the Johnson administration pressured the unpopular South Vietnamese government to adopt democratic reforms, including a new constitution and popular elections. In September 1967 U.S. officials helped to elect General Nguyen Van Thieu president of South Vietnam. Thieu's regime, the administration hoped, would stabilize politics in South Vietnam, advance the military struggle against the Communists, and legitimize the South Vietnamese government in the eyes of the American public.

The Tet Offensive. The administration's hopes evaporated on January 30, 1968, when the Viet Cong unleashed a massive, well-coordinated assault on major urban areas in South Vietnam. Known as the "Tet" offensive, the assault was timed to coincide with the lunar new year, a festive Vietnamese holiday. Viet Cong forces struck thirty-six of the forty-four provincial capitals and five of the six major cities, including Saigon, where they raided the supposedly impregnable U.S. embassy (see Map 29.1). In strict military terms the Tet offensive was a failure for the Viet Cong since it did not provoke the intended collapse of the South Vietnamese government. But its long-term effect was quite different. The daring attack made a mockery of official pronouncements that the United States was winning the war and swung American public opinion more strongly against the war. Just before the offensive a Gallup poll found that 56 percent of Americans considered themselves "hawks" (supporters of the war), while only 28 percent identified with the "doves" (opponents). Three months after Tet the doves outnumbered the hawks 42 to 41 percent. This turnaround in public opinion did not mean that a majority of Americans supported the peace movement, however. Many who called themselves doves had simply concluded that the war was unwinnable and were therefore opposed to it on pragmatic rather than moral grounds. As a housewife told a pollster, "I want to get out, but I don't want to give up."

Political Turmoil. The growing opposition to the war spilled over into the 1968 presidential campaign. Even before Tet, Senator Eugene J. McCarthy of Minnesota had entered the Democratic primaries as an antiwar candidate. President Johnson won the early New Hampshire primary, but McCarthy received a stunning 42.2 percent of the vote. His strong showing against the president reflected profound public dissatisfaction with the course of the war, even among those who were hawks.

Johnson realized that his political support was evaporating. On March 31 and at the end of an otherwise mundane televised address, he stunned the nation by announcing that he would not seek reelection. Johnson had already reversed his policy of incremental escalation of the war. Now he called a partial bombing halt and vowed to devote his remaining months in office to the search for peace. On May 10, 1968, preliminary peace talks between the United States and North Vietnam opened in Paris.

Just four days after Johnson's withdrawal from the presidential race, Martin Luther King Jr. was assassinated in Memphis. The ensuing riots in cities across the country left forty-three people dead. Soon afterward, students protesting Columbia University's plans for expanding into a neighboring ghetto and displacing its residents occupied several campus buildings. The brutal response of the New York City police helped to radicalize even more students. The next month a massive strike by students and labor unions toppled the French government. Student unrest seemed likely to become a world-wide phenomenon.

Then came the final tragedy of the year. Senator Robert Kennedy, who had entered the Democratic presidential primaries in March, had quickly become a front-runner. On June 5, 1968, as he celebrated his victory in the California primary, he was shot dead by a young Palestinian who was thought to oppose Kennedy's pro-Israeli stance. Robert Kennedy's assassination shattered the dreams of many who had hoped that social change could be achieved by working through the political system. His death also weakened the Democratic Party. In his brief but dramatic campaign, Kennedy had excited and energized the traditional members of the New Deal coalition, including blue-collar workers and black voters, in a way that the more cerebral Eugene McCarthy, who appealed mostly to the antiwar movement, never did.

The Democratic Party never fully recovered from Johnson's withdrawal and Kennedy's assassination. McCarthy's campaign limped along, while Senator George S. McGovern of South Dakota entered the Democratic race in an effort to keep the Kennedy forces together. Meanwhile, Vice President Hubert H. Humphrey lined up pledges from traditional Democratic constituencies—unions, urban machines, and state political organizations. Democrats found themselves on the verge of nominating not an antiwar candidate but a public figure closely associated with Johnson's war policies.

The Siege of Chicago. At the August Democratic nominating convention, the political divisions generated by the war consumed the party. Most of the drama occurred not in the convention hall but outside on the streets of Chicago. Led by activists Jerry Rubin and Abbie Hoffman, around 10,000 protesters descended on the city, calling for an end to the war, the legalization of marijuana, and the abolition of money. To mock those inside the convention hall, these "Yippies," as the group called themselves, nominated a pig for president. Their

RFK

Bobby Kennedy inspired strong passions during his 1968 campaign. Followers often tore off his cuff links as they tried to touch him or shake his hand. Steve Schapiro / Black Star.

stunts, geared toward maximizing their media exposure, diverted attention from the more serious and far more numerous antiwar activists who had come to Chicago as convention delegates or volunteers.

Richard J. Daley, the Democratic mayor of Chicago who had grown increasingly angry as protesters disrupted his convention, called out the police to break up the demonstrations. Several nights of skirmishes between protesters and police culminated on the evening of the nominations. In what an official report later described as a "police riot," patrolmen attacked protesters with mace, tear gas, and clubs as demonstrators chanted, "The whole world is watching!" Television networks broadcast a film of the riot as the nominating speeches were being made, cementing a popular impression of the Democrats as the party of disorder. Inside the hall the Democrats dispiritedly nominated Hubert H. Humphrey, who chose Senator Edmund S. Muskie of

Maine as his running mate. The delegates approved a middle-of-the-road platform that endorsed continued fighting in Vietnam while the administration explored diplomatic means of ending the conflict.

Backlash. The disruptive Democratic convention unleashed a backlash against antiwar protesters. The general public did not differentiate between the disruptive antics of the Yippies and the more responsible behavior of those activists who were trying to work within the system. Polls showed overwhelming support for Mayor Daley and the police.

The turmoil surrounding the New Left and the antiwar movement strengthened support for proponents of "law and order," which became a conservative catch phrase for the next several years. Indeed, many Americans, though opposed to the war, were fed up with protest and dissent. Governor George C. Wallace of Alabama, a third-party candidate, skillfully exploited their growing disapproval of the antiwar movement by making student protests and urban riots his chief campaign issues. But Wallace, who in 1963 had promised to enforce "segregation now . . . segregation tomorrow . . . and segregation forever," also exploited the mounting backlash against the civil rights movement. Articulating the resentments of many working-class whites, he combined attacks on liberal intellectuals and government elites with strident denunciations of school desegregation and forced busing.

Even more than George Wallace, Richard Nixon tapped the increasingly conservative mood of the electorate. After his unsuccessful presidential campaign in 1960 and his loss in the California gubernatorial race in 1962, Nixon engineered an amazing political comeback and in 1968 won the Republican presidential nomination. As part of what his advisors called the "southern strategy," he chose Spiro Agnew, the conservative governor of Maryland, as his running mate to help him make inroads into the once solidly Democratic South. Nixon hoped to attract southern voters, especially Wallace supporters, who opposed Democratic civil rights legislation. He also used traditional populist appeals, pledging, to represent the "quiet voice" of the "great majority of Americans, the forgotten Americans, the nonshouters, the nondemonstrators."

Despite the Democratic debacle in Chicago, the election was a close one. In the last weeks of the campaign, Humphrey rallied by gingerly disassociating himself from Johnson's war policies. Then in a televised address on October 31, President Johnson announced a complete halt to the bombing of North Vietnam. Nixon countered by intimating that he had his own plan to end the war—although in reality no such plan existed. On election day Nixon received 43.4 percent of the vote to Humphrey's 42.7 percent, defeating him by a scant 510,000 votes out

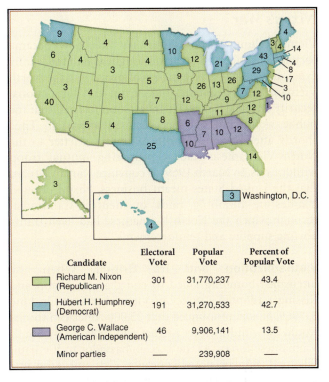

Candidate	Electoral Vote	Popular Vote	Percent of Popular Vote
Richard M. Nixon (Republican)	301	31,770,237	43.4
Hubert H. Humphrey (Democrat)	191	31,270,533	42.7
George C. Wallace (American Independent)	46	9,906,141	13.5
Minor parties	—	239,908	—

MAP 29.3 Presidential Election of 1968

With Lyndon B. Johnson's surprise decision not to run for another term and, less than three month's later, the assassination of the party's most charismatic contender for the presidential nomination, Robert Kennedy, the Democrats faced the election of 1968 in disarray. Controversy over the Vietnam War fractured the party, as did the appeal of Governor George Wallace of Alabama, who left the Democrats to run as a third-party candidate and campaigned on the backlash against the civil rights movement. As late as mid-September Wallace held the support of 21 percent of the voters. But in November he received only 13.5 percent of the vote, winning five states and showing that the South was no longer solidly Democratic. Republican Richard M. Nixon, who like Wallace emphasized "law and order" in his campaign, defeated Hubert H. Humphrey with only 43.4 percent of the popular vote.

of the 73 million that were cast (Map 29.3). Wallace finished with 13.5 percent of the popular vote. Though Nixon owed his election largely to the split in the Democratic coalition, the success of his southern strategy presaged the emergence of a new Republican majority. In the meantime, however, the Democrats retained a majority in both houses of Congress.

The closeness of the 1968 election suggested how polarized American society had become. Nixon appealed to a segment of society that came to be known as the **silent majority**—hard-working, nonprotesting, generally white Americans. Although his victory suggested a growing consensus among voters who were "unblack, unpoor, and unyoung," heated protest and controversy would persist until the war ended.

Nixon's War

Vietnam, long Lyndon Johnson's war, now became Richard Nixon's. At first Nixon sought to end the war by expanding its scope, as a means of pressuring the North Vietnamese to negotiate. But Nixon and his national security advisor, Henry Kissinger, soon realized that the public would not support such an approach. Thus shortly after Nixon took office, he sent a letter to the North Vietnamese leaders proposing mutual troop withdrawals. In March 1969, to convince North Vietnam that the United States meant business, Nixon ordered clandestine bombing raids on neutral Cambodia, through which the North Vietnamese had been transporting supplies and reinforcements.

Vietnamization and Its Critics. When the intensified bombing failed to end the war, Nixon and Kissinger adopted a policy of Vietnamization. On June 8, 1969, Nixon announced that 25,000 American troops would be withdrawn by August and replaced by South Vietnamese forces. As the U.S. ambassador to Vietnam, Ellsworth Bunker, noted cynically, Vietnamization was just a matter of changing "the color of the bodies." Antiwar demonstrators denounced the new policy, which protected American lives at the expense of the Vietnamese but would not end the war. On October 15, 1969, in cities across the country, millions of Americans joined a one-day "moratorium" against the war. A month later more than a quarter of a million people mobilized in Washington in the largest antiwar demonstration to date.

To discredit his critics Nixon denounced student demonstrators as "bums" and stated that "North Vietnam cannot defeat or humiliate the United States. Only Americans can do that." Vice President Spiro Agnew attacked dissenters as "ideological eunuchs" and "nattering nabobs of negativism." Nixon staunchly insisted that he would not be swayed by the mounting protests against the war. During the November 1969 March on Washington, the president barricaded himself in the White House and watched football on television.

Invasion in Cambodia. On April 30, 1970, the bombing of Cambodia, which Nixon had kept secret from both the public and from Congress, culminated in an "incursion" into Cambodia by American ground forces to destroy enemy havens there. The invasion proved only a short-term setback for the North Vietnamese. More critically, the American action in Cambodia—along with the ongoing North Vietnamese intervention there—destabilized the country, exposing it to a takeover by the ruthless Khmer Rouge later in the 1970s.

When the *New York Times* uncovered the secret invasion of Cambodia, outrage led antiwar leaders to organize a national student strike. On May 4 at Kent State University outside Cleveland, panicky National Guardsmen fired into a crowd of students at an antiwar rally. Four people were killed and eleven more wounded. Only two of those who were killed had been attending the demonstration; the other two were just passing by on their way to class. Soon afterward, National Guardsmen stormed a dormitory at Jackson State College in Mississippi, killing two black students. More than 450 colleges closed in protest, and 80 percent of all campuses experienced some kind of disturbance. In June 1970, immediately after the Kent State slayings, a Gallup poll identified campus unrest as the issue that most troubled Americans.

At the same time, however, dissatisfaction with the war continued to spread. Congressional opposition to the war, which had been growing since the Fulbright hearings in 1966, intensified with the invasion of Cambodia. In June 1970 the Senate expressed its disapproval by voting to repeal the Gulf of Tonkin resolution and by cutting off funding for operations in Cambodia. Even the soldiers in Vietnam were showing mounting opposition to their mission. The number of troops who refused to follow combat orders increased steadily, and thousands of U.S. soldiers deserted. Among the majority who fought on, many sewed peace symbols on their uniforms. In the heat of battle, a number of overbearing junior officers were sometimes "fragged"—killed or wounded in grenade attacks by their own soldiers. At home, members of a group called Vietnam Veterans Against the War turned in their combat medals at demonstrations outside the U.S. Capitol.

The My Lai Massacre. In 1971 Americans were appalled by revelations of the sheer brutality of the war when Lieutenant William L. Calley was court-martialed for atrocities committed in the village of My Lai. In March 1968 Calley and the platoon under his command had apparently murdered 350 Vietnamese villagers in retaliation for casualties sustained in an earlier engagement. The incident came to light because one member of the platoon refused to go along with a military cover-up; investigative reporter Seymour Hersh of the *New York Times* broke the story in November 1969. The military court sentenced Calley to life in prison for his part in the massacre. Yet George Wallace and some congressional conservatives called him a hero. President Nixon had Calley's sentence reduced; he was paroled in 1974.

The Decline of Antiwar Protest. After a final outbreak of protest and violence following the incident at Kent State, antiwar activism began to ebb. The antiwar movement was weakened in part by internal divisions within the New Left. In the late 1960s SDS and other antiwar groups fell victim to police harassment, and Federal Bureau of Investigation (FBI) and Central Intelligence Agency (CIA) agents infiltrated and disrupted

Passing the Buck

Highlighting the long and tortured history of the war, Jules Feiffer's 1975 cartoon offered a biting commentary on the lack of presidential accountability for U.S. policies in Vietnam.

radical organizations. After 1968 the New Left splintered into factions, its energy spent. One radical faction broke off from SDS and formed the Weathermen, a tiny band of self-styled revolutionaries who embraced terrorist tactics that alienated more moderate activists.

Nixon's Vietnamization policy also played a role in the decline of antiwar protest by dramatically reducing the number of soldiers in combat. When Nixon took office, more than 543,000 American soldiers were serving in Vietnam; by the end of 1970, there were 334,000, and two years later there were 24,200. Nixon's promise to continue troop withdrawals, end the draft, and institute an all-volunteer army by 1973 further deprived the antiwar movement of important organizing issues, particularly on college campuses. Student commitment to social causes, however, did not disappear altogether. In the early 1970s many student activists refocused their energies on issues such as feminism and environmentalism.

Withdrawal from Vietnam and Détente

At the same time Nixon had been prosecuting the war in Vietnam, ostensibly to halt the spread of communism, he had been formulating a new policy toward the Soviet Union and China. Known as **détente** (the French word for a relaxation of tensions), Nixon's policy was to seek peaceful coexistence with the two Communist powers and to link his overtures of friendship with a plan to end the Vietnam War. In his talks with Chinese and Soviet leaders, Nixon urged them to reduce their military aid to the North Vietnamese as a means of pressuring the North Vietnamese to the negotiating table.

A lifelong anti-Communist crusader, Nixon was better able to reach out to the two Communist superpowers without arousing American mistrust than a Democratic president would have been. Since the Chinese revolution of 1949, the United States had refused to recognize the government of the People's Republic of China. Instead, the State Department had recognized the Nationalist Chinese government in Taiwan. Nixon moved away from that policy, reasoning that the United States could exploit the growing rift between the People's Republic of China and the Soviet Union. In February 1972 Nixon journeyed to China in a symbolic visit that set the stage for the establishment of formal diplomatic relations in 1979.

In a similar spirit Nixon journeyed to Moscow in May 1972 to sign the first Strategic Arms Limitations Treaty (SALT I) between the United States and the Soviet Union. Although SALT I fell far short of ending the arms race, it did limit the production and deployment of intercontinental ballistic missiles (ICBMs) and antiballistic missile systems (ABMs). The treaty also signified that the United States could no longer afford the massive military spending that would have been necessary to regain the

The Fall of Saigon

After the 1973 U.S. withdrawal from Vietnam, the South Vietnamese government lasted another two years. In March 1975 the North Vietnamese forces launched a final offensive against the south and by April had surrounded the capital of Saigon. Here, panicked Vietnamese seek sanctuary at the U.S. embassy compound. Vietnam was united on April 29, 1975. Nik Wheeler / Sipa.

nuclear and military superiority it had enjoyed immediately following World War II. By the early 1970s inflation, domestic dissent, and the decline in American hegemony had limited and reshaped American aims and options in international relations. Most of all Nixon hoped that a rapprochement with the Soviets would help to resolve the prolonged crisis in Vietnam.

The Paris peace talks had been in stalemate since 1968. Though the war had been "Vietnamized," and American casualties had decreased, the South Vietnamese military proved unable to hold its own. In late 1971, as American troops withdrew from the region, Communist forces stepped up their attacks on Laos, Cambodia, and South Vietnam. The next spring North Vietnamese forces launched a major new offensive against South Vietnam. In April, as the fighting intensified, Nixon ordered B-52 bombing raids against North Vietnam, and a month later he approved the mining of North Vietnamese ports (see American Lives, "John Paul Vann: Dissident Patriot," p. 874).

That spring the increased combat activity and growing political pressure at home helped revive the Paris peace negotiations. Nixon hoped to undercut antiwar critics by making concessions to the North Vietnamese in the peace talks. In October Henry Kissinger and the North Vietnamese negotiator Le Duc Tho reached a cease-fire agreement calling for the withdrawal of the remaining U.S. troops, the return of all American prisoners of war, and the continued presence of North Vietnamese troops in South Vietnam. Nixon and Kissinger also promised the North Vietnamese substantial aid for postwar reconstruction. On the eve of the 1972 presidential election, Kissinger announced "peace is at hand," and Nixon returned to the White House with a resounding electoral victory (see Chapter 30).

The peace initiative, however, soon stalled when the South Vietnamese rejected the provision concerning North Vietnamese troop positions, and the North declined to compromise further. With negotiations deadlocked, Nixon stepped up military action once more. From December 17 to December 30, 1972, American planes subjected civilian and military targets in Hanoi and Haiphong to the most devastating bombing of the war, referred to in the press as the "Christmas bombings."

Finally, on January 27, 1973, representatives of the United States, North and South Vietnam, and the Viet Cong signed a cease-fire in Paris. But the Paris Peace accords, which differed little from the proposal that had been rejected in October, did not fulfill Nixon's promise of "peace with honor." Basically, they mandated the unilateral withdrawal of American troops in exchange for the return of American prisoners of war from North Vietnam. For most Americans that was enough.

Without massive U.S. military and economic aid and with North Vietnamese guerrillas operating freely throughout the countryside, the South Vietnamese government of General Nguyen Van Thieu soon fell to the more disciplined and popular Communist forces. In March 1975 North Vietnamese forces launched a final offensive. Horrified American television viewers watched as South Vietnamese officials and soldiers struggled with American embassy personnel to board the last helicopters that would fly out of Saigon before

North Vietnamese troops entered the city. On April 29, 1975, Vietnam was reunited, and Saigon was renamed Ho Chi Minh City in honor of the Communist leader who had died in 1969.

The Legacy of Vietnam

Spanning nearly thirty years, the American involvement in Vietnam occupied administrations from Truman to Nixon's successor Gerald Ford. U.S. troops fought in Vietnam for more than eleven years, from 1961 to 1973. In human terms the nation's longest war exacted an enormous cost. Some 58,000 U.S. troops died, and another 300,000 were wounded. Even those who returned unharmed encountered a sometimes hostile or indifferent reception. Arriving home alone without the fanfare that had greeted soldiers of America's victorious wars, most Vietnam veterans found the transition to civilian life abrupt and disorienting. The psychological tensions

The Vietnam Veterans' Memorial
Conceived and funded by a small group of veterans, the Vietnam Veterans' Memorial was dedicated in Washington, D.C., in November 1982. The memorial, designed by Maya Ling Lin, a Yale architecture student, consists of two walls of black granite inscribed with the names of 58,183 men and women who died in the war. The wall of names has tremendous emotional impact on viewers and has become one of the most popular tourist destinations in the nation's capital. Peter Marlow / Magnum Photos, Inc.

John Paul Vann: Dissident Patriot

The divisions caused by the Vietnam War haunted Arlington National Cemetery on June 16, 1972, when three hundred mourners assembled for the funeral of John Paul Vann. "The soldier of the war in Vietnam," Vann had been killed in a helicopter crash in the Central Highlands the week before. Politicians and military leaders closely associated with the war effort were very much in evidence—General William Westmoreland, CIA Director William Colby, the conservative journalist Joseph Alsop, and Secretary of State William Rogers. But so were Daniel Ellsberg, a former Pentagon official who had publicly turned against the war, and Senator Edward Kennedy, another war opponent who had shared Vann's concern about the plight of Vietnamese refugees. In a time of intense polarization over a war that was still going on, this assemblage of hawks and doves was an exceptional sight.

Vann's family also showed the rifts over Vietnam that day. His wife of twenty-six years, Mary Jane, had requested two pieces of music: the upbeat "Colonel Bogie March" from the film *The Bridge on the River Kwai*, one of her husband's favorites, and the haunting antiwar ballad "Where Have All the Flowers Gone?" to express her opposition to the war. One of Vann's sons, twenty-one-year-old Jesse, hated the war so profoundly that he tore his draft card in two at the funeral, placing half of it on his father's casket. He planned to give the other half to President Richard Nixon at the White House ceremony after the funeral, where his father would be presented posthumously with the Presidential Medal of Freedom. Only at the last moment was Jesse talked out of his act of defiance, agreeing that this was, after all, his father's day.

Also at the funeral was *New York Times* reporter Neil Sheehan, who decided at that moment to write a biography of Vann, which he published sixteen years later, *A Bright and Shining Lie*. Sheehan, along with David Halberstam and other reporters, had fallen under Vann's spell during his first tour of duty in Vietnam in 1963, when Vann seemed to be the only American official who was willing to admit that the war was not going well. Sheehan had continued to rely on Vann's outspoken assessments for the rest of the war. "In this war without heroes, this man had been the one compelling figure," Sheehan concluded. "By an obsession, by an unyielding dedication to the war, he had come to personify the American endeavor in Vietnam."

John Paul Vann was an enormously complicated person—a born leader, a visionary, a man who knew no physical fear, but most of all a true believer in America's mission to share democracy with countries "less fortunate" than the United States. His early years were shaped by poverty and lack of opportunity. Born in 1924 to a working-class family in Norfolk, Virginia, he grew up poor during the Great Depression. A colleague later remembered him as a "cocky little red-necked guy with a rural Virginia twang." World War II offered a ticket out; when Vann turned eighteen in 1943, he enlisted and made the army his career. He served with distinction in the Korean War and then took assignments in West Germany and the United States. But in 1959 his service record was stained by accusations of the statutory rape of a fifteen-year-old girl. Even though the army eventually dropped the charges, the scandal effectively prevented him from moving up in the military bureaucracy. Neil Sheehan later concluded that Vann's "moral heroism" in speaking out against the conduct of the war to the seeming detriment of his career was rooted in his awareness that he had nothing to lose, although reporters did not know the full story at the time.

In 1963 thirty-nine-year-old Lieutenant Colonel Vann was sent to Vietnam, where he served as a senior advisor to a South Vietnamese infantry division in the Mekong Delta. At the battle of Ap Bac, he watched his South Vietnamese counterpart purposely refuse to fight the battle the way it had been planned and let the enemy escape. In a moment of epiphany, Vann realized that the rosy reports being fed to Saigon and Washington were false and that Saigon suffered from "an institutionalized unwillingness to fight." After unsuccessful attempts to enlighten his superiors, he leaked his meticulously documented assessments to reporters such as Halberstam and Sheehan. His candor won him few friends in the military, and at the end of his tour of duty, he was reassigned to the Pentagon. He tried to alert the Joint Chiefs of Staff that the war was not being won, but at the last moment the scheduled briefing was canceled, in large

Planning Strategy

Lieutenant Colonel John P. Vann (left) shown during his tour of duty in Vietnam in 1963, discussing a tactical decision.
U.S. Army Photo / U.S. Department of Defense, Still Media Records Center, Washington, DC.

For more help analyzing this image, see the ONLINE STUDY GUIDE at bedfordstmartins.com/henretta.

part because the Joint Chiefs did not want to hear his version of the problem. Frustrated and disillusioned, Vann resigned from the army soon afterward and went to work for a civilian defense contractor.

Before long, however, Vann grew restless with stateside life and tried to rejoin the military. Wary of Vann's public criticism of the war, the army refused to accept him. In 1965 Vann found civilian employment with the Agency for International Development in a pacification program to win over the peasants to the South Vietnamese side rather than the National Liberation Front. Arriving just as the major escalation of the war was getting underway, Vann would stay in Vietnam (except for brief trips home) until his death. His honesty and unmatched familiarity with conditions in the countryside led him to conclude that the Communists were doing a far better job at appealing to the local population than was the corrupt Saigon government. As he wrote to a friend in 1965, "If I were a lad of eighteen faced with the same choice—whether to support the GVN [Government of Vietnam] or the NLF—and a member of a rural community, I would surely choose the NLF." His concern for winning over the local peasantry made him an outspoken opponent of the heavy bombing inflicted on the Vietnamese countryside to roust Vietcong sympathizers. He also strongly criticized General Westmoreland's strategy of sending in more American troops to wear down the Vietcong in a war of attrition, arguing that this would be useless without major reforms in the Saigon government.

Despite his role as a gadfly and even though he was now a civilian, Vann assumed more and more responsibility in the day-to-day conduct of the war. In 1971 he was given authority over all the U.S. military forces in the Central Highlands, the equivalent of the position of major general. But by then, according to Sheehan, Vann had "lost his compass." He was no longer able to assess realistically the ability or will of the South Vietnamese to fight without American aid. He continued to insist that the war could be won through pacification and reform in Saigon despite evidence of growing Vietcong strength. When his helicopter went down at Kontum in 1972, he had almost single-handedly saved the Central Highlands from a North Vietnamese offensive. Within six months the United States formally ended its involvement. Two years later Vietnam was reunited under Communist rule.

John Paul Vann never wavered in his belief that in Vietnam America's cause was just and its intentions good. He had no quarrel with the war itself, just with the way it was fought. Vann thought he knew the answers, but Saigon and Washington chose not to listen. His life and death serve as a reminder of the complexities of the Vietnam experience: could it ever really have been "won," and what would "winning" have meant? Neil Sheehan is convinced that Vann "died believing he had won his war."

of serving in Vietnam and the difficulty of reentry sowed the seeds of what is now recognized as posttraumatic stress disorder—recurring physical and psychological problems that often lead to divorce, unemployment, and suicide. Only in the 1980s did America begin to make its peace with those who had served in the nation's most unpopular war.

In Southeast Asia the damage was far greater. The war claimed an estimated 1.5 million Vietnamese lives and devastated the country's physical and economic infrastructure. Neighboring Laos and Cambodia also suffered, particularly Cambodia, where between 1975 and 1979 the Khmer Rouge killed an estimated 2 million Cambodians—a quarter of the population—in a brutal relocation campaign. All told, the war produced nearly 10 million refugees, many of whom immigrated to the United States. Among them were thousands of Amerasians, the offspring of American soldiers and Vietnamese women. Spurned by their fathers and by most Vietnamese, more than 30,000 Amerasians arrived in the 1990s.

The defeat in Vietnam prompted Americans to think differently about foreign affairs and to acknowledge the limits of U.S. power abroad. The United States became less willing to plunge into overseas military commitments, a controversial change that conservatives dubbed the "Vietnam syndrome." In 1973 Congress declared its hostility to undeclared wars like those in Vietnam and Korea by passing the War Powers Act, which required the president to report any use of military force within forty-eight hours and directed that without a declaration of war by Congress hostilities must cease within sixty days. On those occasions when Congress did agree to foreign intervention, as in the Persian Gulf War of 1990 to 1991, American leaders would insist on obtainable military objectives and

carefully channeled information to the news media. In the future any foreign entanglement would be evaluated in terms of its potential to become "another Vietnam."

The Vietnam War also distorted American economic and social affairs. At a total price of over $150 billion, the war siphoned resources from domestic needs, added to the deficit, and fueled inflation. Lyndon Johnson's Great Society programs had been pared down, and domestic reform efforts slowed thereafter. Moreover, the war shattered the liberal consensus that had supported the Democratic coalition. Even more seriously, the conduct of the war—the questionable representation of events in the Gulf of Tonkin, the lies about American successes on the battlefield, the secret war in Cambodia—spawned a deep distrust of government among American citizens. The discrediting of liberalism, the increased cynicism toward government, and the growing social turmoil that accompanied the war would continue into the next decade, paving the way for a resurgence of the Republican Party and a new mood of conservatism.

FOR FURTHER EXPLORATION

▶ For definitions of key terms boldfaced in this chapter, see the glossary at the end of the book.

▶ To assess your mastery of the material covered in this chapter, see the Online Study Guide at **bedfordstmartins.com/henretta**.

▶ For suggested references, including Web sites, see page SR-32 at the end of the book.

▶ For map resources and primary documents, see **bedfordstmartins.com/henretta**.

SUMMARY

America's involvement in Vietnam lasted nearly thirty years. Under Truman, Eisenhower, and Kennedy, the United States threw its support behind the French and later the South Vietnamese government in an effort to contain the Communist threat in Asia. Lyndon Johnson transformed the war in 1965 to an offensive combat mission. Between 1965 and 1968 sustained bombing attacks on North Vietnam were accompanied by ever larger infusions of U.S. ground troops. But the Tet offensive of January 1968 highlighted the discrepancy between the administration's glowing accounts of the war and its tortuous reality and marked the beginning of U.S. efforts to disengage from the conflict. Richard Nixon spent another five years trying to end the war, promising Americans "peace with honor." Under his program of Vietnamization, Nixon gradually withdrew U.S. troops while secretly bombing and later invading Cambodia in a futile attempt to destroy enemy havens. The final withdrawal of American troops took place in 1973 under the terms of the Paris Peace accords. The war marked a turning point in U.S. foreign relations, revealing the limitations of American military power in a complex postwar world.

The war also had serious consequences at home, as different viewpoints bitterly divided Americans. Galvanized by opposition to military escalation and the draft, the antiwar movement spread rapidly among young people who staged a series of mass protests between 1967 and 1971. The spirit of rebellion was not limited to the antiwar movement. The New Left challenged university policies and corporate dominance of society, while the more apolitical counterculture preached personal liberation through sex, drugs, music, and spirituality. As the civil rights struggle moved beyond the South, rising militancy and racial strife divided the movement and fueled white opposition to change. At the same time, however, the new black-power movement encouraged racial pride and assertiveness, serving as a model for Mexican Americans, Native Americans, and other ethnic groups. The civil rights movement also helped to inspire a resurgence of feminism and the birth of the gay liberation movement.

The domestic struggle over the war and other issues divided the Democratic Party, resulting in a Democratic National Convention riven with protest and violence in the summer of 1968. The assassinations of Martin Luther King Jr. and Robert Kennedy and a series of urban riots that year further shocked the nation, fueling a growing public desire for law and order. Although antiwar protests continued into the early 1970s, a new mood of conservatism took hold in the country, contributing to the resurgence of the Republican Party under Richard Nixon.

TIMELINE

1946 War begins between French and Vietminh over control of Vietnam

1950 United States recognizes French-backed government of Bao Dai and sends military aid

1954 French defeat at Dienbienphu

Geneva accords partition Vietnam at 17th parallel

1962 Students for a Democratic Society (SDS) founded

1963 Coup ousts Ngo Dinh Diem in South Vietnam

Presidential Commission on the Status of Women

1964 Free Speech Movement at Berkeley

Gulf of Tonkin Resolution authorizes military action in Vietnam

1965 Malcolm X assassinated

Operation Rolling Thunder escalates war through mass bombing campaigns

First U.S. combat troops arrive in Vietnam

Race riot in Watts district of Los Angeles

1966 National Organization for Women (NOW) founded

Stokely Carmichael proclaims black power

1967 Hippie counterculture's "Summer of Love"

Race riots in Detroit and Newark

100,000 march in antiwar protest in Washington, D.C.

1968 Tet offensive dashes American hopes of victory

Martin Luther King Jr. and Robert F. Kennedy assassinated

Riot at Democratic National Convention in Chicago

Women's liberation movement emerges

American Indian Movement (AIM) organized

1969 Stonewall riot leads to gay liberation movement

Woodstock Music and Art Fair

Vietnam moratorium called in protest of war

1970 Nixon orders invasion of Cambodia; renewed antiwar protests

Killings at Kent State and Jackson State

1972 Nixon visits People's Republic of China

SALT I Treaty with Soviet Union

1973 Paris Peace accords

War Powers Act

1975 Fall of Saigon

CHAPTER 30

The Lean Years

1969–1980

The Nixon Years
The Republican Domestic Agenda
The 1972 Election
Watergate

An Economy of Diminished Expectations
Energy Crisis
Economic Woes

Reform and Reaction in the 1970s
The New Activism: Environmental and Consumer Movements
Challenges to Tradition: The Women's Movement and Gay Rights
Racial Minorities
The Politics of Resentment

Politics in the Wake of Watergate
Ford's Caretaker Presidency
Jimmy Carter: The Outsider as President
The Reagan Revolution

"THE UNITED STATES STEEL CORPORATION ANNOUNCED yesterday that it was closing 14 plants and mills in 8 states. About 13,000 production and white-collar workers will lose their jobs." "Weyerhaeuser Co. may trim about 1,000 salaried employees from its 11,000 member workforce over the next year." "Philadelphia: Food Fair Inc. plans to close 89 supermarkets in New York and Connecticut." Newspaper articles in the 1970s told the story of the widespread downsizing that cost millions of workers their jobs when rising oil prices, runaway inflation, declining productivity, and stagnating incomes caused the biggest economic downturn in three decades. Beyond the individual hard-luck stories of demeaning low-paid jobs, lost homes, forced relocations, broken marriages, and alcoholism, the economic uncertainties facing working- and middle-class Americans in this period created a sense of disillusionment about the nation's future. Already reeling from the nation's withdrawal from Vietnam and its implications for the United States' international power, many people also grew disenchanted with their political leadership in the 1970s, as one public official after another, including President Richard Nixon, resigned for misconduct. In the wake of Nixon's resignation, the lackluster administrations of Presidents Gerald Ford and Jimmy Carter failed to provide

◄ **No Gas**

During the energy crisis of 1973 to 1974, American motorists faced widespread gasoline shortages for the first time since World War II. Although gas was not rationed, gas stations were closed on Sundays, and some communities instituted further restrictions such as creating systems by which motorists with license plates ending in even numbers could purchase gas on certain days, with alternate days being reserved for odd numbers. Ken Regan.

the leadership necessary to cope with the nation's economic and international insecurities—failure that fed Americans' growing skepticism about government and its capacity to improve people's lives.

Paradoxically, in the midst of this growing disaffection and skepticism, a commitment to social change persisted. Some of the social movements born in the 1960s, such as feminism and environmentalism, had their greatest impact in the 1970s. As former student radicals moved into the political mainstream, they took their struggles with them, from streets and campuses into courts, schools, workplaces, and community organizations. But like the civil rights and antiwar movements of the 1960s, the social activism of the 1970s stirred fears and uncertainties among many Americans. Furthermore, the darkening economic climate of the new decade undercut the sense of social generosity that had characterized the 1960s, fueling a new conservatism that would become a potent political force by the decade's end.

The Nixon Years

Richard Nixon set the stage for the conservative political resurgence. His election gave impetus to a long-standing Republican effort to trim back the Great Society and shift some federal responsibilities back to the states. At the same time facing a Democratic Congress, Nixon embraced the use of federal power—within limits—to uphold governmental responsibility for social welfare, environmental protection, and economic stability. The president's domestic accomplishments, however, as well as his international initiatives, were ultimately overshadowed by the Watergate scandal, which swept him from office in disgrace and undermined Americans' confidence in their political leaders.

The Republican Domestic Agenda

In a 1968 campaign pledge to "the average American," Nixon vowed to "reverse the flow of power and resources from the states and communities to Washington and start power and resources flowing back . . . to the people." One hallmark of this approach was the 1972 revenue-sharing program, which distributed a portion of federal tax revenues to the states as block grants to be spent as state officials saw fit. In later years revenue sharing would become a key Republican strategy for reducing federal social programs and federal bureaucracy.

Nixon also worked to scale down certain government programs that had grown dramatically during the Johnson administration. Viewing many Democratic social programs as bloated and inefficient, he reduced funding for most of the War on Poverty and dismantled the Office of Economic Opportunity altogether in 1971. Nixon also **impounded** (refused to spend) billions of

dollars appropriated by Congress for urban renewal, pollution control, and other environmental initiatives. Although his administration claimed to support civil rights, Nixon adopted a cautious approach toward racial issues so as not to alienate southern white voters. In a leaked 1970 memo, presidential advisor Daniel Patrick Moynihan, a Democrat who had joined the Nixon White House, suggested that "the issue of race could benefit from a period of benign neglect"—a revelation that scandalized liberals and embarrassed the administration. Nixon also vetoed a 1971 bill to establish a comprehensive national child-care system, fearing that such "communal approaches to child rearing" would "Sovietize" American children.

As an alternative to Democratic social legislation, the administration put forward its own antipoverty program in an ambitious attempt to overhaul the jerrybuilt welfare system. In 1969, following the advice of Moynihan, Nixon proposed a Family Assistance Plan that would provide a family of four a small but guaranteed annual income. The appeal of this proposal lay in its simplicity: it would eliminate the multiple layers of bureaucrats (caseworkers, local and state officials, and federal employees) who administered Aid to Families with Dependent Children (AFDC), the nation's largest welfare program. But the bill floundered in the Senate: conservatives attacked it for putting the federal government too deeply into the welfare business, and liberals and social welfare activists opposed it for not going far enough. Welfare reform would remain a contentious political issue for the next thirty years.

Although Nixon sought to streamline or scale back certain antipoverty programs, he actively expanded federal entitlement programs and the regulatory apparatus. Facing Democratic majorities in both houses of Congress, Nixon agreed to the growth of major entitlement programs such as Medicare, Medicaid, and Social Security. In 1970 he signed a bill establishing the Environmental Protection Agency (EPA) to coordinate the growing federal responsibilities for environmental action. In 1972, to monitor the health and safety of workers and consumers, Nixon approved legislation creating the Occupational Safety and Health Administration (OSHA) and the Consumer Products Safety Commission. As inflation spiraled upward in 1971, he also made use of the federal powers granted under the Economic Stabilization Act of 1970 to institute wage and price controls, the first such measures since World War II. Although Nixon offered only lukewarm support for much of this legislation, his administration generally continued the expansion of federal power that had been under way since the New Deal.

Nixon demonstrated his conservative social values most clearly in his appointments to the Supreme Court. The liberal thrust of the Court under the direction of Chief Justice Earl Warren (1953–1969) had disturbed many conservatives. Its *Brown v. Board of Education* decision in 1954 requiring the desegregation of public schools (see Chapter 27) was followed by other landmark decisions in the 1960s. The *Miranda v. Arizona* (1966) decision reinforced defendants' rights by requiring arresting officers to notify suspects of their legal rights. In *Baker v. Carr* (1962) and *Reynolds v. Sims* (1964), the Court put forth the doctrine of "one person, one vote," meaning that all citizens' votes should have equal weight, no matter where they lived, a challenge to disproportionately rural weighted voting districts. The ruling substantially increased the representation in state legislatures and Congress of both suburban and urban areas (with their concentrations of African American and Spanish-speaking residents) at the expense of rural regions. One of the most controversial decisions was *Engel v. Vitale* (1962), which banned organized prayer in public schools as a violation of the First Amendment. When Justice Warren retired in 1969, President Nixon took the opportunity to begin reshaping the Court and nominated conservative Warren Burger to become chief justice. After some difficulties in getting nominees confirmed by the Senate, Nixon eventually named three other justices: Harry Blackmun (who proved more liberal than expected), Lewis F. Powell Jr., and William Rehnquist.

Nixon's appointees did not always hand down decisions the president approved, however. Despite attempts by the Justice Department to halt further desegregation in the face of determined white opposition, the Court ordered busing of public school students to nonneighborhood schools in order to achieve racial balance in the classroom. In 1972 it issued restrictions on the implementation of capital punishment, though it did not rule the death penalty unconstitutional. And in the controversial 1973 case *Roe v. Wade*, Justice Blackmun wrote the decision that struck down laws prohibiting abortion in Texas and Georgia.

The 1972 Election

Nixon's reelection in 1972 was never much in doubt. In May the threat of a conservative third-party challenge from Alabama governor George Wallace ended abruptly when an assailant shot Wallace, paralyzing him from the waist down. With Wallace out of the picture, Nixon's strategy of wooing southern white voters away from the Democrats got a boost. Nixon also benefited from the disarray of the Democratic Party. Divided over Vietnam and civil rights, the Democrats were plagued by tensions between their newer, more liberal constituencies— women, minorities, and young adults—and the old-line officeholders and labor union leaders who had always dominated the party. Recent changes in the party's system of selecting delegates and candidates benefited the newer groups, and they helped to nominate Senator

Nixon Triumphant

One of the most resilient political figures in American history, Richard Nixon won the presidential elections of 1968 and 1972 after losing campaigns for president in 1960 and for governor of California in 1962. Even after his resignation in 1974, Nixon reemerged as an elder statesman and was frequently consulted for his views on foreign affairs. Here, he exults in an enthusiastic welcome from supporters in Savannah, Georgia, in 1970. Charles Moore / Black Star.

George McGovern of South Dakota, a noted liberal and an outspoken opponent of the Vietnam War.

McGovern's campaign quickly ran into trouble. On learning that his running mate, Senator Thomas F. Eagleton of Missouri, had undergone electroshock therapy for depression some years earlier, McGovern first supported him and then abruptly insisted that he quit the ticket. But McGovern's waffling on the matter made him appear weak and indecisive. Moreover, he was far too liberal for many traditional Democrats, who rejected his ill-defined proposals for welfare reform and his call for unilateral withdrawal from Vietnam.

Nixon's campaign took full advantage of McGovern's weaknesses. Although the president had failed to end the war, his Vietnamization policy had virtually eliminated American combat deaths by 1972. Henry Kissinger's premature declaration that "peace is at hand" raised voters' hopes for a negotiated settlement (see Chapter 29). Not only did those initiatives rob the Democrats of their greatest appeal—their antiwar stance—but a short-term upturn in the economy further favored the Republicans. Nixon won handily, receiving nearly 61 percent of the popular vote and carrying every state except Massachusetts and the District of Columbia. Yet the president failed to kindle strong loyalty in the electorate. Only 55.7 percent of eligible voters bothered to go to the polls, and the Democrats maintained control of both houses of Congress. A far graver threat to Nixon's leadership would emerge shortly after the election, when the news broke that the White House was implicated in the 1972 break-in at the Democratic National Committee's headquarters at the Watergate apartment complex in Washington, D.C.

Watergate

Watergate, one of the great constitutional crises of the twentieth century, was a direct result of Nixon's ruthless political tactics, his secretive style of governing, and his obsession with the antiwar movement. But though many Americans saw Watergate as consisting of only the evil deeds of one person (Richard Nixon) and one unlawful act (obstruction of justice), Watergate was not an isolated incident. It was part of a broad pattern of illegality and misuse of power that flourished in the crisis atmosphere of the Vietnam War.

Before the Break-In.   Though the Watergate scandal began in 1972, its roots lay in the early years of Nixon's first administration. Obsessed with the antiwar movement, the White House had repeatedly authorized illegal surveillance—opening mail, tapping phones, arranging break-ins—of citizens such as Daniel Ellsberg, a former Defense Department analyst who had become disillusioned with the war. In 1971 Ellsberg had leaked the so-called Pentagon Papers to the *New York Times*. This secret study, commissioned by Secretary of Defense McNamara in 1967, detailed so many American blunders in Vietnam that, after reading it, McNamara had commented, "You know, they could hang people for what is in there." To discredit Ellsberg, White House underlings broke into his psychiatrist's office in an unsuccessful search for damaging personal information. When their break-in was revealed, the court dismissed the government's case against Ellsberg.

In another abuse of presidential power, the White House had established a clandestine intelligence group known as the "plumbers" that was supposed to plug leaks of government information. The plumbers relied on tactics such as using the Internal Revenue Service to harass the administration's opponents, who were named on an "enemies list" drawn up by presidential counsel John Dean. One of the plumbers' major targets was the Democratic Party, whose front-running primary candidate in 1972, Senator Edmund Muskie of Maine,

became the object of several of their "dirty tricks," including the distribution of phony campaign posters reading "Help Muskie in Busing More Children Now."

These secret and highly questionable activities were financed by massive illegal fund-raising efforts by Nixon's Committee to Re-Elect the President (known as CREEP). To obtain contributions from major corporations, Nixon's fund-raisers had used high-pressure tactics that included implied threats of federal tax audits if companies failed to cooperate. CREEP raised over $20 million, a portion of which was used to finance the plumbers' dirty tricks, including the Watergate break-in.

The Break-In.   Early in the morning of June 17, 1972, police arrested five men carrying cameras, wiretapping equipment, and a large amount of cash and charged them with breaking into the Democratic National Committee's headquarters at the Watergate apartment complex in Washington, D.C. Two accomplices were apprehended soon afterward. Three of the men had worked in the White House or for CREEP, and four had CIA connections. Nixon later claimed that White House counsel John Dean had conducted a full investigation of the incident (no such investigation ever took place) and that "no one on the White House staff, no one in this administration, presently employed, was involved in this very bizarre incident."

Subsequent investigations revealed that shortly after the break-in the president had ordered his chief of staff, H. R. Haldeman, to instruct the CIA to tell the FBI not to probe too deeply into connections between the White House and the burglars. When the burglars were convicted in January 1973, John Dean, with Nixon's approval, tried to buy their continued silence with $400,000 in hush money and hints of presidential pardons.

The cover-up of the White House's involvement began to unravel when one of the convicted burglars began to talk. Two tenacious investigative reporters at the *Washington Post*, Carl Bernstein and Bob Woodward, exposed the attempt to hide the truth and traced it back to the White House. Reports of CREEP's "dirty tricks" and illegal fund-raising soon compounded the public's suspicions about the president. In February the Senate voted 77 to 0 to establish an investigative committee. Two months later Nixon accepted the resignations of Haldeman, Assistant Secretary of Commerce Jeb Stuart Magruder, and Chief Domestic Advisor John Ehrlichman, all of whom had been implicated in the cover-up. He fired Dean, who had agreed to testify in the case in exchange for immunity from prosecution. In May the Senate Watergate committee began holding nationally televised hearings. In June Magruder testified before the committee, confessing his guilt and implicating former Attorney General John Mitchell, Dean, and others. Dean, in turn, implicated Nixon in the plot. Even more startling testimony from a Nixon aide revealed that Nixon had installed a secret taping system in the Oval Office.

The president steadfastly "stonewalled" the committee's demand that he surrender the tapes, citing executive privilege and national security. But Archibald Cox, a special prosecutor whom Nixon had appointed to investigate the case, successfully petitioned a federal court to order the president to hand the tapes over. Still Nixon refused to comply. After receiving additional federal subpoenas the following spring, Nixon finally released a heavily edited transcript of the tapes, peppered with the words "expletive deleted." Senate Republican leader Hugh Scott called the transcripts "deplorable, disgusting, shabby, immoral." Most suspicious was an eighteen-minute gap in the tape covering a crucial meeting between Nixon, Haldeman, and Ehrlichman on June 20, 1972—three days after the break-in.

The Final Days.   The Watergate affair moved into its final phase when on June 30 the House of Representatives' Judiciary Committee voted three articles of impeachment against Richard Nixon: obstruction of justice, abuse of power, and acting to subvert the Constitution. Two days later the Supreme Court ruled unanimously that Nixon could not claim executive privilege as a justification for refusing to turn over additional tapes. Under duress, on August 5 Nixon released the unexpurgated tapes, which contained evidence that he had ordered the cover-up as early as six days after the break-in. Facing certain conviction if impeached, on August 9, 1974, Nixon became the first U.S. president to resign.

The next day Vice President Gerald Ford was sworn in as president. Ford, a former Michigan congressman and house minority leader, had replaced Vice President Spiro Agnew in 1973 after Agnew resigned under indictment for accepting kickbacks on construction contracts. The transfer of power proceeded smoothly. A month later, however, Ford stunned the nation by granting Nixon a "full, free, and absolute" pardon "for all offenses he had committed or might have committed during his presidency." Ford took that action, he said, to spare the country the agony of rehashing Watergate in a criminal prosecution. Twenty-five members of Nixon's administration went to prison, but he refused to admit guilt for what had happened, conceding only that he had made an error in judgment.

The Aftermath.   In response to the abuses of the Nixon administration and to contain the power of what the historian Arthur M. Schlesinger Jr. called "the imperial presidency," Congress adopted several reforms. In 1974 a strengthened Freedom of Information Act gave citizens greater access to files federal agencies had amassed on them. The Fair Campaign Practices Act of 1974 limited campaign contributions and provided for stricter accountability and public financing of presidential

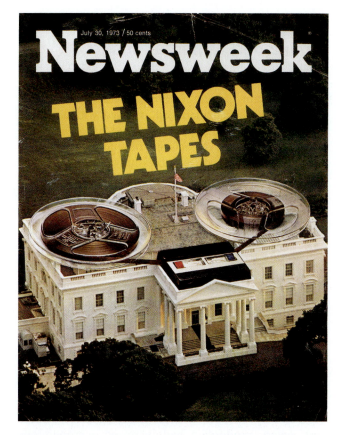

Watergate

In July 1973 White House aide Alexander Butterfield testified before the Senate Watergate Committee that all Oval Office telephone communications had been recorded on a secret taping system. Although Nixon tried in vain to suppress the tapes by claiming executive privilege, their eventual release—including statements directly implicating the president in the Watergate cover-up—led to Nixon's resignation in August of 1974.

campaigns. Ironically, because the act allowed an unlimited number of political action committees (PACs) to donate up to $5,000 per candidate, corporations and lobbying groups found they could actually increase their influence by making multiple donations. By the end of the decade, close to 3,000 PACs were playing an increasingly pivotal—and some would argue unethical—role in national elections.

Perhaps the most significant legacy of Watergate, however, was the wave of cynicism that swept the country in its wake. Beginning with Lyndon Johnson's "credibility gap" during the Vietnam War, public distrust of government had risen steadily with the disclosure of the secret bombing of Cambodia and the illegal surveillance and harassment of antiwar protesters and other political opponents. The saga of Watergate confirmed what many Americans had long suspected: that politicians were hopelessly corrupt and that the federal government was out of control.

An Economy of Diminished Expectations

Economic difficulties compounded Americans' political disillusionment. Growing international demand for natural resources, particularly oil, coupled with unstable access to foreign oil supplies wreaked havoc with the American economy. At the same time foreign competitors in varied industries successfully expanded their share of the world market, edging out American-made products. The resulting sharp downturn in the domestic economy marked the end of America's twenty-five-year dominance of the world economy.

Energy Crisis

Until the mid-twentieth century the United States was the world's leading producer and consumer of oil. During World War II the nation had produced two-thirds of the world's oil, but by 1972 its share had fallen to only 22 percent, even though domestic production had continued to rise. By the late 1960s the United States was buying more and more of its oil on the world market to keep up with shrinking domestic reserves and growing demand.

The imported oil came primarily from the Middle East, where production had increased a stupendous 1,500 percent in the twenty-five years following World War II. The rise of nationalism and the corresponding decline of colonialism in the postwar era had encouraged the Persian Gulf nations to wrest control from the European and American oil companies that once dominated petroleum exploration and production in that region. In 1960, joining with other oil-producing developing countries, they had formed the Organization of Petroleum Exporting Countries (OPEC). Just five of the founding countries—the Middle Eastern states of Saudi Arabia, Kuwait, Iran, and Iraq, plus Venezuela—were the source of more than 80 percent of the world's crude oil exports. During the early 1970s, when world demand climbed and oil reserves fell, they took advantage of market forces to maximize their profits. Between 1973 and 1975 OPEC raised the price of a barrel of oil from $3 to $12. By the end of the decade, the price had peaked at $34 a barrel, setting off a round of furious inflation in the oil-dependent United States.

OPEC members also found that oil could be used as a weapon in global politics. In 1973 OPEC instituted an oil embargo against the United States, Western Europe, and Japan in retaliation for their aid to Israel during the Yom Kippur War, which had begun when Egypt and Syria invaded Israel. The embargo, which lasted six months, forced Americans to curtail their driving or spend long hours in line at the pumps; in a matter of months, gas prices climbed 40 percent. Since the U.S. automobile industry had little to offer except "gas-guzzlers" built to run on cheap fuel, Americans turned to cheaper, more fuel-efficient foreign cars manufactured in Japan and West Germany. Soon the auto industry was in a slump, weakening the American economy.

The energy crisis was an enormous shock to the American psyche. Suddenly, Americans felt like hostages to economic forces that were beyond their control. As OPEC's leaders pushed prices higher and higher, they seemed to be able to determine whether Western economies would grow or stagnate. Despite an extensive public conservation campaign and a second gas shortage in 1979 caused by the Iranian revolution, Americans could not wean themselves from foreign oil. In fact, they used even more foreign oil after the energy crisis than they had before—a testimony to the enormous thirst of modern industrial and consumer societies for petroleum (Figure 30.1).

Economic Woes

While the energy crisis dealt a swift blow to the U.S. economy, other developments had equally damaging results. The high cost of the Vietnam War and the Great Society had contributed to a steadily growing federal deficit and spiraling inflation. A business downturn in 1970 had led to rising unemployment and declining productivity. In the industrial sector the reviving economies of West Germany and Japan over time had reduced demand for American goods worldwide. As a result, in 1971 the dollar fell to its lowest level on the world market since 1949, and the United States posted its first **trade deficit**, importing more than it exported, in almost a century.

Nixon's Remedies. That year Nixon took several bold steps to turn the economy around. To stem the decline in currency and trade, he suspended the Bretton Woods system that had been established at the United Nations monetary conference in 1944 (see Chapter 28). Once again the dollar would fluctuate in relation to the price of an ounce of gold. The change, which effectively devalued the dollar in hopes of encouraging foreign trade, represented a frank acknowledgment that America's currency was no longer the world's strongest. Nixon also instituted wage and price controls to curb inflation, and to boost the sluggish economy he offered a "full employment" budget for 1972, including $11 billion in deficit spending.

Though these measures brought a temporary improvement in the economy, the general decline persisted. Overall economic growth, as measured by the gross domestic product (GDP), had averaged 4.1 percent per year in the 1960s; in the 1970s it dropped to only 2.9 percent, contributing to a noticeable decline in most Americans' standard of living. At the same time galloping inflation forced consumer prices upward (Figure 30.2). Housing prices, in particular, rose rapidly: the average

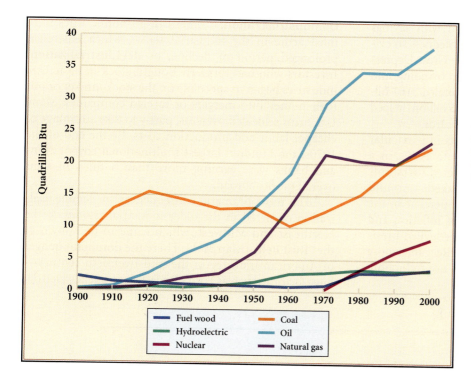

FIGURE 30.1 U.S. Energy Consumption, 1900–2000

Coal was the nation's primary source of energy until the 1950s, when oil and natural gas became the dominant fuels. The use of nuclear and hydroelectric power also rose substantially in the postwar era. During the 1980s fuel-efficient automobiles and conservation measures reduced total energy use, but in the 1990s energy consumption rose significantly.

Source: World Almanac 2002.

cost of a single-family home more than doubled in the 1970s, making homeownership inaccessible to a growing segment of the working and middle classes.

The inflationary crisis helped to forge new attitudes about saving and spending. With bank savings accounts' interests rates unable to keep up with inflation, many Americans turned to the stock market, taking advantage of the appearance of new discount brokerage firms like

Charles Schwab, whose low commission fees made it easier for small investors to take the plunge. The money market mutual fund also emerged in this decade, offering investors uninsured but relatively safe investment opportunities overseen by a fund manager. The inflation-afflicted middle class responded enthusiastically, and by 1982 more than $200 billion dollars were in mutual funds. While these investors sought new ways to increase their

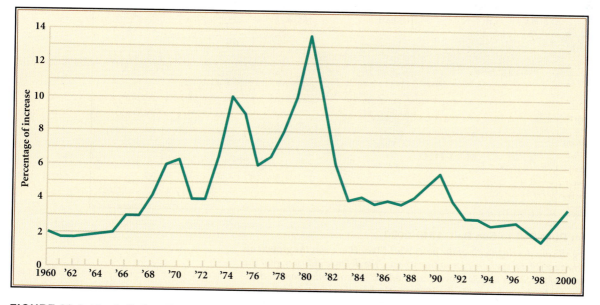

FIGURE 30.2 The Inflation Rate, 1960–2000

One common measure of inflation is the percent change per year in the consumer price index as calculated by the Bureau of Labor Statistics. The annual inflation rate peaked in 1980, the last year of Carter's presidency. Source: Statistical Abstract of the United States, 2000.

savings, millions of Americans dispensed with savings altogether. Putting behind the fear of indebtedness so evident in people who had lived through the Great Depression, now Americans coped with inflation by going into debt. By mid-1975 consumer borrowing totaled $167 billion, but by 1979 it had skyrocketed to $315 billion, helped by a dramatic increase in the use of credit cards.

In addition to inflation young adults in particular faced a constricted job market in the late 1970s, as a record number of baby boomers competed for a limited number of jobs. Unemployment peaked at around 9 percent in 1975 and hovered at 6 to 7 percent in the late 1970s. A devastating combination of inflation and unemployment—dubbed **stagflation**—bedeviled presidential administrations from Nixon to Reagan, whose remedies, such as deficit spending and tax reduction, failed to eradicate the double scourge.

Deindustrialization.   American economic woes were most acute in the industrial sector, which entered a prolonged period of decline, or **deindustrialization**. Investors who had formerly bought stock in basic U.S. industries began to speculate on the stock market or put their money into mergers or foreign companies. Many U.S. firms relocated overseas, partly to take advantage of cheaper labor and production costs. By the end of the 1970s, the hundred largest multinational corporations and banks were earning more than a third of their overall profits abroad.

The most dramatic consequences of deindustrialization occurred in the older industrial regions of the Northeast and Midwest, which came to be known as the "Rust Belt" (Map 30.1). There the dominant images of American industry in the mid-twentieth century— huge factories such as Ford's River Rouge outside Detroit;

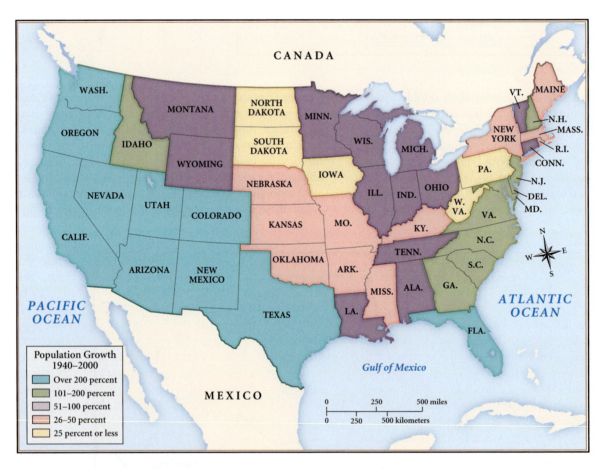

MAP 30.1 From Rust Belt to Sun Belt, 1940–2000

One of the most significant developments of the post–World War II era was the growth of the Sun Belt. Sparked by federal spending for military bases, the defense industry, and the space program, states of the South and Southwest experienced an economic boom in the 1950s. This growth was further enhanced in the 1970s, as the heavily industrialized regions of the Northeast and Midwest declined, and migrants from what was quickly dubbed the "Rust Belt" headed to the South and West in search of jobs. Rising political influence accompanied the economic and demographic growth of the Sun Belt: since Lyndon B. Johnson, all presidents but Gerald Ford have hailed from a Sun Belt state, and the region has provided an important base for the conservative wing of the Republican Party.

Deindustrialization

Scores of industrial plants closed in the 1970s, putting many Americans out of work. At the same time more Americans were buying cheaper imported cars, fueling anger toward foreign competitors. David Helfferich of Greenburg, Pennsylvania, bashed this Japanese-made Honda Civic and urged others to "buy American" as a means of protecting U.S. jobs. Wide World Photos, Inc.

the United States Steel Corporation compound in Gary, Indiana; and the General Electric plant in Lynn, Massachusetts—were fast becoming relics.

When a community's major employer closed up shop and left town, the effect was devastating. In 1977 the Lykes Corporation shut the Campbell Works of the Youngstown Sheet and Tube Company, laying off 4,100 Ohio steelworkers. Two years later Youngstown was still reeling. A third of the displaced workers, considered too old to retrain for new positions, had been forced to take early retirement at half of their previous salaries. Ten percent had moved. Another 15 percent were still looking for work, their unemployment compensation long since exhausted. Among the 40 percent who were the "success stories" (those who had found other jobs), many had taken huge wage cuts. A former rigger, for instance, was selling women's shoes for $2.37 an hour. The impact of such plant closings rippled through communities across America's heartland.

Many of the displaced workers relocated to the Sun Belt, which continued its postwar expansion with the spectacular growth of cities like Houston, Los Angeles, San Diego, and Atlanta (see Chapter 28). Even the least booming of the southern rim states—Alabama—saw its job rolls expanding at four times the rate of New York and Pennsylvania. As the *New York Times* described the out-migration from the North, "All day and through the lonely night, the moving vans push southward, the 14-wheeled boxcars of the highway, changing the demographic face of America." The growth of the Sun Belt owed much to federal spending for defense contracts, military bases, and the space program in the region. The oil industry and agribusiness also benefited from federal

subsidies and tax breaks. Equally important, however, in the creation of new jobs were low labor costs. "Right-to-work" laws that made it difficult to build strong labor unions made these states, unlike those of the Rust Belt, inhospitable to organized labor.

Deindustrialization, the population shift to the Sun Belt, and the changing economic conditions of the 1970s posed a critical problem for the labor movement. In the heyday of labor during the 1940s and 1950s, American managers had often cooperated with unions; with profits high there was room for accommodation. But as foreign competition cut into corporate profits in the 1970s, industry became less willing to bargain, and the labor movement's power declined. In the 1970s union membership dropped from 28 to 23 percent of the American workforce. In the South membership was 14 percent. By the end of the 1980s, only 16 percent of American workers were organized. Operations moving abroad also hurt labor, as the new overseas workforce was beyond American labor's organizing influence. In a competitive global environment, labor's prospects seemed dim.

Reform and Reaction in the 1970s

The nation's economic problems and growing cynicism about government led to deep public anxiety and resentment. Many Americans turned inward to private satisfactions, prompting the journalist Tom Wolfe to label the 1970s the "Me Decade." Yet such a label hardly does justice to a decade in which environmentalism, feminism, lesbian and gay rights, and other social movements blossomed. Furthermore, such characterizations neglect the growing social conservatism that was in part a response to such movements. In fact, the confluence of these trends produced a pattern of shifting crosscurrents that made the 1970s a complex transitional decade.

The New Activism: Environmental and Consumer Movements

After 1970 many baby boomers left the counterculture behind and settled down to pursue careers and material goods. But these young adults sought personal fulfillment as well. In a quest for physical well-being, millions of Americans began jogging, riding bicycles, and working out at the gym. The fitness craze coincided with a heightened environmental awareness that spurred the demand for pesticide-free foods and vegetarian cookbooks. For spiritual support some young people embraced the self-help techniques of the human-potential, or New Age, movement; others turned to alternative religious groups such as the Hare Krishna, the Church of Scientology, and the Unification Church of Reverend Sun Myung Moon.

A few baby boomers continued to pursue the unfinished social and political agendas of the 1960s. Moving into law, education, social work, medicine, and other fields, these former radicals continued their activism on a grassroots level. Some joined the left wing of the Democratic Party; others helped to establish community-based organizations, including health clinics, food co-ops, and day-care centers. On the local level, at least, the progressive spirit of the 1960s lived on.

Environmental Awareness. Many of these 1960s-style activists helped to invigorate the environmental movement, which had been energized by the publication in 1962 of Rachel Carson's *Silent Spring*, a powerful analysis of the impact of pesticides on the food chain. Activists brought their radical political sensibilities to the environmental movement, using sit-ins and other protest tactics developed in the civil rights and antiwar movements to mobilize mass support and infuse the movement with new life. For example, they construed the search for alternative technologies (especially solar power) as a political statement against a corporate structure that was increasingly inhospitable to human-scale technology—and to humans as well.

Other issues that galvanized public opinion included the environmental impact of industrial projects such as an Alaskan oil pipeline and the harmful effects of chlorofluorocarbons and increased carbon dioxide levels on the earth's atmosphere. In January 1969 a huge oil spill off the coast of Santa Barbara, California, provoked an outcry, as did the discovery in 1978 that a housing development outside Niagara Falls,

Rachel Carson
A pioneer of the modern environmental movement, biologist Rachel Carson documented the adverse effects of DDT and other pesticides in her 1962 best-seller, Silent Spring. *This photograph, taken in 1961, shows Carson conducting fieldwork.*
Alfred Eisenstadt / LIFE Magazine © Time, Inc.

New York, had been built on a toxic waste site. Lois Gibbs and other residents became aware of abnormally high rates of illness, miscarriage, and birth defects among Love Canal families, and the New York State government paid homeowners to relocate (see American Lives, "Lois Marie Gibbs: Environmental Activist," p. 890).

Nuclear Power. Nuclear energy became the subject of citizen action in the 1970s, when rising prices and oil shortages led to the expansion of nuclear power, pitting environmental concerns against the need for alternative energy sources. By January 1974 forty-two nuclear power plants were in operation, and over a hundred more were planned. Suddenly the proliferation of nuclear power plants and reactors, which had gone largely unchallenged in the 1950s and 1960s, raised public concerns about safety. Community activists protested plans for new reactors, citing inadequate evacuation plans and the unresolved problem of the disposal of radioactive waste.

Their fears seemed to be confirmed in March 1979 when a nuclear plant at Three Mile Island near Harrisburg, Pennsylvania, came critically close to a meltdown of its central core reactor. A prompt shutdown of the plant brought the problem under control before radioactive material seeped into the environment, but as a member of the panel who investigated the accident admitted, "We were damn lucky." Ultimately, Three Mile Island caused Americans to rethink the question of whether nuclear power could be a viable solution to the nation's energy needs. Grassroots activism, combined with public fear of the potential dangers of nuclear energy, convinced many utility companies to abandon nuclear power, despite its short-term economic advantages.

Environmental Legislation. Americans' concerns about nuclear power, chemical contamination, pesticides, and other environmental issues helped to turn environmentalism into a mass movement. On the first Earth Day, April 22, 1970, 20 million citizens gathered in communities across the country to show their support for the endangered planet. Their efforts helped to create bipartisan support for a spate of new federal legislation. In 1969 Congress passed the National Environmental Policy Act, which required the developers of public projects to file an environmental impact statement. The next year Nixon established the Environmental Protection Agency (EPA) and signed the Clean Air Act, which toughened standards for auto emissions in order to reduce smog and air pollution. Two years later Congress banned the use of the pesticide DDT. And in 1973 the Endangered Species Act expanded the protection provided by the Endangered Animals Act of 1964, granting species such as snail darters and spotted owls protected status. Thus environmental protection joined social welfare, defense, and national security as areas of federal intervention.

The environmental movement did not go uncontested. The EPA-mandated fuel-economy standards for cars provoked criticism for threatening the health of the auto industry as it struggled to keep up with foreign competitors. Corporations resented environmental regulations, but so did many of their workers, who believed that tightened standards threatened their jobs and privileged nature over human beings. "IF YOU'RE HUNGRY AND OUT OF WORK, EAT AN ENVIRONMENTALIST" read one labor union's bumper sticker. In a time of rising unemployment and deindustrialization, activists clashed head-on with proponents of economic development, full employment, and global competitiveness.

The Consumer Movement. Paralleling the rise of environmentalism was a growing consumer protection movement to eliminate harmful consumer products and curb dangerous practices by American corporations. The consumer movement had originated in the Progressive Era with the founding of government agencies such as the Food and Drug Administration (see Chapter 20). After decades of inertia, the consumer movement reemerged in the 1960s under the leadership of Ralph Nader, a young Harvard-educated lawyer whose book *Unsafe at Any Speed* (1965) attacked General Motors for putting flashy style ahead of safe

handling and fuel economy in its engineering of the Chevrolet Corvair.

In 1969 Nader launched a Washington-based consumer protection organization that gave rise to the Public Interest Research Group, a national network of consumer groups that focused on issues ranging from product safety to consumer fraud and environmental pollution. Staffed by a handful of lawyers and hundreds of student volunteers known as "Nader's Raiders," the organization pioneered legal tactics such as the class-action suit, which allowed people with common grievances to sue as a group. Nader's organization became a model for dozens of other groups that emerged in the 1970s and afterward to combat the health hazards of smoking, unethical insurance and credit practices, and other consumer problems. The establishment of the federal Consumer Products Safety Commission in 1972 reflected the growing importance of consumer protection in American life.

Challenges to Tradition: The Women's Movement and Gay Rights

Feminism proved the most enduring movement to emerge from the 1960s. In the next decade the women's movement grew more sophisticated, generating an array of services and organizations, from rape crisis centers and battered women's shelters to feminist health collectives and women's bookstores. In 1972 Gloria Steinem and other journalists founded *Ms.* magazine, the first consumer magazine aimed at a feminist audience. Formerly all-male bastions, such as Yale, Princeton, and the U.S. Military Academy, admitted women undergraduates for the first time, while the proportion of women attending graduate and professional schools rose markedly. Several new national women's organizations emerged, and established groups such as the National Organization for Women (NOW) continued to grow. In 1977, 20,000 women went to Houston for the first National Women's Conference. Their "National Plan of Action" represented a hard-won consensus on topics ranging from violence against women to homemakers' rights, the needs of older women, and, most controversially, abortion and other reproductive issues.

Women were also increasingly visible in politics and public life. The National Women's Political Caucus, founded in 1971, actively promoted the election of women to public office. Their success stories included Shirley Chisholm, Patricia Schroeder, and Geraldine Ferraro, all of whom served in Congress, and Ella T. Grasso, who won election as Connecticut's governor in 1974.

Women's political mobilization produced significant legislative and administrative gains. With the passage of Title IX of the Educational Amendments Act of 1972, which broadened the 1964 Civil Rights Act to include educational institutions, Congress prohibited colleges and

Lois Marie Gibbs: Environmental Activist

In 1978 Lois Gibbs was a twenty-seven-year-old housewife living in Niagara Falls, New York. A chemical worker's wife and the mother of two children, Gibbs spent her days cooking, shopping, and cleaning the family's modest three-bedroom home. Two years later Gibbs was a nationally known figure. As leader of the fight against toxic waste at Love Canal, she organized hundreds of local families, squared off with the governor of New York State, testified before Congress, appeared on national television, and was recognized by President Jimmy Carter for her efforts. She was, as she liked to put it, "the housewife who went to Washington."

Born in Grand Island, New York, in 1951, Lois Conn was one of six children in a blue-collar family in the industrial region surrounding Buffalo. After graduating from high school in 1969, she worked as a nurse's aide at a convalescent home and married Harry Gibbs, a worker at a local chemical plant. After the birth of their first child, Michael, they purchased a home in a quiet, tree-lined neighborhood. Lois quit her job to stay at home and in 1975 gave birth to a daughter. With no inkling of what lay beneath them, the Gibbses finished their basement, tended their garden, and enjoyed a peaceful suburban existence.

The first sign of trouble came in 1977, when their son Michael entered kindergarten at the neighborhood school. Within three months he developed epilepsy and soon contracted asthma and chronic urinary and ear infections. The following spring Gibbs read newspaper reports about toxic chemicals buried beneath the school and tried to have her son transferred. When school officials rejected her request, insisting that the school was safe, Gibbs launched a petition drive to have the school closed.

At first Gibbs was reticent about approaching her neighbors, afraid of having doors slammed in her face. But what she found surprised her. Not only were people interested in and concerned about the dangers of chemicals, but many of them had health problems of their own, including respiratory ailments, cancer, miscarriages, and birth defects. "The more I heard, the more

frightened I became," said Gibbs. "The entire community seemed to be sick."

Gibbs set out to educate herself about the area's history. Consulting local newspaper files, she learned about Love Canal, a six-mile-long canal project developed by William T. Love in the 1890s to connect the upper and lower branches of the Niagara River. Construction had been under way when the depression of 1893 doomed the project, leaving a partially dug trench. The land later became a dump site used mainly by the Hooker Chemical Corporation, which disposed of 22,000 tons of chemical wastes there between 1942 and 1953. (Health officials eventually identified over 200 different compounds at the site, including highly toxic substances such as dioxin—used in the herbicide Agent Orange—toluene, and benzene.) After filling and covering over the site in 1953, Hooker sold the land to the Board of Education for one dollar, stipulating that the company not be held responsible for any future injury or death. Housing subdivisions soon sprang up around the site, and a new elementary school near the corner of the canal opened in 1955.

By the time Gibbs began meeting with her neighbors in 1978, rusted metal drums were surfacing in backyards, chemical sludge was seeping into basements, and residents were complaining about dead trees, burned feet, and a recurring stench. In June of that year, the New York State Health Department began collecting air, soil, and blood samples from households closest to the canal. After finding abnormally high rates of birth defects and miscarriages, the health department issued an order on August 2 for reconstruction of the canal site and recommended the evacuation of all pregnant women and children under age two. Soon afterward, concerned residents established the Love Canal Homeowners Association (LCHA) to fight for permanent relocation of Love Canal families and elected Lois Gibbs as LCHA president. Under pressure from Gibbs and the LCHA, New York's governor, Hugh Carey, agreed a few days later to relocate the 239 families closest to the canal, purchasing their homes at the replacement value.

While Gibbs and the LCHA applauded Carey's action, they worried about the other 810 families remaining in the neighborhood, many of whose homes also showed dangerous levels of chemicals. Gibbs appealed to federal and local officials for further action but encountered repeated delays, denials, and rebuffs. The mayor of Niagara Falls denounced Gibbs's efforts, claiming that the adverse publicity would destroy the

Lois Marie Gibbs

A twenty-seven-year-old housewife in Niagara Falls, New York, Lois Gibbs became the leader of a campaign against toxic waste in her neighborhood in 1978. As president of the Love Canal Homeowners Association, Gibbs fought successfully for the permanent relocation of more than a thousand Love Canal families. Corbis-Bettmann.

city's tourist industry. Meanwhile, the state health department refused to relocate more families until it could complete further studies. At one point in 1979, the department claimed to have lost the residents' health records and instructed them to start the lengthy documentation process all over again.

Faced with bureaucratic inertia, Gibbs sought out sympathetic scientists to help the residents conduct their own studies. Their most important finding came from a neighborhood survey showing health problems clustered around swales—underground drainage ditches that led away from the canal—and suggesting more widespread contamination. The LCHA promptly released the findings to the media. Gibbs got publicity in other ways as well: she appeared on talk shows, organized picketing at the canal construction site, and was arrested for blocking truck traffic. When state officials still failed to take action, Gibbs led a group of citizens to the state capitol in Albany, bearing cardboard coffins symbolizing

Love Canal victims. Throughout the Love Canal crisis Gibbs made frequent trips to Albany and Washington to negotiate with state officials, the governor's office, Senator Daniel Patrick Moynihan, and other federal representatives.

Like other housewives involved in the crisis, Gibbs gained a new independence through her activities outside the home. Those activities, however, also caused tension in her marriage. "My husband was getting upset with me," she recalled. "I was never home . . . dinner was never on time." She and her husband divorced in 1980.

In May of that year, events at Love Canal came to a head when the U.S. Environmental Protection Agency released a study showing abnormally high levels of chromosome breakage in Love Canal residents (suggesting increased risks of cancer, miscarriage, and birth defects). In an act of desperation, Gibbs and two other housewives took two EPA officials hostage in the LCHA office while hundreds of angry residents surrounded the building, demanding federal relocation of Love Canal families. Coming in the middle of the Iranian hostage crisis, the women's ploy brought national media coverage but also a threat of reprisal from the FBI. To avoid violence Gibbs released the officials, but she also demanded a response from President Jimmy Carter within forty-eight hours. Two days later, on May 21, Carter declared a health emergency at Love Canal, authorizing the temporary relocation of the remaining 810 families. Later that year he signed a bill permitting the permanent relocation of those families and the purchase of their homes; he also signed a bill establishing a "Superfund" to clean up Love Canal and thousands of other toxic waste sites identified by the EPA.

Using part of the $30,000 the state paid for her home, Gibbs and her children moved to Washington, D.C., in 1981. There she founded the Citizens Clearinghouse for Hazardous Waste, a consulting group for grassroots organizations working on problems related to pesticides, solid waste, asbestos, and other toxic substances. She married a toxicologist, gave birth to two more children, and continues to work as director of the Citizens Clearinghouse.

One of the communities the Citizens Clearinghouse has been watching is Love Canal. In 1990 the EPA declared Love Canal habitable again after a twelve-year, $250 million cleanup. The elementary school and the 239 houses closest to the canal had been demolished, but 236 other homes were rehabilitated and sold at discount prices to eager buyers. Public officials insist the new containment system has safely and permanently sealed off the dump. Lois Gibbs is not so sure.

universities that received federal funds from discriminating on the basis of sex, a change that particularly benefited women athletes. Another federal initiative was **affirmative action**. Originally instituted in 1966 under Lyndon Johnson's administration to redress a history of discrimination against nonwhites in employment and education, affirmative action procedures—hiring and enrollment goals and recruitment training programs—were extended to women the following year and gave many women, especially educated white ones, more opportunities for educational and career advancement. In 1972 Congress authorized child-care deductions for working parents; in 1974 it passed the Equal Credit Opportunity Act, which significantly improved women's access to credit.

Abortion Rights. The Supreme Court also significantly advanced women's rights. In several rulings the Court gave women more control over their reproductive lives by reading a right of privacy into the Ninth and Fourteenth Amendments' concept of personal liberty. In 1965 *Griswold v. Connecticut* had overturned state laws against the sale of contraceptive devices to married adults, an option that was later extended to single persons. In 1973, in *Roe v. Wade*, the Court struck down Texas and Georgia statutes that allowed an abortion only if the mother's life was in danger. According to this seven-to-two decision, states could no longer outlaw abortions performed during the first trimester of pregnancy.

Roe v. Wade nationalized the liberalization of state abortion laws, which had begun in New York in 1970, but also fueled the development of a powerful antiabortion movement. Charging that the rights of a fetus took precedence over a woman's right to decide whether or not to terminate a pregnancy, abortion opponents worked to circumvent or overturn *Roe v. Wade*. In 1976 they convinced Congress to deny Medicaid funds for abortions for poor women, one of the opening rounds in a protracted legislative and judicial campaign to chip away at the *Roe* decision.

The Equal Rights Amendment. Another battlefront for the women's movement was the proposed Equal Rights Amendment (ERA) to the Constitution. The ERA, first introduced in Congress in 1923 by the National Woman's Party, stated in its entirety, "Equality of rights under the law shall not be denied or abridged by the United States or any State on the basis of sex." In 1970 feminists revived the amendment, which passed the House but died in the Senate. In the next session it passed both houses and was submitted to the states for ratification.

Thirty-four states quickly passed the ERA between 1972 and the end of 1974, but then the momentum stopped (Map 30.2). Only Indiana ratified after that point, leaving the amendment three states short of the necessary three-fourths' majority. Most of the nonratifying states were in the South and the West; Illinois also held out

despite spirited campaigns there by ERA supporters. Congress extended the deadline for ratification until June 30, 1982, but the Equal Rights Amendment still fell short.

Challenges to Feminism. The fate of the ERA and the battle over abortion rights showed that by the mid-1970s the women's movement was beginning to weaken. Increasingly its members were divided by issues of race, class, age, and sexual orientation. For many nonwhite and working-class women, the feminist movement seemed to stand for the interests of self-seeking white career women. At the same time, the women's movement faced growing social conservatism among Americans in general. Although 63 percent of women polled in 1975 said they favored "efforts to strengthen and change women's status in society," a growing minority of both sexes expressed concern over what seemed to be revolutionary changes in women's traditional roles.

Lawyer Phyllis Schlafly, long active in conservative causes, led the antifeminist backlash. Despite the active career she had pursued while raising five children, Schlafly advocated traditional roles for women. Schlafly's STOP ERA organization claimed that the amendment

The Expanding Women's Movement
By the late 1970s the feminist movement had broadened its base, attracting women of all ages and backgrounds, such as this delegate to the 1977 National Women's Conference in Houston, Texas. As the slogan on her hat implies, though, the movement was already on the defensive against right-wing claims that it undermined traditional values. Bettye Lane.

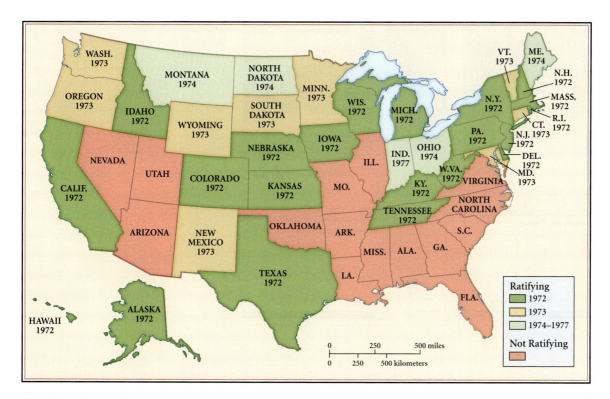

MAP 30.2 States Ratifying the Equal Rights Amendment, 1972–1977

The Equal Rights Amendment (ERA) quickly won support in 1972 and 1973 but then stalled. ERAmerica, a coalition of women's groups formed in 1976, lobbied extensively, particularly in Florida, North Carolina, and Illinois, but failed to sway the conservative legislatures in those states. After Indiana ratified in 1977, the amendment still lacked three votes toward the three-fourths majority needed to pass. Efforts to revive the ERA in the 1980s were unsuccessful, and it remains a dead issue.

would create a "unisex society" in which women could be drafted, homosexuals could be married, and separate toilets for men and women would be prohibited. Alarmed, conservative women in grassroots networks mobilized, showing up at statehouses with home-baked bread and apple pies, symbols of their traditional domestic role. As labels on baked goods at one anti-ERA rally expressed it, "My heart and hand went into this dough / For the sake of the family please vote no." Their message, that women would lose more than they would gain if the ERA passed, resonated with many men and women, especially those who were troubled by the rapid pace of social change.

Women's Changing Roles. Although the feminist movement was on the defensive by the mid-1970s, women's lives showed no signs of returning to the patterns of the 1950s. Because of increasing economic pressures, the proportion of women in the paid workforce continued to rise, from 44 percent in 1970 to 51 percent in 1980. In their private lives easier access to birth control permitted married and unmarried women to enjoy greater sexual freedom (although they also became more vulnerable to male sexual pressure). With a growing number of career options available to them, many women, particularly educated white women, stayed single or delayed marriage and childrearing. The birthrate continued its postwar decline, reaching an all-time low in the mid-1970s. At the same time the divorce rate rose 82 percent in the 1970s, as more men and women elected to leave unhappy marriages.

Although such changes brought increased autonomy for many women, they also caused new hardships, particularly in poor and working-class families. Divorce left many women with low-paying jobs and inadequate child care. Meanwhile, more tolerant attitudes toward premarital sex, along with other social and economic factors, had contributed to rising teenage pregnancy rates. The rise in divorce and adolescent pregnancy produced a sharp increase in the number of female-headed families, contributing to the "feminization" of poverty. By 1980 women accounted for 66 percent of adults who lived below the poverty line, a development that fueled a growing wave of social reaction.

Gays and Lesbians. Another major focus of social activism, the gay liberation movement, achieved heightened visibility in the 1970s. Thousands of gay men and lesbians "came out," publicly proclaiming their sexual

The Income Gap

Although the feminist movement helped create greater opportunities for women, it could not redress the long-standing economic inequalities between men and women. Cartoonist Doug Marlette offered this satirical look at the income gap in 1982, when women earned only fifty-nine cents for every dollar men earned.
Doug Marlette. © The *Charlotte Observer.*

orientation (see American Voices, "David Kopay: The Real Score: A Gay Athlete Comes Out," p. 895). In New York's Greenwich Village, San Francisco's Castro neighborhood, and other urban enclaves, growing gay communities gave rise to hundreds of new gay and lesbian clubs, churches, businesses, and political organizations. In 1973 the National Gay Task Force launched a campaign to include gay men and lesbians as a protected group under laws covering employment and housing rights. Such efforts were most successful on the local level; during the 1970s Detroit, Boston, Los Angeles, Miami, San Francisco, and other cities passed laws barring discrimination on the basis of sexual preference.

Like abortion and the ERA, gay rights came under attack from conservatives, who believed that granting gay lifestyles legal protection would encourage immoral behavior. When the Miami city council passed a measure banning discrimination against gay men and lesbians in 1977, the singer Anita Bryant led a campaign to repeal the law by popular referendum. Later that year voters overturned the measure by a two-to-one majority, prompting similar antigay campaigns around the country.

Racial Minorities

Although the civil rights movement was in disarray by the late 1960s, continued minority-group protests brought social and economic gains in the next decade. Native Americans realized some of the most significant changes. In 1971 the Alaska Native Land Claims Act

An Antibusing Confrontation in Boston

Tensions over court-ordered busing ran high in Boston in 1976. When a black lawyer tried to cross the city hall plaza during an antibusing demonstration, he became a victim of Boston's climate of racial hatred and violence. This Pulitzer Prize-winning photograph by Stanley Forman for the Boston Herald American *shows a protester trying to impale the man with a flagstaff.* Stanley Forman.

David Kopay

The Real Score: A Gay Athlete Comes Out

For ten years David Kopay played professional football for the San Francisco Forty-Niners, the Detroit Lions, the Washington Redskins, the New Orleans Saints, and the Green Bay Packers. In 1975, at the end of his playing career, Kopay publicly acknowledged his homosexuality, creating a national furor in the sports world.

I always knew I was a bit different, but I kept it kind of quiet. I didn't think of myself as queer. In fact I couldn't even say that word for years and years. . . .

When I thought about the future, I assumed I'd be able to get a job in coaching because I was a player-coach my last few years playing. I was always working behind the scenes with the young ballplayers, coaching them. But I wasn't getting any interviews. There were all kinds of rumors about me being gay. . . .

By the time I spoke out, I really had nothing left to lose. It felt like I didn't have a choice—I just had to do it. Then one morning in 1975 I saw an article in the *Washington Star* about homosexual athletes and why they had everything to lose. There was an interview in the article with Jerry Smith [Washington Redskins tight end who died of AIDS in 1986]. . . .

. . . I was at a time and place in my own coming out where I felt that if I was going to survive, I had to speak out. It was do that or maybe go crazy.

So I called Lynn Rosellini, who was the reporter for the article that quoted Jerry Smith. Lynn was doing an entire series on gay athletes. . . .

Everybody said there was going to be a terrible backlash against me when Lynn's article was published. But there wasn't a backlash against me personally: There was a backlash against all the television shows and radio stations that I went on. And the newspapers. The *Washington Star* said they had never received more negative mail for anything they'd ever done—hundreds of horrible hate letters. Only two or three were addressed to me directly; the rest were addressed to the *Washington Star* editor and Lynn Rosellini for doing the series on gay athletes. The letters said things like, "It doesn't belong on the sports page as a model for our young boys and girls." "How could the *Washington Star* run an article like this?" I got letters that said, "I hope you never get a coaching job. Yours in Christ. Love. . . ." Just horrible things.

I never did get a coaching job. I was really quite frightened because I didn't know what I was going to do. No one would hire me to be a coach, I think, because of the image problem. They didn't think I could fill the role of the coach as guardian of the morals of the young students—the father figure. I also knew that I probably wouldn't get that really good sales-rep job that a lot of the other guys got. I had to make a spot for myself somehow, so I wound up working with Perry Young for a year on my book, *The Dave Kopay Story*.

I think we knew we were doing something good. . . .

A lot of kids still write. They say that the book meant so much to them. They remember that it changed them a lot or made a difference.

Source: Eric Marcus, *Making History* (New York: Harper Collins, 1992), 275–77.

restored 40 million acres to Eskimos, Aleuts, and other native peoples, along with $960 million in compensation. Most important, the federal government abandoned the tribal termination program of the 1950s (see Chapter 28). Under the Indian Self-Determination Act of 1974, Congress restored the tribes' right to govern themselves and gave them authority over federal programs on their reservations (Map 30.3).

Busing. The busing of children to achieve school desegregation proved the most disruptive social issue of the 1970s. Progress in achieving the desegregation

mandated by *Brown v. Board of Education of Topeka* had been slow. In the 1970s both the courts and the Justice Department pushed for more action, not just in the South but in other parts of the country. In *Milliken v. Bradley* (1974), the Supreme Court ordered cities with deeply ingrained patterns of residential segregation to use busing of black and white students from segregated neighborhoods to nonneighborhood schools to integrate their classrooms.

The decision sparked intense and sometimes violent opposition. In Boston in 1974 and 1975, the strongly Irish-Catholic working-class neighborhood of

MAP 30.3 American Indian Reservations

Although Native Americans have been able to preserve small enclaves in the northeastern states, most Indian reservations are in the West. Beginning in the 1970s various nations filed land claims against federal and state governments.

For more help analyzing this map, see the ONLINE STUDY GUIDE at bedfordstmartins.com/henretta.

South Boston responded to the arrival of African American students from Roxbury with mob action reminiscent of that in Little Rock in 1957 (see American Voices, "Phyllis Ellison: Busing in Boston," p. 897). Threatened by court-ordered busing, many white parents transferred their children to private schools or moved to the suburbs. The resulting "white flight" exacerbated the racial imbalance busing was supposed to redress. Some black parents also opposed busing, calling instead for better schools in predominantly black neighborhoods. By the late 1970s federal courts had begun to back away from their insistence on busing to achieve racial balance.

Affirmative Action. Almost as divisive as busing was the issue of affirmative action procedures, which had expanded opportunities for blacks and Latinos. The number of African American students enrolled in colleges and universities doubled between 1970 and 1977 to 1.1 million, or 9.3 percent of the total student enrollment. A small but growing number of African Americans moved into white-collar professions in corporations and universities. Others found new opportunities in civil service occupations such as law enforcement or entered apprenticeships in the skilled construction trades. Latinos experienced similar gains in education and employment. On the whole, however, both groups enjoyed only marginal economic improvement, since poor and working-class nonwhites bore the brunt of job loss and unemployment in the 1970s.

Nevertheless, many whites, who were also feeling the economic pinch, came to resent affirmative action programs as an infringement of their rights. White men especially complained of "reverse discrimination" against them. In 1978 Allan Bakke, a white man, sued the University of California Medical School at Davis for rejecting him in favor of less qualified minority candidates.

Phyllis Ellison

Busing in Boston

Nowhere in the North was busing more divisive than in Boston from 1974 to 1975. Phyllis Ellison was one of fifty-six black students from the predominantly black neighborhoods of Columbia Point and Roxbury who were assigned to South Boston High School. In this interview she describes incidents from her sophomore year, including the day a white student was stabbed by a black student during a melee at the school. The student's wound was not fatal, but the incident led to heightened resistance and recriminations.

I remember my first day going on the bus to South Boston High School. I wasn't afraid because I felt important. I didn't know what to expect, what was waiting for me up the hill. We had police escorts. I think there was three motorcycle cops and then two police cruisers in front of the bus, and so I felt really important at that time, not knowing what was on the other side of the hill.

Well, when we started up the hill you could hear people saying, "Niggers go home." There were signs, they had made a sign saying, "Black people stay out. We don't want any niggers in our school." And there were people on the corners holding bananas like we were apes, monkeys. "Monkeys get out, get them out of our neighborhood. We don't want you in our schools.". . .

You can't imagine how tense it was inside the classroom. A teacher was almost afraid to say the wrong thing, because they knew that that would excite the whole class, a disturbance in the classroom. The black students sat on one side of the classes. The white students sat on the other side of the classes. . . . In the lunchrooms . . . [it] was the same thing. . . . So really, it was separate, I mean, we attended the same school, but we really never did anything together. . . .

I remember the day Michael Faith got stabbed vividly, because I was in the principal's office and all of a sudden you heard a lot of commotion and you heard kids screaming and yelling and saying, "He's dead, he's dead. That black nigger killed him. He's dead, he's dead." And then the principal running out of the office. There was a lot of commotion and screaming, yelling, hollering, "Get the niggers at Southie." I was really afraid. And the principal came back into the office and said, Call the ambulance and tell all the black students that were in the office to stay there. A police officer was in there and they were trying to get the white students out of the building, because they had just gone on a rampage and they were just going to hurt the first black student that they saw. . . . The black students were locked in their rooms and all the white students were let go out of their classrooms. I remember us going into a room, and outside you just saw a crowd of people, I mean, just so many people, I can't even count. . . . I remember the police cars coming up the street, attempting to, and people turning over the police cars, and I was just amazed that they could do something like that. The police tried to get horses up. They wouldn't let the horses get up. They stoned the horses. They stoned the cars. And I thought that day that we would never get out of South Boston High School. . . .

Source: Henry Hampton and Steve Fayer, *Voices of Freedom: An Oral History of the Civil Rights Movement from the 1950s through the 1980s* (New York: Bantam, 1990), 600, 610, 612–13.

The Supreme Court ruling in *Bakke v. University of California* was inconclusive. Though it branded the medical school's strict quota system illegal and ordered Bakke admitted, it stated that racial factors could be considered in hiring and admission decisions, thus upholding the principle of affirmative action. But the *Bakke* decision was a setback for proponents of affirmative action, and it prepared the way for subsequent efforts to eliminate those programs.

Though activists who supported racial minorities, women, gays, consumers, and the environment had distinct agendas, they also had much in common. They were part of "a rights revolution"—a wide-ranging movement in the 1960s and 1970s to bring issues of social justice and welfare to the forefront of public policy. Influenced by the Great Society's liberalism, they invariably turned to the federal government for protection of individual rights and—in the case of environmentalists—the world's natural resources. The activists of this period made substantial progress in widening the notion of the federal government's responsibilities, but by the end of the 1970s their movements faced growing opposition.

The Politics of Resentment

Together with the rapidly growing antiabortion movement, the often vociferous public opposition to busing, affirmative action, gay rights ordinances, and the Equal Rights Amendment constituted a broad backlash against the social changes of the previous decade. Many Americans believed that their interests had been slighted by the rights revolution and resented a federal government that protected women who sought abortions or minorities who benefited from affirmative action. The economic changes of the 1970s, which left many working- and middle-class Americans with lower disposable incomes, rising prices, and higher taxes, further fueled what the conservative writer Alan Crawford has termed the *politics of resentment*—a grassroots revolt against "special-interest groups" (women, minorities, gays, and so on) and growing expenditures on social welfare. Special groups and programs, conservatives believed, robbed other Americans of educational and employment opportunities and saddled the working and middle classes with an extra financial burden.

One manifestation of the politics of resentment was a wave of local taxpayers' revolts. In 1978 California voters passed Proposition 13, a measure that reduced property taxes and eventually undercut local governments' ability to maintain schools and other essential services. Promising tax relief to middle-class homeowners and reduced funding for busing and other programs to benefit the poor—who were invariably assumed to be nonwhite—Proposition 13 became the model for similar tax measures around the country in the late 1970s and 1980s.

Evangelical Religion. The rising popularity of evangelical religion also fueled the conservative resurgence of the 1970s. Fundamentalist groups that fostered a "born-again" experience had been growing steadily since World War II, under the leadership of charismatic preachers such as Billy Graham. According to a Gallup poll conducted in 1976, some 50 million Americans—about a quarter of the population—were affiliated with evangelical movements. These groups set up their own school systems and newspapers. Through broadcasting networks like the Christian Broadcasting Network, founded by the Virginia preacher Pat Robertson, a new breed of televangelists such as Jerry Falwell built vast and influential electronic ministries.

Many of these evangelicals spoke out on a broad range of issues, denouncing abortion, busing, sex education, pornography, feminism, and gay rights and bringing their religious values to a wider public. In 1979 Jerry Falwell founded the Moral Majority, a political pressure group that promoted Christian "family values"—traditional gender roles, heterosexuality, family cohesion—and staunch anticommunism. The extensive

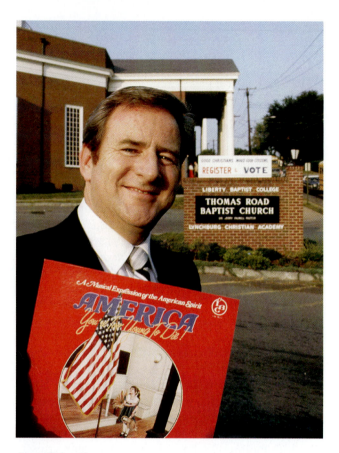

Jerry Falwell

The resurgence of evangelical religion in the 1970s was accompanied by a conservative movement in politics known as the "New Right." Founded in 1979 by televangelist Jerry Falwell, the Moral Majority was one of the earliest New Right groups, committed to promoting "family values" in American society and politics. Dennis Brack / Black Star.

media and fund-raising networks of the Christian right contributed to the organizational base for a larger conservative movement known as the "**New Right**."

The New Right. The New Right's constituency was complex. Conservatives of the early cold war era had focused on resisting creeping socialism at home and abroad and were often identified with corporate business interests. In the 1970s they were joined not only by evangelical Christian groups but by "neoconservatives," intellectuals such as sociologist Nathan Glazier and Norman Podhoretz, editor of *Commentary* magazine, who had been associated with radical or liberal agendas in the past and now vehemently recanted their former political views. Articulate in their criticisms of affirmative action, the welfare state, and changing gender and sexual values, they helped to give conservative values a heightened respectability and reinforced much of the "politics of resentment." The New Right's diverse constituents shared a hostility toward a powerful federal government and a fear of declining social morality. Backed by wealthy corporate interests and using sophisticated computerized mass-mailing campaigns, a variety of New Right political groups mobilized thousands of followers and millions of dollars to support conservative candidates and causes.

Politics in the Wake of Watergate

It is not surprising that in the wake of Watergate many citizens had become cynical about the federal government and about politicians in general. "Don't vote. It only encourages them" read one bumper sticker during the 1976 campaign. Nixon's successors, Gerald Ford and Jimmy Carter, plagued by foreign-policy crises and continued economic woes, did little to restore public confidence. In the 1980 elections voter apathy persisted, but Ronald Reagan's lopsided presidential victory signified a hope that the charismatic former actor could restore America's traditional values and its economic and international power.

Ford's Caretaker Presidency

During the two years Gerald Ford held the nation's highest office, he failed to establish his legitimacy as president. Ford's pardon of Nixon hurt his credibility as a political leader, but an even bigger problem was his handling of the economy, which was reeling from the inflation set in motion by the Vietnam War, rising oil prices, and the growing trade deficit. In 1974 the inflation rate soared to almost 12 percent, and in the following year the economy entered its deepest downturn since the Great Depression. Though many of the nation's economic problems were beyond the president's control, Ford's failure to take more vigorous action made him appear timid and powerless.

In foreign policy Ford was equally lacking in leadership. He maintained Nixon's détente initiatives by asking Henry Kissinger to stay on as secretary of state. Though Ford met with Soviet leaders hoping to hammer out the details of a SALT II (Strategic Arms Limitation Treaty) agreement, he made little progress. Ford and Kissinger also continued Nixon's policy of increasing support for the shah of Iran, ignoring the bitter opposition and anti-Western sentiment that the shah's policy of rapid modernization was provoking among the growing Muslim fundamentalist population in Iran.

Jimmy Carter: The Outsider as President

The 1976 presidential campaign was one of the blandest in years. President Ford chose as his running mate the conservative Senator Robert J. Dole of Kansas. The Democratic choice, James E. (Jimmy) Carter, governor of Georgia, shared the ticket with Senator Walter F. Mondale of Minnesota, who had ties to the traditional Democratic constituencies of labor, liberals, blacks, and big-city machines. Avoiding issues and controversy, Carter played up his role as a Washington outsider, pledging to restore morality to government. "I will never lie to you," he earnestly told voters. Carter won the election with 50 percent of the popular vote to Ford's 48 percent.

Despite his efforts to overcome the post-Watergate climate of skepticism and apathy, Carter never became an effective leader. His outsider strategy distanced him from traditional sources of power, and he did little to heal the breach. Shying away from established Democratic leaders, Carter turned to advisors and friends who had worked with him in Georgia, none of whom had national experience. When his budget director, Bert Lance, was questioned about financial irregularities at the Atlanta bank he had headed, Carter's campaign pledge to restore integrity and morality to the government rang hollow.

Coping with Hard Economic Times.   Inflation was Carter's major domestic challenge. When he took office, the nation was still recovering from the severe recession of 1975 and 1976. Carter embarked on a fiscal policy that eroded both business and consumer confidence. To counter inflation the Federal Reserve Board raised interest rates repeatedly; in 1980 they topped 20 percent, a historic high. A deep recession finally broke the inflationary spiral in 1982, a year after Carter left office.

The Carter administration expanded the federal bureaucracy in some cases and limited its reach in others. Carter enlarged the cabinet by creating the Departments of Energy and Education and approved new environmental protection measures, such as the $1.6 billion "Superfund" to clean up chemical pollution sites as well as new park and forest lands in Alaska. But he continued President Nixon's efforts to reduce the scope of federal activities by reforming the civil service and deregulating the airline, trucking, and railroad industries. With deregulation, prices often dropped, but the resulting cutthroat competition drove many firms out of business and encouraged corporate consolidation. Carter also failed in his effort to decontrol oil and natural gas prices as a spur to domestic production and conservation.

Carter's attempt to provide leadership during the energy crisis also faltered. He called energy conservation efforts "the moral equivalent of war," but the media reduced the phrase to "MEOW" (see Voices from Abroad, "Fei Xiaotong: America's Crisis of Faith," p. 900). In early 1979 a revolution in Iran again raised oil prices, and gas lines again reminded Americans of their dependence on foreign oil. That summer, Carter's approval rating dropped to 26 percent—lower than Richard Nixon's during the worst part of the Watergate scandal.

Fei Xiaotong

America's Crisis of Faith

Fei Xiaotong, a Chinese anthropologist and sociologist, wrote influential books on the United States during World War II and the 1950s. Despite his criticism of U.S. foreign policy, his often sympathetic treatment of America contributed to twenty years of political ostracism in China. Returning to prominence in the late 1970s, he joined an official delegation to the United States in 1979. In this passage written shortly after his return to China, Fei responds to President Jimmy Carter's assessment of the problems Americans faced as a spiritual crisis. Despite Fei's Marxist critique of American capitalism, his concluding remarks indicate a broadly positive attitude about the United States.

I read in the newspaper that the energy crisis in the United States is getting worse and worse. I hear that after spending several days of quiet thought in his mountain retreat, President Carter decided that America's real problem is not the energy crisis but a "crisis of faith." The way it is told is that vast numbers of people have lost their faith in the present government and in the political system, and do not believe that the people in the government working with current government methods can solve the present series of crises. Even more serious, he believes that the masses have come to have doubts about traditional American values, and if this continues, in his opinion, the future of America is terrible to imagine. He made a sad and worried speech. I have not had an opportunity to read the text of his speech, but if he has truly realized that the present American social system has lost popular support, that should be considered a good thing because at least it shows that the old method of just treating the symptoms will no longer work.

In fact, loss of faith in the present social system on the part of the broad masses of the American people did not begin with the energy crisis. The spectacular advances in science and technology in America in the last decade or two and the unceasing rise in the forces of production are good. But the social system remains unchanged, and the relations of production are basically the same old capitalism. This contradiction between the forces of production and the relations of production has not lessened but become deeper. The ruling class, to be sure, still has the power to keep on finding ways of dealing with the endless series of crises, but the masses of people are coming increasingly to feel that they have fallen unwittingly into a situation where their fate is controlled by others, like a moth in a spiderweb, unable to struggle free. Not only the blacks of Harlem—who are clearly able to earn their own living but still have to rely on welfare to support themselves without dignity—but even well-off families in garden-like suburban residences worry all day that some accident may suddenly rob them of everything. As the dependence of individuals on others grows heavier and heavier, each person feels in his heart that this society is no longer to be relied on. . . . No wonder people complain that civilization was created by humans, but humans have been enslaved by it. Such a feeling is natural in a society like America's. Carter is right to call this feeling of helplessness a "crisis of faith," for it is a doubting of the present culture. Only he should realize that the present crisis has been long in the making and is already deep. . . .

These "Glimpses of America" essays may be brought to a close here, but to end with the crisis of faith does violence to my original intention. History is a stream that flows on and cannot be stopped. Words must be cut off, but history goes bubbling on. It is inconceivable that America will come to a standstill at any crisis point. I have full faith in the great American people and hope that they will continue to make even greater contributions to the progress of mankind. . . .

Source: R. David Arkush and Leo O. Lee, trans. and eds., *Land Without Ghosts: Chinese Impressions of America From the Mid-Nineteenth Century to the Present* (Berkeley: University of California Press, 1989).

Foreign Policy and Diplomacy. In foreign affairs President Carter made human rights the centerpiece of his policy. He criticized the suppression of dissent in the Soviet Union—especially as it affected the right of Jewish citizens to emigrate—and withdrew economic and military aid from Argentina, Uruguay, Ethiopia, and other countries that violated human rights. Carter also established the Office of Human Rights in the State Department. Unable to change the internal policies of longtime U.S. allies who were serious violators of human rights, such as the Philippines, South Korea, and South Africa, he did manage to raise public awareness of the human rights issue, making it one future administrations would have to address.

In Latin America Carter's most important contribution was the resolution of the lingering dispute over control of the Panama Canal. In a treaty signed on September 7, 1977, the United States agreed to turn over control of the canal to Panama on December 31, 1999. In return the United States retained the right to send its ships through the canal in case of war, even though the canal itself would be declared neutral territory. Despite a conservative outcry that the United States was giving away more than it got, the Senate narrowly approved the treaty.

Though Carter had campaigned to free the United States from its "inordinate fear of Communism," relations with the Soviet Union soon became tense, largely because of problems surrounding arms-limitation talks. Eventually the Soviet leader Leonid Brezhnev signed SALT II (1979), but hopes for Senate ratification of the treaty collapsed when the Soviet Union invaded Afghanistan that December. In retaliation for this aggression, which Carter viewed as a threat to Middle Eastern oil supplies, the United States curtailed grain sales to the Soviet Union and boycotted the 1980 summer Olympics in Moscow. (The Soviets returned the gesture by boycotting the 1984 summer games in Los Angeles.) In a move with more long-term impact, Carter and his successor Ronald Reagan also provided covert assistance to an Afghan group who called themselves *mujahideen*, or holy warriors. With funding provided by Saudia Arabia and Pakistan, the CIA supported these radical Islamic fundamentalists, whose numbers would eventually include Osama bin Laden, in their efforts to drive the Russians from Afghanistan in the 1980s, thereby helping to establish the now infamous Taliban.

President Carter achieved both his most stunning success and his greatest failure in the Middle East. Relations between Egypt and Israel had remained tense since the 1973 Yom Kippur War. In 1978 Carter helped

A Framework for Peace

President Jimmy Carter's greatest foreign-policy achievement was the personal diplomacy he exerted to persuade President Anwar al-Sadat of Egypt (left) and Prime Minister Menachem Begin of Israel (right) to sign a peace treaty in 1978. The signing of the Camp David accords marked an important first step in constructing a framework for peace in the Middle East. In 2002 Carter received the Nobel Peace Prize in recognition of his "untiring effort to find peaceful solutions to international conflicts, to advance democracy and human rights, and to promote economic and social development."

Jimmy Carter Presidential Library.

to break the diplomatic stalemate by inviting Israel's prime minister Menachem Begin and Egyptian president Anwar al-Sadat to Camp David, the presidential retreat in Maryland. Two weeks of discussions and Carter's promise of additional foreign aid to Egypt persuaded Sadat and Begin to adopt a "framework for peace." The framework included Egypt's recognition of Israel's right to exist and Israel's return of the Sinai Peninsula, which it had occupied since 1967. Transfer of the territory to Egypt took place from 1979 to 1982.

The Iranian Hostage Crisis. Dramatically less successful was U.S. foreign policy toward Iran. Ever since the CIA had helped to install Muhammad Reza Pahlavi on the throne in 1953, the United States had counted Iran as a faithful ally in the troubled Middle East. Overlooking the repressive tactics of Iran's CIA-trained secret police, SAVAK, Carter followed in the footsteps of previous cold war policymakers for whom access to Iranian oil reserves and the shah's consistently anti-Communist stance outweighed all other considerations.

Early in 1979, however, the shah's government was overthrown and driven into exile by a revolution led by fundamentalist Muslim leader Ayatollah Ruhollah Khomeini. In late October 1979 the Carter administration admitted the deposed shah, who was suffering from incurable cancer, to the United States for medical treatment. Though Iran's new leaders had warned that such an action would provoke retaliation, Henry Kissinger and other foreign-policy leaders had argued

that the United States should assist the shah, both for humanitarian reasons and in return for his years of support for American policy. In response, on November 4, 1979, fundamentalist Muslim students under Khomeini's direction seized the U.S. embassy in Tehran, taking Americans there hostage in a flagrant violation of the principle of diplomatic immunity. The hostage takers demanded that the shah be returned to Iran for trial and punishment, but the United States refused. Instead, President Carter suspended arms sales to Iran, froze Iranian assets in American banks, and threatened to deport Iranian students in the United States.

For the next fourteen months, the Iranian hostage crisis paralyzed Jimmy Carter's presidency. Night after night, humiliating pictures of blindfolded hostages appeared on television newscasts. The extensive media coverage and Carter's insistence that the safe return of the fifty-two hostages was his top priority enhanced the value of the hostages to their captors. An attempt to mount a military rescue of the hostages failed miserably in April 1980, six months into the crisis, because of helicopter equipment failures in the desert. The abortive rescue mission reinforced the public's view of Carter as a bumbling and ineffective executive.

The Reagan Revolution

With Carter embroiled in the hostage crisis, the Republicans gained momentum by nominating former California governor Ronald Reagan. A movie actor from the late 1930s to the early 1950s, Reagan had served as president of

American Hostages in Iran
Images of blindfolded, handcuffed American hostages seized by Iranian militants at the American embassy in Tehran in November 1979 shocked the nation and created a foreign-policy crisis that eventually cost President Carter his chance for reelection.
Mingam / Liaison.

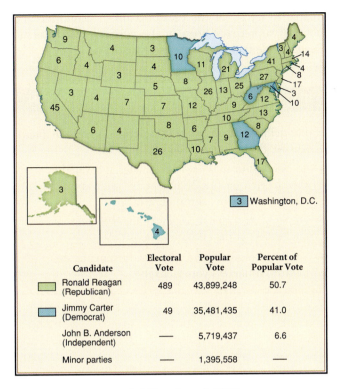

MAP 30.4 Presidential Election of 1980

Ronald Reagan defeated Democratic incumbent Jimmy Carter, winning all but six states and the District of Columbia. Winning 51 percent of the popular vote, Reagan cut deeply into the traditional Democratic coalition by wooing many southern whites, urban ethnics, and blue-collar workers and setting the stage for the "Reagan Revolution" and the conservative swing in American politics that characterized the 1980s and 1990s. Republicans also won control of the Senate for the first time since 1954.

the Screen Actors Guild and had been active in the postwar anti-Communist crusade in Hollywood. He had endorsed conservative presidential candidate Barry Goldwater in 1964 and had begun his own political career shortly thereafter, serving as governor of California from 1967 to 1975. After losing a bid for the Republican nomination in 1976, Reagan secured it easily in 1980 and chose former CIA director George Bush as his running mate.

In the final months of the campaign, Carter took on an embattled and defensive tone, while Reagan remained upbeat and decisive. The Republicans benefited from superior financial resources, which allowed them to make sophisticated use of television and direct-mail appeals. Reagan also had a powerful issue to exploit: the hostage stalemate. Calling the Iranians "barbarians" and "common criminals," he hinted that he would take strong action to win the hostages' return. More important, Reagan effectively appealed to the politics of resentment that flourished during the lean years of the 1970s. In a televised debate between the candidates, Reagan emphasized the

economic plight of working- and middle-class Americans when he posed the rhetorical question, "Are you better off today than you were four years ago?"

In November Reagan won easily, with 51 percent of the popular vote to Carter's 41 percent (Map 30.4). The landslide also gave the Republicans control of the Senate for the first time since 1954, though the Democrats maintained their hold on the House. Voter turnout, however, was at its lowest since the 1920s: only 53 percent of those eligible to vote went to the polls. Many poor and working-class voters stayed home. Nevertheless, the election confirmed the growth in the power of the Republican Party since Richard Nixon's victory in 1968.

Superior financial resources and a realignment of the electorate contributed to the Republican resurgence of the 1970s. The political action committees that had proliferated under the Fair Compaign Practices Act of 1974 collected large sums for both parties, but particularly for the Republicans. While the Democratic Party saw its key constituency—organized labor—dwindle, the GOP's financial superiority enabled it to make sophisticated and effective use of television and direct mail to reach voters. This aggressive outreach helped bring about a realignment of the electorate. The core of the Republican Party that elected Ronald Reagan remained the upper-middle-class white Protestant voters who supported balanced budgets, disliked government activism, feared crime and communism, and believed in a strong national defense. But new groups had gravitated toward the Republican vision: southern whites disaffected by big government and black civil rights gains; blue-collar workers, especially culturally conservative Catholics; young voters who identified themselves as conservatives; and residents in the West, especially those in the rapidly growing suburbs. By wooing these "Reagan Democrats," the Republican Party made deep inroads into Democratic territory, eroding that party's traditional coalition of southerners, blacks, laborers, and urban ethnics.

The New Right was another significant contributor to the Republican victory, especially the religious right, associated with groups like the Moral Majority, whose emphasis on traditional values and Christian morality dovetailed well with conservative Republican ideology. In 1980 these concerns formed the basis for the party's platform, which called for a constitutional ban on abortion, voluntary prayer in public schools, and a mandatory death penalty for certain crimes. The Republicans also demanded an end to court-mandated busing and for the first time in forty years opposed the Equal Rights Amendment. A key factor in the 1980 election, the New Right contributed to the rebirth of the Republican Party under Ronald Reagan.

On January 20, 1981, at the moment Carter turned over the presidency to Ronald Reagan, the Iranian government released the American hostages. After 444 days of captivity, the hostages returned home to an ecstatic welcome, a reflection of the public's frustration over their long ordeal. While most Americans continued to maintain "We're Number One," the hostage crisis in Iran came to symbolize the loss of America's power to control world affairs. Its psychological impact was enhanced by its occurrence at the end of a decade that had witnessed Watergate, the American defeat in Vietnam, and the OPEC embargo.

To a great extent, the decline in American influence had been magnified by the unusual predominance the United States had enjoyed after World War II—an advantage that should not have been expected to last forever. The return of Japan and Western Europe to economic and political power, the control of vital oil resources by Middle Eastern countries, and the industrialization of some developing nations had widened the cast of characters on the international stage. Still, many Americans were unable to let go of the presumption of economic and political supremacy born in the postwar years. Ronald Reagan rode their frustrations to victory in 1980.

FOR FURTHER EXPLORATION

▶ For definitions of key terms boldfaced in this chapter, see the glossary at the end of the book.

▶ To assess your mastery of the material covered in this chapter, see the Online Study Guide at **bedfordstmartins.com/henretta.**

▶ For suggested references, including Web sites, see page SR-33 at the end of the book.

▶ For map resources and primary documents, see **bedfordstmartins.com/henretta.**

With his election to the presidency in 1968, Richard Nixon became a harbinger of more conservative times in American social and political life. During his five years in the White House, Nixon sought to trim back the welfare state through federal revenue sharing, cutbacks in Great Society antipoverty programs, and a reduced commitment to civil rights. But when he deemed it necessary, Nixon did not shrink from the use of executive power; he implemented wage and price controls to fight inflation, periodically impounded federal funds, and expanded the role of the government in environmental and consumer affairs. Nixon's plans, however, were cut short after his administration took part in a series of illegal acts during his campaign for reelection in 1972. The resulting Watergate scandal forced him to resign in 1974.

For much of the decade, the United States struggled with economic problems, including high inflation, skyrocketing energy costs, stagnation of income, and a diminished position in world trade. A series of gas shortages during the Arab oil embargo of 1973 to 1974 and the Iranian revolution in 1979 had a devastating impact on American society and caused many people to question the country's voracious pattern of energy consumption.

Although many Americans became cynical about politics after Watergate and Vietnam, some continued to pursue the unfinished social agendas of the 1960s. Most notably, the environmental and women's movements showed dynamic growth and activism at the grassroots level. Movements for consumer protection, gay and lesbian rights, and racial equality also continued to make modest gains. By the late 1970s, however, a new, more conservative social mood—based in part on the resurgence of evangelical Christianity—limited activists' advances on issues such as abortion rights, the Equal Rights Amendment, gay and lesbian rights, busing, and affirmative action.

On the national level ineffective political leadership by Gerald Ford led to his defeat in 1976 by Jimmy Carter of Georgia, who campaigned as a Washington outsider. Taking a high moral tone, Carter made human rights a priority of his administration and helped to negotiate the Camp David Peace accords between Egypt and Israel in 1978. But his own inexperience, mounting economic problems, and growing troubles abroad plagued his administration. The end of the decade was dominated by the Iranian hostage crisis, as Islamic fundamentalists held fifty-two hostages at the U.S. embassy in Tehran for 444 days. The hostage crisis virtually paralyzed Carter's presidency, helping Ronald Reagan to win election in 1980.

1968 Richard Nixon elected president

1970 Earth Day first observed

Environmental Protection Agency established

1971 Pentagon Papers published

Nixon suspends Bretton Woods system

Swann v. Charlotte-Mecklenburg institutes busing

1972– 1974 Watergate investigation

1972 Revenue sharing begins

Watergate break-in; Nixon reelected

Congress passes Equal Rights Amendment

Ms. magazine founded

1973 Spiro Agnew resigns; Gerald Ford appointed vice president

Roe v. Wade legalizes abortion

Endangered Species Act

1973– 1974 Arab oil embargo; gas shortages

Nixon resigns; Ford becomes president and pardons Nixon

Freedom of Information Act strengthened

Fair Campaign Practices Act passed

1974– 1975 Busing controversy in Boston

1975– 1976 Recession

Jimmy Carter elected president

First National Women's Conference in Houston

Voters overturn a Miami city council's gay rights measure

Carter brokers Camp David accords between Egypt and Israel

Proposition 13 reduces California taxes

Bakke v. University of California limits affirmative action

Love Canal crisis begins

1979 Three Mile Island nuclear accident

Moral Majority founded

Second oil crisis triggered by revolution in Iran

Hostages seized at American embassy in Teheran, Iran

Soviet Union invades Afghanistan

1980 "Superfund" created to clean up chemical pollution

Ronald Reagan elected president

CHAPTER 31

A New Domestic and World Order

1981–2001

The Reagan-Bush Years, 1981–1993
Reaganomics
Reagan's Second Term
The Bush Presidency

Foreign Relations under Reagan and Bush
Interventions in Developing Countries
The End of the Cold War
War in the Persian Gulf, 1990–1991

Uncertain Times: Economic and Social Trends, 1980–2000
The Economy
Popular Culture and Popular Technology
An Increasingly Pluralistic Society
Backlash against Women's and Gay Rights
The AIDS Epidemic
The Environmental Movement at Twenty-five

Restructuring the Domestic Order: Public Life, 1992–2001
Clinton's First Term
"The Era of Big Government Is Over"
Second-Term Stalemates
An Unprecedented Election
George W. Bush's Early Presidency

ON NOVEMBER 9, 1989, MILLIONS of television viewers worldwide watched jubilant Germans swarm through the Berlin Wall after the East German government lifted all restrictions on passage between the eastern and western sectors of the city. The Berlin Wall, which had divided the city since 1961, was the foremost symbol of Communist repression and the cold war division of Europe. Over the years, more than 400 East Germans had lost their lives trying to escape to the freedom of the other side. Now East and West Berliners, young and old, danced and mingled on what remained of the structure.

When the Berlin Wall came down, it brought communism's grip over Eastern Europe down with it. The Soviet Union would dissolve in 1991, ending the cold war. But new sources of conflict soon threatened world peace. International terrorism, instability in developing nations, and ethnic conflict loomed as potentially serious threats. In the new world order, the United States was increasingly linked to a global economy that directly affected American interest rates, consumption patterns, and job opportunities. At home, Americans grappled with racial, ethnic, and cultural conflict; crime and economic inequities; the shrinking role of the federal government; and disenchantment with political leaders' failure to solve many of the nation's pressing social problems.

◄ **The Wall Comes Tumbling Down**
The destruction of the Berlin Wall in November 1989 symbolized the end of the cold war.
Alexandra Avakian / Woodfin Camp & Associates.

The Reagan-Bush Years, 1981–1993

First elected at age sixty-nine, Ronald Reagan was the oldest man ever to serve as president, yet he conveyed a sense of physical vigor. By capitalizing on his skills as an actor and public speaker and by winning the support of the emerging New Right within the Republican Party, Reagan became one of the most popular presidents of the twentieth century. George Bush paled in comparison. His one term as president often seems indistinguishable from the two terms of his predecessor, in part because Bush was overshadowed by Reagan's extraordinary charisma but also because he followed the basic policies of the previous administration. Distrustful of the federal government, both Bush and Reagan turned away from the state as a source of solutions to America's social problems, calling into question almost a half cen-

tury of governmental activism. "Government is not the solution to our problem," Reagan declared. "Government is the problem."

Reaganomics

The economic and tax policies that emerged under Reagan, quickly dubbed **Reaganomics**, were based on supply-side economics theory. According to the theory, high taxes siphoned off capital that would otherwise be invested, stimulating growth. Tax cuts would therefore promote investment, causing an economic expansion that would increase tax revenues. Together with reductions in government spending, tax cuts would also shrink the federal budget deficit. Critics charged that conservative Republicans deliberately cut taxes to force reductions in federal funding for the social programs they disliked.

The Economic Recovery Tax Act passed in 1981 reduced income tax rates by 25 percent over three years. The reductions were supposed to be linked to drastic cutbacks in federal expenditures. But while cuts were made in food stamps, unemployment compensation, and welfare programs such as Aid to Families with Dependent Children (AFDC), congressional resistance kept the Social Security and Medicare programs intact. The net impact of Reaganomics was to further the redistribution of income from the poor to the wealthy.

Another tenet of Reaganomics was that many federal regulations impeded economic growth and productivity. The administration moved to abolish or reduce federal regulation of the workplace, health care, consumer protection, and the environment. The responsibility for and cost of such regulations were transferred to the states. One of the results of this policy was the deinstitutionalization of many of the mentally ill, forcing them onto the streets.

The money saved by these means—and more—was plowed into a five-year, $1.2 trillion defense buildup. This huge increase fulfilled Reagan's campaign pledge to "make America number one again," a slogan that tapped anxieties about the nation's foreign-policy failures, most recently symbolized by the Iranian hostage fiasco. The B-1 bomber, which President Carter had canceled, was resurrected, and development of a new missile system, the MX, was begun. Reagan's most ambitious and controversial weapons plan, proposed in 1983, was the Strategic Defense Initiative (SDI), popularly known as "Star Wars." A computerized satellite and laser shield for detecting and intercepting incoming missiles, SDI would supposedly render nuclear war obsolete.

Reagan's programs benefited from the Federal Reserve Board's tight money policies as well as a serendipitous drop in world oil prices, which reduced the disastrous inflation rates that had bedeviled the nation in the 1970s. Between 1980 and 1982 the inflation rate

Festive Times at the Reagan White House

Since Ronald and Nancy Reagan were both former actors, perhaps they thought of Fred Astaire and Ginger Rogers (see p. 705) when they struck this pose at a White House state dinner in May 1985. Some former White House staffers now suspect that Reagan was showing signs of early Alzheimer's disease by that point.

Photo by Harry Benson. Cover courtesy VANITY FAIR. © 1985 by Condé-Nast Publications, Inc.

dropped from 12.4 percent to just 4 percent. Unfortunately, the Fed's tightening of the money supply also brought on the "Reagan recession" of 1981 to 1982, which threw some 10 million Americans out of work. But as the recession bottomed out in early 1983 the economy began to grow, and for the rest of the decade, inflation remained low. Despite rather unexceptional growth in the gross domestic product, the Reagan administration presided over the longest peacetime economic expansion in American history.

Reagan's Second Term

Economic growth played a role in the 1984 elections. Reagan campaigned on the theme "It's Morning in America," suggesting that a new day of prosperity and pride was dawning. The Democrats nominated former vice president Walter Mondale of Minnesota to run against Reagan. With strong ties to labor unions, minority groups, and party leaders, Mondale epitomized the New Deal coalition that had dominated the Democratic Party since Roosevelt. To appeal to women voters, Mondale selected Representative Geraldine Ferraro of New York as his running mate—the first woman to run on a major party ticket. Nevertheless, Reagan won a landslide victory, carrying the entire nation except for Minnesota and the District of Columbia. Democrats, however, held onto the House and in 1986 would regain control of the Senate.

The Iran-Contra Affair. A major scandal marred Reagan's second term when in 1986 news leaked out that the administration had negotiated an arms-for-hostages deal with the revolutionary government of Iran—the same government Reagan had denounced during the 1980 hostage crisis. In an attempt to gain Iran's help in freeing some American hostages held by pro-Iranian forces in Lebanon, the United States had covertly sold arms to Iran. Some of the profits generated by the arms sales were diverted to the **Contras**, counterrevolutionaries in Nicaragua, whom the administration supported over the leftist regime of the Sandinistas. The covert diversion of funds, which was both illegal and unconstitutional, seemed to have been the brainstorm of Marine Lieutenant Colonel Oliver North, a National Security Council aide at the time. One key memo linked the White House to his plan. But when Congress investigated the mounting scandal in 1986 and 1987, White House officials testified that the president knew nothing about the diversion. Ronald Reagan's defense remained simple and consistent: "I don't remember."

The scandal bore many similarities to Watergate, including the possibility that the president had acted illegally. Yet early in Reagan's administration, one of his critics had coined the phrase "Teflon presidency" to describe Reagan's resiliency: bad news did not stick; it

just rolled off. The public seemed untroubled that the president was often confused or ill informed. Even the news that Nancy Reagan was in the habit of consulting an astrologer before planning major White House events failed to shake public confidence in the president. Reagan weathered "Iran-Contragate," but the scandal weakened his presidency.

The Reagan Legacy. The president proposed no bold domestic policy initiatives in his last two years in office. He had promised to place drastic limits on the federal government and to give free-market forces freer reign. Despite reordering the federal government's priorities, he failed to reduce its size or scope. Social Security and other entitlement programs remained untouched, and the military buildup counteracted cuts in other programs. Nevertheless, those spending cuts and Reagan's antigovernment rhetoric shaped the terms of political debate for the rest of the century.

One of Reagan's most significant legacies was his conservative judicial appointments. In 1981 he appointed Sandra Day O'Connor, the first woman ever to serve on the Supreme Court. In his second term he appointed two more justices, Antonin Scalia (1986) and Anthony Kennedy (1988), both far more conservative than the moderate O'Connor. Justice William Rehnquist, a noted conservative, was elevated to Chief Justice of the

Another Barrier Falls

In 1981 Sandra Day O'Connor (shown here with Chief Justice Warren Burger) became the first woman appointed to the Supreme Court. In 1993 she was joined by Ruth Bader Ginsburg.
Fred Ward / Black Star.

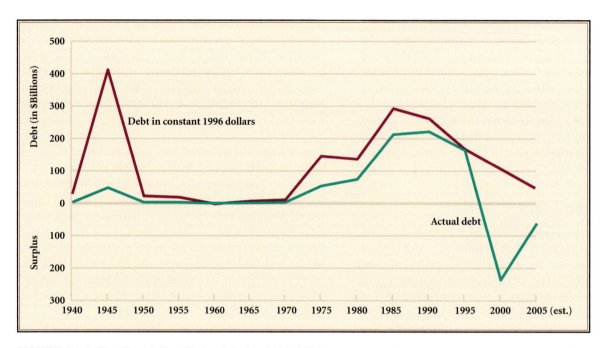

FIGURE 31.1 The Escalating Federal Debt, 1939–2000

The federal debt, which soared during World War II, remained fairly stable until the huge annual deficits of the 1980s. Deficits remained high in the 1990s, but political pressure to balance the budget promised reductions in the national debt.

Source: *Statistical Abstract of the United States, 2000* and Historical Tables, Budget for Fiscal Year 2003.

United States in 1986. Under his leadership the Court, often by a five-to-four margin, chipped away at the Warren Court's legacy in decisions on individual liberties, affirmative action, and the rights of criminal defendants.

Ironically, though Reagan had promised to balance the budget by 1984, his most enduring legacy was the national debt, which tripled during his two terms. The huge deficit reflected the combined effects of increased military spending, tax reductions for high-income taxpayers, and Congress's refusal to approve deep cuts in domestic programs (Figure 31.1). By 1989 the national debt had climbed to $2.8 trillion—more than $11,000 for every American citizen.

The nation was also running an annual deficit in its trade with other nations. Exports had been falling since the 1970s, when American products began to encounter increasing competition in world markets. In the early 1980s a high exchange rate for dollars made U.S. goods more expensive for foreign buyers and imports more affordable for Americans. The budget and trade deficits contributed to a major shift in 1985: for the first time since 1915, the United States became a debtor rather than a creditor nation.

The Bush Presidency

George Bush won the Republican nomination in 1988 and chose for his vice president a young conservative Indiana senator, Dan Quayle. In the Democratic primaries the

Patriotism and Politics

At a confetti parade for the 1988 Summer Olympic team held at Disneyland, California, in September 1988, Republican presidential candidate George Bush and his wife Barbara bask in the glow of America's success. Cynthia Johnson. © TIME Magazine.

most important contest was between Governor Michael Dukakis of Massachusetts and the charismatic civil rights leader Jesse Jackson, whose populist Rainbow Coalition had embraced the diversity of Democratic constituencies. Dukakis received the party's nomination and chose Senator Lloyd Bentsen of Texas as his running mate.

The 1988 campaign had a harsh tone: brief televised attack ads replaced meaningful discussion of the issues. The sound bite "Read My Lips: No New Taxes," drawn from George Bush's acceptance speech at the Republican convention, became the party's campaign mantra. In a racially charged television ad featuring Willie Horton, a black man convicted of murder who had killed again while on furlough from a Massachusetts prison, Republicans charged Dukakis with being soft on crime. Dukakis, forced on the defensive, failed to mount an effective counterattack. Bush carried thirty-eight states, winning the popular vote by 53.4 percent to 45.6 percent.

Supreme Court Conservatism. The judiciary rather than the executive branch determined some of the more significant domestic trends of the Bush era. Under Reagan's appointees the Supreme Court continued to move away from liberal activism toward a more conservative stance, especially on the issue of abortion. The 1989 *Webster v. Reproductive Health Services* decision upheld the right of states to limit the use of public funds and institutions for abortions. The next year the Court upheld a federal regulation barring personnel at federally funded health clinics from discussing abortion with their clients. In 1992 the Court upheld a Pennsylvania law mandating informed consent and a twenty-four-hour waiting period before an abortion could be performed. But the justices also reaffirmed the "essential holding" in *Roe v. Wade:* women had a constitutional right to abortion.

In 1990 David Souter, a little-known federal judge from New Hampshire, easily won confirmation to the Supreme Court. But the next year a major controversy erupted over President Bush's nomination of Clarence Thomas, an African American conservative with little judicial experience. Just as Thomas's confirmation hearings were drawing to a close, a former colleague, Anita Hill, testified publicly that Thomas had sexually harassed her in the early 1980s. After widely watched and widely debated televised testimony by both Thomas and Hill before the all-male Senate Judiciary Committee, the Senate confirmed Thomas by a narrow margin. In the wake of the hearings, national polls confirmed the pervasiveness of sexual harassment on the job: four out of ten women said that they had been the object of unwanted sexual advances from men at work.

Domestic and Economic Policy. Bush's record on the economy was crippled by his predecessor's failed economic policies, especially the budget deficit. The

A Woman of Conscience
Accusations by University of Oklahoma law professor Anita Hill that Supreme Court nominee Clarence Thomas had sexually harassed her sparked fierce debate. Many felt that had there been more women in the Senate, Hill's charges would have been treated more seriously. After the 1992 election women's representation did in fact increase to six women in the Senate and forty-seven in the House of Representatives. Markel / Gamma Liaison.

Gramm-Rudman Act, passed in 1985, had mandated automatic cuts if budget targets were not met in 1991. Facing the prospect of a halt in nonessential government services and the layoff of thousands of government employees, Congress resorted to new spending cuts and one of the largest tax increases in history. Bush's failure to keep his "No New Taxes" promise earned him the enmity of Republican conservatives, which dramatically hurt his chances for reelection in 1992.

Reagan's decision to shift the cost of many federal programs—including housing, education, public works, and social services—to state and local governments caused problems for Bush. In 1990 a recession began to erode state and local tax revenues. As incomes declined and industrial and white-collar layoffs increased, poverty and homelessness increased sharply. In 1991 unemployment approached 7 percent nationwide. To save money, state and local governments laid off workers even as demand for social services climbed.

The Savings and Loan Crisis.   Another drag on the economy was the collapse of the savings and loan industry. Savings and loan associations (S & Ls), also called "thrifts," invested depositors' savings in home mortgages. Since 1934 deposits in S & Ls had been insured by the Federal Savings and Loan Insurance Corporation (FSLIC). After S & Ls complained in 1982 that high inflation and soaring interest rates were reducing their profits, Reagan's deregulation program permitted them to invest in commercial real estate and businesses. The real estate market boomed for most of the 1980s, so the loans and investments were profitable. But when construction and the oil boom in the Southwest slowed and the stock market tumbled sharply in 1987, savings and loan associations' losses mounted, and the value of their assets plummeted. Some S & Ls were taken over by commercial banks, but many simply went bankrupt, forcing the federal government to make good its guarantee to depositors. To recoup some of the massive losses, the Bush administration set up a temporary agency in 1989 to sell the remaining assets—primarily defaulted real estate. It took the Resolution Trust Corporation six years to clean up the mess, at a total cost to American taxpayers of $150 billion.

Foreign Relations under Reagan and Bush

The collapse of détente during the Carter administration, after the Soviet invasion of Afghanistan, prompted Reagan's confrontational approach to what he called the "evil empire." Backed by Republican hard-liners and determined to reduce Communist influence in developing nations, Reagan articulated some of the harshest anti-Soviet rhetoric since the 1950s. The collapse of the Soviet Union in 1991 removed that nation as a credible threat, but new post–cold war challenges quickly appeared.

Interventions in Developing Countries

Despite Reagan's rhetoric, not all his international problems involved U.S.-Soviet confrontations. In 1983, after Israel invaded Lebanon, the U.S. Embassy in Beirut was bombed by anti-Israeli Muslim fundamentalists. A second bombing killed 241 marine peacekeepers barracked in the city. Around the world, terrorist assassins struck down Indira Gandhi in India and Anwar al-Sadat in Egypt. But it was the airplane hijackings and numerous terrorist incidents in the Middle East that led Reagan to order air strikes against one highly visible source of terrorism, Muammar al-Qaddafi of Libya.

The administration reserved its most concerted attention for Central America. Halting what was seen as the spread of communism in that region became an obsession. In 1983 Reagan ordered the marines to invade the tiny Caribbean island of Grenada, claiming that its Cuban-supported Communist regime posed a threat to other states in the region. Reagan's top priority, however, was to topple the leftist Sandinista government in Nicaragua (Map 31.1). In 1981 the United States suspended aid to Nicaragua, charging that the Sandinistas were supplying arms to rebels against a repressive but non-Communist right-wing regime in El Salvador. At the same time the CIA began to provide extensive covert support to the Nicaraguan opposition, the Contras, who Reagan called "freedom fighters." Congress, wary of the assumption of unconstitutional powers by the executive branch, responded in 1984 by passing the Boland Amendment, which banned the CIA and other intelligence agencies from providing military support to the Contras—a provision violated in the Iran-Contra affair.

The End of the Cold War

Surprisingly, given Reagan's rhetoric, his second term brought a reduction in tensions with the Soviet Union. In 1985 Reagan met with the new Soviet premier, Mikhail Gorbachev, at the first superpower summit meeting since 1979. Two years later the two leaders agreed to eliminate all intermediate-range missiles based in Europe. During the Bush administration even more dramatic changes abroad brought an end to the cold war. In 1989 the grip of communism on Eastern Europe eroded in a series of mostly nonviolent revolutions that climaxed in the destruction of the Berlin Wall in November. Soon the Soviet Union itself began to succumb to the forces of change.

The background for these dramatic upheavals was established by Soviet president Mikhail Gorbachev. His policies of *glasnost* (openness) and *perestroika* (economic restructuring) after 1985 signaled a willingness to tolerate significant changes in Soviet society.

Alarmed by Gorbachev's shift, on August 19, 1991, Soviet military leaders seized Gorbachev and attempted unsuccessfully to oust him. The failure of the coup broke the Communist Party's dominance over the Soviet Union. In December the Union of Soviet Socialist Republics formally dissolved itself to make way for an eleven-member Commonwealth of Independent States (CIS) (Map 31.2). Gorbachev resigned, and Boris Yeltsin, president of the new state of Russia, the largest and most populous republic, became the preeminent leader in the region.

The unexpected collapse of the Soviet Union and the end of the cold war stunned America and the world. In the absence of bipolar superpower confrontations, future international conflicts would arise from varied regional, religious, and ethnic differences. Suddenly, the United States faced unfamiliar military and diplomatic challenges.

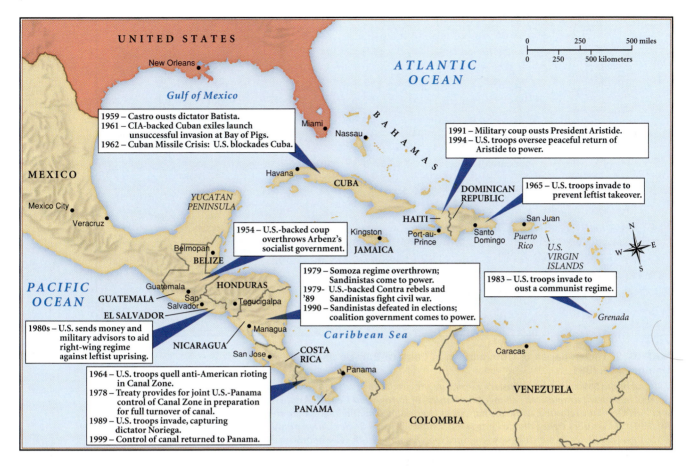

MAP 31.1 U.S. Involvement in Latin America and the Caribbean, 1954–2000

*Ever since the Monroe Doctrine (1823), the United States has claimed a special interest in
Latin America. During the cold war, U.S. foreign policy throughout Latin America
focused on containing instability and the appeal of communism in a region plagued by
poverty and military dictatorships. Providing foreign aid was one approach to addressing
social and economic needs, but, more typically, U.S. policy concentrated on supporting
U.S. business interests. The desire for stability and governments friendly to the United
States also led to repeated military interventions, both overt and covert, throughout the
cold war decades.*

War in the Persian Gulf, 1990–1991

The first challenge had already surfaced in the Middle
East. On August 2, 1990, Iraq, led by Saddam Hussein,
invaded Kuwait, its small but oil-rich neighbor, and
threatened Saudi Arabia, the site of one-fifth of the
world's known oil reserves (see Voices from Abroad,
"Saddam Hussein: Calling for a Holy War against the
United States," p. 915). Concerned about this threat to
Middle East stability as well as to U.S. access to oil, President Bush sponsored a series of resolutions in the
United Nations Security Council condemning Iraq,
calling for its withdrawal, and imposing an embargo and
trade sanctions. When Hussein showed no signs of
yielding, Bush prodded the international organization
to create a legal framework for a military offensive
against the man he called "the butcher of Baghdad." In
November the Security Council voted to use force if Iraq

did not withdraw by January 15. In a close vote of 52 to
48 on January 12, the U.S. Senate authorized military
action. Four days later President Bush announced to the
nation that "the liberation of Kuwait has begun."

The forty-two-day war was a resounding success for
the United Nations' coalition forces, which were predominantly American. Under the leadership of General
Colin Powell, chairman of the Joint Chiefs of Staff, and
the commanding general, H. Norman Schwarzkopf,
Operation Desert Storm opened with a month of air
strikes to crush communications, destroy armaments,
and pummel Iraqi ground troops. A land offensive
followed. Within days, thousands of Iraqi troops had
fled or surrendered, and the fighting quickly ended,
although Hussein remained in power (Map 31.3).

Operation Desert Storm's success and the few U.S.
casualties (145 Americans were killed in action) produced
a euphoric reaction at home. For many the American

MAP 31.2 The Collapse of Communism in Eastern Europe and the Soviet Union, 1989–1991

The end of the Soviet empire in Eastern Europe and the collapse of communism in the Soviet Union itself dramatically changed the borders of Europe and Central Asia. West and East Germany reunited, while the nations of Czechoslovakia and Yugoslavia, created by the 1919 Versailles treaty, divided into smaller states. The old Soviet Union produced fifteen new countries, of which eleven remained loosely bound in the Commonwealth of Independent States (CIS).

Women at War

Women played key and visible roles in the Persian Gulf War, comprising approximately 10 percent of the American troops. Increasing numbers of women are choosing military careers, despite widespread reports of sexual harassment and other forms of discrimination. Luc Delahaye / SIPA Press.

victory over a vastly inferior fighting force seemed to banish the ghost of Vietnam. "By God, we've kicked the Vietnam syndrome once and for all," Bush gloated. The president's approval rating shot up precipitously but declined almost as quickly when a new recession showed that the easy victory had masked the country's serious economic problems.

Uncertain Times: Economic and Social Trends, 1980–2000

Opinion polls taken in the early 1990s showed that Americans were deeply concerned about the future. They worried about crime in the streets, increases in poverty and homelessness, the decline of the inner cities, illegal immigration, the environment, the failure of public schools, the unresolved abortion issue, and AIDS. But above all they worried about their own economic security—whether they would be able to keep their jobs in an era of global competition. By the end of the decade, a vastly improved economic picture would lessen—but not erase—Americans' concerns for the future.

Saddam Hussein

Calling for a Holy War against the United States

After Iraq invaded Kuwait in August 1990, President Saddam Hussein of Iraq justified the action in the language of jihad, *the Muslim holy war. Coming from a secular ruler committed to the suppression of religion in public life, Hussein's call for a holy war against the United States suggested the ways in which Islamic fundamentalism had become part of the larger political discourse of the Arab world, particularly in political relations with Western nations.*

This great crisis started on the 2nd of August, between the faithful rulers and presidents of these nations—the unjust rulers who have abused everything that is noble and holy until they are now standing in a position which enables the devil to manipulate them. This is the great crisis of this age in this great part of the world where the material side of life has surpassed the spiritual one and the moral one. . . . This is the war of right against wrong and is a crisis between Allah's teachings and the devil.

Allah the Almighty has made his choice—the choice for the fighters and the strugglers who are in favor of principles, God has chosen the arena for this crisis to be the Arab World, and has put the Arabs in a progressive position in which the Iraqis are among the foremost. And to confirm once more the meaning that God taught us ever since the first light of faith and belief, which is that the arena of the Arab world is the arena of the first belief and Arabs have always been an example and a model for belief and faith in God Almighty and are the ones who are worthy of true happiness.

It is now your turn, Arabs, to save all humanity and not just save yourselves, and to show the principles and meanings of the message of Islam, of which you are all believers and of which you are all leaders.

It is now your turn to save humanity from the unjust powers who are corrupt and exploit us and are so proud of their positions, and these are led by the United States of America. . . .

For, as we know out of a story from the Holy Koran, the rulers, the corrupt rulers, have always been ousted by their people for it is a right on all of us to carry out the holy jihad, the holy war of Islam, to liberate the holy shrines of Islam. While the ruler of Saudi Arabia called himself the custodian of the two holy shrines, while in fact he is an agent, for he has given away his land to the foreigners.

We call upon all Arabs, each according to his potentials and capabilities within the teachings of Allah and according to the Muslim holy war of jihad, to fight this U.S. presence of nonbelievers and to fight the stance taken by the Arab agents who have followed these foreigners. And we hail the people of Saudi Arabia who are being fooled by their rulers, as well as the people of dear Egypt, as well as all the people of the Arab nations who are not of the same position as their leaders, and they believe in their pride and their sovereignty over their land. We call on them to revolt against their traitors, their rulers, and to fight foreign presence in the holy lands. And we support them, and more important, that God is with them.

Source: New York Times, September 6, 1990, A19.

The Economy

Between 1980 and 2000, the nation's economic mood swung from despairing to optimistic. At the beginning of this two-decade period, Americans struggled with such problems as growing trade deficits, declining productivity, and a widening gap between rich and poor. By 2000, productivity had improved, the federal deficit had disappeared, and the stock market boomed. Despite Americans' optimism, however, many observers warned of danger signs that threatened to reverse the country's future economic outlook.

Economic Pressures. In the 1980s and early 1990s, Americans viewed with alarm the economic success of Germany and Japan, the growing U.S. trade deficit, and the infusion of foreign workers and investment money into the United States. While other nations improved their competitive edge, Americans grappled with a worrisome decline in productivity. In contrast to the period of 1945 to 1973, when productivity had grown 2.8 percent annually, in the next quarter century that figure had dropped to less than 1 percent annually.

As productivity declined, economic inequality increased: the rich got richer, the poor got poorer, and

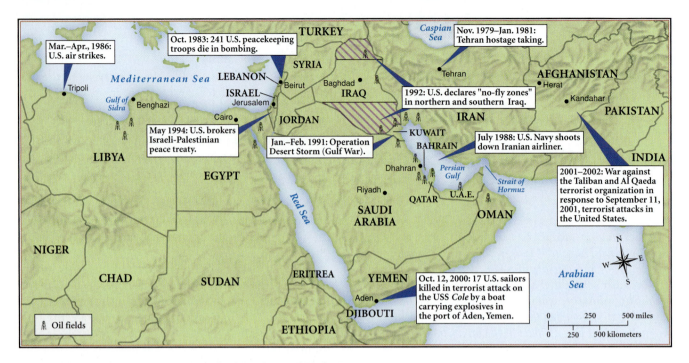

MAP 31.3 U.S. Involvement in the Middle East, 1980–2002
The United States has long played an active role in the Middle East, pursuing the twin goals of protecting Israel's security and ensuring a reliable supply of low-cost oil from the Persian Gulf states. The Middle East has also been the site of terrorist activities targeting U.S. interests, most notably the suicide attack, presumably by Al Qaeda operatives, on the USS Cole *refueling in Yemen. Al Qaeda terrorism against sites in the United States on September 11, 2001, provoked a U.S.-led United Nations attack on Afghanistan that drove the Islamic fundamentalist Taliban government from power.*

the middle class shrank (Figure 31.2). By 1996 the United States was the most economically stratified industrial nation in the world. Statistics from the Congressional Budget Office showed that the richest 1 percent of American families reaped most of the gains of Reaganomics.

Even relatively well-advantaged Americans felt a sense of diminished expectations, in part from changes in the job market. Following an established pattern, the number of minimum-wage service jobs continued to grow, while the number of union-protected manufacturing jobs was shrinking. One-fifth of the labor force in 1994 held only part-time or temporary work. Moreover, in the 1980s and 1990s the downsizing trend, in which companies deliberately shed permanent workers to cut wage costs, spread to middle management. From 1980 to 1995 IBM shrank its mostly white-collar workforce from 400,000 to 220,000. Although most laid-off middle managers eventually found new jobs, many took a large pay cut.

These economic trends put even more pressure on women to seek paid employment. In 1994, 58.8 percent of women were in the labor force, up from 38 percent in 1962, compared with 75.1 percent of men. The stereotypical nuclear family of employed father, homemaker wife, and children characterized less than 15 percent of U.S.

households. Although women continued to make inroads in traditionally male-dominated fields—medicine, law, law enforcement, the military, and skilled trades—one out of five held a clerical or secretarial job, the same proportion as in 1950. Women's pay lagged behind men's; for black and Latino women, the gender gap in pay was especially wide.

At the same time, the labor movement—hurt by downsizing, foreign competition, fear of layoffs, government hostility during the Reagan-Bush years, and its own failure to organize unskilled workers—continued to decline. The number of union members dropped from 20 million in 1978 to 16.2 million in 1998, representing only 13.9 percent of the labor force. Although union membership was more than one-third female and one-fifth black, union leadership remained overwhelmingly white and male.

Economic Turnaround.   The discouraging economic picture began to improve by the mid-1980s. To compete with the economic success of Germany and Japan, American corporations had adopted new technologies, including microelectronics, biotechnology, computers, and robots, and by the late 1990s saw their competi-

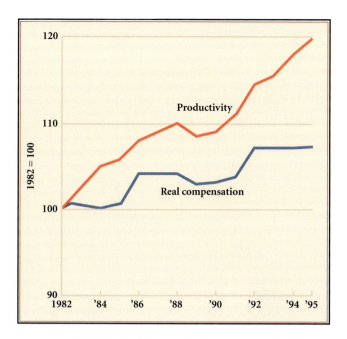

FIGURE 31.2 Productivity and Wages, 1982–1995

Usually as productivity increases, so does labor's share of national income. In the 1990s, however, workers failed to reap the rewards of the increased productivity shown here. Labor's relative loss in real compensation in turn contributed to a rise in corporate profits.

Source: *New York Times,* January 2, 1996, C20. Copyright © 1996 by The New York Times Co. Reprinted by permission.

tiveness return (see New Technology, "The Biotech Revolution," p. 918). Bethlehem Steel, which invested $6 billion to modernize its operations, doubled its productivity between 1989 and 1997. By 1997, U.S. economic growth, measured at 4 percent, was among the healthiest in the world, while one of the country's most serious competitors in the 1980s, Japan, limped along with only a 1.1 percent growth rate.

Working Americans benefited from these developments: new jobs were added to the economy at the rate of 213,000 per month in 1997, and unemployment dropped from 7.5 percent in 1992 to barely over 4 percent in the first half of 2000. A booming stock market, energized by a flow of funds into the high-tech sector and the highly touted emergence of e-commerce (firms doing business over the Internet), seemed to reach new highs daily and fueled the wealth and retirement savings of middle- and upper-income Americans. By 2000, as a result of the economy's strong performance and the spending cuts in the federal budget, the nagging deficit was wiped out: the Congressional Budget Office projected an astonishing surplus of $4.6 trillion in the next ten years.

But there were downsides to the picture as well. Many stock market analysts worried that a steep drop in the stock market might create a recession, although the country weathered a stunning market plunge of 554 points in 1997. Other experts warned that the consumer spending fueling economic growth was tied to growing debts. The median family indebtedness was $33,300 in 1998, up from $23,400 in 1995. An economic downturn could have serious repercussions for overextended families' ability to repay their debts. Moreover, prosperity was not equally distributed. A federal survey released in January 2000 reported that the earnings of the top one-fifth of Americans grew 15 percent in the preceding decade, while the bottom one-fifth grew less than 1 percent. By the end of 2000, the collapse of many e-commerce enterprises and the declining value of many blue-chip technology stocks signaled that the boom was over. In the final quarter of that year, economic growth slowed to 2.2 percent, a pattern that would intensify in 2001.

Popular Culture and Popular Technology

Image was everything in the 1980s and 1990s—or so commentators said, pointing to rock stars Michael Jackson and Madonna and even to President Reagan. One strong influence on popular culture was MTV, a television channel that premiered in 1981 and featured short visual pieces accompanying popular songs. The MTV style—with its creative choreography, flashy colors, and rapid cuts—soon showed up in mainstream media and even political campaigns, which adapted the 30-second sound bites common on television news shows to campaigning purposes. The national newspaper *USA Today*, which debuted in 1982, also adopted the style, featuring eye-catching graphics, color photographs, and short, easy-to-read articles. Soon more staid newspapers followed suit.

At the same time, new technology, especially satellite transmission and live "minicam" broadcasting, reshaped the television industry. Cable and satellite dishes were increasingly available. By the mid-1990s viewers could choose from well over 100 channels, including upstarts such as Ted Turner's Cable News Network (CNN) and the Entertainment Sports Network (ESPN), an all-sports channel. Media, communications, and entertainment were big business, increasingly drawn into global financial networks, markets, and mergers.

Technology also reshaped the home in the late twentieth century. The 1980s saw the introduction of video-cassette recorders (VCRs), compact disc (CD) players, cellular telephones, and inexpensive fax machines. By 1993 more than three-quarters of American households had VCRs. Video was everywhere—stores, airplanes, tennis courts, operating rooms. With the introduction of camcorders, the family photo album could be supplemented by a video of a high school graduation, a marriage, or a birth.

The Biotech Revolution

Was Zachary Taylor poisoned? Did Abraham Lincoln have a rare disease called Marfan's syndrome? Were Tsar Nicholas II and his family executed during the Bolshevik Revolution in 1918? Was the Vietnam serviceman buried in Arlington National Cemetery's Tomb of the Unknowns really Air Force Lieutenant Michael Blassie? Recent advances in DNA testing, part of the dramatic growth in biotechnology in the 1980s and 1990s, mean that these historical questions, plus a host of contemporary ones, can be answered. With promises of breakthroughs in medicine (gene therapy and cancer research), the environment (genetically altered microorganisms for pollution cleanup), and agriculture (genetically engineered foods), biotechnology offers the possibility not just to understand but also to manipulate the processes of life.

The essence of biotechnology is exploiting genes, a process revolutionized by the 1953 discovery of DNA by scientists James Watson and Francis Crick. DNA (deoxyribonucleic acid) is the molecule that carries the genetic blueprint of all living things; genes are DNA chains made up of hundreds or sometimes thousands of simple molecules. Like fingerprints, no two people (other than identical twins) have the same genetic characteristics. Once DNA's structure was understood, it became theoretically possible to isolate the genetic codes that control everything from hair color to height to inherited diseases and certain cancers. But DNA samples were often too meager to work with. Then in the 1980s laboratory advances such as PCR (polymerase chain reaction, polymerase being the enzyme that triggers the replication of DNA) made it possible to take a single fragment of DNA and copy it infinitely. One immediate result of PCR was the introduction of the most sensitive test yet for the AIDS virus.

DNA research in criminal justice cases was one of its earliest applications. From blood, saliva, semen, or hair samples, it became possible to show whether the genetic profile of a suspect matched the DNA information gathered at the crime scene. By 1995 DNA testing had been used in more than twenty-four thousand criminal cases. Some of its most dramatic results proved the innocence of individuals convicted before this technology was available; DNA testing established that their genetic makeup was so markedly different from the surviving evidence that they could not possibly have committed the crimes for which they were imprisoned. Even so, as the 1995 murder trial and acquittal of former football star O. J. Simpson showed, DNA testing remained controversial. Simpson's defense team was able to raise doubts about possible contamination of Simpson's blood samples by faulty laboratory procedures and to counter seemingly overwhelming DNA-based medical evidence that linked bloodstains on Simpson's socks, gloves, and car to the victims.

DNA testing was just one of many promising medical and scientific discoveries to emerge in the 1980s and 1990s. Biotech companies such as Genentech, Amgen, and Biogen pioneered in finding practical—and potentially profitable—applications for the new technology, making biotech companies hot tickets for investors.

But it was the personal computer that revolutionized the home and office. The big breakthrough came in 1977 when the Apple Computer Company offered the Apple II personal computer for $1,195—a price middle-class Americans could afford. When the Apple II became a runaway success, other companies scrambled to get into the market. IBM offered its first personal computer in the summer of 1981. Software companies such as Microsoft, whose founder Bill Gates is now the richest person in America (see American Lives, "Bill Gates: Microsoft's Leader in the Computer Revolution," p. 922) grew rapidly by providing operating systems and other software for the expanding personal-computer market. By 2000, 77 percent of American households had at least one personal computer.

More than any other technological advance, the computer created the modern electronic office. Even the smallest business could afford to keep its records and do all its correspondence, billing, and other business on a single desktop machine. The very concept of the office was changing as a new class of telecommuters worked at home via computer, fax machine, and electronic mail. Today, new technologies utilizing fiberoptics, microwave relays, and satellites can transmit massive quantities of information to and from almost any place on earth, even in outer space.

By 2000, almost 300 million people—approximately 43 percent of them in the United States—used the Internet. At first scientists and other professionals, who communicated with their peers through electronic mail (e-mail), were the primary users of the Internet. But the

Cracking the Genetic Code
A researcher enters DNA sequences into a computer as part of the effort to map the human genome.
© J. Griffin / The Image Works.

Nowhere was the promise of this research more evident than in medical technology, where biotechnology became the driving force in the creation of genetically engineered drugs and vaccines, the identification of specific genes that cause cystic fibrosis and sickle-cell anemia, and the transplantation of either healthy or genetically altered cells to treat cancer. But initial excitement palled as companies found it difficult to translate this new understanding into products that could actually be shown in clinical trials to benefit humans. So volatile has the biotech business been that one analyst called it "free fall" rather than free enterprise—bungee jumping without the bungee.

One of the most ambitious projects undertaken to date is the Human Genome Project, launched in 1988 with the goal of deciphering the entire human genetic code (the entirety of the DNA in an organism is called its genome). In June 2000 scientists on the project announced that they had produced a "Book of Life," a genetic blueprint that would serve a purpose not unlike the periodic table of elements, the basis for twentieth-century research in chemistry. Given that there are approximately three billion nucleic acid–base pairs in a set of human chromosomes, the success of this project was intricately linked to the expanding capacities of modern computers. Biochemistry, medical research, and computer science are increasingly intertwined as earlier technological revolutions spawn new ones.

debut of the World Wide Web in 1991 enhanced the commercial possibilities of the Internet. The Web allowed companies, organizations, political campaigns, and even the White House to create their own "home pages," incorporating both visual and textual information. Businesses and entrepreneurs began to use the Internet to sell their products and services.

The glories of cyberspace are still limited mostly to those who can afford them: in 1997, 65 percent of Americans who used the Internet had incomes of $50,000 or more. But the trend continues to change. In 1998 only 25 percent of all households had access to cyberspace, but by 2000 the figure had grown to 50 percent. Additionally, programs to wire public schools and libraries have significantly increased access to the new technology. In 2000, 63 percent of public classrooms were connected to the Internet.

An Increasingly Pluralistic Society

As technological change reshaped the nation, significant demographic developments emerged as well. Ethnic and racial diversity, always a source of conflict in American culture, became a defining theme of the 1990s. Between 1981 and 1996 almost 13.5 million immigrants entered the country.

Latino and Asian Immigration. The greatest number of newcomers were Latinos. Although Mexico continued to provide the largest group of Spanish-speaking

Honey, Where's the Remote?
How many channels can you watch? How many Web sites can you visit? In the 1990s Americans began to complain of information overload. This image of a person viewing 500 cable TV stations simultaneously was created by photographer Louis Psihoyos for an article on technology that appeared in National Geographic.
© 1995 Louis Psihoyos / Matrix.

immigrants, many also arrived from El Salvador and the Dominican Republic. The Latino population grew at a rate of 18 percent in the 1990s to reach 31 million in 1999, making Latinos the second-largest minority group in the United States after African Americans and the second fastest-growing after Asians. Once concentrated in California, Texas, and New Mexico, Latinos now lived in urban areas throughout the country and made up about 16 percent of the population of Florida and New York (Map 31.4). Their growing numbers have increased their significance as consumers and voters and have led advertisers and politicians alike to vie for their loyalty.

Asia was the other major source of new immigrants. Asian migration, which increased almost 108 percent from 1980 to 1990, consisted mainly of people from China, the Philippines, Vietnam, Laos, Cambodia, Korea, India, and Pakistan. More than 700,000 Indochinese refugees came to escape upheavals in Southeast Asia in the decade following the Vietnam War. The first arrivals, many of them well educated, adapted successfully to their new homeland. Later refugees lacked professional or vocational skills and took low-paying jobs where they could find them.

The Face of Ethnic Pluralism. The new immigrants' impact on the country's social, economic, and cultural landscape has been tremendous. In many places they have

created thriving ethnic communities, such as Koreatown in Los Angeles. In the 1980s tens of thousands of Jews

New Immigrants
In the 1980s many Korean immigrants got their start by opening small grocery stores in urban neighborhoods. Their success sometimes led to conflicts with other racial groups, such as blacks and Hispanics, who were often their customers as well as competitors. Kay Chernush / The Image Bank.

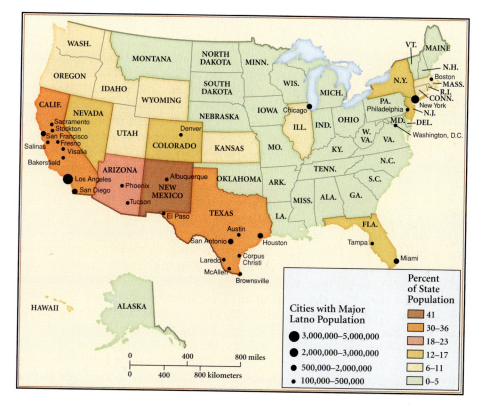

MAP 31.4 Latino Population and Asian Population, 2000

In 2000 Latinos made up over 11 percent of the U.S. population and Asian Americans 4 percent. Demographers predict that Latinos will overtake African Americans as the largest minority group early in the twenty-first century and that by the year 2050 only about half the U.S. population will be composed of non-Latino whites.

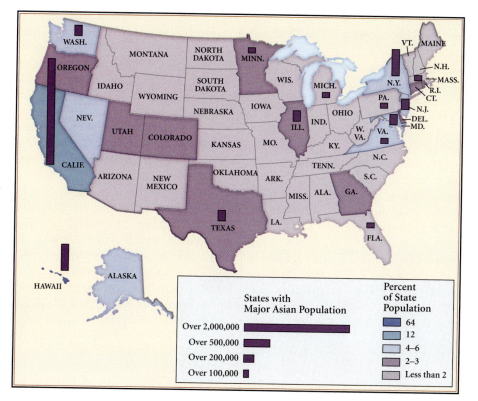

fleeing religious and political persecution in the Soviet Union created Little Odessa in Brooklyn, New York. Ethnic restaurants and shops have sprung up across the country, while some 300 specialized periodicals serve immigrant readers.

The U.S. Census Bureau predicts that in the year 2050, whites will make up 52.7 percent of the American population (down from 75.7 percent in 1990), with Latinos accounting for 21.1 percent, blacks 15 percent, and Asians 10.1 percent. If projected intermarriage is

Bill Gates: Microsoft's Leader in the Computer Revolution

In the eleventh grade Bill Gates told a friend that he would be a millionaire by the time he was thirty. When Gates went to Harvard two years later, he revised his prediction downward to twenty-five. He was being far too modest. At the age of thirty-one, Bill Gates became the youngest self-made billionaire ever. In 1992 *Forbes* magazine named him the richest person in America. What was the source of all this wealth? Microsoft Corporation, whose software runs on nine of every ten personal computers sold in the United States. Microsoft is the most successful start-up company in the history of American business.

This is no Horatio Alger, rags-to-riches story. William Henry Gates III was born into a wealthy Seattle family on October 28, 1955. His father, William Gates Jr., is a successful corporate lawyer and former president of the Washington State Bar Association; his mother, Mary, was a prominent United Way volunteer who also served as a regent of the University of Washington. Gates attended the exclusive Lakeside School, one of the first schools in the country to offer students computer access, thanks to a time-sharing arrangement paid for by the school's mothers' club. The eighth-grader was hooked. Another Lakeside classmate and computer whiz was tenth-grader Paul Allen, who joined Gates in 1972 to found a company called Traf-O-Data, which counted vehicles at busy intersections by using a rudimentary computer device. In 1975 these two former classmates founded Microsoft. Allen was twenty-one; Gates, who would soon drop out of Harvard, was all of nineteen.

Gates looked even younger. When Miriam Lubow became Microsoft's office manager in 1977, she was appalled when some "kid" whipped by her desk into the office of "Mr. Gates" and began playing with the computer terminal. That kid was Bill Gates. In the early days of Microsoft, Gates was too young to rent a car or have a drink with prospective clients on a business trip. His smudged glasses and unkempt hair became trademarks. But looks can be deceiving, as competitors have found out ever since.

In certain ways Gates and Allen were classic hackers—nerdy, mathematically inclined, and fascinated by the possibilities for computation (and mischief) that early computers provided. But most hackers saw computers as a hobby or a game. Back then, the thought of owning a computer seemed as far-fetched as owning a nuclear submarine. But right from the start, Gates and Allen saw commercial possibilities in the new field, long before the personal computer revolution of the 1980s. They anticipated that there would be money to be made writing, and especially marketing, software for the new machines. Microsoft's domination has resulted less from developing innovative products than from anticipating trends in the industry, getting products quickly into the marketplace, and then using its market share to bludgeon the competition. The phenomenal success of products such as MS-DOS and Windows was due as much to Microsoft's relentless marketing barrage as to any inherent technological superiority of its products. One Microsoft veteran described the corporate strategy in this way: "See where everybody's headed then catch up and go past them."

In the early days Microsoft was more like a college dorm than the billion-dollar business it later became. The "Microkids" were barely out of their teens, and some were still in high school. Nobody kept regular hours (in fact, the walls lacked clocks), and they existed on junk food, rock music, and free Coke, a tradition that Microsoft still maintains. A married employee was an oddity, and almost all the programmers were men. Parking slots were unnumbered as a way to reward early arrivals. Gates's competitive and confrontational managerial style set the tone: "That's the stupidest thing I ever heard" was a frequently heard comment.

Gates literally could not sit still, and Seattle-based Microsoft continued to grow at a fantastic rate. Gates had once thought it might employ 20 people; by 1982 Microsoft had 200 employees and sales of $32 million. In 1985, when the company went public, Gates, Allen (who had left the company in 1983 after a bout with Hodgkin's disease), and many Microsoft employees became overnight millionaires. Allen later cashed in some of his stock to buy the Portland Trailblazers. Gates used some of his personal wealth to build a $53 million house on Lake Washington outside Seattle, whose property taxes alone (estimated at $620,000 in 1998) would buy a luxury home in most U.S. cities. The house is a series of interconnected pavilions set deep into a hillside, with its own salmon estuary, a twenty-car subterranean garage, a trampoline room, and video "walls" in every room to

Microsoft Employees, 1978

This group portrait shows eleven of Microsoft's thirteen employees as the company was about to relocate from Albuquerque, New Mexico, to Seattle, Washington. Bill Gates is in the front row, far left; Paul Allen is in the front row, far right. They may look geeky or weird, but they built Microsoft into a multibillion-dollar corporation.

Courtesy, Bob Wallace.

display changing electronic images of art (for which Gates has bought the rights from major museums). "Working for Bill, you design for change," said the architect. That sums up Gates's approach to business as well.

The next step for Gates and Microsoft was onto the information superhighway. Internet commerce was projected to generate $180 billion of business a year by the beginning of the twenty-first century, and Gates wanted Microsoft to be part of that connection. But if Microsoft was able to use its market share to force consumers to use its applications and links to the World Wide Web rather than competitors' browsers, thereby controlling access to the information, entertainment, shopping, real estate, and travel services that the Web provides, its dominance would increase even more. When the Justice Department took Microsoft to court in 1998 for violating antitrust laws, Gates brashly replied that he was simply giving consumers what they wanted. The fact that Attorney General Janet Reno did not even use a personal computer seemed to confirm Microsoft's view that the Department of Justice was out

of touch with the importance of computers to modern life.

Friends note Bill Gates's "extraordinary bandwidth"—that is, the amount of information he can absorb—but it is his insights into business rather than technology that set Gates apart. His entrepreneurial streak would have made Henry Ford or John D. Rockefeller proud. The future, however, comes quickly in the computer field, and Gates keenly worries about being left behind in the next stage of the revolution: "It's a little scary that as computer technology has moved ahead there's never been a leader from one era who was also a leader in the next." He takes this as a warning and a challenge: "I want to defy historical tradition."

"Software is cool," Gates told CNN's Larry King to explain the hoopla surrounding the release of Microsoft's Windows 95. To the computer crowd, cool is the opposite of random, which means out of it, wrong, or inane. No one, especially not his competitors, has ever accused Bill Gates of being random.

factored in (Latinos and Asians marry outside their racial groups much more frequently than blacks), the estimated white "majority" will probably slip to a white "minority." At the close of the twentieth century, already one out of twenty-five married couples were interracial, and at least 3 million children were of mixed-race parentage in the country.

Anti-Immigrant Sentiment. While many Americans celebrated the nation's ethnic pluralism as a source of strength, others viewed the new immigrants as scapegoats for all that was wrong with the United States. Though a 1997 study by the National Academy of Science reported that immigration has benefited the nation, adding some $10 billion a year to the economy, many American-born workers felt threatened by immigrants. The unfounded assumption that immigrants were lured to the United States by generous public services influenced provisions of a 1996 welfare reform act (see p. 930), which severely curtailed legal immigrants' access to welfare benefits, especially food stamps. Also in 1996, Congress enacted legislation that increased the financial requirements for sponsors of new immigrants.

The most dramatic challenges to immigrants have emerged on the state level. In the 1980s California absorbed far more immigrants than any other state: more than a third of its population growth in that decade came from foreign immigration. In 1994 California voters overwhelmingly approved Proposition 187, a ballot initiative provocatively named "Save Our State," which barred undocumented aliens from public schools, non-emergency care at public health clinics, and all other state social services. The initiative also required law enforcement officers, school administrators, and social workers to report suspected illegal immigrants to the Immigration and Naturalization Service. Though opponents challenged the constitutionality of Proposition 187, anti-immigrant feeling soon spread to other parts of the country, becoming a hotly debated issue in the 1996 election.

The Plight of Urban America. Though the National Academy of Sciences report did find that "some black workers have lost their jobs to immigrants," for the most part African Americans were not adversely affected by the new immigration. But in the cities, African Americans and new immigrants were forced by economic necessity and entrenched segregation patterns to fight for space in decaying, crime-ridden ghettos, where unemployment rates sometimes hit 60 percent. Overcrowded and underfunded, inner-city schools had fallen into disrepair and were unable to provide a proper education.

In April 1992 the frustration and anger of impoverished urban Americans erupted in five days of race riots in Los Angeles. The worst civil disorder since the 1960s, the violence took sixty lives and caused $850 million in damage. The riot was set off by the acquittal (on all but one

To Live and Die in L.A.
The images from South-Central Los Angeles in the wake of the 1992 riots looked eerily similar to those from Watts in 1965. The underlying causes of both riots were similar as well—police brutality, racism, and frustration about lack of jobs and opportunity. Sylvie Kreiss / Liaison.

charge) of four white Los Angeles police officers accused of using excessive force in arresting a black motorist, Rodney King. A graphic amateur video showing the policemen kicking, clubbing, and beating King had not swayed the predominantly white jury. Three of the officers were later convicted on federal civil rights charges.

The Los Angeles riot exposed the rifts in urban neighborhoods. Trapped in the nation's inner cities, many blacks resented recent immigrants who were struggling to get ahead and often succeeding. As a result some blacks had targeted Korean-owned stores during the arson and looting. Latinos were also frustrated by high unemployment and crowded housing conditions. According to the Los Angeles Police Department, Latinos accounted for more than half of those arrested and a third of those killed during the rioting. Thus the riots were not simply a case of black rage at white injustice; they contained a strong element of class-based protest against the failure of the American system to address the needs of all poor people.

One of the ways federal and state governments tried to help poor blacks and Latinos was through the establishment of affirmative action programs in government hiring, contracts, and university admissions. In 1995, however, under pressure from the Republican governor, Pete Wilson, the Regents of the University of California voted to scrap the university's twenty-year-old policy of affirmative action, despite protests from the faculty and from university presidents. In the November 1996 elections, the struggle over affirmative action was intensified by California's passage of Proposition 209. It banned all preference based on race or gender in state government hiring and contracting and in public education. As appeals worked their way through the federal courts and black and Latino enrollments declined, the University of California sought new admissions criteria that would circumvent the restrictions imposed by Proposition 209.

One reason affirmative action became a political issue in the 1990s was that many people, including prominent conservatives like George F. Will, William Bennett, and Patrick Buchanan, saw it as a threat to core American values. Lumping affirmative action together with multiculturalism—the attempt to represent the diversity of American society and its peoples—critics feared that all this counting by race, gender, sexual preference, and age would lead to a "balkanization," or fragmentation, of American society. Attempts to revise American history textbooks along multicultural lines aroused much anger, as did efforts by universities such as Stanford to revise college curricula to include the study of non-European cultures. Conservatives also took aim at the antiracist and antisexist regulations and speech codes that had been adopted by many colleges. Arguing for the need to protect First Amendment rights, conservatives derided the attempt to regulate hate speech as "politically correct" (PC).

Backlash against Women's and Gay Rights

Conservative critics also targeted the women's movement. In the widely read *Backlash: The Undeclared War on American Women* (1991), the journalist Susan Faludi described a powerful reaction against the gains American women had won in the 1960s and 1970s. Spearheaded by New Right leaders and aided by the media, conservatives held the women's movement responsible for every ill afflicting modern women, from infertility to rising divorce rates. Yet polls showed strong support for many feminist demands, including equal pay, reproductive rights, and a more equitable distribution of household and child-care responsibilities.

Feminism was also weakened by racial and generational fault lines. Despite the attempts of prominent feminist organizations such as the National Organization for Women (NOW) to focus on racial and ethnic differences among women, African Americans and other women of color often felt themselves to be tokens in a predominantly white movement. Many young women felt that the movement had become too obsessed with women as passive victims (of date rape, discrimination, sexual harassment, the media's beauty myth, and so forth) rather than offering women models of empowerment. Other young women, influenced by women's studies programs and the explosion of feminist scholarship, forged a third wave of feminism in the 1990s (see

American Voices, "Laurie Ouellette: A Third-Wave Feminist," p. 926).

The deep national divide over abortion, one of the main issues associated with feminism, continued to polarize the country. In the 1980s and 1990s, harassment and violence toward those who sought or provided abortions became common. In 1994 two workers were gunned down at Massachusetts abortion clinics, and five people were wounded in the attacks. Although only a fraction of antiabortion activists supported such extreme acts, disruptive confrontational tactics made receiving what was still a woman's legal right more dangerous.

Gay rights was another field of battle. As gays and lesbians gained legal protection against housing and job discrimination across the country, Pat Robertson, North Carolina senator Jesse Helms, and others denounced these civil rights gains as undeserved "special rights." To conservatives, gay rights threatened America's traditional family values. In 1992 Coloradans passed a referendum (overturned by the Supreme Court in 1996) that barred local jurisdictions from passing ordinances protecting gays and lesbians. Across the nation, "gay bashing" and other forms of violence against homosexuals continued.

The AIDS Epidemic

A grim backdrop to gay men's struggle against discrimination was the AIDS epidemic. Acquired immune deficiency syndrome (AIDS) was first recognized by physicians in 1981 in the gay male population and its cause identified as the human immunodeficiency virus (HIV). At first, little government funding was directed toward AIDS research or treatment; critics charged that the lack of attention to the syndrome reflected society's antipathy toward gay men. Only when heterosexuals, such as hemophiliacs who had received the virus through blood transfusions, began to be affected did AIDS gain significant public attention. The death of the film star Rock Hudson from AIDS in 1985 finally broke the barrier of public apathy. Another galvanizing moment came in 1991, when the basketball great Earvin "Magic" Johnson announced that he was HIV-positive.

To date more Americans have died of AIDS than were killed in the Korean and Vietnam wars combined. Between 1995 and 1999, however, deaths from AIDS in the United States dropped 30 percent. This decline—in part the result of new treatment strategies using a combination of drugs, or a "cocktail"—has led to cautious optimism about controlling the disease. Yet the drugs' high costs limit their availability and make distribution particularly limited in poor nations. As AIDS deaths decline in developed countries like the United States, the epidemic has reached crisis proportions in sub-Saharan Africa, which accounts for 30 million of the 40 million infections worldwide. Approximately 95 percent of people infected with HIV live in the developing world.

Mandela, who had spent twenty-seven years in prison for challenging apartheid, as the country's first black president. And in a move that was seen as the symbolic end to the American experience in Vietnam, the United States established diplomatic relations with Hanoi in July 1995, two decades after the fall of Saigon.

"The Era of Big Government Is Over"

In the 1994 midterm elections, Republicans gained fifty-two seats in the House of Representatives, which gave them a majority in the House as well as the Senate. In the House the centerpiece of the new Republican majority was the "Contract with America," a list of proposals that Newt Gingrich of Georgia, the new Speaker of the House, vowed would be voted on in the first 100 days of the new session. The contract included constitutional amendments to balance the budget and set term limits for congressional office, significant tax cuts, reductions in welfare and other entitlement programs, anticrime initiatives, and cutbacks in federal regulations. President Clinton, bowing to political reality, acknowledged in his State of the Union message in January 1996 that "the era of big government is over."

Balancing the Budget. But the Republicans were frustrated in their commitment to cut taxes and balance the budget by the year 2002 because both practical and political considerations made many items in the budget immune to serious reductions. Interest on the national debt had to be paid. Defense spending had declined only slightly in the post–cold war world. Since Social Security was considered as being untouchable, Congress looked to health care and discretionary spending as places to save.

In the fall of 1995, Congress passed a budget that cut $270 billion from projected spending on Medicare and $170 billion from spending on Medicaid over the next seven years. Other savings came from cuts in discretionary programs, including education and the environment. Clinton accepted Congress's resolve to balance the budget in seven years but, vowing to protect the nation from an "extremist" Congress, vetoed the budget itself. In the standoff that followed, nonessential departments of the government were forced to shut down twice for lack of funding, but polls showed that a majority of Americans held Congress, not the president, responsible. The budget that Clinton finally signed in April 1996 left Medicare and Social Security intact, though it did meet the Republicans' goal of cutting $23 billion from discretionary spending.

As part of the Contract with America, House Republicans were especially determined to cut welfare, a joint federal-state program that represented a fairly small part of the budget. The benefits of the main welfare program, Aid for Dependent Children (AFDC), were far from generous: the average annual welfare payment to families (including food stamps) was $7,740, well below the established poverty line. Still, in the 1990s both Democratic and Republican statehouses sought ways to change the behavior of welfare recipients by imposing work requirements or denying benefits for additional children born to women on AFDC. In August 1996, after vetoing two Republican-authored bills, President Clinton signed into law the Personal Responsibility and Work Opportunity Act, a historic overhaul of federal entitlements. The 1996 law ended the federal guarantee of cash assistance to poor children by abolishing AFDC, required most adult recipients to find work within two years, set a five-year limit on payments to any one family, and gave states wide discretion in running their welfare programs.

The 1996 Election. The Republican takeover of Congress had one unintended consequence: it united the usually fractious Democrats behind the president. Unopposed in the 1996 primaries, Clinton was able to burnish his image as a moderate "New Democrat." His political fortunes were aided by the unpopularity of the Republican Congress following the government shutdowns. He also benefited from the continuing strength of the economy. Economic indicators released shortly before election day showed that the "misery index"—a combination of the unemployment rate and inflation—was the lowest it had been in twenty-seven years.

The Republicans settled on Senate Majority Leader Bob Dole of Kansas as their presidential candidate. Acceptable to both the conservative and the moderate wings of the party, Dole selected former representative Jack Kemp, a leading proponent of supply-side economics, as his running mate. Dole made a 15 percent across-the-board tax cut the centerpiece of his campaign, while Clinton emphasized an improved economy. Americans seemed to have made up their minds early about the candidates. With the lowest voter turnout since Calvin Coolidge won the presidency in 1924, Clinton became the first Democratic president since Franklin Roosevelt to win reelection. Republicans retained control of a majority of the nation's statehouses and the House of Representatives and increased their majority in the Senate. Thus a key factor in Bill Clinton's second term was the necessity, as a Democratic president working with a Republican-dominated Congress, of pursuing bipartisan policies or facing stalemate.

Second-Term Stalemates

In his 1998 State of the Union address, Bill Clinton outlined an impressive program of federal spending for schools, tax credits for child care, a hike in the minimum wage, and protection for the beleaguered Social Security system. His ability to pursue this domestic agenda was seriously compromised, however, by a scandal

A Bipartisan Balanced Budget
On August 5, 1997, a smiling President Clinton signed the balanced budget bill,
surrounded by congressional leaders including House Speaker Newt Gingrich of Georgia
(second from right) and House Budget Committee Chairman John Kasich of Ohio (far
right). Also looking on with satisfaction was Vice President Al Gore, who already had
hopes for the presidency in 2000. Ron Edmonds / Wide World Photos, Inc.

that eventually led to his impeachment and by international crises.

Crises Abroad. The first of these foreign crises emerged in Iraq, where Saddam Hussein was still in power despite his 1991 defeat in Operation Desert Storm and the United Nations' imposition of economic sanctions. In late 1997 Hussein ejected American members of a UN inspection team that was searching Iraqi sites for hidden "weapons of mass destruction," which included nuclear, biological, and chemical warfare materials. In response, the United States, with limited international support, began a military buildup in the Gulf. The threatened air strike against Iraq was averted when United Nations Secretary-General Kofi Annan brokered an agreement that temporarily put an end to the crisis. But in December 1998 the same issues led to an intense four-day joint U.S.-British bombing campaign, "Desert Fox." Neither that effort, periodic missile strikes against Iraq, nor economic sanctions seem to have compromised the Iraqis' ability to build "weapons of mass destruction" or to have undercut Hussein's regime.

The second major international crisis began in March 1999 in Kosovo, a province of the Serbian-dominated Federal Republic of Yugoslavia (FRY). There, NATO, strongly influenced by the United States, intervened to protect ethnic Albanians from the Serbians who were determined to drive them out of the region. Three months of bombing eventually forced the Serbians to agree to remove their troops from Kosovo and to agree to a multinational peacekeeping force. Yet, as in the Middle East, no long-term solutions were found to the problems generated by ethnic conflict. The region was devastated and its people impoverished, and a year later most observers considered the war a "hollow triumph" for NATO and the United States. Only in 2000 was the brutal Serbian president Slobodan Milosevic pushed from office (Map 31.6).

In the post–cold war era, terrorism constituted yet another challenge to world peace. In October 2000 a suicide attack on the USS *Cole*, a navy guided-missile destroyer that was refueling in the Yemeni port of Aden, blew a huge hole in the ship's hull, killing seventeen sailors. The United States immediately lay the blame on Saudi exile and Muslim extremist Osama bin Laden. In Yemen six suspects were arrested on suspicion of complicity in the attack, but bin Laden remained at large. The Iraqi and Kosovo crises and the *Cole* incident served as potent reminders that despite its position as the most powerful nation in the world, the United States was limited in its ability to achieve its foreign-policy aims.

Clinton's Impeachment. Although international events deflected President Clinton from his domestic agenda, far more damaging was the crisis that stemmed from a problem that had plagued him since 1992: allegations of sexual misconduct. In January 1998 attorneys representing Paula Jones, who claimed that the then-governor Clinton had propositioned her when she was an Arkansas state employee, revealed that they planned to depose a former White House intern, Monica Lewinsky, about an alleged affair with President Clinton. Kenneth Starr, the independent counsel initially charged with investigating the Whitewater scandal, widened his investigation to explore whether Clinton or his aides had encouraged Lewinsky to lie in her statement. Clinton consistently denied having a sexual relationship with Lewinsky—both on national television and in deposition before a federal grand jury.

In September 1998, after Starr issued a report that concluded that the president had committed impeachable offenses, the House of Representatives began its inquiry. On December 20 the House narrowly approved two articles of impeachment against Clinton, one for perjury before a grand jury concerning his liaison with Lewinsky and a second for obstruction of justice, in which he was accused of encouraging others to lie on his behalf. Yet on the evening of the House vote, a CBS news poll reported that 58 percent of its respondents opposed impeachment, while only 38 percent supported it.

Throughout the ensuing trial conducted by the Senate, Clinton's approval rating remained exceptionally high, perhaps because most Americans doubted the political motives of his attackers and almost certainly because a strong economy kept most citizens content with the

MAP 31.6 Ethnic Conflict in the Balkans: The Breakup of Yugoslavia, 1991–1992

The collapse of the Soviet Union and the end of the cold war released a wave of ethnic conflicts in the Balkans among rival groups forced to live together under Communist rule. Fanned by ethnic hatreds, in the early 1990s Yugoslavia splintered into warring states, with Serbs, Croats, and Muslims fighting for control of their own territories. Serbian president Slobodan Milosevic's brutal aggression against Muslims in Bosnia and later in Kosovo, a province of Serbia, prompted NATO to launch its first offensive war to end the conflict.

For more help analyzing this map, see the ONLINE STUDY GUIDE at bedfordstmartins.com/henretta.

president's performance, even if they disapproved of his personal morality. Finally, after a five-week trial and hours of televised debate, with Democrats voting solidly against impeachment and enough Republicans breaking with their party, the Senate acquitted Clinton on both charges. Like Andrew Johnson, the only other president to be impeached (see Chapter 15), Bill Clinton survived the process, but the scandal, the trial, and the profoundly partisan sentiments that surrounded it limited his ability to be an effective president and deepened public cynicism about politics and its practitioners.

For if Clinton had been hampered by the controversy, so too had Republicans. The November 1998 elections took place while the House was considering impeachment. Despite polls that indicated that Americans did not place much emphasis on the Lewinsky scandal, in many localities and on the national level Republican leaders made Clinton's moral character the focus of the campaign. The Democrats, in contrast, focused on issues like Social Security and education. They also employed vigorous get-out-the-vote drives, particularly among traditional Democratic constituencies—labor unions and African Americans. When the ballots were counted, for the first time since 1934 the party of the incumbent president gained seats—five—in a midterm election, shrinking the Republican majority in Congress to twelve. Although a variety of factors influenced voting patterns, including the improving economy, many observers pointed to a backlash against the drive for impeachment.

Because of the controversies surrounding Clinton and the weakened state of the Republicans, neither party was able to secure significant legislation. For the rest of Clinton's term, shoring up Social Security, addressing the high cost of medical care, and passing an effective gun-control law eluded the president and his supporters, while Republicans were stymied in their efforts to cut taxes and further roll back the federal government. The stalemate was exacerbated by politicians' focus on positioning themselves for the election of 2000. As Senator Joseph I. Lieberman, a Democrat from Connecticut, described the 106th Congress in November 1999, "This was not a session of great initiatives. . . . This was a session that was post-impeachment and preelection."

An Unprecedented Election

Lieberman was to become much better known when the Democratic Party nominated him as Vice President Al Gore's running mate for the 2000 presidential election. The Republicans chose Governor George W. Bush of Texas to head their ticket and Richard Cheney for their vice presidential nominee. Although both Bush and Gore were considered moderate centrists, they had ideological differences over the role of the federal government and how best to use the large projected budget surpluses. Bush proposed a major tax cut that critics claimed would benefit primarily the wealthiest 10 percent of Americans, a partial privatization of Social Security, and the use of government-issued vouchers to pay for private education. Gore argued for using the surplus to shore up the Social Security funds, for a tax-break incentive for college tuition, and for expansion of Medicare. The two candidates disagreed on the abortion issue, with Bush opposing abortion and Gore supporting a woman's right to choose. While Pat Buchanan of the Reform Party fared poorly and was not able to make significant inroads among conservative Republicans, Ralph Nader, the Green Party representative, did appeal to many in the left wing of the Democratic Party who were disenchanted with Gore's centrist position. Nader received over two and a half million votes and detracted enough ballots from Gore in New Hampshire, New Mexico, and Florida to give those states to Bush. Nader's 97,419 votes in Florida (2 percent) contributed to making that state's presidential election a virtual tie between Bush and Gore.

As Florida hung in the balance, returns from the rest of the country showed that Gore had a lead of 337,000 in the popular vote and had won the District of Columbia and twenty states, mostly in the Northeast and Far West, with 267 electoral votes, while Bush had triumphed in twenty-nine states, mostly in the South and Midwest, with 246 electoral votes. In four states, however, fewer than 7,500 votes separated the two major candidates. In such a tight election, the results in Florida became crucial because the electoral college victory would come down to which candidate could claim that state's twenty-five electoral votes (Map 31.7).

At stake were protested "butterfly ballots," which had apparently misled some Gore voters into voting for Buchanan, and "under votes," (ballots not clearly marked)

Recount Nightmare

In the aftermath of the 2000 presidential election, the eyes of the nation, and indeed the world, were riveted on Florida's challenged election result. When the Democrats demanded a hand recount, a crucial issue became how to evaluate dimpled, pregnant, and hanging "chads"— the tiny cardboard pieces punched from the ballot. Here, Judge Robert Rosenberg of the electoral canvassing board of Broward County scrutinizes a Fort Lauderdale ballot. When the Supreme Court put an end to the hand-count process, Vice President Gore conceded the election and George W. Bush announced his victory— 37 days after the election.

AFP Photo / Pool / Allen Eyestone / Corbis.

which resulted from antiquated voting machines and inattentive voters (see American Voices, "John Lewis: We Marched to Be Counted," p. 935). To make certain all votes were tabulated, Gore forces demanded hand recounts in several counties. How to evaluate dimpled, pregnant, and hanging "chads"—the tiny cardboard pieces punched from the ballot—became a hotly contested issue. On November 27, Florida's Secretary of State Katherine Harris halted the recount process and declared Governor Bush the winner by a mere 537 votes. The struggle, however, continued. Gore appealed twice to the Florida Supreme Court in an attempt to get a hand recount. When that court ordered the hand count to continue, Bush went to the United States Supreme Court, which then ordered it stopped.

Finally, on December 12, a deeply divided Supreme Court, in a 5-to-4 decision marked by acrimonious dissenting opinions, declared that the equal protection clause of the Fourteenth Amendment required that all ballots had to be counted in the same way and that time did not permit a statewide hand count. Justice Stephen G. Breyer in dissent angrily pointed out that the majority's opinion was clearly a political one that "runs the risk of undermining the public's confidence in the Court itself." On the following day Vice President Gore gave his concession speech, and George W. Bush announced his victory to become the forty-third president. It took thirty-seven dramatic days and the intervention of the Supreme Court to resolve the controversies surrounding the Florida vote and determine the new president, making the election one of the most remarkable in American history.

George W. Bush's Early Presidency

As President Bush took office, the nation witnessed one more Clinton scandal. In the last hours of his administration, Clinton granted a series of dubious pardons, including most notoriously one for fugitive financier Mark Rich, the ex-husband of Denise Rich, who had contributed heavily to Clinton's political campaign. The incident not only further tarnished Clinton's reputation but also deepened Americans' cynicism about politicians that had been fueled by the 2000 election.

In his first seven months in office, Bush compiled a mixed record of success. He pleased the right wing of his party on his first day in office when he banned the use of foreign-aid funds for family-planning programs abroad that included abortion counseling among their services. Then, despite vigorous opposition, he secured Senate approval for his appointment of John Ashcroft, noted for his conservative social values concerning homosexuality, abortion, and religion, as Attorney General. Other major Bush appointees were Donald Rumsfeld as Secretary of Defense, a position he had also filled under President Gerald Ford, and the widely regarded Gulf War hero Colin Powell as the first black Secretary of State.

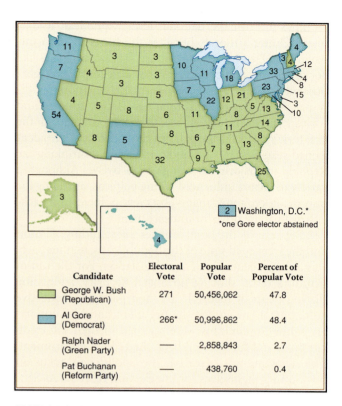

Candidate	Electoral Vote	Popular Vote	Percent of Popular Vote
George W. Bush (Republican)	271	50,456,062	47.8
Al Gore (Democrat)	266*	50,996,862	48.4
Ralph Nader (Green Party)	—	2,858,843	2.7
Pat Buchanan (Reform Party)	—	438,760	0.4

2 Washington, D.C.*
*one Gore elector abstained

MAP 31.7 Presidential Election of 2000

This map illustrates clearly the closeness of the 2000 presidential contest. Democrat Al Gore tallied 337,576 more popular votes than his opponent, Republican George W. Bush, but lost the election. Bush, drawing upon solid support in the South and Midwest, and assisted by Green Party candidate Ralph Nader's drawing votes away from the Democrats, won in the electoral college by only four votes, thus securing the presidency. What the map does not reveal is the extraordinary controversy over Florida's 25 electoral votes that eventually was resolved—37 days after the election—by the United States Supreme Court.

Bush also made good on his campaign pledge to cut taxes, which he claimed would stimulate the slowing economy. The tax act refunded money retroactively to taxpayers ($300–$600 per person). However, it not only failed to stimulate the economy but contributed to the rapid decline of the federal budget surplus, which opened Bush to significant criticism. His economic headaches intensified in March, when the stock market took a dive, marking the greatest loss in eleven years. In September another market dive—the Dow Jones Industrial Average dropped 234 points—coupled with a jump in unemployment figures and slowing economic growth (0.7 percent in the third quarter) led to serious fears that a recession lurked just around the corner.

Other economic woes emerged in the summer, when sharply escalating gasoline prices alarmed consumers, and severe power shortages on the West Coast led to rolling blackouts and increased energy costs there. President Bush resisted calls for federal price controls and emphasized instead the need for the creation of more

John Lewis

We Marched to Be Counted

Emerging from the furor over apparent voting irregularities in Florida in the 2000 presidential election is a concern that uncounted and disqualified voters were more likely to be poor people, especially African Americans. John Lewis, a civil rights activist who had marched from Selma to Montgomery in 1965 to demonstrate for African American voting rights in Alabama, reflects on the relationship between the 1960s civil rights movement and the Florida voting controversy. Lewis is now a congressman from Atlanta.

What's happening in Florida and in Washington is more than a game for pundits. The whole mess reminds African Americans of an era when we had to pass literacy tests, pay poll taxes, and cross every *t* and dot every *i* to get to be able to vote. . . . For all the political maneuvering and legal wrangling, many people have missed an important point: the story of the 2000 election is about more than George W. Bush and Al Gore. It's about the right to vote. And you cannot understand the true implications of this campaign and the subsequent litigation without grasping how deeply many minorities feel about the seemingly simple matter of the sanctity of the ballot box.

There is a lot of troubling new talk of "political profiling"—allegations that officials tried to suppress the black vote on Election Day and may be maneuvering now to make sure it isn't counted. There are reports that officials put new voting machines in white areas but not black ones and that African Americans were asked to present two, not just one, forms of identification to be allowed to vote. These charges should be looked into. But I like to believe that no one met in some smoke-filled room and said, "We're going to keep black voters out, we're going to keep Jewish voters out." . . .

My greatest fear today is that the perception our votes were not counted may usher in a period of great cynicism. On the other hand—and I bet this is more likely—it may give people a greater sense of the importance of voting and of vigilance. The vote, after all, is the real heart of the movement. Younger people shouldn't think civil rights was just about water fountains or stirring speeches on TV. Late in the summer of 1961, after the Freedom Rides, we realized it was not enough to integrate lunch counters and buses. We had to get the vote.

Source: John Lewis, "We Marched to Be Counted," *Newsweek* (December 11, 2000), 38.

power plants and for oil drilling in Alaska and the Arctic, a move that infuriated environmentalists. The political falling-out was compounded by complaints that President Bush's and Vice President Cheney's close personal ties to the energy industry were guiding administration policies. Many observers claimed that energy companies were manipulating the market, pointing for example to Enron Corporation, a Houston-based firm that had been a major contributor to Bush's campaign.

A major political challenge to the administration erupted in late May when Vermont Republican senator Jim Jeffords announced that he was leaving the party to become an independent. The moderate Jeffords had grown disenchanted with the rising influence of the right wing in his party and announced he feared that in the future "I can see more and more instances where I'll disagree with the president on very fundamental issues—the issues of choice, the direction of the judiciary, tax and spending decisions, missile defense, energy and the environment, and a host of other issues, large and small." Jeffords's decision was not only an embarrassment to the president but also had dramatic consequences, as it meant that the Republicans lost their majority status in the Senate. Democrat Tom Daschle then stepped into the position of Senate majority leader, ensuring that Bush's ability to implement his policies would be severely hampered.

Abroad, Bush took steps to heighten his credibility as a world leader, a task made difficult both by the controversial nature of his election and his total inexperience in foreign affairs. Indeed, before he took office, he had barely been outside the United States. His major initiatives were to call for maintaining UN sanctions against Iraq and for increased efforts to destabilize Saddam Hussein's regime. In contrast to his predecessor, Bush decided that the United States would withdraw from active

"We Are under Attack"

On September 11, 2001, President Bush learned that a plane had crashed into one of New York's World Trade Center towers shortly before he entered Emma T. Booker Elementary School in Sarasota, Florida, where he listened to second graders read from the story "Pet Goat." As he listened an aide informed him of a second plane's crash into the other tower and that "America was under attack." Bush waited until the lesson was finished before complimenting the students on their reading and leaving the room. He later recounted his thoughts at this dramatic moment: "I'm being briefed about a reading program that works and I was looking at these little children and, all of the sudden, we were at war. So, I had to maintain my composure. I can remember noticing the press pool and the press corps beginning to get the calls and seeing the look on their face, and it became evident that we were, you know, that the world had changed." Doug Mills.

participation in negotiations in the Palestinian-Israeli conflict. He also announced that the United States would return to creating a missile defense shield, an updated version of Ronald Reagan's discredited "Star Wars." Implementing the plan would violate the 1972 Antiballistic Missile Treaty signed between the United States and Russia, a move that disturbed many U.S. allies.

The domestic and foreign issues that shaped the Bush administration in its first days would soon take a backseat to a sobering challenge when terrorists, later identified as members of Osama bin Laden's Al Qaeda, hijacked four commercial airliners on September 11, 2001. Two plowed into New York's World Trade Center, destroying its twin towers and killing over 2,700 persons. A third plane seriously damaged the Pentagon, but the fourth, headed for the White House, crashed in Pennsylvania when passengers thwarted the hijackers' efforts. As discussed in the Epilogue, the events of September 11 not only

profoundly altered the problems the nation and the world faced in maintaining a stable world order but also affected the domestic economic, political, and social landscape.

FOR FURTHER EXPLORATION

▶ For definitions of key terms boldfaced in this chapter, see the glossary at the end of the book.

▶ To assess your mastery of the material covered in this chapter, see the Online Study Guide at **bedfordstmartins.com/henretta**.

▶ For suggested references, including Web sites, see page SR-35 at the end of the book.

▶ For map resources and primary documents, see **bedfordstmartins.com/henretta**.

The last two decades of the twentieth century brought enormous changes. In the international arena, the collapse of the Soviet Union and the end of the cold war produced repercussions that are still evolving. The United States became the world's only superpower, but as the conflict in Iraq suggested, the nation's dominance in the new world order was limited, and the problem of global terrorism loomed menacingly, its implications not yet fully understood.

In politics, Republican Presidents Ronald Reagan and George Bush advocated a smaller role for the federal government in domestic programs. Though the Democrats regained the White House with the election of Bill Clinton in 1992, the Republican congressional landslide of 1994 helped continue the drive toward a balanced budget, tax cuts, deregulation, and federal government retrenchment. In other political developments, low voter turnout, the popularity of third-party candidates like Ralph Nader, and the controversies surrounding the impeachment of Bill Clinton and the 2000 election of George W. Bush pointed to widespread cynicism about politics.

In social and economic developments, increased immigration, notably from Latin America and Asia, changed the demographic balance of many areas, especially the cities, and the strains of an increasingly diverse society were reflected in debates over affirmative action and multiculturalism. Slow productivity growth, wage stagnation, and growing income inequality were the major domestic economic trends in the 1980s and early 1990s. By the late 1990s the United States had dramatically improved its position in the world economy, but decisions made beyond its borders continued to affect the daily lives of American workers, managers, and consumers.

Despite the problems the nation faced, Americans were relatively confident as the twentieth century ended. Economic prosperity deflected serious discontent. Following the September 11, 2001, terrorist attacks, fears about terrorism and concern about instability around the globe have made Americans and the rest of the world worried and uncertain. Moreover, economic problems—the slowing of the economy and the repercussions from immense corporate scandals—have undercut the confidence the nation felt at the end of the 1990s. How Americans come to interpret the last two decades of the twentieth century in the future will certainly be shaped by their experiences in the twenty-first century.

1981	Sandra Day O'Connor nominated to Supreme Court
	MTV premieres
	Beginning of AIDS epidemic
	IBM markets its first personal computer
1981–1983	Recession
1981–1989	National debt triples
1983	Star Wars proposed
1985	Gramm-Rudman Balanced Budget Act
	United States becomes a debtor nation
	Mikhail Gorbachev takes power in Soviet Union
1986	Iran-Contra affair
	Simpson-Mazzoli Immigration Act
1987	Montreal environmental protocol
	Stock market collapse
1988	George Bush elected president
1989	Savings and loan crisis
	Webster v. Reproductive Health Services
1990–1991	Persian Gulf War
1990–1992	Recession
1991	Dissolution of Soviet Union ends cold war
	Clarence Thomas–Anita Hill hearings
	Susan Faludi, *Backlash: The Undeclared War on American Women*
1992	Los Angeles riots
	Earth Summit in Rio de Janeiro
	Bill Clinton elected president
1993	Family and Medical Leave Act
	North American Free Trade Agreement (NAFTA)
1994	Health-care reform fails
	Republicans gain control of Congress
1995	U.S. troops enforce peace in Bosnia
1996	Personal Responsibility and Work Opportunity Act
	Clinton reelected
1998–1999	Bill Clinton impeached and acquitted
2000	Terrorists attack USS *Cole* in Yemen
	George W. Bush elected president in contested election
2001	Tax-cut refunds $300–$600 to taxpayers
	Worst stock market loss in eleven years
	Terrorists destroy New York's World Trade Center and attack Pentagon

Thinking about Contemporary History

WHEN YOU GO TO SEE A MOVIE AND THE FILM ENDS, the credits roll, the lights come on, and you go home. The movie is over. But for the writers of a history textbook, there is no "end" because history does not stop. The process of creating the next edition is already under way when the last sentence is written and the product of their work is sent to the printer. But which events should be included in the next edition? Just as a movie editor has to determine which sequences to follow and which scenes to cut or include, the authors of the next edition of *America's History* must determine which events will be thought important enough to warrant inclusion in a broad synthesis of American history and culture and which events will be judged as merely interesting occurrences of passing significance. Today's headlines do not always become tomorrow's history.

◄ **A Poignant Symbol**

This striking photograph captures one of the nation's most revered symbols, the Statue of Liberty, against a backdrop of smoke from the collapse of New York's World Trade Center following the terrorist attacks of September 11, 2001.
Daniel Hulshizer / AP / Wide World.

In a 1992 interview, former president Richard M. Nixon stated bluntly, "In my view, history is never worth reading until it's fifty years old. It takes fifty years before you're able to come back and evaluate a man or a period of time." Yet if textbook writers took Nixon's advice literally, they would end their books just after World War II and the onset of the cold war. Of course, this isn't desirable, and the enormous outpouring of

September 11, 2001

Photographers capturing the aftermath of a plane crash into the north tower of New York's World Trade Center found themselves recording an extraordinary moment in the nation's history. When a second plane approached and then slammed into the building's south tower at 9:03 A.M., which erupted into flames, the nation knew it was under attack. Of the estimated 2,843 people who died in the September 11 terrorist attacks, 2,617 were at the World Trade Center. Robert Clark / AURORA.

excellent scholarship that informs Part Six of this textbook demonstrates that it is indeed possible to assess and interpret historically events of the fairly recent past such as the cold war, the civil rights movement, the growth of suburbia, and the changing contours of the global economy.

The closer the past gets to the present, however, the harder the task becomes. Consider the terrorist attacks of September 11, 2001. No reader of this text could possibly have missed the television images of the two Boeing 767s hurtling into New York City's World Trade Center, or the Twin Towers collapsing into rubble, or the crowds fleeing the cascading clouds of dust, and then, as the cameras

switched to Washington, D.C., the flames engulfing a wing of the Pentagon. Few will forget the accounts of survivors who, clambering down the staircases, encountered firefighters laboring upward overloaded with equipment, some to their death, or of the passengers of United Airlines Flight 93 who, learning on their cell phones about what had happened, took on the terrorists and brought down the plane in rural Pennsylvania before it could reach its probable target, the White House. Given the emotional impact of those searing images and the poignant stories of courage and mourning that continue to unfold, historians have a daunting task in trying to

Americans, Think!

For extremist Islamic groups in Pakistan, neighbor to Taliban-controlled Afghanistan, the terrorist attacks on the United States on September 11, 2001, brought to the fore long-standing resentment toward the United States. Their resentment is based in part on U.S. support for Israel, but also stems from the way in which America—with its great power and wealth—exemplifies the corrosive effects of Western capitalism and modernism. Here, Pakistani activists demonstrate at an anti-America rally in Islamabad held on September 15, 2001.

B. K. Bangash / AP / Wide World.

step back from their experience as witnesses of contemporary events to place the trauma of September 11 into a broad historical perspective.

What follows in this epilogue is a preview, to follow our movie analogy, of how we anticipate incorporating the terrorist attacks and their aftermath into the final chapter of the next edition of *America's History*. We offer an overview of the key areas in modern American life that have been traced throughout this book—politics, society and culture, the economy, and diplomacy—in light of September 11, a day that has led many contemporary observers to conclude that "the world will never be the same again." Just as in earlier chapters, we will examine the larger themes, shifting perspectives, and emerging syntheses in these areas but with a more tentative and open-ended perspective. Think of this part of *America's History* as a historical document: how a group of American historians viewed the nation during a heightened time of crisis. Look at the choice of issues and mode of analysis they used to gather and evaluate evidence, how they linked complex events surrounding the terrorist attacks to larger patterns and themes.

We are writing this epilogue in April 2003, nearly eighteen months after the events of September 11. By the time you read this you will know how some of the themes we touch upon have turned out. To reiterate Nixon's remark, "It takes fifty years before you're able to come back and evaluate a man or a period of time." Perhaps, many years from now, you will look back over your copy of *America's History* and judge how well we did.

September 11 and International Affairs

Almost three thousand men and women from over eighty countries perished in the terrorist attacks on the United States on September 11, 2001. For the first time since the War of 1812, foreign agents attacked the continental United States, targeting symbols of American capitalism and government. Within minutes of the first plane's collision into one of the Twin Towers, television crews were on the scene; by the time the second plane hit the other tower, seventeen minutes later, the event was covered live. America was under attack in living color for the entire world to see.

The Search for Al Qaeda

After the terrorist attacks on New York's World Trade Center and the Pentagon, the United States succeeded in marshalling a multinational force to attack Afghanistan, where the repressive anti-American Taliban regime harbored a significant component of the Al Qaeda network. Here, Canadian infantry soldiers board a U.S. Army Ch-47 Chinook helicopter in the Shahi Kot mountains of Afghanistan in March 2002. Later they teamed up with U.S. Army soldiers to search remote mountain regions for Taliban and Al Qaeda personnel. © Jim Hollander / AFP / Corbis.

Within hours, the United States had traced the origins of the attack to a militant Muslim sect, Al Qaeda, under the leadership of Osama bin Laden, a Saudi exile living among and supported by Taliban leaders in Afghanistan. The Taliban was itself a fundamentalist Muslim organization that had seized control of Afghanistan in 1996, following the overthrow of a Soviet-backed regime by forces supplied and assisted by the United States in the heat of the cold war.

In response to the attacks, President George W. Bush and his advisors proclaimed a "war on terrorism," working to forge a broad international coalition that included Great Britain, Canada, Russia, most of Europe, and many Muslim countries, notably Pakistan and Saudi Arabia. In seeking international assistance against terror as a common enemy to all, the Bush administration shifted away from its preference for unilateral action, which had earlier prompted its withdrawal from the Kyoto environmental agreements, the Comprehensive Test Ban Treaty, and participation in the International Criminal Court. These international treaties, which

sought worldwide participation to end global warming, an end to atomic testing and proliferation, and the establishment of a world court, all ran counter to Bush's policies. As the world's only superpower following the collapse of the Soviet Union in 1991, the failure of the United States to participate deeply undermined these international goals and provoked much criticism of its go-it-alone stance.

In response to the September 11 attacks, the United States successfully called upon its allies to support military strikes against Osama bin Laden and the Taliban. Within weeks, the United States and its allies, relying on massive air power and deployment of special forces, routed the Taliban and rolled up the Al Qaeda network's center of operations. Afghanistan was liberated from its Taliban dictators, who had squelched all civil liberties in the name of their fundamentalist beliefs. As television news reported on the change in regime, it particularly celebrated how Afghani women were freed from an exceptionally repressive way of life. In the wake of this victory, the United States and its allies attacked terrorist

Surrender

After a week of being surrounded by 50,000 rival Afghani troops and being subjected to intense American bombing, Taliban forces in Kunduz surrendered on November 25, 2001, marking a significant gain in America's fight against the Taliban. Here a Taliban fighter gives up a rocket launcher to a soldier of the Northern Alliance, a rebel Islamic faction that had resisted the Taliban since its takeover in 1996. The Northern Alliance became a major component of the American strategy to destroy the Taliban.

© Jean-Philippe Ksiazak / AFP / Corbis.

networks throughout the world, destroying many of their secret cells and capturing and killing large numbers of anti-American militants. Despite these successes in the war on terrorism, however, U.S. officials as of this writing believe Osama bin Laden to be alive and the Al Qaeda network active once again in "holy war" against the United States and its allies.

In his State of the Union address on January 29, 2002, President Bush stressed that the world still faced the threat of an international web of radical Muslim terrorists, ranging from Somalia to Bosnia to the Philippines and beyond. He signaled an intention to carry the fight to other nations that harbor terrorists or develop weapons of mass destruction—hence his characterization of Iran, Iraq, and North Korea as "an axis of evil." By the first anniversary of September 11, President Bush was threatening to attack Iraq, a controversial plan that divided his advisors and provoked heated public debate.

To quiet some of the opposition, and more importantly to garner international support for the war on Iraq, President Bush presented his case to the United Nations. On November 8, the Security Council approved Resolution 1441, which included the return of UN weapons inspectors to Iraq and a requirement that

Saddam Hussein's government submit to the Security Council a full account of its weapons, stockpiles, facilities, and delivery capabilities. To achieve passage of the resolution, the United States stepped back from its demand for regime change in Iraq, but it has still reserved the right of unilateral action. As weapons inspections proceeded in December 2002, the Bush administration continued its war preparations, and when it failed to obtain international, UN-sanctioned support for a preemptive strike, the United States and Britain launched an armed attack against Iraq without it. Whatever the results, how the United States chooses to exercise its immense power will undoubtedly be a major theme in future editions of *America's History*.

We will also have to assess the impact of the events of September 11 on other simmering hot spots in the world, where U.S. leadership will play an important role. The long-brewing crisis in the Middle East over Israeli resistance to demands for a Palestinian homeland has deepened since the attacks on the United States, with both sides adopting a harder position, particularly regarding Israeli settlements in the West Bank and the Palestinian use of terrorism, including suicide bombings against Israeli citizens. The Palestinian-Israeli conflict

Antiwar Voices

As President Bush accelerated his calls for war on Iraq in fall 2002, a peace movement emerged in communities throughout the country. These Maine residents were part of a crowd of 2,500 who turned out for an antiwar protest in Augusta, Maine, on October 26, 2002. Jill Brady / Maine Sunday Telegram.

Preparing for War

En route to the Middle East as part of the build-up for what the United States called a possible "pre-emptive strike" against Iraq, the aircraft carrier USS Constellation *made a routine stop in Hong Kong where a crew member worked on one of the fighter jets in November 2002. By mid-January 2003, more than 65,000 U.S. military personnel were in the Persian Gulf region in preparation for war with Iraq.*

Anat Givon / AP / Wide World.

affects the entire Middle East; thus its escalation adds to the enormous problems that face the United States in formulating an effective policy in the region.

Observers also question the stability of other Middle Eastern countries. Saudi Arabia has been an invaluable ally to the United States, but its ruling elite has engaged in a delicate balancing act of maintaining good relations with America while placating militant fundamentalist clerics within the country. Some observers worry that Saudi Arabia could be ripe for a fundamentalist revolution on the order of the Iranian revolution of the 1970s. Moreover, they fear that anger over the U.S. bombing of Muslims in Afghanistan could deepen anti-American sentiment throughout the Muslim world.

Another area of major concern is the continuing threat of war between India, a predominately Hindu nation, and Pakistan, a mostly Muslim state. Both countries possess atomic weapons that they have expressed willingness to use. For many years armed conflicts have erupted along the borders between the two nations, particularly over the issue of Kashmir, a region that lies between them and has both Hindu and Muslim populations. Following India's achievement of independence in 1947, Kashmir declared itself a sovereign nation. Since then, in three Indian-Pakistani wars over Kashmir, some 70,000 Kashmiris have been killed, another 40,000 have been placed in Indian jails, and over 150,000 have become homeless. Tensions in Kashmir have greatly accelerated since September 11, with relations between Pakistan and India strained as well over the issue of Muslim terrorists based in Pakistan.

That so much international anxiety about the future is tied to Muslim extremists also raises the alarming specter of a world divided in two, of the followers of Islam pitted against the rest of the world. Such a division is certainly the goal of the terrorists, who hope to galvanize Muslims into a holy war against the capitalist West. With few exceptions, leaders in Muslim nations have roundly condemned extremism and terrorism in the name of Islam, while the United States and its allies have insisted that their targets are terrorists, not Muslims. President Bush emphasized this point in a highly publicized speech given on September 17, 2001, just days after the attacks. Standing in a mosque in Washington, D.C., the president commented, "These acts of violence against innocents violate the fundamental tenets of the Islamic faith, and it's important for my fellow Americans to understand that."

How can the growth of such religious extremism be understood? As historians grapple with this question, they will need to take into consideration U.S. foreign policy, including its efforts to secure and protect American access to Middle Eastern oil, an objective made clear by its role in unseating Muhammad Mossadegh in Iran in 1954 as well as by its support for Kuwait against Iraq in the Gulf War of 1991. And, despite U.S. efforts to broker peace between Israel and the Palestinians, long-standing American support of Israelis constitutes yet another major source of resentment throughout the Muslim world that historians will have to consider. So, too, they will have to assess the circumstances that led the United States during Jimmy Carter's and Ronald Reagan's presidential administrations to support radical Islamic fundamentalists, including Osama bin Laden, in their efforts to drive the Russians out of Afghanistan in the 1980s. As part of the long-standing cold war tactic of resisting Communist encroachment in developing countries, the CIA trained and partially funded many leaders who eventually formed the Taliban. This is certainly one of the tragic ironies of recent history.

Mideast Crisis
With extremist Palestinian suicide bombers wreaking havoc and killing hundreds in Israel and Israeli officials mounting an aggressive offensive against Palestinians, a solution to the long-standing crisis seems remote. Here, Palestinians survey the rubble in Jenin on the West Bank after an intense Israeli attack in April 2002. In eight days of close-range bloody fighting, twenty-three Israeli soldiers and over fifty Palestinians died. VII Photo Agency.

September 11 and Domestic Issues

The implications of September 11 for international stability are far reaching. Perhaps of less long-term importance but nonetheless significant is the impact on the nation's domestic politics and policies. Put simply, the crisis has been a boon to George W. Bush's administration. Prior to the attacks, Bush was being lampooned in the media for the "dyselection of 2000." Jokes that Vice President Dick Cheney, a far more experienced and sophisticated policymaker, was the real president abounded. Opinion polls in Europe indicated that Bush was not taken seriously as a world leader, while the president's approval rating at home sagged steadily during the summer of 2001, registering only 52 percent in early July. By January 2002, however, Bush's approval rating had soared to an exceptional 83 percent. Some critics flinched at Bush's Wild West rhetoric—"bring them back dead or alive"—and promotion of strident nationalism, but the majority of the public approved the president's handling of the crisis.

As during any war, the power and influence of the executive have increased, and many observers agree that Bush's demeanor has become more "presidential."

Beyond the direction of foreign policy, however, Bush's new strength may have significant effects on domestic policy as well. Most indices suggested that Americans have more confidence in Bush than in his Democratic opposition in Congress. And although the Republicans have not yet been able to use the president's popularity to make substantial progress on their conservative domestic agenda concerning the economy, abortion, and education, this may change as a result of the November 2002 elections. With Republicans gaining two seats, the Senate reverted to Republican control, and in the House they picked up five seats, increasing their majority to 228 out of the total of 435 representatives.

The election results were striking, as this was the first time since 1934 that the party of the president scored gains in both houses of Congress in his administration's first midterm election. In 1934 Democratic candidates rode Franklin D. Roosevelt's coattails into office; in 2002 Republican candidates clearly benefited from President Bush's personal popularity and the voting public's belief that he handled the terrorist crisis well. Moreover, the administration's aggressive posture in challenging Saddam Hussein and success in pushing a resolution through

Minority Whip

San Francisco representative Nancy Pelosi made history when she became the Democrat's House of Representatives leader, the "Minority Whip," and the first woman of either party to hold that position. The selection of the liberal Pelosi came on the heels of significant Republican victories in the 2002 elections and may indicate a shift away from the centrist politics of Democrats in the Clinton era.
Joe Marquette / AP / Wide World.

Congress authorizing military action against Iraq reinforced Bush's status as a forceful leader in uncertain times.

For their part, the Democrats suffered from unimaginative leadership and an inability to offer little that seemed distinctive from the Republicans. Moreover, Republicans mounted an unprecedented get-out-the-vote effort, while Democrats proved unable to energize their constituents to get to the polls. Already looking to the 2004 elections, and perhaps a sign that they are rejecting their move toward the more centrist leanings of the Clinton years, the Democrats have revamped their leadership, selecting Nancy Pelosi, a liberal San Francisco congressional representative, as the House Democratic leader—the first time a woman of either party has held this position.

International issues will undoubtedly remain a crucial factor in partisan politics in the near future. The Democrats will be particularly challenged to find a way of presenting themselves as supporting a forceful U.S. presence in the world—something the American public seems to want—while simultaneously challenging the Republican leadership in charge of that policy. Two other issues—the economy and corporate corruption—were expected, incorrectly, to be important factors in the 2002 midterm elections, but they may yet surface as vital issues in future political confrontations.

Figures released in August 2002 by the Commerce Department reveal that the economy was in recession months before the terrorist attacks and had begun to recover by the end of 2001. By the summer of 2002, however, that recovery had stalled, with most economic indicators looking bleak, leading *The Economist* to describe the outlook as "decidedly wobbly." Certainly, September 11 contributed to the economic woes, most noticeably in damage to the airline industry. Faced with reluctant air travelers, airlines cut schedules between 15 and 20 percent after September 11; within a year, in August 2002, U.S. Airways announced that it had filed for bankruptcy protection. In the same week, United Airlines indicated it was considering the same option, and American Airlines reported that it was overhauling its operation and eliminating 7,000 jobs, or 6 percent of its workforce.

But the fragility of the airline industry paled in comparison to broader economic problems that were unconnected to the terrorist attacks. Just weeks after the destruction of the Twin Towers, the energy giant Enron, a company that brokered electricity and natural gas, collapsed on Wall Street after its announcement of a $618 million third-quarter loss. The Securities and Exchange Commission discovered that the auditing firm Arthur Andersen, which handled Enron's accounts, had been shredding and destroying documents related to the company's collapse. A scandal of huge proportions, it reached into centers of government, including the White House. Kenneth Lay, the CEO of Enron, with a long history of involvement in Republican Party affairs, had been a strong financial backer and personal friend of President Bush, donating over $290,000 to his presidential campaign.

During the summer of 2002, other corporate giants, including WorldCom and Adelphia Communications, fell with regularity, costing thousands of jobs and threatening the nation's economy. By midsummer the unemployment rate stood at 5.9 percent as compared to 4.6 percent the previous year. The accompanying decline in the stock market wiped out $7.7 trillion of paper wealth—an outcome devastating for many Americans, roughly half of whom owned stock. As falling stock prices depleted 401(k) accounts and retirement funds, the elderly found their real incomes reduced and for many their hopes of retirement put on hold.

Hard Times for the Airlines

The most obvious economic impact of the terrorist attacks of September 11 has been on the airline industry since many Americans are now reluctant to fly. The industry has witnessed significant cutbacks in schedules, layoffs of employees, and declarations of bankruptcy. Symbolic of the industry's woes is this photograph of a virtually empty United Airlines terminal at Boston's Logan Airport on the first anniversary of the attacks. Indicative of the increased security precautions for airports, State Police Trooper Maureen Lewis patrols with Bara, a dog trained to detect explosives. Charles Krupa / AP / Wide World.

The corporate scandals and their economic fallout have helped to erode the nation's trust in corporate America. Polls also suggest that they have deflected some attention away from the issues connected to the events of September 11, as economic anxieties are supplanting Americans' fears about terrorism as their number one concern. Recognizing the importance of turning the economy around, the Bush administration instituted a dramatic shakeup of economic appointees in December 2002, replacing the secretary of the treasury, the head of the Securities and Exchange Commission, and the chief economic advisor to the president. Although the faltering economy, corporate scandals, and the terrorist attacks of September 11 are unrelated issues, together they have fostered a widespread uneasiness and have undermined Americans' confidence about the future.

In addition to assessing the impact of September 11 on politics and the economy, future editions of *America's History* will need to analyze another important domestic ramification of the terrorist attacks: the efforts to ensure "homeland security." To improve the nation's domestic defenses, the Bush administration increased security at

The Fall of Enron

Two weeks after the terrorist attacks of September 11, Americans faced more unsettling news as they learned that the energy firm Enron, one of the nation's ten largest corporations, had collapsed on Wall Street, taking the investments and retirement funds of many thousands of people with it. Subsequent investigation revealed the firm had lied about its losses and that its auditing firm had shredded and destroyed documents related to the company's collapse. The full impact of the scandal has yet to be evaluated, but in Texas, one quick result was the change of the name for the Houston Astros' baseball park—from Enron Field to Minute Maid Park. Brett Coomer / AP / Wide World.

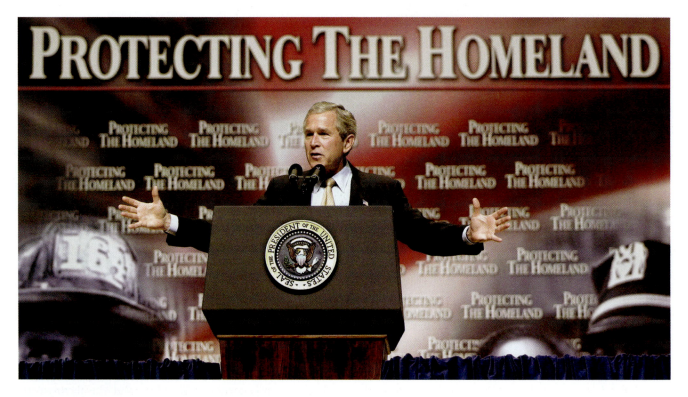

Homeland Security

One of the most far-reaching domestic results of the terrorist attacks on the World Trade Center and the Pentagon was the call for heightened defense at home. At a July 2002 speech in Washington, D.C., President Bush outlined his plan for an Office of Homeland Security designed to thwart the terrorist threat and control the nation's borders. The following November, Congress approved the president's proposal, which combined approximately twenty-two different government departments under a single cabinet-level agency, making it the largest federal government reorganization since 1947. President Bush nominated former Pennsylvania governor Thomas Ridge to head up the new office.
Paul J. Richards / AFP / Corbis.

airports, government buildings, and popular tourist attractions, while proposing legislation that would enhance federal investigative capabilities. The USA PATRIOT (Uniting and Strengthening America by Providing Appropriate Tools Required to Intercept and Obstruct Terrorism) Act of 2002, which passed with only one dissenting vote, gave unparalleled powers to the federal government to investigate and detain immigrants suspected of terrorist activity, all surrounded by a high degree of secrecy in the name of national security. One result of these powers was that the hunt for suspected terrorists threatened to bring about a new type of racial profiling, whereby young Muslim men could become subject to investigations not bound by traditional protections of civil liberties. Other threats to civil liberties included President Bush's executive order of November 2001 that suspected terrorists be tried in military tribunals rather than in the civil courts where they would have the full protections provided in the Constitution.

Similarly, programs such as TIPS (Terrorism Information and Prevention System) put forth by Attorney General John D. Ashcroft have drawn fire for proposing a citizen-spy network that would use mail carriers, utility workers, truckers, dock workers, and others to report on suspicious activities. Responding to criticism, the Justice Department has scaled back its program, but it remains worrisome to many civil liberty advocates. The Justice Department also suffered setbacks in August 2002, when a Federal Appeals Court ruled that the Justice Department's "blanket" policy of secret deportation hearings was unconstitutional and the United States Foreign Intelligence Surveillance Court (created in 1978) placed limits on the USA PATRIOT Act's authorization of electronic surveillance of people accused of spying.

Another important domestic initiative called for the creation of the Office of Homeland Security, which Congress approved in November 2002. The initiative combines approximately twenty-two different government departments into a single cabinet-level agency operating with a budget of $40 billion, with about 170,000 employees. The largest governmental reorganization since the creation of the Department of Defense in 1947, this centralized agency will be responsible for the protection

Stars and Stripes

After September 11, 2001, American flags abounded—from car windows to T-shirts. Less conventional ways to display the stars and stripes also emerged, such as this painted lawn in South Mitford, Indiana. While many Americans praised the pervasive appearance of the flag as a sign of much-needed unity and patriotism, some criticized it as excessive nationalism that did little to address the serious problems the nation faced.

Samuel Hoffman / The Fort Wayne Journal Gazette / AP / Wide World.

of American life and property from terrorist activities and for controlling the nation's borders. It will bring together the U.S. Customs Service, the Coast Guard, the Immigration and Naturalization Service, and the Transportation Security Administration but not the CIA and FBI, even though in the aftermath of September 11 the two agencies were chastened for their mishandling of information relevant to the attacks.

Supporters hope that this monumental reorganization will bring efficiency and coordination to the myriad government agencies engaged in national security. Critics worry that it will create a bureaucracy too unwieldy to operate effectively and that it will center too much power in the president and the executive branch. Historians in the future not only will need to analyze the effectiveness of the USA PATRIOT Act and the new cabinet position in the efforts to weed out terrorism, but they also will need to evaluate the costs entailed in enhanced governmental authority and the reduction of Americans' civil liberties and privacy rights.

September 11 and the American People

Both in the passage of the USA PATRIOT Act and in approval of U.S. bombing in Afghanistan, President Bush enjoyed bipartisan support. This bipartisan spirit formed part of what commentators described as a new sense of unity in the nation. Observers praised the renewed spirit of patriotism—most obviously in the display of the American flag everywhere from taxi cabs to football fields.

It is not surprising that Americans would crave expressions of unity and higher purpose in the aftermath of September 11. During any war, such spirit helps individuals to cope with the vulnerability and uncertainty they face. In the case of America's war on terrorism, moreover, rallying around the flag gave the nation a respite from the disruptions that characterized its recent domestic history. In focusing on coming together for a victory against

terrorism, the American people could ignore, at least for a while, underlying sources of disunity—racial and ethnic conflict and disparate views on issues ranging from taxes and welfare reform to affirmative action and abortion to health care and immigration. They also could hope to have moved beyond such disheartening political controversies as the impeachment of Bill Clinton, the divisive nature of the 2000 elections, and the three-ring circus of media coverage of political sex scandals. But as uplifting as the spirit of a new America might be, historians know that this sort of war-inspired sentiment rarely lasts when the war is over. But the war on terrorism is a different kind of war. How long will it last? How long will the American people—and the rest of the world—support its current trajectories?

Many observers have compared the September 11 attacks to the December 7, 1941, attack on Pearl Harbor. Indeed, within days of September 11 the authors of this textbook were exchanging e-mails and debating the usefulness of the World War II analogy. Certainly, like December 7, 1941, and November 22, 1963, the day John F. Kennedy was shot, September 11, 2001, will be one of those defining dates that contemporaries are sure to remember in precise detail. And, like the bombing of Pearl Harbor, the terrorist attacks touched off an exceptional sense of American unity and determination to defeat the enemy. But important differences stand out. This war is against an elusive enemy—not nation-states with explicit territory and armed forces to be attacked but scattered cells of determined people who can wreak destruction cheaply and quickly and then virtually disappear.

Thus the aftermath of September 11 resembles not so much World War II as the cold war between the United States and the Soviet Union. Certainly, the rhetoric of the current war against terrorists evokes the cold war—a rhetoric of simple dichotomies, of good versus evil, and a tendency to dismiss criticism of U.S. policy as "un-American." And, like containing the Communists, containing the terrorists requires attention to wide-ranging parts of the world and will, according to the nation's leaders, require a long, sustained effort of constant vigilance.

Further parallels with the cold war may be seen in the advent of new weapons. Following the Soviet Union's explosion of the atomic bomb in 1949, Americans experienced a new vulnerability. Despite their extraordinary power and prosperity, for the first time they faced the prospect of possible annihilation—brought about by events far beyond their control or their borders. Although with time the intensity of those fears subsided, the shadow of the bomb became a fact of life that Americans, indeed the entire world, had to live with. The new fears unleashed by the terrorist attacks of September 11—not just of airplanes imploding buildings but of anthrax and other, more sophisticated, biological weapons and germ warfare—suggest the start of a new era that in some ways seems more threatening than the period of the cold war. Despite the arms race and the saber rattling of the cold war, atomic weaponry was never used after the Hiroshima and Nagasaki attacks of 1945. The potential for worldwide destruction set limits on the bomb's deployment. Terrorists have fewer limits, however. Will Americans reach a point where they can feel that the possibility of future attacks has been contained, that they have achieved a clear-cut victory? Or are they beginning a new cold war–like era in which the threat of attack pervades the culture? Contemporary observers are no doubt correct when they say that "the world will never be the same again," but the nature and extent of that transformation has yet to be defined. Students reading *America's History* will be witnesses to that process.

The Declaration of Independence

In Congress, July 4, 1776, The Unanimous Declaration of the Thirteen United States of America

When in the Course of human events, it becomes necessary for one people to dissolve the political bands which have connected them with another, and to assume among the Powers of the earth, the separate and equal station to which the Laws of Nature and of Nature's God entitle them, a decent respect to the opinions of mankind requires that they should declare the causes which impel them to the separation.

We hold these truths to be self-evident, that all men are created equal, that they are endowed by their Creator with certain unalienable rights, that among these are Life, Liberty, and the pursuit of Happiness. That to secure these rights, Governments are instituted among Men, deriving their just powers from the consent of the governed. That whenever any Form of Government becomes destructive of these ends, it is the Right of the People to alter or to abolish it, and to institute new Government, laying its foundation on such principles and organizing its powers in such form, as to them shall seem most likely to effect their Safety and Happiness. Prudence, indeed, will dictate that Governments long established should not be changed for light and transient causes; and accordingly all experience hath shown, that mankind are more disposed to suffer, while evils are sufferable, than to right themselves by abolishing the forms to which they are accustomed. But when a long train of abuses and usurpations, pursuing invariably the same Object evinces a design to reduce them under absolute Despotism, it is their right, it is their duty, to throw off such Government, and to provide new Guards for their future security.—Such has been the patient sufferance of these Colonies; and such is now the necessity which constrains them to alter their former Systems of Government. The history of the present King of Great Britain is a history of repeated injuries and usurpations, all having in direct object the establishment of an absolute Tyranny over these States. To prove this, let Facts be submitted to a candid world.

He has refused his Assent to Laws, the most wholesome and necessary for the public good.

He has forbidden his Governors to pass Laws of immediate and pressing importance, unless suspended in their operation till his Assent should be obtained; and, when so suspended, he has utterly neglected to attend to them.

He has refused to pass other Laws for the accommodation of large districts of people, unless those people would relinquish the right of Representation in the Legislature, a right inestimable to them and formidable to tyrants only.

He has called together legislative bodies at places unusual, uncomfortable, and distant from the depository of their public Records, for the sole purpose of fatiguing them into compliance with his measures.

He has dissolved Representative Houses repeatedly, for opposing with manly firmness his invasions on the rights of the people.

He has refused for a long time, after such dissolutions, to cause others to be elected; whereby the Legislative powers, incapable of Annihilation, have returned to the People at large for their exercise; the State remaining in the mean time exposed to all the dangers of invasion from without and convulsions within.

He has endeavoured to prevent the population of these States; for that purpose obstructing the Laws of Naturalization of Foreigners; refusing to pass others to encourage their migrations hither, and raising the conditions of new Appropriations of Lands.

He has obstructed the Administration of Justice, by refusing his Assent to Laws for establishing Judiciary powers.

He has made Judges dependent on his Will alone, for the tenure of their offices, and the amount and payment of their salaries.

He has erected a multitude of New Offices, and sent hither swarms of Officers to harass our People, and eat out their substance.

He has kept among us, in times of peace, Standing Armies without the Consent of our legislature.

He has combined with others to subject us to a jurisdiction foreign to our constitution, and unacknowledged by our laws; giving his Assent to their Acts of pretended Legislation:

For quartering large bodies of armed troops among us:

For protecting them, by a mock Trial, from Punishment for any Murders which they should commit on the Inhabitants of these States:

For cutting off our Trade with all parts of the world:

For imposing taxes on us without our Consent:

For depriving us, in many cases, of the benefits of Trial by jury:

For transporting us beyond Seas to be tried for pretended offences:

For abolishing the free System of English Laws in a neighbouring Province, establishing therein an Arbitrary government, and enlarging its Boundaries so as to render it at once an example and fit instrument for introducing the same absolute rule into these Colonies:

For taking away our Charters, abolishing our most valuable Laws, and altering fundamentally the Forms of our Governments:

For suspending our own Legislatures, and declaring themselves invested with Power to legislate for us in all cases whatsoever.

He has abdicated Government here, by declaring us out of his Protection and waging War against us.

He has plundered our seas, ravaged our Coasts, burnt our towns, and destroyed the lives of our people.

He is at this time transporting large armies of foreign mercenaries to compleat the works of death, desolation, and tyranny, already begun with circumstances of Cruelty & perfidy scarcely paralleled in the most barbarous ages, and totally unworthy the Head of a civilized nation.

He has constrained our fellow Citizens taken Captive on the high Seas to bear Arms against their Country, to become the executioners of their friends and Brethren, or to fall themselves by their Hands.

He has excited domestic insurrections amongst us, and has endeavoured to bring on the inhabitants of our frontiers, the merciless Indian Savages, whose known rule of warfare, is an undistinguished destruction of all ages, sexes, and conditions.

In every stage of these Oppressions We have Petitioned for Redress in the most humble terms: Our repeated Petitions have been answered only by repeated injury. A Prince, whose character is thus marked by every act which may define a Tyrant, is unfit to be the ruler of a free people.

Nor have We been wanting in attention to our British brethren. We have warned them from time to time of attempts by their legislature to extend an unwarrantable jurisdiction over us. We have reminded them of the circumstances of our emigration and settlement here. We have appealed to their native justice and magnanimity, and we have conjured them by the ties of our common kindred to disavow these usurpations, which would inevitably interrupt our connections and correspondence. They too have been deaf to the voice of justice and of consanguinity. We must, therefore, acquiesce in the necessity, which denounces our Separation, and hold them, as we hold the rest of mankind, Enemies in War, in Peace Friends.

We, therefore, the Representatives of the United States of America, in General Congress, Assembled, appealing to the Supreme Judge of the world for the rectitude of our intentions, do, in the Name, and by Authority of the good People of these Colonies, solemnly publish and declare, That these United Colonies are, and of Right ought to be FREE AND INDEPENDENT STATES; that they are Absolved from all Allegiance to the British Crown, and that all political connection between them and the State of Great Britain, is and ought to be totally dissolved; and that as Free and Independent States, they have full Power to levy War, conclude Peace, contract Alliances, establish Commerce, and to do all other Acts and Things which Independent States may of right do. And for the support of this Declaration, with a firm reliance on the Protection of Divine Providence, we mutually pledge to each other our Lives, our Fortunes, and our sacred Honor.

John Hancock

Button Gwinnett	**George Wythe**	**James Wilson**	**Josiah Bartlett**
Lyman Hall	**Richard Henry Lee**	**Geo. Ross**	**Wm. Whipple**
Geo. Walton	**Th. Jefferson**	**Caesar Rodney**	**Matthew Thornton**
Wm. Hooper	**Benja. Harrison**	**Geo. Read**	**Saml. Adams**
Joseph Hewes	**Thos. Nelson, Jr.**	**Thos. M'Kean**	**John Adams**
John Penn	**Francis Lightfoot Lee**	**Wm. Floyd**	**Robt. Treat Paine**
Edward Rutledge	**Carter Braxton**	**Phil. Livingston**	**Elbridge Gerry**
Thos. Heyward, Junr.	**Robt. Morris**	**Frans. Lewis**	**Step. Hopkins**
Thomas Lynch, Junr.	**Benjamin Rush**	**Lewis Morris**	**William Ellery**
Arthur Middleton	**Benja. Franklin**	**Richd. Stockton**	**Roger Sherman**
Samuel Chase	**John Morton**	**John Witherspoon**	**Sam'el Huntington**
Wm. Paca	**Geo. Clymer**	**Fras. Hopkinson**	**Wm. Williams**
Thos. Stone	**Jas. Smith**	**John Hart**	**Oliver Wolcott**
Charles Carroll of Carrollton	**Geo. Taylor**	**Abra. Clark**	

The Articles of Confederation and Perpetual Union

Agreed to in Congress, November 15, 1777; Ratified March 1781

BETWEEN THE STATES OF NEW HAMPSHIRE, MASSACHUSETTS BAY, RHODE ISLAND AND PROVIDENCE PLANTATIONS, CONNECTICUT, NEW YORK, NEW JERSEY, PENNSYLVANIA, DELAWARE, MARYLAND, VIRGINIA, NORTH CAROLINA, SOUTH CAROLINA, GEORGIA.*

Article 1.

The stile of this confederacy shall be "The United States of America."

Article 2.

Each State retains its sovereignty, freedom and independence, and every power, jurisdiction, and right, which is not by this confederation expressly delegated to the United States, in Congress assembled.

Article 3.

The said states hereby severally enter into a firm league of friendship with each other for their common defence, the security of their liberties and their mutual and general welfare; binding themselves to assist each other against all force offered to, or attacks made upon them, or any of them, on account of religion, sovereignty, trade, or any other pretence whatever.

Article 4.

The better to secure and perpetuate mutual friendship and intercourse among the people of the different states in this union, the free inhabitants of each of these states, paupers, vagabonds, and fugitives from justice excepted, shall be entitled to all privileges and immunities of free citizens in the several states; and the people of each State shall have free ingress and regress to and from any other State, and shall enjoy therein all the privileges of trade and commerce, subject to the same duties, impositions, and restrictions, as the inhabitants thereof respectively; provided, that such restrictions shall not extend so far as to prevent the removal of property, imported into any State, to any

*This copy of the final draft of the Articles of Confederation is taken from the *Journals*, 9:907-25, November 15, 1777.

other State of which the owner is an inhabitant; provided also, that no imposition, duties, or restriction, shall be laid by any State on the property of the United States, or either of them.

If any person guilty of, or charged with treason, felony, or other high misdemeanor in any State, shall flee from justice and be found in any of the United States, he shall, upon demand of the governor or executive power of the State from which he fled, be delivered up and removed to the State having jurisdiction of his offence.

Full faith and credit shall be given in each of these states to the records, acts, and judicial proceedings of the courts and magistrates of every other State.

Article 5.

For the more convenient management of the general interests of the United States, delegates shall be annually appointed, in such manner as the legislature of each State shall direct, to meet in Congress, on the 1st Monday in November in every year, with a power reserved to each State to recall its delegates, or any of them, at any time within the year, and to send others in their stead for the remainder of the year.

No State shall be represented in Congress by less than two, nor by more than seven members; and no person shall be capable of being a delegate for more than three years in any term of six years; nor shall any person, being a delegate, be capable of holding any office under the United States, for which he, or any other for his benefit, receives any salary, fees, or emolument of any kind.

Each State shall maintain its own delegates in a meeting of the states, and while they act as members of the committee of the states.

In determining questions in the United States, in Congress assembled, each State shall have one vote.

Freedom of speech and debate in Congress shall not be impeached or questioned in any court or place out of Congress: and the members of Congress shall be protected in their persons from arrests and imprisonments, during the time of their going to and from, and attendance on Congress, except for treason, felony, or breach of the peace.

Article 6.

No State, without the consent of the United States, in Congress assembled, shall send any embassy to, or receive any embassy from, or enter into any conference, agreement, alliance, or treaty with any king, prince, or state; nor shall any person, holding any office of profit or trust under the United States, or any of them, accept of any present, emolument, office or title, of any kind whatever, from any king, prince, or foreign state; nor shall the United States, in Congress assembled, or any of them, grant any title of nobility.

No two or more states shall enter into any treaty, confederation, or alliance, whatever, between them, without the consent of the United States, in Congress assembled, specifying accurately the purposes for which the same is to be entered into, and how long it shall continue.

No state shall lay any imposts or duties which may interfere with any stipulations in treaties entered into by the United States, in Congress assembled, with any king, prince, or state, in pursuance of any treaties already proposed by Congress to the courts of France and Spain.

No vessels of war shall be kept up in time of peace by any State, except such number only as shall be deemed necessary by the United States, in Congress assembled, for the defence of such State or its trade; nor shall any body of forces be kept up by any State, in time of peace, except such number only as, in the judgment of the United States, in Congress assembled, shall be deemed requisite to garrison the forts necessary for the defence of such State; but every State shall always keep up a well regulated and disciplined militia, sufficiently armed and accoutred, and shall provide, and constantly have ready for use, in public stores, a due number of field pieces and tents, and a proper quantity of arms, ammunition and camp equipage.

No State shall engage in any war without the consent of the United States, in Congress assembled, unless such State be actually invaded by enemies, or shall have received certain advice of a resolution being formed by some nation of Indians to invade such State, and the danger is so imminent as not to admit of a delay till the United States, in Congress assembled, can be consulted; nor shall any State grant commissions to any ships or vessels of war, nor letters of marque or reprisal, except it be after a declaration of war by the United States, in Congress assembled, and then only against the kingdom or state, and the subjects thereof, against which war has been so declared, and under such regulations as shall be established by the United States, in Congress assembled, unless such State be infested by pirates, in which case vessels of war may be fitted out for that occasion, and kept so long as the danger shall continue, or until the United States, in Congress assembled, shall determine otherwise.

Article 7.

When land forces are raised by any State for the common defence, all officers of or under the rank of colonel, shall be appointed by the legislature of each State respectively, by whom such forces shall be raised, or in such manner as such State shall direct; and all vacancies shall be filled up by the State which first made the appointment.

Article 8.

All charges of war and all other expences, that shall be incurred for the common defence or general welfare, and allowed by the United States, in Congress assembled, shall be defrayed out of a common treasury, which shall be supplied by the several states, in proportion to the value of all land within each State, granted to or surveyed for any person, as such land and the buildings and improvements thereon shall be estimated according to such mode as the United States, in Congress assembled, shall, from time to time, direct and appoint.

The taxes for paying that proportion shall be laid and levied by the authority and direction of the legislatures of the several states, within the time agreed upon by the United States, in Congress assembled.

Article 9.

The United States, in Congress assembled, shall have the sole and exclusive right and power of determining on peace and war, except in the cases mentioned in the 6th article; of sending and receiving ambassadors; entering into treaties and alliances, provided that no treaty of commerce shall be made, whereby the legislative power of the respective states shall be restrained from imposing such imposts and duties on foreigners as their own people are subjected to, or from prohibiting the exportation or importation of any species of goods or commodities whatsoever; of establishing rules for deciding, in all cases, what captures on land or water shall be legal, and in what manner prizes, taken by land or naval forces in the service of the United States, shall be divided or appropriated; of granting letters of marque and reprisal in times of peace; appointing courts for the trial of piracies and felonies committed on the high seas, and establishing courts for receiving and determining, finally, appeals in all cases of captures; provided, that no member of Congress shall be appointed a judge of any of the said courts.

The United States, in Congress assembled, shall also be the last resort on appeal in all disputes and differences now subsisting, or that hereafter may arise between two or more states concerning boundary, jurisdiction or any other cause whatever; which authority shall always be exercised in the manner following: whenever the legislative or executive authority, or lawful agent of any State, in controversy with another, shall present a petition to Congress, stating the matter in question, and praying for a hearing, notice thereof shall be given, by order of Congress, to the legislative or executive authority of the other State in controversy, and a day assigned for the appearance of the parties by their lawful agents, who shall then be directed to appoint, by joint consent, commissioners or judges to constitute a court for hearing and determining the matter in question; but, if they cannot agree, Congress shall name three persons out of each of the United States, and from the list of such persons each party shall alternately strike out one, the petitioners beginning, until the number shall be reduced to thirteen; and from that number not less than seven, nor more than nine names, as Congress shall direct, shall, in the presence of Congress, be drawn out by lot; and the persons whose names shall be so drawn, or any five of them, shall be commissioners or judges to hear and finally determine the controversy, so always as a major part of the judges who shall hear the cause shall agree in the determination; and if either party shall neglect to attend at the day appointed, without shewing reasons which Congress shall judge sufficient, or, being present, shall refuse to strike, the Congress shall proceed to nominate three persons out of each State, and the secretary of Congress shall strike in behalf of such party absent or refusing; and the judgment and sentence of the court to be appointed, in the manner before prescribed, shall be final and conclusive; and if any of the parties shall refuse to submit to the authority of such court, or to appear or defend their claim or cause, the court shall nevertheless proceed to pronounce sentence or judgment, which shall, in like manner, be final and decisive, the judgment or sentence and other proceedings begin, in either case, transmitted to Congress, and lodged among the acts of Congress for the security of the parties concerned: provided, that every commissioner, before he sits in judgment, shall take an oath, to be administered by one of the judges of the supreme or superior court of the State where the cause shall be tried, "well and truly to hear and determine the matter in question, according to the best of his judgment, without favour, affection, or hope of reward:" provided, also, that no State shall be deprived of territory for the benefit of the United States.

All controversies concerning the private right of soil, claimed under different grants of two or more states, whose jurisdictions, as they may respect such lands and the states which passed such grants, are adjusted, the said grants, or either of them, being at the same time claimed to have originated antecedent to such settlement of jurisdiction, shall, on the petition of either party to the Congress of the United States, be finally determined, as near as may be, in the same manner as is before prescribed for deciding disputes respecting territorial jurisdiction between different states.

The United States, in Congress assembled, shall also have the sole and exclusive right and power of regulating the alloy and value of coin struck by their own authority, or by that of the respective states; fixing the standard of weights and measures throughout the United States; regulating the trade and managing all affairs with the Indians not members of any of the states; provided that the legislative right of any State within its own limits be not infringed or violated; establishing and regulating post offices from one State to another throughout all the United States, and exacting such postage on the papers passing through the same as may be requisite to defray the expences of the said office; appointing all officers of the land forces in the service of the United States, excepting regimental officers; appointing all the officers of the naval forces, and commissioning all officers whatever in the service of the United States; making rules for the government and regulation of the said land and naval forces, and directing their operations.

The United States, in Congress assembled, shall have authority to appoint a committee to sit in the recess of Congress, to be denominated "a Committee of the States," and to consist of one delegate from each State, and to appoint such other committees and civil officers as may be necessary for managing the general affairs of the United States, under their direction; to appoint one of their number to preside; provided that no person be allowed to serve in the office of president more than one year in any term of three years; to ascertain the necessary sums of money to be raised for the service of the United States, and to appropriate and apply the same for defraying the public expences; to borrow money or emit bills on the credit of the United States, transmitting, every half year, to the respective states, an account of the sums of money so borrowed or emitted; to build and equip a navy; to agree upon the number of land forces, and to make requisitions from each State for its quota, in proportion to the number of white inhabitants in such State; which requisitions shall be binding; and thereupon, the legislature of each State shall appoint the regimental officers, raise the men, and cloathe, arm, and equip them in a soldier-like manner, at the expence of the United States; and the officers and men so cloathed, armed, and equipped, shall march to the place appointed and within the time agreed on by the United States, in Congress assembled;

but if the United States, in Congress assembled, shall, on consideration of circumstances, judge proper that any State should not raise men, or should raise a smaller number than its quota, and that any other State should raise a greater number of men than the quota thereof, such extra number shall be raised, officered, cloathed, armed, and equipped in the same manner as the quota of such State, unless the legislature of such State shall judge that such extra number cannot be safely spared out of the same, in which case they shall raise, officer, cloathe, arm, and equip as many of such extra number as they judge can be safely spared. And the officers and men so cloathed, armed, and equipped, shall march to the place appointed and within the time agreed on by the United States, in Congress assembled.

The United States, in Congress assembled, shall never engage in a war, nor grant letters of marque and reprisal in time of peace, nor enter into any treaties or alliances, nor coin money, nor regulate the value thereof, nor ascertain the sums and expences necessary for the defence and welfare of the United States, or any of them: nor emit bills, nor borrow money on the credit of the United States, nor appropriate money, nor agree upon the number of vessels of war to be built or purchased, or the number of land or sea forces to be raised, nor appoint a commander in chief of the army or navy, unless nine states assent to the same; nor shall a question on any other point, except for adjourning from day to day, be determined, unless by the votes of a majority of the United States, in Congress assembled.

The Congress of the United States shall have power to adjourn to any time within the year, and to any place within the United States, so that no period of adjournment be for a longer duration than the space of six months, and shall publish the journal of their proceedings monthly, except such parts thereof, relating to treaties, alliances or military operations, as, in their judgment, require secrecy; and the yeas and nays of the delegates of each State on any question shall be entered on the journal, when it is desired by any delegate; and the delegates of a State, or any of them, at his, or their request, shall be furnished with a transcript of the said journal, except such parts as are above excepted, to lay before the legislatures of the several states.

Article 10.

The committee of the states, or any nine of them, shall be authorized to execute, in the recess of Congress, such of the powers of Congress as the United States, in Congress assembled, by the consent of nine states, shall, from time to time, think expedient to vest them with; provided, that no power be delegated to the said committee, for the exercise of which, by the articles of confederation, the voice of nine states, in the Congress of the United States assembled, is requisite.

Article 11.

Canada acceding to this confederation, and joining in the measures of the United States, shall be admitted into and entitled to all the advantages of this union; but no other colony shall be admitted into the same, unless such admission be agreed to by nine states.

Article 12.

All bills of credit emitted, monies borrowed and debts contracted by, or under the authority of Congress before the assembling of the United States, in pursuance of the present confederation, shall be deemed and considered as a charge against the United States, for payment and satisfaction whereof the said United States and the public faith are hereby solemnly pledged.

Article 13.

Every State shall abide by the determinations of the United States, in Congress assembled, on all questions which, by this confederation, are submitted to them. And the articles of this confederation shall be inviolably observed by every State, and the union shall be perpetual; nor shall any alteration at any time hereafter be made in any of them, unless such alteration be agreed to in a Congress of the United States, and be afterwards confirmed by the legislatures of every State.

These articles shall be proposed to the legislatures of all the United States, to be considered, and if approved of by them, they are advised to authorize their delegates to ratify the same in the Congress of the United States; which being done, the same shall become conclusive.

The Constitution of the United States of America

Agreed to by Philadelphia Convention, September 17, 1787
Implemented March 4, 1789

We the People of the United States, in Order to form a more perfect Union, establish Justice, insure domestic Tranquility, provide for the common defence, promote the general Welfare, and secure the Blessings of Liberty to ourselves and our Posterity, do ordain and establish this Constitution for the United States of America.

Article I

Section 1. All legislative Powers herein granted shall be vested in a Congress of the United States, which shall consist of a Senate and a House of Representatives.

Section 2. The House of Representatives shall be composed of Members chosen every second Year by the People of the several States, and the Electors in each State shall have the Qualifications requisite for Electors of the most numerous Branch of the State Legislature.

No Person shall be a Representative who shall not have attained to the Age of twenty-five Years, and been seven Years a Citizen of the United States, and who shall not, when elected, be an Inhabitant of that State in which he shall be chosen.

Representatives and direct Taxes shall be apportioned among the several States which may be included within this Union, according to their respective Numbers, *which shall be determined by adding to the whole Number of free Persons, including those bound to Service for a Term of Years, and excluding Indians not taxed, three fifths of all other Persons.*[*] The actual Enumeration shall be made within three Years after the first Meeting of the Congress of the United States, and within every subsequent Term of ten Years, in such Manner as they shall by Law direct. The Number of Representatives shall not exceed one for every thirty Thousand, but each State shall have at Least one Representative; and *until such enumeration shall be made, the State of New Hampshire shall be entitled to chuse three, Massachusetts eight, Rhode Island and Providence Plantations one, Connecticut five, New York six, New Jersey four, Pennsylvania eight, Delaware one, Maryland six, Virginia ten, North Carolina five, South Carolina five, and Georgia three.*

When vacancies happen in the Representation from any State, the Executive Authority thereof shall issue Writs of Election to fill such Vacancies.

The House of Representatives shall chuse their Speaker and other Officers; and shall have the sole Power of Impeachment.

Section 3. The Senate of the United States shall be composed of two Senators from each State, *chosen by the Legislature thereof,*[†] for six Years; and each Senator shall have one Vote.

Immediately after they shall be assembled in Consequence of the first Election, they shall be divided as equally as may be into three Classes. The Seats of the Senators of the first Class shall be vacated at the Expiration of the second Year, of the second Class at the Expiration of the fourth Year, and of the third Class at the Expiration of the sixth Year, so that one-third may be chosen every second Year; and if Vacancies happen by Resignation, or otherwise, during the Recess of the Legislature of any State, the Executive thereof may make temporary Appointments until the next Meeting of the Legislature, which shall then fill such Vacancies.[‡]

No person shall be a Senator who shall not have attained to the Age of thirty Years, and been nine Years a Citizen of the United States, and who shall not, when elected, be an Inhabitant of that State for which he shall be chosen.

The Vice President of the United States shall be President of the Senate, but shall have no Vote, unless they be equally divided.

The Senate shall chuse their other Officers, and also a President pro tempore, in the absence of the Vice President, or when he shall exercise the Office of President of the United States.

The Senate shall have the sole Power to try all Impeachments. When sitting for that Purpose, they shall be on Oath or Affirmation. When the President of the United States is tried, the Chief Justice shall preside: And no Person shall be convicted without the Concurrence of two-thirds of the Members present.

Judgment in Cases of Impeachment shall not extend further than to removal from Office, and disqualification to hold and enjoy any Office of honor, Trust or Profit under the United States: but the Party convicted shall nevertheless be liable and subject to Indictment, Trial, Judgment and Punishment, according to Law.

Section 4. The Times, Places and Manner of holding Elections for Senators and Representatives, shall be prescribed in each State by the Legislature thereof; but the Congress may at any time by Law make or alter such Regulations, except as to the Places of Chusing Senators.

Note: The Constitution became effective March 4, 1789. Provisions in italics are no longer relevant or have been changed by constitutional amendment.

[*]Changed by Section 2 of the Fourteenth Amendment.

[†]Changed by Section 1 of the Seventeenth Amendment.
[‡]Changed by Clause 2 of the Seventeenth Amendment.

The Congress shall assemble at least once in every Year, and such Meeting *shall be on the first Monday in December, unless they shall by Law appoint a different Day.*[*]

Section 5.   Each House shall be the Judge of the Elections, Returns and Qualifications of its own Members, and a Majority of each shall constitute a Quorum to do Business; but a smaller number may adjourn from day to day, and may be authorized to compel the Attendance of absent Members, in such Manner, and under such Penalties, as each House may provide.

Each House may determine the Rules of its Proceedings, punish its Members for disorderly Behavior, and, with the Concurrence of two-thirds, expel a Member.

Each House shall keep a Journal of its Proceedings, and from time to time publish the same, excepting such Parts as may in their Judgment require Secrecy; and the Yeas and Nays of the Members of either House on any question shall, at the Desire of one-fifth of those Present, be entered on the Journal.

Neither House, during the Session of Congress, shall, without the Consent of the other, adjourn for more than three days, nor to any other Place than that in which the two Houses shall be sitting.

Section 6.   The Senators and Representatives shall receive a Compensation for their Services, to be ascertained by Law, and paid out of the Treasury of the United States. They shall in all Cases, except Treason, Felony and Breach of the Peace, be privileged from Arrest during their Attendance at the Session of their respective Houses, and in going to and returning from the same; and for any Speech or Debate in either House, they shall not be questioned in any other Place.

No Senator or Representative shall, during the Time for which he was elected, be appointed to any civil Office under the Authority of the United States, which shall have been created, or the Emoluments whereof shall have been increased, during such time; and no Person holding any Office under the United States, shall be a Member of either House during his Continuance in Office.

Section 7.   All Bills for raising Revenue shall originate in the House of Representatives; but the Senate may propose or concur with Amendments as on other Bills.

Every Bill which shall have passed the House of Representatives and the Senate, shall, before it becomes a Law, be presented to the President of the United States; If he approve he shall sign it, but if not he shall return it, with his Objections to that House in which it shall have originated, who shall enter the Objections at large on their Journal, and proceed to reconsider it. If after such Reconsideration two-thirds of that House shall agree to pass the Bill, it shall be sent, together with the Objections, to the other House, by which it shall likewise be reconsidered, and if approved by two-thirds of that House, it shall become a Law. But in all such Cases the Votes of both Houses shall be determined by Yeas and Nays, and the Names of the Persons voting for and against the Bill shall be entered on the Journal of each House respectively. If any Bill shall not be returned by the President within ten Days (Sundays excepted) after it shall

have been presented to him, the Same shall be a Law, in like Manner as if he had signed it, unless the Congress by their Adjournment prevent its Return, in which Case it shall not be a Law.

Every Order, Resolution, or Vote to which the Concurrence of the Senate and the House of Representatives may be necessary (except on a question of Adjournment) shall be presented to the President of the United States; and before the Same shall take Effect, shall be approved by him, or being disapproved by him, shall be repassed by two-thirds of the Senate and House of Representatives, according to the Rules and Limitations prescribed in the Case of a Bill.

Section 8.   The Congress shall have Power To lay and collect Taxes, Duties, Imposts and Excises, to pay the Debts and provide for the common Defence and general Welfare of the United States; but all Duties, Imposts and Excises shall be uniform throughout the United States;

To borrow money on the credit of the United States;

To regulate Commerce with foreign Nations, and among the several States, and with the Indian Tribes;

To establish an uniform Rule of Naturalization, and uniform Laws on the subject of Bankruptcies throughout the United States;

To coin Money, regulate the Value thereof, and of foreign Coin, and fix the Standard of Weights and Measures;

To provide for the Punishment of counterfeiting the Securities and current Coin of the United States;

To establish Post Offices and post Roads;

To promote the Progress of Science and useful Arts, by securing for limited Times to Authors and Inventors the exclusive Right to their respective Writings and Discoveries;

To constitute Tribunals inferior to the supreme Court;

To define and punish Piracies and Felonies committed on the high Seas, and Offenses against the Law of Nations;

To declare War, grant Letters of Marque and Reprisal, and make Rules concerning Captures on Land and Water;

To raise and support Armies, but no Appropriation of Money to that Use shall be for a longer Term than two Years;

To provide and maintain a Navy;

To make Rules for the Government and Regulation of the land and naval Forces;

To provide for calling forth the Militia to execute the Laws of the Union, suppress Insurrections and repel Invasions;

To provide for organizing, arming, and disciplining the Militia, and for governing such Part of them as may be employed in the Service of the United States, reserving to the States respectively, the Appointment of the Officers, and the Authority of training the Militia according to the discipline prescribed by Congress;

To exercise exclusive Legislation in all Cases whatsoever, over such District (not exceeding ten Miles square) as may, by Cession of particular States, and the acceptance of Congress, become the Seat of Government of the United States, and to exercise like Authority over all Places purchased by the Consent of the Legislature of the State in which the Same shall be, for the Erection of Forts, Magazines, Arsenals, dock-Yards, and other needful Buildings;—And

To make all Laws which shall be necessary and proper for carrying into Execution the foregoing Powers, and all other Powers vested by this Constitution in the Government of the United States, or in any Department or Officer thereof.

---

*Changed by Section 2 of the Twentieth Amendment.

Section 9.   The Migration or Importation of such Persons as any of the States now existing shall think proper to admit, shall not be prohibited by the Congress prior to the Year one thousand eight hundred and eight but a tax or duty may be imposed on such Importation, not exceeding ten dollars for each Person.

The privilege of the Writ of Habeas Corpus shall not be suspended, unless when in Cases of Rebellion or Invasion the public Safety may require it.

No Bill of Attainder or ex post facto Law shall be passed.

*No capitation, or other direct, Tax shall be laid, unless in Proportion to the Census or Enumeration herein before directed to be taken.**

No Tax or Duty shall be laid on Articles exported from any State.

No Preference shall be given by any Regulation of Commerce or Revenue to the Ports of one State over those of another: nor shall Vessels bound to, or from, one State, be obliged to enter, clear, or pay Duties in another.

No Money shall be drawn from the Treasury, but in Consequence of Appropriations made by law; and a regular Statement and Account of the Receipts and Expenditures of all public Money shall be published from time to time.

No Title of Nobility shall be granted by the United States: And no Person holding any Office of Profit or Trust under them, shall, without the Consent of the Congress, accept of any present, Emolument, Office, or Title, of any kind whatever, from any King, Prince, or foreign State.

Section 10.   No State shall enter into any Treaty, Alliance, or Confederation; grant Letters of Marque and Reprisal; coin Money; emit Bills of Credit; make any Thing but gold and silver Coin a Tender in Payment of Debts; pass any Bill of Attainder, ex post facto Law, or Law impairing the Obligation of Contracts, or grant any Title of Nobility.

No State shall, without the Consent of the Congress, lay any Imposts or Duties on Imports or Exports, except what may be absolutely necessary for executing its inspection Laws: and the net Produce of all Duties and Imposts, laid by any State on Imports or Exports, shall be for the Use of the Treasury of the United States; and all such Laws shall be subject to the Revision and Control of the Congress.

No State shall, without the Consent of the Congress, lay any duty of Tonnage, keep Troops, or Ships of War in time of Peace, enter into any Agreement or Compact with another State, or with a foreign Power, or engage in War, unless actually invaded, or in such imminent Danger as will not admit of delay.

Article II

Section 1.   The executive Power shall be vested in a President of the United States of America. He shall hold his Office during the Term of four Years, and, together with the Vice President, chosen for the same Term, be elected, as follows:

Each State shall appoint, in such Manner as the Legislature thereof may direct, a Number of Electors, equal to the whole Number of Senators and Representatives to which the State may be entitled in the Congress; but no Senator or Representative, or Person holding an Office of Trust or Profit under the United States, shall be appointed an Elector.

The Electors shall meet in their respective States, and vote by Ballot for two Persons, of whom one at least shall not be an Inhabitant of the same State with themselves. And they shall make a List of all the Persons voted for, and of the Number of Votes for each; which List they shall sign and certify, and transmit sealed to the Seat of the Government of the United States, directed to the President of the Senate. The President of the Senate shall, in the Presence of the Senate and House of Representatives, open all the Certificates, and the Votes shall then be counted. The Person having the greatest Number of Votes shall be the President, if such Number be a Majority of the whole Number of Electors appointed; and if there be more than one who have such Majority, and have an equal Number of Votes, then the House of Representatives shall immediately chuse by Ballot one of them for President; and if no Person have a Majority, then from the five highest on the List the said House shall in like Manner chuse the President. But in chusing the President, the Votes shall be taken by States, the Representation from each State having one Vote; a quorum for this Purpose shall consist of a Member or Members from two thirds of the States, and a Majority of all the States shall be necessary to a Choice. In every Case, after the Choice of the President, the Person having the greatest Number of Votes of the Electors shall be the Vice President. But if there should remain two or more who have equal Votes, the Senate shall chuse from them by Ballot the Vice President.†

The Congress may determine the Time of chusing the Electors, and the Day on which they shall give their Votes; which Day shall be the same throughout the United States.

No Person except a natural born Citizen, or a Citizen of the United States, at the time of the Adoption of this Constitution, shall be eligible to the Office of President; neither shall any Person be eligible to that Office who shall not have attained to the Age of thirty five Years, and been fourteen Years a Resident within the United States.

In Case of the Removal of the President from Office, or of his Death, Resignation, or Inability to discharge the Powers and Duties of the said Office, the same shall devolve on the Vice President, *and the Congress may by Law provide for the Case of Removal, Death, Resignation, or Inability, both of the President and Vice President, declaring what Officer shall then act as President, and such Officer shall act accordingly, until the Disability be removed, or a President shall be elected.‡*

The President shall, at stated Times, receive for his Services a Compensation, which shall neither be increased nor diminished during the Period for which he shall have been elected, and he shall not receive within that Period any other Emolument from the United States, or any of them.

Before he enter on the Execution of his Office, he shall take the following Oath or Affirmation:—"I do solemnly swear (or affirm) that I will faithfully execute the Office of President of the United States, and will to the best of my Ability, preserve, protect and defend the Constitution of the United States."

Section 2.   The President shall be Commander in Chief of the Army and Navy of the United States, and of the Militia of the several States, when called into the actual Service of the United

---

*Changed by the Sixteenth Amendment.

†Superseded by the Twelfth Amendment.

‡Modified by the Twenty-fifth Amendment.

States; he may require the Opinion, in writing, of the principal Officer in each of the executive Departments, upon any Subject relating to the Duties of their respective Offices, and he shall have Power to Grant Reprieves and Pardons for Offences against the United States, except in Cases of Impeachment.

He shall have Power, by and with the Advice and Consent of the Senate, to make Treaties, provided two thirds of the Senators present concur; and he shall nominate, and by and with the Advice and Consent of the Senate, shall appoint Ambassadors, other public Ministers and Consuls, Judges of the supreme Court, and all other Officers of the United States, whose Appointments are not herein otherwise provided for, and which shall be established by Law: but the Congress may by Law vest the Appointment of such inferior Officers, as they think proper, in the President alone, in the Courts of Law, or in the Heads of Departments.

The President shall have Power to fill up all Vacancies that may happen during the Recess of the Senate, by granting Commissions which shall expire at the End of their next Session.

Section 3. He shall from time to time give to the Congress Information of the State of the Union, and recommend to their Consideration such Measures as he shall judge necessary and expedient; he may, on extraordinary Occasions, convene both Houses, or either of them, and in Case of Disagreement between them, with Respect to the Time of Adjournment, he may adjourn them to such Time as he shall think proper; he shall receive Ambassadors and other public Ministers; he shall take Care that the Laws be faithfully executed, and shall Commission all the Officers of the United States.

Section 4. The President, Vice President and all civil Officers of the United States, shall be removed from Office on Impeachment for, and Conviction of, Treason, Bribery, or other high Crimes and Misdemeanors.

Article III

Section 1. The judicial Power of the United States, shall be vested in one supreme Court, and in such inferior Courts as the Congress may from time to time ordain and establish. The Judges, both of the supreme and inferior Courts, shall hold their Offices during good Behaviour, and shall, at stated Times, receive for their Services a Compensation, which shall not be diminished during their Continuance in Office.

Section 2. The judicial Power shall extend to all Cases, in Law and Equity, arising under this Constitution, the Laws of the United States, and Treaties made, or which shall be made, under their Authority;—to all Cases affecting Ambassadors, other public Ministers and Consuls;—to all Cases of admiralty and maritime Jurisdiction;—to Controversies to which the United States shall be a Party;—to Controversies between two or more States;—*between a State and Citizens of another State;**— between Citizens of different States;—between Citizens of the same State claiming Lands under Grants of different States, and between a State, or the Citizens thereof, and foreign States, Citizens or Subjects.

In all Cases affecting Ambassadors, other public Ministers and Consuls, and those in which a State shall be Party, the supreme Court shall have original Jurisdiction. In all the other Cases before mentioned, the supreme Court shall have appellate Jurisdiction, both as to Law and Fact, with such Exceptions, and under such Regulations as the Congress shall make.

The trial of all Crimes, except in Cases of Impeachment, shall be by Jury; and such Trial shall be held in the State where said Crimes shall have been committed; but when not committed within any State, the Trial shall be at such Place or Places as the Congress may by Law have directed.

Section 3. Treason against the United States, shall consist only in levying War against them, or in adhering to their Enemies, giving them Aid and Comfort. No Person shall be convicted of Treason unless on the Testimony of two Witnesses to the same overt Act, or on Confession in open Court.

The Congress shall have Power to declare the Punishment of Treason, but no Attainder of Treason shall work Corruption of Blood, or Forefeiture except during the Life of the Person attainted.

Article IV

Section 1. Full Faith and Credit shall be given in each State to the public Acts, Records, and judicial Proceedings of every other State. And the Congress may by general Laws prescribe the Manner in which such Acts, Records, and Proceedings shall be proved, and the Effect thereof.

Section 2. The Citizens of each State shall be entitled to all Privileges and Immunities of Citizens in the several States.

A Person charged in any State with Treason, Felony, or other Crime, who shall flee from Justice, and be found in another State, shall on demand of the executive Authority of the State from which he fled, be delivered up, to be removed to the State having Jurisdiction of the Crime.

No Person held to Service or Labour in one State, under the Laws thereof, escaping into another, shall, in Consequence of any Law or Regulation therein, be discharged from such Service or Labour, but shall be delivered up on Claim of the Party to whom such Service or Labour may be due.†

Section 3. New States may be admitted by the Congress into this Union; but no new State shall be formed or erected within the Jurisdiction of any other State; nor any State be formed by the Junction of two or more States, or parts of States, without the Consent of the Legislatures of the States concerned as well as of the Congress.

The Congress shall have Power to dispose of and make all needful Rules and Regulations respecting the Territory or other Property belonging to the United States; and nothing in this Constitution shall be so construed as to Prejudice any Claims of the United States, or of any particular State.

Section 4. The United States shall guarantee to every State in this Union a Republican Form of Government, and shall

---

*Restricted by the Eleventh Amendment.

†Superseded by the Thirteenth Amendment.

protect each of them against Invasion; and on Application of the Legislature, or of the Executive (when the Legislature cannot be convened) against domestic Violence.

Article V

The Congress, whenever two-thirds of both Houses shall deem it necessary, shall propose Amendments to this Constitution, or, on the Application of the Legislatures of two-thirds of the several States, shall call a Convention for proposing Amendments, which, in either Case, shall be valid to all Intents and Purposes, as Part of this Constitution, when ratified by the Legislatures of three-fourths of the several States, or by Conventions in three-fourths thereof, as the one or the other Mode of Ratification may be proposed by the Congress; Provided that no Amendment which may be made prior to the Year One thousand eight hundred and eight shall in any Manner affect the first and fourth Clauses in the Ninth Section of the first Article; and that no State, without its Consent, shall be deprived of its equal Suffrage in the Senate.

Article VI

All Debts contracted and Engagements entered into, before the Adoption of this Constitution, shall be as valid against the United States under this Constitution, as under the Confederation.

This Constitution, and the Laws of the United States which shall be made in Pursuance thereof; and all Treaties made, or which shall be made, under the Authority of the United States, shall be the supreme Law of the Land; and the Judges in every State shall be bound thereby, any Thing in the Constitution or Laws of any State to the Contrary notwithstanding.

The Senators and Representatives before mentioned, and the Members of the several State Legislatures, and all executive and judicial Officers, both of the United States and of the several States, shall be bound by Oath or Affirmation, to support this Constitution; but no religious Test shall ever be required as a Qualification to any Office or public Trust under the United States.

Article VII

The Ratification of the Conventions of nine States shall be sufficient for the Establishment of this Constitution between the States so ratifying the Same.

Done in Convention by the Unanimous Consent of the States present the Seventeenth Day of September in the Year of our Lord one thousand seven hundred and Eighty seven and of the Independence of the United States of America the Twelfth. In Witness whereof We have hereunto subscribed our Names.

Go. Washington
President and deputy from Virginia

New Hampshire	*New Jersey*	*Delaware*	*North Carolina*
John Langdon	Wil. Livingston	Geo. Read	Wm. Blount
Nicholas Gilman	David Brearley	Gunning Bedford jun	Richd. Dobbs Spaight
Massachusetts	Wm. Paterson	John Dickinson	Hu Williamson
Nathaniel Gorham	Jona. Dayton	Richard Bassett	*South Carolina*
Rufus King	*Pennsylvania*	Jaco. Broom	J. Rutledge
Connecticut	B. Franklin	*Maryland*	Charles Cotesworth Pinckney
Wm. Saml. Johnson	Thomas Mifflin	James McHenry	Pierce Butler
Roger Sherman	Robt. Morris	Dan. of St. Thos. Jenifer	*Georgia*
New York	Geo. Clymer	Danl. Carroll	William Few
Alexander Hamilton	Thos. FitzSimons	*Virginia*	Abr. Baldwin
	Jared Ingersoll	John Blair	
	James Wilson	James Madison, Jr.	
	Gouv. Morris		

and no fact tried by a jury, shall be otherwise reexamined in any Court of the United States, than according to the Rules of the common law.

• • •

This amendment guarantees people the same right to a trial by jury as was guaranteed by English common law in 1791. Under common law, in civil trials (those involving money damages) the role of the judge was to settle questions of law and that of the jury was to settle questions of fact. The amendment does not specify the size of the jury or its role in a trial, however. The Supreme Court has generally held that those issues be determined by English common law of 1791, which stated that a jury consists of twelve people, that a trial must be conducted before a judge who instructs the jury on the law and advises it on facts, and that a verdict must be unanimous.

Amendment VIII [1791]

Excessive bail shall not be required, nor excessive fines imposed, nor cruel and unusual punishments inflicted.

• • •

The language used to guarantee the three rights in this amendment was inspired by the English Bill of Rights of 1689. The Supreme Court has not had a lot to say about "excessive fines." In recent years it has agreed that despite the provision against "excessive bail," persons who are believed to be dangerous to others can be held without bail even before they have been convicted.

Although opponents of the death penalty have not succeeded in using the Eighth Amendment to achieve the end of capital punishment, the clause regarding "cruel and unusual punishments" has been used to prohibit capital punishment in certain cases.

Amendment IX [1791]

The enumeration in the Constitution, of certain rights, shall not be construed to deny or disparage others retained by the people.

• • •

Some Federalists feared that inclusion of the Bill of Rights in the Constitution would allow later generations of interpreters to claim that the people had surrendered all rights not specifically enumerated there. To guard against this, James Madison added language that became the Ninth Amendment. Interest in this heretofore largely ignored amendment revived in 1965 when it was used in a concurring opinion in Griswold v. Connecticut (1965). While Justice William O. Douglas called on the Third Amendment to support the right to privacy in deciding that case, Justice Arthur Goldberg, in the concurring opinion, argued that the right to privacy regarding contraception was an unenumerated right that was protected by the Ninth Amendment.

In 1980 the Court ruled that the right of the press to attend a public trial was protected by the Ninth Amendment. Although some scholars argue that modern judges cannot identify the unenumerated rights that the framers were trying to protect, others argue that the Ninth Amendment should be read as providing a constitutional "presumption of liberty" that allows people to act in any way that does not violate the rights of others.

Amendment X [1791]

The powers not delegated to the United States by the Constitution, nor prohibited by it to the States, are reserved to the States respectively, or to the people.

• • •

The Antifederalists were especially eager to see a "reserved powers clause" explicitly guaranteeing the states control over their internal affairs. Not surprisingly, the Tenth Amendment has been a frequent battleground in the struggle over states' rights and federal supremacy. Prior to the Civil War, the Jeffersonian Republican Party and Jacksonian Democrats invoked the Tenth Amendment to prohibit the federal government from making decisions about whether people in individual states could own slaves. The Tenth Amendment was virtually suspended during Reconstruction following the Civil War. In 1883, however, the Supreme Court declared the Civil Rights Act of 1875 unconstitutional on the grounds that it violated the Tenth Amendment. Business interests also called on the amendment to block efforts at federal regulation.

The Court was inconsistent over the next several decades as it attempted to resolve the tension between the restrictions of the Tenth Amendment and the powers the Constitution granted to Congress to regulate interstate commerce and levy taxes. The Court upheld the Pure Food and Drug Act (1906), the Meat Inspection Acts (1906 and 1907), and the White Slave Traffic Act (1910), all of which affected the states, but it struck down an act prohibiting interstate shipment of goods produced through child labor. Between 1934 and 1935 a number of New Deal programs created by Franklin D. Roosevelt were declared unconstitutional on the grounds that they violated the Tenth Amendment. As Roosevelt appointees changed the composition of the Court, the Tenth Amendment was declared to have no substantive meaning. Generally, the amendment is held to protect the rights of states to regulate internal matters such as local government, education, commerce, labor, and business as well as matters involving families such as marriage, divorce, and inheritance within the state.

Unratified Amendment

Reapportionment Amendment (proposed by Congress September 25, 1789, along with the Bill of Rights)

After the first enumeration required by the first article of the Constitution, there shall be one Representative for every thirty thousand, until the number shall amount to one hundred, after which the proportion shall be so regulated by Congress, that there shall be not less than one hundred Representatives, nor less than one Representative for every forty thousand persons, until the number of Representatives shall amount to two hundred; after which the proportion shall be so regulated by Congress, that there shall not be less than two hundred Representatives, nor more than one Representative for every fifty thousand persons.

• • •

If the Reapportionment Amendment had passed and remained in effect, the House of Representatives today would have more than 5,000 members rather than 435 to reflect the current U.S. population.

Amendment XI [1798]

The Judicial power of the United States shall not be construed to extend to any suit in law or equity, commenced or prosecuted against one of the United States by Citizens of another State, or by Citizens or subjects of any foreign state.

• • •

In 1793 the Supreme Court ruled in favor of Alexander Chisholm, executor of the estate of a deceased South Carolina merchant. Chisholm was suing the state of Georgia because the merchant had never been paid for provisions he had supplied during the Revolution. Many regarded this Court decision as an error that violated the intent of the Constitution.

Antifederalists and many other Americans feared a powerful federal court system because they worried that it would become like the British courts of this period, which were accountable only to the monarch. Furthermore, Chisholm v. Georgia prompted a series of suits against state governments by creditors and suppliers who had made loans during the war.

In addition, state legislators and Congress feared that the shaky economies of the new states, as well as the country as a whole, would be destroyed, especially if Loyalists who had fled to other countries sought reimbursement for land and property that had been seized. The day after the Supreme Court announced its decision, a resolution proposing the Eleventh Amendment, which overturned the decision in Chisholm v. Georgia, *was introduced in the U.S. Senate.*

Amendment XII [1804]

The Electors shall meet in their respective States and vote by ballot for President and Vice-President, one of whom, at least, shall not be an inhabitant of the same State with themselves; they shall name in their ballots the person voted for as President, and in distinct ballots the person voted for as Vice-President, and they shall make distinct lists of all persons voted for as President, and of all persons voted for as Vice-President, and of the number of votes for each, which lists they shall sign and certify, and transmit sealed to the seat of government of the United States, directed to the President of the Senate;—the President of the Senate shall, in the presence of the Senate and House of Representatives, open all the certificates and the votes shall then be counted;—The person having the greatest number of votes for President, shall be the President, if such number be a majority of the whole number of Electors appointed; and if no person have such majority, then from the persons having the highest numbers not exceeding three on the list of those voted for as President, the House of Representatives shall choose immediately, by ballot, the President. But in choosing the President, the votes shall be taken by States, the representation from each State having one vote; a quorum for this purpose shall consist of a member or members from two-thirds of the States, and a majority of all the States shall be necessary to a choice. And if the House of Representatives shall not choose a President whenever the right of choice shall devolve upon them, before *the fourth day of March* next following, then the Vice-President shall act as President, as in the case of the death or other constitutional disability of the President.*—The person having the greatest number of votes as Vice-President, shall be the Vice-

President, if such number be a majority of the whole number of Electors appointed; and if no person have a majority, then from the two highest numbers on the list, the Senate shall choose the Vice-President; a quorum for the purpose shall consist of two-thirds of the whole number of Senators, and a majority of the whole number shall be necessary to a choice. But no person constitutionally ineligible to the office of President shall be eligible to that of Vice-President of the United States.

• • •

The framers of the Constitution disliked political parties and assumed that none would ever form. Under the original system, electors chosen by the states would each vote for two candidates. The candidate who won the most votes would become president, and the person who won the second-highest number of votes would become vice president. Rivalries between Federalists and Republicans led to the formation of political parties, however, even before George Washington had left office. In 1796 Federalist John Adams was chosen as president, and his great rival, Thomas Jefferson (whose party was called the Republican Party), became his vice president. In 1800 all the electors cast their two votes as one of two party blocs. Jefferson and his fellow Republican nominee, Aaron Burr, were tied with seventy-three votes each. The contest went to the House of Representatives, which finally elected Jefferson after thirty-six ballots. The Twelfth Amendment prevents these problems by requiring electors to vote separately for the president and vice president.

Unratified Amendment

Titles of Nobility Amendment (proposed by Congress May 1, 1810)

If any citizen of the United States shall accept, claim, receive or retain any title of nobility or honor or shall, without the consent of Congress, accept and retain any present, pension, office or emolument of any kind whatever, from any emperor, king, prince or foreign power, such person shall cease to be a citizen of the United States, and shall be incapable of holding any office of trust or profit under them, or either of them.

• • •

This amendment would have extended Article I, Section 9, Clause 8 of the Constitution, which prevents the awarding of titles by the United States and the acceptance of such awards from foreign powers without congressional consent. Historians speculate that general nervousness about the power of the Emperor Napoleon, who was at that time extending France's empire throughout Europe, may have prompted the proposal. Though it fell one vote short of ratification, Congress and the American people thought the proposal had been ratified, and it was included in many nineteenth-century editions of the Constitution.

The Civil War and Reconstruction Amendments
(Thirteenth, Fourteenth, and Fifteenth Amendments)

In the four months between the election of Abraham Lincoln and his inauguration, more than two hundred proposed constitutional amendments were presented to Congress as part of a desperate attempt to hold the rapidly dissolving Union together. Most of these were efforts to appease the southern states by protecting

---

*Superseded by Section 3 of the Twentieth Amendment.

Amendment XVII [1913]

Section 1. The Senate of the United States shall be composed of two Senators from each State, elected by the people thereof, for six years; and each Senator shall have one vote. The electors in each State shall have the qualifications requisite for electors of [voters for] the most numerous branch of the State legislatures.

Section 2. When vacancies happen in the representation of any State in the Senate, the executive authority of such State shall issue writs of election to fill such vacancies: Provided, that the Legislature of any State may empower the executive thereof to make temporary appointments until the people fill the vacancies by election as the Legislature may direct.

Section 3. This amendment shall not be so construed as to affect the election or term of any Senator chosen before it becomes valid as part of the Constitution.

• • •

The framers of the Constitution saw the members of the House as the representatives of the people and the members of the Senate as the representatives of the states. Originally, senators were to be chosen by the state legislators. According to reform advocates, however, the growth of private industry and transportation conglomerates during the late nineteenth century had created a network of corruption in which wealth and power were exchanged for influence and votes in the Senate. Senator Nelson Aldrich, who represented Rhode Island in this period, for example, was known as "the senator from Standard Oil" because of his open support of special business interests.

Efforts to amend the Constitution to allow direct election of senators had begun in 1826, but because any proposal had to be approved by the Senate, reform seemed impossible. Progressives tried to gain influence in the Senate by instituting party caucuses and primary elections, which gave citizens the chance to express their choice of a senator who could then be officially elected by the state legislature. By 1910 fourteen of the country's thirty senators received popular votes through a state primary before the state legislature made its selection. Despairing of getting a proposal through the Senate, supporters of a direct-election amendment had begun in 1893 to seek a convention of representatives from two-thirds of the states to propose an amendment that could then be ratified. By 1905 thirty-one of forty-five states had endorsed such an amendment. Finally, in 1911, despite extraordinary opposition, a proposed amendment passed the Senate; by 1913 it had been ratified.

Amendment XVIII [1919; repealed 1933 by Amendment XXI]

Section 1. After one year from the ratification of this article the manufacture, sale, or transportation of intoxicating liquors within, the importation thereof into, or the exportation thereof from the United States and all territory subject to the jurisdiction thereof, for beverage purposes, is hereby prohibited.

Section 2. The Congress and the several States shall have concurrent power to enforce this article by appropriate legislation.

Section 3. This article shall be inoperative unless it shall have been ratified as an amendment to the Constitution by the legislatures of the several States, as provided by the Constitution, within seven years from the date of the submission thereof to the States by the Congress.

• • •

The Prohibition Party, formed in 1869, began calling for a constitutional amendment to outlaw alcoholic beverages in 1872. A prohibition amendment was first proposed in the Senate in 1876 and was revived eighteen times before 1913. Between 1913 and 1919 another thirty-nine attempts were made to prohibit liquor in the United States through a constitutional amendment. Prohibition became a key element of the Progressive agenda as reformers linked alcohol and drunkenness to numerous social problems, including the corruption of immigrant voters. Whereas opponents of such an amendment argued that it was undemocratic, supporters claimed that their efforts had widespread public support. The admission of twelve "dry" western states to the Union in the early twentieth century and the spirit of sacrifice during World War I laid the groundwork for passage and ratification of the Eighteenth Amendment in 1919. Opponents added a time limit to the amendment in the hope that they could thereby block ratification, but this effort failed. (See also Amendment XXI.)

Amendment XIX [1920]

Section 1. The right of citizens of the United States to vote shall not be denied or abridged by the United States or by any State on account of sex.

Section 2. Congress shall have the power to enforce this article by appropriate legislation.

• • •

Advocates of women's rights tried and failed to link woman suffrage to the Fourteenth and Fifteenth Amendments. Nonetheless, the effort for woman suffrage continued. Between 1878 and 1912 at least one and sometimes as many as four proposed amendments were introduced in Congress each year to grant women the right to vote. Although over time women won very limited voting rights in some states, at both the state and federal levels opposition to an amendment for woman suffrage remained very strong. President Woodrow Wilson and other officials felt that the federal government should not interfere with the power of the states in this matter. And many people were concerned that giving women the vote would result in their abandoning traditional gender roles. In 1919, following a protracted and often bitter campaign of protest in which women went on hunger strikes and chained themselves to fences, an amendment was introduced with the backing of President Wilson. It narrowly passed the Senate (after efforts to limit the suffrage to white women failed) and was adopted in 1920 after Tennessee became the thirty-sixth state to ratify it.

Unratified Amendment

Child Labor Amendment (proposed by Congress June 2, 1924)

Section 1. The Congress shall have power to limit, regulate, and prohibit the labor of persons under eighteen years of age.

Section 2. The power of the several States is unimpaired by this article except that the operation of State laws shall be suspended to the extent necessary to give effect to legislation enacted by Congress.

• • •

Throughout the late nineteenth and early twentieth centuries, alarm over the condition of child workers grew. Opponents of child labor argued that children worked in dangerous and unhealthy conditions, that they took jobs from adult workers, that they depressed wages in certain industries, and that states that allowed child labor had an economic advantage over those that did not. Defenders of child labor claimed that children provided needed income in many families, that working at a young age helped to develop character, and that the effort to prohibit the practice constituted an invasion of family privacy.

In 1916 Congress passed a law that made it illegal to sell through interstate commerce goods made by children. The Supreme Court, however, ruled that the law violated the limits on the power of Congress to regulate interstate commerce. Congress then tried to penalize industries that used child labor by taxing such goods. This measure was also thrown out by the courts. In response, reformers set out to amend the Constitution. The proposed amendment was ratified by twenty-eight states, but by 1925 thirteen states had rejected it. Passage of the Fair Labor Standards Act in 1938, which was upheld by the Supreme Court in 1941, made the amendment irrelevant.

Amendment XX [1933]

Section 1. The terms of the President and Vice-President shall end at noon on the 20th day of January, and the terms of Senators and Representatives at noon on the 3rd day of January, of the years in which such terms would have ended if this article had not been ratified; and the terms of their successors shall then begin.

Section 2. The Congress shall assemble at least once in every year, and such meeting shall begin at noon on the 3rd day of January, unless they shall by law appoint a different day.

Section 3. If, at the time fixed for the beginning of the term of the President, the President-elect shall have died, the Vice-President-elect shall become President. If a President shall not have been chosen before the time fixed for the beginning of his term, or if the President-elect shall have failed to qualify, then the Vice-President-elect shall act as President until a President shall have qualified; and the Congress may by law provide for the case wherein neither a President-elect nor a Vice-President-elect shall have qualified, declaring who shall then act as President, or the manner in which one who is to act shall be selected, and such person shall act accordingly until a President or Vice-President shall have qualified.

Section 4. The Congress may by law provide for the case of the death of any of the persons from whom the House of Representatives may choose a President whenever the right of choice shall have devolved upon them, and for the case of the death of any of the persons from whom the Senate may choose a Vice-President whenever the right of choice shall have devolved upon them.

Section 5. Sections 1 and 2 shall take effect on the 15th day of October following the ratification of this article.

Section 6. This article shall be inoperative unless it shall have been ratified as an amendment to the Constitution by the Legislatures of three-fourths of the several States within seven years from the date of its submission.

• • •

Until 1933, presidents took office on March 4. Because elections are held in early November and electoral votes are counted in mid-December, this meant that more than three months passed between the time a new president was elected and when he took office. Moving the inauguration to January shortened the transition period and allowed Congress to begin its term closer to the time of the president's inauguration. Although this seems like a minor change, an amendment was required because the Constitution specifies terms of office. This amendment also deals with questions of succession in the event that a president- or vice-president-elect dies before assuming office. Section 3 also clarifies a method for resolving a deadlock in the electoral college.

Amendment XXI [1933]

Section 1. The eighteenth article of amendment to the Constitution of the United States is hereby repealed.

Section 2. The transportation or importation into any State, Territory, or Possession of the United States for delivery or use therein of intoxicating liquors, in violation of the laws thereof, is hereby prohibited.

Section 3. This article shall be inoperative unless it shall have been ratified as an amendment to the Constitution by conventions in the several States, as provided in the Constitution, within seven years from the date of the submission thereof to the States by the Congress.

• • •

Widespread violation of the Volstead Act, the law enacted to enforce prohibition, made the United States a nation of lawbreakers. Prohibition caused more problems than it solved by encouraging crime, bribery, and corruption. Further, a coalition of liquor and beer manufacturers, personal liberty advocates, and constitutional scholars joined forces to challenge the amendment. By 1929 thirty proposed repeal amendments had been introduced in Congress, and the Democratic Party made repeal part of its platform in the 1932 presidential campaign. The Twenty-first Amendment was proposed in February 1933 and ratified less than a year later. The failure of the effort to enforce prohibition through a constitutional amendment has often been cited by opponents of subsequent efforts to shape public virtue and private morality.

Amendment XXII [1951]

Section 1. No person shall be elected to the office of the President more than twice, and no person who has held the office of President, or acted as President, for more than two years of a term to which some other person was elected President shall be elected to the office of President more than once. But this article shall not apply to any person holding the office of President when this Article was proposed by the Congress, and shall not prevent any person who may be holding the office of President, or acting as President, during the term within which this Article becomes operative from holding the office of President or acting as President during the remainder of such term.

Section 2. This article shall be inoperative unless it shall have been ratified as an amendment to the Constitution by the legislatures of three-fourths of the several States within seven years from the date of its submission to the States by the Congress.

• • •

George Washington's refusal to seek a third term of office set a precedent that stood until 1912, when former president Theodore Roosevelt sought, without success, another term as an independent candidate. Democrat Franklin Roosevelt was the only president to seek and win a fourth term, though he did so amid great controversy. Roosevelt died in April 1945, a few months after the beginning of his fourth term. In 1946 Republicans won control of the House and the Senate, and early in 1947 a proposal for an amendment to limit future presidents to two four-year terms was offered to the states for ratification. Democratic critics of the Twenty-second Amendment charged that it was a partisan posthumous jab at Roosevelt.

Since the Twenty-second Amendment was adopted, two of the three presidents who might have been able to seek a third term, had it not existed, were Republicans Dwight Eisenhower and Ronald Reagan. Since 1826, Congress has entertained 160 proposed amendments to limit the president to one six-year term. Such amendments have been backed by fifteen presidents, including Gerald Ford and Jimmy Carter.

Amendment XXIII [1961]

Section 1. The District constituting the seat of Government of the United States shall appoint in such manner as the Congress may direct: A number of electors of President and Vice-President equal to the whole number of Senators and Representatives in Congress to which the District would be entitled if it were a State, but in no event more than the least populous State; they shall be in addition to those appointed by the States, but they shall be considered for the purposes of the election of President and Vice-President, to be electors appointed by a State; and they shall meet in the District and perform such duties as provided by the twelfth article of amendment.

Section 2. The Congress shall have the power to enforce this article by appropriate legislation.

• • •

When Washington, D.C., was established as a federal district, no one expected that a significant number of people would make it their permanent and primary residence. A proposal to allow citizens of the district to vote in presidential elections was approved by Congress in June 1960 and was ratified on March 29, 1961.

Amendment XXIV [1964]

Section 1. The right of citizens of the United States to vote in any primary or other election for President or Vice-President, for electors for President or Vice-President, or for Senator or Representative in Congress, shall not be denied or abridged by the United States or any State by reason of failure to pay any poll tax or other tax.

Section 2. The Congress shall have the power to enforce this article by appropriate legislation.

• • •

In the colonial and Revolutionary eras, financial independence was seen as necessary to political independence, and the poll tax was used as a requirement for voting. By the twentieth century, however, the poll tax was used mostly to bar poor people, especially southern blacks, from voting. Although conservatives complained that the amendment interfered with states' rights, liberals thought that the amendment did not go far enough because it barred the poll tax only in national elections and not in state or local elections. The amendment was ratified in 1964, however, and two years later the Supreme Court ruled that poll taxes in state and local elections also violated the equal protection clause of the Fourteenth Amendment.

Amendment XXV [1967]

Section 1. In case of the removal of the President from office or of his death or resignation, the Vice-President shall become President.

Section 2. Whenever there is a vacancy in the office of the Vice-President, the President shall nominate a Vice-President who shall take office upon confirmation by a majority vote of both Houses of Congress.

Section 3. Whenever the President transmits to the President pro tempore of the Senate and the Speaker of the House of Representatives his written declaration that he is unable to discharge the powers and duties of his office, and until he transmits to them a written declaration to the contrary, such powers and duties shall be discharged by the Vice-President as Acting President.

Section 4. Whenever the Vice-President and a majority of either the principal officers of the executive departments or of such other body as Congress may by law provide, transmit to the President pro tempore of the Senate and the Speaker of the House of Representatives their written declaration that the President is unable to discharge the powers and duties of his office, the Vice-President shall immediately assume the powers and duties of the office as Acting President.

Thereafter, when the President transmits to the President pro tempore of the Senate and the Speaker of the House of Representatives his written declaration that no inability exists, he shall resume the powers and duties of his office unless the Vice-President and a majority of either the principal officers of the executive department[s] or of such other body as Congress may by law provide, transmit within four days to the President pro tempore of the Senate and the Speaker of the House of Representatives their written declaration that the President is unable to discharge the powers and duties of his office. Thereupon Congress shall decide the issue, assembling within forty-eight hours for that purpose if not in session. If the Congress, within twenty-one days after receipt of the latter written declaration, or, if Congress is not in session, within twenty-one days after Congress is required to assemble, determines by two-thirds vote of both Houses that the President is unable to discharge the powers and duties of his office, the Vice-President shall continue to discharge the same as Acting President; otherwise, the President shall resume the powers and duties of his office.

• • •

The framers of the Constitution established the office of vice president because someone was needed to preside over the Senate. The first president to die in office was William Henry Harrison, in 1841. Vice President John Tyler had himself sworn in as president, setting a precedent that was followed when seven later presidents died in office. The assassination of President James A. Garfield in 1881 posed a new problem, however. After he was shot, the president was incapacitated for two months before he died; he was unable to lead the country, and his vice president, Chester A. Arthur, was unable to assume leadership. Efforts to resolve questions of succession in the event of a presidential disability thus began with the death of Garfield.

In 1963 the assassination of President John F. Kennedy galvanized Congress to action. Vice President Lyndon Johnson was a chain-smoker with a history of heart trouble. According to the 1947 Presidential Succession Act, the two men who stood in line to succeed him were the seventy-two-year-old Speaker of the House and the eighty-six-year-old president of the Senate. There were serious concerns that any of these men might become incapacitated while serving as chief executive. The first time the Twenty-fifth Amendment was used, however, was not in the case of presidential death or illness, but during the Watergate crisis. When Vice President Spiro T. Agnew was forced to resign following allegations of bribery and tax violations, President Richard M. Nixon appointed House Minority Leader Gerald R. Ford vice president. Ford became president following Nixon's resignation eight months later and named Nelson A. Rockefeller as his vice president. Thus, for more than two years, the two highest offices in the country were held by people who had not been elected to them.

Amendment XXVI [1971]

Section 1.   The right of citizens of the United States, who are eighteen years of age or older, to vote shall not be denied or abridged by the United States or by any State on account of age.

Section 2.   The Congress shall have power to enforce this article by appropriate legislation.

• • •

Efforts to lower the voting age from twenty-one to eighteen began during World War II. Recognizing that those who were old enough to fight a war should have some say in the government policies that involved them in the war, Presidents Eisenhower, Johnson, and Nixon endorsed the idea. In 1970 the combined pressure of the antiwar movement and the demographic pressure of the baby-boom generation led to a Voting Rights Act lowering the voting age in federal, state, and local elections.

In Oregon v. Mitchell (1970), the state of Oregon challenged the right of Congress to determine the age at which people could vote in state or local elections. The Supreme Court agreed with Oregon. Because the Voting Rights Act was ruled unconstitutional, the Constitution had to be amended to allow passage of a law that would lower the voting age. The amendment was ratified in a little more than three months, making it the most rapidly ratified amendment in U.S. history.

Unratified Amendment

Equal Rights Amendment (proposed by Congress March 22, 1972; seven-year deadline for ratification extended, June 30, 1982)

Section 1.   Equality of rights under the law shall not be denied or abridged by the United States or by any State on account of sex.

Section 2.   The Congress shall have the power to enforce, by appropriate legislation, the provisions of this article.

Section 3.   This amendment shall take effect two years after the date of ratification.

• • •

In 1923, soon after women had won the right to vote, Alice Paul, a leading activist in the woman suffrage movement, proposed an amendment requiring equal treatment of men and women. Opponents of the proposal argued that such an amendment would invalidate laws that protected women and would make women subject to the military draft. After the 1964 Civil Rights Act was adopted, protective workplace legislation was removed anyway.

The renewal of the women's movement, as a by-product of the civil rights and antiwar movements, led to a revival of the Equal Rights Amendment (ERA) in Congress. Disagreements over language held up congressional passage of the proposed amendment, but on March 22, 1972, the Senate approved the ERA by a vote of 84 to 8, and it was sent to the states. Six states ratified the amendment within two days, and by the middle of 1973 the amendment seemed well on its way to adoption, with thirty of the needed thirty-eight states having ratified it. In the mid-1970s, however, a powerful "Stop ERA" campaign developed. The campaign portrayed the ERA as a threat to "family values" and traditional relationships between men and women. Although thirty-five states ratified the ERA, five of those state legislatures voted to rescind ratification, and the amendment was never adopted.

Unratified Amendment

D.C. Statehood Amendment
(proposed by Congress August 22, 1978)

Section 1.   For purposes of representation in the Congress, election of the President and Vice President, and article V of this Constitution, the District constituting the seat of government of the United States shall be treated as though it were a State.

Section 2.   The exercise of the rights and powers conferred under this article shall be by the people of the District constituting the seat of government, and as shall be provided by Congress.

Section 3.   The twenty-third article of amendment to the Constitution of the United States is hereby repealed.

Section 4.   This article shall be inoperative, unless it shall have been ratified as an amendment to the Constitution by the legislatures of three-fourths of the several states within seven years from the date of its submission.

• • •

The 1961 ratification of the Twenty-third Amendment, giving residents of the District of Columbia the right to vote for a president and vice president, inspired an effort to give residents of the district full voting rights. In 1966 President Lyndon Johnson appointed a mayor and city council; in 1971 D.C. residents were allowed to name a nonvoting delegate to the House; and in 1981 residents were allowed to elect the mayor and city council. Congress retained the right to overrule laws that might affect commuters, the height of federal buildings, and selection of judges and prosecutors. The district's nonvoting delegate to Congress, Walter Fauntroy, lobbied fiercely for a congressional amendment granting statehood to the district. In 1978 a proposed amendment was approved and sent to the states. A number of states quickly ratified the amendment, but, like the ERA, the D.C. Statehood Amendment ran into trouble. Opponents argued that Section 2 created a separate category of "nominal" statehood. They argued that the federal district should be eliminated and that the territory should be reabsorbed into the state of Maryland. Most scholars believe that the fears of Republicans that the predominantly black population of the city would consistently elect Democratic senators constituted a major factor leading to the defeat of the amendment.

Amendment XXVII [1992]

No law varying the compensation for the services of the Senators and Representatives, shall take effect, until an election of Representatives shall have intervened.

• • •

Whereas the Twenty-sixth Amendment was the most rapidly ratified amendment in U.S. history, the Twenty-seventh Amendment had the longest journey to ratification. First proposed by James Madison in 1789 as part of the package that included the Bill of Rights, this amendment had been ratified by only six states by 1791. In 1873, however, it was ratified by Ohio to protest a massive retroactive salary increase by the federal government. Unlike later proposed amendments, this one came with no time limit on ratification. In the early 1980s Gregory D. Watson, a University of Texas economics major, discovered the "lost" amendment and began a single-handed campaign to get state legislators to introduce it for ratification. In 1983 it was accepted by Maine. In 1984 it passed the Colorado legislature. Ratifications trickled in slowly until May 1992, when Michigan and New Jersey became the thirty-eighth and thirty-ninth states, respectively, to ratify. This amendment prevents members of Congress from raising their own salaries without giving voters a chance to vote them out of office before they can benefit from the raises.

The American Nation

Admission of States into the Union

State	Date of Admission	State	Date of Admission	State	Date of Admission
1. Delaware	December 7, 1787	18. Louisiana	April 30, 1812	35. West Virginia	June 20, 1863
2. Pennsylvania	December 12, 1787	19. Indiana	December 11, 1816	36. Nevada	October 31, 1864
3. New Jersey	December 18, 1787	20. Mississippi	December 10, 1817	37. Nebraska	March 1, 1867
4. Georgia	January 2, 1788	21. Illinois	December 3, 1818	38. Colorado	August 1, 1876
5. Connecticut	January 9, 1788	22. Alabama	December 14, 1819	39. North Dakota	November 2, 1889
6. Massachusetts	February 6, 1788	23. Maine	March 15, 1820	40. South Dakota	November 2, 1889
7. Maryland	April 28, 1788	24. Missouri	August 10, 1821	41. Montana	November 8, 1889
8. South Carolina	May 23, 1788	25. Arkansas	June 15, 1836	42. Washington	November 11, 1889
9. New Hampshire	June 21, 1788	26. Michigan	January 26, 1837	43. Idaho	July 3, 1890
10. Virginia	June 25, 1788	27. Florida	March 3, 1845	44. Wyoming	July 10, 1890
11. New York	July 26, 1788	28. Texas	December 29, 1845	45. Utah	January 4, 1896
12. North Carolina	November 21, 1789	29. Iowa	December 28, 1846	46. Oklahoma	November 16, 1907
13. Rhode Island	May 29, 1790	30. Wisconsin	May 29, 1848	47. New Mexico	January 6, 1912
14. Vermont	March 4, 1791	31. California	September 9, 1850	48. Arizona	February 14, 1912
15. Kentucky	June 1, 1792	32. Minnesota	May 11, 1858	49. Alaska	January 3, 1959
16. Tennessee	June 1, 1796	33. Oregon	February 14, 1859	50. Hawaii	August 21, 1959
17. Ohio	March 1, 1803	34. Kansas	January 29, 1861		

Territorial Expansion

Territory	Date Acquired	Square Miles	How Acquired
Original states and territories	1783	888,685	Treaty of Paris
Louisiana Purchase	1803	827,192	Purchased from France
Florida	1819	72,003	Adams-Onís Treaty
Texas	1845	390,143	Annexation of independent country
Oregon	1846	285,580	Oregon Boundary Treaty
Mexican cession	1848	529,017	Treaty of Guadalupe Hidalgo
Gadsden Purchase	1853	29,640	Purchased from Mexico
Midway Islands	1867	2	Annexation of uninhabited islands
Alaska	1867	589,757	Purchased from Russia
Hawaii	1898	6,450	Annexation of independent country
Wake Island	1898	3	Annexation of uninhabited island
Puerto Rico	1899	3,435	Treaty of Paris
Guam	1899	212	Treaty of Paris
The Philippines	1899–1946	115,600	Treaty of Paris; granted independence
American Samoa	1900	76	Treaty with Germany and Great Britain
Panama Canal Zone	1904–1978	553	Hay–Bunau-Varilla Treaty
U.S. Virgin Islands	1917	133	Purchased from Denmark
Trust Territory of the Pacific Islands*	1947	717	United Nations Trusteeship

*A number of these islands have recently been granted independence: Federated States of Micronesia, 1990; Marshall Islands, 1991; Palau, 1994.

The American People:
A Demographic Survey

A Demographic Profile of the American People

Year	Life Expectancy from Birth		Average Age at First Marriage		Number of Children Under 5 (per 1,000 Women Aged 20–44)	Percentage of Women in Paid Employment	Percentage of Paid Workers Who Are Women
	White	Black	Men	Women			
1820					1,295	6.2	7.3
1830					1,145	6.4	7.4
1840					1,085	8.4	9.6
1850					923	10.1	10.8
1860					929	9.7	10.2
1870					839	13.7	14.8
1880					822	14.7	15.2
1890			26.1	22.0	716	18.2	17.0
1900	47.6	33.0	25.9	21.9	688	21.2	18.1
1910	50.3	35.6	25.1	21.6	643	24.8	20.0
1920	54.9	45.3	24.6	21.2	604	23.9	20.4
1930	61.4	48.1	24.3	21.3	511	24.4	21.9
1940	64.2	53.1	24.3	21.5	429	25.4	24.6
1950	69.1	60.8	22.8	20.3	589	29.1	27.8
1960	70.6	63.6	22.8	20.3	737	34.8	32.3
1970	71.7	65.3	22.5	20.6	530	43.3	38.0
1980	74.4	68.1	24.7	22.0	440	51.5	42.6
1990	76.2	71.4	26.1	23.9	377	57.4	45.2
1999	77.5	72.2	27.0	25.0	375	60.0	46.6

Source: Historical Statistics of the United States, Colonial Times to 1970 (1975); Statistical Abstract of the United States, 2001.

American Population

Year	Population	Percentage Increase	Year	Population	Percentage Increase
1610	350	—	1810	7,239,881	36.4
1620	2,300	557.1	1820	9,638,453	33.1
1630	4,600	100.0	1830	12,866,020	33.5
1640	26,600	478.3	1840	17,069,453	32.7
1650	50,400	90.8	1850	23,191,876	35.9
1660	75,100	49.0	1860	31,443,321	35.6
1670	111,900	49.0	1870	39,818,449	26.6
1680	151,500	35.4	1880	50,155,783	26.0
1690	210,400	38.9	1890	62,947,714	25.5
1700	250,900	19.2	1900	75,994,575	20.7
1710	331,700	32.2	1910	91,972,266	21.0
1720	466,200	40.5	1920	105,710,620	14.9
1730	629,400	35.0	1930	122,775,046	16.1
1740	905,600	43.9	1940	131,669,275	7.2
1750	1,170,800	29.3	1950	150,697,361	14.5
1760	1,593,600	36.1	1960	179,323,175	19.0
1770	2,148,100	34.8	1970	203,235,298	13.3
1780	2,780,400	29.4	1980	226,545,805	11.5
1790	3,929,214	41.3	1990	248,709,873	9.8
1800	5,308,483	35.1	2000	281,421,906	13.2

Note: These figures largely ignore the Native American population. Census takers never made any effort to count the Native American population that lived outside their political jurisdictions and compiled only casual and incomplete enumerations of those living within their jurisdictions until 1890. In that year the federal government attempted a full count of the Indian population: the Census found 125,719 Indians in 1890, compared with only 12,543 in 1870 and 33,985 in 1880.

Source: Historical Statistics of the United States, Colonial Times to 1970 (1975); Statistical Abstract of the United States, 2001.

White/Nonwhite Population

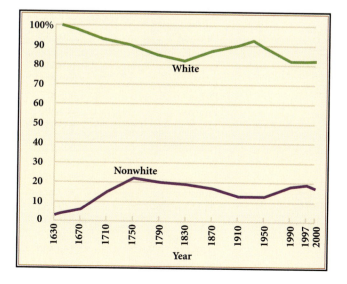

Urban/Rural Population

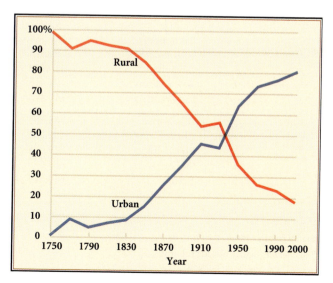

The Ten Largest Cities by Population, 1700–2000

		City	Population			City	Population
1700	1.	Boston	6,700		6.	Cleveland	560,663
	2.	New York	4,937*		7.	Baltimore	558,485
	3.	Philadelphia	4,400†		8.	Pittsburgh	533,905
1790	1.	Philadelphia	42,520		9.	Detroit	465,766
	2.	New York	33,131		10.	Buffalo	423,715
	3.	Boston	18,038	1930	1.	New York	6,930,446
	4.	Charleston, S.C.	16,359		2.	Chicago	3,376,438
	5.	Baltimore	13,503		3.	Philadelphia	1,950,961
	6.	Salem, Mass.	7,921		4.	Detroit	1,568,662
	7.	Newport, R.I.	6,716		5.	Los Angeles	1,238,048
	8.	Providence, R.I.	6,380		6.	Cleveland	900,429
	9.	Marblehead, Mass.	5,661		7.	St. Louis	821,960
	10.	Portsmouth, N.H.	4,720		8.	Baltimore	804,874
1830	1.	New York	197,112		9.	Boston	781,188
	2.	Philadelphia	161,410		10.	Pittsburgh	669,817
	3.	Baltimore	80,620	1950	1.	New York	7,891,957
	4.	Boston	61,392		2.	Chicago	3,620,962
	5.	Charleston, S.C.	30,289		3.	Philadelphia	2,071,605
	6.	New Orleans	29,737		4.	Los Angeles	1,970,358
	7.	Cincinnati	24,831		5.	Detroit	1,849,568
	8.	Albany, N.Y.	24,209		6.	Baltimore	949,708
	9.	Brooklyn, N.Y.	20,535		7.	Cleveland	914,808
	10.	Washington, D.C.	18,826		8.	St. Louis	856,796
1850	1.	New York	515,547		9.	Washington, D.C.	802,178
	2.	Philadelphia	340,045		10.	Boston	801,444
	3.	Baltimore	169,054	1970	1.	New York	7,895,563
	4.	Boston	136,881		2.	Chicago	3,369,357
	5.	New Orleans	116,375		3.	Los Angeles	2,811,801
	6.	Cincinnati	115,435		4.	Philadelphia	1,949,996
	7.	Brooklyn, N.Y.	96,838		5.	Detroit	1,514,063
	8.	St. Louis	77,860		6.	Houston	1,233,535
	9.	Albany, N.Y.	50,763		7.	Baltimore	905,787
	10.	Pittsburgh	46,601		8.	Dallas	844,401
1870	1.	New York	942,292		9.	Washington, D.C.	756,668
	2.	Philadelphia	674,022		10.	Cleveland	750,879
	3.	Brooklyn, N.Y.	419,921‡	1990	1.	New York	7,322,564
	4.	St. Louis	310,864		2.	Los Angeles	3,485,398
	5.	Chicago	298,977		3.	Chicago	2,783,726
	6.	Baltimore	267,354		4.	Houston	1,630,553
	7.	Boston	250,526		5.	Philadelphia	1,585,577
	8.	Cincinnati	216,239		6.	San Diego	1,110,549
	9.	New Orleans	191,418		7.	Detroit	1,027,974
	10.	San Francisco	149,473		8.	Dallas	1,006,877
1910	1.	New York	4,766,883		9.	Phoenix	983,403
	2.	Chicago	2,185,283		10.	San Antonio	935,933
	3.	Philadelphia	1,549,008	2000	1.	New York	8,008,278
	4.	St. Louis	687,029		2.	Los Angeles	3,694,820
	5.	Boston	670,585		3.	Chicago	2,896,016
					4.	Houston	1,953,631
					5.	Philadelphia	1,517,550
					6.	Phoenix	1,321,045
					7.	San Diego	1,223,400
					8.	Dallas	1,188,580
					9.	San Antonio	1,144,646
					10.	Detroit	951,270

*Figure from a census taken in 1698.

†Philadelphia figures include suburbs.

‡Annexed to New York in 1898.

Source: U.S. Census data.

Immigration by Decade

Year	Number	Percentage of Total Population	Year	Number	Percentage of Total Population
1821–1830	151,824	1.6	1921–1930	4,107,209	3.9
1831–1840	599,125	4.6	1931–1940	528,431	0.4
1841–1850	1,713,251	10.0	1941–1950	1,035,039	0.7
1851–1860	2,598,214	11.2	1951–1960	2,515,479	1.6
1861–1870	2,314,824	7.4	1961–1970	3,321,677	1.8
1871–1880	2,812,191	7.1	1971–1980	4,493,000	2.2
1881–1890	5,246,613	10.5	1981–1990	7,338,000	3.0
1891–1900	3,687,546	5.8	1991–2000	9,095,083	3.66
1901–1910	8,795,386	11.6	**Total**	**32,433,918**	
1911–1920	5,735,811	6.2			
Total	**33,654,785**		1821–2000 **GRAND TOTAL**	**66,088,703**	

Sources: U.S. Bureau of the Census, *Historical Statistics of the United States, Colonial Times to 1970* (1975), part 1,105–106; *Statistical Abstract of the United States, 2001.*

Regional Origins

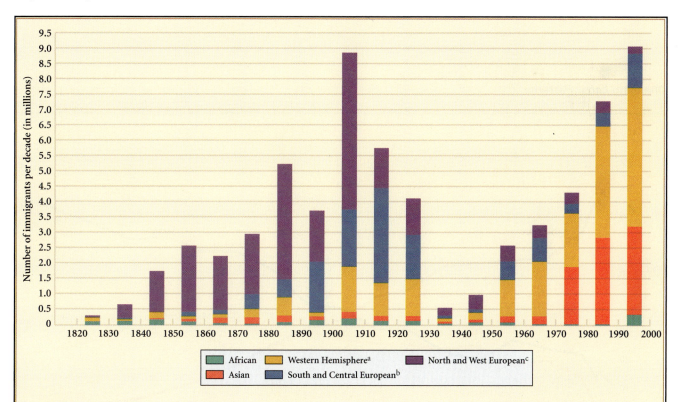

a Canada and all countries in South America and Central America.
b Italy, Spain, Portugal, Greece, Germany (Austria included, 1938–1945), Poland, Czechoslovakia (since 1920), Yugoslavia (since1920), Hungary (since 1861), Austria (since 1861, except 1938–1945), former USSR (excludes Asian USSR between 1931 and 1963), Latvia, Estonia, Lithuania, Finland, Romania, Bulgaria, Turkey (in Europe), and other European countries not classified elsewhere.
c Great Britain, Ireland, Norway, Sweden, Denmark, Iceland, Netherlands, Belgium, Luxembourg, Switzerland, France.
Source: Stephan Thernstrom, ed., *Harvard Encyclopedia of American Ethnic Groups* (1980), 480; U.S. Bureau of the Census, *Statistical Abstract of the United States, 1991;* U.S. Immigration and Naturalization Service, *Statistical Yearbook, 2000.*

The Labor Force (Thousands of Workers)

Year	Agriculture	Mining	Manufacturing	Construction	Trade	Other	Total
1810	1,950	11	75	—	—	294	2,330
1840	3,570	32	500	290	350	918	5,660
1850	4,520	102	1,200	410	530	1,488	8,250
1860	5,880	176	1,530	520	890	2,114	11,110
1870	6,790	180	2,470	780	1,310	1,400	12,930
1880	8,920	280	3,290	900	1,930	2,070	17,390
1890	9,960	440	4,390	1,510	2,960	4,060	23,320
1900	11,680	637	5,895	1,665	3,970	5,223	29,070
1910	11,770	1,068	8,332	1,949	5,320	9,041	37,480
1920	10,790	1,180	11,190	1,233	5,845	11,372	41,610
1930	10,560	1,009	9,884	1,988	8,122	17,267	48,830
1940	9,575	925	11,309	1,876	9,328	23,277	56,290
1950	7,870	901	15,648	3,029	12,152	25,870	65,470
1960	5,970	709	17,145	3,640	14,051	32,545	74,060
1970	3,463	516	20,746	4,818	15,008	34,127	78,678
1980	3,364	979	21,942	6,215	20,191	46,612	99,303
1990	3,223	724	21,346	7,764	24,622	60,849	118,793
1999	3,281	565	20,070	8,987	27,572	74,733	135,208

Source: Historical Statistics of the United States, Colonial Times to 1970 (1975), 139; Statistical Abstract of the United States, 1998, table 675.

Changing Labor Patterns

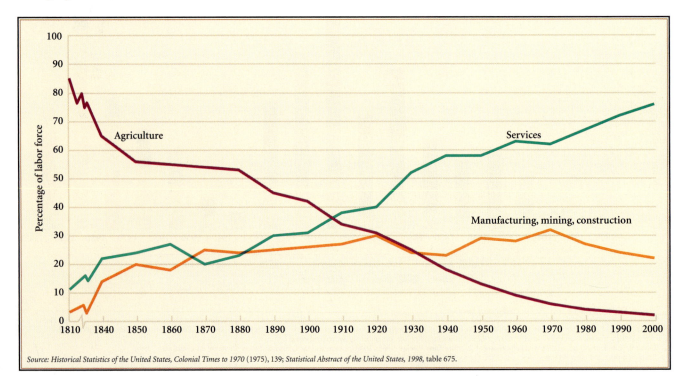

Source: Historical Statistics of the United States, Colonial Times to 1970 (1975), 139; Statistical Abstract of the United States, 1998, table 675.

Birth Rate, 1820–2000

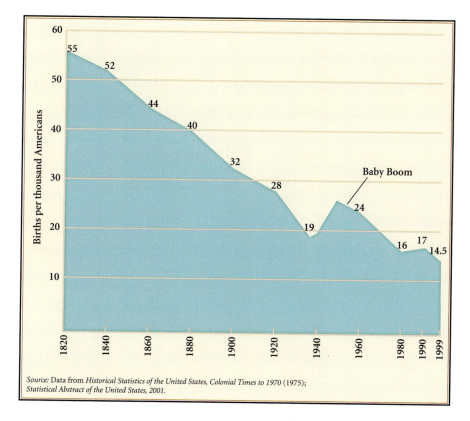

Source: Data from *Historical Statistics of the United States, Colonial Times to 1970* (1975); *Statistical Abstract of the United States, 2001.*

Death Rate, 1900–2000

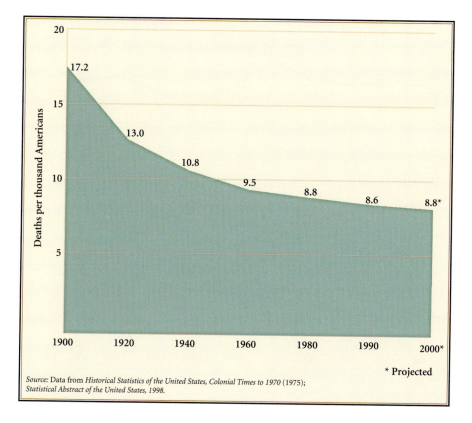

Source: Data from *Historical Statistics of the United States, Colonial Times to 1970* (1975); *Statistical Abstract of the United States, 1998.*

Life Expectancy (at birth), 1900–2000

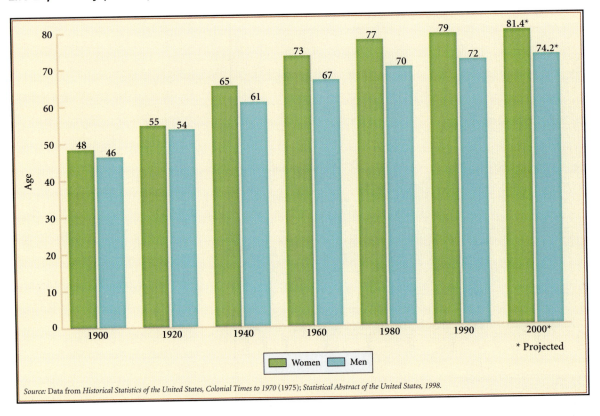

Source: Data from *Historical Statistics of the United States, Colonial Times to 1970* (1975); *Statistical Abstract of the United States, 1998.*

The Aging of the U.S. Population, 1850–1999

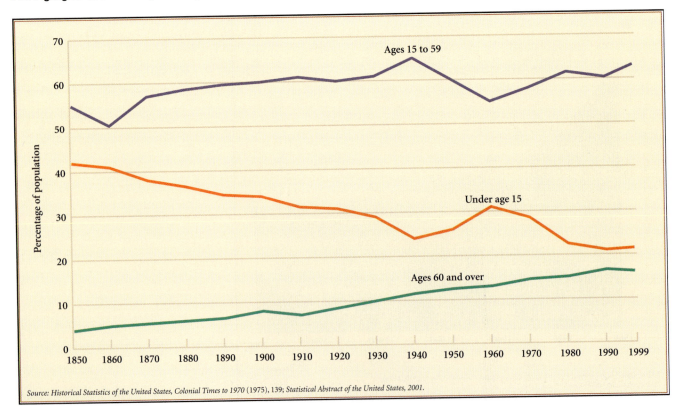

Source: Historical Statistics of the United States, Colonial Times to 1970 (1975), 139; *Statistical Abstract of the United States, 2001.*

The American Government and Economy

The Growth of the Federal Government

Year	Employees (millions)		Receipts and Outlays ($ millions)	
	Civilian	Military	Receipts	Outlays
1900	0.23	0.12	567	521
1910	0.38	0.13	676	694
1920	0.65	0.34	6,649	6,358
1930	0.61	0.25	4,058	3,320
1940	1.04	0.45	6,900	9,600
1950	1.96	1.46	40,900	43,100
1960	2.38	2.47	92,500	92,200
1970	3.00	3.06	193,700	196,600
1980	2.99	2.05	517,112	590,920
1990	3.13	2.07	1,031,321	1,252,705
2000	2.88	1.38	2,025,200	1,788,800

Source: Statistical Profile of the United States, 1900-1980; Statistical Abstract of the United States, 2001.

Gross Domestic Product, 1840–2000

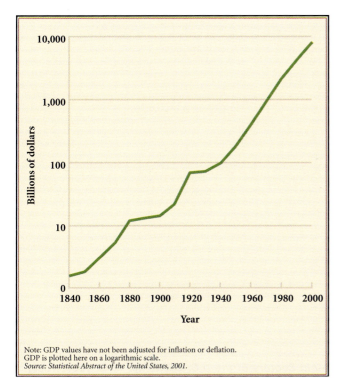

Note: GDP values have not been adjusted for inflation or deflation.
GDP is plotted here on a logarithmic scale.
Source: Statistical Abstract of the United States, 2001.

GDP per Capita, 1840–2000

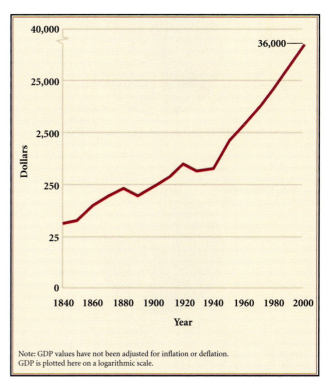

Note: GDP values have not been adjusted for inflation or deflation.
GDP is plotted here on a logarithmic scale.

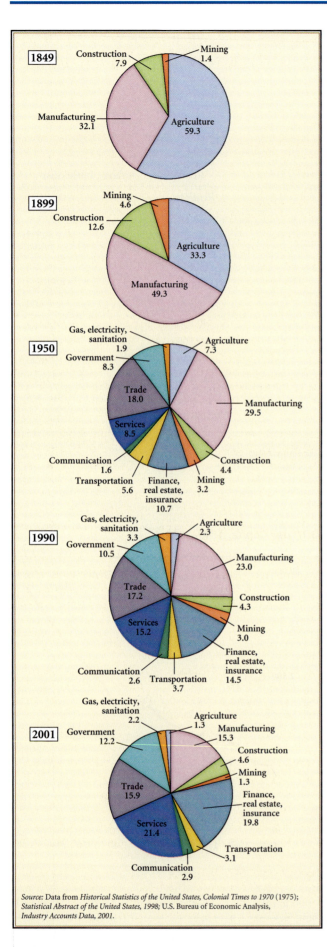

Source: Data from *Historical Statistics of the United States, Colonial Times to 1970* (1975); *Statistical Abstract of the United States, 1998*; U.S. Bureau of Economic Analysis, *Industry Accounts Data, 2001*.

◀ *Main Sectors of the U.S. Economy: 1849, 1899, 1950, 1990, and 2001*

Consumer Price Index

$100 in the year		is equivalent to		in 2001
	1790		$1,920	
	1800		1,400	
	1810		1,430	
	1820		1,500	
	1830		1,900	
	1840		2,030	
	1850		2,250	
	1860		2,110	
	1870		1,340	
	1880		1,720	
	1890		1,940	
	1900		2,090	
	1910		1,850	
	1920		882	
	1930		1,050	
	1940		1,260	
	1950		735	
	1960		598	
	1970		456	
	1980		215	
	1990		135	

This index provides a very rough guide to the purchasing power of $100 in various periods of American history. For example, in the early 1830s, day laborers earned about $1 a day or about $300 a year. This sum is the equivalent of about $5,700 a year in 2001 (3 × $1,900 = $5,700), or about one-half the gross income of a worker earning the federal government-designated minimum wage of $5.15 per hour.

Source: Samuel H. Williamson, "What Is the Relative Value?" Economic History Services, April 2002, <http://www.eh.net/ hmit/compare/>

affirmative action Government mandates beginning in the 1970s that unions, businesses, and educational institutions make a deliberate effort to achieve a better measure of racial and gender equality in their recruitment and hiring. While the civil rights movement had achieved significant legal and political victories, historic patterns of racial and gender discrimination proved difficult to overcome without the assistance of government.

alphabet soup agencies Nickname for the vast number of new federal agencies created by the New Deal that were usually referred to by their initial letters, for example, the AAA, CCC, NRA, and TVA.

America First Committee A committee organized by isolationists in 1940 to oppose American entrance into the war. The membership of the committee included senators, journalists, and publishers. Perhaps the most well-known member was Charles Lindbergh, the famous aviator.

American Lyceum A lecture circuit beginning in 1826 that sent ministers, transcendentalists, and scientists all across the north on speaking tours. The Lyceum movement helped to spread transcendentalism and reform ideas in the nineteenth century.

American System Federal government program to expand economic development through federally funded system of internal improvements (roads and canals), tariffs, and a national bank. Brainchild of Henry Clay and supported by John Quincy Adams in 1824.

anarchism Advocates the revolutionary creation of a stateless society. Anarchists' revolutionary views made them scapegoats for the 1886 Haymarket Square bombing.

Anglo-Saxonism A theory that the English, and by extension their American cousins, were successful because of racial superiority. Combined with Social Darwinism, this notion fueled American expansionism in the late nineteenth century.

Antifederalists Opponents of the Constitution who argued against the new plan of government proposed in 1787. Antifederalists believed that the Constitution would diminish the power of the states, create a new merchant based aristocracy, that republican institutions of government would not function in a territory as large as the United States, and that because the Constitution lacked a declaration of individual rights, personal liberty would be threatened.

appeasement Pacifying an enemy by making concessions. In the context of the coming of World War II, it refers specifically to the agreement reached at Munich in 1938 when England and France agreed to allow Hitler to annex the Sudetenland in exchange for his promise not to take more territory.

armistice The equivalent of a cease-fire during which peace negotiations take place. Signed on November 11, 1918, an armistice marked the effective end to World War I.

assumption In 1790 Alexander Hamilton wanted the federal government to take over the war debts of the states and the states' creditors. By doing so, the national government quickly increased its national debt while relieving the state governments of their debts.

bank holiday State or federal government closure of lending institutions to prevent their going broke; President Franklin Roosevelt's use of this euphemism during the Great Depression was an attempt to put a positive face on an unpleasant reality.

Benevolent Empire A broad-ranging campaign of moral and institutional reform inspired by evangelical Christian ideals and created by middle-class men and women in the 1820s. "Benevolence" became a seminal concept in American spiritual thinking during the Second Great Awakening. Promoters of benevolent reform suggested that people who had experienced saving grace should provide charity to the less fortunate.

bicameral A two-house assembly, usually a house of representatives and a senate, suggested by John Adams in his *Thoughts on Government* (1776). Different qualifications, procedures, term lengths, and means of election differentiate the two. Its existence ensures that each piece of legislation is reviewed and debated by two different groups.

bills of exchange Credit slips that British manufacturers, West Indian planters, and American merchants used to trade among themselves in the eighteenth century.

Black Codes After the Civil War, southern states passed these laws to keep African Americans in conditions close to slavery, forcing them back to the plantations and denying them civil rights.

blacklist Procedure used by employers to label and identify undesirable workers.

blitzkrieg Literally "lightning war," this expression describes the tactics followed by the Germans in 1939–1940 when they used massed armored and air forces to overrun Poland and the countries of Western Europe.

blue laws Term used to refer to the legal restriction of activity on Sundays. In the late nineteenth century, Sunday closings were encouraged by Protestants as part of their crusade to uphold social values, but considered by immigrant Catholics as a violation of their personal freedom.

Bolsheviks Russia's communist revolutionary party in the early twentieth century. Led by Lenin, they took Russia out of the war in early 1917, giving up huge territories to the Germans in the Treaty of Brest-Litovsk.

boomtowns Mid-to-late nineteenth-century frontier settlements created virtually overnight following the news of a gold strike. A high ratio of men to women and a transient population added to their rough-and-tumble atmosphere.

buffalo soldiers   The name Native Americans gave to African American U.S. cavalrymen, most of them Civil War veterans stationed in the West to fight the Indian wars of the 1870s and 1880s.

cabinet   George Washington organized bureaucratic departments to carry out the work of the executive branch and appointed secretaries to run those departments in 1788. These secretaries formed the cabinet, a small group of the president's closest advisors on matters of policy.

capital goods   Products used by manufacturers to add to the productive capacity of the economy, such as machinery. In the late nineteenth century, the dramatic increase in products used by businesses drove industrial expansion.

carpetbaggers   A derisive name given by Southerners to Northerners who moved to the South during Reconstruction to help develop the region's economic potential. Former Confederates despised these Northerners as transient exploiters. Carpetbaggers included former Union army officers and also educated professionals.

caucus   An informal meeting of politicians held by political parties to make majority decisions and enforce party discipline. First put into practice by Martin Van Buren in the early nineteenth century.

civic humanism   A concept that stressed service to the state and government in order to promote the good of the community. During the Renaissance, this idea of selfless service was thought to be critical in a republic where control was vested in a politically active and committed citizenry.

clan   A group of related families who share a common ancestor. In the sixteenth century many native peoples north of the Rio Grande organized their societies around these groups, which often combined to form tribes.

closed shop   Workplace in which one had to be a union member to gain employment. In the late nineteenth century, craft unions began using them to keep out incompetent and lower-wage workers.

closed-shop agreement   Labor agreement in which an employer agrees to hire only union members. Many employers viewed these agreements as illegal and worked to overturn them in the courts.

collective bargaining   A process of negotiation between labor unions and employers, particularly followed by the American Federation of Labor (AFL) in the late nineteenth century. Led by Samuel Gompers, the AFL accepted the new industrial order, but fought for a bigger share of the profits for the workers.

Columbian Exchange   The sixteenth-century transfer of the agricultural products of the Western Hemisphere—maize, tomatoes, potatoes, manioc—to the people of other continents, and the transfer of African and Eurasian crops and diseases to the Americas.

common law   Centuries-old body of English legal rules and procedures that protected the king's subjects against arbitrary acts by the government.

commutation   Fees allowed by both northern and southern governments to hire substitutes for the draft during the Civil War. In the North, Democrats and their immigrant supporters attacked the law for favoring the rich at their expense. In the South, poor southern yeomen complained that commutation made it "a rich man's war and a poor man's fight."

companionate marriage   Empowered by republican ideas, women in the early nineteenth century pressed for legal equality in matrimony. Even though husbands retained significant power as patriarchs, they increasingly viewed their wives as loving partners rather than as inferiors or dependents.

complex marriage   John Humphrey Noyes led his Oneida Community in this practice in the 1830s, based on the belief that all members of the community were wedded to one another. Noyes believed complex marriage was liberating for women.

conglomerate   The business structure created when firms in different industries are purchased and combined into a single large firm. One purpose of this process is to assure an overall profit even if one part of the firm operates at a loss.

conquistadors   Spanish "conquerors," veterans of the wars against the Muslims, who followed the first Spanish explorers to the Americas in the early sixteenth century. The Spanish crown offered them plunder, estates in the conquered territory, and titles in return for creating an empire.

Conscience Whigs   Term used to describe politicians who opposed the Mexican War in the 1840s on moral grounds, arguing that the purpose of the war was to acquire more land for the expansion of slavery. They believed that more slave states would destroy yeoman freeholder society and put slaveholders in charge of the federal government.

conservation   The process of protecting the natural environment for sustained use. As applied by Theodore Roosevelt at the start of the twentieth century, conservation protected public lands from development that was not in the public interest, in contrast to preservationists and later environmentalists, who sought to prevent almost all exploitation of wilderness land.

containment   American cold war policy designed to prevent Soviet expansionism, articulated most forcefully in 1946 by American diplomatic advisor George Kennan. For over forty years, American defense policy was guided by Kennan's argument that the Soviets would stop only when met with "unanswerable force."

contrabands   Term for the thousands of slaves who fled the plantations for protection behind Union lines during the Civil War. General Benjamin Butler refused to return them to their owners, and Congress regularized this policy in the First Confiscation Act, which authorized Union troops to seize all property, including slaves, used on behalf of the Confederacy.

convoy   In the face of threatening submarine warfare during World War I, U.S. and British merchant and troop ships traveled in large numbers bunched together and escorted by armed naval vessels. Organization in convoys greatly reduced the number of ships lost to the U-boats.

corporation   A business organization in which stockholders own the company and that has the ability to issue interest-bearing bonds to raise money. In the late nineteenth century, corporate charters allowed businesses of all sorts—especially the railroads—to raise large amounts of capital to finance expansion.

cost-plus provisions   Agreement between business and government in which industries were guaranteed a profit no matter what the cost of war production turned out to be; designed to enlist American industry in the World War II effort.

counterinsurgency A military operation using specially trained forces to defend against guerrilla warfare. The U.S. military created the Green Berets in the early 1960s to fight this type of nontraditional warfare, characteristic of the fighting in Vietnam.

Court (or Crown) Party The select group in eighteenth-century British Parliament that Robert Walpole favored in patronage appointments, leading to charges of corruption from the Whig Party.

covert interventions Secret undertakings by a country in pursuit of foreign policy goals, as evidenced by the Central Intelligence Agency, started in the 1950s, when operating in the interests of the United States. Knowledge of these acts, like U.S. participation in the overthrow of the government of Guatemala in 1954 and support for the Contras in Nicaragua in the 1980s, was kept from the American people and most members of Congress.

credibility gap Term referring to the wide discrepancy between what was actually happening in Vietnam and what the public was being told. With the war dragging on in the late 1960s, the credibility of the U.S. position was increasingly undermined as more factual details were made public.

cyberspace The information superhighway exists in this virtual world, the vast universe behind a computer screen. By 2000, 50 percent of all American households and 63 percent of public classrooms were connected to the Internet.

deficit spending High government spending based on the ideas of economist John Maynard Keynes, who proposed in the 1930s that governments should be prepared to go into debt to stimulate a stagnant economy.

deindustrialization A long period of decline in the industrial sector. In the 1970s American business reduced its investment in domestic production: capital was diverted to speculation, mergers and acquisitions, and foreign investment, resulting in massive unemployment and a decline in the labor movement.

deism A religious belief associated with the Enlightenment in which a rational, "watchmaker" God did not intervene directly in history or in people's lives. Deists like Benjamin Franklin rejected the authority of the Bible and relied on people's "natural reason" to define a moral code.

détente From a French word for a relaxation of tension, this term was used to signify the new foreign policy of President Nixon, which sought a reduction of tension and hostility between the United States and the Soviet Union and China in the early 1970s.

discount rate The interest level charged by the Federal Reserve for money it loans to member banks. Since its establishment in 1913, the Federal Reserve's ability to manipulate the discount rate has given the "Fed" a powerful influence in the U.S. economy.

division of labor The separation of tasks in a larger manufacturing process designed to improve efficiency and productivity but which also eroded the workers' control over the conditions of labor. The shoe factories in Lynn, Massachusetts, in the 1820s and 1830s are some of the first places where managers put this method of production into practice.

documentary impulse Desire to present real-life situations in such a way as to evoke an emotional response; creating a document such as a film or photograph intended to elicit an empathetic reaction from its audience. During the New Deal, the WPA arts projects were influenced by documentary impulse.

dole Expression referring to direct payment of relief to recipients during the Great Depression, suggesting recipients got relief money without having to perform work.

dollar-a-year men Leading businessmen called to Washington to help organize war mobilization at the beginning of World War II. Many of them stayed on the payrolls of their corporations and volunteered their services to the administration.

dollar diplomacy Term coined to describe the U.S. government's diplomatic initiatives to protect and enhance America's expanding business interests abroad in the early twentieth century.

domino effect President Eisenhower used this metaphor to illustrate what would happen if the United States allowed Vietnam to be united, most assuredly under Communist rule, in free elections in 1956 as called for in the Geneva Accords. Once one country in a region became Communist, others would topple under the Soviet Union's influence almost automatically. The metaphor was used to support an aggressive American foreign policy.

dower right A legal right originating in medieval Europe and carried to the American colonies that extended to a woman following the death of her husband the use of one-third of the family's land and goods during her lifetime.

downsizing The deliberate laying off of permanent employees to cut company costs and raise profits. In the 1980s and 1990s the downsizing trend spread to middle management.

electoral college As set forth in the Constitution, the president was to be elected indirectly. A group of electors, chosen state by state, were appointed each election year, to vote for the president and vice president according to the majority of popular votes cast. This was done to give individual states a greater role in the choosing of a president.

electronic mail (e-mail) This electronic message system operating on the Internet gives individuals the ability to communicate directly with each other through cyberspace.

eminent domain Under the law, this principle gives a government control of all property within its sovereign jurisdiction, and grants it the power to take and use property for public purposes provided that compensation is given to the owners. In the early nineteenth century, states granted this power to private corporations so that, like the states themselves, they could seize property for public use—for example, to build roads, bridges, and canals.

enclosure acts The laws passed in England in the sixteenth century that gave landowners the right to fence open land for their sheep to graze. This prevented peasants from sharing and farming what traditionally had been open lands and dispossessed many of England's poor.

encomenderos Privileged Spanish landholders in America with land grants from the king. In the sixteenth century they collected tribute from the resident Native American population, both in goods and through forced labor.

encomiendas   Land grants in America from the king given to privileged Spanish landholders in the sixteenth century. The *encomiendas* gave the landholders legal control over the native population in the New World.

Ethiopian Regiment   Loyalist military unit that consisted of 1,000 escaped slaves, organized by Virginia's royal governor in the 1770s. This action, coupled with the governor's proclamation offering freedom to any slave who joined the Loyalist cause, pushed Virginia slaveholders to support the Patriot cause.

ethnic cleansing   The practice of entering a populated area during a time of civil strife and killing or driving away a significant portion of the population based on their ethnicity. The term was first used by Serbs seeking to seize territory from Muslims and Croats in the former Yugoslav provinces of Croatia and Bosnia.

excess-profits tax   This levy on corporate profits and the wealthiest individuals during World War I accounted for more than half of all federal taxes, and was a new source of federal government revenue.

excise levies   Taxes imposed on goods such as salt, beer, and distilled spirits in late eighteenth-century Britain. These taxes passed on the cost of imperial management to the king's subjects.

Exodusters   Term used to describe the thousands of African Americans who migrated to Kansas in the spring of 1879 to escape from the post-Reconstruction violence of the South. By 1880, 40,000 blacks lived in Kansas.

faction   A small political group or alliance organized around a single issue or person. Factions often become the basis for political parties. In the eighteenth century, many considered factions dangerous because they were thought to undermine the stability of a community or nation.

factory   Manufacturing businesses first created in the late eighteenth century that concentrated all the aspects of production under one roof, reorganized production, and divided work into specialized tasks. Factories made production faster and more efficient, while narrowing the range of worker activities and skills.

fascism   Right-wing antidemocratic movements that began in Europe after World War I, characterized by strong dictators backed by the military. The dictatorships of Benito Mussolini in Italy, Adolph Hitler in Germany, and Francisco Franco in Spain represent three fascist states.

Federalists   Supporters of the Constitution of 1787, who called for a strong central government. The core of the Federalist argument appeared in the *Federalist*, a collection of writings by James Madison, Alexander Hamilton, and John Jay, published in New York newspapers in support of ratification. In answer to Antifederalist critics, Federalists argued that a strong central government would preserve rather than corrupt liberty and was especially necessary to conduct foreign affairs.

fee-simple   The legal status of land titles in seventeenth-century Puritan society. This term meant that landowners possessed their land outright, free from manorial obligations or feudal dues.

feminine mystique   The title of Betty Friedan's influential 1963 book, this expression refers to the ideal whereby women were encouraged to confine themselves to roles within the domestic sphere. The feminist movements of recent years emerged in reaction to this ideology.

feminism (feminists)   This theory developed in the early twentieth century among female activists who believed that women should be equal to men in all areas of life. Many women activists had accepted the notion of separate spheres for men and women, but feminists sought to overcome all barriers to equality.

fire-eaters   Southern politicians who sought secession. They organized secession conventions in several southern states in 1850 but backed away because of a lack of support and the promise of moderate southern backing for secession if Congress tried to outlaw slavery in the future.

fireside chat   President Franklin Roosevelt's regularly scheduled talks with the public in the 1930s and 1940s; the name suggested an intimate conversation and demonstrated the president's effective use of the new electronic political medium of radio.

flapper   A young woman of the 1920s who defied conventional standards of conduct. She wore short skirts and makeup, danced to jazz, and flaunted her liberated lifestyle. The flapper was a cultural icon of the era, but actually represented only a small minority of women.

flexible response   Strategy adopted by the Kennedy administration in the early 1960s that called for a military establishment that had to be prepared to fight any foe, large or small, conventional- or nuclear-armed, which was seen as a threat to American interests.

Fourteen Points   President Wilson proposed these as a basis for peace negotiations at Versailles in 1919. Among them were open diplomacy, freedom of the seas, free trade, territorial integrity, arms reduction, national self-determination, and the League of Nations.

franchise   The right to vote. Extended to all adult white males in the early nineteenth century by most new states and most older states as well.

freedom rides   A form of civil rights protest for which the Congress of Racial Equality (CORE) organized racially mixed groups to travel by bus through the South in 1961 to test compliance with federal laws banning racial segregation on interstate transportation. These activists were subjected to violence in several southern cities and drew the Kennedy administration further into the struggle for equal rights.

freehold   Ownership of a plot of land and possession of the title or deed. Freeholders have the legal right to improve, transfer, or sell their property. This type of landholding characterized New England in the seventeenth and eighteenth centuries, as its founders attempted to avoid the concentration of land in the hands of an elite—an undesirable characteristic of the England that they had left.

free soil   Term describing the belief that slavery should be kept out of the territories because it threatened republican institutions and yeoman farming. In the 1840s, the short-lived Free Soil Party's slogan stated "free soil, free labor, free men."

Fundamentalists (Fundamentalism)   Conservative Protestants who believe in a literal interpretation of the Bible. In the 1920s, Fundamentalists opposed modernist Protestants, who tried to reconcile Christianity with Darwin's theory of evolution and recent technological and scientific discoveries, and instigated the famous Scopes trial of 1925.

gag rule   Procedure in the House of Representatives from 1836–1844 by which antislavery petitions were automatically tabled when they were received, so that they could not become the subject of debate in the House.

gentry   A class of English men and women who were substantial landholders but lacked the social privileges and titles of nobility that marked the aristocracy. During the Price Revolution of the sixteenth century, the wealth and status of the gentry rose while that of the aristocracy declined.

ghetto   Term describing an urban neighborhood composed of the poor, and occasionally used to describe any tight-knit community containing a single ethnic or class group. Ghettos came into being in the nineteenth century, in tandem with the enormous influx of immigrants to American cities.

Ghost Dance   A religious movement that swept the Plains Indians in 1890. It stemmed from the preaching of the Paiute prophet Wovoka who claimed that the whites would disappear from the Great Plains and that Indians would reclaim their lands.

Gibson girl   Image of the "new woman" created during the 1890s, which represented a stronger, more independent vision of women, as well as a more sexual one.

glasnost and *perestroika*   Policies introduced by Soviet president Mikhail Gorbachev during the 1980s that referred to openness and economic restructuring, respectively. Gorbachev's policies contributed to the freeing of Eastern Europe from Soviet domination and led, unintentionally, to the breakup of the Soviet Union.

Great American Desert   The name given to the drought-stricken Great Plains by Euro-Americans in the early nineteenth century. Believing the region was unfit for cultivation or agriculture, Congress designated the Great Plains as permanent Indian country in 1834.

greenbacks   First issued by the Union during the Civil War to finance the war effort, greenbacks became a general term to describe any paper currency issued by the federal government as legal tender. The value of greenbacks is supported by the good faith of the government rather than specie: gold or silver.

habeas corpus   Constitutional right that protects citizens against arbitrary arrest and detention. During the Civil War, Lincoln suspended *habeas corpus* to stop protests against the draft and other disloyal activities. Lincoln also transferred cases of disloyalty from civilian to military jurisdiction, fearing that local juries would have been lenient toward Confederate sympathizers.

headright   A program begun by the Virginia Company in 1617 that granted the head of a household 50 acres for himself and 50 additional acres for every adult family member or servant brought into the Virginia colony.

hegemony   Dominance in global affairs by a nation. The United States and Soviet Union emerged from World War II as the world's leading powers, each exercising a tremendous influence within their respective spheres of influence.

heresies   Religious doctrines inconsistent with the teaching of an established, official Christian church. Some of the Crusades between 1096 and 1291 stand as examples of Christians attempting to crush groups spreading these "unauthorized" doctrines.

hippie   Young person who participated in the 1960s counterculture, a lifestyle in which drug use, rock music, uninhibited sexuality, and vivid self-expression were celebrated.

home rule   White southern Democrats referred to their desire to overthrow legitimately elected Reconstruction governments and replace them with white supremacy with this euphemism. By 1876, both national parties favored home rule.

homespun   Yarn and cloth produced by American women. During political boycotts in the 1760s it allowed the colonies to escape dependence on British textile manufactures and creating a space for women to make a unique contribution to the colonial resistance.

honest graft   This notion, described by George Washington Plunkitt of Tammany Hall in the 1890s, indicates one aspect of machine politics. It refers to the financial advantages of insider information in the awarding of city contracts.

household mode of production   System of exchanging goods and labor that helped eighteenth-century New England freeholders survive on ever-shrinking farms as available land became more scarce.

impeachment   First step in the constitutional process for removing the president from office in which charges of wrongdoing (articles of impeachment) are passed by the House of Representatives and then judged in a trial conducted by the Senate.

imperial presidency   Historian Arthur M. Schlesinger Jr. used this phrase to describe the growth of executive power, which up to that time reached its highest point in President Nixon's attempts in 1972 to subvert the constitutional restraints on his authority.

impoundment   President Nixon hoped to slow the growth of the federal government and reduce funding for programs he opposed by refusing to spend money appropriated by the Democratic-controlled Congress for urban renewal and pollution control in the early 1970s.

impressment   Forcible, unwilling draft into military service. The British navy forced American merchant sailors into service in the years preceding the War of 1812, greatly increasing tensions between the two nations.

indenture   A seventeenth-century labor contract that promised service for a period of time in return for passage to North America. Indentures were typically for a term of four or five years, provided room and board in exchange for labor, and granted free status at the successful completion of the contract period.

individualism   Term coined by Alexis de Tocqueville in 1835 that described Americans as people no longer bound by social attachments to classes, castes, associations, and families. Some observers worried that this was a cause of social disorder; others saw it as liberating.

indulgences   Catholic Church certificates pardoning a sinner from punishments in the afterlife. In his *Ninety-Five Theses*, written in 1517, Martin Luther condemned the sale of indulgences, a common practice among Catholic clergy.

industrial union   A group of workers in a single industry (for example, automobile, railroad, or mining) organized into a single association, regardless of skill, rather than into separate craft-based associations. The American Railway

Union, formed in the 1880s, was one of the first industrial unions in the nation.

inmates New class of the poor in the eighteenth century, made up of Scots-Irish single men or families who possessed little property and existed as tenants or day laborers with little hope of earning economic independence.

Internet A vast network of communication technology made possible by the computer revolution and supporting tools like e-mail and the World Wide Web that became increasingly popular in the 1990s.

isolationism Supporting the withdrawal of the United States from involvement with nations beyond its borders, especially avoidance of entangling diplomatic relations. The common view of post–World War I U.S. foreign policy is one of isolationism, when in fact the United States played an active role in world affairs, especially in trade and finance.

Jim Crow The system of racial segregation in the South that was created in the late nineteenth century following the end of slavery. Jim Crow laws written in the 1880s and 1890s mandated segregation in public facilities.

jingoism This term came to refer to superpatriotism in the late nineteenth and early twentieth centuries that favored a military solution to all international disputes.

joint-stock company A financial arrangement established by the British to facilitate the colonization of the New World in the seventeenth century. These agreements allowed merchants to band together as stockholders, raising large amounts of money while sharing the risks and profits in proportion to their part of the total investment.

judicial review The right of the courts to judge the constitutionality of laws passed by Congress and the state legislatures. This power is implicit within the federal Constitution and was first practiced by the Supreme Court in *Marbury v. Madison* in 1803.

kamikaze Aerial Japanese suicide attacks during World War II in which pilots crashed their planes into U.S. ships in a last-ditch effort to destroy the American naval forces. This tactic became more common as the war in the Pacific turned more desperate for Japan.

King Cotton In the 1860s, many Confederates believed that cotton would not only provide enough money to fight the war, but the potential threat to supplies would convince the British, whose textile industry was dependent on southern cotton, to recognize the South as an independent nation.

labor theory of value The belief that the price of a product should reflect the work that went into making it and should be paid mostly to the person who produced it. This idea was popularized by the National Trades' Union in the mid-nineteenth century.

laissez-faire Doctrine characterized by the belief that the less government does, the better. This was the philosophy of American government in the late nineteenth century and the guiding light of "conservative" politics in the twentieth. In 1980, Republican Party candidate Ronald Reagan ran for the presidency under the slogan, "The government is the problem, not the solution."

lien (crop lien) Southern redemption governments passed laws in the late nineteenth century allowing furnishing merchants to assume ownership, or lien, of a borrower's (usually sharecroppers) crops as collateral for loans of seed, tools, and fertilizer. This system trapped farmers in a cycle of debt and prevented economic diversification away from the increasingly unprofitable cotton-based agriculture.

limited liability A contractual clause that ensures that the personal assets of shareholders cannot be seized to cover the debts of a corporation. By 1800, state governments had granted more than three hundred corporate charters, many of which included limited liability.

Long Drive The moving of wild longhorn cattle hundreds of miles from Texas to the railheads of Kansas, where they could be shipped to eastern markets. This seemingly colorful event was actually a makeshift means of bridging a gap in the developing transportation system, and was abandoned when the railroads reached the Texas range country during the 1870s.

los pobres Literally, "the poor ones"; Hispanic residents of New Mexico who were displaced when Anglo ranchers fenced communal lands. They organized themselves as masked raiders and in 1889 and 1890 mounted an effective campaign of harassment against the interloping ranchers.

machine tools Machines that are used to produce other machines with standardized parts at a low cost. The development of machine tools by American inventors in the early nineteenth century facilitated the rapid spread of the Industrial Revolution.

MAD (Mutually Assured Destruction) policy This U.S. nuclear policy, purportedly a theory of nuclear deterrence, called for a massive and unstoppable nuclear response if the Soviet Union were to launch an attack on the United States in the 1950s. This program of nuclear reciprocation would result in the total annihilation of both countries.

managed competition This idea was the heart of the failed Clinton health-care-reform initiative in the early 1990s. This policy would have depended on market forces rather than government controls to reduce the cost of health insurance and medical care.

Manifest Destiny Term coined by John L. O'Sullivan in 1845, based on an American sense of cultural and racial superiority. It describes the idea that Americans were fated by Providence to develop the continent from the Atlantic to the Pacific and bring "inferior" peoples under American dominion.

manumission The act of a master liberating a slave. In 1782 the Virginia assembly passed an act allowing manumission; within a decade planters had freed 10,000 slaves.

margin buying The purchase of stocks or securities with a small down payment while financing the rest with a broker loan. When stock prices started to fall in 1929, brokers requested repayment of the loans and the funds were often not forthcoming, leading to the crash of the stock market in October of that year.

Market Revolution The combined impact of the rapidly increased production of goods and the development of a transportation network to distribute them. In the early nineteenth century this led to the growth of urban production and distribution centers, western migration, and the construction of a variety of transportation methods including canals, roads, steamboats, and railroads.

marriage portion Parcel of land, livestock, farm equipment, or household goods that eighteenth-century New England parents gave to their children as a marriage gift to help them start life on their own. Parents expected children to repay this gift by caring for them in their old age.

mass production In contrast to custom or handwork, this industrial process was designed to produce a great number of identical items to be sold to the public on a large scale. In the late nineteenth century most factories came to use the assembly line to maintain high volume.

mechanics Class of skilled craftsmen and inventors who built and improved machinery and developed machine tools for industry in the nineteenth century. They developed a professional identity and established institutes to spread their skills and knowledge.

mercantilism A set of policies that regulated colonial commerce and manufacturing for the enrichment of the mother country. These policies insured that the American colonies in the mid-seventeenth century produced agricultural goods and raw materials, which would then be carried to Britain, where they would be reexported or made into finished goods.

mercenary A soldier for hire; one who cares nothing for the principles or values behind the war, but will fight for either side for money. Thousands of German mercenaries joined the British troops during the Revolutionary War in 1776.

mestizo A person of mixed blood, the offspring of intermarriage or sexual liaison between white Europeans and native people, usually a white man and an Indian woman. In sixteenth-century Mesoamerica, nearly 90 percent of the Spanish settlers were men who took Indian women as wives or mistresses; the result was a substantial mixed-race population.

Middle Passage The brutal sea voyage from Africa to the Americas in the eighteenth and nineteenth centuries in which nearly a million Africans lost their lives.

military-industrial complex Term used to describe the close relationship of military spending and defense contractors that emerged during World War II and grew with the cold war. In the 1950s and 1960s, federal defense spending came to have a tremendous influence on the national economy, particularly in the South and West where many defense contractors were located. In his farewell address in 1961, President Eisenhower raised troubling questions about the influence of this new power in a democracy and warned the nation to be vigilant.

Minutemen In the 1770s colonists organized into voluntary militia units that would be ready to face British troops in a battle on short notice. These soldiers formed the core of the citizen army that met the British at Lexington.

misery index Derived by adding the national unemployment rate and the average annual rate of inflation, the misery index first appeared in the 1970s to measure economic suffering. It reappeared during the 1996 election to underscore a healthy economy. The rate at that time was the lowest it had been in twenty-seven years.

mixed government John Adams's 1776 plan called for three branches of government, each representing one function: executive, legislative, and judicial. This system of dispersed authority was devised to maintain a balance of power and ensure the legitimacy of governmental procedures.

modernist movement (modernism) A literary and artistic style and movement in the 1920s that broke sharply with past traditions and was marked by skepticism and stylistic experimentation. Modernist writers included Gertrude Stein, T. S. Eliot, and F. Scott Fitzgerald.

muckrakers These journalists in the early twentieth century were crusaders who exposed the corruption of big business and government. Theodore Roosevelt gave them the name as a term of reproach. The term comes from a character in *Pilgrim's Progress*, a religious allegory by John Bunyan.

multiculturalism The policy of promoting diversity—gender, race, ethnicity, and sexual preference.

national debt First created in the late eighteenth century by borrowing money from the wealthy through the sale of bonds. Alexander Hamilton believed that drawing on this source of capital to finance government would create ties of loyalty between the government and the business community.

nativism Antiforeign sentiment in the United States that fueled a drive against immigration. In the 1920s, many native-born white Protestants reacted with bitter animosity to the more than 23 million immigrants who had come to America during the previous forty years.

New Freedom President Woodrow Wilson's domestic agenda that called for a limitation of the abuses of economic power by large corporations. Wilson's program differed from Teddy Roosevelt's "New Nationalism" in that it sought to revive competition rather than regulate large corporations.

New Frontier President John F. Kennedy's activist program "to get America moving again" after the Eisenhower administration of the 1950s. In his inaugural speech, Kennedy called for vigorous activism at home and abroad. Although his legislative achievements were limited, Kennedy's example proved inspirational, particularly to the young.

New Left Radical students of the 1960s and 1970s adopted this term to refer to their activist movement, distinguishing themselves from the "Old Left"—the communists and socialists of the 1930s and 1940s. They turned to grassroots organizing in cities and college campuses in their protest against the status quo and what they saw as the accommodationist stance of older generations.

New Nationalism Theodore Roosevelt's program for reform and the cause of social justice, first articulated in 1910 after he left the presidency. Roosevelt called for a strong central government concerned with the interests of the common person.

New Negro Term taken from the title of an anthology of writings from the Harlem Renaissance, edited by Alain Locke; the expression was used to describe the artists and intellectuals of Black America who came to prominence in the 1920s.

new politics The shift in political campaigning from issues-based to image-based strategies. Mass media played a major role in this transformation during the election of 1960.

New Right Conservative political movement that achieved considerable success beginning in the 1970s, helping to elect Ronald Reagan president in 1980 and enabling the Republican Party to retake both houses of Congress in the 1994 elections. Riding the support of evangelical Christians and organizations like Jerry Falwell's Moral Majority, New Right activists mobilized thousands of followers and millions of dollars to combat federal activism and declining social morality.

Niagara Movement   Brought together in 1906 by the black activists William Monroe Trotter and W. E. B. Du Bois, this organization defined the agenda for the racial struggle in the early twentieth century.

nickelodeon   In the early days of the film industry, the late 1890s, this was the most common movie spot: a working-class theater with a five-cent admission charge.

nullification   Idea supported by many southerners starting in the 1820s that a state convention could declare unconstitutional any federal law. John C. Calhoun based this concept on the earlier writings of Jefferson and Madison as published in the Virginia and Kentucky resolutions.

oligopolies   Situations in which a few large corporations control an industry. This became the norm in the 1920s.

Open-Door Notes   Sent by U.S. Secretary of State John Hay to Japan, Russia, Germany, and France in 1899, this policy claimed the right of equal trade for all nations that wanted to do business in China. Because it lacked colonial possessions in China, free trade was crucial to the United States to gain access to China's large markets.

outwork   A system of manufacturing, also known as "putting out," used in the English woolen industry. Merchants in the sixteenth and seventeenth centuries bought wool and provided it to landless peasants, who spun and wove it into cloth, which the merchants in turn sold in English and foreign markets.

Pan-Americanism   In the abstract, this phrase suggests a belief in a community of all Western Hemisphere nations, north and south. In practical terms, it encompassed early twentieth-century theories that ranged from a political confederation to international arbitration.

party (party system)   An organized political body with specific ideologies or interests, established with the goal of organizing the electorate and directing the policies of a government. While not part of the Constitution, competitive political parties appeared quickly in the United States during the election of 1796.

patronage   The power of elected officials to grant government jobs to party members to create and maintain strong party loyalties. In the United States, patronage was first used extensively by Martin Van Buren in early nineteenth-century New York.

peaceful coercion   Thomas Jefferson's strategy designed to force the British and the French to accept the American definition of neutral rights by forbidding American trade with Europe. The centerpiece of this flawed policy was the Embargo Act of 1807.

peaceful coexistence   Premier Khrushchev of the Soviet Union used this term in 1956 to call for diminished tensions between capitalist and communist nations in the cold war. As a sign of the reduced hostility, Khrushchev and Vice President Nixon exchanged official visits.

peasant   A farm laborer who often worked land held by a landlord. In 1450 Europe, these laborers sometimes owned or leased a small plot in the town and worked collectively with other village laborers on the landlord's land.

peonage (debt peonage)   As cotton prices declined during the 1870s, many sharecroppers fell into permanent debt. Merchants often conspired with landowners to make the debt a pretext for forced labor, or peonage.

perfectionism   The religious belief that people could be without flaws, or free from sin, because the Second Coming of Christ had already occurred. This evangelical movement attracted thousands of followers during the 1830s.

personal-liberty laws   Laws passed by northern legislatures in the 1850s to challenge the federal Fugitive Slave Act and extend legal rights to escaped slaves.

phalanxes   Cooperative work groups in the 1840s organized as part of the Fourierist movement in which all members were shareholders in a community as an alternative to capitalist wage labor.

pietism   A European spiritual outlook emphasizing devout behavior and an emotional effort to achieve a personal, mystical union with God that reached America in the mid-eighteenth century. Unlike Puritans and most other Protestants, adherents avoided debates over theological dogma or doctrine.

pocket veto   Presidential way to kill a piece of legislation without issuing a formal veto. When congressional Republicans passed the Wade-Davis Bill in 1864, a harsher alternative to President Lincoln's restoration plan, Lincoln used this method to kill it by simply not signing the bill and letting it expire after Congress adjourned.

police action   A military action, undertaken without a formal declaration of war, by regular armed forces against perceived violators of international peace. This term was applied to the participation of U.N. authorized troops in the Korean War against communist North Korea.

political machine   Nineteenth-century term for a highly organized political party, which was often compared to new technological innovations because of its efficiency and complexity.

politics of resentment   The various social reform movements of the 1960s and 1970s aroused animosity on the part of those who felt change had gone too far, spurring a grassroots conservative backlash against social reform, special-interest groups, and governmental activism.

poll tax   Legal device used throughout the South beginning during Reconstruction to prevent freedmen from voting. Nationally, the northern states used poll taxes to keep immigrants and others deemed unworthy from the polls.

polygamy   The practice of a man having multiple wives. Adopted by some Mormons in the 1840s and practiced until outlawed in 1890 under pressure from the federal government.

popular sovereignty   Michigan senator and Democratic presidential candidate Lewis Cass introduced this solution to the problem of slavery in the territories in 1848 by proposing that territorial residents should have the right to determine the status of slavery locally. This policy alienated free-soil Democrats, but it was later adopted by Senator Stephen Douglas of Illinois, who gave it its final name in the Kansas–Nebraska Act.

Populism (Populist Party)   Late-nineteenth-century movement of farmers, most notably in the West and South, that identified laissez-faire capitalism and big business, especially the giant railroad companies, as responsible for the worsening economic circumstances in rural America. In 1892, the People's or Populist Party captured a million votes and carried four western states, representing the first agrarian protest to truly challenge the entrenched two-party system.

pragmatism Philosophy popular with Progressives, developed by Harvard psychologist William James in the early twentieth century. It judged ideas by their consequences and was concerned with solving problems rather than seeking ultimate truths.

Praying towns Native American settlements supervised by New England Puritans. In these seventeenth-century settlements, Puritans attempted to Christianize Indians, in part, through an Algonquian-language Bible.

predestination The idea that God had chosen certain people for salvation even before they were born. This strict belief was preached by John Calvin in the sixteenth century and became a fundamental tenet of Puritan theology.

Preservationists Early-twentieth-century activists like John Muir who fought to protect the natural environment from commercial exploitation, particularly in the American West. Notable achievements include the establishment of many national parks like Yosemite, Sequoia, and King's Canyon in California.

Price Revolution A term that describes the significance of the high rate of inflation in Europe in the mid-1500s resulting from the introduction of American wealth into the European economy by the Spanish, which doubled the money supply in Europe. It brought about profound social changes by reducing the political power of the aristocracy and leaving many peasant families on the brink of poverty, setting the stage for a substantial migration to America.

primogeniture An inheritance practice by which a family's estate was passed on to the eldest son, forcing many younger children into poverty. In the Revolutionary era, republican Americans increasingly felt this was unfair. As a result, most state legislatures rejected the practice by passing laws requiring the equal distribution of estates.

progressivism This term embraces a widespread, many-sided effort in the years after 1900 to build a better society. The movement rejected the fatalism of earlier social thought in analyzing social problems and replaced it with empirical social science and a belief in administrative efficiency.

Promontory Point Site in Utah where the railway lines built by the Union Pacific and Central Pacific met in 1869, completing the first transcontinental railroad line and contributing to the integration of the western territories into the rest of the Union and the development of the Great Plains.

propaganda The spreading of ideas that support a particular cause. Although this process does not require a distortion of the facts, it usually involves a misrepresentation of the views or policies of one's opponents. During World War I, the U.S. Committee on Public Information, led by George Creel, published literature and sponsored speeches to increase public hostility toward Germany.

proprietors A group of settlers, in seventeenth-century Puritan society, who determined how the land of a township would be distributed. To guarantee a wide distribution of property, the General Courts of Massachusetts Bay and Connecticut gave the title of a township to a group of proprietors and allowed them to distribute land among the settlers.

pump priming Term first used during the Great Depression of the 1930s to describe the practice of pouring money into the financial system and the industrial structure in the hope that it will generate economic activity throughout the system; the beginning of the process that is supposed to lead to significant economic recovery.

Radical Whigs Eighteenth-century opposition party in the British Parliament that challenged the cost of the growing British empire and the subsequent increase in tax collector positions that were used for patronage. They demanded that British government include more representatives of the propertied classes.

Reaganomics The policy enacted by the Reagan administration in the 1980s calling for tax cuts and reductions in domestic spending in order to reduce the size of the federal government.

reconquista The centuries-long campaign by Spanish Catholics to drive African Moors (Muslims) from the European mainland. After a long effort to recover control of their lands, the Spanish defeated the Moors at the battle of Granada in 1492 and drove them back to Africa.

Reconstruction Post–Civil War policies whereby the freedmen, abolitionists, and radical Republican politicians hoped to make changes in the South that would ensure political equality for the freedmen and grant them greater economic rights.

red-baiting Tactics used to identify, accuse, or raise suspicion of communist sympathies. In the 1930s, critics of the New Deal charged the Federal Theatre Project with being under the influence of communists, leading to its termination in 1939.

Redeemers Ex-Confederates who sought to return the political and economic control of the South to white southerners in the decades after the Civil War. They believed that Union support of the freedmen had deprived the South of democratic self-government and organized secret societies and campaigns of terror to regain it, leading to the undoing of Reconstruction.

reparations Payments by a defeated enemy to the victors following a war. After World War I, the European Allies required Germany to pay vast sums for expenses incurred during the war and as a long-term punishment.

republic A state without a monarch and with a representative system of government. In Revolutionary America, "republicanism" became a social philosophy that embodied a sense of community and called individuals to act selflessly for the public good.

republican motherhood The idea that American women's moral superiority gave them a special role to play in the new political and social system. In the early-to-mid-nineteenth century, republican mothers were to instill the values of patriotic duty and republican virtue in their children and mold them into exemplary American citizens with moral and religious education.

Restoration   The name given to the reign of Charles II, King of England, the monarch whom Parliament crowned in 1660, following a decade of Puritan rule under Oliver Cromwell.

restrictive covenant   Limiting clauses in real estate transactions intended to prevent the sale or rental of properties to classes of the population considered "undesirable," such as African Americans, Jews, or Asians. Such clauses were declared unenforceable by the Supreme Court decision in *Shelley v. Kraemer* (1948), but continued to be instituted informally in spite of the ruling.

revenue sharing   The return of federal tax money to the states for use as they saw fit. President Nixon sought to reverse the concentration of power in Washington by initiating a decentralization of governmental functions in 1972.

rock 'n' roll   Style of popular music, an amalgam of white country-and-western music and urban black rhythm and blues. White performers, like Elvis Presley, dramatically increased its popularity with white audiences in the 1950s.

Roosevelt corollary   This 1904 assertion by President Theodore Roosevelt expanded the Monroe Doctrine. It stated that the United States would act as a "policeman" in the Caribbean region and intervene in the affairs of nations that were guilty of "wrongdoing or impotence," in order to protect U.S. interests in Latin America.

rotten boroughs   Tiny electoral districts for Parliament whose voters were controlled by wealthy aristocrats or merchants. In the 1760s Radical Whig John Wilkes called for their elimination to make Parliament more representative of the property-owning classes.

salutary neglect   British colonial policy during the reigns of George I (r. 1714–1727) and George II (r. 1727–1760). Relaxed supervision of internal colonial affairs by royal bureaucrats contributed significantly to the rise of American self-government.

scalawags   Southern whites who joined the Republicans during Reconstruction and were ridiculed by ex-Confederates as worthless traitors. They included wealthy ex-Whigs and yeomen farmers who had not supported the Confederacy and who believed that an alliance with the Republicans was the best way to attract northern capital to the South.

scientific management   A system of organizing work, developed by Frederick W. Taylor in the late nineteenth century, designed to get the maximum output from the individual worker and reduce the cost of production, using methods such as the time-and-motion study to determine how factory work should be organized. The rigid structure of the system was never applied in its totality in any industry, but it contributed to the rise of the "efficiency expert" and the field of industrial psychology.

secondary labor boycott   Technique used by unions during a strike in which force is applied on a second party to bring pressure on the primary target and force it to accept demands. A secondary labor boycott was used in the Great Pullman Boycott of 1894 and failed when the government intervened.

self-made man   This middle-class icon was based on an ideal that became a central theme of American popular culture in the nineteenth century. The ideology of the self-made man held that hard work, temperate habits, and honesty in business was the key to a high standard of living for the nation and social mobility and prosperity for individuals.

sentimentalism   European-spawned idea that emphasized feelings and emotions, a physical appreciation of God, nature, and other people, rather than reason and logic. Sentimentalism had an impact on the American people starting in the early nineteenth century, as love became as important in marriage as financial considerations.

sex typing   Process by which occupations become categorized as either "male" or "female" jobs. In the late nineteenth century, jobs characterized as "female" came to be seen as having feminine attributes, even if the same work had been done by men before.

sharecropping   Labor system developed during Reconstruction by which freedmen agreed to work the land and pay a portion of their harvested crops to the landowner in exchange for land, a house, and tools. A compromise between freedmen and white landowners, this system developed in the cash-strapped South because the freedmen wanted to work their own land but lacked the money to buy it, while the white landowners needed agricultural laborers, but did not have money to pay wages.

silent majority   This term, derived from Ben J. Wattenberg and Richard Scammon's book, applies to the segment of American society to whom Nixon appealed—generally the "unblack, unpoor, and unyoung."

sit-in   Nonviolent protest tactic first popularized by African American students for civil rights in Greensboro, North Carolina, in 1960. As protest in the 1960s spread beyond civil rights, many groups adopted the sit-in as their method of activism.

slave power   Term used by antislavery advocates in the 1850s to describe a suspected conspiracy of southern politicians and their northern business allies. It was believed that these groups planned to expand the bounds of slavery into new territories.

social Darwinism   A social application of Charles Darwin's biological theory of evolution by natural selection, this late-nineteenth-century theory encouraged the notion of human competition and opposed intervention in the natural human order. Social Darwinists justified the increasing inequality of late-nineteenth-century industrial American society as natural.

socialized medicine   Label applied by the American Medical Association in the early 1950s in a campaign against Truman's recommendation that a federally underwritten national health-care system be enacted. The attempt to link Truman's program with leftist politics was successful in arousing congressional and public opinion against the plan.

Sons of Liberty   Carefully directed and well-disciplined mobs that sought to channel popular discontent against British rule toward terrorizing local British officials and other symbols of colonial authority in the decade of hostilities leading up to the American Revolution.

speakeasies   Illegal saloons that sold alcohol to the public during Prohibition (starting in 1920).

specie   Gold or silver coins used by banks to back paper currency. In the early nineteenth century most American money consisted of notes and bills of credit, which were redeemed on demand with specie by the Second Bank of the United States.

speculator Someone who enters a market to buy and then resell at a higher price with the sole goal of making money. The eighteenth-century western land market was dominated by people who acquired land at a low price through political influence, then sold it for a profit to settlers.

sphere of influence A geographical area beyond a nation's borders over which it claims control. The Soviet Union's domination of Eastern European countries after World War II, which created a communist buffer zone between the USSR and Western Europe, extended the Soviet sphere of influence dangerously close to the U.S. sphere of influence.

spoils system Andrew Jackson began this practice in 1829 of awarding public jobs to political supporters to fulfill his campaign promise to introduce rotation in office and open public service to his supporters.

Square Deal President Theodore Roosevelt's domestic reform program, begun in 1904, calling for government control of corporate abuses.

squatter Someone who settles on land they do not own. Many eighteenth- and nineteenth-century settlers established themselves on land before it was surveyed and entered for sale, requesting the first right to purchase the land when sales began.

stagflation An economic condition that results when inflation and unemployment rise at the same time. This condition does not respond to traditional governmental remedies, such as deficit spending and tax reduction.

states' rights An interpretation of the Constitution that argues that the states hold the ultimate sovereignty and have power over the federal government. Expressed in the Virginia and Kentucky resolutions of 1798, the states' rights philosophy became the basis for resistance by the South against attempts to control slavery.

"subtreasury" system A scheme under which the federal government would provide localized banking functions for farmers, allowing them credit and marketing opportunities not controlled by private firms. This banking reform was promoted by the Populist Party in the late nineteenth century.

suburbanization The movement of the upper and middle classes beyond city limits to less crowded areas with larger homes and that are connected to city centers by streetcar or subway lines. By 1910, 25 percent of the population lived in these new communities. The 1990 census revealed that the majority of Americans lived in the suburbs.

suffrage The right to vote. In the early national period suffrage was limited by property restrictions. Gradually state constitutions gave the vote to all white men over the age of twenty-one. Over the course of American history, suffrage has expanded as barriers of race, gender, and age have fallen.

suffragists Those (mostly female) who were active in seeking voting rights for women as an inherent right for all individuals in the nineteenth and early twentieth centuries.

Sun Belt The southern and western United States in the 1950s and 1960s, where many firms moved their operations during the industrial development of the postwar era. Population followed this industrial migration and led to an enormous growth in economic activity and political influence of the Sun Belt states.

Sun Dance Sioux Indian ceremony in which an entire tribe celebrated the rites of coming of age, fertility, the hunt, and combat. The ritual involved four days of fasting and dancing in supplication to Wi, the sun.

supply-side economics This theory, the basis for Reaganomics, argued that a large tax cut would empower individuals and businesses to invest more money. Otherwise known as "trickle-down economics," the subsequent increase in economic activity, the reasoning went, would create jobs, generate more taxable income, and increase government revenues.

syndicalism A revolutionary movement that, like socialism, believed in the Marxist principle of class struggle and advocated the organization of society on the basis of industrial unionism. This approach was advocated by the Industrial Workers of the World (IWW) at the start of the twentieth century.

tariff A tax on imports, which has two purposes: raising revenue for the government and protecting domestic products from foreign competition. A hot political issue throughout much of American history, in the late nineteenth century the tariff became particularly controversial as Republicans, who viewed it as a protective system, and Democrats, who were free traders by tradition, made the tariff the centerpiece of their political campaigns.

task system Unlike the gang-labor system, the privilege of working unsupervised on an assigned daily task allowed slaves in the nineteenth century the opportunity to pace themselves according to their other obligations. Once the specific job was finished, the slaves could do what they wished, including cultivate their own small plots.

teach-in University gatherings in the 1960s where the political, diplomatic, and moral aspects of the nation's involvement in Vietnam were debated. College students and faculty abandoned structured class time to explore these issues.

telecommuters People who perform their jobs at home with the use of electronic communication devices (computers, modems, faxes). Telecommuting became common in the 1990s as the growth and development of the Internet and World Wide Web revolutionized communications.

tenements High-density, cheap, five- or six-story housing units designed for large urban populations built in the late nineteenth century. New York's tenements were known for their horrible crowding and lack of ventilation or plumbing.

time-and-motion study An engineer's study of a particular industrial task to determine the most efficient method for producing the greatest amount in the least amount of time. The factory would then set this time as the standard to which workers would be expected to conform.

total war Traditionally, armies fought each other and left civilians alone, but as the Civil War progressed, Lincoln and Grant realized that to force the Confederacy to surrender, they would have to break the will of the southern people using this style of warfare. Total war required a struggle that mobilized the nation's entire resources against the whole of southern society, not just against the Confederacy's troops.

trade deficit The importation by a nation of more than it exports. Contributing to the economic problems of the 1970s, the United States posted its first trade deficit in more than a century as the emerging industrial economies of Germany and Japan began to provide stiff international competition.

trade slaves A small proportion of unfree West Africans who were sold from one African kingdom to another and not considered members of the society that had enslaved them. European traders began buying trade slaves from African princes and warlords in the early sixteenth century.

transcendentalism A nineteenth-century intellectual movement that espoused an ideal world of mystical knowledge and harmony beyond the world of the senses. Proponents included intellectuals such as Emerson and Thoreau, who emphasized individuality, self-reliance, and nonconformity.

trusts Large business mergers in the late nineteenth and early twentieth centuries. These combinations became a problem because their size gave them the ability to inhibit competition and control the market for their products.

unicameral A one-house assembly in which the elected legislators directly represent the people. Considered efficient and democratic, this type of assembly was established in Pennsylvania during the Revolution.

Upper South Eight states of the Union that did not immediately secede following Lincoln's election in 1860. Following the seizure of Fort Sumter, four of these Upper South states (Virginia, North Carolina, Tennessee, Arkansas) joined the Confederacy; the other four remained in the Union.

urban liberalism An early twentieth-century reform movement organized by unions and politicians who sought state measures to improve the life of the working class of the cities.

urban renewal Process by which city planners, politicians, and real estate developers leveled urban tenements and replaced them with modern construction projects in the 1950s and 1960s. High-rise housing projects, however, destroyed community bonds and led to an increase in crime.

utopias (utopian communities) Reformers and transcendentalists founded numerous communities to help realize their spiritual and moral potential and to escape from the competition of modern industrial society. The most famous communal experiment was Brook Farm, founded by the transcendentalists outside of Boston, Massachusetts, in 1841.

vaudeville A professional stage show composed of singing, dancing, and comedy routines that changed live entertainment from its seedier predecessors like minstrel shows to family entertainment for the urban masses. Vaudeville became popular in the 1880s and 1890s, the years just before the introduction of movies.

vertical integration A national company's capability of handling, within its own structure, all the functions of an industry. Pioneered in the late nineteenth century by Gustavus F. Swift in the meatpacking industry, his Swift & Co. was organized so that it could manage all of the aspects of its operations, from obtaining raw materials to marketing the final product.

vice-admiralty courts Military tribunals composed only of a judge with no local common-law jury. The Sugar Act of 1764 required that offenders be tried before this tribunal rather than in local courts, provoking opposition from smugglers accustomed to acquittal before sympathetic local juries.

virtual representation Claim made by British politicians in 1754 that merchants and others in Parliament with interest in the colonies could provide adequate support for colonial concerns, rather than having Americans serve in Parliament.

ward The basic unit of municipal government in the late nineteenth century. City councils were made up of representatives from these districts, and it was through the ward system that the urban political machine operated.

War Democrats Faction of the northern opposition party that opposed emancipation but backed a policy of continuing with the fighting. George McClellan was part of this faction, but initially, during the 1864 presidential campaign, he backed an immediate cessation of hostilities.

wars of national liberation Leftist movements rebelling against colonial or oligarchic governments in the Third World. In the 1960s the United States saw many of these struggles as attempts to extend the reach of Soviet communism, while the Soviet Union saw them, as legitimate struggles for freedom and national self-determination.

welfare state A nation that provides for the basic needs of its citizens, including such provisions as old-age pensions, unemployment compensation, child-care facilities, education, and other social policies. Unlike the major European countries, such provisions appeared in the United States only with the coming of the New Deal in the 1930s.

Whigs A British political party with a reputation for supporting liberal principles and reform. They rose in power during the Glorious Revolution of 1688 and favored "mixed government" in which the House of Commons would have a voice in shaping policies, especially the power of taxation.

white-collar Middle-class professionals, who are salaried workers as opposed to business owners or wage laborers; they first appeared in large numbers during the industrial expansion in the late nineteenth century. Their ranks were composed of lawyers, engineers, and chemists, as well as salesmen, accountants, and advertising managers.

white primary Southern states accepted the progressive idea of a direct selection of party candidates in the early twentieth century but used this device as a way of reducing the effect of black voting in the general election.

yellow-dog contract When a worker, as a condition of employment, promises not to join a union. Employers in the late nineteenth century used this along with the blacklist and violent strikebreaking to fight unionization of their workforce.

yellow journalism Term that refers to newspapers that specialize in sensationalistic reporting. The name came from the ink used in Hearst's *New York Journal* to print the first comic strip to appear in color in 1895 and is generally associated with the inflammatory reporting leading up to the Spanish-American War of 1898.

yeoman In medieval England, a farmer below the level of gentry, but above the peasantry. A freeholder, he owned his own land, which released him from economic obligations to a landlord. In America, Thomas Jefferson envisioned a nation based on democracy and a thriving agrarian society, built on the labor and prosperity of the yeomen.

Chapter 1: Worlds Collide: Europe, Africa, and America, 1450–1620

Two works by Kenneth Pomeranz, *The Great Divergence: Europe, China, and the Making of the Modern World Economy* (2000) and (with Steven Topek) *The World That Trade Created: Society, Culture, and the World Economy* (1999), set the settlement of America in the perspective of world history. A fine study of the interaction of European and Native American peoples is Eric Wolf, *Europe and the People without History* (1982). See also Noble David Cook, *Born to Die: Disease and the New World Conquest (1492–1650)* (1998); Alfred W. Crosby Jr., *Ecological Imperialism: The Biological Expansion of Europe, 900–1900* (1986); G. V. Scammell, *The World Encompassed: The First European Maritime Empires* (1981); and Roger Schlesinger, *In the Wake of Columbus: The Impact of the New World on Europe, 1492–1650* (1996).

Native American Worlds

Brian M. Fagan, *The Great Journey: The People of Ancient America* (1987), synthesizes recent scholarship on prehistoric American Indians, and his *Kingdoms of Gold, Kingdoms of Jade: The Americas before Columbus* (1991) does the same for the Mesoamerican peoples. See also Stuart J. Fiedel, *Prehistory of the Americas* (1992); Inga Clendinnen, *Aztecs: An Interpretation* (1991); John S. Henderson, *The World of the Maya* (1981); and David Carrasco, *Quetzalcoatl and the Irony of Empire* (1982). Two fine supplements are Michael Coe et al., *Atlas of Ancient America* (1986), and Manuel Lucena Salmoral, *America in 1492* (1991), a photographic survey of dress, artifacts, and architecture. Alfred W. Crosby Jr., *The Columbian Exchange: Biological and Cultural Consequences of 1492* (1972), traces the impact of European diseases. See also Russell Thornton, *American Indian Holocaust and Survival: A Population History since 1492* (1987). Two interesting Public Broadcasting Service (PBS) videos examine the ancient civilizations of Mesoamerica: *Odyssey: Maya Lords of the Jungle* (1 hour); *Odyssey: The Incas* (1 hour). For additional information log on to "1492: An Ongoing Voyage" <http://lcweb.loc.gov/exhibits/1492/intro.html>, which provides a survey of the native cultures of the Western Hemisphere, the impact of discovery, and full-color images of artifacts and art.

On North America consult the following general works: *The Cambridge History of the Native Peoples of the Americas, Volume 1: North America*, ed. Bruce G. Trigger and Wilcomb Washburn (1996); Alvin M. Josephy Jr., ed., *America in 1492* (1993); Philip Kopper, *The Smithsonian Book of North American Indians before the Coming of the Europeans* (1986); and Carl Waldman and Molly Braun, *Atlas of the North American Indian* (1985). Good specialized studies include Linda S. Cordell, *Ancient Pueblo Peoples* (1994); Bruce D. Smith, ed., *The Mississippian Emergence* (1990); and Robert Silverberg,

Mound Builders of Ancient America: The Archaeology of a Myth (1968). Roger Kennedy, *Hidden Cities* (1994), surveys the early Indian civilizations of the Mississippi Valley, and Samuel W. Wilson, ed., *The Indigenous People of the Caribbean* (1997), offers important essays on that topic. Material on an early Indian civilization in the southwestern United States is available at "Sipapu: The Anasazi Emergence into the Cyber World" <http://sipapu.gsu.edu>.

Traditional European Society in 1450

Barbara W. Tuchman, *A Distant Mirror: The Calamitous Fourteenth Century* (1978), presents a vivid portrait of the late medieval world. Two wide-ranging studies of subsequent developments are George Huppert, *After the Black Death: A Social History of Modern Europe* (1986), and Henry Kamen, *European Society, 1500–1700* (1984). Illuminating specialized studies include Peter Burke, *Popular Culture in Early Modern Europe* (1978); Pierre Goubert, *The French Peasantry in the Seventeenth Century* (1986); B. H. Slicher Van Bath, *The Agrarian History of Western Europe, A.D. 500–1850* (1963); and Emanuel Le Roy Ladurie, *The Peasants of Languedoc* (1974). See also Joel Mokyr, *The Lever of Riches: Technological Creativity and Economic Progress* (1990), and E. P. Thompson, *Customs in Common: Studies in Traditional Popular Culture* (1991).

Europe Encounters Africa and the Americas, 1450–1550

The preconditions for European expansion are treated in James D. Tracy, ed., *Rise of Merchant Empires: Long Distance Trade in the Early Modern World, 1350–1750* (1990). For southern Europe, read selectively in Fernand Braudel's stimulating *The Mediterranean and the Mediterranean World in the Age of Philip II* (1949).

Paul H. Chapman, *The Norse Discovery of America* (1981), and Boies Penrose, *Travel and Discovery in the Renaissance, 1420–1620* (1952), illuminate the growth of geographical knowledge. For the expansion of Portugal and Spain, see Bailey W. Diffie and George Winius, *Foundations of the Portuguese Empire, 1415–1580* (1977), and Henry Kamen, *Crisis and Change in Early Modern Spain* (1993). A good short biography of Columbus and his times is Felipe Fernández-Armesto, *Columbus* (1991), but also see William D. Phillips Jr. and Carla Rahn Phillips, *The Worlds of Christopher Columbus* (1992).

For the Spanish and Portuguese colonial empires, see Charles R. Boxer, *The Portuguese Seaborne Empire* (1969), and James Lockhart and Stuart B. Schwartz, *Early Latin America: Colonial Spanish America and Brazil* (1984). Fine accounts of the Spanish conquest include the memorable firsthand report by Bernal Díaz del Castillo, *The Discovery and Conquest of Mexico* (ed. I. A. Leonard, 1956); Leon Portilla, *Broken Spears:*

The Aztec Account of the Conquest of Mexico (1962); and Hugh Thomas, *Conquest: Montezuma, Cortés, and the Fall of Old Mexico* (1994). The decline of native society in New Spain is outlined in Daniel T. Reff, *Disease, Depopulation, and Culture Change in Northwestern New Spain, 1518–1764* (1991). Thomas C. Patterson, *The Inca Empire* (1991); Nigel Davies, *The Incas* (1995); and R. Tom Zuidema, *Inca Civilization in Cuzco* (1992), explore the native civilization of Peru. Susan E. Ramírez, *The World Upside Down: Cross-Cultural Contact and Conflict in Sixteenth-Century Peru* (1996), offers a close analysis of Inca life after the conquest.

The Protestant Reformation and the Rise of England

On the European Reformation, consult William J. Bouwsma, *John Calvin* (1987), and De Lamar Jensen, *Reformation Europe: Age of Reform and Revolution* (1981). For England, see Patrick Collinson, *The Religion of the Protestants: The Church in English Society, 1559–1625* (1982), and Susan Doran and Christopher Durston, *Princes, Pastors, and People: The Church and Religion in England, 1529–1689* (1991). "Martin Luther" <http://www.luther.de/e/index.html> offers biographies of the leading figures of the Protestant Reformation and striking images of the era.

On the decline of Spain, consult Henry Kamen, *Spain: A Society in Conflict, 1479–1714* (2nd ed., 1991), and John Lynch, *The Hispanic World in Crisis and Change, 1598–1700* (1992), which also traces the growing economic independence of New Spain.

A brilliant and forceful portrait of English preindustrial society is offered by Peter Laslett, *The World We Have Lost* (3rd ed., 1984). Other important works are Keith Wrightson, *English Society, 1580–1680* (1982), and Lawrence Stone, *The Crisis of the Aristocracy* (1965). On the movement of people, see Ida Altman and James Horn, eds., *"To Make America": European Emigration in the Early Modern Period* (1991).

Chapter 2: The Invasion and Settlement of North America, 1550–1700

David Weber, *The Spanish Frontier in North America* (1992), and Richard White, *The Middle Ground: Indians, Empires, and Republics in the Great Lakes Region, 1650–1815* (1991), are important studies while Bernard Bailyn, *The Peopling of British North America* (1986), and Colin G. Calloway, *New Worlds for All: Indians, Europeans, and the Remaking of Early America* (1997), offer incisive overviews of two important topics.

Imperial Conflicts and Rival Colonial Models

For a discussion of Spain's northern empire in America, see Ramón Gutiérrez, *When Jesus Came, the Corn Mothers Went Away: Marriage, Sexuality, and Power in New Mexico, 1500–1846* (1991). The French threat to Spain's domain is traced by Robert S. Weddle, *The French Thorn: Rival Explorers in the Spanish Sea, 1682–1762* (1991), and Daniel H. Usner Jr., *Indians, Settlers, and Slaves in a Frontier Exchange Economy: The Lower Mississippi Valley before 1783* (1991).

The best general studies of French Canada are by W. J. Eccles: *The Canadian Frontier, 1534–1760* (1983) and *France in America* (rev. ed., 1990). French interaction with Native Americans is covered by Bruce G. Trigger, *The Children of Aataentsic: A History of the Huron People to 1660* (1976); Daniel K. Richter, *The Ordeal of the Long House: The Peoples of the Iroquois League in the Era of European Colonization* (1992); and Olive Patricia Dickason, *Canada's First Nations: A History of the Founding Peoples from Earliest Times* (1992).

Two works by Jonathan I. Israel, *The Dutch Republic: Its Rise, Greatness and Fall* (1995) and *Dutch Primacy in World Trade, 1585–1740* (1989), show the impressive reach of Dutch commerce. For its American component, consult Oliver A. Rink, *Holland on the Hudson: An Economic and Social History of Dutch New York* (1986).

For a discussion of English expansion, see Kenneth Andrews, *Trade, Plunder, and Settlement: Maritime Enterprise and the Genesis of the British Empire, 1480–1630* (1984); Nicholas Canny, *Kingdom and Colony: Ireland in the Atlantic World, 1560–1800* (1988); A. L. Rowse, *Sir Walter Raleigh* (1962); David B. Quinn, *England and the Discovery of America, 1481–1620* (1974); and Karen O. Kupperman, *Roanoke* (1984). The interaction of the English and Dutch with Native Americans can be followed in Gary B. Nash, *Red, White, and Black: The Peoples of Early America* (1982); Francis Jennings, *The Invasion of America* (1975); and two works by James Axtell, *The European and the Indian* (1981) and *The Invasion Within: The Contest of Cultures in Colonial North America* (1985).

The Chesapeake Experience

Alden Vaughan, *American Genesis: Captain John Smith and the Founding of Virginia* (1975), covers the earliest years, while Edmund S. Morgan, *American Slavery, American Freedom: The Ordeal of Colonial Virginia* (1975), provides a brilliant analysis of the rest of the seventeenth century. Important essays appear in Thad W. Tate and David L. Ammerman, eds., *The Chesapeake in the Seventeenth Century* (1979), and Lois Green Carr, Philip D. Morgan, and Jean B. Russo, *Colonial Chesapeake Society* (1989). Other significant studies include Lois Green Carr et al., *Robert Cole's World: Agriculture and Society in Early Maryland* (1991); Kathleen Brown, *Good Wives, Nasty Wenches, and Anxious Patriarchs: Gender, Race, and Power in Colonial Virginia* (1996); and James Horn, *Adapting to a New World: English Society in the Seventeenth-Century Chesapeake* (1994). For a discussion of political institutions, see W. F. Craven, *The Southern Colonies in the Seventeenth Century, 1607–1689* (1949), and David W. Jordan, *Foundations of Representative Government in Maryland, 1632–1715* (1988). Contrasting accounts of Bacon's Rebellion can be found in T. J. Wertenbaker, *Torchbearer of the Revolution* (1940), and Wilcomb B. Washburn, *The Governor and the Rebel* (1958). "Colonial Williamsburg" <http://www.history.org/> offers an extensive collection of documents, illustrations, and secondary texts about colonial life, as well as information about the archeological excavations at Williamsburg.

Puritan New England

For the Puritan migration, see Virginia DeJohn Anderson, *New England's Generation: The Great Migration and the Formation of Society and Culture in the Seventeenth Century* (1991); Edmund Morgan, *The Puritan Dilemma: The Story of*

John Winthrop (1955); David Grayson Allen, *In English Ways: The Movement of Societies and the Transferral of English Local Law and Custom to Massachusetts Bay in the Seventeenth Century* (1981); and David Cressy, *Coming Over: Migration and Communication between England and New England in the Seventeenth Century* (1987). A highly acclaimed site on the Pilgrims at Plymouth is "Caleb Johnson's Mayflower Web Pages" <http://members.aol.com/calebj/mayflower.html>.

Puritanism as an intellectual movement is best explored in the works of Perry Miller; see especially *The New England Mind: The Seventeenth Century* (1939). Charles Hambrick-Stowe, *The Practice of Piety: Puritan Devotional Disciplines* (1982), discusses the emotional dimension of Puritanism, while David D. Hall, *World of Wonder, Days of Judgment: Popular Religious Belief in Early New England* (1989), explores its supernatural aspects. See also Andrew Delbanco, *The Puritan Ordeal* (1989).

For a discussion of dissent in early New England, consult Philip Gura, *A Glimpse of Sion's Glory: Puritan Radicalism in New England, 1620–1660* (1984); Edwin S. Gaustad, *Liberty of Conscience: Roger Williams in America* (1991); Amy Schrager Lang, *Prophetic Woman: Anne Hutchinson and the Problem of Dissent in the Literature of New England* (1987); Paul Boyer and Steven Nissenbaum, *Salem Possessed: The Social Origins of Witchcraft* (1974); and Carol F. Karlsen, *The Devil in the Shape of a Woman: Witchcraft in New England* (1987). Extensive materials on the Salem witchcraft episode can be viewed at <http://etext.lib.virginia.edu/salem/witchcraft/>.

Community studies that describe the lives of ordinary New England men and women include John Demos, *The Little Commonwealth: Family Life in Plymouth Colony* (1971), and Kenneth A. Lockridge, *A New England Town . . . Dedham, Massachusetts, 1636–1736* (1970). See also John Demos, *The Unredeemed Captive: A Family Story from Early America* (1994), and Stephen Innes, *Creating the Commonwealth: The Economic Culture of Puritan New England* (1995).

The Indians' New World

James H. Merrell, *The Indians' New World: Catawbas and Their Neighbors from European Contact through the Era of Removal* (1989), is a pathbreaking study. Alfred Cave, *The Pequot War* (1996), explores the first war in New England. Three fine studies of subsequent conflicts are Jill Lepore, *The Name of War: King Philip's War and the Origins of American Identity* (1998); Patrick M. Malone, *The Skulking Way of War: Technology and Techniques among New England Indians* (1991); and Russell Bourne, *Red King's Rebellion* (1995). See also Karen Ordahl Kupperman, *Settling with the Indians: The Meeting of English and Indian Cultures in America, 1580–1640* (1981); Bernard Sheehan, *Savagism and Civility: Indians and Englishmen in Colonial Virginia* (1980); and Daniel K. Richter and James H. Merrell, *Beyond the Covenant Chain: The Iroquois and Their Neighbors in Indian North America* (1987). A PBS video, *Surviving Columbus* (2 hours), traces the experiences of the Pueblo Indians over 450 years. "First Nations Histories" <http://www.dickshovel.com/Compacts.html> presents short histories of many North American Indian peoples and information on their politics, language, culture, and demography. A fine ecological study is William Cronon, *Changes in the Land: Indians, Colonists, and the Ecology of New England* (1983).

Chapter 3: The British Empire in America, 1660–1750

The best overview of England's empire is Michael Kammen, *Empire and Interest: The American Colonies and the Politics of Mercantilism* (1970); for more recent accounts, see Alison Olson, *Making the Empire Work: London and American Interest Groups, 1690–1790* (1992), and Linda Colley, *Britons: Forging the Nation, 1707–1837* (1992). On Africa, consult Paul Bohannan and Philip Curtin, *Africa and the Africans* (3rd ed., 1988). Two fine syntheses of the African American experience are Philip D. Morgan, *Slave Counterpoint: Black Culture in the Eighteenth-Century Chesapeake and Low Country* (1998), and Ira Berlin, *Many Thousands Gone: The First Two Centuries of Slavery in North America* (1999).

The Politics of Empire, 1660–1713

Jonathan Scott, *England's Troubles* (2000), sets the European context for imperial politics, while Robert Bliss, *Revolution and Empire: English Politics and the American Colonies in the Seventeenth Century* (1990), and Jack M. Sosin, *English America and the Restoration Monarchy of Charles II: Transatlantic Politics, Commerce, and Kinship* (1980), explore their impact in the colonies. See also Stephen S. Webb, *1676: The End of American Independence* (1984).

For the events of 1688–1689, consult W. A. Speck, *Reluctant Revolutionaries: Englishmen and the Revolution of 1688* (1989), and David S. Lovejoy, *The Glorious Revolution in America* (1972). A good case study is Lois Green Carr and David W. Jordan, *Maryland's Revolution of Government, 1689–1692* (1974). Ethnic tension in New York can be traced in Robert C. Ritchie, *The Duke's Province: Politics and Society in New York, 1660–1691* (1977); Donna Merwick, *Possessing Albany, 1630–1710: The Dutch and English Experiences* (1990); and Joyce Goodfriend, *Before the Melting Pot: Society and Culture in Colonial New York City, 1664–1730* (1992). Jack M. Sosin, *English America and Imperial Inconstancy: The Rise of Provincial Autonomy, 1696–1715* (1985), outlines the new imperial system.

The Imperial Slave Economy

For the African background, see John Thornton, *Africa and Africans in the Making of the Atlantic World, 1400–1680* (1992), and Richard Olaniyan, *African History and Culture* (1982). Specialized studies of forced African migration include Patrick Manning, *Slavery and African Life* (1990); Philip Curtin, *The Atlantic Slave Trade: A Census* (1969); Paul Lovejoy, ed., *Africans in Bondage: Studies in Slavery and the Slave Trade* (1986); Hugh Thomas, *The Slave Trade* (1991); and Barbara L. Solow, ed., *Slavery and the Rise of the Atlantic System* (1991).

Richard S. Dunn, *Sugar and Slaves: The Rise of the Planter Class in the English West Indies, 1624–1713* (1972), provides a graphic portrait of the brutal slave-based economy, while Sidney W. Mintz, *Sweetness and Power: The Place of Sugar in Modern History* (1985), explores the impact of the major crop of the slave economy. Winthrop D. Jordan, *White over Black, 1550–1812* (1968), remains the best account of Virginia's decision for slavery, but see also Thomas D. Morris, *Southern Slavery and the Law, 1619–1860* (1996).

Victory: The Pitt-Newcastle Ministry and the Conduct of the Seven Years' War, 1757–1762 (1985); Howard H. Peckham, *Pontiac and the Indian Uprising* (1947); and Joseph A. Ernst, *Money and Politics in America, 1755–1775* (1973). Marc Egnal, *A Mighty Empire: The Origins of the Revolution* (1988), shows the links to western expansion.

British politics and imperial reform can be traced in John Brewer, *Party Ideology and Popular Politics at the Accession of George III* (1976); P. D. G. Thomas, *British Politics and the Stamp Act Crisis: The First Phase of the American Revolution, 1763–1767* (1975); Thomas C. Barrow, *Trade and Empire: The British Customs Service in Colonial America, 1660–1775* (1967); John L. Bullion, *A Great and Necessary Measure: George Grenville and the Genesis of the Stamp Act, 1763–1765* (1982); Carl Ubbelohde, *The Vice-Admiralty Courts and the American Revolution* (1960); and Philip Lawson, *George Grenville* (1984).

The Dynamics of Rebellion, 1765–1766

For the American response to the British reform laws, see Edmund S. Morgan and Helen M. Morgan, *The Stamp Act Crisis* (1963); Pauline Maier, *From Resistance to Revolution: Colonial Radicals and the Development of Colonial Opposition to Britain, 1765–1776* (1972); and Gary B. Nash, *The Urban Crucible: Social Change, Political Consciousness, and the Origins of the American Revolution* (1979). Merrill Jensen, *The Founding of a Nation: A History of the American Revolution, 1763–1776* (1968), and Robert Middlekauff, *The Glorious Cause: The American Revolution, 1763–1789* (1982), provide detailed narratives of the Revolutionary era.

Studies of individual colonies capture the spirit of the resistance movement. See Woody Holton, *Forced Founders: Indians, Debtors, Slaves, and the Making of the American Revolution in Virginia* (1999); Joseph S. Tiedemann, *Reluctant Revolutionaries: New York City and the Road to Independence, 1963–1976* (1997); and Ronald Hoffman, *A Spirit of Dissension: Economics, Politics, and the Revolution in Maryland* (1973). The motives of Patriots are best addressed through biographies. See Francis Jennings, *Benjamin Franklin, Politician* (1996); Pauline Maier, *The Old Revolutionaries: Political Lives in the Age of Samuel Adams* (1980); Milton E. Flower, *John Dickinson, Conservative Revolutionary* (1983); Richard R. Beeman, *Patrick Henry: A Biography* (1974); John R. Alden, *George Washington: A Biography* (1984); Helen Hill Miller, *George Mason: Gentleman Revolutionary* (1975); and John Ferling, *John Adams: A Life* (1992).

The most important single study of Patriot ideology is Bernard Bailyn, *The Ideological Origins of the American Revolution* (1967), but see also Robert M. Calhoon, *Dominion and Liberty: Ideology in Anglo-American Political Thought, 1660–1801* (1994). Other works include Caroline Robbins, *The Eighteenth-Century Commonwealthman* (1959); Morton White, *The Philosophy of the American Revolution* (1978); Garry Wills, *Inventing America: Jefferson's Declaration of Independence* (1978); and H. T. Dickinson, *Liberty and Property: Political Ideology in Eighteenth-Century Britain* (1978). For a discussion of the legal tradition, see Charles H. McIlwain, *The American Revolution: A Constitutional Interpretation* (1923), and John Philip Reid's *Constitutional History of the American Revolution* (1986–1996).

The Growing Confrontation, 1767–1770

Peter D. G. Thomas, *The Townshend Duties Crisis: The Second Phase of the American Revolution, 1767–1773* (1987), is the most comprehensive treatment, but see also Colin Bonwick, *English Radicals and the American Revolution* (1977). On American resistance consult Richard Alan Ryerson, *The Revolution Is Now Begun: The Radical Committees of Philadelphia, 1765–1776* (1978); Peter Shaw, *American Patriots and the Rituals of Revolution* (1981); and Stanley Godbold Jr. and Robert W. Woody, *Christopher Gadsden* (1982). The military confrontation is covered in John Shy, *Toward Lexington: The Role of the British Army in the Coming of the American Revolution* (1965), and Hiller B. Zobel, *The Boston Massacre* (1970). *Liberty! The American Revolution* (6 hours), a six-part video available through PBS, provides a coherent narrative of the movement for independence. Contrasting firsthand accounts of the Boston Massacre are available on the Web site "From Revolution to Reconstruction" at the University of Groningen <http://odur.let.rug.nl/~usa/> which also contains other materials on the Revolutionary era.

The Road to War, 1771–1775

Benjamin Labaree, *The Boston Tea Party* (1964), is a stimulating account. See also Peter D. G. Thomas, *Tea Party to Independence* (1991); Bernard Donoughue, *British Politics and the American Revolution: The Path to War, 1773–75* (1972); and David Ammerman, *In the Common Cause: American Response to the Coercive Acts of 1774* (1968). A fine study of the resistance movement is Edward F. Countryman, *A People in Revolution: The American Revolution and Political Society in New York* (1983). On prewar Loyalism, see Bernard Bailyn, *The Ordeal of Thomas Hutchinson* (1974), and Janice Potter, *The Liberty We Seek: Loyalist Ideology in Colonial New York and Massachusetts* (1983). For the rising of the countryside, see David Hackett Fischer, *Paul Revere's Ride* (1994); Gregory H. Nobles, *Divisions throughout the Whole: Politics and Society in Hampshire County, Massachusetts, 1740–1775* (1983); and Richard Bushman, *King and People in Provincial Massachusetts* (1985). The transfer of authority is described in Jerrilyn Greene Marston, *King and Congress: The Transfer of Political Legitimacy, 1774–1776* (1987).

Chapter 6: War and Revolution, 1775–1783

Gordon Wood, *The Radicalism of the American Revolution* (1992), offers a fine overview. For contrasting interpretations, see the essays in Alfred F. Young, ed., *Beyond the American Revolution: Explorations in the History of American Radicalism* (1993). Jack P. Greene and J. R. Pole, eds., *The Blackwell Encyclopedia of the American Revolution* (1991), provides illuminating essays on important topics. Colin G. Calloway, *The American Revolution in Indian Country: Crisis and Diversity in Native American Communities* (1995), traces the Revolution's impact on the native peoples, while Robin Blackburn, *The Overthrow of Colonial Slavery, 1776–1848* (1988), shows how it aided the decline of racial bondage in the Western Hemisphere. *Liberty! The American Revolution* (PBS video; 6 hours) and the companion Web site

<http://www.pbs.org/ktca/liberty/> cover the war and the making of the Constitution.

Toward Independence, 1775–1776

Jerrilyn Greene Marston, *King and Congress: The Transfer of Political Legitimacy, 1774–1776* (1987), and Jack N. Rakove, *The Beginnings of National Politics* (1979), discuss the movement toward independence. See also Eric Foner, *Tom Paine and Revolutionary America* (1976); Jack Fruchtman Jr., *Thomas Paine: Apostle of Freedom* (1994); and Pauline Maier, *American Scripture: Making the Declaration of Independence* (1997). To explore the political philosophy of Thomas Jefferson, log on to "Quotations from the Writings of Thomas Jefferson" <http://etext.virginia.edu/jefferson/quotations/>, which are conveniently arranged by topic. On Loyalism, read William N. Nelson, *The American Tory* (1961), and the essays collected in Robert M. Calhoon et al., eds., *Loyalists and Community in North America* (1994).

The Trials of War, 1776–1778

The military history of the war is covered in James L. Stokesbury, *A Short History of the American Revolution* (1991), and Piers Mackesy, *The War for America, 1775–1783* (1964). Don Higginbotham, *George Washington and the American Military Tradition* (1985), and Ronald Hoffman and Peter Albert, eds., *Arms and Independence: The Military Character of the American Revolution* (1984), offer a more analytical perspective. Mark V. Kwasny, *Washington's Partisan War, 1775–1783* (1997), stresses Washington's increasing use of the militia. The war in the North can be followed in Ira D. Gruber, *The Howe Brothers and the American Revolution* (1972), and Richard J. Hargrove Jr., *General John Burgoyne* (1983). "Virtual Marching Tour of the Philadelphia Campaign 1777" <http://www.ushistory.org/march/index.html> offers a multimedia view of Howe's attack on Philadelphia and subsequent events.

Studies of ordinary soldiers include Rodney Attwood, *The Hessians* (1980); Sylvia R. Frey, *The British Soldier in America* (1981); Robert K. Wright Jr., *The Continental Army* (1983); Charles P. Neimeyer, *America Goes to War: A Social History of the Continental Army* (1996); and John C. Dann, ed., *The Revolution Remembered: Eyewitness Accounts of the War for Independence* (1980). For the military bureaucracy, see R. Arthur Bowler, *Logistics and the Failure of the British Army in America, 1775–1783* (1975), and E. Wayne Carp, *To Starve the Army at Pleasure: Continental Army Administration and American Political Culture, 1775–1783* (1984).

Local studies include Jean Butenhoff Lee, *The Price of Nationhood: The American Revolution in Charles County* (1994); David Hackett Fischer, *Paul Revere's Ride* (1994); Richard Buel Jr., *Dear Liberty: Connecticut's Mobilization for the Revolutionary War* (1980); and Donald Wallace White, *A Village at War: Chatham, New Jersey, and the American Revolution* (1979).

African American participation in the war is discussed in Sidney Kaplan, *The Black Presence in the Era of the American Revolution* (rev. ed., 1989), and Gary B. Nash, *Race and Revolution* (1990). A fine, data-rich source on the black experience is "Africans in America: Revolution" <http://www.pbs.org/wgbh/aia/part2/title.html>; other parts of this Web site cover the entire African American experience. The Native American response is described in Colin G. Calloway, *The American Revolution in Indian Country* (1995); Barbara Graymont, *The Iroquois in the American Revolution* (1972); Isabel T. Kelsey, *Joseph Brant, 1743–1807* (1984); and James H. O'Donnell III, *Southern Indians in the American Revolution* (1973).

A classic discussion of the fiscal problems created by the war is E. James Ferguson, *The Power of the Purse* (1961); a more recent study is William G. Anderson, *The Price of Liberty: The Public Debt of the American Revolution* (1983).

The Path to Victory, 1778–1783

Bradford Perkins, *The Creation of a Republican Empire, 1776–1865* (1993), and Jonathan R. Dull, *A Diplomatic History of the American Revolution* (1985), provide good overviews. More specialized studies include James H. Hutson, *John Adams and the Diplomacy of the American Revolution* (1980); Richard B. Morris, *The Peacemakers: The Great Powers and American Independence* (1965); and Ronald Hoffman and Peter J. Albert, eds., *Peace and the Peacemakers: The Treaty of 1783* (1986).

For the southern campaign, consult W. Robert Higgins, ed., *The Revolutionary War in the South* (1979); Ronald Hoffman, Thad W. Tate, and Peter J. Albert, eds., *An Uncivil War: The Southern Backcountry during the American Revolution* (1985); and Jeffrey J. Crow and Larry E. Tise, eds., *The Southern Experience in the American Revolution* (1978). Studies of military action include Hugh F. Rankin, *Francis Marion: The Swamp Fox* (1973), and John S. Pancake, *The Destructive War, 1780–1782* (1985).

Republicanism Defined and Challenged

Milton M. Klein et al., *The Republican Synthesis Revisited* (1992), explores the debate over the importance of republican thought. See also Charles Royster, *A Revolutionary People at War: The Continental Army and American Character, 1775–1783* (1979). On women's lives, see Ronald Hoffman and Peter J. Albert, eds., *Women in the Age of the American Revolution* (1989); Mary Beth Norton, *Liberty's Daughters: The Revolutionary Experience of American Women, 1750–1800* (1980); and Joy Day Buel and Richard Buel Jr., *The Way of Duty: A Woman and Her Family in Revolutionary America* (1984).

On the black experience, consult Sylvia R. Frey, *Water from the Rock: Black Resistance in a Revolutionary Age* (1991); Ira Berlin and Ronald Hoffman, eds., *Slavery and Freedom in the Age of the American Revolution* (1983); and Gary B. Nash, *Forging Freedom: The Formation of Philadelphia's Black Community, 1720–1840* (1988). See also James W. St. G. Walker, *The Black Loyalists: The Search for a Promised Land in Nova Scotia and Sierra Leone, 1783–1870* (1976), and Shane White, *Somewhat More Independent: The End of Slavery in New York City, 1770–1810* (1991).

On changes in American religion, see Dee E. Andrews, *The Methodists and Revolutionary America, 1760–1800* (2000); Ronald Hoffman and Peter J. Albert, eds., *Religion in a Revolutionary Age* (1994); Rhys Isaac, *The Transformation of Virginia, 1740–1790* (1982); Fred Hood, *Reformed America, 1783–1837* (1980); and Nathan O. Hatch, *The Democratization of American Christianity* (1989). The spiritual roots of a new secular religion are traced by Catharine Albanese, *Sons of the Fathers: The Civil Religion of the American Revolution* (1976), and Ruth Bloch, *Visionary Republic: Millennial Themes in American Thought* (1985).

Chapter 7: The New Political Order, 1776–1800

Jack N. Rakove, *Original Meaning: Politics and Ideas in the Making of the Constitution* (1996), and Richard B. Bernstein and Kym S. Rice, *Are We to Be a Nation? The Making of the Constitution* (1987), are the best recent overviews of the creation of a national republic. Stanley Elkins and Eric McKitrick, *The Age of Federalism: The Early Republic, 1788–1800* (1993), offers a comprehensive assessment of the 1790s. Three interesting cultural studies of political life are Simon P. Newman, *Parades and the Politics of the Street: Festive Culture in the Early American Republic* (1997); David Waldstreicher, *In the Midst of Perpetual Fetes: The Making of American Nationalism, 1776–1820* (1997); and Len Travers, *Celebrating the Fourth: Independence Day and the Rise of Nationalism in the Early Republic* (1997).

Creating Republican Institutions, 1776–1787

Elisha P. Douglass, *Rebels and Democrats* (1965), documents the struggle for equal political rights while Gordon Wood, *The Creation of the American Republic, 1776–1790* (1965), provides a magisterial analysis of state and national constitutional development. For a contrary view, see Thomas Pangle, *The Spirit of Modern Republicanism: The Moral Vision of the American Founder and the Philosophy of Locke* (1988). See also Merrill Jensen, *The New Nation* (1950), and Jackson T. Main, *The Sovereign States, 1775–1783* (1973). Important studies of state constitutions include Willi Paul Adams, *The First American Constitutions* (1980); Edward F. Countryman, *A People in Revolution: The American Revolution and Political Society in New York, 1760–1790* (1981); and Donald Lutz, *Popular Consent and Popular Control: Whig Political Theory in the Early State Constitutions* (1980).

On women and republicanism, see Linda K. Kerber, *Women of the Republic* (1980), and *No Constitutional Right to Be Ladies: Women and the Obligations of Citizenship* (1999). Fine in-depth studies include Ronald Hoffman and Peter J. Albert, eds., *Women in the Age of the American Revolution* (1989); Rosemarie Zagarri, *A Woman's Dilemma: Mercy Otis Warren and the American Revolution* (1995); Judith Sargent Murray, *The Gleaner*, ed. Nina Baym (1992); and Lynn Withey, *Dearest Friend: A Life of Abigail Adams* (1982).

Important works on the 1780s include Peter S. Onuf, *The Origins of the Federal Republic: Jurisdictional Controversies in the United States, 1775–1787* (1983); Roger H. Brown, *Redeeming the Republic: Federalists, Taxation, and the Origins of the Constitution* (1993); Richard B. Morris, *The Forging of the Union, 1781–1789* (1987); and Robert A. Gross, ed., *In Debt to Shays* (1993).

The Constitution of 1787

In 1913 two studies initiated the modern analysis of the Constitution: Charles A. Beard, *An Economic Interpretation of the Constitution of the United States*, and Max Farrand, *The Framing of the Constitution*, which presented a detailed analysis of the Philadelphia convention. For critiques of Beard's work, see Leonard Levy, ed., *Essays on the Making of the Constitution* (rev. ed., 1987); for an update of Farrand, read Christopher Collier and James L. Collier, *Decision in Philadelphia* (1987).

Other significant works include Forrest McDonald, *Novus Ordo Seculorum: The Intellectual Origins of the Constitution* (1985); Edmund S. Morgan, *Inventing the People: The Rise of Popular Sovereignty in England and America* (1988); and Michael Kammen, *A Machine That Would Go by Itself: The Constitution in American Culture* (1986). Three fine collections of essays are Richard R. Beeman et al., eds., *Beyond Confederation: Origins of the Constitution and American National Identity* (1987); Ellen Frankel Paul and Howard Dickman, eds., *Liberty, Property and the Foundations of the American Constitution* (1989); and Herman Belz et al., eds., *To Form a More Perfect Union: The Critical Ideas of the Constitution* (1992).

On the Antifederalists and ratification, see Saul Cornell, *The Other Founders: The Antifederalists and the American Dissenting Tradition* (1999); Patrick T. Conley and John P. Kaminski, eds., *The Constitution and the States* (1988); Stephen L. Schechter, *The Reluctant Pillar: New York and the Adoption of the Federal Constitution* (1985); and Herbert Storing, *The Antifederalists* (1985). Two insightful studies of the Federalist papers are David F. Epstein, *The Political Theory of "The Federalist"* (1984), and Charles R. Kesler, ed., *Saving the Revolution* (1987).

R. A. Rutland, *The Birth of the Bill of Rights, 1776–1791* (rev. ed., 1983), offers the basic narrative; more analytic treatments include Michael J. Lacey and Knud Haakonssen, *A Culture of Rights* (1991), and Joyce Lee Malcolm, *To Keep and Bear Arms: The Origins of an Anglo-American Right* (1993). Akhil Reed Amar, *The Bill of Rights: Creation and Reconstruction* (1998), offers a persuasive "republican" interpretation.

The Political Crisis of the 1790s

Two good syntheses are John C. Miller, *The Federalist Age* (1957), and James Rogers Sharp, *American Politics in the Early Republic* (1993). Studies of important statesmen include Forrest McDonald, *Alexander Hamilton: A Biography* (1979), and two works by James T. Flexner, *George Washington and the New Nation, 1783–1793* (1970) and *George Washington: Anguish and Farewell, 1793–1799* (1972). William Martin wrote the documentary *George Washington—The Man Who Wouldn't Be King* (PBS video, 1 hour). Additional material, including Washington's published correspondence, is available online at "The Papers of George Washington" <http://www.virginia.edu/gwpapers/>. For Jeffersonian ideology, see Joyce Appleby, *Capitalism and a New Social Order: The Republican Vision of the 1790s* (1984); Drew McCoy, *The Elusive Republic: Political Economy in Jeffersonian America* (1982); Lance Banning, *The Jeffersonian Persuasion: The Evolution of a Party Ideology* (1978); and John R. Nelson Jr., *Liberty and Property: Political Economy and Policymaking in the New Nation, 1789–1812* (1987). For more information on Thomas Jefferson consult the PBS Web site, "Thomas Jefferson" <http://www.pbs.org/jefferson>, which contains information on the documentary (PBS video, 3 hours), transcripts of interviews with Jefferson scholars, and a collection of documents relating to Jefferson's personal and public life.

Richard Hofstadter, *The Idea of a Party System: The Rise of Legitimate Opposition in the United States, 1790–1840* (1969), offers an overview; see also John F. Hoadley, *Origins of American Political Parties, 1789–1803* (1993), and Thomas P. Slaughter, *The Whiskey Rebellion* (1986). On diplomatic and military history, consult Harry Ammon, *The Genêt*

Mission (1973); Jerald A. Combs, *The Jay Treaty* (1970); Richard H. Kohn, *Eagle and Sword* (1975); and Lawrence D. Cress, *Citizens in Arms: The Army and the Military to the War of 1812* (1982).

On Adams's administration, see Ralph Brown Adams, *The Presidency of John Adams* (1975). More specialized studies are William Sinchcombe, *The XYZ Affair* (1980); Leonard Levy, *The Emergence of a Free Press* (1985); and James M. Smith, *Freedom's Fetters: The Alien and Sedition Laws and American Civil Liberties* (rev. ed., 1966).

Good state histories include Patricia Watlington, *The Partisan Spirit: Kentucky Politics, 1779–1792* (1972); Richard R. Beeman, *The Old Dominion and the New Nation, 1788–1801* (1972); and Mary K. Bonsteel Tachau, *Federal Courts in the Early Republic: Kentucky, 1789–1816* (1978).

Chapter 8: Dynamic Change: Western Settlement and Eastern Capitalism, 1790–1820

Gregory Evans Dowd, *A Spirited Resistance: The North American Indian Struggle for Unity, 1745–1815* (1992), presents a fine survey of the Indian peoples, while Gregory Nobles, *American Frontiers: Cultural Encounters and Continental Conquest* (1997), traces the course of western expansion. Donald R. Hickey, *The War of 1812: A Forgotten Conflict* (1989), places the conflict in an economic and diplomatic context. R. Kent Newmyer, *The Supreme Court under Marshall and Taney* (1968), concisely analyzes early constitutional development, and Jack Larkin, *The Reshaping of Everyday Life, 1790–1840* (1989), demonstrates the impact of economic change on material culture.

Westward Expansion

For studies of white policy toward Native Americans, see Bernard Sheehan, *Seeds of Extinction: Jeffersonian Philanthropy and the American Indian* (1973); Reginald Horsman, *Expansion and American Indian Policy, 1783–1812* (1967); Richard Slotkin, *Regeneration through Violence* (1973); and Dorothy Jones, *License for Empire: Colonialism by Treaty in Early America* (1982). Works dealing with the impact of Christian missions include William W. Fitzhugh, ed., *Cultures in Contact* (1985); William G. McLoughlin, *Cherokees and Missionaries, 1789–1839* (1984); and Earl P. Olmstead, *Blackcoats among the Delaware* (1991). Other analyses of cultural interaction are Theda Perdue, *Cherokee Women: Gender and Culture Change, 1700–1835* (1998); William G. McLoughlin, *Cherokee Renascence in the New Republic* (1986); J. Leitch Wright Jr., *Creeks and Seminoles: The Destruction and Regeneration of the Muscogulge People* (1986); and Kathryn E. Holland Braund, *Deerskins and Duffels* (1993). Two recent studies of white expansion are Eric Hinderaker, *Elusive Empires: Constructing Colonialism in the Ohio Valley, 1673–1800* (1999), and Claudio Saunt, *A New Order of Things: Property, Power, and the Transformation of the Creek Indians, 1733–1816* (1999). The "Chickasaw Historical Research Page" <http://home.flash.net/~kma/> compiled by K. M. Armstrong, contains a collection of letters written by or about Chickasaw Indians between 1792 and 1849; the texts of more than thirty treaties, and other documents.

On the activities of speculators and settlers in the Northeast, see two works by Alan Taylor: *Liberty Men and Great Proprietors* (1990) and *William Cooper's Town* (1995). For developments west of the Appalachians, read Malcolm J. Rohrbough, *The Trans-Appalachian Frontier: Peoples, Societies, and Institutions, 1775–1850* (1978); John Mack Faragher, *Sugar Creek: Life on the Illinois Prairie* (1986); and Andrew R. L. Cayton, *The Frontier Republic: Ideology and Politics in the Ohio Country, 1789–1812* (1986).

The Republicans' Political Revolution

Two good general accounts are Marshall Smelser, *The Democratic Republic, 1801–1815* (1968), and Ralph Ketcham, *Presidents above Party: The First American Presidency, 1789–1829* (1984). Detailed studies of Jefferson's presidency include Daniel Sisson, *The Revolution of 1800* (1974); Dumas Malone, *Jefferson the President* (2 vols., 1970 and 1974); and Richard E. Ellis, *The Jeffersonian Crisis: Courts and Politics in the New Republic* (1971). On the Louisiana Purchase, see James P. Ronda, *Lewis and Clark among the Indians* (1984) and Donald Jackson, *The Letters of the Lewis and Clark Expedition* (1963). *Lewis and Clark: The Journey of the Corps of Discovery* (PBS video, 4 hours) tells the story of the initial European exploration of the Louisiana Purchase; the companion Web site, <http://www.pbs.org/lewisandclark/> contains a rich body of material on the explorers and the Indian peoples of the region.

The activities of Aaron Burr are covered in Milton Lomask, *Aaron Burr* (1979). *The Duel* (PBS video, 1 hour) reenacts the confrontation between Alexander Hamilton and Aaron Burr. For the Federalists, see David Hackett Fischer, *The Revolution of American Conservatism: The Federalist Party in the Age of Jeffersonian Democracy* (1965), and James Banner, *To the Hartford Convention: The Federalists and the Origins of Party Politics in the Early Republic, 1789–1815* (1970). American attempts to avoid involvement in the Napoleonic Wars are traced in Lawrence Kaplan, *"Entangling Alliances with None": American Foreign Policy in the Age of Jefferson* (1987), and Bradford Perkins, *Prologue to War: England and the United States, 1805–1812* (1961). See also Clifford L. Egan, *Neither Peace nor War: Franco-American Relations, 1803–1812* (1983), and Doron S. Ben-Atar, *The Origins of Jeffersonian Commercial Policy and Diplomacy* (1993). On James Madison, see Robert A. Rutland, *The Presidency of James Madison* (1990); J. C. A. Stagg, *Mr. Madison's War: Politics, Diplomacy, and Warfare in the Early Republic, 1783–1830* (1983); and Drew McCoy, *The Last of the Fathers: James Madison and the Republican Legacy* (1989). For Native Americans and the War of 1812, consult R. David Edmunds, *Tecumseh and the Quest for Indian Leadership* (1984), and H. S. Halbert and T. H. Ball, *The Creek War of 1813 and 1814* (1970). "A Century of Lawmaking for a New Nation" <http://memory.loc.gov/ammem/amlaw/lawhome.html>, part of the Library of Congress's American Memory project, contains congressional documents and debates, including discussions of the Northwest Ordinance, the ban on slave imports, the Embargo of 1807, and the decision for war in 1812. The site also contains information and maps of Indian land cessions from 1784 to 1894.

On Spain's northern empire, see David Weber, *The Spanish Frontier in North America* (1992), and Walter La Feber, ed., *John Quincy Adams and American Continental Empire* (1965).

The Capitalist Commonwealth

Thomas M. Doerflinger, *A Vigorous Spirit of Enterprise: Merchants and Economic Development in Revolutionary Philadelphia* (1986); John Denis Haeger, *John Jacob Astor* (1991); and Stuart Bruchey, *Robert Oliver: Merchant of Baltimore* (1956), are fine studies of merchant enterprise. The standard history is Curtis R. Nettels, *The Emergence of a National Economy, 1775–1815* (1965). See also Ronald Hoffman, John J. McCusker, and Peter J. Albert, eds., *The Economy of Revolutionary America* (1987), and Daniel P. Jones, *The Economic and Social Transformation of Rhode Island, 1780–1850* (1992).

On banking, consult the classic study by Bray Hammond, *Banks and Politics in America* (1957), and Richard H. Timberlake, *Monetary Policy in the United States* (1992). Studies of manufacturing include Thomas C. Cochran, *Frontiers of Change: Early Industrialism in America* (1981), and David J. Jeremy, *Transatlantic Industrial Revolution: The Diffusion of Textile Technology between Britain and America, 1790–1830* (1981).

The classic studies of state mercantilism are Oscar Handlin and Mary Handlin, *Commonwealth: A Study of the Role of Government in the American Economy: Massachusetts, 1774–1861* (1947), and Louis Hartz, *Economic Policy and Democratic Thought: Pennsylvania, 1776–1860* (1948). State support for transportation can be traced in Carter Goodrich, *Government Promotion of American Canals and Railroads* (1960); Erik F. Hiates et al., *Western River Transportation: The Era of Early Internal Development, 1810–1860* (1975); and Harry N. Scheiber, *Ohio Canal Era: A Case Study of Government and the Economy* (1969). See also David Gilchrist, ed., *The Growth of the Seaport Cities, 1790–1825* (1967), and Winifred Barr Rothenberg, *From Market-Places to Market Economy: The Transformation of Rural Massachusetts, 1750–1850* (1994).

The legal implications of commonwealth ideology are analyzed in Leonard Levy, *The Law of the Commonwealth and Chief Justice Shaw* (1955), and Morton J. Horwitz, *The Transformation of American Law, 1780–1860* (1976). On the Supreme Court, see Robert K. Faulkner, *The Jurisprudence of John Marshall* (1968); Francis N. Stites, *John Marshall: Defender of the Constitution* (1981); Thomas C. Shevory, ed., *John Marshall's Achievement* (1989); and C. Peter McGrath, *Yazoo: Law and Politics in the New Republic* (1966). See also William J. Novak, *The People's Welfare: Law and Regulation in Nineteenth-Century America* (1996).

Chapter 9: The Quest for a Republican Society, 1790–1820

Two fine local studies—Alan Taylor, *William Cooper's Town: Power and Persuasion on the Frontier of the Early American Republic* (1995), and Laurel Thatcher Ulrich, *The Age of Homespun: Objects and Stories in the Creation of an American Myth* (2000)—capture the texture of northern life in the early republic. James Oakes, *The Ruling Race: A History of American Slaveholders* (1982), offers an important perspective on the expansion of slavery, while Nathan O. Hatch, *The Democratization of American Christianity* (1987), presents an interpretation of religious change.

Democratic Republicanism

Warren S. Tryon, *A Mirror for Americans: Life and Manners in the United States, 1790–1870, as Recorded by European Travelers* (3 vols., 1952), suggests the distinctive features of republican society. Clement Eaton, *Henry Clay and the Art of American Politics* (1957), perceptively describes the coming of political democracy, while more detailed studies are Ronald Formisano, *The Transformation of Political Culture: Massachusetts Parties, 1790s–1840s* (1983), and Chilton Williamson, *American Suffrage from Property to Democracy* (1960).

Michael Grossberg, *Governing the Hearth* (1985), discusses changing marriage rules. Catherine M. Scholten, *Childrearing in American Society, 1650–1850* (1985), should be supplemented by Philip Greven's pathbreaking analysis, *The Protestant Temperament: Patterns of Childrearing, Religious Experience, and the Self in Early America* (1977). On sentimentalism, see Shirley Samuels, *The Culture of Sentiment: Race, Gender, and Sentimentality in Nineteenth-Century America* (1992). Other important works include Daniel Blake Smith, *Inside the Great House: Planter Family Life in Eighteenth-Century Chesapeake Society* (1980); Bernard W. Wishy, *The Child and the Republic* (1970); and Jan Lewis, *The Pursuit of Happiness: Family and Values in Jefferson's Virginia* (1983).

Aristocratic Republicanism and Slavery, 1780–1820

On the expansion of slavery, see Ira Berlin, *Many Thousands Gone: The First Two Centuries of Slavery in North America* (1999), and the essays in Berlin and Ronald Hoffman, eds., *Slavery and Freedom in the Age of the American Revolution* (1983). Other important studies of pre-1820 slavery include Robert McColley, *Slavery and Jeffersonian Virginia* (2nd ed., 1973); Donald L. Robinson, *Slavery in the Structure of American Politics, 1765–1820* (1971); Joyce E. Chaplin, *Agricultural Innovation and Modernity in the Lower South, 1730–1815* (1993); and Peter A. Coclanis, *The Shadow of a Dream: Economic Life and Death in the South Carolina Low Country, 1670–1920* (1988). Other works that include material on this period are Charles Joyner, *Down by the Riverside: A South Carolina Slave Community* (1984), and Jacqueline Jones, *Labor of Love, Labor of Sorrow: Black Women, Work, and the Family from Slavery to the Present* (1986). The complex religious lives of African Americans are treated in Albert Raboteau, *Slave Religion* (1968); Mechal Sobel, *Trabelin' On: The Slave Journey to an Afro Baptist Faith* (1979) and Margaret Washington Creel, *"A Peculiar People," Slave Religion and Community-Culture among the Gullahs* (1988).

For slave revolts, consult Douglas R. Egerton, *Gabriel's Rebellion* (1993); James Sidbury, *Ploughs into Swords: Race, Rebellion, and Identity in Gabriel's Virginia, 1730–1810* (1997); Douglas R. Egerton, *He Shall Go Out Free: The Lives of Denmark Vesey* (1999). On the ambiguous position of free blacks in a slave society, consult Ira Berlin, *Slaves without Masters: The Free Negro in the Antebellum South* (1974). For blacks in the northern states, see Gary B. Nash, *Forging Freedom: Philadelphia's Black Community, 1720–1840* (1988). For primary documents that illustrate the ways in which African Americans acquired and transformed the doctrines and beliefs of Protestant Christianity, log on to Documenting the

American South, "The Church in the Southern Black Community" <http://metalab.unc.edu/docsouth/>.

Glover Moore, *The Missouri Compromise* (1953), provides a detailed analysis of that crisis. See also Merton L. Dillon, *Slavery Attacked: Southern Slaves and Their Allies, 1619–1865* (1990).

Protestant Christianity as a Social Force

Perry Miller, *The Life of the Mind in America* (1966), offers a good overview of the Second Great Awakening. For revivalism, see Stephen A. Marini, *Radical Sects of Revolutionary New England* (1982); Bernard A. Weisberger, *They Gathered at the River* (1958); John B. Boles, *The Great Revival, 1787–1805* (1972); and Paul Conkin, *Cane Ridge: America's Pentecost* (1990). The course of religious thought in New England is traced in Daniel Walker Howe, *The Unitarian Conscience* (1970).

Recent studies focusing on evangelical religion include Christine L. Heyrman, *Southern Cross: The Beginnings of the Bible Belt* (1997); Diana Hockstedt Butler, *Standing against the Whirlwind: Evangelical Episcopalians in Nineteenth-Century America* (1995); Randy J. Sparks, *On Jordan's Stormy Banks: Evangelicalism in Mississippi, 1773–1876* (1994); John G. West Jr., *The Politics of Revelation and Reason: Religion and Civic Life in the New Nation* (1996); and Ian H. Murray, *Revival and Revivalism: The Making and Marring of American Evangelicalism, 1750–1858* (1994).

For women's lives, see Susan Juster, *Disorderly Women: Sexual Politics and Evangelicalism in Revolutionary New England* (1994); Harriet B. Applewhite and Darline G. Levy, eds., *Women and Politics in the Age of Democratic Revolution* (1990); and Linda Kerber, *Women of the Republic: Intellect and Ideology in Revolutionary America* (1980). Specialized studies include Joan M. Jensen, *Loosening the Bonds: Mid-Atlantic Farm Women, 1750–1850* (1986); Jeanne Boydston, *Home and Work* (1990); and Laurel Thatcher Ulrich, *A Midwife's Tale: The Life of Martha Ballard, Based on Her Diary, 1785–1812* (1990), which has also been made into a PBS dramatic documentary, *A Midwife's Tale* (1.5 hours). Additional materials on Ballard's experiences and women's lives are available on the Web at <http://www.pbs.org/amex/midwife> and <http://www.DoHistory.org>.

Women's religious initiatives are discussed in Mary P. Ryan, *Cradle of the Middle Class* (1981); Barbara Epstein, *The Politics of Domesticity: Women, Evangelism, and Temperance* (1978); and Keith Melder, *Beginnings of Sisterhood: The American Women's Rights Movement, 1800–1850* (1977), which also traces the growth of female academies.

Chapter 10: The Economic Revolution, 1820–1860

Three important studies of the economic revolution and its consequences are Stuart Bruchey, *Enterprise: The Dynamic Economy of a Free People* (1990); Charles G. Sellers Jr., *The Market Revolution: Jacksonian America, 1815–1840* (1991); and Stuart M. Blumin, *The Emergence of the Middle Class: Social Experience in the American City, 1760–1900* (1989). See also Carolyn Merchant, *Ecological Revolutions: Nature, Gender, and Science in New England* (1989).

The Coming of Industry: Northeastern Manufacturing

Surveys of the Industrial Revolution in America include W. Elliot Brownlee, *Dynamics of Ascent: A History of the American Economy* (1979), and Thomas C. Cochran, *Frontiers of Change: Early Industrialism in America* (1981). See also the pioneering work in economic geography by Donald W. Meinig, *The Shaping of America: A Geographical Perspective, Vol. 2: Continental America, 1800–1867* (1993). Good regional studies are Peter J. Coleman, *The Transformation of Rhode Island* (1963), and Anthony F. C. Wallace, *Rockdale: The Growth of an American Village in the Early Industrial Revolution* (1978).

Books on technological change include Judith A. McGaw, ed., *Early American Technology* (1994); Gary Cross and Rick Szostak, *Technology and American Society: A History* (1995); David Freeman Hawke, *Nuts and Bolts of the Past: A History of American Technology, 1776–1860* (1988); David A. Hounshell, *From the American System to Mass Production, 1800–1932: The Development of Manufacturing Technology in the United States* (1984); and Barbara M. Tucker, *Samuel Slater and the Origins of the American Textile Industry* (1984).

On American workers during this period, see Mary H. Blewett, *Men, Women, and Work: Class, Gender, and Protest in the New England Shoe Industry, 1780–1910* (1990); Alan Dawley, *Class and Community: The Industrial Revolution in Lynn* (1976); Jonathan Prude, *The Coming of Industrial Order: Town and Factory Life in Rural Massachusetts* (1983); Jeanne Boydston, *Home and Work: Housework, Wages, and the Ideology of Labor in the Early Republic* (1990); and Thomas Dublin, *Transforming Women's Work: New England Lives in the Industrial Revolution* (1994). Other useful analyses are Paul A. Gilje and Howard B. Rock, eds., *Keepers of the Revolution: New Yorkers at Work in the Early Republic* (1992) and Paul Faler, *Mechanics and Manufacturers in the Early Industrial Revolution* (1983).

The Expansion of Markets

For the development of the Midwest, see Stephen Aron, *How the West Was Lost: The Transformation of Kentucky from Daniel Boone to Henry Clay* (1996); Andrew R. L. Cayton and Peter S. Onuf, *The Midwest and the Nation* (1990); and John Mack Faragher, *Sugar Creek: Life on the Illinois Prairie* (1986). On agricultural expansion, consult Paul W. Gates, *The Farmer's Age: Agriculture, 1815–1860* (1960). For the settlement of the Great Lakes region, log on to "Pioneering the Upper Midwest: Books from Michigan, Minnesota, and Wisconsin, 1820–1910" <http://memory.loc.gov/ammem/umhtml/umhome.html>, which offers the full text of first-person accounts, biographies, and promotional literature from the collections of the Library of Congress. An excellent tool for tracking social changes is the United States Historical Census Data Browser <http://fisher.lib.virginia.edu/census>, which has mined the censuses (especially the rich returns for 1850 and 1860) for information on race, slavery, immigration, religion, and other topics.

For urban development, see the classic study by R. G. Albion, *The Rise of New York Port, 1815–1860* (1939), and the fine analysis of Chicago by William Cronon, *Nature's Metrop-*

World of Early Mormonism (1993); and Kenneth H. Winn, *Exiles in a Land of Liberty: Mormons in America, 1830–1846* (1989). On the linkages between religion and the utopians, see Paul E. Johnson and Sean Wilentz, *The Kingdom of Matthias: A Story of Sex and Salvation in Nineteenth-Century America* (1995); and Timothy L. Smith, *Revivalism and Social Reform: American Protestantism on the Eve of the Civil War* (1980).

Abolitionism

Two interesting new studies of abolitionism are James Oliver Horton and Lois E. Horton, *In Hope of Liberty: Culture, Community, and Protest among Northern Free Blacks, 1700–1860* (1996), and Paul Goodman, *Of One Blood: Abolitionism and the Origins of Racial Equality* (1998). Other important works include Robert H. Abzug, *Passionate Liberator: Theodore Dwight Weld and the Dilemma of Reform* (1980); David Brion Davis, *The Problems of Slavery in the Age of Revolution, 1770–1823* (1975); Stanley Harrold, *The Abolitionists and the South, 1831–1861* (1995); Leon F. Litwack, *North of Slavery: The Negro in the Free States, 1790–1860* (1961); Lewis Perry, *Childhood, Marriage, and Reform: Henry Clarke Wright, 1797–1870* (1980); James B. Stewart, *Holy Warriors: The Abolitionists and American Slavery* (1976); and John L. Thomas, *The Liberator: William Lloyd Garrison* (1963). Important studies of Frederick Douglass include Nathan I. Huggins, *Slave and Citizen: The Life of Frederick Douglass* (1980), and William S. McFeely, *Frederick Douglass* (1991); for Douglass's own accounts, read the *Narrative of the Life of Frederick Douglass, an American Slave* (1845) and *Life and Times of Frederick Douglass, Written by Himself* (1881).

For the role of women in the antislavery movement, consult Julie Roy Jeffrey, *The Great Silent Army of Abolitionism: Ordinary Women in the Antislavery Movement* (1998); Dorothy Sterling, *Ahead of Her Time: Abby Kelley and the Politics of Anti-Slavery* (1991); Blanche Hersh, *The Slavery of Sex: Female Abolitionists in Nineteenth-Century America* (1978); and Gerda Lerner, *The Grimké Sisters from South Carolina: Pioneers for Women's Rights and Abolition* (1967). On northern hostility to abolition, see Leonard L. Richards, *"Gentlemen of Property and Standing": Anti-Abolition Mobs in Jacksonian America* (1970).

The Women's Rights Movement

The most comprehensive history of women in the United States is Nancy Woloch, *Women and the American Experience* (1992). On the social history of women, see Nancy F. Cott, *The Bonds of Womanhood: "Women's Sphere" in New England, 1780–1835* (1977); Carl N. Degler, *At Odds: Women and the Family in America from the Revolution to the Present* (1980); and Mary P. Ryan, *Cradle of the Middle Class: The Family in Oneida County, New York, 1790–1865* (1981). The most complete discussion of women in education and benevolent reform is Keith Melder, *Beginnings of Sisterhood: The American Women's Rights Movement, 1800–1850* (1977). For studies of specific aspects of women's involvement in reform, see Barbara J. Berg, *The Remembered Gate: Origins of American Feminism: The Woman and the City, 1800–1860* (1978); Estelle B. Freedman, *Their Sisters' Keepers: Women's Prison Reform in America, 1830–1860* (1981); Lori D. Ginzberg, *Women and the*

Work of Benevolence: Morality, Politics, and Class in the Nineteenth-Century United States (1990); Nancy A. Hewitt, *Women's Activism and Social Change: Rochester, New York, 1822–1872* (1984); and Jean F. Yellin, *Women and Sisters: The Antislavery Feminists in American Culture* (1989). But see also Jeanne Boydston et al., *The Limits of Sisterhood: The Beecher Sisters on Women's Rights and Woman's Sphere* (1990).

On Dorothea Dix, see David Gollaher, *Voice for the Mad: The Life of Dorothea Dix* (1995); and Charles M. Snyder, *The Lady and the President: The Letters of Dorothea Dix and Millard Fillmore* (1975). The leading studies of the early women's rights movement include Kathleen Barry, *Susan B. Anthony—A Biography: A Singular Feminist* (1988); Ellen Du Bois, *Feminism and Suffrage: The Emergence of an Independent Women's Movement, 1848–1869* (1978); and Nancy Isenberg, *Sex and Citizenship in Antebellum America* (1998). See also Elizabeth R. Varon, *We Mean to Be Counted: White Women and Politics in Antebellum Virginia* (1996). "Women and Social Movements in the United States, 1830–1930," prepared by Kathryn Kish Sklar and Thomas Dublin <http://womhist.binghamton.edu./> provides a fine introductory essay and an extensive selection of primary documents. Additional source materials (newspapers and periodicals, with an index to articles and contributors) for the period 1830 to 1877 are available through Cornell University's "Making of America" project <http://moa.cit.cornell.edu/> and its companion site at the University of Michigan <http://moa.umdl.umich.edu/>.

Chapter 13: The Crisis of the Union, 1844–1860

Histories that trace the disruption of the Union between the time of the Mexican War and the election of Lincoln are rare. The best is David M. Potter, *The Impending Crisis, 1848–1861* (1976), but see also Michael A. Morrison, *Slavery and the American West: The Eclipse of Manifest Destiny and the Coming of the Civil War* (1995), and the relevant sections of William W. Freehling, *The Road to Disunion: Secessionists at Bay, 1776–1854* (1990), and Leonard L. Richards, *The Slave Power: The Free North and Southern Domination, 1780–1860* (2000). A fine social history that sheds light on the coming of the war is Stephanie McCurry, *Masters of Small Worlds: Yeoman Households, Gender Relations, and the Political Culture of the Antebellum South Carolina Low Country* (1995).

Manifest Destiny

Peter Kolchin, *American Slavery, 1619–1877* (1993), traces the expansion of the cotton South, while the essays in Ira Berlin and Philip D. Morgan, eds., *Cultivation and Culture: Labor and the Shaping of Slave Life* (1993), suggest the distinct characteristics of the cotton regime. See also Robert W. Fogel, *Without Consent or Contract: The Rise and Fall of American Slavery* (1989). Important studies of slave owners include James Oakes, *The Ruling Race: A History of American Slaveholders* (1982), Eugene D. Genovese, *The Political Economy of Slavery*, 2nd ed. (1989), and J. Mills Thornton III, *Politics and Power in a Slave Society: Alabama, 1800–1860* (1978). For slaveholding women, see Catherine Clinton, *The Plantation Mistress* (1983), and Elizabeth Fox-Genovese, *Within the Plantation Household: Black and White Women of the Old South* (1988).

Slave life is treated in Lawrence W. Levine, *Black Culture and Black Consciousness* (1977); Eugene Genovese, *Roll, Jordan, Roll* (1974); and Dena J. Epstein, *Sinful Tunes and Spirituals: Black Folk Music to the Civil War* (1977). On slave revolts, see Stephen B. Oates, *The Fires of Jubilee: Nat Turner's Fierce Rebellion* (1975). The culture of the planter class and non-slaveholding whites can be explored in O. Vernon Burton, *In My Father's House Are Many Mansions: Family and Community in Edgefield, South Carolina* (1985), and J. William Harris, *Plain Folk and Gentry in a Slave Society: White Liberty and Black Slavery in Augusta's Hinterlands* (1985). "*Uncle Tom's Cabin* and American Culture: A Multi-Media Archive" <http://jefferson.village.virginia.edu/utc/> is an extremely rich Web site that explores the literary and cultural context of the time through essays, original documents, and recordings of minstrel music.

Historians have recently focused attention on the trans-Appalachian West. See Gregory N. Nobles, *American Frontiers* (1996); Nicole Etcheson, *The Emerging Midwest: Upland Southerners and the Political Culture of the Old Northwest, 1787–1861* (1996); William Cronon, *Nature's Metropolis* (1992); and Malcolm J. Rohrbough, *The Trans-Appalachian Frontier: People, Societies, and Institutions, 1775–1850* (1978). A fine video documentary on *The West* (6 hours) by Ken Burns and Stephen Ives has a useful Web site, "New Perspectives on the West" <http://www.pbs.org/thewest>, that includes a good collection of maps, biographical essays, original documents, and images.

The ideology of Manifest Destiny is discussed in Norman Graebner, *Empire on the Pacific: A Study of American Continental Expansion* (1955), and Reginald Horsman, *Race and Manifest Destiny: The Origins of American Racial Anglo-Saxonism* (1981).

New approaches to the history of the trans-Mississippi West include Patricia Nelson Limerick, *The Legacy of Conquest: The Unbroken Past of the Unbroken West* (1987); David J. Weber, *The Mexican Frontier, 1821–1846* (1982); and Richard White, *"It's Your Misfortune and None of My Own": A History of the American West* (1991). This newer scholarship presents a more complete view of women. See Susan Armitage and Elizabeth Jameson, eds., *The Women's West* (1987); John Mack Faragher, *Women and Men on the Overland Trail* (1979); and Julie R. Jeffrey, *Frontier Women: The Trans-Mississippi West, 1840–1860* (1979).

War, Expansion, and Slavery, 1846–1850

Study of expansionism in the 1840s should begin with Frederick Merk, *The Monroe Doctrine and American Expansion, 1843–1849* (1972), and William J. Cooper, *The South and the Politics of Slavery, 1828–1856* (1978). On the coming of the Mexican War, consult Paul H. Bergeron, *The Presidency of James K. Polk* (1987); David Pletcher, *The Diplomacy of Annexation: Texas, Oregon, and the Mexican War* (1973); and Charles G. Sellers, *James K. Polk: Continentalist, 1843–1846* (1966). On the fighting of the war, see K. Jack Bauer, *The Mexican War, 1846–1848* (1974), and John S. D. Eisenhower, *So Far from God: The U.S. War with Mexico, 1846–1848* (1989). Richard Bruce Winders, *Mr. Polk's Army* (1977), discusses the experience of American soldiers. For the impact of the war on American expansionists, see Robert W. Johannsen, *To the Halls of the Montezumas: The Mexican War in the American Imagination* (1985). For the Mexican viewpoint, see Gene M. Brack, *Mexico Views Manifest Destiny, 1821–1846: An Essay on the Origins of the Mexican War* (1975). The PBS documentary *The U.S.-Mexican War* (4 hours) and its Web site <http://www.pbs.org/usmexicanwar> view the war both from the American and the Mexican perspective, drawing upon the expertise of historians from each country.

On congressional politics during the 1840s, see Chaplain Morrison, *Democratic Politics and Sectionalism: The Wilmot Proviso Controversy* (1967); Merrill Peterson, *The Great Triumvirate: Webster, Clay, and Calhoun* (1987); and Richard H. Sewell, *Ballots for Freedom: Antislavery Politics in the United States, 1837–1860* (1976). Holman Hamilton, *Prologue to Conflict: The Crisis and Compromise of 1850* (1964), covers the outcome of the political debate.

The End of the Second Party System, 1850–1858

An older but still valuable study of sectional conflict is Avery O. Craven, *The Growth of Southern Nationalism, 1848–1861* (1953). On the Fugitive Slave Act, consult Stanley W. Campbell, *The Slave Catchers* (1970). For the politics of southern expansionism, read Robert E. May, *The Southern Dream of a Caribbean Empire, 1854–1861* (1973).

On the development of the Republican Party, see Eric Foner, *Free Soil, Free Labor, Free Men: The Ideology of the Republican Party before the Civil War* (1970), and William E. Gienapp, *The Origins of the Republican Party, 1852–1856* (1987). The crisis over Kansas is discussed in James A. Rawley, *Race and Politics: Bleeding Kansas and the Coming of the Civil War* (1969), and Gerald W. Wolff, *The Kansas-Nebraska Bill: Party, Section, and the Coming of the Civil War* (1977). On the Buchanan administration, see Kenneth M. Stampp, *America in 1857: A Nation on the Brink* (1990), and Philip S. Klein, *President James Buchanan* (1962). On Dred Scott, see Don E. Fehrenbacher, *The Dred Scott Case: Its Significance in American Law and Politics* (1978). Good biographies include Robert W. Johannsen, *Stephen A. Douglas* (1973), and Stephen Oates, *To Purge This Land with Blood: A Biography of John Brown* (1970).

Abraham Lincoln and the Republican Triumph, 1858–1860

Abraham Lincoln has inspired a host of biographies. See Benjamin P. Thomas, *Abraham Lincoln: A Biography* (1952); Stephen B. Oates, *With Malice toward None* (1977); Mark E. Neely Jr., *The Last Best Hope of Earth* (1993); and David Herbert Donald, *Lincoln* (1995). On Lincoln's formative political years see Don E. Fehrenbacher, *Prelude to Greatness: Lincoln in the 1850s* (1962), and George B. Forgie, *Patricide and the House Divided* (1979). The fate of the Democratic Party is discussed in Michael Holt, *The Political Crisis of the 1850s* (1978).

Chapter 14: Two Societies at War, 1861–1865

The best up-to-date, comprehensive one-volume survey of the Civil War is James M. McPherson, *Battle Cry of Freedom: The Civil War Era* (1988), while Charles P. Roland, *An American Iliad:*

The Story of the Civil War (1991) is an excellent brief study. For the Confederacy, see George C. Rable, *The Confederate Republic* (1994). Charles Royster, *The Destructive War* (1991) explores the increasing dynamic of military violence. Two award-winning Web sites treat the events of these years. "The Valley of the Shadow" <http://jefferson.village.virginia.edu/vshadow2/> traces the experiences of two communities—one northern, one southern—during the prewar era using a multitude of hyperlinked sources—newspapers, letters, diaries, photographs, maps, etc. "The Freedmen and Southern Society Project" <http://www.inform.umd.edu/ARHU/Depts/History/Freedman/home.html> captures the drama of war and emancipation in the words of the participants: liberated slaves and defeated masters, soldiers and civilians, common folk and leaders.

Secession and Military Stalemate, 1861–1862

Classic studies of the secession crisis include Richard N. Current, *Lincoln and the First Shot* (1963); David M. Potter, *Lincoln and His Party in the Secession Crisis, 1860–61* (1962); and Kenneth M. Stampp, *And the War Came: The North and the Secession Crisis, 1860–61* (1950). Histories of the secession of the Deep South include William L. Barney, *The Secessionist Impulse: Alabama and Mississippi in 1860* (1974), and Michael P. Johnson, *Toward a Patriarchal Republic: The Secession of Georgia* (1977). On the Upper South, see Daniel Crofts, *Reluctant Confederates: Upper South Unionists in the Secession Crisis* (1989).

Toward Total War

To study northern society and politics during the war, consult Iver Bernstein, *The New York City Draft Riots* (1990); Gabor S. Boritt, ed., *Lincoln the War President: The Gettysburg Lectures* (1992); George M. Fredrickson, *The Inner Civil War: Northern Intellectuals and the Crisis of Union* (2nd ed., 1993); J. Matthew Gallman, *The North Fights the Civil War: The Home Front* (1994); Mark E. Neely Jr., *The Fate of Liberty: Abraham Lincoln and Civil Liberties* (1991); Phillip S. Paludan, *The Presidency of Abraham Lincoln* (1994); Joel Silbey, *A Respectable Minority: The Democratic Party in the Civil War Era* (1977); Hans Trefousse, *The Radical Republicans* (1969); and Garry Wills, *Lincoln at Gettysburg* (1992).

Important biographies of Union leaders include Michael Fellman, *Citizen Sherman: A Life of William Tecumseh Sherman* (1995); Jean Edward Smith, *Ulysses S. Grant* (2001); Stephen B. Oates, *With Malice toward None: A Life of Abraham Lincoln* (1977); Stephen W. Sears, *George B. McClellan: The Young Napoleon* (1988); and the Abraham Lincoln studies cited in Chapter 13.

Important studies of the Confederacy include Emory M. Thomas, *The Confederate Nation: 1861–1865* (1979), and Douglas B. Ball, *Financial Failure and Confederate Defeat* (1980). Good biographies of leading Confederates include William J. Cooper Jr., *Jefferson Davis, American* (2000); Emory M. Thomas, *Robert E. Lee, A Biography* (1997); and Thomas E. Schott, *Alexander H. Stephens of Georgia: A Biography* (1988). Three significant works on women are Drew Gilpin Faust,

Mothers of Invention: Southern Slaveholding Women in the Civil War (1996); Catherine Clinton and Nina Silber, eds., *Divided Houses: Gender and the Civil War* (1992); and Jeanie Artie, *Patriotic Toil: Northern Women and the American Civil War* (1998).

Other probing books on the Confederacy are Paul Escott, *After Secession: Jefferson Davis and the Failure of Southern Nationalism* (1978); Drew Gilpin Faust, *The Creation of Confederate Nationalism: Ideology and Identity in the Civil War* (1988); and Philip S. Paludan, *Victims: A True History of the Civil War* (1981).

The Turning Point: 1863

Studies of wartime emancipation include Ira Berlin, Barbara Fields, et al. *Slaves No More: Three Essays on Emancipation and the Civil War* (1992); Clarence R. Mohr, *On the Threshold of Freedom: Masters and Slaves in Civil War Georgia* (1986); and Willie Lee Rose, *Rehearsal for Reconstruction: The Port Royal Experiment* (1964). See also James M. McPherson, *The Struggle for Equality: Abolitionists and the Negro in the Civil War and Reconstruction* (1964). The best scholarship on the lives of slaves and black soldiers during the war is found in Ira Berlin et al., eds., *Freedom: A Documentary History of Emancipation, 1861–1867*, series 1, vol. 1: *The Destruction of Slavery* (1985), series 1, vol. 3: *The Wartime Genesis of Free Labor: The Lower South* (1990), and series 2: *The Black Military Experience* (1982).

The Union Victorious, 1864–1865

The most useful introduction to the military aspects of the war is T. Harry Williams, *The History of American Wars* (1981). On the experiences of Civil War soldiers, consult Albert Castel, *Decision in the West: The Atlanta Campaign* (1992); Gerald F. Linderman, *Embattled Courage: The Experience of Combat in the American Civil War* (1987); James M. McPherson, *What They Fought For, 1861–1865* (1994); and Reid Mitchell, *The Vacant Chair: The Northern Soldier Leaves Home* (1993) and Earl J. Hess, *The Union Soldier in Battle: Enduring the Ordeal of Combat* (1997). On the participation of African Americans in the war, see Noah Andre Trudeau, *Like Men of War: Black Troops in the Civil War, 1862–1865*. For Confederate military tactics, refer to Grady McWhiney and Perry D. Jamieson, *Attack and Die: Civil War Military Tactics and the Southern Heritage* (1982), and Steven E. Woodworth, *Jefferson Davis and His Generals: The Failure of Confederate Command in the West* (1990). For graphic accounts of two crucial battles, see Stephen W. Sears, *Landscape Turned Red: The Battle of Antietam* (1983), and Michael Shaara's novel, *Killer Angels* (1974). On the Civil War in the Far West, consult Alvin M. Josephy Jr., *The Civil War in the American West* (1991). For insightful analyses of the war's outcome, see William W. Freehling, *The South vs. the South : How Anti-Confederate Southerners Shaped the Course of the Civil War* (2001); Richard E. Beringer et al., *Why the South Lost the Civil War* (1986); Herman Hattaway and Archer Jones, *How the North Won: A Military History of the Civil War* (1983); and Archer Jones, *Civil War Command and Strategy: The Process of Victory and Defeat* (1992).

Absorbing firsthand accounts of the war years include C. Vann Woodward, ed., *Mary Chesnut's Civil War* (1981); David Donald, ed., *Inside Lincoln's Cabinet: The Civil War Diaries of Salmon P. Chase* (1959); T. W. Higginson, *Army Life in a Black Regiment* (1867); and W. T. Sherman, *Memoirs* (1990).

Chapter 15: Reconstruction, 1865–1877

The starting point for the study of Reconstruction is Eric Foner's major synthesis, *Reconstruction: America's Unfinished Revolution, 1863–1877* (1988), which is also available in a shorter version. Two older surveys that provide useful introductions are John Hope Franklin, *Reconstruction: After the Civil War* (1961), and Kenneth M. Stampp, *The Era of Reconstruction* (1965). *Black Reconstruction in America* (1935), by the black activist and scholar W. E. B. Du Bois, deserves attention as the first book to challenge traditional racist interpretations of Reconstruction as carpetbagger rule unjustly imposed on the defeated South by radical Republicans. The Web site <http://lcweb2.loc.gov/ammem/aaohtml/exhibit/aopart5.html> provides Library of Congress documents and illustrations on African Americans during Reconstruction.

Presidential Reconstruction

For important studies of presidential efforts to rebuild the Union, see the books on Abraham Lincoln listed in Chapter 14 and the following works on Andrew Johnson: Albert Castel, *The Presidency of Andrew Johnson* (1979); Eric L. McKitrick, *Andrew Johnson and Reconstruction* (1960); and James Sefton, *Andrew Johnson and the Uses of Constitutional Power* (1979). On the radical resistance to presidential Reconstruction, see James M. McPherson, *The Struggle for Equality: Abolitionists and the Negro in the Civil War and Reconstruction* (1965). Books that focus on Congress include LaWanda Cox and John H. Cox, *Politics, Principle, and Prejudice, 1865–1867* (1963); David Donald, *The Politics of Reconstruction, 1863–1867* (1965); and William B. Brock, *An American Crisis: Congress and Reconstruction, 1865–1867* (1963). For insight into developments in the South, see Dan T. Carter, *When the War Was Over: The Failure of Self-Reconstruction in the South, 1865–1867* (1985). Michael Perman, *Reunion without Compromise: The South and Reconstruction, 1865–1868* (1973), stresses the South's relations with Johnson. On the freedmen, see Willie Lee Rose, *Rehearsal for Reconstruction: The Port Royal Experiment* (1964); Peter Kolchin, *First Freedom: The Responses of Alabama's Blacks to Emancipation and Reconstruction* (1972); and Leon F. Litwack, *Been in the Storm So Long: The Aftermath of Slavery* (1979). More recent emancipation studies emphasize slavery as a labor system: Barbara Fields, *Slavery and Freedom on the Middle Ground: Maryland during the Nineteenth Century* (1985); Julie Saville, *The Work of Reconstruction: From Slave to Wage Laborer in South Carolina, 1860–1870* (1994); Ira Berlin et al., *Slaves No More: Three Essays on Emancipation and the Civil War* (1992); and Amy Dru Stanley, *From Bondage to Contract: Wage Labor, Marriage, and the Market in the Age of Slave Emancipation* (1999), which ex-

pands the discussion to show what the onset of wage labor meant for freedwomen. Other books that deal with the impact of emancipation on black women are Jacqueline Jones, *Labor of Love, Labor of Sorrow: Black Women, Work, and the Family from Slavery to the Present* (1985), a pioneering work, and an important case study, Leslie A. Schwalm, *A Hard Fight for We: Women's Transition from Slavery to Freedom in South Carolina* (1997). For a Web site that explores how white northern women attempted to assist freed people during Reconstruction, see <http://womhist.binghamton.edu/aid/intro.htm>. Eric Foner, *Nothing But Freedom: Emancipation and Its Legacy* (1983), helpfully places emancipation in a comparative context.

Radical Reconstruction

For Congress's role in radical Reconstruction, see Michael Les Benedict, *A Compromise of Principle: Congressional Republicans and Reconstruction* (1974), and Hans L. Trefousse, *Impeachment of a President: Andrew Johnson, the Blacks, and Reconstruction* (1975). William S. McFeely, *Grant: A Biography* (1981), deftly explains the politics of Reconstruction. Also helpful is Brooks D. Simpson, *Let Us Have Peace: Ulysses S. Grant and the Politics of War and Reconstruction, 1861–1868* (1991). State studies of Reconstruction include Richard Lowe, *Republicans and Reconstruction in Virginia, 1856–1870* (1991), and Otto Olsen, ed., *Reconstruction and Redemption in the South* (1980). The best account of carpetbaggers is Richard N. Current, *Those Terrible Carpetbaggers: A Reinterpretation* (1988). On blacks during radical Reconstruction, see Joel Williamson, *After Slavery: The Negro in South Carolina during Reconstruction, 1861–1877* (1965); Robert Cruden, *The Negro in Reconstruction* (1969); John Blassingame, *Black New Orleans, 1860–1880* (1973); Thomas Holt, *Black over White: Negro Political Leadership in South Carolina during Reconstruction* (1977); and Barry A. Crouch, *The Freedmen's Bureau and Black Texans* (1992). The emergence of the sharecropping system is explored in Roger L. Ransom and Richard Sutch, *One Kind of Freedom: The Economic Consequences of Emancipation* (1977); Jay Mandle, *The Roots of Black Poverty: The Southern Plantation Economy after the Civil War* (1978); Gavin Wright, *Old South, New South: Revolutions in the Southern Economy since the Civil War* (1986); Edward Royce, *The Origins of Southern Sharecropping* (1993); Harold Woodman, *New South, New Law: The Legal Foundations of Credit and Labor Relations in the Postbellum Agricultural South* (1995).

The Undoing of Reconstruction

The most thorough study of the Ku Klux Klan is Allen W. Trelease, *White Terror: The Ku Klux Klan Conspiracy and Southern Reconstruction* (1972), and on its founder, Brian S. Wills, *A Battle from the Start: The Life of Nathan Bedford Forrest* (1992). To survey Reconstruction politics in the South, consult Michael Perman, *The Road to Redemption: Southern Politics, 1869–1879* (1984). On politics in the North, see James Mohr, ed., *The Radical Republicans in the North: State Politics during Reconstruction* (1976), and William Gillette, *Retreat from Reconstruction, 1863–1879* (1979). Laura F. Edwards, *Gendered Strife and Confusion: The Political Culture of Reconstruction*

(1997) is an innovative study that explores the gendered dimension of Reconstruction politics in a North Carolina county. Equally illuminating as a more traditional political narrative is Jonathan M. Bryant, *How Curious a Land: Conflict and Change in Greene County, Georgia, 1850–1885* (1996). For the impact of Reconstruction on the national state, see Morton Keller, *Affairs of State: Public Life in Late Nineteenth-Century America* (1977), and Richard F. Bensel, *Yankee Leviathan: The Origins of Central State Authority in America, 1859–1877* (1990). On political corruption, see Mark W. Summers, *The Era of Good Stealings* (1993). On the Compromise of 1877, see C. Vann Woodward's classic *Reunion and Reaction* (1956), and K. I. Polakoff, *The Politics of Inertia: The Election of 1876 and the End of Reconstruction* (1973).

Chapter 16: The American West

Western history has become a bitterly contested ground in recent years. The fountainhead of the voluminous traditional scholarship is Frederick Jackson Turner's famous essay "The Significance of the Frontier in American History" (1893), reprinted in Ray A. Billington, ed., *Frontier and Section: Selected Essays of Frederick Jackson Turner* (1961). The "new" western history is critical of Turnerian scholarship for being "Eurocentric"—for seeing western history only through the eyes of frontiersmen and settlers—and for masking the rapacious and environmentally destructive underside of western settlement. Patricia N. Limerick's skillfully argued *The Legacy of Conquest: The Unbroken Past of the American West* (1987) opened the debate. Richard White, *"It's Your Misfortune and None of My Own": A New History of the American West* (1991), provides the fullest synthesis of the new scholarship. For an authoritative, balanced treatment of the main themes of western history, see the essays in Clyde A. Milner II et al., *The Oxford History of the American West* (1994); and, for some of the most debated issues, Clyde A. Milner II, ed., *A New Significance: Re-Envisioning the History of the American West* (1996). On women's experience—another primary concern of the new western history—the starting point is Susan Armitage and Elizabeth Jameson, eds., *The Women's West* (1987). There are incisive environmental essays in Donald Worster, *Under Western Skies: Nature and History in the American West* (1992). D. W. Meinig, *Transcontinental America, 1850–1915* (1998), the third volume of his monumental *The Shaping of America: A Geographical Perspective on 500 Years of History*, is illuminating on the geography of western development. A comprehensive Web site with many links is <http://americanwest.com>.

The Great Plains

The classic book, stressing the settlers' adaptation to climate and environment, is Walter P. Webb, *The Great Plains* (1931). There is an excellent chapter on the ecological history of the southern plains in Donald Worster, *The Great Plains* (1979). Robert M. Utley, *The Indian Frontier of the American West, 1846–1890* (1984), is a good introduction; Robert H. Lowie, *Indians of the Great Plains* (1954), is a classic anthropological study. On the religious life of the Plains Indians, see Howard L. Harrod, *Renewing the World: Plains Indian Religion and Morality* (1987). The assault on Indian culture is recounted in Fred-

erick E. Hoxie, *A Final Promise: The Campaign to Assimilate the Indians, 1880–1920* (1984). On phases of plains settlement see Oscar Winther, *The Transportation Frontier: The Trans-Mississippi West, 1865–1890* (1964); Lewis Atherton, *The Cattle Kings* (1964); Gilbert Fite, *The Farmer's Frontier, 1865–1900* (1966); and Mary W. M. Hargreaves, *Dry-Farming in the Northern Great Plains* (1954). The ecological impact is subtly probed in Frieda Knobloch, *The Culture of Wilderness: Agriculture as Colonization in the American West* (1996). One facet of this subject is reconsidered in Andrew C. Isenberg, *The Destruction of the Bison: An Environmental History* (2000). Richard Slotkin, *The Fatal Environment: The Myth of the Frontier in the Age of Industrialization, 1800–1890* (1985), deals with the process by which Americans translated the hard realities of conquering the West into a national mythology. A case in point is Joy Kasson, *Buffalo Bill's Wild West: Celebrity, Memory, and Popular History* (2000).

The peopling of the plains can be explored in Craig Miner, *West of Wichita: Settling the High Plains of Kansas, 1865–1890* (1986); Frederick C. Luebke, ed., *Ethnicity and the Great Plains* (1980); Jon Gjerde, *The Minds of the West: Ethnocultural Evolution in the Rural Middle West, 1830–1917* (1997); Nell Irvin Painter, *Exodusters: Black Migration to Kansas after Reconstruction* (1976); Julie Roy Jeffrey, *Frontier Women: The Trans-Mississippi West, 1840–1880* (1979); Deborah Fink, *Agrarian Women: Wives and Mothers in Rural Nebraska, 1880–1940* (1992); and Elaine Lindgren, *Land in Her Own Name: Women as Homesteaders in North Dakota* (1991). On the integration of the plains economy with the wider world, an especially rich book is William Cronon, *Nature's Metropolis: Chicago and the Great West* (1991).

The Far West

Two valuable regional histories are David Alan Johnson, *Founding the Far West: California, Oregon, and Nevada* (1992), and Carlos A. Schwantes, *The Pacific Northwest: An Interpretive History* (1989). The best book on western mining is Rodman Paul, *Mining Frontiers of the Far West: 1848–1880* (1963). Two case studies of life in mining towns are Paula Petrik, *Women and Family on the Rocky Mountain Frontier: Helena, Montana, 1865–1900* (1987), and Elizabeth Jameson, *All That Glitters: Class, Conflict, and Community in Cripple Creek* (1998). An imaginative treatment of the New Mexico peasantry is Sarah Deutsch, *No Separate Refuge* (1987). On Hispanic Texas an important book is David Montejano, *Anglos and Mexicans in the Making of Texas* (1987). Local studies of laboring Hispanics and their communities are Mario T. Garcia, *Desert Immigrants: The Mexicans of El Paso, 1880–1920* (1981), and Richard Griswold del Castillo, *The Los Angeles Barrio, 1850–1890* (1979). On the Asian migration to America, the best introduction is Ronald Takaki, *Strangers from a Different Shore: A History of Asian Americans* (1989), which can be supplemented with Sucheng Chan, *This Bittersweet Soil: The Chinese in California Agriculture, 1860–1910* (1986); Yong Chen, *Chinese San Francisco, 1850–1943: A Trans-Pacific Community* (2000); and, on the impact of the exclusion laws, Lucy E. Salyer, *Laws Harsh as Tigers: Chinese Immigrants and the Shaping of Modern Immigration Law* (1995). Labor's opposition to the Chinese is skillfully treated in Alexander Saxton, *The Indispensable Enemy: Labor and the Anti-Chinese Movement in California* (1971). Kevin Starr, *California and the American Dream, 1850–1915* (1973), provides a comprehensive account of the emergence of a distinctive California culture. On John Muir and the California wilderness, see Michael L. Smith, *Pacific Visions: California Scientists and the Environment, 1850–1915* (1987), and on water, with special emphasis on California, Donald J. Pisani, *Water, Land, and Law in the West: The Limits of Public Policy, 1850–1920* (1996).

Chapter 17: Capital and Labor in the Age of Enterprise, 1877–1900

The most useful introduction to the economic history of this period is Edward C. Kirkland, *Industry Comes of Age, 1860–1897* (1961). A more sophisticated analysis can be found in W. Elliot Brownlee, *Dynamics of Ascent* (rev. ed., 1979). For essays on many of the topics covered in this chapter, consult Glenn Porter, ed., *Encyclopedia of American Economic History* (3 vols., 1980).

Industrial Capitalism Triumphant

On railroads a convenient introduction is John F. Stover, *American Railroads* (1970). The growth of the railroads as an integrated system has been treated in George R. Taylor and Irene D. Neu, *The American Railway Network, 1861–1890* (1956). On the key link to the Pacific, see David Haward Bain, *Empire Express: Building the First Transcontinental Railroad* (1999). Julius Grodinsky, *Jay Gould: His Business Career, 1867–1892* (1957), is a complex study demonstrating the contributions this railroad buccaneer made to the transportation system. Books such as Cochran's and Grodinsky's have gone a long way to resurrect Gilded Age businessmen from the debunking tradition first set forth with great power in Matthew Josephson, *Robber Barons: Great American Fortunes* (1934). Important business biographies include Joseph F. Wall, *Andrew Carnegie* (1970); Ron Chernow, *Titan: The Life of John D. Rockefeller* (1998); and Jean Strouse, *Morgan: American Financier* (1999). There is an excellent Web site on Andrew Carnegie <http://pbs.org/wgbh/amex/carnegie/>. Peter Temin, *Iron and Steel in the Nineteenth Century* (1964), is the best treatment of that industry. On the development of mass production the key book is David A. Hounshell, *From the American System to Mass Production, 1800–1932* (1984). Alfred D. Chandler, *The Visible Hand: The Managerial Revolution in American Business* (1977), is not an easy book but will amply repay the labors of interested students.

On the New South, the standard work has long been C. Vann Woodward, *Origins of the New South, 1877–1913* (1951). Equally essential as a modern reconsideration is Edward L. Ayers, *The Promise of the New South: Life after Reconstruction* (1992). A brilliant reinterpretation of the causes of the South's economic retardation is Gavin Wright, *Old South, New South* (1986). Jacqueline Jones, *The Dispossessed: America's Underclasses from the Civil War to the Present* (1992), contains an excellent treatment of southern labor.

The World of Work

To understand the impact of industrialism on American workers, three collections of essays make the best starting points: Herbert G. Gutman, *Work, Culture and Society in In-* *dustrializing America* (1976); Michael S. Frisch and Daniel J. Walkowitz, eds., *Working-Class America: Essays on Labor, Community and American Society* (1983); and Leon Fink, *In Search of the Working Class* (1994). On the introduction of Taylorism, the most useful books are Daniel Nelson, *Managers and Workers: Origins of the New Factory System* (2nd ed., 1995); and Robert Kanigel, *The One Best Way: Frederick W. Taylor and the Enigma of Efficiency* (1997). The impact of Taylorism on American workers is treated with insight in David Montgomery, *The Fall of the House of Labor: The Workplace, the State, and American Labor Activism, 1865–1925* (1987).

Two valuable collections of essays on immigrant workers are Richard Ehrlich, ed., *Immigrants in Industrial America* (1977), and Dirk Hoerder, ed., *American Labor and Immigration History, 1877–1920: Recent European Research* (1983). John Bodnar, *Immigration and Industrialization: Ethnicity in an American Mill Town* (1977), and David M. Emmons, *The Butte Irish: Class and Ethnicity in an American Mining Town* (1989), are important case studies of single communities. On women workers, the best introduction is Alice Kessler-Harris, *Out to Work* (1982). Ava Baron, ed., *Work Engendered: Toward a New History of American Labor* (1991), is a rich collection of essays that apply gender analysis to the history of working people. Two excellent case studies in this vein are Mary Blewett, *Men, Women, and Work: Class, Gender, and Protest in the New England Shoe Industry, 1780–1910* (1988), and Stephen H. Norwood, *Labor's Flaming Youth: Telephone Operators and Worker Militancy, 1878–1923* (1990). On black workers useful introductions are William H. Harris, *The Harder We Run: Black Workers Since the Civil War* (1982), and Philip S. Foner, *Organized Labor and the Black Worker* (1974). Walter Licht, *Getting Work: Philadelphia, 1840–1950* (1992), is a pioneering history of a labor market in operation.

The Labor Movement

The standard book on the struggle between labor reform and trade unionism is Gerald N. Grob, *Workers and Utopia, 1865–1900* (1961). For the Knights of Labor, it should be supplemented by Leon Fink, *Workingmen's Democracy: The Knights of Labor and American Politics* (1983), which captures the cultural dimensions of labor reform not seen by earlier historians. Labor's place in the political environment is the subject of David Montgomery, *Citizen Worker* (1993), and, in an innovative comparative study of a single occupation, John H. M. Laslett, *Colliers Across the Seas: A Comparative Study of Class Formation in Scotland and the American Midwest, 1880–1924* (2000). On the emergence of a political strategy, see Julie Greene, *Pure and Simple Politics: The American Federation of Labor, 1881–1915* (1997). Paul Krause, *The Battle for Homestead, 1880–1892* (1992), puts the great strike in a larger social context. Another landmark conflict is considered from many angles in Richard Schneirov et al., ed., *The Pullman Strike and the Crisis of the 1890s* (1999).

The founder of the AFL is the subject of a lively brief biography by Harold Livesay, *Samuel Gompers and Organized Labor in America* (1978). Among the many books on individual unions, Robert Christie, *Empire in Wood* (1956), best reveals the way pure-and-simple unionism worked out in practice. On the western labor movement, important new interpretations are David Brundage, *The Making of Western Working-Class Radicalism: Denver's Organized Workers,*

emerging city culture are studied in Gunther Barth, *City People: The Rise of Modern City Culture in Nineteenth-Century America* (1982); Susan Porter Benson, *Counter Cultures: Saleswomen, Managers, and Customers in American Department Stores, 1890–1940* (1986); John F. Kasson, *Amusing the Million: Coney Island at the Turn of the Century* (1978); Timothy J. Gilfoyle, *City of Eros: New York City, Prostitution and the Commercialization of Sex, 1790–1920* (1991); Kathy Peiss, *Cheap Amusements: Working Women and Leisure in Turn-of-the-Century New York* (1986); Robert W. Snyder, *The Voice of the City: Vaudeville and Popular Culture in New York City, 1880–1930* (1998); and David Nasaw, *Going Out: The Rise and Fall of Public Amusements* (1993). George Chauncey, *Gay New York: Gender, Urban Culture, and the Making of the Gay New York World, 1890–1940* (1994), reveals a terrain hitherto invisible to the historian. On the fostering of high culture in the American city, see Daniel M. Fox, *Engines of Culture: Philanthropy and Art Museums* (1963). The best introduction to intellectual currents in the emerging urban society is Alan Trachtenberg, *The Incorporation of America: Culture and Society, 1865–1893* (1983).

Chapter 20: The Progressive Era

A good survey of the Progressive Era is John Milton Cooper, *Pivotal Decades: The United States, 1900–1920* (1990). Two older but still serviceable narrative accounts are George E. Mowry, *The Era of Theodore Roosevelt, 1900–1912* (1958), and Arthur S. Link, *Woodrow Wilson and the Progressive Era, 1910–1917* (1954). A highly influential interpretation of progressive reform that is worth reading despite its disputed central arguments is Richard Hofstadter, *Age of Reform* (1955). Robert H. Wiebe, *The Search for Order, 1877–1920* (1967), places progressive reform in a broader context of organizational development.

The Course of Reform

Nancy Cohen, *The Reconstruction of American Liberalism: 1865–1914* (2002), is a good introduction to the intellectual origins of progressivism. The religious underpinnings are stressed in Robert M. Crunden, *Ministers of Reform: The Progressives' Achievement in American Civilization, 1889–1920* (1982). In *The New Radicalism in America, 1889–1963* (1965), Christopher Lasch sees progressivism as a form of cultural revolt. Most useful on political thinkers are Charles Forcey, *The Crossroads of Liberalism: Croly, Weyl, Lippmann, and the Progressive Era* (1961), and Leon Fink, *Progressive Intellectuals and the Dilemmas of Democratic Commitment* (1997). Albert W. Alschuler, *Law Without Values: The Life, Work, and Legacy of Justice Holmes* (2000), is the most recent study of the towering figure in legal realism. Two provocative studies set in an international context are James T. Kloppenberg, *Uncertain Victory: Social Democracy and Progressivism in European and American Thought, 1870–1920* (1986), and Daniel T. Rodgers, *Atlantic Crossings: Social Politics in a Progressive Age* (1998). On the journalists, see David M. Chalmers, *The Social and Political Ideas of the Muckrakers* (1964), and Harold S. Wilson, *McClure's Magazine and the Muckrakers* (1970).

Political reform has been the subject of a voluminous literature. Wisconsin progressivism can be studied in David P. Thelen, *The New Citizenship: Origins of Progressivism in Wis-*

consin, 1885–1900 (1972). Important progressives are discussed in Spencer C. Olin, *California's Prodigal Son: Hiram Johnson and the Progressive Movement* (1968), and Richard Lowitt, *George W. Norris: The Making of a Progressive* (1963). On city reform see Bradley R. Rice, *Progressive Cities: The Commission Government Movement* (1972); Jack Tager, *The Intellectual as Urban Reformer: Brand Whitlock and the Progressive Movement* (1968); and Melvin G. Holli, *Reform in Detroit: Hazen S. Pingree and Urban Politics* (1969). The best treatment of the settlement-house movement is Allen F. Davis, *Spearheads of Reform* (1967). Allen F. Davis, *American Heroine: Jane Addams* (1973); George Martin, *Madame Secretary: Frances Perkins* (1976); and Kathryn Kish Sklar, *Florence Kelley and the Nation's Work: The Rise of Women's Political Culture* (1995), deal with leading women progressives. The connection to working women is effectively treated in Nancy S. Dye, *As Equals and Sisters: Feminism, the Labor Movement, and the Women's Trade Union League of New York* (1980). Women garment workers, the key labor constituency for women progressives, are studied with great skill and insight in Susan A. Glenn, *Daughters of the Shtetl: Life and Labor in the Immigrant Generation* (1990). Two path-breaking books on the origins of American feminism are Rosalind Rosenberg, *Beyond Separate Spheres: The Intellectual Origins of Modern Feminism* (1982), and Nancy F. Cott, *The Grounding of Modern Feminism* (1987). Sara Hunter Graham, *Woman Suffrage and the New Democracy* (1996), treats the battle for the suffrage as a precocious exercise of single-issue pressure politics. "Votes for Women: Selections from the National American Woman Suffrage Association Collection, 1848–1921" at <http://memory.loc.gov/ammem/naw/nawshome.html> is a searchable archive of over 160 documents pertaining to the campaign for suffrage. Ellen Carol DuBois, *Harriot Stanton Blatch and the Winning of Woman Suffrage* (1997), studies one of the key suffragist leaders. The most prominent social reformer to spring from feminism is treated in Ellen Chesler, *Woman of Valor: Margaret Sanger and the Birth Control Movement* (1992).

On urban liberalism, the standard book is John D. Buenker, *Urban Liberalism and Progressive Reform* (1973). Richard Schneirov, *Labor and Urban Politics: Class Conflict and the Origins of Modern Liberalism in Chicago, 1864–97* (1998), traces the origins of urban liberalism back into the nineteenth century. The relationship to organized labor can be followed in Irwin Yellowitz, *Labor and the Progressive Movement in New York State* (1965). An incisive study of labor's legal problems is William E. Forbath, *Law and the Shaping of the American Labor Movement* (1991). Two important books by historical sociologists treat the halting progress toward the welfare state: Theda Skocpol, *Protecting Soldiers and Mothers* (1992), and, in a comparison of the United States with Canada and Britain, Ann Shola Orloff, *The Politics of Pensions* (1993). Linda Gordon, *Pitied but Not Entitled: Single Mothers and the History of Welfare, 1890–1935* (1994), brilliantly uses the contemporary crisis over welfare reform as a lens for probing the tangled history of this central concern of social progressives. The most comprehensive survey is Morton Keller, *Regulating a New Society: Public Policy and Social Change in America, 1900–1933* (1994). On the South, see Jack Temple Kirby, *Darkness at the Dawning: Race and Reform in the Progressive South* (1972), and Dewey Grantham, *Southern Progressivism* (1983); on southern black women as social reformers, Glenda Elizabeth

Gilmore, *Gender and Jim Crow: Women and the Politics of White Supremacy in North Carolina, 1869–1920* (1996); and on the racial conservatism of social progressives, Elizabeth Lasch-Quinn, *Black Neighbors: Race and the Limits of Reform in the American Settlement-House Movement* (1993). The revival of black protest is vigorously described in Stephen R. Fox, *The Guardian of Boston: William Monroe Trotter* (1971), and David Levering Lewis, *W. E. B. Du Bois: Biography of a Race, 1868–1919* (1993).

Progressivism and National Politics

National progressivism is best approached through its leading figures. John Milton Cooper, *The Warrior and the Priest* (1983), is a provocative joint biography of Roosevelt and Wilson that emphasizes their shared worldview. Lewis S. Gould, *The Presidency of Theodore Roosevelt* (1991), provides a useful synthesis. "Theodore Roosevelt: Icon of the American Century" at <http://www.npg.si.edu/exh/roosevelt/maver.htm> presents pictures from the National Portrait Gallery, a biographical narrative, and information on Roosevelt's family and friends. Aspects of national progressive politics can be followed in James Penick, *Progressive Politics and Conservation: The Ballinger-Pinchot Affair* (1968); James Holt, *Congressional Insurgents and the Party System* (1969); and David Sarasohn, *The Party of Reform: The Democrats in the Progressive Era* (1989). "The Evolution of the Conservation Movement" at <http://memory.loc.gov/ammem/amrvhtml/conspref.html> offers a timeline and archive of materials on the movement's development from 1850 to 1920. Naomi Lamoreaux, *The Great Merger Movement in American Business, 1895–1904* (1985), offers a sophisticated modern analysis of trust activity; Thomas K. McCraw, ed., *Regulation in Perspective* (1981), contains valuable interpretative essays on the problems of trust regulation; and James Livingston, *Origins of the Federal Reserve System: Money, Class, and Corporate Capitalism, 1890–1913* (1986), treats banking reform. A comprehensive rethinking of the progressive struggle to fashion a regulatory policy for big business is offered in Martin J. Sklar, *The Corporate Reconstruction of American Capitalism, 1890–1916: The Market, the Law, and Politics* (1988).

Chapter 21: An Emerging World Power, 1877–1914

Two useful surveys of late-nineteenth-century diplomatic history are Charles S. Campbell, *The Transformation of American Foreign Relations, 1865–1900* (1976), and Walter LaFeber, *The American Search for Opportunity, 1865–1913* (vol. II, *The Cambridge History of American Foreign Relations*, 1993). Invaluable as a historiographical guide is Robert L. Beisner, *From the Old Diplomacy to the New, 1865–1900* (2nd ed., 1986).

The Roots of Expansion

Standard works on the preexpansionist era are David M. Pletcher, *The Awkward Years: American Foreign Relations under Garfield and Arthur* (1963), and Milton Plesur, *America's Outward Thrust: Approaches to American Foreign Affairs, 1865–1890* (1971). Walter La Feber's highly influential *The New Empire, 1860–1898* (1963) places economic interest—especially the need for overseas markets—at the center of schol-

arly debate over the sources of American expansionism. A robust counterpoint is Fareed Zakaria, *From Wealth to Power* (1998), which asks why the United States was so slow (compared to other imperial nations) to translate its economic power into international muscle. On American business overseas the definitive work is Myra Wilkins, *The Emergence of the Multinational Enterprise: American Business Abroad from the Colonial Era to 1914* (1970). Other important books dealing with aspects of American expansionism are David Healy, *U.S. Expansionism: The Imperialist Urge in the 1890s* (1970); Robert Seager, *Alfred Thayer Mahan* (1977); Michael Hunt, *Ideology and U.S. Foreign Policy* (1987); Mark R. Shulman, *Navalism and the Emergence of American Sea Power, 1882–1893* (1995); and Kenneth J. Hagan, *This People's Navy: The Making of American Seapower* (1991). Emily S. Rosenberg, *Spreading the American Dream: American Economic and Cultural Expansionism* (1982), and Matthew Fry Jacobson, *Barbarian Virtues: The United States Encounters Foreign Peoples at Home and Abroad* (2000), explore the home roots of expansionism.

An American Empire

On the war with Spain, the liveliest narrative is still Frank Freidel, *A Splendid Little War* (1958). For fuller treatments, see John Offner, *An Unwanted War: The Diplomacy of the United States and Spain over Cuba, 1895–1898* (1988); David S. Trask, *The War with Spain in 1898* (1981); Ivan Musicant, *Empire by Default* (1998); and Lewis Gould, *The Spanish-American War and President McKinley* (1982), which emphasizes McKinley's strong leadership. Ernest R. May, *Imperial Democracy: The Emergence of America as a Great Power* (1961), exemplifies the earlier view that McKinley was a weak figure driven to war by jingoistic pressures. David Nasaw, *The Chief: The Life of William Randolph Hearst* (2000), is a fine new biography of the prime exponent of jingoism. The Library of Congress maintains an excellent Web site, "The Spanish-American War," at <http://lcweb.loc.gov/rr/hispanic/1898/> with separate sections on the war in Cuba, the Philippines, Puerto Rico, and Spain. On the Philippines, see Richard E. Welch, *Response to Imperialism: The United States and the Philippine-American War, 1898–1903* (1979), and, for the subsequent history, Peter Stanley, *A Nation in the Making: The Philippines and the United States, 1899–1921* (1974). Robert L. Beisner, *Twelve against Empire: The Anti-Imperialists, 1898–1900* (1968) remains the best book on that subject. "Anti-Imperialism in the United States" at <http://www.boondocksnet.com/ai/index.html> includes an extensive collection of documents, political cartoons, maps, and photographs from the period.

Onto the World Stage

On the European context a useful introduction can be found in the early chapters of Felix Gilbert, *The End of the European Era, 1890 to the Present* (4th ed., 1991). For a stimulating interpretation see L. C. B. Seaman, *From Vienna to Versailles* (1955). On American relations with Britain the standard work is Bradford Perkins, *The Great Rapprochement: England and the United States, 1895–1914* (1968). On Roosevelt's diplomacy, the starting point remains Howard K. Beale, *Theodore Roosevelt and the Rise of America to World Power* (1956). There are keen insights into the diplomatic views of both Roosevelt

Sport (1994). The Negro Leagues are covered in Robert W. Peterson, *Only the Ball Was White* (1970), and Donn Rogosin, *Invisible Men* (1985).

Dissenting Values and Cultural Conflict

Paul Carter, *Another Part of the Twenties* (1977), outlines the decade's deeply felt cultural controversies. Background on rural and urban life is provided by Don Kirschner, *City and Country: Rural Responses to Urbanization in the 1920s* (1970); Zane Miller, *The Urbanization of America* (1973); and Jon Teaford, *The Twentieth-Century American City* (1986). John Higham, *Strangers in the Land* (1955), describes immigration restriction and nativism. Richard K. Tucker, *The Dragon and the Cross* (1991), and Leonard Moore, *Citizen Klansmen* (1991), cover the Klan's rise and fall, and Kathleen M. Blee, *Women of the Klan* (1991), and Nancy MacLean, *Behind the Mask of Chivalry* (1994), offer a provocative discussion of racism and gender in the 1920s. George M. Marsden, *Fundamentalism and American Culture* (1980), and William G. McLoughlin, *Fundamentalism in American Culture* (1983), cover religion; Edward J. Larson, *Summer of the Gods* (1997), treats the Scopes trial. Douglas O. Linder of the University of Missouri-Kansas City maintains a "Famous Trials" Web site at <http://www.law.umkc.edu/faculty/projects/ftrials/scopes/scopes.htm> that offers photos, cartoons, biographies of the participants, and firsthand accounts of the Scopes trial. On intellectual development, see Robert Crunden, *Body and Soul: The Making of American Modernism: Art, Music and Letters in the Jazz Age, 1919–1926* (2000); Roderick Nash, *The Nervous Generation: American Thought, 1917–1930* (1969); and Daniel Singal, ed., *Modernist Culture in America* (1991). Virginia Sanchez Korrol, *From Colonia to Community* (1983), covers the history of Puerto Ricans in New York City. On the Harlem Renaissance, see George Hutchinson, *The Harlem Renaissance in Black and White* (1995); David Levering Lewis, *When Harlem Was in Vogue* (1981); Nathan Huggins, *Harlem Renaissance* (1971); and Cheryl A. Wall, *Women of the Harlem Renaissance* (1995). For jazz and blues, see Burton Peretti, *The Creation of Jazz* (1992), Daphne Duval Harrison, *Black Pearls: Blues Queens of the 1920s* (1990); and Angela Y. Davis, *Blues Legacies and Black Feminism* (1998). Judith Stein, *The World of Marcus Garvey* (1985), describes the reformer. On Prohibition, see Andrew Sinclair, *Prohibition: The Era of Excess* (1962), and Norman Clark, *Deliver Us from Evil* (1976). The 1928 election is covered in Oscar Handlin, *Al Smith and His America* (1958); Kristi Andersen, *The Creation of a Democratic Majority, 1928–1936* (1979); and Allan J. Lichtman's quantitative study, *Prejudice and the Old Politics* (1979).

Chapter 24: The Great Depression

Useful overviews of the Great Depression are T. H. Watkins, *The Great Depression: America in the 1930s* (1993); John A. Garraty, *The Great Depression* (1987); and Robert S. McElvaine, *The Great Depression, 1929–1941* (1984).

The Coming of the Great Depression

Historians and economists continue to debate the causes of the Great Depression. See John Kenneth Galbraith, *The Great Crash* (1954); Milton Friedman and Anna Schwartz, *The Great Contraction, 1929–1933* (1965); Charles Kindleberger, *The World in Depression* (1974); and Michael Bernstein, *The Great Depression: Delayed Recovery and Economic Change in America, 1929–1939* (1988). Irving Bernstein, *The Lean Years* (1960), offers a compelling portrait of hard times during the Hoover years.

Hard Times

A wealth of material brings the voices of the 1930s to life. The Federal Writers' Project, *These Are Our Lives* (1939); Tom Terrill and Jerrold Hirsch, eds., *Such as Us: Southern Voices of the Thirties* (1978); and Ann Banks, ed., *First-Person America* (1980), all draw on oral histories collected by the Works Progress Administration during the 1930s. See also Robert S. McElvaine, ed., *Down and Out in the Great Depression* (1983). Evocative secondary sources include Studs Terkel, *Hard Times: An Oral History of the Great Depression* (1970), and Caroline Bird, *The Invisible Scar* (1966).

Descriptions of family life in the 1930s include Robert and Helen Lynd, *Middletown in Transition* (1937); Mirra Komarovsky, *The Unemployed Man and His Family* (1940); and Roger Angell, *The Family Encounters the Depression* (1936). Russell Baker's autobiography, *Growing Up* (1982), provides an often humorous description of family life in the 1930s. Glen H. Elder Jr., *Children of the Great Depression* (1974), and John A. Clausen, *American Lives: Looking Back at the Children of the Great Depression* (1993), consider the long-term effects. For more on youth, see Maxine Davis, *The Lost Generation* (1936); and John Modell, *Into One's Own: From Youth to Adulthood, 1920–1975* (1989).

Frederick Lewis Allen, *Since Yesterday* (1939), provides an impressionistic overview of popular culture in the 1930s. See also the essays in Lawrence W. Levine, *The Unpredictable Past* (1993), and Michael Denning, *Cultural Front: The Laboring of American Culture in the Twentieth Century* (1996). Much valuable material can be found on the University of Utrecht's "American Culture in the 1930s" site at <http://www.let.uu.nl/ams/xroads/1930link.htm>, which provides an invaluable list of "Internet Resources on the 1930s." Specific studies of movies and Hollywood include Andrew Bergman, *We're in the Money* (1971); Molly Haskell, *From Reverence to Rape: The Treatment of Women in the Movies* (2nd ed., 1987); and Thomas Schatz, *The Genius of the System: Hollywood Film Making in the Studio Era* (1988). On radio, see Arthur Frank Wertheim, *Radio Comedy* (1979). The University of Virginia's "America in the 1930s" is a comprehensive site. See especially "On the Air," which offers audio clips of *Amos 'n' Andy* and other series at <http://xroads.virginia.edu/~1930s/home_1.html>. Much valuable material can be found on the University of Utrecht's "American Culture in the 1930s" site at <http://www.let.uu.nl/ams/xroads/1930proj.htm>, which in turn points to other sites dealing with literature, film, and other aspects of American culture during the depression.

Material on women in the 1930s can be found in Susan Ware, *Holding Their Own* (1982); Winifred Wandersee, *Women's Work and Family Values, 1920–1940* (1981); and Lois Scharf, *To Work and to Wed* (1981). For the special dimensions of white rural women's lives, see Margaret Hagood, *Mothers of the South* (1939). Jeane Westin, *Making Do: How Women*

Survived the '30s (1976), is a lively account drawn from interviews. The birth control movement is surveyed in Linda Gordon, *Woman's Body, Woman's Right* (2nd ed., 1990); Estelle Freedman and John D'Emilio, *Intimate Matters: A History of Sexuality in America* (1988); and Ellen Chesler, *Woman of Valor: Margaret Sanger and the Birth Control Movement in America* (1992).

Harder Times

Developments in the black community during the 1930s are covered in Cheryl Lyn Greenberg, *"Or Does It Explode?" Harlem in the Great Depression* (1991); Jervis Anderson, *This Was Harlem, 1900–1950* (1982); and Robert Weisbrot, *Father Divine and the Struggle for Racial Equality* (1983). James Goodman, *Stories of Scottsboro* (1994), and Dan T. Carter, *Scottsboro* (1969), discuss that case. Donald Grubbs, *Cry from Cotton* (1971), tells the story of the Southern Tenant Farmers Union. Robin D. G. Kelley, *Hammer and Hoe* (1990), is an excellent account of Alabama communists during the Great Depression. Donald Worster, *Dust Bowl* (1979), evokes the plains during the "Dirty Thirties." James N. Gregory, *American Exodus: The Dust Bowl Migration and Okie Culture in California* (1989), treats the experiences of migrants and their impact on California culture and the economy. The Library of Congress's American Memory collection has extensive material on the depression, including a multimedia presentation, "Voices from the Dust Bowl: The Charles L. Todd and Robert Sonkin Migrant Worker Collection, 1940–41" at <http://lcweb2.loc.gov/ammem/afctshtml/tshome.html>. See also Kevin Starr, *Endangered Dreams: The Great Depression in California* (1996).

On the experiences of Mexican Americans during the 1930s, see Mario T. Garcia, *Mexican Americans: Leadership, Ideology, and Identity, 1930–1960* (1989), and *Memories of Chicano History: The Life and Narrative of Bert Corona* (1994). George J. Sanchez, *Becoming Mexican American* (1993), examines Chicano Los Angeles from 1900 to 1945; and David Gutierrez, *Walls and Mirrors* (1995), looks at Mexican immigration and the politics of ethnicity. See also Richard A. Garcia, *The Rise of the Mexican-American Middle Class* (1990). For Mexican American women's lives in the twentieth century, see Vicki Ruiz's overview, *From Out of the Shadows* (1998), as well as her *Cannery Women, Cannery Lives* (1987), and Patricia Zavella, *Women's Work and Chicano Families* (1987). On Asian Americans, see Judy Yung, *Unbound Feet: A Social History of Chinese Women in San Francisco* (1995) and Ronald Takaki, *Strangers from a Different Shore: A History of Asian Americans* (1989).

Herbert Hoover and the Great Depression

Hoover's response to the depression is chronicled in Alfred Romasco, *The Poverty of Abundance* (1965), and Jordan Schwartz, *The Interregnum of Despair* (1970). Eliot Rosen, *Hoover, Roosevelt, and the Brain Trust* (1977), treats the transition between the two administrations, as does Frank Freidel, *Launching the New Deal* (1973). On the 1932 election and the beginnings of the New Deal coalition, see David Burner, *The Politics of Provincialism* (1967); Samuel Lubell, *The Future of*

American Politics (1952); and John Allswang, *The New Deal in American Politics* (1978).

Chapter 25: The New Deal, 1933–1939

Comprehensive introductions to the New Deal include Robert S. McElvaine, *The Great Depression* (1984); William E. Leuchtenburg, *Franklin D. Roosevelt and the New Deal* (1963); John A. Garraty, *The Great Depression* (1987); Roger Biles, *A New Deal for the American People* (1991); and Harvard Sitkoff, ed., *Fifty Years Later: The New Deal Evaluated* (1985). On the appeal of Roosevelt and his fireside chats, see Lawrence Levine and Cornelia Levine, *The People and the President: America's Conversation with FDR* (2002).

The New Deal Takes Over, 1933–1935

The New Deal has inspired a voluminous bibliography. Frank Freidel, *Launching the New Deal* (1973), covers the first hundred days in detail. Monographs include Bernard Bellush, *The Failure of the NRA* (1975); Thomas K. McCraw, *TVA and the Power Fight* (1970); John Salmond, *The Civilian Conservation Corps* (1967); Roy Lubove, *The Struggle for Social Security* (1968); Mark Leff, *The Limits of Symbolic Reform: The New Deal and Taxation, 1933–1939* (1984); and Bonnie Fox Schwartz, *The Civilian Works Administration, 1933–1934* (1984). Ellis Hawley, *The New Deal and the Problem of Monopoly* (1966), provides a stimulating account of economic policy. Claire Bond Potter, *War on Crime* (1998), analyzes the Federal Bureau of Investigation and state building in the 1930s. Agricultural developments are covered in Theodore Saloutos, *The American Farmer and the New Deal* (1982); and Sidney Baldwin, *Poverty and Politics: The Rise and Decline of the Farm Security Administration* (1968). Alan Brinkley, *Voices of Protest* (1982), covers the Coughlin and Long movements.

The Second New Deal, 1935–1938

Roosevelt's second term has drawn far less attention than has the 1933–1936 period. James MacGregor Burns, *Roosevelt: The Lion and the Fox* (1956), provides an overview, as does Barry Karl, *The Uneasy State* (1983). Alan Brinkley, *The End of Reform* (1995), discusses the New Deal and liberalism between 1937 and 1945. The growing opposition to the New Deal is treated in Clyde P. Weed, *The Nemesis of Reform: The Republican Party during the New Deal* (1994), and James T. Patterson, *Congressional Conservatism and the New Deal* (1967).

The New Deal's Impact on Society

Katie Louchheim, ed., *The Making of the New Deal: The Insiders Speak* (1983), provides an engaging introduction to some of the men and women who shaped the New Deal. "The New Deal Network," sponsored by the Franklin and Eleanor Roosevelt Institute and the Institute for Learning Technologies, has an impressive site at <http://newdeal.feri.org/index.htm> with extensive images, features such as "Work-Study-Live: The

Resident Youth Centers of the NYA," and links to other New Deal sites. On women in the New Deal, see Susan Ware, *Beyond Suffrage* (1981). Blanche Cook, *Eleanor Roosevelt* (1991), takes the story to 1933; see also Lois Scharf, *Eleanor Roosevelt* (1987). Also of interest is Frances Perkins's memoir, *The Roosevelt I Knew* (1946).

On minorities and the New Deal, see Harvard Sitkoff, *A New Deal for Blacks* (1978); John B. Kirby, *Black Americans in the Roosevelt Era* (1980); Robert Zangrando, *The NAACP Crusade against Lynching, 1909–1950* (1980); and Nancy J. Weiss, *Farewell to the Party of Lincoln* (1983). For material on Mary McLeod Bethune, see Darline Clark Hine, ed., *Black Women in America: An Historical Encyclopedia* (1993). George J. Sanchez, *Becoming Mexican American: Ethnicity, Culture and Identity in Chicano Los Angeles, 1900–1945* (1993), and David G. Gutierrez, *Walls and Mirrors: Mexican Americans, Mexican Immigrants, and the Politics of Ethnicity* (1995), describe the politicization of Mexican Americans in the 1930s.

Irving Bernstein, *The Turbulent Years* (1970) and *A Caring Society: The New Deal, the Worker, and the Great Depression* (1985), chronicle the story of the labor movement through 1941 in compelling detail. Additional studies include Ronald Schatz, *The Electrical Workers* (1983); Bruce Nelson, *Workers on the Waterfront* (1988); and Lizabeth Cohen, *Making a New Deal: Industrial Workers in Chicago, 1919–1939* (1990). Steven Fraser, *Labor Will Rule* (1991), is a fine biography of CIO leader Sidney Hillman. A number of Web sites offer resources for local and state history. An excellent example is the Michigan State History Museum's "The Great Depression," with material on the Flint sit-down strike and New Deal relief programs at <http://www.sos.state.mi.us/history/museum/explore/museums/hismus/hismus.html>. For women and the labor movement, see Annelise Orleck, *Common Sense and a Little Fire* (1995).

On Indian policy, see Donald Parman, *Navajos and the New Deal* (1976); Laurence Hauptman, *The Iroquois and the New Deal* (1981); and Laurence C. Kelly, *The Assault on Assimilation: John Collier and the Origins of Indian Policy Reform* (1983). For rural electrification, see D. Clayton Brown, *Electricity for Rural America* (1980).

The various New Deal programs have found historians in Jerry Mangione, *The Dream and the Deal: The Federal Writers' Project, 1935–1943* (1972); Richard McKinzie, *The New Deal for Artists* (1973); and Jane DeHart Mathews, *The Federal Theater, 1935–1939* (1967). The Library of Congress page on the "Federal Theater Project 1933–1939" at <http://memory.loc.gov/ammem/fedtp/fthome.html> offers scripts, still photographs, costumes, and production materials for several plays put on by the Federal Theater Project. See also the library's excellent posting of over 55,000 photographs from the Farm Security Administration and Office of War Information Collection at <http://memory.loc.gov/ammem/fsowhome.html>. Marlene Park and Gerald Markowitz, *Democratic Vistas* (1984), survey New Deal murals and art, and Barbara Melosh, *Engendering Culture* (1991), looks at New Deal public art and theater. General studies of cultural expression include William Stott, *Documentary Expression and Thirties America* (1973), and Richard Pells, *Radical Visions and American Dreams* (1973). The creation of the New Deal's welfare system is treated in James T. Patterson, *America's Struggle against Poverty* (1981), which carries the story through 1980.

See also Michael Katz, *In the Shadow of the Poorhouse: A Social History of Welfare in America* (1986). Linda Gordon, *Pitied but Not Entitled: Single Mothers and the History of Welfare* (1994), assesses the impact of gender on welfare. For the enduring impact of Franklin Roosevelt on the political system, see William Leuchtenburg, *In the Shadow of FDR* (1983).

Chapter 26: The World at War, 1939–1945

John Morton Blum, *V Was for Victory* (1976); William O'Neill, *A Democracy at War* (1993); and Michael C. C. Adams, *The Best War Ever* (1994), offer good introductions to American politics and culture during the war years. A valuable collection of articles is found in Lewis A. Erenberg and Susan E. Hirsch, eds., *The War in American Culture* (1996). Studs Terkel, *"The Good War"* (1984), offers a powerful and provocative oral history of the war. John Keegan, *The Second World War* (1990), offers the best one-volume account of the battlefront aspects.

The Road to War

Depression and wartime diplomacy are covered in Robert Dallek, *Franklin D. Roosevelt and American Foreign Policy, 1932–1945* (1979), and Akira Iriye, *The Globalizing of America, 1913–1945* (1993). On American isolationism, see Wayne Cole, *Roosevelt and the Isolationists, 1932–1945* (1983). Warren T. Kimball, *The Most Unsordid Act* (1969), describes the lend-lease controversy of 1939–1941, whereas Kimball's *The Juggler: Franklin Roosevelt as Wartime Statesman* (1991), provides an overview of Roosevelt's leadership. Roberta Wohlstetter, *Pearl Harbor* (1962); Herbert Feis, *The Road to Pearl Harbor* (1950); and Gordon W. Prange, *At Dawn We Slept* (1981), describe the events that led to American entry into the war.

Organizing for Victory

George Flynn, *The Mess in Washington* (1979), and Harold G. Vatter, *The U.S. Economy in World War II* (1985), discuss America's economic mobilization. Mark S. Foster, *Henry J. Kaiser: Builder in the Modern American West* (1989), and Stephen B. Adams, *Mr. Kaiser Goes to Washington: The Rise of a Government Entrepreneur* (1997), are comprehensive accounts of Kaiser's career. Alan Winkler, *The Politics of Propaganda* (1978), covers the Office of War Information. On labor's role during war, see George Lipsitz, *Rainbow at Midnight: Labor and Culture in the 1940s* (1994); and Nelson Lichtenstein, *Labor's War at Home: The CIO in World War II* (1982). The National Archives Administration at <http://www.archives.gov/exhibit_hall/index.html?page =2> has two World War II sites. "A People at War" offers a number of documents, including a letter about the Navajo Code Talkers. "Powers of Persuasion: Poster Art from World War II" contains thirty-three color posters and a sound file of the song "Any Bonds Today." For more on politics in wartime, see James McGregor Burns, *Roosevelt: The Soldier of Freedom* (1970); Doris Kearns Goodwin, *No Ordinary Time* (1994); and Alan Brinkley, *The End of Reform* (1995).

Women's roles in wartime are covered by Susan Hartmann, *The Home Front and Beyond* (1982); Karen Anderson, *Wartime*

Women (1980); D'Ann Campbell, *Women at War with America* (1984); Ruth Milkman, *Gender at Work* (1987); and Sherna B. Gluck, *Rosie the Riveter Revisited: Women, the War, and Social Change* (1987). Judy Barrett Litoff and David C. Smith, *We're in This War, Too* (1994), includes letters from American women in uniform, and Leisa D. Meyer, *Creating GI Jane* (1996), discusses the Women's Army Corps. The Library of Congress at <http://lcweb.loc.gov/exhibits/wcf/wcf0001.html> has an on-line exhibit, "Women Come to the Front: Journalists, Photographers, and Broadcasters during World War II," that features articles, biographies, and photographs of eight women who covered the war. See also "Rosie Pictures: Select Images Relating to American Women Workers during World War II" at <http://lcweb.loc.gov/rr/print/126_rosi.html>.

Life on the Home Front

William M. Tuttle Jr., *"Daddy's Gone to War"* (1993), describes World War II from the perspective of the nation's children. Alan Clive, *State of War* (1979), provides a case study of Michigan during the war; Marilynn S. Johnson, *The Second Gold Rush* (1993), describes Oakland, California, and the East Bay. See also Gerald D. Nash, *The American West Transformed: The Impact of the Second World War* (1985). The Rutgers Oral History Archive of World War II at <http://fas-history.rutgers.edu/oralhistory/orlhom.htm> offers over 100 oral histories that cover not just the interviewees' war experiences but their life histories as well, providing valuable insights into community life in depression and wartime New Jersey. Clayton R. Koppes and Gregory D. Black, *Hollywood Goes to War* (1987), and Thomas Doherty, *Projections of War* (1993), cover the film industry. On racial tensions and the war, see Ronald Takaki, *Double Victory: A Multicultural History of America in World War II* (2001). The experience of black Americans is treated in Albert Russell Buchanan, *Black Americans in World War II* (1977), and Neil Wynn, *The Afro-American and the Second World War* (1975). On racial tensions, see Dominic Capeci Jr., *Race Relations in Wartime Detroit* (1984), and Mauricio Mazan, *The Zoot Suit Riots* (1984). Richard Dalfiume, *Desegregation of the U.S. Armed Forces* (1969), covers black soldiers in the military, and Phillip McGuire, *Taps for a Jim Crow Army* (1993), offers a collection of letters from black soldiers. Alan Berube, *Coming Out under Fire* (1990), is an oral history of gay men and lesbians in the military; see also John D'Emilio, *Sexual Politics, Sexual Communities* (1983), for the impact of the war on gay Americans. Maurice Isserman, *Which Side Were You On?* (1982), analyzes the American Communist Party during the war. Two compelling accounts of Japanese relocation are Audre Girdner and Anne Loftus, *The Great Betrayal* (1969), and Roger Daniels, *Prisoners without Trial: Japanese-Americans in World War II* (1993). See also John Tateishi, ed., *And Justice for All: An Oral History of the Japanese-American Detention Camps* (1984); Peter Irons, *Justice at War: The Story of the Japanese-American Internment Cases* (1983); and Page Smith, *Democracy on Trial: The Japanese-American Evacuation and Relocation in World War II* (1995). There are many Web sites on Japanese internment. The University of Washington provides a particularly interesting one at <http://www.lib.washington.edu/exhibits/harmony/default.htm> on the experiences of the Seattle Japanese American community's incarceration at the Puyallup Assembly Center; it includes letters, photographs, and other documents.

Fighting and Winning the War

Extensive material chronicles the American military experience during World War II. Williamson Murray and Allan R. Millett, *A War to Be Won: Fighting the Second World War* (2000); Gerald Linderman, *The World within War: America's Combat Experience in World War 2* (1999); and Russell F. Weigley, *The American Way of War* (1973), provide overviews. Ronald Schaffer, *Wings of Judgement: American Bombing in World War II* (1985), and Bradley F. Smith, *The Shadow Warriors: OSS and the Origins of the CIA* (1983), are more specialized. Stephen Ambrose, *D-Day, June 6, 1944* (1994) and *Citizen Soldiers* (1997), describe the end of the fighting in Europe. David S. Wyman, *The Abandonment of the Jews* (1984), describes the lack of American response to the Holocaust from 1941 to 1945. On East Asia, see John W. Dower, *War without Mercy: Race and Power in the Pacific War* (1986); Ronald H. Spector, *Eagle against the Sun: The American War with Japan* (1984); and John Toland, *Rising Sun: The Decline and Fall of the Japanese Empire* (1970).

American diplomacy and the strategy of the Grand Alliance are surveyed in Lloyd Gardner, *Spheres of Influence* (1993). The relationship between the wartime conferences and the onset of the cold war is treated in Walter La Feber, *America, Russia, and the Cold War* (8th ed., 1996), and Stephen Ambrose and Douglas Brinkley, *Rise to Globalism* (8th ed., 1997). Richard Rhodes, *The Making of the Atomic Bomb* (1987), and Martin Sherwin, *A World Destroyed* (1975), provide compelling accounts of the development of the bomb. See also Gar Alperovitz, *The Decision to Use the Atomic Bomb* (1995); Ronald Takaki, *Hiroshima: Why America Dropped the Atomic Bomb* (1995); and Robert Jay Lifton and Greg Mitchell, *Hiroshima in America: Fifty Years of Denial* (1995).

Chapter 27: Cold War America, 1945–1960

General works on the politics and diplomacy of the cold war era include James T. Patterson, *Grand Expectations: The United States, 1945–1974* (1997); William Chafe, *The Unfinished Journey* (4th ed., 1999), and Paul Boyer, *Promises to Keep* (1995). The Woodrow Wilson International Center for Scholars has established the "Cold War International History Project" at <http://cwihp.si.edu/default.htm>, an exceptionally rich Web site offering documents on the cold war, including materials from former communist-bloc countries.

The Cold War Abroad

The best overviews of the cold war are Walter La Feber, *America, Russia, and the Cold War, 1945–1990* (8th ed., 1997); Thomas G. Paterson, *On Every Front: The Making and Unmaking of the Cold War* (rev. ed., 1992); and Stephen Ambrose and Douglas Brinkley, *Rise to Globalism* (8th ed., 1997). Melvyn P. Leffler presents a masterful and exhaustive synthesis of Truman's foreign policy in *A Preponderance of Power* (1992). For critical views of American aims, see H. W. Brands, *The Devil We Knew* (1993), and Richard Ned Lebow and Janice Gross Stein, *We All Lost the Cold War* (1994). John Lewis

Gaddis blames the cold war on both the United States and the Soviet Union in *Strategies of Containment* (1982), although his more recent works, *The Long Peace* (1987) and *The United States and the End of the cold war* (1992), are more sympathetic to American policymaking. For international perspectives on the cold war, see Melvyn P. Leffler and David S. Painter, eds., *Origins of the Cold War: An International History* (1994), and Thomas J. McCormick, *America's Half-Century* (1989). Specialized studies include Ernest R. May, ed., *American Cold War Strategy: Interpreting NSC-68* (1993); Laurence S. Kaplan, *The United States and NATO* (1984); Michael Hogan, *The Marshall Plan* (1987); and Richard Freeland, *The Truman Doctrine and the Origins of McCarthyism* (1972).

McGeorge Bundy, *Danger and Survival* (1989); Martin J. Sherwin, *A World Destroyed* (1975); and Gar Alperovitz, *Atomic Diplomacy* (2nd ed., 1994), cover the impact of atomic weapons on American policy. For developments in Asia, see Akira Iriye, *The Cold War in Asia* (1974); William Borden, *The Pacific Alliance* (1984); Warren I. Cohen, *America's Response to China* (2nd ed., 1980); and Michael Schaller, *The United States and China in the Twentieth Century* (1979) and *The American Occupation of Japan* (1985).

There is an abundance of scholarship on the Korean War, including William Stueck, *The Korean War: An International History* (1995); Clay Blair, *The Forgotten War* (1988); Max Hastings, *The Korean War* (1987); Callum McDonald, *Korea: The War before Vietnam* (1987); Burton Kaufman, *The Korean War* (1986); and Rosemary Foot, *The Wrong War* (1985). Especially influential are the two volumes of *The Origins of the Korean War* by Bruce Cumings: *Liberation and the Emergence of Separate Regions, 1945–1947* (1981) and *The Roaring of the Cataract, 1947–1950* (1990).

On Eisenhower's foreign policy, see Robert A. Divine, *Eisenhower and the Cold War* (1981). On American involvement in the Middle East, see Jarmo Oikarinen, *The Middle East in the American Question for World Order* (1999), and Michael Stoff, *Oil, War, and American Security* (1980). On Latin America, see Stephen Rabe, *Eisenhower and Latin America: The Foreign Policy of Anticommunism* (1988).

The Cold War at Home

Harry Truman, *Memoirs* (1952–1962), tells Truman's story in characteristically pointed language; see also Merle Miller's oral history, *Plain Speaking* (1980); David McCullough, *Truman* (1992), offers a generally sympathetic biography; Alonzo Hamby presents a more mixed view in *Man of the People: A Life of Harry S. Truman* (1995). The Truman Presidential Museum and Library provides a searchable collection of images and documents regarding the Truman presidency at <http://www.trumanlibrary.org/>. This collection is organized into categories such as the origins of the Truman Doctrine, the Berlin airlift, the desegregation of the armed forces, and the 1948 presidential campaign. Users can also browse through the president's correspondence. General accounts of the Truman presidency can be found in Robert J. Donovan, *Tumultuous Years: The Presidency of Harry S. Truman, 1949–1953* (1982); Donald R. McCoy, *The Presidency of Harry S. Truman* (1984); and William Pemberton, *Harry S. Truman* (1989). Critical perspectives are presented in Barton J. Bern-stein, ed., *Politics and Policies of the Truman Administration* (1970). On Eisenhower's presidency, see Fred I. Greenstein, *The Hidden-Hand Presidency* (1982); Stephen Ambrose, *Eisenhower the President* (1984); Herbert S. Parmet, *Eisenhower and the American Crusades* (1972); and Charles C. Alexander, *Holding the Line* (1975).

The literature on McCarthyism is voluminous. Recent works include Richard Gid Powers, *Not without Honor* (1996); Richard Fried, *Nightmare in Red: The McCarthy Era in Perspective* (1990); and Stephen J. Whitfield, *The Culture of the Cold War* (1991). David Caute, *The Great Fear* (1978), provides a detailed account, which can be supplemented by Victor Navasky, *Naming Names* (1980), and Athan Theoharis, *Spying on Americans* (1978). The Center for the Study of the Pacific Northwest's site, "The Cold War and Red Scare in Washington State" at <http://www.washington.edu/uwired/outreach/cspn/curcan/main.html> provides detailed information on how the Great Fear operated in one state. Its bibliography includes books, documents, and videos. Two useful biographies are Thomas C. Reeves, *The Life and Times of Joe McCarthy* (1982), and David Oshinsky, *A Conspiracy So Immense* (1983).

The Emergence of Civil Rights as a National Issue

For the importance of the cold war for race relations, see Mary L. Dudziak, *Cold War Civil Rights: Race and the Image of American Democracy* (2000). Robert F. Burk, *The Eisenhower Administration and Black Civil Rights* (1984), looks at what the administration did and did not do. Richard Kluger, *Simple Justice* (1975), and Mark Tushnet, *The NAACP's Legal Strategy against Segregated Education* (1987), analyze the Brown decision and its context. Pete Daniels, *Lost Revolutions: The South in the 1950s* (2000), offers valuable insights about the emergence of the civil rights movement and the white response. Taylor Branch, *Parting the Waters: America in the King Years, 1954–1963* (1988), provides a good account of King's early years.

The Impact of the Cold War

For the impact of the cold war on American culture, see Tom Engelhardt, *The End of Victory Culture: Cold War America and the Disillusioning of a Generation* (1998) and Richard M. Fried, *The Russians are Coming, The Russians are Coming! Pageanty and Patriotism in Cold War America* (1999). On Americans' response to the bomb, see Paul Boyer, *By the Bomb's Early Light* (1985), and Allan M. Winkler, *Life Under a Cloud* (1993). Howard Ball, *Justice Downwind* (1986), covers nuclear testing in the 1950s. On the military-industrial complex, see Gregory Michael Hooks, *Forging the Military-Industrial Complex* (1991).

Chapter 28: The Affluent Society and the Liberal Consensus, 1945–1965

General introductions to postwar society include Paul Boyer, *Promises to Keep* (1995); James T. Patterson, *Grand Expectations: The United States, 1945–1974* (1996); and David Halberstam, *The Fifties* (1993).

The Affluent Society

For overviews of the economic changes of the postwar period, see David P. Calleo, *The Imperious Economy* (1982). Herman P. Miller, *Rich Man, Poor Man* (1971), and Gabriel Kolko, *Wealth and Power in America* (1962), discuss inequality in income distribution. Michael Harrington, *The Other America* (1962), documents the persistence of poverty in the postwar era.

Kenneth Jackson, *Crabgrass Frontier* (1985), provides an overview of suburban development. Herbert Gans, *The Levittowners* (1967), and Bennett M. Berger, *Working-Class Suburb* (1960), are sociological studies of suburbia written by contemporaries. On postwar development in the South and West, see Carl Abbott, *The Metropolitan Frontier: Cities in the Modern American West* (1993); Numan V. Bartley, *The New South, 1945–1980* (1995); and Richard Bernard and Bradley Rice, eds., *Sunbelt Cities* (1983).

Books that highlight the social and cultural history of the 1950s include Larry May, ed., *Recasting America* (1989), and Douglas T. Miller and Marion Nowak, *The Fifties* (1977). "Literary Kicks: The Beat Generation" at <http://www.charm.net/~brooklyn/LitKicks.html> is an independent site created by New York writer Levi Asher devoted to the literature of the Beat generation. The site includes writings by Jack Kerouac, Allen Ginsberg, Neil Cassidy, and others; material on Beats, music, religion, and film; an extensive bibliography; biographical information; and photographs. For popular culture, George Lipsitz, *Time Passages* (1991), surveys postwar television, music, film, and popular culture, and his *Rainbow at Midnight* (2nd ed., 1994) looks at working-class culture and rock 'n' roll. Other treatments of the mass media include James L. Baughman, *The Republic of Mass Culture* (1992); Peter Biskind, *Seeing Is Believing* (1983); and Larry May, *The Big Tomorrow: Hollywood and the Politics of the American Way* (2000). Vance Packard's influential unmasking of the advertising industry, *The Hidden Persuaders* (1957), can be supplemented by Stephen Fox, *The Mirror Makers* (1984).

Richard Easterlin, *American Baby Boom in Historical Perspective* (1962), analyzes the demographic changes, as does Landon Y. Jones, *Great Expectations* (1980). Elaine May's *Homeward Bound* (1988) is the classic introduction to postwar family life, providing a historical corollary to Betty Friedan's *Feminine Mystique* (1963). Recent revisionist work challenging this view can be found in Joanne Meyerowitz, ed., *Not June Cleaver* (1994) and Daniel Horowitz, *Betty Friedan and the Making of the Feminine Mystique* (1998).

Youth culture is the subject of William Graeber's *Coming of Age in Buffalo* (1990). James Gilbert, *A Cycle of Outrage* (1986), looks at juvenile delinquency in the 1950s. Peter Guralnick, *Last Train to Memphis* (1994), is the definitive biography of Elvis Presley's early years. Discussions of cultural dissent in the 1950s can be found in Bruce Cook, *The Beat Generation* (1971), and Dan Wakefield, *New York in the Fifties* (1992).

The Other America

Reed Ueda, *Postwar Immigrant America* (1994), examines new trends in immigration since 1945. Jacqueline Jones compares black and white urban migrants in *The Dispossessed* (1992). Thomas Sugrue, *Origins of the Urban Crisis* (1996), analyzes the economic decline and racial antagonism that plagued postwar Detroit. Donald Fixico, *Termination and Relocation* (1986), looks at federal Indian policy from 1945 to 1970.

Jon C. Teaford, *Rough Road to Renaissance* (1990); John Mollenkopf, *The Contested City* (1983); and Kenneth Fox, *Metropolitan America* (1985), offer the most complete accounts of postwar urban development.

John F. Kennedy and the Politics of Expectation

The literature on the Kennedy years is voluminous. Among the best general accounts are Richard Reeves, *President Kennedy: Profile of Power* (1993); James Giglio, *The Presidency of JFK* (1991); David Burner, *JFK and a New Generation* (1988); and Jim F. Heath, *Decade of Disillusionment: The Kennedy-Johnson Years* (1975). Critical views appear in Seymour Hersh, *The Dark Side of Camelot* (1997); and David Halberstam, *The Best and the Brightest* (1972). The John F. Kennedy Library and Museum's site at <http://www.cs.umb.edu/jfklibrary/> provides a large collection of records from Kennedy's presidency. The Reference Desk area contains frequently requested information, including transcripts and recordings of JFK's speeches, a database of his executive orders, and a number of other resources.

On foreign policy in the Kennedy years, see Michael Beschloss, *The Crisis Years: Kennedy and Khrushchev, 1960–1963* (1990), and Thomas Paterson, *Kennedy's Quest for Victory* (1989). Ernest R. May and Philip D. Zelikow, eds., *The Kennedy Tapes: Inside the White House during the Cuban Missile Crisis* (1997), provide verbatim accounts of the Cuban missile crisis. The Avalon Project at the Yale Law School's site, "Foreign Relations of the United States: 1961–1963 Cuban Missile Crisis and Aftermath" at <http://www.yale.edu/lawweb/avalon/diplomacy/forrel/cuba/cubamenu.htm> contains almost 300 official documents related to the crisis, including State Department memoranda, records of telephone conversations, transcripts of conversations in the White House, and CIA reports. Secondary treatments include James Nathan, *The Cuban Missile Crisis Revisited* (1992), and Thomas Paterson, *Contesting Castro* (1994). Gerald Posner, *Case Closed* (1993), provides the most definitive treatment of the Kennedy assassination.

The best overviews of the postwar civil rights movement are Robert Weisbrot, *Freedom Bound* (1990); Harvard Sitkoff, *The Struggle for Black Equality* (2nd ed., 1993); and Clayborne Carson et al., *The Eyes on the Prize Civil Rights Reader* (1991). On the relationship between foreign policy and civil rights, see Mary L. Dudziak, *Cold War Civil Rights: Race and the Image of Democracy* (2000). Histories of the major civil rights organizations include Carson's study of SNCC, *In Struggle* (1981), and August Meier and Elliot Rudwick, *CORE* (1973). Doug McAdam, *Freedom Summer* (1988), describes the experiences of northern volunteers during Freedom Summer and Henry Hampton and Steve Fayer, *Voices of Freedom* (1990) is an oral history of the movement.

Local accounts of grassroots organizing include William H. Chafe's superb study of Greensboro, North Carolina, *Civilities and Civil Rights* (1980), and two recent studies of Mississippi: John Dittmer, *Local People* (1994), and Charles M. Payne, *I've Got the Light of Freedom* (1995). The role of women in the civil rights movement is examined in Vicki L. Crawford et al., *Women in the Civil Rights Movement: Trailblazers and*

Torchbearers, 1941–1965 (1990). Martin Luther King Jr. told his own story in *Why We Can't Wait* (1964). His biographers include David Garrow, *Bearing the Cross* (1986), and Taylor Branch, *Parting the Waters* (1988) and *Pillar of Fire* (1998).

Lyndon B. Johnson and the Great Society

Lyndon Johnson's account of his presidency can be found in *The Vantage Point* (1971). Doris Kearns Goodwin, *Lyndon Johnson and the American Dream* (1976), and Merle Miller, *Lyndon: An Oral Biography* (1980), are based on extensive conversations with LBJ. Robert A. Caro focuses on Johnson's early career in *The Path to Power* (1982) and *Means of Ascent* (1989); Robert Dallek offers his own exhaustive account in *Lone Star Rising* (1991) and *Flawed Giant* (1998). Irwin Unger, *The Best of Intentions: The Triumph and Failure of the Great Society under Kennedy, Johnson, and Nixon* (1996) offers a critical overview of that ambitious program.

Chapter 29: War Abroad and at Home: The Vietnam Era, 1961–1975

Among the best general accounts of the Vietnam War are George Herring, *America's Longest War* (3rd ed., 1996); Stanley Karnow, *Vietnam: A History* (rev. ed., 1991); and Marilyn Young, *The Vietnam Wars, 1945–1990* (1991). Guenter Lewy offers a controversial defense of American involvement in *America in Vietnam* (1978). A useful Vietnam site is edited by Professor Vincent Ferraro of Mount Holyoke College and includes state papers and official correspondence from 1941 to the fall of Saigon, <http://www.mtholyoke.edu/acad/intrel/vietnam.htm>.

Into the Quagmire, 1945–1968

The origins of American involvement in Vietnam are covered in Loren Baritz, *Backfire: A History of How American Culture Led Us into Vietnam* (1985); Larry Berman, *Planning a Tragedy* (1982); H. R. McMaster, *Dereliction of Duty: Johnson, McNamara, the Joint Chiefs of Staff, and the Lies That Led to Vietnam* (1998); Lloyd Gardner, *Approaching Vietnam* (1988); David Halberstam, *The Making of a Quagmire* (rev. ed., 1988); and Brian VanDeMark, *Into the Quagmire* (1991). A fascinating insight into Vietnam policymaking in the 1960s can be found in Neil Sheehan, *The Pentagon Papers* (1971). Secretary of Defense Robert McNamara offers an insider's view and belated apologia in *In Retrospect* (1995).

For a sense of what the war felt like to the soldiers who fought it, see Mark Baker, *Nam* (1982); Philip Caputo, *Rumor of War* (1977); Michael Herr, *Dispatches* (1977); and Tim O'Brien, *If I Die in a Combat Zone* (1973). Wallace Terry, *Bloods* (1984), surveys the experiences of black veterans, and Keith Walker, *A Piece of My Heart* (1985), introduces the often forgotten stories of the women who served in Vietnam. Christian G. Appy offers a class analysis of the Vietnam experience in *Working-Class War* (1993). Neil Sheehan surveys the entire Vietnam experience through the life of career soldier John Paul Vann in *A Bright and Shining Lie* (1988).

The Cold War Consensus Unravels

There are a growing number of survey works on the 1960s, including David Steigerwald, *The Sixties and the End of Modern America* (1995); Terry Anderson, *The Movement and the Sixties* (1994); David Farber, *The Age of Great Dreams: America in the 1960s* (1994); Todd Gitlin, *The Sixties: Years of Hope, Days of Rage* (1987); and Maurice Isserman and Michael Kazin, *America Divided: The Civil War of the 1960s* (2000). A valuable anthology is Alexander Bloom and Wini Breines, eds., *Takin' It to the Streets* (2nd ed., 2002). "The Sixties Project," which is hosted by the University of Virginia at Charlottesville, offers personal narratives, special exhibits, and a bibliography of articles published in "Vietnam Generation" at <http://lists.village.virginia.edu/sixties/>.

The student activism of the 1960s is the subject of dozens of eyewitness accounts and scholarly works. See Nathan Glazer, *Remembering the Answers* (1970); and Philip Slater, *The Pursuit of Loneliness* (1970). On student revolt see W. J. Rorabaugh, *Berkeley at War* (1989); Kirkpatrick Sale, *SDS* (1973); Wini Breines, *Community and Organization in the New Left, 1962–1968* (1982); and James Miller, *Democracy Is in the Streets* (1987). The University of California Library's site, "Free Speech Movement Digital Archive: Student Protest-U.C. Berkeley" at <http://bancroft.berkeley.edu/FSM/>, offers newsletters, oral histories, student newspaper accounts, legal defense material, and audio recordings, as well as good links to related sites. The definitive book on the antiwar movement is Charles DeBenedetti, with Charles Chatfield, *An American Ordeal* (1990).

Morris Dickstein, *Gates of Eden* (1977), is an excellent account of cultural developments in the 1960s. Other sources include Roger Kimball, *The Long March: How the Cultural Revolution of the 1960s Changed America* (2000); Theodore Roszak, *The Making of a Counter-Culture* (1969); and Charles Reich, *The Greening of America* (1970). Gerald Howard, ed., *The Sixties* (1982), is a good anthology of the decade's art, politics, and culture. Philip Norman, *Shout! The Beatles in Their Generation* (1981), and Jon Weiner, *Come Together: John Lennon in His Times* (1984), cover developments in popular music.

Major texts of the black power movement include Stokely Carmichael and Charles Hamilton, *Black Power* (1967); James Baldwin, *The Fire Next Time* (1963); and Eldridge Cleaver, *Soul on Ice* (1968). *The Autobiography of Malcolm X* (cowritten with Alex Haley, 1966) has become a black literary classic; it can be supplemented by Michael Eric Dyson, *Making Malcolm: The Myth and Meaning of Malcolm X* (1995). William L. Van Deburg, *New Day in Babylon* (1992), provides a general historical account of the black-power movement.

Report of the National Advisory Commission on Civil Disorders (1968) analyzes the decade's major race riots. See also Joe R. Feagin and Harlan Hahn, *Ghetto Revolts* (1973), and Robert Fogelson, *Violence as Protest* (1971). Sidney Fine's book on the Detroit riot, *Violence in the Model City* (1989), provides the most thorough historical treatment of race rioting in this period.

Carlos Muñoz Jr., *Youth, Identity and Power: The Chicano Movement* (1989), and Juan Gomez-Quiñones, *Chicano Politics* (1990), examine the rise of the Chicano movement in the 1960s. Peter Matthiessen, *In the Spirit of Crazy Horse* (1983), chronicles the American Indian Movement's ongoing conflict with the FBI and the federal government. Historians at the University of Michigan maintain "A Study and Timeline of the Lakota Nation" at <http://www-personal.umich.edu/~jamarcus/new/>, which includes material on the American Indian Movement, the occupation of Wounded Knee in 1973, and the confrontation at the Bureau of Indian Affairs office in 1972. Martin Duberman, *Stonewall* (1993), looks at the birth of the gay movement in the late 1960s.

General histories of women's activism in the 1960s include Cynthia Harrison, *On Account of Sex: The Politics of Women's Issues, 1945–1968* (1988), and Susan M. Hartmann, *From Margin to Mainstream: American Women and Politics since 1960* (1989). The revival of feminism is examined in Blanche Linden-Ward and Carol Hurd Green, *Changing the Future: American Women in the 1960s* (1992); Jo Freeman, *The Politics of Women's Liberation* (1975), and Judith Hole and Ellen Levine, *The Rebirth of Feminism* (1971). Sara Evans, *Personal Politics* (1979), traces the roots of feminism in the civil rights movement and the New Left.

The Long Road Home, 1968–1975

The Tet offensive is the subject of Don Oberdoffer's *Tet! The Turning Point in the Vietnam War* (1971). The domestic events of 1968 are covered in David Caute, *The Year of the Barricades* (1968), and David Farber, *Chicago '68* (1988). Norman Mailer provides a contemporary view of the national political conventions in *Miami and the Siege of Chicago* (1968). William C. Berman, *America's Right Turn* (2nd ed., 1998), chronicles the rightward shift in politics. Kevin Phillips, *The Emerging Republican Majority* (1969), and Richard Scammon and Ben J. Wattenberg, *The Real Majority* (1970), describe the voters Richard Nixon tried to reach. Dan Carter, *The Politics of Rage* (1996), examines the political career of George Wallace.

William Bundy, *The Tangled Web* (1998), and Robert S. Litwak, *Détente and the Nixon Doctrine* (1984), are overviews of Nixon's foreign policy. On his Vietnam policy, see the general works on Vietnam listed above as well as the highly critical study by William Shawcross, *Sideshow: Kissinger, Nixon, and the Destruction of Cambodia* (1979). An account of the My Lai massacre can be found in Seymour Hersh, *Cover-Up* (1972). Robert Jay Lifton, *Home from the War* (1973); Paul Starr, *The Discarded Army* (1973); and Lawrence Baskir and William A. Strauss, *Chance and Circumstance* (1978), discuss the problems of returning Vietnam veterans.

Chapter 30: The Lean Years, 1969–1980

Bruce J. Schulman, *The Seventies: The Great Shift in American Culture, Society, and Politics* (2001), provides a provocative overview of the political and cultural issues of the 1970s. For a popular history of the period, see Peter N. Carroll's. *It Seemed Like Nothing Happened* (1982).

The Nixon Years

Herbert Parmet's *Richard Nixon and His America* (1990) and Stephen Ambrose's three-volume *Nixon* (1987, 1991) are two of many biographies of a complex political leader. Kim McQuaid, *The Anxious Years: America in the Vietnam-Watergate*

Era (1989), is an overview of the Nixon era. See also Garry Wills, *Nixon Agonistes* (rev. ed., 1990), and Nixon's own recollections in *RN: The Memoirs of Richard Nixon* (1978). On Nixon's economic policies, see Allen J. Matusow, *Nixon's Economy: Booms, Busts, Dollars, and Votes* (1998). On the Warren Court, see Morton J. Horwitz, *The Warren Court and the Pursuit of Justice: A Critical Issue* (1998).

Stanley Kutler, *The Wars of Watergate* (1990); Anthony Lukas, *Nightmare: The Underside of the Nixon Years* (1976); and Theodore H. White, *Breach of Faith* (1975), are comprehensive accounts of the Watergate scandal. For the Watergate scandal, a useful Web site is the National Archives and Record Administration's "Watergate Trial Tapes and Transcripts" at <http://www.archives.gov/nixon/tapes/tapes.html>, which provides transcripts of the infamous tapes as well as other useful links to archival holdings concerning Richard Nixon's presidency. Also of interest are the books by the *Washington Post* journalists who broke the story, Carl Bernstein and Bob Woodward: *All the President's Men* (1974) and *The Final Days* (1976). Stanley Kutler, *Abuse of Power: The New Nixon Tapes* (1997), is a collection of transcripts from the White House tapes relating to Watergate and other Nixon-era scandals.

An Economy of Diminished Expectations

Barry Commoner, *The Poverty of Power* (1976), and Robert Heilbroner, *An Inquiry into the Human Prospect* (1974), cogently assess the origins of the energy crisis and the prospects for the future. See also Lester C. Thurow, *The Zero-Sum Society* (1980), and Robert Stobaugh and Daniel Yergin, *Energy Future* (1980). Daniel Yergin, *The Prize* (1991), and John M. Blair, *The Control of Oil* (1976), treat OPEC developments.

General introductions to the economic developments of the decade are Barry Bluestone and Bennett Harrison, *The Deindustrialization of America* (1982); Richard J. Barnet and Ronald E. Muller, *Global Reach* (1974); Richard J. Barnet, *The Lean Years* (1980); John P. Hoerr, *And the Wolf Finally Came: The Decline of the Steel Industry* (1988); and Robert Calleo, *The Imperious Economy* (1982).

Reform and Reaction in the 1970s

Tom Wolfe gave the decade its name in "The Me Decade and the Third Great Awakening," *New York Magazine* (August 23, 1976). Influential books include Christopher Lasch, *The Culture of Narcissism* (1978), and Gail Sheehy, *Passages* (1976).

For a general overview of the environmental movement, see Samuel P. Hays, *Beauty, Health, and Permanence: Environmental Politics in the United States, 1955–1985* (1987). Roderick Nash provides a history of environmental ethics in *The Rights of Nature* (1989). Books that were influential in shaping public awareness of ecological issues include Rachel Carson, *Silent Spring* (1962); Paul R. Ehrlich, *The Population Bomb* (1968); Frances Moore Lappé, *Diet for a Small Planet* (1971); and Philip Slater, *Earthwalk* (1974). Lois Marie Gibbs describes her experience with the Love Canal crisis in *Love Canal: My Story* (1982). Charles McCarry chronicles Ralph Nader's crusade for consumer protection in *Citizen Nader* (1972).

On women and feminism in the 1970s, see Alice Echols, *Daring to Be Bad* (1989); Susan M. Hartmann, *From Margin to Mainstream: American Women and Politics since 1960*

(1989); and Winifred D. Wandersee, *On the Move: American Women in the 1970s* (1988). "Documents from the Women's Liberation Movement," culled from the Duke University Special Collections Library, emphasizes the women's movement of the late 1960s and early 1970s. This searchable site at <http://scriptorium.lib.duke.edu/wlm/> includes books, pamphlets, and other written materials on categories that include theoretical writings, reproductive health, women of color, and women's work and roles. Donald G. Mathews and Jane S. De Hart analyze the struggle over the ERA in *Sex, Gender, and the Politics of ERA* (1990), and Carol Felsenthal examines the life of the ERA opponent Phyllis Schlafly in *The Sweetheart of the Silent Majority* (1981). David Garrow, *Liberty and Sexuality: The Right to Privacy and the Making of Roe v. Wade* (1994), is an in-depth examination of the 1973 abortion decision. On the public abortion debate, see Faye Ginsberg, *Contested Lives* (1989), and Kristen Luker, *Abortion and the Politics of Motherhood* (1984). The Oyez Project at Northwestern University at <http://oyez.nwu.edu/> is an invaluable resource for over 1,000 Supreme Court cases, with audio transcripts, voting records, and summaries. For this period, see, for example, its materials on *Roe v. Wade, Bakke v. University of California,* and *Griswold v. Connecticut.*

Leigh W. Rutledge surveys the gay and lesbian movement in *The Gay Decades: From Stonewall to the Present* (1992). Thomas Byrne Edsall with Mary D. Edsall, *Chain Reaction: The Impact of Race, Rights and Taxes on American Politics* (1991), examines some of the divisive social issues of the 1970s. J. Anthony Lukas, *Common Ground* (1985), tells the story of the Boston busing crisis through the biographies of three families. Paul Moreno, *From Direct Action to Affirmative Action* (1997); Robert J. Weiss, *We Want Jobs* (1997); and Lydia Chavez, *The Color Blind* (1998), treat the controversial topic of affirmative action.

Alan Crawford, *Thunder on the Right* (1980), and Jerome L. Himmelstein, *To the Right: The Transformation of American Conservatism* (1990) survey the new conservatism. John Woodridge, *The Evangelicals* (1975), analyzes the rise of evangelical religion, and Quentin J. Schultze looks at evangelicals' use of the media in *Televangelism and American Culture* (1991). On the political role of the Christian right, see Michael Liensch, *Redeeming America: Piety and Politics in the New Christian Right* (1993).

Politics in the Wake of Watergate

John R. Greene examines the Ford administration in *The Presidency of Gerald R. Ford* (1995), as do James Cannon, *Time and Chance: Gerald Ford's Appointment with History* (1993), and Richard Reeves, *A Ford, Not a Lincoln* (1975).

Peter G. Bourne, *Jimmy Carter* (1997), is a comprehensive biography. Generally unfavorable portraits of the Carter presidency are found in Burton Kaufman, *The Presidency of James Earl Carter Jr.* (1993); Robert Shogan, *Promises to Keep* (1977); and Haynes Johnson, *In the Absence of Power* (1980). See also Gary M. Fink, ed., *The Carter Presidency: Policy Choices in the Post–New Deal Era* (1998); Erwin Hargrove, *Jimmy Carter as President* (1989); Charles Jones, *The Trusteeship Presidency* (1988); and Jimmy Carter's presidential memoirs, *Keeping Faith* (rev. ed., 1995). James Fallows, *National Defense* (1981),

provides an incisive overview of defense developments. See also A. Glenn Mower Jr., *Human Rights and American Foreign Policy: The Carter and Reagan Experiences* (1987). Gary Sick, *All Fall Down: America's Tragic Encounter with Iran* (1986), provides an account of the Iranian hostage crisis, and Jack Germond, *Blue Smoke and Mirrors* (1981), examines the presidential election of 1980.

Chapter 31: A New Domestic and World Order, 1981–2001

Few historians have turned their attention to the period after 1980, leaving the field to journalists, economists, and political scientists. The Bureau of the Census offers a fine introduction to the period in its *Statistical Abstract of the United States* (117th ed., 1997). Essays on important issues are available in the *Congressional Quarterly Researcher.*

The Reagan-Bush Years, 1981–1993

Haynes Johnson, *Sleepwalking through History* (1991), provides an excellent overview of America in the Reagan years. See also Michael Rogin, *Ronald Reagan: The Movie* (1987); Lou Cannon, *President Reagan: A Role of a Lifetime* (1991); Michael Schaller, *Reckoning with Reagan: America and Its President in the 1980s* (1992); and Peggy Noonan, *What I Saw at the Revolution* (1990).

On Reaganomics, George Gilder's *Wealth and Poverty* (1981) represents the views held by many in the Reagan administration, but David Stockman's memoir, *The Triumph of Politics* (1986), is more revealing. See also Benjamin Friedman, *Day of Reckoning: The Consequences of American Economic Policy under Reagan and After* (1988).

On the Bush administration, see James A. Baker, *The Politics of Diplomacy* (1995), and Stephen R. Graubard, *Mr. Bush's War: Adventures in the Politics of Illusion* (1992). "The Gulf War" at <http://www.pbs.org/wgbh/pages/frontline/gulf/> is an online documentary treatment of the Gulf War conflict. A companion to the Gulf War documentary produced by the PBS series *Frontline,* the site includes maps, a chronology, interviews with decision makers and soldiers from the various sides of the conflict, audio clips, and a section on weapons and technology. On politics, see E. J. Dionne, *Why Americans Hate Politics* (1992); William Greider, *Who Will Tell the People?* (1992); and Kevin Phillips, *The Politics of Rich and Poor: Wealth and the American Electorate in the Reagan Aftermath* (1990).

Foreign Relations under Reagan and Bush

For foreign policy, Stephen Ambrose and Douglas Brinkley, *Rise to Globalism* (8th ed., 1997), provide a comprehensive overview of the Reagan and Bush years. The Iran-Contra scandal is covered in Jane Hunter et al., *The Iran-Contra Connection* (1987). Good introductions to U.S. foreign relations with Central and South America include Walter La Feber, *Inevitable Revolutions* (1984), and Thomas Carothers, *In the Name of Democracy: U.S. Policy toward Latin America in the Reagan Years* (1991).

The emergence of a new world order has provoked commentary from economists, journalists, and historians, including

Paul Kennedy, *The Rise and Fall of the Great Powers* (1987); Joseph Nye, *Bound to Lead: The Changing Nature of American Power* (1990); Robert Kuttner, *The End of Laissez Faire* (1991); and Henry R. Nau, *The Myth of America's Decline* (1990). See also Michael Beschloss and Strobe Talbott, *At the Highest Levels: The Inside Story of the End of the Cold War* (1994), and Michael J. Hogan, ed., *The End of the Cold War: Its Meanings and Implications* (1992).

Uncertain Times: Economic and Social Trends, 1980–2000

Paul Krugman, *Peddling Prosperity: Economic Sense and Nonsense in the Age of Diminished Expectations* (1994), and Jeffrey Madrick, *The End of Affluence* (1995), provide overviews of economic trends since the 1970s. Lester C. Thurow offers an insightful analysis of the world economic changes accompanying the collapse of communism in *The Future of Capitalism* (1996). For overviews of U.S. competitiveness in the global marketplace, see Daniel Yergin and Joseph Stanislaw, *The Commanding Heights* (1998); Hedrick Smith, *Rethinking America* (1995). Books that address the growing inequality in American life include William J. Wilson, *The Truly Disadvantaged* (1987); Nicholas Lemann, *The Promised Land* (1989); and Andrew Hacker, *Two Nations: Black and White, Separate, Hostile, Unequal* (1992).

On women, work, and families, see Hilda Scott, *Working Your Way to the Bottom: The Feminization of Poverty* (1985), and Arlie Hochschild, *The Second Shift: Working Parents and the Revolution at Home* (1989). For feminism and its critics, see Susan Faludi, *Backlash: The Undeclared War on American Women* (1991). Toni Morrison, ed., *Race-ing Justice, En-Gendering Power* (1992), covers the Clarence Thomas–Anita Hill hearings.

David Reimers, *Still the Golden Door* (2nd ed., 1992), covers immigration policy in the postwar period. Roberto Suro, *Strangers among Us* (1998), shows how Latino immigration is transforming America. Ronald Takaki, *Strangers from a Different Shore* (1989), covers Asian Americans. On race and politics in California since 1978, see Peter Schrag, *Paradise Lost* (1998).

Randy Shilts, *And the Band Played On: Politics, People, and the AIDS Epidemic* (1987), is a controversial critique of inaction in the early years of the AIDS epidemic. Allan Bloom, *The Closing of the American Mind* (1987), and E. D. Hirsch Jr., *Cultural Literacy* (1988), deal with issues of curriculum, learning, and literacy. Lawrence W. Levine, *The Opening of the American Mind* (1996), challenges many of their assumptions. For differing views on affirmative action, see Stephen L. Carter, *Reflections of an Affirmative Action Baby* (1991), and Gertrude Ezorsky, *Racism and Justice: The Case for Affirmative Action* (1991). Gregg Easterbrook provides a general overview of the environment in *A Moment on the Earth* (1995). Daniel Yergin, *The Prize* (1991), chronicles how oil dominates modern life, with both economic and environmental consequences. The Gallup

Organization has been conducting public opinion surveys since 1935. Its site at <http://www.gallup.com> provides access to recent polls on politics, family, religion, crime, and lifestyle. This searchable site is an invaluable guide to contemporary American opinion. The United States Census Bureau's Web page at <http://www.census.gov/population/www/index.html> offers a rich variety of data—on health insurance, racial and ethnic composition, poverty, work environment, and marriage and family—providing insight into the major demographic changes transforming American society.

For the story of Bill Gates and Microsoft, see Steven Manes, *Gates* (1993), and James Wallace, *Hard Drive* (1992). Also of interest is Joshua Quittner and Michelle Slatalla, *Speeding the Net: The Inside Story of Netscape and How It Challenged Microsoft* (1998). For biotechnology, see Robert Cook-Deegan, *The Gene Wars* (1994); Arthur Kornberg, *The Golden Helix: Inside Biotech Ventures* (1996); and Eric S. Grace, *Biotechnology Unzipped* (1997).

Restructuring the Domestic Order: Public Life, 1992–2001

For an excellent overview of the Clinton administration's first year, see Elizabeth Drew, *Finding His Voice* (1994). Other sources include Joe Klein, *The Natural: The Misunderstood Presidency of Bill Clinton* (2002), and Roger Morris, *Partners in Power: The Clintons and Their America* (1996). Jurist, the Law Professors' Network, provides a "Guide to Impeachment and Censure Materials Online" at <http://jurist.law.pitt.edu/impeach.htm>, which offers extensive links to materials on the constitutional issues raised by impeachment and on public opinion polls, documents, and analysis specific to the Clinton impeachment. Richard Holbrooke, *To End a War* (1998), provides a compelling insider's account of the Dayton peace talks on Bosnia. William Greider, *Fortress America* (1998), examines the American military in the post–cold war era. On the Republican agenda, see Newt Gingrich, *To Renew America* (1995). See also Dan Balz and Ronald Brownstein, *Storming the Gates: Protest Politics and the Republican Revival* (1996), and Ralph Reed, *Active Faith: How Christians Are Changing the Soul of American Politics* (1996). On the 2000 election, see Alan M. Dershowitz, *Supreme Injustice: How the High Court Hijacked Election 2000*, and Bruce Akerman, ed., *Bush v. Gore: The Question of Legitimacy* (2002).

"The September 11 Digital Archive" at <http://911digitalarchive.org/> is cosponsored by the American Social History Project at the City University of New York Graduate Center and the Center for History and New Media at George Mason University. The site is part of an ongoing project to collect and preserve firsthand accounts of Americans' responses to the terrorist attack of September 11, 2001. The site includes oral histories, video and still images, and a valuable guide to Web sites on the topic.

Tocqueville. Copyright © 1945 and renewed 1973 by Alfred A. Knopf, a division of Random House, Inc. Used by permission of Alfred A. Knopf, a division of Random House, Inc.

Fig. 11.1. "The Surge in Immigration, 1842–1855." Adapted from *Division and the Stresses of Reunion 1845–1876* by David M. Potter. Copyright © David M. Potter. Reprinted by permission.

Chapter 12

American Voices: Keziah Kendall, "A Farm Woman Defends the Grimké Sisters." Excerpt from "The Daughters of Job: Property Rights and Women's Lives in Mid-Nineteenth-Century Massachusetts" by Diane Avery and Alfred S. Konefsky in *Law and History Review* 10 (Fall 1992). Reprinted by permission of University of Illinois Press.

Chapter 13

American Voices: Excerpt from pp. 29–30, 245–46 in *Mary Boykin Chesnut: A Slaveholder's Diary* by C. Vann Woodward. Copyright © 1981 by C. Vann Woodward. Reprinted by permission of Yale University Press.

Voices from Abroad: Colonel José Enrique de la Peña, "A Mexican View of the Battle of the Alamo." Excerpt from pp. 40–57 in *With Santa Anna in Texas: A Personal Narrative of the Revolution* by José Enrique de la Peña, and translated by Carmen Perry. Copyright © 1975 by Carmen Perry. Reprinted by permission of Texas A & M University Press.

American Voices: Axalla John Hoole, "'Bleeding Kansas': A Southern View." Excerpt from "A Southerner's Viewpoint of the Kansas Situation, 1856–1857" (pp. 43–65, 149–71) in *Kansas Historical Quarterly* 3 (1934): 149–71, edited by William Stanley Harris. Reprinted by permission of the Kansas State Historical Society.

Fig. 13.1. "The Surge in Cotton Production, 1835–1860." Adapted from fig. 25 in *Time on the Cross* by Robert William Fogel and Stanley L. Engerman. Copyright © 1974 by Robert William Fogel and Stanley L. Engerman. Reprinted by permission of the publisher.

Chapter 14

American Voices: Elizabeth Mary Meade Ingraham, "A Vicksburg Diary." Excerpt from *The Vicksburg Diary of Mrs. Alfred Ingraham* by W. Maury Darst in the *Journal of Mississippi History*, vol. 44 (May 1982): 148–79. Reprinted by permission of the Mississippi Department of Archives and History.

American Voices: Spotswood Rice, "Freeing My Children from Slavery." From pp. 131–33 in *Freedom's Soldiers: The Black Military Experience in the Civil War* by Ira Berlin, Joseph P. Reidy, and Leslie S. Rowland, eds. Copyright © 1998 by Ira Berlin, Joseph P. Reidy, and Leslie S. Rowland. Reprinted by permission of Cambridge University Press.

Chapter 15

Voices from Abroad: David Macrae, "The Devastated South." From *America through British Eyes* by Allan Nevins, editor. Copyright © 1968 by Allan Nevins. Reprinted by permission of Peter Smith Publisher, Inc.

American Voices: Jourdon Anderson, "Relishing Freedom." From pp. 4–6 in *Looking for America*, Second Edition, Volume 1, by Stanley I. Kutler. Copyright © 1979, 1976 by Stanley I. Kutler. Used by permission of W. W. Norton & Company, Inc.

Chapter 16

American Voices: Ida Lindgren, "Swedish Emigrant in Frontier Kansas." From *Letters from the Promised Land: Swedes in America, 1840–1914* by H. Arnold Barton, editor. Copyright © 1975 by H. Arnold Barton. Reprinted by permission of the University of Minnesota Press.

Fig. 16.1. "Freight Rates for Transporting Nebraska Crops." Adapted from data on p. 352 in *The Nation Transformed* by Sigmund Diamond, editor. Reprinted by permission of George Braziller, Inc.

Chapter 18

Fig. 18.2. "Distributions of Weekly Wages for Black and White Workers in Virginia, 1907." Adapted from p. 184 in *Old South, New South: Revolutions in the Southern Economy since the Civil War* by Gavin Wright. Copyright © 1986 by Gavin Wright. Reprinted by permission of Basic Books, a division of Perseus Books Group.

Chapter 19

Voices from Abroad: José Martí, "Coney Island, 1881." Excerpt from *The America of José Martí: Selected Writings* by José Martí, and translated by Juan de Onis. Copyright © 1954 by Juan de Onis. Reprinted by permission.

Chapter 20

American Voices: Charles Edward Russell, "Muckraking." From *Bare Hands and Stone Walls* by Charles Edward Russell. Copyright © 1933 by Charles Scribner's Sons. Copyright © renewed 1961 by Charles Edward Russell. Reprinted by permission of Scribner, an imprint of Simon & Schuster Adult Publishing Group.

American Voices: Dr. Alice Hamilton, "Tracking Down Lead Poisoning." From *Exploring the Dangerous Trades: The Autobiography of Alice Hamilton* by Alice Hamilton. Copyright © 1943 by Alice Hamilton. Reprinted by permission of Little, Brown and Company.

Voices from Abroad: James Bryce, "Business Is King." Excerpt from pp. 384–87 in *America through British Eyes* by Allan Nevins, editor. Copyright © 1968 by Allan Nevins. Reprinted by permission of Peter Smith Publisher, Inc.

Fig. 20.1: "Growth in Federal Employees." From p. 41 in *The Federal Government Service*, edited by W. S. Sayre. The American Assembly, Prentice-Hall, Englewood Cliffs, NJ.

Chapter 21

American Voices: George W. Prioleau, "Black Soldiers in a White Man's War." Excerpt from *Smoked Yankees and the Struggle for Empire, 1898–1902* by Willard B. Gatewood. Copyright © 1987 by the Board of Trustees of the University of Arkansas. Reprinted by permission of the University of Arkansas Press.

Voices from Abroad: Jean Hess, Émile Zola, Ruben Dario. Excerpts from *The Anti-Imperialist Reader: A Documentary History of Anti-Imperialism in the United States*, volume 1, edited by Philip S. Foner and Robert C. Winchester. Copyright © 1984 by Holmes and Meier Publishers, Inc. Reproduced with the permission of the publisher. From *Major Problems in American Foreign Relations*, 2 volumes, by Thomas G. Paterson and Dennis Merrill, eds., and from *Selected Poems of Ruben*

Dario, translated by Lysander Kemp. Copyright © 1965; renewed 1993 by Lysander Kemp. Reprinted by permission of the University of Texas Press.

Chapter 24

Song lyrics from *Duck Soup*. Four lines from "Freedom Hymn" written by Burt Kalmar and Harry Ruby and sung by Groucho Marx in the movie *Duck Soup*. Copyright © 1933 by Famous Music Corporation. Reprinted with permission.

American Voices: Larry Van Dusen, "A Working-Class Family Encounters the Great Depression." From *Hard Times* by Studs Terkel. Copyright 1986 by Studs Terkel. Reprinted by permission of Donadio & Olson, Inc.

Voices from Abroad: Mary Agnes Hamilton, "Breadlines and Beggars." Excerpt from pp. 443–44 in *America through British Eyes* by Allan Nevins, editor. Copyright © 1968 by Allan Nevins. Reprinted by permission of Peter Smith Publisher, Inc.

Chapter 25

American Voices: Joe Marcus, "A New Deal Activist." From *Hard Times* by Studs Terkel. Copyright 1986 by Studs Terkel. Reprinted by permission of Donadio & Olson, Inc.

American Voices: Susana Archuleta, "A Chicana Youth Gets New Deal Work." From "But I Remember Susana Archuleta" in *Las Mujeres: Conversations from a Hispanic Community* by Nan Elsasser, Kyle MacKenzie, and Yvonne Tixier y Vigil. Copyright © 1980 by The Feminist Press at The City University of New York. Reprinted by permission of the publisher.

Chapter 26

American Voices: Monica Sone, "Japanese Relocation." Excerpt from pp. 176–78 in *Nisei Daughter* by Monica Sone. Copyright 1953; renewed 1981 by Monica Sone. Reprinted by permission of Little, Brown and Company.

American Voices: Anton Bilek, "The War in the Pacific." Excerpt from *An Oral History of World War Two: The Good War* by Studs Terkel. Copyright 1986 by Studs Terkel. Reprinted by permission of Donadio & Olson, Inc.

Chapter 27

Voices from Abroad: Jean Monnet, "Truman's Generous Proposal." Excerpt from pp. 264–65 in *Memoirs* by Jean Monnet, translated by Richard Mayne. Translation copyright © 1978 by Doubleday, a division of Bantam Doubleday Dell, a division of Random House, Inc.

American Voices: Mark Goodson, "Red Hunting on the Quiz Shows; or, What's My Party Line?" Excerpt from pp. 320–24 in *Memories of the American Inquisition: An Oral History* by Griffin Fariello. Copyright © 1995 by Griffin Fariello. Reprinted by permission of W. W. Norton & Company, Inc.

American Voices: Isaac Nelson, "Atomic Witness." Excerpt from pp. 133–35 in *American Ground Zero: The Secret Nuclear War* by Carole Gallagher. Copyright © 1993 by Carole Gallagher. Reprinted by permission of the author.

Chapter 28

Voices from Abroad: Hanoch Bartov "Everyone Has a Car." Excerpt from *Arbaah Isrealim Vekhol America* (Four Israelis and the Whole of America) by Hanoch Bartov. Copyright © Hanoch Bartov, Acum House, Israel. Reprinted by permission of the author and Acum House.

American Voices: "A Woman Encounters the Feminine Mystique." Excerpt from pp. 154–56 in *The Fifties: A Woman's Oral History* by Brett Harvey. Copyright © 1993 by Brett Harvey. Reprinted by permission of HarperCollins Publishers, Inc.

Chapter 29

American Voices: Dave Cline, "A Vietnam Vet Remembers." Excerpt from pp. 135–41 in *Winter Soldiers: An Oral History of the Vietnam Veterans against the War* by Richard Stacewicz. Copyright © 1997 by Richard Stacewicz. Reprinted by permission of the Gale Group.

Voices from Abroad: Che Guevara, "Vietnam and the World Freedom Struggle." Excerpt from pp. 144–49, "Message to the Tricontinental," from *Che Guevara Speaks* by Ernesto Che Guevara. Copyright © 2000 by Pathfinder Press. Reprinted by permission.

American Voices: Mary Crow Dog, "The Trail of Broken Treaties." Excerpt from pp. 86–91 in *Lakota Woman* by Mary Crow Dog and Richard Erdos. Copyright © 1990 by Mary Crow Dog and Richard Erdos. Reprinted by permission of St. Martin's Press.

Chapter 30

American Voices: David Kopay, "The Real Score: A Gay Athlete Comes Out." Excerpt from *The David Kopay Story: An Extraordinary Self-Revelation* by David Kopay and Perry D. Young. Copyright © 1988 by David Kopay and Perry D. Young. Reprinted by permission of Donadio & Olson, Inc.

American Voices: Phyllis Ellison, "Busing in Boston." Excerpt from *Voices of Freedom: An Oral History of the Civil Rights Movement from the 1950s through the 1980s* by Henry Hampton and Steve Fayer. Copyright © 1990 by Blackside, Inc. Used by permission of Bantam Books, a division of Random House, Inc.

Voices from Abroad: Fei Xiaotong, "America's Crisis of Faith." Excerpt from *Land Without Ghosts: Chinese Impressions of America from the Mid-Nineteenth Century to the Present* translated and edited by R. David Arkush and Leo O. Lee. Copyright © 1989 The Regents of the University of California. Reprinted by permission of the University of California Press.

Chapter 31

Voices from Abroad: Saddam Hussein, "Calling for a Holy War against the United States." From *The New York Times*, September 6, 1990, p. A20. Copyright © 1990 by The New York Times Company. Reprinted by permission.

American Voices: Laurie Ouellette, "A Third-Wave Feminist." Originally published in *Utne Reader* (July–August 1992). Reprinted by permission.

Fig. 31.2. "Productivity and Wages, 1982–1995." From *The New York Times*, January 2, 1996, C20. Copyright © 1996 by The New York Times Company. Reprinted by permission.

Afghanistan, 939(*i*), 940(*i*), 941(*i*),
    943, 947
    Soviet invasion of, 901, 912, 941
    U.S. aid to, 901
    U.S. attack on, 916(*m*)
AFL-CIO, 817, 863. *See also* American
    Federation of Labor; Congress of
    Industrial Organizations
Africa. *See also* West Africa
    African American migration
        to, 691
    AIDS in, 925
    Arab civilization in, 17–18
    Atlantic slave trade with, 5–6,
        21(*m*), 22, 37, 78(*m*), 265(*t*)
    colonization by freed slaves in,
        134(*m*), 262, 270–271, 354, 393
    gender relations in, 80
    Guinea company in, 35
    jazz and, 677
    migration from, 37. *See also* Middle
        Passage
    modern migration from, 844
    North, 768(*m*), 769
    post-WWI colonialism in, 658–659
    Protestant missions in, 275(*m*)
    slave trade in, 6, 20, 22
    society of, 20–21, 80
    trade with, 14, 20, 22(*m*), 97(*i*)
African Americans. *See also* abolition;
        abolitionism; civil rights
        movement; desegregation;
        emancipation; free blacks;
        racism; segregation; slavery;
        slaves
    affirmative action and,
        896–897, 925
    alleged inferiority of, 369, 580
    Baptists and, 121, 130, 274–275, 279
    in baseball, 680
    Black Power and, 849, 861, 877
    as buffalo soldiers, 470
    in cattle industry, 464, 464(*i*)
    changing demographics and, 921,
        921(*m*), 924
    civil rights movement and, 804,
        806, 856, 860–863, 862(*m*), 877
    Civil War and, 178, 398, 417,
        423(*i*)
    in colonial America, 101, 105–106,
        108, 110(*m*), 119
    Communist Party and, 708–709
    community of, 85–88, 99
    Congressional Delegation (1872) of,
        441(*i*)
    culture of, 85–89
    culture of slavery and,
        265–267, 279
    Democratic Party and, 440,
        746, 933
    Dred Scott and, 391

economic expansion and
    (1920s), 670
education of, 258, 260, 277, 369,
    442(*i*), 531, 534
1852 election and, 388(*i*)
equality of, 160–161, 268, 273,
    527–528
as Exodusters, 465, 468(*i*)
feminism and, 925
Fourteenth Amendment and, 519,
    525, 529
Fifteenth Amendment and, 525,
    529–530, 530(*i*)
in France, 689
freedom and, 187(*i*)
Fugitive Slave Act and, 385–386
German propaganda toward, 648
Great Depression and, 699, 704,
    707–709, 719
Great Migration of, 650–651,
    650(*m*), 652
Great Society and, 846
in Haiti, 271, 337
Harlem Renaissance and,
    690–691, 690(*i*)
hostility to, 408, 408(*i*), 448
in industrial jobs, 650–651
jazz and, 677, 677(*i*), 680
JFK and, 831
Korean immigrants and, 920(*i*)
labor unions and, 507, 733
LBJ and, 840
leadership of, 440–441
lynchings of, 530–534, 531(*i*),
    532(*i*), 660
Methodism and, 270, 274
militancy of, 532–534, 660, 691,
    861–862, 866, 877
in military, 617–619, 618(*i*),
    646, 758
music of, 826
Muslim, 861
New Deal and, 724, 735–738, 747
in New South, 496, 525–534, 541
1920s and, 693
1936 election and, 729
nominating process and, 587
northern, 667
northward migration of, 560,
    650–652, 650(*m*), 681(*m*)
origins of, 265–266, 265(*t*), 279
as percent of population, 170,
    178, 560
post-WWI, 660, 660(*i*)
in public life, 338
Republican Party and, 440, 518, 667
resettlement in Africa of, 134(*m*),
    262, 270–271, 354, 393, 533
revivalism and, 272–275
Revolutionary War and, 156, 170,
    178–179, 179(*i*), 187–190

rights of, 379. *See also* civil rights
rock 'n' roll and, 825–827
rural, 88
sex ratio of, 86
Shakers and, 347
social class and, 50, 53
Social Security Act and, 728
in South Carolina, 321–322, 323(*i*)
in Spanish-American War,
    617–619, 618(*i*)
stereotypes of, 387
on Supreme Court, 911
on television, 822
in Union Army, 381, 418(*i*),
    425, 427
urban, 560–561, 799
urban migration of, 681, 681(*m*),
    690–691, 708, 746, 779,
    828–829, 847
urban rioting of, 849, 861–862,
    862(*m*), 867, 869, 877. *See also*
    race riots
Vietnam War (1961–1975) and, 854
violence against, 445–448, 839
voting districts and, 881
voting rights and, 355, 381, 518,
    529–531, 529(*m*), 530(*i*), 533,
    541, 668, 935
War on Poverty and, 844
welfare system and, 778–779
white supremacy movement and,
    528–534, 541
white women as caretakers of, 370
women, 668, 704, 708, 735, 916
WWII and, 750, 763–765, 777
youth of, 765
African Methodist Episcopal Church
    (AME), 262, 268, 268(*i*), 270,
    271(*i*), 442
Afrika Korps, 769
Agawam Indians, 14
Agency for International Development,
    833, 875
Agent Orange, 853, 858
The Age of Innocence
    (Wharton), 690
Agnew, Spiro, 869–870, 883
Agreda, Maria de Jesus de, 44(*i*)
Agricultural Adjustment Act (AAA),
    724, 730, 731(*t*)
Agricultural Marketing Act
    (1929), 715
agricultural societies, 6, 14–15, 20, 37,
    241
agriculture. *See also* corn; cotton;
        farmers; freehold society; grain;
        maize; sugar; tobacco; wheat
    African, 20, 84, 86–87
    Asian Americans and, 714
    biotechnology and, 918
    in California, 479–482

capital for, 467–469
capitalists in, 106
Columbian Exchange and, 27, 28(*m*)
commercialized, 710
crop rotation in, 214, 227
dry-farming, 466–467
in Dust Bowl, 709–710
in the East, 227–228
in England, 32
in English colonies, 40, 40(*t*), 49–52, 52(*i*), 54, 67, 241
in Europe, 14–16
evangelicalism and, 112, 114–115, 118, 275(*m*)
expansion of, 230, 248, 411
exports of, 105, 105(*f*), 105(*i*), 111, 127, 137, 138(*m*), 149, 285, 303
farm life and, 102, 105–106, 112, 114–115, 118
Granger movement and, 468–469, 535
Great Depression and, 697, 698–699, 715, 719
on Great Plains, 458–460, 458(*m*), 464–469, 467(*m*), 468(*i*), 483
the Great Plains, 458(*m*)
household mode of production and, 102, 105
Indian use-rights and, 11
irrigation for, 9, 11, 466, 478, 482
laborers in, 103, 290–291. *See also* farmers
land as commodity and, 465–467
medieval methods of, 14–16
in Middle Atlantic colonies, 105–106, 128(*i*)
migrant labor and, 478–479, 483
for Native Americans, 471, 473
Native Americans and, 9–14, 15(*i*), 224, 460, 471, 473
Native American women and, 14–15, 224
natural disasters and, 464–466, 473. *See also* drought
nesters and, 464
New Deal and, 746
in New England, 102–105, 131
in 1920s, 668, 693
orchards and, 479–481
outwork and, 106
in Pacific Northwest, 477
prices for, 535, 540
in the South, 301–302, 495, 497, 708, 828
in Southwest, 478–479
subsidies to, 887
subtreasury system and, 535
tariffs and, 290
technology for, 106, 227, 288, 300–301, 465–467

in Texas, 478–479, 518
transportation and, 286, 297–302
TVA and, 741
welfare system and, 778
in the West, 265
Aguilar, Father Geronimo de, 30–31
Aguinaldo, Emilio, 618, 620(*i*)
AIDS (acquired immune deficiency syndrome)/HIV (human immunodeficiency virus), 914, 918, 925
Aid to Dependent Children (ADC), 778(*i*), 779, 844
Aid to Families with Dependent Children (AFDC), 845, 880, 908, 930
Air and Water Quality Acts (1965), 841(*t*)
airline industry, 682–683, 828, 945, 946(*i*). *See also* aviation industry
Aix-la-Chapelle, Treaty of (1748), 97
Ajacán, 42–43
Alabama
    admission to Union of (1818), 262
    coal mining in, 487, 487(*m*), 489, 497
    migration to, 225–226, 296, 297(*m*)
    secession and, 385
    slavery in, 262–263, 272(*m*), 368
    voting rights in, 252
Alabama (Confederate warship), 416, 604
the Alamo, 371–372, 371(*i*)
Alaska, 375, 605–606, 888
    oil drilling in, 935
    parks in, 899
Alaska Native Land Claims Act (1971), 894–895
Albanians, 931
Albany Argus (newspaper), 317
Albany Congress (1754), 123, 139
Albany, New York, 172, 227, 229
    Dutch in, 47–48, 101(*i*)
    Erie Canal and, 298(*m*), 299, 303
Albany Plan (Plan of Union; 1754), 123, 154
Albemarle, duke of, 69
Albigensians, 18
Albright, Madeleine K., 928
Albuquerque, New Mexico, 40
alcohol
    abuse of, 309(*i*)
    blue laws and, 521
    Native American use of, 236
    production of, 287(*t*)
    taxes on, 517
    temperance and, 306–311, 309(*i*), 313, 522, 524–525, 526(*i*). *See also* Prohibition

Aldrich, Nelson W., 596
Aleut peoples, 7
Alexandria, Egypt, 19, 22(*m*)
Alexis, Grand Duke of Russia, 462
Alger, Horatio, 518, 518(*i*), 564, 757
Algonquian Indians, 42–43, 45, 47, 61. *See also* Powhatan Indians
    beaver bowl, 65(*i*)
    "praying towns" of, 62–63
Alien Act (1798), 218–219, 230
Alien and Sedition Acts (1798), 217–219, 230
Alien Land Law (1913; California), 686
Allegheny River, 64, 229
Allen, Ethan, 180
Allen, Gracie, 706
Allen, James, 352
Allen, Paul, 922–923, 923(*i*)
Allen, Richard, 262, 268, 271(*i*)
    biographical information, 270–271
Allen, Thomas, 440
Alliance for Progress, 833
Allies (World War II), 752, 768–773, 777
Almeida, Don Joas Theolomico de, 183
alphabet-soup agencies (New Deal), 726
Al Qaeda, 916(*m*), 936, 940(*i*), 941–942
Alsberg, Henry, 743
Alsop, Joseph, 874
Amar, Akhil Reed, 453
America First Committee, 752
American and Foreign Anti-Slavery Society, 357, 379
American Anti-Slavery Society, 354–355, 365, 381
American Arbitration Association, 581
American Automobile Association (AAA), 675
American Bible Society (1816), 277
American Civil Liberties Union (ACLU)
    Scopes trial and, 687
American colonies. *See also* colonization; *individual colonies by name*
    agriculture in, 40, 40(*t*), 49–52, 52(*i*), 54, 67, 105–106, 128(*i*), 241
    Anglicanism in, 107, 112(*m*), 113, 118–121, 119(*f*), 119(*t*), 131, 157
    British reform measures in (1763–1765), 134–140
    British Restoration and, 70–72
    British troops in, 133(*i*), 134, 139–140
    colonial assemblies in, 93–94, 99

American colonies (Continued):
constitutional rights of, 139–140, 145–146, 159
control of trade by, 93(m)
economic growth in, 127–128
elite in, 93–94
Enlightenment in (1740–1765), 112–115, 121, 131, 143, 159
European spheres of influence in, 122(m)
evangelicalism in, 120–121, 131
freehold society in, 105, 106(m), 119–120, 128–129, 131
French and Indian War and, 121–126, 154
governments of, 48–50, 55–61, 67
independence of. See Revolutionary War
land conflicts in, 128–129
mercantilism and, 19, 35, 37, 72–73, 93(m), 95–99
Navigation Acts and, 97–98
patronage in, 90, 95
population of, 127(f)
proprietary, 69(i), 70, 75, 99
royal, 70
salutary neglect and, 95, 95(i), 98–99
seaport society in, 91–93
self-government in, 93–98, 133
slave labor in, 76–93
tenant farmers in, 105, 128(i), 129
tobacco in, 48–55, 67
urban growth in, 91
women in, 15, 60, 91
American Colonization Society, 262, 271, 354
The American Commonwealth (Bryce), 515, 594
American Diplomacy, 1900–1950 (Kennan), 787
American Education Society (1815), 277
American Expeditionary Force (AEF), 643
American Federation of Labor (AFL), 509, 513, 586–587, 714, 733, 817
American Female Moral Reform Society, 358
American Home Missionary Society (1826), 275(m), 277
American Indian Movment (AIM), 863
American Indians, National Council of, 863
American Justice, 1933 (painting; Jones), 708(i)
American Legion, 647
American Lyceum, 343
American Medical Association (AMA), 799
birth control and, 704
Medicare and Medicaid and, 845

American Mercury, 690
American Notes (Dickens), 348
American Party. See Know-Nothing Party
American Philosophical Society, 114
American Plan, meaning of, 670
American Protective League, 655
American Railway Union (ARU), 510–511
"The American Scholar" (Emerson), 344
American Slavery, American Freedom: The Ordeal of Colonial Virginia (Morgan), 161
American Slavery as It Is: Testimony of a Thousand Witnesses, 354
American Smelting and Refining Company, 477
American Sunday School Union (1824), 277
American System (Clay), 323, 338–339, 376, 427
Adams and, 318–319, 331
Jackson and, 320–321, 325, 328, 330
American Union against Militarism, 640
The American Woman's Home (Beecher), 553
American Woman Suffrage Association, 439
Ames, Adelbert, 448
Ames, Fisher, 201
Amherst, Jeffrey, 125
Amos 'n' Andy (radio program), 680, 707
amusement parks, 567
Disneyland, 821, 910(i)
Long Beach, California, 566(i)
Anabaptists, 29
Anaconda Copper Corporation, 477, 670
anarchism, 508, 510
Anasazi Indians, 6, 11–12
Ancona, Victor, 758(i)
Anderson, Alexander, 214(i)
Anderson, Jourdon, 433
Anderson, Robert, 400
Anderson, Sherwood, 690
Andover, Massachusetts, 60, 62(m)
André, John, 180–181, 181(i)
Andros, Edmund, 73–74
Angelo, Giovanni, 344(i)
Angelou, Maya, 708
Anglicanism (Church of England), 32, 50, 56, 73–74, 273(t)
American, 190
in American colonies, 70–71, 107, 112(m), 113, 118–121, 119(f), 119(t), 131, 157

Columbia University and, 118, 119(t)
as established church, 75, 119–121, 131, 157
Quakers and, 341(i)
slavery and, 160
William and Mary and, 119(t)
Anglo-Dutch Wars (1552–1554, 1664, 1673), 75(t)
Anglo-Saxonism, 609
Angola, West Africa, 20
Annan, Kofi, 931
Ann, Mother, 277
Anschutz, Thomas P., 502(i)
Anthony, Susan B. (1820–1906), 364, 439
anti-Americanism, 943
Antiballistic Missile Treaty (1972), 936
Anti-Comintern Pact, 751
anticommunism, 787, 797, 799–802, 813. See also McCarthy, Joseph R.
in Hollywood, 903
Antietam, battle of, 397(i), 403(i), 404(m), 405, 407, 413, 427
Antifederalists, 204–205, 208–210, 280–281
at Philadelphia convention, 203
Anti-Imperialist Leagues, 620
Anti-Inflation Act, 755
anti-Masonry, 330–331, 339
Anti-Saloon League, 586, 653
anti-Semitism. See also Jews, discrimination against
Holocaust and, 770
racism and, 760
Anti-Slavery Conventions of American Women, 354
Anti-Slavery Society, 357
antitrust laws, 599, 666
Microsoft and, 923
New Deal and, 725
Sherman Antitrust Act (1890), 586, 592–593, 595–596, 599
wartime suspension of, 648, 755
antiwar movement (Vietnam War), 849, 856–858, 882–883
backlash against, 869
Chicago Democratic convention (1968), 868–869
decline of, 870–871
draft and, 854, 858, 866, 874, 877
Kent State and, 870
student protests and, 858–859, 858(i), 877
teach-in and, 858
women in, 857, 866
ANZUS (Australia, New Zealand, United States; 1951), 795(m)

Apache Indians, 7, 469–470, 470(*m*), 471
Apalachee Indians, 12, 40
apartheid, 930
Appalachia, 702(*m*), 841(*t*), 845
  migration from, 828
  War on Poverty and, 844
Appalachian Mountains, 61, 182, 199(*m*), 228, 234(*m*), 235, 249
  western expansion and, 129, 129(*m*), 131, 138(*m*), 265, 296
  as western frontier, 121, 126, 138(*m*), 151(*m*)
Appalachian Regional Development Act (1965), 841(*t*), 845
An Appeal . . . to the Colored Citizens of the World (Walker), 352, 353(*i*)
appeasement (World War II), 750–751
Apple Computer Company, 918
Appleton, Nathan, 290
Appomattox Court House, Virginia, 426, 430
Arab League, 796
Arabs, 17–21, 37. *See also* Middle East; Muslims
  effect on Europe of, 19
  Islamic fundamentalism and, 915
  Mediterranean commerce and, 18, 22(*m*)
  scholarship of, 18–19, 19(*i*)
Arafat, Yasir, 929
Arapaho Indians, 459, 469, 470(*m*)
Arawak Indians, 24
Arbella (ship), 57
architecture, 20(*i*), 193
  Aztec, 9–10
  Federal style, 213
Archuleta, Susana, 739
Arctic, oil drilling in, 935
Arent, Arthur, 721(*i*)
Argentina, 670, 900
Arikara Indians, 459, 470(*m*)
Aristide, Jean-Bertrand, 929
Aristocratic-Republicanism, 252, 261–269, 274, 279
Aristotle, 343
Arizona, 11, 40, 382(*m*)
  copper mining in, 478
  Hispanic settlement in, 478
  Japanese internment in, 765
  Latino immigrants in, 828
Arkansas, 47, 401, 424
  drought in, 709–710
  Japanese internment in, 765
  migration to, 296, 297(*m*)
  slavery in, 369
Arkwright, Richard, 288
Armistead, James, 179(*i*)
arms control, 787, 912. *See also* weapons of mass destruction

Antiballistic Missile Treaty (1972), 936
  Carter and, 901
  nuclear test ban treaty (1963), 834, 857
  SALT I, 871
  SALT II, 899, 901
  Washington Naval Arms Conference (1921), 673
arms race, 783. *See also* atomic bomb; nuclear weapons
  nuclear, 783(*i*), 785, 787, 808
  nuclear proliferation and, 807–810
Armstrong, Louis, 677
Army Corps of Engineers, U.S., 625
Army of the Potomoc, 403–404, 415, 419
Army, U.S., 603
  frontier posts of, 462
  Indian wars and, 462–463, 470–471, 470(*m*), 473
  in Philippines, 620
  in Pullman boycott, 511
  racial segregation in, 646
  racial violence in, 646
  Special Forces of, 831, 833
Arnold, Benedict, 179, 180(*i*)
  biographical information, 180–181
Arnold, Margaret Shippen, 257
art, 18(*i*), 37. *See also* Mayas
  cultural dissent and, 825
  establishment of museums, 569
  modernist, 689
  Native American, 9, 9(*i*), 11, 11(*i*), 12(*i*), 65(*i*)
  New Deal and, 741, 743, 745, 747
  in 1920s, 688–691
  Renaissance, 19
Arthur Anderson Company, 945
Arthur, Chester A. (1829–1886)
  as president (1881–1885), 516, 604
Arthur, Jean, 706(*i*)
Articles of Confederation (1777), 196–203, 219
  provisions of, 196–197
  revision of, 202–203
artisan republicanism, 332
artisans, 242, 332. *See also* mechanics
  in colonial America, 105, 112–114
  education for, 259
  European, 17(*i*), 19
  in industrial age, 292–293, 293(*i*), 296, 303, 313, 486, 498, 501–502, 502(*i*)
  Native American, 9, 11–12, 12(*i*), 65
  on plantations, 261
  as Sons of Liberty, 142–143, 149–150
  South Atlantic system and, 91–92
  taxation on, 252
  trade unionism and, 506–507

Asante people, 79–80
Asbury, Francis, 270
Ashby, Robert, 121
Ashcroft, John D., 934, 946
Asia, 5–6, 22, 37, 387. *See also particular countries*
  European empires in, 604, 607, 626, 626(*m*)
  foreign powers in (1898–1910), 627(*m*)
  immigrants from, 828(*f*), 920, 937
  post-WWI colonialism in, 658–659
  U.S. foreign investment in, 673
Asian Americans, 605(*i*)
  discrimination against, 818
  in Great Depression, 707, 714, 719
  increase of, 921, 921(*m*)
  intermarriage of, 924
assemblies, colonial, 93–94, 99
  restrictions on, 145–146, 149, 154, 155(*t*), 159
  self-government and, 134, 140, 143, 145–146, 149, 154, 157, 159
  struggle with royal government and, 123, 134, 136, 140, 145–146
  support for self-government and, 149, 154, 159
  taxation and, 94
assembly line, 287(*i*), 288, 505(*i*). *See also* mass production
assimilation, cultural, 44
  Franciscans and, 41
  Native Americans and, 28, 41, 44, 222, 471–474, 472(*i*), 473, 829
Astaire, Fred, 705(*i*), 706, 908(*i*)
Astor, John Jacob, 241
astronomy
  Arabic, 19(*i*)
  Mayan, 9
Aswan Dam, 796–797
asylum reform
  abolitionism and, 357
  Dix and, 360–361
  women's rights and, 358
Atchison, David R., 389
Atgeld, John P., 510
Atherton, Joshua, 208
Atlanta, Georgia, 410, 421
  fall of (1864), 424, 425(*m*)
  as railroad hub, 301(*m*)
  Sherman and, 423
Atlantic Charter (1941), 752(*m*), 753, 768, 773
Atlantic Monthly, 570
atomic bomb, 750, 777, 783, 785, 791, 793, 808(*m*)
  Soviet Union and, 948
  testing of, 941
  U.S., 775–776
  use of, 773(*m*)

Atomic Energy Commission (AEC), 809
Attucks, Crispus, 149
Augsberg, Peace of (1555), 29
Auld, Hugh, 380–381
Auld, Thomas, 380–381
Auschwitz concentration camp, 770
Austin, Moses, 370
Austin, Stephen F., 370–371, 371(m)
Australia, 606
    Chinese immigration to, 479
    gold rush in, 475
    secret ballot from, 523, 524(m)
    WWII and, 771
An Australian Looks at America (Adams), 671
Austria, 658, 751
Austria-Hungary, 638–639
Autobiography (Franklin), 113, 305, 344
automobile
    culture of, 675, 817, 819
    foreign, 884, 887(i)
    fuel-efficient, 885(f)
    Great Depression and, 702
    interstate highways and, 820(m)
    1950s culture and, 821
    political campaigns and, 667(i)
    rural life and, 675, 682
    suburbs and, 817, 819–820
automobile industry
    consumer culture and, 673
    energy crisis and, 884
    environmentalism and, 889
    labor unions and, 733
    mass production in, 503, 505, 671, 675
    in 1920s, 668, 693
    steel production for, 489
aviation industry, 682–683
axis of evil (Iran, Iraq, and North Korea), 942
Axis, Rome-Berlin (WWII), 750
Ayres, Thomas A., 457(i)
Azores, 20
Aztecs, 27(i), 30–31, 37
    culture of, 6, 9–10, 12
    European diseases and, 25–27
    human sacrifice among, 10, 12
    social structure of, 9–10, 25
    Spanish conquest of, 24–28, 27(i), 30–31, 37

Babcock, Orville, 449
baby-boom generation, 820–825, 928
    unemployment and, 886
Backlash: The Undeclared War on American Women (Faludi), 925
Backus, Isaac, 115, 118, 190
Bacon, Nathaniel, 55–56, 55(i), 61, 67

Bacon's Rebellion (1676), 55–56, 67, 71, 90, 161
Bad Axe Massacre, 326
Badger, Joseph, 116(i)
Baez, Joan, 860
Bahamas, 24
Bahía de Santa María (Chesapeake Bay), 42–43
Bainbridge, Joseph, 735(i)
Baker, Ella, 839, 866
Baker, Josephine, 689
Baker v. Carr (1962), 881
Bakke, Allan, 896–897
Bakke v. University of California (1978), 897
balance of power, 623, 627
Balboa, Vasco Núñez de, 24
Balkans, 638
Ball, Charles, 274
Ballinger, Richard A., 596
Baltimore, Lord. *See* **Calvert, Cecilius; Calvert, George**
Baltimore, Maryland, 92(i), 289, 305
    British attack on, in War of 1812, 235, 238(m)
    flight of Congress to, 171
    free blacks in, 269
    secessionists in, 401
    transportation and, 299, 300(m), 303
    West Indian trade and, 91
Bangs, Isaac, 169(i)
bank holiday, meaning of, 724
Banking Act (1863), 537
Banking Act (1935), 726, 731(t)
Bank of England, 333, 334(m)
Bank of North America, 206, 241
Bank of the United States, 230, 249
    First, 146, 241–242, 411
    Jackson's attack on Second, 324–326, 326(i), 337
    Second, 242, 246, 318–319, 326(i), 333, 337–339, 411, 416
    Washington and, 211
banks
    American System and, 318–319
    bankers and, 302–303, 324
    in Civil War, 409
    consumer lending and, 674
    economic expansion and (1920s), 670
    failures of, 334(m), 697, 698–699
    gold standard and, 538–540, 538(i)
    Great Depression and, 697, 699, 707, 715, 718
    Hamilton on, 211, 242
    national, 335, 338, 376
    National Banking Acts and, 412, 537
    New Deal and, 724, 724(t), 726
    postwar, 816

private, 332
    reform of, 598–599
Bank War, 242, 246, 318–319, 326(i), 333, 337–339, 411, 416
Banneker, Benjamin, 188, 268
Bao Dai, emperor of Vietnam, 850
Baptists, 103, 188, 190
    abolitionism and, 353, 359
    African Americans and, 121, 130, 274–275, 279
    Brown University and, 118, 119(t)
    child rearing and, 258
    in colonial America, 102, 111, 112(m), 118, 119(f), 131
    egalitarianism of, 120–121, 131, 160, 272–274, 273(t), 274(i), 277
    evangelicalism of, 275, 275(m), 278–279
    fundamentalist, 686
    National Convention of, 442
    separation of church and state and, 115
Barbados, 71, 78, 80–81
Barbary States, 230
Barnum, P. T., 569
Barron v. Baltimore, 210
Barry, Leonora M., 507
Barton, Bruce, 667(i)
Barton, Clara, 409
Bartov, Hanoch, 821
Baruch, Bernard, 648, 725
Baruch Plan, 785
baseball, 568, 568(i), 680
Basel Convention (1994), 927
Bataan death march, 771, 774
Bates, Blanche, 656–657
Batista, Fulgencio, 828, 833
Bayard, James, 218
Bayard, Thomas F., 604
Bay of Pigs invasion (1961), 833, 834(m)
Beard, Ithamar A., 305
the Beatles, 860
Beats, 825
Beauregard, P.G.T., 379, 403, 406
bebop, 825
Beckley, John, 235
Beckwith, Abijah, 379, 389
Beecher, Catharine, 358–359, 362, 553
Beecher, Henry Ward, 333, 563, 570
Beecher, Lyman, 275, 306, 308
Begin, Menachem, 901–902, 901(i)
Beirut, Lebanon, 912
Belgium, 639, 752, 770
Bell, Alexander Graham, 548
Bellamy, Edward, 575
Bellamy, Francis, 452
Belleau Wood, Battle of, 644
Bell, John, 392(m), 394
Bellow, Saul, 743
Bellows, Henry W., 341

Bell, Rex, 678
Below, Ernst, 522
Benevolent Empire activities, 306–311, 313, 336
Benezet, Anthony, 188
Benin, Africa, 80–81
Bennett, James Gordon, 568
Bennett, William, 925
Bennington, Vermont, 171(m), 173
Benny, Jack, 706–707, 822
Benton, Thomas Hart, 324
Bentsen, Lloyd, 911
Bergen, Edgar, 706
Berger, Victor, 586, 655
Bering Strait, 7
Berkeley, William, 54–56, 67
Berle, Adoph A., Jr., 723
Berlin Airlift, 789, 789(i), 790–791
Berlin Conference (1884), 607
Berlin, Germany, 784(i), 789
    compared to Chicago, 550
    division of, 774, 788(m)
    JFK and, 833, 840
Berlin, Ira, 80, 160
Berlin Wall, 833
    fall of, 907, 907(i), 912
Bernard, Francis, 138
Bernard, S., 323
Bernard, Thomas, 257
Bernstein, Carl, 882
Berry, Chuck, 827
Bessemer, Henry, 486, 488
Bethel African Methodist Episcopal Church, 262, 270, 271(i)
Bethlehem Steel Company, 489(i)
Bethune-Cookman College, 736–737
Bethune, Joanna, 308
Bethune, Mary McLeod, 735, 736(i)
    biographical information, 736–737
Beveridge, Alfred J., 613
Bevin, Ernest, 790
The Bible against Slavery (Weld), 354
Bidault, Georges, 790
Biddle, Nicholas, 324, 326(i)
Big Foot, chief of Sioux, 473
Bilek, Anton, 774
Bill for Establishing Religious Freedom (1786), 190
Bill of Rights, 281. See also individual amendments
    Madison and, 209–210, 235
    ratification of Constitution and, 205, 209–210
    of William and Mary, 73
The Bill of Rights (Amar), 453
Bingham, Caleb, 259
Bingham, William, 242
bin Laden, Osama, 932, 936, 941–943
    aid to Afghanistan and, 901
    biotechnology, 918–919

Birch, William, 193(i)
Bird, Caroline, 699
Birmingham, Alabama
    racial violence in, 838, 838(i)
    steel production in, 487(m), 489, 497
Birney, James G., 357, 376
birth control, 892
    declining birth rate and, 255–256, 277–278, 865
    folk medicine and, 256–257
    Great Depression and, 702–704
    information about, 554–555, 582–583, 702–703
    pill, 865
    rhythm method of, 554
    women's rights and, 893
Birth of a Nation (film), 589, 684
birthrate. See also population
    declining, 255–256, 277–278, 865
    of European peasants, 15
    Great Depression and, 702
    increasing, 491
    in 1950s, 823, 823(f)
    women and, 102, 255–257
    women's rights and, 893
Black Ball Line, 303
black churches, 262, 268, 268(i), 270, 271(i), 442, 560, 562. See also particular denominations under African Americans
    in New York, 560–561
Black Codes, 431, 441, 451
Black Death, 14
Black Elk, Sioux holy man, 472(i)
Blackfeet Indians, 459, 470(m)
Black Hawk (1767–1838), 326, 328(i), 329
Black Hills, South Dakota, gold in, 471, 475
Black, Hugo, 453, 731
blacklist, 813
    meaning of, 800, 802
Blackmun, Harry, 881
Black Muslims, 861
black nationalism, 691
Black Panthers, 861, 863
Black Robes. See Jesuits
Black Star Line steamship company, 691
"Black Thursday" (Oct. 24, 1929), 696(i), 697
"Black Tuesday" (Oct. 29, 1929), 696(i), 697
Blaine, James G., 518, 521, 605
Blair, Francis Preston, 321
Blake, William, 215(i)
Bland-Allison Act (1878), 538
Bland, Richard, 137
Blassie, Michael, 918

"Bleeding Kansas," 389–390, 389(i), 392(m), 395
The Blithedale Romance (Hawthorne), 346
blitzkrieg, meaning of, 752
Boardman, Elijah, 241(i)
Board of Trade, British, 123–124, 134, 145
Boeing (company), 749(i)
Boland Amendment, 912
Bolivia, 605
Bolshevism, 658, 661, 668. See also communism
Bonaparte, Charles J., 583
Bonnin, Gertrude Simmons (Zitkala-Ša), 471, 473
Bonsack, James A., 496
Bonus Army (1932), 717
Bonus Bill (1817), 246, 319
The Book of Mormon (Smith), 350
Book-of-the-Month Club, 680
Boone, Daniel, 410
Booth, John Wilkes, 430
Booth, Nathaniel, 252
Borah, William E., 659
Bosnia, 639, 929, 932(m), 942
Boston, Absalom, 268(i)
Boston Guardian, 589
Boston Harbor
    tea in, 152–153, 153(i), 155(t)
Boston Manufacturing Company, 290–291, 302
Boston, Massachusetts, 40(t), 73(m), 180, 180(i), 187
    British troops in, 147, 148(m), 152, 154, 155(t), 157–158, 185
    elite in, 550–551
    news of Glorious Revolution in, 74
    occupation by British, 154
    painting of, 92(i)
    popular power in, 94
    school busing in, 894(i), 895–897
    skyline of, 549
    South Atlantic system and, 93(m)
    transportation and, 298(m), 300, 300(m), 301(m), 302(m), 303
    West Indian trade and, 91, 93(m)
Boston Massacre, 149, 152
Boston Tea Party, 142(i), 150–153, 153(i), 155(t)
Bougainville, Louis Antoine de, 125–126
Bourke-White, Margaret, 745
Bow, Clara, 676, 679(i)
    biographical information, 678–679
Bowdoin, James, 201
the Bowery, New York City, 565, 565(i), 568
Bowie, Jim, 371
Bowles, Chester, 806
Boxer rebellion (China; 1900), 627, 627(m)

Boyce, Ed, 512
boycotts. *See also* nonimportation
    of 1765, 141, 144–145, 147(*i*), 149,
        149(*f*), 154, 157(*i*)
    of 1768, 146
    by Atlanta African Americans, 531
    of British goods, 157(*i*), 159
    of California grapes, 863
    civil rights movement and, 856
    effects of, 144–145
    pre-Revolutionary War, 144–146,
        147(*i*), 149, 149(*f*), 154, 157(*i*),
        159
    Pullman, 510–511, 538, 573
Boyleston, Thomas, 175
bracero program, 828
Braddock, Edward, 124
Bradford, Perry, 677(*i*)
Bradford, William, 56
Bradley, Joseph P., 450
Brady, Matthew, 393(*i*)
Branch Davidians, 929
Brandeis, Louis D., 577, 583, 599
Brant, Joseph (Thayendanegea; Chief
        Joseph; Mohawk chief), 170,
        173(*i*)
Brauckmiller, John R., 764(*i*)
Braxton, Carter, 196
Brazil, 76, 77(*t*), 78, 80
    African slaves in, 47–48
    colonization of, 134(*m*)
    trade with, 303
breadlines, 700
    women in, 699, 701(*i*)
Breckinridge, John C., 392(*m*), 394
Brest-Litovsk, Treaty of, 644
Bretton Woods system, 816, 884
Breyer, Stephen G., 934
Brezhnev, Leonid, 901
Bright, John, 713
A Bright and Shining Lie (Sheehan),
        874
Brisbane, Arthur, 347
Briscoe v. Bank of Kentucky (1837), 329
Bristol, England, 97(*i*), 98
British Columbia, gold in, 475
British East India Company, 35, 125,
        150–151
British Empire. *See also* England; Great
        Britain
    in America (1660–1750), 69–99
    in American colonies, 134, 139–140
    in Boston, 152, 154, 155(*t*), 157–158
    colonial land grants and, 104
    debts of, 124, 127, 134, 136, 141,
        154, 159
    expansion of, 101, 121–126, 138(*m*)
    impressment and, 142
    in India, 124–125, 134(*m*), 150
    Industrial Revolution in, 127
    mercantilism and, 98

Navigation Acts and, 136–138
navy and, 125, 136, 137(*f*), 142, 154
politics of, 93–98
reforms in, 134–139, 142, 145,
        147(*i*), 159
taxation and, 136–155, 137(*f*)
trade in, 134, 134(*m*). *See also* trade,
        Anglo-American
in West Africa, 124–125, 134(*m*)
WWII and, 773
Brook Farm, 345–346, 346(*m*), 365
Brookfield, Massachusetts, 243
Brooklyn, New York, 921
Brooks, Louise, 678
Brooks, Phillips, 563
Brooks, Preston, 367
Brophy, John, 501, 504
Brown Berets, 863
Brown, James, 827
Brown, John, 381, 389, 395
    raid of (1859), 394
Brown, Joseph, 407
Brown, Moses, 288
Brown, Ron, 928
Brownson, Orestes, 332
Brown, Susan, 290–291
Brownlow, William G., 446–447
Brown University, 119(*t*)
    founding of, 118
Brown v. Board of Education (1954),
        804–805, 836(*m*), 861,
        881, 895
Bruce, Blanche K., 440
Bruce, William, 682
Brunelleschi, Filippo, 19
Brush, Charles F., 548
Bryan, Charles W., 667
Bryan, William Jennings, 538–539,
        539(*i*), 540(*m*), 596–598, 620,
        630, 687
Bryant, Anita, 894
Bryce, James, 515–516, 518, 606
    on America, 594
Buchanan, James (1791–1868), 387,
        392(*m*), 395
    Mormons and, 352
    as president (1857–1861), 391, 398
    as Secretary of State, 377, 379
    on slave vs. free state conflict, 383,
        391
Buchanan, Patrick, 925, 933
Buchenwald concentration camp, 770
Buck, Pearl, 707
buffalo, 458, 483
    hunting of, 459, 459(*i*), 460–462,
        463(*i*)
    increase in, 632
    slaughter of, 460(*i*), 461
Buffalo Bill, the King of the Border Men
        (Buntline), 462
Buffalo, New York, 227

transportation and, 298(*m*),
        299–302, 300(*m*), 301(*m*),
        302(*m*)
buffalo soldiers, 470
Bulge, Battle of, 770
Bulkley, William Lewis, 591
Bull Moose Party, 597
Bull Run (Manassas Creek), battle of,
        403–404, 423
Bundy, McGeorge, 834
Bunker, Ellsworth, 870
Buntline, Ned, 462
Bunyan, John, 576
Burger, Warren, 881, 909(*i*)
Burgess, John W., 589
Burgoyne, John, 171(*m*), 172–174, 182
burial mounds, Native American,
        11–12
Burke, Edmund, 95
Burkitt, Frank, 528
Burlage, Dorothy, 866
Burma, 771
Burns, George, 706
Burnside, Ambrose E., 403(*i*)
Burr, Aaron, 212(*i*), 218
    duel with Hamilton, 233
Burroughs, Edgar Rice, 554
Burton, James S., 410
Bush, Barbara, 910(*i*)
Bush, George H. W. (1924–), 281(*i*),
        903
    approval ratings of, 914
    missile attack on Iraq and, 929
    Persian Gulf War and, 913–914
    as president (1989–1993), 910–912
    vs. Reagan, 908
    renomination of, 928
    rollback of federal government and,
        927
    signing of NAFTA and, 928–929
Bush, George W. (1946–)
    approval ratings of, 944
    energy industry and, 935
    Enron and, 945
    Office of Homeland Security and,
        947(*i*)
    as president (2001–), 934–936, 944
    religion and, 452–453
    rollback of federal government and,
        937
    September 11 attacks and, 936(*i*),
        941, 943
    State of the Union address of 2002,
        942
    2000 election and, 933–934, 933(*i*),
        934(*m*)
Bushnell, Horace, 570
business. *See also* corporations
    consolidation of, 670, 899
    credit for, 715
    failures in, 698(*f*), 699

government cooperation with, 666–673, 692–693, 732
Great Depression and, 715
intellectual life and, 690
mobilization for war and, 754–755
modern management and, 503–505, 513, 668, 670
New Deal and, 725, 728–729
in 1920s, 669–670, 693
U.S. interventions and, 913(*m*)
welfare system and, 778
busing, school, 881, 883, 894(*i*), 895–896, 905
1980 election and, 903
opposition to, 898
Bussell, Joshua H., 347(*i*)
Bute, Lord, 136, 144(*t*)
Butler, Andrew P., 367
Butler, Benjamin, 413
Butler, Pierce, 203, 216
Butterfield, Alexander, 883(*i*)
Butterfield Overland Mail, 374(*m*)
butterfly ballots, 933
Byrd, Harry F., 831(*i*)
Byrd, Richard, 682
Byrnes, James, 731, 786
Byrnes, Thomas F., 564
Byzantine civilization, 19

Cabot, John, 23(*m*)
Cagney, James, 706
Cahan, Abraham, 562
Cahill, Holger, 743
Cahokia (Mississippian civilization), 12
Caldwell, James, 152
calendar
Catholic, 17
Mayan, 9
Calhoun, John C. (1782–1850), 235, 324, 368, 387, 391, 398
Bonus Bill and, 246, 319
expansionism and, 379, 395
on majority rule, 322–323
as presidential candidate, 317–318, 320
as secretary of state, 375
on slave vs. free state conflict, 383, 387
as vice-president, 322–323
Whig Party and, 330–331, 339
California, 44, 184(*m*), 387, 395
affirmative action in, 896–897, 925
agricultural strikes in, 711, 711(*i*)
agriculture in, 479–482, 710
annexation of, 374–375, 379
Asian Americans in, 714
attempt to buy, 376–377
Catholic missions in, 481
cession of, 382(*m*)
China trade and, 374

climate of, 481, 483
Compromise of 1850 and, 382(*m*), 384, 386(*m*)
culture of, 481–483
gold rush in (1849–1857), 382–383, 384(*i*), 385(*m*), 477, 479, 483
immigration to, 686, 920, 924
internal migration to, 374–375, 460, 483, 710–711, 710(*m*), 724, 764, 818, 847
Japanese internment in, 765
labor movement in, 480
Mexican culture in, 374–375
Mexican War and, 378
migrant workers in, 710–711
mining frontier and, 474–476, 474(*m*), 475(*i*)
movie industry in, 675
national parks in, 482
Native Americans in, 478
Proposition 13 in, 898
statehood for, 383
California Trail, 374, 374(*m*)
Californios, 374, 478
Calley, William, 870
Calvert, Benedict, 75
Calvert, Cecilius (Cecil; 2nd Baron Baltimore), 50, 69(*i*), 70
Calvert, George (1st Baron Baltimore), 69(*i*), 70
Calvert, Leonard, 50
Calvinism, 33, 56, 258, 308
in Europe, 29, 32, 32(*m*)
Jonathan Edwards and, 116–117
predestination and, 272, 275, 277
Quakers and, 71
transcendentalism and, 343
Calvin, John, 29, 32
Cambodia
immigrants from, 920
Khmer Rouge in, 870, 876
secret bombing of, 883
Vietnam War and, 851(*m*), 853, 870, 872, 876–877
Cambridge, Massachusetts, 157
Camden, South Carolina, 178(*m*), 179, 185
Camino Real, 374(*m*)
campaign finance reform, 883, 903
Camp David accords (1978), 901–902, 901(*i*), 905
camp followers, 172
Canada, 13, 44, 67, 604. *See also* Montreal; Quebec
American invasion of, 166, 170
British conquest of (1754–1760), 124–126, 131, 136
Burgoyne's army and, 173
Douglass and, 381
French loss of, 175, 182
immigrants from, 288(*m*), 296

Loyalist emigration to, 187
NAFTA and, 929
settlement of boundaries with, 240, 249, 623
underground railroad and, 356(*m*)
War of 1812 and, 235, 240(*m*)
war on terrorism and, 941
WWII and, 770
canals, 286, 297–300, 298(*m*), 299(*t*), 302, 305, 313
Erie, 228, 275(*m*), 298(*i*), 303, 308–309, 308(*i*), 350
foreign investment in, 297, 299
as state enterprises, 488
Canandaigua, New York, 229
Canary Islands, 20, 22
Canby, Henry Seidel, 553
Cane (Toomer), 690
Cane Ridge revival, 273, 275(*m*)
Cannon, "Uncle Joe," 596
Cape Breton Island, 123(*i*)
Cape of Good Hope, 22
capitalism, 939(*i*), 940
in agriculture, 106
business cycles in, 697
communalism and, 347, 784
vs. communism, 815
corporate, 816
critiques of, 900
Fourierism and, 347
free-market, 207, 241–245, 249, 331
industrialization and, 485–513
Mormons and, 350, 352
New Deal and, 724, 726, 732
1932 election and, 718(*m*)
in 1950s, 815
Oneida Community and, 349
postwar liberalism and, 816
robber barons and, 489, 492–493
Social Darwinism and, 519
utopian reformers and, 336, 365
welfare, 670, 732, 757
WWII and, 758
capital, labor and, 331, 485–513
capital punishment, 881, 903
Capone, Al, 688
Capra, Frank, 706, 706(*i*)
captives, Indian, 64–65
Carey, Hugh, 890
Caribbean Islands (West Indies)
Columbus in, 24
communism in, 816
expansionist foreign policy and, 387, 622(*m*), 631
French, 70, 98–99, 176–177, 179, 213–214, 234
governance of, 26, 75
Molasses Act and, 96
Navigation Acts and, 98

Caribbean Islands (Continued):
    Revolutionary War and, 176–177,
        179, 182, 184
    slavery in, 15, 69, 76, 77(t), 78, 80,
        84, 88, 99, 321, 385, 395
    South Atlantic system in, 76
    sugar and, 105–106, 105(f), 125,
        134(m), 136–137, 138(m), 154
    trade with, 71, 72(t), 91, 93(m),
        97(i), 200, 241
    U.S. as power in, 613
    U.S. intervention in, 913(m)
    War of Austrian Succession and, 97
Caribbean Sea
    "policing" of, 626, 626(m)
    strategic importance of, 608–609,
        622(m), 631
Carib Indians, 24
Carmichael, Stokely, 861
Carnegie, Andrew, 485(i), 486, 510,
        518, 569, 620
Carolinas, 75–76, 79. See also North
        Carolina; South Carolina
    British occupation of, 70
    as proprietary colonies, 99
    rebellion in, 71
Carpenter, Francis Bicknell, 414(i)
carpetbaggers, 440
Carranza, Venustiano, 628–629
Carroll, Charles, 54, 83, 86
Carroll, James, 849
Carson, Rachel, 888, 888(i)
Cartagena, Colombia, 41, 96
Carter, Jimmy (James E.; 1924–), 787,
        879, 905, 943
    Camp David accords and, 901–902,
        901(i)
    defeat of, 903, 903(m)
    defense spending of, 908
    Love Canal and, 890–891
    Nobel Peace Prize and, 901(i)
    as president (1977–1981), 899–902
Carter, Landon, 155, 161
Carter, Robert, III, 89, 91
Cartier, Jacques, 44
cartoons, political, 326(i), 493(i),
        506(i), 516(i), 725(i), 871(i)
Cartwright, Peter, 296
Caruso, Enrico, 674(i)
Casablanca (film), 762
Cass, Lewis, 379, 382–383, 383(i), 387,
        392(m)
Castro, Fidel, 828, 833, 834(m)
Catharine of Aragon, 32
Catholicism, 330, 453
    in America, 40, 44, 47, 50, 65
    Americanism and, 562–563
    birth control and, 703
    in California, 374
    conversions to, 42–44, 44(i), 236
    ethnic identity and, 563

in Europe, 17–18, 18(i), 73
in Maryland, 74–75, 82(i), 83
missions of, 41–42, 44, 65, 67
mob revolt against, 312–313
1928 election and, 691–692
presidential elections and, 718, 830
vs. Protestantism, 28–29, 32–33, 35,
        50, 452
rhetoric against, 371, 518
riots against, 313
of slaves, 89
Spanish conquest and, 27–28
Catholics, 107, 110, 119(f), 272,
        273(t)
    Acadians and, 124
    anti-Catholicism and, 151, 151(m),
        311–312, 311(i), 313
    California missions and, 481
    Democratic party and, 520–521,
        521(f)
    discrimination against, 691–692
    immigration restriction and,
        682–683
    Irish, 563
    JFK and, 831
    Know-Nothing Party and, 389
    Ku Klux Klan and, 447, 684
    in 1920s, 693
    1936 election and, 729
    in 1950s, 822
    prejudice against, 142, 151, 151(m),
        311–312, 311(i), 313
    in Southwest, 478
Catt, Carrie Chapman, 579, 652
cattle industry, 494(m). See also meat-
        packing industry; ranching
    African Americans in, 464, 464(i)
    on Great Plains, 461, 464, 464(i),
        466–467
    Hispanics in, 464, 464(i)
    and Long Drive, 464
Caverly, Azariah, 304(i)
Cayuga Indians, 64
"The Celebrated Jumping Frog of
        Calaveras County" (Twain), 481
Cemetery Ridge, 415, 417(m)
CENTO. See Central Treaty
        Organization
Central America. See also Mesoamerica
    U.S. intervention in, 623–625, 670,
        673, 912
Central Asia, 914(m)
Central Intelligence Agency (CIA), 947
    Afghanistan and, 901, 943
    antiwar movement and, 870
    covert operations of, 795–796, 813,
        912
    Cuba and, 833
    Iran and, 902
    Nixon's dirty tricks and, 882
    Vietnam and, 850, 874

Central Pacific Railroad, 476
    building of, 460, 461(m)
    Chinese labor for, 479–480, 480(i)
Central Treaty Organization
        (CENTO), 795(m)
A Century of Dishonor (Jackson), 472
Cervera, Pascual, 616–617
Chaco Canyon, 11–12
Chamberlain, Neville, 750
Chambers, Sergeant, 152
Chambers, Whittaker, 800
Champlain, Samuel de, 44–45
Chancellorsville, Virginia, 415, 417(m)
Chandler, Samuel, 104
Chaney, James, 840
Channing, William Ellery, 275, 360
Chaplin, Charlie, 673, 676, 676(i)
charitable activities
    of Benevolent Empire, 306–311, 313
    Great Depression and, 701, 702(m),
        715, 718–719
    New Deal and, 725
    of women, 257, 308
Charles, Robert, 532(i)
    biographical information, 532–533
Charles I, king of England
        (r. 1625–1649), 56, 59, 69,
        140, 142
Charles I, king of Spain
        (r. 1516–1556), 29(t)
Charles II, king of England
        (r. 1660–1685), 59, 70–71,
        99, 128
*Charles River Bridge Co. v. Warren
        Bridge Co.* (1837), 328
Charles Schwab (company), 885
Charleston, South Carolina, 178(m),
        179, 187, 225(i), 398
    vs. Boston, 92(i)
    free blacks in, 268(i), 269
    South Atlantic system and, 93(m)
    transportation and, 298(m),
        300(m), 301(m), 302(m), 303
    West Indian trade and, 91
Charlestown, Massachusetts, 157, 312
charters, 244–245, 249
    contracts and, 246
Chase, Salmon P., 384, 394, 409, 413,
        414(i), 438
Chastellux, marquis de, 261
Chateau-Thierry, Battle of, 644
Chatham, earl of. See Pitt, William
Chattanooga, Tennessee, 419, 425(m)
chattel slavery, meaning of, 53
Chauncy, Charles, 115
Chautauqua, New York, 569
Chávez, César, 711, 863
Chavin culture, 6
checks and balances, 205, 438
Cheever, John, 743
Cheney, Richard, 933, 935, 944

Cherokee Indians, 12, 129, 170, 179, 469, 470(m), 745(i)
    removal of, 326–328, 327(m)
Cherokee Nation v. Georgia (1831), 328
Cherry family, 560(i)
Chesapeake (ship), 234
Chesapeake Bay
    in Civil War, 403
    class in, 90–91
    colonies of, 37, 41–42, 48–55, 67
    economy of, 69(i)
    governance of, 70
    planters of, 105, 121, 155–156, 160, 160(f), 263, 263(i), 265–266, 265(m)
    Revolutionary War and, 182, 185
    slavery in, 69(i), 80, 84–86, 99, 105, 160, 263, 263(i), 265–266, 265(m)
    tobacco in, 50–55, 67
    peoples of, 50, 55
    in War of 1812, 235
Chesnut, James, 370
Chesnut, Mary Boykin, 370, 424
Cheyenne Indians, 459, 462, 469, 470(m), 471
Cheyenne, Wyoming, 460
Chiang Kai-shek (Jiang Jieshi), 791
Chicago Columbian Exposition (1893), 549
Chicago Democratic Convention (1968), 868–869, 877
Chicago, Illinois, 223, 544–545
    African Americans in, 560, 681(m)
    Berlin and, 550
    as center of meat industry, 464, 467, 491, 505(i)
    expansion in, 547(m)
    fire of 1871, 548
    jazz and, 677
    mass transit in, 546(i)
    migration to, 681(m), 828–829
    race riots in, 660, 660(i)
    skyline of, 549
    transportation and, 298(m), 300–303, 300(m), 301(m), 302(m), 467
Chicanos. See Mexican Americans
Chickasaw Indians, 12, 326, 470, 470(m)
Chigabe (Chippewa chief), 13
child care programs, 930
    in 1970s, 892
    Nixon and, 880
    WWII and, 759
child labor, 290–291, 290(i), 500–501, 501(i)
    New Deal and, 725, 731
Child, Lydia Maria, 258–259, 277, 439
children
    attitudes toward, 556
    as indentured servants, 103, 109

interracial, 924
labor of, 501(i)
"latchkey," 764
in medieval Europe, 16–17
in 1950s culture, 822–823
rearing of, 258–259, 260(i), 278–279
republicanism and, 257–261, 260(i), 261(i)
republican motherhood and, 255–259, 258(i), 279, 358
Sheppard-Towner Act and, 669
social reform and, 358–359
WWII and, 764
Children's Bureau, 728, 778(i), 779
Chile, 605, 670
China, 14, 22, 24. See also People's Republic of China; Taiwan
    Boxer rebellion in, 627, 627(m)
    civil war in, 791
    European spheres of influence in, 607, 616, 626–628, 627(m), 631
    Japanese invasion of, 750, 753
    lobby for, 791
    Nationalist, 628, 791, 793, 871
    trade with, 373–374, 607, 626–628
    WWI and, 639
    in WWII, 768, 772(m), 773(m)
Chinatown, San Francisco, 479
Chinese Exclusion Act (1882), 480, 714
    repeal of, 825
Chinese immigrants, 384(i), 476, 828, 920
    discrimination against, 476, 480–481, 483, 765
    Great Depression and, 714
    immigration restriction and, 480, 686, 714, 825
    as migrant workers, 710
    in the West, 476, 479–480, 480(i)
Chipewyan Indians, 223
Chippewa Indians, 13, 236
Chisholm, Shirley, 889
Chittendon, Ebenezer, 102
Choctaw Indians, 12, 326, 469, 470(m)
Cholulans, 30
Chou En-lai (Zhou Enlai), 791
Christiana, Pennsylvania, 385
The Christian Evangelist (periodical), 309
Christianity. See also evangelicalism; Protestant Reformation; revivalism; particular denominations
    African American, 121, 130, 262, 268, 268(i), 270, 271(i), 274–275, 279, 442, 560–562
    in Europe, 16–18, 18(i), 37
    French Revolution and, 213
    fundamentalist, 686–688, 691
    Inquisition and, 22
    vs. Islam, 17–18, 20, 28

vs. Judaism, 28
muscular, 566
Native Americans and, 224
in New World, 24, 43–44
vs. paganism, 17
slave imports and, 80
Christopher, Warren, 929
church and state, separation of, 190–191, 251, 452–453, 563
Churchill, Winston
    Atlantic Charter and, 752(m), 753, 768
    at Potsdam Conference, 785
    wartime planning and, 768–769
    at Yalta, 773–775, 775(i)
Church of England. See Anglicanism
Church of Jesus Christ of Latter-day Saints. See Mormons
Church of Scotland, 32
Churubusco, battle of (1847), 379
Cíbola (mythical seven golden cities), 40
Cincinnati, Ohio, 228, 228(i)
    migration to, 828
    slaughterhouses of, 287, 287(i)
    transportation and, 298(m), 300(m), 301(m), 302, 302(m)
CIO. See Congress of Industrial Organizations
circus, 463
Cisneros, Henry, 928
cities. See also urbanization
    African American migration to, 681, 681(m), 690–691, 708, 746, 779, 828–829, 847
    American vs. European, 546
    amusements in, 566–569
    in art and literature, 570
    as commercial hubs, 302–303
    decaying inner, 820, 825, 829–830, 847, 914, 924
    Democratic Party and, 667, 718, 732, 762
    flapper in, 678
    gay communities in, 894
    Great Depression protests in, 717
    growth of, 91, 544–545, 545(m), 571, 819(m)
    high culture in, 569–571
    immigrants in, 543, 543(i), 557, 920
    industrialization and, 457
    Korean immigrants in, 920(i)
    Ku Klux Klan in, 684, 685(m)
    liberalism in, 668
    life in, 556–571
    lighting of, 547–548
    mass media and, 677
    Mexican Americans in, 711
    middle class and, 304–305, 304(i), 313
    move to suburbs from, 815, 817

cities (Continued):
　　1928 election and, 692
　　1932 election and, 718
　　political machines in, 667
　　population growth and, 302–303,
　　　　302(m), 313, 543
　　population shift to, 681, 681(m),
　　　　724, 825, 828–830
　　poverty in, 305–306, 312–313, 924
　　private/public, 548–549
　　Prohibition in, 688
　　race riots in, 660, 660(i), 849,
　　　　861–862, 862(m), 867, 869, 877,
　　　　924
　　riots in, 764, 861–862, 862(m)
　　skyscrapers in, 547
　　sprawl of, 821
　　Summer of Love (1967) in, 860
　　in Sun Belt, 818
　　ten largest U.S., 544(t)
　　transportation in, 546–547, 546(i),
　　　　571
　　urban development and, 841(t), 842
　　urban renewal and, 829–830, 880
　　voting districts and, 881
　　West Indian trade and, 91
Citizens Clearinghouse for Hazardous
　　　Waste, 891
city-states, 13, 19, 37
civic humanism, 19
Civil Aeronautics Act (1938), 682
Civil Defense Agency, 783(i), 807(i)
civil disobedience, 344–345
"Civil Disobedience" (Thoreau), 356
Civilian Conservation Corps (CCC),
　　　724, 730(m), 731(t)
　　environment and, 741
　　Mexican Americans and, 739
　　Native Americans and, 740
　　WWII and, 761
civil liberties, 801(i), 946–947
civil rights
　　conservative opposition to, 846, 925
　　Eisenhower and, 805
　　federal government and, 816
　　Fourteenth Amendment and, 210,
　　　　435–437, 438(t), 519, 525, 529
　　Fifteenth Amendment and,
　　　　438–439, 438(t), 525, 529–530,
　　　　530(i), 589–591
　　for homosexuals, 864–865, 867, 877
　　individual, 74, 203, 205, 331
　　JFK and, 830, 840
　　LBJ and, 840–842, 847
　　legislation on, 841(t)
　　for Mexican Americans, 863, 877
　　for Native Americans, 863–864, 877
　　New Deal and, 735, 746
　　in 1970s, 905
　　1972 election and, 881
　　1980 election and, 903

Nixon and, 880
　　nonviolent protest and, 805
　　Truman and, 804
　　for women, 864–867, 877
　　WWII and, 750, 760–761, 760(i),
　　　　765–767, 777
Civil Rights Act (1866), 431, 435–436,
　　　438(t)
Civil Rights Act (1964), 840, 841(t)
　　Title IX and, 889
　　women and, 866
Civil Rights Bill (1870), 449
Civil Rights Commission, National, 804
civil rights movement, 160, 836–839,
　　　836(m), 838(i), 842(i), 847, 856,
　　　860–867, 935, 939
　　African Americans and, 804, 806,
　　　　856, 860–863, 862(m), 877
　　anticommunism and, 800
　　cold war and, 784, 797–798, 804,
　　　　806–807
　　conflicts within, 839
　　federal government and, 813, 838
　　Freedom Summer and, 857, 866
　　Harlem Renaissance and, 691
　　in 1970s, 894
　　school busing and, 869
　　sit-ins and, 836–837
　　television and, 838, 842
　　violence against, 839
　　WWII and, 761
Civil Service Commission, 516
civil service reform, 449, 516–517
Civil War (1861–1865), 397–427
　　African Americans and, 178, 398,
　　　　417, 423(i)
　　Antietam, 397(i), 403(i), 404(m),
　　　　405, 407, 413, 427
　　black soldiers in, 381, 417–418,
　　　　418(i)
　　Bull Run, 403–404, 423
　　casualties of, 405, 426
　　civilian war effort in, 408–409
　　comparison of economies in,
　　　　409(f)
　　Constitution and, 201
　　cost of, 411, 412(t), 426
　　crisis of Union and, 367–395
　　disease in, 408
　　Eastern campaigns of, 404(m)
　　financing of, 537
　　Gettysburg, 397, 408, 415–416,
　　　　417(m), 427
　　military draft in, 407–408, 408(i),
　　　　427
　　mobilizing resources in, 409
　　nurses in, 408–409, 408(i)
　　prisoners in, 423(i)
　　Reconstruction and, 429–430, 451
　　religion and, 452
　　roles of France and Britain in, 604

secession and stalemate
　　　　(1861–1862), 398–407
　　Shiloh, 397(i), 406–407
　　slavery and, 160, 397, 402, 413–415,
　　　　419
　　taxation in, 411, 413, 427
　　as total war, 407–413
　　trench warfare in, 421
　　turning point of (1863), 413–417
　　Union victory in (1864–1865),
　　　　417–427
　　Vicksburg, 423
　　Virginia campaign (1864–1865),
　　　　421(m)
　　war bonds in, 412
　　warships of, 610–611
　　in the West, 405–407, 406(m), 415
　　women in, 361, 407–409, 408(i),
　　　　412(i), 416
Civil Works Administration (CWA),
　　　725–726, 731(t)
　　Native Americans and, 740
　　women and, 735
Clark, Champ, 597(i)
Clarke, Edward H., 555
Clarke family, 105
Clark, George Rogers, 177(m)
Clark, William, 233, 233(i), 234(m)
class. See social structure
class-action suits, 889
Clausewitz, Karl Von, 410
Clay, Henry, 262, 387, 399
　　American System of, 318–321, 325,
　　　　328, 330–331, 339, 376, 427
　　Compromise of 1850 and, 384
　　election of 1824 and, 317–318,
　　　　318(m), 339
　　election of 1832 and, 324
　　election of 1840 and, 334
　　election of 1844 and, 375–376
　　freemasonry and, 331
　　Missouri Compromise and, 269
　　national mercantilism and, 409, 411
　　Second Bank and, 246, 324–326
　　War of 1812 and, 235, 240
Clayton Antitrust Act (1914), 599
Clean Air Act (1970), 889
Clemenceau, Georges, 658
Clemens, Samuel. See Twain, Mark
Clermont (ship), 300
Cleveland, Grover (1837–1908), 592
　　election of 1884 and, 518, 523
　　election of 1888 and, 515(i)
　　as passive president (1885–1889),
　　　　516(i)
　　as president (1885–1889;
　　　　1893–1897), 516–518, 516(i),
　　　　520, 520(i), 535, 538, 605,
　　　　612–613
　　Pullman boycott and, 510–511, 538
　　as reformer, 518

Cleveland, Ohio
    transportation and, 298(m),
        300(m), 301(m), 302, 302(m)
The Cliff-Dwellers (Fuller), 570
Clifford, Clark, 798(m)
Clinton, Bill (William Jefferson;
        1946–), 281
    approval rating of, 932
    balanced budget and, 931(i)
    big government and, 930
    first term of, 928
    gays in the military and, 928
    impeachment of, 931–932, 937, 948
    Kyoto Treaty and, 927
    scandals in administration of,
        930–932, 934
    welfare system and, 779, 779(i)
Clinton, De Witt, 235, 297
Clinton, George, 205
Clinton, Henry, 178–179, 181
Clinton, Hilary Rodham, 929, 929(i)
Clinton, James, 177(m)
closed-shop agreements, 332–333
coal mining, 487, 487(m), 489, 497,
        513, 587
    breaker boys and, 501(i)
    decline of (1920s), 668
    strikes and, 599
Coast Guard, 947
    women in, 758
Cobbett, William (Peter Porcupine),
        217
Cody, William F. (Buffalo Bill), 461
    biographical information, 462–463,
        463(i)
Coercive Acts (1774), 150–151,
        154–155, 155(t), 159, 169, 172
Cohan, George M., 643
Cohen, Lizabeth, 673
Colbert, Claudette, 762
Colby, William, 874
Colden, Cadwallader, 143
Cold Harbor, battle of, 420(i)
cold war, 452, 783–813, 871–872, 948
    affluent society and, 815
    in Afghanistan, 941
    arms race in, 834
    assessment of, 939
    beginning of, 790
    Berlin Wall and, 833
    and civil rights movement, 806–807
    civil rights movement and, 784,
        797–798, 804, 806–807
    Cuba in, 833, 834(m)
    domino effect and, 850, 855
    economy and, 847
    end of, 907, 912, 932(m), 937
    in Europe, 788, 788(m)
    impact of, 807–812
    Iran and, 902
    JFK and, 847

    in Middle East, 796–797
    nuclear test ban treaties and, 834
    Peace Corps and, 833
    tactics of, 943
    Third World and, 833(m)
    Vietnam War and, 849–877
    WWII and, 750, 769, 777
    Yalta and, 775(i)
Cold Water movement, 309, 309(i)
Cole, Joseph, 152(i)
Cole, Nathan, 115, 118
Coleridge, Samuel Taylor, 342
Cole, USS, attack on, 916(m), 932
collective security, 753, 795–796
College of New Jersey. *See* Princeton
        College
College of Philadelphia. *See* University
        of Pennsylvania
College of Rhode Island. *See* Brown
        University
Collier, John, 740, 740(i)
Collier's magazine, 575, 595
Collins, R. M., 397
Collins, Samuel W., 292
Colman, Benjamin, 108
colonialism, 784
colonization. *See also* British Empire;
        Dutch colonization; English
        colonization; French
        colonization; Spanish
        colonization
    of African Americans in Africa, 691
    end of, 833(m)
    of Florida, 125, 136, 138(m), 154
    by freed slaves in Africa, 134(m),
        262, 270–271, 354, 393
    Portuguese, 134(m)
    of Quebec, 121, 136, 138(m), 154
    slavery and, 134(m), 262, 270–271,
        354, 393
    by Spain, 474, 478
Colorado, 382(m), 474
    drought in, 709–710
    Japanese internment in, 765
    mining in, 480, 540
Colored Farmers' Alliance, 526–527
Colored Women, National Association
        of (NACW), 736
Colored Women's Clubs, National
        Association of, 591
Colored Women's League of
        Washington, D.C., 590(i)
Colt, Samuel, 288
Columbia Broadcasting Service (CBS),
        680
Columbian Exchange, 27, 28(m), 37,
        50
The Columbian Orator, 380
Columbia plateau, 474
Columbia River, 233, 233(i)
Columbia, South Carolina, 425

Columbia University, 119(t), 133
    founding of, 118
    student demonstrations at, 858(i),
        868
Columbus, Christopher, 5, 22(m), 37
    slave trade and, 24
Comanche Indians, 459, 470(m)
Commentary magazine, 898
Committee Against Jim Crow in
        Military Service, 804
Committee on Public Information,
        654, 656–657
Committees of Correspondence,
        150–151, 155(t)
Committees of Safety and Inspection,
        154
Committee to Defend America by
        Aiding the Allies, 752
Committee to Re-Elect the President
        (CREEP), 882
common law, 103, 137, 143, 244–245,
        249
    inheritance and, 257
    worker's rights and, 293, 332–333
Common Sense (Paine), 167–169, 191
Commonwealth of Independent States
        (CIS), 912, 914(m)
commonwealth system, 244–245, 249
Commonwealth v. Hunt (1842), 333
communalism. *See* utopian
        communities
communism, 452, 943. *See also*
        anticommunism
    vs. capitalism, 784, 786, 815
    Carter and, 901
    Chinese, 791, 851
    cold war and, 816, 850, 854–857,
        871–873, 877
    collapse of, 914(m)
    conservative opposition to, 898
    containment of, 785, 786, 791, 948
    in developing countries, 912
    European economy and, 788
    in Germany, 750
    godless, 822
    Great Fear of, 799–800
    Greece and, 788
    international, 794, 806
    Iran and, 902
    JFK and, 830–831, 840, 847
    Peace Corps and, 833
    Soviet, 797, 799–800, 806, 912
    U.S. interventions and, 913(m)
    Vietnam War and, 849–877
    in WWII, 765
Communist Labor Party, 661
Communist Party
    African Americans and, 708–709
    in Great Depression, 717
    influence of, 745
    labor unions and, 733

Communist Party (Continued):
  1932 election and, 718, 718(m)
  popular protests and, 734(m)
  Scottsboro case and, 708
  in Soviet Union, 912
  U.S., 661
Community Action Program, 845
Comprehensive Orders for New
    Discoveries (1573), 41
Comprehensive Test Ban Treaty, 941
Compromise of 1850, 382(m),
    384–385, 386(m), 395
  political realignment and, 392(m)
computer technology, 810–811,
    918–919, 922–923
Comstock, Anthony, 554
Comstock Lode (1859), 476–477
concentration camps, 750, 770, 770(i)
Concord, Massachusetts, 243, 343–344
  British troops in, 133(i), 155(t),
    157–159
  Patriot movement in, 154, 157
  Revolutionary War battle (1775),
    166, 180, 185
Conestoga Indians, 129
Coney Island, 567
Confederate States of America,
    196–200, 203, 401(t), 402, 427.
    See also Civil War; secession
  collapse of, 425–426
  inflation in, 412–413
  proclamation of, 398
Confederation Congress, 223
Confiscation Acts (1861 and 1862), 413
conglomerates, meaning of, 816
Congo, Africa, 20
Congregationalism, 58, 73, 190
  abolitionism and, 354
  in British colonies, 70
  in colonial America, 102, 112(m),
    114, 117, 119(f), 119(t)
  politics of, 521(f)
  as rationalist, 273, 273(t), 275
  "separatists" and, 115
  social reform and, 306
  women in, 277
Congreso Nacional del Pueblo de
    Habla Español (National
    Congress of Spanish-Speaking
    Peoples), 713, 740
Congress. See also House of
    Representatives, U.S.; Senate, U.S.
  abolitionism and, 355, 357, 359(m)
  asylum reform and, 360–361
  civil rights movement and, 839
  Democratic control of, 798, 880,
    882, 928, 944
  FDR and, 730–731
  Great Depression and, 700
  Gulf of Tonkin Resolution (1964),
    852, 870, 876

labor unions and, 760
  Native Americans and, 829
  New Deal and, 721, 724, 726
  Republicans in, 935, 944
  slave vs. free state conflict in, 383
  Supreme Court and, 667
  War Powers Act (1973), 876
  Wilmot Proviso and, 379
  women in, 643, 643(i), 668, 911(i)
Congress Hall, Philadelphia, 193(i)
Congressional Medal of Honor, 646
Congress of Industrial Organizations
    (CIO), 732–733, 817, 863
  Democratic Party and, 762
  Mexican Americans and, 713, 739
Congress of Racial Equality (CORE),
    761, 838, 861
Conkling, Roscoe, 449, 518, 521
Connecticut
  birth control in, 703
  claims to Western lands, 197
  as corporate colony, 73, 75
  land grants in, 104
  lawyers in, 253(t)
  migration from, 128
  voting rights in, 316
Connecticut Land Company, 241(i)
Connecticut River Valley, 59
  religious revival in, 114–118
Connor, Eugene ("Bull"), 838, 838(i)
conquistadors, 24, 26
conscience Whigs, 379, 389
conscription, 643. See also draft,
    military
conservation. See also environment
  JFK and, 835
  LBJ and, 843
  New Deal and, 740–741
  T. Roosevelt and, 591
conservatism, 928, 934
  affirmative action and, 925
  vs. feminism, 892–893
  gay rights and, 894
  Great Society and, 846
  in 1970s, 880, 888, 898–899, 905
  1980 election and, 903, 903(m)
  resurgence of, 869, 877
  on Supreme Court, 911
Constitution, 201–210, 230, 235, 381
  abolitionism and, 357
  acquired territories and, 621
  amendments to, 383, 652–654. See
    also particular amendments
  Bill of Rights and, 205, 209–210, 281
  Civil War and, 201
  contract clause of, 248
  evolution of, 246
  Federalism and, 204–205, 207–209,
    218, 280
  Garrison and, 354
  implementation of, 209–210

on interstate commerce, 247
  New Deal and, 726
  ratification of, 203–205, 208(m),
    209–210, 219
  revision of, 239–240
  secession and, 430
  as secular document, 452–453
  slave vs. free states and, 383
Constitutional Convention (1787),
    202–204, 219, 248, 269
  Great Compromise in, 203–204
  New Jersey Plan of, 202
  protest against, 203
  Virginia Plan of, 202
Constitutional Crisis (1798–1800),
    216–218
constitutional monarchy, 93, 95
constitutional rights, 149, 154
  of colonies, 139–140, 145–146, 159
  of Southern states, 269
Constitutional Union Party, 392(m),
    394
constitutions, state, 194–196, 219, 330,
    437, 453
construction industry, 486, 489, 698(f),
    699
construction materials, 489
consumerism, 127, 673–675
  foreign investment and, 670
  Great Depression and, 704(i)
  industrial expansion and, 668
  intellectual life and, 688
  interstate highways and, 820
  leisure and, 673, 680
  in literature, 689
  in 1920s, 665, 693
  in 1950s, 815, 820–821, 847
  women and, 665(i), 824
consumer price index (CPI), 699, 755,
    885(f)
Consumer Products Safety
    Commission, 880, 889
consumers
  goods for, 486
  protection of, 595
  rights of, 889, 905
Consumers' League, National, 577
consumer spending
  advertising and, 820
  economic development and, 823
  growth in, 917
  postwar, 817
  television and, 822(i)
consumption, rates of
  Great Depression and, 699, 702, 715
  increased, 847
  WWII and, 762–763
containment, policy of, 673, 787, 948
  in Asia, 791, 794, 797
  meaning of, 785
  militarization of (NSC-68), 786

Third World and, 796
in Truman administration, 813
Continental army, 172, 182, 185, 191, 198, 201
Continental Congress, First (1774), 154, 155(t), 157, 159
Continental Congress, Second (1775), 155(t), 185
    affairs of colonies and, 196, 201
    alliance with France, 175–176
    Articles of Confederation and, 196–203, 219
    Britain and, 166–167, 169, 172–173, 177
    delegates to, 206
    finances of, 174
    independence and, 169–171, 191
    new governing institutions and, 194
contrabands, 413, 417–418
Contract Air Mail Act (1925), 682
Contras, 909, 912
Conversations on Common Things (Dix), 360
Conwell, Russell H., 519, 552
Cooke, Jay, 412, 449
Coolidge, Calvin, 661
    Boston police strike (1919) and, 661
    on factories, 670
    Garvey and, 691
    as president (1923–1929), 667, 667(i)
    as vice-presidential candidate, 666
    on wartime debts, 672
Cooper, Gary, 678
Cooper, Thomas, 319
Coosas Indians, 40
Copernicus, 112
Copland, Aaron, 743
Copley, John Singleton, 144(i), 198(i)
Coral Sea, Battle of, 771, 772(m)
CORE. *See* Congress of Racial Equality
corn, 9, 14–15, 28(m). *See also* grain; maize
    on Great Plains, 459
    prices for, 540
    production of, 104–105, 160, 265, 296–298, 297(m)
Cornell, Saul, 280
Cornish, Samuel D., 352
Cornwallis, Charles, Lord, 165, 178(m), 179, 181–182
Corona, Bert, 711, 712(i)
    biographical information, 712–713
Coronado, Francisco Vasquez de, 40, 41(m)
corporations. *See also* business
    campaign contributions of, 883
    consolidation of, 574, 670, 899
    consumer rights movement and, 889
    corruption in, 944

downsizing of, 879, 916
foreign competition and, 887
foreign investment and, 670
mergers of, 816
multinational, 886
new technology and, 917
power of, 574, 599
rise of, 488–489
scandals in, 937
taxation of, 647
Corrigan, Michael A., 563
corruption
    corporate, 944
    in Harding administration, 667, 690
    Ku Klux Klan and, 684
    in Nixon administration, 882–883
    political, 441, 449, 574
Cortés, Hernán, 24–25, 31(i), 33
    biographical information, 30–31
Costa Rica, 670
cost-plus provisions, 755
cotton
    Civil War and, 409
    as diplomatic weapon, 409, 416
    exports of, 213, 285, 303, 413
    Panic of 1837 and, 333
    prices for, 535, 540
    production of, 368–369, 368(f), 443
    sharecropping and, 443–444, 495
    slavery and, 226, 262–264, 368–369
    the South and, 262–263, 263(f), 265, 265(m), 279, 288(m), 290, 296, 297(m), 301, 313, 368–369, 495, 496(m), 497
    tariff battle and, 319, 319(i)
    technology for, 226, 289–292, 289(i), 295, 295(i)
    in Texas, 465, 478–479, 497(i), 530, 535
    textile industry and, 285(i), 288–292, 288(m), 295(i)
cotton gin, 213, 295, 295(i)
cotton production
    in Texas, 478–479, 497(i), 530, 535
Coughlin, Father Charles, 726–727, 729
Council for Mutual Economic Assistance (COMECON), 791
Council of Economic Advisors, 797
Council of National Defense, 641, 752
counterculture, 349. *See also* Utopian communities
    drugs and, 860, 877
    of 1950s, 825
    of 1960s, 856, 859–860, 877
    1970s activism and, 888
    vs. social conformity, 847
counterinsurgency, 831, 833
Country Party (England), 136
Court of International Justice (World Court), 673

court system, 209, 230. *See also* judiciary; Supreme Court
    trial by jury and, 137, 140–141, 143, 210, 268
    vice-admiralty, 137–138, 140–141, 143, 145, 159
covenant, meaning of, 58
covert interventions, meaning of, 795–796
Covey, Edward, 380
cowboys, 461, 463–464, 464(i)
Cox, Archibald, 883
Cox, Ida, 677
Cox, James M., 666
Coxey, Jacob S., 538
craftsmen. *See* artisans
Crane, Stephen, 465, 570
Crawford, Alan, 898
Crawford, William H., 317–318, 318(m), 339
Crazy Horse, 471
credit. *See also* debt
    consumer, 820, 886
    Great Depression and, 715
Creek Indians, 12, 76, 238(m), 239, 319–320, 326–328, 327(m), 470, 470(m)
Creel, George, 654, 656(i)
    biographical information, 656–657
Crehen, C. G., 349(i)
Crèvecoeur, St. Jean de, 252
Crick, Francis, 918
Crimean War, 408
The Crisis, 589(i), 590, 690(i), 691
Crittenden Plan, 398–400
Croats, 929, 932(m)
Crocker, Charles, 480
Crockett, Davy, 371–372
Croker, Richard, 564–565
Cromwell, Oliver, 59, 73
crops. *See* agriculture
Crow Dog, Mary, 863–864
Crow Indians, 459, 470(m)
Crusades, 18, 37
Crystal Palace Exhibition, London, 292
Cuba, 76, 125, 375
    Bay of Pigs in, 833, 834(m)
    expansionism and, 379, 387, 605
    Grenada and, 912
    independence of, 616
    JFK and, 833–834, 840
    refugees from, 828
    sensationalist journalism and, 612, 612(i), 613(i), 614–615
    vs. Spain, 609, 612–619
    Spanish "reconcentration" camps in, 612–613, 616
    U.S. relations with, 625–626, 626(m), 751
Cuban missile crisis (1962), 833–834, 834(m), 835(i)

Cullen, Countee, 690
cultural values
    automobile and, 675
    conflict and, 681–692
    conservative (1920s), 666
    industrialization and, 681
    legislation of, 686–688
culture, 940. See also multiculturalism;
        popular culture
    automobile, 675, 817, 819
    of California, 481–483
    dissent and, 825
    modern American (1920s),
        665–693
    national, 673–681, 693
    of 1950s, 820–825
Cumberland River, 406
Cummins, Albert B., 584
currency
    free silver and, 536–540, 538(i)
    land banks and, 98
    paper, 72(t), 174(i), 175, 186, 200,
        412–413
    state, 206, 329
    U.S. as dominant, 816, 884
Currency Acts
    of 1751, 72(t), 98–99
    of 1764, 136
Currier and Ives, 400(i), 441(i)
Curtin, Harry, 641
Custer, George Armstrong
    Battle of Little Big Horn and,
        463, 471
Czechoslovakia, 658, 788–789, 790,
        796, 914(m)
    German invasion of, 751
Czekalinski, Steve, 815(i)
Czolgosz, Leon F., 591

Dachau concentration camp, 750, 770
Dahomey, Africa, 78(m), 79
Daily Worker, 802
Dakota territory
    Indian reservations in, 469–473,
        470(m), 471(m), 864
Dale, Thomas, 49
Daley, Richard J., 868–869
Damrosch, Leopold, 569
Danbury Hatters case (1908), 586
Dancing Mothers (film), 678
The Dangers of an Unconverted
        Ministry (Tennent), 115, 118
Daniel, Jackson, 414
Dario, Ruben, 624
Darrow, Clarence, 687
Dartmouth (ship), 150
Dartmouth College, 119(t)
    founding of, 120(i)
Dartmouth College v. Woodward
        (1819), 248, 328–329

Dartmouth, Lord, 157
Darwin, Charles, 519, 609, 686–687
Daschle, Tom, 935
Daughters of Bilitis, 825
Daughters of Liberty, 146, 147(i), 159.
        See also Sons of Liberty
The Dave Kopay Story (Kopay and
        Young), 895
Davis, David, 450
Davis, Jefferson (1808–1889), 394
    black soldiers and, 425
    as Confederate president, 398
    continuance of war and, 432
    elections of 1863 and, 415
    on Emancipation Proclamation, 414
    expansionism and, 379
    Fort Sumter and, 400
    General Sherman and, 424–425
    inauguration of (1861), 401–402
    resources of the South and, 407, 411
    rifle-muskets and, 410
    strategy of, 415
Davis, John W., 667
Davis, Maxine, 705
Davis, Robert, 174
Dawes, Charles G., 672
Dawes Act (1887), 472–473, 740
Dawes Plan (1924), 672
Day, William R., 618
D-Day (June 6, 1944), 769(m), 770,
        771(i)
DDT, 888(i), 889
Deane, Silas, 175
Dean, John, 882
death. See also disease
    AIDS and, 925
    Civil War, 405, 426
    Columbian Exchange and, 27
    gravestones, 59(i)
    seasonal patterns of, 15–16, 16(f)
    slavery and, 77, 78(m), 80–81, 84–85
Debs, Eugene V., 510–511, 513, 575,
        640, 655
debt
    of British Empire, 124, 127, 134,
        136, 141, 154, 159
    of colonists, 200
    consumer, 673–674, 820, 886, 917
    creditors and, 204
    of farmers, 201
    foreign, 201, 672
    imprisonment for, 194, 200–201,
        207, 332
    of Mexico, 375
    national, 204, 210, 231, 249. See also
        deficit spending
    public, 201, 412(t)
    war, 206, 211, 219
Declaration of Independence, 169–170,
        169(i), 184, 194, 216, 336
    women's rights and, 363

Declaration of Rights (1689), 93–94
Declaration of Rights and Grievances
        (1774), 154
Declaration of Sentiments (1848;
        Seneca Falls), 365
Declaration of the Causes and
        Necessities of Taking Up Arms,
        166
Declaratory Act of 1766, 145, 154
decolonization, 833(m), 884
Deere, John, 300
defense spending, 755(f), 794, 930
    economy and, 762, 847, 886(m),
        887
    Eisenhower and, 807, 809, 831
    JFK and, 831
    postwar development and, 818
    Reagan and, 908–910
    Republicans and, 804
    WWII, 753
deficit spending, 886. See also debt
    economy and, 884, 911, 917
    meaning of, 732
    in New Deal, 835
    by Nixon, 884
    Reaganomics and, 908, 910, 910(f)
Degener, Edward, 440
deindustrialization, 886–887, 887(i)
    environmentalism and, 889
deinstitutionalization of mentally ill,
        908
deism, 113–114, 130, 336–337
de Kooning, Willem, 743
Delaney, Martin, 352
Delaware, 71, 160, 401
Delaware Indians, 123–126, 129,
        223–224
Delaware Iron Works, 300
Delaware River, 63
De Leon, Daniel, 511
De Lesseps, Ferdinand, 605
de Lôme, Dupuy, 613
DeMille, Cecil B., 682
democracy
    demagogues and, 727
    direct, 584
    in education, 825
    in England, 93
    Great Depression and, 700
    immigrants and, 402
    Japanese internment and, 767
    meaning of, 316
    movies and, 675, 706
    Native Americans and, 740
    New Deal and, 742, 745
    political evolution of, 316–321, 339
    transcendentalism and, 344
    views of, 194, 202, 207, 315, 345
    WWII as defense of, 753
Democracy in America (Tocqueville),
        247, 286, 315, 325, 452, 515

Democratic Party. *See also* elections;
    Peace Democrats
    African Americans and, 709, 738,
        804
    black political leaders and, 440
    Catholics and, 520–521, 521(*f*)
    Chicago convention of (1968),
        868–869, 877
    in Clinton era, 945
    coalition of, 732, 746–747, 762, 831,
        846–847, 899, 903, 903(*m*)
    Compromise of 1850 and, 384
    in Congress, 882
    control of Congress by, 798, 880,
        882, 928, 944
    divisions in, 387, 394
    in 1870s, 448, 451
    FDR and, 732
    free trade and, 517
    Great Depression and, 719
    Ku Klux Klan and, 445, 447
    labor and, 333, 587, 599, 733–734
    LBJ and, 840
    leadership of, 944
    left wing of, 888
    liberalism and, 849, 876
    "Lost Cause" and, 518, 520, 526
    Mexican Americans and, 740
    Mexican War and, 378–379
    as minority party, 667
    National Committee of, 882
    New Deal and, 746–747, 868
    in New South, 526–534
    1910 election and, 598
    1920s and, 693
    1928 election and, 691–692
    1932 election and, 717–718
    1936 election and, 729
    1964 election and, 843(*m*)
    1972 election and, 881–882
    1980 election and, 903, 903(*m*)
    1984 election and, 909
    1998 election and, 933
    Nixon's dirty tricks and, 882
    Northern, 400, 407–408
    origins of, 317, 320
    presidency and, 666
    progressive politics and, 596
    Reagan and, 903
    realignment of, 392(*m*)
    slave vs. free states and, 382–383,
        395
    social welfare and, 815
    in the South, 746
    Southern, 394, 731, 798, 834
    split in (1948), 798
    states' rights and, 517
    Texas and, 372
    urban liberalism and, 586
    vs. Whigs, 248, 330–332, 335,
        338–339

    Whitman and, 345
    in WWII, 761–762
Democratic-Republicans, 220,
        252–261, 279, 281, 312. *See also*
        Republican Party
    political equality and, 252–253,
        274, 278
Democratic Review (periodical), 372
Dempsey, Jack, 680
Denmark, 752
Dennison, William, 400
Denver, Colorado, 475
deportation, 711, 828, 947
    Mexican American activism and, 712
depressions, 280, 296, 346, 348. *See also*
        Great Depression; panics;
        recessions
    of 1837–1843, 332
    of 1839, 333, 339
    of 1873, 449, 451
    of 1890s, 573, 592
deregulation, 899, 937
    under Reagan, 908
    Savings and Loan crisis and, 912
desegregation, 840, 861
    school busing and, 881, 883, 894(*i*),
        895–898, 903, 905
Deseret, Mormon state of, 350(*m*), 352
Desert Fox campaign, 931
Detroit, Michigan, 126, 223, 235
    riots in, 764, 861–862, 862(*m*)
    tranportation and, 300–302,
        301(*m*), 302(*m*)
Dewey, George, 616–617, 617(*m*), 622,
        623(*i*)
Dewey, Thomas E., 762, 798
DeWitt, John, 765
Dewson, Molly, 735
The Dial (journal), 344
Dias, Bartholomeu, 22, 22(*m*)
Diaz del Castillo, Bernal, 27, 30–31
Diaz, Porfirio, 628
Dickens, Charles, 348
Dickinson, G. Lowes, 569
Dickinson, John, 144, 146, 166
*Diedrich Knickerbocker's History of New
        York* (Irving), 260
Diem, Ngo Dinh, 850–852, 852(*i*), 867
Dies, Martin, 800
dime novels, 462, 464(*i*)
Dinwiddie, Robert, 123–124
diplomacy, 787, 940
    Carter and, 900–902
    cotton and, 409, 416
    dollar, 628
    economic, 607, 751
    in Latin America, 604–605
    Senate and, 604
    U.S. expansion and, 604–607
    U.S. foreign service and, 604
    wartime, 777

discount rate, meaning of, 698
discrimination, 926. *See also* racism
    affirmative action and, 892
    against African Americans, 476,
        480, 498, 500, 525–534, 707,
        761, 863
    against Chinese, 476, 480–481, 483
    against Hispanics, 476, 479–480,
        483
    against Japanese, 480, 483
    Mexican American activism
        and, 712
    against Mexican Americans, 739
    in military, 758
    reverse, 896–897
    against women, 865–866
    against women in military, 914(*i*)
    against women in workforce, 759
disease. *See also* influenza; smallpox
    AIDS, 925
    Bataan death march and, 774
    cholera, 311
    Columbian Exchange and, 27,
        28(*m*), 37, 50
    diphtheria, 28(*m*)
    dysentery, 15, 21, 109
    effect on Native Americans, 25–26,
        28(*m*), 30, 37, 40, 44, 46, 56,
        63–67
    environment and, 51, 51(*t*), 343(*f*)
    epidemic, 80, 84, 112–113, 311, 459
    of Europeans in Africa, 20–21
    industrialization and, 343(*f*)
    malaria, 21, 28(*m*), 625(*i*), 774
    measles, 25, 112, 459
    seasonal cycle and, 15–16
    sexually transmitted, 653
    tuberculosis, 12
    yellow fever, 21, 28(*m*)
Displaced Persons Act, 825
Dissertation on the English Language
        (Webster), 260
District of Columbia (Washington,
        D.C.)
    abolitionism and, 355, 357
    as capital, 268
    Compromise of 1850 and, 384
    slavery in, 262, 393
    War of 1812 and, 238(*m*), 239
Divine, Father, 709
Divine Peace Mission, 709
divine right, 74
divorce, 702, 822, 893
Dix, Dorothea (1802–1887), 358–359,
        361(*i*), 409
    biographical information, 360–361
Dixiecrats. *See* States' Rights Party
DNA (deoxyribonucleic acid), 918,
        919(*i*)
documentary impulse, 745, 822
Doeg Indians, 55

the dole, 725. *See also* welfare
Dole, Robert J. (Bob), 899, 930
dollar-a-year men, meaning of, 755
Domestic Manners of the Americans (Trollope), 276, 307, 315
domestic manufacture, 106, 146. *See also* household production
Dominican Republic, 24
    immigrants from, 920
    U.S. military intervention in, 673
Dominion of New England, 73, 73(*m*), 94, 99, 140
Domino, Fats, 827
domino theory, 788
Doniphan, Alfred A., 378(*m*)
Donner party, 375(*i*)
Doolittle, James H., 771
Dorr, Retha Childe, 523
Dorsey, Tommy, 706
Dos Passos, John, 689, 745
Doubleday, Abner, 568
Douglas, Stephen A. (1813–1861), 161, 393(*i*), 400
    Compromise of 1850 and, 384
    debates with Lincoln, 393
    1852 election and, 387
    1860 election and, 392(*m*), 394
    expansionism and, 379
    on Kansas, 391
    Kansas-Nebraska Act and, 387–388
    popular sovereignty and, 389, 395
    on slave vs. free state conflict, 383
Douglas, William O., 731
Douglass, Frederick (1818–1895), 355, 380(*i*), 413, 417
    biographical information, 380–381
    death of, 531
    Free Soil Party and, 379
    Fugitive Slave Act and, 385–386
    home of, 590(*i*)
Dow Chemical Company, 858
dower right, 104
Downing, Andrew Jackson, 552
Doy, Dr. John, 389(*i*)
draft, military
    Civil War and, 407–408, 408(*i*), 427
    peacetime, 807
    Selective Service Act (1917), 643
    Vietnam War and, 854, 858, 866, 874, 877
    WWII and, 753, 758, 762
draft riots (Civil War), 407–408, 408(*i*), 427
Drake, Samuel, 229
Drake, Sir Francis, 41
Drayton, William Henry, 222, 281
Dred Scott decision (*Dred Scott v. Sandford*; 1857), 246, 391, 393–395
Dreier, Mary, 581
Dreiser, Theodore, 543, 551, 690

Drinker, Elizabeth, 256
drought
    conservation and, 740
    in Dust Bowl, 709–711
    Great Depression and, 719
    on Great Plains, 464–466, 473, 633, 709–710
    in Texas, 518
Du Bois, W. E. B., 534, 589, 589(*i*), 590, 690, 690(*i*), 713
Duck Soup (film), 706
Duer, William, 211
Dukakis, Michael, 911
Duke, James B., 496
Dulles, John Foster, 794–796
    on containment, 787
Dunmore, Lord, 167, 177
Dunsmore, John Ward, 172(*i*)
Durán, Diego, 27(*i*)
Durr, Virginia Foster, 866
Dust Bowl (Oklahoma, Texas, New Mexico, Colorado, Arkansas, Kansas), 709–711, 710(*m*), 719
    conservation and, 740–741
Dutch colonization, 47(*m*), 63, 101, 101(*i*), 115, 118, 119(*f*), 134(*m*), 149–150
    vs. British, 48, 54, 69, 75(*t*), 98, 179, 182
    commercial activities of, 22(*m*), 29, 33–34, 37, 106, 127
    fur trade and, 40, 47–48, 64, 67
    in Hudson River Valley, 74(*i*), 105, 128–129
    Molasses Act and, 96
    Navigation Acts and, 72
    New Amsterdam, 40(*t*), 47–48
    New Netherlands, 7, 34, 47–48, 69–70, 72, 75(*t*), 105, 106(*m*)
    in New World, 6, 34, 40(*t*), 67
    slaves and, 74(*i*), 77
    sugar plantations and, 78
Dutch East India Company, 47
Dutch Reformed Protestants
    in colonial America, 105, 115, 118, 119(*f*), 119(*t*)
    Rutgers University and, 118, 119(*t*)
Dutch West India Company, 105
Duveyier de Hauranne, Ernest, 402
Dwight, John, 71(*i*)
Dwight, Timothy, 103, 216(*i*)
Dylan, Bob, 860

Eagleton, Thomas F., 881
Earhart, Amelia, 682
Earl, Ralph, 216(*i*), 241(*i*)
Early, Jubal, 421
Earth Day, 889, 927, 927(*i*)
Eastern Europe, 785, 789–790, 794, 813

    end of cold war and, 907, 912, 914(*m*)
    Germany and, 750
    Soviet Union and, 773–775, 777
Eastern State Penitentiary, 306(*i*)
eastern woodland Indians, 12, 14, 65
East Germany. *See* German Democratic Republic
East India Company. *See* British East India Company
East Indians
    as migrant workers, 710
    as strikebreakers, 714
East Indies, 18, 124
    Japanese invasion of, 763
Easton, Hosea, 352
East St. Louis, Illinois, 660
Eaton, Peggy, 324
e-commerce, 917
economic development, 246, 330. *See also* agriculture; industrialization; manufacturing; mining; ranching
    capital goods and, 486
    colonial, 102, 105–106, 127–128
    consumerism and, 820
    consumer spending and, 823
    eastern, 221
    government spending and, 797, 799
    industrial capitalism and, 485–513
    John Q. Adams and, 318–319
    nonimportation and, 146, 147(*i*), 149, 149(*f*), 154, 155(*t*), 156
    in Sun Belt, 818–819
    tax cuts and, 835
    of Third World countries, 816
    Whig program for, 394, 517
Economic Opportunity Act (1964), 841(*t*)
Economic Opportunity, Office of (OEO), 845, 880
economic policy, 186, 320, 390, 394
Economic Recovery Tax Act (1981), 908
economic sanctions, 403, 931
    Persian Gulf War and, 913
    in South America, 751
Economic Stabilization Act (1970), 880
economic theory, 574
    Keynesian, 732, 755
    supply-side, 715, 908, 930
    tax cuts and, 835
economy, 940, 945. *See also* business; capitalism; depressions; inflation; market economy; mercantilism; panics; recessions; trade, foreign
    agricultural, 77, 213, 225–228, 301–302, 444, 486, 540
    balanced budget and, 722, 835, 903, 930, 931(*i*), 937

barter, 343
British imperial, 76–93, 244
budget deficits and, 908, 910–911, 910(*f*), 917
under (G. H. W.) Bush, 911–912
business cycles in, 697
business-government partnership and, 666, 668
as campaign issue, 928, 930, 933, 944
change in U.S., 647
changing (1790–1820), 225–228
of Chesapeake Bay, 69(*i*)
Civil War, 409(*f*)
commonwealth system, 244–245, 249
of communal utopias, 345–347, 349
concentration of, 592
cotton, 368–369
of diminished expectations, 884–887
downsizing and, 879, 916
emancipation and, 443–444
Embargo Act of 1807 and, 234
expansionism and, 606
fascism and, 742
federal role in, 745, 755–758
Ford and, 899
free-market capitalist, 207, 241–245, 249, 331
of Germany, 750
Great Deflation and, 486, 486(*f*)
growth of, 909, 916–917
health and, 343(*f*)
Holocaust and, 770
industrial, 574
inequality and, 105–107, 131
international, 670, 672, 698, 719, 847, 884, 887, 907, 937, 939
Japanese, 772
laissez-faire, 330, 333, 518, 536, 541, 574
living standards and, 229, 342, 343(*f*)
mass-consumption, 695
merchant-based, 241–244
of Mexico, 376
Middle Atlantic (1720–1765), 105–107, 131
military power and, 70
of Mormons, 352
in 1920s, 665, 668, 693
1928 election and, 692
in 1950s, 825
in 1970s, 879–905
1972 election and, 882
in 1990s, 914–917
Nixon and, 880
Northern maritime, 91–93
plantation, 368–369, 388
politics and, 93, 375

postwar, 816–820
productivity in, 915, 917(*f*), 937
Reagan and, 908–909
reform and, 342
regulation of, 666, 745
Republicans and, 944
slave, 69(*i*), 76–93, 160–161, 161(*i*), 261–267, 263(*f*), 263(*i*), 265(*m*), 265(*t*), 266(*i*), 269, 273, 279
slowing, 934
social structure and, 92–93
South Atlantic system, 76–80
Southern, 213, 301–302
structural weaknesses of, 697
tobacco, 54–55
trends in, 937
"trickle down," 715
U.S., 927
U.S. dominance of international, 847, 884, 904
West German, 788–789
westward migration and, 228
women's rights and, 362–363, 893
WWII and, 755–758, 763(*i*), 777
Eddy, Frances, 580
Eddy, Mary, 580
Ederle, Gertrude, 680
Edgar Thompson Works, 486
Edison, Thomas A., 546, 548, 548(*i*)
Ed Sullivan Show (TV program), 826
education, 928, 944
abolitionism and, 359
affirmative action in, 896–897, 925
of African Americans, 258, 260, 277, 369, 442(*i*), 531, 534, 736–737
child-care, 577, 577(*i*)
in cities, 924
computer technology and, 919
cuts in, 930
democratization of, 825
elementary, 194
federal aid to, 799, 816
GI Bill and, 762, 817, 865
Great Depression and, 705
high school graduates, 557(*t*)
Japanese internment and, 766
JFK and, 830, 835
LBJ and, 842–843
legislation on, 841(*t*)
middle class culture and, 304
in New England, 258–259, 261, 261(*i*), 301
in 1950s, 823
in 1990s, 914
in 1998 elections, 933
prayer in public schools and, 453, 881
public, 258–260, 441
reforms in, 260, 358–359
republicanism and, 257–261, 260(*i*), 261(*i*)

school segregation and, 525, 861
states and, 911
teachers and, 260, 261(*i*), 278–279
vouchers and, 933
of women, 196, 256, 261(*i*), 277–278, 555, 889
Educational Amendments Act (1972)
Title IX, 889, 892
Education, Department of, 899
Edwards, Henrietta, 295
Edwards, Jonathan, 102, 114, 116(*i*), 118, 236, 295
biographical information, 116–117
Edwards, Pierpont, 295
Egypt, 19, 796
Camp David accords and, 901–902, 901(*i*), 905
invasion of Israel by, 884
Iraq and, 915
Eighteenth Amendment (Prohibition), 654, 654(*m*), 688
Eisenhower, Dwight D. (1890–1969), 830
Bonus Army and, 717
civil rights and, 805
cold war policies of, 816
communism and, 794, 796
covert intervention and, 796
Cuba and, 833
defense spending and, 807, 809, 831
domino theory and, 788
Korea and, 794
McCarthy and, 800
on military-industrial complex, 811–812
New Look in foreign policy of, 794–795
1952 election and, 810
as president (1953–1961), 794–795, 801, 813
Suez crisis and, 797
U-2 spy plane and, 809–810
Vietnam and, 850, 877
in WWII, 769–770
Eisenhower Doctrine, 797
elderly
poverty and, 829, 830(*i*), 844
in stock market, 945
elections. *See also* presidential elections
in Eastern Europe, 774
local, 316
voter turnout for, 520, 668
of 1818, 248
of 1800, 218, 222
of 1824, 317–318, 318(*m*), 339
of 1828, 319–321, 320(*i*), 321(*i*), 321(*m*)
of 1832, 324
of 1836, 331–332
of 1840, 333–338, 335(*i*), 338
of 1844, 375–376, 395

elections (*Continued*):
of 1846, 379
of 1848, 379, 382, 392(*m*)
of 1852, 387, 388(*i*), 392(*m*)
of 1854, 389
of 1856, 390–391, 392(*m*)
of 1858, 393–394
of 1860, 392(*m*), 393(*i*), 394–395, 427
of 1862, 414–415
of 1863, 415
of 1864, 418, 421, 424
of 1866, 436
of 1868, 438
of 1872, 449
of 1874, 449
of 1876, 450–451
of 1896, 573
of 1916, 641–642
of 1938, 732
of 1942, 762
of 1994, 930
of 1998, 930
of 2002, 944
electoral college, 204, 209, 218, 339, 438, 449–450
abolition of, 667
1824 election and, 317–318, 318(*m*)
1828 election and, 321(*m*)
2000 election and, 933–934, 933(*i*), 934(*m*)
electricity, 487, 487(*i*), 513
electrification, 731(*t*)
consumer culture and, 674
rural, 744
TVA and, 741, 741(*m*)
Elementary and Secondary Education Act (1965), 841–842
Elgin, Lord, 301(*m*)
Eliot, John, 61
Eliot, Martha, 779
Eliot, T. S., 689
elite, 93–94, 94(*f*). *See also* middle class; social structure
African American intellectual, 691
business, 296, 303, 313
national, 551
1928 election and, 692
planter-merchant, 79
Southern, 89–91, 368–369
urban, 550–551, 571
Elizabeth I, queen of England (r. 1558–1603), 32–33, 34(*i*), 48, 72
Elkins, William L., 548
Elkins Act (1903), 595
Ellington, Edward "Duke," 677, 706
Ellison, Phyllis, 897
Ellison, Ralph, 680, 743
Ellsberg, Daniel, 874, 882
Ellsworth, Abigail Wolcott, 216

Ellsworth, Oliver, 216(*i*)
El Paso, Texas, 478, 828
El Salvador, 912, 920
Ely, Ezra Stiles, 277
e-mail, 918
emancipation, 430. *See also* Emancipation Proclamation
economic consequences of, 443–444
government power and, 331, 429
Emancipation Proclamation (1862), 413–417, 414(*i*), 424, 427. *See also* abolition
Douglass and, 381
outcome of, 444, 451
Embargo Act (1807), 214, 234–235, 245, 249
Emergency Banking Act (1933), 724, 731(*t*)
Emerson, Ralph Waldo (1803–1882), 342(*i*), 365
at Brook Farm, 346
on children, 556
on industrial revolution, 286
literary influence of, 344–345
on slavery, 355
transcendentalism and, 342–344
emigration. *See also* immigrants; immigration; migration
of Loyalists, 186–187, 186(*i*), 191
eminent domain, 244–245
empiricism, 112, 117
employment. *See also* unemployment
changing patterns of, 915–916
equal opportunity in, 804
gay rights and, 894
Employment Act (1946), 797
Employment Agency (painting; Soyer), 695(*i*)
enclosure acts, 35
encomenderos (land owners), 44
encomiendas (grants), 26–27
Endangered Species Act (1973), 889
End Poverty in California (EPIC), 734(*m*)
energy, 934–935. *See also* oil industry
alternative sources of, 888
consumption of, 885(*f*)
electrical, 487, 487(*i*), 513, 731(*t*)
for manufacturing, 487–488, 513
in 1970s, 905
nuclear, 819, 885(*f*), 888–889
per capita use of, 927
in Sun Belt, 818–819
energy crisis (1973–1974), 879(*i*), 884, 888, 899–900
Energy, Department of, 899
Engel v. Vitale (1962), 453, 881
England. *See also* British empire; Great Britain
agriculture in, 32
democracy in, 93

vs. Dutch, 48, 54, 69, 75(*t*), 98, 179, 182
duties on goods and, 136–138, 154
enclosure acts of, 35, 37
France and, 75
Industrial Revolution and, 127, 285
industry in, 34–35
mercantilism in, 35
merchants in, 148–149
migration to America from, 36, 40, 43, 48
new world trade monopolies of, 54
Price Revolution in, 35, 37
Protestant Reformation and, 28–29, 32–33
Puritan exodus from, 56–57, 57(*m*)
religious civil war in, 59, 70
social structure of, 35(*f*)
vs. Spain, 33–35, 40–41
Whig Party in, 93, 134(*i*), 136, 143–145, 194
in WWII, 749(*i*)
English colonization, 49(*m*), 63, 67, 110(*m*), 122(*m*)
colonial self-government and, 133–134
conflict and, 130
early attempts, 48–50
fur trade and, 63–66
migration of ideas and traditions and, 29, 37, 40, 56
Native Americans and, 6, 61–66
in New England, 56–61, 62(*m*), 102–105
population growth and, 101
social causes of, 35–36
in Virginia, 51(*m*), 51(*t*)
English language, 85–86
ENIAC (Electronic Numerical Integrator and Computer), 810–811
Enlightenment, 167, 169, 190, 199, 212
in American colonies (1740–1765), 112–115, 121, 131, 143, 159
American revolutionary thought and, 131, 143, 159
child rearing and, 258–259, 260(*i*), 279
religious thought and, 275–277
slavery and, 188
transcendentalism and, 342
witchcraft accusations and, 60
women and, 337, 362
Enrollment Act (1863), 407, 408(*i*)
Enron Corporation, 935, 945, 946(*i*)
entrepreneurial enterprise, 207, 242, 331
environment, 9, 12, 27, 37, 243, 928, 930. *See also* national park system
biotechnology and, 918

Dust Bowl and, 709–710
effects of fur trade on, 66
effects of mining on, 475(i), 481
global warming and, 927, 941
of Great Plains, 458, 458(m)
health and, 51, 51(t), 343(f)
LBJ and, 843
legislation on, 841(t), 843, 889
New Deal and, 740–741
in 1990s, 914
Nixon and, 880
preservation of, 483
in Sun Belt, 818–819
urban, 549, 571
environmentalism, 482–483, 871,
    927, 935
Love Canal, 890–891
in 1970s, 880, 887–889, 897, 905
recycling and, 927
Sierra Club and, 482
Environmental Policy Act, National
    (1969), 889
Environmental Protection Agency
    (EPA), 880, 889, 891
Episcopal Church, 258, 272–273,
    273(t). See also Anglicanism
Equal Credit Opportunity Act
    (1974), 892
Equal Employment Opportunity
    Commission (EEOC), 866
equality
    of African Americans, 160–161,
        268, 273, 527–528
    before the law, 432, 436
    within marriage, 252, 254, 279
    Quakers and, 106, 107(f), 108, 160,
        270, 303
    republicanism and, 149, 251–253,
        269, 274, 278–279
equal opportunity, 207, 331, 804
equal rights, 332, 338
Equal Rights Amendment (ERA),
    892–893, 892(i), 893(m), 905
    1980 election and, 903
    opposition to, 898
Equal Rights Association, 439
Equiano, Olaudah (Gustavus Vassa),
    80(i), 81
Era of Good Feeling, 248
Erdman Mediation Act (1898), 573
Erie Canal, 228, 275(m), 297–300,
    298(i), 298(m), 299(t), 303
    Mormons and, 350
    revivalism on, 308–309, 308(i)
Erie Indians, 64
Erie Railroad, 300, 489, 492–493
Erlichman, John, 882–883
Espinel, Luisa Ronstadt, 676(i)
Espionage Act (1917), 655
Essay Concerning Human Understanding
    (Locke), 112–113, 117

Estonia, 658
Ethiopia, 750, 900
Ethiopian Regiment, 167
ethnic cleansing, 929
ethnic conflict, 907, 948. See also race
    riots
    in the Balkans, 932, 932(m)
ethnic diversity, 72, 102, 105, 107–111
    in nineteenth-century America,
        498–499, 513, 521(f)
    politics and, 520–521, 521(f), 539
    and recent immigration, 919–921
    in rural America, 467(m)
    in the West, 464, 464(i)
ethnicity, 557, 561. See also race
    consumer culture and, 673
    Democratic Party and, 718, 732,
        746, 762
    Great Depression and, 699
    immigration restriction and,
        682–684
    politics and, 691–692
    television and, 821
    urbanization and, 692
Eurasian trade system, 22(m), 47(m)
Europe, 14–20, 22(i). See also
    migration; Protestant
    Reformation
    agriculture in, 668
    American colonies and, 40–61,
        40(t)
    American politics and, 315–316
    American writers in, 569, 689
    artisans in, 17(i), 19
    Chinese spheres of influence and,
        607, 616, 626–628, 627(m), 631
    communism in, 816
    economic recovery of, 904
    Great Depression and, 698
    growth of industrial regions in, 545
    immigration from, 101–105, 107,
        828(f)
    immigration restriction and,
        682–683
    impact on new world of, 37, 39
    jazz and, 677, 680
    maritime expansion and, 19–20,
        22(i)
    mass transit in, 552
    medieval era in, 14–18
    movies in, 675
    nineteenth-century alliances in, 629
    oil embargo vs., 884
    opinion polls in, 944
    political innovation and, 19
    vs. postwar U.S., 816
    Price Revolution in, 34(f), 35
    religion in, 16–18, 18(i), 29, 32,
        32(m), 37, 73
    Renaissance in, 19
    rural life in, 14–16, 16(f)

social values of, 17, 37
transcendentalism and, 342, 344
urban development in, 546
U.S. foreign investment in, 673
war on terrorism and, 941
war reparations of, 715
welfare system in, 745, 778
WWII in, 746, 768(m), 769(m),
    769–771, 777
European Recovery Program. See
    Marshall Plan
evangelicalism, 112, 279, 566, 711. See
    also Protestantism; revivalism
    abolitionism and, 353–356, 358
    camp meetings and, 273–276,
        275(m)
    child rearing and, 258–259,
        260(i), 278
    Great Awakening and, 112–120,
        131, 142, 274, 277
    in Middle Atlantic colonies,
        120–121, 131
    in New England, 114–115, 119(f),
        272, 275(m)
    in 1950s, 822
    in 1970s, 898, 905
    Oneida Community and, 348–349
    political freedom and, 115,
        118–119, 140(i), 142, 159
    republicanism and, 272–279
    Second Great Awakening and, 258,
        272–278, 275(m), 279, 308,
        311, 313
    social reform and, 308–311,
        313, 342
    transcendentalism and, 344
    women's rights and, 273–274,
        277–278
    women's role and, 102, 115,
        272–274, 277–278
Evans, Daniel J., 621
Evans, Oliver, 287
Evans, Walker, 745
Everett, Edward, 331
Evers, Medgar, 839
Everson v. Board of Education (1947),
    453
"evil empire," 912
evolution, 686–688, 688(i)
Ewell, Richard B., 415
Ewing, Thomas, 422–423
exceptionalism, of U.S., 638
Executive Order 9066 (Japanese
    internment), 765
executive privilege, 883, 883(i)
Expanding Liberties: Freedom's
    Gains in Postwar America
    (Konvitz), 453
expansionism, 378, 622, 622(m). See
    also westward expansion
    economy of, 606–607

expansionism (Continued):
  as foreign policy, 379, 387, 395,
    603–606
  ideology of, 609
  Manifest Destiny and, 368–376,
    395, 609
  opposition to, 619–620
  Ostend Manifesto and, 387
  roots of, 603–609
  slavery and, 376–385
exports, 606–607. *See also* trade
  colonial, 105, 105(*f*), 105(*i*), 111, 127,
    137, 138(*m*), 149, 154, 285, 303
  cotton, 213, 285, 303, 413
  grain, 105, 105(*f*), 111, 303
  manufactured goods, 288
  rice, 127, 138(*m*), 149
  sugar, 137, 138(*m*), 154
  tobacco, 127, 138(*m*), 149

factory system, 670. *See also*
    industrialization;
    manufacturing; mills
  assembly line and, 287(*i*), 505(*i*)
  division of labor and, 286–288, 287(*i*)
  industrialization and, 457
  mass-production techniques in, 300
  technology and, 287–295, 287(*i*),
    289(*i*), 295(*i*)
Fairbanks, Douglas, 676, 676(*i*)
Fair Campaign Practices Act (1974),
  883, 903
Fair Deal, 799, 802, 813
Fair Employment Practices
    Commission (FEPC), 760
Fairfax, Lord, 129
Fair Labor Standards Act (FLSA;
  1938), 731, 731(*t*), 735
Fall, Albert, 667
Fallen Timbers, battle of, 223
Faludi, Susan, 925
Falwell, Jerry, 898, 898(*i*)
family, 86, 103(*i*). *See also* birth
    control; children; women
  abolitionism and, 355(*i*)
  changing patterns in, 916
  child rearing and, 258–259, 260(*i*),
    278–279
  farm life and, 102–103
  feminism and, 893
  Great Depression and, 701–705
  inheritance and, 104, 131, 253–257,
    303
  marriage and, 103–104, 107,
    109–111, 252–255, 266, 279
  middle class culture and, 304–305,
    304(*i*), 313
  in 1950s, 820, 822–823, 847
  republican motherhood and,
    255–259, 258(*i*), 278–279

  slavery and, 263–267, 362
  television and, 822(*i*)
  working-class, 499–502
  WWI insurance for, 653
Family and Medical Leave Act (1993),
  928
Family Assistance Plan (Nixon), 880
family values, 898, 898(*i*), 928
  gay rights and, 925
family wage, 779
A Farewell to Arms (Hemingway), 689
Farmer, James, 761
farmers. *See also* agriculture; tenant
    farmers; yeomen farmers
  African American, 735
  bankruptcy of, 130
  debt of, 201
  economic problems of, 681
  education for, 259
  Great Depression and, 698,
    716, 719
  Jackson and, 320, 324
  land sales for, 296, 297(*m*)
  as loyalists, 156
  New Deal and, 724
  1920s and, 693
  1936 election and, 729
  Populism and, 511, 535–540
  protests by, 716, 734(*m*)
  Republican Party and, 667
  revolution and, 159
  rural electrification and, 744
  Social Security and, 746
  tariffs and, 319–320
  taxation and, 142, 154
  War on Poverty and, 844
Farmers' Alliance of the Northwest,
  535
Farm Holiday Association, 716, 734(*m*)
farming. *See* agriculture
Farm Security Administration (FSA),
  695, 731(*t*), 745
Farragut, David G., 407
fascism, 733, 742, 750. *See also* Nazi
    (National Socialist) Party
  in movies, 762
Fasel, G. N., 349(*i*)
Fast Horse, Fred, 647(*i*)
Father Knows Best (TV program), 820,
  822
Faubus, Orval, 805
Faucit, Walter, 108
Faulkner, William, 690
Fauset, Jessie, 690
FBI. *See* Federal Bureau of
    Investigation
Federal Art Project (WPA), 729(*i*), 741
Federal Bureau of Indian Affairs,
  863–864
Federal Bureau of Investigation (FBI),
  864, 870, 947

  Love Canal and, 891
  Nixon's dirty tricks and, 882
Federal Council of Churches, 648
Federal Deposit Insurance
    Corporation (FDIC), 724
Federal Emergency Relief
    Administration (FERA), 702(*m*),
    725, 729, 731(*t*)
  Native Americans and, 740
Federal Farm Loan Act (1916), 600
federal government, 19
  activism of, 830, 846, 903
  AIDS and, 925
  automobile and, 675
  big, 843(*m*), 930
  as broker state, 732
  bureaucracy of, 600, 600(*f*), 732,
    745, 755, 880, 899, 947
  business and, 666–673, 692–693,
    732, 757
  Carter and, 899
  centralized system of, 203
  civil rights movement and, 813, 838
  discrimination against women by,
    704
  economy and, 648, 668, 755–758,
    797, 799, 847
  emancipation and, 331, 429
  environmental legislation
    and, 889
  expansion of, 648, 715, 722, 728,
    732, 745, 754–755, 761–762,
    777, 845
  Fuel Administration of, 649
  Great Depression and, 701, 715
  highways and, 819
  housing and, 818
  Indian removal and, 326
  LBJ and, 842, 845–846
  mining interests and, 511–512
  New Deal and, 722, 728, 732
  New Right and, 898
  in 1920s, 693
  in 1970s, 897, 905
  Nixon and, 880
  photography and, 745
  postwar reforms and, 651–652
  powers of, 321–323, 379, 386, 668,
    927, 946
  public cynicism and, 880, 883, 899
  radio and, 680
  railroads and, 488–489, 510–511,
    519
  Reagan and, 908
  Republican Party and, 880
  resentment of, 898
  role of, 905, 933
  Second Bank and, 324–326
  shrinking of, 907, 909, 927, 933, 937
  slavery and, 393
  small, 330

states and, 246–247, 880
wartime propaganda of, 654–655
welfare and, 779
welfare capitalism and, 670
WWII and, 754, 762
Federal Housing Administration (FHA), 818
Federal Housing Authority, 737
The Federalist, 182–183, 198, 201, 205
Federalists, 217, 253, 260, 280–281, 317
  commonwealth idea and, 245
  Constitution and, 204–205, 207–209, 218
  declaration of War of 1812 and, 235
  decline of, 248–249
  financial policy and, 210, 212, 219
  the judiciary and, 230
  New England, 233, 239
  opening of West and, 222
  pro-British foreign policy of, 235
  vs. Republicans, 212, 216–217
Federal Music Project, 743
Federal Reserve Act (1913), 599
Federal Reserve system, 647, 719, 745
  establishment of, 598–599
  Great Depression and, 698
  inflation and, 908–909
  New Deal and, 726
  1970s recessions and, 899
  Roosevelt recession and, 732
Federal Savings and Loan Insurance Corporation (FSLIC), 912
Federal Theatre Project (FTP), 721(i), 743, 745
Federal Trade Commission (FTC), 599, 666
Federal Writers' Project (FWP), 743
fee simple, 61
Feiffer, Jules, 871(i)
Fei Xiaotong, 900
Fell, Margaret, 71
Fellowship for Reconciliation, 857
fellow travelers, 800, 806
Female Charitable Society, 257
Female Guardian Society, 358
feminine mystique, 823–824
The Feminine Mystique (Friedan), 823, 865–866, 926
feminism, 337, 439, 871, 877, 892(i)
  backlash against, 925
  historiography and, 778
  in 1970s, 880, 888–889, 892–893, 905
  opposition to, 892–893, 898
  revival of, 849, 856, 864–867
  rise of, 579, 582–583, 601
  third-wave, 925–926
Ferdinand, king of Spain (r. 1474–1516), 22, 24, 29(t)
Ferraro, Geraldine, 889, 909
Field, David Dudley, 341

Field, Stephen J., 519
Field Workers Union, 714
Fierro, Josefina, 713
Fifteenth Amendment, 438–439, 438(t), 525, 529–530, 530(i)
  African Americans and, 589
Fifth Amendment, 391
fifties. *See* affluent society (1950s)
"Fifty-four forty or fight!", 376, 378
Filipinos. *See also* Philippines
  Bataan death march and, 774
  Great Depression and, 714
  as migrant workers, 710
  treatment of insurrectionists, 621
Fillmore, Millard (1800–1874), 330, 382, 390–391, 392(m)
  as president (1850–1853), 301(m), 361, 387
"final solution," 770, 770(i)
Finland, 658
Finley, James, 273
Finney, Charles Grandison, 308–310, 308(i), 313, 344, 348, 354, 358
Finney, Lydia, 309, 358
firearms industry, 288, 292, 295
fireside chats, 722, 724
First Amendment, 218, 452, 800
  Establishment Clause of, 453
  political correctness and, 925
  prayer in public schools and, 881
First Party System (1794–1815), 319(i)
fishing industry, 91, 137, 149, 477
Fish, Nathaniel, 61
Fiske, John, 609
Fithian, Philip, 89, 104
Fitzgerald, F. Scott, 689, 695
Fitzhugh, George, 370
Five Nations, Iroquois, 12, 45, 64–65. *See also* Iroquois Indians
Flanagan, Hallie, 721(i), 743, 745
flappers, 676, 676(i), 678, 681
Fleetwood, Sara Iredell, 590(i)
Fleming, Victor, 678
Fletcher v. Peck (1810), 248
flexible response policy, 831
Florentine Codex: General History of New Spain (Sahagún), 26
Florida
  British colonization of, 125, 136, 138(m), 154
  Latino immigration to, 920
  migration to, 818, 847
  Republican government in, 449–450
  as sanctuary for escaped slaves, 267
  Seminole Indians in, 327(i), 327(m), 328
  slavery and, 71, 179, 191, 383
  Spain and, 24, 40–42, 41(m), 44, 67, 70, 76, 89, 177, 185(m), 235, 240–241, 249

  2000 election in, 933, 933(i), 934(m), 935
Foch, Ferdinand, 644
Food Administration (World War I), 649
Food and Drug Administration (FDA), 595, 889
Food for Peace program, 833
Food Stamps, 845, 908, 924
Foote, Edward Bliss, 555
Forbes, John Murray, 489
Force Act, 234
Force Bill (1833), 323
Ford, Gerald R. (1913–), 873, 879, 883, 905
  as president (1974–1977), 899
Ford, Henry, 287(i), 640, 669
  assembly line and, 505(i)
Ford Model T, 665(i)
  consumer culture and, 673
  sexuality and, 675
Ford Motor Company, 606, 665(i)
  foreign investment and, 670
  mass production and, 671, 675
  strikes at, 716
Fordney-McCumber Tariff (1922), 672
Foreign Affairs, 786
foreign aid, 816, 833, 913(m). *See also* foreign investment
Foreign Conspiracy against the Liberties of the United States (Morse), 311–312
Foreign Intelligence Surveillance Court, 947
foreign investment, 672
  in Asia, 673
  in canals, 297, 299
  in Europe, 673
  Great Depression and, 698
  in South America, 670, 672–673
foreign policy, 943. *See also* international relations
  acquisition of territories and, 621–622
  Adams, 218
  anti-imperialism in, 619–620
  in Asia, 626–628
  bipartisan, 798
  Bush (George H. W.), 912–914
  Bush (George W.), 935, 944
  in Caribbean, 387, 622(m), 631
  Carter, 900–902
  cold war and, 849–877
  crises in, 931
  1852 election and, 387
  Eisenhower, 794–795
  expansionist, 379, 387, 395, 603–609, 622(m), 631
  Ford, 899
  globalization and, 608, 622
  global strategy in, 608, 622

foreign policy (Continued):
    imperial experiment in, 618–619
    JFK, 831–834, 840, 847
    lack of purpose in, 603–606, 631
    "large," 608, 613
    New Deal and, 746
    in 1920s, 672–673, 693
    1928 election and, 692
    nonalignment, 604
    oil and, 797
    post–cold war, 929–930
    pro-British, 215–216, 218, 235
    Reagan, 908, 912
    Spanish, 387
    trade and, 607–608, 626
    unilateral, 941
    Venezuela and, 609
    Wilson's philosophy of reform and,
        628, 663
Forman, Stanley, 894(i)
Forrest, Nathan Bedford, 445, 446(i)
    biographical information, 446–447
Fort Beauséjour, Nova Scotia,
        122(m), 124
Fort Carrillon, 126
Fort Christina, 40(t)
Fort Corcoran, 418
Fort Donelson, 406
Fort Duquesne, 122(m), 123–125,
        125(m). See also Pittsburgh,
        Pennsylvania
Fort Fisher, 418
Fort George, 142
Fort Hall, 460
Fort Henry, 406
Fort Leavenworth, 462
Fort McHenry, 235
Fort Niagara, 126
Fort Orange, 47
Fort Pillow, Tennessee, massacre at, 446
Fort Pitt. See Pittsburgh, Pennsylvania
Fort Stanwix, Treaty of (1784), 223
Fort Sumter, 398–399, 427
    bombardment (1861) of, 400(i)
    seizure of, 400–401
Fort Ticonderoga, 173, 180
Fort Wagner, 418
Forten, James, 352
"forty-niners," 383. See also gold rush,
        California
Foster, Mark, 756
Foster, William Z., 718
Foundations of American
        Consitutionalism (Richards), 280
The Four Hundred, 552
Fourier, Charles (1777–1837), 347
Fourierism, 347–348, 365
Four-Power Conference (1947), 790
Fourteenth Amendment (1868), 210,
        435–437, 438(t), 519, 525, 529,
        804, 934

abortion rights and, 892
Fowler, Philemon, 358
Fox, George, 71
Fox, Henry, 333
Fox Indians, 65, 326, 328(i), 329
Frame of Government (1681;
        Pennsylvania), 72
France, 18, 37. See also French
        colonization; New France; Paris,
        Treaty of; Versailles, Treaty of
    American writers in, 689
    England and, 69, 75, 95
    Germany and, 750–752, 774
    in Indochina, 850, 877
    jazz and, 680
    liberation of, 770
    loan from, 175
    Mexico and, 375
    migration to New World from, 44
    peace talks with, 182–183
    slave trade and, 77–78
    vs. Spain, 40–41
    Spanish civil war and, 751
    Suez Canal and, 796
    sugar islands and, 125, 134(m),
        136–137, 138(m)
    Texas and, 369
    trade with, 73
    U.S. alliance with, 174–177, 182, 191
    U.S. isolationism and, 752
    War of Austrian Succession and, 97
    Washington Naval Arms
        Conference and, 673
    WWI and, 639, 672
    WWII role of, 768
    XYZ Affair, 216
Francesca, Piero della, 20(i)
Franciscan friars, 47
    cultural assimilation and, 41
    exploitation of Native Americans
        by, 40–41, 44, 67
    forced labor of, 44
    missions and churches of, 41, 65, 67
Franco, Francisco, 750–751
Franco-Prussian War (1870), 629
Frankfurter, Felix, 574, 731
Franklin, Benjamin (1706–1790), 111,
        115, 129, 186
    Albany Plan (Plan of Union)
        and, 123
    Constitution and, 202, 204
    Declaration of Independence
        and, 169(i)
    as diplomat, 175, 182–183, 201
    in England, 139–140, 144
    Enlightenment and, 113–114,
        131, 190
    George III and, 167
    pre-Revolutionary views of,
        146–147, 149–150
    as scientist, 113(i), 292

on slavery, 113
    transcendentalism and, 344
    on work ethic, 305, 310
Franklin Institute, 292
Franz Ferdinand, archduke of Austria
    assassination of (1914), 639
Freake, Elizabeth, 60(i)
Fredericksburg, Virginia, 405, 415
Free African Society, 268, 270–271
free blacks, 88, 267–269, 268(i)
    abolitionism and, 267, 352–358
    accomplishments of, 82–83,
        270–271, 271(i)
    black churches and, 262, 268,
        268(i), 270, 271(i), 279, 442
    in Charleston, 269
    Douglass and, 380–381
    Dred Scott and, 391
    education of, 442(i)
    Fugitive Slave Act and, 385–386
    labor of, 298(i), 434, 435(i)
    Patriot cause and, 188
    prejudice against, 262
    Reconstruction and, 431–435,
        440–441
    sharecropping and, 442–444
    terrorism against, 445–448
    Utopias and, 336
    voting rights for, 253, 267–268, 355,
        438–439
    women, 443
Freed, Alan, 825
Freedman's Savings and Trust
        Company, 449–450
Freedmen's Bureau, 431, 434–435, 440,
        442, 446
Freedom of Information Act, 883
freedom of speech, 218, 857–858,
        857(i)
    limits on, 655
Freedom of the Will (Edwards), 117
Freedom Rides, 836, 838, 935
Freedom's Journal, 271, 352
Freedom Summer (1964), 840, 857,
        866
The Free Enquirer, 337
freehold society, 130, 148, 227, 279
    in Middle Atlantic colonies, 105,
        106(m), 119–120, 128–129, 131
    in New England, 101–105, 131
    property rights and, 102–105,
        106(m), 119–120, 128–129, 131
    republicanism and, 155, 160–161
Freeman, Elizabeth, 187(i)
Freemasonry, Order of, 330–331, 339
Freeport Doctrine (Douglas), 393
Free Presbyterian Church, 309
free silver, 573, 597
Free Soil Party, 379, 382–383, 394–395
    "Bleeding Kansas" and, 389
    Compromise of 1850 and, 386(m)

Douglass and, 381
elections and, 387, 390
Fugitive Slave Act and, 388
in Kansas, 462
political realignment and, 392(m)
Republican Party and, 389
Free Speech Movement (FSM),
    857–858, 857(i)
Frelinghuysen, Theodore Jacob, 114
Frémont, John C., 377–378, 378(m),
    390–391, 392(m), 402
French and Indian War, 121–126, 154,
    170, 175, 180. *See also* Seven
    Years' War
French colonization, 5–6, 12, 102,
    121–126, 122(m), 123(i), 131,
    134, 136–137, 138(m)
    before 1660, 40(t)
    British Empire and, 98
    in Canada, 175, 182
    Christianization and, 47, 65–66
    fur trade and, 11, 40, 44–47, 63–64
    Iroquois and, 65
    in Louisiana, 13, 47, 67
    Molasses Act and, 96
    trade system and, 134(m)
    in West Indies, 70, 98–99, 176–177,
        179, 213–214, 234
French Revolution, 184
    division of Americans and, 213
    ideological impact of, 210, 219
    Jefferson and, 212, 217
Frethorne, Richard, 53
Freudian psychology, 690
Freund, Paul, 723
Frick, Henry Clay, 510, 569
Friedan, Betty, 823, 865–866, 926
frontier
    Appalachian Mountains as, 121,
        126, 138(m), 151(m)
    concept of, 609
    mythic, 457(i), 462–464, 482(i)
Frost, Robert, 690
Fuel Administration, 649
Fugitive Slave Acts
    of 1793, 271, 355
    of 1850, 384–387, 388(i), 395
    resistance to, 385–386
Fujita, Jan, 660(i)
Fulani Indians, 22(i)
Fulbright, J. William, 856, 870
Fuller, Henry Blake, 570
Fuller, Margaret (1810–1850), 344(i),
    344–346
Fulton, Robert, 300
Fundamental Constitutions (Carolina;
    1669), 71
fur trade, 39, 40(t), 121, 124(i)
    Dutch, 40, 47–48, 64, 67
    environmental effects of, 66
    French, 44–47

Indian wars and, 45, 47, 63–65, 67
inland peoples and, 63–66
F.W. Woolworth Company, 495

Gadsden, James, 387–388
Gadsden Purchase (1853), 382(m)
Gagarin, Yuri, 835
Gage, Thomas, 129, 140, 145, 147, 154,
    157–158, 180, 182
gag rule, 357
Gaines, Edmund, 460
Gallatin, Albert, 231, 240, 242
Galloway, James, 477
Galloway, Joseph, 154
Gallup polls. *See* opinion polls
Gama, Vasco da, 22, 22(m)
Gandhi, Indira, assassination of, 912
gang-labor system, 342, 368, 434,
    442–443
"**Gansevoort Limner**" (painter),
    101(i)
Garcia, Mario, 713
Garfield, James A. (1831–1881), 517
    assassination of (1881), 516
Garland, Hamlin, 465, 556
Garretson, Freeborn, 270
Garrison, William Lloyd (1805–1879),
    341, 353–359, 354(i), 365
    Douglass and, 381
    Free Soil Party and, 379
Garsed, Richard, 292
Garson, Aaron Henry, 485(i)
Garvey, Amy Jacques, 691
Garvey, Marcus, 691, 861
Gary, Elbert H., 594
Gary, Indiana, 666(i)
Garza, Elizo de la, 863
Gaspée (ship), 150, 155(t)
Gassaway, Robert, 165
Gates, Bill, 918, 923(i)
    biographical information, 922–923
Gates, Horatio, 171(m), 173–174,
    176(i), 179, 181
gay rights, 864–865, 867, 877, 888,
    893–894
    in military, 928
    in 1970s, 905
    opposition to, 898, 925
    in sports, 895
Gay Task Force, National, 894
Gaza Strip, 916(m), 929
Gazette of the United States, 217
Gellhorn, Martha, 745
gender
    Great Depression and, 699
    historiography and, 778
    welfare system and, 778–779
gender roles. *See also* women;
    masculinity
    in Africa, 80

conservative view of, 898
employment and, 704
feminism and, 892–893
of free blacks, 434
Great Depression and, 701–702
in military, 758
Native American, 12–14, 15(i), 224
New Deal and, 735, 746
in 1950s, 823–825, 847
reform and, 342
sex-typing and, 499–500, 500(i),
    513
on television, 822
traditional, 783(i)
transcendentalism and, 344–345
Utopian communalism and,
    346–348, 365
welfare system and, 778–779
wives and, 553–554
women's rights and, 358, 362
General Agreement on Tariffs and
    Trade (GATT), 816
General Union for Promoting the
    Observance of the Christian
    Sabbath, 308
Geneva, Switzerland, 29, 32
Genius of Universal Emancipation
    (newspaper), 354
*Gentle Measures in the Management
    and Training of the Young*
    (Abbott), 556
gentry class, 71, 89–91. *See also* elite
    defined, 35
George, David Lloyd, 658, 660
George, Henry, 480, 575
George I, king of England
    (r. 1714–1727), 95, 95(i)
George II, king of England
    (r. 1727–1760), 95, 95(i)
George III, king of England
    (r. 1760–1820), 134(i), 166(i),
    167, 176, 181, 187, 248
    Declaration of Independence and,
        169–170, 169(i)
    policies of, 136, 139, 144–145,
        150–151
    rebellion against, 140
    repeal of Stamp Act and, 167
Georgia
    as colony, 70, 87(i), 95–97, 154
    economy of, 213
    evangelicals in, 121
    migrants from, 371
    Native Americans and, 326
    plantations in, 226
    secession and, 385
    Sherman's march through,
        423–424
    slavery in, 95, 121, 160, 262–264,
        265(m), 272(m), 368
    war with Spain and, 95–97

Germain, George, 172–173

German Americans
in WWII, 765

German Democratic Republic (East Germany), 785, 790–791

German immigrants, 72, 83, 130, 303, 311, 313, 388(i), 389, 479, 498
in colonial America, 101, 105, 128–129, 131
as Loyalists, 156
in Pennsylvania, 72, 106–110, 110(m), 111(i), 156
Pietism and, 114
political activism of, 508, 511, 521, 521(f)
unionism of, 506

Germantown, Pennsylvania, 72

Germany, 29, 97, 638–645. See also Berlin; German Democratic Republic
anti-Semitism in, 760
automobile industry in, 884
cartels in, 599
colonies of, 750
declaration of war on U.S. by, 754
defeat of, 784
division of, 774
economic growth of, 915, 917
fascism in, 742
Japan and, 751
Mexico and, 642
Nazi, 160, 750
in 1920s, 693
propaganda efforts of, 648
reunification of, 914(m)
Soviet Union and, 751, 753
Spanish civil war and, 750–751
war reparations of, 658–659, 672, 693, 750, 774
welfare system in, 728
in WWI, 638–645
in WWII, 749, 777
zones of occupation in, 785

Germany, Federal Republic of (West Germany), 785, 790

Geronimo, Chief, 471

Gettysburg, battle of (1863), 397, 408, 410, 415–416, 417(m), 420, 427

Ghent, Treaty of (1814), 240

ghettos, 557, 560, 560(i), 562. See also cities

ghost dance, 473

Gibbons, Thomas, 247

Gibbons v. Ogden (1824), 247, 300

Gibbs, Lois Marie, 888, 891(i)
biographical information, 890–891

GI Bill of Rights (Servicemen's Readjustment Act; 1944), 762, 797, 817, 865

Gibraltar, 76, 177, 184

Gibson, Charles Dana, 555–556

Gibson girl, 556

Giddings, Joshua, 379

Gilbert, Humphrey, 48

Gilbert, John, 676

Gilded Age (late nineteenth century), 569, 574, 583, 591, 604–606

The Gilded Age (Warner), 569

Giles, John, 121

Gilman, Charlotte Perkins, 575, 582

Gingrich, Newt, 930, 931(i)

Ginsberg, Allen, 825, 860

Ginsburg, Ruth Bader, 909(i), 928

glasnost, meaning of, 912

Glass, Carter, 599

Glass-Steagall Banking Act (1932), 715, 724, 731(t)

Glazer, Tom, 844(i)

Glazier, Nathan, 898

Glenn, John, 835

globalization, 887, 907, 927. See also economy, international
foreign policy and, 608, 622
terrorism and, 937

global warming, 927, 941

Glorious Revolution (1688), 73–75, 93, 95, 98–99, 143

Glyn, Elinor, 678

Godey's Lady's Book, 358

Godkin, Edwin L., 523, 550, 552

Goethals, George W., 625(i)

gold
monetary system and, 538–540, 538(i)
Spanish conquests and, 24, 27, 33, 35, 37, 40, 41(m)
trade in, 20, 21(m)
Virginia company and, 48–49

gold mining, 474–477, 474(m), 475(i), 479, 483, 540

gold rush, California (1849–1857), 382–383, 384(i), 385(m)

gold standard, 538–540, 538(i), 698, 726

Goldwater, Barry, 842, 843(m), 903

Goliad, Texas, 371

Gompers, Samuel, 508, 508(i), 509–510, 586, 620

Gone with the Wind (Mitchell), 707

González, Henry, 863

The Good Earth (Buck), 707

Good Housekeeping, 553

Goodman, Andrew, 840

Goodman, Benny, 706

Good Neighbor Policy, 751

Goodrich, Carter, 280

Goodson, Mark, 802

Gorbachev, Mikhail, 912

Gordon, Linda, 778–779

Gore, Albert (Al), Jr., 928, 931(i), 933, 933(i), 934, 934(m)

Gorgas, William C., 625(i)

Gorges, Ferdinando, 48

Gough, John (1817–1886), 310

Gould, Jay, 489, 508
biographical information, 492–493, 492(i), 493(i)

Grable, Betty, 758

Graham, Billy, 822, 898

Graham, Isabella, 308

grain, 32(f). See also corn; rice; wheat
exports of, 105, 105(f), 111, 303
prices of, 34(f). See also Price Revolution
production of, 106, 313, 467
transportation for, 299–300, 302–303

grain production. See also wheat

Gramm-Rudman Act (1985), 911

Grand Canyon, 40

Grand Ole Opry, 826

Grange, Red, 680

Granger movement, 468–469, 535

Grant, Ulysses S. (1822–1885), 377, 401, 420(i), 523
1868 election and, 438
Ku Klux Klan Act of 1871 and, 445
Lee's surrender and, 426
at Petersburg, 425
as president (1869–1877), 448–449, 521, 605
Reconstruction and, 437, 441, 451
Richmond campaign (1864) and, 421(m)
scorched earth campaign of, 421
Sherman and, 423
Shiloh and, 397(i), 406–407
as Union Army commander, 418–421
Vicksburg campaign of, 416, 427
in the West, 406–407, 415, 418, 427

The Grapes of Wrath (Steinbeck), 709(i), 710

Grasso, Ella T., 889

Grateful Dead, 860

Graves, Elizabeth, 83

Grayson, Andrew Jackson (1819–1869), 375(i)

Great American Desert, 458(m), 460, 464, 632–633. See also Great Plains

Great Atlantic and Pacific Tea Company (A & P), 495

Great Awakening, 112–120, 131, 142, 272, 274, 277. See also evangelicalism; revivalism; Second Great Awakening
Edwards and, 114, 116–117
political aspects of, 115, 118–119
religious fervor of, 114–118, 131
Whitefield and, 114–115, 118

Great Basin, 474

Great Britain, 609. *See also* British Empire; England; English colonization
American empire of (1713), 77(*m*)
appeasement of Hitler (1938), 750–751, 785
boundaries of western lands and, 240(*m*)
civil war in, 70
colonial trade of, 69
control of trade by, 93(*m*)
Desert Fox campaign and, 931
division of Germany and, 774
France and, 76
Mexico and, 375
nineteenth-century migration from, 311, 477
nuclear test ban treaties and, 834
Oregon and, 373, 373(*m*), 378
Palestine and, 796
slave trade and, 77
Spain and, 76, 89
Spanish civil war and, 751
Suez Canal and, 796
territorial disputes with, 230
U.S. aid to, 752–753
U.S. relations with, 623, 631, 752
War of Austrian Succession and, 97
war on terrorism and, 941
Washington Naval Arms Conference and, 673
welfare system in, 728
West Indian trade and, 91
WWI and, 639–640, 672
WWII role of, 749(*i*), 768–770, 777
Great Deflation (nineteenth century), 486
Great Depression, 280, 586–587, 657, 663, 695–719, 695(*i*), 698(*f*)
African Americans in, 707–710
beginning of, 697–699
causes of, 697
discontent and, 716–717
fiscal policy and, 715
Harlem Renaissance and, 691
Hoover and, 714–717
immigration and, 684
intellectual life and, 690
1920s economy and, 668, 693
popular protests in, 734(*m*)
Prohibition and, 688
Republican Party and, 692
self-perpetuation of, 697–698
welfare system and, 778–779
WWII and, 749–750, 762, 777
The Great Gatsby (Fitzgerald), 689
Great Lakes, 11, 64, 182, 223, 240, 331
iron ore in, 487
migration to, 296, 297(*m*)
transportation to, 298(*m*), 299
Great Migration, 650–651, 650(*m*), 652

Great Plains, 27, 369
climate of, 458, 458(*m*), 464–467
drought on, 464–466, 473, 633, 709–710
ecosystem of, 458, 458(*m*), 464, 632–633
federal subsidies for, 633
as Great American Desert, 458(*m*), 460, 464, 632–633
homesteaders on, 464–469, 467(*m*), 468(*i*), 474, 483
increase in buffalo on, 632
as Indian country, 460, 462, 469, 474, 632
marketing of, 460–461, 463(*i*), 464
modern population losses of, 632–633, 632(*m*), 633(*i*)
new historical view of, 632–633
railroads and, 460–461, 460(*i*), 461(*m*), 467, 470–471, 490(*m*)
ranching on, 458, 461, 464, 467, 483
settlement of, 458–474, 632–633
sheep raising on, 464
shelter on, 459, 459(*i*), 465
sod houses on, 465, 468(*i*)
wildlife on, 458, 460
Great Salt Lake, 466, 474
Great Society, 816, 840–847, 849, 859, 876
declining economy and, 884
funding for, 845–846
legislation of, 841(*t*)
in 1970s, 897, 905
Nixon and, 880
Great Strike of 1877, 485–486
The Great Train Robbery (film), 675
Great War for Empire. *See* Seven Years' War
Great White Fleet, 611
Greece, 19–20
and Truman Doctrine, 785–786, 790
Greeley, Horace, 347, 413, 449, 458, 460
greenbacks, 412, 537. *See also* currency
Greene, Catherine, 294
Greene, Nathanael, 179, 294
Greenleaf, Simon, 363
Green Party, 933–934, 934(*m*)
Greenstein, Fred, 803
Greenville, Ohio, 236
Greenville, Treaty of (1795), 223
Grenada, 912
Grenville, George, 136–140, 139(*i*), 144(*t*), 145, 159
Gresham, Walter Q., 607
Grey Panthers, 864
Griffin, James B., 407
Griffith, Beatrice, 739
Griffith, D. W., 589, 676(*i*)
Grimes County, Texas, 530–531

Grimké, Angelina, 353–354, 357, 359, 362–363
Grimké, Sarah, 353–354, 357, 359, 363
Grimké, Thomas, 257
Griswold v. Connecticut (1965), 892
Gropper, William, 725(*i*)
gross domestic product (GDP), 668
decline of, 884
defense spending and, 755(*f*)
Great Depression and, 699
late-nineteenth-century boom in, 486(*f*)
postwar, 817, 817(*f*)
under Reagan, 909
Roosevelt recession and, 731
WWII and, 755, 758
Gruening, Ernest, 852
Guadalcanal, 772
Guadalupe Hidalgo, Treaty of (1848), 379, 382(*m*)
Guam, 617, 622, 622(*m*), 771
Guantanamo Bay, Cuba, 618, 622(*m*), 626, 626(*m*), 751
Guarani language (Paraguay), 28
Guatemala, 6, 9, 605, 670, 796
Guevara, Che (Ernesto C.), 859
guilds, 19
Guinea Company, 35
Guiteau, Charles, 516
Gulf of Mexico, 11–12, 47, 183
Gulf of Tonkin Resolution (1964), 852, 870, 876
Gullah dialect, 85, 265
guns
Gatling machine, 470
Remington rifles, 292
repeating rifles, 470
Rifle Clubs, 448
rifle-muskets, 410, 415
Guttridge, Molly, 185(*i*)
Guy Fawkes Day, 142–143
Guy, Seymour J., 551(*i*)
Guzman, Jacobo Arbenz, 796
Gypsies, Holocaust and, 750, 770

habeas corpus, meaning of, 407
The Hague (Netherlands), 183
Hague Peace Conference (1899), 630
Haiti, 24, 26, 231, 605, 929
African Americans and, 271, 337, 381
U.S. military intervention in, 673
Haitian Emigration Society, 271
Halberstam, David, 874
Haldeman, H. R., 882–883
Haldimand, General, 150
Hale, John P., 392(*m*)
Haley, Bill, 825
Halifax, Lord, 124
Hall, Basil, 315

Hall, Fayrer, 96
Hall, G. Stanley, 554
Hall, John H., 292
Hall, Prince, 352
Hamilton, Alexander (1755–1804), 181(i), 325
    assumption plan of, 211–212
    Constitution and, 246
    duel with Aaron Burr, 233
    as Federalist, 281
    The Federalist and and, 205
    fiscal program of, 206, 210–212, 211(f), 219
    Jefferson and, 210–211, 212(i)
    on national bank, 211, 242
    at Philadelphia Convention, 202
    plan for Northern Confederacy and, 233
    pro-British foreign policy of, 216, 218
    program of national mercantilism, 246
    on public credit, 210
    as secretary of the treasury, 209–210
Hamilton, Alice, 588
Hamilton Manufacturing Company, 305
Hamilton, Mary Agnes, 700
Hammond, John Henry, 369
Hancock, John, 137, 143, 153, 169(i), 205
Handlin, Oscar, 280
Handsome Lake (Seneca chief), 224, 236
Hanna, Mark, 539, 573, 591
Harding, Chester, 245(i)
Harding, Warren G. (1865–1923), 655
    corruption and, 667, 690
    as president (1921–1923), 666, 680, 683
Hard, William, 576
Hare Krishna, 888
Hargreaves, James, 289
Harlan County, Kentucky, 716
Harlem, New York City, 560, 709, 738
Harlem Renaissance, 690–691, 690(i)
Harpers Ferry, Virginia, 292, 295, 405
    Brown's raid on (1859), 394
Harper's Weekly, 502(i), 597(i)
Harriman, Averell, 786, 790
Harrington, Michael, 825, 830(i)
Harris, Anna, 263
Harris, David, 425
Harris, Katherine, 934
Harrison, Benjamin (1833–1901)
    1892 election and, 516, 516(i), 540(m)
    as president (1889–1893), 520, 520(i), 525(i), 535, 608
    on protective tariffs, 517

Harrison, William Henry (1773–1841), 235–237, 238(m), 516(i)
    death of, 338–339
    1836 election and, 331
    1840 election and, 334–335, 335(i), 338
    inauguration of, 315(i)
    as military commander, 383(i)
    as president (1841), 335, 338
Harris, William, 63
Harte, Bret, 481
Hartford, Connecticut, 40(t), 59, 185, 239–240
    manufacturing in, 288
    transportation and, 302, 302(m)
Hartz, Louis, 280
Harvard College, 119(t), 141
Harvey, George, 597(i)
Hass, Philip, 317(i)
Hat Act (1732), 72(t)
hat making, 242–243
Hawaii, 275(m)
    annexation of, 616–617, 622, 622(m)
    Chinese immigration to, 479
    Japanese internment and, 766
    strategic importance of, 608, 622(m)
    sugarcane in, 605, 605(i)
Hawikuh Indians, 44
Hawley-Smoot Tariff (1930), 672, 698
Hawthorne, Nathaniel, 299, 345–346
Hayden, Casey, 866
Hayden, Tom, 857
Hayes, Rutherford B. (1822–1893)
    1876 election and, 516
    as president (1877–1881), 450–451
    Strike of 1877 and, 485–486
Hay, John, 627
Haymarket affair, 508–509
Hay-Pauncefote Agreement (1901), 623
Hayworth, Rita, 758
A Hazard of New Fortunes (Howells), 570
Heade, Martin Johnson, 373(i)
Head Start, 844(i), 845
health care, 928, 948
    alternative methods, 926
    attempts to reform, 929, 929(i)
    biotechnology and, 918–919
    federal government and, 816
    folk medicine and, 256–257
    JFK and, 830
    1970s fitness craze and, 888
    socialized, 799
    for women, 257, 257(i)
Health, Education, and Welfare, Department of (HEW), 803
health insurance, 587

    elderly without, 830(i)
    JFK and, 835
    national, 728, 799, 929
    Social Security and, 746
    welfare capitalism and, 670
health maintenance organizations (HMOs), 757
Hearst, George, 614
Hearst, William Randolph, 569, 615(i), 700
    biographical information, 614–615
    sensationalist journalism of, 612–615
Heaton, Hannah, 102, 115
hegemony, meaning of, 783
Helfferich, David, 887(i)
Helms, Jesse, 925
Helper, Hinton, 398
Hemingway, Ernest, 689
Henderson, Charles, 588
Hendrix, Jimi, 860, 861(i)
Henrietta Maria, queen of England (r. 1625–1649), 50
Henry, Patrick (1736–1799), 140, 140(i), 149, 155, 166–167, 202
    church taxes and, 190
    on Hamilton's financial program, 210
    on ratification of Constitution, 205, 208
Henry, prince of Portugal (r. 1394–1460), 19–20
Henry VIII, king of England (r. 1509–1547), 32
Hepburn Railway Act (1906), 595
heresy, 17–18, 29, 60
Heritage Foundation, 280
Hernandes, Harriet, 448
Hersh, Seymour, 870
Her Wedding Night (film), 679(i)
Herzegovina, 639, 929
Hess, Jean, 624
HEW. *See* Health, Education, and Welfare, Department of
Hewes, George Robert Twelves, 151, 152(i), 206
    biographical information, 152–153
Hewitt, Abram, 584
Heyrman, Christine, 452
Hickok, Lorena, 745
Hickok, Wild Bill, 462
Hicks, Clarence J., 587
Hicks, Thomas, 344(i)
Higginson, Francis, 39
Higginson, Thomas Wentworth, 417–418
Higher Education Act (1965), 841, 841(t), 842
Highway Act, National Interstate and Defense (1956), 819, 820(m)
Highway Beautification Act (1965), 843

highways
    automobile and, 675
    interstate, 819–820, 820(m)
    Kaiser and, 756
    move to suburbs and, 817
    1950s culture and, 820
    postwar growth of, 819–820,
        820(m)
    Route 66, 710(m)
Hill, Anita, 911, 911(i)
Hill, James J., 489
Hillsborough, Lord, 147, 149
Hilton, James, 707
Hine, Lewis, 587(i)
hippies, 859. See also counterculture
Hirabayashi v. United States (1943),
    767
Hiroshima, 773(m), 775–776, 776(i),
    791, 948
Hirschfeld, Al, 801(i)
Hispanics. See Latinos
Hispaniola (Haiti), 24, 26
Hiss, Alger, 800–801
History of the Conquest of New Spain
    (Diaz del Castillo), 30–31
"The History of the Standard Oil
    Company" (Tarbell), 575(i)
Hitler, Adolph, 731, 750, 770
    Holocaust and, 770(i), 796(i)
HIV. See AIDS
Hoar, George F., 620
Ho Chi Minh, 850, 873
Hoff, John, 242
Hoffman, Abbie, 868
hog production, 265, 287, 287(i), 296,
    299
Hohokam culture, 6, 11–12
Holland. See Dutch colonization
Holland Land Company, 227
Holly, Buddy, 825
Hollywood, 675, 903. See also Los
    Angeles, California; movies
Hollywood Ten, 800
Holmes, Isaac, 265
Holmes, Oliver Wendell, Jr., 420, 574,
    655
Holocaust, 749, 770(i), 770–771, 796(i)
    homosexuals and, 750
Holy Roman Empire, 29
homeland security, 945, 947(i)
Homeland Security, Office of, 947,
    947(i)
homelessness (1990s), 911, 914
Home Owners Loan Corporation, 724
Homestead Act (1862), 411, 464, 465,
    471
homesteaders, 464–469, 467(m),
    468(i), 474, 483
homestead laws, 464
Homestead steel strike (1892),
    457, 510

homosexuals, 568, 934. See also gay
    rights; lesbians
    cultural dissent and, 825
    gay liberation movement and,
        893–894
    Holocaust and, 750, 770
    in military, 758
    1950s culture and, 824
    violence against, 925
Honduras, 30, 670
The Honeymooners (TV program), 822
Hong Kong, 771, 772(m), 773(m)
Hood, John B., 424, 425(m)
Hooker, Joseph ("Fighting Joe"), 405,
    415
Hooker, Thomas, 59
Hoole, Axalla John, 367, 390
Hooper's Female Pills, 257, 257(i)
Hoover, Herbert (1874–1964), 649
    at Department of Commerce,
        666–667
    Great Depression and, 698,
        714–717, 719, 722, 747
    New Deal and, 724
    as president (1929–1933), 692,
        714–717
    Roosevelt recession and, 732
Hoovervilles, 716, 717(i)
Hope, James, 403(i)
Hopewell Indians, 6, 11, 11(i), 12, 37
Hopi Indians, 12
Hopkins, Harry, 723, 725, 729
Hopkins, Samuel, 276
Horne, Lena, 758
horses, 27
    Indian acquisition of, 459, 459(i),
        483
Horseshoe Bend, battle of (1814),
    238(m), 239
Horton, Willie, 911
Horwitz, Morton, 280
Housatonic Indians, 117
House Committee on Un-American
    Activities (HUAC), 800
House, Edward, 640
household production
    in colonial America, 102, 105, 146
    as early manufacturing, 214(i)
    outwork and, 106, 146, 286, 293
Houseman, John, 743
House of Burgesses, Virginia, 49–50,
    54–55
House of Commons, England, 35,
    139–141
House of Lords, England, 35
House of Representatives, U.S.
    abolitionism and, 357
    Democratic control of, 909
    Republican gains in, 930, 944
    Wilmot Proviso and, 379
    women in, 911(i)

housing
    in cities, 829, 847
    discrimination in, 818
    gay rights and, 894
    inflation and, 884–885
    lack of, 911, 914
    LBJ and, 842
    legislation on, 721(i), 731, 731(t),
        799, 803, 841(t)
    postwar boom in, 817–818
    public, 845
    states and, 911
    wartime migration and, 764
Housing and Urban Development,
    Department of (HUD), 928
Houston, Sam, 371, 373(i)
Hovenden, Thomas, 429(i)
Howard, Oliver O., 434
Howe, Frederic, 538
Howe, Julia Ward, 439
Howells, William Dean, 570
Howe, Marie Jenny, 582
Howe, William, 125, 170–173,
    182, 191
    in Philadelphia, 175
"Howl" (Ginsberg), 825
How the Other Half Lives (Riis), 557
How We Advertised America (Creel),
    657
HUAC. See House Committee on
    Un-American Activities
Hubbard, Maria Cadman, 341(i)
Hübner, Joseph Alexander von, 476
HUD. See Housing and Urban
    Development, Department of
Hudson Bay, 75(t), 76
Hudson, Henry, 47
Hudson River, 47, 63, 170–171, 173,
    180, 247
    Erie Canal and, 228
    manors on, 227
Hudson River Valley
    Dutch in, 74(i), 105, 128–129
    land conflicts in, 128–129,
        129(m)
    loyalists in, 156
    settlement of, 106(m)
Hudson, Rock, 925
Hudson's Bay Company, 373
Huerta, Victoriano, 628
Hughes, Charles Evans, 642
Hughes, Langston, 689–691, 707
Huguenots, 32, 44, 73, 107
Hull, Cordell, 751
Hull House, 577–578, 580, 588
Human Genome Project, 919, 919(i)
human rights, 787
    Carter and, 900–901, 905
Human Rights, Office of, 900
human sacrifice, 10, 12
Hume, David, 143

Humphrey, Hubert H., 798, 842
    1968 election and, 868–869, 869(m)
Hundred Days (New Deal), 724–726
Hungary, 658, 789, 794, 796–797
hunter-gatherers, 6–7, 37
Huntington, Susan, 102
Hunt, Thomas, 309(i)
Huron Indians, 14, 45–46, 64–65
Hurston, Zora Neale, 690–691, 743
Husband, Herman, 130
Hus, Jan, 29
Hussein, King of Jordan, 797
Hussein, Saddam, 913, 915, 931, 935,
    942, 944
Hutcheson, Francis, 143
Hutchinson, Anne, 58–59
Hutchinson, Thomas, 141, 150, 154
hydrogen bomb, 791, 794. *See also*
    nuclear weapons

IBM corporation, 918
Ice Age, 6, 8(m)
Ickes, Harold, 722, 725, 730(m), 740
Idaho
    gold in, 475
    Japanese internment in, 765
    mining in, 477, 480, 511
idealism, 833
    progressive, 574–575
Illinois, 223–224
    Lincoln and, 393
    migration to, 296, 297(m)
    Mormons and, 351
    Northwest Ordinance and, 232(m)
    secession in, 401
    voting rights in, 252
Illinois Indians, 65
immigrants, 217, 338, 338(f), 401–402,
    601, 948. *See also* Chinese
        immigrants; German
        immigrants; immigration; Irish
        immigrants; migration
    Asian, 714, 828(f), 843–844, 920,
        937
    in British America, 103, 105
    Canadian, 288(m), 296
    as cheap labor, 498–499, 513
    in cities, 543, 543(i), 557–560, 920
    class distinctions and, 303, 311–312
    cultural conflict and, 681
    democracy and, 402
    Democratic Party and, 520–521,
        521(f), 718, 746
    deportation of, 711, 828, 947
    discrimination against, 691–692,
        843–844
    earliest, 6–7, 8(m)
    Eastern European, 843–844
    English, 29, 36–37, 40, 43, 48–50,
        56, 311, 477

European, 101–105, 107, 498–499,
    499(f), 558(m), 828(f)
    experience of, 686
    Filipino, 710, 828
    French Canadian, 288(m), 296
    hostility to, 924
    illegal, 685(i), 713
    Italian, 499–500, 557(i)
    Japanese, 480, 483, 682–683, 686, 828
    Jewish, 682–683, 920–921
    Know-Nothing Party and, 389
    Korean, 825, 828, 920, 920(i), 924
    Ku Klux Klan and, 447
    Latino, 828, 919–920
    legal, 828(f)
    Mexican, 478–480, 479(i), 480, 483,
        684, 685(i), 711–714, 919
    movies and, 675
    New Deal and, 739
    newspapers and, 559
    from New York City, 743(i)
    in New York City, 545, 581
    nineteenth century, 311, 477
    Norwegian, 465, 467(m)
    Patriot Act and, 946
    politics and, 691–692
    poverty of, 305, 311–312
    Puerto Rican, 683–684, 828
    Puritan, 56–58
    Red Scare and, 683
    South American, 684, 828(f), 844,
        937
    Southeast Asian, 828
    Swedish, 465, 499
    U.S. fear of anarchy and, 661
immigration
    to California, 686, 920, 924
    changing demographics and,
        919–921, 937
    Democratic Party and, 667
    to Florida, 920
    Great Depression and, 684
    to Hawaii, 479
    legislation on, 841(t), 843–844
    in 1920s, 670, 693
    in 1950s, 824–825, 828
    in 1990s, 914, 946
    opposition to, 924
    rates of, 684(f)
    restrictions on, 586, 667, 682–684
Immigration Act (1965), 843–844
Immigration and Naturalization
    Service (INS), 924, 947
immigration laws, 217–219, 230, 828(f)
    LBJ and, 843–844
    in 1950s, 825, 828
Immigration Restriction League, 586
impeachment
    Clinton, 931–932, 937, 948
    Johnson, 437–438, 932
    Nixon, 883

imperialism, U.S., 603–604, 618–622,
    622(m), 623(i)
    opposition to, 619–620, 624, 631
imports, 110, 127, 127(f), 290. *See also*
    boycotts; exports;
        nonimportation; trade, foreign
impoundment, meaning of, 880
impressment, 262. *See also* draft,
    military
In a Defiant Stance (Reed), 281
Inca civilization, 6, 25, 37
Incidents in the Life of a Slave Girl
    (Jacobs), 362
indentured servants, 36, 108, 136, 161,
    285
    in Chesapeake, 50, 52–56, 67
    children sold as, 103, 109
    laws against, 479
    replaced by slaves, 56, 160(f)
Independence, Missouri, 373
Independent Order of Good Templars,
    358
Independent Treasury Act (1840),
    333–334
India, 17–18, 22, 22(m), 943
    as British colony, 124–125, 134(m),
        150
    immigrants from, 920
    Protestant mission in, 275(m)
    WWII and, 771, 773
Indiana, 224
    Ku Klux Klan in, 684
    migration to, 227, 296, 297(m)
    Northwest Ordinance and, 232(m)
    revivals in, 276, 310
    Shakers in, 277
Indian Affairs, Bureau of, 829
Indian Affairs, Office of, 469, 471–472
Indian Confederation, 237
Indian Ocean, 22
Indian Removal Act (1830), 326,
    328(i), 339
Indian Reorganization Act (1934), 740
Indian reservations. *See* Native
    Americans, reservation system
        and
Indian Rights Association, 472
Indian Self-Determination Act (1974),
    895
indigo, 99, 127, 265(m)
individualism, 342–346, 594
    big business and, 669
    democratic, 423
    Great Depression and, 700–701, 715
    ideology of, 518–519
    Kaiser and, 757
    mass production and, 671
    meaning of, 342
    Mormons and, 350, 352
    in movies, 706
    1928 election and, 692

Prohibition and, 688
technology and, 680
transcendentalism and, 342–344
Utopian communalism and,
 345–349
Indochina, 794. *See also* Cambodia;
 Vietnam
France in, 850, 877
Japanese invasion of, 753
Indonesia, 17, 22, 22(*m*), 134(*m*)
Industrialism, Age of, 632
industrialization, 409, 411(*i*). *See also*
 factory system; manufacturing;
 mills
accumulation of wealth and,
 518–519
artisans and, 292–293, 293(*i*), 296,
 303, 313
environmental pollution and, 485(*i*)
health and, 343(*f*)
immigrant labor and, 498–499
integrated systems within, 487–488,
 491, 493–494, 497, 513
intellectual life and, 689
in late nineteenth century, 457,
 485–505, 485(*i*), 487(*i*), 489(*i*)
living standards and, 343(*f*)
market economy and, 311, 313
middle class and, 552–553
mining and, 477, 483
in New South, 495–497, 496(*m*)
1928 election and, 692
Republican Party and, 389
reversal of, 886–887
robber barons and, 492–493
skills for, 498, 501
traditional values and, 681
transcendentalism and, 343, 346
unemployment and, 296
urbanization and, 302–303, 302(*m*),
 544–545, 571, 601
U.S. dominance and, 904
voting patterns and, 692
working conditions and, 342
Industrial Revolution, 170, 331, 338
in America, 285–296, 313
in Britain, 488
in England, 127, 242, 285
labor for, 285(*i*), 286, 288(*m*),
 289–291, 290(*i*)
political parties and, 317
social structure and, 286, 303–307,
 304(*i*), 313
U.S. Patent Office and, 292
industrial unionism, 732–733. *See also*
 labor unions
Industrial Workers of the World
 (IWW; Wobblies), 512–513, 655,
 661
industry
decline of, 886–887

development of, 594, 818
employment in, 817
gender roles in, 704
Great Depression and, 697, 718
growth of, 604, 631
interstate highways and, 820(*m*)
labor unions and, 732–733
managerial revolution and, 670
Mexican Americans in, 711
New Deal and, 724–725
new techniques in, 668
pollution and, 666(*i*)
postwar, 817–818
product standardization in, 667
wage and price controls in, 667
inflation, 34(*f*), 35, 37, 797
during American Revolution, 186
in Confederacy, 412–413
energy crisis and, 884
excess of currency and, 175, 191
federal government and, 880
housing and, 884–885
in 1920s, 668
1960–2000, 885(*f*)
in 1970s, 899, 905
postwar, 817
Reagan and, 908–909
Roosevelt recession and, 732
Savings and Loan crisis and, 912
WWII and, 755, 759
The Influence of Seapower upon History
 (Mahan), 608
influenza, 25
1918–1919 epidemic of, 644, 645(*i*)
Ingersoll, Jared, 142
Ingraham, Elizabeth Mary Meade, 416
inheritance, 58, 104, 131, 256, 303
marriage and, 103, 255
primogeniture and, 257
women's rights to, 253–255
In His Steps (Sheldon), 566
Inquisition, 22
In Re Jacobs (1885), 519
installment plans, 673–674, 702. *See
 also* credit
Institutes of the Christian Religion
 (Calvin), 29
Inter-American Treaty of Reciprocal
 Assistance (Rio Treaty; 1947),
 795(*m*)
Internal Revenue Service (IRS), 882.
 See also taxation
International Bank for Reconstruction
 and Development (World Bank),
 816
International Criminal Court, 941
internationalism, 750, 762. *See also*
 globalization; isolationism
economic, 784, 816
International Labor Defense (ILD),
 708

International Longshoremen's and
 Warehousemen's Union (ILWU),
 713
International Migration Society, 533
International Monetary Fund (IMF),
 816
international relations, 622–626, 644,
 662–663, 940. *See also under
 particular countries*
cold war, 794–797, 795(*m*)
economic, 670, 672–673
overseas bases and, 608, 631
International Telephone and Telegraph
 Corporation, 670, 816
Internet, 811, 918–919
economy and, 917
Microsoft and, 923
Interstate Commerce Commission
 (ICC), 595
segregation and, 838
Interstate Highway Act (1956),
 803–804
Intolerable Acts (1774), 151
Inuit Indians, 7
Iowa, 296, 297(*m*), 383
Iran, 785, 796, 942–943
modernization in, 899
oil production in, 884, 902
revolution in, 884, 899, 905, 943
shah of, 899, 902
Iran-Contra affair, 909, 912
Iranian hostage crisis, 902–904, 902(*i*),
 905
1980 election and, 903
Reagan and, 908
Iraq, 937, 942
Congress and, 944
invasion of Kuwait by, 915
oil production in, 884
Persian Gulf War and (1990–1991),
 876, 913–914, 916(*m*), 943
preemptive strike against, 943(*i*)
UN sanctions against, 931, 935
Ireland, 73, 154
famine in, 311, 498, 564
Ireland, John, 563
Irish immigrants, 109–110, 217, 338,
 389. *See also* Scots-Irish
cultural conflict and, 311–313
Democratic Party and, 521, 521(*f*),
 564
1852 election and, 388(*i*)
nineteenth century, 288(*m*),
 296–298, 298(*i*), 303, 309,
 479–480, 498–499, 564
Irish Test Act (1704), 110
Iron Act (1750), 72(*t*)
iron industry, 287(*t*), 292, 300, 502(*i*),
 505, 513
coal in, 544
in Great Britain, 457

iron industry *(Continued)*:
  steel and, 486, 487*(m)*, 488, 496*(m)*
  tariffs on, 290, 319
Ironworkers—Noontime (painting),
    502*(i)*
Iroquois Indians, 6, 63–66, 121, 123, 131
  adopted captives of, 65
  "covenant chain" of military
    alliances, 76
  Five Nations of, 12, 45, 64–65, 76,
    170, 172–173, 177*(m)*, 222–224
  French and, 65, 76
  fur trade wars of, 47, 65
irrigation, 9, 11, 86–87
  water resources and, 466, 478, 482
Irving, Washington, 260
Isabella, queen of Spain
    (r. 1474–1516), 22, 24, 29, 29*(t)*
Islam, 22, 939*(i)*
  African American, 861
  vs. Christianity, 17–18, 20, 28
  fundamentalist, 899, 901, 905, 912,
    915, 916*(m)*, 941, 943
  slavery and, 87
isolationism, 604, 606, 630
  opposition to, 752–753
  post-WWI, 672–673
  Republican Party and, 762
  retreat from, 751–753
  WWII and, 750, 777
Israel, 939*(i)*
  Camp David accords and, 901–902,
    901*(i)*, 905
  in international politics, 884
  in Lebanon, 912
  oil embargo and, 884
  Palestinians and, 796, 916*(m)*, 929,
    936, 942–943, 944*(i)*
  West Bank and, 942
Issei (first-generation Japanese
    Americans), 765
Isthmus of Darien (Panama), 24
It (film), 678–679
Italian Americans
  in WWII, 765
Italian Revolution (1848), 344*(i)*, 345
Italy, 19, 37, 638
  fall of, 770
  invasion of Ethiopia by, 750
  migration from, 499–500, 557*(i)*
  Revolution in (1848), 345
  Spanish civil war and, 751
  Washington Naval Arms
    Conference and, 673
  WWII and, 750, 754, 768*(m)*, 777
It's News to Me (TV show), 802
I've Got a Secret (TV show), 802
Iwo Jima, 772–773, 773*(m)*
IWW. *See* Industrial Workers of the
    World
Izard, Ralph, 183

Jackson, Andrew (1829–1836)
  abolitionism and, 357
  American System and, 320–321,
    325, 328, 330
  antimonopoly policies of, 328
  Democratic Party and, 317, 333
  election of 1824 and, 317–318,
    318*(m)*, 339
  election of 1828, 320–321, 321*(i)*,
    339
  election of 1844 and, 375
  freemasonry and, 331
  Harrison and, 335
  inauguration of, 322
  Indian Removal Act of, 326,
    328*(m)*, 339
  as military commander, 238*(m)*,
    239–240, 249, 383*(i)*
  Native Americans and, 320, 326
  nullification and, 320–323, 323*(i)*,
    331, 399–400
  as president (1829–1837), 293,
    321–331, 330*(i)*, 372
  on religion in public life, 452
  Second Bank and, 324–326, 326*(i)*,
    337
  on states' rights, 323, 328
  Supreme Court and, 328–329
Jackson, Helen Hunt, 472, 481
Jackson, Jesse, 911
Jackson, Michael, 917
Jackson, Patrick Tracy, 290
Jackson, Rebecca Cox, 347
Jackson, Thomas J. ("Stonewall"),
    403–405
Jackson, William Henry, 546*(i)*
Jacksonian Democrats, 317
Jackson State College, killing at, 870
Jacobins, 213
Jacobs, Harriet, 362
Jamaica, 79
James, duke of York, 70, 99
James, Frank, 401
James, Henry, 569
James I, king of England
    (r. 1603–1625), 48, 56
James II, king of England
    (r. 1685–1688), 73–74, 99, 140
James, Jesse, 401
James River, 49, 179, 403, 411*(i)*
Jamestown, 40*(t)*, 43, 48–49, 56
James, William, 574, 620–621
Japan, 22, 387, 607
  automobile industry in, 884
  containment of, 673
  defeat of, 784
  economic growth of, 915, 917
  economic recovery of, 904
  Germany and, 751
  invasion of China by, 750, 753
  invasion of Manchuria by, 750

  mass transit in, 547
  oil embargo vs., 884
  Pearl Harbor and, 753–754
  vs. postwar U.S., 816
  Soviet Union and, 768
  surrender of, 776
  U.S. relations with, 627–628, 631,
    714
  Washington Naval Arms
    Conference and, 673
  WWII and, 746, 749–750, 770–773,
    776–777
Japanese Americans
  Great Depression and, 714
  internment of, 750, 765–767, 766*(i)*,
    766*(m)*, 777
  Issei (first-generation), 765
  Nisei (second-generation), 765
  WWII and, 777
Jaramillo, Juan, 31
Jay, John (1745–1829), 316
  The Federalist and, 182–183, 198,
    201
Jay's Treaty (1795), 214–215, 224
jazz, 677, 677*(i)*, 680, 690, 825
Jazz Age (1920s), 677, 693, 695
The Jazz Singer (film), 676–677
Jefferson, Thomas (1743–1826), 88,
    155, 161, 295, 336
  agrarian vision of, 212–214, 328
  as Anti-Federalist, 281
  Bill for Establishing Religious
    Freedom (1786), 190
  Constitution and, 233
  death of, 251
  Declaration of Independence and,
    169–170, 184, 188, 280
  as diplomat, 202
  on education, 259, 261
  Embargo act and, 234
  Enlightenment and, 143
  First Bank and, 146
  Hamilton and, 210–211, 212*(i)*, 218
  on John Q. Adams, 319
  on manufacturing, 292, 295
  on Missouri crisis, 269, 272
  Mormons and, 351
  new Republican Party and, 388
  Northwest Ordinance and, 198, 200,
    212
  as president (1801–1809), 222,
    230–234
  primacy of statute law and, 247
  republicanism and, 217, 219, 277
  Revolution of 1800 and, 230
  rights and, 160, 188
  as Secretary of State, 209
  slavery and, 189, 212, 352
  states' rights and, 218
  technology and, 214
  the West and, 231, 241, 249

Jefferson Airplane, 860
Jeffords, Jim, 935
Jenkins' Ear, War of (1740), 75(*t*), 95–96
Jenney, William, 547
Jennings, Dr. Samuel, 256
Jericho, Israel, 929
Jerome, Chauncey, 285–286
Jeske, Mary, 83
Jesuits, 42–43, 47, 65–67
Jewett, William S., 375(*i*)
Jewish Daily Forward, 559
    bintel brief (bundle of letters) of, 561
Jews, 22, 28, 447, 557–558, 562
    discrimination against, 691, 727, 750, 761, 818
    Holocaust and, 770–771
    immigration of, 920–921
    immigration restrictions and, 682–683
    Ku Klux Klan and, 684
    Nazi view of, 750
    in New Deal, 723
    1936 election and, 729
    in 1950s, 822
    Scottsboro case and, 709
    in Soviet Union, 900
    voting rights and, 935
    Yiddish theater and, 559
Jiang Jieshi (Chiang Kai-shek), 791
jihad, meaning of, 915
Jim Crow laws, 381, 529–531, 668, 863
jingoism, 612–615
Job Corps, 845
Joffre, Joseph, 643
Johnson, Andrew (1808–1875)
    Fourteenth Amendment and, 436
    impeachment of, 437–438, 932
    Ku Klux Klan and, 447
    as Lincoln's running mate, 424
    as president (1865–1869), 430–438
    Reconstruction plan of, 430–431, 431(*i*), 434–436, 442, 451
    veto of civil rights bill by, 435
    veto of Reconstruction Act by, 437
Johnson, Earvin "Magic," 925
Johnson, Gabriel, 95
Johnson, Hiram W., 584, 659
Johnson, Lady Bird, 843
Johnson, Lyndon B. (1908–1973), 830, 847
    affirmative action and, 892
    civil rights movement and, 842
    credibility gap of, 883
    federal power and, 816
    Great Society of, 840–846, 849, 859, 876
    Mexican Americans and, 713
    as president (1963–1969), 840–846, 852–854

    tax cuts and, 835
    Vietnam policy of, 852–854, 854(*f*), 858–859, 867–869, 877
Johnson, Samuel, 160, 187
Johnson, Sir William, 123
Johnston, Albert Sidney, 406
Johnston, Joseph E., 421
Johnston, Joshua, 268
Jolson, Al, 676
Jones, Absalom, 270
Jones, Bobby, 680
Jones, Jacqueline, 704
Jones, Joe, 708(*i*)
Jones, Nathaniel, 165
Jones, Paula, 932
Jones Act (1916; 1917), 621, 683
Jordan, 796–797
Jordan, Winthrop, 160
Joseph, Chief (Mohawk chief). *See* **Brant, Joseph**
Joseph, chief of Nez Percé, 470, 470(*m*)
Josephson, Matthew, 492
journalism, 568–569. *See also* mass media
    national culture and, 680
    photo, 745
    reform, 575–576
    sensationalist, 612–615, 612(*i*), 613(*i*)
    yellow, 569
Journey to Pennsylvania (Mettelberger), 109
Joyce, Cornet George, 142
J.P. Morgan & Co., 491
Judaism, 562. *See also* Jews
judicial review, 218, 246, 248
    meaning of, 230
judiciary, 194, 436. *See also* common law; court system; law; Supreme Court
    on rights of private property, 519
    trial by jury and, 137, 140–141, 143, 210, 268
Judiciary Act
    of 1789, 209
    of 1801, 230
Judson, Edward Zane Carroll. *See* **Buntline, Ned**
Julian, George, 436
July Fourth, 251, 251(*i*)
    Lincoln's speech on, 402–403
The Jungle (Sinclair), 595
the Junta (Cuban exiles), 612
Justice Department, U.S., 928, 946
    Microsoft and, 923
    secret deportation hearings of, 947
juvenile delinquency, 750
    music and, 825–826
    WWII and, 764–765

Kaiser, Henry J., 755, 756(*i*)
    biographical information, 756–757
Kaiser Corporation, 764
Kaiser Permanente Medical Care Program, 757
kamikaze missions, 772
Kansas, 40, 237
    abolitionism in, 368
    admission of, 391
    African American exodus to, 465
    "Bleeding Kansas," 389–390, 389(*i*), 392(*m*), 395
    conflict over slavery and, 462
    drought in, 709
    popular sovereignty in, 386(*m*)
Kansas City, 461, 549
Kansas City Independent, 656
Kansas-Nebraska Act (1854), 386(*m*), 387–391, 393
Kansas Pacific Railroad, 460(*i*), 462
Kant, Immanuel, 342
Kashmir, 943
Kasich, John, 931(*i*)
Kawai, Kazuo, 686
Kearney, Denis, 480
Kearney, Stephen, 378(*m*)
Keaton, Buster, 676
Keegan, John, 767
Kelley, Abby, 357
Kelley, Fanny, 459
Kelley, Florence, 577–578
Kelley, Oliver H., 468
Kellogg-Briand Peace Pact (1928), 673
Kellor, Frances, 581(*i*)
    biographical information, 580–581
Kemp, Jack, 930
Kempe, John Tabor, 186–187
Kendall, Amos, 321
Kendall, Keziah, 363
Kennan, George F., 785, 787(*i*), 790
    biographical information, 786–787
    containment theory of, 786
    and Joseph Stalin, 787
Kennedy, Anthony, 909
Kennedy, Edward, 874
Kennedy, Jacqueline, 840
Kennedy, John Fitzgerald (1917–1963), 787, 830(*i*), 847
    assassination of, 839–840, 852, 860, 948
    civil rights and, 838
    domestic policies of, 834–836
    federal power and, 816
    foreign policy of, 831–834
    Mexican Americans and, 713, 863
    as president (1961–1963), 830–840
    Vietnam policy and, 851–852, 856, 877
Kennedy, Robert F., 838, 863
    assassination of, 868, 868(*i*), 869(*m*), 877

Kennesaw Mountain, battle of, 421
Kent State University, killings at, 870
Kentucky, 225, 229
    migration from, 296, 297(m)
    revivals in, 273, 275(i)
    secession in, 401, 405
    Shakers in, 277
    slavery in, 262, 272(m)
Kentucky Resolution (1798), 281
Kenyon, Cecilia, 280
Kerner Commission. See National
    Advisory Commission (1968)
Kerouac, Jack, 825
Kessler-Harris, Alice, 778
Keun, Odette, 742
Keynes, John Maynard, 732, 755, 797,
    799
Khomeini, Ayatollah Ruhollah, 902
Khrushchev, Nikita, 815, 833
Kickapoo Indians, 65
Kim Il Sung, 791–792
King, Charles Bird, 328(i)
King, Larry, 923
King, Martin Luther, Jr. (1929–1968),
    805–806, 836, 838–839, 839(i),
    840, 846
    assassination of, 862, 868, 877
    in Montgomery, 806(i)
    philosophy of, 861, 863
King, Mary, 866
King Philip's War (Metacom's
    Rebellion), 63, 63(i), 67
King, Rodney, 924
King George's War (War of the
    Austrian Succession;
    1740–1748), 75(t), 97
King's Canyon National Park, 482
King's College. See Columbia
    University
King's Mountain, South Carolina, 179
King William's War (War of the League
    of Augsburg; 1689–1697), 75(t)
Kiowa Indians, 459, 470(m)
Kissinger, Henry, 881, 899
    Iran and, 902
    Vietnam cease-fire agreement and,
        870, 872–873
"kitchen debate" (Nixon-Khrushchev),
    815
Kline, Dave, 854–855
Knickerbocker Trust Company, 599
Knights of Labor, 506–509, 506(i), 513
Knowland, William S., 791
Know-Nothing (American) Party,
    388–391, 388(i), 392(m), 395
Knox, Henry, 201, 209, 222
Knox, John, 32
Knox, William, 136
Kodak, 606
Koehler, Karl, 758(i)
Kongo, Africa, 89

Konvitz, Milton R., 453
Kopay, David, 895
Korea. See also North Korea; South
    Korea
    immigrants from, 825, 828, 920,
        920(i), 924
    Japanese and Chinese claims to, 607
    thirty-eighth parallel in, 791–794,
        793(m)
Korean War (1950–1953), 791–794,
    792(i), 793(m), 797
    beginning of, 791–792, 799
    defense spending and, 755(f)
    end of, 794, 801
    impact of, 794, 801
    public support in U.S. for, 793, 802
    veterans of, 762
Korematsu v. United States (1944), 767
Kosovo, 931–932, 932(m)
Krimmel, J., 251(i)
Ku Klux Klan, 445–449, 445(i), 447(i),
    530(i), 805
    civil rights movement and, 840
    Democratic Party and, 667
    leader of, 446–447
    1920s revival of, 684–686, 685(m)
    Reconstruction and, 589
    terrorism of, 445–448
    women in, 687(i)
Ku Klux Klan Act (1871), 438(t)
    failure to enforce, 445, 448–449
Kuwait, 943
    Iraq's invasion of, 915
    oil production in, 884
    Persian Gulf War and, 913,
        916(m)
Kyoto accord (1997), 927, 941

labor. See also indentured servants;
    labor unions; slavery
    Adamson eight-hour law for, 600
    antiunion movement and, 650
    capital and, 331, 485–513
    division of, 286–288, 287(i)
    forced, 44, 443
    free black, 298(i), 434, 435(i)
    gang, 342, 368, 434, 442–443
    Industrial Revolution and, 285(i),
        286, 288(m), 289–291, 290(i)
    manufacturing and, 290, 303, 312
    overseas, 887
    sex-typing and, 499–500, 500(i),
        513
    shortage of, 766
    systematic control of, 502–505
    wage, 331, 370, 434, 435(i), 442–444
    welfare system and, 778
    work week and, 670, 680, 820
    in WWII, 759–760
    yellow-dog contracts and, 509

laborers
    Chinese, 710
    education for, 259
    factory, 587(i)
    farm, 103, 290–291, 778–779
    Jewish garment, 502, 509
    as journeymen, 292–293
    Mexican, 478–480, 479(i), 483,
        710–711, 713, 929
    migrant, 478–480, 479(i), 483,
        710–711, 713, 825–826, 828, 863
    Pietism and, 112, 114
    railroad, 600
    rights of, 293, 332–333
    as Sons of Liberty, 142, 150
    urbanization and, 305, 311, 313
    women, 285(i), 296, 704, 759, 779,
        823(i), 824
Labor's Nonpartisan League, 734
labor theory of value, 296
labor unions, 296, 505–513, 587, 802.
    See also strikes
    African Americans in, 507
    Amalgamated Association of Iron
        and Steel Workers, 510
    American Federation of Labor, 509,
        586–587
    arbitration and, 507(i)
    Asian Americans in, 714
    Brotherhood of Locomotive
        Firemen, 507(i), 511
    in California, 480
    closed-shop agreements and,
        332–333
    collective bargaining and, 510, 513
    communism and, 800
    decline of, 916
    Democratic Party and, 746, 762,
        881, 933
    emergence of, 292–293, 313, 332, 505
    employer attacks on, 660–661
    in Germany, 750
    identification with radicals of, 660
    immigration and, 684
    industrial, 511
    Mexican Americans and, 711–714,
        863
    in mining industry, 477
    movie industry and, 675
    NAFTA and, 929
    need for, 504
    New Deal and, 725, 728, 732–734,
        747
    1936 election and, 729
    1980 election and, 903
    1984 election and, 909
    in 1990s, 915
    Panic of 1837 and, 333, 339
    Populist Party and, 536
    post-WWI antiunion movement
        and, 650, 660–661, 661(i)

Progressive Party and, 667
public image of, 660
reform and, 336, 505–506, 513, 574
seniority systems in, 732
strength of, 649–650, 817, 817(f)
in Sun Belt, 887
utopian reformers and, 579, 579(i)
wages and, 759
welfare capitalism and, 670
women in, 507, 714
working hours and, 293, 333, 508, 600
WWII and, 759–760, 777
Laclotte, Jean Hyacinthe de, 239(i)
Ladies' Home Journal, 553, 665(i), 680, 704(i)
Lafayette, marquis de, 178(m), 179, 179(i), 207, 336
La Follette, Robert M., 574, 583–584, 583(i), 586–587, 591, 596, 601, 659, 667
Lake Champlain, 63, 126
battle of, 239
Lake Erie, 235
Lake Texcoco, 9
Lamparde, William, 36
Lancaster, Ohio, 422
Lancaster, Pennsylvania, 91, 244
Lancaster Turnpike Company, 244
Lance, Bert, 899
land
grants of, 104, 123, 128
ownership of, 432, 434, 443–444.
See also freehold society;
property rights
policies on, 44, 49–50, 54, 60–61
sales of, 231(t)
taxation of, 369
Land Acts (1796 and 1820), 231
land banks, 98
land grants
for railroads, 460, 488
from Spain, 478
Landon, Alfred M., 729
Lane, Dutton, 121
Lange, Dorothea, 709(i), 745, 745(i)
Lanham Act (1940), 759
Lansing, John, 202–203
Laos
immigrants from, 920
Vietnam War and, 851(m), 853, 872, 876
Larcom, Lucy, 290–291
Larkin, Thomas O., 377
Larkin, Thomas Oliver, 374
La Salle, Robert de, 47
Latin America. *See* South America
Latinos
affirmative action and, 896–897, 925
in cattle industry, 464, 464(i)

culture of, 481
increase of, 921, 921(m)
intermarriage of, 924
Korean immigrants and, 920(i)
migration to cities of, 829, 847
migratory work and, 478
national culture and, 676(i)
political activism of, 713
race riots and, 924
in Southwest, 474, 478–479, 479(i), 483
on television, 822
in Texas, 478–479
voting districts and, 881
women, 916
youth gangs of, 765
Latter-day Saints, Church of Jesus
Christ of. *See* Mormons
Latvia, 658
Laud, William, 56, 59
Laurens, Henry, 185
law, 845. *See also* common law; court
system; immigration laws;
judiciary; Supreme Court
anti-immigrant, 686
antilynching, 668
antimiscegenation, 82
antitrust, 586, 592–596, 599, 648, 666, 725, 755, 923
blue, 521, 539
child labor, 577, 597, 600
DNA and, 918
eight-hour, 600
equality before, 432, 436
experience and, 574
homestead, 464
inheritance, 58
international, 941
Jim Crow, 381, 529–531, 668, 863
minimum wage, 577, 583, 597, 799, 803, 930
Nuremberg, 769
right-to-work, 798
statute, 247
The Law of Civilization and Decay
(B. Adams), 609
Lawrence, Kansas, 389
Lawrence, William, 518
lawyers, 143, 252, 253(t), 538
Lay, Kenneth, 945
lead mining, 477
lead poisoning, 588
League of Armed Neutrality, 182
League of Nations, 655, 658–660, 663, 785, 795(m)
Democratic Party and, 666
U.S. and, 659–660, 673
WWII and, 750
League of United Latin American
Citizens (LULAC), 713, 760
League of Women Voters, 668

Leahy, William D., 774
Leary, Timothy, 860
Lease, Mary Elizabeth, 536, 537(i)
Leave It to Beaver (TV program), 822
Leaves of Grass (Whitman), 345
Lebanon, 797, 909
Israeli invasion of, 912
Lecompton constitution (Kansas), 391
Lee, Anna, 802
Lee, Arthur, 168, 175
Lee, Charles, 210
Lee, Mother Ann, 277
Lee, Richard Henry, 169, 187
Lee, Robert E.
black soldiers and, 425
Gettysburg and, 415
Grant and, 419, 421(m)
invasion of North by, 404–405, 417(m)
Lincoln and, 401
in Mexican War, 379
surrender of, 421(m), 426, 430
Union advance on Richmond and, 427
Leeward Islands, 79
Legal Services Program, 845
Legal Tender Act (1862), 412
Leggett, William, 332
Leisler, Jacob, 75
Leisler's revolt (1689), 130
leisure, 566–569, 566(i), 568(i)
automobile and, 665(i), 675
consumerism and, 673
in Great Depression, 707
mass media and, 568–569, 569(f) 675–681
national culture and, 680
in 1920s, 665, 670, 693
Lemke, William, 729
Lend-Lease Act (1941), 752(m), 753
Lenglen, Suzanne, 680
Lenin, Vladimir Ilych, 644
Leningrad, Soviet Union, 768(m)
Lenroot, Katherine, 779
Leo X, Pope (1513–1521), 29
Le Paon, J. B., 179(i)
lesbians, 888, 893–894
LeSueur, Meridel, 699
Le Temps (newspaper), 622
Letters from a Farmer in Pennsylvania
(Dickenson), 146
Letters from an American Farmer
(Crèvecoeur), 252
Levant Company (Turkey), 34
Levelers, Christian, 161
Levitt, Arthur, 817
Levittown, Long Island, 818, 818(i)
Lewinsky, Monica, 932
Lewis, Benjamin, 419
Lewis, John (civil rights movement), 839, 935

Lewis, John L. (labor movement), 733, 759–760

Lewis, Maureen, 946

Lewis, Meriwether, 233, 233(i), 234(m)

Lewis, Sinclair, 690

Lexington, battle of (1775), 133(i), 155(t), 157(i), 158–159, 180, 185, 234

Lexington, Massachusetts, 180, 185

Leyte Gulf, Battle of, 772

Libby, Owen, 208(m)

liberalism, 330, 849, 876
    in cities, 668
    Fair Deal, 799
    New Deal and, 742
    1970s activism and, 897
    postwar coalition of, 816
    role of the state and, 799
    urban, 584–586, 601

Liberal Republican Party, 449, 451

The Liberator (newspaper), 354–355, 358

Liberia, Africa, 262, 533, 737

Liberty League, 726

liberty of contract, 574

Liberty Party, 357, 365, 376, 379

libraries, public, 707

Libya, 912

Lieberman, Joseph, 452, 933

Life magazine, 623(i), 745

The Life of George Washington (Weems), 260

Liliuokalani, queen of Hawaii (r. 1891–1893), 605

Limerick, Patricia Nelson, 633

Lincoln, Abraham (1809–1865), 393(i), 405(i), 738, 918. See also Civil War; Emancipation Proclamation
    assassination of, 430, 451
    debates with Douglas of, 393
    early life of, 391–393
    1864 campaign of, 424, 438
    election (1860) of, 392(m), 394–395, 398, 427
    Grant and, 407, 418
    national mercantilism under, 409
    Reconstruction and, 430
    Republican Party and, 389, 391–394
    Sherman and, 423
    slavery and, 394, 398
    the South and, 397
    speeches of, 393, 399, 402–403, 429
    suspension of habeas corpus by, 407
    Union victory and, 417–427, 451

Lincoln, Benjamin, 176(i), 179

Lincoln, Mary Todd, 392

Lincoln Brigade, American, 751

Lindbergh, Charles, 680–683, 683(i), 752

Lindgren, Ida, 465–466

Lindsey, Ben, 656

Lin, Maya Ling, 873(i)

Lisbon, Portugal, 22

literacy, 353, 389
    voting rights and, 529, 842

literature
    anti-slavery, 362, 370, 386, 387(i)
    cultural dissent and, 825
    documentary, 745
    genteel tradition in, 570
    modernist, 689
    New Deal and, 747
    in 1920s, 688–691
    republican, 260–261
    transcendental, 344–345

Lithuania, 658

Little Big Horn, Battle of (1876), 463, 471

Little Richard, 827

Little Rock, Arkansas, 805

Little Round Top, 415

Little Turtle (Miami chief), 223

living standards, 229, 342, 343(f), 784
    decline of, 884
    Great Society and, 846
    improved nutrition and, 815(i)
    postwar, 815, 817

Livingston family, 105, 128

Livingston, Robert, 169(i), 231, 233

Lloyd, Harold, 676

Lloyd, Henry Demarest, 575

Lochner v. New York (1905), 574, 578(t)

Locke, Alain, 690

Locke, John, 74, 112–113, 117, 188, 191, 258–259
    on natural rights, 113, 143, 184

Loco-Foco (Equal Rights) Party, 332

Lodge, Henry Cabot, 608, 613, 616, 618, 659

Lodge, Henry Cabot, Jr., 852

log cabin campaign (1840), 335(i), 339

Lombroso, Cesare, 580

London, England, 14, 98

London Times (newspaper), 622

Long, Huey, 726–727, 734(m), 747
    assassination of, 727(i), 729
    New Deal and, 728

Long, Stephen H., 369, 460

Long Island, New York, 48, 75, 820
    battle of, 171, 185
    Levittown in, 818, 818(i)

Longstreet, James, 415

Looking Backward (Bellamy), 575

Look magazine, 745

Lorentz, Pare, 745

Los Alamos, New Mexico, 775

Los Angeles, California
    automobile in, 821
    Latino immigrants in, 828
    movie industry in, 675

population in, 477(m)
real estate boom in, 481
riots in, 836(m), 861, 862(m), 924, 924(i)
youth gangs in, 765

lost colony. *See* Roanoke

Lost Horizon (Hilton), 707

Lott, Trent, 798(m)

Louisbourg, siege of (1745), 97, 123(i), 125

Louisiana, 11, 430
    Acadians in, 124
    admission to Union, 241, 262
    as French colony, 13, 47, 67
    migration to, 226, 226(m), 296, 297(m)
    Napoleon and, 184(m), 231
    Republican government in, 449–451
    slavery in, 263, 265, 265(m), 272(m), 424
    as Spanish colony, 125, 198
    voting rights in, 316

Louisiana Military Seminary, 422

Louisiana Purchase (1803), 222, 231, 233, 234(m), 240(m)
    slavery and, 271(m), 279, 383, 387–388
    Texas and, 241, 369

Louisville, Kentucky, 298(m), 300(m), 301(m), 302, 302(m)

Louis XIV, king of France (r. 1643–1715), 47, 73, 95

Louis XVI, king of France (r. 1774–1792), 175, 179, 207
    execution of, 213, 217

Loutherbourg, Philip Makes de, 215(i)

L'Ouverture, Toussaint, 231

Love, William T., 890

Love Canal, 888, 890–891

Love Canal Homeowners Association (LCHA), 890–891

Lovejoy, Elijah P., 357

Low, Thomas, 260

Lowell, Francis Cabot, 290

Lowell, Josephine Shaw, 577

Lowell, Massachusetts, 285(i), 290–291, 296, 302

Loyalists, 152, 155–157, 168
    British strategies and, 177
    emigration of, 186–187, 186(i), 191
    vs. Patriots, 165, 167, 169–170, 174
    strongholds of, 170(m)

Loyalists, Spanish, 751

loyalty oaths, 800, 813

Lubow, Miriam, 922

Luce, Henry R., 756, 791

"The Luck of Roaring Camp" (Harte), 481

Ludlow, Noah M. (1795–1886), 229

lumber industry, 137, 287(t)

in New South, 496–497, 496(m)
in Pacific Northwest, 477
Lundy, Benjamin, 354
Lutheranism, 272, 273(t)
    in colonial America, 105, 107, 109,
        111, 112(m), 119(f), 119(t)
Luther, Martin, 28–29, 115, 118
Luxembourg, 752
Luzon (Philippines), 618
lynching, 708(i), 709, 806
    laws against, 668
    New Deal and, 735
    in New South, 530–534, 531(i),
        532(i)
Lynd, Helen Merrell, 665, 702
Lynd, Robert, 665, 702
Lynn, Massachusetts, 242

McAdoo, William, 647
MacAllister, Alexander, 101
McAllister, Ward, 551–552
MacArthur, Douglas (1897–1978),
        791–792
    Bonus Army and, 717
    Truman and, 793–794
    in WWII, 771
McCarran-Walter Act (1952), 828
McCarthy, Eugene, 867–868
McCarthy, Joseph R., 799–801, 813
    censure of, 801
McCarthyism, 787, 799
McClellan, George B., 401, 403,
        405, 424
McClure's magazine, 575–576
McColl, Ada, 468(i)
McCormick and Hussey, 300, 508
McCormick, Cyrus, 288, 303
McCulloch v. Maryland (1819), 246,
        248
McDonald's, 821
McDougall, Alexander, 142
McDowell, Gary L., 280
McDowell, Irwin, 403
McGovern, George, 881
    1968 election, 868–869, 869(m)
McGready, James, 273
McGuire, Thomas B., 505
Machiavelli, Niccolò, 19
machinery, 287(t)
    as capital goods, 486
    interchangeable parts and, 285, 295
    tool making and, 292, 295
machinists, 498, 501, 503
McIlvaine, Bishop, 452
McKay, Claude, 690
McKim's Cotton Factory, 289
McKinley, William (1843–1901), 573,
        591–592, 595(i)
    1896 election and, 538–540, 539(i),
        540(m)

as president (1897–1901), 612,
        614–618, 620–622, 631
    war aims of, 616–617
McKinley Tariff (1890), 535, 538, 605
McNamara, Robert, 852, 856, 882
Macon, Nathaniel, 269
McPherson, Aimee Semple, 686
Macrae, David, 432
Madagascar, 79
Madero, Francisco, 628
Madeira Islands, 20, 22
Madison, James (1751–1836), 156,
        167, 201–202. *See also* Virginia
        Plan
    as Anti-Federalist, 281
    Bill of Rights and, 209–210, 235
    Bonus Bill and, 246, 319
    Embargo Act and, 234–235
    The Federalist and, 205
    First Bank and, 242
    on Hamilton's financial plan, 210,
        212
    Marbury case and, 230
    political theory of, 114
    as president (1809–1817), 230, 235,
        249
    religion and, 190
    Republican Party and, 219
    as secretary of state, 235
    unconstitutional laws and, 218
Madonna, 917
MAD (Mutually Assured Destruction)
        policy, 809
magazines, 575–576, 595, 623(i), 680,
        745, 889, 898
Maggie: Girl of the Streets (Crane), 570
Magna Charta, 143
Magnum, W. P., 331
Magruder, Jeb Stuart, 882
Mahan, Alfred T., 608, 611, 618,
        622, 631
Maine, 45, 48, 267, 347(i), 363
    admission as free state, 269, 272(m)
    Massachusetts and, 74
    peace movement in, 942(i)
    settlement of, 226
Maine (battleship), 613–615
Main Poc, 236
maize, 9, 12, 14–15, 20. *See also* corn
Malaya, 670, 771
Malaysia, 763
Malcolm, John, 142(i)
Malcolm X, 861
Malinche (Malinali, Marina), 31(i)
    biographical information, 30–31
management techniques, 668, 670
    scientific, 503–505, 513
Manassas Creek (Bull Run), 403–404
Manchester, England, 214–215
Manchuria, 750
Mandan Indians, 459–460, 470(m)

Mandela, Nelson, 930
Manhattan Island, 47. *See also* New
        York City
Manhattan Project, 775
Manifest Destiny, 368–376, 395, 609,
        631
Manifesto and Declaration of the
        Indians (Bacon), 56
Mann, Horace, 359
Mansfield, Sir James, 144
Mantrap (film), 678
manufacturing. *See also* factory system;
        industrialization; mills
    American System and, 318–319
    business elite and, 296, 303, 313
    distribution for, 491, 494–495, 513
    education and, 260
    energy for, 487–488, 513
    labor force for, 498–512, 498(f)
    mass production and, 502–505, 513
    in Midwest, 300, 302–303
    mining and, 477
    in Northeast, 285–292, 285(i),
        287(t)
    rural, 242
Manzanar (Japanese internment
        camp), 766(i)
Mao Zedong (Mao Tse-tung), 791, 851
Marbury v. Madison (1803), 230, 246
Marbury, William, 230
March on Washington (1963), 839
March on Washington (1941), 804
Marcus, Joe, 723
Marcy, William L., 321, 387
margin buying, meaning of, 697, 726
Marina. *See* **Malinche**
Marianas Islands, 617
Marine Corps Women's Reserve, 758
Marion, Francis (Swamp Fox), 176(i),
        179
market economy, 338
    big business and, 592
    class divisions and, 286, 303–306,
        304(i)
    expansion of, 296–303
    industrialization and, 311, 313
    laissez-faire, 574
    mass marketing and, 491, 494–495,
        495(i)
    trade with Native Americans and,
        460
Markham, Edwin, 656
Marlette, Doug, 894(i)
Marquette, Jacques, 47
marriage. *See also* women
    arranged, 103–104, 254
    companionate, 255
    complex, 349, 365
    divorce and, 255, 865
    domestic abuse and, 255
    dower right and, 104

marriage *(Continued)*:
equality within, 252, 254, 279
within ethnic group, 107, 109–111
farming's dual economy and, 465
Great Depression and, 702
inheritance and, 103–104, 253–255
interracial, 65*(i)*, 356, 398, 921, 924
in late twentieth century, 865
medieval, 16–17
in 1950s, 822
polygamous, 351–352, 365
republican, 253–255
slaves and, 266, 434
utopian communalism and, 336, 346–347
women's rights and, 358, 362, 705, 891, 893
marriage portion, 103
The Married Lady's Companion (Jennings), 256
Married Women's Property Acts (1839–1845), 363
Marshall, George C., 786, 788, 789*(i)*, 790
Marshall, John (1755–1835), 30, 233, 245–246, 245*(i)*, 246*(t)*, 249, 300. *See also* Supreme Court
on commerce clause, 329
death of, 328
Fletcher v. Peck (1810), 248
McCulloch v. Maryland (1819), 246, 248
Marbury v. Madison (1803), 230, 246
Native American cases and, 328
three principles of, 246
Marshall Islands, 772
Marshall Plan, 786, 788–789, 789*(i)*
Marshall, Thomas R., 597
Marshall, Thurgood, 804
Marshall, William, 83
Marsham, Richard, 82–83
Martí, José, 567, 609
Martineau, Harriet, 315
Martin, Henry Byam, 225*(i)*
Martinique, 125
Martin, Joseph J., 793
Martin, Josiah, 167
Marx Brothers, 706
Marx, Groucho, 706
Marxism, 511–512
Marx, Karl, 511
Mary II, queen of England (r. 1688–1694), 73, 75, 93
Maryland. *See also* Baltimore, Maryland
Catholicism in, 50, 74–75, 82*(i)*, 83
Civil War and, 401, 405, 424
claims to western lands and, 197–198
as colony, 50, 54, 56, 69*(i)*, 70, 73*(m)*, 75, 86
First Bank and, 246

land division in, 232*(m)*
law against miscegenation in, 82
ratification of Constitution and, 205
revolts in, 73*(m)*, 74, 99
Scots-Irish in, 110
slavery in, 56, 80, 84, 86, 160, 160*(f)*, 263
South Atlantic system and, 91
voting rights in, 252
wheat production in, 127
Maryland Gazette, 225, 259
masculinity
cult of, 554
politics and, 523
Mason, George, 161, 190, 204
Masons. *See* Freemasonry, Order of
Massachusetts
birth control in, 703
claims to Western lands, 197
lawyers in, 253*(t)*
1928 election and, 692
ratification convention in, 205
revivals in, 272
transportation in, 228
voting rights in, 316
War of 1812 and, 239
women in, 196, 363
Massachusetts Bay Colony, 73. *See also* Boston, Massachusetts
assembly of, 94
Dominion of New England and, 73
General Court of, 57, 134
government of, 56–58
House of Representatives in, 140, 157
inheritance law of, 58
land grants in, 104
Native American attacks on, 76
Navigation Acts and, 72–73
religious intolerance in, 57
revolts in, 74, 99
"taxation without representation" and, 137–138, 146–147, 150, 155*(t)*
Massachusetts Charter (1692), 144*(i)*
Massachusetts Gazette, 146
Massachusetts Spy, 150
Massacre of Saint George Fields, 148
Massatamohtnock. *See* **Opechancanough**
mass media. *See also* magazines; movies; newspapers; radio; television
cities and, 681
environmentalism and, 891
vs. feminism, 867, 925
Great Depression and, 702
Holocaust and, 770
Iranian hostage crisis and, 902
JFK's election and, 830

leisure and, 675–681
in 1920s, 693
1980 election and, 903
in 1990s, 917
mass production
of automobiles, 671, 675
big business and, 669
critique of, 671
in housing, 817–818
industrial expansion and, 668
Kaiser and, 757
in manufacturing, 502–505, 513
1920s and, 693
WWII and, 755–757
Mather, Cotton, 60, 112–113
matrilineal societies, 12, 14
Mattachine Society, 825
Maxim, Hiram, 639–640
Maximilian, Ferdinand, archduke of Mexico (r. 1864–1867), 604
Maxwell, Thompson, 153
Mayas, 6, 9, 12, 30, 37
Mayflower Compact, 56
Mayor of New York v. Miln (1837), 329
Meade, George G., 379, 415–416, 417*(m)*, 427
Meat Inspection Acts, 595
meatpacking industry, 505*(i)*
refrigeration and, 491, 494, 494*(m)*
mechanics, 292, 307, 312–313. *See also* artisans
trade union for, 506
Mechanics' Union of Trade Association, 293
Medicaid, 841–842, 845, 930
abortion rights and, 892
Nixon and, 880
Medical Care Act (1965), 841*(t)*
Medicare, 841–842, 845, 930, 933
Nixon and, 880
Reagan and, 908
medicine. *See* health care
medieval period, 14–18
agriculture in, 14–16
marriage in, 16–17
religion in, 17–18
seasonal cycle in, 15–16
social order in, 16–17
Mediterranean Sea, 17–21, 21*(m)*, 22*(m)*
Mein Kampf (Hitler), 750
Melbourne, Australia, gold rush in, 475
Mellon, Andrew W., 666, 697
Melville, Herman, 345
Memoirs (Kennan), 789
Memorial Day Massacre (1937), 733
Mencken, H. L., 690
Menéndez de Avilés, Pedro, 42–43
Mennonites, 108
mercantilism, 93*(m)*, 95–99. *See also* South Atlantic system

American, 246, 409, 411
British, 35, 37, 95
in British colonies, 72–73
commonwealth system and, 244–245, 249
meaning of, 19, 35
politics of, 97–98
merchant marine, 608
merchants, 93(m), 94(f), 106. See also shopkeepers
as business elite, 296, 302–303, 313
Dutch, 73
education and, 260
in England, 148–149
Enlightenment and, 112–114
as loyalists, 146, 147(i), 149, 156
Navigation Acts and, 98
of New England, 136–137
revolution and, 142–143, 150, 155, 155(t)
Six Companies and, 479
South Atlantic system and, 91–93, 99
textile industry and, 286
trade with Britain and, 127
Merriam, Daniel, 243
Merriam, Ebenezer, 243
Merrill, Michael, 105
Mesabi Range, 487, 489
Mesoamerica, 8(m), 9–12. See also Aztecs
Mayan Indians of, 6, 9, 12, 30, 37
slave imports in, 77(t)
trade with, 95
mestizos, 28, 31, 374, 478
Metacom's Rebellion (King Philip's War), 63, 63(i), 67
Metcalf, Seth, 133
Methodism, 114, 273(t)
abolitionism and, 353, 359
African Americans and, 270, 274
child rearing and, 258
evangelical, 272–273, 275–277, 275(m), 279
politics of, 521, 521(f)
Meuse-Argonne campaign, 644–645
Mexican American Political Association (MAPA), 713, 863
Mexican Americans. See also Hispanics
in cities, 828
civil rights for, 849, 863, 867, 877
discrimination against, 476
Great Depression and, 699, 707, 719
labor activism of, 711–714, 733
and migrant labor, 479(i), 483
as migrant workers, 478–480, 479(i), 483, 710–711, 713
in military, 758
movement into industrial jobs, 651
national culture and, 676(i)
New Deal and, 738–740, 747

in 1920s, 693
race riots and, 765
strikes by, 711(i)
War on Poverty and, 844
women, 735
WWII and, 750, 777
Mexican Revolution (1911–1917), 642, 684, 712
U.S. intervention in, 628–629, 631, 673
Mexican War (1846–1848), 367(i), 368, 376–379, 378(m), 395, 460
Democratic Party and, 378–379
Lincoln and, 393
presidential candidates and, 387
Sherman and, 422
slavery and, 356
Taylor and, 383(i)
victory in, 379, 382
Mexico, 6, 9, 40, 240(m), 447, 605
California and, 373–375
cession of land from, 382(m)
economy of, 376
foreign debts of, 375
France and, 375
independence of, 370, 374
Mexican Americans and, 739
Mormons in, 351–352
NAFTA and, 929
Spanish civil war and, 751
Spanish conquests in, 24–26, 30–31, 37
Texas and, 370–372
U.S. involvement in, 628–629, 670
Mexico City, 9, 379
Miami, Florida, Cuban refugees in, 828
Miami Indians, 65
Miantonomi (Narragansett chief), 39–40
Michelangelo, 19
Michigan, 232(m), 296, 297(m)
Micmac Indians, 11
Microsoft Corporation, 918, 922–923
Middle Atlantic colonies (1720–1765), 105–111
economic inequality in, 105–107, 131
religious diversity in, 102, 105–111, 112(m)
Middlebury Female Seminary, 278
middle class, 552–556, 571
abolitionism and, 355(i)
African American, 691, 846
birth control and, 703–704
conservatism of, 898
consumerism of, 673–675
culture of, 304–305, 304(i), 313
Democratic Party and, 746
education legislation and, 843
European, 552
in government, 195(f), 331

Great Depression and, 697, 701–702, 719, 724
Great Society and, 846
housing and, 552–553, 885
industrial expansion and, 668
intellectual life and, 690
JFK and, 831
Lincoln and, 391–392
Mexican American, 713
movie industry and, 676
in 1920s, 693
1936 election and, 729
in 1970s, 879
1980 election and, 903
in 1990s, 915
politics and, 316–317
postwar, 815, 815(i)
Protestant, 667
racism and, 357
Republican Party and, 389, 667
South Atlantic system and, 92
strikes and, 733
suburban, 552–553, 847
on television, 822
transcendentalism and, 342(i), 343
women of, 304, 304(i), 358, 553–556, 824
Middle East. See also particular countries
Carter and, 901
cold war in, 796
crisis in, 942, 944(i)
declining British influence in, 797
oil production in, 884, 901, 904
post-WWI colonialism in, 658–659
U.S. involvement in, 916(m)
in WWI, 639
Middle Passage, 78(m), 80–81, 84(i), 263(i)
Middlesex County Congress (1774), 157
Middletown (Lynd and Lynd), 665, 702
Midway, Battle of, 771, 772(m)
the Midwest
democracy in, 316
Jackson and, 320
John Q. Adams and, 319
Ku Klux Klan in, 685(m)
manufacturing in, 300, 302–303
migration from, 724
migration to, 227, 291, 296–297, 297(m), 313
wheat production in, 296–299, 297(m), 313
migrant labor, 479(i), 483
migration. See also emigration; immigrants
to Africa, 691
African American, 560, 650–652, 650(m), 681(m), 690–691, 708, 746, 779, 828–829, 847

migration *(Continued)*:
    Asian, 479–480
    to California, 374–375, 460, 483,
        710–711, 710(*m*), 724, 764, 818,
        847
    difficulties of, 109, 465–466, 503
    of farmers, 724
    to Florida, 818, 847
    internal, 8(*m*), 225–228, 828–829
    to and from Midwest, 227, 291,
        296–297, 297(*m*), 313, 724
    Native American, 7–8
    from New England, 128, 226–227,
        291, 296, 297(*m*), 300, 313
    to old Southwest, 262–263, 263(*f*),
        263(*i*), 264(*m*), 265(*t*), 296,
        297(*m*), 313
    postwar, 817
    religious conflict and, 28, 32(*m*)
    social causes of, 16, 35–37
    to and from the South, 225–226,
        226(*m*), 296, 297(*m*), 498
    to Sun Belt, 818–819, 819(*m*)
    trans-Appalachian, 126, 129,
        129(*m*), 131, 136, 138(*m*), 155,
        256, 275(*m*), 296, 297(*m*)
    urban, 708, 746, 779, 828–829, 847.
        See also urbanization
    to the West, 368–369, 372–375,
        374(*m*), 478, 483, 632–633,
        817–819, 829, 886(*m*), 887
    WWII and, 763–764, 777
    of yeomen, 37
military. *See also* Army, U.S.; defense
        spending; draft, military;
        missiles; Navy, U.S.; weapons of
        mass destruction
    African Americans in, 381,
        417–418, 418(*i*), 425, 618(*i*), 619,
        646, 760
    economic growth and, 886(*m*), 887
    gays in, 928
    growth of, 604, 631
    Japanese internment and, 766
    JFK and, 830–831
    racism in, 619, 645–646, 758
    segregation in, 646, 760
    U.S. interventions and, 913(*m*)
    women in, 914(*i*)
    WWII mobilization of, 758
military-industrial complex, 750,
        810–812, 812(*m*), 831
    WWII and, 755
militia, 173(*i*), 182, 185. *See also*
        Minutemen
    colonial, 123(*i*), 124, 129–130,
        133(*i*), 134, 157, 157(*i*), 158
    mob control and, 311(*i*), 312
    service in, 254(*m*)
Militia Act (1862), 407
Mill Dam Act (1795), 245

Miller, Arthur, 743
Millerites, 362(*i*)
Miller, Lewis, 263(*i*)
Milliken v. Bradley (1974), 895
mills, 129(*i*), 544. *See also* factory
        system
    colonial, 101, 106, 129(*i*)
    steel, 485(*i*), 486–489, 489(*i*), 498,
        501
    textile, 288–292, 296, 302, 495–496,
        496(*m*)
    on waterways, 242–243
Milosevic, Slobodan, 932, 932(*m*)
Mimbres Valley, 11
minimum wage
    JFK and, 835
    laws on, 577, 583, 597, 799, 803, 930
    New Deal and, 725, 731
    Supreme Court on, 730
    for women, 597, 735
Minimum Wage Act (1966), 841(*t*)
mining
    in Arizona, 478
    boom towns and, 474–477
    capital for, 476–477
    Chinese labor for, 479–480
    coal, 487–488, 487(*m*), 496(*m*),
        497, 504
    copper, 477
    environmental pollution of,
        475(*i*), 481
    gold, 474–477, 474(*m*), 475(*i*), 479,
        483, 540. *See also* gold rush,
        California
    industrialization of, 477, 483
    labor force for, 498(*f*), 505
    migrant labor and, 478, 479(*i*), 498
    1902 strike and, 591–592, 596
    silver, 474(*m*), 476–477, 538–540
    strikes and, 508(*i*), 511–512, 536,
        591–592, 596
    technology for, 475(*i*), 477
    zinc, 477
Mink, Gwendolyn, 778
Minneconjou Indians, 473
Minnesota, 232(*m*)
minorities. *See also particular groups*
    consumer culture and, 673
    Great Depression and, 704
    1950s culture and, 824
    rights of, 894–897
    women, 735
Minow, Newton, 822
Minutemen, 155(*t*), 157
Miranda v. Arizona (1966), 881
missiles
    defense shield against, 936
    intercontinental ballistic (ICBMs),
        794
    Polaris, 794
    "Star Wars" and, 908

missionaries, 47, 65. *See also* Jesuits
    Catholic, 41–42, 44, 65, 67
    Franciscan, 65, 67
    missions of, 41, 47
    to Native Americans, 39, 41–42, 47,
        65, 120(*i*)
    Protestant, 275(*m*), 277
Mississippi, 225–226, 448
    admission to Union, 262
    migration to, 296, 297(*m*)
    secession and, 385, 398
    slavery in, 262–263, 265–266,
        265(*m*), 266, 272(*m*), 368
    women's rights and, 363
Mississippian civilization, 6, 12–13, 26
Mississippi Freedom Democratic Party,
        840
Mississippi River, 198, 234(*m*), 241
    Civil War and, 401, 405–406,
        406(*m*), 415, 427
    early explorers and, 47, 64
    navigation of, 183, 228, 231
    resettlement of Indians and, 326
    Treaty of Paris and, 182, 191
Mississippi River Valley
    cotton production in, 265, 265(*m*)
    land sales in, 297(*m*)
    Native Americans in, 5–6, 9, 10(*m*),
        11–13, 67, 121, 122(*m*)
Missouri
    Civil War and, 394, 401–402
    emancipation in, 424
    migration to, 296, 297(*m*)
    slavery in, 368–369
    statehood for, 269, 272(*m*), 279
Missouri Compromise (1821), 269,
        272(*m*), 279, 383, 387, 399
    Dred Scott and, 391
    Kansas-Nebraska Act and, 388
Missouri River, 233, 405
Mitchell, John, 591, 882
Mitchell, Margaret, 707
Mittelberger, Gottlieb, 109, 111
Miyatake, Toyo, 766(*i*)
mobs. *See also* draft riots; race riots;
        riots; Sons of Liberty
    anti-abolitionist, 356–357
    antiblack, 352, 533
    anti-Catholic, 311(*i*), 312–313
    anti-Mormon, 349(*i*), 351
    in Britain, 147–149, 147(*i*)
    British troops and, 130, 144–145,
        147–148
    colonial land rights and, 129–130
    colonial taxation and, 134, 141–143,
        142(*i*), 155, 157, 159
    in San Francisco, 480
Moby Dick (Melville), 345
Mochica culture, 6
Moctezuma, 24, 26, 27(*i*), 30–31
Moderators, 129

A Modern Instance (Howells), 570
modernism, 689, 939(*i*)
    Protestant, 686–688
Mogollon culture, 6, 11–12
Mohawk Indians, 47, 63–65, 76
    language of, 48
Mohawk River, 63
Mohegan Indians, 63
Molasses Act (1733), 96, 98–99,
    136–137
Moley, Raymond, 723–724
Molotov, Vyacheslav, 768, 785, 790
Mondale, Walter F., 899, 909
Mongolia, 18
Monnet, Jean, 790
monopolies, chartered, 328, 332
Monroe Doctrine (1823), 609, 913(*m*)
    Roosevelt Corollary to, 626
Monroe, James (1758–1831), 262
    Era of Good Feeling and, 248
    Louisiana Purchase and, 231, 233
    as president (1817–1825), 230, 240
Montana, 475, 477, 480
Montauk Indians, 39
Montcalm, marquis de, 126
Monterrey, Mexico, 377(*i*), 378
Montesquieu, Charles-Louis de, 143,
    205
Montgomery, Alabama, 806(*i*)
    bus boycott in, 805
Montgomery, Richard, 180
Montgomery Ward, 468, 495
Monticello, Virginia, 214–215
Montreal, 121, 180
    capture of (1760), 125, 125(*m*)
Montreal protocol (1987), 927
Moody, Anne, 837
Moody, Dwight L., 566
Moody, Paul, 290
Moon, Reverend Sun Myung, 888
Moore, Colleen, 678, 682
Moore, John Bassett, 622
Moore, Marianne, 690
Moore's Creek Bridge, battle of, 167
Moral Majority, 898, 898(*i*)
    1980 election and, 903
Moreno, Luisa, 713
Morgan, Daniel, 179
Morgan, Edmund, 161
Morgan, J. P., 538, 591–592, 593(*i*)
Morgan, William, 331
Morgenthau, Henry, Jr., 722
Morla, Jennifer, 927(*i*)
Mormons, 346(*m*), 349–352, 350(*m*),
    474
    as farmers, 466
    polygamy of, 351–352, 365
    in Utah, 351–352
    violence against, 349(*i*), 351
Mormon Trail, 374(*m*)
Moroccan crisis, 629–631

Morris, Gouverneur (1752–1814),
    106(*m*), 204, 207(*i*), 248
    biographical information, 206–207
Morris, Lewis, 206
Morris, Lewis, Jr., 206
Morris, Robert, 174, 186, 198,
    201–202, 206–207, 227
Morris, Samuel, 120
Morris, Thomas, 320, 379
Morristown, New Jersey, 185
Morse, Samuel F. B., 294(*i*), 311–312
Morse, Wayne, 852
Morton, Ferdinand "Jelly Roll," 677
Morton, Oliver, 436
Mossadegh, Muhammad, 796, 943
The Mother's Book (Child), 259
Mother's Magazine, 277
Mott, Lucretia, 354, 357, 363
mound building, 11–12
movies, 565, 567
    aviation and, 682
    documentary, 745
    Elvis in, 827
    in Great Depression, 705–706,
        705(*i*)
    mass culture and, 675–679
    self-censorship of, 706
    women and, 676
    WWII and, 762
Moynihan, Daniel Patrick, 880, 891
*Mr. and Mrs. Isaac Newton Phelps
    Stokes* (painting; Sargent), 556(*i*)
Mr. Smith Goes to Washington (film),
    706, 706(*i*)
Ms. magazine, 889
MTV (TV channel), 917
muckrakers, 575–576, 587
Mugwumps, 523, 583, 591, 620
Muhammad, Elijah, 861
Muir, John, 481–482, 591
mujahideen (holy warriors), 901
mulattos, 83
Mulberry Street, New York City,
    543(*i*)
Muller v. Oregon (1908), 577, 578(*t*),
    583, 599
**Mulligan, Catherine Connelly
    Sullivan**, 564
multiculturalism, 925, 937. *See also*
    ethnic diversity
Muncie, Indiana, 665
Mundt, Karl, 791
Munich Conference (1938), 751
Murphy, Charles F., 565
Murray, Anna, 381
Murray, Judith Sargent, 196(*i*)
Murrow, Edward R., 762, 810
music, 569
    African, 88(*i*)
    African American, 825–826
    the Beatles, 860

bebop, 825
    of counterculture, 856, 859–860,
        877
    country, 711, 826
    cultural dissent and, 825
    documentaries and, 745
    Elvis in, 827
    folk, 859–860
    gospel, 826
    jazz, 677, 680
    modernist, 689
    New Deal and, 743
    Okie, 711
    phonograph and, 674(*i*)
    rhythm and blues, 826
    rock 'n' roll, 856, 859–860
    of youth culture, 825–827
Muskie, Edmund S., 868–869, 882
Muslims, 17–22, 28, 29(*t*), 37, 929,
    932(*m*). *See also* Arabs; Islam
    African American, 861
    fundamentalist, 899, 901, 905, 912,
        915, 916(*m*), 941, 943
    racial profiling and, 946
Mussolini, Benito, 750, 770
Mutual Benefit Society, 293
mutual funds, 885
My Lai massacre, 870
My Life in the South (Stroyer), 267
mysticism, 342–344

NAACP. *See* National Association for
    the Advancement of Colored
    People
Nader, Ralph, 889, 933, 934(*m*), 937
NAFTA. *See* North American Free
    Trade Agreement
Nagasaki, 773(*m*), 775–776, 791, 948
Nahuatl language, 30–31
Nanking, sack of (1937), 753
Nantucket, Massachusetts, 268(*i*)
Napoleon Bonaparte, 184(*m*), 231
Napoleonic Wars (1802–1815), 233
Narragansett Indians, 39, 58, 63
*Narrative of the Life of Frederick
    Douglass* (Douglass), 380
NASA. *See* National Aeronautics and
    Space Administration
Nashoba, Tennessee, 336–337, 337(*i*)
Nashoka, 346(*m*)
Nasser, Gamal Abdel, 796–797
Nast, Thomas, 439(*i*)
Natchez Indians, 5, 12–13
National Advisory Commission
    (1968), 862, 862(*m*)
National Aeronautics and Space
    Administration (NASA), 803,
    834–835
National Association for the
    Advancement of Colored People
    (NAACP), 589(*i*), 591, 601,

National Association for the
    Advancement of Colored People
    (*Continued*):
    690(*i*), 691, 709, 836(*m*), 839,
    866
    Communists and, 800
    formation of (1909), 590
    segregation and, 804, 806
    on segregation in military, 758
    in WWII, 760–761
National Banking Acts (1863, 1864),
    412
National Broadcasting Company
    (NBC), 680
National Defense Act (1916), 641
National Defense Advisory
    Commission, 752
National Endowment for the Arts
    (NEA), 841(*t*), 843
National Endowment for the
    Humanities (NEH), 841(*t*), 843
National Grange of the Patrons of
    Husbandry, 468
National Housing Acts
    of 1937, 731, 731(*t*)
    of 1949, 799
National Industrial Recovery Act
    (NIRA; 1933), 724–725,
    731(*t*)
    Supreme Court on, 726
nationalism, 201, 884, 944
    black, 691
    jingoistic, 612–615
    New, 581, 596–598, 601
National Labor Relations Act, 798
National Labor Relations Board
    (NLRB), 728, 731(*t*)
National Liberation Front (NLF), 851,
    851(*m*), 875
national liberation, wars of, 831, 833
National Organization for Women
    (NOW), 866–867, 889, 925
National Origins Act (1924), 683, 686
national park system, 482, 592(*m*),
    821, 843, 899
National Progressive Republican
    League, 596
National Progressive Service, 581
National Recovery Administration
    (NRA), 724–725
    Supreme Court on, 726, 728, 730
    women and, 735
National Republicans, 330
National Road, 297, 319, 321
National Security Council (NSC), 791
National Trades' Union, 293
National Union for Social Justice, 726
National Union Party, 424, 436
National Urban League, 590–591,
    601, 839
    Communists and, 800

National War Labor Board
    (NWLB), 759
National Woman's Party, 579,
    652–653, 892
National Woman Suffrage Association,
    439
National Women's Conference (1977),
    889, 892(*i*)
National Women's Liberation Party,
    866–867, 866(*i*)
National Women's Political Caucus, 889
National Women's Trade Union
    League, 579
National Youth Administration (NYA),
    705, 737
    Mexican Americans and, 739
    WWII and, 761
Nation of Islam, 861
Native American Clubs, 312
Native Americans, 5–14, 609. *See also*
    individual peoples/tribes
    adopted prisoners of, 64–65
    agriculture of, 9–14, 15(*i*), 224, 460,
        471, 473
    alleged inferiority of, 373
    art of, 9(*i*), 11(*i*), 12(*i*), 65(*i*)
    assimilation of, 41, 44, 740
    buffalo and, 459–461, 459(*i*)
    changed world of, 61–67
    citizenship for, 472
    civil rights of, 863–864, 877,
        894–895
    cultural destruction of, 27–28,
        39–41, 44, 47, 63, 65, 67
    cultural diversity of, 6(*t*), 65
    defense against, 136, 145, 148(*m*)
    of eastern woodlands, 12–13
    education of, 471–473, 472(*i*), 863
    encounters with immigrants and,
        102, 108, 111, 128–129, 136
    English settlers and, 43, 49–50,
        49(*m*), 61
    enslavement of, 61, 63
    European diseases and, 25–26,
        28(*m*), 37, 40, 44, 46, 56, 63–67,
        236
    vs. European military technology, 24
    European wars and, 75–76
    as farmers, 34
    French and Indian War and,
        125–126, 131
    fur trade and, 44–45, 47–48,
        63–66
    in Great Depression, 745(*i*)
    on Great Plains, 458(*m*), 459–460,
        459(*i*), 483, 632
    homelands of (1492), 10(*m*)
    Kansas-Nebraska Act and, 388
    land of, 11, 56, 221
    languages of, 28, 30–31, 48
    maize's importance to, 14–15

Marshall Court and, 328
    matrilineal societies of, 12
    medicine men of, 459
    in Mesoamerica (Central America),
        6, 8(*m*), 9–10
    migrations of, 6–8, 763
    migration to cities of, 829, 847
    in military, 645, 647, 758
    missionaries to, 39, 41–42, 47, 65,
        120(*i*)
    mission life and, 481
    in Mississippi valley, 5–6, 10(*m*),
        11–13
    mixed-blood, 326
    mythic West and, 463
    New Deal and, 740, 740(*i*)
    policies towards, 319–320
    political status of, 338
    Pontiac's uprising and, 124(*i*),
        125–126, 136
    population changes of, 55, 65
    Puritan treatment of, 61
    religions of, 9–10, 12–13, 459–460
    removal of (1820–1843), 326–329,
        327(*m*), 339
    reservation system and, 469–474,
        470(*m*), 471(*m*), 483, 829, 864,
        896(*m*)
    resistance of, 43–44, 50, 55, 61, 67,
        222–224
    Revolutionary War and, 170(*m*),
        182
    self-government and, 740
    Sherman and, 423
    in southwest U.S., 11–12
    Spanish conquest of, 24–28, 30–31,
        40–41, 44, 67
    termination policy and, 863
    trade with, 71, 76, 460
    tribal politics of, 65
    unemployment among, 863
    War on Poverty and, 844
    as warriors, 459, 470–471
    wars with, 457, 462, 470–471,
        470(*m*)
    women's role among, 12, 14, 15(*i*),
        65–66, 459
Native Son (Wright), 743
nativism, 311–313, 389, 681–686. *See
    also* Know-Nothing Party
    anti-Catholic, 390
    meaning of, 682
    politics and, 691
NATO. *See* North Atlantic Treaty
    Organization
Naturalization Act (1798), 217, 230
natural resources. *See* environment
natural rights, 113, 143–144, 184, 188
Nauvoo, Illinois, 350–351
Navajo Code Talkers, 758
Navajo Indians, 6–7, 470, 470(*m*), 478

naval power. *See* Navy, U.S.
naval technology, 610–611
Naval War College, 604
Navigation Acts (Acts of Trade and
    Navigation; 1651–1751), 54,
    72–73, 72(*t*), 146, 244
    British Empire and, 136–138
    British mercantilism and, 69–70, 95
    resistance to, 97–98
    South Atlantic system and, 79, 91,
        99
    vice-admiralty courts and, 137–138
    West Indian trade and, 96, 200
Navy, U.S., 603–604
    battleships and, 603(*i*), 610–611,
        631
    building of, 608, 623
    power of, 608, 623, 628, 631
    strategy of, 616–618
    technology of, 610–611
NAWSA. *See* Woman Suffrage
    Association, National American
Nazca culture, 6
Nazi (National Socialist) Party, 160,
    750
    stereotypes of, 758(*i*)
Nebraska, 386(*m*), 395
Neel, Alice, 743
Negro Labor Relations League, 760(*i*)
Negro leagues, 680
Negro Women, National Council of
    (NCNW), 736–737
Negro World, 691
Neighborhood Youth Corps, 845
Nelson, Horatio, 610
Nelson, Isaac, 809
neoconservatives, 898
Neolin, 125
Nestor, Agnes, 579
Netherlands. *See also* Dutch
    colonization
    German invasion of, 752
neutrality, 182, 213, 640–641
Neutrality Acts, 777
    of 1935, 751, 753
    of 1937, 753
Nevada, 382(*m*)
Nevelson, Louise, 743
New Amsterdam, 40(*t*), 47–48, 48(*i*).
    See also New York City
Newark, New Jersey, rioting in, 861,
    862(*m*)
New Deal (1933–1939), 280, 653, 657,
    702(*m*), 721–747, 784, 802, 868
    African Americans and, 724,
        735–738, 747
    anticommunism and, 800
    art and, 741, 743, 745, 747
    Asian Americans and, 714
    attacks on, 726–727
    banks and, 724, 724(*t*), 726

business and, 725, 728–729
    capitalism and, 724, 726, 732
    cartoons of, 725(*i*)
    coalition of, 846, 909
    conservation and, 740–741
    deficit spending and, 835
    Democratic Party and, 692
    first (1933–1935), 722–727
    first Hundred Days of, 724–726
    gender roles and, 735, 746
    Great Society and, 840, 844
    labor unions and, 725, 728,
        732–734, 747
    legacies of, 745–746, 797–798
    legislation of, 731(*t*)
    Mexican Americans and, 738–740,
        747
    Native Americans and, 740, 740(*i*)
    1932 election and, 718
    official end of, 747
    postwar programs and, 815
    Republican Party and, 727, 746, 798
    rollback of, 803, 813
    second (1935–1938), 728–732
    society and, 732–746
    stalemate in, 730–732
    Supreme Court on, 726, 728, 746
    vs. Truman's Fair Deal, 799
    welfare system and, 778
    women and, 734–735, 746–747
    WWII and, 761
Newdow v. U.S. Congress et al. (2002),
    452–453
New England
    California and, 374
    China trade and, 374
    Currency Act and, 98
    currency in, 72(*t*)
    Dominion of, 73, 73(*m*), 94, 99, 140
    economy of, 91–93
    education in, 258–259, 261, 261(*i*),
        301
    elite politics in, 94
    evangelicalism in, 114–115, 119(*f*),
        272, 275, 275(*m*)
    fishing industry in, 185
    governance of, 70
    manufacturing in, 285–292, 285(*i*)
    migration from, 128, 226–227, 291,
        296, 297(*m*), 300, 313
    settlement patterns in, 52(*m*)
    tenant farmers in, 103, 267
    textile industry in, 286–292,
        288(*m*), 302, 496
    War of 1812 and, 235, 249
New England (colonial)
    agriculture in, 102–105, 131
    English colonization in, 56–61,
        62(*m*), 102–105
    farm life in, 102–105, 131
    freehold society in, 101–105, 131

merchants of, 136–137
    population of, 101, 104
    Puritans in, 102, 105, 112–115, 124,
        133, 143, 146, 151, 159–160. *See
        also* Pietism
    republicanism and, 143, 146, 151,
        159
New England Anti-Slavery Society, 354
New England Emigrant Aid Society,
    389
Newfoundland, 48, 76, 77(*m*), 182
    as British colony, 125, 148(*m*),
        151(*m*), 154
New France, 44. *See also* Canada
    Company of, 45
New Freedom, 600–601
    meaning of, 598
New Frontier, 830, 847
    domestic policies of, 834–836
New Hampshire, 73, 104, 226, 248
    constitution of, 185
    migration from, 296, 297(*m*)
    ratification of Constitution by, 205,
        208
    as royal colony, 70
    Shakers in, 277
    South Atlantic system and, 91
New Harmony, Indiana, 336–337,
    337(*i*), 346(*m*)
New Haven, Connecticut, 180
New Jersey, 185, 247
    as colony, 70, 73, 94
    elite politics in, 94(*f*)
    land disputes in, 129
    popular power in, 94
    Quaker settlements in, 105–107
    revivalism in, 114
    in Revolutionary War, 171(*m*), 174
    rioting in, 861, 862(*m*)
    settlement of, 105–106
    voting rights in, 196, 252
    West Indian trade and, 91
Newlands Reclamation Act, 591
New Lebanon, New York, 348
New Left, 857–859, 866, 869–871, 877.
    See also Students for a
    Democratic Society (SDS)
New Lights, 115, 117–118, 120–121,
    131, 167
New London, Connecticut, 181
New Mexico, 11, 40, 44, 67, 121
    annexation of, 379
    attempt to buy, 376
    cession of, 382(*m*)
    Compromise of 1850 and, 384,
        386(*m*)
    drought in, 709–710
    expansionist foreign policy
        and, 387
    grazing rights in, 478
    Hispanic culture in, 478

New Mexico (Continued):
  immigration to, 920
  Mexican War and, 378
New Nationalism, 581, 596, 598, 601
  meaning of, 597
New Negro, 690
The New Negro, 690
New Netherlands, 7, 34, 47, 69, 72,
  75(t). See also New York
  British occupation of, 70
New Orleans, battle of, 238(m), 239(i),
  240, 249
New Orleans, Louisiana, 47, 228(i),
  231, 239, 407
  in Civil War, 412(i)
  free blacks in, 269
  jazz in, 677
  railroad connections to, 461
  transportation and, 298(m),
    300–303, 300(m), 301(m),
    302(m)
Newport, Rhode Island, 58, 91, 93(m),
  179
New Right, 898–899, 898(i), 928
  vs. feminism, 925
  1980 election and, 903
  Reagan and, 908
newspapers, 144, 317, 320, 622. See also
    journalism; *New York Times*;
    New York Tribune
  abolitionist, 354–355, 358
  African American, 381
  circulation of, 569(t)
  delivery of, 300, 300(m)
  immigrants and, 559
  New York, 568–569, 612–615
  political cartoons in, 319(i), 326(i)
  printing industry and, 300, 300(m)
Newton, Huey, 861
Newton, Isaac, 112, 114, 117
New York
  African Americans in, 88
  British occupation of, 70, 185
  colonial, 7, 14, 34, 47–48, 69–75,
    75(t), 99
  constitution of (1777), 206
  Dutch in, 47–48, 105, 106(m)
  immigration to, 920
  land in, 105, 129, 131
  machine politics in, 518
  politics in, 317, 382
  popular power in, 94
  ratification of Constitution by, 205
  representative assembly in, 75
  revivals in, 275(m)
  revolts in, 74, 99
  in Revolutionary War, 171(m), 178
  voting rights in, 252, 316
  West Indian trade and, 91
  wheat production in, 127
  women's rights and, 363

New York Central Railroad, 489,
  492–493
New York City
  African American migration to,
    681(m)
  vs. Boston, 92(i)
  colonial, 40(t), 47–48, 48(i), 73(m),
    75
  foreign trade and, 303, 313
  Great Depression in, 700, 717(i)
  housing in, 721(i)
  immigrants from, 743(i)
  immigrants in, 545, 557(i)
  jazz and, 677
  liberalism in, 668
  Lower East Side in, 559(m)
  Metropolitan Opera in, 551, 551(i)
  Prohibition in, 688
  Puerto Ricans in, 684
  reform movement in, 310–311
  during Revolutionary era, 148(m)
  slavery in, 92
  slums of, 305
  Stonewall riot in, 864
  subway in, 546
  as temporary capital, 209
  as transportation hub, 297–303,
    298(m), 301(m), 302(m)
  war of the opera houses in, 551
  West Indian trade and, 91, 93(m)
New York Elevated, 493
New York Female Moral Reform
    Society, 358
New York Herald, 568
New York Humane Society, 276
New York Journal, 612–615
New York Stock Exchange, 303
New York Sun, 568
New York Times
  Pentagon Papers and, 882
  Vietnam War and, 870, 874
New York Tribune, 303, 413, 440, 449
  Fourierism and, 347
  Fuller and, 345
New York World, 569, 612, 614
Nez Percé Indians, 470, 470(m)
Niagara Falls, New York
  Love Canal, 888, 890–891
Niagara Movement, 589–590
Nicaragua
  Contras in, 909
  U.S. intervention in, 673, 912
Nicholas II, tsar of Russia
    (r. 1894–1917), 918
Nicholson, Lieutenant Governor, 75
nickelodeons, 567
Niles' Weekly Register (periodical), 286
Nimitz, Chester W., 771
Nineteenth Amendment, 652–653
Ninety-five Theses (Luther), 29
Ninth Amendment, 892

Nipmuck Indians, 63
NIRA. *See* National Industrial
    Recovery Act
Nisei (second-generation Japanese
    Americans), 765
Nisei Daughter (Sone), 767
Nixon, Richard M. (1913–1994), 815,
    879, 905
  Alger Hiss and, 800
  antiwar movement and, 882–883
  approval ratings of, 899
  as Eisenhower's running mate, 801
  environment and, 889
  on history, 938, 940
  1968 election and, 867–869, 868(i),
    869(m)
  pardon of, 899
  as president (1969–1974), 880–883,
    881(i)
  recognition of China, 871
  on television, 830–831
  Vietnamization and, 854(i),
    870–872, 877
  Watergate and, 880, 882–883
nobility
  in medieval Europe, 16–17
  Price Revolution and, 35
Nonaggression Pact, Nazi-Soviet
    (1939), 751, 753
nonimportation, 146, 147(i), 149,
    149(f), 154, 155(t), 156. See also
    boycotts
Normandy, France
  D-Day (June 6, 1944) in, 769(m),
    770, 771(i)
the North
  African American migration to,
    560, 650–651, 650(m), 652,
    681(m), 708
  education in, 359
  Fugitive Slave Act and, 386
  maritime economy of, 91–93
  vs. the South, 368
  Uncle Tom's Cabin and, 386
North, Lord, 144(t), 159, 170, 172, 176,
    182, 191
  compromises of, 147–150
  naval blockade and, 154
North, Oliver, 909
North Africa, WWII in, 768(m), 769
North American Free Trade Agreement
    (NAFTA), 929
North Atlantic Treaty Organization
    (NATO), 788(m), 795, 795(m),
    797, 850
  creation of (1949), 789, 790–791
  division of Europe under, 786
  Kosovo and, 931–932, 932(m)
  peacekeeping forces of, 929
North Carolina
  as colony, 48, 70, 76, 79, 94

industrial capacity in, 409
land disputes in, 129, 131
migration from, 296, 297(m)
ratification of Constitution
by, 205
Regulators in, 129(m), 130–131,
130(i), 177, 200(i), 225
revivalism in, 310
salutary neglect and, 95
secession and, 401
slave labor in, 160, 263, 272(m)
voting rights in, 316
the Northeast, 319–320. *See also* New
England; New York
manufacturing in, 285–292, 285(i),
287(t)
Northern Alliance, 941(i)
North Korea, 791–792, 794, 942
North Star (newspaper), 381
Northwest Land Ordinance (1785),
198–200, 199(m), 212, 232(m),
391, 467(m)
Northwest Territory, 215, 229, 232(m),
383
Norton, Charles Eliot, 620
Norton, Seiward J., 621
Norway, German invasion of, 752
Norwood (Beecher), 570
notables, 316–319
Notes on the State of Virginia
(Jefferson), 188, 212, 214, 231
Nova Scotia (Acadia), 11, 75(t), 76,
77(m), 175, 182
as British colony, 70, 124, 148(m),
151(m), 154
control of fisheries off, 183
Noyes, John Humphrey (1811–1886),
348–349
NRA. *See* National Recovery
Administration
NSC-68 (report of National Security
Council), 786, 791
nuclear power, 819, 885(f)
environmentalism and, 888–889
nuclear weapons, 787, 791, 794–795,
797, 801, 943. *See also* atomic
bomb
radioactive fallout from, 808–809,
813
testing of, 808–809, 808(m)
U.S. monopoly of, 785
Nueces River, 376
Nuevo Mexico, 21, 21(m)
nuevo mundo (new world), 24
nullification of tariffs, 322–323, 323(i),
325, 331, 339
Nuremberg Laws, 770
nurses
Civil War, 408–409, 408(i)
in military, 758
Nye, Gerald P., 751

Oakley, Annie, 463
Oberlin College, 308(i)
Occupational Safety and Health
Administration (OSHA), 880
Ochasteguins. *See* Huron Indians
O'Connor, Sandra Day, 909, 909(i)
Ogden, Aaron, 247
Oglethorpe, James, 96
Ohio, 11, 223–224, 229, 236
land division in, 232(m)
migration to, 227, 296, 297(m)
Northwest Ordinance and, 232(m)
voting rights in, 253, 316
Ohio Company, 123–124, 129(m)
Ohio River, 64–65, 67, 228–229, 228(i),
235, 401, 405, 406(m)
Ohio River Valley
expansion of Quebec and, 151
French and Indian War and,
121–124, 122(m)
migration to, 313
oil
embargo on (1970s), 904–905
foreign policy and, 797
in Mexico, 673
in Middle East, 904, 916(m), 943
in Persian Gulf, 670, 884, 943
prices of, 899, 908
oil industry
energy consumption and, 885(f)
energy crisis and, 879(i), 884
environmentalism and, 888
foreign investment and, 670, 673
markets for, 494
subsidies to, 887
in Sun Belt, 887
Okies, 710. *See also* Dust Bowl
Okinawa, 772–773, 773(m)
Oklahoma
drought in, 709–710
Indian reservations in, 469–473,
470(m), 472(i)
Ku Klux Klan in, 684
Old Age Assistance, 844
Old Age Revolving Pension Plan, 726
Old Lights, 115, 131
Old Republicans, 319
Old Southwest (Alabama, Mississippi,
Louisiana), 226
migration to, 262–263, 263(f),
263(i), 264(m), 265(t), 296,
297(m), 313
Old Whigs, 143–144. *See also* Whig
Party (England)
oligopolies, meaning of, 670, 816
Olive Branch petition, 166
Oliver, Andrew, 141
Oliver, Robert, 241
Olmec Indians, 6, 9
Olmsted, Frederick Law, 549
Olney, Richard, 510–511, 573, 608–609

Olsen, Tillie, 743
Olympics, boycotts of, 901
Omaha, Nebraska, 460
Oñate, Juan de, 44
Oneida Community, 346(m),
348–349, 365
Oneida Indians, 64, 170
O'Neill, Eugene, 690
One Third of a Nation (play; Arent),
721(i)
Onondaga Indians, 64
"On The Equality of the Sexes"
(Murray), 196
On the Origin of Species
(Darwin), 519
On the Road (Kerouac), 825
OPA. *See* Price Administration,
Office of
OPEC. *See* Organization of Petroleum
Exporting Countries
Opechancanough (Luis de Velasco;
Massatamohtnock), 42(i),
50, 54, 63
biographical information, 42–43
Capt. John Smith and, 42(i), 43
open-door policy, 753
Operation Desert Storm, 913–914, 931
Operation Rolling Thunder, 853
Operation Wetback, 828
opinion polls, 746, 750, 756, 944. *See
also* public opinion
Orbis Typus Universalis, 5(m)
Order of the Star-Spangled
Banner, 389
Ordinance of Nullification, 322–323,
323(i), 325, 331, 339
Oregon, 373(m), 395
annexation of, 375–376, 382
economy of, 477
1844 election and, 375–376
Japanese internment in, 765
Ku Klux Klan in, 684
migration to, 373–374
wartime migration to, 764(i)
Oregon territory
British ceding of, 460
settlement of, 474, 477
Oregon Trail, 373–374, 374(m), 460
Organization of Petroleum Exporting
Countries (OPEC), 884
Orlando, Vittorio, 658
Orpen, William, 658
Orphan Asylum Society, 308
Ostend Manifesto (1854), 387
Osterhaus' Division, 416
Ostram, Mary Walker, 358
O'Sullivan, John L., 372–373
Oswald, Lee Harvey, 840
Oswald, Richard, 183
*The Other Founders: Anti-Federalism
and the Dissenting Tradition in*

America, 1788–1828 (Cornell), 280

Otis, James, 140, 143

Ottawa Indians, 65, 124(*i*), 125–126, 223

Ouellette, Laurie, 926

"The Outcasts of Poker Flat" (Harte), 481

Out of Work (Kellor), 581

outwork system, 242, 249, 286, 293
  in agriculture, 106
  household production and, 106, 146, 286, 293

Ovington, Mary White, 590–591

Owen, Reba, 573(*i*)

Owen, Robert, 336, 337(*i*)

Owen, Robert Dale, 336–337

Owens Valley, California, 482

"Oxford Pledge," 705

pachuco (youth) gangs, 765

Pacific Mail Steamship Company, 480

Pacific region
  strategic importance of, 622(*m*)
  U.S. in, 605–606, 621–622, 626–628, 627(*m*)
  WWII in, 771–773, 772(*m*), 773(*m*), 777

Pacific slope, 477(*m*)
  ranches in, 477–478

pacifism
  abolitionism and, 357
  in Pennsylvania, 72
  Quakers and, 108, 111, 129, 156
  Vietnam War and, 856–857

Pago Pago (Samoa), 606

Pahlavi, Muhammad Reza, shah of Iran, 796, 902

Paige, Satchel, 680

Paine, Sarah Cobb, 186

Paine, Thomas (1737–1809), 167–171.
    See also Common Sense
  attack on George III, 168
  on word "republic," 185

Paiute Indians, 470(*m*), 473

Pakistan, 939(*i*), 941, 943
  Afghanistan and, 901
  immigrants from, 920

Palestine, 18, 796, 942, 944(*i*)

Palestine Liberation Organization (PLO), 929

Palestinian-Israeli conflict, 916(*m*), 936, 942

Palladio, Andrea, 19

Palmer, A. Mitchell, 661–662

Palmer raids (1919–1920), 661–662, 661(*i*)

Panama (Isthmus of Darien), 24, 605

Panama Canal, 622(*m*), 623, 631
  Colombia and, 625

design of, 626(*m*)
  malaria at, 625(*i*)
  U.S. return of, 901

Pan American Airlines, 683

Pan-American Union, 605

panics. *See also* depressions
  of 1819, 242
  of 1837, 333, 334(*m*), 339, 346–347
  of 1857, 296, 304, 394
  of 1873, 447, 460, 485
  of 1893, 490, 510, 535, 538, 607

Paraguay, 28

Paris, France, 14
  liberation of, 768

Paris, Treaty of (1763), 125, 138(*m*), 151(*m*), 182, 184, 191, 198, 221, 223(*m*)
  western lands and, 222–224

Paris, Treaty of (1899), 619

Parker, Alton B., 593

Parks, Rosa, 805, 806(*i*)

Parliament, English, 35, 134
  taxation and, 134–154, 159

Pascall, Elizabeth Coates, 256

Paterson, William, 202

patriarchy, 15–16, 90, 102
  vs. republicanism, 253

patriotism, American flag and, 949, 949(*i*)

Patriots, 134, 140, 165–167. *See also* Sons of Liberty
  alliance with France and, 176
  Continental army and, 182
  ideological roots of, 143–144, 149
  vs. Loyalists, 165, 167, 169–170, 174
  radical Whig, 172, 210
  strongholds of, 170(*m*)

patronage, 320–321
  in colonies, 90, 95
  politics and, 516
  Republican Party and, 521
  Van Buren and, 317, 339

Patterson, John, 584, 838

Patton, George S., 717, 769

Paul, Alice, 579, 652

Pawnee Indians, 459–460, 470(*m*)

Pax Americana, 816

Paxton Boys, 129, 129(*m*), 130

Payne-Aldrich Tariff Act (1909), 596

Peabody, George H., 512

Peace Corps, 831(*i*), 833

Peace Democrats, 421, 424

peaceful coexistence, meaning of, 794

peace movement, 630, 942(*i*). *See also* antiwar movement

Peale, Charles Willson, 173(*i*)

Peale, James, 258(*i*)

Peale, Norman Vincent, 822

Pearce, Charles H., 442

Pearle, Ann, 83

Pearle, Daniel, 83

Pearle, James, 82

Pearle, Robert
  biographical information, 82–83

Pearl Harbor, attack on (December 7, 1941), 605, 611, 749, 753–754, 754(*i*), 948
  WWII and, 777

peasants, 9, 14–17

pedlars, Yankee, 242, 243(*i*)

Pelham, Henry, 124

Pelosi, Nancy, 944, 945(*i*)

Peña, Frederico, 928

Peña, José Enrique de la, 372

Pendleton Act (1883), 516

Pendleton, Edmund, 167

Penn, John, 129

Pennsylvania
  African Americans in, 88
  assembly of, 94
  coal mining in, 487, 487(*m*), 489, 501(*i*)
  as colony, 14, 55, 70–72, 75, 99
  German settlements in, 105–111
  land disputes in, 131
  Quakers in, 71–72, 106–108
  revivalism in, 114, 310
  slavery in, 160
  social inequality in, 107(*f*)
  transportation in, 228
  West Indian trade and, 91
  wheat production in, 127

Pennsylvania Constitution (1776), 156

Pennsylvania Gazette, 106, 115

Pennsylvania Railroad, 485–486, 493

Penn, William, 71–72, 71(*i*), 94, 99, 128, 341(*i*)

Pentagon, 810–811

Pentagon Papers, 882

People's Party. *See* Populist Party

People's Republic of China
  establishment of (1949), 791
  Korean War and, 792
  support for Vietnam by, 850
  U.N. and, 791–792
  U.S. recognition of, 871–872

Peoria Indians, 47

Pequot Indians, 61

perestroika, meaning of, 912

perfectionism, 348–349

Perkins, Frances, 586, 722, 728, 735
  welfare system and, 778(*i*)

Perot, H. Ross, 928

Perry, Oliver Hazard, 235, 238(*m*)

Pershing, John J., 629, 629(*i*), 643–644

Persia, 19. *See also* Iran

Persian Gulf, 670, 884, 943(*i*)

Persian Gulf War (1990–1991), 876, 913–914, 916(*m*), 943
  women in, 914(*i*)

Personal Narrative (Edwards), 116

Personal Responsibility and Work Opportunity Act (1996), 779, 779(i), 930
Peru, 6, 9, 25–26, 25(m), 37, 605
Petersburg, Virginia, 410, 421, 424, 427
petrochemical industry, 818
petroleum industry. See oil industry
phalanxes (Fourierist communities), 347–348
Phelps-Stokes Fund, 648
Philadelphia Centennial (1876), 487(i)
Philadelphia Convention (1787), 261
Philadelphia Female Anti-Slavery Society, 354
Philadelphia, Pennsylvania, 72, 92(i)
    agitation against George III in, 167
    antiabolitionism in, 357
    architecture of, 193
    Benedict Arnold in, 181
    British occupation of, 178, 185
    as center of American Enlightenment, 114(i)
    Committee of Resistance in, 167
    Committee on Prices in, 186
    Continental Army in, 171
    free blacks in, 262, 270–271, 271(i)
    Howe's attack on, 171(m), 173
    industrial development in, 545–546
    Patriot traders in, 187
    during Revolutionary era, 148(m)
    slavery in, 92
    South Atlantic system and, 92
    Tom Paine in, 168
    transportation and, 244, 298(m), 299–303, 300(m), 301(m), 302(m)
    unions in, 293
    West Indian trade and, 91, 93(m)
Philip, King (Metacom; Wamponoag chief), 63, 63(i), 67
Philippines, 125, 616–622, 942. See also Filipinos
    acquisition from Spain of, 618–620, 631
    human rights in, 901
    immigrants from, 714, 828, 920
    Spanish-American war in, 616–620, 617(m)
    vs. United States, 620–621
    U.S. foreign investment in, 670
    in WWII, 770, 772, 772(m), 773(m)
Philipse Manor, 128(i)
Phillip II, king of Spain (r. 1556–1598), 29(t), 33, 35, 40, 42
Phillips, David Graham, 576
Phillips, Sam, 826
Phillips, Wendell, 353, 414
phonograph, 674(i), 680
photography, 695, 707, 745
photojournalism, 745

Phyfe, Duncan, 213(i)
Physicians for Social Responsibility, 809, 857
Pickett, George E., 415
Pickford, Mary, 676, 676(i)
Piedmont region, 127
Pierce, Franklin (1804–1869), 361, 387, 388(i), 392(m)
    as president (1853–1857), 388–389
"Pieties Quilt" (Hubbard), 341(i)
Pietism, 102, 112, 114–115, 121, 131, 520, 535
Pike, James M., 449
Pike's Peak, 475
Pike, Zebulon, 234(m)
Pilgrims, 56–57. See also Puritans
Pilgrim's Progress (Bunyan), 576
Pinchot, Gifford, 596
Pinckney's Treaty (1795), 231
Pinckney, Thomas, 434
Pine Ridge reservation, South Dakota, 864
Pinkerton Detective Agency, 510
Pittsburgh, Pennsylvania, 228(i), 229, 544, 549. See also Fort Duquesne
    Catholic church in, 563(i)
    railroad strike and, 485
    steel production and, 485(i), 486, 503
    transportation and, 298(m), 300–302, 300(m), 301(m), 302(m)
Pitt, William, 124, 127, 134(i), 139, 144(t), 145, 154
Pius IX, Pope, 311
Pizarro, Francisco, 25
Plain Home Talk on Love, Marriage, and Parentage (Foote), 555
plantation life. See also South, the
plantations, 121, 127. See also South, the
    cotton and, 296, 301, 368–369
    culture of, 127, 294, 313, 495
    impact of sharecropping on, 444(m)
    Kansas-Nebraska Act and, 388
    religion of, 112, 119–121
    slavery and, 80, 160–161, 161(i), 261–269, 263(f), 263(i), 265(m), 265(t), 266(i), 273, 279
    Southern gentry and, 90
    sugar production and, 79
Platt Amendment, 626
    repeal of, 751
Platt, Orville, 606
Pledge of Allegiance, 452–453, 822
Plessy v. Ferguson (1896), 529, 804
PLO. See Palestine Liberation Organization
plumbers, Watergate, 882
Plunkitt, George Washington, 562
pluralism. See also ethnic diversity

    cultural, 586, 919–925
    ethnic, 920–921, 924
    religious, 102, 105–111, 112(m), 119(f)
Plymouth colony, 40(t), 73–74
    legal code in, 56
Poague, William, 401
Pocohontas, 43, 49, 65(i)
Podhoretz, Norman, 898
Poland, 658, 785, 789
    German invasion of, 751–752
    Holocaust in, 770
    Yalta and, 773
Poland Hill, Maine, 347(i)
police action, meaning of, 792, 793(m), 801
police brutality, 924(i)
Polish National Catholic Church of America, 563
political action committees (PACs), 883, 903
political campaigns, 518, 521, 538–539
    automobile and, 667(i)
    economy as issue in, 538–539, 538(i), 928, 930, 933, 944
    finance reform and, 883, 903
    fundraising for, 882–883
    popular culture and, 917
    presidential, 802–803, 803(i), 928
    racism in, 911
    television and, 830–831, 903
political crisis of 1790s, 210–218
political parties. See also elections; particular parties
    fragmentation of, 393–394
    loyalty to, 520
    male-dominated, 525(i)
    new, 387–388
    nineteenth-century changes in, 385–391
    political machines and, 518, 521–523, 541, 562
    priorities of, 517–518
    realignment of (1848–1860), 392(m)
    regional vs. national, 392(m)
    rise of, 216–218, 316–317, 339
    Tocqueville on, 325
    workingmen's, 332, 339
political theory, 113
politics, 940
    abolitionism and, 357, 367–368
    African Americans in, 562
    American, 315–316
    British, 93–98
    corruption in, 441, 449, 574
    cynicism about, 937
    Depression-era movies on, 706
    direct primary in, 584, 587
    elite, 94
    energy crisis and, 884
    of expectation, 830–840, 847

politics (*Continued*):
  government-business cooperation
    in, 666–667
  imperial, 70–76
  initiative and recall in, 584
  international, 884
  Ku Klux Klan and, 684
  labor unions in, 733–734
  of late nineteenth century, 515–541
  machine, 518, 521–523, 541, 574,
    584, 601
  new, 830
  in "New Era" (1920s), 666–668
  patronage and, 516
  post-Watergate, 899–904
  power, 584
  race and, 525–534
  reform in, 523, 524(*m*), 541
  of resentment, 898–899, 903
  rise of popular, 316–321
  slavery and, 365, 368, 383–385
  students in, 705
  ward, 561
  women in, 335, 889
  in WWII, 761–762
Polk, James K. (1795–1849), 375,
  382(*m*), 383, 395
  expansionism of, 376–379, 387
  as president (1845–1849), 376–379
Pollock, Jackson, 743, 825
poll taxes, 252, 529
  voting rights and, 842
pollution, 927. *See also*
    environmentalism
  highways and, 819
  industrial, 485(*i*), 666(*i*)
  at Love Canal, 888, 890–891
  from mining, 475(*i*), 481
  in Sun Belt, 819
  TVA and, 741
Ponce de León, Juan, 24
Pontiac (Ottawa chief), 124(*i*)
  rebellion of, 125–126, 136
Pony Express, 374(*m*), 460, 462
Poor Richard's Almanack (Franklin), 114
Popé (shaman), 44
Popper, Deborah, 632
Popper, Frank, 632
popular culture. *See also* advertising;
    mass media; movies; television
  Great Depression and, 705–707, 719
  intellectual life and, 690
  leisure and, 680
  in 1990s, 917–919
  WWII and, 762
popular front, Communist, 733
popular sovereignty, 216, 247, 328
  original meaning of, 194–195
  slavery decisions and, 383–384,
    386(*m*), 387–389, 391, 393, 395
  population

changes in, 919–921, 921(*m*)
  in colonial America, 104, 127(*f*),
    128, 129(*m*), 131, 138(*m*)
  Columbian Exchange and, 27
  disease and, 25–27
  in England, 34
  environment and, 9
  first census (1790) and, 222
  Great Depression and, 702
  on Great Plains, 632, 632(*f*)
  immigration and, 491
  life expectancy and, 823
  Louisiana Purchase and, 234(*m*)
  in Middle Atlantic colonies, 105,
    105(*f*)
  Native American, 9, 12, 25–28, 65
  seasonal patterns and, 15–16, 16(*f*)
  Spanish conquests and, 26
  urbanization and, 302–303, 302(*m*)
  in the West, 474–479, 477(*m*), 481,
    483
Populism, 511–512, 533–537, 536(*i*),
  537(*i*), 537(*m*), 632
  of American West, 511–512,
    537(*m*), 540
  among farmers, 511, 535–537,
    536(*i*)
  Father Coughlin and, 726
  one party rule and, 526–531,
    533–534, 541
  women's rights and, 535–536,
    537(*i*)
Populist Party
  free silver and, 536–540
  platform of (1892), 536
Port Bill (1774), 151
Portland, Oregon, 477
Portugal, 6, 19–22, 22(*m*), 37,
  77–78, 183
  colonies of, 134(*m*)
  maritime expansion and, 19–22,
    21(*m*), 22(*m*)
Postlethwayt, Malachy, 69
Post Office Act (1792), 300
Potawatomi Indians, 236
Potomack Indians, 43
Potomac River, 403
Potsdam Conference, 785
Pottawatomie massacre (1856), 389
Potter, Helen, 525, 527
Pound, Roscoe, 574
poverty, 845(*f*)
  in California, 734(*m*)
  in cities, 305–306, 312–313, 924,
    926
  of elderly, 829, 830(*i*), 844
  feminization of, 893
  Hoover on, 715
  of immigrants, 305, 311–312
  LBJ's war on, 844–846
  New Deal and, 746

in nineteenth-century America,
  305–306
  1928 election and, 692
  in 1950s, 825–830
  in 1990s, 911, 914
  private control of land and, 575
  in Sun Belt, 818
  welfare and, 779
  of women, 305, 926
Powderly, Terence V., 506–507,
  506(*i*), 509
Powell, Adam Clayton, Sr., 690, 736
Powell, Colin, 913, 934
Powell, Lewis F., Jr., 881
The Power of Positive Thinking
  (Peale), 822
Powers, Francis Gary, 809
Powhatan, 49
Powhatan Indians, 42
POWs. *See* prisoners of war
pragmatism, 574
prairies, 458, 458(*m*)
prairie, short grama grass,
  458(*m*)
Pratt, Zadock, 492
praying towns, 62–63. *See also*
  Algonquian Indians
predestination, 58
Preemption Act (1841), 338
Presbyterians, 32, 190, 273, 273(*t*)
  abolitionism and, 354
  in colonial America, 105, 107,
    110–111, 112(*m*), 114,
    118–119(*f*), 119(*t*)
  egalitarianism of, 120, 160, 303
  Enlightenment and, 258
  fundamentalist, 686
  New Lights, 118, 120–121
  Old Lights, 131
  Princeton and, 118, 119(*t*)
  Republican Party and, 521
  social reform and, 306, 308–310
  synods of, 272
presidency, 230, 666
  expanded powers of, 722
  FDR and, 731
  imperial, 883
  LBJ and, 842
  New Deal and, 722
  Watergate and, 883
Presidential Commission on the Status
  of Women (1963), 865
presidential elections
  of 2004, 944
  radio and, 680
  Adams, John (1796), 216
  Adams, John Quincy (1824), 318,
    318(*m*)
  Arthur, Chester A. (1880),
    517(*m*), 604
  Buchanan, James (1856), 391

Bush, George H. W. (1988), 910–911, 910(i)

Bush, George W. (2000), 933–935, 933(i), 934(m), 937, 948

Cleveland, Grover (1884), 517, 517(m), 518, 523, 605

Cleveland, Grover (1892), 516, 516(i), 517(m), 518, 540(m), 605

Clinton, William Jefferson (1992), 927–928, 937

Clinton, William Jefferson (1996), 924, 930

Coolidge, Calvin (1924), 667–668

Eisenhower, Dwight D. (1952), 787, 794, 801–803, 803(i)

Garfield, James A. (1880), 517

Grant, Ulysses S. (1868), 438

Grant, Ulysses S. (1872), 449, 523

Harding, Warren G. (1920), 666, 680

Harrison, Benjamin (1888), 515(i), 517, 517(m), 520(i), 535, 608

Harrison, William Henry (1840), 334–335, 335(i), 338

Hayes, Rutherford B. (1876), 450–451, 516

Hoover, Herbert (1928), 691–693, 692(m), 715

Jackson, Andrew (1828), 320–321, 320(i), 321(i), 339

Jackson, Andrew (1832), 324

Jefferson, Thomas (1800), 218, 222

Johnson, Lyndon B. (1964), 840, 842, 843(m), 852

Kennedy, John F. (1960), 830–831, 831(m)

Lincoln, Abraham (1860), 392(m), 393(i), 394–395, 427

Lincoln, Abraham (1864), 418, 421, 424

McKinley, William (1896), 538–541, 539(i), 540(m), 595(i), 597, 612, 620

Madison, James (1808), 235

Madison, James (1812), 235

Nixon, Richard M. (1968), 867–869, 868(i), 869(m), 880

Nixon, Richard M. (1972), 872, 881–882, 881(i)

Pierce, Franklin (1852), 387, 388(i), 392(m)

Polk, James K. (1844), 375–376, 395

Reagan, Ronald (1980), 903, 903(m)

Reagan, Ronald (1984), 909

Roosevelt, Franklin D. (1932), 717–718, 718(m)

Roosevelt, Franklin D. (1936), 727, 729, 747

Roosevelt, Franklin D. (1940), 753

Roosevelt, Franklin D. (1944), 762

Roosevelt, Theodore (1904), 593, 595, 595(i)

Taft, William Howard (1908), 628

Taylor, Zachary (1848), 379, 382, 392(m)

Truman, Harry S (1948), 798, 798(m)

Van Buren, Martin (1836), 331–332

Washington, George (1788), 209

Wilson, Woodrow (1912), 598(m), 628, 642

Wilson, Woodrow (1916), 628, 642

presidios, 374, 478

Presley, Elvis, 825, 827(i)
biographical information, 826–827

Price Administration, Office of (OPA), 755, 763, 797

Price Revolution, 34(f), 35, 37

prices. *See also* consumer price index
agricultural, 212–213, 535, 540
controls on, 667, 797, 880, 884, 905, 934
New Deal and, 726
of oil, 899, 908
WWII and, 755, 797

Priestly, Joseph, 114

primogeniture, 17, 257

The Prince (Machiavelli), 19

Princeton College, 117, 119(t)
founding of, 118

Princeton, New Jersey, battle of, 171, 191

Princip, Gavrilo, 639

Principia Mathematica (Newton), 112

printing industry, 113–114, 143–144, 146
newspapers and, 300, 300(m)

Prioleau, George W., 619

Prison Discipline Society, 306

prisoners of war (POWs)
Bataan death march and, 771
in Civil War, 423(i)
German, 761
Japanese internment and, 766(i)
in Vietnam War, 853, 872–873

prisons
debtors', 194, 200–201, 207, 332
as reforming institutions, 306(i), 307
reform of, 357–358, 360

Privy Council (British), 146, 151

Proclamation for Suppressing Rebellion and Sedition, 166

Proclamation Line (1763), 126, 136, 138(m), 151(m), 155, 155(t)

Production Code Administration, 706

Progress and Poverty (George), 575

Progressive Era (1900–1914), 280, 570, 573–601, 799
academic expertise in, 574
consumer rights and, 889

end of, 666
New Deal and, 745
shift from Republican dominance in, 586

Progressive Party, 581, 596, 667
new, 597, 798

progressivism, 601
fracturing of Republican, 595
national politics and, 591–600
of 1970s, 888
Prohibition and, 653
reform and, 651–654, 656–657
science and, 574
white supremacy and, 589, 591
women and, 576–577, 651–654
in WWI, 651–652, 654

Prohibition, 522, 524–525, 526(i), 586, 689(i), 693
Al Smith on, 718
Democratic Party and, 667
Eighteenth Amendment on, 654, 654(m), 688
politics and, 691
progressive reform and, 653
repeal of (1933), 724
rural areas vs. cities in, 653–654, 654(m)
WWI impetus for, 654

Prohibitionist Party, 535, 539

Prohibitory Act (1775), 167, 176

The Promised Land—The Grayson Family (Jewett), 375(i)

Promontory Point, Utah, 460

propaganda
George Creel and, 657
German, 648
vigilante groups and, 655
wartime, 654–655

property
common ownership of, 347
ownership of, 222–224, 432
political rights and, 93
private, 161, 241, 336
protection of, 206–207, 434, 442
slaves as, 434
voting rights and, 94, 316

property rights, 146, 247, 249, 365
conflicts over, 128–131
corporate, 248
Dred Scott and, 391
freeholders and, 102–105, 106(m), 119–120
inheritance and, 103–104, 131, 255
slavery and, 383
of women, 90, 102–104, 110, 131, 362–364

Prophetstown, Indiana, 235–237

Proposition 13 (California), 898

Proposition 187 (California), 924

Proposition 209 (California), 925

proprietorships, 69(i), 70, 75, 99

prospectors, 475–476, 479
Prosser, Gabriel, 189, 266
Prosser, Martin, 266, 274
prostitution, 358, 365, 568, 653
The Prostrate State (Pike), 449
protectionism, 517, 672. *See also* tariffs:
    protective
Protestantism, 74, 88. *See also*
    evangelicalism; *individual
    denominations*
    accumulation of wealth and,
        518–519
    anti-Catholicism of, 142, 151,
        151(*m*), 311–312, 311(*i*), 313
    in city, 563, 565
    French (Huguenots), 32, 44, 73, 107
    Manifest Destiny and, 373
    missionary action and, 275(*m*), 277
    modernist vs. fundamentalist,
        686–688
    in New World, 40–41, 44, 50
    in 1950s, 822
    Republican Party, 520–521, 521(*f*)
    social reform and, 272, 276–278,
        306, 313, 575, 586
    Whigs and, 330
    women and, 256–257, 277–278
    work ethic and, 305, 665
Protestant Reformation, 28–29, 37. *See
    also* Calvinism; Luther, Martin
    in England, 32
    in Holland, 29
    Roman Catholic Church and, 29,
        32–33, 50
Providence, Rhode Island, 40(*t*), 58, 91,
    288
Psihoyos, Louis, 920(*i*)
public assistance. *See* welfare
Public Interest Research Group, 889
public opinion
    on civil rights, 839
    in 1990s, 914
    WWII and, 750, 777
public works
    Great Depression and, 715
    Kaiser and, 756
    Long and, 727
    in New Deal, 725, 730(*m*), 731(*t*),
        735
    Roosevelt recession and, 732
    states and, 911
    War on Poverty and, 844
Public Works Administration (PWA),
    725, 730(*m*), 731(*t*), 735
publishing industry, 691, 707. *See also*
    printing industry
Pueblo Indians, 11–12, 26, 37, 40,
    470(*m*), 478
    revolt of, 44, 67
Puertocarrero, Alonso, 30
Puerto Ricans, 844

Puerto Rico
    annexation of, 617, 622, 622(*m*)
    immigrants from, 683–684, 828
Puget Sound, 373
Pulaski, Tennessee, 446
Pulitzer, Joseph, 569, 612, 614
Pulitzer Prize, 787
Pullman boycott (1894), 510–511, 538,
    573
Pullman, George M., 510, 544
pump priming, meaning of, 715
Pure Food and Drug Act, 595
Puritans, 33, 56–63, 57(*m*), 67, 105,
    133
    coercive policies of, 58–59
    education and, 119(*t*)
    vs. English, 59
    as freeholders, 102
    during French and Indian War, 124
    gravestones of, 59, 59(*i*)
    Great Awakening and, 112–115
    vs. hierarchichal institutions, 59, 61,
        67
    Mormons and, 350
    Plymouth colony and, 40(*t*), 56,
        73–74
    republicanism and, 143, 146, 151,
        159–161
    Revolution of, 59, 140, 142, 161
    seizure of Indian lands by, 58, 61
    transcendentalism and, 342
    witchcraft fears of, 59
    women and, 58–59, 102–103
    work ethic and, 305
putting-out system, 242

al-Qaddafi, Muammar, 912
Quaker Oats Company, 495(*i*)
Quakers, 102, 106–111, 190, 255(*i*),
    273
    abolitionism and, 188, 353–354, 359
    Anglicanism and, 341(*i*)
    Calvinism and, 71
    as merchants, 303
    in Nantucket, 268(*i*)
    Native Americans and, 224
    in New Jersey, 105–107
    pacifism of, 108, 111, 129, 131, 156,
        277, 857
    in Pennsylvania, 71–72, 106–108,
        193(*i*)
    social equality and, 106, 107(*f*), 108,
        160, 270, 303
    women of, 71, 108(*i*)
Quantrill, William, 401
Quartering Acts
    of 1765, 140, 145–146, 154, 155(*t*)
    of 1771, 140, 154
    of 1774, 151
Quayle, Dan, 910, 928

Quebec, 40(*t*), 44–45, 63–64, 69, 76,
    121, 180–181
    battle for (1758), 126
    capture of (1759), 125, 125(*m*),
        134(*i*)
    colonization of, 121, 136, 138(*m*),
        154
Quebec Act (1774), 151, 151(*m*),
    154–155, 155(*t*)
Queen Anne's War (War of the Spanish
    Succession; 1702–1713), 75(*t*),
    76, 77(*m*)
Queen's College. *See* Rutgers
    University
Queen's Own Loyal Virginians, 167
Quetzalcoatl, 24
quilting, 341(*i*)
Quinn, Anthony, 762
Quitman, John A., 387

Rabin, Yitzhak, 929
race. *See also* ethnicity; *particular
    groups*
    Democratic coalition and, 746–747
    feminism and, 892, 925
    Great Depression and, 699
    lynchings and, 660
    in military, 645–646
    status and, 6, 28, 53
race riots
    African Americans and, 849,
        861–862, 862(*m*), 867, 869, 877
    in Chicago, 660, 660(*i*)
    in Harlem (1935), 709
    Latinos and, 924
    in Los Angeles, 924
    Mexican Americans and, 765
    police brutality and, 924(*i*)
    post-WWI, 660, 660(*i*), 663
    social structure and, 924
    Springfield (1908), 590
    in Watts (1965), 836(*m*), 924(*i*)
    WWII and, 764–765
racial profiling, 946
racism, 80, 83, 160–161, 252–253,
    270–271, 381, 393. *See also*
    lynching; segregation
    abolitionism and, 357
    anti-Asian, 627–628, 714
    anti-Semitism and, 760
    anti-Vietnamese, 854–855
    atom bomb and, 776
    in California, 480–481, 483
    in cities, 560–561, 829
    cultural conflict and, 681
    environmental, 927
    France and, 689
    Free-Soil Party and, 379
    immigration restriction and,
        627–628, 682–684

interracial marriage and, 65(i), 356, 398
Jim Crow laws and, 529–531, 863
Ku Klux Klan and, 684
Mexican Americans and, 711–712
middle-class, 357
in military, 619, 645–646, 758
National Advisory Commission (1968) and, 862, 862(m)
in New South, 525–534, 531(i), 532(i)
in 1920s, 693
in 1950s, 847
1988 campaign and, 911
Ninth Cavalry experience of, 619
opposition to, 856–857, 860–863, 877
Philippine annexation and, 620
post-WWI, 660, 660(i)
race riots and, 924(i)
on radio, 707
reform and, 342, 587, 589, 591
Scottsboro case and, 708
in the South, 465, 525–526, 541, 863
in Spanish-American War, 617–619, 618(i)
in suburbs, 818
toward African American soldiers, 619
welfare system and, 778–779
in WWI, 645–646
in WWII, 761
radar, 794
radicalism, 513, 536
fear of, 661–662
in the West, 511–512, 537(m), 540
Radical movement, southern, 394, 398
Radical Republicans, 413, 430, 436, 451
radio
Father Coughlin on, 726
FDR and, 722
in Great Depression, 706–707, 707(m)
JFK-Nixon debates on, 831
music and, 826
national culture and, 680
religion and, 822
rural electrification and, 744
television and, 821
WWII and, 762, 763(i)
radioactive fallout, 808–809, 813
railroads, 285(i), 286, 300–302, 301(m), 390, 411, 418–419, 488–491, 489(m), 513. See also Central Pacific Railroad; Union Pacific Railroad
Adamson eight-hour law and, 600
advertising by, 464, 471
aviation and, 682
Baltimore and Ohio, 485
bankruptcy of, 535

Brotherhood of Locomotive Firemen, 507(i), 511
cattle industry and, 464
Chicago, Burlington, and Quincy, 489
completion of transcontinental (1869), 460
destruction of, 424
development of California and, 481
elevated, 546, 546(i)
Erie, 300, 489, 492–493
expansion of, 300–302, 301(m), 313, 544
federal government and, 510–511, 519
freight rates for, 469, 469(f), 490, 497
government support for, 488–489, 510–511, 518–519
Great Depression and, 697
Great Northern, 489
in Great Plains, 460–461, 461(i), 461(m), 467, 470–471, 490(m)
hub for, 301(m)
industrialization and, 485–491, 487(m), 490(m), 491(i)
investment in, 296, 488–493
Kansas Pacific, 460(i), 462
labor unions and, 507(i), 510–511, 573
land grants for, 460, 488
migrant labor and, 478–479
Missouri Pacific, 461, 461(m), 489, 493
nationalization of, 667
New York Central, 489, 492–493
Northern Pacific, 449, 461, 461(m)
Pennsylvania, 485–486, 493
Pullman boycott (1894) of, 510–511, 538, 573
regulation of, 516–517, 595
Rock Island, 464
Santa Fe, 461, 461(m), 481
segregation laws and, 525, 529
in the South, 495, 496(m), 497
Southern Pacific, 461, 461(m), 481, 614
in Southwest, 478
strikes against, 485, 508, 510–511, 536, 797–798
transcontinental, 387–388, 460–461, 461(m), 476, 479–480, 480(i)
Wabash, 489
Wall Street and, 491–493, 493(i)
western expansion and, 471, 483, 488–489, 490(m)
Railroad War Board, 649
Rainbow Coalition, 911
Rainey, Ma, 677
Raleigh, Walter, 48
Ramona (Jackson), 481

Ramsay, David, 166, 222
ranching
barbed wire and, 465, 467, 483
cattle, 299, 313, 374
on Great Plains, 458, 461, 464, 467, 483
range right and, 464
sheep, 464, 467, 478
in Texas, 461, 464, 478
in the West, 477–478
Randolph, A. Philip, 640, 760, 804, 839
Randolph, Edward, 72
Ranke, Leopold von, 193
Rankin, Christopher, 269
Rankin, Jeannette, 643, 643(i), 754
Ranney, William T., 176(i)
Raphael, 18
Raskob, John J., 697
Rathbone, William, 360
ratification conventions, 205–206
rationing, World War II, 762–763, 777
Rauschenbush, Walter, 575
La Raza Unida (The United Race), 863
Reagan Democrats, 903
Reagan, Nancy, 908(i), 909
Reaganomics, 908–909, 915
budget deficits and, 908, 910, 910(f)
Reagan, Ronald (1911–), 280–281, 899, 902–905, 908(i), 943
aid to Afghanistan and, 901
Alzheimer's of, 908(i)
arms build-up of, 787
Iran-Contra Affair and, 909
as president (1981–1989), 908–910
rollback of federal power and, 927, 937
Star Wars of, 936
realism, legal, 574
Reason and Republicanism: Thomas Jefferson's Legacy of Liberty (McDowell), 280
recessions, 945
of FDR, 731–732
foreign trade and, 816
vs. Great Depression, 697
migrant workers and, 828
of 1920–1921, 668, 693, 697
of 1975–1976, 899
of 1990s, 911, 914, 928
postwar, 817
of Reagan (1981–1982), 909
reconquista, 22, 24
Reconstruction (1865–1877), 429–451, 589
Douglass and, 381
end of (1877), 525, 541
Fourteenth Amendment and, 519
Presidential, 430–436
quest for land in, 442–444
Radical, 436–444, 437(m), 449, 451
Republicans and, 429, 518

Reconstruction (Continued):
  role of black churches in, 442
  southern resistance to, 465
  undoing of, 444–450
Reconstruction Act (1867), 436,
  438(t)
Reconstruction Finance Corporation
  (RFC), 715, 719, 757
red-baiting, 743, 745. See also
  anticommunism
Red Cloud, Chief of the Sioux, 469
Red Cross, 652
Redeemers, 445, 448, 451
  home rule and, 526
  one party system and, 530, 541
redemptioners, 108
Red Jacket (Sagoyewatha;
  c.1758–1830), 222(i), 224
Red River Valley, North Dakota, 466
Red Scare, 661, 663. See also
  anticommunism
  nativism and, 683
  power of federal government and,
  668
Red Shirts, 448
reform, 573–574, 601. See also social
  reform
  British (1763–1765), 134–140, 142,
  145, 147(i), 159
  civil service, 449
  economic, 342
  educational, 260, 358–359
  government, 329–330
  labor, 584–585
  moral, 315(i), 358, 521, 539, 653
  municipal, 584
  party, 584
  progressive, 692
  racism and, 587, 589
  Republican Party and, 596
  tariff, 598–599
Reform Party, 933
refugees
  Cuban, 828
  Holocaust and, 770
  in 1950s, 825
regionalism, 226(m), 318, 318(m),
  392(m)
  interstate highways and, 820(m)
  television and, 821
regulation. See also deregulation
  of economy, 666, 745
  public, 574
  of railroads, 516–517, 595
Regulators, 129–131, 156, 177
  in North Carolina, 129(m),
  130–131, 130(i), 177, 200(i), 225
Rehnquist, William, 881, 909
Reid, John Phillip, 281
Reid, Wallace, 676
relief. See welfare

religion, 28–29, 32–36, 32(m), 37, 40,
  58–60. See also evangelicalism;
  Great Awakening; Protestant
  Reformation; revivalism; Second
  Great Awakening; particular
  denominations
  abolitionism and, 277, 352–359, 452
  African, 87–88
  African American, 121, 130, 262,
  268, 268(i), 270, 271(i), 274–275,
  279, 442, 560–562
  in American public life, 452–453,
  562–563, 565
  anti-Masonry and, 331
  (G. W.) Bush and, 452–453
  conservative social values and, 934
  Crusades and, 17
  cultural conflict and, 681, 686–688
  diversity of, 102, 105–111, 112(m),
  119(f)
  English civil war and, 59, 70
  Enlightenment and, 275–277
  established church and, 251
  in Europe, 17–18, 28–29, 32–33,
  32(m), 37
  evolution and, 688(i)
  extremism in, 943
  freedom of, 58, 72, 190–191
  intolerance and, 57
  justification of slavery and, 369
  kinship and, 83
  vs. laws of nature, 60
  leisure and, 707
  medieval, 17–18
  in Middle Atlantic colonies
  (1720–1765), 102, 105–111,
  112(m)
  Native American, 9–10, 12–13, 44–45
  New Age, 888
  in 1920s, 693
  in 1950s, 822, 847
  Okie, 711
  parochial schools and, 521
  on plantations, 112, 119–121
  politics and, 316
  prayer in public schools and, 881, 903
  progressive idealism and, 575
  reform and, 341–365
  separation of church and state,
  190–191, 251, 452–453
  social meaning and, 566
  society and, 58–60
  taxation and, 190, 453
  utopian reformers and, 336
  wars of, 17–18, 37, 59
  women's rights and, 358, 362
religious factions. See Native
  Americans
Religious Right, 453
  1980 election and, 903
"Remember the *Maine*," 613(i)

Renaissance, 37
  American, 261
  impact of, 19, 37
  Muslim influences on, 18–19
Reno, Janet, 923, 928
rent riots, 717
Reorganized Church of Jesus Christ of
  Latter-day Saints, 352
los repatriados, 712–713
representative government, 137–141
republicanism, 184–191, 193, 316
  artisan, 332
  charters and, 245
  classical, 206
  condemnation of, 311
  education of children and, 257–261,
  260(i), 261(i)
  evangelical Christianity and, 272–279
  ideals of, under wartime pressure,
  185–186
  institutions of, 194–219
  literary culture of, 260–261
  modern, 801–803
  of Puritans, 143, 146, 151, 159, 161
  religion and, 190
  as representative government, 251
  rights of women and, 253–259,
  257(i), 258(i)
  social classes and, 303–307
  the South and, 440
  testing of, 185
  Virginia Plan and, 203
republican motherhood, 255–259,
  258(i), 278–279, 358
Republican Party (Jeffersonian), 240
  agricultural expansion and, 230,
  248
  commonwealth idea and, 245–246
  vs. Federalists, 212, 216, 249
  War of 1812 and, 235
Republican Party (1850s–on), 415,
  642, 945
  African Americans and, 738
  agricultural expansion and, 411
  anticommunism and, 800
  on big government, 804, 843(m)
  candidates of, 928
  Clinton and, 933
  in Congress, 935, 944
  conservatism of, 869, 869(m), 876
  constituents of, 667
  "Contract with America" and, 930
  defense expenditures and, 804
  Democrats and, 320, 424
  domestic policies of, 880–881
  Douglass and, 381
  draft riots and, 408
  factions of, 248, 317
  free silver and, 573
  free-soil policy of, 413
  Halfbreeds in, 521, 523

isolationism in, 787
JFK and, 834
Ku Klux Klan and, 445, 447
law and order campaign of, 869, 869(m), 877
liberal, 449
Lincoln and, 391–394
as majority party, 667, 903, 903(m)
modern, 801–803
Mugwumps and, 523
national mercantilism and, 409
New Deal and, 727, 746, 798
in 1920s, 693
1928 election and, 692
1932 election and, 717–718
1936 election and, 729
1938 election and, 732
1980 election and, 903
origins of, 388–389, 395
Peace Democrats and, 424
pietism and, 520, 535
presidency and, 666
protectionism and, 517, 672
Protestants and, 520–521, 521(f)
realignment of, 392(m)
Reconstruction and, 429, 435–436, 451
reform and, 596
in Senate, 930, 944
silent majority and, 869
slavery and, 394, 397, 399
social welfare and, 804
in the South, 439–440, 450, 880–881
Stalwarts in, 521, 523
Theodore Roosevelt and, 591, 598
veterans' benefits and, 518
white supremacy and, 589
women's rights groups and, 439, 441
in WWII, 761–762
republic, meaning of, 185
reservations
of Dakota territory, 469–471, 470(m), 471(m), 473, 864
of Oklahoma territory, 470(m)
Resettlement Administration, 745
African Americans and, 735
Resolution Trust Corporation, 912
Restoration (Great Britain), 70–72
Restraining Act (1767), 146
restrictive covenants, 818
Revels, Hiram, 441(i)
Revenue Acts
of 1673, 72, 72(t)
of 1762, 136, 145, 155(t)
of 1767, 145
of 1935, 729, 731(t)
of 1942, 755
tax cuts and, 666
revenue-sharing program, 880
Revere, Paul, 158

revivalism, 252, 254, 308–311, 308(i), 313, 335, 566, 686. See also evangelicalism; Great Awakening; Second Great Awakening
abolitionism and, 355
in colonial America, 114–121
in postcolonial America, 252, 254
Second Great Awakening and, 275(m), 279
social reform and, 308–311, 308(i), 313
Revolutionary War
armies and strategies in, 171–172
battles in, 133(i), 155(t), 157(i), 158–159, 166–167, 171–176, 171(m), 179–182, 185, 191, 234
British strategies in, 177
causes of. See Revolutionary War (prewar events)
diplomatic triumph in, 182, 184
financial crisis in, 174–175
in the North, 170–171
paper money in, 412
partisan warfare in Carolinas, 179, 182
Patriot advantage in, 182
Patriot and Loyalist strongholds in, 170(m)
political legacy of, 195
publishing and, 144
response in Britain to, 176–177
rights of man and, 112–113, 143–144
social and financial perils in, 174
in the South, 177–182, 178(m)
Treaty of Alliance with France (1778), 175, 177
women in, 185(i)
Revolutionary War (prewar events)
Boston Massacre, 149
Boston Tea Party, 142(i), 150–153, 153(i), 155(t)
boycotts, 141, 144–146, 147(i), 149, 149(f), 154, 157(i), 159
Committees of Correspondence, 150–151, 155(t)
Daughters of Liberty, 146, 147(i), 159
Intolerable Acts (1774), 151
Loyalists, 152, 155–157
militia, 124, 129–130, 133(i), 134, 155(t), 157–158, 157(i)
Quartering Acts, 140, 145–146, 151, 154, 155(t)
Sons of Liberty, 141, 142(i), 143, 147(i), 150, 153, 155(t), 159
Stamp Act (1765), 134, 138–146, 149, 155(t), 159
taxation, 134–150, 154–155, 159
Tea Act (1773), 150, 155(t), 159

Reyneau, Betsy Graves, 736(i)
Reynolds v. Sims (1964), 881
Rhee, Syngman, 791
Rhett, Robert Barnwell, 394, 398
Rhoads, Molly, 256
Rhode Island, 58, 198, 202, 204–205
as corporate government, 75
currency in, 98
1928 election and, 692
revocation of corporate charters, 73
voting rights in, 316
Rhodes, Elisha Hunt, 397, 407
rice
African knowledge of, 84, 86–87
colonial production of, 129, 138(m), 160, 160(f)
exporting of, 127, 138(m), 149
hulling of, 87(i)
production, 265(m), 266
slavery and, 84–87, 160
South Atlantic system and, 99
in South Carolina, 86, 95, 129
Southern production of, 263, 265(m), 266
Rice, Spotswood, 419
Richards, David A. J., 280
Rich, Denise, 934
Richelieu River (River of the Iroquois), 45, 63
Rich, Mark, 934
Richmond, Virginia, 181
in Civil War, 403, 409–410, 420, 424–425
food riots in, 413
free blacks in, 269
manufacturing in, 292, 298(m), 301, 301(m), 302(m), 411(i)
trolley cars in, 546
Rickenbacker, Eddie, 645
Ridge, Thomas, 947
Riis, Jacob, 557, 576
Rio Grande (river), 11, 121, 376, 478
Rio Grande Valley, Hispanic settlement in, 474, 478
Rio Treaty (Inter-American Treaty of Reciprocal Assistance; 1947), 795(m)
riots. See also mobs
anti-U.S., 605
armory construction and, 486
in Detroit, 764, 861–862, 862(m)
draft, 407–408, 408(i), 427
food, 413
by homosexuals, 864
in Los Angeles, 836(m), 861, 862(m), 924, 924(i)
in Newark, 861, 862(m)
rent, 717
school busing and, 894(i), 897
Stonewall, 864

riots (Continued):
   urban, 849, 861–862, 862(m), 867, 869, 877, 924
The Rise of David Levinsky (Cahan), 562
The Rise of Silas Lapham (Howells), 570
Roanoke (lost colony), 48
Roaring Twenties, 688, 693
The Robber Barons (Josephson), 492
Robertson, Pat, 898, 925
Robeson, Paul, 806
Robespierre, Maximilien, 213
Robinson, Edward G., 706
Robinson, Jackie, 804
Robinson, John, 59
Rochambeau, comte de, 179, 182
Rochester, New York, 309
   transportation and, 301(m), 302, 302(m)
Rockefeller, John D., 494, 575(i), 580
Rockingham, Lord, 144(t), 145
rock 'n' roll, 825–826, 856, 859–860
Rockwell, Norman, 759
Rocky Mountains, 11, 233, 241, 474
   formation of, 458
rodeos, 463
Rodgers, John, 276
Roe v. Wade (1973), 881, 892, 911, 926
Rogers, Ginger, 705(i), 706, 908(i)
Rogers, Robert, 124(i)
Rogers, William, 874
Rolfe, John, 43, 49
Rolling Stones, 860
Roman Catholic Church. See Catholicism; Catholics
Roman Catholics. See Catholics
Romanticism, 254, 342
Rome, ancient, 19–20
Rommel, Erwin, 769
Roosevelt Corollary (to Monroe Doctrine), 626
Roosevelt, Eleanor, 718, 735, 735(i)
   African Americans and, 737–738
   civil rights and, 760
   Great Depression and, 701–702
   Stevenson and, 802
   travels of, 738(m)
   Truman and, 783
Roosevelt family, 106(m)
Roosevelt, Franklin Delano (1882–1945), 657, 743(i), 783. See also New Deal
   aid to Britain and, 752
   Alger Hiss and, 800
   Atlantic Charter and, 752(m), 753
   death of, 775, 785
   four terms of, 830
   Great Depression and, 701, 702(m), 719
   Holocaust and, 770–771
   isolationism and, 751

   Japanese internment and, 765
   Kaiser and, 756
   labor unions and, 734, 760
   leadership of, 722–723
   1932 election and, 717–718
   1934 Democratic candidates and, 944
   on Pearl Harbor, 754
   popularity of, 722, 722(i)
   presidency and, 731
   as president (1933–1945), 717–718, 718(m), 721–747, 749–775
   reforms of, 761–762
   second term of, 799
   Soviet Union and, 786
   Stalin and, 784, 786
   third term of, 753
   as vice-presidential candidate, 666
   wartime planning and, 768–769
   welfare system and, 778, 778(i)
   WWII and, 750, 761–762, 777
   at Yalta, 773–775, 775(i)
Roosevelt, New Jersey, 743(i)
Roosevelt, Theodore (1858–1919), 523, 554, 575–576, 581, 591–595, 599, 642
   attack on legal system, 597
   balance of power philosophy of, 623
   "bully pulpit" of, 595(i)
   conservation and, 591
   "Great White Fleet" and, 611
   Japanese immigration and, 682
   popular vote of, 928
   presidency and, 722
   as president (1901–1909), 608, 622–623, 627–630, 632
   as rancher, 464
   as "Rough Rider," 616
   Spanish-American War and, 609, 611, 616
   Square Deal of, 595, 595(i), 601
   Taft and, 596
   trust-busting and, 593–594, 596
   U.S. expansion and, 604
   Wall Street Giants and, 593(i)
Root, Elihu, 625, 629–630
Rosebud reservation, South Dakota, 864
Rosellini, Lynn, 895
Rosenberg, Ethel, 800
Rosenberg, Julius, 800–801
Rosenberg, Robert, 933(i)
Rosie the Riveter, 759
Ross, Edward A., 586
Rough Riders, 616–617
Route 66, 710(m)
Rowlandson, Mary, 64
Royal African Company, 79
Roybal, Edward, 863
Rubin, Jerry, 868
Ruckle, Thomas Cole, 221(i)

Ruef, Abe, 584
Ruffin, Thomas, 369
rum, 91, 97(i), 98
Rumsfeld, Donald, 934
Rural Electrification Administration, 741, 744
rural life
   of African Americans, 88
   automobile and, 675, 682
   electrification and, 744, 744(i)
   ethnic diversity and, 467(m)
   in Europe, 14–16, 16(f)
   Ku Klux Klan in, 684
   manufacturing and, 242
   mass media and, 681–682
   on mid-nineteenth-century plains, 459–460
   Prohibition and, 653–654, 654(m)
   urbanization and, 681
   in the West, 474–477
Rush-Bagot Treaty, 240
Rush, Benjamin, 167, 185, 256–257, 259
Russell, Charles Edward, 576
Russia. See also Soviet Union
   in Afghanistan, 943
   Alaska and, 375
   claims on China of, 607
   Germany and, 644
   immigration restriction and, 683
   1917 revolution in, 644, 918
   post–Soviet Union, 912, 936
   war on terrorism and, 941
   in WWI, 638–639, 644
Russia Leaves the War (Kennan), 787
Russo-Japanese War (1904–1905), 627, 627(m)
Russwurm, John, 352
Rust Belt, 886–887, 886(m)
Rustin, Bayard, 839
Rutgers University, 119(t)
   founding of, 118
Ruth, Babe, 680

Sacco, Nicola, 662
Sacco-Vanzetti case, 662
Sackville-West, Lionel, 603
Sacramento, California, 460, 477(m)
Sacramento Valley, California, 375(i)
al-Sadat, Anwar
   assassination of, 912
   Camp David accords and, 901–902, 901(i)
Sagoyewatha (Red Jacket; c.1758–1830), 222(i), 224
Sahagún, Friar Bernardino de, 26
Saigon, Vietnam, 850–852, 854, 856(i), 867, 873
   fall of, 872(i)
St. Augustine, 41, 41(m), 42

St. Lawrence River, 44–45, 121, 125
St. Leger, Colonel Barry, 171(*m*), 172–173
St. Louis, Missouri, 12
    transportation and, 298(*m*), 300–303, 300(*m*), 301(*m*), 302(*m*)
St. Louis Post-Dispatch, 569
St. Mary's (first settlement), 40(*t*), 50
St. Paul, Minnesota, 461
St. Thomas's African Church, 270
Salem, Massachusetts, 58
    popular power in, 94
    witchcraft trials in, 60
Salisbury, Stephan, 200
Salmagundi (Irving), 260
saloons, 306. *See also* taverns
    temperance movement and, 522, 524, 526(*i*)
    in Wild West, 477
Salter, John, 837
SALT I (Strategic Arms Limitations Treaty), 871
SALT II (Strategic Arms Limitation Treaty), 899, 901
Salt Lake City, Utah, 476
salutary neglect, 95, 95(*i*), 98–99
Salvation Army, 566
Samoa, 606
    U.S. acquisition of (1900), 622
San Diego, California
    population in, 477(*m*)
    tourism in, 481
Sandinistas, 909, 912
SANE (National Committee for a Sane Nuclear Policy), 809, 857
San Francisco, California
    Anglo migration to, 478
    anti-Chinese agitation in, 480
    Asian Americans in, 714
    Chinatown in, 479
    connected to East, 460
    earthquake (1906) in, 548
    Eastern connections of, 460
    as economic hub of the West, 477, 477(*m*)
    elite in, 550
    gold rush and, 383, 385(*m*), 551
    growth of, 474–475, 477(*m*)
    strikes in, 728(*i*)
    water needs of, 482
San Francisco Examiner, 614
Sanger, Margaret, 582, 703–704
San Jacinto, battle of (1836), 371
San Juan Hill, battle of (1898), 591, 617, 617(*i*), 618(*i*)
Santa Anna, Antonio López de, 371–372, 378, 378(*m*), 379
Santa Fe, New Mexico, 41(*m*), 44, 378
    Hispanic culture of, 478, 481
Santa Fe Railroad, 461, 461(*m*), 481

Santa Fe Trail, 374(*m*)
Santiago (Cuba), 615, 617
Santiago de Cuba, battle of (1898), 603(*i*)
Santo Domingo, 605
Sarajevo, Serbia, 639, 929
Saratoga, battle of (1777), 171(*m*), 172–176, 179, 182, 185, 191
    Benedict Arnold at, 180–181
Sargent, John Singer, 556(*i*)
Saturday Evening Post, 823(*i*)
Saudi Arabia, 941, 943
    Afghanistan and, 901
    Iraq and, 915
    oil production in, 884
    Persian Gulf War and, 913
Sauer, Christopher, 257
Sauk Indians, 65, 236, 326, 328(*i*), 329
Savage, Augusta, 690
Savannah, Georgia, 178, 178(*m*), 187, 424
Saving Private Ryan (film), 771(*i*)
Savings and Loan crisis, 912
scalawags, 440
Scalia, Antonin, 909
The Scarlet Letter (Hawthorne), 345
Schechter v. United States, 726, 730
Schenck, Charles T., 655
Schenck v. United States (1919), 655
Schlafly, Phyllis, 892–893
Schlesinger, Arthur, Jr., 778, 883
Schneebeli, Heinrich, 108
Schneiderman, Rose, 508–509, 579, 579(*i*)
Schroeder, Patricia, 889
Schulberg, B. P., 678
Schurz, Carl, 523, 620
Schuyler, Philip, 172
Schwarzkopf, H. Norman, 913
Schwerner, Michael, 840
Schwerner, Rita, 840
science
    art and, 569
    of management, 503–505, 513
    progressivism and, 574
    social, 580
Scientology, Church of, 888
SCLC. *See* Southern Christian Leadership Conference
Scopes, John T., 687
Scopes ("monkey") trial (1925), 687–688, 688(*i*)
Scots-Irish
    in colonial America, 101, 109, 110, 110(*m*), 120, 123, 127
    as inmates, 106
    in Middle Atlantic colonies, 110–111, 110(*m*), 114, 127
    in Pennsylvania colony, 105–106
    against Quaker pacifism, 106
Scott, Hugh, 883

Scott, Julian, 423(*i*)
Scottsboro case, 708–709
Scott, Winfield, 328, 378–379, 378(*m*), 401, 403
    1852 election and, 388(*i*), 392(*m*)
    as presidential nominee, 387
The Scouts of the Prairie (Buntline), 462
Scudder, Vida, 554
Sea Islands, 434
Seale, Bobby, 861
Seamen's Act (1916), 600
Sears, Isaac, 142
Sears, Roebuck, 467, 495
SEATO. *See* Southeast Asia Treaty Organization
Seattle, Washington, 477, 477(*m*)
secession, 395, 398–407, 416
    Compromise of 1850 and, 384–385
    Constitution and, 430
    end of, 427
    insurrection and, 399
    Lincoln and, 391, 394
    process of, 399(*m*)
    Sherman on, 422–423
    slave vs. free state conflict and, 383
    southern leaders and, 394
    Upper South states and, 398–401, 399(*m*)
Second Amendment, 210
Second Bank of the United States, 246
    war against, 324–326, 326(*i*), 337
Second Great Awakening (1820–1860), 272–279, 275(*m*), 308, 311, 313, 452. *See also* evangelicalism; Great Awakening; revivalism
    abolitionism and, 352
    child rearing and, 258
    women's rights and, 358
Second Party System, 330, 332, 335(*i*), 339, 395
    end of, 385–391
secret ballot, 523, 524(*m*)
secularism
    Constitution and, 452–453
    evolution and, 687–688
Securities and Exchange Commission (SEC), 726, 731(*t*), 945
Sedition Act (1918), 655
Seeger, Charles, 743
Seeger, Pete, 859–860
Seeger, Ruth Crawford, 743
segregation, 534, 869. *See also* busing, school; desegregation
    in cities, 924
    Jim Crow and, 529–531, 863
    laws supporting, 525, 531, 541
    in military, 750, 758, 760
    opposition to, 804
    residential, 709

segregation (Continued):
school, 760, 836(m)
of transportation, 838
Seguara, Juan Baptista de, 43
Selassie, Haile, 750
Selective Service Act (1917), 643
self-determination, national, 796
Atlantic Charter and, 753
movements for, 833(m)
Yalta and, 773
self-government
colonial assemblies and, 140, 143,
145–146, 149, 154, 157, 159
Sellars, John, 292
Sellars, Samuel, 292
Selma, Alabama
civil rights protests in, 842,
842(i)
A Seminary for Young Ladies, 261(i)
Seminole Indians, 12, 267, 326, 327(i),
327(m), 328, 470, 470(m)
Senate, U.S.
Clinton's impeachment trial and, 932
conduct of diplomacy and, 604
Democratic Party control of, 909
Joint Committee on Reconstruction
of, 431
Kyoto Treaty and, 927
Republican control of, 903, 903(m)
Republican gains in, 930, 944
Watergate Committee of, 882–883,
883(i)
Wilmot Proviso and, 379
women in, 911(i)
Seneca Falls convention (1848),
362–364, 381, 653
Seneca Falls Declaration (1848), 364
Seneca Indians, 14, 64, 224, 236
self-government and, 740
Senegal, Africa, 20
Senegambia, Africa, 21
sentimentalism, 254, 255(i), 259, 279
Seoul, South Korea, 792–793
separation of powers, 219, 730. *See also*
checks and balances
September 11, 2001, terrorist attacks,
452, 916(m), 936–940, 936(i),
938(i), 939(i)
economy and, 945
Sequoia National Park, 482
Sequoyah, 326
Serbia, 639, 929, 931–932, 932(m)
Servicemen's Readjustment Act (GI
Bill; 1944), 762, 797
settlement houses, 573(i), 575,
577–578, 577(i)
Seven Years' War, 121, 124–126, 130,
133–134, 134(i), 138(m), 145,
159, 170. *See also* French and
Indian War
Sewall, Samuel, 60

Seward, William H., 384, 391, 394,
414(i), 604
Sex in Education (Clarke), 555
sexual harassment, 911, 911(i)
feminism and, 925
against women in military, 914(i)
sexuality
automobile and, 675
changing views of, 554–556, 571
cultural conflict and, 681
disease and, 653
flapper and, 676
jazz and, 677
music and, 826
Oneida Community and, 348–349
rock 'n' roll and, 825
Shakers and, 346–347
slavery and, 362
women's rights and, 358, 893
Sexual Politics (Millett), 926
Seymour, Horatio, 414, 438
Shahn, Ben, 733(i), 743(i), 745
Shakers, 277, 346–347, 346(m), 365
Dickens on, 348
Shakespeare, William, 570
Shalala, Donna E., 928
shaman, 44
sharecropping, 442–444, 443(i)
African Americans and, 708, 735
New Deal and, 724, 746
Share Our Wealth Society, 727, 727(i),
729, 734(m), 747
Sharpsburg, Maryland, 405
Shaw, Lemuel, 333
Shawnee Indians, 123–124, 129, 222,
224, 236–237
Shays, Daniel, 200(i), 201, 205
Shaysites, 214
Shays's Rebellion, 200–201, 200(i),
201–202, 219
Sheehan, Neil, 874–875
Sheen, Bishop Fulton, 822
Shelburne, earl of, 145
Sheldon, Charles M., 566
Sheldon, Lucy, 227(i)
Shelley v. Kraemer (1948), 804, 818
shell shock, 639(i)
Shepard, Alan, 835
Sheppard-Towner Act (1921), 668–669
Sheridan, Philip H., 421, 461, 604
Sheridan, Robert, 268
Sherman Antitrust Act (1890), 586,
592–593, 595–596, 599
Sherman, John, 423
Sherman, Roger, 169(i)
Sherman Silver Purchase Act (1890), 538
Sherman, William Tecumseh
(1820–1891), 419–420, 422(i),
450
as architect of modern war, 422–423
biographical information, 422–423

capture of Atlanta, 424, 427
land for liberated slaves and, 434
march to the sea, 424–425, 425(m),
427, 432
total war and, 424–425
Shiloh, battle of, 397(i), 406–407, 423,
446
shipbuilding industry, 91
arms control and, 673
Kaiser and, 756(i), 757
wartime migration and, 764(i)
Shippen, Margaret, 181
shoemaking, 286, 287(t)
*The Shop and Warehouse of Duncan
Phyfe* (painting), 213
shopkeepers, 105–106, 142, 161
shopping malls, 820
Shore, Dinah, 822(i)
Shores, Jerry, 468(i)
*A Short Narrative of the Horrid
Massacre in Boston* (1770), 152
Shriver, Sargent, 845
Shuttlesworth, Fred, 838
Siberia, 6
Sicily, WWII in, 768(m), 770
Sierra Club, 482
Sierra Leone, Africa, 187
as African American colony,
270–271
Sierra Nevada (mountains), 474–475,
479–483, 480(i), 483(i)
*The Significance of the Frontier in
American History* (Turner), 609
Silent Spring (Carson), 888, 888(i)
Silliman, Benjamin, 214
Simpson, O. J., 918
Sinai Peninsula, 902
Sinclair, Upton, 595, 734(m)
Singer Sewing Machine Company, 292,
494, 606, 606(i)
Sinners in the Hands of an Angry God
(Edwards), 116
Sino-Japanese War (1894–1895), 607,
627
Sioux Indians, 470(m), 471(m)
AIM and, 863–864, 865(i)
Battle of Little Big Horn and, 463,
471
religion of, 459–460
Teton, 459–460, 459(i), 469, 473
wars with, 462–463
Wounded Knee massacre and, 457,
470(m), 472–473, 472(i)
Sister Carrie (Dreiser), 543
Sisterhood Is Powerful (Morgan, ed.), 926
sit-ins
civil rights movement and, 836–837
1970s activism and, 888
Sitting Bull, chief of Sioux, 463
Six Companies, 479
Six Nations. *See* Iroquois Indians

skyscrapers, 547
Slater, Samuel, 288–289, 289(i)
"Slave-Power" conspiracy, 379, 387, 390–391, 393
slave rebellion, 85, 262, 266, 268(i), 274, 381, 394
    abolitionism and, 352–353
    fear of, 83, 321, 323(i)
    in Haiti, 231
slavery, 76–93, 187(i). See also cotton; Emancipation Proclamation; Middle Passage; plantations; the South
    abolition of, 191, 424, 429–430, 443
    antislavery movement and. See abolitionism
    British Empire and, 69, 98
    in Chesapeake colony, 69(i), 80, 84–86, 99, 105, 160, 263, 263(i), 265–266, 265(m)
    Civil War and, 160, 397, 402, 413–415, 419
    in colonial America, 50, 53, 56, 61, 63, 67, 101, 121, 129, 131, 155–156, 157(i), 160–161
    colonization and, 134(m), 262, 270–271, 354, 393
    Constitutional Convention and, 204
    cotton and, 226, 262–264, 368–369
    economics of, 305
    in 1800, 189(m)
    expansion of, 198, 262–263, 263(f), 263(i), 264(m), 279, 296, 297(m), 376–385, 386(m), 389, 395, 462
    family life and, 263–267
    fugitive slave laws and, 262, 271
    justifications for, 369
    legalization of, 56
    Lincoln and, 393–394
    Mexican War and, 379
    in Mexico, 370
    in Middle Atlantic colonies, 105–106
    Mormons and, 352
    Northwest Ordinance and, 200
    politics and, 339, 365, 375, 383–385, 392(m), 394
    positions on, 113, 317(i), 318, 422
    in postcolonial America, 261–272, 263(f), 263(i), 265(m), 265(t), 266(i), 272(m)
    property rights and, 269
    protection of, 394, 399
    Quakers and, 108
    reform movement and, 342, 361
    republicanism and, 187–188
    Republican Party and, 389
    resettlement to old Southwest and, 263(f), 263(i), 264(m), 265(t), 296, 297(m)

Revolutionary War and, 170, 178–179, 179(i), 187–190
    sadism under, 89
    secession and, 401(t), 414
    slave vs. free states and, 382–384, 391, 395
    in West Indies, 69, 76, 77(t), 78, 80, 84, 88, 99, 321
    westward expansion and, 387–388
    white south and, 526
    women and, 84, 362, 370
slaves
    African, 24, 52–53, 56, 85(t)
    arming, 425
    auctions of, 225(i)
    British and, 177, 191
    denial of education to, 88, 353
    Dutch and, 74(i), 77
    emancipation of, 188–189, 262, 269, 274, 433, 440
    fugitive, 204, 271, 355, 384–387, 388(i), 395, 413, 415
    Indian peoples and, 88
    labor gang system and, 342, 368, 434, 442–443
    in Middle Atlantic colonies, 105–106
    Muslim beliefs and, 87
    Native American, 50, 61, 63
    as property, 206, 413
    relocation of, 263, 263(f), 263(i), 264(m), 296
    resettlement of freed, 134(m), 262, 270–271, 354, 393
    resistance by, 88–89, 369
    three-fifths rule for, 218
    westward migration and, 226
slave trade
    abolition of, 204, 262, 265, 271, 384
    in Africa, 20–22, 21(m), 37
    with Africa, 5–6, 20–22, 21(m), 37, 78(m), 93(m), 265(t)
    South Atlantic system and, 76–80, 77(m), 92, 99
Slavs, Holocaust and, 750, 770
Slidell, John, 376–377
Sloan, Alfred P., Jr., 670
Sloan, John, 689(i)
Sloat, John, 378, 378(m)
The Small Herbal of Little Cost (Sauer), 256–257
smallpox, 25–26, 28(m), 56, 61, 64, 459
    inoculation for, 113, 117
Smallwood, William, 172
Smibert, John, 92(i)
Smith, Adam, 79, 212
Smith, Alfred E. (Al), 585–586, 668, 691–692, 718
Smith, Bessie, 677, 680
Smith-Connally Labor Act (1943), 760
Smith, Franklin, 158

Smith, Hiram, 349(i)
Smith, Jerry, 895
Smith, John Rubens, 213(i)
Smith, Joseph (1805–1844), 349–351, 365
Smith, Joseph, III, 352
Smith, Mamie, 677, 677(i)
Smith, Margaret Bayard, 322
Smith, Melancton, 205
Smith, Seba (Major Jack Downing), 326, 326(i)
Smith, William, 269
Smith, William, Jr., 206
smuggling, 98, 136–137, 149
SNCC. See Student Non-Violent Coordinating Committee
Social Darwinism, 574, 609, 631
The Social Destiny of Man (Brisbane), 347
social insurance, 587. See also health insurance; welfare
socialism, 336–337, 346, 348, 511–513
    conservative opposition to, 898
    "creeping," 799
    New Deal and, 726
    pan-Arab, 796
    utopian reformers and, 575
    women activists and, 509, 511
Socialist Labor Party (1877), 511
Socialist Party, 511, 575, 586, 598(m), 640, 661
    1932 election and, 718, 718(m)
social mobility
    African, 53
    downward, 701
    Great Depression and, 705
    as republican ideal, 252, 279
    Republican Party and, 389
    transcendentalism and, 344
    work ethic and, 305, 311
social reform
    activism in, 813
    asylums and, 357–358, 360–361
    blue laws and, 521, 539
    children and, 358–359
    Dix and, 361
    evangelicalism and, 308–311, 313, 342
    of nineteenth century, 306–311, 313
    in 1920s, 666, 668
    1964 election and, 843(m)
    in 1970s, 880, 887–897, 905
    opposition to, 668, 898–899
    prisons and, 306(i), 307, 357–358, 360
    Protestantism and, 272, 276–278, 306, 313
    religion and, 341–365
    revivalism and, 308–311, 308(i), 313
    sexually transmitted diseases and, 653

social reform (Continued):
    urban liberalism and, 668
    utopian, 336–337
    welfare system and, 778
    women and, 315(i), 358. See also
        women activists
    women's rights and, 358, 364, 509,
        651–653
    WWII and, 761
Social Security Act (1935), 726, 728,
    731(t), 747
    limitations of, 746
    Supreme Court on, 730
    welfare system and, 778, 778(i),
        779
    women and, 735
Social Security system, 280
    in Clinton administration, 930, 933
    expansion of, 844
    increase in, 803
    JFK and, 835
    Nixon and, 880
    Reagan and, 908–909
    in Truman administration, 799
    vs. welfare, 778
social structure, 550. See also elite;
        gentry class; middle class;
        working class
    in Africa, 20
    African Americans and, 50, 53
    Aztec, 9–10, 25
    of British colonies, 70–71
    in Chesapeake colonies, 90–91
    English, 35–36
    European medieval, 14–19, 37
    Great Depression and, 699
    hierarchy in, 17
    immigrants and, 303, 311–312
    Inca, 25
    Industrial Revolution and, 286,
        303–307, 304(i), 313
    market economy and, 286, 303–306,
        304(i)
    matrilineal societies and, 12
    Native American, 9, 12
    Oneida Community and, 349
    peasants in, 35
    politics and, 316
    race and, 6, 28, 53, 357
    race riots and, 924
    Republican Party and, 389
    revolt and, 54–56, 573
    social order and, 571
    in the South, 252, 261, 312, 369,
        526, 529, 541
    South Atlantic system and, 91–93
    in Spanish America, 25–28
    wealth and, 94(f)
    yeoman, 35–37, 54, 60–61
social values
    in new world, 37, 56

Society for Promoting Christian
        Knowledge, 277
Society for the Free Instruction of
        African Females, 277
Society for the Promotion of
        Industry, 308
Society for the Relief of Poor
        Widows, 277
Society for the Relief of the Poor
        Widows with Small Children, 308
Society of Friends. See Quakers
Sociology for the South; or, the Failure of
        Free Society (Fitzhugh), 370
sod houses, 465, 468(i)
Soest, Gerard, 69(i)
Sokoloff, Nicholas, 743
Solemn League and Covenant, 154
Solomon Islands, 771, 772, 772(m)
Somalia, 929, 942
Sone, Monica, 767
Sonntag, W. Louis Jr., 565(i)
Sons of Liberty, 141, 142(i), 143,
        147(i), 150, 153, 155, 155(t), 159,
        214. See also mobs
Soto, Hernán de, 12, 40, 41(m)
The Souls of Black Folk (Du Bois),
        534, 589
The Sound and the Fury (Faulkner), 690
Souter, David, 911
the South. See also Civil War; cotton;
        plantations; slavery
    abolitionism and, 357, 359, 367–368
    African American migration from,
        650–652, 650(m), 690
    African Americans in, 708
    agricultural economy of, 301–302,
        495
    American System and, 318
    civil rights movement and, 839
    class distinctions in, 252, 261, 312,
        526, 529, 541
    cotton and, 495, 497, 497(i)
    Democratic Party in, 394, 667, 718,
        731, 746, 798, 834
    economic growth of, 847, 886(m),
        887
    elite life in, 368–369
    FDR and, 735
    Fugitive Slave Act and, 386
    gentry class in, 89–91
    Great Depression and, 702(m)
    Jim Crow laws in, 529–531, 863
    labor unions in, 887
    low wages in, 495–497, 513, 526,
        535(f)
    migration to and from, 225–226,
        226(m), 296, 297(m), 498, 724,
        817–819, 828, 886(m), 887
    New Deal and, 735
    New South (1900) and, 495–498,
        496(m), 497(i), 529(m)

    1928 election and, 691
    1936 election and, 729
    1980 election and, 903
    Nixon and, 880–881
    vs. the North, 368
    policies of John Q. Adams and, 319,
        319(i)
    Populism in, 526–531, 533–534
    race in, 252
    racism in, 525–526, 541, 863
    segregation in, 525, 531, 541, 869
    slavery in, 261–269, 331, 402
    slave vs. free states and, 383–384
    tariffs and, 323
    tenant farmers of, 131, 261, 526
    urbanization of, 681(m)
    voter registration in, 843(m)
South Africa, 929
    apartheid in, 930
    human rights in, 901
South America, 28, 605
    Chinese immigration to, 479
    colonization of, 134(m)
    foreign aid in, 833
    foreign investment in, 670, 672–673
    immigrants from, 684, 828(f), 844,
        937
    slave imports in, 77(t)
    trade with, 303
    U.S. intervention in, 604–605, 607,
        673, 913(m)
    U.S. relations with, 751, 901
South Atlantic system, 76–80, 99
    Navigation Acts and, 98
    social structure and, 91–93
    urbanization and, 91
South Carolina
    abolitionism and, 367–368
    Acadians in, 124
    African culture in, 88(i)
    Civil War and, 424–425
    class in, 90–91
    as colony, 70, 75–76, 85
    economy of, 213
    evangelicals in, 121
    indigo production in, 127
    kinship in, 86
    Ku Klux Klan in, 445
    land disputes in, 131
    lawyers in, 253(t)
    migration to and from, 226, 296,
        297(m)
    nullification and, 322–323, 323(i),
        339
    ratification of Constitution and,
        205
    Regulators and, 129, 129(m), 131
    Republican government in, 449–451
    revivals in, 273
    rice in, 86, 95
    secession and, 385, 398

slavery in, 80, 84–85, 85(f), 88–89, 99, 121, 160, 261–267, 265(m), 272(m), 321, 323(i), 368
tariffs and, 321–323, 323(i)
voting rights in, 252
war with Spain and, 96
Southeast Asia Treaty Organization (SEATO), 795, 795(m)
Southern Christian Leadership Conference (SCLC), 806, 837, 839
Southern Cross: The Beginnings of the Bible Belt (Heyrman), 452
Southern Homestead Act (1866), 442
Southern Manifesto, 805
Southern Rights Democrats, 394
Southern Tenant Farmers Union (STFU), 708, 734(m)
Southgate, Eliza, 254
South Korea, 791–792, 794
    human rights in, 901
South, the. *See also* slavery
South Vietnam. *See* Vietnam War
Southwest. *See also* Old Southwest
    Anglo-Hispanic conflict in, 478
    economic growth of, 886(m), 887
    Hispanic settlement in, 474, 478–479, 479(i), 483
Southwest, Old (Alabama, Mississippi, Louisiana)
    migration to, 263(f), 263(i), 264(m), 265(t), 296, 297(m), 313
Soviet Union, 657–658. *See also* Russia
    in Afghanistan, 901, 912, 941
    arms race with, 871–872
    atomic bomb and, 776, 948
    Carter and, 901
    collapse of (1991), 787, 907, 912, 914(m), 932(m), 937, 941
    communism in, 733, 765, 797, 799–800, 806, 912
    Cuba and, 833
    Eastern Europe and, 773–775, 777
    FDR and, 786
    Germany and, 751, 753, 774
    Greece and, 785–788
    human rights in, 900
    immigrants from, 921
    intraparty struggle in, 794
    Japan and, 769
    Jews in, 900
    JFK and, 831
    Marshall Plan and, 787
    Nasser and, 796
    nuclear test ban treaties and, 834
    vs. postwar U.S., 816
    satellite states of, 773
    space program of, 803, 803(i)
    Spanish civil war and, 751
    Third World and, 797
    U.S. recognition of, 751

U.S. relations with, 783–785, 791, 813
Vietnam and, 850
war in Pacific and, 769, 773, 773(m)
in WWII, 768(m), 768–769, 769(m), 777
Soyer, Moses, 695(i)
space program, 834–835
    economic growth and, 886(m), 887
    JFK and, 830
    Soviet, 803, 803(i)
Spain. *See also* Spanish-American war
    acquisition of territories from, 617–619
    Cuba and, 375, 609, 612–619
    vs. England, 33, 35, 40–41, 95, 98
    expansionist foreign policy of, 387
    fascism in, 742
    vs. France, 40–41
    Islam in, 17
    maritime expansion of, 19, 22, 22(m)
    Mexican independence from, 370
    missions of, 41, 47
    Napoleon and, 231
    in North America, 474, 478
    peace talks with, 182–184
    Portugal and, 33
    vs. Protestantism, 33
    in Revolutionary War, 177, 182
    rulers of (1474–1598), 29(t)
    South American empire of, 609
    territorial disputes with, 230
    Texas and, 369–370
    wars with, 89, 95–97
    the West and, 198, 240(m), 374
    WWII and, 750
Spanish-American War (1898), 591, 603, 609–617, 612(i), 613(i), 622(m), 623, 631, 751
    Hearst newspapers and, 614–615
Spanish Armada, 33, 610
Spanish civil war (1936–1939), 750–751
Spanish colonization, 19, 22, 22(m), 40–44, 40(t), 41(m), 76, 134(m), 138(m), 267
    Carolinas and, 70
    Catholicism and, 27–28, 41–42, 44, 65, 67
    conquest of Aztecs and Incas, 9, 12, 24–28, 25(m), 27(i), 30–31, 37
    Florida and, 70–71
    gold and, 24, 27, 33, 35, 37, 40
    Louisiana and, 125, 198
    in Mexico, 24–26, 30–31, 37
    in North America, 102, 121, 122(m), 125, 136, 138(m), 151(m), 184(m), 240(m)
    in Texas, 241, 249
Spanish Netherlands, 33. *See also* Dutch colonization

Sparkman, John A., 802
SPARs (women in Coast Guard), 758
speakeasies, 688, 689(i)
Special Forces, Army, 831, 833
special interest groups, 898
specie, 324
    meaning of, 537
Specie Circular (1836), 333
Spencer, Herbert, 519
spheres of influence
    in American colonies, 122(m)
    in China, 607, 616, 626–628, 627(m), 631
    meaning of, 785
Spielberg, Steven, 771(i)
spinning, 242
Spirit of St. Louis (airplane), 680, 683(i)
spoils system, 330, 338
sports
    baseball, 568, 568(i), 680
    gay rights and, 895
    national culture and, 680
    radio and, 680
    in Sun Belt, 818
    Title IX and, 889–890
Spotsylvania Court House, battle of, 420
Sprague, Frank J., 546
Springfield race riot (1908), 590
Sputnik (Soviet satellite), 803, 803(i)
Square Deal, 595(i), 601
    meaning of, 595
squatter sovereignty, 383
Staël, Madame de, 207
Stage Door Canteen (film), 763(i)
stagflation, 886
Stalin, Joseph
    Berlin blockade and, 790
    death of, 794, 801
    FDR and, 784
    Kim Il Sung and, 792
    wartime planning and, 768–769
    at Yalta, 773(m), 773–775, 775(i)
Stalingrad, Battle of, 768(m), 769
Stamp Act (1765), 134, 138–143, 146, 149, 155(t), 159, 177, 201
    repeal of, 144–145, 167
    resistance to, 140–144
Stamp Act Congress (1765), 140, 143, 155(t), 159
Standard Metropolitan Statistical Area (SMSA), 819(m)
Standard Oil case (1911), 596
Standard Oil Company, 494, 606, 670
    monopoly of, 575–576
Stanford-Binet test, 645–646
Stanley, Ann Lee (Mother Ann), 346–347
Stanton, Edward M., 437
Stanton, Elizabeth Cady, 357, 362, 381, 439
    Seneca Falls and, 363–364

Staple Act (1663), 72(t)
Starr, Ellen Gates, 577
Starr, Kenneth, 932
"Star Wars" (Strategic Defense Initiative; SDI), 908
State Department, U.S., 604
state governments, 244
    business and, 666
    vs. federal, 732
    Great Depression and, 701, 702(m)
    reform of, 329–330
    shift of costs to, 908, 911
    shift of powers to, 880
    Social Security and, 746
states
    block grants to, 880
    constitutions of, 194–196, 219, 330, 437, 453
    formation and Indian cessions, 223(m)
    slave vs. free, 382–384, 391, 395
    welfare and, 779, 930
    women's rights and, 363
states' rights, 269, 280, 328, 331, 338
    Calhoun on, 323
    Fourteenth Amendment and, 519
    Fugitive Slave Act and, 386
    Indian removal and, 326
    interstate commerce and, 300, 519
    Second Bank and, 324
States' Rights Party (Dixiecrats), 798
Statue of Liberty, 938(i)
Statute of Wills, 102
steam power, 513
    manufacturing and, 286–287, 313, 487
    steamboats and, 297, 300, 302
steel industry
    Bessemer furnace and, 486, 488
    British, 457
    Homestead strike and, 457, 510
    labor unions and, 733
    in late nineteenth century, 485(i), 486–489, 487(m), 489(i), 503, 510, 513
    mills for, 485(i), 486–489, 489(i)
    in New South, 497
    puddlers and, 486–488, 498, 501, 506
    rolling mills and, 488, 498, 501
Steel Workers Organizing Committee (SWOC), 733, 733(i)
Steffens, Lincoln, 576
Steichen, Edward, 593(i)
Steinbeck, John, 709(i), 710, 745
Steinem, Gloria, 889
Stein, Gertrude, 689
Stephens, Alexander, 402, 415, 424, 431
Stephenson, David, 684

Steuben, baron von, 175
Stevenson, Adlai E., 802–803
Stevens, Thaddeus, 389, 413, 436
Stevens, Wallace, 690
Stewart, Jimmy, 706(i)
Stewart, Maria W., 359
Stiles, Ezra, 130, 194
Stimson, Henry, 755
stock market, 303, 934
    crash of (1929), 696(i), 697, 715, 719, 724
    elderly and, 945
    government regulation of, 745
    Great Depression and, 697
    growth in, 917
    increased investment in, 885–886
    margin buying in, 697, 726
    Roosevelt recession and, 732
    Savings and Loan crisis and, 912
Stoddard, Solomon, 116–117
Stone, Lucy, 357, 439
Stone, Samuel, 253
Stonewall riot (1969), 864–865
Stono Rebellion (1739), 89, 96
Story, Joseph, 246, 248, 321
Stowe, Harriet Beecher, 362, 370, 386
Strachey, Richard, 183
Strategic Air Command, 794
Strategic Arms Limitation Treaties (SALT I & II), 871, 899, 901
Strategic Defense Initiative (SDI; "Star Wars"), 908
strikes, 285(i), 293, 296, 506(i)
    agricultural, 711, 711(i), 714
    by Asian Americans, 714
    in automobile industry, 716
    Boston police (1919), 661
    in California, 728(i)
    of 1877, 485–486
    in Great Depression, 716
    Haymarket affair, 508–509
    Homestead (1892), 457, 510
    injunctions against, 586–587
    Memphis sanitation workers, 862
    by Mexican Americans, 711(i)
    middle class and, 733
    in mining industry, 508(i), 511–512, 536, 591–592, 596, 599
    New Deal and, 728, 728(i)
    in 1902, 591–592, 596
    in 1919, 660–661, 661(i), 663, 733
    post-WWII, 817
    Pullman boycott, 510–511, 538
    railroad, 485, 508, 510–511, 536, 797–798
    sit-down, 733
    in steel industry, 733
    strikebreakers in, 714
    by suffrage movement, 652–653
    in textile industry, 599
    welfare capitalism and, 670

women and, 502, 711(i)
    in WWII, 759–760
Strong, Josiah, 544
Stroyer, Jacob, 266–267
Student Non-Violent Coordinating Committee (SNCC), 837, 839, 861, 866
Students for a Democratic Society (SDS), 857, 870. *See also* New Left
Student Strike against War (1936), 705
Stuyvesant, Peter, 48
submarines
    nuclear, 794
    in WWII, 752(m), 769, 771
suburbs, 815–820, 818(i), 939
    automobile and, 675, 817, 819–820
    decay of inner cities and, 829
    growth of, 552–553, 817–820, 847
    in 1950s, 825
    racism in, 818
    voting districts and, 881
    white flight to, 896
Suckley, Margaret, 756
Sudetenland, German invasion of, 751
Suez Canal, 769, 796–797
suffrage movement, 527, 535–536, 541, 582(m), 668. *See also* voting rights
    activists in, 523–525, 525(i), 579(i), 582, 601
    American politics and, 582, 601
    hunger strikes and, 652–653
    organizations in, 439, 523, 579, 652–653
    revival of, 578–579
suffrage, universal, 338, 449
sugar
    Asian laborers and, 605(i)
    duties on, 136–138, 154
    migrant labor and, 478
    Molasses Act and, 98
    plantations and, 78, 80, 605, 605(i)
    planter-merchant elite and, 79
    Puerto Rican immigrants and, 828
    related industries and, 79
    slavery and, 69, 71, 76–78, 77(m), 77(t), 80, 84, 88, 125, 134(m), 137
    in the South, 262–263, 265, 265(m), 266(i)
    South Atlantic system and, 99
    U.S. foreign investment in, 670
    West Indies trade and, 91, 93(m), 97(i), 105, 105(f), 106, 125, 134(m), 136–137, 138(m), 154
    WWI rationing of, 763
Sugar Act (1764), 136–138, 140, 143, 145, 155(t), 159, 177
sugarcane farming, 605(i)

Sullivan, Big Tim
    biographical information, 564–565
Sullivan, John, 177(*m*)
Sumatra, 670
*A Summary View of the Rights of
    British America* (Jefferson), 169
Summer, Sally, 152
Summit Springs, battle of (1869), 462
Sumner, Charles, 367, 413, 436, 439, 449
Sumner, Willliam Graham, 519
Sun Belt, 818–819
    migration to, 847, 886(*m*), 887
Sun Dance, 459–460
Sunday, Billy, 566, 686
Superfunds, 899
    Love Canal and, 891
Supreme Court, 204, 209, 218, 230,
    249, 438, 928
    abortion rights and, 892. *See also
        Roe v. Wade*
    on affirmative action, 897
    antitrust laws and, 666
    Congress and, 667
    conservatism of, 911
    constitutionality of Civil Rights Bill
        (1870) and, 449
    decisions of, 578(*t*)
    Dred Scott and, 391, 393
    FDR and, 730–731
    Fugitive Slave Act and, 386
    gay rights and, 925
    Gibbons v. Ogden, 300
    on housing discrimination, 818
    on Japanese internment, 767
    labor unions and, 734
    Marshall and, 245–246, 246(*t*)
    Native American cases and, 328
    New Deal and, 726, 728, 746
    on New York subway, 548
    Nixon appointments to, 880–881
    on prayer in public schools, 881
    Reagan and, 909–910
    Roger Taney and, 328–329
    school busing and, 895
    Scottsboro case and, 708
    on segregation, 836(*m*)
    slavery and, 393
    strikes and, 733
    2000 election and, 933–934, 934(*m*)
    welfare capitalism and, 670
Susquehanna Company, 128
Susquehannock Indians, 55, 64
Sutter, John A., 383
Sutter's Mill, discovery of gold (1848)
    at, 477
Swamp Fox. *See* Marion, Francis
Sweden, 40(*t*), 48
    homesteaders from, 465–466
Swift, Gustavus F., 491, 494
syndicalism, 512
Syria, invasion of Israel by, 884

Taff, Blanche, 713
Taft, William Howard (1857–1930),
    589, 595, 598–599
    as president (1909–1913), 620, 628,
        630
    Roosevelt and, 596
Taft-Hartley Act, 798
Taino Indians, 24
Taiwan, 791, 793, 871. *See also* China:
    Nationalist
Taliban, 901, 916(*m*), 939(*i*), 940(*i*),
    941, 941(*i*), 943
Tall Bull, chief of Cheyenne, 462
Tallender, Lydia, 256
Talleyrand, Charles, 216
Tallmadge, James, 269
Tammany Hall, 564–565, 585–586, 667
    1928 election and, 691
Taney, Roger B., 321, 328–329
    Dred Scott and, 391
    Fugitive Slave Act and, 386
    Second Bank and, 324
Taos, New Mexico
    Hispanic culture of, 481
    Tappan, Arthur, 309, 354, 357
Tappan, Lewis, 309, 354, 357
Tarbell, Ida, 575(*i*), 576
Tardieu, Andre, 630
Tariff of Abominations, 319(*i*), 320, 322
tariffs, 201, 205–206, 212, 331
    during Adams's administration,
        318–319, 319(*i*)
    in Civil War, 409, 411
    of 1816, 319
    of 1828, 319, 339
    Jackson and, 320–323, 323(*i*)
    McKinley and, 573
    for manufacturing, 290–291
    nullification of, 321–323
    post-WWI, 672
    protective, 332, 335, 338, 517, 535,
        538, 596
    Tocqueville on, 325
Tarzan of the Apes (Burroughs), 554
Tatch, Kitty, 482(*i*)
taverns
    as political centers, 142
    woman-run, 104(*i*)
taxation, 137(*f*), 948. *See also* Shays's
        Rebellion
    under (G. H. W.) Bush, 911
    of business, 666
    in Civil War, 411, 413, 427
    in cold war, 791
    in colonial America, 134–150,
        154–155, 159
    colonial assemblies and, 94
    Confederacy and, 198, 200, 413
    of corporations, 647
    decay of inner cities and, 829
    excess-profits, 647

excise levies and, 136, 303, 517
    federal surplus and, 517
    Great Depression and, 697, 715
    hidden currency, 186, 191
    of income, 519, 647, 649
    increases in, 74, 647, 668, 797
    Jefferson and, 230, 249
    land, 369
    legislation on, 841(*t*)
    Long on, 727
    mass, 755
    in New England colonies, 73
    1988 campaign and, 911
    occupation tax, 252
    political rights and, 93
    poll tax, 252, 529, 842
    power of, 246
    property, 441
    Reaganomics and, 908, 910
    rebellion and, 71
    in Reconstruction, 441
    reductions in, 666, 797, 835, 886,
        908, 930, 933–934, 937
    religion and, 190, 453
    self-government and, 251
    smuggling and, 136–137, 149
    Southern gentry and, 90
    of stocks and bonds, 332
    taxpayers' revolts against, 898
    of wealthy, 332
    welfare and, 779
    without representation, 137–138,
        140–141, 363
    WWII and, 755
Tax Reduction Act (1964), 835
Taylor, Alan, 144
Taylor, Frederick W., 574, 632, 670
    scientific management and,
        503–505, 513
Taylor, Zachary (1784–1850), 376, 387,
        918
    1848 election and, 382, 392(*m*)
    Mexican War and, 378, 378(*m*)
    as president (1849–1850), 383,
        383(*i*)
    slave vs. free states and, 383
Tea Act (1773), 150, 155(*t*), 159, 176
Teapot Dome scandal (1924), 667
technology. *See also* machinery
    advances in, 513, 810–811
    in agriculture, 106, 288, 300–301,
        465–467, 483
    alternative, 888
    aviation, 682–683
    biotechnology, 918–919
    capitalism and, 900
    computer, 810–811, 918–919,
        922–923
    consumer culture and, 674
    cotton production and, 226,
        289–292, 289(*i*), 295, 295(*i*)

technology (Continued):
　economic growth and, 917
　in factories, 287–295, 287(i), 289(i), 295(i)
　fundamentalists and, 686
　individualism and, 680
　in mining, 475(i), 477
　naval, 610–611
　1950s culture and, 820
　in 1990s, 917–919
　postwar development and, 818
　in railroad system, 490
　Republican values and, 214, 215(i)
　rural life and, 682
　in steel production, 486–487, 489(i)
　textile industry and, 215
　tidal, 86
　tobacco production and, 496
　video, 917
Tecumseh (Shawnee chief), 235–237
Teedyuscung, 76
teenagers. See adolescence; youth
Tejanos, 478
telegraph, 294(i), 300(m), 470, 491
　transcontinental (1861), 460, 604
television, 940–941
　civil rights movement and, 838, 842
　documentaries on, 822
　influence of, 917
　JFK-Nixon debates on, 830–831
　JFK's election and, 830
　1950s culture and, 820–822
　1980 election and, 903
　proliferation of channels, 920(i)
　religion and, 822
　sitcoms on, 822
　as "vast wasteland," 822
Teller, Henry M., 616
temperance movement, 306–311, 309(i), 313, 331, 335, 367, 452, 522, 524–525, 526(i)
　abolitionism and, 354
　reform and, 342
　societies of, 306, 310
　women's rights and, 358, 364
tenant farmers, 225. See also sharecropping
　African American, 708, 735
　in England, 148
　in Hudson River Valley, 106(m), 128–129, 156
　in Middle Atlantic colonies, 105, 128(i), 129
　New Deal and, 724
　in New England, 103, 267
　in Pennsylvania, 106
　Populist party and, 526
　in Virginia, 120–121, 131, 261
Tenement House Law (1901; New York), 549
tenements, dumbbell, 549(f)

Tennent, Gilbert, 114–115, 118, 167
Tennent, William, 114
Tennessee, 225, 239, 398, 401, 415
　emancipation in, 424
　industrial capacity in, 409
　Ku Klux Klan in, 446–447, 447(i)
　public education in, 441
　Reconstruction and, 436
　revivals in, 273, 310
　Scopes trial in, 687–688
Tennessee Coal and Iron Company, 596
Tennessee River, 228, 406, 406(m)
Tennessee Valley Authority (TVA), 724, 731(t), 740–742, 741(m)
　Supreme Court on, 730
Tenochtitlán, 9–10, 24–25, 27, 30
Ten Percent Plan, 430
Tenskwatawa (Lalawethika), 235, 237(i)
　biographical information, 236–237
Tenth Amendment, 210
Tenure of Office Act (1867), 437–438, 438(t)
Teotihuacán culture, 6, 9, 14
tepees, 459, 459(i)
Terkel, Studs, 703, 723, 749
terrorism, 907, 942–943, 946
　against blacks, 445, 448
　fears about, 937, 945
　global, 937
　in Middle East, 916(m)
　in 1980s, 912
　1993 World Trade Center bombing, 929
　Palestinian use of, 942
　September 11, 2001, 452, 916(m), 936–940, 936(i), 938(i), 939(i), 945
　USS Cole attack, 916(m), 932
　war on, 941, 948
Terrorism Information and Prevention System (TIPS), 946
Terry, Eli, 285–286
Texas, 184(m), 395
　admission to Union of, 368
　American settlement in, 369–371, 371(m)
　annexation of, 372, 375–377, 382(m)
　cattle ranching in, 461, 464, 478
　Compromise of 1850 and, 384
　cotton production in, 465, 478–479, 497(i), 530
　drought in, 709–710
　farming in, 466, 478–479
　Hispanics in, 478–479
　immigration and, 685(i), 920
　independence of, 369–372
　migration to, 818, 847
　rebellion in, 371–372
　Republic of, 382(m)

　segregation in, 760
　slavery in, 371–372, 383
　Spanish, 241, 249
textile industry, 285(i), 287(t), 296, 302, 505
　British competition and, 288–292
　decline of (1920s), 668
　Great Depression and, 697
　growth of, 302
　innovations in, 289–292, 289(i), 295(i)
　Jewish garment workers and, 502, 509
　Navigation Acts and, 98
　in the South, 495–496, 496(m), 497
　strikes in, 599
　tariffs and, 319, 319(i)
　technological innovation and, 215
　trade in, 79, 241(i), 242–243
　women in, 285(i), 286, 288(m), 289–291, 290(i), 496, 500
Thames, battle of, 235
Thayendanegea (Mohawk chief). See Brant, Joseph
Thayer, Webster, 662
theater
　in New Deal, 721(i), 743, 745
　vaudeville, 567
　Yiddish, 559
Their Eyes Were Watching God (Hurston), 743
The South Carolina Exposition and Protest (Calhoun), 322
Thieu, Nguyen Van, 867, 873
Third World
　AIDS in, 925
　cold war and, 796, 807, 813
　decolonization in, 833(m)
　development of, 816
　meaning of, 833(m)
　Soviet influence in, 797
　U.S. intervention in, 912
Thirteenth Amendment, 424, 427, 431, 438(t)
Tho, Le Duc, 872
Thomas, Clarence, 911, 911(i)
Thomas, M. Carey, 555
Thomas, Norman, 718
Thomas, Theodore, 569
Thompson, Dorothy, 729
Thompson, Florence, 745(i)
Thompson, LaMarcus, 566
Thompson, Virgil, 745
Thoreau, Henry David (1817–1862), 344, 346, 356, 394
Thoughts on Female Education (Rush), 256
Thoughts on Government (John Adams), 194, 205
Three Mile Island, Pennsylvania, 888–889

Thurman, A.G., 515(i)
Thurmond, J. Strom, 798, 798(m)
Tidewater region, 110(m), 120, 127
Tikal, 9
Tilden, Bill, 680
Tilden, Samuel J., 450
Timucua Indians, 12
Tippecanoe, battle of, 235, 334
Tippecanoe River, 236–237
TIPS. See Terrorism Information and
    Prevention System
The Titan (Dreiser), 551
Title IX, Educational Amendments Act
    (1972), 889–890
Tiwanaku culture, 6
tobacco, 74, 79–80, 84
    colonial production of, 130,
        138(m), 155, 160, 160(f)
    decline of, 262
    duties on, 136, 517
    economy based on, 54–55
    exports of, 127, 138(m), 149
    South Atlantic system and, 99
    Southern gentry and, 90
    Southern production of, 263,
        265(m), 496, 496(m)
    trade in, 93(m)
    transportation for, 298(m)
Tobago, 184
Tocqueville, Alexis de, 207, 286,
    306(i), 315, 342, 452
    on American democracy, 515
    on American political parties, 325
    on law and lawyers in United States,
        248
Tojo, Hideki, 753
Toleration Act (1649), 50
Toltec culture, 6
Toomer, Jean, 690
Tories, 182–183
Tory Association, 157
town meetings, 60–61, 67
Townsend, Francis, 726–729
Townshend Act (1767), 145–147,
    147(i), 149–150, 149(f), 155(t),
    159, 167
Townshend, Charles, 98, 144(t),
    145–146, 159
Tracy, Benjamin F., 608
Tracy, Spencer, 762
trade, 19, 22(m). See also exports;
    imports; South Atlantic system;
    particular commodities
    American colonies as source of, 75
    Anglo-American, 121, 127–128,
        127(f), 137, 144–146, 149,
        149(f), 154
    British empire and, 124, 134,
        134(m)
    with California, 374
    control of, 93(m)

duties on, 110, 136–138, 154
    free, 753, 816
    of manufactured goods, 303
    restraint of, 599
    slave, 72, 79–80, 84(i), 226
    West Indian, 91, 97(i), 105, 105(f),
        106, 125, 134(m), 136–137,
        138(m), 154
trade deficits, 884
    in 1970s, 899
    in 1990s, 915
    Reaganomics and, 910
trade, foreign, 628
    automobile and, 884, 887(i)
    balance of, 606–607, 607(f), 698,
        816, 884. See also trade deficits
    corporations and, 887
    Great Depression and, 698
    New York City and, 303, 313
    in 1970s, 905
    opening of, to U.S. goods, 928
    postwar, 816
    recessions and, 816
    restrictions on, 698
    surpluses in, 816
trade routes, 20, 21(m), 22, 22(m),
    24, 47
trade unionism. See labor unions
Trafalgar, battle of, 610
Trail of Tears, 328
transcendentalism, 342–344, 365
    abolitionism and, 355–356, 358
    industrialization and, 343(f), 346
The Transformation of American Law
    1780–1860 (Horwitz), 280
Trans-Missouri case (1897), 593
Transportation, Department of, 928
Transportation Security
    Administration, 947
transportation system. See also airline
    industry; canals; highways;
    railroads
    automobile and, 675
    bottleneck in, 228–230
    financing of roads, 319, 321
    freight lines and, 460
    JFK and, 835
    legislation on, 841(t)
    public, 821
    revolution in, 286, 297–303,
        298(i), 298(m), 299(t), 300(m),
        313
    segregation of, 838
    subways and, 489
    trolley and, 486, 489
    wartime migration and, 764
    water, 229, 488
    WWII and, 763(i)
Trans World Airlines (TWA), 683
Travis, William B., 372
Treasury Department, U.S., 724

treaties. See also arms control;
    particular treaties by name
    mutual defense, 795(m)
    nuclear test ban, 834
    Strategic Arms Limitation, 871, 899,
        901
A Treatise Concerning Religious
    Affections (Edwards), 117
Treatise on Domestic Economy
    (Beecher), 358
Tredegar Iron Works, 292, 409, 411(i)
Treitschke, Heinrich von, 550
trench warfare, 639(i), 640–641
Trenton, battle of, 171, 191
trial by jury, 137, 140–141, 143, 210,
    268
Triangle Shirtwaist factory fire,
    584–586, 585(i)
tribal termination program, 895
Tri-Partite Pact (Germany, Japan, Italy;
    1940), 753
Triple Alliance, 629, 638
Triple Entente, 629, 638
Triumphant Democracy (Carnegie),
    518
Trollope, Frances, 273, 276, 307, 315
Trotter, William Monroe, 589
Troup, George M., 319–320
Truax, Susanna, 101(i)
Truman, Harry S (1884–1972), 762
    atom bomb and, 775
    civil rights and, 799, 804
    cold war policies of, 816
    communism and, 792, 796, 813
    death of Roosevelt and, 783
    desegregation of armed forces, 804
    Fair Deal of, 799, 802, 813
    George Kennan and, 786
    Japan and, 791
    Korean War and, 792–794
    loyalty program of, 800
    Marshall Plan and, 788
    McCarthy and, 800
    NATO and, 790
    1948 election of, 798, 799(i)
    1949 State of the Union address,
        799
    in 1952, 801–802
    postwar price controls and, 797
    at Potsdam, 785
    as president (1945–1953), 783–794,
        800
    railroad strike and, 797–798
    recognition of Israel, 796
    Soviet Union and, 785
    veto of Taft-Hartley bill, 798
    Vietnam policy of, 850, 873, 877
Truman Doctrine (1947)
    containment and, 785, 788
    National Security Act and, 785
Trumbull, John, 165, 169(i), 435

Trumbull, Lyman, 431, 435
Trumpauer, Joan, 837
trust-busting, 593–594. *See also* antitrust laws
trusts, 593–594
Truth, Sojourner, 362, 362(i)
Tryon, William, 130
Tubman, Harriet, 355
Tubman, William, 737
Tucson, Arizona, 478
Tugwell, Rexford, 723
Tunney, Gene, 680
Turkey, 19(i), 34, 785–788, 790
    colonies of, 750
Turnbow, Hartman, 842
Turner, Frederick Jackson, 609, 632
Turner, Henry M., 434, 533
Turner, Nat, 352–353
Turner, Randolph, 367
Turner, Ted, 917
turnpikes, 286, 297
Tuscarora Indians, 6, 76, 170
Twain, Mark (Samuel Clemens), 481, 546, 548, 569
    on New York, 556–557
"Tweed Days in St. Louis" (Steffens), 576
Tweed Ring, 450
Twelfth Amendment, 218
Twentieth Amendment (1933), 718
Twenty-fourth Amendment (1964), 841(t), 842
Twenty-second Amendment (1951), 830
Two Treatises on Government (Locke), 74, 113
Tydings-McDuffie Act (1934), 714
Tyler, James G., 603(i)
Tyler, John (1790–1862), 334, 395
    1844 election and, 375
    as president (1841–1845), 338–339
Typographical Union (1852), 507

Udall, Stewart, 843
Ukraine, 769
Uncle Sam, 725(i)
Uncle Tom's Cabin (Stowe), 362, 370, 386, 387(i)
underground railroad, 355, 356(m)
Underwood Company, 304
Underwood Tariff Act (1913), 598
unemployment, 296, 305, 312–313, 695(i)
    African American, 709
    Asian American, 714
    baby boom and, 886
    in cities, 847, 924
    compensation for, 587, 728, 803
    decay of inner cities and, 829
    decline of, 917
declining economy and, 884
Democratic Party and, 746
environmentalism and, 889
in Germany, 750
Great Depression and, 699, 699(f), 715, 718
imported automobiles and, 887(i)
in late nineteenth century, 535
migrant workers and, 828
Native American, 740, 863
New Deal and, 725–726
in 1920s, 668
postwar, 817
race riots and, 924(i)
rise in, 934, 945
Roosevelt recession and, 731
in Rust Belt, 887
study of, 581
welfare system and, 778
of women, 704, 714
workers' compensation and, 587
WWII and, 759, 762
Unification Church, 888
Union Army, 418–421
    African Americans in, 381, 418(i), 425, 427
Unionists, 398, 401
Union Manufactory, 289
Union Pacific Railroad, 476, 489, 491(i)
    building of, 460, 461(m)
Union Party
    1936 election and, 729
    vs. Peace Democrats, 421, 424
Union Trade Society of Journeymen Tailors, 332
Unitarianism, 342–343
United Artists, 676(i)
United Automobile Workers (UAW), 733
United Farm Workers (UFW), 863
United Fruit Company, 670
United Mine Workers (UMW), 591, 733, 759, 798
United Nations, 785
    China and, 791–792
    founding of, 774–775
    General Assembly of, 796
    Iraq and economic sanctions, 931, 935
    Iraq and Resolution 1441, 942
    Korean War and, 792
    partitioning of Palestine, 796(i)
    peacekeeping forces of, 792, 929
    Persian Gulf War and, 913, 916(m)
    Security Council of, 774–775, 792
    Suez Canal and, 797
United Nations Earth Summit (1992), 927
United States. *See also* foreign trade
    in Latin America, 607
United States Steel Company, 594, 596
    antitrust laws and, 666
    strikes against, 733
United States Travel Bureau, 729(i)
United States v. Minoru Yasui (1943), 767
United States v. One Package of Japanese Pessaries (1936), 702–703
UNIVAC (Universal Automatic Computer), 810
Universalists, 272, 275(m)
Universal Negro Improvement Association (UNIA), 691
University of California
    affirmative action and, 924–925
    Free Speech Movement and, 857–858, 857(i)
University of Chicago, 580
University of Michigan
    antiwar movement at, 858
University of Pennsylvania, 119(t)
Unsafe at Any Speed (Nader), 889
Upward Bound, 845
urbanization, 543–571, 681(m). *See also* cities
    ethnicity and, 692
    industrialization and, 302–303, 302(m), 544–545, 571, 601
    intellectual life and, 689
    postwar, 817
    in the West, 475–477
U'Ren, Harold, 584
Uruguay, 900
USA Patriot (Uniting and Strengthening America by Providing Appropriate Tools Required to Intercept and Obstruct Terrorism) Act of 2002, 945–947
USA Today, 917
USA trilogy (Dos Passos), 689, 745
Utah
    cession of, 382(m)
    Compromise of 1850 and, 384, 386(m)
    Japanese internment in, 765
    Mormons in, 351–352, 365
Ute Indians, 470, 470(m)
utopian communities, 345–352
    Brook Farm, 345–346, 346(m), 365
    Fourierist, 347–348, 365
    Mormon, 346(m), 349–352, 350(m), 365
    Oneida, 346(m), 348–349, 365
    Shaker, 277, 346–347, 346(m), 348, 365
    Wright and, 336–337
Utrecht, Treaty of (1713), 76, 77(m), 138(m)

Vallejo, Mariano Guadalupe, 376(i)
Valley Forge, Pennsylvania, 170, 175, 191
Valparaiso (Chile), anti-U.S. riot in, 605
Van Bergen, Martin, 74(i)
Van Buren, Martin (1782–1862), 316, 372
    1840 election and, 333–335
    1844 election and, 375
    1848 election and, 382, 392(m)
    1852 election and, 387
    Independent Treasury Act of 1840 and, 333–334
    Jackson and, 319–321
    party government and, 317
    patronage and, 317, 339
    as president (1837–1841), 328, 331–332, 332(i)
    as vice-presidential candidate, 324
    Wilmot Proviso and, 379
    Wright and, 337
Vance, Zebulon, 407
Vanderbilt, Cornelius, 489, 492–493, 551(i), 569
Vanderbilt, George W., 569
Vanderbilt, William Hl, 551(i)
Van Dusen, Larry, 703
Vann, James, 326
Vann, John Paul, 872, 874
    biographical information, 874–875, 875(i)
Van Rensselaer family, 127
Van Rensselaer, Kiliaen, 47
Vanzetti, Bartolomeo, 662
Vassa, Gustavus (Olaudah Equiano), 80(i), 81
vaudeville, 567
Vaya, Count Vay de, 499, 503
V-E (Victory in Europe) Day, 770
Velasco, Don Luis de (Spanish viceroy), 43
Velasco, Luis de. See **Opechancanough**
Venezuela, 303, 605, 609
    oil production in, 884
    U.S. foreign investment in, 670
Venice, Italy, 19
Vergennes, comte de, 175
Vermont
    land grants in, 104
    migration from, 296, 297(m)
    settlement of, 226
    voting rights in, 252, 267
Versailles, Treaty of (1783), 184
Versailles, Treaty of (1919), 633, 658–659, 658(i), 795(m)
    Senate refusal to ratify, 659–660
    states created by, 914(m)
    WWII and, 750
vertical integration, 491, 494, 513
Vesey, Denmark, 266, 268(i)

Vespucci, Amerigo, 22(m), 24
veterans
    benefits for, 587, 762, 803
    benefits for women, 758
    protests by, 717
Veterans Administration, 818
Vicksburg, battle of, 423
Vicksburg, Mississippi, 415–416, 418
Victory gardens, 762
Vietcong, 851, 852(i), 854, 867, 873, 875
Vietminh, 850
Vietnam
    communism in, 816
    diplomatic relations with, 930
    immigrants from, 920
Vietnam Veterans Against the War, 870
Vietnam Veterans Memorial, 873(i)
Vietnam War (1961–1975), 849–877, 858(i), 904. See also antiwar movement
    African Americans in, 854
    aftermath of, 879
    Agent Orange and, 853, 858
    bombing campaigns in, 853, 853(i), 868–869, 872, 875, 877
    Buddhist opposition to, 851, 852(i)
    Cambodian attacks and, 870, 872
    credibility gap in, 856
    defense spending and, 755(f)
    détente and, 871–873
    economy and, 884, 899
    Eisenhower administration and, 850–851, 877
    fall of Saigon and, 872(i)
    Ford administration and, 873
    Great Society and, 847
    guerrilla tactics in, 851, 851(m), 854, 873
    Gulf of Tonkin resolution and, 852–853, 870, 876
    immigration and, 920
    Johnson administration and, 852–854, 854(f), 858–859, 877
    Kennedy administration and, 851–852, 856, 877
    legacy of, 873, 876
    mass media and, 856, 856(i), 870, 872(i), 873, 876
    My Lai massacre and, 870
    1968 presidential election and, 868–869, 869(m)
    1972 election and, 881–882
    Nixon administration and, 854(i), 870–873, 876–877
    Operation Rolling Thunder and, 853
    opposition to, 787. See also antiwar movement
    Paris peace talks and, 872–873, 877
    Persian Gulf War and, 914

    poverty and, 845(f), 846
    prisoners of war in, 853, 872–873
    public cynicism and, 883
    Tet offensive and, 856(i), 867, 877
    troops in, 849(i), 853–854, 854(f), 877
    veterans and, 854–855, 870, 873, 873(i), 876
    Vietnamization policy in, 854(i), 870–872, 877, 881
    women in, 854–856
Views of Society and Manners in America (Wright), 336
Vinci, Leonardo da, 19
vigilantism, WWI, 655
Villa, Pancho, 628–629, 629(i), 712
A Vindication of the Rights of Women (Wollstonecraft), 196(i)
Virginia
    vs. Chesapeake peoples, 50, 55
    claims to Western lands, 197–198, 225
    as colony, 48–50, 53–56, 67, 75
    elite politics in, 94
    end of Civil War and, 425
    evangelicals in, 120–121
    House of Burgesses of, 53–55, 90, 140, 146, 150, 155
    industrial capacity in, 409
    land disputes in, 129, 131
    migration from, 296, 297(m)
    presidency and, 230
    ratification of Constitution and, 205, 208
    rebellion in, 71
    Scots-Irish in, 110
    secession and, 398, 401, 427
    slavery in, 53–56, 67, 80–81, 88, 156, 160–161, 263, 274, 353
    tenant farmers of, 120–121, 131, 261
    voting rights in, 316
    wheat production in, 127
Virginia City, Nevada, 476–477
Virginia Company, 48–50
The Virginian (Wister), 554
Virginia Plan, 202–203
Virginia planters. See also plantations
    culture of, 113–114, 119
    revolution and, 143, 146, 155, 159
    slavery and, 160
Virgin of Guadalupe, 27
V-J (Victory over Japan) Day (August 15, 1945), 749
Voice of Missions, 533
voluntarism
    trade unions and, 586
    in WWI, 647, 649
Volunteers in Service to America (VISTA), 845
voter registration

voter registration (Continued):
    civil rights movement and, 840
    labor unions and, 762
    in the South, 843(m)
voting patterns
    African American, 738
    changes in, 320(f)
    ethnicity and, 692
    in 2000 election, 933
    urbanization and, 692
voting rights, 244(i), 432, 438. See also
        Fifteenth Amendment
    African American, 381, 436, 448,
        525–534, 529(m), 530(i), 840
    federal protection of, 804
    for free blacks, 267–268, 355
    intimidation and, 448
    Know-Nothing Party and, 389
    literacy tests and, 529, 530(i), 531
    poll tax and, 529, 530(i)
    property qualifications for, 94,
        194–195, 206, 219
    republicanism and, 252–253,
        254(m), 278–279
    Southern gentry and, 90
    Supreme Court on, 881
    2000 election and, 933–934, 933(i)
    universal suffrage, 338, 449
    white male, 316
    for women, 219, 364, 439. See also
        suffrage movement
Voting Rights Act (1965), 836(m),
        840–842, 841(t), 843(m)

Waco, Texas, Branch Davidian
        compound in, 929
WACs (Women's Army Corps), 758,
        759(i)
Wade-Davis Bill (1864), 430
Wadsworth, Benjamin, 102
Wadsworth family, 227
wages. See also minimum wage
    controls on, 667
    family, 779
    gender gap in, 499–502, 500(i), 513,
        527, 894(i), 916
    labor for, 331, 370, 434, 435(i),
        442–444
    labor unions and, 759
    productivity and, 917(f)
    in the South, 495–497, 513, 526,
        535(f)
Wagner Act (1935), 728, 731(t)
    labor unions and, 734
    Supreme Court on, 730
Wagner, Robert F., 585–586, 728
wagon trains, 460, 474
Wake Island, 771
Walden, or Life in the Woods
        (Thoreau), 344

Walden Pond, 344
Walker, David (1785–1830), 352,
        353(i)
Walker, Francis, 586
Walker, John, 269
Walker, Jonathan, 357(i)
Wallace, George C., 869, 869(m), 870,
        881
Wallace, Henry A., 722, 753, 762, 798
Waller, John, 121
Wall Street, New York City, 696(i). See
        also stock market
    gold purchases on, 538
    railroad building and, 491–493,
        493(i)
Walpole, Sir Robert, 95–97, 95(i)
Waltham plan, 290
Wampanoag Indians, 56, 63. See also
        Metacom's Rebellion
Wanamaker, John, 495
Wappinger Indians, 128–129
War Brides Act (1945), 825
Ward, Lester F., 574
War Industries Board, 725
War Information, Office of (OWI),
        657, 762
Warner, Charles Dudley, 569
War News from Mexico (painting;
        Woodville), 367(i)
War of 1812, 214, 230, 246, 249, 334,
        610
    causes of, 235
    Congressional vote on declaration
        of, 235
    Indian peoples and, 326
    manufacture of weapons for, 295
    terms of, 262
    Washington, D.C., and, 238(m), 239
War of the Austrian Succession (King
        George's War; 1740–1748), 75(t),
        97
War of the League of Augsburg (King
        William's War; 1689–1697), 75(t)
War of the Spanish Succession (Queen
        Anne's War; 1702–1713),
        75(t), 76
War on Poverty, 844–846, 880
War Powers Act (1941), 754
War Powers Act (1973), 876
War Production Board (WPB), 755
War Refugee Board, 770
War Relocation Authority, 765
Warren, Earl, 798, 804, 880–881, 910
Warren, Joseph, 144
Warren, Mercy Otis, 253–254
War Risk Insurance Act (1917), 653
Warsaw Pact, 788(m), 791, 794
Wartime Industries Board, 648
Washington, Booker T., 589
    Atlanta compromise and, 531, 534,
        534(i), 541

Washington, D.C. See District of
        Columbia
Washington, George (1732–1799),
        155, 161
    attacks on, 217
    in battle of Long Island, 171
    Benedict Arnold and, 180–181
    cabinet of, 209
    church taxes and, 190
    on closing of Boston Harbor, 151
    as commander of Continental
        army, 166, 170–172, 176(m),
        182, 191, 383(i)
    creation of national bank and, 211
    as delegate to Constitutional
        Convention, 202
    on expansion of West, 221
    Federalists and, 216
    on foreign alliances, 795(m)
    freemasonry and, 331
    in French and Indian War, 124
    Gouverneur Morris and, 206
    John Jay and, 215
    nationalist faction and, 201
    on national system of taxation, 198
    Native American resistance and, 223
    as president (1789–1797), 209, 219
    Proclamation of Neutrality, 213
    return to plantation, 193–194
    soldiers' pensions and, 176
    southern strategy of, 179, 182
    at Valley Forge, 175
    at Verplanck's Point, 165(i)
    Whiskey Rebellion and, 214
    Zachary Taylor and, 382
Washington Globe, 321
Washington Naval Arms Conference
        (1921), 673
Washington Post, Watergate and, 882
Washington Star, gay rights and, 895
Washington state, Japanese internment
        in, 765
WASPs (Women Airforce Service
        Pilots), 758
The Waste Land (Eliot), 689
Watergate scandal, 880, 882–883,
        883(i), 904–905
    Iran-Contra and, 909
water power, 302
    manufacturing and, 287–289,
        288(m), 289(i), 291–292, 313,
        487
    mills and, 242–243
water resources
    agriculture and, 466–467, 478, 482
    dams and, 482
    preservation of, 841(t)
    in Sun Belt, 818–819
    transportation and, 229, 488
Waters, Ethel, 677
Watson, James, 918

Watson, Tom, 527–529, 536
Watts Riot (1965), 836(m), 924(i)
WAVES (Women Accepted for Volunteer Emergency Service), 758
Wayne, John, 762
Wayne, "Mad Anthony," 223
wealth. See also economy
  of business elite, 296, 303, 313
  creed of individualism and, 518
  distribution of, 846, 908, 915
  increase of, 594
  inheritance and, 303
  per capita income and, 286, 486, 762
  unequal distribution of, 697, 719, 727
Wealth against Commonwealth (Lloyd), 575
The Wealth of Nations (Smith), 79, 212
weapons of mass destruction (WMD), 916(m), 931, 942. See also atomic bomb; nuclear weapons
  biological, 948
Weathermen, 871
Weaver, James B., 535, 537(m), 540(m)
Webster, Daniel, 235, 248, 330
  Compromise of 1850 and, 384
  election of 1836 and, 331
  election of 1840 and, 334
  on Jackson, 320
  Second Bank and, 324
  Whig Party and, 335, 339
Webster, Noah, 260
Webster v. Reproductive Health Service (1989), 911
Wedemeyer, Albert, 791
Weed, Thurlow, 331, 335
Weems, Parson Mason, 260
Weir, Robert W., 222(i)
Weld, Theodore, 353–354, 357
welfare
  Asian Americans and, 714
  categorical, 728
  conservative opposition to, 846
  cuts in, 908, 930
  Democratic Party and, 815
  in Europe, 745, 778
  expansion of, 815–816
  federal involvement with, 803, 880
  gender and, 778–779
  Great Depression and, 702(m), 715–716, 718
  immigrants and, 924
  job training and, 779, 779(i)
  labor unions and, 734
  legislation on, 778(i), 778–779, 779(i), 841(t), 930
  maternalist, 577
  Nixon and, 880

  reform of, 779, 779(i), 881, 924, 930, 948
  Republican Party and, 804
  resentment of, 898
  vs. social security, 778
  states and, 779, 930
  of Truman, 799
  War on Poverty and, 844
  women and, 601
welfare capitalism, 670, 732, 757
welfare state, 745–747
  conservative opposition to, 898
  New Deal and, 728
  in 1970s, 905
  welfare system and, 779
  WWII and, 761–762
Welles, Orson, 615, 743
The Well-Ordered Family (Wadsworth), 102
Wells, Ida B., 531–533, 531(i), 532(i)
Wentworth, Governor, 157
Wesley, John, 114–115
the West, 183, 184(m), 197. See also westward expansion
  American sovereignty and, 235
  American System and, 318
  Asian Americans in, 714
  cession to U.S. of, 237, 239
  Civil War in, 405–407, 415
  claims to, 198–200, 199(m)
  closing of frontier in, 609
  drought cycles in, 633
  economic growth of, 847, 886(m), 887
  environmental issues in, 632–633
  ethnic diversity in, 464, 464(i)
  federal land policy and, 633
  Free Soil Party and, 379
  geology of, 474, 474(i)
  industrial revolution and, 633
  Jackson as first president from, 320
  Kaiser and, 756–757
  Ku Klux Klan in, 685(m)
  migration to, 368–369, 372–375, 374(m), 817–819, 829, 886(m), 887
  movement of regional cultures to, 226(m)
  1928 election and, 691
  1932 election and, 718
  1980 election and, 903
  opening up of, 198–200, 206, 221–222
  population losses in, 632–633, 632(m)
  removal of Indians to, 326, 327(m), 329, 339
  Second Bank and, 324
  settlement of, 219, 227, 457–483, 632–633
  slavery in, 385

  transmountain, 457–483, 457(i), 474(i), 482(i). See also California; Pacific slope
  urbanization of, 681(m)
West Africa, 85, 87. See also Africa
  as British colony, 124–125, 134(m)
  culture of, 20–21
  Dutch trade in, 47
  Mediterranean trade and, 21, 21(m)
  slave trade in, 21–22, 21(m)
West Bank, 916(m)
West, Benjamin, 165
Western Confederacy (Shawnees, Miamis, and Potawatomis), 223, 235
Western Federation of Miners (WFM), 511–512
Western Front (World War I), 640, 643–644, 644(m), 663
Western Trail (periodical), 464
Western Union, 493
West Germany. See Germany, Federal Republic of
West India Company, 34, 47
West Indies. See Caribbean Islands
Westinghouse, George, 490
Westinghouse turbine, 487(i)
West, Mae, 706
Westmoreland, William, 874–875
West Point, New York, 180–181, 422
West Virginia, creation of, 401
westward expansion, 129(m), 136, 151, 155, 160, 222–230, 233, 248–249. See also migration
  Louisiana Purchase and, 271(m), 279
  Manifest Destiny and, 368–376, 395
  migration and, 121, 126, 227, 296, 297(m), 313, 368–369, 372–375, 374(m)
  Missouri Compromise and, 269, 272(m), 279
  Native Americans and, 102, 121–123, 128–129, 131
  postcolonial, 256, 313
  slavery and, 226, 387–388
  of slavery to old Southwest, 262–263, 263(f), 263(i), 264(m), 265(t), 296, 297(m)
  slave vs. free states and, 382–384, 391, 395
  Treaty of Paris and, 125, 138(m), 151(m)
Wethersfield, Connecticut, 59, 62(m)
Wetmore, Ephraim, 200
Weyler, Valeriano, 609, 613
whaling industry, 268(i), 302(m)
Wharton, Edith, 550, 690
What's My Line? (TV show), 802
wheat, 297(m), 298–299, 313
  in California, 480–481

wheat (Continued):
  colonial production of, 104–106, 111(i), 127
  exports of, 127, 137, 138(m), 285
  on Great Plains, 465–467, 469
  Midwest production of, 296–299, 297(m), 313
  from North in Civil War, 416
  prices of, 212–213, 535, 540
  western, 227
Wheeler, Adam, 200
Wheelock, Eleazar, 120(i)
Whig Party, 383(i), 409, 422
  Compromise of 1850 and, 384
  creation of, 330, 339
  decline of, 387
  vs. Democratic Party, 248, 330–332, 335, 338–339
  economic program of, 390, 394
  first national convention of, 334
  ideology of, 330–331
  Lincoln in, 393
  Mexican War and, 378–379
  Radical, 136, 142, 144, 147(i), 148–149, 159, 172, 210
  realignment of, 392(m)
  salutary neglect and, 95
  slave vs. free states and, 383, 395
  support in the South, 331
  women and, 315(i)
Whig Party (England), 93, 134(i), 136, 143–145, 194
Whiskey Rebellion (1794), 213–214, 230
Whiskey Ring, 449
White, Hugh L., 331
White, Richard, 633
White, Walter, 737
White, William Allen, 520, 752
White Citizens' Councils, 805
white collar jobs, 552. See also middle class
Whitefield, George, 114–116, 115(i), 118, 121, 131, 273, 277
White House, first, 209(i)
White Man's Union, 530–531
White over Black: American Attitudes towards the Negro, 1550–1812 (Jordan), 160–161
white supremacy, 393, 431, 435, 445, 451, 528–534, 541. See also Ku Klux Klan; racism
  in Progressive vein, 589, 591
Whitewater investigation, 928, 932
Whitlock, Brand, 520, 586
Whitman, Walt (1819–1892), 336, 345, 382
Whitney, Eli, 226, 292, 294(i)
  biographical information, 294–295
Whyte, William, 817
Wickersham, George, 596
Widener, Peter A. B., 548

Wilderness, battle of the, 420
Wilderness Preservation Act (1964), 841(t)
Wild, John Casper, 228(i)
Wild West Show, 463
Wilhelm II, emperor of Germany (r. 1888–1918), 622, 629
Wilkes, Charles, 373
Wilkes, John, 136, 147(i), 148–149
Wilkinson, Eliza, 195
Wilkinson, James, 233
Wilkinson, Jemima, 277
Wilkins, Roy, 839
Willamette Valley, Oregon, 373, 460, 474, 477
Willard, Emma, 278
Willard, Frances, 524–525
Will, George F., 925
William III, king of England, 73(m), 75, 93
William and Mary College, 119(t)
Williams, Charles, 648
Williams, Roger, 58–59
Williams, William Carlos, 690
Williams v. Mississippi (1898), 530
Willkie, Wendell, 753
Wills, Helen, 680
Wilmington, North Carolina, 418
Wilmot, David, 379
Wilmot Proviso, 379, 382, 393, 413
Wilson, Charles E., 794
Wilson, Edith Bolling Galt, 660
Wilson, Pete, 924
Wilson, Woodrow (1856–1924), 666
  banks and, 599
  blacks and, 589
  as Democratic Party nominee, 597(i), 598
  "Fourteen Points" of, 655, 658
  immigration restriction and, 683
  isolationism and, 751
  League of Nations and, 655–656, 658–659
  neutrality in WWI and, 640–641
  the New Freedom and, 597–598
  presidency and, 722
  as president (1913–1921), 628–629, 631, 643, 648–649, 653–655, 663
  social program of, 599–600
  suffragists and, 579(i)
  trusts and, 599
Wilson-Gorman Tariff (1894), 538
Windsor, Connecticut, 59, 61
Winnebago Indians, 236
The Winning of the West (T. Roosevelt), 609
Winthrop, James, 205, 281
Winthrop, John, 56–57, 58(i), 61
Wisconsin, 11, 47
  Fugitive Slave Act and, 386
  Northwest Ordinance and, 232(m)

slavery in, 383
Wise, John, 113
Wissler, Clark, 459
Wister, Owen, 554
witchcraft executions, 60
WMD. See weapons of mass destruction
Wobbelin concentration camp, 770(i)
Wobblies. See Industrial Workers of the World
Wolcott, Oliver, 295
Wolfe, James, 125, 134
Wolfe, Tom, 887
Wollstonecraft, Mary, 196(i), 257
Wolof Indians, 21
Woman in the Nineteenth Century (Fuller), 344
Woman Suffrage Association, National American (NAWSA), 523, 579, 652–653
women. See also children; marriage
  abolitionism and, 336, 356–357, 359–362, 359(m), 364–365, 439, 865
  Afghani, 941
  African American, 443, 668, 680, 704, 708
  in antiwar movement, 857, 866
  Baptists and, 121, 273–274
  birthrates and, 102, 255–257, 865
  in breadlines, 701(i)
  changing roles of, 893
  charitable institutions and, 308
  Children's Bureau and, 669
  in Civil War, 361, 407–409, 408(i), 412(i), 416
  clothing of, 337(i)
  in colonies, 15, 60
  in Congress, 643, 643(i), 668, 911(i), 944
  consumer culture and, 665(i), 674
  discrimination against, 704, 866–867
  divorce and, 255, 865
  as domestic servants, 307, 498, 500
  dower right and, 104
  education of, 196, 256, 261(i), 277–278, 555, 705
  employment of, 704–705
  equality of, 196(i), 197, 354, 643, 652–653
  evangelicalism and, 102
  on farms, 102–103, 109, 111(i), 146
  feminist movement and, 849, 856, 865–867, 877
  Fourierism and, 347
  free black, 443
  Free Soil Party and, 379
  gentry, 89–91
  in government, 643, 643(i)

Great Depression and, 699,
701–705, 704(i), 716, 719
handicrafts and, 341(i)
in Hispanic culture, 478
household production and,
185–186
jazz and, 680
Ku Klux Klan and, 684
labor unions and, 507, 714, 733
legal status of married, 554
in medieval Europe, 16–17
Mexican American, 711, 714
middle class, 304, 304(i), 674
midwifery and, 926
in military, 758, 914(i)
minimum wage for, 597, 735
minority, 735
moral reform and, 315(i), 358
mysticism and, 344
Native American, 12–14, 15(i),
65–66, 224
New Deal and, 734–735, 746–747
in 1920s, 668
in 1950s, 823–825, 823(i), 847
1984 election and, 909
in the North, 359
Oneida Community and, 349
opportunities for, 829
political status of, 195, 219, 335,
338, 643, 668
popular protests and, 734(m)
poverty and, 305, 926
as Progressives, 576–577
prostitution and, 475, 477, 479
Puritan, 58–59, 102–103
Quaker, 71, 108(i)
Radical Reconstruction program
and, 439, 441
republican motherhood and,
255–259, 258(i), 278–279
in Revolutionary War, 185, 185(i)
rural electrification and, 744, 744(i)
slavery and, 84, 266, 266(i), 370
social reform and, 315(i), 358, 365,
509, 511
Social Security Act and, 728
in South Atlantic system, 92–93
strikes and, 711(i)
as teachers, 261(i), 278–279
in textile industry, 285(i), 286,
288(m), 289–291, 290(i), 296,
496, 500
transcendentalism and, 344–345
unemployment of, 714
utopian communalism and, 347,
349
Vietnam War and, 854–856
wage gap and, 499–502, 500(i), 513,
527, 916
War on Poverty and, 844
in wartime jobs, 651, 651(i)

welfare and, 601, 778–779
westward migration and, 374,
465–466
in workforce, 750, 759, 779, 817,
823(i), 824, 847, 893, 894(i), 916,
926
WWII and, 750, 777
women activists
Dorr, Retha Childe, 523
Friedan, Betty, 865–866
Gibbs, Lois, 890–891
Lease, Mary Elizabeth, 536, 537(i)
Potter, Helen, 525, 527
Schneiderman, Rose, 508–509
Steinem, Gloria, 889
Wells, Ida B., 531–533, 531(i),
532(i)
Willard, Frances, 524–525
Women's Christian Temperance Union
(WCTU), 524–525, 526(i), 653
Women's Division of Democratic
National Committee, 735, 746
Women's International League for
Peace and Freedom, 673, 857
Women's Joint Congressional
Committee, 668
Women's Peace Party, 640
women's rights, 535–536. See also
feminism; suffrage movement
activists in movement for, 508–509,
523–525, 527, 536, 537(i)
Adams on, 197, 253
Douglass on, 381
economic, 499–502, 500(i), 513,
527, 916
equal, 704
evangelicalism and, 115, 272–274,
277–278
feminist movement and, 864–867
German settlers and, 110
in Great Depression, 704–705
inheritances and, 253–255
in labor force, 285(i), 296, 509
media and, 867, 925
movement for, 336, 358–364
to property, 102–104, 110, 130
Quakers and, 108(i)
sex typing and, 499–500, 500(i), 513
social reform and, 358, 364
Title IX and, 889–890
Title VII and, 866
voting, 219, 253, 439, 440(i),
523–525, 525(i), 651–653,
653(i), 663
women's liberation and, 866–867,
866(i)
Women Strike for Peace, 857
Wood, Jethro, 300
Woodstock, rock concert at, 860, 861(i)
Woodville, Richard Caton
(1825–1855), 367(i)

Woodward, Bob, 882
Woodward, C. Vann, 160
Woolen Act (1699), 72(t)
Woolman, John, 188
Woolworth Building, 547
Worcester v. Georgia (1832), 328
work ethic, 310–311
Protestant, 305, 665
welfare system and, 779
working class. See also laborers
African American, 691
birth control and, 703
conservatism of, 898
feminism and, 892–893
Great Depression and, 703
housing and, 885
labor unions and, 713
movie industry and, 676
in 1950s, 825
in 1970s, 879
1980 election and, 903
school busing and, 895
on television, 822
women, 823
Working Men's Party, 293, 337, 480
Works Progress Administration
(WPA), 728–729, 729(i), 730(m),
731(t), 747
African Americans and, 735
environment and, 741
Federal One of, 741
Mexican Americans and, 739
Roosevelt recession and, 731–732
World Anti-Slavery Convention
(London; 1840), 363
World Bank (International Bank for
Reconstruction and
Development), 816
WorldCom, 945
World's Work (periodical), 660
World Trade Center, 936. See also
September 11, 2001, terrorist
attacks
1993 bombing of, 929
World War I (1914–1918), 410, 421,
611, 637–652, 785, 795(m)
Allied Powers in, 639
aviation and, 682
business-government partnership
and, 666
Central Powers in, 639
civilians in, 639–640
civil rights in, 655
domestic efforts during, 636(i), 637,
649
Dust Bowl and, 710
ethnic loyalties during, 640
European alliances in, 638(m)
federal government and, 638–649,
668
flying aces in, 645

World War I (Continued):
  growth of trade during, 640
  immigration and, 684
  intellectual life and, 688–689
  international balance of power and, 637–638, 647
  isolationism and, 751
  liberty bonds of, 647
  Lusitania and, 640
  modern bureaucratic state and, 649
  neutrality on the seas in, 640
  new military technology in, 639–640
  1920s and, 665, 693
  progressive reforms and, 654
  Prohibition and, 654
  propaganda in, 648, 654–655
  quasi-vigilantism in, 655
  racism in, 645–646
  Red Scare after, 800
  reparations for, 672
  scope of, 639
  ship convoys in, 643
  social divisions and, 638, 660–662
  student activism and, 705
  trench warfare in, 639(i), 640–641, 643
  U-boats in, 640
  Uncle Sam and, 704(i)
  unresolved issues of, 660
  U.S. involvement in, 643–644, 750
  Verdun, battles of, 640, 644
  veterans of, 717
  voluntarism in, 647, 649
  war profiteers in, 751
  Western Front in, 640, 643–644, 644(m), 663
  Western Front of, 643–644
  WWII and, 660, 768
World War II (1939–1945), 405, 749–779
  African American rights and, 709
  budget deficits in, 910(f)
  casualties in, 768
  D-Day (June 6, 1944) in, 769(m), 770, 771(i)
  decolonization and, 833(m)
  defense spending and, 755, 755(f)
  electronic calculators in, 810
  in Europe (1941–1944), 768(m), 769(m)
  as "good war," 749, 749(i)
  Great Depression and, 697, 732
  on home front, 762–767

  mobilization for, 754–762, 777
  in North Atlantic, 752(m)
  Office of War Information in, 657
  in Pacific, 772(m), 773(m)
  postwar world and, 749, 777
  prelude to, 750–754
  rationing in, 762–763, 777
  reparations and, 785
  role of battleships in, 611
  second front in, 768–769
  social unrest in, 750
  strategies of, 768–769
  unemployment and, 729
  U.S. power and, 749
  U.S. role in, 644, 768, 783, 813
  WWI and, 660, 768
World Wide Web, 919, 923. See also Internet
Wounded Knee, South Dakota
  massacre at, 457, 470(m), 472–473, 472(i)
  occupation of (1973), 863–864, 865(i)
Wovoka, Indian holy man, 473
Wright, Frances, 332, 337(i)
  biographical information, 336–337
Wright, Richard, 743
Wyandot Indians, 223, 236
Wyoming, 374
  gold in, 475
  Japanese internment in, 765
Wyoming Valley, Pennsylvania, 128, 129(m)

Yale College, 117, 119(t), 275(m), 294–295
Yalta meeting (1945), 773, 773(m), 773–775, 775(i), 785, 800
Yalu River, 792
Yamasee people, 71
Yancey, William Lowndes, 394
Yates, Robert, 202–203
Yellow Bird, Sioux medicine man, 472(i), 473
Yellow Hand, chief of Sioux, 463
The Yellow Kid (comic strip), 569
Yellowstone region, 11
Yeltsin, Boris, 912
Yemen, 932
yeomen farmers, 35–37, 54–56, 369, 398
  Free Soil Party and, 379
  Lincoln and, 391

  migration to America, 35, 37
  secession and, 399, 401
  slavery and, 379
  social structure of, 60–61
  Southern, 90, 331, 440
  taxation of, 413
yippies, 868–869
YMCA. See Young Men's Christian Association
Yom Kippur War (1973), 884, 901
York, Alvin, 645
York River, Virginia, 403
Yorktown, battle of (1781), 182–183, 191
Yoruba, 88(i)
Yosemite National Park, 482
Yosemite Valley, 481–482, 482(i)
  lithograph of, 457(i)
Young, Alfred, 153
Young, Brigham, 349(i), 350(m), 351–352
Young Men's Christian Association (YMCA), 522, 566, 653
Young, Perry, 895
Young, Whitney, 839
Young Women's Christian Association (YWCA), 566, 653
youth, 556, 571, 845, 893. See also National Youth Administration
  Great Depression and, 705
  WWII and, 765
youth culture, 556. See also counterculture
  music of, 825–827
  in 1950s, 825
Yucatán Peninsula, 9, 12
Yugoslavia, 658, 787, 914(m), 929, 932(m)
  Federal Republic of (FRY), 931
Yukon, gold discovery in, 540
YWCA. See Young Women's Christian Association

Zhou Enlai (Chou En-lai), 791
Zimmerman, Arthur, 642
Zionism, 796
Zitkala-Ša (Gertrude Simmons Bonnin), 471, 473
Zoffany, Johann, 166
Zola, Émile, 624
zoot suits, 765, 765(i)
Zuni Indians, 12

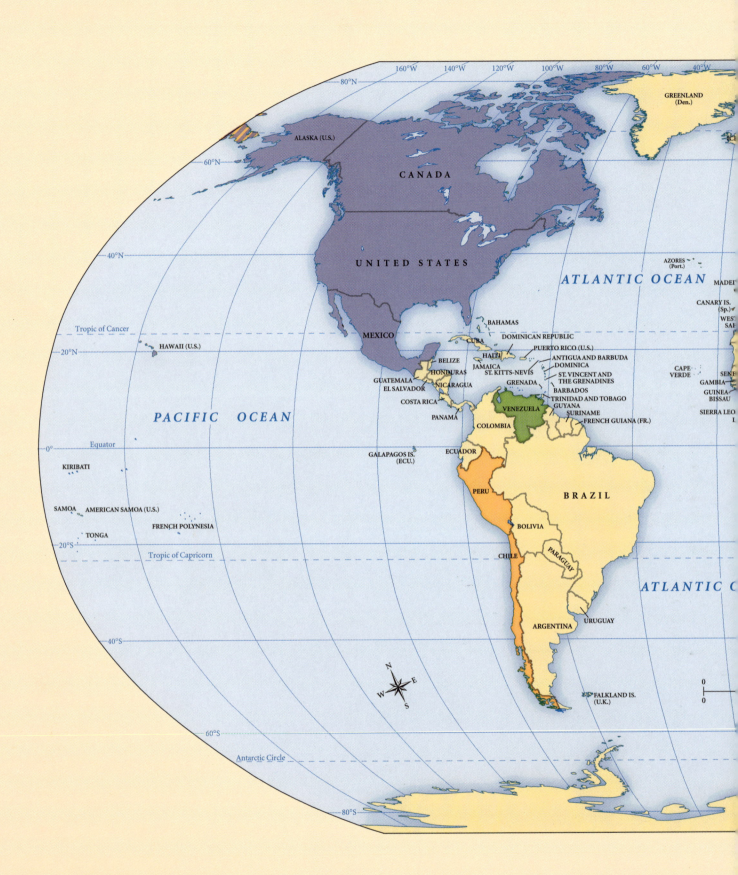

80°N

160°W 140°W 120°W 100°W 80°W 60°W 40°W

GREENLAND
(Den.)

ICI

ALASKA (U.S.)

60°N

CANADA

UNITED STATES

40°N

ATLANTIC OCEAN

AZORES
(Port.)

MADEI

Tropic of Cancer

20°N

HAWAII (U.S.)

MEXICO

CANARY IS.
(Sp.)

WEST
SAH

BAHAMAS

CUBA DOMINICAN REPUBLIC

HAITI PUERTO RICO (U.S.)

BELIZE JAMAICA

HONDURAS ST. KITTS-NEVIS

GUATEMALA

EL SALVADOR NICARAGUA

COSTA RICA

PANAMA

ANTIGUA AND BARBUDA
DOMINICA

ST. VINCENT AND
THE GRENADINES

GRENADA

BARBADOS

TRINIDAD AND TOBAGO

GUYANA

SURINAME

FRENCH GUIANA (FR.)

CAPE
VERDE

SEN

GAMBIA

GUINEA-
BISSAU

SIERRA LEO

PACIFIC OCEAN

VENEZUELA

COLOMBIA

GALAPAGOS IS.
(ECU.)

ECUADOR

Equator 0°

KIRIBATI

PERU

BRAZIL

SAMOA AMERICAN SAMOA (U.S.)

FRENCH POLYNESIA

BOLIVIA

TONGA

20°S

Tropic of Capricorn

PARAGUAY

CHILE

ATLANTIC O

URUGUAY

ARGENTINA

40°S

N
W E
S

FALKLAND IS.
(U.K.)

0
0

60°S

Antarctic Circle

80°S

Political divisions as of April 2003